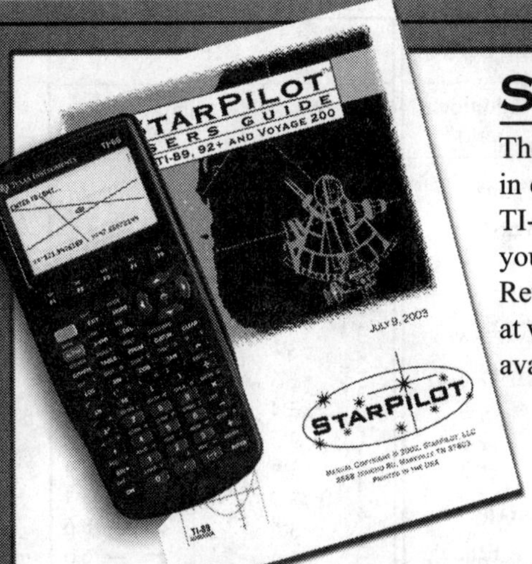

STARP

The state of the
in celestial navigation and coastal piloting, built into a TI-89 calculator. All programs stored in ROM. Makes your navigation more accurate and more efficient. Review features and compare to other nav calculators at www.starpilotllc.com. $379, plus shipping. Software available for download for $129.

STARPILOT - PC

Performs all standard coastal piloting, route planning, and celestial computations, instantly, accurately, and most conveniently on your desktop PC; has special features like 3-body sextant plotting, lunar distance for GMT, and much more. $139 plus shipping or available for download for $129.

For more info on StarPilot please visit **www.starpilotllc.com**, email **info@starpilotllc.com** or call **877.379.8723**

XGATE

EXTRAORDINARY GATEWAY FOR WIRELESS EMAIL

XGate provides fast wireless e-mail for satellite and cellular phones. Its cost-effective user-friendly interface saves users time, money and frustration from dealing with "free" Internet based e-mail systems that burn excessive air time minutes with each painfully slow connection. With XGate, users experience fast connections (up to 50+ emails per minute) with tremendous $$$ savings and leading edge efficiency. Review XGate's design features and testimonials at www.globalmarinenet.net.

Sail Magazines "Freeman K. Pittman Editor's Choice" award for 2003!

OCENS WEATHERNET

WEATHER-ON-DEMAND

Download weather on demand over your cell phone, satellite phone, or SSB radio reliably, fast, and inexpensively. There are over 7,000 conveniently indexed weather products from which to select, including weather charts, ocean charts, text forecasts, satellite imagery, GRIB, Nexrad radar, buoy information and aviation charts. Several weather display systems are available for quick viewing and enhanced analysis of downloaded graphical products.

For more info on services from Global Marine Networks visit **www.globalmarinenet.net**, email **info@globalmarinenet.net** or call **877.379.8723**

A2 ALTITUDE CORRECTION TABLES 10°-90°—SUN, STARS, PLANETS

SUN

OCT.—MAR. App. Alt.	Lower Limb	Upper Limb	APR.—SEPT. App. Alt.	Lower Limb	Upper Limb
° ′	′	′	° ′	′	′
9 33	+10·8	−21·5	9 39	+10·6	−21·2
9 45	+10·9	−21·4	9 50	+10·7	−21·1
9 56	+11·0	−21·3	10 02	+10·8	−21·0
10 08	+11·1	−21·2	10 14	+10·9	−20·9
10 20	+11·2	−21·1	10 27	+11·0	−20·8
10 33	+11·3	−21·0	10 40	+11·1	−20·7
10 46	+11·4	−20·9	10 53	+11·2	−20·6
11 00	+11·5	−20·8	11 07	+11·3	−20·5
11 15	+11·6	−20·7	11 22	+11·4	−20·4
11 30	+11·7	−20·6	11 37	+11·5	−20·3
11 45	+11·8	−20·5	11 53	+11·6	−20·2
12 01	+11·9	−20·4	12 10	+11·7	−20·1
12 18	+12·0	−20·3	12 27	+11·8	−20·0
12 36	+12·1	−20·2	12 45	+11·9	−19·9
12 54	+12·2	−20·1	13 04	+12·0	−19·8
13 14	+12·3	−20·0	13 24	+12·1	−19·7
13 34	+12·4	−19·9	13 44	+12·2	−19·6
13 55	+12·5	−19·8	14 06	+12·3	−19·5
14 17	+12·6	−19·7	14 29	+12·4	−19·4
14 41	+12·7	−19·6	14 53	+12·5	−19·3
15 05	+12·8	−19·5	15 18	+12·6	−19·2
15 31	+12·9	−19·4	15 45	+12·7	−19·1
15 59	+13·0	−19·3	16 13	+12·8	−19·0
16 27	+13·1	−19·2	16 43	+12·9	−18·9
16 58	+13·2	−19·1	17 14	+13·0	−18·8
17 30	+13·3	−19·0	17 47	+13·1	−18·7
18 05	+13·4	−18·9	18 23	+13·2	−18·6
18 41	+13·5	−18·8	19 00	+13·3	−18·5
19 20	+13·6	−18·7	19 41	+13·4	−18·4
20 02	+13·7	−18·6	20 24	+13·5	−18·3
20 46	+13·8	−18·5	21 10	+13·6	−18·2
21 34	+13·9	−18·4	21 59	+13·7	−18·1
22 25	+14·0	−18·3	22 52	+13·8	−18·0
23 20	+14·1	−18·2	23 49	+13·9	−17·9
24 20	+14·2	−18·1	24 51	+14·0	−17·8
25 24	+14·3	−18·0	25 58	+14·1	−17·7
26 34	+14·4	−17·9	27 11	+14·2	−17·6
27 50	+14·5	−17·8	28 31	+14·3	−17·5
29 13	+14·6	−17·7	29 58	+14·4	−17·4
30 44	+14·7	−17·6	31 33	+14·5	−17·3
32 24	+14·8	−17·5	33 18	+14·6	−17·2
34 15	+14·9	−17·4	35 15	+14·7	−17·1
36 17	+15·0	−17·3	37 24	+14·8	−17·0
38 34	+15·1	−17·2	39 48	+14·9	−16·9
41 06	+15·2	−17·1	42 28	+15·0	−16·8
43 56	+15·3	−17·0	45 29	+15·1	−16·7
47 07	+15·4	−16·9	48 52	+15·2	−16·6
50 43	+15·5	−16·8	52 41	+15·3	−16·5
54 46	+15·6	−16·7	56 59	+15·4	−16·4
59 21	+15·7	−16·6	61 50	+15·5	−16·3
64 28	+15·8	−16·5	67 15	+15·6	−16·2
70 10	+15·9	−16·4	73 14	+15·7	−16·1
76 24	+16·0	−16·3	79 42	+15·8	−16·0
83 05	+16·1	−16·2	86 31	+15·9	−15·9
90 00			90 00		

STARS AND PLANETS

App Alt.	Corrⁿ
° ′	′
9 55	−5·3
10 07	−5·2
10 20	−5·1
10 32	−5·0
10 46	−4·9
10 59	−4·8
11 14	−4·7
11 29	−4·6
11 44	−4·5
12 00	−4·4
12 17	−4·3
12 35	−4·2
12 53	−4·1
13 12	−4·0
13 32	−3·9
13 53	−3·8
14 16	−3·7
14 39	−3·6
15 03	−3·5
15 29	−3·4
15 56	−3·3
16 25	−3·2
16 55	−3·1
17 27	−3·0
18 01	−2·9
18 37	−2·8
19 16	−2·7
19 56	−2·6
20 40	−2·5
21 27	−2·4
22 17	−2·3
23 11	−2·2
24 09	−2·1
25 12	−2·0
26 20	−1·9
27 34	−1·8
28 54	−1·7
30 22	−1·6
31 58	−1·5
33 43	−1·4
35 38	−1·3
37 45	−1·2
40 06	−1·1
42 42	−1·0
45 34	−0·9
48 45	−0·8
52 16	−0·7
56 09	−0·6
60 26	−0·5
65 06	−0·4
70 09	−0·3
75 32	−0·2
81 12	−0·1
87 03	0·0
90 00	

App. Alt.	Additional Corrⁿ
2008	
VENUS	
Jan. 1–Dec. 5	
°	′
0	
60	+0·1
Dec. 6–Dec. 31	
°	′
0	
41	+0·2
76	+0·1
MARS	
Jan. 1–Feb. 23	
°	′
0	
41	+0·2
76	+0·1
Feb. 24–Dec. 31	
°	′
0	
60	+0·1

DIP

Ht. of Eye	Corrⁿ	Ht. of Eye
m	′	ft.
2·4	−2·8	8·0
2·6	−2·9	8·6
2·8	−3·0	9·2
3·0	−3·1	9·8
3·2	−3·2	10·5
3·4	−3·3	11·2
3·6	−3·4	11·9
3·8	−3·5	12·6
4·0	−3·6	13·3
4·3	−3·7	14·1
4·5	−3·8	14·9
4·7	−3·9	15·7
5·0	−4·0	16·5
5·2	−4·1	17·4
5·5	−4·2	18·3
5·8	−4·3	19·1
6·1	−4·4	20·1
6·3	−4·5	21·0
6·6	−4·6	22·0
6·9	−4·7	22·9
7·2	−4·8	23·9
7·5	−4·9	24·9
7·9	−5·0	26·0
8·2	−5·1	27·1
8·5	−5·2	28·1
8·8	−5·3	29·2
9·2	−5·4	30·4
9·5	−5·5	31·5
9·9	−5·6	32·7
10·3	−5·7	33·9
10·6	−5·8	35·1
11·0	−5·9	36·3
11·4	−6·0	37·6
11·8	−6·1	38·9
12·2	−6·2	40·1
12·6	−6·3	41·5
13·0	−6·4	42·8
13·4	−6·5	44·2
13·8	−6·6	45·5
14·2	−6·7	46·9
14·7	−6·8	48·4
15·1	−6·9	49·8
15·5	−7·0	51·3
16·0	−7·1	52·8
16·5	−7·2	54·3
16·9	−7·3	55·8
17·4	−7·4	57·4
17·9	−7·5	58·9
18·4	−7·6	60·5
18·8	−7·7	62·1
19·3	−7·8	63·8
19·8	−7·9	65·4
20·4	−8·0	67·1
20·9	−8·1	68·8
21·4		70·5

Ht. of Eye	Corrⁿ
m	′
1·0	− 1·8
1·5	− 2·2
2·0	− 2·5
2·5	− 2·8
3·0	− 3·0
See table ←	
m	′
20	− 7·9
22	− 8·3
24	− 8·6
26	− 9·0
28	− 9·3
30	− 9·6
32	−10·0
34	−10·3
36	−10·6
38	−10·8
40	−11·1
42	−11·4
44	−11·7
46	−11·9
48	−12·2
ft.	
2	− 1·4
4	− 1·9
6	− 2·4
8	− 2·7
10	− 3·1
See table ←	
ft.	′
70	− 8·1
75	− 8·4
80	− 8·7
85	− 8·9
90	− 9·2
95	− 9·5
100	− 9·7
105	− 9·9
110	−10·2
115	−10·4
120	−10·6
125	−10·8
130	−11·1
135	−11·3
140	−11·5
145	−11·7
150	−11·9
155	−12·1

App. Alt. = Apparent altitude = Sextant altitude corrected for index error and dip.

ALTITUDE CORRECTION TABLES 0°-10°—SUN, STARS, PLANETS A3

App. Alt.	OCT.—MAR. SUN Lower Limb	OCT.—MAR. SUN Upper Limb	APR.—SEPT. SUN Lower Limb	APR.—SEPT. SUN Upper Limb	STARS PLANETS
° ′	′	′	′	′	′
0 00	−17·5	−49·8	−17·8	−49·6	−33·8
0 03	16·9	49·2	17·2	49·0	33·2
0 06	16·3	48·6	16·6	48·4	32·6
0 09	15·7	48·0	16·0	47·8	32·0
0 12	15·2	47·5	15·4	47·2	31·5
0 15	14·6	46·9	14·8	46·6	30·9
0 18	−14·1	−46·4	−14·3	−46·1	−30·4
0 21	13·5	45·8	13·8	45·6	29·8
0 24	13·0	45·3	13·3	45·1	29·3
0 27	12·5	44·8	12·8	44·6	28·8
0 30	12·0	44·3	12·3	44·1	28·3
0 33	11·6	43·9	11·8	43·6	27·9
0 36	−11·1	−43·4	−11·3	−43·1	−27·4
0 39	10·6	42·9	10·9	42·7	26·9
0 42	10·2	42·5	10·5	42·3	26·5
0 45	9·8	42·1	10·0	41·8	26·1
0 48	9·4	41·7	9·6	41·4	25·7
0 51	9·0	41·3	9·2	41·0	25·3
0 54	− 8·6	−40·9	− 8·8	−40·6	−24·9
0 57	8·2	40·5	8·4	40·2	24·5
1 00	7·8	40·1	8·0	39·8	24·1
1 03	7·4	39·7	7·7	39·5	23·7
1 06	7·1	39·4	7·3	39·1	23·4
1 09	6·7	39·0	7·0	38·8	23·0
1 12	− 6·4	−38·7	− 6·6	−38·4	−22·7
1 15	6·0	38·3	6·3	38·1	22·3
1 18	5·7	38·0	6·0	37·8	22·0
1 21	5·4	37·7	5·7	37·5	21·7
1 24	5·1	37·4	5·3	37·1	21·4
1 27	4·8	37·1	5·0	36·8	21·1
1 30	− 4·5	−36·8	− 4·7	−36·5	−20·8
1 35	4·0	36·3	4·3	36·1	20·3
1 40	3·6	35·9	3·8	35·6	19·9
1 45	3·1	35·4	3·4	35·2	19·4
1 50	2·7	35·0	2·9	34·7	19·0
1 55	2·3	34·6	2·5	34·3	18·6
2 00	− 1·9	−34·2	− 2·1	−33·9	−18·2
2 05	1·5	33·8	1·7	33·5	17·8
2 10	1·1	33·4	1·4	33·2	17·4
2 15	0·8	33·1	1·0	32·8	17·1
2 20	0·4	32·7	0·7	32·5	16·7
2 25	− 0·1	32·4	− 0·3	32·1	16·4
2 30	+ 0·2	−32·1	0·0	−31·8	−16·1
2 35	0·5	31·8	+ 0·3	31·5	15·8
2 40	0·8	31·5	0·6	31·2	15·4
2 45	1·1	31·2	0·9	30·9	15·2
2 50	1·4	30·9	1·2	30·6	14·9
2 55	1·7	30·6	1·4	30·4	14·6
3 00	+ 2·0	−30·3	+ 1·7	−30·1	−14·3
3 05	2·2	30·1	2·0	29·8	14·1
3 10	2·5	29·8	2·2	29·6	13·8
3 15	2·7	29·6	2·5	29·3	13·6
3 20	2·9	29·4	2·7	29·1	13·4
3 25	3·2	29·1	2·9	28·9	13·1
3 30	+ 3·4	−28·9	+ 3·1	−28·7	−12·9

App. Alt.	OCT.—MAR. SUN Lower Limb	OCT.—MAR. SUN Upper Limb	APR.—SEPT. SUN Lower Limb	APR.—SEPT. SUN Upper Limb	STARS PLANETS
° ′	′	′	′	′	′
3 30	+ 3·4	−28·9	+ 3·1	−28·7	−12·9
3 35	3·6	28·7	3·3	28·5	12·7
3 40	3·8	28·5	3·6	28·2	12·5
3 45	4·0	28·3	3·8	28·0	12·3
3 50	4·2	28·1	4·0	27·8	12·1
3 55	4·4	27·9	4·1	27·7	11·9
4 00	+ 4·6	−27·7	+ 4·3	−27·5	−11·7
4 05	4·8	27·5	4·5	27·3	11·5
4 10	4·9	27·4	4·7	27·1	11·4
4 15	5·1	27·2	4·9	26·9	11·2
4 20	5·3	27·0	5·0	26·8	11·0
4 25	5·4	26·9	5·2	26·6	10·9
4 30	+ 5·6	−26·7	+ 5·3	−26·5	−10·7
4 35	5·7	26·6	5·5	26·3	10·6
4 40	5·9	26·4	5·6	26·2	10·4
4 45	6·0	26·3	5·8	26·0	10·3
4 50	6·2	26·1	5·9	25·9	10·1
4 55	6·3	26·0	6·1	25·7	10·0
5 00	+ 6·4	−25·9	+ 6·2	−25·6	− 9·8
5 05	6·6	25·7	6·3	25·5	9·7
5 10	6·7	25·6	6·5	25·3	9·6
5 15	6·8	25·5	6·6	25·2	9·5
5 20	7·0	25·3	6·7	25·1	9·3
5 25	7·1	25·2	6·8	25·0	9·2
5 30	+ 7·2	−25·1	+ 6·9	−24·9	− 9·1
5 35	7·3	25·0	7·1	24·7	9·0
5 40	7·4	24·9	7·2	24·6	8·9
5 45	7·5	24·8	7·3	24·5	8·8
5 50	7·6	24·7	7·4	24·4	8·7
5 55	7·7	24·6	7·5	24·3	8·6
6 00	+ 7·8	−24·5	+ 7·6	−24·2	− 8·5
6 10	8·0	24·3	7·8	24·0	8·3
6 20	8·2	24·1	8·0	23·8	8·1
6 30	8·4	23·9	8·2	23·6	7·9
6 40	8·6	23·7	8·3	23·5	7·7
6 50	8·7	23·6	8·5	23·3	7·6
7 00	+ 8·9	−23·4	+ 8·7	−23·1	− 7·4
7 10	9·1	23·2	8·8	23·0	7·2
7 20	9·2	23·1	9·0	22·8	7·1
7 30	9·3	23·0	9·1	22·7	6·9
7 40	9·5	22·8	9·2	22·6	6·8
7 50	9·6	22·7	9·4	22·4	6·7
8 00	+ 9·7	−22·6	+ 9·5	−22·3	− 6·6
8 10	9·9	22·4	9·6	22·2	6·4
8 20	10·0	22·3	9·7	22·1	6·3
8 30	10·1	22·2	9·9	21·9	6·2
8 40	10·2	22·1	10·0	21·8	6·1
8 50	10·3	22·0	10·1	21·7	6·0
9 00	+10·4	−21·9	+10·2	−21·6	− 5·9
9 10	10·5	21·8	10·3	21·5	5·8
9 20	10·6	21·7	10·4	21·4	5·7
9 30	10·7	21·6	10·5	21·3	5·6
9 40	10·8	21·5	10·6	21·2	5·5
9 50	10·9	21·4	10·6	21·2	5·4
10 00	+11·0	−21·3	+10·7	−21·1	− 5·3

Additional corrections for temperature and pressure are given on the following page.

For bubble sextant observations ignore dip and use the star corrections for Sun, planets and stars.

ALTITUDE CORRECTION TABLES—ADDITIONAL CORRECTIONS

ADDITIONAL REFRACTION CORRECTIONS FOR NON-STANDARD CONDITIONS

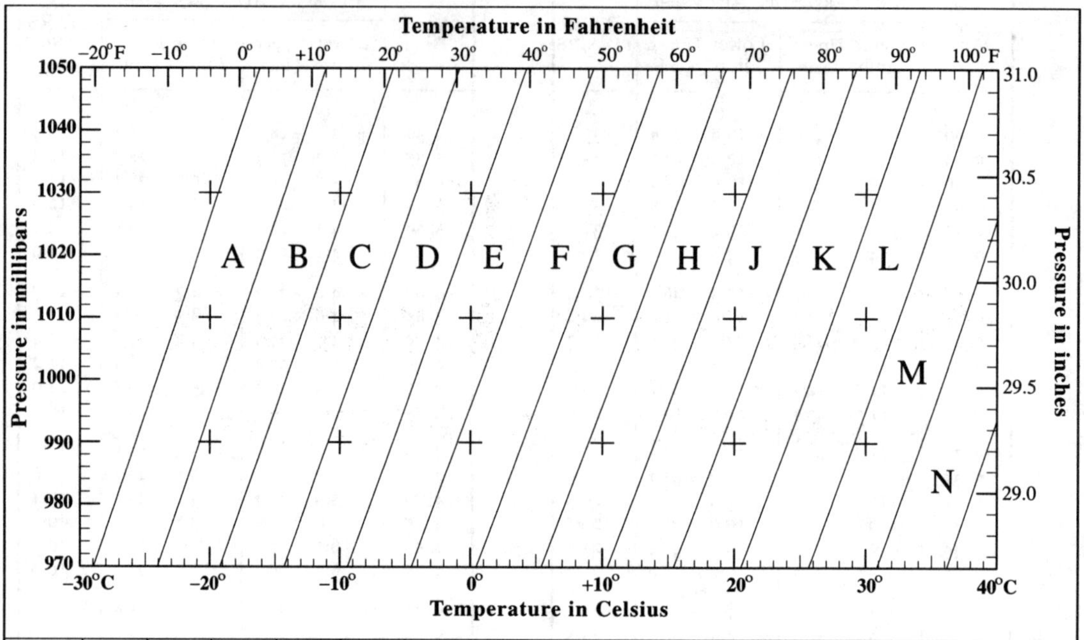

Temperature in Fahrenheit: −20°F −10° 0° +10° 20° 30° 40° 50° 60° 70° 80° 90° 100°F

Pressure in millibars: 1050 1040 1030 1020 1010 1000 990 980 970

Pressure in inches: 31.0 30.5 30.0 29.5 29.0

Zones: A B C D E F G H J K L M N

Temperature in Celsius: −30°C −20° −10° 0° +10° 20° 30° 40°C

App. Alt.	A	B	C	D	E	F	G	H	J	K	L	M	N	P	App. Alt.
° ′	′	′	′	′	′	′	′	′	′	′	′	′	′	′	° ′
00 00	−7·3	−5·9	−4·6	−3·4	−2·2	−1·1	0·0	+1·0	+2·0	+3·0	+4·0	+4·9	+5·9	+6·9	**00 00**
00 30	5·5	4·5	3·5	2·6	1·7	0·8	0·0	0·8	1·6	2·3	3·1	3·8	4·5	5·3	**00 30**
01 00	4·4	3·5	2·8	2·0	1·3	0·7	0·0	0·6	1·2	1·8	2·4	3·0	3·6	4·2	**01 00**
01 30	3·5	2·9	2·2	1·7	1·1	0·5	0·0	0·5	1·0	1·5	2·0	2·5	2·9	3·4	**01 30**
02 00	2·9	2·4	1·9	1·4	0·9	0·4	0·0	0·4	0·8	1·3	1·7	2·0	2·4	2·8	**02 00**
02 30	−2·5	−2·0	−1·6	−1·2	−0·8	−0·4	0·0	+0·4	+0·7	+1·1	+1·4	+1·7	+2·1	+2·4	**02 30**
03 00	2·1	1·7	1·4	1·0	0·7	0·3	0·0	0·3	0·6	0·9	1·2	1·5	1·8	2·1	**03 00**
03 30	1·9	1·5	1·2	0·9	0·6	0·3	0·0	0·3	0·5	0·8	1·1	1·3	1·6	1·8	**03 30**
04 00	1·6	1·3	1·1	0·8	0·5	0·3	0·0	0·2	0·5	0·7	0·9	1·2	1·4	1·6	**04 00**
04 30	1·5	1·2	0·9	0·7	0·5	0·2	0·0	0·2	0·4	0·6	0·8	1·0	1·3	1·5	**04 30**
05 00	−1·3	−1·1	−0·9	−0·6	−0·4	−0·2	0·0	+0·2	+0·4	+0·6	+0·8	+0·9	+1·1	+1·3	**05 00**
06	1·1	0·9	0·7	0·5	0·3	0·2	0·0	0·2	0·3	0·5	0·6	0·8	0·9	1·1	**06**
07	1·0	0·8	0·6	0·5	0·3	0·1	0·0	0·1	0·3	0·4	0·5	0·7	0·8	0·9	**07**
08	0·8	0·7	0·5	0·4	0·3	0·1	0·0	0·1	0·2	0·4	0·5	0·6	0·7	0·8	**08**
09	0·7	0·6	0·5	0·4	0·2	0·1	0·0	0·1	0·2	0·3	0·4	0·5	0·6	0·7	**09**
10 00	−0·7	−0·5	−0·4	−0·3	−0·2	−0·1	0·0	+0·1	+0·2	+0·3	+0·4	+0·5	+0·6	+0·7	**10 00**
12	0·6	0·5	0·4	0·3	0·2	0·1	0·0	0·1	0·2	0·2	0·3	0·4	0·5	0·5	**12**
14	0·5	0·4	0·3	0·2	0·1	0·1	0·0	0·1	0·1	0·2	0·3	0·3	0·4	0·5	**14**
16	0·4	0·3	0·3	0·2	0·1	0·1	0·0	0·1	0·1	0·2	0·2	0·3	0·3	0·4	**16**
18	0·4	0·3	0·2	0·2	0·1	−0·1	0·0	+0·1	0·1	0·2	0·2	0·3	0·3	0·4	**18**
20 00	−0·3	−0·3	−0·2	−0·2	−0·1	0·0	0·0	0·0	+0·1	+0·1	+0·2	+0·2	+0·3	+0·3	**20 00**
25	0·3	0·2	0·2	0·1	0·1	0·0	0·0	0·0	0·1	0·1	0·1	0·2	0·2	0·2	**25**
30	0·2	0·2	0·1	0·1	0·1	0·0	0·0	0·0	+0·1	0·1	0·1	0·1	0·2	0·2	**30**
35	0·2	0·1	0·1	0·1	−0·1	0·0	0·0	0·0	0·0	0·1	0·1	0·1	0·1	0·2	**35**
40	0·1	0·1	0·1	−0·1	0·0	0·0	0·0	0·0	0·0	+0·1	0·1	0·1	0·1	0·1	**40**
50 00	−0·1	−0·1	−0·1	0·0	0·0	0·0	0·0	0·0	0·0	0·0	+0·1	+0·1	+0·1	+0·1	**50 00**

The graph is entered with arguments temperature and pressure to find a zone letter; using as arguments this zone letter and apparent altitude (sextant altitude corrected for index error and dip), a correction is taken from the table. This correction is to be applied to the sextant altitude in addition to the corrections for standard conditions (for the Sun, stars and planets from page A2-A3 and for the Moon from pages xxxiv and xxxv).

2008
Nautical Almanac
COMMERCIAL EDITION

PUBLISHED BY:

Paradise Cay Publications, Inc.
Post Office Box 29
Arcata, CA 95518-0029
Tel: 1-707-822-9063
Fax: 1-707-822-9163
www.paracay.com

ISBN-13: 978-0-939837-76-2
ISBN-10: 0-939837-76-5

Printed and distributed with permission by Paradise Cay Publications, Inc.

NOTE

Every care is taken to prevent errors in the production of this publication. As a final precaution it is recommended that the sequence of pages in this copy be examined on receipt. If faulty, it should be returned for replacement.

PREFACE

The first three sections of this book are a complete and accurate duplication from *The Nautical Almanac* produced jointly by Her Majesty's Nautical Almanac Office, United Kingdom Hydrographic Office, Admiralty Way, Taunton, Somerset, TA1 2DN, United Kingdom and the Nautical Almanac Office of the US Naval Observatory.

We gratefully acknowledge the United Kingdom Hydrographic Office and the United States Naval Observatory for permission to use the material contained in the almanac sections of this publication.

The 2008 Nautical Almanac
Commercial Edition

Pages

RELIGIOUS CALENDARS

Epiphany	Jan. 6	Low Sunday	Mar. 30
Septuagesima Sunday	Jan. 20	Rogation Sunday	Apr. 27
Quinquagesima Sunday	Feb. 3	Ascension Day—Holy Thursday	May 1
Ash Wednesday	Feb. 6	Whit Sunday—Pentecost	May 11
Quadragesima Sunday	Feb. 10	Trinity Sunday	May 18
Palm Sunday	Mar. 16	Corpus Christi	May 22
Good Friday	Mar. 21	First Sunday in Advent	Nov. 30
Easter Day	Mar. 23	Christmas Day (Thursday)	Dec. 25
First Day of Passover (Pesach)	Apr. 20	Day of Atonement (Yom Kippur)	Oct. 9
Feast of Weeks (Shavuot)	June 9	First day of Tabernacles (Succoth)	Oct. 14
Jewish New Year 5769 (Rosh Hashanah)	Sept. 30		
Islamic New Year (1429)	Jan. 10	Ramadân, First day of (tabular)	Sept. 2
and (1430)	Dec. 29		

The Jewish and Islamic dates above are tabular dates, which begin at sunset on the previous evening and end at sunset on the date tabulated. In practice, the dates of Islamic fasts and festivals are determined by an actual sighting of the appropriate new moon.

CIVIL CALENDAR—UNITED KINGDOM

Accession of Queen Elizabeth II	Feb. 6	Birthday of Prince Philip, Duke of Edinburgh	June 10
St David (Wales)	Mar. 1	The Queen's Official Birthday†	June 14
Commonwealth Day	Mar. 10	Remembrance Sunday	Nov. 9
St Patrick (Ireland)	Mar. 17	Birthday of the Prince of Wales	Nov. 14
Birthday of Queen Elizabeth II	Apr. 21	St Andrew (Scotland)	Nov. 30
St George (England)	Apr. 23		
Coronation Day	June 2		

PUBLIC HOLIDAYS

England and Wales—Jan. 1†, Mar. 21, Mar. 24, May 5†, May 26, Aug. 25, Dec. 25, Dec. 26
Northern Ireland—Jan. 1†, Mar. 17, Mar. 21, Mar. 24, May 5†, May 26, July 14†, Aug. 25, Dec. 25, Dec. 26
Scotland—Jan. 1, Jan. 2, Mar. 21, May 5, May 26†, Aug. 4, Dec. 25, Dec. 26†

CIVIL CALENDAR—UNITED STATES OF AMERICA

New Year's Day	Jan. 1	Labor Day	Sept. 1
Martin Luther King's Birthday	Jan. 21	Columbus Day	Oct. 13
Lincoln's Birthday	Feb. 12	General Election Day	Nov. 4
Washington's Birthday	Feb. 18	Veterans Day	Nov. 11
Memorial Day	May 26	Thanksgiving Day	Nov. 27
Independence Day	July 4		

†Dates subject to confirmation

PHASES OF THE MOON

New Moon	d h m	First Quarter	d h m	Full Moon	d h m	Last Quarter	d h m
Jan.	8 11 37	Jan.	15 19 46	Jan.	22 13 35	Jan.	30 05 03
Feb.	7 03 44	Feb.	14 03 33	Feb.	21 03 30	Feb.	29 02 18
Mar.	7 17 14	Mar.	14 10 46	Mar.	21 18 40	Mar.	29 21 47
Apr.	6 03 55	Apr.	12 18 32	Apr.	20 10 25	Apr.	28 14 12
May	5 12 18	May	12 03 47	May	20 02 11	May	28 02 57
June	3 19 23	June	10 15 04	June	18 17 30	June	26 12 10
July	3 02 19	July	10 04 35	July	18 07 59	July	25 18 42
Aug.	1 10 13	Aug.	8 20 20	Aug.	16 21 16	Aug.	23 23 50
Aug.	30 19 58	Sept.	7 14 04	Sept.	15 09 13	Sept.	22 05 04
Sept.	29 08 12	Oct.	7 09 04	Oct.	14 20 02	Oct.	21 11 55
Oct.	28 23 14	Nov.	6 04 03	Nov.	13 06 17	Nov.	19 21 31
Nov.	27 16 55	Dec.	5 21 26	Dec.	12 16 37	Dec.	19 10 29
Dec.	27 12 22						

DAYS OF THE WEEK AND DAYS OF THE YEAR

	JAN.		FEB.		MAR.		APR.		MAY		JUNE		JULY		AUG.		SEPT.		OCT.		NOV.		DEC.	
Day	Wk	Yr	Wk	Yr	Wk	Yr	Wk	Yr	Wk	Yr	Wk	Yr	Wk	Yr	Wk	Yr	Wk	Yr	Wk	Yr	Wk	Yr	Wk	Yr
1	Tu.	1	F.	32	Sa.	61	Tu.	92	Th.	122	Su.	153	Tu.	183	F.	214	M.	245	W.	275	Sa.	306	M.	336
2	W.	2	Sa.	33	Su.	62	W.	93	F.	123	M.	154	W.	184	Sa.	215	Tu.	246	Th.	276	Su.	307	Tu.	337
3	Th.	3	Su.	34	M.	63	Th.	94	Sa.	124	Tu.	155	Th.	185	Su.	216	W.	247	F.	277	M.	308	W.	338
4	F.	4	M.	35	Tu.	64	F.	95	Su.	125	W.	156	F.	186	M.	217	Th.	248	Sa.	278	Tu.	309	Th.	339
5	Sa.	5	Tu.	36	W.	65	Sa.	96	M.	126	Th.	157	Sa.	187	Tu.	218	F.	249	Su.	279	W.	310	F.	340
6	Su.	6	W.	37	Th.	66	Su.	97	Tu.	127	F.	158	Su.	188	W.	219	Sa.	250	M.	280	Th.	311	Sa.	341
7	M.	7	Th.	38	F.	67	M.	98	W.	128	Sa.	159	M.	189	Th.	220	Su.	251	Tu.	281	F.	312	Su.	342
8	Tu.	8	F.	39	Sa.	68	Tu.	99	Th.	129	Su.	160	Tu.	190	F.	221	M.	252	W.	282	Sa.	313	M.	343
9	W.	9	Sa.	40	Su.	69	W.	100	F.	130	M.	161	W.	191	Sa.	222	Tu.	253	Th.	283	Su.	314	Tu.	344
10	Th.	10	Su.	41	M.	70	Th.	101	Sa.	131	Tu.	162	Th.	192	Su.	223	W.	254	F.	284	M.	315	W.	345
11	F.	11	M.	42	Tu.	71	F.	102	Su.	132	W.	163	F.	193	M.	224	Th.	255	Sa.	285	Tu.	316	Th.	346
12	Sa.	12	Tu.	43	W.	72	Sa.	103	M.	133	Th.	164	Sa.	194	Tu.	225	F.	256	Su.	286	W.	317	F.	347
13	Su.	13	W.	44	Th.	73	Su.	104	Tu.	134	F.	165	Su.	195	W.	226	Sa.	257	M.	287	Th.	318	Sa.	348
14	M.	14	Th.	45	F.	74	M.	105	W.	135	Sa.	166	M.	196	Th.	227	Su.	258	Tu.	288	F.	319	Su.	349
15	Tu.	15	F.	46	Sa.	75	Tu.	106	Th.	136	Su.	167	Tu.	197	F.	228	M.	259	W.	289	Sa.	320	M.	350
16	W.	16	Sa.	47	Su.	76	W.	107	F.	137	M.	168	W.	198	Sa.	229	Tu.	260	Th.	290	Su.	321	Tu.	351
17	Th.	17	Su.	48	M.	77	Th.	108	Sa.	138	Tu.	169	Th.	199	Su.	230	W.	261	F.	291	M.	322	W.	352
18	F.	18	M.	49	Tu.	78	F.	109	Su.	139	W.	170	F.	200	M.	231	Th.	262	Sa.	292	Tu.	323	Th.	353
19	Sa.	19	Tu.	50	W.	79	Sa.	110	M.	140	Th.	171	Sa.	201	Tu.	232	F.	263	Su.	293	W.	324	F.	354
20	Su.	20	W.	51	Th.	80	Su.	111	Tu.	141	F.	172	Su.	202	W.	233	Sa.	264	M.	294	Th.	325	Sa.	355
21	M.	21	Th.	52	F.	81	M.	112	W.	142	Sa.	173	M.	203	Th.	234	Su.	265	Tu.	295	F.	326	Su.	356
22	Tu.	22	F.	53	Sa.	82	Tu.	113	Th.	143	Su.	174	Tu.	204	F.	235	M.	266	W.	296	Sa.	327	M.	357
23	W.	23	Sa.	54	Su.	83	W.	114	F.	144	M.	175	W.	205	Sa.	236	Tu.	267	Th.	297	Su.	328	Tu.	358
24	Th.	24	Su.	55	M.	84	Th.	115	Sa.	145	Tu.	176	Th.	206	Su.	237	W.	268	F.	298	M.	329	W.	359
25	F.	25	M.	56	Tu.	85	F.	116	Su.	146	W.	177	F.	207	M.	238	Th.	269	Sa.	299	Tu.	330	Th.	360
26	Sa.	26	Tu.	57	W.	86	Sa.	117	M.	147	Th.	178	Sa.	208	Tu.	239	F.	270	Su.	300	W.	331	F.	361
27	Su.	27	W.	58	Th.	87	Su.	118	Tu.	148	F.	179	Su.	209	W.	240	Sa.	271	M.	301	Th.	332	Sa.	362
28	M.	28	Th.	59	F.	88	M.	119	W.	149	Sa.	180	M.	210	Th.	241	Su.	272	Tu.	302	F.	333	Su.	363
29	Tu.	29	F.	60	Sa.	89	Tu.	120	Th.	150	Su.	181	Tu.	211	F.	242	M.	273	W.	303	Sa.	334	M.	364
30	W.	30			Su.	90	W.	121	F.	151	M.	182	W.	212	Sa.	243	Tu.	274	Th.	304	Su.	335	Tu.	365
31	Th.	31			M.	91			Sa.	152			Th.	213	Su.	244			F.	305			W.	366

ECLIPSES

There are two eclipses of the Sun and two of the Moon.

1. *An annular eclipse of the Sun*, February 7. See map on page 6. The eclipse begins at $01^h\ 38^m$ and ends at $06^h\ 12^m$; the annular phase begins at $03^h\ 24^m$ and ends at $04^h\ 27^m$. The maximum duration of the annular phase is $2^m\ 11^s$.

2. *A total eclipse of the Moon*, February 21. The umbral eclipse begins at $01^h\ 43^m$ and ends at $05^h\ 09^m$; totality lasts from $03^h\ 01^m$ to $03^h\ 51^m$. It is visible from the Arctic, western parts of Russia, most of Arabia, Africa except Madagascar, Europe and the Americas.

3. *A total eclipse of the Sun*, August 1. See map on page 7. The eclipse begins at $08^h\ 04^m$ and ends at $12^h\ 38^m$; the total phase begins at $09^h\ 23^m$ and ends at $11^h\ 20^m$. The maximum duration of totality is $2^m\ 30^s$.

4. *A partial eclipse of the Moon*, August 16. The umbral eclipse begins at $19^h\ 36^m$ and ends at $22^h\ 45^m$. The time of maximum eclipse is $21^h\ 10^m$ when 0·81 of the Moon's diameter is obscured. It is visible from Antarctica, Australasia except New Zealand, Asia except the north-eastern part, Europe, Africa and South America except the north-eastern part.

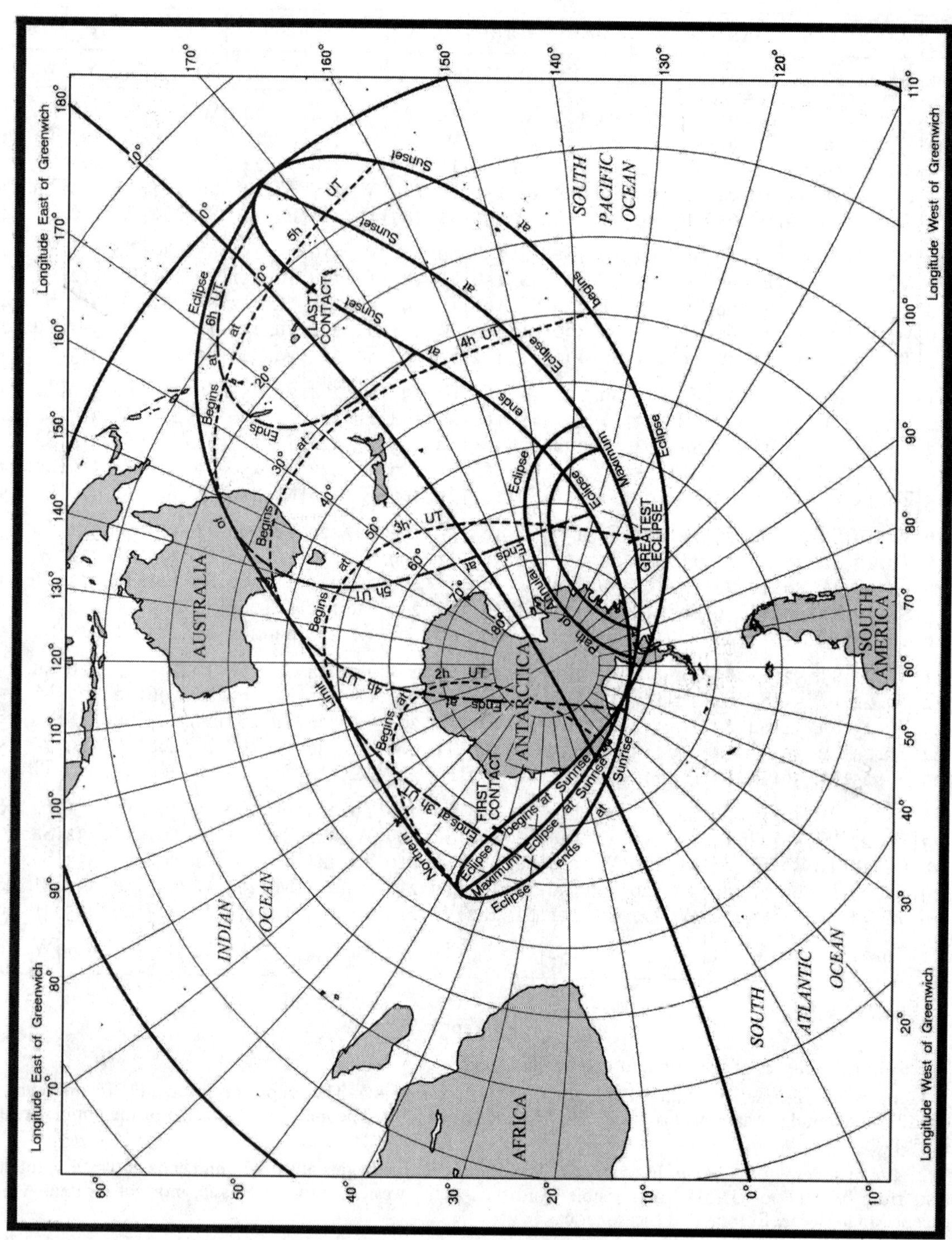

SOLAR ECLIPSE DIAGRAMS

The principal features shown on the above diagrams are: the paths of total and annular eclipses; the northern and southern limits of partial eclipse; the sunrise and sunset curves; dashed lines which show the times of beginning and end of partial eclipse at hourly intervals.

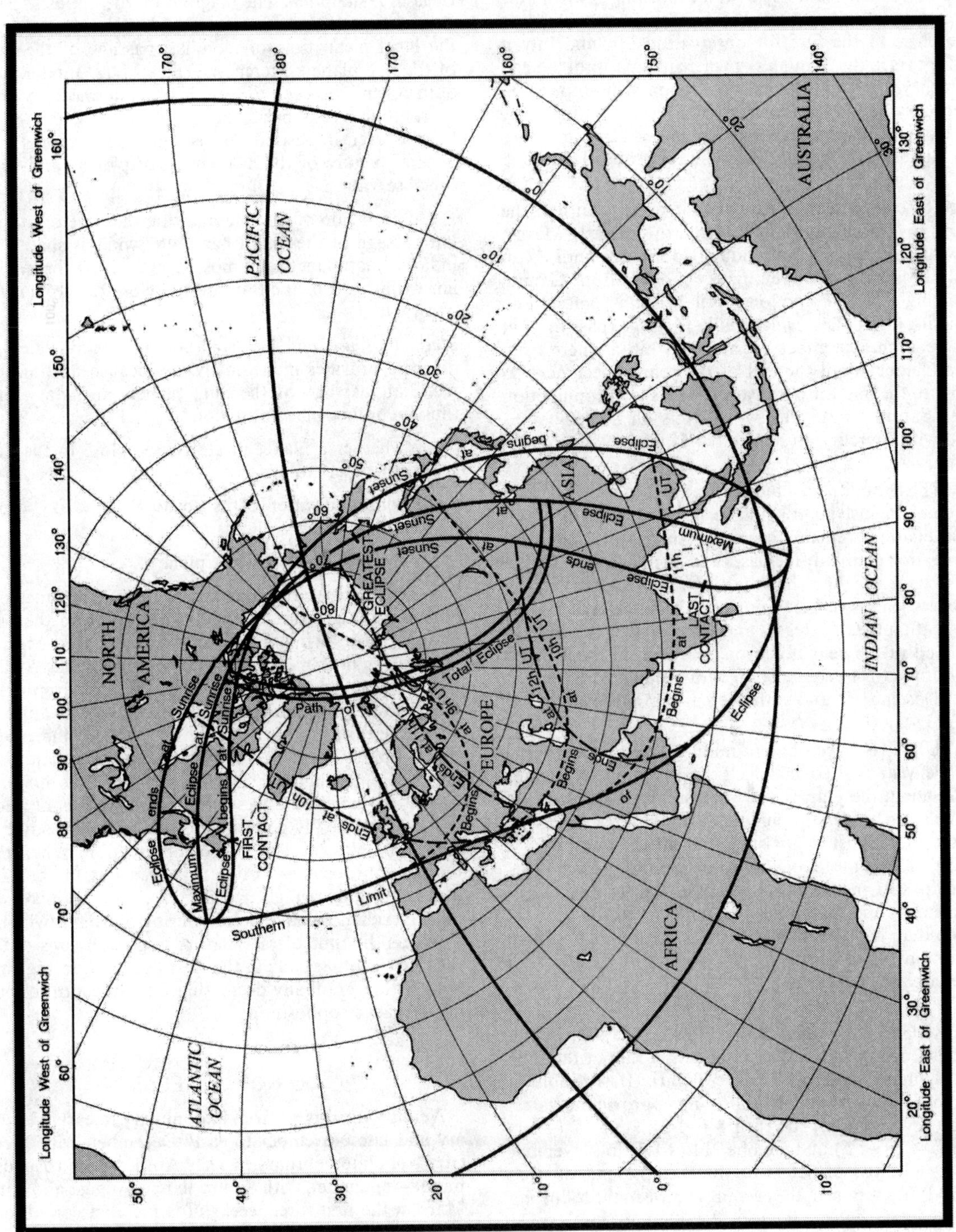

SOLAR ECLIPSE DIAGRAMS

Further details of the paths and times of central eclipse are given in *The Astronomical Almanac*.

VISIBILITY OF PLANETS

VENUS is a brilliant object in the morning sky from the beginning of the year until early May when it becomes too close to the Sun for observation. In mid-July it reappears in the evening sky where it stays until the end of the year. Venus is in conjunction with Jupiter on February 1 and December 1, with Mercury on February 26, March 23, August 23 and September 11, with Saturn on August 13 and with Mars on September 11.

MARS can be seen in January for more than half the night in Taurus and then in Gemini from early March. Its eastward elongation gradually decreases until it can only be seen in the evening sky moving from Gemini (passing 5° S of *Pollux* on April 28) into Cancer, Leo (passing 0°7 N of *Regulus* on July 1), Virgo (passing 2° N of *Spica* on September 23) and into Libra where from mid-October until the end of the year it becomes too close to the Sun for observation. Mars is in conjunction with Saturn on July 11, with Venus on September 11 and with Mercury on September 12 and 19.

JUPITER can be seen towards the end of the first week of January just before sunrise in Sagittarius in which constellation it remains throughout the year. Its westward elongation gradually increases and from mid-April it can be seen for more than half the night. It is at opposition on July 9 when it is visible throughout the night. Its eastward elongation then decreases and from early October until the end of the year it can only be seen in the evening sky. Jupiter is in conjunction with Venus on February 1 and December 1 and with Mercury on December 31.

SATURN rises well before midnight at the beginning of the year in Leo in which constellation it remains throughout the year. It is at opposition on February 24 when it can be seen throughout the night. From late May until mid-August it is visible only in the evening sky, and then becomes too close to the Sun for observation. It reappears in the morning sky in the second half of September and from mid-December it can be seen for more than half the night. Saturn is in conjunction with Mars on July 11, with Venus on August 13 and with Mercury on August 16.

MERCURY can only be seen low in the east before sunrise, or low in the west after sunset (about the time of beginning or end of civil twilight). It is visible in the mornings between the following approximate dates: February 13 (+2·2) to April 8 (−1·2), June 17 (+3·1) to July 22 (−1·5) and October 14 (+1·4) to November 10 (−0·9); the planet is brighter at the end of each period. It is visible in the evenings between the following approximate dates: January 2 (−0·9) to January 31 (+1·4), April 24 (−1·5) to May 29 (+3·1), August 8 (−1·0) to September 30 (+2·1) and December 13 (−0·8) to December 31 (−0·7); the planet is brighter at the beginning of each period. The figures in parentheses are the magnitudes.

PLANET DIAGRAM

General Description. The diagram on the opposite page shows, in graphical form for any date during the year, the local mean time of meridian passage of the Sun, of the five planets Mercury, Venus, Mars, Jupiter, and Saturn, and of each 30° of SHA; intermediate lines corresponding to particular stars, may be drawn in by the user if desired. It is intended to provide a general picture of the availability of planets and stars for observation.

On each side of the line marking the time of meridian passage of the Sun a band, 45^m wide, is shaded to indicate that planets and most stars crossing the meridian within 45^m of the Sun are too close to the Sun for observation.

Method of use and interpretation. For any date the diagram provides immediately the local mean times of meridian passage of the Sun, planets and stars, and thus the following information:

(a) whether a planet or star is too close to the Sun for observation;

(b) some indication of its position in the sky, especially during twilight;

(c) the proximity of other planets.

When the meridian passage of an outer planet occurs at midnight the body is in opposition to the Sun and is visible all night; a planet may then be observable during both morning and evening twilights. As the time of meridian passage decreases, the body eventually ceases to be observable in the morning, but its altitude above the eastern horizon at sunset gradually increases; this continues until the body is on the meridian during evening twilight. From then onwards the body is observable above the western horizon and its altitude at sunset gradually decreases; eventually the body becomes too close to the Sun for observation. When the body again becomes visible it is seen low in the east during morning twilight; its altitude at sunrise increases until meridian passage occurs during morning twilight. Then, as the time of meridian passage decreases to 0^h, the body is observable in the west during morning twilight with a gradually decreasing altitude, until it once again reaches opposition.

DO NOT CONFUSE

Venus with Jupiter from late January to early February and late November to early December, with Mercury from late February to early April and mid-August to mid-September, with Saturn in mid-August and with Mars in the first three weeks of September; on all occasions Venus is the brighter object.

Mars with Saturn for the first three weeks of July when Saturn is the brighter object.

Mercury with Saturn in mid-August and with Mars for most of September; on both occasions Mercury is the brighter object.

Jupiter with Mercury in late December when Jupiter is the brighter object.

LOCAL MEAN TIME OF MERIDIAN PASSAGE

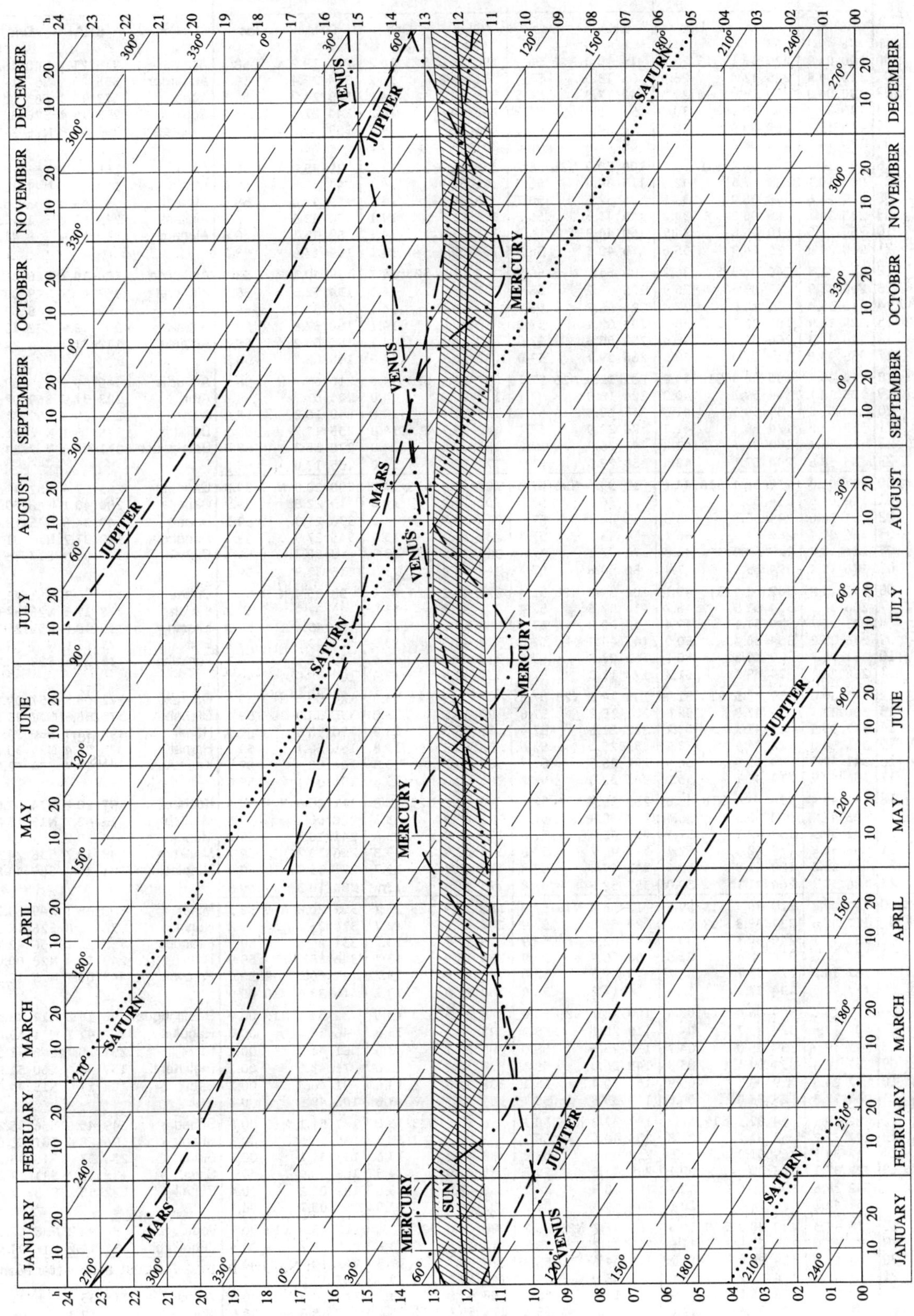

	UT	ARIES	VENUS −4.1		MARS −1.5		JUPITER −1.8		SATURN +0.6	
		GHA	GHA	Dec	GHA	Dec	GHA	Dec	GHA	Dec
	d h	° ′	° ′	° ′	° ′	° ′	° ′	° ′	° ′	° ′
	1 00	100 01.9	220 12.1	S18 28.2	10 10.0	N26 56.5	186 45.0	S23 14.2	299 19.9	N 9 58.3
	01	115 04.4	235 11.4	28.9	25 13.5	56.5	201 46.8	14.2	314 22.4	58.3
	02	130 06.8	250 10.8	29.5	40 17.0	56.5	216 48.7	14.2	329 24.9	58.3
	03	145 09.3	265 10.1	. . 30.2	55 20.5	. . 56.6	231 50.5	. . 14.2	344 27.5	. . 58.3
	04	160 11.8	280 09.5	30.9	70 24.0	56.6	246 52.3	14.2	359 30.0	58.4
	05	175 14.2	295 08.8	31.6	85 27.4	56.6	261 54.2	14.2	14 32.5	58.4
	06	190 16.7	310 08.2	S18 32.2	100 30.9	N26 56.7	276 56.0	S23 14.2	29 35.0	N 9 58.4
	07	205 19.1	325 07.5	32.9	115 34.4	56.7	291 57.9	14.1	44 37.5	58.5
T	08	220 21.6	340 06.9	33.6	130 37.8	56.7	306 59.7	14.1	59 40.0	58.5
U	09	235 24.1	355 06.2	. . 34.2	145 41.3	. . 56.8	322 01.5	. . 14.1	74 42.5	. . 58.5
E	10	250 26.5	10 05.6	34.9	160 44.8	56.8	337 03.4	14.1	89 45.1	58.6
S	11	265 29.0	25 04.9	35.6	175 48.3	56.8	352 05.2	14.1	104 47.6	58.6
D	12	280 31.5	40 04.3	S18 36.2	190 51.7	N26 56.9	7 07.1	S23 14.1	119 50.1	N 9 58.6
A	13	295 33.9	55 03.6	36.9	205 55.2	56.9	22 08.9	14.1	134 52.6	58.7
Y	14	310 36.4	70 03.0	37.6	220 58.7	56.9	37 10.8	14.1	149 55.1	58.7
	15	325 38.9	85 02.3	. . 38.2	236 02.1	. . 57.0	52 12.6	. . 14.1	164 57.6	. . 58.7
	16	340 41.3	100 01.7	38.9	251 05.6	57.0	67 14.4	14.1	180 00.2	58.8
	17	355 43.8	115 01.0	39.5	266 09.1	57.0	82 16.3	14.0	195 02.7	58.8
	18	10 46.3	130 00.3	S18 40.2	281 12.5	N26 57.1	97 18.1	S23 14.0	210 05.2	N 9 58.8
	19	25 48.7	144 59.7	40.9	296 16.0	57.1	112 20.0	14.0	225 07.7	58.8
	20	40 51.2	159 59.0	41.5	311 19.5	57.1	127 21.8	14.0	240 10.2	58.9
	21	55 53.6	174 58.4	. . 42.2	326 22.9	. . 57.1	142 23.7	. . 14.0	255 12.7	. . 58.9
	22	70 56.1	189 57.7	42.8	341 26.4	57.2	157 25.5	14.0	270 15.3	58.9
	23	85 58.6	204 57.1	43.5	356 29.8	57.2	172 27.3	14.0	285 17.8	59.0
	2 00	101 01.0	219 56.4	S18 44.1	11 33.3	N26 57.2	187 29.2	S23 14.0	300 20.3	N 9 59.0
	01	116 03.5	234 55.7	44.8	26 36.8	57.3	202 31.0	14.0	315 22.8	59.0
	02	131 06.0	249 55.1	45.5	41 40.2	57.3	217 32.9	14.0	330 25.3	59.1
	03	146 08.4	264 54.4	. . 46.1	56 43.7	. . 57.3	232 34.7	. . 13.9	345 27.9	. . 59.1
	04	161 10.9	279 53.8	46.8	71 47.1	57.4	247 36.5	13.9	0 30.4	59.1
	05	176 13.4	294 53.1	47.4	86 50.6	57.4	262 38.4	13.9	15 32.9	59.2
	06	191 15.8	309 52.4	S18 48.1	101 54.0	N26 57.4	277 40.2	S23 13.9	30 35.4	N 9 59.2
W	07	206 18.3	324 51.8	48.7	116 57.5	57.4	292 42.1	13.9	45 37.9	59.2
E	08	221 20.7	339 51.1	49.4	132 00.9	57.5	307 43.9	13.9	60 40.4	59.3
D	09	236 23.2	354 50.4	. . 50.0	147 04.4	. . 57.5	322 45.8	. . 13.9	75 43.0	. . 59.3
N	10	251 25.7	9 49.8	50.7	162 07.8	57.5	337 47.6	13.9	90 45.5	59.3
E	11	266 28.1	24 49.1	51.3	177 11.3	57.5	352 49.4	13.9	105 48.0	59.4
S	12	281 30.6	39 48.5	S18 51.9	192 14.7	N26 57.6	7 51.3	S23 13.8	120 50.5	N 9 59.4
D	13	296 33.1	54 47.8	52.6	207 18.2	57.6	22 53.1	13.8	135 53.0	59.4
A	14	311 35.5	69 47.1	53.2	222 21.6	57.6	37 55.0	13.8	150 55.6	59.5
Y	15	326 38.0	84 46.5	. . 53.9	237 25.1	. . 57.6	52 56.8	. . 13.8	165 58.1	. . 59.5
	16	341 40.5	99 45.8	54.5	252 28.5	57.7	67 58.7	13.8	181 00.6	59.5
	17	356 42.9	114 45.1	55.2	267 32.0	57.7	83 00.5	13.8	196 03.1	59.6
	18	11 45.4	129 44.4	S18 55.8	282 35.4	N26 57.7	98 02.3	S23 13.8	211 05.6	N 9 59.6
	19	26 47.9	144 43.8	56.4	297 38.9	57.7	113 04.2	13.8	226 08.2	59.6
	20	41 50.3	159 43.1	57.1	312 42.3	57.8	128 06.0	13.8	241 10.7	59.7
	21	56 52.8	174 42.4	. . 57.7	327 45.7	. . 57.8	143 07.9	. . 13.8	256 13.2	. . 59.7
	22	71 55.2	189 41.8	58.4	342 49.2	57.8	158 09.7	13.7	271 15.7	59.7
	23	86 57.7	204 41.1	59.0	357 52.6	57.8	173 11.6	13.7	286 18.3	59.8
	3 00	102 00.2	219 40.4	S18 59.6	12 56.0	N26 57.9	188 13.4	S23 13.7	301 20.8	N 9 59.8
	01	117 02.6	234 39.8	19 00.3	27 59.5	57.9	203 15.2	13.7	316 23.3	59.8
	02	132 05.1	249 39.1	00.9	43 02.9	57.9	218 17.1	13.7	331 25.8	59.9
	03	147 07.6	264 38.4	. . 01.5	58 06.4	. . 57.9	233 18.9	. . 13.7	346 28.3	. . 59.9
	04	162 10.0	279 37.7	02.2	73 09.8	58.0	248 20.8	13.7	1 30.9	9 59.9
	05	177 12.5	294 37.1	02.8	88 13.2	58.0	263 22.6	13.7	16 33.4	10 00.0
	06	192 15.0	309 36.4	S19 03.4	103 16.7	N26 58.0	278 24.5	S23 13.6	31 35.9	N10 00.0
	07	207 17.4	324 35.7	04.1	118 20.1	58.0	293 26.3	13.6	46 38.4	00.0
T	08	222 19.9	339 35.0	04.7	133 23.5	58.0	308 28.1	13.6	61 41.0	00.1
H	09	237 22.4	354 34.4	. . 05.3	148 26.9	. . 58.1	323 30.0	. . 13.6	76 43.5	. . 00.1
U	10	252 24.8	9 33.7	05.9	163 30.4	58.1	338 31.8	13.6	91 46.0	00.1
R	11	267 27.3	24 33.0	06.6	178 33.8	58.1	353 33.7	13.6	106 48.5	00.2
S	12	282 29.7	39 32.3	S19 07.2	193 37.2	N26 58.1	8 35.5	S23 13.6	121 51.1	N10 00.2
D	13	297 32.2	54 31.7	07.8	208 40.6	58.1	23 37.4	13.6	136 53.6	00.3
A	14	312 34.7	69 31.0	08.5	223 44.1	58.2	38 39.2	13.6	151 56.1	00.3
Y	15	327 37.1	84 30.3	. . 09.1	238 47.5	. . 58.2	53 41.0	. . 13.5	166 58.6	. . 00.3
	16	342 39.6	99 29.6	09.7	253 50.9	58.2	68 42.9	13.5	182 01.2	00.4
	17	357 42.1	114 28.9	10.3	268 54.3	58.2	83 44.7	13.5	197 03.7	00.4
	18	12 44.5	129 28.3	S19 10.9	283 57.7	N26 58.2	98 46.6	S23 13.5	212 06.2	N10 00.4
	19	27 47.0	144 27.6	11.6	299 01.2	58.3	113 48.4	13.5	227 08.7	00.5
	20	42 49.5	159 26.9	12.2	314 04.6	58.3	128 50.3	13.5	242 11.3	00.5
	21	57 51.9	174 26.2	. . 12.8	329 08.0	. . 58.3	143 52.1	. . 13.5	257 13.8	. . 00.5
	22	72 54.4	189 25.5	13.4	344 11.4	58.3	158 53.9	13.5	272 16.3	00.6
	23	87 56.9	204 24.8	14.0	359 14.8	58.3	173 55.8	13.4	287 18.8	00.6
	Mer. Pass.	h m 17 13.1	v −0.7	d 0.6	v 3.4	d 0.0	v 1.8	d 0.0	v 2.5	d 0.0

STARS		
Name	SHA	Dec
	° ′	° ′
Acamar	315 21.1	S40 16.5
Achernar	335 29.4	S57 12.0
Acrux	173 14.3	S63 08.4
Adhara	255 15.4	S28 58.9
Aldebaran	290 53.8	N16 31.7
Alioth	166 24.1	N55 54.6
Alkaid	153 02.1	N49 16.0
Al Na'ir	27 49.0	S46 55.5
Alnilam	275 50.2	S 1 11.7
Alphard	217 59.9	S 8 41.6
Alphecca	126 14.7	N26 41.0
Alpheratz	357 47.9	N29 08.3
Altair	62 12.6	N 8 53.3
Ankaa	353 19.6	S42 15.9
Antares	112 31.7	S26 27.0
Arcturus	145 59.6	N19 08.2
Atria	107 37.9	S69 02.5
Avior	234 19.3	S59 31.9
Bellatrix	278 36.1	N 6 21.5
Betelgeuse	271 05.4	N 7 24.6
Canopus	263 57.4	S52 41.9
Capella	280 40.1	N46 00.5
Deneb	49 34.8	N45 18.6
Denebola	182 37.7	N14 31.5
Diphda	349 00.0	S17 56.6
Dubhe	193 56.1	N61 42.1
Elnath	278 17.5	N28 37.0
Eltanin	90 48.6	N51 29.1
Enif	33 51.5	N 9 54.7
Fomalhaut	15 28.6	S29 34.9
Gacrux	172 05.8	S57 09.3
Gienah	175 56.6	S17 35.2
Hadar	148 54.3	S60 24.5
Hamal	328 05.4	N23 30.2
Kaus Aust.	83 49.7	S34 22.9
Kochab	137 20.0	N74 07.0
Markab	13 42.7	N15 15.0
Menkar	314 19.2	N 4 07.4
Menkent	148 12.7	S36 24.5
Miaplacidus	221 40.2	S69 44.8
Mirfak	308 46.1	N49 53.7
Nunki	76 03.8	S26 17.3
Peacock	53 26.1	S56 42.7
Pollux	243 32.4	N28 00.4
Procyon	245 03.7	N 5 12.3
Rasalhague	96 10.6	N12 33.1
Regulus	207 47.7	N11 55.6
Rigel	281 15.7	S 8 11.5
Rigil Kent.	139 58.0	S60 51.9
Sabik	102 17.6	S15 44.2
Schedar	349 45.6	N56 35.2
Shaula	96 28.0	S37 06.6
Sirius	258 37.0	S16 43.6
Spica	158 35.7	S11 12.2
Suhail	222 55.2	S43 27.7
Vega	80 42.2	N38 47.3
Zuben'ubi	137 10.2	S16 04.5

	SHA	Mer. Pass.
	° ′	h m
Venus	118 55.4	9 21
Mars	270 32.3	23 08
Jupiter	86 28.1	11 29
Saturn	199 19.3	3 58

UT d h	SUN GHA ° ′	SUN Dec ° ′	MOON GHA ° ′	v ′	MOON Dec ° ′	d ′	HP ′
1 00 (TUESDAY)	179 13.8	S23 04.1	265 32.6	16.2	S10 20.8	13.2	54.5
01	194 13.5	04.0	280 07.8	16.1	10 34.0	13.1	54.5
02	209 13.2	03.8	294 42.9	16.1	10 47.1	13.0	54.5
03	224 12.9	. . 03.6	309 18.0	16.1	11 00.1	13.0	54.5
04	239 12.6	03.4	323 53.1	16.1	11 13.1	13.0	54.5
05	254 12.3	03.2	338 28.2	16.0	11 26.1	12.9	54.5
06	269 12.0	S23 03.0	353 03.2	16.0	S11 39.0	12.8	54.5
07	284 11.7	02.8	7 38.2	16.0	11 51.8	12.8	54.4
08	299 11.4	02.6	22 13.2	15.9	12 04.6	12.8	54.4
09	314 11.1	. . 02.4	36 48.1	15.9	12 17.4	12.7	54.4
10	329 10.8	02.2	51 23.0	15.9	12 30.1	12.6	54.4
11	344 10.5	02.0	65 57.9	15.8	12 42.7	12.6	54.4
12	359 10.2	S23 01.8	80 32.7	15.8	S12 55.3	12.6	54.4
13	14 09.9	01.6	95 07.5	15.8	13 07.9	12.4	54.4
14	29 09.6	01.4	109 42.3	15.8	13 20.3	12.5	54.3
15	44 09.3	. . 01.2	124 17.1	15.7	13 32.8	12.4	54.3
16	59 09.0	01.0	138 51.8	15.6	13 45.2	12.3	54.3
17	74 08.7	00.8	153 26.4	15.6	13 57.5	12.2	54.3
18	89 08.4	S23 00.6	168 01.0	15.6	S14 09.7	12.2	54.3
19	104 08.1	00.4	182 35.6	15.6	14 21.9	12.2	54.3
20	119 07.8	00.2	197 10.2	15.5	14 34.1	12.1	54.3
21	134 07.5	23 00.0	211 44.7	15.4	14 46.2	12.0	54.3
22	149 07.2	22 59.8	226 19.1	15.4	14 58.2	12.0	54.3
23	164 06.9	59.6	240 53.5	15.4	15 10.2	11.9	54.2
2 00 (WEDNESDAY)	179 06.6	S22 59.4	255 27.9	15.3	S15 22.1	11.8	54.2
01	194 06.3	59.1	270 02.2	15.3	15 33.9	11.8	54.2
02	209 06.0	58.9	284 36.5	15.2	15 45.7	11.7	54.2
03	224 05.8	. . 58.7	299 10.7	15.2	15 57.4	11.6	54.2
04	239 05.5	58.5	313 44.9	15.1	16 09.0	11.6	54.2
05	254 05.2	58.3	328 19.0	15.1	16 20.6	11.5	54.2
06	269 04.9	S22 58.1	342 53.1	15.0	S16 32.1	11.5	54.2
07	284 04.6	57.9	357 27.1	15.0	16 43.6	11.4	54.2
08	299 04.3	57.7	12 01.1	14.9	16 55.0	11.3	54.2
09	314 04.0	. . 57.4	26 35.0	14.9	17 06.3	11.2	54.2
10	329 03.7	57.2	41 08.9	14.8	17 17.5	11.2	54.2
11	344 03.4	57.0	55 42.7	14.8	17 28.7	11.1	54.2
12	359 03.1	S22 56.8	70 16.5	14.7	S17 39.8	11.1	54.2
13	14 02.8	56.6	84 50.2	14.7	17 50.9	10.9	54.1
14	29 02.5	56.3	99 23.9	14.5	18 01.8	10.9	54.1
15	44 02.2	. . 56.1	113 57.4	14.6	18 12.7	10.8	54.1
16	59 01.9	55.9	128 31.0	14.5	18 23.5	10.8	54.1
17	74 01.6	55.7	143 04.5	14.4	18 34.3	10.7	54.1
18	89 01.4	S22 55.5	157 37.9	14.4	S18 45.0	10.6	54.1
19	104 01.1	55.2	172 11.3	14.3	18 55.6	10.5	54.1
20	119 00.8	55.0	186 44.6	14.2	19 06.1	10.4	54.1
21	134 00.5	. . 54.8	201 17.8	14.2	19 16.5	10.4	54.1
22	149 00.2	54.6	215 51.0	14.1	19 26.9	10.3	54.1
23	163 59.9	54.3	230 24.1	14.1	19 37.2	10.2	54.1
3 00 (THURSDAY)	178 59.6	S22 54.1	244 57.2	14.0	S19 47.4	10.1	54.1
01	193 59.3	53.9	259 30.2	13.9	19 57.5	10.0	54.1
02	208 59.0	53.6	274 03.1	13.9	20 07.5	10.0	54.1
03	223 58.7	. . 53.4	288 36.0	13.8	20 17.5	9.9	54.1
04	238 58.4	53.2	303 08.8	13.7	20 27.4	9.8	54.1
05	253 58.1	53.0	317 41.5	13.7	20 37.2	9.7	54.1
06	268 57.9	S22 52.7	332 14.2	13.6	S20 46.9	9.6	54.1
07	283 57.6	52.5	346 46.8	13.6	20 56.5	9.5	54.1
08	298 57.3	52.3	1 19.4	13.4	21 06.0	9.5	54.1
09	313 57.0	. . 52.0	15 51.8	13.5	21 15.5	9.4	54.1
10	328 56.7	51.8	30 24.3	13.3	21 24.9	9.2	54.1
11	343 56.4	51.5	44 56.6	13.3	21 34.1	9.2	54.1
12	358 56.1	S22 51.3	59 28.9	13.2	S21 43.3	9.1	54.1
13	13 55.8	51.1	74 01.1	13.1	21 52.4	9.0	54.1
14	28 55.5	50.8	88 33.2	13.1	22 01.4	8.9	54.1
15	43 55.2	. . 50.6	103 05.3	13.0	22 10.3	8.8	54.1
16	58 55.0	50.4	117 37.3	12.9	22 19.1	8.8	54.1
17	73 54.7	50.1	132 09.2	12.9	22 27.9	8.6	54.1
18	88 54.4	S22 49.9	146 41.1	12.8	S22 36.5	8.5	54.1
19	103 54.1	49.6	161 12.9	12.7	22 45.0	8.5	54.1
20	118 53.8	49.4	175 44.6	12.7	22 53.5	8.3	54.1
21	133 53.5	. . 49.1	190 16.3	12.6	23 01.8	8.3	54.1
22	148 53.2	48.9	204 47.9	12.5	23 10.1	8.1	54.1
23	163 52.9	48.6	219 19.4	12.4	S23 18.2	8.0	54.1
	SD 16.3	*d* 0.2	SD 14.8		14.8		14.7

Lat. °	Twilight Naut. h m	Twilight Civil h m	Sunrise h m	Moonrise 1 h m	Moonrise 2 h m	Moonrise 3 h m	Moonrise 4 h m
N 72	08 24	10 41	■	02 51	05 32	■	■
N 70	08 05	09 49	■	02 31	04 42	■	■
68	07 50	09 16	■	02 16	04 10	06 39	■
66	07 37	08 53	10 27	02 04	03 48	05 46	■
64	07 27	08 34	09 49	01 54	03 30	05 14	07 14
62	07 17	08 19	09 23	01 45	03 15	04 50	06 31
60	07 09	08 05	09 02	01 38	03 03	04 31	06 02
N 58	07 02	07 54	08 45	01 31	02 53	04 16	05 40
56	06 56	07 44	08 31	01 26	02 44	04 03	05 22
54	06 50	07 36	08 19	01 21	02 35	03 51	05 07
52	06 44	07 28	08 08	01 16	02 28	03 41	04 54
50	06 39	07 20	07 59	01 12	02 22	03 32	04 43
45	06 28	07 05	07 38	01 03	02 08	03 14	04 19
N 40	06 18	06 52	07 22	00 56	01 57	02 58	04 00
35	06 09	06 40	07 08	00 50	01 47	02 46	03 45
30	06 00	06 30	06 56	00 44	01 39	02 34	03 31
20	05 44	06 11	06 35	00 35	01 24	02 15	03 08
N 10	05 28	05 54	06 17	00 26	01 12	01 59	02 48
0	05 11	05 38	06 00	00 19	01 00	01 44	02 30
S 10	04 53	05 20	05 43	00 11	00 49	01 28	02 11
20	04 31	05 00	05 24	00 03	00 36	01 12	01 52
30	04 02	04 35	05 03	24 23	00 23	00 54	01 29
35	03 44	04 20	04 50	24 14	00 14	00 43	01 16
40	03 21	04 03	04 35	24 05	00 05	00 31	01 01
45	02 52	03 41	04 18	23 55	24 17	00 17	00 43
S 50	02 08	03 12	03 56	23 42	23 59	24 21	00 21
52	01 42	02 57	03 45	23 36	23 51	24 11	00 11
54	01 02	02 40	03 33	23 30	23 42	23 59	24 23
56	////	02 18	03 19	23 22	23 32	23 45	24 06
58	////	01 51	03 03	23 14	23 20	23 30	23 46
S 60	////	01 07	02 44	23 05	23 07	23 11	23 20

Lat. °	Sunset h m	Twilight Civil h m	Twilight Naut. h m	Moonset 1 h m	Moonset 2 h m	Moonset 3 h m	Moonset 4 h m
N 72	■	13 27	15 44	09 41	08 28	■	■
N 70	■	14 19	16 03	10 03	09 20	■	■
68	■	14 51	16 18	10 20	09 52	08 56	■
66	13 41	15 15	16 31	10 34	10 16	09 50	■
64	14 19	15 34	16 41	10 45	10 35	10 23	09 59
62	14 45	15 49	16 51	10 55	10 51	10 47	10 43
60	15 06	16 02	16 59	11 03	11 04	11 06	11 12
N 58	15 22	16 14	17 06	11 11	11 15	11 22	11 34
56	15 37	16 23	17 12	11 17	11 25	11 36	11 53
54	15 49	16 32	17 18	11 23	11 34	11 48	12 08
52	16 00	16 40	17 24	11 29	11 42	11 59	12 22
50	16 09	16 47	17 29	11 33	11 49	12 08	12 33
45	16 29	17 03	17 40	11 44	12 04	12 28	12 58
N 40	16 46	17 16	17 50	11 53	12 17	12 44	13 17
35	17 00	17 28	17 59	12 00	12 27	12 58	13 34
30	17 12	17 38	18 08	12 07	12 37	13 10	13 48
20	17 32	17 56	18 24	12 19	12 53	13 31	14 12
N 10	17 50	18 13	18 39	12 29	13 07	13 49	14 33
0	18 08	18 30	18 56	12 39	13 21	14 06	14 53
S 10	18 25	18 48	19 15	12 48	13 34	14 22	15 13
20	18 43	19 08	19 37	12 59	13 49	14 41	15 34
30	19 05	19 32	20 05	13 10	14 05	15 02	15 59
35	19 17	19 47	20 23	13 17	14 15	15 14	16 13
40	19 32	20 05	20 46	13 25	14 26	15 28	16 30
45	19 50	20 27	21 16	13 34	14 40	15 45	16 50
S 50	20 12	20 55	21 59	13 46	14 56	16 06	17 16
52	20 22	21 10	22 25	13 51	15 03	16 16	17 28
54	20 34	21 27	23 04	13 57	15 12	16 28	17 42
56	20 48	21 48	////	14 03	15 21	16 41	17 59
58	21 04	22 16	////	14 10	15 32	16 56	18 19
S 60	21 23	22 58	////	14 18	15 45	17 14	18 44

Day	SUN Eqn. of Time 00^h	SUN Eqn. of Time 12^h	SUN Mer. Pass.	MOON Mer. Pass. Upper	MOON Mer. Pass. Lower	MOON Age	MOON Phase
d	m s	m s	h m	h m	h m	d	%
1	03 04	03 19	12 03	06 29	18 49	23	39
2	03 33	03 47	12 04	07 10	19 32	24	30
3	04 01	04 15	12 04	07 55	20 18	25	22

UT	ARIES	VENUS −4.0		MARS −1.4		JUPITER −1.8		SATURN +0.6		STARS		
	GHA	GHA	Dec	GHA	Dec	GHA	Dec	GHA	Dec	Name	SHA	Dec
d h	° ′	° ′	° ′	° ′	° ′	° ′	° ′	° ′	° ′		° ′	° ′
4 00	102 59.3	219 24.2	S19 14.6	14 18.2	N26 58.3	188 57.6	S23 13.4	302 21.4	N10 00.6	Acamar	315 21.1	S40 16.5
01	118 01.8	234 23.5	15.3	29 21.7	58.4	203 59.5	13.4	317 23.9	00.7	Achernar	335 29.4	S57 12.0
02	133 04.2	249 22.8	15.9	44 25.1	58.4	219 01.3	13.4	332 26.4	00.7	Acrux	173 14.2	S63 08.4
03	148 06.7	264 22.1	. . 16.5	59 28.5	. . 58.4	234 03.2	. . 13.4	347 28.9	. . 00.7	Adhara	255 15.4	S28 58.9
04	163 09.2	279 21.4	17.1	74 31.9	58.4	249 05.0	13.4	2 31.5	00.8	Aldebaran	290 53.8	N16 31.6
05	178 11.6	294 20.7	17.7	89 35.3	58.4	264 06.8	13.4	17 34.0	00.8			
06	193 14.1	309 20.0	S19 18.3	104 38.7	N26 58.4	279 08.7	S23 13.4	32 36.5	N10 00.9	Alioth	166 24.0	N55 54.6
07	208 16.6	324 19.4	18.9	119 42.1	58.5	294 10.5	13.3	47 39.0	00.9	Alkaid	153 02.1	N49 16.0
08	223 19.0	339 18.7	19.5	134 45.5	58.5	309 12.4	13.3	62 41.6	00.9	Al Na'ir	27 49.0	S46 55.5
F 09	238 21.5	354 18.0	. . 20.1	149 48.9	. . 58.5	324 14.2	. . 13.3	77 44.1	. . 01.0	Alnilam	275 50.2	S 1 11.7
R 10	253 24.0	9 17.3	20.8	164 52.3	58.5	339 16.1	13.3	92 46.6	01.0	Alphard	217 59.9	S 8 41.6
I 11	268 26.4	24 16.6	21.4	179 55.7	58.5	354 17.9	13.3	107 49.2	01.0			
D 12	283 28.9	39 15.9	S19 22.0	194 59.1	N26 58.5	9 19.8	S23 13.3	122 51.7	N10 01.1	Alphecca	126 14.7	N26 41.0
A 13	298 31.3	54 15.2	22.6	210 02.5	58.6	24 21.6	13.3	137 54.2	01.1	Alpheratz	357 48.0	N29 08.3
Y 14	313 33.8	69 14.5	23.2	225 05.9	58.6	39 23.4	13.3	152 56.7	01.1	Altair	62 12.6	N 8 53.3
15	328 36.3	84 13.8	. . 23.8	240 09.3	. . 58.6	54 25.3	. . 13.2	167 59.3	. . 01.2	Ankaa	353 19.6	S42 15.9
16	343 38.7	99 13.2	24.4	255 12.7	58.6	69 27.1	13.2	183 01.8	01.2	Antares	112 31.7	S26 27.0
17	358 41.2	114 12.5	25.0	270 16.1	58.6	84 29.0	13.2	198 04.3	01.3			
18	13 43.7	129 11.8	S19 25.6	285 19.5	N26 58.6	99 30.8	S23 13.2	213 06.9	N10 01.3	Arcturus	145 59.6	N19 08.2
19	28 46.1	144 11.1	26.2	300 22.9	58.6	114 32.7	13.2	228 09.4	01.3	Atria	107 37.9	S69 02.5
20	43 48.6	159 10.4	26.8	315 26.3	58.6	129 34.5	13.2	243 11.9	01.4	Avior	234 19.3	S59 32.0
21	58 51.1	174 09.7	. . 27.4	330 29.7	. . 58.7	144 36.3	. . 13.2	258 14.5	. . 01.4	Bellatrix	278 36.1	N 6 21.5
22	73 53.5	189 09.0	28.0	345 33.1	58.7	159 38.2	13.2	273 17.0	01.4	Betelgeuse	271 05.4	N 7 24.6
23	88 56.0	204 08.3	28.6	0 36.5	58.7	174 40.0	13.1	288 19.5	01.5			
5 00	103 58.5	219 07.6	S19 29.2	15 39.8	N26 58.7	189 41.9	S23 13.1	303 22.0	N10 01.5	Canopus	263 57.4	S52 42.0
01	119 00.9	234 06.9	29.8	30 43.2	58.7	204 43.7	13.1	318 24.6	01.5	Capella	280 40.1	N46 00.5
02	134 03.4	249 06.2	30.4	45 46.6	58.7	219 45.6	13.1	333 27.1	01.6	Deneb	49 34.8	N45 18.6
03	149 05.8	264 05.5	. . 30.9	60 50.0	. . 58.7	234 47.4	. . 13.1	348 29.6	. . 01.6	Denebola	182 37.7	N14 31.5
04	164 08.3	279 04.8	31.5	75 53.4	58.7	249 49.3	13.1	3 32.2	01.7	Diphda	349 00.0	S17 56.6
05	179 10.8	294 04.1	32.1	90 56.8	58.7	264 51.1	13.1	18 34.7	01.7			
06	194 13.2	309 03.4	S19 32.7	106 00.1	N26 58.8	279 52.9	S23 13.0	33 37.2	N10 01.7	Dubhe	193 56.0	N61 42.1
S 07	209 15.7	324 02.7	33.3	121 03.5	58.8	294 54.8	13.0	48 39.8	01.8	Elnath	278 17.5	N28 37.0
08	224 18.2	339 02.0	33.9	136 06.9	58.8	309 56.6	13.0	63 42.3	01.8	Eltanin	90 48.6	N51 29.1
A 09	239 20.6	354 01.3	. . 34.5	151 10.3	. . 58.8	324 58.5	. . 13.0	78 44.8	. . 01.8	Enif	33 51.5	N 9 54.7
T 10	254 23.1	9 00.6	35.1	166 13.6	58.8	340 00.3	13.0	93 47.4	01.9	Fomalhaut	15 28.6	S29 34.9
U 11	269 25.6	23 59.9	35.7	181 17.0	58.8	355 02.2	13.0	108 49.9	01.9			
R 12	284 28.0	38 59.2	S19 36.2	196 20.4	N26 58.8	10 04.0	S23 13.0	123 52.4	N10 02.0	Gacrux	172 05.8	S57 09.3
D 13	299 30.5	53 58.5	36.8	211 23.8	58.8	25 05.9	13.0	138 55.0	02.0	Gienah	175 56.6	S17 35.2
A 14	314 33.0	68 57.8	37.4	226 27.1	58.8	40 07.7	12.9	153 57.5	02.0	Hadar	148 54.3	S60 24.5
Y 15	329 35.4	83 57.1	. . 38.0	241 30.5	. . 58.8	55 09.5	. . 12.9	169 00.0	. . 02.1	Hamal	328 05.4	N23 30.2
16	344 37.9	98 56.4	38.6	256 33.9	58.8	70 11.4	12.9	184 02.6	02.1	Kaus Aust.	83 49.7	S34 22.9
17	359 40.3	113 55.7	39.2	271 37.3	58.9	85 13.2	12.9	199 05.1	02.1			
18	14 42.8	128 55.0	S19 39.7	286 40.6	N26 58.9	100 15.1	S23 12.9	214 07.6	N10 02.2	Kochab	137 20.0	N74 06.9
19	29 45.3	143 54.3	40.3	301 44.0	58.9	115 16.9	12.9	229 10.2	02.2	Markab	13 42.7	N15 15.0
20	44 47.7	158 53.6	40.9	316 47.3	58.9	130 18.8	12.9	244 12.7	02.3	Menkar	314 19.2	N 4 07.4
21	59 50.2	173 52.9	. . 41.5	331 50.7	. . 58.9	145 20.6	. . 12.8	259 15.2	. . 02.3	Menkent	148 12.7	S36 24.5
22	74 52.7	188 52.2	42.0	346 54.1	58.9	160 22.5	12.8	274 17.8	02.3	Miaplacidus	221 40.1	S69 44.8
23	89 55.1	203 51.5	42.6	1 57.4	58.9	175 24.3	12.8	289 20.3	02.4			
6 00	104 57.6	218 50.8	S19 43.2	17 00.8	N26 58.9	190 26.1	S23 12.8	304 22.8	N10 02.4	Mirfak	308 46.1	N49 53.7
01	120 00.1	233 50.1	43.8	32 04.2	58.9	205 28.0	12.8	319 25.4	02.5	Nunki	76 03.8	S26 17.3
02	135 02.5	248 49.4	44.3	47 07.5	58.9	220 29.8	12.8	334 27.9	02.5	Peacock	53 26.1	S56 42.7
03	150 05.0	263 48.6	. . 44.9	62 10.9	. . 58.9	235 31.7	. . 12.8	349 30.4	. . 02.5	Pollux	243 32.3	N28 00.4
04	165 07.5	278 47.9	45.5	77 14.2	58.9	250 33.5	12.7	4 33.0	02.6	Procyon	245 03.7	N 5 12.3
05	180 09.9	293 47.2	46.0	92 17.6	58.9	265 35.4	12.7	19 35.5	02.6			
06	195 12.4	308 46.5	S19 46.6	107 20.9	N26 58.9	280 37.2	S23 12.7	34 38.0	N10 02.7	Rasalhague	96 10.6	N12 33.1
07	210 14.8	323 45.8	47.2	122 24.3	58.9	295 39.1	12.7	49 40.6	02.7	Regulus	207 47.6	N11 55.6
08	225 17.3	338 45.1	47.7	137 27.6	58.9	310 40.9	12.7	64 43.1	02.7	Rigel	281 15.7	S 8 11.5
S 09	240 19.8	353 44.4	. . 48.3	152 31.0	. . 58.9	325 42.8	. . 12.7	79 45.6	. . 02.8	Rigil Kent.	139 58.0	S60 51.9
U 10	255 22.2	8 43.7	48.9	167 34.3	58.9	340 44.6	12.7	94 48.2	02.8	Sabik	102 17.6	S15 44.2
N 11	270 24.7	23 43.0	49.4	182 37.7	59.0	355 46.4	12.6	109 50.7	02.8			
D 12	285 27.2	38 42.2	S19 50.0	197 41.0	N26 59.0	10 48.3	S23 12.6	124 53.3	N10 02.9	Schedar	349 45.6	N56 35.2
A 13	300 29.6	53 41.5	50.6	212 44.4	59.0	25 50.1	12.6	139 55.8	02.9	Shaula	96 27.9	S37 06.6
Y 14	315 32.1	68 40.8	51.1	227 47.7	59.0	40 52.0	12.6	154 58.3	03.0	Sirius	258 37.0	S16 43.6
15	330 34.6	83 40.1	. . 51.7	242 51.1	. . 59.0	55 53.8	. . 12.6	170 00.9	. . 03.0	Spica	158 35.7	S11 12.2
16	345 37.0	98 39.4	52.2	257 54.4	59.0	70 55.7	12.6	185 03.4	03.0	Suhail	222 55.2	S43 27.8
17	0 39.5	113 38.7	52.8	272 57.7	59.0	85 57.5	12.6	200 05.9	03.1			
18	15 42.0	128 38.0	S19 53.4	288 01.1	N26 59.0	100 59.4	S23 12.5	215 08.5	N10 03.1	Vega	80 42.2	N38 47.3
19	30 44.4	143 37.2	53.9	303 04.4	59.0	116 01.2	12.5	230 11.0	03.2	Zuben'ubi	137 10.2	S16 04.6
20	45 46.9	158 36.5	54.5	318 07.7	59.0	131 03.1	12.5	245 13.5	03.2		SHA	Mer. Pass.
21	60 49.3	173 35.8	. . 55.0	333 11.1	. . 59.0	146 04.9	. . 12.5	260 16.1	. . 03.2		° ′	h m
22	75 51.8	188 35.1	55.6	348 14.4	59.0	161 06.7	12.5	275 18.6	03.3	Venus	115 09.2	9 24
23	90 54.3	203 34.4	56.1	3 17.7	59.0	176 08.6	12.5	290 21.2	03.3	Mars	271 41.4	22 52
Mer. Pass.	h m 17 01.3	v −0.7	d 0.6	v 3.4	d 0.0	v 1.8	d 0.0	v 2.5	d 0.0	Jupiter	85 43.4	11 20
										Saturn	199 23.6	3 46

UT		SUN GHA	SUN Dec	MOON GHA	v	MOON Dec	d	HP
d	h	° ′	° ′	° ′	′	° ′	′	′
4	00	178 52.6	S22 48.4	233 50.8	12.4	S23 26.2	8.0	54.1
	01	193 52.4	48.2	248 22.2	12.3	23 34.2	7.8	54.1
	02	208 52.1	47.9	262 53.5	12.2	23 42.0	7.8	54.1
	03	223 51.8	. . 47.7	277 24.7	12.2	23 49.8	7.6	54.1
	04	238 51.5	47.4	291 55.9	12.1	23 57.4	7.5	54.1
	05	253 51.2	47.2	306 27.0	12.0	24 04.9	7.5	54.2
	06	268 50.9	S22 46.9	320 58.0	12.0	S24 12.4	7.3	54.2
	07	283 50.6	46.7	335 29.0	11.9	24 19.7	7.2	54.2
	08	298 50.3	46.4	349 59.9	11.8	24 26.9	7.1	54.2
FRIDAY	09	313 50.1	. . 46.1	4 30.7	11.7	24 34.0	7.0	54.2
	10	328 49.8	45.9	19 01.4	11.7	24 41.0	6.9	54.2
	11	343 49.5	45.6	33 32.1	11.6	24 47.9	6.8	54.2
	12	358 49.2	S22 45.4	48 02.7	11.6	S24 54.7	6.6	54.2
	13	13 48.9	45.1	62 33.3	11.4	25 01.3	6.6	54.2
	14	28 48.6	44.9	77 03.7	11.4	25 07.9	6.4	54.2
	15	43 48.3	. . 44.6	91 34.1	11.4	25 14.3	6.4	54.2
	16	58 48.1	44.3	106 04.5	11.2	25 20.7	6.2	54.2
	17	73 47.8	44.1	120 34.7	11.2	25 26.9	6.1	54.2
	18	88 47.5	S22 43.8	135 04.9	11.2	S25 33.0	6.0	54.2
	19	103 47.2	43.6	149 35.1	11.0	25 39.0	5.8	54.2
	20	118 46.9	43.3	164 05.1	11.0	25 44.8	5.8	54.3
	21	133 46.6	. . 43.0	178 35.1	11.0	25 50.6	5.6	54.3
	22	148 46.3	42.8	193 05.1	10.8	25 56.2	5.5	54.3
	23	163 46.1	42.5	207 34.9	10.8	26 01.7	5.4	54.3
5	00	178 45.8	S22 42.2	222 04.7	10.8	S26 07.1	5.3	54.3
	01	193 45.5	42.0	236 34.5	10.6	26 12.4	5.2	54.3
	02	208 45.2	41.7	251 04.1	10.6	26 17.6	5.0	54.3
	03	223 44.9	. . 41.4	265 33.7	10.6	26 22.6	4.9	54.3
	04	238 44.6	41.2	280 03.3	10.5	26 27.5	4.8	54.3
	05	253 44.4	40.9	294 32.8	10.4	26 32.3	4.6	54.3
	06	268 44.1	S22 40.6	309 02.2	10.4	S26 36.9	4.6	54.4
SATURDAY	07	283 43.8	40.4	323 31.6	10.3	26 41.5	4.4	54.4
	08	298 43.5	40.1	338 00.9	10.2	26 45.9	4.2	54.4
	09	313 43.2	. . 39.8	352 30.1	10.2	26 50.1	4.2	54.4
	10	328 43.0	39.5	6 59.3	10.2	26 54.3	4.0	54.4
	11	343 42.7	39.3	21 28.5	10.0	26 58.3	3.9	54.4
	12	358 42.4	S22 39.0	35 57.5	10.1	S27 02.2	3.8	54.4
	13	13 42.1	38.7	50 26.6	9.9	27 06.0	3.6	54.4
	14	28 41.8	38.4	64 55.5	10.0	27 09.6	3.5	54.4
	15	43 41.5	. . 38.2	79 24.5	9.8	27 13.1	3.4	54.5
	16	58 41.3	37.9	93 53.3	9.8	27 16.5	3.2	54.5
	17	73 41.0	37.6	108 22.1	9.8	27 19.7	3.1	54.5
	18	88 40.7	S22 37.3	122 50.9	9.7	S27 22.8	3.0	54.5
	19	103 40.4	37.0	137 19.6	9.7	27 25.8	2.8	54.5
	20	118 40.1	36.8	151 48.3	9.6	27 28.6	2.7	54.5
	21	133 39.9	. . 36.5	166 16.9	9.6	27 31.3	2.6	54.5
	22	148 39.6	36.2	180 45.5	9.5	27 33.9	2.4	54.5
	23	163 39.3	35.9	195 14.0	9.5	27 36.3	2.3	54.6
6	00	178 39.0	S22 35.6	209 42.5	9.4	S27 38.6	2.2	54.6
	01	193 38.7	35.3	224 10.9	9.4	27 40.8	2.0	54.6
	02	208 38.5	35.1	238 39.3	9.4	27 42.8	1.9	54.6
	03	223 38.2	. . 34.8	253 07.7	9.3	27 44.7	1.7	54.6
	04	238 37.9	34.5	267 36.0	9.3	27 46.4	1.6	54.6
	05	253 37.6	34.2	282 04.3	9.2	27 48.0	1.5	54.6
	06	268 37.3	S22 33.9	296 32.5	9.2	S27 49.5	1.3	54.7
	07	283 37.1	33.6	311 00.7	9.2	27 50.8	1.2	54.7
	08	298 36.8	33.3	325 28.9	9.1	27 52.0	1.0	54.7
SUNDAY	09	313 36.5	. . 33.0	339 57.0	9.1	27 53.0	0.9	54.7
	10	328 36.2	32.7	354 25.1	9.1	27 53.9	0.7	54.7
	11	343 36.0	32.5	8 53.2	9.1	27 54.6	0.7	54.7
	12	358 35.7	S22 32.2	23 21.3	9.0	S27 55.3	0.4	54.7
	13	13 35.4	31.9	37 49.3	9.0	27 55.7	0.4	54.8
	14	28 35.1	31.6	52 17.3	9.0	27 56.1	0.1	54.8
	15	43 34.8	. . 31.3	66 45.3	8.9	27 56.2	0.1	54.8
	16	58 34.6	31.0	81 13.2	9.0	27 56.3	0.1	54.8
	17	73 34.3	30.7	95 41.2	8.9	27 56.2	0.3	54.8
	18	88 34.0	S22 30.4	110 09.1	8.9	S27 55.9	0.4	54.8
	19	103 33.7	30.1	124 37.0	8.8	27 55.5	0.5	54.9
	20	118 33.5	29.8	139 04.8	8.9	27 55.0	0.7	54.9
	21	133 33.2	. . 29.5	153 32.7	8.8	27 54.3	0.8	54.9
	22	148 32.9	29.2	168 00.5	8.9	27 53.5	1.0	54.9
	23	163 32.6	28.9	182 28.4	8.8	S27 52.5	1.1	54.9
		SD 16.3	*d* 0.3	SD 14.8		14.8		14.9

Lat.	Twilight Naut.	Twilight Civil	Sunrise	Moonrise 4	Moonrise 5	Moonrise 6	Moonrise 7
°	h m	h m	h m	h m	h m	h m	h m
N 72	08 20	10 32	▬	▬	▬	▬	▬
N 70	08 02	09 44	▬	▬	▬	▬	▬
68	07 48	09 13	11 34	▬	▬	▬	▬
66	07 35	08 50	10 21	▬	▬	▬	▬
64	07 25	08 32	09 45	07 14	▬	▬	▬
62	07 16	08 17	09 20	06 31	08 18	▬	10 34
60	07 08	08 04	09 00	06 02	07 32	08 48	09 34
N 58	07 01	07 53	08 44	05 40	07 02	08 11	09 00
56	06 55	07 44	08 30	05 22	06 39	07 45	08 35
54	06 49	07 35	08 18	05 07	06 20	07 25	08 15
52	06 44	07 27	08 07	04 54	06 05	07 07	07 59
50	06 39	07 20	07 58	04 43	05 51	06 53	07 44
45	06 28	07 05	07 38	04 19	05 23	06 23	07 15
N 40	06 18	06 52	07 22	04 00	05 02	06 00	06 52
35	06 09	06 41	07 09	03 45	04 44	05 40	06 33
30	06 01	06 30	06 57	03 31	04 28	05 24	06 17
20	05 45	06 12	06 36	03 08	04 02	04 56	05 49
N 10	05 29	05 56	06 18	02 48	03 40	04 33	05 26
0	05 13	05 39	06 01	02 30	03 19	04 10	05 04
S 10	04 55	05 22	05 44	02 11	02 58	03 48	04 42
20	04 33	05 02	05 26	01 52	02 36	03 25	04 18
30	04 05	04 38	05 05	01 29	02 10	02 57	03 50
35	03 47	04 23	04 52	01 16	01 55	02 41	03 34
40	03 24	04 05	04 38	01 01	01 38	02 22	03 15
45	02 55	03 44	04 21	00 43	01 17	01 59	02 52
S 50	02 13	03 15	03 59	00 21	00 51	01 30	02 23
52	01 48	03 01	03 49	00 11	00 38	01 16	02 08
54	01 11	02 44	03 37	24 23	00 23	00 59	01 51
56	////	02 24	03 23	24 06	00 06	00 40	01 31
58	////	01 57	03 08	23 46	24 15	00 15	01 06
S 60	////	01 17	02 49	23 20	23 42	24 31	00 31

Lat.	Sunset	Twilight Civil	Twilight Naut.	Moonset 4	Moonset 5	Moonset 6	Moonset 7
°	h m	h m	h m	h m	h m	h m	h m
N 72	▬	13 39	15 51	▬	▬	▬	▬
N 70	▬	14 27	16 09	▬	▬	▬	▬
68	12 37	14 58	16 23	▬	▬	▬	▬
66	13 50	15 21	16 35	▬	▬	▬	▬
64	14 25	15 39	16 46	09 59	▬	▬	▬
62	14 51	15 54	16 54	10 43	10 38	▬	12 03
60	15 10	16 06	17 02	11 12	11 25	11 58	13 03
N 58	15 27	16 17	17 09	11 34	11 56	12 34	13 36
56	15 41	16 27	17 16	11 53	12 19	13 00	14 01
54	15 53	16 36	17 21	12 08	12 38	13 21	14 21
52	16 03	16 43	17 27	12 22	12 53	13 38	14 37
50	16 13	16 50	17 32	12 33	13 07	13 53	14 51
45	16 32	17 06	17 43	12 58	13 35	14 23	15 20
N 40	16 48	17 19	17 53	13 17	13 58	14 46	15 43
35	17 02	17 30	18 01	13 34	14 16	15 05	16 02
30	17 14	17 40	18 10	13 48	14 32	15 22	16 18
20	17 34	17 58	18 25	14 12	14 59	15 50	16 45
N 10	17 52	18 15	18 41	14 33	15 22	16 14	17 08
0	18 09	18 31	18 57	14 53	15 43	16 36	17 29
S 10	18 26	18 49	19 16	15 13	16 05	16 58	17 51
20	18 44	19 08	19 37	15 34	16 28	17 22	18 14
30	19 05	19 32	20 05	15 59	16 55	17 50	18 40
35	19 18	19 47	20 23	16 13	17 11	18 06	18 56
40	19 32	20 05	20 46	16 30	17 30	18 25	19 14
45	19 49	20 26	21 15	16 50	17 52	18 48	19 36
S 50	20 11	20 54	21 57	17 16	18 21	19 18	20 04
52	20 21	21 09	22 21	17 28	18 35	19 33	20 17
54	20 33	21 25	22 57	17 42	18 52	19 49	20 33
56	20 46	21 46	////	17 59	19 11	20 10	20 51
58	21 02	22 12	////	18 19	19 36	20 35	21 13
S 60	21 21	22 51	////	18 44	20 08	21 10	21 42

Day	SUN Eqn. of Time 00^h	SUN Eqn. of Time 12^h	SUN Mer. Pass.	MOON Mer. Pass. Upper	MOON Mer. Pass. Lower	MOON Age	MOON Phase
d	m s	m s	h m	h m	h m	d %	
4	04 29	04 43	12 05	08 41	21 06	26 15	
5	04 56	05 10	12 05	09 31	21 57	27 9	
6	05 23	05 37	12 06	10 23	22 50	28 4	

UT	ARIES	VENUS −4.0		MARS −1.3		JUPITER −1.8		SATURN +0.5	
	GHA	GHA	Dec	GHA	Dec	GHA	Dec	GHA	Dec
d h	° ′	° ′	° ′	° ′	° ′	° ′	° ′	° ′	° ′
7 00	105 56.7	218 33.7	S19 56.7	18 21.1	N26 59.0	191 10.4	S23 12.4	305 23.7	N10 03.4
01	120 59.2	233 32.9	57.2	33 24.4	59.0	206 12.3	12.4	320 26.2	03.4
02	136 01.7	248 32.2	57.8	48 27.7	59.0	221 14.1	12.4	335 28.8	03.4
03	151 04.1	263 31.5	. . 58.3	63 31.1	. . 59.0	236 16.0	. . 12.4	350 31.3	. . 03.5
04	166 06.6	278 30.8	58.9	78 34.4	59.0	251 17.8	12.4	5 33.9	03.5
05	181 09.1	293 30.1	19 59.4	93 37.7	59.0	266 19.7	12.4	20 36.4	03.6
06	196 11.5	308 29.3	S20 00.0	108 41.0	N26 59.0	281 21.5	S23 12.4	35 38.9	N10 03.6
07	211 14.0	323 28.6	00.5	123 44.4	59.0	296 23.4	12.3	50 41.5	03.6
08	226 16.5	338 27.9	01.1	138 47.7	59.0	311 25.2	12.3	65 44.0	03.7
M 09	241 18.9	353 27.2	. . 01.6	153 51.0	. . 59.0	326 27.0	. . 12.3	80 46.6	. . 03.7
O 10	256 21.4	8 26.5	02.2	168 54.3	59.0	341 28.9	12.3	95 49.1	03.8
N 11	271 23.8	23 25.7	02.7	183 57.6	59.0	356 30.7	12.3	110 51.6	03.8
D 12	286 26.3	38 25.0	S20 03.3	199 00.9	N26 59.0	11 32.6	S23 12.3	125 54.2	N10 03.9
A 13	301 28.8	53 24.3	03.8	214 04.3	59.0	26 34.4	12.2	140 56.7	03.9
Y 14	316 31.2	68 23.6	04.3	229 07.6	59.0	41 36.3	12.2	155 59.3	03.9
15	331 33.7	83 22.8	. . 04.9	244 10.9	. . 59.0	56 38.1	. . 12.2	171 01.8	. . 04.0
16	346 36.2	98 22.1	05.4	259 14.2	59.0	71 40.0	12.2	186 04.3	04.0
17	1 38.6	113 21.4	05.9	274 17.5	59.0	86 41.8	12.2	201 06.9	04.1
18	16 41.1	128 20.6	S20 06.5	289 20.8	N26 59.0	101 43.7	S23 12.2	216 09.4	N10 04.1
19	31 43.6	143 19.9	07.0	304 24.1	59.0	116 45.5	12.2	231 12.0	04.1
20	46 46.0	158 19.2	07.6	319 27.4	59.0	131 47.4	12.1	246 14.5	04.2
21	61 48.5	173 18.5	. . 08.1	334 30.7	. . 59.0	146 49.2	. . 12.1	261 17.1	. . 04.2
22	76 50.9	188 17.7	08.6	349 34.0	59.0	161 51.1	12.1	276 19.6	04.3
23	91 53.4	203 17.0	09.1	4 37.3	58.9	176 52.9	12.1	291 22.1	04.3
8 00	106 55.9	218 16.3	S20 09.7	19 40.6	N26 58.9	191 54.7	S23 12.1	306 24.7	N10 04.3
01	121 58.3	233 15.5	10.2	34 43.9	58.9	206 56.6	12.1	321 27.2	04.4
02	137 00.8	248 14.8	10.7	49 47.2	58.9	221 58.4	12.0	336 29.8	04.4
03	152 03.3	263 14.1	. . 11.3	64 50.5	. . 58.9	237 00.3	. . 12.0	351 32.3	. . 04.5
04	167 05.7	278 13.4	11.8	79 53.8	58.9	252 02.1	12.0	6 34.9	04.5
05	182 08.2	293 12.6	12.3	94 57.1	58.9	267 04.0	12.0	21 37.4	04.6
06	197 10.7	308 11.9	S20 12.8	110 00.4	N26 58.9	282 05.8	S23 12.0	36 39.9	N10 04.6
07	212 13.1	323 11.2	13.4	125 03.7	58.9	297 07.7	12.0	51 42.5	04.6
T 08	227 15.6	338 10.4	13.9	140 07.0	58.9	312 09.5	11.9	66 45.0	04.7
U 09	242 18.1	353 09.7	. . 14.4	155 10.3	. . 58.9	327 11.4	. . 11.9	81 47.6	. . 04.7
E 10	257 20.5	8 09.0	14.9	170 13.6	58.9	342 13.2	11.9	96 50.1	04.8
S 11	272 23.0	23 08.2	15.5	185 16.9	58.9	357 15.1	11.9	111 52.7	04.8
D 12	287 25.4	38 07.5	S20 16.0	200 20.1	N26 58.9	12 16.9	S23 11.9	126 55.2	N10 04.9
A 13	302 27.9	53 06.8	16.5	215 23.4	58.9	27 18.8	11.9	141 57.7	04.9
Y 14	317 30.4	68 06.0	17.0	230 26.7	58.9	42 20.6	11.8	157 00.3	04.9
15	332 32.8	83 05.3	. . 17.5	245 30.0	. . 58.9	57 22.4	. . 11.8	172 02.8	. . 05.0
16	347 35.3	98 04.5	18.0	260 33.3	58.9	72 24.3	11.8	187 05.4	05.0
17	2 37.8	113 03.8	18.6	275 36.5	58.8	87 26.1	11.8	202 07.9	05.1
18	17 40.2	128 03.1	S20 19.1	290 39.8	N26 58.8	102 28.0	S23 11.8	217 10.5	N10 05.1
19	32 42.7	143 02.3	19.6	305 43.1	58.8	117 29.8	11.8	232 13.0	05.2
20	47 45.2	158 01.6	20.1	320 46.4	58.8	132 31.7	11.7	247 15.6	05.2
21	62 47.6	173 00.9	. . 20.6	335 49.6	. . 58.8	147 33.5	. . 11.7	262 18.1	. . 05.2
22	77 50.1	188 00.1	21.1	350 52.9	58.8	162 35.4	11.7	277 20.7	05.3
23	92 52.6	202 59.4	21.6	5 56.2	58.8	177 37.2	11.7	292 23.2	05.3
9 00	107 55.0	217 58.6	S20 22.1	20 59.5	N26 58.8	192 39.1	S23 11.7	307 25.8	N10 05.4
01	122 57.5	232 57.9	22.6	36 02.7	58.8	207 40.9	11.7	322 28.3	05.4
02	137 59.9	247 57.2	23.1	51 06.0	58.8	222 42.8	11.6	337 30.8	05.5
03	153 02.4	262 56.4	. . 23.6	66 09.3	. . 58.8	237 44.6	. . 11.6	352 33.4	. . 05.5
04	168 04.9	277 55.7	24.2	81 12.5	58.8	252 46.5	11.6	7 35.9	05.5
05	183 07.3	292 54.9	24.7	96 15.8	58.8	267 48.3	11.6	22 38.5	05.6
06	198 09.8	307 54.2	S20 25.2	111 19.0	N26 58.7	282 50.2	S23 11.6	37 41.0	N10 05.6
W 07	213 12.3	322 53.4	25.7	126 22.3	58.7	297 52.0	11.6	52 43.6	05.7
E 08	228 14.7	337 52.7	26.2	141 25.6	58.7	312 53.9	11.5	67 46.1	05.7
D 09	243 17.2	352 52.0	. . 26.7	156 28.8	. . 58.7	327 55.7	. . 11.5	82 48.7	. . 05.8
N 10	258 19.7	7 51.2	27.2	171 32.1	58.7	342 57.6	11.5	97 51.2	05.8
E 11	273 22.1	22 50.5	27.7	186 35.3	58.7	357 59.4	11.5	112 53.8	05.8
S 12	288 24.6	37 49.7	S20 28.1	201 38.6	N26 58.7	13 01.2	S23 11.5	127 56.3	N10 05.9
D 13	303 27.1	52 49.0	28.6	216 41.8	58.7	28 03.1	11.5	142 58.9	05.9
A 14	318 29.5	67 48.2	29.1	231 45.1	58.7	43 04.9	11.4	158 01.4	06.0
Y 15	333 32.0	82 47.5	. . 29.6	246 48.3	. . 58.6	58 06.8	. . 11.4	173 04.0	. . 06.0
16	348 34.4	97 46.7	30.1	261 51.6	58.6	73 08.6	11.4	188 06.5	06.1
17	3 36.9	112 46.0	30.6	276 54.8	58.6	88 10.5	11.4	203 09.1	06.1
18	18 39.4	127 45.2	S20 31.1	291 58.1	N26 58.6	103 12.3	S23 11.4	218 11.6	N10 06.2
19	33 41.8	142 44.5	31.6	307 01.3	58.6	118 14.2	11.3	233 14.2	06.2
20	48 44.3	157 43.7	32.1	322 04.6	58.6	133 16.0	11.3	248 16.7	06.2
21	63 46.8	172 43.0	. . 32.6	337 07.8	. . 58.6	148 17.9	. . 11.3	263 19.3	. . 06.3
22	78 49.2	187 42.2	33.1	352 11.0	58.6	163 19.7	11.3	278 21.8	06.3
23	93 51.7	202 41.5	33.5	7 14.3	58.6	178 21.6	11.3	293 24.4	06.4
Mer. Pass.	h m 16 49.5	v −0.7	d 0.5	v 3.3	d 0.0	v 1.8	d 0.0	v 2.5	d 0.0

STARS

Name	SHA	Dec
	° ′	° ′
Acamar	315 21.1	S40 16.5
Achernar	335 29.5	S57 12.0
Acrux	173 14.2	S63 08.4
Adhara	255 15.4	S28 58.9
Aldebaran	290 53.8	N16 31.6
Alioth	166 24.0	N55 54.6
Alkaid	153 02.0	N49 16.0
Al Na'ir	27 49.0	S46 55.5
Alnilam	275 50.2	S 1 11.8
Alphard	217 59.9	S 8 41.6
Alphecca	126 14.7	N26 41.0
Alpheratz	357 48.0	N29 08.3
Altair	62 12.6	N 8 53.3
Ankaa	353 19.6	S42 15.9
Antares	112 31.6	S26 27.0
Arcturus	145 59.5	N19 08.2
Atria	107 37.8	S69 02.5
Avior	234 19.3	S59 32.0
Bellatrix	278 36.1	N 6 21.5
Betelgeuse	271 05.4	N 7 24.6
Canopus	263 57.4	S52 42.0
Capella	280 40.1	N46 00.5
Deneb	49 34.8	N45 18.6
Denebola	182 37.7	N14 31.5
Diphda	349 00.0	S17 56.6
Dubhe	193 56.0	N61 42.1
Elnath	278 17.5	N28 37.0
Eltanin	90 48.6	N51 29.1
Enif	33 51.5	N 9 54.7
Fomalhaut	15 28.6	S29 34.9
Gacrux	172 05.7	S57 09.3
Gienah	175 56.5	S17 35.2
Hadar	148 54.2	S60 24.5
Hamal	328 05.4	N23 30.2
Kaus Aust.	83 49.7	S34 22.9
Kochab	137 19.9	N74 06.9
Markab	13 42.7	N15 15.0
Menkar	314 19.2	N 4 07.4
Menkent	148 12.7	S36 24.5
Miaplacidus	221 40.1	S69 44.8
Mirfak	308 46.1	N49 53.7
Nunki	76 03.8	S26 17.3
Peacock	53 26.1	S56 42.7
Pollux	243 32.3	N28 00.4
Procyon	245 03.7	N 5 12.3
Rasalhague	96 10.6	N12 33.1
Regulus	207 47.6	N11 55.6
Rigel	281 15.7	S 8 11.5
Rigil Kent.	139 57.9	S60 51.9
Sabik	102 17.6	S15 44.2
Schedar	349 45.6	N56 35.2
Shaula	96 27.9	S37 06.6
Sirius	258 37.0	S16 43.6
Spica	158 35.7	S11 12.3
Suhail	222 55.2	S43 27.8
Vega	80 42.2	N38 47.3
Zuben'ubi	137 10.2	S16 04.6

	SHA	Mer. Pass.
	° ′	h m
Venus	111 20.4	9 27
Mars	272 44.8	22 36
Jupiter	84 58.9	11 11
Saturn	199 28.8	3 34

UT (d h)		SUN GHA	SUN Dec	MOON GHA	v	MOON Dec	d	HP
		° ′	° ′	° ′	′	° ′	′	′
7 00	MONDAY	178 32.4	S22 28.6	196 56.2	8.8	S27 51.4	1.3	54.9
01		193 32.1	28.3	211 24.0	8.8	27 50.1	1.4	55.0
02		208 31.8	28.0	225 51.8	8.8	27 48.7	1.5	55.0
03		223 31.5	. . 27.7	240 19.6	8.8	27 47.2	1.7	55.0
04		238 31.3	27.4	254 47.4	8.8	27 45.5	1.9	55.0
05		253 31.0	27.0	269 15.2	8.7	27 43.6	1.9	55.0
06		268 30.7	S22 26.7	283 42.9	8.8	S27 41.7	2.2	55.0
07		283 30.4	26.4	298 10.7	8.8	27 39.5	2.3	55.1
08		298 30.2	26.1	312 38.5	8.8	27 37.2	2.4	55.1
09		313 29.9	. . 25.8	327 06.3	8.7	27 34.8	2.6	55.1
10		328 29.6	25.5	341 34.0	8.8	27 32.2	2.7	55.1
11		343 29.4	25.2	356 01.8	8.8	27 29.5	2.8	55.1
12		358 29.1	S22 24.9	10 29.6	8.8	S27 26.7	3.1	55.1
13		13 28.8	24.6	24 57.4	8.8	27 23.6	3.1	55.2
14		28 28.5	24.3	39 25.2	8.8	27 20.5	3.3	55.2
15		43 28.3	. . 23.9	53 53.0	8.9	27 17.2	3.4	55.2
16		58 28.0	23.6	68 20.9	8.8	27 13.8	3.6	55.2
17		73 27.7	23.3	82 48.7	8.9	27 10.2	3.8	55.2
18		88 27.4	S22 23.0	97 16.6	8.8	S27 06.4	3.8	55.3
19		103 27.2	22.7	111 44.4	8.9	27 02.6	4.1	55.3
20		118 26.9	22.4	126 12.3	8.9	26 58.5	4.1	55.3
21		133 26.6	. . 22.0	140 40.2	8.9	26 54.4	4.3	55.3
22		148 26.4	21.7	155 08.1	9.0	26 50.1	4.5	55.3
23		163 26.1	21.4	169 36.1	9.0	26 45.6	4.6	55.3
8 00	TUESDAY	178 25.8	S22 21.1	184 04.1	8.9	S26 41.0	4.7	55.4
01		193 25.6	20.7	198 32.0	9.1	26 36.3	4.9	55.4
02		208 25.3	20.4	213 00.1	9.0	26 31.4	5.0	55.4
03		223 25.0	. . 20.1	227 28.1	9.1	26 26.4	5.2	55.4
04		238 24.7	19.8	241 56.2	9.1	26 21.2	5.3	55.4
05		253 24.5	19.5	256 24.3	9.1	26 15.9	5.4	55.5
06		268 24.2	S22 19.1	270 52.4	9.1	S26 10.5	5.6	55.5
07		283 23.9	18.8	285 20.5	9.2	26 04.9	5.7	55.5
08		298 23.7	18.5	299 48.7	9.2	25 59.2	5.9	55.5
09		313 23.4	. . 18.1	314 16.9	9.3	25 53.3	6.0	55.5
10		328 23.1	17.8	328 45.2	9.3	25 47.3	6.1	55.6
11		343 22.9	17.5	343 13.5	9.3	25 41.2	6.3	55.6
12		358 22.6	S22 17.2	357 41.8	9.3	S25 34.9	6.4	55.6
13		13 22.3	16.8	12 10.1	9.4	25 28.5	6.6	55.6
14		28 22.1	16.5	26 38.5	9.5	25 21.9	6.6	55.6
15		43 21.8	. . 16.2	41 07.0	9.4	25 15.3	6.9	55.7
16		58 21.5	15.8	55 35.4	9.5	25 08.4	6.9	55.7
17		73 21.3	15.5	70 03.9	9.6	25 01.5	7.1	55.7
18		88 21.0	S22 15.2	84 32.5	9.6	S24 54.4	7.2	55.7
19		103 20.7	14.8	99 01.1	9.6	24 47.2	7.4	55.7
20		118 20.5	14.5	113 29.7	9.7	24 39.8	7.5	55.8
21		133 20.2	. . 14.1	127 58.4	9.7	24 32.3	7.6	55.8
22		148 19.9	13.8	142 27.1	9.8	24 24.7	7.7	55.8
23		163 19.7	13.5	156 55.9	9.8	24 17.0	7.9	55.8
9 00	WEDNESDAY	178 19.4	S22 13.1	171 24.7	9.9	S24 09.1	8.0	55.8
01		193 19.1	12.8	185 53.6	9.9	24 01.1	8.1	55.9
02		208 18.9	12.4	200 22.5	9.9	23 53.0	8.3	55.9
03		223 18.6	. . 12.1	214 51.4	10.0	23 44.7	8.4	55.9
04		238 18.4	11.8	229 20.4	10.1	23 36.3	8.5	55.9
05		253 18.1	11.4	243 49.5	10.1	23 27.8	8.6	55.9
06		268 17.8	S22 11.1	258 18.6	10.1	S23 19.2	8.7	56.0
07		283 17.6	10.7	272 47.7	10.2	23 10.5	8.9	56.0
08		298 17.3	10.4	287 16.9	10.3	23 01.6	9.0	56.0
09		313 17.0	. . 10.0	301 46.2	10.3	22 52.6	9.2	56.0
10		328 16.8	09.7	316 15.5	10.4	22 43.4	9.2	56.0
11		343 16.5	09.3	330 44.9	10.4	22 34.2	9.4	56.1
12		358 16.3	S22 09.0	345 14.3	10.4	S22 24.8	9.4	56.1
13		13 16.0	08.6	359 43.7	10.5	22 15.4	9.6	56.1
14		28 15.7	08.3	14 13.2	10.6	22 05.8	9.8	56.1
15		43 15.5	. . 07.9	28 42.8	10.6	21 56.0	9.8	56.1
16		58 15.2	07.6	43 12.4	10.7	21 46.2	9.9	56.2
17		73 14.9	07.2	57 42.1	10.7	21 36.3	10.1	56.2
18		88 14.7	S22 06.9	72 11.8	10.8	S21 26.2	10.2	56.2
19		103 14.4	06.5	86 41.6	10.8	21 16.0	10.3	56.2
20		118 14.2	06.2	101 11.4	10.9	21 05.7	10.4	56.2
21		133 13.9	. . 05.8	115 41.3	10.9	20 55.3	10.5	56.3
22		148 13.6	05.5	130 11.2	11.0	20 44.8	10.6	56.3
23		163 13.4	05.1	144 41.2	11.1	S20 34.2	10.7	56.3
		SD 16.3	*d* 0.3	SD 15.0		15.1		15.3

Lat.	Twilight Naut.	Twilight Civil	Sunrise	Moonrise 7	Moonrise 8	Moonrise 9	Moonrise 10
°	h m	h m	h m	h m	h m	h m	h m
N 72	08 16	10 21	▬	▬	▬	▬	13 29
N 70	07 59	09 38	▬	▬	▬	▬	12 06
68	07 45	09 09	11 13	▬	▬	▬	11 26
66	07 33	08 47	10 14	▬	▬	11 35	10 59
64	07 23	08 29	09 41	▬	11 33	10 53	10 38
62	07 15	08 15	09 17	10 34	10 29	10 24	10 20
60	07 07	08 02	08 57	09 34	09 54	10 02	10 06
N 58	07 00	07 52	08 42	09 00	09 29	09 44	09 54
56	06 54	07 42	08 28	08 35	09 08	09 29	09 43
54	06 48	07 34	08 17	08 15	08 51	09 16	09 33
52	06 43	07 26	08 06	07 59	08 37	09 05	09 25
50	06 38	07 19	07 57	07 44	08 24	08 54	09 17
45	06 28	07 04	07 38	07 15	07 58	08 33	09 01
N 40	06 18	06 52	07 22	06 52	07 37	08 15	08 48
35	06 09	06 41	07 09	06 33	07 20	08 01	08 36
30	06 01	06 31	06 57	06 17	07 05	07 48	08 26
20	05 46	06 13	06 37	05 49	06 40	07 26	08 08
N 10	05 31	05 57	06 19	05 26	06 17	07 07	07 53
0	05 14	05 40	06 03	05 04	05 57	06 49	07 39
S 10	04 56	05 23	05 46	04 42	05 36	06 31	07 25
20	04 35	05 04	05 28	04 18	05 14	06 12	07 09
30	04 07	04 40	05 07	03 50	04 48	05 49	06 51
35	03 50	04 26	04 55	03 34	04 33	05 36	06 41
40	03 28	04 08	04 41	03 15	04 15	05 21	06 29
45	02 59	03 47	04 24	02 52	03 54	05 03	06 15
S 50	02 18	03 19	04 03	02 23	03 27	04 40	05 57
52	01 54	03 06	03 53	02 08	03 14	04 29	05 49
54	01 20	02 49	03 41	01 51	02 58	04 17	05 40
56	////	02 29	03 28	01 31	02 40	04 02	05 29
58	////	02 04	03 13	01 06	02 18	03 46	05 18
S 60	////	01 27	02 54	00 31	01 50	03 25	05 04

Lat.	Sunset	Twilight Civil	Twilight Naut.	Moonset 7	Moonset 8	Moonset 9	Moonset 10
°	h m	h m	h m	h m	h m	h m	h m
N 72	▬	13 52	15 58	▬	▬	▬	14 34
N 70	▬	14 36	16 15	▬	▬	▬	15 56
68	13 01	15 05	16 29	▬	▬	▬	16 34
66	13 59	15 27	16 40	▬	▬	14 41	17 00
64	14 33	15 44	16 50	▬	12 55	15 22	17 20
62	14 57	15 59	16 59	12 03	13 59	15 50	17 36
60	15 16	16 11	17 06	13 03	14 33	16 11	17 50
N 58	15 32	16 22	17 13	13 36	14 58	16 29	18 01
56	15 45	16 31	17 19	14 01	15 18	16 43	18 11
54	15 57	16 39	17 25	14 21	15 34	16 56	18 20
52	16 07	16 47	17 30	14 37	15 48	17 07	18 28
50	16 16	16 54	17 35	14 51	16 01	17 17	18 35
45	16 35	17 09	17 46	15 20	16 26	17 37	18 50
N 40	16 51	17 21	17 55	15 43	16 46	17 53	19 02
35	17 05	17 32	18 04	16 02	17 03	18 07	19 12
30	17 16	17 42	18 12	16 18	17 17	18 19	19 21
20	17 36	18 00	18 27	16 45	17 42	18 39	19 36
N 10	17 54	18 16	18 42	17 08	18 03	18 57	19 50
0	18 10	18 33	18 59	17 29	18 22	19 13	20 02
S 10	18 27	18 50	19 16	17 51	18 41	19 29	20 14
20	18 45	19 09	19 38	18 14	19 02	19 47	20 27
30	19 06	19 33	20 05	18 40	19 26	20 06	20 42
35	19 18	19 47	20 23	18 56	19 40	20 18	20 51
40	19 32	20 04	20 45	19 14	19 56	20 31	21 00
45	19 49	20 25	21 13	19 36	20 15	20 46	21 12
S 50	20 10	20 53	21 54	20 04	20 39	21 05	21 25
52	20 20	21 07	22 17	20 17	20 50	21 14	21 31
54	20 31	21 23	22 50	20 33	21 03	21 24	21 38
56	20 44	21 42	////	20 51	21 18	21 35	21 46
58	20 59	22 07	////	21 13	21 35	21 47	21 55
S 60	21 17	22 43	////	21 42	21 56	22 02	22 05

Day	SUN Eqn. of Time 00^h	SUN Eqn. of Time 12^h	SUN Mer. Pass.	MOON Mer. Pass. Upper	MOON Mer. Pass. Lower	MOON Age	MOON Phase
d	m s	m s	h m	h m	h m	d %	
7	05 50	06 03	12 06	11 16	23 43	29 1	●
8	06 16	06 29	12 06	12 10	24 36	00 0	
9	06 42	06 54	12 07	13 01	00 36	01 1	

UT		ARIES	VENUS −4.0		MARS −1.2		JUPITER −1.8		SATURN +0.5		STARS		
		GHA	GHA	Dec	GHA	Dec	GHA	Dec	GHA	Dec	Name	SHA	Dec
d	h	° ′	° ′	° ′	° ′	° ′	° ′	° ′	° ′	° ′		° ′	° ′
10	00	108 54.2	217 40.7	S20 34.0	22 17.5	N26 58.5	193 23.4	S23 11.3	308 26.9	N10 06.4	Acamar	315 21.1	S40 16.5
	01	123 56.6	232 40.0	34.5	37 20.7	58.5	208 25.3	11.2	323 29.5	06.5	Achernar	335 29.5	S57 12.0
	02	138 59.1	247 39.2	35.0	52 24.0	58.5	223 27.1	11.2	338 32.0	06.5	Acrux	173 14.1	S63 08.4
	03	154 01.6	262 38.5	. . 35.5	67 27.2	. . 58.5	238 29.0	. . 11.2	353 34.6	. . 06.6	Adhara	255 15.4	S28 59.0
	04	169 04.0	277 37.7	36.0	82 30.4	58.5	253 30.8	11.2	8 37.1	06.6	Aldebaran	290 53.8	N16 31.6
	05	184 06.5	292 37.0	36.4	97 33.7	58.5	268 32.7	11.2	23 39.7	06.7			
	06	199 08.9	307 36.2	S20 36.9	112 36.9	N26 58.5	283 34.5	S23 11.1	38 42.2	N10 06.7	Alioth	166 23.9	N55 54.6
	07	214 11.4	322 35.5	37.4	127 40.1	58.4	298 36.4	11.1	53 44.8	06.7	Alkaid	153 02.0	N49 16.0
T	08	229 13.9	337 34.7	37.9	142 43.3	58.4	313 38.2	11.1	68 47.3	06.8	Al Na'ir	27 49.0	S46 55.5
H	09	244 16.3	352 34.0	. . 38.4	157 46.6	. . 58.4	328 40.1	. . 11.1	83 49.9	. . 06.8	Alnilam	275 50.2	S 1 11.8
U	10	259 18.8	7 33.2	38.8	172 49.8	58.4	343 41.9	11.1	98 52.4	06.9	Alphard	217 59.9	S 8 41.6
R	11	274 21.3	22 32.5	39.3	187 53.0	58.4	358 43.8	11.1	113 55.0	06.9			
S	12	289 23.7	37 31.7	S20 39.8	202 56.2	N26 58.4	13 45.6	S23 11.0	128 57.5	N10 07.0	Alphecca	126 14.6	N26 41.0
D	13	304 26.2	52 31.0	40.3	217 59.4	58.4	28 47.5	11.0	144 00.1	07.0	Alpheratz	357 48.0	N29 08.3
A	14	319 28.7	67 30.2	40.7	233 02.7	58.3	43 49.3	11.0	159 02.6	07.1	Altair	62 12.6	N 8 53.3
Y	15	334 31.1	82 29.4	. . 41.2	248 05.9	. . 58.3	58 51.2	. . 11.0	174 05.2	. . 07.1	Ankaa	353 19.7	S42 15.9
	16	349 33.6	97 28.7	41.7	263 09.1	58.3	73 53.0	11.0	189 07.8	07.2	Antares	112 31.6	S26 27.0
	17	4 36.0	112 27.9	42.1	278 12.3	58.3	88 54.9	10.9	204 10.3	07.2			
	18	19 38.5	127 27.2	S20 42.6	293 15.5	N26 58.3	103 56.7	S23 10.9	219 12.9	N10 07.2	Arcturus	145 59.5	N19 08.2
	19	34 41.0	142 26.4	43.1	308 18.7	58.3	118 58.6	10.9	234 15.4	07.3	Atria	107 37.8	S69 02.4
	20	49 43.4	157 25.6	43.5	323 21.9	58.3	134 00.4	10.9	249 18.0	07.3	Avior	234 19.2	S59 32.0
	21	64 45.9	172 24.9	. . 44.0	338 25.1	. . 58.2	149 02.3	. . 10.9	264 20.5	. . 07.4	Bellatrix	278 36.1	N 6 21.5
	22	79 48.4	187 24.1	44.5	353 28.3	58.2	164 04.1	10.9	279 23.1	07.4	Betelgeuse	271 05.4	N 7 24.6
	23	94 50.8	202 23.4	44.9	8 31.5	58.2	179 06.0	10.8	294 25.6	07.5			
11	00	109 53.3	217 22.6	S20 45.4	23 34.7	N26 58.2	194 07.8	S23 10.8	309 28.2	N10 07.5	Canopus	263 57.4	S52 42.0
	01	124 55.8	232 21.8	45.8	38 37.9	58.2	209 09.7	10.8	324 30.7	07.6	Capella	280 40.1	N46 00.5
	02	139 58.2	247 21.1	46.3	53 41.1	58.2	224 11.5	10.8	339 33.3	07.6	Deneb	49 34.9	N45 18.6
	03	155 00.7	262 20.3	. . 46.8	68 44.3	. . 58.1	239 13.4	. . 10.8	354 35.9	. . 07.7	Denebola	182 37.7	N14 31.4
	04	170 03.2	277 19.6	47.2	83 47.5	58.1	254 15.2	10.7	9 38.4	07.7	Diphda	349 00.0	S17 56.6
	05	185 05.6	292 18.8	47.7	98 50.7	58.1	269 17.1	10.7	24 41.0	07.8			
	06	200 08.1	307 18.0	S20 48.1	113 53.9	N26 58.1	284 18.9	S23 10.7	39 43.5	N10 07.8	Dubhe	193 55.9	N61 42.1
	07	215 10.5	322 17.3	48.6	128 57.1	58.1	299 20.8	10.7	54 46.1	07.8	Elnath	278 17.5	N28 37.0
	08	230 13.0	337 16.5	49.0	144 00.3	58.1	314 22.6	10.7	69 48.6	07.9	Eltanin	90 48.6	N51 29.0
F	09	245 15.5	352 15.7	. . 49.5	159 03.5	. . 58.0	329 24.5	. . 10.6	84 51.2	. . 07.9	Enif	33 51.5	N 9 54.7
R	10	260 17.9	7 15.0	49.9	174 06.7	58.0	344 26.3	10.6	99 53.7	08.0	Fomalhaut	15 28.6	S29 34.9
I	11	275 20.4	22 14.2	50.4	189 09.9	58.0	359 28.2	10.6	114 56.3	08.0			
D	12	290 22.9	37 13.5	S20 50.8	204 13.1	N26 58.0	14 30.0	S23 10.6	129 58.9	N10 08.1	Gacrux	172 05.7	S57 09.3
A	13	305 25.3	52 12.7	51.3	219 16.2	58.0	29 31.9	10.6	145 01.4	08.1	Gienah	175 56.5	S17 35.2
Y	14	320 27.8	67 11.9	51.7	234 19.4	57.9	44 33.7	10.5	160 04.0	08.2	Hadar	148 54.2	S60 24.5
	15	335 30.3	82 11.2	. . 52.2	249 22.6	. . 57.9	59 35.6	. . 10.5	175 06.5	. . 08.2	Hamal	328 05.4	N23 30.2
	16	350 32.7	97 10.4	52.6	264 25.8	57.9	74 37.4	10.5	190 09.1	08.3	Kaus Aust.	83 49.6	S34 22.9
	17	5 35.2	112 09.6	53.1	279 29.0	57.9	89 39.3	10.5	205 11.6	08.3			
	18	20 37.7	127 08.9	S20 53.5	294 32.1	N26 57.9	104 41.1	S23 10.5	220 14.2	N10 08.4	Kochab	137 19.8	N74 06.9
	19	35 40.1	142 08.1	54.0	309 35.3	57.8	119 43.0	10.4	235 16.8	08.4	Markab	13 42.7	N15 15.0
	20	50 42.6	157 07.3	54.4	324 38.5	57.8	134 44.8	10.4	250 19.3	08.5	Menkar	314 19.2	N 4 07.4
	21	65 45.0	172 06.5	. . 54.9	339 41.7	. . 57.8	149 46.7	. . 10.4	265 21.9	. . 08.5	Menkent	148 12.6	S36 24.5
	22	80 47.5	187 05.8	55.3	354 44.8	57.8	164 48.5	10.4	280 24.4	08.6	Miaplacidus	221 40.1	S69 44.8
	23	95 50.0	202 05.0	55.7	9 48.0	57.8	179 50.4	10.4	295 27.0	08.6			
12	00	110 52.4	217 04.2	S20 56.2	24 51.2	N26 57.7	194 52.2	S23 10.3	310 29.5	N10 08.6	Mirfak	308 46.1	N49 53.7
	01	125 54.9	232 03.5	56.6	39 54.3	57.7	209 54.1	10.3	325 32.1	08.7	Nunki	76 03.8	S26 17.3
	02	140 57.4	247 02.7	57.0	54 57.5	57.7	224 55.9	10.3	340 34.7	08.7	Peacock	53 26.1	S56 42.7
	03	155 59.8	262 01.9	. . 57.5	70 00.7	. . 57.7	239 57.8	. . 10.3	355 37.2	. . 08.8	Pollux	243 32.3	N28 00.4
	04	171 02.3	277 01.2	57.9	85 03.8	57.7	254 59.6	10.3	10 39.8	08.8	Procyon	245 03.7	N 5 12.3
	05	186 04.8	292 00.4	58.3	100 07.0	57.6	270 01.5	10.2	25 42.3	08.9			
	06	201 07.2	306 59.6	S20 58.8	115 10.1	N26 57.6	285 03.3	S23 10.2	40 44.9	N10 08.9	Rasalhague	96 10.6	N12 33.1
	07	216 09.7	321 58.8	59.2	130 13.3	57.6	300 05.2	10.2	55 47.5	09.0	Regulus	207 47.6	N11 55.6
S	08	231 12.1	336 58.1	20 59.6	145 16.4	57.6	315 07.0	10.2	70 50.0	09.0	Rigel	281 15.7	S 8 11.5
A	09	246 14.6	351 57.3	21 00.1	160 19.6	. . 57.6	330 08.9	. . 10.2	85 52.6	. . 09.1	Rigil Kent.	139 57.9	S60 51.9
T	10	261 17.1	6 56.5	00.5	175 22.7	57.5	345 10.7	10.1	100 55.1	09.1	Sabik	102 17.6	S15 44.2
U	11	276 19.5	21 55.7	00.9	190 25.9	57.5	0 12.6	10.1	115 57.7	09.2			
R	12	291 22.0	36 55.0	S21 01.3	205 29.0	N26 57.5	15 14.4	S23 10.1	131 00.3	N10 09.2	Schedar	349 45.6	N56 35.2
D	13	306 24.5	51 54.2	01.8	220 32.2	57.5	30 16.3	10.1	146 02.8	09.3	Shaula	96 27.9	S37 06.6
A	14	321 26.9	66 53.4	02.2	235 35.3	57.5	45 18.1	10.1	161 05.4	09.3	Sirius	258 37.0	S16 43.6
Y	15	336 29.4	81 52.6	. . 02.6	250 38.5	. . 57.4	60 20.0	. . 10.0	176 07.9	. . 09.4	Spica	158 35.6	S11 12.3
	16	351 31.9	96 51.9	03.0	265 41.6	57.4	75 21.8	10.0	191 10.5	09.4	Suhail	222 55.2	S43 27.8
	17	6 34.3	111 51.1	03.5	280 44.8	57.4	90 23.7	10.0	206 13.1	09.5			
	18	21 36.8	126 50.3	S21 03.9	295 47.9	N26 57.4	105 25.5	S23 10.0	221 15.6	N10 09.5	Vega	80 42.2	N38 47.3
	19	36 39.3	141 49.5	04.3	310 51.1	57.3	120 27.4	10.0	236 18.2	09.6	Zuben'ubi	137 10.2	S16 04.6
	20	51 41.7	156 48.8	04.7	325 54.2	57.3	135 29.3	09.9	251 20.7	09.6			
	21	66 44.2	171 48.0	. . 05.1	340 57.3	. . 57.3	150 31.1	. . 09.9	266 23.3	. . 09.7			
	22	81 46.6	186 47.2	05.6	356 00.5	57.3	165 33.0	09.9	281 25.9	09.7			
	23	96 49.1	201 46.4	06.0	11 03.6	57.2	180 34.8	09.9	296 28.4	09.8			
Mer. Pass.		h m 16 37.7	*v* −0.8	*d* 0.4	*v* 3.2	*d* 0.0	*v* 1.9	*d* 0.0	*v* 2.6	*d* 0.0			

	SHA	Mer. Pass.
	° ′	h m
Venus	107 29.3	9 31
Mars	273 41.4	22 21
Jupiter	84 14.5	11 02
Saturn	199 34.9	3 22

	UT d h	SUN GHA ° ′	SUN Dec ° ′	MOON GHA ° ′	v ′	Dec ° ′	d ′	HP ′
	10 00	178 13.1	S22 04.8	159 11.3	11.1	S20 23.5	10.8	56.3
	01	193 12.9	04.4	173 41.4	11.1	20 12.7	11.0	56.3
	02	208 12.6	04.0	188 11.5	11.2	20 01.7	11.0	56.4
	03	223 12.3	. . 03.7	202 41.7	11.3	19 50.7	11.2	56.4
	04	238 12.1	03.3	217 12.0	11.3	19 39.5	11.2	56.4
	05	253 11.8	03.0	231 42.3	11.4	19 28.3	11.4	56.4
	06	268 11.6	S22 02.6	246 12.7	11.4	S19 16.9	11.4	56.4
	07	283 11.3	02.2	260 43.1	11.5	19 05.5	11.6	56.5
T	08	298 11.1	01.9	275 13.6	11.5	18 53.9	11.6	56.5
H	09	313 10.8	. . 01.5	289 44.1	11.6	18 42.3	11.8	56.5
U	10	328 10.5	01.1	304 14.7	11.6	18 30.5	11.8	56.5
R	11	343 10.3	00.8	318 45.3	11.7	18 18.7	12.0	56.5
S	12	358 10.0	S22 00.4	333 16.0	11.7	S18 06.7	12.0	56.6
D	13	13 09.8	22 00.0	347 46.7	11.8	17 54.7	12.1	56.6
A	14	28 09.5	21 59.7	2 17.5	11.8	17 42.6	12.3	56.6
Y	15	43 09.3	. . 59.3	16 48.3	11.9	17 30.3	12.3	56.6
	16	58 09.0	58.9	31 19.2	12.0	17 18.0	12.4	56.6
	17	73 08.8	58.6	45 50.2	12.0	17 05.6	12.5	56.7
	18	88 08.5	S21 58.2	60 21.2	12.0	S16 53.1	12.6	56.7
	19	103 08.2	57.8	74 52.2	12.1	16 40.5	12.6	56.7
	20	118 08.0	57.4	89 23.3	12.1	16 27.9	12.8	56.7
	21	133 07.7	. . 57.1	103 54.4	12.2	16 15.1	12.8	56.7
	22	148 07.5	56.7	118 25.6	12.2	16 02.3	13.0	56.8
	23	163 07.2	56.3	132 56.8	12.3	15 49.3	13.0	56.8
	11 00	178 07.0	S21 55.9	147 28.1	12.3	S15 36.3	13.1	56.8
	01	193 06.7	55.6	161 59.4	12.4	15 23.2	13.1	56.8
	02	208 06.5	55.2	176 30.8	12.4	15 10.1	13.3	56.8
	03	223 06.2	. . 54.8	191 02.2	12.5	14 56.8	13.3	56.9
	04	238 06.0	54.4	205 33.7	12.5	14 43.5	13.4	56.9
	05	253 05.7	54.1	220 05.2	12.5	14 30.1	13.5	56.9
	06	268 05.5	S21 53.7	234 36.7	12.6	S14 16.6	13.6	56.9
	07	283 05.2	53.3	249 08.3	12.6	14 03.0	13.6	56.9
	08	298 05.0	52.9	263 39.9	12.7	13 49.4	13.7	57.0
F	09	313 04.7	. . 52.5	278 11.6	12.7	13 35.7	13.8	57.0
R	10	328 04.5	52.1	292 43.3	12.8	13 21.9	13.9	57.0
I	11	343 04.2	51.8	307 15.1	12.8	13 08.0	13.9	57.0
D	12	358 04.0	S21 51.4	321 46.9	12.8	S12 54.1	14.0	57.0
A	13	13 03.7	51.0	336 18.7	12.9	12 40.1	14.0	57.1
Y	14	28 03.5	50.6	350 50.6	12.9	12 26.1	14.1	57.1
	15	43 03.2	. . 50.2	5 22.5	12.9	12 12.0	14.2	57.1
	16	58 03.0	49.8	19 54.4	13.0	11 57.8	14.3	57.1
	17	73 02.7	49.4	34 26.4	13.0	11 43.5	14.3	57.1
	18	88 02.5	S21 49.1	48 58.4	13.0	S11 29.2	14.4	57.2
	19	103 02.2	48.7	63 30.4	13.1	11 14.8	14.4	57.2
	20	118 02.0	48.3	78 02.5	13.1	11 00.4	14.5	57.2
	21	133 01.7	. . 47.9	92 34.6	13.1	10 45.9	14.5	57.2
	22	148 01.5	47.5	107 06.7	13.2	10 31.4	14.6	57.2
	23	163 01.2	47.1	121 38.9	13.2	10 16.8	14.7	57.3
	12 00	178 01.0	S21 46.7	136 11.1	13.2	S10 02.1	14.7	57.3
	01	193 00.7	46.3	150 43.3	13.2	9 47.4	14.8	57.3
	02	208 00.5	45.9	165 15.5	13.3	9 32.6	14.8	57.3
	03	223 00.2	. . 45.5	179 47.8	13.3	9 17.8	14.9	57.3
	04	238 00.0	45.1	194 20.1	13.3	9 02.9	14.9	57.4
	05	252 59.7	44.7	208 52.4	13.3	8 48.0	15.0	57.4
	06	267 59.5	S21 44.3	223 24.7	13.4	S 8 33.0	15.0	57.4
	07	282 59.3	43.9	237 57.1	13.4	8 18.0	15.1	57.4
S	08	297 59.0	43.5	252 29.5	13.4	8 02.9	15.1	57.4
A	09	312 58.8	. . 43.1	267 01.9	13.4	7 47.8	15.2	57.5
T	10	327 58.5	42.7	281 34.3	13.4	7 32.6	15.2	57.5
U	11	342 58.3	42.3	296 06.7	13.5	7 17.4	15.3	57.5
R	12	357 58.0	S21 41.9	310 39.2	13.4	S 7 02.1	15.2	57.5
D	13	12 57.8	41.5	325 11.6	13.5	6 46.9	15.4	57.5
A	14	27 57.5	41.1	339 44.1	13.5	6 31.5	15.3	57.6
Y	15	42 57.3	. . 40.7	354 16.6	13.5	6 16.2	15.5	57.6
	16	57 57.1	40.3	8 49.1	13.5	6 00.7	15.4	57.6
	17	72 56.8	39.9	23 21.6	13.5	5 45.3	15.5	57.6
	18	87 56.6	S21 39.5	37 54.1	13.6	S 5 29.8	15.5	57.6
	19	102 56.3	39.1	52 26.7	13.5	5 14.3	15.5	57.7
	20	117 56.1	38.7	66 59.2	13.6	4 58.8	15.6	57.7
	21	132 55.9	. . 38.3	81 31.8	13.5	4 43.2	15.6	57.7
	22	147 55.6	37.9	96 04.3	13.6	4 27.6	15.7	57.7
	23	162 55.4	37.5	110 36.9	13.5	S 4 11.9	15.6	57.7
		SD 16.3	*d* 0.4	SD 15.4		15.5		15.7

Lat. °	Twilight Naut. h m	Twilight Civil h m	Sunrise h m	Moonrise 10 h m	11 h m	12 h m	13 h m
N 72	08 11	10 10	■	13 29	11 36	10 50	10 15
N 70	07 54	09 30	■	12 06	11 12	10 40	10 13
68	07 41	09 03	10 56	11 26	10 54	10 31	10 12
66	07 30	08 42	10 06	10 59	10 39	10 24	10 11
64	07 20	08 26	09 35	10 38	10 27	10 18	10 10
62	07 12	08 12	09 12	10 20	10 16	10 13	10 09
60	07 05	08 00	08 54	10 06	10 07	10 08	10 08
N 58	06 59	07 50	08 39	09 54	10 00	10 04	10 07
56	06 53	07 40	08 26	09 43	09 53	10 00	10 06
54	06 47	07 32	08 15	09 33	09 46	09 57	10 06
52	06 42	07 25	08 05	09 25	09 41	09 54	10 05
50	06 38	07 18	07 56	09 17	09 35	09 51	10 05
45	06 27	07 04	07 37	09 01	09 24	09 45	10 04
N 40	06 18	06 51	07 21	08 48	09 15	09 40	10 03
35	06 09	06 41	07 08	08 36	09 07	09 35	10 02
30	06 02	06 31	06 57	08 26	09 00	09 31	10 01
20	05 46	06 14	06 37	08 08	08 48	09 24	10 00
N 10	05 32	05 58	06 20	07 53	08 37	09 18	09 59
0	05 16	05 42	06 04	07 39	08 27	09 13	09 58
S 10	04 58	05 25	05 48	07 25	08 16	09 07	09 57
20	04 37	05 06	05 30	07 09	08 06	09 01	09 56
30	04 10	04 43	05 10	06 51	07 53	08 54	09 55
35	03 53	04 28	04 58	06 41	07 46	08 50	09 54
40	03 31	04 12	04 44	06 29	07 37	08 46	09 54
45	03 04	03 51	04 27	06 15	07 28	08 40	09 53
S 50	02 24	03 24	04 07	05 57	07 16	08 34	09 52
52	02 01	03 11	03 57	05 49	07 10	08 31	09 51
54	01 30	02 55	03 46	05 40	07 04	08 28	09 51
56	00 23	02 36	03 33	05 29	06 57	08 24	09 50
58	////	02 12	03 18	05 18	06 49	08 20	09 50
S 60	////	01 38	03 01	05 04	06 41	08 15	09 49

Lat. °	Sunset h m	Twilight Civil h m	Twilight Naut. h m	Moonset 10 h m	11 h m	12 h m	13 h m
N 72	■	14 06	16 06	14 34	18 08	20 31	22 45
N 70	■	14 46	16 22	15 56	18 29	20 38	22 42
68	13 20	15 13	16 35	16 34	18 45	20 44	22 40
66	14 10	15 34	16 46	17 00	18 58	20 49	22 38
64	14 41	15 50	16 56	17 20	19 09	20 53	22 36
62	15 03	16 04	17 04	17 36	19 18	20 57	22 35
60	15 22	16 16	17 11	17 50	19 26	21 00	22 34
N 58	15 37	16 26	17 17	18 01	19 33	21 03	22 33
56	15 50	16 35	17 23	18 11	19 39	21 05	22 32
54	16 01	16 43	17 29	18 20	19 44	21 07	22 31
52	16 11	16 51	17 34	18 28	19 49	21 09	22 30
50	16 20	16 57	17 38	18 35	19 53	21 11	22 29
45	16 39	17 12	17 49	18 50	20 02	21 15	22 28
N 40	16 54	17 24	17 58	19 02	20 10	21 18	22 27
35	17 07	17 35	18 06	19 12	20 17	21 21	22 25
30	17 19	17 45	18 14	19 21	20 22	21 23	22 24
20	17 38	18 02	18 29	19 36	20 32	21 27	22 23
N 10	17 55	18 18	18 44	19 50	20 41	21 31	22 21
0	18 11	18 34	19 00	20 02	20 49	21 34	22 20
S 10	18 28	18 50	19 17	20 14	20 57	21 38	22 18
20	18 45	19 09	19 38	20 27	21 05	21 41	22 17
30	19 06	19 33	20 05	20 42	21 15	21 45	22 15
35	19 18	19 47	20 22	20 51	21 20	21 47	22 14
40	19 31	20 03	20 43	21 00	21 26	21 50	22 13
45	19 48	20 24	21 11	21 12	21 33	21 53	22 12
S 50	20 08	20 51	21 50	21 25	21 42	21 56	22 10
52	20 18	21 04	22 12	21 31	21 46	21 58	22 09
54	20 29	21 19	22 42	21 38	21 50	21 59	22 08
56	20 41	21 38	23 40	21 46	21 55	22 01	22 08
58	20 56	22 02	////	21 55	22 00	22 03	22 07
S 60	21 13	22 34	////	22 05	22 06	22 06	22 06

Day	SUN Eqn. of Time 00^h	SUN Eqn. of Time 12^h	SUN Mer. Pass.	MOON Mer. Pass. Upper	MOON Mer. Pass. Lower	Age	Phase
d	m s	m s	h m	h m	h m	d	%
10	07 07	07 19	12 07	13 51	01 26	02	4
11	07 32	07 44	12 08	14 38	02 14	03	9
12	07 56	08 07	12 08	15 24	03 01	04	17

UT d	h		ARIES GHA	VENUS −4.0 GHA	Dec	MARS −1.1 GHA	Dec	JUPITER −1.8 GHA	Dec	SATURN +0.5 GHA	Dec
			° ′	° ′	° ′	° ′	° ′	° ′	° ′	° ′	° ′
13	00		111 51.6	216 45.6	S21 06.4	26 06.7	N26 57.2	195 36.7	S23 09.9	311 31.0	N10 09.8
	01		126 54.0	231 44.9	06.8	41 09.9	57.2	210 38.5	09.8	326 33.6	09.9
	02		141 56.5	246 44.1	07.2	56 13.0	57.2	225 40.4	09.8	341 36.1	09.9
	03		156 59.0	261 43.3	. . 07.6	71 16.1	. . 57.2	240 42.2	. . 09.8	356 38.7	. . 10.0
	04		172 01.4	276 42.5	08.0	86 19.2	57.1	255 44.1	09.8	11 41.2	10.0
	05		187 03.9	291 41.7	08.4	101 22.4	57.1	270 45.9	09.8	26 43.8	10.1
	06		202 06.4	306 41.0	S21 08.8	116 25.5	N26 57.1	285 47.8	S23 09.7	41 46.4	N10 10.1
	07		217 08.8	321 40.2	09.3	131 28.6	57.1	300 49.6	09.7	56 48.9	10.2
	08		232 11.3	336 39.4	09.7	146 31.7	57.0	315 51.5	09.7	71 51.5	10.2
	09	S	247 13.8	351 38.6	. . 10.1	161 34.8	. . 57.0	330 53.3	. . 09.7	86 54.1	. . 10.3
	10	U	262 16.2	6 37.8	10.5	176 38.0	57.0	345 55.2	09.7	101 56.6	10.3
	11	N	277 18.7	21 37.0	10.9	191 41.1	57.0	0 57.0	09.6	116 59.2	10.4
	12	D	292 21.1	36 36.3	S21 11.3	206 44.2	N26 56.9	15 58.9	S23 09.6	132 01.8	N10 10.4
	13	A	307 23.6	51 35.5	11.7	221 47.3	56.9	31 00.7	09.6	147 04.3	10.5
	14	Y	322 26.1	66 34.7	12.1	236 50.4	56.9	46 02.6	09.6	162 06.9	10.5
	15		337 28.5	81 33.9	. . 12.5	251 53.5	. . 56.9	61 04.5	. . 09.5	177 09.4	. . 10.6
	16		352 31.0	96 33.1	12.9	266 56.6	56.8	76 06.3	09.5	192 12.0	10.6
	17		7 33.5	111 32.3	13.3	281 59.7	56.8	91 08.2	09.5	207 14.6	10.7
	18		22 35.9	126 31.5	S21 13.7	297 02.8	N26 56.8	106 10.0	S23 09.5	222 17.1	N10 10.7
	19		37 38.4	141 30.8	14.1	312 05.9	56.8	121 11.9	09.5	237 19.7	10.8
	20		52 40.9	156 30.0	14.4	327 09.0	56.7	136 13.7	09.4	252 22.3	10.8
	21		67 43.3	171 29.2	. . 14.8	342 12.1	. . 56.7	151 15.6	. . 09.4	267 24.8	. . 10.9
	22		82 45.8	186 28.4	15.2	357 15.2	56.7	166 17.4	09.4	282 27.4	10.9
	23		97 48.2	201 27.6	15.6	12 18.3	56.7	181 19.3	09.4	297 30.0	11.0
14	00		112 50.7	216 26.8	S21 16.0	27 21.4	N26 56.6	196 21.1	S23 09.4	312 32.5	N10 11.0
	01		127 53.2	231 26.0	16.4	42 24.5	56.6	211 23.0	09.3	327 35.1	11.1
	02		142 55.6	246 25.2	16.8	57 27.6	56.6	226 24.8	09.3	342 37.7	11.1
	03		157 58.1	261 24.5	. . 17.2	72 30.7	. . 56.5	241 26.7	. . 09.3	357 40.2	. . 11.2
	04		173 00.6	276 23.7	17.6	87 33.8	56.5	256 28.5	09.3	12 42.8	11.2
	05		188 03.0	291 22.9	17.9	102 36.9	56.5	271 30.4	09.2	27 45.4	11.3
	06		203 05.5	306 22.1	S21 18.3	117 40.0	N26 56.5	286 32.3	S23 09.2	42 47.9	N10 11.3
	07		218 08.0	321 21.3	18.7	132 43.0	56.4	301 34.1	09.2	57 50.5	11.4
	08		233 10.4	336 20.5	19.1	147 46.1	56.4	316 36.0	09.2	72 53.1	11.4
	09	M	248 12.9	351 19.7	. . 19.5	162 49.2	. . 56.4	331 37.8	. . 09.2	87 55.6	. . 11.5
	10	O	263 15.4	6 18.9	19.9	177 52.3	56.4	346 39.7	09.1	102 58.2	11.5
	11	N	278 17.8	21 18.1	20.2	192 55.4	56.3	1 41.5	09.1	118 00.8	11.6
	12	D	293 20.3	36 17.3	S21 20.6	207 58.4	N26 56.3	16 43.4	S23 09.1	133 03.3	N10 11.6
	13	A	308 22.7	51 16.5	21.0	223 01.5	56.3	31 45.2	09.1	148 05.9	11.7
	14	Y	323 25.2	66 15.7	21.4	238 04.6	56.2	46 47.1	09.0	163 08.5	11.7
	15		338 27.7	81 15.0	. . 21.7	253 07.7	. . 56.2	61 48.9	. . 09.0	178 11.0	. . 11.8
	16		353 30.1	96 14.2	22.1	268 10.7	56.2	76 50.8	09.0	193 13.6	11.8
	17		8 32.6	111 13.4	22.5	283 13.8	56.2	91 52.7	09.0	208 16.2	11.9
	18		23 35.1	126 12.6	S21 22.8	298 16.9	N26 56.1	106 54.5	S23 09.0	223 18.7	N10 11.9
	19		38 37.5	141 11.8	23.2	313 19.9	56.1	121 56.4	08.9	238 21.3	12.0
	20		53 40.0	156 11.0	23.6	328 23.0	56.1	136 58.2	08.9	253 23.9	12.0
	21		68 42.5	171 10.2	. . 24.0	343 26.1	. . 56.0	152 00.1	. . 08.9	268 26.5	. . 12.1
	22		83 44.9	186 09.4	24.3	358 29.1	56.0	167 01.9	08.9	283 29.0	12.1
	23		98 47.4	201 08.6	24.7	13 32.2	56.0	182 03.8	08.8	298 31.6	12.2
15	00		113 49.9	216 07.8	S21 25.1	28 35.2	N26 56.0	197 05.6	S23 08.8	313 34.2	N10 12.2
	01		128 52.3	231 07.0	25.4	43 38.3	55.9	212 07.5	08.8	328 36.7	12.3
	02		143 54.8	246 06.2	25.8	58 41.3	55.9	227 09.3	08.8	343 39.3	12.3
	03		158 57.2	261 05.4	. . 26.1	73 44.4	. . 55.9	242 11.2	. . 08.8	358 41.9	. . 12.4
	04		173 59.7	276 04.6	26.5	88 47.5	55.8	257 13.1	08.7	13 44.4	12.4
	05		189 02.2	291 03.8	26.9	103 50.5	55.8	272 14.9	08.7	28 47.0	12.5
	06		204 04.6	306 03.0	S21 27.2	118 53.6	N26 55.8	287 16.8	S23 08.7	43 49.6	N10 12.5
	07		219 07.1	321 02.2	27.6	133 56.6	55.8	302 18.6	08.7	58 52.2	12.6
	08	T	234 09.6	336 01.4	27.9	148 59.6	55.7	317 20.5	08.6	73 54.7	12.7
	09	U	249 12.0	351 00.6	. . 28.3	164 02.7	. . 55.7	332 22.3	. . 08.6	88 57.3	. . 12.7
	10	E	264 14.5	5 59.8	28.6	179 05.7	55.7	347 24.2	08.6	103 59.9	12.8
	11	S	279 17.0	20 59.0	29.0	194 08.8	55.6	2 26.0	08.6	119 02.4	12.8
	12		294 19.4	35 58.2	S21 29.3	209 11.8	N26 55.6	17 27.9	S23 08.6	134 05.0	N10 12.9
	13	D	309 21.9	50 57.4	29.7	224 14.8	55.6	32 29.8	08.5	149 07.6	12.9
	14	A	324 24.3	65 56.6	30.0	239 17.9	55.5	47 31.6	08.5	164 10.2	13.0
	15	Y	339 26.8	80 55.8	. . 30.4	254 20.9	. . 55.5	62 33.5	. . 08.5	179 12.7	. . 13.0
	16		354 29.3	95 55.0	30.7	269 24.0	55.5	77 35.3	08.5	194 15.3	13.1
	17		9 31.7	110 54.2	31.1	284 27.0	55.5	92 37.2	08.4	209 17.9	13.1
	18		24 34.2	125 53.4	S21 31.4	299 30.0	N26 55.4	107 39.0	S23 08.4	224 20.4	N10 13.2
	19		39 36.7	140 52.6	31.8	314 33.0	55.4	122 40.9	08.4	239 23.0	13.2
	20		54 39.1	155 51.8	32.1	329 36.1	55.4	137 42.8	08.4	254 25.6	13.3
	21		69 41.6	170 51.0	. . 32.5	344 39.1	. . 55.3	152 44.6	. . 08.3	269 28.2	. . 13.3
	22		84 44.1	185 50.2	32.8	359 42.1	55.3	167 46.5	08.3	284 30.7	13.4
	23		99 46.5	200 49.4	33.2	14 45.1	55.3	182 48.3	08.3	299 33.3	13.4
Mer. Pass.			h m 16 25.9	v −0.8	d 0.4	v 3.1	d 0.0	v 1.9	d 0.0	v 2.6	d 0.1

STARS Name	SHA	Dec
	° ′	° ′
Acamar	315 21.2	S40 16.5
Achernar	335 29.5	S57 12.0
Acrux	173 14.1	S63 08.4
Adhara	255 15.4	S28 59.0
Aldebaran	290 53.9	N16 31.6
Alioth	166 23.9	N55 54.6
Alkaid	153 02.0	N49 16.0
Al Na'ir	27 49.0	S46 55.5
Alnilam	275 50.2	S 1 11.8
Alphard	217 59.8	S 8 41.6
Alphecca	126 14.6	N26 41.0
Alpheratz	357 48.0	N29 08.3
Altair	62 12.6	N 8 53.3
Ankaa	353 19.7	S42 15.9
Antares	112 31.6	S26 27.0
Arcturus	145 59.5	N19 08.2
Atria	107 37.7	S69 02.4
Avior	234 19.2	S59 32.0
Bellatrix	278 36.1	N 6 21.5
Betelgeuse	271 05.4	N 7 24.6
Canopus	263 57.5	S52 42.0
Capella	280 40.1	N46 00.6
Deneb	49 34.9	N45 18.5
Denebola	182 37.6	N14 31.4
Diphda	349 00.0	S17 56.6
Dubhe	193 55.9	N61 42.2
Elnath	278 17.5	N28 37.0
Eltanin	90 48.5	N51 29.0
Enif	33 51.5	N 9 54.7
Fomalhaut	15 28.6	S29 34.9
Gacrux	172 05.6	S57 09.3
Gienah	175 56.5	S17 35.2
Hadar	148 54.1	S60 24.5
Hamal	328 05.4	N23 30.2
Kaus Aust.	83 49.6	S34 22.9
Kochab	137 19.8	N74 06.9
Markab	13 42.7	N15 15.0
Menkar	314 19.2	N 4 07.4
Menkent	148 12.6	S36 24.5
Miaplacidus	221 40.1	S69 44.9
Mirfak	308 46.1	N49 53.7
Nunki	76 03.7	S26 17.3
Peacock	53 26.1	S56 42.7
Pollux	243 32.3	N28 00.4
Procyon	245 03.7	N 5 12.3
Rasalhague	96 10.6	N12 33.1
Regulus	207 47.6	N11 55.6
Rigel	281 15.7	S 8 11.5
Rigil Kent.	139 57.8	S60 51.9
Sabik	102 17.5	S15 44.2
Schedar	349 45.6	N56 35.2
Shaula	96 27.9	S37 06.6
Sirius	258 37.0	S16 43.6
Spica	158 35.6	S11 12.3
Suhail	222 55.2	S43 27.8
Vega	80 42.2	N38 47.3
Zuben'ubi	137 10.1	S16 04.6

	SHA	Mer. Pass.
	° ′	h m
Venus	103 36.1	9 35
Mars	274 30.7	22 06
Jupiter	83 30.4	10 53
Saturn	199 41.8	3 09

	UT	SUN GHA	SUN Dec	MOON GHA	v	MOON Dec	d	HP
	d h	° ′	° ′	° ′	′	° ′	′	′
	13 00	177 55.1	S21 37.0	125 09.4	13.6	S 3 56.3	15.7	57.8
	01	192 54.9	36.6	139 42.0	13.5	3 40.6	15.8	57.8
	02	207 54.7	36.2	154 14.5	13.6	3 24.8	15.7	57.8
	03	222 54.4	. . 35.8	168 47.1	13.5	3 09.1	15.8	57.8
	04	237 54.2	35.4	183 19.6	13.6	2 53.3	15.8	57.8
	05	252 53.9	35.0	197 52.2	13.5	2 37.5	15.8	57.9
	06	267 53.7	S21 34.6	212 24.7	13.5	S 2 21.7	15.8	57.9
	07	282 53.5	34.1	226 57.2	13.6	2 05.9	15.9	57.9
	08	297 53.2	33.7	241 29.8	13.5	1 50.0	15.8	57.9
S	09	312 53.0	. . 33.3	256 02.3	13.5	1 34.2	15.9	57.9
U	10	327 52.7	32.9	270 34.8	13.5	1 18.3	15.9	58.0
N	11	342 52.5	32.5	285 07.3	13.5	1 02.4	16.0	58.0
D	12	357 52.3	S21 32.1	299 39.8	13.4	S 0 46.4	15.9	58.0
A	13	12 52.0	31.6	314 12.2	13.5	0 30.5	15.9	58.0
Y	14	27 51.8	31.2	328 44.7	13.4	S 0 14.6	16.0	58.0
	15	42 51.6	. . 30.8	343 17.1	13.5	N 0 01.4	15.9	58.1
	16	57 51.3	30.4	357 49.6	13.4	0 17.3	16.0	58.1
	17	72 51.1	29.9	12 22.0	13.3	0 33.3	16.0	58.1
	18	87 50.8	S21 29.5	26 54.3	13.4	N 0 49.3	16.0	58.1
	19	102 50.6	29.1	41 26.7	13.3	1 05.3	16.0	58.1
	20	117 50.4	28.7	55 59.0	13.3	1 21.3	16.0	58.1
	21	132 50.1	. . 28.2	70 31.3	13.3	1 37.3	16.0	58.2
	22	147 49.9	27.8	85 03.6	13.3	1 53.3	16.0	58.2
	23	162 49.7	27.4	99 35.9	13.2	2 09.3	16.0	58.2
	14 00	177 49.4	S21 27.0	114 08.1	13.2	N 2 25.3	15.9	58.2
	01	192 49.2	26.5	128 40.3	13.2	2 41.2	16.0	58.2
	02	207 49.0	26.1	143 12.5	13.1	2 57.2	16.0	58.3
	03	222 48.7	. . 25.7	157 44.6	13.1	3 13.2	16.0	58.3
	04	237 48.5	25.2	172 16.7	13.1	3 29.2	16.0	58.3
	05	252 48.3	24.8	186 48.8	13.0	3 45.2	15.9	58.3
	06	267 48.0	S21 24.4	201 20.8	13.0	N 4 01.1	16.0	58.3
	07	282 47.8	23.9	215 52.8	13.0	4 17.1	15.9	58.4
	08	297 47.6	23.5	230 24.8	12.9	4 33.0	16.0	58.4
M	09	312 47.3	. . 23.1	244 56.7	12.9	4 49.0	15.9	58.4
O	10	327 47.1	22.6	259 28.6	12.8	5 04.9	15.9	58.4
N	11	342 46.9	22.2	274 00.4	12.8	5 20.8	15.9	58.4
D	12	357 46.7	S21 21.8	288 32.2	12.7	N 5 36.7	15.9	58.4
A	13	12 46.4	21.3	303 03.9	12.7	5 52.6	15.8	58.5
Y	14	27 46.2	20.9	317 35.6	12.7	6 08.4	15.9	58.5
	15	42 46.0	. . 20.5	332 07.3	12.5	6 24.3	15.8	58.5
	16	57 45.7	20.0	346 38.8	12.6	6 40.1	15.8	58.5
	17	72 45.5	19.6	1 10.4	12.5	6 55.9	15.7	58.5
	18	87 45.3	S21 19.1	15 41.9	12.4	N 7 11.6	15.8	58.6
	19	102 45.1	18.7	30 13.3	12.4	7 27.4	15.7	58.6
	20	117 44.8	18.2	44 44.7	12.3	7 43.1	15.7	58.6
	21	132 44.6	. . 17.8	59 16.0	12.3	7 58.8	15.6	58.6
	22	147 44.4	17.4	73 47.3	12.2	8 14.4	15.6	58.6
	23	162 44.1	16.9	88 18.5	12.1	8 30.0	15.6	58.6
	15 00	177 43.9	S21 16.5	102 49.6	12.1	N 8 45.6	15.6	58.7
	01	192 43.7	16.0	117 20.7	12.0	9 01.2	15.5	58.7
	02	207 43.5	15.6	131 51.7	12.0	9 16.7	15.5	58.7
	03	222 43.2	. . 15.1	146 22.7	11.9	9 32.2	15.5	58.7
	04	237 43.0	14.7	160 53.6	11.8	9 47.7	15.4	58.7
	05	252 42.8	14.2	175 24.4	11.8	10 03.1	15.3	58.8
	06	267 42.6	S21 13.8	189 55.2	11.7	N10 18.4	15.4	58.8
	07	282 42.3	13.3	204 25.9	11.6	10 33.8	15.2	58.8
T	08	297 42.1	12.9	218 56.5	11.5	10 49.0	15.3	58.8
U	09	312 41.9	. . 12.4	233 27.0	11.5	11 04.3	15.2	58.8
E	10	327 41.7	12.0	247 57.5	11.4	11 19.5	15.1	58.8
S	11	342 41.4	11.5	262 27.9	11.3	11 34.6	15.1	58.9
	12	357 41.2	S21 11.1	276 58.2	11.2	N11 49.7	15.0	58.9
D	13	12 41.0	10.6	291 28.4	11.2	12 04.7	15.0	58.9
A	14	27 40.8	10.2	305 58.6	11.1	12 19.7	14.9	58.9
Y	15	42 40.5	. . 09.7	320 28.7	11.0	12 34.6	14.9	58.9
	16	57 40.3	09.2	334 58.7	10.9	12 49.5	14.8	58.9
	17	72 40.1	08.8	349 28.6	10.8	13 04.3	14.8	59.0
	18	87 39.9	S21 08.3	3 58.4	10.8	N13 19.1	14.7	59.0
	19	102 39.7	07.9	18 28.2	10.6	13 33.8	14.6	59.0
	20	117 39.4	07.4	32 57.8	10.6	13 48.4	14.5	59.0
	21	132 39.2	. . 07.0	47 27.4	10.5	14 02.9	14.5	59.0
	22	147 39.0	06.5	61 56.9	10.4	14 17.4	14.5	59.0
	23	162 38.8	06.0	76 26.3	10.3	N14 31.9	14.3	59.1
		SD 16.3	d 0.4	SD		15.8	15.9	16.0

Lat.	Twilight Naut.	Twilight Civil	Sunrise	Moonrise 13	Moonrise 14	Moonrise 15	Moonrise 16
°	h m	h m	h m	h m	h m	h m	h m
N 72	08 04	09 58	▬	10 15	09 41	09 00	07 51
N 70	07 49	09 22	▬	10 13	09 47	09 18	08 34
68	07 37	08 57	10 41	10 12	09 53	09 32	09 03
66	07 26	08 37	09 58	10 11	09 57	09 43	09 25
64	07 17	08 21	09 29	10 10	10 01	09 53	09 43
62	07 09	08 08	09 08	10 09	10 05	10 01	09 57
60	07 02	07 57	08 50	10 08	10 08	10 08	10 10
N 58	06 56	07 47	08 36	10 07	10 10	10 15	10 21
56	06 51	07 38	08 23	10 06	10 13	10 20	10 30
54	06 46	07 30	08 12	10 06	10 15	10 25	10 39
52	06 41	07 23	08 03	10 05	10 17	10 30	10 46
50	06 36	07 17	07 54	10 05	10 19	10 34	10 53
45	06 26	07 03	07 36	10 04	10 23	10 43	11 08
N 40	06 17	06 51	07 21	10 03	10 26	10 51	11 20
35	06 09	06 40	07 08	10 02	10 29	10 58	11 30
30	06 02	06 31	06 57	10 01	10 32	11 04	11 39
20	05 47	06 14	06 38	10 00	10 36	11 14	11 55
N 10	05 33	05 58	06 21	09 59	10 40	11 23	12 10
0	05 17	05 43	06 05	09 58	10 44	11 32	12 23
S 10	05 00	05 27	05 49	09 57	10 48	11 40	12 36
20	04 39	05 08	05 32	09 56	10 52	11 50	12 51
30	04 13	04 45	05 12	09 55	10 57	12 01	13 07
35	03 56	04 32	05 00	09 54	11 00	12 07	13 17
40	03 35	04 15	04 47	09 54	11 03	12 14	13 28
45	03 08	03 55	04 31	09 53	11 07	12 22	13 41
S 50	02 30	03 29	04 11	09 52	11 11	12 33	13 58
52	02 09	03 16	04 01	09 51	11 13	12 37	14 05
54	01 41	03 01	03 51	09 51	11 15	12 43	14 14
56	00 53	02 43	03 38	09 50	11 18	12 49	14 23
58	////	02 20	03 24	09 50	11 21	12 55	14 34
S 60	////	01 50	03 07	09 49	11 24	13 03	14 47

Lat.	Sunset	Twilight Civil	Twilight Naut.	Moonset 13	Moonset 14	Moonset 15	Moonset 16
°	h m	h m	h m	h m	h m	h m	h m
N 72	▬	14 21	16 14	22 45	25 06	01 06	04 01
N 70	▬	14 56	16 30	22 42	24 51	00 51	03 20
68	13 38	15 21	16 42	22 40	24 40	00 40	02 53
66	14 21	15 41	16 52	22 38	24 30	00 30	02 32
64	14 49	15 57	17 01	22 36	24 23	00 23	02 16
62	15 11	16 10	17 09	22 35	24 16	00 16	02 02
60	15 28	16 21	17 16	22 34	24 10	00 10	01 51
N 58	15 43	16 31	17 22	22 33	24 05	00 05	01 41
56	15 55	16 40	17 28	22 32	24 00	00 00	01 33
54	16 06	16 48	17 33	22 31	23 56	25 25	01 25
52	16 16	16 55	17 37	22 30	23 53	25 19	01 19
50	16 24	17 01	17 42	22 29	23 50	25 13	01 13
45	16 42	17 15	17 52	22 28	23 42	25 00	01 00
N 40	16 57	17 27	18 01	22 27	23 37	24 49	00 49
35	17 10	17 38	18 09	22 25	23 31	24 40	00 40
30	17 21	17 47	18 16	22 24	23 27	24 32	00 32
20	17 40	18 04	18 31	22 23	23 19	24 18	00 18
N 10	17 57	18 19	18 45	22 21	23 13	24 07	00 07
0	18 13	18 35	19 01	22 20	23 06	23 56	24 48
S 10	18 28	18 51	19 18	22 18	23 00	23 45	24 33
20	18 45	19 10	19 38	22 17	22 54	23 33	24 17
30	19 05	19 32	20 04	22 15	22 46	23 20	23 58
35	19 17	19 46	20 21	22 14	22 42	23 12	23 47
40	19 30	20 02	20 42	22 13	22 37	23 03	23 34
45	19 46	20 22	21 08	22 12	22 31	22 53	23 20
S 50	20 06	20 48	21 46	22 10	22 24	22 41	23 02
52	20 16	21 01	22 07	22 09	22 21	22 35	22 54
54	20 26	21 16	22 34	22 08	22 18	22 29	22 44
56	20 38	21 33	23 19	22 08	22 14	22 22	22 34
58	20 52	21 56	////	22 07	22 10	22 15	22 22
S 60	21 09	22 25	////	22 06	22 06	22 06	22 08

Day	SUN Eqn. of Time 00^h	SUN Eqn. of Time 12^h	SUN Mer. Pass.	MOON Mer. Pass. Upper	MOON Mer. Pass. Lower	MOON Age	MOON Phase
d	m s	m s	h m	h m	h m	d %	
13	08 19	08 30	12 09	16 09	03 46	05 25	
14	08 42	08 53	12 09	16 55	04 32	06 35	
15	09 04	09 15	12 09	17 44	05 19	07 46	

	UT	ARIES	VENUS −4.0		MARS −1.0		JUPITER −1.8		SATURN +0.5		STARS		
		GHA	GHA	Dec	GHA	Dec	GHA	Dec	GHA	Dec	Name	SHA	Dec
	d h	° ′	° ′	° ′	° ′	° ′	° ′	° ′	° ′	° ′		° ′	° ′
	16 00	114 49.0	215 48.6	S21 33.5	29 48.2	N26 55.2	197 50.2	S23 08.3	314 35.9	N10 13.5	Acamar	315 21.2	S40 16.5
	01	129 51.5	230 47.8	33.8	44 51.2	55.2	212 52.0	08.2	329 38.5	13.6	Achernar	335 29.5	S57 12.0
	02	144 53.9	245 47.0	34.2	59 54.2	55.2	227 53.9	08.2	344 41.0	13.6	Acrux	173 14.0	S63 08.4
	03	159 56.4	260 46.2	. . 34.5	74 57.2	. . 55.1	242 55.7	. . 08.2	359 43.6	. . 13.7	Adhara	255 15.4	S28 59.0
	04	174 58.8	275 45.4	34.8	90 00.2	55.1	257 57.6	08.2	14 46.2	13.7	Aldebaran	290 53.9	N16 31.6
	05	190 01.3	290 44.5	35.2	105 03.2	55.1	272 59.5	08.2	29 48.7	13.8			
	06	205 03.8	305 43.7	S21 35.5	120 06.2	N26 55.0	288 01.3	S23 08.1	44 51.3	N10 13.8	Alioth	166 23.9	N55 54.6
W	07	220 06.2	320 42.9	35.8	135 09.3	55.0	303 03.2	08.1	59 53.9	13.9	Alkaid	153 01.9	N49 16.0
E	08	235 08.7	335 42.1	36.2	150 12.3	55.0	318 05.0	08.1	74 56.5	13.9	Al Na'ir	27 49.1	S46 55.5
D	09	250 11.2	350 41.3	. . 36.5	165 15.3	. . 54.9	333 06.9	. . 08.1	89 59.0	. . 14.0	Alnilam	275 50.2	S 1 11.8
N	10	265 13.6	5 40.5	36.8	180 18.3	54.9	348 08.7	08.0	105 01.6	14.0	Alphard	217 59.8	S 8 41.6
E	11	280 16.1	20 39.7	37.2	195 21.3	54.9	3 10.6	08.0	120 04.2	14.1			
S	12	295 18.6	35 38.9	S21 37.5	210 24.3	N26 54.9	18 12.5	S23 08.0	135 06.8	N10 14.1	Alphecca	126 14.6	N26 41.0
D	13	310 21.0	50 38.1	37.8	225 27.3	54.8	33 14.3	08.0	150 09.3	14.2	Alpheratz	357 48.0	N29 08.3
A	14	325 23.5	65 37.3	38.1	240 30.3	54.8	48 16.2	07.9	165 11.9	14.2	Altair	62 12.6	N 8 53.3
Y	15	340 26.0	80 36.5	. . 38.5	255 33.3	. . 54.8	63 18.0	. . 07.9	180 14.5	. . 14.3	Ankaa	353 19.7	S42 15.9
	16	355 28.4	95 35.7	38.8	270 36.3	54.7	78 19.9	07.9	195 17.1	14.4	Antares	112 31.6	S26 27.0
	17	10 30.9	110 34.8	39.1	285 39.3	54.7	93 21.7	07.9	210 19.6	14.4			
	18	25 33.3	125 34.0	S21 39.4	300 42.3	N26 54.7	108 23.6	S23 07.8	225 22.2	N10 14.5	Arcturus	145 59.5	N19 08.2
	19	40 35.8	140 33.2	39.7	315 45.2	54.6	123 25.5	07.8	240 24.8	14.5	Atria	107 37.7	S69 02.4
	20	55 38.3	155 32.4	40.1	330 48.2	54.6	138 27.3	07.8	255 27.4	14.6	Avior	234 19.2	S59 32.0
	21	70 40.7	170 31.6	. . 40.4	345 51.2	. . 54.6	153 29.2	. . 07.8	270 30.0	. . 14.6	Bellatrix	278 36.1	N 6 21.5
	22	85 43.2	185 30.8	40.7	0 54.2	54.5	168 31.0	07.7	285 32.5	14.7	Betelgeuse	271 05.4	N 7 24.6
	23	100 45.7	200 30.0	41.0	15 57.2	54.5	183 32.9	07.7	300 35.1	14.7			
	17 00	115 48.1	215 29.2	S21 41.3	31 00.2	N26 54.5	198 34.8	S23 07.7	315 37.7	N10 14.8	Canopus	263 57.5	S52 42.0
	01	130 50.6	230 28.4	41.6	46 03.2	54.4	213 36.6	07.7	330 40.3	14.8	Capella	280 40.1	N46 00.6
	02	145 53.1	245 27.5	42.0	61 06.1	54.4	228 38.5	07.6	345 42.8	14.9	Deneb	49 34.9	N45 18.5
	03	160 55.5	260 26.7	. . 42.3	76 09.1	. . 54.4	243 40.3	. . 07.6	0 45.4	. . 15.0	Denebola	182 37.6	N14 31.4
	04	175 58.0	275 25.9	42.6	91 12.1	54.3	258 42.2	07.6	15 48.0	15.0	Diphda	349 00.0	S17 56.6
	05	191 00.4	290 25.1	42.9	106 15.1	54.3	273 44.0	07.6	30 50.6	15.1			
	06	206 02.9	305 24.3	S21 43.2	121 18.0	N26 54.3	288 45.9	S23 07.6	45 53.1	N10 15.1	Dubhe	193 55.9	N61 42.2
	07	221 05.4	320 23.5	43.5	136 21.0	54.2	303 47.8	07.5	60 55.7	15.2	Elnath	278 17.5	N28 37.0
T	08	236 07.8	335 22.7	43.8	151 24.0	54.2	318 49.6	07.5	75 58.3	15.2	Eltanin	90 48.5	N51 29.0
H	09	251 10.3	350 21.8	. . 44.1	166 26.9	. . 54.2	333 51.5	. . 07.5	91 00.9	. . 15.3	Enif	33 51.5	N 9 54.7
U	10	266 12.8	5 21.0	44.4	181 29.9	54.1	348 53.3	07.5	106 03.5	15.3	Fomalhaut	15 28.6	S29 34.9
R	11	281 15.2	20 20.2	44.7	196 32.9	54.1	3 55.2	07.4	121 06.0	15.4			
S	12	296 17.7	35 19.4	S21 45.0	211 35.8	N26 54.0	18 57.1	S23 07.4	136 08.6	N10 15.4	Gacrux	172 05.6	S57 09.3
D	13	311 20.2	50 18.6	45.3	226 38.8	54.0	33 58.9	07.4	151 11.2	15.5	Gienah	175 56.5	S17 35.2
A	14	326 22.6	65 17.8	45.6	241 41.8	54.0	49 00.8	07.4	166 13.8	15.6	Hadar	148 54.1	S60 24.5
Y	15	341 25.1	80 16.9	. . 45.9	256 44.7	. . 53.9	64 02.6	. . 07.3	181 16.4	. . 15.6	Hamal	328 05.4	N23 30.2
	16	356 27.6	95 16.1	46.2	271 47.7	53.9	79 04.5	07.3	196 18.9	15.7	Kaus Aust.	83 49.6	S34 22.9
	17	11 30.0	110 15.3	46.5	286 50.6	53.9	94 06.3	07.3	211 21.5	15.7			
	18	26 32.5	125 14.5	S21 46.8	301 53.6	N26 53.8	109 08.2	S23 07.3	226 24.1	N10 15.8	Kochab	137 19.7	N74 06.9
	19	41 34.9	140 13.7	47.1	316 56.5	53.8	124 10.1	07.2	241 26.7	15.8	Markab	13 42.7	N15 15.0
	20	56 37.4	155 12.9	47.4	331 59.5	53.8	139 11.9	07.2	256 29.3	15.9	Menkar	314 19.2	N 4 07.3
	21	71 39.9	170 12.0	. . 47.7	347 02.4	. . 53.7	154 13.8	. . 07.2	271 31.8	. . 15.9	Menkent	148 12.6	S36 24.5
	22	86 42.3	185 11.2	48.0	2 05.4	53.7	169 15.6	07.2	286 34.4	16.0	Miaplacidus	221 40.0	S69 44.9
	23	101 44.8	200 10.4	48.3	17 08.3	53.7	184 17.5	07.1	301 37.0	16.1			
	18 00	116 47.3	215 09.6	S21 48.5	32 11.3	N26 53.6	199 19.4	S23 07.1	316 39.6	N10 16.1	Mirfak	308 46.1	N49 53.7
	01	131 49.7	230 08.8	48.8	47 14.2	53.6	214 21.2	07.1	331 42.2	16.2	Nunki	76 03.7	S26 17.3
	02	146 52.2	245 07.9	49.1	62 17.2	53.6	229 23.1	07.1	346 44.7	16.2	Peacock	53 26.1	S56 42.7
	03	161 54.7	260 07.1	. . 49.4	77 20.1	. . 53.5	244 24.9	. . 07.0	1 47.3	. . 16.3	Pollux	243 32.3	N28 00.4
	04	176 57.1	275 06.3	49.7	92 23.0	53.5	259 26.8	07.0	16 49.9	16.3	Procyon	245 03.7	N 5 12.3
	05	191 59.6	290 05.5	50.0	107 26.0	53.5	274 28.7	07.0	31 52.5	16.4			
	06	207 02.1	305 04.7	S21 50.3	122 28.9	N26 53.4	289 30.5	S23 07.0	46 55.1	N10 16.4	Rasalhague	96 10.5	N12 33.1
	07	222 04.5	320 03.8	50.5	137 31.8	53.4	304 32.4	06.9	61 57.6	16.5	Regulus	207 47.6	N11 55.6
	08	237 07.0	335 03.0	50.8	152 34.8	53.3	319 34.2	06.9	77 00.2	16.6	Rigel	281 15.7	S 8 11.5
F	09	252 09.4	350 02.2	. . 51.1	167 37.7	. . 53.3	334 36.1	. . 06.9	92 02.8	. . 16.6	Rigil Kent.	139 57.8	S60 51.9
R	10	267 11.9	5 01.4	51.4	182 40.6	53.3	349 38.0	06.9	107 05.4	16.7	Sabik	102 17.5	S15 44.2
I	11	282 14.4	20 00.5	51.7	197 43.6	53.2	4 39.8	06.8	122 08.0	16.7			
D	12	297 16.8	34 59.7	S21 51.9	212 46.5	N26 53.2	19 41.7	S23 06.8	137 10.5	N10 16.8	Schedar	349 45.7	N56 35.2
A	13	312 19.3	49 58.9	52.2	227 49.4	53.2	34 43.5	06.8	152 13.1	16.8	Shaula	96 27.9	S37 06.6
Y	14	327 21.8	64 58.1	52.5	242 52.3	53.1	49 45.4	06.7	167 15.7	16.9	Sirius	258 37.0	S16 43.6
	15	342 24.2	79 57.3	. . 52.7	257 55.3	. . 53.1	64 47.3	. . 06.7	182 18.3	. . 17.0	Spica	158 35.6	S11 12.3
	16	357 26.7	94 56.4	53.0	272 58.2	53.1	79 49.1	06.7	197 20.9	17.0	Suhail	222 55.2	S43 27.8
	17	12 29.2	109 55.6	53.3	288 01.1	53.0	94 51.0	06.7	212 23.5	17.1			
	18	27 31.6	124 54.8	S21 53.6	303 04.0	N26 53.0	109 52.9	S23 06.6	227 26.0	N10 17.1	Vega	80 42.2	N38 47.3
	19	42 34.1	139 54.0	53.8	318 06.9	53.0	124 54.7	06.6	242 28.6	17.2	Zuben'ubi	137 10.1	S16 04.6
	20	57 36.6	154 53.1	54.1	333 09.8	52.9	139 56.6	06.6	257 31.2	17.2		SHA	Mer. Pass.
	21	72 39.0	169 52.3	. . 54.4	348 12.7	. . 52.9	154 58.4	. . 06.6	272 33.8	. . 17.3		° ′	h m
	22	87 41.5	184 51.5	54.6	3 15.7	52.8	170 00.3	06.5	287 36.4	17.3	Venus	99 41.0	9 39
	23	102 43.9	199 50.7	54.9	18 18.6	52.8	185 02.2	06.5	302 39.0	17.4	Mars	275 12.0	21 52
	Mer. Pass.	h m 16 14.1	v −0.8	d 0.3	v 3.0	d 0.0	v 1.9	d 0.0	v 2.6	d 0.1	Jupiter	82 46.6	10 44
											Saturn	199 49.6	2 57

UT d h	SUN GHA ° ′	SUN Dec ° ′	MOON GHA ° ′	v ′	MOON Dec ° ′	d ′	HP ′
16 00 (WEDNESDAY)	177 38.6	S21 05.6	90 55.6	10.2	N14 46.2	14.3	59.1
01	192 38.3	05.1	105 24.8	10.1	15 00.5	14.2	59.1
02	207 38.1	04.6	119 53.9	10.1	15 14.7	14.2	59.1
03	222 37.9	. . 04.2	134 23.0	9.9	15 28.9	14.0	59.1
04	237 37.7	03.7	148 51.9	9.9	15 42.9	14.0	59.1
05	252 37.5	03.2	163 20.8	9.7	15 56.9	13.9	59.2
06	267 37.2	S21 02.8	177 49.5	9.7	N16 10.8	13.9	59.2
07	282 37.0	02.3	192 18.2	9.5	16 24.7	13.7	59.2
08	297 36.8	01.8	206 46.7	9.5	16 38.4	13.7	59.2
09	312 36.6	. . 01.4	221 15.2	9.3	16 52.1	13.6	59.2
10	327 36.4	00.9	235 43.5	9.3	17 05.7	13.4	59.2
11	342 36.2	00.4	250 11.8	9.1	17 19.1	13.4	59.2
12	357 35.9	S21 00.0	264 39.9	9.1	N17 32.5	13.3	59.3
13	12 35.7	20 59.5	279 08.0	8.9	17 45.8	13.2	59.3
14	27 35.5	59.0	293 35.9	8.8	17 59.0	13.2	59.3
15	42 35.3	. . 58.5	308 03.7	8.8	18 12.2	13.0	59.3
16	57 35.1	58.1	322 31.5	8.6	18 25.2	12.9	59.3
17	72 34.9	57.6	336 59.1	8.5	18 38.1	12.8	59.3
18	87 34.7	S20 57.1	351 26.6	8.4	N18 50.9	12.7	59.3
19	102 34.4	56.7	5 54.0	8.4	19 03.6	12.6	59.4
20	117 34.2	56.2	20 21.4	8.2	19 16.2	12.5	59.4
21	132 34.0	. . 55.7	34 48.6	8.1	19 28.7	12.4	59.4
22	147 33.8	55.2	49 15.7	7.9	19 41.1	12.3	59.4
23	162 33.6	54.7	63 42.6	7.9	19 53.4	12.2	59.4
17 00 (THURSDAY)	177 33.4	S20 54.3	78 09.5	7.8	N20 05.6	12.1	59.4
01	192 33.2	53.8	92 36.3	7.7	20 17.7	11.9	59.4
02	207 33.0	53.3	107 03.0	7.5	20 29.6	11.8	59.5
03	222 32.7	. . 52.8	121 29.5	7.4	20 41.4	11.7	59.5
04	237 32.5	52.3	135 55.9	7.4	20 53.1	11.6	59.5
05	252 32.3	51.9	150 22.3	7.2	21 04.7	11.5	59.5
06	267 32.1	S20 51.4	164 48.5	7.1	N21 16.2	11.3	59.5
07	282 31.9	50.9	179 14.6	7.0	21 27.5	11.3	59.5
08	297 31.7	50.4	193 40.6	6.9	21 38.8	11.0	59.5
09	312 31.5	. . 49.9	208 06.5	6.8	21 49.8	11.0	59.5
10	327 31.3	49.4	222 32.3	6.6	22 00.8	10.8	59.6
11	342 31.1	48.9	236 57.9	6.6	22 11.6	10.7	59.6
12	357 30.9	S20 48.5	251 23.5	6.4	N22 22.3	10.6	59.6
13	12 30.6	48.0	265 48.9	6.4	22 32.9	10.4	59.6
14	27 30.4	47.5	280 14.3	6.2	22 43.3	10.3	59.6
15	42 30.2	. . 47.0	294 39.5	6.1	22 53.6	10.1	59.6
16	57 30.0	46.5	309 04.6	6.0	23 03.7	10.0	59.6
17	72 29.8	46.0	323 29.6	5.9	23 13.7	9.9	59.6
18	87 29.6	S20 45.5	337 54.5	5.8	N23 23.6	9.7	59.6
19	102 29.4	45.0	352 19.3	5.7	23 33.3	9.5	59.6
20	117 29.2	44.5	6 44.0	5.6	23 42.8	9.4	59.7
21	132 29.0	. . 44.0	21 08.6	5.5	23 52.2	9.3	59.7
22	147 28.8	43.6	35 33.1	5.4	24 01.5	9.1	59.7
23	162 28.6	43.1	49 57.5	5.2	24 10.6	9.0	59.7
18 00 (FRIDAY)	177 28.4	S20 42.6	64 21.7	5.2	N24 19.6	8.8	59.7
01	192 28.2	42.1	78 45.9	5.1	24 28.4	8.6	59.7
02	207 28.0	41.6	93 10.0	4.9	24 37.0	8.5	59.7
03	222 27.8	. . 41.1	107 33.9	4.9	24 45.5	8.3	59.7
04	237 27.6	40.6	121 57.8	4.8	24 53.8	8.1	59.7
05	252 27.4	40.1	136 21.6	4.6	25 01.9	8.0	59.7
06	267 27.1	S20 39.6	150 45.2	4.6	N25 09.9	7.8	59.7
07	282 26.9	39.1	165 08.8	4.5	25 17.7	7.7	59.7
08	297 26.7	38.6	179 32.3	4.4	25 25.4	7.5	59.8
09	312 26.5	. . 38.1	193 55.7	4.3	25 32.9	7.3	59.8
10	327 26.3	37.6	208 19.0	4.2	25 40.2	7.1	59.8
11	342 26.1	37.1	222 42.2	4.1	25 47.3	7.0	59.8
12	357 25.9	S20 36.6	237 05.3	4.0	N25 54.3	6.7	59.8
13	12 25.7	36.1	251 28.3	4.0	26 01.0	6.7	59.8
14	27 25.5	35.6	265 51.3	3.8	26 07.7	6.4	59.8
15	42 25.3	. . 35.0	280 14.1	3.8	26 14.1	6.2	59.8
16	57 25.1	34.5	294 36.9	3.7	26 20.3	6.1	59.8
17	72 24.9	34.0	308 59.6	3.6	26 26.4	5.9	59.8
18	87 24.7	S20 33.5	323 22.2	3.6	N26 32.3	5.7	59.8
19	102 24.5	33.0	337 44.8	3.4	26 38.0	5.5	59.8
20	117 24.3	32.5	352 07.2	3.4	26 43.5	5.3	59.8
21	132 24.1	. . 32.0	6 29.6	3.4	26 48.8	5.2	59.8
22	147 23.9	31.5	20 52.0	3.2	26 54.0	4.9	59.8
23	162 23.7	31.0	35 14.2	3.2	N26 58.9	4.8	59.8
	SD 16.3	d 0.5	SD	16.1		16.2	16.3

Lat. °	Twilight Naut. h m	Twilight Civil h m	Sunrise h m	Moonrise 16 h m	Moonrise 17 h m	Moonrise 18 h m	Moonrise 19 h m
N 72	07 57	09 46	■	07 51	□	□	□
N 70	07 43	09 14	11 58	08 34	□	□	□
68	07 31	08 50	10 26	09 03	07 57	□	□
66	07 22	08 32	09 49	09 25	08 55	□	□
64	07 13	08 17	09 22	09 43	09 29	08 58	□
62	07 06	08 04	09 02	09 57	09 54	09 51	09 53
60	06 59	07 53	08 46	10 10	10 14	10 24	10 51
N 58	06 54	07 44	08 32	10 21	10 30	10 48	11 24
56	06 48	07 35	08 20	10 30	10 45	11 08	11 49
54	06 43	07 28	08 09	10 39	10 57	11 25	12 08
52	06 39	07 21	08 00	10 46	11 08	11 39	12 25
50	06 35	07 15	07 52	10 53	11 17	11 51	12 40
45	06 25	07 01	07 34	11 08	11 38	12 17	13 09
N 40	06 17	06 50	07 20	11 20	11 54	12 38	13 32
35	06 09	06 40	07 07	11 30	12 09	12 55	13 51
30	06 01	06 31	06 56	11 39	12 21	13 10	14 07
20	05 47	06 14	06 38	11 55	12 42	13 35	14 35
N 10	05 33	05 59	06 22	12 10	13 01	13 57	14 59
0	05 18	05 44	06 06	12 23	13 18	14 18	15 21
S 10	05 02	05 28	05 51	12 36	13 36	14 39	15 44
20	04 42	05 10	05 34	12 51	13 55	15 01	16 08
30	04 16	04 48	05 15	13 07	14 17	15 27	16 36
35	03 59	04 35	05 03	13 17	14 30	15 43	16 53
40	03 39	04 19	04 50	13 28	14 45	16 01	17 12
45	03 13	03 59	04 35	13 41	15 02	16 23	17 36
S 50	02 37	03 34	04 15	13 58	15 25	16 50	18 06
52	02 17	03 22	04 06	14 05	15 36	17 04	18 21
54	01 51	03 07	03 56	14 14	15 48	17 20	18 38
56	01 11	02 50	03 44	14 23	16 02	17 38	19 00
58	////	02 29	03 31	14 34	16 18	18 01	19 26
S 60	////	02 01	03 15	14 47	16 39	18 31	20 04

Lat. °	Sunset h m	Twilight Civil h m	Twilight Naut. h m	Moonset 16 h m	Moonset 17 h m	Moonset 18 h m	Moonset 19 h m
N 72	■	14 35	16 24	04 01	□	□	□
N 70	12 23	15 07	16 38	03 20	□	□	□
68	13 54	15 31	16 49	02 53	05 51	□	□
66	14 32	15 49	16 59	02 32	04 55	□	□
64	14 58	16 04	17 07	02 16	04 22	06 56	□
62	15 18	16 16	17 15	02 02	03 58	06 02	08 12
60	15 35	16 27	17 21	01 51	03 38	05 30	07 15
N 58	15 49	16 37	17 27	01 41	03 23	05 07	06 42
56	16 01	16 45	17 32	01 33	03 09	04 47	06 17
54	16 11	16 52	17 37	01 25	02 58	04 31	05 58
52	16 20	16 59	17 42	01 19	02 48	04 18	05 41
50	16 29	17 05	17 46	01 13	02 39	04 06	05 27
45	16 46	17 19	17 55	01 00	02 20	03 41	04 58
N 40	17 01	17 30	18 04	00 49	02 04	03 21	04 35
35	17 13	17 40	18 11	00 40	01 51	03 04	04 16
30	17 24	17 49	18 19	00 32	01 40	02 50	04 00
20	17 42	18 06	18 33	00 18	01 21	02 26	03 33
N 10	17 58	18 21	18 47	00 07	01 04	02 05	03 10
0	18 14	18 36	19 01	24 48	00 48	01 46	02 48
S 10	18 29	18 52	19 18	24 33	00 33	01 27	02 26
20	18 46	19 10	19 38	24 17	00 17	01 06	02 03
30	19 05	19 31	20 04	23 58	24 43	00 43	01 36
35	19 16	19 45	20 20	23 47	24 29	00 29	01 20
40	19 29	20 01	20 40	23 34	24 13	00 13	01 01
45	19 45	20 20	21 06	23 20	23 54	24 39	00 39
S 50	20 04	20 45	21 41	23 02	23 30	24 10	00 10
52	20 13	20 57	22 01	22 54	23 19	23 57	24 52
54	20 23	21 11	22 26	22 44	23 06	23 41	24 35
56	20 34	21 28	23 04	22 34	22 51	23 22	24 13
58	20 48	21 49	////	22 22	22 34	22 58	23 47
S 60	21 04	22 16	////	22 08	22 14	22 28	23 09

Day	SUN Eqn. of Time 00^h	SUN Eqn. of Time 12^h	SUN Mer. Pass.	MOON Mer. Pass. Upper	MOON Mer. Pass. Lower	MOON Age	MOON Phase
d	m s	m s	h m	h m	h m	d	%
16	09 25	09 36	12 10	18 36	06 09	08	58
17	09 46	09 56	12 10	19 32	07 03	09	69
18	10 06	10 16	12 10	20 33	08 02	10	79

	UT	ARIES	VENUS −4.0		MARS −0.9		JUPITER −1.8		SATURN +0.5	
		GHA	GHA	Dec	GHA	Dec	GHA	Dec	GHA	Dec
	d h	° ′	° ′	° ′	° ′	° ′	° ′	° ′	° ′	° ′
	19 00	117 46.4	214 49.8	S21 55.2	33 21.5	N26 52.8	200 04.0	S23 06.5	317 41.5	N10 17.5
	01	132 48.9	229 49.0	55.4	48 24.4	52.7	215 05.9	06.5	332 44.1	17.5
	02	147 51.3	244 48.2	55.7	63 27.3	52.7	230 07.7	06.4	347 46.7	17.6
	03	162 53.8	259 47.3	. . 55.9	78 30.2	. . 52.7	245 09.6	. . 06.4	2 49.3	. . 17.6
	04	177 56.3	274 46.5	56.2	93 33.1	52.6	260 11.5	06.4	17 51.9	17.7
	05	192 58.7	289 45.7	56.4	108 36.0	52.6	275 13.3	06.4	32 54.5	17.7
	06	208 01.2	304 44.9	S21 56.7	123 38.9	N26 52.5	290 15.2	S23 06.3	47 57.1	N10 17.8
	07	223 03.7	319 44.0	57.0	138 41.8	52.5	305 17.0	06.3	62 59.6	17.9
S	08	238 06.1	334 43.2	57.2	153 44.7	52.5	320 18.9	06.3	78 02.2	17.9
A	09	253 08.6	349 42.4	. . 57.5	168 47.6	. . 52.4	335 20.8	. . 06.3	93 04.8	. . 18.0
T	10	268 11.1	4 41.5	57.7	183 50.4	52.4	350 22.6	06.2	108 07.4	18.0
U	11	283 13.5	19 40.7	58.0	198 53.3	52.4	5 24.5	06.2	123 10.0	18.1
R	12	298 16.0	34 39.9	S21 58.2	213 56.2	N26 52.3	20 26.4	S23 06.2	138 12.6	N10 18.2
D	13	313 18.4	49 39.1	58.5	228 59.1	52.3	35 28.2	06.1	153 15.1	18.2
A	14	328 20.9	64 38.2	58.7	244 02.0	52.2	50 30.1	06.1	168 17.7	18.3
Y	15	343 23.4	79 37.4	. . 59.0	259 04.9	. . 52.2	65 31.9	. . 06.1	183 20.3	. . 18.3
	16	358 25.8	94 36.6	59.2	274 07.8	52.2	80 33.8	06.1	198 22.9	18.4
	17	13 28.3	109 35.7	59.4	289 10.6	52.1	95 35.7	06.0	213 25.5	18.4
	18	28 30.8	124 34.9	S21 59.7	304 13.5	N26 52.1	110 37.5	S23 06.0	228 28.1	N10 18.5
	19	43 33.2	139 34.1	21 59.9	319 16.4	52.1	125 39.4	06.0	243 30.7	18.6
	20	58 35.7	154 33.2	22 00.2	334 19.3	52.0	140 41.3	06.0	258 33.3	18.6
	21	73 38.2	169 32.4	. . 00.4	349 22.1	. . 52.0	155 43.1	. . 05.9	273 35.8	. . 18.7
	22	88 40.6	184 31.6	00.7	4 25.0	51.9	170 45.0	05.9	288 38.4	18.7
	23	103 43.1	199 30.8	00.9	19 27.9	51.9	185 46.8	05.9	303 41.0	18.8
	20 00	118 45.6	214 29.9	S22 01.1	34 30.7	N26 51.9	200 48.7	S23 05.9	318 43.6	N10 18.8
	01	133 48.0	229 29.1	01.4	49 33.6	51.8	215 50.6	05.8	333 46.2	18.9
	02	148 50.5	244 28.3	01.6	64 36.5	51.8	230 52.4	05.8	348 48.8	19.0
	03	163 52.9	259 27.4	. . 01.8	79 39.3	. . 51.8	245 54.3	. . 05.8	3 51.4	. . 19.0
	04	178 55.4	274 26.6	02.1	94 42.2	51.7	260 56.2	05.7	18 54.0	19.1
	05	193 57.9	289 25.8	02.3	109 45.1	51.7	275 58.0	05.7	33 56.5	19.1
	06	209 00.3	304 24.9	S22 02.5	124 47.9	N26 51.6	290 59.9	S23 05.7	48 59.1	N10 19.2
	07	224 02.8	319 24.1	02.8	139 50.8	51.6	306 01.8	05.7	64 01.7	19.3
	08	239 05.3	334 23.3	03.0	154 53.6	51.6	321 03.6	05.6	79 04.3	19.3
S	09	254 07.7	349 22.4	. . 03.2	169 56.5	. . 51.5	336 05.5	. . 05.6	94 06.9	. . 19.4
U	10	269 10.2	4 21.6	03.4	184 59.3	51.5	351 07.3	05.6	109 09.5	19.4
N	11	284 12.7	19 20.7	03.7	200 02.2	51.5	6 09.2	05.6	124 12.1	19.5
D	12	299 15.1	34 19.9	S22 03.9	215 05.0	N26 51.4	21 11.1	S23 05.5	139 14.7	N10 19.5
A	13	314 17.6	49 19.1	04.1	230 07.9	51.4	36 12.9	05.5	154 17.2	19.6
Y	14	329 20.1	64 18.2	04.3	245 10.7	51.3	51 14.8	05.5	169 19.8	19.7
	15	344 22.5	79 17.4	. . 04.5	260 13.6	. . 51.3	66 16.7	. . 05.4	184 22.4	. . 19.7
	16	359 25.0	94 16.6	04.8	275 16.4	51.3	81 18.5	05.4	199 25.0	19.8
	17	14 27.4	109 15.7	05.0	290 19.3	51.2	96 20.4	05.4	214 27.6	19.8
	18	29 29.9	124 14.9	S22 05.2	305 22.1	N26 51.2	111 22.3	S23 05.4	229 30.2	N10 19.9
	19	44 32.4	139 14.1	05.4	320 24.9	51.1	126 24.1	05.3	244 32.8	20.0
	20	59 34.8	154 13.2	05.6	335 27.8	51.1	141 26.0	05.3	259 35.4	20.0
	21	74 37.3	169 12.4	. . 05.8	350 30.6	. . 51.1	156 27.8	. . 05.3	274 38.0	. . 20.1
	22	89 39.8	184 11.5	06.0	5 33.4	51.0	171 29.7	05.3	289 40.6	20.1
	23	104 42.2	199 10.7	06.3	20 36.3	51.0	186 31.6	05.2	304 43.1	20.2
	21 00	119 44.7	214 09.9	S22 06.5	35 39.1	N26 50.9	201 33.4	S23 05.2	319 45.7	N10 20.3
	01	134 47.2	229 09.0	06.7	50 41.9	50.9	216 35.3	05.2	334 48.3	20.3
	02	149 49.6	244 08.2	06.9	65 44.8	50.9	231 37.2	05.1	349 50.9	20.4
	03	164 52.1	259 07.4	. . 07.1	80 47.6	. . 50.8	246 39.0	. . 05.1	4 53.5	. . 20.4
	04	179 54.6	274 06.5	07.3	95 50.4	50.8	261 40.9	05.1	19 56.1	20.5
	05	194 57.0	289 05.7	07.5	110 53.2	50.8	276 42.8	05.1	34 58.7	20.6
	06	209 59.5	304 04.8	S22 07.7	125 56.1	N26 50.7	291 44.6	S23 05.0	50 01.3	N10 20.6
	07	225 01.9	319 04.0	07.9	140 58.9	50.7	306 46.5	05.0	65 03.9	20.7
	08	240 04.4	334 03.2	08.1	156 01.7	50.6	321 48.4	05.0	80 06.5	20.7
M	09	255 06.9	349 02.3	. . 08.3	171 04.5	. . 50.6	336 50.2	. . 05.0	95 09.1	. . 20.8
O	10	270 09.3	4 01.5	08.5	186 07.3	50.6	351 52.1	04.9	110 11.7	20.9
N	11	285 11.8	19 00.6	08.7	201 10.1	50.5	6 54.0	04.9	125 14.2	20.9
D	12	300 14.3	33 59.8	S22 08.9	216 12.9	N26 50.5	21 55.8	S23 04.9	140 16.8	N10 21.0
A	13	315 16.7	48 58.9	09.1	231 15.8	50.4	36 57.7	04.8	155 19.4	21.0
Y	14	330 19.2	63 58.1	09.3	246 18.6	50.4	51 59.6	04.8	170 22.0	21.1
	15	345 21.7	78 57.3	. . 09.5	261 21.4	. . 50.4	67 01.4	. . 04.8	185 24.6	. . 21.2
	16	0 24.1	93 56.4	09.7	276 24.2	50.3	82 03.3	04.8	200 27.2	21.2
	17	15 26.6	108 55.6	09.9	291 27.0	50.3	97 05.2	04.7	215 29.8	21.3
	18	30 29.0	123 54.7	S22 10.1	306 29.8	N26 50.2	112 07.0	S23 04.7	230 32.4	N10 21.3
	19	45 31.5	138 53.9	10.2	321 32.6	50.2	127 08.9	04.7	245 35.0	21.4
	20	60 34.0	153 53.1	10.4	336 35.4	50.2	142 10.8	04.6	260 37.6	21.5
	21	75 36.4	168 52.2	. . 10.6	351 38.2	. . 50.1	157 12.6	. . 04.6	275 40.2	. . 21.5
	22	90 38.9	183 51.4	10.8	6 41.0	50.1	172 14.5	04.6	290 42.8	21.6
	23	105 41.4	198 50.5	11.0	21 43.8	50.0	187 16.4	04.6	305 45.4	21.6
	Mer. Pass.	h m 16 02.3	*v* −0.8	*d* 0.2	*v* 2.8	*d* 0.0	*v* 1.9	*d* 0.0	*v* 2.6	*d* 0.1

STARS		
Name	SHA	Dec
	° ′	° ′
Acamar	315 21.2	S40 16.5
Achernar	335 29.6	S57 12.0
Acrux	173 14.0	S63 08.5
Adhara	255 15.4	S28 59.0
Aldebaran	290 53.9	N16 31.6
Alioth	166 23.8	N55 54.6
Alkaid	153 01.9	N49 16.0
Al Na'ir	27 49.1	S46 55.5
Alnilam	275 50.2	S 1 11.8
Alphard	217 59.8	S 8 41.7
Alphecca	126 14.6	N26 40.9
Alpheratz	357 48.0	N29 08.3
Altair	62 12.6	N 8 53.3
Ankaa	353 19.7	S42 15.9
Antares	112 31.5	S26 27.0
Arcturus	145 59.4	N19 08.1
Atria	107 37.6	S69 02.4
Avior	234 19.2	S59 32.1
Bellatrix	278 36.1	N 6 21.5
Betelgeuse	271 05.4	N 7 24.6
Canopus	263 57.5	S52 42.0
Capella	280 40.1	N46 00.6
Deneb	49 34.9	N45 18.5
Denebola	182 37.6	N14 31.4
Diphda	349 00.0	S17 56.6
Dubhe	193 55.8	N61 42.2
Elnath	278 17.5	N28 37.0
Eltanin	90 48.5	N51 29.0
Enif	33 51.5	N 9 54.7
Fomalhaut	15 28.6	S29 34.9
Gacrux	172 05.6	S57 09.3
Gienah	175 56.4	S17 35.2
Hadar	148 54.0	S60 24.5
Hamal	328 05.4	N23 30.2
Kaus Aust.	83 49.6	S34 22.9
Kochab	137 19.7	N74 06.9
Markab	13 42.7	N15 15.0
Menkar	314 19.2	N 4 07.3
Menkent	148 12.5	S36 24.5
Miaplacidus	221 40.0	S69 44.9
Mirfak	308 46.1	N49 53.7
Nunki	76 03.7	S26 17.3
Peacock	53 26.1	S56 42.7
Pollux	243 32.3	N28 00.4
Procyon	245 03.7	N 5 12.2
Rasalhague	96 10.5	N12 33.0
Regulus	207 47.5	N11 55.5
Rigel	281 15.7	S 8 11.5
Rigil Kent.	139 57.7	S60 51.9
Sabik	102 17.5	S15 44.2
Schedar	349 45.7	N56 35.2
Shaula	96 27.8	S37 06.6
Sirius	258 37.0	S16 43.6
Spica	158 35.6	S11 12.3
Suhail	222 55.1	S43 27.9
Vega	80 42.2	N38 47.3
Zuben'ubi	137 10.1	S16 04.6

	SHA	Mer. Pass.
	° ′	h m
Venus	95 44.4	9 43
Mars	275 45.2	21 38
Jupiter	82 03.2	10 35
Saturn	199 58.1	2 45

2008 JANUARY 19, 20, 21 (SAT., SUN., MON.)

Day	UT (d h)	SUN GHA (° ′)	SUN Dec (° ′)	MOON GHA (° ′)	v (′)	MOON Dec (° ′)	d (′)	HP (′)
SATURDAY	19 00	177 23.5	S20 30.5	49 36.4	3.2	N27 03.7	4.6	59.8
	01	192 23.4	30.0	63 58.6	3.0	27 08.3	4.4	59.8
	02	207 23.2	29.4	78 20.6	3.0	27 12.7	4.1	59.8
	03	222 23.0	. . 28.9	92 42.6	3.0	27 16.8	4.0	59.8
	04	237 22.8	28.4	107 04.6	2.9	27 20.8	3.8	59.8
	05	252 22.6	27.9	121 26.5	2.9	27 24.6	3.7	59.8
	06	267 22.4	S20 27.4	135 48.4	2.8	N27 28.3	3.4	59.8
	07	282 22.2	26.9	150 10.2	2.8	27 31.7	3.2	59.8
	08	297 22.0	26.4	164 32.0	2.7	27 34.9	3.0	59.8
	09	312 21.8	. . 25.8	178 53.7	2.7	27 37.9	2.8	59.8
	10	327 21.6	25.3	193 15.4	2.6	27 40.7	2.6	59.8
	11	342 21.4	24.8	207 37.0	2.6	27 43.3	2.4	59.8
	12	357 21.2	S20 24.3	221 58.6	2.6	N27 45.7	2.3	59.8
	13	12 21.0	23.8	236 20.2	2.6	27 48.0	2.0	59.8
	14	27 20.8	23.2	250 41.8	2.5	27 50.0	1.8	59.8
	15	42 20.6	. . 22.7	265 03.3	2.5	27 51.8	1.6	59.8
	16	57 20.4	22.2	279 24.8	2.5	27 53.4	1.4	59.8
	17	72 20.2	21.7	293 46.3	2.5	27 54.8	1.2	59.8
	18	87 20.1	S20 21.1	308 07.8	2.5	N27 56.0	1.0	59.8
	19	102 19.9	20.6	322 29.3	2.4	27 57.0	0.8	59.8
	20	117 19.7	20.1	336 50.7	2.5	27 57.8	0.6	59.8
	21	132 19.5	. . 19.6	351 12.2	2.4	27 58.4	0.4	59.8
	22	147 19.3	19.0	5 33.6	2.5	27 58.8	0.2	59.8
	23	162 19.1	18.5	19 55.1	2.4	27 59.0	0.0	59.8
SUNDAY	20 00	177 18.9	S20 18.0	34 16.5	2.4	N27 59.0	0.2	59.8
	01	192 18.7	17.5	48 37.9	2.5	27 58.8	0.4	59.8
	02	207 18.5	16.9	62 59.4	2.5	27 58.4	0.6	59.8
	03	222 18.3	. . 16.4	77 20.9	2.5	27 57.8	0.8	59.8
	04	237 18.2	15.9	91 42.4	2.5	27 57.0	1.1	59.8
	05	252 18.0	15.3	106 03.9	2.5	27 55.9	1.2	59.8
	06	267 17.8	S20 14.8	120 25.4	2.5	N27 54.7	1.4	59.8
	07	282 17.6	14.3	134 46.9	2.6	27 53.3	1.6	59.8
	08	297 17.4	13.7	149 08.5	2.6	27 51.7	1.9	59.8
	09	312 17.2	. . 13.2	163 30.1	2.6	27 49.8	2.0	59.7
	10	327 17.0	12.7	177 51.7	2.7	27 47.8	2.2	59.7
	11	342 16.8	12.1	192 13.4	2.7	27 45.6	2.5	59.7
	12	357 16.7	S20 11.6	206 35.1	2.8	N27 43.1	2.6	59.7
	13	12 16.5	11.1	220 56.9	2.7	27 40.5	2.8	59.7
	14	27 16.3	10.5	235 18.6	2.9	27 37.7	3.0	59.7
	15	42 16.1	. . 10.0	249 40.5	2.9	27 34.7	3.2	59.7
	16	57 15.9	09.5	264 02.4	2.9	27 31.5	3.4	59.7
	17	72 15.7	08.9	278 24.3	3.0	27 28.1	3.6	59.7
	18	87 15.6	S20 08.4	292 46.3	3.1	N27 24.5	3.8	59.7
	19	102 15.4	07.8	307 08.4	3.1	27 20.7	4.0	59.7
	20	117 15.2	07.3	321 30.5	3.1	27 16.7	4.2	59.6
	21	132 15.0	. . 06.8	335 52.6	3.3	27 12.5	4.4	59.6
	22	147 14.8	06.2	350 14.9	3.3	27 08.1	4.6	59.6
	23	162 14.6	05.7	4 37.2	3.4	27 03.5	4.7	59.6
MONDAY	21 00	177 14.5	S20 05.1	18 59.6	3.4	N26 58.8	4.9	59.6
	01	192 14.3	04.6	33 22.0	3.5	26 53.9	5.2	59.6
	02	207 14.1	04.0	47 44.5	3.7	26 48.7	5.3	59.6
	03	222 13.9	. . 03.5	62 07.2	3.6	26 43.4	5.5	59.6
	04	237 13.7	03.0	76 29.8	3.8	26 37.9	5.6	59.5
	05	252 13.6	02.4	90 52.6	3.9	26 32.3	5.9	59.5
	06	267 13.4	S20 01.9	105 15.5	3.9	N26 26.4	6.0	59.5
	07	282 13.2	01.3	119 38.4	4.0	26 20.4	6.2	59.5
	08	297 13.0	00.8	134 01.4	4.1	26 14.2	6.4	59.5
	09	312 12.8	20 00.2	148 24.5	4.2	26 07.8	6.6	59.5
	10	327 12.7	19 59.7	162 47.7	4.3	26 01.2	6.7	59.4
	11	342 12.5	59.1	177 11.0	4.4	25 54.5	6.9	59.4
	12	357 12.3	S19 58.6	191 34.4	4.5	N25 47.6	7.1	59.4
	13	12 12.1	58.0	205 57.9	4.6	25 40.5	7.2	59.4
	14	27 12.0	57.5	220 21.5	4.7	25 33.3	7.4	59.4
	15	42 11.8	. . 56.9	234 45.2	4.8	25 25.9	7.6	59.4
	16	57 11.6	56.3	249 09.0	4.9	25 18.3	7.8	59.3
	17	72 11.4	55.8	263 32.9	5.0	25 10.5	7.9	59.3
	18	87 11.2	S19 55.2	277 56.9	5.1	N25 02.6	8.0	59.3
	19	102 11.1	54.7	292 21.0	5.2	24 54.6	8.2	59.3
	20	117 10.9	54.1	306 45.2	5.4	24 46.4	8.4	59.3
	21	132 10.7	. . 53.6	321 09.6	5.4	24 38.0	8.5	59.2
	22	147 10.5	53.0	335 34.0	5.5	24 29.5	8.7	59.2
	23	162 10.4	52.5	349 58.5	5.7	N24 20.8	8.9	59.2
		SD 16.3	*d* 0.5	SD	16.3		16.3	16.2

Lat. (°)	Twilight Naut. (h m)	Twilight Civil (h m)	Sunrise (h m)	Moonrise 19 (h m)	Moonrise 20 (h m)	Moonrise 21 (h m)	Moonrise 22 (h m)
N 72	07 49	09 33	■	□	□	□	□
N 70	07 36	09 04	11 11	□	□	□	□
68	07 26	08 42	10 13	□	□	□	□
66	07 17	08 25	09 39	□	□	□	14 00
64	07 09	08 11	09 15	□	□	11 54	14 39
62	07 02	07 59	08 56	09 53	10 53	13 01	15 05
60	06 56	07 49	08 40	10 51	11 55	13 36	15 26
N 58	06 50	07 40	08 27	11 24	12 29	14 01	15 43
56	06 45	07 32	08 16	11 49	12 54	14 21	15 57
54	06 41	07 25	08 06	12 08	13 14	14 38	16 09
52	06 37	07 18	07 57	12 25	13 31	14 52	16 20
50	06 33	07 13	07 49	12 40	13 45	15 04	16 30
45	06 24	07 00	07 32	13 09	14 14	15 30	16 50
N 40	06 15	06 49	07 18	13 32	14 37	15 50	17 06
35	06 08	06 39	07 06	13 51	14 56	16 07	17 20
30	06 01	06 30	06 56	14 07	15 13	16 22	17 31
20	05 47	06 14	06 38	14 35	15 40	16 47	17 51
N 10	05 34	06 00	06 22	14 59	16 04	17 08	18 09
0	05 20	05 45	06 07	15 21	16 26	17 28	18 25
S 10	05 03	05 30	05 52	15 44	16 48	17 47	18 41
20	04 44	05 12	05 36	16 08	17 11	18 08	18 58
30	04 19	04 51	05 17	16 36	17 39	18 33	19 18
35	04 03	04 38	05 06	16 53	17 55	18 47	19 30
40	03 44	04 22	04 54	17 12	18 14	19 03	19 43
45	03 19	04 04	04 39	17 36	18 36	19 23	19 58
S 50	02 44	03 39	04 20	18 06	19 05	19 47	20 17
52	02 25	03 27	04 11	18 21	19 19	19 59	20 26
54	02 01	03 14	04 02	18 38	19 36	20 12	20 36
56	01 28	02 57	03 50	19 00	19 55	20 28	20 47
58	////	02 38	03 37	19 26	20 19	20 46	20 59
S 60	////	02 12	03 22	20 04	20 51	21 08	21 14

Lat. (°)	Sunset (h m)	Twilight Civil (h m)	Twilight Naut. (h m)	Moonset 19 (h m)	Moonset 20 (h m)	Moonset 21 (h m)	Moonset 22 (h m)
N 72	■	14 49	16 33	□	□	□	□
N 70	13 12	15 19	16 46	□	□	□	□
68	14 10	15 40	16 57	□	□	□	□
66	14 43	15 57	17 06	□	□	□	10 36
64	15 07	16 11	17 14	□	□	10 39	09 57
62	15 26	16 23	17 21	08 12	09 28	09 32	09 29
60	15 42	16 33	17 27	07 15	08 26	08 56	09 08
N 58	15 55	16 42	17 32	06 42	07 52	08 31	08 50
56	16 07	16 50	17 37	06 17	07 27	08 10	08 35
54	16 16	16 57	17 42	05 58	07 06	07 53	08 22
52	16 25	17 04	17 46	05 41	06 49	07 38	08 11
50	16 33	17 10	17 50	05 27	06 35	07 25	08 01
45	16 50	17 23	17 59	04 58	06 05	06 59	07 40
N 40	17 04	17 34	18 07	04 35	05 42	06 38	07 22
35	17 16	17 43	18 14	04 16	05 23	06 20	07 08
30	17 26	17 52	18 21	04 00	05 06	06 05	06 55
20	17 44	18 08	18 34	03 33	04 39	05 39	06 33
N 10	18 00	18 22	18 48	03 10	04 15	05 17	06 14
0	18 15	18 37	19 02	02 48	03 52	04 56	05 56
S 10	18 29	18 52	19 18	02 26	03 30	04 35	05 37
20	18 45	19 09	19 38	02 03	03 06	04 12	05 18
30	19 04	19 31	20 02	01 36	02 37	03 45	04 55
35	19 15	19 43	20 18	01 20	02 21	03 29	04 42
40	19 27	19 59	20 37	01 01	02 01	03 11	04 26
45	19 42	20 17	21 02	00 39	01 38	02 49	04 08
S 50	20 01	20 41	21 36	00 10	01 07	02 21	03 44
52	20 09	20 53	21 55	24 52	00 52	02 07	03 33
54	20 19	21 07	22 18	24 35	00 35	01 51	03 20
56	20 30	21 23	22 50	24 13	00 13	01 31	03 05
58	20 43	21 42	////	23 47	25 08	01 08	02 48
S 60	20 58	22 07	////	23 09	24 36	00 36	02 27

Day	SUN Eqn. of Time 00^h (m s)	SUN Eqn. of Time 12^h (m s)	SUN Mer. Pass. (h m)	MOON Mer. Pass. Upper (h m)	MOON Mer. Pass. Lower (h m)	MOON Age (d)	MOON Phase (%)
19	10 25	10 35	12 11	21 37	09 05	11	88
20	10 44	10 53	12 11	22 41	10 09	12	94 ○
21	11 02	11 10	12 11	23 42	11 12	13	98

UT	ARIES	VENUS −4.0		MARS −0.9		JUPITER −1.8		SATURN +0.4	
d h	GHA ° ′	GHA ° ′	Dec ° ′	GHA ° ′	Dec ° ′	GHA ° ′	Dec ° ′	GHA ° ′	Dec ° ′
22 00	120 43.8	213 49.7	S22 11.2	36 46.6	N26 50.0	202 18.2	S23 04.5	320 48.0	N10 21.7
01	135 46.3	228 48.8	11.4	51 49.3	50.0	217 20.1	04.5	335 50.5	21.8
02	150 48.8	243 48.0	11.5	66 52.1	49.9	232 22.0	04.5	350 53.1	21.8
03	165 51.2	258 47.2	. . 11.7	81 54.9	. . 49.9	247 23.8	. . 04.4	5 55.7	. . 21.9
04	180 53.7	273 46.3	11.9	96 57.7	49.8	262 25.7	04.4	20 58.3	21.9
05	195 56.2	288 45.5	12.1	112 00.5	49.8	277 27.6	04.4	36 00.9	22.0
06	210 58.6	303 44.6	S22 12.3	127 03.3	N26 49.8	292 29.4	S23 04.4	51 03.5	N10 22.1
07	226 01.1	318 43.8	12.4	142 06.1	49.7	307 31.3	04.3	66 06.1	22.1
T 08	241 03.5	333 42.9	12.6	157 08.8	49.7	322 33.2	04.3	81 08.7	22.2
U 09	256 06.0	348 42.1	. . 12.8	172 11.6	. . 49.6	337 35.0	. . 04.3	96 11.3	. . 22.2
E 10	271 08.5	3 41.2	12.9	187 14.4	49.6	352 36.9	04.2	111 13.9	22.3
S 11	286 10.9	18 40.4	13.1	202 17.2	49.6	7 38.8	04.2	126 16.5	22.4
D 12	301 13.4	33 39.5	S22 13.3	217 19.9	N26 49.5	22 40.6	S23 04.2	141 19.1	N10 22.4
A 13	316 15.9	48 38.7	13.5	232 22.7	49.5	37 42.5	04.2	156 21.7	22.5
Y 14	331 18.3	63 37.9	13.6	247 25.5	49.4	52 44.4	04.1	171 24.3	22.5
15	346 20.8	78 37.0	. . 13.8	262 28.2	. . 49.4	67 46.2	. . 04.1	186 26.9	. . 22.6
16	1 23.3	93 36.2	14.0	277 31.0	49.4	82 48.1	04.1	201 29.5	22.7
17	16 25.7	108 35.3	14.1	292 33.8	49.3	97 50.0	04.0	216 32.1	22.7
18	31 28.2	123 34.5	S22 14.3	307 36.5	N26 49.3	112 51.8	S23 04.0	231 34.7	N10 22.8
19	46 30.7	138 33.6	14.4	322 39.3	49.2	127 53.7	04.0	246 37.3	22.9
20	61 33.1	153 32.8	14.6	337 42.1	49.2	142 55.6	04.0	261 39.9	22.9
21	76 35.6	168 31.9	. . 14.8	352 44.8	. . 49.2	157 57.4	. . 03.9	276 42.5	. . 23.0
22	91 38.0	183 31.1	14.9	7 47.6	49.1	172 59.3	03.9	291 45.1	23.0
23	106 40.5	198 30.2	15.1	22 50.3	49.1	188 01.2	03.9	306 47.6	23.1
23 00	121 43.0	213 29.4	S22 15.2	37 53.1	N26 49.0	203 03.0	S23 03.8	321 50.2	N10 23.2
01	136 45.4	228 28.5	15.4	52 55.8	49.0	218 04.9	03.8	336 52.8	23.2
02	151 47.9	243 27.7	15.5	67 58.6	49.0	233 06.8	03.8	351 55.4	23.3
03	166 50.4	258 26.8	. . 15.7	83 01.3	. . 48.9	248 08.7	. . 03.7	6 58.0	. . 23.3
04	181 52.8	273 26.0	15.9	98 04.1	48.9	263 10.5	03.7	22 00.6	23.4
05	196 55.3	288 25.1	16.0	113 06.8	48.8	278 12.4	03.7	37 03.2	23.5
06	211 57.8	303 24.3	S22 16.2	128 09.6	N26 48.8	293 14.3	S23 03.7	52 05.8	N10 23.5
W 07	227 00.2	318 23.4	16.3	143 12.3	48.8	308 16.1	03.6	67 08.4	23.6
E 08	242 02.7	333 22.6	16.5	158 15.1	48.7	323 18.0	03.6	82 11.0	23.7
D 09	257 05.2	348 21.7	. . 16.6	173 17.8	. . 48.7	338 19.9	. . 03.6	97 13.6	. . 23.7
N 10	272 07.6	3 20.9	16.7	188 20.5	48.6	353 21.7	03.5	112 16.2	23.8
E 11	287 10.1	18 20.0	16.9	203 23.3	48.6	8 23.6	03.5	127 18.8	23.8
S 12	302 12.5	33 19.2	S22 17.0	218 26.0	N26 48.6	23 25.5	S23 03.5	142 21.4	N10 23.9
D 13	317 15.0	48 18.3	17.2	233 28.8	48.5	38 27.3	03.5	157 24.0	24.0
A 14	332 17.5	63 17.5	17.3	248 31.5	48.5	53 29.2	03.4	172 26.6	24.0
Y 15	347 19.9	78 16.6	. . 17.5	263 34.2	. . 48.4	68 31.1	. . 03.4	187 29.2	. . 24.1
16	2 22.4	93 15.8	17.6	278 36.9	48.4	83 33.0	03.4	202 31.8	24.2
17	17 24.9	108 14.9	17.7	293 39.7	48.3	98 34.8	03.3	217 34.4	24.2
18	32 27.3	123 14.1	S22 17.9	308 42.4	N26 48.3	113 36.7	S23 03.3	232 37.0	N10 24.3
19	47 29.8	138 13.2	18.0	323 45.1	48.3	128 38.6	03.3	247 39.6	24.3
20	62 32.3	153 12.4	18.1	338 47.8	48.2	143 40.4	03.2	262 42.2	24.4
21	77 34.7	168 11.5	. . 18.3	353 50.6	. . 48.2	158 42.3	. . 03.2	277 44.8	. . 24.5
22	92 37.2	183 10.7	18.4	8 53.3	48.1	173 44.2	03.2	292 47.4	24.5
23	107 39.7	198 09.8	18.5	23 56.0	48.1	188 46.0	03.2	307 50.0	24.6
24 00	122 42.1	213 09.0	S22 18.7	38 58.7	N26 48.1	203 47.9	S23 03.1	322 52.6	N10 24.7
01	137 44.6	228 08.1	18.8	54 01.4	48.0	218 49.8	03.1	337 55.2	24.7
02	152 47.0	243 07.3	18.9	69 04.1	48.0	233 51.7	03.1	352 57.8	24.8
03	167 49.5	258 06.4	. . 19.0	84 06.9	. . 47.9	248 53.5	. . 03.0	8 00.4	. . 24.8
04	182 52.0	273 05.6	19.2	99 09.6	47.9	263 55.4	03.0	23 03.0	24.9
05	197 54.4	288 04.7	19.3	114 12.3	47.9	278 57.3	03.0	38 05.6	25.0
06	212 56.9	303 03.8	S22 19.4	129 15.0	N26 47.8	293 59.1	S23 02.9	53 08.2	N10 25.0
07	227 59.4	318 03.0	19.5	144 17.7	47.8	309 01.0	02.9	68 10.8	25.1
T 08	243 01.8	333 02.1	19.6	159 20.4	47.7	324 02.9	02.9	83 13.4	25.2
H 09	258 04.3	348 01.3	. . 19.8	174 23.1	. . 47.7	339 04.8	. . 02.9	98 16.0	. . 25.2
U 10	273 06.8	3 00.4	19.9	189 25.8	47.7	354 06.6	02.8	113 18.6	25.3
R 11	288 09.2	17 59.6	20.0	204 28.5	47.6	9 08.5	02.8	128 21.2	25.3
S 12	303 11.7	32 58.7	S22 20.1	219 31.2	N26 47.6	24 10.4	S23 02.8	143 23.8	N10 25.4
D 13	318 14.1	47 57.9	20.2	234 33.9	47.5	39 12.2	02.7	158 26.4	25.5
A 14	333 16.6	62 57.0	20.3	249 36.6	47.5	54 14.1	02.7	173 29.0	25.5
Y 15	348 19.1	77 56.2	. . 20.5	264 39.3	. . 47.4	69 16.0	. . 02.7	188 31.6	. . 25.6
16	3 21.5	92 55.3	20.6	279 42.0	47.4	84 17.9	02.6	203 34.2	25.7
17	18 24.0	107 54.5	20.7	294 44.7	47.4	99 19.7	02.6	218 36.8	25.7
18	33 26.5	122 53.6	S22 20.8	309 47.4	N26 47.3	114 21.6	S23 02.6	233 39.4	N10 25.8
19	48 28.9	137 52.7	20.9	324 50.0	47.3	129 23.5	02.5	248 42.0	25.9
20	63 31.4	152 51.9	21.0	339 52.7	47.2	144 25.3	02.5	263 44.6	25.9
21	78 33.9	167 51.0	. . 21.1	354 55.4	. . 47.2	159 27.2	. . 02.5	278 47.2	. . 26.0
22	93 36.3	182 50.2	21.2	9 58.1	47.2	174 29.1	02.5	293 49.8	26.0
23	108 38.8	197 49.3	21.3	25 00.8	47.1	189 31.0	02.4	308 52.5	26.1
Mer. Pass.	h m 15 50.5	v −0.9	d 0.1	v 2.7	d 0.0	v 1.9	d 0.0	v 2.6	d 0.1

STARS

Name	SHA ° ′	Dec ° ′
Acamar	315 21.2	S40 16.5
Achernar	335 29.6	S57 12.0
Acrux	173 13.9	S63 08.5
Adhara	255 15.4	S28 59.0
Aldebaran	290 53.9	N16 31.6
Alioth	166 23.8	N55 54.6
Alkaid	153 01.9	N49 16.0
Al Na'ir	27 49.0	S46 55.5
Alnilam	275 50.2	S 1 11.8
Alphard	217 59.8	S 8 41.7
Alphecca	126 14.5	N26 40.9
Alpheratz	357 48.0	N29 08.2
Altair	62 12.6	N 8 53.2
Ankaa	353 19.7	S42 15.9
Antares	112 31.5	S26 27.0
Arcturus	145 59.4	N19 08.1
Atria	107 37.5	S69 02.4
Avior	234 19.2	S59 32.1
Bellatrix	278 36.1	N 6 21.5
Betelgeuse	271 05.4	N 7 24.6
Canopus	263 57.5	S52 42.1
Capella	280 40.1	N46 00.6
Deneb	49 34.8	N45 18.5
Denebola	182 37.6	N14 31.4
Diphda	349 00.0	S17 56.6
Dubhe	193 55.8	N61 42.2
Elnath	278 17.5	N28 37.0
Eltanin	90 48.5	N51 29.0
Enif	33 51.4	N 9 54.7
Fomalhaut	15 28.6	S29 34.9
Gacrux	172 05.5	S57 09.4
Gienah	175 56.4	S17 35.3
Hadar	148 54.0	S60 24.6
Hamal	328 05.4	N23 30.2
Kaus Aust.	83 49.6	S34 22.9
Kochab	137 19.6	N74 06.9
Markab	13 42.7	N15 15.0
Menkar	314 19.2	N 4 07.3
Menkent	148 12.5	S36 24.5
Miaplacidus	221 40.0	S69 44.9
Mirfak	308 46.2	N49 53.7
Nunki	76 03.7	S26 17.3
Peacock	53 26.0	S56 42.6
Pollux	243 32.3	N28 00.4
Procyon	245 03.6	N 5 12.2
Rasalhague	96 10.5	N12 33.0
Regulus	207 47.5	N11 55.5
Rigel	281 15.7	S 8 11.5
Rigil Kent.	139 57.7	S60 51.9
Sabik	102 17.5	S15 44.2
Schedar	349 45.7	N56 35.2
Shaula	96 27.8	S37 06.6
Sirius	258 37.0	S16 43.7
Spica	158 35.5	S11 12.3
Suhail	222 55.1	S43 27.9
Vega	80 42.1	N38 47.2
Zuben'ubi	137 10.0	S16 04.6

	SHA ° ′	Mer. Pass. h m
Venus	91 46.4	9 47
Mars	276 10.1	21 25
Jupiter	81 20.1	10 26
Saturn	200 07.3	2 32

Day	UT (h)	SUN GHA (° ′)	SUN Dec (° ′)	MOON GHA (° ′)	v (′)	MOON Dec (° ′)	d (′)	HP (′)
22	00	177 10.2	S19 51.9	4 23.2	5.8	N24 11.9	8.9	59.2
	01	192 10.0	51.3	18 48.0	5.9	24 03.0	9.2	59.2
	02	207 09.9	50.8	33 12.9	6.0	23 53.8	9.3	59.1
	03	222 09.7	. . 50.2	47 37.9	6.1	23 44.5	9.4	59.1
	04	237 09.5	49.7	62 03.0	6.2	23 35.1	9.5	59.1
	05	252 09.3	49.1	76 28.2	6.4	23 25.6	9.7	59.1
	06	267 09.2	S19 48.5	90 53.6	6.5	N23 15.9	9.9	59.1
	07	282 09.0	48.0	105 19.1	6.5	23 06.0	10.0	59.0
T	08	297 08.8	47.4	119 44.6	6.8	22 56.0	10.1	59.0
U	09	312 08.6	. . 46.8	134 10.4	6.8	22 45.9	10.2	59.0
E	10	327 08.5	46.3	148 36.2	6.9	22 35.7	10.4	59.0
S	11	342 08.3	45.7	163 02.1	7.1	22 25.3	10.5	58.9
D	12	357 08.1	S19 45.1	177 28.2	7.2	N22 14.8	10.6	58.9
A	13	12 08.0	44.6	191 54.4	7.3	22 04.2	10.7	58.9
Y	14	27 07.8	44.0	206 20.7	7.4	21 53.5	10.9	58.9
	15	42 07.6	. . 43.4	220 47.1	7.6	21 42.6	11.0	58.8
	16	57 07.5	42.9	235 13.7	7.7	21 31.6	11.1	58.8
	17	72 07.3	42.3	249 40.4	7.8	21 20.5	11.3	58.8
	18	87 07.1	S19 41.7	264 07.2	7.9	N21 09.2	11.3	58.8
	19	102 07.0	41.2	278 34.1	8.0	20 57.9	11.4	58.7
	20	117 06.8	40.6	293 01.1	8.2	20 46.5	11.6	58.7
	21	132 06.6	. . 40.0	307 28.3	8.3	20 34.9	11.7	58.7
	22	147 06.5	39.4	321 55.6	8.4	20 23.2	11.8	58.7
	23	162 06.3	38.9	336 23.0	8.5	20 11.4	11.9	58.6
23	00	177 06.1	S19 38.3	350 50.5	8.6	N19 59.5	11.9	58.6
	01	192 06.0	37.7	5 18.1	8.8	19 47.6	12.1	58.6
	02	207 05.8	37.1	19 45.9	8.9	19 35.5	12.2	58.6
	03	222 05.6	. . 36.6	34 13.8	9.0	19 23.3	12.3	58.5
	04	237 05.5	36.0	48 41.8	9.1	19 11.0	12.4	58.5
	05	252 05.3	35.4	63 09.9	9.3	18 58.6	12.5	58.5
	06	267 05.1	S19 34.8	77 38.2	9.3	N18 46.1	12.5	58.5
W	07	282 05.0	34.3	92 06.5	9.5	18 33.6	12.7	58.4
E	08	297 04.8	33.7	106 35.0	9.6	18 20.9	12.7	58.4
D	09	312 04.6	. . 33.1	121 03.6	9.7	18 08.2	12.8	58.4
N	10	327 04.5	32.5	135 32.3	9.8	17 55.4	13.0	58.3
E	11	342 04.3	31.9	150 01.1	10.0	17 42.4	13.0	58.3
S	12	357 04.2	S19 31.4	164 30.1	10.0	N17 29.4	13.0	58.3
D	13	12 04.0	30.8	178 59.1	10.2	17 16.4	13.2	58.3
A	14	27 03.8	30.2	193 28.3	10.3	17 03.2	13.2	58.2
Y	15	42 03.7	. . 29.6	207 57.6	10.4	16 50.0	13.3	58.2
	16	57 03.5	29.0	222 27.0	10.5	16 36.7	13.4	58.2
	17	72 03.4	28.4	236 56.5	10.6	16 23.3	13.4	58.1
	18	87 03.2	S19 27.9	251 26.1	10.8	N16 09.9	13.6	58.1
	19	102 03.0	27.3	265 55.9	10.8	15 56.3	13.5	58.1
	20	117 02.9	26.7	280 25.7	10.9	15 42.8	13.7	58.0
	21	132 02.7	. . 26.1	294 55.6	11.1	15 29.1	13.7	58.0
	22	147 02.6	25.5	309 25.7	11.1	15 15.4	13.8	58.0
	23	162 02.4	24.9	323 55.8	11.3	15 01.6	13.8	58.0
24	00	177 02.2	S19 24.3	338 26.1	11.4	N14 47.8	13.9	57.9
	01	192 02.1	23.7	352 56.5	11.4	14 33.9	14.0	57.9
	02	207 01.9	23.1	7 26.9	11.6	14 19.9	14.0	57.9
	03	222 01.8	. . 22.6	21 57.5	11.7	14 05.9	14.0	57.8
	04	237 01.6	22.0	36 28.2	11.8	13 51.9	14.2	57.8
	05	252 01.5	21.4	50 59.0	11.8	13 37.7	14.1	57.8
	06	267 01.3	S19 20.8	65 29.8	12.0	N13 23.6	14.2	57.7
T	07	282 01.2	20.2	80 00.8	12.1	13 09.4	14.3	57.7
H	08	297 01.0	19.6	94 31.9	12.2	12 55.1	14.3	57.7
U	09	312 00.8	. . 19.0	109 03.1	12.2	12 40.8	14.4	57.6
R	10	327 00.7	18.4	123 34.3	12.4	12 26.4	14.4	57.6
S	11	342 00.5	17.8	138 05.7	12.4	12 12.0	14.4	57.6
D	12	357 00.4	S19 17.2	152 37.1	12.5	N11 57.6	14.5	57.5
A	13	12 00.2	16.6	167 08.6	12.7	11 43.1	14.5	57.5
Y	14	27 00.1	16.0	181 40.3	12.7	11 28.6	14.5	57.5
	15	41 59.9	. . 15.4	196 12.0	12.8	11 14.1	14.6	57.5
	16	56 59.8	14.8	210 43.8	12.9	10 59.5	14.7	57.4
	17	71 59.6	14.2	225 15.7	13.0	10 44.8	14.6	57.4
	18	86 59.5	S19 13.6	239 47.7	13.0	N10 30.2	14.7	57.4
	19	101 59.3	13.0	254 19.7	13.2	10 15.5	14.7	57.3
	20	116 59.2	12.4	268 51.9	13.2	10 00.8	14.8	57.3
	21	131 59.0	. . 11.8	283 24.1	13.3	9 46.0	14.7	57.3
	22	146 58.9	11.2	297 56.4	13.4	9 31.3	14.8	57.2
	23	161 58.7	10.6	312 28.8	13.5	N 9 16.5	14.8	57.2
		SD 16.3	*d* 0.6	SD		16.1	15.9	15.7

Lat. (°)	Twilight Naut. (h m)	Twilight Civil (h m)	Sunrise (h m)	Moonrise 22 (h m)	Moonrise 23 (h m)	Moonrise 24 (h m)	Moonrise 25 (h m)
N 72	07 41	09 21	■	□	14 34	17 42	19 59
N 70	07 29	08 54	10 45	□	15 30	18 00	20 05
68	07 19	08 34	09 59	□	16 02	18 14	20 09
66	07 11	08 18	09 29	14 00	16 26	18 26	20 13
64	07 04	08 05	09 07	14 39	16 44	18 35	20 17
62	06 57	07 54	08 49	15 05	16 59	18 43	20 19
60	06 52	07 44	08 35	15 26	17 12	18 50	20 22
N 58	06 47	07 36	08 22	15 43	17 23	18 56	20 24
56	06 42	07 28	08 11	15 57	17 32	19 01	20 26
54	06 38	07 22	08 02	16 09	17 40	19 06	20 28
52	06 34	07 15	07 53	16 20	17 47	19 11	20 29
50	06 30	07 10	07 46	16 30	17 54	19 14	20 31
45	06 22	06 57	07 30	16 50	18 08	19 23	20 34
N 40	06 14	06 47	07 16	17 06	18 20	19 30	20 36
35	06 07	06 38	07 05	17 20	18 29	19 36	20 38
30	06 00	06 29	06 55	17 31	18 38	19 41	20 40
20	05 47	06 14	06 38	17 51	18 53	19 50	20 44
N 10	05 35	06 00	06 22	18 09	19 06	19 58	20 47
0	05 21	05 46	06 08	18 25	19 17	20 05	20 50
S 10	05 05	05 31	05 54	18 41	19 29	20 13	20 52
20	04 46	05 14	05 38	18 58	19 42	20 20	20 55
30	04 22	04 54	05 20	19 18	19 56	20 29	20 59
35	04 07	04 41	05 09	19 30	20 05	20 34	21 01
40	03 48	04 26	04 57	19 43	20 14	20 40	21 03
45	03 24	04 08	04 43	19 58	20 25	20 47	21 05
S 50	02 51	03 45	04 25	20 17	20 38	20 55	21 08
52	02 33	03 34	04 17	20 26	20 44	20 58	21 10
54	02 12	03 21	04 07	20 36	20 51	21 02	21 11
56	01 42	03 05	03 57	20 47	20 58	21 07	21 13
58	00 48	02 47	03 44	20 59	21 07	21 11	21 15
S 60	////	02 23	03 30	21 14	21 16	21 17	21 17

Lat. (°)	Sunset (h m)	Twilight Civil (h m)	Twilight Naut. (h m)	Moonset 22 (h m)	Moonset 23 (h m)	Moonset 24 (h m)	Moonset 25 (h m)
N 72	■	15 04	16 44	□	11 58	10 33	09 51
N 70	13 39	15 30	16 55	□	11 02	10 13	09 42
68	14 25	15 50	17 05	□	10 27	09 56	09 35
66	14 55	16 06	17 13	10 36	10 02	09 43	09 29
64	15 17	16 19	17 21	09 57	09 42	09 32	09 23
62	15 35	16 30	17 27	09 29	09 26	09 23	09 19
60	15 49	16 40	17 32	09 08	09 13	09 14	09 15
N 58	16 02	16 48	17 37	08 50	09 01	09 07	09 11
56	16 13	16 56	17 42	08 35	08 51	09 01	09 08
54	16 22	17 02	17 46	08 22	08 42	08 55	09 05
52	16 30	17 09	17 50	08 11	08 33	08 50	09 02
50	16 38	17 14	17 54	08 01	08 26	08 45	09 00
45	16 54	17 26	18 02	07 40	08 10	08 35	08 55
N 40	17 08	17 37	18 10	07 22	07 57	08 26	08 50
35	17 19	17 46	18 17	07 08	07 46	08 19	08 46
30	17 29	17 54	18 23	06 55	07 37	08 12	08 43
20	17 46	18 09	18 36	06 33	07 20	08 00	08 37
N 10	18 01	18 23	18 49	06 14	07 05	07 50	08 32
0	18 15	18 37	19 03	05 56	06 51	07 41	08 27
S 10	18 30	18 52	19 18	05 37	06 36	07 31	08 22
20	18 45	19 09	19 37	05 18	06 21	07 21	08 16
30	19 03	19 29	20 01	04 55	06 04	07 09	08 10
35	19 14	19 42	20 16	04 42	05 53	07 02	08 06
40	19 26	19 56	20 35	04 26	05 41	06 54	08 02
45	19 40	20 14	20 58	04 08	05 27	06 44	07 57
S 50	19 57	20 37	21 31	03 44	05 10	06 33	07 51
52	20 06	20 49	21 48	03 33	05 02	06 28	07 49
54	20 15	21 01	22 09	03 20	04 53	06 22	07 46
56	20 26	21 16	22 38	03 05	04 42	06 15	07 42
58	20 38	21 35	23 26	02 48	04 31	06 08	07 39
S 60	20 52	21 57	////	02 27	04 17	05 59	07 34

Day	SUN Eqn. of Time 00^h (m s)	SUN Eqn. of Time 12^h (m s)	SUN Mer. Pass. (h m)	MOON Mer. Pass. Upper (h m)	MOON Mer. Pass. Lower (h m)	MOON Age (d)	MOON Phase (%)
22	11 19	11 27	12 11	24 38	12 11	14	100
23	11 35	11 43	12 12	00 38	13 04	15	99
24	11 51	11 58	12 12	01 29	13 53	16	95

	UT	ARIES	VENUS −4.0		MARS −0.8		JUPITER −1.9		SATURN +0.4		STARS		
	d h	GHA ° ′	GHA ° ′	Dec ° ′	GHA ° ′	Dec ° ′	GHA ° ′	Dec ° ′	GHA ° ′	Dec ° ′	Name	SHA ° ′	Dec ° ′
	25 00	123 41.3	212 48.5	S22 21.4	40 03.4	N26 47.1	204 32.8	S23 02.4	323 55.1	N10 26.2	Acamar	315 21.2	S40 16.5
	01	138 43.7	227 47.6	21.5	55 06.1	47.0	219 34.7	02.4	338 57.7	26.2	Achernar	335 29.6	S57 12.0
	02	153 46.2	242 46.7	21.6	70 08.8	47.0	234 36.6	02.3	354 00.3	26.3	Acrux	173 13.9	S63 08.5
	03	168 48.6	257 45.9	21.7	85 11.5	47.0	249 38.4	02.3	9 02.9	26.4	Adhara	255 15.4	S28 59.0
	04	183 51.1	272 45.0	21.8	100 14.1	46.9	264 40.3	02.3	24 05.5	26.4	Aldebaran	290 53.9	N16 31.6
	05	198 53.6	287 44.2	21.9	115 16.8	46.9	279 42.2	02.2	39 08.1	26.5			
	06	213 56.0	302 43.3	S22 22.0	130 19.5	N26 46.8	294 44.1	S23 02.2	54 10.7	N10 26.6	Alioth	166 23.7	N55 54.6
	07	228 58.5	317 42.5	22.1	145 22.2	46.8	309 45.9	02.2	69 13.3	26.6	Alkaid	153 01.8	N49 16.0
	08	244 01.0	332 41.6	22.2	160 24.8	46.8	324 47.8	02.1	84 15.9	26.7	Al Na'ir	27 49.0	S46 55.5
F	09	259 03.4	347 40.7	22.3	175 27.5	46.7	339 49.7	02.1	99 18.5	26.7	Alnilam	275 50.2	S 1 11.8
R	10	274 05.9	2 39.9	22.4	190 30.2	46.7	354 51.6	02.1	114 21.1	26.8	Alphard	217 59.8	S 8 41.7
I	11	289 08.4	17 39.0	22.5	205 32.8	46.6	9 53.4	02.1	129 23.7	26.9			
D	12	304 10.8	32 38.2	S22 22.6	220 35.5	N26 46.6	24 55.3	S23 02.0	144 26.3	N10 26.9	Alphecca	126 14.5	N26 40.9
A	13	319 13.3	47 37.3	22.6	235 38.1	46.5	39 57.2	02.0	159 28.9	27.0	Alpheratz	357 48.0	N29 08.2
Y	14	334 15.7	62 36.5	22.7	250 40.8	46.5	54 59.1	02.0	174 31.5	27.1	Altair	62 12.6	N 8 53.2
	15	349 18.2	77 35.6	22.8	265 43.4	46.5	70 00.9	01.9	189 34.1	27.1	Ankaa	353 19.7	S42 15.9
	16	4 20.7	92 34.7	22.9	280 46.1	46.4	85 02.8	01.9	204 36.7	27.2	Antares	112 31.5	S26 27.1
	17	19 23.1	107 33.9	23.0	295 48.8	46.4	100 04.7	01.9	219 39.3	27.3			
	18	34 25.6	122 33.0	S22 23.1	310 51.4	N26 46.3	115 06.5	S23 01.8	234 41.9	N10 27.3	Arcturus	145 59.4	N19 08.1
	19	49 28.1	137 32.2	23.1	325 54.1	46.3	130 08.4	01.8	249 44.5	27.4	Atria	107 37.5	S69 02.4
	20	64 30.5	152 31.3	23.2	340 56.7	46.3	145 10.3	01.8	264 47.1	27.5	Avior	234 19.2	S59 32.1
	21	79 33.0	167 30.4	23.3	355 59.4	46.2	160 12.2	01.7	279 49.8	27.5	Bellatrix	278 36.1	N 6 21.5
	22	94 35.5	182 29.6	23.4	11 02.0	46.2	175 14.0	01.7	294 52.4	27.6	Betelgeuse	271 05.4	N 7 24.6
	23	109 37.9	197 28.7	23.4	26 04.6	46.1	190 15.9	01.7	309 55.0	27.7			
	26 00	124 40.4	212 27.9	S22 23.5	41 07.3	N26 46.1	205 17.8	S23 01.6	324 57.6	N10 27.7	Canopus	263 57.5	S52 42.1
	01	139 42.9	227 27.0	23.6	56 09.9	46.1	220 19.7	01.6	340 00.2	27.8	Capella	280 40.2	N46 00.6
	02	154 45.3	242 26.2	23.7	71 12.6	46.0	235 21.5	01.6	355 02.8	27.8	Deneb	49 34.8	N45 18.5
	03	169 47.8	257 25.3	23.7	86 15.2	46.0	250 23.4	01.5	10 05.4	27.9	Denebola	182 37.5	N14 31.4
	04	184 50.2	272 24.4	23.8	101 17.8	45.9	265 25.3	01.5	25 08.0	28.0	Diphda	349 00.0	S17 56.6
	05	199 52.7	287 23.6	23.9	116 20.5	45.9	280 27.2	01.5	40 10.6	28.0			
	06	214 55.2	302 22.7	S22 23.9	131 23.1	N26 45.8	295 29.0	S23 01.5	55 13.2	N10 28.1	Dubhe	193 55.8	N61 42.2
S	07	229 57.6	317 21.9	24.0	146 25.7	45.8	310 30.9	01.4	70 15.8	28.2	Elnath	278 17.5	N28 37.0
A	08	245 00.1	332 21.0	24.1	161 28.4	45.8	325 32.8	01.4	85 18.4	28.2	Eltanin	90 48.5	N51 29.0
T	09	260 02.6	347 20.1	24.1	176 31.0	45.7	340 34.7	01.4	100 21.0	28.3	Enif	33 51.5	N 9 54.7
U	10	275 05.0	2 19.3	24.2	191 33.6	45.7	355 36.5	01.3	115 23.6	28.4	Fomalhaut	15 28.6	S29 34.9
R	11	290 07.5	17 18.4	24.3	206 36.2	45.6	10 38.4	01.3	130 26.2	28.4			
D	12	305 10.0	32 17.6	S22 24.3	221 38.9	N26 45.6	25 40.3	S23 01.3	145 28.9	N10 28.5	Gacrux	172 05.5	S57 09.4
A	13	320 12.4	47 16.7	24.4	236 41.5	45.6	40 42.2	01.2	160 31.5	28.6	Gienah	175 56.4	S17 35.3
Y	14	335 14.9	62 15.8	24.4	251 44.1	45.5	55 44.0	01.2	175 34.1	28.6	Hadar	148 54.0	S60 24.6
	15	350 17.4	77 15.0	24.5	266 46.7	45.5	70 45.9	01.2	190 36.7	28.7	Hamal	328 05.4	N23 30.2
	16	5 19.8	92 14.1	24.6	281 49.3	45.4	85 47.8	01.1	205 39.3	28.8	Kaus Aust.	83 49.5	S34 22.9
	17	20 22.3	107 13.2	24.6	296 52.0	45.4	100 49.7	01.1	220 41.9	28.8			
	18	35 24.7	122 12.4	S22 24.7	311 54.6	N26 45.3	115 51.6	S23 01.1	235 44.5	N10 28.9	Kochab	137 19.5	N74 06.9
	19	50 27.2	137 11.5	24.7	326 57.2	45.3	130 53.4	01.0	250 47.1	29.0	Markab	13 42.7	N15 14.9
	20	65 29.7	152 10.7	24.8	341 59.8	45.3	145 55.3	01.0	265 49.7	29.0	Menkar	314 19.2	N 4 07.3
	21	80 32.1	167 09.8	24.8	357 02.4	45.2	160 57.2	01.0	280 52.3	29.1	Menkent	148 12.5	S36 24.5
	22	95 34.6	182 08.9	24.9	12 05.0	45.2	175 59.1	00.9	295 54.9	29.2	Miaplacidus	221 40.0	S69 44.9
	23	110 37.1	197 08.1	24.9	27 07.6	45.1	191 00.9	00.9	310 57.5	29.2			
	27 00	125 39.5	212 07.2	S22 25.0	42 10.2	N26 45.1	206 02.8	S23 00.9	326 00.2	N10 29.3	Mirfak	308 46.2	N49 53.7
	01	140 42.0	227 06.4	25.0	57 12.8	45.1	221 04.7	00.8	341 02.8	29.4	Nunki	76 03.7	S26 17.3
	02	155 44.5	242 05.5	25.1	72 15.4	45.0	236 06.6	00.8	356 05.4	29.4	Peacock	53 26.0	S56 42.6
	03	170 46.9	257 04.6	25.1	87 18.0	45.0	251 08.4	00.8	11 08.0	29.5	Pollux	243 32.3	N28 00.4
	04	185 49.4	272 03.8	25.1	102 20.6	44.9	266 10.3	00.7	26 10.6	29.5	Procyon	245 03.6	N 5 12.2
	05	200 51.8	287 02.9	25.2	117 23.2	44.9	281 12.2	00.7	41 13.2	29.6			
	06	215 54.3	302 02.0	S22 25.2	132 25.8	N26 44.9	296 14.1	S23 00.7	56 15.8	N10 29.7	Rasalhague	96 10.5	N12 33.0
	07	230 56.8	317 01.2	25.3	147 28.4	44.8	311 16.0	00.6	71 18.4	29.7	Regulus	207 47.5	N11 55.5
	08	245 59.2	332 00.3	25.3	162 31.0	44.8	326 17.8	00.6	86 21.0	29.8	Rigel	281 15.7	S 8 11.5
S	09	261 01.7	346 59.5	25.3	177 33.6	44.7	341 19.7	00.6	101 23.6	29.9	Rigil Kent.	139 57.6	S60 51.9
U	10	276 04.2	1 58.6	25.4	192 36.2	44.7	356 21.6	00.6	116 26.3	29.9	Sabik	102 17.5	S15 44.2
N	11	291 06.6	16 57.7	25.4	207 38.8	44.6	11 23.5	00.5	131 28.9	30.0			
D	12	306 09.1	31 56.9	S22 25.4	222 41.4	N26 44.6	26 25.3	S23 00.5	146 31.5	N10 30.1	Schedar	349 45.7	N56 35.2
A	13	321 11.6	46 56.0	25.5	237 44.0	44.6	41 27.2	00.5	161 34.1	30.1	Shaula	96 27.8	S37 06.6
Y	14	336 14.0	61 55.1	25.5	252 46.5	44.5	56 29.1	00.4	176 36.7	30.2	Sirius	258 37.0	S16 43.7
	15	351 16.5	76 54.3	25.5	267 49.1	44.5	71 31.0	00.4	191 39.3	30.3	Spica	158 35.5	S11 12.3
	16	6 19.0	91 53.4	25.6	282 51.7	44.4	86 32.9	00.4	206 41.9	30.3	Suhail	222 55.1	S43 27.9
	17	21 21.4	106 52.5	25.6	297 54.3	44.4	101 34.7	00.3	221 44.5	30.4			
	18	36 23.9	121 51.7	S22 25.6	312 56.9	N26 44.4	116 36.6	S23 00.3	236 47.1	N10 30.5	Vega	80 42.1	N38 47.2
	19	51 26.3	136 50.8	25.6	327 59.4	44.3	131 38.5	00.3	251 49.8	30.5	Zuben'ubi	137 10.0	S16 04.6
	20	66 28.8	151 50.0	25.7	343 02.0	44.3	146 40.4	00.2	266 52.4	30.6		SHA	Mer. Pass.
	21	81 31.3	166 49.1	25.7	358 04.6	44.2	161 42.2	00.2	281 55.0	30.7		° ′	h m
	22	96 33.7	181 48.2	25.7	13 07.1	44.2	176 44.1	00.2	296 57.6	30.7	Venus	87 47.5	9 51
	23	111 36.2	196 47.4	25.7	28 09.7	44.2	191 46.0	00.1	312 00.2	30.8	Mars	276 26.9	21 12
	Mer. Pass.	h m 15 38.7	v −0.9	d 0.1	v 2.6	d 0.0	v 1.9	d 0.0	v 2.6	d 0.1	Jupiter	80 37.4	10 18
											Saturn	200 17.2	2 20

UT (d h)	SUN GHA ° ′	SUN Dec ° ′	MOON GHA ° ′	v ′	MOON Dec ° ′	d ′	HP ′
25 00	176 58.6	S19 10.0	327 01.3	13.5	N 9 01.7	14.9	57.2
01	191 58.4	09.4	341 33.8	13.6	8 46.8	14.9	57.1
02	206 58.3	08.8	356 06.4	13.7	8 31.9	14.8	57.1
03	221 58.1	. . 08.2	10 39.1	13.8	8 17.1	14.9	57.1
04	236 58.0	07.6	25 11.9	13.8	8 02.2	15.0	57.0
05	251 57.8	07.0	39 44.7	13.9	7 47.2	14.9	57.0
06	266 57.7	S19 06.4	54 17.6	14.0	N 7 32.3	15.0	57.0
07	281 57.5	05.8	68 50.6	14.1	7 17.3	14.9	56.9
08	296 57.4	05.1	83 23.7	14.1	7 02.4	15.0	56.9
F 09	311 57.2	. . 04.5	97 56.8	14.2	6 47.4	15.0	56.9
R 10	326 57.1	03.9	112 30.0	14.2	6 32.4	15.0	56.8
I 11	341 56.9	03.3	127 03.2	14.3	6 17.4	15.0	56.8
D 12	356 56.8	S19 02.7	141 36.5	14.4	N 6 02.4	15.0	56.8
A 13	11 56.6	02.1	156 09.9	14.4	5 47.4	15.0	56.7
Y 14	26 56.5	01.5	170 43.3	14.5	5 32.4	15.1	56.7
15	41 56.4	. . 00.9	185 16.8	14.5	5 17.3	15.0	56.7
16	56 56.2	19 00.3	199 50.3	14.7	5 02.3	15.1	56.6
17	71 56.1	18 59.6	214 24.0	14.6	4 47.2	15.0	56.6
18	86 55.9	S18 59.0	228 57.6	14.7	N 4 32.2	15.0	56.6
19	101 55.8	58.4	243 31.3	14.8	4 17.2	15.1	56.6
20	116 55.6	57.8	258 05.1	14.8	4 02.1	15.0	56.5
21	131 55.5	. . 57.2	272 38.9	14.9	3 47.1	15.1	56.5
22	146 55.4	56.6	287 12.8	14.9	3 32.0	15.0	56.5
23	161 55.2	55.9	301 46.7	15.0	3 17.0	15.0	56.4
26 00	176 55.1	S18 55.3	316 20.7	15.0	N 3 02.0	15.0	56.4
01	191 54.9	54.7	330 54.7	15.1	2 47.0	15.1	56.4
02	206 54.8	54.1	345 28.8	15.1	2 31.9	15.0	56.3
03	221 54.7	. . 53.5	0 02.9	15.1	2 16.9	15.0	56.3
04	236 54.5	52.8	14 37.0	15.2	2 01.9	15.0	56.3
05	251 54.4	52.2	29 11.2	15.3	1 46.9	15.0	56.2
06	266 54.2	S18 51.6	43 45.5	15.2	N 1 31.9	14.9	56.2
07	281 54.1	51.0	58 19.7	15.3	1 17.0	15.0	56.2
S 08	296 54.0	50.4	72 54.0	15.4	1 02.0	14.9	56.2
A 09	311 53.8	. . 49.7	87 28.4	15.4	0 47.1	15.0	56.1
T 10	326 53.7	49.1	102 02.8	15.4	0 32.1	14.9	56.1
U 11	341 53.5	48.5	116 37.2	15.4	0 17.2	14.9	56.1
R 12	356 53.4	S18 47.9	131 11.6	15.5	N 0 02.3	14.9	56.0
D 13	11 53.3	47.2	145 46.1	15.5	S 0 12.6	14.9	56.0
A 14	26 53.1	46.6	160 20.6	15.6	0 27.5	14.8	56.0
Y 15	41 53.0	. . 46.0	174 55.2	15.6	0 42.3	14.8	55.9
16	56 52.9	45.3	189 29.8	15.6	0 57.1	14.9	55.9
17	71 52.7	44.7	204 04.4	15.6	1 12.0	14.7	55.9
18	86 52.6	S18 44.1	218 39.0	15.6	S 1 26.7	14.8	55.9
19	101 52.4	43.5	233 13.6	15.7	1 41.5	14.8	55.8
20	116 52.3	42.8	247 48.3	15.7	1 56.3	14.7	55.8
21	131 52.2	. . 42.2	262 23.0	15.7	2 11.0	14.7	55.8
22	146 52.0	41.6	276 57.7	15.8	2 25.7	14.6	55.7
23	161 51.9	40.9	291 32.5	15.7	2 40.3	14.7	55.7
27 00	176 51.8	S18 40.3	306 07.2	15.8	S 2 55.0	14.6	55.7
01	191 51.6	39.7	320 42.0	15.8	3 09.6	14.6	55.7
02	206 51.5	39.0	335 16.8	15.8	3 24.2	14.6	55.6
03	221 51.4	. . 38.4	349 51.6	15.8	3 38.8	14.5	55.6
04	236 51.2	37.8	4 26.4	15.9	3 53.3	14.5	55.6
05	251 51.1	37.1	19 01.3	15.8	4 07.8	14.5	55.6
06	266 51.0	S18 36.5	33 36.1	15.9	S 4 22.3	14.4	55.5
07	281 50.9	35.9	48 11.0	15.9	4 36.7	14.4	55.5
08	296 50.7	35.2	62 45.9	15.8	4 51.1	14.4	55.5
S 09	311 50.6	. . 34.6	77 20.7	15.9	5 05.5	14.3	55.4
U 10	326 50.5	33.9	91 55.6	15.9	5 19.8	14.3	55.4
N 11	341 50.3	33.3	106 30.5	15.9	5 34.1	14.3	55.4
D 12	356 50.2	S18 32.7	121 05.4	15.9	S 5 48.4	14.2	55.4
A 13	11 50.1	32.0	135 40.3	15.9	6 02.6	14.2	55.3
Y 14	26 49.9	31.4	150 15.2	15.9	6 16.8	14.2	55.3
15	41 49.8	. . 30.7	164 50.1	15.9	6 31.0	14.1	55.3
16	56 49.7	30.1	179 25.0	15.9	6 45.1	14.1	55.3
17	71 49.6	29.4	193 59.9	15.9	6 59.2	14.0	55.2
18	86 49.4	S18 28.8	208 34.8	15.9	S 7 13.2	14.0	55.2
19	101 49.3	28.2	223 09.7	15.9	7 27.2	14.0	55.2
20	116 49.2	27.5	237 44.6	15.9	7 41.2	13.9	55.2
21	131 49.1	. . 26.9	252 19.5	15.9	7 55.1	13.9	55.2
22	146 48.9	26.2	266 54.4	15.9	8 09.0	13.8	55.1
23	161 48.8	25.6	281 29.3	15.9	S 8 22.8	13.8	55.1
	SD 16.3	d 0.6	SD 15.5		15.3		15.1

Lat. °	Twilight Naut. h m	Twilight Civil h m	Sunrise h m	Moonrise 25 h m	Moonrise 26 h m	Moonrise 27 h m	Moonrise 28 h m
N 72	07 32	09 08	11 58	19 59	22 04	24 09	00 09
N 70	07 21	08 44	10 24	20 05	22 00	23 55	25 59
68	07 12	08 26	09 46	20 09	21 57	23 44	25 36
66	07 05	08 11	09 19	20 13	21 55	23 35	25 18
64	06 58	07 59	08 59	20 17	21 53	23 27	25 03
62	06 53	07 48	08 42	20 19	21 51	23 20	24 51
60	06 47	07 39	08 29	20 22	21 49	23 15	24 41
N 58	06 43	07 31	08 17	20 24	21 48	23 10	24 32
56	06 38	07 24	08 07	20 26	21 47	23 06	24 24
54	06 34	07 18	07 58	20 28	21 46	23 02	24 17
52	06 31	07 12	07 50	20 29	21 45	22 58	24 11
50	06 27	07 07	07 42	20 31	21 44	22 55	24 06
45	06 19	06 55	07 27	20 34	21 42	22 48	23 54
N 40	06 12	06 45	07 14	20 36	21 40	22 42	23 44
35	06 06	06 36	07 03	20 38	21 39	22 37	23 36
30	05 59	06 28	06 54	20 40	21 37	22 33	23 28
20	05 47	06 14	06 37	20 44	21 35	22 26	23 16
N 10	05 35	06 00	06 23	20 47	21 33	22 19	23 05
0	05 22	05 47	06 09	20 50	21 32	22 13	22 55
S 10	05 07	05 33	05 55	20 52	21 30	22 07	22 45
20	04 48	05 16	05 40	20 55	21 28	22 01	22 34
30	04 25	04 57	05 23	20 59	21 26	21 54	22 22
35	04 10	04 44	05 13	21 01	21 25	21 50	22 15
40	03 52	04 30	05 01	21 03	21 24	21 45	22 07
45	03 29	04 13	04 47	21 05	21 23	21 40	21 58
S 50	02 58	03 51	04 30	21 08	21 21	21 33	21 47
52	02 42	03 40	04 22	21 10	21 20	21 31	21 42
54	02 22	03 28	04 13	21 11	21 19	21 27	21 37
56	01 55	03 13	04 03	21 13	21 18	21 24	21 30
58	01 15	02 56	03 52	21 15	21 17	21 20	21 24
S 60	////	02 34	03 38	21 17	21 16	21 16	21 16

Lat. °	Sunset h m	Twilight Civil h m	Twilight Naut. h m	Moonset 25 h m	Moonset 26 h m	Moonset 27 h m	Moonset 28 h m
N 72	12 28	15 18	16 54	09 51	09 18	08 46	08 09
N 70	14 01	15 42	17 05	09 42	09 17	08 53	08 26
68	14 40	16 00	17 14	09 35	09 16	08 58	08 39
66	15 06	16 15	17 21	09 29	09 16	09 03	08 50
64	15 27	16 27	17 28	09 23	09 15	09 07	08 59
62	15 43	16 37	17 33	09 19	09 15	09 11	09 07
60	15 57	16 46	17 38	09 15	09 15	09 14	09 14
N 58	16 09	16 54	17 43	09 11	09 14	09 17	09 20
56	16 19	17 01	17 47	09 08	09 14	09 20	09 25
54	16 28	17 08	17 51	09 05	09 14	09 22	09 30
52	16 36	17 13	17 55	09 02	09 13	09 24	09 35
50	16 43	17 19	17 58	09 00	09 13	09 26	09 39
45	16 58	17 30	18 06	08 55	09 13	09 30	09 48
N 40	17 11	17 40	18 13	08 50	09 12	09 33	09 55
35	17 22	17 49	18 20	08 46	09 12	09 36	10 01
30	17 31	17 57	18 26	08 43	09 12	09 39	10 07
20	17 48	18 11	18 38	08 37	09 11	09 44	10 16
N 10	18 02	18 24	18 50	08 32	09 10	09 48	10 25
0	18 16	18 38	19 03	08 27	09 10	09 52	10 33
S 10	18 30	18 52	19 18	08 22	09 09	09 55	10 41
20	18 45	19 08	19 36	08 16	09 09	10 00	10 50
30	19 02	19 28	19 59	08 10	09 08	10 04	11 00
35	19 12	19 40	20 14	08 06	09 08	10 07	11 05
40	19 23	19 54	20 32	08 02	09 07	10 10	11 12
45	19 37	20 11	20 54	07 57	09 07	10 14	11 20
S 50	19 54	20 33	21 25	07 51	09 06	10 18	11 29
52	20 02	20 44	21 41	07 49	09 06	10 20	11 33
54	20 10	20 56	22 01	07 46	09 05	10 22	11 38
56	20 20	21 10	22 26	07 42	09 05	10 25	11 43
58	20 32	21 27	23 04	07 39	09 04	10 27	11 49
S 60	20 45	21 48	////	07 34	09 04	10 30	11 56

Day	SUN Eqn. of Time 00^h	SUN Eqn. of Time 12^h	SUN Mer. Pass.	MOON Mer. Pass. Upper	MOON Mer. Pass. Lower	MOON Age	MOON Phase
d	m s	m s	h m	h m	h m	d %	
25	12 05	12 13	12 12	02 16	14 38	17 90	
26	12 19	12 26	12 12	03 00	15 21	18 83	
27	12 33	12 39	12 13	03 42	16 02	19 75	

2008 JANUARY 28, 29, 30 (MON., TUES., WED.)

	UT	ARIES	VENUS −3.9		MARS −0.7		JUPITER −1.9		SATURN +0.4	
		GHA	GHA	Dec	GHA	Dec	GHA	Dec	GHA	Dec
	d h	° ′	° ′	° ′	° ′	° ′	° ′	° ′	° ′	° ′
	28 00	126 38.7	211 46.5	S22 25.8	43 12.3	N26 44.1	206 47.9	S23 00.1	327 02.8	N10 30.9
	01	141 41.1	226 45.6	25.8	58 14.9	44.1	221 49.8	00.1	342 05.4	30.9
	02	156 43.6	241 44.8	25.8	73 17.4	44.0	236 51.6	00.0	357 08.0	31.0
	03	171 46.1	256 43.9	25.8	88 20.0	44.0	251 53.5	00.0	12 10.7	31.1
	04	186 48.5	271 43.0	25.8	103 22.5	44.0	266 55.4	23 00.0	27 13.3	31.1
	05	201 51.0	286 42.2	25.8	118 25.1	43.9	281 57.3	22 59.9	42 15.9	31.2
	06	216 53.4	301 41.3	S22 25.8	133 27.7	N26 43.9	296 59.2	S22 59.9	57 18.5	N10 31.3
	07	231 55.9	316 40.5	25.9	148 30.2	43.8	312 01.0	59.9	72 21.1	31.3
	08	246 58.4	331 39.6	25.9	163 32.8	43.8	327 02.9	59.8	87 23.7	31.4
M	09	262 00.8	346 38.7	25.9	178 35.3	43.7	342 04.8	59.8	102 26.3	31.5
O	10	277 03.3	1 37.9	25.9	193 37.9	43.7	357 06.7	59.8	117 28.9	31.5
N	11	292 05.8	16 37.0	25.9	208 40.4	43.7	12 08.6	59.7	132 31.6	31.6
D	12	307 08.2	31 36.1	S22 25.9	223 43.0	N26 43.6	27 10.4	S22 59.7	147 34.2	N10 31.7
A	13	322 10.7	46 35.3	25.9	238 45.5	43.6	42 12.3	59.7	162 36.8	31.7
Y	14	337 13.2	61 34.4	25.9	253 48.1	43.5	57 14.2	59.6	177 39.4	31.8
	15	352 15.6	76 33.5	25.9	268 50.6	43.5	72 16.1	59.6	192 42.0	31.9
	16	7 18.1	91 32.7	25.9	283 53.2	43.5	87 18.0	59.6	207 44.6	32.0
	17	22 20.6	106 31.8	25.9	298 55.7	43.4	102 19.8	59.5	222 47.2	32.0
	18	37 23.0	121 30.9	S22 25.9	313 58.3	N26 43.4	117 21.7	S22 59.5	237 49.9	N10 32.1
	19	52 25.5	136 30.1	25.9	329 00.8	43.3	132 23.6	59.5	252 52.5	32.2
	20	67 27.9	151 29.2	25.9	344 03.3	43.3	147 25.5	59.4	267 55.1	32.2
	21	82 30.4	166 28.3	25.9	359 05.9	43.3	162 27.4	59.4	282 57.7	32.3
	22	97 32.9	181 27.5	25.9	14 08.4	43.2	177 29.2	59.4	298 00.3	32.4
	23	112 35.3	196 26.6	25.9	29 10.9	43.2	192 31.1	59.3	313 02.9	32.4
	29 00	127 37.8	211 25.8	S22 25.9	44 13.5	N26 43.1	207 33.0	S22 59.3	328 05.5	N10 32.5
	01	142 40.3	226 24.9	25.9	59 16.0	43.1	222 34.9	59.3	343 08.2	32.6
	02	157 42.7	241 24.0	25.9	74 18.5	43.1	237 36.8	59.2	358 10.8	32.6
	03	172 45.2	256 23.2	25.8	89 21.1	43.0	252 38.6	59.2	13 13.4	32.7
	04	187 47.7	271 22.3	25.8	104 23.6	43.0	267 40.5	59.2	28 16.0	32.8
	05	202 50.1	286 21.4	25.8	119 26.1	42.9	282 42.4	59.1	43 18.6	32.8
	06	217 52.6	301 20.6	S22 25.8	134 28.6	N26 42.9	297 44.3	S22 59.1	58 21.2	N10 32.9
	07	232 55.1	316 19.7	25.8	149 31.2	42.8	312 46.2	59.0	73 23.8	33.0
T	08	247 57.5	331 18.8	25.8	164 33.7	42.8	327 48.1	59.0	88 26.5	33.0
U	09	263 00.0	346 18.0	25.7	179 36.2	42.8	342 49.9	59.0	103 29.1	33.1
E	10	278 02.4	1 17.1	25.7	194 38.7	42.7	357 51.8	58.9	118 31.7	33.2
S	11	293 04.9	16 16.2	25.7	209 41.2	42.7	12 53.7	58.9	133 34.3	33.2
D	12	308 07.4	31 15.4	S22 25.7	224 43.7	N26 42.6	27 55.6	S22 58.9	148 36.9	N10 33.3
A	13	323 09.8	46 14.5	25.7	239 46.3	42.6	42 57.5	58.8	163 39.5	33.4
Y	14	338 12.3	61 13.6	25.6	254 48.8	42.6	57 59.3	58.8	178 42.2	33.4
	15	353 14.8	76 12.8	25.6	269 51.3	42.5	73 01.2	58.8	193 44.8	33.5
	16	8 17.2	91 11.9	25.6	284 53.8	42.5	88 03.1	58.7	208 47.4	33.6
	17	23 19.7	106 11.0	25.6	299 56.3	42.4	103 05.0	58.7	223 50.0	33.6
	18	38 22.2	121 10.2	S22 25.5	314 58.8	N26 42.4	118 06.9	S22 58.7	238 52.6	N10 33.7
	19	53 24.6	136 09.3	25.5	330 01.3	42.4	133 08.8	58.6	253 55.2	33.8
	20	68 27.1	151 08.4	25.5	345 03.8	42.3	148 10.6	58.6	268 57.9	33.9
	21	83 29.5	166 07.6	25.4	0 06.3	42.3	163 12.5	58.6	284 00.5	33.9
	22	98 32.0	181 06.7	25.4	15 08.8	42.2	178 14.4	58.5	299 03.1	34.0
	23	113 34.5	196 05.8	25.4	30 11.3	42.2	193 16.3	58.5	314 05.7	34.1
	30 00	128 36.9	211 05.0	S22 25.3	45 13.8	N26 42.2	208 18.2	S22 58.5	329 08.3	N10 34.1
	01	143 39.4	226 04.1	25.3	60 16.3	42.1	223 20.1	58.4	344 10.9	34.2
	02	158 41.9	241 03.2	25.2	75 18.8	42.1	238 21.9	58.4	359 13.6	34.3
	03	173 44.3	256 02.4	25.2	90 21.3	42.0	253 23.8	58.4	14 16.2	34.3
	04	188 46.8	271 01.5	25.2	105 23.8	42.0	268 25.7	58.3	29 18.8	34.4
	05	203 49.3	286 00.6	25.1	120 26.3	42.0	283 27.6	58.3	44 21.4	34.5
	06	218 51.7	300 59.8	S22 25.1	135 28.7	N26 41.9	298 29.5	S22 58.3	59 24.0	N10 34.5
W	07	233 54.2	315 58.9	25.0	150 31.2	41.9	313 31.4	58.2	74 26.7	34.6
E	08	248 56.7	330 58.0	25.0	165 33.7	41.8	328 33.2	58.2	89 29.3	34.7
D	09	263 59.1	345 57.2	24.9	180 36.2	41.8	343 35.1	58.2	104 31.9	34.7
N	10	279 01.6	0 56.3	24.9	195 38.7	41.8	358 37.0	58.1	119 34.5	34.8
E	11	294 04.0	15 55.4	24.9	210 41.2	41.7	13 38.9	58.1	134 37.1	34.9
S	12	309 06.5	30 54.6	S22 24.8	225 43.6	N26 41.7	28 40.8	S22 58.0	149 39.7	N10 35.0
D	13	324 09.0	45 53.7	24.8	240 46.1	41.6	43 42.7	58.0	164 42.4	35.0
A	14	339 11.4	60 52.8	24.7	255 48.6	41.6	58 44.6	58.0	179 45.0	35.1
Y	15	354 13.9	75 52.0	24.6	270 51.1	41.6	73 46.4	57.9	194 47.6	35.2
	16	9 16.4	90 51.1	24.6	285 53.5	41.5	88 48.3	57.9	209 50.2	35.2
	17	24 18.8	105 50.2	24.5	300 56.0	41.5	103 50.2	57.9	224 52.8	35.3
	18	39 21.3	120 49.4	S22 24.5	315 58.5	N26 41.4	118 52.1	S22 57.8	239 55.5	N10 35.4
	19	54 23.8	135 48.5	24.4	331 00.9	41.4	133 54.0	57.8	254 58.1	35.4
	20	69 26.2	150 47.6	24.4	346 03.4	41.4	148 55.9	57.8	270 00.7	35.5
	21	84 28.7	165 46.8	24.3	1 05.9	41.3	163 57.8	57.7	285 03.3	35.6
	22	99 31.2	180 45.9	24.2	16 08.3	41.3	178 59.6	57.7	300 05.9	35.6
	23	114 33.6	195 45.1	24.2	31 10.8	41.2	194 01.5	57.7	315 08.6	35.7
	Mer. Pass.	h m 15 26.9	*v* −0.9	*d* 0.0	*v* 2.5	*d* 0.0	*v* 1.9	*d* 0.0	*v* 2.6	*d* 0.1

STARS

Name	SHA	Dec
	° ′	° ′
Acamar	315 21.2	S40 16.5
Achernar	335 29.6	S57 12.0
Acrux	173 13.9	S63 08.5
Adhara	255 15.4	S28 59.0
Aldebaran	290 53.9	N16 31.6
Alioth	166 23.7	N55 54.6
Alkaid	153 01.8	N49 16.0
Al Na'ir	27 49.1	S46 55.5
Alnilam	275 50.2	S 1 11.8
Alphard	217 59.8	S 8 41.7
Alphecca	126 14.5	N26 40.9
Alpheratz	357 48.0	N29 08.2
Altair	62 12.5	N 8 53.2
Ankaa	353 19.7	S42 15.9
Antares	112 31.5	S26 27.1
Arcturus	145 59.4	N19 08.1
Atria	107 37.4	S69 02.4
Avior	234 19.2	S59 32.1
Bellatrix	278 36.1	N 6 21.5
Betelgeuse	271 05.4	N 7 24.6
Canopus	263 57.5	S52 42.1
Capella	280 40.2	N46 00.6
Deneb	49 34.8	N45 18.5
Denebola	182 37.5	N14 31.4
Diphda	349 00.0	S17 56.6
Dubhe	193 55.7	N61 42.2
Elnath	278 17.5	N28 37.0
Eltanin	90 48.4	N51 28.9
Enif	33 51.5	N 9 54.7
Fomalhaut	15 28.6	S29 34.9
Gacrux	172 05.5	S57 09.4
Gienah	175 56.4	S17 35.3
Hadar	148 53.9	S60 24.6
Hamal	328 05.5	N23 30.2
Kaus Aust.	83 49.5	S34 22.9
Kochab	137 19.5	N74 06.9
Markab	13 42.7	N15 14.9
Menkar	314 19.3	N 4 07.3
Menkent	148 12.5	S36 24.6
Miaplacidus	221 40.0	S69 45.0
Mirfak	308 46.2	N49 53.7
Nunki	76 03.7	S26 17.3
Peacock	53 26.0	S56 42.6
Pollux	243 32.3	N28 00.4
Procyon	245 03.6	N 5 12.2
Rasalhague	96 10.5	N12 33.0
Regulus	207 47.5	N11 55.5
Rigel	281 15.7	S 8 11.5
Rigil Kent.	139 57.6	S60 51.9
Sabik	102 17.4	S15 44.2
Schedar	349 45.7	N56 35.2
Shaula	96 27.8	S37 06.6
Sirius	258 37.0	S16 43.7
Spica	158 35.5	S11 12.3
Suhail	222 55.1	S43 27.9
Vega	80 42.1	N38 47.2
Zuben'ubi	137 10.0	S16 04.6

	SHA	Mer. Pass.
	° ′	h m
Venus	83 47.9	9 55
Mars	276 35.7	21 00
Jupiter	79 55.2	10 09
Saturn	200 27.7	2 07

INDEX TO SELECTED STARS, 2008

Name	No	Mag	SHA	Dec
			°	°
Acamar	**7**	3·2	315	S 40
Achernar	**5**	0·5	335	S 57
Acrux	**30**	1·3	173	S 63
Adhara	**19**	1·5	255	S 29
Aldebaran	**10**	0·9	291	N 17
Alioth	**32**	1·8	166	N 56
Alkaid	**34**	1·9	153	N 49
Al Na'ir	**55**	1·7	28	S 47
Alnilam	**15**	1·7	276	S 1
Alphard	**25**	2·0	218	S 9
Alphecca	**41**	2·2	126	N 27
Alpheratz	**1**	2·1	358	N 29
Altair	**51**	0·8	62	N 9
Ankaa	**2**	2·4	353	S 42
Antares	**42**	1·0	113	S 26
Arcturus	**37**	0·0	146	N 19
Atria	**43**	1·9	108	S 69
Avior	**22**	1·9	234	S 60
Bellatrix	**13**	1·6	279	N 6
Betelgeuse	**16**	Var.*	271	N 7
Canopus	**17**	−0·7	264	S 53
Capella	**12**	0·1	281	N 46
Deneb	**53**	1·3	50	N 45
Denebola	**28**	2·1	183	N 15
Diphda	**4**	2·0	349	S 18
Dubhe	**27**	1·8	194	N 62
Elnath	**14**	1·7	278	N 29
Eltanin	**47**	2·2	91	N 51
Enif	**54**	2·4	34	N 10
Fomalhaut	**56**	1·2	15	S 30
Gacrux	**31**	1·6	172	S 57
Gienah	**29**	2·6	176	S 18
Hadar	**35**	0·6	149	S 60
Hamal	**6**	2·0	328	N 24
Kaus Australis	**48**	1·9	84	S 34
Kochab	**40**	2·1	137	N 74
Markab	**57**	2·5	14	N 15
Menkar	**8**	2·5	314	N 4
Menkent	**36**	2·1	148	S 36
Miaplacidus	**24**	1·7	222	S 70
Mirfak	**9**	1·8	309	N 50
Nunki	**50**	2·0	76	S 26
Peacock	**52**	1·9	53	S 57
Pollux	**21**	1·1	244	N 28
Procyon	**20**	0·4	245	N 5
Rasalhague	**46**	2·1	96	N 13
Regulus	**26**	1·4	208	N 12
Rigel	**11**	0·1	281	S 8
Rigil Kentaurus	**38**	−0·3	140	S 61
Sabik	**44**	2·4	102	S 16
Schedar	**3**	2·2	350	N 57
Shaula	**45**	1·6	96	S 37
Sirius	**18**	−1·5	259	S 17
Spica	**33**	1·0	159	S 11
Suhail	**23**	2·2	223	S 43
Vega	**49**	0·0	81	N 39
Zubenelgenubi	**39**	2·8	137	S 16

No	Name	Mag	SHA	Dec
			°	°
1	*Alpheratz*	2·1	358	N 29
2	*Ankaa*	2·4	353	S 42
3	*Schedar*	2·2	350	N 57
4	*Diphda*	2·0	349	S 18
5	*Achernar*	0·5	335	S 57
6	*Hamal*	2·0	328	N 24
7	*Acamar*	3·2	315	S 40
8	*Menkar*	2·5	314	N 4
9	*Mirfak*	1·8	309	N 50
10	*Aldebaran*	0·9	291	N 17
11	*Rigel*	0·1	281	S 8
12	*Capella*	0·1	281	N 46
13	*Bellatrix*	1·6	279	N 6
14	*Elnath*	1·7	278	N 29
15	*Alnilam*	1·7	276	S 1
16	*Betelgeuse*	Var.*	271	N 7
17	*Canopus*	−0·7	264	S 53
18	*Sirius*	−1·5	259	S 17
19	*Adhara*	1·5	255	S 29
20	*Procyon*	0·4	245	N 5
21	*Pollux*	1·1	244	N 28
22	*Avior*	1·9	234	S 60
23	*Suhail*	2·2	223	S 43
24	*Miaplacidus*	1·7	222	S 70
25	*Alphard*	2·0	218	S 9
26	*Regulus*	1·4	208	N 12
27	*Dubhe*	1·8	194	N 62
28	*Denebola*	2·1	183	N 15
29	*Gienah*	2·6	176	S 18
30	*Acrux*	1·3	173	S 63
31	*Gacrux*	1·6	172	S 57
32	*Alioth*	1·8	166	N 56
33	*Spica*	1·0	159	S 11
34	*Alkaid*	1·9	153	N 49
35	*Hadar*	0·6	149	S 60
36	*Menkent*	2·1	148	S 36
37	*Arcturus*	0·0	146	N 19
38	*Rigil Kentaurus*	−0·3	140	S 61
39	*Zubenelgenubi*	2·8	137	S 16
40	*Kochab*	2·1	137	N 74
41	*Alphecca*	2·2	126	N 27
42	*Antares*	1·0	113	S 26
43	*Atria*	1·9	108	S 69
44	*Sabik*	2·4	102	S 16
45	*Shaula*	1·6	96	S 37
46	*Rasalhague*	2·1	96	N 13
47	*Eltanin*	2·2	91	N 51
48	*Kaus Australis*	1·9	84	S 34
49	*Vega*	0·0	81	N 39
50	*Nunki*	2·0	76	S 26
51	*Altair*	0·8	62	N 9
52	*Peacock*	1·9	53	S 57
53	*Deneb*	1·3	50	N 45
54	*Enif*	2·4	34	N 10
55	*Al Na'ir*	1·7	28	S 47
56	*Fomalhaut*	1·2	15	S 30
57	*Markab*	2·5	14	N 15

*0·1 — 1·2

ALTITUDE CORRECTION TABLES 10°-90°—SUN, STARS, PLANETS

OCT.—MAR. SUN			APR.—SEPT. SUN			STARS AND PLANETS		DIP		
App. Alt.	Lower Limb	Upper Limb	App. Alt.	Lower Limb	Upper Limb	App Alt.	Corrn	Ht. of Eye	Corrn	Ht. of Eye
° ′	′	′	° ′	′	′	° ′	′	m	′	ft.
9 33			9 39			9 55		2.4		8.0
	+10.8	−21.5		+10.6	−21.2		−5.3		−2.8	
9 45			9 50			10 07		2.6		8.6
	+10.9	−21.4		+10.7	−21.1		−5.2		−2.9	
9 56			10 02			10 20		2.8		9.2
	+11.0	−21.3		+10.8	−21.0		−5.1		−3.0	
10 08			10 14			10 32		3.0		9.8
	+11.1	−21.2		+10.9	−20.9		−5.0		−3.1	
10 20			10 27			10 46		3.2		10.5
	+11.2	−21.1		+11.0	−20.8		−4.9		−3.2	
10 33			10 40			10 59		3.4		11.2
	+11.3	−21.0		+11.1	−20.7		−4.8		−3.3	
10 46			10 53			11 14		3.6		11.9
	+11.4	−20.9		+11.2	−20.6		−4.7		−3.4	
11 00			11 07			11 29		3.8		12.6
	+11.5	−20.8		+11.3	−20.5		−4.6		−3.5	
11 15			11 22			11 44		4.0		13.3
	+11.6	−20.7		+11.4	−20.4		−4.5		−3.6	
11 30			11 37			12 00		4.3		14.1
	+11.7	−20.6		+11.5	−20.3		−4.4		−3.7	
11 45			11 53			12 17		4.5		14.9
	+11.8	−20.5		+11.6	−20.2		−4.3		−3.8	
12 01			12 10			12 35		4.7		15.7
	+11.9	−20.4		+11.7	−20.1		−4.2		−3.9	
12 18			12 27			12 53		5.0		16.5
	+12.0	−20.3		+11.8	−20.0		−4.1		−4.0	
12 36			12 45			13 12		5.2		17.4
	+12.1	−20.2		+11.9	−19.9		−4.0		−4.1	
12 54			13 04			13 32		5.5		18.3
	+12.2	−20.1		+12.0	−19.8		−3.9		−4.2	
13 14			13 24			13 53		5.8		19.1
	+12.3	−20.0		+12.1	−19.7		−3.8		−4.3	
13 34			13 44			14 16		6.1		20.1
	+12.4	−19.9		+12.2	−19.6		−3.7		−4.4	
13 55			14 06			14 39		6.3		21.0
	+12.5	−19.8		+12.3	−19.5		−3.6		−4.5	
14 17			14 29			15 03		6.6		22.0
	+12.6	−19.7		+12.4	−19.4		−3.5		−4.6	
14 41			14 53			15 29		6.9		22.9
	+12.7	−19.6		+12.5	−19.3		−3.4		−4.7	
15 05			15 18			15 56		7.2		23.9
	+12.8	−19.5		+12.6	−19.2		−3.3		−4.8	
15 31			15 45			16 25		7.5		24.9
	+12.9	−19.4		+12.7	−19.1		−3.2		−4.9	
15 59			16 13			16 55		7.9		26.0
	+13.0	−19.3		+12.8	−19.0		−3.1		−5.0	
16 27			16 43			17 27		8.2		27.1
	+13.1	−19.2		+12.9	−18.9		−3.0		−5.1	
16 58			17 14			18 01		8.5		28.1
	+13.2	−19.1		+13.0	−18.8		−2.9		−5.2	
17 30			17 47			18 37		8.8		29.2
	+13.3	−19.0		+13.1	−18.7		−2.8		−5.3	
18 05			18 23			19 16		9.2		30.4
	+13.4	−18.9		+13.2	−18.6		−2.7		−5.4	
18 41			19 00			19 56		9.5		31.5
	+13.5	−18.8		+13.3	−18.5		−2.6		−5.5	
19 20			19 41			20 40		9.9		32.7
	+13.6	−18.7		+13.4	−18.4		−2.5		−5.6	
20 02			20 24			21 27		10.3		33.9
	+13.7	−18.6		+13.5	−18.3		−2.4		−5.7	
20 46			21 10			22 17		10.6		35.1
	+13.8	−18.5		+13.6	−18.2		−2.3		−5.8	
21 34			21 59			23 11		11.0		36.3
	+13.9	−18.4		+13.7	−18.1		−2.2		−5.9	
22 25			22 52			24 09		11.4		37.6
	+14.0	−18.3		+13.8	−18.0		−2.1		−6.0	
23 20			23 49			25 12		11.8		38.9
	+14.1	−18.2		+13.9	−17.9		−2.0		−6.1	
24 20			24 51			26 20		12.2		40.1
	+14.2	−18.1		+14.0	−17.8		−1.9		−6.2	
25 24			25 58			27 34		12.6		41.5
	+14.3	−18.0		+14.1	−17.7		−1.8		−6.3	
26 34			27 11			28 54		13.0		42.8
	+14.4	−17.9		+14.2	−17.6		−1.7		−6.4	
27 50			28 31			30 22		13.4		44.2
	+14.5	−17.8		+14.3	−17.5		−1.6		−6.5	
29 13			29 58			31 58		13.8		45.5
	+14.6	−17.7		+14.4	−17.4		−1.5		−6.6	
30 44			31 33			33 43		14.2		46.9
	+14.7	−17.6		+14.5	−17.3		−1.4		−6.7	
32 24			33 18			35 38		14.7		48.4
	+14.8	−17.5		+14.6	−17.2		−1.3		−6.8	
34 15			35 15			37 45		15.1		49.8
	+14.9	−17.4		+14.7	−17.1		−1.2		−6.9	
36 17			37 24			40 06		15.5		51.3
	+15.0	−17.3		+14.8	−17.0		−1.1		−7.0	
38 34			39 48			42 42		16.0		52.8
	+15.1	−17.2		+14.9	−16.9		−1.0		−7.1	
41 06			42 28			45 34		16.5		54.3
	+15.2	−17.1		+15.0	−16.8		−0.9		−7.2	
43 56			45 29			48 45		16.9		55.8
	+15.3	−17.0		+15.1	−16.7		−0.8		−7.3	
47 07			48 52			52 16		17.4		57.4
	+15.4	−16.9		+15.2	−16.6		−0.7		−7.4	
50 43			52 41			56 09		17.9		58.9
	+15.5	−16.8		+15.3	−16.5		−0.6		−7.5	
54 46			56 59			60 26		18.4		60.5
	+15.6	−16.7		+15.4	−16.4		−0.5		−7.6	
59 21			61 50			65 06		18.8		62.1
	+15.7	−16.6		+15.5	−16.3		−0.4		−7.7	
64 28			67 15			70 09		19.3		63.8
	+15.8	−16.5		+15.6	−16.2		−0.3		−7.8	
70 10			73 14			75 32		19.8		65.4
	+15.9	−16.4		+15.7	−16.1		−0.2		−7.9	
76 24			79 42			81 12		20.4		67.1
	+16.0	−16.3		+15.8	−16.0		−0.1		−8.0	
83 05			86 31			87 03		20.9		68.8
	+16.1	−16.2		+15.9	−15.9		0.0		−8.1	
90 00			90 00			90 00		21.4		70.5

STARS AND PLANETS — App. Alt. / Additional Corrn

2008

VENUS

App. Alt.	Additional Corrn
Jan. 1–Dec. 5	
°	′
0	
	+0.1
60	
Dec. 6–Dec. 31	
°	′
0	
	+0.2
41	
	+0.1
76	

MARS

App. Alt.	Additional Corrn
Jan. 1–Feb. 23	
°	′
0	
	+0.2
41	
	+0.1
76	
Feb. 24–Dec. 31	
°	′
0	
	+0.1
60	

DIP

Ht. of Eye	Corrn
m	′
1.0	− 1.8
1.5	− 2.2
2.0	− 2.5
2.5	− 2.8
3.0	− 3.0
See table ←	
m	′
20	− 7.9
22	− 8.3
24	− 8.6
26	− 9.0
28	− 9.3
30	− 9.6
32	−10.0
34	−10.3
36	−10.6
38	−10.8
40	−11.1
42	−11.4
44	−11.7
46	−11.9
48	−12.2
ft.	′
2	− 1.4
4	− 1.9
6	− 2.4
8	− 2.7
10	− 3.1
See table ←	
ft.	′
70	− 8.1
75	− 8.4
80	− 8.7
85	− 8.9
90	− 9.2
95	− 9.5
100	− 9.7
105	− 9.9
110	−10.2
115	−10.4
120	−10.6
125	−10.8
130	−11.1
135	−11.3
140	−11.5
145	−11.7
150	−11.9
155	−12.1

App. Alt. = Apparent altitude = Sextant altitude corrected for index error and dip.

	UT	SUN GHA	SUN Dec	MOON GHA	v	MOON Dec	d	HP
	d h	° ′	° ′	° ′	′	° ′	′	′
	28 00	176 48.7	S18 24.9	296 04.2	15.8	S 8 36.6	13.7	55.1
	01	191 48.6	24.3	310 39.0	15.9	8 50.3	13.7	55.1
	02	206 48.4	23.6	325 13.9	15.8	9 04.0	13.7	55.0
	03	221 48.3	. . 23.0	339 48.7	15.9	9 17.7	13.6	55.0
	04	236 48.2	22.3	354 23.6	15.8	9 31.3	13.5	55.0
	05	251 48.1	21.7	8 58.4	15.8	9 44.8	13.6	55.0
	06	266 47.9	S18 21.0	23 33.2	15.8	S 9 58.4	13.4	55.0
	07	281 47.8	20.4	38 08.0	15.7	10 11.8	13.4	54.9
	08	296 47.7	19.7	52 42.7	15.8	10 25.2	13.4	54.9
M	09	311 47.6	. . 19.1	67 17.5	15.7	10 38.6	13.3	54.9
O	10	326 47.4	18.4	81 52.2	15.7	10 51.9	13.2	54.9
N	11	341 47.3	17.8	96 26.9	15.7	11 05.1	13.2	54.9
D	12	356 47.2	S18 17.1	111 01.6	15.7	S11 18.3	13.2	54.8
A	13	11 47.1	16.5	125 36.3	15.6	11 31.5	13.1	54.8
Y	14	26 47.0	15.8	140 10.9	15.7	11 44.6	13.0	54.8
	15	41 46.8	. . 15.2	154 45.6	15.6	11 57.6	13.0	54.8
	16	56 46.7	14.5	169 20.2	15.5	12 10.6	13.0	54.8
	17	71 46.6	13.8	183 54.7	15.6	12 23.6	12.8	54.7
	18	86 46.5	S18 13.2	198 29.3	15.5	S12 36.4	12.8	54.7
	19	101 46.4	12.5	213 03.8	15.5	12 49.2	12.8	54.7
	20	116 46.3	11.9	227 38.3	15.5	13 02.0	12.7	54.7
	21	131 46.1	. . 11.2	242 12.8	15.4	13 14.7	12.6	54.7
	22	146 46.0	10.6	256 47.2	15.4	13 27.3	12.6	54.7
	23	161 45.9	09.9	271 21.6	15.4	13 39.9	12.5	54.6
	29 00	176 45.8	S18 09.2	285 56.0	15.3	S13 52.4	12.5	54.6
	01	191 45.7	08.6	300 30.3	15.3	14 04.9	12.4	54.6
	02	206 45.5	07.9	315 04.6	15.3	14 17.3	12.3	54.6
	03	221 45.4	. . 07.2	329 38.9	15.2	14 29.6	12.3	54.6
	04	236 45.3	06.6	344 13.1	15.2	14 41.9	12.2	54.6
	05	251 45.2	05.9	358 47.3	15.2	14 54.1	12.2	54.5
	06	266 45.1	S18 05.3	13 21.5	15.1	S15 06.3	12.0	54.5
	07	281 45.0	04.6	27 55.6	15.1	15 18.3	12.1	54.5
T	08	296 44.9	03.9	42 29.7	15.1	15 30.4	11.9	54.5
U	09	311 44.7	. . 03.3	57 03.8	15.0	15 42.3	11.9	54.5
E	10	326 44.6	02.6	71 37.8	14.9	15 54.2	11.8	54.5
S	11	341 44.5	01.9	86 11.7	14.9	16 06.0	11.7	54.5
D	12	356 44.4	S18 01.3	100 45.6	14.9	S16 17.7	11.7	54.5
A	13	11 44.3	18 00.6	115 19.5	14.8	16 29.4	11.6	54.4
Y	14	26 44.2	17 59.9	129 53.3	14.8	16 41.0	11.5	54.4
	15	41 44.1	. . 59.3	144 27.1	14.8	16 52.5	11.5	54.4
	16	56 44.0	58.6	159 00.9	14.7	17 04.0	11.4	54.4
	17	71 43.8	57.9	173 34.6	14.6	17 15.4	11.3	54.4
	18	86 43.7	S17 57.2	188 08.2	14.6	S17 26.7	11.2	54.4
	19	101 43.6	56.6	202 41.8	14.6	17 37.9	11.2	54.4
	20	116 43.5	55.9	217 15.4	14.5	17 49.1	11.1	54.4
	21	131 43.4	. . 55.2	231 48.9	14.4	18 00.2	11.0	54.4
	22	146 43.3	54.6	246 22.3	14.4	18 11.2	10.9	54.3
	23	161 43.2	53.9	260 55.7	14.4	18 22.1	10.9	54.3
	30 00	176 43.1	S17 53.2	275 29.1	14.3	S18 33.0	10.8	54.3
	01	191 43.0	52.5	290 02.4	14.2	18 43.8	10.7	54.3
	02	206 42.9	51.9	304 35.6	14.2	18 54.5	10.6	54.3
	03	221 42.8	. . 51.2	319 08.8	14.2	19 05.1	10.5	54.3
	04	236 42.7	50.5	333 42.0	14.1	19 15.6	10.5	54.3
	05	251 42.5	49.8	348 15.1	14.0	19 26.1	10.4	54.3
	06	266 42.4	S17 49.1	2 48.1	14.0	S19 36.5	10.3	54.3
W	07	281 42.3	48.5	17 21.1	13.9	19 46.8	10.2	54.3
E	08	296 42.2	47.8	31 54.0	13.8	19 57.0	10.1	54.3
D	09	311 42.1	. . 47.1	46 26.8	13.9	20 07.1	10.1	54.3
N	10	326 42.0	46.4	60 59.7	13.7	20 17.2	9.9	54.3
E	11	341 41.9	45.7	75 32.4	13.7	20 27.1	9.9	54.3
S	12	356 41.8	S17 45.1	90 05.1	13.6	S20 37.0	9.8	54.2
D	13	11 41.7	44.4	104 37.7	13.6	20 46.8	9.7	54.2
A	14	26 41.6	43.7	119 10.3	13.5	20 56.5	9.6	54.2
Y	15	41 41.5	. . 43.0	133 42.8	13.5	21 06.1	9.5	54.2
	16	56 41.4	42.3	148 15.3	13.3	21 15.6	9.5	54.2
	17	71 41.3	41.7	162 47.6	13.4	21 25.1	9.3	54.2
	18	86 41.2	S17 41.0	177 20.0	13.2	S21 34.4	9.3	54.2
	19	101 41.1	40.3	191 52.2	13.2	21 43.7	9.1	54.2
	20	116 41.0	39.6	206 24.4	13.2	21 52.8	9.1	54.2
	21	131 40.9	. . 38.9	220 56.6	13.1	22 01.9	9.0	54.2
	22	146 40.8	38.2	235 28.7	13.0	22 10.9	8.8	54.2
	23	161 40.7	37.5	250 00.7	12.9	S22 19.7	8.8	54.2
		SD 16.3	d 0.7	SD	14.9	14.8		14.8

Lat.	Twilight Naut.	Twilight Civil	Sunrise	Moonrise 28	Moonrise 29	Moonrise 30	Moonrise 31
°	h m	h m	h m	h m	h m	h m	h m
N 72	07 22	08 54	11 02	00 09	02 31	▬	▬
N 70	07 13	08 33	10 06	25 59	01 59	04 54	▬
68	07 05	08 17	09 33	25 36	01 36	03 45	▬
66	06 58	08 03	09 09	25 18	01 18	03 10	05 36
64	06 52	07 52	08 50	25 03	01 03	02 44	04 37
62	06 47	07 42	08 35	24 51	00 51	02 25	04 04
60	06 42	07 34	08 22	24 41	00 41	02 09	03 39
N 58	06 38	07 26	08 11	24 32	00 32	01 55	03 20
56	06 34	07 20	08 02	24 24	00 24	01 44	03 04
54	06 31	07 14	07 53	24 17	00 17	01 34	02 50
52	06 27	07 08	07 45	24 11	00 11	01 25	02 38
50	06 24	07 03	07 39	24 06	00 06	01 17	02 28
45	06 17	06 52	07 24	23 54	25 00	01 00	02 06
N 40	06 10	06 43	07 12	23 44	24 46	00 46	01 48
35	06 04	06 35	07 01	23 36	24 34	00 34	01 33
30	05 58	06 27	06 52	23 28	24 24	00 24	01 21
20	05 47	06 13	06 37	23 16	24 07	00 07	00 59
N 10	05 35	06 01	06 23	23 05	23 52	24 40	00 40
0	05 22	05 48	06 09	22 55	23 38	24 23	00 23
S 10	05 08	05 34	05 56	22 45	23 24	24 06	00 06
20	04 51	05 18	05 42	22 34	23 09	23 47	24 29
30	04 28	04 59	05 25	22 22	22 52	23 26	24 05
35	04 14	04 48	05 16	22 15	22 43	23 14	23 50
40	03 57	04 34	05 05	22 07	22 32	23 00	23 34
45	03 35	04 18	04 51	21 58	22 19	22 43	23 14
S 50	03 05	03 57	04 35	21 47	22 03	22 23	22 49
52	02 50	03 46	04 28	21 42	21 56	22 13	22 37
54	02 32	03 35	04 19	21 37	21 48	22 02	22 23
56	02 08	03 21	04 10	21 30	21 39	21 50	22 08
58	01 35	03 05	03 59	21 24	21 28	21 36	21 49
S 60	////	02 45	03 46	21 16	21 17	21 19	21 26

Lat.	Sunset	Twilight Civil	Twilight Naut.	Moonset 28	Moonset 29	Moonset 30	Moonset 31
°	h m	h m	h m	h m	h m	h m	h m
N 72	13 25	15 33	17 06	08 09	07 15	▬	▬
N 70	14 21	15 54	17 15	08 26	07 50	06 25	▬
68	14 54	16 11	17 22	08 39	08 15	07 35	▬
66	15 18	16 24	17 29	08 50	08 34	08 12	07 21
64	15 37	16 35	17 35	08 59	08 50	08 38	08 20
62	15 52	16 45	17 40	09 07	09 03	08 59	08 54
60	16 05	16 53	17 45	09 14	09 14	09 16	09 19
N 58	16 16	17 00	17 49	09 20	09 24	09 30	09 39
56	16 25	17 07	17 53	09 25	09 33	09 42	09 56
54	16 34	17 13	17 56	09 30	09 40	09 53	10 10
52	16 41	17 18	17 59	09 35	09 47	10 02	10 22
50	16 48	17 23	18 03	09 39	09 53	10 11	10 33
45	17 03	17 34	18 10	09 48	10 07	10 29	10 56
N 40	17 15	17 44	18 16	09 55	10 18	10 44	11 15
35	17 25	17 52	18 22	10 01	10 27	10 57	11 30
30	17 34	17 59	18 28	10 07	10 36	11 08	11 44
20	17 50	18 13	18 39	10 16	10 50	11 27	12 07
N 10	18 04	18 26	18 51	10 25	11 03	11 44	12 27
0	18 17	18 38	19 04	10 33	11 15	11 59	12 46
S 10	18 30	18 52	19 18	10 41	11 27	12 15	13 04
20	18 44	19 07	19 35	10 50	11 40	12 32	13 25
30	19 00	19 26	19 57	11 00	11 55	12 51	13 48
35	19 10	19 38	20 11	11 05	12 04	13 03	14 02
40	19 21	19 51	20 28	11 12	12 14	13 16	14 18
45	19 34	20 08	20 50	11 20	12 25	13 31	14 37
S 50	19 50	20 28	21 19	11 29	12 40	13 51	15 01
52	19 57	20 38	21 34	11 33	12 46	14 00	15 13
54	20 06	20 50	21 52	11 38	12 54	14 10	15 26
56	20 15	21 03	22 15	11 43	13 02	14 22	15 41
58	20 26	21 19	22 46	11 49	13 12	14 35	16 00
S 60	20 38	21 38	23 53	11 56	13 22	14 51	16 22

Day	SUN Eqn. of Time 00^h	SUN Eqn. of Time 12^h	SUN Mer. Pass.	MOON Mer. Pass. Upper	MOON Mer. Pass. Lower	MOON Age	MOON Phase
d	m s	m s	h m	h m	h m	d	%
28	12 45	12 51	12 13	04 23	16 44	20	66
29	12 57	13 02	12 13	05 05	17 26	21	57
30	13 07	13 13	12 13	05 48	18 11	22	47

	UT	ARIES	VENUS −3.9		MARS −0.6		JUPITER −1.9		SATURN +0.4	
		GHA	GHA	Dec	GHA	Dec	GHA	Dec	GHA	Dec
	d h	° ′	° ′	° ′	° ′	° ′	° ′	° ′	° ′	° ′
	31 00	129 36.1	210 44.2	S22 24.1	46 13.3	N26 41.2	209 03.4	S22 57.6	330 11.2	N10 35.8
	01	144 38.5	225 43.3	24.0	61 15.7	41.2	224 05.3	57.6	345 13.8	35.9
	02	159 41.0	240 42.5	24.0	76 18.2	41.1	239 07.2	57.6	0 16.4	35.9
	03	174 43.5	255 41.6	. . 23.9	91 20.6	. . 41.1	254 09.1	. . 57.5	15 19.0	. . 36.0
	04	189 45.9	270 40.7	23.8	106 23.1	41.0	269 11.0	57.5	30 21.7	36.1
	05	204 48.4	285 39.9	23.8	121 25.5	41.0	284 12.8	57.5	45 24.3	36.1
	06	219 50.9	300 39.0	S22 23.7	136 28.0	N26 41.0	299 14.7	S22 57.4	60 26.9	N10 36.2
	07	234 53.3	315 38.1	23.6	151 30.4	40.9	314 16.6	57.4	75 29.5	36.3
T	08	249 55.8	330 37.3	23.6	166 32.9	40.9	329 18.5	57.3	90 32.1	36.3
H	09	264 58.3	345 36.4	. . 23.5	181 35.3	. . 40.8	344 20.4	. . 57.3	105 34.8	. . 36.4
U	10	280 00.7	0 35.5	23.4	196 37.8	40.8	359 22.3	57.3	120 37.4	36.5
R	11	295 03.2	15 34.7	23.3	211 40.2	40.8	14 24.2	57.2	135 40.0	36.6
S	12	310 05.7	30 33.8	S22 23.3	226 42.7	N26 40.7	29 26.1	S22 57.2	150 42.6	N10 36.6
D	13	325 08.1	45 32.9	23.2	241 45.1	40.7	44 27.9	57.2	165 45.3	36.7
A	14	340 10.6	60 32.1	23.1	256 47.6	40.6	59 29.8	57.1	180 47.9	36.8
Y	15	355 13.0	75 31.2	. . 23.0	271 50.0	. . 40.6	74 31.7	. . 57.1	195 50.5	. . 36.8
	16	10 15.5	90 30.3	22.9	286 52.4	40.6	89 33.6	57.1	210 53.1	36.9
	17	25 18.0	105 29.5	22.8	301 54.9	40.5	104 35.5	57.0	225 55.7	37.0
	18	40 20.4	120 28.6	S22 22.8	316 57.3	N26 40.5	119 37.4	S22 57.0	240 58.4	N10 37.0
	19	55 22.9	135 27.7	22.7	331 59.7	40.4	134 39.3	57.0	256 01.0	37.1
	20	70 25.4	150 26.9	22.6	347 02.2	40.4	149 41.2	56.9	271 03.6	37.2
	21	85 27.8	165 26.0	. . 22.5	2 04.6	. . 40.4	164 43.0	. . 56.9	286 06.2	. . 37.3
	22	100 30.3	180 25.1	22.4	17 07.0	40.3	179 44.9	56.8	301 08.9	37.3
	23	115 32.8	195 24.3	22.3	32 09.5	40.3	194 46.8	56.8	316 11.5	37.4
	1 00	130 35.2	210 23.4	S22 22.2	47 11.9	N26 40.2	209 48.7	S22 56.8	331 14.1	N10 37.5
	01	145 37.7	225 22.5	22.1	62 14.3	40.2	224 50.6	56.7	346 16.7	37.5
	02	160 40.1	240 21.7	22.0	77 16.7	40.2	239 52.5	56.7	1 19.3	37.6
	03	175 42.6	255 20.8	. . 21.9	92 19.1	. . 40.1	254 54.4	. . 56.7	16 22.0	. . 37.7
	04	190 45.1	270 19.9	21.9	107 21.6	40.1	269 56.3	56.6	31 24.6	37.7
	05	205 47.5	285 19.1	21.8	122 24.0	40.0	284 58.1	56.6	46 27.2	37.8
	06	220 50.0	300 18.2	S22 21.7	137 26.4	N26 40.0	300 00.0	S22 56.6	61 29.8	N10 37.9
	07	235 52.5	315 17.3	21.6	152 28.8	40.0	315 01.9	56.5	76 32.5	38.0
	08	250 54.9	330 16.5	21.5	167 31.2	39.9	330 03.8	56.5	91 35.1	38.0
F	09	265 57.4	345 15.6	. . 21.4	182 33.6	. . 39.9	345 05.7	. . 56.4	106 37.7	. . 38.1
R	10	280 59.9	0 14.7	21.2	197 36.1	39.8	0 07.6	56.4	121 40.3	38.2
I	11	296 02.3	15 13.9	21.1	212 38.5	39.8	15 09.5	56.4	136 43.0	38.2
D	12	311 04.8	30 13.0	S22 21.0	227 40.9	N26 39.8	30 11.4	S22 56.3	151 45.6	N10 38.3
A	13	326 07.3	45 12.1	20.9	242 43.3	39.7	45 13.3	56.3	166 48.2	38.4
Y	14	341 09.7	60 11.3	20.8	257 45.7	39.7	60 15.2	56.3	181 50.8	38.4
	15	356 12.2	75 10.4	. . 20.7	272 48.1	. . 39.6	75 17.0	. . 56.2	196 53.5	. . 38.5
	16	11 14.6	90 09.5	20.6	287 50.5	39.6	90 18.9	56.2	211 56.1	38.6
	17	26 17.1	105 08.7	20.5	302 52.9	39.6	105 20.8	56.2	226 58.7	38.7
	18	41 19.6	120 07.8	S22 20.4	317 55.3	N26 39.5	120 22.7	S22 56.1	242 01.3	N10 38.7
	19	56 22.0	135 07.0	20.3	332 57.7	39.5	135 24.6	56.1	257 04.0	38.8
	20	71 24.5	150 06.1	20.2	348 00.1	39.5	150 26.5	56.0	272 06.6	38.9
	21	86 27.0	165 05.2	. . 20.0	3 02.5	. . 39.4	165 28.4	. . 56.0	287 09.2	. . 38.9
	22	101 29.4	180 04.4	19.9	18 04.9	39.4	180 30.3	56.0	302 11.8	39.0
	23	116 31.9	195 03.5	19.8	33 07.3	39.3	195 32.2	55.9	317 14.5	39.1
	2 00	131 34.4	210 02.6	S22 19.7	48 09.7	N26 39.3	210 34.1	S22 55.9	332 17.1	N10 39.2
	01	146 36.8	225 01.8	19.6	63 12.0	39.3	225 35.9	55.9	347 19.7	39.2
	02	161 39.3	240 00.9	19.4	78 14.4	39.2	240 37.8	55.8	2 22.3	39.3
	03	176 41.8	255 00.0	. . 19.3	93 16.8	. . 39.2	255 39.7	. . 55.8	17 25.0	. . 39.4
	04	191 44.2	269 59.2	19.2	108 19.2	39.1	270 41.6	55.8	32 27.6	39.4
	05	206 46.7	284 58.3	19.1	123 21.6	39.1	285 43.5	55.7	47 30.2	39.5
	06	221 49.1	299 57.4	S22 18.9	138 24.0	N26 39.1	300 45.4	S22 55.7	62 32.8	N10 39.6
	07	236 51.6	314 56.6	18.8	153 26.4	39.0	315 47.3	55.6	77 35.5	39.7
S	08	251 54.1	329 55.7	18.7	168 28.7	39.0	330 49.2	55.6	92 38.1	39.7
A	09	266 56.5	344 54.8	. . 18.6	183 31.1	. . 38.9	345 51.1	. . 55.6	107 40.7	. . 39.8
T	10	281 59.0	359 54.0	18.4	198 33.5	38.9	0 53.0	55.5	122 43.3	39.9
U	11	297 01.5	14 53.1	18.3	213 35.9	38.9	15 54.9	55.5	137 46.0	39.9
R	12	312 03.9	29 52.3	S22 18.2	228 38.2	N26 38.8	30 56.8	S22 55.5	152 48.6	N10 40.0
D	13	327 06.4	44 51.4	18.0	243 40.6	38.8	45 58.6	55.4	167 51.2	40.1
A	14	342 08.9	59 50.5	17.9	258 43.0	38.8	61 00.5	55.4	182 53.8	40.2
Y	15	357 11.3	74 49.7	. . 17.7	273 45.3	. . 38.7	76 02.4	. . 55.3	197 56.5	. . 40.2
	16	12 13.8	89 48.8	17.6	288 47.7	38.7	91 04.3	55.3	212 59.1	40.3
	17	27 16.3	104 47.9	17.5	303 50.1	38.6	106 06.2	55.3	228 01.7	40.4
	18	42 18.7	119 47.1	S22 17.3	318 52.4	N26 38.6	121 08.1	S22 55.2	243 04.3	N10 40.4
	19	57 21.2	134 46.2	17.2	333 54.8	38.6	136 10.0	55.2	258 07.0	40.5
	20	72 23.6	149 45.3	17.0	348 57.2	38.5	151 11.9	55.2	273 09.6	40.6
	21	87 26.1	164 44.5	. . 16.9	3 59.5	. . 38.5	166 13.8	. . 55.1	288 12.2	. . 40.7
	22	102 28.6	179 43.6	16.8	19 01.9	38.4	181 15.7	55.1	303 14.9	40.7
	23	117 31.0	194 42.8	16.6	34 04.3	38.4	196 17.6	55.1	318 17.5	40.8
	Mer. Pass.	h m 15 15.1	*v* −0.9	*d* 0.1	*v* 2.4	*d* 0.0	*v* 1.9	*d* 0.0	*v* 2.6	*d* 0.1

STARS

Name	SHA	Dec
	° ′	° ′
Acamar	315 21.3	S40 16.5
Achernar	335 29.7	S57 12.0
Acrux	173 13.8	S63 08.5
Adhara	255 15.4	S28 59.0
Aldebaran	290 53.9	N16 31.6
Alioth	166 23.7	N55 54.6
Alkaid	153 01.8	N49 16.0
Al Na'ir	27 49.1	S46 55.5
Alnilam	275 50.2	S 1 11.8
Alphard	217 59.8	S 8 41.7
Alphecca	126 14.5	N26 40.9
Alpheratz	357 48.0	N29 08.2
Altair	62 12.5	N 8 53.2
Ankaa	353 19.7	S42 15.9
Antares	112 31.5	S26 27.1
Arcturus	145 59.3	N19 08.1
Atria	107 37.4	S69 02.4
Avior	234 19.2	S59 32.1
Bellatrix	278 36.1	N 6 21.5
Betelgeuse	271 05.4	N 7 24.5
Canopus	263 57.5	S52 42.1
Capella	280 40.2	N46 00.6
Deneb	49 34.8	N45 18.5
Denebola	182 37.5	N14 31.4
Diphda	349 00.1	S17 56.6
Dubhe	193 55.7	N61 42.2
Elnath	278 17.5	N28 37.0
Eltanin	90 48.4	N51 28.9
Enif	33 51.5	N 9 54.7
Fomalhaut	15 28.6	S29 34.9
Gacrux	172 05.4	S57 09.4
Gienah	175 56.3	S17 35.3
Hadar	148 53.9	S60 24.6
Hamal	328 05.5	N23 30.2
Kaus Aust.	83 49.5	S34 22.9
Kochab	137 19.4	N74 06.9
Markab	13 42.7	N15 14.9
Menkar	314 19.3	N 4 07.3
Menkent	148 12.4	S36 24.6
Miaplacidus	221 40.0	S69 45.0
Mirfak	308 46.2	N49 53.7
Nunki	76 03.6	S26 17.3
Peacock	53 26.0	S56 42.6
Pollux	243 32.3	N28 00.4
Procyon	245 03.6	N 5 12.2
Rasalhague	96 10.4	N12 33.0
Regulus	207 47.5	N11 55.5
Rigel	281 15.7	S 8 11.6
Rigil Kent.	139 57.6	S60 51.9
Sabik	102 17.4	S15 44.2
Schedar	349 45.8	N56 35.2
Shaula	96 27.7	S37 06.6
Sirius	258 37.0	S16 43.7
Spica	158 35.5	S11 12.3
Suhail	222 55.1	S43 27.9
Vega	80 42.1	N38 47.2
Zuben'ubi	137 10.0	S16 04.6

	SHA	Mer. Pass.
	° ′	h m
Venus	79 48.2	9 59
Mars	276 36.7	20 48
Jupiter	79 13.5	9 59
Saturn	200 38.9	1 55

Day	UT (d h)	SUN GHA (° ′)	SUN Dec (° ′)	MOON GHA (° ′)	MOON v (′)	MOON Dec (° ′)	MOON d (′)	MOON HP (′)
31 THURSDAY	00	176 40.6	S17 36.9	264 32.6	12.9	S22 28.5	8.7	54.2
	01	191 40.5	36.2	279 04.5	12.9	22 37.2	8.6	54.2
	02	206 40.4	35.5	293 36.4	12.7	22 45.8	8.5	54.2
	03	221 40.3	. . 34.8	308 08.1	12.7	22 54.3	8.4	54.2
	04	236 40.2	34.1	322 39.8	12.7	23 02.7	8.3	54.2
	05	251 40.1	33.4	337 11.5	12.5	23 11.0	8.2	54.2
	06	266 40.0	S17 32.7	351 43.0	12.5	S23 19.2	8.0	54.2
	07	281 39.9	32.0	6 14.5	12.5	23 27.2	8.0	54.2
	08	296 39.8	31.3	20 46.0	12.3	23 35.2	7.9	54.2
	09	311 39.7	. . 30.6	35 17.3	12.3	23 43.1	7.8	54.2
	10	326 39.6	29.9	49 48.6	12.3	23 50.9	7.7	54.2
	11	341 39.5	29.3	64 19.9	12.2	23 58.6	7.6	54.2
	12	356 39.4	S17 28.6	78 51.1	12.1	S24 06.2	7.4	54.2
	13	11 39.3	27.9	93 22.2	12.0	24 13.6	7.4	54.2
	14	26 39.2	27.2	107 53.2	12.0	24 21.0	7.3	54.2
	15	41 39.1	. . 26.5	122 24.2	11.9	24 28.3	7.1	54.2
	16	56 39.0	25.8	136 55.1	11.9	24 35.4	7.1	54.2
	17	71 38.9	25.1	151 26.0	11.8	24 42.5	6.9	54.2
	18	86 38.8	S17 24.4	165 56.8	11.7	S24 49.4	6.8	54.2
	19	101 38.7	23.7	180 27.5	11.7	24 56.2	6.7	54.2
	20	116 38.6	23.0	194 58.2	11.5	25 02.9	6.6	54.2
	21	131 38.6	. . 22.3	209 28.7	11.6	25 09.5	6.5	54.2
	22	146 38.5	21.6	223 59.3	11.4	25 16.0	6.4	54.3
	23	161 38.4	20.9	238 29.7	11.4	25 22.4	6.3	54.3
1 FRIDAY	00	176 38.3	S17 20.2	253 00.1	11.4	S25 28.7	6.1	54.3
	01	191 38.2	19.5	267 30.5	11.2	25 34.8	6.0	54.3
	02	206 38.1	18.8	282 00.7	11.2	25 40.8	6.0	54.3
	03	221 38.0	. . 18.1	296 30.9	11.2	25 46.8	5.7	54.3
	04	236 37.9	17.4	311 01.1	11.1	25 52.5	5.7	54.3
	05	251 37.8	16.7	325 31.2	11.0	25 58.2	5.6	54.3
	06	266 37.7	S17 16.0	340 01.2	11.0	S26 03.8	5.4	54.3
	07	281 37.6	15.3	354 31.2	10.8	26 09.2	5.4	54.3
	08	296 37.6	14.6	9 01.0	10.9	26 14.6	5.2	54.3
	09	311 37.5	. . 13.9	23 30.9	10.8	26 19.8	5.0	54.3
	10	326 37.4	13.2	38 00.7	10.7	26 24.8	5.0	54.3
	11	341 37.3	12.4	52 30.4	10.6	26 29.8	4.8	54.3
	12	356 37.2	S17 11.7	67 00.0	10.6	S26 34.6	4.7	54.4
	13	11 37.1	11.0	81 29.6	10.6	26 39.3	4.6	54.4
	14	26 37.0	10.3	95 59.2	10.4	26 43.9	4.5	54.4
	15	41 36.9	. . 09.6	110 28.6	10.5	26 48.4	4.3	54.4
	16	56 36.9	08.9	124 58.1	10.3	26 52.7	4.2	54.4
	17	71 36.8	08.2	139 27.4	10.3	26 56.9	4.1	54.4
	18	86 36.7	S17 07.5	153 56.7	10.3	S27 01.0	4.0	54.4
	19	101 36.6	06.8	168 26.0	10.2	27 05.0	3.8	54.4
	20	116 36.5	06.1	182 55.2	10.1	27 08.8	3.7	54.4
	21	131 36.4	. . 05.4	197 24.3	10.1	27 12.5	3.6	54.4
	22	146 36.3	04.6	211 53.4	10.1	27 16.1	3.4	54.5
	23	161 36.3	03.9	226 22.5	9.9	27 19.5	3.3	54.5
2 SATURDAY	00	176 36.2	S17 03.2	240 51.4	10.0	S27 22.8	3.2	54.5
	01	191 36.1	02.5	255 20.4	9.9	27 26.0	3.0	54.5
	02	206 36.0	01.8	269 49.3	9.8	27 29.0	2.9	54.5
	03	221 35.9	. . 01.1	284 18.1	9.8	27 31.9	2.8	54.5
	04	236 35.8	17 00.4	298 46.9	9.7	27 34.7	2.6	54.5
	05	251 35.8	16 59.6	313 15.6	9.7	27 37.3	2.6	54.5
	06	266 35.7	S16 58.9	327 44.3	9.7	S27 39.9	2.3	54.6
	07	281 35.6	58.2	342 13.0	9.6	27 42.2	2.3	54.6
	08	296 35.5	57.5	356 41.6	9.6	27 44.5	2.1	54.6
	09	311 35.4	. . 56.8	11 10.2	9.5	27 46.6	1.9	54.6
	10	326 35.4	56.1	25 38.7	9.5	27 48.5	1.9	54.6
	11	341 35.3	55.3	40 07.2	9.4	27 50.4	1.6	54.6
	12	356 35.2	S16 54.6	54 35.6	9.4	S27 52.0	1.6	54.6
	13	11 35.1	53.9	69 04.0	9.4	27 53.6	1.4	54.7
	14	26 35.0	53.2	83 32.4	9.3	27 55.0	1.3	54.7
	15	41 35.0	. . 52.5	98 00.7	9.3	27 56.3	1.1	54.7
	16	56 34.9	51.7	112 29.0	9.3	27 57.4	1.0	54.7
	17	71 34.8	51.0	126 57.3	9.2	27 58.4	0.8	54.7
	18	86 34.7	S16 50.3	141 25.5	9.2	S27 59.2	0.8	54.7
	19	101 34.7	49.6	155 53.7	9.1	28 00.0	0.5	54.8
	20	116 34.6	48.8	170 21.8	9.2	28 00.5	0.5	54.8
	21	131 34.5	. . 48.1	184 50.0	9.1	28 01.0	0.2	54.8
	22	146 34.4	47.4	199 18.1	9.0	28 01.2	0.2	54.8
	23	161 34.4	46.7	213 46.1	9.1	S28 01.4	0.0	54.8
		SD 16.3	d 0.7	SD 14.8		14.8		14.9

Lat. (°)	Twilight Naut. (h m)	Twilight Civil (h m)	Sunrise (h m)	Moonrise 31 (h m)	Moonrise 1 (h m)	Moonrise 2 (h m)	Moonrise 3 (h m)
N 72	07 12	08 41	10 32	■	■	■	■
N 70	07 04	08 22	09 49	■	■	■	■
68	06 57	08 07	09 20	■	■	■	■
66	06 51	07 55	08 58	05 36	■	■	■
64	06 46	07 45	08 41	04 37	■	■	■
62	06 41	07 36	08 27	04 04	05 49	07 45	■
60	06 37	07 28	08 15	03 39	05 10	06 34	07 33
N 58	06 33	07 21	08 05	03 20	04 43	05 59	06 56
56	06 30	07 15	07 56	03 04	04 22	05 33	06 30
54	06 27	07 09	07 48	02 50	04 05	05 13	06 09
52	06 24	07 04	07 41	02 38	03 50	04 56	05 52
50	06 21	07 00	07 35	02 28	03 37	04 41	05 37
45	06 14	06 49	07 21	02 06	03 11	04 12	05 07
N 40	06 08	06 41	07 09	01 48	02 50	03 49	04 44
35	06 02	06 33	06 59	01 33	02 32	03 30	04 24
30	05 57	06 26	06 51	01 21	02 18	03 14	04 08
20	05 46	06 13	06 36	00 59	01 52	02 47	03 40
N 10	05 35	06 01	06 22	00 40	01 31	02 23	03 16
0	05 23	05 48	06 10	00 23	01 11	02 01	02 54
S 10	05 09	05 35	05 57	00 06	00 51	01 39	02 31
20	04 53	05 20	05 44	24 29	00 29	01 16	02 07
30	04 31	05 02	05 28	24 05	00 05	00 49	01 40
35	04 18	04 51	05 19	23 50	24 33	00 33	01 23
40	04 01	04 38	05 08	23 34	24 15	00 15	01 04
45	03 40	04 22	04 56	23 14	23 52	24 41	00 41
S 50	03 13	04 02	04 41	22 49	23 24	24 11	00 11
52	02 58	03 53	04 33	22 37	23 10	23 56	24 57
54	02 41	03 42	04 25	22 23	22 54	23 39	24 40
56	02 20	03 29	04 16	22 08	22 35	23 18	24 21
58	01 52	03 14	04 06	21 49	22 12	22 53	23 57
S 60	01 04	02 56	03 55	21 26	21 41	22 17	23 25

Lat. (°)	Sunset (h m)	Twilight Civil (h m)	Twilight Naut. (h m)	Moonset 31 (h m)	Moonset 1 (h m)	Moonset 2 (h m)	Moonset 3 (h m)
N 72	13 56	15 47	17 17	■	■	■	■
N 70	14 39	16 06	17 25	■	■	■	■
68	15 08	16 21	17 32	■	■	■	■
66	15 30	16 33	17 37	07 21	■	■	■
64	15 47	16 44	17 42	08 20	■	■	■
62	16 01	16 52	17 47	08 54	08 49	08 39	■
60	16 12	17 00	17 51	09 19	09 29	09 51	10 42
N 58	16 23	17 07	17 55	09 39	09 56	10 26	11 19
56	16 32	17 13	17 58	09 56	10 17	10 52	11 45
54	16 40	17 18	18 01	10 10	10 35	11 12	12 05
52	16 47	17 23	18 04	10 22	10 50	11 29	12 23
50	16 53	17 28	18 07	10 33	11 03	11 44	12 37
45	17 07	17 38	18 13	10 56	11 30	12 14	13 07
N 40	17 18	17 47	18 19	11 15	11 52	12 37	13 30
35	17 28	17 55	18 25	11 30	12 10	12 56	13 49
30	17 37	18 02	18 30	11 44	12 25	13 12	14 06
20	17 52	18 15	18 41	12 07	12 51	13 40	14 34
N 10	18 05	18 27	18 52	12 27	13 14	14 04	14 57
0	18 17	18 39	19 04	12 46	13 35	14 26	15 19
S 10	18 30	18 52	19 17	13 04	13 56	14 49	15 41
20	18 43	19 06	19 34	13 25	14 19	15 12	16 05
30	18 59	19 24	19 55	13 48	14 45	15 40	16 32
35	19 08	19 35	20 09	14 02	15 00	15 57	16 49
40	19 18	19 48	20 25	14 18	15 19	16 16	17 07
45	19 30	20 04	20 45	14 37	15 40	16 39	17 30
S 50	19 45	20 23	21 13	15 01	16 08	17 09	17 59
52	19 53	20 33	21 27	15 13	16 22	17 23	18 13
54	20 00	20 44	21 43	15 26	16 38	17 40	18 29
56	20 09	20 56	22 04	15 41	16 57	18 01	18 49
58	20 19	21 11	22 31	16 00	17 20	18 27	19 13
S 60	20 31	21 28	23 14	16 22	17 50	19 02	19 45

Day (d)	SUN Eqn. of Time 00^h (m s)	SUN Eqn. of Time 12^h (m s)	SUN Mer. Pass. (h m)	MOON Mer. Pass. Upper (h m)	MOON Mer. Pass. Lower (h m)	MOON Age (d)	MOON Phase (%)
31	13 17	13 22	12 13	06 34	18 58	23	38
1	13 27	13 31	12 14	07 23	19 48	24	29
2	13 35	13 39	12 14	08 14	20 40	25	21

UT	ARIES	VENUS −3.9		MARS −0.5		JUPITER −1.9		SATURN +0.3	
	GHA	GHA	Dec	GHA	Dec	GHA	Dec	GHA	Dec
d h	° ′	° ′	° ′	° ′	° ′	° ′	° ′	° ′	° ′
3 00	132 33.5	209 41.9	S22 16.5	49 06.6	N26 38.4	211 19.5	S22 55.0	333 20.1	N10 40.9
01	147 36.0	224 41.0	16.3	64 09.0	38.3	226 21.4	55.0	348 22.7	40.9
02	162 38.4	239 40.2	16.2	79 11.3	38.3	241 23.3	54.9	3 25.4	41.0
03	177 40.9	254 39.3	. . 16.0	94 13.7	. . 38.3	256 25.2	. . 54.9	18 28.0	. . 41.1
04	192 43.4	269 38.4	15.9	109 16.0	38.2	271 27.0	54.9	33 30.6	41.2
05	207 45.8	284 37.6	15.7	124 18.4	38.2	286 28.9	54.8	48 33.2	41.2
06	222 48.3	299 36.7	S22 15.6	139 20.7	N26 38.1	301 30.8	S22 54.8	63 35.9	N10 41.3
07	237 50.8	314 35.9	15.4	154 23.1	38.1	316 32.7	54.8	78 38.5	41.4
08	252 53.2	329 35.0	15.2	169 25.4	38.1	331 34.6	54.7	93 41.1	41.4
S 09	267 55.7	344 34.1	. . 15.1	184 27.8	. . 38.0	346 36.5	. . 54.7	108 43.8	. . 41.5
U 10	282 58.1	359 33.3	14.9	199 30.1	38.0	1 38.4	54.6	123 46.4	41.6
N 11	298 00.6	14 32.4	14.8	214 32.4	37.9	16 40.3	54.6	138 49.0	41.7
D 12	313 03.1	29 31.5	S22 14.6	229 34.8	N26 37.9	31 42.2	S22 54.6	153 51.6	N10 41.7
A 13	328 05.5	44 30.7	14.4	244 37.1	37.9	46 44.1	54.5	168 54.3	41.8
Y 14	343 08.0	59 29.8	14.3	259 39.5	37.8	61 46.0	54.5	183 56.9	41.9
15	358 10.5	74 29.0	. . 14.1	274 41.8	. . 37.8	76 47.9	. . 54.5	198 59.5	. . 42.0
16	13 12.9	89 28.1	13.9	289 44.1	37.8	91 49.8	54.4	214 02.2	42.0
17	28 15.4	104 27.2	13.8	304 46.5	37.7	106 51.7	54.4	229 04.8	42.1
18	43 17.9	119 26.4	S22 13.6	319 48.8	N26 37.7	121 53.6	S22 54.3	244 07.4	N10 42.2
19	58 20.3	134 25.5	13.4	334 51.1	37.6	136 55.5	54.3	259 10.1	42.2
20	73 22.8	149 24.6	13.3	349 53.4	37.6	151 57.4	54.3	274 12.7	42.3
21	88 25.2	164 23.8	. . 13.1	4 55.8	. . 37.6	166 59.3	. . 54.2	289 15.3	. . 42.4
22	103 27.7	179 22.9	12.9	19 58.1	37.5	182 01.2	54.2	304 17.9	42.5
23	118 30.2	194 22.1	12.8	35 00.4	37.5	197 03.1	54.2	319 20.6	42.5
4 00	133 32.6	209 21.2	S22 12.6	50 02.7	N26 37.5	212 05.0	S22 54.1	334 23.2	N10 42.6
01	148 35.1	224 20.3	12.4	65 05.1	37.4	227 06.8	54.1	349 25.8	42.7
02	163 37.6	239 19.5	12.2	80 07.4	37.4	242 08.7	54.0	4 28.5	42.7
03	178 40.0	254 18.6	. . 12.0	95 09.7	. . 37.3	257 10.6	. . 54.0	19 31.1	. . 42.8
04	193 42.5	269 17.8	11.9	110 12.0	37.3	272 12.5	54.0	34 33.7	42.9
05	208 45.0	284 16.9	11.7	125 14.3	37.3	287 14.4	53.9	49 36.3	43.0
06	223 47.4	299 16.0	S22 11.5	140 16.7	N26 37.2	302 16.3	S22 53.9	64 39.0	N10 43.0
07	238 49.9	314 15.2	11.3	155 19.0	37.2	317 18.2	53.8	79 41.6	43.1
08	253 52.4	329 14.3	11.1	170 21.3	37.2	332 20.1	53.8	94 44.2	43.2
M 09	268 54.8	344 13.5	. . 11.0	185 23.6	. . 37.1	347 22.0	. . 53.8	109 46.9	. . 43.3
O 10	283 57.3	359 12.6	10.8	200 25.9	37.1	2 23.9	53.7	124 49.5	43.3
N 11	298 59.7	14 11.7	10.6	215 28.2	37.0	17 25.8	53.7	139 52.1	43.4
D 12	314 02.2	29 10.9	S22 10.4	230 30.5	N26 37.0	32 27.7	S22 53.7	154 54.8	N10 43.5
A 13	329 04.7	44 10.0	10.2	245 32.8	37.0	47 29.6	53.6	169 57.4	43.5
Y 14	344 07.1	59 09.2	10.0	260 35.1	36.9	62 31.5	53.6	185 00.0	43.6
15	359 09.6	74 08.3	. . 09.8	275 37.4	. . 36.9	77 33.4	. . 53.5	200 02.7	. . 43.7
16	14 12.1	89 07.4	09.6	290 39.7	36.9	92 35.3	53.5	215 05.3	43.8
17	29 14.5	104 06.6	09.4	305 42.0	36.8	107 37.2	53.5	230 07.9	43.8
18	44 17.0	119 05.7	S22 09.2	320 44.3	N26 36.8	122 39.1	S22 53.4	245 10.6	N10 43.9
19	59 19.5	134 04.9	09.0	335 46.6	36.7	137 41.0	53.4	260 13.2	44.0
20	74 21.9	149 04.0	08.8	350 48.9	36.7	152 42.9	53.4	275 15.8	44.1
21	89 24.4	164 03.1	. . 08.6	5 51.2	. . 36.7	167 44.8	. . 53.3	290 18.4	. . 44.1
22	104 26.9	179 02.3	08.4	20 53.5	36.6	182 46.7	53.3	305 21.1	44.2
23	119 29.3	194 01.4	08.2	35 55.8	36.6	197 48.6	53.2	320 23.7	44.3
5 00	134 31.8	209 00.6	S22 08.0	50 58.1	N26 36.6	212 50.5	S22 53.2	335 26.3	N10 44.4
01	149 34.2	223 59.7	07.8	66 00.4	36.5	227 52.4	53.2	350 29.0	44.4
02	164 36.7	238 58.9	07.6	81 02.7	36.5	242 54.3	53.1	5 31.6	44.5
03	179 39.2	253 58.0	. . 07.4	96 04.9	. . 36.4	257 56.2	. . 53.1	20 34.2	. . 44.6
04	194 41.6	268 57.1	07.2	111 07.2	36.4	272 58.1	53.0	35 36.9	44.6
05	209 44.1	283 56.3	07.0	126 09.5	36.4	288 00.0	53.0	50 39.5	44.7
06	224 46.6	298 55.4	S22 06.8	141 11.8	N26 36.3	303 01.9	S22 53.0	65 42.1	N10 44.8
07	239 49.0	313 54.6	06.6	156 14.1	36.3	318 03.8	52.9	80 44.8	44.9
T 08	254 51.5	328 53.7	06.4	171 16.3	36.3	333 05.7	52.9	95 47.4	44.9
U 09	269 54.0	343 52.9	. . 06.2	186 18.6	. . 36.2	348 07.6	. . 52.9	110 50.0	. . 45.0
E 10	284 56.4	358 52.0	05.9	201 20.9	36.2	3 09.5	52.8	125 52.7	45.1
S 11	299 58.9	13 51.1	05.7	216 23.2	36.2	18 11.4	52.8	140 55.3	45.2
D 12	315 01.4	28 50.3	S22 05.5	231 25.4	N26 36.1	33 13.3	S22 52.7	155 57.9	N10 45.2
A 13	330 03.8	43 49.4	05.3	246 27.7	36.1	48 15.2	52.7	171 00.6	45.3
Y 14	345 06.3	58 48.6	05.1	261 30.0	36.0	63 17.1	52.7	186 03.2	45.4
15	0 08.7	73 47.7	. . 04.9	276 32.3	. . 36.0	78 19.0	. . 52.6	201 05.8	. . 45.5
16	15 11.2	88 46.9	04.6	291 34.5	36.0	93 20.9	52.6	216 08.5	45.5
17	30 13.7	103 46.0	04.4	306 36.8	35.9	108 22.8	52.5	231 11.1	45.6
18	45 16.1	118 45.1	S22 04.2	321 39.1	N26 35.9	123 24.7	S22 52.5	246 13.7	N10 45.7
19	60 18.6	133 44.3	04.0	336 41.3	35.9	138 26.6	52.5	261 16.4	45.7
20	75 21.1	148 43.4	03.7	351 43.6	35.8	153 28.5	52.4	276 19.0	45.8
21	90 23.5	163 42.6	. . 03.5	6 45.8	. . 35.8	168 30.4	. . 52.4	291 21.6	. . 45.9
22	105 26.0	178 41.7	03.3	21 48.1	35.7	183 32.3	52.3	306 24.3	46.0
23	120 28.5	193 40.9	03.1	36 50.4	35.7	198 34.2	52.3	321 26.9	46.0
Mer. Pass.	h m 15 03.4	v −0.9	d 0.2	v 2.3	d 0.0	v 1.9	d 0.0	v 2.6	d 0.1

STARS Name	SHA	Dec
	° ′	° ′
Acamar	315 21.3	S40 16.5
Achernar	335 29.7	S57 12.0
Acrux	173 13.8	S63 08.5
Adhara	255 15.4	S28 59.1
Aldebaran	290 53.9	N16 31.6
Alioth	166 23.6	N55 54.6
Alkaid	153 01.7	N49 16.0
Al Na'ir	27 49.0	S46 55.4
Alnilam	275 50.3	S 1 11.8
Alphard	217 59.8	S 8 41.7
Alphecca	126 14.4	N26 40.9
Alpheratz	357 48.0	N29 08.2
Altair	62 12.5	N 8 53.2
Ankaa	353 19.8	S42 15.9
Antares	112 31.4	S26 27.1
Arcturus	145 59.3	N19 08.1
Atria	107 37.3	S69 02.4
Avior	234 19.2	S59 32.2
Bellatrix	278 36.1	N 6 21.5
Betelgeuse	271 05.4	N 7 24.5
Canopus	263 57.5	S52 42.1
Capella	280 40.2	N46 00.6
Deneb	49 34.8	N45 18.4
Denebola	182 37.5	N14 31.4
Diphda	349 00.1	S17 56.6
Dubhe	193 55.7	N61 42.2
Elnath	278 17.5	N28 37.0
Eltanin	90 48.4	N51 28.9
Enif	33 51.4	N 9 54.6
Fomalhaut	15 28.6	S29 34.9
Gacrux	172 05.4	S57 09.4
Gienah	175 56.3	S17 35.3
Hadar	148 53.8	S60 24.6
Hamal	328 05.5	N23 30.2
Kaus Aust.	83 49.5	S34 22.9
Kochab	137 19.3	N74 06.9
Markab	13 42.7	N15 14.9
Menkar	314 19.3	N 4 07.3
Menkent	148 12.4	S36 24.6
Miaplacidus	221 40.0	S69 45.0
Mirfak	308 46.2	N49 53.7
Nunki	76 03.6	S26 17.3
Peacock	53 26.0	S56 42.6
Pollux	243 32.3	N28 00.4
Procyon	245 03.6	N 5 12.2
Rasalhague	96 10.4	N12 33.0
Regulus	207 47.5	N11 55.5
Rigel	281 15.7	S 8 11.6
Rigil Kent.	139 57.5	S60 52.0
Sabik	102 17.4	S15 44.2
Schedar	349 45.8	N56 35.2
Shaula	96 27.7	S37 06.6
Sirius	258 37.0	S16 43.7
Spica	158 35.4	S11 12.3
Suhail	222 55.1	S43 27.9
Vega	80 42.1	N38 47.2
Zuben'ubi	137 09.9	S16 04.6

	SHA	Mer. Pass.
	° ′	h m
Venus	75 48.6	10 03
Mars	276 30.1	20 37
Jupiter	78 32.3	9 50
Saturn	200 50.6	1 42

	UT	SUN GHA	SUN Dec	MOON GHA	v	MOON Dec	d	HP
	d h	° ′	° ′	° ′	′	° ′	′	′
	3 00	176 34.3	S16 45.9	228 14.2	9.0	S28 01.4	0.2	54.8
	01	191 34.2	45.2	242 42.2	9.0	28 01.2	0.2	54.9
	02	206 34.1	44.5	257 10.2	9.0	28 01.0	0.5	54.9
	03	221 34.1	. . 43.8	271 38.2	9.0	28 00.5	0.6	54.9
	04	236 34.0	43.0	286 06.2	8.9	27 59.9	0.7	54.9
	05	251 33.9	42.3	300 34.1	8.9	27 59.2	0.8	54.9
	06	266 33.8	S16 41.6	315 02.0	8.9	S27 58.4	1.0	55.0
	07	281 33.8	40.8	329 29.9	8.9	27 57.4	1.2	55.0
	08	296 33.7	40.1	343 57.8	8.9	27 56.2	1.3	55.0
S	09	311 33.6	. . 39.4	358 25.7	8.8	27 54.9	1.4	55.0
U	10	326 33.5	38.7	12 53.5	8.9	27 53.5	1.6	55.0
N	11	341 33.5	37.9	27 21.4	8.8	27 51.9	1.8	55.1
D	12	356 33.4	S16 37.2	41 49.2	8.8	S27 50.1	1.8	55.1
A	13	11 33.3	36.5	56 17.0	8.8	27 48.3	2.1	55.1
Y	14	26 33.3	35.7	70 44.8	8.9	27 46.2	2.1	55.1
	15	41 33.2	. . 35.0	85 12.7	8.8	27 44.1	2.4	55.1
	16	56 33.1	34.3	99 40.5	8.8	27 41.7	2.4	55.2
	17	71 33.1	33.5	114 08.3	8.8	27 39.3	2.6	55.2
	18	86 33.0	S16 32.8	128 36.1	8.8	S27 36.7	2.8	55.2
	19	101 32.9	32.1	143 03.9	8.8	27 33.9	2.9	55.2
	20	116 32.8	31.3	157 31.7	8.8	27 31.0	3.0	55.2
	21	131 32.8	. . 30.6	171 59.5	8.8	27 28.0	3.2	55.3
	22	146 32.7	29.8	186 27.3	8.8	27 24.8	3.4	55.3
	23	161 32.6	29.1	200 55.1	8.8	27 21.4	3.4	55.3
	4 00	176 32.6	S16 28.4	215 22.9	8.8	S27 18.0	3.7	55.3
	01	191 32.5	27.6	229 50.7	8.8	27 14.3	3.8	55.4
	02	206 32.4	26.9	244 18.5	8.8	27 10.5	3.9	55.4
	03	221 32.4	. . 26.2	258 46.3	8.9	27 06.6	4.0	55.4
	04	236 32.3	25.4	273 14.2	8.8	27 02.6	4.3	55.4
	05	251 32.2	24.7	287 42.0	8.9	26 58.3	4.3	55.4
	06	266 32.2	S16 23.9	302 09.9	8.9	S26 54.0	4.5	55.5
	07	281 32.1	23.2	316 37.8	8.9	26 49.5	4.7	55.5
	08	296 32.1	22.5	331 05.7	8.9	26 44.8	4.7	55.5
M	09	311 32.0	. . 21.7	345 33.6	8.9	26 40.1	5.0	55.5
O	10	326 31.9	21.0	0 01.5	9.0	26 35.1	5.1	55.6
N	11	341 31.9	20.2	14 29.5	8.9	26 30.0	5.2	55.6
D	12	356 31.8	S16 19.5	28 57.4	9.0	S26 24.8	5.3	55.6
A	13	11 31.7	18.7	43 25.4	9.0	26 19.5	5.5	55.6
Y	14	26 31.7	18.0	57 53.4	9.1	26 14.0	5.7	55.7
	15	41 31.6	. . 17.2	72 21.5	9.0	26 08.3	5.8	55.7
	16	56 31.6	16.5	86 49.5	9.1	26 02.5	5.9	55.7
	17	71 31.5	15.8	101 17.6	9.1	25 56.6	6.1	55.7
	18	86 31.4	S16 15.0	115 45.7	9.1	S25 50.5	6.2	55.8
	19	101 31.4	14.3	130 13.8	9.2	25 44.3	6.3	55.8
	20	116 31.3	13.5	144 42.0	9.2	25 38.0	6.5	55.8
	21	131 31.3	. . 12.8	159 10.2	9.2	25 31.5	6.7	55.8
	22	146 31.2	12.0	173 38.4	9.3	25 24.8	6.7	55.8
	23	161 31.1	11.3	188 06.7	9.2	25 18.1	6.9	55.9
	5 00	176 31.1	S16 10.5	202 34.9	9.4	S25 11.2	7.1	55.9
	01	191 31.0	09.8	217 03.3	9.3	25 04.1	7.2	55.9
	02	206 31.0	09.0	231 31.6	9.4	24 56.9	7.3	55.9
	03	221 30.9	. . 08.3	246 00.0	9.4	24 49.6	7.4	56.0
	04	236 30.8	07.5	260 28.4	9.5	24 42.2	7.6	56.0
	05	251 30.8	06.8	274 56.9	9.5	24 34.6	7.7	56.0
	06	266 30.7	S16 06.0	289 25.4	9.5	S24 26.9	7.9	56.0
	07	281 30.7	05.3	303 53.9	9.6	24 19.0	8.0	56.1
T	08	296 30.6	04.5	318 22.5	9.6	24 11.0	8.1	56.1
U	09	311 30.6	. . 03.7	332 51.1	9.6	24 02.9	8.3	56.1
E	10	326 30.5	03.0	347 19.7	9.7	23 54.6	8.3	56.1
S	11	341 30.5	02.2	1 48.4	9.7	23 46.3	8.6	56.2
D	12	356 30.4	S16 01.5	16 17.1	9.8	S23 37.7	8.6	56.2
A	13	11 30.4	00.7	30 45.9	9.8	23 29.1	8.8	56.2
Y	14	26 30.3	16 00.0	45 14.7	9.9	23 20.3	8.9	56.2
	15	41 30.2	15 59.2	59 43.6	9.8	23 11.4	9.0	56.3
	16	56 30.2	58.5	74 12.4	10.0	23 02.4	9.2	56.3
	17	71 30.1	57.7	88 41.4	10.0	22 53.2	9.3	56.3
	18	86 30.1	S15 56.9	103 10.4	10.0	S22 43.9	9.4	56.4
	19	101 30.0	56.2	117 39.4	10.1	22 34.5	9.5	56.4
	20	116 30.0	55.4	132 08.5	10.1	22 25.0	9.6	56.4
	21	131 29.9	. . 54.7	146 37.6	10.2	22 15.4	9.8	56.4
	22	146 29.9	53.9	161 06.8	10.2	22 05.6	9.9	56.5
	23	161 29.8	53.1	175 36.0	10.2	S21 55.7	10.0	56.5
		SD 16.3	d 0.7	SD	15.0	15.2		15.3

Lat.	Twilight Naut.	Twilight Civil	Sunrise	Moonrise 3	Moonrise 4	Moonrise 5	Moonrise 6
°	h m	h m	h m	h m	h m	h m	h m
N 72	07 01	08 28	10 08	■	■	■	■
N 70	06 54	08 11	09 32	■	■	■	11 15
68	06 48	07 57	09 07	■	■	■	10 00
66	06 43	07 46	08 48	■	■	10 35	09 22
64	06 39	07 37	08 32	■	■	09 16	08 55
62	06 35	07 29	08 19	■	08 44	08 39	08 34
60	06 31	07 22	08 08	07 33	08 01	08 12	08 17
N 58	06 28	07 15	07 59	06 56	07 32	07 52	08 03
56	06 25	07 10	07 50	06 30	07 09	07 34	07 50
54	06 22	07 05	07 43	06 09	06 51	07 20	07 40
52	06 19	07 00	07 36	05 52	06 35	07 07	07 30
50	06 17	06 56	07 30	05 37	06 22	06 56	07 21
45	06 11	06 46	07 17	05 07	05 54	06 32	07 03
N 40	06 06	06 38	07 06	04 44	05 32	06 13	06 48
35	06 00	06 31	06 57	04 24	05 14	05 57	06 35
30	05 55	06 24	06 49	04 08	04 58	05 43	06 24
20	05 45	06 12	06 35	03 40	04 31	05 20	06 04
N 10	05 35	06 00	06 22	03 16	04 08	04 59	05 47
0	05 24	05 49	06 10	02 54	03 47	04 40	05 31
S 10	05 11	05 36	05 58	02 31	03 26	04 21	05 16
20	04 55	05 22	05 46	02 07	03 03	04 00	04 58
30	04 34	05 05	05 31	01 40	02 36	03 36	04 39
35	04 21	04 55	05 22	01 23	02 20	03 22	04 27
40	04 06	04 42	05 12	01 04	02 01	03 06	04 14
45	03 46	04 27	05 00	00 41	01 39	02 46	03 58
S 50	03 20	04 08	04 46	00 11	01 11	02 21	03 38
52	03 06	03 59	04 39	24 57	00 57	02 09	03 29
54	02 51	03 49	04 32	24 40	00 40	01 55	03 18
56	02 31	03 37	04 23	24 21	00 21	01 40	03 06
58	02 07	03 23	04 14	23 57	25 21	01 21	02 53
S 60	01 30	03 07	04 03	23 25	24 57	00 57	02 36

Lat.	Sunset	Twilight Civil	Twilight Naut.	Moonset 3	Moonset 4	Moonset 5	Moonset 6
°	h m	h m	h m	h m	h m	h m	h m
N 72	14 21	16 01	17 29	■	■	■	■
N 70	14 57	16 18	17 35	■	■	■	12 31
68	15 22	16 32	17 41	■	■	■	13 45
66	15 41	16 43	17 46	■	■	11 22	14 22
64	15 57	16 52	17 50	■	■	12 41	14 47
62	16 09	17 00	17 54	■	11 22	13 17	15 07
60	16 20	17 07	17 57	10 42	12 05	13 43	15 24
N 58	16 30	17 13	18 01	11 19	12 34	14 03	15 37
56	16 38	17 19	18 04	11 45	12 56	14 20	15 49
54	16 46	17 24	18 06	12 05	13 14	14 34	15 59
52	16 52	17 29	18 09	12 23	13 30	14 46	16 08
50	16 58	17 33	18 12	12 37	13 43	14 57	16 16
45	17 11	17 42	18 17	13 07	14 10	15 20	16 33
N 40	17 22	17 50	18 23	13 30	14 31	15 38	16 47
35	17 31	17 58	18 28	13 49	14 49	15 53	16 59
30	17 39	18 04	18 33	14 06	15 04	16 06	17 09
20	17 53	18 16	18 42	14 34	15 30	16 28	17 26
N 10	18 06	18 27	18 53	14 57	15 52	16 47	17 41
0	18 17	18 39	19 04	15 19	16 13	17 05	17 55
S 10	18 29	18 51	19 17	15 41	16 33	17 23	18 09
20	18 42	19 05	19 33	16 05	16 55	17 41	18 24
30	18 57	19 22	19 53	16 32	17 20	18 03	18 41
35	19 05	19 33	20 06	16 49	17 35	18 15	18 50
40	19 15	19 45	20 21	17 07	17 52	18 30	19 01
45	19 27	20 00	20 41	17 30	18 12	18 47	19 14
S 50	19 41	20 18	21 06	17 59	18 38	19 07	19 30
52	19 48	20 27	21 19	18 13	18 50	19 17	19 37
54	19 55	20 37	21 35	18 29	19 04	19 28	19 45
56	20 03	20 49	21 53	18 49	19 21	19 41	19 54
58	20 12	21 02	22 17	19 13	19 40	19 55	20 04
S 60	20 23	21 19	22 51	19 45	20 04	20 12	20 16

Day	SUN Eqn. of Time 00^h	SUN Eqn. of Time 12^h	SUN Mer. Pass.	MOON Mer. Pass. Upper	MOON Mer. Pass. Lower	Age	Phase
d	m s	m s	h m	h m	h m	d	%
3	13 43	13 46	12 14	09 07	21 33	26	14
4	13 50	13 53	12 14	10 00	22 26	27	8
5	13 56	13 58	12 14	10 53	23 18	28	3

UT d	h	ARIES GHA	VENUS −3.9 GHA	VENUS Dec	MARS −0.4 GHA	MARS Dec	JUPITER −1.9 GHA	JUPITER Dec	SATURN +0.3 GHA	SATURN Dec
		° ′	° ′	° ′	° ′	° ′	° ′	° ′	° ′	° ′
6	00	135 30.9	208 40.0	S22 02.8	51 52.6	N26 35.7	213 36.1	S22 52.3	336 29.5	N10 46.1
	01	150 33.4	223 39.2	02.6	66 54.9	35.6	228 38.0	52.2	351 32.2	46.2
	02	165 35.9	238 38.3	02.4	81 57.1	35.6	243 39.9	52.2	6 34.8	46.3
	03	180 38.3	253 37.5	. . 02.1	96 59.4	. . 35.6	258 41.8	. . 52.2	21 37.4	. . 46.3
	04	195 40.8	268 36.6	01.9	112 01.6	35.5	273 43.7	52.1	36 40.1	46.4
	05	210 43.2	283 35.7	01.7	127 03.9	35.5	288 45.6	52.1	51 42.7	46.5
	06	225 45.7	298 34.9	S22 01.4	142 06.1	N26 35.5	303 47.5	S22 52.0	66 45.3	N10 46.6
W	07	240 48.2	313 34.0	01.2	157 08.4	35.4	318 49.4	52.0	81 48.0	46.6
E	08	255 50.6	328 33.2	00.9	172 10.6	35.4	333 51.3	52.0	96 50.6	46.7
D	09	270 53.1	343 32.3	. . 00.7	187 12.9	. . 35.3	348 53.2	. . 51.9	111 53.2	. . 46.8
N	10	285 55.6	358 31.5	00.5	202 15.1	35.3	3 55.1	51.9	126 55.9	46.9
E	11	300 58.0	13 30.6	00.2	217 17.4	35.3	18 57.0	51.8	141 58.5	46.9
S	12	316 00.5	28 29.8	S22 00.0	232 19.6	N26 35.2	33 58.9	S22 51.8	157 01.2	N10 47.0
D	13	331 03.0	43 28.9	21 59.7	247 21.8	35.2	49 00.8	51.8	172 03.8	47.1
A	14	346 05.4	58 28.1	59.5	262 24.1	35.2	64 02.7	51.7	187 06.4	47.1
Y	15	1 07.9	73 27.2	. . 59.2	277 26.3	. . 35.1	79 04.6	. . 51.7	202 09.1	. . 47.2
	16	16 10.3	88 26.4	59.0	292 28.5	35.1	94 06.6	51.6	217 11.7	47.3
	17	31 12.8	103 25.5	58.7	307 30.8	35.1	109 08.5	51.6	232 14.3	47.4
	18	46 15.3	118 24.7	S21 58.5	322 33.0	N26 35.0	124 10.4	S22 51.6	247 17.0	N10 47.4
	19	61 17.7	133 23.8	58.2	337 35.2	35.0	139 12.3	51.5	262 19.6	47.5
	20	76 20.2	148 23.0	58.0	352 37.5	35.0	154 14.2	51.5	277 22.2	47.6
	21	91 22.7	163 22.1	. . 57.7	7 39.7	. . 34.9	169 16.1	. . 51.4	292 24.9	. . 47.7
	22	106 25.1	178 21.2	57.5	22 41.9	34.9	184 18.0	51.4	307 27.5	47.7
	23	121 27.6	193 20.4	57.2	37 44.1	34.8	199 19.9	51.4	322 30.1	47.8
7	00	136 30.1	208 19.5	S21 57.0	52 46.4	N26 34.8	214 21.8	S22 51.3	337 32.8	N10 47.9
	01	151 32.5	223 18.7	56.7	67 48.6	34.8	229 23.7	51.3	352 35.4	48.0
	02	166 35.0	238 17.8	56.4	82 50.8	34.7	244 25.6	51.2	7 38.0	48.0
	03	181 37.5	253 17.0	. . 56.2	97 53.0	. . 34.7	259 27.5	. . 51.2	22 40.7	. . 48.1
	04	196 39.9	268 16.1	55.9	112 55.3	34.7	274 29.4	51.2	37 43.3	48.2
	05	211 42.4	283 15.3	55.7	127 57.5	34.6	289 31.3	51.1	52 46.0	48.3
	06	226 44.8	298 14.4	S21 55.4	142 59.7	N26 34.6	304 33.2	S22 51.1	67 48.6	N10 48.3
	07	241 47.3	313 13.6	55.1	158 01.9	34.6	319 35.1	51.0	82 51.2	48.4
T	08	256 49.8	328 12.7	54.9	173 04.1	34.5	334 37.0	51.0	97 53.9	48.5
H	09	271 52.2	343 11.9	. . 54.6	188 06.3	. . 34.5	349 38.9	. . 51.0	112 56.5	. . 48.6
U	10	286 54.7	358 11.0	54.3	203 08.5	34.4	4 40.8	50.9	127 59.1	48.6
R	11	301 57.2	13 10.2	54.1	218 10.8	34.4	19 42.7	50.9	143 01.8	48.7
S	12	316 59.6	28 09.4	S21 53.8	233 13.0	N26 34.4	34 44.7	S22 50.8	158 04.4	N10 48.8
D	13	332 02.1	43 08.5	53.5	248 15.2	34.3	49 46.6	50.8	173 07.1	48.9
A	14	347 04.6	58 07.7	53.2	263 17.4	34.3	64 48.5	50.8	188 09.7	48.9
Y	15	2 07.0	73 06.8	. . 53.0	278 19.6	. . 34.3	79 50.4	. . 50.7	203 12.3	. . 49.0
	16	17 09.5	88 06.0	52.7	293 21.8	34.2	94 52.3	50.7	218 15.0	49.1
	17	32 12.0	103 05.1	52.4	308 24.0	34.2	109 54.2	50.6	233 17.6	49.2
	18	47 14.4	118 04.3	S21 52.1	323 26.2	N26 34.2	124 56.1	S22 50.6	248 20.2	N10 49.2
	19	62 16.9	133 03.4	51.9	338 28.4	34.1	139 58.0	50.6	263 22.9	49.3
	20	77 19.3	148 02.6	51.6	353 30.6	34.1	154 59.9	50.5	278 25.5	49.4
	21	92 21.8	163 01.7	. . 51.3	8 32.8	. . 34.1	170 01.8	. . 50.5	293 28.2	. . 49.5
	22	107 24.3	178 00.9	51.0	23 35.0	34.0	185 03.7	50.4	308 30.8	49.5
	23	122 26.7	193 00.0	50.7	38 37.2	34.0	200 05.6	50.4	323 33.4	49.6
8	00	137 29.2	207 59.2	S21 50.4	53 39.4	N26 34.0	215 07.5	S22 50.4	338 36.1	N10 49.7
	01	152 31.7	222 58.3	50.2	68 41.6	33.9	230 09.4	50.3	353 38.7	49.8
	02	167 34.1	237 57.5	49.9	83 43.7	33.9	245 11.4	50.3	8 41.3	49.8
	03	182 36.6	252 56.6	. . 49.6	98 45.9	. . 33.8	260 13.3	. . 50.2	23 44.0	. . 49.9
	04	197 39.1	267 55.8	49.3	113 48.1	33.8	275 15.2	50.2	38 46.6	50.0
	05	212 41.5	282 55.0	49.0	128 50.3	33.8	290 17.1	50.2	53 49.3	50.1
	06	227 44.0	297 54.1	S21 48.7	143 52.5	N26 33.7	305 19.0	S22 50.1	68 51.9	N10 50.1
	07	242 46.4	312 53.3	48.4	158 54.7	33.7	320 20.9	50.1	83 54.5	50.2
	08	257 48.9	327 52.4	48.1	173 56.9	33.7	335 22.8	50.0	98 57.2	50.3
F	09	272 51.4	342 51.6	. . 47.8	188 59.0	. . 33.6	350 24.7	. . 50.0	113 59.8	. . 50.4
R	10	287 53.8	357 50.7	47.5	204 01.2	33.6	5 26.6	50.0	129 02.4	50.4
I	11	302 56.3	12 49.9	47.2	219 03.4	33.6	20 28.5	49.9	144 05.1	50.5
D	12	317 58.8	27 49.0	S21 46.9	234 05.6	N26 33.5	35 30.4	S22 49.9	159 07.7	N10 50.6
A	13	333 01.2	42 48.2	46.6	249 07.8	33.5	50 32.4	49.8	174 10.4	50.7
Y	14	348 03.7	57 47.4	46.3	264 09.9	33.5	65 34.3	49.8	189 13.0	50.7
	15	3 06.2	72 46.5	. . 46.0	279 12.1	. . 33.4	80 36.2	. . 49.8	204 15.6	. . 50.8
	16	18 08.6	87 45.7	45.7	294 14.3	33.4	95 38.1	49.7	219 18.3	50.9
	17	33 11.1	102 44.8	45.4	309 16.4	33.4	110 40.0	49.7	234 20.9	51.0
	18	48 13.6	117 44.0	S21 45.1	324 18.6	N26 33.3	125 41.9	S22 49.6	249 23.6	N10 51.0
	19	63 16.0	132 43.1	44.8	339 20.8	33.3	140 43.8	49.6	264 26.2	51.1
	20	78 18.5	147 42.3	44.5	354 22.9	33.3	155 45.7	49.6	279 28.8	51.2
	21	93 20.9	162 41.5	. . 44.2	9 25.1	. . 33.2	170 47.6	. . 49.5	294 31.5	. . 51.3
	22	108 23.4	177 40.6	43.9	24 27.3	33.2	185 49.5	49.5	309 34.1	51.3
	23	123 25.9	192 39.8	43.6	39 29.4	33.1	200 51.5	49.4	324 36.8	51.4
Mer. Pass.		h m 14 51.6	v −0.8	d 0.3	v 2.2	d 0.0	v 1.9	d 0.0	v 2.6	d 0.1

STARS Name	SHA	Dec
	° ′	° ′
Acamar	315 21.3	S40 16.5
Achernar	335 29.7	S57 11.9
Acrux	173 13.8	S63 08.5
Adhara	255 15.4	S28 59.1
Aldebaran	290 53.9	N16 31.6
Alioth	166 23.6	N55 54.6
Alkaid	153 01.7	N49 16.0
Al Na'ir	27 49.0	S46 55.4
Alnilam	275 50.3	S 1 11.8
Alphard	217 59.7	S 8 41.7
Alphecca	126 14.4	N26 40.9
Alpheratz	357 48.1	N29 08.2
Altair	62 12.5	N 8 53.2
Ankaa	353 19.8	S42 15.9
Antares	112 31.4	S26 27.1
Arcturus	145 59.3	N19 08.1
Atria	107 37.3	S69 02.4
Avior	234 19.2	S59 32.2
Bellatrix	278 36.1	N 6 21.5
Betelgeuse	271 05.4	N 7 24.5
Canopus	263 57.5	S52 42.1
Capella	280 40.2	N46 00.6
Deneb	49 34.8	N45 18.4
Denebola	182 37.5	N14 31.4
Diphda	349 00.1	S17 56.6
Dubhe	193 55.6	N61 42.2
Elnath	278 17.5	N28 37.0
Eltanin	90 48.4	N51 28.9
Enif	33 51.4	N 9 54.6
Fomalhaut	15 28.6	S29 34.9
Gacrux	172 05.4	S57 09.4
Gienah	175 56.3	S17 35.3
Hadar	148 53.8	S60 24.6
Hamal	328 05.5	N23 30.2
Kaus Aust.	83 49.5	S34 22.9
Kochab	137 19.3	N74 06.9
Markab	13 42.7	N15 14.9
Menkar	314 19.3	N 4 07.3
Menkent	148 12.4	S36 24.6
Miaplacidus	221 40.0	S69 45.0
Mirfak	308 46.2	N49 53.7
Nunki	76 03.6	S26 17.3
Peacock	53 26.0	S56 42.6
Pollux	243 32.3	N28 00.4
Procyon	245 03.6	N 5 12.2
Rasalhague	96 10.4	N12 33.0
Regulus	207 47.4	N11 55.5
Rigel	281 15.7	S 8 11.6
Rigil Kent.	139 57.5	S60 52.0
Sabik	102 17.4	S15 44.2
Schedar	349 45.8	N56 35.2
Shaula	96 27.7	S37 06.6
Sirius	258 37.0	S16 43.7
Spica	158 35.4	S11 12.4
Suhail	222 55.1	S43 28.0
Vega	80 42.1	N38 47.2
Zuben'ubi	137 09.9	S16 04.6

	SHA	Mer. Pass.
	° ′	h m
Venus	71 49.5	10 07
Mars	276 16.3	20 26
Jupiter	77 51.7	9 41
Saturn	201 02.7	1 30

Day	UT d h	SUN GHA ° ′	SUN Dec ° ′	MOON GHA ° ′	MOON v ′	MOON Dec ° ′	MOON d ′	MOON HP ′
WEDNESDAY	6 00	176 29.8	S15 52.4	190 05.2	10.3	S21 45.7	10.2	56.5
	01	191 29.7	51.6	204 34.5	10.4	21 35.5	10.2	56.5
	02	206 29.7	50.9	219 03.9	10.4	21 25.3	10.4	56.6
	03	221 29.6	. . 50.1	233 33.3	10.4	21 14.9	10.5	56.6
	04	236 29.6	49.3	248 02.7	10.5	21 04.4	10.6	56.6
	05	251 29.5	48.6	262 32.2	10.5	20 53.8	10.8	56.6
	06	266 29.5	S15 47.8	277 01.7	10.6	S20 43.0	10.8	56.7
	07	281 29.4	47.0	291 31.3	10.6	20 32.2	11.0	56.7
	08	296 29.4	46.3	306 00.9	10.7	20 21.2	11.0	56.7
	09	311 29.3	. . 45.5	320 30.6	10.7	20 10.2	11.2	56.7
	10	326 29.3	44.7	335 00.3	10.8	19 59.0	11.3	56.8
	11	341 29.3	44.0	349 30.1	10.8	19 47.7	11.4	56.8
	12	356 29.2	S15 43.2	3 59.9	10.9	S19 36.3	11.5	56.8
	13	11 29.2	42.4	18 29.8	10.9	19 24.8	11.6	56.8
	14	26 29.1	41.7	32 59.7	11.0	19 13.2	11.7	56.9
	15	41 29.1	. . 40.9	47 29.7	11.0	19 01.5	11.8	56.9
	16	56 29.0	40.1	61 59.7	11.1	18 49.7	12.0	56.9
	17	71 29.0	39.4	76 29.8	11.1	18 37.7	12.0	56.9
	18	86 28.9	S15 38.6	90 59.9	11.1	S18 25.7	12.1	57.0
	19	101 28.9	37.8	105 30.0	11.2	18 13.6	12.3	57.0
	20	116 28.9	37.1	120 00.2	11.3	18 01.3	12.3	57.0
	21	131 28.8	. . 36.3	134 30.5	11.3	17 49.0	12.4	57.0
	22	146 28.8	35.5	149 00.8	11.3	17 36.6	12.6	57.1
	23	161 28.7	34.7	163 31.1	11.4	S17 24.0	12.6	57.1
THURSDAY	7 00	176 28.7	S15 34.0	An annular eclipse of the Sun occurs on this date. See page 5.				
	01	191 28.6	33.2					
	02	206 28.6	32.4					
	03	221 28.6	. . 31.6					
	04	236 28.5	30.9					
	05	251 28.5	30.1					
	06	266 28.4	S15 29.3	265 04.7	11.7	S15 53.7	13.3	57.3
	07	281 28.4	28.5	279 35.4	11.8	15 40.4	13.4	57.3
	08	296 28.4	27.8	294 06.2	11.8	15 27.0	13.4	57.3
	09	311 28.3	. . 27.0	308 37.0	11.8	15 13.6	13.5	57.3
	10	326 28.3	26.2	323 07.8	11.8	15 00.1	13.7	57.4
	11	341 28.2	25.4	337 38.6	11.9	14 46.4	13.7	57.4
	12	356 28.2	S15 24.7	352 09.5	12.0	S14 32.7	13.7	57.4
	13	11 28.2	23.9	6 40.5	12.0	14 19.0	13.9	57.4
	14	26 28.1	23.1	21 11.5	12.0	14 05.1	13.9	57.4
	15	41 28.1	. . 22.3	35 42.5	12.1	13 51.2	14.1	57.5
	16	56 28.1	21.5	50 13.6	12.1	13 37.1	14.0	57.5
	17	71 28.0	20.8	64 44.7	12.1	13 23.1	14.2	57.5
	18	86 28.0	S15 20.0	79 15.8	12.2	S13 08.9	14.3	57.5
	19	101 28.0	19.2	93 47.0	12.2	12 54.6	14.3	57.6
	20	116 27.9	18.4	108 18.2	12.2	12 40.3	14.4	57.6
	21	131 27.9	. . 17.6	122 49.4	12.3	12 25.9	14.4	57.6
	22	146 27.9	16.9	137 20.7	12.3	12 11.5	14.5	57.6
	23	161 27.8	16.1	151 52.0	12.3	11 57.0	14.6	57.7
FRIDAY	8 00	176 27.8	S15 15.3	166 23.3	12.4	S11 42.4	14.7	57.7
	01	191 27.8	14.5	180 54.7	12.4	11 27.7	14.7	57.7
	02	206 27.7	13.7	195 26.1	12.4	11 13.0	14.8	57.7
	03	221 27.7	. . 12.9	209 57.5	12.5	10 58.2	14.9	57.7
	04	236 27.7	12.2	224 29.0	12.5	10 43.3	14.9	57.8
	05	251 27.6	11.4	239 00.5	12.5	10 28.4	15.0	57.8
	06	266 27.6	S15 10.6	253 32.0	12.6	S10 13.4	15.0	57.8
	07	281 27.6	09.8	268 03.6	12.5	9 58.4	15.1	57.8
	08	296 27.5	09.0	282 35.1	12.6	9 43.3	15.2	57.8
	09	311 27.5	. . 08.2	297 06.7	12.7	9 28.1	15.2	57.9
	10	326 27.5	07.4	311 38.4	12.6	9 12.9	15.2	57.9
	11	341 27.4	06.6	326 10.0	12.7	8 57.7	15.3	57.9
	12	356 27.4	S15 05.9	340 41.7	12.7	S 8 42.4	15.4	57.9
	13	11 27.4	05.1	355 13.4	12.7	8 27.0	15.4	57.9
	14	26 27.4	04.3	9 45.1	12.7	8 11.6	15.5	58.0
	15	41 27.3	. . 03.5	24 16.8	12.8	7 56.1	15.5	58.0
	16	56 27.3	02.7	38 48.6	12.7	7 40.6	15.6	58.0
	17	71 27.3	01.9	53 20.3	12.8	7 25.0	15.6	58.0
	18	86 27.2	S15 01.1	67 52.1	12.8	S 7 09.4	15.6	58.0
	19	101 27.2	15 00.3	82 23.9	12.8	6 53.8	15.7	58.1
	20	116 27.2	14 59.5	96 55.7	12.9	6 38.1	15.7	58.1
	21	131 27.2	. . 58.7	111 27.6	12.8	6 22.4	15.8	58.1
	22	146 27.1	57.9	125 59.4	12.9	6 06.6	15.8	58.1
	23	161 27.1	57.2	140 31.3	12.8	S 5 50.8	15.8	58.1
		SD 16.2	*d* 0.8	SD 15.5		15.6		15.8

Lat.	Twilight Naut.	Twilight Civil	Sunrise	Moonrise 6	Moonrise 7	Moonrise 8	Moonrise 9
°	h m	h m	h m	h m	h m	h m	h m
N 72	06 50	08 14	09 47	■	10 12	09 17	08 38
N 70	06 44	07 59	09 17	11 15	09 40	09 02	08 34
68	06 39	07 47	08 54	10 00	09 16	08 51	08 30
66	06 35	07 37	08 37	09 22	08 58	08 41	08 27
64	06 31	07 29	08 23	08 55	08 43	08 33	08 24
62	06 28	07 21	08 11	08 34	08 30	08 26	08 22
60	06 25	07 15	08 01	08 17	08 19	08 20	08 20
N 58	06 22	07 09	07 52	08 03	08 10	08 14	08 18
56	06 20	07 04	07 44	07 50	08 01	08 10	08 16
54	06 17	06 59	07 37	07 40	07 54	08 05	08 15
52	06 15	06 55	07 31	07 30	07 47	08 01	08 13
50	06 13	06 51	07 25	07 21	07 41	07 58	08 12
45	06 08	06 42	07 13	07 03	07 28	07 50	08 10
N 40	06 03	06 35	07 03	06 48	07 17	07 43	08 07
35	05 58	06 28	06 55	06 35	07 08	07 37	08 05
30	05 54	06 22	06 47	06 24	07 00	07 32	08 03
20	05 45	06 11	06 34	06 04	06 45	07 24	08 00
N 10	05 35	06 00	06 22	05 47	06 33	07 16	07 58
0	05 24	05 49	06 11	05 31	06 21	07 09	07 55
S 10	05 12	05 38	05 59	05 16	06 09	07 01	07 53
20	04 57	05 24	05 47	04 58	05 56	06 53	07 50
30	04 37	05 08	05 33	04 39	05 42	06 44	07 47
35	04 25	04 58	05 25	04 27	05 33	06 39	07 45
40	04 10	04 46	05 16	04 14	05 23	06 33	07 43
45	03 52	04 32	05 05	03 58	05 12	06 26	07 41
S 50	03 27	04 14	04 51	03 38	04 58	06 18	07 38
52	03 14	04 06	04 45	03 29	04 51	06 14	07 37
54	03 00	03 56	04 38	03 18	04 44	06 10	07 35
56	02 42	03 45	04 30	03 06	04 36	06 05	07 34
58	02 20	03 32	04 21	02 53	04 27	06 00	07 32
S 60	01 50	03 17	04 11	02 36	04 16	05 54	07 30

Lat.	Sunset	Twilight Civil	Twilight Naut.	Moonset 6	Moonset 7	Moonset 8	Moonset 9
°	h m	h m	h m	h m	h m	h m	h m
N 72	14 43	16 16	17 40	■	15 19	17 55	20 14
N 70	15 13	16 30	17 46	12 31	15 49	18 07	20 14
68	15 35	16 42	17 50	13 45	16 11	18 16	20 15
66	15 52	16 52	17 54	14 22	16 28	18 23	20 15
64	16 06	17 01	17 58	14 47	16 41	18 30	20 15
62	16 18	17 08	18 01	15 07	16 53	18 35	20 16
60	16 28	17 14	18 04	15 24	17 03	18 40	20 16
N 58	16 37	17 20	18 07	15 37	17 11	18 44	20 16
56	16 45	17 25	18 09	15 49	17 18	18 47	20 16
54	16 52	17 30	18 12	15 59	17 25	18 51	20 16
52	16 58	17 34	18 14	16 08	17 31	18 54	20 16
50	17 03	17 38	18 16	16 16	17 36	18 56	20 16
45	17 16	17 46	18 21	16 33	17 48	19 02	20 16
N 40	17 26	17 54	18 26	16 47	17 57	19 07	20 17
35	17 34	18 00	18 30	16 59	18 05	19 11	20 17
30	17 42	18 07	18 35	17 09	18 12	19 14	20 17
20	17 55	18 18	18 44	17 26	18 24	19 21	20 17
N 10	18 07	18 28	18 53	17 41	18 34	19 26	20 17
0	18 18	18 39	19 04	17 55	18 44	19 31	20 17
S 10	18 29	18 51	19 16	18 09	18 53	19 36	20 17
20	18 41	19 04	19 31	18 24	19 04	19 41	20 17
30	18 55	19 20	19 50	18 41	19 15	19 47	20 17
35	19 03	19 30	20 02	18 50	19 22	19 50	20 17
40	19 12	19 41	20 17	19 01	19 29	19 54	20 18
45	19 23	19 55	20 35	19 14	19 38	19 58	20 18
S 50	19 36	20 13	21 00	19 30	19 48	20 03	20 18
52	19 42	20 21	21 12	19 37	19 53	20 06	20 18
54	19 49	20 31	21 26	19 45	19 58	20 08	20 18
56	19 57	20 41	21 43	19 54	20 04	20 11	20 18
58	20 05	20 54	22 04	20 04	20 10	20 14	20 18
S 60	20 15	21 09	22 33	20 16	20 17	20 18	20 18

Day	SUN Eqn. of Time 00^h	SUN Eqn. of Time 12^h	SUN Mer. Pass.	MOON Mer. Pass. Upper	MOON Mer. Pass. Lower	Age	Phase
d	m s	m s	h m	h m	h m	d %	
6	14 01	14 03	12 14	11 43	24 08	29 1	●
7	14 05	14 07	12 14	12 32	00 08	00 0	
8	14 09	14 10	12 14	13 20	00 56	01 2	

UT	ARIES	VENUS −3.9		MARS −0.3		JUPITER −1.9		SATURN +0.3	
	GHA	GHA	Dec	GHA	Dec	GHA	Dec	GHA	Dec
d h	° ′	° ′	° ′	° ′	° ′	° ′	° ′	° ′	° ′
9 00	138 28.3	207 38.9	S21 43.3	54 31.6	N26 33.1	215 53.4	S22 49.4	339 39.4	N10 51.5
01	153 30.8	222 38.1	42.9	69 33.8	33.1	230 55.3	49.4	354 42.0	51.6
02	168 33.3	237 37.2	42.6	84 35.9	33.0	245 57.2	49.3	9 44.7	51.6
03	183 35.7	252 36.4	42.3	99 38.1	33.0	260 59.1	49.3	24 47.3	51.7
04	198 38.2	267 35.6	42.0	114 40.2	33.0	276 01.0	49.2	39 50.0	51.8
05	213 40.7	282 34.7	41.7	129 42.4	32.9	291 02.9	49.2	54 52.6	51.9
06	228 43.1	297 33.9	S21 41.4	144 44.5	N26 32.9	306 04.8	S22 49.2	69 55.2	N10 51.9
07	243 45.6	312 33.0	41.0	159 46.7	32.9	321 06.7	49.1	84 57.9	52.0
S 08	258 48.0	327 32.2	40.7	174 48.8	32.8	336 08.7	49.1	100 00.5	52.1
A 09	273 50.5	342 31.4	40.4	189 51.0	32.8	351 10.6	49.0	115 03.2	52.2
T 10	288 53.0	357 30.5	40.1	204 53.1	32.8	6 12.5	49.0	130 05.8	52.2
U 11	303 55.4	12 29.7	39.8	219 55.3	32.7	21 14.4	48.9	145 08.4	52.3
R 12	318 57.9	27 28.9	S21 39.4	234 57.4	N26 32.7	36 16.3	S22 48.9	160 11.1	N10 52.4
D 13	334 00.4	42 28.0	39.1	249 59.6	32.7	51 18.2	48.9	175 13.7	52.5
A 14	349 02.8	57 27.2	38.8	265 01.7	32.6	66 20.1	48.8	190 16.4	52.5
Y 15	4 05.3	72 26.3	38.4	280 03.9	32.6	81 22.0	48.8	205 19.0	52.6
16	19 07.8	87 25.5	38.1	295 06.0	32.6	96 24.0	48.7	220 21.6	52.7
17	34 10.2	102 24.7	37.8	310 08.1	32.5	111 25.9	48.7	235 24.3	52.8
18	49 12.7	117 23.8	S21 37.5	325 10.3	N26 32.5	126 27.8	S22 48.7	250 26.9	N10 52.8
19	64 15.2	132 23.0	37.1	340 12.4	32.5	141 29.7	48.6	265 29.6	52.9
20	79 17.6	147 22.2	36.8	355 14.6	32.4	156 31.6	48.6	280 32.2	53.0
21	94 20.1	162 21.3	36.5	10 16.7	32.4	171 33.5	48.5	295 34.8	53.1
22	109 22.5	177 20.5	36.1	25 18.8	32.4	186 35.4	48.5	310 37.5	53.1
23	124 25.0	192 19.6	35.8	40 21.0	32.3	201 37.4	48.5	325 40.1	53.2
10 00	139 27.5	207 18.8	S21 35.4	55 23.1	N26 32.3	216 39.3	S22 48.4	340 42.8	N10 53.3
01	154 29.9	222 18.0	35.1	70 25.2	32.3	231 41.2	48.4	355 45.4	53.4
02	169 32.4	237 17.1	34.8	85 27.4	32.2	246 43.1	48.3	10 48.1	53.5
03	184 34.9	252 16.3	34.4	100 29.5	32.2	261 45.0	48.3	25 50.7	53.5
04	199 37.3	267 15.5	34.1	115 31.6	32.1	276 46.9	48.2	40 53.3	53.6
05	214 39.8	282 14.6	33.7	130 33.7	32.1	291 48.8	48.2	55 56.0	53.7
06	229 42.3	297 13.8	S21 33.4	145 35.9	N26 32.1	306 50.8	S22 48.2	70 58.6	N10 53.8
07	244 44.7	312 13.0	33.0	160 38.0	32.0	321 52.7	48.1	86 01.3	53.8
08	259 47.2	327 12.1	32.7	175 40.1	32.0	336 54.6	48.1	101 03.9	53.9
S 09	274 49.7	342 11.3	32.3	190 42.2	32.0	351 56.5	48.0	116 06.5	54.0
U 10	289 52.1	357 10.5	32.0	205 44.3	31.9	6 58.4	48.0	131 09.2	54.1
N 11	304 54.6	12 09.6	31.6	220 46.4	31.9	22 00.3	48.0	146 11.8	54.1
D 12	319 57.0	27 08.8	S21 31.3	235 48.6	N26 31.9	37 02.2	S22 47.9	161 14.5	N10 54.2
A 13	334 59.5	42 08.0	30.9	250 50.7	31.8	52 04.2	47.9	176 17.1	54.3
Y 14	350 02.0	57 07.1	30.6	265 52.8	31.8	67 06.1	47.8	191 19.8	54.4
15	5 04.4	72 06.3	30.2	280 54.9	31.8	82 08.0	47.8	206 22.4	54.4
16	20 06.9	87 05.5	29.9	295 57.0	31.7	97 09.9	47.8	221 25.0	54.5
17	35 09.4	102 04.6	29.5	310 59.1	31.7	112 11.8	47.7	236 27.7	54.6
18	50 11.8	117 03.8	S21 29.1	326 01.2	N26 31.7	127 13.7	S22 47.7	251 30.3	N10 54.7
19	65 14.3	132 03.0	28.8	341 03.3	31.6	142 15.7	47.6	266 33.0	54.7
20	80 16.8	147 02.1	28.4	356 05.4	31.6	157 17.6	47.6	281 35.6	54.8
21	95 19.2	162 01.3	28.1	11 07.6	31.6	172 19.5	47.5	296 38.3	54.9
22	110 21.7	177 00.5	27.7	26 09.7	31.5	187 21.4	47.5	311 40.9	55.0
23	125 24.1	191 59.7	27.3	41 11.8	31.5	202 23.3	47.5	326 43.5	55.0
11 00	140 26.6	206 58.8	S21 27.0	56 13.9	N26 31.5	217 25.2	S22 47.4	341 46.2	N10 55.1
01	155 29.1	221 58.0	26.6	71 16.0	31.4	232 27.2	47.4	356 48.8	55.2
02	170 31.5	236 57.2	26.2	86 18.1	31.4	247 29.1	47.3	11 51.5	55.3
03	185 34.0	251 56.3	25.9	101 20.2	31.4	262 31.0	47.3	26 54.1	55.4
04	200 36.5	266 55.5	25.5	116 22.2	31.3	277 32.9	47.2	41 56.8	55.4
05	215 38.9	281 54.7	25.1	131 24.3	31.3	292 34.8	47.2	56 59.4	55.5
06	230 41.4	296 53.9	S21 24.8	146 26.4	N26 31.3	307 36.8	S22 47.2	72 02.0	N10 55.6
07	245 43.9	311 53.0	24.4	161 28.5	31.2	322 38.7	47.1	87 04.7	55.7
08	260 46.3	326 52.2	24.0	176 30.6	31.2	337 40.6	47.1	102 07.3	55.7
M 09	275 48.8	341 51.4	23.6	191 32.7	31.2	352 42.5	47.0	117 10.0	55.8
O 10	290 51.3	356 50.5	23.3	206 34.8	31.1	7 44.4	47.0	132 12.6	55.9
N 11	305 53.7	11 49.7	22.9	221 36.9	31.1	22 46.3	47.0	147 15.3	56.0
D 12	320 56.2	26 48.9	S21 22.5	236 39.0	N26 31.1	37 48.3	S22 46.9	162 17.9	N10 56.0
A 13	335 58.6	41 48.1	22.1	251 41.1	31.0	52 50.2	46.9	177 20.5	56.1
Y 14	351 01.1	56 47.2	21.7	266 43.1	31.0	67 52.1	46.8	192 23.2	56.2
15	6 03.6	71 46.4	21.4	281 45.2	31.0	82 54.0	46.8	207 25.8	56.3
16	21 06.0	86 45.6	21.0	296 47.3	30.9	97 55.9	46.7	222 28.5	56.3
17	36 08.5	101 44.8	20.6	311 49.4	30.9	112 57.9	46.7	237 31.1	56.4
18	51 11.0	116 43.9	S21 20.2	326 51.5	N26 30.9	127 59.8	S22 46.7	252 33.8	N10 56.5
19	66 13.4	131 43.1	19.8	341 53.5	30.8	143 01.7	46.6	267 36.4	56.6
20	81 15.9	146 42.3	19.4	356 55.6	30.8	158 03.6	46.6	282 39.1	56.7
21	96 18.4	161 41.5	19.0	11 57.7	30.8	173 05.5	46.5	297 41.7	56.7
22	111 20.8	176 40.6	18.7	26 59.8	30.7	188 07.5	46.5	312 44.3	56.8
23	126 23.3	191 39.8	18.3	42 01.8	30.7	203 09.4	46.5	327 47.0	56.9
Mer. Pass. (h m)	14 39.8	v −0.8	d 0.4	v 2.1	d 0.0	v 1.9	d 0.0	v 2.6	d 0.1

STARS

Name	SHA	Dec
	° ′	° ′
Acamar	315 21.3	S40 16.5
Achernar	335 29.7	S57 11.9
Acrux	173 13.7	S63 08.6
Adhara	255 15.4	S28 59.1
Aldebaran	290 53.9	N16 31.6
Alioth	166 23.6	N55 54.6
Alkaid	153 01.7	N49 16.0
Al Na'ir	27 49.0	S46 55.4
Alnilam	275 50.3	S 1 11.8
Alphard	217 59.7	S 8 41.7
Alphecca	126 14.4	N26 40.9
Alpheratz	357 48.1	N29 08.2
Altair	62 12.5	N 8 53.2
Ankaa	353 19.8	S42 15.9
Antares	112 31.4	S26 27.1
Arcturus	145 59.3	N19 08.1
Atria	107 37.2	S69 02.4
Avior	234 19.2	S59 32.2
Bellatrix	278 36.2	N 6 21.5
Betelgeuse	271 05.5	N 7 24.5
Canopus	263 57.6	S52 42.1
Capella	280 40.2	N46 00.6
Deneb	49 34.8	N45 18.4
Denebola	182 37.5	N14 31.4
Diphda	349 00.1	S17 56.6
Dubhe	193 55.6	N61 42.2
Elnath	278 17.5	N28 37.0
Eltanin	90 48.4	N51 28.9
Enif	33 51.4	N 9 54.6
Fomalhaut	15 28.6	S29 34.9
Gacrux	172 05.3	S57 09.4
Gienah	175 56.3	S17 35.3
Hadar	148 53.8	S60 24.6
Hamal	328 05.5	N23 30.2
Kaus Aust.	83 49.4	S34 22.9
Kochab	137 19.2	N74 06.9
Markab	13 42.7	N15 14.9
Menkar	314 19.3	N 4 07.3
Menkent	148 12.4	S36 24.6
Miaplacidus	221 40.0	S69 45.0
Mirfak	308 46.3	N49 53.7
Nunki	76 03.6	S26 17.3
Peacock	53 26.0	S56 42.6
Pollux	243 32.3	N28 00.4
Procyon	245 03.6	N 5 12.2
Rasalhague	96 10.4	N12 33.0
Regulus	207 47.4	N11 55.5
Rigel	281 15.8	S 8 11.6
Rigil Kent.	139 57.4	S60 52.0
Sabik	102 17.3	S15 44.2
Schedar	349 45.8	N56 35.2
Shaula	96 27.6	S37 06.6
Sirius	258 37.0	S16 43.7
Spica	158 35.4	S11 12.4
Suhail	222 55.1	S43 28.0
Vega	80 42.0	N38 47.2
Zuben'ubi	137 09.9	S16 04.7

	SHA	Mer. Pass.
	° ′	h m
Venus	67 51.3	10 11
Mars	275 55.6	20 16
Jupiter	77 11.8	9 32
Saturn	201 15.3	1 17

UT d h	SUN GHA ° ′	SUN Dec ° ′	MOON GHA ° ′	v ′	MOON Dec ° ′	d ′	HP ′
9 00 (SATURDAY)	176 27.1	S14 56.4	155 03.1	12.9	S 5 35.0	15.9	58.2
01	191 27.1	55.6	169 35.0	12.9	5 19.1	15.9	58.2
02	206 27.0	54.8	184 06.9	12.9	5 03.2	16.0	58.2
03	221 27.0	. . 54.0	198 38.8	12.9	4 47.2	16.0	58.2
04	236 27.0	53.2	213 10.7	12.9	4 31.2	16.0	58.2
05	251 27.0	52.4	227 42.6	12.9	4 15.2	16.0	58.3
06	266 26.9	S14 51.6	242 14.5	12.9	S 3 59.2	16.1	58.3
07	281 26.9	50.8	256 46.4	12.9	3 43.1	16.1	58.3
08	296 26.9	50.0	271 18.3	12.9	3 27.0	16.1	58.3
09	311 26.9	. . 49.2	285 50.2	12.9	3 10.9	16.1	58.3
10	326 26.9	48.4	300 22.1	13.0	2 54.8	16.2	58.3
11	341 26.8	47.6	314 54.1	12.9	2 38.6	16.2	58.4
12	356 26.8	S14 46.8	329 26.0	12.9	S 2 22.4	16.2	58.4
13	11 26.8	46.0	343 57.9	12.9	2 06.2	16.2	58.4
14	26 26.8	45.2	358 29.8	12.9	1 50.0	16.2	58.4
15	41 26.8	. . 44.4	13 01.7	12.9	1 33.8	16.3	58.4
16	56 26.7	43.6	27 33.6	12.8	1 17.5	16.3	58.4
17	71 26.7	42.8	42 05.4	12.9	1 01.2	16.2	58.5
18	86 26.7	S14 42.0	56 37.3	12.9	S 0 45.0	16.3	58.5
19	101 26.7	41.2	71 09.2	12.8	0 28.7	16.3	58.5
20	116 26.7	40.4	85 41.0	12.9	S 0 12.4	16.3	58.5
21	131 26.6	. . 39.6	100 12.9	12.8	N 0 03.9	16.4	58.5
22	146 26.6	38.8	114 44.7	12.8	0 20.3	16.3	58.5
23	161 26.6	38.0	129 16.5	12.8	0 36.6	16.3	58.5
10 00 (SUNDAY)	176 26.6	S14 37.2	143 48.3	12.8	N 0 52.9	16.3	58.6
01	191 26.6	36.4	158 20.1	12.7	1 09.2	16.4	58.6
02	206 26.6	35.6	172 51.8	12.8	1 25.6	16.3	58.6
03	221 26.5	. . 34.8	187 23.6	12.7	1 41.9	16.3	58.6
04	236 26.5	34.0	201 55.3	12.7	1 58.2	16.4	58.6
05	251 26.5	33.1	216 27.0	12.7	2 14.6	16.3	58.6
06	266 26.5	S14 32.3	230 58.7	12.6	N 2 30.9	16.3	58.6
07	281 26.5	31.5	245 30.3	12.6	2 47.2	16.3	58.7
08	296 26.5	30.7	260 01.9	12.6	3 03.5	16.3	58.7
09	311 26.5	. . 29.9	274 33.5	12.6	3 19.8	16.3	58.7
10	326 26.4	29.1	289 05.1	12.5	3 36.1	16.3	58.7
11	341 26.4	28.3	303 36.6	12.5	3 52.4	16.2	58.7
12	356 26.4	S14 27.5	318 08.1	12.5	N 4 08.6	16.3	58.7
13	11 26.4	26.7	332 39.6	12.4	4 24.9	16.2	58.7
14	26 26.4	25.9	347 11.0	12.5	4 41.1	16.2	58.8
15	41 26.4	. . 25.1	1 42.5	12.3	4 57.3	16.2	58.8
16	56 26.4	24.2	16 13.8	12.4	5 13.5	16.2	58.8
17	71 26.4	23.4	30 45.2	12.3	5 29.7	16.2	58.8
18	86 26.4	S14 22.6	45 16.5	12.2	N 5 45.9	16.1	58.8
19	101 26.3	21.8	59 47.7	12.2	6 02.0	16.1	58.8
20	116 26.3	21.0	74 18.9	12.2	6 18.1	16.1	58.8
21	131 26.3	. . 20.2	88 50.1	12.1	6 34.2	16.0	58.8
22	146 26.3	19.4	103 21.2	12.1	6 50.2	16.1	58.8
23	161 26.3	18.6	117 52.3	12.1	7 06.3	16.0	58.9
11 00 (MONDAY)	176 26.3	S14 17.7	132 23.4	11.9	N 7 22.3	15.9	58.9
01	191 26.3	16.9	146 54.3	12.0	7 38.2	16.0	58.9
02	206 26.3	16.1	161 25.3	11.9	7 54.2	15.9	58.9
03	221 26.3	. . 15.3	175 56.2	11.8	8 10.1	15.8	58.9
04	236 26.3	14.5	190 27.0	11.8	8 25.9	15.8	58.9
05	251 26.3	13.7	204 57.8	11.8	8 41.7	15.8	58.9
06	266 26.3	S14 12.8	219 28.6	11.7	N 8 57.5	15.7	58.9
07	281 26.2	12.0	233 59.3	11.6	9 13.2	15.7	58.9
08	296 26.2	11.2	248 29.9	11.6	9 28.9	15.7	58.9
09	311 26.2	. . 10.4	263 00.5	11.5	9 44.6	15.6	59.0
10	326 26.2	09.6	277 31.0	11.5	10 00.2	15.6	59.0
11	341 26.2	08.8	292 01.5	11.4	10 15.8	15.5	59.0
12	356 26.2	S14 07.9	306 31.9	11.3	N10 31.3	15.4	59.0
13	11 26.2	07.1	321 02.2	11.3	10 46.7	15.4	59.0
14	26 26.2	06.3	335 32.5	11.2	11 02.1	15.4	59.0
15	41 26.2	. . 05.5	350 02.7	11.2	11 17.5	15.3	59.0
16	56 26.2	04.7	4 32.9	11.1	11 32.8	15.2	59.0
17	71 26.2	03.8	19 03.0	11.0	11 48.0	15.2	59.0
18	86 26.2	S14 03.0	33 33.0	10.9	N12 03.2	15.1	59.0
19	101 26.2	02.2	48 02.9	10.9	12 18.3	15.1	59.0
20	116 26.2	01.4	62 32.8	10.8	12 33.4	15.0	59.0
21	131 26.2	14 00.5	77 02.6	10.8	12 48.4	14.9	59.0
22	146 26.2	13 59.7	91 32.4	10.7	13 03.3	14.9	59.1
23	161 26.2	S13 58.9	106 02.1	10.6	N13 18.2	14.8	59.1
	SD 16.2	*d* 0.8	SD		15.9	16.0	16.1

Lat. °	Twilight Naut. h m	Twilight Civil h m	Sunrise h m	Moonrise 9 h m	Moonrise 10 h m	Moonrise 11 h m	Moonrise 12 h m
N 72	06 38	08 00	09 28	08 38	08 04	07 26	06 30
N 70	06 34	07 47	09 01	08 34	08 08	07 39	07 01
68	06 30	07 37	08 42	08 30	08 11	07 50	07 24
66	06 27	07 28	08 26	08 27	08 14	07 59	07 43
64	06 24	07 20	08 13	08 24	08 16	08 07	07 58
62	06 21	07 14	08 02	08 22	08 18	08 14	08 10
60	06 19	07 08	07 53	08 20	08 20	08 20	08 21
N 58	06 16	07 03	07 45	08 18	08 21	08 25	08 30
56	06 14	06 58	07 38	08 16	08 23	08 30	08 39
54	06 12	06 54	07 32	08 15	08 24	08 34	08 46
52	06 10	06 50	07 26	08 13	08 25	08 38	08 53
50	06 08	06 47	07 21	08 12	08 26	08 41	08 59
45	06 04	06 39	07 09	08 10	08 29	08 49	09 12
N 40	06 00	06 32	07 00	08 07	08 31	08 56	09 23
35	05 56	06 26	06 52	08 05	08 33	09 01	09 32
30	05 52	06 20	06 45	08 03	08 34	09 06	09 41
20	05 43	06 10	06 32	08 00	08 37	09 15	09 55
N 10	05 35	06 00	06 21	07 58	08 39	09 22	10 08
0	05 25	05 49	06 11	07 55	08 42	09 30	10 20
S 10	05 13	05 38	06 00	07 53	08 44	09 37	10 32
20	04 59	05 26	05 49	07 50	08 47	09 45	10 45
30	04 40	05 10	05 36	07 47	08 50	09 54	11 00
35	04 29	05 01	05 28	07 45	08 51	09 59	11 09
40	04 15	04 50	05 19	07 43	08 53	10 05	11 19
45	03 57	04 37	05 09	07 41	08 56	10 12	11 31
S 50	03 34	04 20	04 56	07 38	08 58	10 21	11 45
52	03 22	04 12	04 51	07 37	09 00	10 25	11 52
54	03 09	04 03	04 44	07 35	09 01	10 29	11 59
56	02 53	03 53	04 37	07 34	09 03	10 34	12 08
58	02 33	03 41	04 29	07 32	09 05	10 39	12 18
S 60	02 07	03 27	04 19	07 30	09 06	10 45	12 29

Lat. °	Sunset h m	Twilight Civil h m	Twilight Naut. h m	Moonset 9 h m	Moonset 10 h m	Moonset 11 h m	Moonset 12 h m
N 72	15 02	16 30	17 53	20 14	22 34	25 15	01 15
N 70	15 28	16 43	17 57	20 14	22 24	24 46	00 46
68	15 48	16 53	18 00	20 15	22 15	24 24	00 24
66	16 04	17 02	18 03	20 15	22 08	24 08	00 08
64	16 16	17 09	18 06	20 15	22 02	23 54	25 56
62	16 27	17 16	18 09	20 16	21 57	23 43	25 36
60	16 36	17 21	18 11	20 16	21 53	23 33	25 19
N 58	16 44	17 27	18 13	20 16	21 49	23 25	25 05
56	16 51	17 31	18 15	20 16	21 46	23 18	24 53
54	16 58	17 35	18 17	20 16	21 43	23 11	24 43
52	17 03	17 39	18 19	20 16	21 40	23 06	24 34
50	17 09	17 43	18 21	20 16	21 37	23 00	24 26
45	17 20	17 50	18 25	20 16	21 32	22 49	24 08
N 40	17 29	17 57	18 29	20 17	21 27	22 40	23 54
35	17 37	18 03	18 33	20 17	21 23	22 32	23 42
30	17 44	18 09	18 37	20 17	21 20	22 25	23 32
20	17 57	18 19	18 45	20 17	21 14	22 13	23 14
N 10	18 07	18 29	18 54	20 17	21 09	22 03	22 59
0	18 18	18 39	19 04	20 17	21 04	21 53	22 45
S 10	18 28	18 50	19 15	20 17	20 59	21 43	22 31
20	18 39	19 02	19 29	20 17	20 54	21 33	22 15
30	18 52	19 17	19 47	20 17	20 48	21 21	21 58
35	19 00	19 27	19 59	20 17	20 45	21 15	21 48
40	19 08	19 38	20 13	20 18	20 41	21 07	21 37
45	19 19	19 51	20 30	20 18	20 37	20 58	21 23
S 50	19 31	20 07	20 53	20 18	20 32	20 48	21 07
52	19 37	20 15	21 04	20 18	20 30	20 43	21 00
54	19 43	20 24	21 17	20 18	20 27	20 38	20 51
56	19 50	20 34	21 33	20 18	20 24	20 32	20 42
58	19 58	20 45	21 52	20 18	20 21	20 25	20 31
S 60	20 07	20 59	22 17	20 18	20 17	20 18	20 19

Day	SUN Eqn. of Time 00^h	SUN Eqn. of Time 12^h	SUN Mer. Pass.	MOON Mer. Pass. Upper	MOON Mer. Pass. Lower	MOON Age	MOON Phase
d	m s	m s	h m	h m	h m	d	%
9	14 12	14 13	12 14	14 06	01 43	02	6
10	14 14	14 14	12 14	14 53	02 29	03	13
11	14 15	14 15	12 14	15 41	03 17	04	22

Day	UT (d h)	ARIES GHA	VENUS −3.9 GHA	VENUS Dec	MARS −0.2 GHA	MARS Dec	JUPITER −1.9 GHA	JUPITER Dec	SATURN +0.3 GHA	SATURN Dec	STARS Name	SHA	Dec
		° ′	° ′	° ′	° ′	° ′	° ′	° ′	° ′	° ′		° ′	° ′
TUESDAY	12 00	141 25.7	206 39.0	S21 17.9	57 03.9	N26 30.7	218 11.3	S22 46.4	342 49.6	N10 57.0	Acamar	315 21.3	S40 16.5
	01	156 28.2	221 38.2	17.5	72 06.0	30.6	233 13.2	46.4	357 52.3	57.0	Achernar	335 29.7	S57 11.9
	02	171 30.7	236 37.3	17.1	87 08.1	30.6	248 15.1	46.3	12 54.9	57.1	Acrux	173 13.7	S63 08.6
	03	186 33.1	251 36.5	. . 16.7	102 10.1	. . 30.6	263 17.1	. . 46.3	27 57.6	. . 57.2	Adhara	255 15.4	S28 59.1
	04	201 35.6	266 35.7	16.3	117 12.2	30.5	278 19.0	46.2	43 00.2	57.3	Aldebaran	290 53.9	N16 31.6
	05	216 38.1	281 34.9	15.9	132 14.3	30.5	293 20.9	46.2	58 02.9	57.3			
	06	231 40.5	296 34.1	S21 15.5	147 16.3	N26 30.5	308 22.8	S22 46.2	73 05.5	N10 57.4	Alioth	166 23.6	N55 54.6
	07	246 43.0	311 33.2	15.1	162 18.4	30.4	323 24.8	46.1	88 08.1	57.5	Alkaid	153 01.6	N49 16.0
	08	261 45.5	326 32.4	14.7	177 20.4	30.4	338 26.7	46.1	103 10.8	57.6	Al Na'ir	27 49.0	S46 55.4
	09	276 47.9	341 31.6	. . 14.3	192 22.5	. . 30.4	353 28.6	. . 46.0	118 13.4	. . 57.6	Alnilam	275 50.3	S 1 11.8
	10	291 50.4	356 30.8	13.9	207 24.6	30.3	8 30.5	46.0	133 16.1	57.7	Alphard	217 59.7	S 8 41.7
	11	306 52.9	11 30.0	13.5	222 26.6	30.3	23 32.4	45.9	148 18.7	57.8			
	12	321 55.3	26 29.1	S21 13.1	237 28.7	N26 30.3	38 34.4	S22 45.9	163 21.4	N10 57.9	Alphecca	126 14.4	N26 40.9
	13	336 57.8	41 28.3	12.7	252 30.7	30.2	53 36.3	45.9	178 24.0	58.0	Alpheratz	357 48.1	N29 08.2
	14	352 00.2	56 27.5	12.3	267 32.8	30.2	68 38.2	45.8	193 26.7	58.0	Altair	62 12.5	N 8 53.2
	15	7 02.7	71 26.7	. . 11.9	282 34.8	. . 30.2	83 40.1	. . 45.8	208 29.3	. . 58.1	Ankaa	353 19.8	S42 15.9
	16	22 05.2	86 25.9	11.4	297 36.9	30.1	98 42.1	45.7	223 32.0	58.2	Antares	112 31.3	S26 27.1
	17	37 07.6	101 25.0	11.0	312 38.9	30.1	113 44.0	45.7	238 34.6	58.3			
	18	52 10.1	116 24.2	S21 10.6	327 41.0	N26 30.1	128 45.9	S22 45.6	253 37.2	N10 58.3	Arcturus	145 59.2	N19 08.1
	19	67 12.6	131 23.4	10.2	342 43.0	30.0	143 47.8	45.6	268 39.9	58.4	Atria	107 37.2	S69 02.4
	20	82 15.0	146 22.6	09.8	357 45.1	30.0	158 49.7	45.6	283 42.5	58.5	Avior	234 19.2	S59 32.2
	21	97 17.5	161 21.8	. . 09.4	12 47.1	. . 30.0	173 51.7	. . 45.5	298 45.2	. . 58.6	Bellatrix	278 36.2	N 6 21.5
	22	112 20.0	176 21.0	09.0	27 49.2	29.9	188 53.6	45.5	313 47.8	58.6	Betelgeuse	271 05.5	N 7 24.5
	23	127 22.4	191 20.1	08.5	42 51.2	29.9	203 55.5	45.4	328 50.5	58.7			
WEDNESDAY	13 00	142 24.9	206 19.3	S21 08.1	57 53.3	N26 29.9	218 57.4	S22 45.4	343 53.1	N10 58.8	Canopus	263 57.6	S52 42.1
	01	157 27.4	221 18.5	07.7	72 55.3	29.8	233 59.4	45.3	358 55.8	58.9	Capella	280 40.2	N46 00.6
	02	172 29.8	236 17.7	07.3	87 57.3	29.8	249 01.3	45.3	13 58.4	59.0	Deneb	49 34.8	N45 18.4
	03	187 32.3	251 16.9	. . 06.9	102 59.4	. . 29.8	264 03.2	. . 45.3	29 01.1	. . 59.0	Denebola	182 37.4	N14 31.4
	04	202 34.7	266 16.1	06.4	118 01.4	29.7	279 05.1	45.2	44 03.7	59.1	Diphda	349 00.1	S17 56.6
	05	217 37.2	281 15.2	06.0	133 03.5	29.7	294 07.1	45.2	59 06.3	59.2			
	06	232 39.7	296 14.4	S21 05.6	148 05.5	N26 29.7	309 09.0	S22 45.1	74 09.0	N10 59.3	Dubhe	193 55.6	N61 42.2
	07	247 42.1	311 13.6	05.2	163 07.5	29.6	324 10.9	45.1	89 11.6	59.3	Elnath	278 17.5	N28 37.0
	08	262 44.6	326 12.8	04.7	178 09.6	29.6	339 12.8	45.0	104 14.3	59.4	Eltanin	90 48.3	N51 28.9
	09	277 47.1	341 12.0	. . 04.3	193 11.6	. . 29.6	354 14.8	. . 45.0	119 16.9	. . 59.5	Enif	33 51.4	N 9 54.6
	10	292 49.5	356 11.2	03.9	208 13.6	29.5	9 16.7	45.0	134 19.6	59.6	Fomalhaut	15 28.6	S29 34.9
	11	307 52.0	11 10.4	03.5	223 15.7	29.5	24 18.6	44.9	149 22.2	59.6			
	12	322 54.5	26 09.6	S21 03.0	238 17.7	N26 29.5	39 20.5	S22 44.9	164 24.9	N10 59.7	Gacrux	172 05.3	S57 09.5
	13	337 56.9	41 08.7	02.6	253 19.7	29.4	54 22.5	44.8	179 27.5	59.8	Gienah	175 56.3	S17 35.3
	14	352 59.4	56 07.9	02.2	268 21.7	29.4	69 24.4	44.8	194 30.2	10 59.9	Hadar	148 53.7	S60 24.6
	15	8 01.8	71 07.1	. . 01.7	283 23.8	. . 29.4	84 26.3	. . 44.7	209 32.8	11 00.0	Hamal	328 05.5	N23 30.2
	16	23 04.3	86 06.3	01.3	298 25.8	29.3	99 28.2	44.7	224 35.5	00.0	Kaus Aust.	83 49.4	S34 22.9
	17	38 06.8	101 05.5	00.9	313 27.8	29.3	114 30.2	44.7	239 38.1	00.1			
	18	53 09.2	116 04.7	S21 00.4	328 29.8	N26 29.3	129 32.1	S22 44.6	254 40.7	N11 00.2	Kochab	137 19.1	N74 06.9
	19	68 11.7	131 03.9	21 00.0	343 31.9	29.2	144 34.0	44.6	269 43.4	00.3	Markab	13 42.7	N15 14.9
	20	83 14.2	146 03.1	20 59.5	358 33.9	29.2	159 35.9	44.5	284 46.0	00.3	Menkar	314 19.3	N 4 07.3
	21	98 16.6	161 02.3	. . 59.1	13 35.9	. . 29.2	174 37.9	. . 44.5	299 48.7	. . 00.4	Menkent	148 12.3	S36 24.6
	22	113 19.1	176 01.4	58.7	28 37.9	29.1	189 39.8	44.4	314 51.3	00.5	Miaplacidus	221 40.0	S69 45.1
	23	128 21.6	191 00.6	58.2	43 39.9	29.1	204 41.7	44.4	329 54.0	00.6			
THURSDAY	14 00	143 24.0	205 59.8	S20 57.8	58 41.9	N26 29.1	219 43.7	S22 44.4	344 56.6	N11 00.6	Mirfak	308 46.3	N49 53.7
	01	158 26.5	220 59.0	57.3	73 44.0	29.0	234 45.6	44.3	359 59.3	00.7	Nunki	76 03.6	S26 17.3
	02	173 29.0	235 58.2	56.9	88 46.0	29.0	249 47.5	44.3	15 01.9	00.8	Peacock	53 25.9	S56 42.6
	03	188 31.4	250 57.4	. . 56.4	103 48.0	. . 29.0	264 49.4	. . 44.2	30 04.6	. . 00.9	Pollux	243 32.3	N28 00.4
	04	203 33.9	265 56.6	56.0	118 50.0	28.9	279 51.4	44.2	45 07.2	01.0	Procyon	245 03.6	N 5 12.2
	05	218 36.3	280 55.8	55.5	133 52.0	28.9	294 53.3	44.1	60 09.9	01.0			
	06	233 38.8	295 55.0	S20 55.1	148 54.0	N26 28.9	309 55.2	S22 44.1	75 12.5	N11 01.1	Rasalhague	96 10.4	N12 33.0
	07	248 41.3	310 54.2	54.6	163 56.0	28.8	324 57.2	44.1	90 15.2	01.2	Regulus	207 47.4	N11 55.5
	08	263 43.7	325 53.4	54.2	178 58.0	28.8	339 59.1	44.0	105 17.8	01.3	Rigel	281 15.8	S 8 11.6
	09	278 46.2	340 52.6	. . 53.7	194 00.0	. . 28.8	355 01.0	. . 44.0	120 20.5	. . 01.3	Rigil Kent.	139 57.4	S60 52.0
	10	293 48.7	355 51.8	53.3	209 02.0	28.7	10 02.9	43.9	135 23.1	01.4	Sabik	102 17.3	S15 44.2
	11	308 51.1	10 51.0	52.8	224 04.0	28.7	25 04.9	43.9	150 25.8	01.5			
	12	323 53.6	25 50.1	S20 52.4	239 06.0	N26 28.7	40 06.8	S22 43.8	165 28.4	N11 01.6	Schedar	349 45.8	N56 35.1
	13	338 56.1	40 49.3	51.9	254 08.0	28.6	55 08.7	43.8	180 31.0	01.6	Shaula	96 27.6	S37 06.6
	14	353 58.5	55 48.5	51.4	269 10.0	28.6	70 10.7	43.8	195 33.7	01.7	Sirius	258 37.0	S16 43.7
	15	9 01.0	70 47.7	. . 51.0	284 12.0	. . 28.6	85 12.6	. . 43.7	210 36.3	. . 01.8	Spica	158 35.4	S11 12.4
	16	24 03.5	85 46.9	50.5	299 14.0	28.5	100 14.5	43.7	225 39.0	01.9	Suhail	222 55.1	S43 28.0
	17	39 05.9	100 46.1	50.1	314 16.0	28.5	115 16.4	43.6	240 41.6	02.0			
	18	54 08.4	115 45.3	S20 49.6	329 18.0	N26 28.5	130 18.4	S22 43.6	255 44.3	N11 02.0	Vega	80 42.0	N38 47.2
	19	69 10.8	130 44.5	49.1	344 20.0	28.5	145 20.3	43.5	270 46.9	02.1	Zuben'ubi	137 09.9	S16 04.7
	20	84 13.3	145 43.7	48.7	359 22.0	28.4	160 22.2	43.5	285 49.6	02.2			
	21	99 15.8	160 42.9	. . 48.2	14 24.0	. . 28.4	175 24.2	. . 43.5	300 52.2	. . 02.3			
	22	114 18.2	175 42.1	47.7	29 26.0	28.4	190 26.1	43.4	315 54.9	02.3			
	23	129 20.7	190 41.3	47.3	44 28.0	28.3	205 28.0	43.4	330 57.5	02.4			
	Mer. Pass.	h m 14 28.0	v −0.8	d 0.4	v 2.0	d 0.0	v 1.9	d 0.0	v 2.6	d 0.1			

	SHA	Mer. Pass.
	° ′	h m
Venus	63 54.4	10 15
Mars	275 28.4	20 06
Jupiter	76 32.6	9 23
Saturn	201 28.2	1 04

UT		SUN GHA	SUN Dec	MOON GHA	v	MOON Dec	d	HP
d h		° ′	° ′	° ′	′	° ′	′	′
12 00		176 26.2	S13 58.1	120 31.7	10.5	N13 33.0	14.7	59.1
01		191 26.2	57.3	135 01.2	10.5	13 47.7	14.7	59.1
02		206 26.2	56.4	149 30.7	10.3	14 02.4	14.6	59.1
03		221 26.2	. . 55.6	164 00.0	10.4	14 17.0	14.5	59.1
04		236 26.2	54.8	178 29.4	10.2	14 31.5	14.4	59.1
05		251 26.2	54.0	192 58.6	10.1	14 45.9	14.4	59.1
06		266 26.2	S13 53.1	207 27.7	10.1	N15 00.3	14.3	59.1
07		281 26.2	52.3	221 56.8	10.0	15 14.6	14.2	59.1
08	T	296 26.2	51.5	236 25.8	9.9	15 28.8	14.1	59.1
09	U	311 26.2	. . 50.6	250 54.7	9.8	15 42.9	14.0	59.1
10	E	326 26.2	49.8	265 23.5	9.8	15 56.9	14.0	59.1
11	S	341 26.2	49.0	279 52.3	9.6	16 10.9	13.9	59.1
12	D	356 26.2	S13 48.2	294 20.9	9.6	N16 24.8	13.7	59.1
13	A	11 26.2	47.3	308 49.5	9.5	16 38.5	13.7	59.1
14	Y	26 26.2	46.5	323 18.0	9.4	16 52.2	13.6	59.1
15		41 26.2	. . 45.7	337 46.4	9.3	17 05.8	13.5	59.2
16		56 26.2	44.8	352 14.7	9.3	17 19.3	13.4	59.2
17		71 26.2	44.0	6 43.0	9.1	17 32.7	13.3	59.2
18		86 26.2	S13 43.2	21 11.1	9.1	N17 46.0	13.2	59.2
19		101 26.3	42.3	35 39.2	9.0	17 59.2	13.1	59.2
20		116 26.3	41.5	50 07.2	8.8	18 12.3	13.0	59.2
21		131 26.3	. . 40.7	64 35.0	8.8	18 25.3	12.9	59.2
22		146 26.3	39.8	79 02.8	8.7	18 38.2	12.8	59.2
23		161 26.3	39.0	93 30.5	8.7	18 51.0	12.7	59.2
13 00		176 26.3	S13 38.2	107 58.2	8.5	N19 03.7	12.6	59.2
01		191 26.3	37.3	122 25.7	8.4	19 16.3	12.5	59.2
02		206 26.3	36.5	136 53.1	8.3	19 28.8	12.3	59.2
03		221 26.3	. . 35.7	151 20.4	8.3	19 41.1	12.3	59.2
04		236 26.3	34.8	165 47.7	8.1	19 53.4	12.1	59.2
05		251 26.3	34.0	180 14.8	8.1	20 05.5	12.0	59.2
06		266 26.3	S13 33.2	194 41.9	8.0	N20 17.5	11.9	59.2
07	W	281 26.4	32.3	209 08.9	7.8	20 29.4	11.8	59.2
08	E	296 26.4	31.5	223 35.7	7.8	20 41.2	11.7	59.2
09	D	311 26.4	. . 30.7	238 02.5	7.7	20 52.9	11.5	59.2
10	N	326 26.4	29.8	252 29.2	7.6	21 04.4	11.4	59.2
11	E	341 26.4	29.0	266 55.8	7.5	21 15.8	11.3	59.2
12	S	356 26.4	S13 28.1	281 22.3	7.4	N21 27.1	11.1	59.2
13	D	11 26.4	27.3	295 48.7	7.3	21 38.2	11.1	59.2
14	A	26 26.4	26.5	310 15.0	7.2	21 49.3	10.9	59.2
15	Y	41 26.4	. . 25.6	324 41.2	7.2	22 00.2	10.7	59.2
16		56 26.5	24.8	339 07.4	7.0	22 10.9	10.6	59.2
17		71 26.5	24.0	353 33.4	6.9	22 21.5	10.5	59.2
18		86 26.5	S13 23.1	7 59.3	6.9	N22 32.0	10.4	59.2
19		101 26.5	22.3	22 25.2	6.7	22 42.4	10.2	59.2
20		116 26.5	21.4	36 50.9	6.7	22 52.6	10.1	59.2
21		131 26.5	. . 20.6	51 16.6	6.6	23 02.7	9.9	59.2
22		146 26.5	19.7	65 42.2	6.5	23 12.6	9.8	59.2
23		161 26.6	18.9	80 07.7	6.3	23 22.4	9.6	59.2
14 00		176 26.6	S13 18.1	94 33.0	6.3	N23 32.0	9.5	59.2
01		191 26.6	17.2	108 58.3	6.3	23 41.5	9.4	59.2
02		206 26.6	16.4	123 23.6	6.1	23 50.9	9.2	59.2
03		221 26.6	. . 15.5	137 48.7	6.0	24 00.1	9.0	59.2
04		236 26.6	14.7	152 13.7	6.0	24 09.1	8.9	59.2
05		251 26.7	13.8	166 38.7	5.8	24 18.0	8.7	59.2
06		266 26.7	S13 13.0	181 03.5	5.8	N24 26.7	8.6	59.2
07	T	281 26.7	12.2	195 28.3	5.7	24 35.3	8.4	59.2
08	H	296 26.7	11.3	209 53.0	5.6	24 43.7	8.3	59.2
09	U	311 26.7	. . 10.5	224 17.6	5.5	24 52.0	8.1	59.2
10	R	326 26.8	09.6	238 42.1	5.5	25 00.1	8.0	59.2
11	S	341 26.8	08.8	253 06.6	5.3	25 08.1	7.8	59.2
12	D	356 26.8	S13 07.9	267 30.9	5.3	N25 15.9	7.6	59.2
13	A	11 26.8	07.1	281 55.2	5.2	25 23.5	7.4	59.2
14	Y	26 26.8	06.2	296 19.4	5.1	25 30.9	7.3	59.2
15		41 26.9	. . 05.4	310 43.5	5.1	25 38.2	7.1	59.2
16		56 26.9	04.5	325 07.6	5.0	25 45.3	7.0	59.2
17		71 26.9	03.7	339 31.6	4.9	25 52.3	6.8	59.2
18		86 26.9	S13 02.8	353 55.5	4.8	N25 59.1	6.6	59.2
19		101 26.9	02.0	8 19.3	4.8	26 05.7	6.4	59.2
20		116 27.0	01.1	22 43.1	4.7	26 12.1	6.3	59.2
21		131 27.0	13 00.3	37 06.8	4.6	26 18.4	6.1	59.2
22		146 27.0	12 59.4	51 30.4	4.6	26 24.5	5.9	59.2
23		161 27.0	S12 58.6	65 54.0	4.5	N26 30.4	5.8	59.2
		SD 16.2	d 0.8	SD		16.1	16.1	16.1

Lat.	Twilight Naut.	Twilight Civil	Sunrise	Moonrise 12	Moonrise 13	Moonrise 14	Moonrise 15
°	h m	h m	h m	h m	h m	h m	h m
N 72	06 26	07 47	09 09	06 30	▭	▭	▭
N 70	06 23	07 35	08 47	07 01	05 10	▭	▭
68	06 20	07 26	08 29	07 24	06 38	▭	▭
66	06 18	07 18	08 15	07 43	07 18	▭	▭
64	06 16	07 12	08 04	07 58	07 45	07 23	▭
62	06 14	07 06	07 54	08 10	08 07	08 03	08 01
60	06 12	07 01	07 45	08 21	08 24	08 31	08 50
N 58	06 10	06 56	07 38	08 30	08 39	08 53	09 21
56	06 08	06 52	07 31	08 39	08 51	09 11	09 44
54	06 07	06 48	07 25	08 46	09 02	09 26	10 03
52	06 05	06 45	07 20	08 53	09 12	09 39	10 19
50	06 04	06 42	07 15	08 59	09 21	09 51	10 33
45	06 00	06 35	07 05	09 12	09 40	10 15	11 02
N 40	05 57	06 28	06 56	09 23	09 55	10 35	11 24
35	05 53	06 23	06 49	09 32	10 08	10 51	11 43
30	05 49	06 18	06 42	09 41	10 20	11 06	11 59
20	05 42	06 08	06 31	09 55	10 40	11 30	12 26
N 10	05 34	05 59	06 21	10 08	10 57	11 51	12 50
0	05 25	05 50	06 11	10 20	11 13	12 11	13 12
S 10	05 14	05 39	06 01	10 32	11 30	12 31	13 34
20	05 01	05 28	05 50	10 45	11 48	12 53	13 58
30	04 43	05 13	05 38	11 00	12 08	13 18	14 26
35	04 32	05 04	05 31	11 09	12 20	13 32	14 42
40	04 19	04 54	05 23	11 19	12 34	13 50	15 01
45	04 02	04 42	05 13	11 31	12 51	14 10	15 25
S 50	03 41	04 26	05 02	11 45	13 11	14 37	15 54
52	03 30	04 19	04 56	11 52	13 21	14 49	16 09
54	03 18	04 10	04 50	11 59	13 32	15 04	16 26
56	03 03	04 01	04 44	12 08	13 45	15 22	16 47
58	02 45	03 50	04 36	12 18	14 00	15 43	17 13
S 60	02 23	03 37	04 28	12 29	14 18	16 09	17 50

Lat.	Sunset	Twilight Civil	Twilight Naut.	Moonset 12	Moonset 13	Moonset 14	Moonset 15
°	h m	h m	h m	h m	h m	h m	h m
N 72	15 21	16 43	18 05	01 15	▭	▭	▭
N 70	15 43	16 55	18 08	00 46	04 27	▭	▭
68	16 01	17 04	18 10	00 24	03 00	▭	▭
66	16 15	17 11	18 12	00 08	02 22	▭	▭
64	16 26	17 18	18 14	25 56	01 56	04 16	▭
62	16 36	17 24	18 16	25 36	01 36	03 37	05 45
60	16 44	17 29	18 18	25 19	01 19	03 09	04 56
N 58	16 52	17 33	18 19	25 05	01 05	02 48	04 26
56	16 58	17 37	18 21	24 53	00 53	02 31	04 03
54	17 04	17 41	18 23	24 43	00 43	02 16	03 44
52	17 09	17 44	18 24	24 34	00 34	02 03	03 28
50	17 14	17 47	18 25	24 26	00 26	01 52	03 14
45	17 24	17 54	18 29	24 08	00 08	01 29	02 46
N 40	17 33	18 01	18 32	23 54	25 10	01 10	02 24
35	17 40	18 06	18 36	23 42	24 55	00 55	02 06
30	17 47	18 11	18 39	23 32	24 41	00 41	01 50
20	17 58	18 21	18 47	23 14	24 18	00 18	01 24
N 10	18 08	18 30	18 55	22 59	23 59	25 01	01 01
0	18 18	18 39	19 04	22 45	23 40	24 40	00 40
S 10	18 27	18 49	19 14	22 31	23 22	24 19	00 19
20	18 38	19 01	19 27	22 15	23 03	23 56	24 55
30	18 50	19 15	19 45	21 58	22 40	23 30	24 27
35	18 57	19 23	19 55	21 48	22 27	23 14	24 10
40	19 05	19 34	20 08	21 37	22 12	22 56	23 51
45	19 14	19 46	20 25	21 23	21 54	22 35	23 27
S 50	19 26	20 01	20 46	21 07	21 33	22 08	22 57
52	19 31	20 09	20 57	21 00	21 22	21 55	22 42
54	19 37	20 17	21 09	20 51	21 10	21 39	22 25
56	19 43	20 26	21 23	20 42	20 57	21 22	22 04
58	19 51	20 37	21 40	20 31	20 41	21 00	21 38
S 60	19 59	20 49	22 02	20 19	20 23	20 33	21 01

Day	SUN Eqn. of Time 00^h	SUN Eqn. of Time 12^h	SUN Mer. Pass.	MOON Mer. Pass. Upper	MOON Mer. Pass. Lower	MOON Age	MOON Phase
d	m s	m s	h m	h m	h m	d %	
12	14 15	14 15	12 14	16 32	04 06	05 32	
13	14 15	14 14	12 14	17 27	04 59	06 43	◐
14	14 14	14 13	12 14	18 25	05 56	07 54	

UT	ARIES	VENUS −3.9		MARS −0.2		JUPITER −1.9		SATURN +0.3	
	GHA	GHA	Dec	GHA	Dec	GHA	Dec	GHA	Dec
d h	° ′	° ′	° ′	° ′	° ′	° ′	° ′	° ′	° ′
15 00	144 23.2	205 40.5	S20 46.8	59 29.9	N26 28.3	220 30.0	S22 43.3	346 00.2	N11 02.5
01	159 25.6	220 39.7	46.3	74 31.9	28.3	235 31.9	43.3	1 02.8	02.6
02	174 28.1	235 38.9	45.8	89 33.9	28.2	250 33.8	43.2	16 05.5	02.7
03	189 30.6	250 38.1	45.4	104 35.9	28.2	265 35.8	43.2	31 08.1	02.7
04	204 33.0	265 37.3	44.9	119 37.9	28.2	280 37.7	43.1	46 10.8	02.8
05	219 35.5	280 36.5	44.4	134 39.9	28.1	295 39.6	43.1	61 13.4	02.9
06	234 38.0	295 35.7	S20 43.9	149 41.8	N26 28.1	310 41.5	S22 43.1	76 16.1	N11 03.0
07	249 40.4	310 34.9	43.5	164 43.8	28.1	325 43.5	43.0	91 18.7	03.0
08	264 42.9	325 34.1	43.0	179 45.8	28.0	340 45.4	43.0	106 21.4	03.1
F 09	279 45.3	340 33.3	42.5	194 47.8	28.0	355 47.3	42.9	121 24.0	03.2
R 10	294 47.8	355 32.5	42.0	209 49.8	28.0	10 49.3	42.9	136 26.7	03.3
I 11	309 50.3	10 31.7	41.5	224 51.7	27.9	25 51.2	42.8	151 29.3	03.3
D 12	324 52.7	25 30.9	S20 41.1	239 53.7	N26 27.9	40 53.1	S22 42.8	166 32.0	N11 03.4
A 13	339 55.2	40 30.1	40.6	254 55.7	27.9	55 55.1	42.8	181 34.6	03.5
Y 14	354 57.7	55 29.3	40.1	269 57.6	27.8	70 57.0	42.7	196 37.3	03.6
15	10 00.1	70 28.5	39.6	284 59.6	27.8	85 58.9	42.7	211 39.9	03.7
16	25 02.6	85 27.7	39.1	300 01.6	27.8	101 00.9	42.6	226 42.5	03.7
17	40 05.1	100 26.9	38.6	315 03.6	27.7	116 02.8	42.6	241 45.2	03.8
18	55 07.5	115 26.2	S20 38.1	330 05.5	N26 27.7	131 04.7	S22 42.5	256 47.8	N11 03.9
19	70 10.0	130 25.4	37.7	345 07.5	27.7	146 06.7	42.5	271 50.5	04.0
20	85 12.5	145 24.6	37.2	0 09.5	27.6	161 08.6	42.4	286 53.1	04.0
21	100 14.9	160 23.8	36.7	15 11.4	27.6	176 10.5	42.4	301 55.8	04.1
22	115 17.4	175 23.0	36.2	30 13.4	27.6	191 12.5	42.4	316 58.4	04.2
23	130 19.8	190 22.2	35.7	45 15.3	27.5	206 14.4	42.3	332 01.1	04.3
16 00	145 22.3	205 21.4	S20 35.2	60 17.3	N26 27.5	221 16.3	S22 42.3	347 03.7	N11 04.4
01	160 24.8	220 20.6	34.7	75 19.3	27.5	236 18.3	42.2	2 06.4	04.4
02	175 27.2	235 19.8	34.2	90 21.2	27.4	251 20.2	42.2	17 09.0	04.5
03	190 29.7	250 19.0	33.7	105 23.2	27.4	266 22.1	42.1	32 11.7	04.6
04	205 32.2	265 18.2	33.2	120 25.1	27.4	281 24.1	42.1	47 14.3	04.7
05	220 34.6	280 17.4	32.7	135 27.1	27.3	296 26.0	42.1	62 17.0	04.7
06	235 37.1	295 16.6	S20 32.2	150 29.0	N26 27.3	311 28.0	S22 42.0	77 19.6	N11 04.8
S 07	250 39.6	310 15.8	31.7	165 31.0	27.3	326 29.9	42.0	92 22.3	04.9
A 08	265 42.0	325 15.1	31.2	180 32.9	27.2	341 31.8	41.9	107 24.9	05.0
T 09	280 44.5	340 14.3	30.7	195 34.9	27.2	356 33.8	41.9	122 27.6	05.0
U 10	295 46.9	355 13.5	30.2	210 36.8	27.2	11 35.7	41.8	137 30.2	05.1
R 11	310 49.4	10 12.7	29.7	225 38.8	27.1	26 37.6	41.8	152 32.9	05.2
D 12	325 51.9	25 11.9	S20 29.2	240 40.7	N26 27.1	41 39.6	S22 41.7	167 35.5	N11 05.3
A 13	340 54.3	40 11.1	28.7	255 42.7	27.1	56 41.5	41.7	182 38.2	05.4
Y 14	355 56.8	55 10.3	28.1	270 44.6	27.1	71 43.4	41.7	197 40.8	05.4
15	10 59.3	70 09.5	27.6	285 46.6	27.0	86 45.4	41.6	212 43.5	05.5
16	26 01.7	85 08.8	27.1	300 48.5	27.0	101 47.3	41.6	227 46.1	05.6
17	41 04.2	100 08.0	26.6	315 50.5	27.0	116 49.2	41.5	242 48.8	05.7
18	56 06.7	115 07.2	S20 26.1	330 52.4	N26 26.9	131 51.2	S22 41.5	257 51.4	N11 05.7
19	71 09.1	130 06.4	25.6	345 54.3	26.9	146 53.1	41.4	272 54.1	05.8
20	86 11.6	145 05.6	25.1	0 56.3	26.9	161 55.1	41.4	287 56.7	05.9
21	101 14.1	160 04.8	24.5	15 58.2	26.8	176 57.0	41.3	302 59.4	06.0
22	116 16.5	175 04.0	24.0	31 00.1	26.8	191 58.9	41.3	318 02.0	06.1
23	131 19.0	190 03.3	23.5	46 02.1	26.8	207 00.9	41.3	333 04.7	06.1
17 00	146 21.4	205 02.5	S20 23.0	61 04.0	N26 26.7	222 02.8	S22 41.2	348 07.3	N11 06.2
01	161 23.9	220 01.7	22.5	76 06.0	26.7	237 04.8	41.2	3 10.0	06.3
02	176 26.4	235 00.9	21.9	91 07.9	26.7	252 06.7	41.1	18 12.6	06.4
03	191 28.8	250 00.1	21.4	106 09.8	26.6	267 08.6	41.1	33 15.3	06.4
04	206 31.3	264 59.3	20.9	121 11.7	26.6	282 10.6	41.0	48 17.9	06.5
05	221 33.8	279 58.5	20.4	136 13.7	26.6	297 12.5	41.0	63 20.6	06.6
06	236 36.2	294 57.8	S20 19.8	151 15.6	N26 26.5	312 14.4	S22 40.9	78 23.2	N11 06.7
07	251 38.7	309 57.0	19.3	166 17.5	26.5	327 16.4	40.9	93 25.9	06.8
08	266 41.2	324 56.2	18.8	181 19.5	26.5	342 18.3	40.9	108 28.5	06.8
S 09	281 43.6	339 55.4	18.3	196 21.4	26.4	357 20.3	40.8	123 31.2	06.9
U 10	296 46.1	354 54.6	17.7	211 23.3	26.4	12 22.2	40.8	138 33.8	07.0
N 11	311 48.6	9 53.9	17.2	226 25.2	26.4	27 24.1	40.7	153 36.5	07.1
D 12	326 51.0	24 53.1	S20 16.7	241 27.1	N26 26.3	42 26.1	S22 40.7	168 39.1	N11 07.1
A 13	341 53.5	39 52.3	16.1	256 29.1	26.3	57 28.0	40.6	183 41.8	07.2
Y 14	356 55.9	54 51.5	15.6	271 31.0	26.3	72 30.0	40.6	198 44.4	07.3
15	11 58.4	69 50.7	15.1	286 32.9	26.2	87 31.9	40.5	213 47.1	07.4
16	27 00.9	84 50.0	14.5	301 34.8	26.2	102 33.8	40.5	228 49.7	07.5
17	42 03.3	99 49.2	14.0	316 36.7	26.2	117 35.8	40.5	243 52.4	07.5
18	57 05.8	114 48.4	S20 13.4	331 38.6	N26 26.1	132 37.7	S22 40.4	258 55.0	N11 07.6
19	72 08.3	129 47.6	12.9	346 40.6	26.1	147 39.7	40.4	273 57.7	07.7
20	87 10.7	144 46.9	12.4	1 42.5	26.1	162 41.6	40.3	289 00.3	07.8
21	102 13.2	159 46.1	11.8	16 44.4	26.0	177 43.5	40.3	304 03.0	07.8
22	117 15.7	174 45.3	11.3	31 46.3	26.0	192 45.5	40.2	319 05.6	07.9
23	132 18.1	189 44.5	10.7	46 48.2	26.0	207 47.4	40.2	334 08.3	08.0
Mer. Pass.	h m 14 16.2	v −0.8	d 0.5	v 1.9	d 0.0	v 1.9	d 0.0	v 2.6	d 0.1

STARS		
Name	SHA	Dec
	° ′	° ′
Acamar	315 21.3	S40 16.5
Achernar	335 29.8	S57 11.9
Acrux	173 13.7	S63 08.6
Adhara	255 15.4	S28 59.1
Aldebaran	290 53.9	N16 31.6
Alioth	166 23.5	N55 54.6
Alkaid	153 01.6	N49 16.0
Al Na'ir	27 49.0	S46 55.4
Alnilam	275 50.3	S 1 11.8
Alphard	217 59.7	S 8 41.7
Alphecca	126 14.3	N26 40.9
Alpheratz	357 48.1	N29 08.2
Altair	62 12.5	N 8 53.2
Ankaa	353 19.8	S42 15.9
Antares	112 31.3	S26 27.1
Arcturus	145 59.2	N19 08.1
Atria	107 37.1	S69 02.4
Avior	234 19.3	S59 32.2
Bellatrix	278 36.2	N 6 21.4
Betelgeuse	271 05.5	N 7 24.5
Canopus	263 57.6	S52 42.2
Capella	280 40.2	N46 00.6
Deneb	49 34.8	N45 18.4
Denebola	182 37.4	N14 31.4
Diphda	349 00.1	S17 56.6
Dubhe	193 55.6	N61 42.2
Elnath	278 17.6	N28 37.0
Eltanin	90 48.3	N51 28.9
Enif	33 51.4	N 9 54.6
Fomalhaut	15 28.6	S29 34.9
Gacrux	172 05.3	S57 09.5
Gienah	175 56.2	S17 35.3
Hadar	148 53.7	S60 24.6
Hamal	328 05.5	N23 30.2
Kaus Aust.	83 49.4	S34 22.9
Kochab	137 19.1	N74 06.9
Markab	13 42.7	N15 14.9
Menkar	314 19.3	N 4 07.3
Menkent	148 12.3	S36 24.6
Miaplacidus	221 40.0	S69 45.1
Mirfak	308 46.3	N49 53.7
Nunki	76 03.5	S26 17.3
Peacock	53 25.9	S56 42.5
Pollux	243 32.3	N28 00.4
Procyon	245 03.6	N 5 12.2
Rasalhague	96 10.3	N12 33.0
Regulus	207 47.4	N11 55.5
Rigel	281 15.8	S 8 11.6
Rigil Kent.	139 57.3	S60 52.0
Sabik	102 17.3	S15 44.2
Schedar	349 45.8	N56 35.1
Shaula	96 27.6	S37 06.6
Sirius	258 37.0	S16 43.7
Spica	158 35.4	S11 12.4
Suhail	222 55.1	S43 28.0
Vega	80 42.0	N38 47.1
Zuben'ubi	137 09.8	S16 04.7

	SHA	Mer. Pass.
	° ′	h m
Venus	59 59.1	10 19
Mars	274 55.0	19 56
Jupiter	75 54.0	9 14
Saturn	201 41.4	0 52

Day	UT (h)	SUN GHA (° ′)	SUN Dec (° ′)	MOON GHA (° ′)	v (′)	MOON Dec (° ′)	d (′)	HP (′)
15 FRIDAY	00	176 27.1	S12 57.7	80 17.5	4.4	N26 36.2	5.5	59.2
	01	191 27.1	56.9	94 40.9	4.4	26 41.7	5.4	59.2
	02	206 27.1	56.0	109 04.3	4.3	26 47.1	5.2	59.2
	03	221 27.1	. . 55.2	123 27.6	4.3	26 52.3	5.0	59.2
	04	236 27.2	54.3	137 50.9	4.2	26 57.3	4.9	59.2
	05	251 27.2	53.5	152 14.1	4.2	27 02.2	4.6	59.2
	06	266 27.2	S12 52.6	166 37.3	4.1	N27 06.8	4.5	59.2
	07	281 27.2	51.8	181 00.4	4.0	27 11.3	4.3	59.2
	08	296 27.3	50.9	195 23.4	4.0	27 15.6	4.1	59.2
	09	311 27.3	. . 50.1	209 46.4	4.0	27 19.7	4.0	59.2
	10	326 27.3	49.2	224 09.4	3.9	27 23.7	3.7	59.2
	11	341 27.3	48.3	238 32.3	3.9	27 27.4	3.5	59.2
	12	356 27.4	S12 47.5	252 55.2	3.9	N27 30.9	3.4	59.1
	13	11 27.4	46.6	267 18.1	3.8	27 34.3	3.2	59.1
	14	26 27.4	45.8	281 40.9	3.8	27 37.5	3.0	59.1
	15	41 27.5	. . 44.9	296 03.7	3.8	27 40.5	2.8	59.1
	16	56 27.5	44.1	310 26.5	3.7	27 43.3	2.6	59.1
	17	71 27.5	43.2	324 49.2	3.7	27 45.9	2.4	59.1
	18	86 27.5	S12 42.3	339 11.9	3.7	N27 48.3	2.3	59.1
	19	101 27.6	41.5	353 34.6	3.6	27 50.6	2.0	59.1
	20	116 27.6	40.6	7 57.2	3.7	27 52.6	1.8	59.1
	21	131 27.6	. . 39.8	22 19.9	3.6	27 54.4	1.7	59.1
	22	146 27.7	38.9	36 42.5	3.6	27 56.1	1.5	59.1
	23	161 27.7	38.0	51 05.1	3.6	27 57.6	1.2	59.1
16 SATURDAY	00	176 27.7	S12 37.2	65 27.7	3.6	N27 58.8	1.1	59.1
	01	191 27.8	36.3	79 50.3	3.6	27 59.9	0.9	59.1
	02	206 27.8	35.5	94 12.9	3.6	28 00.8	0.7	59.1
	03	221 27.8	. . 34.6	108 35.5	3.5	28 01.5	0.5	59.1
	04	236 27.9	33.7	122 58.0	3.6	28 02.0	0.4	59.1
	05	251 27.9	32.9	137 20.6	3.6	28 02.4	0.1	59.1
	06	266 27.9	S12 32.0	151 43.2	3.6	N28 02.5	0.1	59.0
	07	281 28.0	31.2	166 05.8	3.6	28 02.4	0.2	59.0
	08	296 28.0	30.3	180 28.4	3.6	28 02.2	0.5	59.0
	09	311 28.0	. . 29.4	194 51.0	3.6	28 01.7	0.6	59.0
	10	326 28.1	28.6	209 13.6	3.7	28 01.1	0.9	59.0
	11	341 28.1	27.7	223 36.3	3.7	28 00.2	1.0	59.0
	12	356 28.1	S12 26.8	237 59.0	3.6	N27 59.2	1.2	59.0
	13	11 28.2	26.0	252 21.6	3.8	27 58.0	1.4	59.0
	14	26 28.2	25.1	266 44.4	3.7	27 56.6	1.6	59.0
	15	41 28.2	. . 24.2	281 07.1	3.8	27 55.0	1.8	59.0
	16	56 28.3	23.4	295 29.9	3.8	27 53.2	2.0	59.0
	17	71 28.3	22.5	309 52.7	3.8	27 51.2	2.1	59.0
	18	86 28.3	S12 21.7	324 15.5	3.9	N27 49.1	2.4	58.9
	19	101 28.4	20.8	338 38.4	3.9	27 46.7	2.5	58.9
	20	116 28.4	19.9	353 01.3	3.9	27 44.2	2.7	58.9
	21	131 28.5	. . 19.1	7 24.2	4.0	27 41.5	2.9	58.9
	22	146 28.5	18.2	21 47.2	4.0	27 38.6	3.1	58.9
	23	161 28.5	17.3	36 10.2	4.1	27 35.5	3.3	58.9
17 SUNDAY	00	176 28.6	S12 16.4	50 33.3	4.2	N27 32.2	3.5	58.9
	01	191 28.6	15.6	64 56.5	4.2	27 28.7	3.6	58.9
	02	206 28.7	14.7	79 19.7	4.2	27 25.1	3.9	58.9
	03	221 28.7	. . 13.8	93 42.9	4.3	27 21.2	4.0	58.9
	04	236 28.7	13.0	108 06.2	4.4	27 17.2	4.2	58.9
	05	251 28.8	12.1	122 29.6	4.4	27 13.0	4.3	58.8
	06	266 28.8	S12 11.2	136 53.0	4.5	N27 08.7	4.6	58.8
	07	281 28.9	10.4	151 16.5	4.5	27 04.1	4.7	58.8
	08	296 28.9	09.5	165 40.0	4.6	26 59.4	4.9	58.8
	09	311 28.9	. . 08.6	180 03.6	4.7	26 54.5	5.1	58.8
	10	326 29.0	07.7	194 27.3	4.8	26 49.4	5.2	58.8
	11	341 29.0	06.9	208 51.1	4.8	26 44.2	5.5	58.8
	12	356 29.1	S12 06.0	223 14.9	4.9	N26 38.7	5.5	58.8
	13	11 29.1	05.1	237 38.8	5.0	26 33.2	5.8	58.8
	14	26 29.2	04.3	252 02.8	5.1	26 27.4	6.0	58.7
	15	41 29.2	. . 03.4	266 26.9	5.1	26 21.4	6.1	58.7
	16	56 29.2	02.5	280 51.0	5.2	26 15.3	6.2	58.7
	17	71 29.3	01.6	295 15.2	5.3	26 09.1	6.5	58.7
	18	86 29.3	S12 00.8	309 39.5	5.4	N26 02.6	6.6	58.7
	19	101 29.4	11 59.9	324 03.9	5.5	25 56.0	6.7	58.7
	20	116 29.4	59.0	338 28.4	5.5	25 49.3	7.0	58.7
	21	131 29.5	. . 58.1	352 52.9	5.7	25 42.3	7.0	58.7
	22	146 29.5	57.3	7 17.6	5.7	25 35.3	7.3	58.6
	23	161 29.6	56.4	21 42.3	5.8	N25 28.0	7.4	58.6
		SD 16.2	*d* 0.9	SD 16.1		16.1		16.0

Lat. (°)	Twilight Naut. (h m)	Twilight Civil (h m)	Sunrise (h m)	Moonrise 15 (h m)	Moonrise 16 (h m)	Moonrise 17 (h m)	Moonrise 18 (h m)
N 72	06 13	07 33	08 51	▭	▭	▭	▭
N 70	06 11	07 23	08 32	▭	▭	▭	▭
68	06 10	07 15	08 17	▭	▭	▭	▭
66	06 09	07 09	08 04	▭	▭	▭	10 36
64	06 07	07 03	07 54	▭	▭	▭	11 49
62	06 06	06 58	07 45	08 01	08 22	10 20	12 25
60	06 05	06 53	07 37	08 50	09 37	11 05	12 51
N 58	06 04	06 49	07 30	09 21	10 13	11 34	13 11
56	06 02	06 46	07 25	09 44	10 38	11 56	13 28
54	06 01	06 43	07 19	10 03	10 59	12 15	13 42
52	06 00	06 39	07 14	10 19	11 16	12 30	13 54
50	05 59	06 37	07 10	10 33	11 31	12 44	14 05
45	05 56	06 30	07 01	11 02	12 01	13 11	14 28
N 40	05 53	06 25	06 53	11 24	12 24	13 33	14 46
35	05 50	06 20	06 46	11 43	12 43	13 51	15 01
30	05 47	06 15	06 40	11 59	13 00	14 06	15 14
20	05 41	06 07	06 29	12 26	13 28	14 32	15 36
N 10	05 33	05 58	06 20	12 50	13 52	14 55	15 55
0	05 25	05 50	06 11	13 12	14 14	15 15	16 13
S 10	05 15	05 40	06 02	13 34	14 37	15 36	16 31
20	05 02	05 29	05 52	13 58	15 01	15 59	16 50
30	04 46	05 16	05 41	14 26	15 29	16 24	17 12
35	04 36	05 08	05 34	14 42	15 45	16 40	17 25
40	04 23	04 58	05 27	15 01	16 05	16 57	17 39
45	04 08	04 46	05 18	15 25	16 28	17 18	17 56
S 50	03 48	04 32	05 07	15 54	16 58	17 45	18 18
52	03 38	04 25	05 02	16 09	17 13	17 58	18 28
54	03 26	04 17	04 57	16 26	17 30	18 12	18 39
56	03 13	04 08	04 51	16 47	17 50	18 29	18 52
58	02 57	03 58	04 44	17 13	18 16	18 50	19 07
S 60	02 37	03 47	04 36	17 50	18 52	19 16	19 24

Lat. (°)	Sunset (h m)	Twilight Civil (h m)	Twilight Naut. (h m)	Moonset 15 (h m)	Moonset 16 (h m)	Moonset 17 (h m)	Moonset 18 (h m)
N 72	15 38	16 57	18 17	▭	▭	▭	▭
N 70	15 58	17 07	18 19	▭	▭	▭	▭
68	16 13	17 14	18 20	▭	▭	▭	▭
66	16 25	17 21	18 21	▭	▭	▭	09 34
64	16 36	17 27	18 22	▭	▭	▭	08 20
62	16 45	17 32	18 24	05 45	07 35	07 46	07 43
60	16 52	17 36	18 25	04 56	06 20	07 01	07 17
N 58	16 59	17 40	18 26	04 26	05 44	06 32	06 56
56	17 05	17 43	18 27	04 03	05 18	06 09	06 39
54	17 10	17 47	18 28	03 44	04 57	05 50	06 24
52	17 15	17 50	18 29	03 28	04 40	05 34	06 12
50	17 19	17 52	18 30	03 14	04 25	05 21	06 00
45	17 28	17 59	18 33	02 46	03 56	04 52	05 37
N 40	17 36	18 04	18 36	02 24	03 32	04 30	05 18
35	17 43	18 09	18 39	02 06	03 13	04 12	05 01
30	17 49	18 13	18 42	01 50	02 56	03 56	04 48
20	17 59	18 22	18 48	01 24	02 28	03 29	04 24
N 10	18 09	18 30	18 55	01 01	02 04	03 06	04 03
0	18 18	18 39	19 03	00 40	01 42	02 44	03 44
S 10	18 26	18 48	19 13	00 19	01 19	02 22	03 24
20	18 36	18 59	19 25	24 55	00 55	01 58	03 03
30	18 47	19 12	19 41	24 27	00 27	01 31	02 38
35	18 54	19 20	19 52	24 10	00 10	01 15	02 24
40	19 01	19 30	20 04	23 51	24 56	00 56	02 07
45	19 10	19 41	20 19	23 27	24 32	00 32	01 47
S 50	19 20	19 55	20 39	22 57	24 03	00 03	01 21
52	19 25	20 02	20 49	22 42	23 48	25 09	01 09
54	19 30	20 10	21 00	22 25	23 31	24 55	00 55
56	19 36	20 18	21 13	22 04	23 11	24 38	00 38
58	19 43	20 28	21 29	21 38	22 45	24 18	00 18
S 60	19 51	20 39	21 48	21 01	22 10	23 52	25 41

Day	SUN Eqn. of Time 00^h (m s)	SUN Eqn. of Time 12^h (m s)	SUN Mer. Pass. (h m)	MOON Mer. Pass. Upper (h m)	MOON Mer. Pass. Lower (h m)	MOON Age (d)	MOON Phase (%)
15	14 12	14 11	12 14	19 27	06 56	08	65
16	14 09	14 08	12 14	20 29	07 58	09	76
17	14 06	14 04	12 14	21 30	09 00	10	85

Day	UT (d h)	ARIES GHA (° ′)	VENUS −3.9 GHA (° ′)	VENUS Dec (° ′)	MARS −0.1 GHA (° ′)	MARS Dec (° ′)	JUPITER −1.9 GHA (° ′)	JUPITER Dec (° ′)	SATURN +0.2 GHA (° ′)	SATURN Dec (° ′)
	18 00	147 20.6	204 43.7	S20 10.2	61 50.1	N26 25.9	222 49.4	S22 40.1	349 10.9	N11 08.1
	01	162 23.1	219 43.0	09.6	76 52.0	25.9	237 51.3	40.1	4 13.6	08.2
	02	177 25.5	234 42.2	09.1	91 53.9	25.9	252 53.3	40.1	19 16.2	08.2
	03	192 28.0	249 41.4	. . 08.5	106 55.8	. . 25.9	267 55.2	. . 40.0	34 18.9	. . 08.3
	04	207 30.4	264 40.7	08.0	121 57.7	25.8	282 57.1	40.0	49 21.6	08.4
	05	222 32.9	279 39.9	07.4	136 59.6	25.8	297 59.1	39.9	64 24.2	08.5
	06	237 35.4	294 39.1	S20 06.9	152 01.5	N26 25.8	313 01.0	S22 39.9	79 26.9	N11 08.5
	07	252 37.8	309 38.3	06.3	167 03.4	25.7	328 03.0	39.8	94 29.5	08.6
	08	267 40.3	324 37.6	05.8	182 05.3	25.7	343 04.9	39.8	109 32.2	08.7
M	09	282 42.8	339 36.8	. . 05.2	197 07.2	. . 25.7	358 06.9	. . 39.7	124 34.8	. . 08.8
O	10	297 45.2	354 36.0	04.7	212 09.1	25.6	13 08.8	39.7	139 37.5	08.9
N	11	312 47.7	9 35.2	04.1	227 11.0	25.6	28 10.7	39.7	154 40.1	08.9
D	12	327 50.2	24 34.5	S20 03.6	242 12.9	N26 25.6	43 12.7	S22 39.6	169 42.8	N11 09.0
A	13	342 52.6	39 33.7	03.0	257 14.8	25.5	58 14.6	39.6	184 45.4	09.1
Y	14	357 55.1	54 32.9	02.4	272 16.7	25.5	73 16.6	39.5	199 48.1	09.2
	15	12 57.6	69 32.2	. . 01.9	287 18.6	. . 25.5	88 18.5	. . 39.5	214 50.7	. . 09.2
	16	28 00.0	84 31.4	01.3	302 20.5	25.4	103 20.5	39.4	229 53.4	09.3
	17	43 02.5	99 30.6	00.8	317 22.4	25.4	118 22.4	39.4	244 56.0	09.4
	18	58 04.9	114 29.9	S20 00.2	332 24.3	N26 25.4	133 24.3	S22 39.3	259 58.7	N11 09.5
	19	73 07.4	129 29.1	19 59.6	347 26.2	25.3	148 26.3	39.3	275 01.3	09.5
	20	88 09.9	144 28.3	59.1	2 28.1	25.3	163 28.2	39.3	290 04.0	09.6
	21	103 12.3	159 27.5	. . 58.5	17 30.0	. . 25.3	178 30.2	. . 39.2	305 06.6	. . 09.7
	22	118 14.8	174 26.8	57.9	32 31.8	25.2	193 32.1	39.2	320 09.3	09.8
	23	133 17.3	189 26.0	57.4	47 33.7	25.2	208 34.1	39.1	335 11.9	09.9
	19 00	148 19.7	204 25.2	S19 56.8	62 35.6	N26 25.2	223 36.0	S22 39.1	350 14.6	N11 09.9
	01	163 22.2	219 24.5	56.2	77 37.5	25.1	238 38.0	39.0	5 17.2	10.0
	02	178 24.7	234 23.7	55.6	92 39.4	25.1	253 39.9	39.0	20 19.9	10.1
	03	193 27.1	249 22.9	. . 55.1	107 41.3	. . 25.1	268 41.9	. . 38.9	35 22.5	. . 10.2
	04	208 29.6	264 22.2	54.5	122 43.1	25.0	283 43.8	38.9	50 25.2	10.2
	05	223 32.0	279 21.4	53.9	137 45.0	25.0	298 45.7	38.8	65 27.8	10.3
	06	238 34.5	294 20.7	S19 53.3	152 46.9	N26 25.0	313 47.7	S22 38.8	80 30.5	N11 10.4
	07	253 37.0	309 19.9	52.8	167 48.8	24.9	328 49.6	38.8	95 33.1	10.5
T	08	268 39.4	324 19.1	52.2	182 50.6	24.9	343 51.6	38.7	110 35.8	10.6
U	09	283 41.9	339 18.4	. . 51.6	197 52.5	. . 24.9	358 53.5	. . 38.7	125 38.4	. . 10.6
E	10	298 44.4	354 17.6	51.0	212 54.4	24.8	13 55.5	38.6	140 41.1	10.7
S	11	313 46.8	9 16.8	50.5	227 56.3	24.8	28 57.4	38.6	155 43.7	10.8
	12	328 49.3	24 16.1	S19 49.9	242 58.1	N26 24.8	43 59.4	S22 38.5	170 46.4	N11 10.9
D	13	343 51.8	39 15.3	49.3	258 00.0	24.7	59 01.3	38.5	185 49.1	10.9
A	14	358 54.2	54 14.6	48.7	273 01.9	24.7	74 03.3	38.4	200 51.7	11.0
Y	15	13 56.7	69 13.8	. . 48.1	288 03.7	. . 24.7	89 05.2	. . 38.4	215 54.4	. . 11.1
	16	28 59.2	84 13.0	47.5	303 05.6	24.6	104 07.2	38.4	230 57.0	11.2
	17	44 01.6	99 12.3	46.9	318 07.5	24.6	119 09.1	38.3	245 59.7	11.3
	18	59 04.1	114 11.5	S19 46.4	333 09.3	N26 24.6	134 11.1	S22 38.3	261 02.3	N11 11.3
	19	74 06.5	129 10.8	45.8	348 11.2	24.5	149 13.0	38.2	276 05.0	11.4
	20	89 09.0	144 10.0	45.2	3 13.1	24.5	164 15.0	38.2	291 07.6	11.5
	21	104 11.5	159 09.2	. . 44.6	18 14.9	. . 24.5	179 16.9	. . 38.1	306 10.3	. . 11.6
	22	119 13.9	174 08.5	44.0	33 16.8	24.4	194 18.9	38.1	321 12.9	11.6
	23	134 16.4	189 07.7	43.4	48 18.7	24.4	209 20.8	38.0	336 15.6	11.7
	20 00	149 18.9	204 07.0	S19 42.8	63 20.5	N26 24.4	224 22.8	S22 38.0	351 18.2	N11 11.8
	01	164 21.3	219 06.2	42.2	78 22.4	24.3	239 24.7	37.9	6 20.9	11.9
	02	179 23.8	234 05.5	41.6	93 24.2	24.3	254 26.7	37.9	21 23.5	12.0
	03	194 26.3	249 04.7	. . 41.0	108 26.1	. . 24.3	269 28.6	. . 37.9	36 26.2	. . 12.0
	04	209 28.7	264 03.9	40.4	123 27.9	24.2	284 30.6	37.8	51 28.8	12.1
	05	224 31.2	279 03.2	39.8	138 29.8	24.2	299 32.5	37.8	66 31.5	12.2
	06	239 33.7	294 02.4	S19 39.2	153 31.7	N26 24.2	314 34.5	S22 37.7	81 34.1	N11 12.3
W	07	254 36.1	309 01.7	38.6	168 33.5	24.2	329 36.4	37.7	96 36.8	12.3
E	08	269 38.6	324 00.9	38.0	183 35.4	24.1	344 38.4	37.6	111 39.4	12.4
D	09	284 41.0	339 00.2	. . 37.4	198 37.2	. . 24.1	359 40.3	. . 37.6	126 42.1	. . 12.5
N	10	299 43.5	353 59.4	36.8	213 39.1	24.1	14 42.3	37.5	141 44.7	12.6
E	11	314 46.0	8 58.7	36.2	228 40.9	24.0	29 44.2	37.5	156 47.4	12.7
	12	329 48.4	23 57.9	S19 35.6	243 42.8	N26 24.0	44 46.2	S22 37.4	171 50.1	N11 12.7
S	13	344 50.9	38 57.2	35.0	258 44.6	24.0	59 48.1	37.4	186 52.7	12.8
D	14	359 53.4	53 56.4	34.4	273 46.4	23.9	74 50.1	37.4	201 55.4	12.9
A	15	14 55.8	68 55.7	. . 33.8	288 48.3	. . 23.9	89 52.0	. . 37.3	216 58.0	. . 13.0
Y	16	29 58.3	83 54.9	33.2	303 50.1	23.9	104 54.0	37.3	232 00.7	13.0
	17	45 00.8	98 54.2	32.6	318 52.0	23.8	119 55.9	37.2	247 03.3	13.1
	18	60 03.2	113 53.4	S19 31.9	333 53.8	N26 23.8	134 57.9	S22 37.2	262 06.0	N11 13.2
	19	75 05.7	128 52.7	31.3	348 55.7	23.8	149 59.8	37.1	277 08.6	13.3
	20	90 08.1	143 51.9	30.7	3 57.5	23.7	165 01.8	37.1	292 11.3	13.4
	21	105 10.6	158 51.2	. . 30.1	18 59.3	. . 23.7	180 03.7	. . 37.0	307 13.9	. . 13.4
	22	120 13.1	173 50.4	29.5	34 01.2	23.7	195 05.7	37.0	322 16.6	13.5
	23	135 15.5	188 49.7	28.9	49 03.0	23.6	210 07.6	36.9	337 19.2	13.6
	Mer. Pass. (h m)	14 04.4	v −0.8	d 0.6	v 1.9	d 0.0	v 1.9	d 0.0	v 2.7	d 0.1

STARS Name	SHA (° ′)	Dec (° ′)
Acamar	315 21.3	S40 16.5
Achernar	335 29.8	S57 11.9
Acrux	173 13.6	S63 08.6
Adhara	255 15.4	S28 59.1
Aldebaran	290 53.9	N16 31.6
Alioth	166 23.5	N55 54.6
Alkaid	153 01.6	N49 16.0
Al Na'ir	27 49.0	S46 55.4
Alnilam	275 50.3	S 1 11.8
Alphard	217 59.7	S 8 41.7
Alphecca	126 14.3	N26 40.9
Alpheratz	357 48.1	N29 08.2
Altair	62 12.4	N 8 53.2
Ankaa	353 19.8	S42 15.8
Antares	112 31.3	S26 27.1
Arcturus	145 59.2	N19 08.1
Atria	107 37.0	S69 02.4
Avior	234 19.3	S59 32.2
Bellatrix	278 36.2	N 6 21.4
Betelgeuse	271 05.5	N 7 24.5
Canopus	263 57.6	S52 42.2
Capella	280 40.2	N46 00.6
Deneb	49 34.8	N45 18.4
Denebola	182 37.4	N14 31.4
Diphda	349 00.1	S17 56.6
Dubhe	193 55.6	N61 42.2
Elnath	278 17.6	N28 37.0
Eltanin	90 48.3	N51 28.9
Enif	33 51.4	N 9 54.6
Fomalhaut	15 28.6	S29 34.9
Gacrux	172 05.2	S57 09.5
Gienah	175 56.2	S17 35.4
Hadar	148 53.6	S60 24.6
Hamal	328 05.5	N23 30.2
Kaus Aust.	83 49.4	S34 22.9
Kochab	137 19.0	N74 06.9
Markab	13 42.7	N15 14.9
Menkar	314 19.3	N 4 07.3
Menkent	148 12.3	S36 24.6
Miaplacidus	221 40.0	S69 45.1
Mirfak	308 46.3	N49 53.7
Nunki	76 03.5	S26 17.3
Peacock	53 25.9	S56 42.5
Pollux	243 32.3	N28 00.4
Procyon	245 03.6	N 5 12.2
Rasalhague	96 10.3	N12 33.0
Regulus	207 47.4	N11 55.5
Rigel	281 15.8	S 8 11.6
Rigil Kent.	139 57.3	S60 52.0
Sabik	102 17.3	S15 44.2
Schedar	349 45.8	N56 35.1
Shaula	96 27.6	S37 06.6
Sirius	258 37.0	S16 43.7
Spica	158 35.3	S11 12.4
Suhail	222 55.1	S43 28.0
Vega	80 42.0	N38 47.1
Zuben'ubi	137 09.8	S16 04.7
	SHA (° ′)	**Mer. Pass. (h m)**
Venus	56 05.5	10 23
Mars	274 15.9	19 47
Jupiter	75 16.3	9 04
Saturn	201 54.8	0 39

	UT	SUN GHA	SUN Dec	MOON GHA	*v*	MOON Dec	*d*	HP
	d h	° ′	° ′	° ′	′	° ′	′	′
	18 00	176 29.6	S11 55.5	36 07.1	6.0	N25 20.6	7.6	58.6
	01	191 29.7	54.6	50 32.1	6.0	25 13.0	7.7	58.6
	02	206 29.7	53.8	64 57.1	6.1	25 05.3	7.8	58.6
	03	221 29.8	. . 52.9	79 22.2	6.2	24 57.5	8.1	58.6
	04	236 29.8	52.0	93 47.4	6.3	24 49.4	8.1	58.6
	05	251 29.8	51.1	108 12.7	6.4	24 41.3	8.3	58.5
	06	266 29.9	S11 50.2	122 38.1	6.5	N24 33.0	8.5	58.5
	07	281 29.9	49.4	137 03.6	6.6	24 24.5	8.6	58.5
	08	296 30.0	48.5	151 29.2	6.7	24 15.9	8.8	58.5
M	09	311 30.0	. . 47.6	165 54.9	6.8	24 07.1	8.9	58.5
O	10	326 30.1	46.7	180 20.7	6.9	23 58.2	9.0	58.5
N	11	341 30.1	45.9	194 46.6	7.0	23 49.2	9.2	58.4
D	12	356 30.2	S11 45.0	209 12.6	7.1	N23 40.0	9.3	58.4
A	13	11 30.2	44.1	223 38.7	7.2	23 30.7	9.4	58.4
Y	14	26 30.3	43.2	238 04.9	7.3	23 21.3	9.6	58.4
	15	41 30.3	. . 42.3	252 31.2	7.4	23 11.7	9.7	58.4
	16	56 30.4	41.5	266 57.6	7.5	23 02.0	9.9	58.4
	17	71 30.5	40.6	281 24.1	7.6	22 52.1	10.0	58.4
	18	86 30.5	S11 39.7	295 50.7	7.8	N22 42.1	10.1	58.3
	19	101 30.6	38.8	310 17.5	7.8	22 32.0	10.2	58.3
	20	116 30.6	37.9	324 44.3	8.0	22 21.8	10.3	58.3
	21	131 30.7	. . 37.0	339 11.3	8.0	22 11.5	10.5	58.3
	22	146 30.7	36.2	353 38.3	8.2	22 01.0	10.6	58.3
	23	161 30.8	35.3	8 05.5	8.2	21 50.4	10.7	58.3
	19 00	176 30.8	S11 34.4	22 32.7	8.4	N21 39.7	10.9	58.2
	01	191 30.9	33.5	37 00.1	8.5	21 28.8	10.9	58.2
	02	206 30.9	32.6	51 27.6	8.5	21 17.9	11.1	58.2
	03	221 31.0	. . 31.7	65 55.1	8.7	21 06.8	11.2	58.2
	04	236 31.0	30.9	80 22.8	8.8	20 55.6	11.2	58.2
	05	251 31.1	30.0	94 50.6	8.9	20 44.4	11.4	58.1
	06	266 31.2	S11 29.1	109 18.5	9.0	N20 33.0	11.5	58.1
	07	281 31.2	28.2	123 46.5	9.1	20 21.5	11.7	58.1
T	08	296 31.3	27.3	138 14.6	9.3	20 09.8	11.7	58.1
U	09	311 31.3	. . 26.4	152 42.9	9.3	19 58.1	11.8	58.1
E	10	326 31.4	25.5	167 11.2	9.4	19 46.3	11.9	58.0
S	11	341 31.4	24.6	181 39.6	9.5	19 34.4	12.0	58.0
D	12	356 31.5	S11 23.8	196 08.1	9.7	N19 22.4	12.1	58.0
A	13	11 31.6	22.9	210 36.8	9.7	19 10.3	12.2	58.0
Y	14	26 31.6	22.0	225 05.5	9.9	18 58.1	12.3	58.0
	15	41 31.7	. . 21.1	239 34.4	9.9	18 45.8	12.4	58.0
	16	56 31.7	20.2	254 03.3	10.1	18 33.4	12.5	57.9
	17	71 31.8	19.3	268 32.4	10.1	18 20.9	12.6	57.9
	18	86 31.8	S11 18.4	283 01.5	10.3	N18 08.3	12.6	57.9
	19	101 31.9	17.5	297 30.8	10.3	17 55.7	12.8	57.9
	20	116 32.0	16.6	312 00.1	10.5	17 42.9	12.8	57.8
	21	131 32.0	. . 15.8	326 29.6	10.6	17 30.1	12.9	57.8
	22	146 32.1	14.9	340 59.2	10.6	17 17.2	13.0	57.8
	23	161 32.1	14.0	355 28.8	10.8	17 04.2	13.0	57.8
	20 00	176 32.2	S11 13.1	9 58.6	10.8	N16 51.2	13.2	57.8
	01	191 32.3	12.2	24 28.4	11.0	16 38.0	13.2	57.7
	02	206 32.3	11.3	38 58.4	11.0	16 24.8	13.3	57.7
	03	221 32.4	. . 10.4	53 28.4	11.2	16 11.5	13.4	57.7
	04	236 32.5	09.5	67 58.6	11.2	15 58.1	13.4	57.7
	05	251 32.5	08.6	82 28.8	11.4	15 44.7	13.5	57.7
	06	266 32.6	S11 07.7	96 59.2	11.4	N15 31.2	13.6	57.6
W	07	281 32.6	06.8	111 29.6	11.5	15 17.6	13.6	57.6
E	08	296 32.7	05.9	126 00.1	11.6	15 04.0	13.7	57.6
D	09	311 32.8	. . 05.1	140 30.7	11.7	14 50.3	13.8	57.6
N	10	326 32.8	04.2	155 01.4	11.8	14 36.5	13.8	57.5
E	11	341 32.9	03.3	169 32.2	11.9	14 22.7	13.9	57.5
S	12	356 33.0	S11 02.4	184 03.1	12.0	N14 08.8	13.9	57.5
D	13	11 33.0	01.5	198 34.1	12.0	13 54.9	14.0	57.5
A	14	26 33.1	11 00.6	213 05.1	12.2	13 40.9	14.1	57.5
Y	15	41 33.2	10 59.7	227 36.3	12.2	13 26.8	14.1	57.4
	16	56 33.2	58.8	242 07.5	12.3	13 12.7	14.1	57.4
	17	71 33.3	57.9	256 38.8	12.4	12 58.6	14.2	57.4
	18	86 33.4	S10 57.0	271 10.2	12.5	N12 44.4	14.3	57.4
	19	101 33.4	56.1	285 41.7	12.6	12 30.1	14.3	57.3
	20	116 33.5	55.2	300 13.3	12.6	12 15.8	14.3	57.3
	21	131 33.6	. . 54.3	314 44.9	12.8	12 01.5	14.4	57.3
	22	146 33.6	53.4	329 16.7	12.8	11 47.1	14.5	57.3
	23	161 33.7	52.5	343 48.5	12.8	N11 32.6	14.5	57.2
		SD 16.2	*d* 0.9	SD 15.9		15.8		15.7

Lat.	Twilight Naut.	Twilight Civil	Sunrise	Moonrise 18	Moonrise 19	Moonrise 20	Moonrise 21
°	h m	h m	h m	h m	h m	h m	h m
N 72	06 00	07 19	08 34	▭	▭	14 40	17 10
N 70	06 00	07 11	08 17	▭	12 02	15 08	17 21
68	05 59	07 04	08 04	▭	13 03	15 29	17 29
66	05 59	06 59	07 53	10 36	13 38	15 45	17 36
64	05 58	06 54	07 44	11 49	14 02	15 58	17 42
62	05 58	06 49	07 36	12 25	14 22	16 09	17 48
60	05 57	06 46	07 29	12 51	14 37	16 18	17 52
N 58	05 57	06 42	07 23	13 11	14 51	16 26	17 56
56	05 56	06 39	07 18	13 28	15 02	16 33	17 59
54	05 55	06 36	07 13	13 42	15 12	16 39	18 02
52	05 55	06 34	07 08	13 54	15 21	16 45	18 05
50	05 54	06 31	07 04	14 05	15 29	16 50	18 08
45	05 52	06 26	06 56	14 28	15 45	17 01	18 13
N 40	05 49	06 21	06 49	14 46	15 59	17 10	18 18
35	05 47	06 17	06 42	15 01	16 11	17 18	18 22
30	05 45	06 13	06 37	15 14	16 21	17 24	18 25
20	05 39	06 05	06 27	15 36	16 38	17 36	18 31
N 10	05 33	05 57	06 19	15 55	16 53	17 46	18 36
0	05 25	05 49	06 11	16 13	17 07	17 56	18 41
S 10	05 16	05 41	06 02	16 31	17 20	18 05	18 46
20	05 04	05 31	05 53	16 50	17 35	18 15	18 51
30	04 49	05 18	05 43	17 12	17 52	18 27	18 57
35	04 39	05 11	05 37	17 25	18 02	18 33	19 01
40	04 28	05 02	05 30	17 39	18 13	18 40	19 04
45	04 13	04 51	05 22	17 56	18 26	18 49	19 09
S 50	03 54	04 37	05 12	18 18	18 41	18 59	19 14
52	03 45	04 31	05 08	18 28	18 49	19 04	19 16
54	03 34	04 24	05 03	18 39	18 57	19 09	19 19
56	03 22	04 16	04 57	18 52	19 06	19 15	19 22
58	03 07	04 07	04 51	19 07	19 16	19 22	19 25
S 60	02 50	03 56	04 44	19 24	19 28	19 29	19 29

Lat.	Sunset	Twilight Civil	Twilight Naut.	Moonset 18	Moonset 19	Moonset 20	Moonset 21
°	h m	h m	h m	h m	h m	h m	h m
N 72	15 55	17 11	18 30	▭	▭	09 13	08 21
N 70	16 12	17 19	18 30	▭	10 05	08 43	08 07
68	16 25	17 25	18 30	▭	09 02	08 21	07 56
66	16 36	17 31	18 31	09 34	08 26	08 03	07 47
64	16 45	17 35	18 31	08 20	08 00	07 49	07 39
62	16 53	17 40	18 31	07 43	07 40	07 36	07 33
60	17 00	17 43	18 32	07 17	07 23	07 26	07 27
N 58	17 06	17 47	18 32	06 56	07 09	07 17	07 21
56	17 11	17 50	18 33	06 39	06 57	07 09	07 17
54	17 16	17 52	18 34	06 24	06 46	07 01	07 13
52	17 20	17 55	18 34	06 12	06 37	06 55	07 09
50	17 24	17 57	18 35	06 00	06 28	06 49	07 05
45	17 33	18 03	18 37	05 37	06 10	06 36	06 58
N 40	17 40	18 07	18 39	05 18	05 55	06 26	06 51
35	17 46	18 12	18 41	05 01	05 42	06 17	06 46
30	17 51	18 16	18 44	04 48	05 31	06 09	06 41
20	18 01	18 23	18 49	04 24	05 12	05 55	06 33
N 10	18 09	18 31	18 55	04 03	04 55	05 42	06 25
0	18 17	18 38	19 03	03 44	04 39	05 31	06 18
S 10	18 25	18 47	19 12	03 24	04 23	05 19	06 11
20	18 34	18 57	19 23	03 03	04 06	05 06	06 03
30	18 44	19 09	19 38	02 38	03 46	04 52	05 54
35	18 50	19 17	19 48	02 24	03 34	04 43	05 49
40	18 57	19 25	19 59	02 07	03 21	04 33	05 43
45	19 05	19 36	20 14	01 47	03 05	04 22	05 36
S 50	19 14	19 49	20 32	01 21	02 45	04 08	05 28
52	19 19	19 55	20 41	01 09	02 35	04 01	05 24
54	19 24	20 02	20 51	00 55	02 25	03 54	05 19
56	19 29	20 10	21 03	00 38	02 12	03 46	05 15
58	19 35	20 19	21 18	00 18	01 58	03 36	05 09
S 60	19 42	20 30	21 35	25 41	01 41	03 26	05 03

Day	SUN Eqn. of Time 00^h	SUN Eqn. of Time 12^h	SUN Mer. Pass.	MOON Mer. Pass. Upper	MOON Mer. Pass. Lower	MOON Age	MOON Phase
d	m s	m s	h m	h m	h m	d %	
18	14 02	13 59	12 14	22 26	09 59	11 92	○
19	13 57	13 54	12 14	23 19	10 53	12 97	
20	13 51	13 48	12 14	24 07	11 43	13 100	

UT	ARIES	VENUS −3.9		MARS +0.0		JUPITER −1.9		SATURN +0.2	
	GHA	GHA	Dec	GHA	Dec	GHA	Dec	GHA	Dec
d h	° ′	° ′	° ′	° ′	° ′	° ′	° ′	° ′	° ′
21 00	150 18.0	203 48.9	S19 28.3	64 04.8	N26 23.6	225 09.6	S22 36.9	352 21.9	N11 13.7
01	165 20.5	218 48.2	27.6	79 06.7	23.6	240 11.5	36.9	7 24.5	13.7
02	180 22.9	233 47.4	27.0	94 08.5	23.5	255 13.5	36.8	22 27.2	13.8
03	195 25.4	248 46.7	26.4	109 10.3	23.5	270 15.4	36.8	37 29.8	13.9
04	210 27.9	263 45.9	25.8	124 12.2	23.5	285 17.4	36.7	52 32.5	14.0
05	225 30.3	278 45.2	25.2	139 14.0	23.4	300 19.3	36.7	67 35.2	14.1
06	240 32.8	293 44.4	S19 24.5	154 15.8	N26 23.4	315 21.3	S22 36.6	82 37.8	N11 14.1
07	255 35.3	308 43.7	23.9	169 17.7	23.4	330 23.3	36.6	97 40.5	14.2
T 08	270 37.7	323 42.9	23.3	184 19.5	23.3	345 25.2	36.5	112 43.1	14.3
H 09	285 40.2	338 42.2	22.7	199 21.3	23.3	0 27.2	36.5	127 45.8	14.4
U 10	300 42.6	353 41.5	22.0	214 23.2	23.3	15 29.1	36.4	142 48.4	14.4
R 11	315 45.1	8 40.7	21.4	229 25.0	23.2	30 31.1	36.4	157 51.1	14.5
S 12	330 47.6	23 40.0	S19 20.8	244 26.8	N26 23.2	45 33.0	S22 36.4	172 53.7	N11 14.6
D 13	345 50.0	38 39.2	20.1	259 28.6	23.2	60 35.0	36.3	187 56.4	14.7
A 14	0 52.5	53 38.5	19.5	274 30.4	23.1	75 36.9	36.3	202 59.0	14.8
Y 15	15 55.0	68 37.7	18.9	289 32.3	23.1	90 38.9	36.2	218 01.7	14.8
16	30 57.4	83 37.0	18.2	304 34.1	23.1	105 40.9	36.2	233 04.3	14.9
17	45 59.9	98 36.3	17.6	319 35.9	23.0	120 42.8	36.1	248 07.0	15.0
18	61 02.4	113 35.5	S19 17.0	334 37.7	N26 23.0	135 44.8	S22 36.1	263 09.6	N11 15.1
19	76 04.8	128 34.8	16.3	349 39.5	23.0	150 46.7	36.0	278 12.3	15.1
20	91 07.3	143 34.0	15.7	4 41.4	22.9	165 48.7	36.0	293 14.9	15.2
21	106 09.8	158 33.3	15.1	19 43.2	22.9	180 50.6	35.9	308 17.6	15.3
22	121 12.2	173 32.6	14.4	34 45.0	22.9	195 52.6	35.9	323 20.3	15.4
23	136 14.7	188 31.8	13.8	49 46.8	22.8	210 54.5	35.9	338 22.9	15.5
22 00	151 17.1	203 31.1	S19 13.1	64 48.6	N26 22.8	225 56.5	S22 35.8	353 25.6	N11 15.5
01	166 19.6	218 30.4	12.5	79 50.4	22.8	240 58.5	35.8	8 28.2	15.6
02	181 22.1	233 29.6	11.9	94 52.2	22.7	256 00.4	35.7	23 30.9	15.7
03	196 24.5	248 28.9	11.2	109 54.0	22.7	271 02.4	35.7	38 33.5	15.8
04	211 27.0	263 28.1	10.6	124 55.9	22.7	286 04.3	35.6	53 36.2	15.8
05	226 29.5	278 27.4	09.9	139 57.7	22.6	301 06.3	35.6	68 38.8	15.9
06	241 31.9	293 26.7	S19 09.3	154 59.5	N26 22.6	316 08.2	S22 35.5	83 41.5	N11 16.0
07	256 34.4	308 25.9	08.6	170 01.3	22.5	331 10.2	35.5	98 44.1	16.1
08	271 36.9	323 25.2	08.0	185 03.1	22.5	346 12.2	35.4	113 46.8	16.2
F 09	286 39.3	338 24.5	07.3	200 04.9	22.5	1 14.1	35.4	128 49.4	16.2
R 10	301 41.8	353 23.7	06.7	215 06.7	22.4	16 16.1	35.3	143 52.1	16.3
I 11	316 44.2	8 23.0	06.0	230 08.5	22.4	31 18.0	35.3	158 54.7	16.4
D 12	331 46.7	23 22.3	S19 05.4	245 10.3	N26 22.4	46 20.0	S22 35.3	173 57.4	N11 16.5
A 13	346 49.2	38 21.5	04.7	260 12.1	22.3	61 22.0	35.2	189 00.1	16.5
Y 14	1 51.6	53 20.8	04.1	275 13.9	22.3	76 23.9	35.2	204 02.7	16.6
15	16 54.1	68 20.1	03.4	290 15.7	22.3	91 25.9	35.1	219 05.4	16.7
16	31 56.6	83 19.3	02.7	305 17.5	22.2	106 27.8	35.1	234 08.0	16.8
17	46 59.0	98 18.6	02.1	320 19.3	22.2	121 29.8	35.0	249 10.7	16.9
18	62 01.5	113 17.9	S19 01.4	335 21.1	N26 22.2	136 31.8	S22 35.0	264 13.3	N11 16.9
19	77 04.0	128 17.2	00.8	350 22.9	22.1	151 33.7	34.9	279 16.0	17.0
20	92 06.4	143 16.4	19 00.1	5 24.7	22.1	166 35.7	34.9	294 18.6	17.1
21	107 08.9	158 15.7	18 59.4	20 26.5	22.1	181 37.6	34.8	309 21.3	17.2
22	122 11.4	173 15.0	58.8	35 28.3	22.0	196 39.6	34.8	324 23.9	17.2
23	137 13.8	188 14.2	58.1	50 30.0	22.0	211 41.6	34.8	339 26.6	17.3
23 00	152 16.3	203 13.5	S18 57.5	65 31.8	N26 22.0	226 43.5	S22 34.7	354 29.2	N11 17.4
01	167 18.7	218 12.8	56.8	80 33.6	21.9	241 45.5	34.7	9 31.9	17.5
02	182 21.2	233 12.1	56.1	95 35.4	21.9	256 47.4	34.6	24 34.5	17.5
03	197 23.7	248 11.3	55.5	110 37.2	21.9	271 49.4	34.6	39 37.2	17.6
04	212 26.1	263 10.6	54.8	125 39.0	21.8	286 51.4	34.5	54 39.9	17.7
05	227 28.6	278 09.9	54.1	140 40.8	21.8	301 53.3	34.5	69 42.5	17.8
06	242 31.1	293 09.2	S18 53.5	155 42.6	N26 21.8	316 55.3	S22 34.4	84 45.2	N11 17.9
07	257 33.5	308 08.4	52.8	170 44.3	21.7	331 57.3	34.4	99 47.8	17.9
S 08	272 36.0	323 07.7	52.1	185 46.1	21.7	346 59.2	34.3	114 50.5	18.0
A 09	287 38.5	338 07.0	51.4	200 47.9	21.7	2 01.2	34.3	129 53.1	18.1
T 10	302 40.9	353 06.3	50.8	215 49.7	21.6	17 03.1	34.2	144 55.8	18.2
U 11	317 43.4	8 05.5	50.1	230 51.5	21.6	32 05.1	34.2	159 58.4	18.2
R 12	332 45.8	23 04.8	S18 49.4	245 53.2	N26 21.6	47 07.1	S22 34.2	175 01.1	N11 18.3
D 13	347 48.3	38 04.1	48.7	260 55.0	21.5	62 09.0	34.1	190 03.7	18.4
A 14	2 50.8	53 03.4	48.1	275 56.8	21.5	77 11.0	34.1	205 06.4	18.5
Y 15	17 53.2	68 02.6	47.4	290 58.6	21.5	92 13.0	34.0	220 09.0	18.6
16	32 55.7	83 01.9	46.7	306 00.3	21.4	107 14.9	34.0	235 11.7	18.6
17	47 58.2	98 01.2	46.0	321 02.1	21.4	122 16.9	33.9	250 14.4	18.7
18	63 00.6	113 00.5	S18 45.3	336 03.9	N26 21.4	137 18.8	S22 33.9	265 17.0	N11 18.8
19	78 03.1	127 59.8	44.7	351 05.7	21.3	152 20.8	33.8	280 19.7	18.9
20	93 05.6	142 59.0	44.0	6 07.4	21.3	167 22.8	33.8	295 22.3	18.9
21	108 08.0	157 58.3	43.3	21 09.2	21.2	182 24.7	33.7	310 25.0	19.0
22	123 10.5	172 57.6	42.6	36 11.0	21.2	197 26.7	33.7	325 27.6	19.1
23	138 13.0	187 56.9	41.9	51 12.8	21.2	212 28.7	33.6	340 30.3	19.2
Mer. Pass.	h m 13 52.6	v −0.7	d 0.7	v 1.8	d 0.0	v 2.0	d 0.0	v 2.7	d 0.1

STARS

Name	SHA	Dec
	° ′	° ′
Acamar	315 21.4	S40 16.5
Achernar	335 29.8	S57 11.9
Acrux	173 13.6	S63 08.6
Adhara	255 15.4	S28 59.1
Aldebaran	290 54.0	N16 31.6
Alioth	166 23.5	N55 54.6
Alkaid	153 01.6	N49 16.0
Al Na'ir	27 49.0	S46 55.4
Alnilam	275 50.3	S 1 11.8
Alphard	217 59.7	S 8 41.8
Alphecca	126 14.3	N26 40.9
Alpheratz	357 48.1	N29 08.2
Altair	62 12.4	N 8 53.2
Ankaa	353 19.8	S42 15.8
Antares	112 31.3	S26 27.1
Arcturus	145 59.2	N19 08.1
Atria	107 37.0	S69 02.4
Avior	234 19.3	S59 32.3
Bellatrix	278 36.2	N 6 21.4
Betelgeuse	271 05.5	N 7 24.5
Canopus	263 57.6	S52 42.2
Capella	280 40.3	N46 00.6
Deneb	49 34.8	N45 18.4
Denebola	182 37.4	N14 31.4
Diphda	349 00.1	S17 56.6
Dubhe	193 55.5	N61 42.3
Elnath	278 17.6	N28 37.0
Eltanin	90 48.2	N51 28.9
Enif	33 51.4	N 9 54.6
Fomalhaut	15 28.6	S29 34.9
Gacrux	172 05.2	S57 09.5
Gienah	175 56.2	S17 35.4
Hadar	148 53.6	S60 24.7
Hamal	328 05.5	N23 30.2
Kaus Aust.	83 49.3	S34 22.9
Kochab	137 19.0	N74 06.9
Markab	13 42.7	N15 14.9
Menkar	314 19.3	N 4 07.3
Menkent	148 12.2	S36 24.6
Miaplacidus	221 40.0	S69 45.1
Mirfak	308 46.3	N49 53.7
Nunki	76 03.5	S26 17.3
Peacock	53 25.9	S56 42.5
Pollux	243 32.3	N28 00.4
Procyon	245 03.7	N 5 12.2
Rasalhague	96 10.3	N12 33.0
Regulus	207 47.4	N11 55.5
Rigel	281 15.8	S 8 11.6
Rigil Kent.	139 57.3	S60 52.0
Sabik	102 17.2	S15 44.2
Schedar	349 45.9	N56 35.1
Shaula	96 27.5	S37 06.6
Sirius	258 37.0	S16 43.7
Spica	158 35.3	S11 12.4
Suhail	222 55.1	S43 28.0
Vega	80 42.0	N38 47.1
Zuben'ubi	137 09.8	S16 04.7

	SHA	Mer. Pass.
	° ′	h m
Venus	52 13.9	10 26
Mars	273 31.5	19 38
Jupiter	74 39.4	8 55
Saturn	202 08.4	0 26

UT	SUN GHA	SUN Dec	MOON GHA	v	MOON Dec	d	HP
d h	° ′	° ′	° ′	′	° ′	′	′
21 00	176 33.8	S10 51.6	358 20.3	13.0	N11 18.1	14.5	57.2
01	191 33.8	50.7	12 52.3	13.0	11 03.6	14.5	57.2
02	206 33.9	49.8	27 24.3	13.1	10 49.1	14.6	57.2
03	221 34.0	. . 48.9	41 56.4	13.2	10 34.5	14.7	57.2
04	236 34.0	48.0	56 28.6	13.3	10 19.8	14.6	57.1
05	251 34.1	47.1	71 00.9	13.3	10 05.2	14.7	57.1
06	266 34.2	S10 46.2	85 33.2	13.4	N 9 50.5	14.7	57.1
T 07	281 34.2	45.3	100 05.6	13.5	9 35.8	14.8	57.1
H 08	296 34.3	44.4	114 38.1	13.5	9 21.0	14.8	57.0
U 09	311 34.4	. . 43.5	129 10.6	13.6	9 06.2	14.8	57.0
R 10	326 34.5	42.6	143 43.2	13.7	8 51.4	14.9	57.0
S 11	341 34.5	41.7	158 15.9	13.7	8 36.5	14.8	57.0
D 12	356 34.6	S10 40.8	172 48.6	13.8	N 8 21.7	14.9	56.9
A 13	11 34.7	39.9	187 21.4	13.9	8 06.8	14.9	56.9
Y 14	26 34.7	39.0	201 54.3	13.9	7 51.9	15.0	56.9
15	41 34.8	. . 38.1	216 27.2	14.0	7 36.9	14.9	56.9
16	56 34.9	37.2	231 00.2	14.0	7 22.0	15.0	56.8
17	71 35.0	36.3	245 33.2	14.1	7 07.0	15.0	56.8
18	86 35.0	S10 35.4	260 06.3	14.2	N 6 52.0	15.0	56.8
19	101 35.1	34.5	274 39.5	14.2	6 37.0	15.0	56.8
20	116 35.2	33.6	289 12.7	14.3	6 22.0	15.1	56.7
21	131 35.2	. . 32.7	303 46.0	14.3	6 06.9	15.0	56.7
22	146 35.3	31.8	318 19.3	14.4	5 51.9	15.1	56.7
23	161 35.4	30.9	332 52.7	14.4	5 36.8	15.0	56.7
22 00	176 35.5	S10 30.0	347 26.1	14.5	N 5 21.8	15.1	56.6
01	191 35.5	29.1	1 59.6	14.5	5 06.7	15.1	56.6
02	206 35.6	28.2	16 33.1	14.6	4 51.6	15.1	56.6
03	221 35.7	. . 27.2	31 06.7	14.6	4 36.5	15.1	56.6
04	236 35.8	26.3	45 40.3	14.7	4 21.4	15.1	56.5
05	251 35.8	25.4	60 14.0	14.7	4 06.3	15.1	56.5
06	266 35.9	S10 24.5	74 47.7	14.7	N 3 51.2	15.1	56.5
07	281 36.0	23.6	89 21.4	14.8	3 36.1	15.1	56.5
08	296 36.1	22.7	103 55.2	14.9	3 21.0	15.1	56.4
F 09	311 36.2	. . 21.8	118 29.1	14.8	3 05.9	15.2	56.4
R 10	326 36.2	20.9	133 02.9	15.0	2 50.7	15.1	56.4
I 11	341 36.3	20.0	147 36.9	14.9	2 35.6	15.1	56.4
D 12	356 36.4	S10 19.1	162 10.8	15.0	N 2 20.5	15.1	56.3
A 13	11 36.5	18.2	176 44.8	15.0	2 05.4	15.1	56.3
Y 14	26 36.5	17.3	191 18.8	15.1	1 50.3	15.0	56.3
15	41 36.6	. . 16.4	205 52.9	15.1	1 35.3	15.1	56.3
16	56 36.7	15.4	220 27.0	15.1	1 20.2	15.1	56.2
17	71 36.8	14.5	235 01.1	15.2	1 05.1	15.1	56.2
18	86 36.9	S10 13.6	249 35.3	15.2	N 0 50.0	15.0	56.2
19	101 36.9	12.7	264 09.5	15.2	0 35.0	15.0	56.2
20	116 37.0	11.8	278 43.7	15.3	0 20.0	15.1	56.1
21	131 37.1	. . 10.9	293 18.0	15.2	N 0 04.9	15.0	56.1
22	146 37.2	10.0	307 52.2	15.3	S 0 10.1	15.0	56.1
23	161 37.3	09.1	322 26.5	15.4	0 25.1	14.9	56.1
23 00	176 37.3	S10 08.2	337 00.9	15.3	S 0 40.0	15.0	56.0
01	191 37.4	07.2	351 35.2	15.4	0 55.0	15.0	56.0
02	206 37.5	06.3	6 09.6	15.4	1 10.0	14.9	56.0
03	221 37.6	. . 05.4	20 44.0	15.4	1 24.9	14.9	56.0
04	236 37.7	04.5	35 18.4	15.4	1 39.8	14.9	55.9
05	251 37.8	03.6	49 52.8	15.5	1 54.7	14.8	55.9
06	266 37.8	S10 02.7	64 27.3	15.5	S 2 09.5	14.9	55.9
S 07	281 37.9	01.8	79 01.8	15.4	2 24.4	14.8	55.9
A 08	296 38.0	10 00.8	93 36.2	15.5	2 39.2	14.8	55.8
T 09	311 38.1	9 59.9	108 10.7	15.6	2 54.0	14.8	55.8
U 10	326 38.2	59.0	122 45.3	15.5	3 08.8	14.7	55.8
R 11	341 38.3	58.1	137 19.8	15.5	3 23.5	14.7	55.8
D 12	356 38.3	S 9 57.2	151 54.3	15.6	S 3 38.2	14.7	55.7
A 13	11 38.4	56.3	166 28.9	15.5	3 52.9	14.7	55.7
Y 14	26 38.5	55.4	181 03.4	15.6	4 07.6	14.6	55.7
15	41 38.6	. . 54.4	195 38.0	15.6	4 22.2	14.6	55.7
16	56 38.7	53.5	210 12.6	15.6	4 36.8	14.6	55.6
17	71 38.8	52.6	224 47.2	15.5	4 51.4	14.5	55.6
18	86 38.9	S 9 51.7	239 21.7	15.6	S 5 05.9	14.5	55.6
19	101 38.9	50.8	253 56.3	15.6	5 20.4	14.5	55.6
20	116 39.0	49.9	268 30.9	15.6	5 34.9	14.4	55.6
21	131 39.1	. . 48.9	283 05.5	15.6	5 49.3	14.4	55.5
22	146 39.2	48.0	297 40.1	15.6	6 03.7	14.3	55.5
23	161 39.3	47.1	312 14.7	15.6	S 6 18.0	14.4	55.5
	SD 16.2	*d* 0.9	SD 15.5		15.3		15.2

Lat.	Twilight Naut.	Twilight Civil	Sunrise	Moonrise 21	Moonrise 22	Moonrise 23	Moonrise 24
°	h m	h m	h m	h m	h m	h m	h m
N 72	05 46	07 05	08 18	17 10	19 19	21 24	23 37
N 70	05 48	06 58	08 03	17 21	19 20	21 15	23 15
68	05 48	06 53	07 51	17 29	19 20	21 08	22 58
66	05 49	06 48	07 42	17 36	19 21	21 02	22 44
64	05 49	06 44	07 34	17 42	19 21	20 57	22 33
62	05 50	06 41	07 27	17 48	19 21	20 52	22 23
60	05 50	06 38	07 21	17 52	19 21	20 49	22 15
N 58	05 50	06 35	07 15	17 56	19 22	20 45	22 08
56	05 49	06 32	07 10	17 59	19 22	20 42	22 02
54	05 49	06 30	07 06	18 02	19 22	20 40	21 56
52	05 49	06 28	07 02	18 05	19 22	20 37	21 51
50	05 48	06 26	06 59	18 08	19 22	20 35	21 47
45	05 47	06 21	06 51	18 13	19 23	20 30	21 37
N 40	05 46	06 17	06 45	18 18	19 23	20 26	21 29
35	05 44	06 13	06 39	18 22	19 23	20 23	21 22
30	05 42	06 10	06 34	18 25	19 23	20 20	21 16
20	05 37	06 03	06 25	18 31	19 24	20 15	21 06
N 10	05 32	05 56	06 18	18 36	19 24	20 11	20 57
0	05 25	05 49	06 10	18 41	19 25	20 07	20 48
S 10	05 16	05 41	06 03	18 46	19 25	20 02	20 40
20	05 06	05 32	05 55	18 51	19 25	19 58	20 31
30	04 52	05 21	05 45	18 57	19 26	19 53	20 21
35	04 43	05 14	05 40	19 01	19 26	19 51	20 16
40	04 32	05 05	05 34	19 04	19 26	19 48	20 09
45	04 18	04 55	05 26	19 09	19 27	19 44	20 02
S 50	04 01	04 43	05 18	19 14	19 27	19 40	19 53
52	03 52	04 37	05 13	19 16	19 27	19 38	19 49
54	03 42	04 31	05 09	19 19	19 28	19 36	19 44
56	03 31	04 23	05 04	19 22	19 28	19 33	19 39
58	03 18	04 15	04 58	19 25	19 28	19 31	19 34
S 60	03 02	04 05	04 52	19 29	19 28	19 28	19 28

Lat.	Sunset	Twilight Civil	Twilight Naut.	Moonset 21	Moonset 22	Moonset 23	Moonset 24
°	h m	h m	h m	h m	h m	h m	h m
N 72	16 11	17 25	18 43	08 21	07 45	07 12	06 38
N 70	16 26	17 31	18 42	08 07	07 40	07 16	06 50
68	16 37	17 36	18 41	07 56	07 37	07 19	07 00
66	16 47	17 40	18 40	07 47	07 34	07 21	07 08
64	16 55	17 44	18 39	07 39	07 31	07 23	07 15
62	17 02	17 48	18 39	07 33	07 29	07 25	07 21
60	17 08	17 51	18 39	07 27	07 27	07 26	07 26
N 58	17 13	17 53	18 39	07 21	07 25	07 28	07 31
56	17 18	17 56	18 39	07 17	07 23	07 29	07 35
54	17 22	17 58	18 39	07 13	07 22	07 30	07 38
52	17 26	18 00	18 39	07 09	07 20	07 31	07 42
50	17 29	18 02	18 40	07 05	07 19	07 32	07 45
45	17 37	18 07	18 41	06 58	07 17	07 34	07 51
N 40	17 43	18 11	18 42	06 51	07 14	07 36	07 57
35	17 49	18 14	18 44	06 46	07 12	07 37	08 02
30	17 54	18 18	18 46	06 41	07 11	07 39	08 06
20	18 02	18 24	18 50	06 33	07 07	07 41	08 14
N 10	18 10	18 31	18 56	06 25	07 05	07 43	08 20
0	18 17	18 38	19 02	06 18	07 02	07 45	08 27
S 10	18 24	18 46	19 11	06 11	07 00	07 47	08 33
20	18 32	18 55	19 21	06 03	06 57	07 49	08 40
30	18 41	19 06	19 35	05 54	06 53	07 51	08 47
35	18 47	19 13	19 44	05 49	06 52	07 52	08 52
40	18 53	19 21	19 55	05 43	06 49	07 54	08 57
45	19 00	19 31	20 08	05 36	06 47	07 55	09 03
S 50	19 09	19 43	20 25	05 28	06 44	07 57	09 10
52	19 13	19 49	20 33	05 24	06 42	07 58	09 13
54	19 17	19 55	20 43	05 19	06 41	07 59	09 16
56	19 22	20 02	20 54	05 15	06 39	08 01	09 20
58	19 27	20 10	21 07	05 09	06 37	08 02	09 25
S 60	19 33	20 20	21 22	05 03	06 35	08 03	09 30

Day	SUN Eqn. of Time 00^h	SUN Eqn. of Time 12^h	SUN Mer. Pass.	MOON Mer. Pass. Upper	MOON Mer. Pass. Lower	MOON Age	MOON %	Phase
d	m s	m s	h m	h m	h m	d	%	
21	13 45	13 42	12 14	00 07	12 30	14	100	○
22	13 38	13 35	12 14	00 52	13 13	15	98	
23	13 31	13 27	12 13	01 35	13 56	16	94	

UT d h	ARIES GHA ° ′	VENUS −3.9 GHA ° ′	VENUS Dec ° ′	MARS +0.1 GHA ° ′	MARS Dec ° ′	JUPITER −2.0 GHA ° ′	JUPITER Dec ° ′	SATURN +0.2 GHA ° ′	SATURN Dec ° ′
24 00	153 15.4	202 56.2	S18 41.2	66 14.5	N26 21.1	227 30.6	S22 33.6	355 32.9	N11 19.3
01	168 17.9	217 55.5	40.5	81 16.3	21.1	242 32.6	33.6	10 35.6	19.3
02	183 20.3	232 54.7	39.9	96 18.1	21.1	257 34.6	33.5	25 38.2	19.4
03	198 22.8	247 54.0	. . 39.2	111 19.8	. . 21.0	272 36.5	. . 33.5	40 40.9	. . 19.5
04	213 25.3	262 53.3	38.5	126 21.6	21.0	287 38.5	33.4	55 43.5	19.6
05	228 27.7	277 52.6	37.8	141 23.3	21.0	302 40.5	33.4	70 46.2	19.6
06	243 30.2	292 51.9	S18 37.1	156 25.1	N26 20.9	317 42.4	S22 33.3	85 48.9	N11 19.7
07	258 32.7	307 51.2	36.4	171 26.9	20.9	332 44.4	33.3	100 51.5	19.8
08	273 35.1	322 50.4	35.7	186 28.6	20.9	347 46.4	33.2	115 54.2	19.9
S 09	288 37.6	337 49.7	. . 35.0	201 30.4	. . 20.8	2 48.3	. . 33.2	130 56.8	. . 19.9
U 10	303 40.1	352 49.0	34.3	216 32.1	20.8	17 50.3	33.1	145 59.5	20.0
N 11	318 42.5	7 48.3	33.6	231 33.9	20.8	32 52.3	33.1	161 02.1	20.1
D 12	333 45.0	22 47.6	S18 32.9	246 35.7	N26 20.7	47 54.2	S22 33.0	176 04.8	N11 20.2
A 13	348 47.4	37 46.9	32.2	261 37.4	20.7	62 56.2	33.0	191 07.4	20.3
Y 14	3 49.9	52 46.2	31.5	276 39.2	20.7	77 58.2	32.9	206 10.1	20.3
15	18 52.4	67 45.5	. . 30.8	291 40.9	. . 20.6	93 00.1	. . 32.9	221 12.7	. . 20.4
16	33 54.8	82 44.7	30.1	306 42.7	20.6	108 02.1	32.9	236 15.4	20.5
17	48 57.3	97 44.0	29.4	321 44.4	20.5	123 04.1	32.8	251 18.0	20.6
18	63 59.8	112 43.3	S18 28.7	336 46.2	N26 20.5	138 06.0	S22 32.8	266 20.7	N11 20.6
19	79 02.2	127 42.6	28.0	351 47.9	20.5	153 08.0	32.7	281 23.4	20.7
20	94 04.7	142 41.9	27.3	6 49.7	20.4	168 10.0	32.7	296 26.0	20.8
21	109 07.2	157 41.2	. . 26.6	21 51.4	. . 20.4	183 11.9	. . 32.6	311 28.7	. . 20.9
22	124 09.6	172 40.5	25.9	36 53.2	20.4	198 13.9	32.6	326 31.3	21.0
23	139 12.1	187 39.8	25.2	51 54.9	20.3	213 15.9	32.5	341 34.0	21.0
25 00	154 14.6	202 39.1	S18 24.5	66 56.7	N26 20.3	228 17.8	S22 32.5	356 36.6	N11 21.1
01	169 17.0	217 38.4	23.7	81 58.4	20.3	243 19.8	32.4	11 39.3	21.2
02	184 19.5	232 37.7	23.0	97 00.2	20.2	258 21.8	32.4	26 41.9	21.3
03	199 21.9	247 37.0	. . 22.3	112 01.9	. . 20.2	273 23.8	. . 32.3	41 44.6	. . 21.3
04	214 24.4	262 36.3	21.6	127 03.7	20.2	288 25.7	32.3	56 47.2	21.4
05	229 26.9	277 35.5	20.9	142 05.4	20.1	303 27.7	32.3	71 49.9	21.5
06	244 29.3	292 34.8	S18 20.2	157 07.1	N26 20.1	318 29.7	S22 32.2	86 52.5	N11 21.6
07	259 31.8	307 34.1	19.5	172 08.9	20.0	333 31.6	32.2	101 55.2	21.6
08	274 34.3	322 33.4	18.8	187 10.6	20.0	348 33.6	32.1	116 57.9	21.7
M 09	289 36.7	337 32.7	. . 18.0	202 12.4	. . 20.0	3 35.6	. . 32.1	132 00.5	. . 21.8
O 10	304 39.2	352 32.0	17.3	217 14.1	19.9	18 37.5	32.0	147 03.2	21.9
N 11	319 41.7	7 31.3	16.6	232 15.8	19.9	33 39.5	32.0	162 05.8	22.0
D 12	334 44.1	22 30.6	S18 15.9	247 17.6	N26 19.9	48 41.5	S22 31.9	177 08.5	N11 22.0
A 13	349 46.6	37 29.9	15.2	262 19.3	19.8	63 43.5	31.9	192 11.1	22.1
Y 14	4 49.1	52 29.2	14.4	277 21.0	19.8	78 45.4	31.8	207 13.8	22.2
15	19 51.5	67 28.5	. . 13.7	292 22.8	. . 19.8	93 47.4	. . 31.8	222 16.4	. . 22.3
16	34 54.0	82 27.8	13.0	307 24.5	19.7	108 49.4	31.7	237 19.1	22.3
17	49 56.4	97 27.1	12.3	322 26.2	19.7	123 51.3	31.7	252 21.7	22.4
18	64 58.9	112 26.4	S18 11.5	337 28.0	N26 19.6	138 53.3	S22 31.6	267 24.4	N11 22.5
19	80 01.4	127 25.7	10.8	352 29.7	19.6	153 55.3	31.6	282 27.0	22.6
20	95 03.8	142 25.0	10.1	7 31.4	19.6	168 57.3	31.6	297 29.7	22.6
21	110 06.3	157 24.3	. . 09.4	22 33.1	. . 19.5	183 59.2	. . 31.5	312 32.4	. . 22.7
22	125 08.8	172 23.6	08.6	37 34.9	19.5	199 01.2	31.5	327 35.0	22.8
23	140 11.2	187 22.9	07.9	52 36.6	19.5	214 03.2	31.4	342 37.7	22.9
26 00	155 13.7	202 22.2	S18 07.2	67 38.3	N26 19.4	229 05.2	S22 31.4	357 40.3	N11 23.0
01	170 16.2	217 21.5	06.4	82 40.1	19.4	244 07.1	31.3	12 43.0	23.0
02	185 18.6	232 20.8	05.7	97 41.8	19.4	259 09.1	31.3	27 45.6	23.1
03	200 21.1	247 20.1	. . 05.0	112 43.5	. . 19.3	274 11.1	. . 31.2	42 48.3	. . 23.2
04	215 23.5	262 19.5	04.2	127 45.2	19.3	289 13.0	31.2	57 50.9	23.3
05	230 26.0	277 18.8	03.5	142 46.9	19.2	304 15.0	31.1	72 53.6	23.3
06	245 28.5	292 18.1	S18 02.8	157 48.7	N26 19.2	319 17.0	S22 31.1	87 56.2	N11 23.4
07	260 30.9	307 17.4	02.0	172 50.4	19.2	334 19.0	31.0	102 58.9	23.5
T 08	275 33.4	322 16.7	01.3	187 52.1	19.1	349 20.9	31.0	118 01.5	23.6
U 09	290 35.9	337 16.0	18 00.5	202 53.8	. . 19.1	4 22.9	. . 30.9	133 04.2	. . 23.6
E 10	305 38.3	352 15.3	17 59.8	217 55.5	19.1	19 24.9	30.9	148 06.9	23.7
S 11	320 40.8	7 14.6	59.1	232 57.2	19.0	34 26.9	30.9	163 09.5	23.8
D 12	335 43.3	22 13.9	S17 58.3	247 59.0	N26 19.0	49 28.8	S22 30.8	178 12.2	N11 23.9
A 13	350 45.7	37 13.2	57.6	263 00.7	19.0	64 30.8	30.8	193 14.8	24.0
Y 14	5 48.2	52 12.5	56.8	278 02.4	18.9	79 32.8	30.7	208 17.5	24.0
15	20 50.7	67 11.8	. . 56.1	293 04.1	. . 18.9	94 34.8	. . 30.7	223 20.1	. . 24.1
16	35 53.1	82 11.1	55.3	308 05.8	18.8	109 36.8	30.6	238 22.8	24.2
17	50 55.6	97 10.5	54.6	323 07.5	18.8	124 38.7	30.6	253 25.4	24.3
18	65 58.0	112 09.8	S17 53.8	338 09.2	N26 18.8	139 40.7	S22 30.5	268 28.1	N11 24.3
19	81 00.5	127 09.1	53.1	353 10.9	18.7	154 42.7	30.5	283 30.7	24.4
20	96 03.0	142 08.4	52.3	8 12.7	18.7	169 44.7	30.4	298 33.4	24.5
21	111 05.4	157 07.7	. . 51.6	23 14.4	. . 18.7	184 46.6	. . 30.4	313 36.0	. . 24.6
22	126 07.9	172 07.0	50.8	38 16.1	18.6	199 48.6	30.3	328 38.7	24.6
23	141 10.4	187 06.3	50.1	53 17.8	18.6	214 50.6	30.3	343 41.4	24.7
Mer. Pass.	h m 13 40.8	*v* −0.7	*d* 0.7	*v* 1.7	*d* 0.0	*v* 2.0	*d* 0.0	*v* 2.7	*d* 0.1

STARS

Name	SHA ° ′	Dec ° ′
Acamar	315 21.4	S40 16.5
Achernar	335 29.8	S57 11.9
Acrux	173 13.6	S63 08.6
Adhara	255 15.5	S28 59.1
Aldebaran	290 54.0	N16 31.6
Alioth	166 23.4	N55 54.6
Alkaid	153 01.5	N49 16.0
Al Na'ir	27 49.0	S46 55.4
Alnilam	275 50.3	S 1 11.8
Alphard	217 59.7	S 8 41.8
Alphecca	126 14.3	N26 40.9
Alpheratz	357 48.1	N29 08.2
Altair	62 12.4	N 8 53.2
Ankaa	353 19.8	S42 15.8
Antares	112 31.2	S26 27.1
Arcturus	145 59.2	N19 08.1
Atria	107 36.9	S69 02.4
Avior	234 19.3	S59 32.3
Bellatrix	278 36.2	N 6 21.4
Betelgeuse	271 05.5	N 7 24.5
Canopus	263 57.7	S52 42.2
Capella	280 40.3	N46 00.6
Deneb	49 34.8	N45 18.3
Denebola	182 37.4	N14 31.4
Diphda	349 00.1	S17 56.6
Dubhe	193 55.5	N61 42.3
Elnath	278 17.6	N28 37.0
Eltanin	90 48.2	N51 28.8
Enif	33 51.4	N 9 54.6
Fomalhaut	15 28.6	S29 34.8
Gacrux	172 05.2	S57 09.5
Gienah	175 56.2	S17 35.4
Hadar	148 53.6	S60 24.7
Hamal	328 05.5	N23 30.2
Kaus Aust.	83 49.3	S34 22.9
Kochab	137 18.9	N74 06.9
Markab	13 42.7	N15 14.9
Menkar	314 19.4	N 4 07.3
Menkent	148 12.2	S36 24.6
Miaplacidus	221 40.1	S69 45.1
Mirfak	308 46.4	N49 53.7
Nunki	76 03.5	S26 17.3
Peacock	53 25.8	S56 42.5
Pollux	243 32.3	N28 00.4
Procyon	245 03.7	N 5 12.2
Rasalhague	96 10.3	N12 32.9
Regulus	207 47.4	N11 55.5
Rigel	281 15.8	S 8 11.6
Rigil Kent.	139 57.2	S60 52.0
Sabik	102 17.2	S15 44.2
Schedar	349 45.9	N56 35.1
Shaula	96 27.5	S37 06.6
Sirius	258 37.1	S16 43.7
Spica	158 35.3	S11 12.4
Suhail	222 55.1	S43 28.1
Vega	80 41.9	N38 47.1
Zuben'ubi	137 09.8	S16 04.7

	SHA ° ′	Mer. Pass. h m
Venus	48 24.5	10 30
Mars	272 42.1	19 30
Jupiter	74 03.3	8 46
Saturn	202 22.1	0 14

UT	SUN GHA	SUN Dec	MOON GHA	*v*	MOON Dec	*d*	HP
d h	° ′	° ′	° ′	′	° ′	′	′
24 00	176 39.4	S 9 46.2	326 49.3	15.6	S 6 32.4	14.2	55.5
01	191 39.5	45.3	341 23.9	15.6	6 46.6	14.3	55.4
02	206 39.6	44.4	355 58.5	15.6	7 00.9	14.2	55.4
03	221 39.6	. . 43.4	10 33.1	15.6	7 15.1	14.2	55.4
04	236 39.7	42.5	25 07.7	15.6	7 29.3	14.1	55.4
05	251 39.8	41.6	39 42.3	15.5	7 43.4	14.1	55.3
06	266 39.9	S 9 40.7	54 16.8	15.6	S 7 57.5	14.0	55.3
07	281 40.0	39.8	68 51.4	15.6	8 11.5	14.0	55.3
08	296 40.1	38.8	83 26.0	15.5	8 25.5	13.9	55.3
S 09	311 40.2	. . 37.9	98 00.5	15.6	8 39.4	13.9	55.3
U 10	326 40.3	37.0	112 35.1	15.5	8 53.3	13.9	55.2
N 11	341 40.4	36.1	127 09.6	15.5	9 07.2	13.8	55.2
D 12	356 40.4	S 9 35.2	141 44.1	15.5	S 9 21.0	13.7	55.2
A 13	11 40.5	34.2	156 18.6	15.5	9 34.7	13.8	55.2
Y 14	26 40.6	33.3	170 53.1	15.5	9 48.5	13.6	55.2
15	41 40.7	. . 32.4	185 27.6	15.4	10 02.1	13.6	55.1
16	56 40.8	31.5	200 02.0	15.4	10 15.7	13.6	55.1
17	71 40.9	30.5	214 36.4	15.5	10 29.3	13.5	55.1
18	86 41.0	S 9 29.6	229 10.9	15.4	S10 42.8	13.4	55.1
19	101 41.1	28.7	243 45.3	15.4	10 56.2	13.4	55.1
20	116 41.2	27.8	258 19.7	15.3	11 09.6	13.4	55.0
21	131 41.3	. . 26.8	272 54.0	15.4	11 23.0	13.3	55.0
22	146 41.4	25.9	287 28.4	15.3	11 36.3	13.2	55.0
23	161 41.5	25.0	302 02.7	15.3	11 49.5	13.2	55.0
25 00	176 41.6	S 9 24.1	316 37.0	15.2	S12 02.7	13.1	55.0
01	191 41.6	23.2	331 11.2	15.3	12 15.8	13.1	54.9
02	206 41.7	22.2	345 45.5	15.2	12 28.9	13.0	54.9
03	221 41.8	. . 21.3	0 19.7	15.2	12 41.9	12.9	54.9
04	236 41.9	20.4	14 53.9	15.2	12 54.8	12.9	54.9
05	251 42.0	19.4	29 28.1	15.1	13 07.7	12.8	54.9
06	266 42.1	S 9 18.5	44 02.2	15.1	S13 20.5	12.8	54.9
07	281 42.2	17.6	58 36.3	15.1	13 33.3	12.7	54.8
08	296 42.3	16.7	73 10.4	15.0	13 46.0	12.6	54.8
M 09	311 42.4	. . 15.7	87 44.4	15.0	13 58.6	12.6	54.8
O 10	326 42.5	14.8	102 18.4	15.0	14 11.2	12.5	54.8
N 11	341 42.6	13.9	116 52.4	15.0	14 23.7	12.4	54.8
D 12	356 42.7	S 9 13.0	131 26.4	14.9	S14 36.1	12.4	54.7
A 13	11 42.8	12.0	146 00.3	14.9	14 48.5	12.3	54.7
Y 14	26 42.9	11.1	160 34.2	14.8	15 00.8	12.2	54.7
15	41 43.0	. . 10.2	175 08.0	14.8	15 13.0	12.2	54.7
16	56 43.1	09.3	189 41.8	14.8	15 25.2	12.1	54.7
17	71 43.2	08.3	204 15.6	14.7	15 37.3	12.0	54.7
18	86 43.3	S 9 07.4	218 49.3	14.7	S15 49.3	12.0	54.7
19	101 43.4	06.5	233 23.0	14.7	16 01.3	11.9	54.6
20	116 43.5	05.5	247 56.7	14.6	16 13.2	11.8	54.6
21	131 43.6	. . 04.6	262 30.3	14.6	16 25.0	11.7	54.6
22	146 43.7	03.7	277 03.9	14.5	16 36.7	11.7	54.6
23	161 43.8	02.7	291 37.4	14.5	16 48.4	11.6	54.6
26 00	176 43.9	S 9 01.8	306 10.9	14.4	S17 00.0	11.5	54.6
01	191 44.0	00.9	320 44.3	14.4	17 11.5	11.5	54.6
02	206 44.1	9 00.0	335 17.7	14.4	17 23.0	11.3	54.5
03	221 44.2	8 59.0	349 51.1	14.3	17 34.3	11.3	54.5
04	236 44.3	58.1	4 24.4	14.3	17 45.6	11.2	54.5
05	251 44.4	57.2	18 57.7	14.2	17 56.8	11.2	54.5
06	266 44.5	S 8 56.2	33 30.9	14.2	S18 08.0	11.0	54.5
07	281 44.6	55.3	48 04.1	14.1	18 19.0	11.0	54.5
T 08	296 44.7	54.4	62 37.2	14.1	18 30.0	10.9	54.5
U 09	311 44.8	. . 53.4	77 10.3	14.0	18 40.9	10.8	54.5
E 10	326 44.9	52.5	91 43.3	14.0	18 51.7	10.7	54.4
S 11	341 45.0	51.6	106 16.3	14.0	19 02.4	10.6	54.4
D 12	356 45.1	S 8 50.6	120 49.3	13.9	S19 13.0	10.6	54.4
A 13	11 45.2	49.7	135 22.2	13.8	19 23.6	10.5	54.4
Y 14	26 45.3	48.8	149 55.0	13.8	19 34.1	10.4	54.4
15	41 45.4	. . 47.8	164 27.8	13.7	19 44.5	10.3	54.4
16	56 45.5	46.9	179 00.5	13.7	19 54.8	10.2	54.4
17	71 45.6	46.0	193 33.2	13.6	20 05.0	10.1	54.4
18	86 45.7	S 8 45.0	208 05.8	13.6	S20 15.1	10.1	54.4
19	101 45.8	44.1	222 38.4	13.6	20 25.2	9.9	54.4
20	116 45.9	43.2	237 11.0	13.4	20 35.1	9.9	54.3
21	131 46.0	. . 42.2	251 43.4	13.4	20 45.0	9.7	54.3
22	146 46.1	41.3	266 15.8	13.4	20 54.7	9.7	54.3
23	161 46.2	40.4	280 48.2	13.3	S21 04.4	9.6	54.3
	SD 16.2	*d* 0.9	SD 15.0		14.9		14.8

Lat.	Twilight Naut.	Twilight Civil	Sunrise	Moonrise 24	Moonrise 25	Moonrise 26	Moonrise 27
°	h m	h m	h m	h m	h m	h m	h m
N 72	05 32	06 50	08 01	23 37	26 53	02 53	■
N 70	05 35	06 45	07 49	23 15	25 36	01 36	■
68	05 37	06 41	07 39	22 58	24 58	00 58	■
66	05 39	06 38	07 30	22 44	24 32	00 32	02 38
64	05 40	06 35	07 23	22 33	24 13	00 13	02 00
62	05 41	06 32	07 17	22 23	23 56	25 34	01 34
60	05 42	06 30	07 12	22 15	23 43	25 13	01 13
N 58	05 42	06 27	07 07	22 08	23 32	24 57	00 57
56	05 42	06 25	07 03	22 02	23 22	24 42	00 42
54	05 43	06 24	06 59	21 56	23 13	24 30	00 30
52	05 43	06 22	06 56	21 51	23 05	24 20	00 20
50	05 43	06 20	06 53	21 47	22 58	24 10	00 10
45	05 42	06 16	06 46	21 37	22 44	23 50	24 56
N 40	05 42	06 13	06 40	21 29	22 32	23 34	24 36
35	05 40	06 10	06 35	21 22	22 21	23 21	24 20
30	05 39	06 07	06 31	21 16	22 12	23 09	24 06
20	05 35	06 01	06 23	21 06	21 57	22 49	23 42
N 10	05 31	05 55	06 16	20 57	21 44	22 32	23 22
0	05 25	05 49	06 10	20 48	21 31	22 16	23 03
S 10	05 17	05 42	06 03	20 40	21 19	22 00	22 44
20	05 07	05 33	05 56	20 31	21 06	21 43	22 23
30	04 54	05 23	05 48	20 21	20 51	21 24	22 00
35	04 46	05 17	05 43	20 16	20 43	21 12	21 47
40	04 36	05 09	05 37	20 09	20 33	21 00	21 31
45	04 23	05 00	05 31	20 02	20 21	20 44	21 12
S 50	04 07	04 49	05 23	19 53	20 08	20 26	20 49
52	03 59	04 43	05 19	19 49	20 02	20 17	20 38
54	03 50	04 37	05 15	19 44	19 55	20 08	20 26
56	03 40	04 31	05 11	19 39	19 47	19 57	20 11
58	03 28	04 23	05 06	19 34	19 38	19 44	19 55
S 60	03 13	04 14	05 00	19 28	19 28	19 30	19 34

Lat.	Sunset	Twilight Civil	Twilight Naut.	Moonset 24	Moonset 25	Moonset 26	Moonset 27
°	h m	h m	h m	h m	h m	h m	h m
N 72	16 27	17 38	18 56	06 38	05 55	04 09	■
N 70	16 39	17 43	18 53	06 50	06 19	05 29	■
68	16 49	17 47	18 51	07 00	06 38	06 07	■
66	16 57	17 50	18 49	07 08	06 53	06 35	06 03
64	17 04	17 53	18 48	07 15	07 06	06 56	06 41
62	17 10	17 56	18 47	07 21	07 17	07 13	07 08
60	17 15	17 58	18 46	07 26	07 26	07 27	07 29
N 58	17 20	18 00	18 45	07 31	07 34	07 39	07 47
56	17 24	18 02	18 45	07 35	07 41	07 50	08 01
54	17 28	18 04	18 45	07 38	07 48	07 59	08 14
52	17 31	18 05	18 45	07 42	07 53	08 07	08 25
50	17 34	18 07	18 44	07 45	07 59	08 15	08 35
45	17 41	18 11	18 45	07 51	08 10	08 31	08 56
N 40	17 47	18 14	18 45	07 57	08 20	08 45	09 13
35	17 51	18 17	18 46	08 02	08 28	08 56	09 28
30	17 56	18 20	18 48	08 06	08 35	09 06	09 40
20	18 03	18 26	18 51	08 14	08 48	09 23	10 02
N 10	18 10	18 31	18 56	08 20	08 59	09 38	10 21
0	18 16	18 37	19 02	08 27	09 09	09 52	10 38
S 10	18 23	18 44	19 09	08 33	09 19	10 07	10 56
20	18 30	18 53	19 19	08 40	09 30	10 22	11 15
30	18 38	19 03	19 32	08 47	09 43	10 40	11 37
35	18 43	19 09	19 40	08 52	09 51	10 50	11 49
40	18 48	19 16	19 50	08 57	09 59	11 02	12 04
45	18 55	19 25	20 02	09 03	10 09	11 16	12 22
S 50	19 03	19 36	20 18	09 10	10 21	11 33	12 44
52	19 06	19 42	20 26	09 13	10 27	11 41	12 55
54	19 10	19 48	20 34	09 16	10 33	11 50	13 07
56	19 14	19 54	20 44	09 20	10 40	12 00	13 21
58	19 19	20 02	20 56	09 25	10 48	12 12	13 37
S 60	19 25	20 10	21 10	09 30	10 57	12 26	13 56

Day	SUN Eqn. of Time 00^h	SUN Eqn. of Time 12^h	SUN Mer. Pass.	MOON Mer. Pass. Upper	MOON Mer. Pass. Lower	MOON Age	MOON Phase %
d	m s	m s	h m	h m	h m	d	%
24	13 23	13 18	12 13	02 17	14 38	17	89
25	13 14	13 09	12 13	02 59	15 20	18	82
26	13 05	13 00	12 13	03 42	16 04	19	74

UT	ARIES	VENUS −3.9		MARS +0.1		JUPITER −2.0		SATURN +0.2	
	GHA	GHA	Dec	GHA	Dec	GHA	Dec	GHA	Dec
d h	° ′	° ′	° ′	° ′	° ′	° ′	° ′	° ′	° ′
27 00 (WEDNESDAY)	156 12.8	202 05.6	S17 49.3	68 19.5	N26 18.5	229 52.6	S22 30.2	358 44.0	N11 24.8
01	171 15.3	217 05.0	48.6	83 21.2	18.5	244 54.5	30.2	13 46.7	24.9
02	186 17.8	232 04.3	47.8	98 22.9	18.5	259 56.5	30.1	28 49.3	24.9
03	201 20.2	247 03.6	. . 47.1	113 24.6	. . 18.4	274 58.5	. . 30.1	43 52.0	. . 25.0
04	216 22.7	262 02.9	46.3	128 26.3	18.4	290 00.5	30.1	58 54.6	25.1
05	231 25.2	277 02.2	45.6	143 28.0	18.4	305 02.5	30.0	73 57.3	25.2
06	246 27.6	292 01.5	S17 44.8	158 29.7	N26 18.3	320 04.4	S22 30.0	88 59.9	N11 25.3
07	261 30.1	307 00.9	44.0	173 31.4	18.3	335 06.4	29.9	104 02.6	25.3
08	276 32.5	322 00.2	43.3	188 33.1	18.2	350 08.4	29.9	119 05.2	25.4
09	291 35.0	336 59.5	. . 42.5	203 34.8	. . 18.2	5 10.4	. . 29.8	134 07.9	. . 25.5
10	306 37.5	351 58.8	41.8	218 36.5	18.2	20 12.4	29.8	149 10.5	25.6
11	321 39.9	6 58.1	41.0	233 38.2	18.1	35 14.3	29.7	164 13.2	25.6
12	336 42.4	21 57.4	S17 40.2	248 39.9	N26 18.1	50 16.3	S22 29.7	179 15.9	N11 25.7
13	351 44.9	36 56.8	39.5	263 41.6	18.1	65 18.3	29.6	194 18.5	25.8
14	6 47.3	51 56.1	38.7	278 43.3	18.0	80 20.3	29.6	209 21.2	25.9
15	21 49.8	66 55.4	. . 37.9	293 44.9	. . 18.0	95 22.3	. . 29.5	224 23.8	. . 25.9
16	36 52.3	81 54.7	37.2	308 46.6	17.9	110 24.2	29.5	239 26.5	26.0
17	51 54.7	96 54.1	36.4	323 48.3	17.9	125 26.2	29.4	254 29.1	26.1
18	66 57.2	111 53.4	S17 35.6	338 50.0	N26 17.9	140 28.2	S22 29.4	269 31.8	N11 26.2
19	81 59.6	126 52.7	34.9	353 51.7	17.8	155 30.2	29.4	284 34.4	26.2
20	97 02.1	141 52.0	34.1	8 53.4	17.8	170 32.2	29.3	299 37.1	26.3
21	112 04.6	156 51.3	. . 33.3	23 55.1	. . 17.7	185 34.1	. . 29.3	314 39.7	. . 26.4
22	127 07.0	171 50.7	32.6	38 56.8	17.7	200 36.1	29.2	329 42.4	26.5
23	142 09.5	186 50.0	31.8	53 58.5	17.7	215 38.1	29.2	344 45.0	26.6
28 00 (THURSDAY)	157 12.0	201 49.3	S17 31.0	69 00.1	N26 17.6	230 40.1	S22 29.1	359 47.7	N11 26.6
01	172 14.4	216 48.6	30.2	84 01.8	17.6	245 42.1	29.1	14 50.3	26.7
02	187 16.9	231 48.0	29.5	99 03.5	17.6	260 44.0	29.0	29 53.0	26.8
03	202 19.4	246 47.3	. . 28.7	114 05.2	. . 17.5	275 46.0	. . 29.0	44 55.7	. . 26.9
04	217 21.8	261 46.6	27.9	129 06.9	17.5	290 48.0	28.9	59 58.3	26.9
05	232 24.3	276 45.9	27.1	144 08.5	17.4	305 50.0	28.9	75 01.0	27.0
06	247 26.8	291 45.3	S17 26.3	159 10.2	N26 17.4	320 52.0	S22 28.8	90 03.6	N11 27.1
07	262 29.2	306 44.6	25.6	174 11.9	17.4	335 54.0	28.8	105 06.3	27.2
08	277 31.7	321 43.9	24.8	189 13.6	17.3	350 55.9	28.7	120 08.9	27.2
09	292 34.1	336 43.3	. . 24.0	204 15.3	. . 17.3	5 57.9	. . 28.7	135 11.6	. . 27.3
10	307 36.6	351 42.6	23.2	219 16.9	17.2	20 59.9	28.6	150 14.2	27.4
11	322 39.1	6 41.9	22.4	234 18.6	17.2	36 01.9	28.6	165 16.9	27.5
12	337 41.5	21 41.2	S17 21.7	249 20.3	N26 17.2	51 03.9	S22 28.6	180 19.5	N11 27.5
13	352 44.0	36 40.6	20.9	264 22.0	17.1	66 05.9	28.5	195 22.2	27.6
14	7 46.5	51 39.9	20.1	279 23.6	17.1	81 07.8	28.5	210 24.8	27.7
15	22 48.9	66 39.2	. . 19.3	294 25.3	. . 17.0	96 09.8	. . 28.4	225 27.5	. . 27.8
16	37 51.4	81 38.6	18.5	309 27.0	17.0	111 11.8	28.4	240 30.2	27.8
17	52 53.9	96 37.9	17.7	324 28.6	17.0	126 13.8	28.3	255 32.8	27.9
18	67 56.3	111 37.2	S17 16.9	339 30.3	N26 16.9	141 15.8	S22 28.3	270 35.5	N11 28.0
19	82 58.8	126 36.6	16.1	354 32.0	16.9	156 17.8	28.2	285 38.1	28.1
20	98 01.3	141 35.9	15.4	9 33.7	16.9	171 19.8	28.2	300 40.8	28.2
21	113 03.7	156 35.2	. . 14.6	24 35.3	. . 16.8	186 21.7	. . 28.1	315 43.4	. . 28.2
22	128 06.2	171 34.6	13.8	39 37.0	16.8	201 23.7	28.1	330 46.1	28.3
23	143 08.6	186 33.9	13.0	54 38.7	16.7	216 25.7	28.0	345 48.7	28.4
29 00 (FRIDAY)	158 11.1	201 33.2	S17 12.2	69 40.3	N26 16.7	231 27.7	S22 28.0	0 51.4	N11 28.5
01	173 13.6	216 32.6	11.4	84 42.0	16.7	246 29.7	27.9	15 54.0	28.5
02	188 16.0	231 31.9	10.6	99 43.6	16.6	261 31.7	27.9	30 56.7	28.6
03	203 18.5	246 31.3	. . 09.8	114 45.3	. . 16.6	276 33.7	. . 27.8	45 59.3	. . 28.7
04	218 21.0	261 30.6	09.0	129 47.0	16.5	291 35.6	27.8	61 02.0	28.8
05	233 23.4	276 29.9	08.2	144 48.6	16.5	306 37.6	27.8	76 04.6	28.8
06	248 25.9	291 29.3	S17 07.4	159 50.3	N26 16.5	321 39.6	S22 27.7	91 07.3	N11 28.9
07	263 28.4	306 28.6	06.6	174 51.9	16.4	336 41.6	27.7	106 10.0	29.0
08	278 30.8	321 27.9	05.8	189 53.6	16.4	351 43.6	27.6	121 12.6	29.1
09	293 33.3	336 27.3	. . 05.0	204 55.3	. . 16.3	6 45.6	. . 27.6	136 15.3	. . 29.1
10	308 35.7	351 26.6	04.2	219 56.9	16.3	21 47.6	27.5	151 17.9	29.2
11	323 38.2	6 26.0	03.4	234 58.6	16.3	36 49.6	27.5	166 20.6	29.3
12	338 40.7	21 25.3	S17 02.6	250 00.2	N26 16.2	51 51.5	S22 27.4	181 23.2	N11 29.4
13	353 43.1	36 24.6	01.8	265 01.9	16.2	66 53.5	27.4	196 25.9	29.4
14	8 45.6	51 24.0	01.0	280 03.5	16.1	81 55.5	27.3	211 28.5	29.5
15	23 48.1	66 23.3	17 00.2	295 05.2	. . 16.1	96 57.5	. . 27.3	226 31.2	. . 29.6
16	38 50.5	81 22.7	16 59.4	310 06.8	16.1	111 59.5	27.2	241 33.8	29.7
17	53 53.0	96 22.0	58.5	325 08.5	16.0	127 01.5	27.2	256 36.5	29.7
18	68 55.5	111 21.4	S16 57.7	340 10.1	N26 16.0	142 03.5	S22 27.1	271 39.1	N11 29.8
19	83 57.9	126 20.7	56.9	355 11.8	15.9	157 05.5	27.1	286 41.8	29.9
20	99 00.4	141 20.0	56.1	10 13.4	15.9	172 07.5	27.0	301 44.4	30.0
21	114 02.9	156 19.4	. . 55.3	25 15.1	. . 15.8	187 09.5	. . 27.0	316 47.1	. . 30.0
22	129 05.3	171 18.7	54.5	40 16.7	15.8	202 11.4	27.0	331 49.7	30.1
23	144 07.8	186 18.1	53.7	55 18.4	15.8	217 13.4	26.9	346 52.4	30.2
Mer. Pass.	h m 13 29.0	*v* −0.7	*d* 0.8	*v* 1.7	*d* 0.0	*v* 2.0	*d* 0.0	*v* 2.7	*d* 0.1

STARS Name	SHA	Dec
	° ′	° ′
Acamar	315 21.4	S40 16.5
Achernar	335 29.8	S57 11.9
Acrux	173 13.6	S63 08.7
Adhara	255 15.5	S28 59.1
Aldebaran	290 54.0	N16 31.6
Alioth	166 23.4	N55 54.6
Alkaid	153 01.5	N49 16.0
Al Na'ir	27 49.0	S46 55.3
Alnilam	275 50.3	S 1 11.8
Alphard	217 59.7	S 8 41.8
Alphecca	126 14.3	N26 40.9
Alpheratz	357 48.1	N29 08.2
Altair	62 12.4	N 8 53.2
Ankaa	353 19.8	S42 15.8
Antares	112 31.2	S26 27.1
Arcturus	145 59.1	N19 08.1
Atria	107 36.9	S69 02.4
Avior	234 19.3	S59 32.3
Bellatrix	278 36.2	N 6 21.4
Betelgeuse	271 05.5	N 7 24.5
Canopus	263 57.7	S52 42.2
Capella	280 40.3	N46 00.6
Deneb	49 34.7	N45 18.3
Denebola	182 37.4	N14 31.4
Diphda	349 00.1	S17 56.6
Dubhe	193 55.5	N61 42.3
Elnath	278 17.6	N28 37.0
Eltanin	90 48.2	N51 28.8
Enif	33 51.4	N 9 54.6
Fomalhaut	15 28.6	S29 34.8
Gacrux	172 05.2	S57 09.5
Gienah	175 56.2	S17 35.4
Hadar	148 53.5	S60 24.7
Hamal	328 05.6	N23 30.2
Kaus Aust.	83 49.3	S34 22.9
Kochab	137 18.8	N74 06.9
Markab	13 42.7	N15 14.9
Menkar	314 19.4	N 4 07.3
Menkent	148 12.2	S36 24.7
Miaplacidus	221 40.1	S69 45.2
Mirfak	308 46.4	N49 53.7
Nunki	76 03.5	S26 17.3
Peacock	53 25.8	S56 42.5
Pollux	243 32.3	N28 00.4
Procyon	245 03.7	N 5 12.2
Rasalhague	96 10.3	N12 32.9
Regulus	207 47.4	N11 55.5
Rigel	281 15.8	S 8 11.6
Rigil Kent.	139 57.2	S60 52.0
Sabik	102 17.2	S15 44.2
Schedar	349 45.9	N56 35.1
Shaula	96 27.5	S37 06.6
Sirius	258 37.1	S16 43.7
Spica	158 35.3	S11 12.4
Suhail	222 55.1	S43 28.1
Vega	80 41.9	N38 47.1
Zuben'ubi	137 09.8	S16 04.7

	SHA	Mer. Pass.
	° ′	h m
Venus	44 37.3	10 33
Mars	271 48.2	19 22
Jupiter	73 28.1	8 36
Saturn	202 35.7	0 01

UT	SUN GHA	SUN Dec	MOON GHA	*v*	MOON Dec	*d*	HP
d h	° ′	° ′	° ′	′	° ′	′	′
27 00 (WEDNESDAY)	176 46.3	S 8 39.4	295 20.5	13.3	S21 14.0	9.5	54.3
01	191 46.4	38.5	309 52.8	13.2	21 23.5	9.4	54.3
02	206 46.6	37.6	324 25.0	13.1	21 32.9	9.3	54.3
03	221 46.7	. . 36.6	338 57.1	13.1	21 42.2	9.2	54.3
04	236 46.8	35.7	353 29.2	13.1	21 51.4	9.1	54.3
05	251 46.9	34.7	8 01.3	12.9	22 00.5	9.1	54.3
06	266 47.0	S 8 33.8	22 33.2	13.0	S22 09.6	8.9	54.3
07	281 47.1	32.9	37 05.2	12.8	22 18.5	8.8	54.3
08	296 47.2	31.9	51 37.0	12.8	22 27.3	8.7	54.3
09	311 47.3	. . 31.0	66 08.8	12.8	22 36.0	8.7	54.3
10	326 47.4	30.1	80 40.6	12.7	22 44.7	8.5	54.3
11	341 47.5	29.1	95 12.3	12.6	22 53.2	8.4	54.2
12	356 47.6	S 8 28.2	109 43.9	12.6	S23 01.6	8.4	54.2
13	11 47.7	27.2	124 15.5	12.5	23 10.0	8.2	54.2
14	26 47.8	26.3	138 47.0	12.5	23 18.2	8.1	54.2
15	41 47.9	. . 25.4	153 18.5	12.4	23 26.3	8.0	54.2
16	56 48.1	24.4	167 49.9	12.3	23 34.3	7.9	54.2
17	71 48.2	23.5	182 21.2	12.3	23 42.2	7.8	54.2
18	86 48.3	S 8 22.5	196 52.5	12.2	S23 50.0	7.7	54.2
19	101 48.4	21.6	211 23.7	12.2	23 57.7	7.6	54.2
20	116 48.5	20.7	225 54.9	12.1	24 05.3	7.5	54.2
21	131 48.6	. . 19.7	240 26.0	12.1	24 12.8	7.4	54.2
22	146 48.7	18.8	254 57.1	12.0	24 20.2	7.3	54.2
23	161 48.8	17.8	269 28.1	11.9	24 27.5	7.1	54.2
28 00 (THURSDAY)	176 48.9	S 8 16.9	283 59.0	11.9	S24 34.6	7.1	54.2
01	191 49.1	16.0	298 29.9	11.8	24 41.7	6.9	54.2
02	206 49.2	15.0	313 00.7	11.8	24 48.6	6.9	54.2
03	221 49.3	. . 14.1	327 31.5	11.7	24 55.5	6.7	54.2
04	236 49.4	13.1	342 02.2	11.6	25 02.2	6.6	54.2
05	251 49.5	12.2	356 32.8	11.6	25 08.8	6.5	54.2
06	266 49.6	S 8 11.2	11 03.4	11.6	S25 15.3	6.4	54.2
07	281 49.7	10.3	25 34.0	11.4	25 21.7	6.2	54.2
08	296 49.8	09.4	40 04.4	11.5	25 27.9	6.2	54.2
09	311 49.9	. . 08.4	54 34.9	11.3	25 34.1	6.0	54.2
10	326 50.1	07.5	69 05.2	11.3	25 40.1	5.9	54.2
11	341 50.2	06.5	83 35.5	11.3	25 46.0	5.8	54.2
12	356 50.3	S 8 05.6	98 05.8	11.2	S25 51.8	5.7	54.2
13	11 50.4	04.6	112 36.0	11.1	25 57.5	5.6	54.2
14	26 50.5	03.7	127 06.1	11.1	26 03.1	5.4	54.2
15	41 50.6	. . 02.8	141 36.2	11.1	26 08.5	5.3	54.2
16	56 50.7	01.8	156 06.3	10.9	26 13.8	5.2	54.2
17	71 50.9	8 00.9	170 36.2	11.0	26 19.0	5.1	54.3
18	86 51.0	S 7 59.9	185 06.2	10.8	S26 24.1	5.0	54.3
19	101 51.1	59.0	199 36.0	10.9	26 29.1	4.8	54.3
20	116 51.2	58.0	214 05.9	10.7	26 33.9	4.7	54.3
21	131 51.3	. . 57.1	228 35.6	10.7	26 38.6	4.6	54.3
22	146 51.4	56.1	243 05.3	10.7	26 43.2	4.5	54.3
23	161 51.6	55.2	257 35.0	10.6	26 47.7	4.3	54.3
29 00 (FRIDAY)	176 51.7	S 7 54.3	272 04.6	10.6	S26 52.0	4.2	54.3
01	191 51.8	53.3	286 34.2	10.5	26 56.2	4.1	54.3
02	206 51.9	52.4	301 03.7	10.5	27 00.3	4.0	54.3
03	221 52.0	. . 51.4	315 33.2	10.4	27 04.3	3.8	54.3
04	236 52.1	50.5	330 02.6	10.4	27 08.1	3.7	54.3
05	251 52.3	49.5	344 32.0	10.3	27 11.8	3.6	54.3
06	266 52.4	S 7 48.6	359 01.3	10.3	S27 15.4	3.4	54.3
07	281 52.5	47.6	13 30.6	10.2	27 18.8	3.4	54.3
08	296 52.6	46.7	27 59.8	10.2	27 22.2	3.1	54.4
09	311 52.7	. . 45.7	42 29.0	10.2	27 25.3	3.1	54.4
10	326 52.8	44.8	56 58.2	10.1	27 28.4	2.9	54.4
11	341 53.0	43.8	71 27.3	10.1	27 31.3	2.8	54.4
12	356 53.1	S 7 42.9	85 56.4	10.0	S27 34.1	2.7	54.4
13	11 53.2	41.9	100 25.4	10.0	27 36.8	2.5	54.4
14	26 53.3	41.0	114 54.4	9.9	27 39.3	2.4	54.4
15	41 53.4	. . 40.0	129 23.3	9.9	27 41.7	2.3	54.4
16	56 53.6	39.1	143 52.2	9.9	27 44.0	2.1	54.4
17	71 53.7	38.1	158 21.1	9.8	27 46.1	2.0	54.5
18	86 53.8	S 7 37.2	172 49.9	9.8	S27 48.1	1.9	54.5
19	101 53.9	36.2	187 18.7	9.8	27 50.0	1.7	54.5
20	116 54.0	35.3	201 47.5	9.7	27 51.7	1.6	54.5
21	131 54.2	. . 34.3	216 16.2	9.7	27 53.3	1.4	54.5
22	146 54.3	33.4	230 44.9	9.7	27 54.7	1.3	54.5
23	161 54.4	32.4	245 13.6	9.6	S27 56.0	1.2	54.5
	SD 16.2	*d* 0.9	SD	14.8	14.8		14.8

Lat.	Twilight Naut.	Twilight Civil	Sunrise	Moonrise 27	Moonrise 28	Moonrise 29	Moonrise 1
°	h m	h m	h m	h m	h m	h m	h m
N 72	05 18	06 36	07 45	▬	▬	▬	▬
N 70	05 22	06 32	07 35	▬	▬	▬	▬
68	05 26	06 30	07 26	▬	▬	▬	▬
66	05 28	06 27	07 19	02 38	▬	▬	▬
64	05 30	06 25	07 13	02 00	04 09	▬	▬
62	05 32	06 23	07 08	01 34	03 17	05 06	▬
60	05 33	06 21	07 03	01 13	02 45	04 13	05 23
N 58	05 34	06 20	06 59	00 57	02 21	03 41	04 46
56	05 35	06 18	06 56	00 42	02 02	03 17	04 20
54	05 36	06 17	06 52	00 30	01 46	02 58	03 59
52	05 37	06 16	06 50	00 20	01 33	02 41	03 41
50	05 37	06 14	06 47	00 10	01 21	02 27	03 27
45	05 37	06 11	06 41	24 56	00 56	01 59	02 57
N 40	05 37	06 09	06 36	24 36	00 36	01 37	02 33
35	05 37	06 06	06 32	24 20	00 20	01 18	02 14
30	05 36	06 04	06 28	24 06	00 06	01 03	01 57
20	05 33	05 59	06 21	23 42	24 36	00 36	01 29
N 10	05 29	05 54	06 15	23 22	24 13	00 13	01 05
0	05 24	05 48	06 09	23 03	23 52	24 43	00 43
S 10	05 17	05 42	06 03	22 44	23 31	24 21	00 21
20	05 09	05 35	05 57	22 23	23 08	23 57	24 50
30	04 57	05 25	05 50	22 00	22 42	23 29	24 23
35	04 49	05 20	05 45	21 47	22 26	23 13	24 06
40	04 40	05 13	05 41	21 31	22 09	22 54	23 47
45	04 28	05 04	05 35	21 12	21 47	22 31	23 24
S 50	04 13	04 54	05 28	20 49	21 20	22 01	22 55
52	04 06	04 49	05 25	20 38	21 07	21 47	22 40
54	03 58	04 44	05 21	20 26	20 52	21 30	22 24
56	03 48	04 38	05 17	20 11	20 34	21 10	22 03
58	03 37	04 31	05 13	19 55	20 13	20 44	21 38
S 60	03 24	04 23	05 08	19 34	19 45	20 10	21 03

Lat.	Sunset	Twilight Civil	Twilight Naut.	Moonset 27	Moonset 28	Moonset 29	Moonset 1
°	h m	h m	h m	h m	h m	h m	h m
N 72	16 42	17 52	19 10	▬	▬	▬	▬
N 70	16 52	17 55	19 05	▬	▬	▬	▬
68	17 01	17 57	19 02	▬	▬	▬	▬
66	17 08	18 00	18 59	06 03	▬	▬	▬
64	17 14	18 02	18 57	06 41	06 10	▬	▬
62	17 19	18 04	18 55	07 08	07 04	06 57	▬
60	17 23	18 05	18 53	07 29	07 36	07 51	08 28
N 58	17 27	18 07	18 52	07 47	08 00	08 23	09 05
56	17 31	18 08	18 51	08 01	08 19	08 47	09 32
54	17 34	18 09	18 50	08 14	08 36	09 07	09 52
52	17 37	18 11	18 50	08 25	08 50	09 23	10 10
50	17 39	18 12	18 49	08 35	09 02	09 37	10 25
45	17 45	18 15	18 49	08 56	09 27	10 06	10 55
N 40	17 50	18 17	18 49	09 13	09 48	10 29	11 18
35	17 54	18 20	18 49	09 28	10 05	10 48	11 38
30	17 58	18 22	18 50	09 40	10 19	11 04	11 54
20	18 04	18 27	18 52	10 02	10 44	11 31	12 22
N 10	18 10	18 32	18 56	10 21	11 06	11 54	12 46
0	18 16	18 37	19 01	10 38	11 26	12 16	13 08
S 10	18 22	18 43	19 08	10 56	11 46	12 38	13 31
20	18 28	18 50	19 16	11 15	12 08	13 02	13 55
30	18 35	18 59	19 28	11 37	12 33	13 29	14 22
35	18 39	19 05	19 36	11 49	12 48	13 45	14 39
40	18 44	19 12	19 45	12 04	13 06	14 04	14 58
45	18 50	19 20	19 56	12 22	13 27	14 27	15 21
S 50	18 56	19 30	20 11	12 44	13 53	14 56	15 51
52	19 00	19 35	20 18	12 55	14 06	15 11	16 05
54	19 03	19 40	20 26	13 07	14 21	15 28	16 22
56	19 07	19 46	20 35	13 21	14 38	15 48	16 42
58	19 11	19 53	20 46	13 37	14 59	16 13	17 08
S 60	19 16	20 00	20 58	13 56	15 26	16 47	17 43

Day	SUN Eqn. of Time 00^h	SUN Eqn. of Time 12^h	SUN Mer. Pass.	MOON Mer. Pass. Upper	MOON Mer. Pass. Lower	MOON Age	MOON Phase
d	m s	m s	h m	h m	h m	d	%
27	12 55	12 50	12 13	04 27	16 50	20	65
28	12 44	12 39	12 13	05 14	17 39	21	56 ◑
29	12 34	12 28	12 12	06 04	18 30	22	46

	UT	ARIES	VENUS −3.9		MARS +0.2		JUPITER −2.0		SATURN +0.2		STARS		
		GHA	GHA	Dec	GHA	Dec	GHA	Dec	GHA	Dec	Name	SHA	Dec
	d h	° ′	° ′	° ′	° ′	° ′	° ′	° ′	° ′	° ′		° ′	° ′
	1 00	159 10.2	201 17.4	S16 52.9	70 20.0	N26 15.7	232 15.4	S22 26.9	1 55.1	N11 30.3	Acamar	315 21.4	S40 16.5
	01	174 12.7	216 16.8	52.0	85 21.7	15.7	247 17.4	26.8	16 57.7	30.3	Achernar	335 29.9	S57 11.9
	02	189 15.2	231 16.1	51.2	100 23.3	15.6	262 19.4	26.8	32 00.4	30.4	Acrux	173 13.5	S63 08.7
	03	204 17.6	246 15.5	. . 50.4	115 25.0	. . 15.6	277 21.4	. . 26.7	47 03.0	. . 30.5	Adhara	255 15.5	S28 59.1
	04	219 20.1	261 14.8	49.6	130 26.6	15.6	292 23.4	26.7	62 05.7	30.6	Aldebaran	290 54.0	N16 31.6
	05	234 22.6	276 14.2	48.8	145 28.2	15.5	307 25.4	26.6	77 08.3	30.6			
	06	249 25.0	291 13.5	S16 48.0	160 29.9	N26 15.5	322 27.4	S22 26.6	92 11.0	N11 30.7	Alioth	166 23.4	N55 54.6
	07	264 27.5	306 12.9	47.1	175 31.5	15.4	337 29.4	26.5	107 13.6	30.8	Alkaid	153 01.5	N49 16.0
S	08	279 30.0	321 12.2	46.3	190 33.2	15.4	352 31.4	26.5	122 16.3	30.9	Al Na'ir	27 49.0	S46 55.3
A	09	294 32.4	336 11.6	. . 45.5	205 34.8	. . 15.4	7 33.3	. . 26.4	137 18.9	. . 31.0	Alnilam	275 50.3	S 1 11.8
T	10	309 34.9	351 10.9	44.7	220 36.4	15.3	22 35.3	26.4	152 21.6	31.0	Alphard	217 59.7	S 8 41.8
U	11	324 37.4	6 10.3	43.8	235 38.1	15.3	37 37.3	26.3	167 24.2	31.1			
R	12	339 39.8	21 09.6	S16 43.0	250 39.7	N26 15.2	52 39.3	S22 26.3	182 26.9	N11 31.2	Alphecca	126 14.2	N26 40.9
D	13	354 42.3	36 09.0	42.2	265 41.3	15.2	67 41.3	26.2	197 29.5	31.3	Alpheratz	357 48.1	N29 08.1
A	14	9 44.7	51 08.3	41.4	280 43.0	15.1	82 43.3	26.2	212 32.2	31.3	Altair	62 12.4	N 8 53.2
Y	15	24 47.2	66 07.7	. . 40.5	295 44.6	. . 15.1	97 45.3	. . 26.2	227 34.8	. . 31.4	Ankaa	353 19.8	S42 15.8
	16	39 49.7	81 07.0	39.7	310 46.3	15.1	112 47.3	26.1	242 37.5	31.5	Antares	112 31.2	S26 27.1
	17	54 52.1	96 06.4	38.9	325 47.9	15.0	127 49.3	26.1	257 40.1	31.6			
	18	69 54.6	111 05.7	S16 38.1	340 49.5	N26 15.0	142 51.3	S22 26.0	272 42.8	N11 31.6	Arcturus	145 59.1	N19 08.1
	19	84 57.1	126 05.1	37.2	355 51.1	14.9	157 53.3	26.0	287 45.5	31.7	Atria	107 36.8	S69 02.4
	20	99 59.5	141 04.5	36.4	10 52.8	14.9	172 55.3	25.9	302 48.1	31.8	Avior	234 19.3	S59 32.3
	21	115 02.0	156 03.8	. . 35.6	25 54.4	. . 14.9	187 57.3	. . 25.9	317 50.8	. . 31.9	Bellatrix	278 36.2	N 6 21.4
	22	130 04.5	171 03.2	34.7	40 56.0	14.8	202 59.3	25.8	332 53.4	31.9	Betelgeuse	271 05.5	N 7 24.5
	23	145 06.9	186 02.5	33.9	55 57.7	14.8	218 01.3	25.8	347 56.1	32.0			
	2 00	160 09.4	201 01.9	S16 33.1	70 59.3	N26 14.7	233 03.3	S22 25.7	2 58.7	N11 32.1	Canopus	263 57.7	S52 42.2
	01	175 11.9	216 01.2	32.2	86 00.9	14.7	248 05.3	25.7	18 01.4	32.2	Capella	280 40.3	N46 00.6
	02	190 14.3	231 00.6	31.4	101 02.5	14.6	263 07.2	25.6	33 04.0	32.2	Deneb	49 34.7	N45 18.3
	03	205 16.8	246 00.0	. . 30.6	116 04.2	. . 14.6	278 09.2	. . 25.6	48 06.7	. . 32.3	Denebola	182 37.4	N14 31.4
	04	220 19.2	260 59.3	29.7	131 05.8	14.6	293 11.2	25.5	63 09.3	32.4	Diphda	349 00.1	S17 56.6
	05	235 21.7	275 58.7	28.9	146 07.4	14.5	308 13.2	25.5	78 12.0	32.5			
	06	250 24.2	290 58.0	S16 28.0	161 09.0	N26 14.5	323 15.2	S22 25.4	93 14.6	N11 32.5	Dubhe	193 55.5	N61 42.3
	07	265 26.6	305 57.4	27.2	176 10.7	14.4	338 17.2	25.4	108 17.3	32.6	Elnath	278 17.6	N28 37.0
	08	280 29.1	320 56.8	26.4	191 12.3	14.4	353 19.2	25.3	123 19.9	32.7	Eltanin	90 48.2	N51 28.8
S	09	295 31.6	335 56.1	. . 25.5	206 13.9	. . 14.3	8 21.2	. . 25.3	138 22.6	. . 32.8	Enif	33 51.4	N 9 54.6
U	10	310 34.0	350 55.5	24.7	221 15.5	14.3	23 23.2	25.3	153 25.2	32.8	Fomalhaut	15 28.6	S29 34.8
N	11	325 36.5	5 54.8	23.8	236 17.1	14.3	38 25.2	25.2	168 27.9	32.9			
D	12	340 39.0	20 54.2	S16 23.0	251 18.7	N26 14.2	53 27.2	S22 25.2	183 30.5	N11 33.0	Gacrux	172 05.2	S57 09.6
A	13	355 41.4	35 53.6	22.1	266 20.4	14.2	68 29.2	25.1	198 33.2	33.1	Gienah	175 56.2	S17 35.4
Y	14	10 43.9	50 52.9	21.3	281 22.0	14.1	83 31.2	25.1	213 35.8	33.1	Hadar	148 53.5	S60 24.7
	15	25 46.3	65 52.3	. . 20.4	296 23.6	. . 14.1	98 33.2	. . 25.0	228 38.5	. . 33.2	Hamal	328 05.6	N23 30.2
	16	40 48.8	80 51.7	19.6	311 25.2	14.0	113 35.2	25.0	243 41.1	33.3	Kaus Aust.	83 49.3	S34 22.9
	17	55 51.3	95 51.0	18.8	326 26.8	14.0	128 37.2	24.9	258 43.8	33.4			
	18	70 53.7	110 50.4	S16 17.9	341 28.4	N26 14.0	143 39.2	S22 24.9	273 46.5	N11 33.4	Kochab	137 18.8	N74 06.9
	19	85 56.2	125 49.8	17.1	356 30.0	13.9	158 41.2	24.8	288 49.1	33.5	Markab	13 42.7	N15 14.9
	20	100 58.7	140 49.1	16.2	11 31.7	13.9	173 43.2	24.8	303 51.8	33.6	Menkar	314 19.4	N 4 07.3
	21	116 01.1	155 48.5	. . 15.4	26 33.3	. . 13.8	188 45.2	. . 24.7	318 54.4	. . 33.7	Menkent	148 12.2	S36 24.7
	22	131 03.6	170 47.9	14.5	41 34.9	13.8	203 47.2	24.7	333 57.1	33.7	Miaplacidus	221 40.1	S69 45.2
	23	146 06.1	185 47.2	13.6	56 36.5	13.7	218 49.2	24.6	348 59.7	33.8			
	3 00	161 08.5	200 46.6	S16 12.8	71 38.1	N26 13.7	233 51.2	S22 24.6	4 02.4	N11 33.9	Mirfak	308 46.4	N49 53.7
	01	176 11.0	215 46.0	11.9	86 39.7	13.6	248 53.2	24.5	19 05.0	33.9	Nunki	76 03.4	S26 17.3
	02	191 13.5	230 45.3	11.1	101 41.3	13.6	263 55.2	24.5	34 07.7	34.0	Peacock	53 25.8	S56 42.5
	03	206 15.9	245 44.7	. . 10.2	116 42.9	. . 13.6	278 57.2	. . 24.5	49 10.3	. . 34.1	Pollux	243 32.3	N28 00.4
	04	221 18.4	260 44.1	09.4	131 44.5	13.5	293 59.2	24.4	64 13.0	34.2	Procyon	245 03.7	N 5 12.2
	05	236 20.8	275 43.4	08.5	146 46.1	13.5	309 01.2	24.4	79 15.6	34.2			
	06	251 23.3	290 42.8	S16 07.7	161 47.7	N26 13.4	324 03.2	S22 24.3	94 18.3	N11 34.3	Rasalhague	96 10.2	N12 32.9
	07	266 25.8	305 42.2	06.8	176 49.3	13.4	339 05.2	24.3	109 20.9	34.4	Regulus	207 47.4	N11 55.5
	08	281 28.2	320 41.6	05.9	191 50.9	13.3	354 07.2	24.2	124 23.6	34.5	Rigel	281 15.8	S 8 11.6
M	09	296 30.7	335 40.9	. . 05.1	206 52.5	. . 13.3	9 09.2	. . 24.2	139 26.2	. . 34.5	Rigil Kent.	139 57.1	S60 52.0
O	10	311 33.2	350 40.3	04.2	221 54.1	13.3	24 11.2	24.1	154 28.9	34.6	Sabik	102 17.2	S15 44.2
N	11	326 35.6	5 39.7	03.4	236 55.7	13.2	39 13.2	24.1	169 31.5	34.7			
D	12	341 38.1	20 39.1	S16 02.5	251 57.3	N26 13.2	54 15.2	S22 24.0	184 34.2	N11 34.8	Schedar	349 45.9	N56 35.1
A	13	356 40.6	35 38.4	01.6	266 58.9	13.1	69 17.2	24.0	199 36.8	34.8	Shaula	96 27.4	S37 06.6
Y	14	11 43.0	50 37.8	16 00.8	282 00.5	13.1	84 19.2	23.9	214 39.5	34.9	Sirius	258 37.1	S16 43.8
	15	26 45.5	65 37.2	15 59.9	297 02.1	. . 13.0	99 21.2	. . 23.9	229 42.1	. . 35.0	Spica	158 35.3	S11 12.4
	16	41 48.0	80 36.6	59.0	312 03.7	13.0	114 23.2	23.8	244 44.8	35.1	Suhail	222 55.1	S43 28.1
	17	56 50.4	95 35.9	58.2	327 05.3	12.9	129 25.2	23.8	259 47.4	35.1			
	18	71 52.9	110 35.3	S15 57.3	342 06.9	N26 12.9	144 27.2	S22 23.7	274 50.1	N11 35.2	Vega	80 41.9	N38 47.1
	19	86 55.3	125 34.7	56.4	357 08.5	12.8	159 29.2	23.7	289 52.7	35.3	Zuben'ubi	137 09.7	S16 04.7
	20	101 57.8	140 34.1	55.6	12 10.1	12.8	174 31.2	23.6	304 55.4	35.4		SHA	Mer. Pass.
	21	117 00.3	155 33.4	. . 54.7	27 11.7	. . 12.8	189 33.2	. . 23.6	319 58.0	. . 35.4		° ′	h m
	22	132 02.7	170 32.8	53.8	42 13.3	12.7	204 35.2	23.6	335 00.7	35.5	Venus	40 52.5	10 36
	23	147 05.2	185 32.2	52.9	57 14.9	12.7	219 37.3	23.5	350 03.3	35.6	Mars	270 49.9	19 14
		h m									Jupiter	72 53.9	8 27
	Mer. Pass.	13 17.2	v −0.6	d 0.8	v 1.6	d 0.0	v 2.0	d 0.0	v 2.7	d 0.1	Saturn	202 49.3	23 44

UT		SUN GHA	SUN Dec	MOON GHA	v	MOON Dec	d	HP
d h		° ′	° ′	° ′	′	° ′	′	′
1 00		176 54.5	S 7 31.5	259 42.2	9.6	S27 57.2	1.1	54.5
01		191 54.6	30.5	274 10.8	9.6	27 58.3	0.9	54.6
02		206 54.8	29.6	288 39.4	9.5	27 59.2	0.7	54.6
03		221 54.9	. . 28.6	303 07.9	9.5	27 59.9	0.6	54.6
04		236 55.0	27.7	317 36.4	9.5	28 00.5	0.5	54.6
05		251 55.1	26.7	332 04.9	9.5	28 01.0	0.4	54.6
06		266 55.3	S 7 25.8	346 33.4	9.4	S28 01.4	0.2	54.6
07		281 55.4	24.8	1 01.8	9.5	28 01.6	0.1	54.7
08	SATURDAY	296 55.5	23.9	15 30.3	9.4	28 01.7	0.1	54.7
09		311 55.6	. . 22.9	29 58.7	9.3	28 01.6	0.2	54.7
10		326 55.8	22.0	44 27.0	9.4	28 01.4	0.4	54.7
11		341 55.9	21.0	58 55.4	9.3	28 01.0	0.5	54.7
12		356 56.0	S 7 20.1	73 23.7	9.4	S28 00.5	0.6	54.7
13		11 56.1	19.1	87 52.1	9.3	27 59.9	0.8	54.8
14		26 56.3	18.2	102 20.4	9.2	27 59.1	0.9	54.8
15		41 56.4	. . 17.2	116 48.6	9.3	27 58.2	1.0	54.8
16		56 56.5	16.2	131 16.9	9.3	27 57.2	1.2	54.8
17		71 56.6	15.3	145 45.2	9.2	27 56.0	1.4	54.8
18		86 56.8	S 7 14.3	160 13.4	9.3	S27 54.6	1.5	54.8
19		101 56.9	13.4	174 41.7	9.2	27 53.1	1.6	54.9
20		116 57.0	12.4	189 09.9	9.2	27 51.5	1.7	54.9
21		131 57.1	. . 11.5	203 38.1	9.2	27 49.8	2.0	54.9
22		146 57.3	10.5	218 06.3	9.2	27 47.8	2.0	54.9
23		161 57.4	09.6	232 34.5	9.2	27 45.8	2.2	54.9
2 00		176 57.5	S 7 08.6	247 02.7	9.2	S27 43.6	2.3	55.0
01		191 57.6	07.7	261 30.9	9.2	27 41.3	2.5	55.0
02		206 57.8	06.7	275 59.1	9.2	27 38.8	2.6	55.0
03		221 57.9	. . 05.7	290 27.3	9.2	27 36.2	2.8	55.0
04		236 58.0	04.8	304 55.5	9.2	27 33.4	2.9	55.1
05		251 58.1	03.8	319 23.7	9.2	27 30.5	3.0	55.1
06		266 58.3	S 7 02.9	333 51.9	9.2	S27 27.5	3.2	55.1
07		281 58.4	01.9	348 20.1	9.2	27 24.3	3.4	55.1
08		296 58.5	01.0	2 48.3	9.2	27 20.9	3.4	55.1
09	SUNDAY	311 58.7	7 00.0	17 16.5	9.2	27 17.5	3.7	55.2
10		326 58.8	6 59.0	31 44.7	9.2	27 13.8	3.7	55.2
11		341 58.9	58.1	46 12.9	9.2	27 10.1	3.9	55.2
12		356 59.0	S 6 57.1	60 41.1	9.3	S27 06.2	4.1	55.2
13		11 59.2	56.2	75 09.4	9.2	27 02.1	4.1	55.3
14		26 59.3	55.2	89 37.6	9.2	26 58.0	4.4	55.3
15		41 59.4	. . 54.3	104 05.8	9.3	26 53.6	4.4	55.3
16		56 59.6	53.3	118 34.1	9.3	26 49.2	4.7	55.3
17		71 59.7	52.3	133 02.4	9.3	26 44.5	4.7	55.4
18		86 59.8	S 6 51.4	147 30.7	9.3	S26 39.8	4.9	55.4
19		101 59.9	50.4	161 59.0	9.3	26 34.9	5.0	55.4
20		117 00.1	49.5	176 27.3	9.3	26 29.9	5.2	55.4
21		132 00.2	. . 48.5	190 55.6	9.4	26 24.7	5.3	55.5
22		147 00.3	47.6	205 24.0	9.4	26 19.4	5.5	55.5
23		162 00.5	46.6	219 52.4	9.3	26 13.9	5.6	55.5
3 00		177 00.6	S 6 45.6	234 20.7	9.5	S26 08.3	5.7	55.5
01		192 00.7	44.7	248 49.2	9.4	26 02.6	5.9	55.6
02		207 00.9	43.7	263 17.6	9.4	25 56.7	6.0	55.6
03		222 01.0	. . 42.8	277 46.0	9.5	25 50.7	6.1	55.6
04		237 01.1	41.8	292 14.5	9.5	25 44.6	6.3	55.6
05		252 01.3	40.8	306 43.0	9.5	25 38.3	6.4	55.7
06		267 01.4	S 6 39.9	321 11.5	9.6	S25 31.9	6.6	55.7
07		282 01.5	38.9	335 40.1	9.5	25 25.3	6.7	55.7
08		297 01.7	38.0	350 08.6	9.6	25 18.6	6.8	55.8
09	MONDAY	312 01.8	. . 37.0	4 37.2	9.7	25 11.8	7.0	55.8
10		327 01.9	36.0	19 05.9	9.6	25 04.8	7.1	55.8
11		342 02.1	35.1	33 34.5	9.7	24 57.7	7.2	55.8
12		357 02.2	S 6 34.1	48 03.2	9.7	S24 50.5	7.4	55.9
13		12 02.3	33.1	62 31.9	9.8	24 43.1	7.5	55.9
14		27 02.5	32.2	77 00.7	9.7	24 35.6	7.6	55.9
15		42 02.6	. . 31.2	91 29.4	9.8	24 28.0	7.8	56.0
16		57 02.7	30.3	105 58.2	9.9	24 20.2	7.9	56.0
17		72 02.9	29.3	120 27.1	9.8	24 12.3	8.1	56.0
18		87 03.0	S 6 28.3	134 55.9	9.9	S24 04.2	8.1	56.0
19		102 03.1	27.4	149 24.8	10.0	23 56.1	8.3	56.1
20		117 03.3	26.4	163 53.8	9.9	23 47.8	8.5	56.1
21		132 03.4	. . 25.4	178 22.7	10.0	23 39.3	8.5	56.1
22		147 03.5	24.5	192 51.7	10.1	23 30.8	8.7	56.2
23		162 03.7	23.5	207 20.8	10.0	S23 22.1	8.8	56.2
		SD 16.2	*d* 1.0	SD 14.9		15.0		15.2

Lat.	Twilight Naut.	Twilight Civil	Sunrise	Moonrise 1	Moonrise 2	Moonrise 3	Moonrise 4
°	h m	h m	h m	h m	h m	h m	h m
N 72	05 03	06 21	07 30	■	■	■	■
N 70	05 09	06 19	07 21	■	■	■	■
68	05 14	06 18	07 14	■	■	■	09 08
66	05 17	06 16	07 08	■	■	■	07 52
64	05 20	06 15	07 03	■	■	07 48	07 15
62	05 23	06 14	06 58	■	07 00	06 53	06 48
60	05 25	06 13	06 55	05 23	06 03	06 20	06 28
N 58	05 27	06 12	06 51	04 46	05 30	05 56	06 10
56	05 28	06 11	06 48	04 20	05 06	05 36	05 56
54	05 29	06 10	06 45	03 59	04 46	05 20	05 43
52	05 30	06 09	06 43	03 41	04 30	05 06	05 32
50	05 31	06 08	06 41	03 27	04 15	04 53	05 22
45	05 32	06 06	06 36	02 57	03 46	04 28	05 01
N 40	05 33	06 04	06 32	02 33	03 24	04 07	04 44
35	05 33	06 02	06 28	02 14	03 05	03 50	04 30
30	05 33	06 01	06 25	01 57	02 49	03 36	04 18
20	05 31	05 57	06 19	01 29	02 21	03 10	03 56
N 10	05 28	05 53	06 14	01 05	01 58	02 49	03 38
0	05 24	05 48	06 09	00 43	01 36	02 28	03 20
S 10	05 18	05 43	06 04	00 21	01 14	02 08	03 02
20	05 10	05 36	05 58	24 50	00 50	01 46	02 44
30	04 59	05 28	05 52	24 23	00 23	01 21	02 22
35	04 52	05 22	05 48	24 06	00 06	01 06	02 09
40	04 43	05 16	05 44	23 47	24 48	00 48	01 54
45	04 33	05 09	05 39	23 24	24 27	00 27	01 36
S 50	04 19	05 00	05 33	22 55	24 00	00 00	01 14
52	04 12	04 55	05 30	22 40	23 47	25 04	01 04
54	04 05	04 50	05 27	22 24	23 32	24 52	00 52
56	03 56	04 45	05 24	22 03	23 15	24 38	00 38
58	03 46	04 39	05 20	21 38	22 53	24 22	00 22
S 60	03 35	04 31	05 16	21 03	22 26	24 02	00 02

Lat.	Sunset	Twilight Civil	Twilight Naut.	Moonset 1	Moonset 2	Moonset 3	Moonset 4
°	h m	h m	h m	h m	h m	h m	h m
N 72	16 57	18 05	19 24	■	■	■	■
N 70	17 05	18 07	19 18	■	■	■	■
68	17 12	18 08	19 13	■	■	■	10 12
66	17 18	18 09	19 09	■	■	■	11 27
64	17 23	18 11	19 06	■	■	09 43	12 03
62	17 27	18 12	19 03	■	08 41	10 37	12 29
60	17 31	18 13	19 01	08 28	09 38	11 10	12 49
N 58	17 34	18 13	18 59	09 05	10 10	11 34	13 06
56	17 37	18 14	18 57	09 32	10 34	11 53	13 20
54	17 40	18 15	18 56	09 52	10 54	12 09	13 32
52	17 42	18 16	18 55	10 10	11 10	12 23	13 42
50	17 44	18 17	18 54	10 25	11 24	12 35	13 51
45	17 49	18 19	18 53	10 55	11 53	12 59	14 11
N 40	17 53	18 20	18 52	11 18	12 15	13 19	14 27
35	17 57	18 22	18 52	11 38	12 34	13 36	14 40
30	18 00	18 24	18 52	11 54	12 50	13 50	14 52
20	18 06	18 28	18 53	12 22	13 17	14 14	15 11
N 10	18 11	18 32	18 56	12 46	13 40	14 34	15 28
0	18 15	18 36	19 00	13 08	14 01	14 53	15 44
S 10	18 20	18 41	19 06	13 31	14 22	15 12	16 00
20	18 26	18 48	19 14	13 55	14 45	15 33	16 17
30	18 32	18 56	19 24	14 22	15 12	15 56	16 36
35	18 35	19 01	19 31	14 39	15 27	16 10	16 47
40	18 40	19 07	19 40	14 58	15 45	16 25	16 59
45	18 44	19 14	19 50	15 21	16 07	16 44	17 14
S 50	18 50	19 23	20 04	15 51	16 34	17 07	17 32
52	18 53	19 28	20 10	16 05	16 47	17 18	17 41
54	18 56	19 32	20 18	16 22	17 02	17 31	17 50
56	18 59	19 38	20 26	16 42	17 20	17 45	18 01
58	19 03	19 44	20 36	17 08	17 42	18 01	18 13
S 60	19 07	19 51	20 47	17 43	18 10	18 22	18 27

Day	SUN Eqn. of Time 00^h	SUN Eqn. of Time 12^h	SUN Mer. Pass.	MOON Mer. Pass. Upper	MOON Mer. Pass. Lower	MOON Age	MOON Phase
d	m s	m s	h m	h m	h m	d %	
1	12 22	12 16	12 12	06 56	19 22	23 37	
2	12 10	12 04	12 12	07 48	20 15	24 28	
3	11 58	11 51	12 12	08 41	21 07	25 19	

	UT	ARIES	VENUS −3.8		MARS +0.3		JUPITER −2.0		SATURN +0.2	
		GHA	GHA	Dec	GHA	Dec	GHA	Dec	GHA	Dec
	d h	° ′	° ′	° ′	° ′	° ′	° ′	° ′	° ′	° ′
	4 00	162 07.7	200 31.6	S15 52.1	72 16.5	N26 12.6	234 39.3	S22 23.5	5 06.0	N11 35.7
	01	177 10.1	215 31.0	51.2	87 18.1	12.6	249 41.3	23.4	20 08.6	35.7
	02	192 12.6	230 30.3	50.3	102 19.6	12.5	264 43.3	23.4	35 11.3	35.8
	03	207 15.1	245 29.7	. . 49.5	117 21.2	. . 12.5	279 45.3	. . 23.3	50 13.9	. . 35.9
	04	222 17.5	260 29.1	48.6	132 22.8	12.4	294 47.3	23.3	65 16.6	36.0
	05	237 20.0	275 28.5	47.7	147 24.4	12.4	309 49.3	23.2	80 19.2	36.0
	06	252 22.5	290 27.9	S15 46.8	162 26.0	N26 12.3	324 51.3	S22 23.2	95 21.9	N11 36.1
	07	267 24.9	305 27.2	45.9	177 27.6	12.3	339 53.3	23.1	110 24.5	36.2
T	08	282 27.4	320 26.6	45.1	192 29.2	12.3	354 55.3	23.1	125 27.2	36.2
U	09	297 29.8	335 26.0	. . 44.2	207 30.7	. . 12.2	9 57.3	. . 23.0	140 29.9	. . 36.3
E	10	312 32.3	350 25.4	43.3	222 32.3	12.2	24 59.3	23.0	155 32.5	36.4
S	11	327 34.8	5 24.8	42.4	237 33.9	12.1	40 01.3	22.9	170 35.2	36.5
D	12	342 37.2	20 24.2	S15 41.5	252 35.5	N26 12.1	55 03.3	S22 22.9	185 37.8	N11 36.5
A	13	357 39.7	35 23.5	40.7	267 37.1	12.0	70 05.3	22.8	200 40.5	36.6
Y	14	12 42.2	50 22.9	39.8	282 38.7	12.0	85 07.3	22.8	215 43.1	36.7
	15	27 44.6	65 22.3	. . 38.9	297 40.2	. . 11.9	100 09.4	. . 22.8	230 45.8	. . 36.8
	16	42 47.1	80 21.7	38.0	312 41.8	11.9	115 11.4	22.7	245 48.4	36.8
	17	57 49.6	95 21.1	37.1	327 43.4	11.8	130 13.4	22.7	260 51.1	36.9
	18	72 52.0	110 20.5	S15 36.2	342 45.0	N26 11.8	145 15.4	S22 22.6	275 53.7	N11 37.0
	19	87 54.5	125 19.9	35.4	357 46.5	11.7	160 17.4	22.6	290 56.4	37.1
	20	102 56.9	140 19.3	34.5	12 48.1	11.7	175 19.4	22.5	305 59.0	37.1
	21	117 59.4	155 18.6	. . 33.6	27 49.7	. . 11.7	190 21.4	. . 22.5	321 01.7	. . 37.2
	22	133 01.9	170 18.0	32.7	42 51.3	11.6	205 23.4	22.4	336 04.3	37.3
	23	148 04.3	185 17.4	31.8	57 52.8	11.6	220 25.4	22.4	351 07.0	37.4
	5 00	163 06.8	200 16.8	S15 30.9	72 54.4	N26 11.5	235 27.4	S22 22.3	6 09.6	N11 37.4
	01	178 09.3	215 16.2	30.0	87 56.0	11.5	250 29.4	22.3	21 12.3	37.5
	02	193 11.7	230 15.6	29.1	102 57.6	11.4	265 31.4	22.2	36 14.9	37.6
	03	208 14.2	245 15.0	. . 28.2	117 59.1	. . 11.4	280 33.5	. . 22.2	51 17.6	. . 37.6
	04	223 16.7	260 14.4	27.3	133 00.7	11.3	295 35.5	22.1	66 20.2	37.7
	05	238 19.1	275 13.8	26.4	148 02.3	11.3	310 37.5	22.1	81 22.9	37.8
	06	253 21.6	290 13.2	S15 25.5	163 03.8	N26 11.2	325 39.5	S22 22.0	96 25.5	N11 37.9
W	07	268 24.1	305 12.6	24.6	178 05.4	11.2	340 41.5	22.0	111 28.2	37.9
E	08	283 26.5	320 12.0	23.8	193 07.0	11.1	355 43.5	21.9	126 30.8	38.0
D	09	298 29.0	335 11.4	. . 22.9	208 08.5	. . 11.1	10 45.5	. . 21.9	141 33.5	. . 38.1
N	10	313 31.4	350 10.7	22.0	223 10.1	11.0	25 47.5	21.9	156 36.1	38.2
E	11	328 33.9	5 10.1	21.1	238 11.7	11.0	40 49.5	21.8	171 38.8	38.2
S	12	343 36.4	20 09.5	S15 20.2	253 13.2	N26 10.9	55 51.6	S22 21.8	186 41.4	N11 38.3
D	13	358 38.8	35 08.9	19.3	268 14.8	10.9	70 53.6	21.7	201 44.1	38.4
A	14	13 41.3	50 08.3	18.4	283 16.4	10.8	85 55.6	21.7	216 46.7	38.5
Y	15	28 43.8	65 07.7	. . 17.5	298 17.9	. . 10.8	100 57.6	. . 21.6	231 49.4	. . 38.5
	16	43 46.2	80 07.1	16.6	313 19.5	10.7	115 59.6	21.6	246 52.0	38.6
	17	58 48.7	95 06.5	15.6	328 21.0	10.7	131 01.6	21.5	261 54.7	38.7
	18	73 51.2	110 05.9	S15 14.7	343 22.6	N26 10.6	146 03.6	S22 21.5	276 57.3	N11 38.7
	19	88 53.6	125 05.3	13.8	358 24.2	10.6	161 05.6	21.4	292 00.0	38.8
	20	103 56.1	140 04.7	12.9	13 25.7	10.6	176 07.7	21.4	307 02.6	38.9
	21	118 58.6	155 04.1	. . 12.0	28 27.3	. . 10.5	191 09.7	. . 21.3	322 05.2	. . 39.0
	22	134 01.0	170 03.5	11.1	43 28.8	10.5	206 11.7	21.3	337 07.9	39.0
	23	149 03.5	185 02.9	10.2	58 30.4	10.4	221 13.7	21.2	352 10.5	39.1
	6 00	164 05.9	200 02.3	S15 09.3	73 31.9	N26 10.4	236 15.7	S22 21.2	7 13.2	N11 39.2
	01	179 08.4	215 01.7	08.4	88 33.5	10.3	251 17.7	21.1	22 15.8	39.3
	02	194 10.9	230 01.1	07.5	103 35.0	10.3	266 19.7	21.1	37 18.5	39.3
	03	209 13.3	245 00.5	. . 06.6	118 36.6	. . 10.2	281 21.8	. . 21.1	52 21.1	. . 39.4
	04	224 15.8	259 59.9	05.7	133 38.2	10.2	296 23.8	21.0	67 23.8	39.5
	05	239 18.3	274 59.3	04.8	148 39.7	10.1	311 25.8	21.0	82 26.4	39.5
	06	254 20.7	289 58.7	S15 03.8	163 41.3	N26 10.1	326 27.8	S22 20.9	97 29.1	N11 39.6
	07	269 23.2	304 58.1	02.9	178 42.8	10.0	341 29.8	20.9	112 31.7	39.7
T	08	284 25.7	319 57.6	02.0	193 44.4	10.0	356 31.8	20.8	127 34.4	39.8
H	09	299 28.1	334 57.0	. . 01.1	208 45.9	. . 09.9	11 33.9	. . 20.8	142 37.0	. . 39.8
U	10	314 30.6	349 56.4	15 00.2	223 47.5	09.9	26 35.9	20.7	157 39.7	39.9
R	11	329 33.0	4 55.8	14 59.3	238 49.0	09.8	41 37.9	20.7	172 42.3	40.0
S	12	344 35.5	19 55.2	S14 58.3	253 50.5	N26 09.8	56 39.9	S22 20.6	187 45.0	N11 40.1
D	13	359 38.0	34 54.6	57.4	268 52.1	09.7	71 41.9	20.6	202 47.6	40.1
A	14	14 40.4	49 54.0	56.5	283 53.6	09.7	86 43.9	20.5	217 50.3	40.2
Y	15	29 42.9	64 53.4	. . 55.6	298 55.2	. . 09.6	101 46.0	. . 20.5	232 52.9	. . 40.3
	16	44 45.4	79 52.8	54.7	313 56.7	09.6	116 48.0	20.4	247 55.6	40.3
	17	59 47.8	94 52.2	53.8	328 58.3	09.5	131 50.0	20.4	262 58.2	40.4
	18	74 50.3	109 51.6	S14 52.8	343 59.8	N26 09.5	146 52.0	S22 20.3	278 00.9	N11 40.5
	19	89 52.8	124 51.0	51.9	359 01.4	09.4	161 54.0	20.3	293 03.5	40.6
	20	104 55.2	139 50.4	51.0	14 02.9	09.4	176 56.0	20.3	308 06.2	40.6
	21	119 57.7	154 49.9	. . 50.1	29 04.4	. . 09.3	191 58.1	. . 20.2	323 08.8	. . 40.7
	22	135 00.2	169 49.3	49.1	44 06.0	09.3	207 00.1	20.2	338 11.5	40.8
	23	150 02.6	184 48.7	48.2	59 07.5	09.2	222 02.1	20.1	353 14.1	40.9
	Mer. Pass.	h m 13 05.4	v −0.6	d 0.9	v 1.6	d 0.0	v 2.0	d 0.0	v 2.6	d 0.1

STARS

Name	SHA	Dec
	° ′	° ′
Acamar	315 21.4	S40 16.5
Achernar	335 29.9	S57 11.9
Acrux	173 13.5	S63 08.7
Adhara	255 15.5	S28 59.1
Aldebaran	290 54.0	N16 31.6
Alioth	166 23.4	N55 54.6
Alkaid	153 01.5	N49 16.0
Al Na'ir	27 49.0	S46 55.3
Alnilam	275 50.4	S 1 11.8
Alphard	217 59.7	S 8 41.8
Alphecca	126 14.2	N26 40.9
Alpheratz	357 48.1	N29 08.1
Altair	62 12.4	N 8 53.2
Ankaa	353 19.8	S42 15.8
Antares	112 31.2	S26 27.1
Arcturus	145 59.1	N19 08.1
Atria	107 36.7	S69 02.4
Avior	234 19.4	S59 32.3
Bellatrix	278 36.2	N 6 21.4
Betelgeuse	271 05.5	N 7 24.5
Canopus	263 57.7	S52 42.2
Capella	280 40.3	N46 00.6
Deneb	49 34.7	N45 18.3
Denebola	182 37.3	N14 31.4
Diphda	349 00.1	S17 56.6
Dubhe	193 55.5	N61 42.3
Elnath	278 17.6	N28 37.0
Eltanin	90 48.1	N51 28.8
Enif	33 51.4	N 9 54.6
Fomalhaut	15 28.6	S29 34.8
Gacrux	172 05.1	S57 09.6
Gienah	175 56.2	S17 35.4
Hadar	148 53.5	S60 24.7
Hamal	328 05.6	N23 30.1
Kaus Aust.	83 49.2	S34 22.9
Kochab	137 18.7	N74 06.9
Markab	13 42.7	N15 14.9
Menkar	314 19.4	N 4 07.3
Menkent	148 12.1	S36 24.7
Miaplacidus	221 40.1	S69 45.2
Mirfak	308 46.4	N49 53.7
Nunki	76 03.4	S26 17.3
Peacock	53 25.8	S56 42.5
Pollux	243 32.3	N28 00.4
Procyon	245 03.7	N 5 12.2
Rasalhague	96 10.2	N12 32.9
Regulus	207 47.4	N11 55.5
Rigel	281 15.9	S 8 11.6
Rigil Kent.	139 57.1	S60 52.1
Sabik	102 17.1	S15 44.3
Schedar	349 45.9	N56 35.1
Shaula	96 27.4	S37 06.6
Sirius	258 37.1	S16 43.8
Spica	158 35.2	S11 12.4
Suhail	222 55.1	S43 28.1
Vega	80 41.9	N38 47.1
Zuben'ubi	137 09.7	S16 04.7

	SHA	Mer. Pass.
	° ′	h m
Venus	37 10.0	10 39
Mars	269 47.6	19 06
Jupiter	72 20.6	8 17
Saturn	203 02.8	23 31

UT	SUN GHA	SUN Dec	MOON GHA	v	Dec	d	HP
d h	° ′	° ′	° ′	′	° ′	′	′
4 00 (TUESDAY)	177 03.8	S 6 22.6	221 49.8	10.1	S23 13.3	9.0	56.2
01	192 04.0	21.6	236 18.9	10.2	23 04.3	9.0	56.3
02	207 04.1	20.6	250 48.1	10.1	22 55.3	9.2	56.3
03	222 04.2	. . 19.7	265 17.2	10.2	22 46.1	9.4	56.3
04	237 04.4	18.7	279 46.4	10.3	22 36.7	9.4	56.3
05	252 04.5	17.7	294 15.7	10.3	22 27.3	9.6	56.4
06	267 04.6	S 6 16.8	308 45.0	10.3	S22 17.7	9.7	56.4
07	282 04.8	15.8	323 14.3	10.3	22 08.0	9.8	56.4
08	297 04.9	14.8	337 43.6	10.4	21 58.2	9.9	56.5
09	312 05.0	. . 13.9	352 13.0	10.5	21 48.3	10.1	56.5
10	327 05.2	12.9	6 42.5	10.4	21 38.2	10.2	56.5
11	342 05.3	11.9	21 11.9	10.6	21 28.0	10.3	56.6
12	357 05.5	S 6 11.0	35 41.5	10.5	S21 17.7	10.4	56.6
13	12 05.6	10.0	50 11.0	10.6	21 07.3	10.6	56.6
14	27 05.7	09.1	64 40.6	10.6	20 56.7	10.6	56.7
15	42 05.9	. . 08.1	79 10.2	10.7	20 46.1	10.8	56.7
16	57 06.0	07.1	93 39.9	10.7	20 35.3	10.9	56.7
17	72 06.2	06.2	108 09.6	10.7	20 24.4	11.0	56.8
18	87 06.3	S 6 05.2	122 39.3	10.8	S20 13.4	11.1	56.8
19	102 06.4	04.2	137 09.1	10.8	20 02.3	11.2	56.8
20	117 06.6	03.3	151 38.9	10.8	19 51.1	11.4	56.8
21	132 06.7	. . 02.3	166 08.7	10.9	19 39.7	11.4	56.9
22	147 06.9	01.3	180 38.6	10.9	19 28.3	11.6	56.9
23	162 07.0	6 00.4	195 08.5	11.0	19 16.7	11.7	56.9
5 00 (WEDNESDAY)	177 07.1	S 5 59.4	209 38.5	11.0	S19 05.0	11.8	57.0
01	192 07.3	58.4	224 08.5	11.0	18 53.2	11.9	57.0
02	207 07.4	57.5	238 38.5	11.1	18 41.3	12.0	57.0
03	222 07.6	. . 56.5	253 08.6	11.1	18 29.3	12.1	57.1
04	237 07.7	55.5	267 38.7	11.2	18 17.2	12.2	57.1
05	252 07.8	54.6	282 08.9	11.2	18 05.0	12.3	57.1
06	267 08.0	S 5 53.6	296 39.1	11.2	S17 52.7	12.4	57.2
07	282 08.1	52.6	311 09.3	11.2	17 40.3	12.6	57.2
08	297 08.3	51.7	325 39.5	11.3	17 27.7	12.6	57.2
09	312 08.4	. . 50.7	340 09.8	11.4	17 15.1	12.7	57.3
10	327 08.5	49.7	354 40.2	11.3	17 02.4	12.8	57.3
11	342 08.7	48.7	9 10.5	11.4	16 49.6	12.9	57.3
12	357 08.8	S 5 47.8	23 40.9	11.5	S16 36.7	13.1	57.4
13	12 09.0	46.8	38 11.4	11.4	16 23.6	13.1	57.4
14	27 09.1	45.8	52 41.8	11.5	16 10.5	13.2	57.4
15	42 09.3	. . 44.9	67 12.3	11.5	15 57.3	13.3	57.5
16	57 09.4	43.9	81 42.8	11.6	15 44.0	13.4	57.5
17	72 09.5	42.9	96 13.4	11.6	15 30.6	13.5	57.5
18	87 09.7	S 5 42.0	110 44.0	11.6	S15 17.1	13.6	57.6
19	102 09.8	41.0	125 14.6	11.7	15 03.5	13.6	57.6
20	117 10.0	40.0	139 45.3	11.7	14 49.9	13.8	57.6
21	132 10.1	. . 39.1	154 16.0	11.7	14 36.1	13.8	57.6
22	147 10.3	38.1	168 46.7	11.7	14 22.3	14.0	57.7
23	162 10.4	37.1	183 17.4	11.8	14 08.3	14.0	57.7
6 00 (THURSDAY)	177 10.6	S 5 36.1	197 48.2	11.8	S13 54.3	14.1	57.7
01	192 10.7	35.2	212 19.0	11.8	13 40.2	14.2	57.8
02	207 10.8	34.2	226 49.8	11.9	13 26.0	14.2	57.8
03	222 11.0	. . 33.2	241 20.7	11.9	13 11.8	14.4	57.8
04	237 11.1	32.3	255 51.6	11.9	12 57.4	14.4	57.9
05	252 11.3	31.3	270 22.5	11.9	12 43.0	14.5	57.9
06	267 11.4	S 5 30.3	284 53.4	12.0	S12 28.5	14.6	57.9
07	282 11.6	29.3	299 24.4	11.9	12 13.9	14.6	58.0
08	297 11.7	28.4	313 55.3	12.0	11 59.3	14.8	58.0
09	312 11.9	. . 27.4	328 26.3	12.1	11 44.5	14.8	58.0
10	327 12.0	26.4	342 57.4	12.0	11 29.7	14.8	58.1
11	342 12.2	25.5	357 28.4	12.1	11 14.9	15.0	58.1
12	357 12.3	S 5 24.5	11 59.5	12.1	S10 59.9	15.0	58.1
13	12 12.5	23.5	26 30.6	12.1	10 44.9	15.1	58.1
14	27 12.6	22.5	41 01.7	12.1	10 29.8	15.1	58.2
15	42 12.8	. . 21.6	55 32.8	12.1	10 14.7	15.3	58.2
16	57 12.9	20.6	70 03.9	12.2	9 59.4	15.2	58.2
17	72 13.0	19.6	84 35.1	12.1	9 44.2	15.4	58.3
18	87 13.2	S 5 18.7	99 06.2	12.2	S 9 28.8	15.4	58.3
19	102 13.3	17.7	113 37.4	12.2	9 13.4	15.5	58.3
20	117 13.5	16.7	128 08.6	12.2	8 57.9	15.5	58.3
21	132 13.6	. . 15.7	142 39.8	12.2	8 42.4	15.6	58.4
22	147 13.8	14.8	157 11.0	12.3	8 26.8	15.6	58.4
23	162 13.9	13.8	171 42.3	12.2	S 8 11.2	15.7	58.4
	SD 16.1	*d* 1.0	SD 15.4		15.6		15.8

Lat.	Twilight Naut.	Twilight Civil	Sunrise	Moonrise 4	Moonrise 5	Moonrise 6	Moonrise 7
°	h m	h m	h m	h m	h m	h m	h m
N 72	04 48	06 06	07 14	■	09 15	07 50	07 07
N 70	04 55	06 06	07 07	■	08 19	07 30	06 58
68	05 01	06 06	07 01	09 08	07 45	07 14	06 51
66	05 06	06 05	06 57	07 52	07 20	07 00	06 45
64	05 10	06 05	06 52	07 15	07 00	06 49	06 40
62	05 13	06 05	06 49	06 48	06 44	06 40	06 36
60	05 16	06 04	06 46	06 28	06 31	06 32	06 32
N 58	05 19	06 04	06 43	06 10	06 19	06 25	06 29
56	05 21	06 03	06 41	05 56	06 09	06 18	06 26
54	05 22	06 03	06 38	05 43	06 00	06 12	06 23
52	05 24	06 03	06 36	05 32	05 52	06 07	06 20
50	05 25	06 02	06 34	05 22	05 45	06 02	06 18
45	05 27	06 01	06 30	05 01	05 29	05 52	06 13
N 40	05 29	06 00	06 27	04 44	05 16	05 44	06 09
35	05 29	05 59	06 24	04 30	05 05	05 36	06 05
30	05 30	05 57	06 21	04 18	04 55	05 30	06 02
20	05 29	05 54	06 17	03 56	04 39	05 18	05 56
N 10	05 27	05 51	06 12	03 38	04 24	05 08	05 51
0	05 23	05 47	06 08	03 20	04 10	04 59	05 47
S 10	05 18	05 43	06 04	03 02	03 56	04 50	05 42
20	05 11	05 37	05 59	02 44	03 42	04 39	05 37
30	05 01	05 30	05 54	02 22	03 25	04 28	05 31
35	04 55	05 25	05 51	02 09	03 15	04 21	05 28
40	04 47	05 20	05 47	01 54	03 03	04 13	05 24
45	04 37	05 13	05 43	01 36	02 50	04 04	05 20
S 50	04 25	05 05	05 38	01 14	02 33	03 53	05 15
52	04 19	05 01	05 36	01 04	02 25	03 48	05 12
54	04 12	04 57	05 33	00 52	02 16	03 43	05 10
56	04 04	04 52	05 30	00 38	02 07	03 36	05 07
58	03 55	04 46	05 27	00 22	01 55	03 29	05 03
S 60	03 45	04 40	05 23	00 02	01 42	03 21	05 00

Lat.	Sunset	Twilight Civil	Twilight Naut.	Moonset 4	Moonset 5	Moonset 6	Moonset 7
°	h m	h m	h m	h m	h m	h m	h m
N 72	17 11	18 19	19 38	■	11 53	15 00	17 26
N 70	17 18	18 19	19 30	■	12 47	15 18	17 31
68	17 23	18 19	19 24	10 12	13 20	15 32	17 35
66	17 28	18 19	19 19	11 27	13 44	15 44	17 39
64	17 32	18 19	19 15	12 03	14 02	15 53	17 42
62	17 35	18 20	19 11	12 29	14 17	16 01	17 44
60	17 38	18 20	19 08	12 49	14 29	16 08	17 46
N 58	17 41	18 20	19 06	13 06	14 40	16 14	17 48
56	17 43	18 21	19 04	13 20	14 49	16 19	17 50
54	17 46	18 21	19 02	13 32	14 57	16 24	17 51
52	17 47	18 21	19 00	13 42	15 05	16 28	17 52
50	17 49	18 22	18 59	13 51	15 11	16 32	17 54
45	17 53	18 23	18 57	14 11	15 25	16 40	17 56
N 40	17 57	18 24	18 55	14 27	15 37	16 47	17 58
35	17 59	18 25	18 54	14 40	15 46	16 53	18 00
30	18 02	18 26	18 54	14 52	15 55	16 58	18 02
20	18 07	18 29	18 54	15 11	16 09	17 07	18 05
N 10	18 11	18 32	18 56	15 28	16 22	17 15	18 07
0	18 15	18 35	19 00	15 44	16 34	17 22	18 09
S 10	18 19	18 40	19 04	16 00	16 45	17 29	18 11
20	18 23	18 45	19 11	16 17	16 58	17 36	18 14
30	18 28	18 53	19 21	16 36	17 12	17 45	18 16
35	18 31	18 57	19 27	16 47	17 20	17 50	18 18
40	18 35	19 02	19 35	16 59	17 29	17 55	18 20
45	18 39	19 09	19 44	17 14	17 39	18 01	18 21
S 50	18 44	19 17	19 57	17 32	17 52	18 09	18 24
52	18 46	19 21	20 03	17 41	17 58	18 12	18 25
54	18 49	19 25	20 09	17 50	18 05	18 16	18 26
56	18 51	19 30	20 17	18 01	18 12	18 20	18 27
58	18 54	19 35	20 26	18 13	18 20	18 25	18 28
S 60	18 58	19 41	20 36	18 27	18 29	18 30	18 30

Day	SUN Eqn. of Time 00^h	SUN Eqn. of Time 12^h	SUN Mer. Pass.	MOON Mer. Pass. Upper	MOON Mer. Pass. Lower	Age	Phase
d	m s	m s	h m	h m	h m	d %	
4	11 45	11 38	12 12	09 32	21 57	26 12	
5	11 32	11 25	12 11	10 22	22 46	27 6	
6	11 18	11 11	12 11	11 10	23 34	28 2	

	UT	ARIES	VENUS −3.8		MARS +0.4		JUPITER −2.0		SATURN +0.3		STARS		
		GHA	GHA	Dec	GHA	Dec	GHA	Dec	GHA	Dec	Name	SHA	Dec
	d h	° ′	° ′	° ′	° ′	° ′	° ′	° ′	° ′	° ′		° ′	° ′
	7 00	165 05.1	199 48.1	S14 47.3	74 09.1	N26 09.2	237 04.1	S22 20.1	8 16.8	N11 40.9	Acamar	315 21.5	S40 16.5
	01	180 07.5	214 47.5	46.4	89 10.6	09.1	252 06.1	20.0	23 19.4	41.0	Achernar	335 29.9	S57 11.8
	02	195 10.0	229 46.9	45.4	104 12.1	09.1	267 08.2	20.0	38 22.1	41.1	Acrux	173 13.5	S63 08.7
	03	210 12.5	244 46.3	. . 44.5	119 13.7	. . 09.0	282 10.2	. . 19.9	53 24.7	. . 41.1	Adhara	255 15.5	S28 59.2
	04	225 14.9	259 45.7	43.6	134 15.2	09.0	297 12.2	19.9	68 27.4	41.2	Aldebaran	290 54.0	N16 31.6
	05	240 17.4	274 45.2	42.6	149 16.7	08.9	312 14.2	19.8	83 30.0	41.3			
	06	255 19.9	289 44.6	S14 41.7	164 18.3	N26 08.8	327 16.2	S22 19.8	98 32.7	N11 41.4	Alioth	166 23.4	N55 54.6
	07	270 22.3	304 44.0	40.8	179 19.8	08.8	342 18.3	19.7	113 35.3	41.4	Alkaid	153 01.4	N49 16.0
	08	285 24.8	319 43.4	39.9	194 21.3	08.7	357 20.3	19.7	128 37.9	41.5	Al Na'ir	27 49.0	S46 55.3
F	09	300 27.3	334 42.8	. . 38.9	209 22.9	. . 08.7	12 22.3	. . 19.6	143 40.6	. . 41.6	Alnilam	275 50.4	S 1 11.8
R	10	315 29.7	349 42.2	38.0	224 24.4	08.6	27 24.3	19.6	158 43.2	41.6	Alphard	217 59.7	S 8 41.8
I	11	330 32.2	4 41.7	37.1	239 25.9	08.6	42 26.3	19.5	173 45.9	41.7			
D	12	345 34.6	19 41.1	S14 36.1	254 27.5	N26 08.5	57 28.4	S22 19.5	188 48.5	N11 41.8	Alphecca	126 14.2	N26 40.9
A	13	0 37.1	34 40.5	35.2	269 29.0	08.5	72 30.4	19.5	203 51.2	41.9	Alpheratz	357 48.1	N29 08.1
Y	14	15 39.6	49 39.9	34.2	284 30.5	08.4	87 32.4	19.4	218 53.8	41.9	Altair	62 12.3	N 8 53.2
	15	30 42.0	64 39.3	. . 33.3	299 32.1	. . 08.4	102 34.4	. . 19.4	233 56.5	. . 42.0	Ankaa	353 19.8	S42 15.8
	16	45 44.5	79 38.7	32.4	314 33.6	08.3	117 36.5	19.3	248 59.1	42.1	Antares	112 31.1	S26 27.1
	17	60 47.0	94 38.2	31.4	329 35.1	08.3	132 38.5	19.3	264 01.8	42.2			
	18	75 49.4	109 37.6	S14 30.5	344 36.6	N26 08.2	147 40.5	S22 19.2	279 04.4	N11 42.2	Arcturus	145 59.1	N19 08.1
	19	90 51.9	124 37.0	29.6	359 38.2	08.2	162 42.5	19.2	294 07.1	42.3	Atria	107 36.7	S69 02.4
	20	105 54.4	139 36.4	28.6	14 39.7	08.1	177 44.5	19.1	309 09.7	42.4	Avior	234 19.4	S59 32.3
	21	120 56.8	154 35.9	. . 27.7	29 41.2	. . 08.1	192 46.6	. . 19.1	324 12.4	. . 42.4	Bellatrix	278 36.3	N 6 21.4
	22	135 59.3	169 35.3	26.7	44 42.7	08.0	207 48.6	19.0	339 15.0	42.5	Betelgeuse	271 05.5	N 7 24.5
	23	151 01.8	184 34.7	25.8	59 44.3	08.0	222 50.6	19.0	354 17.7	42.6			
	8 00	166 04.2	199 34.1	S14 24.9	74 45.8	N26 07.9	237 52.6	S22 18.9	9 20.3	N11 42.7	Canopus	263 57.8	S52 42.2
	01	181 06.7	214 33.5	23.9	89 47.3	07.9	252 54.7	18.9	24 22.9	42.7	Capella	280 40.4	N46 00.6
	02	196 09.1	229 33.0	23.0	104 48.8	07.8	267 56.7	18.8	39 25.6	42.8	Deneb	49 34.7	N45 18.3
	03	211 11.6	244 32.4	. . 22.0	119 50.3	. . 07.7	282 58.7	. . 18.8	54 28.2	. . 42.9	Denebola	182 37.3	N14 31.4
	04	226 14.1	259 31.8	21.1	134 51.9	07.7	298 00.7	18.7	69 30.9	42.9	Diphda	349 00.1	S17 56.6
	05	241 16.5	274 31.2	20.1	149 53.4	07.6	313 02.8	18.7	84 33.5	43.0			
	06	256 19.0	289 30.7	S14 19.2	164 54.9	N26 07.6	328 04.8	S22 18.7	99 36.2	N11 43.1	Dubhe	193 55.5	N61 42.3
	07	271 21.5	304 30.1	18.2	179 56.4	07.5	343 06.8	18.6	114 38.8	43.2	Elnath	278 17.6	N28 37.0
S	08	286 23.9	319 29.5	17.3	194 57.9	07.5	358 08.8	18.6	129 41.5	43.2	Eltanin	90 48.1	N51 28.8
A	09	301 26.4	334 28.9	. . 16.3	209 59.4	. . 07.4	13 10.9	. . 18.5	144 44.1	. . 43.3	Enif	33 51.4	N 9 54.6
T	10	316 28.9	349 28.4	15.4	225 01.0	07.4	28 12.9	18.5	159 46.8	43.4	Fomalhaut	15 28.6	S29 34.8
U	11	331 31.3	4 27.8	14.4	240 02.5	07.3	43 14.9	18.4	174 49.4	43.4			
R	12	346 33.8	19 27.2	S14 13.5	255 04.0	N26 07.3	58 17.0	S22 18.4	189 52.1	N11 43.5	Gacrux	172 05.1	S57 09.6
D	13	1 36.3	34 26.7	12.5	270 05.5	07.2	73 19.0	18.3	204 54.7	43.6	Gienah	175 56.2	S17 35.4
A	14	16 38.7	49 26.1	11.6	285 07.0	07.2	88 21.0	18.3	219 57.4	43.7	Hadar	148 53.4	S60 24.7
Y	15	31 41.2	64 25.5	. . 10.6	300 08.5	. . 07.1	103 23.0	. . 18.2	235 00.0	. . 43.7	Hamal	328 05.6	N23 30.1
	16	46 43.6	79 24.9	09.7	315 10.0	07.0	118 25.1	18.2	250 02.6	43.8	Kaus Aust.	83 49.2	S34 22.9
	17	61 46.1	94 24.4	08.7	330 11.6	07.0	133 27.1	18.1	265 05.3	43.9			
	18	76 48.6	109 23.8	S14 07.8	345 13.1	N26 06.9	148 29.1	S22 18.1	280 07.9	N11 43.9	Kochab	137 18.7	N74 06.9
	19	91 51.0	124 23.2	06.8	0 14.6	06.9	163 31.1	18.0	295 10.6	44.0	Markab	13 42.7	N15 14.9
	20	106 53.5	139 22.7	05.9	15 16.1	06.8	178 33.2	18.0	310 13.2	44.1	Menkar	314 19.4	N 4 07.3
	21	121 56.0	154 22.1	. . 04.9	30 17.6	. . 06.8	193 35.2	. . 17.9	325 15.9	. . 44.1	Menkent	148 12.1	S36 24.7
	22	136 58.4	169 21.5	03.9	45 19.1	06.7	208 37.2	17.9	340 18.5	44.2	Miaplacidus	221 40.1	S69 45.2
	23	152 00.9	184 21.0	03.0	60 20.6	06.7	223 39.3	17.9	355 21.2	44.3			
	9 00	167 03.4	199 20.4	S14 02.0	75 22.1	N26 06.6	238 41.3	S22 17.8	10 23.8	N11 44.4	Mirfak	308 46.4	N49 53.7
	01	182 05.8	214 19.8	01.1	90 23.6	06.6	253 43.3	17.8	25 26.5	44.4	Nunki	76 03.4	S26 17.3
	02	197 08.3	229 19.3	14 00.1	105 25.1	06.5	268 45.4	17.7	40 29.1	44.5	Peacock	53 25.7	S56 42.5
	03	212 10.7	244 18.7	13 59.1	120 26.6	. . 06.4	283 47.4	. . 17.7	55 31.7	. . 44.6	Pollux	243 32.3	N28 00.4
	04	227 13.2	259 18.1	58.2	135 28.1	06.4	298 49.4	17.6	70 34.4	44.6	Procyon	245 03.7	N 5 12.2
	05	242 15.7	274 17.6	57.2	150 29.6	06.3	313 51.4	17.6	85 37.0	44.7			
	06	257 18.1	289 17.0	S13 56.3	165 31.1	N26 06.3	328 53.5	S22 17.5	100 39.7	N11 44.8	Rasalhague	96 10.2	N12 32.9
	07	272 20.6	304 16.5	55.3	180 32.6	06.2	343 55.5	17.5	115 42.3	44.9	Regulus	207 47.4	N11 55.5
	08	287 23.1	319 15.9	54.3	195 34.1	06.2	358 57.5	17.4	130 45.0	44.9	Rigel	281 15.9	S 8 11.6
S	09	302 25.5	334 15.3	. . 53.4	210 35.6	. . 06.1	13 59.6	. . 17.4	145 47.6	. . 45.0	Rigil Kent.	139 57.1	S60 52.1
U	10	317 28.0	349 14.8	52.4	225 37.1	06.0	29 01.6	17.3	160 50.3	45.1	Sabik	102 17.1	S15 44.3
N	11	332 30.5	4 14.2	51.4	240 38.6	06.0	44 03.6	17.3	175 52.9	45.1			
D	12	347 32.9	19 13.6	S13 50.5	255 40.1	N26 05.9	59 05.7	S22 17.2	190 55.6	N11 45.2	Schedar	349 45.9	N56 35.0
A	13	2 35.4	34 13.1	49.5	270 41.6	05.9	74 07.7	17.2	205 58.2	45.3	Shaula	96 27.4	S37 06.6
Y	14	17 37.9	49 12.5	48.5	285 43.1	05.8	89 09.7	17.2	221 00.8	45.3	Sirius	258 37.1	S16 43.8
	15	32 40.3	64 12.0	. . 47.6	300 44.6	. . 05.8	104 11.8	. . 17.1	236 03.5	. . 45.4	Spica	158 35.2	S11 12.4
	16	47 42.8	79 11.4	46.6	315 46.1	05.7	119 13.8	17.1	251 06.1	45.5	Suhail	222 55.1	S43 28.1
	17	62 45.2	94 10.9	45.6	330 47.6	05.7	134 15.8	17.0	266 08.8	45.6			
	18	77 47.7	109 10.3	S13 44.6	345 49.1	N26 05.6	149 17.9	S22 17.0	281 11.4	N11 45.6	Vega	80 41.8	N38 47.1
	19	92 50.2	124 09.7	43.7	0 50.6	05.5	164 19.9	16.9	296 14.1	45.7	Zuben'ubi	137 09.7	S16 04.7
	20	107 52.6	139 09.2	42.7	15 52.1	05.5	179 21.9	16.9	311 16.7	45.8			
	21	122 55.1	154 08.6	. . 41.7	30 53.6	. . 05.4	194 24.0	. . 16.8	326 19.4	. . 45.8			
	22	137 57.6	169 08.1	40.8	45 55.1	05.4	209 26.0	16.8	341 22.0	45.9			
	23	153 00.0	184 07.5	39.8	60 56.6	05.3	224 28.0	16.7	356 24.6	46.0			
	Mer. Pass. (h m)	12 53.6	*v* −0.6	*d* 1.0	*v* 1.5	*d* 0.1	*v* 2.0	*d* 0.0	*v* 2.6	*d* 0.1			

	SHA	Mer. Pass.
	° ′	h m
Venus	33 29.9	10 42
Mars	268 41.6	18 59
Jupiter	71 48.4	8 07
Saturn	203 16.1	23 19

UT d	h	SUN GHA ° ′	SUN Dec ° ′	MOON GHA ° ′	v ′	MOON Dec ° ′	d ′	HP ′
7	00	177 14.1	S 5 12.8	186 13.5	12.3	S 7 55.5	15.8	58.5
	01	192 14.2	11.8	200 44.8	12.2	7 39.7	15.8	58.5
	02	207 14.4	10.9	215 16.0	12.3	7 23.9	15.8	58.5
	03	222 14.5	. . 09.9	229 47.3	12.2	7 08.1	15.9	58.5
	04	237 14.7	08.9	244 18.5	12.3	6 52.2	16.0	58.6
	05	252 14.8	08.0	258 49.8	12.3	6 36.2	16.0	58.6
	06	267 15.0	S 5 07.0	273 21.1	12.3	S 6 20.2	16.0	58.6
	07	282 15.1	06.0	287 52.4	12.3	6 04.2	16.1	58.7
	08	297 15.3	05.0	302 23.7	12.2	5 48.1	16.2	58.7
F	09	312 15.4	. . 04.1	316 54.9	12.3	5 31.9	16.1	58.7
R	10	327 15.6	03.1	331 26.2	12.3	5 15.8	16.3	58.7
I	11	342 15.7	02.1	345 57.5	12.3	4 59.5	16.2	58.8
D	12	357 15.9	S 5 01.1	0 28.8	12.3	S 4 43.3	16.3	58.8
A	13	12 16.0	5 00.2	15 00.1	12.3	4 27.0	16.3	58.8
Y	14	27 16.2	4 59.2	29 31.4	12.2	4 10.7	16.4	58.8
	15	42 16.3	. . 58.2	44 02.6	12.3	3 54.3	16.4	58.9
	16	57 16.5	57.2	58 33.9	12.2	3 37.9	16.4	58.9
	17	72 16.6	56.3	73 05.1	12.3	3 21.5	16.5	58.9
	18	87 16.8	S 4 55.3	87 36.4	12.2	S 3 05.0	16.5	58.9
	19	102 16.9	54.3	102 07.6	12.3	2 48.5	16.5	59.0
	20	117 17.1	53.3	116 38.9	12.2	2 32.0	16.5	59.0
	21	132 17.2	. . 52.4	131 10.1	12.2	2 15.5	16.6	59.0
	22	147 17.4	51.4	145 41.3	12.2	1 58.9	16.6	59.0
	23	162 17.6	50.4	160 12.5	12.2	1 42.3	16.6	59.0
8	00	177 17.7	S 4 49.4	174 43.7	12.1	S 1 25.7	16.6	59.1
	01	192 17.9	48.4	189 14.8	12.2	1 09.1	16.6	59.1
	02	207 18.0	47.5	203 46.0	12.1	0 52.5	16.7	59.1
	03	222 18.2	. . 46.5	218 17.1	12.1	0 35.8	16.7	59.1
	04	237 18.3	45.5	232 48.2	12.1	0 19.1	16.7	59.2
	05	252 18.5	44.5	247 19.3	12.0	S 0 02.4	16.7	59.2
	06	267 18.6	S 4 43.6	261 50.3	12.1	N 0 14.3	16.7	59.2
	07	282 18.8	42.6	276 21.4	12.0	0 31.0	16.7	59.2
S	08	297 18.9	41.6	290 52.4	12.0	0 47.7	16.7	59.2
A	09	312 19.1	. . 40.6	305 23.4	12.0	1 04.4	16.7	59.3
T	10	327 19.2	39.7	319 54.4	11.9	1 21.1	16.8	59.3
U	11	342 19.4	38.7	334 25.3	11.9	1 37.9	16.7	59.3
R	12	357 19.6	S 4 37.7	348 56.2	11.9	N 1 54.6	16.7	59.3
D	13	12 19.7	36.7	3 27.1	11.8	2 11.3	16.8	59.3
A	14	27 19.9	35.8	17 57.9	11.9	2 28.1	16.7	59.4
Y	15	42 20.0	. . 34.8	32 28.8	11.7	2 44.8	16.7	59.4
	16	57 20.2	33.8	46 59.5	11.8	3 01.5	16.8	59.4
	17	72 20.3	32.8	61 30.3	11.7	3 18.3	16.7	59.4
	18	87 20.5	S 4 31.8	76 01.0	11.7	N 3 35.0	16.7	59.4
	19	102 20.6	30.9	90 31.7	11.6	3 51.7	16.7	59.4
	20	117 20.8	29.9	105 02.3	11.6	4 08.4	16.6	59.5
	21	132 21.0	. . 28.9	119 32.9	11.6	4 25.0	16.7	59.5
	22	147 21.1	27.9	134 03.5	11.5	4 41.7	16.7	59.5
	23	162 21.3	26.9	148 34.0	11.5	4 58.4	16.6	59.5
9	00	177 21.4	S 4 26.0	163 04.5	11.4	N 5 15.0	16.6	59.5
	01	192 21.6	25.0	177 34.9	11.4	5 31.6	16.6	59.5
	02	207 21.7	24.0	192 05.3	11.4	5 48.2	16.5	59.6
	03	222 21.9	. . 23.0	206 35.7	11.3	6 04.7	16.6	59.6
	04	237 22.1	22.1	221 06.0	11.2	6 21.3	16.5	59.6
	05	252 22.2	21.1	235 36.2	11.2	6 37.8	16.5	59.6
	06	267 22.4	S 4 20.1	250 06.4	11.2	N 6 54.3	16.5	59.6
	07	282 22.5	19.1	264 36.6	11.1	7 10.8	16.4	59.6
	08	297 22.7	18.1	279 06.7	11.0	7 27.2	16.4	59.6
S	09	312 22.8	. . 17.2	293 36.7	11.0	7 43.6	16.3	59.6
U	10	327 23.0	16.2	308 06.7	11.0	7 59.9	16.3	59.7
N	11	342 23.2	15.2	322 36.7	10.9	8 16.2	16.3	59.7
D	12	357 23.3	S 4 14.2	337 06.6	10.8	N 8 32.5	16.3	59.7
A	13	12 23.5	13.2	351 36.4	10.8	8 48.8	16.2	59.7
Y	14	27 23.6	12.3	6 06.2	10.7	9 05.0	16.1	59.7
	15	42 23.8	. . 11.3	20 35.9	10.6	9 21.1	16.1	59.7
	16	57 23.9	10.3	35 05.5	10.6	9 37.2	16.1	59.7
	17	72 24.1	09.3	49 35.1	10.5	9 53.3	16.0	59.7
	18	87 24.3	S 4 08.3	64 04.6	10.5	N10 09.3	16.0	59.7
	19	102 24.4	07.4	78 34.1	10.4	10 25.3	15.9	59.7
	20	117 24.6	06.4	93 03.5	10.4	10 41.2	15.8	59.8
	21	132 24.7	. . 05.4	107 32.9	10.2	10 57.0	15.8	59.8
	22	147 24.9	04.4	122 02.1	10.2	11 12.8	15.8	59.8
	23	162 25.1	03.4	136 31.3	10.2	N11 28.6	15.6	59.8
		SD 16.1	*d* 1.0	SD		16.0	16.2	16.3

Lat. °	Twilight Naut. h m	Twilight Civil h m	Sunrise h m	Moonrise 7 h m	Moonrise 8 h m	Moonrise 9 h m	Moonrise 10 h m
N 72	04 32	05 51	06 58	07 07	06 31	05 54	05 07
N 70	04 41	05 53	06 53	06 58	06 31	06 04	05 30
68	04 48	05 53	06 49	06 51	06 31	06 11	05 48
66	04 55	05 54	06 45	06 45	06 32	06 18	06 02
64	05 00	05 55	06 42	06 40	06 32	06 23	06 14
62	05 04	05 55	06 39	06 36	06 32	06 28	06 24
60	05 07	05 56	06 37	06 32	06 32	06 32	06 33
N 58	05 10	05 56	06 35	06 29	06 32	06 36	06 41
56	05 13	05 56	06 33	06 26	06 32	06 40	06 48
54	05 15	05 56	06 31	06 23	06 33	06 43	06 54
52	05 17	05 56	06 30	06 20	06 33	06 45	07 00
50	05 19	05 56	06 28	06 18	06 33	06 48	07 05
45	05 22	05 56	06 25	06 13	06 33	06 53	07 16
N 40	05 24	05 55	06 22	06 09	06 33	06 58	07 25
35	05 25	05 55	06 20	06 05	06 33	07 02	07 33
30	05 26	05 54	06 18	06 02	06 33	07 06	07 40
20	05 27	05 52	06 14	05 56	06 34	07 12	07 53
N 10	05 25	05 50	06 11	05 51	06 34	07 18	08 03
0	05 23	05 47	06 07	05 47	06 34	07 23	08 14
S 10	05 18	05 43	06 04	05 42	06 35	07 28	08 24
20	05 12	05 38	06 00	05 37	06 35	07 34	08 35
30	05 04	05 32	05 56	05 31	06 35	07 41	08 48
35	04 58	05 28	05 53	05 28	06 36	07 45	08 56
40	04 51	05 23	05 50	05 24	06 36	07 49	09 04
45	04 42	05 17	05 47	05 20	06 36	07 54	09 14
S 50	04 31	05 10	05 43	05 15	06 37	08 00	09 27
52	04 25	05 07	05 41	05 12	06 37	08 03	09 32
54	04 19	05 03	05 39	05 10	06 37	08 07	09 39
56	04 12	04 58	05 37	05 07	06 37	08 10	09 46
58	04 04	04 54	05 34	05 03	06 38	08 14	09 54
S 60	03 54	04 48	05 31	05 00	06 38	08 18	10 03

Lat. °	Sunset h m	Twilight Civil h m	Twilight Naut. h m	Moonset 7 h m	Moonset 8 h m	Moonset 9 h m	Moonset 10 h m
N 72	17 25	18 33	19 53	17 26	19 48	22 22	▭
N 70	17 30	18 31	19 43	17 31	19 42	22 02	24 53
68	17 34	18 30	19 35	17 35	19 38	21 46	24 13
66	17 38	18 29	19 29	17 39	19 34	21 34	23 45
64	17 41	18 28	19 24	17 42	19 30	21 23	23 25
62	17 44	18 28	19 19	17 44	19 28	21 15	23 08
60	17 46	18 27	19 16	17 46	19 25	21 07	22 54
N 58	17 48	18 27	19 13	17 48	19 23	21 01	22 42
56	17 50	18 27	19 10	17 50	19 21	20 55	22 32
54	17 51	18 27	19 08	17 51	19 19	20 50	22 23
52	17 53	18 26	19 06	17 52	19 18	20 45	22 15
50	17 54	18 26	19 04	17 54	19 16	20 41	22 08
45	17 57	18 27	19 01	17 56	19 13	20 32	21 53
N 40	18 00	18 27	18 58	17 58	19 11	20 25	21 41
35	18 02	18 27	18 57	18 00	19 08	20 18	21 30
30	18 04	18 28	18 56	18 02	19 06	20 13	21 21
20	18 08	18 30	18 55	18 05	19 03	20 03	21 05
N 10	18 11	18 32	18 56	18 07	19 00	19 55	20 52
0	18 14	18 35	18 59	18 09	18 57	19 47	20 39
S 10	18 17	18 38	19 03	18 11	18 54	19 39	20 26
20	18 21	18 43	19 09	18 14	18 51	19 31	20 13
30	18 25	18 49	19 17	18 16	18 48	19 21	19 57
35	18 27	18 53	19 23	18 18	18 46	19 16	19 49
40	18 30	18 58	19 30	18 20	18 44	19 10	19 38
45	18 34	19 03	19 38	18 21	18 41	19 02	19 27
S 50	18 37	19 10	19 50	18 24	18 38	18 54	19 13
52	18 39	19 14	19 55	18 25	18 37	18 50	19 06
54	18 41	19 17	20 01	18 26	18 35	18 46	18 59
56	18 44	19 22	20 08	18 27	18 34	18 41	18 51
58	18 46	19 26	20 16	18 28	18 32	18 36	18 42
S 60	18 49	19 32	20 25	18 30	18 30	18 30	18 31

Day	SUN Eqn. of Time 00^h	SUN Eqn. of Time 12^h	SUN Mer. Pass.	MOON Mer. Pass. Upper	MOON Mer. Pass. Lower	MOON Age	MOON Phase
d	m s	m s	h m	h m	h m	d	%
7	11 04	10 57	12 11	11 58	24 22	29	0
8	10 49	10 42	12 11	12 46	00 22	01	1
9	10 35	10 27	12 10	13 35	01 10	02	4

UT	ARIES	VENUS −3.8		MARS +0.4		JUPITER −2.0		SATURN +0.3	
	GHA	GHA	Dec	GHA	Dec	GHA	Dec	GHA	Dec
d h	° ′	° ′	° ′	° ′	° ′	° ′	° ′	° ′	° ′
10 00	168 02.5	199 07.0	S13 38.8	75 58.1	N26 05.3	239 30.1	S22 16.7	11 27.3	N11 46.1
01	183 05.0	214 06.4	37.8	90 59.5	05.2	254 32.1	16.6	26 29.9	46.1
02	198 07.4	229 05.8	36.9	106 01.0	05.1	269 34.1	16.6	41 32.6	46.2
03	213 09.9	244 05.3	. . 35.9	121 02.5	. . 05.1	284 36.2	. . 16.5	56 35.2	. . 46.3
04	228 12.3	259 04.7	34.9	136 04.0	05.0	299 38.2	16.5	71 37.9	46.3
05	243 14.8	274 04.2	33.9	151 05.5	05.0	314 40.2	16.5	86 40.5	46.4
06	258 17.3	289 03.6	S13 32.9	166 07.0	N26 04.9	329 42.3	S22 16.4	101 43.2	N11 46.5
07	273 19.7	304 03.1	32.0	181 08.5	04.8	344 44.3	16.4	116 45.8	46.5
08	288 22.2	319 02.5	31.0	196 10.0	04.8	359 46.3	16.3	131 48.4	46.6
M 09	303 24.7	334 02.0	. . 30.0	211 11.4	. . 04.7	14 48.4	. . 16.3	146 51.1	. . 46.7
O 10	318 27.1	349 01.4	29.0	226 12.9	04.7	29 50.4	16.2	161 53.7	46.7
N 11	333 29.6	4 00.9	28.0	241 14.4	04.6	44 52.5	16.2	176 56.4	46.8
D 12	348 32.1	19 00.3	S13 27.1	256 15.9	N26 04.6	59 54.5	S22 16.1	191 59.0	N11 46.9
A 13	3 34.5	33 59.8	26.1	271 17.4	04.5	74 56.5	16.1	207 01.7	47.0
Y 14	18 37.0	48 59.2	25.1	286 18.9	04.4	89 58.6	16.0	222 04.3	47.0
15	33 39.5	63 58.7	. . 24.1	301 20.3	. . 04.4	105 00.6	. . 16.0	237 06.9	. . 47.1
16	48 41.9	78 58.1	23.1	316 21.8	04.3	120 02.6	15.9	252 09.6	47.2
17	63 44.4	93 57.6	22.1	331 23.3	04.3	135 04.7	15.9	267 12.2	47.2
18	78 46.8	108 57.0	S13 21.2	346 24.8	N26 04.2	150 06.7	S22 15.8	282 14.9	N11 47.3
19	93 49.3	123 56.5	20.2	1 26.3	04.1	165 08.8	15.8	297 17.5	47.4
20	108 51.8	138 55.9	19.2	16 27.7	04.1	180 10.8	15.8	312 20.2	47.4
21	123 54.2	153 55.4	. . 18.2	31 29.2	. . 04.0	195 12.8	. . 15.7	327 22.8	. . 47.5
22	138 56.7	168 54.8	17.2	46 30.7	04.0	210 14.9	15.7	342 25.4	47.6
23	153 59.2	183 54.3	16.2	61 32.2	03.9	225 16.9	15.6	357 28.1	47.7
11 00	169 01.6	198 53.8	S13 15.2	76 33.6	N26 03.8	240 19.0	S22 15.6	12 30.7	N11 47.7
01	184 04.1	213 53.2	14.2	91 35.1	03.8	255 21.0	15.5	27 33.4	47.8
02	199 06.6	228 52.7	13.2	106 36.6	03.7	270 23.0	15.5	42 36.0	47.9
03	214 09.0	243 52.1	. . 12.2	121 38.1	. . 03.7	285 25.1	. . 15.4	57 38.7	. . 47.9
04	229 11.5	258 51.6	11.3	136 39.5	03.6	300 27.1	15.4	72 41.3	48.0
05	244 13.9	273 51.0	10.3	151 41.0	03.5	315 29.2	15.3	87 43.9	48.1
06	259 16.4	288 50.5	S13 09.3	166 42.5	N26 03.5	330 31.2	S22 15.3	102 46.6	N11 48.1
07	274 18.9	303 49.9	08.3	181 44.0	03.4	345 33.2	15.2	117 49.2	48.2
T 08	289 21.3	318 49.4	07.3	196 45.4	03.4	0 35.3	15.2	132 51.9	48.3
U 09	304 23.8	333 48.9	. . 06.3	211 46.9	. . 03.3	15 37.3	. . 15.1	147 54.5	. . 48.3
E 10	319 26.3	348 48.3	05.3	226 48.4	03.2	30 39.4	15.1	162 57.2	48.4
S 11	334 28.7	3 47.8	04.3	241 49.8	03.2	45 41.4	15.1	177 59.8	48.5
D 12	349 31.2	18 47.2	S13 03.3	256 51.3	N26 03.1	60 43.5	S22 15.0	193 02.4	N11 48.5
A 13	4 33.7	33 46.7	02.3	271 52.8	03.1	75 45.5	15.0	208 05.1	48.6
Y 14	19 36.1	48 46.2	01.3	286 54.2	03.0	90 47.5	14.9	223 07.7	48.7
15	34 38.6	63 45.6	13 00.3	301 55.7	. . 02.9	105 49.6	. . 14.9	238 10.4	. . 48.8
16	49 41.1	78 45.1	12 59.3	316 57.2	02.9	120 51.6	14.8	253 13.0	48.8
17	64 43.5	93 44.6	58.3	331 58.6	02.8	135 53.7	14.8	268 15.6	48.9
18	79 46.0	108 44.0	S12 57.3	347 00.1	N26 02.7	150 55.7	S22 14.7	283 18.3	N11 49.0
19	94 48.4	123 43.5	56.3	2 01.6	02.7	165 57.8	14.7	298 20.9	49.0
20	109 50.9	138 42.9	55.3	17 03.0	02.6	180 59.8	14.6	313 23.6	49.1
21	124 53.4	153 42.4	. . 54.3	32 04.5	. . 02.6	196 01.8	. . 14.6	328 26.2	. . 49.2
22	139 55.8	168 41.9	53.3	47 05.9	02.5	211 03.9	14.5	343 28.9	49.2
23	154 58.3	183 41.3	52.3	62 07.4	02.4	226 05.9	14.5	358 31.5	49.3
12 00	170 00.8	198 40.8	S12 51.3	77 08.9	N26 02.4	241 08.0	S22 14.5	13 34.1	N11 49.4
01	185 03.2	213 40.3	50.3	92 10.3	02.3	256 10.0	14.4	28 36.8	49.4
02	200 05.7	228 39.7	49.3	107 11.8	02.2	271 12.1	14.4	43 39.4	49.5
03	215 08.2	243 39.2	. . 48.2	122 13.2	. . 02.2	286 14.1	. . 14.3	58 42.1	. . 49.6
04	230 10.6	258 38.7	47.2	137 14.7	02.1	301 16.2	14.3	73 44.7	49.6
05	245 13.1	273 38.1	46.2	152 16.2	02.1	316 18.2	14.2	88 47.3	49.7
06	260 15.6	288 37.6	S12 45.2	167 17.6	N26 02.0	331 20.3	S22 14.2	103 50.0	N11 49.8
W 07	275 18.0	303 37.1	44.2	182 19.1	01.9	346 22.3	14.1	118 52.6	49.8
E 08	290 20.5	318 36.5	43.2	197 20.5	01.9	1 24.3	14.1	133 55.3	49.9
D 09	305 22.9	333 36.0	. . 42.2	212 22.0	. . 01.8	16 26.4	. . 14.0	148 57.9	. . 50.0
N 10	320 25.4	348 35.5	41.2	227 23.4	01.7	31 28.4	14.0	164 00.5	50.1
E 11	335 27.9	3 34.9	40.2	242 24.9	01.7	46 30.5	13.9	179 03.2	50.1
S 12	350 30.3	18 34.4	S12 39.2	257 26.3	N26 01.6	61 32.5	S22 13.9	194 05.8	N11 50.2
D 13	5 32.8	33 33.9	38.1	272 27.8	01.5	76 34.6	13.8	209 08.5	50.3
A 14	20 35.3	48 33.4	37.1	287 29.2	01.5	91 36.6	13.8	224 11.1	50.3
Y 15	35 37.7	63 32.8	. . 36.1	302 30.7	. . 01.4	106 38.7	. . 13.8	239 13.7	. . 50.4
16	50 40.2	78 32.3	35.1	317 32.2	01.4	121 40.7	13.7	254 16.4	50.5
17	65 42.7	93 31.8	34.1	332 33.6	01.3	136 42.8	13.7	269 19.0	50.5
18	80 45.1	108 31.2	S12 33.1	347 35.1	N26 01.2	151 44.8	S22 13.6	284 21.7	N11 50.6
19	95 47.6	123 30.7	32.1	2 36.5	01.2	166 46.9	13.6	299 24.3	50.7
20	110 50.1	138 30.2	31.0	17 37.9	01.1	181 48.9	13.5	314 26.9	50.7
21	125 52.5	153 29.7	. . 30.0	32 39.4	. . 01.0	196 51.0	. . 13.5	329 29.6	. . 50.8
22	140 55.0	168 29.1	29.0	47 40.8	01.0	211 53.0	13.4	344 32.2	50.9
23	155 57.4	183 28.6	28.0	62 42.3	00.9	226 55.1	13.4	359 34.9	50.9
Mer. Pass. (h m)	12 41.8	v −0.5	d 1.0	v 1.5	d 0.1	v 2.0	d 0.0	v 2.6	d 0.1

STARS

Name	SHA	Dec
	° ′	° ′
Acamar	315 21.5	S40 16.5
Achernar	335 29.9	S57 11.8
Acrux	173 13.5	S63 08.7
Adhara	255 15.5	S28 59.2
Aldebaran	290 54.0	N16 31.6
Alioth	166 23.4	N55 54.7
Alkaid	153 01.4	N49 16.0
Al Na'ir	27 48.9	S46 55.3
Alnilam	275 50.4	S 1 11.8
Alphard	217 59.7	S 8 41.8
Alphecca	126 14.2	N26 40.9
Alpheratz	357 48.1	N29 08.1
Altair	62 12.3	N 8 53.2
Ankaa	353 19.8	S42 15.8
Antares	112 31.1	S26 27.1
Arcturus	145 59.1	N19 08.1
Atria	107 36.6	S69 02.4
Avior	234 19.4	S59 32.3
Bellatrix	278 36.3	N 6 21.4
Betelgeuse	271 05.6	N 7 24.5
Canopus	263 57.8	S52 42.2
Capella	280 40.4	N46 00.6
Deneb	49 34.7	N45 18.3
Denebola	182 37.3	N14 31.4
Diphda	349 00.1	S17 56.6
Dubhe	193 55.5	N61 42.3
Elnath	278 17.7	N28 37.0
Eltanin	90 48.1	N51 28.8
Enif	33 51.4	N 9 54.6
Fomalhaut	15 28.6	S29 34.8
Gacrux	172 05.1	S57 09.6
Gienah	175 56.1	S17 35.4
Hadar	148 53.4	S60 24.7
Hamal	328 05.6	N23 30.1
Kaus Aust.	83 49.2	S34 22.9
Kochab	137 18.6	N74 06.9
Markab	13 42.7	N15 14.9
Menkar	314 19.4	N 4 07.3
Menkent	148 12.1	S36 24.7
Miaplacidus	221 40.2	S69 45.2
Mirfak	308 46.5	N49 53.7
Nunki	76 03.4	S26 17.3
Peacock	53 25.7	S56 42.5
Pollux	243 32.3	N28 00.4
Procyon	245 03.7	N 5 12.2
Rasalhague	96 10.2	N12 32.9
Regulus	207 47.4	N11 55.5
Rigel	281 15.9	S 8 11.6
Rigil Kent.	139 57.0	S60 52.1
Sabik	102 17.1	S15 44.3
Schedar	349 45.9	N56 35.0
Shaula	96 27.4	S37 06.6
Sirius	258 37.1	S16 43.8
Spica	158 35.2	S11 12.4
Suhail	222 55.2	S43 28.1
Vega	80 41.8	N38 47.1
Zuben'ubi	137 09.7	S16 04.7

	SHA	Mer. Pass.
	° ′	h m
Venus	29 52.1	10 45
Mars	267 32.0	18 52
Jupiter	71 17.3	7 58
Saturn	203 29.1	23 06

UT		SUN		MOON				
		GHA	Dec	GHA	v	Dec	d	HP
d	h	° ′	° ′	° ′	′	° ′	′	′
10	00	177 25.2	S 4 02.5	151 00.5	10.0	N11 44.2	15.7	59.8
	01	192 25.4	01.5	165 29.5	10.0	11 59.9	15.5	59.8
	02	207 25.5	4 00.5	179 58.5	10.0	12 15.4	15.5	59.8
	03	222 25.7	3 59.5	194 27.5	9.8	12 30.9	15.4	59.8
	04	237 25.9	58.5	208 56.3	9.8	12 46.3	15.4	59.8
	05	252 26.0	57.6	223 25.1	9.7	13 01.7	15.2	59.8
	06	267 26.2	S 3 56.6	237 53.8	9.7	N13 16.9	15.2	59.8
	07	282 26.4	55.6	252 22.5	9.5	13 32.1	15.2	59.8
	08	297 26.5	54.6	266 51.0	9.5	13 47.3	15.0	59.8
MONDAY	09	312 26.7	. . 53.6	281 19.5	9.4	14 02.3	15.0	59.8
	10	327 26.8	52.6	295 47.9	9.4	14 17.3	14.9	59.8
	11	342 27.0	51.7	310 16.3	9.2	14 32.2	14.8	59.8
	12	357 27.2	S 3 50.7	324 44.5	9.2	N14 47.0	14.7	59.8
	13	12 27.3	49.7	339 12.7	9.1	15 01.7	14.7	59.9
	14	27 27.5	48.7	353 40.8	9.0	15 16.4	14.5	59.9
	15	42 27.6	. . 47.7	8 08.8	8.9	15 30.9	14.5	59.9
	16	57 27.8	46.8	22 36.7	8.9	15 45.4	14.4	59.9
	17	72 28.0	45.8	37 04.6	8.8	15 59.8	14.3	59.9
	18	87 28.1	S 3 44.8	51 32.4	8.7	N16 14.1	14.2	59.9
	19	102 28.3	43.8	66 00.1	8.6	16 28.3	14.1	59.9
	20	117 28.5	42.8	80 27.7	8.5	16 42.4	13.9	59.9
	21	132 28.6	. . 41.8	94 55.2	8.4	16 56.3	13.9	59.9
	22	147 28.8	40.9	109 22.6	8.4	17 10.2	13.8	59.9
	23	162 29.0	39.9	123 50.0	8.2	17 24.0	13.7	59.9
11	00	177 29.1	S 3 38.9	138 17.2	8.2	N17 37.7	13.6	59.9
	01	192 29.3	37.9	152 44.4	8.1	17 51.3	13.5	59.9
	02	207 29.4	36.9	167 11.5	8.0	18 04.8	13.3	59.9
	03	222 29.6	. . 36.0	181 38.5	8.0	18 18.1	13.3	59.9
	04	237 29.8	35.0	196 05.5	7.8	18 31.4	13.1	59.9
	05	252 29.9	34.0	210 32.3	7.8	18 44.5	13.1	59.9
	06	267 30.1	S 3 33.0	224 59.1	7.6	N18 57.6	12.9	59.9
	07	282 30.3	32.0	239 25.7	7.6	19 10.5	12.8	59.8
TUESDAY	08	297 30.4	31.0	253 52.3	7.5	19 23.3	12.6	59.8
	09	312 30.6	. . 30.1	268 18.8	7.4	19 35.9	12.6	59.8
	10	327 30.8	29.1	282 45.2	7.3	19 48.5	12.4	59.8
	11	342 30.9	28.1	297 11.5	7.2	20 00.9	12.3	59.8
	12	357 31.1	S 3 27.1	311 37.7	7.2	N20 13.2	12.2	59.8
	13	12 31.3	26.1	326 03.9	7.0	20 25.4	12.0	59.8
	14	27 31.4	25.1	340 29.9	7.0	20 37.4	11.9	59.8
	15	42 31.6	. . 24.2	354 55.9	6.9	20 49.3	11.8	59.8
	16	57 31.8	23.2	9 21.8	6.8	21 01.1	11.7	59.8
	17	72 31.9	22.2	23 47.6	6.7	21 12.8	11.5	59.8
	18	87 32.1	S 3 21.2	38 13.3	6.6	N21 24.3	11.4	59.8
	19	102 32.3	20.2	52 38.9	6.5	21 35.7	11.2	59.8
	20	117 32.4	19.2	67 04.4	6.5	21 46.9	11.1	59.8
	21	132 32.6	. . 18.2	81 29.9	6.3	21 58.0	10.9	59.8
	22	147 32.8	17.3	95 55.2	6.3	22 08.9	10.9	59.8
	23	162 32.9	16.3	110 20.5	6.2	22 19.8	10.6	59.8
12	00	177 33.1	S 3 15.3	124 45.7	6.1	N22 30.4	10.5	59.8
	01	192 33.3	14.3	139 10.8	6.0	22 40.9	10.4	59.8
	02	207 33.4	13.3	153 35.8	6.0	22 51.3	10.2	59.7
	03	222 33.6	. . 12.3	168 00.8	5.8	23 01.5	10.1	59.7
	04	237 33.8	11.4	182 25.6	5.8	23 11.6	9.9	59.7
	05	252 33.9	10.4	196 50.4	5.7	23 21.5	9.8	59.7
	06	267 34.1	S 3 09.4	211 15.1	5.6	N23 31.3	9.6	59.7
WEDNESDAY	07	282 34.3	08.4	225 39.7	5.6	23 40.9	9.5	59.7
	08	297 34.4	07.4	240 04.3	5.5	23 50.4	9.3	59.7
	09	312 34.6	. . 06.4	254 28.8	5.3	23 59.7	9.1	59.7
	10	327 34.8	05.5	268 53.1	5.4	24 08.8	9.0	59.7
	11	342 34.9	04.5	283 17.5	5.2	24 17.8	8.8	59.7
	12	357 35.1	S 3 03.5	297 41.7	5.2	N24 26.6	8.6	59.7
	13	12 35.3	02.5	312 05.9	5.1	24 35.2	8.5	59.6
	14	27 35.4	01.5	326 30.0	5.0	24 43.7	8.3	59.6
	15	42 35.6	3 00.5	340 54.0	4.9	24 52.0	8.2	59.6
	16	57 35.8	2 59.5	355 17.9	4.9	25 00.2	7.9	59.6
	17	72 35.9	58.6	9 41.8	4.8	25 08.1	7.8	59.6
	18	87 36.1	S 2 57.6	24 05.6	4.8	N25 15.9	7.7	59.6
	19	102 36.3	56.6	38 29.4	4.7	25 23.6	7.4	59.6
	20	117 36.5	55.6	52 53.1	4.6	25 31.0	7.3	59.6
	21	132 36.6	. . 54.6	67 16.7	4.6	25 38.3	7.1	59.6
	22	147 36.8	53.6	81 40.3	4.5	25 45.4	7.0	59.5
	23	162 37.0	52.6	96 03.8	4.4	N25 52.4	6.7	59.5
		SD 16.1	d 1.0	SD 16.3		16.3		16.3

Lat.	Twilight Naut.	Twilight Civil	Sunrise	Moonrise 10	Moonrise 11	Moonrise 12	Moonrise 13
°	h m	h m	h m	h m	h m	h m	h m
N 72	04 15	05 36	06 43	05 07	▭	▭	▭
N 70	04 26	05 39	06 39	05 30	04 30	▭	▭
68	04 35	05 41	06 36	05 48	05 12	▭	▭
66	04 43	05 43	06 34	06 02	05 41	04 56	▭
64	04 49	05 44	06 31	06 14	06 03	05 46	▭
62	04 54	05 46	06 30	06 24	06 21	06 18	06 16
60	04 58	05 47	06 28	06 33	06 36	06 42	06 56
N 58	05 02	05 47	06 26	06 41	06 48	07 01	07 24
56	05 05	05 48	06 25	06 48	07 00	07 17	07 46
54	05 08	05 49	06 24	06 54	07 09	07 31	08 04
52	05 10	05 49	06 23	07 00	07 18	07 43	08 19
50	05 12	05 50	06 22	07 05	07 26	07 54	08 32
45	05 16	05 50	06 19	07 16	07 43	08 16	09 00
N 40	05 19	05 51	06 18	07 25	07 57	08 35	09 21
35	05 21	05 51	06 16	07 33	08 09	08 50	09 39
30	05 23	05 50	06 14	07 40	08 19	09 03	09 55
20	05 24	05 50	06 12	07 53	08 37	09 26	10 22
N 10	05 24	05 48	06 09	08 03	08 53	09 47	10 45
0	05 22	05 46	06 07	08 14	09 08	10 05	11 06
S 10	05 19	05 43	06 04	08 24	09 23	10 24	11 28
20	05 13	05 39	06 01	08 35	09 39	10 45	11 51
30	05 06	05 34	05 58	08 48	09 58	11 08	12 18
35	05 01	05 31	05 56	08 56	10 09	11 23	12 34
40	04 54	05 26	05 54	09 04	10 21	11 39	12 53
45	04 46	05 21	05 51	09 14	10 36	11 58	13 16
S 50	04 36	05 15	05 48	09 27	10 55	12 23	13 45
52	04 31	05 12	05 46	09 32	11 04	12 35	13 59
54	04 25	05 09	05 45	09 39	11 14	12 49	14 16
56	04 19	05 05	05 43	09 46	11 25	13 04	14 36
58	04 12	05 01	05 41	09 54	11 38	13 23	15 00
S 60	04 03	04 56	05 39	10 03	11 53	13 47	15 34

Lat.	Sunset	Twilight Civil	Twilight Naut.	Moonset 10	Moonset 11	Moonset 12	Moonset 13
°	h m	h m	h m	h m	h m	h m	h m
N 72	17 39	18 46	20 09	▭	▭	▭	▭
N 70	17 43	18 43	19 57	24 53	00 53	▭	▭
68	17 45	18 41	19 47	24 13	00 13	▭	▭
66	17 48	18 39	19 40	23 45	26 29	02 29	▭
64	17 50	18 37	19 33	23 25	25 40	01 40	▭
62	17 52	18 36	19 28	23 08	25 09	01 09	03 17
60	17 53	18 35	19 23	22 54	24 46	00 46	02 37
N 58	17 55	18 34	19 20	22 42	24 27	00 27	02 09
56	17 56	18 33	19 16	22 32	24 12	00 12	01 48
54	17 57	18 32	19 13	22 23	23 59	25 30	01 30
52	17 58	18 32	19 11	22 15	23 47	25 15	01 15
50	17 59	18 31	19 09	22 08	23 37	25 02	01 02
45	18 01	18 30	19 05	21 53	23 15	24 36	00 36
N 40	18 03	18 30	19 01	21 41	22 58	24 14	00 14
35	18 05	18 30	18 59	21 30	22 44	23 57	25 06
30	18 06	18 30	18 58	21 21	22 31	23 42	24 50
20	18 09	18 31	18 56	21 05	22 10	23 16	24 22
N 10	18 11	18 32	18 56	20 52	21 52	22 54	23 58
0	18 13	18 34	18 58	20 39	21 35	22 34	23 36
S 10	18 16	18 37	19 01	20 26	21 18	22 14	23 14
20	18 18	18 40	19 06	20 13	20 59	21 52	22 50
30	18 21	18 45	19 13	19 57	20 39	21 27	22 22
35	18 23	18 49	19 18	19 49	20 27	21 12	22 06
40	18 25	18 53	19 25	19 38	20 13	20 55	21 46
45	18 28	18 58	19 32	19 27	19 56	20 34	21 23
S 50	18 31	19 04	19 42	19 13	19 36	20 09	20 54
52	18 32	19 07	19 47	19 06	19 27	19 56	20 39
54	18 34	19 10	19 53	18 59	19 16	19 42	20 23
56	18 36	19 13	19 59	18 51	19 04	19 26	20 02
58	18 38	19 17	20 06	18 42	18 50	19 06	19 37
S 60	18 40	19 22	20 14	18 31	18 34	18 42	19 03

Day	SUN Eqn. of Time 00^h	SUN Eqn. of Time 12^h	SUN Mer. Pass.	MOON Mer. Pass. Upper	MOON Mer. Pass. Lower	MOON Age	MOON Phase
d	m s	m s	h m	h m	h m	d	%
10	10 19	10 12	12 10	14 26	02 00	03	10
11	10 04	09 56	12 10	15 21	02 53	04	19
12	09 48	09 40	12 10	16 20	03 50	05	28

UT d h	ARIES GHA ° ′	VENUS −3.8 GHA ° ′	VENUS Dec ° ′	MARS +0.5 GHA ° ′	MARS Dec ° ′	JUPITER −2.0 GHA ° ′	JUPITER Dec ° ′	SATURN +0.3 GHA ° ′	SATURN Dec ° ′
13 00	170 59.9	198 28.1	S12 27.0	77 43.7	N26 00.8	241 57.1	S22 13.3	14 37.5	N11 51.0
01	186 02.4	213 27.6	25.9	92 45.2	00.8	256 59.2	13.3	29 40.1	51.1
02	201 04.8	228 27.0	24.9	107 46.6	00.7	272 01.2	13.2	44 42.8	51.1
03	216 07.3	243 26.5	· · 23.9	122 48.1	· · 00.6	287 03.3	· · 13.2	59 45.4	· · 51.2
04	231 09.8	258 26.0	22.9	137 49.5	00.6	302 05.3	13.2	74 48.1	51.3
05	246 12.2	273 25.5	21.9	152 51.0	00.5	317 07.4	13.1	89 50.7	51.3
06	261 14.7	288 25.0	S12 20.8	167 52.4	N26 00.4	332 09.4	S22 13.1	104 53.3	N11 51.4
07	276 17.2	303 24.4	19.8	182 53.8	00.4	347 11.5	13.0	119 56.0	51.5
08	291 19.6	318 23.9	18.8	197 55.3	00.3	2 13.5	13.0	134 58.6	51.5
09	306 22.1	333 23.4	· · 17.8	212 56.7	· · 00.3	17 15.6	· · 12.9	150 01.3	· · 51.6
10	321 24.5	348 22.9	16.7	227 58.2	00.2	32 17.6	12.9	165 03.9	51.7
11	336 27.0	3 22.4	15.7	242 59.6	00.1	47 19.7	12.8	180 06.5	51.7
12	351 29.5	18 21.8	S12 14.7	258 01.0	N26 00.1	62 21.7	S22 12.8	195 09.2	N11 51.8
13	6 31.9	33 21.3	13.7	273 02.5	26 00.0	77 23.8	12.7	210 11.8	51.9
14	21 34.4	48 20.8	12.6	288 03.9	25 59.9	92 25.9	12.7	225 14.4	51.9
15	36 36.9	63 20.3	· · 11.6	303 05.4	· · 59.9	107 27.9	· · 12.6	240 17.1	· · 52.0
16	51 39.3	78 19.8	10.6	318 06.8	59.8	122 30.0	12.6	255 19.7	52.1
17	66 41.8	93 19.2	09.5	333 08.2	59.7	137 32.0	12.6	270 22.4	52.1
18	81 44.3	108 18.7	S12 08.5	348 09.7	N25 59.7	152 34.1	S22 12.5	285 25.0	N11 52.2
19	96 46.7	123 18.2	07.5	3 11.1	59.6	167 36.1	12.5	300 27.6	52.3
20	111 49.2	138 17.7	06.5	18 12.5	59.5	182 38.2	12.4	315 30.3	52.3
21	126 51.7	153 17.2	· · 05.4	33 14.0	· · 59.5	197 40.2	· · 12.4	330 32.9	· · 52.4
22	141 54.1	168 16.7	04.4	48 15.4	59.4	212 42.3	12.3	345 35.6	52.5
23	156 56.6	183 16.1	03.4	63 16.8	59.3	227 44.3	12.3	0 38.2	52.5
14 00	171 59.0	198 15.6	S12 02.3	78 18.3	N25 59.2	242 46.4	S22 12.2	15 40.8	N11 52.6
01	187 01.5	213 15.1	01.3	93 19.7	59.2	257 48.5	12.2	30 43.5	52.7
02	202 04.0	228 14.6	12 00.3	108 21.1	59.1	272 50.5	12.1	45 46.1	52.7
03	217 06.4	243 14.1	11 59.2	123 22.6	· · 59.0	287 52.6	· · 12.1	60 48.7	· · 52.8
04	232 08.9	258 13.6	58.2	138 24.0	59.0	302 54.6	12.1	75 51.4	52.9
05	247 11.4	273 13.1	57.1	153 25.4	58.9	317 56.7	12.0	90 54.0	52.9
06	262 13.8	288 12.5	S11 56.1	168 26.9	N25 58.8	332 58.7	S22 12.0	105 56.7	N11 53.0
07	277 16.3	303 12.0	55.1	183 28.3	58.8	348 00.8	11.9	120 59.3	53.1
08	292 18.8	318 11.5	54.0	198 29.7	58.7	3 02.9	11.9	136 01.9	53.1
09	307 21.2	333 11.0	· · 53.0	213 31.1	· · 58.6	18 04.9	· · 11.8	151 04.6	· · 53.2
10	322 23.7	348 10.5	52.0	228 32.6	58.6	33 07.0	11.8	166 07.2	53.3
11	337 26.2	3 10.0	50.9	243 34.0	58.5	48 09.0	11.7	181 09.8	53.3
12	352 28.6	18 09.5	S11 49.9	258 35.4	N25 58.4	63 11.1	S22 11.7	196 12.5	N11 53.4
13	7 31.1	33 09.0	48.8	273 36.8	58.4	78 13.2	11.6	211 15.1	53.5
14	22 33.5	48 08.5	47.8	288 38.3	58.3	93 15.2	11.6	226 17.7	53.5
15	37 36.0	63 08.0	· · 46.8	303 39.7	· · 58.2	108 17.3	· · 11.5	241 20.4	· · 53.6
16	52 38.5	78 07.5	45.7	318 41.1	58.1	123 19.3	11.5	256 23.0	53.7
17	67 40.9	93 06.9	44.7	333 42.5	58.1	138 21.4	11.5	271 25.7	53.7
18	82 43.4	108 06.4	S11 43.6	348 44.0	N25 58.0	153 23.5	S22 11.4	286 28.3	N11 53.8
19	97 45.9	123 05.9	42.6	3 45.4	57.9	168 25.5	11.4	301 30.9	53.9
20	112 48.3	138 05.4	41.5	18 46.8	57.9	183 27.6	11.3	316 33.6	53.9
21	127 50.8	153 04.9	· · 40.5	33 48.2	· · 57.8	198 29.6	· · 11.3	331 36.2	· · 54.0
22	142 53.3	168 04.4	39.4	48 49.6	57.7	213 31.7	11.2	346 38.8	54.1
23	157 55.7	183 03.9	38.4	63 51.1	57.7	228 33.8	11.2	1 41.5	54.1
15 00	172 58.2	198 03.4	S11 37.4	78 52.5	N25 57.6	243 35.8	S22 11.1	16 44.1	N11 54.2
01	188 00.7	213 02.9	36.3	93 53.9	57.5	258 37.9	11.1	31 46.7	54.3
02	203 03.1	228 02.4	35.3	108 55.3	57.4	273 39.9	11.0	46 49.4	54.3
03	218 05.6	243 01.9	· · 34.2	123 56.7	· · 57.4	288 42.0	· · 11.0	61 52.0	· · 54.4
04	233 08.0	258 01.4	33.2	138 58.1	57.3	303 44.1	11.0	76 54.6	54.5
05	248 10.5	273 00.9	32.1	153 59.6	57.2	318 46.1	10.9	91 57.3	54.5
06	263 13.0	288 00.4	S11 31.1	169 01.0	N25 57.2	333 48.2	S22 10.9	106 59.9	N11 54.6
07	278 15.4	302 59.9	30.0	184 02.4	57.1	348 50.3	10.8	122 02.6	54.6
08	293 17.9	317 59.4	29.0	199 03.8	57.0	3 52.3	10.8	137 05.2	54.7
09	308 20.4	332 58.9	· · 27.9	214 05.2	· · 56.9	18 54.4	· · 10.7	152 07.8	· · 54.8
10	323 22.8	347 58.4	26.9	229 06.6	56.9	33 56.4	10.7	167 10.5	54.8
11	338 25.3	2 57.9	25.8	244 08.0	56.8	48 58.5	10.6	182 13.1	54.9
12	353 27.8	17 57.4	S11 24.8	259 09.5	N25 56.7	64 00.6	S22 10.6	197 15.7	N11 55.0
13	8 30.2	32 56.9	23.7	274 10.9	56.7	79 02.6	10.5	212 18.4	55.0
14	23 32.7	47 56.4	22.6	289 12.3	56.6	94 04.7	10.5	227 21.0	55.1
15	38 35.2	62 55.9	· · 21.6	304 13.7	· · 56.5	109 06.8	· · 10.5	242 23.6	· · 55.2
16	53 37.6	77 55.4	20.5	319 15.1	56.4	124 08.8	10.4	257 26.3	55.2
17	68 40.1	92 54.9	19.5	334 16.5	56.4	139 10.9	10.4	272 28.9	55.3
18	83 42.5	107 54.4	S11 18.4	349 17.9	N25 56.3	154 13.0	S22 10.3	287 31.5	N11 55.4
19	98 45.0	122 53.9	17.4	4 19.3	56.2	169 15.0	10.3	302 34.2	55.4
20	113 47.5	137 53.4	16.3	19 20.7	56.2	184 17.1	10.2	317 36.8	55.5
21	128 49.9	152 52.9	· · 15.2	34 22.1	· · 56.1	199 19.2	· · 10.2	332 39.4	· · 55.6
22	143 52.4	167 52.4	14.2	49 23.5	56.0	214 21.2	10.1	347 42.1	55.6
23	158 54.9	182 51.9	13.1	64 25.0	55.9	229 23.3	10.1	2 44.7	55.7
Mer. Pass. (h m)	12 30.0	*v* −0.5	*d* 1.0	*v* 1.4	*d* 0.1	*v* 2.1	*d* 0.0	*v* 2.6	*d* 0.1

STARS

Name	SHA ° ′	Dec ° ′
Acamar	315 21.5	S40 16.5
Achernar	335 29.9	S57 11.8
Acrux	173 13.5	S63 08.8
Adhara	255 15.5	S28 59.2
Aldebaran	290 54.0	N16 31.6
Alioth	166 23.3	N55 54.7
Alkaid	153 01.4	N49 16.0
Al Na'ir	27 48.9	S46 55.3
Alnilam	275 50.4	S 1 11.8
Alphard	217 59.7	S 8 41.8
Alphecca	126 14.1	N26 40.9
Alpheratz	357 48.1	N29 08.1
Altair	62 12.3	N 8 53.2
Ankaa	353 19.8	S42 15.8
Antares	112 31.1	S26 27.1
Arcturus	145 59.0	N19 08.1
Atria	107 36.5	S69 02.4
Avior	234 19.4	S59 32.4
Bellatrix	278 36.3	N 6 21.4
Betelgeuse	271 05.6	N 7 24.5
Canopus	263 57.8	S52 42.2
Capella	280 40.4	N46 00.6
Deneb	49 34.6	N45 18.3
Denebola	182 37.3	N14 31.4
Diphda	349 00.1	S17 56.6
Dubhe	193 55.5	N61 42.3
Elnath	278 17.7	N28 37.0
Eltanin	90 48.0	N51 28.8
Enif	33 51.3	N 9 54.6
Fomalhaut	15 28.6	S29 34.8
Gacrux	172 05.1	S57 09.6
Gienah	175 56.1	S17 35.4
Hadar	148 53.4	S60 24.8
Hamal	328 05.6	N23 30.1
Kaus Aust.	83 49.1	S34 22.9
Kochab	137 18.6	N74 06.9
Markab	13 42.7	N15 14.9
Menkar	314 19.4	N 4 07.3
Menkent	148 12.1	S36 24.7
Miaplacidus	221 40.2	S69 45.2
Mirfak	308 46.5	N49 53.6
Nunki	76 03.3	S26 17.3
Peacock	53 25.7	S56 42.4
Pollux	243 32.3	N28 00.4
Procyon	245 03.7	N 5 12.2
Rasalhague	96 10.1	N12 32.9
Regulus	207 47.4	N11 55.5
Rigel	281 15.9	S 8 11.6
Rigil Kent.	139 57.0	S60 52.1
Sabik	102 17.1	S15 44.3
Schedar	349 45.9	N56 35.0
Shaula	96 27.3	S37 06.6
Sirius	258 37.1	S16 43.8
Spica	158 35.2	S11 12.4
Suhail	222 55.2	S43 28.1
Vega	80 41.8	N38 47.1
Zuben'ubi	137 09.7	S16 04.7

	SHA ° ′	Mer. Pass. h m
Venus	26 16.6	10 47
Mars	266 19.2	18 45
Jupiter	70 47.4	7 48
Saturn	203 41.8	22 53

	UT	SUN GHA	SUN Dec	MOON GHA	v	MOON Dec	d	HP
	d h	° ′	° ′	° ′	′	° ′	′	′
THURSDAY	13 00	177 37.1	S 2 51.7	110 27.2	4.4	N25 59.1	6.6	59.5
	01	192 37.3	50.7	124 50.6	4.4	26 05.7	6.4	59.5
	02	207 37.5	49.7	139 14.0	4.2	26 12.1	6.3	59.5
	03	222 37.6	. . 48.7	153 37.2	4.3	26 18.4	6.0	59.5
	04	237 37.8	47.7	168 00.5	4.2	26 24.4	5.9	59.5
	05	252 38.0	46.7	182 23.7	4.1	26 30.3	5.7	59.5
	06	267 38.2	S 2 45.7	196 46.8	4.1	N26 36.0	5.5	59.4
	07	282 38.3	44.8	211 09.9	4.1	26 41.5	5.3	59.4
	08	297 38.5	43.8	225 33.0	4.0	26 46.8	5.1	59.4
	09	312 38.7	. . 42.8	239 56.0	3.9	26 51.9	4.9	59.4
	10	327 38.8	41.8	254 18.9	4.0	26 56.8	4.8	59.4
	11	342 39.0	40.8	268 41.9	3.9	27 01.6	4.6	59.4
	12	357 39.2	S 2 39.8	283 04.8	3.8	N27 06.2	4.4	59.4
	13	12 39.4	38.8	297 27.6	3.9	27 10.6	4.2	59.4
	14	27 39.5	37.9	311 50.5	3.8	27 14.8	4.0	59.3
	15	42 39.7	. . 36.9	326 13.3	3.8	27 18.8	3.8	59.3
	16	57 39.9	35.9	340 36.1	3.7	27 22.6	3.6	59.3
	17	72 40.0	34.9	354 58.8	3.8	27 26.2	3.5	59.3
	18	87 40.2	S 2 33.9	9 21.6	3.7	N27 29.7	3.2	59.3
	19	102 40.4	32.9	23 44.3	3.7	27 32.9	3.1	59.3
	20	117 40.6	31.9	38 07.0	3.7	27 36.0	2.8	59.2
	21	132 40.7	. . 31.0	52 29.7	3.7	27 38.8	2.7	59.2
	22	147 40.9	30.0	66 52.4	3.6	27 41.5	2.5	59.2
	23	162 41.1	29.0	81 15.0	3.7	27 44.0	2.3	59.2
FRIDAY	14 00	177 41.3	S 2 28.0	95 37.7	3.6	N27 46.3	2.1	59.2
	01	192 41.4	27.0	110 00.3	3.7	27 48.4	1.9	59.2
	02	207 41.6	26.0	124 23.0	3.6	27 50.3	1.8	59.2
	03	222 41.8	. . 25.0	138 45.6	3.7	27 52.1	1.5	59.1
	04	237 41.9	24.0	153 08.3	3.6	27 53.6	1.3	59.1
	05	252 42.1	23.1	167 30.9	3.7	27 54.9	1.2	59.1
	06	267 42.3	S 2 22.1	181 53.6	3.7	N27 56.1	0.9	59.1
	07	282 42.5	21.1	196 16.3	3.7	27 57.0	0.8	59.1
	08	297 42.6	20.1	210 39.0	3.7	27 57.8	0.6	59.1
	09	312 42.8	. . 19.1	225 01.7	3.7	27 58.4	0.4	59.0
	10	327 43.0	18.1	239 24.4	3.7	27 58.8	0.2	59.0
	11	342 43.2	17.1	253 47.1	3.8	27 59.0	0.0	59.0
	12	357 43.3	S 2 16.1	268 09.9	3.8	N27 59.0	0.2	59.0
	13	12 43.5	15.2	282 32.7	3.8	27 58.8	0.4	59.0
	14	27 43.7	14.2	296 55.5	3.8	27 58.4	0.5	59.0
	15	42 43.9	. . 13.2	311 18.3	3.9	27 57.9	0.8	58.9
	16	57 44.0	12.2	325 41.2	3.9	27 57.1	0.9	58.9
	17	72 44.2	11.2	340 04.1	3.9	27 56.2	1.2	58.9
	18	87 44.4	S 2 10.2	354 27.0	4.0	N27 55.0	1.3	58.9
	19	102 44.6	09.2	8 50.0	4.0	27 53.7	1.5	58.9
	20	117 44.7	08.3	23 13.0	4.0	27 52.2	1.7	58.8
	21	132 44.9	. . 07.3	37 36.0	4.1	27 50.5	1.8	58.8
	22	147 45.1	06.3	51 59.1	4.2	27 48.7	2.1	58.8
	23	162 45.3	05.3	66 22.3	4.2	27 46.6	2.2	58.8
SATURDAY	15 00	177 45.4	S 2 04.3	80 45.5	4.2	N27 44.4	2.5	58.8
	01	192 45.6	03.3	95 08.7	4.3	27 41.9	2.6	58.8
	02	207 45.8	02.3	109 32.0	4.4	27 39.3	2.7	58.7
	03	222 46.0	. . 01.3	123 55.4	4.4	27 36.6	3.0	58.7
	04	237 46.1	2 00.4	138 18.8	4.5	27 33.6	3.2	58.7
	05	252 46.3	1 59.4	152 42.3	4.5	27 30.4	3.3	58.7
	06	267 46.5	S 1 58.4	167 05.8	4.6	N27 27.1	3.5	58.7
	07	282 46.7	57.4	181 29.4	4.7	27 23.6	3.7	58.7
	08	297 46.9	56.4	195 53.1	4.7	27 19.9	3.8	58.6
	09	312 47.0	. . 55.4	210 16.8	4.8	27 16.1	4.1	58.6
	10	327 47.2	54.4	224 40.6	4.9	27 12.0	4.2	58.6
	11	342 47.4	53.4	239 04.5	4.9	27 07.8	4.4	58.6
	12	357 47.6	S 1 52.5	253 28.4	5.0	N27 03.4	4.5	58.6
	13	12 47.7	51.5	267 52.4	5.1	26 58.9	4.7	58.5
	14	27 47.9	50.5	282 16.5	5.2	26 54.2	4.9	58.5
	15	42 48.1	. . 49.5	296 40.7	5.2	26 49.3	5.1	58.5
	16	57 48.3	48.5	311 04.9	5.3	26 44.2	5.2	58.5
	17	72 48.4	47.5	325 29.2	5.5	26 39.0	5.4	58.5
	18	87 48.6	S 1 46.5	339 53.7	5.4	N26 33.6	5.6	58.4
	19	102 48.8	45.5	354 18.1	5.6	26 28.0	5.7	58.4
	20	117 49.0	44.5	8 42.7	5.7	26 22.3	5.9	58.4
	21	132 49.2	. . 43.6	23 07.4	5.7	26 16.4	6.0	58.4
	22	147 49.3	42.6	37 32.1	5.9	26 10.4	6.2	58.4
	23	162 49.5	41.6	51 57.0	5.9	N26 04.2	6.4	58.4
		SD 16.1	d 1.0	SD 16.2		16.1		16.0

Lat.	Twilight Naut.	Twilight Civil	Sunrise	Moonrise 13	Moonrise 14	Moonrise 15	Moonrise 16
°	h m	h m	h m	h m	h m	h m	h m
N 72	03 57	05 21	06 27	▭	▭	▭	▭
N 70	04 11	05 25	06 25	▭	▭	▭	▭
68	04 22	05 29	06 24	▭	▭	▭	▭
66	04 30	05 31	06 22	▭	▭	▭	▭
64	04 38	05 34	06 21	▭	▭	▭	09 13
62	04 44	05 36	06 20	06 16	06 24	07 56	09 59
60	04 49	05 38	06 19	06 56	07 32	08 48	10 29
N 58	04 53	05 39	06 18	07 24	08 07	09 20	10 52
56	04 57	05 40	06 17	07 46	08 33	09 44	11 11
54	05 00	05 41	06 17	08 04	08 53	10 03	11 26
52	05 03	05 42	06 16	08 19	09 11	10 19	11 40
50	05 06	05 43	06 15	08 32	09 25	10 33	11 51
45	05 11	05 45	06 14	09 00	09 55	11 02	12 15
N 40	05 14	05 46	06 13	09 21	10 18	11 24	12 35
35	05 17	05 47	06 12	09 39	10 37	11 42	12 51
30	05 19	05 47	06 11	09 55	10 54	11 58	13 05
20	05 22	05 47	06 09	10 22	11 22	12 25	13 28
N 10	05 22	05 46	06 07	10 45	11 46	12 48	13 49
0	05 21	05 45	06 06	11 06	12 08	13 10	14 07
S 10	05 19	05 43	06 04	11 28	12 31	13 31	14 26
20	05 14	05 40	06 02	11 51	12 55	13 54	14 46
30	05 08	05 36	06 00	12 18	13 23	14 21	15 10
35	05 03	05 33	05 58	12 34	13 40	14 36	15 23
40	04 58	05 30	05 57	12 53	13 59	14 54	15 39
45	04 51	05 26	05 55	13 16	14 23	15 16	15 57
S 50	04 41	05 20	05 53	13 45	14 53	15 44	16 20
52	04 37	05 18	05 52	13 59	15 08	15 58	16 31
54	04 32	05 15	05 50	14 16	15 25	16 13	16 44
56	04 26	05 12	05 49	14 36	15 46	16 31	16 58
58	04 20	05 08	05 48	15 00	16 13	16 54	17 14
S 60	04 12	05 04	05 46	15 34	16 50	17 22	17 34

Lat.	Sunset	Twilight Civil	Twilight Naut.	Moonset 13	Moonset 14	Moonset 15	Moonset 16
°	h m	h m	h m	h m	h m	h m	h m
N 72	17 53	19 01	20 25	▭	▭	▭	▭
N 70	17 55	18 56	20 11	▭	▭	▭	▭
68	17 56	18 52	19 59	▭	▭	▭	▭
66	17 58	18 49	19 50	▭	▭	▭	▭
64	17 59	18 46	19 43	▭	▭	▭	06 43
62	18 00	18 44	19 37	03 17	05 19	05 56	05 56
60	18 01	18 42	19 31	02 37	04 10	05 04	05 25
N 58	18 01	18 41	19 27	02 09	03 35	04 32	05 02
56	18 02	18 39	19 23	01 48	03 10	04 08	04 43
54	18 03	18 38	19 19	01 30	02 50	03 48	04 27
52	18 03	18 37	19 16	01 15	02 33	03 32	04 13
50	18 04	18 36	19 14	01 02	02 18	03 18	04 01
45	18 05	18 34	19 09	00 36	01 48	02 49	03 36
N 40	18 06	18 33	19 05	00 14	01 25	02 26	03 16
35	18 07	18 32	19 02	25 06	01 06	02 07	02 59
30	18 08	18 32	19 00	24 50	00 50	01 51	02 45
20	18 09	18 31	18 57	24 22	00 22	01 24	02 20
N 10	18 11	18 32	18 56	23 58	25 00	01 00	01 58
0	18 12	18 33	18 57	23 36	24 38	00 38	01 38
S 10	18 14	18 35	18 59	23 14	24 16	00 16	01 17
20	18 16	18 38	19 03	22 50	23 52	24 55	00 55
30	18 18	18 42	19 10	22 22	23 24	24 30	00 30
35	18 19	18 44	19 14	22 06	23 07	24 15	00 15
40	18 21	18 48	19 20	21 46	22 48	23 57	25 09
45	18 22	18 52	19 27	21 23	22 25	23 36	24 52
S 50	18 25	18 57	19 35	20 54	21 55	23 09	24 30
52	18 26	18 59	19 40	20 39	21 40	22 56	24 19
54	18 27	19 02	19 45	20 23	21 22	22 40	24 07
56	18 28	19 05	19 50	20 02	21 02	22 22	23 54
58	18 29	19 09	19 57	19 37	20 35	22 00	23 38
S 60	18 31	19 13	20 04	19 03	19 58	21 32	23 19

Day	SUN Eqn. of Time 00h	SUN Eqn. of Time 12h	SUN Mer. Pass.	MOON Mer. Pass. Upper	MOON Mer. Pass. Lower	MOON Age	MOON Phase
d	m s	m s	h m	h m	h m	d %	
13	09 32	09 24	12 09	17 21	04 50	06 39	
14	09 15	09 07	12 09	18 23	05 52	07 51	◐
15	08 59	08 50	12 09	19 24	06 54	08 62	

	UT d h	ARIES GHA ° ′	VENUS −3.8 GHA ° ′	VENUS Dec ° ′	MARS +0.5 GHA ° ′	MARS Dec ° ′	JUPITER −2.1 GHA ° ′	JUPITER Dec ° ′	SATURN +0.3 GHA ° ′	SATURN Dec ° ′
	16 00	173 57.3	197 51.4	S11 12.1	79 26.4	N25 55.9	244 25.4	S22 10.1	17 47.3	N11 55.8
	01	188 59.8	212 50.9	11.0	94 27.8	55.8	259 27.4	10.0	32 50.0	55.8
	02	204 02.3	227 50.4	10.0	109 29.2	55.7	274 29.5	10.0	47 52.6	55.9
	03	219 04.7	242 49.9	. . 08.9	124 30.6	. . 55.6	289 31.6	. . 09.9	62 55.2	. . 55.9
	04	234 07.2	257 49.4	07.8	139 32.0	55.6	304 33.6	09.9	77 57.9	56.0
	05	249 09.6	272 48.9	06.8	154 33.4	55.5	319 35.7	09.8	93 00.5	56.1
	06	264 12.1	287 48.4	S11 05.7	169 34.8	N25 55.4	334 37.8	S22 09.8	108 03.1	N11 56.1
	07	279 14.6	302 47.9	04.6	184 36.2	55.3	349 39.8	09.7	123 05.8	56.2
	08	294 17.0	317 47.5	03.6	199 37.6	55.3	4 41.9	09.7	138 08.4	56.3
S	09	309 19.5	332 47.0	. . 02.5	214 39.0	. . 55.2	19 44.0	. . 09.6	153 11.0	. . 56.3
U	10	324 22.0	347 46.5	01.4	229 40.4	55.1	34 46.0	09.6	168 13.7	56.4
N	11	339 24.4	2 46.0	11 00.4	244 41.8	55.0	49 48.1	09.6	183 16.3	56.5
D	12	354 26.9	17 45.5	S10 59.3	259 43.2	N25 55.0	64 50.2	S22 09.5	198 18.9	N11 56.5
A	13	9 29.4	32 45.0	58.3	274 44.6	54.9	79 52.3	09.5	213 21.6	56.6
Y	14	24 31.8	47 44.5	57.2	289 46.0	54.8	94 54.3	09.4	228 24.2	56.7
	15	39 34.3	62 44.0	. . 56.1	304 47.4	. . 54.7	109 56.4	. . 09.4	243 26.8	. . 56.7
	16	54 36.8	77 43.5	55.0	319 48.8	54.7	124 58.5	09.3	258 29.5	56.8
	17	69 39.2	92 43.0	54.0	334 50.2	54.6	140 00.5	09.3	273 32.1	56.8
	18	84 41.7	107 42.6	S10 52.9	349 51.6	N25 54.5	155 02.6	S22 09.2	288 34.7	N11 56.9
	19	99 44.1	122 42.1	51.8	4 53.0	54.4	170 04.7	09.2	303 37.4	57.0
	20	114 46.6	137 41.6	50.8	19 54.4	54.4	185 06.7	09.1	318 40.0	57.0
	21	129 49.1	152 41.1	. . 49.7	34 55.8	. . 54.3	200 08.8	. . 09.1	333 42.6	. . 57.1
	22	144 51.5	167 40.6	48.6	49 57.1	54.2	215 10.9	09.1	348 45.3	57.2
	23	159 54.0	182 40.1	47.6	64 58.5	54.1	230 13.0	09.0	3 47.9	57.2
	17 00	174 56.5	197 39.6	S10 46.5	79 59.9	N25 54.1	245 15.0	S22 09.0	18 50.5	N11 57.3
	01	189 58.9	212 39.1	45.4	95 01.3	54.0	260 17.1	08.9	33 53.2	57.4
	02	205 01.4	227 38.7	44.3	110 02.7	53.9	275 19.2	08.9	48 55.8	57.4
	03	220 03.9	242 38.2	. . 43.3	125 04.1	. . 53.8	290 21.3	. . 08.8	63 58.4	. . 57.5
	04	235 06.3	257 37.7	42.2	140 05.5	53.8	305 23.3	08.8	79 01.0	57.5
	05	250 08.8	272 37.2	41.1	155 06.9	53.7	320 25.4	08.7	94 03.7	57.6
	06	265 11.3	287 36.7	S10 40.0	170 08.3	N25 53.6	335 27.5	S22 08.7	109 06.3	N11 57.7
	07	280 13.7	302 36.2	39.0	185 09.7	53.5	350 29.6	08.7	124 08.9	57.7
	08	295 16.2	317 35.8	37.9	200 11.1	53.5	5 31.6	08.6	139 11.6	57.8
M	09	310 18.6	332 35.3	. . 36.8	215 12.4	. . 53.4	20 33.7	. . 08.6	154 14.2	. . 57.9
O	10	325 21.1	347 34.8	35.7	230 13.8	53.3	35 35.8	08.5	169 16.8	57.9
N	11	340 23.6	2 34.3	34.7	245 15.2	53.2	50 37.9	08.5	184 19.5	58.0
D	12	355 26.0	17 33.8	S10 33.6	260 16.6	N25 53.1	65 39.9	S22 08.4	199 22.1	N11 58.1
A	13	10 28.5	32 33.3	32.5	275 18.0	53.1	80 42.0	08.4	214 24.7	58.1
Y	14	25 31.0	47 32.9	31.4	290 19.4	53.0	95 44.1	08.3	229 27.4	58.2
	15	40 33.4	62 32.4	. . 30.3	305 20.8	. . 52.9	110 46.2	. . 08.3	244 30.0	. . 58.2
	16	55 35.9	77 31.9	29.3	320 22.2	52.8	125 48.2	08.3	259 32.6	58.3
	17	70 38.4	92 31.4	28.2	335 23.5	52.8	140 50.3	08.2	274 35.2	58.4
	18	85 40.8	107 30.9	S10 27.1	350 24.9	N25 52.7	155 52.4	S22 08.2	289 37.9	N11 58.4
	19	100 43.3	122 30.5	26.0	5 26.3	52.6	170 54.5	08.1	304 40.5	58.5
	20	115 45.8	137 30.0	24.9	20 27.7	52.5	185 56.5	08.1	319 43.1	58.6
	21	130 48.2	152 29.5	. . 23.9	35 29.1	. . 52.4	200 58.6	. . 08.0	334 45.8	. . 58.6
	22	145 50.7	167 29.0	22.8	50 30.5	52.4	216 00.7	08.0	349 48.4	58.7
	23	160 53.1	182 28.6	21.7	65 31.8	52.3	231 02.8	07.9	4 51.0	58.7
	18 00	175 55.6	197 28.1	S10 20.6	80 33.2	N25 52.2	246 04.9	S22 07.9	19 53.7	N11 58.8
	01	190 58.1	212 27.6	19.5	95 34.6	52.1	261 06.9	07.9	34 56.3	58.9
	02	206 00.5	227 27.1	18.4	110 36.0	52.0	276 09.0	07.8	49 58.9	58.9
	03	221 03.0	242 26.6	. . 17.4	125 37.4	. . 52.0	291 11.1	. . 07.8	65 01.5	. . 59.0
	04	236 05.5	257 26.2	16.3	140 38.7	51.9	306 13.2	07.7	80 04.2	59.1
	05	251 07.9	272 25.7	15.2	155 40.1	51.8	321 15.2	07.7	95 06.8	59.1
	06	266 10.4	287 25.2	S10 14.1	170 41.5	N25 51.7	336 17.3	S22 07.6	110 09.4	N11 59.2
	07	281 12.9	302 24.7	13.0	185 42.9	51.6	351 19.4	07.6	125 12.1	59.2
T	08	296 15.3	317 24.3	11.9	200 44.2	51.6	6 21.5	07.5	140 14.7	59.3
U	09	311 17.8	332 23.8	. . 10.8	215 45.6	. . 51.5	21 23.6	. . 07.5	155 17.3	. . 59.4
E	10	326 20.2	347 23.3	09.7	230 47.0	51.4	36 25.6	07.5	170 19.9	59.4
S	11	341 22.7	2 22.8	08.7	245 48.4	51.3	51 27.7	07.4	185 22.6	59.5
D	12	356 25.2	17 22.4	S10 07.6	260 49.7	N25 51.2	66 29.8	S22 07.4	200 25.2	N11 59.6
A	13	11 27.6	32 21.9	06.5	275 51.1	51.2	81 31.9	07.3	215 27.8	59.6
Y	14	26 30.1	47 21.4	05.4	290 52.5	51.1	96 34.0	07.3	230 30.5	59.7
	15	41 32.6	62 21.0	. . 04.3	305 53.9	. . 51.0	111 36.1	. . 07.2	245 33.1	. . 59.7
	16	56 35.0	77 20.5	03.2	320 55.2	50.9	126 38.1	07.2	260 35.7	59.8
	17	71 37.5	92 20.0	02.1	335 56.6	50.8	141 40.2	07.1	275 38.3	59.9
	18	86 40.0	107 19.5	S10 01.0	350 58.0	N25 50.8	156 42.3	S22 07.1	290 41.0	N11 59.9
	19	101 42.4	122 19.1	9 59.9	5 59.3	50.7	171 44.4	07.1	305 43.6	12 00.0
	20	116 44.9	137 18.6	58.8	21 00.7	50.6	186 46.5	07.0	320 46.2	00.0
	21	131 47.4	152 18.1	. . 57.7	36 02.1	. . 50.5	201 48.6	. . 07.0	335 48.9	. . 00.1
	22	146 49.8	167 17.7	56.6	51 03.5	50.4	216 50.6	06.9	350 51.5	00.2
	23	161 52.3	182 17.2	55.6	66 04.8	50.3	231 52.7	06.9	5 54.1	00.2
	Mer. Pass.	h m 12 18.2	v −0.5	d 1.1	v 1.4	d 0.1	v 2.1	d 0.0	v 2.6	d 0.1

STARS

Name	SHA ° ′	Dec ° ′
Acamar	315 21.5	S40 16.4
Achernar	335 29.9	S57 11.8
Acrux	173 13.5	S63 08.8
Adhara	255 15.6	S28 59.2
Aldebaran	290 54.1	N16 31.6
Alioth	166 23.3	N55 54.7
Alkaid	153 01.4	N49 16.0
Al Na'ir	27 48.9	S46 55.3
Alnilam	275 50.4	S 1 11.8
Alphard	217 59.7	S 8 41.8
Alphecca	126 14.1	N26 40.9
Alpheratz	357 48.1	N29 08.1
Altair	62 12.3	N 8 53.2
Ankaa	353 19.8	S42 15.7
Antares	112 31.0	S26 27.1
Arcturus	145 59.0	N19 08.1
Atria	107 36.5	S69 02.4
Avior	234 19.5	S59 32.4
Bellatrix	278 36.3	N 6 21.4
Betelgeuse	271 05.6	N 7 24.5
Canopus	263 57.8	S52 42.2
Capella	280 40.4	N46 00.6
Deneb	49 34.6	N45 18.3
Denebola	182 37.3	N14 31.4
Diphda	349 00.1	S17 56.6
Dubhe	193 55.5	N61 42.3
Elnath	278 17.7	N28 37.0
Eltanin	90 48.0	N51 28.8
Enif	33 51.3	N 9 54.6
Fomalhaut	15 28.6	S29 34.8
Gacrux	172 05.1	S57 09.6
Gienah	175 56.1	S17 35.4
Hadar	148 53.3	S60 24.8
Hamal	328 05.6	N23 30.1
Kaus Aust.	83 49.1	S34 22.9
Kochab	137 18.5	N74 06.9
Markab	13 42.7	N15 14.9
Menkar	314 19.4	N 4 07.3
Menkent	148 12.1	S36 24.7
Miaplacidus	221 40.2	S69 45.3
Mirfak	308 46.5	N49 53.6
Nunki	76 03.3	S26 17.3
Peacock	53 25.6	S56 42.4
Pollux	243 32.3	N28 00.4
Procyon	245 03.7	N 5 12.2
Rasalhague	96 10.1	N12 32.9
Regulus	207 47.4	N11 55.5
Rigel	281 15.9	S 8 11.6
Rigil Kent.	139 57.0	S60 52.1
Sabik	102 17.0	S15 44.3
Schedar	349 45.9	N56 35.0
Shaula	96 27.3	S37 06.6
Sirius	258 37.1	S16 43.8
Spica	158 35.2	S11 12.5
Suhail	222 55.2	S43 28.2
Vega	80 41.8	N38 47.1
Zuben'ubi	137 09.6	S16 04.7

	SHA ° ′	Mer. Pass. h m
Venus	22 43.2	10 50
Mars	265 03.5	18 38
Jupiter	70 18.6	7 38
Saturn	203 54.1	22 41

UT d	h	SUN GHA ° ′	SUN Dec ° ′	MOON GHA ° ′	v ′	MOON Dec ° ′	d ′	HP ′
16	00	177 49.7	S 1 40.6	66 21.9	6.0	N25 57.8	6.5	58.3
	01	192 49.9	39.6	80 46.9	6.1	25 51.3	6.7	58.3
	02	207 50.0	38.6	95 12.0	6.2	25 44.6	6.8	58.3
	03	222 50.2	. . 37.6	109 37.2	6.3	25 37.8	7.0	58.3
	04	237 50.4	36.6	124 02.5	6.4	25 30.8	7.1	58.3
	05	252 50.6	35.7	138 27.9	6.5	25 23.7	7.3	58.2
	06	267 50.8	S 1 34.7	152 53.4	6.6	N25 16.4	7.4	58.2
	07	282 50.9	33.7	167 19.0	6.7	25 09.0	7.6	58.2
	08	297 51.1	32.7	181 44.7	6.8	25 01.4	7.8	58.2
S	09	312 51.3	. . 31.7	196 10.5	6.9	24 53.6	7.8	58.2
U	10	327 51.5	30.7	210 36.4	7.0	24 45.8	8.0	58.1
N	11	342 51.7	29.7	225 02.4	7.0	24 37.8	8.2	58.1
D	12	357 51.8	S 1 28.7	239 28.4	7.2	N24 29.6	8.3	58.1
A	13	12 52.0	27.8	253 54.6	7.3	24 21.3	8.4	58.1
Y	14	27 52.2	26.8	268 20.9	7.4	24 12.9	8.6	58.1
	15	42 52.4	. . 25.8	282 47.3	7.5	24 04.3	8.7	58.0
	16	57 52.6	24.8	297 13.8	7.6	23 55.6	8.8	58.0
	17	72 52.7	23.8	311 40.4	7.7	23 46.8	9.0	58.0
	18	87 52.9	S 1 22.8	326 07.1	7.8	N23 37.8	9.1	58.0
	19	102 53.1	21.8	340 33.9	7.9	23 28.7	9.2	58.0
	20	117 53.3	20.8	355 00.8	8.0	23 19.5	9.4	57.9
	21	132 53.5	. . 19.8	9 27.8	8.1	23 10.1	9.5	57.9
	22	147 53.6	18.9	23 54.9	8.3	23 00.6	9.6	57.9
	23	162 53.8	17.9	38 22.2	8.3	22 51.0	9.7	57.9
17	00	177 54.0	S 1 16.9	52 49.5	8.4	N22 41.3	9.9	57.9
	01	192 54.2	15.9	67 16.9	8.5	22 31.4	9.9	57.8
	02	207 54.4	14.9	81 44.4	8.7	22 21.5	10.1	57.8
	03	222 54.5	. . 13.9	96 12.1	8.7	22 11.4	10.2	57.8
	04	237 54.7	12.9	110 39.8	8.9	22 01.2	10.3	57.8
	05	252 54.9	11.9	125 07.7	8.9	21 50.9	10.5	57.8
	06	267 55.1	S 1 11.0	139 35.6	9.1	N21 40.4	10.5	57.7
	07	282 55.3	10.0	154 03.7	9.2	21 29.9	10.7	57.7
	08	297 55.4	09.0	168 31.9	9.2	21 19.2	10.7	57.7
M	09	312 55.6	. . 08.0	183 00.1	9.4	21 08.5	10.9	57.7
O	10	327 55.8	07.0	197 28.5	9.5	20 57.6	11.0	57.7
N	11	342 56.0	06.0	211 57.0	9.6	20 46.6	11.1	57.6
D	12	357 56.2	S 1 05.0	226 25.6	9.6	N20 35.5	11.2	57.6
A	13	12 56.4	04.0	240 54.2	9.8	20 24.3	11.3	57.6
Y	14	27 56.5	03.0	255 23.0	9.9	20 13.0	11.3	57.6
	15	42 56.7	. . 02.1	269 51.9	10.0	20 01.7	11.5	57.6
	16	57 56.9	01.1	284 20.9	10.1	19 50.2	11.6	57.5
	17	72 57.1	1 00.1	298 50.0	10.2	19 38.6	11.7	57.5
	18	87 57.3	S 0 59.1	313 19.2	10.3	N19 26.9	11.8	57.5
	19	102 57.4	58.1	327 48.5	10.4	19 15.1	11.8	57.5
	20	117 57.6	57.1	342 17.9	10.5	19 03.3	12.0	57.5
	21	132 57.8	. . 56.1	356 47.4	10.6	18 51.3	12.0	57.4
	22	147 58.0	55.1	11 17.0	10.7	18 39.3	12.1	57.4
	23	162 58.2	54.2	25 46.7	10.7	18 27.2	12.2	57.4
18	00	177 58.4	S 0 53.2	40 16.4	10.9	N18 15.0	12.3	57.4
	01	192 58.5	52.2	54 46.3	11.0	18 02.7	12.4	57.4
	02	207 58.7	51.2	69 16.3	11.1	17 50.3	12.5	57.3
	03	222 58.9	. . 50.2	83 46.4	11.1	17 37.8	12.5	57.3
	04	237 59.1	49.2	98 16.5	11.3	17 25.3	12.6	57.3
	05	252 59.3	48.2	112 46.8	11.4	17 12.7	12.7	57.3
	06	267 59.5	S 0 47.2	127 17.2	11.4	N17 00.0	12.8	57.3
	07	282 59.6	46.2	141 47.6	11.6	16 47.2	12.9	57.2
T	08	297 59.8	45.3	156 18.2	11.6	16 34.3	12.9	57.2
U	09	313 00.0	. . 44.3	170 48.8	11.7	16 21.4	13.0	57.2
E	10	328 00.2	43.3	185 19.5	11.8	16 08.4	13.0	57.2
S	11	343 00.4	42.3	199 50.3	11.9	15 55.4	13.2	57.2
D	12	358 00.5	S 0 41.3	214 21.2	12.0	N15 42.2	13.2	57.1
A	13	13 00.7	40.3	228 52.2	12.1	15 29.0	13.2	57.1
Y	14	28 00.9	39.3	243 23.3	12.2	15 15.8	13.3	57.1
	15	43 01.1	. . 38.3	257 54.5	12.2	15 02.5	13.4	57.1
	16	58 01.3	37.4	272 25.7	12.3	14 49.1	13.5	57.1
	17	73 01.5	36.4	286 57.0	12.5	14 35.6	13.5	57.0
	18	88 01.7	S 0 35.4	301 28.5	12.5	N14 22.1	13.5	57.0
	19	103 01.8	34.4	316 00.0	12.5	14 08.6	13.7	57.0
	20	118 02.0	33.4	330 31.5	12.7	13 54.9	13.6	57.0
	21	133 02.2	. . 32.4	345 03.2	12.7	13 41.3	13.8	57.0
	22	148 02.4	31.4	359 34.9	12.8	13 27.5	13.8	56.9
	23	163 02.6	30.4	14 06.7	12.9	N13 13.7	13.8	56.9
		SD 16.1	*d* 1.0	SD 15.8		15.7		15.6

Lat.	Twilight Naut.	Twilight Civil	Sunrise	Moonrise 16	Moonrise 17	Moonrise 18	Moonrise 19
°	h m	h m	h m	h m	h m	h m	h m
N 72	03 39	05 05	06 12	□	□	11 44	14 29
N 70	03 55	05 11	06 12	□	□	12 25	14 44
68	04 08	05 16	06 11	□	10 10	12 53	14 57
66	04 18	05 20	06 11	□	11 01	13 13	15 07
64	04 26	05 23	06 10	09 13	11 33	13 30	15 15
62	04 33	05 26	06 10	09 59	11 56	13 43	15 22
60	04 39	05 28	06 10	10 29	12 14	13 54	15 29
N 58	04 44	05 31	06 10	10 52	12 30	14 04	15 34
56	04 49	05 32	06 09	11 11	12 43	14 13	15 39
54	04 52	05 34	06 09	11 26	12 54	14 20	15 43
52	04 56	05 35	06 09	11 40	13 04	14 27	15 47
50	04 59	05 37	06 09	11 51	13 13	14 33	15 50
45	05 05	05 39	06 08	12 15	13 31	14 46	15 58
N 40	05 10	05 41	06 08	12 35	13 47	14 57	16 04
35	05 13	05 42	06 08	12 51	13 59	15 06	16 10
30	05 16	05 43	06 07	13 05	14 10	15 14	16 14
20	05 19	05 45	06 07	13 28	14 29	15 28	16 23
N 10	05 20	05 45	06 06	13 49	14 46	15 39	16 30
0	05 20	05 44	06 05	14 07	15 01	15 51	16 36
S 10	05 19	05 43	06 04	14 26	15 16	16 02	16 43
20	05 15	05 41	06 03	14 46	15 33	16 13	16 50
30	05 10	05 38	06 02	15 10	15 51	16 27	16 58
35	05 06	05 36	06 01	15 23	16 02	16 34	17 03
40	05 01	05 33	06 00	15 39	16 14	16 43	17 08
45	04 55	05 30	05 59	15 57	16 29	16 53	17 14
S 50	04 47	05 25	05 58	16 20	16 46	17 05	17 21
52	04 43	05 23	05 57	16 31	16 54	17 11	17 24
54	04 38	05 21	05 56	16 44	17 04	17 17	17 28
56	04 33	05 18	05 55	16 58	17 14	17 24	17 32
58	04 27	05 15	05 54	17 14	17 25	17 32	17 36
S 60	04 21	05 12	05 53	17 34	17 39	17 41	17 41

Lat.	Sunset	Twilight Civil	Twilight Naut.	Moonset 16	Moonset 17	Moonset 18	Moonset 19
°	h m	h m	h m	h m	h m	h m	h m
N 72	18 07	19 15	20 42	□	□	07 56	06 49
N 70	18 07	19 08	20 25	□	□	07 13	06 31
68	18 07	19 03	20 12	□	07 42	06 44	06 17
66	18 08	18 59	20 01	□	06 50	06 22	06 05
64	18 08	18 55	19 53	06 43	06 17	06 04	05 55
62	18 08	18 52	19 45	05 56	05 53	05 50	05 46
60	18 08	18 50	19 39	05 25	05 34	05 37	05 39
N 58	18 08	18 47	19 34	05 02	05 18	05 27	05 32
56	18 08	18 45	19 29	04 43	05 04	05 17	05 26
54	18 08	18 44	19 25	04 27	04 52	05 09	05 21
52	18 09	18 42	19 22	04 13	04 42	05 01	05 16
50	18 09	18 41	19 19	04 01	04 32	04 55	05 12
45	18 09	18 38	19 13	03 36	04 12	04 40	05 02
N 40	18 09	18 36	19 08	03 16	03 56	04 28	04 54
35	18 10	18 35	19 04	02 59	03 42	04 17	04 48
30	18 10	18 34	19 01	02 45	03 30	04 08	04 42
20	18 10	18 32	18 58	02 20	03 09	03 52	04 31
N 10	18 11	18 32	18 56	01 58	02 51	03 38	04 22
0	18 12	18 32	18 56	01 38	02 34	03 25	04 13
S 10	18 12	18 33	18 58	01 17	02 16	03 12	04 04
20	18 13	18 35	19 01	00 55	01 58	02 58	03 54
30	18 14	18 38	19 06	00 30	01 36	02 41	03 43
35	18 15	18 40	19 10	00 15	01 24	02 32	03 37
40	18 16	18 43	19 15	25 09	01 09	02 20	03 30
45	18 17	18 46	19 21	24 52	00 52	02 07	03 21
S 50	18 18	18 50	19 29	24 30	00 30	01 51	03 10
52	18 19	18 52	19 32	24 19	00 19	01 44	03 06
54	18 19	18 55	19 37	24 07	00 07	01 35	03 00
56	18 20	18 57	19 42	23 54	25 26	01 26	02 54
58	18 21	19 00	19 47	23 38	25 15	01 15	02 48
S 60	18 22	19 03	19 54	23 19	25 02	01 02	02 40

Day	SUN Eqn. of Time 00^h	SUN Eqn. of Time 12^h	SUN Mer. Pass.	MOON Mer. Pass. Upper	MOON Mer. Pass. Lower	MOON Age	MOON Phase
d	m s	m s	h m	h m	h m	d %	
16	08 42	08 33	12 09	20 21	07 53	09 72	
17	08 24	08 16	12 08	21 13	08 48	10 81	
18	08 07	07 58	12 08	22 02	09 38	11 89	

UT d	UT h	ARIES GHA	VENUS −3.8 GHA	VENUS Dec	MARS +0.6 GHA	MARS Dec	JUPITER −2.1 GHA	JUPITER Dec	SATURN +0.3 GHA	SATURN Dec
		° ′	° ′	° ′	° ′	° ′	° ′	° ′	° ′	° ′
19	00	176 54.7	197 16.7	S 9 54.5	81 06.2	N25 50.3	246 54.8	S22 06.8	20 56.7	N12 00.3
	01	191 57.2	212 16.3	53.4	96 07.6	50.2	261 56.9	06.8	35 59.4	00.4
	02	206 59.7	227 15.8	52.3	111 08.9	50.1	276 59.0	06.7	51 02.0	00.4
	03	222 02.1	242 15.3	. . 51.2	126 10.3	. . 50.0	292 01.1	. . 06.7	66 04.6	. . 00.5
	04	237 04.6	257 14.9	50.1	141 11.7	49.9	307 03.1	06.7	81 07.2	00.5
	05	252 07.1	272 14.4	49.0	156 13.0	49.8	322 05.2	06.6	96 09.9	00.6
	06	267 09.5	287 13.9	S 9 47.9	171 14.4	N25 49.8	337 07.3	S22 06.6	111 12.5	N12 00.7
W	07	282 12.0	302 13.5	46.8	186 15.8	49.7	352 09.4	06.5	126 15.1	00.7
E	08	297 14.5	317 13.0	45.7	201 17.1	49.6	7 11.5	06.5	141 17.8	00.8
D	09	312 16.9	332 12.5	. . 44.6	216 18.5	. . 49.5	22 13.6	. . 06.4	156 20.4	. . 00.8
N	10	327 19.4	347 12.1	43.5	231 19.9	49.4	37 15.7	06.4	171 23.0	00.9
E	11	342 21.8	2 11.6	42.4	246 21.2	49.3	52 17.7	06.3	186 25.6	01.0
S	12	357 24.3	17 11.1	S 9 41.3	261 22.6	N25 49.3	67 19.8	S22 06.3	201 28.3	N12 01.0
D	13	12 26.8	32 10.7	40.2	276 23.9	49.2	82 21.9	06.3	216 30.9	01.1
A	14	27 29.2	47 10.2	39.1	291 25.3	49.1	97 24.0	06.2	231 33.5	01.2
Y	15	42 31.7	62 09.7	. . 38.0	306 26.7	. . 49.0	112 26.1	. . 06.2	246 36.1	. . 01.2
	16	57 34.2	77 09.3	36.9	321 28.0	48.9	127 28.2	06.1	261 38.8	01.3
	17	72 36.6	92 08.8	35.8	336 29.4	48.8	142 30.3	06.1	276 41.4	01.3
	18	87 39.1	107 08.4	S 9 34.7	351 30.8	N25 48.8	157 32.4	S22 06.0	291 44.0	N12 01.4
	19	102 41.6	122 07.9	33.6	6 32.1	48.7	172 34.4	06.0	306 46.6	01.5
	20	117 44.0	137 07.4	32.5	21 33.5	48.6	187 36.5	06.0	321 49.3	01.5
	21	132 46.5	152 07.0	. . 31.3	36 34.8	. . 48.5	202 38.6	. . 05.9	336 51.9	. . 01.6
	22	147 49.0	167 06.5	30.2	51 36.2	48.4	217 40.7	05.9	351 54.5	01.6
	23	162 51.4	182 06.0	29.1	66 37.5	48.3	232 42.8	05.8	6 57.1	01.7
20	00	177 53.9	197 05.6	S 9 28.0	81 38.9	N25 48.2	247 44.9	S22 05.8	21 59.8	N12 01.8
	01	192 56.3	212 05.1	26.9	96 40.3	48.2	262 47.0	05.7	37 02.4	01.8
	02	207 58.8	227 04.7	25.8	111 41.6	48.1	277 49.1	05.7	52 05.0	01.9
	03	223 01.3	242 04.2	. . 24.7	126 43.0	. . 48.0	292 51.2	. . 05.6	67 07.6	. . 01.9
	04	238 03.7	257 03.7	23.6	141 44.3	47.9	307 53.3	05.6	82 10.3	02.0
	05	253 06.2	272 03.3	22.5	156 45.7	47.8	322 55.3	05.6	97 12.9	02.1
	06	268 08.7	287 02.8	S 9 21.4	171 47.0	N25 47.7	337 57.4	S22 05.5	112 15.5	N12 02.1
T	07	283 11.1	302 02.4	20.3	186 48.4	47.6	352 59.5	05.5	127 18.1	02.2
H	08	298 13.6	317 01.9	19.2	201 49.7	47.6	8 01.6	05.4	142 20.8	02.2
U	09	313 16.1	332 01.5	. . 18.1	216 51.1	. . 47.5	23 03.7	. . 05.4	157 23.4	. . 02.3
R	10	328 18.5	347 01.0	16.9	231 52.4	47.4	38 05.8	05.3	172 26.0	02.4
S	11	343 21.0	2 00.5	15.8	246 53.8	47.3	53 07.9	05.3	187 28.6	02.4
D	12	358 23.5	17 00.1	S 9 14.7	261 55.1	N25 47.2	68 10.0	S22 05.3	202 31.3	N12 02.5
A	13	13 25.9	31 59.6	13.6	276 56.5	47.1	83 12.1	05.2	217 33.9	02.5
Y	14	28 28.4	46 59.2	12.5	291 57.9	47.0	98 14.2	05.2	232 36.5	02.6
	15	43 30.8	61 58.7	. . 11.4	306 59.2	. . 46.9	113 16.3	. . 05.1	247 39.1	. . 02.7
	16	58 33.3	76 58.3	10.3	322 00.6	46.9	128 18.4	05.1	262 41.7	02.7
	17	73 35.8	91 57.8	09.2	337 01.9	46.8	143 20.5	05.0	277 44.4	02.8
	18	88 38.2	106 57.4	S 9 08.0	352 03.2	N25 46.7	158 22.6	S22 05.0	292 47.0	N12 02.8
	19	103 40.7	121 56.9	06.9	7 04.6	46.6	173 24.6	04.9	307 49.6	02.9
	20	118 43.2	136 56.5	05.8	22 05.9	46.5	188 26.7	04.9	322 52.2	03.0
	21	133 45.6	151 56.0	. . 04.7	37 07.3	. . 46.4	203 28.8	. . 04.9	337 54.9	. . 03.0
	22	148 48.1	166 55.5	03.6	52 08.6	46.3	218 30.9	04.8	352 57.5	03.1
	23	163 50.6	181 55.1	02.5	67 10.0	46.2	233 33.0	04.8	8 00.1	03.1
21	00	178 53.0	196 54.6	S 9 01.4	82 11.3	N25 46.1	248 35.1	S22 04.7	23 02.7	N12 03.2
	01	193 55.5	211 54.2	9 00.2	97 12.7	46.1	263 37.2	04.7	38 05.4	03.3
	02	208 57.9	226 53.7	8 59.1	112 14.0	46.0	278 39.3	04.6	53 08.0	03.3
	03	224 00.4	241 53.3	. . 58.0	127 15.4	. . 45.9	293 41.4	. . 04.6	68 10.6	. . 03.4
	04	239 02.9	256 52.8	56.9	142 16.7	45.8	308 43.5	04.6	83 13.2	03.4
	05	254 05.3	271 52.4	55.8	157 18.1	45.7	323 45.6	04.5	98 15.8	03.5
	06	269 07.8	286 51.9	S 8 54.6	172 19.4	N25 45.6	338 47.7	S22 04.5	113 18.5	N12 03.6
	07	284 10.3	301 51.5	53.5	187 20.7	45.5	353 49.8	04.4	128 21.1	03.6
	08	299 12.7	316 51.0	52.4	202 22.1	45.4	8 51.9	04.4	143 23.7	03.7
F	09	314 15.2	331 50.6	. . 51.3	217 23.4	. . 45.3	23 54.0	. . 04.3	158 26.3	. . 03.7
R	10	329 17.7	346 50.1	50.2	232 24.8	45.2	38 56.1	04.3	173 29.0	03.8
I	11	344 20.1	1 49.7	49.0	247 26.1	45.2	53 58.2	04.3	188 31.6	03.8
D	12	359 22.6	16 49.2	S 8 47.9	262 27.4	N25 45.1	69 00.3	S22 04.2	203 34.2	N12 03.9
A	13	14 25.1	31 48.8	46.8	277 28.8	45.0	84 02.4	04.2	218 36.8	04.0
Y	14	29 27.5	46 48.3	45.7	292 30.1	44.9	99 04.5	04.1	233 39.4	04.0
	15	44 30.0	61 47.9	. . 44.6	307 31.5	. . 44.8	114 06.6	. . 04.1	248 42.1	. . 04.1
	16	59 32.4	76 47.4	43.4	322 32.8	44.7	129 08.7	04.0	263 44.7	04.1
	17	74 34.9	91 47.0	42.3	337 34.1	44.6	144 10.8	04.0	278 47.3	04.2
	18	89 37.4	106 46.6	S 8 41.2	352 35.5	N25 44.5	159 12.9	S22 04.0	293 49.9	N12 04.3
	19	104 39.8	121 46.1	40.1	7 36.8	44.4	174 15.0	03.9	308 52.5	04.3
	20	119 42.3	136 45.7	38.9	22 38.1	44.3	189 17.1	03.9	323 55.2	04.4
	21	134 44.8	151 45.2	. . 37.8	37 39.5	. . 44.2	204 19.2	. . 03.8	338 57.8	. . 04.4
	22	149 47.2	166 44.8	36.7	52 40.8	44.2	219 21.3	03.8	354 00.4	04.5
	23	164 49.7	181 44.3	35.6	67 42.2	44.1	234 23.4	03.7	9 03.0	04.5
Mer. Pass.		h m 12 06.4	v −0.5	d 1.1	v 1.4	d 0.1	v 2.1	d 0.0	v 2.6	d 0.1

STARS

Name	SHA	Dec
	° ′	° ′
Acamar	315 21.5	S40 16.4
Achernar	335 29.9	S57 11.8
Acrux	173 13.5	S63 08.8
Adhara	255 15.6	S28 59.2
Aldebaran	290 54.1	N16 31.6
Alioth	166 23.3	N55 54.7
Alkaid	153 01.4	N49 16.0
Al Na'ir	27 48.9	S46 55.2
Alnilam	275 50.4	S 1 11.8
Alphard	217 59.8	S 8 41.8
Alphecca	126 14.1	N26 40.9
Alpheratz	357 48.1	N29 08.1
Altair	62 12.3	N 8 53.2
Ankaa	353 19.8	S42 15.7
Antares	112 31.0	S26 27.1
Arcturus	145 59.0	N19 08.1
Atria	107 36.4	S69 02.4
Avior	234 19.5	S59 32.4
Bellatrix	278 36.3	N 6 21.4
Betelgeuse	271 05.6	N 7 24.5
Canopus	263 57.9	S52 42.2
Capella	280 40.4	N46 00.6
Deneb	49 34.6	N45 18.3
Denebola	182 37.3	N14 31.4
Diphda	349 00.1	S17 56.6
Dubhe	193 55.5	N61 42.4
Elnath	278 17.7	N28 37.0
Eltanin	90 48.0	N51 28.8
Enif	33 51.3	N 9 54.6
Fomalhaut	15 28.6	S29 34.8
Gacrux	172 05.1	S57 09.7
Gienah	175 56.1	S17 35.4
Hadar	148 53.3	S60 24.8
Hamal	328 05.6	N23 30.1
Kaus Aust.	83 49.1	S34 22.9
Kochab	137 18.5	N74 06.9
Markab	13 42.6	N15 14.9
Menkar	314 19.4	N 4 07.3
Menkent	148 12.1	S36 24.7
Miaplacidus	221 40.3	S69 45.3
Mirfak	308 46.5	N49 53.6
Nunki	76 03.3	S26 17.3
Peacock	53 25.6	S56 42.4
Pollux	243 32.4	N28 00.5
Procyon	245 03.7	N 5 12.2
Rasalhague	96 10.1	N12 32.9
Regulus	207 47.4	N11 55.5
Rigel	281 15.9	S 8 11.6
Rigil Kent.	139 56.9	S60 52.1
Sabik	102 17.0	S15 44.3
Schedar	349 45.9	N56 35.0
Shaula	96 27.3	S37 06.6
Sirius	258 37.2	S16 43.8
Spica	158 35.2	S11 12.5
Suhail	222 55.2	S43 28.2
Vega	80 41.7	N38 47.1
Zuben'ubi	137 09.6	S16 04.7

	SHA	Mer. Pass.
	° ′	h m
Venus	19 11.7	10 52
Mars	263 45.0	18 32
Jupiter	69 51.0	7 28
Saturn	204 05.9	22 28

UT	SUN GHA	SUN Dec	MOON GHA	v	MOON Dec	d	HP
d h	° ′	° ′	° ′	′	° ′	′	′
19 00	178 02.8	S 0 29.4	28 38.6	13.0	N12 59.9	13.9	56.9
01	193 02.9	28.5	43 10.6	13.0	12 46.0	13.9	56.9
02	208 03.1	27.5	57 42.6	13.2	12 32.1	14.0	56.9
03	223 03.3	. . 26.5	72 14.8	13.2	12 18.1	14.0	56.8
04	238 03.5	25.5	86 47.0	13.2	12 04.1	14.1	56.8
05	253 03.7	24.5	101 19.2	13.4	11 50.0	14.1	56.8
06	268 03.9	S 0 23.5	115 51.6	13.4	N11 35.9	14.2	56.8
W 07	283 04.0	22.5	130 24.0	13.4	11 21.7	14.2	56.8
E 08	298 04.2	21.5	144 56.4	13.6	11 07.5	14.3	56.7
D 09	313 04.4	. . 20.6	159 29.0	13.6	10 53.2	14.2	56.7
N 10	328 04.6	19.6	174 01.6	13.7	10 39.0	14.4	56.7
E 11	343 04.8	18.6	188 34.3	13.7	10 24.6	14.3	56.7
S 12	358 05.0	S 0 17.6	203 07.0	13.8	N10 10.3	14.4	56.7
D 13	13 05.2	16.6	217 39.8	13.9	9 55.9	14.4	56.6
A 14	28 05.3	15.6	232 12.7	13.9	9 41.5	14.5	56.6
Y 15	43 05.5	. . 14.6	246 45.6	14.0	9 27.0	14.5	56.6
16	58 05.7	13.6	261 18.6	14.1	9 12.5	14.5	56.6
17	73 05.9	12.7	275 51.7	14.1	8 58.0	14.5	56.6
18	88 06.1	S 0 11.7	290 24.8	14.1	N 8 43.5	14.6	56.5
19	103 06.3	10.7	304 57.9	14.3	8 28.9	14.6	56.5
20	118 06.5	09.7	319 31.2	14.2	8 14.3	14.6	56.5
21	133 06.6	. . 08.7	334 04.4	14.4	7 59.7	14.7	56.5
22	148 06.8	07.7	348 37.8	14.4	7 45.0	14.7	56.5
23	163 07.0	06.7	3 11.2	14.4	7 30.3	14.7	56.4
20 00	178 07.2	S 0 05.7	17 44.6	14.5	N 7 15.6	14.7	56.4
01	193 07.4	04.7	32 18.1	14.5	7 00.9	14.7	56.4
02	208 07.6	03.8	46 51.6	14.6	6 46.2	14.8	56.4
03	223 07.8	. . 02.8	61 25.2	14.6	6 31.4	14.7	56.4
04	238 07.9	01.8	75 58.8	14.7	6 16.7	14.8	56.3
05	253 08.1	S 00.8	90 32.5	14.7	6 01.9	14.8	56.3
06	268 08.3	N 0 00.2	105 06.2	14.8	N 5 47.1	14.9	56.3
07	283 08.5	01.2	119 40.0	14.8	5 32.2	14.8	56.3
T 08	298 08.7	02.2	134 13.8	14.9	5 17.4	14.8	56.2
H 09	313 08.9	. . 03.2	148 47.7	14.9	5 02.6	14.9	56.2
U 10	328 09.1	04.1	163 21.6	14.9	4 47.7	14.8	56.2
R 11	343 09.2	05.1	177 55.5	15.0	4 32.9	14.9	56.2
S 12	358 09.4	N 0 06.1	192 29.5	15.0	N 4 18.0	14.9	56.2
D 13	13 09.6	07.1	207 03.5	15.1	4 03.1	14.9	56.1
A 14	28 09.8	08.1	221 37.6	15.0	3 48.2	14.9	56.1
Y 15	43 10.0	. . 09.1	236 11.6	15.2	3 33.3	14.8	56.1
16	58 10.2	10.1	250 45.8	15.1	3 18.5	14.9	56.1
17	73 10.4	11.1	265 19.9	15.2	3 03.6	14.9	56.1
18	88 10.6	N 0 12.0	279 54.1	15.2	N 2 48.7	14.9	56.0
19	103 10.7	13.0	294 28.3	15.3	2 33.8	14.9	56.0
20	118 10.9	14.0	309 02.6	15.2	2 18.9	14.9	56.0
21	133 11.1	. . 15.0	323 36.8	15.3	2 04.0	14.9	56.0
22	148 11.3	16.0	338 11.1	15.4	1 49.1	14.9	56.0
23	163 11.5	17.0	352 45.5	15.3	1 34.2	14.9	55.9
21 00	178 11.7	N 0 18.0	7 19.8	15.4	N 1 19.3	14.9	55.9
01	193 11.9	18.9	21 54.2	15.4	1 04.4	14.9	55.9
02	208 12.0	19.9	36 28.6	15.5	0 49.5	14.8	55.9
03	223 12.2	. . 20.9	51 03.1	15.4	0 34.7	14.9	55.9
04	238 12.4	21.9	65 37.5	15.5	0 19.8	14.8	55.8
05	253 12.6	22.9	80 12.0	15.5	N 0 05.0	14.9	55.8
06	268 12.8	N 0 23.9	94 46.5	15.5	S 0 09.9	14.8	55.8
07	283 13.0	24.9	109 21.0	15.5	0 24.7	14.8	55.8
08	298 13.2	25.9	123 55.5	15.5	0 39.5	14.8	55.8
F 09	313 13.4	. . 26.8	138 30.0	15.6	0 54.3	14.8	55.7
R 10	328 13.5	27.8	153 04.6	15.6	1 09.1	14.8	55.7
I 11	343 13.7	28.8	167 39.2	15.6	1 23.9	14.8	55.7
D 12	358 13.9	N 0 29.8	182 13.8	15.6	S 1 38.7	14.7	55.7
A 13	13 14.1	30.8	196 48.4	15.6	1 53.4	14.7	55.7
Y 14	28 14.3	31.8	211 23.0	15.6	2 08.1	14.7	55.7
15	43 14.5	. . 32.8	225 57.6	15.6	2 22.8	14.7	55.6
16	58 14.7	33.7	240 32.2	15.6	2 37.5	14.7	55.6
17	73 14.9	34.7	255 06.8	15.7	2 52.2	14.6	55.6
18	88 15.0	N 0 35.7	269 41.5	15.6	S 3 06.8	14.7	55.6
19	103 15.2	36.7	284 16.1	15.7	3 21.5	14.6	55.6
20	118 15.4	37.7	298 50.8	15.7	3 36.1	14.5	55.5
21	133 15.6	. . 38.7	313 25.5	15.6	3 50.6	14.6	55.5
22	148 15.8	39.7	328 00.1	15.7	4 05.2	14.5	55.5
23	163 16.0	40.7	342 34.8	15.7	S 4 19.7	14.5	55.5
	SD 16.1	d 1.0	SD 15.4		15.3		15.2

Lat.	Twilight Naut.	Twilight Civil	Sunrise	Moonrise 19	Moonrise 20	Moonrise 21	Moonrise 22
°	h m	h m	h m	h m	h m	h m	h m
N 72	03 19	04 49	05 57	14 29	16 41	18 45	20 52
N 70	03 38	04 56	05 58	14 44	16 45	18 40	20 36
68	03 53	05 03	05 59	14 57	16 49	18 36	20 24
66	04 05	05 08	05 59	15 07	16 52	18 32	20 13
64	04 14	05 12	06 00	15 15	16 54	18 30	20 05
62	04 23	05 16	06 00	15 22	16 56	18 27	19 58
60	04 29	05 19	06 01	15 29	16 58	18 25	19 51
N 58	04 35	05 22	06 01	15 34	17 00	18 23	19 46
56	04 40	05 24	06 01	15 39	17 01	18 22	19 41
54	04 45	05 27	06 02	15 43	17 03	18 20	19 37
52	04 49	05 28	06 02	15 47	17 04	18 19	19 33
50	04 52	05 30	06 02	15 50	17 05	18 18	19 29
45	04 59	05 33	06 03	15 58	17 07	18 15	19 22
N 40	05 05	05 36	06 03	16 04	17 09	18 13	19 15
35	05 09	05 38	06 03	16 10	17 11	18 11	19 10
30	05 12	05 40	06 04	16 14	17 13	18 09	19 05
20	05 16	05 42	06 04	16 23	17 15	18 06	18 57
N 10	05 19	05 43	06 04	16 30	17 18	18 04	18 50
0	05 19	05 43	06 04	16 36	17 20	18 02	18 43
S 10	05 19	05 43	06 04	16 43	17 22	17 59	18 37
20	05 16	05 42	06 04	16 50	17 24	17 57	18 30
30	05 12	05 40	06 04	16 58	17 27	17 54	18 22
35	05 09	05 38	06 03	17 03	17 28	17 53	18 18
40	05 04	05 36	06 03	17 08	17 30	17 51	18 13
45	04 59	05 33	06 03	17 14	17 32	17 49	18 07
S 50	04 52	05 30	06 02	17 21	17 34	17 47	18 00
52	04 48	05 28	06 02	17 24	17 35	17 46	17 57
54	04 45	05 26	06 02	17 28	17 37	17 45	17 53
56	04 40	05 24	06 02	17 32	17 38	17 43	17 49
58	04 35	05 22	06 01	17 36	17 39	17 42	17 45
S 60	04 29	05 19	06 01	17 41	17 41	17 40	17 40

Lat.	Sunset	Twilight Civil	Twilight Naut.	Moonset 19	Moonset 20	Moonset 21	Moonset 22
°	h m	h m	h m	h m	h m	h m	h m
N 72	18 21	19 29	21 01	06 49	06 10	05 38	05 06
N 70	18 19	19 21	20 40	06 31	06 03	05 38	05 14
68	18 18	19 14	20 25	06 17	05 56	05 38	05 20
66	18 17	19 09	20 13	06 05	05 51	05 39	05 26
64	18 17	19 04	20 03	05 55	05 46	05 39	05 31
62	18 16	19 00	19 54	05 46	05 43	05 39	05 35
60	18 15	18 57	19 47	05 39	05 39	05 39	05 39
N 58	18 15	18 54	19 41	05 32	05 36	05 39	05 42
56	18 14	18 52	19 36	05 26	05 33	05 39	05 45
54	18 14	18 49	19 31	05 21	05 31	05 39	05 47
52	18 14	18 48	19 27	05 16	05 28	05 39	05 50
50	18 13	18 46	19 24	05 12	05 26	05 39	05 52
45	18 13	18 42	19 17	05 02	05 22	05 39	05 57
N 40	18 12	18 39	19 11	04 54	05 18	05 39	06 01
35	18 12	18 37	19 07	04 48	05 14	05 40	06 04
30	18 12	18 36	19 03	04 42	05 11	05 40	06 07
20	18 11	18 33	18 59	04 31	05 06	05 40	06 13
N 10	18 11	18 32	18 56	04 22	05 02	05 40	06 17
0	18 11	18 31	18 55	04 13	04 57	05 40	06 22
S 10	18 11	18 32	18 56	04 04	04 53	05 40	06 26
20	18 11	18 33	18 58	03 54	04 48	05 40	06 31
30	18 11	18 35	19 02	03 43	04 43	05 40	06 36
35	18 11	18 36	19 05	03 37	04 39	05 40	06 39
40	18 11	18 38	19 10	03 30	04 36	05 40	06 43
45	18 11	18 40	19 15	03 21	04 32	05 40	06 47
S 50	18 12	18 44	19 22	03 10	04 27	05 40	06 52
52	18 12	18 45	19 25	03 06	04 24	05 40	06 54
54	18 12	18 47	19 29	03 00	04 22	05 40	06 57
56	18 12	18 49	19 33	02 54	04 19	05 40	07 00
58	18 12	18 51	19 38	02 48	04 15	05 40	07 03
S 60	18 13	18 54	19 44	02 40	04 12	05 40	07 06

Day	SUN Eqn. of Time 00^h	SUN Eqn. of Time 12^h	SUN Mer. Pass.	MOON Mer. Pass. Upper	MOON Mer. Pass. Lower	MOON Age	MOON Phase (%)
d	m s	m s	h m	h m	h m	d	%
19	07 49	07 40	12 08	22 47	10 25	12	95
20	07 32	07 23	12 07	23 30	11 09	13	98
21	07 14	07 05	12 07	24 12	11 51	14	100

UT d h	ARIES GHA	VENUS −3.8 GHA	VENUS Dec	MARS +0.7 GHA	MARS Dec	JUPITER −2.1 GHA	JUPITER Dec	SATURN +0.3 GHA	SATURN Dec
	° ′	° ′	° ′	° ′	° ′	° ′	° ′	° ′	° ′
22 00 (SATURDAY)	179 52.2	196 43.9	S 8 34.4	82 43.5	N25 44.0	249 25.5	S22 03.7	24 05.6	N12 04.6
01	194 54.6	211 43.4	33.3	97 44.8	43.9	264 27.6	03.7	39 08.3	04.7
02	209 57.1	226 43.0	32.2	112 46.2	43.8	279 29.7	03.6	54 10.9	04.7
03	224 59.5	241 42.6	31.0	127 47.5	43.7	294 31.8	03.6	69 13.5	04.8
04	240 02.0	256 42.1	29.9	142 48.8	43.6	309 33.9	03.5	84 16.1	04.8
05	255 04.5	271 41.7	28.8	157 50.2	43.5	324 36.0	03.5	99 18.7	04.9
06	270 06.9	286 41.2	S 8 27.7	172 51.5	N25 43.4	339 38.1	S22 03.4	114 21.4	N12 05.0
07	285 09.4	301 40.8	26.5	187 52.8	43.3	354 40.2	03.4	129 24.0	05.0
08	300 11.9	316 40.3	25.4	202 54.2	43.2	9 42.3	03.4	144 26.6	05.1
09	315 14.3	331 39.9	24.3	217 55.5	43.1	24 44.4	03.3	159 29.2	05.1
10	330 16.8	346 39.5	23.1	232 56.8	43.0	39 46.5	03.3	174 31.8	05.2
11	345 19.3	1 39.0	22.0	247 58.1	42.9	54 48.6	03.2	189 34.5	05.2
12	0 21.7	16 38.6	S 8 20.9	262 59.5	N25 42.8	69 50.7	S22 03.2	204 37.1	N12 05.3
13	15 24.2	31 38.1	19.7	278 00.8	42.8	84 52.8	03.1	219 39.7	05.4
14	30 26.7	46 37.7	18.6	293 02.1	42.7	99 54.9	03.1	234 42.3	05.4
15	45 29.1	61 37.3	17.5	308 03.5	42.6	114 57.0	03.1	249 44.9	05.5
16	60 31.6	76 36.8	16.3	323 04.8	42.5	129 59.2	03.0	264 47.5	05.5
17	75 34.0	91 36.4	15.2	338 06.1	42.4	145 01.3	03.0	279 50.2	05.6
18	90 36.5	106 35.9	S 8 14.1	353 07.4	N25 42.3	160 03.4	S22 02.9	294 52.8	N12 05.6
19	105 39.0	121 35.5	12.9	8 08.8	42.2	175 05.5	02.9	309 55.4	05.7
20	120 41.4	136 35.1	11.8	23 10.1	42.1	190 07.6	02.8	324 58.0	05.8
21	135 43.9	151 34.6	10.7	38 11.4	42.0	205 09.7	02.8	340 00.6	05.8
22	150 46.4	166 34.2	09.5	53 12.7	41.9	220 11.8	02.8	355 03.3	05.9
23	165 48.8	181 33.7	08.4	68 14.1	41.8	235 13.9	02.7	10 05.9	05.9
23 00 (SUNDAY)	180 51.3	196 33.3	S 8 07.3	83 15.4	N25 41.7	250 16.0	S22 02.7	25 08.5	N12 06.0
01	195 53.8	211 32.9	06.1	98 16.7	41.6	265 18.1	02.6	40 11.1	06.0
02	210 56.2	226 32.4	05.0	113 18.0	41.5	280 20.2	02.6	55 13.7	06.1
03	225 58.7	241 32.0	03.9	128 19.4	41.4	295 22.3	02.5	70 16.3	06.2
04	241 01.1	256 31.6	02.7	143 20.7	41.3	310 24.4	02.5	85 19.0	06.2
05	256 03.6	271 31.1	01.6	158 22.0	41.2	325 26.6	02.5	100 21.6	06.3
06	271 06.1	286 30.7	S 8 00.4	173 23.3	N25 41.1	340 28.7	S22 02.4	115 24.2	N12 06.3
07	286 08.5	301 30.3	7 59.3	188 24.7	41.0	355 30.8	02.4	130 26.8	06.4
08	301 11.0	316 29.8	58.2	203 26.0	40.9	10 32.9	02.3	145 29.4	06.4
09	316 13.5	331 29.4	57.0	218 27.3	40.8	25 35.0	02.3	160 32.0	06.5
10	331 15.9	346 29.0	55.9	233 28.6	40.7	40 37.1	02.3	175 34.7	06.6
11	346 18.4	1 28.5	54.7	248 29.9	40.6	55 39.2	02.2	190 37.3	06.6
12	1 20.9	16 28.1	S 7 53.6	263 31.3	N25 40.5	70 41.3	S22 02.2	205 39.9	N12 06.7
13	16 23.3	31 27.7	52.5	278 32.6	40.5	85 43.4	02.1	220 42.5	06.7
14	31 25.8	46 27.2	51.3	293 33.9	40.4	100 45.5	02.1	235 45.1	06.8
15	46 28.3	61 26.8	50.2	308 35.2	40.3	115 47.7	02.0	250 47.7	06.8
16	61 30.7	76 26.4	49.0	323 36.5	40.2	130 49.8	02.0	265 50.4	06.9
17	76 33.2	91 25.9	47.9	338 37.8	40.1	145 51.9	02.0	280 53.0	07.0
18	91 35.6	106 25.5	S 7 46.8	353 39.2	N25 40.0	160 54.0	S22 01.9	295 55.6	N12 07.0
19	106 38.1	121 25.1	45.6	8 40.5	39.9	175 56.1	01.9	310 58.2	07.1
20	121 40.6	136 24.6	44.5	23 41.8	39.8	190 58.2	01.8	326 00.8	07.1
21	136 43.0	151 24.2	43.3	38 43.1	39.7	206 00.3	01.8	341 03.4	07.2
22	151 45.5	166 23.8	42.2	53 44.4	39.6	221 02.4	01.7	356 06.1	07.2
23	166 48.0	181 23.3	41.0	68 45.7	39.5	236 04.6	01.7	11 08.7	07.3
24 00 (MONDAY)	181 50.4	196 22.9	S 7 39.9	83 47.0	N25 39.4	251 06.7	S22 01.7	26 11.3	N12 07.3
01	196 52.9	211 22.5	38.7	98 48.4	39.3	266 08.8	01.6	41 13.9	07.4
02	211 55.4	226 22.0	37.6	113 49.7	39.2	281 10.9	01.6	56 16.5	07.5
03	226 57.8	241 21.6	36.4	128 51.0	39.1	296 13.0	01.5	71 19.1	07.5
04	242 00.3	256 21.2	35.3	143 52.3	39.0	311 15.1	01.5	86 21.7	07.6
05	257 02.7	271 20.8	34.2	158 53.6	38.9	326 17.2	01.5	101 24.4	07.6
06	272 05.2	286 20.3	S 7 33.0	173 54.9	N25 38.8	341 19.4	S22 01.4	116 27.0	N12 07.7
07	287 07.7	301 19.9	31.9	188 56.2	38.7	356 21.5	01.4	131 29.6	07.7
08	302 10.1	316 19.5	30.7	203 57.5	38.6	11 23.6	01.3	146 32.2	07.8
09	317 12.6	331 19.0	29.6	218 58.8	38.5	26 25.7	01.3	161 34.8	07.8
10	332 15.1	346 18.6	28.4	234 00.2	38.4	41 27.8	01.2	176 37.4	07.9
11	347 17.5	1 18.2	27.3	249 01.5	38.3	56 29.9	01.2	191 40.0	08.0
12	2 20.0	16 17.8	S 7 26.1	264 02.8	N25 38.2	71 32.1	S22 01.2	206 42.7	N12 08.0
13	17 22.5	31 17.3	25.0	279 04.1	38.1	86 34.2	01.1	221 45.3	08.1
14	32 24.9	46 16.9	23.8	294 05.4	38.0	101 36.3	01.1	236 47.9	08.1
15	47 27.4	61 16.5	22.7	309 06.7	37.9	116 38.4	01.0	251 50.5	08.2
16	62 29.9	76 16.1	21.5	324 08.0	37.8	131 40.5	01.0	266 53.1	08.2
17	77 32.3	91 15.6	20.4	339 09.3	37.7	146 42.6	01.0	281 55.7	08.3
18	92 34.8	106 15.2	S 7 19.2	354 10.6	N25 37.6	161 44.8	S22 00.9	296 58.3	N12 08.3
19	107 37.2	121 14.8	18.1	9 11.9	37.5	176 46.9	00.9	312 00.9	08.4
20	122 39.7	136 14.4	16.9	24 13.2	37.3	191 49.0	00.8	327 03.6	08.5
21	137 42.2	151 13.9	15.8	39 14.5	37.2	206 51.1	00.8	342 06.2	08.5
22	152 44.6	166 13.5	14.6	54 15.8	37.1	221 53.2	00.7	357 08.8	08.6
23	167 47.1	181 13.1	13.4	69 17.1	37.0	236 55.4	00.7	12 11.4	08.6
Mer. Pass. (h m)	11 54.6	*v* −0.4	*d* 1.1	*v* 1.3	*d* 0.1	*v* 2.1	*d* 0.0	*v* 2.6	*d* 0.1

STARS

Name	SHA	Dec
	° ′	° ′
Acamar	315 21.5	S40 16.4
Achernar	335 30.0	S57 11.8
Acrux	173 13.4	S63 08.8
Adhara	255 15.6	S28 59.2
Aldebaran	290 54.1	N16 31.6
Alioth	166 23.3	N55 54.7
Alkaid	153 01.3	N49 16.0
Al Na'ir	27 48.9	S46 55.2
Alnilam	275 50.4	S 1 11.8
Alphard	217 59.8	S 8 41.8
Alphecca	126 14.1	N26 40.9
Alpheratz	357 48.1	N29 08.1
Altair	62 12.2	N 8 53.2
Ankaa	353 19.8	S42 15.7
Antares	112 31.0	S26 27.1
Arcturus	145 59.0	N19 08.1
Atria	107 36.4	S69 02.4
Avior	234 19.5	S59 32.4
Bellatrix	278 36.3	N 6 21.4
Betelgeuse	271 05.6	N 7 24.5
Canopus	263 57.9	S52 42.2
Capella	280 40.5	N46 00.6
Deneb	49 34.6	N45 18.3
Denebola	182 37.3	N14 31.4
Diphda	349 00.1	S17 56.6
Dubhe	193 55.5	N61 42.4
Elnath	278 17.7	N28 37.0
Eltanin	90 47.9	N51 28.8
Enif	33 51.3	N 9 54.6
Fomalhaut	15 28.6	S29 34.8
Gacrux	172 05.1	S57 09.7
Gienah	175 56.1	S17 35.5
Hadar	148 53.3	S60 24.8
Hamal	328 05.6	N23 30.1
Kaus Aust.	83 49.1	S34 22.9
Kochab	137 18.4	N74 06.9
Markab	13 42.6	N15 14.9
Menkar	314 19.4	N 4 07.3
Menkent	148 12.0	S36 24.7
Miaplacidus	221 40.3	S69 45.3
Mirfak	308 46.5	N49 53.6
Nunki	76 03.3	S26 17.3
Peacock	53 25.6	S56 42.4
Pollux	243 32.4	N28 00.5
Procyon	245 03.8	N 5 12.2
Rasalhague	96 10.1	N12 32.9
Regulus	207 47.4	N11 55.5
Rigel	281 15.9	S 8 11.6
Rigil Kent.	139 56.9	S60 52.1
Sabik	102 17.0	S15 44.3
Schedar	349 45.9	N56 35.0
Shaula	96 27.2	S37 06.6
Sirius	258 37.2	S16 43.8
Spica	158 35.2	S11 12.5
Suhail	222 55.2	S43 28.2
Vega	80 41.7	N38 47.1
Zuben'ubi	137 09.6	S16 04.7

	SHA	Mer. Pass.
	° ′	h m
Venus	15 42.0	10 54
Mars	262 24.1	18 25
Jupiter	69 24.7	7 18
Saturn	204 17.2	22 16

	UT	SUN GHA	SUN Dec	MOON GHA	v	MOON Dec	d	HP
	d h	° ′	° ′	° ′	′	° ′	′	′
	22 00	178 16.2	N 0 41.6	357 09.5	15.6	S 4 34.2	14.5	55.5
	01	193 16.4	42.6	11 44.1	15.7	4 48.7	14.4	55.4
	02	208 16.6	43.6	26 18.8	15.7	5 03.1	14.4	55.4
	03	223 16.7	. . 44.6	40 53.5	15.6	5 17.5	14.4	55.4
	04	238 16.9	45.6	55 28.1	15.7	5 31.9	14.3	55.4
	05	253 17.1	46.6	70 02.8	15.6	5 46.2	14.3	55.4
	06	268 17.3	N 0 47.6	84 37.4	15.7	S 6 00.5	14.3	55.3
	07	283 17.5	48.5	99 12.1	15.6	6 14.8	14.3	55.3
S	08	298 17.7	49.5	113 46.7	15.7	6 29.1	14.2	55.3
A	09	313 17.9	. . 50.5	128 21.4	15.6	6 43.3	14.2	55.3
T	10	328 18.1	51.5	142 56.0	15.6	6 57.5	14.1	55.3
U	11	343 18.2	52.5	157 30.6	15.6	7 11.6	14.1	55.3
R	12	358 18.4	N 0 53.5	172 05.2	15.6	S 7 25.7	14.0	55.2
D	13	13 18.6	54.5	186 39.8	15.6	7 39.7	14.1	55.2
A	14	28 18.8	55.4	201 14.4	15.6	7 53.8	13.9	55.2
Y	15	43 19.0	. . 56.4	215 49.0	15.5	8 07.7	14.0	55.2
	16	58 19.2	57.4	230 23.5	15.6	8 21.7	13.9	55.2
	17	73 19.4	58.4	244 58.1	15.5	8 35.6	13.8	55.1
	18	88 19.6	N 0 59.4	259 32.6	15.5	S 8 49.4	13.8	55.1
	19	103 19.8	1 00.4	274 07.1	15.5	9 03.2	13.8	55.1
	20	118 19.9	01.4	288 41.6	15.5	9 17.0	13.7	55.1
	21	133 20.1	. . 02.3	303 16.1	15.4	9 30.7	13.7	55.1
	22	148 20.3	03.3	317 50.5	15.5	9 44.4	13.6	55.1
	23	163 20.5	04.3	332 25.0	15.4	9 58.0	13.6	55.0
	23 00	178 20.7	N 1 05.3	346 59.4	15.4	S10 11.6	13.5	55.0
	01	193 20.9	06.3	1 33.8	15.4	10 25.1	13.5	55.0
	02	208 21.1	07.3	16 08.2	15.3	10 38.6	13.4	55.0
	03	223 21.3	. . 08.3	30 42.5	15.3	10 52.0	13.4	55.0
	04	238 21.5	09.2	45 16.8	15.3	11 05.4	13.3	55.0
	05	253 21.6	10.2	59 51.1	15.3	11 18.7	13.3	54.9
	06	268 21.8	N 1 11.2	74 25.4	15.3	S11 32.0	13.2	54.9
	07	283 22.0	12.2	88 59.7	15.2	11 45.2	13.2	54.9
	08	298 22.2	13.2	103 33.9	15.2	11 58.4	13.1	54.9
S	09	313 22.4	. . 14.2	118 08.1	15.2	12 11.5	13.0	54.9
U	10	328 22.6	15.1	132 42.3	15.1	12 24.5	13.0	54.9
N	11	343 22.8	16.1	147 16.4	15.1	12 37.5	13.0	54.8
D	12	358 23.0	N 1 17.1	161 50.5	15.1	S12 50.5	12.8	54.8
A	13	13 23.2	18.1	176 24.6	15.0	13 03.3	12.9	54.8
Y	14	28 23.3	19.1	190 58.6	15.0	13 16.2	12.7	54.8
	15	43 23.5	. . 20.1	205 32.6	15.0	13 28.9	12.7	54.8
	16	58 23.7	21.1	220 06.6	15.0	13 41.6	12.6	54.8
	17	73 23.9	22.0	234 40.6	14.9	13 54.2	12.6	54.8
	18	88 24.1	N 1 23.0	249 14.5	14.8	S14 06.8	12.5	54.7
	19	103 24.3	24.0	263 48.3	14.9	14 19.3	12.4	54.7
	20	118 24.5	25.0	278 22.2	14.8	14 31.7	12.4	54.7
	21	133 24.7	. . 26.0	292 56.0	14.7	14 44.1	12.3	54.7
	22	148 24.9	27.0	307 29.7	14.8	14 56.4	12.3	54.7
	23	163 25.1	27.9	322 03.5	14.7	15 08.7	12.1	54.7
	24 00	178 25.2	N 1 28.9	336 37.2	14.6	S15 20.8	12.1	54.7
	01	193 25.4	29.9	351 10.8	14.6	15 32.9	12.1	54.6
	02	208 25.6	30.9	5 44.4	14.6	15 45.0	11.9	54.6
	03	223 25.8	. . 31.9	20 18.0	14.5	15 56.9	11.9	54.6
	04	238 26.0	32.9	34 51.5	14.5	16 08.8	11.8	54.6
	05	253 26.2	33.8	49 25.0	14.5	16 20.6	11.8	54.6
	06	268 26.4	N 1 34.8	63 58.5	14.4	S16 32.4	11.6	54.6
	07	283 26.6	35.8	78 31.9	14.3	16 44.0	11.6	54.6
	08	298 26.8	36.8	93 05.2	14.3	16 55.6	11.6	54.5
M	09	313 26.9	. . 37.8	107 38.5	14.3	17 07.2	11.4	54.5
O	10	328 27.1	38.8	122 11.8	14.2	17 18.6	11.4	54.5
N	11	343 27.3	39.7	136 45.0	14.2	17 30.0	11.3	54.5
D	12	358 27.5	N 1 40.7	151 18.2	14.1	S17 41.3	11.2	54.5
A	13	13 27.7	41.7	165 51.3	14.1	17 52.5	11.1	54.5
Y	14	28 27.9	42.7	180 24.4	14.1	18 03.6	11.1	54.5
	15	43 28.1	. . 43.7	194 57.5	14.0	18 14.7	10.9	54.5
	16	58 28.3	44.7	209 30.5	13.9	18 25.6	10.9	54.4
	17	73 28.5	45.6	224 03.4	13.9	18 36.5	10.8	54.4
	18	88 28.7	N 1 46.6	238 36.3	13.9	S18 47.3	10.8	54.4
	19	103 28.8	47.6	253 09.2	13.8	18 58.1	10.6	54.4
	20	118 29.0	48.6	267 42.0	13.7	19 08.7	10.6	54.4
	21	133 29.2	. . 49.6	282 14.7	13.7	19 19.3	10.4	54.4
	22	148 29.4	50.6	296 47.4	13.7	19 29.7	10.4	54.4
	23	163 29.6	51.5	311 20.1	13.6	S19 40.1	10.3	54.4
		SD 16.1	*d* 1.0	SD 15.1		14.9		14.8

Lat.	Twilight Naut.	Twilight Civil	Sunrise	Moonrise 22	Moonrise 23	Moonrise 24	Moonrise 25
°	h m	h m	h m	h m	h m	h m	h m
N 72	02 58	04 32	05 41	20 52	23 22	■	■
N 70	03 21	04 42	05 44	20 36	22 44	■	■
68	03 38	04 50	05 46	20 24	22 18	24 36	00 36
66	03 51	04 56	05 48	20 13	21 58	23 54	26 52
64	04 02	05 01	05 49	20 05	21 43	23 26	25 22
62	04 12	05 06	05 51	19 58	21 30	23 05	24 45
60	04 19	05 10	05 52	19 51	21 19	22 48	24 19
N 58	04 26	05 13	05 53	19 46	21 09	22 34	23 59
56	04 32	05 16	05 54	19 41	21 01	22 21	23 42
54	04 37	05 19	05 54	19 37	20 54	22 11	23 28
52	04 41	05 21	05 55	19 33	20 47	22 01	23 15
50	04 45	05 23	05 56	19 29	20 41	21 53	23 04
45	04 53	05 28	05 57	19 22	20 28	21 35	22 42
N 40	04 59	05 31	05 58	19 15	20 18	21 21	22 23
35	05 04	05 34	05 59	19 10	20 09	21 09	22 08
30	05 08	05 36	06 00	19 05	20 01	20 58	21 55
20	05 14	05 39	06 01	18 57	19 48	20 40	21 33
N 10	05 17	05 41	06 02	18 50	19 37	20 24	21 14
0	05 19	05 43	06 03	18 43	19 26	20 10	20 56
S 10	05 19	05 43	06 04	18 37	19 15	19 55	20 38
20	05 17	05 43	06 05	18 30	19 04	19 40	20 19
30	05 14	05 42	06 05	18 22	18 51	19 23	19 58
35	05 11	05 41	06 06	18 18	18 44	19 12	19 45
40	05 08	05 39	06 06	18 13	18 35	19 01	19 30
45	05 03	05 37	06 07	18 07	18 26	18 47	19 13
S 50	04 57	05 35	06 07	18 00	18 14	18 31	18 52
52	04 54	05 34	06 07	17 57	18 09	18 23	18 42
54	04 51	05 32	06 07	17 53	18 03	18 15	18 31
56	04 47	05 31	06 08	17 49	17 56	18 05	18 18
58	04 42	05 29	06 08	17 45	17 49	17 55	18 03
S 60	04 37	05 27	06 08	17 40	17 41	17 42	17 46

Lat.	Sunset	Twilight Civil	Twilight Naut.	Moonset 22	Moonset 23	Moonset 24	Moonset 25
°	h m	h m	h m	h m	h m	h m	h m
N 72	18 34	19 44	21 21	05 06	04 28	03 28	■
N 70	18 31	19 34	20 57	05 14	04 46	04 08	■
68	18 29	19 26	20 39	05 20	05 01	04 35	03 50
66	18 27	19 19	20 25	05 26	05 13	04 56	04 33
64	18 25	19 14	20 13	05 31	05 23	05 13	05 01
62	18 24	19 09	20 04	05 35	05 31	05 27	05 24
60	18 23	19 05	19 56	05 39	05 39	05 39	05 41
N 58	18 22	19 01	19 49	05 42	05 45	05 50	05 56
56	18 21	18 58	19 43	05 45	05 51	05 59	06 09
54	18 20	18 55	19 38	05 47	05 56	06 07	06 21
52	18 19	18 53	19 33	05 50	06 01	06 14	06 31
50	18 18	18 51	19 29	05 52	06 05	06 21	06 39
45	18 17	18 46	19 21	05 57	06 15	06 35	06 58
N 40	18 15	18 43	19 14	06 01	06 23	06 47	07 14
35	18 14	18 40	19 09	06 04	06 29	06 57	07 27
30	18 13	18 37	19 05	06 07	06 35	07 06	07 39
20	18 12	18 34	19 00	06 13	06 46	07 21	07 58
N 10	18 11	18 32	18 56	06 17	06 55	07 34	08 16
0	18 10	18 30	18 54	06 22	07 04	07 47	08 32
S 10	18 09	18 30	18 54	06 26	07 12	08 00	08 48
20	18 08	18 30	18 55	06 31	07 22	08 13	09 06
30	18 07	18 31	18 59	06 36	07 32	08 29	09 26
35	18 07	18 32	19 01	06 39	07 39	08 38	09 38
40	18 06	18 33	19 05	06 43	07 46	08 48	09 51
45	18 06	18 35	19 09	06 47	07 54	09 01	10 07
S 50	18 05	18 37	19 15	06 52	08 04	09 16	10 27
52	18 05	18 38	19 18	06 54	08 08	09 23	10 37
54	18 04	18 40	19 21	06 57	08 14	09 31	10 48
56	18 04	18 41	19 25	07 00	08 19	09 39	11 00
58	18 04	18 43	19 29	07 03	08 26	09 49	11 14
S 60	18 03	18 45	19 34	07 06	08 33	10 01	11 31

Day	SUN Eqn. of Time 00^h	SUN Eqn. of Time 12^h	SUN Mer. Pass.	MOON Mer. Pass. Upper	MOON Mer. Pass. Lower	MOON Age	MOON Phase
d	m s	m s	h m	h m	h m	d %	
22	06 56	06 47	12 07	00 12	12 33	15 99	
23	06 38	06 29	12 06	00 54	13 15	16 97	○
24	06 19	06 10	12 06	01 36	13 58	17 93	

UT	ARIES	VENUS −3.8		MARS +0.7		JUPITER −2.1		SATURN +0.3	
	GHA	GHA	Dec	GHA	Dec	GHA	Dec	GHA	Dec
d h	° ′	° ′	° ′	° ′	° ′	° ′	° ′	° ′	° ′
25 00	182 49.6	196 12.7	S 7 12.3	84 18.4	N25 36.9	251 57.5	S22 00.7	27 14.0	N12 08.7
01	197 52.0	211 12.2	11.1	99 19.8	36.8	266 59.6	00.6	42 16.6	08.7
02	212 54.5	226 11.8	10.0	114 21.1	36.7	282 01.7	00.6	57 19.2	08.8
03	227 57.0	241 11.4	. . 08.8	129 22.4	. . 36.6	297 03.8	. . 00.5	72 21.8	. . 08.8
04	242 59.4	256 11.0	07.7	144 23.7	36.5	312 06.0	00.5	87 24.5	08.9
05	258 01.9	271 10.5	06.5	159 25.0	36.4	327 08.1	00.5	102 27.1	08.9
06	273 04.4	286 10.1	S 7 05.4	174 26.3	N25 36.3	342 10.2	S22 00.4	117 29.7	N12 09.0
07	288 06.8	301 09.7	04.2	189 27.6	36.2	357 12.3	00.4	132 32.3	09.1
T 08	303 09.3	316 09.3	03.1	204 28.9	36.1	12 14.4	00.3	147 34.9	09.1
U 09	318 11.7	331 08.9	. . 01.9	219 30.2	. . 36.0	27 16.6	. . 00.3	162 37.5	. . 09.2
E 10	333 14.2	346 08.4	7 00.7	234 31.5	35.9	42 18.7	00.2	177 40.1	09.2
S 11	348 16.7	1 08.0	6 59.6	249 32.8	35.8	57 20.8	00.2	192 42.7	09.3
D 12	3 19.1	16 07.6	S 6 58.4	264 34.1	N25 35.7	72 22.9	S22 00.2	207 45.3	N12 09.3
A 13	18 21.6	31 07.2	57.3	279 35.4	35.6	87 25.1	00.1	222 48.0	09.4
Y 14	33 24.1	46 06.8	56.1	294 36.7	35.5	102 27.2	00.1	237 50.6	09.4
15	48 26.5	61 06.3	. . 54.9	309 38.0	. . 35.4	117 29.3	. . 00.0	252 53.2	. . 09.5
16	63 29.0	76 05.9	53.8	324 39.3	35.3	132 31.4	00.0	267 55.8	09.5
17	78 31.5	91 05.5	52.6	339 40.5	35.2	147 33.6	22 00.0	282 58.4	09.6
18	93 33.9	106 05.1	S 6 51.5	354 41.8	N25 35.1	162 35.7	S21 59.9	298 01.0	N12 09.6
19	108 36.4	121 04.7	50.3	9 43.1	35.0	177 37.8	59.9	313 03.6	09.7
20	123 38.8	136 04.2	49.2	24 44.4	34.8	192 39.9	59.8	328 06.2	09.8
21	138 41.3	151 03.8	. . 48.0	39 45.7	. . 34.7	207 42.1	. . 59.8	343 08.8	. . 09.8
22	153 43.8	166 03.4	46.8	54 47.0	34.6	222 44.2	59.8	358 11.4	09.9
23	168 46.2	181 03.0	45.7	69 48.3	34.5	237 46.3	59.7	13 14.1	09.9
26 00	183 48.7	196 02.6	S 6 44.5	84 49.6	N25 34.4	252 48.4	S21 59.7	28 16.7	N12 10.0
01	198 51.2	211 02.2	43.3	99 50.9	34.3	267 50.6	59.6	43 19.3	10.0
02	213 53.6	226 01.7	42.2	114 52.2	34.2	282 52.7	59.6	58 21.9	10.1
03	228 56.1	241 01.3	. . 41.0	129 53.5	. . 34.1	297 54.8	. . 59.6	73 24.5	. . 10.1
04	243 58.6	256 00.9	39.9	144 54.8	34.0	312 56.9	59.5	88 27.1	10.2
05	259 01.0	271 00.5	38.7	159 56.1	33.9	327 59.1	59.5	103 29.7	10.2
06	274 03.5	286 00.1	S 6 37.5	174 57.4	N25 33.8	343 01.2	S21 59.4	118 32.3	N12 10.3
W 07	289 06.0	300 59.7	36.4	189 58.7	33.7	358 03.3	59.4	133 34.9	10.3
E 08	304 08.4	315 59.2	35.2	205 00.0	33.6	13 05.4	59.3	148 37.5	10.4
D 09	319 10.9	330 58.8	. . 34.0	220 01.2	. . 33.5	28 07.6	. . 59.3	163 40.1	. . 10.4
N 10	334 13.3	345 58.4	32.9	235 02.5	33.3	43 09.7	59.3	178 42.8	10.5
E 11	349 15.8	0 58.0	31.7	250 03.8	33.2	58 11.8	59.2	193 45.4	10.5
S 12	4 18.3	15 57.6	S 6 30.5	265 05.1	N25 33.1	73 14.0	S21 59.2	208 48.0	N12 10.6
D 13	19 20.7	30 57.2	29.4	280 06.4	33.0	88 16.1	59.1	223 50.6	10.7
A 14	34 23.2	45 56.8	28.2	295 07.7	32.9	103 18.2	59.1	238 53.2	10.7
Y 15	49 25.7	60 56.3	. . 27.0	310 09.0	. . 32.8	118 20.4	. . 59.1	253 55.8	. . 10.8
16	64 28.1	75 55.9	25.9	325 10.3	32.7	133 22.5	59.0	268 58.4	10.8
17	79 30.6	90 55.5	24.7	340 11.5	32.6	148 24.6	59.0	284 01.0	10.9
18	94 33.1	105 55.1	S 6 23.5	355 12.8	N25 32.5	163 26.7	S21 58.9	299 03.6	N12 10.9
19	109 35.5	120 54.7	22.4	10 14.1	32.4	178 28.9	58.9	314 06.2	11.0
20	124 38.0	135 54.3	21.2	25 15.4	32.3	193 31.0	58.9	329 08.8	11.0
21	139 40.5	150 53.9	. . 20.0	40 16.7	. . 32.1	208 33.1	. . 58.8	344 11.4	. . 11.1
22	154 42.9	165 53.5	18.9	55 18.0	32.0	223 35.3	58.8	359 14.0	11.1
23	169 45.4	180 53.1	17.7	70 19.3	31.9	238 37.4	58.7	14 16.6	11.2
27 00	184 47.8	195 52.6	S 6 16.5	85 20.5	N25 31.8	253 39.5	S21 58.7	29 19.3	N12 11.2
01	199 50.3	210 52.2	15.4	100 21.8	31.7	268 41.7	58.7	44 21.9	11.3
02	214 52.8	225 51.8	14.2	115 23.1	31.6	283 43.8	58.6	59 24.5	11.3
03	229 55.2	240 51.4	. . 13.0	130 24.4	. . 31.5	298 45.9	. . 58.6	74 27.1	. . 11.4
04	244 57.7	255 51.0	11.9	145 25.7	31.4	313 48.1	58.5	89 29.7	11.4
05	260 00.2	270 50.6	10.7	160 27.0	31.3	328 50.2	58.5	104 32.3	11.5
06	275 02.6	285 50.2	S 6 09.5	175 28.2	N25 31.2	343 52.3	S21 58.5	119 34.9	N12 11.5
07	290 05.1	300 49.8	08.3	190 29.5	31.0	358 54.5	58.4	134 37.5	11.6
T 08	305 07.6	315 49.4	07.2	205 30.8	30.9	13 56.6	58.4	149 40.1	11.6
H 09	320 10.0	330 48.9	. . 06.0	220 32.1	. . 30.8	28 58.7	. . 58.3	164 42.7	. . 11.7
U 10	335 12.5	345 48.5	04.8	235 33.4	30.7	44 00.9	58.3	179 45.3	11.7
R 11	350 14.9	0 48.1	03.6	250 34.6	30.6	59 03.0	58.3	194 47.9	11.8
S 12	5 17.4	15 47.7	S 6 02.5	265 35.9	N25 30.5	74 05.1	S21 58.2	209 50.5	N12 11.9
D 13	20 19.9	30 47.3	01.3	280 37.2	30.4	89 07.3	58.2	224 53.1	11.9
A 14	35 22.3	45 46.9	6 00.1	295 38.5	30.3	104 09.4	58.1	239 55.7	12.0
Y 15	50 24.8	60 46.5	5 59.0	310 39.8	. . 30.1	119 11.6	. . 58.1	254 58.3	. . 12.0
16	65 27.3	75 46.1	57.8	325 41.0	30.0	134 13.7	58.1	270 00.9	12.1
17	80 29.7	90 45.7	56.6	340 42.3	29.9	149 15.8	58.0	285 03.5	12.1
18	95 32.2	105 45.3	S 5 55.4	355 43.6	N25 29.8	164 18.0	S21 58.0	300 06.2	N12 12.2
19	110 34.7	120 44.9	54.3	10 44.9	29.7	179 20.1	57.9	315 08.8	12.2
20	125 37.1	135 44.5	53.1	25 46.1	29.6	194 22.2	57.9	330 11.4	12.3
21	140 39.6	150 44.1	. . 51.9	40 47.4	. . 29.5	209 24.4	. . 57.9	345 14.0	. . 12.3
22	155 42.1	165 43.7	50.7	55 48.7	29.3	224 26.5	57.8	0 16.6	12.4
23	170 44.5	180 43.2	49.6	70 50.0	29.2	239 28.7	57.8	15 19.2	12.4
Mer. Pass.	h m 11 42.8	*v* −0.4	*d* 1.2	*v* 1.3	*d* 0.1	*v* 2.1	*d* 0.0	*v* 2.6	*d* 0.1

STARS

Name	SHA	Dec
	° ′	° ′
Acamar	315 21.5	S40 16.4
Achernar	335 30.0	S57 11.8
Acrux	173 13.4	S63 08.8
Adhara	255 15.6	S28 59.2
Aldebaran	290 54.1	N16 31.6
Alioth	166 23.3	N55 54.7
Alkaid	153 01.3	N49 16.1
Al Na'ir	27 48.9	S46 55.2
Alnilam	275 50.4	S 1 11.8
Alphard	217 59.8	S 8 41.8
Alphecca	126 14.1	N26 40.9
Alpheratz	357 48.1	N29 08.1
Altair	62 12.2	N 8 53.2
Ankaa	353 19.8	S42 15.7
Antares	112 31.0	S26 27.1
Arcturus	145 59.0	N19 08.1
Atria	107 36.3	S69 02.4
Avior	234 19.5	S59 32.4
Bellatrix	278 36.3	N 6 21.4
Betelgeuse	271 05.6	N 7 24.5
Canopus	263 57.9	S52 42.2
Capella	280 40.5	N46 00.6
Deneb	49 34.6	N45 18.3
Denebola	182 37.3	N14 31.4
Diphda	349 00.1	S17 56.5
Dubhe	193 55.5	N61 42.4
Elnath	278 17.7	N28 37.0
Eltanin	90 47.9	N51 28.8
Enif	33 51.3	N 9 54.6
Fomalhaut	15 28.6	S29 34.7
Gacrux	172 05.1	S57 09.7
Gienah	175 56.1	S17 35.5
Hadar	148 53.3	S60 24.8
Hamal	328 05.6	N23 30.1
Kaus Aust.	83 49.0	S34 22.9
Kochab	137 18.4	N74 07.0
Markab	13 42.6	N15 14.8
Menkar	314 19.4	N 4 07.3
Menkent	148 12.0	S36 24.8
Miaplacidus	221 40.3	S69 45.3
Mirfak	308 46.5	N49 53.6
Nunki	76 03.2	S26 17.3
Peacock	53 25.5	S56 42.4
Pollux	243 32.4	N28 00.5
Procyon	245 03.8	N 5 12.2
Rasalhague	96 10.1	N12 32.9
Regulus	207 47.4	N11 55.5
Rigel	281 15.9	S 8 11.6
Rigil Kent.	139 56.9	S60 52.1
Sabik	102 17.0	S15 44.3
Schedar	349 45.9	N56 35.0
Shaula	96 27.2	S37 06.6
Sirius	258 37.2	S16 43.8
Spica	158 35.2	S11 12.5
Suhail	222 55.2	S43 28.2
Vega	80 41.7	N38 47.1
Zuben'ubi	137 09.6	S16 04.7

	SHA	Mer. Pass.
	° ′	h m
Venus	12 13.9	10 56
Mars	261 00.9	18 19
Jupiter	68 59.7	7 08
Saturn	204 28.0	22 03

UT		SUN		MOON				
		GHA	Dec	GHA	*v*	Dec	*d*	HP
d	h	° ′	° ′	° ′	′	° ′	′	′
25	00	178 29.8	N 1 52.5	325 52.7	13.5	S19 50.4	10.2	54.4
	01	193 30.0	53.5	340 25.2	13.5	20 00.6	10.2	54.4
	02	208 30.2	54.5	354 57.7	13.5	20 10.8	10.0	54.3
	03	223 30.4	. . 55.5	9 30.2	13.3	20 20.8	9.9	54.3
	04	238 30.5	56.4	24 02.5	13.4	20 30.7	9.9	54.3
	05	253 30.7	57.4	38 34.9	13.3	20 40.6	9.7	54.3
	06	268 30.9	N 1 58.4	53 07.2	13.2	S20 50.3	9.7	54.3
	07	283 31.1	1 59.4	67 39.4	13.2	21 00.0	9.6	54.3
T	08	298 31.3	2 00.4	82 11.6	13.1	21 09.6	9.5	54.3
U	09	313 31.5	. . 01.4	96 43.7	13.1	21 19.1	9.4	54.3
E	10	328 31.7	02.3	111 15.8	13.0	21 28.5	9.2	54.3
S	11	343 31.9	03.3	125 47.8	13.0	21 37.7	9.2	54.3
D	12	358 32.1	N 2 04.3	140 19.8	12.9	S21 46.9	9.1	54.3
A	13	13 32.3	05.3	154 51.7	12.9	21 56.0	9.0	54.2
Y	14	28 32.4	06.3	169 23.6	12.8	22 05.0	8.9	54.2
	15	43 32.6	. . 07.2	183 55.4	12.8	22 13.9	8.8	54.2
	16	58 32.8	08.2	198 27.2	12.7	22 22.7	8.7	54.2
	17	73 33.0	09.2	212 58.9	12.6	22 31.4	8.6	54.2
	18	88 33.2	N 2 10.2	227 30.5	12.6	S22 40.0	8.5	54.2
	19	103 33.4	11.2	242 02.1	12.5	22 48.5	8.4	54.2
	20	118 33.6	12.1	256 33.6	12.5	22 56.9	8.3	54.2
	21	133 33.8	. . 13.1	271 05.1	12.4	23 05.2	8.2	54.2
	22	148 34.0	14.1	285 36.5	12.4	23 13.4	8.1	54.2
	23	163 34.2	15.1	300 07.9	12.3	23 21.5	8.0	54.2
26	00	178 34.3	N 2 16.1	314 39.2	12.3	S23 29.5	7.9	54.2
	01	193 34.5	17.0	329 10.5	12.2	23 37.4	7.7	54.2
	02	208 34.7	18.0	343 41.7	12.2	23 45.1	7.7	54.2
	03	223 34.9	. . 19.0	358 12.9	12.1	23 52.8	7.6	54.2
	04	238 35.1	20.0	12 44.0	12.1	24 00.4	7.4	54.2
	05	253 35.3	21.0	27 15.1	12.0	24 07.8	7.3	54.2
	06	268 35.5	N 2 21.9	41 46.1	11.9	S24 15.1	7.3	54.2
W	07	283 35.7	22.9	56 17.0	11.9	24 22.4	7.1	54.2
E	08	298 35.9	23.9	70 47.9	11.8	24 29.5	7.0	54.1
D	09	313 36.1	. . 24.9	85 18.7	11.8	24 36.5	6.9	54.1
N	10	328 36.2	25.9	99 49.5	11.8	24 43.4	6.8	54.1
E	11	343 36.4	26.8	114 20.3	11.6	24 50.2	6.6	54.1
S	12	358 36.6	N 2 27.8	128 50.9	11.7	S24 56.8	6.6	54.1
D	13	13 36.8	28.8	143 21.6	11.5	25 03.4	6.4	54.1
A	14	28 37.0	29.8	157 52.1	11.6	25 09.8	6.4	54.1
Y	15	43 37.2	. . 30.8	172 22.7	11.5	25 16.2	6.2	54.1
	16	58 37.4	31.7	186 53.2	11.4	25 22.4	6.1	54.1
	17	73 37.6	32.7	201 23.6	11.4	25 28.5	5.9	54.1
	18	88 37.8	N 2 33.7	215 54.0	11.3	S25 34.4	5.9	54.1
	19	103 37.9	34.7	230 24.3	11.3	25 40.3	5.7	54.1
	20	118 38.1	35.7	244 54.6	11.2	25 46.0	5.7	54.1
	21	133 38.3	. . 36.6	259 24.8	11.2	25 51.7	5.5	54.1
	22	148 38.5	37.6	273 55.0	11.1	25 57.2	5.3	54.1
	23	163 38.7	38.6	288 25.1	11.1	26 02.5	5.3	54.1
27	00	178 38.9	N 2 39.6	302 55.2	11.0	S26 07.8	5.2	54.1
	01	193 39.1	40.6	317 25.2	11.0	26 13.0	5.0	54.1
	02	208 39.3	41.5	331 55.2	11.0	26 18.0	4.9	54.1
	03	223 39.5	. . 42.5	346 25.2	10.9	26 22.9	4.7	54.1
	04	238 39.7	43.5	0 55.1	10.9	26 27.6	4.7	54.1
	05	253 39.8	44.5	15 25.0	10.8	26 32.3	4.5	54.1
	06	268 40.0	N 2 45.4	29 54.8	10.7	S26 36.8	4.4	54.1
T	07	283 40.2	46.4	44 24.5	10.8	26 41.2	4.3	54.1
H	08	298 40.4	47.4	58 54.3	10.7	26 45.5	4.2	54.1
U	09	313 40.6	. . 48.4	73 24.0	10.6	26 49.7	4.0	54.2
R	10	328 40.8	49.4	87 53.6	10.6	26 53.7	3.9	54.2
S	11	343 41.0	50.3	102 23.2	10.6	26 57.6	3.7	54.2
D	12	358 41.2	N 2 51.3	116 52.8	10.5	S27 01.3	3.7	54.2
A	13	13 41.4	52.3	131 22.3	10.5	27 05.0	3.5	54.2
Y	14	28 41.6	53.3	145 51.8	10.4	27 08.5	3.4	54.2
	15	43 41.7	. . 54.2	160 21.2	10.5	27 11.9	3.3	54.2
	16	58 41.9	55.2	174 50.7	10.3	27 15.2	3.1	54.2
	17	73 42.1	56.2	189 20.0	10.4	27 18.3	3.0	54.2
	18	88 42.3	N 2 57.2	203 49.4	10.3	S27 21.3	2.9	54.2
	19	103 42.5	58.1	218 18.7	10.3	27 24.2	2.7	54.2
	20	118 42.7	2 59.1	232 48.0	10.2	27 26.9	2.6	54.2
	21	133 42.9	3 00.1	247 17.2	10.2	27 29.5	2.5	54.2
	22	148 43.1	01.1	261 46.4	10.2	27 32.0	2.3	54.2
	23	163 43.3	02.1	276 15.6	10.2	S27 34.3	2.3	54.2
		SD 16.1	*d* 1.0	SD 14.8		14.8		14.8

Lat.	Twilight Naut.	Twilight Civil	Sunrise	Moonrise 25	Moonrise 26	Moonrise 27	Moonrise 28
°	h m	h m	h m	h m	h m	h m	h m
N 72	02 34	04 15	05 26	■	■	■	■
N 70	03 02	04 27	05 30	■	■	■	■
68	03 22	04 36	05 33	00 36	■	■	■
66	03 37	04 44	05 36	26 52	02 52	■	■
64	03 50	04 50	05 39	25 22	01 22	■	■
62	04 00	04 56	05 41	24 45	00 45	02 30	04 19
60	04 09	05 01	05 43	24 19	00 19	01 49	03 07
N 58	04 17	05 05	05 44	23 59	25 21	01 21	02 32
56	04 23	05 08	05 46	23 42	24 59	00 59	02 07
54	04 29	05 11	05 47	23 28	24 41	00 41	01 46
52	04 34	05 14	05 48	23 15	24 26	00 26	01 30
50	04 38	05 17	05 49	23 04	24 13	00 13	01 15
45	04 47	05 22	05 51	22 42	23 46	24 46	00 46
N 40	04 54	05 26	05 53	22 23	23 25	24 23	00 23
35	05 00	05 30	05 55	22 08	23 07	24 04	00 04
30	05 04	05 32	05 56	21 55	22 52	23 47	24 40
20	05 11	05 37	05 59	21 33	22 27	23 20	24 12
N 10	05 15	05 40	06 01	21 14	22 05	22 56	23 48
0	05 18	05 42	06 02	20 56	21 44	22 34	23 26
S 10	05 19	05 43	06 04	20 38	21 24	22 13	23 04
20	05 18	05 44	06 06	20 19	21 02	21 49	22 40
30	05 16	05 43	06 07	19 58	20 37	21 22	22 13
35	05 14	05 43	06 08	19 45	20 22	21 06	21 56
40	05 11	05 42	06 09	19 30	20 06	20 47	21 37
45	05 07	05 41	06 10	19 13	19 45	20 25	21 14
S 50	05 02	05 40	06 12	18 52	19 20	19 57	20 45
52	04 59	05 39	06 12	18 42	19 07	19 43	20 30
54	04 56	05 38	06 13	18 31	18 53	19 26	20 13
56	04 53	05 37	06 14	18 18	18 37	19 07	19 53
58	04 49	05 35	06 15	18 03	18 18	18 44	19 27
S 60	04 45	05 34	06 15	17 46	17 54	18 12	18 53

Lat.	Sunset	Twilight Civil	Twilight Naut.	Moonset 25	Moonset 26	Moonset 27	Moonset 28
°	h m	h m	h m	h m	h m	h m	h m
N 72	18 48	20 00	21 44	■	■	■	■
N 70	18 44	19 47	21 14	■	■	■	■
68	18 40	19 38	20 53	03 50	■	■	■
66	18 37	19 30	20 37	04 33	03 12	■	■
64	18 34	19 23	20 24	05 01	04 42	■	■
62	18 32	19 17	20 13	05 24	05 20	05 16	05 13
60	18 30	19 12	20 04	05 41	05 46	05 58	06 25
N 58	18 28	19 08	19 56	05 56	06 07	06 26	07 00
56	18 27	19 04	19 50	06 09	06 25	06 48	07 25
54	18 25	19 01	19 44	06 21	06 39	07 06	07 46
52	18 24	18 58	19 39	06 31	06 52	07 22	08 03
50	18 23	18 55	19 34	06 39	07 03	07 35	08 17
45	18 20	18 50	19 25	06 58	07 27	08 03	08 47
N 40	18 18	18 46	19 18	07 14	07 46	08 24	09 10
35	18 17	18 42	19 12	07 27	08 02	08 42	09 29
30	18 15	18 39	19 07	07 39	08 16	08 58	09 46
20	18 13	18 35	19 01	07 58	08 39	09 24	10 13
N 10	18 11	18 32	18 56	08 16	09 00	09 47	10 37
0	18 09	18 30	18 54	08 32	09 19	10 08	10 59
S 10	18 07	18 28	18 52	08 48	09 38	10 30	11 21
20	18 05	18 27	18 53	09 06	09 59	10 52	11 45
30	18 03	18 27	18 55	09 26	10 23	11 19	12 13
35	18 02	18 28	18 57	09 38	10 37	11 35	12 29
40	18 01	18 28	19 00	09 51	10 53	11 53	12 48
45	18 00	18 29	19 03	10 07	11 13	12 15	13 11
S 50	17 58	18 31	19 08	10 27	11 38	12 43	13 41
52	17 58	18 31	19 11	10 37	11 49	12 57	13 55
54	17 57	18 32	19 13	10 48	12 03	13 13	14 12
56	17 56	18 33	19 17	11 00	12 19	13 32	14 33
58	17 55	18 34	19 20	11 14	12 38	13 55	14 58
S 60	17 54	18 36	19 25	11 31	13 02	14 27	15 33

Day	SUN Eqn. of Time 00^h	SUN Eqn. of Time 12^h	SUN Mer. Pass.	MOON Mer. Pass. Upper	MOON Mer. Pass. Lower	MOON Age	MOON Phase
d	m s	m s	h m	h m	h m	d %	
25	06 01	05 52	12 06	02 21	14 44	18 87	
26	05 43	05 34	12 06	03 07	15 32	19 80	
27	05 25	05 16	12 05	03 56	16 21	20 72	

	UT d h	ARIES GHA ° ′	VENUS −3.8 GHA ° ′	VENUS Dec ° ′	MARS +0.8 GHA ° ′	MARS Dec ° ′	JUPITER −2.1 GHA ° ′	JUPITER Dec ° ′	SATURN +0.4 GHA ° ′	SATURN Dec ° ′
	28 00	185 47.0	195 42.8	S 5 48.4	85 51.3	N25 29.1	254 30.8	S21 57.7	30 21.8	N12 12.5
	01	200 49.4	210 42.4	47.2	100 52.5	29.0	269 32.9	57.7	45 24.4	12.5
	02	215 51.9	225 42.0	46.0	115 53.8	28.9	284 35.1	57.7	60 27.0	12.6
	03	230 54.4	240 41.6	. . 44.8	130 55.1	. . 28.8	299 37.2	. . 57.6	75 29.6	. . 12.6
	04	245 56.8	255 41.2	43.7	145 56.3	28.7	314 39.3	57.6	90 32.2	12.7
	05	260 59.3	270 40.8	42.5	160 57.6	28.5	329 41.5	57.5	105 34.8	12.7
	06	276 01.8	285 40.4	S 5 41.3	175 58.9	N25 28.4	344 43.6	S21 57.5	120 37.4	N12 12.8
	07	291 04.2	300 40.0	40.1	191 00.2	28.3	359 45.8	57.5	135 40.0	12.8
	08	306 06.7	315 39.6	39.0	206 01.4	28.2	14 47.9	57.4	150 42.6	12.9
F	09	321 09.2	330 39.2	. . 37.8	221 02.7	. . 28.1	29 50.1	. . 57.4	165 45.2	. . 12.9
R	10	336 11.6	345 38.8	36.6	236 04.0	28.0	44 52.2	57.3	180 47.8	13.0
I	11	351 14.1	0 38.4	35.4	251 05.3	27.9	59 54.3	57.3	195 50.4	13.0
D	12	6 16.6	15 38.0	S 5 34.2	266 06.5	N25 27.7	74 56.5	S21 57.3	210 53.0	N12 13.1
A	13	21 19.0	30 37.6	33.1	281 07.8	27.6	89 58.6	57.2	225 55.6	13.1
Y	14	36 21.5	45 37.2	31.9	296 09.1	27.5	105 00.8	57.2	240 58.2	13.2
	15	51 23.9	60 36.8	. . 30.7	311 10.3	. . 27.4	120 02.9	. . 57.2	256 00.8	. . 13.2
	16	66 26.4	75 36.4	29.5	326 11.6	27.3	135 05.0	57.1	271 03.4	13.3
	17	81 28.9	90 36.0	28.3	341 12.9	27.2	150 07.2	57.1	286 06.0	13.3
	18	96 31.3	105 35.6	S 5 27.2	356 14.1	N25 27.0	165 09.3	S21 57.0	301 08.6	N12 13.4
	19	111 33.8	120 35.2	26.0	11 15.4	26.9	180 11.5	57.0	316 11.2	13.4
	20	126 36.3	135 34.8	24.8	26 16.7	26.8	195 13.6	57.0	331 13.8	13.5
	21	141 38.7	150 34.4	. . 23.6	41 17.9	. . 26.7	210 15.8	. . 56.9	346 16.4	. . 13.5
	22	156 41.2	165 34.0	22.4	56 19.2	26.6	225 17.9	56.9	1 19.0	13.6
	23	171 43.7	180 33.6	21.2	71 20.5	26.4	240 20.1	56.8	16 21.6	13.6
	29 00	186 46.1	195 33.2	S 5 20.1	86 21.7	N25 26.3	255 22.2	S21 56.8	31 24.2	N12 13.7
	01	201 48.6	210 32.8	18.9	101 23.0	26.2	270 24.3	56.8	46 26.8	13.7
	02	216 51.1	225 32.4	17.7	116 24.3	26.1	285 26.5	56.7	61 29.4	13.8
	03	231 53.5	240 32.0	. . 16.5	131 25.5	. . 26.0	300 28.6	. . 56.7	76 32.0	. . 13.8
	04	246 56.0	255 31.6	15.3	146 26.8	25.9	315 30.8	56.6	91 34.6	13.9
	05	261 58.4	270 31.2	14.1	161 28.1	25.7	330 32.9	56.6	106 37.2	13.9
	06	277 00.9	285 30.8	S 5 13.0	176 29.3	N25 25.6	345 35.1	S21 56.6	121 39.8	N12 14.0
	07	292 03.4	300 30.4	11.8	191 30.6	25.5	0 37.2	56.5	136 42.4	14.0
S	08	307 05.8	315 30.0	10.6	206 31.8	25.4	15 39.4	56.5	151 45.0	14.1
A	09	322 08.3	330 29.6	. . 09.4	221 33.1	. . 25.3	30 41.5	. . 56.4	166 47.6	. . 14.1
T	10	337 10.8	345 29.2	08.2	236 34.4	25.1	45 43.7	56.4	181 50.2	14.2
U	11	352 13.2	0 28.8	07.0	251 35.6	25.0	60 45.8	56.4	196 52.8	14.2
R	12	7 15.7	15 28.4	S 5 05.9	266 36.9	N25 24.9	75 48.0	S21 56.3	211 55.4	N12 14.3
D	13	22 18.2	30 28.0	04.7	281 38.2	24.8	90 50.1	56.3	226 58.0	14.3
A	14	37 20.6	45 27.6	03.5	296 39.4	24.7	105 52.3	56.3	242 00.6	14.4
Y	15	52 23.1	60 27.2	. . 02.3	311 40.7	. . 24.5	120 54.4	. . 56.2	257 03.2	. . 14.4
	16	67 25.5	75 26.8	5 01.1	326 41.9	24.4	135 56.6	56.2	272 05.8	14.5
	17	82 28.0	90 26.4	4 59.9	341 43.2	24.3	150 58.7	56.1	287 08.4	14.5
	18	97 30.5	105 26.0	S 4 58.7	356 44.5	N25 24.2	166 00.9	S21 56.1	302 11.0	N12 14.5
	19	112 32.9	120 25.6	57.5	11 45.7	24.1	181 03.0	56.1	317 13.6	14.6
	20	127 35.4	135 25.2	56.4	26 47.0	23.9	196 05.2	56.0	332 16.2	14.6
	21	142 37.9	150 24.8	. . 55.2	41 48.2	. . 23.8	211 07.3	. . 56.0	347 18.8	. . 14.7
	22	157 40.3	165 24.4	54.0	56 49.5	23.7	226 09.5	55.9	2 21.4	14.7
	23	172 42.8	180 24.0	52.8	71 50.7	23.6	241 11.6	55.9	17 24.0	14.8
	30 00	187 45.3	195 23.6	S 4 51.6	86 52.0	N25 23.4	256 13.8	S21 55.9	32 26.6	N12 14.8
	01	202 47.7	210 23.2	50.4	101 53.3	23.3	271 15.9	55.8	47 29.2	14.9
	02	217 50.2	225 22.8	49.2	116 54.5	23.2	286 18.1	55.8	62 31.8	14.9
	03	232 52.7	240 22.4	. . 48.0	131 55.8	. . 23.1	301 20.2	. . 55.8	77 34.4	. . 15.0
	04	247 55.1	255 22.0	46.8	146 57.0	23.0	316 22.4	55.7	92 37.0	15.0
	05	262 57.6	270 21.6	45.7	161 58.3	22.8	331 24.5	55.7	107 39.6	15.1
	06	278 00.0	285 21.2	S 4 44.5	176 59.5	N25 22.7	346 26.7	S21 55.6	122 42.2	N12 15.1
	07	293 02.5	300 20.9	43.3	192 00.8	22.6	1 28.8	55.6	137 44.8	15.2
	08	308 05.0	315 20.5	42.1	207 02.0	22.5	16 31.0	55.6	152 47.4	15.2
S	09	323 07.4	330 20.1	. . 40.9	222 03.3	. . 22.3	31 33.1	. . 55.5	167 50.0	. . 15.3
U	10	338 09.9	345 19.7	39.7	237 04.6	22.2	46 35.3	55.5	182 52.6	15.3
N	11	353 12.4	0 19.3	38.5	252 05.8	22.1	61 37.5	55.5	197 55.2	15.4
D	12	8 14.8	15 18.9	S 4 37.3	267 07.1	N25 22.0	76 39.6	S21 55.4	212 57.8	N12 15.4
A	13	23 17.3	30 18.5	36.1	282 08.3	21.8	91 41.8	55.4	228 00.4	15.5
Y	14	38 19.8	45 18.1	34.9	297 09.6	21.7	106 43.9	55.3	243 03.0	15.5
	15	53 22.2	60 17.7	. . 33.7	312 10.8	. . 21.6	121 46.1	. . 55.3	258 05.6	. . 15.6
	16	68 24.7	75 17.3	32.5	327 12.1	21.5	136 48.2	55.3	273 08.1	15.6
	17	83 27.2	90 16.9	31.4	342 13.3	21.3	151 50.4	55.2	288 10.7	15.6
	18	98 29.6	105 16.5	S 4 30.2	357 14.6	N25 21.2	166 52.5	S21 55.2	303 13.3	N12 15.7
	19	113 32.1	120 16.1	29.0	12 15.8	21.1	181 54.7	55.1	318 15.9	15.7
	20	128 34.5	135 15.7	27.8	27 17.1	21.0	196 56.9	55.1	333 18.5	15.8
	21	143 37.0	150 15.4	. . 26.6	42 18.3	. . 20.8	211 59.0	. . 55.1	348 21.1	. . 15.8
	22	158 39.5	165 15.0	25.4	57 19.6	20.7	227 01.2	55.0	3 23.7	15.9
	23	173 41.9	180 14.6	24.2	72 20.8	20.6	242 03.3	55.0	18 26.3	15.9
	Mer. Pass. h m	11 31.0	v −0.4	d 1.2	v 1.3	d 0.1	v 2.1	d 0.0	v 2.6	d 0.0

STARS

Name	SHA ° ′	Dec ° ′
Acamar	315 21.5	S40 16.4
Achernar	335 30.0	S57 11.7
Acrux	173 13.4	S63 08.8
Adhara	255 15.6	S28 59.2
Aldebaran	290 54.1	N16 31.6
Alioth	166 23.3	N55 54.7
Alkaid	153 01.3	N49 16.1
Al Na'ir	27 48.8	S46 55.2
Alnilam	275 50.5	S 1 11.8
Alphard	217 59.8	S 8 41.8
Alphecca	126 14.0	N26 40.9
Alpheratz	357 48.1	N29 08.1
Altair	62 12.2	N 8 53.2
Ankaa	353 19.8	S42 15.7
Antares	112 31.0	S26 27.1
Arcturus	145 59.0	N19 08.1
Atria	107 36.3	S69 02.4
Avior	234 19.6	S59 32.4
Bellatrix	278 36.3	N 6 21.4
Betelgeuse	271 05.6	N 7 24.5
Canopus	263 58.0	S52 42.2
Capella	280 40.5	N46 00.6
Deneb	49 34.5	N45 18.3
Denebola	182 37.3	N14 31.4
Diphda	349 00.1	S17 56.5
Dubhe	193 55.5	N61 42.4
Elnath	278 17.7	N28 37.0
Eltanin	90 47.9	N51 28.8
Enif	33 51.3	N 9 54.6
Fomalhaut	15 28.5	S29 34.7
Gacrux	172 05.1	S57 09.7
Gienah	175 56.1	S17 35.5
Hadar	148 53.2	S60 24.8
Hamal	328 05.6	N23 30.1
Kaus Aust.	83 49.0	S34 22.9
Kochab	137 18.4	N74 07.0
Markab	13 42.6	N15 14.8
Menkar	314 19.4	N 4 07.3
Menkent	148 12.0	S36 24.8
Miaplacidus	221 40.4	S69 45.3
Mirfak	308 46.5	N49 53.6
Nunki	76 03.2	S26 17.2
Peacock	53 25.5	S56 42.4
Pollux	243 32.4	N28 00.5
Procyon	245 03.8	N 5 12.2
Rasalhague	96 10.0	N12 32.9
Regulus	207 47.4	N11 55.5
Rigel	281 16.0	S 8 11.6
Rigil Kent.	139 56.9	S60 52.2
Sabik	102 17.0	S15 44.3
Schedar	349 45.9	N56 35.0
Shaula	96 27.2	S37 06.6
Sirius	258 37.2	S16 43.8
Spica	158 35.1	S11 12.5
Suhail	222 55.2	S43 28.2
Vega	80 41.7	N38 47.1
Zuben'ubi	137 09.6	S16 04.8

	SHA ° ′	Mer. Pass. h m
Venus	8 47.0	10 58
Mars	259 35.6	18 13
Jupiter	68 36.1	6 58
Saturn	204 38.1	21 51

	UT	SUN GHA	SUN Dec	MOON GHA	v	MOON Dec	d	HP
	d h	° ′	° ′	° ′	′	° ′	′	′
	28 00	178 43.4	N 3 03.0	290 44.8	10.1	S27 36.6	2.0	54.2
	01	193 43.6	04.0	305 13.9	10.1	27 38.6	2.0	54.2
	02	208 43.8	05.0	319 43.0	10.0	27 40.6	1.8	54.2
	03	223 44.0	. . 06.0	334 12.0	10.1	27 42.4	1.7	54.3
	04	238 44.2	06.9	348 41.1	10.0	27 44.1	1.5	54.3
	05	253 44.4	07.9	3 10.1	10.0	27 45.6	1.5	54.3
	06	268 44.6	N 3 08.9	17 39.1	9.9	S27 47.1	1.2	54.3
	07	283 44.8	09.9	32 08.0	10.0	27 48.3	1.2	54.3
	08	298 45.0	10.8	46 37.0	9.9	27 49.5	1.0	54.3
F	09	313 45.1	. . 11.8	61 05.9	9.9	27 50.5	0.9	54.3
R	10	328 45.3	12.8	75 34.8	9.9	27 51.4	0.7	54.3
I	11	343 45.5	13.8	90 03.7	9.9	27 52.1	0.6	54.3
D	12	358 45.7	N 3 14.7	104 32.6	9.8	S27 52.7	0.5	54.3
A	13	13 45.9	15.7	119 01.4	9.8	27 53.2	0.3	54.4
Y	14	28 46.1	16.7	133 30.2	9.8	27 53.5	0.2	54.4
	15	43 46.3	. . 17.7	147 59.0	9.8	27 53.7	0.1	54.4
	16	58 46.5	18.6	162 27.8	9.8	27 53.8	0.1	54.4
	17	73 46.7	19.6	176 56.6	9.8	27 53.7	0.2	54.4
	18	88 46.8	N 3 20.6	191 25.4	9.7	S27 53.5	0.3	54.4
	19	103 47.0	21.6	205 54.1	9.8	27 53.2	0.5	54.4
	20	118 47.2	22.5	220 22.9	9.7	27 52.7	0.6	54.4
	21	133 47.4	. . 23.5	234 51.6	9.8	27 52.1	0.8	54.5
	22	148 47.6	24.5	249 20.4	9.7	27 51.3	0.9	54.5
	23	163 47.8	25.5	263 49.1	9.7	27 50.4	1.0	54.5
	29 00	178 48.0	N 3 26.4	278 17.8	9.7	S27 49.4	1.2	54.5
	01	193 48.2	27.4	292 46.5	9.7	27 48.2	1.3	54.5
	02	208 48.4	28.4	307 15.2	9.7	27 46.9	1.4	54.5
	03	223 48.5	. . 29.3	321 43.9	9.7	27 45.5	1.6	54.5
	04	238 48.7	30.3	336 12.6	9.7	27 43.9	1.7	54.6
	05	253 48.9	31.3	350 41.3	9.7	27 42.2	1.9	54.6
	06	268 49.1	N 3 32.3	5 10.0	9.7	S27 40.3	2.0	54.6
S	07	283 49.3	33.2	19 38.7	9.7	27 38.3	2.1	54.6
A	08	298 49.5	34.2	34 07.4	9.7	27 36.2	2.3	54.6
T	09	313 49.7	. . 35.2	48 36.1	9.7	27 33.9	2.4	54.6
U	10	328 49.9	36.2	63 04.8	9.7	27 31.5	2.5	54.7
R	11	343 50.1	37.1	77 33.5	9.7	27 29.0	2.7	54.7
D	12	358 50.2	N 3 38.1	92 02.2	9.7	S27 26.3	2.8	54.7
A	13	13 50.4	39.1	106 30.9	9.8	27 23.5	3.0	54.7
Y	14	28 50.6	40.0	120 59.7	9.7	27 20.5	3.1	54.7
	15	43 50.8	. . 41.0	135 28.4	9.7	27 17.4	3.2	54.8
	16	58 51.0	42.0	149 57.1	9.8	27 14.2	3.4	54.8
	17	73 51.2	43.0	164 25.9	9.8	27 10.8	3.5	54.8
	18	88 51.4	N 3 43.9	178 54.7	9.7	S27 07.3	3.6	54.8
	19	103 51.6	44.9	193 23.4	9.8	27 03.7	3.8	54.8
	20	118 51.7	45.9	207 52.2	9.8	26 59.9	3.9	54.9
	21	133 51.9	. . 46.8	222 21.0	9.8	26 56.0	4.1	54.9
	22	148 52.1	47.8	236 49.8	9.9	26 51.9	4.2	54.9
	23	163 52.3	48.8	251 18.7	9.8	26 47.7	4.3	54.9
	30 00	178 52.5	N 3 49.8	265 47.5	9.9	S26 43.4	4.4	54.9
	01	193 52.7	50.7	280 16.4	9.8	26 39.0	4.6	55.0
	02	208 52.9	51.7	294 45.2	9.9	26 34.4	4.8	55.0
	03	223 53.1	. . 52.7	309 14.1	10.0	26 29.6	4.8	55.0
	04	238 53.2	53.6	323 43.1	9.9	26 24.8	5.0	55.0
	05	253 53.4	54.6	338 12.0	10.0	26 19.8	5.2	55.0
	06	268 53.6	N 3 55.6	352 41.0	9.9	S26 14.6	5.2	55.1
	07	283 53.8	56.6	7 09.9	10.0	26 09.4	5.4	55.1
	08	298 54.0	57.5	21 38.9	10.1	26 04.0	5.5	55.1
S	09	313 54.2	. . 58.5	36 08.0	10.0	25 58.5	5.7	55.1
U	10	328 54.4	3 59.5	50 37.0	10.1	25 52.8	5.8	55.2
N	11	343 54.6	4 00.4	65 06.1	10.1	25 47.0	5.9	55.2
D	12	358 54.7	N 4 01.4	79 35.2	10.1	S25 41.1	6.1	55.2
A	13	13 54.9	02.4	94 04.3	10.1	25 35.0	6.2	55.2
Y	14	28 55.1	03.3	108 33.4	10.2	25 28.8	6.3	55.3
	15	43 55.3	. . 04.3	123 02.6	10.2	25 22.5	6.5	55.3
	16	58 55.5	05.3	137 31.8	10.2	25 16.0	6.6	55.3
	17	73 55.7	06.2	152 01.0	10.3	25 09.4	6.7	55.3
	18	88 55.9	N 4 07.2	166 30.3	10.3	S25 02.7	6.8	55.4
	19	103 56.1	08.2	180 59.6	10.3	24 55.9	7.0	55.4
	20	118 56.2	09.2	195 28.9	10.3	24 48.9	7.1	55.4
	21	133 56.4	. . 10.1	209 58.2	10.4	24 41.8	7.2	55.5
	22	148 56.6	11.1	224 27.6	10.4	24 34.6	7.4	55.5
	23	163 56.8	12.1	238 57.0	10.4	S24 27.2	7.5	55.5
		SD 16.0	d 1.0	SD 14.8		14.9		15.0

Lat.	Twilight Naut.	Twilight Civil	Sunrise	Moonrise 28	29	30	31
°	h m	h m	h m	h m	h m	h m	h m
N 72	02 07	03 57	05 10	▬	▬	▬	▬
N 70	02 41	04 11	05 16	▬	▬	▬	▬
68	03 05	04 23	05 21	▬	▬	▬	▬
66	03 23	04 32	05 25	▬	▬	▬	06 33
64	03 37	04 39	05 28	▬	▬	▬	05 34
62	03 49	04 46	05 31	04 19	05 07	05 04	05 00
60	03 59	04 51	05 33	03 07	04 00	04 25	04 35
N 58	04 07	04 56	05 36	02 32	03 25	03 57	04 15
56	04 14	05 00	05 38	02 07	02 59	03 36	03 59
54	04 21	05 04	05 40	01 46	02 39	03 18	03 45
52	04 26	05 07	05 41	01 30	02 22	03 03	03 32
50	04 31	05 10	05 43	01 15	02 08	02 49	03 21
45	04 41	05 16	05 46	00 46	01 38	02 22	02 58
N 40	04 49	05 21	05 48	00 23	01 15	02 01	02 40
35	04 56	05 25	05 51	00 04	00 56	01 43	02 24
30	05 01	05 29	05 53	24 40	00 40	01 28	02 11
20	05 08	05 34	05 56	24 12	00 12	01 02	01 48
N 10	05 13	05 38	05 59	23 48	24 39	00 39	01 28
0	05 17	05 41	06 01	23 26	24 18	00 18	01 09
S 10	05 18	05 43	06 04	23 04	23 57	24 50	00 50
20	05 19	05 44	06 06	22 40	23 34	24 30	00 30
30	05 17	05 45	06 09	22 13	23 08	24 07	00 07
35	05 16	05 45	06 11	21 56	22 52	23 53	24 56
40	05 14	05 45	06 12	21 37	22 34	23 37	24 43
45	05 11	05 45	06 14	21 14	22 12	23 18	24 28
S 50	05 07	05 44	06 16	20 45	21 44	22 53	24 09
52	05 05	05 44	06 17	20 30	21 31	22 42	24 00
54	05 02	05 43	06 19	20 13	21 15	22 29	23 49
56	04 59	05 43	06 20	19 53	20 56	22 13	23 38
58	04 56	05 42	06 21	19 27	20 33	21 55	23 25
S 60	04 52	05 41	06 23	18 53	20 03	21 32	23 09

Lat.	Sunset	Twilight Civil	Twilight Naut.	Moonset 28	29	30	31
°	h m	h m	h m	h m	h m	h m	h m
N 72	19 02	20 16	22 10	▬	▬	▬	▬
N 70	18 56	20 01	21 34	▬	▬	▬	▬
68	18 51	19 50	21 09	▬	▬	▬	▬
66	18 47	19 40	20 50	▬	▬	▬	08 21
64	18 43	19 32	20 35	▬	▬	▬	09 20
62	18 40	19 26	20 23	05 13	06 12	08 03	09 53
60	18 37	19 20	20 13	06 25	07 20	08 43	10 17
N 58	18 35	19 15	20 04	07 00	07 55	09 10	10 37
56	18 33	19 11	19 57	07 25	08 20	09 31	10 53
54	18 31	19 07	19 50	07 46	08 40	09 48	11 06
52	18 29	19 03	19 45	08 03	08 57	10 03	11 18
50	18 28	19 00	19 39	08 17	09 11	10 16	11 29
45	18 24	18 54	19 29	08 47	09 41	10 43	11 51
N 40	18 22	18 49	19 21	09 10	10 03	11 03	12 08
35	18 19	18 45	19 14	09 29	10 22	11 21	12 23
30	18 17	18 41	19 09	09 46	10 39	11 36	12 36
20	18 14	18 36	19 01	10 13	11 06	12 01	12 57
N 10	18 11	18 32	18 56	10 37	11 29	12 23	13 16
0	18 08	18 29	18 53	10 59	11 51	12 43	13 33
S 10	18 05	18 26	18 51	11 21	12 13	13 03	13 50
20	18 03	18 25	18 50	11 45	12 36	13 24	14 09
30	18 00	18 24	18 51	12 13	13 03	13 49	14 30
35	17 58	18 23	18 53	12 29	13 19	14 03	14 42
40	17 56	18 23	18 55	12 48	13 38	14 20	14 56
45	17 54	18 24	18 58	13 11	14 00	14 40	15 12
S 50	17 52	18 24	19 02	13 41	14 28	15 05	15 33
52	17 51	18 24	19 04	13 55	14 42	15 17	15 42
54	17 50	18 25	19 06	14 12	14 58	15 30	15 53
56	17 48	18 25	19 09	14 33	15 17	15 46	16 05
58	17 47	18 26	19 12	14 58	15 40	16 05	16 19
S 60	17 45	18 27	19 15	15 33	16 11	16 28	16 36

Day	SUN Eqn. of Time 00^h	SUN Eqn. of Time 12^h	SUN Mer. Pass.	MOON Mer. Pass. Upper	MOON Mer. Pass. Lower	MOON Age	MOON Phase
d	m s	m s	h m	h m	h m	d %	
28	05 07	04 58	12 05	04 47	17 13	21 63	
29	04 48	04 39	12 05	05 39	18 05	22 54	◑
30	04 30	04 21	12 04	06 30	18 56	23 44	

	UT	ARIES	VENUS −3.8		MARS +0.8		JUPITER −2.2		SATURN +0.4	
	d h	GHA ° ′	GHA ° ′	Dec ° ′	GHA ° ′	Dec ° ′	GHA ° ′	Dec ° ′	GHA ° ′	Dec ° ′
	31 00	188 44.4	195 14.2	S 4 23.0	87 22.1	N25 20.5	257 05.5	S21 55.0	33 28.9	N12 16.0
	01	203 46.9	210 13.8	21.8	102 23.3	20.3	272 07.6	54.9	48 31.5	16.0
	02	218 49.3	225 13.4	20.6	117 24.6	20.2	287 09.8	54.9	63 34.1	16.1
	03	233 51.8	240 13.0	. . 19.4	132 25.8	. . 20.1	302 12.0	. . 54.8	78 36.7	. . 16.1
	04	248 54.3	255 12.6	18.2	147 27.1	20.0	317 14.1	54.8	93 39.3	16.2
	05	263 56.7	270 12.2	17.0	162 28.3	19.8	332 16.3	54.8	108 41.9	16.2
	06	278 59.2	285 11.8	S 4 15.8	177 29.5	N25 19.7	347 18.4	S21 54.7	123 44.5	N12 16.3
	07	294 01.7	300 11.4	14.6	192 30.8	19.6	2 20.6	54.7	138 47.1	16.3
	08	309 04.1	315 11.1	13.4	207 32.0	19.5	17 22.8	54.7	153 49.7	16.4
M	09	324 06.6	330 10.7	. . 12.2	222 33.3	. . 19.3	32 24.9	. . 54.6	168 52.3	. . 16.4
O	10	339 09.0	345 10.3	11.0	237 34.5	19.2	47 27.1	54.6	183 54.8	16.4
N	11	354 11.5	0 09.9	09.8	252 35.8	19.1	62 29.2	54.5	198 57.4	16.5
D	12	9 14.0	15 09.5	S 4 08.6	267 37.0	N25 18.9	77 31.4	S21 54.5	214 00.0	N12 16.5
A	13	24 16.4	30 09.1	07.4	282 38.3	18.8	92 33.6	54.5	229 02.6	16.6
Y	14	39 18.9	45 08.7	06.3	297 39.5	18.7	107 35.7	54.4	244 05.2	16.6
	15	54 21.4	60 08.3	. . 05.1	312 40.7	. . 18.6	122 37.9	. . 54.4	259 07.8	. . 16.7
	16	69 23.8	75 07.9	03.9	327 42.0	18.4	137 40.1	54.4	274 10.4	16.7
	17	84 26.3	90 07.6	02.7	342 43.2	18.3	152 42.2	54.3	289 13.0	16.8
	18	99 28.8	105 07.2	S 4 01.5	357 44.5	N25 18.2	167 44.4	S21 54.3	304 15.6	N12 16.8
	19	114 31.2	120 06.8	4 00.3	12 45.7	18.0	182 46.5	54.2	319 18.2	16.9
	20	129 33.7	135 06.4	3 59.1	27 47.0	17.9	197 48.7	54.2	334 20.8	16.9
	21	144 36.1	150 06.0	. . 57.9	42 48.2	. . 17.8	212 50.9	. . 54.2	349 23.4	. . 16.9
	22	159 38.6	165 05.6	56.7	57 49.4	17.7	227 53.0	54.1	4 26.0	17.0
	23	174 41.1	180 05.2	55.5	72 50.7	17.5	242 55.2	54.1	19 28.5	17.0
	1 00	189 43.5	195 04.8	S 3 54.3	87 51.9	N25 17.4	257 57.4	S21 54.1	34 31.1	N12 17.1
	01	204 46.0	210 04.5	53.1	102 53.2	17.3	272 59.5	54.0	49 33.7	17.1
	02	219 48.5	225 04.1	51.9	117 54.4	17.1	288 01.7	54.0	64 36.3	17.2
	03	234 50.9	240 03.7	. . 50.7	132 55.6	. . 17.0	303 03.9	. . 54.0	79 38.9	. . 17.2
	04	249 53.4	255 03.3	49.5	147 56.9	16.9	318 06.0	53.9	94 41.5	17.3
	05	264 55.9	270 02.9	48.3	162 58.1	16.7	333 08.2	53.9	109 44.1	17.3
	06	279 58.3	285 02.5	S 3 47.1	177 59.3	N25 16.6	348 10.4	S21 53.8	124 46.7	N12 17.4
	07	295 00.8	300 02.1	45.9	193 00.6	16.5	3 12.5	53.8	139 49.3	17.4
T	08	310 03.3	315 01.8	44.7	208 01.8	16.3	18 14.7	53.8	154 51.9	17.4
U	09	325 05.7	330 01.4	. . 43.5	223 03.1	. . 16.2	33 16.9	. . 53.7	169 54.5	. . 17.5
E	10	340 08.2	345 01.0	42.3	238 04.3	16.1	48 19.0	53.7	184 57.0	17.5
S	11	355 10.6	0 00.6	41.1	253 05.5	15.9	63 21.2	53.7	199 59.6	17.6
D	12	10 13.1	15 00.2	S 3 39.9	268 06.8	N25 15.8	78 23.4	S21 53.6	215 02.2	N12 17.6
	13	25 15.6	29 59.8	38.7	283 08.0	15.7	93 25.5	53.6	230 04.8	17.7
A	14	40 18.0	44 59.4	37.5	298 09.2	15.6	108 27.7	53.6	245 07.4	17.7
Y	15	55 20.5	59 59.1	. . 36.2	313 10.5	. . 15.4	123 29.9	. . 53.5	260 10.0	. . 17.8
	16	70 23.0	74 58.7	35.0	328 11.7	15.3	138 32.0	53.5	275 12.6	17.8
	17	85 25.4	89 58.3	33.8	343 12.9	15.2	153 34.2	53.4	290 15.2	17.9
	18	100 27.9	104 57.9	S 3 32.6	358 14.2	N25 15.0	168 36.4	S21 53.4	305 17.8	N12 17.9
	19	115 30.4	119 57.5	31.4	13 15.4	14.9	183 38.6	53.4	320 20.3	17.9
	20	130 32.8	134 57.1	30.2	28 16.6	14.8	198 40.7	53.3	335 22.9	18.0
	21	145 35.3	149 56.8	. . 29.0	43 17.9	. . 14.6	213 42.9	. . 53.3	350 25.5	. . 18.0
	22	160 37.8	164 56.4	27.8	58 19.1	14.5	228 45.1	53.3	5 28.1	18.1
	23	175 40.2	179 56.0	26.6	73 20.3	14.4	243 47.2	53.2	20 30.7	18.1
	2 00	190 42.7	194 55.6	S 3 25.4	88 21.6	N25 14.2	258 49.4	S21 53.2	35 33.3	N12 18.2
	01	205 45.1	209 55.2	24.2	103 22.8	14.1	273 51.6	53.2	50 35.9	18.2
	02	220 47.6	224 54.8	23.0	118 24.0	13.9	288 53.8	53.1	65 38.5	18.2
	03	235 50.1	239 54.5	. . 21.8	133 25.3	. . 13.8	303 55.9	. . 53.1	80 41.0	. . 18.3
	04	250 52.5	254 54.1	20.6	148 26.5	13.7	318 58.1	53.0	95 43.6	18.3
	05	265 55.0	269 53.7	19.4	163 27.7	13.5	334 00.3	53.0	110 46.2	18.4
	06	280 57.5	284 53.3	S 3 18.2	178 29.0	N25 13.4	349 02.4	S21 53.0	125 48.8	N12 18.4
W	07	295 59.9	299 52.9	17.0	193 30.2	13.3	4 04.6	52.9	140 51.4	18.5
E	08	311 02.4	314 52.5	15.8	208 31.4	13.1	19 06.8	52.9	155 54.0	18.5
D	09	326 04.9	329 52.2	. . 14.6	223 32.6	. . 13.0	34 09.0	. . 52.9	170 56.6	. . 18.6
N	10	341 07.3	344 51.8	13.4	238 33.9	12.9	49 11.1	52.8	185 59.2	18.6
E	11	356 09.8	359 51.4	12.2	253 35.1	12.7	64 13.3	52.8	201 01.7	18.6
S	12	11 12.2	14 51.0	S 3 11.0	268 36.3	N25 12.6	79 15.5	S21 52.8	216 04.3	N12 18.7
D	13	26 14.7	29 50.6	09.7	283 37.6	12.5	94 17.7	52.7	231 06.9	18.7
A	14	41 17.2	44 50.2	08.5	298 38.8	12.3	109 19.8	52.7	246 09.5	18.8
Y	15	56 19.6	59 49.9	. . 07.3	313 40.0	. . 12.2	124 22.0	. . 52.6	261 12.1	. . 18.8
	16	71 22.1	74 49.5	06.1	328 41.2	12.0	139 24.2	52.6	276 14.7	18.9
	17	86 24.6	89 49.1	04.9	343 42.5	11.9	154 26.4	52.6	291 17.3	18.9
	18	101 27.0	104 48.7	S 3 03.7	358 43.7	N25 11.8	169 28.5	S21 52.5	306 19.8	N12 18.9
	19	116 29.5	119 48.3	02.5	13 44.9	11.6	184 30.7	52.5	321 22.4	19.0
	20	131 32.0	134 48.0	01.3	28 46.1	11.5	199 32.9	52.5	336 25.0	19.0
	21	146 34.4	149 47.6	3 00.1	43 47.4	. . 11.4	214 35.1	. . 52.4	351 27.6	. . 19.1
	22	161 36.9	164 47.2	2 58.9	58 48.6	11.2	229 37.3	52.4	6 30.2	19.1
	23	176 39.4	179 46.8	S 2 57.7	73 49.8	11.1	244 39.4	52.4	21 32.8	19.2
	Mer. Pass.	h m 11 19.2	v −0.4	d 1.2	v 1.2	d 0.1	v 2.2	d 0.0	v 2.6	d 0.0

STARS

Name	SHA ° ′	Dec ° ′
Acamar	315 21.6	S40 16.4
Achernar	335 30.0	S57 11.7
Acrux	173 13.4	S63 08.9
Adhara	255 15.6	S28 59.2
Aldebaran	290 54.1	N16 31.6
Alioth	166 23.3	N55 54.7
Alkaid	153 01.3	N49 16.1
Al Na'ir	27 48.8	S46 55.2
Alnilam	275 50.5	S 1 11.8
Alphard	217 59.8	S 8 41.8
Alphecca	126 14.0	N26 40.9
Alpheratz	357 48.1	N29 08.1
Altair	62 12.2	N 8 53.2
Ankaa	353 19.8	S42 15.7
Antares	112 30.9	S26 27.1
Arcturus	145 59.0	N19 08.1
Atria	107 36.2	S69 02.4
Avior	234 19.6	S59 32.4
Bellatrix	278 36.4	N 6 21.4
Betelgeuse	271 05.6	N 7 24.5
Canopus	263 58.0	S52 42.2
Capella	280 40.5	N46 00.6
Deneb	49 34.5	N45 18.3
Denebola	182 37.3	N14 31.4
Diphda	349 00.1	S17 56.5
Dubhe	193 55.5	N61 42.4
Elnath	278 17.7	N28 37.0
Eltanin	90 47.8	N51 28.8
Enif	33 51.2	N 9 54.6
Fomalhaut	15 28.5	S29 34.7
Gacrux	172 05.1	S57 09.7
Gienah	175 56.1	S17 35.5
Hadar	148 53.2	S60 24.8
Hamal	328 05.6	N23 30.1
Kaus Aust.	83 49.0	S34 22.9
Kochab	137 18.3	N74 07.0
Markab	13 42.6	N15 14.8
Menkar	314 19.4	N 4 07.3
Menkent	148 12.0	S36 24.8
Miaplacidus	221 40.4	S69 45.3
Mirfak	308 46.5	N49 53.6
Nunki	76 03.2	S26 17.2
Peacock	53 25.5	S56 42.4
Pollux	243 32.4	N28 00.5
Procyon	245 03.8	N 5 12.2
Rasalhague	96 10.0	N12 32.9
Regulus	207 47.4	N11 55.5
Rigel	281 16.0	S 8 11.6
Rigil Kent.	139 56.8	S60 52.2
Sabik	102 16.9	S15 44.3
Schedar	349 45.9	N56 35.0
Shaula	96 27.2	S37 06.6
Sirius	258 37.2	S16 43.8
Spica	158 35.1	S11 12.5
Suhail	222 55.2	S43 28.2
Vega	80 41.6	N38 47.1
Zuben'ubi	137 09.5	S16 04.8

	SHA ° ′	Mer. Pass. h m
Venus	5 21.3	11 00
Mars	258 08.4	18 07
Jupiter	68 13.8	6 47
Saturn	204 47.6	21 38

UT d h	SUN GHA ° ′	SUN Dec ° ′	MOON GHA ° ′	v ′	MOON Dec ° ′	d ′	HP ′
31 00	178 57.0	N 4 13.0	253 26.4	10.5	S24 19.7	7.6	55.5
01	193 57.2	14.0	267 55.9	10.5	24 12.1	7.7	55.6
02	208 57.4	15.0	282 25.4	10.5	24 04.4	7.9	55.6
03	223 57.6	. . 15.9	296 54.9	10.5	23 56.5	8.0	55.6
04	238 57.7	16.9	311 24.4	10.6	23 48.5	8.1	55.6
05	253 57.9	17.9	325 54.0	10.7	23 40.4	8.2	55.7
06	268 58.1	N 4 18.8	340 23.7	10.6	S23 32.2	8.4	55.7
07	283 58.3	19.8	354 53.3	10.7	23 23.8	8.5	55.7
M 08	298 58.5	20.8	9 23.0	10.7	23 15.3	8.6	55.8
O 09	313 58.7	. . 21.7	23 52.7	10.8	23 06.7	8.7	55.8
N 10	328 58.9	22.7	38 22.5	10.8	22 58.0	8.9	55.8
D 11	343 59.0	23.7	52 52.3	10.8	22 49.1	8.9	55.9
A 12	358 59.2	N 4 24.6	67 22.1	10.8	S22 40.2	9.1	55.9
Y 13	13 59.4	25.6	81 51.9	10.9	22 31.1	9.3	55.9
14	28 59.6	26.6	96 21.8	11.0	22 21.8	9.3	56.0
15	43 59.8	. . 27.5	110 51.8	10.9	22 12.5	9.4	56.0
16	59 00.0	28.5	125 21.7	11.0	22 03.1	9.6	56.0
17	74 00.2	29.5	139 51.7	11.0	21 53.5	9.7	56.0
18	89 00.3	N 4 30.4	154 21.7	11.1	S21 43.8	9.8	56.1
19	104 00.5	31.4	168 51.8	11.1	21 34.0	9.9	56.1
20	119 00.7	32.4	183 21.9	11.1	21 24.1	10.1	56.1
21	134 00.9	. . 33.3	197 52.0	11.2	21 14.0	10.1	56.2
22	149 01.1	34.3	212 22.2	11.2	21 03.9	10.3	56.2
23	164 01.3	35.3	226 52.4	11.2	20 53.6	10.4	56.2
1 00	179 01.5	N 4 36.2	241 22.6	11.3	S20 43.2	10.4	56.3
01	194 01.6	37.2	255 52.9	11.3	20 32.8	10.7	56.3
02	209 01.8	38.1	270 23.2	11.3	20 22.1	10.7	56.3
03	224 02.0	. . 39.1	284 53.5	11.4	20 11.4	10.8	56.4
04	239 02.2	40.1	299 23.9	11.4	20 00.6	10.9	56.4
05	254 02.4	41.0	313 54.3	11.4	19 49.7	11.1	56.4
06	269 02.6	N 4 42.0	328 24.7	11.5	S19 38.6	11.1	56.5
07	284 02.8	43.0	342 55.2	11.4	19 27.5	11.3	56.5
T 08	299 02.9	43.9	357 25.6	11.6	19 16.2	11.4	56.5
U 09	314 03.1	. . 44.9	11 56.2	11.5	19 04.8	11.4	56.6
E 10	329 03.3	45.9	26 26.7	11.6	18 53.4	11.6	56.6
S 11	344 03.5	46.8	40 57.3	11.6	18 41.8	11.7	56.7
D 12	359 03.7	N 4 47.8	55 27.9	11.7	S18 30.1	11.8	56.7
A 13	14 03.9	48.7	69 58.6	11.7	18 18.3	11.9	56.7
Y 14	29 04.1	49.7	84 29.3	11.7	18 06.4	12.0	56.8
15	44 04.2	. . 50.7	99 00.0	11.7	17 54.4	12.1	56.8
16	59 04.4	51.6	113 30.7	11.8	17 42.3	12.2	56.8
17	74 04.6	52.6	128 01.5	11.8	17 30.1	12.3	56.9
18	89 04.8	N 4 53.6	142 32.3	11.8	S17 17.8	12.4	56.9
19	104 05.0	54.5	157 03.1	11.9	17 05.4	12.5	56.9
20	119 05.2	55.5	171 34.0	11.9	16 52.9	12.6	57.0
21	134 05.3	. . 56.4	186 04.9	11.9	16 40.3	12.6	57.0
22	149 05.5	57.4	200 35.8	11.9	16 27.7	12.8	57.0
23	164 05.7	58.4	215 06.7	12.0	16 14.9	12.9	57.1
2 00	179 05.9	N 4 59.3	229 37.7	12.0	S16 02.0	13.0	57.1
01	194 06.1	5 00.3	244 08.7	12.0	15 49.0	13.0	57.2
02	209 06.3	01.2	258 39.7	12.0	15 36.0	13.2	57.2
03	224 06.4	. . 02.2	273 10.7	12.1	15 22.8	13.3	57.2
04	239 06.6	03.2	287 41.8	12.0	15 09.5	13.3	57.3
05	254 06.8	04.1	302 12.8	12.1	14 56.2	13.4	57.3
06	269 07.0	N 5 05.1	316 43.9	12.2	S14 42.8	13.5	57.3
W 07	284 07.2	06.0	331 15.1	12.1	14 29.3	13.6	57.4
E 08	299 07.4	07.0	345 46.2	12.2	14 15.7	13.7	57.4
D 09	314 07.5	. . 08.0	0 17.4	12.2	14 02.0	13.8	57.5
N 10	329 07.7	08.9	14 48.6	12.2	13 48.2	13.9	57.5
E 11	344 07.9	09.9	29 19.8	12.2	13 34.3	13.9	57.5
S 12	359 08.1	N 5 10.8	43 51.0	12.2	S13 20.4	14.1	57.6
D 13	14 08.3	11.8	58 22.2	12.3	13 06.3	14.1	57.6
A 14	29 08.5	12.8	72 53.5	12.2	12 52.2	14.2	57.6
Y 15	44 08.6	. . 13.7	87 24.7	12.3	12 38.0	14.2	57.7
16	59 08.8	14.7	101 56.0	12.3	12 23.8	14.4	57.7
17	74 09.0	15.6	116 27.3	12.3	12 09.4	14.4	57.8
18	89 09.2	N 5 16.6	130 58.6	12.3	S11 55.0	14.5	57.8
19	104 09.4	17.6	145 29.9	12.4	11 40.5	14.6	57.8
20	119 09.6	18.5	160 01.3	12.3	11 25.9	14.7	57.9
21	134 09.7	. . 19.5	174 32.6	12.4	11 11.2	14.7	57.9
22	149 09.9	20.4	189 04.0	12.3	10 56.5	14.8	57.9
23	164 10.1	21.4	203 35.3	12.4	S10 41.7	14.9	58.0
	SD 16.0	*d* 1.0	SD		15.2	15.4	15.7

Lat. °	Twilight Naut. h m	Twilight Civil h m	Sunrise h m	Moonrise 31 h m	Moonrise 1 h m	Moonrise 2 h m	Moonrise 3 h m
N 72	01 34	03 39	04 54	▬	▬	06 30	05 37
N 70	02 18	03 56	05 02	▬	07 17	06 00	05 24
68	02 47	04 09	05 08	▬	06 17	05 38	05 13
66	03 08	04 19	05 13	06 33	05 42	05 20	05 04
64	03 24	04 28	05 17	05 34	05 17	05 05	04 56
62	03 37	04 35	05 21	05 00	04 57	04 53	04 49
60	03 48	04 42	05 24	04 35	04 40	04 42	04 43
N 58	03 57	04 47	05 27	04 15	04 26	04 33	04 38
56	04 05	04 52	05 30	03 59	04 14	04 25	04 33
54	04 12	04 56	05 32	03 45	04 04	04 18	04 29
52	04 19	05 00	05 34	03 32	03 54	04 11	04 26
50	04 24	05 03	05 36	03 21	03 46	04 05	04 22
45	04 35	05 11	05 40	02 58	03 28	03 53	04 14
N 40	04 44	05 16	05 44	02 40	03 13	03 42	04 08
35	04 51	05 21	05 47	02 24	03 01	03 33	04 03
30	04 57	05 25	05 49	02 11	02 50	03 25	03 58
20	05 06	05 31	05 53	01 48	02 31	03 11	03 49
N 10	05 12	05 36	05 57	01 28	02 14	02 59	03 42
0	05 16	05 40	06 00	01 09	01 59	02 47	03 35
S 10	05 18	05 43	06 04	00 50	01 43	02 36	03 28
20	05 20	05 45	06 07	00 30	01 27	02 23	03 20
30	05 19	05 47	06 11	00 07	01 07	02 09	03 12
35	05 18	05 48	06 13	24 56	00 56	02 01	03 07
40	05 17	05 48	06 15	24 43	00 43	01 51	03 01
45	05 15	05 49	06 18	24 28	00 28	01 40	02 54
S 50	05 11	05 49	06 21	24 09	00 09	01 27	02 46
52	05 10	05 49	06 23	24 00	00 00	01 20	02 43
54	05 08	05 49	06 24	23 49	25 13	01 13	02 39
56	05 06	05 49	06 26	23 38	25 05	01 05	02 34
58	05 03	05 49	06 28	23 25	24 56	00 56	02 29
S 60	05 00	05 48	06 30	23 09	24 46	00 46	02 23

Lat. °	Sunset h m	Twilight Civil h m	Twilight Naut. h m	Moonset 31 h m	Moonset 1 h m	Moonset 2 h m	Moonset 3 h m
N 72	19 16	20 33	22 46	▬	▬	11 54	14 28
N 70	19 08	20 15	21 56	▬	09 24	12 22	14 38
68	19 02	20 02	21 26	▬	10 22	12 43	14 47
66	18 57	19 51	21 04	08 21	10 56	12 59	14 54
64	18 52	19 42	20 47	09 20	11 20	13 12	15 00
62	18 48	19 34	20 33	09 53	11 39	13 23	15 05
60	18 45	19 28	20 22	10 17	11 55	13 32	15 09
N 58	18 42	19 22	20 12	10 37	12 08	13 40	15 13
56	18 39	19 17	20 04	10 53	12 19	13 47	15 17
54	18 37	19 13	19 57	11 06	12 29	13 54	15 20
52	18 34	19 09	19 50	11 18	12 38	13 59	15 22
50	18 32	19 05	19 45	11 29	12 46	14 05	15 25
45	18 28	18 58	19 33	11 51	13 02	14 16	15 30
N 40	18 25	18 52	19 24	12 08	13 16	14 25	15 35
35	18 22	18 47	19 17	12 23	13 27	14 32	15 39
30	18 19	18 43	19 11	12 36	13 37	14 39	15 42
20	18 14	18 37	19 02	12 57	13 54	14 51	15 48
N 10	18 11	18 32	18 56	13 16	14 09	15 01	15 53
0	18 07	18 28	18 52	13 33	14 22	15 10	15 57
S 10	18 04	18 25	18 49	13 50	14 36	15 19	16 02
20	18 00	18 22	18 48	14 09	14 50	15 29	16 07
30	17 56	18 20	18 48	14 30	15 07	15 40	16 12
35	17 54	18 19	18 49	14 42	15 16	15 47	16 16
40	17 52	18 19	18 50	14 56	15 27	15 54	16 19
45	17 49	18 18	18 52	15 12	15 39	16 02	16 23
S 50	17 46	18 18	18 55	15 33	15 54	16 12	16 28
52	17 44	18 18	18 57	15 42	16 02	16 17	16 30
54	17 42	18 18	18 58	15 53	16 09	16 22	16 32
56	17 41	18 18	19 01	16 05	16 18	16 27	16 35
58	17 39	18 18	19 03	16 19	16 28	16 34	16 38
S 60	17 36	18 18	19 06	16 36	16 39	16 41	16 41

Day	SUN Eqn. of Time 00^h	SUN Eqn. of Time 12^h	SUN Mer. Pass.	MOON Mer. Pass. Upper	MOON Mer. Pass. Lower	MOON Age	MOON Phase
d	m s	m s	h m	h m	h m	d	%
31	04 12	04 03	12 04	07 21	19 46	24	35
1	03 55	03 46	12 04	08 11	20 35	25	25
2	03 37	03 28	12 03	08 59	21 23	26	17

UT	ARIES	VENUS −3.8		MARS +0.9		JUPITER −2.2		SATURN +0.4		STARS		
d h	GHA ° ′	GHA ° ′	Dec ° ′	GHA ° ′	Dec ° ′	GHA ° ′	Dec ° ′	GHA ° ′	Dec ° ′	Name	SHA ° ′	Dec ° ′
3 00 THURSDAY	191 41.8	194 46.4	S 2 56.5	88 51.0	N25 10.9	259 41.6	S21 52.3	36 35.4	N12 19.2	Acamar	315 21.6	S40 16.4
01	206 44.3	209 46.1	55.3	103 52.3	10.8	274 43.8	52.3	51 37.9	19.2	Achernar	335 30.0	S57 11.7
02	221 46.7	224 45.7	54.1	118 53.5	10.7	289 46.0	52.3	66 40.5	19.3	Acrux	173 13.4	S63 08.9
03	236 49.2	239 45.3	. . 52.8	133 54.7	. . 10.5	304 48.2	. . 52.2	81 43.1	. . 19.3	Adhara	255 15.7	S28 59.2
04	251 51.7	254 44.9	51.6	148 55.9	10.4	319 50.3	52.2	96 45.7	19.4	Aldebaran	290 54.1	N16 31.6
05	266 54.1	269 44.5	50.4	163 57.1	10.2	334 52.5	52.2	111 48.3	19.4			
06	281 56.6	284 44.2	S 2 49.2	178 58.4	N25 10.1	349 54.7	S21 52.1	126 50.9	N12 19.5	Alioth	166 23.3	N55 54.8
07	296 59.1	299 43.8	48.0	193 59.6	10.0	4 56.9	52.1	141 53.4	19.5	Alkaid	153 01.3	N49 16.1
08	312 01.5	314 43.4	46.8	209 00.8	09.8	19 59.1	52.0	156 56.0	19.5	Al Na'ir	27 48.8	S46 55.2
09	327 04.0	329 43.0	. . 45.6	224 02.0	. . 09.7	35 01.2	. . 52.0	171 58.6	. . 19.6	Alnilam	275 50.5	S 1 11.8
10	342 06.5	344 42.6	44.4	239 03.3	09.5	50 03.4	52.0	187 01.2	19.6	Alphard	217 59.8	S 8 41.8
11	357 08.9	359 42.3	43.2	254 04.5	09.4	65 05.6	51.9	202 03.8	19.7			
12	12 11.4	14 41.9	S 2 42.0	269 05.7	N25 09.3	80 07.8	S21 51.9	217 06.4	N12 19.7	Alphecca	126 14.0	N26 40.9
13	27 13.9	29 41.5	40.7	284 06.9	09.1	95 10.0	51.9	232 08.9	19.8	Alpheratz	357 48.0	N29 08.1
14	42 16.3	44 41.1	39.5	299 08.1	09.0	110 12.1	51.8	247 11.5	19.8	Altair	62 12.2	N 8 53.2
15	57 18.8	59 40.8	. . 38.3	314 09.4	. . 08.8	125 14.3	. . 51.8	262 14.1	. . 19.8	Ankaa	353 19.8	S42 15.7
16	72 21.2	74 40.4	37.1	329 10.6	08.7	140 16.5	51.8	277 16.7	19.9	Antares	112 30.9	S26 27.1
17	87 23.7	89 40.0	35.9	344 11.8	08.6	155 18.7	51.7	292 19.3	19.9			
18	102 26.2	104 39.6	S 2 34.7	359 13.0	N25 08.4	170 20.9	S21 51.7	307 21.9	N12 20.0	Arcturus	145 58.9	N19 08.1
19	117 28.6	119 39.2	33.5	14 14.2	08.3	185 23.1	51.7	322 24.4	20.0	Atria	107 36.2	S69 02.5
20	132 31.1	134 38.9	32.3	29 15.4	08.1	200 25.2	51.6	337 27.0	20.0	Avior	234 19.6	S59 32.4
21	147 33.6	149 38.5	. . 31.1	44 16.7	. . 08.0	215 27.4	. . 51.6	352 29.6	. . 20.1	Bellatrix	278 36.4	N 6 21.4
22	162 36.0	164 38.1	29.9	59 17.9	07.8	230 29.6	51.6	7 32.2	20.1	Betelgeuse	271 05.7	N 7 24.5
23	177 38.5	179 37.7	28.6	74 19.1	07.7	245 31.8	51.5	22 34.8	20.2			
4 00 FRIDAY	192 41.0	194 37.4	S 2 27.4	89 20.3	N25 07.6	260 34.0	S21 51.5	37 37.3	N12 20.2	Canopus	263 58.0	S52 42.2
01	207 43.4	209 37.0	26.2	104 21.5	07.4	275 36.2	51.5	52 39.9	20.2	Capella	280 40.5	N46 00.6
02	222 45.9	224 36.6	25.0	119 22.7	07.3	290 38.4	51.4	67 42.5	20.3	Deneb	49 34.5	N45 18.2
03	237 48.3	239 36.2	. . 23.8	134 24.0	. . 07.1	305 40.5	. . 51.4	82 45.1	. . 20.3	Denebola	182 37.3	N14 31.4
04	252 50.8	254 35.8	22.6	149 25.2	07.0	320 42.7	51.3	97 47.7	20.4	Diphda	349 00.1	S17 56.5
05	267 53.3	269 35.5	21.4	164 26.4	06.8	335 44.9	51.3	112 50.2	20.4			
06	282 55.7	284 35.1	S 2 20.2	179 27.6	N25 06.7	350 47.1	S21 51.3	127 52.8	N12 20.5	Dubhe	193 55.5	N61 42.4
07	297 58.2	299 34.7	18.9	194 28.8	06.6	5 49.3	51.2	142 55.4	20.5	Elnath	278 17.8	N28 37.0
08	313 00.7	314 34.3	17.7	209 30.0	06.4	20 51.5	51.2	157 58.0	20.5	Eltanin	90 47.8	N51 28.8
09	328 03.1	329 34.0	. . 16.5	224 31.2	. . 06.3	35 53.7	. . 51.2	173 00.6	. . 20.6	Enif	33 51.2	N 9 54.6
10	343 05.6	344 33.6	15.3	239 32.4	06.1	50 55.9	51.1	188 03.1	20.6	Fomalhaut	15 28.5	S29 34.7
11	358 08.1	359 33.2	14.1	254 33.7	06.0	65 58.0	51.1	203 05.7	20.7			
12	13 10.5	14 32.8	S 2 12.9	269 34.9	N25 05.8	81 00.2	S21 51.1	218 08.3	N12 20.7	Gacrux	172 05.1	S57 09.7
13	28 13.0	29 32.5	11.7	284 36.1	05.7	96 02.4	51.0	233 10.9	20.7	Gienah	175 56.1	S17 35.5
14	43 15.5	44 32.1	10.4	299 37.3	05.5	111 04.6	51.0	248 13.5	20.8	Hadar	148 53.2	S60 24.9
15	58 17.9	59 31.7	. . 09.2	314 38.5	. . 05.4	126 06.8	. . 51.0	263 16.0	. . 20.8	Hamal	328 05.6	N23 30.1
16	73 20.4	74 31.3	08.0	329 39.7	05.3	141 09.0	50.9	278 18.6	20.9	Kaus Aust.	83 49.0	S34 22.9
17	88 22.8	89 31.0	06.8	344 40.9	05.1	156 11.2	50.9	293 21.2	20.9			
18	103 25.3	104 30.6	S 2 05.6	359 42.1	N25 05.0	171 13.4	S21 50.9	308 23.8	N12 20.9	Kochab	137 18.3	N74 07.0
19	118 27.8	119 30.2	04.4	14 43.3	04.8	186 15.6	50.8	323 26.4	21.0	Markab	13 42.6	N15 14.8
20	133 30.2	134 29.8	03.2	29 44.6	04.7	201 17.8	50.8	338 28.9	21.0	Menkar	314 19.5	N 4 07.3
21	148 32.7	149 29.5	. . 02.0	44 45.8	. . 04.5	216 19.9	. . 50.8	353 31.5	. . 21.1	Menkent	148 12.0	S36 24.8
22	163 35.2	164 29.1	2 00.7	59 47.0	04.4	231 22.1	50.7	8 34.1	21.1	Miaplacidus	221 40.4	S69 45.3
23	178 37.6	179 28.7	1 59.5	74 48.2	04.2	246 24.3	50.7	23 36.7	21.1			
5 00 SATURDAY	193 40.1	194 28.3	S 1 58.3	89 49.4	N25 04.1	261 26.5	S21 50.7	38 39.3	N12 21.2	Mirfak	308 46.6	N49 53.6
01	208 42.6	209 28.0	57.1	104 50.6	03.9	276 28.7	50.6	53 41.8	21.2	Nunki	76 03.2	S26 17.2
02	223 45.0	224 27.6	55.9	119 51.8	03.8	291 30.9	50.6	68 44.4	21.3	Peacock	53 25.4	S56 42.4
03	238 47.5	239 27.2	. . 54.7	134 53.0	. . 03.6	306 33.1	. . 50.6	83 47.0	. . 21.3	Pollux	243 32.4	N28 00.5
04	253 49.9	254 26.8	53.4	149 54.2	03.5	321 35.3	50.5	98 49.6	21.3	Procyon	245 03.8	N 5 12.2
05	268 52.4	269 26.5	52.2	164 55.4	03.3	336 37.5	50.5	113 52.1	21.4			
06	283 54.9	284 26.1	S 1 51.0	179 56.6	N25 03.2	351 39.7	S21 50.5	128 54.7	N12 21.4	Rasalhague	96 10.0	N12 32.9
07	298 57.3	299 25.7	49.8	194 57.8	03.0	6 41.9	50.4	143 57.3	21.5	Regulus	207 47.4	N11 55.5
08	313 59.8	314 25.3	48.6	209 59.0	02.9	21 44.1	50.4	158 59.9	21.5	Rigel	281 16.0	S 8 11.6
09	329 02.3	329 25.0	. . 47.4	225 00.3	. . 02.7	36 46.3	. . 50.4	174 02.4	. . 21.5	Rigil Kent.	139 56.8	S60 52.2
10	344 04.7	344 24.6	46.2	240 01.5	02.6	51 48.5	50.3	189 05.0	21.6	Sabik	102 16.9	S15 44.3
11	359 07.2	359 24.2	44.9	255 02.7	02.4	66 50.7	50.3	204 07.6	21.6			
12	14 09.7	14 23.9	S 1 43.7	270 03.9	N25 02.3	81 52.9	S21 50.3	219 10.2	N12 21.7	Schedar	349 45.9	N56 34.9
13	29 12.1	29 23.5	42.5	285 05.1	02.1	96 55.0	50.2	234 12.7	21.7	Shaula	96 27.1	S37 06.6
14	44 14.6	44 23.1	41.3	300 06.3	02.0	111 57.2	50.2	249 15.3	21.7	Sirius	258 37.2	S16 43.8
15	59 17.1	59 22.7	. . 40.1	315 07.5	. . 01.8	126 59.4	. . 50.2	264 17.9	. . 21.8	Spica	158 35.1	S11 12.5
16	74 19.5	74 22.4	38.9	330 08.7	01.7	142 01.6	50.1	279 20.5	21.8	Suhail	222 55.3	S43 28.2
17	89 22.0	89 22.0	37.6	345 09.9	01.5	157 03.8	50.1	294 23.1	21.8			
18	104 24.4	104 21.6	S 1 36.4	0 11.1	N25 01.4	172 06.0	S21 50.1	309 25.6	N12 21.9	Vega	80 41.6	N38 47.1
19	119 26.9	119 21.2	35.2	15 12.3	01.2	187 08.2	50.0	324 28.2	21.9	Zuben'ubi	137 09.5	S16 04.8
20	134 29.4	134 20.9	34.0	30 13.5	01.1	202 10.4	50.0	339 30.8	22.0			
21	149 31.8	149 20.5	. . 32.8	45 14.7	. . 00.9	217 12.6	. . 50.0	354 33.4	. . 22.0			
22	164 34.3	164 20.1	31.6	60 15.9	00.8	232 14.8	49.9	9 35.9	22.0			
23	179 36.8	179 19.7	30.3	75 17.1	00.6	247 17.0	49.9	24 38.5	22.1			
Mer. Pass.	h m 11 07.4	v −0.4	d 1.2	v 1.2	d 0.1	v 2.2	d 0.0	v 2.6	d 0.0			

	SHA ° ′	Mer. Pass. h m
Venus	1 56.4	11 02
Mars	256 39.4	18 01
Jupiter	67 53.0	6 37
Saturn	204 56.4	21 26

Day	UT d h	SUN GHA ° ′	SUN Dec ° ′	MOON GHA ° ′	v ′	MOON Dec ° ′	d ′	HP ′
THURSDAY	3 00	179 10.3	N 5 22.3	218 06.7	12.4	S10 26.8	14.9	58.0
	01	194 10.5	23.3	232 38.1	12.4	10 11.9	15.0	58.1
	02	209 10.7	24.3	247 09.5	12.3	9 56.9	15.1	58.1
	03	224 10.8	. . 25.2	261 40.8	12.4	9 41.8	15.2	58.1
	04	239 11.0	26.2	276 12.2	12.4	9 26.6	15.2	58.2
	05	254 11.2	27.1	290 43.6	12.4	9 11.4	15.3	58.2
	06	269 11.4	N 5 28.1	305 15.0	12.4	S 8 56.1	15.3	58.2
	07	284 11.6	29.0	319 46.4	12.4	8 40.8	15.4	58.3
	08	299 11.8	30.0	334 17.8	12.4	8 25.4	15.5	58.3
	09	314 11.9	. . 31.0	348 49.2	12.4	8 09.9	15.5	58.4
	10	329 12.1	31.9	3 20.6	12.4	7 54.4	15.6	58.4
	11	344 12.3	32.9	17 52.0	12.4	7 38.8	15.6	58.4
	12	359 12.5	N 5 33.8	32 23.4	12.4	S 7 23.2	15.7	58.5
	13	14 12.7	34.8	46 54.8	12.4	7 07.5	15.8	58.5
	14	29 12.8	35.7	61 26.2	12.3	6 51.7	15.8	58.5
	15	44 13.0	. . 36.7	75 57.5	12.4	6 35.9	15.9	58.6
	16	59 13.2	37.6	90 28.9	12.4	6 20.0	15.9	58.6
	17	74 13.4	38.6	105 00.3	12.3	6 04.1	15.9	58.6
	18	89 13.6	N 5 39.5	119 31.6	12.3	S 5 48.2	16.1	58.7
	19	104 13.7	40.5	134 02.9	12.4	5 32.1	16.0	58.7
	20	119 13.9	41.5	148 34.3	12.3	5 16.1	16.1	58.8
	21	134 14.1	. . 42.4	163 05.6	12.3	5 00.0	16.2	58.8
	22	149 14.3	43.4	177 36.9	12.2	4 43.8	16.2	58.8
	23	164 14.5	44.3	192 08.1	12.3	4 27.6	16.2	58.9
FRIDAY	4 00	179 14.7	N 5 45.3	206 39.4	12.2	S 4 11.4	16.3	58.9
	01	194 14.8	46.2	221 10.6	12.3	3 55.1	16.3	58.9
	02	209 15.0	47.2	235 41.9	12.2	3 38.8	16.4	59.0
	03	224 15.2	. . 48.1	250 13.1	12.2	3 22.4	16.3	59.0
	04	239 15.4	49.1	264 44.3	12.1	3 06.1	16.5	59.0
	05	254 15.6	50.0	279 15.4	12.2	2 49.6	16.4	59.1
	06	269 15.7	N 5 51.0	293 46.6	12.1	S 2 33.2	16.5	59.1
	07	284 15.9	51.9	308 17.7	12.1	2 16.7	16.6	59.1
	08	299 16.1	52.9	322 48.8	12.0	2 00.1	16.5	59.2
	09	314 16.3	. . 53.8	337 19.8	12.1	1 43.6	16.6	59.2
	10	329 16.5	54.8	351 50.9	12.0	1 27.0	16.6	59.2
	11	344 16.6	55.7	6 21.9	11.9	1 10.4	16.6	59.3
	12	359 16.8	N 5 56.7	20 52.8	12.0	S 0 53.8	16.7	59.3
	13	14 17.0	57.6	35 23.8	11.9	0 37.1	16.7	59.3
	14	29 17.2	58.6	49 54.7	11.9	0 20.4	16.7	59.4
	15	44 17.4	5 59.6	64 25.6	11.8	S 0 03.7	16.7	59.4
	16	59 17.5	6 00.5	78 56.4	11.8	N 0 13.0	16.7	59.4
	17	74 17.7	01.5	93 27.2	11.8	0 29.7	16.8	59.5
	18	89 17.9	N 6 02.4	107 58.0	11.7	N 0 46.5	16.7	59.5
	19	104 18.1	03.4	122 28.7	11.7	1 03.2	16.8	59.5
	20	119 18.3	04.3	136 59.4	11.6	1 20.0	16.8	59.6
	21	134 18.4	. . 05.3	151 30.0	11.6	1 36.8	16.8	59.6
	22	149 18.6	06.2	166 00.6	11.6	1 53.6	16.8	59.6
	23	164 18.8	07.2	180 31.2	11.5	2 10.4	16.8	59.6
SATURDAY	5 00	179 19.0	N 6 08.1	195 01.7	11.5	N 2 27.2	16.8	59.7
	01	194 19.1	09.0	209 32.2	11.4	2 44.0	16.8	59.7
	02	209 19.3	10.0	224 02.6	11.4	3 00.8	16.8	59.7
	03	224 19.5	. . 10.9	238 33.0	11.3	3 17.6	16.9	59.8
	04	239 19.7	11.9	253 03.3	11.3	3 34.5	16.8	59.8
	05	254 19.9	12.8	267 33.6	11.2	3 51.3	16.8	59.8
	06	269 20.0	N 6 13.8	282 03.8	11.1	N 4 08.1	16.8	59.8
	07	284 20.2	14.7	296 33.9	11.2	4 24.9	16.8	59.9
	08	299 20.4	15.7	311 04.1	11.0	4 41.7	16.8	59.9
	09	314 20.6	. . 16.6	325 34.1	11.0	4 58.5	16.7	59.9
	10	329 20.8	17.6	340 04.1	11.0	5 15.2	16.8	60.0
	11	344 20.9	18.5	354 34.1	10.8	5 32.0	16.7	60.0
	12	359 21.1	N 6 19.5	9 03.9	10.9	N 5 48.7	16.8	60.0
	13	14 21.3	20.4	23 33.8	10.7	6 05.5	16.7	60.0
	14	29 21.5	21.4	38 03.5	10.7	6 22.2	16.6	60.1
	15	44 21.6	. . 22.3	52 33.2	10.6	6 38.8	16.7	60.1
	16	59 21.8	23.3	67 02.8	10.6	6 55.5	16.6	60.1
	17	74 22.0	24.2	81 32.4	10.5	7 12.1	16.7	60.1
	18	89 22.2	N 6 25.2	96 01.9	10.4	N 7 28.8	16.5	60.1
	19	104 22.4	26.1	110 31.3	10.4	7 45.3	16.6	60.2
	20	119 22.5	27.0	125 00.7	10.3	8 01.9	16.5	60.2
	21	134 22.7	. . 28.0	139 30.0	10.2	8 18.4	16.5	60.2
	22	149 22.9	28.9	153 59.2	10.2	8 34.9	16.5	60.2
	23	164 23.1	29.9	168 28.4	10.1	N 8 51.4	16.4	60.3
		SD 16.0	*d* 1.0	SD 15.9		16.2		16.3

Lat. °	Twilight Naut. h m	Twilight Civil h m	Sunrise h m	Moonrise 3 h m	Moonrise 4 h m	Moonrise 5 h m	Moonrise 6 h m
N 72	00 40	03 20	04 38	05 37	05 00	04 25	03 45
N 70	01 52	03 39	04 48	05 24	04 56	04 30	04 00
68	02 27	03 54	04 55	05 13	04 53	04 33	04 12
66	02 51	04 06	05 01	05 04	04 50	04 37	04 22
64	03 10	04 16	05 07	04 56	04 48	04 40	04 31
62	03 25	04 25	05 11	04 49	04 46	04 42	04 39
60	03 37	04 32	05 15	04 43	04 44	04 44	04 45
N 58	03 47	04 38	05 19	04 38	04 42	04 46	04 51
56	03 56	04 44	05 22	04 33	04 41	04 48	04 56
54	04 04	04 48	05 25	04 29	04 39	04 49	05 01
52	04 11	04 53	05 27	04 26	04 38	04 51	05 05
50	04 17	04 57	05 30	04 22	04 37	04 52	05 09
45	04 29	05 05	05 35	04 14	04 35	04 55	05 17
N 40	04 39	05 11	05 39	04 08	04 33	04 58	05 24
35	04 47	05 17	05 42	04 03	04 31	05 00	05 30
30	04 53	05 21	05 46	03 58	04 30	05 02	05 36
20	05 03	05 29	05 51	03 49	04 27	05 05	05 45
N 10	05 10	05 34	05 55	03 42	04 25	05 08	05 53
0	05 15	05 39	06 00	03 35	04 22	05 11	06 01
S 10	05 18	05 43	06 04	03 28	04 20	05 14	06 09
20	05 20	05 46	06 08	03 20	04 18	05 17	06 18
30	05 21	05 49	06 13	03 12	04 15	05 20	06 28
35	05 21	05 50	06 15	03 07	04 14	05 22	06 34
40	05 20	05 51	06 18	03 01	04 12	05 25	06 40
45	05 18	05 52	06 22	02 54	04 10	05 28	06 48
S 50	05 16	05 53	06 26	02 46	04 08	05 31	06 57
52	05 15	05 54	06 28	02 43	04 06	05 32	07 02
54	05 13	05 54	06 30	02 39	04 05	05 34	07 07
56	05 12	05 55	06 32	02 34	04 04	05 36	07 12
58	05 10	05 55	06 34	02 29	04 02	05 38	07 18
S 60	05 07	05 55	06 37	02 23	04 01	05 41	07 25

Lat. °	Sunset h m	Twilight Civil h m	Twilight Naut. h m	Moonset 3 h m	Moonset 4 h m	Moonset 5 h m	Moonset 6 h m
N 72	19 31	20 51	////	14 28	16 49	19 16	22 13
N 70	19 21	20 30	22 22	14 38	16 49	19 04	21 38
68	19 13	20 15	21 44	14 47	16 49	18 54	21 13
66	19 06	20 02	21 18	14 54	16 48	18 46	20 54
64	19 01	19 52	20 59	15 00	16 48	18 40	20 39
62	18 56	19 43	20 44	15 05	16 48	18 34	20 26
60	18 52	19 36	20 31	15 09	16 48	18 29	20 16
N 58	18 48	19 29	20 20	15 13	16 47	18 25	20 07
56	18 45	19 24	20 11	15 17	16 47	18 21	19 59
54	18 42	19 19	20 03	15 20	16 47	18 17	19 52
52	18 39	19 14	19 56	15 22	16 47	18 14	19 45
50	18 37	19 10	19 50	15 25	16 47	18 11	19 40
45	18 32	19 02	19 38	15 30	16 47	18 05	19 27
N 40	18 28	18 55	19 28	15 35	16 46	18 00	19 17
35	18 24	18 50	19 20	15 39	16 46	17 56	19 09
30	18 21	18 45	19 13	15 42	16 46	17 52	19 01
20	18 15	18 37	19 03	15 48	16 46	17 46	18 48
N 10	18 10	18 32	18 56	15 53	16 45	17 40	18 37
0	18 06	18 27	18 51	15 57	16 45	17 34	18 26
S 10	18 02	18 23	18 47	16 02	16 45	17 29	18 16
20	17 58	18 20	18 45	16 07	16 44	17 23	18 05
30	17 53	18 17	18 44	16 12	16 44	17 17	17 52
35	17 50	18 15	18 45	16 16	16 44	17 13	17 45
40	17 47	18 14	18 45	16 19	16 43	17 09	17 37
45	17 43	18 13	18 47	16 23	16 43	17 04	17 27
S 50	17 39	18 11	18 49	16 28	16 43	16 58	17 16
52	17 37	18 11	18 50	16 30	16 43	16 56	17 11
54	17 35	18 10	18 51	16 32	16 42	16 53	17 05
56	17 33	18 10	18 53	16 35	16 42	16 49	16 58
58	17 30	18 09	18 55	16 38	16 42	16 46	16 51
S 60	17 27	18 09	18 57	16 41	16 42	16 42	16 43

Day	SUN Eqn. of Time 00^h	SUN Eqn. of Time 12^h	SUN Mer. Pass.	MOON Mer. Pass. Upper	MOON Mer. Pass. Lower	MOON Age	MOON Phase
d	m s	m s	h m	h m	h m	d	%
3	03 19	03 10	12 03	09 46	22 10	27	9
4	03 02	02 53	12 03	10 34	22 58	28	4
5	02 44	02 36	12 03	11 22	23 48	29	1

UT	ARIES	VENUS −3.8		MARS +0.9		JUPITER −2.2		SATURN +0.4	
	GHA	GHA	Dec	GHA	Dec	GHA	Dec	GHA	Dec
d h	° ′	° ′	° ′	° ′	° ′	° ′	° ′	° ′	° ′
6 00	194 39.2	194 19.4	S 1 29.1	90 18.3	N25 00.5	262 19.2	S21 49.9	39 41.1	N12 22.1
01	209 41.7	209 19.0	27.9	105 19.5	00.3	277 21.4	49.8	54 43.6	22.2
02	224 44.2	224 18.6	26.7	120 20.7	00.2	292 23.6	49.8	69 46.2	22.2
03	239 46.6	239 18.3	. . 25.5	135 21.9	25 00.0	307 25.8	. . 49.8	84 48.8	. . 22.2
04	254 49.1	254 17.9	24.2	150 23.1	24 59.9	322 28.0	49.7	99 51.4	22.3
05	269 51.5	269 17.5	23.0	165 24.3	59.7	337 30.2	49.7	114 53.9	22.3
06	284 54.0	284 17.1	S 1 21.8	180 25.5	N24 59.6	352 32.4	S21 49.7	129 56.5	N12 22.3
07	299 56.5	299 16.8	20.6	195 26.7	59.4	7 34.6	49.6	144 59.1	22.4
08	314 58.9	314 16.4	19.4	210 27.9	59.3	22 36.8	49.6	160 01.7	22.4
S 09	330 01.4	329 16.0	. . 18.2	225 29.1	. . 59.1	37 39.0	. . 49.6	175 04.2	. . 22.5
U 10	345 03.9	344 15.7	16.9	240 30.3	59.0	52 41.2	49.5	190 06.8	22.5
N 11	0 06.3	359 15.3	15.7	255 31.5	58.8	67 43.4	49.5	205 09.4	22.5
D 12	15 08.8	14 14.9	S 1 14.5	270 32.7	N24 58.7	82 45.6	S21 49.5	220 12.0	N12 22.6
A 13	30 11.3	29 14.5	13.3	285 33.9	58.5	97 47.8	49.4	235 14.5	22.6
Y 14	45 13.7	44 14.2	12.1	300 35.1	58.3	112 50.0	49.4	250 17.1	22.6
15	60 16.2	59 13.8	. . 10.8	315 36.3	. . 58.2	127 52.3	. . 49.4	265 19.7	. . 22.7
16	75 18.7	74 13.4	09.6	330 37.5	58.0	142 54.5	49.3	280 22.2	22.7
17	90 21.1	89 13.1	08.4	345 38.7	57.9	157 56.7	49.3	295 24.8	22.8
18	105 23.6	104 12.7	S 1 07.2	0 39.9	N24 57.7	172 58.9	S21 49.3	310 27.4	N12 22.8
19	120 26.0	119 12.3	06.0	15 41.1	57.6	188 01.1	49.2	325 30.0	22.8
20	135 28.5	134 11.9	04.8	30 42.3	57.4	203 03.3	49.2	340 32.5	22.9
21	150 31.0	149 11.6	. . 03.5	45 43.5	. . 57.3	218 05.5	. . 49.2	355 35.1	. . 22.9
22	165 33.4	164 11.2	02.3	60 44.6	57.1	233 07.7	49.1	10 37.7	22.9
23	180 35.9	179 10.8	1 01.1	75 45.8	56.9	248 09.9	49.1	25 40.2	23.0
7 00	195 38.4	194 10.5	S 0 59.9	90 47.0	N24 56.8	263 12.1	S21 49.1	40 42.8	N12 23.0
01	210 40.8	209 10.1	58.7	105 48.2	56.6	278 14.3	49.1	55 45.4	23.1
02	225 43.3	224 09.7	57.4	120 49.4	56.5	293 16.5	49.0	70 48.0	23.1
03	240 45.8	239 09.4	. . 56.2	135 50.6	. . 56.3	308 18.7	. . 49.0	85 50.5	. . 23.1
04	255 48.2	254 09.0	55.0	150 51.8	56.2	323 20.9	49.0	100 53.1	23.2
05	270 50.7	269 08.6	53.8	165 53.0	56.0	338 23.1	48.9	115 55.7	23.2
06	285 53.1	284 08.2	S 0 52.6	180 54.2	N24 55.9	353 25.3	S21 48.9	130 58.2	N12 23.2
07	300 55.6	299 07.9	51.3	195 55.4	55.7	8 27.6	48.9	146 00.8	23.3
08	315 58.1	314 07.5	50.1	210 56.6	55.5	23 29.8	48.8	161 03.4	23.3
M 09	331 00.5	329 07.1	. . 48.9	225 57.8	. . 55.4	38 32.0	. . 48.8	176 05.9	. . 23.3
O 10	346 03.0	344 06.8	47.7	240 59.0	55.2	53 34.2	48.8	191 08.5	23.4
N 11	1 05.5	359 06.4	46.5	256 00.2	55.1	68 36.4	48.7	206 11.1	23.4
D 12	16 07.9	14 06.0	S 0 45.2	271 01.3	N24 54.9	83 38.6	S21 48.7	221 13.6	N12 23.5
A 13	31 10.4	29 05.7	44.0	286 02.5	54.7	98 40.8	48.7	236 16.2	23.5
Y 14	46 12.9	44 05.3	42.8	301 03.7	54.6	113 43.0	48.6	251 18.8	23.5
15	61 15.3	59 04.9	. . 41.6	316 04.9	. . 54.4	128 45.2	. . 48.6	266 21.4	. . 23.6
16	76 17.8	74 04.5	40.4	331 06.1	54.3	143 47.4	48.6	281 23.9	23.6
17	91 20.3	89 04.2	39.1	346 07.3	54.1	158 49.7	48.5	296 26.5	23.6
18	106 22.7	104 03.8	S 0 37.9	1 08.5	N24 53.9	173 51.9	S21 48.5	311 29.1	N12 23.7
19	121 25.2	119 03.4	36.7	16 09.7	53.8	188 54.1	48.5	326 31.6	23.7
20	136 27.6	134 03.1	35.5	31 10.9	53.6	203 56.3	48.4	341 34.2	23.7
21	151 30.1	149 02.7	. . 34.3	46 12.0	. . 53.5	218 58.5	. . 48.4	356 36.8	. . 23.8
22	166 32.6	164 02.3	33.0	61 13.2	53.3	234 00.7	48.4	11 39.3	23.8
23	181 35.0	179 02.0	31.8	76 14.4	53.1	249 02.9	48.4	26 41.9	23.8
8 00	196 37.5	194 01.6	S 0 30.6	91 15.6	N24 53.0	264 05.1	S21 48.3	41 44.5	N12 23.9
01	211 40.0	209 01.2	29.4	106 16.8	52.8	279 07.4	48.3	56 47.0	23.9
02	226 42.4	224 00.8	28.1	121 18.0	52.7	294 09.6	48.3	71 49.6	24.0
03	241 44.9	239 00.5	. . 26.9	136 19.2	. . 52.5	309 11.8	. . 48.2	86 52.2	. . 24.0
04	256 47.4	254 00.1	25.7	151 20.3	52.3	324 14.0	48.2	101 54.7	24.0
05	271 49.8	268 59.7	24.5	166 21.5	52.2	339 16.2	48.2	116 57.3	24.1
06	286 52.3	283 59.4	S 0 23.3	181 22.7	N24 52.0	354 18.4	S21 48.1	131 59.9	N12 24.1
07	301 54.8	298 59.0	22.0	196 23.9	51.9	9 20.6	48.1	147 02.4	24.1
T 08	316 57.2	313 58.6	20.8	211 25.1	51.7	24 22.9	48.1	162 05.0	24.2
U 09	331 59.7	328 58.3	. . 19.6	226 26.3	. . 51.5	39 25.1	. . 48.0	177 07.6	. . 24.2
E 10	347 02.1	343 57.9	18.4	241 27.5	51.4	54 27.3	48.0	192 10.1	24.2
S 11	2 04.6	358 57.5	17.2	256 28.6	51.2	69 29.5	48.0	207 12.7	24.3
D 12	17 07.1	13 57.2	S 0 15.9	271 29.8	N24 51.0	84 31.7	S21 48.0	222 15.3	N12 24.3
A 13	32 09.5	28 56.8	14.7	286 31.0	50.9	99 34.0	47.9	237 17.8	24.3
Y 14	47 12.0	43 56.4	13.5	301 32.2	50.7	114 36.2	47.9	252 20.4	24.4
15	62 14.5	58 56.1	. . 12.3	316 33.4	. . 50.6	129 38.4	. . 47.9	267 23.0	. . 24.4
16	77 16.9	73 55.7	11.0	331 34.6	50.4	144 40.6	47.8	282 25.5	24.4
17	92 19.4	88 55.3	09.8	346 35.7	50.2	159 42.8	47.8	297 28.1	24.5
18	107 21.9	103 55.0	S 0 08.6	1 36.9	N24 50.1	174 45.0	S21 47.8	312 30.6	N12 24.5
19	122 24.3	118 54.6	07.4	16 38.1	49.9	189 47.3	47.7	327 33.2	24.5
20	137 26.8	133 54.2	06.2	31 39.3	49.7	204 49.5	47.7	342 35.8	24.6
21	152 29.3	148 53.8	. . 04.9	46 40.5	. . 49.6	219 51.7	. . 47.7	357 38.3	. . 24.6
22	167 31.7	163 53.5	03.7	61 41.6	49.4	234 53.9	47.6	12 40.9	24.6
23	182 34.2	178 53.1	02.5	76 42.8	49.2	249 56.1	47.6	27 43.5	24.7
Mer. Pass.	h m 10 55.6	v −0.4	d 1.2	v 1.2	d 0.2	v 2.2	d 0.0	v 2.6	d 0.0

STARS Name	SHA	Dec
	° ′	° ′
Acamar	315 21.6	S40 16.4
Achernar	335 30.0	S57 11.7
Acrux	173 13.4	S63 08.9
Adhara	255 15.7	S28 59.2
Aldebaran	290 54.1	N16 31.6
Alioth	166 23.3	N55 54.8
Alkaid	153 01.3	N49 16.1
Al Na'ir	27 48.8	S46 55.2
Alnilam	275 50.5	S 1 11.8
Alphard	217 59.8	S 8 41.8
Alphecca	126 14.0	N26 40.9
Alpheratz	357 48.0	N29 08.1
Altair	62 12.1	N 8 53.2
Ankaa	353 19.8	S42 15.6
Antares	112 30.9	S26 27.1
Arcturus	145 58.9	N19 08.1
Atria	107 36.1	S69 02.5
Avior	234 19.7	S59 32.4
Bellatrix	278 36.4	N 6 21.4
Betelgeuse	271 05.7	N 7 24.5
Canopus	263 58.0	S52 42.2
Capella	280 40.5	N46 00.6
Deneb	49 34.5	N45 18.2
Denebola	182 37.3	N14 31.4
Diphda	349 00.1	S17 56.5
Dubhe	193 55.6	N61 42.4
Elnath	278 17.8	N28 37.0
Eltanin	90 47.8	N51 28.8
Enif	33 51.2	N 9 54.6
Fomalhaut	15 28.5	S29 34.7
Gacrux	172 05.1	S57 09.8
Gienah	175 56.1	S17 35.5
Hadar	148 53.2	S60 24.9
Hamal	328 05.6	N23 30.1
Kaus Aust.	83 48.9	S34 22.9
Kochab	137 18.3	N74 07.0
Markab	13 42.6	N15 14.8
Menkar	314 19.5	N 4 07.3
Menkent	148 12.0	S36 24.8
Miaplacidus	221 40.5	S69 45.3
Mirfak	308 46.6	N49 53.6
Nunki	76 03.1	S26 17.2
Peacock	53 25.4	S56 42.4
Pollux	243 32.4	N28 00.5
Procyon	245 03.8	N 5 12.2
Rasalhague	96 10.0	N12 32.9
Regulus	207 47.4	N11 55.5
Rigel	281 16.0	S 8 11.6
Rigil Kent.	139 56.8	S60 52.2
Sabik	102 16.9	S15 44.3
Schedar	349 45.9	N56 34.9
Shaula	96 27.1	S37 06.6
Sirius	258 37.2	S16 43.8
Spica	158 35.1	S11 12.5
Suhail	222 55.3	S43 28.2
Vega	80 41.6	N38 47.1
Zuben'ubi	137 09.5	S16 04.8

	SHA	Mer. Pass.
	° ′	h m
Venus	358 32.1	11 04
Mars	255 08.7	17 55
Jupiter	67 33.7	6 26
Saturn	205 04.4	21 14

UT d h	SUN GHA ° ′	SUN Dec ° ′	MOON GHA ° ′	v ′	MOON Dec ° ′	d ′	HP ′
6 00 (SUNDAY)	179 23.2	N 6 30.8	182 57.5	10.0	N 9 07.8	16.3	60.3
01	194 23.4	31.8	197 26.5	9.9	9 24.1	16.4	60.3
02	209 23.6	32.7	211 55.4	9.9	9 40.5	16.3	60.3
03	224 23.8	. . 33.7	226 24.3	9.7	9 56.8	16.2	60.3
04	239 23.9	34.6	240 53.0	9.7	10 13.0	16.2	60.4
05	254 24.1	35.5	255 21.7	9.7	10 29.2	16.1	60.4
06	269 24.3	N 6 36.5	269 50.4	9.5	N10 45.3	16.1	60.4
07	284 24.5	37.4	284 18.9	9.5	11 01.4	16.1	60.4
08	299 24.6	38.4	298 47.4	9.3	11 17.5	15.9	60.4
09	314 24.8	. . 39.3	313 15.7	9.3	11 33.4	16.0	60.4
10	329 25.0	40.3	327 44.0	9.2	11 49.4	15.8	60.5
11	344 25.2	41.2	342 12.2	9.2	12 05.2	15.8	60.5
12	359 25.3	N 6 42.1	356 40.4	9.0	N12 21.0	15.8	60.5
13	14 25.5	43.1	11 08.4	8.9	12 36.8	15.6	60.5
14	29 25.7	44.0	25 36.3	8.9	12 52.4	15.6	60.5
15	44 25.9	. . 45.0	40 04.2	8.8	13 08.0	15.6	60.5
16	59 26.1	45.9	54 32.0	8.7	13 23.6	15.4	60.5
17	74 26.2	46.8	68 59.7	8.6	13 39.0	15.4	60.6
18	89 26.4	N 6 47.8	83 27.3	8.5	N13 54.4	15.3	60.6
19	104 26.6	48.7	97 54.8	8.4	14 09.7	15.2	60.6
20	119 26.8	49.7	112 22.2	8.3	14 24.9	15.2	60.6
21	134 26.9	. . 50.6	126 49.5	8.2	14 40.1	15.0	60.6
22	149 27.1	51.6	141 16.7	8.2	14 55.1	15.0	60.6
23	164 27.3	52.5	155 43.9	8.0	15 10.1	14.9	60.6
7 00 (MONDAY)	179 27.5	N 6 53.4	170 10.9	8.0	N15 25.0	14.8	60.6
01	194 27.6	54.4	184 37.9	7.8	15 39.8	14.7	60.6
02	209 27.8	55.3	199 04.7	7.8	15 54.5	14.6	60.7
03	224 28.0	. . 56.2	213 31.5	7.6	16 09.1	14.5	60.7
04	239 28.1	57.2	227 58.1	7.6	16 23.6	14.4	60.7
05	254 28.3	58.1	242 24.7	7.5	16 38.0	14.3	60.7
06	269 28.5	N 6 59.1	256 51.2	7.3	N16 52.3	14.2	60.7
07	284 28.7	7 00.0	271 17.5	7.3	17 06.5	14.1	60.7
08	299 28.8	00.9	285 43.8	7.2	17 20.6	14.0	60.7
09	314 29.0	. . 01.9	300 10.0	7.1	17 34.6	13.9	60.7
10	329 29.2	02.8	314 36.1	6.9	17 48.5	13.8	60.7
11	344 29.4	03.8	329 02.0	6.9	18 02.3	13.7	60.7
12	359 29.5	N 7 04.7	343 27.9	6.8	N18 16.0	13.5	60.7
13	14 29.7	05.6	357 53.7	6.7	18 29.5	13.4	60.7
14	29 29.9	06.6	12 19.4	6.6	18 42.9	13.4	60.7
15	44 30.1	. . 07.5	26 45.0	6.5	18 56.3	13.2	60.7
16	59 30.2	08.4	41 10.5	6.3	19 09.5	13.0	60.7
17	74 30.4	09.4	55 35.8	6.3	19 22.5	13.0	60.7
18	89 30.6	N 7 10.3	70 01.1	6.2	N19 35.5	12.8	60.7
19	104 30.7	11.2	84 26.3	6.1	19 48.3	12.7	60.7
20	119 30.9	12.2	98 51.4	6.0	20 01.0	12.5	60.7
21	134 31.1	. . 13.1	113 16.4	5.9	20 13.5	12.4	60.7
22	149 31.3	14.1	127 41.3	5.8	20 25.9	12.3	60.7
23	164 31.4	15.0	142 06.1	5.7	20 38.2	12.1	60.7
8 00 (TUESDAY)	179 31.6	N 7 15.9	156 30.8	5.6	N20 50.3	12.0	60.7
01	194 31.8	16.9	170 55.4	5.5	21 02.3	11.9	60.7
02	209 32.0	17.8	185 19.9	5.4	21 14.2	11.7	60.7
03	224 32.1	. . 18.7	199 44.3	5.3	21 25.9	11.6	60.7
04	239 32.3	19.7	214 08.6	5.3	21 37.5	11.4	60.7
05	254 32.5	20.6	228 32.9	5.1	21 48.9	11.3	60.7
06	269 32.6	N 7 21.5	242 57.0	5.0	N22 00.2	11.1	60.7
07	284 32.8	22.5	257 21.0	5.0	22 11.3	11.0	60.7
08	299 33.0	23.4	271 45.0	4.8	22 22.3	10.8	60.7
09	314 33.2	. . 24.3	286 08.8	4.8	22 33.1	10.6	60.7
10	329 33.3	25.3	300 32.6	4.7	22 43.7	10.5	60.7
11	344 33.5	26.2	314 56.3	4.6	22 54.2	10.4	60.7
12	359 33.7	N 7 27.1	329 19.9	4.5	N23 04.6	10.1	60.7
13	14 33.8	28.1	343 43.4	4.4	23 14.7	10.0	60.7
14	29 34.0	29.0	358 06.8	4.3	23 24.7	9.9	60.6
15	44 34.2	. . 29.9	12 30.1	4.3	23 34.6	9.7	60.6
16	59 34.4	30.8	26 53.4	4.1	23 44.3	9.5	60.6
17	74 34.5	31.8	41 16.5	4.1	23 53.8	9.3	60.6
18	89 34.7	N 7 32.7	55 39.6	4.0	N24 03.1	9.2	60.6
19	104 34.9	33.6	70 02.6	4.0	24 12.3	9.0	60.6
20	119 35.0	34.6	84 25.6	3.8	24 21.3	8.8	60.6
21	134 35.2	. . 35.5	98 48.4	3.8	24 30.1	8.6	60.6
22	149 35.4	36.4	113 11.2	3.7	24 38.7	8.5	60.6
23	164 35.5	37.4	127 33.9	3.7	N24 47.2	8.3	60.6
	SD 16.0	*d* 0.9	SD 16.5		16.5		16.5

Lat. °	Twilight Naut. h m	Twilight Civil h m	Sunrise h m	Moonrise 6 h m	Moonrise 7 h m	Moonrise 8 h m	Moonrise 9 h m
N 72	////	02 59	04 22	03 45	02 40	▭	▭
N 70	01 18	03 22	04 33	04 00	03 18	▭	▭
68	02 05	03 40	04 42	04 12	03 44	02 45	▭
66	02 34	03 53	04 50	04 22	04 05	03 36	▭
64	02 56	04 05	04 56	04 31	04 22	04 09	03 41
62	03 12	04 14	05 02	04 39	04 35	04 33	04 32
60	03 26	04 22	05 06	04 45	04 47	04 52	05 04
N 58	03 37	04 29	05 10	04 51	04 58	05 08	05 28
56	03 47	04 35	05 14	04 56	05 07	05 22	05 47
54	03 56	04 41	05 18	05 01	05 15	05 34	06 03
52	04 03	04 46	05 21	05 05	05 22	05 45	06 17
50	04 10	04 50	05 23	05 09	05 29	05 54	06 30
45	04 23	04 59	05 29	05 17	05 43	06 14	06 55
N 40	04 34	05 07	05 34	05 24	05 54	06 31	07 16
35	04 42	05 13	05 38	05 30	06 05	06 45	07 33
30	04 49	05 18	05 42	05 36	06 13	06 57	07 48
20	05 00	05 26	05 48	05 45	06 29	07 18	08 13
N 10	05 08	05 33	05 54	05 53	06 42	07 36	08 35
0	05 14	05 38	05 59	06 01	06 55	07 53	08 55
S 10	05 18	05 43	06 04	06 09	07 08	08 11	09 16
20	05 21	05 47	06 09	06 18	07 22	08 30	09 38
30	05 23	05 50	06 14	06 28	07 38	08 51	10 04
35	05 23	05 52	06 18	06 34	07 48	09 04	10 20
40	05 23	05 54	06 21	06 40	07 59	09 19	10 38
45	05 22	05 56	06 25	06 48	08 12	09 37	10 59
S 50	05 21	05 58	06 30	06 57	08 27	09 59	11 27
52	05 20	05 59	06 33	07 02	08 35	10 10	11 40
54	05 19	06 00	06 35	07 07	08 43	10 22	11 56
56	05 18	06 01	06 38	07 12	08 52	10 35	12 14
58	05 16	06 01	06 41	07 18	09 03	10 52	12 37
S 60	05 14	06 02	06 44	07 25	09 15	11 11	13 06

Lat. °	Sunset h m	Twilight Civil h m	Twilight Naut. h m	Moonset 6 h m	Moonset 7 h m	Moonset 8 h m	Moonset 9 h m
N 72	19 45	21 10	////	22 13	▭	▭	▭
N 70	19 34	20 46	22 59	21 38	▭	▭	▭
68	19 24	20 28	22 05	21 13	24 12	00 12	▭
66	19 16	20 14	21 34	20 54	23 22	▭	▭
64	19 10	20 02	21 12	20 39	22 50	25 26	01 26
62	19 04	19 52	20 55	20 26	22 27	24 36	00 36
60	18 59	19 44	20 41	20 16	22 09	24 04	00 04
N 58	18 55	19 36	20 29	20 07	21 53	23 41	25 18
56	18 51	19 30	20 19	19 59	21 40	23 22	24 54
54	18 48	19 25	20 10	19 52	21 29	23 06	24 34
52	18 45	19 20	20 03	19 45	21 19	22 53	24 18
50	18 42	19 15	19 56	19 40	21 10	22 41	24 04
45	18 36	19 06	19 42	19 27	20 52	22 16	23 35
N 40	18 31	18 58	19 31	19 17	20 37	21 57	23 12
35	18 26	18 52	19 22	19 09	20 24	21 40	22 54
30	18 23	18 47	19 15	19 01	20 13	21 26	22 38
20	18 16	18 38	19 04	18 48	19 54	21 02	22 11
N 10	18 10	18 32	18 56	18 37	19 38	20 42	21 47
0	18 05	18 26	18 50	18 26	19 22	20 22	21 26
S 10	18 00	18 21	18 46	18 16	19 07	20 03	21 04
20	17 55	18 17	18 43	18 05	18 51	19 43	20 41
30	17 49	18 13	18 41	17 52	18 33	19 19	20 14
35	17 46	18 11	18 41	17 45	18 22	19 06	19 58
40	17 42	18 09	18 41	17 37	18 10	18 50	19 40
45	17 38	18 07	18 41	17 27	17 55	18 31	19 17
S 50	17 33	18 05	18 42	17 16	17 38	18 08	18 49
52	17 30	18 04	18 43	17 11	17 30	17 56	18 36
54	17 28	18 03	18 44	17 05	17 21	17 44	18 20
56	17 25	18 02	18 45	16 58	17 11	17 29	18 01
58	17 22	18 01	18 47	16 51	16 59	17 12	17 38
S 60	17 19	18 00	18 48	16 43	16 46	16 52	17 08

Day	SUN Eqn. of Time 00^h	SUN Eqn. of Time 12^h	SUN Mer. Pass.	MOON Mer. Pass. Upper	MOON Mer. Pass. Lower	MOON Age	MOON Phase
d	m s	m s	h m	h m	h m	d	%
6	02 27	02 19	12 02	12 14	24 41	00	0 ●
7	02 11	02 02	12 02	13 09	00 41	01	3
8	01 54	01 46	12 02	14 08	01 38	02	8

UT d h	ARIES GHA ° ′	VENUS −3.8 GHA ° ′	Dec ° ′	MARS +0.9 GHA ° ′	Dec ° ′	JUPITER −2.2 GHA ° ′	Dec ° ′	SATURN +0.4 GHA ° ′	Dec ° ′
9 00	197 36.6	193 52.7	S 0 01.3	91 44.0	N24 49.1	264 58.4	S21 47.6	42 46.0	N12 24.7
01	212 39.1	208 52.4	00.0	106 45.2	48.9	280 00.6	47.6	57 48.6	24.7
02	227 41.6	223 52.0	N 01.2	121 46.4	48.7	295 02.8	47.5	72 51.2	24.8
03	242 44.0	238 51.6	. . 02.4	136 47.5	. . 48.6	310 05.0	. . 47.5	87 53.7	. . 24.8
04	257 46.5	253 51.3	03.6	151 48.7	48.4	325 07.3	47.5	102 56.3	24.8
05	272 49.0	268 50.9	04.8	166 49.9	48.2	340 09.5	47.4	117 58.8	24.9
06	287 51.4	283 50.5	N 0 06.1	181 51.1	N24 48.1	355 11.7	S21 47.4	133 01.4	N12 24.9
W 07	302 53.9	298 50.2	07.3	196 52.3	47.9	10 13.9	47.4	148 04.0	24.9
E 08	317 56.4	313 49.8	08.5	211 53.4	47.7	25 16.1	47.3	163 06.5	25.0
D 09	332 58.8	328 49.4	. . 09.7	226 54.6	. . 47.6	40 18.4	. . 47.3	178 09.1	. . 25.0
N 10	348 01.3	343 49.1	11.0	241 55.8	47.4	55 20.6	47.3	193 11.7	25.0
E 11	3 03.7	358 48.7	12.2	256 57.0	47.2	70 22.8	47.3	208 14.2	25.1
S 12	18 06.2	13 48.3	N 0 13.4	271 58.2	N24 47.1	85 25.0	S21 47.2	223 16.8	N12 25.1
D 13	33 08.7	28 48.0	14.6	286 59.3	46.9	100 27.3	47.2	238 19.3	25.1
A 14	48 11.1	43 47.6	15.8	302 00.5	46.7	115 29.5	47.2	253 21.9	25.2
Y 15	63 13.6	58 47.2	. . 17.1	317 01.7	. . 46.6	130 31.7	. . 47.1	268 24.5	. . 25.2
16	78 16.1	73 46.9	18.3	332 02.9	46.4	145 33.9	47.1	283 27.0	25.2
17	93 18.5	88 46.5	19.5	347 04.0	46.2	160 36.2	47.1	298 29.6	25.3
18	108 21.0	103 46.1	N 0 20.7	2 05.2	N24 46.1	175 38.4	S21 47.0	313 32.1	N12 25.3
19	123 23.5	118 45.8	22.0	17 06.4	45.9	190 40.6	47.0	328 34.7	25.3
20	138 25.9	133 45.4	23.2	32 07.6	45.7	205 42.8	47.0	343 37.3	25.4
21	153 28.4	148 45.0	. . 24.4	47 08.7	. . 45.6	220 45.1	. . 47.0	358 39.8	. . 25.4
22	168 30.9	163 44.6	25.6	62 09.9	45.4	235 47.3	46.9	13 42.4	25.4
23	183 33.3	178 44.3	26.8	77 11.1	45.2	250 49.5	46.9	28 44.9	25.5
10 00	198 35.8	193 43.9	N 0 28.1	92 12.3	N24 45.0	265 51.8	S21 46.9	43 47.5	N12 25.5
01	213 38.2	208 43.5	29.3	107 13.4	44.9	280 54.0	46.8	58 50.1	25.5
02	228 40.7	223 43.2	30.5	122 14.6	44.7	295 56.2	46.8	73 52.6	25.6
03	243 43.2	238 42.8	. . 31.7	137 15.8	. . 44.5	310 58.4	. . 46.8	88 55.2	. . 25.6
04	258 45.6	253 42.4	33.0	152 16.9	44.4	326 00.7	46.8	103 57.7	25.6
05	273 48.1	268 42.1	34.2	167 18.1	44.2	341 02.9	46.7	119 00.3	25.7
06	288 50.6	283 41.7	N 0 35.4	182 19.3	N24 44.0	356 05.1	S21 46.7	134 02.9	N12 25.7
T 07	303 53.0	298 41.3	36.6	197 20.5	43.9	11 07.4	46.7	149 05.4	25.7
H 08	318 55.5	313 41.0	37.9	212 21.6	43.7	26 09.6	46.6	164 08.0	25.8
U 09	333 58.0	328 40.6	. . 39.1	227 22.8	. . 43.5	41 11.8	. . 46.6	179 10.5	. . 25.8
R 10	349 00.4	343 40.2	40.3	242 24.0	43.3	56 14.1	46.6	194 13.1	25.8
S 11	4 02.9	358 39.9	41.5	257 25.2	43.2	71 16.3	46.5	209 15.6	25.9
D 12	19 05.4	13 39.5	N 0 42.7	272 26.3	N24 43.0	86 18.5	S21 46.5	224 18.2	N12 25.9
A 13	34 07.8	28 39.1	44.0	287 27.5	42.8	101 20.7	46.5	239 20.8	25.9
Y 14	49 10.3	43 38.8	45.2	302 28.7	42.7	116 23.0	46.5	254 23.3	25.9
15	64 12.7	58 38.4	. . 46.4	317 29.8	. . 42.5	131 25.2	. . 46.4	269 25.9	. . 26.0
16	79 15.2	73 38.0	47.6	332 31.0	42.3	146 27.4	46.4	284 28.4	26.0
17	94 17.7	88 37.7	48.9	347 32.2	42.1	161 29.7	46.4	299 31.0	26.0
18	109 20.1	103 37.3	N 0 50.1	2 33.3	N24 42.0	176 31.9	S21 46.3	314 33.5	N12 26.1
19	124 22.6	118 36.9	51.3	17 34.5	41.8	191 34.1	46.3	329 36.1	26.1
20	139 25.1	133 36.6	52.5	32 35.7	41.6	206 36.4	46.3	344 38.7	26.1
21	154 27.5	148 36.2	. . 53.7	47 36.8	. . 41.4	221 38.6	. . 46.3	359 41.2	. . 26.2
22	169 30.0	163 35.8	55.0	62 38.0	41.3	236 40.9	46.2	14 43.8	26.2
23	184 32.5	178 35.5	56.2	77 39.2	41.1	251 43.1	46.2	29 46.3	26.2
11 00	199 34.9	193 35.1	N 0 57.4	92 40.4	N24 40.9	266 45.3	S21 46.2	44 48.9	N12 26.3
01	214 37.4	208 34.7	58.6	107 41.5	40.7	281 47.6	46.1	59 51.4	26.3
02	229 39.9	223 34.4	0 59.9	122 42.7	40.6	296 49.8	46.1	74 54.0	26.3
03	244 42.3	238 34.0	1 01.1	137 43.9	. . 40.4	311 52.0	. . 46.1	89 56.6	. . 26.3
04	259 44.8	253 33.6	02.3	152 45.0	40.2	326 54.3	46.1	104 59.1	26.4
05	274 47.2	268 33.3	03.5	167 46.2	40.0	341 56.5	46.0	120 01.7	26.4
06	289 49.7	283 32.9	N 1 04.8	182 47.4	N24 39.9	356 58.7	S21 46.0	135 04.2	N12 26.4
07	304 52.2	298 32.5	06.0	197 48.5	39.7	12 01.0	46.0	150 06.8	26.5
08	319 54.6	313 32.2	07.2	212 49.7	39.5	27 03.2	45.9	165 09.3	26.5
F 09	334 57.1	328 31.8	. . 08.4	227 50.9	. . 39.3	42 05.5	. . 45.9	180 11.9	. . 26.5
R 10	349 59.6	343 31.4	09.6	242 52.0	39.2	57 07.7	45.9	195 14.4	26.6
I 11	5 02.0	358 31.1	10.9	257 53.2	39.0	72 09.9	45.9	210 17.0	26.6
D 12	20 04.5	13 30.7	N 1 12.1	272 54.3	N24 38.8	87 12.2	S21 45.8	225 19.5	N12 26.6
A 13	35 07.0	28 30.3	13.3	287 55.5	38.6	102 14.4	45.8	240 22.1	26.6
Y 14	50 09.4	43 30.0	14.5	302 56.7	38.5	117 16.6	45.8	255 24.7	26.7
15	65 11.9	58 29.6	. . 15.8	317 57.8	. . 38.3	132 18.9	. . 45.8	270 27.2	. . 26.7
16	80 14.4	73 29.2	17.0	332 59.0	38.1	147 21.1	45.7	285 29.8	26.7
17	95 16.8	88 28.9	18.2	348 00.2	37.9	162 23.4	45.7	300 32.3	26.8
18	110 19.3	103 28.5	N 1 19.4	3 01.3	N24 37.7	177 25.6	S21 45.7	315 34.9	N12 26.8
19	125 21.7	118 28.1	20.6	18 02.5	37.6	192 27.9	45.6	330 37.4	26.8
20	140 24.2	133 27.7	21.9	33 03.7	37.4	207 30.1	45.6	345 40.0	26.9
21	155 26.7	148 27.4	. . 23.1	48 04.8	. . 37.2	222 32.3	. . 45.6	0 42.5	. . 26.9
22	170 29.1	163 27.0	24.3	63 06.0	37.0	237 34.6	45.6	15 45.1	26.9
23	185 31.6	178 26.6	25.5	78 07.1	36.8	252 36.8	45.5	30 47.6	26.9
Mer. Pass. (h m)	10 43.9	v −0.4	d 1.2	v 1.2	d 0.2	v 2.2	d 0.0	v 2.6	d 0.0

STARS

Name	SHA ° ′	Dec ° ′
Acamar	315 21.6	S40 16.4
Achernar	335 30.0	S57 11.7
Acrux	173 13.4	S63 08.9
Adhara	255 15.7	S28 59.2
Aldebaran	290 54.1	N16 31.6
Alioth	166 23.3	N55 54.8
Alkaid	153 01.3	N49 16.1
Al Na'ir	27 48.7	S46 55.2
Alnilam	275 50.5	S 1 11.8
Alphard	217 59.8	S 8 41.8
Alphecca	126 14.0	N26 40.9
Alpheratz	357 48.0	N29 08.1
Altair	62 12.1	N 8 53.2
Ankaa	353 19.8	S42 15.6
Antares	112 30.9	S26 27.1
Arcturus	145 58.9	N19 08.1
Atria	107 36.0	S69 02.5
Avior	234 19.7	S59 32.4
Bellatrix	278 36.4	N 6 21.4
Betelgeuse	271 05.7	N 7 24.5
Canopus	263 58.1	S52 42.2
Capella	280 40.5	N46 00.6
Deneb	49 34.4	N45 18.2
Denebola	182 37.3	N14 31.4
Diphda	349 00.1	S17 56.5
Dubhe	193 55.6	N61 42.5
Elnath	278 17.8	N28 37.0
Eltanin	90 47.8	N51 28.9
Enif	33 51.2	N 9 54.6
Fomalhaut	15 28.5	S29 34.7
Gacrux	172 05.0	S57 09.8
Gienah	175 56.1	S17 35.5
Hadar	148 53.2	S60 24.9
Hamal	328 05.6	N23 30.1
Kaus Aust.	83 48.9	S34 22.9
Kochab	137 18.3	N74 07.0
Markab	13 42.6	N15 14.8
Menkar	314 19.5	N 4 07.3
Menkent	148 12.0	S36 24.8
Miaplacidus	221 40.5	S69 45.3
Mirfak	308 46.6	N49 53.6
Nunki	76 03.1	S26 17.2
Peacock	53 25.4	S56 42.4
Pollux	243 32.5	N28 00.5
Procyon	245 03.8	N 5 12.2
Rasalhague	96 09.9	N12 33.0
Regulus	207 47.4	N11 55.5
Rigel	281 16.0	S 8 11.6
Rigil Kent.	139 56.8	S60 52.2
Sabik	102 16.9	S15 44.3
Schedar	349 45.9	N56 34.9
Shaula	96 27.1	S37 06.6
Sirius	258 37.3	S16 43.8
Spica	158 35.1	S11 12.5
Suhail	222 55.3	S43 28.2
Vega	80 41.5	N38 47.1
Zuben'ubi	137 09.5	S16 04.8

	SHA ° ′	Mer. Pass. h m
Venus	355 08.1	11 05
Mars	253 36.5	17 50
Jupiter	67 16.0	6 16
Saturn	205 11.7	21 01

UT (d h)	SUN GHA ° ′	SUN Dec ° ′	MOON GHA ° ′	v ′	MOON Dec ° ′	d ′	HP ′
9 00	179 35.7	N 7 38.3	141 56.6	3.5	N24 55.5	8.1	60.5
01	194 35.9	39.2	156 19.1	3.5	25 03.6	7.9	60.5
02	209 36.1	40.1	170 41.6	3.5	25 11.5	7.7	60.5
03	224 36.2	. . 41.1	185 04.1	3.3	25 19.2	7.6	60.5
04	239 36.4	42.0	199 26.4	3.3	25 26.8	7.3	60.5
05	254 36.6	42.9	213 48.7	3.3	25 34.1	7.2	60.5
06	269 36.7	N 7 43.9	228 11.0	3.2	N25 41.3	7.0	60.5
W 07	284 36.9	44.8	242 33.2	3.1	25 48.3	6.8	60.4
E 08	299 37.1	45.7	256 55.3	3.1	25 55.1	6.6	60.4
D 09	314 37.2	. . 46.6	271 17.4	3.0	26 01.7	6.4	60.4
N 10	329 37.4	47.6	285 39.4	3.0	26 08.1	6.2	60.4
E 11	344 37.6	48.5	300 01.4	3.0	26 14.3	6.1	60.4
S 12	359 37.7	N 7 49.4	314 23.4	2.9	N26 20.4	5.8	60.4
D 13	14 37.9	50.4	328 45.3	2.8	26 26.2	5.6	60.3
A 14	29 38.1	51.3	343 07.1	2.8	26 31.8	5.5	60.3
Y 15	44 38.2	. . 52.2	357 28.9	2.8	26 37.3	5.2	60.3
16	59 38.4	53.1	11 50.7	2.8	26 42.5	5.1	60.3
17	74 38.6	54.1	26 12.5	2.7	26 47.6	4.8	60.3
18	89 38.7	N 7 55.0	40 34.2	2.7	N26 52.4	4.7	60.3
19	104 38.9	55.9	54 55.9	2.6	26 57.1	4.5	60.2
20	119 39.1	56.8	69 17.5	2.7	27 01.6	4.2	60.2
21	134 39.3	. . 57.8	83 39.2	2.6	27 05.8	4.1	60.2
22	149 39.4	58.7	98 00.8	2.6	27 09.9	3.8	60.2
23	164 39.6	7 59.6	112 22.4	2.6	27 13.7	3.7	60.2
10 00	179 39.8	N 8 00.5	126 44.0	2.5	N27 17.4	3.4	60.1
01	194 39.9	01.5	141 05.5	2.6	27 20.8	3.3	60.1
02	209 40.1	02.4	155 27.1	2.5	27 24.1	3.0	60.1
03	224 40.3	. . 03.3	169 48.6	2.6	27 27.1	2.9	60.1
04	239 40.4	04.2	184 10.2	2.5	27 30.0	2.6	60.1
05	254 40.6	05.1	198 31.7	2.6	27 32.6	2.5	60.0
06	269 40.8	N 8 06.1	212 53.3	2.5	N27 35.1	2.2	60.0
07	284 40.9	07.0	227 14.8	2.6	27 37.3	2.1	60.0
T 08	299 41.1	07.9	241 36.4	2.5	27 39.4	1.8	60.0
H 09	314 41.3	. . 08.8	255 57.9	2.6	27 41.2	1.7	59.9
U 10	329 41.4	09.8	270 19.5	2.6	27 42.9	1.4	59.9
R 11	344 41.6	10.7	284 41.1	2.6	27 44.3	1.2	59.9
S 12	359 41.7	N 8 11.6	299 02.7	2.7	N27 45.5	1.1	59.9
D 13	14 41.9	12.5	313 24.4	2.6	27 46.6	0.8	59.9
A 14	29 42.1	13.4	327 46.0	2.7	27 47.4	0.6	59.8
Y 15	44 42.2	. . 14.4	342 07.7	2.7	27 48.0	0.5	59.8
16	59 42.4	15.3	356 29.4	2.8	27 48.5	0.2	59.8
17	74 42.6	16.2	10 51.2	2.7	27 48.7	0.0	59.8
18	89 42.7	N 8 17.1	25 12.9	2.9	N27 48.7	0.1	59.7
19	104 42.9	18.0	39 34.8	2.8	27 48.6	0.4	59.7
20	119 43.1	19.0	53 56.6	2.9	27 48.2	0.5	59.7
21	134 43.2	. . 19.9	68 18.5	2.9	27 47.7	0.8	59.7
22	149 43.4	20.8	82 40.4	3.0	27 46.9	0.9	59.6
23	164 43.6	21.7	97 02.4	3.1	27 46.0	1.2	59.6
11 00	179 43.7	N 8 22.6	111 24.5	3.1	N27 44.8	1.3	59.6
01	194 43.9	23.5	125 46.6	3.1	27 43.5	1.6	59.5
02	209 44.1	24.5	140 08.7	3.2	27 41.9	1.7	59.5
03	224 44.2	. . 25.4	154 30.9	3.3	27 40.2	1.9	59.5
04	239 44.4	26.3	168 53.2	3.3	27 38.3	2.1	59.5
05	254 44.5	27.2	183 15.5	3.4	27 36.2	2.3	59.4
06	269 44.7	N 8 28.1	197 37.9	3.5	N27 33.9	2.5	59.4
07	284 44.9	29.0	212 00.4	3.5	27 31.4	2.7	59.4
08	299 45.0	30.0	226 22.9	3.6	27 28.7	2.9	59.4
F 09	314 45.2	. . 30.9	240 45.5	3.7	27 25.8	3.0	59.3
R 10	329 45.4	31.8	255 08.2	3.7	27 22.8	3.3	59.3
I 11	344 45.5	32.7	269 30.9	3.9	27 19.5	3.4	59.3
D 12	359 45.7	N 8 33.6	283 53.8	3.9	N27 16.1	3.6	59.3
A 13	14 45.9	34.5	298 16.7	4.0	27 12.5	3.8	59.2
Y 14	29 46.0	35.5	312 39.7	4.0	27 08.7	3.9	59.2
15	44 46.2	. . 36.4	327 02.7	4.2	27 04.8	4.2	59.2
16	59 46.3	37.3	341 25.9	4.3	27 00.6	4.3	59.1
17	74 46.5	38.2	355 49.2	4.3	26 56.3	4.5	59.1
18	89 46.7	N 8 39.1	10 12.5	4.4	N26 51.8	4.7	59.1
19	104 46.8	40.0	24 35.9	4.6	26 47.1	4.8	59.1
20	119 47.0	40.9	38 59.5	4.6	26 42.3	5.0	59.0
21	134 47.2	. . 41.9	53 23.1	4.7	26 37.3	5.2	59.0
22	149 47.3	42.8	67 46.8	4.8	26 32.1	5.4	59.0
23	164 47.5	43.7	82 10.6	4.9	N26 26.7	5.5	58.9
	SD 16.0	d 0.9	SD	16.4	16.3		16.1

Lat. °	Twilight Naut. h m	Twilight Civil h m	Sunrise h m	Moonrise 9 h m	Moonrise 10 h m	Moonrise 11 h m	Moonrise 12 h m
N 72	////	02 37	04 06	▭	▭	▭	▭
N 70	////	03 04	04 19	▭	▭	▭	▭
68	01 39	03 24	04 29	▭	▭	▭	▭
66	02 15	03 40	04 38	▭	▭	▭	▭
64	02 40	03 53	04 46	03 41	▭	▭	06 36
62	02 59	04 04	04 52	04 32	04 38	05 39	07 39
60	03 15	04 13	04 57	05 04	05 32	06 36	08 13
N 58	03 27	04 20	05 02	05 28	06 04	07 09	08 38
56	03 38	04 27	05 06	05 47	06 28	07 33	08 57
54	03 47	04 33	05 10	06 03	06 48	07 53	09 14
52	03 55	04 39	05 14	06 17	07 05	08 10	09 28
50	04 02	04 43	05 17	06 30	07 19	08 24	09 41
45	04 17	04 54	05 24	06 55	07 48	08 53	10 06
N 40	04 29	05 02	05 29	07 16	08 11	09 15	10 26
35	04 38	05 08	05 34	07 33	08 30	09 34	10 43
30	04 46	05 14	05 39	07 48	08 46	09 50	10 57
20	04 57	05 24	05 46	08 13	09 13	10 17	11 22
N 10	05 06	05 31	05 52	08 35	09 37	10 41	11 43
0	05 13	05 37	05 58	08 55	09 59	11 03	12 03
S 10	05 18	05 42	06 04	09 16	10 22	11 25	12 22
20	05 22	05 47	06 10	09 38	10 46	11 48	12 43
30	05 24	05 52	06 16	10 04	11 13	12 15	13 08
35	05 25	05 55	06 20	10 20	11 30	12 31	13 22
40	05 26	05 57	06 24	10 38	11 49	12 50	13 38
45	05 26	06 00	06 29	10 59	12 13	13 12	13 58
S 50	05 25	06 03	06 35	11 27	12 43	13 41	14 22
52	05 25	06 04	06 38	11 40	12 57	13 55	14 34
54	05 24	06 05	06 41	11 56	13 15	14 11	14 47
56	05 23	06 06	06 44	12 14	13 35	14 30	15 02
58	05 22	06 08	06 48	12 37	14 02	14 54	15 20
S 60	05 21	06 09	06 52	13 06	14 38	15 25	15 42

Lat. °	Sunset h m	Twilight Civil h m	Twilight Naut. h m	Moonset 9 h m	Moonset 10 h m	Moonset 11 h m	Moonset 12 h m
N 72	20 00	21 31	////	▭	▭	▭	▭
N 70	19 47	21 02	////	▭	▭	▭	▭
68	19 36	20 42	22 31	▭	▭	▭	▭
66	19 27	20 25	21 52	▭	▭	▭	▭
64	19 19	20 12	21 26	01 26	▭	▭	05 08
62	19 12	20 01	21 06	00 36	02 44	03 57	04 05
60	19 07	19 52	20 51	00 04	01 50	03 00	03 30
N 58	19 02	19 44	20 38	25 18	01 18	02 27	03 05
56	18 57	19 37	20 27	24 54	00 54	02 02	02 45
54	18 53	19 31	20 17	24 34	00 34	01 42	02 28
52	18 50	19 25	20 09	24 18	00 18	01 25	02 13
50	18 47	19 20	20 01	24 04	00 04	01 11	02 01
45	18 40	19 10	19 46	23 35	24 42	00 42	01 34
N 40	18 34	19 02	19 35	23 12	24 19	00 19	01 13
35	18 29	18 55	19 25	22 54	24 00	00 00	00 56
30	18 24	18 49	19 17	22 38	23 44	24 41	00 41
20	18 17	18 39	19 05	22 11	23 16	24 15	00 15
N 10	18 10	18 32	18 56	21 47	22 52	23 53	24 48
0	18 05	18 25	18 50	21 26	22 30	23 32	24 30
S 10	17 59	18 20	18 44	21 04	22 08	23 11	24 12
20	17 53	18 15	18 40	20 41	21 44	22 48	23 52
30	17 46	18 10	18 38	20 14	21 16	22 22	23 29
35	17 42	18 07	18 37	19 58	20 59	22 06	23 16
40	17 38	18 05	18 36	19 40	20 40	21 48	23 00
45	17 33	18 02	18 36	19 17	20 16	21 26	22 42
S 50	17 27	17 59	18 36	18 49	19 46	20 58	22 19
52	17 24	17 58	18 37	18 36	19 32	20 45	22 07
54	17 21	17 56	18 37	18 20	19 14	20 29	21 55
56	17 18	17 55	18 38	18 01	18 54	20 10	21 40
58	17 14	17 53	18 39	17 38	18 27	19 47	21 23
S 60	17 10	17 52	18 40	17 08	17 51	19 16	21 01

Day	SUN Eqn. of Time 00^h m s	SUN Eqn. of Time 12^h m s	SUN Mer. Pass. h m	MOON Mer. Pass. Upper h m	MOON Mer. Pass. Lower h m	MOON Age d	MOON Phase %
9	01 37	01 29	12 01	15 11	02 39	03	16
10	01 21	01 13	12 01	16 15	03 43	04	25
11	01 05	00 58	12 01	17 17	04 46	05	36

UT	ARIES GHA	VENUS −3.8 GHA	VENUS Dec	MARS +1.0 GHA	MARS Dec	JUPITER −2.2 GHA	JUPITER Dec	SATURN +0.5 GHA	SATURN Dec
d h	° ′	° ′	° ′	° ′	° ′	° ′	° ′	° ′	° ′
12 00	200 34.1	193 26.3	N 1 26.8	93 08.3	N24 36.7	267 39.1	S21 45.5	45 50.2	N12 27.0
01	215 36.5	208 25.9	28.0	108 09.5	36.5	282 41.3	45.5	60 52.7	27.0
02	230 39.0	223 25.5	29.2	123 10.6	36.3	297 43.6	45.5	75 55.3	27.0
03	245 41.5	238 25.2	. . 30.4	138 11.8	. . 36.1	312 45.8	. . 45.4	90 57.8	. . 27.1
04	260 43.9	253 24.8	31.6	153 13.0	36.0	327 48.0	45.4	106 00.4	27.1
05	275 46.4	268 24.4	32.9	168 14.1	35.8	342 50.3	45.4	121 02.9	27.1
06	290 48.9	283 24.1	N 1 34.1	183 15.3	N24 35.6	357 52.5	S21 45.3	136 05.5	N12 27.1
07	305 51.3	298 23.7	35.3	198 16.4	35.4	12 54.8	45.3	151 08.0	27.2
S 08	320 53.8	313 23.3	36.5	213 17.6	35.2	27 57.0	45.3	166 10.6	27.2
A 09	335 56.2	328 23.0	. . 37.8	228 18.8	. . 35.0	42 59.3	. . 45.3	181 13.1	. . 27.2
T 10	350 58.7	343 22.6	39.0	243 19.9	34.9	58 01.5	45.2	196 15.7	27.3
U 11	6 01.2	358 22.2	40.2	258 21.1	34.7	73 03.8	45.2	211 18.2	27.3
R 12	21 03.6	13 21.9	N 1 41.4	273 22.2	N24 34.5	88 06.0	S21 45.2	226 20.8	N12 27.3
D 13	36 06.1	28 21.5	42.6	288 23.4	34.3	103 08.2	45.2	241 23.3	27.3
A 14	51 08.6	43 21.1	43.9	303 24.5	34.1	118 10.5	45.1	256 25.9	27.4
Y 15	66 11.0	58 20.8	. . 45.1	318 25.7	. . 34.0	133 12.7	. . 45.1	271 28.4	. . 27.4
16	81 13.5	73 20.4	46.3	333 26.9	33.8	148 15.0	45.1	286 31.0	27.4
17	96 16.0	88 20.0	47.5	348 28.0	33.6	163 17.2	45.0	301 33.5	27.5
18	111 18.4	103 19.7	N 1 48.8	3 29.2	N24 33.4	178 19.5	S21 45.0	316 36.1	N12 27.5
19	126 20.9	118 19.3	50.0	18 30.3	33.2	193 21.7	45.0	331 38.6	27.5
20	141 23.3	133 18.9	51.2	33 31.5	33.0	208 24.0	45.0	346 41.2	27.5
21	156 25.8	148 18.6	. . 52.4	48 32.7	. . 32.9	223 26.2	. . 44.9	1 43.7	. . 27.6
22	171 28.3	163 18.2	53.6	63 33.8	32.7	238 28.5	44.9	16 46.3	27.6
23	186 30.7	178 17.8	54.9	78 35.0	32.5	253 30.7	44.9	31 48.8	27.6
13 00	201 33.2	193 17.5	N 1 56.1	93 36.1	N24 32.3	268 33.0	S21 44.9	46 51.4	N12 27.7
01	216 35.7	208 17.1	57.3	108 37.3	32.1	283 35.2	44.8	61 53.9	27.7
02	231 38.1	223 16.7	58.5	123 38.4	31.9	298 37.5	44.8	76 56.5	27.7
03	246 40.6	238 16.3	. . 1 59.7	138 39.6	. . 31.8	313 39.7	. . 44.8	91 59.0	. . 27.7
04	261 43.1	253 16.0	2 01.0	153 40.7	31.6	328 42.0	44.8	107 01.6	27.8
05	276 45.5	268 15.6	02.2	168 41.9	31.4	343 44.2	44.7	122 04.1	27.8
06	291 48.0	283 15.2	N 2 03.4	183 43.1	N24 31.2	358 46.5	S21 44.7	137 06.7	N12 27.8
07	306 50.5	298 14.9	04.6	198 44.2	31.0	13 48.7	44.7	152 09.2	27.8
08	321 52.9	313 14.5	05.9	213 45.4	30.8	28 51.0	44.6	167 11.8	27.9
S 09	336 55.4	328 14.1	. . 07.1	228 46.5	. . 30.6	43 53.3	. . 44.6	182 14.3	. . 27.9
U 10	351 57.8	343 13.8	08.3	243 47.7	30.5	58 55.5	44.6	197 16.9	27.9
N 11	7 00.3	358 13.4	09.5	258 48.8	30.3	73 57.8	44.6	212 19.4	28.0
D 12	22 02.8	13 13.0	N 2 10.7	273 50.0	N24 30.1	89 00.0	S21 44.5	227 21.9	N12 28.0
A 13	37 05.2	28 12.7	12.0	288 51.1	29.9	104 02.3	44.5	242 24.5	28.0
Y 14	52 07.7	43 12.3	13.2	303 52.3	29.7	119 04.5	44.5	257 27.0	28.0
15	67 10.2	58 11.9	. . 14.4	318 53.4	. . 29.5	134 06.8	. . 44.5	272 29.6	. . 28.1
16	82 12.6	73 11.6	15.6	333 54.6	29.3	149 09.0	44.4	287 32.1	28.1
17	97 15.1	88 11.2	16.8	348 55.7	29.2	164 11.3	44.4	302 34.7	28.1
18	112 17.6	103 10.8	N 2 18.1	3 56.9	N24 29.0	179 13.5	S21 44.4	317 37.2	N12 28.1
19	127 20.0	118 10.5	19.3	18 58.0	28.8	194 15.8	44.4	332 39.8	28.2
20	142 22.5	133 10.1	20.5	33 59.2	28.6	209 18.1	44.3	347 42.3	28.2
21	157 25.0	148 09.7	. . 21.7	49 00.3	. . 28.4	224 20.3	. . 44.3	2 44.9	. . 28.2
22	172 27.4	163 09.3	22.9	64 01.5	28.2	239 22.6	44.3	17 47.4	28.2
23	187 29.9	178 09.0	24.2	79 02.7	28.0	254 24.8	44.3	32 49.9	28.3
14 00	202 32.3	193 08.6	N 2 25.4	94 03.8	N24 27.8	269 27.1	S21 44.2	47 52.5	N12 28.3
01	217 34.8	208 08.2	26.6	109 05.0	27.7	284 29.3	44.2	62 55.0	28.3
02	232 37.3	223 07.9	27.8	124 06.1	27.5	299 31.6	44.2	77 57.6	28.3
03	247 39.7	238 07.5	. . 29.0	139 07.3	. . 27.3	314 33.9	. . 44.2	93 00.1	. . 28.4
04	262 42.2	253 07.1	30.3	154 08.4	27.1	329 36.1	44.1	108 02.7	28.4
05	277 44.7	268 06.8	31.5	169 09.6	26.9	344 38.4	44.1	123 05.2	28.4
06	292 47.1	283 06.4	N 2 32.7	184 10.7	N24 26.7	359 40.6	S21 44.1	138 07.7	N12 28.5
07	307 49.6	298 06.0	33.9	199 11.9	26.5	14 42.9	44.1	153 10.3	28.5
08	322 52.1	313 05.6	35.1	214 13.0	26.3	29 45.2	44.0	168 12.8	28.5
M 09	337 54.5	328 05.3	. . 36.4	229 14.1	. . 26.1	44 47.4	. . 44.0	183 15.4	. . 28.5
O 10	352 57.0	343 04.9	37.6	244 15.3	25.9	59 49.7	44.0	198 17.9	28.6
N 11	7 59.4	358 04.5	38.8	259 16.4	25.8	74 51.9	44.0	213 20.5	28.6
D 12	23 01.9	13 04.2	N 2 40.0	274 17.6	N24 25.6	89 54.2	S21 43.9	228 23.0	N12 28.6
A 13	38 04.4	28 03.8	41.2	289 18.7	25.4	104 56.5	43.9	243 25.5	28.6
Y 14	53 06.8	43 03.4	42.5	304 19.9	25.2	119 58.7	43.9	258 28.1	28.7
15	68 09.3	58 03.1	. . 43.7	319 21.0	. . 25.0	135 01.0	. . 43.9	273 30.6	. . 28.7
16	83 11.8	73 02.7	44.9	334 22.2	24.8	150 03.2	43.8	288 33.2	28.7
17	98 14.2	88 02.3	46.1	349 23.3	24.6	165 05.5	43.8	303 35.7	28.7
18	113 16.7	103 01.9	N 2 47.3	4 24.5	N24 24.4	180 07.8	S21 43.8	318 38.3	N12 28.8
19	128 19.2	118 01.6	48.6	19 25.6	24.2	195 10.0	43.8	333 40.8	28.8
20	143 21.6	133 01.2	49.8	34 26.8	24.0	210 12.3	43.7	348 43.3	28.8
21	158 24.1	148 00.8	. . 51.0	49 27.9	. . 23.8	225 14.6	. . 43.7	3 45.9	. . 28.8
22	173 26.6	163 00.5	52.2	64 29.1	23.6	240 16.8	43.7	18 48.4	28.9
23	188 29.0	178 00.1	53.4	79 30.2	23.4	255 19.1	43.7	33 51.0	28.9
Mer. Pass.	h m 10 32.1	v −0.4	d 1.2	v 1.2	d 0.2	v 2.3	d 0.0	v 2.5	d 0.0

STARS

Name	SHA	Dec
	° ′	° ′
Acamar	315 21.6	S40 16.3
Achernar	335 30.0	S57 11.6
Acrux	173 13.4	S63 08.9
Adhara	255 15.7	S28 59.2
Aldebaran	290 54.1	N16 31.6
Alioth	166 23.3	N55 54.8
Alkaid	153 01.3	N49 16.1
Al Na'ir	27 48.7	S46 55.1
Alnilam	275 50.5	S 1 11.8
Alphard	217 59.8	S 8 41.8
Alphecca	126 14.0	N26 40.9
Alpheratz	357 48.0	N29 08.1
Altair	62 12.1	N 8 53.2
Ankaa	353 19.8	S42 15.6
Antares	112 30.8	S26 27.1
Arcturus	145 58.9	N19 08.1
Atria	107 36.0	S69 02.5
Avior	234 19.7	S59 32.4
Bellatrix	278 36.4	N 6 21.4
Betelgeuse	271 05.7	N 7 24.5
Canopus	263 58.1	S52 42.2
Capella	280 40.6	N46 00.6
Deneb	49 34.4	N45 18.2
Denebola	182 37.3	N14 31.4
Diphda	349 00.1	S17 56.5
Dubhe	193 55.6	N61 42.5
Elnath	278 17.8	N28 37.0
Eltanin	90 47.7	N51 28.9
Enif	33 51.2	N 9 54.6
Fomalhaut	15 28.5	S29 34.7
Gacrux	172 05.0	S57 09.8
Gienah	175 56.1	S17 35.5
Hadar	148 53.1	S60 24.9
Hamal	328 05.6	N23 30.1
Kaus Aust.	83 48.9	S34 22.9
Kochab	137 18.2	N74 07.0
Markab	13 42.5	N15 14.9
Menkar	314 19.5	N 4 07.3
Menkent	148 11.9	S36 24.8
Miaplacidus	221 40.6	S69 45.4
Mirfak	308 46.6	N49 53.6
Nunki	76 03.1	S26 17.2
Peacock	53 25.3	S56 42.3
Pollux	243 32.5	N28 00.5
Procyon	245 03.8	N 5 12.2
Rasalhague	96 09.9	N12 33.0
Regulus	207 47.4	N11 55.5
Rigel	281 16.0	S 8 11.6
Rigil Kent.	139 56.7	S60 52.2
Sabik	102 16.8	S15 44.3
Schedar	349 45.9	N56 34.9
Shaula	96 27.0	S37 06.6
Sirius	258 37.3	S16 43.8
Spica	158 35.1	S11 12.5
Suhail	222 55.3	S43 28.2
Vega	80 41.5	N38 47.1
Zuben'ubi	137 09.5	S16 04.8

	SHA	Mer. Pass.
	° ′	h m
Venus	351 44.2	11 07
Mars	252 02.9	17 44
Jupiter	66 59.8	6 05
Saturn	205 18.2	20 49

UT d h	SUN GHA ° ′	SUN Dec ° ′	MOON GHA ° ′	v ′	MOON Dec ° ′	d ′	HP ′
12 00	179 47.6	N 8 44.6	96 34.5	5.0	N26 21.2	5.7	58.9
01	194 47.8	45.5	110 58.5	5.1	26 15.5	5.8	58.9
02	209 48.0	46.4	125 22.6	5.3	26 09.7	6.0	58.9
03	224 48.1	. . 47.3	139 46.9	5.3	26 03.7	6.2	58.8
04	239 48.3	48.2	154 11.2	5.4	25 57.5	6.4	58.8
05	254 48.4	49.1	168 35.6	5.6	25 51.1	6.5	58.8
06	269 48.6	N 8 50.1	183 00.2	5.6	N25 44.6	6.6	58.7
S 07	284 48.8	51.0	197 24.8	5.7	25 38.0	6.8	58.7
A 08	299 48.9	51.9	211 49.5	5.9	25 31.2	7.0	58.7
T 09	314 49.1	. . 52.8	226 14.4	6.0	25 24.2	7.1	58.7
U 10	329 49.2	53.7	240 39.4	6.1	25 17.1	7.3	58.6
R 11	344 49.4	54.6	255 04.5	6.2	25 09.8	7.4	58.6
D 12	359 49.6	N 8 55.5	269 29.7	6.3	N25 02.4	7.5	58.6
A 13	14 49.7	56.4	283 55.0	6.4	24 54.9	7.7	58.5
Y 14	29 49.9	57.3	298 20.4	6.5	24 47.2	7.9	58.5
15	44 50.0	. . 58.2	312 45.9	6.7	24 39.3	8.0	58.5
16	59 50.2	8 59.1	327 11.6	6.8	24 31.3	8.1	58.5
17	74 50.4	9 00.1	341 37.4	6.8	24 23.2	8.3	58.4
18	89 50.5	N 9 01.0	356 03.2	7.0	N24 14.9	8.4	58.4
19	104 50.7	01.9	10 29.2	7.2	24 06.5	8.5	58.4
20	119 50.8	02.8	24 55.4	7.2	23 58.0	8.7	58.3
21	134 51.0	. . 03.7	39 21.6	7.3	23 49.3	8.8	58.3
22	149 51.2	04.6	53 47.9	7.5	23 40.5	8.9	58.3
23	164 51.3	05.5	68 14.4	7.6	23 31.6	9.1	58.2
13 00	179 51.5	N 9 06.4	82 41.0	7.7	N23 22.5	9.2	58.2
01	194 51.6	07.3	97 07.7	7.8	23 13.3	9.3	58.2
02	209 51.8	08.2	111 34.5	8.0	23 04.0	9.4	58.2
03	224 51.9	. . 09.1	126 01.5	8.0	22 54.6	9.6	58.1
04	239 52.1	10.0	140 28.5	8.2	22 45.0	9.7	58.1
05	254 52.3	10.9	154 55.7	8.3	22 35.3	9.8	58.1
06	269 52.4	N 9 11.8	169 23.0	8.4	N22 25.5	9.9	58.0
07	284 52.6	12.7	183 50.4	8.5	22 15.6	10.0	58.0
08	299 52.7	13.6	198 17.9	8.7	22 05.6	10.2	58.0
S 09	314 52.9	. . 14.5	212 45.6	8.7	21 55.4	10.2	58.0
U 10	329 53.0	15.4	227 13.3	8.9	21 45.2	10.4	57.9
N 11	344 53.2	16.3	241 41.2	9.0	21 34.8	10.5	57.9
D 12	359 53.4	N 9 17.2	256 09.2	9.1	N21 24.3	10.6	57.9
A 13	14 53.5	18.1	270 37.3	9.2	21 13.7	10.7	57.8
Y 14	29 53.7	19.0	285 05.5	9.4	21 03.0	10.7	57.8
15	44 53.8	. . 20.0	299 33.9	9.4	20 52.3	10.9	57.8
16	59 54.0	20.9	314 02.3	9.6	20 41.4	11.0	57.8
17	74 54.1	21.8	328 30.9	9.7	20 30.4	11.1	57.7
18	89 54.3	N 9 22.7	342 59.6	9.8	N20 19.3	11.2	57.7
19	104 54.5	23.6	357 28.4	9.9	20 08.1	11.3	57.7
20	119 54.6	24.5	11 57.3	10.0	19 56.8	11.4	57.6
21	134 54.8	. . 25.4	26 26.3	10.1	19 45.4	11.5	57.6
22	149 54.9	26.3	40 55.4	10.3	19 33.9	11.5	57.6
23	164 55.1	27.2	55 24.7	10.3	19 22.4	11.7	57.6
14 00	179 55.2	N 9 28.1	69 54.0	10.5	N19 10.7	11.7	57.5
01	194 55.4	29.0	84 23.5	10.6	18 59.0	11.8	57.5
02	209 55.5	29.9	98 53.1	10.6	18 47.2	11.9	57.5
03	224 55.7	. . 30.7	113 22.7	10.8	18 35.3	12.0	57.4
04	239 55.8	31.6	127 52.5	10.9	18 23.3	12.1	57.4
05	254 56.0	32.5	142 22.4	11.0	18 11.2	12.2	57.4
06	269 56.2	N 9 33.4	156 52.4	11.1	N17 59.0	12.2	57.4
07	284 56.3	34.3	171 22.5	11.2	17 46.8	12.3	57.3
08	299 56.5	35.2	185 52.7	11.3	17 34.5	12.4	57.3
M 09	314 56.6	. . 36.1	200 23.0	11.4	17 22.1	12.5	57.3
O 10	329 56.8	37.0	214 53.4	11.5	17 09.6	12.5	57.3
N 11	344 56.9	37.9	229 23.9	11.6	16 57.1	12.6	57.2
D 12	359 57.1	N 9 38.8	243 54.5	11.7	N16 44.5	12.7	57.2
A 13	14 57.2	39.7	258 25.2	11.8	16 31.8	12.7	57.2
Y 14	29 57.4	40.6	272 56.0	11.9	16 19.1	12.8	57.1
15	44 57.5	. . 41.5	287 26.9	12.0	16 06.3	12.9	57.1
16	59 57.7	42.4	301 57.9	12.1	15 53.4	12.9	57.1
17	74 57.8	43.3	316 29.0	12.2	15 40.5	13.0	57.1
18	89 58.0	N 9 44.2	331 00.2	12.2	N15 27.5	13.1	57.0
19	104 58.1	45.1	345 31.4	12.4	15 14.4	13.1	57.0
20	119 58.3	46.0	0 02.8	12.5	15 01.3	13.2	57.0
21	134 58.5	. . 46.9	14 34.3	12.5	14 48.1	13.3	57.0
22	149 58.6	47.8	29 05.8	12.6	14 34.8	13.2	56.9
23	164 58.8	48.7	43 37.4	12.7	N14 21.6	13.4	56.9
	SD 16.0	*d* 0.9	SD 16.0		15.8		15.6

Lat. °	Twilight Naut. h m	Twilight Civil h m	Sunrise h m	Moonrise 12 h m	Moonrise 13 h m	Moonrise 14 h m	Moonrise 15 h m
N 72	////	02 13	03 49	▭	▭	08 45	11 58
N 70	////	02 45	04 04	▭	▭	09 50	12 18
68	01 06	03 09	04 16	▭	▭	10 26	12 34
66	01 55	03 27	04 26	▭	08 31	10 51	12 46
64	02 24	03 41	04 35	06 36	09 10	11 10	12 57
62	02 46	03 53	04 42	07 39	09 37	11 26	13 06
60	03 03	04 03	04 48	08 13	09 58	11 39	13 13
N 58	03 17	04 11	04 54	08 38	10 15	11 50	13 20
56	03 29	04 19	04 59	08 57	10 29	11 59	13 26
54	03 39	04 26	05 03	09 14	10 41	12 08	13 31
52	03 47	04 32	05 07	09 28	10 52	12 16	13 35
50	03 55	04 37	05 11	09 41	11 02	12 22	13 40
45	04 11	04 48	05 18	10 06	11 22	12 37	13 49
N 40	04 24	04 57	05 25	10 26	11 38	12 49	13 56
35	04 34	05 04	05 30	10 43	11 52	12 59	14 03
30	04 42	05 11	05 35	10 57	12 04	13 08	14 08
20	04 55	05 21	05 43	11 22	12 24	13 23	14 18
N 10	05 04	05 29	05 51	11 43	12 42	13 36	14 27
0	05 12	05 36	05 57	12 03	12 58	13 48	14 35
S 10	05 18	05 42	06 04	12 22	13 14	14 01	14 43
20	05 22	05 48	06 10	12 43	13 32	14 14	14 51
30	05 26	05 54	06 18	13 08	13 51	14 28	15 01
35	05 27	05 57	06 22	13 22	14 03	14 37	15 06
40	05 29	06 00	06 27	13 38	14 16	14 47	15 12
45	05 29	06 03	06 33	13 58	14 32	14 58	15 20
S 50	05 30	06 07	06 40	14 22	14 51	15 12	15 28
52	05 29	06 09	06 43	14 34	15 00	15 18	15 32
54	05 29	06 10	06 46	14 47	15 10	15 25	15 36
56	05 29	06 12	06 50	15 02	15 21	15 33	15 41
58	05 29	06 14	06 54	15 20	15 34	15 42	15 47
S 60	05 28	06 16	06 59	15 42	15 49	15 52	15 53

Lat. °	Sunset h m	Twilight Civil h m	Twilight Naut. h m	Moonset 12 h m	Moonset 13 h m	Moonset 14 h m	Moonset 15 h m
N 72	20 16	21 55	////	▭	▭	06 50	05 15
N 70	20 00	21 20	////	▭	▭	05 42	04 53
68	19 47	20 56	23 09	▭	▭	05 05	04 35
66	19 37	20 37	22 13	▭	05 12	04 39	04 21
64	19 28	20 23	21 41	05 08	04 32	04 18	04 09
62	19 21	20 10	21 19	04 05	04 04	04 02	03 59
60	19 14	20 00	21 01	03 30	03 43	03 48	03 50
N 58	19 08	19 51	20 47	03 05	03 25	03 36	03 42
56	19 03	19 44	20 34	02 45	03 10	03 25	03 35
54	18 59	19 37	20 24	02 28	02 57	03 16	03 29
52	18 55	19 31	20 15	02 13	02 45	03 08	03 24
50	18 51	19 25	20 07	02 01	02 35	03 00	03 19
45	18 43	19 14	19 51	01 34	02 14	02 44	03 08
N 40	18 37	19 05	19 38	01 13	01 57	02 31	02 59
35	18 31	18 57	19 28	00 56	01 42	02 19	02 51
30	18 26	18 51	19 20	00 41	01 29	02 09	02 44
20	18 18	18 40	19 06	00 15	01 07	01 52	02 32
N 10	18 10	18 32	18 57	24 48	00 48	01 37	02 21
0	18 04	18 25	18 49	24 30	00 30	01 23	02 11
S 10	17 57	18 18	18 43	24 12	00 12	01 08	02 01
20	17 50	18 12	18 38	23 52	24 53	00 53	01 50
30	17 42	18 07	18 34	23 29	24 35	00 35	01 37
35	17 38	18 04	18 33	23 16	24 24	00 24	01 30
40	17 33	18 00	18 32	23 00	24 12	00 12	01 22
45	17 27	17 57	18 31	22 42	23 58	25 12	01 12
S 50	17 20	17 53	18 30	22 19	23 40	25 00	01 00
52	17 17	17 51	18 30	22 07	23 32	24 54	00 54
54	17 14	17 50	18 30	21 55	23 23	24 48	00 48
56	17 10	17 48	18 31	21 40	23 12	24 41	00 41
58	17 06	17 46	18 31	21 23	23 00	24 33	00 33
S 60	17 01	17 43	18 31	21 01	22 46	24 24	00 24

Day	SUN Eqn. of Time 00^h	SUN Eqn. of Time 12^h	SUN Mer. Pass.	MOON Mer. Pass. Upper	MOON Mer. Pass. Lower	MOON Age	MOON Phase
d	m s	m s	h m	h m	h m	d %	
12	00 50	00 42	12 01	18 16	05 48	06 47	
13	00 34	00 27	12 00	19 10	06 44	07 58	◐
14	00 19	00 12	12 00	20 00	07 36	08 68	

UT		ARIES	VENUS −3.8		MARS +1.0		JUPITER −2.3		SATURN +0.5	
		GHA	GHA	Dec	GHA	Dec	GHA	Dec	GHA	Dec
d h		° ′	° ′	° ′	° ′	° ′	° ′	° ′	° ′	° ′
15 00		203 31.5	192 59.7	N 2 54.6	94 31.4	N24 23.3	270 21.4	S21 43.6	48 53.5	N12 28.9
01		218 33.9	207 59.4	55.9	109 32.5	23.1	285 23.6	43.6	63 56.0	28.9
02		233 36.4	222 59.0	57.1	124 33.6	22.9	300 25.9	43.6	78 58.6	29.0
03		248 38.9	237 58.6	. . 58.3	139 34.8	. . 22.7	315 28.2	. . 43.6	94 01.1	. . 29.0
04		263 41.3	252 58.2	2 59.5	154 35.9	22.5	330 30.4	43.5	109 03.7	29.0
05		278 43.8	267 57.9	3 00.7	169 37.1	22.3	345 32.7	43.5	124 06.2	29.0
06		293 46.3	282 57.5	N 3 02.0	184 38.2	N24 22.1	0 35.0	S21 43.5	139 08.7	N12 29.0
07		308 48.7	297 57.1	03.2	199 39.4	21.9	15 37.2	43.5	154 11.3	29.1
08	TUESDAY	323 51.2	312 56.8	04.4	214 40.5	21.7	30 39.5	43.4	169 13.8	29.1
09		338 53.7	327 56.4	. . 05.6	229 41.7	. . 21.5	45 41.8	. . 43.4	184 16.4	. . 29.1
10		353 56.1	342 56.0	06.8	244 42.8	21.3	60 44.0	43.4	199 18.9	29.1
11		8 58.6	357 55.6	08.0	259 43.9	21.1	75 46.3	43.4	214 21.4	29.2
12		24 01.1	12 55.3	N 3 09.3	274 45.1	N24 20.9	90 48.6	S21 43.4	229 24.0	N12 29.2
13		39 03.5	27 54.9	10.5	289 46.2	20.7	105 50.8	43.3	244 26.5	29.2
14		54 06.0	42 54.5	11.7	304 47.4	20.5	120 53.1	43.3	259 29.1	29.2
15		69 08.4	57 54.2	. . 12.9	319 48.5	. . 20.3	135 55.4	. . 43.3	274 31.6	. . 29.3
16		84 10.9	72 53.8	14.1	334 49.7	20.1	150 57.6	43.3	289 34.1	29.3
17		99 13.4	87 53.4	15.3	349 50.8	19.9	165 59.9	43.2	304 36.7	29.3
18		114 15.8	102 53.0	N 3 16.6	4 51.9	N24 19.7	181 02.2	S21 43.2	319 39.2	N12 29.3
19		129 18.3	117 52.7	17.8	19 53.1	19.5	196 04.5	43.2	334 41.7	29.4
20		144 20.8	132 52.3	19.0	34 54.2	19.3	211 06.7	43.2	349 44.3	29.4
21		159 23.2	147 51.9	. . 20.2	49 55.4	. . 19.2	226 09.0	. . 43.1	4 46.8	. . 29.4
22		174 25.7	162 51.6	21.4	64 56.5	19.0	241 11.3	43.1	19 49.3	29.4
23		189 28.2	177 51.2	22.6	79 57.6	18.8	256 13.5	43.1	34 51.9	29.4
16 00		204 30.6	192 50.8	N 3 23.9	94 58.8	N24 18.6	271 15.8	S21 43.1	49 54.4	N12 29.5
01		219 33.1	207 50.4	25.1	109 59.9	18.4	286 18.1	43.0	64 57.0	29.5
02		234 35.5	222 50.1	26.3	125 01.1	18.2	301 20.4	43.0	79 59.5	29.5
03		249 38.0	237 49.7	. . 27.5	140 02.2	. . 18.0	316 22.6	. . 43.0	95 02.0	. . 29.5
04		264 40.5	252 49.3	28.7	155 03.3	17.8	331 24.9	43.0	110 04.6	29.6
05		279 42.9	267 48.9	29.9	170 04.5	17.6	346 27.2	43.0	125 07.1	29.6
06		294 45.4	282 48.6	N 3 31.2	185 05.6	N24 17.4	1 29.5	S21 42.9	140 09.6	N12 29.6
07	WEDNESDAY	309 47.9	297 48.2	32.4	200 06.8	17.2	16 31.7	42.9	155 12.2	29.6
08		324 50.3	312 47.8	33.6	215 07.9	17.0	31 34.0	42.9	170 14.7	29.7
09		339 52.8	327 47.5	. . 34.8	230 09.0	. . 16.8	46 36.3	. . 42.9	185 17.2	. . 29.7
10		354 55.3	342 47.1	36.0	245 10.2	16.6	61 38.6	42.8	200 19.8	29.7
11		9 57.7	357 46.7	37.2	260 11.3	16.4	76 40.8	42.8	215 22.3	29.7
12		25 00.2	12 46.3	N 3 38.4	275 12.5	N24 16.2	91 43.1	S21 42.8	230 24.8	N12 29.7
13		40 02.7	27 46.0	39.7	290 13.6	16.0	106 45.4	42.8	245 27.4	29.8
14		55 05.1	42 45.6	40.9	305 14.7	15.8	121 47.7	42.7	260 29.9	29.8
15		70 07.6	57 45.2	. . 42.1	320 15.9	. . 15.6	136 50.0	. . 42.7	275 32.4	. . 29.8
16		85 10.0	72 44.8	43.3	335 17.0	15.4	151 52.2	42.7	290 35.0	29.8
17		100 12.5	87 44.5	44.5	350 18.1	15.2	166 54.5	42.7	305 37.5	29.9
18		115 15.0	102 44.1	N 3 45.7	5 19.3	N24 15.0	181 56.8	S21 42.7	320 40.1	N12 29.9
19		130 17.4	117 43.7	46.9	20 20.4	14.8	196 59.1	42.6	335 42.6	29.9
20		145 19.9	132 43.3	48.2	35 21.6	14.6	212 01.3	42.6	350 45.1	29.9
21		160 22.4	147 43.0	. . 49.4	50 22.7	. . 14.4	227 03.6	. . 42.6	5 47.6	. . 29.9
22		175 24.8	162 42.6	50.6	65 23.8	14.1	242 05.9	42.6	20 50.2	30.0
23		190 27.3	177 42.2	51.8	80 25.0	13.9	257 08.2	42.5	35 52.7	30.0
17 00		205 29.8	192 41.8	N 3 53.0	95 26.1	N24 13.7	272 10.5	S21 42.5	50 55.2	N12 30.0
01		220 32.2	207 41.5	54.2	110 27.2	13.5	287 12.7	42.5	65 57.8	30.0
02		235 34.7	222 41.1	55.4	125 28.4	13.3	302 15.0	42.5	81 00.3	30.0
03		250 37.1	237 40.7	. . 56.6	140 29.5	. . 13.1	317 17.3	. . 42.5	96 02.8	. . 30.1
04		265 39.6	252 40.3	57.9	155 30.6	12.9	332 19.6	42.4	111 05.4	30.1
05		280 42.1	267 40.0	3 59.1	170 31.8	12.7	347 21.9	42.4	126 07.9	30.1
06		295 44.5	282 39.6	N 4 00.3	185 32.9	N24 12.5	2 24.2	S21 42.4	141 10.4	N12 30.1
07		310 47.0	297 39.2	01.5	200 34.0	12.3	17 26.4	42.4	156 13.0	30.1
08	THURSDAY	325 49.5	312 38.8	02.7	215 35.2	12.1	32 28.7	42.3	171 15.5	30.2
09		340 51.9	327 38.5	. . 03.9	230 36.3	. . 11.9	47 31.0	. . 42.3	186 18.0	. . 30.2
10		355 54.4	342 38.1	05.1	245 37.4	11.7	62 33.3	42.3	201 20.6	30.2
11		10 56.9	357 37.7	06.3	260 38.6	11.5	77 35.6	42.3	216 23.1	30.2
12		25 59.3	12 37.3	N 4 07.6	275 39.7	N24 11.3	92 37.9	S21 42.3	231 25.6	N12 30.3
13		41 01.8	27 37.0	08.8	290 40.8	11.1	107 40.1	42.2	246 28.2	30.3
14		56 04.3	42 36.6	10.0	305 42.0	10.9	122 42.4	42.2	261 30.7	30.3
15		71 06.7	57 36.2	. . 11.2	320 43.1	. . 10.7	137 44.7	. . 42.2	276 33.2	. . 30.3
16		86 09.2	72 35.8	12.4	335 44.2	10.5	152 47.0	42.2	291 35.7	30.3
17		101 11.6	87 35.4	13.6	350 45.4	10.3	167 49.3	42.2	306 38.3	30.4
18		116 14.1	102 35.1	N 4 14.8	5 46.5	N24 10.1	182 51.6	S21 42.1	321 40.8	N12 30.4
19		131 16.6	117 34.7	16.0	20 47.6	09.8	197 53.9	42.1	336 43.3	30.4
20		146 19.0	132 34.3	17.2	35 48.8	09.6	212 56.1	42.1	351 45.9	30.4
21		161 21.5	147 33.9	. . 18.5	50 49.9	. . 09.4	227 58.4	. . 42.1	6 48.4	. . 30.4
22		176 24.0	162 33.6	19.7	65 51.0	09.2	243 00.7	42.0	21 50.9	30.5
23		191 26.4	177 33.2	20.9	80 52.2	09.0	258 03.0	42.0	36 53.4	30.5
Mer. Pass.		h m 10 20.3	*v* −0.4	*d* 1.2	*v* 1.1	*d* 0.2	*v* 2.3	*d* 0.0	*v* 2.5	*d* 0.0

STARS

Name	SHA	Dec
	° ′	° ′
Acamar	315 21.6	S40 16.3
Achernar	335 30.0	S57 11.6
Acrux	173 13.4	S63 08.9
Adhara	255 15.7	S28 59.2
Aldebaran	290 54.1	N16 31.6
Alioth	166 23.3	N55 54.8
Alkaid	153 01.3	N49 16.1
Al Na'ir	27 48.7	S46 55.1
Alnilam	275 50.5	S 1 11.8
Alphard	217 59.8	S 8 41.8
Alphecca	126 13.9	N26 40.9
Alpheratz	357 48.0	N29 08.1
Altair	62 12.1	N 8 53.2
Ankaa	353 19.8	S42 15.6
Antares	112 30.8	S26 27.2
Arcturus	145 58.9	N19 08.1
Atria	107 35.9	S69 02.5
Avior	234 19.7	S59 32.4
Bellatrix	278 36.4	N 6 21.4
Betelgeuse	271 05.7	N 7 24.5
Canopus	263 58.1	S52 42.2
Capella	280 40.6	N46 00.6
Deneb	49 34.4	N45 18.2
Denebola	182 37.3	N14 31.4
Diphda	349 00.1	S17 56.5
Dubhe	193 55.6	N61 42.5
Elnath	278 17.8	N28 37.0
Eltanin	90 47.7	N51 28.9
Enif	33 51.1	N 9 54.6
Fomalhaut	15 28.4	S29 34.7
Gacrux	172 05.0	S57 09.8
Gienah	175 56.1	S17 35.5
Hadar	148 53.1	S60 24.9
Hamal	328 05.6	N23 30.1
Kaus Aust.	83 48.8	S34 22.9
Kochab	137 18.2	N74 07.1
Markab	13 42.5	N15 14.9
Menkar	314 19.5	N 4 07.3
Menkent	148 11.9	S36 24.8
Miaplacidus	221 40.6	S69 45.4
Mirfak	308 46.6	N49 53.6
Nunki	76 03.0	S26 17.2
Peacock	53 25.3	S56 42.3
Pollux	243 32.5	N28 00.5
Procyon	245 03.8	N 5 12.2
Rasalhague	96 09.9	N12 33.0
Regulus	207 47.5	N11 55.5
Rigel	281 16.0	S 8 11.6
Rigil Kent.	139 56.7	S60 52.2
Sabik	102 16.8	S15 44.3
Schedar	349 45.9	N56 34.9
Shaula	96 27.0	S37 06.6
Sirius	258 37.3	S16 43.8
Spica	158 35.1	S11 12.5
Suhail	222 55.3	S43 28.2
Vega	80 41.5	N38 47.1
Zuben'ubi	137 09.5	S16 04.8

	SHA	Mer. Pass.
	° ′	h m
Venus	348 20.2	11 09
Mars	250 28.2	17 39
Jupiter	66 45.2	5 54
Saturn	205 23.8	20 37

	UT (d h)	SUN GHA	SUN Dec	MOON GHA	*v*	MOON Dec	*d*	HP
		° ′	° ′	° ′	′	° ′	′	′
	15 00	179 58.9	N 9 49.6	58 09.1	12.9	N14 08.2	13.4	56.9
	01	194 59.1	50.4	72 41.0	12.8	13 54.8	13.5	56.9
	02	209 59.2	51.3	87 12.8	13.0	13 41.3	13.5	56.8
	03	224 59.4	. . 52.2	101 44.8	13.1	13 27.8	13.5	56.8
	04	239 59.5	53.1	116 16.9	13.1	13 14.3	13.6	56.8
	05	254 59.7	54.0	130 49.0	13.2	13 00.7	13.7	56.8
	06	269 59.8	N 9 54.9	145 21.2	13.3	N12 47.0	13.7	56.7
	07	285 00.0	55.8	159 53.5	13.4	12 33.3	13.7	56.7
T	08	300 00.1	56.7	174 25.9	13.4	12 19.6	13.8	56.7
U	09	315 00.3	. . 57.6	188 58.3	13.6	12 05.8	13.8	56.7
E	10	330 00.4	58.5	203 30.9	13.6	11 52.0	13.9	56.6
S	11	345 00.6	9 59.3	218 03.5	13.7	11 38.1	13.9	56.6
D	12	0 00.7	N10 00.2	232 36.2	13.7	N11 24.2	14.0	56.6
A	13	15 00.9	01.1	247 08.9	13.8	11 10.2	14.0	56.6
Y	14	30 01.0	02.0	261 41.7	13.9	10 56.2	14.0	56.5
	15	45 01.2	. . 02.9	276 14.6	14.0	10 42.2	14.0	56.5
	16	60 01.3	03.8	290 47.6	14.0	10 28.2	14.1	56.5
	17	75 01.5	04.7	305 20.6	14.1	10 14.1	14.2	56.5
	18	90 01.6	N10 05.6	319 53.7	14.1	N 9 59.9	14.1	56.4
	19	105 01.8	06.5	334 26.8	14.3	9 45.8	14.2	56.4
	20	120 01.9	07.3	349 00.1	14.2	9 31.6	14.2	56.4
	21	135 02.1	. . 08.2	3 33.3	14.4	9 17.4	14.3	56.4
	22	150 02.2	09.1	18 06.7	14.4	9 03.1	14.2	56.3
	23	165 02.4	10.0	32 40.1	14.4	8 48.9	14.3	56.3
	16 00	180 02.5	N10 10.9	47 13.5	14.6	N 8 34.6	14.3	56.3
	01	195 02.6	11.8	61 47.1	14.5	8 20.3	14.4	56.3
	02	210 02.8	12.7	76 20.6	14.7	8 05.9	14.4	56.2
	03	225 02.9	. . 13.5	90 54.3	14.7	7 51.5	14.4	56.2
	04	240 03.1	14.4	105 28.0	14.7	7 37.1	14.4	56.2
	05	255 03.2	15.3	120 01.7	14.8	7 22.7	14.4	56.2
	06	270 03.4	N10 16.2	134 35.5	14.8	N 7 08.3	14.5	56.2
W	07	285 03.5	17.1	149 09.3	14.9	6 53.8	14.4	56.1
E	08	300 03.7	18.0	163 43.2	15.0	6 39.4	14.5	56.1
D	09	315 03.8	. . 18.8	178 17.2	15.0	6 24.9	14.5	56.1
N	10	330 04.0	19.7	192 51.2	15.0	6 10.4	14.5	56.1
E	11	345 04.1	20.6	207 25.2	15.1	5 55.9	14.6	56.0
S	12	0 04.3	N10 21.5	221 59.3	15.1	N 5 41.3	14.5	56.0
D	13	15 04.4	22.4	236 33.4	15.2	5 26.8	14.5	56.0
A	14	30 04.6	23.2	251 07.6	15.2	5 12.3	14.6	56.0
Y	15	45 04.7	. . 24.1	265 41.8	15.2	4 57.7	14.6	56.0
	16	60 04.8	25.0	280 16.0	15.3	4 43.1	14.6	55.9
	17	75 05.0	25.9	294 50.3	15.3	4 28.5	14.6	55.9
	18	90 05.1	N10 26.8	309 24.6	15.4	N 4 13.9	14.6	55.9
	19	105 05.3	27.7	323 59.0	15.4	3 59.3	14.6	55.9
	20	120 05.4	28.5	338 33.4	15.4	3 44.7	14.6	55.9
	21	135 05.6	. . 29.4	353 07.8	15.5	3 30.1	14.6	55.8
	22	150 05.7	30.3	7 42.3	15.5	3 15.5	14.6	55.8
	23	165 05.9	31.2	22 16.8	15.5	3 00.9	14.6	55.8
	17 00	180 06.0	N10 32.0	36 51.3	15.6	N 2 46.3	14.6	55.8
	01	195 06.2	32.9	51 25.9	15.5	2 31.7	14.6	55.7
	02	210 06.3	33.8	66 00.4	15.7	2 17.1	14.7	55.7
	03	225 06.4	. . 34.7	80 35.1	15.6	2 02.4	14.6	55.7
	04	240 06.6	35.6	95 09.7	15.7	1 47.8	14.6	55.7
	05	255 06.7	36.4	109 44.4	15.6	1 33.2	14.6	55.7
	06	270 06.9	N10 37.3	124 19.0	15.8	N 1 18.6	14.6	55.6
	07	285 07.0	38.2	138 53.8	15.7	1 04.0	14.6	55.6
T	08	300 07.2	39.1	153 28.5	15.7	0 49.4	14.6	55.6
H	09	315 07.3	. . 39.9	168 03.2	15.8	0 34.8	14.6	55.6
U	10	330 07.4	40.8	182 38.0	15.8	0 20.2	14.6	55.6
R	11	345 07.6	41.7	197 12.8	15.8	N 0 05.6	14.5	55.5
S	12	0 07.7	N10 42.6	211 47.6	15.8	S 0 08.9	14.6	55.5
D	13	15 07.9	43.4	226 22.4	15.9	0 23.5	14.5	55.5
A	14	30 08.0	44.3	240 57.3	15.8	0 38.0	14.6	55.5
Y	15	45 08.1	. . 45.2	255 32.1	15.9	0 52.6	14.5	55.5
	16	60 08.3	46.1	270 07.0	15.9	1 07.1	14.5	55.5
	17	75 08.4	46.9	284 41.9	15.9	1 21.6	14.5	55.4
	18	90 08.6	N10 47.8	299 16.8	15.9	S 1 36.1	14.5	55.4
	19	105 08.7	48.7	313 51.7	15.9	1 50.6	14.4	55.4
	20	120 08.9	49.5	328 26.6	15.9	2 05.0	14.5	55.4
	21	135 09.0	. . 50.4	343 01.5	15.9	2 19.5	14.4	55.4
	22	150 09.1	51.3	357 36.4	16.0	2 33.9	14.4	55.3
	23	165 09.3	52.2	12 11.4	15.9	S 2 48.3	14.4	55.3
		SD 16.0	*d* 0.9	SD 15.4		15.3		15.1

Lat.	Twilight Naut.	Twilight Civil	Sunrise	Moonrise 15	Moonrise 16	Moonrise 17	Moonrise 18
°	h m	h m	h m	h m	h m	h m	h m
N 72	////	01 44	03 31	11 58	14 13	16 16	18 19
N 70	////	02 25	03 49	12 18	14 20	16 14	18 07
68	////	02 52	04 03	12 34	14 26	16 13	17 58
66	01 30	03 13	04 15	12 46	14 31	16 11	17 50
64	02 06	03 29	04 24	12 57	14 36	16 10	17 44
62	02 31	03 42	04 33	13 06	14 39	16 09	17 38
60	02 51	03 53	04 40	13 13	14 43	16 09	17 34
N 58	03 06	04 03	04 46	13 20	14 45	16 08	17 29
56	03 19	04 11	04 51	13 26	14 48	16 07	17 26
54	03 30	04 18	04 56	13 31	14 50	16 07	17 22
52	03 40	04 25	05 01	13 35	14 52	16 06	17 19
50	03 48	04 30	05 05	13 40	14 54	16 06	17 17
45	04 05	04 42	05 13	13 49	14 58	16 05	17 11
N 40	04 19	04 52	05 20	13 56	15 01	16 04	17 06
35	04 29	05 00	05 26	14 03	15 04	16 03	17 02
30	04 38	05 07	05 32	14 08	15 06	16 03	16 58
20	04 52	05 19	05 41	14 18	15 11	16 02	16 52
N 10	05 03	05 28	05 49	14 27	15 15	16 01	16 46
0	05 11	05 35	05 56	14 35	15 18	16 00	16 41
S 10	05 18	05 42	06 04	14 43	15 22	15 59	16 36
20	05 23	05 49	06 11	14 51	15 26	15 58	16 31
30	05 28	05 56	06 20	15 01	15 30	15 57	16 25
35	05 30	05 59	06 25	15 06	15 32	15 57	16 21
40	05 31	06 03	06 30	15 12	15 35	15 56	16 17
45	05 33	06 07	06 37	15 20	15 38	15 56	16 13
S 50	05 34	06 11	06 44	15 28	15 42	15 55	16 08
52	05 34	06 13	06 48	15 32	15 44	15 54	16 05
54	05 34	06 16	06 52	15 36	15 46	15 54	16 02
56	05 35	06 18	06 56	15 41	15 48	15 54	16 00
58	05 35	06 20	07 01	15 47	15 50	15 53	15 56
S 60	05 35	06 23	07 06	15 53	15 53	15 53	15 53

Lat.	Sunset	Twilight Civil	Twilight Naut.	Moonset 15	Moonset 16	Moonset 17	Moonset 18
°	h m	h m	h m	h m	h m	h m	h m
N 72	20 32	22 24	////	05 15	04 33	04 00	03 29
N 70	20 13	21 40	////	04 53	04 22	03 58	03 34
68	19 59	21 11	////	04 35	04 14	03 56	03 39
66	19 47	20 50	22 38	04 21	04 07	03 54	03 43
64	19 37	20 33	21 58	04 09	04 01	03 53	03 46
62	19 29	20 20	21 32	03 59	03 55	03 52	03 48
60	19 21	20 08	21 12	03 50	03 51	03 51	03 51
N 58	19 15	19 59	20 56	03 42	03 47	03 50	03 53
56	19 10	19 50	20 43	03 35	03 43	03 49	03 55
54	19 05	19 43	20 31	03 29	03 40	03 48	03 57
52	19 00	19 36	20 22	03 24	03 37	03 48	03 58
50	18 56	19 30	20 13	03 19	03 34	03 47	04 00
45	18 47	19 18	19 55	03 08	03 28	03 46	04 03
N 40	18 40	19 08	19 42	02 59	03 23	03 45	04 06
35	18 34	19 00	19 31	02 51	03 18	03 44	04 08
30	18 28	18 53	19 22	02 44	03 14	03 43	04 10
20	18 19	18 41	19 08	02 32	03 08	03 41	04 14
N 10	18 11	18 32	18 57	02 21	03 02	03 40	04 17
0	18 03	18 24	18 48	02 11	02 56	03 38	04 20
S 10	17 56	18 17	18 42	02 01	02 50	03 37	04 23
20	17 48	18 10	18 36	01 50	02 44	03 35	04 26
30	17 39	18 03	18 31	01 37	02 37	03 34	04 29
35	17 34	18 00	18 29	01 30	02 33	03 33	04 32
40	17 29	17 56	18 27	01 22	02 28	03 32	04 34
45	17 22	17 52	18 26	01 12	02 22	03 30	04 37
S 50	17 14	17 47	18 25	01 00	02 16	03 29	04 40
52	17 11	17 45	18 24	00 54	02 13	03 28	04 41
54	17 07	17 43	18 24	00 48	02 09	03 27	04 43
56	17 03	17 41	18 24	00 41	02 05	03 26	04 45
58	16 58	17 38	18 23	00 33	02 01	03 25	04 47
S 60	16 52	17 35	18 23	00 24	01 56	03 24	04 49

Day	SUN Eqn. of Time 00^h	SUN Eqn. of Time 12^h	SUN Mer. Pass.	MOON Mer. Pass. Upper	MOON Mer. Pass. Lower	MOON Age	MOON Phase
d	m s	m s	h m	h m	h m	d %	
15	00 05	00 03	12 00	20 45	08 23	09 78	
16	00 10	00 17	12 00	21 28	09 07	10 86	
17	00 24	00 31	11 59	22 10	09 49	11 92	

UT	ARIES	VENUS −3.8		MARS +1.1		JUPITER −2.3		SATURN +0.5	
	GHA	GHA	Dec	GHA	Dec	GHA	Dec	GHA	Dec
d h	° ′	° ′	° ′	° ′	° ′	° ′	° ′	° ′	° ′
18 00	206 28.9	192 32.8	N 4 22.1	95 53.3	N24 08.8	273 05.3	S21 42.0	51 56.0	N12 30.5
01	221 31.4	207 32.4	23.3	110 54.4	08.6	288 07.6	42.0	66 58.5	30.5
02	236 33.8	222 32.1	24.5	125 55.6	08.4	303 09.9	42.0	82 01.0	30.5
03	251 36.3	237 31.7	. . 25.7	140 56.7	. . 08.2	318 12.2	. . 41.9	97 03.6	. . 30.6
04	266 38.8	252 31.3	26.9	155 57.8	08.0	333 14.4	41.9	112 06.1	30.6
05	281 41.2	267 30.9	28.1	170 59.0	07.8	348 16.7	41.9	127 08.6	30.6
06	296 43.7	282 30.5	N 4 29.3	186 00.1	N24 07.6	3 19.0	S21 41.9	142 11.1	N12 30.6
07	311 46.1	297 30.2	30.5	201 01.2	07.4	18 21.3	41.9	157 13.7	30.6
08	326 48.6	312 29.8	31.8	216 02.3	07.1	33 23.6	41.8	172 16.2	30.6
F 09	341 51.1	327 29.4	. . 33.0	231 03.5	. . 06.9	48 25.9	. . 41.8	187 18.7	. . 30.7
R 10	356 53.5	342 29.0	34.2	246 04.6	06.7	63 28.2	41.8	202 21.3	30.7
I 11	11 56.0	357 28.6	35.4	261 05.7	06.5	78 30.5	41.8	217 23.8	30.7
D 12	26 58.5	12 28.3	N 4 36.6	276 06.9	N24 06.3	93 32.8	S21 41.8	232 26.3	N12 30.7
A 13	42 00.9	27 27.9	37.8	291 08.0	06.1	108 35.1	41.7	247 28.8	30.7
Y 14	57 03.4	42 27.5	39.0	306 09.1	05.9	123 37.4	41.7	262 31.4	30.8
15	72 05.9	57 27.1	. . 40.2	321 10.2	. . 05.7	138 39.6	. . 41.7	277 33.9	. . 30.8
16	87 08.3	72 26.7	41.4	336 11.4	05.5	153 41.9	41.7	292 36.4	30.8
17	102 10.8	87 26.4	42.6	351 12.5	05.3	168 44.2	41.7	307 38.9	30.8
18	117 13.2	102 26.0	N 4 43.8	6 13.6	N24 05.0	183 46.5	S21 41.6	322 41.5	N12 30.8
19	132 15.7	117 25.6	45.0	21 14.8	04.8	198 48.8	41.6	337 44.0	30.9
20	147 18.2	132 25.2	46.2	36 15.9	04.6	213 51.1	41.6	352 46.5	30.9
21	162 20.6	147 24.8	. . 47.5	51 17.0	. . 04.4	228 53.4	. . 41.6	7 49.0	. . 30.9
22	177 23.1	162 24.5	48.7	66 18.1	04.2	243 55.7	41.5	22 51.6	30.9
23	192 25.6	177 24.1	49.9	81 19.3	04.0	258 58.0	41.5	37 54.1	30.9
19 00	207 28.0	192 23.7	N 4 51.1	96 20.4	N24 03.8	274 00.3	S21 41.5	52 56.6	N12 30.9
01	222 30.5	207 23.3	52.3	111 21.5	03.6	289 02.6	41.5	67 59.1	31.0
02	237 33.0	222 22.9	53.5	126 22.6	03.3	304 04.9	41.5	83 01.7	31.0
03	252 35.4	237 22.6	. . 54.7	141 23.8	. . 03.1	319 07.2	. . 41.4	98 04.2	. . 31.0
04	267 37.9	252 22.2	55.9	156 24.9	02.9	334 09.5	41.4	113 06.7	31.0
05	282 40.4	267 21.8	57.1	171 26.0	02.7	349 11.8	41.4	128 09.2	31.0
06	297 42.8	282 21.4	N 4 58.3	186 27.1	N24 02.5	4 14.1	S21 41.4	143 11.8	N12 31.1
S 07	312 45.3	297 21.0	4 59.5	201 28.3	02.3	19 16.4	41.4	158 14.3	31.1
A 08	327 47.7	312 20.7	5 00.7	216 29.4	02.1	34 18.7	41.3	173 16.8	31.1
T 09	342 50.2	327 20.3	. . 01.9	231 30.5	. . 01.8	49 21.0	. . 41.3	188 19.3	. . 31.1
U 10	357 52.7	342 19.9	03.1	246 31.6	01.6	64 23.3	41.3	203 21.8	31.1
R 11	12 55.1	357 19.5	04.3	261 32.8	01.4	79 25.6	41.3	218 24.4	31.1
D 12	27 57.6	12 19.1	N 5 05.5	276 33.9	N24 01.2	94 27.9	S21 41.3	233 26.9	N12 31.2
A 13	43 00.1	27 18.7	06.7	291 35.0	01.0	109 30.2	41.3	248 29.4	31.2
Y 14	58 02.5	42 18.4	07.9	306 36.1	00.8	124 32.5	41.2	263 31.9	31.2
15	73 05.0	57 18.0	. . 09.1	321 37.3	. . 00.6	139 34.8	. . 41.2	278 34.5	. . 31.2
16	88 07.5	72 17.6	10.3	336 38.4	00.3	154 37.1	41.2	293 37.0	31.2
17	103 09.9	87 17.2	11.6	351 39.5	24 00.1	169 39.4	41.2	308 39.5	31.2
18	118 12.4	102 16.8	N 5 12.8	6 40.6	N23 59.9	184 41.7	S21 41.2	323 42.0	N12 31.3
19	133 14.8	117 16.4	14.0	21 41.8	59.7	199 44.0	41.1	338 44.5	31.3
20	148 17.3	132 16.1	15.2	36 42.9	59.5	214 46.3	41.1	353 47.1	31.3
21	163 19.8	147 15.7	. . 16.4	51 44.0	. . 59.3	229 48.6	. . 41.1	8 49.6	. . 31.3
22	178 22.2	162 15.3	17.6	66 45.1	59.0	244 50.9	41.1	23 52.1	31.3
23	193 24.7	177 14.9	18.8	81 46.3	58.8	259 53.2	41.1	38 54.6	31.3
20 00	208 27.2	192 14.5	N 5 20.0	96 47.4	N23 58.6	274 55.5	S21 41.0	53 57.2	N12 31.4
01	223 29.6	207 14.1	21.2	111 48.5	58.4	289 57.8	41.0	68 59.7	31.4
02	238 32.1	222 13.7	22.4	126 49.6	58.2	305 00.1	41.0	84 02.2	31.4
03	253 34.6	237 13.4	. . 23.6	141 50.7	. . 57.9	320 02.4	. . 41.0	99 04.7	. . 31.4
04	268 37.0	252 13.0	24.8	156 51.9	57.7	335 04.7	41.0	114 07.2	31.4
05	283 39.5	267 12.6	26.0	171 53.0	57.5	350 07.0	40.9	129 09.8	31.4
06	298 42.0	282 12.2	N 5 27.2	186 54.1	N23 57.3	5 09.3	S21 40.9	144 12.3	N12 31.5
07	313 44.4	297 11.8	28.4	201 55.2	57.1	20 11.6	40.9	159 14.8	31.5
08	328 46.9	312 11.4	29.6	216 56.4	56.9	35 13.9	40.9	174 17.3	31.5
S 09	343 49.3	327 11.0	. . 30.8	231 57.5	. . 56.6	50 16.2	. . 40.9	189 19.8	. . 31.5
U 10	358 51.8	342 10.7	32.0	246 58.6	56.4	65 18.5	40.9	204 22.3	31.5
N 11	13 54.3	357 10.3	33.2	261 59.7	56.2	80 20.9	40.8	219 24.9	31.5
D 12	28 56.7	12 09.9	N 5 34.4	277 00.8	N23 56.0	95 23.2	S21 40.8	234 27.4	N12 31.6
A 13	43 59.2	27 09.5	35.6	292 02.0	55.8	110 25.5	40.8	249 29.9	31.6
Y 14	59 01.7	42 09.1	36.8	307 03.1	55.5	125 27.8	40.8	264 32.4	31.6
15	74 04.1	57 08.7	. . 38.0	322 04.2	. . 55.3	140 30.1	. . 40.8	279 34.9	. . 31.6
16	89 06.6	72 08.3	39.2	337 05.3	55.1	155 32.4	40.7	294 37.5	31.6
17	104 09.1	87 08.0	40.4	352 06.4	54.9	170 34.7	40.7	309 40.0	31.6
18	119 11.5	102 07.6	N 5 41.6	7 07.6	N23 54.7	185 37.0	S21 40.7	324 42.5	N12 31.7
19	134 14.0	117 07.2	42.8	22 08.7	54.4	200 39.3	40.7	339 45.0	31.7
20	149 16.5	132 06.8	44.0	37 09.8	54.2	215 41.6	40.7	354 47.5	31.7
21	164 18.9	147 06.4	. . 45.2	52 10.9	. . 54.0	230 43.9	. . 40.7	9 50.0	. . 31.7
22	179 21.4	162 06.0	46.4	67 12.0	53.8	245 46.2	40.6	24 52.6	31.7
23	194 23.8	177 05.6	47.6	82 13.1	53.5	260 48.6	40.6	39 55.1	31.7
Mer. Pass. (h m)	10 08.5	*v* −0.4	*d* 1.2	*v* 1.1	*d* 0.2	*v* 2.3	*d* 0.0	*v* 2.5	*d* 0.0

STARS

Name	SHA	Dec
	° ′	° ′
Acamar	315 21.6	S40 16.3
Achernar	335 30.0	S57 11.6
Acrux	173 13.4	S63 09.0
Adhara	255 15.7	S28 59.2
Aldebaran	290 54.2	N16 31.6
Alioth	166 23.3	N55 54.8
Alkaid	153 01.3	N49 16.2
Al Na'ir	27 48.7	S46 55.1
Alnilam	275 50.5	S 1 11.8
Alphard	217 59.8	S 8 41.8
Alphecca	126 13.9	N26 40.9
Alpheratz	357 48.0	N29 08.1
Altair	62 12.0	N 8 53.2
Ankaa	353 19.8	S42 15.6
Antares	112 30.8	S26 27.2
Arcturus	145 58.9	N19 08.1
Atria	107 35.9	S69 02.5
Avior	234 19.8	S59 32.4
Bellatrix	278 36.4	N 6 21.4
Betelgeuse	271 05.7	N 7 24.5
Canopus	263 58.1	S52 42.2
Capella	280 40.6	N46 00.6
Deneb	49 34.3	N45 18.2
Denebola	182 37.3	N14 31.4
Diphda	349 00.1	S17 56.5
Dubhe	193 55.6	N61 42.5
Elnath	278 17.8	N28 37.0
Eltanin	90 47.7	N51 28.9
Enif	33 51.1	N 9 54.6
Fomalhaut	15 28.4	S29 34.7
Gacrux	172 05.1	S57 09.8
Gienah	175 56.1	S17 35.5
Hadar	148 53.1	S60 24.9
Hamal	328 05.6	N23 30.1
Kaus Aust.	83 48.8	S34 22.9
Kochab	137 18.2	N74 07.1
Markab	13 42.5	N15 14.9
Menkar	314 19.5	N 4 07.3
Menkent	148 11.9	S36 24.8
Miaplacidus	221 40.6	S69 45.4
Mirfak	308 46.6	N49 53.6
Nunki	76 03.0	S26 17.2
Peacock	53 25.2	S56 42.3
Pollux	243 32.5	N28 00.5
Procyon	245 03.9	N 5 12.2
Rasalhague	96 09.9	N12 33.0
Regulus	207 47.5	N11 55.5
Rigel	281 16.0	S 8 11.6
Rigil Kent.	139 56.7	S60 52.3
Sabik	102 16.8	S15 44.3
Schedar	349 45.8	N56 34.9
Shaula	96 27.0	S37 06.6
Sirius	258 37.3	S16 43.8
Spica	158 35.1	S11 12.5
Suhail	222 55.3	S43 28.2
Vega	80 41.5	N38 47.1
Zuben'ubi	137 09.5	S16 04.8

	SHA	Mer. Pass.
	° ′	h m
Venus	344 55.7	11 11
Mars	248 52.4	17 33
Jupiter	66 32.3	5 43
Saturn	205 28.6	20 25

	UT	SUN GHA	SUN Dec	MOON GHA	v	MOON Dec	d	HP
	d h	° ′	° ′	° ′	′	° ′	′	′
	18 00	180 09.4	N10 53.0	26 46.3	15.9	S 3 02.7	14.4	55.3
	01	195 09.6	53.9	41 21.2	16.0	3 17.1	14.3	55.3
	02	210 09.7	54.8	55 56.2	15.9	3 31.4	14.4	55.3
	03	225 09.8	. . 55.6	70 31.1	16.0	3 45.8	14.3	55.3
	04	240 10.0	56.5	85 06.1	15.9	4 00.1	14.3	55.2
	05	255 10.1	57.4	99 41.0	15.9	4 14.4	14.2	55.2
	06	270 10.3	N10 58.3	114 15.9	16.0	S 4 28.6	14.2	55.2
	07	285 10.4	10 59.1	128 50.9	15.9	4 42.8	14.2	55.2
	08	300 10.5	11 00.0	143 25.8	15.9	4 57.0	14.2	55.2
F	09	315 10.7	. . 00.9	158 00.7	16.0	5 11.2	14.2	55.1
R	10	330 10.8	01.7	172 35.7	15.9	5 25.4	14.1	55.1
I	11	345 10.9	02.6	187 10.6	15.9	5 39.5	14.1	55.1
D	12	0 11.1	N11 03.5	201 45.5	15.9	S 5 53.6	14.0	55.1
A	13	15 11.2	04.3	216 20.4	15.9	6 07.6	14.1	55.1
Y	14	30 11.4	05.2	230 55.3	15.9	6 21.7	14.0	55.1
	15	45 11.5	. . 06.1	245 30.2	15.8	6 35.7	13.9	55.0
	16	60 11.6	06.9	260 05.0	15.9	6 49.6	14.0	55.0
	17	75 11.8	07.8	274 39.9	15.8	7 03.6	13.9	55.0
	18	90 11.9	N11 08.7	289 14.7	15.9	S 7 17.5	13.8	55.0
	19	105 12.0	09.5	303 49.6	15.8	7 31.3	13.8	55.0
	20	120 12.2	10.4	318 24.4	15.8	7 45.1	13.8	55.0
	21	135 12.3	. . 11.2	332 59.2	15.8	7 58.9	13.8	55.0
	22	150 12.5	12.1	347 34.0	15.7	8 12.7	13.7	54.9
	23	165 12.6	13.0	2 08.7	15.8	8 26.4	13.6	54.9
	19 00	180 12.7	N11 13.8	16 43.5	15.7	S 8 40.0	13.7	54.9
	01	195 12.9	14.7	31 18.2	15.7	8 53.7	13.6	54.9
	02	210 13.0	15.6	45 52.9	15.7	9 07.3	13.5	54.9
	03	225 13.1	. . 16.4	60 27.6	15.7	9 20.8	13.5	54.9
	04	240 13.3	17.3	75 02.3	15.6	9 34.3	13.5	54.8
	05	255 13.4	18.2	89 36.9	15.6	9 47.8	13.4	54.8
	06	270 13.5	N11 19.0	104 11.5	15.6	S10 01.2	13.3	54.8
	07	285 13.7	19.9	118 46.1	15.6	10 14.5	13.4	54.8
S	08	300 13.8	20.7	133 20.7	15.5	10 27.9	13.2	54.8
A	09	315 13.9	. . 21.6	147 55.2	15.6	10 41.1	13.2	54.8
T	10	330 14.1	22.5	162 29.8	15.4	10 54.3	13.2	54.8
U	11	345 14.2	23.3	177 04.2	15.5	11 07.5	13.1	54.7
R	12	0 14.4	N11 24.2	191 38.7	15.4	S11 20.6	13.1	54.7
D	13	15 14.5	25.0	206 13.1	15.4	11 33.7	13.0	54.7
A	14	30 14.6	25.9	220 47.5	15.4	11 46.7	13.0	54.7
Y	15	45 14.8	. . 26.8	235 21.9	15.3	11 59.7	12.9	54.7
	16	60 14.9	27.6	249 56.2	15.3	12 12.6	12.9	54.7
	17	75 15.0	28.5	264 30.5	15.3	12 25.5	12.8	54.7
	18	90 15.2	N11 29.3	279 04.8	15.2	S12 38.3	12.8	54.6
	19	105 15.3	30.2	293 39.0	15.2	12 51.1	12.6	54.6
	20	120 15.4	31.0	308 13.2	15.2	13 03.7	12.7	54.6
	21	135 15.5	. . 31.9	322 47.4	15.1	13 16.4	12.6	54.6
	22	150 15.7	32.8	337 21.5	15.1	13 29.0	12.5	54.6
	23	165 15.8	33.6	351 55.6	15.1	13 41.5	12.4	54.6
	20 00	180 15.9	N11 34.5	6 29.7	15.0	S13 53.9	12.4	54.6
	01	195 16.1	35.3	21 03.7	15.0	14 06.3	12.4	54.6
	02	210 16.2	36.2	35 37.7	14.9	14 18.7	12.3	54.5
	03	225 16.3	. . 37.0	50 11.6	14.9	14 31.0	12.2	54.5
	04	240 16.5	37.9	64 45.5	14.8	14 43.2	12.1	54.5
	05	255 16.6	38.7	79 19.3	14.9	14 55.3	12.1	54.5
	06	270 16.7	N11 39.6	93 53.2	14.7	S15 07.4	12.0	54.5
	07	285 16.9	40.4	108 26.9	14.8	15 19.4	12.0	54.5
	08	300 17.0	41.3	123 00.7	14.6	15 31.4	11.9	54.5
S	09	315 17.1	. . 42.1	137 34.3	14.7	15 43.3	11.8	54.5
U	10	330 17.3	43.0	152 08.0	14.6	15 55.1	11.7	54.5
N	11	345 17.4	43.9	166 41.6	14.5	16 06.8	11.7	54.4
D	12	0 17.5	N11 44.7	181 15.1	14.5	S16 18.5	11.6	54.4
A	13	15 17.6	45.6	195 48.6	14.5	16 30.1	11.5	54.4
Y	14	30 17.8	46.4	210 22.1	14.4	16 41.6	11.5	54.4
	15	45 17.9	. . 47.3	224 55.5	14.4	16 53.1	11.4	54.4
	16	60 18.0	48.1	239 28.9	14.3	17 04.5	11.3	54.4
	17	75 18.2	49.0	254 02.2	14.3	17 15.8	11.2	54.4
	18	90 18.3	N11 49.8	268 35.5	14.2	S17 27.0	11.2	54.4
	19	105 18.4	50.7	283 08.7	14.1	17 38.2	11.1	54.4
	20	120 18.5	51.5	297 41.8	14.2	17 49.3	11.0	54.3
	21	135 18.7	. . 52.4	312 15.0	14.0	18 00.3	10.9	54.3
	22	150 18.8	53.2	326 48.0	14.1	18 11.2	10.9	54.3
	23	165 18.9	54.0	341 21.1	13.9	S18 22.1	10.8	54.3
		SD 15.9	*d* 0.9	SD 15.0		14.9		14.8

Lat.	Twilight Naut.	Twilight Civil	Sunrise	Moonrise 18	Moonrise 19	Moonrise 20	Moonrise 21
°	h m	h m	h m	h m	h m	h m	h m
N 72	////	01 07	03 13	18 19	20 34	▬	▬
N 70	////	02 02	03 34	18 07	20 08	22 38	▬
68	////	02 35	03 50	17 58	19 48	21 51	▬
66	00 58	02 58	04 03	17 50	19 32	21 22	23 32
64	01 47	03 16	04 14	17 44	19 19	20 59	22 48
62	02 16	03 31	04 23	17 38	19 08	20 42	22 19
60	02 38	03 43	04 31	17 34	18 59	20 27	21 57
N 58	02 55	03 54	04 38	17 29	18 51	20 15	21 39
56	03 09	04 03	04 44	17 26	18 44	20 04	21 24
54	03 21	04 11	04 49	17 22	18 38	19 55	21 11
52	03 32	04 18	04 54	17 19	18 33	19 46	21 00
50	03 41	04 24	04 59	17 17	18 28	19 39	20 50
45	03 59	04 37	05 08	17 11	18 17	19 23	20 30
N 40	04 14	04 48	05 16	17 06	18 08	19 10	20 13
35	04 25	04 56	05 23	17 02	18 00	18 59	19 59
30	04 35	05 04	05 29	16 58	17 54	18 50	19 47
20	04 50	05 16	05 39	16 52	17 42	18 33	19 26
N 10	05 01	05 26	05 48	16 46	17 32	18 19	19 08
0	05 10	05 35	05 56	16 41	17 23	18 06	18 51
S 10	05 18	05 42	06 04	16 36	17 14	17 53	18 35
20	05 24	05 50	06 12	16 31	17 04	17 39	18 17
30	05 29	05 57	06 22	16 25	16 53	17 23	17 57
35	05 32	06 01	06 27	16 21	16 47	17 14	17 45
40	05 34	06 06	06 33	16 17	16 40	17 04	17 32
45	05 36	06 10	06 40	16 13	16 31	16 52	17 16
S 50	05 38	06 16	06 49	16 08	16 21	16 37	16 57
52	05 39	06 18	06 53	16 05	16 17	16 30	16 48
54	05 40	06 21	06 57	16 02	16 12	16 23	16 38
56	05 40	06 23	07 02	16 00	16 06	16 15	16 26
58	05 41	06 27	07 07	15 56	16 00	16 05	16 13
S 60	05 41	06 30	07 13	15 53	15 53	15 54	15 58

Lat.	Sunset	Twilight Civil	Twilight Naut.	Moonset 18	Moonset 19	Moonset 20	Moonset 21
°	h m	h m	h m	h m	h m	h m	h m
N 72	20 49	23 07	////	03 29	02 55	02 08	▬
N 70	20 27	22 02	////	03 34	03 09	02 37	01 38
68	20 11	21 28	////	03 39	03 21	02 58	02 25
66	19 57	21 03	23 15	03 43	03 30	03 16	02 56
64	19 46	20 45	22 17	03 46	03 38	03 30	03 20
62	19 37	20 30	21 46	03 48	03 45	03 42	03 38
60	19 29	20 17	21 23	03 51	03 51	03 52	03 54
N 58	19 22	20 06	21 06	03 53	03 56	04 01	04 07
56	19 16	19 57	20 51	03 55	04 01	04 09	04 18
54	19 10	19 49	20 39	03 57	04 05	04 16	04 28
52	19 05	19 42	20 28	03 58	04 09	04 22	04 37
50	19 01	19 35	20 19	04 00	04 13	04 28	04 45
45	18 51	19 22	20 00	04 03	04 21	04 40	05 02
N 40	18 43	19 11	19 45	04 06	04 27	04 50	05 16
35	18 36	19 02	19 34	04 08	04 33	04 59	05 28
30	18 30	18 55	19 24	04 10	04 38	05 07	05 39
20	18 20	18 42	19 09	04 14	04 46	05 21	05 57
N 10	18 11	18 32	18 57	04 17	04 54	05 32	06 13
0	18 02	18 23	18 48	04 20	05 01	05 44	06 28
S 10	17 54	18 16	18 40	04 23	05 08	05 55	06 43
20	17 46	18 08	18 34	04 26	05 16	06 07	06 59
30	17 36	18 00	18 28	04 29	05 25	06 21	07 17
35	17 30	17 56	18 26	04 32	05 30	06 29	07 28
40	17 24	17 52	18 23	04 34	05 36	06 38	07 40
45	17 17	17 47	18 21	04 37	05 43	06 49	07 55
S 50	17 08	17 42	18 19	04 40	05 51	07 02	08 13
52	17 04	17 39	18 18	04 41	05 55	07 08	08 22
54	17 00	17 36	18 18	04 43	05 59	07 15	08 32
56	16 55	17 34	18 17	04 45	06 03	07 23	08 42
58	16 50	17 31	18 16	04 47	06 09	07 31	08 55
S 60	16 44	17 27	18 16	04 49	06 14	07 41	09 10

Day	SUN Eqn. of Time 00^h	SUN Eqn. of Time 12^h	SUN Mer. Pass.	MOON Mer. Pass. Upper	MOON Mer. Pass. Lower	Age	Phase
d	m s	m s	h m	h m	h m	d %	
18	00 37	00 44	11 59	22 51	10 30	12 96	
19	00 51	00 57	11 59	23 33	11 12	13 99	○
20	01 04	01 10	11 59	24 17	11 55	14 100	

UT		ARIES	VENUS −3.8		MARS +1.1		JUPITER −2.3		SATURN +0.5	
		GHA	GHA	Dec	GHA	Dec	GHA	Dec	GHA	Dec
d	h	° ′	° ′	° ′	° ′	° ′	° ′	° ′	° ′	° ′
21	00	209 26.3	192 05.2	N 5 48.8	97 14.3	N23 53.3	275 50.9	S21 40.6	54 57.6	N12 31.7
	01	224 28.8	207 04.9	50.0	112 15.4	53.1	290 53.2	40.6	70 00.1	31.8
	02	239 31.2	222 04.5	51.2	127 16.5	52.9	305 55.5	40.6	85 02.6	31.8
	03	254 33.7	237 04.1	. . 52.3	142 17.6	. . 52.7	320 57.8	. . 40.5	100 05.1	. . 31.8
	04	269 36.2	252 03.7	53.5	157 18.7	52.4	336 00.1	40.5	115 07.7	31.8
	05	284 38.6	267 03.3	54.7	172 19.9	52.2	351 02.4	40.5	130 10.2	31.8
	06	299 41.1	282 02.9	N 5 55.9	187 21.0	N23 52.0	6 04.7	S21 40.5	145 12.7	N12 31.8
	07	314 43.6	297 02.5	57.1	202 22.1	51.8	21 07.1	40.5	160 15.2	31.8
	08	329 46.0	312 02.1	58.3	217 23.2	51.5	36 09.4	40.5	175 17.7	31.9
M	09	344 48.5	327 01.7	5 59.5	232 24.3	. . 51.3	51 11.7	. . 40.4	190 20.2	. . 31.9
O	10	359 50.9	342 01.3	6 00.7	247 25.4	51.1	66 14.0	40.4	205 22.7	31.9
N	11	14 53.4	357 01.0	01.9	262 26.6	50.9	81 16.3	40.4	220 25.3	31.9
D	12	29 55.9	12 00.6	N 6 03.1	277 27.7	N23 50.6	96 18.6	S21 40.4	235 27.8	N12 31.9
A	13	44 58.3	27 00.2	04.3	292 28.8	50.4	111 20.9	40.4	250 30.3	31.9
Y	14	60 00.8	41 59.8	05.5	307 29.9	50.2	126 23.3	40.4	265 32.8	31.9
	15	75 03.3	56 59.4	. . 06.7	322 31.0	. . 50.0	141 25.6	. . 40.3	280 35.3	. . 32.0
	16	90 05.7	71 59.0	07.9	337 32.1	49.7	156 27.9	40.3	295 37.8	32.0
	17	105 08.2	86 58.6	09.1	352 33.3	49.5	171 30.2	40.3	310 40.3	32.0
	18	120 10.7	101 58.2	N 6 10.3	7 34.4	N23 49.3	186 32.5	S21 40.3	325 42.9	N12 32.0
	19	135 13.1	116 57.8	11.5	22 35.5	49.1	201 34.8	40.3	340 45.4	32.0
	20	150 15.6	131 57.4	12.7	37 36.6	48.8	216 37.2	40.3	355 47.9	32.0
	21	165 18.1	146 57.0	. . 13.9	52 37.7	. . 48.6	231 39.5	. . 40.2	10 50.4	. . 32.0
	22	180 20.5	161 56.6	15.0	67 38.8	48.4	246 41.8	40.2	25 52.9	32.1
	23	195 23.0	176 56.3	16.2	82 39.9	48.1	261 44.1	40.2	40 55.4	32.1
22	00	210 25.4	191 55.9	N 6 17.4	97 41.1	N23 47.9	276 46.4	S21 40.2	55 57.9	N12 32.1
	01	225 27.9	206 55.5	18.6	112 42.2	47.7	291 48.8	40.2	71 00.4	32.1
	02	240 30.4	221 55.1	19.8	127 43.3	47.5	306 51.1	40.2	86 03.0	32.1
	03	255 32.8	236 54.7	. . 21.0	142 44.4	. . 47.2	321 53.4	. . 40.1	101 05.5	. . 32.1
	04	270 35.3	251 54.3	22.2	157 45.5	47.0	336 55.7	40.1	116 08.0	32.1
	05	285 37.8	266 53.9	23.4	172 46.6	46.8	351 58.0	40.1	131 10.5	32.1
	06	300 40.2	281 53.5	N 6 24.6	187 47.7	N23 46.6	7 00.4	S21 40.1	146 13.0	N12 32.2
	07	315 42.7	296 53.1	25.8	202 48.9	46.3	22 02.7	40.1	161 15.5	32.2
T	08	330 45.2	311 52.7	27.0	217 50.0	46.1	37 05.0	40.1	176 18.0	32.2
U	09	345 47.6	326 52.3	. . 28.1	232 51.1	. . 45.9	52 07.3	. . 40.0	191 20.5	. . 32.2
E	10	0 50.1	341 51.9	29.3	247 52.2	45.6	67 09.6	40.0	206 23.0	32.2
S	11	15 52.6	356 51.5	30.5	262 53.3	45.4	82 12.0	40.0	221 25.6	32.2
D	12	30 55.0	11 51.1	N 6 31.7	277 54.4	N23 45.2	97 14.3	S21 40.0	236 28.1	N12 32.2
A	13	45 57.5	26 50.7	32.9	292 55.5	44.9	112 16.6	40.0	251 30.6	32.2
Y	14	60 59.9	41 50.3	34.1	307 56.6	44.7	127 18.9	40.0	266 33.1	32.3
	15	76 02.4	56 49.9	. . 35.3	322 57.8	. . 44.5	142 21.3	. . 39.9	281 35.6	. . 32.3
	16	91 04.9	71 49.5	36.5	337 58.9	44.3	157 23.6	39.9	296 38.1	32.3
	17	106 07.3	86 49.1	37.7	353 00.0	44.0	172 25.9	39.9	311 40.6	32.3
	18	121 09.8	101 48.8	N 6 38.8	8 01.1	N23 43.8	187 28.2	S21 39.9	326 43.1	N12 32.3
	19	136 12.3	116 48.4	40.0	23 02.2	43.6	202 30.6	39.9	341 45.6	32.3
	20	151 14.7	131 48.0	41.2	38 03.3	43.3	217 32.9	39.9	356 48.1	32.3
	21	166 17.2	146 47.6	. . 42.4	53 04.4	. . 43.1	232 35.2	. . 39.8	11 50.7	. . 32.3
	22	181 19.7	161 47.2	43.6	68 05.5	42.9	247 37.5	39.8	26 53.2	32.4
	23	196 22.1	176 46.8	44.8	83 06.6	42.6	262 39.9	39.8	41 55.7	32.4
23	00	211 24.6	191 46.4	N 6 46.0	98 07.8	N23 42.4	277 42.2	S21 39.8	56 58.2	N12 32.4
	01	226 27.0	206 46.0	47.2	113 08.9	42.2	292 44.5	39.8	72 00.7	32.4
	02	241 29.5	221 45.6	48.3	128 10.0	41.9	307 46.9	39.8	87 03.2	32.4
	03	256 32.0	236 45.2	. . 49.5	143 11.1	. . 41.7	322 49.2	. . 39.8	102 05.7	. . 32.4
	04	271 34.4	251 44.8	50.7	158 12.2	41.5	337 51.5	39.7	117 08.2	32.4
	05	286 36.9	266 44.4	51.9	173 13.3	41.2	352 53.8	39.7	132 10.7	32.4
	06	301 39.4	281 44.0	N 6 53.1	188 14.4	N23 41.0	7 56.2	S21 39.7	147 13.2	N12 32.5
W	07	316 41.8	296 43.6	54.3	203 15.5	40.8	22 58.5	39.7	162 15.7	32.5
E	08	331 44.3	311 43.2	55.5	218 16.6	40.5	38 00.8	39.7	177 18.2	32.5
D	09	346 46.8	326 42.8	. . 56.6	233 17.7	. . 40.3	53 03.2	. . 39.7	192 20.7	. . 32.5
N	10	1 49.2	341 42.4	57.8	248 18.8	40.1	68 05.5	39.6	207 23.3	32.5
E	11	16 51.7	356 42.0	6 59.0	263 20.0	39.8	83 07.8	39.6	222 25.8	32.5
S	12	31 54.2	11 41.6	N 7 00.2	278 21.1	N23 39.6	98 10.1	S21 39.6	237 28.3	N12 32.5
D	13	46 56.6	26 41.2	01.4	293 22.2	39.4	113 12.5	39.6	252 30.8	32.5
A	14	61 59.1	41 40.8	02.6	308 23.3	39.1	128 14.8	39.6	267 33.3	32.5
Y	15	77 01.5	56 40.4	. . 03.7	323 24.4	. . 38.9	143 17.1	. . 39.6	282 35.8	. . 32.5
	16	92 04.0	71 40.0	04.9	338 25.5	38.7	158 19.5	39.6	297 38.3	32.6
	17	107 06.5	86 39.6	06.1	353 26.6	38.4	173 21.8	39.5	312 40.8	32.6
	18	122 08.9	101 39.2	N 7 07.3	8 27.7	N23 38.2	188 24.1	S21 39.5	327 43.3	N12 32.6
	19	137 11.4	116 38.8	08.5	23 28.8	38.0	203 26.5	39.5	342 45.8	32.6
	20	152 13.9	131 38.4	09.6	38 29.9	37.7	218 28.8	39.5	357 48.3	32.6
	21	167 16.3	146 38.0	. . 10.8	53 31.0	. . 37.5	233 31.1	. . 39.5	12 50.8	. . 32.6
	22	182 18.8	161 37.6	12.0	68 32.1	37.2	248 33.5	39.5	27 53.3	32.6
	23	197 21.3	176 37.2	13.2	83 33.2	37.0	263 35.8	39.5	42 55.8	32.6
Mer. Pass.		h m 9 56.7	*v* −0.4	*d* 1.2	*v* 1.1	*d* 0.2	*v* 2.3	*d* 0.0	*v* 2.5	*d* 0.0

STARS Name	SHA	Dec
	° ′	° ′
Acamar	315 21.6	S40 16.3
Achernar	335 30.0	S57 11.6
Acrux	173 13.4	S63 09.0
Adhara	255 15.8	S28 59.2
Aldebaran	290 54.2	N16 31.6
Alioth	166 23.3	N55 54.8
Alkaid	153 01.3	N49 16.2
Al Na'ir	27 48.6	S46 55.1
Alnilam	275 50.5	S 1 11.8
Alphard	217 59.9	S 8 41.8
Alphecca	126 13.9	N26 40.9
Alpheratz	357 48.0	N29 08.1
Altair	62 12.0	N 8 53.2
Ankaa	353 19.7	S42 15.6
Antares	112 30.8	S26 27.2
Arcturus	145 58.9	N19 08.1
Atria	107 35.9	S69 02.5
Avior	234 19.8	S59 32.4
Bellatrix	278 36.4	N 6 21.4
Betelgeuse	271 05.7	N 7 24.5
Canopus	263 58.2	S52 42.2
Capella	280 40.6	N46 00.6
Deneb	49 34.3	N45 18.3
Denebola	182 37.3	N14 31.4
Diphda	349 00.0	S17 56.5
Dubhe	193 55.7	N61 42.5
Elnath	278 17.8	N28 37.0
Eltanin	90 47.7	N51 28.9
Enif	33 51.1	N 9 54.6
Fomalhaut	15 28.4	S29 34.6
Gacrux	172 05.1	S57 09.8
Gienah	175 56.1	S17 35.5
Hadar	148 53.1	S60 24.9
Hamal	328 05.6	N23 30.1
Kaus Aust.	83 48.8	S34 22.9
Kochab	137 18.2	N74 07.1
Markab	13 42.5	N15 14.9
Menkar	314 19.5	N 4 07.3
Menkent	148 11.9	S36 24.8
Miaplacidus	221 40.7	S69 45.4
Mirfak	308 46.6	N49 53.5
Nunki	76 03.0	S26 17.2
Peacock	53 25.2	S56 42.3
Pollux	243 32.5	N28 00.5
Procyon	245 03.9	N 5 12.2
Rasalhague	96 09.9	N12 33.0
Regulus	207 47.5	N11 55.5
Rigel	281 16.0	S 8 11.6
Rigil Kent.	139 56.7	S60 52.3
Sabik	102 16.8	S15 44.3
Schedar	349 45.8	N56 34.9
Shaula	96 27.0	S37 06.6
Sirius	258 37.3	S16 43.8
Spica	158 35.1	S11 12.5
Suhail	222 55.4	S43 28.2
Vega	80 41.5	N38 47.1
Zuben'ubi	137 09.5	S16 04.8

	SHA	Mer. Pass.
	° ′	h m
Venus	341 30.4	11 13
Mars	247 15.6	17 28
Jupiter	66 21.0	5 32
Saturn	205 32.5	20 13

	UT	SUN GHA	SUN Dec	MOON GHA	v	MOON Dec	d	HP
	d h	° ′	° ′	° ′	′	° ′	′	′
	21 00	180 19.0	N11 54.9	355 54.0	13.9	S18 32.9	10.7	54.3
	01	195 19.2	55.7	10 26.9	13.9	18 43.6	10.6	54.3
	02	210 19.3	56.6	24 59.8	13.8	18 54.2	10.5	54.3
	03	225 19.4	. . 57.4	39 32.6	13.8	19 04.7	10.4	54.3
	04	240 19.6	58.3	54 05.4	13.7	19 15.1	10.4	54.3
	05	255 19.7	11 59.1	68 38.1	13.7	19 25.5	10.3	54.3
	06	270 19.8	N12 00.0	83 10.8	13.6	S19 35.8	10.2	54.3
	07	285 19.9	00.8	97 43.4	13.5	19 46.0	10.1	54.2
	08	300 20.1	01.7	112 15.9	13.5	19 56.1	10.0	54.2
M	09	315 20.2	. . 02.5	126 48.4	13.5	20 06.1	9.9	54.2
O	10	330 20.3	03.4	141 20.9	13.4	20 16.0	9.8	54.2
N	11	345 20.4	04.2	155 53.3	13.3	20 25.8	9.8	54.2
D	12	0 20.6	N12 05.0	170 25.6	13.3	S20 35.6	9.7	54.2
A	13	15 20.7	05.9	184 57.9	13.2	20 45.3	9.5	54.2
Y	14	30 20.8	06.7	199 30.1	13.2	20 54.8	9.5	54.2
	15	45 20.9	. . 07.6	214 02.3	13.1	21 04.3	9.4	54.2
	16	60 21.1	08.4	228 34.4	13.1	21 13.7	9.3	54.2
	17	75 21.2	09.3	243 06.5	13.0	21 23.0	9.2	54.2
	18	90 21.3	N12 10.1	257 38.5	12.9	S21 32.2	9.1	54.2
	19	105 21.4	10.9	272 10.4	12.9	21 41.3	9.0	54.2
	20	120 21.6	11.8	286 42.3	12.9	21 50.3	8.9	54.1
	21	135 21.7	. . 12.6	301 14.2	12.8	21 59.2	8.8	54.1
	22	150 21.8	13.5	315 46.0	12.7	22 08.0	8.7	54.1
	23	165 21.9	14.3	330 17.7	12.7	22 16.7	8.6	54.1
	22 00	180 22.0	N12 15.1	344 49.4	12.6	S22 25.3	8.5	54.1
	01	195 22.2	16.0	359 21.0	12.6	22 33.8	8.4	54.1
	02	210 22.3	16.8	13 52.6	12.5	22 42.2	8.3	54.1
	03	225 22.4	. . 17.6	28 24.1	12.4	22 50.5	8.2	54.1
	04	240 22.5	18.5	42 55.5	12.4	22 58.7	8.1	54.1
	05	255 22.7	19.3	57 26.9	12.4	23 06.8	8.0	54.1
	06	270 22.8	N12 20.2	71 58.3	12.3	S23 14.8	7.9	54.1
	07	285 22.9	21.0	86 29.6	12.2	23 22.7	7.8	54.1
T	08	300 23.0	21.8	101 00.8	12.2	23 30.5	7.7	54.1
U	09	315 23.1	. . 22.7	115 32.0	12.1	23 38.2	7.5	54.1
E	10	330 23.3	23.5	130 03.1	12.1	23 45.7	7.5	54.1
S	11	345 23.4	24.3	144 34.2	12.0	23 53.2	7.4	54.1
D	12	0 23.5	N12 25.2	159 05.2	12.0	S24 00.6	7.2	54.1
A	13	15 23.6	26.0	173 36.2	11.9	24 07.8	7.2	54.1
Y	14	30 23.7	26.8	188 07.1	11.9	24 15.0	7.0	54.1
	15	45 23.9	. . 27.7	202 38.0	11.8	24 22.0	6.9	54.0
	16	60 24.0	28.5	217 08.8	11.8	24 28.9	6.8	54.0
	17	75 24.1	29.3	231 39.6	11.7	24 35.7	6.7	54.0
	18	90 24.2	N12 30.2	246 10.3	11.6	S24 42.4	6.6	54.0
	19	105 24.3	31.0	260 40.9	11.6	24 49.0	6.5	54.0
	20	120 24.5	31.8	275 11.5	11.6	24 55.5	6.3	54.0
	21	135 24.6	. . 32.7	289 42.1	11.5	25 01.8	6.3	54.0
	22	150 24.7	33.5	304 12.6	11.5	25 08.1	6.1	54.0
	23	165 24.8	34.3	318 43.1	11.4	25 14.2	6.0	54.0
	23 00	180 24.9	N12 35.2	333 13.5	11.3	S25 20.2	5.9	54.0
	01	195 25.0	36.0	347 43.8	11.4	25 26.1	5.7	54.0
	02	210 25.2	36.8	2 14.2	11.2	25 31.8	5.7	54.0
	03	225 25.3	. . 37.7	16 44.4	11.3	25 37.5	5.5	54.0
	04	240 25.4	38.5	31 14.7	11.1	25 43.0	5.4	54.0
	05	255 25.5	39.3	45 44.8	11.2	25 48.4	5.3	54.0
	06	270 25.6	N12 40.1	60 15.0	11.1	S25 53.7	5.2	54.0
W	07	285 25.7	41.0	74 45.1	11.0	25 58.9	5.1	54.0
E	08	300 25.9	41.8	89 15.1	11.0	26 04.0	4.9	54.0
D	09	315 26.0	. . 42.6	103 45.1	11.0	26 08.9	4.8	54.0
N	10	330 26.1	43.5	118 15.1	10.9	26 13.7	4.7	54.0
E	11	345 26.2	44.3	132 45.0	10.8	26 18.4	4.6	54.0
S	12	0 26.3	N12 45.1	147 14.8	10.9	S26 23.0	4.4	54.0
D	13	15 26.4	45.9	161 44.7	10.8	26 27.4	4.3	54.0
A	14	30 26.6	46.8	176 14.5	10.7	26 31.7	4.2	54.0
Y	15	45 26.7	. . 47.6	190 44.2	10.7	26 35.9	4.1	54.0
	16	60 26.8	48.4	205 13.9	10.7	26 40.0	3.9	54.0
	17	75 26.9	49.2	219 43.6	10.7	26 43.9	3.8	54.0
	18	90 27.0	N12 50.1	234 13.3	10.6	S26 47.7	3.7	54.0
	19	105 27.1	50.9	248 42.9	10.5	26 51.4	3.6	54.0
	20	120 27.2	51.7	263 12.4	10.6	26 55.0	3.4	54.0
	21	135 27.4	. . 52.5	277 42.0	10.5	26 58.4	3.3	54.0
	22	150 27.5	53.4	292 11.5	10.5	27 01.7	3.2	54.0
	23	165 27.6	54.2	306 41.0	10.4	S27 04.9	3.0	54.0
		SD 15.9	d 0.8	SD 14.8		14.7		14.7

Lat.	Twilight Naut.	Twilight Civil	Sunrise	Moonrise 21	Moonrise 22	Moonrise 23	Moonrise 24
°	h m	h m	h m	h m	h m	h m	h m
N 72	////	////	02 55	■	■	■	■
N 70	////	01 36	03 19	■	■	■	■
68	////	02 16	03 37	■	■	■	■
66	////	02 43	03 51	23 32	■	■	■
64	01 24	03 04	04 03	22 48	25 02	01 02	■
62	02 00	03 20	04 14	22 19	24 01	00 01	01 43
60	02 25	03 33	04 22	21 57	23 27	24 50	00 50
N 58	02 44	03 45	04 30	21 39	23 02	24 18	00 18
56	03 00	03 55	04 36	21 24	22 43	23 54	24 52
54	03 13	04 03	04 42	21 11	22 26	23 35	24 32
52	03 24	04 11	04 48	21 00	22 12	23 18	24 15
50	03 34	04 18	04 53	20 50	22 00	23 04	24 00
45	03 53	04 32	05 03	20 30	21 35	22 36	23 31
N 40	04 09	04 43	05 12	20 13	21 15	22 14	23 08
35	04 21	04 53	05 19	19 59	20 58	21 55	22 49
30	04 31	05 01	05 26	19 47	20 44	21 39	22 33
20	04 47	05 14	05 37	19 26	20 19	21 13	22 05
N 10	04 59	05 25	05 46	19 08	19 58	20 50	21 42
0	05 09	05 34	05 55	18 51	19 39	20 29	21 20
S 10	05 18	05 42	06 04	18 35	19 20	20 07	20 58
20	05 25	05 51	06 13	18 17	18 59	19 45	20 34
30	05 31	05 59	06 24	17 57	18 35	19 18	20 07
35	05 34	06 04	06 30	17 45	18 21	19 03	19 50
40	05 37	06 09	06 36	17 32	18 05	18 45	19 31
45	05 40	06 14	06 44	17 16	17 46	18 23	19 09
S 50	05 42	06 20	06 53	16 57	17 22	17 56	18 40
52	05 43	06 23	06 58	16 48	17 11	17 42	18 25
54	05 44	06 26	07 03	16 38	16 58	17 27	18 09
56	05 46	06 29	07 08	16 26	16 43	17 09	17 49
58	05 47	06 33	07 14	16 13	16 26	16 47	17 24
S 60	05 48	06 36	07 20	15 58	16 04	16 19	16 51

Lat.	Sunset	Twilight Civil	Twilight Naut.	Moonset 21	Moonset 22	Moonset 23	Moonset 24
°	h m	h m	h m	h m	h m	h m	h m
N 72	21 07	////	////	■	■	■	■
N 70	20 42	22 29	////	01 38	■	■	■
68	20 23	21 46	////	02 25	■	■	■
66	20 08	21 17	////	02 56	02 21	■	■
64	19 56	20 56	22 41	03 20	03 06	02 31	■
62	19 45	20 39	22 01	03 38	03 35	03 33	03 35
60	19 36	20 26	21 35	03 54	03 58	04 08	04 28
N 58	19 29	20 14	21 16	04 07	04 16	04 33	05 01
56	19 22	20 04	21 00	04 18	04 32	04 53	05 25
54	19 16	19 55	20 46	04 28	04 45	05 09	05 44
52	19 10	19 47	20 35	04 37	04 57	05 24	06 01
50	19 05	19 41	20 25	04 45	05 07	05 36	06 15
45	18 55	19 26	20 05	05 02	05 29	06 02	06 43
N 40	18 46	19 15	19 49	05 16	05 47	06 23	07 06
35	18 38	19 05	19 37	05 28	06 02	06 40	07 25
30	18 32	18 57	19 26	05 39	06 15	06 55	07 41
20	18 21	18 43	19 10	05 57	06 37	07 20	08 08
N 10	18 11	18 32	18 58	06 13	06 56	07 42	08 31
0	18 02	18 23	18 48	06 28	07 14	08 03	08 53
S 10	17 53	18 14	18 39	06 43	07 32	08 23	09 15
20	17 44	18 06	18 32	06 59	07 52	08 45	09 38
30	17 33	17 57	18 25	07 17	08 14	09 11	10 06
35	17 27	17 53	18 22	07 28	08 27	09 26	10 22
40	17 20	17 48	18 19	07 40	08 43	09 43	10 40
45	17 12	17 42	18 17	07 55	09 01	10 05	11 03
S 50	17 03	17 36	18 14	08 13	09 24	10 31	11 32
52	16 58	17 33	18 13	08 22	09 35	10 45	11 46
54	16 53	17 30	18 11	08 32	09 48	11 00	12 03
56	16 48	17 27	18 10	08 42	10 02	11 17	12 23
58	16 42	17 23	18 09	08 55	10 19	11 39	12 47
S 60	16 36	17 19	18 08	09 10	10 40	12 07	13 20

Day	SUN Eqn. of Time 00^h	SUN Eqn. of Time 12^h	SUN Mer. Pass.	MOON Mer. Pass. Upper	MOON Mer. Pass. Lower	Age	Phase
d	m s	m s	h m	h m	h m	d %	
21	01 16	01 22	11 59	00 17	12 40	15 99	
22	01 28	01 34	11 58	01 03	13 26	16 96	○
23	01 39	01 45	11 58	01 51	14 16	17 92	

UT	ARIES	VENUS −3.9		MARS +1.1		JUPITER −2.3		SATURN +0.5	
	GHA	GHA	Dec	GHA	Dec	GHA	Dec	GHA	Dec
d h	° ′	° ′	° ′	° ′	° ′	° ′	° ′	° ′	° ′
24 00	212 23.7	191 36.8	N 7 14.4	98 34.4	N23 36.8	278 38.1	S21 39.4	57 58.3	N12 32.6
01	227 26.2	206 36.3	15.5	113 35.5	36.5	293 40.5	39.4	73 00.8	32.7
02	242 28.7	221 35.9	16.7	128 36.6	36.3	308 42.8	39.4	88 03.3	32.7
03	257 31.1	236 35.5	. . 17.9	143 37.7	. . 36.1	323 45.2	. . 39.4	103 05.8	. . 32.7
04	272 33.6	251 35.1	19.1	158 38.8	35.8	338 47.5	39.4	118 08.3	32.7
05	287 36.0	266 34.7	20.3	173 39.9	35.6	353 49.8	39.4	133 10.8	32.7
06	302 38.5	281 34.3	N 7 21.4	188 41.0	N23 35.3	8 52.2	S21 39.4	148 13.3	N12 32.7
07	317 41.0	296 33.9	22.6	203 42.1	35.1	23 54.5	39.3	163 15.9	32.7
T 08	332 43.4	311 33.5	23.8	218 43.2	34.9	38 56.8	39.3	178 18.4	32.7
H 09	347 45.9	326 33.1	. . 25.0	233 44.3	. . 34.6	53 59.2	. . 39.3	193 20.9	. . 32.7
U 10	2 48.4	341 32.7	26.2	248 45.4	34.4	69 01.5	39.3	208 23.4	32.7
R 11	17 50.8	356 32.3	27.3	263 46.5	34.1	84 03.9	39.3	223 25.9	32.7
S 12	32 53.3	11 31.9	N 7 28.5	278 47.6	N23 33.9	99 06.2	S21 39.3	238 28.4	N12 32.8
D 13	47 55.8	26 31.5	29.7	293 48.7	33.7	114 08.5	39.3	253 30.9	32.8
A 14	62 58.2	41 31.1	30.9	308 49.8	33.4	129 10.9	39.2	268 33.4	32.8
Y 15	78 00.7	56 30.7	. . 32.0	323 50.9	. . 33.2	144 13.2	. . 39.2	283 35.9	. . 32.8
16	93 03.2	71 30.3	33.2	338 52.0	32.9	159 15.5	39.2	298 38.4	32.8
17	108 05.6	86 29.9	34.4	353 53.1	32.7	174 17.9	39.2	313 40.9	32.8
18	123 08.1	101 29.5	N 7 35.6	8 54.3	N23 32.5	189 20.2	S21 39.2	328 43.4	N12 32.8
19	138 10.5	116 29.0	36.7	23 55.4	32.2	204 22.6	39.2	343 45.9	32.8
20	153 13.0	131 28.6	37.9	38 56.5	32.0	219 24.9	39.2	358 48.4	32.8
21	168 15.5	146 28.2	. . 39.1	53 57.6	. . 31.7	234 27.3	. . 39.1	13 50.9	. . 32.8
22	183 17.9	161 27.8	40.3	68 58.7	31.5	249 29.6	39.1	28 53.4	32.8
23	198 20.4	176 27.4	41.4	83 59.8	31.3	264 31.9	39.1	43 55.9	32.9
25 00	213 22.9	191 27.0	N 7 42.6	99 00.9	N23 31.0	279 34.3	S21 39.1	58 58.4	N12 32.9
01	228 25.3	206 26.6	43.8	114 02.0	30.8	294 36.6	39.1	74 00.9	32.9
02	243 27.8	221 26.2	45.0	129 03.1	30.5	309 39.0	39.1	89 03.4	32.9
03	258 30.3	236 25.8	. . 46.1	144 04.2	. . 30.3	324 41.3	. . 39.1	104 05.9	. . 32.9
04	273 32.7	251 25.4	47.3	159 05.3	30.0	339 43.7	39.1	119 08.4	32.9
05	288 35.2	266 25.0	48.5	174 06.4	29.8	354 46.0	39.0	134 10.9	32.9
06	303 37.6	281 24.5	N 7 49.6	189 07.5	N23 29.6	9 48.3	S21 39.0	149 13.4	N12 32.9
07	318 40.1	296 24.1	50.8	204 08.6	29.3	24 50.7	39.0	164 15.9	32.9
08	333 42.6	311 23.7	52.0	219 09.7	29.1	39 53.0	39.0	179 18.4	32.9
F 09	348 45.0	326 23.3	. . 53.2	234 10.8	. . 28.8	54 55.4	. . 39.0	194 20.9	. . 32.9
R 10	3 47.5	341 22.9	54.3	249 11.9	28.6	69 57.7	39.0	209 23.4	32.9
I 11	18 50.0	356 22.5	55.5	264 13.0	28.3	85 00.1	39.0	224 25.9	33.0
D 12	33 52.4	11 22.1	N 7 56.7	279 14.1	N23 28.1	100 02.4	S21 39.0	239 28.4	N12 33.0
A 13	48 54.9	26 21.7	57.8	294 15.2	27.8	115 04.8	38.9	254 30.9	33.0
Y 14	63 57.4	41 21.3	7 59.0	309 16.3	27.6	130 07.1	38.9	269 33.4	33.0
15	78 59.8	56 20.8	8 00.2	324 17.4	. . 27.4	145 09.5	. . 38.9	284 35.9	. . 33.0
16	94 02.3	71 20.4	01.3	339 18.5	27.1	160 11.8	38.9	299 38.4	33.0
17	109 04.8	86 20.0	02.5	354 19.6	26.9	175 14.2	38.9	314 40.8	33.0
18	124 07.2	101 19.6	N 8 03.7	9 20.7	N23 26.6	190 16.5	S21 38.9	329 43.3	N12 33.0
19	139 09.7	116 19.2	04.9	24 21.8	26.4	205 18.9	38.9	344 45.8	33.0
20	154 12.1	131 18.8	06.0	39 22.9	26.1	220 21.2	38.9	359 48.3	33.0
21	169 14.6	146 18.4	. . 07.2	54 24.0	. . 25.9	235 23.6	. . 38.8	14 50.8	. . 33.0
22	184 17.1	161 17.9	08.4	69 25.1	25.6	250 25.9	38.8	29 53.3	33.0
23	199 19.5	176 17.5	09.5	84 26.2	25.4	265 28.3	38.8	44 55.8	33.0
26 00	214 22.0	191 17.1	N 8 10.7	99 27.3	N23 25.1	280 30.6	S21 38.8	59 58.3	N12 33.1
01	229 24.5	206 16.7	11.9	114 28.4	24.9	295 33.0	38.8	75 00.8	33.1
02	244 26.9	221 16.3	13.0	129 29.5	24.6	310 35.3	38.8	90 03.3	33.1
03	259 29.4	236 15.9	. . 14.2	144 30.6	. . 24.4	325 37.7	. . 38.8	105 05.8	. . 33.1
04	274 31.9	251 15.5	15.3	159 31.7	24.1	340 40.0	38.8	120 08.3	33.1
05	289 34.3	266 15.0	16.5	174 32.8	23.9	355 42.4	38.8	135 10.8	33.1
06	304 36.8	281 14.6	N 8 17.7	189 33.9	N23 23.6	10 44.7	S21 38.7	150 13.3	N12 33.1
07	319 39.3	296 14.2	18.8	204 35.0	23.4	25 47.1	38.7	165 15.8	33.1
S 08	334 41.7	311 13.8	20.0	219 36.1	23.2	40 49.4	38.7	180 18.3	33.1
A 09	349 44.2	326 13.4	. . 21.2	234 37.2	. . 22.9	55 51.8	. . 38.7	195 20.8	. . 33.1
T 10	4 46.6	341 13.0	22.3	249 38.3	22.7	70 54.1	38.7	210 23.3	33.1
U 11	19 49.1	356 12.5	23.5	264 39.4	22.4	85 56.5	38.7	225 25.8	33.1
R 12	34 51.6	11 12.1	N 8 24.7	279 40.5	N23 22.2	100 58.9	S21 38.7	240 28.3	N12 33.1
D 13	49 54.0	26 11.7	25.8	294 41.6	21.9	116 01.2	38.7	255 30.8	33.1
A 14	64 56.5	41 11.3	27.0	309 42.7	21.7	131 03.6	38.6	270 33.2	33.1
Y 15	79 59.0	56 10.9	. . 28.1	324 43.8	. . 21.4	146 05.9	. . 38.6	285 35.7	. . 33.1
16	95 01.4	71 10.4	29.3	339 44.9	21.2	161 08.3	38.6	300 38.2	33.2
17	110 03.9	86 10.0	30.5	354 46.0	20.9	176 10.6	38.6	315 40.7	33.2
18	125 06.4	101 09.6	N 8 31.6	9 47.1	N23 20.7	191 13.0	S21 38.6	330 43.2	N12 33.2
19	140 08.8	116 09.2	32.8	24 48.2	20.4	206 15.3	38.6	345 45.7	33.2
20	155 11.3	131 08.8	33.9	39 49.3	20.1	221 17.7	38.6	0 48.2	33.2
21	170 13.8	146 08.3	. . 35.1	54 50.4	. . 19.9	236 20.1	. . 38.6	15 50.7	. . 33.2
22	185 16.2	161 07.9	36.3	69 51.5	19.6	251 22.4	38.6	30 53.2	33.2
23	200 18.7	176 07.5	37.4	84 52.6	19.4	266 24.8	38.5	45 55.7	33.2
Mer. Pass. (h m)	9 44.9	v −0.4	d 1.2	v 1.1	d 0.2	v 2.3	d 0.0	v 2.5	d 0.0

STARS

Name	SHA	Dec
	° ′	° ′
Acamar	315 21.6	S40 16.3
Achernar	335 30.0	S57 11.6
Acrux	173 13.4	S63 09.0
Adhara	255 15.8	S28 59.2
Aldebaran	290 54.2	N16 31.6
Alioth	166 23.3	N55 54.8
Alkaid	153 01.3	N49 16.2
Al Na'ir	27 48.6	S46 55.1
Alnilam	275 50.5	S 1 11.8
Alphard	217 59.9	S 8 41.8
Alphecca	126 13.9	N26 41.0
Alpheratz	357 47.9	N29 08.1
Altair	62 12.0	N 8 53.2
Ankaa	353 19.7	S42 15.5
Antares	112 30.8	S26 27.2
Arcturus	145 58.9	N19 08.1
Atria	107 35.8	S69 02.5
Avior	234 19.8	S59 32.4
Bellatrix	278 36.4	N 6 21.4
Betelgeuse	271 05.7	N 7 24.5
Canopus	263 58.2	S52 42.2
Capella	280 40.6	N46 00.5
Deneb	49 34.3	N45 18.3
Denebola	182 37.3	N14 31.4
Diphda	349 00.0	S17 56.4
Dubhe	193 55.7	N61 42.5
Elnath	278 17.8	N28 37.0
Eltanin	90 47.6	N51 28.9
Enif	33 51.1	N 9 54.6
Fomalhaut	15 28.4	S29 34.6
Gacrux	172 05.1	S57 09.8
Gienah	175 56.1	S17 35.5
Hadar	148 53.1	S60 25.0
Hamal	328 05.6	N23 30.1
Kaus Aust.	83 48.8	S34 22.9
Kochab	137 18.2	N74 07.1
Markab	13 42.5	N15 14.9
Menkar	314 19.5	N 4 07.3
Menkent	148 11.9	S36 24.9
Miaplacidus	221 40.7	S69 45.4
Mirfak	308 46.6	N49 53.5
Nunki	76 03.0	S26 17.2
Peacock	53 25.2	S56 42.3
Pollux	243 32.5	N28 00.5
Procyon	245 03.9	N 5 12.2
Rasalhague	96 09.8	N12 33.0
Regulus	207 47.5	N11 55.5
Rigel	281 16.0	S 8 11.6
Rigil Kent.	139 56.7	S60 52.3
Sabik	102 16.8	S15 44.3
Schedar	349 45.8	N56 34.9
Shaula	96 26.9	S37 06.6
Sirius	258 37.3	S16 43.8
Spica	158 35.1	S11 12.5
Suhail	222 55.4	S43 28.2
Vega	80 41.4	N38 47.1
Zuben'ubi	137 09.5	S16 04.8

	SHA	Mer. Pass.
	° ′	h m
Venus	338 04.1	11 15
Mars	245 38.0	17 23
Jupiter	66 11.4	5 21
Saturn	205 35.5	20 01

	UT d h	SUN GHA	SUN Dec	MOON GHA	v	MOON Dec	d	HP
		° ′	° ′	° ′	′	° ′	′	′
	24 00	180 27.7	N12 55.0	321 10.4	10.4	S27 07.9	3.0	54.0
	01	195 27.8	55.8	335 39.8	10.4	27 10.9	2.7	54.0
	02	210 27.9	56.6	350 09.2	10.4	27 13.6	2.7	54.0
	03	225 28.0	. . 57.5	4 38.6	10.3	27 16.3	2.5	54.0
	04	240 28.1	58.3	19 07.9	10.3	27 18.8	2.4	54.1
	05	255 28.3	59.1	33 37.2	10.3	27 21.2	2.3	54.1
	06	270 28.4	N12 59.9	48 06.5	10.2	S27 23.5	2.1	54.1
	07	285 28.5	13 00.7	62 35.7	10.3	27 25.6	2.0	54.1
T	08	300 28.6	01.6	77 05.0	10.2	27 27.6	1.9	54.1
H	09	315 28.7	. . 02.4	91 34.2	10.1	27 29.5	1.8	54.1
U	10	330 28.8	03.2	106 03.3	10.2	27 31.3	1.6	54.1
R	11	345 28.9	04.0	120 32.5	10.2	27 32.9	1.4	54.1
S	12	0 29.0	N13 04.8	135 01.7	10.1	S27 34.3	1.4	54.1
D	13	15 29.1	05.7	149 30.8	10.1	27 35.7	1.2	54.1
A	14	30 29.3	06.5	163 59.9	10.1	27 36.9	1.1	54.1
Y	15	45 29.4	. . 07.3	178 29.0	10.1	27 38.0	0.9	54.1
	16	60 29.5	08.1	192 58.1	10.0	27 38.9	0.8	54.1
	17	75 29.6	08.9	207 27.1	10.1	27 39.7	0.7	54.1
	18	90 29.7	N13 09.7	221 56.2	10.0	S27 40.4	0.6	54.1
	19	105 29.8	10.6	236 25.2	10.0	27 41.0	0.4	54.1
	20	120 29.9	11.4	250 54.2	10.1	27 41.4	0.2	54.1
	21	135 30.0	. . 12.2	265 23.3	10.0	27 41.6	0.2	54.1
	22	150 30.1	13.0	279 52.3	10.0	27 41.8	0.0	54.2
	23	165 30.2	13.8	294 21.3	10.0	27 41.8	0.1	54.2
	25 00	180 30.3	N13 14.6	308 50.3	9.9	S27 41.7	0.3	54.2
	01	195 30.4	15.4	323 19.2	10.0	27 41.4	0.4	54.2
	02	210 30.6	16.2	337 48.2	10.0	27 41.0	0.5	54.2
	03	225 30.7	. . 17.1	352 17.2	10.0	27 40.5	0.7	54.2
	04	240 30.8	17.9	6 46.2	10.0	27 39.8	0.8	54.2
	05	255 30.9	18.7	21 15.2	9.9	27 39.0	0.9	54.2
	06	270 31.0	N13 19.5	35 44.1	10.0	S27 38.1	1.1	54.2
	07	285 31.1	20.3	50 13.1	10.0	27 37.0	1.2	54.2
	08	300 31.2	21.1	64 42.1	10.0	27 35.8	1.3	54.2
F	09	315 31.3	. . 21.9	79 11.1	10.0	27 34.5	1.5	54.3
R	10	330 31.4	22.7	93 40.1	10.0	27 33.0	1.6	54.3
I	11	345 31.5	23.5	108 09.1	10.0	27 31.4	1.8	54.3
D	12	0 31.6	N13 24.4	122 38.1	10.0	S27 29.6	1.8	54.3
A	13	15 31.7	25.2	137 07.1	10.0	27 27.8	2.0	54.3
Y	14	30 31.8	26.0	151 36.1	10.0	27 25.8	2.2	54.3
	15	45 31.9	. . 26.8	166 05.1	10.0	27 23.6	2.3	54.3
	16	60 32.0	27.6	180 34.1	10.1	27 21.3	2.4	54.3
	17	75 32.1	28.4	195 03.2	10.0	27 18.9	2.5	54.4
	18	90 32.2	N13 29.2	209 32.2	10.1	S27 16.4	2.7	54.4
	19	105 32.3	30.0	224 01.3	10.1	27 13.7	2.8	54.4
	20	120 32.4	30.8	238 30.4	10.1	27 10.9	3.0	54.4
	21	135 32.5	. . 31.6	252 59.5	10.1	27 07.9	3.0	54.4
	22	150 32.7	32.4	267 28.6	10.1	27 04.9	3.2	54.4
	23	165 32.8	33.2	281 57.7	10.1	27 01.7	3.4	54.4
	26 00	180 32.9	N13 34.0	296 26.8	10.2	S26 58.3	3.5	54.4
	01	195 33.0	34.8	310 56.0	10.2	26 54.8	3.6	54.5
	02	210 33.1	35.6	325 25.2	10.2	26 51.2	3.7	54.5
	03	225 33.2	. . 36.4	339 54.4	10.2	26 47.5	3.9	54.5
	04	240 33.3	37.2	354 23.6	10.3	26 43.6	4.0	54.5
	05	255 33.4	38.0	8 52.9	10.2	26 39.6	4.1	54.5
	06	270 33.5	N13 38.8	23 22.1	10.3	S26 35.5	4.3	54.5
	07	285 33.6	39.6	37 51.4	10.3	26 31.2	4.4	54.6
S	08	300 33.7	40.4	52 20.7	10.4	26 26.8	4.5	54.6
A	09	315 33.8	. . 41.2	66 50.1	10.3	26 22.3	4.6	54.6
T	10	330 33.9	42.0	81 19.4	10.4	26 17.7	4.8	54.6
U	11	345 34.0	42.8	95 48.8	10.4	26 12.9	4.9	54.6
R	12	0 34.1	N13 43.6	110 18.2	10.5	S26 08.0	5.1	54.6
D	13	15 34.2	44.4	124 47.7	10.5	26 02.9	5.1	54.7
A	14	30 34.3	45.2	139 17.2	10.5	25 57.8	5.3	54.7
Y	15	45 34.4	. . 46.0	153 46.7	10.5	25 52.5	5.5	54.7
	16	60 34.5	46.8	168 16.2	10.6	25 47.0	5.5	54.7
	17	75 34.6	47.6	182 45.8	10.6	25 41.5	5.7	54.7
	18	90 34.7	N13 48.4	197 15.4	10.6	S25 35.8	5.8	54.8
	19	105 34.8	49.2	211 45.0	10.6	25 30.0	5.9	54.8
	20	120 34.9	50.0	226 14.6	10.7	25 24.1	6.1	54.8
	21	135 35.0	. . 50.8	240 44.3	10.8	25 18.0	6.2	54.8
	22	150 35.1	51.6	255 14.1	10.7	25 11.8	6.3	54.8
	23	165 35.2	52.4	269 43.8	10.8	S25 05.5	6.4	54.9
		SD 15.9	*d* 0.8	SD 14.7		14.8		14.9

Lat.	Twilight Naut.	Twilight Civil	Sunrise	Moonrise 24	Moonrise 25	Moonrise 26	Moonrise 27
°	h m	h m	h m	h m	h m	h m	h m
N 72	////	////	02 35	▬	▬	▬	▬
N 70	////	01 02	03 03	▬	▬	▬	▬
68	////	01 56	03 23	▬	▬	▬	▬
66	////	02 28	03 40	▬	▬	▬	▬
64	00 54	02 51	03 53	▬	▬	▬	03 52
62	01 42	03 09	04 04	01 43	02 59	03 10	03 10
60	02 11	03 24	04 14	00 50	01 52	02 26	02 41
N 58	02 33	03 36	04 22	00 18	01 17	01 56	02 19
56	02 50	03 47	04 29	24 52	00 52	01 33	02 01
54	03 04	03 56	04 36	24 32	00 32	01 15	01 45
52	03 16	04 04	04 42	24 15	00 15	00 59	01 32
50	03 26	04 11	04 47	24 00	00 00	00 46	01 21
45	03 48	04 27	04 58	23 31	24 18	00 18	00 56
N 40	04 04	04 39	05 08	23 08	23 56	24 37	00 37
35	04 17	04 49	05 16	22 49	23 38	24 20	00 20
30	04 28	04 58	05 23	22 33	23 22	24 06	00 06
20	04 45	05 12	05 35	22 05	22 55	23 42	24 25
N 10	04 58	05 23	05 45	21 42	22 32	23 21	24 08
0	05 09	05 33	05 55	21 20	22 11	23 02	23 51
S 10	05 18	05 42	06 04	20 58	21 49	22 42	23 34
20	05 25	05 51	06 14	20 34	21 26	22 21	23 16
30	05 33	06 01	06 25	20 07	21 00	21 56	22 55
35	05 36	06 06	06 32	19 50	20 44	21 42	22 43
40	05 40	06 11	06 39	19 31	20 25	21 25	22 29
45	05 43	06 17	06 48	19 09	20 03	21 05	22 12
S 50	05 46	06 24	06 58	18 40	19 35	20 40	21 51
52	05 48	06 28	07 03	18 25	19 21	20 27	21 41
54	05 49	06 31	07 08	18 09	19 05	20 13	21 30
56	05 51	06 35	07 14	17 49	18 46	19 57	21 17
58	05 52	06 39	07 20	17 24	18 22	19 37	21 02
S 60	05 54	06 43	07 28	16 51	17 50	19 12	20 44

Lat.	Sunset	Twilight Civil	Twilight Naut.	Moonset 24	Moonset 25	Moonset 26	Moonset 27
°	h m	h m	h m	h m	h m	h m	h m
N 72	21 26	////	////	▬	▬	▬	▬
N 70	20 57	23 08	////	▬	▬	▬	▬
68	20 36	22 06	////	▬	▬	▬	▬
66	20 19	21 32	////	▬	▬	▬	▬
64	20 05	21 08	23 15	▬	▬	▬	06 45
62	19 54	20 50	22 19	03 35	04 06	05 41	07 27
60	19 44	20 34	21 48	04 28	05 13	06 26	07 55
N 58	19 35	20 22	21 26	05 01	05 47	06 55	08 16
56	19 28	20 11	21 08	05 25	06 13	07 17	08 34
54	19 21	20 01	20 54	05 44	06 33	07 36	08 49
52	19 15	19 53	20 42	06 01	06 50	07 51	09 02
50	19 10	19 46	20 31	06 15	07 04	08 05	09 13
45	18 58	19 30	20 09	06 43	07 33	08 32	09 37
N 40	18 49	19 18	19 53	07 06	07 56	08 53	09 55
35	18 41	19 08	19 40	07 25	08 15	09 11	10 11
30	18 34	18 59	19 29	07 41	08 32	09 27	10 25
20	18 22	18 44	19 11	08 08	08 59	09 53	10 47
N 10	18 11	18 33	18 58	08 31	09 22	10 15	11 07
0	18 01	18 23	18 47	08 53	09 44	10 35	11 25
S 10	17 52	18 13	18 38	09 15	10 06	10 56	11 44
20	17 41	18 04	18 30	09 38	10 30	11 18	12 03
30	17 30	17 55	18 23	10 06	10 57	11 44	12 26
35	17 23	17 49	18 19	10 22	11 13	11 59	12 39
40	17 16	17 44	18 16	10 40	11 32	12 16	12 53
45	17 07	17 38	18 12	11 03	11 54	12 37	13 11
S 50	16 57	17 31	18 09	11 32	12 23	13 03	13 33
52	16 52	17 27	18 07	11 46	12 37	13 15	13 44
54	16 47	17 24	18 06	12 03	12 53	13 30	13 55
56	16 41	17 20	18 04	12 23	13 12	13 46	14 09
58	16 35	17 16	18 02	12 47	13 36	14 06	14 24
S 60	16 27	17 12	18 01	13 20	14 08	14 32	14 43

Day	SUN Eqn. of Time 00^h	SUN Eqn. of Time 12^h	SUN Mer. Pass.	MOON Mer. Pass. Upper	MOON Mer. Pass. Lower	MOON Age	MOON Phase
d	m s	m s	h m	h m	h m	d %	
24	01 51	01 56	11 58	02 41	15 06	18 86	
25	02 01	02 06	11 58	03 32	15 58	19 78	
26	02 11	02 16	11 58	04 23	16 49	20 70	

UT d h	ARIES GHA	VENUS −3.9 GHA	VENUS Dec	MARS +1.2 GHA	MARS Dec	JUPITER −2.3 GHA	JUPITER Dec	SATURN +0.5 GHA	SATURN Dec
	° ′	° ′	° ′	° ′	° ′	° ′	° ′	° ′	° ′
27 00	215 21.1	191 07.1	N 8 38.6	99 53.7	N23 19.1	281 27.1	S21 38.5	60 58.2	N12 33.2
01	230 23.6	206 06.7	39.7	114 54.8	18.9	296 29.5	38.5	76 00.7	33.2
02	245 26.1	221 06.2	40.9	129 55.9	18.6	311 31.9	38.5	91 03.2	33.2
03	260 28.5	236 05.8	· · 42.1	144 56.9	· · 18.4	326 34.2	· · 38.5	106 05.6	· · 33.2
04	275 31.0	251 05.4	43.2	159 58.0	18.1	341 36.6	38.5	121 08.1	33.2
05	290 33.5	266 05.0	44.4	174 59.1	17.9	356 38.9	38.5	136 10.6	33.2
06	305 35.9	281 04.5	N 8 45.5	190 00.2	N23 17.6	11 41.3	S21 38.5	151 13.1	N12 33.2
07	320 38.4	296 04.1	46.7	205 01.3	17.4	26 43.7	38.5	166 15.6	33.2
S 08	335 40.9	311 03.7	47.8	220 02.4	17.1	41 46.0	38.5	181 18.1	33.2
U 09	350 43.3	326 03.3	· · 49.0	235 03.5	· · 16.9	56 48.4	· · 38.4	196 20.6	· · 33.2
N 10	5 45.8	341 02.9	50.2	250 04.6	16.6	71 50.7	38.4	211 23.1	33.2
D 11	20 48.2	356 02.4	51.3	265 05.7	16.4	86 53.1	38.4	226 25.6	33.3
A 12	35 50.7	11 02.0	N 8 52.5	280 06.8	N23 16.1	101 55.5	S21 38.4	241 28.1	N12 33.3
Y 13	50 53.2	26 01.6	53.6	295 07.9	15.8	116 57.8	38.4	256 30.5	33.3
14	65 55.6	41 01.2	54.8	310 09.0	15.6	132 00.2	38.4	271 33.0	33.3
15	80 58.1	56 00.7	· · 55.9	325 10.1	· · 15.3	147 02.6	· · 38.4	286 35.5	· · 33.3
16	96 00.6	71 00.3	57.1	340 11.2	15.1	162 04.9	38.4	301 38.0	33.3
17	111 03.0	85 59.9	58.2	355 12.3	14.8	177 07.3	38.4	316 40.5	33.3
18	126 05.5	100 59.5	N 8 59.4	10 13.4	N23 14.6	192 09.7	S21 38.4	331 43.0	N12 33.3
19	141 08.0	115 59.0	9 00.5	25 14.5	14.3	207 12.0	38.3	346 45.5	33.3
20	156 10.4	130 58.6	01.7	40 15.6	14.1	222 14.4	38.3	1 48.0	33.3
21	171 12.9	145 58.2	· · 02.8	55 16.7	· · 13.8	237 16.8	· · 38.3	16 50.5	· · 33.3
22	186 15.4	160 57.7	04.0	70 17.7	13.5	252 19.1	38.3	31 52.9	33.3
23	201 17.8	175 57.3	05.1	85 18.8	13.3	267 21.5	38.3	46 55.4	33.3
28 00	216 20.3	190 56.9	N 9 06.3	100 19.9	N23 13.0	282 23.9	S21 38.3	61 57.9	N12 33.3
01	231 22.7	205 56.5	07.4	115 21.0	12.8	297 26.2	38.3	77 00.4	33.3
02	246 25.2	220 56.0	08.6	130 22.1	12.5	312 28.6	38.3	92 02.9	33.3
03	261 27.7	235 55.6	· · 09.7	145 23.2	· · 12.3	327 31.0	· · 38.3	107 05.4	· · 33.3
04	276 30.1	250 55.2	10.9	160 24.3	12.0	342 33.3	38.3	122 07.9	33.3
05	291 32.6	265 54.7	12.0	175 25.4	11.7	357 35.7	38.3	137 10.4	33.3
06	306 35.1	280 54.3	N 9 13.2	190 26.5	N23 11.5	12 38.1	S21 38.2	152 12.8	N12 33.3
07	321 37.5	295 53.9	14.3	205 27.6	11.2	27 40.4	38.2	167 15.3	33.3
08	336 40.0	310 53.5	15.5	220 28.7	11.0	42 42.8	38.2	182 17.8	33.3
M 09	351 42.5	325 53.0	· · 16.6	235 29.8	· · 10.7	57 45.2	· · 38.2	197 20.3	· · 33.3
O 10	6 44.9	340 52.6	17.8	250 30.9	10.4	72 47.5	38.2	212 22.8	33.3
N 11	21 47.4	355 52.2	18.9	265 31.9	10.2	87 49.9	38.2	227 25.3	33.3
D 12	36 49.9	10 51.7	N 9 20.1	280 33.0	N23 09.9	102 52.3	S21 38.2	242 27.8	N12 33.3
A 13	51 52.3	25 51.3	21.2	295 34.1	09.7	117 54.7	38.2	257 30.2	33.3
Y 14	66 54.8	40 50.9	22.4	310 35.2	09.4	132 57.0	38.2	272 32.7	33.3
15	81 57.2	55 50.4	· · 23.5	325 36.3	· · 09.1	147 59.4	· · 38.2	287 35.2	· · 33.4
16	96 59.7	70 50.0	24.7	340 37.4	08.9	163 01.8	38.2	302 37.7	33.4
17	112 02.2	85 49.6	25.8	355 38.5	08.6	178 04.2	38.1	317 40.2	33.4
18	127 04.6	100 49.1	N 9 26.9	10 39.6	N23 08.4	193 06.5	S21 38.1	332 42.7	N12 33.4
19	142 07.1	115 48.7	28.1	25 40.7	08.1	208 08.9	38.1	347 45.1	33.4
20	157 09.6	130 48.3	29.2	40 41.8	07.8	223 11.3	38.1	2 47.6	33.4
21	172 12.0	145 47.8	· · 30.4	55 42.9	· · 07.6	238 13.6	· · 38.1	17 50.1	· · 33.4
22	187 14.5	160 47.4	31.5	70 44.0	07.3	253 16.0	38.1	32 52.6	33.4
23	202 17.0	175 47.0	32.7	85 45.0	07.0	268 18.4	38.1	47 55.1	33.4
29 00	217 19.4	190 46.5	N 9 33.8	100 46.1	N23 06.8	283 20.8	S21 38.1	62 57.6	N12 33.4
01	232 21.9	205 46.1	34.9	115 47.2	06.5	298 23.1	38.1	78 00.1	33.4
02	247 24.4	220 45.7	36.1	130 48.3	06.3	313 25.5	38.1	93 02.5	33.4
03	262 26.8	235 45.2	· · 37.2	145 49.4	· · 06.0	328 27.9	· · 38.1	108 05.0	· · 33.4
04	277 29.3	250 44.8	38.4	160 50.5	05.7	343 30.3	38.1	123 07.5	33.4
05	292 31.7	265 44.3	39.5	175 51.6	05.5	358 32.7	38.0	138 10.0	33.4
06	307 34.2	280 43.9	N 9 40.6	190 52.7	N23 05.2	13 35.0	S21 38.0	153 12.5	N12 33.4
07	322 36.7	295 43.5	41.8	205 53.8	04.9	28 37.4	38.0	168 14.9	33.4
T 08	337 39.1	310 43.0	42.9	220 54.8	04.7	43 39.8	38.0	183 17.4	33.4
U 09	352 41.6	325 42.6	· · 44.1	235 55.9	· · 04.4	58 42.2	· · 38.0	198 19.9	· · 33.4
E 10	7 44.1	340 42.2	45.2	250 57.0	04.2	73 44.5	38.0	213 22.4	33.4
S 11	22 46.5	355 41.7	46.3	265 58.1	03.9	88 46.9	38.0	228 24.9	33.4
D 12	37 49.0	10 41.3	N 9 47.5	280 59.2	N23 03.6	103 49.3	S21 38.0	243 27.4	N12 33.4
A 13	52 51.5	25 40.8	48.6	296 00.3	03.4	118 51.7	38.0	258 29.8	33.4
Y 14	67 53.9	40 40.4	49.8	311 01.4	03.1	133 54.1	38.0	273 32.3	33.4
15	82 56.4	55 40.0	· · 50.9	326 02.5	· · 02.8	148 56.4	· · 38.0	288 34.8	· · 33.4
16	97 58.8	70 39.5	52.0	341 03.6	02.6	163 58.8	38.0	303 37.3	33.4
17	113 01.3	85 39.1	53.2	356 04.6	02.3	179 01.2	38.0	318 39.8	33.4
18	128 03.8	100 38.6	N 9 54.3	11 05.7	N23 02.0	194 03.6	S21 37.9	333 42.2	N12 33.4
19	143 06.2	115 38.2	55.4	26 06.8	01.8	209 06.0	37.9	348 44.7	33.4
20	158 08.7	130 37.8	56.6	41 07.9	01.5	224 08.4	37.9	3 47.2	33.4
21	173 11.2	145 37.3	· · 57.7	56 09.0	· · 01.2	239 10.7	· · 37.9	18 49.7	· · 33.4
22	188 13.6	160 36.9	9 58.8	71 10.1	01.0	254 13.1	37.9	33 52.2	33.4
23	203 16.1	175 36.4	N10 00.0	86 11.2	00.7	269 15.5	37.9	48 54.6	33.4
Mer. Pass. (h m)	9 33.1	v −0.4	d 1.1	v 1.1	d 0.3	v 2.4	d 0.0	v 2.5	d 0.0

STARS

Name	SHA	Dec
	° ′	° ′
Acamar	315 21.6	S40 16.3
Achernar	335 30.0	S57 11.6
Acrux	173 13.4	S63 09.0
Adhara	255 15.8	S28 59.2
Aldebaran	290 54.2	N16 31.6
Alioth	166 23.3	N55 54.9
Alkaid	153 01.3	N49 16.2
Al Na'ir	27 48.6	S46 55.1
Alnilam	275 50.6	S 1 11.8
Alphard	217 59.9	S 8 41.8
Alphecca	126 13.9	N26 41.0
Alpheratz	357 47.9	N29 08.1
Altair	62 12.0	N 8 53.2
Ankaa	353 19.7	S42 15.5
Antares	112 30.8	S26 27.2
Arcturus	145 58.9	N19 08.2
Atria	107 35.8	S69 02.5
Avior	234 19.9	S59 32.4
Bellatrix	278 36.4	N 6 21.4
Betelgeuse	271 05.7	N 7 24.5
Canopus	263 58.2	S52 42.2
Capella	280 40.6	N46 00.5
Deneb	49 34.3	N45 18.3
Denebola	182 37.3	N14 31.4
Diphda	349 00.0	S17 56.4
Dubhe	193 55.7	N61 42.5
Elnath	278 17.8	N28 37.0
Eltanin	90 47.6	N51 28.9
Enif	33 51.1	N 9 54.6
Fomalhaut	15 28.4	S29 34.6
Gacrux	172 05.1	S57 09.9
Gienah	175 56.1	S17 35.5
Hadar	148 53.1	S60 25.0
Hamal	328 05.6	N23 30.1
Kaus Aust.	83 48.7	S34 22.9
Kochab	137 18.2	N74 07.1
Markab	13 42.5	N15 14.9
Menkar	314 19.5	N 4 07.3
Menkent	148 11.9	S36 24.9
Miaplacidus	221 40.8	S69 45.4
Mirfak	308 46.6	N49 53.5
Nunki	76 02.9	S26 17.2
Peacock	53 25.1	S56 42.3
Pollux	243 32.5	N28 00.5
Procyon	245 03.9	N 5 12.2
Rasalhague	96 09.8	N12 33.0
Regulus	207 47.5	N11 55.5
Rigel	281 16.0	S 8 11.6
Rigil Kent.	139 56.7	S60 52.3
Sabik	102 16.7	S15 44.3
Schedar	349 45.8	N56 34.9
Shaula	96 26.9	S37 06.6
Sirius	258 37.3	S16 43.8
Spica	158 35.1	S11 12.5
Suhail	222 55.4	S43 28.2
Vega	80 41.4	N38 47.1
Zuben'ubi	137 09.4	S16 04.8

	SHA	Mer. Pass.
	° ′	h m
Venus	334 36.6	11 17
Mars	243 59.6	17 17
Jupiter	66 03.6	5 10
Saturn	205 37.6	19 49

UT d	UT h	SUN GHA ° ′	SUN Dec ° ′	MOON GHA ° ′	MOON *v* ′	MOON Dec ° ′	MOON *d* ′	MOON HP ′
27	00	180 35.2	N13 53.2	284 13.6	10.8	S24 59.1	6.5	54.9
	01	195 35.3	54.0	298 43.4	10.9	24 52.6	6.7	54.9
	02	210 35.4	54.8	313 13.3	10.9	24 45.9	6.8	54.9
	03	225 35.5	. . 55.6	327 43.2	10.9	24 39.1	6.9	54.9
	04	240 35.6	56.4	342 13.1	11.0	24 32.2	7.1	55.0
	05	255 35.7	57.2	356 43.1	11.0	24 25.1	7.1	55.0
	06	270 35.8	N13 58.0	11 13.1	11.0	S24 18.0	7.3	55.0
	07	285 35.9	58.8	25 43.1	11.1	24 10.7	7.4	55.0
	08	300 36.0	13 59.6	40 13.2	11.1	24 03.3	7.5	55.0
S	09	315 36.1	14 00.3	54 43.3	11.1	23 55.8	7.7	55.1
U	10	330 36.2	01.1	69 13.4	11.2	23 48.1	7.7	55.1
N	11	345 36.3	01.9	83 43.6	11.2	23 40.4	7.9	55.1
D	12	0 36.4	N14 02.7	98 13.8	11.3	S23 32.5	8.0	55.1
A	13	15 36.5	03.5	112 44.1	11.3	23 24.5	8.1	55.2
Y	14	30 36.6	04.3	127 14.4	11.3	23 16.4	8.2	55.2
	15	45 36.7	. . 05.1	141 44.7	11.4	23 08.2	8.4	55.2
	16	60 36.8	05.9	156 15.1	11.4	22 59.8	8.4	55.2
	17	75 36.9	06.7	170 45.5	11.5	22 51.4	8.6	55.3
	18	90 37.0	N14 07.4	185 16.0	11.5	S22 42.8	8.7	55.3
	19	105 37.1	08.2	199 46.5	11.5	22 34.1	8.8	55.3
	20	120 37.1	09.0	214 17.0	11.6	22 25.3	8.9	55.3
	21	135 37.2	. . 09.8	228 47.6	11.6	22 16.4	9.0	55.4
	22	150 37.3	10.6	243 18.2	11.6	22 07.4	9.2	55.4
	23	165 37.4	11.4	257 48.8	11.7	21 58.2	9.2	55.4
28	00	180 37.5	N14 12.2	272 19.5	11.7	S21 49.0	9.4	55.5
	01	195 37.6	13.0	286 50.2	11.8	21 39.6	9.4	55.5
	02	210 37.7	13.7	301 21.0	11.8	21 30.2	9.6	55.5
	03	225 37.8	. . 14.5	315 51.8	11.8	21 20.6	9.7	55.5
	04	240 37.9	15.3	330 22.6	11.9	21 10.9	9.8	55.6
	05	255 38.0	16.1	344 53.5	11.9	21 01.1	9.9	55.6
	06	270 38.1	N14 16.9	359 24.4	11.9	S20 51.2	10.0	55.6
	07	285 38.1	17.7	13 55.3	12.0	20 41.2	10.1	55.6
	08	300 38.2	18.4	28 26.3	12.1	20 31.1	10.2	55.7
M	09	315 38.3	. . 19.2	42 57.4	12.0	20 20.9	10.4	55.7
O	10	330 38.4	20.0	57 28.4	12.1	20 10.5	10.4	55.7
N	11	345 38.5	20.8	71 59.5	12.1	20 00.1	10.5	55.8
D	12	0 38.6	N14 21.6	86 30.6	12.2	S19 49.6	10.6	55.8
A	13	15 38.7	22.3	101 01.8	12.2	19 39.0	10.8	55.8
Y	14	30 38.8	23.1	115 33.0	12.2	19 28.2	10.8	55.9
	15	45 38.9	. . 23.9	130 04.2	12.3	19 17.4	10.9	55.9
	16	60 38.9	24.7	144 35.5	12.3	19 06.5	11.1	55.9
	17	75 39.0	25.5	159 06.8	12.3	18 55.4	11.1	55.9
	18	90 39.1	N14 26.2	173 38.1	12.4	S18 44.3	11.2	56.0
	19	105 39.2	27.0	188 09.5	12.4	18 33.1	11.4	56.0
	20	120 39.3	27.8	202 40.9	12.5	18 21.7	11.4	56.0
	21	135 39.4	. . 28.6	217 12.4	12.4	18 10.3	11.5	56.1
	22	150 39.5	29.3	231 43.8	12.5	17 58.8	11.6	56.1
	23	165 39.6	30.1	246 15.3	12.6	17 47.2	11.7	56.1
29	00	180 39.6	N14 30.9	260 46.9	12.5	S17 35.5	11.8	56.2
	01	195 39.7	31.7	275 18.4	12.6	17 23.7	11.9	56.2
	02	210 39.8	32.4	289 50.0	12.6	17 11.8	12.0	56.2
	03	225 39.9	. . 33.2	304 21.6	12.7	16 59.8	12.1	56.3
	04	240 40.0	34.0	318 53.3	12.7	16 47.7	12.2	56.3
	05	255 40.1	34.8	333 25.0	12.7	16 35.5	12.3	56.3
	06	270 40.2	N14 35.5	347 56.7	12.7	S16 23.2	12.3	56.4
	07	285 40.2	36.3	2 28.4	12.7	16 10.9	12.4	56.4
T	08	300 40.3	37.1	17 00.1	12.8	15 58.5	12.6	56.4
U	09	315 40.4	. . 37.9	31 31.9	12.8	15 45.9	12.6	56.5
E	10	330 40.5	38.6	46 03.7	12.9	15 33.3	12.7	56.5
S	11	345 40.6	39.4	60 35.6	12.8	15 20.6	12.8	56.6
D	12	0 40.7	N14 40.2	75 07.4	12.9	S15 07.8	12.9	56.6
A	13	15 40.7	40.9	89 39.3	12.9	14 54.9	12.9	56.6
Y	14	30 40.8	41.7	104 11.2	12.9	14 42.0	13.1	56.7
	15	45 40.9	. . 42.5	118 43.1	13.0	14 28.9	13.1	56.7
	16	60 41.0	43.2	133 15.1	12.9	14 15.8	13.2	56.7
	17	75 41.1	44.0	147 47.0	13.0	14 02.6	13.3	56.8
	18	90 41.1	N14 44.8	162 19.0	13.0	S13 49.3	13.4	56.8
	19	105 41.2	45.5	176 51.0	13.0	13 35.9	13.4	56.8
	20	120 41.3	46.3	191 23.0	13.0	13 22.5	13.5	56.9
	21	135 41.4	. . 47.1	205 55.0	13.1	13 09.0	13.7	56.9
	22	150 41.5	47.8	220 27.1	13.0	12 55.3	13.6	57.0
	23	165 41.6	48.6	234 59.1	13.1	S12 41.7	13.8	57.0
		SD 15.9	*d* 0.8	SD		15.0	15.2	15.4

Lat. °	Twilight Naut. h m	Twilight Civil h m	Sunrise h m	Moonrise 27 h m	Moonrise 28 h m	Moonrise 29 h m	Moonrise 30 h m
N 72	////	////	02 13	▬	▬	05 15	04 07
N 70	////	////	02 46	▬	▬	04 30	03 48
68	////	01 33	03 10	▬	04 53	04 00	03 33
66	////	02 11	03 28	▬	04 03	03 37	03 20
64	////	02 37	03 43	03 52	03 31	03 19	03 10
62	01 22	02 58	03 55	03 10	03 07	03 04	03 01
60	01 57	03 14	04 05	02 41	02 48	02 52	02 53
N 58	02 21	03 27	04 14	02 19	02 32	02 41	02 46
56	02 40	03 39	04 22	02 01	02 19	02 31	02 40
54	02 55	03 49	04 29	01 45	02 07	02 23	02 35
52	03 08	03 57	04 36	01 32	01 57	02 15	02 30
50	03 19	04 05	04 41	01 21	01 47	02 08	02 25
45	03 42	04 21	04 54	00 56	01 27	01 53	02 16
N 40	03 59	04 35	05 04	00 37	01 11	01 41	02 08
35	04 13	04 45	05 12	00 20	00 58	01 31	02 01
30	04 25	04 54	05 20	00 06	00 46	01 22	01 54
20	04 43	05 10	05 33	24 25	00 25	01 06	01 44
N 10	04 57	05 22	05 44	24 08	00 08	00 52	01 34
0	05 08	05 33	05 54	23 51	24 39	00 39	01 25
S 10	05 18	05 43	06 04	23 34	24 25	00 25	01 16
20	05 26	05 52	06 15	23 16	24 11	00 11	01 06
30	05 34	06 03	06 27	22 55	23 55	24 55	00 55
35	05 38	06 08	06 34	22 43	23 46	24 49	00 49
40	05 42	06 14	06 42	22 29	23 35	24 42	00 42
45	05 46	06 21	06 51	22 12	23 22	24 33	00 33
S 50	05 50	06 29	07 03	21 51	23 06	24 23	00 23
52	05 52	06 32	07 08	21 41	22 59	24 18	00 18
54	05 54	06 36	07 13	21 30	22 51	24 13	00 13
56	05 56	06 40	07 20	21 17	22 41	24 07	00 07
58	05 58	06 45	07 27	21 02	22 31	24 00	00 00
S 60	06 00	06 50	07 35	20 44	22 19	23 53	25 27

Lat. °	Sunset h m	Twilight Civil h m	Twilight Naut. h m	Moonset 27 h m	Moonset 28 h m	Moonset 29 h m	Moonset 30 h m
N 72	21 48	////	////	▬	▬	08 48	11 34
N 70	21 13	////	////	▬	▬	09 31	11 51
68	20 48	22 30	////	▬	07 28	10 00	12 04
66	20 30	21 48	////	▬	08 17	10 21	12 14
64	20 14	21 21	////	06 45	08 48	10 38	12 23
62	20 02	21 00	22 40	07 27	09 11	10 52	12 31
60	19 51	20 43	22 03	07 55	09 29	11 03	12 37
N 58	19 42	20 30	21 37	08 16	09 44	11 13	12 43
56	19 34	20 18	21 18	08 34	09 57	11 22	12 48
54	19 27	20 08	21 02	08 49	10 08	11 30	12 52
52	19 20	19 59	20 48	09 02	10 18	11 36	12 56
50	19 15	19 51	20 37	09 13	10 27	11 43	13 00
45	19 02	19 34	20 14	09 37	10 45	11 56	13 08
N 40	18 52	19 21	19 57	09 55	11 00	12 07	13 14
35	18 43	19 10	19 42	10 11	11 13	12 16	13 20
30	18 36	19 01	19 31	10 25	11 24	12 24	13 25
20	18 23	18 46	19 13	10 47	11 43	12 38	13 33
N 10	18 11	18 33	18 58	11 07	11 59	12 50	13 40
0	18 01	18 22	18 47	11 25	12 14	13 01	13 47
S 10	17 50	18 12	18 37	11 44	12 29	13 12	13 54
20	17 40	18 02	18 28	12 03	12 45	13 24	14 01
30	17 27	17 52	18 20	12 26	13 03	13 37	14 09
35	17 20	17 46	18 16	12 39	13 14	13 45	14 13
40	17 12	17 40	18 12	12 53	13 25	13 53	14 19
45	17 03	17 33	18 08	13 11	13 40	14 03	14 25
S 50	16 52	17 25	18 04	13 33	13 57	14 16	14 32
52	16 46	17 22	18 02	13 44	14 05	14 21	14 35
54	16 41	17 18	18 00	13 55	14 14	14 27	14 38
56	16 34	17 14	17 58	14 09	14 23	14 34	14 42
58	16 27	17 09	17 56	14 24	14 35	14 42	14 47
S 60	16 19	17 04	17 54	14 43	14 48	14 50	14 52

Day	SUN Eqn. of Time 00^h	SUN Eqn. of Time 12^h	SUN Mer. Pass.	MOON Mer. Pass. Upper	MOON Mer. Pass. Lower	MOON Age	MOON Phase
d	m s	m s	h m	h m	h m	d	%
27	02 21	02 25	11 58	05 14	17 38	21	61
28	02 30	02 34	11 57	06 02	18 26	22	51
29	02 38	02 42	11 57	06 50	19 13	23	41

Day	UT	ARIES GHA	VENUS −3.9 GHA	VENUS Dec	MARS +1.2 GHA	MARS Dec	JUPITER −2.4 GHA	JUPITER Dec	SATURN +0.6 GHA	SATURN Dec
	d h	° ′	° ′	° ′	° ′	° ′	° ′	° ′	° ′	° ′
	30 00	218 18.6	190 36.0	N10 01.1	101 12.3	N23 00.4	284 17.9	S21 37.9	63 57.1	N12 33.4
	01	233 21.0	205 35.5	02.2	116 13.3	23 00.2	299 20.3	37.9	78 59.6	33.4
	02	248 23.5	220 35.1	03.4	131 14.4	22 59.9	314 22.7	37.9	94 02.1	33.4
	03	263 26.0	235 34.7	. . 04.5	146 15.5	. . 59.6	329 25.0	. . 37.9	109 04.6	. . 33.4
	04	278 28.4	250 34.2	05.6	161 16.6	59.4	344 27.4	37.9	124 07.0	33.4
	05	293 30.9	265 33.8	06.8	176 17.7	59.1	359 29.8	37.9	139 09.5	33.4
	06	308 33.3	280 33.3	N10 07.9	191 18.8	N22 58.8	14 32.2	S21 37.9	154 12.0	N12 33.4
W	07	323 35.8	295 32.9	09.0	206 19.9	58.6	29 34.6	37.9	169 14.5	33.4
E	08	338 38.3	310 32.4	10.1	221 20.9	58.3	44 37.0	37.9	184 16.9	33.4
	09	353 40.7	325 32.0	. . 11.3	236 22.0	. . 58.0	59 39.4	. . 37.8	199 19.4	. . 33.4
D	10	8 43.2	340 31.5	12.4	251 23.1	57.7	74 41.7	37.8	214 21.9	33.4
N	11	23 45.7	355 31.1	13.5	266 24.2	57.5	89 44.1	37.8	229 24.4	33.4
E	12	38 48.1	10 30.6	N10 14.7	281 25.3	N22 57.2	104 46.5	S21 37.8	244 26.9	N12 33.4
S	13	53 50.6	25 30.2	15.8	296 26.4	56.9	119 48.9	37.8	259 29.3	33.4
D	14	68 53.1	40 29.8	16.9	311 27.5	56.7	134 51.3	37.8	274 31.8	33.4
A	15	83 55.5	55 29.3	. . 18.0	326 28.5	. . 56.4	149 53.7	. . 37.8	289 34.3	. . 33.4
Y	16	98 58.0	70 28.9	19.2	341 29.6	56.1	164 56.1	37.8	304 36.8	33.4
	17	114 00.5	85 28.4	20.3	356 30.7	55.9	179 58.5	37.8	319 39.2	33.4
	18	129 02.9	100 28.0	N10 21.4	11 31.8	N22 55.6	195 00.8	S21 37.8	334 41.7	N12 33.4
	19	144 05.4	115 27.5	22.5	26 32.9	55.3	210 03.2	37.8	349 44.2	33.4
	20	159 07.8	130 27.1	23.7	41 34.0	55.0	225 05.6	37.8	4 46.7	33.4
	21	174 10.3	145 26.6	. . 24.8	56 35.1	. . 54.8	240 08.0	. . 37.8	19 49.1	. . 33.4
	22	189 12.8	160 26.2	25.9	71 36.1	54.5	255 10.4	37.8	34 51.6	33.4
	23	204 15.2	175 25.7	27.0	86 37.2	54.2	270 12.8	37.8	49 54.1	33.4
	1 00	219 17.7	190 25.3	N10 28.2	101 38.3	N22 53.9	285 15.2	S21 37.8	64 56.6	N12 33.4
	01	234 20.2	205 24.8	29.3	116 39.4	53.7	300 17.6	37.8	79 59.0	33.4
	02	249 22.6	220 24.4	30.4	131 40.5	53.4	315 20.0	37.7	95 01.5	33.4
	03	264 25.1	235 23.9	. . 31.5	146 41.6	. . 53.1	330 22.4	. . 37.7	110 04.0	. . 33.4
	04	279 27.6	250 23.5	32.7	161 42.6	52.9	345 24.8	37.7	125 06.5	33.4
	05	294 30.0	265 23.0	33.8	176 43.7	52.6	0 27.2	37.7	140 08.9	33.4
	06	309 32.5	280 22.5	N10 34.9	191 44.8	N22 52.3	15 29.6	S21 37.7	155 11.4	N12 33.4
	07	324 34.9	295 22.1	36.0	206 45.9	52.0	30 31.9	37.7	170 13.9	33.4
T	08	339 37.4	310 21.6	37.1	221 47.0	51.8	45 34.3	37.7	185 16.4	33.4
H	09	354 39.9	325 21.2	. . 38.3	236 48.1	. . 51.5	60 36.7	. . 37.7	200 18.8	. . 33.4
U	10	9 42.3	340 20.7	39.4	251 49.1	51.2	75 39.1	37.7	215 21.3	33.4
R	11	24 44.8	355 20.3	40.5	266 50.2	50.9	90 41.5	37.7	230 23.8	33.4
S	12	39 47.3	10 19.8	N10 41.6	281 51.3	N22 50.7	105 43.9	S21 37.7	245 26.2	N12 33.4
D	13	54 49.7	25 19.4	42.7	296 52.4	50.4	120 46.3	37.7	260 28.7	33.4
A	14	69 52.2	40 18.9	43.8	311 53.5	50.1	135 48.7	37.7	275 31.2	33.4
Y	15	84 54.7	55 18.5	. . 45.0	326 54.6	. . 49.8	150 51.1	. . 37.7	290 33.7	. . 33.4
	16	99 57.1	70 18.0	46.1	341 55.6	49.6	165 53.5	37.7	305 36.1	33.4
	17	114 59.6	85 17.5	47.2	356 56.7	49.3	180 55.9	37.7	320 38.6	33.4
	18	130 02.1	100 17.1	N10 48.3	11 57.8	N22 49.0	195 58.3	S21 37.7	335 41.1	N12 33.4
	19	145 04.5	115 16.6	49.4	26 58.9	48.7	211 00.7	37.7	350 43.6	33.4
	20	160 07.0	130 16.2	50.5	42 00.0	48.5	226 03.1	37.7	5 46.0	33.4
	21	175 09.4	145 15.7	. . 51.7	57 01.1	. . 48.2	241 05.5	. . 37.7	20 48.5	. . 33.4
	22	190 11.9	160 15.3	52.8	72 02.1	47.9	256 07.9	37.6	35 51.0	33.4
	23	205 14.4	175 14.8	53.9	87 03.2	47.6	271 10.3	37.6	50 53.4	33.4
	2 00	220 16.8	190 14.3	N10 55.0	102 04.3	N22 47.3	286 12.7	S21 37.6	65 55.9	N12 33.3
	01	235 19.3	205 13.9	56.1	117 05.4	47.1	301 15.1	37.6	80 58.4	33.3
	02	250 21.8	220 13.4	57.2	132 06.5	46.8	316 17.5	37.6	96 00.8	33.3
	03	265 24.2	235 13.0	. . 58.3	147 07.5	. . 46.5	331 19.9	. . 37.6	111 03.3	. . 33.3
	04	280 26.7	250 12.5	10 59.4	162 08.6	46.2	346 22.3	37.6	126 05.8	33.3
	05	295 29.2	265 12.0	11 00.5	177 09.7	46.0	1 24.7	37.6	141 08.3	33.3
	06	310 31.6	280 11.6	N11 01.7	192 10.8	N22 45.7	16 27.1	S21 37.6	156 10.7	N12 33.3
	07	325 34.1	295 11.1	02.8	207 11.9	45.4	31 29.5	37.6	171 13.2	33.3
	08	340 36.5	310 10.7	03.9	222 12.9	45.1	46 31.9	37.6	186 15.7	33.3
F	09	355 39.0	325 10.2	. . 05.0	237 14.0	. . 44.8	61 34.3	. . 37.6	201 18.1	. . 33.3
R	10	10 41.5	340 09.7	06.1	252 15.1	44.6	76 36.7	37.6	216 20.6	33.3
I	11	25 43.9	355 09.3	07.2	267 16.2	44.3	91 39.1	37.6	231 23.1	33.3
D	12	40 46.4	10 08.8	N11 08.3	282 17.3	N22 44.0	106 41.5	S21 37.6	246 25.5	N12 33.3
A	13	55 48.9	25 08.3	09.4	297 18.3	43.7	121 43.9	37.6	261 28.0	33.3
Y	14	70 51.3	40 07.9	10.5	312 19.4	43.4	136 46.3	37.6	276 30.5	33.3
	15	85 53.8	55 07.4	. . 11.6	327 20.5	. . 43.2	151 48.7	. . 37.6	291 32.9	. . 33.3
	16	100 56.3	70 07.0	12.7	342 21.6	42.9	166 51.2	37.6	306 35.4	33.3
	17	115 58.7	85 06.5	13.8	357 22.7	42.6	181 53.6	37.6	321 37.9	33.3
	18	131 01.2	100 06.0	N11 14.9	12 23.7	N22 42.3	196 56.0	S21 37.6	336 40.4	N12 33.3
	19	146 03.7	115 05.6	16.1	27 24.8	42.0	211 58.4	37.6	351 42.8	33.3
	20	161 06.1	130 05.1	17.2	42 25.9	41.8	227 00.8	37.6	6 45.3	33.3
	21	176 08.6	145 04.6	. . 18.3	57 27.0	. . 41.5	242 03.2	. . 37.6	21 47.8	. . 33.3
	22	191 11.0	160 04.2	19.4	72 28.1	41.2	257 05.6	37.6	36 50.2	33.3
	23	206 13.5	175 03.7	20.5	87 29.1	40.9	272 08.0	37.6	51 52.7	33.3
	Mer. Pass.	h m 9 21.3	*v* −0.5	*d* 1.1	*v* 1.1	*d* 0.3	*v* 2.4	*d* 0.0	*v* 2.5	*d* 0.0

STARS

Name	SHA	Dec
	° ′	° ′
Acamar	315 21.6	S40 16.2
Achernar	335 29.9	S57 11.5
Acrux	173 13.5	S63 09.0
Adhara	255 15.8	S28 59.2
Aldebaran	290 54.2	N16 31.6
Alioth	166 23.3	N55 54.9
Alkaid	153 01.3	N49 16.2
Al Na'ir	27 48.6	S46 55.1
Alnilam	275 50.6	S 1 11.8
Alphard	217 59.9	S 8 41.8
Alphecca	126 13.9	N26 41.0
Alpheratz	357 47.9	N29 08.1
Altair	62 11.9	N 8 53.2
Ankaa	353 19.7	S42 15.5
Antares	112 30.7	S26 27.2
Arcturus	145 58.9	N19 08.2
Atria	107 35.7	S69 02.5
Avior	234 19.9	S59 32.4
Bellatrix	278 36.4	N 6 21.5
Betelgeuse	271 05.7	N 7 24.5
Canopus	263 58.2	S52 42.2
Capella	280 40.6	N46 00.5
Deneb	49 34.2	N45 18.3
Denebola	182 37.3	N14 31.4
Diphda	349 00.0	S17 56.4
Dubhe	193 55.7	N61 42.5
Elnath	278 17.8	N28 37.0
Eltanin	90 47.6	N51 28.9
Enif	33 51.0	N 9 54.6
Fomalhaut	15 28.3	S29 34.6
Gacrux	172 05.1	S57 09.9
Gienah	175 56.1	S17 35.5
Hadar	148 53.1	S60 25.0
Hamal	328 05.6	N23 30.1
Kaus Aust.	83 48.7	S34 22.9
Kochab	137 18.2	N74 07.1
Markab	13 42.4	N15 14.9
Menkar	314 19.5	N 4 07.3
Menkent	148 11.9	S36 24.9
Miaplacidus	221 40.8	S69 45.4
Mirfak	308 46.6	N49 53.5
Nunki	76 02.9	S26 17.2
Peacock	53 25.1	S56 42.3
Pollux	243 32.5	N28 00.5
Procyon	245 03.9	N 5 12.2
Rasalhague	96 09.8	N12 33.0
Regulus	207 47.5	N11 55.5
Rigel	281 16.1	S 8 11.5
Rigil Kent.	139 56.7	S60 52.3
Sabik	102 16.7	S15 44.3
Schedar	349 45.8	N56 34.9
Shaula	96 26.9	S37 06.6
Sirius	258 37.3	S16 43.7
Spica	158 35.1	S11 12.5
Suhail	222 55.4	S43 28.2
Vega	80 41.4	N38 47.1
Zuben'ubi	137 09.4	S16 04.8

	SHA	Mer. Pass.
	° ′	h m
Venus	331 07.6	11 19
Mars	242 20.6	17 12
Jupiter	65 57.5	4 58
Saturn	205 38.9	19 37

UT d	h	SUN GHA	SUN Dec	MOON GHA	v	MOON Dec	d	HP
		° ′	° ′	° ′	′	° ′	′	′
30	00	180 41.6	N14 49.4	249 31.2	13.1	S12 27.9	13.8	57.0
	01	195 41.7	50.1	264 03.3	13.1	12 14.1	13.9	57.1
	02	210 41.8	50.9	278 35.4	13.1	12 00.2	14.0	57.1
	03	225 41.9	. . 51.7	293 07.5	13.1	11 46.2	14.1	57.1
	04	240 42.0	52.4	307 39.6	13.1	11 32.1	14.1	57.2
	05	255 42.0	53.2	322 11.7	13.1	11 18.0	14.2	57.2
	06	270 42.1	N14 54.0	336 43.8	13.2	S11 03.8	14.3	57.3
W	07	285 42.2	54.7	351 16.0	13.1	10 49.5	14.3	57.3
E	08	300 42.3	55.5	5 48.1	13.2	10 35.2	14.4	57.3
D	09	315 42.3	. . 56.2	20 20.3	13.1	10 20.8	14.5	57.4
N	10	330 42.4	57.0	34 52.4	13.2	10 06.3	14.5	57.4
E	11	345 42.5	57.8	49 24.6	13.1	9 51.8	14.6	57.4
S	12	0 42.6	N14 58.5	63 56.7	13.2	S 9 37.2	14.7	57.5
D	13	15 42.7	14 59.3	78 28.9	13.2	9 22.5	14.7	57.5
A	14	30 42.7	15 00.0	93 01.1	13.1	9 07.8	14.8	57.6
Y	15	45 42.8	. . 00.8	107 33.2	13.2	8 53.0	14.9	57.6
	16	60 42.9	01.6	122 05.4	13.1	8 38.1	14.9	57.6
	17	75 43.0	02.3	136 37.5	13.2	8 23.2	15.0	57.7
	18	90 43.0	N15 03.1	151 09.7	13.1	S 8 08.2	15.0	57.7
	19	105 43.1	03.8	165 41.8	13.1	7 53.2	15.1	57.8
	20	120 43.2	04.6	180 13.9	13.2	7 38.1	15.1	57.8
	21	135 43.3	. . 05.4	194 46.1	13.1	7 23.0	15.2	57.8
	22	150 43.3	06.1	209 18.2	13.1	7 07.8	15.3	57.9
	23	165 43.4	06.9	223 50.3	13.1	6 52.5	15.3	57.9
1	00	180 43.5	N15 07.6	238 22.4	13.1	S 6 37.2	15.4	58.0
	01	195 43.6	08.4	252 54.5	13.1	6 21.8	15.4	58.0
	02	210 43.6	09.1	267 26.6	13.0	6 06.4	15.5	58.0
	03	225 43.7	. . 09.9	281 58.6	13.0	5 50.9	15.5	58.1
	04	240 43.8	10.6	296 30.6	13.1	5 35.4	15.6	58.1
	05	255 43.9	11.4	311 02.7	13.0	5 19.8	15.6	58.2
	06	270 43.9	N15 12.1	325 34.7	13.0	S 5 04.2	15.6	58.2
T	07	285 44.0	12.9	340 06.7	12.9	4 48.6	15.7	58.2
H	08	300 44.1	13.6	354 38.6	13.0	4 32.9	15.8	58.3
U	09	315 44.2	. . 14.4	9 10.6	12.9	4 17.1	15.8	58.3
R	10	330 44.2	15.1	23 42.5	12.9	4 01.3	15.8	58.4
S	11	345 44.3	15.9	38 14.4	12.8	3 45.5	15.9	58.4
D	12	0 44.4	N15 16.6	52 46.2	12.9	S 3 29.6	15.9	58.4
A	13	15 44.4	17.4	67 18.1	12.8	3 13.7	16.0	58.5
Y	14	30 44.5	18.1	81 49.9	12.8	2 57.7	15.9	58.5
	15	45 44.6	. . 18.9	96 21.7	12.7	2 41.8	16.1	58.6
	16	60 44.7	19.6	110 53.4	12.8	2 25.7	16.0	58.6
	17	75 44.7	20.4	125 25.2	12.6	2 09.7	16.1	58.6
	18	90 44.8	N15 21.1	139 56.8	12.7	S 1 53.6	16.1	58.7
	19	105 44.9	21.9	154 28.5	12.6	1 37.5	16.2	58.7
	20	120 44.9	22.6	169 00.1	12.6	1 21.3	16.2	58.8
	21	135 45.0	. . 23.4	183 31.7	12.5	1 05.1	16.2	58.8
	22	150 45.1	24.1	198 03.2	12.5	0 48.9	16.2	58.8
	23	165 45.1	24.9	212 34.7	12.5	0 32.7	16.3	58.9
2	00	180 45.2	N15 25.6	227 06.2	12.4	S 0 16.4	16.3	58.9
	01	195 45.3	26.4	241 37.6	12.4	S 0 00.1	16.3	59.0
	02	210 45.3	27.1	256 09.0	12.3	N 0 16.2	16.3	59.0
	03	225 45.4	. . 27.8	270 40.3	12.3	0 32.5	16.4	59.0
	04	240 45.5	28.6	285 11.6	12.2	0 48.9	16.3	59.1
	05	255 45.5	29.3	299 42.8	12.2	1 05.2	16.4	59.1
	06	270 45.6	N15 30.1	314 14.0	12.2	N 1 21.6	16.4	59.2
	07	285 45.7	30.8	328 45.2	12.0	1 38.0	16.4	59.2
	08	300 45.8	31.6	343 16.2	12.1	1 54.4	16.5	59.2
F	09	315 45.8	. . 32.3	357 47.3	12.0	2 10.9	16.4	59.3
R	10	330 45.9	33.0	12 18.3	11.9	2 27.3	16.5	59.3
I	11	345 45.9	33.8	26 49.2	11.8	2 43.8	16.4	59.3
D	12	0 46.0	N15 34.5	41 20.0	11.8	N 3 00.2	16.5	59.4
A	13	15 46.1	35.3	55 50.8	11.8	3 16.7	16.5	59.4
Y	14	30 46.1	36.0	70 21.6	11.7	3 33.2	16.4	59.5
	15	45 46.2	. . 36.7	84 52.3	11.6	3 49.6	16.5	59.5
	16	60 46.3	37.5	99 22.9	11.6	4 06.1	16.5	59.5
	17	75 46.3	38.2	113 53.5	11.4	4 22.6	16.4	59.6
	18	90 46.4	N15 38.9	128 23.9	11.5	N 4 39.0	16.5	59.6
	19	105 46.5	39.7	142 54.4	11.3	4 55.5	16.5	59.6
	20	120 46.5	40.4	157 24.7	11.3	5 12.0	16.4	59.7
	21	135 46.6	. . 41.1	171 55.0	11.2	5 28.4	16.5	59.7
	22	150 46.7	41.9	186 25.2	11.2	5 44.9	16.4	59.7
	23	165 46.7	42.6	200 55.4	11.1	N 6 01.3	16.5	59.8
		SD 15.9	*d* 0.7	SD 15.7		15.9		16.2

Lat.	Twilight Naut.	Twilight Civil	Sunrise	Moonrise 30	Moonrise 1	Moonrise 2	Moonrise 3
°	h m	h m	h m	h m	h m	h m	h m
N 72	////	////	01 50	04 07	03 27	02 53	02 17
N 70	////	////	02 29	03 48	03 19	02 53	02 27
68	////	01 03	02 56	03 33	03 12	02 54	02 34
66	////	01 53	03 16	03 20	03 07	02 54	02 41
64	////	02 24	03 32	03 10	03 02	02 54	02 47
62	00 56	02 46	03 46	03 01	02 58	02 54	02 51
60	01 41	03 04	03 57	02 53	02 54	02 55	02 56
N 58	02 09	03 18	04 07	02 46	02 51	02 55	02 59
56	02 30	03 31	04 15	02 40	02 48	02 55	03 03
54	02 46	03 42	04 23	02 35	02 45	02 55	03 06
52	03 00	03 51	04 30	02 30	02 43	02 55	03 09
50	03 12	03 59	04 36	02 25	02 41	02 56	03 11
45	03 36	04 17	04 49	02 16	02 36	02 56	03 17
N 40	03 55	04 30	05 00	02 08	02 32	02 56	03 21
35	04 09	04 42	05 09	02 01	02 29	02 56	03 26
30	04 21	04 52	05 17	01 54	02 26	02 57	03 29
20	04 40	05 08	05 31	01 44	02 20	02 57	03 36
N 10	04 55	05 21	05 43	01 34	02 16	02 57	03 41
0	05 07	05 32	05 54	01 25	02 11	02 58	03 47
S 10	05 18	05 43	06 05	01 16	02 07	02 58	03 52
20	05 27	05 53	06 16	01 06	02 02	02 59	03 58
30	05 36	06 04	06 29	00 55	01 57	02 59	04 04
35	05 40	06 10	06 37	00 49	01 53	03 00	04 08
40	05 45	06 17	06 45	00 42	01 50	03 00	04 13
45	05 50	06 24	06 55	00 33	01 46	03 00	04 18
S 50	05 54	06 33	07 07	00 23	01 41	03 01	04 24
52	05 57	06 37	07 13	00 18	01 39	03 01	04 27
54	05 59	06 41	07 19	00 13	01 36	03 01	04 30
56	06 01	06 45	07 26	00 07	01 33	03 02	04 34
58	06 04	06 50	07 33	00 00	01 30	03 02	04 38
S 60	06 06	06 56	07 42	25 27	01 27	03 02	04 42

Lat.	Sunset	Twilight Civil	Twilight Naut.	Moonset 30	Moonset 1	Moonset 2	Moonset 3
°	h m	h m	h m	h m	h m	h m	h m
N 72	22 12	////	////	11 34	13 54	16 13	18 47
N 70	21 30	////	////	11 51	13 58	16 07	18 27
68	21 02	23 03	////	12 04	14 02	16 02	18 11
66	20 41	22 06	////	12 14	14 05	15 58	17 58
64	20 24	21 34	////	12 23	14 08	15 54	17 48
62	20 10	21 11	23 09	12 31	14 10	15 52	17 39
60	19 59	20 53	22 18	12 37	14 12	15 49	17 32
N 58	19 49	20 38	21 49	12 43	14 13	15 47	17 25
56	19 40	20 25	21 27	12 48	14 15	15 45	17 19
54	19 32	20 14	21 10	12 52	14 16	15 43	17 14
52	19 25	20 05	20 56	12 56	14 17	15 41	17 10
50	19 19	19 56	20 43	13 00	14 19	15 40	17 05
45	19 06	19 38	20 19	13 08	14 21	15 37	16 56
N 40	18 55	19 24	20 00	13 14	14 23	15 34	16 49
35	18 46	19 13	19 45	13 20	14 25	15 32	16 42
30	18 38	19 03	19 33	13 25	14 26	15 30	16 37
20	18 24	18 47	19 14	13 33	14 29	15 26	16 27
N 10	18 12	18 33	18 59	13 40	14 31	15 23	16 19
0	18 00	18 22	18 47	13 47	14 33	15 21	16 11
S 10	17 49	18 11	18 36	13 54	14 35	15 18	16 03
20	17 38	18 01	18 27	14 01	14 37	15 15	15 54
30	17 25	17 49	18 18	14 09	14 40	15 11	15 45
35	17 17	17 43	18 13	14 13	14 41	15 09	15 40
40	17 08	17 37	18 09	14 19	14 43	15 07	15 33
45	16 58	17 29	18 04	14 25	14 44	15 04	15 26
S 50	16 46	17 21	17 59	14 32	14 46	15 01	15 18
52	16 41	17 17	17 57	14 35	14 47	15 00	15 14
54	16 35	17 12	17 54	14 38	14 48	14 58	15 10
56	16 28	17 08	17 52	14 42	14 49	14 57	15 05
58	16 20	17 03	17 50	14 47	14 51	14 55	15 00
S 60	16 11	16 57	17 47	14 52	14 52	14 53	14 54

Day	SUN Eqn. of Time 00^h	SUN Eqn. of Time 12^h	SUN Mer. Pass.	MOON Mer. Pass. Upper	MOON Mer. Pass. Lower	Age	Phase
d	m s	m s	h m	h m	h m	d %	
30	02 46	02 50	11 57	07 36	19 59	24 31	
1	02 54	02 57	11 57	08 22	20 45	25 21	
2	03 01	03 04	11 57	09 09	21 33	26 13	

	UT	ARIES	VENUS −3.9		MARS +1.2		JUPITER −2.4		SATURN +0.6	
		GHA	GHA	Dec	GHA	Dec	GHA	Dec	GHA	Dec
	d h	° ′	° ′	° ′	° ′	° ′	° ′	° ′	° ′	° ′
	3 00	221 16.0	190 03.2	N11 21.6	102 30.2	N22 40.6	287 10.4	S21 37.5	66 55.2	N12 33.3
	01	236 18.4	205 02.8	22.7	117 31.3	40.3	302 12.8	37.5	81 57.6	33.3
	02	251 20.9	220 02.3	23.8	132 32.4	40.1	317 15.2	37.5	97 00.1	33.3
	03	266 23.4	235 01.8	. . 24.9	147 33.5	. . 39.8	332 17.6	. . 37.5	112 02.6	. . 33.2
	04	281 25.8	250 01.4	26.0	162 34.5	39.5	347 20.0	37.5	127 05.0	33.2
	05	296 28.3	265 00.9	27.1	177 35.6	39.2	2 22.5	37.5	142 07.5	33.2
	06	311 30.8	280 00.4	N11 28.2	192 36.7	N22 38.9	17 24.9	S21 37.5	157 09.9	N12 33.2
	07	326 33.2	294 59.9	29.3	207 37.8	38.6	32 27.3	37.5	172 12.4	33.2
S	08	341 35.7	309 59.5	30.4	222 38.8	38.4	47 29.7	37.5	187 14.9	33.2
A	09	356 38.1	324 59.0	. . 31.5	237 39.9	. . 38.1	62 32.1	. . 37.5	202 17.3	. . 33.2
T	10	11 40.6	339 58.5	32.6	252 41.0	37.8	77 34.5	37.5	217 19.8	33.2
U	11	26 43.1	354 58.1	33.7	267 42.1	37.5	92 36.9	37.5	232 22.3	33.2
R	12	41 45.5	9 57.6	N11 34.8	282 43.2	N22 37.2	107 39.3	S21 37.5	247 24.7	N12 33.2
D	13	56 48.0	24 57.1	35.9	297 44.2	36.9	122 41.8	37.5	262 27.2	33.2
A	14	71 50.5	39 56.6	37.0	312 45.3	36.6	137 44.2	37.5	277 29.7	33.2
Y	15	86 52.9	54 56.2	. . 38.0	327 46.4	. . 36.4	152 46.6	. . 37.5	292 32.1	. . 33.2
	16	101 55.4	69 55.7	39.1	342 47.5	36.1	167 49.0	37.5	307 34.6	33.2
	17	116 57.9	84 55.2	40.2	357 48.5	35.8	182 51.4	37.5	322 37.1	33.2
	18	132 00.3	99 54.7	N11 41.3	12 49.6	N22 35.5	197 53.8	S21 37.5	337 39.5	N12 33.2
	19	147 02.8	114 54.3	42.4	27 50.7	35.2	212 56.2	37.5	352 42.0	33.2
	20	162 05.3	129 53.8	43.5	42 51.8	34.9	227 58.7	37.5	7 44.4	33.2
	21	177 07.7	144 53.3	. . 44.6	57 52.8	. . 34.6	243 01.1	. . 37.5	22 46.9	. . 33.2
	22	192 10.2	159 52.9	45.7	72 53.9	34.3	258 03.5	37.5	37 49.4	33.1
	23	207 12.6	174 52.4	46.8	87 55.0	34.1	273 05.9	37.5	52 51.8	33.1
	4 00	222 15.1	189 51.9	N11 47.9	102 56.1	N22 33.8	288 08.3	S21 37.5	67 54.3	N12 33.1
	01	237 17.6	204 51.4	49.0	117 57.2	33.5	303 10.7	37.5	82 56.8	33.1
	02	252 20.0	219 50.9	50.1	132 58.2	33.2	318 13.2	37.5	97 59.2	33.1
	03	267 22.5	234 50.5	. . 51.2	147 59.3	. . 32.9	333 15.6	. . 37.5	113 01.7	. . 33.1
	04	282 25.0	249 50.0	52.2	163 00.4	32.6	348 18.0	37.5	128 04.1	33.1
	05	297 27.4	264 49.5	53.3	178 01.5	32.3	3 20.4	37.5	143 06.6	33.1
	06	312 29.9	279 49.0	N11 54.4	193 02.5	N22 32.0	18 22.8	S21 37.5	158 09.1	N12 33.1
	07	327 32.4	294 48.6	55.5	208 03.6	31.8	33 25.2	37.5	173 11.5	33.1
	08	342 34.8	309 48.1	56.6	223 04.7	31.5	48 27.7	37.5	188 14.0	33.1
S	09	357 37.3	324 47.6	. . 57.7	238 05.8	. . 31.2	63 30.1	. . 37.5	203 16.4	. . 33.1
U	10	12 39.8	339 47.1	58.8	253 06.8	30.9	78 32.5	37.5	218 18.9	33.1
N	11	27 42.2	354 46.6	11 59.8	268 07.9	30.6	93 34.9	37.5	233 21.4	33.1
D	12	42 44.7	9 46.2	N12 00.9	283 09.0	N22 30.3	108 37.3	S21 37.5	248 23.8	N12 33.1
A	13	57 47.1	24 45.7	02.0	298 10.1	30.0	123 39.8	37.5	263 26.3	33.1
Y	14	72 49.6	39 45.2	03.1	313 11.1	29.7	138 42.2	37.5	278 28.8	33.0
	15	87 52.1	54 44.7	. . 04.2	328 12.2	. . 29.4	153 44.6	. . 37.5	293 31.2	. . 33.0
	16	102 54.5	69 44.2	05.3	343 13.3	29.1	168 47.0	37.5	308 33.7	33.0
	17	117 57.0	84 43.7	06.4	358 14.4	28.8	183 49.5	37.5	323 36.1	33.0
	18	132 59.5	99 43.3	N12 07.4	13 15.4	N22 28.6	198 51.9	S21 37.5	338 38.6	N12 33.0
	19	148 01.9	114 42.8	08.5	28 16.5	28.3	213 54.3	37.5	353 41.0	33.0
	20	163 04.4	129 42.3	09.6	43 17.6	28.0	228 56.7	37.5	8 43.5	33.0
	21	178 06.9	144 41.8	. . 10.7	58 18.7	. . 27.7	243 59.2	. . 37.5	23 46.0	. . 33.0
	22	193 09.3	159 41.3	11.8	73 19.7	27.4	259 01.6	37.5	38 48.4	33.0
	23	208 11.8	174 40.8	12.8	88 20.8	27.1	274 04.0	37.5	53 50.9	33.0
	5 00	223 14.2	189 40.4	N12 13.9	103 21.9	N22 26.8	289 06.4	S21 37.5	68 53.3	N12 33.0
	01	238 16.7	204 39.9	15.0	118 22.9	26.5	304 08.9	37.5	83 55.8	33.0
	02	253 19.2	219 39.4	16.1	133 24.0	26.2	319 11.3	37.5	98 58.3	33.0
	03	268 21.6	234 38.9	. . 17.2	148 25.1	. . 25.9	334 13.7	. . 37.5	114 00.7	. . 32.9
	04	283 24.1	249 38.4	18.2	163 26.2	25.6	349 16.1	37.5	129 03.2	32.9
	05	298 26.6	264 37.9	19.3	178 27.2	25.3	4 18.6	37.5	144 05.6	32.9
	06	313 29.0	279 37.4	N12 20.4	193 28.3	N22 25.0	19 21.0	S21 37.5	159 08.1	N12 32.9
	07	328 31.5	294 37.0	21.5	208 29.4	24.7	34 23.4	37.5	174 10.5	32.9
	08	343 34.0	309 36.5	22.5	223 30.5	24.5	49 25.8	37.5	189 13.0	32.9
M	09	358 36.4	324 36.0	. . 23.6	238 31.5	. . 24.2	64 28.3	. . 37.5	204 15.5	. . 32.9
O	10	13 38.9	339 35.5	24.7	253 32.6	23.9	79 30.7	37.5	219 17.9	32.9
N	11	28 41.4	354 35.0	25.8	268 33.7	23.6	94 33.1	37.5	234 20.4	32.9
D	12	43 43.8	9 34.5	N12 26.8	283 34.7	N22 23.3	109 35.6	S21 37.5	249 22.8	N12 32.9
A	13	58 46.3	24 34.0	27.9	298 35.8	23.0	124 38.0	37.5	264 25.3	32.9
Y	14	73 48.7	39 33.5	29.0	313 36.9	22.7	139 40.4	37.5	279 27.7	32.9
	15	88 51.2	54 33.0	. . 30.0	328 38.0	. . 22.4	154 42.8	. . 37.5	294 30.2	. . 32.8
	16	103 53.7	69 32.5	31.1	343 39.0	22.1	169 45.3	37.5	309 32.6	32.8
	17	118 56.1	84 32.1	32.2	358 40.1	21.8	184 47.7	37.5	324 35.1	32.8
	18	133 58.6	99 31.6	N12 33.3	13 41.2	N22 21.5	199 50.1	S21 37.5	339 37.6	N12 32.8
	19	149 01.1	114 31.1	34.3	28 42.3	21.2	214 52.6	37.5	354 40.0	32.8
	20	164 03.5	129 30.6	35.4	43 43.3	20.9	229 55.0	37.5	9 42.5	32.8
	21	179 06.0	144 30.1	. . 36.5	58 44.4	. . 20.6	244 57.4	. . 37.5	24 44.9	. . 32.8
	22	194 08.5	159 29.6	37.5	73 45.5	20.3	259 59.9	37.5	39 47.4	32.8
	23	209 10.9	174 29.1	38.6	88 46.5	20.0	275 02.3	37.5	54 49.8	32.8
	Mer. Pass.	h m 9 09.5	*v* −0.5	*d* 1.1	*v* 1.1	*d* 0.3	*v* 2.4	*d* 0.0	*v* 2.5	*d* 0.0

STARS

Name	SHA	Dec
	° ′	° ′
Acamar	315 21.6	S40 16.2
Achernar	335 29.9	S57 11.5
Acrux	173 13.5	S63 09.0
Adhara	255 15.8	S28 59.1
Aldebaran	290 54.2	N16 31.6
Alioth	166 23.3	N55 54.9
Alkaid	153 01.3	N49 16.2
Al Na'ir	27 48.5	S46 55.1
Alnilam	275 50.6	S 1 11.8
Alphard	217 59.9	S 8 41.8
Alphecca	126 13.9	N26 41.0
Alpheratz	357 47.9	N29 08.1
Altair	62 11.9	N 8 53.2
Ankaa	353 19.7	S42 15.5
Antares	112 30.7	S26 27.2
Arcturus	145 58.9	N19 08.2
Atria	107 35.7	S69 02.6
Avior	234 19.9	S59 32.4
Bellatrix	278 36.4	N 6 21.5
Betelgeuse	271 05.7	N 7 24.5
Canopus	263 58.2	S52 42.2
Capella	280 40.6	N46 00.5
Deneb	49 34.2	N45 18.3
Denebola	182 37.3	N14 31.4
Diphda	349 00.0	S17 56.4
Dubhe	193 55.7	N61 42.5
Elnath	278 17.9	N28 37.0
Eltanin	90 47.6	N51 28.9
Enif	33 51.0	N 9 54.6
Fomalhaut	15 28.3	S29 34.6
Gacrux	172 05.1	S57 09.9
Gienah	175 56.1	S17 35.5
Hadar	148 53.1	S60 25.0
Hamal	328 05.6	N23 30.1
Kaus Aust.	83 48.7	S34 22.9
Kochab	137 18.2	N74 07.2
Markab	13 42.4	N15 14.9
Menkar	314 19.5	N 4 07.4
Menkent	148 11.9	S36 24.9
Miaplacidus	221 40.9	S69 45.4
Mirfak	308 46.6	N49 53.5
Nunki	76 02.9	S26 17.2
Peacock	53 25.1	S56 42.3
Pollux	243 32.6	N28 00.5
Procyon	245 03.9	N 5 12.2
Rasalhague	96 09.8	N12 33.0
Regulus	207 47.5	N11 55.5
Rigel	281 16.1	S 8 11.5
Rigil Kent.	139 56.7	S60 52.3
Sabik	102 16.7	S15 44.3
Schedar	349 45.7	N56 34.8
Shaula	96 26.9	S37 06.6
Sirius	258 37.4	S16 43.7
Spica	158 35.1	S11 12.5
Suhail	222 55.4	S43 28.2
Vega	80 41.4	N38 47.2
Zuben'ubi	137 09.4	S16 04.8

	SHA	Mer. Pass.
	° ′	h m
Venus	327 36.8	11 21
Mars	240 41.0	17 07
Jupiter	65 53.2	4 47
Saturn	205 39.2	19 25

Day	UT (d h)	SUN GHA (° ′)	SUN Dec (° ′)	MOON GHA (° ′)	v (′)	MOON Dec (° ′)	d (′)	HP (′)
3	00	180 46.8	N15 43.3	215 25.5	11.0	N 6 17.8	16.4	59.8
	01	195 46.8	44.1	229 55.5	10.9	6 34.2	16.4	59.9
	02	210 46.9	44.8	244 25.4	10.8	6 50.6	16.4	59.9
	03	225 47.0	. . 45.5	258 55.2	10.8	7 07.0	16.3	59.9
	04	240 47.0	46.3	273 25.0	10.7	7 23.3	16.4	60.0
	05	255 47.1	47.0	287 54.7	10.6	7 39.7	16.3	60.0
	06	270 47.2	N15 47.7	302 24.3	10.5	N 7 56.0	16.3	60.0
	07	285 47.2	48.5	316 53.8	10.5	8 12.3	16.3	60.1
S	08	300 47.3	49.2	331 23.3	10.3	8 28.6	16.2	60.1
A	09	315 47.3	. . 49.9	345 52.6	10.3	8 44.8	16.2	60.1
T	10	330 47.4	50.7	0 21.9	10.2	9 01.0	16.2	60.2
U	11	345 47.5	51.4	14 51.1	10.1	9 17.2	16.1	60.2
R	12	0 47.5	N15 52.1	29 20.2	10.0	N 9 33.3	16.2	60.2
D	13	15 47.6	52.8	43 49.2	9.9	9 49.5	16.0	60.2
A	14	30 47.6	53.6	58 18.1	9.8	10 05.5	16.1	60.3
Y	15	45 47.7	. . 54.3	72 46.9	9.7	10 21.6	16.0	60.3
	16	60 47.8	55.0	87 15.6	9.7	10 37.6	15.9	60.3
	17	75 47.8	55.8	101 44.3	9.5	10 53.5	15.9	60.4
	18	90 47.9	N15 56.5	116 12.8	9.5	N11 09.4	15.9	60.4
	19	105 47.9	57.2	130 41.3	9.3	11 25.3	15.8	60.4
	20	120 48.0	57.9	145 09.6	9.3	11 41.1	15.7	60.5
	21	135 48.1	. . 58.7	159 37.9	9.1	11 56.8	15.7	60.5
	22	150 48.1	15 59.4	174 06.0	9.0	12 12.5	15.7	60.5
	23	165 48.2	16 00.1	188 34.0	9.0	12 28.2	15.6	60.5
4	00	180 48.2	N16 00.8	203 02.0	8.8	N12 43.8	15.5	60.6
	01	195 48.3	01.5	217 29.8	8.8	12 59.3	15.4	60.6
	02	210 48.3	02.3	231 57.6	8.6	13 14.7	15.4	60.6
	03	225 48.4	. . 03.0	246 25.2	8.5	13 30.1	15.4	60.6
	04	240 48.4	03.7	260 52.7	8.4	13 45.5	15.2	60.7
	05	255 48.5	04.4	275 20.1	8.3	14 00.7	15.2	60.7
	06	270 48.6	N16 05.2	289 47.4	8.2	N14 15.9	15.1	60.7
	07	285 48.6	05.9	304 14.6	8.1	14 31.0	15.1	60.7
	08	300 48.7	06.6	318 41.7	8.0	14 46.1	14.9	60.8
S	09	315 48.7	. . 07.3	333 08.7	7.9	15 01.0	14.9	60.8
U	10	330 48.8	08.0	347 35.6	7.8	15 15.9	14.8	60.8
N	11	345 48.8	08.7	2 02.4	7.6	15 30.7	14.7	60.8
D	12	0 48.9	N16 09.5	16 29.0	7.5	N15 45.4	14.6	60.9
A	13	15 48.9	10.2	30 55.5	7.5	16 00.0	14.6	60.9
Y	14	30 49.0	10.9	45 22.0	7.3	16 14.6	14.4	60.9
	15	45 49.0	. . 11.6	59 48.3	7.2	16 29.0	14.4	60.9
	16	60 49.1	12.3	74 14.5	7.0	16 43.4	14.2	60.9
	17	75 49.2	13.0	88 40.5	7.0	16 57.6	14.2	61.0
	18	90 49.2	N16 13.8	103 06.5	6.8	N17 11.8	14.0	61.0
	19	105 49.3	14.5	117 32.3	6.8	17 25.8	14.0	61.0
	20	120 49.3	15.2	131 58.1	6.6	17 39.8	13.8	61.0
	21	135 49.4	. . 15.9	146 23.7	6.5	17 53.6	13.7	61.0
	22	150 49.4	16.6	160 49.2	6.4	18 07.3	13.7	61.0
	23	165 49.5	17.3	175 14.6	6.2	18 21.0	13.5	61.1
5	00	180 49.5	N16 18.0	189 39.8	6.2	N18 34.5	13.4	61.1
	01	195 49.6	18.7	204 05.0	6.0	18 47.9	13.2	61.1
	02	210 49.6	19.5	218 30.0	5.9	19 01.1	13.2	61.1
	03	225 49.7	. . 20.2	232 54.9	5.8	19 14.3	13.0	61.1
	04	240 49.7	20.9	247 19.7	5.7	19 27.3	12.9	61.1
	05	255 49.8	21.6	261 44.4	5.5	19 40.2	12.8	61.1
	06	270 49.8	N16 22.3	276 08.9	5.5	N19 53.0	12.7	61.2
	07	285 49.9	23.0	290 33.4	5.3	20 05.7	12.5	61.2
	08	300 49.9	23.7	304 57.7	5.2	20 18.2	12.4	61.2
M	09	315 50.0	. . 24.4	319 21.9	5.1	20 30.6	12.2	61.2
O	10	330 50.0	25.1	333 46.0	4.9	20 42.8	12.1	61.2
N	11	345 50.1	25.8	348 09.9	4.9	20 54.9	12.0	61.2
D	12	0 50.1	N16 26.5	2 33.8	4.7	N21 06.9	11.8	61.2
A	13	15 50.2	27.2	16 57.5	4.7	21 18.7	11.7	61.2
Y	14	30 50.2	28.0	31 21.2	4.5	21 30.4	11.5	61.2
	15	45 50.3	. . 28.7	45 44.7	4.4	21 41.9	11.4	61.2
	16	60 50.3	29.4	60 08.1	4.3	21 53.3	11.3	61.3
	17	75 50.4	30.1	74 31.4	4.2	22 04.6	11.0	61.3
	18	90 50.4	N16 30.8	88 54.6	4.1	N22 15.6	11.0	61.3
	19	105 50.4	31.5	103 17.7	3.9	22 26.6	10.7	61.3
	20	120 50.5	32.2	117 40.6	3.9	22 37.3	10.6	61.3
	21	135 50.5	. . 32.9	132 03.5	3.7	22 47.9	10.5	61.3
	22	150 50.6	33.6	146 26.2	3.7	22 58.4	10.2	61.3
	23	165 50.6	34.3	160 48.9	3.5	N23 08.6	10.1	61.3
		SD 15.9	d 0.7	SD 16.4		16.6		16.7

Lat.	Twilight Naut.	Twilight Civil	Sunrise	Moonrise 3	Moonrise 4	Moonrise 5	Moonrise 6
°	h m	h m	h m	h m	h m	h m	h m
N 72	////	////	01 21	02 17	01 31	▭	▭
N 70	////	////	02 11	02 27	01 54	00 53	▭
68	////	////	02 42	02 34	02 12	01 36	▭
66	////	01 33	03 04	02 41	02 26	02 06	01 19
64	////	02 09	03 22	02 47	02 38	02 28	02 13
62	////	02 34	03 37	02 51	02 49	02 46	02 45
60	01 23	02 54	03 49	02 56	02 58	03 01	03 10
N 58	01 56	03 10	04 00	02 59	03 05	03 14	03 30
56	02 19	03 23	04 09	03 03	03 12	03 26	03 46
54	02 38	03 35	04 17	03 06	03 19	03 35	04 00
52	02 53	03 45	04 24	03 09	03 24	03 44	04 12
50	03 06	03 53	04 31	03 11	03 29	03 52	04 23
45	03 31	04 12	04 45	03 17	03 40	04 09	04 46
N 40	03 50	04 27	04 56	03 21	03 50	04 23	05 05
35	04 06	04 39	05 06	03 26	03 58	04 35	05 20
30	04 18	04 49	05 14	03 29	04 05	04 46	05 34
20	04 38	05 06	05 29	03 36	04 17	05 04	05 57
N 10	04 54	05 20	05 42	03 41	04 28	05 20	06 18
0	05 07	05 32	05 53	03 47	04 39	05 35	06 37
S 10	05 18	05 43	06 05	03 52	04 49	05 50	06 56
20	05 28	05 54	06 17	03 58	05 00	06 07	07 17
30	05 38	06 06	06 31	04 04	05 13	06 26	07 41
35	05 42	06 13	06 39	04 08	05 21	06 37	07 55
40	05 47	06 20	06 48	04 13	05 29	06 50	08 11
45	05 53	06 28	06 59	04 18	05 40	07 05	08 31
S 50	05 58	06 37	07 12	04 24	05 52	07 24	08 56
52	06 01	06 41	07 17	04 27	05 58	07 33	09 08
54	06 03	06 46	07 24	04 30	06 04	07 43	09 22
56	06 06	06 51	07 31	04 34	06 12	07 54	09 38
58	06 09	06 56	07 40	04 38	06 20	08 08	09 58
S 60	06 12	07 02	07 49	04 42	06 29	08 23	10 22

Lat.	Sunset	Twilight Civil	Twilight Naut.	Moonset 3	Moonset 4	Moonset 5	Moonset 6
°	h m	h m	h m	h m	h m	h m	h m
N 72	22 43	////	////	18 47	▭	▭	▭
N 70	21 48	////	////	18 27	21 23	▭	▭
68	21 16	////	////	18 11	20 41	▭	▭
66	20 52	22 27	////	17 58	20 13	23 06	▭
64	20 34	21 48	////	17 48	19 52	22 13	▭
62	20 19	21 22	////	17 39	19 35	21 41	23 53
60	20 06	21 02	22 36	17 32	19 21	21 18	23 12
N 58	19 55	20 46	22 01	17 25	19 10	20 59	22 45
56	19 46	20 32	21 37	17 19	18 59	20 43	22 23
54	19 38	20 20	21 18	17 14	18 50	20 30	22 05
52	19 30	20 10	21 03	17 10	18 42	20 18	21 50
50	19 24	20 01	20 50	17 05	18 35	20 07	21 37
45	19 10	19 43	20 24	16 56	18 20	19 46	21 10
N 40	18 58	19 28	20 04	16 49	18 07	19 28	20 49
35	18 48	19 15	19 48	16 42	17 57	19 14	20 31
30	18 40	19 05	19 36	16 37	17 47	19 01	20 16
20	18 25	18 48	19 15	16 27	17 31	18 40	19 50
N 10	18 12	18 34	19 00	16 19	17 18	18 21	19 28
0	18 00	18 22	18 47	16 11	17 05	18 04	19 07
S 10	17 48	18 10	18 36	16 03	16 52	17 47	18 47
20	17 36	17 59	18 25	15 54	16 38	17 28	18 25
30	17 22	17 47	18 16	15 45	16 23	17 07	17 59
35	17 14	17 40	18 11	15 40	16 14	16 55	17 44
40	17 05	17 33	18 06	15 33	16 04	16 41	17 27
45	16 54	17 25	18 00	15 26	15 52	16 24	17 06
S 50	16 41	17 16	17 54	15 18	15 38	16 04	16 40
52	16 35	17 12	17 52	15 14	15 31	15 54	16 28
54	16 29	17 07	17 49	15 10	15 24	15 43	16 14
56	16 21	17 02	17 47	15 05	15 15	15 31	15 57
58	16 13	16 56	17 44	15 00	15 06	15 17	15 37
S 60	16 04	16 50	17 40	14 54	14 56	15 01	15 12

Day	SUN Eqn. of Time 00^h	SUN Eqn. of Time 12^h	SUN Mer. Pass.	MOON Mer. Pass. Upper	MOON Mer. Pass. Lower	MOON Age	MOON Phase
d	m s	m s	h m	h m	h m	d %	
3	03 07	03 10	11 57	09 58	22 24	27 6	
4	03 13	03 15	11 57	10 52	23 20	28 2	●
5	03 18	03 20	11 57	11 49	24 20	29 0	

	UT	ARIES	VENUS −3.9		MARS +1.3		JUPITER −2.4		SATURN +0.6	
	d h	GHA ° ′	GHA ° ′	Dec ° ′	GHA ° ′	Dec ° ′	GHA ° ′	Dec ° ′	GHA ° ′	Dec ° ′
TUESDAY	6 00	224 13.4	189 28.6	N12 39.7	103 47.6	N22 19.7	290 04.7	S21 37.5	69 52.3	N12 32.8
	01	239 15.9	204 28.1	40.7	118 48.7	19.4	305 07.2	37.5	84 54.7	32.8
	02	254 18.3	219 27.6	41.8	133 49.8	19.1	320 09.6	37.5	99 57.2	32.7
	03	269 20.8	234 27.1	. . 42.9	148 50.8	. . 18.8	335 12.0	. . 37.5	114 59.6	. . 32.7
	04	284 23.2	249 26.6	43.9	163 51.9	18.5	350 14.5	37.5	130 02.1	32.7
	05	299 25.7	264 26.1	45.0	178 53.0	18.2	5 16.9	37.5	145 04.5	32.7
	06	314 28.2	279 25.6	N12 46.1	193 54.0	N22 17.9	20 19.3	S21 37.5	160 07.0	N12 32.7
	07	329 30.6	294 25.1	47.1	208 55.1	17.6	35 21.8	37.5	175 09.4	32.7
	08	344 33.1	309 24.6	48.2	223 56.2	17.3	50 24.2	37.5	190 11.9	32.7
	09	359 35.6	324 24.1	. . 49.2	238 57.2	. . 17.0	65 26.7	. . 37.5	205 14.4	. . 32.7
	10	14 38.0	339 23.6	50.3	253 58.3	16.7	80 29.1	37.5	220 16.8	32.7
	11	29 40.5	354 23.1	51.4	268 59.4	16.4	95 31.5	37.5	235 19.3	32.7
	12	44 43.0	9 22.6	N12 52.4	284 00.5	N22 16.1	110 34.0	S21 37.5	250 21.7	N12 32.7
	13	59 45.4	24 22.1	53.5	299 01.5	15.8	125 36.4	37.5	265 24.2	32.6
	14	74 47.9	39 21.6	54.6	314 02.6	15.5	140 38.8	37.5	280 26.6	32.6
	15	89 50.4	54 21.1	. . 55.6	329 03.7	. . 15.2	155 41.3	. . 37.5	295 29.1	. . 32.6
	16	104 52.8	69 20.6	56.7	344 04.7	14.9	170 43.7	37.5	310 31.5	32.6
	17	119 55.3	84 20.1	57.7	359 05.8	14.6	185 46.2	37.5	325 34.0	32.6
	18	134 57.7	99 19.6	N12 58.8	14 06.9	N22 14.3	200 48.6	S21 37.5	340 36.4	N12 32.6
	19	150 00.2	114 19.1	12 59.8	29 07.9	14.0	215 51.0	37.5	355 38.9	32.6
	20	165 02.7	129 18.6	13 00.9	44 09.0	13.7	230 53.5	37.5	10 41.3	32.6
	21	180 05.1	144 18.1	. . 02.0	59 10.1	. . 13.4	245 55.9	. . 37.5	25 43.8	. . 32.6
	22	195 07.6	159 17.6	03.0	74 11.2	13.1	260 58.4	37.5	40 46.2	32.5
	23	210 10.1	174 17.1	04.1	89 12.2	12.8	276 00.8	37.5	55 48.7	32.5
WEDNESDAY	7 00	225 12.5	189 16.6	N13 05.1	104 13.3	N22 12.5	291 03.3	S21 37.5	70 51.1	N12 32.5
	01	240 15.0	204 16.1	06.2	119 14.4	12.2	306 05.7	37.5	85 53.6	32.5
	02	255 17.5	219 15.6	07.2	134 15.4	11.9	321 08.1	37.5	100 56.0	32.5
	03	270 19.9	234 15.1	. . 08.3	149 16.5	. . 11.6	336 10.6	. . 37.5	115 58.5	. . 32.5
	04	285 22.4	249 14.6	09.3	164 17.6	11.3	351 13.0	37.5	131 00.9	32.5
	05	300 24.9	264 14.1	10.4	179 18.6	11.0	6 15.5	37.5	146 03.4	32.5
	06	315 27.3	279 13.6	N13 11.4	194 19.7	N22 10.7	21 17.9	S21 37.5	161 05.8	N12 32.5
	07	330 29.8	294 13.1	12.5	209 20.8	10.4	36 20.4	37.5	176 08.3	32.4
	08	345 32.2	309 12.6	13.5	224 21.8	10.1	51 22.8	37.5	191 10.7	32.4
	09	0 34.7	324 12.1	. . 14.6	239 22.9	. . 09.8	66 25.2	. . 37.5	206 13.2	. . 32.4
	10	15 37.2	339 11.6	15.6	254 24.0	09.4	81 27.7	37.5	221 15.6	32.4
	11	30 39.6	354 11.0	16.7	269 25.1	09.1	96 30.1	37.5	236 18.0	32.4
	12	45 42.1	9 10.5	N13 17.7	284 26.1	N22 08.8	111 32.6	S21 37.5	251 20.5	N12 32.4
	13	60 44.6	24 10.0	18.8	299 27.2	08.5	126 35.0	37.5	266 22.9	32.4
	14	75 47.0	39 09.5	19.8	314 28.3	08.2	141 37.5	37.5	281 25.4	32.4
	15	90 49.5	54 09.0	. . 20.9	329 29.3	. . 07.9	156 39.9	. . 37.5	296 27.8	. . 32.4
	16	105 52.0	69 08.5	21.9	344 30.4	07.6	171 42.4	37.5	311 30.3	32.3
	17	120 54.4	84 08.0	23.0	359 31.5	07.3	186 44.8	37.6	326 32.7	32.3
	18	135 56.9	99 07.5	N13 24.0	14 32.5	N22 07.0	201 47.3	S21 37.6	341 35.2	N12 32.3
	19	150 59.3	114 07.0	25.0	29 33.6	06.7	216 49.7	37.6	356 37.6	32.3
	20	166 01.8	129 06.5	26.1	44 34.7	06.4	231 52.2	37.6	11 40.1	32.3
	21	181 04.3	144 05.9	. . 27.1	59 35.7	. . 06.1	246 54.6	. . 37.6	26 42.5	. . 32.3
	22	196 06.7	159 05.4	28.2	74 36.8	05.8	261 57.1	37.6	41 45.0	32.3
	23	211 09.2	174 04.9	29.2	89 37.9	05.5	276 59.5	37.6	56 47.4	32.3
THURSDAY	8 00	226 11.7	189 04.4	N13 30.3	104 38.9	N22 05.1	292 02.0	S21 37.6	71 49.9	N12 32.2
	01	241 14.1	204 03.9	31.3	119 40.0	04.8	307 04.4	37.6	86 52.3	32.2
	02	256 16.6	219 03.4	32.3	134 41.1	04.5	322 06.9	37.6	101 54.7	32.2
	03	271 19.1	234 02.9	. . 33.4	149 42.1	. . 04.2	337 09.3	. . 37.6	116 57.2	. . 32.2
	04	286 21.5	249 02.3	34.4	164 43.2	03.9	352 11.8	37.6	131 59.6	32.2
	05	301 24.0	264 01.8	35.5	179 44.3	03.6	7 14.2	37.6	147 02.1	32.2
	06	316 26.5	279 01.3	N13 36.5	194 45.3	N22 03.3	22 16.7	S21 37.6	162 04.5	N12 32.2
	07	331 28.9	294 00.8	37.5	209 46.4	03.0	37 19.1	37.6	177 07.0	32.2
	08	346 31.4	309 00.3	38.6	224 47.5	02.7	52 21.6	37.6	192 09.4	32.1
	09	1 33.8	323 59.8	. . 39.6	239 48.5	. . 02.4	67 24.0	. . 37.6	207 11.9	. . 32.1
	10	16 36.3	338 59.2	40.6	254 49.6	02.1	82 26.5	37.6	222 14.3	32.1
	11	31 38.8	353 58.7	41.7	269 50.7	01.7	97 28.9	37.6	237 16.7	32.1
	12	46 41.2	8 58.2	N13 42.7	284 51.7	N22 01.4	112 31.4	S21 37.6	252 19.2	N12 32.1
	13	61 43.7	23 57.7	43.7	299 52.8	01.1	127 33.9	37.6	267 21.6	32.1
	14	76 46.2	38 57.2	44.8	314 53.9	00.8	142 36.3	37.6	282 24.1	32.1
	15	91 48.6	53 56.6	. . 45.8	329 54.9	. . 00.5	157 38.8	. . 37.6	297 26.5	. . 32.0
	16	106 51.1	68 56.1	46.8	344 56.0	22 00.2	172 41.2	37.6	312 29.0	32.0
	17	121 53.6	83 55.6	47.9	359 57.1	21 59.9	187 43.7	37.6	327 31.4	32.0
	18	136 56.0	98 55.1	N13 48.9	14 58.1	N21 59.6	202 46.1	S21 37.6	342 33.8	N12 32.0
	19	151 58.5	113 54.6	49.9	29 59.2	59.3	217 48.6	37.7	357 36.3	32.0
	20	167 01.0	128 54.0	51.0	45 00.3	58.9	232 51.0	37.7	12 38.7	32.0
	21	182 03.4	143 53.5	. . 52.0	60 01.3	. . 58.6	247 53.5	. . 37.7	27 41.2	. . 32.0
	22	197 05.9	158 53.0	53.0	75 02.4	58.3	262 56.0	37.7	42 43.6	32.0
	23	212 08.3	173 52.5	54.0	90 03.4	58.0	277 58.4	37.7	57 46.0	31.9
	Mer. Pass.	h m 8 57.7	v −0.5	d 1.0	v 1.1	d 0.3	v 2.4	d 0.0	v 2.4	d 0.0

STARS

Name	SHA ° ′	Dec ° ′
Acamar	315 21.6	S40 16.2
Achernar	335 29.9	S57 11.5
Acrux	173 13.5	S63 09.0
Adhara	255 15.8	S28 59.1
Aldebaran	290 54.2	N16 31.6
Alioth	166 23.3	N55 54.9
Alkaid	153 01.3	N49 16.2
Al Na'ir	27 48.5	S46 55.1
Alnilam	275 50.6	S 1 11.8
Alphard	217 59.9	S 8 41.8
Alphecca	126 13.9	N26 41.0
Alpheratz	357 47.9	N29 08.1
Altair	62 11.9	N 8 53.2
Ankaa	353 19.7	S42 15.5
Antares	112 30.7	S26 27.2
Arcturus	145 58.9	N19 08.2
Atria	107 35.7	S69 02.6
Avior	234 19.9	S59 32.4
Bellatrix	278 36.4	N 6 21.5
Betelgeuse	271 05.8	N 7 24.5
Canopus	263 58.3	S52 42.2
Capella	280 40.6	N46 00.5
Deneb	49 34.2	N45 18.3
Denebola	182 37.4	N14 31.4
Diphda	349 00.0	S17 56.4
Dubhe	193 55.8	N61 42.5
Elnath	278 17.9	N28 37.0
Eltanin	90 47.5	N51 28.9
Enif	33 51.0	N 9 54.6
Fomalhaut	15 28.3	S29 34.6
Gacrux	172 05.1	S57 09.9
Gienah	175 56.1	S17 35.5
Hadar	148 53.1	S60 25.0
Hamal	328 05.5	N23 30.1
Kaus Aust.	83 48.7	S34 22.9
Kochab	137 18.2	N74 07.2
Markab	13 42.4	N15 14.9
Menkar	314 19.4	N 4 07.4
Menkent	148 11.9	S36 24.9
Miaplacidus	221 40.9	S69 45.4
Mirfak	308 46.6	N49 53.5
Nunki	76 02.9	S26 17.2
Peacock	53 25.0	S56 42.3
Pollux	243 32.6	N28 00.5
Procyon	245 03.9	N 5 12.2
Rasalhague	96 09.8	N12 33.0
Regulus	207 47.5	N11 55.5
Rigel	281 16.1	S 8 11.5
Rigil Kent.	139 56.7	S60 52.3
Sabik	102 16.7	S15 44.3
Schedar	349 45.7	N56 34.8
Shaula	96 26.9	S37 06.6
Sirius	258 37.4	S16 43.7
Spica	158 35.1	S11 12.5
Suhail	222 55.4	S43 28.2
Vega	80 41.3	N38 47.2
Zuben'ubi	137 09.4	S16 04.8

	SHA ° ′	Mer. Pass. h m
Venus	324 04.1	11 23
Mars	239 00.8	17 02
Jupiter	65 50.7	4 35
Saturn	205 38.6	19 13

Day	UT (h)	SUN GHA (° ′)	SUN Dec (° ′)	MOON GHA (° ′)	v (′)	MOON Dec (° ′)	d (′)	HP (′)
6	00	180 50.7	N16 35.0	175 11.4	3.5	N23 18.7	10.0	61.3
	01	195 50.7	35.7	189 33.9	3.3	23 28.7	9.8	61.3
	02	210 50.8	36.4	203 56.2	3.2	23 38.5	9.5	61.3
	03	225 50.8	. . 37.1	218 18.4	3.2	23 48.0	9.5	61.3
	04	240 50.9	37.8	232 40.6	3.0	23 57.5	9.2	61.3
	05	255 50.9	38.5	247 02.6	3.0	24 06.7	9.1	61.3
	06	270 50.9	N16 39.2	261 24.6	2.8	N24 15.8	8.9	61.3
	07	285 51.0	39.9	275 46.4	2.8	24 24.7	8.7	61.3
TUESDAY	08	300 51.0	40.6	290 08.2	2.7	24 33.4	8.5	61.3
	09	315 51.1	. . 41.3	304 29.9	2.6	24 41.9	8.3	61.3
	10	330 51.1	42.0	318 51.5	2.5	24 50.2	8.2	61.3
	11	345 51.2	42.7	333 13.0	2.4	24 58.4	7.9	61.3
	12	0 51.2	N16 43.3	347 34.4	2.3	N25 06.3	7.8	61.3
	13	15 51.2	44.0	1 55.7	2.3	25 14.1	7.6	61.3
	14	30 51.3	44.7	16 17.0	2.2	25 21.7	7.3	61.3
	15	45 51.3	. . 45.4	30 38.2	2.1	25 29.0	7.2	61.3
	16	60 51.4	46.1	44 59.3	2.1	25 36.2	7.0	61.2
	17	75 51.4	46.8	59 20.4	2.0	25 43.2	6.8	61.2
	18	90 51.4	N16 47.5	73 41.4	1.9	N25 50.0	6.6	61.2
	19	105 51.5	48.2	88 02.3	1.8	25 56.6	6.4	61.2
	20	120 51.5	48.9	102 23.1	1.8	26 03.0	6.2	61.2
	21	135 51.6	. . 49.6	116 43.9	1.7	26 09.2	6.0	61.2
	22	150 51.6	50.3	131 04.6	1.7	26 15.2	5.8	61.2
	23	165 51.6	51.0	145 25.3	1.7	26 21.0	5.5	61.2
7	00	180 51.7	N16 51.6	159 46.0	1.5	N26 26.5	5.4	61.2
	01	195 51.7	52.3	174 06.5	1.6	26 31.9	5.2	61.2
	02	210 51.8	53.0	188 27.1	1.5	26 37.1	4.9	61.1
	03	225 51.8	. . 53.7	202 47.6	1.4	26 42.0	4.8	61.1
	04	240 51.8	54.4	217 08.0	1.4	26 46.8	4.5	61.1
	05	255 51.9	55.1	231 28.4	1.4	26 51.3	4.3	61.1
	06	270 51.9	N16 55.8	245 48.8	1.3	N26 55.6	4.2	61.1
WEDNESDAY	07	285 52.0	56.5	260 09.1	1.4	26 59.8	3.9	61.1
	08	300 52.0	57.1	274 29.5	1.3	27 03.7	3.7	61.1
	09	315 52.0	. . 57.8	288 49.8	1.2	27 07.4	3.5	61.0
	10	330 52.1	58.5	303 10.0	1.3	27 10.9	3.2	61.0
	11	345 52.1	59.2	317 30.3	1.3	27 14.1	3.1	61.0
	12	0 52.1	N16 59.9	331 50.6	1.2	N27 17.2	2.8	61.0
	13	15 52.2	17 00.6	346 10.8	1.2	27 20.0	2.7	61.0
	14	30 52.2	01.2	0 31.0	1.2	27 22.7	2.4	61.0
	15	45 52.2	. . 01.9	14 51.2	1.3	27 25.1	2.2	60.9
	16	60 52.3	02.6	29 11.5	1.2	27 27.3	2.0	60.9
	17	75 52.3	03.3	43 31.7	1.2	27 29.3	1.7	60.9
	18	90 52.4	N17 04.0	57 51.9	1.3	N27 31.0	1.6	60.9
	19	105 52.4	04.6	72 12.2	1.2	27 32.6	1.3	60.9
	20	120 52.4	05.3	86 32.4	1.3	27 33.9	1.2	60.8
	21	135 52.5	. . 06.0	100 52.7	1.3	27 35.1	0.9	60.8
	22	150 52.5	06.7	115 13.0	1.3	27 36.0	0.7	60.8
	23	165 52.5	07.3	129 33.3	1.3	27 36.7	0.5	60.8
8	00	180 52.6	N17 08.0	143 53.6	1.4	N27 37.2	0.3	60.8
	01	195 52.6	08.7	158 14.0	1.4	27 37.5	0.0	60.7
	02	210 52.6	09.4	172 34.4	1.4	27 37.5	0.1	60.7
	03	225 52.7	. . 10.1	186 54.8	1.5	27 37.4	0.4	60.7
	04	240 52.7	10.7	201 15.3	1.5	27 37.0	0.5	60.7
	05	255 52.7	11.4	215 35.8	1.6	27 36.5	0.8	60.6
	06	270 52.8	N17 12.1	229 56.4	1.6	N27 35.7	1.0	60.6
THURSDAY	07	285 52.8	12.8	244 17.0	1.7	27 34.7	1.2	60.6
	08	300 52.8	13.4	258 37.7	1.7	27 33.5	1.4	60.6
	09	315 52.9	. . 14.1	272 58.4	1.8	27 32.1	1.6	60.5
	10	330 52.9	14.8	287 19.2	1.8	27 30.5	1.8	60.5
	11	345 52.9	15.4	301 40.0	1.9	27 28.7	2.0	60.5
	12	0 52.9	N17 16.1	316 00.9	2.0	N27 26.7	2.2	60.4
	13	15 53.0	16.8	330 21.9	2.0	27 24.5	2.5	60.4
	14	30 53.0	17.5	344 42.9	2.2	27 22.0	2.6	60.4
	15	45 53.0	. . 18.1	359 04.1	2.1	27 19.4	2.8	60.4
	16	60 53.1	18.8	13 25.2	2.3	27 16.6	3.0	60.3
	17	75 53.1	19.5	27 46.5	2.4	27 13.6	3.3	60.3
	18	90 53.1	N17 20.1	42 07.9	2.4	N27 10.3	3.4	60.3
	19	105 53.2	20.8	56 29.3	2.5	27 06.9	3.6	60.2
	20	120 53.2	21.5	70 50.8	2.6	27 03.3	3.8	60.2
	21	135 53.2	. . 22.1	85 12.4	2.7	26 59.5	4.0	60.2
	22	150 53.2	22.8	99 34.1	2.8	26 55.5	4.2	60.2
	23	165 53.3	23.5	113 55.9	2.9	N26 51.3	4.4	60.1
		SD 15.9	d 0.7	SD 16.7		16.6		16.5

Lat. (°)	Twilight Naut. (h m)	Twilight Civil (h m)	Sunrise (h m)	Moonrise 6 (h m)	Moonrise 7 (h m)	Moonrise 8 (h m)	Moonrise 9 (h m)
N 72	////	////	00 40	▭	▭	▭	▭
N 70	////	////	01 51	▭	▭	▭	▭
68	////	////	02 27	▭	▭	▭	▭
66	////	01 09	02 52	01 19	▭	▭	▭
64	////	01 54	03 12	02 13	▭	▭	▭
62	////	02 23	03 28	02 45	02 49	03 23	05 09
60	01 02	02 44	03 41	03 10	03 30	04 20	05 49
N 58	01 42	03 01	03 53	03 30	03 58	04 53	06 16
56	02 09	03 16	04 02	03 46	04 20	05 17	06 38
54	02 29	03 28	04 11	04 00	04 39	05 37	06 55
52	02 45	03 39	04 19	04 12	04 54	05 54	07 10
50	02 59	03 48	04 26	04 23	05 07	06 08	07 24
45	03 26	04 07	04 41	04 46	05 35	06 37	07 50
N 40	03 46	04 23	04 53	05 05	05 57	07 00	08 11
35	04 02	04 36	05 03	05 20	06 15	07 19	08 29
30	04 16	04 46	05 12	05 34	06 31	07 35	08 44
20	04 37	05 04	05 27	05 57	06 57	08 03	09 10
N 10	04 53	05 19	05 41	06 18	07 20	08 26	09 32
0	05 06	05 31	05 53	06 37	07 42	08 48	09 52
S 10	05 18	05 43	06 05	06 56	08 04	09 10	10 13
20	05 29	05 55	06 18	07 17	08 27	09 34	10 35
30	05 39	06 08	06 33	07 41	08 54	10 02	11 00
35	05 45	06 15	06 41	07 55	09 10	10 18	11 15
40	05 50	06 22	06 51	08 11	09 29	10 37	11 32
45	05 56	06 31	07 02	08 31	09 52	11 00	11 53
S 50	06 02	06 41	07 16	08 56	10 21	11 29	12 18
52	06 05	06 46	07 22	09 08	10 35	11 44	12 31
54	06 08	06 51	07 29	09 22	10 52	12 00	12 45
56	06 11	06 56	07 37	09 38	11 12	12 20	13 02
58	06 14	07 02	07 46	09 58	11 36	12 45	13 21
S 60	06 18	07 09	07 56	10 22	12 10	13 18	13 46

Lat. (°)	Sunset (h m)	Twilight Civil (h m)	Twilight Naut. (h m)	Moonset 6 (h m)	Moonset 7 (h m)	Moonset 8 (h m)	Moonset 9 (h m)
N 72	23 41	////	////	▭	▭	▭	▭
N 70	22 08	////	////	▭	▭	▭	▭
68	21 30	////	////	▭	▭	▭	▭
66	21 04	22 52	////	▭	▭	▭	▭
64	20 43	22 03	////	▭	▭	▭	▭
62	20 27	21 34	////	23 53	25 40	01 40	02 10
60	20 14	21 11	22 59	23 12	24 43	00 43	01 29
N 58	20 02	20 54	22 15	22 45	24 10	00 10	01 02
56	19 52	20 39	21 47	22 23	23 45	24 40	00 40
54	19 43	20 27	21 27	22 05	23 25	24 22	00 22
52	19 35	20 16	21 10	21 50	23 09	24 06	00 06
50	19 28	20 06	20 56	21 37	22 54	23 53	24 34
45	19 13	19 47	20 28	21 10	22 25	23 26	24 11
N 40	19 01	19 31	20 08	20 49	22 02	23 04	23 53
35	18 51	19 18	19 51	20 31	21 43	22 46	23 37
30	18 41	19 07	19 38	20 16	21 27	22 30	23 24
20	18 26	18 49	19 17	19 50	20 59	22 04	23 00
N 10	18 12	18 35	19 00	19 28	20 36	21 41	22 40
0	18 00	18 22	18 47	19 07	20 14	21 19	22 21
S 10	17 48	18 10	18 35	18 47	19 52	20 58	22 02
20	17 35	17 58	18 24	18 25	19 28	20 34	21 41
30	17 20	17 45	18 13	17 59	19 00	20 07	21 17
35	17 11	17 38	18 08	17 44	18 44	19 51	21 03
40	17 02	17 30	18 03	17 27	18 25	19 33	20 47
45	16 50	17 21	17 57	17 06	18 02	19 10	20 27
S 50	16 37	17 11	17 50	16 40	17 32	18 41	20 02
52	16 30	17 07	17 47	16 28	17 18	18 27	19 50
54	16 23	17 02	17 44	16 14	17 01	18 10	19 36
56	16 15	16 56	17 41	15 57	16 41	17 51	19 20
58	16 06	16 50	17 38	15 37	16 16	17 26	19 01
S 60	15 56	16 44	17 34	15 12	15 42	16 53	18 37

Day (d)	SUN Eqn. of Time 00^h (m s)	SUN Eqn. of Time 12^h (m s)	SUN Mer. Pass. (h m)	MOON Mer. Pass. Upper (h m)	MOON Mer. Pass. Lower (h m)	MOON Age (d)	MOON Phase (%)
6	03 23	03 25	11 57	12 52	00 20	01	2
7	03 27	03 28	11 57	13 58	01 25	02	6 ●
8	03 30	03 32	11 56	15 04	02 31	03	13

UT d h	ARIES GHA	VENUS −3.9 GHA	VENUS Dec	MARS +1.3 GHA	MARS Dec	JUPITER −2.4 GHA	JUPITER Dec	SATURN +0.6 GHA	SATURN Dec
	° ′	° ′	° ′	° ′	° ′	° ′	° ′	° ′	° ′
9 00	227 10.8	188 51.9	N13 55.1	105 04.5	N21 57.7	293 00.9	S21 37.7	72 48.5	N12 31.9
01	242 13.3	203 51.4	56.1	120 05.6	57.4	308 03.3	37.7	87 50.9	31.9
02	257 15.7	218 50.9	57.1	135 06.6	57.1	323 05.8	37.7	102 53.4	31.9
03	272 18.2	233 50.4	58.1	150 07.7	56.7	338 08.3	37.7	117 55.8	31.9
04	287 20.7	248 49.8	13 59.2	165 08.8	56.4	353 10.7	37.7	132 58.3	31.9
05	302 23.1	263 49.3	14 00.2	180 09.8	56.1	8 13.2	37.7	148 00.7	31.9
06	317 25.6	278 48.8	N14 01.2	195 10.9	N21 55.8	23 15.6	S21 37.7	163 03.1	N12 31.8
07	332 28.1	293 48.3	02.2	210 12.0	55.5	38 18.1	37.7	178 05.6	31.8
08	347 30.5	308 47.7	03.3	225 13.0	55.2	53 20.6	37.7	193 08.0	31.8
F 09	2 33.0	323 47.2	04.3	240 14.1	54.9	68 23.0	37.7	208 10.4	31.8
R 10	17 35.5	338 46.7	05.3	255 15.2	54.5	83 25.5	37.7	223 12.9	31.8
I 11	32 37.9	353 46.2	06.3	270 16.2	54.2	98 27.9	37.7	238 15.3	31.8
D 12	47 40.4	8 45.6	N14 07.3	285 17.3	N21 53.9	113 30.4	S21 37.7	253 17.8	N12 31.7
A 13	62 42.8	23 45.1	08.4	300 18.4	53.6	128 32.9	37.7	268 20.2	31.7
Y 14	77 45.3	38 44.6	09.4	315 19.4	53.3	143 35.3	37.7	283 22.6	31.7
15	92 47.8	53 44.0	10.4	330 20.5	53.0	158 37.8	37.8	298 25.1	31.7
16	107 50.2	68 43.5	11.4	345 21.5	52.6	173 40.3	37.8	313 27.5	31.7
17	122 52.7	83 43.0	12.4	0 22.6	52.3	188 42.7	37.8	328 30.0	31.7
18	137 55.2	98 42.4	N14 13.5	15 23.7	N21 52.0	203 45.2	S21 37.8	343 32.4	N12 31.7
19	152 57.6	113 41.9	14.5	30 24.7	51.7	218 47.7	37.8	358 34.8	31.6
20	168 00.1	128 41.4	15.5	45 25.8	51.4	233 50.1	37.8	13 37.3	31.6
21	183 02.6	143 40.8	16.5	60 26.9	51.1	248 52.6	37.8	28 39.7	31.6
22	198 05.0	158 40.3	17.5	75 27.9	50.7	263 55.1	37.8	43 42.1	31.6
23	213 07.5	173 39.8	18.5	90 29.0	50.4	278 57.5	37.8	58 44.6	31.6
10 00	228 10.0	188 39.2	N14 19.5	105 30.1	N21 50.1	294 00.0	S21 37.8	73 47.0	N12 31.6
01	243 12.4	203 38.7	20.6	120 31.1	49.8	309 02.5	37.8	88 49.5	31.5
02	258 14.9	218 38.2	21.6	135 32.2	49.5	324 04.9	37.8	103 51.9	31.5
03	273 17.3	233 37.6	22.6	150 33.2	49.1	339 07.4	37.8	118 54.3	31.5
04	288 19.8	248 37.1	23.6	165 34.3	48.8	354 09.9	37.8	133 56.8	31.5
05	303 22.3	263 36.6	24.6	180 35.4	48.5	9 12.3	37.8	148 59.2	31.5
06	318 24.7	278 36.0	N14 25.6	195 36.4	N21 48.2	24 14.8	S21 37.8	164 01.6	N12 31.5
S 07	333 27.2	293 35.5	26.6	210 37.5	47.9	39 17.3	37.9	179 04.1	31.5
08	348 29.7	308 35.0	27.6	225 38.6	47.6	54 19.7	37.9	194 06.5	31.4
A 09	3 32.1	323 34.4	28.6	240 39.6	47.2	69 22.2	37.9	209 08.9	31.4
T 10	18 34.6	338 33.9	29.6	255 40.7	46.9	84 24.7	37.9	224 11.4	31.4
U 11	33 37.1	353 33.3	30.6	270 41.7	46.6	99 27.2	37.9	239 13.8	31.4
R 12	48 39.5	8 32.8	N14 31.6	285 42.8	N21 46.3	114 29.6	S21 37.9	254 16.3	N12 31.4
D 13	63 42.0	23 32.3	32.7	300 43.9	45.9	129 32.1	37.9	269 18.7	31.4
A 14	78 44.5	38 31.7	33.7	315 44.9	45.6	144 34.6	37.9	284 21.1	31.3
Y 15	93 46.9	53 31.2	34.7	330 46.0	45.3	159 37.0	37.9	299 23.6	31.3
16	108 49.4	68 30.6	35.7	345 47.1	45.0	174 39.5	37.9	314 26.0	31.3
17	123 51.8	83 30.1	36.7	0 48.1	44.7	189 42.0	37.9	329 28.4	31.3
18	138 54.3	98 29.6	N14 37.7	15 49.2	N21 44.3	204 44.5	S21 37.9	344 30.9	N12 31.3
19	153 56.8	113 29.0	38.7	30 50.2	44.0	219 46.9	37.9	359 33.3	31.3
20	168 59.2	128 28.5	39.7	45 51.3	43.7	234 49.4	37.9	14 35.7	31.2
21	184 01.7	143 27.9	40.7	60 52.4	43.4	249 51.9	38.0	29 38.2	31.2
22	199 04.2	158 27.4	41.7	75 53.4	43.0	264 54.4	38.0	44 40.6	31.2
23	214 06.6	173 26.8	42.7	90 54.5	42.7	279 56.8	38.0	59 43.0	31.2
11 00	229 09.1	188 26.3	N14 43.7	105 55.6	N21 42.4	294 59.3	S21 38.0	74 45.5	N12 31.2
01	244 11.6	203 25.8	44.7	120 56.6	42.1	310 01.8	38.0	89 47.9	31.2
02	259 14.0	218 25.2	45.7	135 57.7	41.8	325 04.3	38.0	104 50.3	31.1
03	274 16.5	233 24.7	46.7	150 58.7	41.4	340 06.7	38.0	119 52.8	31.1
04	289 19.0	248 24.1	47.6	165 59.8	41.1	355 09.2	38.0	134 55.2	31.1
05	304 21.4	263 23.6	48.6	181 00.9	40.8	10 11.7	38.0	149 57.6	31.1
06	319 23.9	278 23.0	N14 49.6	196 01.9	N21 40.5	25 14.2	S21 38.0	165 00.0	N12 31.1
07	334 26.3	293 22.5	50.6	211 03.0	40.1	40 16.7	38.0	180 02.5	31.0
08	349 28.8	308 21.9	51.6	226 04.0	39.8	55 19.1	38.0	195 04.9	31.0
S 09	4 31.3	323 21.4	52.6	241 05.1	39.5	70 21.6	38.0	210 07.3	31.0
U 10	19 33.7	338 20.8	53.6	256 06.2	39.2	85 24.1	38.1	225 09.8	31.0
N 11	34 36.2	353 20.3	54.6	271 07.2	38.8	100 26.6	38.1	240 12.2	31.0
D 12	49 38.7	8 19.7	N14 55.6	286 08.3	N21 38.5	115 29.0	S21 38.1	255 14.6	N12 31.0
A 13	64 41.1	23 19.2	56.6	301 09.3	38.2	130 31.5	38.1	270 17.1	30.9
Y 14	79 43.6	38 18.6	57.6	316 10.4	37.9	145 34.0	38.1	285 19.5	30.9
15	94 46.1	53 18.1	58.6	331 11.5	37.5	160 36.5	38.1	300 21.9	30.9
16	109 48.5	68 17.5	14 59.5	346 12.5	37.2	175 39.0	38.1	315 24.4	30.9
17	124 51.0	83 17.0	15 00.5	1 13.6	36.9	190 41.4	38.1	330 26.8	30.9
18	139 53.4	98 16.4	N15 01.5	16 14.6	N21 36.5	205 43.9	S21 38.1	345 29.2	N12 30.8
19	154 55.9	113 15.9	02.5	31 15.7	36.2	220 46.4	38.1	0 31.6	30.8
20	169 58.4	128 15.3	03.5	46 16.8	35.9	235 48.9	38.1	15 34.1	30.8
21	185 00.8	143 14.8	04.5	61 17.8	35.6	250 51.4	38.1	30 36.5	30.8
22	200 03.3	158 14.2	05.5	76 18.9	35.2	265 53.9	38.2	45 38.9	30.8
23	215 05.8	173 13.7	06.4	91 20.0	34.9	280 56.3	38.2	60 41.4	30.8
Mer. Pass.	h m 8 45.9	v −0.5	d 1.0	v 1.1	d 0.3	v 2.5	d 0.0	v 2.4	d 0.0

STARS

Name	SHA ° ′	Dec ° ′
Acamar	315 21.6	S40 16.2
Achernar	335 29.9	S57 11.5
Acrux	173 13.5	S63 09.0
Adhara	255 15.8	S28 59.1
Aldebaran	290 54.2	N16 31.6
Alioth	166 23.3	N55 54.9
Alkaid	153 01.3	N49 16.2
Al Na'ir	27 48.5	S46 55.0
Alnilam	275 50.6	S 1 11.8
Alphard	217 59.9	S 8 41.8
Alphecca	126 13.9	N26 41.0
Alpheratz	357 47.8	N29 08.1
Altair	62 11.9	N 8 53.2
Ankaa	353 19.6	S42 15.5
Antares	112 30.7	S26 27.2
Arcturus	145 58.9	N19 08.2
Atria	107 35.6	S69 02.6
Avior	234 20.0	S59 32.4
Bellatrix	278 36.4	N 6 21.5
Betelgeuse	271 05.7	N 7 24.5
Canopus	263 58.3	S52 42.1
Capella	280 40.6	N46 00.5
Deneb	49 34.1	N45 18.3
Denebola	182 37.4	N14 31.4
Diphda	349 00.0	S17 56.4
Dubhe	193 55.8	N61 42.5
Elnath	278 17.8	N28 37.0
Eltanin	90 47.5	N51 29.0
Enif	33 51.0	N 9 54.7
Fomalhaut	15 28.3	S29 34.6
Gacrux	172 05.1	S57 09.9
Gienah	175 56.1	S17 35.5
Hadar	148 53.1	S60 25.0
Hamal	328 05.5	N23 30.1
Kaus Aust.	83 48.6	S34 22.9
Kochab	137 18.2	N74 07.2
Markab	13 42.4	N15 14.9
Menkar	314 19.4	N 4 07.4
Menkent	148 11.9	S36 24.9
Miaplacidus	221 40.9	S69 45.4
Mirfak	308 46.5	N49 53.5
Nunki	76 02.8	S26 17.2
Peacock	53 25.0	S56 42.3
Pollux	243 32.6	N28 00.5
Procyon	245 03.9	N 5 12.2
Rasalhague	96 09.7	N12 33.0
Regulus	207 47.5	N11 55.5
Rigel	281 16.1	S 8 11.5
Rigil Kent.	139 56.6	S60 52.4
Sabik	102 16.7	S15 44.3
Schedar	349 45.7	N56 34.8
Shaula	96 26.8	S37 06.6
Sirius	258 37.4	S16 43.7
Spica	158 35.1	S11 12.5
Suhail	222 55.5	S43 28.2
Vega	80 41.3	N38 47.2
Zuben'ubi	137 09.4	S16 04.8

	SHA ° ′	Mer. Pass. h m
Venus	320 29.3	11 26
Mars	237 20.1	16 57
Jupiter	65 50.0	4 23
Saturn	205 37.1	19 02

	UT (d h)	SUN GHA	SUN Dec	MOON GHA	v	MOON Dec	d	HP
		° ′	° ′	° ′	′	° ′	′	′
	9 00	180 53.3	N17 24.1	128 17.8	3.0	N26 46.9	4.5	60.1
	01	195 53.3	24.8	142 39.8	3.1	26 42.4	4.8	60.1
	02	210 53.3	25.4	157 01.9	3.2	26 37.6	4.9	60.0
	03	225 53.4	. . 26.1	171 24.1	3.2	26 32.7	5.1	60.0
	04	240 53.4	26.8	185 46.3	3.4	26 27.6	5.3	60.0
	05	255 53.4	27.4	200 08.7	3.6	26 22.3	5.5	59.9
	06	270 53.5	N17 28.1	214 31.3	3.6	N26 16.8	5.7	59.9
	07	285 53.5	28.8	228 53.9	3.7	26 11.1	5.8	59.9
	08	300 53.5	29.4	243 16.6	3.8	26 05.3	6.0	59.8
F	09	315 53.5	. . 30.1	257 39.4	4.0	25 59.3	6.2	59.8
R	10	330 53.6	30.7	272 02.4	4.1	25 53.1	6.3	59.8
I	11	345 53.6	31.4	286 25.5	4.2	25 46.8	6.5	59.7
D	12	0 53.6	N17 32.1	300 48.7	4.3	N25 40.3	6.7	59.7
A	13	15 53.6	32.7	315 12.0	4.4	25 33.6	6.9	59.7
Y	14	30 53.7	33.4	329 35.4	4.5	25 26.7	7.0	59.6
	15	45 53.7	. . 34.0	343 58.9	4.7	25 19.7	7.2	59.6
	16	60 53.7	34.7	358 22.6	4.8	25 12.5	7.3	59.6
	17	75 53.7	35.3	12 46.4	4.9	25 05.2	7.5	59.5
	18	90 53.8	N17 36.0	27 10.3	5.1	N24 57.7	7.6	59.5
	19	105 53.8	36.7	41 34.4	5.2	24 50.1	7.8	59.5
	20	120 53.8	37.3	55 58.6	5.3	24 42.3	8.0	59.4
	21	135 53.8	. . 38.0	70 22.9	5.4	24 34.3	8.1	59.4
	22	150 53.8	38.6	84 47.3	5.6	24 26.2	8.2	59.4
	23	165 53.9	39.3	99 11.9	5.7	24 18.0	8.4	59.3
	10 00	180 53.9	N17 39.9	113 36.6	5.8	N24 09.6	8.6	59.3
	01	195 53.9	40.6	128 01.4	6.0	24 01.0	8.7	59.3
	02	210 53.9	41.2	142 26.4	6.0	23 52.3	8.8	59.2
	03	225 54.0	. . 41.9	156 51.4	6.3	23 43.5	8.9	59.2
	04	240 54.0	42.5	171 16.7	6.3	23 34.6	9.1	59.1
	05	255 54.0	43.2	185 42.0	6.5	23 25.5	9.3	59.1
	06	270 54.0	N17 43.8	200 07.5	6.6	N23 16.2	9.3	59.1
	07	285 54.0	44.5	214 33.1	6.8	23 06.9	9.5	59.0
S	08	300 54.1	45.1	228 58.9	6.9	22 57.4	9.6	59.0
A	09	315 54.1	. . 45.8	243 24.8	7.0	22 47.8	9.8	59.0
T	10	330 54.1	46.4	257 50.8	7.1	22 38.0	9.9	58.9
U	11	345 54.1	47.1	272 16.9	7.3	22 28.1	10.0	58.9
R	12	0 54.1	N17 47.7	286 43.2	7.4	N22 18.1	10.1	58.9
D	13	15 54.2	48.4	301 09.6	7.6	22 08.0	10.2	58.8
A	14	30 54.2	49.0	315 36.2	7.7	21 57.8	10.3	58.8
Y	15	45 54.2	. . 49.6	330 02.9	7.8	21 47.5	10.5	58.7
	16	60 54.2	50.3	344 29.7	7.9	21 37.0	10.6	58.7
	17	75 54.2	50.9	358 56.6	8.1	21 26.4	10.7	58.7
	18	90 54.2	N17 51.6	13 23.7	8.2	N21 15.7	10.8	58.6
	19	105 54.3	52.2	27 50.9	8.4	21 04.9	10.9	58.6
	20	120 54.3	52.9	42 18.3	8.5	20 54.0	11.0	58.6
	21	135 54.3	. . 53.5	56 45.8	8.6	20 43.0	11.1	58.5
	22	150 54.3	54.1	71 13.4	8.7	20 31.9	11.2	58.5
	23	165 54.3	54.8	85 41.1	8.9	20 20.7	11.3	58.5
	11 00	180 54.3	N17 55.4	100 09.0	9.0	N20 09.4	11.4	58.4
	01	195 54.4	56.1	114 37.0	9.1	19 58.0	11.5	58.4
	02	210 54.4	56.7	129 05.1	9.2	19 46.5	11.6	58.3
	03	225 54.4	. . 57.3	143 33.3	9.4	19 34.9	11.7	58.3
	04	240 54.4	58.0	158 01.7	9.5	19 23.2	11.8	58.3
	05	255 54.4	58.6	172 30.2	9.6	19 11.4	11.9	58.2
	06	270 54.4	N17 59.3	186 58.8	9.8	N18 59.5	11.9	58.2
	07	285 54.5	17 59.9	201 27.6	9.8	18 47.6	12.1	58.2
	08	300 54.5	18 00.5	215 56.4	10.0	18 35.5	12.1	58.1
S	09	315 54.5	. . 01.2	230 25.4	10.2	18 23.4	12.2	58.1
U	10	330 54.5	01.8	244 54.6	10.2	18 11.2	12.3	58.1
N	11	345 54.5	02.4	259 23.8	10.3	17 58.9	12.4	58.0
D	12	0 54.5	N18 03.1	273 53.1	10.5	N17 46.5	12.4	58.0
A	13	15 54.5	03.7	288 22.6	10.6	17 34.1	12.5	57.9
Y	14	30 54.5	04.3	302 52.2	10.7	17 21.6	12.6	57.9
	15	45 54.6	. . 05.0	317 21.9	10.8	17 09.0	12.7	57.9
	16	60 54.6	05.6	331 51.7	11.0	16 56.3	12.7	57.8
	17	75 54.6	06.2	346 21.7	11.0	16 43.6	12.8	57.8
	18	90 54.6	N18 06.9	0 51.7	11.2	N16 30.8	12.9	57.8
	19	105 54.6	07.5	15 21.9	11.3	16 17.9	12.9	57.7
	20	120 54.6	08.1	29 52.2	11.3	16 05.0	13.0	57.7
	21	135 54.6	. . 08.7	44 22.5	11.5	15 52.0	13.1	57.7
	22	150 54.6	09.4	58 53.0	11.6	15 38.9	13.1	57.6
	23	165 54.7	10.0	73 23.6	11.7	N15 25.8	13.2	57.6
		SD 15.9	*d* 0.6	SD 16.3		16.0		15.8

Lat.	Twilight Naut.	Twilight Civil	Sunrise	Moonrise 9	Moonrise 10	Moonrise 11	Moonrise 12
°	h m	h m	h m	h m	h m	h m	h m
N 72	☐	☐	☐	☐	☐	☐	09 26
N 70	////	////	01 28	☐	☐	07 02	09 52
68	////	////	02 12	☐	☐	07 53	10 11
66	////	00 36	02 41	☐	05 43	08 24	10 26
64	////	01 38	03 02	☐	06 39	08 47	10 39
62	////	02 11	03 19	05 09	07 11	09 05	10 49
60	00 32	02 34	03 34	05 49	07 36	09 20	10 58
N 58	01 28	02 53	03 46	06 16	07 55	09 33	11 06
56	01 58	03 08	03 56	06 38	08 11	09 44	11 13
54	02 20	03 21	04 05	06 55	08 24	09 54	11 19
52	02 38	03 33	04 14	07 10	08 36	10 02	11 24
50	02 52	03 43	04 21	07 24	08 47	10 10	11 29
45	03 21	04 03	04 37	07 50	09 08	10 26	11 40
N 40	03 42	04 19	04 49	08 11	09 26	10 39	11 49
35	03 59	04 33	05 00	08 29	09 41	10 50	11 56
30	04 13	04 44	05 10	08 44	09 53	11 00	12 03
20	04 35	05 02	05 26	09 10	10 15	11 17	12 14
N 10	04 52	05 18	05 40	09 32	10 34	11 31	12 24
0	05 06	05 31	05 53	09 52	10 51	11 45	12 33
S 10	05 18	05 44	06 06	10 13	11 09	11 58	12 42
20	05 30	05 56	06 19	10 35	11 27	12 12	12 52
30	05 41	06 10	06 35	11 00	11 48	12 29	13 03
35	05 47	06 17	06 44	11 15	12 01	12 38	13 09
40	05 53	06 25	06 54	11 32	12 15	12 49	13 16
45	05 59	06 34	07 06	11 53	12 32	13 01	13 25
S 50	06 06	06 45	07 20	12 18	12 52	13 16	13 34
52	06 09	06 50	07 27	12 31	13 02	13 23	13 39
54	06 12	06 55	07 34	12 45	13 13	13 31	13 44
56	06 16	07 01	07 43	13 02	13 25	13 40	13 50
58	06 19	07 07	07 52	13 21	13 40	13 50	13 56
S 60	06 23	07 15	08 03	13 46	13 57	14 01	14 03

Lat.	Sunset	Twilight Civil	Twilight Naut.	Moonset 9	Moonset 10	Moonset 11	Moonset 12
°	h m	h m	h m	h m	h m	h m	h m
N 72	☐	☐	☐	☐	☐	☐	03 41
N 70	22 32	////	////	☐	☐	04 20	03 13
68	21 45	////	////	☐	☐	03 28	02 52
66	21 15	23 37	////	☐	03 43	02 56	02 35
64	20 53	22 20	////	☐	02 47	02 31	02 22
62	20 35	21 46	////	02 10	02 13	02 12	02 10
60	20 21	21 21	23 39	01 29	01 48	01 56	02 00
N 58	20 09	21 02	22 30	01 02	01 28	01 43	01 51
56	19 58	20 46	21 58	00 40	01 12	01 31	01 43
54	19 49	20 33	21 35	00 22	00 58	01 21	01 36
52	19 40	20 21	21 17	00 06	00 45	01 11	01 30
50	19 33	20 11	21 02	24 34	00 34	01 03	01 24
45	19 17	19 51	20 33	24 11	00 11	00 46	01 12
N 40	19 04	19 34	20 11	23 53	24 31	00 31	01 02
35	18 53	19 21	19 54	23 37	24 19	00 19	00 53
30	18 43	19 09	19 40	23 24	24 08	00 08	00 45
20	18 27	18 51	19 18	23 00	23 49	24 31	00 31
N 10	18 13	18 35	19 01	22 40	23 33	24 19	00 19
0	18 00	18 22	18 47	22 21	23 17	24 08	00 08
S 10	17 47	18 09	18 34	22 02	23 02	23 57	24 47
20	17 33	17 56	18 23	21 41	22 45	23 44	24 40
30	17 18	17 43	18 12	21 17	22 26	23 30	24 31
35	17 09	17 35	18 06	21 03	22 14	23 22	24 26
40	16 58	17 27	18 00	20 47	22 01	23 13	24 21
45	16 46	17 18	17 53	20 27	21 45	23 02	24 14
S 50	16 32	17 07	17 46	20 02	21 26	22 48	24 06
52	16 25	17 02	17 43	19 50	21 17	22 42	24 02
54	16 18	16 57	17 40	19 36	21 07	22 35	23 58
56	16 09	16 51	17 36	19 20	20 55	22 27	23 53
58	16 00	16 45	17 33	19 01	20 41	22 18	23 48
S 60	15 49	16 37	17 29	18 37	20 25	22 08	23 42

Day	SUN Eqn. of Time 00^h	SUN Eqn. of Time 12^h	SUN Mer. Pass.	MOON Mer. Pass. Upper	MOON Mer. Pass. Lower	MOON Age	MOON Phase
d	m s	m s	h m	h m	h m	d	%
9	03 33	03 34	11 56	16 07	03 36	04	22
10	03 36	03 36	11 56	17 04	04 36	05	32
11	03 37	03 38	11 56	17 56	05 31	06	43

2008 MAY 12, 13, 14 (MON., TUES., WED.)

UT	ARIES	VENUS −3.9		MARS +1.3		JUPITER −2.5		SATURN +0.6	
	GHA	GHA	Dec	GHA	Dec	GHA	Dec	GHA	Dec
d h	° ′	° ′	° ′	° ′	° ′	° ′	° ′	° ′	° ′
12 00	230 08.2	188 13.1	N15 07.4	106 21.0	N21 34.6	295 58.8	S21 38.2	75 43.8	N12 30.7
01	245 10.7	203 12.6	08.4	121 22.1	34.2	311 01.3	38.2	90 46.2	30.7
02	260 13.2	218 12.0	09.4	136 23.1	33.9	326 03.8	38.2	105 48.6	30.7
03	275 15.6	233 11.4	. . 10.4	151 24.2	. . 33.6	341 06.3	. . 38.2	120 51.1	. . 30.7
04	290 18.1	248 10.9	11.4	166 25.3	33.3	356 08.8	38.2	135 53.5	30.7
05	305 20.6	263 10.3	12.3	181 26.3	32.9	11 11.3	38.2	150 55.9	30.6
06	320 23.0	278 09.8	N15 13.3	196 27.4	N21 32.6	26 13.7	S21 38.2	165 58.4	N12 30.6
07	335 25.5	293 09.2	14.3	211 28.4	32.3	41 16.2	38.2	181 00.8	30.6
08	350 27.9	308 08.7	15.3	226 29.5	31.9	56 18.7	38.2	196 03.2	30.6
M 09	5 30.4	323 08.1	. . 16.2	241 30.5	. . 31.6	71 21.2	. . 38.3	211 05.6	. . 30.6
O 10	20 32.9	338 07.5	17.2	256 31.6	31.3	86 23.7	38.3	226 08.1	30.5
N 11	35 35.3	353 07.0	18.2	271 32.7	31.0	101 26.2	38.3	241 10.5	30.5
D 12	50 37.8	8 06.4	N15 19.2	286 33.7	N21 30.6	116 28.7	S21 38.3	256 12.9	N12 30.5
A 13	65 40.3	23 05.9	20.1	301 34.8	30.3	131 31.2	38.3	271 15.3	30.5
Y 14	80 42.7	38 05.3	21.1	316 35.8	30.0	146 33.6	38.3	286 17.8	30.5
15	95 45.2	53 04.7	. . 22.1	331 36.9	. . 29.6	161 36.1	. . 38.3	301 20.2	. . 30.4
16	110 47.7	68 04.2	23.1	346 38.0	29.3	176 38.6	38.3	316 22.6	30.4
17	125 50.1	83 03.6	24.0	1 39.0	29.0	191 41.1	38.3	331 25.0	30.4
18	140 52.6	98 03.0	N15 25.0	16 40.1	N21 28.6	206 43.6	S21 38.3	346 27.5	N12 30.4
19	155 55.1	113 02.5	26.0	31 41.1	28.3	221 46.1	38.3	1 29.9	30.4
20	170 57.5	128 01.9	26.9	46 42.2	28.0	236 48.6	38.4	16 32.3	30.3
21	186 00.0	143 01.3	. . 27.9	61 43.3	. . 27.6	251 51.1	. . 38.4	31 34.7	. . 30.3
22	201 02.4	158 00.8	28.9	76 44.3	27.3	266 53.6	38.4	46 37.2	30.3
23	216 04.9	173 00.2	29.8	91 45.4	27.0	281 56.1	38.4	61 39.6	30.3
13 00	231 07.4	187 59.7	N15 30.8	106 46.4	N21 26.6	296 58.5	S21 38.4	76 42.0	N12 30.3
01	246 09.8	202 59.1	31.8	121 47.5	26.3	312 01.0	38.4	91 44.4	30.2
02	261 12.3	217 58.5	32.7	136 48.6	26.0	327 03.5	38.4	106 46.9	30.2
03	276 14.8	232 58.0	. . 33.7	151 49.6	. . 25.6	342 06.0	. . 38.4	121 49.3	. . 30.2
04	291 17.2	247 57.4	34.7	166 50.7	25.3	357 08.5	38.4	136 51.7	30.2
05	306 19.7	262 56.8	35.6	181 51.7	25.0	12 11.0	38.5	151 54.1	30.2
06	321 22.2	277 56.2	N15 36.6	196 52.8	N21 24.6	27 13.5	S21 38.5	166 56.6	N12 30.1
07	336 24.6	292 55.7	37.6	211 53.8	24.3	42 16.0	38.5	181 59.0	30.1
T 08	351 27.1	307 55.1	38.5	226 54.9	24.0	57 18.5	38.5	197 01.4	30.1
U 09	6 29.5	322 54.5	. . 39.5	241 56.0	. . 23.6	72 21.0	. . 38.5	212 03.8	. . 30.1
10	21 32.0	337 54.0	40.4	256 57.0	23.3	87 23.5	38.5	227 06.3	30.1
E 11	36 34.5	352 53.4	41.4	271 58.1	23.0	102 26.0	38.5	242 08.7	30.0
S 12	51 36.9	7 52.8	N15 42.4	286 59.1	N21 22.6	117 28.5	S21 38.5	257 11.1	N12 30.0
D 13	66 39.4	22 52.3	43.3	302 00.2	22.3	132 31.0	38.5	272 13.5	30.0
A 14	81 41.9	37 51.7	44.3	317 01.3	21.9	147 33.5	38.5	287 15.9	30.0
Y 15	96 44.3	52 51.1	. . 45.2	332 02.3	. . 21.6	162 36.0	. . 38.6	302 18.4	. . 30.0
16	111 46.8	67 50.5	46.2	347 03.4	21.3	177 38.5	38.6	317 20.8	29.9
17	126 49.3	82 50.0	47.1	2 04.4	20.9	192 41.0	38.6	332 23.2	29.9
18	141 51.7	97 49.4	N15 48.1	17 05.5	N21 20.6	207 43.5	S21 38.6	347 25.6	N12 29.9
19	156 54.2	112 48.8	49.1	32 06.5	20.3	222 46.0	38.6	2 28.0	29.9
20	171 56.7	127 48.2	50.0	47 07.6	19.9	237 48.5	38.6	17 30.5	29.8
21	186 59.1	142 47.7	. . 51.0	62 08.7	. . 19.6	252 51.0	. . 38.6	32 32.9	. . 29.8
22	202 01.6	157 47.1	51.9	77 09.7	19.2	267 53.5	38.6	47 35.3	29.8
23	217 04.0	172 46.5	52.9	92 10.8	18.9	282 56.0	38.6	62 37.7	29.8
14 00	232 06.5	187 45.9	N15 53.8	107 11.8	N21 18.6	297 58.5	S21 38.7	77 40.2	N12 29.8
01	247 09.0	202 45.4	54.8	122 12.9	18.2	313 01.0	38.7	92 42.6	29.7
02	262 11.4	217 44.8	55.7	137 13.9	17.9	328 03.5	38.7	107 45.0	29.7
03	277 13.9	232 44.2	. . 56.7	152 15.0	. . 17.6	343 06.0	. . 38.7	122 47.4	. . 29.7
04	292 16.4	247 43.6	57.6	167 16.1	17.2	358 08.5	38.7	137 49.8	29.7
05	307 18.8	262 43.0	58.6	182 17.1	16.9	13 11.0	38.7	152 52.3	29.6
06	322 21.3	277 42.5	N15 59.5	197 18.2	N21 16.5	28 13.5	S21 38.7	167 54.7	N12 29.6
W 07	337 23.8	292 41.9	16 00.5	212 19.2	16.2	43 16.0	38.7	182 57.1	29.6
E 08	352 26.2	307 41.3	01.4	227 20.3	15.9	58 18.5	38.8	197 59.5	29.6
D 09	7 28.7	322 40.7	. . 02.3	242 21.3	. . 15.5	73 21.0	. . 38.8	213 01.9	. . 29.6
10	22 31.1	337 40.1	03.3	257 22.4	15.2	88 23.5	38.8	228 04.3	29.5
N 11	37 33.6	352 39.6	04.2	272 23.5	14.8	103 26.0	38.8	243 06.8	29.5
E 12	52 36.1	7 39.0	N16 05.2	287 24.5	N21 14.5	118 28.5	S21 38.8	258 09.2	N12 29.5
S 13	67 38.5	22 38.4	06.1	302 25.6	14.1	133 31.0	38.8	273 11.6	29.5
D 14	82 41.0	37 37.8	07.1	317 26.6	13.8	148 33.5	38.8	288 14.0	29.4
A 15	97 43.5	52 37.2	. . 08.0	332 27.7	. . 13.5	163 36.0	. . 38.8	303 16.4	. . 29.4
Y 16	112 45.9	67 36.6	08.9	347 28.7	13.1	178 38.5	38.8	318 18.9	29.4
17	127 48.4	82 36.1	09.9	2 29.8	12.8	193 41.0	38.9	333 21.3	29.4
18	142 50.9	97 35.5	N16 10.8	17 30.9	N21 12.4	208 43.5	S21 38.9	348 23.7	N12 29.3
19	157 53.3	112 34.9	11.7	32 31.9	12.1	223 46.0	38.9	3 26.1	29.3
20	172 55.8	127 34.3	12.7	47 33.0	11.8	238 48.5	38.9	18 28.5	29.3
21	187 58.3	142 33.7	. . 13.6	62 34.0	. . 11.4	253 51.1	. . 38.9	33 30.9	. . 29.3
22	203 00.7	157 33.1	14.6	77 35.1	11.1	268 53.6	38.9	48 33.4	29.3
23	218 03.2	172 32.5	15.5	92 36.1	10.7	283 56.1	38.9	63 35.8	29.2
	h m								
Mer. Pass.	8 34.1	v −0.6	d 1.0	v 1.1	d 0.3	v 2.5	d 0.0	v 2.4	d 0.0

STARS Name	SHA	Dec
	° ′	° ′
Acamar	315 21.6	S40 16.2
Achernar	335 29.9	S57 11.5
Acrux	173 13.5	S63 09.1
Adhara	255 15.8	S28 59.1
Aldebaran	290 54.2	N16 31.6
Alioth	166 23.3	N55 54.9
Alkaid	153 01.3	N49 16.3
Al Na'ir	27 48.4	S46 55.0
Alnilam	275 50.6	S 1 11.8
Alphard	217 59.9	S 8 41.8
Alphecca	126 13.8	N26 41.0
Alpheratz	357 47.8	N29 08.1
Altair	62 11.9	N 8 53.2
Ankaa	353 19.6	S42 15.5
Antares	112 30.7	S26 27.2
Arcturus	145 58.9	N19 08.2
Atria	107 35.6	S69 02.6
Avior	234 20.0	S59 32.4
Bellatrix	278 36.4	N 6 21.5
Betelgeuse	271 05.8	N 7 24.5
Canopus	263 58.3	S52 42.1
Capella	280 40.6	N46 00.5
Deneb	49 34.1	N45 18.3
Denebola	182 37.4	N14 31.5
Diphda	348 59.9	S17 56.4
Dubhe	193 55.8	N61 42.5
Elnath	278 17.8	N28 37.0
Eltanin	90 47.5	N51 29.0
Enif	33 50.9	N 9 54.7
Fomalhaut	15 28.2	S29 34.6
Gacrux	172 05.1	S57 09.9
Gienah	175 56.1	S17 35.5
Hadar	148 53.1	S60 25.0
Hamal	328 05.5	N23 30.1
Kaus Aust.	83 48.6	S34 22.9
Kochab	137 18.2	N74 07.2
Markab	13 42.3	N15 14.9
Menkar	314 19.4	N 4 07.4
Menkent	148 11.9	S36 24.9
Miaplacidus	221 41.0	S69 45.4
Mirfak	308 46.5	N49 53.5
Nunki	76 02.8	S26 17.2
Peacock	53 24.9	S56 42.3
Pollux	243 32.6	N28 00.5
Procyon	245 03.9	N 5 12.2
Rasalhague	96 09.7	N12 33.0
Regulus	207 47.5	N11 55.6
Rigel	281 16.1	S 8 11.5
Rigil Kent.	139 56.6	S60 52.4
Sabik	102 16.7	S15 44.3
Schedar	349 45.6	N56 34.8
Shaula	96 26.8	S37 06.6
Sirius	258 37.4	S16 43.7
Spica	158 35.1	S11 12.5
Suhail	222 55.5	S43 28.2
Vega	80 41.3	N38 47.2
Zuben'ubi	137 09.4	S16 04.8

	SHA	Mer. Pass.
	° ′	h m
Venus	316 52.3	11 28
Mars	235 39.1	16 52
Jupiter	65 51.2	4 11
Saturn	205 34.6	18 50

UT		SUN GHA	SUN Dec	MOON GHA	*v*	MOON Dec	*d*	HP
d	h	° ′	° ′	° ′	′	° ′	′	′
12	00	180 54.7	N18 10.6	87 54.3	11.8	N15 12.6	13.2	57.6
	01	195 54.7	11.3	102 25.1	12.0	14 59.4	13.3	57.5
	02	210 54.7	11.9	116 56.1	12.0	14 46.1	13.4	57.5
	03	225 54.7	. . 12.5	131 27.1	12.1	14 32.7	13.4	57.4
	04	240 54.7	13.1	145 58.2	12.2	14 19.3	13.4	57.4
	05	255 54.7	13.8	160 29.4	12.3	14 05.9	13.5	57.4
	06	270 54.7	N18 14.4	175 00.7	12.5	N13 52.4	13.6	57.3
	07	285 54.7	15.0	189 32.2	12.5	13 38.8	13.6	57.3
	08	300 54.7	15.6	204 03.7	12.6	13 25.2	13.7	57.3
MONDAY	09	315 54.7	. . 16.3	218 35.3	12.7	13 11.5	13.6	57.2
	10	330 54.8	16.9	233 07.0	12.8	12 57.9	13.8	57.2
	11	345 54.8	17.5	247 38.8	12.9	12 44.1	13.8	57.2
	12	0 54.8	N18 18.1	262 10.7	12.9	N12 30.3	13.8	57.1
	13	15 54.8	18.7	276 42.6	13.1	12 16.5	13.9	57.1
	14	30 54.8	19.4	291 14.7	13.1	12 02.6	13.9	57.1
	15	45 54.8	. . 20.0	305 46.8	13.3	11 48.7	13.9	57.0
	16	60 54.8	20.6	320 19.1	13.3	11 34.8	14.0	57.0
	17	75 54.8	21.2	334 51.4	13.4	11 20.8	14.0	57.0
	18	90 54.8	N18 21.8	349 23.8	13.5	N11 06.8	14.0	56.9
	19	105 54.8	22.4	3 56.3	13.6	10 52.8	14.1	56.9
	20	120 54.8	23.1	18 28.9	13.6	10 38.7	14.1	56.9
	21	135 54.8	. . 23.7	33 01.5	13.7	10 24.6	14.1	56.8
	22	150 54.8	24.3	47 34.2	13.9	10 10.5	14.2	56.8
	23	165 54.8	24.9	62 07.1	13.8	9 56.3	14.2	56.8
13	00	180 54.8	N18 25.5	76 39.9	14.0	N 9 42.1	14.2	56.7
	01	195 54.8	26.1	91 12.9	14.0	9 27.9	14.3	56.7
	02	210 54.9	26.8	105 45.9	14.1	9 13.6	14.2	56.7
	03	225 54.9	. . 27.4	120 19.0	14.2	8 59.4	14.3	56.6
	04	240 54.9	28.0	134 52.2	14.2	8 45.1	14.3	56.6
	05	255 54.9	28.6	149 25.4	14.3	8 30.8	14.4	56.6
	06	270 54.9	N18 29.2	163 58.7	14.4	N 8 16.4	14.3	56.6
	07	285 54.9	29.8	178 32.1	14.4	8 02.1	14.4	56.5
TUESDAY	08	300 54.9	30.4	193 05.5	14.5	7 47.7	14.4	56.5
	09	315 54.9	. . 31.0	207 39.0	14.6	7 33.3	14.4	56.5
	10	330 54.9	31.6	222 12.6	14.6	7 18.9	14.4	56.4
	11	345 54.9	32.2	236 46.2	14.7	7 04.5	14.5	56.4
	12	0 54.9	N18 32.9	251 19.9	14.7	N 6 50.0	14.4	56.4
	13	15 54.9	33.5	265 53.6	14.8	6 35.6	14.5	56.3
	14	30 54.9	34.1	280 27.4	14.9	6 21.1	14.5	56.3
	15	45 54.9	. . 34.7	295 01.3	14.9	6 06.6	14.4	56.3
	16	60 54.9	35.3	309 35.2	14.9	5 52.2	14.5	56.3
	17	75 54.9	35.9	324 09.1	15.0	5 37.7	14.5	56.2
	18	90 54.9	N18 36.5	338 43.1	15.1	N 5 23.2	14.6	56.2
	19	105 54.9	37.1	353 17.2	15.1	5 08.6	14.5	56.2
	20	120 54.9	37.7	7 51.3	15.2	4 54.1	14.5	56.1
	21	135 54.9	. . 38.3	22 25.5	15.2	4 39.6	14.5	56.1
	22	150 54.9	38.9	36 59.7	15.2	4 25.1	14.6	56.1
	23	165 54.9	39.5	51 33.9	15.3	4 10.5	14.5	56.1
14	00	180 54.9	N18 40.1	66 08.2	15.3	N 3 56.0	14.5	56.0
	01	195 54.9	40.7	80 42.5	15.4	3 41.5	14.6	56.0
	02	210 54.9	41.3	95 16.9	15.4	3 26.9	14.5	56.0
	03	225 54.9	. . 41.9	109 51.3	15.5	3 12.4	14.6	55.9
	04	240 54.9	42.5	124 25.8	15.5	2 57.8	14.5	55.9
	05	255 54.9	43.1	139 00.3	15.5	2 43.3	14.5	55.9
	06	270 54.9	N18 43.7	153 34.8	15.6	N 2 28.8	14.6	55.9
WEDNESDAY	07	285 54.9	44.3	168 09.4	15.6	2 14.2	14.5	55.8
	08	300 54.9	44.9	182 44.0	15.6	1 59.7	14.5	55.8
	09	315 54.9	. . 45.5	197 18.6	15.6	1 45.2	14.6	55.8
	10	330 54.9	46.1	211 53.2	15.7	1 30.6	14.5	55.8
	11	345 54.9	46.7	226 27.9	15.8	1 16.1	14.5	55.7
	12	0 54.9	N18 47.3	241 02.7	15.7	N 1 01.6	14.5	55.7
	13	15 54.9	47.9	255 37.4	15.8	0 47.1	14.5	55.7
	14	30 54.9	48.5	270 12.2	15.8	0 32.6	14.4	55.7
	15	45 54.8	. . 49.1	284 47.0	15.8	0 18.2	14.5	55.6
	16	60 54.8	49.7	299 21.8	15.8	N 0 03.7	14.5	55.6
	17	75 54.8	50.2	313 56.6	15.9	S 0 10.8	14.4	55.6
	18	90 54.8	N18 50.8	328 31.5	15.9	S 0 25.2	14.4	55.6
	19	105 54.8	51.4	343 06.4	15.9	0 39.6	14.4	55.5
	20	120 54.8	52.0	357 41.3	15.9	0 54.0	14.4	55.5
	21	135 54.8	. . 52.6	12 16.2	15.9	1 08.4	14.4	55.5
	22	150 54.8	53.2	26 51.1	16.0	1 22.8	14.4	55.5
	23	165 54.8	53.8	41 26.1	16.0	S 1 37.2	14.3	55.4
		SD 15.9	*d* 0.6	SD	15.6		15.4	15.2

Lat.	Twilight Naut.	Twilight Civil	Sunrise	Moonrise 12	Moonrise 13	Moonrise 14	Moonrise 15
°	h m	h m	h m	h m	h m	h m	h m
N 72	▭	▭	▭	09 26	11 49	13 53	15 54
N 70	////	////	01 01	09 52	11 59	13 54	15 46
68	////	////	01 56	10 11	12 08	13 55	15 39
66	////	////	02 29	10 26	12 14	13 55	15 33
64	////	01 19	02 52	10 39	12 20	13 55	15 28
62	////	01 58	03 11	10 49	12 25	13 56	15 24
60	////	02 24	03 26	10 58	12 29	13 56	15 21
N 58	01 11	02 45	03 39	11 06	12 33	13 56	15 17
56	01 47	03 01	03 50	11 13	12 37	13 57	15 15
54	02 11	03 15	04 00	11 19	12 40	13 57	15 12
52	02 30	03 27	04 09	11 24	12 42	13 57	15 10
50	02 46	03 38	04 17	11 29	12 45	13 57	15 08
45	03 16	03 59	04 33	11 40	12 50	13 58	15 03
N 40	03 38	04 16	04 46	11 49	12 55	13 58	15 00
35	03 56	04 30	04 58	11 56	12 58	13 58	14 56
30	04 10	04 42	05 08	12 03	13 02	13 58	14 54
20	04 33	05 01	05 25	12 14	13 08	13 59	14 49
N 10	04 51	05 17	05 39	12 24	13 13	13 59	14 45
0	05 06	05 31	05 53	12 33	13 17	14 00	14 41
S 10	05 19	05 44	06 06	12 42	13 22	14 00	14 37
20	05 31	05 57	06 21	12 52	13 27	14 00	14 33
30	05 43	06 11	06 37	13 03	13 33	14 01	14 28
35	05 49	06 19	06 46	13 09	13 36	14 01	14 26
40	05 55	06 28	06 57	13 16	13 40	14 02	14 23
45	06 02	06 37	07 09	13 25	13 44	14 02	14 19
S 50	06 10	06 49	07 24	13 34	13 49	14 02	14 15
52	06 13	06 54	07 32	13 39	13 52	14 03	14 13
54	06 16	07 00	07 39	13 44	13 54	14 03	14 11
56	06 20	07 06	07 48	13 50	13 57	14 03	14 09
58	06 24	07 13	07 58	13 56	14 00	14 04	14 07
S 60	06 29	07 21	08 10	14 03	14 04	14 04	14 04

Lat.	Sunset	Twilight Civil	Twilight Naut.	Moonset 12	Moonset 13	Moonset 14	Moonset 15
°	h m	h m	h m	h m	h m	h m	h m
N 72	▭	▭	▭	03 41	02 54	02 20	01 49
N 70	23 03	////	////	03 13	02 41	02 15	01 52
68	22 01	////	////	02 52	02 30	02 12	01 55
66	21 27	////	////	02 35	02 21	02 09	01 57
64	21 03	22 39	////	02 22	02 13	02 06	01 59
62	20 44	21 58	////	02 10	02 07	02 04	02 01
60	20 28	21 31	////	02 00	02 01	02 02	02 02
N 58	20 15	21 10	22 47	01 51	01 56	02 00	02 03
56	20 04	20 53	22 09	01 43	01 52	01 59	02 05
54	19 54	20 39	21 44	01 36	01 48	01 57	02 06
52	19 45	20 27	21 24	01 30	01 44	01 56	02 07
50	19 37	20 16	21 08	01 24	01 41	01 55	02 08
45	19 20	19 55	20 38	01 12	01 33	01 52	02 09
N 40	19 07	19 37	20 15	01 02	01 27	01 50	02 11
35	18 55	19 23	19 57	00 53	01 22	01 48	02 12
30	18 45	19 11	19 43	00 45	01 17	01 46	02 14
20	18 28	18 52	19 20	00 31	01 09	01 43	02 16
N 10	18 14	18 36	19 02	00 19	01 01	01 40	02 18
0	18 00	18 22	18 47	00 08	00 54	01 38	02 19
S 10	17 46	18 08	18 34	24 47	00 47	01 35	02 21
20	17 32	17 55	18 22	24 40	00 40	01 32	02 23
30	17 16	17 41	18 10	24 31	00 31	01 29	02 25
35	17 06	17 33	18 04	24 26	00 26	01 27	02 26
40	16 56	17 25	17 57	24 21	00 21	01 25	02 28
45	16 43	17 15	17 50	24 14	00 14	01 23	02 29
S 50	16 28	17 03	17 43	24 06	00 06	01 20	02 31
52	16 21	16 58	17 39	24 02	00 02	01 18	02 32
54	16 13	16 52	17 36	23 58	25 17	01 17	02 33
56	16 04	16 46	17 32	23 53	25 15	01 15	02 34
58	15 54	16 39	17 28	23 48	25 13	01 13	02 35
S 60	15 42	16 31	17 23	23 42	25 11	01 11	02 37

Day	SUN Eqn. of Time 00^h	SUN Eqn. of Time 12^h	SUN Mer. Pass.	MOON Mer. Pass. Upper	MOON Mer. Pass. Lower	MOON Age	MOON Phase
d	m s	m s	h m	h m	h m	d	%
12	03 39	03 39	11 56	18 44	06 21	07	54
13	03 39	03 40	11 56	19 28	07 06	08	64
14	03 40	03 39	11 56	20 10	07 49	09	73

	UT	ARIES	VENUS −3.9		MARS +1.4		JUPITER −2.5		SATURN +0.6	
		GHA	GHA	Dec	GHA	Dec	GHA	Dec	GHA	Dec
	d h	° ′	° ′	° ′	° ′	° ′	° ′	° ′	° ′	° ′
	15 00	233 05.6	187 32.0	N16 16.4	107 37.2	N21 10.4	298 58.6	S21 38.9	78 38.2	N12 29.2
	01	248 08.1	202 31.4	17.4	122 38.2	10.0	314 01.1	39.0	93 40.6	29.2
	02	263 10.6	217 30.8	18.3	137 39.3	09.7	329 03.6	39.0	108 43.0	29.2
	03	278 13.0	232 30.2	. . 19.2	152 40.4	. . 09.4	344 06.1	. . 39.0	123 45.4	. . 29.1
	04	293 15.5	247 29.6	20.1	167 41.4	09.0	359 08.6	39.0	138 47.8	29.1
	05	308 18.0	262 29.0	21.1	182 42.5	08.7	14 11.1	39.0	153 50.3	29.1
	06	323 20.4	277 28.4	N16 22.0	197 43.5	N21 08.3	29 13.6	S21 39.0	168 52.7	N12 29.1
	07	338 22.9	292 27.8	22.9	212 44.6	08.0	44 16.2	39.0	183 55.1	29.0
T	08	353 25.4	307 27.2	23.9	227 45.6	07.6	59 18.7	39.1	198 57.5	29.0
H	09	8 27.8	322 26.6	. . 24.8	242 46.7	. . 07.3	74 21.2	. . 39.1	213 59.9	. . 29.0
U	10	23 30.3	337 26.1	25.7	257 47.7	06.9	89 23.7	39.1	229 02.3	29.0
R	11	38 32.8	352 25.5	26.6	272 48.8	06.6	104 26.2	39.1	244 04.8	28.9
S	12	53 35.2	7 24.9	N16 27.6	287 49.9	N21 06.2	119 28.7	S21 39.1	259 07.2	N12 28.9
D	13	68 37.7	22 24.3	28.5	302 50.9	05.9	134 31.2	39.1	274 09.6	28.9
A	14	83 40.1	37 23.7	29.4	317 52.0	05.6	149 33.7	39.1	289 12.0	28.9
Y	15	98 42.6	52 23.1	. . 30.3	332 53.0	. . 05.2	164 36.3	. . 39.1	304 14.4	. . 28.8
	16	113 45.1	67 22.5	31.3	347 54.1	04.9	179 38.8	39.2	319 16.8	28.8
	17	128 47.5	82 21.9	32.2	2 55.1	04.5	194 41.3	39.2	334 19.2	28.8
	18	143 50.0	97 21.3	N16 33.1	17 56.2	N21 04.2	209 43.8	S21 39.2	349 21.6	N12 28.8
	19	158 52.5	112 20.7	34.0	32 57.2	03.8	224 46.3	39.2	4 24.1	28.8
	20	173 54.9	127 20.1	34.9	47 58.3	03.5	239 48.8	39.2	19 26.5	28.7
	21	188 57.4	142 19.5	. . 35.9	62 59.4	. . 03.1	254 51.3	. . 39.2	34 28.9	. . 28.7
	22	203 59.9	157 18.9	36.8	78 00.4	02.8	269 53.9	39.2	49 31.3	28.7
	23	219 02.3	172 18.3	37.7	93 01.5	02.4	284 56.4	39.3	64 33.7	28.7
	16 00	234 04.8	187 17.7	N16 38.6	108 02.5	N21 02.1	299 58.9	S21 39.3	79 36.1	N12 28.6
	01	249 07.2	202 17.1	39.5	123 03.6	01.7	315 01.4	39.3	94 38.5	28.6
	02	264 09.7	217 16.5	40.4	138 04.6	01.4	330 03.9	39.3	109 40.9	28.6
	03	279 12.2	232 15.9	. . 41.4	153 05.7	. . 01.0	345 06.5	. . 39.3	124 43.4	. . 28.6
	04	294 14.6	247 15.3	42.3	168 06.7	00.7	0 09.0	39.3	139 45.8	28.5
	05	309 17.1	262 14.7	43.2	183 07.8	00.3	15 11.5	39.3	154 48.2	28.5
	06	324 19.6	277 14.1	N16 44.1	198 08.9	N21 00.0	30 14.0	S21 39.4	169 50.6	N12 28.5
	07	339 22.0	292 13.5	45.0	213 09.9	20 59.6	45 16.5	39.4	184 53.0	28.4
	08	354 24.5	307 12.9	45.9	228 11.0	59.3	60 19.0	39.4	199 55.4	28.4
F	09	9 27.0	322 12.3	. . 46.8	243 12.0	. . 58.9	75 21.6	. . 39.4	214 57.8	. . 28.4
R	10	24 29.4	337 11.7	47.7	258 13.1	58.6	90 24.1	39.4	230 00.2	28.4
I	11	39 31.9	352 11.1	48.6	273 14.1	58.2	105 26.6	39.4	245 02.6	28.3
D	12	54 34.4	7 10.5	N16 49.6	288 15.2	N20 57.9	120 29.1	S21 39.4	260 05.1	N12 28.3
A	13	69 36.8	22 09.9	50.5	303 16.2	57.5	135 31.7	39.5	275 07.5	28.3
Y	14	84 39.3	37 09.3	51.4	318 17.3	57.2	150 34.2	39.5	290 09.9	28.3
	15	99 41.7	52 08.7	. . 52.3	333 18.3	. . 56.8	165 36.7	. . 39.5	305 12.3	. . 28.2
	16	114 44.2	67 08.1	53.2	348 19.4	56.5	180 39.2	39.5	320 14.7	28.2
	17	129 46.7	82 07.4	54.1	3 20.5	56.1	195 41.7	39.5	335 17.1	28.2
	18	144 49.1	97 06.8	N16 55.0	18 21.5	N20 55.8	210 44.3	S21 39.5	350 19.5	N12 28.2
	19	159 51.6	112 06.2	55.9	33 22.6	55.4	225 46.8	39.5	5 21.9	28.1
	20	174 54.1	127 05.6	56.8	48 23.6	55.1	240 49.3	39.6	20 24.3	28.1
	21	189 56.5	142 05.0	. . 57.7	63 24.7	. . 54.7	255 51.8	. . 39.6	35 26.7	. . 28.1
	22	204 59.0	157 04.4	58.6	78 25.7	54.4	270 54.4	39.6	50 29.1	28.1
	23	220 01.5	172 03.8	16 59.5	93 26.8	54.0	285 56.9	39.6	65 31.5	28.0
	17 00	235 03.9	187 03.2	N17 00.4	108 27.8	N20 53.7	300 59.4	S21 39.6	80 34.0	N12 28.0
	01	250 06.4	202 02.6	01.3	123 28.9	53.3	316 01.9	39.6	95 36.4	28.0
	02	265 08.8	217 02.0	02.2	138 29.9	52.9	331 04.5	39.7	110 38.8	28.0
	03	280 11.3	232 01.4	. . 03.1	153 31.0	. . 52.6	346 07.0	. . 39.7	125 41.2	. . 27.9
	04	295 13.8	247 00.7	04.0	168 32.0	52.2	1 09.5	39.7	140 43.6	27.9
	05	310 16.2	262 00.1	04.9	183 33.1	51.9	16 12.0	39.7	155 46.0	27.9
	06	325 18.7	276 59.5	N17 05.8	198 34.2	N20 51.5	31 14.6	S21 39.7	170 48.4	N12 27.8
	07	340 21.2	291 58.9	06.7	213 35.2	51.2	46 17.1	39.7	185 50.8	27.8
S	08	355 23.6	306 58.3	07.5	228 36.3	50.8	61 19.6	39.7	200 53.2	27.8
A	09	10 26.1	321 57.7	. . 08.4	243 37.3	. . 50.5	76 22.2	. . 39.8	215 55.6	. . 27.8
T	10	25 28.6	336 57.1	09.3	258 38.4	50.1	91 24.7	39.8	230 58.0	27.7
U	11	40 31.0	351 56.4	10.2	273 39.4	49.8	106 27.2	39.8	246 00.4	27.7
R	12	55 33.5	6 55.8	N17 11.1	288 40.5	N20 49.4	121 29.7	S21 39.8	261 02.8	N12 27.7
D	13	70 36.0	21 55.2	12.0	303 41.5	49.0	136 32.3	39.8	276 05.2	27.7
A	14	85 38.4	36 54.6	12.9	318 42.6	48.7	151 34.8	39.8	291 07.7	27.6
Y	15	100 40.9	51 54.0	. . 13.8	333 43.6	. . 48.3	166 37.3	. . 39.9	306 10.1	. . 27.6
	16	115 43.3	66 53.4	14.7	348 44.7	48.0	181 39.9	39.9	321 12.5	27.6
	17	130 45.8	81 52.7	15.5	3 45.7	47.6	196 42.4	39.9	336 14.9	27.5
	18	145 48.3	96 52.1	N17 16.4	18 46.8	N20 47.3	211 44.9	S21 39.9	351 17.3	N12 27.5
	19	160 50.7	111 51.5	17.3	33 47.9	46.9	226 47.5	39.9	6 19.7	27.5
	20	175 53.2	126 50.9	18.2	48 48.9	46.5	241 50.0	39.9	21 22.1	27.5
	21	190 55.7	141 50.3	. . 19.1	63 50.0	. . 46.2	256 52.5	. . 40.0	36 24.5	. . 27.4
	22	205 58.1	156 49.6	20.0	78 51.0	45.8	271 55.1	40.0	51 26.9	27.4
	23	221 00.6	171 49.0	20.8	93 52.1	45.5	286 57.6	40.0	66 29.3	27.4
	Mer. Pass.	h m 8 22.3	*v* −0.6	*d* 0.9	*v* 1.1	*d* 0.4	*v* 2.5	*d* 0.0	*v* 2.4	*d* 0.0

STARS

Name	SHA	Dec
	° ′	° ′
Acamar	315 21.6	S40 16.2
Achernar	335 29.9	S57 11.5
Acrux	173 13.5	S63 09.1
Adhara	255 15.8	S28 59.1
Aldebaran	290 54.2	N16 31.6
Alioth	166 23.4	N55 54.9
Alkaid	153 01.3	N49 16.3
Al Na'ir	27 48.4	S46 55.0
Alnilam	275 50.6	S 1 11.8
Alphard	217 59.9	S 8 41.8
Alphecca	126 13.8	N26 41.0
Alpheratz	357 47.8	N29 08.1
Altair	62 11.8	N 8 53.3
Ankaa	353 19.6	S42 15.4
Antares	112 30.7	S26 27.2
Arcturus	145 58.9	N19 08.2
Atria	107 35.6	S69 02.6
Avior	234 20.0	S59 32.4
Bellatrix	278 36.5	N 6 21.5
Betelgeuse	271 05.8	N 7 24.5
Canopus	263 58.3	S52 42.1
Capella	280 40.6	N46 00.5
Deneb	49 34.1	N45 18.3
Denebola	182 37.4	N14 31.5
Diphda	348 59.9	S17 56.4
Dubhe	193 55.8	N61 42.6
Elnath	278 17.9	N28 37.0
Eltanin	90 47.5	N51 29.0
Enif	33 50.9	N 9 54.7
Fomalhaut	15 28.2	S29 34.5
Gacrux	172 05.1	S57 09.9
Gienah	175 56.1	S17 35.5
Hadar	148 53.1	S60 25.1
Hamal	328 05.5	N23 30.1
Kaus Aust.	83 48.6	S34 22.9
Kochab	137 18.2	N74 07.2
Markab	13 42.3	N15 14.9
Menkar	314 19.4	N 4 07.4
Menkent	148 11.9	S36 24.9
Miaplacidus	221 41.0	S69 45.4
Mirfak	308 46.5	N49 53.5
Nunki	76 02.8	S26 17.2
Peacock	53 24.9	S56 42.3
Pollux	243 32.6	N28 00.5
Procyon	245 03.9	N 5 12.2
Rasalhague	96 09.7	N12 33.0
Regulus	207 47.6	N11 55.6
Rigel	281 16.1	S 8 11.5
Rigil Kent.	139 56.6	S60 52.4
Sabik	102 16.6	S15 44.3
Schedar	349 45.6	N56 34.8
Shaula	96 26.8	S37 06.7
Sirius	258 37.4	S16 43.7
Spica	158 35.1	S11 12.5
Suhail	222 55.5	S43 28.2
Vega	80 41.3	N38 47.2
Zuben'ubi	137 09.4	S16 04.8

	SHA	Mer. Pass.
	° ′	h m
Venus	313 12.9	11 31
Mars	233 57.7	16 47
Jupiter	65 54.1	3 59
Saturn	205 31.3	18 39

UT d h	SUN GHA ° ′	SUN Dec ° ′	MOON GHA ° ′	v ′	MOON Dec ° ′	d ′	HP ′
15 00	180 54.8	N18 54.4	56 01.1	15.9	S 1 51.5	14.4	55.4
01	195 54.8	55.0	70 36.0	16.0	2 05.9	14.3	55.4
02	210 54.8	55.6	85 11.0	16.0	2 20.2	14.3	55.4
03	225 54.8	. . 56.1	99 46.0	16.1	2 34.5	14.2	55.4
04	240 54.8	56.7	114 21.1	16.0	2 48.7	14.3	55.3
05	255 54.8	57.3	128 56.1	16.0	3 03.0	14.2	55.3
06	270 54.7	N18 57.9	143 31.1	16.0	S 3 17.2	14.2	55.3
T 07	285 54.7	58.5	158 06.1	16.1	3 31.4	14.2	55.3
H 08	300 54.7	59.1	172 41.2	16.0	3 45.6	14.2	55.2
U 09	315 54.7	18 59.6	187 16.2	16.1	3 59.8	14.1	55.2
R 10	330 54.7	19 00.2	201 51.3	16.0	4 13.9	14.1	55.2
S 11	345 54.7	00.8	216 26.3	16.1	4 28.0	14.1	55.2
D 12	0 54.7	N19 01.4	231 01.4	16.0	S 4 42.1	14.0	55.2
A 13	15 54.7	02.0	245 36.4	16.1	4 56.1	14.1	55.1
Y 14	30 54.7	02.6	260 11.5	16.0	5 10.2	14.0	55.1
15	45 54.7	. . 03.1	274 46.5	16.1	5 24.2	13.9	55.1
16	60 54.7	03.7	289 21.6	16.0	5 38.1	14.0	55.1
17	75 54.6	04.3	303 56.6	16.0	5 52.1	13.9	55.1
18	90 54.6	N19 04.9	318 31.6	16.1	S 6 06.0	13.8	55.0
19	105 54.6	05.4	333 06.7	16.0	6 19.8	13.9	55.0
20	120 54.6	06.0	347 41.7	16.0	6 33.7	13.8	55.0
21	135 54.6	. . 06.6	2 16.7	16.0	6 47.5	13.8	55.0
22	150 54.6	07.2	16 51.7	16.0	7 01.3	13.7	55.0
23	165 54.6	07.7	31 26.7	16.0	7 15.0	13.7	54.9
16 00	180 54.6	N19 08.3	46 01.7	15.9	S 7 28.7	13.7	54.9
01	195 54.5	08.9	60 36.6	16.0	7 42.4	13.6	54.9
02	210 54.5	09.5	75 11.6	15.9	7 56.0	13.6	54.9
03	225 54.5	. . 10.0	89 46.5	15.9	8 09.6	13.5	54.9
04	240 54.5	10.6	104 21.4	15.9	8 23.1	13.5	54.9
05	255 54.5	11.2	118 56.3	15.9	8 36.6	13.5	54.8
06	270 54.5	N19 11.8	133 31.2	15.9	S 8 50.1	13.4	54.8
07	285 54.5	12.3	148 06.1	15.8	9 03.5	13.4	54.8
08	300 54.5	12.9	162 40.9	15.9	9 16.9	13.3	54.8
F 09	315 54.4	. . 13.5	177 15.8	15.8	9 30.2	13.3	54.8
R 10	330 54.4	14.0	191 50.6	15.7	9 43.5	13.3	54.8
I 11	345 54.4	14.6	206 25.3	15.8	9 56.8	13.2	54.7
D 12	0 54.4	N19 15.2	221 00.1	15.7	S10 10.0	13.2	54.7
A 13	15 54.4	15.7	235 34.8	15.7	10 23.2	13.1	54.7
Y 14	30 54.4	16.3	250 09.5	15.7	10 36.3	13.1	54.7
15	45 54.3	. . 16.9	264 44.2	15.7	10 49.4	13.0	54.7
16	60 54.3	17.4	279 18.9	15.6	11 02.4	13.0	54.7
17	75 54.3	18.0	293 53.5	15.6	11 15.4	12.9	54.6
18	90 54.3	N19 18.6	308 28.1	15.6	S11 28.3	12.9	54.6
19	105 54.3	19.1	323 02.7	15.5	11 41.2	12.8	54.6
20	120 54.3	19.7	337 37.2	15.5	11 54.0	12.7	54.6
21	135 54.2	. . 20.3	352 11.7	15.5	12 06.7	12.8	54.6
22	150 54.2	20.8	6 46.2	15.5	12 19.5	12.6	54.6
23	165 54.2	21.4	21 20.7	15.4	12 32.1	12.6	54.6
17 00	180 54.2	N19 21.9	35 55.1	15.3	S12 44.7	12.6	54.5
01	195 54.2	22.5	50 29.4	15.4	12 57.3	12.5	54.5
02	210 54.2	23.1	65 03.8	15.3	13 09.8	12.4	54.5
03	225 54.1	. . 23.6	79 38.1	15.2	13 22.2	12.4	54.5
04	240 54.1	24.2	94 12.3	15.3	13 34.6	12.3	54.5
05	255 54.1	24.7	108 46.6	15.2	13 46.9	12.3	54.5
06	270 54.1	N19 25.3	123 20.8	15.1	S13 59.2	12.2	54.5
S 07	285 54.1	25.9	137 54.9	15.1	14 11.4	12.2	54.4
A 08	300 54.0	26.4	152 29.0	15.1	14 23.6	12.1	54.4
T 09	315 54.0	. . 27.0	167 03.1	15.0	14 35.7	12.0	54.4
U 10	330 54.0	27.5	181 37.1	15.0	14 47.7	11.9	54.4
R 11	345 54.0	28.1	196 11.1	15.0	14 59.6	11.9	54.4
D 12	0 54.0	N19 28.6	210 45.1	14.9	S15 11.5	11.9	54.4
A 13	15 53.9	29.2	225 19.0	14.8	15 23.4	11.7	54.4
Y 14	30 53.9	29.7	239 52.8	14.8	15 35.1	11.7	54.4
15	45 53.9	. . 30.3	254 26.6	14.8	15 46.8	11.7	54.4
16	60 53.9	30.8	269 00.4	14.7	15 58.5	11.5	54.3
17	75 53.8	31.4	283 34.1	14.7	16 10.0	11.5	54.3
18	90 53.8	N19 31.9	298 07.8	14.6	S16 21.5	11.5	54.3
19	105 53.8	32.5	312 41.4	14.6	16 33.0	11.3	54.3
20	120 53.8	33.0	327 15.0	14.6	16 44.3	11.3	54.3
21	135 53.8	. . 33.6	341 48.6	14.4	16 55.6	11.2	54.3
22	150 53.7	34.1	356 22.0	14.5	17 06.8	11.2	54.3
23	165 53.7	34.7	10 55.5	14.4	S17 18.0	11.0	54.3
	SD 15.8	*d* 0.6	SD 15.0		14.9		14.8

Lat. °	Twilight Naut. h m	Twilight Civil h m	Sunrise h m	Moonrise 15 h m	Moonrise 16 h m	Moonrise 17 h m	Moonrise 18 h m
N 72	▭	▭	▭	15 54	18 03	20 53	■
N 70	////	////	00 09	15 46	17 42	19 55	■
68	////	////	01 39	15 39	17 25	19 22	21 56
66	////	////	02 17	15 33	17 13	18 58	20 57
64	////	00 58	02 43	15 28	17 02	18 39	20 23
62	////	01 45	03 03	15 24	16 53	18 24	19 59
60	////	02 15	03 19	15 21	16 45	18 11	19 40
N 58	00 52	02 37	03 33	15 17	16 38	18 00	19 24
56	01 35	02 54	03 45	15 15	16 32	17 51	19 10
54	02 02	03 09	03 55	15 12	16 27	17 43	18 59
52	02 23	03 22	04 04	15 10	16 22	17 35	18 49
50	02 40	03 33	04 12	15 08	16 18	17 29	18 39
45	03 11	03 55	04 30	15 03	16 09	17 14	18 20
N 40	03 35	04 13	04 44	15 00	16 01	17 03	18 05
35	03 53	04 27	04 56	14 56	15 54	16 53	17 52
30	04 08	04 40	05 06	14 54	15 49	16 44	17 40
20	04 32	05 00	05 23	14 49	15 39	16 29	17 21
N 10	04 50	05 16	05 39	14 45	15 30	16 16	17 04
0	05 05	05 31	05 53	14 41	15 22	16 04	16 49
S 10	05 19	05 45	06 07	14 37	15 14	15 53	16 33
20	05 32	05 58	06 22	14 33	15 06	15 40	16 17
30	05 44	06 13	06 39	14 28	14 56	15 26	15 58
35	05 51	06 21	06 48	14 26	14 51	15 17	15 47
40	05 57	06 30	07 00	14 23	14 44	15 08	15 35
45	06 05	06 41	07 13	14 19	14 37	14 57	15 20
S 50	06 13	06 53	07 29	14 15	14 29	14 44	15 02
52	06 17	06 58	07 36	14 13	14 25	14 38	14 54
54	06 20	07 04	07 44	14 11	14 20	14 31	14 45
56	06 25	07 11	07 54	14 09	14 16	14 24	14 34
58	06 29	07 18	08 04	14 07	14 10	14 15	14 22
S 60	06 34	07 26	08 16	14 04	14 05	14 06	14 09

Lat. °	Sunset h m	Twilight Civil h m	Twilight Naut. h m	Moonset 15 h m	Moonset 16 h m	Moonset 17 h m	Moonset 18 h m
N 72	▭	▭	▭	01 49	01 17	{00 37, 23 16}	■
N 70	▭	▭	▭	01 52	01 28	01 00	00 15
68	22 19	////	////	01 55	01 38	01 18	{00 50, 23 49}
66	21 39	////	////	01 57	01 45	01 32	01 16
64	21 12	23 03	////	01 59	01 52	01 44	01 35
62	20 52	22 11	////	02 01	01 58	01 54	01 52
60	20 35	21 41	////	02 02	02 03	02 03	02 05
N 58	20 21	21 18	23 08	02 03	02 07	02 11	02 17
56	20 09	21 00	22 21	02 05	02 11	02 18	02 27
54	19 59	20 45	21 53	02 06	02 14	02 24	02 36
52	19 50	20 32	21 32	02 07	02 18	02 30	02 44
50	19 41	20 21	21 15	02 08	02 21	02 35	02 51
45	19 24	19 58	20 42	02 09	02 27	02 46	03 07
N 40	19 10	19 41	20 19	02 11	02 32	02 55	03 20
35	18 58	19 26	20 00	02 12	02 37	03 03	03 31
30	18 47	19 14	19 45	02 14	02 41	03 10	03 41
20	18 29	18 53	19 21	02 16	02 48	03 22	03 57
N 10	18 14	18 37	19 03	02 18	02 55	03 32	04 12
0	18 00	18 22	18 47	02 19	03 01	03 42	04 26
S 10	17 46	18 08	18 34	02 21	03 06	03 52	04 39
20	17 31	17 54	18 21	02 23	03 13	04 03	04 54
30	17 14	17 39	18 08	02 25	03 20	04 15	05 11
35	17 04	17 31	18 02	02 26	03 24	04 23	05 21
40	16 53	17 22	17 55	02 28	03 29	04 31	05 33
45	16 40	17 12	17 47	02 29	03 35	04 40	05 46
S 50	16 24	17 00	17 39	02 31	03 42	04 52	06 03
52	16 16	16 54	17 36	02 32	03 45	04 57	06 10
54	16 08	16 48	17 32	02 33	03 48	05 03	06 19
56	15 59	16 41	17 28	02 34	03 52	05 10	06 29
58	15 48	16 34	17 23	02 35	03 56	05 18	06 40
S 60	15 36	16 26	17 18	02 37	04 01	05 26	06 53

Day	SUN Eqn. of Time 00^h m s	SUN Eqn. of Time 12^h m s	SUN Mer. Pass. h m	MOON Mer. Pass. Upper h m	MOON Mer. Pass. Lower h m	MOON Age d	MOON Phase %
15	03 39	03 39	11 56	20 51	08 30	10	82
16	03 38	03 38	11 56	21 32	09 11	11	89
17	03 37	03 36	11 56	22 15	09 53	12	94

UT d	UT h	ARIES GHA ° ′	VENUS −3.9 GHA ° ′	VENUS Dec ° ′	MARS +1.4 GHA ° ′	MARS Dec ° ′	JUPITER −2.5 GHA ° ′	JUPITER Dec ° ′	SATURN +0.6 GHA ° ′	SATURN Dec ° ′
18	00	236 03.1	186 48.4	N17 21.7	108 53.1	N20 45.1	302 00.1	S21 40.0	81 31.7	N12 27.3
	01	251 05.5	201 47.8	22.6	123 54.2	44.8	317 02.7	40.0	96 34.1	27.3
	02	266 08.0	216 47.1	23.5	138 55.2	44.4	332 05.2	40.0	111 36.5	27.3
	03	281 10.5	231 46.5	24.4	153 56.3	44.0	347 07.7	40.1	126 38.9	27.3
	04	296 12.9	246 45.9	25.2	168 57.3	43.7	2 10.3	40.1	141 41.3	27.2
	05	311 15.4	261 45.3	26.1	183 58.4	43.3	17 12.8	40.1	156 43.7	27.2
	06	326 17.8	276 44.6	N17 27.0	198 59.4	N20 43.0	32 15.3	S21 40.1	171 46.1	N12 27.2
	07	341 20.3	291 44.0	27.9	214 00.5	42.6	47 17.9	40.1	186 48.5	27.1
	08	356 22.8	306 43.4	28.7	229 01.5	42.2	62 20.4	40.1	201 50.9	27.1
S	09	11 25.2	321 42.8	29.6	244 02.6	41.9	77 22.9	40.2	216 53.3	27.1
U	10	26 27.7	336 42.1	30.5	259 03.6	41.5	92 25.5	40.2	231 55.7	27.1
N	11	41 30.2	351 41.5	31.4	274 04.7	41.2	107 28.0	40.2	246 58.1	27.0
D	12	56 32.6	6 40.9	N17 32.2	289 05.8	N20 40.8	122 30.6	S21 40.2	262 00.5	N12 27.0
A	13	71 35.1	21 40.3	33.1	304 06.8	40.4	137 33.1	40.2	277 02.9	27.0
Y	14	86 37.6	36 39.6	34.0	319 07.9	40.1	152 35.6	40.2	292 05.3	26.9
	15	101 40.0	51 39.0	34.8	334 08.9	39.7	167 38.2	40.3	307 07.7	26.9
	16	116 42.5	66 38.4	35.7	349 10.0	39.4	182 40.7	40.3	322 10.1	26.9
	17	131 45.0	81 37.7	36.6	4 11.0	39.0	197 43.3	40.3	337 12.5	26.9
	18	146 47.4	96 37.1	N17 37.4	19 12.1	N20 38.6	212 45.8	S21 40.3	352 14.9	N12 26.8
	19	161 49.9	111 36.5	38.3	34 13.1	38.3	227 48.3	40.3	7 17.3	26.8
	20	176 52.3	126 35.8	39.2	49 14.2	37.9	242 50.9	40.3	22 19.7	26.8
	21	191 54.8	141 35.2	40.0	64 15.2	37.5	257 53.4	40.4	37 22.1	26.7
	22	206 57.3	156 34.6	40.9	79 16.3	37.2	272 56.0	40.4	52 24.5	26.7
	23	221 59.7	171 33.9	41.8	94 17.3	36.8	287 58.5	40.4	67 26.9	26.7
19	00	237 02.2	186 33.3	N17 42.6	109 18.4	N20 36.5	303 01.0	S21 40.4	82 29.3	N12 26.7
	01	252 04.7	201 32.7	43.5	124 19.4	36.1	318 03.6	40.4	97 31.7	26.6
	02	267 07.1	216 32.0	44.3	139 20.5	35.7	333 06.1	40.5	112 34.1	26.6
	03	282 09.6	231 31.4	45.2	154 21.5	35.4	348 08.7	40.5	127 36.5	26.6
	04	297 12.1	246 30.8	46.1	169 22.6	35.0	3 11.2	40.5	142 38.9	26.5
	05	312 14.5	261 30.1	46.9	184 23.6	34.6	18 13.8	40.5	157 41.3	26.5
	06	327 17.0	276 29.5	N17 47.8	199 24.7	N20 34.3	33 16.3	S21 40.5	172 43.7	N12 26.5
	07	342 19.4	291 28.9	48.6	214 25.7	33.9	48 18.8	40.5	187 46.1	26.4
	08	357 21.9	306 28.2	49.5	229 26.8	33.5	63 21.4	40.6	202 48.5	26.4
M	09	12 24.4	321 27.6	50.3	244 27.8	33.2	78 23.9	40.6	217 50.9	26.4
O	10	27 26.8	336 27.0	51.2	259 28.9	32.8	93 26.5	40.6	232 53.3	26.4
N	11	42 29.3	351 26.3	52.0	274 30.0	32.4	108 29.0	40.6	247 55.7	26.3
D	12	57 31.8	6 25.7	N17 52.9	289 31.0	N20 32.1	123 31.6	S21 40.6	262 58.1	N12 26.3
A	13	72 34.2	21 25.0	53.7	304 32.1	31.7	138 34.1	40.7	278 00.5	26.3
Y	14	87 36.7	36 24.4	54.6	319 33.1	31.3	153 36.7	40.7	293 02.9	26.2
	15	102 39.2	51 23.8	55.4	334 34.2	31.0	168 39.2	40.7	308 05.3	26.2
	16	117 41.6	66 23.1	56.3	349 35.2	30.6	183 41.8	40.7	323 07.7	26.2
	17	132 44.1	81 22.5	57.1	4 36.3	30.2	198 44.3	40.7	338 10.1	26.1
	18	147 46.6	96 21.8	N17 58.0	19 37.3	N20 29.9	213 46.8	S21 40.7	353 12.5	N12 26.1
	19	162 49.0	111 21.2	58.8	34 38.4	29.5	228 49.4	40.8	8 14.9	26.1
	20	177 51.5	126 20.5	17 59.7	49 39.4	29.1	243 51.9	40.8	23 17.3	26.0
	21	192 53.9	141 19.9	18 00.5	64 40.5	28.8	258 54.5	40.8	38 19.7	26.0
	22	207 56.4	156 19.3	01.4	79 41.5	28.4	273 57.0	40.8	53 22.1	26.0
	23	222 58.9	171 18.6	02.2	94 42.6	28.0	288 59.6	40.8	68 24.5	26.0
20	00	238 01.3	186 18.0	N18 03.1	109 43.6	N20 27.7	304 02.1	S21 40.9	83 26.9	N12 25.9
	01	253 03.8	201 17.3	03.9	124 44.7	27.3	319 04.7	40.9	98 29.3	25.9
	02	268 06.3	216 16.7	04.7	139 45.7	26.9	334 07.2	40.9	113 31.7	25.9
	03	283 08.7	231 16.0	05.6	154 46.8	26.6	349 09.8	40.9	128 34.1	25.8
	04	298 11.2	246 15.4	06.4	169 47.8	26.2	4 12.3	40.9	143 36.5	25.8
	05	313 13.7	261 14.7	07.3	184 48.9	25.8	19 14.9	41.0	158 38.9	25.8
	06	328 16.1	276 14.1	N18 08.1	199 49.9	N20 25.5	34 17.4	S21 41.0	173 41.3	N12 25.7
	07	343 18.6	291 13.4	08.9	214 51.0	25.1	49 20.0	41.0	188 43.6	25.7
T	08	358 21.1	306 12.8	09.8	229 52.0	24.7	64 22.6	41.0	203 46.0	25.7
U	09	13 23.5	321 12.1	10.6	244 53.1	24.4	79 25.1	41.0	218 48.4	25.6
E	10	28 26.0	336 11.5	11.4	259 54.1	24.0	94 27.7	41.1	233 50.8	25.6
S	11	43 28.4	351 10.8	12.3	274 55.2	23.6	109 30.2	41.1	248 53.2	25.6
D	12	58 30.9	6 10.2	N18 13.1	289 56.2	N20 23.2	124 32.8	S21 41.1	263 55.6	N12 25.5
A	13	73 33.4	21 09.5	13.9	304 57.3	22.9	139 35.3	41.1	278 58.0	25.5
Y	14	88 35.8	36 08.9	14.8	319 58.3	22.5	154 37.9	41.1	294 00.4	25.5
	15	103 38.3	51 08.2	15.6	334 59.4	22.1	169 40.4	41.1	309 02.8	25.4
	16	118 40.8	66 07.6	16.4	350 00.4	21.8	184 43.0	41.2	324 05.2	25.4
	17	133 43.2	81 06.9	17.3	5 01.5	21.4	199 45.5	41.2	339 07.6	25.4
	18	148 45.7	96 06.3	N18 18.1	20 02.5	N20 21.0	214 48.1	S21 41.2	354 10.0	N12 25.4
	19	163 48.2	111 05.6	18.9	35 03.6	20.6	229 50.7	41.2	9 12.4	25.3
	20	178 50.6	126 05.0	19.7	50 04.6	20.3	244 53.2	41.2	24 14.8	25.3
	21	193 53.1	141 04.3	20.6	65 05.7	19.9	259 55.8	41.3	39 17.2	25.3
	22	208 55.6	156 03.6	21.4	80 06.7	19.5	274 58.3	41.3	54 19.5	25.2
	23	223 58.0	171 03.0	22.2	95 07.8	19.2	290 00.9	41.3	69 21.9	25.2
Mer. Pass.		h m 8 10.5	v −0.6	d 0.9	v 1.1	d 0.4	v 2.5	d 0.0	v 2.4	d 0.0

STARS Name	SHA ° ′	Dec ° ′
Acamar	315 21.6	S40 16.2
Achernar	335 29.9	S57 11.4
Acrux	173 13.5	S63 09.1
Adhara	255 15.9	S28 59.1
Aldebaran	290 54.2	N16 31.6
Alioth	166 23.4	N55 54.9
Alkaid	153 01.3	N49 16.3
Al Na'ir	27 48.4	S46 55.0
Alnilam	275 50.6	S 1 11.8
Alphard	217 59.9	S 8 41.8
Alphecca	126 13.8	N26 41.0
Alpheratz	357 47.8	N29 08.1
Altair	62 11.8	N 8 53.3
Ankaa	353 19.6	S42 15.4
Antares	112 30.7	S26 27.2
Arcturus	145 58.9	N19 08.2
Atria	107 35.5	S69 02.6
Avior	234 20.1	S59 32.4
Bellatrix	278 36.5	N 6 21.5
Betelgeuse	271 05.8	N 7 24.5
Canopus	263 58.3	S52 42.1
Capella	280 40.6	N46 00.5
Deneb	49 34.1	N45 18.3
Denebola	182 37.4	N14 31.5
Diphda	348 59.9	S17 56.4
Dubhe	193 55.9	N61 42.6
Elnath	278 17.9	N28 36.9
Eltanin	90 47.5	N51 29.0
Enif	33 50.9	N 9 54.7
Fomalhaut	15 28.2	S29 34.5
Gacrux	172 05.1	S57 09.9
Gienah	175 56.1	S17 35.5
Hadar	148 53.1	S60 25.1
Hamal	328 05.5	N23 30.1
Kaus Aust.	83 48.6	S34 22.9
Kochab	137 18.2	N74 07.2
Markab	13 42.3	N15 14.9
Menkar	314 19.4	N 4 07.4
Menkent	148 11.9	S36 24.9
Miaplacidus	221 41.1	S69 45.4
Mirfak	308 46.5	N49 53.5
Nunki	76 02.8	S26 17.2
Peacock	53 24.9	S56 42.3
Pollux	243 32.6	N28 00.5
Procyon	245 03.9	N 5 12.2
Rasalhague	96 09.7	N12 33.0
Regulus	207 47.6	N11 55.6
Rigel	281 16.1	S 8 11.5
Rigil Kent.	139 56.6	S60 52.4
Sabik	102 16.6	S15 44.2
Schedar	349 45.6	N56 34.8
Shaula	96 26.8	S37 06.7
Sirius	258 37.4	S16 43.7
Spica	158 35.1	S11 12.5
Suhail	222 55.5	S43 28.2
Vega	80 41.3	N38 47.2
Zuben'ubi	137 09.4	S16 04.8

	SHA ° ′	Mer. Pass. h m
Venus	309 31.1	11 34
Mars	232 16.2	16 42
Jupiter	65 58.8	3 47
Saturn	205 27.1	18 27

UT d h		SUN GHA	SUN Dec	MOON GHA	v	MOON Dec	d	HP
		° ′	° ′	° ′	′	° ′	′	′
18 00		180 53.7	N19 35.2	25 28.9	14.3	S17 29.0	11.0	54.3
01		195 53.7	35.8	40 02.2	14.3	17 40.0	10.9	54.2
02		210 53.6	36.3	54 35.5	14.2	17 50.9	10.9	54.2
03		225 53.6	. . 36.9	69 08.7	14.2	18 01.8	10.7	54.2
04		240 53.6	37.4	83 41.9	14.1	18 12.5	10.7	54.2
05		255 53.6	38.0	98 15.0	14.1	18 23.2	10.6	54.2
06		270 53.5	N19 38.5	112 48.1	14.0	S18 33.8	10.6	54.2
07		285 53.5	39.1	127 21.1	14.0	18 44.4	10.4	54.2
08		300 53.5	39.6	141 54.1	13.9	18 54.8	10.4	54.2
09	S	315 53.5	. . 40.1	156 27.0	13.9	19 05.2	10.3	54.2
10	U	330 53.4	40.7	170 59.9	13.8	19 15.5	10.2	54.2
11	N	345 53.4	41.2	185 32.7	13.7	19 25.7	10.1	54.2
12	D	0 53.4	N19 41.8	200 05.4	13.7	S19 35.8	10.1	54.2
13	A	15 53.4	42.3	214 38.1	13.7	19 45.9	9.9	54.1
14	Y	30 53.3	42.8	229 10.8	13.6	19 55.8	9.9	54.1
15		45 53.3	. . 43.4	243 43.4	13.5	20 05.7	9.8	54.1
16		60 53.3	43.9	258 15.9	13.5	20 15.5	9.7	54.1
17		75 53.2	44.5	272 48.4	13.4	20 25.2	9.6	54.1
18		90 53.2	N19 45.0	287 20.8	13.4	S20 34.8	9.5	54.1
19		105 53.2	45.5	301 53.2	13.3	20 44.3	9.4	54.1
20		120 53.2	46.1	316 25.5	13.2	20 53.7	9.3	54.1
21		135 53.1	. . 46.6	330 57.7	13.2	21 03.0	9.3	54.1
22		150 53.1	47.1	345 29.9	13.2	21 12.3	9.1	54.1
23		165 53.1	47.7	0 02.1	13.0	21 21.4	9.1	54.1
19 00		180 53.0	N19 48.2	14 34.1	13.0	S21 30.5	9.0	54.1
01		195 53.0	48.7	29 06.1	13.0	21 39.5	8.8	54.1
02		210 53.0	49.3	43 38.1	12.9	21 48.3	8.8	54.1
03		225 52.9	. . 49.8	58 10.0	12.9	21 57.1	8.7	54.1
04		240 52.9	50.3	72 41.9	12.8	22 05.8	8.6	54.0
05		255 52.9	50.9	87 13.7	12.7	22 14.4	8.5	54.0
06		270 52.9	N19 51.4	101 45.4	12.7	S22 22.9	8.3	54.0
07		285 52.8	51.9	116 17.1	12.6	22 31.2	8.3	54.0
08		300 52.8	52.4	130 48.7	12.5	22 39.5	8.2	54.0
09	M	315 52.8	. . 53.0	145 20.2	12.6	22 47.7	8.1	54.0
10	O	330 52.7	53.5	159 51.8	12.4	22 55.8	8.0	54.0
11	N	345 52.7	54.0	174 23.2	12.4	23 03.8	7.9	54.0
12	D	0 52.7	N19 54.6	188 54.6	12.3	S23 11.7	7.7	54.0
13	A	15 52.6	55.1	203 25.9	12.3	23 19.4	7.7	54.0
14	Y	30 52.6	55.6	217 57.2	12.2	23 27.1	7.6	54.0
15		45 52.6	. . 56.1	232 28.4	12.2	23 34.7	7.4	54.0
16		60 52.5	56.7	246 59.6	12.1	23 42.1	7.4	54.0
17		75 52.5	57.2	261 30.7	12.0	23 49.5	7.3	54.0
18		90 52.5	N19 57.7	276 01.7	12.0	S23 56.8	7.1	54.0
19		105 52.4	58.2	290 32.7	12.0	24 03.9	7.0	54.0
20		120 52.4	58.7	305 03.7	11.9	24 10.9	6.9	54.0
21		135 52.4	. . 59.3	319 34.6	11.8	24 17.8	6.9	54.0
22		150 52.3	19 59.8	334 05.4	11.8	24 24.7	6.7	54.0
23		165 52.3	20 00.3	348 36.2	11.7	24 31.4	6.6	54.0
20 00		180 52.3	N20 00.8	3 06.9	11.7	S24 38.0	6.4	54.0
01		195 52.2	01.3	17 37.6	11.6	24 44.4	6.4	54.0
02		210 52.2	01.9	32 08.2	11.6	24 50.8	6.3	54.0
03		225 52.2	. . 02.4	46 38.8	11.5	24 57.1	6.1	54.0
04		240 52.1	02.9	61 09.3	11.5	25 03.2	6.0	54.0
05		255 52.1	03.4	75 39.8	11.4	25 09.2	5.9	54.0
06		270 52.0	N20 03.9	90 10.2	11.4	S25 15.1	5.8	54.0
07		285 52.0	04.4	104 40.6	11.3	25 20.9	5.7	54.0
08	T	300 52.0	05.0	119 10.9	11.2	25 26.6	5.6	54.0
09	U	315 51.9	. . 05.5	133 41.1	11.3	25 32.2	5.4	54.0
10	E	330 51.9	06.0	148 11.4	11.1	25 37.6	5.3	54.0
11	S	345 51.9	06.5	162 41.5	11.2	25 42.9	5.2	54.0
12	D	0 51.8	N20 07.0	177 11.7	11.0	S25 48.1	5.1	54.0
13	A	15 51.8	07.5	191 41.7	11.1	25 53.2	5.0	54.0
14	Y	30 51.7	08.0	206 11.8	11.0	25 58.2	4.8	54.0
15		45 51.7	. . 08.5	220 41.8	10.9	26 03.0	4.7	54.0
16		60 51.7	09.0	235 11.7	10.9	26 07.7	4.6	54.0
17		75 51.6	09.6	249 41.6	10.9	26 12.3	4.5	54.0
18		90 51.6	N20 10.1	264 11.5	10.8	S26 16.8	4.3	54.0
19		105 51.5	10.6	278 41.3	10.8	26 21.1	4.3	54.0
20		120 51.5	11.1	293 11.1	10.7	26 25.4	4.1	54.0
21		135 51.5	. . 11.6	307 40.8	10.7	26 29.5	3.9	54.0
22		150 51.4	12.1	322 10.5	10.7	26 33.4	3.9	54.0
23		165 51.4	12.6	336 40.2	10.6	S26 37.3	3.7	54.0
		SD 15.8	*d* 0.5	SD 14.8		14.7		14.7

Lat.	Twilight Naut.	Twilight Civil	Sunrise	Moonrise 18	19	20	21
°	h m	h m	h m	h m	h m	h m	h m
N 72	□	□	□	■	■	■	■
N 70	□	□	□	■	■	■	■
68	////	////	01 21	21 56	■	■	■
66	////	////	02 05	20 57	■	■	■
64	////	00 26	02 33	20 23	22 22	■	■
62	////	01 32	02 55	19 59	21 38	23 19	24 45
60	////	02 05	03 13	19 40	21 09	22 35	23 44
N 58	00 23	02 29	03 27	19 24	20 47	22 05	23 10
56	01 23	02 48	03 40	19 10	20 29	21 43	22 45
54	01 54	03 03	03 50	18 59	20 14	21 25	22 25
52	02 16	03 17	04 00	18 49	20 01	21 09	22 09
50	02 34	03 28	04 08	18 39	19 49	20 56	21 54
45	03 07	03 52	04 26	18 20	19 26	20 28	21 25
N 40	03 32	04 10	04 41	18 05	19 07	20 07	21 03
35	03 50	04 25	04 53	17 52	18 51	19 49	20 44
30	04 06	04 38	05 04	17 40	18 37	19 33	20 28
20	04 30	04 59	05 22	17 21	18 14	19 07	20 00
N 10	04 49	05 16	05 38	17 04	17 54	18 45	19 37
0	05 05	05 31	05 53	16 49	17 35	18 24	19 15
S 10	05 19	05 45	06 07	16 33	17 17	18 04	18 53
20	05 33	05 59	06 23	16 17	16 57	17 42	18 30
30	05 46	06 15	06 40	15 58	16 35	17 16	18 03
35	05 53	06 23	06 51	15 47	16 21	17 01	17 47
40	06 00	06 33	07 02	15 35	16 06	16 44	17 28
45	06 08	06 44	07 16	15 20	15 48	16 23	17 06
S 50	06 16	06 56	07 32	15 02	15 26	15 57	16 37
52	06 20	07 02	07 40	14 54	15 15	15 44	16 23
54	06 24	07 08	07 49	14 45	15 03	15 30	16 07
56	06 29	07 15	07 59	14 34	14 50	15 13	15 48
58	06 34	07 23	08 10	14 22	14 34	14 52	15 24
S 60	06 39	07 32	08 23	14 09	14 15	14 27	14 53

Lat.	Sunset	Twilight Civil	Twilight Naut.	Moonset 18	19	20	21
°	h m	h m	h m	h m	h m	h m	h m
N 72	□	□	□	■	■	■	■
N 70	□	□	□	00 15	■	■	■
68	22 38	////	////	{00 50 / 23 49}	■	■	■
66	21 52	////	////	01 16	00 49	■	■
64	21 22	////	////	01 35	01 24	01 03	■
62	21 00	22 25	////	01 52	01 49	01 48	01 49
60	20 42	21 51	////	02 05	02 09	02 17	02 34
N 58	20 27	21 26	////	02 17	02 25	02 40	03 04
56	20 15	21 07	22 34	02 27	02 39	02 58	03 26
54	20 04	20 51	22 02	02 36	02 52	03 14	03 45
52	19 54	20 38	21 39	02 44	03 02	03 27	04 01
50	19 45	20 26	21 21	02 51	03 12	03 39	04 14
45	19 27	20 02	20 47	03 07	03 32	04 03	04 42
N 40	19 12	19 44	20 22	03 20	03 49	04 23	05 04
35	19 00	19 28	20 03	03 31	04 03	04 40	05 22
30	18 49	19 16	19 47	03 41	04 15	04 54	05 38
20	18 31	18 55	19 23	03 57	04 36	05 18	06 04
N 10	18 15	18 37	19 04	04 12	04 54	05 39	06 27
0	18 00	18 22	18 48	04 26	05 11	05 59	06 49
S 10	17 45	18 08	18 33	04 39	05 28	06 19	07 10
20	17 30	17 53	18 20	04 54	05 47	06 40	07 33
30	17 12	17 38	18 07	05 11	06 08	07 05	08 00
35	17 02	17 29	18 00	05 21	06 20	07 19	08 16
40	16 50	17 20	17 53	05 33	06 35	07 36	08 34
45	16 37	17 09	17 45	05 46	06 52	07 56	08 56
S 50	16 20	16 56	17 36	06 03	07 13	08 22	09 25
52	16 12	16 50	17 32	06 10	07 23	08 34	09 38
54	16 04	16 44	17 28	06 19	07 35	08 48	09 55
56	15 54	16 37	17 24	06 29	07 48	09 05	10 14
58	15 43	16 29	17 19	06 40	08 04	09 25	10 37
S 60	15 30	16 21	17 14	06 53	08 22	09 50	11 08

Day	SUN Eqn. of Time 00^h	SUN Eqn. of Time 12^h	SUN Mer. Pass.	MOON Mer. Pass. Upper	MOON Mer. Pass. Lower	Age	Phase
d	m s	m s	h m	h m	h m	d	%
18	03 35	03 34	11 56	23 00	10 37	13	98
19	03 32	03 31	11 56	23 47	11 23	14	99
20	03 29	03 27	11 57	24 37	12 12	15	100

2008 MAY 21, 22, 23 (WED., THURS., FRI.)

	UT	ARIES	VENUS −3.9		MARS +1.4		JUPITER −2.5		SATURN +0.7	
		GHA	GHA	Dec	GHA	Dec	GHA	Dec	GHA	Dec
	d h	° ′	° ′	° ′	° ′	° ′	° ′	° ′	° ′	° ′
	21 00	239 00.5	186 02.3	N18 23.0	110 08.8	N20 18.8	305 03.4	S21 41.3	84 24.3	N12 25.2
	01	254 02.9	201 01.7	23.8	125 09.9	18.4	320 06.0	41.4	99 26.7	25.1
	02	269 05.4	216 01.0	24.7	140 10.9	18.0	335 08.6	41.4	114 29.1	25.1
	03	284 07.9	231 00.4	. . 25.5	155 12.0	. . 17.7	350 11.1	. . 41.4	129 31.5	. . 25.1
	04	299 10.3	245 59.7	26.3	170 13.0	17.3	5 13.7	41.4	144 33.9	25.0
	05	314 12.8	260 59.0	27.1	185 14.1	16.9	20 16.2	41.4	159 36.3	25.0
	06	329 15.3	275 58.4	N18 27.9	200 15.1	N20 16.5	35 18.8	S21 41.5	174 38.7	N12 25.0
W	07	344 17.7	290 57.7	28.8	215 16.2	16.2	50 21.4	41.5	189 41.1	24.9
E	08	359 20.2	305 57.1	29.6	230 17.3	15.8	65 23.9	41.5	204 43.5	24.9
D	09	14 22.7	320 56.4	. . 30.4	245 18.3	. . 15.4	80 26.5	. . 41.5	219 45.9	. . 24.9
	10	29 25.1	335 55.7	31.2	260 19.4	15.0	95 29.0	41.5	234 48.2	24.8
N	11	44 27.6	350 55.1	32.0	275 20.4	14.7	110 31.6	41.6	249 50.6	24.8
E	12	59 30.0	5 54.4	N18 32.8	290 21.5	N20 14.3	125 34.2	S21 41.6	264 53.0	N12 24.8
S	13	74 32.5	20 53.7	33.6	305 22.5	13.9	140 36.7	41.6	279 55.4	24.7
D	14	89 35.0	35 53.1	34.5	320 23.6	13.5	155 39.3	41.6	294 57.8	24.7
A	15	104 37.4	50 52.4	. . 35.3	335 24.6	. . 13.2	170 41.9	. . 41.6	310 00.2	. . 24.7
Y	16	119 39.9	65 51.8	36.1	350 25.7	12.8	185 44.4	41.7	325 02.6	24.6
	17	134 42.4	80 51.1	36.9	5 26.7	12.4	200 47.0	41.7	340 05.0	24.6
	18	149 44.8	95 50.4	N18 37.7	20 27.8	N20 12.0	215 49.5	S21 41.7	355 07.4	N12 24.6
	19	164 47.3	110 49.8	38.5	35 28.8	11.7	230 52.1	41.7	10 09.7	24.5
	20	179 49.8	125 49.1	39.3	50 29.9	11.3	245 54.7	41.7	25 12.1	24.5
	21	194 52.2	140 48.4	. . 40.1	65 30.9	. . 10.9	260 57.2	. . 41.8	40 14.5	. . 24.5
	22	209 54.7	155 47.8	40.9	80 32.0	10.5	275 59.8	41.8	55 16.9	24.4
	23	224 57.2	170 47.1	41.7	95 33.0	10.1	291 02.4	41.8	70 19.3	24.4
	22 00	239 59.6	185 46.4	N18 42.5	110 34.1	N20 09.8	306 04.9	S21 41.8	85 21.7	N12 24.4
	01	255 02.1	200 45.7	43.3	125 35.1	09.4	321 07.5	41.9	100 24.1	24.3
	02	270 04.5	215 45.1	44.1	140 36.2	09.0	336 10.1	41.9	115 26.5	24.3
	03	285 07.0	230 44.4	. . 44.9	155 37.2	. . 08.6	351 12.6	. . 41.9	130 28.8	. . 24.3
	04	300 09.5	245 43.7	45.7	170 38.3	08.3	6 15.2	41.9	145 31.2	24.2
	05	315 11.9	260 43.1	46.5	185 39.3	07.9	21 17.8	41.9	160 33.6	24.2
	06	330 14.4	275 42.4	N18 47.3	200 40.4	N20 07.5	36 20.3	S21 42.0	175 36.0	N12 24.1
	07	345 16.9	290 41.7	48.1	215 41.4	07.1	51 22.9	42.0	190 38.4	24.1
T	08	0 19.3	305 41.0	48.9	230 42.5	06.7	66 25.5	42.0	205 40.8	24.1
H	09	15 21.8	320 40.4	. . 49.7	245 43.5	. . 06.4	81 28.0	. . 42.0	220 43.2	. . 24.0
U	10	30 24.3	335 39.7	50.5	260 44.6	06.0	96 30.6	42.1	235 45.6	24.0
R	11	45 26.7	350 39.0	51.3	275 45.6	05.6	111 33.2	42.1	250 47.9	24.0
S	12	60 29.2	5 38.4	N18 52.1	290 46.6	N20 05.2	126 35.8	S21 42.1	265 50.3	N12 23.9
D	13	75 31.7	20 37.7	52.9	305 47.7	04.8	141 38.3	42.1	280 52.7	23.9
A	14	90 34.1	35 37.0	53.7	320 48.7	04.5	156 40.9	42.1	295 55.1	23.9
Y	15	105 36.6	50 36.3	. . 54.4	335 49.8	. . 04.1	171 43.5	. . 42.2	310 57.5	. . 23.8
	16	120 39.0	65 35.7	55.2	350 50.8	03.7	186 46.0	42.2	325 59.9	23.8
	17	135 41.5	80 35.0	56.0	5 51.9	03.3	201 48.6	42.2	341 02.3	23.8
	18	150 44.0	95 34.3	N18 56.8	20 52.9	N20 02.9	216 51.2	S21 42.2	356 04.6	N12 23.7
	19	165 46.4	110 33.6	57.6	35 54.0	02.6	231 53.8	42.3	11 07.0	23.7
	20	180 48.9	125 32.9	58.4	50 55.0	02.2	246 56.3	42.3	26 09.4	23.7
	21	195 51.4	140 32.3	18 59.2	65 56.1	. . 01.8	261 58.9	. . 42.3	41 11.8	. . 23.6
	22	210 53.8	155 31.6	19 00.0	80 57.1	01.4	277 01.5	42.3	56 14.2	23.6
	23	225 56.3	170 30.9	00.7	95 58.2	01.0	292 04.1	42.3	71 16.6	23.6
	23 00	240 58.8	185 30.2	N19 01.5	110 59.2	N20 00.6	307 06.6	S21 42.4	86 18.9	N12 23.5
	01	256 01.2	200 29.5	02.3	126 00.3	20 00.3	322 09.2	42.4	101 21.3	23.5
	02	271 03.7	215 28.9	03.1	141 01.3	19 59.9	337 11.8	42.4	116 23.7	23.4
	03	286 06.2	230 28.2	. . 03.9	156 02.4	. . 59.5	352 14.4	. . 42.4	131 26.1	. . 23.4
	04	301 08.6	245 27.5	04.6	171 03.4	59.1	7 16.9	42.5	146 28.5	23.4
	05	316 11.1	260 26.8	05.4	186 04.5	58.7	22 19.5	42.5	161 30.9	23.3
	06	331 13.5	275 26.1	N19 06.2	201 05.5	N19 58.3	37 22.1	S21 42.5	176 33.2	N12 23.3
	07	346 16.0	290 25.4	07.0	216 06.6	58.0	52 24.7	42.5	191 35.6	23.3
	08	1 18.5	305 24.8	07.7	231 07.6	57.6	67 27.2	42.5	206 38.0	23.2
	09	16 20.9	320 24.1	. . 08.5	246 08.7	. . 57.2	82 29.8	. . 42.6	221 40.4	. . 23.2
F	10	31 23.4	335 23.4	09.3	261 09.7	56.8	97 32.4	42.6	236 42.8	23.2
R	11	46 25.9	350 22.7	10.1	276 10.8	56.4	112 35.0	42.6	251 45.2	23.1
I	12	61 28.3	5 22.0	N19 10.8	291 11.8	N19 56.0	127 37.5	S21 42.6	266 47.5	N12 23.1
D	13	76 30.8	20 21.3	11.6	306 12.9	55.7	142 40.1	42.7	281 49.9	23.0
A	14	91 33.3	35 20.6	12.4	321 13.9	55.3	157 42.7	42.7	296 52.3	23.0
Y	15	106 35.7	50 20.0	. . 13.1	336 15.0	. . 54.9	172 45.3	. . 42.7	311 54.7	. . 23.0
	16	121 38.2	65 19.3	13.9	351 16.0	54.5	187 47.9	42.7	326 57.1	22.9
	17	136 40.7	80 18.6	14.7	6 17.1	54.1	202 50.4	42.8	341 59.4	22.9
	18	151 43.1	95 17.9	N19 15.4	21 18.1	N19 53.7	217 53.0	S21 42.8	357 01.8	N12 22.9
	19	166 45.6	110 17.2	16.2	36 19.2	53.3	232 55.6	42.8	12 04.2	22.8
	20	181 48.0	125 16.5	17.0	51 20.2	52.9	247 58.2	42.8	27 06.6	22.8
	21	196 50.5	140 15.8	. . 17.7	66 21.3	. . 52.6	263 00.8	. . 42.9	42 09.0	. . 22.8
	22	211 53.0	155 15.1	18.5	81 22.3	52.2	278 03.3	42.9	57 11.3	22.7
	23	226 55.4	170 14.4	19.3	96 23.4	51.8	293 05.9	42.9	72 13.7	22.7
	Mer. Pass.	h m 7 58.7	v −0.7	d 0.8	v 1.0	d 0.4	v 2.6	d 0.0	v 2.4	d 0.0

STARS

Name	SHA	Dec
	° ′	° ′
Acamar	315 21.5	S40 16.1
Achernar	335 29.8	S57 11.4
Acrux	173 13.6	S63 09.1
Adhara	255 15.9	S28 59.1
Aldebaran	290 54.2	N16 31.6
Alioth	166 23.4	N55 55.0
Alkaid	153 01.3	N49 16.3
Al Na'ir	27 48.3	S46 55.0
Alnilam	275 50.6	S 1 11.8
Alphard	217 59.9	S 8 41.8
Alphecca	126 13.8	N26 41.0
Alpheratz	357 47.8	N29 08.1
Altair	62 11.8	N 8 53.3
Ankaa	353 19.5	S42 15.4
Antares	112 30.6	S26 27.2
Arcturus	145 58.9	N19 08.2
Atria	107 35.5	S69 02.6
Avior	234 20.1	S59 32.4
Bellatrix	278 36.4	N 6 21.5
Betelgeuse	271 05.8	N 7 24.6
Canopus	263 58.3	S52 42.1
Capella	280 40.6	N46 00.5
Deneb	49 34.0	N45 18.3
Denebola	182 37.4	N14 31.5
Diphda	348 59.9	S17 56.3
Dubhe	193 55.9	N61 42.6
Elnath	278 17.8	N28 36.9
Eltanin	90 47.4	N51 29.0
Enif	33 50.9	N 9 54.7
Fomalhaut	15 28.2	S29 34.5
Gacrux	172 05.1	S57 09.9
Gienah	175 56.1	S17 35.5
Hadar	148 53.1	S60 25.1
Hamal	328 05.5	N23 30.1
Kaus Aust.	83 48.5	S34 22.9
Kochab	137 18.2	N74 07.2
Markab	13 42.3	N15 14.9
Menkar	314 19.4	N 4 07.4
Menkent	148 11.9	S36 24.9
Miaplacidus	221 41.1	S69 45.4
Mirfak	308 46.5	N49 53.5
Nunki	76 02.8	S26 17.2
Peacock	53 24.8	S56 42.3
Pollux	243 32.6	N28 00.5
Procyon	245 03.9	N 5 12.2
Rasalhague	96 09.7	N12 33.1
Regulus	207 47.6	N11 55.6
Rigel	281 16.1	S 8 11.5
Rigil Kent.	139 56.6	S60 52.4
Sabik	102 16.6	S15 44.2
Schedar	349 45.6	N56 34.8
Shaula	96 26.8	S37 06.7
Sirius	258 37.4	S16 43.7
Spica	158 35.1	S11 12.5
Suhail	222 55.5	S43 28.2
Vega	80 41.2	N38 47.2
Zuben'ubi	137 09.4	S16 04.8

	SHA	Mer. Pass.
	° ′	h m
Venus	305 46.8	11 37
Mars	230 34.4	16 37
Jupiter	66 05.3	3 35
Saturn	205 22.1	18 16

Day	UT d h	SUN GHA ° ′	SUN Dec ° ′	MOON GHA ° ′	v ′	MOON Dec ° ′	d ′	HP ′
21 WEDNESDAY	00	180 51.3	N20 13.1	351 09.8	10.6	S26 41.0	3.6	54.0
	01	195 51.3	13.6	5 39.4	10.6	26 44.6	3.5	54.0
	02	210 51.3	14.1	20 09.0	10.5	26 48.1	3.3	54.0
	03	225 51.2	. . 14.6	34 38.5	10.5	26 51.4	3.3	54.0
	04	240 51.2	15.1	49 08.0	10.4	26 54.7	3.1	54.0
	05	255 51.1	15.6	63 37.4	10.4	26 57.8	2.9	54.0
	06	270 51.1	N20 16.1	78 06.8	10.4	S27 00.7	2.8	54.0
	07	285 51.1	16.6	92 36.2	10.4	27 03.5	2.7	54.0
	08	300 51.0	17.1	107 05.6	10.3	27 06.2	2.6	54.0
	09	315 51.0	. . 17.6	121 34.9	10.4	27 08.8	2.5	54.0
	10	330 50.9	18.1	136 04.3	10.2	27 11.3	2.3	54.0
	11	345 50.9	18.6	150 33.5	10.3	27 13.6	2.2	54.0
	12	0 50.8	N20 19.1	165 02.8	10.2	S27 15.8	2.0	54.0
	13	15 50.8	19.6	179 32.0	10.2	27 17.8	1.9	54.0
	14	30 50.8	20.1	194 01.2	10.2	27 19.7	1.8	54.0
	15	45 50.7	. . 20.6	208 30.4	10.2	27 21.5	1.7	54.0
	16	60 50.7	21.1	222 59.6	10.1	27 23.2	1.5	54.0
	17	75 50.6	21.6	237 28.7	10.2	27 24.7	1.4	54.0
	18	90 50.6	N20 22.1	251 57.9	10.1	S27 26.1	1.3	54.0
	19	105 50.5	22.6	266 27.0	10.1	27 27.4	1.1	54.0
	20	120 50.5	23.1	280 56.1	10.1	27 28.5	1.0	54.0
	21	135 50.4	. . 23.6	295 25.2	10.0	27 29.5	0.8	54.0
	22	150 50.4	24.1	309 54.2	10.1	27 30.3	0.8	54.0
	23	165 50.3	24.6	324 23.3	10.0	27 31.1	0.6	54.0
22 THURSDAY	00	180 50.3	N20 25.0	338 52.3	10.1	S27 31.7	0.4	54.0
	01	195 50.3	25.5	353 21.4	10.0	27 32.1	0.4	54.1
	02	210 50.2	26.0	7 50.4	10.0	27 32.5	0.2	54.1
	03	225 50.2	. . 26.5	22 19.4	10.0	27 32.7	0.0	54.1
	04	240 50.1	27.0	36 48.4	10.0	27 32.7	0.1	54.1
	05	255 50.1	27.5	51 17.4	10.0	27 32.6	0.2	54.1
	06	270 50.0	N20 28.0	65 46.4	10.0	S27 32.4	0.3	54.1
	07	285 50.0	28.5	80 15.4	10.0	27 32.1	0.5	54.1
	08	300 49.9	28.9	94 44.4	10.0	27 31.6	0.6	54.1
	09	315 49.9	. . 29.4	109 13.4	10.0	27 31.0	0.7	54.1
	10	330 49.8	29.9	123 42.4	10.0	27 30.3	0.9	54.1
	11	345 49.8	30.4	138 11.4	10.0	27 29.4	1.0	54.1
	12	0 49.7	N20 30.9	152 40.4	10.0	S27 28.4	1.2	54.1
	13	15 49.7	31.4	167 09.4	10.0	27 27.2	1.3	54.1
	14	30 49.6	31.8	181 38.4	10.1	27 25.9	1.4	54.1
	15	45 49.6	. . 32.3	196 07.5	10.0	27 24.5	1.5	54.1
	16	60 49.5	32.8	210 36.5	10.0	27 23.0	1.7	54.2
	17	75 49.5	33.3	225 05.5	10.0	27 21.3	1.8	54.2
	18	90 49.4	N20 33.8	239 34.5	10.1	S27 19.5	2.0	54.2
	19	105 49.4	34.2	254 03.6	10.1	27 17.5	2.0	54.2
	20	120 49.3	34.7	268 32.7	10.0	27 15.5	2.2	54.2
	21	135 49.3	. . 35.2	283 01.7	10.1	27 13.3	2.4	54.2
	22	150 49.2	35.7	297 30.8	10.1	27 10.9	2.5	54.2
	23	165 49.2	36.2	311 59.9	10.2	27 08.4	2.6	54.2
23 FRIDAY	00	180 49.1	N20 36.6	326 29.1	10.1	S27 05.8	2.7	54.2
	01	195 49.1	37.1	340 58.2	10.1	27 03.1	2.9	54.2
	02	210 49.0	37.6	355 27.3	10.2	27 00.2	3.0	54.2
	03	225 49.0	. . 38.1	9 56.5	10.2	26 57.2	3.1	54.3
	04	240 48.9	38.5	24 25.7	10.2	26 54.1	3.3	54.3
	05	255 48.9	39.0	38 54.9	10.3	26 50.8	3.4	54.3
	06	270 48.8	N20 39.5	53 24.2	10.2	S26 47.4	3.6	54.3
	07	285 48.8	39.9	67 53.4	10.3	26 43.8	3.6	54.3
	08	300 48.7	40.4	82 22.7	10.3	26 40.2	3.8	54.3
	09	315 48.6	. . 40.9	96 52.0	10.4	26 36.4	3.9	54.3
	10	330 48.6	41.4	111 21.4	10.3	26 32.5	4.1	54.3
	11	345 48.5	41.8	125 50.7	10.4	26 28.4	4.2	54.3
	12	0 48.5	N20 42.3	140 20.1	10.4	S26 24.2	4.3	54.4
	13	15 48.4	42.8	154 49.5	10.5	26 19.9	4.4	54.4
	14	30 48.4	43.2	169 19.0	10.5	26 15.5	4.6	54.4
	15	45 48.3	. . 43.7	183 48.5	10.5	26 10.9	4.7	54.4
	16	60 48.3	44.2	198 18.0	10.5	26 06.2	4.8	54.4
	17	75 48.2	44.6	212 47.5	10.6	26 01.4	4.9	54.4
	18	90 48.2	N20 45.1	227 17.1	10.6	S25 56.5	5.1	54.4
	19	105 48.1	45.6	241 46.7	10.6	25 51.4	5.2	54.4
	20	120 48.0	46.0	256 16.3	10.7	25 46.2	5.3	54.5
	21	135 48.0	. . 46.5	270 46.0	10.7	25 40.9	5.4	54.5
	22	150 47.9	46.9	285 15.7	10.8	25 35.5	5.6	54.5
	23	165 47.9	47.4	299 45.5	10.8	S25 29.9	5.7	54.5
		SD 15.8	*d* 0.5	SD 14.7		14.7		14.8

Lat. °	Twilight Naut. h m	Twilight Civil h m	Sunrise h m	Moonrise 21 h m	Moonrise 22 h m	Moonrise 23 h m	Moonrise 24 h m
N 72	□	□	□	■	■	■	■
N 70	□	□	□	■	■	■	■
68	////	////	00 59	■	■	■	■
66	////	////	01 53	■	■	■	■
64	////	////	02 24	■	■	■	02 10
62	////	01 18	02 48	24 45	00 45	01 15	01 18
60	////	01 56	03 06	23 44	24 26	00 26	00 46
N 58	////	02 22	03 22	23 10	23 55	24 22	00 22
56	01 10	02 42	03 35	22 45	23 32	24 03	00 03
54	01 45	02 58	03 46	22 25	23 13	23 47	24 11
52	02 09	03 12	03 56	22 09	22 57	23 33	24 00
50	02 28	03 24	04 05	21 54	22 43	23 21	23 50
45	03 03	03 48	04 24	21 25	22 15	22 55	23 29
N 40	03 28	04 07	04 39	21 03	21 52	22 35	23 12
35	03 48	04 23	04 52	20 44	21 34	22 18	22 57
30	04 04	04 36	05 03	20 28	21 18	22 04	22 44
20	04 29	04 58	05 22	20 00	20 51	21 39	22 23
N 10	04 49	05 15	05 38	19 37	20 28	21 17	22 04
0	05 05	05 31	05 53	19 15	20 06	20 57	21 47
S 10	05 20	05 46	06 08	18 53	19 45	20 37	21 29
20	05 34	06 01	06 24	18 30	19 22	20 15	21 10
30	05 47	06 17	06 42	18 03	18 55	19 50	20 48
35	05 54	06 25	06 53	17 47	18 39	19 35	20 35
40	06 02	06 35	07 05	17 28	18 20	19 18	20 20
45	06 10	06 46	07 19	17 06	17 58	18 57	20 03
S 50	06 20	07 00	07 36	16 37	17 29	18 31	19 40
52	06 24	07 06	07 44	16 23	17 15	18 19	19 30
54	06 28	07 12	07 53	16 07	16 59	18 04	19 18
56	06 33	07 20	08 04	15 48	16 40	17 47	19 04
58	06 38	07 28	08 15	15 24	16 16	17 26	18 48
S 60	06 43	07 37	08 29	14 53	15 44	16 59	18 28

Lat. °	Sunset h m	Twilight Civil h m	Twilight Naut. h m	Moonset 21 h m	Moonset 22 h m	Moonset 23 h m	Moonset 24 h m
N 72	□	□	□	■	■	■	■
N 70	□	□	□	■	■	■	■
68	23 02	////	////	■	■	■	■
66	22 04	////	////	■	■	■	■
64	21 31	////	////	■	■	■	04 17
62	21 07	22 40	////	01 49	02 09	03 27	05 09
60	20 49	22 01	////	02 34	03 11	04 15	05 40
N 58	20 33	21 34	////	03 04	03 45	04 46	06 03
56	20 20	21 13	22 47	03 26	04 09	05 09	06 22
54	20 08	20 57	22 11	03 45	04 29	05 28	06 38
52	19 58	20 43	21 46	04 01	04 46	05 44	06 52
50	19 49	20 30	21 27	04 14	05 00	05 58	07 04
45	19 30	20 06	20 51	04 42	05 29	06 25	07 28
N 40	19 15	19 46	20 26	05 04	05 52	06 47	07 48
35	19 02	19 31	20 06	05 22	06 11	07 06	08 04
30	18 51	19 18	19 50	05 38	06 27	07 21	08 18
20	18 32	18 56	19 24	06 04	06 55	07 47	08 42
N 10	18 16	18 38	19 05	06 27	07 18	08 10	09 02
0	18 00	18 22	18 48	06 49	07 40	08 31	09 21
S 10	17 45	18 08	18 33	07 10	08 02	08 52	09 40
20	17 29	17 53	18 20	07 33	08 25	09 15	10 00
30	17 11	17 37	18 06	08 00	08 52	09 41	10 24
35	17 00	17 28	17 59	08 16	09 08	09 56	10 37
40	16 48	17 18	17 51	08 34	09 27	10 13	10 53
45	16 34	17 07	17 43	08 56	09 50	10 35	11 12
S 50	16 17	16 53	17 33	09 25	10 18	11 01	11 35
52	16 09	16 47	17 29	09 38	10 33	11 15	11 46
54	15 59	16 41	17 25	09 55	10 49	11 29	11 58
56	15 49	16 33	17 20	10 14	11 08	11 47	12 12
58	15 38	16 25	17 15	10 37	11 32	12 08	12 29
S 60	15 24	16 16	17 09	11 08	12 05	12 35	12 49

Day	SUN Eqn. of Time 00h	SUN Eqn. of Time 12h	SUN Mer. Pass.	MOON Mer. Pass. Upper	MOON Mer. Pass. Lower	MOON Age	MOON Phase
d	m s	m s	h m	h m	h m	d	%
21	03 25	03 23	11 57	00 37	13 02	16	98
22	03 21	03 19	11 57	01 28	13 53	17	95
23	03 17	03 14	11 57	02 19	14 44	18	90

	UT (d h)	ARIES GHA	VENUS −3.9 GHA	VENUS Dec	MARS +1.4 GHA	MARS Dec	JUPITER −2.5 GHA	JUPITER Dec	SATURN +0.7 GHA	SATURN Dec
		° ′	° ′	° ′	° ′	° ′	° ′	° ′	° ′	° ′
	24 00	241 57.9	185 13.7	N19 20.0	111 24.4	N19 51.4	308 08.5	S21 42.9	87 16.1	N12 22.6
	01	257 00.4	200 13.1	20.8	126 25.5	51.0	323 11.1	42.9	102 18.5	22.6
	02	272 02.8	215 12.4	21.5	141 26.5	50.6	338 13.7	43.0	117 20.9	22.6
	03	287 05.3	230 11.7	. . 22.3	156 27.6	. . 50.2	353 16.3	. . 43.0	132 23.2	. . 22.5
	04	302 07.8	245 11.0	23.0	171 28.6	49.8	8 18.8	43.0	147 25.6	22.5
	05	317 10.2	260 10.3	23.8	186 29.7	49.5	23 21.4	43.0	162 28.0	22.5
	06	332 12.7	275 09.6	N19 24.6	201 30.7	N19 49.1	38 24.0	S21 43.1	177 30.4	N12 22.4
	07	347 15.1	290 08.9	25.3	216 31.8	48.7	53 26.6	43.1	192 32.8	22.4
S	08	2 17.6	305 08.2	26.1	231 32.8	48.3	68 29.2	43.1	207 35.1	22.3
A	09	17 20.1	320 07.5	. . 26.8	246 33.9	. . 47.9	83 31.8	. . 43.1	222 37.5	. . 22.3
T	10	32 22.5	335 06.8	27.6	261 34.9	47.5	98 34.4	43.2	237 39.9	22.3
U	11	47 25.0	350 06.1	28.3	276 36.0	47.1	113 36.9	43.2	252 42.3	22.2
R	12	62 27.5	5 05.4	N19 29.1	291 37.0	N19 46.7	128 39.5	S21 43.2	267 44.7	N12 22.2
D	13	77 29.9	20 04.7	29.8	306 38.0	46.3	143 42.1	43.2	282 47.0	22.2
A	14	92 32.4	35 04.0	30.6	321 39.1	46.0	158 44.7	43.3	297 49.4	22.1
Y	15	107 34.9	50 03.3	. . 31.3	336 40.1	. . 45.6	173 47.3	. . 43.3	312 51.8	. . 22.1
	16	122 37.3	65 02.6	32.1	351 41.2	45.2	188 49.9	43.3	327 54.2	22.0
	17	137 39.8	80 01.9	32.8	6 42.2	44.8	203 52.5	43.3	342 56.5	22.0
	18	152 42.3	95 01.2	N19 33.5	21 43.3	N19 44.4	218 55.0	S21 43.4	357 58.9	N12 22.0
	19	167 44.7	110 00.5	34.3	36 44.3	44.0	233 57.6	43.4	13 01.3	21.9
	20	182 47.2	124 59.8	35.0	51 45.4	43.6	249 00.2	43.4	28 03.7	21.9
	21	197 49.6	139 59.1	. . 35.8	66 46.4	. . 43.2	264 02.8	. . 43.4	43 06.0	. . 21.8
	22	212 52.1	154 58.4	36.5	81 47.5	42.8	279 05.4	43.5	58 08.4	21.8
	23	227 54.6	169 57.7	37.3	96 48.5	42.4	294 08.0	43.5	73 10.8	21.8
	25 00	242 57.0	184 57.0	N19 38.0	111 49.6	N19 42.0	309 10.6	S21 43.5	88 13.2	N12 21.7
	01	257 59.5	199 56.3	38.7	126 50.6	41.6	324 13.2	43.5	103 15.6	21.7
	02	273 02.0	214 55.6	39.5	141 51.7	41.3	339 15.8	43.6	118 17.9	21.7
	03	288 04.4	229 54.9	. . 40.2	156 52.7	. . 40.9	354 18.4	. . 43.6	133 20.3	. . 21.6
	04	303 06.9	244 54.2	40.9	171 53.8	40.5	9 21.0	43.6	148 22.7	21.6
	05	318 09.4	259 53.5	41.7	186 54.8	40.1	24 23.5	43.6	163 25.1	21.5
	06	333 11.8	274 52.8	N19 42.4	201 55.9	N19 39.7	39 26.1	S21 43.7	178 27.4	N12 21.5
	07	348 14.3	289 52.1	43.1	216 56.9	39.3	54 28.7	43.7	193 29.8	21.5
	08	3 16.8	304 51.3	43.9	231 58.0	38.9	69 31.3	43.7	208 32.2	21.4
S	09	18 19.2	319 50.6	. . 44.6	246 59.0	. . 38.5	84 33.9	. . 43.7	223 34.6	. . 21.4
U	10	33 21.7	334 49.9	45.3	262 00.1	38.1	99 36.5	43.8	238 36.9	21.3
N	11	48 24.1	349 49.2	46.1	277 01.1	37.7	114 39.1	43.8	253 39.3	21.3
D	12	63 26.6	4 48.5	N19 46.8	292 02.2	N19 37.3	129 41.7	S21 43.8	268 41.7	N12 21.3
A	13	78 29.1	19 47.8	47.5	307 03.2	36.9	144 44.3	43.8	283 44.0	21.2
Y	14	93 31.5	34 47.1	48.2	322 04.3	36.5	159 46.9	43.9	298 46.4	21.2
	15	108 34.0	49 46.4	. . 49.0	337 05.3	. . 36.1	174 49.5	. . 43.9	313 48.8	. . 21.1
	16	123 36.5	64 45.7	49.7	352 06.3	35.7	189 52.1	43.9	328 51.2	21.1
	17	138 38.9	79 45.0	50.4	7 07.4	35.3	204 54.7	43.9	343 53.5	21.1
	18	153 41.4	94 44.2	N19 51.1	22 08.4	N19 34.9	219 57.3	S21 44.0	358 55.9	N12 21.0
	19	168 43.9	109 43.5	51.9	37 09.5	34.6	234 59.9	44.0	13 58.3	21.0
	20	183 46.3	124 42.8	52.6	52 10.5	34.2	250 02.5	44.0	29 00.7	20.9
	21	198 48.8	139 42.1	. . 53.3	67 11.6	. . 33.8	265 05.1	. . 44.1	44 03.0	. . 20.9
	22	213 51.3	154 41.4	54.0	82 12.6	33.4	280 07.7	44.1	59 05.4	20.9
	23	228 53.7	169 40.7	54.7	97 13.7	33.0	295 10.3	44.1	74 07.8	20.8
	26 00	243 56.2	184 40.0	N19 55.5	112 14.7	N19 32.6	310 12.9	S21 44.1	89 10.2	N12 20.8
	01	258 58.6	199 39.2	56.2	127 15.8	32.2	325 15.4	44.2	104 12.5	20.7
	02	274 01.1	214 38.5	56.9	142 16.8	31.8	340 18.0	44.2	119 14.9	20.7
	03	289 03.6	229 37.8	. . 57.6	157 17.9	. . 31.4	355 20.6	. . 44.2	134 17.3	. . 20.7
	04	304 06.0	244 37.1	58.3	172 18.9	31.0	10 23.2	44.2	149 19.6	20.6
	05	319 08.5	259 36.4	59.0	187 20.0	30.6	25 25.8	44.3	164 22.0	20.6
	06	334 11.0	274 35.7	N19 59.7	202 21.0	N19 30.2	40 28.4	S21 44.3	179 24.4	N12 20.5
	07	349 13.4	289 34.9	20 00.4	217 22.1	29.8	55 31.0	44.3	194 26.8	20.5
	08	4 15.9	304 34.2	01.2	232 23.1	29.4	70 33.6	44.3	209 29.1	20.5
M	09	19 18.4	319 33.5	. . 01.9	247 24.2	. . 29.0	85 36.2	. . 44.4	224 31.5	. . 20.4
O	10	34 20.8	334 32.8	02.6	262 25.2	28.6	100 38.9	44.4	239 33.9	20.4
N	11	49 23.3	349 32.1	03.3	277 26.3	28.2	115 41.5	44.4	254 36.2	20.3
D	12	64 25.8	4 31.3	N20 04.0	292 27.3	N19 27.8	130 44.1	S21 44.5	269 38.6	N12 20.3
A	13	79 28.2	19 30.6	04.7	307 28.3	27.4	145 46.7	44.5	284 41.0	20.3
Y	14	94 30.7	34 29.9	05.4	322 29.4	27.0	160 49.3	44.5	299 43.3	20.2
	15	109 33.1	49 29.2	. . 06.1	337 30.4	. . 26.6	175 51.9	. . 44.5	314 45.7	. . 20.2
	16	124 35.6	64 28.5	06.8	352 31.5	26.2	190 54.5	44.6	329 48.1	20.1
	17	139 38.1	79 27.7	07.5	7 32.5	25.8	205 57.1	44.6	344 50.5	20.1
	18	154 40.5	94 27.0	N20 08.2	22 33.6	N19 25.4	220 59.7	S21 44.6	359 52.8	N12 20.1
	19	169 43.0	109 26.3	08.9	37 34.6	25.0	236 02.3	44.6	14 55.2	20.0
	20	184 45.5	124 25.6	09.6	52 35.7	24.6	251 04.9	44.7	29 57.6	20.0
	21	199 47.9	139 24.8	. . 10.3	67 36.7	. . 24.2	266 07.5	. . 44.7	44 59.9	. . 19.9
	22	214 50.4	154 24.1	11.0	82 37.8	23.8	281 10.1	44.7	60 02.3	19.9
	23	229 52.9	169 23.4	11.7	97 38.8	23.4	296 12.7	44.8	75 04.7	19.9
	Mer. Pass.	h m 7 46.9	v −0.7	d 0.7	v 1.0	d 0.4	v 2.6	d 0.0	v 2.4	d 0.0

STARS

Name	SHA	Dec
	° ′	° ′
Acamar	315 21.5	S40 16.1
Achernar	335 29.8	S57 11.4
Acrux	173 13.6	S63 09.1
Adhara	255 15.9	S28 59.1
Aldebaran	290 54.1	N16 31.6
Alioth	166 23.4	N55 55.0
Alkaid	153 01.3	N49 16.3
Al Na'ir	27 48.3	S46 55.0
Alnilam	275 50.6	S 1 11.8
Alphard	218 00.0	S 8 41.8
Alphecca	126 13.8	N26 41.1
Alpheratz	357 47.7	N29 08.1
Altair	62 11.8	N 8 53.3
Ankaa	353 19.5	S42 15.4
Antares	112 30.6	S26 27.2
Arcturus	145 58.9	N19 08.2
Atria	107 35.5	S69 02.6
Avior	234 20.1	S59 32.4
Bellatrix	278 36.4	N 6 21.5
Betelgeuse	271 05.8	N 7 24.6
Canopus	263 58.4	S52 42.1
Capella	280 40.6	N46 00.5
Deneb	49 34.0	N45 18.3
Denebola	182 37.4	N14 31.5
Diphda	348 59.9	S17 56.3
Dubhe	193 55.9	N61 42.6
Elnath	278 17.8	N28 36.9
Eltanin	90 47.4	N51 29.0
Enif	33 50.8	N 9 54.7
Fomalhaut	15 28.1	S29 34.5
Gacrux	172 05.1	S57 10.0
Gienah	175 56.1	S17 35.5
Hadar	148 53.1	S60 25.1
Hamal	328 05.5	N23 30.1
Kaus Aust.	83 48.5	S34 22.9
Kochab	137 18.3	N74 07.3
Markab	13 42.3	N15 14.9
Menkar	314 19.4	N 4 07.4
Menkent	148 11.9	S36 24.9
Miaplacidus	221 41.2	S69 45.4
Mirfak	308 46.5	N49 53.5
Nunki	76 02.7	S26 17.2
Peacock	53 24.8	S56 42.3
Pollux	243 32.6	N28 00.5
Procyon	245 04.0	N 5 12.2
Rasalhague	96 09.7	N12 33.1
Regulus	207 47.6	N11 55.6
Rigel	281 16.1	S 8 11.5
Rigil Kent.	139 56.6	S60 52.4
Sabik	102 16.6	S15 44.2
Schedar	349 45.5	N56 34.8
Shaula	96 26.7	S37 06.7
Sirius	258 37.4	S16 43.7
Spica	158 35.1	S11 12.5
Suhail	222 55.5	S43 28.2
Vega	80 41.2	N38 47.3
Zuben'ubi	137 09.4	S16 04.8

	SHA	Mer. Pass.
	° ′	h m
Venus	302 00.0	11 41
Mars	228 52.5	16 32
Jupiter	66 13.5	3 23
Saturn	205 16.1	18 04

UT		SUN GHA	SUN Dec	MOON GHA	v	MOON Dec	d	HP
d	h	° ′	° ′	° ′	′	° ′	′	′
24 SATURDAY	00	180 47.8	N20 47.9	314 15.3	10.8	S25 24.2	5.8	54.5
	01	195 47.8	48.3	328 45.1	10.9	25 18.4	6.0	54.5
	02	210 47.7	48.8	343 15.0	10.9	25 12.4	6.0	54.5
	03	225 47.6	. . 49.2	357 44.9	10.9	25 06.4	6.2	54.6
	04	240 47.6	49.7	12 14.8	11.0	25 00.2	6.3	54.6
	05	255 47.5	50.2	26 44.8	11.0	24 53.9	6.4	54.6
	06	270 47.5	N20 50.6	41 14.8	11.1	S24 47.5	6.6	54.6
	07	285 47.4	51.1	55 44.9	11.1	24 40.9	6.6	54.6
	08	300 47.3	51.5	70 15.0	11.1	24 34.3	6.8	54.6
	09	315 47.3	. . 52.0	84 45.1	11.2	24 27.5	6.9	54.7
	10	330 47.2	52.4	99 15.3	11.2	24 20.6	7.0	54.7
	11	345 47.2	52.9	113 45.5	11.3	24 13.6	7.2	54.7
	12	0 47.1	N20 53.4	128 15.8	11.3	S24 06.4	7.2	54.7
	13	15 47.0	53.8	142 46.1	11.3	23 59.2	7.4	54.7
	14	30 47.0	54.3	157 16.4	11.4	23 51.8	7.5	54.7
	15	45 46.9	. . 54.7	171 46.8	11.5	23 44.3	7.6	54.8
	16	60 46.9	55.2	186 17.3	11.5	23 36.7	7.7	54.8
	17	75 46.8	55.6	200 47.8	11.5	23 29.0	7.8	54.8
	18	90 46.7	N20 56.1	215 18.3	11.6	S23 21.2	7.9	54.8
	19	105 46.7	56.5	229 48.9	11.6	23 13.3	8.1	54.8
	20	120 46.6	57.0	244 19.5	11.7	23 05.2	8.2	54.8
	21	135 46.6	. . 57.4	258 50.2	11.7	22 57.0	8.2	54.9
	22	150 46.5	57.9	273 20.9	11.7	22 48.8	8.4	54.9
	23	165 46.4	58.3	287 51.6	11.8	22 40.4	8.5	54.9
25 SUNDAY	00	180 46.4	N20 58.7	302 22.4	11.9	S22 31.9	8.6	54.9
	01	195 46.3	59.2	316 53.3	11.9	22 23.3	8.7	54.9
	02	210 46.2	20 59.6	331 24.2	11.9	22 14.6	8.8	55.0
	03	225 46.2	21 00.1	345 55.1	12.0	22 05.8	8.9	55.0
	04	240 46.1	00.5	0 26.1	12.0	21 56.9	9.1	55.0
	05	255 46.1	01.0	14 57.1	12.1	21 47.8	9.1	55.0
	06	270 46.0	N21 01.4	29 28.2	12.1	S21 38.7	9.2	55.0
	07	285 45.9	01.9	43 59.3	12.2	21 29.5	9.4	55.1
	08	300 45.9	02.3	58 30.5	12.2	21 20.1	9.4	55.1
	09	315 45.8	. . 02.7	73 01.7	12.2	21 10.7	9.6	55.1
	10	330 45.7	03.2	87 32.9	12.3	21 01.1	9.6	55.1
	11	345 45.7	03.6	102 04.2	12.4	20 51.5	9.8	55.2
	12	0 45.6	N21 04.1	116 35.6	12.4	S20 41.7	9.8	55.2
	13	15 45.5	04.5	131 07.0	12.4	20 31.9	10.0	55.2
	14	30 45.5	04.9	145 38.4	12.5	20 21.9	10.0	55.2
	15	45 45.4	. . 05.4	160 09.9	12.5	20 11.9	10.2	55.2
	16	60 45.3	05.8	174 41.4	12.6	20 01.7	10.2	55.3
	17	75 45.3	06.2	189 13.0	12.6	19 51.5	10.3	55.3
	18	90 45.2	N21 06.7	203 44.6	12.6	S19 41.2	10.5	55.3
	19	105 45.1	07.1	218 16.2	12.7	19 30.7	10.5	55.3
	20	120 45.1	07.5	232 47.9	12.7	19 20.2	10.6	55.4
	21	135 45.0	. . 08.0	247 19.6	12.8	19 09.6	10.8	55.4
	22	150 44.9	08.4	261 51.4	12.8	18 58.8	10.8	55.4
	23	165 44.9	08.8	276 23.2	12.9	18 48.0	10.9	55.4
26 MONDAY	00	180 44.8	N21 09.3	290 55.1	12.9	S18 37.1	11.0	55.5
	01	195 44.7	09.7	305 27.0	12.9	18 26.1	11.1	55.5
	02	210 44.7	10.1	319 58.9	13.0	18 15.0	11.1	55.5
	03	225 44.6	. . 10.6	334 30.9	13.0	18 03.9	11.3	55.5
	04	240 44.5	11.0	349 02.9	13.0	17 52.6	11.4	55.6
	05	255 44.5	11.4	3 34.9	13.1	17 41.2	11.4	55.6
	06	270 44.4	N21 11.8	18 07.0	13.2	S17 29.8	11.6	55.6
	07	285 44.3	12.3	32 39.2	13.1	17 18.2	11.6	55.6
	08	300 44.3	12.7	47 11.3	13.2	17 06.6	11.7	55.7
	09	315 44.2	. . 13.1	61 43.5	13.2	16 54.9	11.8	55.7
	10	330 44.1	13.5	76 15.7	13.3	16 43.1	11.8	55.7
	11	345 44.1	14.0	90 48.0	13.3	16 31.3	12.0	55.7
	12	0 44.0	N21 14.4	105 20.3	13.4	S16 19.3	12.0	55.8
	13	15 43.9	14.8	119 52.7	13.3	16 07.3	12.2	55.8
	14	30 43.8	15.2	134 25.0	13.4	15 55.1	12.2	55.8
	15	45 43.8	. . 15.7	148 57.4	13.5	15 42.9	12.2	55.9
	16	60 43.7	16.1	163 29.9	13.4	15 30.7	12.4	55.9
	17	75 43.6	16.5	178 02.3	13.5	15 18.3	12.4	55.9
	18	90 43.6	N21 16.9	192 34.8	13.5	S15 05.9	12.6	55.9
	19	105 43.5	17.3	207 07.3	13.6	14 53.3	12.6	56.0
	20	120 43.4	17.8	221 39.9	13.6	14 40.7	12.6	56.0
	21	135 43.3	. . 18.2	236 12.5	13.6	14 28.1	12.8	56.0
	22	150 43.3	18.6	250 45.1	13.6	14 15.3	12.8	56.1
	23	165 43.2	19.0	265 17.7	13.7	S14 02.5	12.9	56.1
		SD 15.8	d 0.4	SD 14.9		15.0		15.2

Lat.	Twilight Naut.	Twilight Civil	Sunrise	Moonrise 24	Moonrise 25	Moonrise 26	Moonrise 27
°	h m	h m	h m	h m	h m	h m	h m
N 72	▭	▭	▭	■	■	04 21	02 34
N 70	▭	▭	▭	■	■	03 00	02 09
68	////	////	00 28	■	■	02 20	01 50
66	////	////	01 40	■	02 23	01 53	01 35
64	////	////	02 16	02 10	01 44	01 32	01 23
62	////	01 02	02 41	01 18	01 17	01 15	01 12
60	////	01 46	03 00	00 46	00 56	01 00	01 03
N 58	////	02 14	03 17	00 22	00 38	00 48	00 55
56	00 56	02 36	03 30	00 03	00 24	00 37	00 47
54	01 37	02 53	03 42	24 11	00 11	00 28	00 41
52	02 03	03 08	03 52	24 00	00 00	00 20	00 35
50	02 23	03 20	04 02	23 50	24 12	00 12	00 30
45	03 00	03 46	04 21	23 29	23 56	24 19	00 19
N 40	03 26	04 05	04 37	23 12	23 42	24 09	00 09
35	03 46	04 21	04 50	22 57	23 31	24 01	00 01
30	04 02	04 35	05 01	22 44	23 21	23 54	24 25
20	04 28	04 57	05 21	22 23	23 03	23 41	24 17
N 10	04 49	05 15	05 38	22 04	22 48	23 30	24 11
0	05 05	05 31	05 53	21 47	22 34	23 20	24 05
S 10	05 20	05 46	06 09	21 29	22 20	23 10	23 59
20	05 35	06 02	06 25	21 10	22 04	22 58	23 52
30	05 49	06 18	06 44	20 48	21 47	22 46	23 45
35	05 56	06 27	06 55	20 35	21 36	22 38	23 40
40	06 04	06 38	07 07	20 20	21 25	22 30	23 35
45	06 13	06 49	07 22	20 03	21 11	22 20	23 30
S 50	06 23	07 03	07 40	19 40	20 53	22 08	23 23
52	06 27	07 09	07 48	19 30	20 45	22 02	23 20
54	06 31	07 16	07 58	19 18	20 36	21 56	23 16
56	06 36	07 24	08 08	19 04	20 26	21 49	23 12
58	06 42	07 32	08 20	18 48	20 14	21 41	23 08
S 60	06 48	07 42	08 35	18 28	20 00	21 32	23 03

Lat.	Sunset	Twilight Civil	Twilight Naut.	Moonset 24	Moonset 25	Moonset 26	Moonset 27
°	h m	h m	h m	h m	h m	h m	h m
N 72	▭	▭	▭	■	■	05 30	08 54
N 70	▭	▭	▭	■	■	06 50	09 16
68	23 49	////	////	■	■	07 28	09 33
66	22 17	////	////	■	05 46	07 54	09 47
64	21 41	////	////	04 17	06 24	08 14	09 58
62	21 15	22 57	////	05 09	06 51	08 30	10 07
60	20 55	22 10	////	05 40	07 12	08 44	10 15
N 58	20 39	21 41	////	06 03	07 28	08 55	10 22
56	20 25	21 20	23 03	06 22	07 43	09 05	10 28
54	20 13	21 02	22 20	06 38	07 55	09 14	10 34
52	20 02	20 47	21 53	06 52	08 05	09 22	10 39
50	19 53	20 35	21 32	07 04	08 15	09 29	10 43
45	19 33	20 09	20 55	07 28	08 35	09 44	10 53
N 40	19 18	19 49	20 29	07 48	08 51	09 56	11 01
35	19 04	19 33	20 08	08 04	09 05	10 06	11 08
30	18 53	19 20	19 52	08 18	09 16	10 15	11 14
20	18 33	18 57	19 26	08 42	09 36	10 30	11 24
N 10	18 16	18 39	19 05	09 02	09 54	10 44	11 33
0	18 01	18 23	18 49	09 21	10 10	10 56	11 41
S 10	17 45	18 07	18 33	09 40	10 26	11 09	11 50
20	17 29	17 52	18 19	10 00	10 43	11 22	11 58
30	17 10	17 36	18 05	10 24	11 02	11 37	12 08
35	16 59	17 26	17 57	10 37	11 13	11 45	12 14
40	16 46	17 16	17 49	10 53	11 26	11 55	12 20
45	16 32	17 04	17 41	11 12	11 41	12 06	12 28
S 50	16 14	16 51	17 31	11 35	12 00	12 20	12 36
52	16 05	16 44	17 27	11 46	12 09	12 26	12 40
54	15 56	16 37	17 22	11 58	12 18	12 33	12 45
56	15 45	16 30	17 17	12 12	12 29	12 41	12 50
58	15 33	16 21	17 12	12 29	12 42	12 50	12 55
S 60	15 19	16 11	17 05	12 49	12 56	13 00	13 01

Day	SUN Eqn. of Time 00^h	SUN Eqn. of Time 12^h	SUN Mer. Pass.	MOON Mer. Pass. Upper	MOON Mer. Pass. Lower	MOON Age	MOON Phase
d	m s	m s	h m	h m	h m	d	%
24	03 11	03 09	11 57	03 09	15 34	19	83
25	03 06	03 03	11 57	03 58	16 22	20	75
26	02 59	02 56	11 57	04 45	17 08	21	66

	UT	ARIES	VENUS −3.9		MARS +1.5		JUPITER −2.6		SATURN +0.7		STARS		
		GHA	GHA	Dec	GHA	Dec	GHA	Dec	GHA	Dec	Name	SHA	Dec
	d h	° ′	° ′	° ′	° ′	° ′	° ′	° ′	° ′	° ′		° ′	° ′
	27 00	244 55.3	184 22.7	N20 12.4	112 39.9	N19 23.0	311 15.3	S21 44.8	90 07.0	N12 19.8	Acamar	315 21.5	S40 16.1
	01	259 57.8	199 21.9	13.1	127 40.9	22.6	326 17.9	44.8	105 09.4	19.8	Achernar	335 29.8	S57 11.4
	02	275 00.2	214 21.2	13.8	142 42.0	22.2	341 20.5	44.8	120 11.8	19.7	Acrux	173 13.6	S63 09.1
	03	290 02.7	229 20.5	. . 14.5	157 43.0	. . 21.8	356 23.1	. . 44.9	135 14.1	. . 19.7	Adhara	255 15.9	S28 59.1
	04	305 05.2	244 19.7	15.1	172 44.1	21.4	11 25.7	44.9	150 16.5	19.6	Aldebaran	290 54.1	N16 31.6
	05	320 07.6	259 19.0	15.8	187 45.1	21.0	26 28.3	44.9	165 18.9	19.6			
	06	335 10.1	274 18.3	N20 16.5	202 46.1	N19 20.6	41 30.9	S21 44.9	180 21.2	N12 19.6	Alioth	166 23.4	N55 55.0
	07	350 12.6	289 17.6	17.2	217 47.2	20.2	56 33.6	45.0	195 23.6	19.5	Alkaid	153 01.3	N49 16.3
T	08	5 15.0	304 16.8	17.9	232 48.2	19.8	71 36.2	45.0	210 26.0	19.5	Al Na'ir	27 48.3	S46 55.0
U	09	20 17.5	319 16.1	. . 18.6	247 49.3	. . 19.4	86 38.8	. . 45.0	225 28.3	. . 19.4	Alnilam	275 50.6	S 1 11.8
E	10	35 20.0	334 15.4	19.3	262 50.3	19.0	101 41.4	45.1	240 30.7	19.4	Alphard	218 00.0	S 8 41.8
S	11	50 22.4	349 14.6	19.9	277 51.4	18.5	116 44.0	45.1	255 33.1	19.4			
D	12	65 24.9	4 13.9	N20 20.6	292 52.4	N19 18.1	131 46.6	S21 45.1	270 35.4	N12 19.3	Alphecca	126 13.8	N26 41.1
A	13	80 27.4	19 13.2	21.3	307 53.5	17.7	146 49.2	45.1	285 37.8	19.3	Alpheratz	357 47.7	N29 08.1
Y	14	95 29.8	34 12.4	22.0	322 54.5	17.3	161 51.8	45.2	300 40.2	19.2	Altair	62 11.8	N 8 53.3
	15	110 32.3	49 11.7	. . 22.7	337 55.6	. . 16.9	176 54.4	. . 45.2	315 42.5	. . 19.2	Ankaa	353 19.5	S42 15.4
	16	125 34.7	64 11.0	23.4	352 56.6	16.5	191 57.0	45.2	330 44.9	19.1	Antares	112 30.6	S26 27.2
	17	140 37.2	79 10.2	24.0	7 57.7	16.1	206 59.7	45.3	345 47.3	19.1			
	18	155 39.7	94 09.5	N20 24.7	22 58.7	N19 15.7	222 02.3	S21 45.3	0 49.6	N12 19.1	Arcturus	145 58.9	N19 08.2
	19	170 42.1	109 08.8	25.4	37 59.8	15.3	237 04.9	45.3	15 52.0	19.0	Atria	107 35.4	S69 02.7
	20	185 44.6	124 08.0	26.1	53 00.8	14.9	252 07.5	45.3	30 54.4	19.0	Avior	234 20.1	S59 32.4
	21	200 47.1	139 07.3	. . 26.7	68 01.9	. . 14.5	267 10.1	. . 45.4	45 56.7	. . 18.9	Bellatrix	278 36.4	N 6 21.5
	22	215 49.5	154 06.6	27.4	83 02.9	14.1	282 12.7	45.4	60 59.1	18.9	Betelgeuse	271 05.8	N 7 24.6
	23	230 52.0	169 05.8	28.1	98 03.9	13.7	297 15.3	45.4	76 01.5	18.8			
	28 00	245 54.5	184 05.1	N20 28.7	113 05.0	N19 13.3	312 17.9	S21 45.5	91 03.8	N12 18.8	Canopus	263 58.4	S52 42.1
	01	260 56.9	199 04.3	29.4	128 06.0	12.9	327 20.6	45.5	106 06.2	18.8	Capella	280 40.6	N46 00.5
	02	275 59.4	214 03.6	30.1	143 07.1	12.5	342 23.2	45.5	121 08.5	18.7	Deneb	49 34.0	N45 18.3
	03	291 01.9	229 02.9	. . 30.8	158 08.1	. . 12.1	357 25.8	. . 45.5	136 10.9	. . 18.7	Denebola	182 37.4	N14 31.5
	04	306 04.3	244 02.1	31.4	173 09.2	11.7	12 28.4	45.6	151 13.3	18.6	Diphda	348 59.8	S17 56.3
	05	321 06.8	259 01.4	32.1	188 10.2	11.2	27 31.0	45.6	166 15.6	18.6			
	06	336 09.2	274 00.6	N20 32.8	203 11.3	N19 10.8	42 33.6	S21 45.6	181 18.0	N12 18.5	Dubhe	193 55.9	N61 42.6
W	07	351 11.7	288 59.9	33.4	218 12.3	10.4	57 36.3	45.7	196 20.4	18.5	Elnath	278 17.8	N28 36.9
E	08	6 14.2	303 59.2	34.1	233 13.4	10.0	72 38.9	45.7	211 22.7	18.5	Eltanin	90 47.4	N51 29.0
D	09	21 16.6	318 58.4	. . 34.7	248 14.4	. . 09.6	87 41.5	. . 45.7	226 25.1	. . 18.4	Enif	33 50.8	N 9 54.7
N	10	36 19.1	333 57.7	35.4	263 15.5	09.2	102 44.1	45.7	241 27.5	18.4	Fomalhaut	15 28.1	S29 34.5
E	11	51 21.6	348 56.9	36.1	278 16.5	08.8	117 46.7	45.8	256 29.8	18.3			
S	12	66 24.0	3 56.2	N20 36.7	293 17.6	N19 08.4	132 49.3	S21 45.8	271 32.2	N12 18.3	Gacrux	172 05.2	S57 10.0
D	13	81 26.5	18 55.4	37.4	308 18.6	08.0	147 52.0	45.8	286 34.5	18.2	Gienah	175 56.1	S17 35.5
A	14	96 29.0	33 54.7	38.0	323 19.6	07.6	162 54.6	45.9	301 36.9	18.2	Hadar	148 53.1	S60 25.1
Y	15	111 31.4	48 54.0	. . 38.7	338 20.7	. . 07.2	177 57.2	. . 45.9	316 39.3	. . 18.1	Hamal	328 05.4	N23 30.1
	16	126 33.9	63 53.2	39.4	353 21.7	06.7	192 59.8	45.9	331 41.6	18.1	Kaus Aust.	83 48.5	S34 22.9
	17	141 36.3	78 52.5	40.0	8 22.8	06.3	208 02.4	45.9	346 44.0	18.1			
	18	156 38.8	93 51.7	N20 40.7	23 23.8	N19 05.9	223 05.1	S21 46.0	1 46.4	N12 18.0	Kochab	137 18.3	N74 07.3
	19	171 41.3	108 51.0	41.3	38 24.9	05.5	238 07.7	46.0	16 48.7	18.0	Markab	13 42.2	N15 14.9
	20	186 43.7	123 50.2	42.0	53 25.9	05.1	253 10.3	46.0	31 51.1	17.9	Menkar	314 19.4	N 4 07.4
	21	201 46.2	138 49.5	. . 42.6	68 27.0	. . 04.7	268 12.9	. . 46.1	46 53.4	. . 17.9	Menkent	148 11.9	S36 24.9
	22	216 48.7	153 48.7	43.3	83 28.0	04.3	283 15.5	46.1	61 55.8	17.8	Miaplacidus	221 41.2	S69 45.4
	23	231 51.1	168 48.0	43.9	98 29.1	03.9	298 18.2	46.1	76 58.2	17.8			
	29 00	246 53.6	183 47.2	N20 44.6	113 30.1	N19 03.5	313 20.8	S21 46.2	92 00.5	N12 17.8	Mirfak	308 46.5	N49 53.4
	01	261 56.1	198 46.5	45.2	128 31.2	03.1	328 23.4	46.2	107 02.9	17.7	Nunki	76 02.7	S26 17.2
	02	276 58.5	213 45.7	45.9	143 32.2	02.6	343 26.0	46.2	122 05.2	17.7	Peacock	53 24.7	S56 42.3
	03	292 01.0	228 45.0	. . 46.5	158 33.2	. . 02.2	358 28.6	. . 46.2	137 07.6	. . 17.6	Pollux	243 32.6	N28 00.5
	04	307 03.5	243 44.2	47.1	173 34.3	01.8	13 31.3	46.3	152 10.0	17.6	Procyon	245 04.0	N 5 12.2
	05	322 05.9	258 43.5	47.8	188 35.3	01.4	28 33.9	46.3	167 12.3	17.5			
	06	337 08.4	273 42.7	N20 48.4	203 36.4	N19 01.0	43 36.5	S21 46.3	182 14.7	N12 17.5	Rasalhague	96 09.7	N12 33.1
	07	352 10.8	288 42.0	49.1	218 37.4	00.6	58 39.1	46.4	197 17.0	17.4	Regulus	207 47.6	N11 55.6
T	08	7 13.3	303 41.2	49.7	233 38.5	19 00.2	73 41.8	46.4	212 19.4	17.4	Rigel	281 16.1	S 8 11.5
H	09	22 15.8	318 40.5	. . 50.3	248 39.5	18 59.8	88 44.4	. . 46.4	227 21.8	. . 17.4	Rigil Kent.	139 56.6	S60 52.4
U	10	37 18.2	333 39.7	51.0	263 40.6	59.3	103 47.0	46.5	242 24.1	17.3	Sabik	102 16.6	S15 44.2
R	11	52 20.7	348 39.0	51.6	278 41.6	58.9	118 49.6	46.5	257 26.5	17.3			
S	12	67 23.2	3 38.2	N20 52.3	293 42.7	N18 58.5	133 52.3	S21 46.5	272 28.8	N12 17.2	Schedar	349 45.5	N56 34.8
D	13	82 25.6	18 37.5	52.9	308 43.7	58.1	148 54.9	46.5	287 31.2	17.2	Shaula	96 26.7	S37 06.7
A	14	97 28.1	33 36.7	53.5	323 44.8	57.7	163 57.5	46.6	302 33.5	17.1	Sirius	258 37.4	S16 43.7
Y	15	112 30.6	48 35.9	. . 54.2	338 45.8	. . 57.3	179 00.1	. . 46.6	317 35.9	. . 17.1	Spica	158 35.1	S11 12.5
	16	127 33.0	63 35.2	54.8	353 46.8	56.9	194 02.8	46.6	332 38.3	17.0	Suhail	222 55.6	S43 28.2
	17	142 35.5	78 34.4	55.4	8 47.9	56.4	209 05.4	46.7	347 40.6	17.0			
	18	157 37.9	93 33.7	N20 56.1	23 48.9	N18 56.0	224 08.0	S21 46.7	2 43.0	N12 16.9	Vega	80 41.2	N38 47.3
	19	172 40.4	108 32.9	56.7	38 50.0	55.6	239 10.7	46.7	17 45.3	16.9	Zuben'ubi	137 09.4	S16 04.8
	20	187 42.9	123 32.2	57.3	53 51.0	55.2	254 13.3	46.8	32 47.7	16.9			
	21	202 45.3	138 31.4	. . 57.9	68 52.1	. . 54.8	269 15.9	. . 46.8	47 50.1	. . 16.8			
	22	217 47.8	153 30.6	58.6	83 53.1	54.4	284 18.5	46.8	62 52.4	16.8			
	23	232 50.3	168 29.9	59.2	98 54.2	54.0	299 21.2	46.9	77 54.8	16.7			
	Mer. Pass.	h m 7 35.1	v −0.7	d 0.7	v 1.0	d 0.4	v 2.6	d 0.0	v 2.4	d 0.0			

	SHA	Mer. Pass.
	° ′	h m
Venus	298 10.6	11 44
Mars	227 10.5	16 27
Jupiter	66 23.5	3 10
Saturn	205 09.4	17 53

UT		SUN GHA	SUN Dec	MOON GHA	v	Dec	d	HP
d h		° ′	° ′	° ′	′	° ′	′	′
27 00		180 43.1	N21 19.4	279 50.4	13.6	S13 49.6	13.0	56.1
01		195 43.0	19.8	294 23.0	13.8	13 36.6	13.0	56.1
02		210 43.0	20.3	308 55.8	13.7	13 23.6	13.1	56.2
03		225 42.9	. . 20.7	323 28.5	13.7	13 10.5	13.2	56.2
04		240 42.8	21.1	338 01.2	13.8	12 57.3	13.3	56.2
05		255 42.8	21.5	352 34.0	13.8	12 44.0	13.3	56.3
06		270 42.7	N21 21.9	7 06.8	13.8	S12 30.7	13.4	56.3
07		285 42.6	22.3	21 39.6	13.8	12 17.3	13.5	56.3
08	T	300 42.5	22.7	36 12.4	13.9	12 03.8	13.5	56.4
09	U	315 42.5	. . 23.1	50 45.3	13.8	11 50.3	13.6	56.4
10	E	330 42.4	23.5	65 18.1	13.9	11 36.7	13.6	56.4
11	S	345 42.3	24.0	79 51.0	13.9	11 23.1	13.8	56.5
12	D	0 42.2	N21 24.4	94 23.9	13.9	S11 09.3	13.8	56.5
13		15 42.2	24.8	108 56.8	13.9	10 55.5	13.8	56.5
14	A	30 42.1	25.2	123 29.7	14.0	10 41.7	13.9	56.6
15	Y	45 42.0	. . 25.6	138 02.7	13.9	10 27.8	14.0	56.6
16		60 41.9	26.0	152 35.6	14.0	10 13.8	14.0	56.6
17		75 41.9	26.4	167 08.6	13.9	9 59.8	14.1	56.7
18		90 41.8	N21 26.8	181 41.5	14.0	S 9 45.7	14.2	56.7
19		105 41.7	27.2	196 14.5	13.9	9 31.5	14.2	56.7
20		120 41.6	27.6	210 47.4	14.0	9 17.3	14.3	56.8
21		135 41.5	. . 28.0	225 20.4	14.0	9 03.0	14.3	56.8
22		150 41.5	28.4	239 53.4	14.0	8 48.7	14.4	56.8
23		165 41.4	28.8	254 26.4	14.0	8 34.3	14.4	56.9
28 00		180 41.3	N21 29.2	268 59.4	14.0	S 8 19.9	14.5	56.9
01		195 41.2	29.6	283 32.4	13.9	8 05.4	14.6	56.9
02		210 41.2	30.0	298 05.3	14.0	7 50.8	14.6	57.0
03		225 41.1	. . 30.4	312 38.3	14.0	7 36.2	14.6	57.0
04		240 41.0	30.8	327 11.3	14.0	7 21.6	14.7	57.0
05		255 40.9	31.2	341 44.3	14.0	7 06.9	14.7	57.1
06		270 40.8	N21 31.6	356 17.3	13.9	S 6 52.2	14.8	57.1
07	W	285 40.8	32.0	10 50.2	14.0	6 37.4	14.9	57.1
08	E	300 40.7	32.4	25 23.2	13.9	6 22.5	14.9	57.2
09	D	315 40.6	. . 32.8	39 56.1	14.0	6 07.6	14.9	57.2
10	N	330 40.5	33.2	54 29.1	13.9	5 52.7	15.0	57.2
11	E	345 40.4	33.6	69 02.0	13.9	5 37.7	15.0	57.3
12	S	0 40.4	N21 34.0	83 34.9	13.9	S 5 22.7	15.1	57.3
13	D	15 40.3	34.4	98 07.8	13.9	5 07.6	15.1	57.4
14	A	30 40.2	34.7	112 40.7	13.9	4 52.5	15.1	57.4
15	Y	45 40.1	. . 35.1	127 13.6	13.8	4 37.4	15.2	57.4
16		60 40.0	35.5	141 46.4	13.9	4 22.2	15.2	57.5
17		75 40.0	35.9	156 19.3	13.8	4 07.0	15.3	57.5
18		90 39.9	N21 36.3	170 52.1	13.8	S 3 51.7	15.3	57.5
19		105 39.8	36.7	185 24.9	13.8	3 36.4	15.3	57.6
20		120 39.7	37.1	199 57.7	13.7	3 21.1	15.4	57.6
21		135 39.6	. . 37.5	214 30.4	13.8	3 05.7	15.4	57.6
22		150 39.5	37.9	229 03.2	13.7	2 50.3	15.5	57.7
23		165 39.5	38.2	243 35.9	13.6	2 34.8	15.4	57.7
29 00		180 39.4	N21 38.6	258 08.5	13.7	S 2 19.4	15.5	57.8
01		195 39.3	39.0	272 41.2	13.6	2 03.9	15.6	57.8
02		210 39.2	39.4	287 13.8	13.6	1 48.3	15.5	57.8
03		225 39.1	. . 39.8	301 46.4	13.5	1 32.8	15.6	57.9
04		240 39.0	40.2	316 18.9	13.5	1 17.2	15.6	57.9
05		255 39.0	40.5	330 51.4	13.5	1 01.6	15.7	57.9
06		270 38.9	N21 40.9	345 23.9	13.5	S 0 45.9	15.7	58.0
07	T	285 38.8	41.3	359 56.4	13.4	0 30.2	15.6	58.0
08	H	300 38.7	41.7	14 28.8	13.3	S 0 14.6	15.8	58.1
09	U	315 38.6	. . 42.1	29 01.1	13.4	N 0 01.2	15.7	58.1
10	R	330 38.5	42.4	43 33.5	13.3	0 16.9	15.7	58.1
11	S	345 38.5	42.8	58 05.8	13.2	0 32.6	15.8	58.2
12	D	0 38.4	N21 43.2	72 38.0	13.2	N 0 48.4	15.8	58.2
13	A	15 38.3	43.6	87 10.2	13.1	1 04.2	15.8	58.3
14	Y	30 38.2	43.9	101 42.3	13.1	1 20.0	15.8	58.3
15		45 38.1	. . 44.3	116 14.4	13.1	1 35.8	15.9	58.3
16		60 38.0	44.7	130 46.5	13.0	1 51.7	15.8	58.4
17		75 37.9	45.1	145 18.5	12.9	2 07.5	15.9	58.4
18		90 37.9	N21 45.4	159 50.4	12.9	N 2 23.4	15.8	58.4
19		105 37.8	45.8	174 22.3	12.9	2 39.2	15.9	58.5
20		120 37.7	46.2	188 54.2	12.8	2 55.1	15.9	58.5
21		135 37.6	. . 46.6	203 26.0	12.7	3 11.0	15.9	58.6
22		150 37.5	46.9	217 57.7	12.7	3 26.9	15.9	58.6
23		165 37.4	47.3	232 29.4	12.6	N 3 42.8	15.9	58.6
		SD 15.8	*d* 0.4	SD	15.4	15.6		15.9

Lat.	Twilight Naut.	Twilight Civil	Sunrise	Moonrise 27	Moonrise 28	Moonrise 29	Moonrise 30
°	h m	h m	h m	h m	h m	h m	h m
N 72	▭	▭	▭	02 34	01 50	01 16	00 43
N 70	▭	▭	▭	02 09	01 39	01 13	00 49
68	▭	▭	▭	01 50	01 29	01 11	00 53
66	////	////	01 28	01 35	01 21	01 09	00 57
64	////	////	02 07	01 23	01 15	01 07	01 00
62	////	00 43	02 34	01 12	01 09	01 06	01 03
60	////	01 37	02 55	01 03	01 04	01 05	01 05
N 58	////	02 08	03 12	00 55	00 59	01 03	01 08
56	00 39	02 30	03 26	00 47	00 55	01 02	01 10
54	01 28	02 49	03 39	00 41	00 52	01 02	01 11
52	01 57	03 04	03 49	00 35	00 48	01 01	01 13
50	02 18	03 17	03 59	00 30	00 45	01 00	01 15
45	02 56	03 43	04 19	00 19	00 39	00 58	01 18
N 40	03 23	04 03	04 35	00 09	00 33	00 57	01 21
35	03 44	04 20	04 49	00 01	00 29	00 56	01 23
30	04 01	04 34	05 00	24 25	00 25	00 55	01 25
20	04 28	04 56	05 20	24 17	00 17	00 53	01 29
N 10	04 48	05 15	05 38	24 11	00 11	00 51	01 32
0	05 06	05 31	05 54	24 05	00 05	00 49	01 36
S 10	05 21	05 47	06 10	23 59	24 48	00 48	01 39
20	05 36	06 03	06 26	23 52	24 46	00 46	01 42
30	05 50	06 20	06 46	23 45	24 44	00 44	01 46
35	05 58	06 29	06 57	23 40	24 43	00 43	01 49
40	06 06	06 40	07 10	23 35	24 42	00 42	01 51
45	06 15	06 52	07 25	23 30	24 41	00 41	01 54
S 50	06 25	07 06	07 43	23 23	24 39	00 39	01 58
52	06 30	07 13	07 52	23 20	24 38	00 38	02 00
54	06 35	07 20	08 02	23 16	24 38	00 38	02 02
56	06 40	07 28	08 13	23 12	24 37	00 37	02 04
58	06 46	07 37	08 25	23 08	24 36	00 36	02 06
S 60	06 52	07 47	08 40	23 03	24 34	00 34	02 09

Lat.	Sunset	Twilight Civil	Twilight Naut.	Moonset 27	Moonset 28	Moonset 29	Moonset 30
°	h m	h m	h m	h m	h m	h m	h m
N 72	▭	▭	▭	08 54	11 13	13 25	15 45
N 70	▭	▭	▭	09 16	11 21	13 23	15 32
68	▭	▭	▭	09 33	11 28	13 22	15 22
66	22 31	////	////	09 47	11 34	13 21	15 13
64	21 50	////	////	09 58	11 39	13 20	15 06
62	21 22	23 19	////	10 07	11 43	13 19	15 00
60	21 01	22 20	////	10 15	11 46	13 19	14 55
N 58	20 44	21 49	////	10 22	11 49	13 18	14 51
56	20 29	21 26	23 22	10 28	11 52	13 18	14 47
54	20 17	21 07	22 29	10 34	11 55	13 17	14 43
52	20 06	20 52	22 00	10 39	11 57	13 17	14 40
50	19 56	20 39	21 38	10 43	11 59	13 16	14 37
45	19 36	20 12	20 59	10 53	12 03	13 16	14 31
N 40	19 20	19 52	20 32	11 01	12 07	13 15	14 25
35	19 06	19 35	20 11	11 08	12 10	13 14	14 21
30	18 54	19 21	19 54	11 14	12 13	13 14	14 17
20	18 34	18 59	19 27	11 24	12 18	13 13	14 10
N 10	18 17	18 40	19 06	11 33	12 22	13 12	14 04
0	18 01	18 23	18 49	11 41	12 26	13 11	13 58
S 10	17 45	18 08	18 34	11 50	12 30	13 10	13 53
20	17 28	17 52	18 19	11 58	12 34	13 09	13 47
30	17 09	17 35	18 04	12 08	12 38	13 08	13 40
35	16 58	17 25	17 56	12 14	12 41	13 08	13 36
40	16 45	17 15	17 48	12 20	12 44	13 07	13 32
45	16 30	17 03	17 39	12 28	12 47	13 06	13 27
S 50	16 11	16 48	17 29	12 36	12 51	13 05	13 21
52	16 02	16 42	17 24	12 40	12 53	13 05	13 18
54	15 53	16 35	17 19	12 45	12 55	13 05	13 15
56	15 41	16 27	17 14	12 50	12 57	13 04	13 11
58	15 29	16 18	17 08	12 55	13 00	13 03	13 08
S 60	15 14	16 08	17 02	13 01	13 02	13 03	13 04

Day	SUN Eqn. of Time 00^h	SUN Eqn. of Time 12^h	SUN Mer. Pass.	MOON Mer. Pass. Upper	MOON Mer. Pass. Lower	MOON Age	MOON Phase
d	m s	m s	h m	h m	h m	d %	
27	02 53	02 49	11 57	05 31	17 53	22 57	
28	02 45	02 42	11 57	06 15	18 38	23 46	◑
29	02 38	02 34	11 57	07 00	19 23	24 35	

UT (d h)	ARIES GHA ° ′	VENUS −4.0 GHA ° ′	VENUS Dec ° ′	MARS +1.5 GHA ° ′	MARS Dec ° ′	JUPITER −2.6 GHA ° ′	JUPITER Dec ° ′	SATURN +0.7 GHA ° ′	SATURN Dec ° ′
30 00 FRIDAY	247 52.7	183 29.1	N20 59.8	113 55.2	N18 53.5	314 23.8	S21 46.9	92 57.1	N12 16.7
01	262 55.2	198 28.4	21 00.4	128 56.3	53.1	329 26.4	46.9	107 59.5	16.6
02	277 57.7	213 27.6	01.1	143 57.3	52.7	344 29.1	46.9	123 01.8	16.6
03	293 00.1	228 26.8	01.7	158 58.3	52.3	359 31.7	47.0	138 04.2	16.5
04	308 02.6	243 26.1	02.3	173 59.4	51.9	14 34.3	47.0	153 06.5	16.5
05	323 05.1	258 25.3	02.9	189 00.4	51.5	29 36.9	47.0	168 08.9	16.4
06	338 07.5	273 24.6	N21 03.5	204 01.5	N18 51.0	44 39.6	S21 47.1	183 11.3	N12 16.4
07	353 10.0	288 23.8	04.2	219 02.5	50.6	59 42.2	47.1	198 13.6	16.3
08	8 12.4	303 23.0	04.8	234 03.6	50.2	74 44.8	47.1	213 16.0	16.3
09	23 14.9	318 22.3	05.4	249 04.6	49.8	89 47.5	47.2	228 18.3	16.3
10	38 17.4	333 21.5	06.0	264 05.7	49.4	104 50.1	47.2	243 20.7	16.2
11	53 19.8	348 20.7	06.6	279 06.7	48.9	119 52.7	47.2	258 23.0	16.2
12	68 22.3	3 20.0	N21 07.2	294 07.8	N18 48.5	134 55.4	S21 47.3	273 25.4	N12 16.1
13	83 24.8	18 19.2	07.8	309 08.8	48.1	149 58.0	47.3	288 27.7	16.1
14	98 27.2	33 18.4	08.4	324 09.9	47.7	165 00.6	47.3	303 30.1	16.0
15	113 29.7	48 17.7	09.1	339 10.9	47.3	180 03.3	47.3	318 32.5	16.0
16	128 32.2	63 16.9	09.7	354 11.9	46.9	195 05.9	47.4	333 34.8	15.9
17	143 34.6	78 16.1	10.3	9 13.0	46.4	210 08.5	47.4	348 37.2	15.9
18	158 37.1	93 15.4	N21 10.9	24 14.0	N18 46.0	225 11.2	S21 47.4	3 39.5	N12 15.8
19	173 39.6	108 14.6	11.5	39 15.1	45.6	240 13.8	47.5	18 41.9	15.8
20	188 42.0	123 13.8	12.1	54 16.1	45.2	255 16.4	47.5	33 44.2	15.7
21	203 44.5	138 13.1	12.7	69 17.2	44.8	270 19.1	47.5	48 46.6	15.7
22	218 46.9	153 12.3	13.3	84 18.2	44.3	285 21.7	47.6	63 48.9	15.6
23	233 49.4	168 11.5	13.9	99 19.3	43.9	300 24.4	47.6	78 51.3	15.6
31 00 SATURDAY	248 51.9	183 10.8	N21 14.5	114 20.3	N18 43.5	315 27.0	S21 47.6	93 53.6	N12 15.6
01	263 54.3	198 10.0	15.1	129 21.4	43.1	330 29.6	47.7	108 56.0	15.5
02	278 56.8	213 09.2	15.7	144 22.4	42.7	345 32.3	47.7	123 58.3	15.5
03	293 59.3	228 08.4	16.3	159 23.4	42.2	0 34.9	47.7	139 00.7	15.4
04	309 01.7	243 07.7	16.9	174 24.5	41.8	15 37.5	47.8	154 03.0	15.4
05	324 04.2	258 06.9	17.5	189 25.5	41.4	30 40.2	47.8	169 05.4	15.3
06	339 06.7	273 06.1	N21 18.1	204 26.6	N18 41.0	45 42.8	S21 47.8	184 07.8	N12 15.3
07	354 09.1	288 05.3	18.7	219 27.6	40.5	60 45.5	47.9	199 10.1	15.2
08	9 11.6	303 04.6	19.2	234 28.7	40.1	75 48.1	47.9	214 12.5	15.2
09	24 14.0	318 03.8	19.8	249 29.7	39.7	90 50.7	47.9	229 14.8	15.1
10	39 16.5	333 03.0	20.4	264 30.8	39.3	105 53.4	48.0	244 17.2	15.1
11	54 19.0	348 02.2	21.0	279 31.8	38.9	120 56.0	48.0	259 19.5	15.0
12	69 21.4	3 01.5	N21 21.6	294 32.9	N18 38.4	135 58.7	S21 48.0	274 21.9	N12 15.0
13	84 23.9	18 00.7	22.2	309 33.9	38.0	151 01.3	48.1	289 24.2	14.9
14	99 26.4	32 59.9	22.8	324 34.9	37.6	166 03.9	48.1	304 26.6	14.9
15	114 28.8	47 59.1	23.4	339 36.0	37.2	181 06.6	48.1	319 28.9	14.8
16	129 31.3	62 58.4	23.9	354 37.0	36.7	196 09.2	48.2	334 31.3	14.8
17	144 33.8	77 57.6	24.5	9 38.1	36.3	211 11.9	48.2	349 33.6	14.7
18	159 36.2	92 56.8	N21 25.1	24 39.1	N18 35.9	226 14.5	S21 48.2	4 36.0	N12 14.7
19	174 38.7	107 56.0	25.7	39 40.2	35.5	241 17.2	48.2	19 38.3	14.6
20	189 41.2	122 55.3	26.3	54 41.2	35.0	256 19.8	48.3	34 40.7	14.6
21	204 43.6	137 54.5	26.8	69 42.3	34.6	271 22.4	48.3	49 43.0	14.6
22	219 46.1	152 53.7	27.4	84 43.3	34.2	286 25.1	48.3	64 45.4	14.5
23	234 48.5	167 52.9	28.0	99 44.4	33.8	301 27.7	48.4	79 47.7	14.5
1 00 SUNDAY	249 51.0	182 52.1	N21 28.6	114 45.4	N18 33.3	316 30.4	S21 48.4	94 50.1	N12 14.4
01	264 53.5	197 51.4	29.1	129 46.4	32.9	331 33.0	48.4	109 52.4	14.4
02	279 55.9	212 50.6	29.7	144 47.5	32.5	346 35.7	48.5	124 54.8	14.3
03	294 58.4	227 49.8	30.3	159 48.5	32.1	1 38.3	48.5	139 57.1	14.3
04	310 00.9	242 49.0	30.9	174 49.6	31.6	16 41.0	48.5	154 59.5	14.2
05	325 03.3	257 48.2	31.4	189 50.6	31.2	31 43.6	48.6	170 01.8	14.2
06	340 05.8	272 47.4	N21 32.0	204 51.7	N18 30.8	46 46.2	S21 48.6	185 04.2	N12 14.1
07	355 08.3	287 46.7	32.6	219 52.7	30.4	61 48.9	48.6	200 06.5	14.1
08	10 10.7	302 45.9	33.1	234 53.8	29.9	76 51.5	48.7	215 08.9	14.0
09	25 13.2	317 45.1	33.7	249 54.8	29.5	91 54.2	48.7	230 11.2	14.0
10	40 15.7	332 44.3	34.3	264 55.8	29.1	106 56.8	48.7	245 13.5	13.9
11	55 18.1	347 43.5	34.8	279 56.9	28.6	121 59.5	48.8	260 15.9	13.9
12	70 20.6	2 42.7	N21 35.4	294 57.9	N18 28.2	137 02.1	S21 48.8	275 18.2	N12 13.8
13	85 23.0	17 41.9	35.9	309 59.0	27.8	152 04.8	48.8	290 20.6	13.8
14	100 25.5	32 41.2	36.5	325 00.0	27.4	167 07.4	48.9	305 22.9	13.7
15	115 28.0	47 40.4	37.1	340 01.1	26.9	182 10.1	48.9	320 25.3	13.7
16	130 30.4	62 39.6	37.6	355 02.1	26.5	197 12.7	48.9	335 27.6	13.6
17	145 32.9	77 38.8	38.2	10 03.2	26.1	212 15.4	49.0	350 30.0	13.6
18	160 35.4	92 38.0	N21 38.7	25 04.2	N18 25.6	227 18.0	S21 49.0	5 32.3	N12 13.5
19	175 37.8	107 37.2	39.3	40 05.3	25.2	242 20.7	49.0	20 34.7	13.5
20	190 40.3	122 36.4	39.8	55 06.3	24.8	257 23.3	49.1	35 37.0	13.4
21	205 42.8	137 35.6	40.4	70 07.3	24.4	272 26.0	49.1	50 39.4	13.4
22	220 45.2	152 34.8	40.9	85 08.4	23.9	287 28.6	49.1	65 41.7	13.3
23	235 47.7	167 34.1	41.5	100 09.4	23.5	302 31.3	49.2	80 44.1	13.3
Mer. Pass. (h m)	7 23.3	*v* −0.8	*d* 0.6	*v* 1.0	*d* 0.4	*v* 2.6	*d* 0.0	*v* 2.4	*d* 0.0

STARS

Name	SHA ° ′	Dec ° ′
Acamar	315 21.5	S40 16.1
Achernar	335 29.8	S57 11.4
Acrux	173 13.6	S63 09.1
Adhara	255 15.9	S28 59.1
Aldebaran	290 54.1	N16 31.6
Alioth	166 23.4	N55 55.0
Alkaid	153 01.3	N49 16.3
Al Na'ir	27 48.2	S46 55.0
Alnilam	275 50.6	S 1 11.8
Alphard	218 00.0	S 8 41.8
Alphecca	126 13.8	N26 41.1
Alpheratz	357 47.7	N29 08.1
Altair	62 11.7	N 8 53.3
Ankaa	353 19.5	S42 15.4
Antares	112 30.6	S26 27.2
Arcturus	145 58.9	N19 08.2
Atria	107 35.4	S69 02.7
Avior	234 20.2	S59 32.4
Bellatrix	278 36.4	N 6 21.5
Betelgeuse	271 05.8	N 7 24.6
Canopus	263 58.4	S52 42.1
Capella	280 40.6	N46 00.5
Deneb	49 34.0	N45 18.4
Denebola	182 37.4	N14 31.5
Diphda	348 59.8	S17 56.3
Dubhe	193 56.0	N61 42.6
Elnath	278 17.8	N28 36.9
Eltanin	90 47.4	N51 29.1
Enif	33 50.8	N 9 54.7
Fomalhaut	15 28.1	S29 34.5
Gacrux	172 05.2	S57 10.0
Gienah	175 56.2	S17 35.5
Hadar	148 53.1	S60 25.1
Hamal	328 05.4	N23 30.1
Kaus Aust.	83 48.5	S34 22.9
Kochab	137 18.3	N74 07.3
Markab	13 42.2	N15 14.9
Menkar	314 19.4	N 4 07.4
Menkent	148 11.9	S36 24.9
Miaplacidus	221 41.2	S69 45.4
Mirfak	308 46.5	N49 53.4
Nunki	76 02.7	S26 17.2
Peacock	53 24.7	S56 42.3
Pollux	243 32.6	N28 00.5
Procyon	245 04.0	N 5 12.2
Rasalhague	96 09.7	N12 33.1
Regulus	207 47.6	N11 55.6
Rigel	281 16.1	S 8 11.5
Rigil Kent.	139 56.7	S60 52.4
Sabik	102 16.6	S15 44.2
Schedar	349 45.5	N56 34.8
Shaula	96 26.7	S37 06.7
Sirius	258 37.4	S16 43.7
Spica	158 35.1	S11 12.5
Suhail	222 55.6	S43 28.2
Vega	80 41.2	N38 47.3
Zuben'ubi	137 09.4	S16 04.8

	SHA ° ′	Mer. Pass. h m
Venus	294 18.9	11 48
Mars	225 28.4	16 22
Jupiter	66 35.1	2 58
Saturn	205 01.8	17 42

UT		SUN GHA	SUN Dec	MOON GHA	v	MOON Dec	d	HP
d	h	° ′	° ′	° ′	′	° ′	′	′
30	00	180 37.3	N21 47.7	247 01.0	12.5	N 3 58.7	15.9	58.7
	01	195 37.2	48.0	261 32.5	12.5	4 14.6	15.9	58.7
	02	210 37.2	48.4	276 04.0	12.4	4 30.5	15.9	58.8
	03	225 37.1	. . 48.8	290 35.4	12.4	4 46.4	15.9	58.8
	04	240 37.0	49.1	305 06.8	12.2	5 02.3	15.9	58.8
	05	255 36.9	49.5	319 38.0	12.3	5 18.2	15.9	58.9
	06	270 36.8	N21 49.9	334 09.3	12.1	N 5 34.1	15.9	58.9
	07	285 36.7	50.2	348 40.4	12.1	5 50.0	15.9	58.9
	08	300 36.6	50.6	3 11.5	12.0	6 05.9	15.8	59.0
F	09	315 36.5	. . 51.0	17 42.5	11.9	6 21.7	15.9	59.0
R	10	330 36.4	51.3	32 13.4	11.8	6 37.6	15.8	59.1
I	11	345 36.4	51.7	46 44.2	11.8	6 53.4	15.9	59.1
D	12	0 36.3	N21 52.0	61 15.0	11.7	N 7 09.3	15.8	59.1
A	13	15 36.2	52.4	75 45.7	11.6	7 25.1	15.8	59.2
Y	14	30 36.1	52.8	90 16.3	11.5	7 40.9	15.8	59.2
	15	45 36.0	. . 53.1	104 46.8	11.5	7 56.7	15.8	59.2
	16	60 35.9	53.5	119 17.3	11.3	8 12.5	15.7	59.3
	17	75 35.8	53.8	133 47.6	11.3	8 28.2	15.7	59.3
	18	90 35.7	N21 54.2	148 17.9	11.2	N 8 43.9	15.7	59.4
	19	105 35.6	54.6	162 48.1	11.1	8 59.6	15.7	59.4
	20	120 35.5	54.9	177 18.2	11.0	9 15.3	15.6	59.4
	21	135 35.5	. . 55.3	191 48.2	10.9	9 30.9	15.6	59.5
	22	150 35.4	55.6	206 18.1	10.8	9 46.5	15.6	59.5
	23	165 35.3	56.0	220 47.9	10.8	10 02.1	15.5	59.5
31	00	180 35.2	N21 56.3	235 17.7	10.6	N10 17.6	15.5	59.6
	01	195 35.1	56.7	249 47.3	10.5	10 33.1	15.5	59.6
	02	210 35.0	57.0	264 16.8	10.5	10 48.6	15.5	59.6
	03	225 34.9	. . 57.4	278 46.3	10.3	11 04.1	15.3	59.7
	04	240 34.8	57.7	293 15.6	10.2	11 19.4	15.4	59.7
	05	255 34.7	58.1	307 44.8	10.2	11 34.8	15.3	59.8
	06	270 34.6	N21 58.4	322 14.0	10.0	N11 50.1	15.3	59.8
	07	285 34.5	58.8	336 43.0	9.9	12 05.4	15.2	59.8
S	08	300 34.4	59.1	351 11.9	9.8	12 20.6	15.1	59.9
A	09	315 34.3	. . 59.5	5 40.7	9.7	12 35.7	15.1	59.9
T	10	330 34.2	21 59.8	20 09.4	9.6	12 50.8	15.1	59.9
U	11	345 34.2	22 00.2	34 38.0	9.5	13 05.9	15.0	60.0
R	12	0 34.1	N22 00.5	49 06.5	9.4	N13 20.9	14.9	60.0
D	13	15 34.0	00.9	63 34.9	9.3	13 35.8	14.9	60.0
A	14	30 33.9	01.2	78 03.2	9.1	13 50.7	14.8	60.1
Y	15	45 33.8	. . 01.5	92 31.3	9.1	14 05.5	14.8	60.1
	16	60 33.7	01.9	106 59.4	8.9	14 20.3	14.6	60.1
	17	75 33.6	02.2	121 27.3	8.8	14 34.9	14.7	60.2
	18	90 33.5	N22 02.6	135 55.1	8.7	N14 49.6	14.5	60.2
	19	105 33.4	02.9	150 22.8	8.6	15 04.1	14.5	60.2
	20	120 33.3	03.3	164 50.4	8.4	15 18.6	14.4	60.3
	21	135 33.2	. . 03.6	179 17.8	8.4	15 33.0	14.3	60.3
	22	150 33.1	03.9	193 45.2	8.2	15 47.3	14.3	60.3
	23	165 33.0	04.3	208 12.4	8.1	16 01.6	14.1	60.3
1	00	180 32.9	N22 04.6	222 39.5	7.9	N16 15.7	14.1	60.4
	01	195 32.8	04.9	237 06.4	7.9	16 29.8	14.0	60.4
	02	210 32.7	05.3	251 33.3	7.7	16 43.8	13.9	60.4
	03	225 32.6	. . 05.6	266 00.0	7.6	16 57.7	13.8	60.5
	04	240 32.5	05.9	280 26.6	7.5	17 11.5	13.7	60.5
	05	255 32.4	06.3	294 53.1	7.3	17 25.2	13.7	60.5
	06	270 32.3	N22 06.6	309 19.4	7.2	N17 38.9	13.5	60.6
	07	285 32.2	06.9	323 45.6	7.1	17 52.4	13.4	60.6
	08	300 32.1	07.3	338 11.7	7.0	18 05.8	13.3	60.6
S	09	315 32.0	. . 07.6	352 37.7	6.8	18 19.1	13.3	60.6
U	10	330 31.9	07.9	7 03.5	6.7	18 32.4	13.1	60.7
N	11	345 31.8	08.3	21 29.2	6.6	18 45.5	13.0	60.7
D	12	0 31.7	N22 08.6	35 54.8	6.4	N18 58.5	12.9	60.7
A	13	15 31.6	08.9	50 20.2	6.4	19 11.4	12.8	60.7
Y	14	30 31.5	09.3	64 45.6	6.1	19 24.2	12.7	60.8
	15	45 31.4	. . 09.6	79 10.7	6.1	19 36.9	12.5	60.8
	16	60 31.3	09.9	93 35.8	5.9	19 49.4	12.5	60.8
	17	75 31.2	10.2	108 00.7	5.8	20 01.9	12.3	60.8
	18	90 31.1	N22 10.6	122 25.5	5.7	N20 14.2	12.2	60.9
	19	105 31.0	10.9	136 50.2	5.5	20 26.4	12.0	60.9
	20	120 30.9	11.2	151 14.7	5.4	20 38.4	11.9	60.9
	21	135 30.8	. . 11.5	165 39.1	5.3	20 50.3	11.8	60.9
	22	150 30.7	11.9	180 03.4	5.2	21 02.1	11.7	60.9
	23	165 30.6	12.2	194 27.6	5.0	N21 13.8	11.5	61.0
		SD 15.8	*d* 0.3	SD	16.1		16.3	16.5

Lat.	Twilight Naut.	Twilight Civil	Sunrise	Moonrise 30	Moonrise 31	Moonrise 1	Moonrise 2
°	h m	h m	h m	h m	h m	h m	h m
N 72	□	□	□	00 43	{00 05 / 23 03}	□	□
N 70	□	□	□	00 49	{00 21 / 23 40}	□	□
68	□	□	□	00 53	00 33	{00 07 / 23 12}	□
66	////	////	01 15	00 57	00 44	00 27	00 01
64	////	////	01 59	01 00	00 53	00 44	00 33
62	////	00 13	02 28	01 03	01 00	00 58	00 57
60	////	01 28	02 50	01 05	01 07	01 10	01 16
N 58	////	02 01	03 08	01 08	01 13	01 20	01 32
56	00 12	02 25	03 23	01 10	01 18	01 29	01 45
54	01 20	02 44	03 35	01 11	01 23	01 37	01 57
52	01 51	03 00	03 47	01 13	01 27	01 44	02 08
50	02 14	03 14	03 56	01 15	01 31	01 51	02 17
45	02 53	03 41	04 17	01 18	01 39	02 05	02 37
N 40	03 21	04 01	04 34	01 21	01 47	02 17	02 53
35	03 43	04 18	04 47	01 23	01 53	02 27	03 07
30	04 00	04 33	05 00	01 25	01 58	02 36	03 19
20	04 27	04 56	05 20	01 29	02 08	02 51	03 40
N 10	04 48	05 15	05 38	01 32	02 16	03 05	03 58
0	05 06	05 32	05 54	01 36	02 24	03 17	04 16
S 10	05 22	05 48	06 10	01 39	02 32	03 30	04 33
20	05 37	06 04	06 28	01 42	02 41	03 44	04 52
30	05 52	06 21	06 47	01 46	02 51	04 00	05 13
35	06 00	06 31	06 59	01 49	02 57	04 10	05 26
40	06 08	06 42	07 12	01 51	03 04	04 20	05 41
45	06 18	06 54	07 27	01 54	03 12	04 33	05 58
S 50	06 28	07 09	07 46	01 58	03 21	04 49	06 20
52	06 33	07 16	07 55	02 00	03 25	04 56	06 31
54	06 38	07 23	08 05	02 02	03 30	05 04	06 43
56	06 43	07 31	08 17	02 04	03 36	05 14	06 56
58	06 49	07 40	08 30	02 06	03 42	05 24	07 13
S 60	06 56	07 51	08 45	02 09	03 49	05 36	07 32

Lat.	Sunset	Twilight Civil	Twilight Naut.	Moonset 30	Moonset 31	Moonset 1	Moonset 2
°	h m	h m	h m	h m	h m	h m	h m
N 72	□	□	□	15 45	18 35	□	□
N 70	□	□	□	15 32	18 00	□	□
68	□	□	□	15 22	17 35	20 29	□
66	22 44	////	////	15 13	17 17	19 41	□
64	21 58	////	////	15 06	17 01	19 10	21 43
62	21 29	////	////	15 00	16 49	18 47	20 56
60	21 06	22 30	////	14 55	16 38	18 29	20 25
N 58	20 49	21 56	////	14 51	16 29	18 14	20 02
56	20 34	21 31	////	14 47	16 21	18 01	19 44
54	20 21	21 12	22 38	14 43	16 14	17 50	19 28
52	20 10	20 56	22 06	14 40	16 08	17 40	19 14
50	20 00	20 42	21 43	14 37	16 02	17 32	19 03
45	19 39	20 15	21 03	14 31	15 50	17 13	18 38
N 40	19 22	19 54	20 35	14 25	15 40	16 58	18 19
35	19 08	19 37	20 13	14 21	15 31	16 45	18 03
30	18 56	19 23	19 56	14 17	15 24	16 34	17 49
20	18 36	19 00	19 29	14 10	15 11	16 16	17 25
N 10	18 18	18 41	19 07	14 04	14 59	15 59	17 04
0	18 01	18 24	18 50	13 58	14 49	15 44	16 45
S 10	17 45	18 08	18 34	13 53	14 38	15 29	16 26
20	17 28	17 51	18 19	13 47	14 27	15 13	16 06
30	17 08	17 34	18 04	13 40	14 15	14 55	15 43
35	16 56	17 24	17 56	13 36	14 07	14 44	15 29
40	16 43	17 13	17 47	13 32	13 59	14 32	15 13
45	16 28	17 01	17 38	13 27	13 50	14 18	14 54
S 50	16 09	16 46	17 27	13 21	13 38	14 00	14 31
52	16 00	16 39	17 22	13 18	13 33	13 52	14 20
54	15 50	16 32	17 17	13 15	13 27	13 43	14 08
56	15 38	16 24	17 12	13 11	13 21	13 33	13 53
58	15 25	16 15	17 06	13 08	13 13	13 22	13 37
S 60	15 10	16 04	16 59	13 04	13 05	13 09	13 16

Day	SUN Eqn. of Time 00h	SUN Eqn. of Time 12h	SUN Mer. Pass.	MOON Mer. Pass. Upper	MOON Mer. Pass. Lower	MOON Age	MOON Phase
d	m s	m s	h m	h m	h m	d	%
30	02 30	02 25	11 58	07 47	20 11	25	25
31	02 21	02 16	11 58	08 36	21 03	26	16
1	02 12	02 07	11 58	09 31	22 00	27	8

	UT	ARIES	VENUS −4.0		MARS +1.5		JUPITER −2.6		SATURN +0.7		STARS		
		GHA	GHA	Dec	GHA	Dec	GHA	Dec	GHA	Dec	Name	SHA	Dec
	d h	° ′	° ′	° ′	° ′	° ′	° ′	° ′	° ′	° ′		° ′	° ′
	2 00	250 50.1	182 33.3	N21 42.0	115 10.5	N18 23.1	317 33.9	S21 49.2	95 46.4	N12 13.2	Acamar	315 21.5	S40 16.1
	01	265 52.6	197 32.5	42.6	130 11.5	22.6	332 36.6	49.3	110 48.7	13.2	Achernar	335 29.7	S57 11.4
	02	280 55.1	212 31.7	43.1	145 12.6	22.2	347 39.2	49.3	125 51.1	13.1	Acrux	173 13.6	S63 09.1
	03	295 57.5	227 30.9	. . 43.7	160 13.6	. . 21.8	2 41.9	. . 49.3	140 53.4	. . 13.1	Adhara	255 15.9	S28 59.1
	04	311 00.0	242 30.1	44.2	175 14.7	21.3	17 44.5	49.4	155 55.8	13.0	Aldebaran	290 54.1	N16 31.6
	05	326 02.5	257 29.3	44.8	190 15.7	20.9	32 47.2	49.4	170 58.1	13.0			
	06	341 04.9	272 28.5	N21 45.3	205 16.7	N18 20.5	47 49.8	S21 49.4	186 00.5	N12 12.9	Alioth	166 23.5	N55 55.0
	07	356 07.4	287 27.7	45.9	220 17.8	20.1	62 52.5	49.5	201 02.8	12.9	Alkaid	153 01.3	N49 16.3
	08	11 09.9	302 26.9	46.4	235 18.8	19.6	77 55.2	49.5	216 05.2	12.8	Al Na'ir	27 48.2	S46 55.0
M	09	26 12.3	317 26.1	. . 46.9	250 19.9	. . 19.2	92 57.8	. . 49.5	231 07.5	. . 12.8	Alnilam	275 50.6	S 1 11.8
O	10	41 14.8	332 25.3	47.5	265 20.9	18.8	108 00.5	49.6	246 09.8	12.7	Alphard	218 00.0	S 8 41.8
N	11	56 17.3	347 24.5	48.0	280 22.0	18.3	123 03.1	49.6	261 12.2	12.7			
D	12	71 19.7	2 23.7	N21 48.6	295 23.0	N18 17.9	138 05.8	S21 49.6	276 14.5	N12 12.6	Alphecca	126 13.8	N26 41.1
A	13	86 22.2	17 22.9	49.1	310 24.1	17.5	153 08.4	49.7	291 16.9	12.6	Alpheratz	357 47.7	N29 08.1
Y	14	101 24.6	32 22.2	49.6	325 25.1	17.0	168 11.1	49.7	306 19.2	12.5	Altair	62 11.7	N 8 53.3
	15	116 27.1	47 21.4	. . 50.2	340 26.1	. . 16.6	183 13.7	. . 49.7	321 21.6	. . 12.5	Ankaa	353 19.4	S42 15.4
	16	131 29.6	62 20.6	50.7	355 27.2	16.2	198 16.4	49.8	336 23.9	12.4	Antares	112 30.6	S26 27.2
	17	146 32.0	77 19.8	51.2	10 28.2	15.7	213 19.1	49.8	351 26.2	12.4			
	18	161 34.5	92 19.0	N21 51.8	25 29.3	N18 15.3	228 21.7	S21 49.8	6 28.6	N12 12.3	Arcturus	145 58.9	N19 08.3
	19	176 37.0	107 18.2	52.3	40 30.3	14.9	243 24.4	49.9	21 30.9	12.3	Atria	107 35.4	S69 02.7
	20	191 39.4	122 17.4	52.8	55 31.4	14.4	258 27.0	49.9	36 33.3	12.2	Avior	234 20.2	S59 32.4
	21	206 41.9	137 16.6	. . 53.3	70 32.4	. . 14.0	273 29.7	. . 49.9	51 35.6	. . 12.2	Bellatrix	278 36.4	N 6 21.5
	22	221 44.4	152 15.8	53.9	85 33.5	13.6	288 32.3	50.0	66 38.0	12.1	Betelgeuse	271 05.8	N 7 24.6
	23	236 46.8	167 15.0	54.4	100 34.5	13.1	303 35.0	50.0	81 40.3	12.1			
	3 00	251 49.3	182 14.2	N21 54.9	115 35.5	N18 12.7	318 37.7	S21 50.0	96 42.6	N12 12.0	Canopus	263 58.4	S52 42.1
	01	266 51.8	197 13.4	55.4	130 36.6	12.3	333 40.3	50.1	111 45.0	12.0	Capella	280 40.6	N46 00.5
	02	281 54.2	212 12.6	56.0	145 37.6	11.8	348 43.0	50.1	126 47.3	11.9	Deneb	49 33.9	N45 18.4
	03	296 56.7	227 11.8	. . 56.5	160 38.7	. . 11.4	3 45.6	. . 50.1	141 49.7	. . 11.8	Denebola	182 37.4	N14 31.5
	04	311 59.1	242 11.0	57.0	175 39.7	11.0	18 48.3	50.2	156 52.0	11.8	Diphda	348 59.8	S17 56.3
	05	327 01.6	257 10.2	57.5	190 40.8	10.5	33 51.0	50.2	171 54.3	11.7			
	06	342 04.1	272 09.3	N21 58.0	205 41.8	N18 10.1	48 53.6	S21 50.3	186 56.7	N12 11.7	Dubhe	193 56.0	N61 42.6
	07	357 06.5	287 08.5	58.6	220 42.9	09.6	63 56.3	50.3	201 59.0	11.6	Elnath	278 17.8	N28 36.9
T	08	12 09.0	302 07.7	59.1	235 43.9	09.2	78 58.9	50.3	217 01.4	11.6	Eltanin	90 47.4	N51 29.1
U	09	27 11.5	317 06.9	21 59.6	250 44.9	. . 08.8	94 01.6	. . 50.4	232 03.7	. . 11.5	Enif	33 50.8	N 9 54.7
E	10	42 13.9	332 06.1	22 00.1	265 46.0	08.3	109 04.3	50.4	247 06.1	11.5	Fomalhaut	15 28.1	S29 34.5
S	11	57 16.4	347 05.3	00.6	280 47.0	07.9	124 06.9	50.4	262 08.4	11.4			
D	12	72 18.9	2 04.5	N22 01.1	295 48.1	N18 07.5	139 09.6	S21 50.5	277 10.7	N12 11.4	Gacrux	172 05.2	S57 10.0
A	13	87 21.3	17 03.7	01.6	310 49.1	07.0	154 12.3	50.5	292 13.1	11.3	Gienah	175 56.2	S17 35.5
Y	14	102 23.8	32 02.9	02.2	325 50.2	06.6	169 14.9	50.5	307 15.4	11.3	Hadar	148 53.1	S60 25.1
	15	117 26.3	47 02.1	. . 02.7	340 51.2	. . 06.1	184 17.6	. . 50.6	322 17.8	. . 11.2	Hamal	328 05.4	N23 30.1
	16	132 28.7	62 01.3	03.2	355 52.3	05.7	199 20.2	50.6	337 20.1	11.2	Kaus Aust.	83 48.5	S34 22.9
	17	147 31.2	77 00.5	03.7	10 53.3	05.3	214 22.9	50.6	352 22.4	11.1			
	18	162 33.6	91 59.7	N22 04.2	25 54.3	N18 04.8	229 25.6	S21 50.7	7 24.8	N12 11.1	Kochab	137 18.3	N74 07.3
	19	177 36.1	106 58.9	04.7	40 55.4	04.4	244 28.2	50.7	22 27.1	11.0	Markab	13 42.2	N15 15.0
	20	192 38.6	121 58.1	05.2	55 56.4	04.0	259 30.9	50.8	37 29.4	11.0	Menkar	314 19.3	N 4 07.4
	21	207 41.0	136 57.3	. . 05.7	70 57.5	. . 03.5	274 33.6	. . 50.8	52 31.8	. . 10.9	Menkent	148 11.9	S36 24.9
	22	222 43.5	151 56.4	06.2	85 58.5	03.1	289 36.2	50.8	67 34.1	10.9	Miaplacidus	221 41.3	S69 45.4
	23	237 46.0	166 55.6	06.7	100 59.6	02.6	304 38.9	50.9	82 36.5	10.8			
	4 00	252 48.4	181 54.8	N22 07.2	116 00.6	N18 02.2	319 41.6	S21 50.9	97 38.8	N12 10.8	Mirfak	308 46.4	N49 53.4
	01	267 50.9	196 54.0	07.7	131 01.7	01.8	334 44.2	50.9	112 41.1	10.7	Nunki	76 02.7	S26 17.2
	02	282 53.4	211 53.2	08.2	146 02.7	01.3	349 46.9	51.0	127 43.5	10.6	Peacock	53 24.7	S56 42.3
	03	297 55.8	226 52.4	. . 08.7	161 03.7	. . 00.9	4 49.6	. . 51.0	142 45.8	. . 10.6	Pollux	243 32.6	N28 00.5
	04	312 58.3	241 51.6	09.2	176 04.8	00.4	19 52.2	51.0	157 48.2	10.5	Procyon	245 04.0	N 5 12.2
	05	328 00.8	256 50.8	09.7	191 05.8	18 00.0	34 54.9	51.1	172 50.5	10.5			
	06	343 03.2	271 50.0	N22 10.2	206 06.9	N17 59.6	49 57.6	S21 51.1	187 52.8	N12 10.4	Rasalhague	96 09.6	N12 33.1
W	07	358 05.7	286 49.1	10.6	221 07.9	59.1	65 00.2	51.1	202 55.2	10.4	Regulus	207 47.6	N11 55.6
E	08	13 08.1	301 48.3	11.1	236 09.0	58.7	80 02.9	51.2	217 57.5	10.3	Rigel	281 16.1	S 8 11.5
D	09	28 10.6	316 47.5	. . 11.6	251 10.0	. . 58.2	95 05.6	. . 51.2	232 59.8	. . 10.3	Rigil Kent.	139 56.7	S60 52.5
N	10	43 13.1	331 46.7	12.1	266 11.1	57.8	110 08.2	51.3	248 02.2	10.2	Sabik	102 16.6	S15 44.2
E	11	58 15.5	346 45.9	12.6	281 12.1	57.4	125 10.9	51.3	263 04.5	10.2			
S	12	73 18.0	1 45.1	N22 13.1	296 13.1	N17 56.9	140 13.6	S21 51.3	278 06.8	N12 10.1	Schedar	349 45.4	N56 34.8
D	13	88 20.5	16 44.3	13.6	311 14.2	56.5	155 16.3	51.4	293 09.2	10.1	Shaula	96 26.7	S37 06.7
A	14	103 22.9	31 43.4	14.0	326 15.2	56.0	170 18.9	51.4	308 11.5	10.0	Sirius	258 37.4	S16 43.7
Y	15	118 25.4	46 42.6	. . 14.5	341 16.3	. . 55.6	185 21.6	. . 51.4	323 13.9	. . 10.0	Spica	158 35.1	S11 12.5
	16	133 27.9	61 41.8	15.0	356 17.3	55.1	200 24.3	51.5	338 16.2	09.9	Suhail	222 55.6	S43 28.2
	17	148 30.3	76 41.0	15.5	11 18.4	54.7	215 26.9	51.5	353 18.5	09.8			
	18	163 32.8	91 40.2	N22 16.0	26 19.4	N17 54.3	230 29.6	S21 51.5	8 20.9	N12 09.8	Vega	80 41.2	N38 47.3
	19	178 35.3	106 39.4	16.4	41 20.5	53.8	245 32.3	51.6	23 23.2	09.7	Zuben'ubi	137 09.4	S16 04.8
	20	193 37.7	121 38.5	16.9	56 21.5	53.4	260 35.0	51.6	38 25.5	09.7			
	21	208 40.2	136 37.7	. . 17.4	71 22.5	. . 52.9	275 37.6	. . 51.7	53 27.9	. . 09.6			
	22	223 42.6	151 36.9	17.9	86 23.6	52.5	290 40.3	51.7	68 30.2	09.6			
	23	238 45.1	166 36.1	18.3	101 24.6	52.0	305 43.0	51.7	83 32.5	09.5			
	Mer. Pass.	h m 7 11.5	*v* −0.8	*d* 0.5	*v* 1.0	*d* 0.4	*v* 2.7	*d* 0.0	*v* 2.3	*d* 0.1			

	SHA	Mer. Pass.
	° ′	h m
Venus	290 24.9	11 52
Mars	223 46.3	16 16
Jupiter	66 48.4	2 45
Saturn	204 53.4	17 30

UT d	h	SUN GHA ° ′	SUN Dec ° ′	MOON GHA ° ′	v ′	MOON Dec ° ′	d ′	HP ′
2	00	180 30.5	N22 12.5	208 51.6	4.9	N21 25.3	11.4	61.0
	01	195 30.4	12.8	223 15.5	4.7	21 36.7	11.3	61.0
	02	210 30.3	13.1	237 39.2	4.7	21 48.0	11.1	61.0
	03	225 30.2	. . 13.5	252 02.9	4.5	21 59.1	10.9	61.0
	04	240 30.1	13.8	266 26.4	4.4	22 10.0	10.9	61.1
	05	255 30.0	14.1	280 49.8	4.2	22 20.9	10.6	61.1
	06	270 29.9	N22 14.4	295 13.0	4.2	N22 31.5	10.5	61.1
	07	285 29.8	14.7	309 36.2	4.0	22 42.0	10.4	61.1
	08	300 29.7	15.0	323 59.2	3.8	22 52.4	10.2	61.1
M	09	315 29.6	. . 15.4	338 22.0	3.8	23 02.6	10.0	61.2
O	10	330 29.5	15.7	352 44.8	3.7	23 12.6	9.9	61.2
N	11	345 29.4	16.0	7 07.5	3.5	23 22.5	9.7	61.2
D	12	0 29.3	N22 16.3	21 30.0	3.4	N23 32.2	9.5	61.2
A	13	15 29.2	16.6	35 52.4	3.3	23 41.7	9.4	61.2
Y	14	30 29.1	16.9	50 14.7	3.2	23 51.1	9.2	61.2
	15	45 29.0	. . 17.2	64 36.9	3.0	24 00.3	9.1	61.2
	16	60 28.9	17.5	78 58.9	3.0	24 09.4	8.8	61.2
	17	75 28.8	17.9	93 20.9	2.8	24 18.2	8.7	61.3
	18	90 28.7	N22 18.2	107 42.7	2.7	N24 26.9	8.5	61.3
	19	105 28.6	18.5	122 04.4	2.7	24 35.4	8.4	61.3
	20	120 28.5	18.8	136 26.1	2.5	24 43.8	8.1	61.3
	21	135 28.4	. . 19.1	150 47.6	2.4	24 51.9	8.0	61.3
	22	150 28.3	19.4	165 09.0	2.3	24 59.9	7.7	61.3
	23	165 28.2	19.7	179 30.3	2.2	25 07.6	7.6	61.3
3	00	180 28.1	N22 20.0	193 51.5	2.1	N25 15.2	7.4	61.3
	01	195 28.0	20.3	208 12.6	2.1	25 22.6	7.2	61.3
	02	210 27.9	20.6	222 33.7	1.9	25 29.8	7.0	61.3
	03	225 27.8	. . 20.9	236 54.6	1.9	25 36.8	6.8	61.3
	04	240 27.7	21.2	251 15.5	1.7	25 43.6	6.7	61.4
	05	255 27.6	21.5	265 36.2	1.7	25 50.3	6.4	61.4
	06	270 27.5	N22 21.8	279 56.9	1.6	N25 56.7	6.2	61.4
	07	285 27.3	22.1	294 17.5	1.5	26 02.9	6.0	61.4
T	08	300 27.2	22.4	308 38.0	1.4	26 08.9	5.8	61.4
U	09	315 27.1	. . 22.7	322 58.4	1.4	26 14.7	5.7	61.4
E	10	330 27.0	23.0	337 18.8	1.3	26 20.4	5.4	61.4
S	11	345 26.9	23.3	351 39.1	1.2	26 25.8	5.2	61.4
D	12	0 26.8	N22 23.6	5 59.3	1.2	N26 31.0	5.0	61.4
A	13	15 26.7	23.9	20 19.5	1.1	26 36.0	4.8	61.4
Y	14	30 26.6	24.2	34 39.6	1.0	26 40.8	4.5	61.4
	15	45 26.5	. . 24.5	48 59.6	1.0	26 45.3	4.4	61.4
	16	60 26.4	24.8	63 19.6	1.0	26 49.7	4.1	61.4
	17	75 26.3	25.1	77 39.6	0.9	26 53.8	4.0	61.4
	18	90 26.2	N22 25.4	91 59.5	0.8	N26 57.8	3.7	61.4
	19	105 26.1	25.7	106 19.3	0.8	27 01.5	3.5	61.4
	20	120 26.0	26.0	120 39.1	0.8	27 05.0	3.3	61.4
	21	135 25.8	. . 26.3	134 58.9	0.7	27 08.3	3.1	61.4
	22	150 25.7	26.5	149 18.6	0.7	27 11.4	2.9	61.4
	23	165 25.6	26.8	163 38.3	0.7	27 14.3	2.6	61.4
4	00	180 25.5	N22 27.1	177 58.0	0.7	N27 16.9	2.4	61.3
	01	195 25.4	27.4	192 17.7	0.6	27 19.3	2.2	61.3
	02	210 25.3	27.7	206 37.3	0.6	27 21.5	2.0	61.3
	03	225 25.2	. . 28.0	220 56.9	0.6	27 23.5	1.8	61.3
	04	240 25.1	28.3	235 16.5	0.6	27 25.3	1.5	61.3
	05	255 25.0	28.6	249 36.1	0.6	27 26.8	1.4	61.3
	06	270 24.9	N22 28.8	263 55.7	0.6	N27 28.2	1.1	61.3
W	07	285 24.8	29.1	278 15.3	0.6	27 29.3	0.9	61.3
E	08	300 24.7	29.4	292 34.9	0.6	27 30.2	0.6	61.3
D	09	315 24.5	. . 29.7	306 54.5	0.6	27 30.8	0.5	61.3
N	10	330 24.4	30.0	321 14.1	0.6	27 31.3	0.2	61.3
E	11	345 24.3	30.3	335 33.7	0.6	27 31.5	0.0	61.2
S	12	0 24.2	N22 30.5	349 53.3	0.7	N27 31.5	0.2	61.2
D	13	15 24.1	30.8	4 13.0	0.7	27 31.3	0.4	61.2
A	14	30 24.0	31.1	18 32.7	0.7	27 30.9	0.6	61.2
Y	15	45 23.9	. . 31.4	32 52.4	0.7	27 30.3	0.9	61.2
	16	60 23.8	31.6	47 12.1	0.8	27 29.4	1.1	61.2
	17	75 23.7	31.9	61 31.9	0.8	27 28.3	1.3	61.2
	18	90 23.6	N22 32.2	75 51.7	0.9	N27 27.0	1.5	61.1
	19	105 23.4	32.5	90 11.6	0.9	27 25.5	1.7	61.1
	20	120 23.3	32.8	104 31.5	0.9	27 23.8	1.9	61.1
	21	135 23.2	. . 33.0	118 51.4	1.0	27 21.9	2.2	61.1
	22	150 23.1	33.3	133 11.4	1.1	27 19.7	2.4	61.1
	23	165 23.0	33.6	147 31.5	1.1	N27 17.3	2.5	61.1
		SD 15.8	*d* 0.3	SD 16.7		16.7		16.7

Lat. °	Twilight Naut. h m	Twilight Civil h m	Sunrise h m	Moonrise 2 h m	Moonrise 3 h m	Moonrise 4 h m	Moonrise 5 h m
N 72	▭	▭	▭	▭	▭	▭	▭
N 70	▭	▭	▭	▭	▭	▭	▭
68	▭	▭	▭	▭	▭	▭	▭
66	////	////	01 02	00 01	▭	▭	▭
64	////	////	01 52	00 33	00 10	▭	▭
62	////	////	02 23	00 57	00 58	01 13	02 27
60	////	01 19	02 46	01 16	01 29	02 02	03 15
N 58	////	01 56	03 04	01 32	01 53	02 34	03 46
56	////	02 21	03 20	01 45	02 12	02 58	04 09
54	01 12	02 41	03 33	01 57	02 28	03 17	04 28
52	01 46	02 57	03 44	02 08	02 42	03 33	04 44
50	02 10	03 11	03 54	02 17	02 54	03 47	04 58
45	02 51	03 39	04 15	02 37	03 20	04 16	05 26
N 40	03 19	04 00	04 32	02 53	03 40	04 38	05 48
35	03 41	04 17	04 47	03 07	03 57	04 57	06 06
30	03 59	04 32	04 59	03 19	04 12	05 13	06 22
20	04 27	04 56	05 20	03 40	04 37	05 41	06 49
N 10	04 48	05 15	05 38	03 58	04 59	06 04	07 12
0	05 06	05 32	05 55	04 16	05 19	06 26	07 33
S 10	05 22	05 48	06 11	04 33	05 40	06 48	07 55
20	05 38	06 05	06 29	04 52	06 02	07 12	08 18
30	05 53	06 23	06 49	05 13	06 28	07 40	08 44
35	06 01	06 33	07 01	05 26	06 43	07 56	09 00
40	06 10	06 44	07 14	05 41	07 01	08 15	09 18
45	06 20	06 56	07 30	05 58	07 22	08 38	09 40
S 50	06 31	07 12	07 49	06 20	07 50	09 08	10 07
52	06 35	07 18	07 59	06 31	08 03	09 22	10 21
54	06 41	07 26	08 09	06 43	08 18	09 39	10 36
56	06 46	07 35	08 21	06 56	08 37	10 00	10 55
58	06 52	07 44	08 34	07 13	08 59	10 25	11 17
S 60	06 59	07 55	08 50	07 32	09 28	10 59	11 45

Lat. °	Sunset h m	Twilight Civil h m	Twilight Naut. h m	Moonset 2 h m	Moonset 3 h m	Moonset 4 h m	Moonset 5 h m
N 72	▭	▭	▭	▭	▭	▭	▭
N 70	▭	▭	▭	▭	▭	▭	▭
68	▭	▭	▭	▭	▭	▭	▭
66	22 59	////	////	▭	▭	▭	▭
64	22 06	////	////	21 43	▭	▭	▭
62	21 35	////	////	20 56	23 01	24 09	00 09
60	21 12	22 40	////	20 25	22 11	23 20	23 51
N 58	20 53	22 02	////	20 02	21 40	22 50	23 28
56	20 38	21 36	////	19 44	21 17	22 26	23 09
54	20 24	21 16	22 46	19 28	20 57	22 07	22 53
52	20 13	21 00	22 12	19 14	20 41	21 51	22 39
50	20 03	20 46	21 48	19 03	20 27	21 37	22 27
45	19 41	20 18	21 06	18 38	19 59	21 08	22 02
N 40	19 24	19 57	20 37	18 19	19 37	20 46	21 42
35	19 10	19 39	20 16	18 03	19 18	20 27	21 25
30	18 58	19 25	19 58	17 49	19 02	20 11	21 11
20	18 37	19 01	19 30	17 25	18 35	19 44	20 46
N 10	18 19	18 42	19 08	17 04	18 12	19 20	20 24
0	18 02	18 24	18 50	16 45	17 51	18 58	20 04
S 10	17 45	18 08	18 34	16 26	17 29	18 36	19 44
20	17 28	17 51	18 19	16 06	17 06	18 13	19 22
30	17 07	17 34	18 03	15 43	16 39	17 45	18 56
35	16 56	17 24	17 55	15 29	16 24	17 29	18 41
40	16 42	17 12	17 46	15 13	16 05	17 10	18 23
45	16 26	17 00	17 37	14 54	15 43	16 47	18 02
S 50	16 07	16 45	17 26	14 31	15 15	16 17	17 35
52	15 58	16 38	17 21	14 20	15 02	16 03	17 22
54	15 47	16 30	17 16	14 08	14 46	15 46	17 07
56	15 36	16 22	17 10	13 53	14 27	15 25	16 49
58	15 22	16 12	17 04	13 37	14 05	15 00	16 27
S 60	15 06	16 01	16 57	13 16	13 36	14 25	15 59

Day	SUN Eqn. of Time 00^h	SUN Eqn. of Time 12^h	SUN Mer. Pass.	MOON Mer. Pass. Upper	MOON Mer. Pass. Lower	MOON Age	MOON Phase
d	m s	m s	h m	h m	h m	d	%
2	02 02	01 58	11 58	10 30	23 02	28	3
3	01 53	01 47	11 58	11 35	24 09	29	0
4	01 42	01 37	11 58	12 42	00 09	01	1

Day	UT (d h)	ARIES GHA	VENUS −4.0 GHA	VENUS Dec	MARS +1.5 GHA	MARS Dec	JUPITER −2.6 GHA	JUPITER Dec	SATURN +0.7 GHA	SATURN Dec
		° ′	° ′	° ′	° ′	° ′	° ′	° ′	° ′	° ′
THURSDAY	5 00	253 47.6	181 35.3	N22 18.8	116 25.7	N17 51.6	320 45.6	S21 51.8	98 34.9	N12 09.5
	01	268 50.0	196 34.5	19.3	131 26.7	51.2	335 48.3	51.8	113 37.2	09.4
	02	283 52.5	211 33.6	19.8	146 27.8	50.7	350 51.0	51.8	128 39.5	09.4
	03	298 55.0	226 32.8	. . 20.2	161 28.8	. . 50.3	5 53.7	. . 51.9	143 41.9	. . 09.3
	04	313 57.4	241 32.0	20.7	176 29.9	49.8	20 56.3	51.9	158 44.2	09.2
	05	328 59.9	256 31.2	21.2	191 30.9	49.4	35 59.0	52.0	173 46.5	09.2
	06	344 02.4	271 30.4	N22 21.6	206 31.9	N17 48.9	51 01.7	S21 52.0	188 48.9	N12 09.1
	07	359 04.8	286 29.5	22.1	221 33.0	48.5	66 04.4	52.0	203 51.2	09.1
	08	14 07.3	301 28.7	22.6	236 34.0	48.0	81 07.0	52.1	218 53.5	09.0
	09	29 09.8	316 27.9	. . 23.0	251 35.1	. . 47.6	96 09.7	. . 52.1	233 55.9	. . 09.0
	10	44 12.2	331 27.1	23.5	266 36.1	47.2	111 12.4	52.1	248 58.2	08.9
	11	59 14.7	346 26.2	23.9	281 37.2	46.7	126 15.1	52.2	264 00.5	08.9
	12	74 17.1	1 25.4	N22 24.4	296 38.2	N17 46.3	141 17.7	S21 52.2	279 02.9	N12 08.8
	13	89 19.6	16 24.6	24.9	311 39.3	45.8	156 20.4	52.3	294 05.2	08.8
	14	104 22.1	31 23.8	25.3	326 40.3	45.4	171 23.1	52.3	309 07.5	08.7
	15	119 24.5	46 22.9	. . 25.8	341 41.3	. . 44.9	186 25.8	. . 52.3	324 09.9	. . 08.6
	16	134 27.0	61 22.1	26.2	356 42.4	44.5	201 28.5	52.4	339 12.2	08.6
	17	149 29.5	76 21.3	26.7	11 43.4	44.0	216 31.1	52.4	354 14.5	08.5
	18	164 31.9	91 20.5	N22 27.1	26 44.5	N17 43.6	231 33.8	S21 52.4	9 16.9	N12 08.5
	19	179 34.4	106 19.6	27.6	41 45.5	43.1	246 36.5	52.5	24 19.2	08.4
	20	194 36.9	121 18.8	28.0	56 46.6	42.7	261 39.2	52.5	39 21.5	08.4
	21	209 39.3	136 18.0	. . 28.5	71 47.6	. . 42.2	276 41.9	. . 52.6	54 23.9	. . 08.3
	22	224 41.8	151 17.2	28.9	86 48.6	41.8	291 44.5	52.6	69 26.2	08.3
	23	239 44.3	166 16.3	29.4	101 49.7	41.3	306 47.2	52.6	84 28.5	08.2
FRIDAY	6 00	254 46.7	181 15.5	N22 29.8	116 50.7	N17 40.9	321 49.9	S21 52.7	99 30.9	N12 08.1
	01	269 49.2	196 14.7	30.3	131 51.8	40.4	336 52.6	52.7	114 33.2	08.1
	02	284 51.6	211 13.9	30.7	146 52.8	40.0	351 55.3	52.7	129 35.5	08.0
	03	299 54.1	226 13.0	. . 31.2	161 53.9	. . 39.6	6 57.9	. . 52.8	144 37.8	. . 08.0
	04	314 56.6	241 12.2	31.6	176 54.9	39.1	22 00.6	52.8	159 40.2	07.9
	05	329 59.0	256 11.4	32.0	191 56.0	38.7	37 03.3	52.9	174 42.5	07.9
	06	345 01.5	271 10.5	N22 32.5	206 57.0	N17 38.2	52 06.0	S21 52.9	189 44.8	N12 07.8
	07	0 04.0	286 09.7	32.9	221 58.0	37.8	67 08.7	52.9	204 47.2	07.8
	08	15 06.4	301 08.9	33.3	236 59.1	37.3	82 11.3	53.0	219 49.5	07.7
	09	30 08.9	316 08.0	. . 33.8	252 00.1	. . 36.9	97 14.0	. . 53.0	234 51.8	. . 07.6
	10	45 11.4	331 07.2	34.2	267 01.2	36.4	112 16.7	53.0	249 54.2	07.6
	11	60 13.8	346 06.4	34.7	282 02.2	36.0	127 19.4	53.1	264 56.5	07.5
	12	75 16.3	1 05.6	N22 35.1	297 03.3	N17 35.5	142 22.1	S21 53.1	279 58.8	N12 07.5
	13	90 18.8	16 04.7	35.5	312 04.3	35.1	157 24.8	53.2	295 01.1	07.4
	14	105 21.2	31 03.9	35.9	327 05.4	34.6	172 27.4	53.2	310 03.5	07.4
	15	120 23.7	46 03.1	. . 36.4	342 06.4	. . 34.2	187 30.1	. . 53.2	325 05.8	. . 07.3
	16	135 26.1	61 02.2	36.8	357 07.4	33.7	202 32.8	53.3	340 08.1	07.3
	17	150 28.6	76 01.4	37.2	12 08.5	33.2	217 35.5	53.3	355 10.5	07.2
	18	165 31.1	91 00.6	N22 37.7	27 09.5	N17 32.8	232 38.2	S21 53.4	10 12.8	N12 07.1
	19	180 33.5	105 59.7	38.1	42 10.6	32.3	247 40.9	53.4	25 15.1	07.1
	20	195 36.0	120 58.9	38.5	57 11.6	31.9	262 43.6	53.4	40 17.4	07.0
	21	210 38.5	135 58.1	. . 38.9	72 12.7	. . 31.4	277 46.2	. . 53.5	55 19.8	. . 07.0
	22	225 40.9	150 57.2	39.3	87 13.7	31.0	292 48.9	53.5	70 22.1	06.9
	23	240 43.4	165 56.4	39.8	102 14.8	30.5	307 51.6	53.5	85 24.4	06.9
SATURDAY	7 00	255 45.9	180 55.5	N22 40.2	117 15.8	N17 30.1	322 54.3	S21 53.6	100 26.7	N12 06.8
	01	270 48.3	195 54.7	40.6	132 16.8	29.6	337 57.0	53.6	115 29.1	06.7
	02	285 50.8	210 53.9	41.0	147 17.9	29.2	352 59.7	53.7	130 31.4	06.7
	03	300 53.2	225 53.0	. . 41.4	162 18.9	. . 28.7	8 02.4	. . 53.7	145 33.7	. . 06.6
	04	315 55.7	240 52.2	41.8	177 20.0	28.3	23 05.1	53.7	160 36.1	06.6
	05	330 58.2	255 51.4	42.3	192 21.0	27.8	38 07.7	53.8	175 38.4	06.5
	06	346 00.6	270 50.5	N22 42.7	207 22.1	N17 27.4	53 10.4	S21 53.8	190 40.7	N12 06.5
	07	1 03.1	285 49.7	43.1	222 23.1	26.9	68 13.1	53.9	205 43.0	06.4
	08	16 05.6	300 48.9	43.5	237 24.1	26.5	83 15.8	53.9	220 45.4	06.3
	09	31 08.0	315 48.0	. . 43.9	252 25.2	. . 26.0	98 18.5	. . 53.9	235 47.7	. . 06.3
	10	46 10.5	330 47.2	44.3	267 26.2	25.5	113 21.2	54.0	250 50.0	06.2
	11	61 13.0	345 46.3	44.7	282 27.3	25.1	128 23.9	54.0	265 52.3	06.2
	12	76 15.4	0 45.5	N22 45.1	297 28.3	N17 24.6	143 26.6	S21 54.1	280 54.7	N12 06.1
	13	91 17.9	15 44.7	45.5	312 29.4	24.2	158 29.3	54.1	295 57.0	06.1
	14	106 20.4	30 43.8	45.9	327 30.4	23.7	173 31.9	54.1	310 59.3	06.0
	15	121 22.8	45 43.0	. . 46.3	342 31.5	. . 23.3	188 34.6	. . 54.2	326 01.6	. . 05.9
	16	136 25.3	60 42.1	46.7	357 32.5	22.8	203 37.3	54.2	341 04.0	05.9
	17	151 27.7	75 41.3	47.1	12 33.5	22.4	218 40.0	54.2	356 06.3	05.8
	18	166 30.2	90 40.5	N22 47.5	27 34.6	N17 21.9	233 42.7	S21 54.3	11 08.6	N12 05.8
	19	181 32.7	105 39.6	47.9	42 35.6	21.4	248 45.4	54.3	26 10.9	05.7
	20	196 35.1	120 38.8	48.3	57 36.7	21.0	263 48.1	54.4	41 13.3	05.7
	21	211 37.6	135 37.9	. . 48.7	72 37.7	. . 20.5	278 50.8	. . 54.4	56 15.6	. . 05.6
	22	226 40.1	150 37.1	49.1	87 38.8	20.1	293 53.5	54.4	71 17.9	05.5
	23	241 42.5	165 36.2	49.5	102 39.8	19.6	308 56.2	54.5	86 20.2	05.5
	Mer. Pass.	h m 6 59.7	*v* −0.8	*d* 0.4	*v* 1.0	*d* 0.5	*v* 2.7	*d* 0.0	*v* 2.3	*d* 0.1

STARS

Name	SHA	Dec
	° ′	° ′
Acamar	315 21.5	S40 16.1
Achernar	335 29.7	S57 11.3
Acrux	173 13.7	S63 09.1
Adhara	255 15.9	S28 59.1
Aldebaran	290 54.1	N16 31.6
Alioth	166 23.5	N55 55.0
Alkaid	153 01.4	N49 16.3
Al Na'ir	27 48.2	S46 55.0
Alnilam	275 50.6	S 1 11.7
Alphard	218 00.0	S 8 41.8
Alphecca	126 13.8	N26 41.1
Alpheratz	357 47.6	N29 08.1
Altair	62 11.7	N 8 53.3
Ankaa	353 19.4	S42 15.3
Antares	112 30.6	S26 27.2
Arcturus	145 58.9	N19 08.3
Atria	107 35.4	S69 02.7
Avior	234 20.2	S59 32.4
Bellatrix	278 36.4	N 6 21.5
Betelgeuse	271 05.7	N 7 24.6
Canopus	263 58.4	S52 42.0
Capella	280 40.6	N46 00.5
Deneb	49 33.9	N45 18.4
Denebola	182 37.4	N14 31.5
Diphda	348 59.8	S17 56.3
Dubhe	193 56.0	N61 42.6
Elnath	278 17.8	N28 36.9
Eltanin	90 47.4	N51 29.1
Enif	33 50.7	N 9 54.7
Fomalhaut	15 28.0	S29 34.5
Gacrux	172 05.2	S57 10.0
Gienah	175 56.2	S17 35.5
Hadar	148 53.1	S60 25.1
Hamal	328 05.4	N23 30.1
Kaus Aust.	83 48.4	S34 22.9
Kochab	137 18.4	N74 07.3
Markab	13 42.2	N15 15.0
Menkar	314 19.3	N 4 07.4
Menkent	148 11.9	S36 24.9
Miaplacidus	221 41.3	S69 45.4
Mirfak	308 46.4	N49 53.4
Nunki	76 02.7	S26 17.2
Peacock	53 24.6	S56 42.3
Pollux	243 32.6	N28 00.5
Procyon	245 04.0	N 5 12.2
Rasalhague	96 09.6	N12 33.1
Regulus	207 47.6	N11 55.6
Rigel	281 16.0	S 8 11.5
Rigil Kent.	139 56.6	S60 52.5
Sabik	102 16.6	S15 44.2
Schedar	349 45.4	N56 34.8
Shaula	96 26.7	S37 06.7
Sirius	258 37.4	S16 43.7
Spica	158 35.1	S11 12.5
Suhail	222 55.6	S43 28.2
Vega	80 41.1	N38 47.3
Zuben'ubi	137 09.4	S16 04.8

	SHA	Mer. Pass.
	° ′	h m
Venus	286 28.8	11 56
Mars	222 04.0	16 11
Jupiter	67 03.2	2 32
Saturn	204 44.1	17 19

UT d	h	SUN GHA	SUN Dec	MOON GHA	v	MOON Dec	d	HP
		° ′	° ′	° ′	′	° ′	′	′
5	00	180 22.9	N22 33.8	161 51.6	1.2	N27 14.8	2.8	61.0
	01	195 22.8	34.1	176 11.8	1.2	27 12.0	3.0	61.0
	02	210 22.7	34.4	190 32.0	1.3	27 09.0	3.2	61.0
	03	225 22.5	. . 34.7	204 52.3	1.4	27 05.8	3.4	61.0
	04	240 22.4	34.9	219 12.7	1.5	27 02.4	3.7	61.0
	05	255 22.3	35.2	233 33.2	1.5	26 58.7	3.8	60.9
	06	270 22.2	N22 35.5	247 53.7	1.7	N26 54.9	4.0	60.9
	07	285 22.1	35.7	262 14.4	1.7	26 50.9	4.2	60.9
T	08	300 22.0	36.0	276 35.1	1.8	26 46.7	4.5	60.9
H	09	315 21.9	. . 36.3	290 55.9	1.8	26 42.2	4.6	60.8
U	10	330 21.8	36.5	305 16.7	2.0	26 37.6	4.8	60.8
R	11	345 21.6	36.8	319 37.7	2.1	26 32.8	5.0	60.8
S	12	0 21.5	N22 37.1	333 58.8	2.2	N26 27.8	5.2	60.8
D	13	15 21.4	37.3	348 20.0	2.2	26 22.6	5.5	60.7
A	14	30 21.3	37.6	2 41.2	2.4	26 17.1	5.6	60.7
Y	15	45 21.2	. . 37.8	17 02.6	2.5	26 11.5	5.7	60.7
	16	60 21.1	38.1	31 24.1	2.6	26 05.8	6.0	60.7
	17	75 21.0	38.4	45 45.7	2.7	25 59.8	6.2	60.6
	18	90 20.9	N22 38.6	60 07.4	2.8	N25 53.6	6.3	60.6
	19	105 20.7	38.9	74 29.2	2.9	25 47.3	6.5	60.6
	20	120 20.6	39.1	88 51.1	3.0	25 40.8	6.8	60.5
	21	135 20.5	. . 39.4	103 13.1	3.2	25 34.0	6.8	60.5
	22	150 20.4	39.7	117 35.3	3.2	25 27.2	7.1	60.5
	23	165 20.3	39.9	131 57.5	3.4	25 20.1	7.2	60.5
6	00	180 20.2	N22 40.2	146 19.9	3.5	N25 12.9	7.4	60.4
	01	195 20.0	40.4	160 42.4	3.7	25 05.5	7.6	60.4
	02	210 19.9	40.7	175 05.1	3.7	24 57.9	7.8	60.4
	03	225 19.8	. . 40.9	189 27.8	3.9	24 50.1	7.9	60.3
	04	240 19.7	41.2	203 50.7	4.0	24 42.2	8.0	60.3
	05	255 19.6	41.4	218 13.7	4.2	24 34.2	8.3	60.3
	06	270 19.5	N22 41.7	232 36.9	4.2	N24 25.9	8.4	60.2
	07	285 19.4	41.9	247 00.1	4.5	24 17.5	8.5	60.2
	08	300 19.2	42.2	261 23.6	4.5	24 09.0	8.7	60.2
F	09	315 19.1	. . 42.4	275 47.1	4.7	24 00.3	8.9	60.1
R	10	330 19.0	42.7	290 10.8	4.8	23 51.4	9.0	60.1
I	11	345 18.9	42.9	304 34.6	4.9	23 42.4	9.2	60.1
D	12	0 18.8	N22 43.2	318 58.5	5.1	N23 33.2	9.3	60.0
A	13	15 18.7	43.4	333 22.6	5.2	23 23.9	9.4	60.0
Y	14	30 18.5	43.7	347 46.8	5.4	23 14.5	9.6	60.0
	15	45 18.4	. . 43.9	2 11.2	5.5	23 04.9	9.8	59.9
	16	60 18.3	44.2	16 35.7	5.6	22 55.1	9.9	59.9
	17	75 18.2	44.4	31 00.3	5.8	22 45.2	10.0	59.9
	18	90 18.1	N22 44.7	45 25.1	5.9	N22 35.2	10.1	59.8
	19	105 18.0	44.9	59 50.0	6.0	22 25.1	10.3	59.8
	20	120 17.8	45.1	74 15.0	6.2	22 14.8	10.4	59.8
	21	135 17.7	. . 45.4	88 40.2	6.3	22 04.4	10.5	59.7
	22	150 17.6	45.6	103 05.5	6.5	21 53.9	10.7	59.7
	23	165 17.5	45.9	117 31.0	6.6	21 43.2	10.8	59.7
7	00	180 17.4	N22 46.1	131 56.6	6.8	N21 32.4	10.9	59.6
	01	195 17.3	46.3	146 22.4	6.9	21 21.5	11.0	59.6
	02	210 17.1	46.6	160 48.3	7.0	21 10.5	11.1	59.5
	03	225 17.0	. . 46.8	175 14.3	7.1	20 59.4	11.3	59.5
	04	240 16.9	47.0	189 40.4	7.3	20 48.1	11.3	59.5
	05	255 16.8	47.3	204 06.7	7.5	20 36.8	11.5	59.4
	06	270 16.7	N22 47.5	218 33.2	7.6	N20 25.3	11.6	59.4
S	07	285 16.5	47.8	232 59.8	7.7	20 13.7	11.7	59.4
A	08	300 16.4	48.0	247 26.5	7.8	20 02.0	11.8	59.3
T	09	315 16.3	. . 48.2	261 53.3	8.0	19 50.2	11.8	59.3
U	10	330 16.2	48.4	276 20.3	8.2	19 38.4	12.0	59.2
R	11	345 16.1	48.7	290 47.5	8.2	19 26.4	12.1	59.2
D	12	0 15.9	N22 48.9	305 14.7	8.4	N19 14.3	12.2	59.2
A	13	15 15.8	49.1	319 42.1	8.6	19 02.1	12.3	59.1
Y	14	30 15.7	49.4	334 09.7	8.6	18 49.8	12.3	59.1
	15	45 15.6	. . 49.6	348 37.3	8.8	18 37.5	12.5	59.1
	16	60 15.5	49.8	3 05.1	9.0	18 25.0	12.5	59.0
	17	75 15.4	50.1	17 33.1	9.0	18 12.5	12.7	59.0
	18	90 15.2	N22 50.3	32 01.1	9.2	N17 59.8	12.7	58.9
	19	105 15.1	50.5	46 29.3	9.3	17 47.1	12.8	58.9
	20	120 15.0	50.7	60 57.6	9.5	17 34.3	12.8	58.9
	21	135 14.9	. . 51.0	75 26.1	9.6	17 21.5	13.0	58.8
	22	150 14.8	51.2	89 54.7	9.7	17 08.5	13.0	58.8
	23	165 14.6	51.4	104 23.4	9.8	N16 55.5	13.1	58.7
		SD 15.8	d 0.2	SD 16.6		16.4		16.1

Lat.	Twilight Naut.	Twilight Civil	Sunrise	Moonrise 5	Moonrise 6	Moonrise 7	Moonrise 8
°	h m	h m	h m	h m	h m	h m	h m
N 72	▭	▭	▭	▭	▭	▭	06 33
N 70	▭	▭	▭	▭	▭	▭	07 10
68	▭	▭	▭	▭	▭	04 53	07 36
66	////	////	00 48	▭	▭	05 40	07 55
64	////	////	01 46	▭	03 46	06 10	08 11
62	////	////	02 19	02 27	04 31	06 32	08 24
60	////	01 11	02 42	03 15	05 00	06 50	08 34
N 58	////	01 51	03 01	03 46	05 23	07 05	08 44
56	////	02 17	03 17	04 09	05 41	07 18	08 52
54	01 05	02 38	03 31	04 28	05 56	07 29	08 59
52	01 42	02 55	03 42	04 44	06 09	07 39	09 06
50	02 06	03 09	03 53	04 58	06 21	07 48	09 12
45	02 49	03 37	04 14	05 26	06 45	08 06	09 24
N 40	03 18	03 59	04 31	05 48	07 04	08 21	09 34
35	03 40	04 17	04 46	06 06	07 20	08 33	09 43
30	03 58	04 31	04 59	06 22	07 34	08 44	09 51
20	04 26	04 55	05 20	06 49	07 58	09 03	10 04
N 10	04 48	05 15	05 38	07 12	08 18	09 19	10 16
0	05 07	05 33	05 55	07 33	08 37	09 34	10 26
S 10	05 23	05 49	06 12	07 55	08 55	09 49	10 37
20	05 39	06 06	06 30	08 18	09 15	10 05	10 48
30	05 54	06 24	06 50	08 44	09 39	10 24	11 01
35	06 03	06 34	07 02	09 00	09 52	10 34	11 09
40	06 12	06 46	07 16	09 18	10 08	10 46	11 17
45	06 22	06 59	07 32	09 40	10 26	11 00	11 27
S 50	06 33	07 14	07 52	10 07	10 49	11 18	11 39
52	06 38	07 21	08 01	10 21	11 00	11 26	11 44
54	06 43	07 29	08 12	10 36	11 12	11 35	11 50
56	06 49	07 37	08 24	10 55	11 26	11 45	11 57
58	06 55	07 47	08 38	11 17	11 43	11 56	12 04
S 60	07 02	07 58	08 54	11 45	12 02	12 09	12 12

Lat.	Sunset	Twilight Civil	Twilight Naut.	Moonset 5	Moonset 6	Moonset 7	Moonset 8
°	h m	h m	h m	h m	h m	h m	h m
N 72	▭	▭	▭	▭	▭	▭	02 19
N 70	▭	▭	▭	▭	▭	▭	01 40
68	▭	▭	▭	▭	▭	02 04	01 12
66	23 14	////	////	▭	▭	01 16	00 51
64	22 13	////	////	▭	01 06	00 45	00 34
62	21 40	////	////	00 09	00 21	00 22	00 20
60	21 16	22 49	////	23 51	24 03	00 03	00 08
N 58	20 57	22 08	////	23 28	23 47	23 58	24 05
56	20 41	21 41	////	23 09	23 34	23 49	23 59
54	20 27	21 20	22 55	22 53	23 22	23 41	23 54
52	20 16	21 03	22 17	22 39	23 11	23 33	23 50
50	20 05	20 49	21 52	22 27	23 02	23 27	23 46
45	19 44	20 21	21 09	22 02	22 42	23 13	23 37
N 40	19 26	19 59	20 40	21 42	22 26	23 01	23 29
35	19 12	19 41	20 18	21 25	22 13	22 51	23 22
30	18 59	19 26	19 59	21 11	22 01	22 42	23 17
20	18 38	19 02	19 31	20 46	21 40	22 26	23 07
N 10	18 19	18 42	19 09	20 24	21 22	22 13	22 58
0	18 02	18 25	18 51	20 04	21 05	22 00	22 49
S 10	17 46	18 08	18 34	19 44	20 48	21 47	22 41
20	17 28	17 51	18 19	19 22	20 29	21 33	22 32
30	17 07	17 33	18 03	18 56	20 08	21 17	22 21
35	16 55	17 23	17 55	18 41	19 55	21 07	22 15
40	16 41	17 12	17 46	18 23	19 41	20 56	22 08
45	16 25	16 59	17 36	18 02	19 23	20 44	22 00
S 50	16 05	16 43	17 25	17 35	19 02	20 28	21 50
52	15 56	16 36	17 20	17 22	18 51	20 21	21 45
54	15 45	16 28	17 14	17 07	18 40	20 12	21 40
56	15 33	16 20	17 08	16 49	18 26	20 03	21 35
58	15 19	16 10	17 02	16 27	18 10	19 52	21 28
S 60	15 03	15 59	16 55	15 59	17 51	19 40	21 21

Day	SUN Eqn. of Time 00^h	SUN Eqn. of Time 12^h	SUN Mer. Pass.	MOON Mer. Pass. Upper	MOON Mer. Pass. Lower	MOON Age	MOON Phase
d	m s	m s	h m	h m	h m	d	%
5	01 32	01 26	11 59	13 49	01 16	02	4
6	01 21	01 15	11 59	14 51	02 21	03	11
7	01 10	01 04	11 59	15 47	03 20	04	19

UT (d h)	ARIES GHA	VENUS −4.0 GHA	VENUS Dec	MARS +1.5 GHA	MARS Dec	JUPITER −2.6 GHA	JUPITER Dec	SATURN +0.7 GHA	SATURN Dec
	° ′	° ′	° ′	° ′	° ′	° ′	° ′	° ′	° ′
8 00 (SUNDAY)	256 45.0	180 35.4	N22 49.9	117 40.9	N17 19.2	323 58.9	S21 54.5	101 22.6	N12 05.4
01	271 47.5	195 34.6	50.3	132 41.9	18.7	339 01.6	54.6	116 24.9	05.4
02	286 49.9	210 33.7	50.7	147 42.9	18.3	354 04.3	54.6	131 27.2	05.3
03	301 52.4	225 32.9	. . 51.1	162 44.0	. . 17.8	9 07.0	. . 54.6	146 29.5	. . 05.2
04	316 54.9	240 32.0	51.5	177 45.0	17.3	24 09.6	54.7	161 31.9	05.2
05	331 57.3	255 31.2	51.8	192 46.1	16.9	39 12.3	54.7	176 34.2	05.1
06	346 59.8	270 30.3	N22 52.2	207 47.1	N17 16.4	54 15.0	S21 54.8	191 36.5	N12 05.1
07	2 02.2	285 29.5	52.6	222 48.2	16.0	69 17.7	54.8	206 38.8	05.0
08	17 04.7	300 28.6	53.0	237 49.2	15.5	84 20.4	54.8	221 41.1	05.0
09	32 07.2	315 27.8	. . 53.4	252 50.2	. . 15.0	99 23.1	. . 54.9	236 43.5	. . 04.9
10	47 09.6	330 27.0	53.8	267 51.3	14.6	114 25.8	54.9	251 45.8	04.8
11	62 12.1	345 26.1	54.1	282 52.3	14.1	129 28.5	55.0	266 48.1	04.8
12	77 14.6	0 25.3	N22 54.5	297 53.4	N17 13.7	144 31.2	S21 55.0	281 50.4	N12 04.7
13	92 17.0	15 24.4	54.9	312 54.4	13.2	159 33.9	55.0	296 52.8	04.7
14	107 19.5	30 23.6	55.3	327 55.5	12.7	174 36.6	55.1	311 55.1	04.6
15	122 22.0	45 22.7	. . 55.6	342 56.5	. . 12.3	189 39.3	. . 55.1	326 57.4	. . 04.5
16	137 24.4	60 21.9	56.0	357 57.6	11.8	204 42.0	55.2	341 59.7	04.5
17	152 26.9	75 21.0	56.4	12 58.6	11.4	219 44.7	55.2	357 02.0	04.4
18	167 29.4	90 20.2	N22 56.8	27 59.6	N17 10.9	234 47.4	S21 55.2	12 04.4	N12 04.4
19	182 31.8	105 19.3	57.1	43 00.7	10.4	249 50.1	55.3	27 06.7	04.3
20	197 34.3	120 18.5	57.5	58 01.7	10.0	264 52.8	55.3	42 09.0	04.2
21	212 36.7	135 17.6	. . 57.9	73 02.8	. . 09.5	279 55.5	. . 55.4	57 11.3	. . 04.2
22	227 39.2	150 16.8	58.2	88 03.8	09.1	294 58.2	55.4	72 13.6	04.1
23	242 41.7	165 15.9	58.6	103 04.9	08.6	310 00.9	55.4	87 16.0	04.1
9 00 (MONDAY)	257 44.1	180 15.1	N22 59.0	118 05.9	N17 08.1	325 03.6	S21 55.5	102 18.3	N12 04.0
01	272 46.6	195 14.2	59.4	133 07.0	07.7	340 06.3	55.5	117 20.6	04.0
02	287 49.1	210 13.4	22 59.7	148 08.0	07.2	355 09.0	55.6	132 22.9	03.9
03	302 51.5	225 12.5	23 00.1	163 09.0	. . 06.8	10 11.7	. . 55.6	147 25.2	. . 03.8
04	317 54.0	240 11.7	00.5	178 10.1	06.3	25 14.4	55.6	162 27.6	03.8
05	332 56.5	255 10.8	00.8	193 11.1	05.8	40 17.1	55.7	177 29.9	03.7
06	347 58.9	270 09.9	N23 01.2	208 12.2	N17 05.4	55 19.8	S21 55.7	192 32.2	N12 03.7
07	3 01.4	285 09.1	01.5	223 13.2	04.9	70 22.5	55.8	207 34.5	03.6
08	18 03.8	300 08.2	01.9	238 14.3	04.4	85 25.2	55.8	222 36.8	03.5
09	33 06.3	315 07.4	. . 02.2	253 15.3	. . 04.0	100 27.9	. . 55.9	237 39.2	. . 03.5
10	48 08.8	330 06.5	02.6	268 16.4	03.5	115 30.6	55.9	252 41.5	03.4
11	63 11.2	345 05.7	02.9	283 17.4	03.1	130 33.3	55.9	267 43.8	03.4
12	78 13.7	0 04.8	N23 03.3	298 18.4	N17 02.6	145 36.0	S21 56.0	282 46.1	N12 03.3
13	93 16.2	15 03.9	03.6	313 19.5	02.1	160 38.7	56.0	297 48.4	03.2
14	108 18.6	30 03.1	03.9	328 20.5	01.7	175 41.4	56.1	312 50.8	03.2
15	123 21.1	45 02.2	. . 04.3	343 21.6	. . 01.2	190 44.1	. . 56.1	327 53.1	. . 03.1
16	138 23.6	60 01.4	04.6	358 22.6	00.7	205 46.8	56.1	342 55.4	03.1
17	153 26.0	75 00.5	05.0	13 23.7	17 00.3	220 49.5	56.2	357 57.7	03.0
18	168 28.5	89 59.7	N23 05.3	28 24.7	N16 59.8	235 52.2	S21 56.2	13 00.0	N12 02.9
19	183 31.0	104 58.8	05.7	43 25.7	59.3	250 55.0	56.3	28 02.3	02.9
20	198 33.4	119 58.0	06.0	58 26.8	58.9	265 57.7	56.3	43 04.7	02.8
21	213 35.9	134 57.1	. . 06.3	73 27.8	. . 58.4	281 00.4	. . 56.3	58 07.0	. . 02.7
22	228 38.3	149 56.3	06.7	88 28.9	57.9	296 03.1	56.4	73 09.3	02.7
23	243 40.8	164 55.4	07.0	103 29.9	57.5	311 05.8	56.4	88 11.6	02.6
10 00 (TUESDAY)	258 43.3	179 54.5	N23 07.4	118 31.0	N16 57.0	326 08.5	S21 56.5	103 13.9	N12 02.6
01	273 45.7	194 53.7	07.7	133 32.0	56.5	341 11.2	56.5	118 16.2	02.5
02	288 48.2	209 52.8	08.0	148 33.1	56.1	356 13.9	56.5	133 18.6	02.4
03	303 50.7	224 52.0	. . 08.4	163 34.1	. . 55.6	11 16.6	. . 56.6	148 20.9	. . 02.4
04	318 53.1	239 51.1	08.7	178 35.1	55.1	26 19.3	56.6	163 23.2	02.3
05	333 55.6	254 50.3	09.0	193 36.2	54.7	41 22.0	56.7	178 25.5	02.3
06	348 58.1	269 49.4	N23 09.3	208 37.2	N16 54.2	56 24.7	S21 56.7	193 27.8	N12 02.2
07	4 00.5	284 48.5	09.7	223 38.3	53.7	71 27.4	56.8	208 30.1	02.1
08	19 03.0	299 47.7	10.0	238 39.3	53.3	86 30.1	56.8	223 32.5	02.1
09	34 05.5	314 46.8	. . 10.3	253 40.4	. . 52.8	101 32.8	. . 56.8	238 34.8	. . 02.0
10	49 07.9	329 46.0	10.7	268 41.4	52.3	116 35.6	56.9	253 37.1	02.0
11	64 10.4	344 45.1	11.0	283 42.5	51.9	131 38.3	56.9	268 39.4	01.9
12	79 12.8	359 44.2	N23 11.3	298 43.5	N16 51.4	146 41.0	S21 57.0	283 41.7	N12 01.8
13	94 15.3	14 43.4	11.6	313 44.5	50.9	161 43.7	57.0	298 44.0	01.8
14	109 17.8	29 42.5	11.9	328 45.6	50.5	176 46.4	57.0	313 46.4	01.7
15	124 20.2	44 41.7	. . 12.3	343 46.6	. . 50.0	191 49.1	. . 57.1	328 48.7	. . 01.7
16	139 22.7	59 40.8	12.6	358 47.7	49.5	206 51.8	57.1	343 51.0	01.6
17	154 25.2	74 39.9	12.9	13 48.7	49.1	221 54.5	57.2	358 53.3	01.5
18	169 27.6	89 39.1	N23 13.2	28 49.8	N16 48.6	236 57.2	S21 57.2	13 55.6	N12 01.5
19	184 30.1	104 38.2	13.5	43 50.8	48.1	252 00.0	57.3	28 57.9	01.4
20	199 32.6	119 37.3	13.8	58 51.9	47.7	267 02.7	57.3	44 00.2	01.3
21	214 35.0	134 36.5	. . 14.1	73 52.9	. . 47.2	282 05.4	. . 57.3	59 02.6	. . 01.3
22	229 37.5	149 35.6	14.5	88 53.9	46.7	297 08.1	57.4	74 04.9	01.2
23	244 39.9	164 34.8	14.8	103 55.0	46.3	312 10.8	57.4	89 07.2	01.2
Mer. Pass. (h m)	6 47.9	v −0.9	d 0.3	v 1.0	d 0.5	v 2.7	d 0.0	v 2.3	d 0.1

STARS Name	SHA	Dec
	° ′	° ′
Acamar	315 21.5	S40 16.0
Achernar	335 29.7	S57 11.3
Acrux	173 13.7	S63 09.1
Adhara	255 15.9	S28 59.0
Aldebaran	290 54.1	N16 31.6
Alioth	166 23.5	N55 55.0
Alkaid	153 01.4	N49 16.4
Al Na'ir	27 48.1	S46 55.0
Alnilam	275 50.5	S 1 11.7
Alphard	218 00.0	S 8 41.8
Alphecca	126 13.8	N26 41.1
Alpheratz	357 47.6	N29 08.1
Altair	62 11.7	N 8 53.3
Ankaa	353 19.4	S42 15.3
Antares	112 30.6	S26 27.2
Arcturus	145 58.9	N19 08.3
Atria	107 35.4	S69 02.7
Avior	234 20.2	S59 32.4
Bellatrix	278 36.4	N 6 21.5
Betelgeuse	271 05.7	N 7 24.6
Canopus	263 58.4	S52 42.0
Capella	280 40.6	N46 00.4
Deneb	49 33.9	N45 18.4
Denebola	182 37.4	N14 31.5
Diphda	348 59.7	S17 56.3
Dubhe	193 56.0	N61 42.6
Elnath	278 17.8	N28 36.9
Eltanin	90 47.4	N51 29.1
Enif	33 50.7	N 9 54.8
Fomalhaut	15 28.0	S29 34.5
Gacrux	172 05.2	S57 10.0
Gienah	175 56.2	S17 35.5
Hadar	148 53.1	S60 25.1
Hamal	328 05.4	N23 30.1
Kaus Aust.	83 48.4	S34 22.9
Kochab	137 18.4	N74 07.3
Markab	13 42.1	N15 15.0
Menkar	314 19.3	N 4 07.4
Menkent	148 11.9	S36 25.0
Miaplacidus	221 41.4	S69 45.4
Mirfak	308 46.4	N49 53.4
Nunki	76 02.6	S26 17.2
Peacock	53 24.6	S56 42.3
Pollux	243 32.6	N28 00.5
Procyon	245 04.0	N 5 12.2
Rasalhague	96 09.6	N12 33.1
Regulus	207 47.6	N11 55.6
Rigel	281 16.0	S 8 11.4
Rigil Kent.	139 56.7	S60 52.5
Sabik	102 16.5	S15 44.2
Schedar	349 45.3	N56 34.8
Shaula	96 26.6	S37 06.7
Sirius	258 37.4	S16 43.7
Spica	158 35.1	S11 12.5
Suhail	222 55.6	S43 28.2
Vega	80 41.1	N38 47.3
Zuben'ubi	137 09.4	S16 04.8

	SHA	Mer. Pass.
	° ′	h m
Venus	282 31.0	12 00
Mars	220 21.8	16 06
Jupiter	67 19.5	2 19
Saturn	204 34.1	17 08

	UT	SUN		MOON				
		GHA	Dec	GHA	v	Dec	d	HP
	d h	° ′	° ′	° ′	′	° ′	′	′
	8 00	180 14.5	N22 51.6	118 52.2	10.0	N16 42.4	13.2	58.7
	01	195 14.4	51.8	133 21.2	10.1	16 29.2	13.2	58.7
	02	210 14.3	52.1	147 50.3	10.2	16 16.0	13.3	58.6
	03	225 14.2	. . 52.3	162 19.5	10.3	16 02.7	13.4	58.6
	04	240 14.0	52.5	176 48.8	10.4	15 49.3	13.4	58.5
	05	255 13.9	52.7	191 18.2	10.6	15 35.9	13.5	58.5
	06	270 13.8	N22 52.9	205 47.8	10.7	N15 22.4	13.6	58.5
	07	285 13.7	53.2	220 17.5	10.8	15 08.8	13.6	58.4
	08	300 13.5	53.4	234 47.3	10.9	14 55.2	13.7	58.4
SUNDAY	09	315 13.4	. . 53.6	249 17.2	11.0	14 41.5	13.7	58.3
	10	330 13.3	53.8	263 47.2	11.2	14 27.8	13.8	58.3
	11	345 13.2	54.0	278 17.4	11.2	14 14.0	13.9	58.3
	12	0 13.1	N22 54.2	292 47.6	11.4	N14 00.1	13.9	58.2
	13	15 12.9	54.5	307 18.0	11.5	13 46.2	13.9	58.2
	14	30 12.8	54.7	321 48.5	11.5	13 32.3	14.0	58.1
	15	45 12.7	. . 54.9	336 19.0	11.7	13 18.3	14.0	58.1
	16	60 12.6	55.1	350 49.7	11.8	13 04.3	14.1	58.1
	17	75 12.4	55.3	5 20.5	11.9	12 50.2	14.1	58.0
	18	90 12.3	N22 55.5	19 51.4	12.0	N12 36.1	14.2	58.0
	19	105 12.2	55.7	34 22.4	12.1	12 21.9	14.2	57.9
	20	120 12.1	55.9	48 53.5	12.2	12 07.7	14.2	57.9
	21	135 12.0	. . 56.1	63 24.7	12.3	11 53.5	14.3	57.9
	22	150 11.8	56.3	77 56.0	12.4	11 39.2	14.3	57.8
	23	165 11.7	56.5	92 27.4	12.5	11 24.9	14.4	57.8
	9 00	180 11.6	N22 56.8	106 58.9	12.6	N11 10.5	14.4	57.7
	01	195 11.5	57.0	121 30.5	12.7	10 56.1	14.4	57.7
	02	210 11.3	57.2	136 02.2	12.8	10 41.7	14.4	57.7
	03	225 11.2	. . 57.4	150 34.0	12.9	10 27.3	14.5	57.6
	04	240 11.1	57.6	165 05.9	12.9	10 12.8	14.5	57.6
	05	255 11.0	57.8	179 37.8	13.0	9 58.3	14.5	57.5
	06	270 10.9	N22 58.0	194 09.8	13.2	N 9 43.8	14.6	57.5
	07	285 10.7	58.2	208 42.0	13.2	9 29.2	14.6	57.5
	08	300 10.6	58.4	223 14.2	13.3	9 14.6	14.6	57.4
MONDAY	09	315 10.5	. . 58.6	237 46.5	13.4	9 00.0	14.6	57.4
	10	330 10.4	58.8	252 18.9	13.4	8 45.4	14.6	57.4
	11	345 10.2	59.0	266 51.3	13.6	8 30.8	14.7	57.3
	12	0 10.1	N22 59.2	281 23.9	13.6	N 8 16.1	14.7	57.3
	13	15 10.0	59.4	295 56.5	13.7	8 01.4	14.6	57.2
	14	30 09.9	59.6	310 29.2	13.7	7 46.8	14.8	57.2
	15	45 09.7	. . 59.7	325 01.9	13.9	7 32.0	14.7	57.2
	16	60 09.6	22 59.9	339 34.8	13.9	7 17.3	14.7	57.1
	17	75 09.5	23 00.1	354 07.7	14.0	7 02.6	14.7	57.1
	18	90 09.4	N23 00.3	8 40.7	14.0	N 6 47.9	14.8	57.1
	19	105 09.2	00.5	23 13.7	14.1	6 33.1	14.8	57.0
	20	120 09.1	00.7	37 46.8	14.2	6 18.3	14.7	57.0
	21	135 09.0	. . 00.9	52 20.0	14.3	6 03.6	14.8	56.9
	22	150 08.9	01.1	66 53.3	14.3	5 48.8	14.8	56.9
	23	165 08.7	01.3	81 26.6	14.4	5 34.0	14.8	56.9
	10 00	180 08.6	N23 01.5	96 00.0	14.4	N 5 19.2	14.8	56.8
	01	195 08.5	01.7	110 33.4	14.5	5 04.4	14.7	56.8
	02	210 08.4	01.8	125 06.9	14.6	4 49.7	14.8	56.8
	03	225 08.2	. . 02.0	139 40.5	14.6	4 34.9	14.8	56.7
	04	240 08.1	02.2	154 14.1	14.6	4 20.1	14.8	56.7
	05	255 08.0	02.4	168 47.7	14.8	4 05.3	14.8	56.7
	06	270 07.9	N23 02.6	183 21.5	14.7	N 3 50.5	14.8	56.6
	07	285 07.7	02.8	197 55.2	14.9	3 35.7	14.8	56.6
	08	300 07.6	03.0	212 29.1	14.8	3 20.9	14.8	56.6
TUESDAY	09	315 07.5	. . 03.1	227 02.9	15.0	3 06.1	14.8	56.5
	10	330 07.4	03.3	241 36.9	14.9	2 51.3	14.7	56.5
	11	345 07.2	03.5	256 10.8	15.0	2 36.6	14.8	56.5
	12	0 07.1	N23 03.7	270 44.8	15.1	N 2 21.8	14.7	56.4
	13	15 07.0	03.9	285 18.9	15.1	2 07.1	14.8	56.4
	14	30 06.9	04.0	299 53.0	15.1	1 52.3	14.7	56.3
	15	45 06.7	. . 04.2	314 27.1	15.2	1 37.6	14.8	56.3
	16	60 06.6	04.4	329 01.3	15.3	1 22.8	14.7	56.3
	17	75 06.5	04.6	343 35.6	15.2	1 08.1	14.7	56.2
	18	90 06.4	N23 04.7	358 09.8	15.3	N 0 53.4	14.7	56.2
	19	105 06.2	04.9	12 44.1	15.3	0 38.7	14.6	56.2
	20	120 06.1	05.1	27 18.4	15.4	0 24.1	14.7	56.2
	21	135 06.0	. . 05.3	41 52.8	15.4	N 0 09.4	14.6	56.1
	22	150 05.8	05.4	56 27.2	15.4	S 0 05.2	14.7	56.1
	23	165 05.7	05.6	71 01.6	15.5	S 0 19.9	14.6	56.1
		SD 15.8	*d* 0.2	SD 15.9		15.6		15.4

Lat.	Twilight Naut.	Twilight Civil	Sunrise	Moonrise 8	Moonrise 9	Moonrise 10	Moonrise 11
°	h m	h m	h m	h m	h m	h m	h m
N 72	▭	▭	▭	06 33	09 16	11 27	13 29
N 70	▭	▭	▭	07 10	09 30	11 30	13 24
68	▭	▭	▭	07 36	09 41	11 33	13 19
66	////	////	00 32	07 55	09 50	11 35	13 15
64	////	////	01 40	08 11	09 58	11 37	13 12
62	////	////	02 15	08 24	10 05	11 39	13 09
60	////	01 04	02 40	08 34	10 11	11 40	13 07
N 58	////	01 47	02 59	08 44	10 16	11 42	13 04
56	////	02 14	03 15	08 52	10 20	11 43	13 03
54	00 58	02 36	03 29	08 59	10 24	11 44	13 01
52	01 38	02 53	03 41	09 06	10 28	11 45	12 59
50	02 04	03 07	03 51	09 12	10 31	11 46	12 58
45	02 47	03 36	04 13	09 24	10 38	11 48	12 55
N 40	03 17	03 58	04 31	09 34	10 44	11 49	12 52
35	03 40	04 16	04 46	09 43	10 49	11 51	12 50
30	03 58	04 31	04 58	09 51	10 53	11 52	12 48
20	04 26	04 55	05 20	10 04	11 01	11 54	12 45
N 10	04 48	05 15	05 38	10 16	11 07	11 56	12 42
0	05 07	05 33	05 56	10 26	11 14	11 57	12 39
S 10	05 24	05 50	06 13	10 37	11 20	11 59	12 37
20	05 40	06 07	06 31	10 48	11 26	12 01	12 34
30	05 56	06 25	06 52	11 01	11 34	12 03	12 31
35	06 04	06 36	07 04	11 09	11 38	12 04	12 29
40	06 13	06 47	07 18	11 17	11 43	12 06	12 27
45	06 23	07 00	07 34	11 27	11 48	12 07	12 25
S 50	06 35	07 16	07 54	11 39	11 55	12 09	12 22
52	06 40	07 23	08 04	11 44	11 58	12 10	12 21
54	06 45	07 31	08 15	11 50	12 01	12 11	12 20
56	06 51	07 40	08 27	11 57	12 05	12 12	12 18
58	06 58	07 50	08 41	12 04	12 09	12 13	12 17
S 60	07 05	08 01	08 58	12 12	12 14	12 14	12 15

Lat.	Sunset	Twilight Civil	Twilight Naut.	Moonset 8	Moonset 9	Moonset 10	Moonset 11
°	h m	h m	h m	h m	h m	h m	h m
N 72	▭	▭	▭	02 19	01 17	00 40	{00 09 / 23 38}
N 70	▭	▭	▭	01 40	01 00	00 33	{00 10 / 23 46}
68	▭	▭	▭	01 12	00 47	00 28	{00 11 / 23 54}
66	23 33	////	////	00 51	00 36	00 23	00 11
64	22 20	////	////	00 34	00 26	00 19	00 12
62	21 45	////	////	00 20	00 18	00 15	00 12
60	21 20	22 57	////	00 08	00 11	00 12	00 13
N 58	21 00	22 13	////	24 05	00 05	00 09	00 13
56	20 44	21 45	////	23 59	24 07	00 07	00 13
54	20 30	21 24	23 02	23 54	24 05	00 05	00 14
52	20 18	21 06	22 22	23 50	24 03	00 03	00 14
50	20 08	20 52	21 56	23 46	24 01	00 01	00 14
45	19 46	20 23	21 12	23 37	23 57	24 15	00 15
N 40	19 28	20 01	20 42	23 29	23 53	24 15	00 15
35	19 13	19 43	20 19	23 22	23 50	24 16	00 16
30	19 00	19 28	20 01	23 17	23 48	24 16	00 16
20	18 39	19 03	19 32	23 07	23 43	24 17	00 17
N 10	18 20	18 43	19 10	22 58	23 39	24 17	00 17
0	18 03	18 25	18 52	22 49	23 35	24 18	00 18
S 10	17 46	18 09	18 35	22 41	23 31	24 18	00 18
20	17 28	17 52	18 19	22 32	23 27	24 19	00 19
30	17 07	17 33	18 03	22 21	23 22	24 19	00 19
35	16 55	17 23	17 54	22 15	23 19	24 19	00 19
40	16 41	17 11	17 45	22 08	23 15	24 20	00 20
45	16 25	16 58	17 35	22 00	23 12	24 20	00 20
S 50	16 04	16 42	17 24	21 50	23 07	24 21	00 21
52	15 55	16 35	17 19	21 45	23 05	24 21	00 21
54	15 44	16 27	17 13	21 40	23 03	24 21	00 21
56	15 32	16 18	17 07	21 35	23 00	24 21	00 21
58	15 17	16 09	17 01	21 28	22 57	24 22	00 22
S 60	15 01	15 57	16 53	21 21	22 54	24 22	00 22

Day	SUN Eqn. of Time 00^h	SUN Eqn. of Time 12^h	SUN Mer. Pass.	MOON Mer. Pass. Upper	MOON Mer. Pass. Lower	MOON Age	MOON Phase
d	m s	m s	h m	h m	h m	d	%
8	00 58	00 52	11 59	16 38	04 13	05	28
9	00 47	00 41	11 59	17 24	05 02	06	38
10	00 35	00 29	12 00	18 08	05 46	07	49

UT d	UT h	ARIES GHA ° ′	VENUS −4.0 GHA ° ′	VENUS Dec ° ′	MARS +1.6 GHA ° ′	MARS Dec ° ′	JUPITER −2.6 GHA ° ′	JUPITER Dec ° ′	SATURN +0.7 GHA ° ′	SATURN Dec ° ′
11 WEDNESDAY	00	259 42.4	179 33.9	N23 15.1	118 56.0	N16 45.8	327 13.5	S21 57.5	104 09.5	N12 01.1
	01	274 44.9	194 33.0	15.4	133 57.1	45.3	342 16.2	57.5	119 11.8	01.0
	02	289 47.3	209 32.2	15.7	148 58.1	44.8	357 18.9	57.5	134 14.1	01.0
	03	304 49.8	224 31.3	. . 16.0	163 59.2	. . 44.4	12 21.7	. . 57.6	149 16.4	. . 00.9
	04	319 52.3	239 30.4	16.3	179 00.2	43.9	27 24.4	57.6	164 18.7	00.8
	05	334 54.7	254 29.6	16.6	194 01.3	43.4	42 27.1	57.7	179 21.1	00.8
	06	349 57.2	269 28.7	N23 16.9	209 02.3	N16 43.0	57 29.8	S21 57.7	194 23.4	N12 00.7
	07	4 59.7	284 27.8	17.2	224 03.3	42.5	72 32.5	57.8	209 25.7	00.7
	08	20 02.1	299 27.0	17.5	239 04.4	42.0	87 35.2	57.8	224 28.0	00.6
	09	35 04.6	314 26.1	. . 17.8	254 05.4	. . 41.5	102 37.9	. . 57.8	239 30.3	. . 00.5
	10	50 07.1	329 25.2	18.1	269 06.5	41.1	117 40.7	57.9	254 32.6	00.5
	11	65 09.5	344 24.4	18.4	284 07.5	40.6	132 43.4	57.9	269 34.9	00.4
	12	80 12.0	359 23.5	N23 18.7	299 08.6	N16 40.1	147 46.1	S21 58.0	284 37.2	N12 00.3
	13	95 14.4	14 22.6	19.0	314 09.6	39.7	162 48.8	58.0	299 39.6	00.3
	14	110 16.9	29 21.8	19.3	329 10.7	39.2	177 51.5	58.1	314 41.9	00.2
	15	125 19.4	44 20.9	. . 19.6	344 11.7	. . 38.7	192 54.2	. . 58.1	329 44.2	. . 00.2
	16	140 21.8	59 20.0	19.8	359 12.7	38.2	207 56.9	58.1	344 46.5	00.1
	17	155 24.3	74 19.2	20.1	14 13.8	37.8	222 59.7	58.2	359 48.8	00.0
	18	170 26.8	89 18.3	N23 20.4	29 14.8	N16 37.3	238 02.4	S21 58.2	14 51.1	N12 00.0
	19	185 29.2	104 17.4	20.7	44 15.9	36.8	253 05.1	58.3	29 53.4	11 59.9
	20	200 31.7	119 16.6	21.0	59 16.9	36.3	268 07.8	58.3	44 55.7	59.8
	21	215 34.2	134 15.7	. . 21.3	74 18.0	. . 35.9	283 10.5	. . 58.3	59 58.0	. . 59.8
	22	230 36.6	149 14.8	21.6	89 19.0	35.4	298 13.3	58.4	75 00.4	59.7
	23	245 39.1	164 14.0	21.8	104 20.1	34.9	313 16.0	58.4	90 02.7	59.7
12 THURSDAY	00	260 41.6	179 13.1	N23 22.1	119 21.1	N16 34.4	328 18.7	S21 58.5	105 05.0	N11 59.6
	01	275 44.0	194 12.2	22.4	134 22.1	34.0	343 21.4	58.5	120 07.3	59.5
	02	290 46.5	209 11.4	22.7	149 23.2	33.5	358 24.1	58.6	135 09.6	59.5
	03	305 48.9	224 10.5	. . 23.0	164 24.2	. . 33.0	13 26.8	. . 58.6	150 11.9	. . 59.4
	04	320 51.4	239 09.6	23.2	179 25.3	32.5	28 29.6	58.6	165 14.2	59.3
	05	335 53.9	254 08.7	23.5	194 26.3	32.1	43 32.3	58.7	180 16.5	59.3
	06	350 56.3	269 07.9	N23 23.8	209 27.4	N16 31.6	58 35.0	S21 58.7	195 18.8	N11 59.2
	07	5 58.8	284 07.0	24.0	224 28.4	31.1	73 37.7	58.8	210 21.1	59.1
	08	21 01.3	299 06.1	24.3	239 29.5	30.6	88 40.4	58.8	225 23.4	59.1
	09	36 03.7	314 05.3	. . 24.6	254 30.5	. . 30.2	103 43.2	. . 58.9	240 25.8	. . 59.0
	10	51 06.2	329 04.4	24.9	269 31.5	29.7	118 45.9	58.9	255 28.1	59.0
	11	66 08.7	344 03.5	25.1	284 32.6	29.2	133 48.6	58.9	270 30.4	58.9
	12	81 11.1	359 02.6	N23 25.4	299 33.6	N16 28.7	148 51.3	S21 59.0	285 32.7	N11 58.8
	13	96 13.6	14 01.8	25.7	314 34.7	28.3	163 54.1	59.0	300 35.0	58.8
	14	111 16.0	29 00.9	25.9	329 35.7	27.8	178 56.8	59.1	315 37.3	58.7
	15	126 18.5	44 00.0	. . 26.2	344 36.8	. . 27.3	193 59.5	. . 59.1	330 39.6	. . 58.6
	16	141 21.0	58 59.1	26.4	359 37.8	26.8	209 02.2	59.2	345 41.9	58.6
	17	156 23.4	73 58.3	26.7	14 38.9	26.4	224 04.9	59.2	0 44.2	58.5
	18	171 25.9	88 57.4	N23 27.0	29 39.9	N16 25.9	239 07.7	S21 59.2	15 46.5	N11 58.4
	19	186 28.4	103 56.5	27.2	44 41.0	25.4	254 10.4	59.3	30 48.8	58.4
	20	201 30.8	118 55.7	27.5	59 42.0	24.9	269 13.1	59.3	45 51.1	58.3
	21	216 33.3	133 54.8	. . 27.7	74 43.0	. . 24.4	284 15.8	. . 59.4	60 53.5	. . 58.3
	22	231 35.8	148 53.9	28.0	89 44.1	24.0	299 18.6	59.4	75 55.8	58.2
	23	246 38.2	163 53.0	28.2	104 45.1	23.5	314 21.3	59.5	90 58.1	58.1
13 FRIDAY	00	261 40.7	178 52.2	N23 28.5	119 46.2	N16 23.0	329 24.0	S21 59.5	106 00.4	N11 58.1
	01	276 43.2	193 51.3	28.7	134 47.2	22.5	344 26.7	59.5	121 02.7	58.0
	02	291 45.6	208 50.4	29.0	149 48.3	22.1	359 29.5	59.6	136 05.0	57.9
	03	306 48.1	223 49.5	. . 29.2	164 49.3	. . 21.6	14 32.2	. . 59.6	151 07.3	. . 57.9
	04	321 50.5	238 48.7	29.5	179 50.4	21.1	29 34.9	59.7	166 09.6	57.8
	05	336 53.0	253 47.8	29.7	194 51.4	20.6	44 37.6	59.7	181 11.9	57.7
	06	351 55.5	268 46.9	N23 30.0	209 52.4	N16 20.1	59 40.4	S21 59.8	196 14.2	N11 57.7
	07	6 57.9	283 46.0	30.2	224 53.5	19.7	74 43.1	59.8	211 16.5	57.6
	08	22 00.4	298 45.2	30.5	239 54.5	19.2	89 45.8	59.9	226 18.8	57.5
	09	37 02.9	313 44.3	. . 30.7	254 55.6	. . 18.7	104 48.5	. . 59.9	241 21.1	. . 57.5
	10	52 05.3	328 43.4	30.9	269 56.6	18.2	119 51.3	21 59.9	256 23.4	57.4
	11	67 07.8	343 42.5	31.2	284 57.7	17.7	134 54.0	22 00.0	271 25.7	57.3
	12	82 10.3	358 41.6	N23 31.4	299 58.7	N16 17.3	149 56.7	S22 00.0	286 28.0	N11 57.3
	13	97 12.7	13 40.8	31.7	314 59.8	16.8	164 59.4	00.1	301 30.3	57.2
	14	112 15.2	28 39.9	31.9	330 00.8	16.3	180 02.2	00.1	316 32.7	57.1
	15	127 17.6	43 39.0	. . 32.1	345 01.9	. . 15.8	195 04.9	. . 00.2	331 35.0	. . 57.1
	16	142 20.1	58 38.1	32.4	0 02.9	15.3	210 07.6	00.2	346 37.3	57.0
	17	157 22.6	73 37.3	32.6	15 03.9	14.9	225 10.4	00.2	1 39.6	57.0
	18	172 25.0	88 36.4	N23 32.8	30 05.0	N16 14.4	240 13.1	S22 00.3	16 41.9	N11 56.9
	19	187 27.5	103 35.5	33.0	45 06.0	13.9	255 15.8	00.3	31 44.2	56.8
	20	202 30.0	118 34.6	33.3	60 07.1	13.4	270 18.5	00.4	46 46.5	56.8
	21	217 32.4	133 33.7	. . 33.5	75 08.1	. . 12.9	285 21.3	. . 00.4	61 48.8	. . 56.7
	22	232 34.9	148 32.9	33.7	90 09.2	12.4	300 24.0	00.5	76 51.1	56.6
	23	247 37.4	163 32.0	33.9	105 10.2	12.0	315 26.7	00.5	91 53.4	56.6
Mer. Pass.		h m 6 36.1	*v* −0.9	*d* 0.3	*v* 1.0	*d* 0.5	*v* 2.7	*d* 0.0	*v* 2.3	*d* 0.1

STARS

Name	SHA ° ′	Dec ° ′
Acamar	315 21.4	S40 16.0
Achernar	335 29.6	S57 11.3
Acrux	173 13.7	S63 09.1
Adhara	255 15.9	S28 59.0
Aldebaran	290 54.1	N16 31.6
Alioth	166 23.5	N55 55.0
Alkaid	153 01.4	N49 16.4
Al Na'ir	27 48.1	S46 55.0
Alnilam	275 50.5	S 1 11.7
Alphard	218 00.0	S 8 41.8
Alphecca	126 13.8	N26 41.1
Alpheratz	357 47.6	N29 08.1
Altair	62 11.7	N 8 53.4
Ankaa	353 19.4	S42 15.3
Antares	112 30.6	S26 27.2
Arcturus	145 58.9	N19 08.3
Atria	107 35.4	S69 02.7
Avior	234 20.2	S59 32.4
Bellatrix	278 36.4	N 6 21.5
Betelgeuse	271 05.7	N 7 24.6
Canopus	263 58.4	S52 42.0
Capella	280 40.6	N46 00.4
Deneb	49 33.9	N45 18.4
Denebola	182 37.4	N14 31.5
Diphda	348 59.7	S17 56.3
Dubhe	193 56.1	N61 42.6
Elnath	278 17.8	N28 36.9
Eltanin	90 47.4	N51 29.1
Enif	33 50.7	N 9 54.8
Fomalhaut	15 28.0	S29 34.5
Gacrux	172 05.3	S57 10.0
Gienah	175 56.2	S17 35.5
Hadar	148 53.1	S60 25.2
Hamal	328 05.3	N23 30.1
Kaus Aust.	83 48.4	S34 22.9
Kochab	137 18.4	N74 07.3
Markab	13 42.1	N15 15.0
Menkar	314 19.3	N 4 07.4
Menkent	148 11.9	S36 25.0
Miaplacidus	221 41.4	S69 45.4
Mirfak	308 46.4	N49 53.4
Nunki	76 02.6	S26 17.2
Peacock	53 24.6	S56 42.3
Pollux	243 32.6	N28 00.5
Procyon	245 04.0	N 5 12.2
Rasalhague	96 09.6	N12 33.1
Regulus	207 47.6	N11 55.6
Rigel	281 16.0	S 8 11.4
Rigil Kent.	139 56.7	S60 52.5
Sabik	102 16.5	S15 44.2
Schedar	349 45.3	N56 34.8
Shaula	96 26.6	S37 06.7
Sirius	258 37.4	S16 43.6
Spica	158 35.1	S11 12.5
Suhail	222 55.6	S43 28.2
Vega	80 41.1	N38 47.3
Zuben'ubi	137 09.4	S16 04.8

	SHA ° ′	Mer. Pass. h m
Venus	278 31.5	12 04
Mars	218 39.6	16 01
Jupiter	67 37.1	2 06
Saturn	204 23.4	16 57

	UT	SUN GHA	SUN Dec	MOON GHA	v	MOON Dec	d	HP
	d h	° ′	° ′	° ′	′	° ′	′	′
	11 00	180 05.6	N23 05.8	85 36.1	15.5	S 0 34.5	14.6	56.0
	01	195 05.5	06.0	100 10.6	15.5	0 49.1	14.5	56.0
	02	210 05.3	06.1	114 45.1	15.5	1 03.6	14.6	56.0
	03	225 05.2	. . 06.3	129 19.6	15.6	1 18.2	14.5	55.9
	04	240 05.1	06.5	143 54.2	15.6	1 32.7	14.5	55.9
	05	255 05.0	06.6	158 28.8	15.6	1 47.2	14.5	55.9
	06	270 04.8	N23 06.8	173 03.4	15.6	S 2 01.7	14.5	55.8
W	07	285 04.7	07.0	187 38.0	15.7	2 16.2	14.4	55.8
E	08	300 04.6	07.1	202 12.7	15.7	2 30.6	14.4	55.8
D	09	315 04.4	. . 07.3	216 47.4	15.6	2 45.0	14.4	55.8
N	10	330 04.3	07.5	231 22.0	15.8	2 59.4	14.4	55.7
E	11	345 04.2	07.6	245 56.8	15.7	3 13.8	14.3	55.7
S	12	0 04.1	N23 07.8	260 31.5	15.7	S 3 28.1	14.3	55.7
D	13	15 03.9	08.0	275 06.2	15.7	3 42.4	14.3	55.6
A	14	30 03.8	08.1	289 40.9	15.8	3 56.7	14.2	55.6
Y	15	45 03.7	. . 08.3	304 15.7	15.8	4 10.9	14.3	55.6
	16	60 03.5	08.4	318 50.5	15.7	4 25.2	14.2	55.6
	17	75 03.4	08.6	333 25.2	15.8	4 39.4	14.1	55.5
	18	90 03.3	N23 08.8	348 00.0	15.8	S 4 53.5	14.1	55.5
	19	105 03.2	08.9	2 34.8	15.8	5 07.6	14.1	55.5
	20	120 03.0	09.1	17 09.6	15.8	5 21.7	14.1	55.4
	21	135 02.9	. . 09.2	31 44.4	15.8	5 35.8	14.0	55.4
	22	150 02.8	09.4	46 19.2	15.8	5 49.8	14.0	55.4
	23	165 02.6	09.5	60 54.0	15.8	6 03.8	13.9	55.4
	12 00	180 02.5	N23 09.7	75 28.8	15.8	S 6 17.7	14.0	55.3
	01	195 02.4	09.8	90 03.6	15.8	6 31.7	13.8	55.3
	02	210 02.3	10.0	104 38.4	15.8	6 45.5	13.9	55.3
	03	225 02.1	. . 10.2	119 13.2	15.8	6 59.4	13.8	55.3
	04	240 02.0	10.3	133 48.0	15.8	7 13.2	13.7	55.2
	05	255 01.9	10.5	148 22.8	15.8	7 26.9	13.8	55.2
	06	270 01.7	N23 10.6	162 57.6	15.8	S 7 40.7	13.6	55.2
	07	285 01.6	10.8	177 32.4	15.7	7 54.3	13.7	55.2
T	08	300 01.5	10.9	192 07.1	15.8	8 08.0	13.6	55.1
H	09	315 01.4	. . 11.1	206 41.9	15.7	8 21.6	13.5	55.1
U	10	330 01.2	11.2	221 16.6	15.8	8 35.1	13.5	55.1
R	11	345 01.1	11.3	235 51.4	15.7	8 48.6	13.5	55.1
S	12	0 01.0	N23 11.5	250 26.1	15.7	S 9 02.1	13.4	55.1
D	13	15 00.8	11.6	265 00.8	15.7	9 15.5	13.4	55.0
A	14	30 00.7	11.8	279 35.5	15.7	9 28.9	13.3	55.0
Y	15	45 00.6	. . 11.9	294 10.2	15.6	9 42.2	13.3	55.0
	16	60 00.4	12.1	308 44.8	15.7	9 55.5	13.3	55.0
	17	75 00.3	12.2	323 19.5	15.6	10 08.8	13.1	54.9
	18	90 00.2	N23 12.4	337 54.1	15.6	S10 21.9	13.2	54.9
	19	105 00.1	12.5	352 28.7	15.6	10 35.1	13.1	54.9
	20	119 59.9	12.6	7 03.3	15.6	10 48.2	13.0	54.9
	21	134 59.8	. . 12.8	21 37.9	15.5	11 01.2	13.0	54.9
	22	149 59.7	12.9	36 12.4	15.6	11 14.2	12.9	54.8
	23	164 59.5	13.1	50 47.0	15.5	11 27.1	12.9	54.8
	13 00	179 59.4	N23 13.2	65 21.5	15.4	S11 40.0	12.8	54.8
	01	194 59.3	13.3	79 55.9	15.5	11 52.8	12.8	54.8
	02	209 59.1	13.5	94 30.4	15.4	12 05.6	12.7	54.8
	03	224 59.0	. . 13.6	109 04.8	15.4	12 18.3	12.7	54.7
	04	239 58.9	13.7	123 39.2	15.4	12 31.0	12.6	54.7
	05	254 58.8	13.9	138 13.6	15.3	12 43.6	12.5	54.7
	06	269 58.6	N23 14.0	152 47.9	15.3	S12 56.1	12.5	54.7
	07	284 58.5	14.1	167 22.2	15.3	13 08.6	12.4	54.7
	08	299 58.4	14.3	181 56.5	15.2	13 21.0	12.4	54.7
F	09	314 58.2	. . 14.4	196 30.7	15.2	13 33.4	12.3	54.6
R	10	329 58.1	14.5	211 04.9	15.2	13 45.7	12.3	54.6
I	11	344 58.0	14.7	225 39.1	15.1	13 58.0	12.1	54.6
D	12	359 57.8	N23 14.8	240 13.2	15.1	S14 10.1	12.2	54.6
A	13	14 57.7	14.9	254 47.3	15.1	14 22.3	12.0	54.6
Y	14	29 57.6	15.0	269 21.4	15.0	14 34.3	12.0	54.6
	15	44 57.4	. . 15.2	283 55.4	15.0	14 46.3	12.0	54.5
	16	59 57.3	15.3	298 29.4	15.0	14 58.3	11.8	54.5
	17	74 57.2	15.4	313 03.4	14.9	15 10.1	11.9	54.5
	18	89 57.1	N23 15.5	327 37.3	14.8	S15 22.0	11.7	54.5
	19	104 56.9	15.7	342 11.1	14.9	15 33.7	11.7	54.5
	20	119 56.8	15.8	356 45.0	14.8	15 45.4	11.6	54.5
	21	134 56.7	. . 15.9	11 18.8	14.7	15 57.0	11.5	54.4
	22	149 56.5	16.0	25 52.5	14.7	16 08.5	11.5	54.4
	23	164 56.4	16.2	40 26.2	14.7	S16 20.0	11.4	54.4
		SD 15.8	d 0.1	SD 15.2		15.0		14.9

Lat.	Twilight Naut.	Twilight Civil	Sunrise	Moonrise 11	Moonrise 12	Moonrise 13	Moonrise 14
°	h m	h m	h m	h m	h m	h m	h m
N 72	□	□	□	13 29	15 35	18 03	■
N 70	□	□	□	13 24	15 18	17 24	■
68	□	□	□	13 19	15 05	16 58	19 12
66	////	////	00 05	13 15	14 54	16 37	18 31
64	////	////	01 36	13 12	14 46	16 21	18 03
62	////	////	02 12	13 09	14 38	16 08	17 42
60	////	00 58	02 37	13 07	14 31	15 57	17 25
N 58	////	01 44	02 57	13 04	14 26	15 48	17 10
56	////	02 12	03 14	13 03	14 21	15 39	16 58
54	00 53	02 34	03 28	13 01	14 16	15 32	16 48
52	01 35	02 51	03 40	12 59	14 12	15 25	16 38
50	02 02	03 06	03 51	12 58	14 09	15 19	16 30
45	02 46	03 36	04 13	12 55	14 01	15 06	16 12
N 40	03 16	03 58	04 31	12 52	13 54	14 56	15 58
35	03 39	04 16	04 45	12 50	13 49	14 47	15 46
30	03 58	04 31	04 58	12 48	13 44	14 39	15 35
20	04 26	04 56	05 20	12 45	13 35	14 26	15 17
N 10	04 49	05 16	05 39	12 42	13 28	14 14	15 01
0	05 08	05 34	05 56	12 39	13 21	14 03	14 47
S 10	05 24	05 51	06 14	12 37	13 14	13 52	14 32
20	05 40	06 08	06 32	12 34	13 07	13 41	14 17
30	05 57	06 27	06 53	12 31	12 59	13 28	13 59
35	06 05	06 37	07 05	12 29	12 54	13 20	13 49
40	06 15	06 49	07 19	12 27	12 49	13 12	13 38
45	06 25	07 02	07 36	12 25	12 43	13 02	13 24
S 50	06 36	07 18	07 56	12 22	12 36	12 50	13 08
52	06 42	07 25	08 06	12 21	12 32	12 45	13 00
54	06 47	07 33	08 17	12 20	12 29	12 39	12 51
56	06 53	07 42	08 29	12 18	12 25	12 32	12 42
58	07 00	07 52	08 44	12 17	12 20	12 25	12 31
S 60	07 07	08 04	09 01	12 15	12 15	12 16	12 19

Lat.	Sunset	Twilight Civil	Twilight Naut.	Moonset 11	Moonset 12	Moonset 13	Moonset 14
°	h m	h m	h m	h m	h m	h m	h m
N 72	□	□	□	{00 09 / 23 38}	23 01	22 02	■
N 70	□	□	□	{00 10 / 23 46}	23 20	22 42	■
68	□	□	□	{00 11 / 23 54}	23 35	23 11	22 28
66	□	□	□	00 11	{00 00 / 23 47}	23 32	23 10
64	22 25	////	////	00 12	{00 05 / 23 57}	23 49	23 39
62	21 49	////	////	00 12	00 09	00 06	00 03
60	21 23	23 04	////	00 13	00 13	00 14	00 15
N 58	21 03	22 17	////	00 13	00 17	00 21	00 26
56	20 46	21 48	////	00 13	00 20	00 27	00 35
54	20 32	21 26	23 09	00 14	00 23	00 32	00 43
52	20 20	21 09	22 26	00 14	00 25	00 37	00 51
50	20 10	20 54	21 59	00 14	00 27	00 41	00 57
45	19 47	20 25	21 14	00 15	00 33	00 51	01 11
N 40	19 29	20 02	20 44	00 15	00 37	00 59	01 23
35	19 15	19 44	20 21	00 16	00 41	01 06	01 33
30	19 02	19 29	20 02	00 16	00 44	01 12	01 42
20	18 40	19 04	19 34	00 17	00 50	01 23	01 58
N 10	18 21	18 44	19 11	00 17	00 55	01 32	02 11
0	18 04	18 26	18 52	00 18	00 59	01 41	02 24
S 10	17 46	18 09	18 35	00 18	01 04	01 50	02 37
20	17 28	17 52	18 19	00 19	01 09	01 59	02 50
30	17 07	17 33	18 03	00 19	01 15	02 10	03 06
35	16 55	17 23	17 54	00 19	01 18	02 17	03 15
40	16 41	17 11	17 45	00 20	01 22	02 24	03 26
45	16 24	16 58	17 35	00 20	01 27	02 32	03 38
S 50	16 04	16 42	17 23	00 21	01 32	02 42	03 53
52	15 54	16 35	17 18	00 21	01 34	02 47	04 00
54	15 43	16 27	17 13	00 21	01 37	02 52	04 08
56	15 30	16 18	17 07	00 21	01 40	02 58	04 17
58	15 16	16 07	17 00	00 22	01 43	03 05	04 27
S 60	14 59	15 56	16 53	00 22	01 47	03 12	04 39

Day	SUN Eqn. of Time 00^h	SUN Eqn. of Time 12^h	SUN Mer. Pass.	MOON Mer. Pass. Upper	MOON Mer. Pass. Lower	Age	Phase
d	m s	m s	h m	h m	h m	d %	
11	00 23	00 16	12 00	18 49	06 29	08 59	
12	00 10	00 04	12 00	19 31	07 10	09 68	
13	00 02	00 08	12 00	20 13	07 52	10 77	

2008 JUNE 14, 15, 16 (SAT., SUN., MON.)

	UT	ARIES	VENUS −4.0		MARS +1.6		JUPITER −2.7		SATURN +0.8	
		GHA	GHA	Dec	GHA	Dec	GHA	Dec	GHA	Dec
	d h	° ′	° ′	° ′	° ′	° ′	° ′	° ′	° ′	° ′
	14 00	262 39.8	178 31.1	N23 34.2	120 11.3	N16 11.5	330 29.5	S22 00.5	106 55.7	N11 56.5
	01	277 42.3	193 30.2	34.4	135 12.3	11.0	345 32.2	00.6	121 58.0	56.4
	02	292 44.8	208 29.3	34.6	150 13.3	10.5	0 34.9	00.6	137 00.3	56.4
	03	307 47.2	223 28.5	34.8	165 14.4	10.0	15 37.7	00.7	152 02.6	56.3
	04	322 49.7	238 27.6	35.1	180 15.4	09.5	30 40.4	00.7	167 04.9	56.2
	05	337 52.1	253 26.7	35.3	195 16.5	09.1	45 43.1	00.8	182 07.2	56.2
	06	352 54.6	268 25.8	N23 35.5	210 17.5	N16 08.6	60 45.9	S22 00.8	197 09.5	N11 56.1
	07	7 57.1	283 24.9	35.7	225 18.6	08.1	75 48.6	00.9	212 11.8	56.0
S	08	22 59.5	298 24.1	35.9	240 19.6	07.6	90 51.3	00.9	227 14.1	56.0
A	09	38 02.0	313 23.2	36.1	255 20.7	07.1	105 54.0	00.9	242 16.4	55.9
T	10	53 04.5	328 22.3	36.3	270 21.7	06.6	120 56.8	01.0	257 18.7	55.8
U	11	68 06.9	343 21.4	36.5	285 22.8	06.2	135 59.5	01.0	272 21.0	55.8
R	12	83 09.4	358 20.5	N23 36.8	300 23.8	N16 05.7	151 02.2	S22 01.1	287 23.3	N11 55.7
D	13	98 11.9	13 19.7	37.0	315 24.8	05.2	166 05.0	01.1	302 25.6	55.6
A	14	113 14.3	28 18.8	37.2	330 25.9	04.7	181 07.7	01.2	317 27.9	55.6
Y	15	128 16.8	43 17.9	37.4	345 26.9	04.2	196 10.4	01.2	332 30.2	55.5
	16	143 19.3	58 17.0	37.6	0 28.0	03.7	211 13.2	01.3	347 32.5	55.4
	17	158 21.7	73 16.1	37.8	15 29.0	03.2	226 15.9	01.3	2 34.8	55.4
	18	173 24.2	88 15.2	N23 38.0	30 30.1	N16 02.8	241 18.6	S22 01.3	17 37.1	N11 55.3
	19	188 26.6	103 14.4	38.2	45 31.1	02.3	256 21.4	01.4	32 39.4	55.2
	20	203 29.1	118 13.5	38.4	60 32.2	01.8	271 24.1	01.4	47 41.7	55.2
	21	218 31.6	133 12.6	38.6	75 33.2	01.3	286 26.9	01.5	62 44.0	55.1
	22	233 34.0	148 11.7	38.8	90 34.2	00.8	301 29.6	01.5	77 46.3	55.0
	23	248 36.5	163 10.8	39.0	105 35.3	16 00.3	316 32.3	01.6	92 48.6	55.0
	15 00	263 39.0	178 09.9	N23 39.2	120 36.3	N15 59.8	331 35.1	S22 01.6	107 50.9	N11 54.9
	01	278 41.4	193 09.1	39.4	135 37.4	59.4	346 37.8	01.7	122 53.2	54.8
	02	293 43.9	208 08.2	39.5	150 38.4	58.9	1 40.5	01.7	137 55.5	54.8
	03	308 46.4	223 07.3	39.7	165 39.5	58.4	16 43.3	01.7	152 57.8	54.7
	04	323 48.8	238 06.4	39.9	180 40.5	57.9	31 46.0	01.8	168 00.1	54.6
	05	338 51.3	253 05.5	40.1	195 41.6	57.4	46 48.7	01.8	183 02.4	54.6
	06	353 53.8	268 04.6	N23 40.3	210 42.6	N15 56.9	61 51.5	S22 01.9	198 04.7	N11 54.5
	07	8 56.2	283 03.8	40.5	225 43.7	56.4	76 54.2	01.9	213 07.0	54.4
	08	23 58.7	298 02.9	40.7	240 44.7	55.9	91 57.0	02.0	228 09.3	54.4
S	09	39 01.1	313 02.0	40.9	255 45.7	55.5	106 59.7	02.0	243 11.6	54.3
U	10	54 03.6	328 01.1	41.0	270 46.8	55.0	122 02.4	02.1	258 13.9	54.2
N	11	69 06.1	343 00.2	41.2	285 47.8	54.5	137 05.2	02.1	273 16.2	54.2
D	12	84 08.5	357 59.3	N23 41.4	300 48.9	N15 54.0	152 07.9	S22 02.1	288 18.5	N11 54.1
A	13	99 11.0	12 58.4	41.6	315 49.9	53.5	167 10.6	02.2	303 20.8	54.0
Y	14	114 13.5	27 57.6	41.8	330 51.0	53.0	182 13.4	02.2	318 23.1	54.0
	15	129 15.9	42 56.7	41.9	345 52.0	52.5	197 16.1	02.3	333 25.4	53.9
	16	144 18.4	57 55.8	42.1	0 53.1	52.0	212 18.9	02.3	348 27.7	53.8
	17	159 20.9	72 54.9	42.3	15 54.1	51.5	227 21.6	02.4	3 30.0	53.8
	18	174 23.3	87 54.0	N23 42.5	30 55.2	N15 51.1	242 24.3	S22 02.4	18 32.3	N11 53.7
	19	189 25.8	102 53.1	42.6	45 56.2	50.6	257 27.1	02.5	33 34.6	53.6
	20	204 28.2	117 52.2	42.8	60 57.2	50.1	272 29.8	02.5	48 36.9	53.5
	21	219 30.7	132 51.4	43.0	75 58.3	49.6	287 32.6	02.5	63 39.2	53.5
	22	234 33.2	147 50.5	43.1	90 59.3	49.1	302 35.3	02.6	78 41.5	53.4
	23	249 35.6	162 49.6	43.3	106 00.4	48.6	317 38.0	02.6	93 43.8	53.3
	16 00	264 38.1	177 48.7	N23 43.5	121 01.4	N15 48.1	332 40.8	S22 02.7	108 46.1	N11 53.3
	01	279 40.6	192 47.8	43.6	136 02.5	47.6	347 43.5	02.7	123 48.4	53.2
	02	294 43.0	207 46.9	43.8	151 03.5	47.1	2 46.3	02.8	138 50.7	53.1
	03	309 45.5	222 46.0	43.9	166 04.6	46.6	17 49.0	02.8	153 53.0	53.1
	04	324 48.0	237 45.1	44.1	181 05.6	46.1	32 51.8	02.9	168 55.3	53.0
	05	339 50.4	252 44.3	44.3	196 06.7	45.7	47 54.5	02.9	183 57.6	52.9
	06	354 52.9	267 43.4	N23 44.4	211 07.7	N15 45.2	62 57.2	S22 03.0	198 59.9	N11 52.9
	07	9 55.4	282 42.5	44.6	226 08.8	44.7	78 00.0	03.0	214 02.2	52.8
	08	24 57.8	297 41.6	44.7	241 09.8	44.2	93 02.7	03.0	229 04.5	52.7
M	09	40 00.3	312 40.7	44.9	256 10.8	43.7	108 05.5	03.1	244 06.8	52.7
O	10	55 02.7	327 39.8	45.0	271 11.9	43.2	123 08.2	03.1	259 09.1	52.6
N	11	70 05.2	342 38.9	45.2	286 12.9	42.7	138 11.0	03.2	274 11.4	52.5
D	12	85 07.7	357 38.0	N23 45.3	301 14.0	N15 42.2	153 13.7	S22 03.2	289 13.7	N11 52.5
A	13	100 10.1	12 37.1	45.5	316 15.0	41.7	168 16.4	03.3	304 16.0	52.4
Y	14	115 12.6	27 36.3	45.6	331 16.1	41.2	183 19.2	03.3	319 18.2	52.3
	15	130 15.1	42 35.4	45.8	346 17.1	40.7	198 21.9	03.4	334 20.5	52.2
	16	145 17.5	57 34.5	45.9	1 18.2	40.2	213 24.7	03.4	349 22.8	52.2
	17	160 20.0	72 33.6	46.1	16 19.2	39.7	228 27.4	03.4	4 25.1	52.1
	18	175 22.5	87 32.7	N23 46.2	31 20.3	N15 39.2	243 30.2	S22 03.5	19 27.4	N11 52.0
	19	190 24.9	102 31.8	46.4	46 21.3	38.8	258 32.9	03.5	34 29.7	52.0
	20	205 27.4	117 30.9	46.5	61 22.3	38.3	273 35.7	03.6	49 32.0	51.9
	21	220 29.9	132 30.0	46.7	76 23.4	37.8	288 38.4	03.6	64 34.3	51.8
	22	235 32.3	147 29.1	46.8	91 24.4	37.3	303 41.1	03.7	79 36.6	51.8
	23	250 34.8	162 28.3	46.9	106 25.5	36.8	318 43.9	03.7	94 38.9	51.7
	Mer. Pass.	h m 6 24.3	*v* −0.9	*d* 0.2	*v* 1.0	*d* 0.5	*v* 2.7	*d* 0.0	*v* 2.3	*d* 0.1

STARS		
Name	SHA	Dec
	° ′	° ′
Acamar	315 21.4	S40 16.0
Achernar	335 29.6	S57 11.3
Acrux	173 13.7	S63 09.1
Adhara	255 15.9	S28 59.0
Aldebaran	290 54.1	N16 31.6
Alioth	166 23.5	N55 55.0
Alkaid	153 01.4	N49 16.4
Al Na'ir	27 48.1	S46 55.0
Alnilam	275 50.5	S 1 11.7
Alphard	218 00.0	S 8 41.8
Alphecca	126 13.8	N26 41.1
Alpheratz	357 47.6	N29 08.1
Altair	62 11.6	N 8 53.4
Ankaa	353 19.3	S42 15.3
Antares	112 30.6	S26 27.2
Arcturus	145 58.9	N19 08.3
Atria	107 35.3	S69 02.7
Avior	234 20.2	S59 32.4
Bellatrix	278 36.4	N 6 21.5
Betelgeuse	271 05.7	N 7 24.6
Canopus	263 58.4	S52 42.0
Capella	280 40.6	N46 00.4
Deneb	49 33.8	N45 18.4
Denebola	182 37.4	N14 31.5
Diphda	348 59.7	S17 56.2
Dubhe	193 56.1	N61 42.6
Elnath	278 17.8	N28 36.9
Eltanin	90 47.3	N51 29.2
Enif	33 50.7	N 9 54.8
Fomalhaut	15 28.0	S29 34.4
Gacrux	172 05.3	S57 10.0
Gienah	175 56.2	S17 35.5
Hadar	148 53.1	S60 25.2
Hamal	328 05.3	N23 30.1
Kaus Aust.	83 48.4	S34 22.9
Kochab	137 18.5	N74 07.3
Markab	13 42.1	N15 15.0
Menkar	314 19.3	N 4 07.4
Menkent	148 11.9	S36 25.0
Miaplacidus	221 41.4	S69 45.4
Mirfak	308 46.3	N49 53.4
Nunki	76 02.6	S26 17.2
Peacock	53 24.5	S56 42.3
Pollux	243 32.6	N28 00.4
Procyon	245 04.0	N 5 12.2
Rasalhague	96 09.6	N12 33.1
Regulus	207 47.6	N11 55.6
Rigel	281 16.0	S 8 11.4
Rigil Kent.	139 56.7	S60 52.5
Sabik	102 16.5	S15 44.2
Schedar	349 45.3	N56 34.8
Shaula	96 26.6	S37 06.7
Sirius	258 37.4	S16 43.6
Spica	158 35.1	S11 12.5
Suhail	222 55.6	S43 28.2
Vega	80 41.1	N38 47.4
Zuben'ubi	137 09.4	S16 04.8

	SHA	Mer. Pass.
	° ′	h m
Venus	274 31.0	12 08
Mars	216 57.4	15 56
Jupiter	67 56.1	1 53
Saturn	204 12.0	16 46

UT		SUN GHA	SUN Dec	MOON GHA	v	MOON Dec	d	HP
d	h	° ′	° ′	° ′	′	° ′	′	′
14	00	179 56.3	N23 16.3	54 59.9	14.6	S16 31.4	11.3	54.4
	01	194 56.1	16.4	69 33.5	14.5	16 42.7	11.2	54.4
	02	209 56.0	16.5	84 07.0	14.6	16 53.9	11.2	54.4
	03	224 55.9	. . 16.6	98 40.6	14.4	17 05.1	11.1	54.4
	04	239 55.7	16.8	113 14.0	14.5	17 16.2	11.1	54.4
	05	254 55.6	16.9	127 47.5	14.4	17 27.3	10.9	54.3
	06	269 55.5	N23 17.0	142 20.9	14.3	S17 38.2	10.9	54.3
	07	284 55.3	17.1	156 54.2	14.3	17 49.1	10.8	54.3
S	08	299 55.2	17.2	171 27.5	14.2	17 59.9	10.7	54.3
A	09	314 55.1	. . 17.3	186 00.7	14.2	18 10.6	10.7	54.3
T	10	329 54.9	17.4	200 33.9	14.1	18 21.3	10.6	54.3
U	11	344 54.8	17.6	215 07.0	14.1	18 31.9	10.5	54.3
R	12	359 54.7	N23 17.7	229 40.1	14.1	S18 42.4	10.4	54.3
D	13	14 54.5	17.8	244 13.2	13.9	18 52.8	10.3	54.2
A	14	29 54.4	17.9	258 46.1	14.0	19 03.1	10.3	54.2
Y	15	44 54.3	. . 18.0	273 19.1	13.8	19 13.4	10.1	54.2
	16	59 54.2	18.1	287 51.9	13.9	19 23.5	10.1	54.2
	17	74 54.0	18.2	302 24.8	13.7	19 33.6	10.0	54.2
	18	89 53.9	N23 18.3	316 57.5	13.7	S19 43.6	9.9	54.2
	19	104 53.8	18.4	331 30.2	13.7	19 53.5	9.9	54.2
	20	119 53.6	18.5	346 02.9	13.6	20 03.4	9.7	54.2
	21	134 53.5	. . 18.6	0 35.5	13.6	20 13.1	9.7	54.2
	22	149 53.4	18.8	15 08.1	13.5	20 22.8	9.6	54.2
	23	164 53.2	18.9	29 40.6	13.4	20 32.4	9.5	54.2
15	00	179 53.1	N23 19.0	44 13.0	13.4	S20 41.9	9.3	54.1
	01	194 53.0	19.1	58 45.4	13.3	20 51.2	9.4	54.1
	02	209 52.8	19.2	73 17.7	13.3	21 00.6	9.2	54.1
	03	224 52.7	. . 19.3	87 50.0	13.2	21 09.8	9.1	54.1
	04	239 52.6	19.4	102 22.2	13.2	21 18.9	9.0	54.1
	05	254 52.4	19.5	116 54.4	13.1	21 27.9	9.0	54.1
	06	269 52.3	N23 19.6	131 26.5	13.0	S21 36.9	8.8	54.1
	07	284 52.2	19.7	145 58.5	13.0	21 45.7	8.8	54.1
	08	299 52.0	19.8	160 30.5	12.9	21 54.5	8.6	54.1
S	09	314 51.9	. . 19.9	175 02.4	12.9	22 03.1	8.6	54.1
U	10	329 51.8	20.0	189 34.3	12.8	22 11.7	8.4	54.1
N	11	344 51.6	20.1	204 06.1	12.8	22 20.1	8.4	54.1
D	12	359 51.5	N23 20.1	218 37.9	12.7	S22 28.5	8.3	54.1
A	13	14 51.4	20.2	233 09.6	12.6	22 36.8	8.1	54.1
Y	14	29 51.2	20.3	247 41.2	12.6	22 44.9	8.1	54.0
	15	44 51.1	. . 20.4	262 12.8	12.5	22 53.0	8.0	54.0
	16	59 51.0	20.5	276 44.3	12.5	23 01.0	7.8	54.0
	17	74 50.8	20.6	291 15.8	12.4	23 08.8	7.8	54.0
	18	89 50.7	N23 20.7	305 47.2	12.4	S23 16.6	7.6	54.0
	19	104 50.6	20.8	320 18.6	12.3	23 24.2	7.6	54.0
	20	119 50.4	20.9	334 49.9	12.2	23 31.8	7.5	54.0
	21	134 50.3	. . 21.0	349 21.1	12.2	23 39.3	7.3	54.0
	22	149 50.2	21.1	3 52.3	12.1	23 46.6	7.2	54.0
	23	164 50.0	21.1	18 23.4	12.1	23 53.8	7.2	54.0
16	00	179 49.9	N23 21.2	32 54.5	12.0	S24 01.0	7.0	54.0
	01	194 49.8	21.3	47 25.5	12.0	24 08.0	6.9	54.0
	02	209 49.6	21.4	61 56.5	11.9	24 14.9	6.8	54.0
	03	224 49.5	. . 21.5	76 27.4	11.8	24 21.7	6.7	54.0
	04	239 49.4	21.6	90 58.2	11.8	24 28.4	6.6	54.0
	05	254 49.2	21.7	105 29.0	11.7	24 35.0	6.5	54.0
	06	269 49.1	N23 21.7	119 59.7	11.7	S24 41.5	6.4	54.0
	07	284 49.0	21.8	134 30.4	11.7	24 47.9	6.2	54.0
	08	299 48.8	21.9	149 01.1	11.5	24 54.1	6.1	54.0
M	09	314 48.7	. . 22.0	163 31.6	11.6	25 00.2	6.1	54.0
O	10	329 48.6	22.1	178 02.2	11.4	25 06.3	5.9	54.0
N	11	344 48.4	22.1	192 32.6	11.4	25 12.2	5.8	54.0
D	12	359 48.3	N23 22.2	207 03.0	11.4	S25 18.0	5.7	54.0
A	13	14 48.2	22.3	221 33.4	11.3	25 23.7	5.5	54.0
Y	14	29 48.0	22.4	236 03.7	11.3	25 29.2	5.5	54.0
	15	44 47.9	. . 22.4	250 34.0	11.2	25 34.7	5.3	54.0
	16	59 47.7	22.5	265 04.2	11.2	25 40.0	5.2	54.0
	17	74 47.6	22.6	279 34.4	11.1	25 45.2	5.1	54.0
	18	89 47.5	N23 22.7	294 04.5	11.1	S25 50.3	5.0	54.0
	19	104 47.3	22.7	308 34.6	11.0	25 55.3	4.8	54.0
	20	119 47.2	22.8	323 04.6	11.0	26 00.1	4.8	54.0
	21	134 47.1	. . 22.9	337 34.6	10.9	26 04.9	4.6	54.0
	22	149 46.9	22.9	352 04.5	10.9	26 09.5	4.5	54.0
	23	164 46.8	23.0	6 34.4	10.8	S26 14.0	4.3	54.0
		SD 15.8	d 0.1	SD 14.8		14.7		14.7

Lat.	Twilight Naut.	Twilight Civil	Sunrise	Moonrise 14	Moonrise 15	Moonrise 16	Moonrise 17
°	h m	h m	h m	h m	h m	h m	h m
N 72	□	□	□	■	■	■	■
N 70	□	□	□	■	■	■	■
68	□	□	□	19 12	■	■	■
66	□	□	□	18 31	21 08	■	■
64	////	////	01 33	18 03	19 55	■	■
62	////	////	02 10	17 42	19 19	21 00	22 34
60	////	00 53	02 36	17 25	18 54	20 21	21 36
N 58	////	01 41	02 56	17 10	18 34	19 54	21 03
56	////	02 11	03 13	16 58	18 17	19 33	20 39
54	00 48	02 33	03 27	16 48	18 03	19 15	20 19
52	01 33	02 51	03 39	16 38	17 51	19 00	20 03
50	02 01	03 06	03 50	16 30	17 40	18 47	19 49
45	02 46	03 35	04 13	16 12	17 18	18 21	19 20
N 40	03 16	03 58	04 31	15 58	17 00	18 00	18 57
35	03 39	04 16	04 46	15 46	16 44	17 43	18 39
30	03 58	04 31	04 59	15 35	16 31	17 28	18 23
20	04 27	04 56	05 20	15 17	16 09	17 03	17 56
N 10	04 49	05 16	05 39	15 01	15 50	16 41	17 33
0	05 08	05 34	05 57	14 47	15 33	16 21	17 11
S 10	05 25	05 51	06 14	14 32	15 15	16 01	16 50
20	05 41	06 09	06 33	14 17	14 56	15 39	16 26
30	05 58	06 28	06 54	13 59	14 35	15 14	16 00
35	06 06	06 38	07 06	13 49	14 22	15 00	15 44
40	06 16	06 50	07 20	13 38	14 08	14 43	15 26
45	06 26	07 03	07 37	13 24	13 51	14 23	15 04
S 50	06 38	07 19	07 58	13 08	13 30	13 58	14 36
52	06 43	07 27	08 08	13 00	13 20	13 46	14 22
54	06 49	07 35	08 19	12 51	13 08	13 32	14 06
56	06 55	07 44	08 31	12 42	12 56	13 16	13 47
58	07 01	07 54	08 46	12 31	12 41	12 57	13 25
S 60	07 09	08 06	09 03	12 19	12 24	12 34	12 55

Lat.	Sunset	Twilight Civil	Twilight Naut.	Moonset 14	Moonset 15	Moonset 16	Moonset 17
°	h m	h m	h m	h m	h m	h m	h m
N 72	□	□	□	■	■	■	■
N 70	□	□	□	■	■	■	■
68	□	□	□	22 28	■	■	■
66	□	□	□	23 10	22 09	■	■
64	22 29	////	////	23 39	23 23	■	■
62	21 52	////	////	00 03	{00 01 / 23 59}	24 00	00 00
60	21 25	23 10	////	00 15	00 19	00 25	00 39
N 58	21 05	22 20	////	00 26	00 34	00 46	01 07
56	20 48	21 51	////	00 35	00 46	01 03	01 28
54	20 34	21 29	23 14	00 43	00 58	01 17	01 46
52	20 22	21 11	22 29	00 51	01 08	01 30	02 01
50	20 11	20 56	22 01	00 57	01 17	01 41	02 14
45	19 49	20 26	21 16	01 11	01 35	02 05	02 41
N 40	19 31	20 04	20 45	01 23	01 51	02 23	03 02
35	19 16	19 45	20 22	01 33	02 04	02 39	03 20
30	19 03	19 30	20 03	01 42	02 15	02 53	03 35
20	18 41	19 05	19 34	01 58	02 35	03 16	04 01
N 10	18 22	18 45	19 12	02 11	02 52	03 37	04 24
0	18 04	18 27	18 53	02 24	03 09	03 56	04 45
S 10	17 47	18 10	18 36	02 37	03 25	04 15	05 06
20	17 28	17 52	18 20	02 50	03 42	04 35	05 28
30	17 07	17 34	18 03	03 06	04 02	04 59	05 55
35	16 55	17 23	17 55	03 15	04 14	05 13	06 10
40	16 41	17 11	17 45	03 26	04 28	05 29	06 28
45	16 24	16 58	17 35	03 38	04 44	05 48	06 50
S 50	16 03	16 42	17 23	03 53	05 04	06 13	07 18
52	15 53	16 34	17 18	04 00	05 13	06 25	07 31
54	15 42	16 26	17 12	04 08	05 24	06 38	07 47
56	15 30	16 17	17 06	04 17	05 36	06 54	08 05
58	15 15	16 07	17 00	04 27	05 50	07 12	08 28
S 60	14 58	15 55	16 52	04 39	06 07	07 35	08 58

Day	SUN Eqn. of Time 00^h	SUN Eqn. of Time 12^h	SUN Mer. Pass.	MOON Mer. Pass. Upper	MOON Mer. Pass. Lower	MOON Age	MOON Phase
d	m s	m s	h m	h m	h m	d %	
14	00 15	00 21	12 00	20 58	08 35	11 85	
15	00 27	00 34	12 01	21 44	09 20	12 91	◐
16	00 40	00 47	12 01	22 33	10 08	13 95	

UT		ARIES	VENUS −4.0		MARS +1.6		JUPITER −2.7		SATURN +0.8	
d h	Day	GHA	GHA	Dec	GHA	Dec	GHA	Dec	GHA	Dec
		° ′	° ′	° ′	° ′	° ′	° ′	° ′	° ′	° ′
17 00		265 37.2	177 27.4	N23 47.1	121 26.5	N15 36.3	333 46.6	S22 03.8	109 41.2	N11 51.6
01		280 39.7	192 26.5	47.2	136 27.6	35.8	348 49.4	03.8	124 43.5	51.6
02		295 42.2	207 25.6	47.3	151 28.6	35.3	3 52.1	03.9	139 45.8	51.5
03		310 44.6	222 24.7	. . 47.5	166 29.7	. . 34.8	18 54.9	. . 03.9	154 48.1	. . 51.4
04		325 47.1	237 23.8	47.6	181 30.7	34.3	33 57.6	03.9	169 50.4	51.3
05		340 49.6	252 22.9	47.7	196 31.8	33.8	49 00.4	04.0	184 52.7	51.3
06		355 52.0	267 22.0	N23 47.9	211 32.8	N15 33.3	64 03.1	S22 04.0	199 55.0	N11 51.2
07		10 54.5	282 21.1	48.0	226 33.9	32.8	79 05.9	04.1	214 57.2	51.1
08	T	25 57.0	297 20.2	48.1	241 34.9	32.3	94 08.6	04.1	229 59.5	51.1
09	U	40 59.4	312 19.3	. . 48.2	256 35.9	. . 31.8	109 11.4	. . 04.2	245 01.8	. . 51.0
10	E	56 01.9	327 18.5	48.4	271 37.0	31.3	124 14.1	04.2	260 04.1	50.9
11	S	71 04.4	342 17.6	48.5	286 38.0	30.8	139 16.9	04.3	275 06.4	50.9
12		86 06.8	357 16.7	N23 48.6	301 39.1	N15 30.3	154 19.6	S22 04.3	290 08.7	N11 50.8
13	D	101 09.3	12 15.8	48.7	316 40.1	29.8	169 22.4	04.4	305 11.0	50.7
14	A	116 11.7	27 14.9	48.8	331 41.2	29.3	184 25.1	04.4	320 13.3	50.6
15	Y	131 14.2	42 14.0	. . 49.0	346 42.2	. . 28.8	199 27.9	. . 04.5	335 15.6	. . 50.6
16		146 16.7	57 13.1	49.1	1 43.3	28.3	214 30.6	04.5	350 17.9	50.5
17		161 19.1	72 12.2	49.2	16 44.3	27.8	229 33.4	04.5	5 20.2	50.4
18		176 21.6	87 11.3	N23 49.3	31 45.4	N15 27.3	244 36.1	S22 04.6	20 22.5	N11 50.4
19		191 24.1	102 10.4	49.4	46 46.4	26.8	259 38.9	04.6	35 24.8	50.3
20		206 26.5	117 09.5	49.5	61 47.4	26.4	274 41.6	04.7	50 27.0	50.2
21		221 29.0	132 08.6	. . 49.6	76 48.5	. . 25.9	289 44.4	. . 04.7	65 29.3	. . 50.2
22		236 31.5	147 07.7	49.7	91 49.5	25.4	304 47.1	04.8	80 31.6	50.1
23		251 33.9	162 06.9	49.9	106 50.6	24.9	319 49.9	04.8	95 33.9	50.0
18 00		266 36.4	177 06.0	N23 50.0	121 51.6	N15 24.4	334 52.6	S22 04.9	110 36.2	N11 49.9
01		281 38.9	192 05.1	50.1	136 52.7	23.9	349 55.4	04.9	125 38.5	49.9
02		296 41.3	207 04.2	50.2	151 53.7	23.4	4 58.1	05.0	140 40.8	49.8
03		311 43.8	222 03.3	. . 50.3	166 54.8	. . 22.9	20 00.9	. . 05.0	155 43.1	. . 49.7
04		326 46.2	237 02.4	50.4	181 55.8	22.4	35 03.6	05.0	170 45.4	49.7
05		341 48.7	252 01.5	50.5	196 56.9	21.9	50 06.4	05.1	185 47.7	49.6
06		356 51.2	267 00.6	N23 50.6	211 57.9	N15 21.4	65 09.1	S22 05.1	200 49.9	N11 49.5
07	W	11 53.6	281 59.7	50.7	226 59.0	20.9	80 11.9	05.2	215 52.2	49.4
08	E	26 56.1	296 58.8	50.8	242 00.0	20.4	95 14.6	05.2	230 54.5	49.4
09	D	41 58.6	311 57.9	. . 50.9	257 01.1	. . 19.9	110 17.4	. . 05.3	245 56.8	. . 49.3
10	N	57 01.0	326 57.0	51.0	272 02.1	19.4	125 20.1	05.3	260 59.1	49.2
11	E	72 03.5	341 56.1	51.1	287 03.1	18.9	140 22.9	05.4	276 01.4	49.2
12	S	87 06.0	356 55.2	N23 51.2	302 04.2	N15 18.4	155 25.6	S22 05.4	291 03.7	N11 49.1
13	D	102 08.4	11 54.3	51.2	317 05.2	17.9	170 28.4	05.5	306 06.0	49.0
14	A	117 10.9	26 53.5	51.3	332 06.3	17.4	185 31.1	05.5	321 08.3	49.0
15	Y	132 13.3	41 52.6	. . 51.4	347 07.3	. . 16.9	200 33.9	. . 05.6	336 10.6	. . 48.9
16		147 15.8	56 51.7	51.5	2 08.4	16.4	215 36.7	05.6	351 12.8	48.8
17		162 18.3	71 50.8	51.6	17 09.4	15.9	230 39.4	05.6	6 15.1	48.7
18		177 20.7	86 49.9	N23 51.7	32 10.5	N15 15.3	245 42.2	S22 05.7	21 17.4	N11 48.7
19		192 23.2	101 49.0	51.8	47 11.5	14.8	260 44.9	05.7	36 19.7	48.6
20		207 25.7	116 48.1	51.8	62 12.6	14.3	275 47.7	05.8	51 22.0	48.5
21		222 28.1	131 47.2	. . 51.9	77 13.6	. . 13.8	290 50.4	. . 05.8	66 24.3	. . 48.5
22		237 30.6	146 46.3	52.0	92 14.7	13.3	305 53.2	05.9	81 26.6	48.4
23		252 33.1	161 45.4	52.1	107 15.7	12.8	320 55.9	05.9	96 28.9	48.3
19 00		267 35.5	176 44.5	N23 52.2	122 16.7	N15 12.3	335 58.7	S22 06.0	111 31.1	N11 48.2
01		282 38.0	191 43.6	52.2	137 17.8	11.8	351 01.5	06.0	126 33.4	48.2
02		297 40.5	206 42.7	52.3	152 18.8	11.3	6 04.2	06.1	141 35.7	48.1
03		312 42.9	221 41.8	. . 52.4	167 19.9	. . 10.8	21 07.0	. . 06.1	156 38.0	. . 48.0
04		327 45.4	236 40.9	52.5	182 20.9	10.3	36 09.7	06.2	171 40.3	47.9
05		342 47.8	251 40.0	52.5	197 22.0	09.8	51 12.5	06.2	186 42.6	47.9
06		357 50.3	266 39.1	N23 52.6	212 23.0	N15 09.3	66 15.2	S22 06.3	201 44.9	N11 47.8
07		12 52.8	281 38.2	52.7	227 24.1	08.8	81 18.0	06.3	216 47.2	47.7
08	T	27 55.2	296 37.3	52.7	242 25.1	08.3	96 20.8	06.3	231 49.4	47.7
09	H	42 57.7	311 36.5	. . 52.8	257 26.2	. . 07.8	111 23.5	. . 06.4	246 51.7	. . 47.6
10	U	58 00.2	326 35.6	52.9	272 27.2	07.3	126 26.3	06.4	261 54.0	47.5
11	R	73 02.6	341 34.7	52.9	287 28.3	06.8	141 29.0	06.5	276 56.3	47.4
12	S	88 05.1	356 33.8	N23 53.0	302 29.3	N15 06.3	156 31.8	S22 06.5	291 58.6	N11 47.4
13	D	103 07.6	11 32.9	53.1	317 30.4	05.8	171 34.5	06.6	307 00.9	47.3
14	A	118 10.0	26 32.0	53.1	332 31.4	05.3	186 37.3	06.6	322 03.2	47.2
15	Y	133 12.5	41 31.1	. . 53.2	347 32.4	. . 04.8	201 40.1	. . 06.7	337 05.4	. . 47.2
16		148 15.0	56 30.2	53.2	2 33.5	04.3	216 42.8	06.7	352 07.7	47.1
17		163 17.4	71 29.3	53.3	17 34.5	03.8	231 45.6	06.8	7 10.0	47.0
18		178 19.9	86 28.4	N23 53.3	32 35.6	N15 03.3	246 48.3	S22 06.8	22 12.3	N11 46.9
19		193 22.3	101 27.5	53.4	47 36.6	02.8	261 51.1	06.9	37 14.6	46.9
20		208 24.8	116 26.6	53.5	62 37.7	02.2	276 53.9	06.9	52 16.9	46.8
21		223 27.3	131 25.7	. . 53.5	77 38.7	. . 01.7	291 56.6	. . 07.0	67 19.2	. . 46.7
22		238 29.7	146 24.8	53.6	92 39.8	01.2	306 59.4	07.0	82 21.4	46.6
23		253 32.2	161 23.9	53.6	107 40.8	00.7	322 02.1	07.0	97 23.7	46.6
Mer. Pass.		h m 6 12.6	*v* −0.9	*d* 0.1	*v* 1.0	*d* 0.5	*v* 2.8	*d* 0.0	*v* 2.3	*d* 0.1

STARS

Name	SHA	Dec
	° ′	° ′
Acamar	315 21.4	S40 16.0
Achernar	335 29.6	S57 11.3
Acrux	173 13.7	S63 09.1
Adhara	255 15.9	S28 59.0
Aldebaran	290 54.1	N16 31.6
Alioth	166 23.6	N55 55.0
Alkaid	153 01.4	N49 16.4
Al Na'ir	27 48.0	S46 55.0
Alnilam	275 50.5	S 1 11.7
Alphard	218 00.0	S 8 41.8
Alphecca	126 13.8	N26 41.1
Alpheratz	357 47.5	N29 08.1
Altair	62 11.6	N 8 53.4
Ankaa	353 19.3	S42 15.3
Antares	112 30.6	S26 27.2
Arcturus	145 58.9	N19 08.3
Atria	107 35.3	S69 02.7
Avior	234 20.3	S59 32.3
Bellatrix	278 36.4	N 6 21.5
Betelgeuse	271 05.7	N 7 24.6
Canopus	263 58.4	S52 42.0
Capella	280 40.5	N46 00.4
Deneb	49 33.8	N45 18.4
Denebola	182 37.5	N14 31.5
Diphda	348 59.7	S17 56.2
Dubhe	193 56.1	N61 42.6
Elnath	278 17.8	N28 36.9
Eltanin	90 47.3	N51 29.2
Enif	33 50.7	N 9 54.8
Fomalhaut	15 27.9	S29 34.4
Gacrux	172 05.3	S57 10.0
Gienah	175 56.2	S17 35.5
Hadar	148 53.2	S60 25.2
Hamal	328 05.3	N23 30.1
Kaus Aust.	83 48.4	S34 22.9
Kochab	137 18.5	N74 07.4
Markab	13 42.1	N15 15.0
Menkar	314 19.3	N 4 07.5
Menkent	148 11.9	S36 25.0
Miaplacidus	221 41.5	S69 45.4
Mirfak	308 46.3	N49 53.4
Nunki	76 02.6	S26 17.2
Peacock	53 24.5	S56 42.3
Pollux	243 32.6	N28 00.4
Procyon	245 04.0	N 5 12.2
Rasalhague	96 09.6	N12 33.1
Regulus	207 47.6	N11 55.6
Rigel	281 16.0	S 8 11.4
Rigil Kent.	139 56.7	S60 52.5
Sabik	102 16.5	S15 44.2
Schedar	349 45.2	N56 34.8
Shaula	96 26.6	S37 06.7
Sirius	258 37.4	S16 43.6
Spica	158 35.1	S11 12.5
Suhail	222 55.6	S43 28.2
Vega	80 41.1	N38 47.4
Zuben'ubi	137 09.4	S16 04.8

	SHA	Mer. Pass.
	° ′	h m
Venus	270 29.6	12 12
Mars	215 15.2	15 51
Jupiter	68 16.2	1 40
Saturn	203 59.8	16 35

UT d h	Day	SUN GHA ° ′	SUN Dec ° ′	MOON GHA ° ′	v ′	MOON Dec ° ′	d ′	HP ′
17 00	TUESDAY	179 46.7	N23 23.1	21 04.2	10.8	S26 18.3	4.3	54.0
01		194 46.5	23.2	35 34.0	10.8	26 22.6	4.1	54.0
02		209 46.4	23.2	50 03.8	10.7	26 26.7	4.0	54.0
03		224 46.3	. . 23.3	64 33.5	10.6	26 30.7	3.9	54.0
04		239 46.1	23.4	79 03.1	10.7	26 34.6	3.7	54.0
05		254 46.0	23.4	93 32.8	10.6	26 38.3	3.6	54.0
06		269 45.9	N23 23.5	108 02.4	10.5	S26 41.9	3.5	54.0
07		284 45.7	23.6	122 31.9	10.5	26 45.4	3.4	54.0
08		299 45.6	23.6	137 01.4	10.5	26 48.8	3.2	54.0
09		314 45.5	. . 23.7	151 30.9	10.5	26 52.0	3.2	54.0
10		329 45.3	23.7	166 00.4	10.4	26 55.2	2.9	54.0
11		344 45.2	23.8	180 29.8	10.3	26 58.1	2.9	54.0
12		359 45.1	N23 23.9	194 59.1	10.4	S27 01.0	2.7	54.0
13		14 44.9	23.9	209 28.5	10.3	27 03.7	2.6	54.0
14		29 44.8	24.0	223 57.8	10.3	27 06.3	2.5	54.0
15		44 44.7	. . 24.0	238 27.1	10.2	27 08.8	2.3	54.0
16		59 44.5	24.1	252 56.3	10.3	27 11.1	2.2	54.0
17		74 44.4	24.2	267 25.6	10.1	27 13.3	2.1	54.0
18		89 44.3	N23 24.2	281 54.7	10.2	S27 15.4	2.0	54.0
19		104 44.1	24.3	296 23.9	10.2	27 17.4	1.8	54.0
20		119 44.0	24.3	310 53.1	10.1	27 19.2	1.6	54.0
21		134 43.8	. . 24.4	325 22.2	10.1	27 20.8	1.6	54.0
22		149 43.7	24.4	339 51.3	10.1	27 22.4	1.4	54.0
23		164 43.6	24.5	354 20.4	10.0	27 23.8	1.3	54.1
18 00	WEDNESDAY	179 43.4	N23 24.5	8 49.4	10.0	S27 25.1	1.2	54.1
01		194 43.3	24.6	23 18.4	10.1	27 26.3	1.0	54.1
02		209 43.2	24.6	37 47.5	10.0	27 27.3	0.9	54.1
03		224 43.0	. . 24.7	52 16.5	10.0	27 28.2	0.7	54.1
04		239 42.9	24.7	66 45.5	9.9	27 28.9	0.6	54.1
05		254 42.8	24.8	81 14.4	10.0	27 29.5	0.5	54.1
06		269 42.6	N23 24.8	95 43.4	9.9	S27 30.0	0.4	54.1
07		284 42.5	24.9	110 12.3	10.0	27 30.4	0.2	54.1
08		299 42.4	24.9	124 41.3	9.9	27 30.6	0.1	54.1
09		314 42.2	. . 25.0	139 10.2	9.9	27 30.7	0.1	54.1
10		329 42.1	25.0	153 39.1	9.9	27 30.6	0.2	54.1
11		344 42.0	25.1	168 08.0	9.9	27 30.4	0.3	54.1
12		359 41.8	N23 25.1	182 36.9	9.9	S27 30.1	0.5	54.1
13		14 41.7	25.1	197 05.8	9.9	27 29.6	0.5	54.1
14		29 41.6	25.2	211 34.7	9.9	27 29.1	0.8	54.1
15		44 41.4	. . 25.2	226 03.6	9.9	27 28.3	0.8	54.1
16		59 41.3	25.3	240 32.5	9.9	27 27.5	1.0	54.2
17		74 41.1	25.3	255 01.4	9.9	27 26.5	1.2	54.2
18		89 41.0	N23 25.3	269 30.3	9.9	S27 25.3	1.2	54.2
19		104 40.9	25.4	283 59.2	9.9	27 24.1	1.4	54.2
20		119 40.7	25.4	298 28.1	9.9	27 22.7	1.6	54.2
21		134 40.6	. . 25.5	312 57.0	9.9	27 21.1	1.6	54.2
22		149 40.5	25.5	327 25.9	9.9	27 19.5	1.8	54.2
23		164 40.3	25.5	341 54.8	9.9	27 17.7	2.0	54.2
19 00	THURSDAY	179 40.2	N23 25.6	356 23.7	10.0	S27 15.7	2.0	54.2
01		194 40.1	25.6	10 52.7	9.9	27 13.7	2.2	54.2
02		209 39.9	25.6	25 21.6	10.0	27 11.5	2.4	54.2
03		224 39.8	. . 25.7	39 50.6	10.0	27 09.1	2.5	54.2
04		239 39.7	25.7	54 19.6	10.0	27 06.6	2.6	54.3
05		254 39.5	25.7	68 48.6	10.0	27 04.0	2.7	54.3
06		269 39.4	N23 25.8	83 17.6	10.0	S27 01.3	2.9	54.3
07		284 39.3	25.8	97 46.6	10.0	26 58.4	3.0	54.3
08		299 39.1	25.8	112 15.6	10.1	26 55.4	3.1	54.3
09		314 39.0	. . 25.8	126 44.7	10.1	26 52.3	3.3	54.3
10		329 38.9	25.9	141 13.8	10.0	26 49.0	3.4	54.3
11		344 38.7	25.9	155 42.8	10.2	26 45.6	3.5	54.3
12		359 38.6	N23 25.9	170 12.0	10.1	S26 42.1	3.7	54.3
13		14 38.4	26.0	184 41.1	10.2	26 38.4	3.8	54.3
14		29 38.3	26.0	199 10.3	10.2	26 34.6	3.9	54.4
15		44 38.2	. . 26.0	213 39.5	10.2	26 30.7	4.1	54.4
16		59 38.0	26.0	228 08.7	10.3	26 26.6	4.2	54.4
17		74 37.9	26.1	242 38.0	10.2	26 22.4	4.3	54.4
18		89 37.8	N23 26.1	257 07.2	10.3	S26 18.1	4.4	54.4
19		104 37.6	26.1	271 36.5	10.4	26 13.7	4.6	54.4
20		119 37.5	26.1	286 05.9	10.3	26 09.1	4.7	54.4
21		134 37.4	. . 26.1	300 35.2	10.4	26 04.4	4.8	54.4
22		149 37.2	26.2	315 04.6	10.5	25 59.6	5.0	54.4
23		164 37.1	26.2	329 34.1	10.4	S25 54.6	5.1	54.5
		SD 15.8	d 0.0	SD 14.7		14.7		14.8

Lat. °	Twilight Naut. h m	Twilight Civil h m	Sunrise h m	Moonrise 17 h m	Moonrise 18 h m	Moonrise 19 h m	Moonrise 20 h m
N 72	□	□	□	■	■	■	■
N 70	□	□	□	■	■	■	■
68	□	□	□	■	■	■	■
66	□	□	□	■	■	■	■
64	////	////	01 31	■	■	■	{00 40 / 23 59}
62	////	////	02 09	22 34	23 21	23 28	23 28
60	////	00 50	02 35	21 36	22 27	22 52	23 04
N 58	////	01 40	02 56	21 03	21 55	22 27	22 45
56	////	02 10	03 13	20 39	21 31	22 06	22 29
54	00 45	02 32	03 27	20 19	21 11	21 49	22 16
52	01 32	02 50	03 39	20 03	20 55	21 34	22 04
50	02 00	03 06	03 50	19 49	20 41	21 22	21 53
45	02 46	03 35	04 13	19 20	20 12	20 55	21 31
N 40	03 16	03 58	04 31	18 57	19 49	20 34	21 13
35	03 39	04 16	04 46	18 39	19 31	20 17	20 58
30	03 58	04 31	04 59	18 23	19 15	20 02	20 44
20	04 27	04 56	05 21	17 56	18 48	19 36	20 22
N 10	04 50	05 17	05 40	17 33	18 24	19 14	20 02
0	05 09	05 35	05 58	17 11	18 02	18 54	19 44
S 10	05 26	05 52	06 15	16 50	17 41	18 33	19 25
20	05 42	06 09	06 34	16 26	17 17	18 11	19 06
30	05 58	06 28	06 55	16 00	16 50	17 45	18 43
35	06 07	06 39	07 07	15 44	16 34	17 30	18 29
40	06 17	06 51	07 21	15 26	16 16	17 12	18 14
45	06 27	07 04	07 38	15 04	15 53	16 51	17 55
S 50	06 39	07 20	07 59	14 36	15 24	16 24	17 32
52	06 44	07 28	08 09	14 22	15 10	16 11	17 20
54	06 50	07 36	08 20	14 06	14 54	15 55	17 07
56	06 56	07 45	08 33	13 47	14 34	15 37	16 53
58	07 03	07 55	08 47	13 25	14 10	15 16	16 35
S 60	07 10	08 07	09 05	12 55	13 38	14 47	16 14

Lat. °	Sunset h m	Twilight Civil h m	Twilight Naut. h m	Moonset 17 h m	Moonset 18 h m	Moonset 19 h m	Moonset 20 h m
N 72	□	□	□	■	■	■	■
N 70	□	□	□	■	■	■	■
68	□	□	□	■	■	■	■
66	□	□	□	■	■	■	■
64	22 32	////	////	■	■	■	01 40
62	21 54	////	////	00 00	00 12	01 12	02 51
60	21 27	23 13	////	00 39	01 09	02 06	03 26
N 58	21 07	22 22	////	01 07	01 42	02 38	03 52
56	20 50	21 52	////	01 28	02 06	03 02	04 12
54	20 36	21 30	23 18	01 46	02 26	03 21	04 28
52	20 23	21 12	22 31	02 01	02 43	03 37	04 43
50	20 12	20 57	22 03	02 14	02 57	03 51	04 55
45	19 50	20 27	21 17	02 41	03 26	04 20	05 21
N 40	19 32	20 05	20 46	03 02	03 48	04 42	05 41
35	19 17	19 46	20 23	03 20	04 07	05 00	05 58
30	19 04	19 31	20 04	03 35	04 23	05 16	06 13
20	18 41	19 06	19 35	04 01	04 51	05 43	06 37
N 10	18 22	18 46	19 13	04 24	05 14	06 06	06 58
0	18 05	18 27	18 54	04 45	05 36	06 27	07 18
S 10	17 47	18 10	18 37	05 06	05 58	06 49	07 38
20	17 29	17 53	18 20	05 28	06 21	07 12	07 59
30	17 08	17 34	18 04	05 55	06 48	07 38	08 23
35	16 55	17 23	17 55	06 10	07 04	07 54	08 37
40	16 41	17 12	17 46	06 28	07 23	08 12	08 53
45	16 24	16 58	17 35	06 50	07 46	08 33	09 13
S 50	16 03	16 42	17 24	07 18	08 14	09 01	09 37
52	15 54	16 35	17 18	07 31	08 29	09 14	09 48
54	15 42	16 26	17 13	07 47	08 45	09 30	10 02
56	15 30	16 17	17 06	08 05	09 05	09 48	10 17
58	15 15	16 07	17 00	08 28	09 29	10 10	10 35
S 60	14 57	15 55	16 52	08 58	10 01	10 39	10 57

Day d	SUN Eqn. of Time 00^h m s	SUN Eqn. of Time 12^h m s	SUN Mer. Pass. h m	MOON Mer. Pass. Upper h m	MOON Mer. Pass. Lower h m	MOON Age d	MOON %	Phase
17	00 53	00 59	12 01	23 23	10 58	14	98	○
18	01 06	01 12	12 01	24 15	11 49	15	100	
19	01 19	01 25	12 01	00 15	12 41	16	99	

UT d	UT h	ARIES GHA	VENUS −3.9 GHA	VENUS Dec	MARS +1.6 GHA	MARS Dec	JUPITER −2.7 GHA	JUPITER Dec	SATURN +0.8 GHA	SATURN Dec
d	h	° ′	° ′	° ′	° ′	° ′	° ′	° ′	° ′	° ′
20	00	268 34.7	176 23.0	N23 53.7	122 41.9	N15 00.2	337 04.9	S22 07.1	112 26.0	N11 46.5
	01	283 37.1	191 22.1	53.7	137 42.9	14 59.7	352 07.7	07.1	127 28.3	46.4
	02	298 39.6	206 21.2	53.7	152 44.0	59.2	7 10.4	07.2	142 30.6	46.4
	03	313 42.1	221 20.3	. . 53.8	167 45.0	. . 58.7	22 13.2	. . 07.2	157 32.9	. . 46.3
	04	328 44.5	236 19.4	53.8	182 46.1	58.2	37 15.9	07.3	172 35.1	46.2
	05	343 47.0	251 18.5	53.9	197 47.1	57.7	52 18.7	07.3	187 37.4	46.1
	06	358 49.5	266 17.6	N23 53.9	212 48.1	N14 57.2	67 21.5	S22 07.4	202 39.7	N11 46.1
	07	13 51.9	281 16.7	54.0	227 49.2	56.7	82 24.2	07.4	217 42.0	46.0
	08	28 54.4	296 15.8	54.0	242 50.2	56.2	97 27.0	07.5	232 44.3	45.9
F	09	43 56.8	311 15.0	. . 54.0	257 51.3	. . 55.7	112 29.8	. . 07.5	247 46.6	. . 45.8
R	10	58 59.3	326 14.1	54.1	272 52.3	55.1	127 32.5	07.6	262 48.9	45.8
I	11	74 01.8	341 13.2	54.1	287 53.4	54.6	142 35.3	07.6	277 51.1	45.7
D	12	89 04.2	356 12.3	N23 54.1	302 54.4	N14 54.1	157 38.0	S22 07.7	292 53.4	N11 45.6
A	13	104 06.7	11 11.4	54.2	317 55.5	53.6	172 40.8	07.7	307 55.7	45.5
Y	14	119 09.2	26 10.5	54.2	332 56.5	53.1	187 43.6	07.7	322 58.0	45.5
	15	134 11.6	41 09.6	. . 54.2	347 57.6	. . 52.6	202 46.3	. . 07.8	338 00.3	. . 45.4
	16	149 14.1	56 08.7	54.3	2 58.6	52.1	217 49.1	07.8	353 02.5	45.3
	17	164 16.6	71 07.8	54.3	17 59.7	51.6	232 51.9	07.9	8 04.8	45.3
	18	179 19.0	86 06.9	N23 54.3	33 00.7	N14 51.1	247 54.6	S22 07.9	23 07.1	N11 45.2
	19	194 21.5	101 06.0	54.3	48 01.8	50.6	262 57.4	08.0	38 09.4	45.1
	20	209 24.0	116 05.1	54.4	63 02.8	50.1	278 00.2	08.0	53 11.7	45.0
	21	224 26.4	131 04.2	. . 54.4	78 03.8	. . 49.5	293 02.9	. . 08.1	68 14.0	. . 45.0
	22	239 28.9	146 03.3	54.4	93 04.9	49.0	308 05.7	08.1	83 16.2	44.9
	23	254 31.3	161 02.4	54.4	108 05.9	48.5	323 08.5	08.2	98 18.5	44.8
21	00	269 33.8	176 01.5	N23 54.4	123 07.0	N14 48.0	338 11.2	S22 08.2	113 20.8	N11 44.7
	01	284 36.3	191 00.6	54.5	138 08.0	47.5	353 14.0	08.3	128 23.1	44.7
	02	299 38.7	205 59.7	54.5	153 09.1	47.0	8 16.8	08.3	143 25.4	44.6
	03	314 41.2	220 58.8	. . 54.5	168 10.1	. . 46.5	23 19.5	. . 08.4	158 27.6	. . 44.5
	04	329 43.7	235 57.9	54.5	183 11.2	46.0	38 22.3	08.4	173 29.9	44.4
	05	344 46.1	250 57.0	54.5	198 12.2	45.5	53 25.0	08.5	188 32.2	44.4
	06	359 48.6	265 56.1	N23 54.5	213 13.3	N14 44.9	68 27.8	S22 08.5	203 34.5	N11 44.3
	07	14 51.1	280 55.2	54.5	228 14.3	44.4	83 30.6	08.6	218 36.8	44.2
S	08	29 53.5	295 54.3	54.5	243 15.4	43.9	98 33.3	08.6	233 39.1	44.1
A	09	44 56.0	310 53.4	. . 54.6	258 16.4	. . 43.4	113 36.1	. . 08.6	248 41.3	. . 44.1
T	10	59 58.5	325 52.5	54.6	273 17.5	42.9	128 38.9	08.7	263 43.6	44.0
U	11	75 00.9	340 51.6	54.6	288 18.5	42.4	143 41.6	08.7	278 45.9	43.9
R	12	90 03.4	355 50.7	N23 54.6	303 19.6	N14 41.9	158 44.4	S22 08.8	293 48.2	N11 43.8
D	13	105 05.8	10 49.8	54.6	318 20.6	41.4	173 47.2	08.8	308 50.5	43.8
A	14	120 08.3	25 48.9	54.6	333 21.6	40.8	188 50.0	08.9	323 52.7	43.7
Y	15	135 10.8	40 48.1	. . 54.6	348 22.7	. . 40.3	203 52.7	. . 08.9	338 55.0	. . 43.6
	16	150 13.2	55 47.2	54.6	3 23.7	39.8	218 55.5	09.0	353 57.3	43.5
	17	165 15.7	70 46.3	54.6	18 24.8	39.3	233 58.3	09.0	8 59.6	43.5
	18	180 18.2	85 45.4	N23 54.6	33 25.8	N14 38.8	249 01.0	S22 09.1	24 01.9	N11 43.4
	19	195 20.6	100 44.5	54.6	48 26.9	38.3	264 03.8	09.1	39 04.1	43.3
	20	210 23.1	115 43.6	54.6	63 27.9	37.8	279 06.6	09.2	54 06.4	43.2
	21	225 25.6	130 42.7	. . 54.5	78 29.0	. . 37.3	294 09.3	. . 09.2	69 08.7	. . 43.2
	22	240 28.0	145 41.8	54.5	93 30.0	36.7	309 12.1	09.3	84 11.0	43.1
	23	255 30.5	160 40.9	54.5	108 31.1	36.2	324 14.9	09.3	99 13.2	43.0
22	00	270 32.9	175 40.0	N23 54.5	123 32.1	N14 35.7	339 17.6	S22 09.4	114 15.5	N11 42.9
	01	285 35.4	190 39.1	54.5	138 33.2	35.2	354 20.4	09.4	129 17.8	42.9
	02	300 37.9	205 38.2	54.5	153 34.2	34.7	9 23.2	09.5	144 20.1	42.8
	03	315 40.3	220 37.3	. . 54.5	168 35.3	. . 34.2	24 25.9	. . 09.5	159 22.4	. . 42.7
	04	330 42.8	235 36.4	54.5	183 36.3	33.6	39 28.7	09.5	174 24.6	42.6
	05	345 45.3	250 35.5	54.4	198 37.4	33.1	54 31.5	09.6	189 26.9	42.6
	06	0 47.7	265 34.6	N23 54.4	213 38.4	N14 32.6	69 34.3	S22 09.6	204 29.2	N11 42.5
	07	15 50.2	280 33.7	54.4	228 39.4	32.1	84 37.0	09.7	219 31.5	42.4
	08	30 52.7	295 32.8	54.4	243 40.5	31.6	99 39.8	09.7	234 33.7	42.3
S	09	45 55.1	310 31.9	. . 54.4	258 41.5	. . 31.1	114 42.6	. . 09.8	249 36.0	. . 42.3
U	10	60 57.6	325 31.0	54.3	273 42.6	30.6	129 45.3	09.8	264 38.3	42.2
N	11	76 00.1	340 30.1	54.3	288 43.6	30.0	144 48.1	09.9	279 40.6	42.1
D	12	91 02.5	355 29.2	N23 54.3	303 44.7	N14 29.5	159 50.9	S22 09.9	294 42.9	N11 42.0
A	13	106 05.0	10 28.3	54.3	318 45.7	29.0	174 53.7	10.0	309 45.1	42.0
Y	14	121 07.4	25 27.4	54.2	333 46.8	28.5	189 56.4	10.0	324 47.4	41.9
	15	136 09.9	40 26.5	. . 54.2	348 47.8	. . 28.0	204 59.2	. . 10.1	339 49.7	. . 41.8
	16	151 12.4	55 25.6	54.2	3 48.9	27.5	220 02.0	10.1	354 52.0	41.7
	17	166 14.8	70 24.7	54.1	18 49.9	26.9	235 04.7	10.2	9 54.2	41.7
	18	181 17.3	85 23.8	N23 54.1	33 51.0	N14 26.4	250 07.5	S22 10.2	24 56.5	N11 41.6
	19	196 19.8	100 22.9	54.1	48 52.0	25.9	265 10.3	10.3	39 58.8	41.5
	20	211 22.2	115 22.0	54.0	63 53.1	25.4	280 13.1	10.3	55 01.1	41.4
	21	226 24.7	130 21.1	. . 54.0	78 54.1	. . 24.9	295 15.8	. . 10.4	70 03.3	. . 41.4
	22	241 27.2	145 20.3	54.0	93 55.2	24.4	310 18.6	10.4	85 05.6	41.3
	23	256 29.6	160 19.4	53.9	108 56.2	23.8	325 21.4	10.5	100 07.9	41.2
Mer. Pass.		h m 6 00.8	*v* −0.9	*d* 0.0	*v* 1.0	*d* 0.5	*v* 2.8	*d* 0.0	*v* 2.3	*d* 0.1

STARS

Name	SHA	Dec
	° ′	° ′
Acamar	315 21.4	S40 16.0
Achernar	335 29.6	S57 11.3
Acrux	173 13.8	S63 09.1
Adhara	255 15.9	S28 59.0
Aldebaran	290 54.0	N16 31.6
Alioth	166 23.6	N55 55.0
Alkaid	153 01.4	N49 16.4
Al Na'ir	27 48.0	S46 54.9
Alnilam	275 50.5	S 1 11.7
Alphard	218 00.0	S 8 41.8
Alphecca	126 13.8	N26 41.2
Alpheratz	357 47.5	N29 08.1
Altair	62 11.6	N 8 53.4
Ankaa	353 19.3	S42 15.3
Antares	112 30.6	S26 27.2
Arcturus	145 58.9	N19 08.3
Atria	107 35.3	S69 02.8
Avior	234 20.3	S59 32.3
Bellatrix	278 36.4	N 6 21.5
Betelgeuse	271 05.7	N 7 24.6
Canopus	263 58.4	S52 42.0
Capella	280 40.5	N46 00.4
Deneb	49 33.8	N45 18.5
Denebola	182 37.5	N14 31.5
Diphda	348 59.7	S17 56.2
Dubhe	193 56.1	N61 42.6
Elnath	278 17.8	N28 36.9
Eltanin	90 47.3	N51 29.2
Enif	33 50.6	N 9 54.8
Fomalhaut	15 27.9	S29 34.4
Gacrux	172 05.3	S57 10.0
Gienah	175 56.2	S17 35.5
Hadar	148 53.2	S60 25.2
Hamal	328 05.3	N23 30.1
Kaus Aust.	83 48.4	S34 22.9
Kochab	137 18.6	N74 07.4
Markab	13 42.0	N15 15.0
Menkar	314 19.2	N 4 07.5
Menkent	148 11.9	S36 25.0
Miaplacidus	221 41.5	S69 45.3
Mirfak	308 46.3	N49 53.4
Nunki	76 02.6	S26 17.2
Peacock	53 24.5	S56 42.3
Pollux	243 32.6	N28 00.4
Procyon	245 04.0	N 5 12.2
Rasalhague	96 09.6	N12 33.2
Regulus	207 47.6	N11 55.6
Rigel	281 16.0	S 8 11.4
Rigil Kent.	139 56.7	S60 52.5
Sabik	102 16.5	S15 44.2
Schedar	349 45.2	N56 34.8
Shaula	96 26.6	S37 06.7
Sirius	258 37.4	S16 43.6
Spica	158 35.1	S11 12.5
Suhail	222 55.7	S43 28.2
Vega	80 41.1	N38 47.4
Zuben'ubi	137 09.4	S16 04.8

	SHA	Mer. Pass.
	° ′	h m
Venus	266 27.7	12 17
Mars	213 33.2	15 46
Jupiter	68 37.4	1 27
Saturn	203 47.0	16 24

UT	SUN GHA	SUN Dec	MOON GHA	v	MOON Dec	d	HP
d h	° ′	° ′	° ′	′	° ′	′	′
20 00	179 37.0	N23 26.2	344 03.5	10.5	S25 49.5	5.2	54.5
01	194 36.8	26.2	358 33.0	10.6	25 44.3	5.3	54.5
02	209 36.7	26.2	13 02.6	10.6	25 39.0	5.5	54.5
03	224 36.6	. . 26.2	27 32.2	10.6	25 33.5	5.6	54.5
04	239 36.4	26.3	42 01.8	10.6	25 27.9	5.7	54.5
05	254 36.3	26.3	56 31.4	10.7	25 22.2	5.8	54.5
06	269 36.1	N23 26.3	71 01.1	10.7	S25 16.4	6.0	54.5
07	284 36.0	26.3	85 30.8	10.8	25 10.4	6.1	54.6
08	299 35.9	26.3	100 00.6	10.8	25 04.3	6.2	54.6
F 09	314 35.7	. . 26.3	114 30.4	10.9	24 58.1	6.3	54.6
R 10	329 35.6	26.3	129 00.3	10.8	24 51.8	6.4	54.6
I 11	344 35.5	26.3	143 30.1	11.0	24 45.4	6.6	54.6
D 12	359 35.3	N23 26.3	158 00.1	11.0	S24 38.8	6.7	54.6
A 13	14 35.2	26.4	172 30.1	11.0	24 32.1	6.8	54.6
Y 14	29 35.1	26.4	187 00.1	11.0	24 25.3	6.9	54.6
15	44 34.9	. . 26.4	201 30.1	11.1	24 18.4	7.1	54.7
16	59 34.8	26.4	216 00.2	11.2	24 11.3	7.1	54.7
17	74 34.7	26.4	230 30.4	11.2	24 04.2	7.3	54.7
18	89 34.5	N23 26.4	245 00.6	11.2	S23 56.9	7.4	54.7
19	104 34.4	26.4	259 30.8	11.3	23 49.5	7.5	54.7
20	119 34.3	26.4	274 01.1	11.4	23 42.0	7.6	54.7
21	134 34.1	. . 26.4	288 31.5	11.4	23 34.4	7.7	54.7
22	149 34.0	26.4	303 01.9	11.4	23 26.7	7.9	54.8
23	164 33.8	26.4	317 32.3	11.5	23 18.8	8.0	54.8
21 00	179 33.7	N23 26.4	332 02.8	11.5	S23 10.8	8.0	54.8
01	194 33.6	26.4	346 33.3	11.6	23 02.8	8.2	54.8
02	209 33.4	26.4	1 03.9	11.6	22 54.6	8.3	54.8
03	224 33.3	. . 26.4	15 34.5	11.7	22 46.3	8.4	54.8
04	239 33.2	26.4	30 05.2	11.7	22 37.9	8.5	54.9
05	254 33.0	26.4	44 35.9	11.8	22 29.4	8.6	54.9
06	269 32.9	N23 26.4	59 06.7	11.8	S22 20.8	8.8	54.9
07	284 32.8	26.4	73 37.5	11.9	22 12.0	8.8	54.9
S 08	299 32.6	26.4	88 08.4	11.9	22 03.2	9.0	54.9
A 09	314 32.5	. . 26.4	102 39.3	12.0	21 54.2	9.0	54.9
T 10	329 32.4	26.4	117 10.3	12.0	21 45.2	9.1	55.0
U 11	344 32.2	26.4	131 41.3	12.1	21 36.1	9.3	55.0
R 12	359 32.1	N23 26.3	146 12.4	12.1	S21 26.8	9.4	55.0
D 13	14 32.0	26.3	160 43.5	12.2	21 17.4	9.4	55.0
A 14	29 31.8	26.3	175 14.7	12.2	21 08.0	9.6	55.0
Y 15	44 31.7	. . 26.3	189 45.9	12.3	20 58.4	9.6	55.0
16	59 31.6	26.3	204 17.2	12.3	20 48.8	9.8	55.1
17	74 31.4	26.3	218 48.5	12.3	20 39.0	9.9	55.1
18	89 31.3	N23 26.3	233 19.8	12.5	S20 29.1	9.9	55.1
19	104 31.2	26.3	247 51.3	12.4	20 19.2	10.1	55.1
20	119 31.0	26.3	262 22.7	12.5	20 09.1	10.1	55.1
21	134 30.9	. . 26.2	276 54.2	12.6	19 59.0	10.3	55.1
22	149 30.7	26.2	291 25.8	12.6	19 48.7	10.3	55.2
23	164 30.6	26.2	305 57.4	12.7	19 38.4	10.4	55.2
22 00	179 30.5	N23 26.2	320 29.1	12.7	S19 28.0	10.6	55.2
01	194 30.3	26.2	335 00.8	12.8	19 17.4	10.6	55.2
02	209 30.2	26.2	349 32.6	12.8	19 06.8	10.7	55.2
03	224 30.1	. . 26.1	4 04.4	12.8	18 56.1	10.8	55.3
04	239 29.9	26.1	18 36.2	12.9	18 45.3	10.9	55.3
05	254 29.8	26.1	33 08.1	13.0	18 34.4	11.0	55.3
06	269 29.7	N23 26.1	47 40.1	12.9	S18 23.4	11.0	55.3
07	284 29.5	26.1	62 12.0	13.1	18 12.4	11.2	55.3
08	299 29.4	26.0	76 44.1	13.1	18 01.2	11.2	55.4
S 09	314 29.3	. . 26.0	91 16.2	13.1	17 50.0	11.4	55.4
U 10	329 29.1	26.0	105 48.3	13.2	17 38.6	11.4	55.4
N 11	344 29.0	26.0	120 20.5	13.2	17 27.2	11.5	55.4
D 12	359 28.9	N23 25.9	134 52.7	13.2	S17 15.7	11.5	55.4
A 13	14 28.7	25.9	149 24.9	13.3	17 04.2	11.7	55.5
Y 14	29 28.6	25.9	163 57.2	13.4	16 52.5	11.8	55.5
15	44 28.5	. . 25.9	178 29.6	13.4	16 40.7	11.8	55.5
16	59 28.3	25.8	193 02.0	13.4	16 28.9	11.9	55.5
17	74 28.2	25.8	207 34.4	13.5	16 17.0	12.0	55.5
18	89 28.1	N23 25.8	222 06.9	13.5	S16 05.0	12.0	55.6
19	104 27.9	25.7	236 39.4	13.5	15 53.0	12.2	55.6
20	119 27.8	25.7	251 11.9	13.6	15 40.8	12.2	55.6
21	134 27.7	. . 25.7	265 44.5	13.6	15 28.6	12.3	55.6
22	149 27.5	25.6	280 17.1	13.7	15 16.3	12.3	55.6
23	164 27.4	25.6	294 49.8	13.7	S15 04.0	12.5	55.7
	SD 15.8	*d* 0.0	SD		14.9	15.0	15.1

Lat.	Twilight Naut.	Twilight Civil	Sunrise	Moonrise 20	Moonrise 21	Moonrise 22	Moonrise 23
°	h m	h m	h m	h m	h m	h m	h m
N 72	□	□	□	■	■	■	01 01
N 70	□	□	□	■	■	01 37	{00 31 / 23 57}
68	□	□	□	■	■	00 43	{00 08 / 23 46}
66	□	□	□	■	00 49	{00 10 / 23 50}	23 36
64	////	////	01 31	{00 40 / 23 59}	23 45	23 36	23 28
62	////	////	02 09	23 28	23 26	23 23	23 21
60	////	00 49	02 36	23 04	23 10	23 13	23 14
N 58	////	01 40	02 56	22 45	22 56	23 04	23 09
56	////	02 10	03 13	22 29	22 45	22 56	23 04
54	00 45	02 33	03 27	22 16	22 34	22 48	23 00
52	01 32	02 51	03 40	22 04	22 25	22 42	22 56
50	02 00	03 06	03 51	21 53	22 17	22 36	22 52
45	02 46	03 36	04 13	21 31	21 59	22 23	22 44
N 40	03 17	03 58	04 31	21 13	21 45	22 13	22 37
35	03 40	04 17	04 46	20 58	21 33	22 04	22 32
30	03 59	04 32	04 59	20 44	21 22	21 56	22 27
20	04 28	04 57	05 22	20 22	21 03	21 42	22 18
N 10	04 50	05 17	05 41	20 02	20 47	21 30	22 10
0	05 09	05 36	05 58	19 44	20 32	21 18	22 03
S 10	05 26	05 53	06 16	19 25	20 17	21 07	21 55
20	05 43	06 10	06 34	19 06	20 00	20 54	21 47
30	05 59	06 29	06 55	18 43	19 41	20 40	21 38
35	06 08	06 40	07 08	18 29	19 30	20 32	21 33
40	06 17	06 51	07 22	18 14	19 18	20 22	21 27
45	06 28	07 05	07 39	17 55	19 02	20 11	21 20
S 50	06 40	07 21	08 00	17 32	18 44	19 58	21 12
52	06 45	07 29	08 10	17 20	18 35	19 51	21 08
54	06 51	07 37	08 21	17 07	18 25	19 44	21 04
56	06 57	07 46	08 33	16 53	18 14	19 36	20 59
58	07 04	07 56	08 48	16 35	18 01	19 28	20 54
S 60	07 11	08 08	09 06	16 14	17 46	19 17	20 48

Lat.	Sunset	Twilight Civil	Twilight Naut.	Moonset 20	Moonset 21	Moonset 22	Moonset 23
°	h m	h m	h m	h m	h m	h m	h m
N 72	□	□	□	■	■	■	06 21
N 70	□	□	□	■	■	04 07	06 49
68	□	□	□	■	■	05 00	07 10
66	□	□	□	■	03 14	05 32	07 27
64	22 33	////	////	01 40	04 03	05 56	07 40
62	21 54	////	////	02 51	04 34	06 14	07 51
60	21 28	23 15	////	03 26	04 57	06 29	08 00
N 58	21 07	22 23	////	03 52	05 15	06 42	08 09
56	20 51	21 53	////	04 12	05 31	06 53	08 16
54	20 36	21 31	23 19	04 28	05 44	07 03	08 22
52	20 24	21 13	22 31	04 43	05 56	07 11	08 28
50	20 13	20 58	22 03	04 55	06 06	07 19	08 33
45	19 50	20 28	21 18	05 21	06 27	07 35	08 44
N 40	19 32	20 05	20 47	05 41	06 44	07 49	08 53
35	19 17	19 47	20 24	05 58	06 58	08 00	09 01
30	19 04	19 32	20 05	06 13	07 11	08 10	09 08
20	18 42	19 07	19 36	06 37	07 32	08 26	09 20
N 10	18 23	18 46	19 13	06 58	07 50	08 41	09 30
0	18 06	18 28	18 54	07 18	08 07	08 54	09 40
S 10	17 48	18 11	18 37	07 38	08 24	09 08	09 49
20	17 30	17 54	18 21	07 59	08 42	09 22	09 59
30	17 08	17 35	18 05	08 23	09 03	09 38	10 10
35	16 56	17 24	17 56	08 37	09 15	09 47	10 17
40	16 42	17 12	17 46	08 53	09 28	09 58	10 24
45	16 25	16 59	17 36	09 13	09 44	10 10	10 33
S 50	16 04	16 43	17 24	09 37	10 04	10 25	10 43
52	15 54	16 35	17 19	09 48	10 14	10 32	10 47
54	15 43	16 27	17 13	10 02	10 24	10 40	10 53
56	15 30	16 18	17 07	10 17	10 36	10 49	10 58
58	15 15	16 07	17 00	10 35	10 49	10 58	11 05
S 60	14 58	15 56	16 53	10 57	11 05	11 10	11 12

Day	SUN Eqn. of Time 00^h	SUN Eqn. of Time 12^h	SUN Mer. Pass.	MOON Mer. Pass. Upper	MOON Mer. Pass. Lower	Age	Phase
d	m s	m s	h m	h m	h m	d %	
20	01 32	01 38	12 02	01 06	13 31	17 97	
21	01 45	01 51	12 02	01 56	14 20	18 93	
22	01 58	02 04	12 02	02 43	15 06	19 87	

UT	ARIES GHA	VENUS −3.9 GHA	VENUS Dec	MARS +1.6 GHA	MARS Dec	JUPITER −2.7 GHA	JUPITER Dec	SATURN +0.8 GHA	SATURN Dec	STARS Name	SHA	Dec
d h	° ′	° ′	° ′	° ′	° ′	° ′	° ′	° ′	° ′		° ′	° ′
23 00	271 32.1	175 18.5	N23 53.9	123 57.3	N14 23.3	340 24.2	S22 10.5	115 10.2	N11 41.1	Acamar	315 21.4	S40 16.0
01	286 34.6	190 17.6	53.8	138 58.3	22.8	355 26.9	10.6	130 12.4	41.1	Achernar	335 29.5	S57 11.3
02	301 37.0	205 16.7	53.8	153 59.4	22.3	10 29.7	10.6	145 14.7	41.0	Acrux	173 13.8	S63 09.1
03	316 39.5	220 15.8	. . 53.8	169 00.4	. . 21.8	25 32.5	. . 10.6	160 17.0	. . 40.9	Adhara	255 15.9	S28 59.0
04	331 41.9	235 14.9	53.7	184 01.4	21.2	40 35.3	10.7	175 19.3	40.8	Aldebaran	290 54.0	N16 31.6
05	346 44.4	250 14.0	53.7	199 02.5	20.7	55 38.0	10.7	190 21.5	40.7			
06	1 46.9	265 13.1	N23 53.6	214 03.5	N14 20.2	70 40.8	S22 10.8	205 23.8	N11 40.7	Alioth	166 23.6	N55 55.0
07	16 49.3	280 12.2	53.6	229 04.6	19.7	85 43.6	10.8	220 26.1	40.6	Alkaid	153 01.4	N49 16.4
08	31 51.8	295 11.3	53.5	244 05.6	19.2	100 46.4	10.9	235 28.4	40.5	Al Na'ir	27 48.0	S46 54.9
M 09	46 54.3	310 10.4	. . 53.5	259 06.7	. . 18.6	115 49.1	. . 10.9	250 30.6	. . 40.4	Alnilam	275 50.5	S 1 11.7
O 10	61 56.7	325 09.5	53.4	274 07.7	18.1	130 51.9	11.0	265 32.9	40.4	Alphard	218 00.0	S 8 41.8
N 11	76 59.2	340 08.6	53.4	289 08.8	17.6	145 54.7	11.0	280 35.2	40.3			
D 12	92 01.7	355 07.7	N23 53.3	304 09.8	N14 17.1	160 57.5	S22 11.1	295 37.5	N11 40.2	Alphecca	126 13.8	N26 41.2
A 13	107 04.1	10 06.8	53.2	319 10.9	16.6	176 00.2	11.1	310 39.7	40.1	Alpheratz	357 47.5	N29 08.2
Y 14	122 06.6	25 05.9	53.2	334 11.9	16.0	191 03.0	11.2	325 42.0	40.1	Altair	62 11.6	N 8 53.4
15	137 09.1	40 05.0	. . 53.1	349 13.0	. . 15.5	206 05.8	. . 11.2	340 44.3	. . 40.0	Ankaa	353 19.2	S42 15.3
16	152 11.5	55 04.1	53.1	4 14.0	15.0	221 08.6	11.3	355 46.6	39.9	Antares	112 30.6	S26 27.2
17	167 14.0	70 03.2	53.0	19 15.1	14.5	236 11.3	11.3	10 48.8	39.8			
18	182 16.4	85 02.3	N23 52.9	34 16.1	N14 14.0	251 14.1	S22 11.4	25 51.1	N11 39.7	Arcturus	145 58.9	N19 08.3
19	197 18.9	100 01.4	52.9	49 17.2	13.4	266 16.9	11.4	40 53.4	39.7	Atria	107 35.3	S69 02.8
20	212 21.4	115 00.5	52.8	64 18.2	12.9	281 19.7	11.5	55 55.7	39.6	Avior	234 20.3	S59 32.3
21	227 23.8	129 59.6	. . 52.7	79 19.3	. . 12.4	296 22.4	. . 11.5	70 57.9	. . 39.5	Bellatrix	278 36.4	N 6 21.5
22	242 26.3	144 58.7	52.7	94 20.3	11.9	311 25.2	11.6	86 00.2	39.4	Betelgeuse	271 05.7	N 7 24.6
23	257 28.8	159 57.9	52.6	109 21.3	11.4	326 28.0	11.6	101 02.5	39.4			
24 00	272 31.2	174 57.0	N23 52.5	124 22.4	N14 10.8	341 30.8	S22 11.7	116 04.8	N11 39.3	Canopus	263 58.4	S52 41.9
01	287 33.7	189 56.1	52.5	139 23.4	10.3	356 33.6	11.7	131 07.0	39.2	Capella	280 40.5	N46 00.4
02	302 36.2	204 55.2	52.4	154 24.5	09.8	11 36.3	11.8	146 09.3	39.1	Deneb	49 33.8	N45 18.5
03	317 38.6	219 54.3	. . 52.3	169 25.5	. . 09.3	26 39.1	. . 11.8	161 11.6	. . 39.1	Denebola	182 37.5	N14 31.5
04	332 41.1	234 53.4	52.2	184 26.6	08.7	41 41.9	11.9	176 13.8	39.0	Diphda	348 59.6	S17 56.2
05	347 43.5	249 52.5	52.2	199 27.6	08.2	56 44.7	11.9	191 16.1	38.9			
06	2 46.0	264 51.6	N23 52.1	214 28.7	N14 07.7	71 47.4	S22 11.9	206 18.4	N11 38.8	Dubhe	193 56.1	N61 42.6
07	17 48.5	279 50.7	52.0	229 29.7	07.2	86 50.2	12.0	221 20.7	38.7	Elnath	278 17.8	N28 36.9
T 08	32 50.9	294 49.8	51.9	244 30.8	06.6	101 53.0	12.0	236 22.9	38.7	Eltanin	90 47.3	N51 29.2
U 09	47 53.4	309 48.9	. . 51.9	259 31.8	. . 06.1	116 55.8	. . 12.1	251 25.2	. . 38.6	Enif	33 50.6	N 9 54.8
E 10	62 55.9	324 48.0	51.8	274 32.9	05.6	131 58.6	12.1	266 27.5	38.5	Fomalhaut	15 27.9	S29 34.4
S 11	77 58.3	339 47.1	51.7	289 33.9	05.1	147 01.3	12.2	281 29.7	38.4			
D 12	93 00.8	354 46.2	N23 51.6	304 35.0	N14 04.6	162 04.1	S22 12.2	296 32.0	N11 38.4	Gacrux	172 05.3	S57 10.0
A 13	108 03.3	9 45.3	51.5	319 36.0	04.0	177 06.9	12.3	311 34.3	38.3	Gienah	175 56.2	S17 35.5
Y 14	123 05.7	24 44.4	51.4	334 37.1	03.5	192 09.7	12.3	326 36.6	38.2	Hadar	148 53.2	S60 25.2
15	138 08.2	39 43.5	. . 51.3	349 38.1	. . 03.0	207 12.5	. . 12.4	341 38.8	. . 38.1	Hamal	328 05.2	N23 30.1
16	153 10.7	54 42.6	51.3	4 39.2	02.5	222 15.2	12.4	356 41.1	38.0	Kaus Aust.	83 48.4	S34 22.9
17	168 13.1	69 41.7	51.2	19 40.2	01.9	237 18.0	12.5	11 43.4	38.0			
18	183 15.6	84 40.8	N23 51.1	34 41.3	N14 01.4	252 20.8	S22 12.5	26 45.6	N11 37.9	Kochab	137 18.6	N74 07.4
19	198 18.0	99 40.0	51.0	49 42.3	00.9	267 23.6	12.6	41 47.9	37.8	Markab	13 42.0	N15 15.0
20	213 20.5	114 39.1	50.9	64 43.4	14 00.4	282 26.4	12.6	56 50.2	37.7	Menkar	314 19.2	N 4 07.5
21	228 23.0	129 38.2	. . 50.8	79 44.4	13 59.8	297 29.1	. . 12.7	71 52.4	. . 37.6	Menkent	148 11.9	S36 25.0
22	243 25.4	144 37.3	50.7	94 45.4	59.3	312 31.9	12.7	86 54.7	37.6	Miaplacidus	221 41.5	S69 45.3
23	258 27.9	159 36.4	50.6	109 46.5	58.8	327 34.7	12.8	101 57.0	37.5			
25 00	273 30.4	174 35.5	N23 50.5	124 47.5	N13 58.3	342 37.5	S22 12.8	116 59.3	N11 37.4	Mirfak	308 46.3	N49 53.4
01	288 32.8	189 34.6	50.4	139 48.6	57.7	357 40.3	12.9	132 01.5	37.3	Nunki	76 02.6	S26 17.2
02	303 35.3	204 33.7	50.3	154 49.6	57.2	12 43.0	12.9	147 03.8	37.3	Peacock	53 24.4	S56 42.3
03	318 37.8	219 32.8	. . 50.2	169 50.7	. . 56.7	27 45.8	. . 13.0	162 06.1	. . 37.2	Pollux	243 32.6	N28 00.4
04	333 40.2	234 31.9	50.1	184 51.7	56.2	42 48.6	13.0	177 08.3	37.1	Procyon	245 04.0	N 5 12.3
05	348 42.7	249 31.0	50.0	199 52.8	55.6	57 51.4	13.1	192 10.6	37.0			
06	3 45.2	264 30.1	N23 49.9	214 53.8	N13 55.1	72 54.2	S22 13.1	207 12.9	N11 36.9	Rasalhague	96 09.6	N12 33.2
W 07	18 47.6	279 29.2	49.8	229 54.9	54.6	87 57.0	13.2	222 15.1	36.9	Regulus	207 47.6	N11 55.6
E 08	33 50.1	294 28.3	49.7	244 55.9	54.0	102 59.7	13.2	237 17.4	36.8	Rigel	281 16.0	S 8 11.4
D 09	48 52.5	309 27.4	. . 49.5	259 57.0	. . 53.5	118 02.5	. . 13.3	252 19.7	. . 36.7	Rigil Kent.	139 56.7	S60 52.5
N 10	63 55.0	324 26.6	49.4	274 58.0	53.0	133 05.3	13.3	267 22.0	36.6	Sabik	102 16.5	S15 44.2
E 11	78 57.5	339 25.7	49.3	289 59.1	52.5	148 08.1	13.3	282 24.2	36.5			
S 12	93 59.9	354 24.8	N23 49.2	305 00.1	N13 51.9	163 10.9	S22 13.4	297 26.5	N11 36.5	Schedar	349 45.2	N56 34.8
D 13	109 02.4	9 23.9	49.1	320 01.2	51.4	178 13.7	13.4	312 28.8	36.4	Shaula	96 26.6	S37 06.7
A 14	124 04.9	24 23.0	49.0	335 02.2	50.9	193 16.4	13.5	327 31.0	36.3	Sirius	258 37.4	S16 43.6
Y 15	139 07.3	39 22.1	. . 48.9	350 03.3	. . 50.4	208 19.2	. . 13.5	342 33.3	. . 36.2	Spica	158 35.1	S11 12.5
16	154 09.8	54 21.2	48.7	5 04.3	49.8	223 22.0	13.6	357 35.6	36.2	Suhail	222 55.7	S43 28.2
17	169 12.3	69 20.3	48.6	20 05.4	49.3	238 24.8	13.6	12 37.8	36.1			
18	184 14.7	84 19.4	N23 48.5	35 06.4	N13 48.8	253 27.6	S22 13.7	27 40.1	N11 36.0	Vega	80 41.1	N38 47.4
19	199 17.2	99 18.5	48.4	50 07.5	48.2	268 30.4	13.7	42 42.4	35.9	Zuben'ubi	137 09.4	S16 04.8
20	214 19.6	114 17.6	48.2	65 08.5	47.7	283 33.1	13.8	57 44.6	35.8			
21	229 22.1	129 16.7	. . 48.1	80 09.6	. . 47.2	298 35.9	. . 13.8	72 46.9	. . 35.8			
22	244 24.6	144 15.8	48.0	95 10.6	46.6	313 38.7	13.9	87 49.2	35.7			
23	259 27.0	159 15.0	47.9	110 11.6	46.1	328 41.5	13.9	102 51.4	35.6			
Mer. Pass.	h m 5 49.0	v −0.9	d 0.1	v 1.0	d 0.5	v 2.8	d 0.0	v 2.3	d 0.1			

	SHA	Mer. Pass.
	° ′	h m
Venus	262 25.7	12 21
Mars	211 51.2	15 41
Jupiter	68 59.5	1 14
Saturn	203 33.5	16 13

Day	UT d h	SUN GHA ° ′	SUN Dec ° ′	MOON GHA ° ′	MOON v ′	MOON Dec ° ′	MOON d ′	MOON HP ′
MONDAY	23 00	179 27.3	N23 25.6	309 22.5	13.7	S14 51.5	12.5	55.7
	01	194 27.1	25.5	323 55.2	13.8	14 39.0	12.6	55.7
	02	209 27.0	25.5	338 28.0	13.8	14 26.4	12.6	55.7
	03	224 26.8	. . 25.5	353 00.8	13.8	14 13.8	12.7	55.8
	04	239 26.7	25.4	7 33.6	13.9	14 01.1	12.8	55.8
	05	254 26.6	25.4	22 06.5	13.9	13 48.3	12.9	55.8
	06	269 26.4	N23 25.4	36 39.4	13.9	S13 35.4	12.9	55.8
	07	284 26.3	25.3	51 12.3	14.0	13 22.5	13.0	55.8
	08	299 26.2	25.3	65 45.3	14.0	13 09.5	13.1	55.9
	09	314 26.0	. . 25.2	80 18.3	14.0	12 56.4	13.1	55.9
	10	329 25.9	25.2	94 51.3	14.0	12 43.3	13.2	55.9
	11	344 25.8	25.2	109 24.3	14.1	12 30.1	13.3	55.9
	12	359 25.6	N23 25.1	123 57.4	14.1	S12 16.8	13.3	56.0
	13	14 25.5	25.1	138 30.5	14.2	12 03.5	13.4	56.0
	14	29 25.4	25.0	153 03.7	14.1	11 50.1	13.4	56.0
	15	44 25.2	. . 25.0	167 36.8	14.2	11 36.7	13.5	56.0
	16	59 25.1	24.9	182 10.0	14.2	11 23.2	13.6	56.1
	17	74 25.0	24.9	196 43.2	14.2	11 09.6	13.6	56.1
	18	89 24.8	N23 24.8	211 16.4	14.3	S10 56.0	13.7	56.1
	19	104 24.7	24.8	225 49.7	14.2	10 42.3	13.7	56.1
	20	119 24.6	24.7	240 22.9	14.3	10 28.6	13.8	56.2
	21	134 24.4	. . 24.7	254 56.2	14.3	10 14.8	13.9	56.2
	22	149 24.3	24.6	269 29.5	14.3	10 00.9	13.9	56.2
	23	164 24.2	24.6	284 02.8	14.4	9 47.0	13.9	56.2
TUESDAY	24 00	179 24.0	N23 24.5	298 36.2	14.3	S 9 33.1	14.0	56.3
	01	194 23.9	24.5	313 09.5	14.4	9 19.1	14.1	56.3
	02	209 23.8	24.4	327 42.9	14.4	9 05.0	14.1	56.3
	03	224 23.6	. . 24.4	342 16.3	14.4	8 50.9	14.2	56.3
	04	239 23.5	24.3	356 49.7	14.4	8 36.7	14.2	56.4
	05	254 23.4	24.3	11 23.1	14.4	8 22.5	14.2	56.4
	06	269 23.2	N23 24.2	25 56.5	14.4	S 8 08.3	14.3	56.4
	07	284 23.1	24.2	40 29.9	14.4	7 54.0	14.4	56.4
	08	299 23.0	24.1	55 03.3	14.5	7 39.6	14.4	56.5
	09	314 22.8	. . 24.1	69 36.8	14.4	7 25.2	14.4	56.5
	10	329 22.7	24.0	84 10.2	14.5	7 10.8	14.5	56.5
	11	344 22.6	23.9	98 43.7	14.4	6 56.3	14.5	56.6
	12	359 22.4	N23 23.9	113 17.1	14.5	S 6 41.8	14.6	56.6
	13	14 22.3	23.8	127 50.6	14.4	6 27.2	14.6	56.6
	14	29 22.2	23.8	142 24.0	14.5	6 12.6	14.6	56.6
	15	44 22.0	. . 23.7	156 57.5	14.4	5 58.0	14.7	56.7
	16	59 21.9	23.6	171 30.9	14.5	5 43.3	14.7	56.7
	17	74 21.8	23.6	186 04.4	14.4	5 28.6	14.8	56.7
	18	89 21.6	N23 23.5	200 37.8	14.5	S 5 13.8	14.8	56.7
	19	104 21.5	23.4	215 11.3	14.4	4 59.0	14.8	56.8
	20	119 21.4	23.4	229 44.7	14.5	4 44.2	14.9	56.8
	21	134 21.2	. . 23.3	244 18.2	14.4	4 29.3	14.9	56.8
	22	149 21.1	23.2	258 51.6	14.4	4 14.4	14.9	56.9
	23	164 21.0	23.2	273 25.0	14.4	3 59.5	15.0	56.9
WEDNESDAY	25 00	179 20.9	N23 23.1	287 58.4	14.4	S 3 44.5	15.0	56.9
	01	194 20.7	23.0	302 31.8	14.4	3 29.5	15.0	56.9
	02	209 20.6	23.0	317 05.2	14.3	3 14.5	15.0	57.0
	03	224 20.5	. . 22.9	331 38.5	14.4	2 59.5	15.1	57.0
	04	239 20.3	22.8	346 11.9	14.3	2 44.4	15.1	57.0
	05	254 20.2	22.8	0 45.2	14.4	2 29.3	15.2	57.1
	06	269 20.1	N23 22.7	15 18.6	14.2	S 2 14.1	15.1	57.1
	07	284 19.9	22.6	29 51.8	14.3	1 59.0	15.2	57.1
	08	299 19.8	22.5	44 25.1	14.3	1 43.8	15.2	57.2
	09	314 19.7	. . 22.5	58 58.4	14.2	1 28.6	15.2	57.2
	10	329 19.5	22.4	73 31.6	14.2	1 13.4	15.3	57.2
	11	344 19.4	22.3	88 04.8	14.2	0 58.1	15.3	57.2
	12	359 19.3	N23 22.2	102 38.0	14.2	S 0 42.8	15.2	57.3
	13	14 19.1	22.2	117 11.2	14.1	0 27.6	15.3	57.3
	14	29 19.0	22.1	131 44.3	14.1	S 0 12.3	15.4	57.3
	15	44 18.9	. . 22.0	146 17.4	14.1	N 0 03.1	15.3	57.4
	16	59 18.7	21.9	160 50.5	14.0	0 18.4	15.4	57.4
	17	74 18.6	21.8	175 23.5	14.0	0 33.8	15.3	57.4
	18	89 18.5	N23 21.8	189 56.5	14.0	N 0 49.1	15.4	57.5
	19	104 18.3	21.7	204 29.5	13.9	1 04.5	15.4	57.5
	20	119 18.2	21.6	219 02.4	13.9	1 19.9	15.4	57.5
	21	134 18.1	. . 21.5	233 35.3	13.8	1 35.3	15.4	57.6
	22	149 18.0	21.4	248 08.1	13.9	1 50.7	15.4	57.6
	23	164 17.8	21.3	262 41.0	13.7	N 2 06.1	15.4	57.6
		SD 15.8	*d* 0.1	SD 15.2		15.4		15.6

Lat. °	Twilight Naut. h m	Twilight Civil h m	Sunrise h m	Moonrise 23 h m	Moonrise 24 h m	Moonrise 25 h m	Moonrise 26 h m
N 72	□	□	□	01 01	{00 12 / 23 37}	23 05	22 31
N 70	□	□	□	{00 31 / 23 57}	23 31	23 08	22 42
68	□	□	□	{00 08 / 23 46}	23 27	23 10	22 51
66	□	□	□	23 36	23 23	23 12	22 59
64	////	////	01 32	23 28	23 20	23 13	23 06
62	////	////	02 10	23 21	23 18	23 15	23 12
60	////	00 51	02 37	23 14	23 15	23 16	23 17
N 58	////	01 42	02 57	23 09	23 13	23 17	23 21
56	////	02 12	03 14	23 04	23 11	23 18	23 25
54	00 47	02 34	03 28	23 00	23 09	23 19	23 29
52	01 33	02 52	03 41	22 56	23 08	23 20	23 32
50	02 01	03 07	03 52	22 52	23 06	23 20	23 35
45	02 47	03 37	04 14	22 44	23 03	23 22	23 42
N 40	03 18	03 59	04 32	22 37	23 00	23 23	23 47
35	03 41	04 17	04 47	22 32	22 58	23 24	23 52
30	03 59	04 33	05 00	22 27	22 56	23 26	23 56
20	04 28	04 58	05 22	22 18	22 53	23 27	24 04
N 10	04 51	05 18	05 41	22 10	22 49	23 29	24 11
0	05 10	05 36	05 59	22 03	22 46	23 31	24 17
S 10	05 27	05 53	06 16	21 55	22 43	23 32	24 23
20	05 43	06 11	06 35	21 47	22 40	23 34	24 30
30	06 00	06 30	06 56	21 38	22 37	23 36	24 38
35	06 09	06 40	07 08	21 33	22 35	23 37	24 42
40	06 18	06 52	07 23	21 27	22 32	23 39	24 48
45	06 28	07 06	07 39	21 20	22 30	23 40	24 54
S 50	06 40	07 22	08 00	21 12	22 26	23 42	25 01
52	06 45	07 29	08 10	21 08	22 25	23 43	25 04
54	06 51	07 37	08 21	21 04	22 23	23 44	25 08
56	06 57	07 46	08 34	20 59	22 21	23 45	25 12
58	07 04	07 57	08 48	20 54	22 19	23 46	25 17
S 60	07 11	08 08	09 06	20 48	22 17	23 48	25 22

Lat. °	Sunset h m	Twilight Civil h m	Twilight Naut. h m	Moonset 23 h m	Moonset 24 h m	Moonset 25 h m	Moonset 26 h m
N 72	□	□	□	06 21	08 44	10 54	13 05
N 70	□	□	□	06 49	08 56	10 55	12 57
68	□	□	□	07 10	09 05	10 56	12 50
66	□	□	□	07 27	09 13	10 58	12 44
64	22 32	////	////	07 40	09 20	10 58	12 40
62	21 54	////	////	07 51	09 25	10 59	12 36
60	21 28	23 13	////	08 00	09 30	11 00	12 32
N 58	21 07	22 23	////	08 09	09 34	11 01	12 29
56	20 51	21 53	////	08 16	09 38	11 01	12 26
54	20 36	21 31	23 17	08 22	09 42	11 02	12 24
52	20 24	21 13	22 31	08 28	09 45	11 02	12 21
50	20 13	20 58	22 03	08 33	09 47	11 02	12 19
45	19 51	20 28	21 18	08 44	09 53	11 03	12 15
N 40	19 33	20 06	20 47	08 53	09 58	11 04	12 11
35	19 18	19 47	20 24	09 01	10 03	11 05	12 08
30	19 05	19 32	20 06	09 08	10 06	11 05	12 05
20	18 43	19 07	19 37	09 20	10 13	11 06	12 01
N 10	18 24	18 47	19 14	09 30	10 18	11 07	11 56
0	18 06	18 29	18 55	09 40	10 24	11 07	11 52
S 10	17 49	18 12	18 38	09 49	10 29	11 08	11 48
20	17 30	17 54	18 22	09 59	10 34	11 09	11 44
30	17 09	17 35	18 05	10 10	10 40	11 10	11 39
35	16 57	17 25	17 57	10 17	10 44	11 10	11 37
40	16 42	17 13	17 47	10 24	10 48	11 10	11 34
45	16 26	17 00	17 37	10 33	10 52	11 11	11 30
S 50	16 05	16 43	17 25	10 43	10 58	11 12	11 26
52	15 55	16 36	17 20	10 47	11 00	11 12	11 24
54	15 44	16 28	17 14	10 53	11 03	11 12	11 22
56	15 31	16 19	17 08	10 58	11 06	11 13	11 19
58	15 17	16 08	17 01	11 05	11 09	11 13	11 17
S 60	14 59	15 57	16 54	11 12	11 13	11 13	11 14

Day	SUN Eqn. of Time 00^h	SUN Eqn. of Time 12^h	SUN Mer. Pass.	MOON Mer. Pass. Upper	MOON Mer. Pass. Lower	MOON Age	MOON Phase
d	m s	m s	h m	h m	h m	d %	
23	02 11	02 17	12 02	03 29	15 51	20 80	
24	02 24	02 30	12 02	04 13	16 35	21 71	
25	02 36	02 43	12 03	04 57	17 19	22 61	

2008 JUNE 26, 27, 28 (THURS., FRI., SAT.)

UT		ARIES	VENUS −3.9		MARS +1.6		JUPITER −2.7		SATURN +0.8	
	d h	GHA	GHA	Dec	GHA	Dec	GHA	Dec	GHA	Dec
		° ′	° ′	° ′	° ′	° ′	° ′	° ′	° ′	° ′
	26 00	274 29.5	174 14.1	N23 47.7	125 12.7	N13 45.6	343 44.3	S22 14.0	117 53.7	N11 35.5
	01	289 32.0	189 13.2	47.6	140 13.7	45.1	358 47.1	14.0	132 56.0	35.4
	02	304 34.4	204 12.3	47.5	155 14.8	44.5	13 49.8	14.1	147 58.2	35.4
	03	319 36.9	219 11.4	. . 47.3	170 15.8	. . 44.0	28 52.6	. . 14.1	163 00.5	. . 35.3
	04	334 39.4	234 10.5	47.2	185 16.9	43.5	43 55.4	14.2	178 02.8	35.2
	05	349 41.8	249 09.6	47.1	200 17.9	42.9	58 58.2	14.2	193 05.0	35.1
	06	4 44.3	264 08.7	N23 46.9	215 19.0	N13 42.4	74 01.0	S22 14.3	208 07.3	N11 35.0
	07	19 46.8	279 07.8	46.8	230 20.0	41.9	89 03.8	14.3	223 09.6	35.0
T	08	34 49.2	294 06.9	46.7	245 21.1	41.3	104 06.6	14.4	238 11.8	34.9
H	09	49 51.7	309 06.0	. . 46.5	260 22.1	. . 40.8	119 09.3	. . 14.4	253 14.1	. . 34.8
U	10	64 54.1	324 05.2	46.4	275 23.2	40.3	134 12.1	14.5	268 16.4	34.7
R	11	79 56.6	339 04.3	46.2	290 24.2	39.8	149 14.9	14.5	283 18.6	34.6
S	12	94 59.1	354 03.4	N23 46.1	305 25.3	N13 39.2	164 17.7	S22 14.6	298 20.9	N11 34.6
D	13	110 01.5	9 02.5	45.9	320 26.3	38.7	179 20.5	14.6	313 23.2	34.5
A	14	125 04.0	24 01.6	45.8	335 27.4	38.2	194 23.3	14.7	328 25.4	34.4
Y	15	140 06.5	39 00.7	. . 45.6	350 28.4	. . 37.6	209 26.1	. . 14.7	343 27.7	. . 34.3
	16	155 08.9	53 59.8	45.5	5 29.5	37.1	224 28.9	14.8	358 30.0	34.2
	17	170 11.4	68 58.9	45.4	20 30.5	36.6	239 31.6	14.8	13 32.2	34.2
	18	185 13.9	83 58.0	N23 45.2	35 31.6	N13 36.0	254 34.4	S22 14.9	28 34.5	N11 34.1
	19	200 16.3	98 57.1	45.0	50 32.6	35.5	269 37.2	14.9	43 36.7	34.0
	20	215 18.8	113 56.3	44.9	65 33.7	35.0	284 40.0	15.0	58 39.0	33.9
	21	230 21.2	128 55.4	. . 44.7	80 34.7	. . 34.4	299 42.8	. . 15.0	73 41.3	. . 33.8
	22	245 23.7	143 54.5	44.6	95 35.8	33.9	314 45.6	15.0	88 43.5	33.8
	23	260 26.2	158 53.6	44.4	110 36.8	33.4	329 48.4	15.1	103 45.8	33.7
	27 00	275 28.6	173 52.7	N23 44.3	125 37.9	N13 32.8	344 51.2	S22 15.1	118 48.1	N11 33.6
	01	290 31.1	188 51.8	44.1	140 38.9	32.3	359 53.9	15.2	133 50.3	33.5
	02	305 33.6	203 50.9	43.9	155 39.9	31.8	14 56.7	15.2	148 52.6	33.4
	03	320 36.0	218 50.0	. . 43.8	170 41.0	. . 31.2	29 59.5	. . 15.3	163 54.9	. . 33.4
	04	335 38.5	233 49.2	43.6	185 42.0	30.7	45 02.3	15.3	178 57.1	33.3
	05	350 41.0	248 48.3	43.5	200 43.1	30.2	60 05.1	15.4	193 59.4	33.2
	06	5 43.4	263 47.4	N23 43.3	215 44.1	N13 29.6	75 07.9	S22 15.4	209 01.7	N11 33.1
	07	20 45.9	278 46.5	43.1	230 45.2	29.1	90 10.7	15.5	224 03.9	33.0
	08	35 48.4	293 45.6	43.0	245 46.2	28.6	105 13.5	15.5	239 06.2	32.9
F	09	50 50.8	308 44.7	. . 42.8	260 47.3	. . 28.0	120 16.3	. . 15.6	254 08.4	. . 32.9
R	10	65 53.3	323 43.8	42.6	275 48.3	27.5	135 19.0	15.6	269 10.7	32.8
I	11	80 55.7	338 42.9	42.4	290 49.4	27.0	150 21.8	15.7	284 13.0	32.7
D	12	95 58.2	353 42.1	N23 42.3	305 50.4	N13 26.4	165 24.6	S22 15.7	299 15.2	N11 32.6
A	13	111 00.7	8 41.2	42.1	320 51.5	25.9	180 27.4	15.8	314 17.5	32.5
Y	14	126 03.1	23 40.3	41.9	335 52.5	25.4	195 30.2	15.8	329 19.8	32.5
	15	141 05.6	38 39.4	. . 41.7	350 53.6	. . 24.8	210 33.0	. . 15.9	344 22.0	. . 32.4
	16	156 08.1	53 38.5	41.6	5 54.6	24.3	225 35.8	15.9	359 24.3	32.3
	17	171 10.5	68 37.6	41.4	20 55.7	23.8	240 38.6	16.0	14 26.5	32.2
	18	186 13.0	83 36.7	N23 41.2	35 56.7	N13 23.2	255 41.4	S22 16.0	29 28.8	N11 32.1
	19	201 15.5	98 35.8	41.0	50 57.8	22.7	270 44.2	16.1	44 31.1	32.1
	20	216 17.9	113 35.0	40.8	65 58.8	22.1	285 46.9	16.1	59 33.3	32.0
	21	231 20.4	128 34.1	. . 40.7	80 59.9	. . 21.6	300 49.7	. . 16.2	74 35.6	. . 31.9
	22	246 22.9	143 33.2	40.5	96 00.9	21.1	315 52.5	16.2	89 37.9	31.8
	23	261 25.3	158 32.3	40.3	111 02.0	20.5	330 55.3	16.3	104 40.1	31.7
	28 00	276 27.8	173 31.4	N23 40.1	126 03.0	N13 20.0	345 58.1	S22 16.3	119 42.4	N11 31.6
	01	291 30.2	188 30.5	39.9	141 04.1	19.5	1 00.9	16.4	134 44.6	31.6
	02	306 32.7	203 29.7	39.7	156 05.1	18.9	16 03.7	16.4	149 46.9	31.5
	03	321 35.2	218 28.8	. . 39.5	171 06.2	. . 18.4	31 06.5	. . 16.5	164 49.2	. . 31.4
	04	336 37.6	233 27.9	39.3	186 07.2	17.8	46 09.3	16.5	179 51.4	31.3
	05	351 40.1	248 27.0	39.1	201 08.3	17.3	61 12.1	16.6	194 53.7	31.2
	06	6 42.6	263 26.1	N23 38.9	216 09.3	N13 16.8	76 14.9	S22 16.6	209 55.9	N11 31.2
	07	21 45.0	278 25.2	38.7	231 10.3	16.2	91 17.6	16.7	224 58.2	31.1
S	08	36 47.5	293 24.3	38.5	246 11.4	15.7	106 20.4	16.7	240 00.5	31.0
A	09	51 50.0	308 23.5	. . 38.3	261 12.4	. . 15.2	121 23.2	. . 16.8	255 02.7	. . 30.9
T	10	66 52.4	323 22.6	38.1	276 13.5	14.6	136 26.0	16.8	270 05.0	30.8
U	11	81 54.9	338 21.7	37.9	291 14.5	14.1	151 28.8	16.9	285 07.2	30.7
R	12	96 57.3	353 20.8	N23 37.7	306 15.6	N13 13.5	166 31.6	S22 16.9	300 09.5	N11 30.7
D	13	111 59.8	8 19.9	37.5	321 16.6	13.0	181 34.4	17.0	315 11.8	30.6
A	14	127 02.3	23 19.0	37.3	336 17.7	12.5	196 37.2	17.0	330 14.0	30.5
Y	15	142 04.7	38 18.2	. . 37.1	351 18.7	. . 11.9	211 40.0	. . 17.0	345 16.3	. . 30.4
	16	157 07.2	53 17.3	36.9	6 19.8	11.4	226 42.8	17.1	0 18.5	30.3
	17	172 09.7	68 16.4	36.7	21 20.8	10.8	241 45.6	17.1	15 20.8	30.2
	18	187 12.1	83 15.5	N23 36.5	36 21.9	N13 10.3	256 48.4	S22 17.2	30 23.1	N11 30.2
	19	202 14.6	98 14.6	36.3	51 22.9	09.8	271 51.2	17.2	45 25.3	30.1
	20	217 17.1	113 13.8	36.1	66 24.0	09.2	286 54.0	17.3	60 27.6	30.0
	21	232 19.5	128 12.9	. . 35.9	81 25.0	. . 08.7	301 56.7	. . 17.3	75 29.8	. . 29.9
	22	247 22.0	143 12.0	35.7	96 26.1	08.1	316 59.5	17.4	90 32.1	29.8
	23	262 24.5	158 11.1	35.4	111 27.1	07.6	332 02.3	17.4	105 34.4	29.8
	Mer. Pass.	h m 5 37.2	v −0.9	d 0.2	v 1.0	d 0.5	v 2.8	d 0.0	v 2.3	d 0.1

STARS

Name	SHA	Dec
	° ′	° ′
Acamar	315 21.3	S40 16.0
Achernar	335 29.5	S57 11.2
Acrux	173 13.8	S63 09.1
Adhara	255 15.9	S28 59.0
Aldebaran	290 54.0	N16 31.6
Alioth	166 23.6	N55 55.0
Alkaid	153 01.5	N49 16.4
Al Na'ir	27 48.0	S46 54.9
Alnilam	275 50.5	S 1 11.7
Alphard	218 00.0	S 8 41.8
Alphecca	126 13.8	N26 41.2
Alpheratz	357 47.5	N29 08.2
Altair	62 11.6	N 8 53.4
Ankaa	353 19.2	S42 15.3
Antares	112 30.6	S26 27.2
Arcturus	145 58.9	N19 08.3
Atria	107 35.3	S69 02.8
Avior	234 20.3	S59 32.3
Bellatrix	278 36.4	N 6 21.5
Betelgeuse	271 05.7	N 7 24.6
Canopus	263 58.4	S52 41.9
Capella	280 40.5	N46 00.4
Deneb	49 33.8	N45 18.5
Denebola	182 37.5	N14 31.5
Diphda	348 59.6	S17 56.2
Dubhe	193 56.2	N61 42.5
Elnath	278 17.7	N28 36.9
Eltanin	90 47.3	N51 29.2
Enif	33 50.6	N 9 54.8
Fomalhaut	15 27.9	S29 34.4
Gacrux	172 05.3	S57 10.0
Gienah	175 56.2	S17 35.5
Hadar	148 53.2	S60 25.2
Hamal	328 05.2	N23 30.1
Kaus Aust.	83 48.3	S34 22.9
Kochab	137 18.7	N74 07.4
Markab	13 42.0	N15 15.0
Menkar	314 19.2	N 4 07.5
Menkent	148 11.9	S36 25.0
Miaplacidus	221 41.6	S69 45.3
Mirfak	308 46.2	N49 53.4
Nunki	76 02.6	S26 17.2
Peacock	53 24.4	S56 42.3
Pollux	243 32.6	N28 00.4
Procyon	245 04.0	N 5 12.3
Rasalhague	96 09.6	N12 33.2
Regulus	207 47.7	N11 55.6
Rigel	281 16.0	S 8 11.4
Rigil Kent.	139 56.7	S60 52.5
Sabik	102 16.5	S15 44.2
Schedar	349 45.1	N56 34.8
Shaula	96 26.6	S37 06.7
Sirius	258 37.4	S16 43.6
Spica	158 35.1	S11 12.5
Suhail	222 55.7	S43 28.1
Vega	80 41.1	N38 47.4
Zuben'ubi	137 09.4	S16 04.8

	SHA	Mer. Pass.
	° ′	h m
Venus	258 24.1	12 25
Mars	210 09.2	15 36
Jupiter	69 22.5	1 00
Saturn	203 19.4	16 02

UT d	h	SUN GHA	SUN Dec	MOON GHA	v	MOON Dec	d	HP
		° ′	° ′	° ′	′	° ′	′	′
26 THURSDAY	00	179 17.7	N23 21.3	277 13.7	13.8	N 2 21.5	15.5	57.6
	01	194 17.6	21.2	291 46.5	13.6	2 37.0	15.4	57.7
	02	209 17.4	21.1	306 19.1	13.7	2 52.4	15.5	57.7
	03	224 17.3	. . 21.0	320 51.8	13.6	3 07.9	15.4	57.7
	04	239 17.2	20.9	335 24.4	13.5	3 23.3	15.4	57.8
	05	254 17.0	20.8	349 56.9	13.5	3 38.7	15.5	57.8
	06	269 16.9	N23 20.7	4 29.4	13.5	N 3 54.2	15.4	57.8
	07	284 16.8	20.6	19 01.9	13.3	4 09.6	15.5	57.9
	08	299 16.6	20.5	33 34.2	13.4	4 25.1	15.4	57.9
	09	314 16.5	. . 20.5	48 06.6	13.3	4 40.5	15.4	57.9
	10	329 16.4	20.4	62 38.9	13.2	4 55.9	15.5	58.0
	11	344 16.3	20.3	77 11.1	13.2	5 11.4	15.4	58.0
	12	359 16.1	N23 20.2	91 43.3	13.1	N 5 26.8	15.4	58.0
	13	14 16.0	20.1	106 15.4	13.0	5 42.2	15.4	58.1
	14	29 15.9	20.0	120 47.4	13.0	5 57.6	15.4	58.1
	15	44 15.7	. . 19.9	135 19.4	12.9	6 13.0	15.4	58.1
	16	59 15.6	19.8	149 51.3	12.9	6 28.4	15.3	58.2
	17	74 15.5	19.7	164 23.2	12.8	6 43.7	15.4	58.2
	18	89 15.3	N23 19.6	178 55.0	12.7	N 6 59.1	15.3	58.2
	19	104 15.2	19.5	193 26.7	12.6	7 14.4	15.4	58.3
	20	119 15.1	19.4	207 58.3	12.6	7 29.8	15.3	58.3
	21	134 14.9	. . 19.3	222 29.9	12.5	7 45.1	15.2	58.3
	22	149 14.8	19.2	237 01.4	12.4	8 00.3	15.3	58.4
	23	164 14.7	19.1	251 32.8	12.4	8 15.6	15.2	58.4
27 FRIDAY	00	179 14.6	N23 19.0	266 04.2	12.3	N 8 30.8	15.3	58.4
	01	194 14.4	18.9	280 35.5	12.2	8 46.1	15.1	58.5
	02	209 14.3	18.8	295 06.7	12.1	9 01.2	15.2	58.5
	03	224 14.2	. . 18.7	309 37.8	12.1	9 16.4	15.1	58.5
	04	239 14.0	18.6	324 08.9	11.9	9 31.5	15.1	58.6
	05	254 13.9	18.5	338 39.8	11.9	9 46.6	15.1	58.6
	06	269 13.8	N23 18.4	353 10.7	11.8	N10 01.7	15.0	58.6
	07	284 13.7	18.2	7 41.5	11.7	10 16.7	15.0	58.6
	08	299 13.5	18.1	22 12.2	11.6	10 31.7	15.0	58.7
	09	314 13.4	. . 18.0	36 42.8	11.5	10 46.7	14.9	58.7
	10	329 13.3	17.9	51 13.3	11.5	11 01.6	14.9	58.7
	11	344 13.1	17.8	65 43.8	11.3	11 16.5	14.9	58.8
	12	359 13.0	N23 17.7	80 14.1	11.3	N11 31.4	14.8	58.8
	13	14 12.9	17.6	94 44.4	11.1	11 46.2	14.8	58.8
	14	29 12.8	17.5	109 14.5	11.1	12 01.0	14.7	58.9
	15	44 12.6	. . 17.4	123 44.6	11.0	12 15.7	14.7	58.9
	16	59 12.5	17.2	138 14.6	10.8	12 30.4	14.6	58.9
	17	74 12.4	17.1	152 44.4	10.8	12 45.0	14.5	59.0
	18	89 12.2	N23 17.0	167 14.2	10.7	N12 59.5	14.6	59.0
	19	104 12.1	16.9	181 43.9	10.6	13 14.1	14.4	59.0
	20	119 12.0	16.8	196 13.5	10.4	13 28.5	14.4	59.1
	21	134 11.9	. . 16.7	210 42.9	10.4	13 42.9	14.4	59.1
	22	149 11.7	16.5	225 12.3	10.2	13 57.3	14.3	59.1
	23	164 11.6	16.4	239 41.5	10.2	14 11.6	14.2	59.2
28 SATURDAY	00	179 11.5	N23 16.3	254 10.7	10.0	N14 25.8	14.2	59.2
	01	194 11.3	16.2	268 39.7	10.0	14 40.0	14.1	59.2
	02	209 11.2	16.1	283 08.7	9.8	14 54.1	14.1	59.3
	03	224 11.1	. . 15.9	297 37.5	9.7	15 08.2	13.9	59.3
	04	239 11.0	15.8	312 06.2	9.6	15 22.1	13.9	59.3
	05	254 10.8	15.7	326 34.8	9.5	15 36.0	13.9	59.4
	06	269 10.7	N23 15.6	341 03.3	9.3	N15 49.9	13.7	59.4
	07	284 10.6	15.5	355 31.6	9.3	16 03.6	13.7	59.4
	08	299 10.4	15.3	9 59.9	9.1	16 17.3	13.6	59.4
	09	314 10.3	. . 15.2	24 28.0	9.0	16 30.9	13.5	59.5
	10	329 10.2	15.1	38 56.0	8.9	16 44.4	13.5	59.5
	11	344 10.1	14.9	53 23.9	8.8	16 57.9	13.4	59.5
	12	359 09.9	N23 14.8	67 51.7	8.7	N17 11.3	13.2	59.6
	13	14 09.8	14.7	82 19.4	8.5	17 24.5	13.2	59.6
	14	29 09.7	14.6	96 46.9	8.4	17 37.7	13.1	59.6
	15	44 09.6	. . 14.4	111 14.3	8.3	17 50.8	13.0	59.7
	16	59 09.4	14.3	125 41.6	8.2	18 03.8	12.9	59.7
	17	74 09.3	14.2	140 08.8	8.1	18 16.7	12.9	59.7
	18	89 09.2	N23 14.0	154 35.9	7.9	N18 29.6	12.7	59.7
	19	104 09.0	13.9	169 02.8	7.8	18 42.3	12.6	59.8
	20	119 08.9	13.8	183 29.6	7.7	18 54.9	12.5	59.8
	21	134 08.8	. . 13.6	197 56.3	7.5	19 07.4	12.5	59.8
	22	149 08.7	13.5	212 22.8	7.4	19 19.9	12.3	59.9
	23	164 08.5	13.4	226 49.2	7.3	N19 32.2	12.2	59.9
		SD 15.8	*d* 0.1	SD 15.8		16.0		16.2

Lat.	Twilight Naut.	Twilight Civil	Sunrise	Moonrise 26	Moonrise 27	Moonrise 28	Moonrise 29
°	h m	h m	h m	h m	h m	h m	h m
N 72	□	□	□	22 31	21 44	□	□
N 70	□	□	□	22 42	22 09	21 05	□
68	□	□	□	22 51	22 29	21 53	□
66	□	□	□	22 59	22 45	22 25	21 37
64	////	////	01 36	23 06	22 58	22 48	22 33
62	////	////	02 13	23 12	23 09	23 07	23 07
60	////	00 55	02 39	23 17	23 19	23 23	23 32
N 58	////	01 44	02 59	23 21	23 27	23 36	23 52
56	////	02 13	03 16	23 25	23 35	23 48	24 08
54	00 51	02 36	03 30	23 29	23 41	23 58	24 22
52	01 36	02 53	03 42	23 32	23 47	24 07	00 07
50	02 03	03 08	03 53	23 35	23 53	24 15	00 15
45	02 48	03 38	04 15	23 42	24 05	00 05	00 33
N 40	03 19	04 00	04 33	23 47	24 15	00 15	00 47
35	03 42	04 18	04 48	23 52	24 23	00 23	00 59
30	04 00	04 34	05 01	23 56	24 31	00 31	01 10
20	04 29	04 59	05 23	24 04	00 04	00 44	01 29
N 10	04 52	05 19	05 42	24 11	00 11	00 55	01 45
0	05 11	05 37	05 59	24 17	00 17	01 06	02 00
S 10	05 28	05 54	06 17	24 23	00 23	01 17	02 16
20	05 44	06 11	06 35	24 30	00 30	01 29	02 32
30	06 00	06 30	06 56	24 38	00 38	01 43	02 52
35	06 09	06 41	07 09	24 42	00 42	01 51	03 03
40	06 18	06 52	07 23	24 48	00 48	02 00	03 16
45	06 28	07 06	07 39	24 54	00 54	02 11	03 32
S 50	06 40	07 22	08 00	25 01	01 01	02 24	03 51
52	06 45	07 29	08 10	25 04	01 04	02 30	04 00
54	06 51	07 37	08 21	25 08	01 08	02 37	04 10
56	06 57	07 46	08 34	25 12	01 12	02 44	04 22
58	07 04	07 56	08 48	25 17	01 17	02 53	04 35
S 60	07 11	08 08	09 05	25 22	01 22	03 03	04 51

Lat.	Sunset	Twilight Civil	Twilight Naut.	Moonset 26	Moonset 27	Moonset 28	Moonset 29
°	h m	h m	h m	h m	h m	h m	h m
N 72	□	□	□	13 05	15 34	□	□
N 70	□	□	□	12 57	15 10	18 04	□
68	□	□	□	12 50	14 53	17 17	□
66	□	□	□	12 44	14 39	16 47	19 36
64	22 30	////	////	12 40	14 27	16 25	18 40
62	21 53	////	////	12 36	14 17	16 07	18 08
60	21 27	23 09	////	12 32	14 09	15 53	17 43
N 58	21 07	22 22	////	12 29	14 02	15 40	17 24
56	20 50	21 52	////	12 26	13 55	15 30	17 08
54	20 36	21 30	23 14	12 24	13 49	15 20	16 55
52	20 24	21 13	22 30	12 21	13 44	15 12	16 43
50	20 13	20 58	22 03	12 19	13 40	15 04	16 32
45	19 51	20 28	21 18	12 15	13 30	14 49	16 11
N 40	19 33	20 06	20 47	12 11	13 22	14 36	15 53
35	19 18	19 48	20 24	12 08	13 15	14 25	15 38
30	19 05	19 32	20 06	12 05	13 08	14 15	15 26
20	18 43	19 08	19 37	12 01	12 58	13 59	15 04
N 10	18 24	18 47	19 14	11 56	12 48	13 44	14 45
0	18 07	18 29	18 56	11 52	12 40	13 31	14 28
S 10	17 49	18 12	18 39	11 48	12 31	13 18	14 10
20	17 31	17 55	18 23	11 44	12 22	13 04	13 52
30	17 10	17 36	18 06	11 39	12 12	12 48	13 31
35	16 58	17 26	17 57	11 37	12 06	12 39	13 18
40	16 44	17 14	17 48	11 34	11 59	12 28	13 04
45	16 27	17 01	17 38	11 30	11 51	12 16	12 47
S 50	16 06	16 45	17 26	11 26	11 42	12 01	12 27
52	15 56	16 37	17 21	11 24	11 37	11 54	12 17
54	15 45	16 29	17 15	11 22	11 33	11 46	12 06
56	15 33	16 20	17 09	11 19	11 27	11 38	11 53
58	15 18	16 10	17 03	11 17	11 22	11 28	11 39
S 60	15 01	15 58	16 55	11 14	11 15	11 17	11 22

Day	SUN Eqn. of Time 00^h	SUN Eqn. of Time 12^h	SUN Mer. Pass.	MOON Mer. Pass. Upper	MOON Mer. Pass. Lower	MOON Age	MOON Phase
d	m s	m s	h m	h m	h m	d %	
26	02 49	02 55	12 03	05 41	18 04	23 50	
27	03 02	03 08	12 03	06 28	18 53	24 39	
28	03 14	03 20	12 03	07 19	19 45	25 28	

UT d	h	ARIES GHA	VENUS −3.9 GHA	VENUS Dec	MARS +1.6 GHA	MARS Dec	JUPITER −2.7 GHA	JUPITER Dec	SATURN +0.8 GHA	SATURN Dec
		° ′	° ′	° ′	° ′	° ′	° ′	° ′	° ′	° ′
29 SUNDAY	00	277 26.9	173 10.2	N23 35.2	126 28.2	N13 07.1	347 05.1	S22 17.5	120 36.6	N11 29.7
	01	292 29.4	188 09.3	35.0	141 29.2	06.5	2 07.9	17.5	135 38.9	29.6
	02	307 31.8	203 08.5	34.8	156 30.3	06.0	17 10.7	17.6	150 41.1	29.5
	03	322 34.3	218 07.6	. . 34.6	171 31.3	. . 05.4	32 13.5	. . 17.6	165 43.4	. . 29.4
	04	337 36.8	233 06.7	34.3	186 32.4	04.9	47 16.3	17.7	180 45.6	29.3
	05	352 39.2	248 05.8	34.1	201 33.4	04.4	62 19.1	17.7	195 47.9	29.3
	06	7 41.7	263 04.9	N23 33.9	216 34.5	N13 03.8	77 21.9	S22 17.8	210 50.2	N11 29.2
	07	22 44.2	278 04.1	33.7	231 35.5	03.3	92 24.7	17.8	225 52.4	29.1
	08	37 46.6	293 03.2	33.4	246 36.6	02.7	107 27.5	17.9	240 54.7	29.0
	09	52 49.1	308 02.3	. . 33.2	261 37.6	. . 02.2	122 30.3	. . 17.9	255 56.9	. . 28.9
	10	67 51.6	323 01.4	33.0	276 38.7	01.7	137 33.1	18.0	270 59.2	28.8
	11	82 54.0	338 00.5	32.8	291 39.7	01.1	152 35.9	18.0	286 01.5	28.8
	12	97 56.5	352 59.7	N23 32.5	306 40.8	N13 00.6	167 38.7	S22 18.1	301 03.7	N11 28.7
	13	112 59.0	7 58.8	32.3	321 41.8	13 00.0	182 41.5	18.1	316 06.0	28.6
	14	128 01.4	22 57.9	32.1	336 42.8	12 59.5	197 44.3	18.2	331 08.2	28.5
	15	143 03.9	37 57.0	. . 31.8	351 43.9	. . 58.9	212 47.1	. . 18.2	346 10.5	. . 28.4
	16	158 06.3	52 56.2	31.6	6 44.9	58.4	227 49.8	18.3	1 12.7	28.3
	17	173 08.8	67 55.3	31.3	21 46.0	57.9	242 52.6	18.3	16 15.0	28.3
	18	188 11.3	82 54.4	N23 31.1	36 47.0	N12 57.3	257 55.4	S22 18.4	31 17.3	N11 28.2
	19	203 13.7	97 53.5	30.9	51 48.1	56.8	272 58.2	18.4	46 19.5	28.1
	20	218 16.2	112 52.6	30.6	66 49.1	56.2	288 01.0	18.5	61 21.8	28.0
	21	233 18.7	127 51.8	. . 30.4	81 50.2	. . 55.7	303 03.8	. . 18.5	76 24.0	. . 27.9
	22	248 21.1	142 50.9	30.1	96 51.2	55.1	318 06.6	18.6	91 26.3	27.8
	23	263 23.6	157 50.0	29.9	111 52.3	54.6	333 09.4	18.6	106 28.5	27.8
30 MONDAY	00	278 26.1	172 49.1	N23 29.6	126 53.3	N12 54.1	348 12.2	S22 18.7	121 30.8	N11 27.7
	01	293 28.5	187 48.3	29.4	141 54.4	53.5	3 15.0	18.7	136 33.0	27.6
	02	308 31.0	202 47.4	29.1	156 55.4	53.0	18 17.8	18.8	151 35.3	27.5
	03	323 33.5	217 46.5	. . 28.9	171 56.5	. . 52.4	33 20.6	. . 18.8	166 37.6	. . 27.4
	04	338 35.9	232 45.6	28.6	186 57.5	51.9	48 23.4	18.9	181 39.8	27.3
	05	353 38.4	247 44.8	28.4	201 58.6	51.3	63 26.2	18.9	196 42.1	27.2
	06	8 40.8	262 43.9	N23 28.1	216 59.6	N12 50.8	78 29.0	S22 19.0	211 44.3	N11 27.2
	07	23 43.3	277 43.0	27.9	232 00.7	50.2	93 31.8	19.0	226 46.6	27.1
	08	38 45.8	292 42.1	27.6	247 01.7	49.7	108 34.6	19.1	241 48.8	27.0
	09	53 48.2	307 41.3	. . 27.4	262 02.8	. . 49.1	123 37.4	. . 19.1	256 51.1	. . 26.9
	10	68 50.7	322 40.4	27.1	277 03.8	48.6	138 40.2	19.1	271 53.3	26.8
	11	83 53.2	337 39.5	26.9	292 04.9	48.1	153 43.0	19.2	286 55.6	26.7
	12	98 55.6	352 38.6	N23 26.6	307 05.9	N12 47.5	168 45.8	S22 19.2	301 57.8	N11 26.7
	13	113 58.1	7 37.8	26.3	322 07.0	47.0	183 48.6	19.3	317 00.1	26.6
	14	129 00.6	22 36.9	26.1	337 08.0	46.4	198 51.4	19.3	332 02.4	26.5
	15	144 03.0	37 36.0	. . 25.8	352 09.1	. . 45.9	213 54.2	. . 19.4	347 04.6	. . 26.4
	16	159 05.5	52 35.1	25.5	7 10.1	45.3	228 57.0	19.4	2 06.9	26.3
	17	174 08.0	67 34.3	25.3	22 11.2	44.8	243 59.8	19.5	17 09.1	26.2
	18	189 10.4	82 33.4	N23 25.0	37 12.2	N12 44.2	259 02.6	S22 19.5	32 11.4	N11 26.2
	19	204 12.9	97 32.5	24.7	52 13.3	43.7	274 05.4	19.6	47 13.6	26.1
	20	219 15.3	112 31.6	24.5	67 14.3	43.1	289 08.2	19.6	62 15.9	26.0
	21	234 17.8	127 30.8	. . 24.2	82 15.4	. . 42.6	304 11.0	. . 19.7	77 18.1	. . 25.9
	22	249 20.3	142 29.9	23.9	97 16.4	42.0	319 13.8	19.7	92 20.4	25.8
	23	264 22.7	157 29.0	23.6	112 17.4	41.5	334 16.6	19.8	107 22.6	25.7
1 TUESDAY	00	279 25.2	172 28.2	N23 23.4	127 18.5	N12 41.0	349 19.4	S22 19.8	122 24.9	N11 25.6
	01	294 27.7	187 27.3	23.1	142 19.5	40.4	4 22.2	19.9	137 27.1	25.6
	02	309 30.1	202 26.4	22.8	157 20.6	39.9	19 25.0	19.9	152 29.4	25.5
	03	324 32.6	217 25.6	. . 22.5	172 21.6	. . 39.3	34 27.8	. . 20.0	167 31.7	. . 25.4
	04	339 35.1	232 24.7	22.3	187 22.7	38.8	49 30.6	20.0	182 33.9	25.3
	05	354 37.5	247 23.8	22.0	202 23.7	38.2	64 33.4	20.1	197 36.2	25.2
	06	9 40.0	262 22.9	N23 21.7	217 24.8	N12 37.7	79 36.2	S22 20.1	212 38.4	N11 25.1
	07	24 42.5	277 22.1	21.4	232 25.8	37.1	94 39.0	20.2	227 40.7	25.0
	08	39 44.9	292 21.2	21.1	247 26.9	36.6	109 41.8	20.2	242 42.9	25.0
	09	54 47.4	307 20.3	. . 20.8	262 27.9	. . 36.0	124 44.6	. . 20.3	257 45.2	. . 24.9
	10	69 49.8	322 19.5	20.6	277 29.0	35.5	139 47.4	20.3	272 47.4	24.8
	11	84 52.3	337 18.6	20.3	292 30.0	34.9	154 50.2	20.4	287 49.7	24.7
	12	99 54.8	352 17.7	N23 20.0	307 31.1	N12 34.4	169 53.0	S22 20.4	302 51.9	N11 24.6
	13	114 57.2	7 16.9	19.7	322 32.1	33.8	184 55.8	20.5	317 54.2	24.5
	14	129 59.7	22 16.0	19.4	337 33.2	33.3	199 58.6	20.5	332 56.4	24.4
	15	145 02.2	37 15.1	. . 19.1	352 34.2	. . 32.7	215 01.4	. . 20.6	347 58.7	. . 24.4
	16	160 04.6	52 14.3	18.8	7 35.3	32.2	230 04.2	20.6	3 00.9	24.3
	17	175 07.1	67 13.4	18.5	22 36.3	31.6	245 07.0	20.7	18 03.2	24.2
	18	190 09.6	82 12.5	N23 18.2	37 37.4	N12 31.1	260 09.8	S22 20.7	33 05.4	N11 24.1
	19	205 12.0	97 11.7	17.9	52 38.4	30.5	275 12.6	20.8	48 07.7	24.0
	20	220 14.5	112 10.8	17.6	67 39.5	30.0	290 15.4	20.8	63 09.9	23.9
	21	235 16.9	127 09.9	. . 17.3	82 40.5	. . 29.4	305 18.2	. . 20.9	78 12.2	. . 23.8
	22	250 19.4	142 09.1	17.0	97 41.6	28.9	320 21.0	20.9	93 14.4	23.8
	23	265 21.9	157 08.2	16.7	112 42.6	28.3	335 23.8	21.0	108 16.7	23.7
Mer. Pass.		h m 5 25.4	v −0.9	d 0.3	v 1.0	d 0.5	v 2.8	d 0.0	v 2.3	d 0.1

STARS

Name	SHA	Dec
	° ′	° ′
Acamar	315 21.3	S40 15.9
Achernar	335 29.5	S57 11.2
Acrux	173 13.9	S63 09.1
Adhara	255 15.9	S28 59.0
Aldebaran	290 54.0	N16 31.6
Alioth	166 23.6	N55 55.0
Alkaid	153 01.5	N49 16.4
Al Na'ir	27 47.9	S46 54.9
Alnilam	275 50.5	S 1 11.7
Alphard	218 00.0	S 8 41.8
Alphecca	126 13.8	N26 41.2
Alpheratz	357 47.4	N29 08.2
Altair	62 11.6	N 8 53.4
Ankaa	353 19.2	S42 15.3
Antares	112 30.6	S26 27.2
Arcturus	145 58.9	N19 08.3
Atria	107 35.3	S69 02.8
Avior	234 20.3	S59 32.3
Bellatrix	278 36.3	N 6 21.5
Betelgeuse	271 05.7	N 7 24.6
Canopus	263 58.4	S52 41.9
Capella	280 40.5	N46 00.4
Deneb	49 33.7	N45 18.5
Denebola	182 37.5	N14 31.5
Diphda	348 59.6	S17 56.2
Dubhe	193 56.2	N61 42.5
Elnath	278 17.7	N28 36.9
Eltanin	90 47.3	N51 29.2
Enif	33 50.6	N 9 54.8
Fomalhaut	15 27.8	S29 34.4
Gacrux	172 05.4	S57 10.0
Gienah	175 56.2	S17 35.5
Hadar	148 53.2	S60 25.2
Hamal	328 05.2	N23 30.1
Kaus Aust.	83 48.3	S34 22.9
Kochab	137 18.7	N74 07.4
Markab	13 42.0	N15 15.0
Menkar	314 19.2	N 4 07.5
Menkent	148 11.9	S36 25.0
Miaplacidus	221 41.6	S69 45.3
Mirfak	308 46.2	N49 53.4
Nunki	76 02.5	S26 17.2
Peacock	53 24.4	S56 42.3
Pollux	243 32.6	N28 00.4
Procyon	245 04.0	N 5 12.3
Rasalhague	96 09.6	N12 33.2
Regulus	207 47.7	N11 55.6
Rigel	281 16.0	S 8 11.4
Rigil Kent.	139 56.8	S60 52.5
Sabik	102 16.5	S15 44.2
Schedar	349 45.1	N56 34.8
Shaula	96 26.6	S37 06.7
Sirius	258 37.4	S16 43.6
Spica	158 35.1	S11 12.5
Suhail	222 55.7	S43 28.1
Vega	80 41.1	N38 47.4
Zuben'ubi	137 09.4	S16 04.8

	SHA	Mer. Pass.
	° ′	h m
Venus	254 23.1	12 29
Mars	208 27.3	15 31
Jupiter	69 46.2	0 47
Saturn	203 04.7	15 52

Day	UT d h	SUN GHA ° ′	SUN Dec ° ′	MOON GHA ° ′	v ′	MOON Dec ° ′	d ′	HP ′
	29 00	179 08.4	N23 13.2	241 15.5	7.2	N19 44.4	12.1	59.9
	01	194 08.3	13.1	255 41.7	7.0	19 56.5	12.0	59.9
	02	209 08.2	13.0	270 07.7	6.9	20 08.5	11.8	60.0
	03	224 08.0	. . 12.8	284 33.6	6.8	20 20.3	11.8	60.0
	04	239 07.9	12.7	298 59.4	6.6	20 32.1	11.6	60.0
	05	254 07.8	12.5	313 25.0	6.6	20 43.7	11.6	60.0
	06	269 07.7	N23 12.4	327 50.6	6.4	N20 55.3	11.4	60.1
	07	284 07.5	12.2	342 16.0	6.2	21 06.7	11.2	60.1
	08	299 07.4	12.1	356 41.2	6.2	21 17.9	11.2	60.1
S	09	314 07.3	. . 12.0	11 06.4	6.0	21 29.1	11.0	60.1
U	10	329 07.2	11.8	25 31.4	5.8	21 40.1	10.9	60.2
N	11	344 07.0	11.7	39 56.2	5.8	21 51.0	10.7	60.2
D	12	359 06.9	N23 11.5	54 21.0	5.6	N22 01.7	10.7	60.2
A	13	14 06.8	11.4	68 45.6	5.5	22 12.4	10.4	60.2
Y	14	29 06.7	11.2	83 10.1	5.4	22 22.8	10.4	60.3
	15	44 06.5	. . 11.1	97 34.5	5.2	22 33.2	10.2	60.3
	16	59 06.4	10.9	111 58.7	5.1	22 43.4	10.0	60.3
	17	74 06.3	10.8	126 22.8	5.0	22 53.4	9.9	60.3
	18	89 06.2	N23 10.6	140 46.8	4.8	N23 03.3	9.8	60.4
	19	104 06.0	10.5	155 10.6	4.8	23 13.1	9.6	60.4
	20	119 05.9	10.3	169 34.4	4.6	23 22.7	9.5	60.4
	21	134 05.8	. . 10.2	183 58.0	4.5	23 32.2	9.3	60.4
	22	149 05.7	10.0	198 21.5	4.3	23 41.5	9.1	60.5
	23	164 05.5	09.9	212 44.8	4.3	23 50.6	9.0	60.5
	30 00	179 05.4	N23 09.7	227 08.1	4.1	N23 59.6	8.9	60.5
	01	194 05.3	09.6	241 31.2	4.0	24 08.5	8.6	60.5
	02	209 05.2	09.4	255 54.2	3.9	24 17.1	8.5	60.5
	03	224 05.0	. . 09.3	270 17.1	3.8	24 25.6	8.4	60.6
	04	239 04.9	09.1	284 39.9	3.6	24 34.0	8.1	60.6
	05	254 04.8	09.0	299 02.5	3.5	24 42.1	8.0	60.6
	06	269 04.7	N23 08.8	313 25.0	3.5	N24 50.1	7.9	60.6
	07	284 04.6	08.6	327 47.5	3.3	24 58.0	7.6	60.6
	08	299 04.4	08.5	342 09.8	3.2	25 05.6	7.5	60.6
M	09	314 04.3	. . 08.3	356 32.0	3.1	25 13.1	7.3	60.7
O	10	329 04.2	08.2	10 54.1	3.0	25 20.4	7.1	60.7
N	11	344 04.1	08.0	25 16.1	2.9	25 27.5	7.0	60.7
D	12	359 03.9	N23 07.8	39 38.0	2.8	N25 34.5	6.7	60.7
A	13	14 03.8	07.7	53 59.8	2.7	25 41.2	6.6	60.7
Y	14	29 03.7	07.5	68 21.5	2.6	25 47.8	6.4	60.7
	15	44 03.6	. . 07.3	82 43.1	2.5	25 54.2	6.2	60.8
	16	59 03.4	07.2	97 04.6	2.4	26 00.4	6.0	60.8
	17	74 03.3	07.0	111 26.0	2.3	26 06.4	5.8	60.8
	18	89 03.2	N23 06.8	125 47.3	2.2	N26 12.2	5.6	60.8
	19	104 03.1	06.7	140 08.5	2.2	26 17.8	5.4	60.8
	20	119 03.0	06.5	154 29.7	2.0	26 23.2	5.3	60.8
	21	134 02.8	. . 06.3	168 50.7	2.0	26 28.5	5.0	60.8
	22	149 02.7	06.2	183 11.7	1.9	26 33.5	4.8	60.9
	23	164 02.6	06.0	197 32.6	1.8	26 38.3	4.7	60.9
	1 00	179 02.5	N23 05.8	211 53.4	1.8	N26 43.0	4.4	60.9
	01	194 02.4	05.7	226 14.2	1.7	26 47.4	4.3	60.9
	02	209 02.2	05.5	240 34.9	1.6	26 51.7	4.0	60.9
	03	224 02.1	. . 05.3	254 55.5	1.5	26 55.7	3.8	60.9
	04	239 02.0	05.1	269 16.0	1.5	26 59.5	3.6	60.9
	05	254 01.9	05.0	283 36.5	1.5	27 03.1	3.4	60.9
	06	269 01.7	N23 04.8	297 57.0	1.3	N27 06.5	3.2	60.9
	07	284 01.6	04.6	312 17.3	1.4	27 09.7	3.0	60.9
T	08	299 01.5	04.4	326 37.7	1.2	27 12.7	2.8	60.9
U	09	314 01.4	. . 04.3	340 57.9	1.3	27 15.5	2.6	61.0
E	10	329 01.3	04.1	355 18.2	1.2	27 18.1	2.4	61.0
S	11	344 01.1	03.9	9 38.4	1.1	27 20.5	2.1	61.0
D	12	359 01.0	N23 03.7	23 58.5	1.2	N27 22.6	1.9	61.0
A	13	14 00.9	03.6	38 18.7	1.0	27 24.5	1.8	61.0
Y	14	29 00.8	03.4	52 38.7	1.1	27 26.3	1.5	61.0
	15	44 00.7	. . 03.2	66 58.8	1.0	27 27.8	1.3	61.0
	16	59 00.5	03.0	81 18.8	1.1	27 29.1	1.1	61.0
	17	74 00.4	02.8	95 38.9	1.0	27 30.2	0.8	61.0
	18	89 00.3	N23 02.6	109 58.9	0.9	N27 31.0	0.7	61.0
	19	104 00.2	02.5	124 18.8	1.0	27 31.7	0.4	61.0
	20	119 00.1	02.3	138 38.8	1.0	27 32.1	0.2	61.0
	21	134 00.0	. . 02.1	152 58.8	1.0	27 32.3	0.0	61.0
	22	148 59.8	01.9	167 18.8	0.9	27 32.3	0.2	61.0
	23	163 59.7	01.7	181 38.7	1.0	N27 32.1	0.4	61.0
		SD 15.8	*d* 0.2	SD 16.4		16.5		16.6

Lat. °	Twilight Naut. h m	Twilight Civil h m	Sunrise h m	Moonrise 29 h m	Moonrise 30 h m	Moonrise 1 h m	Moonrise 2 h m
N 72	▭	▭	▭	▭	▭	▭	▭
N 70	▭	▭	▭	▭	▭	▭	▭
68	▭	▭	▭	▭	▭	▭	▭
66	////	////	00 08	21 37	▭	▭	▭
64	////	////	01 40	22 33	▭	▭	▭
62	////	////	02 16	23 07	23 12	23 49	25 38
60	////	01 02	02 41	23 32	23 53	24 44	00 44
N 58	////	01 48	03 01	23 52	24 21	00 21	01 16
56	////	02 16	03 18	24 08	00 08	00 43	01 41
54	00 57	02 38	03 32	24 22	00 22	01 01	02 00
52	01 39	02 55	03 44	00 07	00 35	01 16	02 17
50	02 06	03 10	03 55	00 15	00 46	01 30	02 31
45	02 50	03 39	04 17	00 33	01 09	01 57	03 00
N 40	03 20	04 02	04 34	00 47	01 27	02 19	03 23
35	03 43	04 20	04 49	00 59	01 43	02 37	03 42
30	04 02	04 35	05 02	01 10	01 57	02 53	03 58
20	04 30	04 59	05 24	01 29	02 20	03 19	04 25
N 10	04 53	05 20	05 43	01 45	02 40	03 42	04 49
0	05 11	05 38	06 00	02 00	03 00	04 04	05 11
S 10	05 28	05 55	06 17	02 16	03 19	04 25	05 33
20	05 44	06 12	06 36	02 32	03 40	04 49	05 56
30	06 00	06 30	06 57	02 52	04 04	05 16	06 24
35	06 09	06 41	07 09	03 03	04 18	05 32	06 40
40	06 18	06 52	07 23	03 16	04 34	05 51	06 59
45	06 28	07 06	07 39	03 32	04 54	06 13	07 22
S 50	06 40	07 21	08 00	03 51	05 19	06 42	07 51
52	06 45	07 29	08 09	04 00	05 31	06 57	08 05
54	06 51	07 37	08 20	04 10	05 45	07 13	08 22
56	06 57	07 46	08 33	04 22	06 02	07 33	08 41
58	07 03	07 56	08 47	04 35	06 21	07 57	09 06
S 60	07 11	08 07	09 04	04 51	06 45	08 31	09 38

Lat. °	Sunset h m	Twilight Civil h m	Twilight Naut. h m	Moonset 29 h m	Moonset 30 h m	Moonset 1 h m	Moonset 2 h m
N 72	▭	▭	▭	▭	▭	▭	▭
N 70	▭	▭	▭	▭	▭	▭	▭
68	▭	▭	▭	▭	▭	▭	▭
66	23 45	////	////	19 36	▭	▭	▭
64	22 26	////	////	18 40	▭	▭	▭
62	21 51	////	////	18 08	20 14	21 58	22 28
60	21 25	23 04	////	17 43	19 34	21 03	21 50
N 58	21 06	22 19	////	17 24	19 07	20 30	21 22
56	20 49	21 51	////	17 08	18 45	20 06	21 01
54	20 35	21 29	23 09	16 55	18 27	19 46	20 43
52	20 23	21 12	22 28	16 43	18 12	19 30	20 28
50	20 13	20 57	22 01	16 32	17 59	19 15	20 15
45	19 51	20 28	21 17	16 11	17 32	18 46	19 48
N 40	19 33	20 05	20 47	15 53	17 11	18 24	19 26
35	19 18	19 48	20 24	15 38	16 53	18 05	19 08
30	19 05	19 33	20 06	15 26	16 38	17 49	18 53
20	18 43	19 08	19 37	15 04	16 12	17 21	18 26
N 10	18 25	18 48	19 15	14 45	15 50	16 58	18 04
0	18 07	18 30	18 56	14 28	15 30	16 36	17 42
S 10	17 50	18 13	18 39	14 10	15 09	16 13	17 21
20	17 32	17 56	18 23	13 52	14 47	15 50	16 58
30	17 11	17 37	18 07	13 31	14 22	15 22	16 31
35	16 59	17 27	17 59	13 18	14 07	15 06	16 15
40	16 45	17 15	17 49	13 04	13 49	14 47	15 56
45	16 28	17 02	17 39	12 47	13 29	14 24	15 34
S 50	16 08	16 46	17 28	12 27	13 03	13 55	15 05
52	15 58	16 39	17 22	12 17	12 50	13 40	14 51
54	15 47	16 31	17 17	12 06	12 36	13 24	14 35
56	15 35	16 22	17 11	11 53	12 19	13 04	14 15
58	15 21	16 12	17 04	11 39	11 59	12 39	13 51
S 60	15 03	16 01	16 57	11 22	11 34	12 06	13 19

Day	SUN Eqn. of Time 00^h	SUN Eqn. of Time 12^h	SUN Mer. Pass.	MOON Mer. Pass. Upper	MOON Mer. Pass. Lower	MOON Age	MOON Phase
d	m s	m s	h m	h m	h m	d	%
29	03 26	03 32	12 04	08 14	20 43	26	18
30	03 38	03 44	12 04	09 14	21 47	27	10
1	03 50	03 56	12 04	10 20	22 53	28	4

UT d h	ARIES GHA	VENUS −3.9 GHA	VENUS Dec	MARS +1.7 GHA	MARS Dec	JUPITER −2.7 GHA	JUPITER Dec	SATURN +0.8 GHA	SATURN Dec
	° ′	° ′	° ′	° ′	° ′	° ′	° ′	° ′	° ′
2 00	280 24.3	172 07.3	N23 16.4	127 43.7	N12 27.8	350 26.6	S22 21.0	123 18.9	N11 23.6
01	295 26.8	187 06.5	16.1	142 44.7	27.2	5 29.4	21.1	138 21.2	23.5
02	310 29.3	202 05.6	15.8	157 45.8	26.7	20 32.2	21.1	153 23.4	23.4
03	325 31.7	217 04.7	15.5	172 46.8	26.1	35 35.0	21.2	168 25.7	23.3
04	340 34.2	232 03.9	15.2	187 47.9	25.6	50 37.8	21.2	183 27.9	23.2
05	355 36.7	247 03.0	14.9	202 48.9	25.0	65 40.6	21.3	198 30.2	23.2
06	10 39.1	262 02.1	N23 14.6	217 50.0	N12 24.5	80 43.4	S22 21.3	213 32.4	N11 23.1
W 07	25 41.6	277 01.3	14.3	232 51.0	23.9	95 46.2	21.3	228 34.7	23.0
E 08	40 44.1	292 00.4	13.9	247 52.1	23.4	110 49.0	21.4	243 36.9	22.9
D 09	55 46.5	306 59.5	13.6	262 53.1	22.8	125 51.8	21.4	258 39.2	22.8
N 10	70 49.0	321 58.7	13.3	277 54.1	22.2	140 54.6	21.5	273 41.4	22.7
E 11	85 51.4	336 57.8	13.0	292 55.2	21.7	155 57.4	21.5	288 43.7	22.6
S 12	100 53.9	351 57.0	N23 12.7	307 56.2	N12 21.1	171 00.2	S22 21.6	303 45.9	N11 22.6
D 13	115 56.4	6 56.1	12.4	322 57.3	20.6	186 03.0	21.6	318 48.2	22.5
A 14	130 58.8	21 55.2	12.0	337 58.3	20.0	201 05.8	21.7	333 50.4	22.4
Y 15	146 01.3	36 54.4	11.7	352 59.4	19.5	216 08.6	21.7	348 52.7	22.3
16	161 03.8	51 53.5	11.4	8 00.4	18.9	231 11.4	21.8	3 54.9	22.2
17	176 06.2	66 52.6	11.1	23 01.5	18.4	246 14.2	21.8	18 57.2	22.1
18	191 08.7	81 51.8	N23 10.7	38 02.5	N12 17.8	261 17.0	S22 21.9	33 59.4	N11 22.0
19	206 11.2	96 50.9	10.4	53 03.6	17.3	276 19.8	21.9	49 01.7	22.0
20	221 13.6	111 50.1	10.1	68 04.6	16.7	291 22.6	22.0	64 03.9	21.9
21	236 16.1	126 49.2	09.8	83 05.7	16.2	306 25.4	22.0	79 06.2	21.8
22	251 18.6	141 48.3	09.4	98 06.7	15.6	321 28.2	22.1	94 08.4	21.7
23	266 21.0	156 47.5	09.1	113 07.8	15.1	336 31.0	22.1	109 10.7	21.6
3 00	281 23.5	171 46.6	N23 08.8	128 08.8	N12 14.5	351 33.8	S22 22.2	124 12.9	N11 21.5
01	296 25.9	186 45.8	08.4	143 09.9	13.9	6 36.6	22.2	139 15.2	21.4
02	311 28.4	201 44.9	08.1	158 10.9	13.4	21 39.4	22.3	154 17.4	21.3
03	326 30.9	216 44.1	07.8	173 12.0	12.8	36 42.2	22.3	169 19.7	21.3
04	341 33.3	231 43.2	07.4	188 13.0	12.3	51 45.0	22.4	184 21.9	21.2
05	356 35.8	246 42.3	07.1	203 14.1	11.7	66 47.8	22.4	199 24.2	21.1
06	11 38.3	261 41.5	N23 06.7	218 15.1	N12 11.2	81 50.6	S22 22.5	214 26.4	N11 21.0
07	26 40.7	276 40.6	06.4	233 16.2	10.6	96 53.4	22.5	229 28.7	20.9
T 08	41 43.2	291 39.8	06.1	248 17.2	10.1	111 56.2	22.6	244 30.9	20.8
H 09	56 45.7	306 38.9	05.7	263 18.3	09.5	126 59.0	22.6	259 33.2	20.7
U 10	71 48.1	321 38.1	05.4	278 19.3	08.9	142 01.8	22.7	274 35.4	20.6
R 11	86 50.6	336 37.2	05.0	293 20.4	08.4	157 04.6	22.7	289 37.6	20.6
S 12	101 53.1	351 36.3	N23 04.7	308 21.4	N12 07.8	172 07.4	S22 22.8	304 39.9	N11 20.5
D 13	116 55.5	6 35.5	04.3	323 22.5	07.3	187 10.3	22.8	319 42.1	20.4
A 14	131 58.0	21 34.6	04.0	338 23.5	06.7	202 13.1	22.9	334 44.4	20.3
Y 15	147 00.4	36 33.8	03.6	353 24.6	06.2	217 15.9	22.9	349 46.6	20.2
16	162 02.9	51 32.9	03.3	8 25.6	05.6	232 18.7	23.0	4 48.9	20.1
17	177 05.4	66 32.1	02.9	23 26.7	05.1	247 21.5	23.0	19 51.1	20.0
18	192 07.8	81 31.2	N23 02.6	38 27.7	N12 04.5	262 24.3	S22 23.1	34 53.4	N11 19.9
19	207 10.3	96 30.4	02.2	53 28.8	03.9	277 27.1	23.1	49 55.6	19.9
20	222 12.8	111 29.5	01.9	68 29.8	03.4	292 29.9	23.2	64 57.9	19.8
21	237 15.2	126 28.7	01.5	83 30.9	02.8	307 32.7	23.2	80 00.1	19.7
22	252 17.7	141 27.8	01.1	98 31.9	02.3	322 35.5	23.3	95 02.4	19.6
23	267 20.2	156 26.9	00.8	113 32.9	01.7	337 38.3	23.3	110 04.6	19.5
4 00	282 22.6	171 26.1	N23 00.4	128 34.0	N12 01.2	352 41.1	S22 23.3	125 06.8	N11 19.4
01	297 25.1	186 25.2	23 00.1	143 35.0	00.6	7 43.9	23.4	140 09.1	19.3
02	312 27.6	201 24.4	22 59.7	158 36.1	12 00.0	22 46.7	23.4	155 11.3	19.2
03	327 30.0	216 23.5	59.3	173 37.1	11 59.5	37 49.5	23.5	170 13.6	19.2
04	342 32.5	231 22.7	59.0	188 38.2	58.9	52 52.3	23.5	185 15.8	19.1
05	357 34.9	246 21.8	58.6	203 39.2	58.4	67 55.1	23.6	200 18.1	19.0
06	12 37.4	261 21.0	N22 58.2	218 40.3	N11 57.8	82 57.9	S22 23.6	215 20.3	N11 18.9
07	27 39.9	276 20.1	57.9	233 41.3	57.2	98 00.7	23.7	230 22.6	18.8
08	42 42.3	291 19.3	57.5	248 42.4	56.7	113 03.5	23.7	245 24.8	18.7
F 09	57 44.8	306 18.4	57.1	263 43.4	56.1	128 06.3	23.8	260 27.0	18.6
R 10	72 47.3	321 17.6	56.8	278 44.5	55.6	143 09.1	23.8	275 29.3	18.5
I 11	87 49.7	336 16.7	56.4	293 45.5	55.0	158 11.9	23.9	290 31.5	18.5
D 12	102 52.2	351 15.9	N22 56.0	308 46.6	N11 54.4	173 14.8	S22 23.9	305 33.8	N11 18.4
A 13	117 54.7	6 15.0	55.6	323 47.6	53.9	188 17.6	24.0	320 36.0	18.3
Y 14	132 57.1	21 14.2	55.3	338 48.7	53.3	203 20.4	24.0	335 38.3	18.2
15	147 59.6	36 13.3	54.9	353 49.7	52.8	218 23.2	24.1	350 40.5	18.1
16	163 02.1	51 12.5	54.5	8 50.8	52.2	233 26.0	24.1	5 42.8	18.0
17	178 04.5	66 11.7	54.1	23 51.8	51.6	248 28.8	24.2	20 45.0	17.9
18	193 07.0	81 10.8	N22 53.7	38 52.9	N11 51.1	263 31.6	S22 24.2	35 47.2	N11 17.8
19	208 09.4	96 10.0	53.4	53 53.9	50.5	278 34.4	24.3	50 49.5	17.7
20	223 11.9	111 09.1	53.0	68 55.0	50.0	293 37.2	24.3	65 51.7	17.7
21	238 14.4	126 08.3	52.6	83 56.0	49.4	308 40.0	24.4	80 54.0	17.6
22	253 16.8	141 07.4	52.2	98 57.1	48.8	323 42.8	24.4	95 56.2	17.5
23	268 19.3	156 06.6	51.8	113 58.1	48.3	338 45.6	24.5	110 58.5	17.4
Mer. Pass.	h m 5 13.6	v −0.9	d 0.3	v 1.0	d 0.6	v 2.8	d 0.0	v 2.2	d 0.1

STARS

Name	SHA	Dec
	° ′	° ′
Acamar	315 21.3	S40 15.9
Achernar	335 29.4	S57 11.2
Acrux	173 13.9	S63 09.2
Adhara	255 15.9	S28 58.9
Aldebaran	290 54.0	N16 31.7
Alioth	166 23.7	N55 55.0
Alkaid	153 01.5	N49 16.4
Al Na'ir	27 47.9	S46 54.9
Alnilam	275 50.5	S 1 11.7
Alphard	218 00.0	S 8 41.7
Alphecca	126 13.8	N26 41.2
Alpheratz	357 47.4	N29 08.2
Altair	62 11.5	N 8 53.4
Ankaa	353 19.2	S42 15.3
Antares	112 30.5	S26 27.2
Arcturus	145 58.9	N19 08.3
Atria	107 35.3	S69 02.8
Avior	234 20.3	S59 32.3
Bellatrix	278 36.3	N 6 21.5
Betelgeuse	271 05.7	N 7 24.6
Canopus	263 58.4	S52 41.9
Capella	280 40.4	N46 00.4
Deneb	49 33.7	N45 18.5
Denebola	182 37.5	N14 31.5
Diphda	348 59.6	S17 56.2
Dubhe	193 56.2	N61 42.5
Elnath	278 17.7	N28 36.9
Eltanin	90 47.3	N51 29.3
Enif	33 50.6	N 9 54.8
Fomalhaut	15 27.8	S29 34.4
Gacrux	172 05.4	S57 10.0
Gienah	175 56.2	S17 35.5
Hadar	148 53.2	S60 25.2
Hamal	328 05.2	N23 30.2
Kaus Aust.	83 48.3	S34 22.9
Kochab	137 18.8	N74 07.4
Markab	13 41.9	N15 15.1
Menkar	314 19.1	N 4 07.5
Menkent	148 11.9	S36 25.0
Miaplacidus	221 41.6	S69 45.3
Mirfak	308 46.2	N49 53.4
Nunki	76 02.5	S26 17.2
Peacock	53 24.4	S56 42.3
Pollux	243 32.6	N28 00.4
Procyon	245 03.9	N 5 12.3
Rasalhague	96 09.6	N12 33.2
Regulus	207 47.7	N11 55.6
Rigel	281 15.9	S 8 11.4
Rigil Kent.	139 56.8	S60 52.5
Sabik	102 16.5	S15 44.2
Schedar	349 45.0	N56 34.9
Shaula	96 26.6	S37 06.7
Sirius	258 37.4	S16 43.6
Spica	158 35.1	S11 12.5
Suhail	222 55.7	S43 28.1
Vega	80 41.1	N38 47.5
Zuben'ubi	137 09.4	S16 04.8

	SHA	Mer. Pass.
	° ′	h m
Venus	250 23.1	12 34
Mars	206 45.3	15 26
Jupiter	70 10.3	0 34
Saturn	202 49.4	15 41

	UT d h	SUN GHA ° ′	SUN Dec ° ′	MOON GHA ° ′	v ′	Dec ° ′	d ′	HP ′
	2 00	178 59.6	N23 01.5	195 58.7	1.0	N27 31.7	0.6	61.0
	01	193 59.5	01.3	210 18.7	0.9	27 31.1	0.9	61.0
	02	208 59.4	01.2	224 38.6	1.0	27 30.2	1.1	61.0
	03	223 59.2	. . 01.0	238 58.6	1.1	27 29.1	1.2	61.0
	04	238 59.1	00.8	253 18.7	1.0	27 27.9	1.5	61.0
	05	253 59.0	00.6	267 38.7	1.1	27 26.4	1.8	61.0
	06	268 58.9	N23 00.4	281 58.8	1.1	N27 24.6	1.9	61.0
W	07	283 58.8	00.2	296 18.9	1.1	27 22.7	2.1	61.0
E	08	298 58.6	23 00.0	310 39.0	1.2	27 20.6	2.4	61.0
D	09	313 58.5	22 59.8	324 59.2	1.1	27 18.2	2.6	61.0
N	10	328 58.4	59.6	339 19.3	1.3	27 15.6	2.7	61.0
E	11	343 58.3	59.4	353 39.6	1.3	27 12.9	3.0	60.9
S	12	358 58.2	N22 59.2	7 59.9	1.3	N27 09.9	3.2	60.9
D	13	13 58.1	59.0	22 20.2	1.4	27 06.7	3.4	60.9
A	14	28 57.9	58.8	36 40.6	1.4	27 03.3	3.6	60.9
Y	15	43 57.8	. . 58.6	51 01.0	1.5	26 59.7	3.9	60.9
	16	58 57.7	58.4	65 21.5	1.6	26 55.8	4.0	60.9
	17	73 57.6	58.2	79 42.1	1.6	26 51.8	4.2	60.9
	18	88 57.5	N22 58.0	94 02.7	1.7	N26 47.6	4.4	60.9
	19	103 57.4	57.8	108 23.4	1.8	26 43.2	4.7	60.9
	20	118 57.2	57.6	122 44.2	1.8	26 38.5	4.8	60.9
	21	133 57.1	. . 57.4	137 05.0	1.9	26 33.7	5.0	60.8
	22	148 57.0	57.2	151 25.9	2.0	26 28.7	5.3	60.8
	23	163 56.9	57.0	165 46.9	2.1	26 23.4	5.4	60.8
	3 00	178 56.8	N22 56.8	180 08.0	2.1	N26 18.0	5.6	60.8
	01	193 56.7	56.6	194 29.1	2.3	26 12.4	5.9	60.8
	02	208 56.6	56.4	208 50.4	2.3	26 06.5	6.0	60.8
	03	223 56.4	. . 56.2	223 11.7	2.4	26 00.5	6.2	60.8
	04	238 56.3	56.0	237 33.1	2.6	25 54.3	6.4	60.8
	05	253 56.2	55.8	251 54.7	2.6	25 47.9	6.6	60.7
	06	268 56.1	N22 55.6	266 16.3	2.7	N25 41.3	6.7	60.7
	07	283 56.0	55.4	280 38.0	2.8	25 34.6	7.0	60.7
T	08	298 55.9	55.2	294 59.8	2.9	25 27.6	7.1	60.7
H	09	313 55.7	. . 55.0	309 21.7	3.1	25 20.5	7.3	60.7
U	10	328 55.6	54.7	323 43.8	3.1	25 13.2	7.5	60.6
R	11	343 55.5	54.5	338 05.9	3.2	25 05.7	7.7	60.6
S	12	358 55.4	N22 54.3	352 28.1	3.4	N24 58.0	7.8	60.6
D	13	13 55.3	54.1	6 50.5	3.4	24 50.2	8.0	60.6
A	14	28 55.2	53.9	21 12.9	3.6	24 42.2	8.2	60.6
Y	15	43 55.1	. . 53.7	35 35.5	3.7	24 34.0	8.4	60.5
	16	58 54.9	53.5	49 58.2	3.8	24 25.6	8.5	60.5
	17	73 54.8	53.2	64 21.0	3.9	24 17.1	8.7	60.5
	18	88 54.7	N22 53.0	78 43.9	4.1	N24 08.4	8.8	60.5
	19	103 54.6	52.8	93 07.0	4.2	23 59.6	9.0	60.5
	20	118 54.5	52.6	107 30.2	4.3	23 50.6	9.2	60.4
	21	133 54.4	. . 52.4	121 53.5	4.4	23 41.4	9.3	60.4
	22	148 54.3	52.2	136 16.9	4.5	23 32.1	9.5	60.4
	23	163 54.2	51.9	150 40.4	4.7	23 22.6	9.6	60.4
	4 00	178 54.0	N22 51.7	165 04.1	4.8	N23 13.0	9.8	60.3
	01	193 53.9	51.5	179 27.9	4.9	23 03.2	10.0	60.3
	02	208 53.8	51.3	193 51.8	5.0	22 53.2	10.0	60.3
	03	223 53.7	. . 51.0	208 15.8	5.2	22 43.2	10.3	60.3
	04	238 53.6	50.8	222 40.0	5.3	22 32.9	10.3	60.2
	05	253 53.5	50.6	237 04.3	5.5	22 22.6	10.5	60.2
	06	268 53.4	N22 50.4	251 28.8	5.5	N22 12.1	10.7	60.2
	07	283 53.3	50.2	265 53.3	5.7	22 01.4	10.7	60.2
	08	298 53.2	49.9	280 18.0	5.9	21 50.7	10.9	60.1
F	09	313 53.0	. . 49.7	294 42.9	5.9	21 39.8	11.1	60.1
R	10	328 52.9	49.5	309 07.8	6.1	21 28.7	11.1	60.1
I	11	343 52.8	49.2	323 32.9	6.3	21 17.6	11.3	60.0
D	12	358 52.7	N22 49.0	337 58.2	6.3	N21 06.3	11.4	60.0
A	13	13 52.6	48.8	352 23.5	6.5	20 54.9	11.6	60.0
Y	14	28 52.5	48.6	6 49.0	6.6	20 43.3	11.6	60.0
	15	43 52.4	. . 48.3	21 14.6	6.8	20 31.7	11.8	59.9
	16	58 52.3	48.1	35 40.4	6.9	20 19.9	11.9	59.9
	17	73 52.2	47.9	50 06.3	7.0	20 08.0	12.0	59.9
	18	88 52.0	N22 47.6	64 32.3	7.2	N19 56.0	12.1	59.8
	19	103 51.9	47.4	78 58.5	7.3	19 43.9	12.2	59.8
	20	118 51.8	47.2	93 24.8	7.4	19 31.7	12.3	59.8
	21	133 51.7	. . 46.9	107 51.2	7.5	19 19.4	12.5	59.7
	22	148 51.6	46.7	122 17.7	7.7	19 06.9	12.5	59.7
	23	163 51.5	46.4	136 44.4	7.8	N18 54.4	12.6	59.7
		SD 15.8	d 0.2	SD		16.6	16.5	16.4

Lat.	Twilight Naut.	Twilight Civil	Sunrise	Moonrise 2	Moonrise 3	Moonrise 4	Moonrise 5
°	h m	h m	h m	h m	h m	h m	h m
N 72	▭	▭	▭	▭	▭	▭	▭
N 70	▭	▭	▭	▭	▭	▭	03 59
68	▭	▭	▭	▭	▭	▭	04 40
66	////	////	00 37	▭	▭	02 28	05 07
64	////	////	01 46	▭	▭	03 15	05 28
62	////	////	02 20	25 38	01 38	03 45	05 44
60	////	01 09	02 45	00 44	02 16	04 08	05 58
N 58	////	01 52	03 04	01 16	02 43	04 26	06 10
56	////	02 20	03 20	01 41	03 04	04 42	06 20
54	01 03	02 41	03 34	02 00	03 21	04 55	06 29
52	01 43	02 58	03 46	02 17	03 36	05 06	06 37
50	02 09	03 13	03 57	02 31	03 49	05 16	06 44
45	02 52	03 41	04 18	03 00	04 16	05 38	06 59
N 40	03 22	04 03	04 36	03 23	04 37	05 55	07 12
35	03 45	04 21	04 51	03 42	04 54	06 09	07 22
30	04 03	04 36	05 03	03 58	05 09	06 21	07 32
20	04 31	05 00	05 25	04 25	05 34	06 43	07 47
N 10	04 53	05 20	05 43	04 49	05 56	07 01	08 01
0	05 12	05 38	06 01	05 11	06 16	07 18	08 14
S 10	05 29	05 55	06 18	05 33	06 37	07 35	08 26
20	05 44	06 12	06 36	05 56	06 58	07 53	08 40
30	06 00	06 30	06 56	06 24	07 23	08 14	08 55
35	06 09	06 41	07 09	06 40	07 38	08 26	09 04
40	06 18	06 52	07 22	06 59	07 55	08 39	09 14
45	06 28	07 05	07 39	07 22	08 15	08 56	09 26
S 50	06 39	07 21	07 59	07 51	08 41	09 16	09 40
52	06 44	07 28	08 08	08 05	08 53	09 25	09 47
54	06 50	07 36	08 19	08 22	09 07	09 36	09 54
56	06 56	07 45	08 31	08 41	09 23	09 48	10 02
58	07 02	07 54	08 45	09 06	09 43	10 01	10 12
S 60	07 10	08 06	09 02	09 38	10 06	10 17	10 22

Lat.	Sunset	Twilight Civil	Twilight Naut.	Moonset 2	Moonset 3	Moonset 4	Moonset 5
°	h m	h m	h m	h m	h m	h m	h m
N 72	▭	▭	▭	▭	▭	▭	23 49
N 70	▭	▭	▭	▭	▭	▭	{00 22 / 23 26}
68	▭	▭	▭	▭	▭	23 40	23 07
66	23 26	////	////	▭	23 52	23 11	22 52
64	22 21	////	////	▭	23 03	22 49	22 40
62	21 48	////	////	22 28	22 32	22 32	22 30
60	21 23	22 57	////	21 50	22 09	22 17	22 21
N 58	21 04	22 15	////	21 22	21 50	22 04	22 13
56	20 48	21 48	////	21 01	21 34	21 53	22 06
54	20 34	21 27	23 03	20 43	21 20	21 43	21 59
52	20 22	21 10	22 24	20 28	21 08	21 35	21 54
50	20 12	20 56	21 59	20 15	20 57	21 27	21 48
45	19 50	20 27	21 16	19 48	20 35	21 10	21 37
N 40	19 32	20 05	20 46	19 26	20 17	20 56	21 28
35	19 18	19 47	20 24	19 08	20 01	20 44	21 20
30	19 05	19 32	20 05	18 53	19 48	20 34	21 12
20	18 44	19 08	19 37	18 26	19 25	20 16	21 00
N 10	18 25	18 48	19 15	18 04	19 05	20 00	20 49
0	18 08	18 30	18 57	17 42	18 46	19 45	20 38
S 10	17 51	18 14	18 40	17 21	18 27	19 30	20 28
20	17 33	17 57	18 24	16 58	18 07	19 14	20 17
30	17 12	17 38	18 08	16 31	17 43	18 55	20 04
35	17 00	17 28	18 00	16 15	17 29	18 44	19 56
40	16 46	17 17	17 51	15 56	17 13	18 32	19 47
45	16 30	17 04	17 41	15 34	16 54	18 17	19 37
S 50	16 10	16 48	17 29	15 05	16 29	17 58	19 25
52	16 00	16 41	17 24	14 51	16 17	17 49	19 19
54	15 50	16 33	17 19	14 35	16 04	17 39	19 12
56	15 37	16 24	17 13	14 15	15 48	17 28	19 05
58	15 23	16 14	17 07	13 51	15 29	17 15	18 57
S 60	15 07	16 03	16 59	13 19	15 06	17 00	18 48

Day	SUN Eqn. of Time 00^h	SUN Eqn. of Time 12^h	SUN Mer. Pass.	MOON Mer. Pass. Upper	MOON Mer. Pass. Lower	MOON Age	MOON Phase
d	m s	m s	h m	h m	h m	d	%
2	04 01	04 07	12 04	11 27	23 59	29	1
3	04 13	04 18	12 04	12 31	25 02	00	0
4	04 24	04 29	12 04	13 32	01 02	01	3

UT d h	ARIES GHA ° ′	VENUS −3.9 GHA ° ′	VENUS Dec ° ′	MARS +1.7 GHA ° ′	MARS Dec ° ′	JUPITER −2.7 GHA ° ′	JUPITER Dec ° ′	SATURN +0.8 GHA ° ′	SATURN Dec ° ′
5 00 (SATURDAY)	283 21.8	171 05.7	N22 51.4	128 59.2	N11 47.7	353 48.4	S22 24.5	126 00.7	N11 17.3
01	298 24.2	186 04.9	51.0	144 00.2	47.2	8 51.2	24.6	141 02.9	17.2
02	313 26.7	201 04.0	50.6	159 01.3	46.6	23 54.0	24.6	156 05.2	17.1
03	328 29.2	216 03.2	. . 50.2	174 02.3	. . 46.0	38 56.8	. . 24.7	171 07.4	. . 17.0
04	343 31.6	231 02.4	49.9	189 03.4	45.5	53 59.6	24.7	186 09.7	16.9
05	358 34.1	246 01.5	49.5	204 04.4	44.9	69 02.4	24.8	201 11.9	16.9
06	13 36.6	261 00.7	N22 49.1	219 05.5	N11 44.4	84 05.3	S22 24.8	216 14.2	N11 16.8
07	28 39.0	275 59.8	48.7	234 06.5	43.8	99 08.1	24.9	231 16.4	16.7
08	43 41.5	290 59.0	48.3	249 07.6	43.2	114 10.9	24.9	246 18.6	16.6
09	58 43.9	305 58.1	. . 47.9	264 08.6	. . 42.7	129 13.7	. . 25.0	261 20.9	. . 16.5
10	73 46.4	320 57.3	47.5	279 09.7	42.1	144 16.5	25.0	276 23.1	16.4
11	88 48.9	335 56.5	47.1	294 10.7	41.5	159 19.3	25.1	291 25.4	16.3
12	103 51.3	350 55.6	N22 46.7	309 11.8	N11 41.0	174 22.1	S22 25.1	306 27.6	N11 16.2
13	118 53.8	5 54.8	46.3	324 12.8	40.4	189 24.9	25.1	321 29.9	16.1
14	133 56.3	20 53.9	45.9	339 13.8	39.9	204 27.7	25.2	336 32.1	16.1
15	148 58.7	35 53.1	. . 45.4	354 14.9	. . 39.3	219 30.5	. . 25.2	351 34.3	. . 16.0
16	164 01.2	50 52.3	45.0	9 15.9	38.7	234 33.3	25.3	6 36.6	15.9
17	179 03.7	65 51.4	44.6	24 17.0	38.2	249 36.1	25.3	21 38.8	15.8
18	194 06.1	80 50.6	N22 44.2	39 18.0	N11 37.6	264 38.9	S22 25.4	36 41.1	N11 15.7
19	209 08.6	95 49.7	43.8	54 19.1	37.0	279 41.7	25.4	51 43.3	15.6
20	224 11.0	110 48.9	43.4	69 20.1	36.5	294 44.5	25.5	66 45.5	15.5
21	239 13.5	125 48.1	. . 43.0	84 21.2	. . 35.9	309 47.4	. . 25.5	81 47.8	. . 15.4
22	254 16.0	140 47.2	42.6	99 22.2	35.3	324 50.2	25.6	96 50.0	15.3
23	269 18.4	155 46.4	42.2	114 23.3	34.8	339 53.0	25.6	111 52.3	15.2
6 00 (SUNDAY)	284 20.9	170 45.6	N22 41.7	129 24.3	N11 34.2	354 55.8	S22 25.7	126 54.5	N11 15.2
01	299 23.4	185 44.7	41.3	144 25.4	33.7	9 58.6	25.7	141 56.7	15.1
02	314 25.8	200 43.9	40.9	159 26.4	33.1	25 01.4	25.8	156 59.0	15.0
03	329 28.3	215 43.0	. . 40.5	174 27.5	. . 32.5	40 04.2	. . 25.8	172 01.2	. . 14.9
04	344 30.8	230 42.2	40.1	189 28.5	32.0	55 07.0	25.9	187 03.5	14.8
05	359 33.2	245 41.4	39.6	204 29.6	31.4	70 09.8	25.9	202 05.7	14.7
06	14 35.7	260 40.5	N22 39.2	219 30.6	N11 30.8	85 12.6	S22 26.0	217 07.9	N11 14.6
07	29 38.2	275 39.7	38.8	234 31.7	30.3	100 15.4	26.0	232 10.2	14.5
08	44 40.6	290 38.9	38.4	249 32.7	29.7	115 18.2	26.1	247 12.4	14.4
09	59 43.1	305 38.0	. . 37.9	264 33.8	. . 29.1	130 21.0	. . 26.1	262 14.7	. . 14.3
10	74 45.5	320 37.2	37.5	279 34.8	28.6	145 23.8	26.2	277 16.9	14.3
11	89 48.0	335 36.4	37.1	294 35.9	28.0	160 26.6	26.2	292 19.1	14.2
12	104 50.5	350 35.5	N22 36.7	309 36.9	N11 27.4	175 29.5	S22 26.3	307 21.4	N11 14.1
13	119 52.9	5 34.7	36.2	324 38.0	26.9	190 32.3	26.3	322 23.6	14.0
14	134 55.4	20 33.9	35.8	339 39.0	26.3	205 35.1	26.4	337 25.9	13.9
15	149 57.9	35 33.0	. . 35.4	354 40.1	. . 25.7	220 37.9	. . 26.4	352 28.1	. . 13.8
16	165 00.3	50 32.2	34.9	9 41.1	25.2	235 40.7	26.5	7 30.3	13.7
17	180 02.8	65 31.4	34.5	24 42.2	24.6	250 43.5	26.5	22 32.6	13.6
18	195 05.3	80 30.6	N22 34.0	39 43.2	N11 24.0	265 46.3	S22 26.6	37 34.8	N11 13.5
19	210 07.7	95 29.7	33.6	54 44.3	23.5	280 49.1	26.6	52 37.1	13.4
20	225 10.2	110 28.9	33.2	69 45.3	22.9	295 51.9	26.6	67 39.3	13.4
21	240 12.7	125 28.1	. . 32.7	84 46.4	. . 22.3	310 54.7	. . 26.7	82 41.5	. . 13.3
22	255 15.1	140 27.2	32.3	99 47.4	21.8	325 57.5	26.7	97 43.8	13.2
23	270 17.6	155 26.4	31.8	114 48.5	21.2	341 00.3	26.8	112 46.0	13.1
7 00 (MONDAY)	285 20.0	170 25.6	N22 31.4	129 49.5	N11 20.6	356 03.1	S22 26.8	127 48.2	N11 13.0
01	300 22.5	185 24.7	31.0	144 50.6	20.1	11 06.0	26.9	142 50.5	12.9
02	315 25.0	200 23.9	30.5	159 51.6	19.5	26 08.8	26.9	157 52.7	12.8
03	330 27.4	215 23.1	. . 30.1	174 52.7	. . 18.9	41 11.6	. . 27.0	172 55.0	. . 12.7
04	345 29.9	230 22.3	29.6	189 53.7	18.4	56 14.4	27.0	187 57.2	12.6
05	0 32.4	245 21.4	29.2	204 54.8	17.8	71 17.2	27.1	202 59.4	12.5
06	15 34.8	260 20.6	N22 28.7	219 55.8	N11 17.2	86 20.0	S22 27.1	218 01.7	N11 12.4
07	30 37.3	275 19.8	28.3	234 56.9	16.7	101 22.8	27.2	233 03.9	12.4
08	45 39.8	290 19.0	27.8	249 57.9	16.1	116 25.6	27.2	248 06.2	12.3
09	60 42.2	305 18.1	. . 27.3	264 58.9	. . 15.5	131 28.4	. . 27.3	263 08.4	. . 12.2
10	75 44.7	320 17.3	26.9	280 00.0	15.0	146 31.2	27.3	278 10.6	12.1
11	90 47.1	335 16.5	26.4	295 01.0	14.4	161 34.0	27.4	293 12.9	12.0
12	105 49.6	350 15.7	N22 26.0	310 02.1	N11 13.8	176 36.8	S22 27.4	308 15.1	N11 11.9
13	120 52.1	5 14.8	25.5	325 03.1	13.2	191 39.6	27.5	323 17.3	11.8
14	135 54.5	20 14.0	25.1	340 04.2	12.7	206 42.5	27.5	338 19.6	11.7
15	150 57.0	35 13.2	. . 24.6	355 05.2	. . 12.1	221 45.3	. . 27.6	353 21.8	. . 11.6
16	165 59.5	50 12.4	24.1	10 06.3	11.5	236 48.1	27.6	8 24.0	11.5
17	181 01.9	65 11.5	23.7	25 07.3	11.0	251 50.9	27.7	23 26.3	11.4
18	196 04.4	80 10.7	N22 23.2	40 08.4	N11 10.4	266 53.7	S22 27.7	38 28.5	N11 11.4
19	211 06.9	95 09.9	22.7	55 09.4	09.8	281 56.5	27.8	53 30.8	11.3
20	226 09.3	110 09.1	22.3	70 10.5	09.3	296 59.3	27.8	68 33.0	11.2
21	241 11.8	125 08.3	. . 21.8	85 11.5	. . 08.7	312 02.1	. . 27.8	83 35.2	. . 11.1
22	256 14.3	140 07.4	21.3	100 12.6	08.1	327 04.9	27.9	98 37.5	11.0
23	271 16.7	155 06.6	20.9	115 13.6	07.5	342 07.7	27.9	113 39.7	10.9
Mer. Pass. (h m)	5 01.8	v −0.8	d 0.4	v 1.0	d 0.6	v 2.8	d 0.0	v 2.2	d 0.1

STARS

Name	SHA ° ′	Dec ° ′
Acamar	315 21.3	S40 15.9
Achernar	335 29.4	S57 11.2
Acrux	173 13.9	S63 09.2
Adhara	255 15.9	S28 58.9
Aldebaran	290 53.9	N16 31.7
Alioth	166 23.7	N55 55.0
Alkaid	153 01.5	N49 16.4
Al Na'ir	27 47.9	S46 54.9
Alnilam	275 50.4	S 1 11.7
Alphard	218 00.0	S 8 41.7
Alphecca	126 13.9	N26 41.2
Alpheratz	357 47.4	N29 08.2
Altair	62 11.5	N 8 53.4
Ankaa	353 19.1	S42 15.2
Antares	112 30.5	S26 27.2
Arcturus	145 58.9	N19 08.3
Atria	107 35.3	S69 02.8
Avior	234 20.3	S59 32.3
Bellatrix	278 36.3	N 6 21.5
Betelgeuse	271 05.6	N 7 24.6
Canopus	263 58.4	S52 41.9
Capella	280 40.4	N46 00.4
Deneb	49 33.7	N45 18.5
Denebola	182 37.5	N14 31.5
Diphda	348 59.5	S17 56.2
Dubhe	193 56.2	N61 42.5
Elnath	278 17.7	N28 36.9
Eltanin	90 47.3	N51 29.3
Enif	33 50.5	N 9 54.9
Fomalhaut	15 27.8	S29 34.4
Gacrux	172 05.4	S57 10.0
Gienah	175 56.2	S17 35.5
Hadar	148 53.3	S60 25.2
Hamal	328 05.1	N23 30.2
Kaus Aust.	83 48.3	S34 22.9
Kochab	137 18.8	N74 07.4
Markab	13 41.9	N15 15.1
Menkar	314 19.1	N 4 07.5
Menkent	148 11.9	S36 25.0
Miaplacidus	221 41.6	S69 45.3
Mirfak	308 46.1	N49 53.4
Nunki	76 02.5	S26 17.2
Peacock	53 24.3	S56 42.3
Pollux	243 32.6	N28 00.4
Procyon	245 03.9	N 5 12.3
Rasalhague	96 09.6	N12 33.2
Regulus	207 47.7	N11 55.6
Rigel	281 15.9	S 8 11.4
Rigil Kent.	139 56.8	S60 52.5
Sabik	102 16.5	S15 44.2
Schedar	349 45.0	N56 34.9
Shaula	96 26.6	S37 06.7
Sirius	258 37.3	S16 43.6
Spica	158 35.2	S11 12.5
Suhail	222 55.7	S43 28.1
Vega	80 41.1	N38 47.5
Zuben'ubi	137 09.4	S16 04.8

	SHA ° ′	Mer. Pass. h m
Venus	246 24.6	12 38
Mars	205 03.4	15 21
Jupiter	70 34.9	0 20
Saturn	202 33.6	15 30

UT	SUN GHA	SUN Dec	MOON GHA	v	MOON Dec	d	HP
d h	° ′	° ′	° ′	′	° ′	′	′
5 00	178 51.4	N22 46.2	151 11.2	8.0	N18 41.8	12.7	59.6
01	193 51.3	46.0	165 38.2	8.1	18 29.1	12.9	59.6
02	208 51.2	45.7	180 05.3	8.2	18 16.2	12.9	59.6
03	223 51.1	. . 45.5	194 32.5	8.3	18 03.3	13.0	59.5
04	238 51.0	45.3	208 59.8	8.5	17 50.3	13.1	59.5
05	253 50.8	45.0	223 27.3	8.5	17 37.2	13.2	59.5
06	268 50.7	N22 44.8	237 54.8	8.8	N17 24.0	13.2	59.4
07	283 50.6	44.5	252 22.6	8.8	17 10.8	13.4	59.4
SATURDAY 08	298 50.5	44.3	266 50.4	9.0	16 57.4	13.4	59.4
09	313 50.4	. . 44.0	281 18.4	9.0	16 44.0	13.5	59.3
10	328 50.3	43.8	295 46.4	9.3	16 30.5	13.6	59.3
11	343 50.2	43.6	310 14.7	9.3	16 16.9	13.6	59.3
12	358 50.1	N22 43.3	324 43.0	9.5	N16 03.3	13.8	59.2
13	13 50.0	43.1	339 11.5	9.5	15 49.5	13.8	59.2
14	28 49.9	42.8	353 40.0	9.7	15 35.7	13.8	59.2
15	43 49.8	. . 42.6	8 08.7	9.8	15 21.9	14.0	59.1
16	58 49.7	42.3	22 37.5	10.0	15 07.9	14.0	59.1
17	73 49.6	42.1	37 06.5	10.0	14 53.9	14.0	59.1
18	88 49.5	N22 41.8	51 35.5	10.2	N14 39.9	14.2	59.0
19	103 49.4	41.6	66 04.7	10.3	14 25.7	14.2	59.0
20	118 49.2	41.3	80 34.0	10.4	14 11.5	14.2	58.9
21	133 49.1	. . 41.1	95 03.4	10.5	13 57.3	14.3	58.9
22	148 49.0	40.8	109 32.9	10.6	13 43.0	14.3	58.9
23	163 48.9	40.6	124 02.5	10.7	13 28.7	14.4	58.8
6 00	178 48.8	N22 40.3	138 32.2	10.8	N13 14.3	14.5	58.8
01	193 48.7	40.1	153 02.0	11.0	12 59.8	14.5	58.8
02	208 48.6	39.8	167 32.0	11.0	12 45.3	14.5	58.7
03	223 48.5	. . 39.5	182 02.0	11.2	12 30.8	14.6	58.7
04	238 48.4	39.3	196 32.2	11.2	12 16.2	14.7	58.6
05	253 48.3	39.0	211 02.4	11.4	12 01.5	14.6	58.6
06	268 48.2	N22 38.8	225 32.8	11.5	N11 46.9	14.7	58.6
07	283 48.1	38.5	240 03.3	11.5	11 32.2	14.8	58.5
08	298 48.0	38.3	254 33.8	11.7	11 17.4	14.8	58.5
SUNDAY 09	313 47.9	. . 38.0	269 04.5	11.7	11 02.6	14.8	58.4
10	328 47.8	37.7	283 35.2	11.9	10 47.8	14.9	58.4
11	343 47.7	37.5	298 06.1	11.9	10 32.9	14.9	58.4
12	358 47.6	N22 37.2	312 37.0	12.1	N10 18.0	14.9	58.3
13	13 47.5	37.0	327 08.1	12.1	10 03.1	14.9	58.3
14	28 47.4	36.7	341 39.2	12.2	9 48.2	15.0	58.3
15	43 47.3	. . 36.4	356 10.4	12.4	9 33.2	15.0	58.2
16	58 47.2	36.2	10 41.8	12.4	9 18.2	15.0	58.2
17	73 47.1	35.9	25 13.2	12.5	9 03.2	15.1	58.1
18	88 47.0	N22 35.6	39 44.7	12.5	N 8 48.1	15.0	58.1
19	103 46.9	35.4	54 16.2	12.7	8 33.1	15.1	58.1
20	118 46.8	35.1	68 47.9	12.7	8 18.0	15.1	58.0
21	133 46.7	. . 34.8	83 19.6	12.9	8 02.9	15.1	58.0
22	148 46.6	34.6	97 51.5	12.9	7 47.8	15.2	57.9
23	163 46.5	34.3	112 23.4	13.0	7 32.6	15.1	57.9
7 00	178 46.4	N22 34.0	126 55.4	13.0	N 7 17.5	15.2	57.9
01	193 46.3	33.7	141 27.4	13.2	7 02.3	15.2	57.8
02	208 46.2	33.5	155 59.6	13.2	6 47.1	15.2	57.8
03	223 46.1	. . 33.2	170 31.8	13.3	6 31.9	15.1	57.8
04	238 46.0	32.9	185 04.1	13.3	6 16.8	15.2	57.7
05	253 45.9	32.7	199 36.4	13.4	6 01.6	15.3	57.7
06	268 45.8	N22 32.4	214 08.8	13.5	N 5 46.3	15.2	57.6
07	283 45.7	32.1	228 41.3	13.6	5 31.1	15.2	57.6
08	298 45.6	31.8	243 13.9	13.6	5 15.9	15.2	57.6
MONDAY 09	313 45.5	. . 31.6	257 46.5	13.7	5 00.7	15.2	57.5
10	328 45.4	31.3	272 19.2	13.8	4 45.5	15.2	57.5
11	343 45.3	31.0	286 52.0	13.8	4 30.3	15.3	57.4
12	358 45.2	N22 30.7	301 24.8	13.9	N 4 15.0	15.2	57.4
13	13 45.1	30.4	315 57.7	13.9	3 59.8	15.2	57.4
14	28 45.0	30.2	330 30.6	14.0	3 44.6	15.2	57.3
15	43 44.9	. . 29.9	345 03.6	14.1	3 29.4	15.2	57.3
16	58 44.8	29.6	359 36.7	14.1	3 14.2	15.2	57.3
17	73 44.7	29.3	14 09.8	14.2	2 59.0	15.2	57.2
18	88 44.6	N22 29.0	28 43.0	14.2	N 2 43.8	15.2	57.2
19	103 44.5	28.8	43 16.2	14.3	2 28.6	15.1	57.1
20	118 44.4	28.5	57 49.5	14.3	2 13.5	15.2	57.1
21	133 44.3	. . 28.2	72 22.8	14.4	1 58.3	15.1	57.1
22	148 44.2	27.9	86 56.2	14.4	1 43.2	15.2	57.0
23	163 44.1	27.6	101 29.6	14.5	N 1 28.0	15.1	57.0
	SD 15.8	*d* 0.3	SD 16.1		15.9		15.6

Lat.	Twilight Naut.	Twilight Civil	Sunrise	Moonrise 5	Moonrise 6	Moonrise 7	Moonrise 8
°	h m	h m	h m	h m	h m	h m	h m
N 72	□	□	□	□	06 23	08 47	10 55
N 70	□	□	□	03 59	06 44	08 54	10 53
68	□	□	□	04 40	07 00	09 00	10 51
66	////	////	00 54	05 07	07 13	09 05	10 49
64	////	////	01 52	05 28	07 24	09 09	10 48
62	////	////	02 25	05 44	07 33	09 13	10 47
60	////	01 18	02 49	05 58	07 41	09 16	10 46
N 58	////	01 57	03 08	06 10	07 48	09 19	10 45
56	////	02 24	03 23	06 20	07 54	09 21	10 44
54	01 11	02 44	03 37	06 29	07 59	09 23	10 43
52	01 48	03 01	03 49	06 37	08 04	09 25	10 43
50	02 13	03 15	03 59	06 44	08 08	09 27	10 42
45	02 55	03 44	04 20	06 59	08 17	09 31	10 41
N 40	03 24	04 05	04 38	07 12	08 25	09 34	10 40
35	03 47	04 23	04 52	07 22	08 32	09 37	10 39
30	04 04	04 37	05 05	07 32	08 38	09 39	10 38
20	04 33	05 02	05 26	07 47	08 48	09 44	10 37
N 10	04 54	05 21	05 44	08 01	08 56	09 47	10 36
0	05 13	05 39	06 01	08 14	09 04	09 51	10 35
S 10	05 29	05 55	06 18	08 26	09 13	09 54	10 34
20	05 45	06 12	06 36	08 40	09 21	09 58	10 33
30	06 00	06 30	06 56	08 55	09 31	10 02	10 32
35	06 09	06 40	07 08	09 04	09 37	10 05	10 31
40	06 18	06 51	07 22	09 14	09 43	10 08	10 30
45	06 27	07 04	07 38	09 26	09 50	10 11	10 29
S 50	06 39	07 20	07 58	09 40	09 59	10 14	10 28
52	06 43	07 27	08 07	09 47	10 03	10 16	10 28
54	06 49	07 34	08 17	09 54	10 08	10 18	10 27
56	06 55	07 43	08 29	10 02	10 12	10 20	10 27
58	07 01	07 53	08 43	10 12	10 18	10 22	10 26
S 60	07 08	08 04	09 00	10 22	10 24	10 25	10 25

Lat.	Sunset	Twilight Civil	Twilight Naut.	Moonset 5	Moonset 6	Moonset 7	Moonset 8
°	h m	h m	h m	h m	h m	h m	h m
N 72	□	□	□	23 49	23 05	22 31	22 00
N 70	□	□	□	{00 22 / 23 26}	22 54	22 29	22 06
68	□	□	□	23 07	22 46	22 28	22 10
66	23 11	////	////	22 52	22 38	22 26	22 15
64	22 16	////	////	22 40	22 32	22 25	22 18
62	21 43	////	////	22 30	22 27	22 24	22 21
60	21 20	22 50	////	22 21	22 22	22 23	22 24
N 58	21 01	22 11	////	22 13	22 18	22 22	22 26
56	20 45	21 45	////	22 06	22 15	22 22	22 28
54	20 32	21 24	22 56	21 59	22 11	22 21	22 30
52	20 21	21 08	22 20	21 54	22 08	22 20	22 32
50	20 10	20 54	21 56	21 48	22 05	22 20	22 33
45	19 49	20 26	21 14	21 37	21 59	22 19	22 37
N 40	19 32	20 04	20 45	21 28	21 54	22 18	22 40
35	19 17	19 47	20 23	21 20	21 50	22 17	22 42
30	19 05	19 32	20 05	21 12	21 46	22 16	22 45
20	18 44	19 08	19 37	21 00	21 39	22 15	22 49
N 10	18 25	18 48	19 15	20 49	21 33	22 13	22 52
0	18 08	18 31	18 57	20 38	21 27	22 12	22 55
S 10	17 52	18 14	18 41	20 28	21 21	22 11	22 58
20	17 34	17 58	18 25	20 17	21 15	22 10	23 02
30	17 14	17 40	18 09	20 04	21 08	22 08	23 06
35	17 02	17 30	18 01	19 56	21 03	22 07	23 08
40	16 48	17 18	17 52	19 47	20 59	22 06	23 11
45	16 32	17 06	17 42	19 37	20 53	22 05	23 14
S 50	16 12	16 50	17 31	19 25	20 46	22 03	23 17
52	16 03	16 43	17 26	19 19	20 43	22 03	23 19
54	15 52	16 35	17 21	19 12	20 40	22 02	23 21
56	15 40	16 27	17 15	19 05	20 36	22 01	23 23
58	15 27	16 17	17 09	18 57	20 32	22 00	23 25
S 60	15 10	16 06	17 02	18 48	20 27	21 59	23 28

Day	SUN Eqn. of Time 00^h	SUN Eqn. of Time 12^h	SUN Mer. Pass.	MOON Mer. Pass. Upper	MOON Mer. Pass. Lower	MOON Age	MOON Phase
d	m s	m s	h m	h m	h m	d %	
5	04 34	04 39	12 05	14 26	02 00	02 8	
6	04 44	04 49	12 05	15 16	02 52	03 15	
7	04 54	04 59	12 05	16 02	03 39	04 24	

	UT	ARIES	VENUS −3.9		MARS +1.7		JUPITER −2.7		SATURN +0.8	
		GHA	GHA	Dec	GHA	Dec	GHA	Dec	GHA	Dec
	d h	° ′	° ′	° ′	° ′	° ′	° ′	° ′	° ′	° ′
	8 00	286 19.2	170 05.8	N22 20.4	130 14.7	N11 07.0	357 10.5	S22 28.0	128 41.9	N11 10.8
	01	301 21.6	185 05.0	19.9	145 15.7	06.4	12 13.3	28.0	143 44.2	10.7
	02	316 24.1	200 04.2	19.4	160 16.8	05.8	27 16.2	28.1	158 46.4	10.6
	03	331 26.6	215 03.3	. . 19.0	175 17.8	. . 05.3	42 19.0	. . 28.1	173 48.6	. . 10.5
	04	346 29.0	230 02.5	18.5	190 18.9	04.7	57 21.8	28.2	188 50.9	10.4
	05	1 31.5	245 01.7	18.0	205 19.9	04.1	72 24.6	28.2	203 53.1	10.3
	06	16 34.0	260 00.9	N22 17.5	220 21.0	N11 03.5	87 27.4	S22 28.3	218 55.3	N11 10.3
	07	31 36.4	275 00.1	17.1	235 22.0	03.0	102 30.2	28.3	233 57.6	10.2
T	08	46 38.9	289 59.3	16.6	250 23.1	02.4	117 33.0	28.4	248 59.8	10.1
U	09	61 41.4	304 58.4	. . 16.1	265 24.1	. . 01.8	132 35.8	. . 28.4	264 02.1	. . 10.0
E	10	76 43.8	319 57.6	15.6	280 25.2	01.3	147 38.6	28.5	279 04.3	09.9
S	11	91 46.3	334 56.8	15.1	295 26.2	00.7	162 41.4	28.5	294 06.5	09.8
D	12	106 48.8	349 56.0	N22 14.6	310 27.3	N11 00.1	177 44.2	S22 28.6	309 08.8	N11 09.7
A	13	121 51.2	4 55.2	14.2	325 28.3	10 59.5	192 47.0	28.6	324 11.0	09.6
Y	14	136 53.7	19 54.4	13.7	340 29.4	59.0	207 49.9	28.7	339 13.2	09.5
	15	151 56.1	34 53.6	. . 13.2	355 30.4	. . 58.4	222 52.7	. . 28.7	354 15.5	. . 09.4
	16	166 58.6	49 52.7	12.7	10 31.5	57.8	237 55.5	28.8	9 17.7	09.3
	17	182 01.1	64 51.9	12.2	25 32.5	57.3	252 58.3	28.8	24 19.9	09.2
	18	197 03.5	79 51.1	N22 11.7	40 33.6	N10 56.7	268 01.1	S22 28.9	39 22.2	N11 09.2
	19	212 06.0	94 50.3	11.2	55 34.6	56.1	283 03.9	28.9	54 24.4	09.1
	20	227 08.5	109 49.5	10.7	70 35.7	55.5	298 06.7	28.9	69 26.6	09.0
	21	242 10.9	124 48.7	. . 10.2	85 36.7	. . 55.0	313 09.5	. . 29.0	84 28.9	. . 08.9
	22	257 13.4	139 47.9	09.7	100 37.8	54.4	328 12.3	29.0	99 31.1	08.8
	23	272 15.9	154 47.1	09.2	115 38.8	53.8	343 15.1	29.1	114 33.3	08.7
	9 00	287 18.3	169 46.2	N22 08.7	130 39.9	N10 53.2	358 17.9	S22 29.1	129 35.6	N11 08.6
	01	302 20.8	184 45.4	08.2	145 40.9	52.7	13 20.7	29.2	144 37.8	08.5
	02	317 23.2	199 44.6	07.7	160 42.0	52.1	28 23.6	29.2	159 40.0	08.4
	03	332 25.7	214 43.8	. . 07.2	175 43.0	. . 51.5	43 26.4	. . 29.3	174 42.3	. . 08.3
	04	347 28.2	229 43.0	06.7	190 44.1	50.9	58 29.2	29.3	189 44.5	08.2
	05	2 30.6	244 42.2	06.2	205 45.1	50.4	73 32.0	29.4	204 46.7	08.1
	06	17 33.1	259 41.4	N22 05.7	220 46.2	N10 49.8	88 34.8	S22 29.4	219 49.0	N11 08.0
W	07	32 35.6	274 40.6	05.2	235 47.2	49.2	103 37.6	29.5	234 51.2	07.9
E	08	47 38.0	289 39.8	04.7	250 48.2	48.6	118 40.4	29.5	249 53.4	07.9
D	09	62 40.5	304 39.0	. . 04.2	265 49.3	. . 48.1	133 43.2	. . 29.6	264 55.7	. . 07.8
N	10	77 43.0	319 38.2	03.7	280 50.3	47.5	148 46.0	29.6	279 57.9	07.7
E	11	92 45.4	334 37.4	03.2	295 51.4	46.9	163 48.8	29.7	295 00.1	07.6
S	12	107 47.9	349 36.6	N22 02.7	310 52.4	N10 46.3	178 51.6	S22 29.7	310 02.4	N11 07.5
D	13	122 50.4	4 35.8	02.2	325 53.5	45.8	193 54.5	29.8	325 04.6	07.4
A	14	137 52.8	19 34.9	01.6	340 54.5	45.2	208 57.3	29.8	340 06.8	07.3
Y	15	152 55.3	34 34.1	. . 01.1	355 55.6	. . 44.6	224 00.1	. . 29.8	355 09.1	. . 07.2
	16	167 57.7	49 33.3	00.6	10 56.6	44.0	239 02.9	29.9	10 11.3	07.1
	17	183 00.2	64 32.5	22 00.1	25 57.7	43.5	254 05.7	29.9	25 13.5	07.0
	18	198 02.7	79 31.7	N21 59.6	40 58.7	N10 42.9	269 08.5	S22 30.0	40 15.8	N11 06.9
	19	213 05.1	94 30.9	59.1	55 59.8	42.3	284 11.3	30.0	55 18.0	06.8
	20	228 07.6	109 30.1	58.5	71 00.8	41.7	299 14.1	30.1	70 20.2	06.7
	21	243 10.1	124 29.3	. . 58.0	86 01.9	. . 41.2	314 16.9	. . 30.1	85 22.4	. . 06.6
	22	258 12.5	139 28.5	57.5	101 02.9	40.6	329 19.7	30.2	100 24.7	06.6
	23	273 15.0	154 27.7	57.0	116 04.0	40.0	344 22.5	30.2	115 26.9	06.5
	10 00	288 17.5	169 26.9	N21 56.4	131 05.0	N10 39.4	359 25.3	S22 30.3	130 29.1	N11 06.4
	01	303 19.9	184 26.1	55.9	146 06.1	38.9	14 28.2	30.3	145 31.4	06.3
	02	318 22.4	199 25.3	55.4	161 07.1	38.3	29 31.0	30.4	160 33.6	06.2
	03	333 24.9	214 24.5	. . 54.9	176 08.2	. . 37.7	44 33.8	. . 30.4	175 35.8	. . 06.1
	04	348 27.3	229 23.7	54.3	191 09.2	37.1	59 36.6	30.5	190 38.1	06.0
	05	3 29.8	244 22.9	53.8	206 10.3	36.5	74 39.4	30.5	205 40.3	05.9
	06	18 32.2	259 22.1	N21 53.3	221 11.3	N10 36.0	89 42.2	S22 30.6	220 42.5	N11 05.8
	07	33 34.7	274 21.3	52.7	236 12.4	35.4	104 45.0	30.6	235 44.8	05.7
T	08	48 37.2	289 20.5	52.2	251 13.4	34.8	119 47.8	30.7	250 47.0	05.6
H	09	63 39.6	304 19.7	. . 51.7	266 14.5	. . 34.2	134 50.6	. . 30.7	265 49.2	. . 05.5
U	10	78 42.1	319 18.9	51.1	281 15.5	33.7	149 53.4	30.7	280 51.4	05.4
R	11	93 44.6	334 18.1	50.6	296 16.6	33.1	164 56.2	30.8	295 53.7	05.3
S	12	108 47.0	349 17.4	N21 50.1	311 17.6	N10 32.5	179 59.0	S22 30.8	310 55.9	N11 05.2
D	13	123 49.5	4 16.6	49.5	326 18.7	31.9	195 01.9	30.9	325 58.1	05.2
A	14	138 52.0	19 15.8	49.0	341 19.7	31.3	210 04.7	30.9	341 00.4	05.1
Y	15	153 54.4	34 15.0	. . 48.4	356 20.8	. . 30.8	225 07.5	. . 31.0	356 02.6	. . 05.0
	16	168 56.9	49 14.2	47.9	11 21.8	30.2	240 10.3	31.0	11 04.8	04.9
	17	183 59.3	64 13.4	47.3	26 22.9	29.6	255 13.1	31.1	26 07.1	04.8
	18	199 01.8	79 12.6	N21 46.8	41 23.9	N10 29.0	270 15.9	S22 31.1	41 09.3	N11 04.7
	19	214 04.3	94 11.8	46.3	56 25.0	28.5	285 18.7	31.2	56 11.5	04.6
	20	229 06.7	109 11.0	45.7	71 26.0	27.9	300 21.5	31.2	71 13.7	04.5
	21	244 09.2	124 10.2	. . 45.2	86 27.1	. . 27.3	315 24.3	. . 31.3	86 16.0	. . 04.4
	22	259 11.7	139 09.4	44.6	101 28.1	26.7	330 27.1	31.3	101 18.2	04.3
	23	274 14.1	154 08.6	44.1	116 29.2	26.1	345 29.9	31.4	116 20.4	04.2
	Mer. Pass.	h m 4 50.0	v −0.8	d 0.5	v 1.0	d 0.6	v 2.8	d 0.0	v 2.2	d 0.1

STARS

Name	SHA	Dec
	° ′	° ′
Acamar	315 21.2	S40 15.9
Achernar	335 29.3	S57 11.2
Acrux	173 13.9	S63 09.1
Adhara	255 15.8	S28 58.9
Aldebaran	290 53.9	N16 31.7
Alioth	166 23.7	N55 55.0
Alkaid	153 01.5	N49 16.4
Al Na'ir	27 47.8	S46 54.9
Alnilam	275 50.4	S 1 11.7
Alphard	218 00.0	S 8 41.7
Alphecca	126 13.9	N26 41.2
Alpheratz	357 47.3	N29 08.2
Altair	62 11.5	N 8 53.4
Ankaa	353 19.1	S42 15.2
Antares	112 30.6	S26 27.2
Arcturus	145 58.9	N19 08.3
Atria	107 35.3	S69 02.8
Avior	234 20.3	S59 32.3
Bellatrix	278 36.3	N 6 21.6
Betelgeuse	271 05.6	N 7 24.6
Canopus	263 58.4	S52 41.9
Capella	280 40.4	N46 00.4
Deneb	49 33.7	N45 18.6
Denebola	182 37.5	N14 31.5
Diphda	348 59.5	S17 56.2
Dubhe	193 56.2	N61 42.5
Elnath	278 17.7	N28 36.9
Eltanin	90 47.3	N51 29.3
Enif	33 50.5	N 9 54.9
Fomalhaut	15 27.7	S29 34.4
Gacrux	172 05.4	S57 10.0
Gienah	175 56.3	S17 35.5
Hadar	148 53.3	S60 25.2
Hamal	328 05.1	N23 30.2
Kaus Aust.	83 48.3	S34 22.9
Kochab	137 18.9	N74 07.4
Markab	13 41.9	N15 15.1
Menkar	314 19.1	N 4 07.5
Menkent	148 12.0	S36 25.0
Miaplacidus	221 41.7	S69 45.3
Mirfak	308 46.1	N49 53.4
Nunki	76 02.5	S26 17.2
Peacock	53 24.3	S56 42.4
Pollux	243 32.6	N28 00.4
Procyon	245 03.9	N 5 12.3
Rasalhague	96 09.6	N12 33.2
Regulus	207 47.7	N11 55.6
Rigel	281 15.9	S 8 11.4
Rigil Kent.	139 56.8	S60 52.5
Sabik	102 16.5	S15 44.2
Schedar	349 45.0	N56 34.9
Shaula	96 26.6	S37 06.7
Sirius	258 37.3	S16 43.6
Spica	158 35.2	S11 12.5
Suhail	222 55.7	S43 28.1
Vega	80 41.1	N38 47.5
Zuben'ubi	137 09.4	S16 04.8

	SHA	Mer. Pass.
	° ′	h m
Venus	242 27.9	12 42
Mars	203 21.5	15 16
Jupiter	70 59.6	0 07
Saturn	202 17.2	15 19

UT	SUN GHA	SUN Dec	MOON GHA	v	MOON Dec	d	HP
d h	° ′	° ′	° ′	′	° ′	′	′
8 00 TUESDAY	178 44.0	N22 27.3	116 03.1	14.5	N 1 12.9	15.1	57.0
01	193 43.9	27.0	130 36.6	14.5	0 57.8	15.1	56.9
02	208 43.8	26.8	145 10.1	14.6	0 42.7	15.0	56.9
03	223 43.7	. . 26.5	159 43.7	14.6	0 27.7	15.1	56.8
04	238 43.6	26.2	174 17.3	14.7	N 0 12.6	15.0	56.8
05	253 43.5	25.9	188 51.0	14.7	S 0 02.4	15.0	56.8
06	268 43.4	N22 25.6	203 24.7	14.8	S 0 17.4	15.0	56.7
07	283 43.3	25.3	217 58.5	14.8	0 32.4	15.0	56.7
08	298 43.2	25.0	232 32.3	14.8	0 47.4	14.9	56.7
09	313 43.1	. . 24.7	247 06.1	14.8	1 02.3	15.0	56.6
10	328 43.0	24.4	261 39.9	14.9	1 17.3	14.9	56.6
11	343 42.9	24.1	276 13.8	14.9	1 32.2	14.8	56.6
12	358 42.8	N22 23.8	290 47.7	15.0	S 1 47.0	14.9	56.5
13	13 42.7	23.6	305 21.7	15.0	2 01.9	14.8	56.5
14	28 42.6	23.3	319 55.7	15.0	2 16.7	14.8	56.5
15	43 42.6	. . 23.0	334 29.7	15.0	2 31.5	14.7	56.4
16	58 42.5	22.7	349 03.7	15.0	2 46.2	14.8	56.4
17	73 42.4	22.4	3 37.7	15.1	3 01.0	14.7	56.4
18	88 42.3	N22 22.1	18 11.8	15.1	S 3 15.7	14.6	56.3
19	103 42.2	21.8	32 45.9	15.1	3 30.3	14.7	56.3
20	118 42.1	21.5	47 20.0	15.1	3 45.0	14.6	56.2
21	133 42.0	. . 21.2	61 54.1	15.2	3 59.6	14.6	56.2
22	148 41.9	20.9	76 28.3	15.1	4 14.2	14.5	56.2
23	163 41.8	20.6	91 02.4	15.2	4 28.7	14.5	56.1
9 00 WEDNESDAY	178 41.7	N22 20.3	105 36.6	15.2	S 4 43.2	14.5	56.1
01	193 41.6	20.0	120 10.8	15.2	4 57.7	14.4	56.1
02	208 41.5	19.7	134 45.0	15.2	5 12.1	14.4	56.1
03	223 41.4	. . 19.4	149 19.2	15.3	5 26.5	14.3	56.0
04	238 41.4	19.0	163 53.5	15.2	5 40.8	14.3	56.0
05	253 41.3	18.7	178 27.7	15.3	5 55.1	14.3	56.0
06	268 41.2	N22 18.4	193 02.0	15.2	S 6 09.4	14.2	55.9
07	283 41.1	18.1	207 36.2	15.3	6 23.6	14.2	55.9
08	298 41.0	17.8	222 10.5	15.2	6 37.8	14.2	55.9
09	313 40.9	. . 17.5	236 44.7	15.3	6 52.0	14.1	55.8
10	328 40.8	17.2	251 19.0	15.3	7 06.1	14.0	55.8
11	343 40.7	16.9	265 53.3	15.3	7 20.1	14.0	55.8
12	358 40.6	N22 16.6	280 27.6	15.2	S 7 34.1	14.0	55.7
13	13 40.5	16.3	295 01.8	15.3	7 48.1	13.9	55.7
14	28 40.4	16.0	309 36.1	15.3	8 02.0	13.9	55.7
15	43 40.4	. . 15.6	324 10.4	15.3	8 15.9	13.8	55.7
16	58 40.3	15.3	338 44.7	15.2	8 29.7	13.8	55.6
17	73 40.2	15.0	353 18.9	15.3	8 43.5	13.7	55.6
18	88 40.1	N22 14.7	7 53.2	15.2	S 8 57.2	13.7	55.6
19	103 40.0	14.4	22 27.4	15.3	9 10.9	13.6	55.5
20	118 39.9	14.1	37 01.7	15.2	9 24.5	13.6	55.5
21	133 39.8	. . 13.8	51 35.9	15.2	9 38.1	13.5	55.5
22	148 39.7	13.4	66 10.1	15.3	9 51.6	13.5	55.5
23	163 39.6	13.1	80 44.4	15.2	10 05.1	13.4	55.4
10 00 THURSDAY	178 39.6	N22 12.8	95 18.6	15.2	S10 18.5	13.4	55.4
01	193 39.5	12.5	109 52.8	15.2	10 31.9	13.3	55.4
02	208 39.4	12.2	124 27.0	15.1	10 45.2	13.2	55.3
03	223 39.3	. . 11.8	139 01.1	15.2	10 58.4	13.2	55.3
04	238 39.2	11.5	153 35.3	15.1	11 11.6	13.2	55.3
05	253 39.1	11.2	168 09.4	15.1	11 24.8	13.1	55.3
06	268 39.0	N22 10.9	182 43.5	15.1	S11 37.9	13.0	55.2
07	283 39.0	10.6	197 17.6	15.1	11 50.9	13.0	55.2
08	298 38.9	10.2	211 51.7	15.1	12 03.9	12.9	55.2
09	313 38.8	. . 09.9	226 25.8	15.0	12 16.8	12.8	55.2
10	328 38.7	09.6	240 59.8	15.0	12 29.6	12.8	55.1
11	343 38.6	09.3	255 33.8	15.0	12 42.4	12.7	55.1
12	358 38.5	N22 08.9	270 07.8	15.0	S12 55.1	12.7	55.1
13	13 38.4	08.6	284 41.8	14.9	13 07.8	12.6	55.1
14	28 38.4	08.3	299 15.7	14.9	13 20.4	12.5	55.0
15	43 38.3	. . 08.0	313 49.6	14.9	13 32.9	12.5	55.0
16	58 38.2	07.6	328 23.5	14.9	13 45.4	12.4	55.0
17	73 38.1	07.3	342 57.4	14.8	13 57.8	12.4	55.0
18	88 38.0	N22 07.0	357 31.2	14.8	S14 10.2	12.2	55.0
19	103 37.9	06.6	12 05.0	14.8	14 22.4	12.3	54.9
20	118 37.8	06.3	26 38.8	14.8	14 34.7	12.1	54.9
21	133 37.8	. . 06.0	41 12.6	14.7	14 46.8	12.1	54.9
22	148 37.7	05.6	55 46.3	14.6	14 58.9	12.0	54.9
23	163 37.6	05.3	70 19.9	14.7	S15 10.9	11.9	54.9
	SD 15.8	*d* 0.3	SD	15.4		15.2	15.0

Lat.	Twilight Naut.	Twilight Civil	Sunrise	Moonrise 8	Moonrise 9	Moonrise 10	Moonrise 11
°	h m	h m	h m	h m	h m	h m	h m
N 72	▭	▭	▭	10 55	13 01	15 20	■
N 70	▭	▭	▭	10 53	12 49	14 51	17 27
68	▭	▭	▭	10 51	12 39	14 30	16 35
66	////	////	01 09	10 49	12 31	14 14	16 04
64	////	////	02 00	10 48	12 24	14 00	15 41
62	////	////	02 30	10 47	12 18	13 49	15 23
60	////	01 27	02 53	10 46	12 13	13 40	15 07
N 58	////	02 03	03 12	10 45	12 09	13 31	14 55
56	////	02 29	03 27	10 44	12 05	13 24	14 44
54	01 20	02 48	03 40	10 43	12 01	13 18	14 34
52	01 53	03 05	03 52	10 43	11 58	13 12	14 26
50	02 17	03 18	04 02	10 42	11 55	13 07	14 18
45	02 58	03 46	04 23	10 41	11 49	12 56	14 02
N 40	03 27	04 07	04 40	10 40	11 44	12 46	13 49
35	03 49	04 25	04 54	10 39	11 39	12 38	13 38
30	04 06	04 39	05 06	10 38	11 35	12 32	13 28
20	04 34	05 03	05 27	10 37	11 29	12 20	13 11
N 10	04 55	05 22	05 45	10 36	11 23	12 09	12 57
0	05 13	05 39	06 02	10 35	11 17	12 00	12 43
S 10	05 29	05 56	06 18	10 34	11 12	11 50	12 30
20	05 45	06 12	06 36	10 33	11 06	11 40	12 16
30	06 00	06 30	06 56	10 32	11 00	11 29	12 00
35	06 08	06 40	07 07	10 31	10 56	11 22	11 50
40	06 17	06 51	07 21	10 30	10 52	11 15	11 40
45	06 26	07 03	07 37	10 29	10 47	11 06	11 27
S 50	06 37	07 18	07 56	10 28	10 42	10 56	11 13
52	06 42	07 25	08 05	10 28	10 39	10 51	11 06
54	06 47	07 33	08 15	10 27	10 36	10 46	10 58
56	06 53	07 41	08 27	10 27	10 33	10 40	10 49
58	06 59	07 50	08 40	10 26	10 30	10 34	10 40
S 60	07 06	08 01	08 56	10 25	10 26	10 27	10 29

Lat.	Sunset	Twilight Civil	Twilight Naut.	Moonset 8	Moonset 9	Moonset 10	Moonset 11
°	h m	h m	h m	h m	h m	h m	h m
N 72	▭	▭	▭	22 00	21 25	20 37	■
N 70	▭	▭	▭	22 06	21 40	21 07	20 04
68	▭	▭	▭	22 10	21 52	21 30	20 56
66	22 57	////	////	22 15	22 02	21 48	21 29
64	22 09	////	////	22 18	22 11	22 03	21 53
62	21 39	////	////	22 21	22 18	22 15	22 12
60	21 16	22 41	////	22 24	22 24	22 26	22 28
N 58	20 58	22 06	////	22 26	22 30	22 35	22 42
56	20 43	21 41	////	22 28	22 35	22 43	22 53
54	20 30	21 21	22 49	22 30	22 39	22 50	23 03
52	20 18	21 05	22 16	22 32	22 44	22 57	23 12
50	20 08	20 51	21 52	22 33	22 47	23 03	23 21
45	19 47	20 24	21 12	22 37	22 55	23 15	23 38
N 40	19 31	20 03	20 43	22 40	23 02	23 26	23 52
35	19 16	19 46	20 22	22 42	23 08	23 35	24 05
30	19 04	19 31	20 04	22 45	23 13	23 43	24 15
20	18 43	19 08	19 37	22 49	23 22	23 57	24 34
N 10	18 26	18 48	19 15	22 52	23 30	24 09	00 09
0	18 09	18 31	18 57	22 55	23 38	24 21	00 21
S 10	17 52	18 15	18 41	22 58	23 45	24 32	00 32
20	17 35	17 59	18 26	23 02	23 53	24 45	00 45
30	17 15	17 41	18 11	23 06	24 02	00 02	00 59
35	17 03	17 31	18 03	23 08	24 08	00 08	01 07
40	16 50	17 20	17 54	23 11	24 14	00 14	01 16
45	16 34	17 08	17 44	23 14	24 21	00 21	01 28
S 50	16 15	16 53	17 34	23 17	24 30	00 30	01 41
52	16 06	16 46	17 29	23 19	24 34	00 34	01 47
54	15 56	16 38	17 24	23 21	24 38	00 38	01 54
56	15 44	16 30	17 18	23 23	24 43	00 43	02 02
58	15 30	16 20	17 12	23 25	24 48	00 48	02 11
S 60	15 15	16 10	17 05	23 28	24 54	00 54	02 21

Day	SUN Eqn. of Time 00^h	SUN Eqn. of Time 12^h	SUN Mer. Pass.	MOON Mer. Pass. Upper	MOON Mer. Pass. Lower	Age	Phase
d	m s	m s	h m	h m	h m	d	%
8	05 04	05 08	12 05	16 45	04 24	05	33
9	05 13	05 17	12 05	17 28	05 06	06	43
10	05 22	05 26	12 05	18 10	05 49	07	53

UT d	h	ARIES GHA	VENUS −3.9 GHA	Dec	MARS +1.7 GHA	Dec	JUPITER −2.7 GHA	Dec	SATURN +0.8 GHA	Dec
		° ′	° ′	° ′	° ′	° ′	° ′	° ′	° ′	° ′
11	00	289 16.6	169 07.8	N21 43.5	131 30.2	N10 25.6	0 32.8	S22 31.4	131 22.7	N11 04.1
	01	304 19.1	184 07.0	43.0	146 31.3	25.0	15 35.6	31.4	146 24.9	04.0
	02	319 21.5	199 06.3	42.4	161 32.3	24.4	30 38.4	31.5	161 27.1	03.9
	03	334 24.0	214 05.5	. . 41.9	176 33.4	. . 23.8	45 41.2	. . 31.5	176 29.3	. . 03.8
	04	349 26.5	229 04.7	41.3	191 34.4	23.2	60 44.0	31.6	191 31.6	03.7
	05	4 28.9	244 03.9	40.7	206 35.5	22.7	75 46.8	31.6	206 33.8	03.6
	06	19 31.4	259 03.1	N21 40.2	221 36.5	N10 22.1	90 49.6	S22 31.7	221 36.0	N11 03.6
	07	34 33.8	274 02.3	39.6	236 37.6	21.5	105 52.4	31.7	236 38.3	03.5
	08	49 36.3	289 01.5	39.1	251 38.6	20.9	120 55.2	31.8	251 40.5	03.4
F	09	64 38.8	304 00.7	. . 38.5	266 39.7	. . 20.3	135 58.0	. . 31.8	266 42.7	. . 03.3
R	10	79 41.2	319 00.0	37.9	281 40.7	19.8	151 00.8	31.9	281 44.9	03.2
I	11	94 43.7	333 59.2	37.4	296 41.8	19.2	166 03.6	31.9	296 47.2	03.1
D	12	109 46.2	348 58.4	N21 36.8	311 42.8	N10 18.6	181 06.5	S22 32.0	311 49.4	N11 03.0
A	13	124 48.6	3 57.6	36.2	326 43.8	18.0	196 09.3	32.0	326 51.6	02.9
Y	14	139 51.1	18 56.8	35.7	341 44.9	17.4	211 12.1	32.1	341 53.9	02.8
	15	154 53.6	33 56.0	. . 35.1	356 45.9	. . 16.8	226 14.9	. . 32.1	356 56.1	. . 02.7
	16	169 56.0	48 55.2	34.5	11 47.0	16.3	241 17.7	32.1	11 58.3	02.6
	17	184 58.5	63 54.5	34.0	26 48.0	15.7	256 20.5	32.2	27 00.5	02.5
	18	200 01.0	78 53.7	N21 33.4	41 49.1	N10 15.1	271 23.3	S22 32.2	42 02.8	N11 02.4
	19	215 03.4	93 52.9	32.8	56 50.1	14.5	286 26.1	32.3	57 05.0	02.3
	20	230 05.9	108 52.1	32.3	71 51.2	13.9	301 28.9	32.3	72 07.2	02.2
	21	245 08.3	123 51.3	. . 31.7	86 52.2	. . 13.4	316 31.7	. . 32.4	87 09.4	. . 02.1
	22	260 10.8	138 50.6	31.1	101 53.3	12.8	331 34.5	32.4	102 11.7	02.0
	23	275 13.3	153 49.8	30.5	116 54.3	12.2	346 37.3	32.5	117 13.9	01.9
12	00	290 15.7	168 49.0	N21 30.0	131 55.4	N10 11.6	1 40.1	S22 32.5	132 16.1	N11 01.8
	01	305 18.2	183 48.2	29.4	146 56.4	11.0	16 43.0	32.6	147 18.4	01.7
	02	320 20.7	198 47.4	28.8	161 57.5	10.4	31 45.8	32.6	162 20.6	01.7
	03	335 23.1	213 46.7	. . 28.2	176 58.5	. . 09.9	46 48.6	. . 32.7	177 22.8	. . 01.6
	04	350 25.6	228 45.9	27.6	191 59.6	09.3	61 51.4	32.7	192 25.0	01.5
	05	5 28.1	243 45.1	27.1	207 00.6	08.7	76 54.2	32.8	207 27.3	01.4
	06	20 30.5	258 44.3	N21 26.5	222 01.7	N10 08.1	91 57.0	S22 32.8	222 29.5	N11 01.3
S	07	35 33.0	273 43.5	25.9	237 02.7	07.5	106 59.8	32.8	237 31.7	01.2
A	08	50 35.4	288 42.8	25.3	252 03.8	06.9	122 02.6	32.9	252 33.9	01.1
T	09	65 37.9	303 42.0	. . 24.7	267 04.8	. . 06.4	137 05.4	. . 32.9	267 36.2	. . 01.0
U	10	80 40.4	318 41.2	24.1	282 05.9	05.8	152 08.2	33.0	282 38.4	00.9
R	11	95 42.8	333 40.4	23.5	297 06.9	05.2	167 11.0	33.0	297 40.6	00.8
D	12	110 45.3	348 39.7	N21 22.9	312 08.0	N10 04.6	182 13.8	S22 33.1	312 42.8	N11 00.7
A	13	125 47.8	3 38.9	22.4	327 09.0	04.0	197 16.6	33.1	327 45.1	00.6
Y	14	140 50.2	18 38.1	21.8	342 10.1	03.4	212 19.5	33.2	342 47.3	00.5
	15	155 52.7	33 37.3	. . 21.2	357 11.1	. . 02.8	227 22.3	. . 33.2	357 49.5	. . 00.4
	16	170 55.2	48 36.6	20.6	12 12.2	02.3	242 25.1	33.3	12 51.7	00.3
	17	185 57.6	63 35.8	20.0	27 13.2	01.7	257 27.9	33.3	27 54.0	00.2
	18	201 00.1	78 35.0	N21 19.4	42 14.3	N10 01.1	272 30.7	S22 33.4	42 56.2	N11 00.1
	19	216 02.6	93 34.3	18.8	57 15.3	10 00.5	287 33.5	33.4	57 58.4	11 00.0
	20	231 05.0	108 33.5	18.2	72 16.4	9 59.9	302 36.3	33.4	73 00.6	10 59.9
	21	246 07.5	123 32.7	. . 17.6	87 17.4	. . 59.3	317 39.1	. . 33.5	88 02.9	. . 59.8
	22	261 09.9	138 31.9	17.0	102 18.5	58.8	332 41.9	33.5	103 05.1	59.7
	23	276 12.4	153 31.2	16.4	117 19.5	58.2	347 44.7	33.6	118 07.3	59.6
13	00	291 14.9	168 30.4	N21 15.8	132 20.6	N 9 57.6	2 47.5	S22 33.6	133 09.5	N10 59.6
	01	306 17.3	183 29.6	15.2	147 21.6	57.0	17 50.3	33.7	148 11.8	59.5
	02	321 19.8	198 28.9	14.6	162 22.7	56.4	32 53.1	33.7	163 14.0	59.4
	03	336 22.3	213 28.1	. . 14.0	177 23.7	. . 55.8	47 56.0	. . 33.8	178 16.2	. . 59.3
	04	351 24.7	228 27.3	13.4	192 24.8	55.2	62 58.8	33.8	193 18.4	59.2
	05	6 27.2	243 26.6	12.7	207 25.8	54.7	78 01.6	33.9	208 20.7	59.1
	06	21 29.7	258 25.8	N21 12.1	222 26.9	N 9 54.1	93 04.4	S22 33.9	223 22.9	N10 59.0
	07	36 32.1	273 25.0	11.5	237 27.9	53.5	108 07.2	34.0	238 25.1	58.9
	08	51 34.6	288 24.3	10.9	252 29.0	52.9	123 10.0	34.0	253 27.3	58.8
S	09	66 37.1	303 23.5	. . 10.3	267 30.0	. . 52.3	138 12.8	. . 34.0	268 29.6	. . 58.7
U	10	81 39.5	318 22.7	09.7	282 31.1	51.7	153 15.6	34.1	283 31.8	58.6
N	11	96 42.0	333 22.0	09.1	297 32.1	51.1	168 18.4	34.1	298 34.0	58.5
D	12	111 44.4	348 21.2	N21 08.5	312 33.2	N 9 50.5	183 21.2	S22 34.2	313 36.2	N10 58.4
A	13	126 46.9	3 20.4	07.8	327 34.2	50.0	198 24.0	34.2	328 38.5	58.3
Y	14	141 49.4	18 19.7	07.2	342 35.3	49.4	213 26.8	34.3	343 40.7	58.2
	15	156 51.8	33 18.9	. . 06.6	357 36.3	. . 48.8	228 29.6	. . 34.3	358 42.9	. . 58.1
	16	171 54.3	48 18.2	06.0	12 37.4	48.2	243 32.4	34.4	13 45.1	58.0
	17	186 56.8	63 17.4	05.4	27 38.4	47.6	258 35.2	34.4	28 47.4	57.9
	18	201 59.2	78 16.6	N21 04.7	42 39.4	N 9 47.0	273 38.1	S22 34.5	43 49.6	N10 57.8
	19	217 01.7	93 15.9	04.1	57 40.5	46.4	288 40.9	34.5	58 51.8	57.7
	20	232 04.2	108 15.1	03.5	72 41.5	45.8	303 43.7	34.5	73 54.0	57.6
	21	247 06.6	123 14.4	. . 02.9	87 42.6	. . 45.3	318 46.5	. . 34.6	88 56.2	. . 57.5
	22	262 09.1	138 13.6	02.2	102 43.6	44.7	333 49.3	34.6	103 58.5	57.4
	23	277 11.6	153 12.8	01.6	117 44.7	44.1	348 52.1	34.7	119 00.7	57.3
Mer. Pass.		h m 4 38.2	*v* −0.8	*d* 0.6	*v* 1.0	*d* 0.6	*v* 2.8	*d* 0.0	*v* 2.2	*d* 0.1

STARS

Name	SHA	Dec
	° ′	° ′
Acamar	315 21.2	S40 15.9
Achernar	335 29.3	S57 11.2
Acrux	173 14.0	S63 09.1
Adhara	255 15.8	S28 58.9
Aldebaran	290 53.9	N16 31.7
Alioth	166 23.7	N55 55.0
Alkaid	153 01.5	N49 16.4
Al Na'ir	27 47.8	S46 54.9
Alnilam	275 50.4	S 1 11.7
Alphard	218 00.0	S 8 41.7
Alphecca	126 13.9	N26 41.2
Alpheratz	357 47.3	N29 08.2
Altair	62 11.5	N 8 53.5
Ankaa	353 19.1	S42 15.2
Antares	112 30.6	S26 27.2
Arcturus	145 59.0	N19 08.3
Atria	107 35.4	S69 02.8
Avior	234 20.3	S59 32.2
Bellatrix	278 36.3	N 6 21.6
Betelgeuse	271 05.6	N 7 24.6
Canopus	263 58.4	S52 41.8
Capella	280 40.4	N46 00.4
Deneb	49 33.7	N45 18.6
Denebola	182 37.5	N14 31.5
Diphda	348 59.5	S17 56.2
Dubhe	193 56.3	N61 42.5
Elnath	278 17.7	N28 36.9
Eltanin	90 47.3	N51 29.3
Enif	33 50.5	N 9 54.9
Fomalhaut	15 27.7	S29 34.4
Gacrux	172 05.4	S57 10.0
Gienah	175 56.3	S17 35.5
Hadar	148 53.3	S60 25.2
Hamal	328 05.1	N23 30.2
Kaus Aust.	83 48.3	S34 22.9
Kochab	137 18.9	N74 07.4
Markab	13 41.9	N15 15.1
Menkar	314 19.1	N 4 07.5
Menkent	148 12.0	S36 25.0
Miaplacidus	221 41.7	S69 45.3
Mirfak	308 46.1	N49 53.4
Nunki	76 02.5	S26 17.2
Peacock	53 24.3	S56 42.4
Pollux	243 32.6	N28 00.4
Procyon	245 03.9	N 5 12.3
Rasalhague	96 09.6	N12 33.2
Regulus	207 47.7	N11 55.6
Rigel	281 15.9	S 8 11.3
Rigil Kent.	139 56.8	S60 52.5
Sabik	102 16.5	S15 44.2
Schedar	349 44.9	N56 34.9
Shaula	96 26.6	S37 06.7
Sirius	258 37.3	S16 43.5
Spica	158 35.2	S11 12.5
Suhail	222 55.7	S43 28.1
Vega	80 41.1	N38 47.5
Zuben'ubi	137 09.4	S16 04.8

	SHA	Mer. Pass.
	° ′	h m
Venus	238 33.3	12 45
Mars	201 39.7	15 11
Jupiter	71 24.4	23 49
Saturn	202 00.4	15 09

UT d	h	SUN GHA	SUN Dec	MOON GHA	v	MOON Dec	d	HP
		° ′	° ′	° ′	′	° ′	′	′
11	00	178 37.5	N22 05.0	84 53.6	14.6	S15 22.8	11.9	54.8
	01	193 37.4	04.6	99 27.2	14.6	15 34.7	11.8	54.8
	02	208 37.4	04.3	114 00.8	14.5	15 46.5	11.7	54.8
	03	223 37.3	. . 04.0	128 34.3	14.5	15 58.2	11.6	54.8
	04	238 37.2	03.6	143 07.8	14.5	16 09.8	11.6	54.8
	05	253 37.1	03.3	157 41.3	14.4	16 21.4	11.5	54.7
	06	268 37.0	N22 03.0	172 14.7	14.4	S16 32.9	11.4	54.7
	07	283 36.9	02.6	186 48.1	14.4	16 44.3	11.4	54.7
	08	298 36.9	02.3	201 21.5	14.3	16 55.7	11.3	54.7
F	09	313 36.8	. . 01.9	215 54.8	14.2	17 07.0	11.2	54.7
R	10	328 36.7	01.6	230 28.0	14.3	17 18.2	11.1	54.6
I	11	343 36.6	01.3	245 01.3	14.2	17 29.3	11.0	54.6
D	12	358 36.5	N22 00.9	259 34.5	14.1	S17 40.3	11.0	54.6
A	13	13 36.5	00.6	274 07.6	14.1	17 51.3	10.9	54.6
Y	14	28 36.4	22 00.2	288 40.7	14.1	18 02.2	10.8	54.6
	15	43 36.3	21 59.9	303 13.8	14.0	18 13.0	10.7	54.6
	16	58 36.2	59.5	317 46.8	13.9	18 23.7	10.7	54.5
	17	73 36.1	59.2	332 19.7	14.0	18 34.4	10.5	54.5
	18	88 36.1	N21 58.8	346 52.7	13.8	S18 44.9	10.5	54.5
	19	103 36.0	58.5	1 25.5	13.9	18 55.4	10.4	54.5
	20	118 35.9	58.1	15 58.4	13.7	19 05.8	10.3	54.5
	21	133 35.8	. . 57.8	30 31.1	13.8	19 16.1	10.2	54.5
	22	148 35.7	57.5	45 03.9	13.7	19 26.3	10.2	54.5
	23	163 35.7	57.1	59 36.6	13.6	19 36.5	10.0	54.4
12	00	178 35.6	N21 56.8	74 09.2	13.6	S19 46.5	10.0	54.4
	01	193 35.5	56.4	88 41.8	13.5	19 56.5	9.9	54.4
	02	208 35.4	56.1	103 14.3	13.5	20 06.4	9.8	54.4
	03	223 35.4	. . 55.7	117 46.8	13.4	20 16.2	9.7	54.4
	04	238 35.3	55.3	132 19.2	13.4	20 25.9	9.6	54.4
	05	253 35.2	55.0	146 51.6	13.4	20 35.5	9.5	54.4
	06	268 35.1	N21 54.6	161 24.0	13.2	S20 45.0	9.4	54.3
	07	283 35.0	54.3	175 56.2	13.3	20 54.4	9.4	54.3
S	08	298 35.0	53.9	190 28.5	13.1	21 03.8	9.2	54.3
A	09	313 34.9	. . 53.6	205 00.6	13.2	21 13.0	9.2	54.3
T	10	328 34.8	53.2	219 32.8	13.0	21 22.2	9.0	54.3
U	11	343 34.7	52.9	234 04.8	13.1	21 31.2	9.0	54.3
R	12	358 34.7	N21 52.5	248 36.9	12.9	S21 40.2	8.9	54.3
D	13	13 34.6	52.1	263 08.8	12.9	21 49.1	8.7	54.3
A	14	28 34.5	51.8	277 40.7	12.9	21 57.8	8.7	54.3
Y	15	43 34.4	. . 51.4	292 12.6	12.8	22 06.5	8.6	54.3
	16	58 34.4	51.1	306 44.4	12.8	22 15.1	8.5	54.2
	17	73 34.3	50.7	321 16.2	12.6	22 23.6	8.3	54.2
	18	88 34.2	N21 50.3	335 47.8	12.7	S22 31.9	8.3	54.2
	19	103 34.1	50.0	350 19.5	12.6	22 40.2	8.2	54.2
	20	118 34.1	49.6	4 51.1	12.5	22 48.4	8.1	54.2
	21	133 34.0	. . 49.3	19 22.6	12.5	22 56.5	7.9	54.2
	22	148 33.9	48.9	33 54.1	12.4	23 04.4	7.9	54.2
	23	163 33.9	48.5	48 25.5	12.4	23 12.3	7.8	54.2
13	00	178 33.8	N21 48.2	62 56.9	12.3	S23 20.1	7.6	54.2
	01	193 33.7	47.8	77 28.2	12.3	23 27.7	7.6	54.2
	02	208 33.6	47.4	91 59.5	12.2	23 35.3	7.5	54.2
	03	223 33.6	. . 47.1	106 30.7	12.1	23 42.8	7.3	54.2
	04	238 33.5	46.7	121 01.8	12.1	23 50.1	7.3	54.2
	05	253 33.4	46.3	135 32.9	12.1	23 57.4	7.1	54.1
	06	268 33.3	N21 46.0	150 04.0	11.9	S24 04.5	7.0	54.1
	07	283 33.3	45.6	164 34.9	12.0	24 11.5	6.9	54.1
	08	298 33.2	45.2	179 05.9	11.9	24 18.4	6.8	54.1
S	09	313 33.1	. . 44.8	193 36.8	11.8	24 25.2	6.7	54.1
U	10	328 33.1	44.5	208 07.6	11.8	24 31.9	6.6	54.1
N	11	343 33.0	44.1	222 38.4	11.7	24 38.5	6.5	54.1
D	12	358 32.9	N21 43.7	237 09.1	11.7	S24 45.0	6.4	54.1
A	13	13 32.9	43.4	251 39.8	11.6	24 51.4	6.2	54.1
Y	14	28 32.8	43.0	266 10.4	11.5	24 57.6	6.2	54.1
	15	43 32.7	. . 42.6	280 40.9	11.6	25 03.8	6.0	54.1
	16	58 32.6	42.2	295 11.5	11.4	25 09.8	5.9	54.1
	17	73 32.6	41.9	309 41.9	11.4	25 15.7	5.8	54.1
	18	88 32.5	N21 41.5	324 12.3	11.4	S25 21.5	5.7	54.1
	19	103 32.4	41.1	338 42.7	11.3	25 27.2	5.5	54.1
	20	118 32.4	40.7	353 13.0	11.3	25 32.7	5.5	54.1
	21	133 32.3	. . 40.3	7 43.3	11.2	25 38.2	5.3	54.1
	22	148 32.2	40.0	22 13.5	11.1	25 43.5	5.2	54.1
	23	163 32.2	39.6	36 43.6	11.1	S25 48.7	5.1	54.1
		SD 15.8	*d* 0.4	SD	14.9	14.8		14.7

Lat.	Twilight Naut.	Twilight Civil	Sunrise	Moonrise 11	Moonrise 12	Moonrise 13	Moonrise 14
°	h m	h m	h m	h m	h m	h m	h m
N 72	□	□	□	■	■	■	■
N 70	□	□	□	17 27	■	■	■
68	□	□	□	16 35	■	■	■
66	////	////	01 23	16 04	18 16	■	■
64	////	////	02 08	15 41	17 29	19 44	■
62	////	00 21	02 37	15 23	16 59	18 40	20 19
60	////	01 36	02 59	15 07	16 37	18 06	19 27
N 58	////	02 10	03 16	14 55	16 19	17 41	18 55
56	00 20	02 34	03 31	14 44	16 03	17 21	18 31
54	01 28	02 53	03 44	14 34	15 50	17 04	18 12
52	01 59	03 08	03 55	14 26	15 39	16 50	17 56
50	02 22	03 22	04 05	14 18	15 29	16 38	17 42
45	03 02	03 49	04 25	14 02	15 08	16 12	17 13
N 40	03 29	04 10	04 42	13 49	14 51	15 52	16 51
35	03 51	04 26	04 56	13 38	14 37	15 36	16 33
30	04 08	04 41	05 08	13 28	14 25	15 21	16 17
20	04 35	05 04	05 28	13 11	14 04	14 57	15 50
N 10	04 56	05 23	05 46	12 57	13 46	14 36	15 27
0	05 14	05 40	06 02	12 43	13 29	14 16	15 06
S 10	05 30	05 56	06 18	12 30	13 12	13 57	14 45
20	05 45	06 12	06 35	12 16	12 54	13 36	14 22
30	06 00	06 29	06 55	12 00	12 34	13 12	13 56
35	06 08	06 39	07 07	11 50	12 22	12 58	13 40
40	06 16	06 50	07 20	11 40	12 08	12 42	13 22
45	06 25	07 02	07 35	11 27	11 52	12 23	13 00
S 50	06 36	07 16	07 54	11 13	11 33	11 59	12 33
52	06 40	07 23	08 03	11 06	11 23	11 47	12 20
54	06 45	07 30	08 13	10 58	11 13	11 34	12 05
56	06 51	07 39	08 24	10 49	11 01	11 19	11 47
58	06 57	07 48	08 37	10 40	10 48	11 02	11 25
S 60	07 03	07 58	08 52	10 29	10 32	10 40	10 56

Lat.	Sunset	Twilight Civil	Twilight Naut.	Moonset 11	Moonset 12	Moonset 13	Moonset 14
°	h m	h m	h m	h m	h m	h m	h m
N 72	□	□	□	■	■	■	■
N 70	□	□	□	20 04	■	■	■
68	□	□	□	20 56	■	■	■
66	22 44	////	////	21 29	20 52	■	■
64	22 01	////	////	21 53	21 39	21 05	■
62	21 33	23 37	////	22 12	22 10	22 09	22 14
60	21 12	22 32	////	22 28	22 33	22 44	23 07
N 58	20 54	22 00	////	22 42	22 52	23 09	23 39
56	20 39	21 36	23 40	22 53	23 08	23 29	24 03
54	20 27	21 18	22 41	23 03	23 21	23 46	24 22
52	20 16	21 02	22 10	23 12	23 33	24 01	00 01
50	20 06	20 49	21 48	23 21	23 43	24 13	00 13
45	19 46	20 22	21 09	23 38	24 05	00 05	00 39
N 40	19 29	20 01	20 41	23 52	24 23	00 23	01 00
35	19 15	19 45	20 20	24 05	00 05	00 38	01 17
30	19 03	19 30	20 03	24 15	00 15	00 51	01 32
20	18 43	19 07	19 36	24 34	00 34	01 14	01 58
N 10	18 26	18 48	19 15	00 09	00 50	01 33	02 20
0	18 09	18 32	18 57	00 21	01 05	01 51	02 40
S 10	17 53	18 16	18 42	00 32	01 20	02 10	03 01
20	17 36	18 00	18 27	00 45	01 36	02 29	03 23
30	17 16	17 42	18 12	00 59	01 55	02 52	03 48
35	17 05	17 33	18 04	01 07	02 06	03 05	04 03
40	16 52	17 22	17 56	01 16	02 19	03 21	04 21
45	16 37	17 10	17 46	01 28	02 34	03 39	04 42
S 50	16 18	16 55	17 36	01 41	02 52	04 02	05 09
52	16 09	16 49	17 31	01 47	03 01	04 13	05 22
54	15 59	16 41	17 26	01 54	03 11	04 26	05 37
56	15 48	16 33	17 21	02 02	03 22	04 41	05 55
58	15 35	16 24	17 15	02 11	03 35	04 58	06 17
S 60	15 19	16 14	17 09	02 21	03 50	05 19	06 44

Day	SUN Eqn. of Time 00^h	SUN Eqn. of Time 12^h	SUN Mer. Pass.	MOON Mer. Pass. Upper	MOON Mer. Pass. Lower	MOON Age	MOON Phase
d	m s	m s	h m	h m	h m	d	%
11	05 30	05 34	12 06	18 54	06 32	08	63
12	05 37	05 41	12 06	19 40	07 17	09	72
13	05 45	05 48	12 06	20 28	08 04	10	80

UT	ARIES	VENUS −3.9		MARS +1.7		JUPITER −2.7		SATURN +0.8	
d h	GHA ° ′	GHA ° ′	Dec ° ′	GHA ° ′	Dec ° ′	GHA ° ′	Dec ° ′	GHA ° ′	Dec ° ′
14 00	292 14.0	168 12.1	N21 01.0	132 45.7	N 9 43.5	3 54.9	S22 34.7	134 02.9	N10 57.2
01	307 16.5	183 11.3	21 00.4	147 46.8	42.9	18 57.7	34.8	149 05.1	57.1
02	322 18.9	198 10.6	20 59.7	162 47.8	42.3	34 00.5	34.8	164 07.4	57.0
03	337 21.4	213 09.8	. . 59.1	177 48.9	. . 41.7	49 03.3	. . 34.9	179 09.6	. . 56.9
04	352 23.9	228 09.1	58.5	192 49.9	41.1	64 06.1	34.9	194 11.8	56.9
05	7 26.3	243 08.3	57.8	207 51.0	40.6	79 08.9	35.0	209 14.0	56.8
06	22 28.8	258 07.5	N20 57.2	222 52.0	N 9 40.0	94 11.7	S22 35.0	224 16.2	N10 56.7
07	37 31.3	273 06.8	56.6	237 53.1	39.4	109 14.5	35.0	239 18.5	56.6
08	52 33.7	288 06.0	55.9	252 54.1	38.8	124 17.3	35.1	254 20.7	56.5
M 09	67 36.2	303 05.3	. . 55.3	267 55.2	. . 38.2	139 20.2	. . 35.1	269 22.9	. . 56.4
O 10	82 38.7	318 04.5	54.7	282 56.2	37.6	154 23.0	35.2	284 25.1	56.3
N 11	97 41.1	333 03.8	54.0	297 57.3	37.0	169 25.8	35.2	299 27.4	56.2
D 12	112 43.6	348 03.0	N20 53.4	312 58.3	N 9 36.4	184 28.6	S22 35.3	314 29.6	N10 56.1
A 13	127 46.0	3 02.3	52.7	327 59.4	35.8	199 31.4	35.3	329 31.8	56.0
Y 14	142 48.5	18 01.5	52.1	343 00.4	35.2	214 34.2	35.4	344 34.0	55.9
15	157 51.0	33 00.8	. . 51.4	358 01.5	. . 34.7	229 37.0	. . 35.4	359 36.2	. . 55.8
16	172 53.4	48 00.0	50.8	13 02.5	34.1	244 39.8	35.5	14 38.5	55.7
17	187 55.9	62 59.3	50.2	28 03.6	33.5	259 42.6	35.5	29 40.7	55.6
18	202 58.4	77 58.5	N20 49.5	43 04.6	N 9 32.9	274 45.4	S22 35.5	44 42.9	N10 55.5
19	218 00.8	92 57.8	48.9	58 05.7	32.3	289 48.2	35.6	59 45.1	55.4
20	233 03.3	107 57.0	48.2	73 06.7	31.7	304 51.0	35.6	74 47.3	55.3
21	248 05.8	122 56.3	. . 47.6	88 07.8	. . 31.1	319 53.8	. . 35.7	89 49.6	. . 55.2
22	263 08.2	137 55.5	46.9	103 08.8	30.5	334 56.6	35.7	104 51.8	55.1
23	278 10.7	152 54.8	46.3	118 09.9	29.9	349 59.4	35.8	119 54.0	55.0
15 00	293 13.2	167 54.0	N20 45.6	133 10.9	N 9 29.3	5 02.2	S22 35.8	134 56.2	N10 54.9
01	308 15.6	182 53.3	45.0	148 12.0	28.8	20 05.0	35.9	149 58.4	54.8
02	323 18.1	197 52.5	44.3	163 13.0	28.2	35 07.8	35.9	165 00.7	54.7
03	338 20.5	212 51.8	. . 43.6	178 14.1	. . 27.6	50 10.7	. . 36.0	180 02.9	. . 54.6
04	353 23.0	227 51.0	43.0	193 15.1	27.0	65 13.5	36.0	195 05.1	54.5
05	8 25.5	242 50.3	42.3	208 16.2	26.4	80 16.3	36.0	210 07.3	54.4
06	23 27.9	257 49.5	N20 41.7	223 17.2	N 9 25.8	95 19.1	S22 36.1	225 09.5	N10 54.3
07	38 30.4	272 48.8	41.0	238 18.3	25.2	110 21.9	36.1	240 11.8	54.2
T 08	53 32.9	287 48.1	40.3	253 19.3	24.6	125 24.7	36.2	255 14.0	54.1
U 09	68 35.3	302 47.3	. . 39.7	268 20.4	. . 24.0	140 27.5	. . 36.2	270 16.2	. . 54.0
E 10	83 37.8	317 46.6	39.0	283 21.4	23.4	155 30.3	36.3	285 18.4	53.9
S 11	98 40.3	332 45.8	38.4	298 22.5	22.8	170 33.1	36.3	300 20.6	53.8
D 12	113 42.7	347 45.1	N20 37.7	313 23.5	N 9 22.2	185 35.9	S22 36.4	315 22.9	N10 53.7
A 13	128 45.2	2 44.4	37.0	328 24.6	21.6	200 38.7	36.4	330 25.1	53.6
Y 14	143 47.7	17 43.6	36.4	343 25.6	21.1	215 41.5	36.4	345 27.3	53.5
15	158 50.1	32 42.9	. . 35.7	358 26.7	. . 20.5	230 44.3	. . 36.5	0 29.5	. . 53.4
16	173 52.6	47 42.1	35.0	13 27.7	19.9	245 47.1	36.5	15 31.7	53.3
17	188 55.0	62 41.4	34.3	28 28.8	19.3	260 49.9	36.6	30 34.0	53.2
18	203 57.5	77 40.7	N20 33.7	43 29.8	N 9 18.7	275 52.7	S22 36.6	45 36.2	N10 53.1
19	219 00.0	92 39.9	33.0	58 30.8	18.1	290 55.5	36.7	60 38.4	53.0
20	234 02.4	107 39.2	32.3	73 31.9	17.5	305 58.3	36.7	75 40.6	53.0
21	249 04.9	122 38.4	. . 31.7	88 32.9	. . 16.9	321 01.1	. . 36.8	90 42.8	. . 52.9
22	264 07.4	137 37.7	31.0	103 34.0	16.3	336 03.9	36.8	105 45.1	52.8
23	279 09.8	152 37.0	30.3	118 35.0	15.7	351 06.7	36.8	120 47.3	52.7
16 00	294 12.3	167 36.2	N20 29.6	133 36.1	N 9 15.1	6 09.5	S22 36.9	135 49.5	N10 52.6
01	309 14.8	182 35.5	28.9	148 37.1	14.5	21 12.3	36.9	150 51.7	52.5
02	324 17.2	197 34.8	28.3	163 38.2	13.9	36 15.2	37.0	165 53.9	52.4
03	339 19.7	212 34.0	. . 27.6	178 39.2	. . 13.3	51 18.0	. . 37.0	180 56.1	. . 52.3
04	354 22.2	227 33.3	26.9	193 40.3	12.7	66 20.8	37.1	195 58.4	52.2
05	9 24.6	242 32.6	26.2	208 41.3	12.2	81 23.6	37.1	211 00.6	52.1
06	24 27.1	257 31.8	N20 25.5	223 42.4	N 9 11.6	96 26.4	S22 37.2	226 02.8	N10 52.0
W 07	39 29.5	272 31.1	24.9	238 43.4	11.0	111 29.2	37.2	241 05.0	51.9
E 08	54 32.0	287 30.4	24.2	253 44.5	10.4	126 32.0	37.2	256 07.2	51.8
D 09	69 34.5	302 29.6	. . 23.5	268 45.5	. . 09.8	141 34.8	. . 37.3	271 09.5	. . 51.7
N 10	84 36.9	317 28.9	22.8	283 46.6	09.2	156 37.6	37.3	286 11.7	51.6
E 11	99 39.4	332 28.2	22.1	298 47.6	08.6	171 40.4	37.4	301 13.9	51.5
S 12	114 41.9	347 27.4	N20 21.4	313 48.7	N 9 08.0	186 43.2	S22 37.4	316 16.1	N10 51.4
D 13	129 44.3	2 26.7	20.7	328 49.7	07.4	201 46.0	37.5	331 18.3	51.3
A 14	144 46.8	17 26.0	20.0	343 50.8	06.8	216 48.8	37.5	346 20.5	51.2
Y 15	159 49.3	32 25.3	. . 19.3	358 51.8	. . 06.2	231 51.6	. . 37.6	1 22.8	. . 51.1
16	174 51.7	47 24.5	18.7	13 52.9	05.6	246 54.4	37.6	16 25.0	51.0
17	189 54.2	62 23.8	18.0	28 53.9	05.0	261 57.2	37.6	31 27.2	50.9
18	204 56.7	77 23.1	N20 17.3	43 55.0	N 9 04.4	277 00.0	S22 37.7	46 29.4	N10 50.8
19	219 59.1	92 22.3	16.6	58 56.0	03.8	292 02.8	37.7	61 31.6	50.7
20	235 01.6	107 21.6	15.9	73 57.1	03.2	307 05.6	37.8	76 33.8	50.6
21	250 04.0	122 20.9	. . 15.2	88 58.1	. . 02.6	322 08.4	. . 37.8	91 36.1	. . 50.5
22	265 06.5	137 20.2	14.5	103 59.2	02.0	337 11.2	37.9	106 38.3	50.4
23	280 09.0	152 19.4	13.8	119 00.2	01.4	352 14.0	37.9	121 40.5	50.3
Mer. Pass.	h m 4 26.4	v −0.7	d 0.7	v 1.0	d 0.6	v 2.8	d 0.0	v 2.2	d 0.1

STARS Name	SHA ° ′	Dec ° ′
Acamar	315 21.2	S40 15.9
Achernar	335 29.3	S57 11.2
Acrux	173 14.0	S63 09.1
Adhara	255 15.8	S28 58.9
Aldebaran	290 53.9	N16 31.7
Alioth	166 23.7	N55 55.0
Alkaid	153 01.6	N49 16.4
Al Na'ir	27 47.8	S46 54.9
Alnilam	275 50.4	S 1 11.7
Alphard	218 00.0	S 8 41.7
Alphecca	126 13.9	N26 41.2
Alpheratz	357 47.3	N29 08.2
Altair	62 11.5	N 8 53.5
Ankaa	353 19.0	S42 15.2
Antares	112 30.6	S26 27.2
Arcturus	145 59.0	N19 08.3
Atria	107 35.4	S69 02.8
Avior	234 20.3	S59 32.2
Bellatrix	278 36.3	N 6 21.6
Betelgeuse	271 05.6	N 7 24.6
Canopus	263 58.3	S52 41.8
Capella	280 40.3	N46 00.4
Deneb	49 33.7	N45 18.6
Denebola	182 37.5	N14 31.5
Diphda	348 59.5	S17 56.1
Dubhe	193 56.3	N61 42.5
Elnath	278 17.6	N28 36.9
Eltanin	90 47.4	N51 29.3
Enif	33 50.5	N 9 54.9
Fomalhaut	15 27.7	S29 34.4
Gacrux	172 05.5	S57 10.0
Gienah	175 56.3	S17 35.5
Hadar	148 53.3	S60 25.2
Hamal	328 05.1	N23 30.2
Kaus Aust.	83 48.3	S34 22.9
Kochab	137 19.0	N74 07.4
Markab	13 41.9	N15 15.1
Menkar	314 19.1	N 4 07.5
Menkent	148 12.0	S36 25.0
Miaplacidus	221 41.7	S69 45.3
Mirfak	308 46.0	N49 53.4
Nunki	76 02.5	S26 17.2
Peacock	53 24.3	S56 42.4
Pollux	243 32.6	N28 00.4
Procyon	245 03.9	N 5 12.3
Rasalhague	96 09.6	N12 33.2
Regulus	207 47.7	N11 55.6
Rigel	281 15.9	S 8 11.3
Rigil Kent.	139 56.8	S60 52.5
Sabik	102 16.5	S15 44.2
Schedar	349 44.9	N56 34.9
Shaula	96 26.6	S37 06.7
Sirius	258 37.3	S16 43.5
Spica	158 35.2	S11 12.5
Suhail	222 55.7	S43 28.1
Vega	80 41.1	N38 47.5
Zuben'ubi	137 09.4	S16 04.8

	SHA ° ′	Mer. Pass. h m
Venus	234 40.9	12 49
Mars	199 57.8	15 06
Jupiter	71 49.1	23 35
Saturn	201 43.1	14 58

UT d h	SUN GHA ° ′	SUN Dec ° ′	MOON GHA ° ′	v ′	MOON Dec ° ′	d ′	HP ′
14 00 (MONDAY)	178 32.1	N21 39.2	51 13.7	11.1	S25 53.8	5.0	54.1
01	193 32.0	38.8	65 43.8	11.0	25 58.8	4.8	54.1
02	208 32.0	38.4	80 13.8	11.0	26 03.6	4.7	54.1
03	223 31.9	. . 38.1	94 43.8	10.9	26 08.3	4.6	54.1
04	238 31.8	37.7	109 13.7	10.9	26 12.9	4.5	54.1
05	253 31.8	37.3	123 43.6	10.9	26 17.4	4.4	54.1
06	268 31.7	N21 36.9	138 13.5	10.7	S26 21.8	4.2	54.1
07	283 31.6	36.5	152 43.2	10.8	26 26.0	4.1	54.1
08	298 31.6	36.1	167 13.0	10.7	26 30.1	4.0	54.1
09	313 31.5	. . 35.7	181 42.7	10.7	26 34.1	3.9	54.1
10	328 31.4	35.4	196 12.4	10.6	26 38.0	3.7	54.1
11	343 31.4	35.0	210 42.0	10.6	26 41.7	3.7	54.1
12	358 31.3	N21 34.6	225 11.6	10.5	S26 45.4	3.4	54.1
13	13 31.2	34.2	239 41.1	10.5	26 48.8	3.4	54.1
14	28 31.2	33.8	254 10.6	10.5	26 52.2	3.2	54.1
15	43 31.1	. . 33.4	268 40.1	10.5	26 55.4	3.1	54.1
16	58 31.0	33.0	283 09.6	10.4	26 58.5	3.0	54.1
17	73 31.0	32.6	297 39.0	10.3	27 01.5	2.9	54.1
18	88 30.9	N21 32.2	312 08.3	10.3	S27 04.4	2.7	54.1
19	103 30.9	31.8	326 37.6	10.3	27 07.1	2.6	54.1
20	118 30.8	31.5	341 06.9	10.3	27 09.7	2.5	54.1
21	133 30.7	. . 31.1	355 36.2	10.2	27 12.2	2.3	54.1
22	148 30.7	30.7	10 05.4	10.2	27 14.5	2.2	54.1
23	163 30.6	30.3	24 34.6	10.2	27 16.7	2.1	54.1
15 00 (TUESDAY)	178 30.5	N21 29.9	39 03.8	10.2	S27 18.8	1.9	54.1
01	193 30.5	29.5	53 33.0	10.1	27 20.7	1.8	54.1
02	208 30.4	29.1	68 02.1	10.1	27 22.5	1.7	54.1
03	223 30.4	. . 28.7	82 31.2	10.1	27 24.2	1.5	54.1
04	238 30.3	28.3	97 00.3	10.0	27 25.7	1.4	54.1
05	253 30.2	27.9	111 29.3	10.0	27 27.1	1.3	54.1
06	268 30.2	N21 27.5	125 58.3	10.0	S27 28.4	1.2	54.2
07	283 30.1	27.1	140 27.3	10.0	27 29.6	1.0	54.2
08	298 30.0	26.7	154 56.3	10.0	27 30.6	0.9	54.2
09	313 30.0	. . 26.3	169 25.3	9.9	27 31.5	0.7	54.2
10	328 29.9	25.9	183 54.2	9.9	27 32.2	0.6	54.2
11	343 29.9	25.5	198 23.1	9.9	27 32.8	0.5	54.2
12	358 29.8	N21 25.1	212 52.0	9.9	S27 33.3	0.3	54.2
13	13 29.7	24.7	227 20.9	9.9	27 33.6	0.3	54.2
14	28 29.7	24.3	241 49.8	9.9	27 33.9	0.0	54.2
15	43 29.6	. . 23.9	256 18.7	9.8	27 33.9	0.0	54.2
16	58 29.6	23.4	270 47.5	9.9	27 33.9	0.2	54.2
17	73 29.5	23.0	285 16.4	9.8	27 33.7	0.4	54.2
18	88 29.5	N21 22.6	299 45.2	9.8	S27 33.3	0.4	54.2
19	103 29.4	22.2	314 14.0	9.9	27 32.9	0.6	54.2
20	118 29.3	21.8	328 42.9	9.8	27 32.3	0.8	54.3
21	133 29.3	. . 21.4	343 11.7	9.8	27 31.5	0.8	54.3
22	148 29.2	21.0	357 40.5	9.8	27 30.7	1.0	54.3
23	163 29.2	20.6	12 09.3	9.8	27 29.7	1.2	54.3
16 00 (WEDNESDAY)	178 29.1	N21 20.2	26 38.1	9.8	S27 28.5	1.3	54.3
01	193 29.1	19.8	41 06.9	9.8	27 27.2	1.4	54.3
02	208 29.0	19.4	55 35.7	9.8	27 25.8	1.5	54.3
03	223 28.9	. . 18.9	70 04.5	9.8	27 24.3	1.7	54.3
04	238 28.9	18.5	84 33.3	9.8	27 22.6	1.8	54.3
05	253 28.8	18.1	99 02.1	9.8	27 20.8	2.0	54.3
06	268 28.8	N21 17.7	113 30.9	9.9	S27 18.8	2.1	54.3
07	283 28.7	17.3	127 59.8	9.8	27 16.7	2.2	54.4
08	298 28.7	16.9	142 28.6	9.8	27 14.5	2.4	54.4
09	313 28.6	. . 16.4	156 57.4	9.9	27 12.1	2.5	54.4
10	328 28.6	16.0	171 26.3	9.9	27 09.6	2.6	54.4
11	343 28.5	15.6	185 55.2	9.8	27 07.0	2.8	54.4
12	358 28.4	N21 15.2	200 24.0	9.9	S27 04.2	2.9	54.4
13	13 28.4	14.8	214 52.9	9.9	27 01.3	3.0	54.4
14	28 28.3	14.4	229 21.8	9.9	26 58.3	3.2	54.4
15	43 28.3	. . 13.9	243 50.7	10.0	26 55.1	3.3	54.4
16	58 28.2	13.5	258 19.7	9.9	26 51.8	3.4	54.4
17	73 28.2	13.1	272 48.6	10.0	26 48.4	3.6	54.5
18	88 28.1	N21 12.7	287 17.6	10.0	S26 44.8	3.7	54.5
19	103 28.1	12.2	301 46.6	10.0	26 41.1	3.8	54.5
20	118 28.0	11.8	316 15.6	10.0	26 37.3	4.0	54.5
21	133 28.0	. . 11.4	330 44.6	10.1	26 33.3	4.1	54.5
22	148 27.9	11.0	345 13.7	10.0	26 29.2	4.2	54.5
23	163 27.9	10.5	359 42.7	10.1	S26 25.0	4.4	54.5
	SD 15.8	*d* 0.4	SD 14.7		14.8		14.8

Lat. °	Twilight Naut. h m	Twilight Civil h m	Sunrise h m	Moonrise 14 h m	Moonrise 15 h m	Moonrise 16 h m	Moonrise 17 h m
N 72	□	□	□	■	■	■	■
N 70	□	□	□	■	■	■	■
68	□	□	□	■	■	■	■
66	////	////	01 37	■	■	■	■
64	////	////	02 16	■	■	■	22 19
62	////	00 52	02 43	20 19	21 27	21 40	21 41
60	////	01 46	03 04	19 27	20 26	20 59	21 14
N 58	////	02 17	03 21	18 55	19 53	20 30	20 52
56	00 48	02 39	03 35	18 31	19 28	20 08	20 35
54	01 37	02 58	03 48	18 12	19 08	19 50	20 20
52	02 06	03 13	03 58	17 56	18 51	19 35	20 07
50	02 27	03 26	04 08	17 42	18 37	19 21	19 56
45	03 05	03 52	04 28	17 13	18 08	18 54	19 32
N 40	03 32	04 12	04 44	16 51	17 45	18 32	19 13
35	03 53	04 29	04 57	16 33	17 26	18 14	18 57
30	04 10	04 42	05 09	16 17	17 10	17 59	18 43
20	04 36	05 05	05 29	15 50	16 43	17 33	18 19
N 10	04 57	05 24	05 46	15 27	16 19	17 10	17 59
0	05 14	05 40	06 02	15 06	15 57	16 49	17 40
S 10	05 30	05 56	06 18	14 45	15 35	16 28	17 20
20	05 44	06 11	06 35	14 22	15 12	16 05	17 00
30	05 59	06 28	06 54	13 56	14 45	15 38	16 36
35	06 07	06 38	07 05	13 40	14 28	15 23	16 21
40	06 15	06 48	07 18	13 22	14 10	15 05	16 05
45	06 24	07 00	07 33	13 00	13 47	14 43	15 45
S 50	06 34	07 14	07 51	12 33	13 18	14 15	15 21
52	06 38	07 21	08 00	12 20	13 04	14 01	15 09
54	06 43	07 28	08 10	12 05	12 48	13 45	14 55
56	06 48	07 36	08 21	11 47	12 28	13 26	14 39
58	06 54	07 45	08 33	11 25	12 04	13 03	14 20
S 60	07 00	07 54	08 48	10 56	11 31	12 33	13 56

Lat. °	Sunset h m	Twilight Civil h m	Twilight Naut. h m	Moonset 14 h m	Moonset 15 h m	Moonset 16 h m	Moonset 17 h m
N 72	□	□	□	■	■	■	■
N 70	□	□	□	■	■	■	■
68	□	□	□	■	■	■	■
66	22 32	////	////	■	■	■	■
64	21 53	////	////	■	■	■	■
62	21 27	23 14	////	22 14	22 54	24 28	00 28
60	21 06	22 23	////	23 07	23 54	25 09	01 09
N 58	20 50	21 54	////	23 39	24 28	00 28	01 37
56	20 36	21 31	23 18	24 03	00 03	00 53	01 59
54	20 24	21 13	22 32	24 22	00 22	01 12	02 17
52	20 13	20 58	22 05	00 01	00 39	01 29	02 32
50	20 04	20 45	21 44	00 13	00 53	01 43	02 45
45	19 44	20 19	21 06	00 39	01 21	02 12	03 12
N 40	19 28	19 59	20 39	01 00	01 44	02 35	03 33
35	19 14	19 43	20 19	01 17	02 02	02 54	03 51
30	19 03	19 29	20 02	01 32	02 18	03 10	04 06
20	18 43	19 07	19 35	01 58	02 45	03 37	04 31
N 10	18 26	18 48	19 15	02 20	03 09	04 00	04 53
0	18 10	18 32	18 58	02 40	03 31	04 22	05 14
S 10	17 54	18 16	18 42	03 01	03 52	04 44	05 34
20	17 37	18 01	18 28	03 23	04 16	05 07	05 56
30	17 18	17 44	18 13	03 48	04 43	05 34	06 21
35	17 07	17 35	18 06	04 03	04 59	05 50	06 35
40	16 54	17 24	17 58	04 21	05 17	06 08	06 52
45	16 39	17 12	17 49	04 42	05 40	06 31	07 13
S 50	16 21	16 58	17 39	05 09	06 09	06 59	07 38
52	16 12	16 52	17 34	05 22	06 23	07 13	07 50
54	16 03	16 45	17 29	05 37	06 39	07 29	08 05
56	15 52	16 37	17 24	05 55	06 59	07 48	08 21
58	15 39	16 28	17 19	06 17	07 23	08 11	08 40
S 60	15 25	16 18	17 12	06 44	07 56	08 42	09 04

Day	SUN Eqn. of Time 00^h	SUN Eqn. of Time 12^h	SUN Mer. Pass.	MOON Mer. Pass. Upper	MOON Mer. Pass. Lower	MOON Age	MOON Phase
d	m s	m s	h m	h m	h m	d %	
14	05 51	05 55	12 06	21 18	08 53	11 87	
15	05 58	06 01	12 06	22 10	09 44	12 93	
16	06 03	06 06	12 06	23 01	10 35	13 97	

	UT	ARIES	VENUS −3.9		MARS +1.7		JUPITER −2.7		SATURN +0.8	
		GHA	GHA	Dec	GHA	Dec	GHA	Dec	GHA	Dec
	d h	° ′	° ′	° ′	° ′	° ′	° ′	° ′	° ′	° ′
	17 00	295 11.4	167 18.7	N20 13.1	134 01.3	N 9 00.8	7 16.8	S22 38.0	136 42.7	N10 50.2
	01	310 13.9	182 18.0	12.4	149 02.3	9 00.2	22 19.6	38.0	151 44.9	50.1
	02	325 16.4	197 17.3	11.7	164 03.4	8 59.6	37 22.4	38.0	166 47.1	50.0
	03	340 18.8	212 16.6	. . 11.0	179 04.4	. . 59.0	52 25.2	. . 38.1	181 49.4	. . 49.9
	04	355 21.3	227 15.8	10.3	194 05.5	58.4	67 28.0	38.1	196 51.6	49.8
	05	10 23.8	242 15.1	09.5	209 06.5	57.9	82 30.8	38.2	211 53.8	49.7
	06	25 26.2	257 14.4	N20 08.8	224 07.6	N 8 57.3	97 33.6	S22 38.2	226 56.0	N10 49.6
	07	40 28.7	272 13.7	08.1	239 08.6	56.7	112 36.4	38.3	241 58.2	49.5
T	08	55 31.2	287 13.0	07.4	254 09.7	56.1	127 39.2	38.3	257 00.4	49.4
H	09	70 33.6	302 12.2	. . 06.7	269 10.7	. . 55.5	142 42.0	. . 38.4	272 02.7	. . 49.3
U	10	85 36.1	317 11.5	06.0	284 11.8	54.9	157 44.8	38.4	287 04.9	49.2
R	11	100 38.5	332 10.8	05.3	299 12.8	54.3	172 47.6	38.4	302 07.1	49.1
S	12	115 41.0	347 10.1	N20 04.6	314 13.8	N 8 53.7	187 50.4	S22 38.5	317 09.3	N10 49.0
D	13	130 43.5	2 09.4	03.9	329 14.9	53.1	202 53.2	38.5	332 11.5	48.9
A	14	145 45.9	17 08.6	03.1	344 15.9	52.5	217 56.0	38.6	347 13.7	48.8
Y	15	160 48.4	32 07.9	. . 02.4	359 17.0	. . 51.9	232 58.8	. . 38.6	2 16.0	. . 48.7
	16	175 50.9	47 07.2	01.7	14 18.0	51.3	248 01.6	38.7	17 18.2	48.6
	17	190 53.3	62 06.5	01.0	29 19.1	50.7	263 04.4	38.7	32 20.4	48.5
	18	205 55.8	77 05.8	N20 00.3	44 20.1	N 8 50.1	278 07.2	S22 38.7	47 22.6	N10 48.4
	19	220 58.3	92 05.1	19 59.6	59 21.2	49.5	293 10.0	38.8	62 24.8	48.3
	20	236 00.7	107 04.3	58.8	74 22.2	48.9	308 12.8	38.8	77 27.0	48.2
	21	251 03.2	122 03.6	. . 58.1	89 23.3	. . 48.3	323 15.6	. . 38.9	92 29.2	. . 48.1
	22	266 05.6	137 02.9	57.4	104 24.3	47.7	338 18.4	38.9	107 31.5	48.0
	23	281 08.1	152 02.2	56.7	119 25.4	47.1	353 21.2	39.0	122 33.7	47.9
	18 00	296 10.6	167 01.5	N19 55.9	134 26.4	N 8 46.5	8 24.0	S22 39.0	137 35.9	N10 47.8
	01	311 13.0	182 00.8	55.2	149 27.5	45.9	23 26.8	39.1	152 38.1	47.7
	02	326 15.5	197 00.1	54.5	164 28.5	45.3	38 29.6	39.1	167 40.3	47.6
	03	341 18.0	211 59.4	. . 53.8	179 29.6	. . 44.7	53 32.4	. . 39.1	182 42.5	. . 47.5
	04	356 20.4	226 58.7	53.0	194 30.6	44.1	68 35.2	39.2	197 44.7	47.4
	05	11 22.9	241 57.9	52.3	209 31.7	43.5	83 38.0	39.2	212 47.0	47.3
	06	26 25.4	256 57.2	N19 51.6	224 32.7	N 8 42.9	98 40.8	S22 39.3	227 49.2	N10 47.2
	07	41 27.8	271 56.5	50.8	239 33.8	42.3	113 43.6	39.3	242 51.4	47.1
	08	56 30.3	286 55.8	50.1	254 34.8	41.7	128 46.4	39.4	257 53.6	47.0
F	09	71 32.8	301 55.1	. . 49.4	269 35.9	. . 41.1	143 49.2	. . 39.4	272 55.8	. . 46.9
R	10	86 35.2	316 54.4	48.6	284 36.9	40.5	158 52.0	39.4	287 58.0	46.8
I	11	101 37.7	331 53.7	47.9	299 38.0	39.9	173 54.8	39.5	303 00.2	46.7
D	12	116 40.1	346 53.0	N19 47.2	314 39.0	N 8 39.3	188 57.6	S22 39.5	318 02.5	N10 46.6
A	13	131 42.6	1 52.3	46.4	329 40.1	38.7	204 00.4	39.6	333 04.7	46.5
Y	14	146 45.1	16 51.6	45.7	344 41.1	38.1	219 03.2	39.6	348 06.9	46.4
	15	161 47.5	31 50.9	. . 44.9	359 42.2	. . 37.5	234 06.0	. . 39.7	3 09.1	. . 46.3
	16	176 50.0	46 50.2	44.2	14 43.2	36.9	249 08.8	39.7	18 11.3	46.2
	17	191 52.5	61 49.5	43.5	29 44.3	36.3	264 11.6	39.7	33 13.5	46.1
	18	206 54.9	76 48.8	N19 42.7	44 45.3	N 8 35.7	279 14.4	S22 39.8	48 15.7	N10 46.0
	19	221 57.4	91 48.1	42.0	59 46.4	35.1	294 17.2	39.8	63 17.9	45.9
	20	236 59.9	106 47.4	41.2	74 47.4	34.5	309 20.0	39.9	78 20.2	45.8
	21	252 02.3	121 46.7	. . 40.5	89 48.4	. . 33.9	324 22.8	. . 39.9	93 22.4	. . 45.7
	22	267 04.8	136 46.0	39.7	104 49.5	33.3	339 25.6	40.0	108 24.6	45.6
	23	282 07.3	151 45.3	39.0	119 50.5	32.7	354 28.4	40.0	123 26.8	45.5
	19 00	297 09.7	166 44.6	N19 38.3	134 51.6	N 8 32.1	9 31.2	S22 40.0	138 29.0	N10 45.4
	01	312 12.2	181 43.9	37.5	149 52.6	31.5	24 34.0	40.1	153 31.2	45.3
	02	327 14.6	196 43.2	36.8	164 53.7	30.9	39 36.8	40.1	168 33.4	45.2
	03	342 17.1	211 42.5	. . 36.0	179 54.7	. . 30.3	54 39.6	. . 40.2	183 35.6	. . 45.1
	04	357 19.6	226 41.8	35.2	194 55.8	29.7	69 42.4	40.2	198 37.9	45.0
	05	12 22.0	241 41.1	34.5	209 56.8	29.1	84 45.2	40.3	213 40.1	44.9
	06	27 24.5	256 40.4	N19 33.7	224 57.9	N 8 28.5	99 48.0	S22 40.3	228 42.3	N10 44.8
	07	42 27.0	271 39.7	33.0	239 58.9	27.9	114 50.8	40.3	243 44.5	44.7
S	08	57 29.4	286 39.0	32.2	255 00.0	27.3	129 53.6	40.4	258 46.7	44.6
A	09	72 31.9	301 38.3	. . 31.5	270 01.0	. . 26.7	144 56.4	. . 40.4	273 48.9	. . 44.5
T	10	87 34.4	316 37.6	30.7	285 02.1	26.1	159 59.2	40.5	288 51.1	44.4
U	11	102 36.8	331 36.9	30.0	300 03.1	25.5	175 02.0	40.5	303 53.3	44.3
R	12	117 39.3	346 36.2	N19 29.2	315 04.2	N 8 24.9	190 04.8	S22 40.6	318 55.6	N10 44.2
D	13	132 41.8	1 35.5	28.4	330 05.2	24.2	205 07.6	40.6	333 57.8	44.1
A	14	147 44.2	16 34.8	27.7	345 06.3	23.6	220 10.4	40.6	349 00.0	44.0
Y	15	162 46.7	31 34.1	. . 26.9	0 07.3	. . 23.0	235 13.2	. . 40.7	4 02.2	. . 43.9
	16	177 49.1	46 33.4	26.1	15 08.4	22.4	250 16.0	40.7	19 04.4	43.8
	17	192 51.6	61 32.7	25.4	30 09.4	21.8	265 18.8	40.8	34 06.6	43.7
	18	207 54.1	76 32.0	N19 24.6	45 10.5	N 8 21.2	280 21.6	S22 40.8	49 08.8	N10 43.6
	19	222 56.5	91 31.4	23.9	60 11.5	20.6	295 24.4	40.9	64 11.0	43.5
	20	237 59.0	106 30.7	23.1	75 12.6	20.0	310 27.2	40.9	79 13.2	43.4
	21	253 01.5	121 30.0	. . 22.3	90 13.6	. . 19.4	325 30.0	. . 40.9	94 15.5	. . 43.3
	22	268 03.9	136 29.3	21.5	105 14.7	18.8	340 32.8	41.0	109 17.7	43.2
	23	283 06.4	151 28.6	20.8	120 15.7	18.2	355 35.6	41.0	124 19.9	43.1
	Mer. Pass.	h m 4 14.6	*v* −0.7	*d* 0.7	*v* 1.0	*d* 0.6	*v* 2.8	*d* 0.0	*v* 2.2	*d* 0.1

STARS

Name	SHA	Dec
	° ′	° ′
Acamar	315 21.2	S40 15.9
Achernar	335 29.2	S57 11.2
Acrux	173 14.0	S63 09.1
Adhara	255 15.8	S28 58.9
Aldebaran	290 53.9	N16 31.7
Alioth	166 23.8	N55 55.0
Alkaid	153 01.6	N49 16.4
Al Na'ir	27 47.8	S46 54.9
Alnilam	275 50.4	S 1 11.6
Alphard	218 00.0	S 8 41.7
Alphecca	126 13.9	N26 41.2
Alpheratz	357 47.3	N29 08.2
Altair	62 11.5	N 8 53.5
Ankaa	353 19.0	S42 15.2
Antares	112 30.6	S26 27.2
Arcturus	145 59.0	N19 08.3
Atria	107 35.4	S69 02.9
Avior	234 20.3	S59 32.2
Bellatrix	278 36.2	N 6 21.6
Betelgeuse	271 05.6	N 7 24.6
Canopus	263 58.3	S52 41.8
Capella	280 40.3	N46 00.4
Deneb	49 33.6	N45 18.6
Denebola	182 37.5	N14 31.5
Diphda	348 59.4	S17 56.1
Dubhe	193 56.3	N61 42.5
Elnath	278 17.6	N28 36.9
Eltanin	90 47.4	N51 29.3
Enif	33 50.5	N 9 54.9
Fomalhaut	15 27.7	S29 34.4
Gacrux	172 05.5	S57 10.0
Gienah	175 56.3	S17 35.5
Hadar	148 53.3	S60 25.2
Hamal	328 05.0	N23 30.2
Kaus Aust.	83 48.3	S34 22.9
Kochab	137 19.0	N74 07.4
Markab	13 41.8	N15 15.1
Menkar	314 19.0	N 4 07.5
Menkent	148 12.0	S36 25.0
Miaplacidus	221 41.7	S69 45.2
Mirfak	308 46.0	N49 53.4
Nunki	76 02.5	S26 17.2
Peacock	53 24.2	S56 42.4
Pollux	243 32.6	N28 00.4
Procyon	245 03.9	N 5 12.3
Rasalhague	96 09.6	N12 33.2
Regulus	207 47.7	N11 55.6
Rigel	281 15.9	S 8 11.3
Rigil Kent.	139 56.9	S60 52.6
Sabik	102 16.5	S15 44.2
Schedar	349 44.9	N56 34.9
Shaula	96 26.6	S37 06.7
Sirius	258 37.3	S16 43.5
Spica	158 35.2	S11 12.5
Suhail	222 55.7	S43 28.1
Vega	80 41.1	N38 47.5
Zuben'ubi	137 09.4	S16 04.8

	SHA	Mer. Pass.
	° ′	h m
Venus	230 50.9	12 53
Mars	198 15.9	15 01
Jupiter	72 13.5	23 22
Saturn	201 25.3	14 47

UT d h	SUN GHA ° ′	SUN Dec ° ′	MOON GHA ° ′	v ′	MOON Dec ° ′	d ′	HP ′
17 00 THURSDAY	178 27.8	N21 10.1	14 11.8	10.2	S26 20.6	4.5	54.5
01	193 27.8	09.7	28 41.0	10.1	26 16.1	4.6	54.6
02	208 27.7	09.3	43 10.1	10.2	26 11.5	4.8	54.6
03	223 27.7	. . 08.8	57 39.3	10.2	26 06.7	4.8	54.6
04	238 27.6	08.4	72 08.5	10.3	26 01.9	5.1	54.6
05	253 27.6	08.0	86 37.8	10.2	25 56.8	5.1	54.6
06	268 27.5	N21 07.5	101 07.0	10.3	S25 51.7	5.3	54.6
07	283 27.5	07.1	115 36.3	10.4	25 46.4	5.4	54.6
08	298 27.4	06.7	130 05.7	10.4	25 41.0	5.5	54.6
09	313 27.4	. . 06.3	144 35.1	10.4	25 35.5	5.7	54.7
10	328 27.3	05.8	159 04.5	10.4	25 29.8	5.7	54.7
11	343 27.3	05.4	173 33.9	10.5	25 24.1	5.9	54.7
12	358 27.2	N21 05.0	188 03.4	10.5	S25 18.2	6.1	54.7
13	13 27.2	04.5	202 32.9	10.5	25 12.1	6.1	54.7
14	28 27.1	04.1	217 02.4	10.6	25 06.0	6.3	54.7
15	43 27.1	. . 03.7	231 32.0	10.6	24 59.7	6.4	54.7
16	58 27.0	03.2	246 01.6	10.7	24 53.3	6.6	54.8
17	73 27.0	02.8	260 31.3	10.7	24 46.7	6.6	54.8
18	88 26.9	N21 02.3	275 01.0	10.8	S24 40.1	6.8	54.8
19	103 26.9	01.9	289 30.8	10.7	24 33.3	6.9	54.8
20	118 26.8	01.5	304 00.5	10.9	24 26.4	7.0	54.8
21	133 26.8	. . 01.0	318 30.4	10.8	24 19.4	7.1	54.8
22	148 26.7	00.6	333 00.2	10.9	24 12.3	7.3	54.8
23	163 26.7	21 00.1	347 30.1	11.0	24 05.0	7.4	54.9
18 00 FRIDAY	178 26.6	N20 59.7	2 00.1	11.0	S23 57.6	7.5	54.9
01	193 26.6	59.3	16 30.1	11.0	23 50.1	7.6	54.9
02	208 26.6	58.8	31 00.1	11.1	23 42.5	7.7	54.9
03	223 26.5	. . 58.4	45 30.2	11.2	23 34.8	7.8	54.9
04	238 26.5	57.9	60 00.4	11.2	23 27.0	8.0	54.9
05	253 26.4	57.5	74 30.6	11.2	23 19.0	8.1	55.0
06	268 26.4	N20 57.0	89 00.8	11.3	S23 10.9	8.2	55.0
07	283 26.3	56.6	103 31.1	11.3	23 02.7	8.3	55.0
08	298 26.3	56.2	118 01.4	11.3	22 54.4	8.4	55.0
09	313 26.2	. . 55.7	132 31.7	11.5	22 46.0	8.5	55.0
10	328 26.2	55.3	147 02.2	11.4	22 37.5	8.7	55.0
11	343 26.2	54.8	161 32.6	11.5	22 28.8	8.7	55.1
12	358 26.1	N20 54.4	176 03.1	11.6	S22 20.1	8.9	55.1
13	13 26.1	53.9	190 33.7	11.6	22 11.2	8.9	55.1
14	28 26.0	53.5	205 04.3	11.6	22 02.3	9.1	55.1
15	43 26.0	. . 53.0	219 34.9	11.8	21 53.2	9.2	55.1
16	58 25.9	52.6	234 05.7	11.7	21 44.0	9.3	55.1
17	73 25.9	52.1	248 36.4	11.8	21 34.7	9.4	55.2
18	88 25.9	N20 51.7	263 07.2	11.9	S21 25.3	9.5	55.2
19	103 25.8	51.2	277 38.1	11.9	21 15.8	9.6	55.2
20	118 25.8	50.8	292 09.0	11.9	21 06.2	9.7	55.2
21	133 25.7	. . 50.3	306 39.9	12.0	20 56.5	9.8	55.2
22	148 25.7	49.8	321 10.9	12.1	20 46.7	9.9	55.2
23	163 25.7	49.4	335 42.0	12.1	20 36.8	10.0	55.3
19 00 SATURDAY	178 25.6	N20 48.9	350 13.1	12.1	S20 26.8	10.1	55.3
01	193 25.6	48.5	4 44.2	12.2	20 16.7	10.3	55.3
02	208 25.5	48.0	19 15.4	12.2	20 06.4	10.3	55.3
03	223 25.5	. . 47.6	33 46.6	12.3	19 56.1	10.4	55.3
04	238 25.5	47.1	48 17.9	12.4	19 45.7	10.5	55.3
05	253 25.4	46.7	62 49.3	12.4	19 35.2	10.6	55.4
06	268 25.4	N20 46.2	77 20.7	12.4	S19 24.6	10.7	55.4
07	283 25.3	45.7	91 52.1	12.5	19 13.9	10.8	55.4
08	298 25.3	45.3	106 23.6	12.5	19 03.1	10.8	55.4
09	313 25.3	. . 44.8	120 55.1	12.6	18 52.3	11.0	55.4
10	328 25.2	44.3	135 26.7	12.7	18 41.3	11.1	55.5
11	343 25.2	43.9	149 58.4	12.6	18 30.2	11.1	55.5
12	358 25.2	N20 43.4	164 30.0	12.8	S18 19.1	11.3	55.5
13	13 25.1	43.0	179 01.8	12.7	18 07.8	11.3	55.5
14	28 25.1	42.5	193 33.5	12.8	17 56.5	11.4	55.5
15	43 25.0	. . 42.0	208 05.3	12.9	17 45.1	11.5	55.5
16	58 25.0	41.6	222 37.2	12.9	17 33.6	11.6	55.6
17	73 25.0	41.1	237 09.1	13.0	17 22.0	11.7	55.6
18	88 24.9	N20 40.6	251 41.1	13.0	S17 10.3	11.8	55.6
19	103 24.9	40.2	266 13.1	13.0	16 58.5	11.8	55.6
20	118 24.9	39.7	280 45.1	13.1	16 46.7	11.9	55.6
21	133 24.8	. . 39.2	295 17.2	13.1	16 34.8	12.0	55.7
22	148 24.8	38.8	309 49.3	13.2	16 22.8	12.1	55.7
23	163 24.8	38.3	324 21.5	13.2	S16 10.7	12.2	55.7
	SD 15.8	d 0.4	SD 14.9		15.0		15.1

Lat. °	Twilight Naut. h m	Twilight Civil h m	Sunrise h m	Moonrise 17 h m	Moonrise 18 h m	Moonrise 19 h m	Moonrise 20 h m
N 72	□	□	□	■	■	23 36	22 36
N 70	□	□	□	■	■	22 56	22 18
68	////	////	00 37	■	23 14	22 29	22 03
66	////	////	01 50	■	22 31	22 07	21 52
64	////	////	02 25	22 19	22 01	21 50	21 42
62	////	01 11	02 50	21 41	21 39	21 36	21 33
60	////	01 56	03 10	21 14	21 21	21 24	21 26
N 58	////	02 24	03 26	20 52	21 06	21 14	21 19
56	01 05	02 45	03 40	20 35	20 53	21 05	21 14
54	01 46	03 03	03 52	20 20	20 41	20 56	21 08
52	02 12	03 17	04 02	20 07	20 31	20 49	21 04
50	02 32	03 30	04 11	19 56	20 22	20 43	20 59
45	03 09	03 55	04 31	19 32	20 03	20 28	20 50
N 40	03 35	04 15	04 46	19 13	19 47	20 17	20 42
35	03 55	04 31	04 59	18 57	19 34	20 06	20 35
30	04 12	04 44	05 11	18 43	19 22	19 58	20 29
20	04 38	05 06	05 30	18 19	19 03	19 42	20 19
N 10	04 58	05 24	05 47	17 59	18 45	19 29	20 10
0	05 15	05 41	06 03	17 40	18 29	19 16	20 01
S 10	05 30	05 56	06 18	17 20	18 13	19 03	19 53
20	05 44	06 11	06 34	17 00	17 55	18 50	19 44
30	05 58	06 27	06 53	16 36	17 35	18 34	19 33
35	06 05	06 36	07 04	16 21	17 23	18 25	19 27
40	06 13	06 47	07 16	16 05	17 09	18 14	19 20
45	06 22	06 58	07 31	15 45	16 53	18 02	19 12
S 50	06 31	07 12	07 49	15 21	16 33	17 47	19 02
52	06 36	07 18	07 57	15 09	16 23	17 40	18 57
54	06 40	07 25	08 06	14 55	16 12	17 32	18 52
56	06 45	07 32	08 17	14 39	16 00	17 23	18 46
58	06 51	07 41	08 29	14 20	15 45	17 13	18 40
S 60	06 57	07 50	08 43	13 56	15 28	17 01	18 33

Lat. °	Sunset h m	Twilight Civil h m	Twilight Naut. h m	Moonset 17 h m	Moonset 18 h m	Moonset 19 h m	Moonset 20 h m
N 72	□	□	□	■	■	■	03 41
N 70	□	□	□	■	■	■	04 19
68	23 24	////	////	■	■	02 23	04 46
66	22 19	////	////	■	■	03 05	05 05
64	21 45	////	////	■	01 35	03 34	05 21
62	21 20	22 56	////	00 28	02 12	03 55	05 34
60	21 01	22 14	////	01 09	02 39	04 13	05 45
N 58	20 45	21 47	////	01 37	03 00	04 27	05 55
56	20 32	21 26	23 03	01 59	03 17	04 39	06 03
54	20 20	21 09	22 24	02 17	03 31	04 50	06 10
52	20 10	20 54	21 58	02 32	03 43	05 00	06 17
50	20 01	20 42	21 39	02 45	03 54	05 08	06 23
45	19 41	20 17	21 02	03 12	04 17	05 26	06 35
N 40	19 26	19 57	20 37	03 33	04 36	05 40	06 46
35	19 13	19 41	20 17	03 51	04 51	05 53	06 55
30	19 01	19 28	20 00	04 06	05 04	06 03	07 02
20	18 42	19 06	19 34	04 31	05 26	06 21	07 16
N 10	18 25	18 48	19 14	04 53	05 46	06 37	07 27
0	18 10	18 32	18 58	05 14	06 04	06 52	07 38
S 10	17 54	18 17	18 43	05 34	06 21	07 06	07 49
20	17 38	18 02	18 29	05 56	06 41	07 22	08 00
30	17 20	17 45	18 15	06 21	07 02	07 39	08 13
35	17 09	17 36	18 07	06 35	07 15	07 50	08 20
40	16 57	17 26	18 00	06 52	07 30	08 01	08 28
45	16 42	17 15	17 51	07 13	07 47	08 15	08 38
S 50	16 24	17 01	17 41	07 38	08 08	08 31	08 50
52	16 16	16 55	17 37	07 50	08 18	08 39	08 55
54	16 07	16 48	17 33	08 05	08 30	08 48	09 01
56	15 56	16 41	17 28	08 21	08 43	08 57	09 08
58	15 44	16 32	17 22	08 40	08 58	09 08	09 15
S 60	15 30	16 23	17 17	09 04	09 15	09 20	09 23

Day d	SUN Eqn. of Time 00^h m s	SUN Eqn. of Time 12^h m s	SUN Mer. Pass. h m	MOON Mer. Pass. Upper h m	MOON Mer. Pass. Lower h m	MOON Age d	MOON %	Phase
17	06 09	06 11	12 06	23 52	11 27	14	99	○
18	06 13	06 15	12 06	24 40	12 16	15	100	
19	06 17	06 19	12 06	00 40	13 04	16	99	

	UT (d h)	ARIES GHA (° ′)	VENUS −3.9 GHA (° ′)	VENUS Dec (° ′)	MARS +1.7 GHA (° ′)	MARS Dec (° ′)	JUPITER −2.7 GHA (° ′)	JUPITER Dec (° ′)	SATURN +0.8 GHA (° ′)	SATURN Dec (° ′)
	20 00	298 08.9	166 27.9	N19 20.0	135 16.7	N 8 17.6	10 38.4	S22 41.1	139 22.1	N10 43.0
	01	313 11.3	181 27.2	19.2	150 17.8	17.0	25 41.2	41.1	154 24.3	42.9
	02	328 13.8	196 26.5	18.5	165 18.8	16.4	40 44.0	41.2	169 26.5	42.8
	03	343 16.2	211 25.8	. . 17.7	180 19.9	. . 15.8	55 46.7	. . 41.2	184 28.7	. . 42.7
	04	358 18.7	226 25.2	16.9	195 20.9	15.2	70 49.5	41.2	199 30.9	42.6
	05	13 21.2	241 24.5	16.1	210 22.0	14.6	85 52.3	41.3	214 33.1	42.5
	06	28 23.6	256 23.8	N19 15.4	225 23.0	N 8 14.0	100 55.1	S22 41.3	229 35.4	N10 42.4
	07	43 26.1	271 23.1	14.6	240 24.1	13.4	115 57.9	41.4	244 37.6	42.3
	08	58 28.6	286 22.4	13.8	255 25.1	12.8	131 00.7	41.4	259 39.8	42.2
S	09	73 31.0	301 21.7	. . 13.0	270 26.2	. . 12.2	146 03.5	. . 41.5	274 42.0	. . 42.1
U	10	88 33.5	316 21.1	12.2	285 27.2	11.6	161 06.3	41.5	289 44.2	42.0
N	11	103 36.0	331 20.4	11.5	300 28.3	11.0	176 09.1	41.5	304 46.4	41.9
D	12	118 38.4	346 19.7	N19 10.7	315 29.3	N 8 10.3	191 11.9	S22 41.6	319 48.6	N10 41.8
A	13	133 40.9	1 19.0	09.9	330 30.4	09.7	206 14.7	41.6	334 50.8	41.7
Y	14	148 43.4	16 18.3	09.1	345 31.4	09.1	221 17.5	41.7	349 53.0	41.5
	15	163 45.8	31 17.7	. . 08.3	0 32.5	. . 08.5	236 20.3	. . 41.7	4 55.2	. . 41.4
	16	178 48.3	46 17.0	07.5	15 33.5	07.9	251 23.1	41.7	19 57.5	41.3
	17	193 50.7	61 16.3	06.8	30 34.6	07.3	266 25.9	41.8	34 59.7	41.2
	18	208 53.2	76 15.6	N19 06.0	45 35.6	N 8 06.7	281 28.7	S22 41.8	50 01.9	N10 41.1
	19	223 55.7	91 14.9	05.2	60 36.7	06.1	296 31.5	41.9	65 04.1	41.0
	20	238 58.1	106 14.3	04.4	75 37.7	05.5	311 34.3	41.9	80 06.3	40.9
	21	254 00.6	121 13.6	. . 03.6	90 38.8	. . 04.9	326 37.1	. . 42.0	95 08.5	. . 40.8
	22	269 03.1	136 12.9	02.8	105 39.8	04.3	341 39.8	42.0	110 10.7	40.7
	23	284 05.5	151 12.2	02.0	120 40.8	03.7	356 42.6	42.0	125 12.9	40.6
	21 00	299 08.0	166 11.6	N19 01.2	135 41.9	N 8 03.1	11 45.4	S22 42.1	140 15.1	N10 40.5
	01	314 10.5	181 10.9	19 00.4	150 42.9	02.5	26 48.2	42.1	155 17.3	40.4
	02	329 12.9	196 10.2	18 59.6	165 44.0	01.9	41 51.0	42.2	170 19.5	40.3
	03	344 15.4	211 09.5	. . 58.8	180 45.0	. . 01.3	56 53.8	. . 42.2	185 21.8	. . 40.2
	04	359 17.9	226 08.9	58.0	195 46.1	00.6	71 56.6	42.3	200 24.0	40.1
	05	14 20.3	241 08.2	57.2	210 47.1	8 00.0	86 59.4	42.3	215 26.2	40.0
	06	29 22.8	256 07.5	N18 56.4	225 48.2	N 7 59.4	102 02.2	S22 42.3	230 28.4	N10 39.9
	07	44 25.2	271 06.8	55.6	240 49.2	58.8	117 05.0	42.4	245 30.6	39.8
	08	59 27.7	286 06.2	54.8	255 50.3	58.2	132 07.8	42.4	260 32.8	39.7
M	09	74 30.2	301 05.5	. . 54.0	270 51.3	. . 57.6	147 10.6	. . 42.5	275 35.0	. . 39.6
O	10	89 32.6	316 04.8	53.2	285 52.4	57.0	162 13.4	42.5	290 37.2	39.5
N	11	104 35.1	331 04.2	52.4	300 53.4	56.4	177 16.2	42.5	305 39.4	39.4
D	12	119 37.6	346 03.5	N18 51.6	315 54.5	N 7 55.8	192 18.9	S22 42.6	320 41.6	N10 39.3
A	13	134 40.0	1 02.8	50.8	330 55.5	55.2	207 21.7	42.6	335 43.8	39.2
Y	14	149 42.5	16 02.1	50.0	345 56.6	54.6	222 24.5	42.7	350 46.0	39.1
	15	164 45.0	31 01.5	. . 49.2	0 57.6	. . 54.0	237 27.3	. . 42.7	5 48.3	. . 39.0
	16	179 47.4	46 00.8	48.4	15 58.7	53.4	252 30.1	42.7	20 50.5	38.9
	17	194 49.9	61 00.1	47.6	30 59.7	52.7	267 32.9	42.8	35 52.7	38.8
	18	209 52.3	75 59.5	N18 46.8	46 00.8	N 7 52.1	282 35.7	S22 42.8	50 54.9	N10 38.7
	19	224 54.8	90 58.8	46.0	61 01.8	51.5	297 38.5	42.9	65 57.1	38.6
	20	239 57.3	105 58.1	45.2	76 02.8	50.9	312 41.3	42.9	80 59.3	38.5
	21	254 59.7	120 57.5	. . 44.4	91 03.9	. . 50.3	327 44.1	. . 43.0	96 01.5	. . 38.4
	22	270 02.2	135 56.8	43.5	106 04.9	49.7	342 46.9	43.0	111 03.7	38.3
	23	285 04.7	150 56.2	42.7	121 06.0	49.1	357 49.7	43.0	126 05.9	38.2
	22 00	300 07.1	165 55.5	N18 41.9	136 07.0	N 7 48.5	12 52.4	S22 43.1	141 08.1	N10 38.1
	01	315 09.6	180 54.8	41.1	151 08.1	47.9	27 55.2	43.1	156 10.3	38.0
	02	330 12.1	195 54.2	40.3	166 09.1	47.3	42 58.0	43.2	171 12.5	37.9
	03	345 14.5	210 53.5	. . 39.5	181 10.2	. . 46.7	58 00.8	. . 43.2	186 14.7	. . 37.8
	04	0 17.0	225 52.8	38.6	196 11.2	46.0	73 03.6	43.2	201 17.0	37.7
	05	15 19.5	240 52.2	37.8	211 12.3	45.4	88 06.4	43.3	216 19.2	37.6
	06	30 21.9	255 51.5	N18 37.0	226 13.3	N 7 44.8	103 09.2	S22 43.3	231 21.4	N10 37.5
	07	45 24.4	270 50.9	36.2	241 14.4	44.2	118 12.0	43.4	246 23.6	37.4
T	08	60 26.8	285 50.2	35.4	256 15.4	43.6	133 14.8	43.4	261 25.8	37.2
U	09	75 29.3	300 49.5	. . 34.5	271 16.5	. . 43.0	148 17.6	. . 43.4	276 28.0	. . 37.1
E	10	90 31.8	315 48.9	33.7	286 17.5	42.4	163 20.3	43.5	291 30.2	37.0
S	11	105 34.2	330 48.2	32.9	301 18.6	41.8	178 23.1	43.5	306 32.4	36.9
D	12	120 36.7	345 47.6	N18 32.1	316 19.6	N 7 41.2	193 25.9	S22 43.6	321 34.6	N10 36.8
A	13	135 39.2	0 46.9	31.2	331 20.7	40.6	208 28.7	43.6	336 36.8	36.7
Y	14	150 41.6	15 46.3	30.4	346 21.7	39.9	223 31.5	43.7	351 39.0	36.6
	15	165 44.1	30 45.6	. . 29.6	1 22.7	. . 39.3	238 34.3	. . 43.7	6 41.2	. . 36.5
	16	180 46.6	45 44.9	28.8	16 23.8	38.7	253 37.1	43.7	21 43.4	36.4
	17	195 49.0	60 44.3	27.9	31 24.8	38.1	268 39.9	43.8	36 45.6	36.3
	18	210 51.5	75 43.6	N18 27.1	46 25.9	N 7 37.5	283 42.7	S22 43.8	51 47.8	N10 36.2
	19	225 54.0	90 43.0	26.3	61 26.9	36.9	298 45.4	43.9	66 50.0	36.1
	20	240 56.4	105 42.3	25.4	76 28.0	36.3	313 48.2	43.9	81 52.3	36.0
	21	255 58.9	120 41.7	. . 24.6	91 29.0	. . 35.7	328 51.0	. . 43.9	96 54.5	. . 35.9
	22	271 01.3	135 41.0	23.8	106 30.1	35.1	343 53.8	44.0	111 56.7	35.8
	23	286 03.8	150 40.4	22.9	121 31.1	34.4	358 56.6	44.0	126 58.9	35.7
	Mer. Pass.	h m 4 02.8	*v* −0.7	*d* 0.8	*v* 1.0	*d* 0.6	*v* 2.8	*d* 0.0	*v* 2.2	*d* 0.1

STARS

Name	SHA (° ′)	Dec (° ′)
Acamar	315 21.1	S40 15.9
Achernar	335 29.2	S57 11.2
Acrux	173 14.0	S63 09.1
Adhara	255 15.8	S28 58.9
Aldebaran	290 53.8	N16 31.7
Alioth	166 23.8	N55 55.0
Alkaid	153 01.6	N49 16.4
Al Na'ir	27 47.7	S46 55.0
Alnilam	275 50.4	S 1 11.6
Alphard	218 00.0	S 8 41.7
Alphecca	126 13.9	N26 41.2
Alpheratz	357 47.2	N29 08.3
Altair	62 11.5	N 8 53.5
Ankaa	353 19.0	S42 15.2
Antares	112 30.6	S26 27.2
Arcturus	145 59.0	N19 08.3
Atria	107 35.4	S69 02.9
Avior	234 20.3	S59 32.2
Bellatrix	278 36.2	N 6 21.6
Betelgeuse	271 05.6	N 7 24.6
Canopus	263 58.3	S52 41.8
Capella	280 40.3	N46 00.4
Deneb	49 33.6	N45 18.6
Denebola	182 37.5	N14 31.5
Diphda	348 59.4	S17 56.1
Dubhe	193 56.3	N61 42.5
Elnath	278 17.6	N28 36.9
Eltanin	90 47.4	N51 29.3
Enif	33 50.5	N 9 54.9
Fomalhaut	15 27.7	S29 34.4
Gacrux	172 05.5	S57 10.0
Gienah	175 56.3	S17 35.5
Hadar	148 53.4	S60 25.2
Hamal	328 05.0	N23 30.2
Kaus Aust.	83 48.3	S34 22.9
Kochab	137 19.1	N74 07.4
Markab	13 41.8	N15 15.1
Menkar	314 19.0	N 4 07.6
Menkent	148 12.0	S36 25.0
Miaplacidus	221 41.7	S69 45.2
Mirfak	308 46.0	N49 53.4
Nunki	76 02.5	S26 17.2
Peacock	53 24.2	S56 42.4
Pollux	243 32.6	N28 00.4
Procyon	245 03.9	N 5 12.3
Rasalhague	96 09.6	N12 33.2
Regulus	207 47.7	N11 55.6
Rigel	281 15.8	S 8 11.3
Rigil Kent.	139 56.9	S60 52.6
Sabik	102 16.5	S15 44.2
Schedar	349 44.8	N56 34.9
Shaula	96 26.6	S37 06.7
Sirius	258 37.3	S16 43.5
Spica	158 35.2	S11 12.5
Suhail	222 55.7	S43 28.1
Vega	80 41.1	N38 47.5
Zuben'ubi	137 09.4	S16 04.8

	SHA (° ′)	Mer. Pass. (h m)
Venus	227 03.6	12 56
Mars	196 33.9	14 56
Jupiter	72 37.4	23 09
Saturn	201 07.1	14 37

UT d	UT h	SUN GHA ° ′	SUN Dec ° ′	MOON GHA ° ′	MOON v ′	MOON Dec ° ′	MOON d ′	MOON HP ′
20 SUNDAY	00	178 24.7	N20 37.8	338 53.7	13.3	S15 58.5	12.2	55.7
	01	193 24.7	37.4	353 26.0	13.3	15 46.3	12.3	55.7
	02	208 24.7	36.9	7 58.3	13.3	15 34.0	12.4	55.8
	03	223 24.6	. . 36.4	22 30.6	13.4	15 21.6	12.5	55.8
	04	238 24.6	35.9	37 03.0	13.4	15 09.1	12.6	55.8
	05	253 24.6	35.5	51 35.4	13.5	14 56.5	12.6	55.8
	06	268 24.5	N20 35.0	66 07.9	13.5	S14 43.9	12.7	55.8
	07	283 24.5	34.5	80 40.4	13.6	14 31.2	12.7	55.9
	08	298 24.5	34.0	95 13.0	13.5	14 18.5	12.9	55.9
	09	313 24.4	. . 33.6	109 45.5	13.6	14 05.6	12.9	55.9
	10	328 24.4	33.1	124 18.1	13.7	13 52.7	13.0	55.9
	11	343 24.4	32.6	138 50.8	13.7	13 39.7	13.0	55.9
	12	358 24.3	N20 32.1	153 23.5	13.7	S13 26.7	13.1	56.0
	13	13 24.3	31.7	167 56.2	13.7	13 13.6	13.2	56.0
	14	28 24.3	31.2	182 28.9	13.8	13 00.4	13.2	56.0
	15	43 24.2	. . 30.7	197 01.7	13.8	12 47.2	13.3	56.0
	16	58 24.2	30.2	211 34.5	13.9	12 33.9	13.4	56.0
	17	73 24.2	29.7	226 07.4	13.9	12 20.5	13.4	56.1
	18	88 24.2	N20 29.3	240 40.3	13.9	S12 07.1	13.5	56.1
	19	103 24.1	28.8	255 13.2	13.9	11 53.6	13.6	56.1
	20	118 24.1	28.3	269 46.1	14.0	11 40.0	13.6	56.1
	21	133 24.1	. . 27.8	284 19.1	14.0	11 26.4	13.7	56.1
	22	148 24.0	27.3	298 52.1	14.0	11 12.7	13.7	56.2
	23	163 24.0	26.8	313 25.1	14.1	10 59.0	13.8	56.2
21 MONDAY	00	178 24.0	N20 26.4	327 58.2	14.0	S10 45.2	13.8	56.2
	01	193 23.9	25.9	342 31.2	14.1	10 31.4	13.9	56.2
	02	208 23.9	25.4	357 04.3	14.2	10 17.5	14.0	56.2
	03	223 23.9	. . 24.9	11 37.5	14.1	10 03.5	14.0	56.3
	04	238 23.9	24.4	26 10.6	14.2	9 49.5	14.0	56.3
	05	253 23.8	23.9	40 43.8	14.2	9 35.5	14.1	56.3
	06	268 23.8	N20 23.4	55 17.0	14.2	S 9 21.4	14.2	56.3
	07	283 23.8	22.9	69 50.2	14.2	9 07.2	14.2	56.3
	08	298 23.8	22.5	84 23.4	14.3	8 53.0	14.2	56.4
	09	313 23.7	. . 22.0	98 56.7	14.2	8 38.8	14.3	56.4
	10	328 23.7	21.5	113 29.9	14.3	8 24.5	14.3	56.4
	11	343 23.7	21.0	128 03.2	14.3	8 10.2	14.4	56.4
	12	358 23.7	N20 20.5	142 36.5	14.3	S 7 55.8	14.5	56.5
	13	13 23.6	20.0	157 09.8	14.3	7 41.3	14.4	56.5
	14	28 23.6	19.5	171 43.1	14.4	7 26.9	14.5	56.5
	15	43 23.6	. . 19.0	186 16.5	14.3	7 12.4	14.6	56.5
	16	58 23.5	18.5	200 49.8	14.4	6 57.8	14.6	56.5
	17	73 23.5	18.0	215 23.2	14.3	6 43.2	14.6	56.6
	18	88 23.5	N20 17.5	229 56.5	14.4	S 6 28.6	14.7	56.6
	19	103 23.5	17.0	244 29.9	14.4	6 13.9	14.7	56.6
	20	118 23.5	16.5	259 03.3	14.4	5 59.2	14.7	56.6
	21	133 23.4	. . 16.0	273 36.7	14.3	5 44.5	14.8	56.6
	22	148 23.4	15.5	288 10.0	14.4	5 29.7	14.8	56.7
	23	163 23.4	15.0	302 43.4	14.4	5 14.9	14.9	56.7
22 TUESDAY	00	178 23.4	N20 14.6	317 16.8	14.4	S 5 00.0	14.9	56.7
	01	193 23.3	14.1	331 50.2	14.4	4 45.1	14.9	56.7
	02	208 23.3	13.6	346 23.6	14.4	4 30.2	14.9	56.8
	03	223 23.3	. . 13.1	0 57.0	14.4	4 15.3	15.0	56.8
	04	238 23.3	12.5	15 30.4	14.4	4 00.3	15.0	56.8
	05	253 23.3	12.0	30 03.8	14.4	3 45.3	15.0	56.8
	06	268 23.2	N20 11.5	44 37.2	14.4	S 3 30.3	15.0	56.8
	07	283 23.2	11.0	59 10.6	14.4	3 15.3	15.1	56.9
	08	298 23.2	10.5	73 44.0	14.4	3 00.2	15.1	56.9
	09	313 23.2	. . 10.0	88 17.4	14.3	2 45.1	15.1	56.9
	10	328 23.1	09.5	102 50.7	14.4	2 30.0	15.1	56.9
	11	343 23.1	09.0	117 24.1	14.3	2 14.9	15.2	57.0
	12	358 23.1	N20 08.5	131 57.4	14.4	S 1 59.7	15.2	57.0
	13	13 23.1	08.0	146 30.8	14.3	1 44.5	15.2	57.0
	14	28 23.1	07.5	161 04.1	14.3	1 29.3	15.2	57.0
	15	43 23.0	. . 07.0	175 37.4	14.3	1 14.1	15.2	57.0
	16	58 23.0	06.5	190 10.7	14.2	0 58.9	15.3	57.1
	17	73 23.0	06.0	204 43.9	14.3	0 43.6	15.2	57.1
	18	88 23.0	N20 05.5	219 17.2	14.2	S 0 28.4	15.3	57.1
	19	103 23.0	05.0	233 50.4	14.3	S 0 13.1	15.3	57.1
	20	118 23.0	04.5	248 23.7	14.2	N 0 02.2	15.3	57.2
	21	133 22.9	. . 03.9	262 56.9	14.1	0 17.5	15.3	57.2
	22	148 22.9	03.4	277 30.0	14.2	0 32.8	15.3	57.2
	23	163 22.9	02.9	292 03.2	14.1	N 0 48.1	15.3	57.2
		SD 15.8	*d* 0.5	SD 15.2		15.4		15.5

Lat. °	Twilight Naut. h m	Twilight Civil h m	Sunrise h m	Moonrise 20 h m	Moonrise 21 h m	Moonrise 22 h m	Moonrise 23 h m
N 72	▭	▭	▭	22 36	21 58	21 26	20 53
N 70	▭	▭	▭	22 18	21 50	21 26	21 01
68	////	////	01 09	22 03	21 44	21 26	21 08
66	////	////	02 02	21 52	21 39	21 27	21 14
64	////	////	02 34	21 42	21 34	21 27	21 20
62	////	01 27	02 58	21 33	21 30	21 27	21 24
60	////	02 05	03 16	21 26	21 27	21 27	21 28
N 58	////	02 31	03 32	21 19	21 24	21 27	21 31
56	01 20	02 52	03 45	21 14	21 21	21 28	21 35
54	01 55	03 08	03 56	21 08	21 18	21 28	21 37
52	02 19	03 22	04 06	21 04	21 16	21 28	21 40
50	02 38	03 34	04 15	20 59	21 14	21 28	21 42
45	03 13	03 58	04 34	20 50	21 09	21 28	21 47
N 40	03 38	04 17	04 49	20 42	21 06	21 28	21 52
35	03 58	04 33	05 02	20 35	21 02	21 29	21 55
30	04 14	04 46	05 13	20 29	20 59	21 29	21 59
20	04 39	05 08	05 31	20 19	20 54	21 29	22 05
N 10	04 59	05 25	05 48	20 10	20 50	21 29	22 10
0	05 15	05 41	06 03	20 01	20 46	21 30	22 15
S 10	05 30	05 55	06 18	19 53	20 41	21 30	22 20
20	05 43	06 10	06 34	19 44	20 37	21 30	22 25
30	05 57	06 26	06 52	19 33	20 32	21 31	22 31
35	06 04	06 35	07 02	19 27	20 29	21 31	22 35
40	06 12	06 45	07 14	19 20	20 25	21 31	22 39
45	06 20	06 56	07 28	19 12	20 21	21 32	22 43
S 50	06 29	07 09	07 45	19 02	20 17	21 32	22 49
52	06 33	07 15	07 53	18 57	20 14	21 32	22 52
54	06 37	07 21	08 02	18 52	20 12	21 32	22 55
56	06 42	07 29	08 12	18 46	20 09	21 33	22 58
58	06 47	07 37	08 24	18 40	20 06	21 33	23 01
S 60	06 53	07 46	08 37	18 33	20 03	21 33	23 05

Lat. °	Sunset h m	Twilight Civil h m	Twilight Naut. h m	Moonset 20 h m	Moonset 21 h m	Moonset 22 h m	Moonset 23 h m
N 72	▭	▭	▭	03 41	06 17	08 29	10 38
N 70	▭	▭	▭	04 19	06 32	08 33	10 33
68	22 57	////	////	04 46	06 44	08 37	10 28
66	22 07	////	////	05 05	06 54	08 39	10 25
64	21 36	////	////	05 21	07 03	08 42	10 22
62	21 13	22 41	////	05 34	07 10	08 44	10 19
60	20 55	22 05	////	05 45	07 16	08 46	10 17
N 58	20 40	21 39	////	05 55	07 21	08 48	10 15
56	20 27	21 20	22 49	06 03	07 26	08 49	10 13
54	20 16	21 03	22 15	06 10	07 30	08 50	10 11
52	20 06	20 50	21 52	06 17	07 34	08 51	10 10
50	19 57	20 38	21 33	06 23	07 38	08 53	10 08
45	19 39	20 14	20 59	06 35	07 45	08 55	10 06
N 40	19 24	19 55	20 34	06 46	07 51	08 57	10 03
35	19 11	19 39	20 14	06 55	07 57	08 58	10 01
30	19 00	19 26	19 58	07 02	08 01	09 00	09 59
20	18 41	19 05	19 33	07 16	08 09	09 02	09 56
N 10	18 25	18 48	19 14	07 27	08 16	09 05	09 53
0	18 10	18 32	18 58	07 38	08 23	09 07	09 51
S 10	17 55	18 17	18 43	07 49	08 29	09 09	09 48
20	17 39	18 03	18 30	08 00	08 36	09 11	09 45
30	17 21	17 47	18 16	08 13	08 43	09 13	09 42
35	17 11	17 38	18 09	08 20	08 48	09 14	09 40
40	16 59	17 28	18 02	08 28	08 53	09 16	09 38
45	16 45	17 17	17 54	08 38	08 59	09 17	09 36
S 50	16 28	17 04	17 44	08 50	09 05	09 19	09 33
52	16 20	16 58	17 40	08 55	09 08	09 20	09 32
54	16 11	16 52	17 36	09 01	09 12	09 21	09 31
56	16 01	16 45	17 31	09 08	09 16	09 22	09 29
58	15 49	16 37	17 26	09 15	09 20	09 24	09 27
S 60	15 36	16 28	17 21	09 23	09 24	09 25	09 25

Day	SUN Eqn. of Time 00^h	SUN Eqn. of Time 12^h	SUN Mer. Pass.	MOON Mer. Pass. Upper	MOON Mer. Pass. Lower	MOON Age	MOON Phase
d	m s	m s	h m	h m	h m	d %	
20	06 21	06 23	12 06	01 27	13 50	17 95	
21	06 24	06 25	12 06	02 12	14 34	18 90	
22	06 27	06 28	12 06	02 56	15 18	19 83	

	UT d h	ARIES GHA ° ′	VENUS −3.9 GHA ° ′	VENUS Dec ° ′	MARS +1.7 GHA ° ′	MARS Dec ° ′	JUPITER −2.7 GHA ° ′	JUPITER Dec ° ′	SATURN +0.8 GHA ° ′	SATURN Dec ° ′
	23 00	301 06.3	165 39.7	N18 22.1	136 32.2	N 7 33.8	13 59.4	S22 44.1	142 01.1	N10 35.6
	01	316 08.7	180 39.1	21.2	151 33.2	33.2	29 02.2	44.1	157 03.3	35.5
	02	331 11.2	195 38.4	20.4	166 34.3	32.6	44 05.0	44.1	172 05.5	35.4
	03	346 13.7	210 37.8	· · 19.6	181 35.3	· · 32.0	59 07.7	· · 44.2	187 07.7	· · 35.3
	04	1 16.1	225 37.1	18.7	196 36.4	31.4	74 10.5	44.2	202 09.9	35.2
	05	16 18.6	240 36.5	17.9	211 37.4	30.8	89 13.3	44.3	217 12.1	35.1
	06	31 21.1	255 35.8	N18 17.0	226 38.4	N 7 30.2	104 16.1	S22 44.3	232 14.3	N10 35.0
W	07	46 23.5	270 35.2	16.2	241 39.5	29.6	119 18.9	44.3	247 16.5	34.9
E	08	61 26.0	285 34.5	15.4	256 40.5	28.9	134 21.7	44.4	262 18.7	34.8
D	09	76 28.4	300 33.9	· · 14.5	271 41.6	· · 28.3	149 24.5	· · 44.4	277 20.9	· · 34.7
N	10	91 30.9	315 33.2	13.7	286 42.6	27.7	164 27.3	44.5	292 23.1	34.6
E	11	106 33.4	330 32.6	12.8	301 43.7	27.1	179 30.0	44.5	307 25.3	34.5
S	12	121 35.8	345 31.9	N18 12.0	316 44.7	N 7 26.5	194 32.8	S22 44.5	322 27.5	N10 34.4
D	13	136 38.3	0 31.3	11.1	331 45.8	25.9	209 35.6	44.6	337 29.7	34.3
A	14	151 40.8	15 30.7	10.3	346 46.8	25.3	224 38.4	44.6	352 31.9	34.1
Y	15	166 43.2	30 30.0	· · 09.4	1 47.9	· · 24.7	239 41.2	· · 44.7	7 34.1	· · 34.0
	16	181 45.7	45 29.4	08.6	16 48.9	24.0	254 44.0	44.7	22 36.4	33.9
	17	196 48.2	60 28.7	07.7	31 50.0	23.4	269 46.8	44.7	37 38.6	33.8
	18	211 50.6	75 28.1	N18 06.9	46 51.0	N 7 22.8	284 49.5	S22 44.8	52 40.8	N10 33.7
	19	226 53.1	90 27.4	06.0	61 52.1	22.2	299 52.3	44.8	67 43.0	33.6
	20	241 55.6	105 26.8	05.2	76 53.1	21.6	314 55.1	44.9	82 45.2	33.5
	21	256 58.0	120 26.2	· · 04.3	91 54.1	· · 21.0	329 57.9	· · 44.9	97 47.4	· · 33.4
	22	272 00.5	135 25.5	03.5	106 55.2	20.4	345 00.7	44.9	112 49.6	33.3
	23	287 02.9	150 24.9	02.6	121 56.2	19.7	0 03.5	45.0	127 51.8	33.2
	24 00	302 05.4	165 24.2	N18 01.7	136 57.3	N 7 19.1	15 06.2	S22 45.0	142 54.0	N10 33.1
	01	317 07.9	180 23.6	00.9	151 58.3	18.5	30 09.0	45.1	157 56.2	33.0
	02	332 10.3	195 23.0	18 00.0	166 59.4	17.9	45 11.8	45.1	172 58.4	32.9
	03	347 12.8	210 22.3	17 59.2	182 00.4	· · 17.3	60 14.6	· · 45.1	188 00.6	· · 32.8
	04	2 15.3	225 21.7	58.3	197 01.5	16.7	75 17.4	45.2	203 02.8	32.7
	05	17 17.7	240 21.1	57.4	212 02.5	16.1	90 20.2	45.2	218 05.0	32.6
	06	32 20.2	255 20.4	N17 56.6	227 03.6	N 7 15.4	105 23.0	S22 45.3	233 07.2	N10 32.5
	07	47 22.7	270 19.8	55.7	242 04.6	14.8	120 25.7	45.3	248 09.4	32.4
T	08	62 25.1	285 19.2	54.9	257 05.7	14.2	135 28.5	45.3	263 11.6	32.3
H	09	77 27.6	300 18.5	· · 54.0	272 06.7	· · 13.6	150 31.3	· · 45.4	278 13.8	· · 32.2
U	10	92 30.0	315 17.9	53.1	287 07.7	13.0	165 34.1	45.4	293 16.0	32.1
R	11	107 32.5	330 17.3	52.3	302 08.8	12.4	180 36.9	45.5	308 18.2	32.0
S	12	122 35.0	345 16.6	N17 51.4	317 09.8	N 7 11.8	195 39.7	S22 45.5	323 20.4	N10 31.9
D	13	137 37.4	0 16.0	50.5	332 10.9	11.1	210 42.4	45.5	338 22.6	31.8
A	14	152 39.9	15 15.4	49.6	347 11.9	10.5	225 45.2	45.6	353 24.8	31.6
Y	15	167 42.4	30 14.7	· · 48.8	2 13.0	· · 09.9	240 48.0	· · 45.6	8 27.0	· · 31.5
	16	182 44.8	45 14.1	47.9	17 14.0	09.3	255 50.8	45.7	23 29.2	31.4
	17	197 47.3	60 13.5	47.0	32 15.1	08.7	270 53.6	45.7	38 31.4	31.3
	18	212 49.8	75 12.8	N17 46.2	47 16.1	N 7 08.1	285 56.3	S22 45.7	53 33.6	N10 31.2
	19	227 52.2	90 12.2	45.3	62 17.2	07.4	300 59.1	45.8	68 35.8	31.1
	20	242 54.7	105 11.6	44.4	77 18.2	06.8	316 01.9	45.8	83 38.0	31.0
	21	257 57.2	120 11.0	· · 43.5	92 19.3	· · 06.2	331 04.7	· · 45.9	98 40.2	· · 30.9
	22	272 59.6	135 10.3	42.7	107 20.3	05.6	346 07.5	45.9	113 42.4	30.8
	23	288 02.1	150 09.7	41.8	122 21.3	05.0	1 10.3	45.9	128 44.7	30.7
	25 00	303 04.5	165 09.1	N17 40.9	137 22.4	N 7 04.4	16 13.0	S22 46.0	143 46.9	N10 30.6
	01	318 07.0	180 08.4	40.0	152 23.4	03.8	31 15.8	46.0	158 49.1	30.5
	02	333 09.5	195 07.8	39.1	167 24.5	03.1	46 18.6	46.1	173 51.3	30.4
	03	348 11.9	210 07.2	· · 38.3	182 25.5	· · 02.5	61 21.4	· · 46.1	188 53.5	· · 30.3
	04	3 14.4	225 06.6	37.4	197 26.6	01.9	76 24.2	46.1	203 55.7	30.2
	05	18 16.9	240 05.9	36.5	212 27.6	01.3	91 26.9	46.2	218 57.9	30.1
	06	33 19.3	255 05.3	N17 35.6	227 28.7	N 7 00.7	106 29.7	S22 46.2	234 00.1	N10 30.0
	07	48 21.8	270 04.7	34.7	242 29.7	7 00.1	121 32.5	46.2	249 02.3	29.9
	08	63 24.3	285 04.1	33.8	257 30.8	6 59.4	136 35.3	46.3	264 04.5	29.8
F	09	78 26.7	300 03.5	· · 33.0	272 31.8	· · 58.8	151 38.1	· · 46.3	279 06.7	· · 29.7
R	10	93 29.2	315 02.8	32.1	287 32.8	58.2	166 40.8	46.4	294 08.9	29.6
I	11	108 31.7	330 02.2	31.2	302 33.9	57.6	181 43.6	46.4	309 11.1	29.4
D	12	123 34.1	345 01.6	N17 30.3	317 34.9	N 6 57.0	196 46.4	S22 46.4	324 13.3	N10 29.3
A	13	138 36.6	0 01.0	29.4	332 36.0	56.3	211 49.2	46.5	339 15.5	29.2
Y	14	153 39.0	15 00.4	28.5	347 37.0	55.7	226 52.0	46.5	354 17.7	29.1
	15	168 41.5	29 59.7	· · 27.6	2 38.1	· · 55.1	241 54.7	· · 46.6	9 19.9	· · 29.0
	16	183 44.0	44 59.1	26.7	17 39.1	54.5	256 57.5	46.6	24 22.1	28.9
	17	198 46.4	59 58.5	25.8	32 40.2	53.9	272 00.3	46.6	39 24.3	28.8
	18	213 48.9	74 57.9	N17 25.0	47 41.2	N 6 53.3	287 03.1	S22 46.7	54 26.5	N10 28.7
	19	228 51.4	89 57.3	24.1	62 42.3	52.6	302 05.8	46.7	69 28.7	28.6
	20	243 53.8	104 56.7	23.2	77 43.3	52.0	317 08.6	46.8	84 30.9	28.5
	21	258 56.3	119 56.0	· · 22.3	92 44.3	· · 51.4	332 11.4	· · 46.8	99 33.1	· · 28.4
	22	273 58.8	134 55.4	21.4	107 45.4	50.8	347 14.2	46.8	114 35.3	28.3
	23	289 01.2	149 54.8	20.5	122 46.4	50.2	2 17.0	46.9	129 37.5	28.2
	Mer. Pass. (h m)	3 51.0	v −0.6	d 0.9	v 1.0	d 0.6	v 2.8	d 0.0	v 2.2	d 0.1

STARS

Name	SHA ° ′	Dec ° ′
Acamar	315 21.1	S40 15.8
Achernar	335 29.2	S57 11.2
Acrux	173 14.1	S63 09.1
Adhara	255 15.8	S28 58.9
Aldebaran	290 53.8	N16 31.7
Alioth	166 23.8	N55 55.0
Alkaid	153 01.6	N49 16.4
Al Na'ir	27 47.7	S46 55.0
Alnilam	275 50.4	S 1 11.6
Alphard	218 00.0	S 8 41.7
Alphecca	126 13.9	N26 41.2
Alpheratz	357 47.2	N29 08.3
Altair	62 11.5	N 8 53.5
Ankaa	353 19.0	S42 15.2
Antares	112 30.6	S26 27.2
Arcturus	145 59.0	N19 08.3
Atria	107 35.4	S69 02.9
Avior	234 20.3	S59 32.2
Bellatrix	278 36.2	N 6 21.6
Betelgeuse	271 05.6	N 7 24.6
Canopus	263 58.3	S52 41.8
Capella	280 40.3	N46 00.4
Deneb	49 33.6	N45 18.6
Denebola	182 37.5	N14 31.5
Diphda	348 59.4	S17 56.1
Dubhe	193 56.3	N61 42.5
Elnath	278 17.6	N28 36.9
Eltanin	90 47.4	N51 29.4
Enif	33 50.4	N 9 54.9
Fomalhaut	15 27.6	S29 34.4
Gacrux	172 05.5	S57 10.0
Gienah	175 56.3	S17 35.5
Hadar	148 53.4	S60 25.2
Hamal	328 05.0	N23 30.2
Kaus Aust.	83 48.3	S34 22.9
Kochab	137 19.1	N74 07.4
Markab	13 41.8	N15 15.1
Menkar	314 19.0	N 4 07.6
Menkent	148 12.0	S36 25.0
Miaplacidus	221 41.7	S69 45.2
Mirfak	308 45.9	N49 53.4
Nunki	76 02.5	S26 17.2
Peacock	53 24.2	S56 42.4
Pollux	243 32.5	N28 00.4
Procyon	245 03.9	N 5 12.3
Rasalhague	96 09.6	N12 33.3
Regulus	207 47.7	N11 55.6
Rigel	281 15.8	S 8 11.3
Rigil Kent.	139 56.9	S60 52.6
Sabik	102 16.5	S15 44.2
Schedar	349 44.8	N56 34.9
Shaula	96 26.6	S37 06.7
Sirius	258 37.3	S16 43.5
Spica	158 35.2	S11 12.5
Suhail	222 55.7	S43 28.0
Vega	80 41.1	N38 47.6
Zuben'ubi	137 09.4	S16 04.8

	SHA ° ′	Mer. Pass. h m
Venus	223 18.8	12 59
Mars	194 51.9	14 51
Jupiter	73 00.8	22 55
Saturn	200 48.6	14 26

UT d	h	SUN GHA ° ′	SUN Dec ° ′	MOON GHA ° ′	v ′	MOON Dec ° ′	d ′	HP ′
23	00	178 22.9	N20 02.4	306 36.3	14.1	N 1 03.4	15.4	57.3
	01	193 22.9	01.9	321 09.4	14.1	1 18.8	15.3	57.3
	02	208 22.9	01.4	335 42.5	14.0	1 34.1	15.3	57.3
	03	223 22.8	. . 00.9	350 15.5	14.0	1 49.4	15.4	57.3
	04	238 22.8	20 00.3	4 48.5	14.0	2 04.8	15.3	57.3
	05	253 22.8	19 59.8	19 21.5	14.0	2 20.1	15.4	57.4
	06	268 22.8	N19 59.3	33 54.5	13.9	N 2 35.5	15.3	57.4
W	07	283 22.8	58.8	48 27.4	13.9	2 50.8	15.4	57.4
E	08	298 22.8	58.3	63 00.3	13.8	3 06.2	15.3	57.4
D	09	313 22.7	. . 57.8	77 33.1	13.8	3 21.5	15.3	57.5
N	10	328 22.7	57.2	92 05.9	13.8	3 36.8	15.4	57.5
E	11	343 22.7	56.7	106 38.7	13.7	3 52.2	15.3	57.5
S	12	358 22.7	N19 56.2	121 11.4	13.7	N 4 07.5	15.3	57.5
D	13	13 22.7	55.7	135 44.1	13.6	4 22.8	15.3	57.6
A	14	28 22.7	55.2	150 16.7	13.6	4 38.1	15.3	57.6
Y	15	43 22.7	. . 54.6	164 49.3	13.6	4 53.4	15.3	57.6
	16	58 22.7	54.1	179 21.9	13.5	5 08.7	15.3	57.6
	17	73 22.6	53.6	193 54.4	13.4	5 24.0	15.3	57.6
	18	88 22.6	N19 53.1	208 26.8	13.5	N 5 39.3	15.3	57.7
	19	103 22.6	52.6	222 59.3	13.3	5 54.6	15.2	57.7
	20	118 22.6	52.0	237 31.6	13.3	6 09.8	15.2	57.7
	21	133 22.6	. . 51.5	252 03.9	13.3	6 25.0	15.2	57.7
	22	148 22.6	51.0	266 36.2	13.2	6 40.2	15.2	57.8
	23	163 22.6	50.4	281 08.4	13.1	6 55.4	15.2	57.8
24	00	178 22.6	N19 49.9	295 40.5	13.1	N 7 10.6	15.1	57.8
	01	193 22.5	49.4	310 12.6	13.0	7 25.7	15.1	57.8
	02	208 22.5	48.9	324 44.6	13.0	7 40.8	15.1	57.9
	03	223 22.5	. . 48.3	339 16.6	12.9	7 55.9	15.1	57.9
	04	238 22.5	47.8	353 48.5	12.9	8 11.0	15.1	57.9
	05	253 22.5	47.3	8 20.4	12.8	8 26.1	15.0	57.9
	06	268 22.5	N19 46.8	22 52.2	12.7	N 8 41.1	15.0	58.0
	07	283 22.5	46.2	37 23.9	12.6	8 56.1	14.9	58.0
T	08	298 22.5	45.7	51 55.5	12.6	9 11.0	14.9	58.0
H	09	313 22.5	. . 45.2	66 27.1	12.5	9 25.9	14.9	58.0
U	10	328 22.5	44.6	80 58.6	12.5	9 40.8	14.9	58.0
R	11	343 22.5	44.1	95 30.1	12.4	9 55.7	14.8	58.1
S	12	358 22.4	N19 43.6	110 01.5	12.3	N10 10.5	14.8	58.1
D	13	13 22.4	43.0	124 32.8	12.2	10 25.3	14.7	58.1
A	14	28 22.4	42.5	139 04.0	12.2	10 40.0	14.7	58.1
Y	15	43 22.4	. . 42.0	153 35.2	12.0	10 54.7	14.7	58.2
	16	58 22.4	41.4	168 06.2	12.0	11 09.4	14.6	58.2
	17	73 22.4	40.9	182 37.2	12.0	11 24.0	14.6	58.2
	18	88 22.4	N19 40.3	197 08.2	11.8	N11 38.6	14.5	58.2
	19	103 22.4	39.8	211 39.0	11.8	11 53.1	14.5	58.3
	20	118 22.4	39.3	226 09.8	11.7	12 07.6	14.5	58.3
	21	133 22.4	. . 38.7	240 40.5	11.6	12 22.1	14.3	58.3
	22	148 22.4	38.2	255 11.1	11.5	12 36.4	14.4	58.3
	23	163 22.4	37.6	269 41.6	11.4	12 50.8	14.2	58.4
25	00	178 22.4	N19 37.1	284 12.0	11.3	N13 05.0	14.3	58.4
	01	193 22.4	36.6	298 42.3	11.3	13 19.3	14.1	58.4
	02	208 22.4	36.0	313 12.6	11.2	13 33.4	14.1	58.4
	03	223 22.4	. . 35.5	327 42.8	11.0	13 47.5	14.1	58.5
	04	238 22.3	34.9	342 12.8	11.0	14 01.6	14.0	58.5
	05	253 22.3	34.4	356 42.8	10.9	14 15.6	13.9	58.5
	06	268 22.3	N19 33.9	11 12.7	10.8	N14 29.5	13.9	58.5
	07	283 22.3	33.3	25 42.5	10.7	14 43.4	13.8	58.5
	08	298 22.3	32.8	40 12.2	10.6	14 57.2	13.7	58.6
F	09	313 22.3	. . 32.2	54 41.8	10.5	15 10.9	13.7	58.6
R	10	328 22.3	31.7	69 11.3	10.4	15 24.6	13.6	58.6
I	11	343 22.3	31.1	83 40.7	10.3	15 38.2	13.5	58.6
D	12	358 22.3	N19 30.6	98 10.0	10.2	N15 51.7	13.4	58.7
A	13	13 22.3	30.0	112 39.2	10.2	16 05.1	13.4	58.7
Y	14	28 22.3	29.5	127 08.4	10.0	16 18.5	13.3	58.7
	15	43 22.3	. . 28.9	141 37.4	9.9	16 31.8	13.2	58.7
	16	58 22.3	28.4	156 06.3	9.8	16 45.0	13.1	58.8
	17	73 22.3	27.8	170 35.1	9.7	16 58.1	13.1	58.8
	18	88 22.3	N19 27.3	185 03.8	9.6	N17 11.2	12.9	58.8
	19	103 22.3	26.7	199 32.4	9.4	17 24.1	12.9	58.8
	20	118 22.3	26.2	214 00.8	9.4	17 37.0	12.8	58.8
	21	133 22.3	. . 25.6	228 29.2	9.3	17 49.8	12.7	58.9
	22	148 22.3	25.1	242 57.5	9.1	18 02.5	12.6	58.9
	23	163 22.3	24.5	257 25.6	9.1	N18 15.1	12.6	58.9
		SD 15.8	*d* 0.5	SD 15.7		15.8		16.0

Lat.	Twilight Naut.	Twilight Civil	Sunrise	Moonrise 23	Moonrise 24	Moonrise 25	Moonrise 26
°	h m	h m	h m	h m	h m	h m	h m
N 72	▭	▭	▭	20 53	20 12	18 51	▭
N 70	▭	▭	▭	21 01	20 32	19 45	▭
68	////	////	01 31	21 08	20 48	20 19	18 54
66	////	////	02 15	21 14	21 01	20 44	20 13
64	////	00 34	02 44	21 20	21 12	21 03	20 51
62	////	01 42	03 05	21 24	21 21	21 19	21 17
60	////	02 15	03 23	21 28	21 29	21 32	21 38
N 58	00 31	02 39	03 37	21 31	21 36	21 44	21 56
56	01 33	02 58	03 50	21 35	21 43	21 54	22 10
54	02 04	03 14	04 01	21 37	21 48	22 03	22 23
52	02 26	03 27	04 10	21 40	21 54	22 11	22 34
50	02 44	03 38	04 19	21 42	21 58	22 18	22 44
45	03 17	04 02	04 37	21 47	22 09	22 34	23 05
N 40	03 42	04 20	04 51	21 52	22 17	22 47	23 23
35	04 01	04 35	05 04	21 55	22 24	22 58	23 37
30	04 16	04 48	05 14	21 59	22 31	23 07	23 50
20	04 41	05 09	05 33	22 05	22 42	23 24	24 11
N 10	05 00	05 26	05 48	22 10	22 52	23 39	24 30
0	05 15	05 41	06 03	22 15	23 02	23 53	24 48
S 10	05 29	05 55	06 17	22 20	23 11	24 07	00 07
20	05 43	06 09	06 33	22 25	23 22	24 22	00 22
30	05 56	06 25	06 50	22 31	23 34	24 39	00 39
35	06 02	06 33	07 00	22 35	23 41	24 50	00 50
40	06 10	06 43	07 12	22 39	23 48	25 01	01 01
45	06 17	06 53	07 25	22 43	23 58	25 15	01 15
S 50	06 26	07 06	07 42	22 49	24 09	00 09	01 32
52	06 30	07 11	07 50	22 52	24 14	00 14	01 41
54	06 34	07 18	07 58	22 55	24 20	00 20	01 50
56	06 38	07 25	08 08	22 58	24 27	00 27	02 00
58	06 43	07 32	08 19	23 01	24 34	00 34	02 12
S 60	06 48	07 41	08 31	23 05	24 42	00 42	02 25

Lat.	Sunset	Twilight Civil	Twilight Naut.	Moonset 23	Moonset 24	Moonset 25	Moonset 26
°	h m	h m	h m	h m	h m	h m	h m
N 72	▭	▭	▭	10 38	12 57	16 02	▭
N 70	▭	▭	▭	10 33	12 40	15 10	▭
68	22 37	////	////	10 28	12 26	14 38	17 56
66	21 55	////	////	10 25	12 15	14 15	16 38
64	21 27	23 26	////	10 22	12 05	13 57	16 02
62	21 06	22 27	////	10 19	11 57	13 42	15 36
60	20 48	21 55	////	10 17	11 51	13 30	15 15
N 58	20 34	21 32	23 30	10 15	11 45	13 19	14 59
56	20 22	21 13	22 36	10 13	11 39	13 10	14 45
54	20 11	20 58	22 07	10 11	11 35	13 02	14 33
52	20 02	20 45	21 45	10 10	11 30	12 55	14 22
50	19 53	20 33	21 27	10 08	11 27	12 48	14 13
45	19 36	20 10	20 55	10 06	11 18	12 34	13 53
N 40	19 21	19 52	20 31	10 03	11 12	12 23	13 37
35	19 09	19 37	20 12	10 01	11 06	12 13	13 24
30	18 58	19 25	19 56	09 59	11 01	12 05	13 12
20	18 40	19 04	19 32	09 56	10 52	11 50	12 52
N 10	18 25	18 47	19 13	09 53	10 44	11 37	12 35
0	18 10	18 32	18 58	09 51	10 37	11 26	12 19
S 10	17 56	18 18	18 44	09 48	10 29	11 14	12 03
20	17 40	18 04	18 31	09 45	10 22	11 01	11 46
30	17 23	17 49	18 18	09 42	10 13	10 47	11 26
35	17 13	17 40	18 11	09 40	10 08	10 39	11 15
40	17 01	17 31	18 04	09 38	10 02	10 30	11 02
45	16 48	17 20	17 56	09 36	09 56	10 19	10 47
S 50	16 32	17 08	17 48	09 33	09 48	10 06	10 28
52	16 24	17 02	17 44	09 32	09 45	10 00	10 19
54	16 15	16 56	17 40	09 31	09 41	09 53	10 09
56	16 06	16 49	17 35	09 29	09 36	09 45	09 58
58	15 55	16 41	17 31	09 27	09 32	09 37	09 46
S 60	15 42	16 33	17 26	09 25	09 26	09 28	09 31

Day	SUN Eqn. of Time 00^h	SUN Eqn. of Time 12^h	SUN Mer. Pass.	MOON Mer. Pass. Upper	MOON Mer. Pass. Lower	Age	Phase
d	m s	m s	h m	h m	h m	d	%
23	06 28	06 29	12 06	03 40	16 03	20	74
24	06 30	06 30	12 07	04 26	16 49	21	64
25	06 31	06 31	12 07	05 14	17 39	22	53

Day	UT d h	ARIES GHA	VENUS −3.9 GHA	VENUS Dec	MARS +1.7 GHA	MARS Dec	JUPITER −2.7 GHA	JUPITER Dec	SATURN +0.8 GHA	SATURN Dec
		° ′	° ′	° ′	° ′	° ′	° ′	° ′	° ′	° ′
	26 00	304 03.7	164 54.2	N17 19.6	137 47.5	N 6 49.6	17 19.7	S22 46.9	144 39.7	N10 28.1
	01	319 06.1	179 53.6	18.7	152 48.5	48.9	32 22.5	46.9	159 41.9	28.0
	02	334 08.6	194 53.0	17.8	167 49.6	48.3	47 25.3	47.0	174 44.1	27.9
	03	349 11.1	209 52.4	16.9	182 50.6	47.7	62 28.1	47.0	189 46.3	27.8
	04	4 13.5	224 51.7	16.0	197 51.7	47.1	77 30.8	47.1	204 48.5	27.7
	05	19 16.0	239 51.1	15.1	212 52.7	46.5	92 33.6	47.1	219 50.7	27.5
	06	34 18.5	254 50.5	N17 14.2	227 53.8	N 6 45.8	107 36.4	S22 47.1	234 52.9	N10 27.4
	07	49 20.9	269 49.9	13.3	242 54.8	45.2	122 39.2	47.2	249 55.1	27.3
S	08	64 23.4	284 49.3	12.4	257 55.8	44.6	137 41.9	47.2	264 57.3	27.2
A	09	79 25.9	299 48.7	11.5	272 56.9	44.0	152 44.7	47.2	279 59.5	27.1
T	10	94 28.3	314 48.1	10.6	287 57.9	43.4	167 47.5	47.3	295 01.7	27.0
U	11	109 30.8	329 47.5	09.6	302 59.0	42.7	182 50.3	47.3	310 03.9	26.9
R	12	124 33.3	344 46.9	N17 08.7	318 00.0	N 6 42.1	197 53.1	S22 47.4	325 06.1	N10 26.8
D	13	139 35.7	359 46.3	07.8	333 01.1	41.5	212 55.8	47.4	340 08.3	26.7
A	14	154 38.2	14 45.6	06.9	348 02.1	40.9	227 58.6	47.4	355 10.5	26.6
Y	15	169 40.6	29 45.0	06.0	3 03.2	40.3	243 01.4	47.5	10 12.7	26.5
	16	184 43.1	44 44.4	05.1	18 04.2	39.6	258 04.2	47.5	25 14.9	26.4
	17	199 45.6	59 43.8	04.2	33 05.2	39.0	273 06.9	47.6	40 17.1	26.3
	18	214 48.0	74 43.2	N17 03.3	48 06.3	N 6 38.4	288 09.7	S22 47.6	55 19.3	N10 26.2
	19	229 50.5	89 42.6	02.4	63 07.3	37.8	303 12.5	47.6	70 21.5	26.1
	20	244 53.0	104 42.0	01.4	78 08.4	37.2	318 15.3	47.7	85 23.7	26.0
	21	259 55.4	119 41.4	17 00.5	93 09.4	36.5	333 18.0	47.7	100 25.9	25.9
	22	274 57.9	134 40.8	16 59.6	108 10.5	35.9	348 20.8	47.7	115 28.1	25.7
	23	290 00.4	149 40.2	58.7	123 11.5	35.3	3 23.6	47.8	130 30.3	25.6
	27 00	305 02.8	164 39.6	N16 57.8	138 12.6	N 6 34.7	18 26.3	S22 47.8	145 32.5	N10 25.5
	01	320 05.3	179 39.0	56.9	153 13.6	34.1	33 29.1	47.9	160 34.7	25.4
	02	335 07.8	194 38.4	55.9	168 14.6	33.4	48 31.9	47.9	175 36.9	25.3
	03	350 10.2	209 37.8	55.0	183 15.7	32.8	63 34.7	47.9	190 39.1	25.2
	04	5 12.7	224 37.2	54.1	198 16.7	32.2	78 37.4	48.0	205 41.3	25.1
	05	20 15.1	239 36.6	53.2	213 17.8	31.6	93 40.2	48.0	220 43.5	25.0
	06	35 17.6	254 36.0	N16 52.3	228 18.8	N 6 31.0	108 43.0	S22 48.0	235 45.7	N10 24.9
	07	50 20.1	269 35.4	51.3	243 19.9	30.3	123 45.8	48.1	250 47.9	24.8
	08	65 22.5	284 34.8	50.4	258 20.9	29.7	138 48.5	48.1	265 50.1	24.7
S	09	80 25.0	299 34.2	49.5	273 22.0	29.1	153 51.3	48.2	280 52.3	24.6
U	10	95 27.5	314 33.6	48.6	288 23.0	28.5	168 54.1	48.2	295 54.5	24.5
N	11	110 29.9	329 33.0	47.6	303 24.0	27.8	183 56.8	48.2	310 56.7	24.4
D	12	125 32.4	344 32.4	N16 46.7	318 25.1	N 6 27.2	198 59.6	S22 48.3	325 58.9	N10 24.3
A	13	140 34.9	359 31.8	45.8	333 26.1	26.6	214 02.4	48.3	341 01.1	24.2
Y	14	155 37.3	14 31.2	44.8	348 27.2	26.0	229 05.2	48.3	356 03.3	24.0
	15	170 39.8	29 30.6	43.9	3 28.2	25.4	244 07.9	48.4	11 05.4	23.9
	16	185 42.3	44 30.0	43.0	18 29.3	24.7	259 10.7	48.4	26 07.6	23.8
	17	200 44.7	59 29.5	42.1	33 30.3	24.1	274 13.5	48.5	41 09.8	23.7
	18	215 47.2	74 28.9	N16 41.1	48 31.4	N 6 23.5	289 16.2	S22 48.5	56 12.0	N10 23.6
	19	230 49.6	89 28.3	40.2	63 32.4	22.9	304 19.0	48.5	71 14.2	23.5
	20	245 52.1	104 27.7	39.3	78 33.4	22.2	319 21.8	48.6	86 16.4	23.4
	21	260 54.6	119 27.1	38.3	93 34.5	21.6	334 24.6	48.6	101 18.6	23.3
	22	275 57.0	134 26.5	37.4	108 35.5	21.0	349 27.3	48.6	116 20.8	23.2
	23	290 59.5	149 25.9	36.5	123 36.6	20.4	4 30.1	48.7	131 23.0	23.1
	28 00	306 02.0	164 25.3	N16 35.5	138 37.6	N 6 19.8	19 32.9	S22 48.7	146 25.2	N10 23.0
	01	321 04.4	179 24.7	34.6	153 38.7	19.1	34 35.6	48.8	161 27.4	22.9
	02	336 06.9	194 24.1	33.6	168 39.7	18.5	49 38.4	48.8	176 29.6	22.8
	03	351 09.4	209 23.5	32.7	183 40.8	17.9	64 41.2	48.8	191 31.8	22.7
	04	6 11.8	224 23.0	31.8	198 41.8	17.3	79 43.9	48.9	206 34.0	22.6
	05	21 14.3	239 22.4	30.8	213 42.8	16.6	94 46.7	48.9	221 36.2	22.4
	06	36 16.7	254 21.8	N16 29.9	228 43.9	N 6 16.0	109 49.5	S22 48.9	236 38.4	N10 22.3
	07	51 19.2	269 21.2	28.9	243 44.9	15.4	124 52.2	49.0	251 40.6	22.2
	08	66 21.7	284 20.6	28.0	258 46.0	14.8	139 55.0	49.0	266 42.8	22.1
M	09	81 24.1	299 20.0	27.0	273 47.0	14.1	154 57.8	49.0	281 45.0	22.0
O	10	96 26.6	314 19.4	26.1	288 48.1	13.5	170 00.5	49.1	296 47.2	21.9
N	11	111 29.1	329 18.9	25.2	303 49.1	12.9	185 03.3	49.1	311 49.4	21.8
D	12	126 31.5	344 18.3	N16 24.2	318 50.1	N 6 12.3	200 06.1	S22 49.2	326 51.6	N10 21.7
A	13	141 34.0	359 17.7	23.3	333 51.2	11.6	215 08.8	49.2	341 53.8	21.6
Y	14	156 36.5	14 17.1	22.3	348 52.2	11.0	230 11.6	49.2	356 56.0	21.5
	15	171 38.9	29 16.5	21.4	3 53.3	10.4	245 14.4	49.3	11 58.2	21.4
	16	186 41.4	44 15.9	20.4	18 54.3	09.8	260 17.1	49.3	27 00.4	21.3
	17	201 43.9	59 15.4	19.5	33 55.4	09.2	275 19.9	49.3	42 02.6	21.2
	18	216 46.3	74 14.8	N16 18.5	48 56.4	N 6 08.5	290 22.7	S22 49.4	57 04.8	N10 21.1
	19	231 48.8	89 14.2	17.6	63 57.4	07.9	305 25.4	49.4	72 07.0	20.9
	20	246 51.2	104 13.6	16.6	78 58.5	07.3	320 28.2	49.5	87 09.2	20.8
	21	261 53.7	119 13.0	15.7	93 59.5	06.7	335 31.0	49.5	102 11.4	20.7
	22	276 56.2	134 12.5	14.7	109 00.6	06.0	350 33.7	49.5	117 13.5	20.6
	23	291 58.6	149 11.9	13.8	124 01.6	05.4	5 36.5	49.6	132 15.7	20.5
	Mer. Pass.	h m 3 39.2	v −0.6	d 0.9	v 1.0	d 0.6	v 2.8	d 0.0	v 2.2	d 0.1

STARS

Name	SHA	Dec
	° ′	° ′
Acamar	315 21.1	S40 15.8
Achernar	335 29.1	S57 11.2
Acrux	173 14.1	S63 09.1
Adhara	255 15.8	S28 58.8
Aldebaran	290 53.8	N16 31.7
Alioth	166 23.8	N55 55.0
Alkaid	153 01.6	N49 16.4
Al Na'ir	27 47.7	S46 55.0
Alnilam	275 50.3	S 1 11.6
Alphard	218 00.0	S 8 41.7
Alphecca	126 13.9	N26 41.2
Alpheratz	357 47.2	N29 08.3
Altair	62 11.5	N 8 53.5
Ankaa	353 18.9	S42 15.2
Antares	112 30.6	S26 27.2
Arcturus	145 59.0	N19 08.3
Atria	107 35.4	S69 02.9
Avior	234 20.3	S59 32.2
Bellatrix	278 36.2	N 6 21.6
Betelgeuse	271 05.5	N 7 24.6
Canopus	263 58.3	S52 41.8
Capella	280 40.2	N46 00.4
Deneb	49 33.6	N45 18.7
Denebola	182 37.5	N14 31.5
Diphda	348 59.4	S17 56.1
Dubhe	193 56.3	N61 42.5
Elnath	278 17.6	N28 36.9
Eltanin	90 47.4	N51 29.4
Enif	33 50.4	N 9 54.9
Fomalhaut	15 27.6	S29 34.4
Gacrux	172 05.5	S57 10.0
Gienah	175 56.3	S17 35.5
Hadar	148 53.4	S60 25.2
Hamal	328 05.0	N23 30.2
Kaus Aust.	83 48.3	S34 22.9
Kochab	137 19.2	N74 07.4
Markab	13 41.8	N15 15.2
Menkar	314 19.0	N 4 07.6
Menkent	148 12.0	S36 25.0
Miaplacidus	221 41.7	S69 45.2
Mirfak	308 45.9	N49 53.4
Nunki	76 02.5	S26 17.2
Peacock	53 24.2	S56 42.4
Pollux	243 32.5	N28 00.4
Procyon	245 03.9	N 5 12.3
Rasalhague	96 09.6	N12 33.3
Regulus	207 47.7	N11 55.6
Rigel	281 15.8	S 8 11.3
Rigil Kent.	139 56.9	S60 52.6
Sabik	102 16.5	S15 44.2
Schedar	349 44.8	N56 34.9
Shaula	96 26.6	S37 06.7
Sirius	258 37.3	S16 43.5
Spica	158 35.2	S11 12.5
Suhail	222 55.7	S43 28.0
Vega	80 41.1	N38 47.6
Zuben'ubi	137 09.5	S16 04.8

	SHA	Mer. Pass.
	° ′	h m
Venus	219 36.8	13 02
Mars	193 09.7	14 46
Jupiter	73 23.5	22 42
Saturn	200 29.6	14 16

UT		SUN GHA	SUN Dec	MOON GHA	v	MOON Dec	d	HP
d	h	° ′	° ′	° ′	′	° ′	′	′
26 SATURDAY	00	178 22.3	N19 24.0	271 53.7	8.9	N18 27.7	12.4	58.9
	01	193 22.3	23.4	286 21.6	8.9	18 40.1	12.3	59.0
	02	208 22.3	22.9	300 49.5	8.7	18 52.4	12.3	59.0
	03	223 22.3	. . 22.3	315 17.2	8.6	19 04.7	12.1	59.0
	04	238 22.3	21.7	329 44.8	8.5	19 16.8	12.0	59.0
	05	253 22.3	21.2	344 12.3	8.4	19 28.8	12.0	59.0
	06	268 22.3	N19 20.6	358 39.7	8.2	N19 40.8	11.8	59.1
	07	283 22.3	20.1	13 06.9	8.2	19 52.6	11.7	59.1
	08	298 22.3	19.5	27 34.1	8.0	20 04.3	11.6	59.1
	09	313 22.3	. . 19.0	42 01.1	7.9	20 15.9	11.5	59.1
	10	328 22.3	18.4	56 28.0	7.9	20 27.4	11.4	59.2
	11	343 22.3	17.8	70 54.9	7.6	20 38.8	11.3	59.2
	12	358 22.4	N19 17.3	85 21.5	7.6	N20 50.1	11.1	59.2
	13	13 22.4	16.7	99 48.1	7.5	21 01.2	11.1	59.2
	14	28 22.4	16.2	114 14.6	7.3	21 12.3	10.9	59.2
	15	43 22.4	. . 15.6	128 40.9	7.3	21 23.2	10.8	59.3
	16	58 22.4	15.0	143 07.2	7.1	21 34.0	10.7	59.3
	17	73 22.4	14.5	157 33.3	7.0	21 44.7	10.5	59.3
	18	88 22.4	N19 13.9	171 59.3	6.9	N21 55.2	10.4	59.3
	19	103 22.4	13.3	186 25.2	6.7	22 05.6	10.3	59.3
	20	118 22.4	12.8	200 50.9	6.7	22 15.9	10.2	59.4
	21	133 22.4	. . 12.2	215 16.6	6.5	22 26.1	10.0	59.4
	22	148 22.4	11.6	229 42.1	6.4	22 36.1	9.9	59.4
	23	163 22.4	11.1	244 07.5	6.3	22 46.0	9.8	59.4
27 SUNDAY	00	178 22.4	N19 10.5	258 32.8	6.2	N22 55.8	9.6	59.5
	01	193 22.4	09.9	272 58.0	6.1	23 05.4	9.5	59.5
	02	208 22.4	09.4	287 23.1	5.9	23 14.9	9.4	59.5
	03	223 22.4	. . 08.8	301 48.0	5.9	23 24.3	9.2	59.5
	04	238 22.4	08.2	316 12.9	5.7	23 33.5	9.0	59.5
	05	253 22.5	07.7	330 37.6	5.6	23 42.5	8.9	59.5
	06	268 22.5	N19 07.1	345 02.2	5.5	N23 51.4	8.8	59.6
	07	283 22.5	06.5	359 26.7	5.4	24 00.2	8.6	59.6
	08	298 22.5	05.9	13 51.1	5.3	24 08.8	8.5	59.6
	09	313 22.5	. . 05.4	28 15.4	5.2	24 17.3	8.3	59.6
	10	328 22.5	04.8	42 39.6	5.0	24 25.6	8.1	59.6
	11	343 22.5	04.2	57 03.6	5.0	24 33.7	8.0	59.7
	12	358 22.5	N19 03.7	71 27.6	4.9	N24 41.7	7.8	59.7
	13	13 22.5	03.1	85 51.5	4.7	24 49.5	7.7	59.7
	14	28 22.5	02.5	100 15.2	4.6	24 57.2	7.5	59.7
	15	43 22.6	. . 01.9	114 38.8	4.6	25 04.7	7.4	59.7
	16	58 22.6	01.4	129 02.4	4.4	25 12.1	7.1	59.7
	17	73 22.6	00.8	143 25.8	4.4	25 19.2	7.1	59.8
	18	88 22.6	N19 00.2	157 49.2	4.2	N25 26.3	6.8	59.8
	19	103 22.6	18 59.6	172 12.4	4.1	25 33.1	6.7	59.8
	20	118 22.6	59.0	186 35.5	4.1	25 39.8	6.5	59.8
	21	133 22.6	. . 58.5	200 58.6	3.9	25 46.3	6.3	59.8
	22	148 22.6	57.9	215 21.5	3.9	25 52.6	6.2	59.8
	23	163 22.6	57.3	229 44.4	3.8	25 58.8	5.9	59.9
28 MONDAY	00	178 22.7	N18 56.7	244 07.2	3.6	N26 04.7	5.8	59.9
	01	193 22.7	56.1	258 29.8	3.6	26 10.5	5.6	59.9
	02	208 22.7	55.6	272 52.4	3.5	26 16.1	5.5	59.9
	03	223 22.7	. . 55.0	287 14.9	3.5	26 21.6	5.2	59.9
	04	238 22.7	54.4	301 37.4	3.3	26 26.8	5.1	59.9
	05	253 22.7	53.8	315 59.7	3.3	26 31.9	4.9	59.9
	06	268 22.7	N18 53.2	330 22.0	3.1	N26 36.8	4.7	60.0
	07	283 22.8	52.6	344 44.1	3.2	26 41.5	4.5	60.0
	08	298 22.8	52.1	359 06.3	3.0	26 46.0	4.3	60.0
	09	313 22.8	. . 51.5	13 28.3	3.0	26 50.3	4.2	60.0
	10	328 22.8	50.9	27 50.3	2.9	26 54.5	3.9	60.0
	11	343 22.8	50.3	42 12.2	2.8	26 58.4	3.7	60.0
	12	358 22.8	N18 49.7	56 34.0	2.8	N27 02.1	3.6	60.0
	13	13 22.9	49.1	70 55.8	2.7	27 05.7	3.4	60.0
	14	28 22.9	48.5	85 17.5	2.6	27 09.1	3.1	60.1
	15	43 22.9	. . 47.9	99 39.1	2.6	27 12.2	3.0	60.1
	16	58 22.9	47.4	114 00.7	2.6	27 15.2	2.8	60.1
	17	73 22.9	46.8	128 22.3	2.5	27 18.0	2.6	60.1
	18	88 22.9	N18 46.2	142 43.8	2.4	N27 20.6	2.3	60.1
	19	103 23.0	45.6	157 05.2	2.4	27 22.9	2.2	60.1
	20	118 23.0	45.0	171 26.6	2.4	27 25.1	2.0	60.1
	21	133 23.0	. . 44.4	185 48.0	2.3	27 27.1	1.8	60.1
	22	148 23.0	43.8	200 09.3	2.3	27 28.9	1.5	60.1
	23	163 23.0	43.2	214 30.6	2.2	N27 30.4	1.4	60.2
		SD 15.8	d 0.6	SD		16.1	16.3	16.4

Lat.	Twilight Naut.	Twilight Civil	Sunrise	Moonrise 26	27	28	29
°	h m	h m	h m	h m	h m	h m	h m
N 72	▭	▭	▭	▭	▭	▭	▭
N 70	▭	▭	▭	▭	▭	▭	▭
68	////	////	01 49	18 54	▭	▭	▭
66	////	////	02 27	20 13	▭	▭	▭
64	////	01 07	02 53	20 51	20 21	▭	▭
62	////	01 55	03 13	21 17	21 19	21 34	22 51
60	////	02 25	03 30	21 38	21 52	22 27	23 40
N 58	01 01	02 47	03 43	21 56	22 17	22 59	24 10
56	01 45	03 05	03 55	22 10	22 37	23 23	24 34
54	02 13	03 19	04 06	22 23	22 54	23 42	24 52
52	02 33	03 32	04 15	22 34	23 08	23 59	25 08
50	02 50	03 43	04 23	22 44	23 21	24 13	00 13
45	03 22	04 06	04 40	23 05	23 47	24 42	00 42
N 40	03 45	04 23	04 54	23 23	24 08	00 08	01 05
35	04 03	04 38	05 06	23 37	24 25	00 25	01 23
30	04 18	04 50	05 16	23 50	24 40	00 40	01 40
20	04 42	05 10	05 34	24 11	00 11	01 06	02 07
N 10	05 00	05 27	05 49	24 30	00 30	01 28	02 31
0	05 16	05 41	06 03	24 48	00 48	01 49	02 53
S 10	05 29	05 55	06 17	00 07	01 06	02 10	03 15
20	05 42	06 08	06 32	00 22	01 26	02 32	03 39
30	05 54	06 23	06 49	00 39	01 48	02 58	04 06
35	06 01	06 31	06 58	00 50	02 01	03 14	04 23
40	06 07	06 40	07 09	01 01	02 17	03 32	04 42
45	06 15	06 50	07 22	01 15	02 35	03 54	05 05
S 50	06 23	07 02	07 38	01 32	02 58	04 21	05 35
52	06 26	07 08	07 45	01 41	03 09	04 35	05 49
54	06 30	07 14	07 54	01 50	03 22	04 51	06 06
56	06 34	07 20	08 03	02 00	03 36	05 10	06 27
58	06 39	07 27	08 13	02 12	03 54	05 32	06 52
S 60	06 43	07 35	08 25	02 25	04 14	06 03	07 27

Lat.	Sunset	Twilight Civil	Twilight Naut.	Moonset 26	27	28	29
°	h m	h m	h m	h m	h m	h m	h m
N 72	▭	▭	▭	▭	▭	▭	▭
N 70	23 31	////	////	▭	▭	▭	▭
68	22 19	////	////	17 56	▭	▭	▭
66	21 43	////	////	16 38	▭	▭	▭
64	21 17	22 58	////	16 02	18 35	▭	▭
62	20 58	22 14	////	15 36	17 37	19 35	20 34
60	20 42	21 45	////	15 15	17 04	18 43	19 46
N 58	20 28	21 24	23 05	14 59	16 40	18 11	19 15
56	20 17	21 07	22 24	14 45	16 20	17 47	18 51
54	20 06	20 52	21 58	14 33	16 04	17 27	18 32
52	19 57	20 40	21 38	14 22	15 50	17 11	18 16
50	19 49	20 29	21 21	14 13	15 38	16 57	18 02
45	19 32	20 07	20 50	13 53	15 13	16 28	17 34
N 40	19 18	19 49	20 27	13 37	14 53	16 06	17 11
35	19 07	19 35	20 09	13 24	14 36	15 47	16 52
30	18 57	19 23	19 54	13 12	14 21	15 31	16 36
20	18 39	19 03	19 31	12 52	13 57	15 04	16 09
N 10	18 24	18 46	19 12	12 35	13 36	14 41	15 46
0	18 10	18 32	18 57	12 19	13 17	14 19	15 24
S 10	17 56	18 18	18 44	12 03	12 57	13 57	15 02
20	17 41	18 05	18 31	11 46	12 36	13 34	14 38
30	17 25	17 50	18 19	11 26	12 12	13 07	14 10
35	17 15	17 42	18 13	11 15	11 58	12 51	13 54
40	17 04	17 33	18 06	11 02	11 42	12 32	13 35
45	16 51	17 23	17 59	10 47	11 23	12 10	13 12
S 50	16 35	17 11	17 51	10 28	10 58	11 42	12 42
52	16 28	17 06	17 47	10 19	10 47	11 28	12 28
54	16 20	17 00	17 44	10 09	10 34	11 12	12 11
56	16 11	16 53	17 40	09 58	10 19	10 53	11 51
58	16 00	16 46	17 35	09 46	10 01	10 30	11 25
S 60	15 48	16 38	17 30	09 31	09 39	09 59	10 50

Day	SUN Eqn. of Time 00^h	SUN Eqn. of Time 12^h	SUN Mer. Pass.	MOON Mer. Pass. Upper	MOON Mer. Pass. Lower	MOON Age	MOON Phase
d	m s	m s	h m	h m	h m	d	%
26	06 31	06 31	12 07	06 06	18 33	23	42
27	06 30	06 30	12 06	07 02	19 32	24	31
28	06 29	06 29	12 06	08 04	20 36	25	21

UT d	h	ARIES GHA	VENUS −3.9 GHA	VENUS Dec	MARS +1.7 GHA	MARS Dec	JUPITER −2.7 GHA	JUPITER Dec	SATURN +0.8 GHA	SATURN Dec
		° ′	° ′	° ′	° ′	° ′	° ′	° ′	° ′	° ′
29 TUESDAY	00	307 01.1	164 11.3	N16 12.8	139 02.7	N 6 04.8	20 39.3	S22 49.6	147 17.9	N10 20.4
	01	322 03.6	179 10.7	11.8	154 03.7	04.2	35 42.0	49.6	162 20.1	20.3
	02	337 06.0	194 10.2	10.9	169 04.7	03.5	50 44.8	49.7	177 22.3	20.2
	03	352 08.5	209 09.6	. . 09.9	184 05.8	. . 02.9	65 47.6	. . 49.7	192 24.5	. . 20.1
	04	7 11.0	224 09.0	09.0	199 06.8	02.3	80 50.3	49.7	207 26.7	20.0
	05	22 13.4	239 08.4	08.0	214 07.9	01.7	95 53.1	49.8	222 28.9	19.9
	06	37 15.9	254 07.9	N16 07.1	229 08.9	N 6 01.0	110 55.9	S22 49.8	237 31.1	N10 19.8
	07	52 18.4	269 07.3	06.1	244 10.0	6 00.4	125 58.6	49.9	252 33.3	19.7
	08	67 20.8	284 06.7	05.1	259 11.0	5 59.8	141 01.4	49.9	267 35.5	19.6
	09	82 23.3	299 06.1	. . 04.2	274 12.0	. . 59.1	156 04.2	. . 49.9	282 37.7	. . 19.4
	10	97 25.7	314 05.6	03.2	289 13.1	58.5	171 06.9	50.0	297 39.9	19.3
	11	112 28.2	329 05.0	02.2	304 14.1	57.9	186 09.7	50.0	312 42.1	19.2
	12	127 30.7	344 04.4	N16 01.3	319 15.2	N 5 57.3	201 12.4	S22 50.0	327 44.3	N10 19.1
	13	142 33.1	359 03.9	16 00.3	334 16.2	56.6	216 15.2	50.1	342 46.5	19.0
	14	157 35.6	14 03.3	15 59.3	349 17.3	56.0	231 18.0	50.1	357 48.7	18.9
	15	172 38.1	29 02.7	. . 58.4	4 18.3	. . 55.4	246 20.7	. . 50.1	12 50.9	. . 18.8
	16	187 40.5	44 02.1	57.4	19 19.3	54.8	261 23.5	50.2	27 53.1	18.7
	17	202 43.0	59 01.6	56.4	34 20.4	54.1	276 26.3	50.2	42 55.3	18.6
	18	217 45.5	74 01.0	N15 55.5	49 21.4	N 5 53.5	291 29.0	S22 50.2	57 57.5	N10 18.5
	19	232 47.9	89 00.4	54.5	64 22.5	52.9	306 31.8	50.3	72 59.6	18.4
	20	247 50.4	103 59.9	53.5	79 23.5	52.3	321 34.5	50.3	88 01.8	18.3
	21	262 52.9	118 59.3	. . 52.6	94 24.6	. . 51.6	336 37.3	. . 50.4	103 04.0	. . 18.1
	22	277 55.3	133 58.7	51.6	109 25.6	51.0	351 40.1	50.4	118 06.2	18.0
	23	292 57.8	148 58.2	50.6	124 26.6	50.4	6 42.8	50.4	133 08.4	17.9
30 WEDNESDAY	00	308 00.2	163 57.6	N15 49.6	139 27.7	N 5 49.8	21 45.6	S22 50.5	148 10.6	N10 17.8
	01	323 02.7	178 57.0	48.7	154 28.7	49.1	36 48.3	50.5	163 12.8	17.7
	02	338 05.2	193 56.5	47.7	169 29.8	48.5	51 51.1	50.5	178 15.0	17.6
	03	353 07.6	208 55.9	. . 46.7	184 30.8	. . 47.9	66 53.9	. . 50.6	193 17.2	. . 17.5
	04	8 10.1	223 55.3	45.7	199 31.9	47.2	81 56.6	50.6	208 19.4	17.4
	05	23 12.6	238 54.8	44.8	214 32.9	46.6	96 59.4	50.6	223 21.6	17.3
	06	38 15.0	253 54.2	N15 43.8	229 33.9	N 5 46.0	112 02.1	S22 50.7	238 23.8	N10 17.2
	07	53 17.5	268 53.7	42.8	244 35.0	45.4	127 04.9	50.7	253 26.0	17.1
	08	68 20.0	283 53.1	41.8	259 36.0	44.7	142 07.7	50.7	268 28.2	17.0
	09	83 22.4	298 52.5	. . 40.8	274 37.1	. . 44.1	157 10.4	. . 50.8	283 30.4	. . 16.9
	10	98 24.9	313 52.0	39.9	289 38.1	43.5	172 13.2	50.8	298 32.6	16.7
	11	113 27.4	328 51.4	38.9	304 39.1	42.8	187 15.9	50.8	313 34.8	16.6
	12	128 29.8	343 50.9	N15 37.9	319 40.2	N 5 42.2	202 18.7	S22 50.9	328 36.9	N10 16.5
	13	143 32.3	358 50.3	36.9	334 41.2	41.6	217 21.5	50.9	343 39.1	16.4
	14	158 34.7	13 49.7	35.9	349 42.3	41.0	232 24.2	51.0	358 41.3	16.3
	15	173 37.2	28 49.2	. . 35.0	4 43.3	. . 40.3	247 27.0	. . 51.0	13 43.5	. . 16.2
	16	188 39.7	43 48.6	34.0	19 44.4	39.7	262 29.7	51.0	28 45.7	16.1
	17	203 42.1	58 48.1	33.0	34 45.4	39.1	277 32.5	51.1	43 47.9	16.0
	18	218 44.6	73 47.5	N15 32.0	49 46.4	N 5 38.4	292 35.2	S22 51.1	58 50.1	N10 15.9
	19	233 47.1	88 47.0	31.0	64 47.5	37.8	307 38.0	51.1	73 52.3	15.8
	20	248 49.5	103 46.4	30.0	79 48.5	37.2	322 40.8	51.2	88 54.5	15.7
	21	263 52.0	118 45.8	. . 29.0	94 49.6	. . 36.6	337 43.5	. . 51.2	103 56.7	. . 15.6
	22	278 54.5	133 45.3	28.0	109 50.6	35.9	352 46.3	51.2	118 58.9	15.4
	23	293 56.9	148 44.7	27.1	124 51.6	35.3	7 49.0	51.3	134 01.1	15.3
31 THURSDAY	00	308 59.4	163 44.2	N15 26.1	139 52.7	N 5 34.7	22 51.8	S22 51.3	149 03.3	N10 15.2
	01	324 01.9	178 43.6	25.1	154 53.7	34.0	37 54.5	51.3	164 05.5	15.1
	02	339 04.3	193 43.1	24.1	169 54.8	33.4	52 57.3	51.4	179 07.6	15.0
	03	354 06.8	208 42.5	. . 23.1	184 55.8	. . 32.8	68 00.0	. . 51.4	194 09.8	. . 14.9
	04	9 09.2	223 42.0	22.1	199 56.8	32.2	83 02.8	51.4	209 12.0	14.8
	05	24 11.7	238 41.4	21.1	214 57.9	31.5	98 05.6	51.5	224 14.2	14.7
	06	39 14.2	253 40.9	N15 20.1	229 58.9	N 5 30.9	113 08.3	S22 51.5	239 16.4	N10 14.6
	07	54 16.6	268 40.3	19.1	245 00.0	30.3	128 11.1	51.5	254 18.6	14.5
	08	69 19.1	283 39.8	18.1	260 01.0	29.6	143 13.8	51.6	269 20.8	14.4
	09	84 21.6	298 39.2	. . 17.1	275 02.1	. . 29.0	158 16.6	. . 51.6	284 23.0	. . 14.2
	10	99 24.0	313 38.7	16.1	290 03.1	28.4	173 19.3	51.7	299 25.2	14.1
	11	114 26.5	328 38.1	15.1	305 04.1	27.7	188 22.1	51.7	314 27.4	14.0
	12	129 29.0	343 37.6	N15 14.1	320 05.2	N 5 27.1	203 24.8	S22 51.7	329 29.6	N10 13.9
	13	144 31.4	358 37.0	13.1	335 06.2	26.5	218 27.6	51.8	344 31.8	13.8
	14	159 33.9	13 36.5	12.1	350 07.3	25.9	233 30.3	51.8	359 34.0	13.7
	15	174 36.4	28 35.9	. . 11.1	5 08.3	. . 25.2	248 33.1	. . 51.8	14 36.1	. . 13.6
	16	189 38.8	43 35.4	10.1	20 09.3	24.6	263 35.8	51.9	29 38.3	13.5
	17	204 41.3	58 34.9	09.1	35 10.4	24.0	278 38.6	51.9	44 40.5	13.4
	18	219 43.7	73 34.3	N15 08.1	50 11.4	N 5 23.3	293 41.3	S22 51.9	59 42.7	N10 13.3
	19	234 46.2	88 33.8	07.1	65 12.5	22.7	308 44.1	52.0	74 44.9	13.2
	20	249 48.7	103 33.2	06.1	80 13.5	22.1	323 46.8	52.0	89 47.1	13.1
	21	264 51.1	118 32.7	. . 05.1	95 14.5	. . 21.4	338 49.6	. . 52.0	104 49.3	. . 12.9
	22	279 53.6	133 32.1	04.1	110 15.6	20.8	353 52.4	52.1	119 51.5	12.8
	23	294 56.1	148 31.6	03.1	125 16.6	20.2	8 55.1	52.1	134 53.7	12.7
Mer. Pass.		h m 3 27.4	*v* −0.6	*d* 1.0	*v* 1.0	*d* 0.6	*v* 2.8	*d* 0.0	*v* 2.2	*d* 0.1

STARS

Name	SHA	Dec
	° ′	° ′
Acamar	315 21.1	S40 15.8
Achernar	335 29.1	S57 11.2
Acrux	173 14.1	S63 09.1
Adhara	255 15.8	S28 58.8
Aldebaran	290 53.8	N16 31.7
Alioth	166 23.8	N55 55.0
Alkaid	153 01.6	N49 16.4
Al Na'ir	27 47.7	S46 55.0
Alnilam	275 50.3	S 1 11.6
Alphard	218 00.0	S 8 41.7
Alphecca	126 13.9	N26 41.2
Alpheratz	357 47.2	N29 08.3
Altair	62 11.5	N 8 53.5
Ankaa	353 18.9	S42 15.2
Antares	112 30.6	S26 27.2
Arcturus	145 59.0	N19 08.3
Atria	107 35.5	S69 02.9
Avior	234 20.3	S59 32.2
Bellatrix	278 36.2	N 6 21.6
Betelgeuse	271 05.5	N 7 24.7
Canopus	263 58.3	S52 41.8
Capella	280 40.2	N46 00.4
Deneb	49 33.6	N45 18.7
Denebola	182 37.5	N14 31.5
Diphda	348 59.3	S17 56.1
Dubhe	193 56.3	N61 42.4
Elnath	278 17.5	N28 36.9
Eltanin	90 47.4	N51 29.4
Enif	33 50.4	N 9 54.9
Fomalhaut	15 27.6	S29 34.4
Gacrux	172 05.5	S57 10.0
Gienah	175 56.3	S17 35.5
Hadar	148 53.4	S60 25.2
Hamal	328 04.9	N23 30.2
Kaus Aust.	83 48.3	S34 22.9
Kochab	137 19.3	N74 07.4
Markab	13 41.8	N15 15.2
Menkar	314 18.9	N 4 07.6
Menkent	148 12.0	S36 25.0
Miaplacidus	221 41.7	S69 45.2
Mirfak	308 45.9	N49 53.4
Nunki	76 02.5	S26 17.2
Peacock	53 24.2	S56 42.4
Pollux	243 32.5	N28 00.4
Procyon	245 03.9	N 5 12.3
Rasalhague	96 09.6	N12 33.3
Regulus	207 47.7	N11 55.6
Rigel	281 15.8	S 8 11.3
Rigil Kent.	139 57.0	S60 52.6
Sabik	102 16.5	S15 44.2
Schedar	349 44.7	N56 35.0
Shaula	96 26.6	S37 06.7
Sirius	258 37.3	S16 43.5
Spica	158 35.2	S11 12.4
Suhail	222 55.7	S43 28.0
Vega	80 41.1	N38 47.6
Zuben'ubi	137 09.5	S16 04.8

	SHA	Mer. Pass.
	° ′	h m
Venus	215 57.4	13 05
Mars	191 27.4	14 41
Jupiter	73 45.3	22 29
Saturn	200 10.4	14 05

Day	UT d h	SUN GHA ° ′	SUN Dec ° ′	MOON GHA ° ′	v ′	MOON Dec ° ′	d ′	HP ′
TUESDAY	29 00	178 23.1	N18 42.6	228 51.8	2.3	N27 31.8	1.2	60.2
	01	193 23.1	42.0	243 13.1	2.1	27 33.0	1.0	60.2
	02	208 23.1	41.4	257 34.2	2.2	27 34.0	0.7	60.2
	03	223 23.1	. . 40.8	271 55.4	2.2	27 34.7	0.6	60.2
	04	238 23.1	40.2	286 16.6	2.1	27 35.3	0.4	60.2
	05	253 23.2	39.6	300 37.7	2.1	27 35.7	0.1	60.2
	06	268 23.2	N18 39.1	314 58.8	2.1	N27 35.8	0.0	60.2
	07	283 23.2	38.5	329 19.9	2.1	27 35.8	0.3	60.2
	08	298 23.2	37.9	343 41.0	2.1	27 35.5	0.4	60.2
	09	313 23.2	. . 37.3	358 02.1	2.1	27 35.1	0.7	60.2
	10	328 23.3	36.7	12 23.2	2.1	27 34.4	0.9	60.2
	11	343 23.3	36.1	26 44.3	2.1	27 33.5	1.0	60.2
	12	358 23.3	N18 35.5	41 05.4	2.1	N27 32.5	1.3	60.2
	13	13 23.3	34.9	55 26.5	2.1	27 31.2	1.5	60.2
	14	28 23.3	34.3	69 47.6	2.1	27 29.7	1.7	60.2
	15	43 23.4	. . 33.7	84 08.7	2.1	27 28.0	1.9	60.2
	16	58 23.4	33.1	98 29.8	2.2	27 26.1	2.1	60.2
	17	73 23.4	32.5	112 51.0	2.1	27 24.0	2.2	60.3
	18	88 23.4	N18 31.8	127 12.1	2.2	N27 21.8	2.5	60.3
	19	103 23.5	31.2	141 33.3	2.2	27 19.3	2.7	60.3
	20	118 23.5	30.6	155 54.5	2.3	27 16.6	2.9	60.3
	21	133 23.5	. . 30.0	170 15.8	2.3	27 13.7	3.1	60.3
	22	148 23.5	29.4	184 37.1	2.3	27 10.6	3.3	60.3
	23	163 23.6	28.8	198 58.4	2.4	27 07.3	3.6	60.3
WEDNESDAY	30 00	178 23.6	N18 28.2	213 19.8	2.4	N27 03.7	3.7	60.3
	01	193 23.6	27.6	227 41.2	2.4	27 00.0	3.9	60.3
	02	208 23.6	27.0	242 02.6	2.5	26 56.1	4.1	60.3
	03	223 23.7	. . 26.4	256 24.1	2.5	26 52.0	4.2	60.3
	04	238 23.7	25.8	270 45.6	2.6	26 47.8	4.5	60.3
	05	253 23.7	25.2	285 07.2	2.7	26 43.3	4.7	60.3
	06	268 23.7	N18 24.6	299 28.9	2.7	N26 38.6	4.9	60.3
	07	283 23.8	24.0	313 50.6	2.8	26 33.7	5.1	60.2
	08	298 23.8	23.3	328 12.4	2.8	26 28.6	5.2	60.2
	09	313 23.8	. . 22.7	342 34.2	2.9	26 23.4	5.5	60.2
	10	328 23.9	22.1	356 56.1	3.0	26 17.9	5.6	60.2
	11	343 23.9	21.5	11 18.1	3.0	26 12.3	5.9	60.2
	12	358 23.9	N18 20.9	25 40.1	3.1	N26 06.4	6.0	60.2
	13	13 23.9	20.3	40 02.2	3.2	26 00.4	6.2	60.2
	14	28 24.0	19.7	54 24.4	3.3	25 54.2	6.4	60.2
	15	43 24.0	. . 19.1	68 46.7	3.3	25 47.8	6.5	60.2
	16	58 24.0	18.4	83 09.0	3.4	25 41.3	6.8	60.2
	17	73 24.1	17.8	97 31.4	3.5	25 34.5	6.9	60.2
	18	88 24.1	N18 17.2	111 53.9	3.6	N25 27.6	7.1	60.2
	19	103 24.1	16.6	126 16.5	3.7	25 20.5	7.3	60.2
	20	118 24.2	16.0	140 39.2	3.8	25 13.2	7.5	60.2
	21	133 24.2	. . 15.4	155 02.0	3.8	25 05.7	7.6	60.2
	22	148 24.2	14.7	169 24.8	4.0	24 58.1	7.9	60.2
	23	163 24.2	14.1	183 47.8	4.0	24 50.2	7.9	60.2
THURSDAY	31 00	178 24.3	N18 13.5	198 10.8	4.2	N24 42.3	8.2	60.1
	01	193 24.3	12.9	212 34.0	4.2	24 34.1	8.3	60.1
	02	208 24.3	12.3	226 57.2	4.3	24 25.8	8.5	60.1
	03	223 24.4	. . 11.7	241 20.5	4.5	24 17.3	8.6	60.1
	04	238 24.4	11.0	255 44.0	4.5	24 08.7	8.8	60.1
	05	253 24.4	10.4	270 07.5	4.7	23 59.9	9.0	60.1
	06	268 24.5	N18 09.8	284 31.2	4.7	N23 50.9	9.1	60.1
	07	283 24.5	09.2	298 54.9	4.9	23 41.8	9.3	60.1
	08	298 24.5	08.5	313 18.8	4.9	23 32.5	9.5	60.1
	09	313 24.6	. . 07.9	327 42.7	5.1	23 23.0	9.6	60.0
	10	328 24.6	07.3	342 06.8	5.2	23 13.4	9.7	60.0
	11	343 24.6	06.7	356 31.0	5.3	23 03.7	9.9	60.0
	12	358 24.7	N18 06.0	10 55.3	5.4	N22 53.8	10.0	60.0
	13	13 24.7	05.4	25 19.7	5.5	22 43.8	10.2	60.0
	14	28 24.7	04.8	39 44.2	5.6	22 33.6	10.3	60.0
	15	43 24.8	. . 04.2	54 08.8	5.7	22 23.3	10.5	60.0
	16	58 24.8	03.5	68 33.5	5.9	22 12.8	10.6	59.9
	17	73 24.9	02.9	82 58.4	5.9	22 02.2	10.8	59.9
	18	88 24.9	N18 02.3	97 23.3	6.1	N21 51.4	10.8	59.9
	19	103 24.9	01.7	111 48.4	6.2	21 40.6	11.1	59.9
	20	118 25.0	01.0	126 13.6	6.3	21 29.5	11.1	59.9
	21	133 25.0	18 00.4	140 38.9	6.4	21 18.4	11.3	59.9
	22	148 25.0	17 59.8	155 04.3	6.6	21 07.1	11.4	59.8
	23	163 25.1	N17 59.1	169 29.9	6.6	N20 55.7	11.5	59.8
		SD 15.8	*d* 0.6	SD 16.4		16.4		16.3

Lat.	Twilight Naut.	Twilight Civil	Sunrise	Moonrise 29	Moonrise 30	Moonrise 31	Moonrise 1
°	h m	h m	h m	h m	h m	h m	h m
N 72	▭	▭	▭	▭	▭	▭	▭
N 70	////	////	01 10	▭	▭	▭	▭
68	////	////	02 06	▭	▭	▭	01 22
66	////	////	02 39	▭	▭	▭	02 07
64	////	01 29	03 03	▭	▭	00 11	02 36
62	////	02 08	03 21	22 51	24 55	00 55	02 58
60	////	02 35	03 37	23 40	25 24	01 24	03 16
N 58	01 21	02 55	03 50	24 10	00 10	01 47	03 31
56	01 57	03 11	04 01	24 34	00 34	02 05	03 44
54	02 21	03 25	04 10	24 52	00 52	02 20	03 54
52	02 40	03 37	04 19	25 08	01 08	02 33	04 04
50	02 56	03 48	04 27	00 13	01 22	02 45	04 13
45	03 26	04 09	04 43	00 42	01 50	03 09	04 31
N 40	03 49	04 26	04 57	01 05	02 13	03 28	04 46
35	04 06	04 40	05 08	01 23	02 31	03 44	04 58
30	04 21	04 52	05 18	01 40	02 47	03 58	05 09
20	04 43	05 11	05 35	02 07	03 13	04 21	05 28
N 10	05 01	05 27	05 49	02 31	03 36	04 41	05 44
0	05 16	05 41	06 03	02 53	03 58	05 00	05 58
S 10	05 29	05 54	06 16	03 15	04 19	05 19	06 13
20	05 41	06 07	06 30	03 39	04 42	05 39	06 29
30	05 52	06 21	06 47	04 06	05 08	06 02	06 47
35	05 59	06 29	06 56	04 23	05 24	06 15	06 58
40	06 05	06 38	07 06	04 42	05 42	06 31	07 10
45	06 12	06 47	07 19	05 05	06 04	06 49	07 24
S 50	06 19	06 58	07 34	05 35	06 31	07 12	07 41
52	06 22	07 04	07 41	05 49	06 45	07 23	07 49
54	06 26	07 09	07 49	06 06	07 00	07 35	07 58
56	06 30	07 15	07 57	06 27	07 18	07 49	08 08
58	06 34	07 22	08 07	06 52	07 40	08 05	08 19
S 60	06 38	07 30	08 19	07 27	08 09	08 25	08 32

Lat.	Sunset	Twilight Civil	Twilight Naut.	Moonset 29	Moonset 30	Moonset 31	Moonset 1
°	h m	h m	h m	h m	h m	h m	h m
N 72	▭	▭	▭	▭	▭	▭	22 35
N 70	22 54	////	////	▭	▭	▭	21 59
68	22 02	////	////	▭	▭	22 24	21 33
66	21 31	////	////	▭	▭	21 38	21 12
64	21 08	22 38	////	▭	21 29	21 07	20 56
62	20 49	22 01	////	20 34	20 44	20 44	20 42
60	20 34	21 36	////	19 46	20 14	20 25	20 31
N 58	20 22	21 16	22 47	19 15	19 51	20 10	20 21
56	20 11	21 00	22 13	18 51	19 32	19 56	20 12
54	20 01	20 46	21 49	18 32	19 16	19 45	20 04
52	19 53	20 34	21 31	18 16	19 03	19 34	19 57
50	19 45	20 24	21 15	18 02	18 51	19 25	19 50
45	19 29	20 03	20 45	17 34	18 26	19 06	19 36
N 40	19 16	19 46	20 23	17 11	18 06	18 49	19 24
35	19 04	19 32	20 06	16 52	17 49	18 36	19 15
30	18 55	19 20	19 52	16 36	17 34	18 24	19 06
20	18 38	19 01	19 29	16 09	17 10	18 03	18 51
N 10	18 23	18 46	19 12	15 46	16 48	17 45	18 37
0	18 10	18 32	18 57	15 24	16 28	17 29	18 24
S 10	17 57	18 19	18 44	15 02	16 08	17 12	18 12
20	17 43	18 06	18 32	14 38	15 46	16 53	17 58
30	17 27	17 52	18 21	14 10	15 20	16 32	17 42
35	17 17	17 44	18 15	13 54	15 05	16 19	17 33
40	17 07	17 36	18 08	13 35	14 47	16 05	17 22
45	16 54	17 26	18 02	13 12	14 26	15 48	17 10
S 50	16 39	17 15	17 54	12 42	13 59	15 26	16 54
52	16 32	17 10	17 51	12 28	13 46	15 16	16 47
54	16 25	17 04	17 47	12 11	13 31	15 04	16 39
56	16 16	16 58	17 44	11 51	13 13	14 51	16 30
58	16 06	16 51	17 40	11 25	12 52	14 35	16 19
S 60	15 55	16 44	17 35	10 50	12 24	14 16	16 07

Day	SUN Eqn. of Time 00^h	SUN Eqn. of Time 12^h	SUN Mer. Pass.	MOON Mer. Pass. Upper	MOON Mer. Pass. Lower	MOON Age	MOON Phase
d	m s	m s	h m	h m	h m	d	%
29	06 28	06 27	12 06	09 08	21 41	26	12
30	06 26	06 24	12 06	10 13	22 44	27	5 ●
31	06 23	06 21	12 06	11 15	23 44	28	1

	UT d h	ARIES GHA ° ′	VENUS −3.9 GHA ° ′	VENUS Dec ° ′	MARS +1.7 GHA ° ′	MARS Dec ° ′	JUPITER −2.7 GHA ° ′	JUPITER Dec ° ′	SATURN +0.8 GHA ° ′	SATURN Dec ° ′
	1 00	309 58.5	163 31.1	N15 02.1	140 17.7	N 5 19.6	23 57.9	S22 52.1	149 55.9	N10 12.6
	01	325 01.0	178 30.5	01.1	155 18.7	18.9	39 00.6	52.2	164 58.1	12.5
	02	340 03.5	193 30.0	15 00.0	170 19.7	18.3	54 03.4	52.2	180 00.3	12.4
	03	355 05.9	208 29.4	14 59.0	185 20.8	. . 17.7	69 06.1	. . 52.2	195 02.4	. . 12.3
	04	10 08.4	223 28.9	58.0	200 21.8	17.0	84 08.9	52.3	210 04.6	12.2
	05	25 10.9	238 28.4	57.0	215 22.9	16.4	99 11.6	52.3	225 06.8	12.1
	06	40 13.3	253 27.8	N14 56.0	230 23.9	N 5 15.8	114 14.4	S22 52.3	240 09.0	N10 12.0
	07	55 15.8	268 27.3	55.0	245 24.9	15.1	129 17.1	52.4	255 11.2	11.9
	08	70 18.2	283 26.7	54.0	260 26.0	14.5	144 19.9	52.4	270 13.4	11.7
F	09	85 20.7	298 26.2	. . 53.0	275 27.0	. . 13.9	159 22.6	. . 52.4	285 15.6	. . 11.6
R	10	100 23.2	313 25.7	51.9	290 28.1	13.2	174 25.4	52.5	300 17.8	11.5
I	11	115 25.6	328 25.1	50.9	305 29.1	12.6	189 28.1	52.5	315 20.0	11.4
D	12	130 28.1	343 24.6	N14 49.9	320 30.1	N 5 12.0	204 30.8	S22 52.5	330 22.2	N10 11.3
A	13	145 30.6	358 24.1	48.9	335 31.2	11.3	219 33.6	52.6	345 24.4	11.2
Y	14	160 33.0	13 23.5	47.9	350 32.2	10.7	234 36.3	52.6	0 26.5	11.1
	15	175 35.5	28 23.0	. . 46.9	5 33.3	. . 10.1	249 39.1	. . 52.6	15 28.7	. . 11.0
	16	190 38.0	43 22.5	45.8	20 34.3	09.4	264 41.8	52.7	30 30.9	10.9
	17	205 40.4	58 21.9	44.8	35 35.3	08.8	279 44.6	52.7	45 33.1	10.8
	18	220 42.9	73 21.4	N14 43.8	50 36.4	N 5 08.2	294 47.3	S22 52.7	60 35.3	N10 10.6
	19	235 45.3	88 20.9	42.8	65 37.4	07.5	309 50.1	52.8	75 37.5	10.5
	20	250 47.8	103 20.3	41.8	80 38.5	06.9	324 52.8	52.8	90 39.7	10.4
	21	265 50.3	118 19.8	. . 40.7	95 39.5	. . 06.3	339 55.6	. . 52.8	105 41.9	. . 10.3
	22	280 52.7	133 19.3	39.7	110 40.5	05.6	354 58.3	52.9	120 44.1	10.2
	23	295 55.2	148 18.7	38.7	125 41.6	05.0	10 01.1	52.9	135 46.3	10.1
	2 00	310 57.7	163 18.2	N14 37.7	140 42.6	N 5 04.4	25 03.8	S22 52.9	150 48.5	N10 10.0
	01	326 00.1	178 17.7	36.6	155 43.7	03.8	40 06.6	53.0	165 50.6	09.9
	02	341 02.6	193 17.1	35.6	170 44.7	03.1	55 09.3	53.0	180 52.8	09.8
	03	356 05.1	208 16.6	. . 34.6	185 45.7	. . 02.5	70 12.0	. . 53.0	195 55.0	. . 09.7
	04	11 07.5	223 16.1	33.6	200 46.8	01.9	85 14.8	53.1	210 57.2	09.6
	05	26 10.0	238 15.6	32.5	215 47.8	01.2	100 17.5	53.1	225 59.4	09.4
	06	41 12.5	253 15.0	N14 31.5	230 48.9	N 5 00.6	115 20.3	S22 53.1	241 01.6	N10 09.3
	07	56 14.9	268 14.5	30.5	245 49.9	5 00.0	130 23.0	53.2	256 03.8	09.2
S	08	71 17.4	283 14.0	29.4	260 50.9	4 59.3	145 25.8	53.2	271 06.0	09.1
A	09	86 19.8	298 13.5	. . 28.4	275 52.0	. . 58.7	160 28.5	. . 53.2	286 08.2	. . 09.0
T	10	101 22.3	313 12.9	27.4	290 53.0	58.0	175 31.3	53.3	301 10.3	08.9
U	11	116 24.8	328 12.4	26.3	305 54.1	57.4	190 34.0	53.3	316 12.5	08.8
R	12	131 27.2	343 11.9	N14 25.3	320 55.1	N 4 56.8	205 36.7	S22 53.3	331 14.7	N10 08.7
D	13	146 29.7	358 11.4	24.3	335 56.1	56.1	220 39.5	53.4	346 16.9	08.6
A	14	161 32.2	13 10.8	23.2	350 57.2	55.5	235 42.2	53.4	1 19.1	08.5
Y	15	176 34.6	28 10.3	. . 22.2	5 58.2	. . 54.9	250 45.0	. . 53.4	16 21.3	. . 08.3
	16	191 37.1	43 09.8	21.2	20 59.2	54.2	265 47.7	53.5	31 23.5	08.2
	17	206 39.6	58 09.3	20.1	36 00.3	53.6	280 50.5	53.5	46 25.7	08.1
	18	221 42.0	73 08.7	N14 19.1	51 01.3	N 4 53.0	295 53.2	S22 53.5	61 27.9	N10 08.0
	19	236 44.5	88 08.2	18.1	66 02.4	52.3	310 55.9	53.6	76 30.1	07.9
	20	251 47.0	103 07.7	17.0	81 03.4	51.7	325 58.7	53.6	91 32.2	07.8
	21	266 49.4	118 07.2	. . 16.0	96 04.4	. . 51.1	341 01.4	. . 53.6	106 34.4	. . 07.7
	22	281 51.9	133 06.7	15.0	111 05.5	50.4	356 04.2	53.7	121 36.6	07.6
	23	296 54.3	148 06.1	13.9	126 06.5	49.8	11 06.9	53.7	136 38.8	07.5
	3 00	311 56.8	163 05.6	N14 12.9	141 07.6	N 4 49.2	26 09.6	S22 53.7	151 41.0	N10 07.4
	01	326 59.3	178 05.1	11.8	156 08.6	48.5	41 12.4	53.8	166 43.2	07.2
	02	342 01.7	193 04.6	10.8	171 09.6	47.9	56 15.1	53.8	181 45.4	07.1
	03	357 04.2	208 04.1	. . 09.7	186 10.7	. . 47.3	71 17.9	. . 53.8	196 47.6	. . 07.0
	04	12 06.7	223 03.6	08.7	201 11.7	46.6	86 20.6	53.9	211 49.8	06.9
	05	27 09.1	238 03.0	07.7	216 12.7	46.0	101 23.3	53.9	226 51.9	06.8
	06	42 11.6	253 02.5	N14 06.6	231 13.8	N 4 45.4	116 26.1	S22 53.9	241 54.1	N10 06.7
	07	57 14.1	268 02.0	05.6	246 14.8	44.7	131 28.8	54.0	256 56.3	06.6
	08	72 16.5	283 01.5	04.5	261 15.9	44.1	146 31.6	54.0	271 58.5	06.5
S	09	87 19.0	298 01.0	. . 03.5	276 16.9	. . 43.5	161 34.3	. . 54.0	287 00.7	. . 06.4
U	10	102 21.4	313 00.5	02.4	291 17.9	42.8	176 37.0	54.1	302 02.9	06.3
N	11	117 23.9	328 00.0	01.4	306 19.0	42.2	191 39.8	54.1	317 05.1	06.1
D	12	132 26.4	342 59.4	N14 00.3	321 20.0	N 4 41.5	206 42.5	S22 54.1	332 07.3	N10 06.0
A	13	147 28.8	357 58.9	13 59.3	336 21.1	40.9	221 45.2	54.2	347 09.4	05.9
Y	14	162 31.3	12 58.4	58.2	351 22.1	40.3	236 48.0	54.2	2 11.6	05.8
	15	177 33.8	27 57.9	. . 57.2	6 23.1	. . 39.6	251 50.7	. . 54.2	17 13.8	. . 05.7
	16	192 36.2	42 57.4	56.1	21 24.2	39.0	266 53.5	54.2	32 16.0	05.6
	17	207 38.7	57 56.9	55.1	36 25.2	38.4	281 56.2	54.3	47 18.2	05.5
	18	222 41.2	72 56.4	N13 54.0	51 26.2	N 4 37.7	296 58.9	S22 54.3	62 20.4	N10 05.4
	19	237 43.6	87 55.9	53.0	66 27.3	37.1	312 01.7	54.3	77 22.6	05.3
	20	252 46.1	102 55.4	51.9	81 28.3	36.5	327 04.4	54.4	92 24.8	05.1
	21	267 48.6	117 54.9	. . 50.9	96 29.4	. . 35.8	342 07.1	. . 54.4	107 26.9	. . 05.0
	22	282 51.0	132 54.3	49.8	111 30.4	35.2	357 09.9	54.4	122 29.1	04.9
	23	297 53.5	147 53.8	48.8	126 31.4	34.6	12 12.6	54.5	137 31.3	04.8
	Mer. Pass.	h m 3 15.6	v −0.5	d 1.0	v 1.0	d 0.6	v 2.7	d 0.0	v 2.2	d 0.1

STARS

Name	SHA ° ′	Dec ° ′
Acamar	315 21.0	S40 15.8
Achernar	335 29.1	S57 11.2
Acrux	173 14.1	S63 09.1
Adhara	255 15.8	S28 58.8
Aldebaran	290 53.8	N16 31.7
Alioth	166 23.8	N55 55.0
Alkaid	153 01.7	N49 16.4
Al Na'ir	27 47.7	S46 55.0
Alnilam	275 50.3	S 1 11.6
Alphard	218 00.0	S 8 41.7
Alphecca	126 13.9	N26 41.2
Alpheratz	357 47.2	N29 08.3
Altair	62 11.5	N 8 53.5
Ankaa	353 18.9	S42 15.2
Antares	112 30.6	S26 27.2
Arcturus	145 59.0	N19 08.3
Atria	107 35.5	S69 02.9
Avior	234 20.3	S59 32.1
Bellatrix	278 36.1	N 6 21.6
Betelgeuse	271 05.5	N 7 24.7
Canopus	263 58.2	S52 41.7
Capella	280 40.2	N46 00.4
Deneb	49 33.6	N45 18.7
Denebola	182 37.5	N14 31.5
Diphda	348 59.3	S17 56.1
Dubhe	193 56.3	N61 42.4
Elnath	278 17.5	N28 36.9
Eltanin	90 47.4	N51 29.4
Enif	33 50.4	N 9 55.0
Fomalhaut	15 27.6	S29 34.4
Gacrux	172 05.6	S57 10.0
Gienah	175 56.3	S17 35.5
Hadar	148 53.4	S60 25.2
Hamal	328 04.9	N23 30.2
Kaus Aust.	83 48.3	S34 22.9
Kochab	137 19.3	N74 07.4
Markab	13 41.7	N15 15.2
Menkar	314 18.9	N 4 07.6
Menkent	148 12.0	S36 25.0
Miaplacidus	221 41.8	S69 45.2
Mirfak	308 45.8	N49 53.4
Nunki	76 02.5	S26 17.2
Peacock	53 24.2	S56 42.4
Pollux	243 32.5	N28 00.4
Procyon	245 03.8	N 5 12.3
Rasalhague	96 09.6	N12 33.3
Regulus	207 47.7	N11 55.6
Rigel	281 15.8	S 8 11.3
Rigil Kent.	139 57.0	S60 52.6
Sabik	102 16.5	S15 44.2
Schedar	349 44.7	N56 35.0
Shaula	96 26.6	S37 06.8
Sirius	258 37.2	S16 43.5
Spica	158 35.2	S11 12.4
Suhail	222 55.7	S43 28.0
Vega	80 41.1	N38 47.6
Zuben'ubi	137 09.5	S16 04.8

	SHA ° ′	Mer. Pass. h m
Venus	212 20.5	13 07
Mars	189 45.0	14 36
Jupiter	74 06.1	22 16
Saturn	199 50.8	13 55

UT d h	SUN GHA ° ′	SUN Dec ° ′	MOON GHA ° ′	MOON v ′	MOON Dec ° ′	MOON d ′	MOON HP ′
1 00 (FRIDAY)	178 25.1	N17 58.5	183 55.5	6.8	N20 44.2	11.7	59.8
01	193 25.2	57.9	198 21.3	6.9	20 32.5	11.7	59.8
02	208 25.2	57.2	212 47.2	7.0	20 20.8	11.9	59.8
03	223 25.2 . .	56.6	227 13.2	7.1	20 08.9	12.0	59.7
04	238 25.3	56.0	241 39.3	7.3	19 56.9	12.1	59.7
05	253 25.3	55.3	256 05.6	7.3	N19 44.8	12.3	59.7
06	268 25.3	N17 54.7	A total eclipse of the Sun occurs on this date. See page 5.				
07	283 25.4	54.1					
08	298 25.4	53.4					
09	313 25.5 . .	52.8					
10	328 25.5	52.2					
11	343 25.5	51.5					
12	358 25.6	N17 50.9	357 12.5	8.2	N18 16.9	13.0	59.5
13	13 25.6	50.3	11 39.7	8.2	18 03.9	13.0	59.5
14	28 25.7	49.6	26 06.9	8.4	17 50.9	13.2	59.5
15	43 25.7 . .	49.0	40 34.3	8.6	17 37.7	13.3	59.5
16	58 25.8	48.3	55 01.9	8.6	17 24.4	13.3	59.4
17	73 25.8	47.7	69 29.5	8.7	17 11.1	13.4	59.4
18	88 25.8	N17 47.1	83 57.2	8.9	N16 57.7	13.5	59.4
19	103 25.9	46.4	98 25.1	8.9	16 44.2	13.6	59.4
20	118 25.9	45.8	112 53.0	9.1	16 30.6	13.7	59.3
21	133 26.0 . .	45.1	127 21.1	9.2	16 16.9	13.8	59.3
22	148 26.0	44.5	141 49.3	9.3	16 03.1	13.8	59.3
23	163 26.1	43.8	156 17.6	9.4	15 49.3	13.9	59.3
2 00 (SATURDAY)	178 26.1	N17 43.2	170 46.0	9.5	N15 35.4	14.0	59.2
01	193 26.1	42.6	185 14.5	9.6	15 21.4	14.1	59.2
02	208 26.2	41.9	199 43.1	9.7	15 07.3	14.1	59.2
03	223 26.2 . .	41.3	214 11.8	9.9	14 53.2	14.2	59.2
04	238 26.3	40.6	228 40.7	9.9	14 39.0	14.2	59.1
05	253 26.3	40.0	243 09.6	10.0	14 24.8	14.4	59.1
06	268 26.4	N17 39.3	257 38.6	10.2	N14 10.4	14.4	59.1
07	283 26.4	38.7	272 07.8	10.2	13 56.0	14.4	59.1
08	298 26.5	38.0	286 37.0	10.4	13 41.6	14.5	59.0
09	313 26.5 . .	37.4	301 06.4	10.4	13 27.1	14.6	59.0
10	328 26.6	36.7	315 35.8	10.6	13 12.5	14.6	59.0
11	343 26.6	36.1	330 05.4	10.6	12 57.9	14.7	58.9
12	358 26.7	N17 35.4	344 35.0	10.8	N12 43.2	14.7	58.9
13	13 26.7	34.8	359 04.8	10.8	12 28.5	14.8	58.9
14	28 26.7	34.1	13 34.6	10.9	12 13.7	14.9	58.8
15	43 26.8 . .	33.5	28 04.5	11.1	11 58.8	14.8	58.8
16	58 26.8	32.8	42 34.6	11.1	11 44.0	14.9	58.8
17	73 26.9	32.2	57 04.7	11.2	11 29.1	15.0	58.8
18	88 26.9	N17 31.5	71 34.9	11.3	N11 14.1	15.0	58.7
19	103 27.0	30.9	86 05.2	11.4	10 59.1	15.1	58.7
20	118 27.0	30.2	100 35.6	11.5	10 44.0	15.0	58.7
21	133 27.1 . .	29.6	115 06.1	11.6	10 29.0	15.2	58.6
22	148 27.1	28.9	129 36.7	11.6	10 13.8	15.1	58.6
23	163 27.2	28.3	144 07.3	11.8	9 58.7	15.2	58.6
3 00 (SUNDAY)	178 27.2	N17 27.6	158 38.1	11.8	N 9 43.5	15.2	58.5
01	193 27.3	27.0	173 08.9	11.9	9 28.3	15.3	58.5
02	208 27.3	26.3	187 39.8	12.0	9 13.0	15.2	58.5
03	223 27.4 . .	25.6	202 10.8	12.1	8 57.8	15.3	58.4
04	238 27.4	25.0	216 41.9	12.1	8 42.5	15.4	58.4
05	253 27.5	24.3	231 13.0	12.3	8 27.1	15.3	58.4
06	268 27.6	N17 23.7	245 44.3	12.3	N 8 11.8	15.4	58.3
07	283 27.6	23.0	260 15.6	12.4	7 56.4	15.4	58.3
08	298 27.7	22.4	274 47.0	12.4	7 41.0	15.4	58.3
09	313 27.7 . .	21.7	289 18.4	12.6	7 25.6	15.4	58.2
10	328 27.8	21.0	303 50.0	12.6	7 10.2	15.5	58.2
11	343 27.8	20.4	318 21.6	12.6	6 54.7	15.4	58.2
12	358 27.9	N17 19.7	332 53.2	12.8	N 6 39.3	15.5	58.1
13	13 27.9	19.1	347 25.0	12.8	6 23.8	15.5	58.1
14	28 28.0	18.4	1 56.8	12.9	6 08.3	15.5	58.1
15	43 28.0 . .	17.7	16 28.7	12.9	5 52.8	15.5	58.0
16	58 28.1	17.1	31 00.6	13.0	5 37.3	15.5	58.0
17	73 28.1	16.4	45 32.6	13.1	5 21.8	15.5	58.0
18	88 28.2	N17 15.7	60 04.7	13.2	N 5 06.3	15.5	57.9
19	103 28.3	15.1	74 36.9	13.1	4 50.8	15.5	57.9
20	118 28.3	14.4	89 09.0	13.3	4 35.3	15.6	57.9
21	133 28.4 . .	13.7	103 41.3	13.3	4 19.7	15.5	57.8
22	148 28.4	13.1	118 13.6	13.4	4 04.2	15.5	57.8
23	163 28.5	12.4	132 46.0	13.4	N 3 48.7	15.5	57.8
	SD 15.8	*d* 0.6	SD		16.2	16.0	15.8

Lat. °	Twilight Naut. h m	Twilight Civil h m	Sunrise h m	Moonrise 1 h m	Moonrise 2 h m	Moonrise 3 h m	Moonrise 4 h m
N 72	▭	▭	▭	▭	03 08	05 53	08 10
N 70	////	////	01 38	▭	03 43	06 06	08 11
68	////	////	02 22	01 22	04 07	06 16	08 13
66	////	00 43	02 51	02 07	04 25	06 25	08 14
64	////	01 47	03 12	02 36	04 40	06 32	08 15
62	////	02 20	03 29	02 58	04 53	06 38	08 16
60	00 39	02 44	03 44	03 16	05 03	06 43	08 17
N 58	01 37	03 03	03 56	03 31	05 12	06 48	08 18
56	02 07	03 18	04 06	03 44	05 20	06 52	08 18
54	02 30	03 31	04 16	03 54	05 27	06 55	08 19
52	02 47	03 43	04 24	04 04	05 34	06 59	08 20
50	03 02	03 53	04 31	04 13	05 39	07 02	08 20
45	03 31	04 13	04 47	04 31	05 51	07 08	08 21
N 40	03 52	04 29	04 59	04 46	06 01	07 13	08 22
35	04 09	04 43	05 10	04 58	06 10	07 18	08 23
30	04 23	04 54	05 20	05 09	06 17	07 22	08 23
20	04 45	05 12	05 36	05 28	06 30	07 29	08 25
N 10	05 02	05 28	05 50	05 44	06 41	07 35	08 26
0	05 16	05 41	06 03	05 58	06 52	07 41	08 27
S 10	05 28	05 54	06 16	06 13	07 02	07 46	08 28
20	05 40	06 06	06 29	06 29	07 13	07 53	08 29
30	05 51	06 19	06 44	06 47	07 26	07 59	08 30
35	05 56	06 27	06 53	06 58	07 33	08 03	08 31
40	06 02	06 35	07 03	07 10	07 41	08 08	08 32
45	06 08	06 44	07 15	07 24	07 51	08 13	08 32
S 50	06 15	06 54	07 29	07 41	08 02	08 19	08 34
52	06 18	06 59	07 36	07 49	08 07	08 22	08 34
54	06 22	07 04	07 43	07 58	08 13	08 25	08 35
56	06 25	07 10	07 52	08 08	08 20	08 28	08 35
58	06 29	07 17	08 01	08 19	08 27	08 32	08 36
S 60	06 33	07 24	08 12	08 32	08 35	08 36	08 37

Lat. °	Sunset h m	Twilight Civil h m	Twilight Naut. h m	Moonset 1 h m	Moonset 2 h m	Moonset 3 h m	Moonset 4 h m
N 72	▭	▭	▭	22 35	21 35	20 57	20 25
N 70	22 28	////	////	21 59	21 19	20 52	20 28
68	21 47	////	////	21 33	21 07	20 47	20 30
66	21 19	23 16	////	21 12	20 56	20 43	20 31
64	20 58	22 21	////	20 56	20 47	20 40	20 33
62	20 41	21 49	////	20 42	20 40	20 37	20 34
60	20 27	21 26	23 21	20 31	20 33	20 34	20 35
N 58	20 15	21 08	22 31	20 21	20 27	20 32	20 36
56	20 05	20 52	22 02	20 12	20 22	20 30	20 37
54	19 56	20 40	21 40	20 04	20 17	20 28	20 38
52	19 48	20 28	21 23	19 57	20 13	20 26	20 38
50	19 40	20 19	21 09	19 50	20 09	20 25	20 39
45	19 25	19 58	20 40	19 36	20 01	20 21	20 40
N 40	19 12	19 42	20 19	19 24	19 53	20 18	20 42
35	19 02	19 29	20 03	19 15	19 47	20 16	20 43
30	18 52	19 18	19 49	19 06	19 42	20 14	20 44
20	18 36	19 00	19 27	18 51	19 32	20 10	20 45
N 10	18 23	18 45	19 11	18 37	19 24	20 06	20 47
0	18 10	18 31	18 57	18 24	19 16	20 03	20 48
S 10	17 57	18 19	18 44	18 12	19 07	20 00	20 49
20	17 44	18 07	18 33	17 58	18 59	19 56	20 50
30	17 28	17 53	18 22	17 42	18 49	19 52	20 52
35	17 19	17 46	18 17	17 33	18 43	19 49	20 53
40	17 09	17 38	18 11	17 22	18 36	19 47	20 54
45	16 58	17 29	18 05	17 10	18 28	19 43	20 55
S 50	16 44	17 19	17 58	16 54	18 19	19 40	20 56
52	16 37	17 14	17 55	16 47	18 15	19 38	20 57
54	16 30	17 09	17 52	16 39	18 10	19 36	20 58
56	16 21	17 03	17 48	16 30	18 04	19 34	20 59
58	16 12	16 57	17 45	16 19	17 58	19 31	20 59
S 60	16 02	16 50	17 41	16 07	17 51	19 28	21 00

Day	SUN Eqn. of Time 00h	SUN Eqn. of Time 12h	SUN Mer. Pass.	MOON Mer. Pass. Upper	MOON Mer. Pass. Lower	MOON Age	MOON Phase
d	m s	m s	h m	h m	h m	d	%
1	06 20	06 18	12 06	12 12	24 38	00	0
2	06 16	06 13	12 06	13 04	00 38	01	2
3	06 11	06 09	12 06	13 52	01 28	02	6

UT	ARIES	VENUS −3.8		MARS +1.7		JUPITER −2.7		SATURN +0.8	
	GHA	GHA	Dec	GHA	Dec	GHA	Dec	GHA	Dec
d h	° ′	° ′	° ′	° ′	° ′	° ′	° ′	° ′	° ′
4 00 MONDAY	312 55.9	162 53.3	N13 47.7	141 32.5	N 4 33.9	27 15.3	S22 54.5	152 33.5	N10 04.7
01	327 58.4	177 52.8	46.6	156 33.5	33.3	42 18.1	54.5	167 35.7	04.6
02	343 00.9	192 52.3	45.6	171 34.5	32.6	57 20.8	54.6	182 37.9	04.5
03	358 03.3	207 51.8	44.5	186 35.6	32.0	72 23.5	54.6	197 40.1	04.4
04	13 05.8	222 51.3	43.5	201 36.6	31.4	87 26.3	54.6	212 42.3	04.3
05	28 08.3	237 50.8	42.4	216 37.7	30.7	102 29.0	54.7	227 44.4	04.1
06	43 10.7	252 50.3	N13 41.4	231 38.7	N 4 30.1	117 31.7	S22 54.7	242 46.6	N10 04.0
07	58 13.2	267 49.8	40.3	246 39.7	29.5	132 34.5	54.7	257 48.8	03.9
08	73 15.7	282 49.3	39.2	261 40.8	28.8	147 37.2	54.8	272 51.0	03.8
09	88 18.1	297 48.8	38.2	276 41.8	28.2	162 39.9	54.8	287 53.2	03.7
10	103 20.6	312 48.3	37.1	291 42.8	27.5	177 42.7	54.8	302 55.4	03.6
11	118 23.0	327 47.8	36.0	306 43.9	26.9	192 45.4	54.8	317 57.6	03.5
12	133 25.5	342 47.3	N13 35.0	321 44.9	N 4 26.3	207 48.1	S22 54.9	332 59.8	N10 03.4
13	148 28.0	357 46.8	33.9	336 46.0	25.6	222 50.9	54.9	348 01.9	03.3
14	163 30.4	12 46.3	32.8	351 47.0	25.0	237 53.6	54.9	3 04.1	03.2
15	178 32.9	27 45.8	31.8	6 48.0	24.4	252 56.3	55.0	18 06.3	03.0
16	193 35.4	42 45.3	30.7	21 49.1	23.7	267 59.1	55.0	33 08.5	02.9
17	208 37.8	57 44.8	29.6	36 50.1	23.1	283 01.8	55.0	48 10.7	02.8
18	223 40.3	72 44.3	N13 28.6	51 51.1	N 4 22.4	298 04.5	S22 55.1	63 12.9	N10 02.7
19	238 42.8	87 43.8	27.5	66 52.2	21.8	313 07.3	55.1	78 15.1	02.6
20	253 45.2	102 43.3	26.4	81 53.2	21.2	328 10.0	55.1	93 17.3	02.5
21	268 47.7	117 42.8	25.4	96 54.2	20.5	343 12.7	55.2	108 19.4	02.4
22	283 50.2	132 42.3	24.3	111 55.3	19.9	358 15.4	55.2	123 21.6	02.3
23	298 52.6	147 41.8	23.2	126 56.3	19.3	13 18.2	55.2	138 23.8	02.2
5 00 TUESDAY	313 55.1	162 41.3	N13 22.2	141 57.4	N 4 18.6	28 20.9	S22 55.3	153 26.0	N10 02.0
01	328 57.5	177 40.8	21.1	156 58.4	18.0	43 23.6	55.3	168 28.2	01.9
02	344 00.0	192 40.3	20.0	171 59.4	17.3	58 26.4	55.3	183 30.4	01.8
03	359 02.5	207 39.8	18.9	187 00.5	16.7	73 29.1	55.3	198 32.6	01.7
04	14 04.9	222 39.3	17.9	202 01.5	16.1	88 31.8	55.4	213 34.7	01.6
05	29 07.4	237 38.8	16.8	217 02.5	15.4	103 34.5	55.4	228 36.9	01.5
06	44 09.9	252 38.3	N13 15.7	232 03.6	N 4 14.8	118 37.3	S22 55.4	243 39.1	N10 01.4
07	59 12.3	267 37.8	14.6	247 04.6	14.2	133 40.0	55.5	258 41.3	01.3
08	74 14.8	282 37.4	13.6	262 05.6	13.5	148 42.7	55.5	273 43.5	01.2
09	89 17.3	297 36.9	12.5	277 06.7	12.9	163 45.4	55.5	288 45.7	01.0
10	104 19.7	312 36.4	11.4	292 07.7	12.2	178 48.2	55.6	303 47.9	00.9
11	119 22.2	327 35.9	10.3	307 08.8	11.6	193 50.9	55.6	318 50.0	00.8
12	134 24.7	342 35.4	N13 09.3	322 09.8	N 4 11.0	208 53.6	S22 55.6	333 52.2	N10 00.7
13	149 27.1	357 34.9	08.2	337 10.8	10.3	223 56.4	55.7	348 54.4	00.6
14	164 29.6	12 34.4	07.1	352 11.9	09.7	238 59.1	55.7	3 56.6	00.5
15	179 32.0	27 33.9	06.0	7 12.9	09.0	254 01.8	55.7	18 58.8	00.4
16	194 34.5	42 33.4	04.9	22 13.9	08.4	269 04.5	55.7	34 01.0	00.3
17	209 37.0	57 32.9	03.9	37 15.0	07.8	284 07.3	55.8	49 03.2	00.1
18	224 39.4	72 32.5	N13 02.8	52 16.0	N 4 07.1	299 10.0	S22 55.8	64 05.3	N10 00.0
19	239 41.9	87 32.0	01.7	67 17.0	06.5	314 12.7	55.8	79 07.5	9 59.9
20	254 44.4	102 31.5	13 00.6	82 18.1	05.8	329 15.4	55.9	94 09.7	59.8
21	269 46.8	117 31.0	12 59.5	97 19.1	05.2	344 18.1	55.9	109 11.9	59.7
22	284 49.3	132 30.5	58.4	112 20.1	04.6	359 20.9	55.9	124 14.1	59.6
23	299 51.8	147 30.0	57.4	127 21.2	03.9	14 23.6	56.0	139 16.3	59.5
6 00 WEDNESDAY	314 54.2	162 29.5	N12 56.3	142 22.2	N 4 03.3	29 26.3	S22 56.0	154 18.5	N 9 59.4
01	329 56.7	177 29.1	55.2	157 23.3	02.6	44 29.0	56.0	169 20.6	59.3
02	344 59.1	192 28.6	54.1	172 24.3	02.0	59 31.8	56.0	184 22.8	59.1
03	0 01.6	207 28.1	53.0	187 25.3	01.4	74 34.5	56.1	199 25.0	59.0
04	15 04.1	222 27.6	51.9	202 26.4	00.7	89 37.2	56.1	214 27.2	58.9
05	30 06.5	237 27.1	50.8	217 27.4	4 00.1	104 39.9	56.1	229 29.4	58.8
06	45 09.0	252 26.6	N12 49.7	232 28.4	N 3 59.4	119 42.7	S22 56.2	244 31.6	N 9 58.7
07	60 11.5	267 26.2	48.7	247 29.5	58.8	134 45.4	56.2	259 33.7	58.6
08	75 13.9	282 25.7	47.6	262 30.5	58.2	149 48.1	56.2	274 35.9	58.5
09	90 16.4	297 25.2	46.5	277 31.5	57.5	164 50.8	56.3	289 38.1	58.4
10	105 18.9	312 24.7	45.4	292 32.6	56.9	179 53.5	56.3	304 40.3	58.3
11	120 21.3	327 24.2	44.3	307 33.6	56.2	194 56.3	56.3	319 42.5	58.1
12	135 23.8	342 23.8	N12 43.2	322 34.6	N 3 55.6	209 59.0	S22 56.3	334 44.7	N 9 58.0
13	150 26.3	357 23.3	42.1	337 35.7	55.0	225 01.7	56.4	349 46.9	57.9
14	165 28.7	12 22.8	41.0	352 36.7	54.3	240 04.4	56.4	4 49.0	57.8
15	180 31.2	27 22.3	39.9	7 37.7	53.7	255 07.1	56.4	19 51.2	57.7
16	195 33.6	42 21.8	38.8	22 38.8	53.0	270 09.9	56.5	34 53.4	57.6
17	210 36.1	57 21.4	37.7	37 39.8	52.4	285 12.6	56.5	49 55.6	57.5
18	225 38.6	72 20.9	N12 36.6	52 40.8	N 3 51.8	300 15.3	S22 56.5	64 57.8	N 9 57.4
19	240 41.0	87 20.4	35.5	67 41.9	51.1	315 18.0	56.5	80 00.0	57.2
20	255 43.5	102 19.9	34.4	82 42.9	50.5	330 20.7	56.6	95 02.1	57.1
21	270 46.0	117 19.5	33.3	97 44.0	49.8	345 23.4	56.6	110 04.3	57.0
22	285 48.4	132 19.0	32.2	112 45.0	49.2	0 26.2	56.6	125 06.5	56.9
23	300 50.9	147 18.5	31.1	127 46.0	48.6	15 28.9	56.7	140 08.7	56.8
Mer. Pass.	h m 3 03.8	*v* −0.5	*d* 1.1	*v* 1.0	*d* 0.6	*v* 2.7	*d* 0.0	*v* 2.2	*d* 0.1

STARS Name	SHA	Dec
	° ′	° ′
Acamar	315 21.0	S40 15.8
Achernar	335 29.0	S57 11.2
Acrux	173 14.1	S63 09.1
Adhara	255 15.7	S28 58.8
Aldebaran	290 53.7	N16 31.7
Alioth	166 23.9	N55 55.0
Alkaid	153 01.7	N49 16.4
Al Na'ir	27 47.7	S46 55.0
Alnilam	275 50.3	S 1 11.6
Alphard	218 00.0	S 8 41.7
Alphecca	126 14.0	N26 41.3
Alpheratz	357 47.1	N29 08.3
Altair	62 11.5	N 8 53.5
Ankaa	353 18.9	S42 15.2
Antares	112 30.6	S26 27.2
Arcturus	145 59.0	N19 08.3
Atria	107 35.5	S69 02.9
Avior	234 20.3	S59 32.1
Bellatrix	278 36.1	N 6 21.6
Betelgeuse	271 05.5	N 7 24.7
Canopus	263 58.2	S52 41.7
Capella	280 40.2	N46 00.4
Deneb	49 33.6	N45 18.7
Denebola	182 37.6	N14 31.5
Diphda	348 59.3	S17 56.1
Dubhe	193 56.4	N61 42.4
Elnath	278 17.5	N28 36.9
Eltanin	90 47.4	N51 29.4
Enif	33 50.4	N 9 55.0
Fomalhaut	15 27.6	S29 34.4
Gacrux	172 05.6	S57 09.9
Gienah	175 56.3	S17 35.5
Hadar	148 53.5	S60 25.2
Hamal	328 04.9	N23 30.3
Kaus Aust.	83 48.3	S34 22.9
Kochab	137 19.4	N74 07.4
Markab	13 41.7	N15 15.2
Menkar	314 18.9	N 4 07.6
Menkent	148 12.1	S36 25.0
Miaplacidus	221 41.8	S69 45.1
Mirfak	308 45.8	N49 53.4
Nunki	76 02.5	S26 17.2
Peacock	53 24.2	S56 42.4
Pollux	243 32.5	N28 00.4
Procyon	245 03.8	N 5 12.3
Rasalhague	96 09.6	N12 33.3
Regulus	207 47.7	N11 55.6
Rigel	281 15.7	S 8 11.3
Rigil Kent.	139 57.0	S60 52.6
Sabik	102 16.5	S15 44.2
Schedar	349 44.7	N56 35.0
Shaula	96 26.6	S37 06.8
Sirius	258 37.2	S16 43.5
Spica	158 35.2	S11 12.4
Suhail	222 55.7	S43 28.0
Vega	80 41.1	N38 47.6
Zuben'ubi	137 09.5	S16 04.8

	SHA	Mer. Pass.
	° ′	h m
Venus	208 46.2	13 10
Mars	188 02.3	14 31
Jupiter	74 25.8	22 03
Saturn	199 30.9	13 44

UT	Day	SUN GHA	SUN Dec	MOON GHA	v	MOON Dec	d	HP
d h		° ′	° ′	° ′	′	° ′	′	′
4 00	MONDAY	178 28.5	N17 11.7	147 18.4	13.5	N 3 33.2	15.5	57.7
01		193 28.6	11.1	161 50.9	13.5	3 17.7	15.6	57.7
02		208 28.7	10.4	176 23.4	13.6	3 02.1	15.5	57.7
03		223 28.7	. . 09.7	190 56.0	13.7	2 46.6	15.5	57.6
04		238 28.8	09.1	205 28.7	13.7	2 31.1	15.5	57.6
05		253 28.8	08.4	220 01.4	13.7	2 15.6	15.4	57.6
06		268 28.9	N17 07.7	234 34.1	13.8	N 2 00.2	15.5	57.5
07		283 28.9	07.1	249 06.9	13.8	1 44.7	15.5	57.5
08		298 29.0	06.4	263 39.7	13.9	1 29.2	15.4	57.5
09		313 29.1	. . 05.7	278 12.6	13.9	1 13.8	15.5	57.4
10		328 29.1	05.0	292 45.5	14.0	0 58.3	15.4	57.4
11		343 29.2	04.4	307 18.5	14.0	0 42.9	15.4	57.4
12		358 29.2	N17 03.7	321 51.5	14.0	N 0 27.5	15.4	57.3
13		13 29.3	03.0	336 24.5	14.1	N 0 12.1	15.3	57.3
14		28 29.4	02.4	350 57.6	14.1	S 0 03.2	15.4	57.2
15		43 29.4	. . 01.7	5 30.7	14.2	0 18.6	15.3	57.2
16		58 29.5	01.0	20 03.9	14.2	0 33.9	15.3	57.2
17		73 29.5	17 00.3	34 37.1	14.2	0 49.2	15.3	57.1
18		88 29.6	N16 59.7	49 10.3	14.3	S 1 04.5	15.2	57.1
19		103 29.7	59.0	63 43.6	14.2	1 19.7	15.3	57.1
20		118 29.7	58.3	78 16.8	14.4	1 35.0	15.2	57.0
21		133 29.8	. . 57.6	92 50.2	14.3	1 50.2	15.1	57.0
22		148 29.9	57.0	107 23.5	14.4	2 05.3	15.2	57.0
23		163 29.9	56.3	121 56.9	14.4	2 20.5	15.1	56.9
5 00	TUESDAY	178 30.0	N16 55.6	136 30.3	14.4	S 2 35.6	15.1	56.9
01		193 30.1	54.9	151 03.7	14.5	2 50.7	15.1	56.9
02		208 30.1	54.2	165 37.2	14.4	3 05.8	15.0	56.8
03		223 30.2	. . 53.6	180 10.6	14.5	3 20.8	15.0	56.8
04		238 30.2	52.9	194 44.1	14.5	3 35.8	14.9	56.8
05		253 30.3	52.2	209 17.6	14.6	3 50.7	15.0	56.7
06		268 30.4	N16 51.5	223 51.2	14.5	S 4 05.7	14.8	56.7
07		283 30.4	50.8	238 24.7	14.6	4 20.5	14.9	56.7
08		298 30.5	50.2	252 58.3	14.6	4 35.4	14.8	56.6
09		313 30.6	. . 49.5	267 31.9	14.6	4 50.2	14.8	56.6
10		328 30.6	48.8	282 05.5	14.6	5 05.0	14.7	56.6
11		343 30.7	48.1	296 39.1	14.6	5 19.7	14.7	56.5
12		358 30.8	N16 47.4	311 12.7	14.7	S 5 34.4	14.7	56.5
13		13 30.8	46.7	325 46.4	14.6	5 49.1	14.6	56.5
14		28 30.9	46.0	340 20.0	14.7	6 03.7	14.5	56.4
15		43 31.0	. . 45.4	354 53.7	14.7	6 18.2	14.6	56.4
16		58 31.0	44.7	9 27.4	14.6	6 32.8	14.4	56.4
17		73 31.1	44.0	24 01.0	14.7	6 47.2	14.5	56.3
18		88 31.2	N16 43.3	38 34.7	14.7	S 7 01.7	14.3	56.3
19		103 31.2	42.6	53 08.4	14.7	7 16.0	14.4	56.3
20		118 31.3	41.9	67 42.1	14.7	7 30.4	14.3	56.2
21		133 31.4	. . 41.2	82 15.8	14.7	7 44.7	14.2	56.2
22		148 31.4	40.6	96 49.5	14.7	7 58.9	14.2	56.2
23		163 31.5	39.9	111 23.2	14.7	8 13.1	14.1	56.2
6 00	WEDNESDAY	178 31.6	N16 39.2	125 56.9	14.7	S 8 27.2	14.1	56.1
01		193 31.7	38.5	140 30.6	14.7	8 41.3	14.1	56.1
02		208 31.7	37.8	155 04.3	14.7	8 55.4	13.9	56.1
03		223 31.8	. . 37.1	169 38.0	14.6	9 09.3	14.0	56.0
04		238 31.9	36.4	184 11.6	14.7	9 23.3	13.8	56.0
05		253 31.9	35.7	198 45.3	14.7	9 37.1	13.9	56.0
06		268 32.0	N16 35.0	213 19.0	14.7	S 9 51.0	13.7	55.9
07		283 32.1	34.3	227 52.7	14.6	10 04.7	13.7	55.9
08		298 32.2	33.6	242 26.3	14.7	10 18.4	13.7	55.9
09		313 32.2	. . 32.9	257 00.0	14.6	10 32.1	13.6	55.9
10		328 32.3	32.3	271 33.6	14.6	10 45.7	13.5	55.8
11		343 32.4	31.6	286 07.2	14.6	10 59.2	13.5	55.8
12		358 32.4	N16 30.9	300 40.8	14.6	S11 12.7	13.4	55.8
13		13 32.5	30.2	315 14.4	14.6	11 26.1	13.3	55.7
14		28 32.6	29.5	329 48.0	14.6	11 39.4	13.3	55.7
15		43 32.7	. . 28.8	344 21.6	14.6	11 52.7	13.2	55.7
16		58 32.7	28.1	358 55.2	14.5	12 05.9	13.2	55.7
17		73 32.8	27.4	13 28.7	14.5	12 19.1	13.1	55.6
18		88 32.9	N16 26.7	28 02.2	14.5	S12 32.2	13.0	55.6
19		103 33.0	26.0	42 35.7	14.5	12 45.2	12.9	55.6
20		118 33.0	25.3	57 09.2	14.5	12 58.1	12.9	55.5
21		133 33.1	. . 24.6	71 42.7	14.4	13 11.0	12.9	55.5
22		148 33.2	23.9	86 16.1	14.4	13 23.9	12.7	55.5
23		163 33.3	23.2	100 49.5	14.4	S13 36.6	12.7	55.5
		SD 15.8	*d* 0.7	SD		15.6	15.4	15.2

Lat.	Twilight Naut.	Twilight Civil	Sunrise	Moonrise 4	Moonrise 5	Moonrise 6	Moonrise 7
°	h m	h m	h m	h m	h m	h m	h m
N 72	////	////	00 45	08 10	10 18	12 32	15 29
N 70	////	////	02 00	08 11	10 10	12 12	14 30
68	////	////	02 36	08 13	10 04	11 56	13 56
66	////	01 18	03 02	08 14	09 59	11 43	13 32
64	////	02 03	03 22	08 15	09 54	11 33	13 13
62	////	02 32	03 38	08 16	09 51	11 24	12 58
60	01 10	02 54	03 51	08 17	09 47	11 16	12 45
N 58	01 51	03 11	04 02	08 18	09 44	11 09	12 34
56	02 18	03 25	04 12	08 18	09 42	11 03	12 25
54	02 38	03 37	04 21	08 19	09 40	10 58	12 16
52	02 54	03 48	04 28	08 20	09 37	10 53	12 09
50	03 08	03 58	04 35	08 20	09 36	10 49	12 02
45	03 35	04 17	04 50	08 21	09 31	10 40	11 48
N 40	03 56	04 32	05 02	08 22	09 28	10 32	11 36
35	04 12	04 45	05 13	08 23	09 25	10 26	11 26
30	04 25	04 56	05 22	08 23	09 23	10 20	11 18
20	04 46	05 14	05 37	08 25	09 18	10 10	11 03
N 10	05 02	05 28	05 50	08 26	09 14	10 02	10 50
0	05 16	05 41	06 02	08 27	09 11	09 54	10 38
S 10	05 27	05 53	06 15	08 28	09 07	09 46	10 26
20	05 38	06 05	06 28	08 29	09 03	09 38	10 13
30	05 49	06 17	06 42	08 30	08 59	09 28	09 59
35	05 54	06 24	06 51	08 31	08 57	09 23	09 51
40	05 59	06 32	07 00	08 32	08 54	09 17	09 41
45	06 05	06 40	07 11	08 32	08 51	09 10	09 30
S 50	06 11	06 50	07 25	08 34	08 47	09 02	09 17
52	06 14	06 55	07 31	08 34	08 46	08 58	09 11
54	06 17	06 59	07 38	08 35	08 44	08 53	09 04
56	06 20	07 05	07 46	08 35	08 42	08 49	08 57
58	06 23	07 11	07 54	08 36	08 40	08 44	08 49
S 60	06 27	07 17	08 04	08 37	08 37	08 38	08 39

Lat.	Sunset	Twilight Civil	Twilight Naut.	Moonset 4	Moonset 5	Moonset 6	Moonset 7
°	h m	h m	h m	h m	h m	h m	h m
N 72	23 10	////	////	20 25	19 52	19 11	17 47
N 70	22 07	////	////	20 28	20 03	19 33	18 48
68	21 32	////	////	20 30	20 12	19 51	19 23
66	21 07	22 47	////	20 31	20 19	20 05	19 49
64	20 48	22 05	////	20 33	20 25	20 17	20 08
62	20 32	21 37	////	20 34	20 31	20 28	20 25
60	20 19	21 16	22 55	20 35	20 35	20 36	20 38
N 58	20 08	20 59	22 17	20 36	20 40	20 44	20 50
56	19 59	20 45	21 51	20 37	20 44	20 51	21 00
54	19 50	20 33	21 32	20 38	20 47	20 57	21 09
52	19 42	20 22	21 16	20 38	20 50	21 03	21 17
50	19 36	20 13	21 02	20 39	20 53	21 08	21 25
45	19 21	19 54	20 35	20 40	20 59	21 19	21 40
N 40	19 09	19 39	20 15	20 42	21 04	21 28	21 53
35	18 59	19 26	19 59	20 43	21 09	21 36	22 04
30	18 50	19 16	19 46	20 44	21 13	21 42	22 14
20	18 35	18 58	19 25	20 45	21 20	21 54	22 31
N 10	18 22	18 44	19 09	20 47	21 26	22 05	22 46
0	18 09	18 31	18 56	20 48	21 31	22 15	22 59
S 10	17 57	18 19	18 44	20 49	21 37	22 25	23 13
20	17 45	18 07	18 34	20 50	21 43	22 36	23 28
30	17 30	17 55	18 24	20 52	21 50	22 48	23 45
35	17 22	17 48	18 18	20 53	21 54	22 55	23 55
40	17 12	17 41	18 13	20 54	21 59	23 03	24 07
45	17 01	17 32	18 07	20 55	22 04	23 13	24 20
S 50	16 48	17 22	18 01	20 56	22 11	23 24	24 37
52	16 41	17 18	17 59	20 57	22 14	23 30	24 45
54	16 35	17 13	17 56	20 58	22 17	23 36	24 53
56	16 27	17 08	17 53	20 59	22 21	23 42	25 03
58	16 18	17 02	17 50	20 59	22 25	23 50	25 15
S 60	16 08	16 56	17 46	21 00	22 30	23 58	25 28

Day	SUN Eqn. of Time 00^h	SUN Eqn. of Time 12^h	SUN Mer. Pass.	MOON Mer. Pass. Upper	MOON Mer. Pass. Lower	MOON Age	MOON Phase
d	m s	m s	h m	h m	h m	d	%
4	06 06	06 03	12 06	14 37	02 15	03	12
5	06 00	05 57	12 06	15 21	02 59	04	19
6	05 54	05 50	12 06	16 04	03 43	05	28

	UT (d h)	ARIES GHA	VENUS −3.8 GHA	VENUS Dec	MARS +1.7 GHA	MARS Dec	JUPITER −2.6 GHA	JUPITER Dec	SATURN +0.8 GHA	SATURN Dec
		° ′	° ′	° ′	° ′	° ′	° ′	° ′	° ′	° ′
	7 00	315 53.4	162 18.0	N12 30.0	142 47.1	N 3 47.9	30 31.6	S22 56.7	155 10.9	N 9 56.7
	01	330 55.8	177 17.6	28.9	157 48.1	47.3	45 34.3	56.7	170 13.1	56.6
	02	345 58.3	192 17.1	27.8	172 49.1	46.6	60 37.0	56.8	185 15.2	56.5
	03	1 00.7	207 16.6	. . 26.7	187 50.2	. . 46.0	75 39.7	. . 56.8	200 17.4	. . 56.3
	04	16 03.2	222 16.2	25.6	202 51.2	45.3	90 42.5	56.8	215 19.6	56.2
	05	31 05.7	237 15.7	24.5	217 52.2	44.7	105 45.2	56.8	230 21.8	56.1
	06	46 08.1	252 15.2	N12 23.4	232 53.3	N 3 44.1	120 47.9	S22 56.9	245 24.0	N 9 56.0
	07	61 10.6	267 14.7	22.3	247 54.3	43.4	135 50.6	56.9	260 26.2	55.9
T	08	76 13.1	282 14.3	21.2	262 55.3	42.8	150 53.3	56.9	275 28.4	55.8
H	09	91 15.5	297 13.8	. . 20.1	277 56.4	. . 42.1	165 56.0	. . 57.0	290 30.5	. . 55.7
U	10	106 18.0	312 13.3	19.0	292 57.4	41.5	180 58.7	57.0	305 32.7	55.6
R	11	121 20.5	327 12.9	17.9	307 58.4	40.9	196 01.5	57.0	320 34.9	55.5
S	12	136 22.9	342 12.4	N12 16.8	322 59.5	N 3 40.2	211 04.2	S22 57.0	335 37.1	N 9 55.3
D	13	151 25.4	357 11.9	15.7	338 00.5	39.6	226 06.9	57.1	350 39.3	55.2
A	14	166 27.9	12 11.5	14.6	353 01.5	38.9	241 09.6	57.1	5 41.5	55.1
Y	15	181 30.3	27 11.0	. . 13.5	8 02.6	. . 38.3	256 12.3	. . 57.1	20 43.6	. . 55.0
	16	196 32.8	42 10.5	12.4	23 03.6	37.6	271 15.0	57.2	35 45.8	54.9
	17	211 35.2	57 10.1	11.3	38 04.6	37.0	286 17.7	57.2	50 48.0	54.8
	18	226 37.7	72 09.6	N12 10.2	53 05.7	N 3 36.4	301 20.5	S22 57.2	65 50.2	N 9 54.7
	19	241 40.2	87 09.1	09.0	68 06.7	35.7	316 23.2	57.2	80 52.4	54.6
	20	256 42.6	102 08.7	07.9	83 07.7	35.1	331 25.9	57.3	95 54.6	54.4
	21	271 45.1	117 08.2	. . 06.8	98 08.8	. . 34.4	346 28.6	. . 57.3	110 56.7	. . 54.3
	22	286 47.6	132 07.7	05.7	113 09.8	33.8	1 31.3	57.3	125 58.9	54.2
	23	301 50.0	147 07.3	04.6	128 10.8	33.1	16 34.0	57.4	141 01.1	54.1
	8 00	316 52.5	162 06.8	N12 03.5	143 11.9	N 3 32.5	31 36.7	S22 57.4	156 03.3	N 9 54.0
	01	331 55.0	177 06.3	02.4	158 12.9	31.9	46 39.4	57.4	171 05.5	53.9
	02	346 57.4	192 05.9	01.3	173 13.9	31.2	61 42.1	57.4	186 07.6	53.8
	03	1 59.9	207 05.4	12 00.1	188 15.0	. . 30.6	76 44.8	. . 57.5	201 09.8	. . 53.7
	04	17 02.4	222 05.0	11 59.0	203 16.0	29.9	91 47.6	57.5	216 12.0	53.5
	05	32 04.8	237 04.5	57.9	218 17.0	29.3	106 50.3	57.5	231 14.2	53.4
	06	47 07.3	252 04.0	N11 56.8	233 18.1	N 3 28.6	121 53.0	S22 57.6	246 16.4	N 9 53.3
	07	62 09.7	267 03.6	55.7	248 19.1	28.0	136 55.7	57.6	261 18.6	53.2
	08	77 12.2	282 03.1	54.6	263 20.1	27.4	151 58.4	57.6	276 20.7	53.1
F	09	92 14.7	297 02.6	. . 53.4	278 21.2	. . 26.7	167 01.1	. . 57.6	291 22.9	. . 53.0
R	10	107 17.1	312 02.2	52.3	293 22.2	26.1	182 03.8	57.7	306 25.1	52.9
I	11	122 19.6	327 01.7	51.2	308 23.2	25.4	197 06.5	57.7	321 27.3	52.7
D	12	137 22.1	342 01.3	N11 50.1	323 24.3	N 3 24.8	212 09.2	S22 57.7	336 29.5	N 9 52.6
A	13	152 24.5	357 00.8	49.0	338 25.3	24.1	227 11.9	57.8	351 31.7	52.5
Y	14	167 27.0	12 00.4	47.8	353 26.3	23.5	242 14.6	57.8	6 33.8	52.4
	15	182 29.5	26 59.9	. . 46.7	8 27.4	. . 22.9	257 17.3	. . 57.8	21 36.0	. . 52.3
	16	197 31.9	41 59.4	45.6	23 28.4	22.2	272 20.1	57.8	36 38.2	52.2
	17	212 34.4	56 59.0	44.5	38 29.4	21.6	287 22.8	57.9	51 40.4	52.1
	18	227 36.8	71 58.5	N11 43.4	53 30.5	N 3 20.9	302 25.5	S22 57.9	66 42.6	N 9 52.0
	19	242 39.3	86 58.1	42.2	68 31.5	20.3	317 28.2	57.9	81 44.8	51.8
	20	257 41.8	101 57.6	41.1	83 32.5	19.6	332 30.9	57.9	96 46.9	51.7
	21	272 44.2	116 57.2	. . 40.0	98 33.6	. . 19.0	347 33.6	. . 58.0	111 49.1	. . 51.6
	22	287 46.7	131 56.7	38.9	113 34.6	18.3	2 36.3	58.0	126 51.3	51.5
	23	302 49.2	146 56.3	37.7	128 35.6	17.7	17 39.0	58.0	141 53.5	51.4
	9 00	317 51.6	161 55.8	N11 36.6	143 36.6	N 3 17.1	32 41.7	S22 58.1	156 55.7	N 9 51.3
	01	332 54.1	176 55.4	35.5	158 37.7	16.4	47 44.4	58.1	171 57.8	51.2
	02	347 56.6	191 54.9	34.4	173 38.7	15.8	62 47.1	58.1	187 00.0	51.1
	03	2 59.0	206 54.4	. . 33.2	188 39.7	. . 15.1	77 49.8	. . 58.1	202 02.2	. . 50.9
	04	18 01.5	221 54.0	32.1	203 40.8	14.5	92 52.5	58.2	217 04.4	50.8
	05	33 04.0	236 53.5	31.0	218 41.8	13.8	107 55.2	58.2	232 06.6	50.7
	06	48 06.4	251 53.1	N11 29.8	233 42.8	N 3 13.2	122 57.9	S22 58.2	247 08.8	N 9 50.6
	07	63 08.9	266 52.6	28.7	248 43.9	12.5	138 00.6	58.2	262 10.9	50.5
S	08	78 11.3	281 52.2	27.6	263 44.9	11.9	153 03.3	58.3	277 13.1	50.4
A	09	93 13.8	296 51.7	. . 26.4	278 45.9	. . 11.3	168 06.0	. . 58.3	292 15.3	. . 50.3
T	10	108 16.3	311 51.3	25.3	293 47.0	10.6	183 08.7	58.3	307 17.5	50.2
U	11	123 18.7	326 50.8	24.2	308 48.0	10.0	198 11.4	58.4	322 19.7	50.0
R	12	138 21.2	341 50.4	N11 23.1	323 49.0	N 3 09.3	213 14.1	S22 58.4	337 21.8	N 9 49.9
D	13	153 23.7	356 50.0	21.9	338 50.1	08.7	228 16.8	58.4	352 24.0	49.8
A	14	168 26.1	11 49.5	20.8	353 51.1	08.0	243 19.5	58.4	7 26.2	49.7
Y	15	183 28.6	26 49.1	. . 19.7	8 52.1	. . 07.4	258 22.2	. . 58.5	22 28.4	. . 49.6
	16	198 31.1	41 48.6	18.5	23 53.2	06.7	273 24.9	58.5	37 30.6	49.5
	17	213 33.5	56 48.2	17.4	38 54.2	06.1	288 27.6	58.5	52 32.7	49.4
	18	228 36.0	71 47.7	N11 16.2	53 55.2	N 3 05.5	303 30.3	S22 58.5	67 34.9	N 9 49.2
	19	243 38.5	86 47.3	15.1	68 56.2	04.8	318 33.0	58.6	82 37.1	49.1
	20	258 40.9	101 46.8	14.0	83 57.3	04.2	333 35.7	58.6	97 39.3	49.0
	21	273 43.4	116 46.4	. . 12.8	98 58.3	. . 03.5	348 38.4	. . 58.6	112 41.5	. . 48.9
	22	288 45.8	131 45.9	11.7	113 59.3	02.9	3 41.1	58.7	127 43.7	48.8
	23	303 48.3	146 45.5	10.6	129 00.4	02.2	18 43.8	58.7	142 45.8	48.7
	Mer. Pass.	h m 2 52.0	v −0.5	d 1.1	v 1.0	d 0.6	v 2.7	d 0.0	v 2.2	d 0.1

STARS

Name	SHA	Dec
	° ′	° ′
Acamar	315 21.0	S40 15.8
Achernar	335 29.0	S57 11.2
Acrux	173 14.2	S63 09.1
Adhara	255 15.7	S28 58.8
Aldebaran	290 53.7	N16 31.7
Alioth	166 23.9	N55 55.0
Alkaid	153 01.7	N49 16.4
Al Na'ir	27 47.6	S46 55.0
Alnilam	275 50.3	S 1 11.6
Alphard	218 00.0	S 8 41.7
Alphecca	126 14.0	N26 41.3
Alpheratz	357 47.1	N29 08.3
Altair	62 11.5	N 8 53.5
Ankaa	353 18.8	S42 15.2
Antares	112 30.6	S26 27.2
Arcturus	145 59.1	N19 08.3
Atria	107 35.5	S69 02.9
Avior	234 20.3	S59 32.1
Bellatrix	278 36.1	N 6 21.6
Betelgeuse	271 05.5	N 7 24.7
Canopus	263 58.2	S52 41.7
Capella	280 40.1	N46 00.4
Deneb	49 33.6	N45 18.7
Denebola	182 37.6	N14 31.5
Diphda	348 59.3	S17 56.1
Dubhe	193 56.4	N61 42.4
Elnath	278 17.5	N28 36.9
Eltanin	90 47.5	N51 29.4
Enif	33 50.4	N 9 55.0
Fomalhaut	15 27.6	S29 34.4
Gacrux	172 05.6	S57 09.9
Gienah	175 56.3	S17 35.4
Hadar	148 53.5	S60 25.2
Hamal	328 04.9	N23 30.3
Kaus Aust.	83 48.3	S34 22.9
Kochab	137 19.4	N74 07.4
Markab	13 41.7	N15 15.2
Menkar	314 18.9	N 4 07.6
Menkent	148 12.1	S36 25.0
Miaplacidus	221 41.8	S69 45.1
Mirfak	308 45.8	N49 53.4
Nunki	76 02.5	S26 17.2
Peacock	53 24.2	S56 42.4
Pollux	243 32.5	N28 00.4
Procyon	245 03.8	N 5 12.3
Rasalhague	96 09.6	N12 33.3
Regulus	207 47.7	N11 55.6
Rigel	281 15.7	S 8 11.3
Rigil Kent.	139 57.0	S60 52.6
Sabik	102 16.5	S15 44.2
Schedar	349 44.6	N56 35.0
Shaula	96 26.6	S37 06.8
Sirius	258 37.2	S16 43.5
Spica	158 35.2	S11 12.4
Suhail	222 55.7	S43 28.0
Vega	80 41.1	N38 47.6
Zuben'ubi	137 09.5	S16 04.8

	SHA	Mer. Pass.
	° ′	h m
Venus	205 14.3	13 12
Mars	186 19.4	14 26
Jupiter	74 44.2	21 50
Saturn	199 10.8	13 34

Day	UT (d h)	SUN GHA (° ′)	SUN Dec (° ′)	MOON GHA (° ′)	v (′)	MOON Dec (° ′)	d (′)	HP (′)
THURSDAY	7 00	178 33.3	N16 22.5	115 22.9	14.4	S13 49.3	12.6	55.4
	01	193 33.4	21.8	129 56.3	14.4	14 01.9	12.6	55.4
	02	208 33.5	21.1	144 29.7	14.3	14 14.5	12.5	55.4
	03	223 33.6	. . 20.4	159 03.0	14.3	14 27.0	12.4	55.4
	04	238 33.6	19.7	173 36.3	14.2	14 39.4	12.3	55.3
	05	253 33.7	19.0	188 09.5	14.3	14 51.7	12.3	55.3
	06	268 33.8	N16 18.3	202 42.8	14.2	S15 04.0	12.1	55.3
	07	283 33.9	17.6	217 16.0	14.2	15 16.1	12.2	55.3
	08	298 34.0	16.9	231 49.2	14.1	15 28.3	12.0	55.2
	09	313 34.0	. . 16.2	246 22.3	14.2	15 40.3	12.0	55.2
	10	328 34.1	15.5	260 55.5	14.1	15 52.3	11.8	55.2
	11	343 34.2	14.7	275 28.6	14.0	16 04.1	11.8	55.2
	12	358 34.3	N16 14.0	290 01.6	14.0	S16 15.9	11.8	55.1
	13	13 34.4	13.3	304 34.6	14.0	16 27.7	11.6	55.1
	14	28 34.4	12.6	319 07.6	14.0	16 39.3	11.6	55.1
	15	43 34.5	. . 11.9	333 40.6	13.9	16 50.9	11.5	55.1
	16	58 34.6	11.2	348 13.5	13.9	17 02.4	11.4	55.0
	17	73 34.7	10.5	2 46.4	13.9	17 13.8	11.3	55.0
	18	88 34.8	N16 09.8	17 19.3	13.8	S17 25.1	11.3	55.0
	19	103 34.8	09.1	31 52.1	13.8	17 36.4	11.1	55.0
	20	118 34.9	08.4	46 24.9	13.7	17 47.5	11.1	55.0
	21	133 35.0	. . 07.7	60 57.6	13.7	17 58.6	11.0	54.9
	22	148 35.1	07.0	75 30.3	13.7	18 09.6	10.9	54.9
	23	163 35.2	06.2	90 03.0	13.6	18 20.5	10.8	54.9
FRIDAY	8 00	178 35.2	N16 05.5	104 35.6	13.6	S18 31.3	10.8	54.9
	01	193 35.3	04.8	119 08.2	13.5	18 42.1	10.6	54.9
	02	208 35.4	04.1	133 40.7	13.5	18 52.7	10.6	54.8
	03	223 35.5	. . 03.4	148 13.2	13.5	19 03.3	10.5	54.8
	04	238 35.6	02.7	162 45.7	13.4	19 13.8	10.4	54.8
	05	253 35.7	02.0	177 18.1	13.4	19 24.2	10.3	54.8
	06	268 35.7	N16 01.3	191 50.5	13.3	S19 34.5	10.2	54.8
	07	283 35.8	16 00.5	206 22.8	13.3	19 44.7	10.1	54.7
	08	298 35.9	15 59.8	220 55.1	13.2	19 54.8	10.0	54.7
	09	313 36.0	. . 59.1	235 27.3	13.2	20 04.8	9.9	54.7
	10	328 36.1	58.4	249 59.5	13.2	20 14.7	9.9	54.7
	11	343 36.2	57.7	264 31.7	13.1	20 24.6	9.7	54.7
	12	358 36.3	N15 57.0	279 03.8	13.0	S20 34.3	9.7	54.7
	13	13 36.3	56.2	293 35.8	13.1	20 44.0	9.5	54.6
	14	28 36.4	55.5	308 07.9	12.9	20 53.5	9.5	54.6
	15	43 36.5	. . 54.8	322 39.8	12.9	21 03.0	9.4	54.6
	16	58 36.6	54.1	337 11.7	12.9	21 12.4	9.2	54.6
	17	73 36.7	53.4	351 43.6	12.9	21 21.6	9.2	54.6
	18	88 36.8	N15 52.7	6 15.5	12.7	S21 30.8	9.1	54.6
	19	103 36.9	51.9	20 47.2	12.8	21 39.9	8.9	54.6
	20	118 37.0	51.2	35 19.0	12.7	21 48.8	8.9	54.5
	21	133 37.0	. . 50.5	49 50.7	12.6	21 57.7	8.8	54.5
	22	148 37.1	49.8	64 22.3	12.6	22 06.5	8.7	54.5
	23	163 37.2	49.0	78 53.9	12.5	22 15.2	8.5	54.5
SATURDAY	9 00	178 37.3	N15 48.3	93 25.4	12.5	S22 23.7	8.5	54.5
	01	193 37.4	47.6	107 56.9	12.5	22 32.2	8.4	54.5
	02	208 37.5	46.9	122 28.4	12.4	22 40.6	8.2	54.5
	03	223 37.6	. . 46.2	136 59.8	12.3	22 48.8	8.2	54.4
	04	238 37.7	45.4	151 31.1	12.3	22 57.0	8.0	54.4
	05	253 37.8	44.7	166 02.4	12.2	23 05.0	8.0	54.4
	06	268 37.8	N15 44.0	180 33.6	12.2	S23 13.0	7.8	54.4
	07	283 37.9	43.3	195 04.8	12.2	23 20.8	7.8	54.4
	08	298 38.0	42.5	209 36.0	12.1	23 28.6	7.6	54.4
	09	313 38.1	. . 41.8	224 07.1	12.0	23 36.2	7.5	54.4
	10	328 38.2	41.1	238 38.1	12.0	23 43.7	7.4	54.4
	11	343 38.3	40.4	253 09.1	12.0	23 51.1	7.3	54.4
	12	358 38.4	N15 39.6	267 40.1	11.9	S23 58.4	7.2	54.4
	13	13 38.5	38.9	282 11.0	11.9	24 05.6	7.1	54.3
	14	28 38.6	38.2	296 41.9	11.8	24 12.7	7.0	54.3
	15	43 38.7	. . 37.4	311 12.7	11.7	24 19.7	6.8	54.3
	16	58 38.8	36.7	325 43.4	11.7	24 26.5	6.8	54.3
	17	73 38.9	36.0	340 14.1	11.7	24 33.3	6.6	54.3
	18	88 38.9	N15 35.3	354 44.8	11.6	S24 39.9	6.5	54.3
	19	103 39.0	34.5	9 15.4	11.6	24 46.4	6.5	54.3
	20	118 39.1	33.8	23 46.0	11.5	24 52.9	6.2	54.3
	21	133 39.2	. . 33.1	38 16.5	11.5	24 59.1	6.2	54.3
	22	148 39.3	32.3	52 47.0	11.4	25 05.3	6.1	54.3
	23	163 39.4	31.6	67 17.4	11.4	S25 11.4	5.9	54.3
		SD 15.8	d 0.7	SD 15.0		14.9		14.8

Lat. (°)	Twilight Naut. (h m)	Twilight Civil (h m)	Sunrise (h m)	Moonrise 7 (h m)	Moonrise 8 (h m)	Moonrise 9 (h m)	Moonrise 10 (h m)
N 72	////	////	01 28	15 29	■	■	■
N 70	////	////	02 19	14 30	■	■	■
68	////	////	02 50	13 56	16 36	■	■
66	////	01 41	03 13	13 32	15 33	■	■
64	////	02 18	03 31	13 13	14 59	17 00	■
62	////	02 43	03 46	12 58	14 34	16 15	17 57
60	01 31	03 03	03 58	12 45	14 15	15 45	17 11
N 58	02 04	03 19	04 09	12 34	13 59	15 23	16 41
56	02 28	03 32	04 18	12 25	13 45	15 05	16 19
54	02 46	03 44	04 26	12 16	13 34	14 49	16 00
52	03 01	03 54	04 33	12 09	13 23	14 36	15 44
50	03 14	04 02	04 40	12 02	13 14	14 25	15 31
45	03 40	04 21	04 54	11 48	12 55	14 01	15 03
N 40	03 59	04 36	05 05	11 36	12 39	13 42	14 42
35	04 15	04 48	05 15	11 26	12 26	13 26	14 24
30	04 27	04 58	05 23	11 18	12 15	13 12	14 08
20	04 47	05 15	05 38	11 03	11 55	12 49	13 42
N 10	05 03	05 29	05 50	10 50	11 39	12 29	13 20
0	05 16	05 41	06 02	10 38	11 23	12 10	12 59
S 10	05 27	05 52	06 14	10 26	11 07	11 51	12 38
20	05 37	06 03	06 26	10 13	10 51	11 32	12 16
30	05 46	06 15	06 40	09 59	10 32	11 09	11 51
35	05 51	06 21	06 48	09 51	10 21	10 56	11 35
40	05 56	06 28	06 57	09 41	10 09	10 40	11 18
45	06 01	06 36	07 07	09 30	09 54	10 22	10 57
S 50	06 07	06 45	07 20	09 17	09 36	10 00	10 31
52	06 09	06 50	07 26	09 11	09 28	09 49	10 18
54	06 12	06 54	07 32	09 04	09 18	09 37	10 03
56	06 15	06 59	07 39	08 57	09 08	09 23	09 46
58	06 17	07 04	07 48	08 49	08 56	09 07	09 26
S 60	06 20	07 11	07 57	08 39	08 42	08 48	09 00

Lat. (°)	Sunset (h m)	Twilight Civil (h m)	Twilight Naut. (h m)	Moonset 7 (h m)	Moonset 8 (h m)	Moonset 9 (h m)	Moonset 10 (h m)
N 72	22 34	////	////	17 47	■	■	■
N 70	21 47	////	////	18 48	■	■	■
68	21 17	23 35	////	19 23	18 18	■	■
66	20 55	22 24	////	19 49	19 21	■	■
64	20 38	21 50	////	20 08	19 57	19 35	■
62	20 23	21 25	23 38	20 25	20 22	20 20	20 21
60	20 11	21 06	22 35	20 38	20 42	20 50	21 07
N 58	20 01	20 50	22 03	20 50	20 59	21 13	21 37
56	19 52	20 37	21 41	21 00	21 13	21 32	22 00
54	19 44	20 26	21 23	21 09	21 25	21 47	22 19
52	19 37	20 16	21 08	21 17	21 36	22 01	22 35
50	19 30	20 08	20 55	21 25	21 46	22 13	22 48
45	19 17	19 49	20 30	21 40	22 06	22 37	23 16
N 40	19 05	19 35	20 11	21 53	22 23	22 57	23 38
35	18 56	19 23	19 56	22 04	22 37	23 14	23 57
30	18 47	19 13	19 43	22 14	22 49	23 28	24 12
20	18 33	18 56	19 23	22 31	23 10	23 53	24 39
N 10	18 21	18 42	19 08	22 46	23 28	24 14	00 14
0	18 09	18 31	18 55	22 59	23 45	24 34	00 34
S 10	17 58	18 19	18 45	23 13	24 03	00 03	00 53
20	17 45	18 08	18 35	23 28	24 21	00 21	01 15
30	17 32	17 57	18 25	23 45	24 43	00 43	01 39
35	17 24	17 50	18 20	23 55	24 55	00 55	01 54
40	17 15	17 43	18 16	24 07	00 07	01 10	02 11
45	17 05	17 35	18 10	24 20	00 20	01 27	02 31
S 50	16 52	17 26	18 05	24 37	00 37	01 48	02 57
52	16 46	17 22	18 03	24 45	00 45	01 59	03 09
54	16 40	17 18	18 00	24 53	00 53	02 10	03 24
56	16 32	17 13	17 57	25 03	01 03	02 24	03 41
58	16 24	17 08	17 55	25 15	01 15	02 39	04 01
S 60	16 15	17 02	17 52	25 28	01 28	02 58	04 26

Day	SUN Eqn. of Time 00^h	SUN Eqn. of Time 12^h	SUN Mer. Pass.	MOON Mer. Pass. Upper	MOON Mer. Pass. Lower	MOON Age	MOON Phase
d	m s	m s	h m	h m	h m	d	%
7	05 47	05 43	12 06	16 49	04 26	06	37
8	05 39	05 35	12 06	17 34	05 11	07	47
9	05 31	05 27	12 05	18 22	05 58	08	56

	UT	ARIES	VENUS −3.8		MARS +1.7		JUPITER −2.6		SATURN +0.8	
		GHA	GHA	Dec	GHA	Dec	GHA	Dec	GHA	Dec
	d h	° ′	° ′	° ′	° ′	° ′	° ′	° ′	° ′	° ′
	10 00	318 50.8	161 45.1	N11 09.4	144 01.4	N 3 01.6	33 46.5	S22 58.7	157 48.0	N 9 48.6
	01	333 53.2	176 44.6	08.3	159 02.4	00.9	48 49.2	58.7	172 50.2	48.5
	02	348 55.7	191 44.2	07.1	174 03.5	3 00.3	63 51.9	58.8	187 52.4	48.3
	03	3 58.2	206 43.7	. . 06.0	189 04.5	2 59.6	78 54.6	. . 58.8	202 54.6	. . 48.2
	04	19 00.6	221 43.3	04.9	204 05.5	59.0	93 57.3	58.8	217 56.7	48.1
	05	34 03.1	236 42.8	03.7	219 06.6	58.4	109 00.0	58.8	232 58.9	48.0
	06	49 05.6	251 42.4	N11 02.6	234 07.6	N 2 57.7	124 02.7	S22 58.9	248 01.1	N 9 47.9
	07	64 08.0	266 42.0	01.4	249 08.6	57.1	139 05.4	58.9	263 03.3	47.8
	08	79 10.5	281 41.5	11 00.3	264 09.6	56.4	154 08.1	58.9	278 05.5	47.7
S	09	94 13.0	296 41.1	10 59.2	279 10.7	. . 55.8	169 10.8	. . 58.9	293 07.6	. . 47.5
U	10	109 15.4	311 40.6	58.0	294 11.7	55.1	184 13.5	59.0	308 09.8	47.4
N	11	124 17.9	326 40.2	56.9	309 12.7	54.5	199 16.2	59.0	323 12.0	47.3
D	12	139 20.3	341 39.8	N10 55.7	324 13.8	N 2 53.8	214 18.9	S22 59.0	338 14.2	N 9 47.2
A	13	154 22.8	356 39.3	54.6	339 14.8	53.2	229 21.6	59.1	353 16.4	47.1
Y	14	169 25.3	11 38.9	53.4	354 15.8	52.5	244 24.2	59.1	8 18.5	47.0
	15	184 27.7	26 38.5	. . 52.3	9 16.9	. . 51.9	259 26.9	. . 59.1	23 20.7	. . 46.9
	16	199 30.2	41 38.0	51.1	24 17.9	51.2	274 29.6	59.1	38 22.9	46.8
	17	214 32.7	56 37.6	50.0	39 18.9	50.6	289 32.3	59.2	53 25.1	46.6
	18	229 35.1	71 37.1	N10 48.8	54 19.9	N 2 49.9	304 35.0	S22 59.2	68 27.3	N 9 46.5
	19	244 37.6	86 36.7	47.7	69 21.0	49.3	319 37.7	59.2	83 29.4	46.4
	20	259 40.1	101 36.3	46.5	84 22.0	48.7	334 40.4	59.2	98 31.6	46.3
	21	274 42.5	116 35.8	. . 45.4	99 23.0	. . 48.0	349 43.1	. . 59.3	113 33.8	. . 46.2
	22	289 45.0	131 35.4	44.2	114 24.1	47.4	4 45.8	59.3	128 36.0	46.1
	23	304 47.4	146 35.0	43.1	129 25.1	46.7	19 48.5	59.3	143 38.2	46.0
	11 00	319 49.9	161 34.5	N10 41.9	144 26.1	N 2 46.1	34 51.2	S22 59.3	158 40.3	N 9 45.8
	01	334 52.4	176 34.1	40.8	159 27.2	45.4	49 53.9	59.4	173 42.5	45.7
	02	349 54.8	191 33.7	39.6	174 28.2	44.8	64 56.5	59.4	188 44.7	45.6
	03	4 57.3	206 33.2	. . 38.5	189 29.2	. . 44.1	79 59.2	. . 59.4	203 46.9	. . 45.5
	04	19 59.8	221 32.8	37.3	204 30.2	43.5	95 01.9	59.4	218 49.1	45.4
	05	35 02.2	236 32.4	36.2	219 31.3	42.8	110 04.6	59.5	233 51.2	45.3
	06	50 04.7	251 31.9	N10 35.0	234 32.3	N 2 42.2	125 07.3	S22 59.5	248 53.4	N 9 45.2
	07	65 07.2	266 31.5	33.9	249 33.3	41.5	140 10.0	59.5	263 55.6	45.0
	08	80 09.6	281 31.1	32.7	264 34.4	40.9	155 12.7	59.5	278 57.8	44.9
M	09	95 12.1	296 30.7	. . 31.6	279 35.4	. . 40.2	170 15.4	. . 59.6	294 00.0	. . 44.8
O	10	110 14.6	311 30.2	30.4	294 36.4	39.6	185 18.1	59.6	309 02.1	44.7
N	11	125 17.0	326 29.8	29.3	309 37.4	38.9	200 20.7	59.6	324 04.3	44.6
D	12	140 19.5	341 29.4	N10 28.1	324 38.5	N 2 38.3	215 23.4	S22 59.6	339 06.5	N 9 44.5
A	13	155 21.9	356 28.9	26.9	339 39.5	37.7	230 26.1	59.7	354 08.7	44.4
Y	14	170 24.4	11 28.5	25.8	354 40.5	37.0	245 28.8	59.7	9 10.9	44.2
	15	185 26.9	26 28.1	. . 24.6	9 41.6	. . 36.4	260 31.5	. . 59.7	24 13.0	. . 44.1
	16	200 29.3	41 27.7	23.5	24 42.6	35.7	275 34.2	59.7	39 15.2	44.0
	17	215 31.8	56 27.2	22.3	39 43.6	35.1	290 36.9	59.8	54 17.4	43.9
	18	230 34.3	71 26.8	N10 21.2	54 44.6	N 2 34.4	305 39.6	S22 59.8	69 19.6	N 9 43.8
	19	245 36.7	86 26.4	20.0	69 45.7	33.8	320 42.2	59.8	84 21.8	43.7
	20	260 39.2	101 25.9	18.8	84 46.7	33.1	335 44.9	59.8	99 23.9	43.6
	21	275 41.7	116 25.5	. . 17.7	99 47.7	. . 32.5	350 47.6	. . 59.9	114 26.1	. . 43.4
	22	290 44.1	131 25.1	16.5	114 48.8	31.8	5 50.3	59.9	129 28.3	43.3
	23	305 46.6	146 24.7	15.4	129 49.8	31.2	20 53.0	59.9	144 30.5	43.2
	12 00	320 49.1	161 24.2	N10 14.2	144 50.8	N 2 30.5	35 55.7	S22 59.9	159 32.7	N 9 43.1
	01	335 51.5	176 23.8	13.0	159 51.8	29.9	50 58.3	23 00.0	174 34.8	43.0
	02	350 54.0	191 23.4	11.9	174 52.9	29.2	66 01.0	00.0	189 37.0	42.9
	03	5 56.4	206 23.0	. . 10.7	189 53.9	. . 28.6	81 03.7	. . 00.0	204 39.2	. . 42.8
	04	20 58.9	221 22.6	09.5	204 54.9	27.9	96 06.4	00.0	219 41.4	42.7
	05	36 01.4	236 22.1	08.4	219 56.0	27.3	111 09.1	00.1	234 43.5	42.5
	06	51 03.8	251 21.7	N10 07.2	234 57.0	N 2 26.6	126 11.8	S23 00.1	249 45.7	N 9 42.4
	07	66 06.3	266 21.3	06.0	249 58.0	26.0	141 14.4	00.1	264 47.9	42.3
T	08	81 08.8	281 20.9	04.9	264 59.0	25.3	156 17.1	00.1	279 50.1	42.2
U	09	96 11.2	296 20.4	. . 03.7	280 00.1	. . 24.7	171 19.8	. . 00.2	294 52.3	. . 42.1
E	10	111 13.7	311 20.0	02.5	295 01.1	24.0	186 22.5	00.2	309 54.4	42.0
S	11	126 16.2	326 19.6	01.4	310 02.1	23.4	201 25.2	00.2	324 56.6	41.9
D	12	141 18.6	341 19.2	N10 00.2	325 03.1	N 2 22.7	216 27.8	S23 00.2	339 58.8	N 9 41.7
A	13	156 21.1	356 18.8	9 59.0	340 04.2	22.1	231 30.5	00.3	355 01.0	41.6
Y	14	171 23.6	11 18.3	57.9	355 05.2	21.4	246 33.2	00.3	10 03.2	41.5
	15	186 26.0	26 17.9	. . 56.7	10 06.2	. . 20.8	261 35.9	. . 00.3	25 05.3	. . 41.4
	16	201 28.5	41 17.5	55.5	25 07.3	20.2	276 38.6	00.3	40 07.5	41.3
	17	216 30.9	56 17.1	54.4	40 08.3	19.5	291 41.2	00.4	55 09.7	41.2
	18	231 33.4	71 16.7	N 9 53.2	55 09.3	N 2 18.9	306 43.9	S23 00.4	70 11.9	N 9 41.0
	19	246 35.9	86 16.3	52.0	70 10.3	18.2	321 46.6	00.4	85 14.0	40.9
	20	261 38.3	101 15.8	50.9	85 11.4	17.6	336 49.3	00.4	100 16.2	40.8
	21	276 40.8	116 15.4	. . 49.7	100 12.4	. . 16.9	351 52.0	. . 00.5	115 18.4	. . 40.7
	22	291 43.3	131 15.0	48.5	115 13.4	16.3	6 54.6	00.5	130 20.6	40.6
	23	306 45.7	146 14.6	47.3	130 14.4	15.6	21 57.3	00.5	145 22.8	40.5
	Mer. Pass.	h m 2 40.2	v −0.4	d 1.2	v 1.0	d 0.6	v 2.7	d 0.0	v 2.2	d 0.1

STARS

Name	SHA	Dec
	° ′	° ′
Acamar	315 21.0	S40 15.8
Achernar	335 29.0	S57 11.2
Acrux	173 14.2	S63 09.1
Adhara	255 15.7	S28 58.8
Aldebaran	290 53.7	N16 31.7
Alioth	166 23.9	N55 55.0
Alkaid	153 01.7	N49 16.4
Al Na'ir	27 47.6	S46 55.0
Alnilam	275 50.2	S 1 11.6
Alphard	218 00.0	S 8 41.7
Alphecca	126 14.0	N26 41.3
Alpheratz	357 47.1	N29 08.3
Altair	62 11.5	N 8 53.5
Ankaa	353 18.8	S42 15.2
Antares	112 30.6	S26 27.2
Arcturus	145 59.1	N19 08.3
Atria	107 35.6	S69 02.9
Avior	234 20.3	S59 32.1
Bellatrix	278 36.1	N 6 21.6
Betelgeuse	271 05.4	N 7 24.7
Canopus	263 58.2	S52 41.7
Capella	280 40.1	N46 00.4
Deneb	49 33.6	N45 18.7
Denebola	182 37.6	N14 31.5
Diphda	348 59.3	S17 56.1
Dubhe	193 56.4	N61 42.4
Elnath	278 17.4	N28 36.9
Eltanin	90 47.5	N51 29.4
Enif	33 50.4	N 9 55.0
Fomalhaut	15 27.5	S29 34.4
Gacrux	172 05.6	S57 09.9
Gienah	175 56.3	S17 35.4
Hadar	148 53.5	S60 25.2
Hamal	328 04.8	N23 30.3
Kaus Aust.	83 48.3	S34 22.9
Kochab	137 19.5	N74 07.4
Markab	13 41.7	N15 15.2
Menkar	314 18.8	N 4 07.6
Menkent	148 12.1	S36 24.9
Miaplacidus	221 41.7	S69 45.1
Mirfak	308 45.7	N49 53.4
Nunki	76 02.5	S26 17.2
Peacock	53 24.2	S56 42.4
Pollux	243 32.5	N28 00.4
Procyon	245 03.8	N 5 12.3
Rasalhague	96 09.6	N12 33.3
Regulus	207 47.7	N11 55.6
Rigel	281 15.7	S 8 11.3
Rigil Kent.	139 57.1	S60 52.5
Sabik	102 16.5	S15 44.2
Schedar	349 44.6	N56 35.0
Shaula	96 26.6	S37 06.8
Sirius	258 37.2	S16 43.5
Spica	158 35.3	S11 12.4
Suhail	222 55.7	S43 28.0
Vega	80 41.1	N38 47.6
Zuben'ubi	137 09.5	S16 04.8

	SHA	Mer. Pass.
	° ′	h m
Venus	201 44.6	13 14
Mars	184 36.2	14 21
Jupiter	75 01.3	21 37
Saturn	198 50.4	13 23

UT d	h	SUN GHA ° ′	SUN Dec ° ′	MOON GHA ° ′	v ′	MOON Dec ° ′	d ′	HP ′
10	00	178 39.5	N15 30.9	81 47.8	11.3	S25 17.3	5.9	54.3
	01	193 39.6	30.1	96 18.1	11.3	25 23.2	5.7	54.3
	02	208 39.7	29.4	110 48.4	11.2	25 28.9	5.6	54.2
	03	223 39.8	. . 28.7	125 18.6	11.2	25 34.5	5.4	54.2
	04	238 39.9	27.9	139 48.8	11.2	25 39.9	5.4	54.2
	05	253 40.0	27.2	154 19.0	11.1	25 45.3	5.2	54.2
	06	268 40.1	N15 26.5	168 49.1	11.0	S25 50.5	5.2	54.2
	07	283 40.2	25.7	183 19.1	11.1	25 55.7	4.9	54.2
	08	298 40.3	25.0	197 49.2	10.9	26 00.6	4.9	54.2
S	09	313 40.4	. . 24.3	212 19.1	11.0	26 05.5	4.8	54.2
U	10	328 40.5	23.5	226 49.1	10.9	26 10.3	4.6	54.2
N	11	343 40.6	22.8	241 19.0	10.8	26 14.9	4.5	54.2
D	12	358 40.7	N15 22.0	255 48.8	10.8	S26 19.4	4.4	54.2
A	13	13 40.8	21.3	270 18.6	10.8	26 23.8	4.3	54.2
Y	14	28 40.9	20.6	284 48.4	10.7	26 28.1	4.1	54.2
	15	43 41.0	. . 19.8	299 18.1	10.7	26 32.2	4.0	54.2
	16	58 41.1	19.1	313 47.8	10.7	26 36.2	3.9	54.2
	17	73 41.2	18.4	328 17.5	10.6	26 40.1	3.7	54.2
	18	88 41.3	N15 17.6	342 47.1	10.6	S26 43.8	3.7	54.2
	19	103 41.4	16.9	357 16.7	10.5	26 47.5	3.5	54.2
	20	118 41.5	16.1	11 46.2	10.5	26 51.0	3.4	54.2
	21	133 41.6	. . 15.4	26 15.7	10.5	26 54.4	3.2	54.2
	22	148 41.7	14.6	40 45.2	10.5	26 57.6	3.2	54.2
	23	163 41.8	13.9	55 14.7	10.4	27 00.8	2.9	54.2
11	00	178 41.9	N15 13.2	69 44.1	10.3	S27 03.7	2.9	54.2
	01	193 42.0	12.4	84 13.4	10.4	27 06.6	2.8	54.2
	02	208 42.1	11.7	98 42.8	10.3	27 09.4	2.6	54.2
	03	223 42.2	. . 10.9	113 12.1	10.3	27 12.0	2.4	54.2
	04	238 42.3	10.2	127 41.4	10.2	27 14.4	2.4	54.2
	05	253 42.4	09.4	142 10.6	10.3	27 16.8	2.2	54.2
	06	268 42.5	N15 08.7	156 39.9	10.2	S27 19.0	2.1	54.2
	07	283 42.6	08.0	171 09.1	10.2	27 21.1	2.0	54.2
	08	298 42.7	07.2	185 38.3	10.1	27 23.1	1.8	54.2
M	09	313 42.8	. . 06.5	200 07.4	10.1	27 24.9	1.7	54.2
O	10	328 42.9	05.7	214 36.5	10.1	27 26.6	1.6	54.2
N	11	343 43.0	05.0	229 05.6	10.1	27 28.2	1.4	54.2
D	12	358 43.1	N15 04.2	243 34.7	10.1	S27 29.6	1.3	54.2
A	13	13 43.2	03.5	258 03.8	10.0	27 30.9	1.1	54.2
Y	14	28 43.3	02.7	272 32.8	10.0	27 32.0	1.1	54.2
	15	43 43.4	. . 02.0	287 01.8	10.0	27 33.1	0.9	54.2
	16	58 43.5	01.2	301 30.8	10.0	27 34.0	0.7	54.3
	17	73 43.6	15 00.5	315 59.8	10.0	27 34.7	0.7	54.3
	18	88 43.7	N14 59.7	330 28.8	9.9	S27 35.4	0.5	54.3
	19	103 43.8	59.0	344 57.7	10.0	27 35.9	0.3	54.3
	20	118 43.9	58.2	359 26.7	9.9	27 36.2	0.3	54.3
	21	133 44.0	. . 57.5	13 55.6	9.9	27 36.5	0.1	54.3
	22	148 44.1	56.7	28 24.5	9.9	27 36.6	0.1	54.3
	23	163 44.3	56.0	42 53.4	9.9	27 36.5	0.1	54.3
12	00	178 44.4	N14 55.2	57 22.3	9.8	S27 36.4	0.4	54.3
	01	193 44.5	54.5	71 51.1	9.9	27 36.0	0.4	54.3
	02	208 44.6	53.7	86 20.0	9.9	27 35.6	0.6	54.3
	03	223 44.7	. . 53.0	100 48.9	9.8	27 35.0	0.7	54.3
	04	238 44.8	52.2	115 17.7	9.9	27 34.3	0.8	54.3
	05	253 44.9	51.4	129 46.6	9.8	27 33.5	1.0	54.3
	06	268 45.0	N14 50.7	144 15.4	9.9	S27 32.5	1.1	54.4
	07	283 45.1	49.9	158 44.3	9.8	27 31.4	1.3	54.4
T	08	298 45.2	49.2	173 13.1	9.9	27 30.1	1.4	54.4
U	09	313 45.3	. . 48.4	187 42.0	9.8	27 28.7	1.5	54.4
E	10	328 45.4	47.7	202 10.8	9.9	27 27.2	1.7	54.4
S	11	343 45.6	46.9	216 39.7	9.8	27 25.5	1.8	54.4
D	12	358 45.7	N14 46.2	231 08.5	9.8	S27 23.7	1.9	54.4
A	13	13 45.8	45.4	245 37.3	9.9	27 21.8	2.1	54.4
Y	14	28 45.9	44.6	260 06.2	9.9	27 19.7	2.2	54.4
	15	43 46.0	. . 43.9	274 35.1	9.8	27 17.5	2.3	54.4
	16	58 46.1	43.1	289 03.9	9.9	27 15.2	2.5	54.5
	17	73 46.2	42.4	303 32.8	9.9	27 12.7	2.6	54.5
	18	88 46.3	N14 41.6	318 01.7	9.9	S27 10.1	2.7	54.5
	19	103 46.4	40.8	332 30.6	9.9	27 07.4	2.9	54.5
	20	118 46.6	40.1	346 59.5	9.9	27 04.5	3.0	54.5
	21	133 46.7	. . 39.3	1 28.4	9.9	27 01.5	3.1	54.5
	22	148 46.8	38.6	15 57.3	10.0	26 58.4	3.3	54.5
	23	163 46.9	37.8	30 26.3	9.9	S26 55.1	3.4	54.5
		SD 15.8	*d* 0.7	SD 14.8		14.8		14.8

Lat.	Twilight Naut.	Twilight Civil	Sunrise	Moonrise 10	Moonrise 11	Moonrise 12	Moonrise 13
°	h m	h m	h m	h m	h m	h m	h m
N 72	////	////	01 56	▬	▬	▬	▬
N 70	////	////	02 37	▬	▬	▬	▬
68	////	01 09	03 04	▬	▬	▬	▬
66	////	02 00	03 24	▬	▬	▬	▬
64	////	02 31	03 40	▬	▬	▬	20 45
62	01 01	02 54	03 54	17 57	19 24	19 51	19 54
60	01 48	03 12	04 05	17 11	18 20	19 02	19 22
N 58	02 16	03 26	04 15	16 41	17 46	18 31	18 58
56	02 37	03 39	04 24	16 19	17 21	18 07	18 39
54	02 54	03 50	04 31	16 00	17 01	17 48	18 23
52	03 08	03 59	04 38	15 44	16 44	17 32	18 09
50	03 20	04 07	04 44	15 31	16 30	17 18	17 56
45	03 45	04 25	04 57	15 03	16 01	16 50	17 31
N 40	04 03	04 39	05 08	14 42	15 38	16 28	17 11
35	04 17	04 50	05 17	14 24	15 19	16 09	16 54
30	04 30	05 00	05 25	14 08	15 03	15 53	16 39
20	04 49	05 16	05 39	13 42	14 35	15 26	16 14
N 10	05 03	05 29	05 51	13 20	14 12	15 03	15 53
0	05 15	05 40	06 02	12 59	13 50	14 41	15 33
S 10	05 26	05 51	06 13	12 38	13 28	14 20	15 13
20	05 35	06 01	06 24	12 16	13 05	13 57	14 51
30	05 44	06 12	06 37	11 51	12 37	13 30	14 26
35	05 48	06 18	06 45	11 35	12 21	13 14	14 11
40	05 53	06 25	06 53	11 18	12 03	12 55	13 54
45	05 57	06 32	07 03	10 57	11 40	12 32	13 33
S 50	06 02	06 41	07 15	10 31	11 12	12 04	13 07
52	06 04	06 44	07 20	10 18	10 58	11 50	12 54
54	06 07	06 49	07 26	10 03	10 41	11 33	12 39
56	06 09	06 53	07 33	09 46	10 22	11 14	12 22
58	06 11	06 58	07 40	09 26	09 58	10 50	12 01
S 60	06 14	07 04	07 49	09 00	09 26	10 17	11 35

Lat.	Sunset	Twilight Civil	Twilight Naut.	Moonset 10	Moonset 11	Moonset 12	Moonset 13
°	h m	h m	h m	h m	h m	h m	h m
N 72	22 07	////	////	▬	▬	▬	▬
N 70	21 29	////	////	▬	▬	▬	▬
68	21 03	22 52	////	▬	▬	▬	▬
66	20 43	22 05	////	▬	▬	▬	▬
64	20 28	21 35	////	▬	▬	▬	22 53
62	20 14	21 14	23 00	20 21	20 40	22 00	23 44
60	20 03	20 56	22 18	21 07	21 44	22 50	24 16
N 58	19 54	20 42	21 51	21 37	22 18	23 20	24 39
56	19 45	20 30	21 30	22 00	22 43	23 44	24 58
54	19 38	20 19	21 14	22 19	23 03	24 03	00 03
52	19 31	20 10	21 00	22 35	23 20	24 19	00 19
50	19 25	20 02	20 48	22 48	23 35	24 32	00 32
45	19 12	19 45	20 25	23 16	24 04	00 04	01 00
N 40	19 02	19 31	20 06	23 38	24 27	00 27	01 22
35	18 53	19 20	19 52	23 57	24 46	00 46	01 41
30	18 45	19 10	19 40	24 12	00 12	01 02	01 56
20	18 31	18 54	19 21	24 39	00 39	01 29	02 23
N 10	18 19	18 41	19 07	00 14	01 02	01 53	02 45
0	18 09	18 30	18 55	00 34	01 23	02 15	03 06
S 10	17 58	18 19	18 45	00 53	01 45	02 37	03 27
20	17 46	18 09	18 35	01 15	02 08	03 00	03 50
30	17 34	17 58	18 27	01 39	02 35	03 27	04 16
35	17 26	17 52	18 22	01 54	02 51	03 44	04 31
40	17 18	17 46	18 18	02 11	03 09	04 02	04 49
45	17 08	17 39	18 13	02 31	03 31	04 25	05 10
S 50	16 56	17 30	18 09	02 57	04 00	04 54	05 37
52	16 51	17 27	18 07	03 09	04 14	05 08	05 50
54	16 45	17 23	18 05	03 24	04 30	05 24	06 05
56	16 38	17 18	18 02	03 41	04 49	05 44	06 22
58	16 31	17 13	18 00	04 01	05 13	06 08	06 44
S 60	16 22	17 08	17 57	04 26	05 45	06 41	07 10

Day	SUN Eqn. of Time 00^h	SUN Eqn. of Time 12^h	SUN Mer. Pass.	MOON Mer. Pass. Upper	MOON Mer. Pass. Lower	MOON Age	MOON Phase
d	m s	m s	h m	h m	h m	d	%
10	05 22	05 18	12 05	19 11	06 46	09	66
11	05 13	05 08	12 05	20 02	07 37	10	74
12	05 03	04 58	12 05	20 54	08 28	11	82

	UT	ARIES	VENUS −3.8		MARS +1.7		JUPITER −2.6		SATURN +0.8		STARS		
		GHA	GHA	Dec	GHA	Dec	GHA	Dec	GHA	Dec	Name	SHA	Dec
	d h	° ′	° ′	° ′	° ′	° ′	° ′	° ′	° ′	° ′		° ′	° ′
	13 00	321 48.2	161 14.2	N 9 46.2	145 15.5	N 2 15.0	37 00.0	S23 00.5	160 24.9	N 9 40.4	Acamar	315 20.9	S40 15.8
	01	336 50.7	176 13.8	45.0	160 16.5	14.3	52 02.7	00.6	175 27.1	40.2	Achernar	335 28.9	S57 11.2
	02	351 53.1	191 13.4	43.8	175 17.5	13.7	67 05.3	00.6	190 29.3	40.1	Acrux	173 14.2	S63 09.1
	03	6 55.6	206 12.9	. . 42.6	190 18.6	. . 13.0	82 08.0	. . 00.6	205 31.5	. . 40.0	Adhara	255 15.7	S28 58.8
	04	21 58.1	221 12.5	41.5	205 19.6	12.4	97 10.7	00.6	220 33.6	39.9	Aldebaran	290 53.7	N16 31.7
	05	37 00.5	236 12.1	40.3	220 20.6	11.7	112 13.4	00.7	235 35.8	39.8			
	06	52 03.0	251 11.7	N 9 39.1	235 21.6	N 2 11.1	127 16.0	S23 00.7	250 38.0	N 9 39.7	Alioth	166 23.9	N55 55.0
W	07	67 05.4	266 11.3	37.9	250 22.7	10.4	142 18.7	00.7	265 40.2	39.6	Alkaid	153 01.7	N49 16.4
E	08	82 07.9	281 10.9	36.8	265 23.7	09.8	157 21.4	00.7	280 42.4	39.4	Al Na'ir	27 47.6	S46 55.0
D	09	97 10.4	296 10.5	. . 35.6	280 24.7	. . 09.1	172 24.1	. . 00.8	295 44.5	. . 39.3	Alnilam	275 50.2	S 1 11.6
N	10	112 12.8	311 10.0	34.4	295 25.7	08.5	187 26.7	00.8	310 46.7	39.2	Alphard	218 00.0	S 8 41.7
E	11	127 15.3	326 09.6	33.2	310 26.8	07.8	202 29.4	00.8	325 48.9	39.1			
S	12	142 17.8	341 09.2	N 9 32.1	325 27.8	N 2 07.2	217 32.1	S23 00.8	340 51.1	N 9 39.0	Alphecca	126 14.0	N26 41.3
D	13	157 20.2	356 08.8	30.9	340 28.8	06.5	232 34.8	00.9	355 53.3	38.9	Alpheratz	357 47.1	N29 08.4
A	14	172 22.7	11 08.4	29.7	355 29.8	05.9	247 37.4	00.9	10 55.4	38.8	Altair	62 11.5	N 8 53.6
Y	15	187 25.2	26 08.0	. . 28.5	10 30.9	. . 05.2	262 40.1	. . 00.9	25 57.6	. . 38.6	Ankaa	353 18.8	S42 15.2
	16	202 27.6	41 07.6	27.3	25 31.9	04.6	277 42.8	00.9	40 59.8	38.5	Antares	112 30.6	S26 27.2
	17	217 30.1	56 07.2	26.2	40 32.9	03.9	292 45.5	00.9	56 02.0	38.4			
	18	232 32.5	71 06.8	N 9 25.0	55 33.9	N 2 03.3	307 48.1	S23 01.0	71 04.1	N 9 38.3	Arcturus	145 59.1	N19 08.3
	19	247 35.0	86 06.4	23.8	70 35.0	02.6	322 50.8	01.0	86 06.3	38.2	Atria	107 35.6	S69 02.9
	20	262 37.5	101 06.0	22.6	85 36.0	02.0	337 53.5	01.0	101 08.5	38.1	Avior	234 20.3	S59 32.1
	21	277 39.9	116 05.5	. . 21.4	100 37.0	. . 01.3	352 56.1	. . 01.0	116 10.7	. . 38.0	Bellatrix	278 36.1	N 6 21.6
	22	292 42.4	131 05.1	20.3	115 38.0	00.7	7 58.8	01.1	131 12.8	37.8	Betelgeuse	271 05.4	N 7 24.7
	23	307 44.9	146 04.7	19.1	130 39.1	2 00.0	23 01.5	01.1	146 15.0	37.7			
	14 00	322 47.3	161 04.3	N 9 17.9	145 40.1	N 1 59.4	38 04.2	S23 01.1	161 17.2	N 9 37.6	Canopus	263 58.2	S52 41.7
	01	337 49.8	176 03.9	16.7	160 41.1	58.7	53 06.8	01.1	176 19.4	37.5	Capella	280 40.1	N46 00.4
	02	352 52.3	191 03.5	15.5	175 42.1	58.1	68 09.5	01.2	191 21.6	37.4	Deneb	49 33.6	N45 18.8
	03	7 54.7	206 03.1	. . 14.3	190 43.2	. . 57.4	83 12.2	. . 01.2	206 23.7	. . 37.3	Denebola	182 37.6	N14 31.5
	04	22 57.2	221 02.7	13.2	205 44.2	56.8	98 14.8	01.2	221 25.9	37.2	Diphda	348 59.2	S17 56.1
	05	37 59.7	236 02.3	12.0	220 45.2	56.1	113 17.5	01.2	236 28.1	37.0			
	06	53 02.1	251 01.9	N 9 10.8	235 46.2	N 1 55.5	128 20.2	S23 01.3	251 30.3	N 9 36.9	Dubhe	193 56.4	N61 42.4
	07	68 04.6	266 01.5	09.6	250 47.3	54.8	143 22.8	01.3	266 32.4	36.8	Elnath	278 17.4	N28 36.9
T	08	83 07.0	281 01.1	08.4	265 48.3	54.2	158 25.5	01.3	281 34.6	36.7	Eltanin	90 47.5	N51 29.4
H	09	98 09.5	296 00.7	. . 07.2	280 49.3	. . 53.5	173 28.2	. . 01.3	296 36.8	. . 36.6	Enif	33 50.4	N 9 55.0
U	10	113 12.0	311 00.3	06.0	295 50.3	52.9	188 30.8	01.3	311 39.0	36.5	Fomalhaut	15 27.5	S29 34.4
R	11	128 14.4	325 59.9	04.8	310 51.4	52.2	203 33.5	01.4	326 41.2	36.3			
S	12	143 16.9	340 59.5	N 9 03.7	325 52.4	N 1 51.6	218 36.2	S23 01.4	341 43.3	N 9 36.2	Gacrux	172 05.6	S57 09.9
D	13	158 19.4	355 59.1	02.5	340 53.4	50.9	233 38.8	01.4	356 45.5	36.1	Gienah	175 56.3	S17 35.4
A	14	173 21.8	10 58.7	01.3	355 54.4	50.2	248 41.5	01.4	11 47.7	36.0	Hadar	148 53.5	S60 25.2
Y	15	188 24.3	25 58.3	9 00.1	10 55.5	. . 49.6	263 44.2	. . 01.5	26 49.9	. . 35.9	Hamal	328 04.8	N23 30.3
	16	203 26.8	40 57.9	8 58.9	25 56.5	48.9	278 46.8	01.5	41 52.0	35.8	Kaus Aust.	83 48.3	S34 22.9
	17	218 29.2	55 57.5	57.7	40 57.5	48.3	293 49.5	01.5	56 54.2	35.7			
	18	233 31.7	70 57.1	N 8 56.5	55 58.5	N 1 47.6	308 52.2	S23 01.5	71 56.4	N 9 35.5	Kochab	137 19.5	N74 07.4
	19	248 34.2	85 56.7	55.3	70 59.6	47.0	323 54.8	01.6	86 58.6	35.4	Markab	13 41.7	N15 15.2
	20	263 36.6	100 56.3	54.1	86 00.6	46.3	338 57.5	01.6	102 00.7	35.3	Menkar	314 18.8	N 4 07.6
	21	278 39.1	115 55.9	. . 52.9	101 01.6	. . 45.7	354 00.2	. . 01.6	117 02.9	. . 35.2	Menkent	148 12.1	S36 24.9
	22	293 41.5	130 55.5	51.8	116 02.6	45.0	9 02.8	01.6	132 05.1	35.1	Miaplacidus	221 41.7	S69 45.1
	23	308 44.0	145 55.1	50.6	131 03.7	44.4	24 05.5	01.6	147 07.3	35.0			
	15 00	323 46.5	160 54.7	N 8 49.4	146 04.7	N 1 43.7	39 08.1	S23 01.7	162 09.4	N 9 34.9	Mirfak	308 45.7	N49 53.4
	01	338 48.9	175 54.3	48.2	161 05.7	43.1	54 10.8	01.7	177 11.6	34.7	Nunki	76 02.5	S26 17.2
	02	353 51.4	190 53.9	47.0	176 06.7	42.4	69 13.5	01.7	192 13.8	34.6	Peacock	53 24.2	S56 42.5
	03	8 53.9	205 53.5	. . 45.8	191 07.8	. . 41.8	84 16.1	. . 01.7	207 16.0	. . 34.5	Pollux	243 32.4	N28 00.4
	04	23 56.3	220 53.1	44.6	206 08.8	41.1	99 18.8	01.8	222 18.2	34.4	Procyon	245 03.8	N 5 12.3
	05	38 58.8	235 52.7	43.4	221 09.8	40.5	114 21.4	01.8	237 20.3	34.3			
	06	54 01.3	250 52.3	N 8 42.2	236 10.8	N 1 39.8	129 24.1	S23 01.8	252 22.5	N 9 34.2	Rasalhague	96 09.6	N12 33.3
	07	69 03.7	265 51.9	41.0	251 11.9	39.2	144 26.8	01.8	267 24.7	34.0	Regulus	207 47.6	N11 55.6
	08	84 06.2	280 51.5	39.8	266 12.9	38.5	159 29.4	01.8	282 26.9	33.9	Rigel	281 15.7	S 8 11.3
F	09	99 08.7	295 51.1	. . 38.6	281 13.9	. . 37.9	174 32.1	. . 01.9	297 29.0	. . 33.8	Rigil Kent.	139 57.1	S60 52.5
R	10	114 11.1	310 50.7	37.4	296 14.9	37.2	189 34.7	01.9	312 31.2	33.7	Sabik	102 16.5	S15 44.2
I	11	129 13.6	325 50.3	36.2	311 15.9	36.6	204 37.4	01.9	327 33.4	33.6			
D	12	144 16.0	340 49.9	N 8 35.0	326 17.0	N 1 35.9	219 40.1	S23 01.9	342 35.6	N 9 33.5	Schedar	349 44.6	N56 35.0
A	13	159 18.5	355 49.5	33.8	341 18.0	35.3	234 42.7	02.0	357 37.7	33.4	Shaula	96 26.6	S37 06.8
Y	14	174 21.0	10 49.1	32.6	356 19.0	34.6	249 45.4	02.0	12 39.9	33.2	Sirius	258 37.2	S16 43.4
	15	189 23.4	25 48.7	. . 31.4	11 20.0	. . 34.0	264 48.0	. . 02.0	27 42.1	. . 33.1	Spica	158 35.3	S11 12.4
	16	204 25.9	40 48.3	30.2	26 21.1	33.3	279 50.7	02.0	42 44.3	33.0	Suhail	222 55.7	S43 28.0
	17	219 28.4	55 48.0	29.0	41 22.1	32.7	294 53.4	02.0	57 46.4	32.9			
	18	234 30.8	70 47.6	N 8 27.8	56 23.1	N 1 32.0	309 56.0	S23 02.1	72 48.6	N 9 32.8	Vega	80 41.1	N38 47.6
	19	249 33.3	85 47.2	26.6	71 24.1	31.3	324 58.7	02.1	87 50.8	32.7	Zuben'ubi	137 09.5	S16 04.8
	20	264 35.8	100 46.8	25.4	86 25.1	30.7	340 01.3	02.1	102 53.0	32.5		SHA	Mer. Pass.
	21	279 38.2	115 46.4	. . 24.2	101 26.2	. . 30.0	355 04.0	. . 02.1	117 55.1	. . 32.4		° ′	h m
	22	294 40.7	130 46.0	23.0	116 27.2	29.4	10 06.6	02.2	132 57.3	32.3	Venus	198 17.0	13 16
	23	309 43.1	145 45.6	21.8	131 28.2	28.7	25 09.3	02.2	147 59.5	32.2	Mars	182 52.8	14 16
		h m									Jupiter	75 16.8	21 24
	Mer. Pass.	2 28.4	*v* −0.4	*d* 1.2	*v* 1.0	*d* 0.7	*v* 2.7	*d* 0.0	*v* 2.2	*d* 0.1	Saturn	198 29.9	13 13

UT d	h	SUN GHA	SUN Dec	MOON GHA	v	MOON Dec	d	HP
		° ′	° ′	° ′	′	° ′	′	′
13 (WEDNESDAY)	00	178 47.0	N14 37.0	44 55.2	10.0	S26 51.7	3.6	54.5
	01	193 47.1	36.3	59 24.2	10.0	26 48.1	3.6	54.6
	02	208 47.2	35.5	73 53.2	10.0	26 44.5	3.8	54.6
	03	223 47.3	. . 34.7	88 22.2	10.0	26 40.7	4.0	54.6
	04	238 47.5	34.0	102 51.2	10.0	26 36.7	4.1	54.6
	05	253 47.6	33.2	117 20.2	10.1	26 32.6	4.2	54.6
	06	268 47.7	N14 32.5	131 49.3	10.1	S26 28.4	4.3	54.6
	07	283 47.8	31.7	146 18.4	10.1	26 24.1	4.5	54.6
	08	298 47.9	30.9	160 47.5	10.1	26 19.6	4.6	54.7
	09	313 48.0	. . 30.2	175 16.6	10.2	26 15.0	4.7	54.7
	10	328 48.1	29.4	189 45.8	10.2	26 10.3	4.9	54.7
	11	343 48.3	28.6	204 15.0	10.2	26 05.4	5.0	54.7
	12	358 48.4	N14 27.9	218 44.2	10.2	S26 00.4	5.1	54.7
	13	13 48.5	27.1	233 13.4	10.3	25 55.3	5.2	54.7
	14	28 48.6	26.3	247 42.7	10.3	25 50.1	5.4	54.7
	15	43 48.7	. . 25.6	262 12.0	10.3	25 44.7	5.5	54.8
	16	58 48.8	24.8	276 41.3	10.3	25 39.2	5.7	54.8
	17	73 49.0	24.0	291 10.6	10.4	25 33.5	5.7	54.8
	18	88 49.1	N14 23.2	305 40.0	10.4	S25 27.8	5.9	54.8
	19	103 49.2	22.5	320 09.4	10.5	25 21.9	6.1	54.8
	20	118 49.3	21.7	334 38.9	10.4	25 15.8	6.1	54.8
	21	133 49.4	. . 20.9	349 08.3	10.5	25 09.7	6.3	54.9
	22	148 49.5	20.2	3 37.8	10.6	25 03.4	6.4	54.9
	23	163 49.7	19.4	18 07.4	10.5	24 57.0	6.5	54.9
14 (THURSDAY)	00	178 49.8	N14 18.6	32 36.9	10.7	S24 50.5	6.6	54.9
	01	193 49.9	17.8	47 06.6	10.6	24 43.9	6.8	54.9
	02	208 50.0	17.1	61 36.2	10.7	24 37.1	6.9	54.9
	03	223 50.1	. . 16.3	76 05.9	10.7	24 30.2	7.0	55.0
	04	238 50.3	15.5	90 35.6	10.8	24 23.2	7.2	55.0
	05	253 50.4	14.8	105 05.4	10.8	24 16.0	7.2	55.0
	06	268 50.5	N14 14.0	119 35.2	10.8	S24 08.8	7.4	55.0
	07	283 50.6	13.2	134 05.0	10.9	24 01.4	7.5	55.0
	08	298 50.7	12.4	148 34.9	10.9	23 53.9	7.6	55.1
	09	313 50.9	. . 11.7	163 04.8	10.9	23 46.3	7.8	55.1
	10	328 51.0	10.9	177 34.7	11.0	23 38.5	7.8	55.1
	11	343 51.1	10.1	192 04.7	11.1	23 30.7	8.0	55.1
	12	358 51.2	N14 09.3	206 34.8	11.0	S23 22.7	8.1	55.1
	13	13 51.3	08.6	221 04.8	11.2	23 14.6	8.2	55.1
	14	28 51.5	07.8	235 35.0	11.1	23 06.4	8.4	55.2
	15	43 51.6	. . 07.0	250 05.1	11.2	22 58.0	8.4	55.2
	16	58 51.7	06.2	264 35.3	11.3	22 49.6	8.6	55.2
	17	73 51.8	05.4	279 05.6	11.2	22 41.0	8.6	55.2
	18	88 52.0	N14 04.7	293 35.8	11.4	S22 32.4	8.8	55.2
	19	103 52.1	03.9	308 06.2	11.3	22 23.6	8.9	55.3
	20	118 52.2	03.1	322 36.5	11.5	22 14.7	9.0	55.3
	21	133 52.3	. . 02.3	337 07.0	11.4	22 05.7	9.2	55.3
	22	148 52.4	01.5	351 37.4	11.5	21 56.5	9.2	55.3
	23	163 52.6	00.8	6 07.9	11.6	21 47.3	9.3	55.3
15 (FRIDAY)	00	178 52.7	N14 00.0	20 38.5	11.6	S21 38.0	9.5	55.4
	01	193 52.8	13 59.2	35 09.1	11.6	21 28.5	9.5	55.4
	02	208 52.9	58.4	49 39.7	11.7	21 19.0	9.7	55.4
	03	223 53.1	. . 57.6	64 10.4	11.7	21 09.3	9.8	55.4
	04	238 53.2	56.9	78 41.1	11.8	20 59.5	9.9	55.4
	05	253 53.3	56.1	93 11.9	11.8	20 49.6	9.9	55.5
	06	268 53.4	N13 55.3	107 42.7	11.8	S20 39.7	10.1	55.5
	07	283 53.6	54.5	122 13.5	11.9	20 29.6	10.2	55.5
	08	298 53.7	53.7	136 44.4	12.0	20 19.4	10.3	55.5
	09	313 53.8	. . 52.9	151 15.4	12.0	20 09.1	10.4	55.5
	10	328 54.0	52.1	165 46.4	12.0	19 58.7	10.5	55.6
	11	343 54.1	51.4	180 17.4	12.1	19 48.2	10.6	55.6
	12	358 54.2	N13 50.6	194 48.5	12.1	S19 37.6	10.7	55.6
	13	13 54.3	49.8	209 19.6	12.2	19 26.9	10.8	55.6
	14	28 54.5	49.0	223 50.8	12.2	19 16.1	10.9	55.7
	15	43 54.6	. . 48.2	238 22.0	12.2	19 05.2	11.0	55.7
	16	58 54.7	47.4	252 53.2	12.3	18 54.2	11.0	55.7
	17	73 54.8	46.6	267 24.5	12.4	18 43.2	11.2	55.7
	18	88 55.0	N13 45.9	281 55.9	12.3	S18 32.0	11.3	55.7
	19	103 55.1	45.1	296 27.2	12.5	18 20.7	11.3	55.8
	20	118 55.2	44.3	310 58.7	12.4	18 09.4	11.5	55.8
	21	133 55.4	. . 43.5	325 30.1	12.5	17 57.9	11.5	55.8
	22	148 55.5	42.7	340 01.6	12.6	17 46.4	11.7	55.8
	23	163 55.6	41.9	354 33.2	12.6	S17 34.7	11.7	55.8
		SD 15.8	*d* 0.8	SD	14.9	15.0		15.2

Lat.	Twilight Naut.	Twilight Civil	Sunrise	Moonrise 13	14	15	16
°	h m	h m	h m	h m	h m	h m	h m
N 72	////	////	02 19	■	■	22 42	21 05
N 70	////	////	02 53	■	■	21 31	20 42
68	////	01 38	03 17	■	22 25	20 54	20 24
66	////	02 17	03 35	■	20 57	20 27	20 09
64	////	02 44	03 50	20 45	20 19	20 06	19 57
62	01 27	03 04	04 02	19 54	19 52	19 50	19 47
60	02 03	03 21	04 12	19 22	19 31	19 36	19 38
N 58	02 27	03 34	04 22	18 58	19 14	19 24	19 30
56	02 47	03 46	04 29	18 39	18 59	19 13	19 23
54	03 02	03 56	04 37	18 23	18 47	19 04	19 17
52	03 15	04 05	04 43	18 09	18 35	18 55	19 11
50	03 26	04 12	04 49	17 56	18 25	18 48	19 06
45	03 49	04 29	05 01	17 31	18 04	18 32	18 55
N 40	04 06	04 42	05 11	17 11	17 47	18 19	18 46
35	04 20	04 53	05 19	16 54	17 33	18 07	18 38
30	04 32	05 02	05 27	16 39	17 21	17 57	18 31
20	04 50	05 17	05 40	16 14	16 59	17 40	18 19
N 10	05 04	05 29	05 51	15 53	16 40	17 25	18 08
0	05 15	05 40	06 01	15 33	16 23	17 11	17 58
S 10	05 25	05 50	06 11	15 13	16 05	16 57	17 48
20	05 33	05 59	06 22	14 51	15 46	16 42	17 37
30	05 41	06 10	06 34	14 26	15 25	16 24	17 24
35	05 45	06 15	06 41	14 11	15 12	16 14	17 17
40	05 49	06 21	06 49	13 54	14 57	16 02	17 09
45	05 53	06 28	06 58	13 33	14 39	15 48	16 59
S 50	05 57	06 36	07 09	13 07	14 17	15 31	16 47
52	05 59	06 39	07 14	12 54	14 06	15 23	16 42
54	06 01	06 43	07 20	12 39	13 54	15 14	16 36
56	06 03	06 47	07 26	12 22	13 41	15 04	16 29
58	06 05	06 51	07 33	12 01	13 25	14 53	16 21
S 60	06 07	06 56	07 41	11 35	13 05	14 39	16 13

Lat.	Sunset	Twilight Civil	Twilight Naut.	Moonset 13	14	15	16
°	h m	h m	h m	h m	h m	h m	h m
N 72	21 44	////	////	■	■	■	00 25
N 70	21 12	////	////	■	■	■	01 34
68	20 49	22 24	////	■	22 59	26 10	02 10
66	20 32	21 47	////	■	■	00 25	02 35
64	20 17	21 22	////	22 53	25 03	01 03	02 55
62	20 05	21 02	22 36	23 44	25 29	01 29	03 11
60	19 55	20 46	22 02	24 16	00 16	01 49	03 24
N 58	19 46	20 33	21 39	24 39	00 39	02 06	03 35
56	19 38	20 22	21 20	24 58	00 58	02 20	03 45
54	19 31	20 12	21 05	00 03	01 14	02 32	03 53
52	19 25	20 03	20 52	00 19	01 28	02 43	04 01
50	19 20	19 56	20 41	00 32	01 39	02 52	04 08
45	19 08	19 40	20 19	01 00	02 04	03 12	04 22
N 40	18 58	19 27	20 02	01 22	02 24	03 28	04 34
35	18 49	19 16	19 48	01 41	02 40	03 42	04 44
30	18 42	19 07	19 37	01 56	02 54	03 53	04 53
20	18 29	18 52	19 19	02 23	03 18	04 13	05 08
N 10	18 18	18 40	19 05	02 45	03 38	04 30	05 21
0	18 08	18 29	18 54	03 06	03 57	04 46	05 34
S 10	17 58	18 19	18 44	03 27	04 16	05 02	05 46
20	17 47	18 10	18 36	03 50	04 36	05 19	05 59
30	17 35	18 00	18 28	04 16	04 59	05 38	06 13
35	17 28	17 54	18 24	04 31	05 13	05 50	06 22
40	17 21	17 49	18 20	04 49	05 29	06 02	06 31
45	17 11	17 42	18 17	05 10	05 47	06 17	06 42
S 50	17 01	17 34	18 12	05 37	06 10	06 36	06 56
52	16 55	17 31	18 11	05 50	06 21	06 44	07 02
54	16 50	17 27	18 09	06 05	06 34	06 54	07 09
56	16 44	17 23	18 07	06 22	06 48	07 05	07 16
58	16 37	17 19	18 05	06 44	07 05	07 17	07 25
S 60	16 29	17 14	18 03	07 10	07 25	07 31	07 35

Day	SUN Eqn. of Time 00h	SUN Eqn. of Time 12h	SUN Mer. Pass.	MOON Mer. Pass. Upper	MOON Mer. Pass. Lower	MOON Age	MOON Phase
d	m s	m s	h m	h m	h m	d %	
13	04 52	04 47	12 05	21 45	09 20	12 89	
14	04 41	04 35	12 05	22 35	10 10	13 94	○
15	04 29	04 23	12 04	23 22	10 59	14 98	

UT d	h	ARIES GHA	VENUS −3.8 GHA	VENUS Dec	MARS +1.7 GHA	MARS Dec	JUPITER −2.6 GHA	JUPITER Dec	SATURN +0.8 GHA	SATURN Dec
		° ′	° ′	° ′	° ′	° ′	° ′	° ′	° ′	° ′
16	00	324 45.6	160 45.2	N 8 20.6	146 29.2	N 1 28.1	40 12.0	S23 02.2	163 01.7	N 9 32.1
	01	339 48.1	175 44.8	19.4	161 30.3	27.4	55 14.6	02.2	178 03.9	32.0
	02	354 50.5	190 44.4	18.2	176 31.3	26.8	70 17.3	02.2	193 06.0	31.9
	03	9 53.0	205 44.0	. . 17.0	191 32.3	. . 26.1	85 19.9	. . 02.3	208 08.2	. . 31.7
	04	24 55.5	220 43.7	15.8	206 33.3	25.5	100 22.6	02.3	223 10.4	31.6
	05	39 57.9	235 43.3	14.6	221 34.3	24.8	115 25.2	02.3	238 12.6	31.5
	06	55 00.4	250 42.9	N 8 13.4	236 35.4	N 1 24.2	130 27.9	S23 02.3	253 14.7	N 9 31.4
	07	70 02.9	265 42.5	12.2	251 36.4	23.5	145 30.5	02.3	268 16.9	31.3
S	08	85 05.3	280 42.1	11.0	266 37.4	22.9	160 33.2	02.4	283 19.1	31.2
A	09	100 07.8	295 41.7	. . 09.8	281 38.4	. . 22.2	175 35.8	. . 02.4	298 21.3	. . 31.0
T	10	115 10.3	310 41.3	08.6	296 39.5	21.6	190 38.5	02.4	313 23.4	30.9
U	11	130 12.7	325 40.9	07.4	311 40.5	20.9	205 41.1	02.4	328 25.6	30.8
R	12	145 15.2	340 40.6	N 8 06.1	326 41.5	N 1 20.3	220 43.8	S23 02.5	343 27.8	N 9 30.7
D	13	160 17.6	355 40.2	04.9	341 42.5	19.6	235 46.4	02.5	358 30.0	30.6
A	14	175 20.1	10 39.8	03.7	356 43.5	18.9	250 49.1	02.5	13 32.1	30.5
Y	15	190 22.6	25 39.4	. . 02.5	11 44.6	. . 18.3	265 51.7	. . 02.5	28 34.3	. . 30.4
	16	205 25.0	40 39.0	01.3	26 45.6	17.6	280 54.4	02.5	43 36.5	30.2
	17	220 27.5	55 38.6	8 00.1	41 46.6	17.0	295 57.0	02.6	58 38.7	30.1
	18	235 30.0	70 38.2	N 7 58.9	56 47.6	N 1 16.3	310 59.7	S23 02.6	73 40.8	N 9 30.0
	19	250 32.4	85 37.9	57.7	71 48.6	15.7	326 02.3	02.6	88 43.0	29.9
	20	265 34.9	100 37.5	56.5	86 49.7	15.0	341 05.0	02.6	103 45.2	29.8
	21	280 37.4	115 37.1	. . 55.3	101 50.7	. . 14.4	356 07.6	. . 02.6	118 47.4	. . 29.7
	22	295 39.8	130 36.7	54.1	116 51.7	13.7	11 10.3	02.7	133 49.5	29.5
	23	310 42.3	145 36.3	52.8	131 52.7	13.1	26 12.9	02.7	148 51.7	29.4
17	00	325 44.8	160 35.9	N 7 51.6	146 53.8	N 1 12.4	41 15.6	S23 02.7	163 53.9	N 9 29.3
	01	340 47.2	175 35.6	50.4	161 54.8	11.8	56 18.2	02.7	178 56.1	29.2
	02	355 49.7	190 35.2	49.2	176 55.8	11.1	71 20.9	02.7	193 58.2	29.1
	03	10 52.1	205 34.8	. . 48.0	191 56.8	. . 10.5	86 23.5	. . 02.8	209 00.4	. . 29.0
	04	25 54.6	220 34.4	46.8	206 57.8	09.8	101 26.2	02.8	224 02.6	28.8
	05	40 57.1	235 34.0	45.6	221 58.9	09.1	116 28.8	02.8	239 04.8	28.7
	06	55 59.5	250 33.6	N 7 44.4	236 59.9	N 1 08.5	131 31.5	S23 02.8	254 06.9	N 9 28.6
	07	71 02.0	265 33.3	43.1	252 00.9	07.8	146 34.1	02.9	269 09.1	28.5
	08	86 04.5	280 32.9	41.9	267 01.9	07.2	161 36.8	02.9	284 11.3	28.4
S	09	101 06.9	295 32.5	. . 40.7	282 02.9	. . 06.5	176 39.4	. . 02.9	299 13.5	. . 28.3
U	10	116 09.4	310 32.1	39.5	297 04.0	05.9	191 42.1	02.9	314 15.6	28.2
N	11	131 11.9	325 31.7	38.3	312 05.0	05.2	206 44.7	02.9	329 17.8	28.0
D	12	146 14.3	340 31.4	N 7 37.1	327 06.0	N 1 04.6	221 47.3	S23 03.0	344 20.0	N 9 27.9
A	13	161 16.8	355 31.0	35.8	342 07.0	03.9	236 50.0	03.0	359 22.2	27.8
Y	14	176 19.2	10 30.6	34.6	357 08.0	03.3	251 52.6	03.0	14 24.3	27.7
	15	191 21.7	25 30.2	. . 33.4	12 09.1	. . 02.6	266 55.3	. . 03.0	29 26.5	. . 27.6
	16	206 24.2	40 29.9	32.2	27 10.1	02.0	281 57.9	03.0	44 28.7	27.5
	17	221 26.6	55 29.5	31.0	42 11.1	01.3	297 00.6	03.1	59 30.9	27.3
	18	236 29.1	70 29.1	N 7 29.8	57 12.1	N 1 00.6	312 03.2	S23 03.1	74 33.0	N 9 27.2
	19	251 31.6	85 28.7	28.5	72 13.1	1 00.0	327 05.8	03.1	89 35.2	27.1
	20	266 34.0	100 28.3	27.3	87 14.1	0 59.3	342 08.5	03.1	104 37.4	27.0
	21	281 36.5	115 28.0	. . 26.1	102 15.2	. . 58.7	357 11.1	. . 03.1	119 39.6	. . 26.9
	22	296 39.0	130 27.6	24.9	117 16.2	58.0	12 13.8	03.2	134 41.7	26.8
	23	311 41.4	145 27.2	23.7	132 17.2	57.4	27 16.4	03.2	149 43.9	26.6
18	00	326 43.9	160 26.8	N 7 22.4	147 18.2	N 0 56.7	42 19.0	S23 03.2	164 46.1	N 9 26.5
	01	341 46.4	175 26.5	21.2	162 19.2	56.1	57 21.7	03.2	179 48.3	26.4
	02	356 48.8	190 26.1	20.0	177 20.3	55.4	72 24.3	03.2	194 50.4	26.3
	03	11 51.3	205 25.7	. . 18.8	192 21.3	. . 54.8	87 27.0	. . 03.3	209 52.6	. . 26.2
	04	26 53.7	220 25.3	17.6	207 22.3	54.1	102 29.6	03.3	224 54.8	26.1
	05	41 56.2	235 25.0	16.3	222 23.3	53.4	117 32.2	03.3	239 56.9	26.0
	06	56 58.7	250 24.6	N 7 15.1	237 24.3	N 0 52.8	132 34.9	S23 03.3	254 59.1	N 9 25.8
	07	72 01.1	265 24.2	13.9	252 25.4	52.1	147 37.5	03.3	270 01.3	25.7
	08	87 03.6	280 23.9	12.7	267 26.4	51.5	162 40.2	03.4	285 03.5	25.6
M	09	102 06.1	295 23.5	. . 11.5	282 27.4	. . 50.8	177 42.8	. . 03.4	300 05.6	. . 25.5
O	10	117 08.5	310 23.1	10.2	297 28.4	50.2	192 45.4	03.4	315 07.8	25.4
N	11	132 11.0	325 22.7	09.0	312 29.4	49.5	207 48.1	03.4	330 10.0	25.3
D	12	147 13.5	340 22.4	N 7 07.8	327 30.4	N 0 48.9	222 50.7	S23 03.4	345 12.2	N 9 25.1
A	13	162 15.9	355 22.0	06.6	342 31.5	48.2	237 53.3	03.5	0 14.3	25.0
Y	14	177 18.4	10 21.6	05.3	357 32.5	47.6	252 56.0	03.5	15 16.5	24.9
	15	192 20.8	25 21.2	. . 04.1	12 33.5	. . 46.9	267 58.6	. . 03.5	30 18.7	. . 24.8
	16	207 23.3	40 20.9	02.9	27 34.5	46.2	283 01.3	03.5	45 20.9	24.7
	17	222 25.8	55 20.5	01.7	42 35.5	45.6	298 03.9	03.5	60 23.0	24.6
	18	237 28.2	70 20.1	N 7 00.4	57 36.6	N 0 44.9	313 06.5	S23 03.6	75 25.2	N 9 24.4
	19	252 30.7	85 19.8	6 59.2	72 37.6	44.3	328 09.2	03.6	90 27.4	24.3
	20	267 33.2	100 19.4	58.0	87 38.6	43.6	343 11.8	03.6	105 29.6	24.2
	21	282 35.6	115 19.0	. . 56.8	102 39.6	. . 43.0	358 14.4	. . 03.6	120 31.7	. . 24.1
	22	297 38.1	130 18.7	55.5	117 40.6	42.3	13 17.1	03.6	135 33.9	24.0
	23	312 40.6	145 18.3	54.3	132 41.6	41.7	28 19.7	03.7	150 36.1	23.9
Mer. Pass.		h m 2 16.6	v −0.4	d 1.2	v 1.0	d 0.7	v 2.6	d 0.0	v 2.2	d 0.1

STARS Name	SHA	Dec
	° ′	° ′
Acamar	315 20.9	S40 15.8
Achernar	335 28.9	S57 11.2
Acrux	173 14.2	S63 09.1
Adhara	255 15.7	S28 58.8
Aldebaran	290 53.6	N16 31.7
Alioth	166 23.9	N55 54.9
Alkaid	153 01.7	N49 16.4
Al Na'ir	27 47.6	S46 55.0
Alnilam	275 50.2	S 1 11.6
Alphard	218 00.0	S 8 41.7
Alphecca	126 14.0	N26 41.3
Alpheratz	357 47.1	N29 08.4
Altair	62 11.5	N 8 53.6
Ankaa	353 18.8	S42 15.2
Antares	112 30.6	S26 27.2
Arcturus	145 59.1	N19 08.3
Atria	107 35.6	S69 02.9
Avior	234 20.3	S59 32.1
Bellatrix	278 36.0	N 6 21.6
Betelgeuse	271 05.4	N 7 24.7
Canopus	263 58.1	S52 41.7
Capella	280 40.0	N46 00.4
Deneb	49 33.6	N45 18.8
Denebola	182 37.6	N14 31.5
Diphda	348 59.2	S17 56.1
Dubhe	193 56.4	N61 42.4
Elnath	278 17.4	N28 36.9
Eltanin	90 47.5	N51 29.4
Enif	33 50.4	N 9 55.0
Fomalhaut	15 27.5	S29 34.4
Gacrux	172 05.7	S57 09.9
Gienah	175 56.3	S17 35.4
Hadar	148 53.6	S60 25.2
Hamal	328 04.8	N23 30.3
Kaus Aust.	83 48.3	S34 22.9
Kochab	137 19.6	N74 07.4
Markab	13 41.7	N15 15.2
Menkar	314 18.8	N 4 07.6
Menkent	148 12.1	S36 24.9
Miaplacidus	221 41.7	S69 45.1
Mirfak	308 45.7	N49 53.4
Nunki	76 02.5	S26 17.2
Peacock	53 24.2	S56 42.5
Pollux	243 32.4	N28 00.4
Procyon	245 03.8	N 5 12.3
Rasalhague	96 09.6	N12 33.3
Regulus	207 47.6	N11 55.6
Rigel	281 15.7	S 8 11.3
Rigil Kent.	139 57.1	S60 52.5
Sabik	102 16.6	S15 44.2
Schedar	349 44.5	N56 35.0
Shaula	96 26.6	S37 06.8
Sirius	258 37.2	S16 43.4
Spica	158 35.3	S11 12.4
Suhail	222 55.7	S43 27.9
Vega	80 41.1	N38 47.6
Zuben'ubi	137 09.5	S16 04.8

	SHA	Mer. Pass.
	° ′	h m
Venus	194 51.2	13 18
Mars	181 09.0	14 11
Jupiter	75 30.8	21 11
Saturn	198 09.1	13 03

UT d	UT h	SUN GHA	SUN Dec	MOON GHA	*v*	MOON Dec	*d*	HP
d	h	° ′	° ′	° ′	′	° ′	′	′
16	00	178 55.7	N13 41.1	9 04.8	12.6	S17 23.0	11.8	55.9
	01	193 55.9	40.3	23 36.4	12.7	17 11.2	11.9	55.9
	02	208 56.0	39.5	38 08.1	12.7	16 59.3	12.0	55.9
	03	223 56.1	. . 38.7	52 39.8	12.7	16 47.3	12.1	55.9
	04	238 56.3	38.0	67 11.5	12.8	16 35.2	12.1	56.0
	05	253 56.4	37.2	81 43.3	12.9	16 23.1	12.3	56.0
	06	268 56.5	N13 36.4	96 15.2	12.8	S16 10.8	12.3	56.0
	07	283 56.7	35.6	110 47.0	12.9	15 58.5	12.4	56.0
S	08	298 56.8	34.8	125 18.9	13.0	15 46.1	12.5	56.0
A	09	313 56.9	. . 34.0	139 50.9	13.0	15 33.6	12.6	56.1
T	10	328 57.1	33.2	154 22.9	13.0	15 21.0	12.6	56.1
U	11	343 57.2	32.4	168 54.9	13.0	15 08.4	12.8	56.1
R	12	358 57.3	N13 31.6	183 26.9	13.1	S14 55.6	12.8	56.1
D	13	13 57.5	30.8	197 59.0	13.2	14 42.8	12.8	56.2
A	14	28 57.6	30.0	212 31.2	13.1	14 30.0	13.0	56.2
Y	15	43 57.7	. . 29.2	227 03.3	13.2	14 17.0	13.0	56.2
	16	58 57.9	28.4	241 35.5	13.2	14 04.0	13.1	56.2
	17	73 58.0	27.6	256 07.7	13.3	13 50.9	13.2	56.2
	18	88 58.1	N13 26.8	270 40.0	13.3	S13 37.7	13.2	56.3
	19	103 58.3	26.0	285 12.3	13.3	13 24.5	13.4	56.3
	20	118 58.4	25.2	299 44.6	13.4	13 11.1	13.3	56.3
	21	133 58.5	. . 24.4	314 17.0	13.4	12 57.8	13.5	56.3
	22	148 58.7	23.6	328 49.4	13.4	12 44.3	13.5	56.4
	23	163 58.8	22.8	343 21.8	13.4	12 30.8	13.6	56.4
17	00	178 58.9	N13 22.0	357 54.2	13.5	S12 17.2	13.7	56.4
	01	193 59.1	21.2	12 26.7	13.5	12 03.5	13.7	56.4
	02	208 59.2	20.4	26 59.2	13.5	11 49.8	13.8	56.5
	03	223 59.3	. . 19.6	41 31.7	13.6	11 36.0	13.8	56.5
	04	238 59.5	18.8	56 04.3	13.5	11 22.2	13.9	56.5
	05	253 59.6	18.0	70 36.8	13.6	11 08.3	14.0	56.5
	06	268 59.7	N13 17.2	85 09.4	13.7	S10 54.3	14.0	56.5
	07	283 59.9	16.4	99 42.1	13.6	10 40.3	14.1	56.6
	08	299 00.0	15.6	114 14.7	13.7	10 26.2	14.1	56.6
S	09	314 00.2	. . 14.8	128 47.4	13.7	10 12.1	14.2	56.6
U	10	329 00.3	14.0	143 20.1	13.7	9 57.9	14.2	56.6
N	11	344 00.4	13.2	157 52.8	13.7	9 43.7	14.3	56.7
D	12	359 00.6	N13 12.4	172 25.5	13.8	S 9 29.4	14.4	56.7
A	13	14 00.7	11.6	186 58.3	13.7	9 15.0	14.4	56.7
Y	14	29 00.8	10.8	201 31.0	13.8	9 00.6	14.5	56.7
	15	44 01.0	. . 10.0	216 03.8	13.8	8 46.1	14.5	56.7
	16	59 01.1	09.2	230 36.6	13.8	8 31.6	14.5	56.8
	17	74 01.3	08.4	245 09.4	13.8	8 17.1	14.6	56.8
	18	89 01.4	N13 07.6	259 42.2	13.9	S 8 02.5	14.7	56.8
	19	104 01.5	06.8	274 15.1	13.8	7 47.8	14.7	56.8
	20	119 01.7	06.0	288 47.9	13.9	7 33.1	14.7	56.9
	21	134 01.8	. . 05.2	303 20.8	13.9	7 18.4	14.8	56.9
	22	149 02.0	04.4	317 53.7	13.9	7 03.6	14.8	56.9
	23	164 02.1	03.6	332 26.6	13.9	6 48.8	14.9	56.9
18	00	179 02.2	N13 02.8	346 59.5	13.9	S 6 33.9	14.9	56.9
	01	194 02.4	01.9	1 32.4	13.9	6 19.0	14.9	57.0
	02	209 02.5	01.1	16 05.3	13.9	6 04.1	15.0	57.0
	03	224 02.7	13 00.3	30 38.2	13.9	5 49.1	15.0	57.0
	04	239 02.8	12 59.5	45 11.1	13.9	5 34.1	15.0	57.0
	05	254 02.9	58.7	59 44.0	14.0	5 19.1	15.1	57.0
	06	269 03.1	N12 57.9	74 17.0	13.9	S 5 04.0	15.1	57.1
	07	284 03.2	57.1	88 49.9	13.9	4 48.9	15.2	57.1
	08	299 03.4	56.3	103 22.8	14.0	4 33.7	15.2	57.1
M	09	314 03.5	. . 55.5	117 55.8	13.9	4 18.5	15.2	57.1
O	10	329 03.7	54.7	132 28.7	13.9	4 03.3	15.2	57.2
N	11	344 03.8	53.8	147 01.6	13.9	3 48.1	15.3	57.2
D	12	359 03.9	N12 53.0	161 34.5	14.0	S 3 32.8	15.3	57.2
A	13	14 04.1	52.2	176 07.5	13.9	3 17.5	15.3	57.2
Y	14	29 04.2	51.4	190 40.4	13.9	3 02.2	15.3	57.2
	15	44 04.4	. . 50.6	205 13.3	13.9	2 46.9	15.4	57.3
	16	59 04.5	49.8	219 46.2	13.9	2 31.5	15.4	57.3
	17	74 04.7	49.0	234 19.1	13.9	2 16.1	15.4	57.3
	18	89 04.8	N12 48.2	248 52.0	13.8	S 2 00.7	15.4	57.3
	19	104 04.9	47.3	263 24.8	13.9	1 45.3	15.4	57.3
	20	119 05.1	46.5	277 57.7	13.9	1 29.9	15.5	57.4
	21	134 05.2	. . 45.7	292 30.6	13.8	1 14.4	15.5	57.4
	22	149 05.4	44.9	307 03.4	13.8	0 58.9	15.5	57.4
	23	164 05.5	44.1	321 36.2	13.8	S 0 43.4	15.5	57.4
		SD 15.8	*d* 0.8	SD	15.3		15.4	15.6

Lat.	Twilight Naut.	Twilight Civil	Sunrise	Moonrise 16	Moonrise 17	Moonrise 18	Moonrise 19
°	h m	h m	h m	h m	h m	h m	h m
N 72	////	////	02 40	21 05	20 22	19 49	19 16
N 70	////	01 04	03 08	20 42	20 12	19 46	19 22
68	////	02 00	03 29	20 24	20 03	19 45	19 27
66	////	02 33	03 45	20 09	19 55	19 43	19 31
64	00 56	02 56	03 59	19 57	19 49	19 42	19 34
62	01 47	03 14	04 10	19 47	19 44	19 41	19 38
60	02 16	03 29	04 20	19 38	19 39	19 40	19 40
N 58	02 38	03 42	04 28	19 30	19 35	19 39	19 43
56	02 55	03 52	04 35	19 23	19 31	19 38	19 45
54	03 10	04 02	04 42	19 17	19 28	19 37	19 47
52	03 22	04 10	04 48	19 11	19 24	19 36	19 49
50	03 32	04 17	04 53	19 06	19 22	19 36	19 50
45	03 54	04 33	05 04	18 55	19 15	19 35	19 54
N 40	04 10	04 45	05 14	18 46	19 10	19 33	19 57
35	04 23	04 55	05 22	18 38	19 06	19 32	19 59
30	04 34	05 04	05 29	18 31	19 02	19 32	20 02
20	04 51	05 18	05 41	18 19	18 55	19 30	20 06
N 10	05 04	05 29	05 51	18 08	18 49	19 29	20 09
0	05 15	05 39	06 01	17 58	18 43	19 28	20 13
S 10	05 24	05 49	06 10	17 48	18 37	19 27	20 16
20	05 32	05 58	06 20	17 37	18 31	19 25	20 20
30	05 39	06 07	06 31	17 24	18 24	19 24	20 25
35	05 42	06 12	06 38	17 17	18 20	19 23	20 27
40	05 46	06 17	06 45	17 09	18 15	19 22	20 30
45	05 49	06 23	06 54	16 59	18 10	19 21	20 33
S 50	05 52	06 30	07 04	16 47	18 03	19 20	20 37
52	05 54	06 33	07 08	16 42	18 00	19 19	20 39
54	05 55	06 37	07 14	16 36	17 57	19 19	20 41
56	05 57	06 40	07 19	16 29	17 53	19 18	20 44
58	05 58	06 44	07 26	16 21	17 49	19 17	20 46
S 60	06 00	06 49	07 33	16 13	17 45	19 16	20 49

Lat.	Sunset	Twilight Civil	Twilight Naut.	Moonset 16	Moonset 17	Moonset 18	Moonset 19
°	h m	h m	h m	h m	h m	h m	h m
N 72	21 23	////	////	00 25	03 39	05 58	08 09
N 70	20 56	22 52	////	01 34	04 00	06 05	08 07
68	20 36	22 02	////	02 10	04 16	06 12	08 05
66	20 20	21 31	////	02 35	04 29	06 17	08 03
64	20 07	21 09	23 01	02 55	04 40	06 21	08 02
62	19 56	20 51	22 16	03 11	04 49	06 25	08 01
60	19 47	20 36	21 48	03 24	04 57	06 28	08 00
N 58	19 38	20 24	21 27	03 35	05 03	06 31	07 59
56	19 31	20 14	21 10	03 45	05 09	06 34	07 58
54	19 25	20 05	20 56	03 53	05 15	06 36	07 58
52	19 19	19 57	20 44	04 01	05 19	06 38	07 57
50	19 14	19 49	20 34	04 08	05 24	06 40	07 57
45	19 03	19 34	20 13	04 22	05 33	06 44	07 55
N 40	18 54	19 22	19 57	04 34	05 41	06 47	07 54
35	18 46	19 12	19 44	04 44	05 47	06 50	07 54
30	18 39	19 04	19 33	04 53	05 53	06 53	07 53
20	18 27	18 50	19 17	05 08	06 03	06 57	07 51
N 10	18 17	18 38	19 04	05 21	06 11	07 01	07 50
0	18 07	18 29	18 53	05 34	06 19	07 04	07 49
S 10	17 58	18 19	18 44	05 46	06 27	07 08	07 48
20	17 48	18 11	18 37	05 59	06 36	07 11	07 47
30	17 37	18 01	18 30	06 13	06 45	07 16	07 45
35	17 31	17 57	18 26	06 22	06 51	07 18	07 45
40	17 23	17 51	18 23	06 31	06 57	07 21	07 44
45	17 15	17 45	18 20	06 42	07 04	07 24	07 43
S 50	17 05	17 38	18 16	06 56	07 12	07 27	07 41
52	17 00	17 35	18 15	07 02	07 16	07 29	07 41
54	16 55	17 32	18 14	07 09	07 21	07 31	07 40
56	16 49	17 28	18 12	07 16	07 25	07 33	07 39
58	16 43	17 25	18 11	07 25	07 31	07 35	07 39
S 60	16 36	17 20	18 09	07 35	07 36	07 37	07 38

Day	SUN Eqn. of Time 00^h	SUN Eqn. of Time 12^h	SUN Mer. Pass.	MOON Mer. Pass. Upper	MOON Mer. Pass. Lower	MOON Age	MOON Phase
d	m s	m s	h m	h m	h m	d %	
16	04 17	04 11	12 04	24 09	11 46	15 100	
17	04 05	03 58	12 04	00 09	12 31	16 100	○
18	03 51	03 45	12 04	00 54	13 16	17 97	

UT		ARIES	VENUS −3.8		MARS +1.7		JUPITER −2.6		SATURN +0.8	
	d h	GHA ° ′	GHA ° ′	Dec ° ′	GHA ° ′	Dec ° ′	GHA ° ′	Dec ° ′	GHA ° ′	Dec ° ′
	19 00	327 43.0	160 17.9	N 6 53.1	147 42.7	N 0 41.0	43 22.3	S23 03.7	165 38.3	N 9 23.7
	01	342 45.5	175 17.5	51.8	162 43.7	40.4	58 25.0	03.7	180 40.4	23.6
	02	357 48.0	190 17.2	50.6	177 44.7	39.7	73 27.6	03.7	195 42.6	23.5
	03	12 50.4	205 16.8	. . 49.4	192 45.7	. . 39.0	88 30.2	. . 03.7	210 44.8	. . 23.4
	04	27 52.9	220 16.4	48.2	207 46.7	38.4	103 32.9	03.7	225 46.9	23.3
	05	42 55.3	235 16.1	46.9	222 47.7	37.7	118 35.5	03.8	240 49.1	23.2
	06	57 57.8	250 15.7	N 6 45.7	237 48.8	N 0 37.1	133 38.1	S23 03.8	255 51.3	N 9 23.0
	07	73 00.3	265 15.3	44.5	252 49.8	36.4	148 40.7	03.8	270 53.5	22.9
	08	88 02.7	280 15.0	43.2	267 50.8	35.8	163 43.4	03.8	285 55.6	22.8
T	09	103 05.2	295 14.6	. . 42.0	282 51.8	. . 35.1	178 46.0	. . 03.8	300 57.8	. . 22.7
U	10	118 07.7	310 14.2	40.8	297 52.8	34.5	193 48.6	03.9	316 00.0	22.6
E	11	133 10.1	325 13.9	39.5	312 53.8	33.8	208 51.3	03.9	331 02.2	22.5
S	12	148 12.6	340 13.5	N 6 38.3	327 54.9	N 0 33.1	223 53.9	S23 03.9	346 04.3	N 9 22.3
D	13	163 15.1	355 13.1	37.1	342 55.9	32.5	238 56.5	03.9	1 06.5	22.2
A	14	178 17.5	10 12.8	35.8	357 56.9	31.8	253 59.1	03.9	16 08.7	22.1
Y	15	193 20.0	25 12.4	. . 34.6	12 57.9	. . 31.2	269 01.8	. . 04.0	31 10.9	. . 22.0
	16	208 22.4	40 12.1	33.4	27 58.9	30.5	284 04.4	04.0	46 13.0	21.9
	17	223 24.9	55 11.7	32.1	42 59.9	29.9	299 07.0	04.0	61 15.2	21.8
	18	238 27.4	70 11.3	N 6 30.9	58 00.9	N 0 29.2	314 09.7	S23 04.0	76 17.4	N 9 21.7
	19	253 29.8	85 11.0	29.7	73 02.0	28.6	329 12.3	04.0	91 19.5	21.5
	20	268 32.3	100 10.6	28.4	88 03.0	27.9	344 14.9	04.1	106 21.7	21.4
	21	283 34.8	115 10.2	. . 27.2	103 04.0	. . 27.2	359 17.5	. . 04.1	121 23.9	. . 21.3
	22	298 37.2	130 09.9	26.0	118 05.0	26.6	14 20.2	04.1	136 26.1	21.2
	23	313 39.7	145 09.5	24.7	133 06.0	25.9	29 22.8	04.1	151 28.2	21.1
	20 00	328 42.2	160 09.1	N 6 23.5	148 07.0	N 0 25.3	44 25.4	S23 04.1	166 30.4	N 9 21.0
	01	343 44.6	175 08.8	22.3	163 08.1	24.6	59 28.0	04.1	181 32.6	20.8
	02	358 47.1	190 08.4	21.0	178 09.1	24.0	74 30.7	04.2	196 34.8	20.7
	03	13 49.6	205 08.1	. . 19.8	193 10.1	. . 23.3	89 33.3	. . 04.2	211 36.9	. . 20.6
	04	28 52.0	220 07.7	18.6	208 11.1	22.6	104 35.9	04.2	226 39.1	20.5
	05	43 54.5	235 07.3	17.3	223 12.1	22.0	119 38.5	04.2	241 41.3	20.4
	06	58 56.9	250 07.0	N 6 16.1	238 13.1	N 0 21.3	134 41.2	S23 04.2	256 43.5	N 9 20.3
W	07	73 59.4	265 06.6	14.8	253 14.1	20.7	149 43.8	04.3	271 45.6	20.1
E	08	89 01.9	280 06.3	13.6	268 15.2	20.0	164 46.4	04.3	286 47.8	20.0
D	09	104 04.3	295 05.9	. . 12.4	283 16.2	. . 19.4	179 49.0	. . 04.3	301 50.0	. . 19.9
N	10	119 06.8	310 05.5	11.1	298 17.2	18.7	194 51.6	04.3	316 52.1	19.8
	11	134 09.3	325 05.2	09.9	313 18.2	18.1	209 54.3	04.3	331 54.3	19.7
E	12	149 11.7	340 04.8	N 6 08.7	328 19.2	N 0 17.4	224 56.9	S23 04.3	346 56.5	N 9 19.6
S	13	164 14.2	355 04.5	07.4	343 20.2	16.7	239 59.5	04.4	1 58.7	19.4
D	14	179 16.7	10 04.1	06.2	358 21.2	16.1	255 02.1	04.4	17 00.8	19.3
A	15	194 19.1	25 03.7	. . 04.9	13 22.3	. . 15.4	270 04.8	. . 04.4	32 03.0	. . 19.2
Y	16	209 21.6	40 03.4	03.7	28 23.3	14.8	285 07.4	04.4	47 05.2	19.1
	17	224 24.1	55 03.0	02.5	43 24.3	14.1	300 10.0	04.4	62 07.4	19.0
	18	239 26.5	70 02.7	N 6 01.2	58 25.3	N 0 13.5	315 12.6	S23 04.5	77 09.5	N 9 18.9
	19	254 29.0	85 02.3	6 00.0	73 26.3	12.8	330 15.2	04.5	92 11.7	18.7
	20	269 31.4	100 02.0	5 58.7	88 27.3	12.1	345 17.9	04.5	107 13.9	18.6
	21	284 33.9	115 01.6	. . 57.5	103 28.3	. . 11.5	0 20.5	. . 04.5	122 16.0	. . 18.5
	22	299 36.4	130 01.2	56.2	118 29.4	10.8	15 23.1	04.5	137 18.2	18.4
	23	314 38.8	145 00.9	55.0	133 30.4	10.2	30 25.7	04.5	152 20.4	18.3
	21 00	329 41.3	160 00.5	N 5 53.8	148 31.4	N 0 09.5	45 28.3	S23 04.6	167 22.6	N 9 18.2
	01	344 43.8	175 00.2	52.5	163 32.4	08.9	60 30.9	04.6	182 24.7	18.0
	02	359 46.2	189 59.8	51.3	178 33.4	08.2	75 33.6	04.6	197 26.9	17.9
	03	14 48.7	204 59.5	. . 50.0	193 34.4	. . 07.5	90 36.2	. . 04.6	212 29.1	. . 17.8
	04	29 51.2	219 59.1	48.8	208 35.4	06.9	105 38.8	04.6	227 31.3	17.7
	05	44 53.6	234 58.7	47.5	223 36.4	06.2	120 41.4	04.6	242 33.4	17.6
	06	59 56.1	249 58.4	N 5 46.3	238 37.5	N 0 05.6	135 44.0	S23 04.7	257 35.6	N 9 17.5
	07	74 58.5	264 58.0	45.1	253 38.5	04.9	150 46.6	04.7	272 37.8	17.3
T	08	90 01.0	279 57.7	43.8	268 39.5	04.3	165 49.2	04.7	287 39.9	17.2
H	09	105 03.5	294 57.3	. . 42.6	283 40.5	. . 03.6	180 51.9	. . 04.7	302 42.1	. . 17.1
U	10	120 05.9	309 57.0	41.3	298 41.5	03.0	195 54.5	04.7	317 44.3	17.0
R	11	135 08.4	324 56.6	40.1	313 42.5	02.3	210 57.1	04.7	332 46.5	16.9
S	12	150 10.9	339 56.3	N 5 38.8	328 43.5	N 0 01.6	225 59.7	S23 04.8	347 48.6	N 9 16.8
D	13	165 13.3	354 55.9	37.6	343 44.5	01.0	241 02.3	04.8	2 50.8	16.6
A	14	180 15.8	9 55.6	36.3	358 45.6	N 00.3	256 04.9	04.8	17 53.0	16.5
Y	15	195 18.3	24 55.2	. . 35.1	13 46.6	S 00.3	271 07.5	. . 04.8	32 55.1	. . 16.4
	16	210 20.7	39 54.9	33.8	28 47.6	01.0	286 10.2	04.8	47 57.3	16.3
	17	225 23.2	54 54.5	32.6	43 48.6	01.6	301 12.8	04.9	62 59.5	16.2
	18	240 25.7	69 54.1	N 5 31.3	58 49.6	S 0 02.3	316 15.4	S23 04.9	78 01.7	N 9 16.0
	19	255 28.1	84 53.8	30.1	73 50.6	03.0	331 18.0	04.9	93 03.8	15.9
	20	270 30.6	99 53.4	28.9	88 51.6	03.6	346 20.6	04.9	108 06.0	15.8
	21	285 33.0	114 53.1	. . 27.6	103 52.6	. . 04.3	1 23.2	. . 04.9	123 08.2	. . 15.7
	22	300 35.5	129 52.7	26.4	118 53.7	04.9	16 25.8	04.9	138 10.4	15.6
	23	315 38.0	144 52.4	25.1	133 54.7	05.6	31 28.4	05.0	153 12.5	15.5
Mer. Pass.		h m 2 04.8	v −0.4	d 1.2	v 1.0	d 0.7	v 2.6	d 0.0	v 2.2	d 0.1

STARS

Name	SHA ° ′	Dec ° ′
Acamar	315 20.9	S40 15.8
Achernar	335 28.9	S57 11.2
Acrux	173 14.2	S63 09.0
Adhara	255 15.7	S28 58.8
Aldebaran	290 53.6	N16 31.7
Alioth	166 24.0	N55 54.9
Alkaid	153 01.8	N49 16.4
Al Na'ir	27 47.6	S46 55.0
Alnilam	275 50.2	S 1 11.6
Alphard	218 00.0	S 8 41.7
Alphecca	126 14.0	N26 41.3
Alpheratz	357 47.0	N29 08.4
Altair	62 11.5	N 8 53.6
Ankaa	353 18.7	S42 15.2
Antares	112 30.7	S26 27.2
Arcturus	145 59.1	N19 08.3
Atria	107 35.7	S69 02.9
Avior	234 20.3	S59 32.0
Bellatrix	278 36.0	N 6 21.6
Betelgeuse	271 05.4	N 7 24.7
Canopus	263 58.1	S52 41.7
Capella	280 40.0	N46 00.4
Deneb	49 33.6	N45 18.8
Denebola	182 37.6	N14 31.5
Diphda	348 59.2	S17 56.1
Dubhe	193 56.4	N61 42.4
Elnath	278 17.4	N28 36.9
Eltanin	90 47.5	N51 29.4
Enif	33 50.4	N 9 55.0
Fomalhaut	15 27.5	S29 34.4
Gacrux	172 05.7	S57 09.9
Gienah	175 56.3	S17 35.4
Hadar	148 53.6	S60 25.2
Hamal	328 04.8	N23 30.3
Kaus Aust.	83 48.3	S34 22.9
Kochab	137 19.6	N74 07.4
Markab	13 41.7	N15 15.2
Menkar	314 18.8	N 4 07.6
Menkent	148 12.1	S36 24.9
Miaplacidus	221 41.7	S69 45.1
Mirfak	308 45.6	N49 53.5
Nunki	76 02.5	S26 17.2
Peacock	53 24.2	S56 42.5
Pollux	243 32.4	N28 00.4
Procyon	245 03.8	N 5 12.3
Rasalhague	96 09.6	N12 33.3
Regulus	207 47.6	N11 55.6
Rigel	281 15.6	S 8 11.2
Rigil Kent.	139 57.1	S60 52.5
Sabik	102 16.6	S15 44.2
Schedar	349 44.5	N56 35.1
Shaula	96 26.6	S37 06.8
Sirius	258 37.1	S16 43.4
Spica	158 35.3	S11 12.4
Suhail	222 55.7	S43 27.9
Vega	80 41.1	N38 47.7
Zuben'ubi	137 09.5	S16 04.7

	SHA ° ′	Mer. Pass. h m
Venus	191 27.0	13 20
Mars	179 24.9	14 07
Jupiter	75 43.3	20 59
Saturn	197 48.3	12 52

	UT	SUN GHA	SUN Dec	MOON GHA	MOON *v*	MOON Dec	MOON *d*	MOON HP
	d h	° ′	° ′	° ′	′	° ′	′	′
	19 00	179 05.7	N12 43.3	336 09.0	13.8	S 0 27.9	15.5	57.4
	01	194 05.8	42.4	350 41.8	13.8	S 0 12.4	15.5	57.5
	02	209 06.0	41.6	5 14.6	13.7	N 0 03.1	15.5	57.5
	03	224 06.1	. . 40.8	19 47.3	13.7	0 18.6	15.6	57.5
	04	239 06.3	40.0	34 20.0	13.8	0 34.2	15.5	57.5
	05	254 06.4	39.2	48 52.8	13.6	0 49.7	15.6	57.5
	06	269 06.5	N12 38.4	63 25.4	13.7	N 1 05.3	15.6	57.6
	07	284 06.7	37.5	77 58.1	13.6	1 20.9	15.5	57.6
T	08	299 06.8	36.7	92 30.7	13.6	1 36.4	15.6	57.6
U	09	314 07.0	. . 35.9	107 03.3	13.6	1 52.0	15.6	57.6
E	10	329 07.1	35.1	121 35.9	13.6	2 07.6	15.5	57.6
S	11	344 07.3	34.3	136 08.5	13.5	2 23.1	15.6	57.7
D	12	359 07.4	N12 33.4	150 41.0	13.5	N 2 38.7	15.6	57.7
A	13	14 07.6	32.6	165 13.5	13.5	2 54.3	15.5	57.7
Y	14	29 07.7	31.8	179 46.0	13.4	3 09.8	15.6	57.7
	15	44 07.9	. . 31.0	194 18.4	13.4	3 25.4	15.5	57.7
	16	59 08.0	30.1	208 50.8	13.4	3 40.9	15.6	57.8
	17	74 08.2	29.3	223 23.2	13.3	3 56.5	15.5	57.8
	18	89 08.3	N12 28.5	237 55.5	13.3	N 4 12.0	15.5	57.8
	19	104 08.5	27.7	252 27.8	13.2	4 27.5	15.5	57.8
	20	119 08.6	26.9	267 00.0	13.2	4 43.0	15.5	57.8
	21	134 08.8	. . 26.0	281 32.2	13.2	4 58.5	15.5	57.9
	22	149 08.9	25.2	296 04.4	13.1	5 14.0	15.5	57.9
	23	164 09.1	24.4	310 36.5	13.1	5 29.5	15.4	57.9
	20 00	179 09.2	N12 23.6	325 08.6	13.0	N 5 44.9	15.5	57.9
	01	194 09.4	22.7	339 40.6	13.0	6 00.4	15.4	57.9
	02	209 09.5	21.9	354 12.6	12.9	6 15.8	15.4	57.9
	03	224 09.7	. . 21.1	8 44.5	12.9	6 31.2	15.3	58.0
	04	239 09.8	20.3	23 16.4	12.9	6 46.5	15.4	58.0
	05	254 10.0	19.4	37 48.3	12.8	7 01.9	15.3	58.0
	06	269 10.1	N12 18.6	52 20.1	12.7	N 7 17.2	15.3	58.0
W	07	284 10.3	17.8	66 51.8	12.7	7 32.5	15.3	58.0
E	08	299 10.4	16.9	81 23.5	12.7	7 47.8	15.2	58.1
D	09	314 10.6	. . 16.1	95 55.2	12.5	8 03.0	15.2	58.1
N	10	329 10.7	15.3	110 26.7	12.6	8 18.2	15.2	58.1
E	11	344 10.9	14.5	124 58.3	12.4	8 33.4	15.1	58.1
S	12	359 11.0	N12 13.6	139 29.7	12.4	N 8 48.5	15.1	58.1
D	13	14 11.2	12.8	154 01.1	12.4	9 03.6	15.1	58.1
A	14	29 11.4	12.0	168 32.5	12.3	9 18.7	15.0	58.2
Y	15	44 11.5	. . 11.1	183 03.8	12.2	9 33.7	15.0	58.2
	16	59 11.7	10.3	197 35.0	12.2	9 48.7	15.0	58.2
	17	74 11.8	09.5	212 06.2	12.1	10 03.7	14.9	58.2
	18	89 12.0	N12 08.7	226 37.3	12.0	N10 18.6	14.9	58.2
	19	104 12.1	07.8	241 08.3	12.0	10 33.5	14.8	58.2
	20	119 12.3	07.0	255 39.3	11.9	10 48.3	14.8	58.3
	21	134 12.4	. . 06.2	270 10.2	11.8	11 03.1	14.7	58.3
	22	149 12.6	05.3	284 41.0	11.8	11 17.8	14.7	58.3
	23	164 12.7	04.5	299 11.8	11.6	11 32.5	14.7	58.3
	21 00	179 12.9	N12 03.7	313 42.4	11.7	N11 47.2	14.5	58.3
	01	194 13.0	02.8	328 13.1	11.5	12 01.7	14.6	58.3
	02	209 13.2	02.0	342 43.6	11.5	12 16.3	14.4	58.4
	03	224 13.4	. . 01.2	357 14.1	11.4	12 30.7	14.5	58.4
	04	239 13.5	12 00.3	11 44.5	11.3	12 45.2	14.3	58.4
	05	254 13.7	11 59.5	26 14.8	11.2	12 59.5	14.3	58.4
	06	269 13.8	N11 58.7	40 45.0	11.2	N13 13.8	14.3	58.4
	07	284 14.0	57.8	55 15.2	11.1	13 28.1	14.1	58.4
T	08	299 14.1	57.0	69 45.3	11.0	13 42.2	14.2	58.5
H	09	314 14.3	. . 56.2	84 15.3	10.9	13 56.4	14.0	58.5
U	10	329 14.5	55.3	98 45.2	10.9	14 10.4	14.0	58.5
R	11	344 14.6	54.5	113 15.1	10.7	14 24.4	13.9	58.5
S	12	359 14.8	N11 53.6	127 44.8	10.7	N14 38.3	13.8	58.5
D	13	14 14.9	52.8	142 14.5	10.6	14 52.1	13.8	58.5
A	14	29 15.1	52.0	156 44.1	10.5	15 05.9	13.7	58.5
Y	15	44 15.2	. . 51.1	171 13.6	10.4	15 19.6	13.6	58.6
	16	59 15.4	50.3	185 43.0	10.4	15 33.2	13.6	58.6
	17	74 15.6	49.5	200 12.4	10.2	15 46.8	13.5	58.6
	18	89 15.7	N11 48.6	214 41.6	10.2	N16 00.3	13.3	58.6
	19	104 15.9	47.8	229 10.8	10.0	16 13.6	13.4	58.6
	20	119 16.0	46.9	243 39.8	10.0	16 27.0	13.2	58.6
	21	134 16.2	. . 46.1	258 08.8	9.9	16 40.2	13.1	58.6
	22	149 16.4	45.3	272 37.7	9.8	16 53.3	13.1	58.7
	23	164 16.5	44.4	287 06.5	9.7	N17 06.4	12.9	58.7
		SD 15.8	*d* 0.8	SD	15.7	15.8		15.9

Lat.	Twilight Naut.	Twilight Civil	Sunrise	Moonrise 19	Moonrise 20	Moonrise 21	Moonrise 22
°	h m	h m	h m	h m	h m	h m	h m
N 72	////	////	02 58	19 16	18 38	17 39	▭
N 70	////	01 38	03 23	19 22	18 54	18 16	▭
68	////	02 20	03 41	19 27	19 07	18 42	17 53
66	////	02 47	03 56	19 31	19 18	19 02	18 38
64	01 26	03 08	04 08	19 34	19 27	19 18	19 07
62	02 04	03 24	04 18	19 38	19 35	19 32	19 30
60	02 29	03 38	04 27	19 40	19 41	19 44	19 49
N 58	02 48	03 49	04 35	19 43	19 47	19 54	20 04
56	03 04	03 59	04 41	19 45	19 53	20 03	20 17
54	03 17	04 08	04 47	19 47	19 57	20 11	20 29
52	03 28	04 15	04 53	19 49	20 02	20 18	20 39
50	03 38	04 22	04 57	19 50	20 06	20 24	20 48
45	03 58	04 37	05 08	19 54	20 14	20 38	21 07
N 40	04 13	04 48	05 17	19 57	20 22	20 50	21 23
35	04 26	04 57	05 24	19 59	20 28	21 00	21 37
30	04 36	05 06	05 30	20 02	20 34	21 09	21 49
20	04 52	05 19	05 41	20 06	20 43	21 24	22 09
N 10	05 04	05 29	05 51	20 09	20 52	21 37	22 27
0	05 14	05 39	06 00	20 13	21 00	21 50	22 43
S 10	05 22	05 47	06 09	20 16	21 08	22 02	23 00
20	05 30	05 55	06 18	20 20	21 17	22 16	23 18
30	05 36	06 04	06 28	20 25	21 27	22 32	23 39
35	05 39	06 08	06 34	20 27	21 33	22 41	23 52
40	05 42	06 13	06 41	20 30	21 40	22 52	24 06
45	05 44	06 19	06 49	20 33	21 48	23 04	24 23
S 50	05 47	06 25	06 58	20 37	21 57	23 20	24 44
52	05 48	06 28	07 02	20 39	22 02	23 27	24 55
54	05 49	06 30	07 07	20 41	22 06	23 35	25 06
56	05 50	06 34	07 12	20 44	22 12	23 44	25 19
58	05 51	06 37	07 18	20 46	22 18	23 54	25 35
S 60	05 52	06 41	07 25	20 49	22 25	24 06	00 06

Lat.	Sunset	Twilight Civil	Twilight Naut.	Moonset 19	Moonset 20	Moonset 21	Moonset 22
°	h m	h m	h m	h m	h m	h m	h m
N 72	21 03	////	////	08 09	10 25	13 08	▭
N 70	20 40	22 20	////	08 07	10 12	12 33	▭
68	20 22	21 42	////	08 05	10 01	12 09	14 47
66	20 08	21 16	////	08 03	09 53	11 50	14 04
64	19 56	20 56	22 33	08 02	09 46	11 35	13 35
62	19 46	20 40	21 59	08 01	09 39	11 23	13 13
60	19 38	20 27	21 34	08 00	09 34	11 12	12 56
N 58	19 31	20 15	21 16	07 59	09 29	11 03	12 41
56	19 24	20 06	21 00	07 58	09 25	10 55	12 29
54	19 18	19 57	20 47	07 58	09 21	10 48	12 18
52	19 13	19 50	20 36	07 57	09 18	10 42	12 08
50	19 08	19 43	20 27	07 57	09 15	10 36	12 00
45	18 58	19 29	20 07	07 55	09 08	10 24	11 42
N 40	18 49	19 18	19 52	07 54	09 03	10 14	11 27
35	18 42	19 08	19 40	07 54	08 58	10 05	11 15
30	18 36	19 01	19 30	07 53	08 54	09 58	11 04
20	18 25	18 47	19 14	07 51	08 47	09 45	10 46
N 10	18 15	18 37	19 02	07 50	08 41	09 34	10 30
0	18 07	18 28	18 52	07 49	08 35	09 23	10 15
S 10	17 58	18 19	18 44	07 48	08 29	09 13	10 00
20	17 49	18 11	18 37	07 47	08 23	09 02	09 44
30	17 39	18 03	18 31	07 45	08 16	08 49	09 26
35	17 33	17 59	18 28	07 45	08 12	08 42	09 16
40	17 26	17 54	18 26	07 44	08 07	08 34	09 04
45	17 18	17 49	18 23	07 43	08 02	08 24	08 50
S 50	17 09	17 43	18 20	07 41	07 56	08 13	08 33
52	17 05	17 40	18 19	07 41	07 53	08 07	08 25
54	17 00	17 37	18 18	07 40	07 50	08 01	08 16
56	16 55	17 34	18 17	07 39	07 46	07 55	08 07
58	16 49	17 30	18 16	07 39	07 43	07 48	07 55
S 60	16 43	17 27	18 15	07 38	07 38	07 40	07 43

Day	SUN Eqn. of Time 00^h	SUN Eqn. of Time 12^h	SUN Mer. Pass.	MOON Mer. Pass. Upper	MOON Mer. Pass. Lower	MOON Age	MOON Phase
d	m s	m s	h m	h m	h m	d	%
19	03 38	03 31	12 04	01 38	14 01	18	92
20	03 23	03 16	12 03	02 24	14 47	19	86
21	03 09	03 01	12 03	03 11	15 36	20	77

UT d	h	ARIES GHA ° ′	VENUS −3.8 GHA ° ′	Dec ° ′	MARS +1.7 GHA ° ′	Dec ° ′	JUPITER −2.6 GHA ° ′	Dec ° ′	SATURN +0.8 GHA ° ′	Dec ° ′
22	00	330 40.4	159 52.0	N 5 23.9	148 55.7	S 0 06.3	46 31.0	S23 05.0	168 14.7	N 9 15.3
	01	345 42.9	174 51.7	22.6	163 56.7	06.9	61 33.6	05.0	183 16.9	15.2
	02	0 45.4	189 51.3	21.4	178 57.7	07.6	76 36.3	05.0	198 19.0	15.1
	03	15 47.8	204 51.0	. . 20.1	193 58.7	. . 08.2	91 38.9	. . 05.0	213 21.2	. . 15.0
	04	30 50.3	219 50.6	18.9	208 59.7	08.9	106 41.5	05.0	228 23.4	14.9
	05	45 52.8	234 50.3	17.6	224 00.7	09.5	121 44.1	05.1	243 25.6	14.8
	06	60 55.2	249 49.9	N 5 16.4	239 01.7	S 0 10.2	136 46.7	S23 05.1	258 27.7	N 9 14.6
	07	75 57.7	264 49.6	15.1	254 02.8	10.9	151 49.3	05.1	273 29.9	14.5
	08	91 00.1	279 49.2	13.9	269 03.8	11.5	166 51.9	05.1	288 32.1	14.4
F	09	106 02.6	294 48.9	. . 12.6	284 04.8	. . 12.2	181 54.5	. . 05.1	303 34.2	. . 14.3
R	10	121 05.1	309 48.5	11.4	299 05.8	12.8	196 57.1	05.1	318 36.4	14.2
I	11	136 07.5	324 48.2	10.1	314 06.8	13.5	211 59.7	05.2	333 38.6	14.1
D	12	151 10.0	339 47.8	N 5 08.8	329 07.8	S 0 14.1	227 02.3	S23 05.2	348 40.8	N 9 13.9
A	13	166 12.5	354 47.5	07.6	344 08.8	14.8	242 04.9	05.2	3 42.9	13.8
Y	14	181 14.9	9 47.1	06.3	359 09.8	15.5	257 07.5	05.2	18 45.1	13.7
	15	196 17.4	24 46.8	. . 05.1	14 10.8	. . 16.1	272 10.1	. . 05.2	33 47.3	. . 13.6
	16	211 19.9	39 46.5	03.8	29 11.8	16.8	287 12.7	05.2	48 49.4	13.5
	17	226 22.3	54 46.1	02.6	44 12.9	17.4	302 15.3	05.2	63 51.6	13.4
	18	241 24.8	69 45.8	N 5 01.3	59 13.9	S 0 18.1	317 18.0	S23 05.3	78 53.8	N 9 13.2
	19	256 27.3	84 45.4	5 00.1	74 14.9	18.7	332 20.6	05.3	93 56.0	13.1
	20	271 29.7	99 45.1	4 58.8	89 15.9	19.4	347 23.2	05.3	108 58.1	13.0
	21	286 32.2	114 44.7	. . 57.6	104 16.9	. . 20.1	2 25.8	. . 05.3	124 00.3	. . 12.9
	22	301 34.6	129 44.4	56.3	119 17.9	20.7	17 28.4	05.3	139 02.5	12.8
	23	316 37.1	144 44.0	55.1	134 18.9	21.4	32 31.0	05.3	154 04.6	12.7
23	00	331 39.6	159 43.7	N 4 53.8	149 19.9	S 0 22.0	47 33.6	S23 05.4	169 06.8	N 9 12.5
	01	346 42.0	174 43.3	52.5	164 20.9	22.7	62 36.2	05.4	184 09.0	12.4
	02	1 44.5	189 43.0	51.3	179 21.9	23.4	77 38.8	05.4	199 11.2	12.3
	03	16 47.0	204 42.6	. . 50.0	194 22.9	. . 24.0	92 41.4	. . 05.4	214 13.3	. . 12.2
	04	31 49.4	219 42.3	48.8	209 24.0	24.7	107 44.0	05.4	229 15.5	12.1
	05	46 51.9	234 42.0	47.5	224 25.0	25.3	122 46.6	05.4	244 17.7	11.9
	06	61 54.4	249 41.6	N 4 46.3	239 26.0	S 0 26.0	137 49.2	S23 05.5	259 19.8	N 9 11.8
S	07	76 56.8	264 41.3	45.0	254 27.0	26.6	152 51.8	05.5	274 22.0	11.7
A	08	91 59.3	279 40.9	43.8	269 28.0	27.3	167 54.4	05.5	289 24.2	11.6
T	09	107 01.8	294 40.6	. . 42.5	284 29.0	. . 28.0	182 57.0	. . 05.5	304 26.4	. . 11.5
U	10	122 04.2	309 40.2	41.2	299 30.0	28.6	197 59.6	05.5	319 28.5	11.4
R	11	137 06.7	324 39.9	40.0	314 31.0	29.3	213 02.2	05.5	334 30.7	11.2
D	12	152 09.1	339 39.5	N 4 38.7	329 32.0	S 0 29.9	228 04.8	S23 05.6	349 32.9	N 9 11.1
A	13	167 11.6	354 39.2	37.5	344 33.0	30.6	243 07.4	05.6	4 35.0	11.0
Y	14	182 14.1	9 38.9	36.2	359 34.0	31.3	258 10.0	05.6	19 37.2	10.9
	15	197 16.5	24 38.5	. . 34.9	14 35.0	. . 31.9	273 12.5	. . 05.6	34 39.4	. . 10.8
	16	212 19.0	39 38.2	33.7	29 36.1	32.6	288 15.1	05.6	49 41.6	10.7
	17	227 21.5	54 37.8	32.4	44 37.1	33.2	303 17.7	05.6	64 43.7	10.5
	18	242 23.9	69 37.5	N 4 31.2	59 38.1	S 0 33.9	318 20.3	S23 05.6	79 45.9	N 9 10.4
	19	257 26.4	84 37.1	29.9	74 39.1	34.5	333 22.9	05.7	94 48.1	10.3
	20	272 28.9	99 36.8	28.7	89 40.1	35.2	348 25.5	05.7	109 50.2	10.2
	21	287 31.3	114 36.5	. . 27.4	104 41.1	. . 35.9	3 28.1	. . 05.7	124 52.4	. . 10.1
	22	302 33.8	129 36.1	26.1	119 42.1	36.5	18 30.7	05.7	139 54.6	10.0
	23	317 36.3	144 35.8	24.9	134 43.1	37.2	33 33.3	05.7	154 56.8	09.8
24	00	332 38.7	159 35.4	N 4 23.6	149 44.1	S 0 37.8	48 35.9	S23 05.7	169 58.9	N 9 09.7
	01	347 41.2	174 35.1	22.3	164 45.1	38.5	63 38.5	05.8	185 01.1	09.6
	02	2 43.6	189 34.8	21.1	179 46.1	39.2	78 41.1	05.8	200 03.3	09.5
	03	17 46.1	204 34.4	. . 19.8	194 47.1	. . 39.8	93 43.7	. . 05.8	215 05.4	. . 09.4
	04	32 48.6	219 34.1	18.6	209 48.1	40.5	108 46.3	05.8	230 07.6	09.2
	05	47 51.0	234 33.7	17.3	224 49.1	41.1	123 48.9	05.8	245 09.8	09.1
	06	62 53.5	249 33.4	N 4 16.0	239 50.1	S 0 41.8	138 51.5	S23 05.8	260 12.0	N 9 09.0
	07	77 56.0	264 33.1	14.8	254 51.2	42.4	153 54.0	05.8	275 14.1	08.9
	08	92 58.4	279 32.7	13.5	269 52.2	43.1	168 56.6	05.9	290 16.3	08.8
S	09	108 00.9	294 32.4	. . 12.3	284 53.2	. . 43.8	183 59.2	. . 05.9	305 18.5	. . 08.7
U	10	123 03.4	309 32.0	11.0	299 54.2	44.4	199 01.8	05.9	320 20.6	08.5
N	11	138 05.8	324 31.7	09.7	314 55.2	45.1	214 04.4	05.9	335 22.8	08.4
D	12	153 08.3	339 31.4	N 4 08.5	329 56.2	S 0 45.7	229 07.0	S23 05.9	350 25.0	N 9 08.3
A	13	168 10.7	354 31.0	07.2	344 57.2	46.4	244 09.6	05.9	5 27.1	08.2
Y	14	183 13.2	9 30.7	05.9	359 58.2	47.1	259 12.2	05.9	20 29.3	08.1
	15	198 15.7	24 30.3	. . 04.7	14 59.2	. . 47.7	274 14.8	. . 06.0	35 31.5	. . 08.0
	16	213 18.1	39 30.0	03.4	30 00.2	48.4	289 17.3	06.0	50 33.7	07.8
	17	228 20.6	54 29.7	02.1	45 01.2	49.0	304 19.9	06.0	65 35.8	07.7
	18	243 23.1	69 29.3	N 4 00.9	60 02.2	S 0 49.7	319 22.5	S23 06.0	80 38.0	N 9 07.6
	19	258 25.5	84 29.0	3 59.6	75 03.2	50.4	334 25.1	06.0	95 40.2	07.5
	20	273 28.0	99 28.7	58.4	90 04.2	51.0	349 27.7	06.0	110 42.3	07.4
	21	288 30.5	114 28.3	. . 57.1	105 05.2	. . 51.7	4 30.3	. . 06.0	125 44.5	. . 07.3
	22	303 32.9	129 28.0	55.8	120 06.2	52.3	19 32.9	06.1	140 46.7	07.1
	23	318 35.4	144 27.6	54.6	135 07.2	53.0	34 35.5	06.1	155 48.9	07.0
Mer. Pass.		h m 1 53.1	v −0.3	d 1.3	v 1.0	d 0.7	v 2.6	d 0.0	v 2.2	d 0.1

STARS

Name	SHA ° ′	Dec ° ′
Acamar	315 20.9	S40 15.8
Achernar	335 28.8	S57 11.2
Acrux	173 14.3	S63 09.0
Adhara	255 15.6	S28 58.8
Aldebaran	290 53.6	N16 31.7
Alioth	166 24.0	N55 54.9
Alkaid	153 01.8	N49 16.4
Al Na'ir	27 47.6	S46 55.0
Alnilam	275 50.2	S 1 11.6
Alphard	218 00.0	S 8 41.7
Alphecca	126 14.0	N26 41.3
Alpheratz	357 47.0	N29 08.4
Altair	62 11.5	N 8 53.6
Ankaa	353 18.7	S42 15.2
Antares	112 30.7	S26 27.2
Arcturus	145 59.1	N19 08.3
Atria	107 35.7	S69 02.9
Avior	234 20.3	S59 32.0
Bellatrix	278 36.0	N 6 21.6
Betelgeuse	271 05.4	N 7 24.7
Canopus	263 58.1	S52 41.7
Capella	280 40.0	N46 00.4
Deneb	49 33.6	N45 18.8
Denebola	182 37.6	N14 31.5
Diphda	348 59.2	S17 56.1
Dubhe	193 56.4	N61 42.3
Elnath	278 17.3	N28 36.9
Eltanin	90 47.6	N51 29.5
Enif	33 50.4	N 9 55.0
Fomalhaut	15 27.5	S29 34.4
Gacrux	172 05.7	S57 09.9
Gienah	175 56.3	S17 35.4
Hadar	148 53.6	S60 25.2
Hamal	328 04.7	N23 30.3
Kaus Aust.	83 48.3	S34 22.9
Kochab	137 19.7	N74 07.4
Markab	13 41.7	N15 15.3
Menkar	314 18.8	N 4 07.6
Menkent	148 12.1	S36 24.9
Miaplacidus	221 41.7	S69 45.1
Mirfak	308 45.6	N49 53.5
Nunki	76 02.5	S26 17.2
Peacock	53 24.2	S56 42.5
Pollux	243 32.4	N28 00.4
Procyon	245 03.8	N 5 12.3
Rasalhague	96 09.7	N12 33.3
Regulus	207 47.6	N11 55.6
Rigel	281 15.6	S 8 11.2
Rigil Kent.	139 57.2	S60 52.5
Sabik	102 16.6	S15 44.2
Schedar	349 44.5	N56 35.1
Shaula	96 26.7	S37 06.8
Sirius	258 37.1	S16 43.4
Spica	158 35.3	S11 12.4
Suhail	222 55.7	S43 27.9
Vega	80 41.2	N38 47.7
Zuben'ubi	137 09.5	S16 04.7

	SHA ° ′	Mer. Pass. h m
Venus	188 04.1	13 21
Mars	177 40.3	14 02
Jupiter	75 54.0	20 46
Saturn	197 27.2	12 42

UT d h	SUN GHA ° ′	SUN Dec ° ′	MOON GHA ° ′	v ′	MOON Dec ° ′	d ′	HP ′
22 00	179 16.7	N11 43.6	301 35.2	9.6	N17 19.3	12.9	58.7
01	194 16.8	42.7	316 03.8	9.5	17 32.2	12.8	58.7
02	209 17.0	41.9	330 32.3	9.4	17 45.0	12.7	58.7
03	224 17.2	. . 41.1	345 00.7	9.4	17 57.7	12.6	58.7
04	239 17.3	40.2	359 29.1	9.2	18 10.3	12.5	58.7
05	254 17.5	39.4	13 57.3	9.1	18 22.8	12.4	58.8
06	269 17.6	N11 38.5	28 25.4	9.1	N18 35.2	12.3	58.8
07	284 17.8	37.7	42 53.5	8.9	18 47.5	12.2	58.8
08	299 18.0	36.8	57 21.4	8.8	18 59.7	12.2	58.8
F 09	314 18.1	. . 36.0	71 49.2	8.8	19 11.9	12.0	58.8
R 10	329 18.3	35.1	86 17.0	8.6	19 23.9	11.9	58.8
I 11	344 18.4	34.3	100 44.6	8.6	19 35.8	11.7	58.8
D 12	359 18.6	N11 33.5	115 12.2	8.4	N19 47.5	11.7	58.8
A 13	14 18.8	32.6	129 39.6	8.3	19 59.2	11.6	58.9
Y 14	29 18.9	31.8	144 06.9	8.3	20 10.8	11.5	58.9
15	44 19.1	. . 30.9	158 34.2	8.1	20 22.3	11.3	58.9
16	59 19.3	30.1	173 01.3	8.1	20 33.6	11.2	58.9
17	74 19.4	29.2	187 28.4	7.9	20 44.8	11.1	58.9
18	89 19.6	N11 28.4	201 55.3	7.9	N20 55.9	11.0	58.9
19	104 19.7	27.5	216 22.2	7.7	21 06.9	10.9	58.9
20	119 19.9	26.7	230 48.9	7.6	21 17.8	10.8	58.9
21	134 20.1	. . 25.8	245 15.5	7.6	21 28.6	10.6	59.0
22	149 20.2	25.0	259 42.1	7.4	21 39.2	10.5	59.0
23	164 20.4	24.1	274 08.5	7.4	21 49.7	10.4	59.0
23 00	179 20.6	N11 23.3	288 34.9	7.2	N22 00.1	10.2	59.0
01	194 20.7	22.5	303 01.1	7.1	22 10.3	10.1	59.0
02	209 20.9	21.6	317 27.2	7.1	22 20.4	10.0	59.0
03	224 21.1	. . 20.8	331 53.3	6.9	22 30.4	9.9	59.0
04	239 21.2	19.9	346 19.2	6.8	22 40.3	9.7	59.0
05	254 21.4	19.1	0 45.0	6.8	22 50.0	9.6	59.0
06	269 21.5	N11 18.2	15 10.8	6.6	N22 59.6	9.4	59.1
07	284 21.7	17.4	29 36.4	6.6	23 09.0	9.3	59.1
S 08	299 21.9	16.5	44 02.0	6.4	23 18.3	9.2	59.1
A 09	314 22.0	. . 15.6	58 27.4	6.4	23 27.5	9.0	59.1
T 10	329 22.2	14.8	72 52.8	6.2	23 36.5	8.9	59.1
U 11	344 22.4	13.9	87 18.0	6.2	23 45.4	8.7	59.1
R 12	359 22.5	N11 13.1	101 43.2	6.0	N23 54.1	8.6	59.1
D 13	14 22.7	12.2	116 08.2	6.0	24 02.7	8.4	59.1
A 14	29 22.9	11.4	130 33.2	5.9	24 11.1	8.3	59.1
Y 15	44 23.0	. . 10.5	144 58.1	5.7	24 19.4	8.1	59.2
16	59 23.2	09.7	159 22.8	5.7	24 27.5	8.0	59.2
17	74 23.4	08.8	173 47.5	5.6	24 35.5	7.8	59.2
18	89 23.5	N11 08.0	188 12.1	5.5	N24 43.3	7.7	59.2
19	104 23.7	07.1	202 36.6	5.4	24 51.0	7.5	59.2
20	119 23.9	06.3	217 01.0	5.4	24 58.5	7.3	59.2
21	134 24.0	. . 05.4	231 25.4	5.2	25 05.8	7.2	59.2
22	149 24.2	04.6	245 49.6	5.1	25 13.0	7.0	59.2
23	164 24.4	03.7	260 13.7	5.1	25 20.0	6.9	59.2
24 00	179 24.6	N11 02.8	274 37.8	5.0	N25 26.9	6.7	59.2
01	194 24.7	02.0	289 01.8	4.9	25 33.6	6.5	59.2
02	209 24.9	01.1	303 25.7	4.8	25 40.1	6.3	59.3
03	224 25.1	11 00.3	317 49.5	4.8	25 46.4	6.2	59.3
04	239 25.2	10 59.4	332 13.3	4.6	25 52.6	6.1	59.3
05	254 25.4	58.6	346 36.9	4.6	25 58.7	5.8	59.3
06	269 25.6	N10 57.7	1 00.5	4.5	N26 04.5	5.7	59.3
07	284 25.7	56.8	15 24.0	4.5	26 10.2	5.5	59.3
08	299 25.9	56.0	29 47.5	4.4	26 15.7	5.3	59.3
S 09	314 26.1	. . 55.1	44 10.9	4.3	26 21.0	5.2	59.3
U 10	329 26.2	54.3	58 34.2	4.2	26 26.2	5.0	59.3
N 11	344 26.4	53.4	72 57.4	4.2	26 31.2	4.8	59.3
D 12	359 26.6	N10 52.5	87 20.6	4.1	N26 36.0	4.6	59.3
A 13	14 26.8	51.7	101 43.7	4.0	26 40.6	4.4	59.3
Y 14	29 26.9	50.8	116 06.7	4.0	26 45.0	4.3	59.3
15	44 27.1	. . 50.0	130 29.7	3.9	26 49.3	4.1	59.3
16	59 27.3	49.1	144 52.6	3.9	26 53.4	3.8	59.4
17	74 27.4	48.2	159 15.5	3.8	26 57.2	3.8	59.4
18	89 27.6	N10 47.4	173 38.3	3.8	N27 01.0	3.5	59.4
19	104 27.8	46.5	188 01.1	3.7	27 04.5	3.3	59.4
20	119 28.0	45.7	202 23.8	3.7	27 07.8	3.2	59.4
21	134 28.1	. . 44.8	216 46.5	3.6	27 11.0	3.0	59.4
22	149 28.3	43.9	231 09.1	3.6	27 14.0	2.7	59.4
23	164 28.5	43.1	245 31.7	3.5	N27 16.7	2.6	59.4
	SD 15.8	*d* 0.9	SD 16.0		16.1		16.2

Lat. °	Twilight Naut. h m	Twilight Civil h m	Sunrise h m	Moonrise 22 h m	Moonrise 23 h m	Moonrise 24 h m	Moonrise 25 h m
N 72	////	01 04	03 16	▭	▭	▭	▭
N 70	////	02 04	03 37	▭	▭	▭	▭
68	////	02 37	03 53	17 53	▭	▭	▭
66	00 56	03 01	04 06	18 38	▭	▭	▭
64	01 48	03 19	04 17	19 07	18 48	▭	▭
62	02 18	03 34	04 26	19 30	19 30	19 37	20 25
60	02 41	03 46	04 34	19 49	19 59	20 24	21 20
N 58	02 58	03 57	04 41	20 04	20 21	20 54	21 52
56	03 12	04 06	04 47	20 17	20 40	21 17	22 17
54	03 24	04 14	04 53	20 29	20 55	21 36	22 36
52	03 35	04 21	04 57	20 39	21 09	21 52	22 53
50	03 44	04 27	05 02	20 48	21 20	22 06	23 07
45	04 03	04 40	05 11	21 07	21 45	22 34	23 36
N 40	04 17	04 51	05 19	21 23	22 05	22 56	23 59
35	04 29	05 00	05 26	21 37	22 21	23 15	24 17
30	04 38	05 07	05 32	21 49	22 36	23 31	24 33
20	04 53	05 20	05 42	22 09	23 00	23 58	25 01
N 10	05 05	05 30	05 51	22 27	23 21	24 21	00 21
0	05 14	05 38	05 59	22 43	23 41	24 43	00 43
S 10	05 21	05 46	06 07	23 00	24 01	00 01	01 05
20	05 27	05 53	06 16	23 18	24 23	00 23	01 28
30	05 33	06 01	06 25	23 39	24 48	00 48	01 56
35	05 35	06 05	06 31	23 52	25 03	01 03	02 12
40	05 38	06 09	06 37	24 06	00 06	01 20	02 31
45	05 40	06 14	06 44	24 23	00 23	01 41	02 54
S 50	05 42	06 19	06 52	24 44	00 44	02 08	03 23
52	05 42	06 22	06 56	24 55	00 55	02 21	03 38
54	05 43	06 24	07 00	25 06	01 06	02 35	03 55
56	05 44	06 27	07 05	25 19	01 19	02 53	04 15
58	05 44	06 30	07 10	25 35	01 35	03 14	04 40
S 60	05 45	06 33	07 16	00 06	01 53	03 41	05 14

Lat. °	Sunset h m	Twilight Civil h m	Twilight Naut. h m	Moonset 22 h m	Moonset 23 h m	Moonset 24 h m	Moonset 25 h m
N 72	20 45	22 47	////	▭	▭	▭	▭
N 70	20 25	21 55	////	▭	▭	▭	▭
68	20 09	21 24	////	14 47	▭	▭	▭
66	19 56	21 01	22 57	14 04	▭	▭	▭
64	19 46	20 43	22 11	13 35	15 53	▭	▭
62	19 37	20 29	21 43	13 13	15 11	17 11	18 35
60	19 29	20 17	21 21	12 56	14 43	16 25	17 40
N 58	19 22	20 06	21 04	12 41	14 21	15 55	17 08
56	19 17	19 58	20 51	12 29	14 03	15 32	16 43
54	19 11	19 50	20 39	12 18	13 48	15 13	16 24
52	19 06	19 43	20 29	12 08	13 35	14 58	16 07
50	19 02	19 37	20 20	12 00	13 24	14 44	15 53
45	18 53	19 24	20 01	11 42	13 00	14 16	15 24
N 40	18 45	19 13	19 47	11 27	12 42	13 54	15 01
35	18 38	19 05	19 36	11 15	12 26	13 36	14 42
30	18 32	18 57	19 26	11 04	12 12	13 21	14 26
20	18 22	18 45	19 12	10 46	11 49	12 54	13 59
N 10	18 14	18 35	19 00	10 30	11 29	12 32	13 35
0	18 06	18 27	18 51	10 15	11 11	12 10	13 13
S 10	17 58	18 19	18 44	10 00	10 52	11 49	12 51
20	17 50	18 12	18 38	09 44	10 32	11 27	12 27
30	17 40	18 05	18 33	09 26	10 10	11 00	11 59
35	17 35	18 01	18 30	09 16	09 56	10 45	11 43
40	17 29	17 56	18 28	09 04	09 41	10 27	11 24
45	17 22	17 52	18 26	08 50	09 23	10 06	11 01
S 50	17 14	17 47	18 24	08 33	09 00	09 38	10 31
52	17 10	17 44	18 24	08 25	08 50	09 25	10 17
54	17 05	17 42	18 23	08 16	08 38	09 10	10 00
56	17 01	17 39	18 22	08 07	08 24	08 52	09 40
58	16 56	17 36	18 22	07 55	08 08	08 31	09 14
S 60	16 50	17 33	18 21	07 43	07 49	08 03	08 40

Day d	SUN Eqn. of Time 00^h m s	SUN Eqn. of Time 12^h m s	SUN Mer. Pass. h m	MOON Mer. Pass. Upper h m	MOON Mer. Pass. Lower h m	MOON Age d	MOON Phase %
22	02 54	02 46	12 03	04 02	16 29	21	67
23	02 38	02 30	12 03	04 57	17 26	22	56
24	02 22	02 14	12 02	05 56	18 27	23	44

UT		ARIES	VENUS −3.8		MARS +1.7		JUPITER −2.5		SATURN +0.8	
		GHA	GHA	Dec	GHA	Dec	GHA	Dec	GHA	Dec
d	h	° ′	° ′	° ′	° ′	° ′	° ′	° ′	° ′	° ′
25	00	333 37.9	159 27.3	N 3 53.3	150 08.2	S 0 53.7	49 38.0	S23 06.1	170 51.0	N 9 06.9
	01	348 40.3	174 27.0	52.0	165 09.3	54.3	64 40.6	06.1	185 53.2	06.8
	02	3 42.8	189 26.6	50.8	180 10.3	55.0	79 43.2	06.1	200 55.4	06.7
	03	18 45.2	204 26.3	. . 49.5	195 11.3	. . 55.6	94 45.8	. . 06.1	215 57.5	. . 06.5
	04	33 47.7	219 26.0	48.2	210 12.3	56.3	109 48.4	06.1	230 59.7	06.4
	05	48 50.2	234 25.6	47.0	225 13.3	56.9	124 51.0	06.2	246 01.9	06.3
	06	63 52.6	249 25.3	N 3 45.7	240 14.3	S 0 57.6	139 53.5	S23 06.2	261 04.1	N 9 06.2
	07	78 55.1	264 25.0	44.4	255 15.3	58.3	154 56.1	06.2	276 06.2	06.1
	08	93 57.6	279 24.6	43.2	270 16.3	58.9	169 58.7	06.2	291 08.4	06.0
M	09	109 00.0	294 24.3	. . 41.9	285 17.3	0 59.6	185 01.3	. . 06.2	306 10.6	. . 05.8
O	10	124 02.5	309 23.9	40.6	300 18.3	1 00.2	200 03.9	06.2	321 12.7	05.7
N	11	139 05.0	324 23.6	39.4	315 19.3	00.9	215 06.5	06.2	336 14.9	05.6
D	12	154 07.4	339 23.3	N 3 38.1	330 20.3	S 1 01.6	230 09.0	S23 06.3	351 17.1	N 9 05.5
A	13	169 09.9	354 22.9	36.8	345 21.3	02.2	245 11.6	06.3	6 19.2	05.4
Y	14	184 12.4	9 22.6	35.6	0 22.3	02.9	260 14.2	06.3	21 21.4	05.3
	15	199 14.8	24 22.3	. . 34.3	15 23.3	. . 03.5	275 16.8	. . 06.3	36 23.6	. . 05.1
	16	214 17.3	39 21.9	33.0	30 24.3	04.2	290 19.4	06.3	51 25.8	05.0
	17	229 19.7	54 21.6	31.7	45 25.3	04.9	305 21.9	06.3	66 27.9	04.9
	18	244 22.2	69 21.3	N 3 30.5	60 26.3	S 1 05.5	320 24.5	S23 06.3	81 30.1	N 9 04.8
	19	259 24.7	84 20.9	29.2	75 27.3	06.2	335 27.1	06.4	96 32.3	04.7
	20	274 27.1	99 20.6	27.9	90 28.3	06.8	350 29.7	06.4	111 34.4	04.5
	21	289 29.6	114 20.3	. . 26.7	105 29.3	. . 07.5	5 32.3	. . 06.4	126 36.6	. . 04.4
	22	304 32.1	129 19.9	25.4	120 30.3	08.2	20 34.8	06.4	141 38.8	04.3
	23	319 34.5	144 19.6	24.1	135 31.3	08.8	35 37.4	06.4	156 40.9	04.2
26	00	334 37.0	159 19.3	N 3 22.9	150 32.3	S 1 09.5	50 40.0	S23 06.4	171 43.1	N 9 04.1
	01	349 39.5	174 18.9	21.6	165 33.3	10.1	65 42.6	06.4	186 45.3	04.0
	02	4 41.9	189 18.6	20.3	180 34.3	10.8	80 45.1	06.5	201 47.5	03.8
	03	19 44.4	204 18.3	. . 19.0	195 35.3	. . 11.5	95 47.7	. . 06.5	216 49.6	. . 03.7
	04	34 46.9	219 17.9	17.8	210 36.3	12.1	110 50.3	06.5	231 51.8	03.6
	05	49 49.3	234 17.6	16.5	225 37.3	12.8	125 52.9	06.5	246 54.0	03.5
	06	64 51.8	249 17.3	N 3 15.2	240 38.3	S 1 13.4	140 55.4	S23 06.5	261 56.1	N 9 03.4
	07	79 54.2	264 16.9	14.0	255 39.3	14.1	155 58.0	06.5	276 58.3	03.2
T	08	94 56.7	279 16.6	12.7	270 40.3	14.8	171 00.6	06.5	292 00.5	03.1
U	09	109 59.2	294 16.3	. . 11.4	285 41.3	. . 15.4	186 03.2	. . 06.5	307 02.6	. . 03.0
E	10	125 01.6	309 15.9	10.1	300 42.3	16.1	201 05.7	06.6	322 04.8	02.9
S	11	140 04.1	324 15.6	08.9	315 43.3	16.7	216 08.3	06.6	337 07.0	02.8
D	12	155 06.6	339 15.3	N 3 07.6	330 44.4	S 1 17.4	231 10.9	S23 06.6	352 09.2	N 9 02.7
A	13	170 09.0	354 15.0	06.3	345 45.4	18.1	246 13.5	06.6	7 11.3	02.5
Y	14	185 11.5	9 14.6	05.1	0 46.4	18.7	261 16.0	06.6	22 13.5	02.4
	15	200 14.0	24 14.3	. . 03.8	15 47.4	. . 19.4	276 18.6	. . 06.6	37 15.7	. . 02.3
	16	215 16.4	39 14.0	02.5	30 48.4	20.0	291 21.2	06.6	52 17.8	02.2
	17	230 18.9	54 13.6	01.2	45 49.4	20.7	306 23.7	06.6	67 20.0	02.1
	18	245 21.4	69 13.3	N 3 00.0	60 50.4	S 1 21.4	321 26.3	S23 06.7	82 22.2	N 9 02.0
	19	260 23.8	84 13.0	2 58.7	75 51.4	22.0	336 28.9	06.7	97 24.3	01.8
	20	275 26.3	99 12.6	57.4	90 52.4	22.7	351 31.5	06.7	112 26.5	01.7
	21	290 28.7	114 12.3	. . 56.1	105 53.4	. . 23.3	6 34.0	. . 06.7	127 28.7	. . 01.6
	22	305 31.2	129 12.0	54.9	120 54.4	24.0	21 36.6	06.7	142 30.9	01.5
	23	320 33.7	144 11.6	53.6	135 55.4	24.7	36 39.2	06.7	157 33.0	01.4
27	00	335 36.1	159 11.3	N 2 52.3	150 56.4	S 1 25.3	51 41.7	S23 06.7	172 35.2	N 9 01.2
	01	350 38.6	174 11.0	51.0	165 57.4	26.0	66 44.3	06.8	187 37.4	01.1
	02	5 41.1	189 10.7	49.8	180 58.4	26.6	81 46.9	06.8	202 39.5	01.0
	03	20 43.5	204 10.3	. . 48.5	195 59.4	. . 27.3	96 49.4	. . 06.8	217 41.7	. . 00.9
	04	35 46.0	219 10.0	47.2	211 00.4	28.0	111 52.0	06.8	232 43.9	00.8
	05	50 48.5	234 09.7	45.9	226 01.4	28.6	126 54.6	06.8	247 46.0	00.7
	06	65 50.9	249 09.3	N 2 44.7	241 02.4	S 1 29.3	141 57.1	S23 06.8	262 48.2	N 9 00.5
W	07	80 53.4	264 09.0	43.4	256 03.4	29.9	156 59.7	06.8	277 50.4	00.4
E	08	95 55.9	279 08.7	42.1	271 04.4	30.6	172 02.3	06.8	292 52.6	00.3
D	09	110 58.3	294 08.4	. . 40.8	286 05.4	. . 31.3	187 04.8	. . 06.9	307 54.7	. . 00.2
N	10	126 00.8	309 08.0	39.6	301 06.4	31.9	202 07.4	06.9	322 56.9	9 00.1
E	11	141 03.2	324 07.7	38.3	316 07.3	32.6	217 10.0	06.9	337 59.1	8 59.9
S	12	156 05.7	339 07.4	N 2 37.0	331 08.3	S 1 33.2	232 12.5	S23 06.9	353 01.2	N 8 59.8
D	13	171 08.2	354 07.0	35.7	346 09.3	33.9	247 15.1	06.9	8 03.4	59.7
A	14	186 10.6	9 06.7	34.5	1 10.3	34.6	262 17.7	06.9	23 05.6	59.6
Y	15	201 13.1	24 06.4	. . 33.2	16 11.3	. . 35.2	277 20.2	. . 06.9	38 07.7	. . 59.5
	16	216 15.6	39 06.1	31.9	31 12.3	35.9	292 22.8	06.9	53 09.9	59.4
	17	231 18.0	54 05.7	30.6	46 13.3	36.5	307 25.3	07.0	68 12.1	59.2
	18	246 20.5	69 05.4	N 2 29.4	61 14.3	S 1 37.2	322 27.9	S23 07.0	83 14.3	N 8 59.1
	19	261 23.0	84 05.1	28.1	76 15.3	37.9	337 30.5	07.0	98 16.4	59.0
	20	276 25.4	99 04.7	26.8	91 16.3	38.5	352 33.0	07.0	113 18.6	58.9
	21	291 27.9	114 04.4	. . 25.5	106 17.3	. . 39.2	7 35.6	. . 07.0	128 20.8	. . 58.8
	22	306 30.3	129 04.1	24.2	121 18.3	39.8	22 38.2	07.0	143 22.9	58.7
	23	321 32.8	144 03.8	23.0	136 19.3	40.5	37 40.7	07.0	158 25.1	58.5
Mer. Pass.		h m 1 41.3	*v* −0.3	*d* 1.3	*v* 1.0	*d* 0.7	*v* 2.6	*d* 0.0	*v* 2.2	*d* 0.1

STARS

Name	SHA	Dec
	° ′	° ′
Acamar	315 20.8	S40 15.8
Achernar	335 28.8	S57 11.2
Acrux	173 14.3	S63 09.0
Adhara	255 15.6	S28 58.7
Aldebaran	290 53.6	N16 31.7
Alioth	166 24.0	N55 54.9
Alkaid	153 01.8	N49 16.4
Al Na'ir	27 47.6	S46 55.0
Alnilam	275 50.1	S 1 11.6
Alphard	218 00.0	S 8 41.7
Alphecca	126 14.0	N26 41.3
Alpheratz	357 47.0	N29 08.4
Altair	62 11.5	N 8 53.6
Ankaa	353 18.7	S42 15.2
Antares	112 30.7	S26 27.2
Arcturus	145 59.1	N19 08.3
Atria	107 35.7	S69 02.9
Avior	234 20.2	S59 32.0
Bellatrix	278 36.0	N 6 21.6
Betelgeuse	271 05.3	N 7 24.7
Canopus	263 58.1	S52 41.6
Capella	280 39.9	N46 00.4
Deneb	49 33.6	N45 18.8
Denebola	182 37.6	N14 31.5
Diphda	348 59.2	S17 56.1
Dubhe	193 56.4	N61 42.3
Elnath	278 17.3	N28 36.9
Eltanin	90 47.6	N51 29.5
Enif	33 50.4	N 9 55.0
Fomalhaut	15 27.5	S29 34.4
Gacrux	172 05.7	S57 09.9
Gienah	175 56.3	S17 35.4
Hadar	148 53.6	S60 25.2
Hamal	328 04.7	N23 30.3
Kaus Aust.	83 48.3	S34 22.9
Kochab	137 19.8	N74 07.4
Markab	13 41.6	N15 15.3
Menkar	314 18.7	N 4 07.6
Menkent	148 12.1	S36 24.9
Miaplacidus	221 41.7	S69 45.0
Mirfak	308 45.6	N49 53.5
Nunki	76 02.5	S26 17.2
Peacock	53 24.2	S56 42.5
Pollux	243 32.4	N28 00.4
Procyon	245 03.7	N 5 12.3
Rasalhague	96 09.7	N12 33.3
Regulus	207 47.6	N11 55.6
Rigel	281 15.6	S 8 11.2
Rigil Kent.	139 57.2	S60 52.5
Sabik	102 16.6	S15 44.2
Schedar	349 44.5	N56 35.1
Shaula	96 26.7	S37 06.8
Sirius	258 37.1	S16 43.4
Spica	158 35.3	S11 12.4
Suhail	222 55.6	S43 27.9
Vega	80 41.2	N38 47.7
Zuben'ubi	137 09.6	S16 04.7

	SHA	Mer. Pass.
	° ′	h m
Venus	184 42.3	13 23
Mars	175 55.3	13 57
Jupiter	76 03.0	20 34
Saturn	197 06.1	12 31

UT d	UT h	SUN GHA	SUN Dec	MOON GHA	v	MOON Dec	d	HP
d	h	° ′	° ′	° ′	′	° ′	′	′
25	00	179 28.6	N10 42.2	259 54.2	3.5	N27 19.3	2.4	59.4
	01	194 28.8	41.3	274 16.7	3.5	27 21.7	2.3	59.4
	02	209 29.0	40.5	288 39.2	3.4	27 24.0	2.0	59.4
	03	224 29.2	. . 39.6	303 01.6	3.4	27 26.0	1.8	59.4
	04	239 29.3	38.7	317 24.0	3.4	27 27.8	1.7	59.4
	05	254 29.5	37.9	331 46.4	3.3	27 29.5	1.4	59.4
	06	269 29.7	N10 37.0	346 08.7	3.4	N27 30.9	1.3	59.4
	07	284 29.9	36.2	0 31.1	3.3	27 32.2	1.0	59.4
	08	299 30.0	35.3	14 53.4	3.2	27 33.2	0.9	59.4
M	09	314 30.2	. . 34.4	29 15.6	3.3	27 34.1	0.7	59.4
O	10	329 30.4	33.6	43 37.9	3.3	27 34.8	0.5	59.4
N	11	344 30.6	32.7	58 00.2	3.2	27 35.3	0.3	59.4
D	12	359 30.7	N10 31.8	72 22.4	3.2	N27 35.6	0.1	59.4
A	13	14 30.9	31.0	86 44.6	3.3	27 35.7	0.1	59.5
Y	14	29 31.1	30.1	101 06.9	3.2	27 35.6	0.3	59.5
	15	44 31.2	. . 29.2	115 29.1	3.2	27 35.3	0.4	59.5
	16	59 31.4	28.4	129 51.3	3.3	27 34.9	0.7	59.5
	17	74 31.6	27.5	144 13.6	3.2	27 34.2	0.9	59.5
	18	89 31.8	N10 26.6	158 35.8	3.2	N27 33.3	1.0	59.5
	19	104 32.0	25.7	172 58.0	3.3	27 32.3	1.3	59.5
	20	119 32.1	24.9	187 20.3	3.2	27 31.0	1.4	59.5
	21	134 32.3	. . 24.0	201 42.5	3.3	27 29.6	1.6	59.5
	22	149 32.5	23.1	216 04.8	3.3	27 28.0	1.9	59.5
	23	164 32.7	22.3	230 27.1	3.3	27 26.1	2.0	59.5
26	00	179 32.8	N10 21.4	244 49.4	3.3	N27 24.1	2.2	59.5
	01	194 33.0	20.5	259 11.7	3.4	27 21.9	2.4	59.5
	02	209 33.2	19.7	273 34.1	3.4	27 19.5	2.6	59.5
	03	224 33.4	. . 18.8	287 56.5	3.4	27 16.9	2.8	59.5
	04	239 33.5	17.9	302 18.9	3.4	27 14.1	2.9	59.5
	05	254 33.7	17.0	316 41.3	3.5	27 11.2	3.2	59.5
	06	269 33.9	N10 16.2	331 03.8	3.5	N27 08.0	3.3	59.5
	07	284 34.1	15.3	345 26.3	3.6	27 04.7	3.6	59.5
T	08	299 34.2	14.4	359 48.9	3.6	27 01.1	3.7	59.5
U	09	314 34.4	. . 13.6	14 11.5	3.6	26 57.4	3.9	59.5
E	10	329 34.6	12.7	28 34.1	3.7	26 53.5	4.1	59.5
S	11	344 34.8	11.8	42 56.8	3.8	26 49.4	4.3	59.5
D	12	359 35.0	N10 10.9	57 19.6	3.8	N26 45.1	4.4	59.5
A	13	14 35.1	10.1	71 42.4	3.8	26 40.7	4.7	59.5
Y	14	29 35.3	09.2	86 05.2	3.9	26 36.0	4.8	59.5
	15	44 35.5	. . 08.3	100 28.1	3.9	26 31.2	5.0	59.5
	16	59 35.7	07.4	114 51.0	4.1	26 26.2	5.2	59.5
	17	74 35.9	06.6	129 14.1	4.0	26 21.0	5.4	59.5
	18	89 36.0	N10 05.7	143 37.1	4.2	N26 15.6	5.6	59.5
	19	104 36.2	04.8	158 00.3	4.2	26 10.0	5.7	59.4
	20	119 36.4	03.9	172 23.5	4.2	26 04.3	5.9	59.4
	21	134 36.6	. . 03.1	186 46.7	4.4	25 58.4	6.1	59.4
	22	149 36.8	02.2	201 10.1	4.4	25 52.3	6.2	59.4
	23	164 36.9	01.3	215 33.5	4.4	25 46.1	6.5	59.4
27	00	179 37.1	N10 00.4	229 56.9	4.6	N25 39.6	6.6	59.4
	01	194 37.3	9 59.5	244 20.5	4.6	25 33.0	6.7	59.4
	02	209 37.5	58.7	258 44.1	4.7	25 26.3	7.0	59.4
	03	224 37.7	. . 57.8	273 07.8	4.8	25 19.3	7.1	59.4
	04	239 37.8	56.9	287 31.6	4.9	25 12.2	7.2	59.4
	05	254 38.0	56.0	301 55.5	4.9	25 05.0	7.5	59.4
	06	269 38.2	N 9 55.2	316 19.4	5.0	N24 57.5	7.6	59.4
W	07	284 38.4	54.3	330 43.4	5.2	24 49.9	7.8	59.4
E	08	299 38.6	53.4	345 07.6	5.2	24 42.1	7.9	59.4
D	09	314 38.7	. . 52.5	359 31.8	5.2	24 34.2	8.1	59.4
N	10	329 38.9	51.6	13 56.0	5.4	24 26.1	8.2	59.4
E	11	344 39.1	50.8	28 20.4	5.5	24 17.9	8.4	59.4
S	12	359 39.3	N 9 49.9	42 44.9	5.5	N24 09.5	8.6	59.4
D	13	14 39.5	49.0	57 09.4	5.7	24 00.9	8.7	59.4
A	14	29 39.7	48.1	71 34.1	5.7	23 52.2	8.8	59.3
Y	15	44 39.8	. . 47.2	85 58.8	5.8	23 43.4	9.0	59.3
	16	59 40.0	46.4	100 23.6	6.0	23 34.4	9.2	59.3
	17	74 40.2	45.5	114 48.6	6.0	23 25.2	9.3	59.3
	18	89 40.4	N 9 44.6	129 13.6	6.1	N23 15.9	9.5	59.3
	19	104 40.6	43.7	143 38.7	6.2	23 06.4	9.6	59.3
	20	119 40.8	42.8	158 03.9	6.3	22 56.8	9.7	59.3
	21	134 40.9	. . 41.9	172 29.2	6.4	22 47.1	9.9	59.3
	22	149 41.1	41.1	186 54.6	6.5	22 37.2	10.0	59.3
	23	164 41.3	40.2	201 20.1	6.6	N22 27.2	10.1	59.3
		SD 15.9	d 0.9	SD 16.2		16.2		16.2

Lat.	Twilight Naut.	Twilight Civil	Sunrise	Moonrise 25	Moonrise 26	Moonrise 27	Moonrise 28
°	h m	h m	h m	h m	h m	h m	h m
N 72	////	01 43	03 32	▭	▭	▭	23 17
N 70	////	02 25	03 50	▭	▭	▭	▭
68	////	02 53	04 05	▭	▭	▭	▭
66	01 29	03 14	04 16	▭	▭	23 07	25 39
64	02 06	03 30	04 26	▭	21 02	23 50	25 59
62	02 32	03 43	04 34	20 25	22 17	24 19	00 19
60	02 52	03 54	04 41	21 20	22 53	24 41	00 41
N 58	03 07	04 04	04 48	21 52	23 19	24 59	00 59
56	03 20	04 12	04 53	22 17	23 39	25 13	01 13
54	03 31	04 20	04 58	22 36	23 56	25 26	01 26
52	03 41	04 26	05 02	22 53	24 10	00 10	01 37
50	03 50	04 32	05 06	23 07	24 23	00 23	01 47
45	04 07	04 44	05 15	23 36	24 49	00 49	02 08
N 40	04 20	04 54	05 22	23 59	25 09	01 09	02 25
35	04 31	05 02	05 28	24 17	00 17	01 27	02 39
30	04 40	05 09	05 34	24 33	00 33	01 41	02 51
20	04 54	05 20	05 43	25 01	01 01	02 06	03 12
N 10	05 05	05 30	05 51	00 21	01 24	02 28	03 29
0	05 13	05 37	05 58	00 43	01 46	02 48	03 46
S 10	05 20	05 44	06 06	01 05	02 08	03 08	04 03
20	05 25	05 51	06 13	01 28	02 31	03 29	04 21
30	05 30	05 58	06 22	01 56	02 58	03 54	04 41
35	05 32	06 01	06 27	02 12	03 14	04 08	04 53
40	05 33	06 05	06 32	02 31	03 33	04 25	05 06
45	05 35	06 09	06 39	02 54	03 56	04 45	05 22
S 50	05 36	06 13	06 46	03 23	04 24	05 09	05 42
52	05 36	06 15	06 50	03 38	04 38	05 21	05 51
54	05 36	06 17	06 53	03 55	04 55	05 35	06 01
56	05 37	06 20	06 58	04 15	05 14	05 51	06 13
58	05 37	06 22	07 02	04 40	05 38	06 09	06 26
S 60	05 37	06 25	07 08	05 14	06 09	06 32	06 42

Lat.	Sunset	Twilight Civil	Twilight Naut.	Moonset 25	Moonset 26	Moonset 27	Moonset 28
°	h m	h m	h m	h m	h m	h m	h m
N 72	20 27	22 12	////	▭	▭	▭	22 00
N 70	20 10	21 33	////	▭	▭	▭	20 41
68	19 56	21 06	////	▭	▭	▭	20 01
66	19 45	20 47	22 27	▭	▭	20 10	19 34
64	19 35	20 31	21 52	▭	20 10	19 26	19 13
62	19 27	20 18	21 28	18 35	18 54	18 57	18 55
60	19 20	20 07	21 09	17 40	18 18	18 34	18 41
N 58	19 14	19 57	20 54	17 08	17 52	18 15	18 29
56	19 09	19 49	20 41	16 43	17 31	18 00	18 18
54	19 04	19 42	20 30	16 24	17 14	17 47	18 08
52	19 00	19 36	20 21	16 07	16 59	17 35	18 00
50	18 56	19 30	20 12	15 53	16 46	17 24	17 52
45	18 47	19 18	19 55	15 24	16 19	17 02	17 36
N 40	18 40	19 08	19 42	15 01	15 58	16 45	17 22
35	18 34	19 00	19 31	14 42	15 40	16 30	17 10
30	18 29	18 54	19 23	14 26	15 25	16 17	17 00
20	18 20	18 43	19 09	13 59	14 59	15 54	16 43
N 10	18 12	18 34	18 59	13 35	14 37	15 34	16 27
0	18 05	18 26	18 50	13 13	14 16	15 16	16 13
S 10	17 58	18 19	18 44	12 51	13 54	14 58	15 58
20	17 50	18 13	18 38	12 27	13 32	14 38	15 42
30	17 42	18 06	18 34	11 59	13 05	14 14	15 24
35	17 37	18 03	18 32	11 43	12 49	14 01	15 13
40	17 32	17 59	18 31	11 24	12 31	13 45	15 01
45	17 25	17 55	18 29	11 01	12 09	13 26	14 46
S 50	17 18	17 51	18 28	10 31	11 41	13 02	14 28
52	17 14	17 49	18 28	10 17	11 27	12 50	14 19
54	17 11	17 47	18 28	10 00	11 11	12 37	14 10
56	17 07	17 45	18 28	09 40	10 52	12 22	13 59
58	17 02	17 42	18 28	09 14	10 28	12 04	13 46
S 60	16 57	17 40	18 28	08 40	09 57	11 42	13 31

Day	SUN Eqn. of Time 00^h	SUN Eqn. of Time 12^h	SUN Mer. Pass.	MOON Mer. Pass. Upper	MOON Mer. Pass. Lower	MOON Age	MOON Phase
d	m s	m s	h m	h m	h m	d %	
25	02 06	01 57	12 02	06 58	19 29	24 33	
26	01 49	01 41	12 02	08 01	20 32	25 23	
27	01 32	01 23	12 01	09 02	21 31	26 14	

UT	ARIES	VENUS −3.8		MARS +1.7		JUPITER −2.5		SATURN +0.8	
	GHA	GHA	Dec	GHA	Dec	GHA	Dec	GHA	Dec
d h	° ′	° ′	° ′	° ′	° ′	° ′	° ′	° ′	° ′
28 00	336 35.3	159 03.4	N 2 21.7	151 20.3	S 1 41.2	52 43.3	S23 07.0	173 27.3	N 8 58.4
01	351 37.7	174 03.1	20.4	166 21.3	41.8	67 45.8	07.0	188 29.4	58.3
02	6 40.2	189 02.8	19.1	181 22.3	42.5	82 48.4	07.1	203 31.6	58.2
03	21 42.7	204 02.5 . .	17.9	196 23.3 . .	43.1	97 51.0 . .	07.1	218 33.8 . .	58.1
04	36 45.1	219 02.1	16.6	211 24.3	43.8	112 53.5	07.1	233 35.9	57.9
05	51 47.6	234 01.8	15.3	226 25.3	44.5	127 56.1	07.1	248 38.1	57.8
06	66 50.1	249 01.5	N 2 14.0	241 26.3	S 1 45.1	142 58.6	S23 07.1	263 40.3	N 8 57.7
07	81 52.5	264 01.2	12.7	256 27.3	45.8	158 01.2	07.1	278 42.5	57.6
T 08	96 55.0	279 00.8	11.5	271 28.3	46.4	173 03.7	07.1	293 44.6	57.5
H 09	111 57.5	294 00.5 . .	10.2	286 29.3 . .	47.1	188 06.3 . .	07.1	308 46.8 . .	57.4
U 10	126 59.9	309 00.2	08.9	301 30.3	47.8	203 08.9	07.2	323 49.0	57.2
R 11	142 02.4	323 59.9	07.6	316 31.3	48.4	218 11.4	07.2	338 51.1	57.1
S 12	157 04.8	338 59.5	N 2 06.3	331 32.3	S 1 49.1	233 14.0	S23 07.2	353 53.3	N 8 57.0
D 13	172 07.3	353 59.2	05.1	346 33.3	49.7	248 16.5	07.2	8 55.5	56.9
A 14	187 09.8	8 58.9	03.8	1 34.3	50.4	263 19.1	07.2	23 57.6	56.8
Y 15	202 12.2	23 58.6 . .	02.5	16 35.3 . .	51.1	278 21.6 . .	07.2	38 59.8 . .	56.6
16	217 14.7	38 58.2	2 01.2	31 36.3	51.7	293 24.2	07.2	54 02.0	56.5
17	232 17.2	53 57.9	1 59.9	46 37.3	52.4	308 26.7	07.2	69 04.1	56.4
18	247 19.6	68 57.6	N 1 58.7	61 38.3	S 1 53.0	323 29.3	S23 07.2	84 06.3	N 8 56.3
19	262 22.1	83 57.3	57.4	76 39.3	53.7	338 31.9	07.3	99 08.5	56.2
20	277 24.6	98 56.9	56.1	91 40.3	54.4	353 34.4	07.3	114 10.7	56.1
21	292 27.0	113 56.6 . .	54.8	106 41.2 . .	55.0	8 37.0 . .	07.3	129 12.8 . .	55.9
22	307 29.5	128 56.3	53.5	121 42.2	55.7	23 39.5	07.3	144 15.0	55.8
23	322 32.0	143 56.0	52.3	136 43.2	56.4	38 42.1	07.3	159 17.2	55.7
29 00	337 34.4	158 55.6	N 1 51.0	151 44.2	S 1 57.0	53 44.6	S23 07.3	174 19.3	N 8 55.6
01	352 36.9	173 55.3	49.7	166 45.2	57.7	68 47.2	07.3	189 21.5	55.5
02	7 39.3	188 55.0	48.4	181 46.2	58.3	83 49.7	07.3	204 23.7	55.3
03	22 41.8	203 54.7 . .	47.1	196 47.2 . .	59.0	98 52.3 . .	07.3	219 25.8 . .	55.2
04	37 44.3	218 54.3	45.9	211 48.2	1 59.7	113 54.8	07.4	234 28.0	55.1
05	52 46.7	233 54.0	44.6	226 49.2	2 00.3	128 57.4	07.4	249 30.2	55.0
06	67 49.2	248 53.7	N 1 43.3	241 50.2	S 2 01.0	143 59.9	S23 07.4	264 32.4	N 8 54.9
07	82 51.7	263 53.4	42.0	256 51.2	01.6	159 02.5	07.4	279 34.5	54.8
08	97 54.1	278 53.0	40.7	271 52.2	02.3	174 05.0	07.4	294 36.7	54.6
F 09	112 56.6	293 52.7 . .	39.4	286 53.2 . .	03.0	189 07.6 . .	07.4	309 38.9 . .	54.5
R 10	127 59.1	308 52.4	38.2	301 54.2	03.6	204 10.1	07.4	324 41.0	54.4
I 11	143 01.5	323 52.1	36.9	316 55.2	04.3	219 12.7	07.4	339 43.2	54.3
D 12	158 04.0	338 51.7	N 1 35.6	331 56.2	S 2 04.9	234 15.2	S23 07.4	354 45.4	N 8 54.2
A 13	173 06.5	353 51.4	34.3	346 57.2	05.6	249 17.8	07.5	9 47.5	54.0
Y 14	188 08.9	8 51.1	33.0	1 58.1	06.3	264 20.3	07.5	24 49.7	53.9
15	203 11.4	23 50.8 . .	31.8	16 59.1 . .	06.9	279 22.9 . .	07.5	39 51.9 . .	53.8
16	218 13.8	38 50.5	30.5	32 00.1	07.6	294 25.4	07.5	54 54.0	53.7
17	233 16.3	53 50.1	29.2	47 01.1	08.2	309 27.9	07.5	69 56.2	53.6
18	248 18.8	68 49.8	N 1 27.9	62 02.1	S 2 08.9	324 30.5	S23 07.5	84 58.4	N 8 53.5
19	263 21.2	83 49.5	26.6	77 03.1	09.6	339 33.0	07.5	100 00.6	53.3
20	278 23.7	98 49.2	25.3	92 04.1	10.2	354 35.6	07.5	115 02.7	53.2
21	293 26.2	113 48.8 . .	24.1	107 05.1 . .	10.9	9 38.1 . .	07.5	130 04.9 . .	53.1
22	308 28.6	128 48.5	22.8	122 06.1	11.5	24 40.7	07.6	145 07.1	53.0
23	323 31.1	143 48.2	21.5	137 07.1	12.2	39 43.2	07.6	160 09.2	52.9
30 00	338 33.6	158 47.9	N 1 20.2	152 08.1	S 2 12.9	54 45.8	S23 07.6	175 11.4	N 8 52.7
01	353 36.0	173 47.6	18.9	167 09.1	13.5	69 48.3	07.6	190 13.6	52.6
02	8 38.5	188 47.2	17.6	182 10.1	14.2	84 50.8	07.6	205 15.7	52.5
03	23 40.9	203 46.9 . .	16.4	197 11.1 . .	14.8	99 53.4 . .	07.6	220 17.9 . .	52.4
04	38 43.4	218 46.6	15.1	212 12.0	15.5	114 55.9	07.6	235 20.1	52.3
05	53 45.9	233 46.3	13.8	227 13.0	16.2	129 58.5	07.6	250 22.2	52.2
06	68 48.3	248 45.9	N 1 12.5	242 14.0	S 2 16.8	145 01.0	S23 07.6	265 24.4	N 8 52.0
07	83 50.8	263 45.6	11.2	257 15.0	17.5	160 03.5	07.6	280 26.6	51.9
S 08	98 53.3	278 45.3	09.9	272 16.0	18.2	175 06.1	07.7	295 28.7	51.8
A 09	113 55.7	293 45.0 . .	08.7	287 17.0 . .	18.8	190 08.6 . .	07.7	310 30.9 . .	51.7
T 10	128 58.2	308 44.7	07.4	302 18.0	19.5	205 11.2	07.7	325 33.1	51.6
U 11	144 00.7	323 44.3	06.1	317 19.0	20.1	220 13.7	07.7	340 35.3	51.4
R 12	159 03.1	338 44.0	N 1 04.8	332 20.0	S 2 20.8	235 16.2	S23 07.7	355 37.4	N 8 51.3
D 13	174 05.6	353 43.7	03.5	347 21.0	21.5	250 18.8	07.7	10 39.6	51.2
A 14	189 08.1	8 43.4	02.2	2 22.0	22.1	265 21.3	07.7	25 41.8	51.1
Y 15	204 10.5	23 43.1	1 00.9	17 22.9 . .	22.8	280 23.9 . .	07.7	40 43.9 . .	51.0
16	219 13.0	38 42.7	0 59.7	32 23.9	23.4	295 26.4	07.7	55 46.1	50.9
17	234 15.4	53 42.4	58.4	47 24.9	24.1	310 28.9	07.7	70 48.3	50.7
18	249 17.9	68 42.1	N 0 57.1	62 25.9	S 2 24.8	325 31.5	S23 07.8	85 50.4	N 8 50.6
19	264 20.4	83 41.8	55.8	77 26.9	25.4	340 34.0	07.8	100 52.6	50.5
20	279 22.8	98 41.5	54.5	92 27.9	26.1	355 36.5	07.8	115 54.8	50.4
21	294 25.3	113 41.1 . .	53.2	107 28.9 . .	26.7	10 39.1 . .	07.8	130 56.9 . .	50.3
22	309 27.8	128 40.8	51.9	122 29.9	27.4	25 41.6	07.8	145 59.1	50.1
23	324 30.2	143 40.5	50.7	137 30.9	28.1	40 44.2	07.8	161 01.3	50.0
Mer. Pass.	h m 1 29.5	*v* −0.3	*d* 1.3	*v* 1.0	*d* 0.7	*v* 2.5	*d* 0.0	*v* 2.2	*d* 0.1

STARS

Name	SHA	Dec
	° ′	° ′
Acamar	315 20.8	S40 15.8
Achernar	335 28.8	S57 11.2
Acrux	173 14.3	S63 09.0
Adhara	255 15.6	S28 58.7
Aldebaran	290 53.5	N16 31.7
Alioth	166 24.0	N55 54.9
Alkaid	153 01.8	N49 16.4
Al Na'ir	27 47.6	S46 55.0
Alnilam	275 50.1	S 1 11.6
Alphard	217 59.9	S 8 41.6
Alphecca	126 14.1	N26 41.3
Alpheratz	357 47.0	N29 08.4
Altair	62 11.5	N 8 53.6
Ankaa	353 18.7	S42 15.2
Antares	112 30.7	S26 27.2
Arcturus	145 59.1	N19 08.3
Atria	107 35.8	S69 02.9
Avior	234 20.2	S59 32.0
Bellatrix	278 35.9	N 6 21.6
Betelgeuse	271 05.3	N 7 24.7
Canopus	263 58.0	S52 41.6
Capella	280 39.9	N46 00.4
Deneb	49 33.6	N45 18.8
Denebola	182 37.6	N14 31.5
Diphda	348 59.1	S17 56.1
Dubhe	193 56.4	N61 42.3
Elnath	278 17.3	N28 36.9
Eltanin	90 47.6	N51 29.5
Enif	33 50.3	N 9 55.0
Fomalhaut	15 27.5	S29 34.4
Gacrux	172 05.7	S57 09.9
Gienah	175 56.3	S17 35.4
Hadar	148 53.7	S60 25.2
Hamal	328 04.7	N23 30.3
Kaus Aust.	83 48.4	S34 22.9
Kochab	137 19.8	N74 07.4
Markab	13 41.6	N15 15.3
Menkar	314 18.7	N 4 07.6
Menkent	148 12.1	S36 24.9
Miaplacidus	221 41.7	S69 45.0
Mirfak	308 45.5	N49 53.5
Nunki	76 02.5	S26 17.2
Peacock	53 24.2	S56 42.5
Pollux	243 32.3	N28 00.4
Procyon	245 03.7	N 5 12.3
Rasalhague	96 09.7	N12 33.3
Regulus	207 47.6	N11 55.6
Rigel	281 15.6	S 8 11.2
Rigil Kent.	139 57.2	S60 52.5
Sabik	102 16.6	S15 44.2
Schedar	349 44.4	N56 35.1
Shaula	96 26.7	S37 06.8
Sirius	258 37.1	S16 43.4
Spica	158 35.3	S11 12.4
Suhail	222 55.6	S43 27.9
Vega	80 41.2	N38 47.7
Zuben'ubi	137 09.6	S16 04.7

	SHA	Mer. Pass.
	° ′	h m
Venus	181 21.2	13 25
Mars	174 09.8	13 52
Jupiter	76 10.2	20 22
Saturn	196 44.9	12 21

2008 AUGUST 28, 29, 30 (THURS., FRI., SAT.)

Day	UT (h)	SUN GHA	SUN Dec	MOON GHA	v	MOON Dec	d	HP
d	h	° ′	° ′	° ′	′	° ′	′	′
28	00	179 41.5	N 9 39.3	215 45.7	6.7	N22 17.1	10.3	59.3
	01	194 41.7	38.4	230 11.4	6.8	22 06.8	10.4	59.2
	02	209 41.9	37.5	244 37.2	6.9	21 56.4	10.6	59.2
	03	224 42.0	. . 36.6	259 03.1	7.1	21 45.8	10.7	59.2
	04	239 42.2	35.8	273 29.2	7.1	21 35.1	10.8	59.2
	05	254 42.4	34.9	287 55.3	7.2	21 24.3	10.9	59.2
	06	269 42.6	N 9 34.0	302 21.5	7.3	N21 13.4	11.1	59.2
	07	284 42.8	33.1	316 47.8	7.4	21 02.3	11.2	59.2
THURSDAY	08	299 43.0	32.2	331 14.2	7.5	20 51.1	11.3	59.2
	09	314 43.1	. . 31.3	345 40.7	7.6	20 39.8	11.4	59.2
	10	329 43.3	30.4	0 07.3	7.7	20 28.4	11.6	59.1
	11	344 43.5	29.5	14 34.0	7.9	20 16.8	11.6	59.1
	12	359 43.7	N 9 28.7	29 00.9	7.9	N20 05.2	11.8	59.1
	13	14 43.9	27.8	43 27.8	8.0	19 53.4	11.9	59.1
	14	29 44.1	26.9	57 54.8	8.1	19 41.5	12.0	59.1
	15	44 44.3	. . 26.0	72 21.9	8.3	19 29.5	12.1	59.1
	16	59 44.5	25.1	86 49.2	8.3	19 17.4	12.2	59.1
	17	74 44.6	24.2	101 16.5	8.4	19 05.2	12.4	59.0
	18	89 44.8	N 9 23.3	115 43.9	8.6	N18 52.8	12.4	59.0
	19	104 45.0	22.4	130 11.5	8.6	18 40.4	12.5	59.0
	20	119 45.2	21.6	144 39.1	8.8	18 27.9	12.6	59.0
	21	134 45.4	. . 20.7	159 06.9	8.8	18 15.3	12.8	59.0
	22	149 45.6	19.8	173 34.7	8.9	18 02.5	12.8	59.0
	23	164 45.8	18.9	188 02.6	9.1	17 49.7	12.9	59.0
29	00	179 45.9	N 9 18.0	202 30.7	9.1	N17 36.8	13.0	58.9
	01	194 46.1	17.1	216 58.8	9.2	17 23.8	13.1	58.9
	02	209 46.3	16.2	231 27.0	9.4	17 10.7	13.2	58.9
	03	224 46.5	. . 15.3	245 55.4	9.4	16 57.5	13.3	58.9
	04	239 46.7	14.4	260 23.8	9.5	16 44.2	13.3	58.9
	05	254 46.9	13.5	274 52.3	9.7	16 30.9	13.5	58.9
	06	269 47.1	N 9 12.7	289 21.0	9.7	N16 17.4	13.5	58.8
	07	284 47.3	11.8	303 49.7	9.8	16 03.9	13.6	58.8
	08	299 47.5	10.9	318 18.5	9.9	15 50.3	13.7	58.8
FRIDAY	09	314 47.6	. . 10.0	332 47.4	10.0	15 36.6	13.8	58.8
	10	329 47.8	09.1	347 16.4	10.1	15 22.8	13.8	58.8
	11	344 48.0	08.2	1 45.5	10.2	15 09.0	13.9	58.8
	12	359 48.2	N 9 07.3	16 14.7	10.3	N14 55.1	14.0	58.7
	13	14 48.4	06.4	30 44.0	10.3	14 41.1	14.0	58.7
	14	29 48.6	05.5	45 13.3	10.5	14 27.1	14.2	58.7
	15	44 48.8	. . 04.6	59 42.8	10.6	14 12.9	14.1	58.7
	16	59 49.0	03.7	74 12.4	10.6	13 58.8	14.3	58.7
	17	74 49.2	02.8	88 42.0	10.7	13 44.5	14.3	58.6
	18	89 49.3	N 9 01.9	103 11.7	10.8	N13 30.2	14.4	58.6
	19	104 49.5	01.0	117 41.5	10.9	13 15.8	14.4	58.6
	20	119 49.7	9 00.1	132 11.4	11.0	13 01.4	14.5	58.6
	21	134 49.9	8 59.3	146 41.4	11.1	12 46.9	14.5	58.6
	22	149 50.1	58.4	161 11.5	11.2	12 32.4	14.6	58.5
	23	164 50.3	57.5	175 41.7	11.2	12 17.8	14.7	58.5
30	00	179 50.5	N 8 56.6	190 11.9	11.3	N12 03.1	14.7	58.5
	01	194 50.7	55.7	204 42.2	11.4	11 48.4	14.8	58.5
	02	209 50.9	54.8	219 12.6	11.5	11 33.6	14.8	58.4
	03	224 51.1	. . 53.9	233 43.1	11.5	11 18.8	14.8	58.4
	04	239 51.3	53.0	248 13.6	11.7	11 04.0	14.9	58.4
	05	254 51.4	52.1	262 44.3	11.7	10 49.1	14.9	58.4
	06	269 51.6	N 8 51.2	277 15.0	11.8	N10 34.2	15.0	58.4
	07	284 51.8	50.3	291 45.8	11.8	10 19.2	15.0	58.3
	08	299 52.0	49.4	306 16.6	12.0	10 04.2	15.1	58.3
	09	314 52.2	. . 48.5	320 47.6	12.0	9 49.1	15.1	58.3
	10	329 52.4	47.6	335 18.6	12.1	9 34.0	15.1	58.3
SATURDAY	11	344 52.6	46.7	349 49.7	12.1	9 18.9	15.1	58.2
	12	359 52.8	N 8 45.8	4 20.8	12.2	N 9 03.8	15.2	58.2
	13	14 53.0	44.9	18 52.0	12.3	8 48.6	15.3	58.2
	14	29 53.2	44.0	33 23.3	12.4	8 33.3	15.2	58.2
	15	44 53.4	. . 43.1	47 54.7	12.4	8 18.1	15.3	58.1
	16	59 53.6	42.2	62 26.1	12.5	8 02.8	15.3	58.1
	17	74 53.8	41.3	76 57.6	12.5	7 47.5	15.3	58.1
	18	89 54.0	N 8 40.4	91 29.1	12.6	N 7 32.2	15.4	58.1
	19	104 54.1	39.5	106 00.7	12.7	7 16.8	15.3	58.0
	20	119 54.3	38.6	120 32.4	12.7	7 01.5	15.4	58.0
	21	134 54.5	. . 37.7	135 04.1	12.8	6 46.1	15.4	58.0
	22	149 54.7	36.8	149 35.9	12.9	6 30.7	15.5	58.0
	23	164 54.9	35.9	164 07.8	12.9	N 6 15.2	15.4	57.9
		SD 15.9	*d* 0.9	SD 16.1		16.0		15.9

Lat.	Twilight Naut.	Twilight Civil	Sunrise	Moonrise 28	Moonrise 29	Moonrise 30	Moonrise 31
°	h m	h m	h m	h m	h m	h m	h m
N 72	////	02 10	03 48	23 17	26 55	02 55	05 19
N 70	////	02 44	04 04	□	00 35	03 15	05 26
68	01 00	03 08	04 16	□	01 13	03 31	05 31
66	01 52	03 26	04 26	25 39	01 39	03 43	05 36
64	02 23	03 40	04 35	25 59	01 59	03 54	05 40
62	02 45	03 52	04 42	00 19	02 15	04 02	05 43
60	03 02	04 03	04 48	00 41	02 28	04 10	05 46
N 58	03 16	04 11	04 54	00 59	02 39	04 16	05 48
56	03 28	04 19	04 59	01 13	02 49	04 22	05 50
54	03 38	04 26	05 03	01 26	02 58	04 27	05 52
52	03 47	04 32	05 07	01 37	03 06	04 32	05 54
50	03 55	04 37	05 11	01 47	03 13	04 36	05 56
45	04 11	04 48	05 19	02 08	03 28	04 45	05 59
N 40	04 24	04 57	05 25	02 25	03 40	04 53	06 02
35	04 34	05 05	05 31	02 39	03 50	04 59	06 05
30	04 42	05 11	05 35	02 51	03 59	05 05	06 07
20	04 55	05 21	05 44	03 12	04 15	05 14	06 11
N 10	05 05	05 30	05 51	03 29	04 28	05 23	06 14
0	05 12	05 37	05 57	03 46	04 40	05 31	06 18
S 10	05 18	05 43	06 04	04 03	04 53	05 38	06 21
20	05 23	05 49	06 11	04 21	05 06	05 47	06 24
30	05 26	05 54	06 18	04 41	05 21	05 56	06 28
35	05 28	05 57	06 23	04 53	05 30	06 02	06 30
40	05 29	06 00	06 28	05 06	05 40	06 08	06 33
45	05 30	06 04	06 33	05 22	05 51	06 15	06 36
S 50	05 30	06 07	06 40	05 42	06 05	06 24	06 39
52	05 30	06 09	06 43	05 51	06 12	06 27	06 41
54	05 30	06 11	06 47	06 01	06 19	06 32	06 42
56	05 30	06 13	06 50	06 13	06 27	06 36	06 44
58	05 29	06 15	06 54	06 26	06 36	06 42	06 46
S 60	05 29	06 17	06 59	06 42	06 46	06 48	06 49

Lat.	Sunset	Twilight Civil	Twilight Naut.	Moonset 28	Moonset 29	Moonset 30	Moonset 31
°	h m	h m	h m	h m	h m	h m	h m
N 72	20 10	21 44	////	22 00	20 10	19 26	18 52
N 70	19 55	21 13	////	20 41	19 47	19 16	18 51
68	19 43	20 50	22 49	20 01	19 30	19 08	18 50
66	19 33	20 33	22 03	19 34	19 15	19 01	18 49
64	19 25	20 19	21 35	19 13	19 03	18 55	18 48
62	19 18	20 07	21 14	18 55	18 53	18 50	18 47
60	19 12	19 57	20 57	18 41	18 44	18 46	18 47
N 58	19 06	19 49	20 43	18 29	18 37	18 42	18 46
56	19 01	19 41	20 31	18 18	18 30	18 39	18 46
54	18 57	19 35	20 21	18 08	18 24	18 35	18 45
52	18 53	19 29	20 13	18 00	18 18	18 32	18 45
50	18 50	19 24	20 05	17 52	18 13	18 30	18 45
45	18 42	19 13	19 49	17 36	18 02	18 24	18 44
N 40	18 36	19 04	19 37	17 22	17 53	18 19	18 43
35	18 30	18 56	19 27	17 10	17 45	18 15	18 42
30	18 26	18 50	19 19	17 00	17 38	18 11	18 42
20	18 18	18 40	19 06	16 43	17 26	18 05	18 41
N 10	18 11	18 32	18 57	16 27	17 15	17 59	18 40
0	18 04	18 25	18 49	16 13	17 05	17 53	18 39
S 10	17 58	18 19	18 44	15 58	16 55	17 48	18 38
20	17 51	18 13	18 39	15 42	16 43	17 42	18 37
30	17 44	18 08	18 36	15 24	16 31	17 35	18 36
35	17 39	18 05	18 34	15 13	16 23	17 31	18 36
40	17 34	18 02	18 33	15 01	16 15	17 26	18 35
45	17 29	17 59	18 33	14 46	16 05	17 21	18 34
S 50	17 22	17 55	18 32	14 28	15 53	17 15	18 33
52	17 19	17 53	18 33	14 19	15 47	17 12	18 32
54	17 16	17 52	18 33	14 10	15 41	17 08	18 32
56	17 12	17 50	18 33	13 59	15 34	17 05	18 31
58	17 08	17 48	18 34	13 46	15 26	17 01	18 31
S 60	17 04	17 46	18 34	13 31	15 17	16 56	18 30

Day	SUN Eqn. of Time 00h	SUN Eqn. of Time 12h	SUN Mer. Pass.	MOON Mer. Pass. Upper	MOON Mer. Pass. Lower	MOON Age	MOON Phase
d	m s	m s	h m	h m	h m	d	%
28	01 14	01 06	12 01	09 59	22 27	27	7
29	00 57	00 48	12 01	10 53	23 18	28	2
30	00 38	00 29	12 00	11 42	24 06	29	0

	UT	ARIES	VENUS −3.8		MARS +1.7		JUPITER −2.5		SATURN +0.8	
		GHA	GHA	Dec	GHA	Dec	GHA	Dec	GHA	Dec
	d h	° ′	° ′	° ′	° ′	° ′	° ′	° ′	° ′	° ′
	31 00	339 32.7	158 40.2	N 0 49.4	152 31.9	S 2 28.7	55 46.7	S23 07.8	176 03.5	N 8 49.9
	01	354 35.2	173 39.8	48.1	167 32.9	29.4	70 49.2	07.8	191 05.6	49.8
	02	9 37.6	188 39.5	46.8	182 33.8	30.0	85 51.8	07.8	206 07.8	49.7
	03	24 40.1	203 39.2 . .	45.5	197 34.8 . .	30.7	100 54.3 . .	07.8	221 10.0 . .	49.6
	04	39 42.5	218 38.9	44.2	212 35.8	31.4	115 56.8	07.8	236 12.1	49.4
	05	54 45.0	233 38.6	42.9	227 36.8	32.0	130 59.4	07.9	251 14.3	49.3
	06	69 47.5	248 38.2	N 0 41.7	242 37.8	S 2 32.7	146 01.9	S23 07.9	266 16.5	N 8 49.2
	07	84 49.9	263 37.9	40.4	257 38.8	33.3	161 04.4	07.9	281 18.6	49.1
	08	99 52.4	278 37.6	39.1	272 39.8	34.0	176 07.0	07.9	296 20.8	49.0
S	09	114 54.9	293 37.3 . .	37.8	287 40.8 . .	34.7	191 09.5 . .	07.9	311 23.0 . .	48.8
U	10	129 57.3	308 37.0	36.5	302 41.8	35.3	206 12.0	07.9	326 25.1	48.7
N	11	144 59.8	323 36.6	35.2	317 42.7	36.0	221 14.6	07.9	341 27.3	48.6
D	12	160 02.3	338 36.3	N 0 33.9	332 43.7	S 2 36.7	236 17.1	S23 07.9	356 29.5	N 8 48.5
A	13	175 04.7	353 36.0	32.7	347 44.7	37.3	251 19.6	07.9	11 31.6	48.4
Y	14	190 07.2	8 35.7	31.4	2 45.7	38.0	266 22.1	07.9	26 33.8	48.3
	15	205 09.7	23 35.4 . .	30.1	17 46.7 . .	38.6	281 24.7 . .	07.9	41 36.0 . .	48.1
	16	220 12.1	38 35.1	28.8	32 47.7	39.3	296 27.2	08.0	56 38.2	48.0
	17	235 14.6	53 34.7	27.5	47 48.7	40.0	311 29.7	08.0	71 40.3	47.9
	18	250 17.0	68 34.4	N 0 26.2	62 49.7	S 2 40.6	326 32.3	S23 08.0	86 42.5	N 8 47.8
	19	265 19.5	83 34.1	24.9	77 50.6	41.3	341 34.8	08.0	101 44.7	47.7
	20	280 22.0	98 33.8	23.7	92 51.6	41.9	356 37.3	08.0	116 46.8	47.5
	21	295 24.4	113 33.5 . .	22.4	107 52.6 . .	42.6	11 39.8 . .	08.0	131 49.0 . .	47.4
	22	310 26.9	128 33.1	21.1	122 53.6	43.3	26 42.4	08.0	146 51.2	47.3
	23	325 29.4	143 32.8	19.8	137 54.6	43.9	41 44.9	08.0	161 53.3	47.2
	1 00	340 31.8	158 32.5	N 0 18.5	152 55.6	S 2 44.6	56 47.4	S23 08.0	176 55.5	N 8 47.1
	01	355 34.3	173 32.2	17.2	167 56.6	45.2	71 49.9	08.0	191 57.7	47.0
	02	10 36.8	188 31.9	15.9	182 57.6	45.9	86 52.5	08.0	206 59.8	46.8
	03	25 39.2	203 31.5 . .	14.6	197 58.5 . .	46.6	101 55.0 . .	08.1	222 02.0 . .	46.7
	04	40 41.7	218 31.2	13.4	212 59.5	47.2	116 57.5	08.1	237 04.2	46.6
	05	55 44.1	233 30.9	12.1	228 00.5	47.9	132 00.0	08.1	252 06.3	46.5
	06	70 46.6	248 30.6	N 0 10.8	243 01.5	S 2 48.5	147 02.6	S23 08.1	267 08.5	N 8 46.4
	07	85 49.1	263 30.3	09.5	258 02.5	49.2	162 05.1	08.1	282 10.7	46.2
	08	100 51.5	278 29.9	08.2	273 03.5	49.9	177 07.6	08.1	297 12.9	46.1
M	09	115 54.0	293 29.6 . .	06.9	288 04.5 . .	50.5	192 10.1 . .	08.1	312 15.0 . .	46.0
O	10	130 56.5	308 29.3	05.6	303 05.4	51.2	207 12.7	08.1	327 17.2	45.9
N	11	145 58.9	323 29.0	04.3	318 06.4	51.9	222 15.2	08.1	342 19.4	45.8
D	12	161 01.4	338 28.7	N 0 03.1	333 07.4	S 2 52.5	237 17.7	S23 08.1	357 21.5	N 8 45.7
A	13	176 03.9	353 28.4	01.8	348 08.4	53.2	252 20.2	08.1	12 23.7	45.5
Y	14	191 06.3	8 28.0	N 00.5	3 09.4	53.8	267 22.8	08.1	27 25.9	45.4
	15	206 08.8	23 27.7	S 00.8	18 10.4 . .	54.5	282 25.3 . .	08.2	42 28.0 . .	45.3
	16	221 11.3	38 27.4	02.1	33 11.4	55.2	297 27.8	08.2	57 30.2	45.2
	17	236 13.7	53 27.1	03.4	48 12.3	55.8	312 30.3	08.2	72 32.4	45.1
	18	251 16.2	68 26.8	S 0 04.7	63 13.3	S 2 56.5	327 32.8	S23 08.2	87 34.5	N 8 44.9
	19	266 18.6	83 26.4	06.0	78 14.3	57.1	342 35.4	08.2	102 36.7	44.8
	20	281 21.1	98 26.1	07.2	93 15.3	57.8	357 37.9	08.2	117 38.9	44.7
	21	296 23.6	113 25.8 . .	08.5	108 16.3 . .	58.5	12 40.4 . .	08.2	132 41.0 . .	44.6
	22	311 26.0	128 25.5	09.8	123 17.3	59.1	27 42.9	08.2	147 43.2	44.5
	23	326 28.5	143 25.2	11.1	138 18.3	2 59.8	42 45.4	08.2	162 45.4	44.4
	2 00	341 31.0	158 24.8	S 0 12.4	153 19.2	S 3 00.4	57 47.9	S23 08.2	177 47.6	N 8 44.2
	01	356 33.4	173 24.5	13.7	168 20.2	01.1	72 50.5	08.2	192 49.7	44.1
	02	11 35.9	188 24.2	15.0	183 21.2	01.8	87 53.0	08.2	207 51.9	44.0
	03	26 38.4	203 23.9 . .	16.3	198 22.2 . .	02.4	102 55.5 . .	08.3	222 54.1 . .	43.9
	04	41 40.8	218 23.6	17.5	213 23.2	03.1	117 58.0	08.3	237 56.2	43.8
	05	56 43.3	233 23.3	18.8	228 24.2	03.7	133 00.5	08.3	252 58.4	43.6
	06	71 45.8	248 22.9	S 0 20.1	243 25.1	S 3 04.4	148 03.0	S23 08.3	268 00.6	N 8 43.5
	07	86 48.2	263 22.6	21.4	258 26.1	05.1	163 05.6	08.3	283 02.7	43.4
T	08	101 50.7	278 22.3	22.7	273 27.1	05.7	178 08.1	08.3	298 04.9	43.3
U	09	116 53.1	293 22.0 . .	24.0	288 28.1 . .	06.4	193 10.6 . .	08.3	313 07.1 . .	43.2
E	10	131 55.6	308 21.7	25.3	303 29.1	07.0	208 13.1	08.3	328 09.2	43.1
S	11	146 58.1	323 21.4	26.6	318 30.1	07.7	223 15.6	08.3	343 11.4	42.9
D	12	162 00.5	338 21.0	S 0 27.9	333 31.0	S 3 08.4	238 18.1	S23 08.3	358 13.6	N 8 42.8
A	13	177 03.0	353 20.7	29.1	348 32.0	09.0	253 20.6	08.3	13 15.7	42.7
Y	14	192 05.5	8 20.4	30.4	3 33.0	09.7	268 23.2	08.3	28 17.9	42.6
	15	207 07.9	23 20.1 . .	31.7	18 34.0 . .	10.3	283 25.7 . .	08.3	43 20.1 . .	42.5
	16	222 10.4	38 19.8	33.0	33 35.0	11.0	298 28.2	08.4	58 22.3	42.3
	17	237 12.9	53 19.4	34.3	48 36.0	11.7	313 30.7	08.4	73 24.4	42.2
	18	252 15.3	68 19.1	S 0 35.6	63 36.9	S 3 12.3	328 33.2	S23 08.4	88 26.6	N 8 42.1
	19	267 17.8	83 18.8	36.9	78 37.9	13.0	343 35.7	08.4	103 28.8	42.0
	20	282 20.2	98 18.5	38.2	93 38.9	13.7	358 38.2	08.4	118 30.9	41.9
	21	297 22.7	113 18.2 . .	39.5	108 39.9 . .	14.3	13 40.7 . .	08.4	133 33.1 . .	41.8
	22	312 25.2	128 17.9	40.7	123 40.9	15.0	28 43.2	08.4	148 35.3	41.6
	23	327 27.6	143 17.5	42.0	138 41.8	15.6	43 45.8	08.4	163 37.4	41.5
	Mer. Pass.	h m 1 17.7	v −0.3	d 1.3	v 1.0	d 0.7	v 2.5	d 0.0	v 2.2	d 0.1

STARS

Name	SHA	Dec
	° ′	° ′
Acamar	315 20.8	S40 15.8
Achernar	335 28.8	S57 11.2
Acrux	173 14.3	S63 09.0
Adhara	255 15.6	S28 58.7
Aldebaran	290 53.5	N16 31.7
Alioth	166 24.0	N55 54.9
Alkaid	153 01.8	N49 16.3
Al Na'ir	27 47.6	S46 55.0
Alnilam	275 50.1	S 1 11.6
Alphard	217 59.9	S 8 41.6
Alphecca	126 14.1	N26 41.3
Alpheratz	357 47.0	N29 08.4
Altair	62 11.5	N 8 53.6
Ankaa	353 18.7	S42 15.2
Antares	112 30.7	S26 27.2
Arcturus	145 59.1	N19 08.3
Atria	107 35.8	S69 02.9
Avior	234 20.2	S59 32.0
Bellatrix	278 35.9	N 6 21.6
Betelgeuse	271 05.3	N 7 24.7
Canopus	263 58.0	S52 41.6
Capella	280 39.9	N46 00.4
Deneb	49 33.6	N45 18.9
Denebola	182 37.6	N14 31.5
Diphda	348 59.1	S17 56.1
Dubhe	193 56.4	N61 42.3
Elnath	278 17.3	N28 36.9
Eltanin	90 47.6	N51 29.5
Enif	33 50.4	N 9 55.0
Fomalhaut	15 27.5	S29 34.4
Gacrux	172 05.7	S57 09.9
Gienah	175 56.4	S17 35.4
Hadar	148 53.7	S60 25.2
Hamal	328 04.7	N23 30.3
Kaus Aust.	83 48.4	S34 23.0
Kochab	137 19.9	N74 07.4
Markab	13 41.6	N15 15.3
Menkar	314 18.7	N 4 07.6
Menkent	148 12.2	S36 24.9
Miaplacidus	221 41.7	S69 45.0
Mirfak	308 45.5	N49 53.5
Nunki	76 02.5	S26 17.2
Peacock	53 24.2	S56 42.5
Pollux	243 32.3	N28 00.4
Procyon	245 03.7	N 5 12.3
Rasalhague	96 09.7	N12 33.3
Regulus	207 47.6	N11 55.6
Rigel	281 15.6	S 8 11.2
Rigil Kent.	139 57.2	S60 52.5
Sabik	102 16.6	S15 44.2
Schedar	349 44.4	N56 35.1
Shaula	96 26.7	S37 06.8
Sirius	258 37.1	S16 43.4
Spica	158 35.3	S11 12.4
Suhail	222 55.6	S43 27.9
Vega	80 41.2	N38 47.7
Zuben'ubi	137 09.6	S16 04.7

	SHA	Mer. Pass.
	° ′	h m
Venus	178 00.7	13 26
Mars	172 23.8	13 47
Jupiter	76 15.6	20 09
Saturn	196 23.7	12 11

	UT	SUN GHA	SUN Dec	MOON GHA	*v*	MOON Dec	*d*	HP
	d h	° ′	° ′	° ′	′	° ′	′	′
	31 00	179 55.1	N 8 35.0	178 39.7	12.9	N 5 59.8	15.5	57.9
	01	194 55.3	34.1	193 11.6	13.1	5 44.3	15.4	57.9
	02	209 55.5	33.2	207 43.7	13.0	5 28.9	15.5	57.9
	03	224 55.7	. . 32.3	222 15.7	13.1	5 13.4	15.5	57.8
	04	239 55.9	31.4	236 47.8	13.2	4 57.9	15.5	57.8
	05	254 56.1	30.5	251 20.0	13.2	4 42.4	15.5	57.8
	06	269 56.3	N 8 29.6	265 52.2	13.3	N 4 26.9	15.5	57.8
	07	284 56.5	28.7	280 24.5	13.3	4 11.4	15.5	57.7
	08	299 56.7	27.8	294 56.8	13.4	3 55.9	15.6	57.7
S	09	314 56.9	. . 26.9	309 29.2	13.4	3 40.3	15.5	57.7
U	10	329 57.1	25.9	324 01.6	13.5	3 24.8	15.5	57.7
N	11	344 57.3	25.0	338 34.1	13.5	3 09.3	15.5	57.6
D	12	359 57.5	N 8 24.1	353 06.6	13.5	N 2 53.8	15.5	57.6
A	13	14 57.7	23.2	7 39.1	13.6	2 38.3	15.6	57.6
Y	14	29 57.9	22.3	22 11.7	13.7	2 22.7	15.5	57.5
	15	44 58.0	. . 21.4	36 44.4	13.6	2 07.2	15.5	57.5
	16	59 58.2	20.5	51 17.0	13.7	1 51.7	15.5	57.5
	17	74 58.4	19.6	65 49.7	13.8	1 36.2	15.5	57.5
	18	89 58.6	N 8 18.7	80 22.5	13.8	N 1 20.7	15.5	57.4
	19	104 58.8	17.8	94 55.3	13.8	1 05.2	15.4	57.4
	20	119 59.0	16.9	109 28.1	13.8	0 49.8	15.5	57.4
	21	134 59.2	. . 16.0	124 00.9	13.9	0 34.3	15.4	57.4
	22	149 59.4	15.1	138 33.8	13.9	0 18.9	15.5	57.3
	23	164 59.6	14.2	153 06.7	14.0	N 0 03.4	15.4	57.3
	1 00	179 59.8	N 8 13.3	167 39.7	13.9	S 0 12.0	15.4	57.3
	01	195 00.0	12.4	182 12.6	14.0	0 27.4	15.4	57.2
	02	210 00.2	11.4	196 45.6	14.0	0 42.8	15.3	57.2
	03	225 00.4	. . 10.5	211 18.6	14.1	0 58.1	15.4	57.2
	04	240 00.6	09.6	225 51.7	14.1	1 13.5	15.3	57.2
	05	255 00.8	08.7	240 24.8	14.1	1 28.8	15.3	57.1
	06	270 01.0	N 8 07.8	254 57.9	14.1	S 1 44.1	15.3	57.1
	07	285 01.2	06.9	269 31.0	14.1	1 59.4	15.2	57.1
	08	300 01.4	06.0	284 04.1	14.2	2 14.6	15.2	57.0
M	09	315 01.6	. . 05.1	298 37.3	14.2	2 29.8	15.2	57.0
O	10	330 01.8	04.2	313 10.5	14.2	2 45.0	15.2	57.0
N	11	345 02.0	03.3	327 43.7	14.2	3 00.2	15.2	57.0
D	12	0 02.2	N 8 02.4	342 16.9	14.2	S 3 15.4	15.1	56.9
A	13	15 02.4	01.4	356 50.1	14.3	3 30.5	15.0	56.9
Y	14	30 02.6	8 00.5	11 23.4	14.2	3 45.5	15.1	56.9
	15	45 02.8	7 59.6	25 56.6	14.3	4 00.6	15.0	56.8
	16	60 03.0	58.7	40 29.9	14.3	4 15.6	15.0	56.8
	17	75 03.2	57.8	55 03.2	14.3	4 30.6	14.9	56.8
	18	90 03.4	N 7 56.9	69 36.5	14.3	S 4 45.5	14.9	56.8
	19	105 03.6	56.0	84 09.8	14.3	5 00.4	14.9	56.7
	20	120 03.8	55.1	98 43.1	14.4	5 15.3	14.8	56.7
	21	135 04.0	. . 54.2	113 16.5	14.3	5 30.1	14.8	56.7
	22	150 04.2	53.2	127 49.8	14.3	5 44.9	14.8	56.6
	23	165 04.4	52.3	142 23.1	14.4	5 59.7	14.7	56.6
	2 00	180 04.6	N 7 51.4	156 56.5	14.3	S 6 14.4	14.6	56.6
	01	195 04.8	50.5	171 29.8	14.4	6 29.0	14.7	56.6
	02	210 05.0	49.6	186 03.2	14.3	6 43.7	14.5	56.5
	03	225 05.2	. . 48.7	200 36.5	14.4	6 58.2	14.6	56.5
	04	240 05.4	47.8	215 09.9	14.3	7 12.8	14.5	56.5
	05	255 05.6	46.8	229 43.2	14.4	7 27.3	14.4	56.4
	06	270 05.8	N 7 45.9	244 16.6	14.3	S 7 41.7	14.4	56.4
	07	285 06.0	45.0	258 49.9	14.4	7 56.1	14.3	56.4
T	08	300 06.2	44.1	273 23.3	14.3	8 10.4	14.3	56.4
U	09	315 06.4	. . 43.2	287 56.6	14.4	8 24.7	14.3	56.3
E	10	330 06.6	42.3	302 30.0	14.3	8 39.0	14.2	56.3
	11	345 06.8	41.4	317 03.3	14.3	8 53.2	14.1	56.3
S	12	0 07.0	N 7 40.4	331 36.6	14.4	S 9 07.3	14.1	56.2
D	13	15 07.2	39.5	346 10.0	14.3	9 21.4	14.0	56.2
A	14	30 07.4	38.6	0 43.3	14.3	9 35.4	14.0	56.2
Y	15	45 07.6	. . 37.7	15 16.6	14.3	9 49.4	13.9	56.2
	16	60 07.8	36.8	29 49.9	14.2	10 03.3	13.9	56.1
	17	75 08.0	35.9	44 23.1	14.3	10 17.2	13.8	56.1
	18	90 08.2	N 7 34.9	58 56.4	14.3	S10 31.0	13.7	56.1
	19	105 08.4	34.0	73 29.7	14.2	10 44.7	13.7	56.1
	20	120 08.6	33.1	88 02.9	14.2	10 58.4	13.6	56.0
	21	135 08.8	. . 32.2	102 36.1	14.2	11 12.0	13.6	56.0
	22	150 09.0	31.3	117 09.3	14.2	11 25.6	13.5	56.0
	23	165 09.2	30.4	131 42.5	14.2	S11 39.1	13.4	55.9
		SD 15.9	*d* 0.9	SD	15.7		15.5	15.3

Lat.	Twilight Naut.	Twilight Civil	Sunrise	Moonrise 31	Moonrise 1	Moonrise 2	Moonrise 3
°	h m	h m	h m	h m	h m	h m	h m
N 72	////	02 33	04 03	05 19	07 31	09 42	12 10
N 70	////	03 01	04 16	05 26	07 27	09 28	11 37
68	01 34	03 22	04 27	05 31	07 25	09 17	11 13
66	02 12	03 38	04 36	05 36	07 23	09 08	10 55
64	02 37	03 51	04 44	05 40	07 21	09 00	10 40
62	02 57	04 01	04 50	05 43	07 19	08 53	10 28
60	03 12	04 11	04 56	05 46	07 18	08 48	10 18
N 58	03 25	04 18	05 00	05 48	07 17	08 43	10 09
56	03 36	04 25	05 05	05 50	07 15	08 39	10 01
54	03 45	04 31	05 09	05 52	07 15	08 35	09 54
52	03 53	04 37	05 12	05 54	07 14	08 31	09 48
50	04 01	04 42	05 15	05 56	07 13	08 28	09 42
45	04 15	04 52	05 22	05 59	07 11	08 21	09 30
N 40	04 27	05 00	05 28	06 02	07 10	08 15	09 20
35	04 36	05 07	05 33	06 05	07 08	08 11	09 12
30	04 44	05 13	05 37	06 07	07 07	08 06	09 05
20	04 56	05 22	05 44	06 11	07 06	07 59	08 52
N 10	05 05	05 30	05 51	06 14	07 04	07 52	08 41
0	05 11	05 36	05 57	06 18	07 03	07 47	08 31
S 10	05 17	05 41	06 02	06 21	07 01	07 41	08 21
20	05 20	05 46	06 08	06 24	07 00	07 34	08 10
30	05 23	05 51	06 15	06 28	06 58	07 27	07 58
35	05 24	05 53	06 19	06 30	06 57	07 23	07 51
40	05 24	05 56	06 23	06 33	06 56	07 19	07 43
45	05 25	05 58	06 28	06 36	06 55	07 13	07 33
S 50	05 24	06 01	06 34	06 39	06 53	07 07	07 22
52	05 24	06 03	06 36	06 41	06 52	07 04	07 17
54	05 23	06 04	06 39	06 42	06 52	07 01	07 12
56	05 22	06 05	06 43	06 44	06 51	06 58	07 06
58	05 21	06 07	06 46	06 46	06 50	06 54	06 59
S 60	05 20	06 08	06 50	06 49	06 49	06 50	06 51

Lat.	Sunset	Twilight Civil	Twilight Naut.	Moonset 31	Moonset 1	Moonset 2	Moonset 3
°	h m	h m	h m	h m	h m	h m	h m
N 72	19 53	21 21	////	18 52	18 20	17 44	16 49
N 70	19 40	20 54	23 33	18 51	18 27	18 00	17 24
68	19 30	20 35	22 18	18 50	18 32	18 13	17 50
66	19 21	20 19	21 43	18 49	18 37	18 24	18 09
64	19 14	20 07	21 19	18 48	18 41	18 33	18 25
62	19 08	19 56	21 00	18 47	18 44	18 41	18 38
60	19 03	19 47	20 45	18 47	18 47	18 48	18 50
N 58	18 58	19 40	20 33	18 46	18 50	18 54	19 00
56	18 54	19 33	20 22	18 46	18 53	19 00	19 08
54	18 50	19 27	20 13	18 45	18 55	19 05	19 16
52	18 46	19 22	20 05	18 45	18 57	19 09	19 23
50	18 43	19 17	19 58	18 45	18 59	19 13	19 29
45	18 37	19 07	19 43	18 44	19 03	19 22	19 43
N 40	18 31	18 59	19 32	18 43	19 06	19 29	19 54
35	18 26	18 52	19 23	18 42	19 09	19 36	20 04
30	18 22	18 46	19 15	18 42	19 11	19 41	20 12
20	18 15	18 37	19 03	18 41	19 16	19 51	20 27
N 10	18 09	18 30	18 55	18 40	19 20	19 59	20 40
0	18 03	18 24	18 48	18 39	19 24	20 08	20 52
S 10	17 58	18 19	18 43	18 38	19 27	20 16	21 04
20	17 52	18 14	18 40	18 37	19 31	20 24	21 17
30	17 45	18 09	18 37	18 36	19 36	20 34	21 32
35	17 41	18 07	18 36	18 36	19 38	20 40	21 41
40	17 37	18 05	18 36	18 35	19 41	20 47	21 51
45	17 32	18 02	18 36	18 34	19 45	20 54	22 03
S 50	17 27	17 59	18 37	18 33	19 49	21 04	22 18
52	17 24	17 58	18 37	18 32	19 51	21 08	22 24
54	17 21	17 57	18 38	18 32	19 53	21 13	22 32
56	17 18	17 56	18 39	18 31	19 55	21 18	22 40
58	17 15	17 54	18 40	18 31	19 58	21 24	22 50
S 60	17 11	17 53	18 41	18 30	20 01	21 31	23 01

Day	SUN Eqn. of Time 00^h	SUN Eqn. of Time 12^h	SUN Mer. Pass.	MOON Mer. Pass. Upper	MOON Mer. Pass. Lower	MOON Age	MOON Phase
d	m s	m s	h m	h m	h m	d	%
31	00 20	00 11	12 00	12 28	00 06	01	1
1	00 01	00 08	12 00	13 13	00 51	02	3
2	00 18	00 28	12 00	13 57	01 35	03	8

UT d	h	ARIES GHA	VENUS −3.8 GHA	VENUS Dec	MARS +1.7 GHA	MARS Dec	JUPITER −2.5 GHA	JUPITER Dec	SATURN +0.8 GHA	SATURN Dec
		° ′	° ′	° ′	° ′	° ′	° ′	° ′	° ′	° ′
3	00	342 30.1	158 17.2	S 0 43.3	153 42.8	S 3 16.3	58 48.3	S23 08.4	178 39.6	N 8 41.4
	01	357 32.6	173 16.9	44.6	168 43.8	17.0	73 50.8	08.4	193 41.8	41.3
	02	12 35.0	188 16.6	45.9	183 44.8	17.6	88 53.3	08.4	208 43.9	41.2
	03	27 37.5	203 16.3	. . 47.2	198 45.8	. . 18.3	103 55.8	. . 08.4	223 46.1	. . 41.0
	04	42 40.0	218 15.9	48.5	213 46.7	18.9	118 58.3	08.4	238 48.3	40.9
	05	57 42.4	233 15.6	49.8	228 47.7	19.6	134 00.8	08.4	253 50.4	40.8
	06	72 44.9	248 15.3	S 0 51.0	243 48.7	S 3 20.3	149 03.3	S23 08.4	268 52.6	N 8 40.7
W	07	87 47.4	263 15.0	52.3	258 49.7	20.9	164 05.8	08.5	283 54.8	40.6
E	08	102 49.8	278 14.7	53.6	273 50.7	21.6	179 08.3	08.5	298 57.0	40.5
D	09	117 52.3	293 14.4	. . 54.9	288 51.7	. . 22.2	194 10.8	. . 08.5	313 59.1	. . 40.3
N	10	132 54.7	308 14.0	56.2	303 52.6	22.9	209 13.3	08.5	329 01.3	40.2
E	11	147 57.2	323 13.7	57.5	318 53.6	23.6	224 15.8	08.5	344 03.5	40.1
S	12	162 59.7	338 13.4	S 0 58.8	333 54.6	S 3 24.2	239 18.3	S23 08.5	359 05.6	N 8 40.0
D	13	178 02.1	353 13.1	1 00.1	348 55.6	24.9	254 20.8	08.5	14 07.8	39.9
A	14	193 04.6	8 12.8	01.4	3 56.6	25.5	269 23.3	08.5	29 10.0	39.7
Y	15	208 07.1	23 12.5	. . 02.6	18 57.5	. . 26.2	284 25.9	. . 08.5	44 12.1	. . 39.6
	16	223 09.5	38 12.1	03.9	33 58.5	26.9	299 28.4	08.5	59 14.3	39.5
	17	238 12.0	53 11.8	05.2	48 59.5	27.5	314 30.9	08.5	74 16.5	39.4
	18	253 14.5	68 11.5	S 1 06.5	64 00.5	S 3 28.2	329 33.4	S23 08.5	89 18.6	N 8 39.3
	19	268 16.9	83 11.2	07.8	79 01.5	28.8	344 35.9	08.5	104 20.8	39.1
	20	283 19.4	98 10.9	09.1	94 02.4	29.5	359 38.4	08.5	119 23.0	39.0
	21	298 21.8	113 10.5	. . 10.4	109 03.4	. . 30.2	14 40.9	. . 08.5	134 25.1	. . 38.9
	22	313 24.3	128 10.2	11.7	124 04.4	30.8	29 43.4	08.6	149 27.3	38.8
	23	328 26.8	143 09.9	13.0	139 05.4	31.5	44 45.9	08.6	164 29.5	38.7
4	00	343 29.2	158 09.6	S 1 14.2	154 06.3	S 3 32.1	59 48.4	S23 08.6	179 31.7	N 8 38.6
	01	358 31.7	173 09.3	15.5	169 07.3	32.8	74 50.9	08.6	194 33.8	38.4
	02	13 34.2	188 09.0	16.8	184 08.3	33.5	89 53.4	08.6	209 36.0	38.3
	03	28 36.6	203 08.6	. . 18.1	199 09.3	. . 34.1	104 55.9	. . 08.6	224 38.2	. . 38.2
	04	43 39.1	218 08.3	19.4	214 10.3	34.8	119 58.4	08.6	239 40.3	38.1
	05	58 41.6	233 08.0	20.7	229 11.2	35.4	135 00.9	08.6	254 42.5	38.0
	06	73 44.0	248 07.7	S 1 22.0	244 12.2	S 3 36.1	150 03.4	S23 08.6	269 44.7	N 8 37.8
	07	88 46.5	263 07.4	23.3	259 13.2	36.8	165 05.9	08.6	284 46.8	37.7
T	08	103 49.0	278 07.1	24.6	274 14.2	37.4	180 08.4	08.6	299 49.0	37.6
H	09	118 51.4	293 06.7	. . 25.8	289 15.1	. . 38.1	195 10.9	. . 08.6	314 51.2	. . 37.5
U	10	133 53.9	308 06.4	27.1	304 16.1	38.7	210 13.4	08.6	329 53.3	37.4
R	11	148 56.3	323 06.1	28.4	319 17.1	39.4	225 15.8	08.6	344 55.5	37.3
S	12	163 58.8	338 05.8	S 1 29.7	334 18.1	S 3 40.1	240 18.3	S23 08.6	359 57.7	N 8 37.1
D	13	179 01.3	353 05.5	31.0	349 19.1	40.7	255 20.8	08.6	14 59.8	37.0
A	14	194 03.7	8 05.1	32.3	4 20.0	41.4	270 23.3	08.7	30 02.0	36.9
Y	15	209 06.2	23 04.8	. . 33.6	19 21.0	. . 42.0	285 25.8	. . 08.7	45 04.2	. . 36.8
	16	224 08.7	38 04.5	34.9	34 22.0	42.7	300 28.3	08.7	60 06.4	36.7
	17	239 11.1	53 04.2	36.1	49 23.0	43.4	315 30.8	08.7	75 08.5	36.5
	18	254 13.6	68 03.9	S 1 37.4	64 23.9	S 3 44.0	330 33.3	S23 08.7	90 10.7	N 8 36.4
	19	269 16.1	83 03.6	38.7	79 24.9	44.7	345 35.8	08.7	105 12.9	36.3
	20	284 18.5	98 03.2	40.0	94 25.9	45.3	0 38.3	08.7	120 15.0	36.2
	21	299 21.0	113 02.9	. . 41.3	109 26.9	. . 46.0	15 40.8	. . 08.7	135 17.2	. . 36.1
	22	314 23.5	128 02.6	42.6	124 27.8	46.7	30 43.3	08.7	150 19.4	36.0
	23	329 25.9	143 02.3	43.9	139 28.8	47.3	45 45.8	08.7	165 21.5	35.8
5	00	344 28.4	158 02.0	S 1 45.2	154 29.8	S 3 48.0	60 48.3	S23 08.7	180 23.7	N 8 35.7
	01	359 30.8	173 01.6	46.5	169 30.8	48.6	75 50.8	08.7	195 25.9	35.6
	02	14 33.3	188 01.3	47.7	184 31.7	49.3	90 53.3	08.7	210 28.0	35.5
	03	29 35.8	203 01.0	. . 49.0	199 32.7	. . 50.0	105 55.7	. . 08.7	225 30.2	. . 35.4
	04	44 38.2	218 00.7	50.3	214 33.7	50.6	120 58.2	08.7	240 32.4	35.2
	05	59 40.7	233 00.4	51.6	229 34.7	51.3	136 00.7	08.7	255 34.6	35.1
	06	74 43.2	248 00.1	S 1 52.9	244 35.7	S 3 51.9	151 03.2	S23 08.7	270 36.7	N 8 35.0
	07	89 45.6	262 59.7	54.2	259 36.6	52.6	166 05.7	08.7	285 38.9	34.9
	08	104 48.1	277 59.4	55.5	274 37.6	53.3	181 08.2	08.8	300 41.1	34.8
F	09	119 50.6	292 59.1	. . 56.8	289 38.6	. . 53.9	196 10.7	. . 08.8	315 43.2	. . 34.7
R	10	134 53.0	307 58.8	58.0	304 39.5	54.6	211 13.2	08.8	330 45.4	34.5
I	11	149 55.5	322 58.5	1 59.3	319 40.5	55.2	226 15.7	08.8	345 47.6	34.4
D	12	164 57.9	337 58.1	S 2 00.6	334 41.5	S 3 55.9	241 18.1	S23 08.8	0 49.7	N 8 34.3
A	13	180 00.4	352 57.8	01.9	349 42.5	56.6	256 20.6	08.8	15 51.9	34.2
Y	14	195 02.9	7 57.5	03.2	4 43.4	57.2	271 23.1	08.8	30 54.1	34.1
	15	210 05.3	22 57.2	. . 04.5	19 44.4	. . 57.9	286 25.6	. . 08.8	45 56.2	. . 33.9
	16	225 07.8	37 56.9	05.8	34 45.4	58.5	301 28.1	08.8	60 58.4	33.8
	17	240 10.3	52 56.6	07.1	49 46.4	59.2	316 30.6	08.8	76 00.6	33.7
	18	255 12.7	67 56.2	S 2 08.3	64 47.3	S 3 59.9	331 33.1	S23 08.8	91 02.7	N 8 33.6
	19	270 15.2	82 55.9	09.6	79 48.3	4 00.5	346 35.5	08.8	106 04.9	33.5
	20	285 17.7	97 55.6	10.9	94 49.3	01.2	1 38.0	08.8	121 07.1	33.4
	21	300 20.1	112 55.3	. . 12.2	109 50.3	. . 01.8	16 40.5	. . 08.8	136 09.3	. . 33.2
	22	315 22.6	127 55.0	13.5	124 51.2	02.5	31 43.0	08.8	151 11.4	33.1
	23	330 25.1	142 54.6	14.8	139 52.2	03.2	46 45.5	08.8	166 13.6	33.0
Mer. Pass.		h m 1 05.9	*v* −0.3	*d* 1.3	*v* 1.0	*d* 0.7	*v* 2.5	*d* 0.0	*v* 2.2	*d* 0.1

STARS

Name	SHA	Dec
	° ′	° ′
Acamar	315 20.8	S40 15.8
Achernar	335 28.7	S57 11.2
Acrux	173 14.3	S63 09.0
Adhara	255 15.6	S28 58.7
Aldebaran	290 53.5	N16 31.7
Alioth	166 24.0	N55 54.9
Alkaid	153 01.8	N49 16.3
Al Na'ir	27 47.6	S46 55.1
Alnilam	275 50.1	S 1 11.6
Alphard	217 59.9	S 8 41.6
Alphecca	126 14.1	N26 41.3
Alpheratz	357 47.0	N29 08.4
Altair	62 11.5	N 8 53.6
Ankaa	353 18.7	S42 15.3
Antares	112 30.7	S26 27.2
Arcturus	145 59.1	N19 08.3
Atria	107 35.9	S69 02.9
Avior	234 20.2	S59 32.0
Bellatrix	278 35.9	N 6 21.6
Betelgeuse	271 05.3	N 7 24.7
Canopus	263 58.0	S52 41.6
Capella	280 39.8	N46 00.4
Deneb	49 33.7	N45 18.9
Denebola	182 37.6	N14 31.5
Diphda	348 59.1	S17 56.1
Dubhe	193 56.4	N61 42.3
Elnath	278 17.2	N28 36.9
Eltanin	90 47.6	N51 29.5
Enif	33 50.4	N 9 55.0
Fomalhaut	15 27.5	S29 34.4
Gacrux	172 05.7	S57 09.8
Gienah	175 56.4	S17 35.4
Hadar	148 53.7	S60 25.1
Hamal	328 04.7	N23 30.3
Kaus Aust.	83 48.4	S34 23.0
Kochab	137 19.9	N74 07.4
Markab	13 41.6	N15 15.3
Menkar	314 18.7	N 4 07.6
Menkent	148 12.2	S36 24.9
Miaplacidus	221 41.7	S69 45.0
Mirfak	308 45.5	N49 53.5
Nunki	76 02.5	S26 17.2
Peacock	53 24.2	S56 42.5
Pollux	243 32.3	N28 00.4
Procyon	245 03.7	N 5 12.3
Rasalhague	96 09.7	N12 33.3
Regulus	207 47.6	N11 55.6
Rigel	281 15.5	S 8 11.2
Rigil Kent.	139 57.3	S60 52.5
Sabik	102 16.6	S15 44.2
Schedar	349 44.4	N56 35.1
Shaula	96 26.7	S37 06.8
Sirius	258 37.0	S16 43.4
Spica	158 35.3	S11 12.4
Suhail	222 55.6	S43 27.9
Vega	80 41.2	N38 47.7
Zuben'ubi	137 09.6	S16 04.7

	SHA	Mer. Pass.
	° ′	h m
Venus	174 40.4	13 28
Mars	170 37.1	13 43
Jupiter	76 19.1	19 57
Saturn	196 02.4	12 00

Day	UT (h)	SUN GHA	SUN Dec	MOON GHA	v	MOON Dec	d	HP
d	h	° ′	° ′	° ′	′	° ′	′	′
3	00	180 09.5	N 7 29.4	146 15.7	14.2	S11 52.5	13.4	55.9
	01	195 09.7	28.5	160 48.9	14.1	12 05.9	13.3	55.9
	02	210 09.9	27.6	175 22.0	14.1	12 19.2	13.2	55.9
	03	225 10.1	. . 26.7	189 55.1	14.2	12 32.4	13.2	55.8
	04	240 10.3	25.8	204 28.3	14.0	12 45.6	13.1	55.8
	05	255 10.5	24.8	219 01.3	14.1	12 58.7	13.0	55.8
	06	270 10.7	N 7 23.9	233 34.4	14.0	S13 11.7	13.0	55.8
W	07	285 10.9	23.0	248 07.4	14.0	13 24.7	12.9	55.7
E	08	300 11.1	22.1	262 40.4	14.0	13 37.6	12.8	55.7
D	09	315 11.3	. . 21.2	277 13.4	14.0	13 50.4	12.7	55.7
N	10	330 11.5	20.3	291 46.4	13.9	14 03.1	12.7	55.7
E	11	345 11.7	19.3	306 19.3	14.0	14 15.8	12.6	55.6
S	12	0 11.9	N 7 18.4	320 52.3	13.9	S14 28.4	12.6	55.6
D	13	15 12.1	17.5	335 25.2	13.8	14 41.0	12.4	55.6
A	14	30 12.3	16.6	349 58.0	13.8	14 53.4	12.4	55.6
Y	15	45 12.5	. . 15.6	4 30.8	13.8	15 05.8	12.3	55.5
	16	60 12.7	14.7	19 03.6	13.8	15 18.1	12.2	55.5
	17	75 12.9	13.8	33 36.4	13.8	15 30.3	12.2	55.5
	18	90 13.1	N 7 12.9	48 09.2	13.7	S15 42.5	12.1	55.5
	19	105 13.3	12.0	62 41.9	13.7	15 54.6	11.9	55.4
	20	120 13.5	11.0	77 14.6	13.6	16 06.5	12.0	55.4
	21	135 13.8	. . 10.1	91 47.2	13.6	16 18.5	11.8	55.4
	22	150 14.0	09.2	106 19.8	13.6	16 30.3	11.7	55.4
	23	165 14.2	08.3	120 52.4	13.6	16 42.0	11.7	55.3
4	00	180 14.4	N 7 07.3	135 25.0	13.5	S16 53.7	11.6	55.3
	01	195 14.6	06.4	149 57.5	13.5	17 05.3	11.5	55.3
	02	210 14.8	05.5	164 30.0	13.4	17 16.8	11.4	55.3
	03	225 15.0	. . 04.6	179 02.4	13.4	17 28.2	11.3	55.3
	04	240 15.2	03.7	193 34.8	13.4	17 39.5	11.3	55.2
	05	255 15.4	02.7	208 07.2	13.3	17 50.8	11.1	55.2
	06	270 15.6	N 7 01.8	222 39.5	13.3	S18 01.9	11.1	55.2
	07	285 15.8	00.9	237 11.8	13.3	18 13.0	11.0	55.2
T	08	300 16.0	7 00.0	251 44.1	13.2	18 24.0	10.9	55.1
H	09	315 16.2	6 59.0	266 16.3	13.2	18 34.9	10.8	55.1
U	10	330 16.4	58.1	280 48.5	13.2	18 45.7	10.7	55.1
R	11	345 16.6	57.2	295 20.7	13.1	18 56.4	10.6	55.1
S	12	0 16.9	N 6 56.3	309 52.8	13.0	S19 07.0	10.6	55.1
D	13	15 17.1	55.3	324 24.8	13.1	19 17.6	10.4	55.0
A	14	30 17.3	54.4	338 56.9	13.0	19 28.0	10.3	55.0
Y	15	45 17.5	. . 53.5	353 28.9	12.9	19 38.3	10.3	55.0
	16	60 17.7	52.6	8 00.8	12.9	19 48.6	10.1	55.0
	17	75 17.9	51.6	22 32.7	12.9	19 58.7	10.1	55.0
	18	90 18.1	N 6 50.7	37 04.6	12.8	S20 08.8	10.0	54.9
	19	105 18.3	49.8	51 36.4	12.8	20 18.8	9.8	54.9
	20	120 18.5	48.8	66 08.2	12.7	20 28.6	9.8	54.9
	21	135 18.7	. . 47.9	80 39.9	12.7	20 38.4	9.7	54.9
	22	150 18.9	47.0	95 11.6	12.7	20 48.1	9.5	54.9
	23	165 19.1	46.1	109 43.3	12.6	20 57.6	9.5	54.8
5	00	180 19.4	N 6 45.1	124 14.9	12.6	S21 07.1	9.4	54.8
	01	195 19.6	44.2	138 46.5	12.5	21 16.5	9.3	54.8
	02	210 19.8	43.3	153 18.0	12.5	21 25.8	9.1	54.8
	03	225 20.0	. . 42.4	167 49.5	12.4	21 34.9	9.1	54.8
	04	240 20.2	41.4	182 20.9	12.4	21 44.0	9.0	54.8
	05	255 20.4	40.5	196 52.3	12.4	21 53.0	8.8	54.7
	06	270 20.6	N 6 39.6	211 23.7	12.3	S22 01.8	8.8	54.7
	07	285 20.8	38.6	225 55.0	12.2	22 10.6	8.6	54.7
	08	300 21.0	37.7	240 26.2	12.2	22 19.2	8.6	54.7
F	09	315 21.2	. . 36.8	254 57.4	12.2	22 27.8	8.4	54.7
R	10	330 21.4	35.9	269 28.6	12.1	22 36.2	8.4	54.7
I	11	345 21.7	34.9	283 59.7	12.1	22 44.6	8.2	54.6
D	12	0 21.9	N 6 34.0	298 30.8	12.1	S22 52.8	8.1	54.6
A	13	15 22.1	33.1	313 01.9	12.0	23 00.9	8.0	54.6
Y	14	30 22.3	32.1	327 32.9	11.9	23 08.9	7.9	54.6
	15	45 22.5	. . 31.2	342 03.8	11.9	23 16.8	7.8	54.6
	16	60 22.7	30.3	356 34.7	11.9	23 24.6	7.7	54.6
	17	75 22.9	29.3	11 05.6	11.8	23 32.3	7.6	54.6
	18	90 23.1	N 6 28.4	25 36.4	11.8	S23 39.9	7.4	54.5
	19	105 23.3	27.5	40 07.2	11.7	23 47.3	7.4	54.5
	20	120 23.5	26.5	54 37.9	11.7	23 54.7	7.2	54.5
	21	135 23.8	. . 25.6	69 08.6	11.7	24 01.9	7.2	54.5
	22	150 24.0	24.7	83 39.3	11.6	24 09.1	7.0	54.5
	23	165 24.2	23.8	98 09.9	11.5	S24 16.1	6.9	54.5
		SD 15.9	d 0.9	SD		15.2	15.0	14.9

Lat.	Twilight Naut.	Twilight Civil	Sunrise	Moonrise 3	Moonrise 4	Moonrise 5	Moonrise 6
°	h m	h m	h m	h m	h m	h m	h m
N 72	////	02 54	04 18	12 10	▬	▬	▬
N 70	01 08	03 17	04 29	11 37	14 44	▬	▬
68	01 58	03 35	04 38	11 13	13 27	▬	▬
66	02 29	03 49	04 46	10 55	12 51	15 19	▬
64	02 51	04 01	04 52	10 40	12 25	14 18	▬
62	03 08	04 10	04 58	10 28	12 05	13 44	15 26
60	03 22	04 18	05 03	10 18	11 48	13 20	14 49
N 58	03 33	04 25	05 07	10 09	11 35	13 00	14 22
56	03 43	04 32	05 11	10 01	11 23	12 44	14 01
54	03 52	04 37	05 14	09 54	11 13	12 30	13 44
52	03 59	04 42	05 17	09 48	11 04	12 18	13 29
50	04 06	04 46	05 20	09 42	10 56	12 08	13 17
45	04 20	04 56	05 26	09 30	10 39	11 46	12 50
N 40	04 30	05 03	05 31	09 20	10 25	11 28	12 30
35	04 39	05 09	05 35	09 12	10 13	11 13	12 13
30	04 46	05 14	05 39	09 05	10 03	11 01	11 58
20	04 57	05 23	05 45	08 52	09 45	10 39	11 33
N 10	05 05	05 29	05 51	08 41	09 30	10 20	11 11
0	05 11	05 35	05 56	08 31	09 16	10 03	10 51
S 10	05 15	05 39	06 01	08 21	09 02	09 45	10 31
20	05 18	05 44	06 06	08 10	08 47	09 27	10 10
30	05 20	05 47	06 11	07 58	08 30	09 06	09 45
35	05 20	05 49	06 15	07 51	08 20	08 53	09 31
40	05 20	05 51	06 18	07 43	08 09	08 39	09 14
45	05 19	05 53	06 22	07 33	07 56	08 22	08 55
S 50	05 18	05 55	06 27	07 22	07 40	08 02	08 30
52	05 17	05 56	06 30	07 17	07 33	07 52	08 18
54	05 16	05 57	06 32	07 12	07 25	07 41	08 04
56	05 15	05 58	06 35	07 06	07 15	07 29	07 49
58	05 13	05 59	06 38	06 59	07 05	07 15	07 30
S 60	05 12	06 00	06 41	06 51	06 53	06 58	07 07

Lat.	Sunset	Twilight Civil	Twilight Naut.	Moonset 3	Moonset 4	Moonset 5	Moonset 6
°	h m	h m	h m	h m	h m	h m	h m
N 72	19 37	20 59	////	16 49	▬	▬	▬
N 70	19 26	20 37	22 38	17 24	15 53	▬	▬
68	19 17	20 20	21 53	17 50	17 10	▬	▬
66	19 10	20 06	21 25	18 09	17 48	16 58	▬
64	19 04	19 55	21 04	18 25	18 15	18 00	▬
62	18 58	19 46	20 47	18 38	18 36	18 34	18 34
60	18 54	19 38	20 34	18 50	18 53	18 59	19 12
N 58	18 49	19 31	20 22	19 00	19 07	19 19	19 39
56	18 46	19 25	20 13	19 08	19 20	19 36	20 00
54	18 43	19 19	20 04	19 16	19 31	19 50	20 17
52	18 40	19 14	19 57	19 23	19 40	20 02	20 32
50	18 37	19 10	19 50	19 29	19 49	20 13	20 45
45	18 31	19 01	19 37	19 43	20 07	20 36	21 12
N 40	18 26	18 54	19 27	19 54	20 22	20 55	21 33
35	18 22	18 48	19 18	20 04	20 35	21 10	21 51
30	18 19	18 43	19 11	20 12	20 46	21 24	22 06
20	18 12	18 35	19 01	20 27	21 06	21 47	22 32
N 10	18 07	18 28	18 53	20 40	21 22	22 07	22 54
0	18 02	18 23	18 47	20 52	21 38	22 26	23 15
S 10	17 57	18 18	18 43	21 04	21 54	22 45	23 36
20	17 52	18 14	18 40	21 17	22 11	23 05	23 59
30	17 47	18 11	18 39	21 32	22 31	23 28	24 25
35	17 44	18 09	18 38	21 41	22 42	23 42	24 40
40	17 40	18 07	18 39	21 51	22 55	23 58	24 58
45	17 36	18 05	18 39	22 03	23 11	24 17	00 17
S 50	17 31	18 04	18 41	22 18	23 30	24 41	00 41
52	17 29	18 03	18 42	22 24	23 40	24 53	00 53
54	17 26	18 02	18 43	22 32	23 50	25 06	01 06
56	17 24	18 01	18 44	22 40	24 02	00 02	01 21
58	17 21	18 00	18 46	22 50	24 16	00 16	01 40
S 60	17 18	17 59	18 48	23 01	24 32	00 32	02 02

Day	SUN Eqn. of Time 00^h	SUN Eqn. of Time 12^h	SUN Mer. Pass.	MOON Mer. Pass. Upper	MOON Mer. Pass. Lower	MOON Age	MOON Phase
d	m s	m s	h m	h m	h m	d %	
3	00 37	00 47	11 59	14 41	02 19	04 15	
4	00 57	01 07	11 59	15 27	03 04	05 22	
5	01 17	01 27	11 59	16 14	03 50	06 31	

UT d h	ARIES GHA ° ′	VENUS −3.8 GHA ° ′	VENUS Dec ° ′	MARS +1.7 GHA ° ′	MARS Dec ° ′	JUPITER −2.5 GHA ° ′	JUPITER Dec ° ′	SATURN +0.9 GHA ° ′	SATURN Dec ° ′
6 00 SATURDAY	345 27.5	157 54.3	S 2 16.1	154 53.2	S 4 03.8	61 48.0	S23 08.8	181 15.8	N 8 32.9
01	0 30.0	172 54.0	17.4	169 54.2	04.5	76 50.4	08.8	196 17.9	32.8
02	15 32.4	187 53.7	18.6	184 55.1	05.1	91 52.9	08.8	211 20.1	32.6
03	30 34.9	202 53.4	. . 19.9	199 56.1	. . 05.8	106 55.4	. . 08.8	226 22.3	. . 32.5
04	45 37.4	217 53.0	21.2	214 57.1	06.5	121 57.9	08.8	241 24.4	32.4
05	60 39.8	232 52.7	22.5	229 58.0	07.1	137 00.4	08.9	256 26.6	32.3
06	75 42.3	247 52.4	S 2 23.8	244 59.0	S 4 07.8	152 02.9	S23 08.9	271 28.8	N 8 32.2
07	90 44.8	262 52.1	25.1	260 00.0	08.4	167 05.3	08.9	286 30.9	32.1
08	105 47.2	277 51.8	26.4	275 01.0	09.1	182 07.8	08.9	301 33.1	31.9
09	120 49.7	292 51.4	. . 27.7	290 01.9	. . 09.8	197 10.3	. . 08.9	316 35.3	. . 31.8
10	135 52.2	307 51.1	28.9	305 02.9	10.4	212 12.8	08.9	331 37.4	31.7
11	150 54.6	322 50.8	30.2	320 03.9	11.1	227 15.2	08.9	346 39.6	31.6
12	165 57.1	337 50.5	S 2 31.5	335 04.8	S 4 11.7	242 17.7	S23 08.9	1 41.8	N 8 31.5
13	180 59.6	352 50.2	32.8	350 05.8	12.4	257 20.2	08.9	16 44.0	31.3
14	196 02.0	7 49.9	34.1	5 06.8	13.1	272 22.7	08.9	31 46.1	31.2
15	211 04.5	22 49.5	. . 35.4	20 07.8	. . 13.7	287 25.2	. . 08.9	46 48.3	. . 31.1
16	226 06.9	37 49.2	36.7	35 08.7	14.4	302 27.6	08.9	61 50.5	31.0
17	241 09.4	52 48.9	37.9	50 09.7	15.0	317 30.1	08.9	76 52.6	30.9
18	256 11.9	67 48.6	S 2 39.2	65 10.7	S 4 15.7	332 32.6	S23 08.9	91 54.8	N 8 30.8
19	271 14.3	82 48.3	40.5	80 11.6	16.4	347 35.1	08.9	106 57.0	30.6
20	286 16.8	97 47.9	41.8	95 12.6	17.0	2 37.5	08.9	121 59.1	30.5
21	301 19.3	112 47.6	. . 43.1	110 13.6	. . 17.7	17 40.0	. . 08.9	137 01.3	. . 30.4
22	316 21.7	127 47.3	44.4	125 14.6	18.3	32 42.5	08.9	152 03.5	30.3
23	331 24.2	142 47.0	45.7	140 15.5	19.0	47 45.0	08.9	167 05.6	30.2
7 00 SUNDAY	346 26.7	157 46.7	S 2 46.9	155 16.5	S 4 19.7	62 47.4	S23 08.9	182 07.8	N 8 30.0
01	1 29.1	172 46.3	48.2	170 17.5	20.3	77 49.9	08.9	197 10.0	29.9
02	16 31.6	187 46.0	49.5	185 18.4	21.0	92 52.4	08.9	212 12.2	29.8
03	31 34.0	202 45.7	. . 50.8	200 19.4	. . 21.6	107 54.9	. . 08.9	227 14.3	. . 29.7
04	46 36.5	217 45.4	52.1	215 20.4	22.3	122 57.3	08.9	242 16.5	29.6
05	61 39.0	232 45.1	53.4	230 21.3	22.9	137 59.8	08.9	257 18.7	29.5
06	76 41.4	247 44.7	S 2 54.7	245 22.3	S 4 23.6	153 02.3	S23 09.0	272 20.8	N 8 29.3
07	91 43.9	262 44.4	55.9	260 23.3	24.3	168 04.8	09.0	287 23.0	29.2
08	106 46.4	277 44.1	57.2	275 24.2	24.9	183 07.2	09.0	302 25.2	29.1
09	121 48.8	292 43.8	. . 58.5	290 25.2	. . 25.6	198 09.7	. . 09.0	317 27.3	. . 29.0
10	136 51.3	307 43.4	2 59.8	305 26.2	26.2	213 12.2	09.0	332 29.5	28.9
11	151 53.8	322 43.1	3 01.1	320 27.2	26.9	228 14.6	09.0	347 31.7	28.7
12	166 56.2	337 42.8	S 3 02.4	335 28.1	S 4 27.6	243 17.1	S23 09.0	2 33.8	N 8 28.6
13	181 58.7	352 42.5	03.7	350 29.1	28.2	258 19.6	09.0	17 36.0	28.5
14	197 01.2	7 42.2	04.9	5 30.1	28.9	273 22.0	09.0	32 38.2	28.4
15	212 03.6	22 41.8	. . 06.2	20 31.0	. . 29.5	288 24.5	. . 09.0	47 40.4	. . 28.3
16	227 06.1	37 41.5	07.5	35 32.0	30.2	303 27.0	09.0	62 42.5	28.2
17	242 08.5	52 41.2	08.8	50 33.0	30.9	318 29.5	09.0	77 44.7	28.0
18	257 11.0	67 40.9	S 3 10.1	65 33.9	S 4 31.5	333 31.9	S23 09.0	92 46.9	N 8 27.9
19	272 13.5	82 40.6	11.4	80 34.9	32.2	348 34.4	09.0	107 49.0	27.8
20	287 15.9	97 40.2	12.6	95 35.9	32.8	3 36.9	09.0	122 51.2	27.7
21	302 18.4	112 39.9	. . 13.9	110 36.8	. . 33.5	18 39.3	. . 09.0	137 53.4	. . 27.6
22	317 20.9	127 39.6	15.2	125 37.8	34.1	33 41.8	09.0	152 55.5	27.4
23	332 23.3	142 39.3	16.5	140 38.8	34.8	48 44.3	09.0	167 57.7	27.3
8 00 MONDAY	347 25.8	157 38.9	S 3 17.8	155 39.7	S 4 35.5	63 46.7	S23 09.0	182 59.9	N 8 27.2
01	2 28.3	172 38.6	19.1	170 40.7	36.1	78 49.2	09.0	198 02.0	27.1
02	17 30.7	187 38.3	20.3	185 41.7	36.8	93 51.6	09.0	213 04.2	27.0
03	32 33.2	202 38.0	. . 21.6	200 42.6	. . 37.4	108 54.1	. . 09.0	228 06.4	. . 26.9
04	47 35.7	217 37.7	22.9	215 43.6	38.1	123 56.6	09.0	243 08.6	26.7
05	62 38.1	232 37.3	24.2	230 44.6	38.8	138 59.0	09.0	258 10.7	26.6
06	77 40.6	247 37.0	S 3 25.5	245 45.5	S 4 39.4	154 01.5	S23 09.0	273 12.9	N 8 26.5
07	92 43.0	262 36.7	26.8	260 46.5	40.1	169 04.0	09.0	288 15.1	26.4
08	107 45.5	277 36.4	28.0	275 47.5	40.7	184 06.4	09.0	303 17.2	26.3
09	122 48.0	292 36.0	. . 29.3	290 48.4	. . 41.4	199 08.9	. . 09.0	318 19.4	. . 26.1
10	137 50.4	307 35.7	30.6	305 49.4	42.1	214 11.4	09.0	333 21.6	26.0
11	152 52.9	322 35.4	31.9	320 50.4	42.7	229 13.8	09.0	348 23.7	25.9
12	167 55.4	337 35.1	S 3 33.2	335 51.3	S 4 43.4	244 16.3	S23 09.0	3 25.9	N 8 25.8
13	182 57.8	352 34.8	34.5	350 52.3	44.0	259 18.7	09.1	18 28.1	25.7
14	198 00.3	7 34.4	35.7	5 53.3	44.7	274 21.2	09.1	33 30.2	25.6
15	213 02.8	22 34.1	. . 37.0	20 54.2	. . 45.3	289 23.7	. . 09.1	48 32.4	. . 25.4
16	228 05.2	37 33.8	38.3	35 55.2	46.0	304 26.1	09.1	63 34.6	25.3
17	243 07.7	52 33.5	39.6	50 56.1	46.7	319 28.6	09.1	78 36.8	25.2
18	258 10.2	67 33.1	S 3 40.9	65 57.1	S 4 47.3	334 31.0	S23 09.1	93 38.9	N 8 25.1
19	273 12.6	82 32.8	42.1	80 58.1	48.0	349 33.5	09.1	108 41.1	25.0
20	288 15.1	97 32.5	43.4	95 59.0	48.6	4 36.0	09.1	123 43.3	24.8
21	303 17.5	112 32.2	. . 44.7	111 00.0	. . 49.3	19 38.4	. . 09.1	138 45.4	. . 24.7
22	318 20.0	127 31.8	46.0	126 01.0	50.0	34 40.9	09.1	153 47.6	24.6
23	333 22.5	142 31.5	47.3	141 01.9	50.6	49 43.3	09.1	168 49.8	24.5
Mer. Pass.	h m 0 54.1	*v* −0.3	*d* 1.3	*v* 1.0	*d* 0.7	*v* 2.5	*d* 0.0	*v* 2.2	*d* 0.1

STARS

Name	SHA ° ′	Dec ° ′
Acamar	315 20.7	S40 15.8
Achernar	335 28.7	S57 11.2
Acrux	173 14.3	S63 09.0
Adhara	255 15.5	S28 58.7
Aldebaran	290 53.5	N16 31.7
Alioth	166 24.0	N55 54.9
Alkaid	153 01.9	N49 16.3
Al Na'ir	27 47.6	S46 55.1
Alnilam	275 50.1	S 1 11.6
Alphard	217 59.9	S 8 41.6
Alphecca	126 14.1	N26 41.3
Alpheratz	357 47.0	N29 08.5
Altair	62 11.5	N 8 53.6
Ankaa	353 18.6	S42 15.3
Antares	112 30.7	S26 27.2
Arcturus	145 59.2	N19 08.3
Atria	107 35.9	S69 02.9
Avior	234 20.1	S59 32.0
Bellatrix	278 35.9	N 6 21.6
Betelgeuse	271 05.3	N 7 24.7
Canopus	263 58.0	S52 41.6
Capella	280 39.8	N46 00.4
Deneb	49 33.7	N45 18.9
Denebola	182 37.6	N14 31.5
Diphda	348 59.1	S17 56.1
Dubhe	193 56.4	N61 42.3
Elnath	278 17.2	N28 36.9
Eltanin	90 47.7	N51 29.5
Enif	33 50.4	N 9 55.1
Fomalhaut	15 27.4	S29 34.4
Gacrux	172 05.7	S57 09.8
Gienah	175 56.4	S17 35.4
Hadar	148 53.7	S60 25.1
Hamal	328 04.6	N23 30.3
Kaus Aust.	83 48.4	S34 23.0
Kochab	137 20.0	N74 07.4
Markab	13 41.6	N15 15.3
Menkar	314 18.7	N 4 07.7
Menkent	148 12.2	S36 24.9
Miaplacidus	221 41.6	S69 45.0
Mirfak	308 45.4	N49 53.5
Nunki	76 02.5	S26 17.2
Peacock	53 24.2	S56 42.5
Pollux	243 32.3	N28 00.4
Procyon	245 03.7	N 5 12.3
Rasalhague	96 09.7	N12 33.3
Regulus	207 47.6	N11 55.6
Rigel	281 15.5	S 8 11.2
Rigil Kent.	139 57.3	S60 52.5
Sabik	102 16.6	S15 44.2
Schedar	349 44.4	N56 35.1
Shaula	96 26.7	S37 06.8
Sirius	258 37.0	S16 43.4
Spica	158 35.3	S11 12.4
Suhail	222 55.6	S43 27.9
Vega	80 41.2	N38 47.7
Zuben'ubi	137 09.6	S16 04.7

	SHA ° ′	Mer. Pass. h m
Venus	171 20.0	13 29
Mars	168 49.8	13 38
Jupiter	76 20.8	19 46
Saturn	195 41.2	11 50

Day	UT d h	SUN GHA ° ′	SUN Dec ° ′	MOON GHA ° ′	*v* ′	MOON Dec ° ′	*d* ′	HP ′
	6 00	180 24.4	N 6 22.8	112 40.4	11.6	S24 23.0	6.7	54.5
	01	195 24.6	21.9	127 11.0	11.4	24 29.7	6.7	54.5
	02	210 24.8	21.0	141 41.4	11.5	24 36.4	6.6	54.5
	03	225 25.0	. . 20.0	156 11.9	11.4	24 43.0	6.4	54.4
	04	240 25.2	19.1	170 42.3	11.3	24 49.4	6.3	54.4
	05	255 25.5	18.2	185 12.6	11.3	24 55.7	6.2	54.4
	06	270 25.7	N 6 17.2	199 42.9	11.3	S25 01.9	6.1	54.4
	07	285 25.9	16.3	214 13.2	11.2	25 08.0	6.0	54.4
SATURDAY	08	300 26.1	15.4	228 43.4	11.2	25 14.0	5.8	54.4
	09	315 26.3	. . 14.4	243 13.6	11.2	25 19.8	5.7	54.4
	10	330 26.5	13.5	257 43.8	11.1	25 25.5	5.6	54.4
	11	345 26.7	12.6	272 13.9	11.1	25 31.1	5.5	54.4
	12	0 26.9	N 6 11.6	286 44.0	11.0	S25 36.6	5.4	54.4
	13	15 27.1	10.7	301 14.0	11.0	25 42.0	5.2	54.3
	14	30 27.4	09.8	315 44.0	11.0	25 47.2	5.2	54.3
	15	45 27.6	. . 08.8	330 14.0	10.9	25 52.4	5.0	54.3
	16	60 27.8	07.9	344 43.9	10.9	25 57.4	4.8	54.3
	17	75 28.0	06.9	359 13.8	10.8	26 02.2	4.8	54.3
	18	90 28.2	N 6 06.0	13 43.6	10.8	S26 07.0	4.6	54.3
	19	105 28.4	05.1	28 13.4	10.8	26 11.6	4.5	54.3
	20	120 28.6	04.1	42 43.2	10.8	26 16.1	4.4	54.3
	21	135 28.9	. . 03.2	57 13.0	10.7	26 20.5	4.3	54.3
	22	150 29.1	02.3	71 42.7	10.7	26 24.8	4.1	54.3
	23	165 29.3	01.3	86 12.4	10.6	26 28.9	4.0	54.3
	7 00	180 29.5	N 6 00.4	100 42.0	10.6	S26 32.9	3.9	54.3
	01	195 29.7	5 59.5	115 11.6	10.6	26 36.8	3.7	54.3
	02	210 29.9	58.5	129 41.2	10.6	26 40.5	3.6	54.3
	03	225 30.1	. . 57.6	144 10.8	10.5	26 44.1	3.5	54.3
	04	240 30.3	56.7	158 40.3	10.5	26 47.6	3.4	54.3
	05	255 30.6	55.7	173 09.8	10.5	26 51.0	3.3	54.3
	06	270 30.8	N 5 54.8	187 39.3	10.4	S26 54.3	3.1	54.3
	07	285 31.0	53.8	202 08.7	10.4	26 57.4	2.9	54.3
	08	300 31.2	52.9	216 38.1	10.4	27 00.3	2.9	54.3
SUNDAY	09	315 31.4	. . 52.0	231 07.5	10.4	27 03.2	2.7	54.3
	10	330 31.6	51.0	245 36.9	10.3	27 05.9	2.6	54.3
	11	345 31.8	50.1	260 06.2	10.3	27 08.5	2.5	54.2
	12	0 32.1	N 5 49.2	274 35.5	10.3	S27 11.0	2.3	54.2
	13	15 32.3	48.2	289 04.8	10.3	27 13.3	2.2	54.2
	14	30 32.5	47.3	303 34.1	10.3	27 15.5	2.1	54.2
	15	45 32.7	. . 46.3	318 03.4	10.2	27 17.6	2.0	54.2
	16	60 32.9	45.4	332 32.6	10.2	27 19.6	1.8	54.2
	17	75 33.1	44.5	347 01.8	10.2	27 21.4	1.7	54.2
	18	90 33.3	N 5 43.5	1 31.0	10.2	S27 23.1	1.5	54.2
	19	105 33.6	42.6	16 00.2	10.1	27 24.6	1.4	54.2
	20	120 33.8	41.6	30 29.3	10.2	27 26.0	1.3	54.3
	21	135 34.0	. . 40.7	44 58.5	10.1	27 27.3	1.2	54.3
	22	150 34.2	39.8	59 27.6	10.1	27 28.5	1.0	54.3
	23	165 34.4	38.8	73 56.7	10.1	27 29.5	0.9	54.3
	8 00	180 34.6	N 5 37.9	88 25.8	10.1	S27 30.4	0.8	54.3
	01	195 34.9	36.9	102 54.9	10.1	27 31.2	0.6	54.3
	02	210 35.1	36.0	117 24.0	10.1	27 31.8	0.5	54.3
	03	225 35.3	. . 35.1	131 53.1	10.0	27 32.3	0.3	54.3
	04	240 35.5	34.1	146 22.1	10.1	27 32.6	0.3	54.3
	05	255 35.7	33.2	160 51.2	10.0	27 32.9	0.1	54.3
	06	270 35.9	N 5 32.2	175 20.2	10.1	S27 33.0	0.1	54.3
	07	285 36.1	31.3	189 49.3	10.0	27 32.9	0.1	54.3
	08	300 36.4	30.4	204 18.3	10.0	27 32.8	0.4	54.3
MONDAY	09	315 36.6	. . 29.4	218 47.3	10.0	27 32.4	0.4	54.3
	10	330 36.8	28.5	233 16.3	10.1	27 32.0	0.6	54.3
	11	345 37.0	27.5	247 45.4	10.0	27 31.4	0.7	54.3
	12	0 37.2	N 5 26.6	262 14.4	10.0	S27 30.7	0.8	54.3
	13	15 37.4	25.6	276 43.4	10.0	27 29.9	1.0	54.3
	14	30 37.7	24.7	291 12.4	10.0	27 28.9	1.1	54.3
	15	45 37.9	. . 23.8	305 41.4	10.0	27 27.8	1.2	54.3
	16	60 38.1	22.8	320 10.4	10.1	27 26.6	1.4	54.3
	17	75 38.3	21.9	334 39.5	10.0	27 25.2	1.5	54.3
	18	90 38.5	N 5 20.9	349 08.5	10.0	S27 23.7	1.6	54.4
	19	105 38.7	20.0	3 37.5	10.1	27 22.1	1.8	54.4
	20	120 39.0	19.0	18 06.6	10.0	27 20.3	1.9	54.4
	21	135 39.2	. . 18.1	32 35.6	10.0	27 18.4	2.1	54.4
	22	150 39.4	17.2	47 04.6	10.1	27 16.3	2.1	54.4
	23	165 39.6	16.2	61 33.7	10.1	S27 14.2	2.3	54.4
		SD 15.9	*d* 0.9	SD 14.8		14.8		14.8

Lat.	Twilight Naut. h m	Twilight Civil h m	Sunrise h m	Moonrise 6 h m	Moonrise 7 h m	Moonrise 8 h m	Moonrise 9 h m
N 72	////	03 12	04 32	■	■	■	■
N 70	01 42	03 32	04 41	■	■	■	■
68	02 19	03 48	04 49	■	■	■	■
66	02 44	04 00	04 55	■	■	■	■
64	03 03	04 10	05 01	■	■	■	■
62	03 18	04 19	05 06	15 26	17 03	17 56	18 04
60	03 31	04 26	05 10	14 49	16 06	16 59	17 27
N 58	03 41	04 32	05 13	14 22	15 33	16 26	17 00
56	03 50	04 38	05 16	14 01	15 09	16 02	16 39
54	03 58	04 43	05 19	13 44	14 49	15 42	16 21
52	04 05	04 47	05 22	13 29	14 33	15 26	16 07
50	04 11	04 51	05 24	13 17	14 19	15 12	15 54
45	04 24	04 59	05 29	12 50	13 50	14 43	15 27
N 40	04 34	05 06	05 34	12 30	13 28	14 20	15 06
35	04 41	05 12	05 37	12 13	13 09	14 01	14 48
30	04 48	05 16	05 40	11 58	12 53	13 45	14 33
20	04 58	05 24	05 46	11 33	12 26	13 18	14 07
N 10	05 05	05 29	05 50	11 11	12 03	12 54	13 45
0	05 10	05 34	05 55	10 51	11 41	12 33	13 24
S 10	05 13	05 38	05 59	10 31	11 20	12 11	13 03
20	05 15	05 41	06 03	10 10	10 57	11 47	12 40
30	05 16	05 44	06 08	09 45	10 30	11 20	12 14
35	05 16	05 45	06 10	09 31	10 15	11 04	11 59
40	05 15	05 46	06 13	09 14	09 56	10 45	11 41
45	05 14	05 48	06 17	08 55	09 34	10 23	11 20
S 50	05 11	05 49	06 21	08 30	09 07	09 54	10 52
52	05 10	05 49	06 23	08 18	08 53	09 40	10 39
54	05 09	05 50	06 25	08 04	08 37	09 23	10 23
56	05 07	05 50	06 27	07 49	08 19	09 04	10 05
58	05 05	05 51	06 30	07 30	07 56	08 39	09 43
S 60	05 03	05 51	06 32	07 07	07 27	08 06	09 13

Lat.	Sunset h m	Twilight Civil h m	Twilight Naut. h m	Moonset 6 h m	Moonset 7 h m	Moonset 8 h m	Moonset 9 h m
N 72	19 21	20 39	23 12	■	■	■	■
N 70	19 12	20 20	22 06	■	■	■	■
68	19 04	20 05	21 32	■	■	■	■
66	18 58	19 53	21 08	■	■	■	■
64	18 53	19 43	20 49	■	■	■	■
62	18 48	19 35	20 35	18 34	18 43	19 36	21 14
60	18 45	19 28	20 22	19 12	19 39	20 33	21 51
N 58	18 41	19 22	20 12	19 39	20 12	21 06	22 18
56	18 38	19 16	20 03	20 00	20 37	21 30	22 39
54	18 35	19 12	19 56	20 17	20 56	21 49	22 56
52	18 33	19 07	19 49	20 32	21 13	22 06	23 10
50	18 30	19 03	19 43	20 45	21 27	22 20	23 23
45	18 26	18 55	19 31	21 12	21 56	22 49	23 49
N 40	18 21	18 49	19 21	21 33	22 19	23 11	24 10
35	18 18	18 44	19 14	21 51	22 37	23 30	24 27
30	18 15	18 39	19 07	22 06	22 54	23 46	24 42
20	18 10	18 32	18 58	22 32	23 21	24 13	00 13
N 10	18 05	18 26	18 51	22 54	23 44	24 36	00 36
0	18 01	18 22	18 46	23 15	24 06	00 06	00 57
S 10	17 57	18 18	18 43	23 36	24 28	00 28	01 19
20	17 53	18 15	18 41	23 59	24 51	00 51	01 42
30	17 48	18 12	18 40	24 25	00 25	01 19	02 08
35	17 46	18 11	18 40	24 40	00 40	01 35	02 24
40	17 43	18 10	18 41	24 58	00 58	01 53	02 42
45	17 40	18 09	18 43	00 17	01 20	02 16	03 04
S 50	17 36	18 08	18 45	00 41	01 47	02 45	03 32
52	17 34	18 07	18 47	00 53	02 00	02 59	03 46
54	17 32	18 07	18 48	01 06	02 16	03 15	04 01
56	17 30	18 07	18 50	01 21	02 34	03 35	04 20
58	17 27	18 06	18 52	01 40	02 57	03 59	04 42
S 60	17 25	18 06	18 54	02 02	03 26	04 32	05 12

Day	SUN Eqn. of Time 00^h	SUN Eqn. of Time 12^h	SUN Mer. Pass.	MOON Mer. Pass. Upper	MOON Mer. Pass. Lower	MOON Age	MOON Phase
d	m s	m s	h m	h m	h m	d %	
6	01 37	01 47	11 58	17 03	04 38	07 40	
7	01 58	02 08	11 58	17 54	05 28	08 49	
8	02 18	02 28	11 58	18 45	06 19	09 59	

Day	UT	ARIES GHA	VENUS −3.8 GHA	VENUS Dec	MARS +1.7 GHA	MARS Dec	JUPITER −2.4 GHA	JUPITER Dec	SATURN +0.9 GHA	SATURN Dec
	d h	° ′	° ′	° ′	° ′	° ′	° ′	° ′	° ′	° ′
	9 00	348 24.9	157 31.2	S 3 48.6	156 02.9	S 4 51.3	64 45.8	S23 09.1	183 51.9	N 8 24.4
	01	3 27.4	172 30.9	49.8	171 03.9	51.9	79 48.2	09.1	198 54.1	24.3
	02	18 29.9	187 30.6	51.1	186 04.8	52.6	94 50.7	09.1	213 56.3	24.1
	03	33 32.3	202 30.2	. . 52.4	201 05.8	. . 53.2	109 53.2	. . 09.1	228 58.4	. . 24.0
	04	48 34.8	217 29.9	53.7	216 06.8	53.9	124 55.6	09.1	244 00.6	23.9
	05	63 37.3	232 29.6	55.0	231 07.7	54.6	139 58.1	09.1	259 02.8	23.8
	06	78 39.7	247 29.3	S 3 56.2	246 08.7	S 4 55.2	155 00.5	S23 09.1	274 05.0	N 8 23.7
	07	93 42.2	262 28.9	57.5	261 09.6	55.9	170 03.0	09.1	289 07.1	23.5
T	08	108 44.6	277 28.6	3 58.8	276 10.6	56.5	185 05.4	09.1	304 09.3	23.4
U	09	123 47.1	292 28.3	4 00.1	291 11.6	. . 57.2	200 07.9	. . 09.1	319 11.5	. . 23.3
E	10	138 49.6	307 28.0	01.4	306 12.5	57.8	215 10.3	09.1	334 13.6	23.2
S	11	153 52.0	322 27.6	02.6	321 13.5	58.5	230 12.8	09.1	349 15.8	23.1
	12	168 54.5	337 27.3	S 4 03.9	336 14.5	S 4 59.2	245 15.2	S23 09.1	4 18.0	N 8 23.0
D	13	183 57.0	352 27.0	05.2	351 15.4	4 59.8	260 17.7	09.1	19 20.1	22.8
A	14	198 59.4	7 26.7	06.5	6 16.4	5 00.5	275 20.1	09.1	34 22.3	22.7
Y	15	214 01.9	22 26.3	. . 07.8	21 17.3	. . 01.1	290 22.6	. . 09.1	49 24.5	. . 22.6
	16	229 04.4	37 26.0	09.0	36 18.3	01.8	305 25.0	09.1	64 26.7	22.5
	17	244 06.8	52 25.7	10.3	51 19.3	02.4	320 27.5	09.1	79 28.8	22.4
	18	259 09.3	67 25.4	S 4 11.6	66 20.2	S 5 03.1	335 29.9	S23 09.1	94 31.0	N 8 22.3
	19	274 11.8	82 25.0	12.9	81 21.2	03.8	350 32.4	09.1	109 33.2	22.1
	20	289 14.2	97 24.7	14.2	96 22.1	04.4	5 34.8	09.1	124 35.3	22.0
	21	304 16.7	112 24.4	. . 15.4	111 23.1	. . 05.1	20 37.3	. . 09.1	139 37.5	. . 21.9
	22	319 19.1	127 24.0	16.7	126 24.1	05.7	35 39.7	09.1	154 39.7	21.8
	23	334 21.6	142 23.7	18.0	141 25.0	06.4	50 42.2	09.1	169 41.8	21.7
	10 00	349 24.1	157 23.4	S 4 19.3	156 26.0	S 5 07.1	65 44.6	S23 09.1	184 44.0	N 8 21.5
	01	4 26.5	172 23.1	20.5	171 26.9	07.7	80 47.1	09.1	199 46.2	21.4
	02	19 29.0	187 22.7	21.8	186 27.9	08.4	95 49.5	09.1	214 48.3	21.3
	03	34 31.5	202 22.4	. . 23.1	201 28.9	. . 09.0	110 52.0	. . 09.1	229 50.5	. . 21.2
	04	49 33.9	217 22.1	24.4	216 29.8	09.7	125 54.4	09.1	244 52.7	21.1
	05	64 36.4	232 21.8	25.7	231 30.8	10.3	140 56.9	09.1	259 54.9	21.0
	06	79 38.9	247 21.4	S 4 26.9	246 31.7	S 5 11.0	155 59.3	S23 09.1	274 57.0	N 8 20.8
W	07	94 41.3	262 21.1	28.2	261 32.7	11.7	171 01.8	09.1	289 59.2	20.7
E	08	109 43.8	277 20.8	29.5	276 33.7	12.3	186 04.2	09.1	305 01.4	20.6
D	09	124 46.3	292 20.5	. . 30.8	291 34.6	. . 13.0	201 06.7	. . 09.1	320 03.5	. . 20.5
N	10	139 48.7	307 20.1	32.0	306 35.6	13.6	216 09.1	09.1	335 05.7	20.4
E	11	154 51.2	322 19.8	33.3	321 36.5	14.3	231 11.5	09.1	350 07.9	20.2
S	12	169 53.6	337 19.5	S 4 34.6	336 37.5	S 5 14.9	246 14.0	S23 09.1	5 10.0	N 8 20.1
	13	184 56.1	352 19.1	35.9	351 38.5	15.6	261 16.4	09.1	20 12.2	20.0
D	14	199 58.6	7 18.8	37.2	6 39.4	16.3	276 18.9	09.1	35 14.4	19.9
A	15	215 01.0	22 18.5	. . 38.4	21 40.4	. . 16.9	291 21.3	. . 09.1	50 16.6	. . 19.8
Y	16	230 03.5	37 18.2	39.7	36 41.3	17.6	306 23.8	09.1	65 18.7	19.7
	17	245 06.0	52 17.8	41.0	51 42.3	18.2	321 26.2	09.1	80 20.9	19.5
	18	260 08.4	67 17.5	S 4 42.3	66 43.3	S 5 18.9	336 28.6	S23 09.1	95 23.1	N 8 19.4
	19	275 10.9	82 17.2	43.5	81 44.2	19.5	351 31.1	09.1	110 25.2	19.3
	20	290 13.4	97 16.8	44.8	96 45.2	20.2	6 33.5	09.1	125 27.4	19.2
	21	305 15.8	112 16.5	. . 46.1	111 46.1	. . 20.8	21 36.0	. . 09.1	140 29.6	. . 19.1
	22	320 18.3	127 16.2	47.4	126 47.1	21.5	36 38.4	09.1	155 31.7	19.0
	23	335 20.8	142 15.9	48.6	141 48.0	22.2	51 40.8	09.1	170 33.9	18.8
	11 00	350 23.2	157 15.5	S 4 49.9	156 49.0	S 5 22.8	66 43.3	S23 09.2	185 36.1	N 8 18.7
	01	5 25.7	172 15.2	51.2	171 50.0	23.5	81 45.7	09.2	200 38.3	18.6
	02	20 28.1	187 14.9	52.5	186 50.9	24.1	96 48.2	09.2	215 40.4	18.5
	03	35 30.6	202 14.5	. . 53.7	201 51.9	. . 24.8	111 50.6	. . 09.2	230 42.6	. . 18.4
	04	50 33.1	217 14.2	55.0	216 52.8	25.4	126 53.0	09.2	245 44.8	18.2
	05	65 35.5	232 13.9	56.3	231 53.8	26.1	141 55.5	09.2	260 46.9	18.1
	06	80 38.0	247 13.5	S 4 57.6	246 54.7	S 5 26.8	156 57.9	S23 09.2	275 49.1	N 8 18.0
	07	95 40.5	262 13.2	4 58.8	261 55.7	27.4	172 00.4	09.2	290 51.3	17.9
T	08	110 42.9	277 12.9	5 00.1	276 56.7	28.1	187 02.8	09.2	305 53.4	17.8
H	09	125 45.4	292 12.6	. . 01.4	291 57.6	. . 28.7	202 05.2	. . 09.2	320 55.6	. . 17.7
U	10	140 47.9	307 12.2	02.6	306 58.6	29.4	217 07.7	09.2	335 57.8	17.5
R	11	155 50.3	322 11.9	03.9	321 59.5	30.0	232 10.1	09.2	351 00.0	17.4
S	12	170 52.8	337 11.6	S 5 05.2	337 00.5	S 5 30.7	247 12.5	S23 09.2	6 02.1	N 8 17.3
D	13	185 55.2	352 11.2	06.5	352 01.4	31.4	262 15.0	09.2	21 04.3	17.2
A	14	200 57.7	7 10.9	07.7	7 02.4	32.0	277 17.4	09.2	36 06.5	17.1
Y	15	216 00.2	22 10.6	. . 09.0	22 03.3	. . 32.7	292 19.8	. . 09.2	51 08.6	. . 17.0
	16	231 02.6	37 10.2	10.3	37 04.3	33.3	307 22.3	09.2	66 10.8	16.8
	17	246 05.1	52 09.9	11.6	52 05.3	34.0	322 24.7	09.2	81 13.0	16.7
	18	261 07.6	67 09.6	S 5 12.8	67 06.2	S 5 34.6	337 27.1	S23 09.2	96 15.1	N 8 16.6
	19	276 10.0	82 09.2	14.1	82 07.2	35.3	352 29.6	09.2	111 17.3	16.5
	20	291 12.5	97 08.9	15.4	97 08.1	35.9	7 32.0	09.2	126 19.5	16.4
	21	306 15.0	112 08.6	. . 16.6	112 09.1	. . 36.6	22 34.4	. . 09.2	141 21.7	. . 16.2
	22	321 17.4	127 08.2	17.9	127 10.0	37.3	37 36.9	09.2	156 23.8	16.1
	23	336 19.9	142 07.9	19.2	142 11.0	37.9	52 39.3	09.2	171 26.0	16.0
	Mer. Pass.	h m 0 42.3	*v* −0.3	*d* 1.3	*v* 1.0	*d* 0.7	*v* 2.4	*d* 0.0	*v* 2.2	*d* 0.1

STARS

Name	SHA	Dec
	° ′	° ′
Acamar	315 20.7	S40 15.8
Achernar	335 28.7	S57 11.2
Acrux	173 14.3	S63 09.0
Adhara	255 15.5	S28 58.7
Aldebaran	290 53.4	N16 31.7
Alioth	166 24.0	N55 54.8
Alkaid	153 01.9	N49 16.3
Al Na'ir	27 47.6	S46 55.1
Alnilam	275 50.0	S 1 11.6
Alphard	217 59.9	S 8 41.6
Alphecca	126 14.1	N26 41.3
Alpheratz	357 47.0	N29 08.5
Altair	62 11.5	N 8 53.6
Ankaa	353 18.6	S42 15.3
Antares	112 30.7	S26 27.2
Arcturus	145 59.2	N19 08.3
Atria	107 35.9	S69 02.9
Avior	234 20.1	S59 32.0
Bellatrix	278 35.9	N 6 21.6
Betelgeuse	271 05.2	N 7 24.7
Canopus	263 57.9	S52 41.6
Capella	280 39.8	N46 00.4
Deneb	49 33.7	N45 18.9
Denebola	182 37.6	N14 31.5
Diphda	348 59.1	S17 56.1
Dubhe	193 56.4	N61 42.2
Elnath	278 17.2	N28 36.9
Eltanin	90 47.7	N51 29.5
Enif	33 50.4	N 9 55.1
Fomalhaut	15 27.4	S29 34.4
Gacrux	172 05.7	S57 09.8
Gienah	175 56.4	S17 35.4
Hadar	148 53.7	S60 25.1
Hamal	328 04.6	N23 30.4
Kaus Aust.	83 48.4	S34 23.0
Kochab	137 20.0	N74 07.3
Markab	13 41.6	N15 15.3
Menkar	314 18.6	N 4 07.7
Menkent	148 12.2	S36 24.9
Miaplacidus	221 41.6	S69 45.0
Mirfak	308 45.4	N49 53.5
Nunki	76 02.6	S26 17.2
Peacock	53 24.2	S56 42.5
Pollux	243 32.3	N28 00.3
Procyon	245 03.6	N 5 12.3
Rasalhague	96 09.7	N12 33.3
Regulus	207 47.6	N11 55.6
Rigel	281 15.5	S 8 11.2
Rigil Kent.	139 57.3	S60 52.5
Sabik	102 16.6	S15 44.2
Schedar	349 44.4	N56 35.2
Shaula	96 26.7	S37 06.8
Sirius	258 37.0	S16 43.4
Spica	158 35.3	S11 12.4
Suhail	222 55.6	S43 27.8
Vega	80 41.3	N38 47.7
Zuben'ubi	137 09.6	S16 04.7

	SHA	Mer. Pass.
	° ′	h m
Venus	167 59.3	13 31
Mars	167 01.9	13 33
Jupiter	76 20.6	19 34
Saturn	195 19.9	11 39

UT d h	SUN GHA ° ′	SUN Dec ° ′	MOON GHA ° ′	v ′	MOON Dec ° ′	d ′	HP ′
9 00 (TUESDAY)	180 39.8	N 5 15.3	76 02.8	10.0	S27 11.9	2.5	54.4
01	195 40.1	14.3	90 31.8	10.1	27 09.4	2.5	54.4
02	210 40.3	13.4	105 00.9	10.1	27 06.9	2.8	54.4
03	225 40.5	. . 12.4	119 30.0	10.2	27 04.1	2.8	54.4
04	240 40.7	11.5	133 59.2	10.1	27 01.3	3.0	54.5
05	255 40.9	10.5	148 28.3	10.1	26 58.3	3.1	54.5
06	270 41.1	N 5 09.6	162 57.4	10.2	S26 55.2	3.2	54.5
07	285 41.4	08.7	177 26.6	10.2	26 52.0	3.3	54.5
08	300 41.6	07.7	191 55.8	10.1	26 48.7	3.5	54.5
09	315 41.8	. . 06.8	206 24.9	10.2	26 45.2	3.7	54.5
10	330 42.0	05.8	220 54.1	10.3	26 41.5	3.7	54.5
11	345 42.2	04.9	235 23.4	10.2	26 37.8	3.9	54.5
12	0 42.4	N 5 03.9	249 52.6	10.3	S26 33.9	4.0	54.5
13	15 42.7	03.0	264 21.9	10.3	26 29.9	4.2	54.6
14	30 42.9	02.0	278 51.2	10.3	26 25.7	4.2	54.6
15	45 43.1	. . 01.1	293 20.5	10.3	26 21.5	4.5	54.6
16	60 43.3	5 00.1	307 49.8	10.4	26 17.0	4.5	54.6
17	75 43.5	4 59.2	322 19.2	10.3	26 12.5	4.7	54.6
18	90 43.8	N 4 58.3	336 48.5	10.5	S26 07.8	4.7	54.6
19	105 44.0	57.3	351 18.0	10.4	26 03.1	5.0	54.6
20	120 44.2	56.4	5 47.4	10.4	25 58.1	5.0	54.7
21	135 44.4	. . 55.4	20 16.8	10.5	25 53.1	5.2	54.7
22	150 44.6	54.5	34 46.3	10.5	25 47.9	5.3	54.7
23	165 44.9	53.5	49 15.8	10.6	25 42.6	5.4	54.7
10 00 (WEDNESDAY)	180 45.1	N 4 52.6	63 45.4	10.5	S25 37.2	5.6	54.7
01	195 45.3	51.6	78 14.9	10.6	25 31.6	5.7	54.7
02	210 45.5	50.7	92 44.5	10.6	25 25.9	5.8	54.8
03	225 45.7	. . 49.7	107 14.1	10.7	25 20.1	5.9	54.8
04	240 45.9	48.8	121 43.8	10.7	25 14.2	6.1	54.8
05	255 46.2	47.8	136 13.5	10.7	25 08.1	6.2	54.8
06	270 46.4	N 4 46.9	150 43.2	10.8	S25 01.9	6.3	54.8
07	285 46.6	45.9	165 13.0	10.7	24 55.6	6.4	54.8
08	300 46.8	45.0	179 42.7	10.8	24 49.2	6.5	54.9
09	315 47.0	. . 44.0	194 12.5	10.9	24 42.7	6.7	54.9
10	330 47.3	43.1	208 42.4	10.9	24 36.0	6.8	54.9
11	345 47.5	42.1	223 12.3	10.9	24 29.2	6.9	54.9
12	0 47.7	N 4 41.2	237 42.2	10.9	S24 22.3	7.1	54.9
13	15 47.9	40.2	252 12.1	11.0	24 15.2	7.1	55.0
14	30 48.1	39.3	266 42.1	11.0	24 08.1	7.3	55.0
15	45 48.4	. . 38.3	281 12.1	11.1	24 00.8	7.4	55.0
16	60 48.6	37.4	295 42.2	11.1	23 53.4	7.5	55.0
17	75 48.8	36.4	310 12.3	11.1	23 45.9	7.7	55.0
18	90 49.0	N 4 35.5	324 42.4	11.2	S23 38.2	7.7	55.1
19	105 49.2	34.5	339 12.6	11.2	23 30.5	7.9	55.1
20	120 49.5	33.6	353 42.8	11.2	23 22.6	8.0	55.1
21	135 49.7	. . 32.6	8 13.0	11.3	23 14.6	8.1	55.1
22	150 49.9	31.7	22 43.3	11.3	23 06.5	8.2	55.1
23	165 50.1	30.7	37 13.6	11.4	22 58.3	8.4	55.2
11 00 (THURSDAY)	180 50.3	N 4 29.8	51 44.0	11.4	S22 49.9	8.4	55.2
01	195 50.6	28.8	66 14.4	11.4	22 41.5	8.6	55.2
02	210 50.8	27.9	80 44.8	11.5	22 32.9	8.6	55.2
03	225 51.0	. . 26.9	95 15.3	11.5	22 24.3	8.8	55.3
04	240 51.2	26.0	109 45.8	11.5	22 15.5	8.9	55.3
05	255 51.4	25.0	124 16.3	11.6	22 06.6	9.0	55.3
06	270 51.7	N 4 24.1	138 46.9	11.6	S21 57.6	9.2	55.3
07	285 51.9	23.1	153 17.5	11.7	21 48.4	9.2	55.3
08	300 52.1	22.2	167 48.2	11.7	21 39.2	9.3	55.4
09	315 52.3	. . 21.2	182 18.9	11.7	21 29.9	9.5	55.4
10	330 52.5	20.3	196 49.6	11.8	21 20.4	9.6	55.4
11	345 52.8	19.3	211 20.4	11.8	21 10.8	9.6	55.4
12	0 53.0	N 4 18.4	225 51.2	11.8	S21 01.2	9.8	55.5
13	15 53.2	17.4	240 22.0	11.9	20 51.4	9.9	55.5
14	30 53.4	16.5	254 52.9	12.0	20 41.5	9.9	55.5
15	45 53.7	. . 15.5	269 23.9	11.9	20 31.6	10.1	55.5
16	60 53.9	14.6	283 54.8	12.0	20 21.5	10.2	55.6
17	75 54.1	13.6	298 25.8	12.1	20 11.3	10.3	55.6
18	90 54.3	N 4 12.7	312 56.9	12.1	S20 01.0	10.4	55.6
19	105 54.5	11.7	327 28.0	12.1	19 50.6	10.5	55.6
20	120 54.8	10.8	341 59.1	12.2	19 40.1	10.6	55.7
21	135 55.0	. . 09.8	356 30.3	12.1	19 29.5	10.7	55.7
22	150 55.2	08.8	11 01.4	12.3	19 18.8	10.8	55.7
23	165 55.4	07.9	25 32.7	12.3	S19 08.0	10.9	55.7
	SD 15.9	*d* 0.9	SD 14.9		15.0		15.1

Lat. °	Twilight Naut. h m	Twilight Civil h m	Sunrise h m	Moonrise 9 h m	Moonrise 10 h m	Moonrise 11 h m	Moonrise 12 h m
N 72	01 19	03 30	04 46	■	■	■	19 43
N 70	02 07	03 47	04 53	■	■	20 31	19 11
68	02 37	04 00	05 00	■	■	19 25	18 47
66	02 58	04 11	05 05	■	19 36	18 49	18 28
64	03 15	04 20	05 10	■	18 38	18 23	18 13
62	03 29	04 27	05 13	18 04	18 04	18 03	18 00
60	03 40	04 34	05 17	17 27	17 40	17 46	17 49
N 58	03 49	04 39	05 20	17 00	17 20	17 32	17 40
56	03 57	04 44	05 22	16 39	17 03	17 20	17 31
54	04 05	04 49	05 25	16 21	16 49	17 09	17 24
52	04 11	04 52	05 27	16 07	16 37	16 59	17 17
50	04 16	04 56	05 29	15 54	16 26	16 51	17 11
45	04 28	05 03	05 33	15 27	16 03	16 33	16 58
N 40	04 37	05 09	05 36	15 06	15 45	16 18	16 47
35	04 44	05 14	05 39	14 48	15 29	16 05	16 37
30	04 50	05 18	05 42	14 33	15 16	15 54	16 29
20	04 58	05 24	05 46	14 07	14 53	15 35	16 15
N 10	05 05	05 29	05 50	13 45	14 33	15 19	16 02
0	05 09	05 33	05 54	13 24	14 14	15 03	15 50
S 10	05 11	05 36	05 57	13 03	13 55	14 47	15 38
20	05 13	05 38	06 00	12 40	13 35	14 30	15 26
30	05 13	05 40	06 04	12 14	13 12	14 11	15 11
35	05 12	05 41	06 06	11 59	12 58	14 00	15 02
40	05 10	05 42	06 09	11 41	12 42	13 47	14 53
45	05 08	05 42	06 11	11 20	12 23	13 31	14 41
S 50	05 05	05 42	06 15	10 52	11 59	13 12	14 27
52	05 03	05 42	06 16	10 39	11 48	13 03	14 21
54	05 02	05 42	06 18	10 23	11 35	12 53	14 13
56	04 59	05 42	06 19	10 05	11 19	12 41	14 05
58	04 57	05 42	06 21	09 43	11 01	12 27	13 56
S 60	04 54	05 42	06 23	09 13	10 39	12 12	13 45

Lat. °	Sunset h m	Twilight Civil h m	Twilight Naut. h m	Moonset 9 h m	Moonset 10 h m	Moonset 11 h m	Moonset 12 h m
N 72	19 05	20 20	22 23	■	■	■	■
N 70	18 58	20 04	21 40	■	■	22 16	25 15
68	18 52	19 51	21 12	■	■	23 21	25 37
66	18 47	19 40	20 52	■	21 27	23 56	25 54
64	18 42	19 32	20 36	■	22 25	24 21	00 21
62	18 39	19 24	20 22	21 14	22 58	24 40	00 40
60	18 35	19 18	20 12	21 51	23 22	24 56	00 56
N 58	18 33	19 13	20 02	22 18	23 41	25 09	01 09
56	18 30	19 08	19 54	22 39	23 57	25 21	01 21
54	18 28	19 04	19 47	22 56	24 11	00 11	01 31
52	18 26	19 00	19 41	23 10	24 23	00 23	01 40
50	18 24	18 57	19 36	23 23	24 33	00 33	01 48
45	18 20	18 50	19 25	23 49	24 55	00 55	02 04
N 40	18 17	18 44	19 16	24 10	00 10	01 13	02 18
35	18 14	18 39	19 09	24 27	00 27	01 28	02 30
30	18 11	18 35	19 03	24 42	00 42	01 40	02 40
20	18 07	18 29	18 55	00 13	01 07	02 02	02 57
N 10	18 03	18 24	18 49	00 36	01 28	02 20	03 12
0	18 00	18 21	18 45	00 57	01 48	02 38	03 26
S 10	17 57	18 18	18 42	01 19	02 08	02 55	03 40
20	17 54	18 16	18 41	01 42	02 29	03 13	03 54
30	17 50	18 14	18 42	02 08	02 54	03 34	04 11
35	17 48	18 13	18 43	02 24	03 08	03 47	04 20
40	17 46	18 13	18 44	02 42	03 25	04 01	04 31
45	17 43	18 12	18 46	03 04	03 44	04 17	04 44
S 50	17 40	18 12	18 50	03 32	04 09	04 38	05 00
52	17 39	18 12	18 51	03 46	04 21	04 47	05 07
54	17 37	18 12	18 53	04 01	04 35	04 58	05 15
56	17 35	18 12	18 56	04 20	04 50	05 10	05 24
58	17 34	18 13	18 58	04 42	05 09	05 24	05 34
S 60	17 31	18 13	19 01	05 12	05 31	05 41	05 45

Day	SUN Eqn. of Time 00^h	SUN Eqn. of Time 12^h	SUN Mer. Pass.	MOON Mer. Pass. Upper	MOON Mer. Pass. Lower	MOON Age	MOON Phase
d	m s	m s	h m	h m	h m	d	%
9	02 39	02 49	11 57	19 36	07 11	10	68
10	03 00	03 10	11 57	20 26	08 01	11	77
11	03 21	03 32	11 56	21 14	08 50	12	84

Day	UT (d h)	ARIES GHA	VENUS −3.8 GHA	VENUS Dec	MARS +1.7 GHA	MARS Dec	JUPITER −2.4 GHA	JUPITER Dec	SATURN +0.9 GHA	SATURN Dec
		° ′	° ′	° ′	° ′	° ′	° ′	° ′	° ′	° ′
FRIDAY	12 00	351 22.4	157 07.6	S 5 20.5	157 11.9	S 5 38.6	67 41.7	S23 09.2	186 28.2	N 8 15.9
	01	6 24.8	172 07.2	21.7	172 12.9	39.2	82 44.2	09.2	201 30.3	15.8
	02	21 27.3	187 06.9	23.0	187 13.8	39.9	97 46.6	09.2	216 32.5	15.7
	03	36 29.7	202 06.6	. . 24.3	202 14.8	. . 40.5	112 49.0	. . 09.2	231 34.7	. . 15.5
	04	51 32.2	217 06.2	25.5	217 15.7	41.2	127 51.5	09.2	246 36.9	15.4
	05	66 34.7	232 05.9	26.8	232 16.7	41.8	142 53.9	09.2	261 39.0	15.3
	06	81 37.1	247 05.6	S 5 28.1	247 17.7	S 5 42.5	157 56.3	S23 09.2	276 41.2	N 8 15.2
	07	96 39.6	262 05.2	29.3	262 18.6	43.2	172 58.7	09.2	291 43.4	15.1
	08	111 42.1	277 04.9	30.6	277 19.6	43.8	188 01.2	09.2	306 45.5	15.0
	09	126 44.5	292 04.6	. . 31.9	292 20.5	. . 44.5	203 03.6	. . 09.2	321 47.7	. . 14.8
	10	141 47.0	307 04.2	33.1	307 21.5	45.1	218 06.0	09.2	336 49.9	14.7
	11	156 49.5	322 03.9	34.4	322 22.4	45.8	233 08.4	09.2	351 52.0	14.6
	12	171 51.9	337 03.6	S 5 35.7	337 23.4	S 5 46.4	248 10.9	S23 09.2	6 54.2	N 8 14.5
	13	186 54.4	352 03.2	37.0	352 24.3	47.1	263 13.3	09.2	21 56.4	14.4
	14	201 56.9	7 02.9	38.2	7 25.3	47.7	278 15.7	09.2	36 58.6	14.2
	15	216 59.3	22 02.6	. . 39.5	22 26.2	. . 48.4	293 18.2	. . 09.2	52 00.7	. . 14.1
	16	232 01.8	37 02.2	40.8	37 27.2	49.1	308 20.6	09.2	67 02.9	14.0
	17	247 04.2	52 01.9	42.0	52 28.1	49.7	323 23.0	09.2	82 05.1	13.9
	18	262 06.7	67 01.6	S 5 43.3	67 29.1	S 5 50.4	338 25.4	S23 09.2	97 07.2	N 8 13.8
	19	277 09.2	82 01.2	44.6	82 30.0	51.0	353 27.8	09.2	112 09.4	13.7
	20	292 11.6	97 00.9	45.8	97 31.0	51.7	8 30.3	09.2	127 11.6	13.5
	21	307 14.1	112 00.6	. . 47.1	112 31.9	. . 52.3	23 32.7	. . 09.1	142 13.8	. . 13.4
	22	322 16.6	127 00.2	48.4	127 32.9	53.0	38 35.1	09.1	157 15.9	13.3
	23	337 19.0	141 59.9	49.6	142 33.8	53.6	53 37.5	09.1	172 18.1	13.2
SATURDAY	13 00	352 21.5	156 59.5	S 5 50.9	157 34.8	S 5 54.3	68 40.0	S23 09.1	187 20.3	N 8 13.1
	01	7 24.0	171 59.2	52.2	172 35.7	55.0	83 42.4	09.1	202 22.4	13.0
	02	22 26.4	186 58.9	53.4	187 36.7	55.6	98 44.8	09.1	217 24.6	12.8
	03	37 28.9	201 58.5	. . 54.7	202 37.6	. . 56.3	113 47.2	. . 09.1	232 26.8	. . 12.7
	04	52 31.3	216 58.2	56.0	217 38.6	56.9	128 49.7	09.1	247 28.9	12.6
	05	67 33.8	231 57.9	57.2	232 39.5	57.6	143 52.1	09.1	262 31.1	12.5
	06	82 36.3	246 57.5	S 5 58.5	247 40.5	S 5 58.2	158 54.5	S23 09.1	277 33.3	N 8 12.4
	07	97 38.7	261 57.2	5 59.8	262 41.4	58.9	173 56.9	09.1	292 35.5	12.3
	08	112 41.2	276 56.8	6 01.0	277 42.4	5 59.5	188 59.3	09.1	307 37.6	12.1
	09	127 43.7	291 56.5	. . 02.3	292 43.3	6 00.2	204 01.7	. . 09.1	322 39.8	. . 12.0
	10	142 46.1	306 56.2	03.5	307 44.3	00.8	219 04.2	09.1	337 42.0	11.9
	11	157 48.6	321 55.8	04.8	322 45.2	01.5	234 06.6	09.1	352 44.1	11.8
	12	172 51.1	336 55.5	S 6 06.1	337 46.2	S 6 02.2	249 09.0	S23 09.1	7 46.3	N 8 11.7
	13	187 53.5	351 55.2	07.3	352 47.1	02.8	264 11.4	09.1	22 48.5	11.6
	14	202 56.0	6 54.8	08.6	7 48.1	03.5	279 13.8	09.1	37 50.7	11.4
	15	217 58.5	21 54.5	. . 09.9	22 49.0	. . 04.1	294 16.3	. . 09.1	52 52.8	. . 11.3
	16	233 00.9	36 54.1	11.1	37 50.0	04.8	309 18.7	09.1	67 55.0	11.2
	17	248 03.4	51 53.8	12.4	52 50.9	05.4	324 21.1	09.1	82 57.2	11.1
	18	263 05.8	66 53.5	S 6 13.7	67 51.9	S 6 06.1	339 23.5	S23 09.1	97 59.3	N 8 11.0
	19	278 08.3	81 53.1	14.9	82 52.8	06.7	354 25.9	09.1	113 01.5	10.8
	20	293 10.8	96 52.8	16.2	97 53.8	07.4	9 28.3	09.1	128 03.7	10.7
	21	308 13.2	111 52.4	. . 17.4	112 54.7	. . 08.0	24 30.8	. . 09.1	143 05.9	. . 10.6
	22	323 15.7	126 52.1	18.7	127 55.7	08.7	39 33.2	09.1	158 08.0	10.5
	23	338 18.2	141 51.8	20.0	142 56.6	09.3	54 35.6	09.1	173 10.2	10.4
SUNDAY	14 00	353 20.6	156 51.4	S 6 21.2	157 57.6	S 6 10.0	69 38.0	S23 09.1	188 12.4	N 8 10.3
	01	8 23.1	171 51.1	22.5	172 58.5	10.7	84 40.4	09.1	203 14.5	10.1
	02	23 25.6	186 50.7	23.7	187 59.4	11.3	99 42.8	09.1	218 16.7	10.0
	03	38 28.0	201 50.4	. . 25.0	203 00.4	. . 12.0	114 45.2	. . 09.1	233 18.9	. . 09.9
	04	53 30.5	216 50.0	26.3	218 01.3	12.6	129 47.6	09.1	248 21.1	09.8
	05	68 32.9	231 49.7	27.5	233 02.3	13.3	144 50.1	09.1	263 23.2	09.7
	06	83 35.4	246 49.4	S 6 28.8	248 03.2	S 6 13.9	159 52.5	S23 09.1	278 25.4	N 8 09.6
	07	98 37.9	261 49.0	30.0	263 04.2	14.6	174 54.9	09.1	293 27.6	09.4
	08	113 40.3	276 48.7	31.3	278 05.1	15.2	189 57.3	09.1	308 29.7	09.3
	09	128 42.8	291 48.3	. . 32.6	293 06.1	. . 15.9	204 59.7	. . 09.1	323 31.9	. . 09.2
	10	143 45.3	306 48.0	33.8	308 07.0	16.5	220 02.1	09.1	338 34.1	09.1
	11	158 47.7	321 47.6	35.1	323 08.0	17.2	235 04.5	09.1	353 36.2	09.0
	12	173 50.2	336 47.3	S 6 36.3	338 08.9	S 6 17.8	250 06.9	S23 09.1	8 38.4	N 8 08.9
	13	188 52.7	351 47.0	37.6	353 09.9	18.5	265 09.3	09.1	23 40.6	08.7
	14	203 55.1	6 46.6	38.9	8 10.8	19.1	280 11.7	09.1	38 42.8	08.6
	15	218 57.6	21 46.3	. . 40.1	23 11.7	. . 19.8	295 14.2	. . 09.1	53 44.9	. . 08.5
	16	234 00.1	36 45.9	41.4	38 12.7	20.5	310 16.6	09.1	68 47.1	08.4
	17	249 02.5	51 45.6	42.6	53 13.6	21.1	325 19.0	09.1	83 49.3	08.3
	18	264 05.0	66 45.2	S 6 43.9	68 14.6	S 6 21.8	340 21.4	S23 09.1	98 51.4	N 8 08.2
	19	279 07.4	81 44.9	45.1	83 15.5	22.4	355 23.8	09.1	113 53.6	08.0
	20	294 09.9	96 44.6	46.4	98 16.5	23.1	10 26.2	09.1	128 55.8	07.9
	21	309 12.4	111 44.2	. . 47.7	113 17.4	. . 23.7	25 28.6	. . 09.1	143 58.0	. . 07.8
	22	324 14.8	126 43.9	48.9	128 18.4	24.4	40 31.0	09.1	159 00.1	07.7
	23	339 17.3	141 43.5	50.2	143 19.3	25.0	55 33.4	09.1	174 02.3	07.6
	Mer. Pass.	h m 0 30.5	v −0.3	d 1.3	v 0.9	d 0.7	v 2.4	d 0.0	v 2.2	d 0.1

STARS

Name	SHA	Dec
	° ′	° ′
Acamar	315 20.7	S40 15.8
Achernar	335 28.7	S57 11.2
Acrux	173 14.3	S63 09.0
Adhara	255 15.5	S28 58.7
Aldebaran	290 53.4	N16 31.8
Alioth	166 24.0	N55 54.8
Alkaid	153 01.9	N49 16.3
Al Na'ir	27 47.6	S46 55.1
Alnilam	275 50.0	S 1 11.5
Alphard	217 59.9	S 8 41.6
Alphecca	126 14.1	N26 41.2
Alpheratz	357 46.9	N29 08.5
Altair	62 11.5	N 8 53.6
Ankaa	353 18.6	S42 15.3
Antares	112 30.7	S26 27.2
Arcturus	145 59.2	N19 08.3
Atria	107 36.0	S69 02.9
Avior	234 20.1	S59 31.9
Bellatrix	278 35.8	N 6 21.6
Betelgeuse	271 05.2	N 7 24.7
Canopus	263 57.9	S52 41.6
Capella	280 39.7	N46 00.4
Deneb	49 33.7	N45 18.9
Denebola	182 37.6	N14 31.5
Diphda	348 59.1	S17 56.1
Dubhe	193 56.3	N61 42.2
Elnath	278 17.1	N28 36.9
Eltanin	90 47.7	N51 29.5
Enif	33 50.4	N 9 55.1
Fomalhaut	15 27.4	S29 34.4
Gacrux	172 05.7	S57 09.8
Gienah	175 56.4	S17 35.4
Hadar	148 53.7	S60 25.1
Hamal	328 04.6	N23 30.4
Kaus Aust.	83 48.4	S34 23.0
Kochab	137 20.1	N74 07.3
Markab	13 41.6	N15 15.3
Menkar	314 18.6	N 4 07.7
Menkent	148 12.2	S36 24.9
Miaplacidus	221 41.6	S69 45.0
Mirfak	308 45.4	N49 53.5
Nunki	76 02.6	S26 17.2
Peacock	53 24.2	S56 42.5
Pollux	243 32.2	N28 00.3
Procyon	245 03.6	N 5 12.3
Rasalhague	96 09.7	N12 33.3
Regulus	207 47.6	N11 55.6
Rigel	281 15.5	S 8 11.2
Rigil Kent.	139 57.3	S60 52.5
Sabik	102 16.7	S15 44.2
Schedar	349 44.4	N56 35.2
Shaula	96 26.8	S37 06.8
Sirius	258 37.0	S16 43.4
Spica	158 35.3	S11 12.4
Suhail	222 55.6	S43 27.8
Vega	80 41.3	N38 47.7
Zuben'ubi	137 09.6	S16 04.7

	SHA	Mer. Pass.
	° ′	h m
Venus	164 38.1	13 32
Mars	165 13.3	13 29
Jupiter	76 18.5	19 22
Saturn	194 58.8	11 29

d	h	SUN GHA ° ′	SUN Dec ° ′	MOON GHA ° ′	v ′	MOON Dec ° ′	d ′	HP ′
12	00	180 55.6	N 4 06.9	40 04.0	12.3	S18 57.1	11.0	55.8
	01	195 55.9	06.0	54 35.3	12.3	18 46.1	11.1	55.8
	02	210 56.1	05.0	69 06.6	12.4	18 35.0	11.2	55.8
	03	225 56.3	. . 04.1	83 38.0	12.4	18 23.8	11.3	55.8
	04	240 56.5	03.1	98 09.4	12.5	18 12.5	11.3	55.9
	05	255 56.8	02.2	112 40.9	12.4	18 01.2	11.5	55.9
	06	270 57.0	N 4 01.2	127 12.3	12.6	S17 49.7	11.6	55.9
	07	285 57.2	4 00.3	141 43.9	12.5	17 38.1	11.6	55.9
	08	300 57.4	3 59.3	156 15.4	12.6	17 26.5	11.8	56.0
F	09	315 57.6	. . 58.4	170 47.0	12.6	17 14.7	11.8	56.0
R	10	330 57.9	57.4	185 18.6	12.7	17 02.9	11.9	56.0
I	11	345 58.1	56.4	199 50.3	12.7	16 51.0	12.0	56.0
D	12	0 58.3	N 3 55.5	214 22.0	12.7	S16 39.0	12.1	56.1
A	13	15 58.5	54.5	228 53.7	12.8	16 26.9	12.2	56.1
Y	14	30 58.8	53.6	243 25.5	12.7	16 14.7	12.3	56.1
	15	45 59.0	. . 52.6	257 57.2	12.9	16 02.4	12.4	56.2
	16	60 59.2	51.7	272 29.1	12.8	15 50.0	12.4	56.2
	17	75 59.4	50.7	287 00.9	12.9	15 37.6	12.5	56.2
	18	90 59.6	N 3 49.8	301 32.8	12.9	S15 25.1	12.7	56.2
	19	105 59.9	48.8	316 04.7	12.9	15 12.4	12.6	56.3
	20	121 00.1	47.8	330 36.6	13.0	14 59.8	12.8	56.3
	21	136 00.3	. . 46.9	345 08.6	13.0	14 47.0	12.9	56.3
	22	151 00.5	45.9	359 40.6	13.0	14 34.1	12.9	56.4
	23	166 00.8	45.0	14 12.6	13.0	14 21.2	13.0	56.4
13	00	181 01.0	N 3 44.0	28 44.6	13.1	S14 08.2	13.1	56.4
	01	196 01.2	43.1	43 16.7	13.1	13 55.1	13.2	56.4
	02	211 01.4	42.1	57 48.8	13.1	13 41.9	13.2	56.5
	03	226 01.6	. . 41.1	72 20.9	13.2	13 28.7	13.3	56.5
	04	241 01.9	40.2	86 53.1	13.1	13 15.4	13.4	56.5
	05	256 02.1	39.2	101 25.2	13.2	13 02.0	13.5	56.5
	06	271 02.3	N 3 38.3	115 57.4	13.2	S12 48.5	13.5	56.6
	07	286 02.5	37.3	130 29.6	13.3	12 35.0	13.6	56.6
S	08	301 02.8	36.4	145 01.9	13.2	12 21.4	13.7	56.6
A	09	316 03.0	. . 35.4	159 34.1	13.3	12 07.7	13.7	56.7
T	10	331 03.2	34.4	174 06.4	13.3	11 54.0	13.9	56.7
U	11	346 03.4	33.5	188 38.7	13.3	11 40.1	13.8	56.7
R	12	1 03.6	N 3 32.5	203 11.0	13.3	S11 26.3	14.0	56.7
D	13	16 03.9	31.6	217 43.3	13.4	11 12.3	14.0	56.8
A	14	31 04.1	30.6	232 15.7	13.3	10 58.3	14.1	56.8
Y	15	46 04.3	. . 29.7	246 48.0	13.4	10 44.2	14.1	56.8
	16	61 04.5	28.7	261 20.4	13.4	10 30.1	14.2	56.9
	17	76 04.8	27.7	275 52.8	13.4	10 15.9	14.3	56.9
	18	91 05.0	N 3 26.8	290 25.2	13.4	S10 01.6	14.3	56.9
	19	106 05.2	25.8	304 57.6	13.5	9 47.3	14.3	56.9
	20	121 05.4	24.9	319 30.1	13.4	9 33.0	14.5	57.0
	21	136 05.7	. . 23.9	334 02.5	13.4	9 18.5	14.5	57.0
	22	151 05.9	22.9	348 34.9	13.5	9 04.0	14.5	57.0
	23	166 06.1	22.0	3 07.4	13.5	8 49.5	14.6	57.1
14	00	181 06.3	N 3 21.0	17 39.9	13.4	S 8 34.9	14.7	57.1
	01	196 06.5	20.1	32 12.3	13.5	8 20.2	14.7	57.1
	02	211 06.8	19.1	46 44.8	13.5	8 05.5	14.7	57.1
	03	226 07.0	. . 18.1	61 17.3	13.5	7 50.8	14.8	57.2
	04	241 07.2	17.2	75 49.8	13.5	7 36.0	14.9	57.2
	05	256 07.4	16.2	90 22.3	13.5	7 21.1	14.9	57.2
	06	271 07.7	N 3 15.3	104 54.8	13.5	S 7 06.2	15.0	57.3
	07	286 07.9	14.3	119 27.3	13.5	6 51.2	15.0	57.3
	08	301 08.1	13.3	133 59.8	13.5	6 36.2	15.0	57.3
S	09	316 08.3	. . 12.4	148 32.3	13.5	6 21.2	15.1	57.3
U	10	331 08.6	11.4	163 04.8	13.5	6 06.1	15.1	57.4
N	11	346 08.8	10.5	177 37.3	13.5	5 51.0	15.2	57.4
D	12	1 09.0	N 3 09.5	192 09.8	13.5	S 5 35.8	15.2	57.4
A	13	16 09.2	08.5	206 42.3	13.5	5 20.6	15.2	57.4
Y	14	31 09.5	07.6	221 14.8	13.5	5 05.4	15.3	57.5
	15	46 09.7	. . 06.6	235 47.3	13.4	4 50.1	15.4	57.5
	16	61 09.9	05.7	250 19.7	13.5	4 34.7	15.3	57.5
	17	76 10.1	04.7	264 52.2	13.5	4 19.4	15.4	57.6
	18	91 10.3	N 3 03.7	279 24.7	13.4	S 4 04.0	15.4	57.6
	19	106 10.6	02.8	293 57.1	13.5	3 48.6	15.5	57.6
	20	121 10.8	01.8	308 29.6	13.4	3 33.1	15.5	57.6
	21	136 11.0	3 00.9	323 02.0	13.4	3 17.6	15.5	57.7
	22	151 11.2	2 59.9	337 34.4	13.4	3 02.1	15.5	57.7
	23	166 11.5	N 2 58.9	352 06.8	13.4	S 2 46.6	15.6	57.7
		SD 15.9	*d* 1.0	SD	15.3	15.5		15.6

Lat. °	Twilight Naut. h m	Twilight Civil h m	Sunrise h m	Moonrise 12 h m	13 h m	14 h m	15 h m
N 72	01 52	03 46	04 59	19 43	18 51	18 14	17 42
N 70	02 28	04 00	05 06	19 11	18 36	18 09	17 44
68	02 53	04 12	05 10	18 47	18 23	18 04	17 47
66	03 12	04 21	05 15	18 28	18 13	18 00	17 48
64	03 26	04 29	05 18	18 13	18 05	17 57	17 50
62	03 38	04 36	05 21	18 00	17 57	17 54	17 51
60	03 48	04 41	05 24	17 49	17 51	17 52	17 53
N 58	03 57	04 46	05 26	17 40	17 45	17 49	17 54
56	04 04	04 50	05 28	17 31	17 40	17 47	17 55
54	04 11	04 54	05 30	17 24	17 35	17 46	17 56
52	04 16	04 58	05 32	17 17	17 31	17 44	17 56
50	04 21	05 01	05 33	17 11	17 27	17 42	17 57
45	04 32	05 07	05 37	16 58	17 19	17 39	17 59
N 40	04 40	05 12	05 39	16 47	17 12	17 36	18 00
35	04 46	05 16	05 42	16 37	17 06	17 34	18 01
30	04 51	05 20	05 44	16 29	17 01	17 32	18 02
20	04 59	05 25	05 47	16 15	16 52	17 28	18 04
N 10	05 04	05 29	05 50	16 02	16 44	17 25	18 06
0	05 08	05 32	05 53	15 50	16 36	17 22	18 08
S 10	05 10	05 34	05 55	15 38	16 29	17 19	18 09
20	05 10	05 36	05 58	15 26	16 20	17 15	18 11
30	05 09	05 37	06 00	15 11	16 11	17 12	18 13
35	05 07	05 37	06 02	15 02	16 06	17 09	18 14
40	05 05	05 37	06 04	14 53	15 59	17 07	18 16
45	05 02	05 36	06 06	14 41	15 52	17 04	18 17
S 50	04 58	05 36	06 08	14 27	15 44	17 01	18 19
52	04 56	05 36	06 09	14 21	15 40	16 59	18 20
54	04 54	05 35	06 10	14 13	15 35	16 57	18 21
56	04 51	05 35	06 11	14 05	15 30	16 55	18 22
58	04 48	05 34	06 13	13 56	15 25	16 53	18 23
S 60	04 45	05 33	06 14	13 45	15 18	16 51	18 25

Lat. °	Sunset h m	Twilight Civil h m	Twilight Naut. h m	Moonset 12 h m	13 h m	14 h m	15 h m
N 72	18 49	20 02	21 51	■	00 44	03 14	05 28
N 70	18 44	19 48	21 18	25 15	01 15	03 26	05 30
68	18 39	19 37	20 54	25 37	01 37	03 36	05 31
66	18 35	19 28	20 37	25 54	01 54	03 45	05 33
64	18 32	19 20	20 22	00 21	02 08	03 51	05 34
62	18 29	19 14	20 11	00 40	02 20	03 57	05 35
60	18 26	19 09	20 01	00 56	02 30	04 02	05 35
N 58	18 24	19 04	19 53	01 09	02 38	04 07	05 36
56	18 22	19 00	19 45	01 21	02 46	04 11	05 37
54	18 20	18 56	19 39	01 31	02 52	04 14	05 37
52	18 19	18 53	19 34	01 40	02 58	04 17	05 38
50	18 17	18 50	19 29	01 48	03 04	04 20	05 38
45	18 14	18 44	19 19	02 04	03 15	04 27	05 39
N 40	18 12	18 39	19 11	02 18	03 25	04 32	05 40
35	18 09	18 35	19 05	02 30	03 33	04 36	05 40
30	18 07	18 31	19 00	02 40	03 40	04 40	05 41
20	18 04	18 26	18 52	02 57	03 52	04 47	05 42
N 10	18 01	18 23	18 47	03 12	04 03	04 53	05 43
0	17 59	18 20	18 44	03 26	04 12	04 58	05 43
S 10	17 57	18 18	18 42	03 40	04 22	05 03	05 44
20	17 54	18 16	18 42	03 54	04 32	05 09	05 45
30	17 52	18 15	18 43	04 11	04 44	05 15	05 46
35	17 50	18 15	18 45	04 20	04 51	05 19	05 46
40	17 48	18 15	18 47	04 31	04 58	05 23	05 47
45	17 47	18 16	18 50	04 44	05 07	05 28	05 47
S 50	17 44	18 17	18 54	05 00	05 18	05 33	05 48
52	17 43	18 17	18 56	05 07	05 23	05 36	05 48
54	17 42	18 18	18 59	05 15	05 28	05 39	05 49
56	17 41	18 18	19 02	05 24	05 34	05 42	05 49
58	17 40	18 19	19 05	05 34	05 40	05 45	05 49
S 60	17 38	18 20	19 09	05 45	05 48	05 49	05 50

Day	SUN Eqn. of Time 00^h	SUN Eqn. of Time 12^h	SUN Mer. Pass.	MOON Mer. Pass. Upper	MOON Mer. Pass. Lower	Age	Phase
d	m s	m s	h m	h m	h m	d %	
12	03 42	03 53	11 56	22 01	09 38	13 91	○
13	04 03	04 14	11 56	22 47	10 24	14 96	
14	04 25	04 36	11 55	23 33	11 10	15 99	

UT	ARIES	VENUS −3.9		MARS +1.7		JUPITER −2.4		SATURN +0.9		STARS		
	GHA	GHA	Dec	GHA	Dec	GHA	Dec	GHA	Dec	Name	SHA	Dec
d h	° ′	° ′	° ′	° ′	° ′	° ′	° ′	° ′	° ′		° ′	° ′
15 00 (MONDAY)	354 19.8	156 43.2	S 6 51.4	158 20.2	S 6 25.7	70 35.8	S23 09.1	189 04.5	N 8 07.5	Acamar	315 20.7	S40 15.8
01	9 22.2	171 42.8	52.7	173 21.2	26.3	85 38.2	09.1	204 06.7	07.3	Achernar	335 28.6	S57 11.2
02	24 24.7	186 42.5	53.9	188 22.1	27.0	100 40.6	09.1	219 08.8	07.2	Acrux	173 14.3	S63 08.9
03	39 27.2	201 42.1	. . 55.2	203 23.1	. . 27.6	115 43.0	. . 09.1	234 11.0	. . 07.1	Adhara	255 15.5	S28 58.7
04	54 29.6	216 41.8	56.5	218 24.0	28.3	130 45.4	09.1	249 13.2	07.0	Aldebaran	290 53.4	N16 31.8
05	69 32.1	231 41.4	57.7	233 25.0	28.9	145 47.8	09.1	264 15.3	06.9			
06	84 34.5	246 41.1	S 6 59.0	248 25.9	S 6 29.6	160 50.2	S23 09.1	279 17.5	N 8 06.8	Alioth	166 24.0	N55 54.8
07	99 37.0	261 40.7	7 00.2	263 26.8	30.2	175 52.6	09.1	294 19.7	06.6	Alkaid	153 01.9	N49 16.3
08	114 39.5	276 40.4	01.5	278 27.8	30.9	190 55.0	09.0	309 21.9	06.5	Al Na'ir	27 47.6	S46 55.1
09	129 41.9	291 40.1	. . 02.7	293 28.7	. . 31.6	205 57.4	. . 09.0	324 24.0	. . 06.4	Alnilam	275 50.0	S 1 11.5
10	144 44.4	306 39.7	04.0	308 29.7	32.2	220 59.8	09.0	339 26.2	06.3	Alphard	217 59.9	S 8 41.6
11	159 46.9	321 39.4	05.2	323 30.6	32.9	236 02.2	09.0	354 28.4	06.2			
12	174 49.3	336 39.0	S 7 06.5	338 31.5	S 6 33.5	251 04.7	S23 09.0	9 30.5	N 8 06.0	Alphecca	126 14.1	N26 41.2
13	189 51.8	351 38.7	07.7	353 32.5	34.2	266 07.1	09.0	24 32.7	05.9	Alpheratz	357 46.9	N29 08.5
14	204 54.3	6 38.3	09.0	8 33.4	34.8	281 09.5	09.0	39 34.9	05.8	Altair	62 11.6	N 8 53.6
15	219 56.7	21 38.0	. . 10.2	23 34.4	. . 35.5	296 11.9	. . 09.0	54 37.1	. . 05.7	Ankaa	353 18.6	S42 15.3
16	234 59.2	36 37.6	11.5	38 35.3	36.1	311 14.3	09.0	69 39.2	05.6	Antares	112 30.8	S26 27.2
17	250 01.7	51 37.3	12.7	53 36.3	36.8	326 16.7	09.0	84 41.4	05.5			
18	265 04.1	66 36.9	S 7 14.0	68 37.2	S 6 37.4	341 19.0	S23 09.0	99 43.6	N 8 05.3	Arcturus	145 59.2	N19 08.3
19	280 06.6	81 36.6	15.2	83 38.1	38.1	356 21.4	09.0	114 45.7	05.2	Atria	107 36.0	S69 02.9
20	295 09.0	96 36.2	16.5	98 39.1	38.7	11 23.8	09.0	129 47.9	05.1	Avior	234 20.1	S59 31.9
21	310 11.5	111 35.9	. . 17.7	113 40.0	. . 39.4	26 26.2	. . 09.0	144 50.1	. . 05.0	Bellatrix	278 35.8	N 6 21.6
22	325 14.0	126 35.5	19.0	128 41.0	40.0	41 28.6	09.0	159 52.3	04.9	Betelgeuse	271 05.2	N 7 24.7
23	340 16.4	141 35.2	20.2	143 41.9	40.7	56 31.0	09.0	174 54.4	04.8			
16 00 (TUESDAY)	355 18.9	156 34.8	S 7 21.5	158 42.8	S 6 41.3	71 33.4	S23 09.0	189 56.6	N 8 04.6	Canopus	263 57.9	S52 41.6
01	10 21.4	171 34.5	22.7	173 43.8	42.0	86 35.8	09.0	204 58.8	04.5	Capella	280 39.7	N46 00.4
02	25 23.8	186 34.1	24.0	188 44.7	42.6	101 38.2	09.0	220 00.9	04.4	Deneb	49 33.7	N45 18.9
03	40 26.3	201 33.8	. . 25.2	203 45.7	. . 43.3	116 40.6	. . 09.0	235 03.1	. . 04.3	Denebola	182 37.6	N14 31.5
04	55 28.8	216 33.4	26.5	218 46.6	43.9	131 43.0	09.0	250 05.3	04.2	Diphda	348 59.1	S17 56.1
05	70 31.2	231 33.1	27.7	233 47.5	44.6	146 45.4	09.0	265 07.5	04.1			
06	85 33.7	246 32.7	S 7 29.0	248 48.5	S 6 45.2	161 47.8	S23 09.0	280 09.6	N 8 03.9	Dubhe	193 56.3	N61 42.2
07	100 36.2	261 32.4	30.2	263 49.4	45.9	176 50.2	09.0	295 11.8	03.8	Elnath	278 17.1	N28 36.9
08	115 38.6	276 32.0	31.5	278 50.4	46.5	191 52.6	09.0	310 14.0	03.7	Eltanin	90 47.7	N51 29.5
09	130 41.1	291 31.6	. . 32.7	293 51.3	. . 47.2	206 55.0	. . 09.0	325 16.2	. . 03.6	Enif	33 50.4	N 9 55.1
10	145 43.5	306 31.3	34.0	308 52.2	47.8	221 57.4	09.0	340 18.3	03.5	Fomalhaut	15 27.4	S29 34.4
11	160 46.0	321 30.9	35.2	323 53.2	48.5	236 59.8	09.0	355 20.5	03.4			
12	175 48.5	336 30.6	S 7 36.5	338 54.1	S 6 49.1	252 02.2	S23 09.0	10 22.7	N 8 03.2	Gacrux	172 05.7	S57 09.8
13	190 50.9	351 30.2	37.7	353 55.0	49.8	267 04.6	09.0	25 24.8	03.1	Gienah	175 56.4	S17 35.4
14	205 53.4	6 29.9	39.0	8 56.0	50.5	282 07.0	09.0	40 27.0	03.0	Hadar	148 53.8	S60 25.1
15	220 55.9	21 29.5	. . 40.2	23 56.9	. . 51.1	297 09.3	. . 08.9	55 29.2	. . 02.9	Hamal	328 04.6	N23 30.4
16	235 58.3	36 29.2	41.5	38 57.9	51.8	312 11.7	08.9	70 31.4	02.8	Kaus Aust.	83 48.4	S34 23.0
17	251 00.8	51 28.8	42.7	53 58.8	52.4	327 14.1	08.9	85 33.5	02.7			
18	266 03.3	66 28.5	S 7 44.0	68 59.7	S 6 53.1	342 16.5	S23 08.9	100 35.7	N 8 02.5	Kochab	137 20.1	N74 07.3
19	281 05.7	81 28.1	45.2	84 00.7	53.7	357 18.9	08.9	115 37.9	02.4	Markab	13 41.6	N15 15.3
20	296 08.2	96 27.8	46.4	99 01.6	54.4	12 21.3	08.9	130 40.1	02.3	Menkar	314 18.6	N 4 07.7
21	311 10.6	111 27.4	. . 47.7	114 02.5	. . 55.0	27 23.7	. . 08.9	145 42.2	. . 02.2	Menkent	148 12.2	S36 24.9
22	326 13.1	126 27.0	48.9	129 03.5	55.7	42 26.1	08.9	160 44.4	02.1	Miaplacidus	221 41.6	S69 44.9
23	341 15.6	141 26.7	50.2	144 04.4	56.3	57 28.5	08.9	175 46.6	02.0			
17 00 (WEDNESDAY)	356 18.0	156 26.3	S 7 51.4	159 05.3	S 6 57.0	72 30.8	S23 08.9	190 48.7	N 8 01.8	Mirfak	308 45.3	N49 53.5
01	11 20.5	171 26.0	52.7	174 06.3	57.6	87 33.2	08.9	205 50.9	01.7	Nunki	76 02.6	S26 17.2
02	26 23.0	186 25.6	53.9	189 07.2	58.3	102 35.6	08.9	220 53.1	01.6	Peacock	53 24.3	S56 42.6
03	41 25.4	201 25.3	. . 55.1	204 08.2	. . 58.9	117 38.0	. . 08.9	235 55.3	. . 01.5	Pollux	243 32.2	N28 00.3
04	56 27.9	216 24.9	56.4	219 09.1	6 59.6	132 40.4	08.9	250 57.4	01.4	Procyon	245 03.6	N 5 12.3
05	71 30.4	231 24.5	57.6	234 10.0	7 00.2	147 42.8	08.9	265 59.6	01.3			
06	86 32.8	246 24.2	S 7 58.9	249 11.0	S 7 00.9	162 45.2	S23 08.9	281 01.8	N 8 01.2	Rasalhague	96 09.8	N12 33.3
07	101 35.3	261 23.8	8 00.1	264 11.9	01.5	177 47.6	08.9	296 04.0	01.0	Regulus	207 47.6	N11 55.6
08	116 37.8	276 23.5	01.4	279 12.8	02.2	192 49.9	08.9	311 06.1	00.9	Rigel	281 15.4	S 8 11.2
09	131 40.2	291 23.1	. . 02.6	294 13.8	. . 02.8	207 52.3	. . 08.9	326 08.3	. . 00.8	Rigil Kent.	139 57.3	S60 52.5
10	146 42.7	306 22.8	03.8	309 14.7	03.5	222 54.7	08.9	341 10.5	00.7	Sabik	102 16.7	S15 44.2
11	161 45.1	321 22.4	05.1	324 15.6	04.1	237 57.1	08.9	356 12.6	00.6			
12	176 47.6	336 22.0	S 8 06.3	339 16.6	S 7 04.8	252 59.5	S23 08.9	11 14.8	N 8 00.5	Schedar	349 44.3	N56 35.2
13	191 50.1	351 21.7	07.6	354 17.5	05.4	268 01.9	08.9	26 17.0	00.3	Shaula	96 26.8	S37 06.8
14	206 52.5	6 21.3	08.8	9 18.4	06.1	283 04.2	08.9	41 19.2	00.2	Sirius	258 37.0	S16 43.4
15	221 55.0	21 21.0	. . 10.0	24 19.4	. . 06.7	298 06.6	. . 08.8	56 21.3	. . 00.1	Spica	158 35.3	S11 12.4
16	236 57.5	36 20.6	11.3	39 20.3	07.4	313 09.0	08.8	71 23.5	8 00.0	Suhail	222 55.5	S43 27.8
17	251 59.9	51 20.2	12.5	54 21.2	08.0	328 11.4	08.8	86 25.7	7 59.9			
18	267 02.4	66 19.9	S 8 13.7	69 22.2	S 7 08.7	343 13.8	S23 08.8	101 27.9	N 7 59.8	Vega	80 41.3	N38 47.7
19	282 04.9	81 19.5	15.0	84 23.1	09.3	358 16.2	08.8	116 30.0	59.6	Zuben'ubi	137 09.6	S16 04.7
20	297 07.3	96 19.2	16.2	99 24.0	10.0	13 18.5	08.8	131 32.2	59.5			
21	312 09.8	111 18.8	. . 17.5	114 25.0	. . 10.6	28 20.9	. . 08.8	146 34.4	. . 59.4			
22	327 12.2	126 18.4	18.7	129 25.9	11.3	43 23.3	08.8	161 36.5	59.3			
23	342 14.7	141 18.1	19.9	144 26.8	11.9	58 25.7	08.8	176 38.7	59.2			
Mer. Pass.	h m 0 18.7	*v* −0.4	*d* 1.2	*v* 0.9	*d* 0.7	*v* 2.4	*d* 0.0	*v* 2.2	*d* 0.1			

	SHA	Mer. Pass.
	° ′	h m
Venus	161 15.9	13 34
Mars	163 23.9	13 24
Jupiter	76 14.5	19 11
Saturn	194 37.7	11 19

UT		SUN GHA	SUN Dec	MOON GHA	*v*	MOON Dec	*d*	HP
d	h	° ′	° ′	° ′	′	° ′	′	′
15	00	181 11.7	N 2 58.0	6 39.2	13.4	S 2 31.0	15.6	57.7
	01	196 11.9	57.0	21 11.6	13.3	2 15.4	15.6	57.8
	02	211 12.1	56.0	35 43.9	13.4	1 59.8	15.7	57.8
	03	226 12.4	. . 55.1	50 16.3	13.3	1 44.1	15.6	57.8
	04	241 12.6	54.1	64 48.6	13.3	1 28.5	15.7	57.8
	05	256 12.8	53.2	79 20.9	13.3	1 12.8	15.7	57.9
	06	271 13.0	N 2 52.2	93 53.2	13.2	S 0 57.1	15.8	57.9
	07	286 13.3	51.2	108 25.4	13.2	0 41.3	15.7	57.9
	08	301 13.5	50.3	122 57.6	13.2	0 25.6	15.8	57.9
M	09	316 13.7	. . 49.3	137 29.8	13.2	S 0 09.8	15.7	58.0
O	10	331 13.9	48.4	152 02.0	13.2	N 0 05.9	15.8	58.0
N	11	346 14.2	47.4	166 34.2	13.1	0 21.7	15.8	58.0
D	12	1 14.4	N 2 46.4	181 06.3	13.1	N 0 37.5	15.8	58.0
A	13	16 14.6	45.5	195 38.4	13.1	0 53.3	15.8	58.1
Y	14	31 14.8	44.5	210 10.5	13.0	1 09.1	15.9	58.1
	15	46 15.0	. . 43.5	224 42.5	13.0	1 25.0	15.8	58.1
	16	61 15.3	42.6	239 14.5	13.0	1 40.8	15.8	58.1
	17	76 15.5	41.6	253 46.5	12.9	1 56.6	15.8	58.2
	18	91 15.7	N 2 40.6	268 18.4	12.9	N 2 12.4	15.9	58.2
	19	106 15.9	39.7	282 50.3	12.9	2 28.3	15.8	58.2
	20	121 16.2	38.7	297 22.2	12.8	2 44.1	15.9	58.2
	21	136 16.4	. . 37.8	311 54.0	12.8	3 00.0	15.8	58.3
	22	151 16.6	36.8	326 25.8	12.8	3 15.8	15.8	58.3
	23	166 16.8	35.8	340 57.6	12.7	3 31.6	15.9	58.3
16	00	181 17.1	N 2 34.9	355 29.3	12.7	N 3 47.5	15.8	58.3
	01	196 17.3	33.9	10 01.0	12.6	4 03.3	15.8	58.3
	02	211 17.5	32.9	24 32.6	12.6	4 19.1	15.8	58.4
	03	226 17.7	. . 32.0	39 04.2	12.5	4 34.9	15.8	58.4
	04	241 18.0	31.0	53 35.7	12.5	4 50.7	15.8	58.4
	05	256 18.2	30.0	68 07.2	12.4	5 06.5	15.7	58.4
	06	271 18.4	N 2 29.1	82 38.6	12.4	N 5 22.2	15.8	58.5
	07	286 18.6	28.1	97 10.0	12.4	5 38.0	15.7	58.5
T	08	301 18.9	27.2	111 41.4	12.3	5 53.7	15.7	58.5
U	09	316 19.1	. . 26.2	126 12.7	12.2	6 09.4	15.7	58.5
E	10	331 19.3	25.2	140 43.9	12.2	6 25.1	15.7	58.5
S	11	346 19.5	24.3	155 15.1	12.1	6 40.8	15.6	58.6
D	12	1 19.8	N 2 23.3	169 46.2	12.1	N 6 56.4	15.7	58.6
A	13	16 20.0	22.3	184 17.3	12.0	7 12.1	15.6	58.6
Y	14	31 20.2	21.4	198 48.3	12.0	7 27.7	15.5	58.6
	15	46 20.4	. . 20.4	213 19.3	11.9	7 43.2	15.6	58.6
	16	61 20.7	19.4	227 50.2	11.9	7 58.8	15.5	58.7
	17	76 20.9	18.5	242 21.1	11.7	8 14.3	15.5	58.7
	18	91 21.1	N 2 17.5	256 51.8	11.8	N 8 29.8	15.4	58.7
	19	106 21.3	16.5	271 22.6	11.6	8 45.2	15.4	58.7
	20	121 21.5	15.6	285 53.2	11.6	9 00.6	15.4	58.7
	21	136 21.8	. . 14.6	300 23.8	11.6	9 16.0	15.3	58.8
	22	151 22.0	13.6	314 54.4	11.4	9 31.3	15.3	58.8
	23	166 22.2	12.7	329 24.8	11.4	9 46.6	15.3	58.8
17	00	181 22.4	N 2 11.7	343 55.2	11.4	N10 01.9	15.2	58.8
	01	196 22.7	10.7	358 25.6	11.2	10 17.1	15.2	58.8
	02	211 22.9	09.8	12 55.8	11.2	10 32.3	15.1	58.8
	03	226 23.1	. . 08.8	27 26.0	11.2	10 47.4	15.1	58.9
	04	241 23.3	07.8	41 56.2	11.0	11 02.5	15.0	58.9
	05	256 23.6	06.9	56 26.2	11.0	11 17.5	15.0	58.9
	06	271 23.8	N 2 05.9	70 56.2	10.9	N11 32.5	14.9	58.9
W	07	286 24.0	04.9	85 26.1	10.8	11 47.4	14.8	58.9
E	08	301 24.2	04.0	99 55.9	10.8	12 02.2	14.8	58.9
D	09	316 24.5	. . 03.0	114 25.7	10.7	12 17.0	14.8	59.0
N	10	331 24.7	02.0	128 55.4	10.6	12 31.8	14.7	59.0
E	11	346 24.9	01.1	143 25.0	10.5	12 46.5	14.6	59.0
S	12	1 25.1	N 2 00.1	157 54.5	10.4	N13 01.1	14.6	59.0
D	13	16 25.4	1 59.1	172 23.9	10.4	13 15.7	14.5	59.0
A	14	31 25.6	58.2	186 53.3	10.3	13 30.2	14.4	59.0
Y	15	46 25.8	. . 57.2	201 22.6	10.2	13 44.6	14.3	59.0
	16	61 26.0	56.2	215 51.8	10.1	13 58.9	14.3	59.1
	17	76 26.3	55.3	230 20.9	10.1	14 13.2	14.3	59.1
	18	91 26.5	N 1 54.3	244 50.0	9.9	N14 27.5	14.1	59.1
	19	106 26.7	53.3	259 18.9	9.9	14 41.6	14.1	59.1
	20	121 26.9	52.4	273 47.8	9.8	14 55.7	14.0	59.1
	21	136 27.1	. . 51.4	288 16.6	9.7	15 09.7	13.9	59.1
	22	151 27.4	50.4	302 45.3	9.6	15 23.6	13.8	59.1
	23	166 27.6	49.5	317 13.9	9.5	N15 37.4	13.8	59.1
		SD 15.9	*d* 1.0	SD 15.8		16.0		16.1

Lat.	Twilight Naut.	Twilight Civil	Sunrise	Moonrise 15	Moonrise 16	Moonrise 17	Moonrise 18
°	h m	h m	h m	h m	h m	h m	h m
N 72	02 18	04 02	05 13	17 42	17 07	16 19	▭
N 70	02 47	04 14	05 17	17 44	17 18	16 45	15 39
68	03 08	04 24	05 21	17 47	17 28	17 05	16 29
66	03 24	04 31	05 24	17 48	17 36	17 21	17 01
64	03 37	04 38	05 27	17 50	17 43	17 35	17 25
62	03 48	04 44	05 29	17 51	17 49	17 46	17 44
60	03 57	04 49	05 31	17 53	17 54	17 56	18 00
N 58	04 04	04 53	05 32	17 54	17 58	18 05	18 14
56	04 11	04 56	05 34	17 55	18 02	18 12	18 25
54	04 17	05 00	05 35	17 56	18 06	18 19	18 36
52	04 22	05 03	05 37	17 56	18 10	18 25	18 45
50	04 26	05 05	05 38	17 57	18 13	18 31	18 53
45	04 36	05 11	05 40	17 59	18 19	18 43	19 10
N 40	04 43	05 15	05 42	18 00	18 25	18 53	19 25
35	04 49	05 18	05 44	18 01	18 30	19 01	19 37
30	04 53	05 21	05 45	18 02	18 34	19 09	19 48
20	05 00	05 26	05 48	18 04	18 42	19 22	20 07
N 10	05 04	05 29	05 50	18 06	18 49	19 34	20 23
0	05 07	05 31	05 51	18 08	18 55	19 45	20 39
S 10	05 08	05 32	05 53	18 09	19 01	19 56	20 54
20	05 07	05 33	05 55	18 11	19 08	20 08	21 11
30	05 05	05 33	05 57	18 13	19 16	20 22	21 30
35	05 03	05 32	05 58	18 14	19 21	20 30	21 41
40	05 00	05 32	05 59	18 16	19 26	20 39	21 55
45	04 57	05 31	06 00	18 17	19 32	20 50	22 10
S 50	04 52	05 29	06 01	18 19	19 40	21 03	22 29
52	04 49	05 29	06 02	18 20	19 43	21 10	22 39
54	04 46	05 28	06 03	18 21	19 47	21 17	22 49
56	04 43	05 27	06 04	18 22	19 51	21 24	23 01
58	04 40	05 25	06 04	18 23	19 56	21 33	23 14
S 60	04 35	05 24	06 05	18 25	20 02	21 43	23 30

Lat.	Sunset	Twilight Civil	Twilight Naut.	Moonset 15	Moonset 16	Moonset 17	Moonset 18
°	h m	h m	h m	h m	h m	h m	h m
N 72	18 34	19 44	21 25	05 28	07 44	10 16	▭
N 70	18 30	19 33	20 57	05 30	07 35	09 52	12 48
68	18 26	19 23	20 38	05 31	07 28	09 34	11 59
66	18 23	19 16	20 22	05 33	07 23	09 19	11 28
64	18 21	19 09	20 10	05 34	07 18	09 07	11 06
62	18 19	19 04	19 59	05 35	07 14	08 57	10 48
60	18 17	18 59	19 51	05 35	07 10	08 49	10 33
N 58	18 16	18 55	19 43	05 36	07 07	08 41	10 20
56	18 14	18 52	19 37	05 37	07 04	08 35	10 09
54	18 13	18 48	19 31	05 37	07 02	08 29	10 00
52	18 12	18 46	19 26	05 38	06 59	08 24	09 52
50	18 11	18 43	19 22	05 38	06 57	08 19	09 44
45	18 08	18 38	19 13	05 39	06 53	08 09	09 28
N 40	18 07	18 34	19 06	05 40	06 49	08 01	09 15
35	18 05	18 30	19 00	05 40	06 46	07 54	09 04
30	18 04	18 28	18 56	05 41	06 43	07 47	08 54
20	18 01	18 24	18 49	05 42	06 38	07 36	08 38
N 10	18 00	18 21	18 45	05 43	06 34	07 27	08 23
0	17 58	18 19	18 43	05 43	06 30	07 18	08 10
S 10	17 56	18 17	18 42	05 44	06 26	07 09	07 57
20	17 55	18 17	18 42	05 45	06 22	07 00	07 42
30	17 53	18 17	18 45	05 46	06 17	06 50	07 26
35	17 52	18 17	18 47	05 46	06 14	06 44	07 17
40	17 51	18 18	18 50	05 47	06 11	06 37	07 06
45	17 50	18 19	18 54	05 47	06 07	06 29	06 54
S 50	17 49	18 21	18 59	05 48	06 03	06 19	06 39
52	17 48	18 22	19 01	05 48	06 01	06 15	06 32
54	17 48	18 23	19 04	05 49	05 59	06 10	06 24
56	17 47	18 24	19 08	05 49	05 56	06 05	06 15
58	17 46	18 25	19 11	05 49	05 54	05 59	06 06
S 60	17 45	18 27	19 16	05 50	05 51	05 52	05 55

Day	SUN Eqn. of Time 00^h	SUN Eqn. of Time 12^h	SUN Mer. Pass.	MOON Mer. Pass. Upper	MOON Mer. Pass. Lower	MOON Age	MOON Phase
d	m s	m s	h m	h m	h m	d %	
15	04 46	04 57	11 55	24 19	11 55	16 100	○
16	05 08	05 19	11 55	00 19	12 42	17 98	
17	05 29	05 40	11 54	01 07	13 31	18 94	

UT d	UT h		ARIES GHA	VENUS −3.9 GHA	VENUS Dec	MARS +1.7 GHA	MARS Dec	JUPITER −2.4 GHA	JUPITER Dec	SATURN +0.9 GHA	SATURN Dec
			° ′	° ′	° ′	° ′	° ′	° ′	° ′	° ′	° ′
18	00		357 17.2	156 17.7	S 8 21.2	159 27.8	S 7 12.6	73 28.1	S23 08.8	191 40.9	N 7 59.1
	01		12 19.6	171 17.3	22.4	174 28.7	13.2	88 30.4	08.8	206 43.1	58.9
	02		27 22.1	186 17.0	23.6	189 29.6	13.9	103 32.8	08.8	221 45.2	58.8
	03		42 24.6	201 16.6	24.9	204 30.6	14.5	118 35.2	08.8	236 47.4	58.7
	04		57 27.0	216 16.3	26.1	219 31.5	15.2	133 37.6	08.8	251 49.6	58.6
	05		72 29.5	231 15.9	27.4	234 32.4	15.8	148 40.0	08.8	266 51.8	58.5
	06		87 32.0	246 15.5	S 8 28.6	249 33.4	S 7 16.4	163 42.3	S23 08.8	281 53.9	N 7 58.4
	07		102 34.4	261 15.2	29.8	264 34.3	17.1	178 44.7	08.8	296 56.1	58.2
	08	T	117 36.9	276 14.8	31.1	279 35.2	17.7	193 47.1	08.8	311 58.3	58.1
	09	H	132 39.4	291 14.4	32.3	294 36.2	18.4	208 49.5	08.8	327 00.5	58.0
	10	U	147 41.8	306 14.1	33.5	309 37.1	19.0	223 51.8	08.8	342 02.6	57.9
	11	R	162 44.3	321 13.7	34.8	324 38.0	19.7	238 54.2	08.8	357 04.8	57.8
	12	S	177 46.7	336 13.3	S 8 36.0	339 38.9	S 7 20.3	253 56.6	S23 08.7	12 07.0	N 7 57.7
	13	D	192 49.2	351 13.0	37.2	354 39.9	21.0	268 59.0	08.7	27 09.1	57.5
	14	A	207 51.7	6 12.6	38.5	9 40.8	21.6	284 01.3	08.7	42 11.3	57.4
	15	Y	222 54.1	21 12.2	39.7	24 41.7	22.3	299 03.7	08.7	57 13.5	57.3
	16		237 56.6	36 11.9	40.9	39 42.7	22.9	314 06.1	08.7	72 15.7	57.2
	17		252 59.1	51 11.5	42.1	54 43.6	23.6	329 08.5	08.7	87 17.8	57.1
	18		268 01.5	66 11.1	S 8 43.4	69 44.5	S 7 24.2	344 10.8	S23 08.7	102 20.0	N 7 57.0
	19		283 04.0	81 10.8	44.6	84 45.5	24.9	359 13.2	08.7	117 22.2	56.8
	20		298 06.5	96 10.4	45.8	99 46.4	25.5	14 15.6	08.7	132 24.4	56.7
	21		313 08.9	111 10.0	47.1	114 47.3	26.2	29 17.9	08.7	147 26.5	56.6
	22		328 11.4	126 09.7	48.3	129 48.2	26.8	44 20.3	08.7	162 28.7	56.5
	23		343 13.9	141 09.3	49.5	144 49.2	27.5	59 22.7	08.7	177 30.9	56.4
19	00		358 16.3	156 08.9	S 8 50.8	159 50.1	S 7 28.1	74 25.1	S23 08.7	192 33.1	N 7 56.3
	01		13 18.8	171 08.6	52.0	174 51.0	28.8	89 27.4	08.7	207 35.2	56.2
	02		28 21.2	186 08.2	53.2	189 52.0	29.4	104 29.8	08.7	222 37.4	56.0
	03		43 23.7	201 07.8	54.4	204 52.9	30.1	119 32.2	08.7	237 39.6	55.9
	04		58 26.2	216 07.5	55.7	219 53.8	30.7	134 34.5	08.7	252 41.8	55.8
	05		73 28.6	231 07.1	56.9	234 54.7	31.4	149 36.9	08.7	267 43.9	55.7
	06		88 31.1	246 06.7	S 8 58.1	249 55.7	S 7 32.0	164 39.3	S23 08.6	282 46.1	N 7 55.6
	07		103 33.6	261 06.3	8 59.4	264 56.6	32.7	179 41.7	08.6	297 48.3	55.5
	08		118 36.0	276 06.0	9 00.6	279 57.5	33.3	194 44.0	08.6	312 50.4	55.3
	09	F	133 38.5	291 05.6	01.8	294 58.4	33.9	209 46.4	08.6	327 52.6	55.2
	10	R	148 41.0	306 05.2	03.0	309 59.4	34.6	224 48.8	08.6	342 54.8	55.1
	11	I	163 43.4	321 04.9	04.3	325 00.3	35.2	239 51.1	08.6	357 57.0	55.0
	12	D	178 45.9	336 04.5	S 9 05.5	340 01.2	S 7 35.9	254 53.5	S23 08.6	12 59.1	N 7 54.9
	13	A	193 48.3	351 04.1	06.7	355 02.2	36.5	269 55.9	08.6	28 01.3	54.8
	14	Y	208 50.8	6 03.7	07.9	10 03.1	37.2	284 58.2	08.6	43 03.5	54.6
	15		223 53.3	21 03.4	09.2	25 04.0	37.8	300 00.6	08.6	58 05.7	54.5
	16		238 55.7	36 03.0	10.4	40 04.9	38.5	315 03.0	08.6	73 07.8	54.4
	17		253 58.2	51 02.6	11.6	55 05.9	39.1	330 05.3	08.6	88 10.0	54.3
	18		269 00.7	66 02.2	S 9 12.8	70 06.8	S 7 39.8	345 07.7	S23 08.6	103 12.2	N 7 54.2
	19		284 03.1	81 01.9	14.0	85 07.7	40.4	0 10.0	08.6	118 14.4	54.1
	20		299 05.6	96 01.5	15.3	100 08.6	41.1	15 12.4	08.6	133 16.5	54.0
	21		314 08.1	111 01.1	16.5	115 09.6	41.7	30 14.8	08.6	148 18.7	53.8
	22		329 10.5	126 00.7	17.7	130 10.5	42.4	45 17.1	08.5	163 20.9	53.7
	23		344 13.0	141 00.4	18.9	145 11.4	43.0	60 19.5	08.5	178 23.1	53.6
20	00		359 15.5	156 00.0	S 9 20.2	160 12.3	S 7 43.7	75 21.9	S23 08.5	193 25.2	N 7 53.5
	01		14 17.9	170 59.6	21.4	175 13.3	44.3	90 24.2	08.5	208 27.4	53.4
	02		29 20.4	185 59.2	22.6	190 14.2	44.9	105 26.6	08.5	223 29.6	53.3
	03		44 22.8	200 58.9	23.8	205 15.1	45.6	120 29.0	08.5	238 31.8	53.1
	04		59 25.3	215 58.5	25.0	220 16.0	46.2	135 31.3	08.5	253 33.9	53.0
	05		74 27.8	230 58.1	26.3	235 16.9	46.9	150 33.7	08.5	268 36.1	52.9
	06		89 30.2	245 57.7	S 9 27.5	250 17.9	S 7 47.5	165 36.0	S23 08.5	283 38.3	N 7 52.8
	07		104 32.7	260 57.4	28.7	265 18.8	48.2	180 38.4	08.5	298 40.5	52.7
	08	S	119 35.2	275 57.0	29.9	280 19.7	48.8	195 40.8	08.5	313 42.6	52.6
	09	A	134 37.6	290 56.6	31.1	295 20.6	49.5	210 43.1	08.5	328 44.8	52.4
	10	T	149 40.1	305 56.2	32.4	310 21.6	50.1	225 45.5	08.5	343 47.0	52.3
	11	U	164 42.6	320 55.8	33.6	325 22.5	50.8	240 47.8	08.5	358 49.2	52.2
	12	R	179 45.0	335 55.5	S 9 34.8	340 23.4	S 7 51.4	255 50.2	S23 08.5	13 51.3	N 7 52.1
	13	D	194 47.5	350 55.1	36.0	355 24.3	52.1	270 52.6	08.5	28 53.5	52.0
	14	A	209 50.0	5 54.7	37.2	10 25.3	52.7	285 54.9	08.4	43 55.7	51.9
	15	Y	224 52.4	20 54.3	38.4	25 26.2	53.3	300 57.3	08.4	58 57.9	51.8
	16		239 54.9	35 53.9	39.7	40 27.1	54.0	315 59.6	08.4	74 00.0	51.6
	17		254 57.3	50 53.6	40.9	55 28.0	54.6	331 02.0	08.4	89 02.2	51.5
	18		269 59.8	65 53.2	S 9 42.1	70 28.9	S 7 55.3	346 04.3	S23 08.4	104 04.4	N 7 51.4
	19		285 02.3	80 52.8	43.3	85 29.9	55.9	1 06.7	08.4	119 06.6	51.3
	20		300 04.7	95 52.4	44.5	100 30.8	56.6	16 09.0	08.4	134 08.7	51.2
	21		315 07.2	110 52.0	45.7	115 31.7	57.2	31 11.4	08.4	149 10.9	51.1
	22		330 09.7	125 51.7	46.9	130 32.6	57.9	46 13.8	08.4	164 13.1	50.9
	23		345 12.1	140 51.3	48.2	145 33.5	58.5	61 16.1	08.4	179 15.3	50.8
Mer. Pass.			h m 0 06.9	v −0.4	d 1.2	v 0.9	d 0.6	v 2.4	d 0.0	v 2.2	d 0.1

STARS

Name	SHA	Dec
	° ′	° ′
Acamar	315 20.6	S40 15.8
Achernar	335 28.6	S57 11.3
Acrux	173 14.3	S63 08.9
Adhara	255 15.5	S28 58.7
Aldebaran	290 53.4	N16 31.8
Alioth	166 24.1	N55 54.8
Alkaid	153 01.9	N49 16.3
Al Na'ir	27 47.6	S46 55.1
Alnilam	275 50.0	S 1 11.5
Alphard	217 59.9	S 8 41.6
Alphecca	126 14.2	N26 41.2
Alpheratz	357 46.9	N29 08.5
Altair	62 11.6	N 8 53.6
Ankaa	353 18.6	S42 15.3
Antares	112 30.8	S26 27.2
Arcturus	145 59.2	N19 08.3
Atria	107 36.0	S69 02.9
Avior	234 20.0	S59 31.9
Bellatrix	278 35.8	N 6 21.6
Betelgeuse	271 05.2	N 7 24.7
Canopus	263 57.8	S52 41.6
Capella	280 39.7	N46 00.4
Deneb	49 33.7	N45 18.9
Denebola	182 37.6	N14 31.5
Diphda	348 59.1	S17 56.1
Dubhe	193 56.3	N61 42.2
Elnath	278 17.1	N28 36.9
Eltanin	90 47.8	N51 29.5
Enif	33 50.4	N 9 55.1
Fomalhaut	15 27.4	S29 34.4
Gacrux	172 05.7	S57 09.8
Gienah	175 56.4	S17 35.4
Hadar	148 53.8	S60 25.1
Hamal	328 04.6	N23 30.4
Kaus Aust.	83 48.5	S34 23.0
Kochab	137 20.2	N74 07.3
Markab	13 41.6	N15 15.3
Menkar	314 18.6	N 4 07.7
Menkent	148 12.2	S36 24.9
Miaplacidus	221 41.5	S69 44.9
Mirfak	308 45.3	N49 53.5
Nunki	76 02.6	S26 17.2
Peacock	53 24.3	S56 42.6
Pollux	243 32.2	N28 00.3
Procyon	245 03.6	N 5 12.3
Rasalhague	96 09.8	N12 33.3
Regulus	207 47.6	N11 55.6
Rigel	281 15.4	S 8 11.2
Rigil Kent.	139 57.4	S60 52.5
Sabik	102 16.7	S15 44.2
Schedar	349 44.3	N56 35.2
Shaula	96 26.8	S37 06.8
Sirius	258 36.9	S16 43.4
Spica	158 35.3	S11 12.4
Suhail	222 55.5	S43 27.8
Vega	80 41.3	N38 47.7
Zuben'ubi	137 09.6	S16 04.7

	SHA	Mer. Pass.
	° ′	h m
Venus	157 52.6	13 36
Mars	161 33.8	13 20
Jupiter	76 08.7	18 59
Saturn	194 16.7	11 08

UT		SUN		MOON				
	d h	GHA	Dec	GHA	v	Dec	d	HP
		° ′	° ′	° ′	′	° ′	′	′
	18 00	181 27.8	N 1 48.5	331 42.4	9.4	N15 51.2	13.6	59.2
	01	196 28.0	47.5	346 10.8	9.4	16 04.8	13.6	59.2
	02	211 28.3	46.6	0 39.2	9.2	16 18.4	13.5	59.2
	03	226 28.5	. . 45.6	15 07.4	9.2	16 31.9	13.4	59.2
	04	241 28.7	44.6	29 35.6	9.1	16 45.3	13.3	59.2
	05	256 28.9	43.7	44 03.7	9.0	16 58.6	13.2	59.2
	06	271 29.2	N 1 42.7	58 31.7	8.9	N17 11.8	13.2	59.2
THURSDAY	07	286 29.4	41.7	72 59.6	8.8	17 25.0	13.0	59.2
	08	301 29.6	40.8	87 27.4	8.7	17 38.0	12.9	59.2
	09	316 29.8	. . 39.8	101 55.1	8.6	17 50.9	12.9	59.2
	10	331 30.1	38.8	116 22.7	8.5	18 03.8	12.7	59.3
	11	346 30.3	37.9	130 50.2	8.4	18 16.5	12.6	59.3
	12	1 30.5	N 1 36.9	145 17.6	8.4	N18 29.1	12.5	59.3
	13	16 30.7	35.9	159 45.0	8.2	18 41.6	12.5	59.3
	14	31 30.9	34.9	174 12.2	8.2	18 54.1	12.3	59.3
	15	46 31.2	. . 34.0	188 39.4	8.0	19 06.4	12.2	59.3
	16	61 31.4	33.0	203 06.4	8.0	19 18.6	12.0	59.3
	17	76 31.6	32.0	217 33.4	7.9	19 30.6	12.0	59.3
	18	91 31.8	N 1 31.1	232 00.3	7.7	N19 42.6	11.9	59.3
	19	106 32.1	30.1	246 27.0	7.7	19 54.5	11.7	59.3
	20	121 32.3	29.1	260 53.7	7.6	20 06.2	11.6	59.3
	21	136 32.5	. . 28.2	275 20.3	7.5	20 17.8	11.5	59.3
	22	151 32.7	27.2	289 46.8	7.4	20 29.3	11.4	59.4
	23	166 33.0	26.2	304 13.2	7.3	20 40.7	11.2	59.4
	19 00	181 33.2	N 1 25.3	318 39.5	7.2	N20 51.9	11.2	59.4
	01	196 33.4	24.3	333 05.7	7.1	21 03.1	11.0	59.4
	02	211 33.6	23.3	347 31.8	7.0	21 14.1	10.8	59.4
	03	226 33.9	. . 22.3	1 57.8	6.9	21 24.9	10.8	59.4
	04	241 34.1	21.4	16 23.7	6.8	21 35.7	10.6	59.4
	05	256 34.3	20.4	30 49.5	6.8	21 46.3	10.5	59.4
	06	271 34.5	N 1 19.4	45 15.3	6.6	N21 56.8	10.3	59.4
	07	286 34.7	18.5	59 40.9	6.6	22 07.1	10.2	59.4
	08	301 35.0	17.5	74 06.5	6.4	22 17.3	10.1	59.4
FRIDAY	09	316 35.2	. . 16.5	88 31.9	6.4	22 27.4	9.9	59.4
	10	331 35.4	15.6	102 57.3	6.3	22 37.3	9.8	59.4
	11	346 35.6	14.6	117 22.6	6.2	22 47.1	9.6	59.4
	12	1 35.9	N 1 13.6	131 47.8	6.1	N22 56.7	9.5	59.4
	13	16 36.1	12.7	146 12.9	6.0	23 06.2	9.3	59.4
	14	31 36.3	11.7	160 37.9	5.9	23 15.5	9.2	59.4
	15	46 36.5	. . 10.7	175 02.8	5.8	23 24.7	9.1	59.4
	16	61 36.8	09.7	189 27.6	5.8	23 33.8	8.8	59.4
	17	76 37.0	08.8	203 52.4	5.6	23 42.6	8.8	59.4
	18	91 37.2	N 1 07.8	218 17.0	5.6	N23 51.4	8.6	59.4
	19	106 37.4	06.8	232 41.6	5.5	24 00.0	8.4	59.4
	20	121 37.6	05.9	247 06.1	5.4	24 08.4	8.3	59.4
	21	136 37.9	. . 04.9	261 30.5	5.3	24 16.7	8.1	59.4
	22	151 38.1	03.9	275 54.8	5.3	24 24.8	7.9	59.4
	23	166 38.3	02.9	290 19.1	5.2	24 32.7	7.8	59.4
	20 00	181 38.5	N 1 02.0	304 43.3	5.1	N24 40.5	7.7	59.4
	01	196 38.8	01.0	319 07.4	5.0	24 48.2	7.4	59.4
	02	211 39.0	1 00.0	333 31.4	4.9	24 55.6	7.3	59.4
	03	226 39.2	0 59.1	347 55.3	4.9	25 02.9	7.2	59.4
	04	241 39.4	58.1	2 19.2	4.8	25 10.1	6.9	59.4
	05	256 39.6	57.1	16 43.0	4.7	25 17.0	6.8	59.4
	06	271 39.9	N 0 56.2	31 06.7	4.7	N25 23.8	6.7	59.4
	07	286 40.1	55.2	45 30.4	4.6	25 30.5	6.4	59.4
SATURDAY	08	301 40.3	54.2	59 54.0	4.5	25 36.9	6.3	59.4
	09	316 40.5	. . 53.2	74 17.5	4.4	25 43.2	6.1	59.4
	10	331 40.8	52.3	88 40.9	4.4	25 49.3	6.0	59.4
	11	346 41.0	51.3	103 04.3	4.4	25 55.3	5.7	59.4
	12	1 41.2	N 0 50.3	117 27.7	4.3	N26 01.0	5.6	59.4
	13	16 41.4	49.4	131 51.0	4.2	26 06.6	5.4	59.4
	14	31 41.6	48.4	146 14.2	4.2	26 12.0	5.2	59.4
	15	46 41.9	. . 47.4	160 37.4	4.1	26 17.2	5.1	59.4
	16	61 42.1	46.4	175 00.5	4.0	26 22.3	4.9	59.4
	17	76 42.3	45.5	189 23.5	4.0	26 27.2	4.6	59.4
	18	91 42.5	N 0 44.5	203 46.5	4.0	N26 31.8	4.5	59.4
	19	106 42.8	43.5	218 09.5	3.9	26 36.3	4.4	59.4
	20	121 43.0	42.6	232 32.4	3.9	26 40.7	4.1	59.4
	21	136 43.2	. . 41.6	246 55.3	3.8	26 44.8	4.0	59.4
	22	151 43.4	40.6	261 18.1	3.8	26 48.8	3.7	59.4
	23	166 43.6	39.6	275 40.9	3.8	N26 52.5	3.6	59.4
		SD 15.9	d 1.0	SD 16.2		16.2		16.2

Lat.	Twilight Naut.	Twilight Civil	Sunrise	Moonrise 18	19	20	21
°	h m	h m	h m	h m	h m	h m	h m
N 72	02 40	04 17	05 26	▭	▭	▭	▭
N 70	03 04	04 27	05 29	15 39	▭	▭	▭
68	03 22	04 35	05 32	16 29	▭	▭	▭
66	03 36	04 42	05 34	17 01	16 15	▭	▭
64	03 48	04 47	05 35	17 25	17 11	▭	▭
62	03 57	04 52	05 37	17 44	17 44	17 49	18 20
60	04 05	04 56	05 38	18 00	18 09	18 29	19 14
N 58	04 12	04 59	05 39	18 14	18 29	18 56	19 46
56	04 18	05 02	05 40	18 25	18 45	19 18	20 10
54	04 23	05 05	05 41	18 36	19 00	19 36	20 30
52	04 27	05 08	05 41	18 45	19 12	19 51	20 46
50	04 31	05 10	05 42	18 53	19 23	20 04	21 00
45	04 40	05 14	05 44	19 10	19 46	20 31	21 29
N 40	04 46	05 18	05 45	19 25	20 04	20 53	21 52
35	04 51	05 21	05 46	19 37	20 20	21 11	22 11
30	04 55	05 23	05 47	19 48	20 34	21 26	22 27
20	05 01	05 26	05 48	20 07	20 57	21 53	22 54
N 10	05 04	05 28	05 49	20 23	21 17	22 16	23 18
0	05 06	05 30	05 50	20 39	21 36	22 37	23 40
S 10	05 06	05 30	05 51	20 54	21 55	22 58	24 01
20	05 05	05 30	05 52	21 11	22 16	23 21	24 25
30	05 01	05 29	05 53	21 30	22 40	23 48	24 52
35	04 59	05 28	05 53	21 41	22 54	24 04	00 04
40	04 55	05 27	05 54	21 55	23 10	24 23	00 23
45	04 51	05 25	05 54	22 10	23 30	24 45	00 45
S 50	04 45	05 23	05 55	22 29	23 55	25 14	01 14
52	04 42	05 22	05 55	22 39	24 07	00 07	01 28
54	04 39	05 20	05 55	22 49	24 21	00 21	01 44
56	04 35	05 19	05 56	23 01	24 37	00 37	02 04
58	04 31	05 17	05 56	23 14	24 56	00 56	02 28
S 60	04 26	05 15	05 56	23 30	25 20	01 20	03 00

Lat.	Sunset	Twilight Civil	Twilight Naut.	Moonset 18	19	20	21
°	h m	h m	h m	h m	h m	h m	h m
N 72	18 18	19 27	21 01	▭	▭	▭	▭
N 70	18 16	19 18	20 39	12 48	▭	▭	▭
68	18 14	19 10	20 22	11 59	▭	▭	▭
66	18 12	19 04	20 08	11 28	14 13	▭	▭
64	18 10	18 58	19 57	11 06	13 18	▭	▭
62	18 09	18 54	19 48	10 48	12 45	14 46	16 26
60	18 08	18 50	19 40	10 33	12 21	14 07	15 32
N 58	18 07	18 46	19 34	10 20	12 02	13 40	15 00
56	18 06	18 43	19 28	10 09	11 46	13 18	14 36
54	18 05	18 41	19 23	10 00	11 32	13 01	14 16
52	18 05	18 38	19 19	09 52	11 20	12 46	14 00
50	18 04	18 36	19 15	09 44	11 10	12 33	13 46
45	18 03	18 32	19 07	09 28	10 48	12 06	13 17
N 40	18 02	18 29	19 00	09 15	10 31	11 45	12 54
35	18 01	18 26	18 56	09 04	10 16	11 28	12 35
30	18 00	18 24	18 52	08 54	10 03	11 13	12 19
20	17 59	18 21	18 46	08 38	09 42	10 47	11 52
N 10	17 58	18 19	18 43	08 23	09 23	10 25	11 29
0	17 57	18 18	18 42	08 10	09 05	10 05	11 07
S 10	17 56	18 17	18 41	07 57	08 48	09 44	10 45
20	17 55	18 17	18 43	07 42	08 30	09 23	10 21
30	17 55	18 19	18 46	07 26	08 08	08 57	09 54
35	17 54	18 20	18 49	07 17	07 56	08 43	09 38
40	17 54	18 21	18 53	07 06	07 42	08 25	09 19
45	17 54	18 23	18 57	06 54	07 25	08 05	08 56
S 50	17 53	18 26	19 03	06 39	07 04	07 39	08 28
52	17 53	18 27	19 06	06 32	06 55	07 27	08 13
54	17 53	18 28	19 10	06 24	06 44	07 13	07 57
56	17 53	18 30	19 14	06 15	06 31	06 56	07 37
58	17 53	18 32	19 18	06 06	06 17	06 36	07 13
S 60	17 52	18 34	19 23	05 55	06 00	06 12	06 41

Day	SUN Eqn. of Time 00^h	SUN Eqn. of Time 12^h	SUN Mer. Pass.	MOON Mer. Pass. Upper	MOON Mer. Pass. Lower	Age	Phase
d	m s	m s	h m	h m	h m	d %	
18	05 51	06 02	11 54	01 57	14 24	19 88	
19	06 12	06 23	11 54	02 52	15 21	20 79	
20	06 34	06 44	11 53	03 50	16 21	21 69	

UT		ARIES	VENUS −3.9		MARS +1.7		JUPITER −2.4		SATURN +0.9		STARS		
d h		GHA	GHA	Dec	GHA	Dec	GHA	Dec	GHA	Dec	Name	SHA	Dec
		° ′	° ′	° ′	° ′	° ′	° ′	° ′	° ′	° ′		° ′	° ′
21 00		0 14.6	155 50.9	S 9 49.4	160 34.5	S 7 59.2	76 18.5	S23 08.4	194 17.4	N 7 50.7	Acamar	315 20.6	S40 15.8
01		15 17.1	170 50.5	50.6	175 35.4	7 59.8	91 20.8	08.4	209 19.6	50.6	Achernar	335 28.6	S57 11.3
02		30 19.5	185 50.1	51.8	190 36.3	8 00.4	106 23.2	08.4	224 21.8	50.5	Acrux	173 14.3	S63 08.9
03		45 22.0	200 49.7	. . 53.0	205 37.2	. . 01.1	121 25.5	. . 08.4	239 24.0	. . 50.4	Adhara	255 15.4	S28 58.7
04		60 24.5	215 49.4	54.2	220 38.1	01.7	136 27.9	08.3	254 26.1	50.3	Aldebaran	290 53.4	N16 31.8
05		75 26.9	230 49.0	55.4	235 39.1	02.4	151 30.2	08.3	269 28.3	50.1			
06		90 29.4	245 48.6	S 9 56.6	250 40.0	S 8 03.0	166 32.6	S23 08.3	284 30.5	N 7 50.0	Alioth	166 24.1	N55 54.8
07		105 31.8	260 48.2	57.8	265 40.9	03.7	181 34.9	08.3	299 32.7	49.9	Alkaid	153 01.9	N49 16.3
08		120 34.3	275 47.8	9 59.1	280 41.8	04.3	196 37.3	08.3	314 34.8	49.8	Al Na'ir	27 47.6	S46 55.1
09	S	135 36.8	290 47.4	10 00.3	295 42.7	. . 05.0	211 39.6	. . 08.3	329 37.0	. . 49.7	Alnilam	275 49.9	S 1 11.5
10	U	150 39.2	305 47.0	01.5	310 43.7	05.6	226 42.0	08.3	344 39.2	49.6	Alphard	217 59.8	S 8 41.6
11	N	165 41.7	320 46.7	02.7	325 44.6	06.2	241 44.3	08.3	359 41.4	49.4			
12	D	180 44.2	335 46.3	S10 03.9	340 45.5	S 8 06.9	256 46.7	S23 08.3	14 43.5	N 7 49.3	Alphecca	126 14.2	N26 41.2
13	A	195 46.6	350 45.9	05.1	355 46.4	07.5	271 49.0	08.3	29 45.7	49.2	Alpheratz	357 46.9	N29 08.5
14	Y	210 49.1	5 45.5	06.3	10 47.3	08.2	286 51.4	08.3	44 47.9	49.1	Altair	62 11.6	N 8 53.6
15		225 51.6	20 45.1	. . 07.5	25 48.3	. . 08.8	301 53.7	. . 08.3	59 50.1	. . 49.0	Ankaa	353 18.6	S42 15.3
16		240 54.0	35 44.7	08.7	40 49.2	09.5	316 56.1	08.3	74 52.2	48.9	Antares	112 30.8	S26 27.2
17		255 56.5	50 44.3	09.9	55 50.1	10.1	331 58.4	08.2	89 54.4	48.8			
18		270 58.9	65 43.9	S10 11.1	70 51.0	S 8 10.8	347 00.8	S23 08.2	104 56.6	N 7 48.6	Arcturus	145 59.2	N19 08.3
19		286 01.4	80 43.6	12.3	85 51.9	11.4	2 03.1	08.2	119 58.8	48.5	Atria	107 36.1	S69 02.9
20		301 03.9	95 43.2	13.5	100 52.8	12.0	17 05.5	08.2	135 00.9	48.4	Avior	234 20.0	S59 31.9
21		316 06.3	110 42.8	. . 14.7	115 53.8	. . 12.7	32 07.8	. . 08.2	150 03.1	. . 48.3	Bellatrix	278 35.8	N 6 21.6
22		331 08.8	125 42.4	15.9	130 54.7	13.3	47 10.2	08.2	165 05.3	48.2	Betelgeuse	271 05.1	N 7 24.7
23		346 11.3	140 42.0	17.2	145 55.6	14.0	62 12.5	08.2	180 07.5	48.1			
22 00		1 13.7	155 41.6	S10 18.4	160 56.5	S 8 14.6	77 14.9	S23 08.2	195 09.6	N 7 47.9	Canopus	263 57.8	S52 41.6
01		16 16.2	170 41.2	19.6	175 57.4	15.3	92 17.2	08.2	210 11.8	47.8	Capella	280 39.6	N46 00.4
02		31 18.7	185 40.8	20.8	190 58.3	15.9	107 19.6	08.2	225 14.0	47.7	Deneb	49 33.7	N45 18.9
03		46 21.1	200 40.4	. . 22.0	205 59.3	. . 16.5	122 21.9	. . 08.2	240 16.2	. . 47.6	Denebola	182 37.6	N14 31.5
04		61 23.6	215 40.0	23.2	221 00.2	17.2	137 24.2	08.2	255 18.3	47.5	Diphda	348 59.1	S17 56.1
05		76 26.1	230 39.7	24.4	236 01.1	17.8	152 26.6	08.1	270 20.5	47.4			
06		91 28.5	245 39.3	S10 25.6	251 02.0	S 8 18.5	167 28.9	S23 08.1	285 22.7	N 7 47.3	Dubhe	193 56.3	N61 42.2
07		106 31.0	260 38.9	26.8	266 02.9	19.1	182 31.3	08.1	300 24.9	47.1	Elnath	278 17.1	N28 36.9
08		121 33.4	275 38.5	28.0	281 03.8	19.8	197 33.6	08.1	315 27.1	47.0	Eltanin	90 47.8	N51 29.5
09	M	136 35.9	290 38.1	. . 29.2	296 04.7	. . 20.4	212 36.0	. . 08.1	330 29.2	. . 46.9	Enif	33 50.4	N 9 55.1
10	O	151 38.4	305 37.7	30.4	311 05.7	21.0	227 38.3	08.1	345 31.4	46.8	Fomalhaut	15 27.4	S29 34.4
11	N	166 40.8	320 37.3	31.6	326 06.6	21.7	242 40.7	08.1	0 33.6	46.7			
12	D	181 43.3	335 36.9	S10 32.8	341 07.5	S 8 22.3	257 43.0	S23 08.1	15 35.8	N 7 46.6	Gacrux	172 05.7	S57 09.8
13	A	196 45.8	350 36.5	34.0	356 08.4	23.0	272 45.3	08.1	30 37.9	46.5	Gienah	175 56.3	S17 35.4
14	Y	211 48.2	5 36.1	35.2	11 09.3	23.6	287 47.7	08.1	45 40.1	46.3	Hadar	148 53.8	S60 25.1
15		226 50.7	20 35.7	. . 36.4	26 10.2	. . 24.3	302 50.0	. . 08.1	60 42.3	. . 46.2	Hamal	328 04.5	N23 30.4
16		241 53.2	35 35.3	37.6	41 11.1	24.9	317 52.4	08.1	75 44.5	46.1	Kaus Aust.	83 48.5	S34 23.0
17		256 55.6	50 34.9	38.8	56 12.1	25.5	332 54.7	08.0	90 46.6	46.0			
18		271 58.1	65 34.5	S10 40.0	71 13.0	S 8 26.2	347 57.0	S23 08.0	105 48.8	N 7 45.9	Kochab	137 20.2	N74 07.3
19		287 00.6	80 34.1	41.2	86 13.9	26.8	2 59.4	08.0	120 51.0	45.8	Markab	13 41.6	N15 15.3
20		302 03.0	95 33.7	42.4	101 14.8	27.5	18 01.7	08.0	135 53.2	45.6	Menkar	314 18.6	N 4 07.7
21		317 05.5	110 33.3	. . 43.5	116 15.7	. . 28.1	33 04.1	. . 08.0	150 55.3	. . 45.5	Menkent	148 12.2	S36 24.9
22		332 07.9	125 32.9	44.7	131 16.6	28.8	48 06.4	08.0	165 57.5	45.4	Miaplacidus	221 41.5	S69 44.9
23		347 10.4	140 32.5	45.9	146 17.5	29.4	63 08.7	08.0	180 59.7	45.3			
23 00		2 12.9	155 32.1	S10 47.1	161 18.4	S 8 30.0	78 11.1	S23 08.0	196 01.9	N 7 45.2	Mirfak	308 45.3	N49 53.5
01		17 15.3	170 31.7	48.3	176 19.4	30.7	93 13.4	08.0	211 04.1	45.1	Nunki	76 02.6	S26 17.2
02		32 17.8	185 31.3	49.5	191 20.3	31.3	108 15.7	08.0	226 06.2	45.0	Peacock	53 24.3	S56 42.6
03		47 20.3	200 30.9	. . 50.7	206 21.2	. . 32.0	123 18.1	. . 08.0	241 08.4	. . 44.8	Pollux	243 32.2	N28 00.3
04		62 22.7	215 30.5	51.9	221 22.1	32.6	138 20.4	08.0	256 10.6	44.7	Procyon	245 03.6	N 5 12.3
05		77 25.2	230 30.1	53.1	236 23.0	33.2	153 22.8	07.9	271 12.8	44.6			
06		92 27.7	245 29.7	S10 54.3	251 23.9	S 8 33.9	168 25.1	S23 07.9	286 14.9	N 7 44.5	Rasalhague	96 09.8	N12 33.3
07		107 30.1	260 29.3	55.5	266 24.8	34.5	183 27.4	07.9	301 17.1	44.4	Regulus	207 47.5	N11 55.5
08	T	122 32.6	275 28.9	56.7	281 25.7	35.2	198 29.8	07.9	316 19.3	44.3	Rigel	281 15.4	S 8 11.2
09	U	137 35.1	290 28.5	. . 57.9	296 26.6	. . 35.8	213 32.1	. . 07.9	331 21.5	. . 44.2	Rigil Kent.	139 57.4	S60 52.4
10	E	152 37.5	305 28.1	10 59.1	311 27.5	36.5	228 34.4	07.9	346 23.6	44.0	Sabik	102 16.7	S15 44.2
11	S	167 40.0	320 27.7	11 00.2	326 28.5	37.1	243 36.8	07.9	1 25.8	43.9			
12	D	182 42.4	335 27.3	S11 01.4	341 29.4	S 8 37.7	258 39.1	S23 07.9	16 28.0	N 7 43.8	Schedar	349 44.3	N56 35.2
13	A	197 44.9	350 26.9	02.6	356 30.3	38.4	273 41.4	07.9	31 30.2	43.7	Shaula	96 26.8	S37 06.8
14	Y	212 47.4	5 26.5	03.8	11 31.2	39.0	288 43.8	07.9	46 32.4	43.6	Sirius	258 36.9	S16 43.4
15		227 49.8	20 26.1	. . 05.0	26 32.1	. . 39.7	303 46.1	. . 07.9	61 34.5	. . 43.5	Spica	158 35.3	S11 12.4
16		242 52.3	35 25.7	06.2	41 33.0	40.3	318 48.4	07.8	76 36.7	43.4	Suhail	222 55.5	S43 27.8
17		257 54.8	50 25.3	07.4	56 33.9	40.9	333 50.8	07.8	91 38.9	43.2			
18		272 57.2	65 24.9	S11 08.6	71 34.8	S 8 41.6	348 53.1	S23 07.8	106 41.1	N 7 43.1	Vega	80 41.3	N38 47.7
19		287 59.7	80 24.5	09.7	86 35.7	42.2	3 55.4	07.8	121 43.2	43.0	Zuben'ubi	137 09.6	S16 04.7
20		303 02.2	95 24.1	10.9	101 36.6	42.9	18 57.7	07.8	136 45.4	42.9			
21		318 04.6	110 23.7	. . 12.1	116 37.5	. . 43.5	34 00.1	. . 07.8	151 47.6	. . 42.8			
22		333 07.1	125 23.3	13.3	131 38.5	44.1	49 02.4	07.8	166 49.8	42.7			
23		348 09.6	140 22.9	14.5	146 39.4	44.8	64 04.7	07.8	181 51.9	42.6			
Mer. Pass.		h m 23 51.2	v −0.4	d 1.2	v 0.9	d 0.6	v 2.3	d 0.0	v 2.2	d 0.1			

	SHA	Mer. Pass.
	° ′	h m
Venus	154 27.9	13 38
Mars	159 42.8	13 15
Jupiter	76 01.1	18 48
Saturn	193 55.9	10 58

	UT	SUN GHA	SUN Dec	MOON GHA	v	MOON Dec	d	HP
	d h	° ′	° ′	° ′	′	° ′	′	′
	21 00	181 43.9	N 0 38.7	290 03.7	3.7	N26 56.1	3.4	59.4
	01	196 44.1	37.7	304 26.4	3.7	26 59.5	3.2	59.4
	02	211 44.3	36.7	318 49.1	3.7	27 02.7	3.1	59.4
	03	226 44.5	. . 35.7	333 11.8	3.6	27 05.8	2.8	59.4
	04	241 44.8	34.8	347 34.4	3.6	27 08.6	2.6	59.4
	05	256 45.0	33.8	1 57.0	3.6	27 11.2	2.5	59.4
	06	271 45.2	N 0 32.8	16 19.6	3.6	N27 13.7	2.3	59.4
	07	286 45.4	31.9	30 42.2	3.5	27 16.0	2.1	59.4
	08	301 45.6	30.9	45 04.7	3.5	27 18.1	1.9	59.4
S	09	316 45.9	. . 29.9	59 27.2	3.6	27 20.0	1.7	59.4
U	10	331 46.1	28.9	73 49.8	3.5	27 21.7	1.5	59.4
N	11	346 46.3	28.0	88 12.3	3.5	27 23.2	1.3	59.4
D	12	1 46.5	N 0 27.0	102 34.8	3.5	N27 24.5	1.1	59.3
A	13	16 46.7	26.0	116 57.3	3.4	27 25.6	1.0	59.3
Y	14	31 47.0	25.1	131 19.7	3.5	27 26.6	0.7	59.3
	15	46 47.2	. . 24.1	145 42.2	3.5	27 27.3	0.6	59.3
	16	61 47.4	23.1	160 04.7	3.5	27 27.9	0.4	59.3
	17	76 47.6	22.1	174 27.2	3.5	27 28.3	0.2	59.3
	18	91 47.8	N 0 21.2	188 49.7	3.5	N27 28.5	0.0	59.3
	19	106 48.1	20.2	203 12.2	3.5	27 28.5	0.2	59.3
	20	121 48.3	19.2	217 34.7	3.6	27 28.3	0.4	59.3
	21	136 48.5	. . 18.2	231 57.3	3.5	27 27.9	0.6	59.3
	22	151 48.7	17.3	246 19.8	3.6	27 27.3	0.8	59.3
	23	166 48.9	16.3	260 42.4	3.5	27 26.5	0.9	59.3
	22 00	181 49.2	N 0 15.3	275 04.9	3.6	N27 25.6	1.2	59.3
	01	196 49.4	14.4	289 27.5	3.7	27 24.4	1.3	59.3
	02	211 49.6	13.4	303 50.2	3.6	27 23.1	1.5	59.3
	03	226 49.8	. . 12.4	318 12.8	3.7	27 21.6	1.7	59.2
	04	241 50.0	11.4	332 35.5	3.7	27 19.9	1.9	59.2
	05	256 50.3	10.5	346 58.2	3.8	27 18.0	2.1	59.2
	06	271 50.5	N 0 09.5	1 21.0	3.8	N27 15.9	2.3	59.2
	07	286 50.7	08.5	15 43.8	3.8	27 13.6	2.4	59.2
	08	301 50.9	07.5	30 06.6	3.9	27 11.2	2.7	59.2
M	09	316 51.1	. . 06.6	44 29.5	3.9	27 08.5	2.8	59.2
O	10	331 51.4	05.6	58 52.4	4.0	27 05.7	3.0	59.2
N	11	346 51.6	04.6	73 15.4	4.0	27 02.7	3.2	59.2
D	12	1 51.8	N 0 03.6	87 38.4	4.0	N26 59.5	3.4	59.2
A	13	16 52.0	02.7	102 01.4	4.1	26 56.1	3.5	59.2
Y	14	31 52.2	01.7	116 24.5	4.2	26 52.6	3.7	59.2
	15	46 52.5	N 00.7	130 47.7	4.2	26 48.9	4.0	59.1
	16	61 52.7	S 00.2	145 10.9	4.3	26 44.9	4.0	59.1
	17	76 52.9	01.2	159 34.2	4.3	26 40.9	4.3	59.1
	18	91 53.1	S 0 02.2	173 57.5	4.4	N26 36.6	4.5	59.1
	19	106 53.3	03.2	188 20.9	4.5	26 32.1	4.6	59.1
	20	121 53.6	04.1	202 44.4	4.5	26 27.5	4.8	59.1
	21	136 53.8	. . 05.1	217 07.9	4.6	26 22.7	4.9	59.1
	22	151 54.0	06.1	231 31.5	4.6	26 17.8	5.2	59.1
	23	166 54.2	07.1	245 55.1	4.8	26 12.6	5.3	59.1
	23 00	181 54.4	S 0 08.0	260 18.9	4.8	N26 07.3	5.5	59.1
	01	196 54.7	09.0	274 42.7	4.9	26 01.8	5.6	59.0
	02	211 54.9	10.0	289 06.6	4.9	25 56.2	5.8	59.0
	03	226 55.1	. . 11.0	303 30.5	5.0	25 50.4	6.0	59.0
	04	241 55.3	11.9	317 54.5	5.1	25 44.4	6.2	59.0
	05	256 55.5	12.9	332 18.6	5.2	25 38.2	6.3	59.0
	06	271 55.8	S 0 13.9	346 42.8	5.3	N25 31.9	6.5	59.0
	07	286 56.0	14.8	1 07.1	5.3	25 25.4	6.6	59.0
T	08	301 56.2	15.8	15 31.4	5.5	25 18.8	6.8	59.0
U	09	316 56.4	. . 16.8	29 55.9	5.5	25 12.0	7.0	59.0
E	10	331 56.6	17.8	44 20.4	5.6	25 05.0	7.1	59.0
S	11	346 56.8	18.7	58 45.0	5.7	24 57.9	7.3	58.9
D	12	1 57.1	S 0 19.7	73 09.7	5.8	N24 50.6	7.4	58.9
A	13	16 57.3	20.7	87 34.5	5.8	24 43.2	7.6	58.9
Y	14	31 57.5	21.7	101 59.3	6.0	24 35.6	7.8	58.9
	15	46 57.7	. . 22.6	116 24.3	6.0	24 27.8	7.8	58.9
	16	61 57.9	23.6	130 49.3	6.2	24 20.0	8.1	58.9
	17	76 58.2	24.6	145 14.5	6.2	24 11.9	8.2	58.9
	18	91 58.4	S 0 25.6	159 39.7	6.3	N24 03.7	8.3	58.9
	19	106 58.6	26.5	174 05.0	6.4	23 55.4	8.5	58.8
	20	121 58.8	27.5	188 30.4	6.5	23 46.9	8.6	58.8
	21	136 59.0	. . 28.5	202 55.9	6.7	23 38.3	8.8	58.8
	22	151 59.2	29.5	217 21.6	6.7	23 29.5	8.9	58.8
	23	166 59.5	30.4	231 47.3	6.8	N23 20.6	9.0	58.8
		SD 16.0	*d* 1.0	SD 16.2		16.1		16.1

Lat.	Twilight Naut.	Twilight Civil	Sunrise	Moonrise 21	22	23	24
°	h m	h m	h m	h m	h m	h m	h m
N 72	03 00	04 31	05 40	▭	▭	▭	▭
N 70	03 20	04 39	05 41	▭	▭	▭	21 25
68	03 35	04 46	05 42	▭	▭	▭	22 29
66	03 48	04 51	05 43	▭	▭	20 10	23 03
64	03 58	04 56	05 44	▭	▭	21 18	23 28
62	04 06	05 00	05 44	18 20	19 55	21 53	23 48
60	04 13	05 03	05 45	19 14	20 36	22 18	24 04
N 58	04 19	05 06	05 45	19 46	21 04	22 38	24 17
56	04 24	05 09	05 46	20 10	21 25	22 55	24 28
54	04 29	05 11	05 46	20 30	21 43	23 09	24 38
52	04 33	05 13	05 46	20 46	21 58	23 21	24 47
50	04 36	05 14	05 47	21 00	22 11	23 32	24 55
45	04 44	05 18	05 47	21 29	22 38	23 54	25 12
N 40	04 49	05 21	05 48	21 52	23 00	24 12	00 12
35	04 53	05 23	05 48	22 11	23 17	24 27	00 27
30	04 57	05 25	05 48	22 27	23 33	24 40	00 40
20	05 01	05 27	05 49	22 54	23 58	25 03	01 03
N 10	05 04	05 28	05 49	23 18	24 20	00 20	01 22
0	05 05	05 29	05 49	23 40	24 41	00 41	01 40
S 10	05 04	05 28	05 49	24 01	00 01	01 02	01 57
20	05 02	05 27	05 49	24 25	00 25	01 24	02 16
30	04 58	05 25	05 49	24 52	00 52	01 49	02 38
35	04 54	05 24	05 49	00 04	01 09	02 04	02 51
40	04 50	05 22	05 49	00 23	01 27	02 22	03 05
45	04 45	05 19	05 49	00 45	01 50	02 42	03 22
S 50	04 38	05 16	05 48	01 14	02 19	03 08	03 44
52	04 35	05 14	05 48	01 28	02 34	03 21	03 54
54	04 31	05 13	05 48	01 44	02 50	03 36	04 05
56	04 27	05 11	05 48	02 04	03 10	03 52	04 18
58	04 22	05 08	05 47	02 28	03 34	04 13	04 33
S 60	04 16	05 06	05 47	03 00	04 07	04 38	04 50

Lat.	Sunset	Twilight Civil	Twilight Naut.	Moonset 21	22	23	24
°	h m	h m	h m	h m	h m	h m	h m
N 72	18 03	19 11	20 40	▭	▭	▭	▭
N 70	18 02	19 03	20 21	▭	▭	▭	19 35
68	18 01	18 57	20 06	▭	▭	▭	18 30
66	18 00	18 52	19 55	▭	▭	18 52	17 54
64	18 00	18 47	19 45	▭	▭	17 43	17 28
62	17 59	18 44	19 37	16 26	17 01	17 07	17 07
60	17 59	18 40	19 30	15 32	16 20	16 41	16 51
N 58	17 59	18 38	19 24	15 00	15 52	16 21	16 36
56	17 58	18 35	19 19	14 36	15 30	16 04	16 24
54	17 58	18 33	19 15	14 16	15 12	15 49	16 13
52	17 58	18 31	19 11	14 00	14 57	15 36	16 04
50	17 57	18 30	19 08	13 46	14 43	15 25	15 55
45	17 57	18 26	19 01	13 17	14 16	15 02	15 37
N 40	17 57	18 24	18 55	12 54	13 54	14 43	15 22
35	17 56	18 22	18 51	12 35	13 36	14 27	15 09
30	17 56	18 20	18 48	12 19	13 20	14 13	14 58
20	17 56	18 18	18 44	11 52	12 54	13 49	14 39
N 10	17 56	18 17	18 41	11 29	12 31	13 29	14 22
0	17 56	18 16	18 40	11 07	12 09	13 09	14 06
S 10	17 56	18 17	18 41	10 45	11 48	12 50	13 50
20	17 56	18 18	18 44	10 21	11 24	12 29	13 33
30	17 56	18 20	18 48	09 54	10 57	12 05	13 13
35	17 57	18 22	18 51	09 38	10 41	11 50	13 01
40	17 57	18 24	18 56	09 19	10 23	11 34	12 47
45	17 57	18 27	19 01	08 56	10 00	11 14	12 31
S 50	17 58	18 30	19 08	08 28	09 32	10 48	12 11
52	17 58	18 32	19 12	08 13	09 17	10 36	12 02
54	17 58	18 34	19 16	07 57	09 01	10 22	11 51
56	17 59	18 36	19 20	07 37	08 41	10 06	11 39
58	17 59	18 38	19 25	07 13	08 17	09 46	11 25
S 60	17 59	18 41	19 31	06 41	07 44	09 21	11 08

Day	SUN Eqn. of Time 00^h	12^h	Mer. Pass.	MOON Mer. Pass. Upper	Lower	Age	Phase
d	m s	m s	h m	h m	h m	d %	
21	06 55	07 06	11 53	04 52	17 23	22 58	
22	07 16	07 27	11 53	05 54	18 25	23 47	
23	07 37	07 48	11 52	06 55	19 25	24 36	

UT		ARIES	VENUS −3.9		MARS +1.7		JUPITER −2.3		SATURN +0.9		STARS		
d h		GHA	GHA	Dec	GHA	Dec	GHA	Dec	GHA	Dec	Name	SHA	Dec
		° ′	° ′	° ′	° ′	° ′	° ′	° ′	° ′	° ′		° ′	° ′
24 00		3 12.0	155 22.5	S11 15.7	161 40.3	S 8 45.4	79 07.1	S23 07.8	196 54.1	N 7 42.4	Acamar	315 20.6	S40 15.8
01		18 14.5	170 22.1	16.9	176 41.2	46.1	94 09.4	07.8	211 56.3	42.3	Achernar	335 28.6	S57 11.3
02		33 16.9	185 21.7	18.0	191 42.1	46.7	109 11.7	07.7	226 58.5	42.2	Acrux	173 14.3	S63 08.9
03		48 19.4	200 21.2	. . 19.2	206 43.0	. . 47.3	124 14.1	. . 07.7	242 00.7	. . 42.1	Adhara	255 15.4	S28 58.7
04		63 21.9	215 20.8	20.4	221 43.9	48.0	139 16.4	07.7	257 02.8	42.0	Aldebaran	290 53.3	N16 31.8
05		78 24.3	230 20.4	21.6	236 44.8	48.6	154 18.7	07.7	272 05.0	41.9			
06		93 26.8	245 20.0	S11 22.8	251 45.7	S 8 49.3	169 21.0	S23 07.7	287 07.2	N 7 41.8	Alioth	166 24.1	N55 54.8
07	W	108 29.3	260 19.6	24.0	266 46.6	49.9	184 23.4	07.7	302 09.4	41.6	Alkaid	153 01.9	N49 16.2
08	E	123 31.7	275 19.2	25.1	281 47.5	50.5	199 25.7	07.7	317 11.5	41.5	Al Na'ir	27 47.6	S46 55.1
09	D	138 34.2	290 18.8	. . 26.3	296 48.4	. . 51.2	214 28.0	. . 07.7	332 13.7	. . 41.4	Alnilam	275 49.9	S 1 11.5
10	N	153 36.7	305 18.4	27.5	311 49.3	51.8	229 30.3	07.7	347 15.9	41.3	Alphard	217 59.8	S 8 41.6
11	E	168 39.1	320 18.0	28.7	326 50.2	52.5	244 32.7	07.7	2 18.1	41.2			
12	S	183 41.6	335 17.6	S11 29.9	341 51.2	S 8 53.1	259 35.0	S23 07.7	17 20.3	N 7 41.1	Alphecca	126 14.2	N26 41.2
13	D	198 44.0	350 17.1	31.0	356 52.1	53.7	274 37.3	07.6	32 22.4	41.0	Alpheratz	357 46.9	N29 08.5
14	A	213 46.5	5 16.7	32.2	11 53.0	54.4	289 39.6	07.6	47 24.6	40.8	Altair	62 11.6	N 8 53.6
15	Y	228 49.0	20 16.3	. . 33.4	26 53.9	. . 55.0	304 42.0	. . 07.6	62 26.8	. . 40.7	Ankaa	353 18.6	S42 15.3
16		243 51.4	35 15.9	34.6	41 54.8	55.7	319 44.3	07.6	77 29.0	40.6	Antares	112 30.8	S26 27.2
17		258 53.9	50 15.5	35.7	56 55.7	56.3	334 46.6	07.6	92 31.1	40.5			
18		273 56.4	65 15.1	S11 36.9	71 56.6	S 8 56.9	349 48.9	S23 07.6	107 33.3	N 7 40.4	Arcturus	145 59.2	N19 08.3
19		288 58.8	80 14.7	38.1	86 57.5	57.6	4 51.3	07.6	122 35.5	40.3	Atria	107 36.1	S69 02.9
20		304 01.3	95 14.3	39.3	101 58.4	58.2	19 53.6	07.6	137 37.7	40.2	Avior	234 20.0	S59 31.9
21		319 03.8	110 13.8	. . 40.4	116 59.3	. . 58.8	34 55.9	. . 07.6	152 39.9	. . 40.0	Bellatrix	278 35.7	N 6 21.7
22		334 06.2	125 13.4	41.6	132 00.2	8 59.5	49 58.2	07.6	167 42.0	39.9	Betelgeuse	271 05.1	N 7 24.7
23		349 08.7	140 13.0	42.8	147 01.1	9 00.1	65 00.5	07.5	182 44.2	39.8			
25 00		4 11.2	155 12.6	S11 44.0	162 02.0	S 9 00.8	80 02.9	S23 07.5	197 46.4	N 7 39.7	Canopus	263 57.8	S52 41.6
01		19 13.6	170 12.2	45.1	177 02.9	01.4	95 05.2	07.5	212 48.6	39.6	Capella	280 39.6	N46 00.4
02		34 16.1	185 11.8	46.3	192 03.8	02.0	110 07.5	07.5	227 50.8	39.5	Deneb	49 33.7	N45 18.9
03		49 18.5	200 11.3	. . 47.5	207 04.7	. . 02.7	125 09.8	. . 07.5	242 52.9	. . 39.4	Denebola	182 37.5	N14 31.4
04		64 21.0	215 10.9	48.7	222 05.6	03.3	140 12.1	07.5	257 55.1	39.2	Diphda	348 59.0	S17 56.1
05		79 23.5	230 10.5	49.8	237 06.5	04.0	155 14.5	07.5	272 57.3	39.1			
06		94 25.9	245 10.1	S11 51.0	252 07.4	S 9 04.6	170 16.8	S23 07.5	287 59.5	N 7 39.0	Dubhe	193 56.3	N61 42.2
07		109 28.4	260 09.7	52.2	267 08.3	05.2	185 19.1	07.5	303 01.6	38.9	Elnath	278 17.0	N28 36.9
08	T	124 30.9	275 09.3	53.3	282 09.2	05.9	200 21.4	07.4	318 03.8	38.8	Eltanin	90 47.8	N51 29.5
09	H	139 33.3	290 08.8	. . 54.5	297 10.1	. . 06.5	215 23.7	. . 07.4	333 06.0	. . 38.7	Enif	33 50.4	N 9 55.1
10	U	154 35.8	305 08.4	55.7	312 11.0	07.1	230 26.1	07.4	348 08.2	38.6	Fomalhaut	15 27.4	S29 34.4
11	R	169 38.3	320 08.0	56.8	327 11.9	07.8	245 28.4	07.4	3 10.4	38.4			
12	S	184 40.7	335 07.6	S11 58.0	342 12.8	S 9 08.4	260 30.7	S23 07.4	18 12.5	N 7 38.3	Gacrux	172 05.7	S57 09.8
13	D	199 43.2	350 07.2	11 59.2	357 13.7	09.1	275 33.0	07.4	33 14.7	38.2	Gienah	175 56.3	S17 35.4
14	A	214 45.7	5 06.7	12 00.4	12 14.6	09.7	290 35.3	07.4	48 16.9	38.1	Hadar	148 53.8	S60 25.1
15	Y	229 48.1	20 06.3	. . 01.5	27 15.5	. . 10.3	305 37.6	. . 07.4	63 19.1	. . 38.0	Hamal	328 04.5	N23 30.4
16		244 50.6	35 05.9	02.7	42 16.4	11.0	320 40.0	07.4	78 21.3	37.9	Kaus Aust.	83 48.5	S34 23.0
17		259 53.0	50 05.5	03.8	57 17.3	11.6	335 42.3	07.3	93 23.4	37.8			
18		274 55.5	65 05.0	S12 05.0	72 18.2	S 9 12.2	350 44.6	S23 07.3	108 25.6	N 7 37.6	Kochab	137 20.3	N74 07.3
19		289 58.0	80 04.6	06.2	87 19.1	12.9	5 46.9	07.3	123 27.8	37.5	Markab	13 41.6	N15 15.3
20		305 00.4	95 04.2	07.3	102 20.0	13.5	20 49.2	07.3	138 30.0	37.4	Menkar	314 18.5	N 4 07.7
21		320 02.9	110 03.8	. . 08.5	117 20.9	. . 14.2	35 51.5	. . 07.3	153 32.1	. . 37.3	Menkent	148 12.2	S36 24.9
22		335 05.4	125 03.4	09.7	132 21.8	14.8	50 53.8	07.3	168 34.3	37.2	Miaplacidus	221 41.4	S69 44.9
23		350 07.8	140 02.9	10.8	147 22.7	15.4	65 56.2	07.3	183 36.5	37.1			
26 00		5 10.3	155 02.5	S12 12.0	162 23.6	S 9 16.1	80 58.5	S23 07.3	198 38.7	N 7 37.0	Mirfak	308 45.2	N49 53.6
01		20 12.8	170 02.1	13.2	177 24.5	16.7	96 00.8	07.3	213 40.9	36.9	Nunki	76 02.6	S26 17.2
02		35 15.2	185 01.7	14.3	192 25.4	17.3	111 03.1	07.2	228 43.0	36.7	Peacock	53 24.3	S56 42.6
03		50 17.7	200 01.2	. . 15.5	207 26.3	. . 18.0	126 05.4	. . 07.2	243 45.2	. . 36.6	Pollux	243 32.1	N28 00.3
04		65 20.1	215 00.8	16.6	222 27.2	18.6	141 07.7	07.2	258 47.4	36.5	Procyon	245 03.5	N 5 12.3
05		80 22.6	230 00.4	17.8	237 28.1	19.2	156 10.0	07.2	273 49.6	36.4			
06		95 25.1	244 59.9	S12 19.0	252 29.0	S 9 19.9	171 12.3	S23 07.2	288 51.8	N 7 36.3	Rasalhague	96 09.8	N12 33.3
07		110 27.5	259 59.5	20.1	267 29.9	20.5	186 14.7	07.2	303 53.9	36.2	Regulus	207 47.5	N11 55.5
08		125 30.0	274 59.1	21.3	282 30.8	21.1	201 17.0	07.2	318 56.1	36.1	Rigel	281 15.4	S 8 11.2
09	F	140 32.5	289 58.7	. . 22.4	297 31.7	. . 21.8	216 19.3	. . 07.2	333 58.3	. . 35.9	Rigil Kent.	139 57.4	S60 52.4
10	R	155 34.9	304 58.2	23.6	312 32.6	22.4	231 21.6	07.2	349 00.5	35.8	Sabik	102 16.7	S15 44.2
11	I	170 37.4	319 57.8	24.8	327 33.5	23.1	246 23.9	07.1	4 02.7	35.7			
12	D	185 39.9	334 57.4	S12 25.9	342 34.4	S 9 23.7	261 26.2	S23 07.1	19 04.8	N 7 35.6	Schedar	349 44.3	N56 35.3
13	A	200 42.3	349 56.9	27.1	357 35.3	24.3	276 28.5	07.1	34 07.0	35.5	Shaula	96 26.8	S37 06.8
14	Y	215 44.8	4 56.5	28.2	12 36.2	25.0	291 30.8	07.1	49 09.2	35.4	Sirius	258 36.9	S16 43.4
15		230 47.3	19 56.1	. . 29.4	27 37.1	. . 25.6	306 33.1	. . 07.1	64 11.4	. . 35.3	Spica	158 35.3	S11 12.4
16		245 49.7	34 55.7	30.5	42 38.0	26.2	321 35.4	07.1	79 13.6	35.2	Suhail	222 55.5	S43 27.8
17		260 52.2	49 55.2	31.7	57 38.9	26.9	336 37.7	07.1	94 15.7	35.0			
18		275 54.6	64 54.8	S12 32.8	72 39.8	S 9 27.5	351 40.0	S23 07.1	109 17.9	N 7 34.9	Vega	80 41.3	N38 47.7
19		290 57.1	79 54.4	34.0	87 40.7	28.1	6 42.3	07.1	124 20.1	34.8	Zuben'ubi	137 09.6	S16 04.7
20		305 59.6	94 53.9	35.2	102 41.6	28.8	21 44.7	07.0	139 22.3	34.7			
21		321 02.0	109 53.5	. . 36.3	117 42.5	. . 29.4	36 47.0	. . 07.0	154 24.5	. . 34.6			
22		336 04.5	124 53.1	37.5	132 43.4	30.0	51 49.3	07.0	169 26.6	34.5			
23		351 07.0	139 52.6	38.6	147 44.2	30.7	66 51.6	07.0	184 28.8	34.4			
Mer. Pass. (h m)		23 39.4	*v* −0.4	*d* 1.2	*v* 0.9	*d* 0.6	*v* 2.3	*d* 0.0	*v* 2.2	*d* 0.1			

	SHA	Mer. Pass.
	° ′	h m
Venus	151 01.4	13 40
Mars	157 50.8	13 11
Jupiter	75 51.7	18 37
Saturn	193 35.2	10 47

UT (d h)		SUN GHA ° ′	SUN Dec ° ′	MOON GHA ° ′	v ′	MOON Dec ° ′	d ′	HP ′
24 00		181 59.7	S 0 31.4	246 13.1	6.9	N23 11.6	9.2	58.8
01		196 59.9	32.4	260 39.0	7.0	23 02.4	9.3	58.8
02		212 00.1	33.3	275 05.0	7.0	22 53.1	9.5	58.8
03		227 00.3	. . 34.3	289 31.0	7.2	22 43.6	9.6	58.7
04		242 00.5	35.3	303 57.2	7.3	22 34.0	9.7	58.7
05		257 00.8	36.3	318 23.5	7.4	22 24.3	9.8	58.7
06		272 01.0	S 0 37.2	332 49.9	7.5	N22 14.5	10.0	58.7
07	W	287 01.2	38.2	347 16.4	7.6	22 04.5	10.1	58.7
08	E	302 01.4	39.2	1 43.0	7.7	21 54.4	10.2	58.7
09	D	317 01.6	. . 40.2	16 09.7	7.8	21 44.2	10.4	58.7
10	N	332 01.8	41.1	30 36.5	7.9	21 33.8	10.4	58.6
11	E	347 02.1	42.1	45 03.4	7.9	21 23.4	10.6	58.6
12	S	2 02.3	S 0 43.1	59 30.3	8.1	N21 12.8	10.8	58.6
13	D	17 02.5	44.1	73 57.4	8.2	21 02.0	10.8	58.6
14	A	32 02.7	45.0	88 24.6	8.3	20 51.2	10.9	58.6
15	Y	47 02.9	. . 46.0	102 51.9	8.4	20 40.3	11.1	58.6
16		62 03.1	47.0	117 19.3	8.5	20 29.2	11.1	58.6
17		77 03.4	48.0	131 46.8	8.6	20 18.1	11.3	58.6
18		92 03.6	S 0 48.9	146 14.4	8.6	N20 06.8	11.4	58.5
19		107 03.8	49.9	160 42.0	8.8	19 55.4	11.5	58.5
20		122 04.0	50.9	175 09.8	8.9	19 43.9	11.6	58.5
21		137 04.2	. . 51.9	189 37.7	9.0	19 32.3	11.7	58.5
22		152 04.4	52.8	204 05.7	9.1	19 20.6	11.8	58.5
23		167 04.7	53.8	218 33.8	9.1	19 08.8	11.9	58.5
25 00		182 04.9	S 0 54.8	233 01.9	9.3	N18 56.9	12.0	58.4
01		197 05.1	55.8	247 30.2	9.4	18 44.9	12.1	58.4
02		212 05.3	56.7	261 58.6	9.4	18 32.8	12.2	58.4
03		227 05.5	. . 57.7	276 27.0	9.6	18 20.6	12.3	58.4
04		242 05.7	58.7	290 55.6	9.6	18 08.3	12.4	58.4
05		257 05.9	0 59.6	305 24.2	9.8	17 55.9	12.5	58.4
06		272 06.2	S 1 00.6	319 53.0	9.8	N17 43.4	12.6	58.4
07		287 06.4	01.6	334 21.8	10.0	17 30.8	12.6	58.3
08	T	302 06.6	02.6	348 50.8	10.0	17 18.2	12.8	58.3
09	H	317 06.8	. . 03.5	3 19.8	10.1	17 05.4	12.8	58.3
10	U	332 07.0	04.5	17 48.9	10.2	16 52.6	12.9	58.3
11	R	347 07.2	05.5	32 18.1	10.3	16 39.7	13.0	58.3
12	S	2 07.5	S 1 06.5	46 47.4	10.4	N16 26.7	13.1	58.3
13	D	17 07.7	07.4	61 16.8	10.5	16 13.6	13.1	58.2
14	A	32 07.9	08.4	75 46.3	10.6	16 00.5	13.3	58.2
15	Y	47 08.1	. . 09.4	90 15.9	10.7	15 47.2	13.3	58.2
16		62 08.3	10.4	104 45.6	10.7	15 33.9	13.3	58.2
17		77 08.5	11.3	119 15.3	10.8	15 20.6	13.5	58.2
18		92 08.7	S 1 12.3	133 45.1	11.0	N15 07.1	13.5	58.2
19		107 09.0	13.3	148 15.1	11.0	14 53.6	13.6	58.1
20		122 09.2	14.3	162 45.1	11.1	14 40.0	13.7	58.1
21		137 09.4	. . 15.2	177 15.2	11.1	14 26.3	13.7	58.1
22		152 09.6	16.2	191 45.3	11.3	14 12.6	13.8	58.1
23		167 09.8	17.2	206 15.6	11.3	13 58.8	13.8	58.1
26 00		182 10.0	S 1 18.2	220 45.9	11.4	N13 45.0	13.9	58.1
01		197 10.2	19.1	235 16.3	11.5	13 31.1	14.0	58.0
02		212 10.4	20.1	249 46.8	11.6	13 17.1	14.0	58.0
03		227 10.7	. . 21.1	264 17.4	11.6	13 03.1	14.1	58.0
04		242 10.9	22.1	278 48.0	11.8	12 49.0	14.2	58.0
05		257 11.1	23.0	293 18.8	11.8	12 34.8	14.2	58.0
06		272 11.3	S 1 24.0	307 49.6	11.9	N12 20.6	14.2	57.9
07		287 11.5	25.0	322 20.5	11.9	12 06.4	14.3	57.9
08		302 11.7	25.9	336 51.4	12.0	11 52.1	14.4	57.9
09	F	317 11.9	. . 26.9	351 22.4	12.1	11 37.7	14.4	57.9
10	R	332 12.1	27.9	5 53.5	12.2	11 23.3	14.4	57.9
11	I	347 12.4	28.9	20 24.7	12.2	11 08.9	14.5	57.9
12	D	2 12.6	S 1 29.8	34 55.9	12.3	N10 54.4	14.6	57.8
13	A	17 12.8	30.8	49 27.2	12.4	10 39.8	14.5	57.8
14	Y	32 13.0	31.8	63 58.6	12.4	10 25.3	14.7	57.8
15		47 13.2	. . 32.8	78 30.0	12.5	10 10.6	14.6	57.8
16		62 13.4	33.7	93 01.5	12.6	9 56.0	14.7	57.8
17		77 13.6	34.7	107 33.1	12.6	9 41.3	14.8	57.7
18		92 13.8	S 1 35.7	122 04.7	12.7	N 9 26.5	14.7	57.7
19		107 14.1	36.7	136 36.4	12.8	9 11.8	14.8	57.7
20		122 14.3	37.6	151 08.2	12.8	8 57.0	14.9	57.7
21		137 14.5	. . 38.6	165 40.0	12.9	8 42.1	14.8	57.7
22		152 14.7	39.6	180 11.9	12.9	8 27.3	14.9	57.6
23		167 14.9	40.6	194 43.8	13.0	N 8 12.4	15.0	57.6
		SD 16.0	*d* 1.0	SD 16.0		15.9		15.8

Lat.	Twilight Naut.	Twilight Civil	Sunrise	Moonrise 24	Moonrise 25	Moonrise 26	Moonrise 27
°	h m	h m	h m	h m	h m	h m	h m
N 72	03 18	04 45	05 53	▭	▭	00 05	02 37
N 70	03 35	04 52	05 53	21 25	24 33	00 33	02 48
68	03 48	04 57	05 53	22 29	24 54	00 54	02 57
66	03 59	05 01	05 52	23 03	25 11	01 11	03 04
64	04 07	05 05	05 52	23 28	25 24	01 24	03 10
62	04 15	05 08	05 52	23 48	25 35	01 35	03 16
60	04 21	05 10	05 52	24 04	00 04	01 45	03 20
N 58	04 26	05 13	05 52	24 17	00 17	01 53	03 24
56	04 31	05 15	05 52	24 28	00 28	02 00	03 28
54	04 35	05 16	05 51	24 38	00 38	02 06	03 31
52	04 38	05 18	05 51	24 47	00 47	02 12	03 34
50	04 41	05 19	05 51	24 55	00 55	02 17	03 37
45	04 47	05 22	05 51	25 12	01 12	02 28	03 42
N 40	04 52	05 24	05 51	00 12	01 26	02 38	03 47
35	04 56	05 25	05 50	00 27	01 37	02 46	03 51
30	04 58	05 26	05 50	00 40	01 48	02 52	03 55
20	05 02	05 28	05 50	01 03	02 05	03 04	04 01
N 10	05 04	05 28	05 49	01 22	02 20	03 15	04 06
0	05 04	05 28	05 48	01 40	02 34	03 24	04 11
S 10	05 02	05 27	05 48	01 57	02 48	03 34	04 16
20	04 59	05 25	05 47	02 16	03 03	03 44	04 22
30	04 54	05 22	05 45	02 38	03 20	03 56	04 28
35	04 50	05 19	05 45	02 51	03 29	04 02	04 31
40	04 45	05 17	05 44	03 05	03 40	04 10	04 35
45	04 39	05 14	05 43	03 22	03 54	04 18	04 40
S 50	04 31	05 09	05 42	03 44	04 09	04 29	04 45
52	04 27	05 07	05 41	03 54	04 17	04 34	04 48
54	04 23	05 05	05 40	04 05	04 25	04 39	04 50
56	04 18	05 02	05 40	04 18	04 34	04 45	04 53
58	04 12	05 00	05 39	04 33	04 44	04 52	04 57
S 60	04 06	04 56	05 38	04 50	04 56	04 59	05 00

Lat.	Sunset	Twilight Civil	Twilight Naut.	Moonset 24	Moonset 25	Moonset 26	Moonset 27
°	h m	h m	h m	h m	h m	h m	h m
N 72	17 47	18 55	20 21	▭	18 44	17 53	17 18
N 70	17 48	18 49	20 04	19 35	18 14	17 39	17 13
68	17 48	18 44	19 52	18 30	17 51	17 28	17 09
66	17 49	18 40	19 42	17 54	17 33	17 18	17 06
64	17 49	18 36	19 33	17 28	17 18	17 10	17 03
62	17 49	18 34	19 26	17 07	17 06	17 04	17 01
60	17 50	18 31	19 20	16 51	16 55	16 57	16 59
N 58	17 50	18 29	19 15	16 36	16 46	16 52	16 57
56	17 50	18 27	19 11	16 24	16 38	16 47	16 55
54	17 50	18 26	19 07	16 13	16 30	16 43	16 54
52	17 51	18 24	19 04	16 04	16 24	16 39	16 52
50	17 51	18 23	19 01	15 55	16 18	16 36	16 51
45	17 51	18 21	18 55	15 37	16 05	16 28	16 48
N 40	17 52	18 19	18 50	15 22	15 54	16 21	16 46
35	17 52	18 17	18 47	15 09	15 45	16 16	16 44
30	17 52	18 16	18 44	14 58	15 37	16 11	16 42
20	17 53	18 15	18 41	14 39	15 23	16 02	16 38
N 10	17 54	18 15	18 39	14 22	15 10	15 54	16 36
0	17 55	18 15	18 39	14 06	14 58	15 47	16 33
S 10	17 56	18 17	18 41	13 50	14 46	15 40	16 30
20	17 57	18 19	18 44	13 33	14 34	15 32	16 27
30	17 58	18 22	18 50	13 13	14 19	15 23	16 24
35	17 59	18 24	18 54	13 01	14 10	15 17	16 22
40	18 00	18 27	18 59	12 47	14 00	15 11	16 19
45	18 01	18 30	19 05	12 31	13 49	15 04	16 17
S 50	18 02	18 35	19 13	12 11	13 35	14 55	16 13
52	18 03	18 37	19 17	12 02	13 28	14 51	16 12
54	18 04	18 39	19 22	11 51	13 21	14 47	16 10
56	18 05	18 42	19 27	11 39	13 12	14 42	16 09
58	18 05	18 45	19 32	11 25	13 03	14 37	16 07
S 60	18 06	18 48	19 39	11 08	12 52	14 31	16 04

Day	SUN Eqn. of Time 00^h	SUN Eqn. of Time 12^h	SUN Mer. Pass.	MOON Mer. Pass. Upper	MOON Mer. Pass. Lower	MOON Age	MOON Phase
d	m s	m s	h m	h m	h m	d %	
24	07 58	08 09	11 52	07 53	20 20	25 25	
25	08 19	08 29	11 52	08 46	21 11	26 16	
26	08 40	08 50	11 51	09 36	21 59	27 9	

	UT d h	ARIES GHA	VENUS −3.9 GHA	VENUS Dec	MARS +1.6 GHA	MARS Dec	JUPITER −2.3 GHA	JUPITER Dec	SATURN +1.0 GHA	SATURN Dec
		° ′	° ′	° ′	° ′	° ′	° ′	° ′	° ′	° ′
	27 00	6 09.4	154 52.2	S12 39.8	162 45.1	S 9 31.3	81 53.9	S23 07.0	199 31.0	N 7 34.2
	01	21 11.9	169 51.8	40.9	177 46.0	31.9	96 56.2	07.0	214 33.2	34.1
	02	36 14.4	184 51.3	42.1	192 46.9	32.6	111 58.5	07.0	229 35.4	34.0
	03	51 16.8	199 50.9	. . 43.2	207 47.8	. . 33.2	127 00.8	. . 07.0	244 37.5	. . 33.9
	04	66 19.3	214 50.5	44.4	222 48.7	33.8	142 03.1	06.9	259 39.7	33.8
	05	81 21.7	229 50.0	45.5	237 49.6	34.5	157 05.4	06.9	274 41.9	33.7
	06	96 24.2	244 49.6	S12 46.7	252 50.5	S 9 35.1	172 07.7	S23 06.9	289 44.1	N 7 33.6
	07	111 26.7	259 49.1	47.8	267 51.4	35.7	187 10.0	06.9	304 46.3	33.5
S	08	126 29.1	274 48.7	49.0	282 52.3	36.4	202 12.3	06.9	319 48.4	33.3
A	09	141 31.6	289 48.3	. . 50.1	297 53.2	. . 37.0	217 14.6	. . 06.9	334 50.6	. . 33.2
T	10	156 34.1	304 47.8	51.2	312 54.1	37.6	232 16.9	06.9	349 52.8	33.1
U	11	171 36.5	319 47.4	52.4	327 55.0	38.3	247 19.2	06.9	4 55.0	33.0
R	12	186 39.0	334 47.0	S12 53.5	342 55.9	S 9 38.9	262 21.5	S23 06.8	19 57.2	N 7 32.9
D	13	201 41.5	349 46.5	54.7	357 56.8	39.5	277 23.8	06.8	34 59.3	32.8
	14	216 43.9	4 46.1	55.8	12 57.6	40.2	292 26.1	06.8	50 01.5	32.7
A	15	231 46.4	19 45.6	. . 57.0	27 58.5	. . 40.8	307 28.4	. . 06.8	65 03.7	. . 32.6
Y	16	246 48.9	34 45.2	58.1	42 59.4	41.4	322 30.7	06.8	80 05.9	32.4
	17	261 51.3	49 44.8	12 59.3	58 00.3	42.1	337 33.0	06.8	95 08.1	32.3
	18	276 53.8	64 44.3	S13 00.4	73 01.2	S 9 42.7	352 35.3	S23 06.8	110 10.2	N 7 32.2
	19	291 56.2	79 43.9	01.5	88 02.1	43.3	7 37.6	06.8	125 12.4	32.1
	20	306 58.7	94 43.4	02.7	103 03.0	44.0	22 39.9	06.7	140 14.6	32.0
	21	322 01.2	109 43.0	. . 03.8	118 03.9	. . 44.6	37 42.2	. . 06.7	155 16.8	. . 31.9
	22	337 03.6	124 42.5	05.0	133 04.8	45.2	52 44.5	06.7	170 19.0	31.8
	23	352 06.1	139 42.1	06.1	148 05.7	45.9	67 46.8	06.7	185 21.2	31.7
	28 00	7 08.6	154 41.7	S13 07.2	163 06.6	S 9 46.5	82 49.1	S23 06.7	200 23.3	N 7 31.5
	01	22 11.0	169 41.2	08.4	178 07.4	47.1	97 51.4	06.7	215 25.5	31.4
	02	37 13.5	184 40.8	09.5	193 08.3	47.8	112 53.7	06.7	230 27.7	31.3
	03	52 16.0	199 40.3	. . 10.7	208 09.2	. . 48.4	127 56.0	. . 06.7	245 29.9	. . 31.2
	04	67 18.4	214 39.9	11.8	223 10.1	49.0	142 58.3	06.6	260 32.1	31.1
	05	82 20.9	229 39.4	12.9	238 11.0	49.7	158 00.6	06.6	275 34.2	31.0
	06	97 23.4	244 39.0	S13 14.1	253 11.9	S 9 50.3	173 02.9	S23 06.6	290 36.4	N 7 30.9
	07	112 25.8	259 38.5	15.2	268 12.8	50.9	188 05.2	06.6	305 38.6	30.8
	08	127 28.3	274 38.1	16.3	283 13.7	51.6	203 07.4	06.6	320 40.8	30.6
S	09	142 30.7	289 37.6	. . 17.5	298 14.6	. . 52.2	218 09.7	. . 06.6	335 43.0	. . 30.5
U	10	157 33.2	304 37.2	18.6	313 15.4	52.8	233 12.0	06.6	350 45.1	30.4
N	11	172 35.7	319 36.7	19.7	328 16.3	53.5	248 14.3	06.5	5 47.3	30.3
D	12	187 38.1	334 36.3	S13 20.9	343 17.2	S 9 54.1	263 16.6	S23 06.5	20 49.5	N 7 30.2
A	13	202 40.6	349 35.8	22.0	358 18.1	54.7	278 18.9	06.5	35 51.7	30.1
Y	14	217 43.1	4 35.4	23.1	13 19.0	55.4	293 21.2	06.5	50 53.9	30.0
	15	232 45.5	19 34.9	. . 24.3	28 19.9	. . 56.0	308 23.5	. . 06.5	65 56.1	. . 29.9
	16	247 48.0	34 34.5	25.4	43 20.8	56.6	323 25.8	06.5	80 58.2	29.7
	17	262 50.5	49 34.0	26.5	58 21.6	57.2	338 28.1	06.5	96 00.4	29.6
	18	277 52.9	64 33.6	S13 27.6	73 22.5	S 9 57.9	353 30.4	S23 06.5	111 02.6	N 7 29.5
	19	292 55.4	79 33.1	28.8	88 23.4	58.5	8 32.7	06.4	126 04.8	29.4
	20	307 57.8	94 32.7	29.9	103 24.3	59.1	23 34.9	06.4	141 07.0	29.3
	21	323 00.3	109 32.2	. . 31.0	118 25.2	9 59.8	38 37.2	. . 06.4	156 09.1	. . 29.2
	22	338 02.8	124 31.8	32.2	133 26.1	10 00.4	53 39.5	06.4	171 11.3	29.1
	23	353 05.2	139 31.3	33.3	148 27.0	01.0	68 41.8	06.4	186 13.5	29.0
	29 00	8 07.7	154 30.9	S13 34.4	163 27.8	S10 01.7	83 44.1	S23 06.4	201 15.7	N 7 28.8
	01	23 10.2	169 30.4	35.5	178 28.7	02.3	98 46.4	06.4	216 17.9	28.7
	02	38 12.6	184 30.0	36.7	193 29.6	02.9	113 48.7	06.3	231 20.1	28.6
	03	53 15.1	199 29.5	. . 37.8	208 30.5	. . 03.5	128 51.0	. . 06.3	246 22.2	. . 28.5
	04	68 17.6	214 29.1	38.9	223 31.4	04.2	143 53.2	06.3	261 24.4	28.4
	05	83 20.0	229 28.6	40.0	238 32.3	04.8	158 55.5	06.3	276 26.6	28.3
	06	98 22.5	244 28.1	S13 41.2	253 33.2	S10 05.4	173 57.8	S23 06.3	291 28.8	N 7 28.2
	07	113 25.0	259 27.7	42.3	268 34.0	06.1	189 00.1	06.3	306 31.0	28.1
	08	128 27.4	274 27.2	43.4	283 34.9	06.7	204 02.4	06.3	321 33.2	27.9
M	09	143 29.9	289 26.8	. . 44.5	298 35.8	. . 07.3	219 04.7	. . 06.2	336 35.3	. . 27.8
O	10	158 32.3	304 26.3	45.6	313 36.7	08.0	234 07.0	06.2	351 37.5	27.7
N	11	173 34.8	319 25.9	46.8	328 37.6	08.6	249 09.2	06.2	6 39.7	27.6
D	12	188 37.3	334 25.4	S13 47.9	343 38.5	S10 09.2	264 11.5	S23 06.2	21 41.9	N 7 27.5
A	13	203 39.7	349 24.9	49.0	358 39.3	09.8	279 13.8	06.2	36 44.1	27.4
Y	14	218 42.2	4 24.5	50.1	13 40.2	10.5	294 16.1	06.2	51 46.3	27.3
	15	233 44.7	19 24.0	. . 51.2	28 41.1	. . 11.1	309 18.4	. . 06.2	66 48.4	. . 27.2
	16	248 47.1	34 23.6	52.4	43 42.0	11.7	324 20.7	06.1	81 50.6	27.0
	17	263 49.6	49 23.1	53.5	58 42.9	12.4	339 22.9	06.1	96 52.8	26.9
	18	278 52.1	64 22.6	S13 54.6	73 43.7	S10 13.0	354 25.2	S23 06.1	111 55.0	N 7 26.8
	19	293 54.5	79 22.2	55.7	88 44.6	13.6	9 27.5	06.1	126 57.2	26.7
	20	308 57.0	94 21.7	56.8	103 45.5	14.2	24 29.8	06.1	141 59.3	26.6
	21	323 59.4	109 21.2	. . 57.9	118 46.4	. . 14.9	39 32.1	. . 06.1	157 01.5	. . 26.5
	22	339 01.9	124 20.8	13 59.1	133 47.3	15.5	54 34.4	06.1	172 03.7	26.4
	23	354 04.4	139 20.3	S14 00.2	148 48.2	16.1	69 36.6	06.0	187 05.9	26.3
	Mer. Pass.	h m 23 27.6	v −0.4	d 1.1	v 0.9	d 0.6	v 2.3	d 0.0	v 2.2	d 0.1

STARS

Name	SHA	Dec
	° ′	° ′
Acamar	315 20.6	S40 15.8
Achernar	335 28.6	S57 11.3
Acrux	173 14.3	S63 08.9
Adhara	255 15.4	S28 58.7
Aldebaran	290 53.3	N16 31.8
Alioth	166 24.1	N55 54.8
Alkaid	153 01.9	N49 16.2
Al Na'ir	27 47.6	S46 55.1
Alnilam	275 49.9	S 1 11.5
Alphard	217 59.8	S 8 41.6
Alphecca	126 14.2	N26 41.2
Alpheratz	357 46.9	N29 08.5
Altair	62 11.6	N 8 53.6
Ankaa	353 18.6	S42 15.3
Antares	112 30.8	S26 27.2
Arcturus	145 59.2	N19 08.3
Atria	107 36.1	S69 02.9
Avior	234 20.0	S59 31.9
Bellatrix	278 35.7	N 6 21.7
Betelgeuse	271 05.1	N 7 24.7
Canopus	263 57.7	S52 41.6
Capella	280 39.6	N46 00.4
Deneb	49 33.8	N45 19.0
Denebola	182 37.5	N14 31.4
Diphda	348 59.0	S17 56.1
Dubhe	193 56.3	N61 42.1
Elnath	278 17.0	N28 37.0
Eltanin	90 47.8	N51 29.5
Enif	33 50.4	N 9 55.1
Fomalhaut	15 27.4	S29 34.4
Gacrux	172 05.7	S57 09.7
Gienah	175 56.3	S17 35.4
Hadar	148 53.8	S60 25.1
Hamal	328 04.5	N23 30.4
Kaus Aust.	83 48.5	S34 23.0
Kochab	137 20.3	N74 07.3
Markab	13 41.6	N15 15.4
Menkar	314 18.5	N 4 07.7
Menkent	148 12.2	S36 24.9
Miaplacidus	221 41.4	S69 44.9
Mirfak	308 45.2	N49 53.6
Nunki	76 02.6	S26 17.2
Peacock	53 24.3	S56 42.6
Pollux	243 32.1	N28 00.3
Procyon	245 03.5	N 5 12.3
Rasalhague	96 09.8	N12 33.3
Regulus	207 47.5	N11 55.5
Rigel	281 15.4	S 8 11.2
Rigil Kent.	139 57.4	S60 52.4
Sabik	102 16.7	S15 44.2
Schedar	349 44.3	N56 35.3
Shaula	96 26.8	S37 06.8
Sirius	258 36.9	S16 43.4
Spica	158 35.3	S11 12.4
Suhail	222 55.5	S43 27.8
Vega	80 41.4	N38 47.7
Zuben'ubi	137 09.6	S16 04.7

	SHA	Mer. Pass.
	° ′	h m
Venus	147 33.1	13 42
Mars	155 58.0	13 07
Jupiter	75 40.5	18 26
Saturn	193 14.8	10 37

UT d	UT h	SUN GHA	SUN Dec	MOON GHA	v	MOON Dec	d	HP
		° ′	° ′	° ′	′	° ′	′	′
27	00	182 15.1	S 1 41.5	209 15.8	13.0	N 7 57.4	14.9	57.6
	01	197 15.3	42.5	223 47.8	13.1	7 42.5	15.0	57.6
	02	212 15.5	43.5	238 19.9	13.2	7 27.5	15.0	57.6
	03	227 15.8	. . 44.5	252 52.1	13.2	7 12.5	15.0	57.5
	04	242 16.0	45.4	267 24.3	13.2	6 57.5	15.1	57.5
	05	257 16.2	46.4	281 56.5	13.3	6 42.4	15.1	57.5
	06	272 16.4	S 1 47.4	296 28.8	13.4	N 6 27.3	15.1	57.5
	07	287 16.6	48.3	311 01.2	13.4	6 12.2	15.1	57.5
SATURDAY	08	302 16.8	49.3	325 33.6	13.5	5 57.1	15.1	57.4
	09	317 17.0	. . 50.3	340 06.1	13.5	5 42.0	15.1	57.4
	10	332 17.2	51.3	354 38.6	13.5	5 26.9	15.2	57.4
	11	347 17.4	52.2	9 11.1	13.6	5 11.7	15.2	57.4
	12	2 17.6	S 1 53.2	23 43.7	13.6	N 4 56.5	15.1	57.4
	13	17 17.9	54.2	38 16.3	13.7	4 41.4	15.2	57.3
	14	32 18.1	55.2	52 49.0	13.7	4 26.2	15.2	57.3
	15	47 18.3	. . 56.1	67 21.7	13.7	4 11.0	15.3	57.3
	16	62 18.5	57.1	81 54.4	13.8	3 55.7	15.2	57.3
	17	77 18.7	58.1	96 27.2	13.8	3 40.5	15.2	57.3
	18	92 18.9	S 1 59.1	111 00.0	13.9	N 3 25.3	15.2	57.2
	19	107 19.1	2 00.0	125 32.9	13.9	3 10.1	15.3	57.2
	20	122 19.3	01.0	140 05.8	13.9	2 54.8	15.2	57.2
	21	137 19.5	. . 02.0	154 38.7	14.0	2 39.6	15.2	57.2
	22	152 19.7	02.9	169 11.7	14.0	2 24.4	15.3	57.2
	23	167 20.0	03.9	183 44.7	14.0	2 09.1	15.2	57.1
28	00	182 20.2	S 2 04.9	198 17.7	14.1	N 1 53.9	15.2	57.1
	01	197 20.4	05.9	212 50.8	14.0	1 38.7	15.2	57.1
	02	212 20.6	06.8	227 23.8	14.1	1 23.5	15.3	57.1
	03	227 20.8	. . 07.8	241 56.9	14.2	1 08.2	15.2	57.0
	04	242 21.0	08.8	256 30.1	14.1	0 53.0	15.2	57.0
	05	257 21.2	09.8	271 03.2	14.2	0 37.8	15.2	57.0
	06	272 21.4	S 2 10.7	285 36.4	14.2	N 0 22.6	15.2	57.0
	07	287 21.6	11.7	300 09.6	14.3	N 0 07.4	15.1	57.0
	08	302 21.8	12.7	314 42.9	14.2	S 0 07.7	15.2	56.9
SUNDAY	09	317 22.0	. . 13.6	329 16.1	14.3	0 22.9	15.2	56.9
	10	332 22.2	14.6	343 49.4	14.3	0 38.1	15.1	56.9
	11	347 22.5	15.6	358 22.7	14.3	0 53.2	15.1	56.9
	12	2 22.7	S 2 16.6	12 56.0	14.3	S 1 08.3	15.1	56.8
	13	17 22.9	17.5	27 29.3	14.3	1 23.4	15.1	56.8
	14	32 23.1	18.5	42 02.6	14.4	1 38.5	15.1	56.8
	15	47 23.3	. . 19.5	56 36.0	14.3	1 53.6	15.0	56.8
	16	62 23.5	20.5	71 09.3	14.4	2 08.6	15.0	56.8
	17	77 23.7	21.4	85 42.7	14.4	2 23.6	15.1	56.7
	18	92 23.9	S 2 22.4	100 16.1	14.4	S 2 38.7	14.9	56.7
	19	107 24.1	23.4	114 49.5	14.4	2 53.6	15.0	56.7
	20	122 24.3	24.3	129 22.9	14.4	3 08.6	14.9	56.7
	21	137 24.5	. . 25.3	143 56.3	14.5	3 23.5	14.9	56.6
	22	152 24.7	26.3	158 29.8	14.4	3 38.4	14.9	56.6
	23	167 24.9	27.3	173 03.2	14.4	3 53.3	14.9	56.6
29	00	182 25.1	S 2 28.2	187 36.6	14.5	S 4 08.2	14.8	56.6
	01	197 25.4	29.2	202 10.1	14.4	4 23.0	14.8	56.6
	02	212 25.6	30.2	216 43.5	14.5	4 37.8	14.7	56.5
	03	227 25.8	. . 31.2	231 17.0	14.4	4 52.5	14.8	56.5
	04	242 26.0	32.1	245 50.4	14.5	5 07.3	14.6	56.5
	05	257 26.2	33.1	260 23.9	14.4	5 21.9	14.7	56.5
	06	272 26.4	S 2 34.1	274 57.3	14.5	S 5 36.6	14.6	56.4
	07	287 26.6	35.0	289 30.8	14.4	5 51.2	14.6	56.4
	08	302 26.8	36.0	304 04.2	14.5	6 05.8	14.6	56.4
MONDAY	09	317 27.0	. . 37.0	318 37.7	14.4	6 20.4	14.5	56.4
	10	332 27.2	38.0	333 11.1	14.4	6 34.9	14.4	56.4
	11	347 27.4	38.9	347 44.5	14.5	6 49.3	14.5	56.3
	12	2 27.6	S 2 39.9	2 18.0	14.4	S 7 03.8	14.3	56.3
	13	17 27.8	40.9	16 51.4	14.4	7 18.1	14.4	56.3
	14	32 28.0	41.8	31 24.8	14.4	7 32.5	14.3	56.3
	15	47 28.2	. . 42.8	45 58.2	14.4	7 46.8	14.2	56.2
	16	62 28.4	43.8	60 31.6	14.4	8 01.0	14.2	56.2
	17	77 28.6	44.8	75 05.0	14.4	8 15.2	14.2	56.2
	18	92 28.8	S 2 45.7	89 38.4	14.3	S 8 29.4	14.1	56.2
	19	107 29.0	46.7	104 11.7	14.4	8 43.5	14.1	56.1
	20	122 29.3	47.7	118 45.1	14.3	8 57.6	14.0	56.1
	21	137 29.5	. . 48.6	133 18.4	14.4	9 11.6	13.9	56.1
	22	152 29.7	49.6	147 51.8	14.3	9 25.5	14.0	56.1
	23	167 29.9	50.6	162 25.1	14.2	S 9 39.5	13.8	56.1
		SD 16.0	d 1.0	SD 15.6		15.5		15.3

Lat.	Twilight Naut.	Twilight Civil	Sunrise	Moonrise 27	Moonrise 28	Moonrise 29	Moonrise 30
°	h m	h m	h m	h m	h m	h m	h m
N 72	03 35	04 59	06 07	02 37	04 49	06 57	09 14
N 70	03 49	05 04	06 05	02 48	04 50	06 48	08 51
68	04 00	05 08	06 03	02 57	04 50	06 41	08 34
66	04 09	05 11	06 02	03 04	04 51	06 35	08 20
64	04 17	05 14	06 01	03 10	04 51	06 30	08 09
62	04 23	05 16	06 00	03 16	04 52	06 25	07 59
60	04 28	05 18	05 59	03 20	04 52	06 22	07 51
N 58	04 33	05 19	05 58	03 24	04 52	06 18	07 44
56	04 37	05 20	05 58	03 28	04 53	06 15	07 38
54	04 40	05 22	05 57	03 31	04 53	06 13	07 32
52	04 43	05 23	05 56	03 34	04 53	06 10	07 27
50	04 46	05 24	05 56	03 37	04 53	06 08	07 22
45	04 51	05 25	05 55	03 42	04 54	06 04	07 13
N 40	04 55	05 27	05 54	03 47	04 54	06 00	07 05
35	04 58	05 27	05 53	03 51	04 54	05 56	06 58
30	05 00	05 28	05 52	03 55	04 55	05 53	06 52
20	05 03	05 28	05 50	04 01	04 55	05 48	06 41
N 10	05 03	05 28	05 49	04 06	04 56	05 44	06 32
0	05 03	05 27	05 47	04 11	04 56	05 40	06 24
S 10	05 00	05 25	05 46	04 16	04 57	05 36	06 16
20	04 56	05 22	05 44	04 22	04 57	05 32	06 07
30	04 50	05 18	05 42	04 28	04 58	05 27	05 57
35	04 45	05 15	05 40	04 31	04 58	05 24	05 51
40	04 40	05 12	05 39	04 35	04 59	05 21	05 45
45	04 33	05 08	05 37	04 40	04 59	05 18	05 37
S 50	04 24	05 03	05 35	04 45	05 00	05 14	05 28
52	04 20	05 00	05 34	04 48	05 00	05 12	05 24
54	04 15	04 57	05 33	04 50	05 00	05 10	05 20
56	04 09	04 54	05 32	04 53	05 00	05 07	05 15
58	04 03	04 51	05 30	04 57	05 01	05 05	05 09
S 60	03 56	04 47	05 29	05 00	05 01	05 02	05 03

Lat.	Sunset	Twilight Civil	Twilight Naut.	Moonset 27	Moonset 28	Moonset 29	Moonset 30
°	h m	h m	h m	h m	h m	h m	h m
N 72	17 32	18 39	20 02	17 18	16 46	16 13	15 30
N 70	17 34	18 35	19 49	17 13	16 50	16 25	15 55
68	17 36	18 31	19 38	17 09	16 52	16 35	16 14
66	17 37	18 28	19 29	17 06	16 54	16 43	16 29
64	17 39	18 26	19 22	17 03	16 56	16 49	16 42
62	17 40	18 24	19 16	17 01	16 58	16 55	16 53
60	17 41	18 22	19 11	16 59	17 00	17 01	17 02
N 58	17 42	18 21	19 06	16 57	17 01	17 05	17 10
56	17 42	18 19	19 03	16 55	17 02	17 09	17 17
54	17 43	18 18	18 59	16 54	17 03	17 13	17 24
52	17 44	18 17	18 57	16 52	17 04	17 16	17 30
50	17 44	18 16	18 54	16 51	17 05	17 19	17 35
45	17 46	18 15	18 49	16 48	17 07	17 26	17 46
N 40	17 47	18 14	18 45	16 46	17 09	17 32	17 56
35	17 48	18 13	18 42	16 44	17 10	17 36	18 04
30	17 49	18 13	18 40	16 42	17 11	17 41	18 11
20	17 51	18 12	18 38	16 38	17 13	17 48	18 24
N 10	17 52	18 13	18 37	16 36	17 15	17 55	18 35
0	17 54	18 14	18 38	16 33	17 17	18 01	18 45
S 10	17 55	18 16	18 41	16 30	17 19	18 07	18 56
20	17 57	18 19	18 45	16 27	17 21	18 14	19 07
30	18 00	18 24	18 52	16 24	17 23	18 22	19 20
35	18 01	18 26	18 56	16 22	17 24	18 26	19 27
40	18 03	18 30	19 02	16 19	17 26	18 31	19 36
45	18 05	18 34	19 09	16 17	17 27	18 37	19 46
S 50	18 07	18 39	19 18	16 13	17 29	18 44	19 58
52	18 08	18 42	19 23	16 12	17 30	18 47	20 04
54	18 09	18 45	19 28	16 10	17 31	18 51	20 10
56	18 11	18 48	19 33	16 09	17 32	18 55	20 17
58	18 12	18 52	19 40	16 07	17 33	18 59	20 25
S 60	18 14	18 56	19 47	16 04	17 35	19 04	20 34

Day	SUN Eqn. of Time 00^h	SUN Eqn. of Time 12^h	SUN Mer. Pass.	MOON Mer. Pass. Upper	MOON Mer. Pass. Lower	MOON Age	MOON Phase
d	m s	m s	h m	h m	h m	d %	
27	09 00	09 10	11 51	10 22	22 45	28 4	
28	09 20	09 30	11 50	11 07	23 29	29 1	●
29	09 40	09 50	11 50	11 51	24 12	00 0	

UT d	UT h	ARIES GHA	VENUS −3.9 GHA	VENUS Dec	MARS +1.6 GHA	MARS Dec	JUPITER −2.3 GHA	JUPITER Dec	SATURN +1.0 GHA	SATURN Dec
		° ′	° ′	° ′	° ′	° ′	° ′	° ′	° ′	° ′
30 TUESDAY	00	9 06.8	154 19.9	S14 01.3	163 49.0	S10 16.7	84 38.9	S23 06.0	202 08.1	N 7 26.2
	01	24 09.3	169 19.4	02.4	178 49.9	17.4	99 41.2	06.0	217 10.3	26.0
	02	39 11.8	184 18.9	03.5	193 50.8	18.0	114 43.5	06.0	232 12.4	25.9
	03	54 14.2	199 18.5	04.6	208 51.7	18.6	129 45.8	06.0	247 14.6	25.8
	04	69 16.7	214 18.0	05.7	223 52.6	19.3	144 48.0	06.0	262 16.8	25.7
	05	84 19.2	229 17.5	06.8	238 53.4	19.9	159 50.3	06.0	277 19.0	25.6
	06	99 21.6	244 17.1	S14 07.9	253 54.3	S10 20.5	174 52.6	S23 05.9	292 21.2	N 7 25.5
	07	114 24.1	259 16.6	09.1	268 55.2	21.1	189 54.9	05.9	307 23.4	25.4
	08	129 26.6	274 16.1	10.2	283 56.1	21.8	204 57.1	05.9	322 25.6	25.3
	09	144 29.0	289 15.7	11.3	298 57.0	22.4	219 59.4	05.9	337 27.7	25.1
	10	159 31.5	304 15.2	12.4	313 57.8	23.0	235 01.7	05.9	352 29.9	25.0
	11	174 33.9	319 14.7	13.5	328 58.7	23.6	250 04.0	05.9	7 32.1	24.9
	12	189 36.4	334 14.2	S14 14.6	343 59.6	S10 24.3	265 06.3	S23 05.9	22 34.3	N 7 24.8
	13	204 38.9	349 13.8	15.7	359 00.5	24.9	280 08.5	05.8	37 36.5	24.7
	14	219 41.3	4 13.3	16.8	14 01.3	25.5	295 10.8	05.8	52 38.7	24.6
	15	234 43.8	19 12.8	17.9	29 02.2	26.2	310 13.1	05.8	67 40.8	24.5
	16	249 46.3	34 12.4	19.0	44 03.1	26.8	325 15.4	05.8	82 43.0	24.4
	17	264 48.7	49 11.9	20.1	59 04.0	27.4	340 17.6	05.8	97 45.2	24.3
	18	279 51.2	64 11.4	S14 21.2	74 04.9	S10 28.0	355 19.9	S23 05.8	112 47.4	N 7 24.1
	19	294 53.7	79 11.0	22.3	89 05.7	28.7	10 22.2	05.8	127 49.6	24.0
	20	309 56.1	94 10.5	23.4	104 06.6	29.3	25 24.5	05.7	142 51.8	23.9
	21	324 58.6	109 10.0	24.5	119 07.5	29.9	40 26.7	05.7	157 53.9	23.8
	22	340 01.0	124 09.5	25.6	134 08.4	30.5	55 29.0	05.7	172 56.1	23.7
	23	355 03.5	139 09.1	26.7	149 09.2	31.2	70 31.3	05.7	187 58.3	23.6
1 WEDNESDAY	00	10 06.0	154 08.6	S14 27.8	164 10.1	S10 31.8	85 33.5	S23 05.7	203 00.5	N 7 23.5
	01	25 08.4	169 08.1	28.9	179 11.0	32.4	100 35.8	05.7	218 02.7	23.4
	02	40 10.9	184 07.6	30.0	194 11.9	33.0	115 38.1	05.6	233 04.9	23.3
	03	55 13.4	199 07.2	31.1	209 12.7	33.7	130 40.4	05.6	248 07.1	23.1
	04	70 15.8	214 06.7	32.2	224 13.6	34.3	145 42.6	05.6	263 09.2	23.0
	05	85 18.3	229 06.2	33.3	239 14.5	34.9	160 44.9	05.6	278 11.4	22.9
	06	100 20.8	244 05.7	S14 34.4	254 15.4	S10 35.5	175 47.2	S23 05.6	293 13.6	N 7 22.8
	07	115 23.2	259 05.2	35.5	269 16.2	36.2	190 49.4	05.6	308 15.8	22.7
	08	130 25.7	274 04.8	36.6	284 17.1	36.8	205 51.7	05.5	323 18.0	22.6
	09	145 28.2	289 04.3	37.7	299 18.0	37.4	220 54.0	05.5	338 20.2	22.5
	10	160 30.6	304 03.8	38.8	314 18.9	38.0	235 56.3	05.5	353 22.3	22.4
	11	175 33.1	319 03.3	39.9	329 19.7	38.7	250 58.5	05.5	8 24.5	22.3
	12	190 35.5	334 02.9	S14 41.0	344 20.6	S10 39.3	266 00.8	S23 05.5	23 26.7	N 7 22.1
	13	205 38.0	349 02.4	42.1	359 21.5	39.9	281 03.1	05.5	38 28.9	22.0
	14	220 40.5	4 01.9	43.2	14 22.4	40.5	296 05.3	05.5	53 31.1	21.9
	15	235 42.9	19 01.4	44.2	29 23.2	41.2	311 07.6	05.4	68 33.3	21.8
	16	250 45.4	34 00.9	45.3	44 24.1	41.8	326 09.9	05.4	83 35.5	21.7
	17	265 47.9	49 00.4	46.4	59 25.0	42.4	341 12.1	05.4	98 37.6	21.6
	18	280 50.3	64 00.0	S14 47.5	74 25.8	S10 43.0	356 14.4	S23 05.4	113 39.8	N 7 21.5
	19	295 52.8	78 59.5	48.6	89 26.7	43.6	11 16.7	05.4	128 42.0	21.4
	20	310 55.3	93 59.0	49.7	104 27.6	44.3	26 18.9	05.4	143 44.2	21.3
	21	325 57.7	108 58.5	50.8	119 28.5	44.9	41 21.2	05.3	158 46.4	21.1
	22	341 00.2	123 58.0	51.9	134 29.3	45.5	56 23.5	05.3	173 48.6	21.0
	23	356 02.6	138 57.5	52.9	149 30.2	46.1	71 25.7	05.3	188 50.8	20.9
2 THURSDAY	00	11 05.1	153 57.1	S14 54.0	164 31.1	S10 46.8	86 28.0	S23 05.3	203 52.9	N 7 20.8
	01	26 07.6	168 56.6	55.1	179 31.9	47.4	101 30.2	05.3	218 55.1	20.7
	02	41 10.0	183 56.1	56.2	194 32.8	48.0	116 32.5	05.3	233 57.3	20.6
	03	56 12.5	198 55.6	57.3	209 33.7	48.6	131 34.8	05.2	248 59.5	20.5
	04	71 15.0	213 55.1	58.4	224 34.6	49.3	146 37.0	05.2	264 01.7	20.4
	05	86 17.4	228 54.6	14 59.4	239 35.4	49.9	161 39.3	05.2	279 03.9	20.3
	06	101 19.9	243 54.1	S15 00.5	254 36.3	S10 50.5	176 41.6	S23 05.2	294 06.1	N 7 20.2
	07	116 22.4	258 53.6	01.6	269 37.2	51.1	191 43.8	05.2	309 08.2	20.0
	08	131 24.8	273 53.2	02.7	284 38.0	51.7	206 46.1	05.2	324 10.4	19.9
	09	146 27.3	288 52.7	03.8	299 38.9	52.4	221 48.3	05.1	339 12.6	19.8
	10	161 29.8	303 52.2	04.8	314 39.8	53.0	236 50.6	05.1	354 14.8	19.7
	11	176 32.2	318 51.7	05.9	329 40.6	53.6	251 52.9	05.1	9 17.0	19.6
	12	191 34.7	333 51.2	S15 07.0	344 41.5	S10 54.2	266 55.1	S23 05.1	24 19.2	N 7 19.5
	13	206 37.1	348 50.7	08.1	359 42.4	54.9	281 57.4	05.1	39 21.4	19.4
	14	221 39.6	3 50.2	09.2	14 43.2	55.5	296 59.6	05.1	54 23.5	19.3
	15	236 42.1	18 49.7	10.2	29 44.1	56.1	312 01.9	05.0	69 25.7	19.2
	16	251 44.5	33 49.2	11.3	44 45.0	56.7	327 04.2	05.0	84 27.9	19.0
	17	266 47.0	48 48.7	12.4	59 45.8	57.3	342 06.4	05.0	99 30.1	18.9
	18	281 49.5	63 48.2	S15 13.5	74 46.7	S10 58.0	357 08.7	S23 05.0	114 32.3	N 7 18.8
	19	296 51.9	78 47.7	14.5	89 47.6	58.6	12 10.9	05.0	129 34.5	18.7
	20	311 54.4	93 47.3	15.6	104 48.5	59.2	27 13.2	05.0	144 36.7	18.6
	21	326 56.9	108 46.8	16.7	119 49.3	10 59.8	42 15.5	04.9	159 38.8	18.5
	22	341 59.3	123 46.3	17.7	134 50.2	11 00.4	57 17.7	04.9	174 41.0	18.4
	23	357 01.8	138 45.8	18.8	149 51.1	S11 01.1	72 20.0	04.9	189 43.2	18.3
Mer. Pass.		h m 23 15.8	v −0.5	d 1.1	v 0.9	d 0.6	v 2.3	d 0.0	v 2.2	d 0.1

STARS

Name	SHA	Dec
	° ′	° ′
Acamar	315 20.6	S40 15.8
Achernar	335 28.6	S57 11.3
Acrux	173 14.3	S63 08.9
Adhara	255 15.4	S28 58.7
Aldebaran	290 53.3	N16 31.8
Alioth	166 24.1	N55 54.7
Alkaid	153 01.9	N49 16.2
Al Na'ir	27 47.6	S46 55.1
Alnilam	275 49.9	S 1 11.5
Alphard	217 59.8	S 8 41.6
Alphecca	126 14.2	N26 41.2
Alpheratz	357 46.9	N29 08.5
Altair	62 11.6	N 8 53.6
Ankaa	353 18.6	S42 15.3
Antares	112 30.8	S26 27.2
Arcturus	145 59.2	N19 08.3
Atria	107 36.2	S69 02.9
Avior	234 19.9	S59 31.9
Bellatrix	278 35.7	N 6 21.6
Betelgeuse	271 05.1	N 7 24.7
Canopus	263 57.7	S52 41.6
Capella	280 39.6	N46 00.4
Deneb	49 33.8	N45 19.0
Denebola	182 37.5	N14 31.4
Diphda	348 59.0	S17 56.1
Dubhe	193 56.3	N61 42.1
Elnath	278 17.0	N28 37.0
Eltanin	90 47.9	N51 29.5
Enif	33 50.4	N 9 55.1
Fomalhaut	15 27.4	S29 34.5
Gacrux	172 05.7	S57 09.7
Gienah	175 56.3	S17 35.4
Hadar	148 53.8	S60 25.0
Hamal	328 04.5	N23 30.4
Kaus Aust.	83 48.5	S34 23.0
Kochab	137 20.3	N74 07.2
Markab	13 41.6	N15 15.4
Menkar	314 18.5	N 4 07.7
Menkent	148 12.2	S36 24.8
Miaplacidus	221 41.4	S69 44.9
Mirfak	308 45.2	N49 53.6
Nunki	76 02.6	S26 17.2
Peacock	53 24.4	S56 42.6
Pollux	243 32.1	N28 00.3
Procyon	245 03.5	N 5 12.3
Rasalhague	96 09.8	N12 33.3
Regulus	207 47.5	N11 55.5
Rigel	281 15.3	S 8 11.2
Rigil Kent.	139 57.4	S60 52.4
Sabik	102 16.7	S15 44.2
Schedar	349 44.3	N56 35.3
Shaula	96 26.8	S37 06.8
Sirius	258 36.8	S16 43.4
Spica	158 35.3	S11 12.4
Suhail	222 55.4	S43 27.8
Vega	80 41.4	N38 47.7
Zuben'ubi	137 09.7	S16 04.7

	SHA	Mer. Pass.
	° ′	h m
Venus	144 02.6	13 44
Mars	154 04.1	13 03
Jupiter	75 27.6	18 15
Saturn	192 54.5	10 26

UT d h	SUN GHA ° ′	SUN Dec ° ′	MOON GHA ° ′	v ′	MOON Dec ° ′	d ′	HP ′
30 00 (TUESDAY)	182 30.1	S 2 51.6	176 58.3	14.3	S 9 53.3	13.8	56.0
01	197 30.3	52.5	191 31.6	14.3	10 07.1	13.8	56.0
02	212 30.5	53.5	206 04.9	14.2	10 20.9	13.7	56.0
03	227 30.7	. . 54.5	220 38.1	14.2	10 34.6	13.6	56.0
04	242 30.9	55.4	235 11.3	14.2	10 48.2	13.6	55.9
05	257 31.1	56.4	249 44.5	14.2	11 01.8	13.5	55.9
06	272 31.3	S 2 57.4	264 17.7	14.2	S11 15.3	13.5	55.9
07	287 31.5	58.4	278 50.9	14.1	11 28.8	13.4	55.9
08	302 31.7	2 59.3	293 24.0	14.1	11 42.2	13.3	55.9
09	317 31.9	3 00.3	307 57.1	14.1	11 55.5	13.3	55.8
10	332 32.1	01.3	322 30.2	14.1	12 08.8	13.2	55.8
11	347 32.3	02.2	337 03.3	14.0	12 22.0	13.2	55.8
12	2 32.5	S 3 03.2	351 36.3	14.0	S12 35.2	13.0	55.8
13	17 32.7	04.2	6 09.3	14.0	12 48.2	13.1	55.7
14	32 32.9	05.1	20 42.3	14.0	13 01.3	12.9	55.7
15	47 33.1	. . 06.1	35 15.3	13.9	13 14.2	12.9	55.7
16	62 33.3	07.1	49 48.2	13.9	13 27.1	12.8	55.7
17	77 33.5	08.1	64 21.1	13.9	13 39.9	12.8	55.7
18	92 33.7	S 3 09.0	78 54.0	13.8	S13 52.7	12.7	55.6
19	107 33.9	10.0	93 26.8	13.8	14 05.4	12.6	55.6
20	122 34.1	11.0	107 59.6	13.8	14 18.0	12.5	55.6
21	137 34.3	. . 11.9	122 32.4	13.7	14 30.5	12.5	55.6
22	152 34.5	12.9	137 05.1	13.8	14 43.0	12.4	55.5
23	167 34.7	13.9	151 37.9	13.6	14 55.4	12.3	55.5
1 00 (WEDNESDAY)	182 34.9	S 3 14.8	166 10.5	13.7	S15 07.7	12.2	55.5
01	197 35.1	15.8	180 43.2	13.6	15 19.9	12.2	55.5
02	212 35.3	16.8	195 15.8	13.6	15 32.1	12.1	55.5
03	227 35.5	. . 17.8	209 48.4	13.5	15 44.2	12.0	55.4
04	242 35.7	18.7	224 20.9	13.5	15 56.2	11.9	55.4
05	257 35.9	19.7	238 53.4	13.5	16 08.1	11.9	55.4
06	272 36.1	S 3 20.7	253 25.9	13.5	S16 20.0	11.7	55.4
07	287 36.3	21.6	267 58.4	13.4	16 31.7	11.7	55.4
08	302 36.5	22.6	282 30.8	13.3	16 43.4	11.6	55.3
09	317 36.7	. . 23.6	297 03.1	13.4	16 55.0	11.5	55.3
10	332 36.9	24.5	311 35.5	13.2	17 06.5	11.5	55.3
11	347 37.1	25.5	326 07.7	13.3	17 18.0	11.3	55.3
12	2 37.3	S 3 26.5	340 40.0	13.2	S17 29.3	11.3	55.3
13	17 37.5	27.4	355 12.2	13.2	17 40.6	11.2	55.2
14	32 37.7	28.4	9 44.4	13.1	17 51.8	11.1	55.2
15	47 37.9	. . 29.4	24 16.5	13.1	18 02.9	11.0	55.2
16	62 38.1	30.4	38 48.6	13.1	18 13.9	10.9	55.2
17	77 38.3	31.3	53 20.7	13.0	18 24.8	10.8	55.2
18	92 38.5	S 3 32.3	67 52.7	12.9	S18 35.6	10.8	55.1
19	107 38.7	33.3	82 24.6	13.0	18 46.4	10.6	55.1
20	122 38.9	34.2	96 56.6	12.9	18 57.0	10.6	55.1
21	137 39.1	. . 35.2	111 28.5	12.8	19 07.6	10.5	55.1
22	152 39.3	36.2	126 00.3	12.8	19 18.1	10.3	55.1
23	167 39.5	37.1	140 32.1	12.8	19 28.4	10.3	55.0
2 00 (THURSDAY)	182 39.7	S 3 38.1	155 03.9	12.7	S19 38.7	10.2	55.0
01	197 39.9	39.1	169 35.6	12.7	19 48.9	10.1	55.0
02	212 40.1	40.0	184 07.3	12.6	19 59.0	10.0	55.0
03	227 40.3	. . 41.0	198 38.9	12.6	20 09.0	9.8	55.0
04	242 40.5	42.0	213 10.5	12.5	20 18.8	9.8	55.0
05	257 40.7	42.9	227 42.0	12.6	20 28.6	9.7	54.9
06	272 40.9	S 3 43.9	242 13.6	12.4	S20 38.3	9.6	54.9
07	287 41.1	44.9	256 45.0	12.4	20 47.9	9.5	54.9
08	302 41.3	45.8	271 16.4	12.4	20 57.4	9.4	54.9
09	317 41.5	. . 46.8	285 47.8	12.3	21 06.8	9.3	54.9
10	332 41.7	47.8	300 19.1	12.3	21 16.1	9.2	54.8
11	347 41.9	48.7	314 50.4	12.3	21 25.3	9.1	54.8
12	2 42.1	S 3 49.7	329 21.7	12.2	S21 34.4	9.0	54.8
13	17 42.3	50.7	343 52.9	12.1	21 43.4	8.9	54.8
14	32 42.5	51.6	358 24.0	12.2	21 52.3	8.7	54.8
15	47 42.7	. . 52.6	12 55.2	12.0	22 01.0	8.7	54.8
16	62 42.8	53.6	27 26.2	12.1	22 09.7	8.6	54.8
17	77 43.0	54.5	41 57.3	11.9	22 18.3	8.4	54.7
18	92 43.2	S 3 55.5	56 28.2	12.0	S22 26.7	8.4	54.7
19	107 43.4	56.5	70 59.2	11.9	22 35.1	8.2	54.7
20	122 43.6	57.4	85 30.1	11.8	22 43.3	8.2	54.7
21	137 43.8	. . 58.4	100 00.9	11.9	22 51.5	8.0	54.7
22	152 44.0	3 59.4	114 31.8	11.7	22 59.5	7.9	54.7
23	167 44.2	S 4 00.3	129 02.5	11.8	S23 07.4	7.8	54.6
	SD 16.0	d 1.0	SD		15.2	15.1	14.9

Lat.	Twilight Naut.	Twilight Civil	Sunrise	Moonrise 30	Moonrise 1	Moonrise 2	Moonrise 3
°	h m	h m	h m	h m	h m	h m	h m
N 72	03 51	05 13	06 20	09 14	12 35	▬	▬
N 70	04 03	05 16	06 17	08 51	11 15	▬	▬
68	04 12	05 18	06 14	08 34	10 37	13 48	▬
66	04 20	05 21	06 12	08 20	10 11	12 17	▬
64	04 26	05 22	06 09	08 09	09 51	11 39	13 43
62	04 31	05 24	06 08	07 59	09 35	11 13	12 54
60	04 36	05 25	06 06	07 51	09 21	10 53	12 23
N 58	04 40	05 26	06 05	07 44	09 10	10 36	12 00
56	04 43	05 26	06 03	07 38	09 00	10 22	11 41
54	04 46	05 27	06 02	07 32	08 51	10 10	11 25
52	04 48	05 28	06 01	07 27	08 43	09 59	11 12
50	04 51	05 28	06 00	07 22	08 36	09 50	11 00
45	04 55	05 29	05 58	07 13	08 22	09 30	10 36
N 40	04 58	05 29	05 56	07 05	08 09	09 14	10 16
35	05 00	05 30	05 55	06 58	07 59	09 00	10 00
30	05 02	05 30	05 53	06 52	07 50	08 48	09 46
20	05 03	05 29	05 51	06 41	07 35	08 28	09 23
N 10	05 03	05 28	05 49	06 32	07 21	08 11	09 02
0	05 02	05 26	05 46	06 24	07 09	07 55	08 43
S 10	04 58	05 23	05 44	06 16	06 56	07 39	08 24
20	04 53	05 19	05 41	06 07	06 43	07 22	08 04
30	04 46	05 14	05 38	05 57	06 28	07 03	07 41
35	04 41	05 11	05 36	05 51	06 20	06 52	07 28
40	04 35	05 07	05 34	05 45	06 10	06 39	07 12
45	04 27	05 02	05 32	05 37	05 59	06 24	06 54
S 50	04 17	04 56	05 28	05 28	05 45	06 05	06 31
52	04 12	04 53	05 27	05 24	05 39	05 57	06 20
54	04 07	04 50	05 25	05 20	05 32	05 47	06 07
56	04 01	04 46	05 24	05 15	05 24	05 36	05 53
58	03 53	04 42	05 22	05 09	05 15	05 24	05 37
S 60	03 45	04 37	05 20	05 03	05 05	05 09	05 17

Lat.	Sunset	Twilight Civil	Twilight Naut.	Moonset 30	Moonset 1	Moonset 2	Moonset 3
°	h m	h m	h m	h m	h m	h m	h m
N 72	17 17	18 24	19 45	15 30	13 44	▬	▬
N 70	17 20	18 21	19 33	15 55	15 06	▬	▬
68	17 23	18 18	19 24	16 14	15 45	14 11	▬
66	17 26	18 17	19 17	16 29	16 12	15 43	▬
64	17 28	18 15	19 11	16 42	16 33	16 22	16 00
62	17 30	18 14	19 06	16 53	16 50	16 49	16 49
60	17 32	18 13	19 01	17 02	17 05	17 10	17 20
N 58	17 33	18 12	18 58	17 10	17 17	17 27	17 44
56	17 34	18 11	18 55	17 17	17 28	17 42	18 03
54	17 36	18 11	18 52	17 24	17 37	17 55	18 19
52	17 37	18 10	18 49	17 30	17 46	18 06	18 33
50	17 38	18 10	18 47	17 35	17 53	18 16	18 45
45	17 40	18 09	18 43	17 46	18 09	18 37	19 10
N 40	17 42	18 09	18 40	17 56	18 23	18 54	19 30
35	17 44	18 09	18 38	18 04	18 34	19 08	19 47
30	17 45	18 09	18 37	18 11	18 44	19 21	20 01
20	17 48	18 10	18 35	18 24	19 02	19 42	20 26
N 10	17 50	18 11	18 36	18 35	19 17	20 01	20 47
0	17 53	18 13	18 38	18 45	19 31	20 18	21 07
S 10	17 55	18 16	18 41	18 56	19 45	20 36	21 27
20	17 58	18 20	18 46	19 07	20 01	20 55	21 49
30	18 01	18 25	18 54	19 20	20 18	21 16	22 14
35	18 03	18 29	18 59	19 27	20 28	21 29	22 28
40	18 06	18 33	19 05	19 36	20 40	21 44	22 46
45	18 08	18 38	19 13	19 46	20 54	22 02	23 06
S 50	18 12	18 44	19 23	19 58	21 12	22 24	23 32
52	18 13	18 47	19 28	20 04	21 20	22 34	23 45
54	18 15	18 51	19 34	20 10	21 29	22 46	23 59
56	18 17	18 54	19 40	20 17	21 39	23 00	24 16
58	18 19	18 59	19 48	20 25	21 51	23 16	24 37
S 60	18 21	19 03	19 56	20 34	22 05	23 35	25 03

Day	SUN Eqn. of Time 00ʰ	SUN Eqn. of Time 12ʰ	SUN Mer. Pass.	MOON Mer. Pass. Upper	MOON Mer. Pass. Lower	MOON Age	%	Phase
d	m s	m s	h m	h m	h m	d	%	
30	10 00	10 10	11 50	12 35	00 12	01	2	
1	10 19	10 29	11 50	13 20	00 57	02	5	●
2	10 38	10 48	11 49	14 07	01 43	03	10	

	UT	ARIES	VENUS −3.9		MARS +1.6		JUPITER −2.3		SATURN +1.0	
	d h	GHA ° ′	GHA ° ′	Dec ° ′	GHA ° ′	Dec ° ′	GHA ° ′	Dec ° ′	GHA ° ′	Dec ° ′
	3 00	12 04.3	153 45.3	S15 19.9	164 51.9	S11 01.7	87 22.2	S23 04.9	204 45.4	N 7 18.2
	01	27 06.7	168 44.8	21.0	179 52.8	02.3	102 24.5	04.9	219 47.6	18.1
	02	42 09.2	183 44.3	22.0	194 53.6	02.9	117 26.7	04.9	234 49.8	17.9
	03	57 11.6	198 43.8	. . 23.1	209 54.5	. . 03.5	132 29.0	. . 04.8	249 52.0	. . 17.8
	04	72 14.1	213 43.3	24.2	224 55.4	04.2	147 31.3	04.8	264 54.2	17.7
	05	87 16.6	228 42.8	25.2	239 56.2	04.8	162 33.5	04.8	279 56.3	17.6
	06	102 19.0	243 42.3	S15 26.3	254 57.1	S11 05.4	177 35.8	S23 04.8	294 58.5	N 7 17.5
	07	117 21.5	258 41.8	27.4	269 58.0	06.0	192 38.0	04.8	310 00.7	17.4
	08	132 24.0	273 41.3	28.4	284 58.8	06.6	207 40.3	04.8	325 02.9	17.3
F	09	147 26.4	288 40.8	. . 29.5	299 59.7	. . 07.3	222 42.5	. . 04.7	340 05.1	. . 17.2
R	10	162 28.9	303 40.3	30.6	315 00.6	07.9	237 44.8	04.7	355 07.3	17.1
I	11	177 31.4	318 39.8	31.6	330 01.4	08.5	252 47.0	04.7	10 09.5	17.0
D	12	192 33.8	333 39.3	S15 32.7	345 02.3	S11 09.1	267 49.3	S23 04.7	25 11.7	N 7 16.8
A	13	207 36.3	348 38.8	33.7	0 03.2	09.7	282 51.5	04.7	40 13.8	16.7
Y	14	222 38.7	3 38.3	34.8	15 04.0	10.4	297 53.8	04.6	55 16.0	16.6
	15	237 41.2	18 37.8	. . 35.9	30 04.9	. . 11.0	312 56.0	. . 04.6	70 18.2	. . 16.5
	16	252 43.7	33 37.3	36.9	45 05.7	11.6	327 58.3	04.6	85 20.4	16.4
	17	267 46.1	48 36.8	38.0	60 06.6	12.2	343 00.5	04.6	100 22.6	16.3
	18	282 48.6	63 36.3	S15 39.0	75 07.5	S11 12.8	358 02.8	S23 04.6	115 24.8	N 7 16.2
	19	297 51.1	78 35.7	40.1	90 08.3	13.4	13 05.0	04.6	130 27.0	16.1
	20	312 53.5	93 35.2	41.2	105 09.2	14.1	28 07.3	04.5	145 29.2	16.0
	21	327 56.0	108 34.7	. . 42.2	120 10.1	. . 14.7	43 09.5	. . 04.5	160 31.3	. . 15.9
	22	342 58.5	123 34.2	43.3	135 10.9	15.3	58 11.8	04.5	175 33.5	15.7
	23	358 00.9	138 33.7	44.3	150 11.8	15.9	73 14.0	04.5	190 35.7	15.6
	4 00	13 03.4	153 33.2	S15 45.4	165 12.6	S11 16.5	88 16.3	S23 04.5	205 37.9	N 7 15.5
	01	28 05.9	168 32.7	46.4	180 13.5	17.2	103 18.5	04.5	220 40.1	15.4
	02	43 08.3	183 32.2	47.5	195 14.4	17.8	118 20.8	04.4	235 42.3	15.3
	03	58 10.8	198 31.7	. . 48.5	210 15.2	. . 18.4	133 23.0	. . 04.4	250 44.5	. . 15.2
	04	73 13.2	213 31.2	49.6	225 16.1	19.0	148 25.3	04.4	265 46.7	15.1
	05	88 15.7	228 30.7	50.6	240 17.0	19.6	163 27.5	04.4	280 48.9	15.0
	06	103 18.2	243 30.2	S15 51.7	255 17.8	S11 20.2	178 29.8	S23 04.4	295 51.0	N 7 14.9
	07	118 20.6	258 29.7	52.8	270 18.7	20.9	193 32.0	04.3	310 53.2	14.8
S	08	133 23.1	273 29.1	53.8	285 19.5	21.5	208 34.3	04.3	325 55.4	14.7
A	09	148 25.6	288 28.6	. . 54.8	300 20.4	. . 22.1	223 36.5	. . 04.3	340 57.6	. . 14.5
T	10	163 28.0	303 28.1	55.9	315 21.2	22.7	238 38.8	04.3	355 59.8	14.4
U	11	178 30.5	318 27.6	56.9	330 22.1	23.3	253 41.0	04.3	11 02.0	14.3
R	12	193 33.0	333 27.1	S15 58.0	345 23.0	S11 23.9	268 43.2	S23 04.2	26 04.2	N 7 14.2
D	13	208 35.4	348 26.6	15 59.0	0 23.8	24.6	283 45.5	04.2	41 06.4	14.1
A	14	223 37.9	3 26.1	16 00.1	15 24.7	25.2	298 47.7	04.2	56 08.5	14.0
Y	15	238 40.4	18 25.5	. . 01.1	30 25.5	. . 25.8	313 50.0	. . 04.2	71 10.7	. . 13.9
	16	253 42.8	33 25.0	02.2	45 26.4	26.4	328 52.2	04.2	86 12.9	13.8
	17	268 45.3	48 24.5	03.2	60 27.3	27.0	343 54.5	04.2	101 15.1	13.7
	18	283 47.7	63 24.0	S16 04.3	75 28.1	S11 27.6	358 56.7	S23 04.1	116 17.3	N 7 13.6
	19	298 50.2	78 23.5	05.3	90 29.0	28.3	13 59.0	04.1	131 19.5	13.5
	20	313 52.7	93 23.0	06.3	105 29.8	28.9	29 01.2	04.1	146 21.7	13.3
	21	328 55.1	108 22.4	. . 07.4	120 30.7	. . 29.5	44 03.4	. . 04.1	161 23.9	. . 13.2
	22	343 57.6	123 21.9	08.4	135 31.5	30.1	59 05.7	04.1	176 26.1	13.1
	23	359 00.1	138 21.4	09.5	150 32.4	30.7	74 07.9	04.0	191 28.3	13.0
	5 00	14 02.5	153 20.9	S16 10.5	165 33.3	S11 31.3	89 10.2	S23 04.0	206 30.4	N 7 12.9
	01	29 05.0	168 20.4	11.5	180 34.1	31.9	104 12.4	04.0	221 32.6	12.8
	02	44 07.5	183 19.9	12.6	195 35.0	32.6	119 14.6	04.0	236 34.8	12.7
	03	59 09.9	198 19.3	. . 13.6	210 35.8	. . 33.2	134 16.9	. . 04.0	251 37.0	. . 12.6
	04	74 12.4	213 18.8	14.7	225 36.7	33.8	149 19.1	03.9	266 39.2	12.5
	05	89 14.9	228 18.3	15.7	240 37.5	34.4	164 21.4	03.9	281 41.4	12.4
	06	104 17.3	243 17.8	S16 16.7	255 38.4	S11 35.0	179 23.6	S23 03.9	296 43.6	N 7 12.3
	07	119 19.8	258 17.2	17.8	270 39.2	35.6	194 25.8	03.9	311 45.8	12.1
	08	134 22.2	273 16.7	18.8	285 40.1	36.2	209 28.1	03.9	326 48.0	12.0
S	09	149 24.7	288 16.2	. . 19.8	300 41.0	. . 36.9	224 30.3	. . 03.9	341 50.1	. . 11.9
U	10	164 27.2	303 15.7	20.9	315 41.8	37.5	239 32.6	03.8	356 52.3	11.8
N	11	179 29.6	318 15.2	21.9	330 42.7	38.1	254 34.8	03.8	11 54.5	11.7
D	12	194 32.1	333 14.6	S16 22.9	345 43.5	S11 38.7	269 37.0	S23 03.8	26 56.7	N 7 11.6
A	13	209 34.6	348 14.1	23.9	0 44.4	39.3	284 39.3	03.8	41 58.9	11.5
Y	14	224 37.0	3 13.6	25.0	15 45.2	39.9	299 41.5	03.8	57 01.1	11.4
	15	239 39.5	18 13.1	. . 26.0	30 46.1	. . 40.5	314 43.7	. . 03.7	72 03.3	. . 11.3
	16	254 42.0	33 12.5	27.0	45 46.9	41.2	329 46.0	03.7	87 05.5	11.2
	17	269 44.4	48 12.0	28.1	60 47.8	41.8	344 48.2	03.7	102 07.7	11.1
	18	284 46.9	63 11.5	S16 29.1	75 48.6	S11 42.4	359 50.4	S23 03.7	117 09.9	N 7 10.9
	19	299 49.3	78 10.9	30.1	90 49.5	43.0	14 52.7	03.7	132 12.1	10.8
	20	314 51.8	93 10.4	31.1	105 50.3	43.6	29 54.9	03.6	147 14.2	10.7
	21	329 54.3	108 09.9	. . 32.2	120 51.2	. . 44.2	44 57.1	. . 03.6	162 16.4	. . 10.6
	22	344 56.7	123 09.4	33.2	135 52.1	44.8	59 59.4	03.6	177 18.6	10.5
	23	359 59.2	138 08.8	34.2	150 52.9	45.4	75 01.6	03.6	192 20.8	10.4
	Mer. Pass.	h m 23 04.0	*v* −0.5	*d* 1.0	*v* 0.9	*d* 0.6	*v* 2.2	*d* 0.0	*v* 2.2	*d* 0.1

STARS

Name	SHA ° ′	Dec ° ′
Acamar	315 20.6	S40 15.9
Achernar	335 28.6	S57 11.3
Acrux	173 14.3	S63 08.9
Adhara	255 15.3	S28 58.7
Aldebaran	290 53.3	N16 31.8
Alioth	166 24.1	N55 54.7
Alkaid	153 01.9	N49 16.2
Al Na'ir	27 47.6	S46 55.1
Alnilam	275 49.9	S 1 11.6
Alphard	217 59.8	S 8 41.6
Alphecca	126 14.2	N26 41.2
Alpheratz	357 46.9	N29 08.5
Altair	62 11.6	N 8 53.6
Ankaa	353 18.6	S42 15.3
Antares	112 30.8	S26 27.2
Arcturus	145 59.2	N19 08.3
Atria	107 36.2	S69 02.9
Avior	234 19.9	S59 31.9
Bellatrix	278 35.7	N 6 21.6
Betelgeuse	271 05.0	N 7 24.7
Canopus	263 57.7	S52 41.6
Capella	280 39.5	N46 00.4
Deneb	49 33.8	N45 19.0
Denebola	182 37.5	N14 31.4
Diphda	348 59.0	S17 56.1
Dubhe	193 56.3	N61 42.1
Elnath	278 17.0	N28 36.9
Eltanin	90 47.9	N51 29.5
Enif	33 50.4	N 9 55.1
Fomalhaut	15 27.4	S29 34.5
Gacrux	172 05.7	S57 09.7
Gienah	175 56.3	S17 35.4
Hadar	148 53.8	S60 25.0
Hamal	328 04.5	N23 30.4
Kaus Aust.	83 48.5	S34 23.0
Kochab	137 20.4	N74 07.2
Markab	13 41.6	N15 15.4
Menkar	314 18.5	N 4 07.7
Menkent	148 12.2	S36 24.8
Miaplacidus	221 41.3	S69 44.9
Mirfak	308 45.2	N49 53.6
Nunki	76 02.7	S26 17.2
Peacock	53 24.4	S56 42.6
Pollux	243 32.1	N28 00.3
Procyon	245 03.5	N 5 12.3
Rasalhague	96 09.8	N12 33.3
Regulus	207 47.5	N11 55.5
Rigel	281 15.3	S 8 11.2
Rigil Kent.	139 57.4	S60 52.4
Sabik	102 16.7	S15 44.2
Schedar	349 44.3	N56 35.3
Shaula	96 26.9	S37 06.8
Sirius	258 36.8	S16 43.4
Spica	158 35.3	S11 12.4
Suhail	222 55.4	S43 27.8
Vega	80 41.4	N38 47.7
Zuben'ubi	137 09.7	S16 04.7

	SHA ° ′	Mer. Pass. h m
Venus	140 29.8	13 46
Mars	152 09.3	12 58
Jupiter	75 12.9	18 04
Saturn	192 34.5	10 16

UT d	h		SUN GHA ° ′	SUN Dec ° ′	MOON GHA ° ′	v ′	MOON Dec ° ′	d ′	HP ′
3	00		182 44.4	S 4 01.3	143 33.3	11.6	S23 15.2	7.7	54.6
	01		197 44.6	02.3	158 03.9	11.7	23 22.9	7.6	54.6
	02		212 44.8	03.2	172 34.6	11.6	23 30.5	7.4	54.6
	03		227 45.0	. . 04.2	187 05.2	11.6	23 37.9	7.4	54.6
	04		242 45.2	05.2	201 35.8	11.5	23 45.3	7.2	54.6
	05		257 45.4	06.1	216 06.3	11.5	23 52.5	7.2	54.6
	06		272 45.6	S 4 07.1	230 36.8	11.4	S23 59.7	7.0	54.5
	07		287 45.8	08.1	245 07.2	11.4	24 06.7	6.9	54.5
	08		302 46.0	09.0	259 37.6	11.4	24 13.6	6.7	54.5
	09	F	317 46.2	. . 10.0	274 08.0	11.3	24 20.3	6.7	54.5
	10	R	332 46.3	11.0	288 38.3	11.3	24 27.0	6.5	54.5
	11	I	347 46.5	11.9	303 08.6	11.2	24 33.5	6.5	54.5
	12	D	2 46.7	S 4 12.9	317 38.8	11.2	S24 40.0	6.3	54.5
	13	A	17 46.9	13.9	332 09.0	11.2	24 46.3	6.2	54.5
	14	Y	32 47.1	14.8	346 39.2	11.1	24 52.5	6.0	54.4
	15		47 47.3	. . 15.8	1 09.3	11.1	24 58.5	6.0	54.4
	16		62 47.5	16.8	15 39.4	11.1	25 04.5	5.8	54.4
	17		77 47.7	17.7	30 09.5	11.0	25 10.3	5.7	54.4
	18		92 47.9	S 4 18.7	44 39.5	11.0	S25 16.0	5.6	54.4
	19		107 48.1	19.7	59 09.5	11.0	25 21.6	5.5	54.4
	20		122 48.3	20.6	73 39.5	10.9	25 27.1	5.3	54.4
	21		137 48.5	. . 21.6	88 09.4	10.9	25 32.4	5.2	54.4
	22		152 48.7	22.5	102 39.3	10.8	25 37.6	5.1	54.4
	23		167 48.8	23.5	117 09.1	10.8	25 42.7	5.0	54.4
4	00		182 49.0	S 4 24.5	131 38.9	10.8	S25 47.7	4.9	54.3
	01		197 49.2	25.4	146 08.7	10.8	25 52.6	4.7	54.3
	02		212 49.4	26.4	160 38.5	10.7	25 57.3	4.6	54.3
	03		227 49.6	. . 27.4	175 08.2	10.7	26 01.9	4.5	54.3
	04		242 49.8	28.3	189 37.9	10.7	26 06.4	4.3	54.3
	05		257 50.0	29.3	204 07.6	10.7	26 10.7	4.3	54.3
	06		272 50.2	S 4 30.3	218 37.3	10.6	S26 15.0	4.1	54.3
	07		287 50.4	31.2	233 06.9	10.6	26 19.1	3.9	54.3
	08	S	302 50.6	32.2	247 36.5	10.5	26 23.0	3.9	54.3
	09	A	317 50.7	. . 33.2	262 06.0	10.6	26 26.9	3.7	54.3
	10	T	332 50.9	34.1	276 35.6	10.5	26 30.6	3.6	54.3
	11	U	347 51.1	35.1	291 05.1	10.5	26 34.2	3.5	54.3
	12	R	2 51.3	S 4 36.0	305 34.6	10.5	S26 37.7	3.3	54.2
	13	D	17 51.5	37.0	320 04.1	10.4	26 41.0	3.2	54.2
	14	A	32 51.7	38.0	334 33.5	10.4	26 44.2	3.1	54.2
	15	Y	47 51.9	. . 38.9	349 02.9	10.5	26 47.3	2.9	54.2
	16		62 52.1	39.9	3 32.4	10.3	26 50.2	2.9	54.2
	17		77 52.3	40.9	18 01.7	10.4	26 53.1	2.6	54.2
	18		92 52.4	S 4 41.8	32 31.1	10.4	S26 55.7	2.6	54.2
	19		107 52.6	42.8	47 00.5	10.3	26 58.3	2.4	54.2
	20		122 52.8	43.7	61 29.8	10.3	27 00.7	2.3	54.2
	21		137 53.0	. . 44.7	75 59.1	10.3	27 03.0	2.2	54.2
	22		152 53.2	45.7	90 28.4	10.3	27 05.2	2.1	54.2
	23		167 53.4	46.6	104 57.7	10.3	27 07.3	1.9	54.2
5	00		182 53.6	S 4 47.6	119 27.0	10.3	S27 09.2	1.8	54.2
	01		197 53.8	48.5	133 56.3	10.2	27 11.0	1.6	54.2
	02		212 53.9	49.5	148 25.5	10.3	27 12.6	1.5	54.2
	03		227 54.1	. . 50.5	162 54.8	10.2	27 14.1	1.4	54.2
	04		242 54.3	51.4	177 24.0	10.2	27 15.5	1.3	54.2
	05		257 54.5	52.4	191 53.2	10.2	27 16.8	1.1	54.2
	06		272 54.7	S 4 53.4	206 22.4	10.3	S27 17.9	1.0	54.2
	07		287 54.9	54.3	220 51.7	10.2	27 18.9	0.9	54.2
	08		302 55.1	55.3	235 20.9	10.2	27 19.8	0.7	54.2
	09	S	317 55.3	. . 56.2	249 50.1	10.2	27 20.5	0.6	54.2
	10	U	332 55.4	57.2	264 19.3	10.1	27 21.1	0.5	54.2
	11	N	347 55.6	58.2	278 48.4	10.2	27 21.6	0.3	54.2
	12	D	2 55.8	S 4 59.1	293 17.6	10.2	S27 21.9	0.2	54.2
	13	A	17 56.0	5 00.1	307 46.8	10.2	27 22.1	0.1	54.2
	14	Y	32 56.2	01.0	322 16.0	10.2	27 22.2	0.1	54.2
	15		47 56.4	. . 02.0	336 45.2	10.2	27 22.1	0.2	54.2
	16		62 56.6	03.0	351 14.4	10.2	27 21.9	0.3	54.2
	17		77 56.7	03.9	5 43.6	10.2	27 21.6	0.4	54.2
	18		92 56.9	S 5 04.9	20 12.8	10.2	S27 21.2	0.6	54.2
	19		107 57.1	05.8	34 42.0	10.2	27 20.6	0.7	54.2
	20		122 57.3	06.8	49 11.2	10.2	27 19.9	0.9	54.2
	21		137 57.5	. . 07.8	63 40.4	10.2	27 19.0	1.0	54.2
	22		152 57.7	08.7	78 09.6	10.3	27 18.0	1.1	54.2
	23		167 57.8	09.7	92 38.9	10.2	S27 16.9	1.2	54.2
			SD 16.0	*d* 1.0	SD 14.8		14.8		14.8

Lat. °	Twilight Naut. h m	Twilight Civil h m	Sunrise h m	Moonrise 3 h m	Moonrise 4 h m	Moonrise 5 h m	Moonrise 6 h m
N 72	04 06	05 26	06 34	■	■	■	■
N 70	04 16	05 28	06 29	■	■	■	■
68	04 24	05 29	06 25	■	■	■	■
66	04 30	05 30	06 21	■	■	■	■
64	04 35	05 31	06 18	13 43	■	■	■
62	04 40	05 31	06 16	12 54	14 32	15 46	16 09
60	04 43	05 32	06 13	12 23	13 46	14 49	15 26
N 58	04 46	05 32	06 11	12 00	13 16	14 17	14 58
56	04 49	05 32	06 09	11 41	12 53	13 52	14 35
54	04 52	05 33	06 08	11 25	12 35	13 33	14 17
52	04 54	05 33	06 06	11 12	12 19	13 16	14 02
50	04 55	05 33	06 05	11 00	12 05	13 02	13 48
45	04 59	05 33	06 02	10 36	11 38	12 33	13 21
N 40	05 01	05 32	05 59	10 16	11 16	12 11	12 59
35	05 03	05 32	05 57	10 00	10 58	11 52	12 41
30	05 04	05 31	05 55	09 46	10 43	11 36	12 25
20	05 04	05 30	05 52	09 23	10 17	11 09	11 59
N 10	05 03	05 27	05 48	09 02	09 54	10 46	11 36
0	05 01	05 25	05 45	08 43	09 33	10 24	11 15
S 10	04 57	05 21	05 42	08 24	09 12	10 02	10 54
20	04 51	05 16	05 39	08 04	08 50	09 39	10 31
30	04 42	05 10	05 34	07 41	08 24	09 12	10 04
35	04 37	05 06	05 32	07 28	08 09	08 56	09 49
40	04 30	05 02	05 29	07 12	07 52	08 38	09 30
45	04 21	04 56	05 26	06 54	07 30	08 15	09 08
S 50	04 10	04 49	05 22	06 31	07 04	07 47	08 41
52	04 05	04 46	05 20	06 20	06 51	07 33	08 27
54	03 59	04 42	05 18	06 07	06 36	07 17	08 11
56	03 52	04 38	05 16	05 53	06 19	06 58	07 52
58	03 44	04 33	05 13	05 37	05 58	06 34	07 29
S 60	03 35	04 28	05 11	05 17	05 32	06 03	06 59

Lat. °	Sunset h m	Twilight Civil h m	Twilight Naut. h m	Moonset 3 h m	Moonset 4 h m	Moonset 5 h m	Moonset 6 h m
N 72	17 01	18 08	19 28	■	■	■	■
N 70	17 06	18 07	19 19	■	■	■	■
68	17 11	18 06	19 11	■	■	■	■
66	17 14	18 05	19 05	■	■	■	■
64	17 18	18 05	19 00	16 00	■	■	■
62	17 20	18 04	18 56	16 49	16 55	17 27	18 50
60	17 23	18 04	18 52	17 20	17 41	18 24	19 32
N 58	17 25	18 04	18 49	17 44	18 11	18 56	20 01
56	17 27	18 04	18 47	18 03	18 34	19 21	20 23
54	17 28	18 03	18 44	18 19	18 53	19 40	20 41
52	17 30	18 03	18 42	18 33	19 09	19 57	20 56
50	17 31	18 03	18 41	18 45	19 22	20 11	21 09
45	17 34	18 04	18 38	19 10	19 50	20 39	21 36
N 40	17 37	18 04	18 35	19 30	20 13	21 02	21 58
35	17 39	18 05	18 34	19 47	20 31	21 21	22 16
30	17 42	18 05	18 33	20 01	20 47	21 37	22 31
20	17 45	18 07	18 33	20 26	21 13	22 04	22 57
N 10	17 49	18 10	18 34	20 47	21 36	22 27	23 19
0	17 52	18 13	18 37	21 07	21 58	22 49	23 39
S 10	17 55	18 16	18 41	21 27	22 19	23 10	24 00
20	17 59	18 21	18 47	21 49	22 42	23 33	24 22
30	18 03	18 27	18 56	22 14	23 09	24 00	00 00
35	18 06	18 31	19 01	22 28	23 25	24 16	00 16
40	18 09	18 36	19 08	22 46	23 43	24 34	00 34
45	18 12	18 42	19 17	23 06	24 05	00 05	00 57
S 50	18 16	18 49	19 29	23 32	24 33	00 33	01 25
52	18 18	18 53	19 34	23 45	24 47	00 47	01 39
54	18 20	18 56	19 40	23 59	25 03	01 03	01 55
56	18 23	19 01	19 47	24 16	00 16	01 22	02 14
58	18 25	19 06	19 55	24 37	00 37	01 46	02 37
S 60	18 28	19 11	20 05	25 03	01 03	02 17	03 07

Day	SUN Eqn. of Time 00h	SUN Eqn. of Time 12h	SUN Mer. Pass.	MOON Mer. Pass. Upper	MOON Mer. Pass. Lower	MOON Age	MOON Phase
d	m s	m s	h m	h m	h m	d %	
3	10 57	11 07	11 49	14 55	02 31	04 17	
4	11 16	11 25	11 49	15 45	03 20	05 24	
5	11 34	11 43	11 48	16 36	04 11	06 33	

Day	UT d h	ARIES GHA	VENUS −3.9 GHA	VENUS Dec	MARS +1.6 GHA	MARS Dec	JUPITER −2.3 GHA	JUPITER Dec	SATURN +1.0 GHA	SATURN Dec
		° ′	° ′	° ′	° ′	° ′	° ′	° ′	° ′	° ′
	6 00	15 01.7	153 08.3	S16 35.2	165 53.8	S11 46.1	90 03.8	S23 03.6	207 23.0	N 7 10.3
	01	30 04.1	168 07.8	36.3	180 54.6	46.7	105 06.1	03.5	222 25.2	10.2
	02	45 06.6	183 07.2	37.3	195 55.5	47.3	120 08.3	03.5	237 27.4	10.1
	03	60 09.1	198 06.7	. . 38.3	210 56.3	. . 47.9	135 10.5	. . 03.5	252 29.6	. . 10.0
	04	75 11.5	213 06.2	39.3	225 57.2	48.5	150 12.8	03.5	267 31.8	09.9
	05	90 14.0	228 05.6	40.3	240 58.0	49.1	165 15.0	03.5	282 34.0	09.8
	06	105 16.5	243 05.1	S16 41.4	255 58.9	S11 49.7	180 17.2	S23 03.4	297 36.2	N 7 09.6
	07	120 18.9	258 04.6	42.4	270 59.7	50.3	195 19.5	03.4	312 38.3	09.5
	08	135 21.4	273 04.0	43.4	286 00.6	50.9	210 21.7	03.4	327 40.5	09.4
MONDAY	09	150 23.8	288 03.5	. . 44.4	301 01.4	. . 51.6	225 23.9	. . 03.4	342 42.7	. . 09.3
	10	165 26.3	303 03.0	45.4	316 02.3	52.2	240 26.2	03.4	357 44.9	09.2
	11	180 28.8	318 02.4	46.4	331 03.1	52.8	255 28.4	03.3	12 47.1	09.1
	12	195 31.2	333 01.9	S16 47.5	346 04.0	S11 53.4	270 30.6	S23 03.3	27 49.3	N 7 09.0
	13	210 33.7	348 01.4	48.5	1 04.8	54.0	285 32.9	03.3	42 51.5	08.9
	14	225 36.2	3 00.8	49.5	16 05.7	54.6	300 35.1	03.3	57 53.7	08.8
	15	240 38.6	18 00.3	. . 50.5	31 06.5	. . 55.2	315 37.3	. . 03.3	72 55.9	. . 08.7
	16	255 41.1	32 59.7	51.5	46 07.4	55.8	330 39.5	03.2	87 58.1	08.6
	17	270 43.6	47 59.2	52.5	61 08.2	56.4	345 41.8	03.2	103 00.3	08.5
	18	285 46.0	62 58.7	S16 53.5	76 09.0	S11 57.0	0 44.0	S23 03.2	118 02.4	N 7 08.4
	19	300 48.5	77 58.1	54.5	91 09.9	57.7	15 46.2	03.2	133 04.6	08.2
	20	315 51.0	92 57.6	55.5	106 10.7	58.3	30 48.4	03.2	148 06.8	08.1
	21	330 53.4	107 57.1	. . 56.5	121 11.6	. . 58.9	45 50.7	. . 03.1	163 09.0	. . 08.0
	22	345 55.9	122 56.5	57.6	136 12.4	11 59.5	60 52.9	03.1	178 11.2	07.9
	23	0 58.3	137 56.0	58.6	151 13.3	12 00.1	75 55.1	03.1	193 13.4	07.8
	7 00	16 00.8	152 55.4	S16 59.6	166 14.1	S12 00.7	90 57.4	S23 03.1	208 15.6	N 7 07.7
	01	31 03.3	167 54.9	17 00.6	181 15.0	01.3	105 59.6	03.1	223 17.8	07.6
	02	46 05.7	182 54.3	01.6	196 15.8	01.9	121 01.8	03.0	238 20.0	07.5
	03	61 08.2	197 53.8	. . 02.6	211 16.7	. . 02.5	136 04.0	. . 03.0	253 22.2	. . 07.4
	04	76 10.7	212 53.3	03.6	226 17.5	03.1	151 06.3	03.0	268 24.4	07.3
	05	91 13.1	227 52.7	04.6	241 18.4	03.7	166 08.5	03.0	283 26.6	07.2
	06	106 15.6	242 52.2	S17 05.6	256 19.2	S12 04.4	181 10.7	S23 03.0	298 28.8	N 7 07.1
	07	121 18.1	257 51.6	06.6	271 20.0	05.0	196 12.9	02.9	313 30.9	07.0
TUESDAY	08	136 20.5	272 51.1	07.6	286 20.9	05.6	211 15.1	02.9	328 33.1	06.8
	09	151 23.0	287 50.5	. . 08.6	301 21.7	. . 06.2	226 17.4	. . 02.9	343 35.3	. . 06.7
	10	166 25.5	302 50.0	09.6	316 22.6	06.8	241 19.6	02.9	358 37.5	06.6
	11	181 27.9	317 49.4	10.6	331 23.4	07.4	256 21.8	02.8	13 39.7	06.5
	12	196 30.4	332 48.9	S17 11.6	346 24.3	S12 08.0	271 24.0	S23 02.8	28 41.9	N 7 06.4
	13	211 32.8	347 48.3	12.6	1 25.1	08.6	286 26.3	02.8	43 44.1	06.3
	14	226 35.3	2 47.8	13.6	16 26.0	09.2	301 28.5	02.8	58 46.3	06.2
	15	241 37.8	17 47.2	. . 14.6	31 26.8	. . 09.8	316 30.7	. . 02.8	73 48.5	. . 06.1
	16	256 40.2	32 46.7	15.6	46 27.6	10.4	331 32.9	02.7	88 50.7	06.0
	17	271 42.7	47 46.1	16.5	61 28.5	11.0	346 35.1	02.7	103 52.9	05.9
	18	286 45.2	62 45.6	S17 17.5	76 29.3	S12 11.6	1 37.4	S23 02.7	118 55.1	N 7 05.8
	19	301 47.6	77 45.0	18.5	91 30.2	12.3	16 39.6	02.7	133 57.3	05.7
	20	316 50.1	92 44.5	19.5	106 31.0	12.9	31 41.8	02.7	148 59.5	05.6
	21	331 52.6	107 43.9	. . 20.5	121 31.9	. . 13.5	46 44.0	. . 02.6	164 01.7	. . 05.4
	22	346 55.0	122 43.4	21.5	136 32.7	14.1	61 46.2	02.6	179 03.8	05.3
	23	1 57.5	137 42.8	22.5	151 33.5	14.7	76 48.5	02.6	194 06.0	05.2
	8 00	16 59.9	152 42.3	S17 23.5	166 34.4	S12 15.3	91 50.7	S23 02.6	209 08.2	N 7 05.1
	01	32 02.4	167 41.7	24.5	181 35.2	15.9	106 52.9	02.5	224 10.4	05.0
	02	47 04.9	182 41.2	25.5	196 36.1	16.5	121 55.1	02.5	239 12.6	04.9
	03	62 07.3	197 40.6	. . 26.4	211 36.9	. . 17.1	136 57.3	. . 02.5	254 14.8	. . 04.8
	04	77 09.8	212 40.1	27.4	226 37.7	17.7	151 59.5	02.5	269 17.0	04.7
	05	92 12.3	227 39.5	28.4	241 38.6	18.3	167 01.8	02.5	284 19.2	04.6
	06	107 14.7	242 38.9	S17 29.4	256 39.4	S12 18.9	182 04.0	S23 02.4	299 21.4	N 7 04.5
WEDNESDAY	07	122 17.2	257 38.4	30.4	271 40.3	19.5	197 06.2	02.4	314 23.6	04.4
	08	137 19.7	272 37.8	31.4	286 41.1	20.1	212 08.4	02.4	329 25.8	04.3
	09	152 22.1	287 37.3	. . 32.3	301 41.9	. . 20.7	227 10.6	. . 02.4	344 28.0	. . 04.2
	10	167 24.6	302 36.7	33.3	316 42.8	21.3	242 12.8	02.4	359 30.2	04.1
	11	182 27.1	317 36.1	34.3	331 43.6	21.9	257 15.1	02.3	14 32.4	04.0
	12	197 29.5	332 35.6	S17 35.3	346 44.5	S12 22.5	272 17.3	S23 02.3	29 34.6	N 7 03.8
	13	212 32.0	347 35.0	36.3	1 45.3	23.1	287 19.5	02.3	44 36.8	03.7
	14	227 34.4	2 34.5	37.2	16 46.1	23.8	302 21.7	02.3	59 38.9	03.6
	15	242 36.9	17 33.9	. . 38.2	31 47.0	. . 24.4	317 23.9	. . 02.2	74 41.1	. . 03.5
	16	257 39.4	32 33.3	39.2	46 47.8	25.0	332 26.1	02.2	89 43.3	03.4
	17	272 41.8	47 32.8	40.2	61 48.7	25.6	347 28.3	02.2	104 45.5	03.3
	18	287 44.3	62 32.2	S17 41.1	76 49.5	S12 26.2	2 30.6	S23 02.2	119 47.7	N 7 03.2
	19	302 46.8	77 31.7	42.1	91 50.3	26.8	17 32.8	02.2	134 49.9	03.1
	20	317 49.2	92 31.1	43.1	106 51.2	27.4	32 35.0	02.1	149 52.1	03.0
	21	332 51.7	107 30.5	. . 44.1	121 52.0	. . 28.0	47 37.2	. . 02.1	164 54.3	. . 02.9
	22	347 54.2	122 30.0	45.0	136 52.8	28.6	62 39.4	02.1	179 56.5	02.8
	23	2 56.6	137 29.4	46.0	151 53.7	29.2	77 41.6	02.1	194 58.7	02.7
	Mer. Pass.	h m 22 52.2	v −0.5	d 1.0	v 0.8	d 0.6	v 2.2	d 0.0	v 2.2	d 0.1

STARS

Name	SHA	Dec
	° ′	° ′
Acamar	315 20.5	S40 15.9
Achernar	335 28.5	S57 11.3
Acrux	173 14.3	S63 08.8
Adhara	255 15.3	S28 58.7
Aldebaran	290 53.2	N16 31.8
Alioth	166 24.1	N55 54.7
Alkaid	153 01.9	N49 16.2
Al Na'ir	27 47.6	S46 55.2
Alnilam	275 49.8	S 1 11.6
Alphard	217 59.8	S 8 41.6
Alphecca	126 14.2	N26 41.2
Alpheratz	357 46.9	N29 08.6
Altair	62 11.6	N 8 53.6
Ankaa	353 18.6	S42 15.4
Antares	112 30.8	S26 27.2
Arcturus	145 59.2	N19 08.3
Atria	107 36.2	S69 02.9
Avior	234 19.8	S59 31.9
Bellatrix	278 35.7	N 6 21.6
Betelgeuse	271 05.0	N 7 24.7
Canopus	263 57.6	S52 41.6
Capella	280 39.5	N46 00.4
Deneb	49 33.8	N45 19.0
Denebola	182 37.5	N14 31.4
Diphda	348 59.0	S17 56.1
Dubhe	193 56.2	N61 42.1
Elnath	278 16.9	N28 37.0
Eltanin	90 47.9	N51 29.5
Enif	33 50.4	N 9 55.1
Fomalhaut	15 27.4	S29 34.5
Gacrux	172 05.7	S57 09.7
Gienah	175 56.3	S17 35.4
Hadar	148 53.8	S60 25.0
Hamal	328 04.5	N23 30.4
Kaus Aust.	83 48.5	S34 23.0
Kochab	137 20.4	N74 07.2
Markab	13 41.6	N15 15.4
Menkar	314 18.5	N 4 07.7
Menkent	148 12.2	S36 24.8
Miaplacidus	221 41.3	S69 44.9
Mirfak	308 45.1	N49 53.6
Nunki	76 02.7	S26 17.2
Peacock	53 24.4	S56 42.6
Pollux	243 32.1	N28 00.3
Procyon	245 03.5	N 5 12.3
Rasalhague	96 09.8	N12 33.3
Regulus	207 47.5	N11 55.5
Rigel	281 15.3	S 8 11.2
Rigil Kent.	139 57.4	S60 52.4
Sabik	102 16.8	S15 44.2
Schedar	349 44.3	N56 35.3
Shaula	96 26.9	S37 06.8
Sirius	258 36.8	S16 43.4
Spica	158 35.3	S11 12.4
Suhail	222 55.4	S43 27.8
Vega	80 41.4	N38 47.7
Zuben'ubi	137 09.7	S16 04.7

	SHA	Mer. Pass.
	° ′	h m
Venus	136 54.6	13 49
Mars	150 13.3	12 54
Jupiter	74 56.5	17 54
Saturn	192 14.8	10 05

Day	UT d h	SUN GHA	SUN Dec	MOON GHA	v	MOON Dec	d	HP
		° ′	° ′	° ′	′	° ′	′	′
MONDAY	6 00	182 58.0	S 5 10.6	107 08.1	10.2	S27 15.7	1.4	54.2
	01	197 58.2	11.6	121 37.3	10.3	27 14.3	1.5	54.2
	02	212 58.4	12.6	136 06.6	10.3	27 12.8	1.6	54.2
	03	227 58.6	. . 13.5	150 35.9	10.2	27 11.2	1.8	54.2
	04	242 58.8	14.5	165 05.1	10.3	27 09.4	1.9	54.2
	05	257 58.9	15.4	179 34.4	10.3	27 07.5	2.0	54.2
	06	272 59.1	S 5 16.4	194 03.7	10.4	S27 05.5	2.1	54.2
	07	287 59.3	17.3	208 33.1	10.3	27 03.4	2.3	54.2
	08	302 59.5	18.3	223 02.4	10.4	27 01.1	2.4	54.2
	09	317 59.7	. . 19.3	237 31.8	10.3	26 58.7	2.6	54.3
	10	332 59.9	20.2	252 01.1	10.4	26 56.1	2.7	54.3
	11	348 00.0	21.2	266 30.5	10.4	26 53.4	2.8	54.3
	12	3 00.2	S 5 22.1	280 59.9	10.4	S26 50.6	2.9	54.3
	13	18 00.4	23.1	295 29.3	10.5	26 47.7	3.0	54.3
	14	33 00.6	24.1	309 58.8	10.5	26 44.7	3.2	54.3
	15	48 00.8	. . 25.0	324 28.3	10.5	26 41.5	3.3	54.3
	16	63 00.9	26.0	338 57.8	10.5	26 38.2	3.5	54.3
	17	78 01.1	26.9	353 27.3	10.5	26 34.7	3.6	54.3
	18	93 01.3	S 5 27.9	7 56.8	10.6	S26 31.1	3.6	54.3
	19	108 01.5	28.8	22 26.4	10.6	26 27.5	3.9	54.3
	20	123 01.7	29.8	36 56.0	10.6	26 23.6	3.9	54.3
	21	138 01.8	. . 30.7	51 25.6	10.6	26 19.7	4.1	54.4
	22	153 02.0	31.7	65 55.2	10.7	26 15.6	4.2	54.4
	23	168 02.2	32.7	80 24.9	10.7	26 11.4	4.3	54.4
TUESDAY	7 00	183 02.4	S 5 33.6	94 54.6	10.7	S26 07.1	4.5	54.4
	01	198 02.6	34.6	109 24.3	10.7	26 02.6	4.6	54.4
	02	213 02.7	35.5	123 54.0	10.8	25 58.0	4.7	54.4
	03	228 02.9	. . 36.5	138 23.8	10.8	25 53.3	4.8	54.4
	04	243 03.1	37.4	152 53.6	10.9	25 48.5	4.9	54.4
	05	258 03.3	38.4	167 23.5	10.8	25 43.6	5.1	54.4
	06	273 03.5	S 5 39.4	181 53.3	10.9	S25 38.5	5.2	54.5
	07	288 03.6	40.3	196 23.2	11.0	25 33.3	5.3	54.5
	08	303 03.8	41.3	210 53.2	10.9	25 28.0	5.5	54.5
	09	318 04.0	. . 42.2	225 23.1	11.0	25 22.5	5.5	54.5
	10	333 04.2	43.2	239 53.1	11.1	25 17.0	5.7	54.5
	11	348 04.3	44.1	254 23.2	11.0	25 11.3	5.8	54.5
	12	3 04.5	S 5 45.1	268 53.2	11.1	S25 05.5	5.9	54.5
	13	18 04.7	46.0	283 23.3	11.1	24 59.6	6.1	54.6
	14	33 04.9	47.0	297 53.4	11.2	24 53.5	6.1	54.6
	15	48 05.1	. . 47.9	312 23.6	11.2	24 47.4	6.3	54.6
	16	63 05.2	48.9	326 53.8	11.3	24 41.1	6.4	54.6
	17	78 05.4	49.9	341 24.1	11.2	24 34.7	6.5	54.6
	18	93 05.6	S 5 50.8	355 54.3	11.3	S24 28.2	6.7	54.6
	19	108 05.8	51.8	10 24.6	11.4	24 21.5	6.7	54.7
	20	123 05.9	52.7	24 55.0	11.4	24 14.8	6.9	54.7
	21	138 06.1	. . 53.7	39 25.4	11.4	24 07.9	7.0	54.7
	22	153 06.3	54.6	53 55.8	11.5	24 00.9	7.1	54.7
	23	168 06.5	55.6	68 26.3	11.4	23 53.8	7.2	54.7
WEDNESDAY	8 00	183 06.6	S 5 56.5	82 56.7	11.6	S23 46.6	7.3	54.7
	01	198 06.8	57.5	97 27.3	11.5	23 39.3	7.5	54.8
	02	213 07.0	58.4	111 57.8	11.7	23 31.8	7.5	54.8
	03	228 07.2	5 59.4	126 28.5	11.6	23 24.3	7.7	54.8
	04	243 07.3	6 00.3	140 59.1	11.7	23 16.6	7.8	54.8
	05	258 07.5	01.3	155 29.8	11.7	23 08.8	7.9	54.8
	06	273 07.7	S 6 02.2	170 00.5	11.8	S23 00.9	8.0	54.9
	07	288 07.9	03.2	184 31.3	11.8	22 52.9	8.1	54.9
	08	303 08.0	04.1	199 02.1	11.8	22 44.8	8.2	54.9
	09	318 08.2	. . 05.1	213 32.9	11.9	22 36.6	8.4	54.9
	10	333 08.4	06.0	228 03.8	11.9	22 28.2	8.4	54.9
	11	348 08.6	07.0	242 34.7	12.0	22 19.8	8.6	55.0
	12	3 08.7	S 6 08.0	257 05.7	11.9	S22 11.2	8.6	55.0
	13	18 08.9	08.9	271 36.6	12.1	22 02.6	8.8	55.0
	14	33 09.1	09.9	286 07.7	12.0	21 53.8	8.9	55.0
	15	48 09.2	. . 10.8	300 38.7	12.1	21 44.9	9.0	55.0
	16	63 09.4	11.8	315 09.8	12.2	21 35.9	9.1	55.1
	17	78 09.6	12.7	329 41.0	12.2	21 26.8	9.2	55.1
	18	93 09.8	S 6 13.7	344 12.2	12.2	S21 17.6	9.3	55.1
	19	108 09.9	14.6	358 43.4	12.3	21 08.3	9.4	55.1
	20	123 10.1	15.6	13 14.7	12.2	20 58.9	9.5	55.2
	21	138 10.3	. . 16.5	27 45.9	12.4	20 49.4	9.6	55.2
	22	153 10.5	17.5	42 17.3	12.3	20 39.8	9.7	55.2
	23	168 10.6	18.4	56 48.6	12.5	S20 30.1	9.8	55.2
		SD 16.0	d 1.0	SD 14.8		14.9		15.0

Lat.	Twilight Naut.	Twilight Civil	Sunrise	Moonrise 6	Moonrise 7	Moonrise 8	Moonrise 9
°	h m	h m	h m	h m	h m	h m	h m
N 72	04 20	05 40	06 48	■	■	■	18 35
N 70	04 28	05 40	06 41	■	■	■	17 43
68	04 35	05 40	06 35	■	■	18 06	17 10
66	04 40	05 40	06 31	■	■	17 11	16 46
64	04 44	05 39	06 27	■	16 56	16 38	16 27
62	04 48	05 39	06 24	16 09	16 13	16 13	16 12
60	04 51	05 39	06 21	15 26	15 45	15 54	15 58
N 58	04 53	05 39	06 18	14 58	15 23	15 37	15 47
56	04 55	05 38	06 16	14 35	15 04	15 24	15 37
54	04 57	05 38	06 13	14 17	14 49	15 12	15 28
52	04 59	05 38	06 11	14 02	14 36	15 01	15 20
50	05 00	05 37	06 10	13 48	14 24	14 52	15 13
45	05 02	05 36	06 06	13 21	14 00	14 32	14 58
N 40	05 04	05 35	06 02	12 59	13 40	14 15	14 45
35	05 05	05 34	06 00	12 41	13 24	14 01	14 35
30	05 05	05 33	05 57	12 25	13 10	13 49	14 25
20	05 05	05 30	05 52	11 59	12 46	13 29	14 09
N 10	05 03	05 27	05 48	11 36	12 25	13 11	13 54
0	05 00	05 24	05 44	11 15	12 05	12 54	13 41
S 10	04 55	05 19	05 40	10 54	11 45	12 37	13 27
20	04 48	05 14	05 36	10 31	11 24	12 19	13 13
30	04 38	05 07	05 31	10 04	11 00	11 58	12 56
35	04 32	05 02	05 28	09 49	10 46	11 45	12 46
40	04 25	04 57	05 24	09 30	10 29	11 31	12 35
45	04 15	04 51	05 20	09 08	10 09	11 14	12 22
S 50	04 03	04 43	05 15	08 41	09 43	10 53	12 06
52	03 57	04 39	05 13	08 27	09 31	10 43	11 58
54	03 50	04 34	05 11	08 11	09 17	10 31	11 50
56	03 43	04 30	05 08	07 52	09 01	10 18	11 40
58	03 34	04 24	05 05	07 29	08 41	10 03	11 29
S 60	03 24	04 18	05 02	06 59	08 17	09 45	11 17

Lat.	Sunset	Twilight Civil	Twilight Naut.	Moonset 6	Moonset 7	Moonset 8	Moonset 9
°	h m	h m	h m	h m	h m	h m	h m
N 72	16 46	17 53	19 12	■	■	■	21 31
N 70	16 53	17 54	19 04	■	■	■	22 21
68	16 58	17 54	18 58	■	■	20 19	22 53
66	17 03	17 54	18 53	■	■	21 13	23 15
64	17 07	17 54	18 49	■	19 47	21 46	23 33
62	17 11	17 55	18 46	18 50	20 29	22 09	23 48
60	17 14	17 55	18 43	19 32	20 57	22 28	24 00
N 58	17 16	17 56	18 41	20 01	21 19	22 44	24 11
56	17 19	17 56	18 39	20 23	21 37	22 57	24 20
54	17 21	17 56	18 37	20 41	21 52	23 08	24 28
52	17 23	17 57	18 36	20 56	22 05	23 18	24 35
50	17 25	17 57	18 34	21 09	22 16	23 27	24 41
45	17 29	17 58	18 32	21 36	22 39	23 46	24 55
N 40	17 32	17 59	18 31	21 58	22 58	24 02	00 02
35	17 35	18 01	18 30	22 16	23 14	24 15	00 15
30	17 38	18 02	18 30	22 31	23 28	24 26	00 26
20	17 43	18 05	18 30	22 57	23 51	24 45	00 45
N 10	17 47	18 08	18 32	23 19	24 10	00 10	01 01
0	17 51	18 12	18 36	23 39	24 29	00 29	01 17
S 10	17 55	18 16	18 41	24 00	00 00	00 47	01 32
20	18 00	18 22	18 48	24 22	00 22	01 07	01 48
30	18 05	18 29	18 58	00 00	00 47	01 29	02 07
35	18 08	18 34	19 04	00 16	01 02	01 42	02 17
40	18 12	18 39	19 12	00 34	01 19	01 57	02 30
45	18 16	18 46	19 22	00 57	01 40	02 15	02 44
S 50	18 21	18 54	19 34	01 25	02 06	02 37	03 01
52	18 23	18 58	19 40	01 39	02 18	02 48	03 10
54	18 26	19 02	19 47	01 55	02 33	02 59	03 19
56	18 29	19 07	19 55	02 14	02 49	03 13	03 29
58	18 32	19 13	20 04	02 37	03 09	03 29	03 41
S 60	18 35	19 19	20 14	03 07	03 34	03 47	03 54

Day	SUN Eqn. of Time 00^h	SUN Eqn. of Time 12^h	SUN Mer. Pass.	MOON Mer. Pass. Upper	MOON Mer. Pass. Lower	MOON Age	MOON Phase
d	m s	m s	h m	h m	h m	d %	
6	11 52	12 01	11 48	17 27	05 02	07 42	
7	12 09	12 18	11 48	18 17	05 52	08 51	
8	12 26	12 35	11 47	19 05	06 41	09 61	

2008 OCTOBER 9, 10, 11 (THURS., FRI., SAT.)

Day	UT d h	ARIES GHA ° ′	VENUS −3.9 GHA ° ′	VENUS Dec ° ′	MARS +1.6 GHA ° ′	MARS Dec ° ′	JUPITER −2.2 GHA ° ′	JUPITER Dec ° ′	SATURN +1.0 GHA ° ′	SATURN Dec ° ′
	9 00	17 59.1	152 28.8	S17 47.0	166 54.5	S12 29.8	92 43.8	S23 02.0	210 00.9	N 7 02.6
	01	33 01.6	167 28.3	47.9	181 55.4	30.4	107 46.0	02.0	225 03.1	02.5
	02	48 04.0	182 27.7	48.9	196 56.2	31.0	122 48.2	02.0	240 05.3	02.4
	03	63 06.5	197 27.1	. . 49.9	211 57.0	. . 31.6	137 50.5	. . 02.0	255 07.5	. . 02.2
	04	78 08.9	212 26.6	50.8	226 57.9	32.2	152 52.7	02.0	270 09.7	02.1
	05	93 11.4	227 26.0	51.8	241 58.7	32.8	167 54.9	01.9	285 11.9	02.0
	06	108 13.9	242 25.4	S17 52.8	256 59.5	S12 33.4	182 57.1	S23 01.9	300 14.1	N 7 01.9
	07	123 16.3	257 24.9	53.7	272 00.4	34.0	197 59.3	01.9	315 16.3	01.8
T	08	138 18.8	272 24.3	54.7	287 01.2	34.6	213 01.5	01.9	330 18.5	01.7
H	09	153 21.3	287 23.7	. . 55.7	302 02.0	. . 35.2	228 03.7	. . 01.8	345 20.7	. . 01.6
U	10	168 23.7	302 23.2	56.6	317 02.9	35.8	243 05.9	01.8	0 22.9	01.5
R	11	183 26.2	317 22.6	57.6	332 03.7	36.4	258 08.1	01.8	15 25.0	01.4
S	12	198 28.7	332 22.0	S17 58.6	347 04.5	S12 37.0	273 10.3	S23 01.8	30 27.2	N 7 01.3
D	13	213 31.1	347 21.4	17 59.5	2 05.4	37.6	288 12.5	01.8	45 29.4	01.2
A	14	228 33.6	2 20.9	18 00.5	17 06.2	38.2	303 14.7	01.7	60 31.6	01.1
Y	15	243 36.1	17 20.3	. . 01.4	32 07.0	. . 38.8	318 17.0	. . 01.7	75 33.8	. . 01.0
	16	258 38.5	32 19.7	02.4	47 07.9	39.4	333 19.2	01.7	90 36.0	00.9
	17	273 41.0	47 19.1	03.3	62 08.7	40.0	348 21.4	01.7	105 38.2	00.8
	18	288 43.4	62 18.6	S18 04.3	77 09.5	S12 40.6	3 23.6	S23 01.6	120 40.4	N 7 00.7
	19	303 45.9	77 18.0	05.3	92 10.4	41.2	18 25.8	01.6	135 42.6	00.5
	20	318 48.4	92 17.4	06.2	107 11.2	41.8	33 28.0	01.6	150 44.8	00.4
	21	333 50.8	107 16.8	. . 07.2	122 12.0	. . 42.4	48 30.2	. . 01.6	165 47.0	. . 00.3
	22	348 53.3	122 16.3	08.1	137 12.9	43.0	63 32.4	01.5	180 49.2	00.2
	23	3 55.8	137 15.7	09.1	152 13.7	43.6	78 34.6	01.5	195 51.4	00.1
	10 00	18 58.2	152 15.1	S18 10.0	167 14.5	S12 44.2	93 36.8	S23 01.5	210 53.6	N 7 00.0
	01	34 00.7	167 14.5	11.0	182 15.4	44.8	108 39.0	01.5	225 55.8	6 59.9
	02	49 03.2	182 14.0	11.9	197 16.2	45.4	123 41.2	01.5	240 58.0	59.8
	03	64 05.6	197 13.4	. . 12.9	212 17.0	. . 46.0	138 43.4	. . 01.4	256 00.2	. . 59.7
	04	79 08.1	212 12.8	13.8	227 17.8	46.6	153 45.6	01.4	271 02.4	59.6
	05	94 10.5	227 12.2	14.8	242 18.7	47.2	168 47.8	01.4	286 04.6	59.5
	06	109 13.0	242 11.6	S18 15.7	257 19.5	S12 47.8	183 50.0	S23 01.4	301 06.8	N 6 59.4
	07	124 15.5	257 11.1	16.7	272 20.3	48.4	198 52.2	01.3	316 09.0	59.3
	08	139 17.9	272 10.5	17.6	287 21.2	49.0	213 54.4	01.3	331 11.2	59.2
F	09	154 20.4	287 09.9	. . 18.5	302 22.0	. . 49.6	228 56.6	. . 01.3	346 13.4	. . 59.1
R	10	169 22.9	302 09.3	19.5	317 22.8	50.2	243 58.8	01.3	1 15.6	59.0
I	11	184 25.3	317 08.7	20.4	332 23.7	50.8	259 01.0	01.2	16 17.8	58.9
D	12	199 27.8	332 08.1	S18 21.4	347 24.5	S12 51.4	274 03.2	S23 01.2	31 20.0	N 6 58.8
A	13	214 30.3	347 07.6	22.3	2 25.3	52.0	289 05.4	01.2	46 22.2	58.6
Y	14	229 32.7	2 07.0	23.3	17 26.1	52.6	304 07.6	01.2	61 24.4	58.5
	15	244 35.2	17 06.4	. . 24.2	32 27.0	. . 53.2	319 09.8	. . 01.1	76 26.6	. . 58.4
	16	259 37.7	32 05.8	25.1	47 27.8	53.8	334 12.0	01.1	91 28.8	58.3
	17	274 40.1	47 05.2	26.1	62 28.6	54.4	349 14.2	01.1	106 31.0	58.2
	18	289 42.6	62 04.6	S18 27.0	77 29.4	S12 55.0	4 16.4	S23 01.1	121 33.2	N 6 58.1
	19	304 45.0	77 04.0	27.9	92 30.3	55.6	19 18.6	01.0	136 35.3	58.0
	20	319 47.5	92 03.5	28.9	107 31.1	56.2	34 20.8	01.0	151 37.5	57.9
	21	334 50.0	107 02.9	. . 29.8	122 31.9	. . 56.8	49 23.0	. . 01.0	166 39.7	. . 57.8
	22	349 52.4	122 02.3	30.8	137 32.8	57.4	64 25.2	01.0	181 41.9	57.7
	23	4 54.9	137 01.7	31.7	152 33.6	58.0	79 27.4	01.0	196 44.1	57.6
	11 00	19 57.4	152 01.1	S18 32.6	167 34.4	S12 58.6	94 29.6	S23 00.9	211 46.3	N 6 57.5
	01	34 59.8	167 00.5	33.5	182 35.2	59.2	109 31.8	00.9	226 48.5	57.4
	02	50 02.3	181 59.9	34.5	197 36.1	12 59.8	124 34.0	00.9	241 50.7	57.3
	03	65 04.8	196 59.3	. . 35.4	212 36.9	13 00.4	139 36.2	. . 00.9	256 52.9	. . 57.2
	04	80 07.2	211 58.7	36.3	227 37.7	00.9	154 38.4	00.8	271 55.1	57.1
	05	95 09.7	226 58.1	37.3	242 38.5	01.5	169 40.6	00.8	286 57.3	57.0
	06	110 12.1	241 57.6	S18 38.2	257 39.4	S13 02.1	184 42.8	S23 00.8	301 59.5	N 6 56.9
	07	125 14.6	256 57.0	39.1	272 40.2	02.7	199 45.0	00.8	317 01.7	56.8
S	08	140 17.1	271 56.4	40.0	287 41.0	03.3	214 47.1	00.7	332 03.9	56.7
A	09	155 19.5	286 55.8	. . 41.0	302 41.8	. . 03.9	229 49.3	. . 00.7	347 06.1	. . 56.5
T	10	170 22.0	301 55.2	41.9	317 42.7	04.5	244 51.5	00.7	2 08.3	56.4
U	11	185 24.5	316 54.6	42.8	332 43.5	05.1	259 53.7	00.7	17 10.5	56.3
R	12	200 26.9	331 54.0	S18 43.7	347 44.3	S13 05.7	274 55.9	S23 00.6	32 12.7	N 6 56.2
D	13	215 29.4	346 53.4	44.7	2 45.1	06.3	289 58.1	00.6	47 14.9	56.1
A	14	230 31.9	1 52.8	45.6	17 45.9	06.9	305 00.3	00.6	62 17.1	56.0
Y	15	245 34.3	16 52.2	. . 46.5	32 46.8	. . 07.5	320 02.5	. . 00.6	77 19.3	. . 55.9
	16	260 36.8	31 51.6	47.4	47 47.6	08.1	335 04.7	00.5	92 21.5	55.8
	17	275 39.3	46 51.0	48.3	62 48.4	08.7	350 06.9	00.5	107 23.7	55.7
	18	290 41.7	61 50.4	S18 49.3	77 49.2	S13 09.3	5 09.1	S23 00.5	122 25.9	N 6 55.6
	19	305 44.2	76 49.8	50.2	92 50.1	09.9	20 11.3	00.5	137 28.1	55.5
	20	320 46.6	91 49.2	51.1	107 50.9	10.5	35 13.4	00.4	152 30.3	55.4
	21	335 49.1	106 48.6	. . 52.0	122 51.7	. . 11.1	50 15.6	. . 00.4	167 32.5	. . 55.3
	22	350 51.6	121 48.0	52.9	137 52.5	11.6	65 17.8	00.4	182 34.7	55.2
	23	5 54.0	136 47.4	53.8	152 53.3	12.2	80 20.0	00.4	197 36.9	55.1
	Mer. Pass.	h m 22 40.4	v −0.6	d 0.9	v 0.8	d 0.6	v 2.2	d 0.0	v 2.2	d 0.1

STARS

Name	SHA ° ′	Dec ° ′
Acamar	315 20.5	S40 15.9
Achernar	335 28.5	S57 11.3
Acrux	173 14.3	S63 08.8
Adhara	255 15.3	S28 58.7
Aldebaran	290 53.2	N16 31.8
Alioth	166 24.1	N55 54.7
Alkaid	153 01.9	N49 16.2
Al Na'ir	27 47.6	S46 55.2
Alnilam	275 49.8	S 1 11.6
Alphard	217 59.7	S 8 41.6
Alphecca	126 14.2	N26 41.2
Alpheratz	357 46.9	N29 08.6
Altair	62 11.6	N 8 53.6
Ankaa	353 18.6	S42 15.4
Antares	112 30.9	S26 27.2
Arcturus	145 59.2	N19 08.2
Atria	107 36.3	S69 02.9
Avior	234 19.8	S59 31.9
Bellatrix	278 35.6	N 6 21.6
Betelgeuse	271 05.0	N 7 24.7
Canopus	263 57.6	S52 41.6
Capella	280 39.5	N46 00.4
Deneb	49 33.8	N45 19.0
Denebola	182 37.5	N14 31.4
Diphda	348 59.0	S17 56.1
Dubhe	193 56.2	N61 42.1
Elnath	278 16.9	N28 37.0
Eltanin	90 47.9	N51 29.5
Enif	33 50.4	N 9 55.1
Fomalhaut	15 27.5	S29 34.5
Gacrux	172 05.7	S57 09.7
Gienah	175 56.3	S17 35.4
Hadar	148 53.8	S60 25.0
Hamal	328 04.5	N23 30.4
Kaus Aust.	83 48.6	S34 23.0
Kochab	137 20.5	N74 07.2
Markab	13 41.6	N15 15.4
Menkar	314 18.5	N 4 07.7
Menkent	148 12.2	S36 24.8
Miaplacidus	221 41.2	S69 44.9
Mirfak	308 45.1	N49 53.6
Nunki	76 02.7	S26 17.2
Peacock	53 24.4	S56 42.6
Pollux	243 32.0	N28 00.3
Procyon	245 03.4	N 5 12.3
Rasalhague	96 09.9	N12 33.3
Regulus	207 47.4	N11 55.5
Rigel	281 15.3	S 8 11.2
Rigil Kent.	139 57.4	S60 52.4
Sabik	102 16.8	S15 44.2
Schedar	349 44.3	N56 35.3
Shaula	96 26.9	S37 06.8
Sirius	258 36.8	S16 43.4
Spica	158 35.3	S11 12.4
Suhail	222 55.4	S43 27.8
Vega	80 41.4	N38 47.7
Zuben'ubi	137 09.7	S16 04.7

	SHA ° ′	Mer. Pass. h m
Venus	133 16.9	13 52
Mars	148 16.3	12 50
Jupiter	74 38.6	17 43
Saturn	191 55.4	9 55

UT		SUN GHA	SUN Dec	MOON GHA	v	MOON Dec	d	HP
d h		° ′	° ′	° ′	′	° ′	′	′
9 00	THURSDAY	183 10.8	S 6 19.4	71 20.1	12.4	S20 20.3	9.9	55.3
01		198 11.0	20.3	85 51.5	12.5	20 10.4	10.0	55.3
02		213 11.1	21.3	100 23.0	12.5	20 00.4	10.1	55.3
03		228 11.3	. . 22.2	114 54.5	12.5	19 50.3	10.2	55.3
04		243 11.5	23.2	129 26.0	12.6	19 40.1	10.3	55.4
05		258 11.6	24.1	143 57.6	12.6	19 29.8	10.4	55.4
06		273 11.8	S 6 25.0	158 29.2	12.7	S19 19.4	10.5	55.4
07		288 12.0	26.0	173 00.9	12.7	19 08.9	10.6	55.4
08		303 12.2	26.9	187 32.6	12.7	18 58.3	10.7	55.5
09		318 12.3	. . 27.9	202 04.3	12.8	18 47.6	10.8	55.5
10		333 12.5	28.8	216 36.1	12.8	18 36.8	10.9	55.5
11		348 12.7	29.8	231 07.9	12.8	18 25.9	11.0	55.5
12		3 12.8	S 6 30.7	245 39.7	12.8	S18 14.9	11.0	55.6
13		18 13.0	31.7	260 11.5	12.9	18 03.9	11.2	55.6
14		33 13.2	32.6	274 43.4	12.9	17 52.7	11.2	55.6
15		48 13.3	. . 33.6	289 15.3	13.0	17 41.5	11.4	55.7
16		63 13.5	34.5	303 47.3	13.0	17 30.1	11.4	55.7
17		78 13.7	35.5	318 19.3	13.0	17 18.7	11.5	55.7
18		93 13.8	S 6 36.4	332 51.3	13.0	S17 07.2	11.6	55.7
19		108 14.0	37.4	347 23.3	13.1	16 55.6	11.7	55.8
20		123 14.2	38.3	1 55.4	13.1	16 43.9	11.8	55.8
21		138 14.3	. . 39.3	16 27.5	13.1	16 32.1	11.9	55.8
22		153 14.5	40.2	30 59.6	13.2	16 20.2	11.9	55.9
23		168 14.7	41.2	45 31.8	13.1	16 08.3	12.1	55.9
10 00	FRIDAY	183 14.8	S 6 42.1	60 03.9	13.2	S15 56.2	12.1	55.9
01		198 15.0	43.0	74 36.1	13.3	15 44.1	12.2	55.9
02		213 15.2	44.0	89 08.4	13.2	15 31.9	12.3	56.0
03		228 15.3	. . 44.9	103 40.6	13.3	15 19.6	12.4	56.0
04		243 15.5	45.9	118 12.9	13.3	15 07.2	12.4	56.0
05		258 15.7	46.8	132 45.2	13.3	14 54.8	12.5	56.1
06		273 15.8	S 6 47.8	147 17.5	13.4	S14 42.3	12.7	56.1
07		288 16.0	48.7	161 49.9	13.3	14 29.6	12.6	56.1
08		303 16.2	49.7	176 22.2	13.4	14 17.0	12.8	56.2
09		318 16.3	. . 50.6	190 54.6	13.4	14 04.2	12.9	56.2
10		333 16.5	51.5	205 27.0	13.5	13 51.3	12.9	56.2
11		348 16.7	52.5	219 59.5	13.4	13 38.4	13.0	56.3
12		3 16.8	S 6 53.4	234 31.9	13.5	S13 25.4	13.1	56.3
13		18 17.0	54.4	249 04.4	13.4	13 12.3	13.1	56.3
14		33 17.1	55.3	263 36.8	13.5	12 59.2	13.2	56.4
15		48 17.3	. . 56.3	278 09.3	13.6	12 46.0	13.3	56.4
16		63 17.5	57.2	292 41.9	13.5	12 32.7	13.4	56.4
17		78 17.6	58.2	307 14.4	13.5	12 19.3	13.4	56.5
18		93 17.8	S 6 59.1	321 46.9	13.6	S12 05.9	13.5	56.5
19		108 18.0	7 00.0	336 19.5	13.5	11 52.4	13.6	56.5
20		123 18.1	01.0	350 52.0	13.6	11 38.8	13.6	56.6
21		138 18.3	. . 01.9	5 24.6	13.6	11 25.2	13.7	56.6
22		153 18.4	02.9	19 57.2	13.6	11 11.5	13.8	56.6
23		168 18.6	03.8	34 29.8	13.6	10 57.7	13.9	56.7
11 00	SATURDAY	183 18.8	S 7 04.8	49 02.4	13.6	S10 43.8	13.9	56.7
01		198 18.9	05.7	63 35.0	13.6	10 29.9	13.9	56.7
02		213 19.1	06.6	78 07.6	13.6	10 16.0	14.1	56.8
03		228 19.3	. . 07.6	92 40.2	13.7	10 01.9	14.1	56.8
04		243 19.4	08.5	107 12.9	13.6	9 47.8	14.1	56.8
05		258 19.6	09.5	121 45.5	13.6	9 33.7	14.2	56.9
06		273 19.7	S 7 10.4	136 18.1	13.7	S 9 19.5	14.3	56.9
07		288 19.9	11.3	150 50.8	13.6	9 05.2	14.4	56.9
08		303 20.1	12.3	165 23.4	13.6	8 50.8	14.3	57.0
09		318 20.2	. . 13.2	179 56.0	13.7	8 36.5	14.5	57.0
10		333 20.4	14.2	194 28.7	13.6	8 22.0	14.5	57.0
11		348 20.5	15.1	209 01.3	13.6	8 07.5	14.6	57.1
12		3 20.7	S 7 16.0	223 33.9	13.7	S 7 52.9	14.6	57.1
13		18 20.9	17.0	238 06.6	13.6	7 38.3	14.6	57.1
14		33 21.0	17.9	252 39.2	13.6	7 23.7	14.8	57.2
15		48 21.2	. . 18.9	267 11.8	13.6	7 08.9	14.7	57.2
16		63 21.3	19.8	281 44.4	13.6	6 54.2	14.8	57.2
17		78 21.5	20.7	296 17.0	13.6	6 39.4	14.9	57.3
18		93 21.6	S 7 21.7	310 49.6	13.6	S 6 24.5	14.9	57.3
19		108 21.8	22.6	325 22.2	13.6	6 09.6	15.0	57.3
20		123 22.0	23.6	339 54.8	13.5	5 54.6	15.0	57.4
21		138 22.1	. . 24.5	354 27.3	13.6	5 39.6	15.1	57.4
22		153 22.3	25.4	8 59.9	13.5	5 24.5	15.0	57.4
23		168 22.4	26.4	23 32.4	13.6	S 5 09.5	15.2	57.5
		SD 16.0	d 0.9	SD 15.1		15.3		15.6

Lat.	Twilight Naut.	Twilight Civil	Sunrise	Moonrise 9	Moonrise 10	Moonrise 11	Moonrise 12
°	h m	h m	h m	h m	h m	h m	h m
N 72	04 34	05 53	07 02	18 35	17 21	16 41	16 08
N 70	04 41	05 51	06 53	17 43	17 00	16 32	16 07
68	04 46	05 50	06 46	17 10	16 44	16 24	16 06
66	04 50	05 49	06 41	16 46	16 30	16 17	16 06
64	04 53	05 48	06 36	16 27	16 19	16 12	16 05
62	04 56	05 47	06 32	16 12	16 09	16 07	16 04
60	04 58	05 46	06 28	15 58	16 01	16 03	16 04
N 58	05 00	05 45	06 25	15 47	15 54	15 59	16 03
56	05 01	05 44	06 22	15 37	15 47	15 55	16 03
54	05 03	05 43	06 19	15 28	15 41	15 52	16 02
52	05 04	05 43	06 17	15 20	15 36	15 49	16 02
50	05 05	05 42	06 14	15 13	15 31	15 47	16 02
45	05 06	05 40	06 10	14 58	15 21	15 41	16 01
N 40	05 07	05 38	06 06	14 45	15 12	15 37	16 01
35	05 07	05 37	06 02	14 35	15 05	15 33	16 00
30	05 07	05 35	05 59	14 25	14 58	15 29	16 00
20	05 06	05 31	05 53	14 09	14 46	15 23	15 59
N 10	05 03	05 27	05 48	13 54	14 36	15 17	15 58
0	04 59	05 23	05 44	13 41	14 27	15 12	15 58
S 10	04 53	05 18	05 39	13 27	14 17	15 07	15 57
20	04 45	05 11	05 33	13 13	14 07	15 01	15 56
30	04 35	05 03	05 27	12 56	13 55	14 55	15 56
35	04 28	04 58	05 24	12 46	13 48	14 51	15 55
40	04 19	04 52	05 20	12 35	13 41	14 47	15 55
45	04 09	04 45	05 15	12 22	13 32	14 42	15 55
S 50	03 56	04 36	05 09	12 06	13 21	14 36	15 54
52	03 49	04 32	05 06	11 58	13 15	14 34	15 54
54	03 42	04 27	05 03	11 50	13 10	14 31	15 53
56	03 33	04 22	05 00	11 40	13 03	14 27	15 53
58	03 24	04 16	04 57	11 29	12 56	14 24	15 53
S 60	03 13	04 09	04 53	11 17	12 48	14 20	15 52

Lat.	Sunset	Twilight Civil	Twilight Naut.	Moonset 9	Moonset 10	Moonset 11	Moonset 12
°	h m	h m	h m	h m	h m	h m	h m
N 72	16 30	17 39	18 57	21 31	24 21	00 21	02 38
N 70	16 39	17 40	18 51	22 21	24 40	00 40	02 44
68	16 46	17 42	18 46	22 53	24 55	00 55	02 50
66	16 52	17 43	18 42	23 15	25 06	01 06	02 54
64	16 57	17 44	18 39	23 33	25 16	01 16	02 58
62	17 01	17 45	18 37	23 48	25 24	01 24	03 01
60	17 05	17 46	18 34	24 00	00 00	01 32	03 03
N 58	17 08	17 47	18 33	24 11	00 11	01 38	03 06
56	17 11	17 48	18 31	24 20	00 20	01 43	03 08
54	17 14	17 49	18 30	24 28	00 28	01 48	03 10
52	17 16	17 50	18 29	24 35	00 35	01 53	03 12
50	17 19	17 51	18 28	24 41	00 41	01 57	03 13
45	17 23	17 53	18 27	24 55	00 55	02 05	03 17
N 40	17 28	17 55	18 26	00 02	01 07	02 12	03 19
35	17 31	17 57	18 26	00 15	01 16	02 19	03 22
30	17 34	17 58	18 26	00 26	01 25	02 24	03 24
20	17 40	18 02	18 28	00 45	01 39	02 33	03 28
N 10	17 45	18 06	18 31	01 01	01 51	02 41	03 31
0	17 50	18 11	18 35	01 17	02 03	02 48	03 34
S 10	17 55	18 16	18 41	01 32	02 15	02 56	03 37
20	18 01	18 23	18 49	01 48	02 27	03 04	03 40
30	18 07	18 31	19 00	02 07	02 41	03 12	03 43
35	18 11	18 36	19 07	02 17	02 49	03 17	03 45
40	18 15	18 42	19 15	02 30	02 58	03 23	03 47
45	18 20	18 50	19 26	02 44	03 08	03 30	03 50
S 50	18 26	18 59	19 40	03 01	03 21	03 38	03 53
52	18 28	19 03	19 46	03 10	03 27	03 41	03 54
54	18 32	19 08	19 54	03 19	03 33	03 45	03 56
56	18 35	19 14	20 02	03 29	03 41	03 49	03 57
58	18 39	19 20	20 12	03 41	03 49	03 54	03 59
S 60	18 43	19 27	20 24	03 54	03 58	04 00	04 01

Day	SUN Eqn. of Time 00h	SUN Eqn. of Time 12h	SUN Mer. Pass.	MOON Mer. Pass. Upper	MOON Mer. Pass. Lower	MOON Age	MOON Phase
d	m s	m s	h m	h m	h m	d %	
9	12 43	12 51	11 47	19 52	07 29	10 70	◐
10	12 59	13 07	11 47	20 38	08 15	11 79	
11	13 15	13 22	11 47	21 23	09 00	12 87	

UT d	h	ARIES GHA ° ′	VENUS −3.9 GHA ° ′	VENUS Dec ° ′	MARS +1.6 GHA ° ′	MARS Dec ° ′	JUPITER −2.2 GHA ° ′	JUPITER Dec ° ′	SATURN +1.0 GHA ° ′	SATURN Dec ° ′
12 SUNDAY	00	20 56.5	151 46.8	S18 54.8	167 54.2	S13 12.8	95 22.2	S23 00.3	212 39.1	N 6 55.0
	01	35 59.0	166 46.2	55.7	182 55.0	13.4	110 24.4	00.3	227 41.3	54.9
	02	51 01.4	181 45.6	56.6	197 55.8	14.0	125 26.6	00.3	242 43.5	54.8
	03	66 03.9	196 45.0	57.5	212 56.6	14.6	140 28.8	00.3	257 45.7	54.7
	04	81 06.4	211 44.4	58.4	227 57.4	15.2	155 31.0	00.2	272 47.9	54.6
	05	96 08.8	226 43.8	18 59.3	242 58.3	15.8	170 33.1	00.2	287 50.1	54.5
	06	111 11.3	241 43.2	S19 00.2	257 59.1	S13 16.4	185 35.3	S23 00.2	302 52.3	N 6 54.4
	07	126 13.8	256 42.6	01.1	272 59.9	17.0	200 37.5	00.2	317 54.5	54.3
	08	141 16.2	271 42.0	02.0	288 00.7	17.6	215 39.7	00.1	332 56.7	54.1
	09	156 18.7	286 41.4	02.9	303 01.5	18.2	230 41.9	00.1	347 58.9	54.0
	10	171 21.1	301 40.8	03.8	318 02.4	18.8	245 44.1	00.1	3 01.1	53.9
	11	186 23.6	316 40.2	04.7	333 03.2	19.3	260 46.3	00.1	18 03.3	53.8
	12	201 26.1	331 39.5	S19 05.6	348 04.0	S13 19.9	275 48.5	S23 00.0	33 05.5	N 6 53.7
	13	216 28.5	346 38.9	06.5	3 04.8	20.5	290 50.6	00.0	48 07.7	53.6
	14	231 31.0	1 38.3	07.4	18 05.6	21.1	305 52.8	00.0	63 09.9	53.5
	15	246 33.5	16 37.7	08.3	33 06.4	21.7	320 55.0	23 00.0	78 12.1	53.4
	16	261 35.9	31 37.1	09.2	48 07.3	22.3	335 57.2	22 59.9	93 14.3	53.3
	17	276 38.4	46 36.5	10.1	63 08.1	22.9	350 59.4	59.9	108 16.5	53.2
	18	291 40.9	61 35.9	S19 11.0	78 08.9	S13 23.5	6 01.6	S22 59.9	123 18.7	N 6 53.1
	19	306 43.3	76 35.3	11.9	93 09.7	24.1	21 03.7	59.9	138 20.9	53.0
	20	321 45.8	91 34.7	12.8	108 10.5	24.7	36 05.9	59.8	153 23.1	52.9
	21	336 48.2	106 34.1	13.7	123 11.3	25.2	51 08.1	59.8	168 25.3	52.8
	22	351 50.7	121 33.4	14.6	138 12.2	25.8	66 10.3	59.8	183 27.5	52.7
	23	6 53.2	136 32.8	15.5	153 13.0	26.4	81 12.5	59.8	198 29.7	52.6
13 MONDAY	00	21 55.6	151 32.2	S19 16.4	168 13.8	S13 27.0	96 14.7	S22 59.7	213 31.9	N 6 52.5
	01	36 58.1	166 31.6	17.3	183 14.6	27.6	111 16.8	59.7	228 34.1	52.4
	02	52 00.6	181 31.0	18.2	198 15.4	28.2	126 19.0	59.7	243 36.3	52.3
	03	67 03.0	196 30.4	19.1	213 16.2	28.8	141 21.2	59.6	258 38.5	52.2
	04	82 05.5	211 29.8	20.0	228 17.1	29.4	156 23.4	59.6	273 40.7	52.1
	05	97 08.0	226 29.1	20.9	243 17.9	30.0	171 25.6	59.6	288 42.9	52.0
	06	112 10.4	241 28.5	S19 21.7	258 18.7	S13 30.5	186 27.7	S22 59.6	303 45.1	N 6 51.9
	07	127 12.9	256 27.9	22.6	273 19.5	31.1	201 29.9	59.5	318 47.3	51.8
	08	142 15.4	271 27.3	23.5	288 20.3	31.7	216 32.1	59.5	333 49.5	51.7
	09	157 17.8	286 26.7	24.4	303 21.1	32.3	231 34.3	59.5	348 51.8	51.6
	10	172 20.3	301 26.1	25.3	318 21.9	32.9	246 36.5	59.5	3 54.0	51.5
	11	187 22.7	316 25.4	26.2	333 22.7	33.5	261 38.6	59.4	18 56.2	51.4
	12	202 25.2	331 24.8	S19 27.1	348 23.6	S13 34.1	276 40.8	S22 59.4	33 58.4	N 6 51.2
	13	217 27.7	346 24.2	27.9	3 24.4	34.7	291 43.0	59.4	49 00.6	51.1
	14	232 30.1	1 23.6	28.8	18 25.2	35.2	306 45.2	59.4	64 02.8	51.0
	15	247 32.6	16 23.0	29.7	33 26.0	35.8	321 47.4	59.3	79 05.0	50.9
	16	262 35.1	31 22.3	30.6	48 26.8	36.4	336 49.5	59.3	94 07.2	50.8
	17	277 37.5	46 21.7	31.4	63 27.6	37.0	351 51.7	59.3	109 09.4	50.7
	18	292 40.0	61 21.1	S19 32.3	78 28.4	S13 37.6	6 53.9	S22 59.3	124 11.6	N 6 50.6
	19	307 42.5	76 20.5	33.2	93 29.2	38.2	21 56.1	59.2	139 13.8	50.5
	20	322 44.9	91 19.8	34.1	108 30.1	38.8	36 58.2	59.2	154 16.0	50.4
	21	337 47.4	106 19.2	35.0	123 30.9	39.4	52 00.4	59.2	169 18.2	50.3
	22	352 49.8	121 18.6	35.8	138 31.7	39.9	67 02.6	59.1	184 20.4	50.2
	23	7 52.3	136 18.0	36.7	153 32.5	40.5	82 04.8	59.1	199 22.6	50.1
14 TUESDAY	00	22 54.8	151 17.3	S19 37.6	168 33.3	S13 41.1	97 06.9	S22 59.1	214 24.8	N 6 50.0
	01	37 57.2	166 16.7	38.4	183 34.1	41.7	112 09.1	59.1	229 27.0	49.9
	02	52 59.7	181 16.1	39.3	198 34.9	42.3	127 11.3	59.0	244 29.2	49.8
	03	68 02.2	196 15.5	40.2	213 35.7	42.9	142 13.5	59.0	259 31.4	49.7
	04	83 04.6	211 14.8	41.1	228 36.5	43.4	157 15.6	59.0	274 33.6	49.6
	05	98 07.1	226 14.2	41.9	243 37.3	44.0	172 17.8	59.0	289 35.8	49.5
	06	113 09.6	241 13.6	S19 42.8	258 38.1	S13 44.6	187 20.0	S22 58.9	304 38.0	N 6 49.4
	07	128 12.0	256 12.9	43.7	273 39.0	45.2	202 22.2	58.9	319 40.2	49.3
	08	143 14.5	271 12.3	44.5	288 39.8	45.8	217 24.3	58.9	334 42.4	49.2
	09	158 17.0	286 11.7	45.4	303 40.6	46.4	232 26.5	58.8	349 44.6	49.1
	10	173 19.4	301 11.1	46.2	318 41.4	47.0	247 28.7	58.8	4 46.8	49.0
	11	188 21.9	316 10.4	47.1	333 42.2	47.5	262 30.8	58.8	19 49.0	48.9
	12	203 24.3	331 09.8	S19 48.0	348 43.0	S13 48.1	277 33.0	S22 58.8	34 51.2	N 6 48.8
	13	218 26.8	346 09.2	48.8	3 43.8	48.7	292 35.2	58.7	49 53.4	48.7
	14	233 29.3	1 08.5	49.7	18 44.6	49.3	307 37.4	58.7	64 55.6	48.6
	15	248 31.7	16 07.9	50.5	33 45.4	49.9	322 39.5	58.7	79 57.8	48.5
	16	263 34.2	31 07.3	51.4	48 46.2	50.5	337 41.7	58.7	95 00.1	48.4
	17	278 36.7	46 06.6	52.3	63 47.0	51.0	352 43.9	58.6	110 02.3	48.3
	18	293 39.1	61 06.0	S19 53.1	78 47.8	S13 51.6	7 46.0	S22 58.6	125 04.5	N 6 48.2
	19	308 41.6	76 05.4	54.0	93 48.6	52.2	22 48.2	58.6	140 06.7	48.1
	20	323 44.1	91 04.7	54.8	108 49.4	52.8	37 50.4	58.5	155 08.9	48.0
	21	338 46.5	106 04.1	55.7	123 50.2	53.4	52 52.5	58.5	170 11.1	47.9
	22	353 49.0	121 03.4	56.5	138 51.1	54.0	67 54.7	58.5	185 13.3	47.8
	23	8 51.4	136 02.8	57.4	153 51.9	54.5	82 56.9	58.5	200 15.5	47.7
Mer. Pass.		22 28.6 (h m)	v −0.6	d 0.9	v 0.8	d 0.6	v 2.2	d 0.0	v 2.2	d 0.1

STARS

Name	SHA ° ′	Dec ° ′
Acamar	315 20.5	S40 15.9
Achernar	335 28.5	S57 11.4
Acrux	173 14.3	S63 08.8
Adhara	255 15.3	S28 58.7
Aldebaran	290 53.2	N16 31.8
Alioth	166 24.0	N55 54.7
Alkaid	153 01.9	N49 16.2
Al Na'ir	27 47.7	S46 55.2
Alnilam	275 49.8	S 1 11.6
Alphard	217 59.7	S 8 41.6
Alphecca	126 14.2	N26 41.2
Alpheratz	357 46.9	N29 08.6
Altair	62 11.7	N 8 53.6
Ankaa	353 18.6	S42 15.4
Antares	112 30.9	S26 27.2
Arcturus	145 59.2	N19 08.2
Atria	107 36.3	S69 02.9
Avior	234 19.8	S59 31.9
Bellatrix	278 35.6	N 6 21.6
Betelgeuse	271 05.0	N 7 24.7
Canopus	263 57.6	S52 41.6
Capella	280 39.4	N46 00.4
Deneb	49 33.9	N45 19.0
Denebola	182 37.5	N14 31.4
Diphda	348 59.0	S17 56.1
Dubhe	193 56.2	N61 42.1
Elnath	278 16.9	N28 37.0
Eltanin	90 48.0	N51 29.5
Enif	33 50.4	N 9 55.1
Fomalhaut	15 27.5	S29 34.5
Gacrux	172 05.7	S57 09.7
Gienah	175 56.3	S17 35.4
Hadar	148 53.8	S60 25.0
Hamal	328 04.5	N23 30.4
Kaus Aust.	83 48.6	S34 23.0
Kochab	137 20.5	N74 07.2
Markab	13 41.6	N15 15.4
Menkar	314 18.4	N 4 07.7
Menkent	148 12.2	S36 24.8
Miaplacidus	221 41.2	S69 44.9
Mirfak	308 45.1	N49 53.6
Nunki	76 02.7	S26 17.2
Peacock	53 24.4	S56 42.6
Pollux	243 32.0	N28 00.3
Procyon	245 03.4	N 5 12.3
Rasalhague	96 09.9	N12 33.3
Regulus	207 47.4	N11 55.5
Rigel	281 15.3	S 8 11.2
Rigil Kent.	139 57.4	S60 52.4
Sabik	102 16.8	S15 44.2
Schedar	349 44.3	N56 35.3
Shaula	96 26.9	S37 06.8
Sirius	258 36.8	S16 43.4
Spica	158 35.3	S11 12.4
Suhail	222 55.3	S43 27.8
Vega	80 41.5	N38 47.7
Zuben'ubi	137 09.7	S16 04.7

	SHA ° ′	Mer. Pass. h m
Venus	129 36.6	13 54
Mars	146 18.2	12 46
Jupiter	74 19.0	17 32
Saturn	191 36.3	9 44

UT d	UT h	SUN GHA ° ′	SUN Dec ° ′	MOON GHA ° ′	MOON *v* ′	MOON Dec ° ′	MOON *d* ′	MOON HP ′
12 SUNDAY	00	183 22.6	S 7 27.3	38 05.0	13.5	S 4 54.3	15.2	57.5
	01	198 22.7	28.2	52 37.5	13.5	4 39.1	15.2	57.6
	02	213 22.9	29.2	67 10.0	13.4	4 23.9	15.2	57.6
	03	228 23.1	. . 30.1	81 42.4	13.5	4 08.7	15.3	57.6
	04	243 23.2	31.1	96 14.9	13.4	3 53.4	15.4	57.7
	05	258 23.4	32.0	110 47.3	13.4	3 38.0	15.3	57.7
	06	273 23.5	S 7 32.9	125 19.7	13.4	S 3 22.7	15.5	57.7
	07	288 23.7	33.9	139 52.1	13.4	3 07.2	15.4	57.8
	08	303 23.8	34.8	154 24.5	13.3	2 51.8	15.5	57.8
	09	318 24.0	. . 35.7	168 56.8	13.3	2 36.3	15.5	57.8
	10	333 24.1	36.7	183 29.1	13.3	2 20.8	15.5	57.9
	11	348 24.3	37.6	198 01.4	13.3	2 05.3	15.6	57.9
	12	3 24.4	S 7 38.5	212 33.7	13.2	S 1 49.7	15.6	57.9
	13	18 24.6	39.5	227 05.9	13.2	1 34.1	15.6	58.0
	14	33 24.8	40.4	241 38.1	13.1	1 18.5	15.6	58.0
	15	48 24.9	. . 41.4	256 10.2	13.2	1 02.9	15.7	58.0
	16	63 25.1	42.3	270 42.4	13.1	0 47.2	15.7	58.1
	17	78 25.2	43.2	285 14.5	13.0	0 31.5	15.7	58.1
	18	93 25.4	S 7 44.2	299 46.5	13.1	S 0 15.8	15.7	58.1
	19	108 25.5	45.1	314 18.6	13.0	S 0 00.1	15.8	58.2
	20	123 25.7	46.0	328 50.6	12.9	N 0 15.7	15.7	58.2
	21	138 25.8	. . 47.0	343 22.5	12.9	0 31.4	15.8	58.2
	22	153 26.0	47.9	357 54.4	12.9	0 47.2	15.8	58.3
	23	168 26.1	48.8	12 26.3	12.8	1 03.0	15.8	58.3
13 MONDAY	00	183 26.3	S 7 49.8	26 58.1	12.8	N 1 18.8	15.8	58.3
	01	198 26.4	50.7	41 29.9	12.7	1 34.6	15.9	58.4
	02	213 26.6	51.6	56 01.6	12.7	1 50.5	15.8	58.4
	03	228 26.7	. . 52.6	70 33.3	12.7	2 06.3	15.9	58.4
	04	243 26.9	53.5	85 05.0	12.6	2 22.2	15.8	58.5
	05	258 27.0	54.4	99 36.6	12.5	2 38.0	15.9	58.5
	06	273 27.2	S 7 55.4	114 08.1	12.5	N 2 53.9	15.9	58.5
	07	288 27.3	56.3	128 39.6	12.5	3 09.8	15.8	58.6
	08	303 27.5	57.2	143 11.1	12.4	3 25.6	15.9	58.6
	09	318 27.6	. . 58.2	157 42.5	12.3	3 41.5	15.9	58.6
	10	333 27.8	7 59.1	172 13.8	12.3	3 57.4	15.8	58.7
	11	348 27.9	8 00.0	186 45.1	12.2	4 13.2	15.9	58.7
	12	3 28.1	S 8 00.9	201 16.3	12.2	N 4 29.1	15.9	58.7
	13	18 28.2	01.9	215 47.5	12.1	4 45.0	15.8	58.8
	14	33 28.4	02.8	230 18.6	12.1	5 00.8	15.9	58.8
	15	48 28.5	. . 03.7	244 49.7	12.0	5 16.7	15.8	58.8
	16	63 28.7	04.7	259 20.7	11.9	5 32.5	15.8	58.9
	17	78 28.8	05.6	273 51.6	11.9	5 48.3	15.8	58.9
	18	93 29.0	S 8 06.5	288 22.5	11.8	N 6 04.1	15.8	58.9
	19	108 29.1	07.5	302 53.3	11.7	6 19.9	15.8	58.9
	20	123 29.3	08.4	317 24.0	11.7	6 35.7	15.8	59.0
	21	138 29.4	. . 09.3	331 54.7	11.6	6 51.5	15.7	59.0
	22	153 29.5	10.2	346 25.3	11.6	7 07.2	15.8	59.0
	23	168 29.7	11.2	0 55.9	11.4	7 23.0	15.7	59.1
14 TUESDAY	00	183 29.8	S 8 12.1	15 26.3	11.4	N 7 38.7	15.6	59.1
	01	198 30.0	13.0	29 56.7	11.3	7 54.3	15.7	59.1
	02	213 30.1	14.0	44 27.0	11.3	8 10.0	15.6	59.1
	03	228 30.3	. . 14.9	58 57.3	11.2	8 25.6	15.6	59.2
	04	243 30.4	15.8	73 27.5	11.1	8 41.2	15.6	59.2
	05	258 30.6	16.7	87 57.6	11.0	8 56.8	15.5	59.2
	06	273 30.7	S 8 17.7	102 27.6	10.9	N 9 12.3	15.5	59.3
	07	288 30.8	18.6	116 57.5	10.9	9 27.8	15.5	59.3
	08	303 31.0	19.5	131 27.4	10.8	9 43.3	15.4	59.3
	09	318 31.1	. . 20.5	145 57.2	10.7	9 58.7	15.4	59.3
	10	333 31.3	21.4	160 26.9	10.6	10 14.1	15.3	59.4
	11	348 31.4	22.3	174 56.5	10.5	10 29.4	15.3	59.4
	12	3 31.6	S 8 23.2	189 26.0	10.5	N10 44.7	15.3	59.4
	13	18 31.7	24.2	203 55.5	10.4	11 00.0	15.2	59.4
	14	33 31.9	25.1	218 24.9	10.3	11 15.2	15.1	59.5
	15	48 32.0	. . 26.0	232 54.2	10.2	11 30.3	15.1	59.5
	16	63 32.1	26.9	247 23.4	10.1	11 45.4	15.1	59.5
	17	78 32.3	27.9	261 52.5	10.0	12 00.5	15.0	59.5
	18	93 32.4	S 8 28.8	276 21.5	9.9	N12 15.5	14.9	59.6
	19	108 32.6	29.7	290 50.4	9.9	12 30.4	14.9	59.6
	20	123 32.7	30.6	305 19.3	9.7	12 45.3	14.8	59.6
	21	138 32.8	. . 31.6	319 48.0	9.7	13 00.1	14.8	59.6
	22	153 33.0	32.5	334 16.7	9.5	13 14.9	14.7	59.6
	23	168 33.1	33.4	348 45.2	9.5	N13 29.6	14.6	59.7
		SD 16.1	*d* 0.9	SD 15.8		16.0		16.2

Lat.	Twilight Naut.	Twilight Civil	Sunrise	Moonrise 12	Moonrise 13	Moonrise 14	Moonrise 15
°	h m	h m	h m	h m	h m	h m	h m
N 72	04 48	06 06	07 16	16 08	15 36	14 56	13 44
N 70	04 52	06 03	07 06	16 07	15 43	15 14	14 30
68	04 56	06 01	06 57	16 06	15 49	15 29	15 01
66	04 59	05 58	06 51	16 06	15 54	15 41	15 25
64	05 01	05 56	06 45	16 05	15 58	15 51	15 43
62	05 03	05 55	06 40	16 04	16 02	16 00	15 58
60	05 05	05 53	06 35	16 04	16 05	16 07	16 11
N 58	05 06	05 52	06 31	16 03	16 08	16 14	16 22
56	05 07	05 50	06 28	16 03	16 11	16 20	16 32
54	05 08	05 49	06 25	16 02	16 13	16 25	16 41
52	05 09	05 48	06 22	16 02	16 15	16 30	16 49
50	05 09	05 47	06 19	16 02	16 17	16 34	16 56
45	05 10	05 44	06 13	16 01	16 22	16 44	17 11
N 40	05 10	05 41	06 09	16 01	16 25	16 52	17 23
35	05 10	05 39	06 04	16 00	16 28	16 59	17 34
30	05 09	05 37	06 01	16 00	16 31	17 05	17 43
20	05 06	05 32	05 54	15 59	16 36	17 16	18 00
N 10	05 03	05 27	05 48	15 58	16 40	17 25	18 14
0	04 58	05 22	05 43	15 58	16 45	17 34	18 28
S 10	04 51	05 16	05 37	15 57	16 49	17 43	18 41
20	04 43	05 09	05 31	15 56	16 53	17 53	18 56
30	04 31	05 00	05 24	15 56	16 59	18 04	19 13
35	04 23	04 54	05 20	15 55	17 02	18 11	19 23
40	04 14	04 47	05 15	15 55	17 05	18 18	19 35
45	04 03	04 39	05 09	15 55	17 09	18 27	19 48
S 50	03 48	04 29	05 03	15 54	17 14	18 38	20 05
52	03 41	04 25	05 00	15 54	17 16	18 43	20 13
54	03 33	04 19	04 56	15 53	17 19	18 48	20 22
56	03 24	04 13	04 53	15 53	17 22	18 54	20 32
58	03 14	04 07	04 48	15 53	17 25	19 01	20 43
S 60	03 01	03 59	04 44	15 52	17 28	19 09	20 56

Lat.	Sunset	Twilight Civil	Twilight Naut.	Moonset 12	Moonset 13	Moonset 14	Moonset 15
°	h m	h m	h m	h m	h m	h m	h m
N 72	16 14	17 24	18 42	02 38	04 52	07 15	10 17
N 70	16 25	17 27	18 37	02 44	04 48	06 59	09 32
68	16 33	17 30	18 34	02 50	04 45	06 47	09 03
66	16 40	17 32	18 31	02 54	04 43	06 37	08 41
64	16 46	17 34	18 29	02 58	04 41	06 28	08 24
62	16 51	17 36	18 27	03 01	04 39	06 21	08 10
60	16 56	17 38	18 26	03 03	04 37	06 15	07 59
N 58	17 00	17 40	18 25	03 06	04 36	06 10	07 49
56	17 04	17 41	18 24	03 08	04 35	06 05	07 40
54	17 07	17 42	18 23	03 10	04 34	06 01	07 32
52	17 10	17 44	18 23	03 12	04 33	05 57	07 25
50	17 12	17 45	18 22	03 13	04 32	05 53	07 19
45	17 18	17 48	18 22	03 17	04 30	05 46	07 05
N 40	17 23	17 50	18 22	03 19	04 28	05 40	06 54
35	17 27	17 53	18 22	03 22	04 27	05 34	06 45
30	17 31	17 55	18 23	03 24	04 26	05 30	06 37
20	17 38	18 00	18 26	03 28	04 23	05 21	06 23
N 10	17 44	18 05	18 29	03 31	04 21	05 14	06 11
0	17 49	18 10	18 35	03 34	04 20	05 08	05 59
S 10	17 55	18 16	18 41	03 37	04 18	05 01	05 48
20	18 02	18 24	18 50	03 40	04 16	04 54	05 36
30	18 09	18 33	19 02	03 43	04 14	04 46	05 22
35	18 13	18 39	19 10	03 45	04 13	04 42	05 14
40	18 18	18 46	19 19	03 47	04 11	04 37	05 05
45	18 24	18 54	19 30	03 50	04 09	04 31	04 55
S 50	18 31	19 04	19 45	03 53	04 08	04 23	04 42
52	18 34	19 09	19 53	03 54	04 07	04 20	04 36
54	18 37	19 14	20 01	03 56	04 06	04 17	04 30
56	18 41	19 21	20 10	03 57	04 05	04 13	04 23
58	18 45	19 27	20 21	03 59	04 03	04 08	04 15
S 60	18 50	19 35	20 34	04 01	04 02	04 03	04 06

Day	SUN Eqn. of Time 00^h	SUN Eqn. of Time 12^h	SUN Mer. Pass.	MOON Mer. Pass. Upper	MOON Mer. Pass. Lower	MOON Age	MOON Phase
d	m s	m s	h m	h m	h m	d %	
12	13 30	13 37	11 46	22 09	09 46	13 93	
13	13 45	13 52	11 46	22 56	10 32	14 98	○
14	13 59	14 06	11 46	23 47	11 21	15 100	

	UT	ARIES	VENUS −3.9		MARS +1.6		JUPITER −2.2		SATURN +1.0	
	d h	GHA ° ′	GHA ° ′	Dec ° ′	GHA ° ′	Dec ° ′	GHA ° ′	Dec ° ′	GHA ° ′	Dec ° ′
	15 00	23 53.9	151 02.2	S19 58.2	168 52.7	S13 55.1	97 59.0	S22 58.4	215 17.7	N 6 47.6
	01	38 56.4	166 01.5	59.1	183 53.5	55.7	113 01.2	58.4	230 19.9	47.5
	02	53 58.8	181 00.9	19 59.9	198 54.3	56.3	128 03.4	58.4	245 22.1	47.4
	03	69 01.3	196 00.3	20 00.8	213 55.1 . .	56.9	143 05.5 . .	58.3	260 24.3 . .	47.3
	04	84 03.8	210 59.6	01.6	228 55.9	57.4	158 07.7	58.3	275 26.5	47.1
	05	99 06.2	225 59.0	02.5	243 56.7	58.0	173 09.9	58.3	290 28.7	47.0
	06	114 08.7	240 58.3	S20 03.3	258 57.5	S13 58.6	188 12.0	S22 58.3	305 30.9	N 6 46.9
W	07	129 11.2	255 57.7	04.2	273 58.3	59.2	203 14.2	58.2	320 33.1	46.8
E	08	144 13.6	270 57.0	05.0	288 59.1	13 59.8	218 16.4	58.2	335 35.3	46.7
D	09	159 16.1	285 56.4 . .	05.9	303 59.9	14 00.3	233 18.5 . .	58.2	350 37.5 . .	46.6
N	10	174 18.6	300 55.8	06.7	319 00.7	00.9	248 20.7	58.2	5 39.7	46.5
E	11	189 21.0	315 55.1	07.5	334 01.5	01.5	263 22.9	58.1	20 41.9	46.4
S	12	204 23.5	330 54.5	S20 08.4	349 02.3	S14 02.1	278 25.0	S22 58.1	35 44.2	N 6 46.3
D	13	219 25.9	345 53.8	09.2	4 03.1	02.7	293 27.2	58.1	50 46.4	46.2
A	14	234 28.4	0 53.2	10.1	19 03.9	03.2	308 29.4	58.0	65 48.6	46.1
Y	15	249 30.9	15 52.5 . .	10.9	34 04.7 . .	03.8	323 31.5 . .	58.0	80 50.8 . .	46.0
	16	264 33.3	30 51.9	11.7	49 05.5	04.4	338 33.7	58.0	95 53.0	45.9
	17	279 35.8	45 51.2	12.6	64 06.3	05.0	353 35.9	58.0	110 55.2	45.8
	18	294 38.3	60 50.6	S20 13.4	79 07.1	S14 05.6	8 38.0	S22 57.9	125 57.4	N 6 45.7
	19	309 40.7	75 50.0	14.2	94 07.9	06.1	23 40.2	57.9	140 59.6	45.6
	20	324 43.2	90 49.3	15.1	109 08.7	06.7	38 42.3	57.9	156 01.8	45.5
	21	339 45.7	105 48.7 . .	15.9	124 09.5 . .	07.3	53 44.5 . .	57.8	171 04.0 . .	45.4
	22	354 48.1	120 48.0	16.7	139 10.3	07.9	68 46.7	57.8	186 06.2	45.3
	23	9 50.6	135 47.4	17.6	154 11.1	08.5	83 48.8	57.8	201 08.4	45.2
	16 00	24 53.1	150 46.7	S20 18.4	169 11.9	S14 09.0	98 51.0	S22 57.8	216 10.6	N 6 45.1
	01	39 55.5	165 46.1	19.2	184 12.7	09.6	113 53.2	57.7	231 12.8	45.0
	02	54 58.0	180 45.4	20.0	199 13.5	10.2	128 55.3	57.7	246 15.0	44.9
	03	70 00.4	195 44.8 . .	20.9	214 14.3 . .	10.8	143 57.5 . .	57.7	261 17.2 . .	44.8
	04	85 02.9	210 44.1	21.7	229 15.1	11.3	158 59.6	57.6	276 19.5	44.7
	05	100 05.4	225 43.5	22.5	244 15.9	11.9	174 01.8	57.6	291 21.7	44.6
	06	115 07.8	240 42.8	S20 23.3	259 16.7	S14 12.5	189 04.0	S22 57.6	306 23.9	N 6 44.5
T	07	130 10.3	255 42.1	24.2	274 17.5	13.1	204 06.1	57.5	321 26.1	44.4
H	08	145 12.8	270 41.5	25.0	289 18.3	13.7	219 08.3	57.5	336 28.3	44.3
U	09	160 15.2	285 40.8 . .	25.8	304 19.1 . .	14.2	234 10.4 . .	57.5	351 30.5 . .	44.2
R	10	175 17.7	300 40.2	26.6	319 19.9	14.8	249 12.6	57.5	6 32.7	44.1
S	11	190 20.2	315 39.5	27.5	334 20.7	15.4	264 14.7	57.4	21 34.9	44.0
D	12	205 22.6	330 38.9	S20 28.3	349 21.5	S14 16.0	279 16.9	S22 57.4	36 37.1	N 6 43.9
A	13	220 25.1	345 38.2	29.1	4 22.3	16.5	294 19.1	57.4	51 39.3	43.8
Y	14	235 27.5	0 37.6	29.9	19 23.1	17.1	309 21.2	57.3	66 41.5	43.7
	15	250 30.0	15 36.9 . .	30.7	34 23.8 . .	17.7	324 23.4 . .	57.3	81 43.7 . .	43.6
	16	265 32.5	30 36.2	31.5	49 24.6	18.3	339 25.5	57.3	96 45.9	43.5
	17	280 34.9	45 35.6	32.3	64 25.4	18.8	354 27.7	57.3	111 48.2	43.4
	18	295 37.4	60 34.9	S20 33.2	79 26.2	S14 19.4	9 29.8	S22 57.2	126 50.4	N 6 43.3
	19	310 39.9	75 34.3	34.0	94 27.0	20.0	24 32.0	57.2	141 52.6	43.2
	20	325 42.3	90 33.6	34.8	109 27.8	20.6	39 34.2	57.2	156 54.8	43.1
	21	340 44.8	105 32.9 . .	35.6	124 28.6 . .	21.1	54 36.3 . .	57.1	171 57.0 . .	43.0
	22	355 47.3	120 32.3	36.4	139 29.4	21.7	69 38.5	57.1	186 59.2	42.9
	23	10 49.7	135 31.6	37.2	154 30.2	22.3	84 40.6	57.1	202 01.4	42.8
	17 00	25 52.2	150 31.0	S20 38.0	169 31.0	S14 22.9	99 42.8	S22 57.0	217 03.6	N 6 42.7
	01	40 54.7	165 30.3	38.8	184 31.8	23.4	114 44.9	57.0	232 05.8	42.6
	02	55 57.1	180 29.6	39.6	199 32.6	24.0	129 47.1	57.0	247 08.0	42.5
	03	70 59.6	195 29.0 . .	40.4	214 33.4 . .	24.6	144 49.2 . .	57.0	262 10.2 . .	42.4
	04	86 02.0	210 28.3	41.2	229 34.2	25.2	159 51.4	56.9	277 12.4	42.3
	05	101 04.5	225 27.6	42.0	244 35.0	25.7	174 53.5	56.9	292 14.7	42.2
	06	116 07.0	240 27.0	S20 42.8	259 35.7	S14 26.3	189 55.7	S22 56.9	307 16.9	N 6 42.1
	07	131 09.4	255 26.3	43.6	274 36.5	26.9	204 57.8	56.8	322 19.1	42.0
	08	146 11.9	270 25.6	44.4	289 37.3	27.4	220 00.0	56.8	337 21.3	41.9
F	09	161 14.4	285 25.0 . .	45.2	304 38.1 . .	28.0	235 02.2 . .	56.8	352 23.5 . .	41.8
R	10	176 16.8	300 24.3	46.0	319 38.9	28.6	250 04.3	56.7	7 25.7	41.7
I	11	191 19.3	315 23.6	46.8	334 39.7	29.2	265 06.5	56.7	22 27.9	41.6
D	12	206 21.8	330 23.0	S20 47.6	349 40.5	S14 29.7	280 08.6	S22 56.7	37 30.1	N 6 41.5
A	13	221 24.2	345 22.3	48.4	4 41.3	30.3	295 10.8	56.7	52 32.3	41.4
Y	14	236 26.7	0 21.6	49.2	19 42.1	30.9	310 12.9	56.6	67 34.5	41.3
	15	251 29.2	15 21.0 . .	50.0	34 42.9 . .	31.5	325 15.1 . .	56.6	82 36.7 . .	41.2
	16	266 31.6	30 20.3	50.8	49 43.7	32.0	340 17.2	56.6	97 39.0	41.1
	17	281 34.1	45 19.6	51.6	64 44.4	32.6	355 19.4	56.5	112 41.2	41.0
	18	296 36.5	60 19.0	S20 52.4	79 45.2	S14 33.2	10 21.5	S22 56.5	127 43.4	N 6 40.9
	19	311 39.0	75 18.3	53.2	94 46.0	33.7	25 23.7	56.5	142 45.6	40.8
	20	326 41.5	90 17.6	54.0	109 46.8	34.3	40 25.8	56.4	157 47.8	40.7
	21	341 43.9	105 16.9 . .	54.8	124 47.6 . .	34.9	55 27.9 . .	56.4	172 50.0 . .	40.6
	22	356 46.4	120 16.3	55.5	139 48.4	35.4	70 30.1	56.4	187 52.2	40.5
	23	11 48.9	135 15.6	56.3	154 49.2	36.0	85 32.2	56.4	202 54.4	40.4
	Mer. Pass.	h m 22 16.8	v −0.7	d 0.8	v 0.8	d 0.6	v 2.2	d 0.0	v 2.2	d 0.1

STARS Name	SHA ° ′	Dec ° ′
Acamar	315 20.5	S40 15.9
Achernar	335 28.5	S57 11.4
Acrux	173 14.3	S63 08.8
Adhara	255 15.2	S28 58.7
Aldebaran	290 53.2	N16 31.8
Alioth	166 24.0	N55 54.6
Alkaid	153 02.0	N49 16.1
Al Na'ir	27 47.7	S46 55.2
Alnilam	275 49.8	S 1 11.6
Alphard	217 59.7	S 8 41.6
Alphecca	126 14.2	N26 41.2
Alpheratz	357 46.9	N29 08.6
Altair	62 11.7	N 8 53.6
Ankaa	353 18.6	S42 15.4
Antares	112 30.9	S26 27.2
Arcturus	145 59.2	N19 08.2
Atria	107 36.3	S69 02.9
Avior	234 19.7	S59 31.9
Bellatrix	278 35.6	N 6 21.6
Betelgeuse	271 05.0	N 7 24.7
Canopus	263 57.6	S52 41.6
Capella	280 39.4	N46 00.4
Deneb	49 33.9	N45 19.0
Denebola	182 37.5	N14 31.4
Diphda	348 59.0	S17 56.1
Dubhe	193 56.2	N61 42.0
Elnath	278 16.9	N28 37.0
Eltanin	90 48.0	N51 29.5
Enif	33 50.4	N 9 55.1
Fomalhaut	15 27.5	S29 34.5
Gacrux	172 05.7	S57 09.7
Gienah	175 56.3	S17 35.4
Hadar	148 53.8	S60 25.0
Hamal	328 04.5	N23 30.4
Kaus Aust.	83 48.6	S34 23.0
Kochab	137 20.5	N74 07.2
Markab	13 41.6	N15 15.4
Menkar	314 18.4	N 4 07.7
Menkent	148 12.2	S36 24.8
Miaplacidus	221 41.1	S69 44.9
Mirfak	308 45.1	N49 53.6
Nunki	76 02.7	S26 17.2
Peacock	53 24.5	S56 42.6
Pollux	243 32.0	N28 00.3
Procyon	245 03.4	N 5 12.3
Rasalhague	96 09.9	N12 33.3
Regulus	207 47.4	N11 55.5
Rigel	281 15.2	S 8 11.2
Rigil Kent.	139 57.5	S60 52.4
Sabik	102 16.8	S15 44.2
Schedar	349 44.3	N56 35.4
Shaula	96 26.9	S37 06.8
Sirius	258 36.7	S16 43.4
Spica	158 35.3	S11 12.4
Suhail	222 55.3	S43 27.8
Vega	80 41.5	N38 47.7
Zuben'ubi	137 09.7	S16 04.7

	SHA ° ′	Mer. Pass. h m
Venus	125 53.7	13 57
Mars	144 18.8	12 43
Jupiter	73 57.9	17 22
Saturn	191 17.6	9 34

UT d h	SUN GHA ° ′	SUN Dec ° ′	MOON GHA ° ′	v ′	MOON Dec ° ′	d ′	HP ′
15 00	183 33.3	S 8 34.3	3 13.7	9.4	N13 44.2	14.6	59.7
01	198 33.4	35.3	17 42.1	9.3	13 58.8	14.5	59.7
02	213 33.5	36.2	32 10.4	9.1	14 13.3	14.4	59.7
03	228 33.7	. . 37.1	46 38.5	9.1	14 27.7	14.4	59.7
04	243 33.8	38.0	61 06.6	9.0	14 42.1	14.2	59.8
05	258 34.0	38.9	75 34.6	8.9	14 56.3	14.2	59.8
06	273 34.1	S 8 39.9	90 02.5	8.8	N15 10.5	14.2	59.8
W 07	288 34.2	40.8	104 30.3	8.7	15 24.7	14.0	59.8
E 08	303 34.4	41.7	118 58.0	8.6	15 38.7	13.9	59.8
D 09	318 34.5	. . 42.6	133 25.6	8.5	15 52.6	13.9	59.9
N 10	333 34.6	43.6	147 53.1	8.4	16 06.5	13.8	59.9
E 11	348 34.8	44.5	162 20.5	8.2	16 20.3	13.7	59.9
S 12	3 34.9	S 8 45.4	176 47.7	8.2	N16 34.0	13.6	59.9
D 13	18 35.1	46.3	191 14.9	8.1	16 47.6	13.5	59.9
A 14	33 35.2	47.2	205 42.0	8.0	17 01.1	13.4	59.9
Y 15	48 35.3	. . 48.2	220 09.0	7.9	17 14.5	13.3	60.0
16	63 35.5	49.1	234 35.9	7.7	17 27.8	13.2	60.0
17	78 35.6	50.0	249 02.6	7.7	17 41.0	13.1	60.0
18	93 35.7	S 8 50.9	263 29.3	7.6	N17 54.1	13.0	60.0
19	108 35.9	51.8	277 55.9	7.4	18 07.1	12.9	60.0
20	123 36.0	52.8	292 22.3	7.4	18 20.0	12.8	60.0
21	138 36.1	. . 53.7	306 48.7	7.2	18 32.8	12.7	60.1
22	153 36.3	54.6	321 14.9	7.2	18 45.5	12.5	60.1
23	168 36.4	55.5	335 41.1	7.0	18 58.0	12.5	60.1
16 00	183 36.5	S 8 56.4	350 07.1	6.9	N19 10.5	12.3	60.1
01	198 36.7	57.4	4 33.0	6.9	19 22.8	12.3	60.1
02	213 36.8	58.3	18 58.9	6.7	19 35.1	12.1	60.1
03	228 36.9	8 59.2	33 24.6	6.6	19 47.2	11.9	60.1
04	243 37.1	9 00.1	47 50.2	6.5	19 59.1	11.9	60.1
05	258 37.2	01.0	62 15.7	6.5	20 11.0	11.7	60.1
06	273 37.3	S 9 01.9	76 41.2	6.3	N20 22.7	11.6	60.2
07	288 37.5	02.9	91 06.5	6.2	20 34.3	11.5	60.2
T 08	303 37.6	03.8	105 31.7	6.1	20 45.8	11.3	60.2
H 09	318 37.7	. . 04.7	119 56.8	6.0	20 57.1	11.2	60.2
U 10	333 37.9	05.6	134 21.8	5.9	21 08.3	11.1	60.2
R 11	348 38.0	06.5	148 46.7	5.8	21 19.4	10.9	60.2
S 12	3 38.1	S 9 07.4	163 11.5	5.7	N21 30.3	10.8	60.2
D 13	18 38.3	08.4	177 36.2	5.5	21 41.1	10.7	60.2
A 14	33 38.4	09.3	192 00.7	5.5	21 51.8	10.5	60.2
Y 15	48 38.5	. . 10.2	206 25.2	5.4	22 02.3	10.4	60.2
16	63 38.7	11.1	220 49.6	5.3	22 12.7	10.2	60.2
17	78 38.8	12.0	235 13.9	5.2	22 22.9	10.0	60.2
18	93 38.9	S 9 12.9	249 38.1	5.1	N22 32.9	10.0	60.2
19	108 39.0	13.9	264 02.2	5.0	22 42.9	9.7	60.2
20	123 39.2	14.8	278 26.2	4.9	22 52.6	9.6	60.2
21	138 39.3	. . 15.7	292 50.1	4.9	23 02.2	9.5	60.3
22	153 39.4	16.6	307 14.0	4.7	23 11.7	9.3	60.3
23	168 39.6	17.5	321 37.7	4.6	23 21.0	9.1	60.3
17 00	183 39.7	S 9 18.4	336 01.3	4.6	N23 30.1	9.0	60.3
01	198 39.8	19.3	350 24.9	4.4	23 39.1	8.8	60.3
02	213 39.9	20.3	4 48.3	4.4	23 47.9	8.7	60.3
03	228 40.1	. . 21.2	19 11.7	4.3	23 56.6	8.4	60.3
04	243 40.2	22.1	33 35.0	4.2	24 05.0	8.4	60.3
05	258 40.3	23.0	47 58.2	4.1	24 13.4	8.1	60.3
06	273 40.4	S 9 23.9	62 21.3	4.0	N24 21.5	8.0	60.3
07	288 40.6	24.8	76 44.3	4.0	24 29.5	7.8	60.3
08	303 40.7	25.7	91 07.3	3.9	24 37.3	7.6	60.3
F 09	318 40.8	. . 26.6	105 30.2	3.8	24 44.9	7.5	60.3
R 10	333 40.9	27.5	119 53.0	3.7	24 52.4	7.2	60.3
I 11	348 41.1	28.5	134 15.7	3.6	24 59.6	7.2	60.3
D 12	3 41.2	S 9 29.4	148 38.3	3.6	N25 06.8	6.9	60.3
A 13	18 41.3	30.3	163 00.9	3.5	25 13.7	6.7	60.3
Y 14	33 41.4	31.2	177 23.4	3.5	25 20.4	6.6	60.3
15	48 41.6	. . 32.1	191 45.9	3.4	25 27.0	6.4	60.3
16	63 41.7	33.0	206 08.3	3.3	25 33.4	6.2	60.3
17	78 41.8	33.9	220 30.6	3.3	25 39.6	6.0	60.2
18	93 41.9	S 9 34.8	234 52.9	3.2	N25 45.6	5.8	60.2
19	108 42.1	35.7	249 15.1	3.1	25 51.4	5.6	60.2
20	123 42.2	36.6	263 37.2	3.1	25 57.0	5.5	60.2
21	138 42.3	. . 37.6	277 59.3	3.0	26 02.5	5.2	60.2
22	153 42.4	38.5	292 21.3	3.0	26 07.7	5.1	60.2
23	168 42.6	39.4	306 43.3	3.0	N26 12.8	4.9	60.2
	SD 16.1	*d* 0.9	SD 16.3		16.4		16.4

Lat.	Twilight Naut.	Twilight Civil	Sunrise	Moonrise 15	Moonrise 16	Moonrise 17	Moonrise 18
°	h m	h m	h m	h m	h m	h m	h m
N 72	05 01	06 19	07 31	13 44	▭	▭	▭
N 70	05 04	06 15	07 18	14 30	▭	▭	▭
68	05 07	06 11	07 09	15 01	13 53	▭	▭
66	05 08	06 08	07 01	15 25	14 57	▭	▭
64	05 10	06 05	06 54	15 43	15 33	15 10	▭
62	05 11	06 02	06 48	15 58	15 58	16 03	16 24
60	05 12	06 00	06 43	16 11	16 19	16 35	17 11
N 58	05 13	05 58	06 38	16 22	16 36	16 59	17 42
56	05 13	05 56	06 34	16 32	16 50	17 19	18 05
54	05 13	05 54	06 30	16 41	17 02	17 35	18 24
52	05 14	05 53	06 27	16 49	17 13	17 49	18 40
50	05 14	05 51	06 24	16 56	17 23	18 01	18 54
45	05 14	05 48	06 17	17 11	17 44	18 27	19 22
N 40	05 13	05 44	06 12	17 23	18 01	18 48	19 45
35	05 12	05 41	06 07	17 34	18 15	19 05	20 03
30	05 11	05 39	06 03	17 43	18 28	19 20	20 19
20	05 07	05 33	05 55	18 00	18 49	19 45	20 46
N 10	05 03	05 27	05 49	18 14	19 08	20 07	21 10
0	04 57	05 21	05 42	18 28	19 26	20 27	21 31
S 10	04 50	05 14	05 36	18 41	19 43	20 48	21 53
20	04 40	05 06	05 29	18 56	20 02	21 10	22 17
30	04 27	04 56	05 21	19 13	20 25	21 36	22 44
35	04 19	04 50	05 16	19 23	20 38	21 51	23 00
40	04 09	04 43	05 10	19 35	20 53	22 09	23 19
45	03 57	04 34	05 04	19 48	21 11	22 31	23 42
S 50	03 41	04 23	04 57	20 05	21 34	22 58	24 10
52	03 34	04 17	04 53	20 13	21 45	23 12	24 25
54	03 25	04 12	04 49	20 22	21 57	23 27	24 41
56	03 15	04 05	04 45	20 32	22 11	23 45	25 01
58	03 03	03 58	04 40	20 43	22 28	24 07	00 07
S 60	02 49	03 49	04 35	20 56	22 48	24 36	00 36

Lat.	Sunset	Twilight Civil	Twilight Naut.	Moonset 15	Moonset 16	Moonset 17	Moonset 18
°	h m	h m	h m	h m	h m	h m	h m
N 72	15 58	17 10	18 27	10 17	▭	▭	▭
N 70	16 11	17 14	18 25	09 32	▭	▭	▭
68	16 21	17 18	18 22	09 03	12 10	▭	▭
66	16 29	17 22	18 21	08 41	11 07	▭	▭
64	16 36	17 25	18 19	08 24	10 33	13 02	▭
62	16 42	17 27	18 18	08 10	10 08	12 10	14 03
60	16 47	17 30	18 18	07 59	09 48	11 39	13 15
N 58	16 52	17 32	18 17	07 49	09 32	11 15	12 45
56	16 56	17 34	18 17	07 40	09 18	10 56	12 22
54	17 00	17 36	18 16	07 32	09 06	10 40	12 03
52	17 03	17 37	18 16	07 25	08 56	10 26	11 47
50	17 06	17 39	18 16	07 19	08 47	10 14	11 33
45	17 13	17 43	18 17	07 05	08 27	09 49	11 05
N 40	17 19	17 46	18 17	06 54	08 12	09 29	10 43
35	17 23	17 49	18 18	06 45	07 59	09 13	10 25
30	17 28	17 52	18 20	06 37	07 47	08 59	10 09
20	17 35	17 58	18 23	06 23	07 27	08 35	09 42
N 10	17 42	18 04	18 28	06 11	07 10	08 14	09 19
0	17 49	18 10	18 34	05 59	06 55	07 55	08 58
S 10	17 55	18 17	18 42	05 48	06 39	07 35	08 36
20	18 03	18 25	18 51	05 36	06 22	07 15	08 13
30	18 11	18 35	19 04	05 22	06 03	06 51	07 47
35	18 16	18 42	19 13	05 14	05 52	06 37	07 31
40	18 21	18 49	19 23	05 05	05 39	06 21	07 13
45	18 28	18 58	19 35	04 55	05 24	06 02	06 51
S 50	18 35	19 09	19 51	04 42	05 06	05 38	06 23
52	18 39	19 15	19 59	04 36	04 57	05 27	06 09
54	18 43	19 21	20 08	04 30	04 48	05 14	05 54
56	18 47	19 27	20 18	04 23	04 37	04 59	05 35
58	18 52	19 35	20 30	04 15	04 25	04 42	05 13
S 60	18 58	19 44	20 44	04 06	04 11	04 21	04 43

Day	SUN Eqn. of Time 00^h	SUN Eqn. of Time 12^h	SUN Mer. Pass.	MOON Mer. Pass. Upper	MOON Mer. Pass. Lower	MOON Age	MOON Phase
d	m s	m s	h m	h m	h m	d %	
15	14 13	14 19	11 46	24 41	12 13	16 99	○
16	14 26	14 32	11 45	00 41	13 10	17 96	
17	14 38	14 45	11 45	01 40	14 11	18 90	

Day	UT (d h)	ARIES GHA	VENUS −3.9 GHA	VENUS Dec	MARS +1.6 GHA	MARS Dec	JUPITER −2.2 GHA	JUPITER Dec	SATURN +1.0 GHA	SATURN Dec
		° ′	° ′	° ′	° ′	° ′	° ′	° ′	° ′	° ′
	18 00	26 51.3	150 14.9	S20 57.1	169 50.0	S14 36.6	100 34.4	S22 56.3	217 56.6	N 6 40.3
	01	41 53.8	165 14.2	57.9	184 50.7	37.2	115 36.5	56.3	232 58.8	40.2
	02	56 56.3	180 13.6	58.7	199 51.5	37.7	130 38.7	56.3	248 01.1	40.1
	03	71 58.7	195 12.9	20 59.5	214 52.3	. . 38.3	145 40.8	. . 56.2	263 03.3	. . 40.0
	04	87 01.2	210 12.2	21 00.2	229 53.1	38.9	160 43.0	56.2	278 05.5	39.9
	05	102 03.7	225 11.5	01.0	244 53.9	39.4	175 45.1	56.2	293 07.7	39.8
	06	117 06.1	240 10.9	S21 01.8	259 54.7	S14 40.0	190 47.3	S22 56.1	308 09.9	N 6 39.7
	07	132 08.6	255 10.2	02.6	274 55.5	40.6	205 49.4	56.1	323 12.1	39.6
S	08	147 11.0	270 09.5	03.3	289 56.2	41.1	220 51.6	56.1	338 14.3	39.5
A	09	162 13.5	285 08.8	. . 04.1	304 57.0	. . 41.7	235 53.7	. . 56.0	353 16.5	. . 39.4
T	10	177 16.0	300 08.2	04.9	319 57.8	42.3	250 55.9	56.0	8 18.7	39.3
U	11	192 18.4	315 07.5	05.7	334 58.6	42.8	265 58.0	56.0	23 21.0	39.2
R	12	207 20.9	330 06.8	S21 06.4	349 59.4	S14 43.4	281 00.1	S22 56.0	38 23.2	N 6 39.1
D	13	222 23.4	345 06.1	07.2	5 00.2	44.0	296 02.3	55.9	53 25.4	39.0
A	14	237 25.8	0 05.4	08.0	20 01.0	44.6	311 04.4	55.9	68 27.6	38.9
Y	15	252 28.3	15 04.8	. . 08.8	35 01.7	. . 45.1	326 06.6	. . 55.9	83 29.8	. . 38.8
	16	267 30.8	30 04.1	09.5	50 02.5	45.7	341 08.7	55.8	98 32.0	38.7
	17	282 33.2	45 03.4	10.3	65 03.3	46.3	356 10.9	55.8	113 34.2	38.6
	18	297 35.7	60 02.7	S21 11.1	80 04.1	S14 46.8	11 13.0	S22 55.8	128 36.4	N 6 38.5
	19	312 38.1	75 02.0	11.8	95 04.9	47.4	26 15.1	55.7	143 38.6	38.4
	20	327 40.6	90 01.3	12.6	110 05.7	48.0	41 17.3	55.7	158 40.9	38.3
	21	342 43.1	105 00.7	. . 13.4	125 06.4	. . 48.5	56 19.4	. . 55.7	173 43.1	. . 38.2
	22	357 45.5	120 00.0	14.1	140 07.2	49.1	71 21.6	55.6	188 45.3	38.1
	23	12 48.0	134 59.3	14.9	155 08.0	49.7	86 23.7	55.6	203 47.5	38.0
	19 00	27 50.5	149 58.6	S21 15.7	170 08.8	S14 50.2	101 25.9	S22 55.6	218 49.7	N 6 37.9
	01	42 52.9	164 57.9	16.4	185 09.6	50.8	116 28.0	55.5	233 51.9	37.8
	02	57 55.4	179 57.2	17.2	200 10.3	51.4	131 30.1	55.5	248 54.1	37.7
	03	72 57.9	194 56.5	. . 17.9	215 11.1	. . 51.9	146 32.3	. . 55.5	263 56.3	. . 37.6
	04	88 00.3	209 55.9	18.7	230 11.9	52.5	161 34.4	55.4	278 58.6	37.5
	05	103 02.8	224 55.2	19.4	245 12.7	53.0	176 36.6	55.4	294 00.8	37.4
	06	118 05.3	239 54.5	S21 20.2	260 13.5	S14 53.6	191 38.7	S22 55.4	309 03.0	N 6 37.3
	07	133 07.7	254 53.8	21.0	275 14.2	54.2	206 40.8	55.4	324 05.2	37.2
	08	148 10.2	269 53.1	21.7	290 15.0	54.7	221 43.0	55.3	339 07.4	37.1
S	09	163 12.6	284 52.4	. . 22.5	305 15.8	. . 55.3	236 45.1	. . 55.3	354 09.6	. . 37.0
U	10	178 15.1	299 51.7	23.2	320 16.6	55.9	251 47.2	55.3	9 11.8	36.9
N	11	193 17.6	314 51.0	24.0	335 17.4	56.4	266 49.4	55.2	24 14.0	36.8
D	12	208 20.0	329 50.3	S21 24.7	350 18.1	S14 57.0	281 51.5	S22 55.2	39 16.3	N 6 36.7
A	13	223 22.5	344 49.6	25.5	5 18.9	57.6	296 53.7	55.2	54 18.5	36.6
Y	14	238 25.0	359 48.9	26.2	20 19.7	58.1	311 55.8	55.1	69 20.7	36.5
	15	253 27.4	14 48.3	. . 27.0	35 20.5	. . 58.7	326 57.9	. . 55.1	84 22.9	. . 36.4
	16	268 29.9	29 47.6	27.7	50 21.3	59.3	342 00.1	55.1	99 25.1	36.3
	17	283 32.4	44 46.9	28.4	65 22.0	14 59.8	357 02.2	55.0	114 27.3	36.2
	18	298 34.8	59 46.2	S21 29.2	80 22.8	S15 00.4	12 04.3	S22 55.0	129 29.5	N 6 36.1
	19	313 37.3	74 45.5	29.9	95 23.6	00.9	27 06.5	55.0	144 31.8	36.0
	20	328 39.8	89 44.8	30.7	110 24.4	01.5	42 08.6	54.9	159 34.0	35.9
	21	343 42.2	104 44.1	. . 31.4	125 25.1	. . 02.1	57 10.7	. . 54.9	174 36.2	. . 35.9
	22	358 44.7	119 43.4	32.2	140 25.9	02.6	72 12.9	54.9	189 38.4	35.8
	23	13 47.1	134 42.7	32.9	155 26.7	03.2	87 15.0	54.8	204 40.6	35.7
	20 00	28 49.6	149 42.0	S21 33.6	170 27.5	S15 03.8	102 17.1	S22 54.8	219 42.8	N 6 35.6
	01	43 52.1	164 41.3	34.4	185 28.2	04.3	117 19.3	54.8	234 45.0	35.5
	02	58 54.5	179 40.6	35.1	200 29.0	04.9	132 21.4	54.7	249 47.3	35.4
	03	73 57.0	194 39.9	. . 35.8	215 29.8	. . 05.4	147 23.6	. . 54.7	264 49.5	. . 35.3
	04	88 59.5	209 39.2	36.6	230 30.6	06.0	162 25.7	54.7	279 51.7	35.2
	05	104 01.9	224 38.5	37.3	245 31.3	06.6	177 27.8	54.6	294 53.9	35.1
	06	119 04.4	239 37.8	S21 38.0	260 32.1	S15 07.1	192 29.9	S22 54.6	309 56.1	N 6 35.0
	07	134 06.9	254 37.1	38.8	275 32.9	07.7	207 32.1	54.6	324 58.3	34.9
	08	149 09.3	269 36.4	39.5	290 33.7	08.2	222 34.2	54.5	340 00.5	34.8
M	09	164 11.8	284 35.7	. . 40.2	305 34.4	. . 08.8	237 36.3	. . 54.5	355 02.8	. . 34.7
O	10	179 14.3	299 35.0	41.0	320 35.2	09.4	252 38.5	54.5	10 05.0	34.6
N	11	194 16.7	314 34.3	41.7	335 36.0	09.9	267 40.6	54.4	25 07.2	34.5
D	12	209 19.2	329 33.6	S21 42.4	350 36.8	S15 10.5	282 42.7	S22 54.4	40 09.4	N 6 34.4
A	13	224 21.6	344 32.9	43.1	5 37.5	11.0	297 44.9	54.4	55 11.6	34.3
Y	14	239 24.1	359 32.2	43.9	20 38.3	11.6	312 47.0	54.3	70 13.8	34.2
	15	254 26.6	14 31.5	. . 44.6	35 39.1	. . 12.2	327 49.1	. . 54.3	85 16.0	. . 34.1
	16	269 29.0	29 30.8	45.3	50 39.8	12.7	342 51.3	54.3	100 18.3	34.0
	17	284 31.5	44 30.1	46.0	65 40.6	13.3	357 53.4	54.2	115 20.5	33.9
	18	299 34.0	59 29.4	S21 46.7	80 41.4	S15 13.8	12 55.5	S22 54.2	130 22.7	N 6 33.8
	19	314 36.4	74 28.7	47.5	95 42.2	14.4	27 57.6	54.2	145 24.9	33.7
	20	329 38.9	89 27.9	48.2	110 42.9	15.0	42 59.8	54.1	160 27.1	33.6
	21	344 41.4	104 27.2	. . 48.9	125 43.7	. . 15.5	58 01.9	. . 54.1	175 29.3	. . 33.5
	22	359 43.8	119 26.5	49.6	140 44.5	16.1	73 04.0	54.1	190 31.6	33.4
	23	14 46.3	134 25.8	50.3	155 45.2	16.6	88 06.2	54.0	205 33.8	33.3
	Mer. Pass.	h m 22 05.0	v −0.7	d 0.7	v 0.8	d 0.6	v 2.1	d 0.0	v 2.2	d 0.1

STARS Name	SHA	Dec
	° ′	° ′
Acamar	315 20.5	S40 15.9
Achernar	335 28.5	S57 11.4
Acrux	173 14.2	S63 08.8
Adhara	255 15.2	S28 58.7
Aldebaran	290 53.2	N16 31.8
Alioth	166 24.0	N55 54.6
Alkaid	153 01.9	N49 16.1
Al Na'ir	27 47.7	S46 55.2
Alnilam	275 49.7	S 1 11.6
Alphard	217 59.7	S 8 41.6
Alphecca	126 14.2	N26 41.2
Alpheratz	357 46.9	N29 08.6
Altair	62 11.7	N 8 53.6
Ankaa	353 18.6	S42 15.4
Antares	112 30.9	S26 27.2
Arcturus	145 59.2	N19 08.2
Atria	107 36.3	S69 02.9
Avior	234 19.7	S59 31.9
Bellatrix	278 35.6	N 6 21.6
Betelgeuse	271 04.9	N 7 24.7
Canopus	263 57.5	S52 41.6
Capella	280 39.4	N46 00.4
Deneb	49 33.9	N45 19.0
Denebola	182 37.5	N14 31.4
Diphda	348 59.0	S17 56.1
Dubhe	193 56.1	N61 42.0
Elnath	278 16.8	N28 37.0
Eltanin	90 48.0	N51 29.5
Enif	33 50.4	N 9 55.1
Fomalhaut	15 27.5	S29 34.5
Gacrux	172 05.7	S57 09.7
Gienah	175 56.3	S17 35.4
Hadar	148 53.8	S60 25.0
Hamal	328 04.4	N23 30.4
Kaus Aust.	83 48.6	S34 23.0
Kochab	137 20.5	N74 07.1
Markab	13 41.6	N15 15.4
Menkar	314 18.4	N 4 07.7
Menkent	148 12.2	S36 24.8
Miaplacidus	221 41.1	S69 44.9
Mirfak	308 45.1	N49 53.6
Nunki	76 02.7	S26 17.2
Peacock	53 24.5	S56 42.6
Pollux	243 32.0	N28 00.3
Procyon	245 03.4	N 5 12.3
Rasalhague	96 09.9	N12 33.3
Regulus	207 47.4	N11 55.5
Rigel	281 15.2	S 8 11.2
Rigil Kent.	139 57.4	S60 52.3
Sabik	102 16.8	S15 44.2
Schedar	349 44.3	N56 35.4
Shaula	96 26.9	S37 06.7
Sirius	258 36.7	S16 43.4
Spica	158 35.3	S11 12.4
Suhail	222 55.3	S43 27.8
Vega	80 41.5	N38 47.7
Zuben'ubi	137 09.7	S16 04.7

	SHA	Mer. Pass.
	° ′	h m
Venus	122 08.1	14 01
Mars	142 18.3	12 39
Jupiter	73 35.4	17 12
Saturn	190 59.2	9 23

	UT	SUN GHA	SUN Dec	MOON GHA	v	MOON Dec	d	HP
	d h	° ′	° ′	° ′	′	° ′	′	′
	18 00	183 42.7	S 9 40.3	321 05.3	2.9	N26 17.7	4.7	60.2
	01	198 42.8	41.2	335 27.2	2.9	26 22.4	4.5	60.2
	02	213 42.9	42.1	349 49.1	2.8	26 26.9	4.3	60.2
	03	228 43.0	. . 43.0	4 10.9	2.8	26 31.2	4.1	60.2
	04	243 43.2	43.9	18 32.7	2.7	26 35.3	3.9	60.2
	05	258 43.3	44.8	32 54.4	2.7	26 39.2	3.7	60.2
	06	273 43.4	S 9 45.7	47 16.1	2.7	N26 42.9	3.6	60.2
	07	288 43.5	46.6	61 37.8	2.7	26 46.5	3.3	60.2
S	08	303 43.6	47.5	75 59.5	2.6	26 49.8	3.1	60.1
A	09	318 43.8	. . 48.4	90 21.1	2.7	26 52.9	3.0	60.1
T	10	333 43.9	49.3	104 42.8	2.6	26 55.9	2.7	60.1
U	11	348 44.0	50.2	119 04.4	2.6	26 58.6	2.5	60.1
R	12	3 44.1	S 9 51.2	133 26.0	2.5	N27 01.1	2.4	60.1
D	13	18 44.2	52.1	147 47.5	2.6	27 03.5	2.1	60.1
A	14	33 44.3	53.0	162 09.1	2.6	27 05.6	2.0	60.1
Y	15	48 44.5	. . 53.9	176 30.7	2.5	27 07.6	1.7	60.1
	16	63 44.6	54.8	190 52.2	2.6	27 09.3	1.6	60.1
	17	78 44.7	55.7	205 13.8	2.5	27 10.9	1.3	60.1
	18	93 44.8	S 9 56.6	219 35.3	2.6	N27 12.2	1.2	60.0
	19	108 44.9	57.5	233 56.9	2.5	27 13.4	0.9	60.0
	20	123 45.0	58.4	248 18.4	2.6	27 14.3	0.8	60.0
	21	138 45.2	9 59.3	262 40.0	2.6	27 15.1	0.5	60.0
	22	153 45.3	10 00.2	277 01.6	2.6	27 15.6	0.4	60.0
	23	168 45.4	01.1	291 23.2	2.6	27 16.0	0.1	60.0
	19 00	183 45.5	S10 02.0	305 44.8	2.7	N27 16.1	0.0	60.0
	01	198 45.6	02.9	320 06.5	2.7	27 16.1	0.2	59.9
	02	213 45.7	03.8	334 28.2	2.6	27 15.9	0.5	59.9
	03	228 45.8	. . 04.7	348 49.8	2.8	27 15.4	0.6	59.9
	04	243 46.0	05.6	3 11.6	2.7	27 14.8	0.8	59.9
	05	258 46.1	06.5	17 33.3	2.8	27 14.0	1.0	59.9
	06	273 46.2	S10 07.4	31 55.1	2.8	N27 13.0	1.3	59.9
	07	288 46.3	08.3	46 16.9	2.9	27 11.7	1.4	59.9
	08	303 46.4	09.2	60 38.8	2.9	27 10.3	1.6	59.8
S	09	318 46.5	. . 10.1	75 00.7	3.0	27 08.7	1.8	59.8
U	10	333 46.6	11.0	89 22.7	3.0	27 06.9	2.0	59.8
N	11	348 46.7	11.9	103 44.7	3.0	27 04.9	2.2	59.8
D	12	3 46.9	S10 12.8	118 06.7	3.1	N27 02.7	2.3	59.8
A	13	18 47.0	13.7	132 28.8	3.2	27 00.4	2.6	59.8
Y	14	33 47.1	14.6	146 51.0	3.2	26 57.8	2.7	59.7
	15	48 47.2	. . 15.5	161 13.2	3.3	26 55.1	3.0	59.7
	16	63 47.3	16.4	175 35.5	3.3	26 52.1	3.1	59.7
	17	78 47.4	17.3	189 57.8	3.4	26 49.0	3.3	59.7
	18	93 47.5	S10 18.2	204 20.2	3.5	N26 45.7	3.5	59.7
	19	108 47.6	19.1	218 42.7	3.5	26 42.2	3.7	59.7
	20	123 47.7	20.0	233 05.2	3.6	26 38.5	3.9	59.6
	21	138 47.8	. . 20.9	247 27.8	3.7	26 34.6	4.0	59.6
	22	153 48.0	21.8	261 50.5	3.7	26 30.6	4.3	59.6
	23	168 48.1	22.7	276 13.2	3.9	26 26.3	4.4	59.6
	20 00	183 48.2	S10 23.6	290 36.1	3.9	N26 21.9	4.6	59.6
	01	198 48.3	24.5	304 59.0	4.0	26 17.3	4.7	59.5
	02	213 48.4	25.4	319 22.0	4.0	26 12.6	5.0	59.5
	03	228 48.5	. . 26.2	333 45.0	4.2	26 07.6	5.1	59.5
	04	243 48.6	27.1	348 08.2	4.2	26 02.5	5.3	59.5
	05	258 48.7	28.0	2 31.4	4.4	25 57.2	5.5	59.5
	06	273 48.8	S10 28.9	16 54.8	4.4	N25 51.7	5.6	59.4
	07	288 48.9	29.8	31 18.2	4.5	25 46.1	5.8	59.4
	08	303 49.0	30.7	45 41.7	4.6	25 40.3	6.0	59.4
M	09	318 49.1	. . 31.6	60 05.3	4.7	25 34.3	6.1	59.4
O	10	333 49.2	32.5	74 29.0	4.8	25 28.2	6.3	59.4
N	11	348 49.3	33.4	88 52.8	4.8	25 21.9	6.5	59.3
D	12	3 49.4	S10 34.3	103 16.6	5.0	N25 15.4	6.6	59.3
A	13	18 49.6	35.2	117 40.6	5.1	25 08.8	6.8	59.3
Y	14	33 49.7	36.1	132 04.7	5.2	25 02.0	6.9	59.3
	15	48 49.8	. . 37.0	146 28.9	5.3	24 55.1	7.1	59.3
	16	63 49.9	37.9	160 53.2	5.4	24 48.0	7.3	59.2
	17	78 50.0	38.7	175 17.6	5.4	24 40.7	7.4	59.2
	18	93 50.1	S10 39.6	189 42.0	5.6	N24 33.3	7.6	59.2
	19	108 50.2	40.5	204 06.6	5.7	24 25.7	7.7	59.2
	20	123 50.3	41.4	218 31.3	5.8	24 18.0	7.9	59.2
	21	138 50.4	. . 42.3	232 56.1	5.9	24 10.1	8.0	59.1
	22	153 50.5	43.2	247 21.0	6.1	24 02.1	8.1	59.1
	23	168 50.6	44.1	261 46.1	6.1	N23 54.0	8.3	59.1
		SD 16.1	d 0.9	SD	16.4		16.3	16.2

Lat.	Twilight Naut.	Twilight Civil	Sunrise	Moonrise 18	Moonrise 19	Moonrise 20	Moonrise 21
°	h m	h m	h m	h m	h m	h m	h m
N 72	05 14	06 33	07 46	□	□	□	□
N 70	05 16	06 26	07 31	□	□	□	□
68	05 17	06 21	07 20	□	□	□	19 52
66	05 18	06 17	07 11	□	□	□	20 37
64	05 18	06 13	07 03	□	□	18 52	21 07
62	05 19	06 10	06 56	16 24	17 40	19 34	21 29
60	05 19	06 07	06 50	17 11	18 23	20 02	21 47
N 58	05 19	06 05	06 45	17 42	18 52	20 24	22 02
56	05 19	06 02	06 40	18 05	19 15	20 42	22 15
54	05 19	06 00	06 36	18 24	19 33	20 57	22 26
52	05 19	05 58	06 32	18 40	19 49	21 10	22 36
50	05 18	05 56	06 29	18 54	20 02	21 21	22 44
45	05 17	05 51	06 21	19 22	20 30	21 45	23 02
N 40	05 16	05 47	06 15	19 45	20 51	22 04	23 17
35	05 14	05 44	06 09	20 03	21 09	22 20	23 30
30	05 13	05 40	06 05	20 19	21 25	22 33	23 41
20	05 08	05 34	05 56	20 46	21 51	22 56	23 59
N 10	05 03	05 27	05 49	21 10	22 14	23 16	24 15
0	04 56	05 21	05 42	21 31	22 35	23 35	24 31
S 10	04 48	05 13	05 34	21 53	22 56	23 53	24 46
20	04 38	05 04	05 26	22 17	23 18	24 13	00 13
30	04 24	04 53	05 17	22 44	23 44	24 36	00 36
35	04 15	04 46	05 12	23 00	24 00	00 00	00 49
40	04 04	04 38	05 06	23 19	24 18	00 18	01 05
45	03 51	04 28	04 59	23 42	24 39	00 39	01 23
S 50	03 34	04 16	04 50	24 10	00 10	01 06	01 45
52	03 26	04 11	04 47	24 25	00 25	01 19	01 56
54	03 16	04 04	04 42	24 41	00 41	01 34	02 08
56	03 05	03 57	04 37	25 01	01 01	01 52	02 22
58	02 53	03 49	04 32	00 07	01 25	02 13	02 38
S 60	02 37	03 39	04 26	00 36	01 58	02 40	02 57

Lat.	Sunset	Twilight Civil	Twilight Naut.	Moonset 18	Moonset 19	Moonset 20	Moonset 21
°	h m	h m	h m	h m	h m	h m	h m
N 72	15 42	16 55	18 13	□	□	□	□
N 70	15 57	17 01	18 12	□	□	□	□
68	16 08	17 07	18 11	□	□	□	16 58
66	16 18	17 11	18 10	□	□	□	16 11
64	16 26	17 15	18 10	□	□	15 57	15 41
62	16 33	17 18	18 10	14 03	15 01	15 15	15 17
60	16 39	17 21	18 10	13 15	14 17	14 46	14 59
N 58	16 44	17 24	18 10	12 45	13 48	14 24	14 43
56	16 49	17 27	18 10	12 22	13 25	14 05	14 30
54	16 53	17 29	18 10	12 03	13 07	13 50	14 18
52	16 57	17 31	18 10	11 47	12 51	13 37	14 08
50	17 00	17 33	18 11	11 33	12 37	13 25	13 58
45	17 08	17 38	18 12	11 05	12 10	13 00	13 39
N 40	17 14	17 42	18 13	10 43	11 47	12 41	13 23
35	17 20	17 45	18 15	10 25	11 29	12 24	13 09
30	17 25	17 49	18 17	10 09	11 13	12 10	12 57
20	17 33	17 56	18 21	09 42	10 47	11 45	12 37
N 10	17 41	18 02	18 27	09 19	10 23	11 24	12 19
0	17 48	18 09	18 34	08 58	10 02	11 04	12 02
S 10	17 56	18 17	18 42	08 36	09 40	10 44	11 45
20	18 04	18 26	18 53	08 13	09 17	10 22	11 27
30	18 13	18 37	19 07	07 47	08 50	09 57	11 06
35	18 18	18 44	19 16	07 31	08 34	09 42	10 53
40	18 24	18 53	19 26	07 13	08 15	09 25	10 39
45	18 32	19 02	19 40	06 51	07 52	09 04	10 22
S 50	18 40	19 15	19 57	06 23	07 24	08 38	10 00
52	18 44	19 21	20 06	06 09	07 09	08 25	09 50
54	18 49	19 27	20 15	05 54	06 53	08 11	09 38
56	18 54	19 34	20 27	05 35	06 33	07 53	09 25
58	18 59	19 43	20 40	05 13	06 09	07 32	09 10
S 60	19 06	19 52	20 55	04 43	05 36	07 06	08 51

Day	SUN Eqn. of Time 00^h	SUN Eqn. of Time 12^h	SUN Mer. Pass.	MOON Mer. Pass. Upper	MOON Mer. Pass. Lower	MOON Age	MOON Phase
d	m s	m s	h m	h m	h m	d	%
18	14 50	14 56	11 45	02 43	15 15	19	82
19	15 02	15 07	11 45	03 47	16 18	20	72
20	15 12	15 18	11 45	04 49	17 20	21	61

UT d h	ARIES GHA ° ′	VENUS −3.9 GHA ° ′	VENUS Dec ° ′	MARS +1.6 GHA ° ′	MARS Dec ° ′	JUPITER −2.2 GHA ° ′	JUPITER Dec ° ′	SATURN +1.1 GHA ° ′	SATURN Dec ° ′
21 00 (TUESDAY)	29 48.8	149 25.1	S21 51.0	170 46.0	S15 17.2	103 08.3	S22 54.0	220 36.0	N 6 33.2
01	44 51.2	164 24.4	51.8	185 46.8	17.7	118 10.4	54.0	235 38.2	33.1
02	59 53.7	179 23.7	52.5	200 47.6	18.3	133 12.5	53.9	250 40.4	33.0
03	74 56.1	194 23.0	. . 53.2	215 48.3	. . 18.9	148 14.7	. . 53.9	265 42.6	. . 32.9
04	89 58.6	209 22.3	53.9	230 49.1	19.4	163 16.8	53.9	280 44.9	32.8
05	105 01.1	224 21.6	54.6	245 49.9	20.0	178 18.9	53.8	295 47.1	32.7
06	120 03.5	239 20.8	S21 55.3	260 50.6	S15 20.5	193 21.1	S22 53.8	310 49.3	N 6 32.6
07	135 06.0	254 20.1	56.0	275 51.4	21.1	208 23.2	53.8	325 51.5	32.5
08	150 08.5	269 19.4	56.7	290 52.2	21.6	223 25.3	53.7	340 53.7	32.4
09	165 10.9	284 18.7	. . 57.4	305 52.9	. . 22.2	238 27.4	. . 53.7	355 55.9	. . 32.3
10	180 13.4	299 18.0	58.1	320 53.7	22.7	253 29.6	53.7	10 58.2	32.3
11	195 15.9	314 17.3	58.8	335 54.5	23.3	268 31.7	53.6	26 00.4	32.2
12	210 18.3	329 16.6	S21 59.5	350 55.2	S15 23.9	283 33.8	S22 53.6	41 02.6	N 6 32.1
13	225 20.8	344 15.9	22 00.2	5 56.0	24.4	298 35.9	53.6	56 04.8	32.0
14	240 23.3	359 15.1	00.9	20 56.8	25.0	313 38.0	53.5	71 07.0	31.9
15	255 25.7	14 14.4	. . 01.6	35 57.5	. . 25.5	328 40.2	. . 53.5	86 09.2	. . 31.8
16	270 28.2	29 13.7	02.3	50 58.3	26.1	343 42.3	53.5	101 11.5	31.7
17	285 30.6	44 13.0	03.0	65 59.1	26.6	358 44.4	53.4	116 13.7	31.6
18	300 33.1	59 12.3	S22 03.7	80 59.8	S15 27.2	13 46.5	S22 53.4	131 15.9	N 6 31.5
19	315 35.6	74 11.6	04.4	96 00.6	27.7	28 48.7	53.4	146 18.1	31.4
20	330 38.0	89 10.8	05.1	111 01.4	28.3	43 50.8	53.3	161 20.3	31.3
21	345 40.5	104 10.1	. . 05.8	126 02.1	. . 28.8	58 52.9	. . 53.3	176 22.5	. . 31.2
22	0 43.0	119 09.4	06.5	141 02.9	29.4	73 55.0	53.3	191 24.8	31.1
23	15 45.4	134 08.7	07.2	156 03.7	30.0	88 57.2	53.2	206 27.0	31.0
22 00 (WEDNESDAY)	30 47.9	149 08.0	S22 07.9	171 04.4	S15 30.5	103 59.3	S22 53.2	221 29.2	N 6 30.9
01	45 50.4	164 07.2	08.6	186 05.2	31.1	119 01.4	53.2	236 31.4	30.8
02	60 52.8	179 06.5	09.3	201 05.9	31.6	134 03.5	53.1	251 33.6	30.7
03	75 55.3	194 05.8	. . 09.9	216 06.7	. . 32.2	149 05.6	. . 53.1	266 35.9	. . 30.6
04	90 57.7	209 05.1	10.6	231 07.5	32.7	164 07.8	53.1	281 38.1	30.5
05	106 00.2	224 04.3	11.3	246 08.2	33.3	179 09.9	53.0	296 40.3	30.4
06	121 02.7	239 03.6	S22 12.0	261 09.0	S15 33.8	194 12.0	S22 53.0	311 42.5	N 6 30.3
07	136 05.1	254 02.9	12.7	276 09.8	34.4	209 14.1	53.0	326 44.7	30.2
08	151 07.6	269 02.2	13.4	291 10.5	34.9	224 16.2	52.9	341 46.9	30.1
09	166 10.1	284 01.4	. . 14.0	306 11.3	. . 35.5	239 18.4	. . 52.9	356 49.2	. . 30.0
10	181 12.5	299 00.7	14.7	321 12.0	36.0	254 20.5	52.8	11 51.4	29.9
11	196 15.0	314 00.0	15.4	336 12.8	36.6	269 22.6	52.8	26 53.6	29.8
12	211 17.5	328 59.3	S22 16.1	351 13.6	S15 37.1	284 24.7	S22 52.8	41 55.8	N 6 29.8
13	226 19.9	343 58.5	16.8	6 14.3	37.7	299 26.8	52.7	56 58.0	29.7
14	241 22.4	358 57.8	17.4	21 15.1	38.2	314 28.9	52.7	72 00.3	29.6
15	256 24.9	13 57.1	. . 18.1	36 15.8	. . 38.8	329 31.1	. . 52.7	87 02.5	. . 29.5
16	271 27.3	28 56.4	18.8	51 16.6	39.3	344 33.2	52.6	102 04.7	29.4
17	286 29.8	43 55.6	19.4	66 17.4	39.9	359 35.3	52.6	117 06.9	29.3
18	301 32.2	58 54.9	S22 20.1	81 18.1	S15 40.4	14 37.4	S22 52.6	132 09.1	N 6 29.2
19	316 34.7	73 54.2	20.8	96 18.9	41.0	29 39.5	52.5	147 11.4	29.1
20	331 37.2	88 53.4	21.5	111 19.6	41.5	44 41.6	52.5	162 13.6	29.0
21	346 39.6	103 52.7	. . 22.1	126 20.4	. . 42.1	59 43.8	. . 52.5	177 15.8	. . 28.9
22	1 42.1	118 52.0	22.8	141 21.2	42.6	74 45.9	52.4	192 18.0	28.8
23	16 44.6	133 51.3	23.5	156 21.9	43.2	89 48.0	52.4	207 20.2	28.7
23 00 (THURSDAY)	31 47.0	148 50.5	S22 24.1	171 22.7	S15 43.7	104 50.1	S22 52.4	222 22.5	N 6 28.6
01	46 49.5	163 49.8	24.8	186 23.4	44.3	119 52.2	52.3	237 24.7	28.5
02	61 52.0	178 49.1	25.4	201 24.2	44.8	134 54.3	52.3	252 26.9	28.4
03	76 54.4	193 48.3	. . 26.1	216 25.0	. . 45.4	149 56.4	. . 52.2	267 29.1	. . 28.3
04	91 56.9	208 47.6	26.8	231 25.7	45.9	164 58.6	52.2	282 31.3	28.2
05	106 59.4	223 46.9	27.4	246 26.5	46.5	180 00.7	52.2	297 33.6	28.1
06	122 01.8	238 46.1	S22 28.1	261 27.2	S15 47.0	195 02.8	S22 52.1	312 35.8	N 6 28.0
07	137 04.3	253 45.4	28.7	276 28.0	47.6	210 04.9	52.1	327 38.0	27.9
08	152 06.7	268 44.7	29.4	291 28.7	48.1	225 07.0	52.1	342 40.2	27.8
09	167 09.2	283 43.9	. . 30.1	306 29.5	. . 48.7	240 09.1	. . 52.0	357 42.4	. . 27.8
10	182 11.7	298 43.2	30.7	321 30.2	49.2	255 11.2	52.0	12 44.7	27.7
11	197 14.1	313 42.4	31.4	336 31.0	49.7	270 13.3	52.0	27 46.9	27.6
12	212 16.6	328 41.7	S22 32.0	351 31.8	S15 50.3	285 15.5	S22 51.9	42 49.1	N 6 27.5
13	227 19.1	343 41.0	32.7	6 32.5	50.8	300 17.6	51.9	57 51.3	27.4
14	242 21.5	358 40.2	33.3	21 33.3	51.4	315 19.7	51.9	72 53.5	27.3
15	257 24.0	13 39.5	. . 34.0	36 34.0	. . 51.9	330 21.8	. . 51.8	87 55.8	. . 27.2
16	272 26.5	28 38.8	34.6	51 34.8	52.5	345 23.9	51.8	102 58.0	27.1
17	287 28.9	43 38.0	35.3	66 35.5	53.0	0 26.0	51.7	118 00.2	27.0
18	302 31.4	58 37.3	S22 35.9	81 36.3	S15 53.6	15 28.1	S22 51.7	133 02.4	N 6 26.9
19	317 33.8	73 36.5	36.5	96 37.0	54.1	30 30.2	51.7	148 04.7	26.8
20	332 36.3	88 35.8	37.2	111 37.8	54.7	45 32.3	51.6	163 06.9	26.7
21	347 38.8	103 35.1	. . 37.8	126 38.5	. . 55.2	60 34.5	. . 51.6	178 09.1	. . 26.6
22	2 41.2	118 34.3	38.5	141 39.3	55.7	75 36.6	51.6	193 11.3	26.5
23	17 43.7	133 33.6	39.1	156 40.0	56.3	90 38.7	51.5	208 13.5	26.4
Mer. Pass. (h m)	21 53.2	v −0.7	d 0.7	v 0.8	d 0.6	v 2.1	d 0.0	v 2.2	d 0.1

STARS

Name	SHA ° ′	Dec ° ′
Acamar	315 20.5	S40 15.9
Achernar	335 28.5	S57 11.4
Acrux	173 14.2	S63 08.8
Adhara	255 15.2	S28 58.7
Aldebaran	290 53.1	N16 31.8
Alioth	166 24.0	N55 54.6
Alkaid	153 01.9	N49 16.1
Al Na'ir	27 47.7	S46 55.2
Alnilam	275 49.7	S 1 11.6
Alphard	217 59.7	S 8 41.7
Alphecca	126 14.2	N26 41.2
Alpheratz	357 46.9	N29 08.6
Altair	62 11.7	N 8 53.6
Ankaa	353 18.6	S42 15.4
Antares	112 30.9	S26 27.2
Arcturus	145 59.2	N19 08.2
Atria	107 36.4	S69 02.8
Avior	234 19.7	S59 31.9
Bellatrix	278 35.6	N 6 21.6
Betelgeuse	271 04.9	N 7 24.7
Canopus	263 57.5	S52 41.6
Capella	280 39.3	N46 00.4
Deneb	49 33.9	N45 19.0
Denebola	182 37.4	N14 31.4
Diphda	348 59.0	S17 56.1
Dubhe	193 56.1	N61 42.0
Elnath	278 16.8	N28 37.0
Eltanin	90 48.0	N51 29.5
Enif	33 50.4	N 9 55.1
Fomalhaut	15 27.5	S29 34.5
Gacrux	172 05.6	S57 09.7
Gienah	175 56.3	S17 35.4
Hadar	148 53.8	S60 25.0
Hamal	328 04.4	N23 30.5
Kaus Aust.	83 48.6	S34 23.0
Kochab	137 20.6	N74 07.1
Markab	13 41.6	N15 15.4
Menkar	314 18.4	N 4 07.7
Menkent	148 12.2	S36 24.8
Miaplacidus	221 41.0	S69 44.9
Mirfak	308 45.0	N49 53.6
Nunki	76 02.7	S26 17.2
Peacock	53 24.5	S56 42.6
Pollux	243 31.9	N28 00.3
Procyon	245 03.3	N 5 12.3
Rasalhague	96 09.9	N12 33.3
Regulus	207 47.4	N11 55.5
Rigel	281 15.2	S 8 11.2
Rigil Kent.	139 57.4	S60 52.3
Sabik	102 16.8	S15 44.2
Schedar	349 44.3	N56 35.4
Shaula	96 26.9	S37 06.7
Sirius	258 36.7	S16 43.4
Spica	158 35.3	S11 12.4
Suhail	222 55.3	S43 27.8
Vega	80 41.5	N38 47.7
Zuben'ubi	137 09.7	S16 04.7

	SHA ° ′	Mer. Pass. h m
Venus	118 20.1	14 04
Mars	140 16.5	12 35
Jupiter	73 11.4	17 02
Saturn	190 41.3	9 13

Day	UT (d h)	SUN GHA (° ′)	SUN Dec (° ′)	MOON GHA (° ′)	MOON *v* (′)	MOON Dec (° ′)	MOON *d* (′)	MOON HP (′)
TUESDAY	21 00	183 50.7	S10 45.0	276 11.2	6.2	N23 45.7	8.5	59.1
	01	198 50.8	45.9	290 36.4	6.4	23 37.2	8.6	59.0
	02	213 50.9	46.8	305 01.8	6.4	23 28.6	8.7	59.0
	03	228 51.0	. . 47.6	319 27.2	6.6	23 19.9	8.9	59.0
	04	243 51.1	48.5	333 52.8	6.6	23 11.0	9.0	59.0
	05	258 51.2	49.4	348 18.4	6.8	23 02.0	9.1	59.0
	06	273 51.3	S10 50.3	2 44.2	6.9	N22 52.9	9.3	58.9
	07	288 51.4	51.2	17 10.1	7.0	22 43.6	9.4	58.9
	08	303 51.5	52.1	31 36.1	7.1	22 34.2	9.5	58.9
	09	318 51.6	. . 53.0	46 02.2	7.3	22 24.7	9.7	58.9
	10	333 51.7	53.9	60 28.5	7.3	22 15.0	9.7	58.8
	11	348 51.8	54.7	74 54.8	7.5	22 05.3	10.0	58.8
	12	3 51.9	S10 55.6	89 21.3	7.5	N21 55.3	10.0	58.8
	13	18 52.0	56.5	103 47.8	7.7	21 45.3	10.1	58.8
	14	33 52.1	57.4	118 14.5	7.8	21 35.2	10.3	58.7
	15	48 52.2	. . 58.3	132 41.3	7.9	21 24.9	10.4	58.7
	16	63 52.3	10 59.2	147 08.2	8.0	21 14.5	10.5	58.7
	17	78 52.3	11 00.1	161 35.2	8.1	21 04.0	10.6	58.7
	18	93 52.4	S11 00.9	176 02.3	8.3	N20 53.4	10.7	58.7
	19	108 52.5	01.8	190 29.6	8.3	20 42.7	10.9	58.6
	20	123 52.6	02.7	204 56.9	8.5	20 31.8	10.9	58.6
	21	138 52.7	. . 03.6	219 24.4	8.5	20 20.9	11.1	58.6
	22	153 52.8	04.5	233 51.9	8.7	20 09.8	11.1	58.6
	23	168 52.9	05.4	248 19.6	8.8	19 58.7	11.3	58.5
WEDNESDAY	22 00	183 53.0	S11 06.2	262 47.4	8.9	N19 47.4	11.4	58.5
	01	198 53.1	07.1	277 15.3	9.0	19 36.0	11.4	58.5
	02	213 53.2	08.0	291 43.3	9.1	19 24.6	11.6	58.5
	03	228 53.3	. . 08.9	306 11.4	9.2	19 13.0	11.7	58.4
	04	243 53.4	09.8	320 39.6	9.4	19 01.3	11.7	58.4
	05	258 53.5	10.7	335 08.0	9.4	18 49.6	11.9	58.4
	06	273 53.6	S11 11.5	349 36.4	9.5	N18 37.7	11.9	58.4
	07	288 53.7	12.4	4 04.9	9.7	18 25.8	12.1	58.3
	08	303 53.7	13.3	18 33.6	9.7	18 13.7	12.1	58.3
	09	318 53.8	. . 14.2	33 02.3	9.9	18 01.6	12.2	58.3
	10	333 53.9	15.1	47 31.2	10.0	17 49.4	12.3	58.3
	11	348 54.0	15.9	62 00.2	10.0	17 37.1	12.4	58.3
	12	3 54.1	S11 16.8	76 29.2	10.2	N17 24.7	12.4	58.2
	13	18 54.2	17.7	90 58.4	10.2	17 12.3	12.6	58.2
	14	33 54.3	18.6	105 27.6	10.4	16 59.7	12.6	58.2
	15	48 54.4	. . 19.4	119 57.0	10.5	16 47.1	12.7	58.2
	16	63 54.5	20.3	134 26.5	10.5	16 34.4	12.8	58.1
	17	78 54.6	21.2	148 56.0	10.7	16 21.6	12.9	58.1
	18	93 54.6	S11 22.1	163 25.7	10.7	N16 08.7	12.9	58.1
	19	108 54.7	23.0	177 55.4	10.9	15 55.8	13.0	58.1
	20	123 54.8	23.8	192 25.3	10.9	15 42.8	13.0	58.0
	21	138 54.9	. . 24.7	206 55.2	11.0	15 29.8	13.2	58.0
	22	153 55.0	25.6	221 25.2	11.2	15 16.6	13.2	58.0
	23	168 55.1	26.5	235 55.4	11.2	15 03.4	13.3	58.0
THURSDAY	23 00	183 55.2	S11 27.3	250 25.6	11.3	N14 50.1	13.3	57.9
	01	198 55.3	28.2	264 55.9	11.4	14 36.8	13.4	57.9
	02	213 55.3	29.1	279 26.3	11.5	14 23.4	13.5	57.9
	03	228 55.4	. . 30.0	293 56.8	11.6	14 09.9	13.5	57.9
	04	243 55.5	30.8	308 27.4	11.6	13 56.4	13.6	57.9
	05	258 55.6	31.7	322 58.0	11.8	13 42.8	13.6	57.8
	06	273 55.7	S11 32.6	337 28.8	11.8	N13 29.2	13.7	57.8
	07	288 55.8	33.5	351 59.6	11.9	13 15.5	13.7	57.8
	08	303 55.8	34.3	6 30.5	12.0	13 01.8	13.8	57.8
	09	318 55.9	. . 35.2	21 01.5	12.1	12 48.0	13.9	57.7
	10	333 56.0	36.1	35 32.6	12.2	12 34.1	13.9	57.7
	11	348 56.1	37.0	50 03.8	12.2	12 20.2	13.9	57.7
	12	3 56.2	S11 37.8	64 35.0	12.3	N12 06.3	14.0	57.7
	13	18 56.3	38.7	79 06.3	12.4	11 52.3	14.1	57.6
	14	33 56.3	39.6	93 37.7	12.5	11 38.2	14.1	57.6
	15	48 56.4	. . 40.4	108 09.2	12.5	11 24.1	14.1	57.6
	16	63 56.5	41.3	122 40.7	12.6	11 10.0	14.2	57.6
	17	78 56.6	42.2	137 12.3	12.7	10 55.8	14.2	57.5
	18	93 56.7	S11 43.0	151 44.0	12.7	N10 41.6	14.2	57.5
	19	108 56.8	43.9	166 15.7	12.9	10 27.4	14.3	57.5
	20	123 56.8	44.8	180 47.6	12.9	10 13.1	14.3	57.5
	21	138 56.9	. . 45.7	195 19.5	12.9	9 58.8	14.4	57.5
	22	153 57.0	46.5	209 51.4	13.1	9 44.4	14.4	57.4
	23	168 57.1	47.4	224 23.5	13.0	N 9 30.0	14.4	57.4
		SD 16.1	*d* 0.9	SD 16.0		15.9		15.7

Lat. (°)	Twilight Naut. (h m)	Twilight Civil (h m)	Sunrise (h m)	Moonrise 21 (h m)	Moonrise 22 (h m)	Moonrise 23 (h m)	Moonrise 24 (h m)
N 72	05 27	06 46	08 01	▭	21 24	24 06	00 06
N 70	05 27	06 38	07 45	▭	22 03	24 21	00 21
68	05 27	06 32	07 32	19 52	22 29	24 33	00 33
66	05 27	06 27	07 21	20 37	22 48	24 43	00 43
64	05 27	06 22	07 12	21 07	23 04	24 51	00 51
62	05 26	06 18	07 04	21 29	23 17	24 58	00 58
60	05 26	06 14	06 58	21 47	23 28	25 04	01 04
N 58	05 25	06 11	06 52	22 02	23 38	25 09	01 09
56	05 25	06 08	06 46	22 15	23 46	25 13	01 13
54	05 24	06 05	06 42	22 26	23 53	25 18	01 18
52	05 24	06 03	06 37	22 36	24 00	00 00	01 21
50	05 23	06 00	06 34	22 44	24 06	00 06	01 25
45	05 21	05 55	06 25	23 02	24 19	00 19	01 32
N 40	05 19	05 51	06 18	23 17	24 29	00 29	01 38
35	05 17	05 46	06 12	23 30	24 38	00 38	01 43
30	05 14	05 42	06 07	23 41	24 46	00 46	01 48
20	05 09	05 35	05 57	23 59	24 59	00 59	01 56
N 10	05 03	05 28	05 49	24 15	00 15	01 11	02 02
0	04 55	05 20	05 41	24 31	00 31	01 22	02 09
S 10	04 47	05 12	05 33	24 46	00 46	01 32	02 15
20	04 35	05 02	05 24	00 13	01 01	01 44	02 22
30	04 20	04 50	05 14	00 36	01 20	01 57	02 30
35	04 11	04 42	05 08	00 49	01 30	02 04	02 34
40	03 59	04 33	05 02	01 05	01 42	02 13	02 39
45	03 45	04 23	04 54	01 23	01 56	02 23	02 45
S 50	03 27	04 10	04 45	01 45	02 14	02 35	02 52
52	03 18	04 04	04 40	01 56	02 22	02 40	02 55
54	03 08	03 57	04 35	02 08	02 31	02 46	02 58
56	02 56	03 49	04 30	02 22	02 41	02 53	03 02
58	02 42	03 40	04 24	02 38	02 52	03 01	03 06
S 60	02 25	03 30	04 17	02 57	03 05	03 09	03 11

Lat. (°)	Sunset (h m)	Twilight Civil (h m)	Twilight Naut. (h m)	Moonset 21 (h m)	Moonset 22 (h m)	Moonset 23 (h m)	Moonset 24 (h m)
N 72	15 26	16 41	18 00	▭	17 17	16 16	15 39
N 70	15 42	16 49	18 00	▭	16 37	15 59	15 32
68	15 56	16 55	18 00	16 58	16 10	15 45	15 26
66	16 07	17 01	18 00	16 11	15 48	15 33	15 21
64	16 16	17 06	18 01	15 41	15 31	15 24	15 17
62	16 23	17 10	18 01	15 17	15 17	15 15	15 13
60	16 30	17 13	18 02	14 59	15 05	15 08	15 10
N 58	16 36	17 17	18 02	14 43	14 54	15 02	15 07
56	16 41	17 20	18 03	14 30	14 45	14 56	15 04
54	16 46	17 23	18 04	14 18	14 37	14 51	15 02
52	16 51	17 25	18 04	14 08	14 30	14 46	15 00
50	16 54	17 27	18 05	13 58	14 23	14 42	14 58
45	17 03	17 33	18 07	13 39	14 09	14 33	14 53
N 40	17 10	17 38	18 09	13 23	13 57	14 25	14 50
35	17 16	17 42	18 11	13 09	13 47	14 18	14 47
30	17 22	17 46	18 14	12 57	13 38	14 12	14 44
20	17 31	17 54	18 19	12 37	13 22	14 02	14 39
N 10	17 40	18 01	18 26	12 19	13 08	13 53	14 35
0	17 48	18 09	18 33	12 02	12 55	13 44	14 30
S 10	17 56	18 17	18 42	11 45	12 42	13 36	14 26
20	18 05	18 27	18 54	11 27	12 28	13 26	14 22
30	18 15	18 40	19 09	11 06	12 12	13 16	14 16
35	18 21	18 47	19 19	10 53	12 03	13 09	14 13
40	18 28	18 56	19 30	10 39	11 52	13 02	14 10
45	18 36	19 07	19 45	10 22	11 39	12 54	14 06
S 50	18 45	19 20	20 03	10 00	11 23	12 44	14 01
52	18 50	19 26	20 13	09 50	11 16	12 39	13 59
54	18 55	19 34	20 23	09 38	11 08	12 34	13 56
56	19 00	19 42	20 35	09 25	10 58	12 28	13 54
58	19 06	19 51	20 50	09 10	10 48	12 22	13 51
S 60	19 13	20 01	21 07	08 51	10 35	12 14	13 47

Day	SUN Eqn. of Time 00^h (m s)	SUN Eqn. of Time 12^h (m s)	SUN Mer. Pass. (h m)	MOON Mer. Pass. Upper (h m)	MOON Mer. Pass. Lower (h m)	MOON Age (d)	MOON Phase (%)
21	15 23	15 27	11 45	05 49	18 16	22	50
22	15 32	15 36	11 44	06 43	19 09	23	39
23	15 41	15 45	11 44	07 33	19 57	24	29

UT		ARIES	VENUS −4.0		MARS +1.5		JUPITER −2.2		SATURN +1.1	
		GHA	GHA	Dec	GHA	Dec	GHA	Dec	GHA	Dec
d h		° ′	° ′	° ′	° ′	° ′	° ′	° ′	° ′	° ′
24 00		32 46.2	148 32.8	S22 39.8	171 40.8	S15 56.8	105 40.8	S22 51.5	223 15.8	N 6 26.3
01		47 48.6	163 32.1	40.4	186 41.5	57.4	120 42.9	51.5	238 18.0	26.2
02		62 51.1	178 31.3	41.0	201 42.3	57.9	135 45.0	51.4	253 20.2	26.1
03		77 53.6	193 30.6	. . 41.7	216 43.0	. . 58.5	150 47.1	. . 51.4	268 22.4	. . 26.1
04		92 56.0	208 29.9	42.3	231 43.8	59.0	165 49.2	51.3	283 24.7	26.0
05		107 58.5	223 29.1	42.9	246 44.5	15 59.6	180 51.3	51.3	298 26.9	25.9
06		123 01.0	238 28.4	S22 43.6	261 45.3	S16 00.1	195 53.4	S22 51.3	313 29.1	N 6 25.8
07		138 03.4	253 27.6	44.2	276 46.0	00.6	210 55.5	51.2	328 31.3	25.7
08		153 05.9	268 26.9	44.8	291 46.8	01.2	225 57.6	51.2	343 33.5	25.6
09	F	168 08.3	283 26.1	. . 45.5	306 47.5	. . 01.7	240 59.7	. . 51.2	358 35.8	. . 25.5
10	R	183 10.8	298 25.4	46.1	321 48.3	02.3	256 01.9	51.1	13 38.0	25.4
11	I	198 13.3	313 24.6	46.7	336 49.0	02.8	271 04.0	51.1	28 40.2	25.3
12	D	213 15.7	328 23.9	S22 47.3	351 49.8	S16 03.3	286 06.1	S22 51.0	43 42.4	N 6 25.2
13	A	228 18.2	343 23.1	48.0	6 50.5	03.9	301 08.2	51.0	58 44.7	25.1
14	Y	243 20.7	358 22.4	48.6	21 51.3	04.4	316 10.3	51.0	73 46.9	25.0
15		258 23.1	13 21.6	. . 49.2	36 52.0	. . 05.0	331 12.4	. . 50.9	88 49.1	. . 24.9
16		273 25.6	28 20.9	49.8	51 52.8	05.5	346 14.5	50.9	103 51.3	24.8
17		288 28.1	43 20.1	50.5	66 53.5	06.1	1 16.6	50.9	118 53.6	24.7
18		303 30.5	58 19.4	S22 51.1	81 54.3	S16 06.6	16 18.7	S22 50.8	133 55.8	N 6 24.6
19		318 33.0	73 18.6	51.7	96 55.0	07.1	31 20.8	50.8	148 58.0	24.6
20		333 35.4	88 17.9	52.3	111 55.8	07.7	46 22.9	50.8	164 00.2	24.5
21		348 37.9	103 17.1	. . 52.9	126 56.5	. . 08.2	61 25.0	. . 50.7	179 02.5	. . 24.4
22		3 40.4	118 16.4	53.5	141 57.3	08.8	76 27.1	50.7	194 04.7	24.3
23		18 42.8	133 15.6	54.2	156 58.0	09.3	91 29.2	50.6	209 06.9	24.2
25 00		33 45.3	148 14.9	S22 54.8	171 58.8	S16 09.8	106 31.3	S22 50.6	224 09.1	N 6 24.1
01		48 47.8	163 14.1	55.4	186 59.5	10.4	121 33.4	50.6	239 11.4	24.0
02		63 50.2	178 13.4	56.0	202 00.3	10.9	136 35.5	50.5	254 13.6	23.9
03		78 52.7	193 12.6	. . 56.6	217 01.0	. . 11.4	151 37.6	. . 50.5	269 15.8	. . 23.8
04		93 55.2	208 11.9	57.2	232 01.7	12.0	166 39.7	50.5	284 18.0	23.7
05		108 57.6	223 11.1	57.8	247 02.5	12.5	181 41.8	50.4	299 20.3	23.6
06		124 00.1	238 10.4	S22 58.4	262 03.2	S16 13.1	196 43.9	S22 50.4	314 22.5	N 6 23.5
07		139 02.6	253 09.6	59.0	277 04.0	13.6	211 46.0	50.3	329 24.7	23.4
08	S	154 05.0	268 08.8	22 59.6	292 04.7	14.1	226 48.1	50.3	344 26.9	23.3
09	A	169 07.5	283 08.1	23 00.2	307 05.5	. . 14.7	241 50.2	. . 50.3	359 29.2	. . 23.3
10	T	184 09.9	298 07.3	00.9	322 06.2	15.2	256 52.3	50.2	14 31.4	23.2
11	U	199 12.4	313 06.6	01.5	337 06.9	15.7	271 54.4	50.2	29 33.6	23.1
12	R	214 14.9	328 05.8	S23 02.1	352 07.7	S16 16.3	286 56.5	S22 50.1	44 35.8	N 6 23.0
13	D	229 17.3	343 05.1	02.7	7 08.4	16.8	301 58.6	50.1	59 38.1	22.9
14	A	244 19.8	358 04.3	03.3	22 09.2	17.4	317 00.7	50.1	74 40.3	22.8
15	Y	259 22.3	13 03.5	. . 03.8	37 09.9	. . 17.9	332 02.8	. . 50.0	89 42.5	. . 22.7
16		274 24.7	28 02.8	04.4	52 10.7	18.4	347 04.9	50.0	104 44.7	22.6
17		289 27.2	43 02.0	05.0	67 11.4	19.0	2 07.0	50.0	119 47.0	22.5
18		304 29.7	58 01.3	S23 05.6	82 12.1	S16 19.5	17 09.1	S22 49.9	134 49.2	N 6 22.4
19		319 32.1	73 00.5	06.2	97 12.9	20.0	32 11.2	49.9	149 51.4	22.3
20		334 34.6	87 59.7	06.8	112 13.6	20.6	47 13.3	49.8	164 53.6	22.2
21		349 37.1	102 59.0	. . 07.4	127 14.4	. . 21.1	62 15.4	. . 49.8	179 55.9	. . 22.1
22		4 39.5	117 58.2	08.0	142 15.1	21.6	77 17.5	49.8	194 58.1	22.0
23		19 42.0	132 57.4	08.6	157 15.8	22.2	92 19.6	49.7	210 00.3	22.0
26 00		34 44.4	147 56.7	S23 09.2	172 16.6	S16 22.7	107 21.7	S22 49.7	225 02.5	N 6 21.9
01		49 46.9	162 55.9	09.8	187 17.3	23.2	122 23.8	49.6	240 04.8	21.8
02		64 49.4	177 55.2	10.3	202 18.1	23.8	137 25.9	49.6	255 07.0	21.7
03		79 51.8	192 54.4	. . 10.9	217 18.8	. . 24.3	152 28.0	. . 49.6	270 09.2	. . 21.6
04		94 54.3	207 53.6	11.5	232 19.5	24.8	167 30.1	49.5	285 11.5	21.5
05		109 56.8	222 52.9	12.1	247 20.3	25.4	182 32.2	49.5	300 13.7	21.4
06		124 59.2	237 52.1	S23 12.7	262 21.0	S16 25.9	197 34.3	S22 49.5	315 15.9	N 6 21.3
07		140 01.7	252 51.3	13.3	277 21.8	26.4	212 36.3	49.4	330 18.1	21.2
08		155 04.2	267 50.6	13.8	292 22.5	27.0	227 38.4	49.4	345 20.4	21.1
09	S	170 06.6	282 49.8	. . 14.4	307 23.2	. . 27.5	242 40.5	. . 49.3	0 22.6	. . 21.0
10	U	185 09.1	297 49.0	15.0	322 24.0	28.0	257 42.6	49.3	15 24.8	20.9
11	N	200 11.5	312 48.3	15.6	337 24.7	28.6	272 44.7	49.3	30 27.0	20.9
12	D	215 14.0	327 47.5	S23 16.1	352 25.4	S16 29.1	287 46.8	S22 49.2	45 29.3	N 6 20.8
13	A	230 16.5	342 46.7	16.7	7 26.2	29.6	302 48.9	49.2	60 31.5	20.7
14	Y	245 18.9	357 46.0	17.3	22 26.9	30.2	317 51.0	49.1	75 33.7	20.6
15		260 21.4	12 45.2	. . 17.8	37 27.7	. . 30.7	332 53.1	. . 49.1	90 36.0	. . 20.5
16		275 23.9	27 44.4	18.4	52 28.4	31.2	347 55.2	49.1	105 38.2	20.4
17		290 26.3	42 43.7	19.0	67 29.1	31.8	2 57.3	49.0	120 40.4	20.3
18		305 28.8	57 42.9	S23 19.6	82 29.9	S16 32.3	17 59.4	S22 49.0	135 42.6	N 6 20.2
19		320 31.3	72 42.1	20.1	97 30.6	32.8	33 01.5	48.9	150 44.9	20.1
20		335 33.7	87 41.3	20.7	112 31.3	33.3	48 03.6	48.9	165 47.1	20.0
21		350 36.2	102 40.6	. . 21.3	127 32.1	. . 33.9	63 05.6	. . 48.9	180 49.3	. . 19.9
22		5 38.7	117 39.8	21.8	142 32.8	34.4	78 07.7	48.8	195 51.6	19.8
23		20 41.1	132 39.0	22.4	157 33.5	34.9	93 09.8	48.8	210 53.8	19.8
Mer. Pass.		h m 21 41.4	v −0.8	d 0.6	v 0.7	d 0.5	v 2.1	d 0.0	v 2.2	d 0.1

STARS		
Name	SHA	Dec
	° ′	° ′
Acamar	315 20.5	S40 15.9
Achernar	335 28.5	S57 11.4
Acrux	173 14.2	S63 08.8
Adhara	255 15.2	S28 58.7
Aldebaran	290 53.1	N16 31.8
Alioth	166 24.0	N55 54.6
Alkaid	153 01.9	N49 16.1
Al Na'ir	27 47.7	S46 55.2
Alnilam	275 49.7	S 1 11.6
Alphard	217 59.6	S 8 41.7
Alphecca	126 14.3	N26 41.1
Alpheratz	357 46.9	N29 08.6
Altair	62 11.7	N 8 53.6
Ankaa	353 18.6	S42 15.4
Antares	112 30.9	S26 27.2
Arcturus	145 59.2	N19 08.2
Atria	107 36.4	S69 02.8
Avior	234 19.6	S59 31.9
Bellatrix	278 35.5	N 6 21.6
Betelgeuse	271 04.9	N 7 24.7
Canopus	263 57.5	S52 41.6
Capella	280 39.3	N46 00.4
Deneb	49 33.9	N45 19.0
Denebola	182 37.4	N14 31.4
Diphda	348 59.0	S17 56.1
Dubhe	193 56.1	N61 42.0
Elnath	278 16.8	N28 37.0
Eltanin	90 48.1	N51 29.4
Enif	33 50.5	N 9 55.1
Fomalhaut	15 27.5	S29 34.5
Gacrux	172 05.6	S57 09.6
Gienah	175 56.2	S17 35.4
Hadar	148 53.8	S60 25.0
Hamal	328 04.4	N23 30.5
Kaus Aust.	83 48.6	S34 23.0
Kochab	137 20.6	N74 07.1
Markab	13 41.6	N15 15.4
Menkar	314 18.4	N 4 07.7
Menkent	148 12.2	S36 24.8
Miaplacidus	221 41.0	S69 44.9
Mirfak	308 45.0	N49 53.7
Nunki	76 02.7	S26 17.2
Peacock	53 24.5	S56 42.6
Pollux	243 31.9	N28 00.3
Procyon	245 03.3	N 5 12.3
Rasalhague	96 09.9	N12 33.3
Regulus	207 47.3	N11 55.5
Rigel	281 15.2	S 8 11.3
Rigil Kent.	139 57.4	S60 52.3
Sabik	102 16.8	S15 44.2
Schedar	349 44.3	N56 35.4
Shaula	96 26.9	S37 06.7
Sirius	258 36.7	S16 43.4
Spica	158 35.3	S11 12.4
Suhail	222 55.2	S43 27.8
Vega	80 41.5	N38 47.7
Zuben'ubi	137 09.7	S16 04.7

	SHA	Mer. Pass.
	° ′	h m
Venus	114 29.6	14 08
Mars	138 13.5	12 31
Jupiter	72 46.0	16 52
Saturn	190 23.8	9 02

UT (d h)	Day	SUN GHA (° ′)	SUN Dec (° ′)	MOON GHA (° ′)	v (′)	MOON Dec (° ′)	d (′)	HP (′)
24 00	FRIDAY	183 57.2	S11 48.3	238 55.5	13.2	N 9 15.6	14.5	57.4
01		198 57.2	49.1	253 27.7	13.2	9 01.1	14.5	57.4
02		213 57.3	50.0	267 59.9	13.3	8 46.6	14.5	57.3
03		228 57.4	. . 50.9	282 32.2	13.3	8 32.1	14.6	57.3
04		243 57.5	51.7	297 04.5	13.4	8 17.5	14.6	57.3
05		258 57.5	52.6	311 36.9	13.5	8 02.9	14.6	57.3
06		273 57.6	S11 53.5	326 09.4	13.5	N 7 48.3	14.6	57.3
07		288 57.7	54.3	340 41.9	13.6	7 33.7	14.6	57.2
08		303 57.8	55.2	355 14.5	13.6	7 19.1	14.7	57.2
09		318 57.8	. . 56.1	9 47.1	13.6	7 04.4	14.7	57.2
10		333 57.9	56.9	24 19.7	13.8	6 49.7	14.7	57.2
11		348 58.0	57.8	38 52.5	13.7	6 35.0	14.7	57.1
12		3 58.1	S11 58.7	53 25.2	13.9	N 6 20.3	14.8	57.1
13		18 58.1	11 59.5	67 58.1	13.8	6 05.5	14.8	57.1
14		33 58.2	12 00.4	82 30.9	14.0	5 50.7	14.7	57.1
15		48 58.3	. . 01.3	97 03.9	13.9	5 36.0	14.8	57.0
16		63 58.4	02.1	111 36.8	14.0	5 21.2	14.8	57.0
17		78 58.4	03.0	126 09.8	14.1	5 06.4	14.9	57.0
18		93 58.5	S12 03.8	140 42.9	14.1	N 4 51.5	14.8	57.0
19		108 58.6	04.7	155 16.0	14.1	4 36.7	14.8	57.0
20		123 58.7	05.6	169 49.1	14.2	4 21.9	14.9	56.9
21		138 58.7	. . 06.4	184 22.3	14.2	4 07.0	14.8	56.9
22		153 58.8	07.3	198 55.5	14.2	3 52.2	14.9	56.9
23		168 58.9	08.1	213 28.7	14.3	3 37.3	14.9	56.9
25 00	SATURDAY	183 59.0	S12 09.0	228 02.0	14.3	N 3 22.4	14.8	56.8
01		198 59.0	09.9	242 35.3	14.4	3 07.6	14.9	56.8
02		213 59.1	10.7	257 08.7	14.4	2 52.7	14.9	56.8
03		228 59.2	. . 11.6	271 42.1	14.4	2 37.8	14.9	56.8
04		243 59.2	12.5	286 15.5	14.4	2 22.9	14.8	56.8
05		258 59.3	13.3	300 48.9	14.5	2 08.1	14.9	56.7
06		273 59.4	S12 14.2	315 22.4	14.5	N 1 53.2	14.9	56.7
07		288 59.4	15.0	329 55.9	14.6	1 38.3	14.9	56.7
08		303 59.5	15.9	344 29.5	14.5	1 23.4	14.8	56.7
09		318 59.6	. . 16.7	359 03.0	14.6	1 08.6	14.9	56.7
10		333 59.6	17.6	13 36.6	14.6	0 53.7	14.8	56.6
11		348 59.7	18.5	28 10.2	14.6	0 38.9	14.9	56.6
12		3 59.8	S12 19.3	42 43.8	14.7	N 0 24.0	14.8	56.6
13		18 59.8	20.2	57 17.5	14.6	N 0 09.2	14.8	56.6
14		33 59.9	21.0	71 51.1	14.7	S 0 05.6	14.9	56.5
15		49 00.0	. . 21.9	86 24.8	14.7	0 20.5	14.8	56.5
16		64 00.0	22.7	100 58.5	14.7	0 35.3	14.8	56.5
17		79 00.1	23.6	115 32.2	14.8	0 50.1	14.7	56.5
18		94 00.2	S12 24.4	130 06.0	14.7	S 1 04.8	14.8	56.5
19		109 00.2	25.3	144 39.7	14.8	1 19.6	14.7	56.4
20		124 00.3	26.2	159 13.5	14.8	1 34.3	14.8	56.4
21		139 00.4	. . 27.0	173 47.3	14.8	1 49.1	14.7	56.4
22		154 00.4	27.9	188 21.1	14.8	2 03.8	14.7	56.4
23		169 00.5	28.7	202 54.9	14.8	2 18.5	14.6	56.4
26 00	SUNDAY	184 00.6	S12 29.6	217 28.7	14.8	S 2 33.1	14.7	56.3
01		199 00.6	30.4	232 02.5	14.8	2 47.8	14.6	56.3
02		214 00.7	31.3	246 36.3	14.8	3 02.4	14.6	56.3
03		229 00.8	. . 32.1	261 10.1	14.8	3 17.0	14.6	56.3
04		244 00.8	33.0	275 43.9	14.9	3 31.6	14.6	56.3
05		259 00.9	33.8	290 17.8	14.8	3 46.2	14.5	56.2
06		274 00.9	S12 34.7	304 51.6	14.9	S 4 00.7	14.5	56.2
07		289 01.0	35.5	319 25.5	14.8	4 15.2	14.5	56.2
08		304 01.1	36.4	333 59.3	14.8	4 29.7	14.5	56.2
09		319 01.1	. . 37.2	348 33.1	14.9	4 44.2	14.4	56.2
10		334 01.2	38.1	3 07.0	14.8	4 58.6	14.4	56.1
11		349 01.2	38.9	17 40.8	14.8	5 13.0	14.4	56.1
12		4 01.3	S12 39.8	32 14.6	14.9	S 5 27.4	14.3	56.1
13		19 01.4	40.6	46 48.5	14.8	5 41.7	14.3	56.1
14		34 01.4	41.5	61 22.3	14.8	5 56.0	14.2	56.0
15		49 01.5	. . 42.3	75 56.1	14.8	6 10.2	14.3	56.0
16		64 01.5	43.2	90 29.9	14.8	6 24.5	14.2	56.0
17		79 01.6	44.0	105 03.7	14.8	6 38.7	14.1	56.0
18		94 01.7	S12 44.9	119 37.5	14.8	S 6 52.8	14.1	56.0
19		109 01.7	45.7	134 11.3	14.7	7 06.9	14.1	56.0
20		124 01.8	46.6	148 45.0	14.8	7 21.0	14.0	55.9
21		139 01.8	. . 47.4	163 18.8	14.7	7 35.0	14.0	55.9
22		154 01.9	48.3	177 52.5	14.8	7 49.0	14.0	55.9
23		169 01.9	49.1	192 26.3	14.7	S 8 03.0	13.9	55.9
		SD 16.1	*d* 0.9	SD 15.6		15.4		15.3

Lat. (°)	Twilight Naut. (h m)	Twilight Civil (h m)	Sunrise (h m)	Moonrise 24 (h m)	Moonrise 25 (h m)	Moonrise 26 (h m)	Moonrise 27 (h m)
N 72	05 39	06 59	08 18	00 06	02 19	04 24	06 33
N 70	05 38	06 50	07 59	00 21	02 23	04 19	06 17
68	05 37	06 42	07 44	00 33	02 26	04 14	06 04
66	05 36	06 36	07 31	00 43	02 29	04 11	05 53
64	05 35	06 30	07 21	00 51	02 31	04 08	05 44
62	05 34	06 26	07 13	00 58	02 33	04 05	05 37
60	05 33	06 21	07 05	01 04	02 34	04 03	05 30
N 58	05 32	06 17	06 59	01 09	02 36	04 01	05 25
56	05 30	06 14	06 53	01 13	02 37	03 59	05 20
54	05 29	06 11	06 48	01 18	02 38	03 57	05 15
52	05 28	06 08	06 43	01 21	02 39	03 56	05 11
50	05 27	06 05	06 39	01 25	02 40	03 54	05 08
45	05 25	05 59	06 29	01 32	02 43	03 51	05 00
N 40	05 22	05 54	06 21	01 38	02 44	03 49	04 53
35	05 19	05 49	06 15	01 43	02 46	03 47	04 48
30	05 16	05 44	06 09	01 48	02 47	03 45	04 43
20	05 10	05 36	05 59	01 56	02 50	03 42	04 34
N 10	05 03	05 28	05 49	02 02	02 52	03 39	04 27
0	04 55	05 19	05 41	02 09	02 53	03 37	04 20
S 10	04 45	05 10	05 32	02 15	02 55	03 34	04 13
20	04 33	05 00	05 22	02 22	02 57	03 32	04 06
30	04 17	04 46	05 11	02 30	03 00	03 29	03 58
35	04 07	04 38	05 05	02 34	03 01	03 27	03 53
40	03 55	04 29	04 58	02 39	03 03	03 25	03 48
45	03 40	04 18	04 49	02 45	03 04	03 23	03 42
S 50	03 20	04 04	04 39	02 52	03 07	03 21	03 35
52	03 10	03 57	04 34	02 55	03 08	03 19	03 32
54	02 59	03 49	04 29	02 58	03 09	03 18	03 28
56	02 46	03 41	04 23	03 02	03 10	03 17	03 24
58	02 31	03 31	04 16	03 06	03 11	03 15	03 20
S 60	02 12	03 20	04 09	03 11	03 12	03 13	03 15

Lat. (°)	Sunset (h m)	Twilight Civil (h m)	Twilight Naut. (h m)	Moonset 24 (h m)	Moonset 25 (h m)	Moonset 26 (h m)	Moonset 27 (h m)
N 72	15 09	16 27	17 47	15 39	15 08	14 37	14 01
N 70	15 28	16 36	17 48	15 32	15 09	14 46	14 20
68	15 43	16 44	17 49	15 26	15 10	14 53	14 35
66	15 55	16 51	17 51	15 21	15 10	14 59	14 47
64	16 06	16 56	17 52	15 17	15 10	15 04	14 57
62	16 14	17 01	17 53	15 13	15 11	15 08	15 06
60	16 22	17 06	17 54	15 10	15 11	15 12	15 14
N 58	16 29	17 10	17 55	15 07	15 11	15 16	15 20
56	16 34	17 13	17 56	15 04	15 12	15 19	15 26
54	16 40	17 16	17 58	15 02	15 12	15 21	15 32
52	16 44	17 19	17 59	15 00	15 12	15 24	15 37
50	16 49	17 22	18 00	14 58	15 12	15 26	15 41
45	16 58	17 28	18 03	14 53	15 12	15 31	15 51
N 40	17 06	17 34	18 05	14 50	15 13	15 35	15 59
35	17 13	17 39	18 08	14 47	15 13	15 39	16 06
30	17 19	17 43	18 11	14 44	15 13	15 42	16 12
20	17 29	17 52	18 18	14 39	15 14	15 48	16 23
N 10	17 39	18 00	18 25	14 35	15 14	15 53	16 32
0	17 47	18 09	18 33	14 30	15 14	15 57	16 41
S 10	17 56	18 18	18 43	14 26	15 15	16 02	16 50
20	18 06	18 29	18 55	14 22	15 15	16 07	16 59
30	18 17	18 42	19 12	14 16	15 15	16 13	17 10
35	18 24	18 50	19 22	14 13	15 15	16 16	17 17
40	18 31	19 00	19 34	14 10	15 16	16 20	17 24
45	18 40	19 11	19 50	14 06	15 16	16 24	17 32
S 50	18 50	19 26	20 10	14 01	15 16	16 29	17 43
52	18 55	19 32	20 20	13 59	15 16	16 32	17 47
54	19 01	19 40	20 31	13 56	15 16	16 35	17 53
56	19 07	19 49	20 44	13 54	15 16	16 38	17 58
58	19 13	19 59	21 00	13 51	15 17	16 41	18 05
S 60	19 21	20 10	21 20	13 47	15 17	16 44	18 12

Day	SUN Eqn. of Time 00^h (m s)	SUN Eqn. of Time 12^h (m s)	SUN Mer. Pass. (h m)	MOON Mer. Pass. Upper (h m)	MOON Mer. Pass. Lower (h m)	MOON Age (d)	MOON Phase (%)
24	15 48	15 52	11 44	08 20	20 42	25	20
25	15 56	15 59	11 44	09 04	21 26	26	12
26	16 02	16 05	11 44	09 47	22 09	27	6

UT		ARIES	VENUS −4.0		MARS +1.5		JUPITER −2.1		SATURN +1.1	
d h		GHA ° ′	GHA ° ′	Dec ° ′	GHA ° ′	Dec ° ′	GHA ° ′	Dec ° ′	GHA ° ′	Dec ° ′
27 00		35 43.6	147 38.2	S23 22.9	172 34.3	S16 35.5	108 11.9	S22 48.8	225 56.0	N 6 19.7
01		50 46.0	162 37.5	23.5	187 35.0	36.0	123 14.0	48.7	240 58.2	19.6
02		65 48.5	177 36.7	24.1	202 35.7	36.5	138 16.1	48.7	256 00.5	19.5
03		80 51.0	192 35.9	. . 24.6	217 36.5	. . 37.1	153 18.2	. . 48.6	271 02.7	. . 19.4
04		95 53.4	207 35.2	25.2	232 37.2	37.6	168 20.3	48.6	286 04.9	19.3
05		110 55.9	222 34.4	25.7	247 37.9	38.1	183 22.4	48.6	301 07.2	19.2
06		125 58.4	237 33.6	S23 26.3	262 38.7	S16 38.6	198 24.4	S22 48.5	316 09.4	N 6 19.1
07		141 00.8	252 32.8	26.8	277 39.4	39.2	213 26.5	48.5	331 11.6	19.0
08		156 03.3	267 32.1	27.4	292 40.1	39.7	228 28.6	48.4	346 13.8	18.9
09	M	171 05.8	282 31.3	. . 27.9	307 40.9	. . 40.2	243 30.7	. . 48.4	1 16.1	. . 18.8
10	O	186 08.2	297 30.5	28.5	322 41.6	40.7	258 32.8	48.4	16 18.3	18.8
11	N	201 10.7	312 29.7	29.0	337 42.3	41.3	273 34.9	48.3	31 20.5	18.7
12	D	216 13.1	327 28.9	S23 29.6	352 43.0	S16 41.8	288 37.0	S22 48.3	46 22.8	N 6 18.6
13	A	231 15.6	342 28.2	30.1	7 43.8	42.3	303 39.1	48.2	61 25.0	18.5
14	Y	246 18.1	357 27.4	30.7	22 44.5	42.9	318 41.1	48.2	76 27.2	18.4
15		261 20.5	12 26.6	. . 31.2	37 45.2	. . 43.4	333 43.2	. . 48.2	91 29.5	. . 18.3
16		276 23.0	27 25.8	31.8	52 46.0	43.9	348 45.3	48.1	106 31.7	18.2
17		291 25.5	42 25.1	32.3	67 46.7	44.4	3 47.4	48.1	121 33.9	18.1
18		306 27.9	57 24.3	S23 32.8	82 47.4	S16 45.0	18 49.5	S22 48.0	136 36.1	N 6 18.0
19		321 30.4	72 23.5	33.4	97 48.2	45.5	33 51.6	48.0	151 38.4	17.9
20		336 32.9	87 22.7	33.9	112 48.9	46.0	48 53.7	47.9	166 40.6	17.9
21		351 35.3	102 21.9	. . 34.4	127 49.6	. . 46.5	63 55.7	. . 47.9	181 42.8	. . 17.8
22		6 37.8	117 21.1	35.0	142 50.3	47.1	78 57.8	47.9	196 45.1	17.7
23		21 40.3	132 20.4	35.5	157 51.1	47.6	93 59.9	47.8	211 47.3	17.6
28 00		36 42.7	147 19.6	S23 36.1	172 51.8	S16 48.1	109 02.0	S22 47.8	226 49.5	N 6 17.5
01		51 45.2	162 18.8	36.6	187 52.5	48.6	124 04.1	47.7	241 51.8	17.4
02		66 47.6	177 18.0	37.1	202 53.2	49.2	139 06.2	47.7	256 54.0	17.3
03		81 50.1	192 17.2	. . 37.6	217 54.0	. . 49.7	154 08.2	. . 47.7	271 56.2	. . 17.2
04		96 52.6	207 16.5	38.2	232 54.7	50.2	169 10.3	47.6	286 58.5	17.1
05		111 55.0	222 15.7	38.7	247 55.4	50.7	184 12.4	47.6	302 00.7	17.0
06		126 57.5	237 14.9	S23 39.2	262 56.2	S16 51.2	199 14.5	S22 47.5	317 02.9	N 6 17.0
07		142 00.0	252 14.1	39.8	277 56.9	51.8	214 16.6	47.5	332 05.2	16.9
08	T	157 02.4	267 13.3	40.3	292 57.6	52.3	229 18.7	47.5	347 07.4	16.8
09	U	172 04.9	282 12.5	. . 40.8	307 58.3	. . 52.8	244 20.7	. . 47.4	2 09.6	. . 16.7
10	E	187 07.4	297 11.7	41.3	322 59.1	53.3	259 22.8	47.4	17 11.9	16.6
11	S	202 09.8	312 11.0	41.8	337 59.8	53.9	274 24.9	47.3	32 14.1	16.5
12	D	217 12.3	327 10.2	S23 42.4	353 00.5	S16 54.4	289 27.0	S22 47.3	47 16.3	N 6 16.4
13	A	232 14.7	342 09.4	42.9	8 01.2	54.9	304 29.1	47.3	62 18.5	16.3
14	Y	247 17.2	357 08.6	43.4	23 01.9	55.4	319 31.1	47.2	77 20.8	16.2
15		262 19.7	12 07.8	. . 43.9	38 02.7	. . 55.9	334 33.2	. . 47.2	92 23.0	. . 16.1
16		277 22.1	27 07.0	44.4	53 03.4	56.5	349 35.3	47.1	107 25.2	16.1
17		292 24.6	42 06.2	45.0	68 04.1	57.0	4 37.4	47.1	122 27.5	16.0
18		307 27.1	57 05.4	S23 45.5	83 04.8	S16 57.5	19 39.5	S22 47.0	137 29.7	N 6 15.9
19		322 29.5	72 04.7	46.0	98 05.6	58.0	34 41.5	47.0	152 31.9	15.8
20		337 32.0	87 03.9	46.5	113 06.3	58.5	49 43.6	47.0	167 34.2	15.7
21		352 34.5	102 03.1	. . 47.0	128 07.0	. . 59.1	64 45.7	. . 46.9	182 36.4	. . 15.6
22		7 36.9	117 02.3	47.5	143 07.7	16 59.6	79 47.8	46.9	197 38.6	15.5
23		22 39.4	132 01.5	48.0	158 08.5	17 00.1	94 49.9	46.8	212 40.9	15.4
29 00		37 41.9	147 00.7	S23 48.5	173 09.2	S17 00.6	109 51.9	S22 46.8	227 43.1	N 6 15.3
01		52 44.3	161 59.9	49.0	188 09.9	01.1	124 54.0	46.8	242 45.3	15.3
02		67 46.8	176 59.1	49.5	203 10.6	01.7	139 56.1	46.7	257 47.6	15.2
03		82 49.2	191 58.3	. . 50.0	218 11.3	. . 02.2	154 58.2	. . 46.7	272 49.8	. . 15.1
04		97 51.7	206 57.5	50.5	233 12.1	02.7	170 00.2	46.6	287 52.0	15.0
05		112 54.2	221 56.7	51.0	248 12.8	03.2	185 02.3	46.6	302 54.3	14.9
06		127 56.6	236 55.9	S23 51.5	263 13.5	S17 03.7	200 04.4	S22 46.5	317 56.5	N 6 14.8
07	W	142 59.1	251 55.2	52.0	278 14.2	04.2	215 06.5	46.5	332 58.8	14.7
08	E	158 01.6	266 54.4	52.5	293 14.9	04.8	230 08.5	46.5	348 01.0	14.6
09	D	173 04.0	281 53.6	. . 53.0	308 15.7	. . 05.3	245 10.6	. . 46.4	3 03.2	. . 14.5
10	N	188 06.5	296 52.8	53.5	323 16.4	05.8	260 12.7	46.4	18 05.5	14.5
11	E	203 09.0	311 52.0	54.0	338 17.1	06.3	275 14.8	46.3	33 07.7	14.4
12	S	218 11.4	326 51.2	S23 54.5	353 17.8	S17 06.8	290 16.9	S22 46.3	48 09.9	N 6 14.3
13	D	233 13.9	341 50.4	55.0	8 18.5	07.3	305 18.9	46.3	63 12.2	14.2
14	A	248 16.4	356 49.6	55.5	23 19.2	07.9	320 21.0	46.2	78 14.4	14.1
15	Y	263 18.8	11 48.8	. . 56.0	38 20.0	. . 08.4	335 23.1	. . 46.2	93 16.6	. . 14.0
16		278 21.3	26 48.0	56.5	53 20.7	08.9	350 25.1	46.1	108 18.9	13.9
17		293 23.7	41 47.2	56.9	68 21.4	09.4	5 27.2	46.1	123 21.1	13.8
18		308 26.2	56 46.4	S23 57.4	83 22.1	S17 09.9	20 29.3	S22 46.0	138 23.3	N 6 13.7
19		323 28.7	71 45.6	57.9	98 22.8	10.4	35 31.4	46.0	153 25.6	13.7
20		338 31.1	86 44.8	58.4	113 23.5	11.0	50 33.4	46.0	168 27.8	13.6
21		353 33.6	101 44.0	. . 58.9	128 24.3	. . 11.5	65 35.5	. . 45.9	183 30.0	. . 13.5
22		8 36.1	116 43.2	59.4	143 25.0	12.0	80 37.6	45.9	198 32.3	13.4
23		23 38.5	131 42.4	59.8	158 25.7	12.5	95 39.7	45.8	213 34.5	13.3
Mer. Pass. (h m)		21 29.6	*v* −0.8	*d* 0.5	*v* 0.7	*d* 0.5	*v* 2.1	*d* 0.0	*v* 2.2	*d* 0.1

STARS

Name	SHA ° ′	Dec ° ′
Acamar	315 20.5	S40 15.9
Achernar	335 28.5	S57 11.4
Acrux	173 14.2	S63 08.8
Adhara	255 15.1	S28 58.7
Aldebaran	290 53.1	N16 31.8
Alioth	166 24.0	N55 54.6
Alkaid	153 01.9	N49 16.1
Al Na'ir	27 47.7	S46 55.2
Alnilam	275 49.7	S 1 11.6
Alphard	217 59.6	S 8 41.7
Alphecca	126 14.3	N26 41.1
Alpheratz	357 46.9	N29 08.6
Altair	62 11.7	N 8 53.6
Ankaa	353 18.6	S42 15.4
Antares	112 30.9	S26 27.2
Arcturus	145 59.2	N19 08.2
Atria	107 36.4	S69 02.8
Avior	234 19.6	S59 31.9
Bellatrix	278 35.5	N 6 21.6
Betelgeuse	271 04.9	N 7 24.7
Canopus	263 57.4	S52 41.7
Capella	280 39.3	N46 00.4
Deneb	49 34.0	N45 19.0
Denebola	182 37.4	N14 31.4
Diphda	348 59.0	S17 56.2
Dubhe	193 56.0	N61 42.0
Elnath	278 16.8	N28 37.0
Eltanin	90 48.1	N51 29.4
Enif	33 50.5	N 9 55.1
Fomalhaut	15 27.5	S29 34.5
Gacrux	172 05.6	S57 09.6
Gienah	175 56.2	S17 35.4
Hadar	148 53.8	S60 24.9
Hamal	328 04.4	N23 30.5
Kaus Aust.	83 48.6	S34 22.9
Kochab	137 20.6	N74 07.1
Markab	13 41.7	N15 15.4
Menkar	314 18.4	N 4 07.7
Menkent	148 12.2	S36 24.8
Miaplacidus	221 40.9	S69 44.9
Mirfak	308 45.0	N49 53.7
Nunki	76 02.8	S26 17.2
Peacock	53 24.6	S56 42.6
Pollux	243 31.9	N28 00.3
Procyon	245 03.3	N 5 12.3
Rasalhague	96 09.9	N12 33.3
Regulus	207 47.3	N11 55.5
Rigel	281 15.2	S 8 11.3
Rigil Kent.	139 57.4	S60 52.3
Sabik	102 16.8	S15 44.2
Schedar	349 44.3	N56 35.4
Shaula	96 27.0	S37 06.7
Sirius	258 36.6	S16 43.4
Spica	158 35.3	S11 12.4
Suhail	222 55.2	S43 27.8
Vega	80 41.5	N38 47.7
Zuben'ubi	137 09.7	S16 04.7

	SHA ° ′	Mer. Pass. h m
Venus	110 36.9	14 11
Mars	136 09.1	12 28
Jupiter	72 19.3	16 42
Saturn	190 06.8	8 51

UT		SUN GHA	SUN Dec	MOON GHA	v	MOON Dec	d	HP
d h		° ′	° ′	° ′	′	° ′	′	′
27 00		184 02.0	S12 49.9	207 00.0	14.7	S 8 16.9	13.9	55.9
01		199 02.1	50.8	221 33.7	14.7	8 30.8	13.8	55.8
02		214 02.1	51.6	236 07.4	14.6	8 44.6	13.8	55.8
03		229 02.2	. . 52.5	250 41.0	14.7	8 58.4	13.7	55.8
04		244 02.2	53.3	265 14.7	14.6	9 12.1	13.7	55.8
05		259 02.3	54.2	279 48.3	14.6	9 25.8	13.6	55.8
06		274 02.3	S12 55.0	294 21.9	14.6	S 9 39.4	13.6	55.7
07		289 02.4	55.8	308 55.5	14.6	9 53.0	13.6	55.7
08		304 02.4	56.7	323 29.1	14.5	10 06.6	13.5	55.7
09	M	319 02.5	. . 57.5	338 02.6	14.5	10 20.1	13.4	55.7
10	O	334 02.5	58.4	352 36.1	14.5	10 33.5	13.4	55.7
11	N	349 02.6	12 59.2	7 09.6	14.5	10 46.9	13.3	55.6
12	D	4 02.6	S13 00.1	21 43.1	14.5	S11 00.2	13.3	55.6
13	A	19 02.7	00.9	36 16.6	14.4	11 13.5	13.2	55.6
14	Y	34 02.7	01.7	50 50.0	14.4	11 26.7	13.2	55.6
15		49 02.8	. . 02.6	65 23.4	14.3	11 39.9	13.1	55.6
16		64 02.8	03.4	79 56.7	14.4	11 53.0	13.0	55.5
17		79 02.9	04.2	94 30.1	14.3	12 06.0	13.0	55.5
18		94 02.9	S13 05.1	109 03.4	14.3	S12 19.0	12.9	55.5
19		109 03.0	05.9	123 36.7	14.2	12 31.9	12.9	55.5
20		124 03.0	06.8	138 09.9	14.2	12 44.8	12.8	55.5
21		139 03.1	. . 07.6	152 43.1	14.2	12 57.6	12.7	55.5
22		154 03.1	08.4	167 16.3	14.1	13 10.3	12.7	55.4
23		169 03.2	09.3	181 49.4	14.2	13 23.0	12.6	55.4
28 00		184 03.2	S13 10.1	196 22.6	14.0	S13 35.6	12.6	55.4
01		199 03.3	10.9	210 55.6	14.1	13 48.2	12.5	55.4
02		214 03.3	11.8	225 28.7	14.0	14 00.7	12.4	55.4
03		229 03.4	. . 12.6	240 01.7	14.0	14 13.1	12.3	55.3
04		244 03.4	13.5	254 34.7	13.9	14 25.4	12.3	55.3
05		259 03.5	14.3	269 07.6	13.9	14 37.7	12.2	55.3
06		274 03.5	S13 15.1	283 40.5	13.9	S14 49.9	12.1	55.3
07		289 03.6	16.0	298 13.4	13.8	15 02.0	12.1	55.3
08	T	304 03.6	16.8	312 46.2	13.8	15 14.1	12.0	55.3
09	U	319 03.7	. . 17.6	327 19.0	13.8	15 26.1	11.9	55.2
10	E	334 03.7	18.5	341 51.8	13.7	15 38.0	11.9	55.2
11	S	349 03.7	19.3	356 24.5	13.7	15 49.9	11.7	55.2
12		4 03.8	S13 20.1	10 57.2	13.6	S16 01.6	11.7	55.2
13	D	19 03.8	21.0	25 29.8	13.6	16 13.3	11.6	55.2
14	A	34 03.9	21.8	40 02.4	13.5	16 24.9	11.6	55.2
15	Y	49 03.9	. . 22.6	54 34.9	13.5	16 36.5	11.4	55.1
16		64 04.0	23.4	69 07.4	13.5	16 47.9	11.4	55.1
17		79 04.0	24.3	83 39.9	13.4	16 59.3	11.3	55.1
18		94 04.0	S13 25.1	98 12.3	13.4	S17 10.6	11.2	55.1
19		109 04.1	25.9	112 44.7	13.3	17 21.8	11.2	55.1
20		124 04.1	26.8	127 17.0	13.3	17 33.0	11.0	55.1
21		139 04.2	. . 27.6	141 49.3	13.3	17 44.0	11.0	55.0
22		154 04.2	28.4	156 21.6	13.2	17 55.0	10.9	55.0
23		169 04.3	29.2	170 53.8	13.1	18 05.9	10.8	55.0
29 00		184 04.3	S13 30.1	185 25.9	13.1	S18 16.7	10.7	55.0
01		199 04.3	30.9	199 58.0	13.1	18 27.4	10.6	55.0
02		214 04.4	31.7	214 30.1	13.0	18 38.0	10.5	55.0
03		229 04.4	. . 32.6	229 02.1	13.0	18 48.5	10.5	54.9
04		244 04.4	33.4	243 34.1	12.9	18 59.0	10.3	54.9
05		259 04.5	34.2	258 06.0	12.9	19 09.3	10.3	54.9
06		274 04.5	S13 35.0	272 37.9	12.9	S19 19.6	10.2	54.9
07	W	289 04.6	35.9	287 09.8	12.8	19 29.8	10.1	54.9
08	E	304 04.6	36.7	301 41.6	12.7	19 39.9	9.9	54.9
09	D	319 04.6	. . 37.5	316 13.3	12.7	19 49.8	9.9	54.8
10		334 04.7	38.3	330 45.0	12.7	19 59.7	9.8	54.8
11	N	349 04.7	39.2	345 16.7	12.6	20 09.5	9.8	54.8
12	E	4 04.7	S13 40.0	359 48.3	12.5	S20 19.3	9.6	54.8
13	S	19 04.8	40.8	14 19.8	12.5	20 28.9	9.5	54.8
14	D	34 04.8	41.6	28 51.3	12.5	20 38.4	9.4	54.8
15	A	49 04.9	. . 42.4	43 22.8	12.4	20 47.8	9.3	54.8
16	Y	64 04.9	43.3	57 54.2	12.4	20 57.1	9.2	54.7
17		79 04.9	44.1	72 25.6	12.3	21 06.3	9.1	54.7
18		94 05.0	S13 44.9	86 56.9	12.3	S21 15.4	9.1	54.7
19		109 05.0	45.7	101 28.2	12.2	21 24.5	8.9	54.7
20		124 05.0	46.5	115 59.4	12.2	21 33.4	8.8	54.7
21		139 05.1	. . 47.4	130 30.6	12.1	21 42.2	8.7	54.7
22		154 05.1	48.2	145 01.7	12.1	21 50.9	8.6	54.7
23		169 05.1	49.0	159 32.8	12.1	S21 59.5	8.5	54.6
		SD 16.1	d 0.8	SD 15.2		15.0		14.9

Lat.	Twilight Naut.	Twilight Civil	Sunrise	Moonrise 27	Moonrise 28	Moonrise 29	Moonrise 30
°	h m	h m	h m	h m	h m	h m	h m
N 72	05 51	07 13	08 35	06 33	09 07	■	■
N 70	05 49	07 02	08 13	06 17	08 27	■	■
68	05 47	06 53	07 56	06 04	08 00	10 19	■
66	05 45	06 45	07 42	05 53	07 40	09 36	12 18
64	05 43	06 39	07 31	05 44	07 23	09 08	11 01
62	05 41	06 33	07 21	05 37	07 10	08 46	10 25
60	05 39	06 28	07 13	05 30	06 59	08 29	09 59
N 58	05 38	06 24	07 06	05 25	06 49	08 15	09 39
56	05 36	06 20	06 59	05 20	06 41	08 02	09 22
54	05 35	06 16	06 53	05 15	06 33	07 51	09 08
52	05 33	06 13	06 48	05 11	06 27	07 42	08 56
50	05 32	06 10	06 43	05 08	06 21	07 34	08 45
45	05 28	06 03	06 33	05 00	06 08	07 16	08 22
N 40	05 25	05 57	06 25	04 53	05 57	07 01	08 04
35	05 22	05 52	06 18	04 48	05 48	06 49	07 49
30	05 18	05 47	06 11	04 43	05 40	06 38	07 36
20	05 11	05 37	06 00	04 34	05 27	06 20	07 14
N 10	05 03	05 28	05 50	04 27	05 15	06 04	06 55
0	04 54	05 19	05 40	04 20	05 04	05 50	06 37
S 10	04 44	05 09	05 31	04 13	04 53	05 35	06 19
20	04 31	04 58	05 20	04 06	04 42	05 20	06 00
30	04 14	04 44	05 09	03 58	04 29	05 02	05 39
35	04 03	04 35	05 02	03 53	04 21	04 52	05 26
40	03 50	04 25	04 54	03 48	04 13	04 40	05 12
45	03 34	04 13	04 44	03 42	04 03	04 26	04 54
S 50	03 13	03 58	04 33	03 35	03 51	04 10	04 33
52	03 02	03 50	04 28	03 32	03 45	04 02	04 23
54	02 50	03 42	04 22	03 28	03 39	03 53	04 12
56	02 36	03 33	04 16	03 24	03 33	03 44	03 59
58	02 19	03 22	04 08	03 20	03 25	03 33	03 44
S 60	01 58	03 10	04 00	03 15	03 17	03 20	03 27

Lat.	Sunset	Twilight Civil	Twilight Naut.	Moonset 27	Moonset 28	Moonset 29	Moonset 30
°	h m	h m	h m	h m	h m	h m	h m
N 72	14 51	16 13	17 34	14 01	13 01	■	■
N 70	15 13	16 24	17 37	14 20	13 42	■	■
68	15 31	16 33	17 39	14 35	14 11	13 28	■
66	15 44	16 41	17 41	14 47	14 32	14 11	13 09
64	15 56	16 47	17 43	14 57	14 50	14 41	14 27
62	16 05	16 53	17 45	15 06	15 04	15 03	15 03
60	16 14	16 58	17 47	15 14	15 16	15 21	15 30
N 58	16 21	17 03	17 49	15 20	15 27	15 36	15 50
56	16 28	17 07	17 50	15 26	15 36	15 49	16 07
54	16 33	17 10	17 52	15 32	15 44	16 00	16 22
52	16 39	17 14	17 53	15 37	15 52	16 10	16 35
50	16 43	17 17	17 55	15 41	15 58	16 19	16 46
45	16 54	17 24	17 58	15 51	16 13	16 38	17 09
N 40	17 02	17 30	18 02	15 59	16 25	16 54	17 28
35	17 10	17 36	18 05	16 06	16 35	17 07	17 44
30	17 16	17 41	18 09	16 12	16 44	17 19	17 58
20	17 27	17 50	18 16	16 23	16 59	17 39	18 21
N 10	17 38	17 59	18 24	16 32	17 13	17 56	18 42
0	17 47	18 08	18 33	16 41	17 26	18 12	19 01
S 10	17 57	18 19	18 44	16 50	17 39	18 28	19 20
20	18 07	18 30	18 57	16 59	17 52	18 46	19 40
30	18 19	18 44	19 14	17 10	18 08	19 06	20 04
35	18 26	18 53	19 25	17 17	18 17	19 18	20 18
40	18 35	19 03	19 38	17 24	18 28	19 32	20 34
45	18 44	19 16	19 55	17 32	18 40	19 48	20 53
S 50	18 55	19 31	20 16	17 43	18 56	20 08	21 18
52	19 01	19 39	20 27	17 47	19 03	20 18	21 30
54	19 07	19 47	20 39	17 53	19 11	20 28	21 43
56	19 13	19 56	20 54	17 58	19 20	20 41	21 59
58	19 21	20 07	21 11	18 05	19 30	20 55	22 17
S 60	19 29	20 20	21 33	18 12	19 42	21 12	22 40

Day	SUN Eqn. of Time 00^h	SUN Eqn. of Time 12^h	SUN Mer. Pass.	MOON Mer. Pass. Upper	MOON Mer. Pass. Lower	Age	Phase
d	m s	m s	h m	h m	h m	d %	
27	16 08	16 10	11 44	10 30	22 52	28 2	
28	16 13	16 15	11 44	11 15	23 38	29 0	●
29	16 17	16 19	11 44	12 01	24 25	01 0	

UT		ARIES	VENUS −4.0		MARS +1.5		JUPITER −2.1		SATURN +1.1		STARS		
		GHA	GHA	Dec	GHA	Dec	GHA	Dec	GHA	Dec	Name	SHA	Dec
d	h	° ′	° ′	° ′	° ′	° ′	° ′	° ′	° ′	° ′		° ′	° ′
30	00	38 41.0	146 41.6	S24 00.3	173 26.4	S17 13.0	110 41.7	S22 45.8	228 36.7	N 6 13.2	Acamar	315 20.4	S40 16.0
	01	53 43.5	161 40.8	00.8	188 27.1	13.5	125 43.8	45.7	243 39.0	13.1	Achernar	335 28.5	S57 11.4
	02	68 45.9	176 40.0	01.3	203 27.8	14.0	140 45.9	45.7	258 41.2	13.0	Acrux	173 14.1	S63 08.8
	03	83 48.4	191 39.2	01.7	218 28.6	14.5	155 47.9	45.7	273 43.5	13.0	Adhara	255 15.1	S28 58.8
	04	98 50.9	206 38.4	02.2	233 29.3	15.1	170 50.0	45.6	288 45.7	12.9	Aldebaran	290 53.1	N16 31.8
	05	113 53.3	221 37.6	02.7	248 30.0	15.6	185 52.1	45.6	303 47.9	12.8			
	06	128 55.8	236 36.8	S24 03.2	263 30.7	S17 16.1	200 54.2	S22 45.5	318 50.2	N 6 12.7	Alioth	166 24.0	N55 54.6
	07	143 58.2	251 36.0	03.6	278 31.4	16.6	215 56.2	45.5	333 52.4	12.6	Alkaid	153 01.9	N49 16.1
T	08	159 00.7	266 35.2	04.1	293 32.1	17.1	230 58.3	45.4	348 54.6	12.5	Al Na'ir	27 47.7	S46 55.2
H	09	174 03.2	281 34.4	04.6	308 32.8	17.6	246 00.4	45.4	3 56.9	12.4	Alnilam	275 49.7	S 1 11.6
U	10	189 05.6	296 33.6	05.0	323 33.5	18.1	261 02.4	45.4	18 59.1	12.3	Alphard	217 59.6	S 8 41.7
R	11	204 08.1	311 32.8	05.5	338 34.3	18.6	276 04.5	45.3	34 01.4	12.3			
S	12	219 10.6	326 32.0	S24 06.0	353 35.0	S17 19.2	291 06.6	S22 45.3	49 03.6	N 6 12.2	Alphecca	126 14.3	N26 41.1
D	13	234 13.0	341 31.2	06.4	8 35.7	19.7	306 08.6	45.2	64 05.8	12.1	Alpheratz	357 46.9	N29 08.6
A	14	249 15.5	356 30.4	06.9	23 36.4	20.2	321 10.7	45.2	79 08.1	12.0	Altair	62 11.7	N 8 53.6
Y	15	264 18.0	11 29.6	07.4	38 37.1	20.7	336 12.8	45.1	94 10.3	11.9	Ankaa	353 18.6	S42 15.4
	16	279 20.4	26 28.8	07.8	53 37.8	21.2	351 14.9	45.1	109 12.5	11.8	Antares	112 30.9	S26 27.2
	17	294 22.9	41 28.0	08.3	68 38.5	21.7	6 16.9	45.1	124 14.8	11.7			
	18	309 25.3	56 27.2	S24 08.7	83 39.2	S17 22.2	21 19.0	S22 45.0	139 17.0	N 6 11.6	Arcturus	145 59.2	N19 08.2
	19	324 27.8	71 26.4	09.2	98 39.9	22.7	36 21.1	45.0	154 19.3	11.6	Atria	107 36.4	S69 02.8
	20	339 30.3	86 25.5	09.6	113 40.7	23.2	51 23.1	44.9	169 21.5	11.5	Avior	234 19.6	S59 31.9
	21	354 32.7	101 24.7	10.1	128 41.4	23.7	66 25.2	44.9	184 23.7	11.4	Bellatrix	278 35.5	N 6 21.6
	22	9 35.2	116 23.9	10.6	143 42.1	24.3	81 27.3	44.8	199 26.0	11.3	Betelgeuse	271 04.9	N 7 24.7
	23	24 37.7	131 23.1	11.0	158 42.8	24.8	96 29.3	44.8	214 28.2	11.2			
31	00	39 40.1	146 22.3	S24 11.5	173 43.5	S17 25.3	111 31.4	S22 44.7	229 30.4	N 6 11.1	Canopus	263 57.4	S52 41.7
	01	54 42.6	161 21.5	11.9	188 44.2	25.8	126 33.5	44.7	244 32.7	11.0	Capella	280 39.3	N46 00.4
	02	69 45.1	176 20.7	12.4	203 44.9	26.3	141 35.5	44.7	259 34.9	10.9	Deneb	49 34.0	N45 19.0
	03	84 47.5	191 19.9	12.8	218 45.6	26.8	156 37.6	44.6	274 37.2	10.9	Denebola	182 37.4	N14 31.3
	04	99 50.0	206 19.1	13.2	233 46.3	27.3	171 39.7	44.6	289 39.4	10.8	Diphda	348 59.0	S17 56.2
	05	114 52.5	221 18.3	13.7	248 47.0	27.8	186 41.7	44.5	304 41.6	10.7			
	06	129 54.9	236 17.5	S24 14.1	263 47.7	S17 28.3	201 43.8	S22 44.5	319 43.9	N 6 10.6	Dubhe	193 56.0	N61 42.0
	07	144 57.4	251 16.7	14.6	278 48.4	28.8	216 45.8	44.4	334 46.1	10.5	Elnath	278 16.8	N28 37.0
	08	159 59.8	266 15.8	15.0	293 49.2	29.3	231 47.9	44.4	349 48.4	10.4	Eltanin	90 48.1	N51 29.4
F	09	175 02.3	281 15.0	15.5	308 49.9	29.8	246 50.0	44.3	4 50.6	10.3	Enif	33 50.5	N 9 55.1
R	10	190 04.8	296 14.2	15.9	323 50.6	30.3	261 52.0	44.3	19 52.8	10.3	Fomalhaut	15 27.5	S29 34.5
I	11	205 07.2	311 13.4	16.3	338 51.3	30.8	276 54.1	44.3	34 55.1	10.2			
D	12	220 09.7	326 12.6	S24 16.8	353 52.0	S17 31.4	291 56.2	S22 44.2	49 57.3	N 6 10.1	Gacrux	172 05.6	S57 09.6
A	13	235 12.2	341 11.8	17.2	8 52.7	31.9	306 58.2	44.2	64 59.6	10.0	Gienah	175 56.2	S17 35.4
Y	14	250 14.6	356 11.0	17.6	23 53.4	32.4	322 00.3	44.1	80 01.8	09.9	Hadar	148 53.8	S60 24.9
	15	265 17.1	11 10.2	18.1	38 54.1	32.9	337 02.4	44.1	95 04.0	09.8	Hamal	328 04.4	N23 30.5
	16	280 19.6	26 09.4	18.5	53 54.8	33.4	352 04.4	44.0	110 06.3	09.7	Kaus Aust.	83 48.6	S34 22.9
	17	295 22.0	41 08.5	18.9	68 55.5	33.9	7 06.5	44.0	125 08.5	09.6			
	18	310 24.5	56 07.7	S24 19.4	83 56.2	S17 34.4	22 08.5	S22 43.9	140 10.8	N 6 09.6	Kochab	137 20.6	N74 07.1
	19	325 27.0	71 06.9	19.8	98 56.9	34.9	37 10.6	43.9	155 13.0	09.5	Markab	13 41.7	N15 15.4
	20	340 29.4	86 06.1	20.2	113 57.6	35.4	52 12.7	43.9	170 15.2	09.4	Menkar	314 18.4	N 4 07.7
	21	355 31.9	101 05.3	20.6	128 58.3	35.9	67 14.7	43.8	185 17.5	09.3	Menkent	148 12.2	S36 24.8
	22	10 34.3	116 04.5	21.1	143 59.0	36.4	82 16.8	43.8	200 19.7	09.2	Miaplacidus	221 40.9	S69 44.9
	23	25 36.8	131 03.7	21.5	158 59.7	36.9	97 18.8	43.7	215 22.0	09.1			
1	00	40 39.3	146 02.8	S24 21.9	174 00.4	S17 37.4	112 20.9	S22 43.7	230 24.2	N 6 09.0	Mirfak	308 45.0	N49 53.7
	01	55 41.7	161 02.0	22.3	189 01.1	37.9	127 23.0	43.6	245 26.4	09.0	Nunki	76 02.8	S26 17.2
	02	70 44.2	176 01.2	22.7	204 01.8	38.4	142 25.0	43.6	260 28.7	08.9	Peacock	53 24.6	S56 42.6
	03	85 46.7	191 00.4	23.2	219 02.5	38.9	157 27.1	43.5	275 30.9	08.8	Pollux	243 31.9	N28 00.3
	04	100 49.1	205 59.6	23.6	234 03.2	39.4	172 29.1	43.5	290 33.2	08.7	Procyon	245 03.3	N 5 12.3
	05	115 51.6	220 58.8	24.0	249 03.9	39.9	187 31.2	43.5	305 35.4	08.6			
	06	130 54.1	235 58.0	S24 24.4	264 04.6	S17 40.4	202 33.3	S22 43.4	320 37.6	N 6 08.5	Rasalhague	96 09.9	N12 33.3
	07	145 56.5	250 57.1	24.8	279 05.3	40.9	217 35.3	43.4	335 39.9	08.4	Regulus	207 47.3	N11 55.5
S	08	160 59.0	265 56.3	25.2	294 06.0	41.4	232 37.4	43.3	350 42.1	08.4	Rigel	281 15.1	S 8 11.3
A	09	176 01.5	280 55.5	25.7	309 06.7	41.9	247 39.4	43.3	5 44.4	08.3	Rigil Kent.	139 57.4	S60 52.3
T	10	191 03.9	295 54.7	26.1	324 07.4	42.4	262 41.5	43.2	20 46.6	08.2	Sabik	102 16.8	S15 44.2
U	11	206 06.4	310 53.9	26.5	339 08.1	42.9	277 43.6	43.2	35 48.9	08.1			
R	12	221 08.8	325 53.0	S24 26.9	354 08.8	S17 43.4	292 45.6	S22 43.1	50 51.1	N 6 08.0	Schedar	349 44.3	N56 35.4
D	13	236 11.3	340 52.2	27.3	9 09.5	43.9	307 47.7	43.1	65 53.3	07.9	Shaula	96 27.0	S37 06.7
A	14	251 13.8	355 51.4	27.7	24 10.2	44.4	322 49.7	43.0	80 55.6	07.9	Sirius	258 36.6	S16 43.5
Y	15	266 16.2	10 50.6	28.1	39 10.9	44.9	337 51.8	43.0	95 57.8	07.8	Spica	158 35.3	S11 12.4
	16	281 18.7	25 49.8	28.5	54 11.6	45.4	352 53.8	43.0	111 00.1	07.7	Suhail	222 55.2	S43 27.8
	17	296 21.2	40 49.0	28.9	69 12.3	45.9	7 55.9	42.9	126 02.3	07.6			
	18	311 23.6	55 48.1	S24 29.3	84 13.0	S17 46.4	22 58.0	S22 42.9	141 04.6	N 6 07.5	Vega	80 41.6	N38 47.7
	19	326 26.1	70 47.3	29.7	99 13.7	46.9	38 00.0	42.8	156 06.8	07.4	Zuben'ubi	137 09.7	S16 04.7
	20	341 28.6	85 46.5	30.1	114 14.4	47.4	53 02.1	42.8	171 09.0	07.3		SHA	Mer. Pass.
	21	356 31.0	100 45.7	30.5	129 15.1	47.9	68 04.1	42.7	186 11.3	07.3		° ′	h m
	22	11 33.5	115 44.9	30.9	144 15.8	48.4	83 06.2	42.7	201 13.5	07.2	Venus	106 42.2	14 15
	23	26 35.9	130 44.0	31.3	159 16.5	48.9	98 08.2	42.6	216 15.8	07.1	Mars	134 03.4	12 25
Mer. Pass.		h m 21 17.8	*v* −0.8	*d* 0.4	*v* 0.7	*d* 0.5	*v* 2.1	*d* 0.0	*v* 2.2	*d* 0.1	Jupiter	71 51.3	16 32
											Saturn	189 50.3	8 41

UT d	h	SUN GHA	SUN Dec	MOON GHA	v	MOON Dec	d	HP
d	h	° ′	° ′	° ′	′	° ′	′	′
30	00	184 05.2	S13 49.8	174 03.9	12.0	S22 08.0	8.4	54.6
	01	199 05.2	50.6	188 34.9	11.9	22 16.4	8.3	54.6
	02	214 05.2	51.5	203 05.8	11.9	22 24.7	8.2	54.6
	03	229 05.2	. . 52.3	217 36.7	11.9	22 32.9	8.0	54.6
	04	244 05.3	53.1	232 07.6	11.8	22 40.9	8.0	54.6
	05	259 05.3	53.9	246 38.4	11.8	22 48.9	7.9	54.6
	06	274 05.3	S13 54.7	261 09.2	11.7	S22 56.8	7.7	54.5
T	07	289 05.4	55.5	275 39.9	11.7	23 04.5	7.6	54.5
H	08	304 05.4	56.4	290 10.6	11.6	23 12.1	7.6	54.5
	09	319 05.4	. . 57.2	304 41.2	11.6	23 19.7	7.4	54.5
U	10	334 05.5	58.0	319 11.8	11.5	23 27.1	7.3	54.5
R	11	349 05.5	58.8	333 42.3	11.6	23 34.4	7.2	54.5
S	12	4 05.5	S13 59.6	348 12.9	11.4	S23 41.6	7.0	54.5
D	13	19 05.5	14 00.4	2 43.3	11.4	23 48.6	7.0	54.5
A	14	34 05.6	01.2	17 13.7	11.4	23 55.6	6.9	54.4
Y	15	49 05.6	. . 02.1	31 44.1	11.4	24 02.5	6.7	54.4
	16	64 05.6	02.9	46 14.5	11.3	24 09.2	6.6	54.4
	17	79 05.6	03.7	60 44.8	11.2	24 15.8	6.5	54.4
	18	94 05.7	S14 04.5	75 15.0	11.2	S24 22.3	6.4	54.4
	19	109 05.7	05.3	89 45.2	11.2	24 28.7	6.3	54.4
	20	124 05.7	06.1	104 15.4	11.2	24 35.0	6.1	54.4
	21	139 05.7	. . 06.9	118 45.6	11.1	24 41.1	6.0	54.4
	22	154 05.8	07.7	133 15.7	11.0	24 47.1	5.9	54.4
	23	169 05.8	08.5	147 45.7	11.1	24 53.0	5.8	54.3
31	00	184 05.8	S14 09.4	162 15.8	10.9	S24 58.8	5.7	54.3
	01	199 05.8	10.2	176 45.7	11.0	25 04.5	5.6	54.3
	02	214 05.9	11.0	191 15.7	10.9	25 10.1	5.4	54.3
	03	229 05.9	. . 11.8	205 45.6	10.9	25 15.5	5.3	54.3
	04	244 05.9	12.6	220 15.5	10.9	25 20.8	5.2	54.3
	05	259 05.9	13.4	234 45.4	10.8	25 26.0	5.0	54.3
	06	274 06.0	S14 14.2	249 15.2	10.8	S25 31.0	5.0	54.3
	07	289 06.0	15.0	263 45.0	10.8	25 36.0	4.8	54.3
	08	304 06.0	15.8	278 14.8	10.7	25 40.8	4.7	54.3
F	09	319 06.0	. . 16.6	292 44.5	10.7	25 45.5	4.5	54.3
R	10	334 06.0	17.4	307 14.2	10.7	25 50.0	4.5	54.2
I	11	349 06.1	18.2	321 43.9	10.6	25 54.5	4.3	54.2
D	12	4 06.1	S14 19.0	336 13.5	10.6	S25 58.8	4.2	54.2
A	13	19 06.1	19.8	350 43.1	10.6	26 03.0	4.1	54.2
Y	14	34 06.1	20.6	5 12.7	10.6	26 07.1	3.9	54.2
	15	49 06.1	. . 21.4	19 42.3	10.5	26 11.0	3.8	54.2
	16	64 06.2	22.3	34 11.8	10.5	26 14.8	3.7	54.2
	17	79 06.2	23.1	48 41.3	10.5	26 18.5	3.6	54.2
	18	94 06.2	S14 23.9	63 10.8	10.5	S26 22.1	3.4	54.2
	19	109 06.2	24.7	77 40.3	10.5	26 25.5	3.3	54.2
	20	124 06.2	25.5	92 09.8	10.4	26 28.8	3.2	54.2
	21	139 06.2	. . 26.3	106 39.2	10.4	26 32.0	3.0	54.2
	22	154 06.3	27.1	121 08.6	10.4	26 35.0	2.9	54.2
	23	169 06.3	27.9	135 38.0	10.4	26 37.9	2.8	54.1
1	00	184 06.3	S14 28.7	150 07.4	10.3	S26 40.7	2.7	54.1
	01	199 06.3	29.5	164 36.7	10.4	26 43.4	2.5	54.1
	02	214 06.3	30.3	179 06.1	10.3	26 45.9	2.4	54.1
	03	229 06.3	. . 31.1	193 35.4	10.4	26 48.3	2.3	54.1
	04	244 06.3	31.9	208 04.8	10.3	26 50.6	2.1	54.1
	05	259 06.4	32.7	222 34.1	10.3	26 52.7	2.0	54.1
	06	274 06.4	S14 33.5	237 03.4	10.2	S26 54.7	1.9	54.1
S	07	289 06.4	34.2	251 32.6	10.3	26 56.6	1.8	54.1
	08	304 06.4	35.0	266 01.9	10.3	26 58.4	1.6	54.1
A	09	319 06.4	. . 35.8	280 31.2	10.3	27 00.0	1.5	54.1
T	10	334 06.4	36.6	295 00.5	10.2	27 01.5	1.3	54.1
U	11	349 06.4	37.4	309 29.7	10.3	27 02.8	1.3	54.1
R	12	4 06.4	S14 38.2	323 59.0	10.2	S27 04.1	1.1	54.1
D	13	19 06.5	39.0	338 28.2	10.3	27 05.2	0.9	54.1
A	14	34 06.5	39.8	352 57.5	10.2	27 06.1	0.9	54.1
Y	15	49 06.5	. . 40.6	7 26.7	10.3	27 07.0	0.7	54.1
	16	64 06.5	41.4	21 56.0	10.2	27 07.7	0.5	54.1
	17	79 06.5	42.2	36 25.2	10.2	27 08.2	0.5	54.1
	18	94 06.5	S14 43.0	50 54.4	10.3	S27 08.7	0.3	54.1
	19	109 06.5	43.8	65 23.7	10.2	27 09.0	0.2	54.1
	20	124 06.5	44.6	79 52.9	10.3	27 09.2	0.0	54.1
	21	139 06.5	. . 45.4	94 22.2	10.3	27 09.2	0.0	54.1
	22	154 06.5	46.1	108 51.5	10.2	27 09.2	0.2	54.1
	23	169 06.5	46.9	123 20.7	10.3	S27 09.0	0.4	54.0
		SD 16.1	*d* 0.8	SD 14.8		14.8		14.7

Lat.	Twilight Naut.	Twilight Civil	Sunrise	Moonrise 30	31	1	2
°	h m	h m	h m	h m	h m	h m	h m
N 72	06 04	07 26	08 53	■	■	■	■
N 70	06 00	07 14	08 27	■	■	■	■
68	05 56	07 03	08 08	■	■	■	■
66	05 53	06 55	07 53	12 18	■	■	■
64	05 51	06 47	07 40	11 01	■	■	■
62	05 48	06 41	07 30	10 25	12 03	13 27	14 09
60	05 46	06 35	07 20	09 59	11 25	12 36	13 23
N 58	05 44	06 30	07 12	09 39	10 58	12 05	12 53
56	05 42	06 26	07 05	09 22	10 37	11 41	12 30
54	05 40	06 22	06 59	09 08	10 20	11 22	12 12
52	05 38	06 18	06 54	08 56	10 05	11 06	11 56
50	05 36	06 15	06 48	08 45	09 52	10 52	11 42
45	05 32	06 07	06 37	08 22	09 26	10 24	11 14
N 40	05 28	06 00	06 28	08 04	09 05	10 02	10 52
35	05 24	05 54	06 20	07 49	08 48	09 44	10 34
30	05 20	05 49	06 13	07 36	08 33	09 28	10 19
20	05 12	05 38	06 01	07 14	08 08	09 01	09 52
N 10	05 04	05 29	05 50	06 55	07 46	08 38	09 29
0	04 54	05 19	05 40	06 37	07 26	08 17	09 08
S 10	04 43	05 08	05 30	06 19	07 06	07 56	08 46
20	04 29	04 56	05 19	06 00	06 45	07 33	08 23
30	04 11	04 41	05 06	05 39	06 20	07 06	07 57
35	03 59	04 32	04 58	05 26	06 06	06 51	07 41
40	03 46	04 21	04 50	05 12	05 49	06 33	07 23
45	03 28	04 08	04 40	04 54	05 29	06 11	07 01
S 50	03 06	03 52	04 28	04 33	05 04	05 43	06 33
52	02 55	03 44	04 22	04 23	04 52	05 30	06 19
54	02 42	03 35	04 16	04 12	04 38	05 14	06 03
56	02 26	03 25	04 09	03 59	04 22	04 56	05 44
58	02 08	03 14	04 01	03 44	04 03	04 34	05 21
S 60	01 43	03 00	03 52	03 27	03 40	04 05	04 51

Lat.	Sunset	Twilight Civil	Twilight Naut.	Moonset 30	31	1	2
°	h m	h m	h m	h m	h m	h m	h m
N 72	14 33	15 59	17 22	■	■	■	■
N 70	14 59	16 12	17 26	■	■	■	■
68	15 18	16 23	17 29	■	■	■	■
66	15 33	16 31	17 32	13 09	■	■	■
64	15 46	16 39	17 35	14 27	■	■	■
62	15 57	16 45	17 38	15 03	15 08	15 30	16 34
60	16 06	16 51	17 40	15 30	15 47	16 21	17 20
N 58	16 14	16 56	17 42	15 50	16 14	16 52	17 50
56	16 21	17 00	17 44	16 07	16 35	17 16	18 12
54	16 27	17 05	17 46	16 22	16 53	17 35	18 31
52	16 33	17 08	17 48	16 35	17 08	17 51	18 46
50	16 38	17 12	17 50	16 46	17 21	18 05	19 00
45	16 49	17 20	17 54	17 09	17 47	18 33	19 27
N 40	16 58	17 27	17 58	17 28	18 09	18 56	19 49
35	17 06	17 33	18 02	17 44	18 26	19 14	20 07
30	17 14	17 38	18 06	17 58	18 42	19 30	20 23
20	17 26	17 48	18 15	18 21	19 07	19 57	20 49
N 10	17 37	17 58	18 23	18 42	19 30	20 20	21 11
0	17 47	18 08	18 33	19 01	19 51	20 41	21 32
S 10	17 57	18 19	18 45	19 20	20 11	21 03	21 53
20	18 09	18 32	18 59	19 40	20 34	21 26	22 15
30	18 22	18 47	19 17	20 04	21 00	21 53	22 41
35	18 29	18 56	19 29	20 18	21 15	22 09	22 56
40	18 38	19 07	19 43	20 34	21 33	22 27	23 14
45	18 48	19 20	20 00	20 53	21 55	22 49	23 35
S 50	19 01	19 37	20 23	21 18	22 22	23 17	24 02
52	19 06	19 45	20 34	21 30	22 35	23 31	24 15
54	19 13	19 54	20 48	21 43	22 51	23 47	24 29
56	19 20	20 04	21 03	21 59	23 09	24 06	00 06
58	19 28	20 16	21 23	22 17	23 31	24 29	00 29
S 60	19 37	20 29	21 48	22 40	24 00	00 00	00 59

Day	SUN Eqn. of Time 00^h	SUN Eqn. of Time 12^h	SUN Mer. Pass.	MOON Mer. Pass. Upper	MOON Mer. Pass. Lower	MOON Age	MOON Phase
d	m s	m s	h m	h m	h m	d	%
30	16 21	16 22	11 44	12 49	00 25	02	2 ●
31	16 23	16 24	11 44	13 38	01 13	03	6
1	16 25	16 26	11 44	14 29	02 04	04	11

UT		ARIES	VENUS −4.0		MARS +1.5		JUPITER −2.1		SATURN +1.1	
	d h	GHA ° ′	GHA ° ′	Dec ° ′	GHA ° ′	Dec ° ′	GHA ° ′	Dec ° ′	GHA ° ′	Dec ° ′
	2 00	41 38.4	145 43.2	S24 31.7	174 17.2	S17 49.4	113 10.3	S22 42.6	231 18.0	N 6 07.0
	01	56 40.9	160 42.4	32.1	189 17.9	49.9	128 12.3	42.5	246 20.3	06.9
	02	71 43.3	175 41.6	32.5	204 18.6	50.4	143 14.4	42.5	261 22.5	06.8
	03	86 45.8	190 40.7	. . 32.8	219 19.3	. . 50.9	158 16.5	. . 42.5	276 24.7	. . 06.7
	04	101 48.3	205 39.9	33.2	234 20.0	51.4	173 18.5	42.4	291 27.0	06.7
	05	116 50.7	220 39.1	33.6	249 20.7	51.9	188 20.6	42.4	306 29.2	06.6
	06	131 53.2	235 38.3	S24 34.0	264 21.4	S17 52.4	203 22.6	S22 42.3	321 31.5	N 6 06.5
	07	146 55.7	250 37.5	34.4	279 22.1	52.9	218 24.7	42.3	336 33.7	06.4
	08	161 58.1	265 36.6	34.8	294 22.8	53.4	233 26.7	42.2	351 36.0	06.3
S	09	177 00.6	280 35.8	. . 35.2	309 23.5	. . 53.9	248 28.8	. . 42.2	6 38.2	. . 06.2
U	10	192 03.1	295 35.0	35.5	324 24.2	54.3	263 30.8	42.1	21 40.4	06.2
N	11	207 05.5	310 34.2	35.9	339 24.9	54.8	278 32.9	42.1	36 42.7	06.1
D	12	222 08.0	325 33.3	S24 36.3	354 25.6	S17 55.3	293 34.9	S22 42.0	51 44.9	N 6 06.0
A	13	237 10.4	340 32.5	36.7	9 26.3	55.8	308 37.0	42.0	66 47.2	05.9
Y	14	252 12.9	355 31.7	37.1	24 26.9	56.3	323 39.0	41.9	81 49.4	05.8
	15	267 15.4	10 30.9	. . 37.4	39 27.6	. . 56.8	338 41.1	. . 41.9	96 51.7	. . 05.7
	16	282 17.8	25 30.0	37.8	54 28.3	57.3	353 43.1	41.8	111 53.9	05.7
	17	297 20.3	40 29.2	38.2	69 29.0	57.8	8 45.2	41.8	126 56.2	05.6
	18	312 22.8	55 28.4	S24 38.5	84 29.7	S17 58.3	23 47.2	S22 41.8	141 58.4	N 6 05.5
	19	327 25.2	70 27.6	38.9	99 30.4	58.8	38 49.3	41.7	157 00.7	05.4
	20	342 27.7	85 26.7	39.3	114 31.1	59.3	53 51.3	41.7	172 02.9	05.3
	21	357 30.2	100 25.9	. . 39.7	129 31.8	17 59.8	68 53.4	. . 41.6	187 05.1	. . 05.2
	22	12 32.6	115 25.1	40.0	144 32.5	18 00.3	83 55.4	41.6	202 07.4	05.2
	23	27 35.1	130 24.2	40.4	159 33.2	00.8	98 57.5	41.5	217 09.6	05.1
	3 00	42 37.6	145 23.4	S24 40.8	174 33.9	S18 01.2	113 59.5	S22 41.5	232 11.9	N 6 05.0
	01	57 40.0	160 22.6	41.1	189 34.5	01.7	129 01.6	41.4	247 14.1	04.9
	02	72 42.5	175 21.8	41.5	204 35.2	02.2	144 03.6	41.4	262 16.4	04.8
	03	87 44.9	190 20.9	. . 41.8	219 35.9	. . 02.7	159 05.7	. . 41.3	277 18.6	. . 04.7
	04	102 47.4	205 20.1	42.2	234 36.6	03.2	174 07.7	41.3	292 20.9	04.7
	05	117 49.9	220 19.3	42.6	249 37.3	03.7	189 09.8	41.2	307 23.1	04.6
	06	132 52.3	235 18.4	S24 42.9	264 38.0	S18 04.2	204 11.8	S22 41.2	322 25.4	N 6 04.5
	07	147 54.8	250 17.6	43.3	279 38.7	04.7	219 13.9	41.1	337 27.6	04.4
	08	162 57.3	265 16.8	43.6	294 39.4	05.2	234 15.9	41.1	352 29.9	04.3
M	09	177 59.7	280 16.0	. . 44.0	309 40.1	. . 05.7	249 18.0	. . 41.1	7 32.1	. . 04.2
O	10	193 02.2	295 15.1	44.3	324 40.7	06.1	264 20.0	41.0	22 34.4	04.2
N	11	208 04.7	310 14.3	44.7	339 41.4	06.6	279 22.1	41.0	37 36.6	04.1
D	12	223 07.1	325 13.5	S24 45.0	354 42.1	S18 07.1	294 24.1	S22 40.9	52 38.8	N 6 04.0
A	13	238 09.6	340 12.6	45.4	9 42.8	07.6	309 26.2	40.9	67 41.1	03.9
Y	14	253 12.1	355 11.8	45.7	24 43.5	08.1	324 28.2	40.8	82 43.3	03.8
	15	268 14.5	10 11.0	. . 46.1	39 44.2	. . 08.6	339 30.3	. . 40.8	97 45.6	. . 03.7
	16	283 17.0	25 10.1	46.4	54 44.9	09.1	354 32.3	40.7	112 47.8	03.7
	17	298 19.4	40 09.3	46.8	69 45.6	09.6	9 34.4	40.7	127 50.1	03.6
	18	313 21.9	55 08.5	S24 47.1	84 46.2	S18 10.0	24 36.4	S22 40.6	142 52.3	N 6 03.5
	19	328 24.4	70 07.6	47.4	99 46.9	10.5	39 38.4	40.6	157 54.6	03.4
	20	343 26.8	85 06.8	47.8	114 47.6	11.0	54 40.5	40.5	172 56.8	03.3
	21	358 29.3	100 06.0	. . 48.1	129 48.3	. . 11.5	69 42.5	. . 40.5	187 59.1	. . 03.2
	22	13 31.8	115 05.1	48.5	144 49.0	12.0	84 44.6	40.4	203 01.3	03.2
	23	28 34.2	130 04.3	48.8	159 49.7	12.5	99 46.6	40.4	218 03.6	03.1
	4 00	43 36.7	145 03.5	S24 49.1	174 50.4	S18 13.0	114 48.7	S22 40.3	233 05.8	N 6 03.0
	01	58 39.2	160 02.6	49.5	189 51.0	13.4	129 50.7	40.3	248 08.1	02.9
	02	73 41.6	175 01.8	49.8	204 51.7	13.9	144 52.8	40.2	263 10.3	02.8
	03	88 44.1	190 01.0	. . 50.1	219 52.4	. . 14.4	159 54.8	. . 40.2	278 12.6	. . 02.7
	04	103 46.5	205 00.1	50.5	234 53.1	14.9	174 56.8	40.1	293 14.8	02.7
	05	118 49.0	219 59.3	50.8	249 53.8	15.4	189 58.9	40.1	308 17.1	02.6
	06	133 51.5	234 58.5	S24 51.1	264 54.5	S18 15.9	205 00.9	S22 40.0	323 19.3	N 6 02.5
	07	148 53.9	249 57.6	51.4	279 55.1	16.4	220 03.0	40.0	338 21.6	02.4
T	08	163 56.4	264 56.8	51.8	294 55.8	16.8	235 05.0	39.9	353 23.8	02.3
U	09	178 58.9	279 56.0	. . 52.1	309 56.5	. . 17.3	250 07.0	. . 39.9	8 26.1	. . 02.3
E	10	194 01.3	294 55.1	52.4	324 57.2	17.8	265 09.1	39.9	23 28.3	02.2
S	11	209 03.8	309 54.3	52.7	339 57.9	18.3	280 11.1	39.8	38 30.6	02.1
D	12	224 06.3	324 53.5	S24 53.1	354 58.5	S18 18.8	295 13.2	S22 39.8	53 32.8	N 6 02.0
A	13	239 08.7	339 52.6	53.4	9 59.2	19.2	310 15.2	39.7	68 35.1	01.9
Y	14	254 11.2	354 51.8	53.7	24 59.9	19.7	325 17.3	39.7	83 37.3	01.8
	15	269 13.7	9 51.0	. . 54.0	40 00.6	. . 20.2	340 19.3	. . 39.6	98 39.6	. . 01.8
	16	284 16.1	24 50.1	54.3	55 01.3	20.7	355 21.3	39.6	113 41.8	01.7
	17	299 18.6	39 49.3	54.6	70 01.9	21.2	10 23.4	39.5	128 44.1	01.6
	18	314 21.0	54 48.5	S24 55.0	85 02.6	S18 21.7	25 25.4	S22 39.5	143 46.3	N 6 01.5
	19	329 23.5	69 47.6	55.3	100 03.3	22.1	40 27.5	39.4	158 48.6	01.4
	20	344 26.0	84 46.8	55.6	115 04.0	22.6	55 29.5	39.4	173 50.8	01.4
	21	359 28.4	99 45.9	. . 55.9	130 04.7	. . 23.1	70 31.5	. . 39.3	188 53.1	. . 01.3
	22	14 30.9	114 45.1	56.2	145 05.3	23.6	85 33.6	39.3	203 55.3	01.2
	23	29 33.4	129 44.3	56.5	160 06.0	24.1	100 35.6	39.2	218 57.6	01.1
	Mer. Pass.	h m 21 06.0	*v* −0.8	*d* 0.3	*v* 0.7	*d* 0.5	*v* 2.0	*d* 0.0	*v* 2.2	*d* 0.1

STARS

Name	SHA ° ′	Dec ° ′
Acamar	315 20.4	S40 16.0
Achernar	335 28.5	S57 11.5
Acrux	173 14.1	S63 08.7
Adhara	255 15.1	S28 58.8
Aldebaran	290 53.1	N16 31.8
Alioth	166 24.0	N55 54.5
Alkaid	153 01.9	N49 16.0
Al Na'ir	27 47.8	S46 55.2
Alnilam	275 49.6	S 1 11.6
Alphard	217 59.6	S 8 41.7
Alphecca	126 14.3	N26 41.1
Alpheratz	357 46.9	N29 08.6
Altair	62 11.7	N 8 53.6
Ankaa	353 18.6	S42 15.5
Antares	112 30.9	S26 27.1
Arcturus	145 59.2	N19 08.2
Atria	107 36.4	S69 02.8
Avior	234 19.5	S59 31.9
Bellatrix	278 35.5	N 6 21.6
Betelgeuse	271 04.8	N 7 24.7
Canopus	263 57.4	S52 41.7
Capella	280 39.2	N46 00.4
Deneb	49 34.0	N45 19.0
Denebola	182 37.4	N14 31.3
Diphda	348 59.0	S17 56.2
Dubhe	193 56.0	N61 41.9
Elnath	278 16.7	N28 37.0
Eltanin	90 48.1	N51 29.4
Enif	33 50.5	N 9 55.1
Fomalhaut	15 27.5	S29 34.5
Gacrux	172 05.6	S57 09.6
Gienah	175 56.2	S17 35.4
Hadar	148 53.8	S60 24.9
Hamal	328 04.4	N23 30.5
Kaus Aust.	83 48.7	S34 22.9
Kochab	137 20.6	N74 07.1
Markab	13 41.7	N15 15.4
Menkar	314 18.4	N 4 07.7
Menkent	148 12.2	S36 24.8
Miaplacidus	221 40.8	S69 44.9
Mirfak	308 45.0	N49 53.7
Nunki	76 02.8	S26 17.2
Peacock	53 24.6	S56 42.6
Pollux	243 31.8	N28 00.3
Procyon	245 03.2	N 5 12.2
Rasalhague	96 09.9	N12 33.3
Regulus	207 47.3	N11 55.4
Rigel	281 15.1	S 8 11.3
Rigil Kent.	139 57.4	S60 52.3
Sabik	102 16.8	S15 44.2
Schedar	349 44.3	N56 35.4
Shaula	96 27.0	S37 06.7
Sirius	258 36.6	S16 43.5
Spica	158 35.3	S11 12.4
Suhail	222 55.1	S43 27.8
Vega	80 41.6	N38 47.7
Zuben'ubi	137 09.6	S16 04.7

	SHA ° ′	Mer. Pass. h m
Venus	102 45.9	14 19
Mars	131 56.3	12 21
Jupiter	71 22.0	16 22
Saturn	189 34.3	8 30

UT	SUN GHA	SUN Dec	MOON GHA	v	MOON Dec	d	HP
d h	° ′	° ′	° ′	′	° ′	′	′
2 00	184 06.6	S14 47.7	137 50.0	10.3	S27 08.6	0.4	54.0
01	199 06.6	48.5	152 19.3	10.3	27 08.2	0.6	54.0
02	214 06.6	49.3	166 48.6	10.3	27 07.6	0.8	54.0
03	229 06.6	. . 50.1	181 17.9	10.3	27 06.8	0.8	54.0
04	244 06.6	50.9	195 47.2	10.3	27 06.0	1.0	54.0
05	259 06.6	51.7	210 16.5	10.4	27 05.0	1.1	54.0
06	274 06.6	S14 52.5	224 45.9	10.3	S27 03.9	1.3	54.0
07	289 06.6	53.2	239 15.2	10.4	27 02.6	1.4	54.0
S 08	304 06.6	54.0	253 44.6	10.4	27 01.2	1.5	54.0
U 09	319 06.6	. . 54.8	268 14.0	10.4	26 59.7	1.6	54.0
N 10	334 06.6	55.6	282 43.4	10.4	26 58.1	1.8	54.0
D 11	349 06.6	56.4	297 12.8	10.4	26 56.3	1.9	54.0
A 12	4 06.6	S14 57.2	311 42.2	10.5	S26 54.4	2.0	54.1
Y 13	19 06.6	58.0	326 11.7	10.5	26 52.4	2.1	54.1
14	34 06.6	58.7	340 41.2	10.5	26 50.3	2.3	54.1
15	49 06.6	14 59.5	355 10.7	10.5	26 48.0	2.4	54.1
16	64 06.6	15 00.3	9 40.2	10.6	26 45.6	2.5	54.1
17	79 06.6	01.1	24 09.8	10.5	26 43.1	2.7	54.1
18	94 06.6	S15 01.9	38 39.3	10.6	S26 40.4	2.8	54.1
19	109 06.6	02.7	53 08.9	10.7	26 37.6	2.9	54.1
20	124 06.6	03.4	67 38.6	10.6	26 34.7	3.0	54.1
21	139 06.6	. . 04.2	82 08.2	10.7	26 31.7	3.2	54.1
22	154 06.6	05.0	96 37.9	10.7	26 28.5	3.3	54.1
23	169 06.6	05.8	111 07.6	10.7	26 25.2	3.4	54.1
3 00	184 06.6	S15 06.6	125 37.3	10.8	S26 21.8	3.5	54.1
01	199 06.6	07.3	140 07.1	10.8	26 18.3	3.7	54.1
02	214 06.6	08.1	154 36.9	10.8	26 14.6	3.8	54.1
03	229 06.6	. . 08.9	169 06.7	10.9	26 10.8	3.9	54.1
04	244 06.6	09.7	183 36.6	10.9	26 06.9	4.0	54.1
05	259 06.6	10.4	198 06.5	10.9	26 02.9	4.2	54.1
06	274 06.6	S15 11.2	212 36.4	11.0	S25 58.7	4.2	54.1
07	289 06.6	12.0	227 06.4	11.0	25 54.5	4.4	54.1
08	304 06.6	12.8	241 36.4	11.0	25 50.1	4.6	54.1
M 09	319 06.6	. . 13.6	256 06.4	11.0	25 45.5	4.6	54.1
O 10	334 06.6	14.3	270 36.4	11.2	25 40.9	4.7	54.2
N 11	349 06.6	15.1	285 06.6	11.1	25 36.2	4.9	54.2
D 12	4 06.6	S15 15.9	299 36.7	11.2	S25 31.3	5.0	54.2
A 13	19 06.6	16.7	314 06.9	11.2	25 26.3	5.1	54.2
Y 14	34 06.6	17.4	328 37.1	11.2	25 21.2	5.3	54.2
15	49 06.6	. . 18.2	343 07.3	11.3	25 15.9	5.3	54.2
16	64 06.6	19.0	357 37.6	11.4	25 10.6	5.5	54.2
17	79 06.6	19.7	12 08.0	11.3	25 05.1	5.6	54.2
18	94 06.5	S15 20.5	26 38.3	11.4	S24 59.5	5.7	54.2
19	109 06.5	21.3	41 08.7	11.5	24 53.8	5.8	54.2
20	124 06.5	22.1	55 39.2	11.5	24 48.0	5.9	54.2
21	139 06.5	. . 22.8	70 09.7	11.5	24 42.1	6.1	54.2
22	154 06.5	23.6	84 40.2	11.6	24 36.0	6.2	54.3
23	169 06.5	24.4	99 10.8	11.6	24 29.8	6.2	54.3
4 00	184 06.5	S15 25.1	113 41.4	11.7	S24 23.6	6.4	54.3
01	199 06.5	25.9	128 12.1	11.7	24 17.2	6.5	54.3
02	214 06.5	26.7	142 42.8	11.7	24 10.7	6.6	54.3
03	229 06.5	. . 27.4	157 13.5	11.8	24 04.1	6.8	54.3
04	244 06.5	28.2	171 44.3	11.8	23 57.3	6.8	54.3
05	259 06.4	29.0	186 15.1	11.9	23 50.5	6.9	54.3
06	274 06.4	S15 29.7	200 46.0	11.9	S23 43.6	7.1	54.4
07	289 06.4	30.5	215 16.9	12.0	23 36.5	7.2	54.4
T 08	304 06.4	31.3	229 47.9	12.0	23 29.3	7.3	54.4
U 09	319 06.4	. . 32.0	244 18.9	12.0	23 22.0	7.3	54.4
E 10	334 06.4	32.8	258 49.9	12.1	23 14.7	7.5	54.4
S 11	349 06.4	33.6	273 21.0	12.2	23 07.2	7.6	54.4
D 12	4 06.4	S15 34.3	287 52.2	12.1	S22 59.6	7.7	54.4
A 13	19 06.3	35.1	302 23.3	12.3	22 51.9	7.8	54.5
Y 14	34 06.3	35.9	316 54.6	12.2	22 44.1	8.0	54.5
15	49 06.3	. . 36.6	331 25.8	12.3	22 36.1	8.0	54.5
16	64 06.3	37.4	345 57.1	12.4	22 28.1	8.1	54.5
17	79 06.3	38.1	0 28.5	12.4	22 20.0	8.2	54.5
18	94 06.3	S15 38.9	14 59.9	12.4	S22 11.8	8.4	54.5
19	109 06.3	39.7	29 31.3	12.5	22 03.4	8.4	54.5
20	124 06.2	40.4	44 02.8	12.5	21 55.0	8.5	54.6
21	139 06.2	. . 41.2	58 34.3	12.6	21 46.5	8.7	54.6
22	154 06.2	41.9	73 05.9	12.6	21 37.8	8.7	54.6
23	169 06.2	42.7	87 37.5	12.7	S21 29.1	8.8	54.6
	SD 16.2	*d* 0.8	SD 14.7		14.8		14.8

Lat.	Twilight Naut.	Twilight Civil	Sunrise	Moonrise 2	Moonrise 3	Moonrise 4	Moonrise 5
°	h m	h m	h m	h m	h m	h m	h m
N 72	06 15	07 40	09 12	▬	▬	▬	▬
N 70	06 10	07 25	08 42	▬	▬	▬	16 19
68	06 06	07 14	08 21	▬	▬	▬	15 33
66	06 02	07 04	08 04	▬	▬	15 33	15 03
64	05 58	06 56	07 50	▬	15 12	14 51	14 40
62	05 55	06 49	07 38	14 09	14 20	14 22	14 21
60	05 53	06 42	07 28	13 23	13 47	14 00	14 06
N 58	05 50	06 37	07 19	12 53	13 23	13 42	13 53
56	05 47	06 32	07 12	12 30	13 04	13 26	13 42
54	05 45	06 27	07 05	12 12	12 48	13 13	13 32
52	05 43	06 23	06 59	11 56	12 34	13 02	13 23
50	05 41	06 19	06 53	11 42	12 22	12 52	13 15
45	05 36	06 11	06 42	11 14	11 56	12 30	12 58
N 40	05 31	06 03	06 32	10 52	11 36	12 13	12 44
35	05 27	05 57	06 23	10 34	11 19	11 58	12 32
30	05 22	05 51	06 16	10 19	11 04	11 45	12 22
20	05 14	05 40	06 03	09 52	10 40	11 23	12 04
N 10	05 04	05 29	05 51	09 29	10 18	11 04	11 48
0	04 54	05 19	05 40	09 08	09 58	10 47	11 33
S 10	04 42	05 07	05 29	08 46	09 38	10 29	11 19
20	04 27	04 54	05 17	08 23	09 16	10 09	11 03
30	04 08	04 38	05 03	07 57	08 51	09 47	10 44
35	03 56	04 28	04 55	07 41	08 36	09 34	10 34
40	03 41	04 17	04 46	07 23	08 19	09 19	10 21
45	03 23	04 03	04 36	07 01	07 58	09 01	10 07
S 50	02 59	03 46	04 22	06 33	07 32	08 39	09 49
52	02 47	03 38	04 16	06 19	07 19	08 28	09 40
54	02 33	03 28	04 10	06 03	07 05	08 15	09 31
56	02 16	03 17	04 02	05 44	06 48	08 01	09 20
58	01 55	03 05	03 53	05 21	06 27	07 45	09 08
S 60	01 27	02 50	03 44	04 51	06 01	07 25	08 53

Lat.	Sunset	Twilight Civil	Twilight Naut.	Moonset 2	Moonset 3	Moonset 4	Moonset 5
°	h m	h m	h m	h m	h m	h m	h m
N 72	14 14	15 46	17 10	▬	▬	▬	▬
N 70	14 43	16 00	17 15	▬	▬	▬	19 28
68	15 05	16 12	17 20	▬	▬	▬	20 12
66	15 22	16 22	17 24	▬	▬	18 35	20 42
64	15 36	16 30	17 27	▬	17 15	19 17	21 04
62	15 48	16 37	17 31	16 34	18 07	19 45	21 21
60	15 58	16 44	17 34	17 20	18 39	20 06	21 36
N 58	16 07	16 49	17 36	17 50	19 03	20 24	21 48
56	16 14	16 54	17 39	18 12	19 22	20 38	21 58
54	16 21	16 59	17 41	18 31	19 37	20 51	22 08
52	16 27	17 03	17 43	18 46	19 51	21 02	22 16
50	16 33	17 07	17 46	19 00	20 03	21 12	22 23
45	16 45	17 16	17 51	19 27	20 28	21 32	22 39
N 40	16 55	17 23	17 55	19 49	20 47	21 49	22 52
35	17 04	17 30	18 00	20 07	21 04	22 03	23 03
30	17 11	17 36	18 04	20 23	21 18	22 15	23 12
20	17 24	17 47	18 13	20 49	21 42	22 35	23 28
N 10	17 36	17 58	18 23	21 11	22 02	22 53	23 42
0	17 47	18 08	18 33	21 32	22 22	23 09	23 55
S 10	17 58	18 20	18 46	21 53	22 41	23 26	24 08
20	18 10	18 33	19 00	22 15	23 01	23 43	24 22
30	18 24	18 49	19 20	22 41	23 24	24 03	00 03
35	18 32	18 59	19 32	22 56	23 38	24 15	00 15
40	18 41	19 11	19 47	23 14	23 54	24 28	00 28
45	18 52	19 25	20 05	23 35	24 13	00 13	00 44
S 50	19 06	19 43	20 30	24 02	00 02	00 36	01 03
52	19 12	19 51	20 42	24 15	00 15	00 47	01 12
54	19 19	20 01	20 56	24 29	00 29	01 00	01 22
56	19 27	20 11	21 14	00 06	00 47	01 14	01 33
58	19 35	20 24	21 35	00 29	01 08	01 31	01 46
S 60	19 45	20 39	22 05	00 59	01 34	01 52	02 01

Day	SUN Eqn. of Time 00^h	SUN Eqn. of Time 12^h	SUN Mer. Pass.	MOON Mer. Pass. Upper	MOON Mer. Pass. Lower	MOON Age	MOON Phase
d	m s	m s	h m	h m	h m	d	%
2	16 26	16 26	11 44	15 20	02 55	05	18
3	16 27	16 26	11 44	16 10	03 45	06	26
4	16 26	16 25	11 44	16 58	04 34	07	34

UT	ARIES	VENUS −4.0		MARS +1.5		JUPITER −2.1		SATURN +1.1		STARS		
	GHA	GHA	Dec	GHA	Dec	GHA	Dec	GHA	Dec	Name	SHA	Dec
d h	° ′	° ′	° ′	° ′	° ′	° ′	° ′	° ′	° ′		° ′	° ′
5 00	44 35.8	144 43.4	S24 56.8	175 06.7	S18 24.5	115 37.7	S22 39.2	233 59.8	N 6 01.0	Acamar	315 20.4	S40 16.0
01	59 38.3	159 42.6	57.1	190 07.4	25.0	130 39.7	39.1	249 02.1	01.0	Achernar	335 28.5	S57 11.5
02	74 40.8	174 41.7	57.4	205 08.0	25.5	145 41.7	39.1	264 04.3	00.9	Acrux	173 14.1	S63 08.7
03	89 43.2	189 40.9	. . 57.7	220 08.7	. . 26.0	160 43.8	. . 39.0	279 06.6	. . 00.8	Adhara	255 15.1	S28 58.8
04	104 45.7	204 40.1	58.0	235 09.4	26.4	175 45.8	39.0	294 08.8	00.7	Aldebaran	290 53.1	N16 31.8
05	119 48.2	219 39.2	58.3	250 10.1	26.9	190 47.8	38.9	309 11.1	00.6			
06	134 50.6	234 38.4	S24 58.6	265 10.8	S18 27.4	205 49.9	S22 38.9	324 13.3	N 6 00.6	Alioth	166 23.9	N55 54.5
W 07	149 53.1	249 37.6	58.9	280 11.4	27.9	220 51.9	38.8	339 15.6	00.5	Alkaid	153 01.9	N49 16.0
E 08	164 55.5	264 36.7	59.2	295 12.1	28.4	235 54.0	38.8	354 17.8	00.4	Al Na'ir	27 47.8	S46 55.2
D 09	179 58.0	279 35.9	. . 59.5	310 12.8	. . 28.8	250 56.0	. . 38.7	9 20.1	. . 00.3	Alnilam	275 49.6	S 1 11.6
N 10	195 00.5	294 35.0	24 59.8	325 13.5	29.3	265 58.0	38.7	24 22.3	00.2	Alphard	217 59.5	S 8 41.7
E 11	210 02.9	309 34.2	25 00.1	340 14.1	29.8	281 00.1	38.6	39 24.6	00.1			
S 12	225 05.4	324 33.4	S25 00.4	355 14.8	S18 30.3	296 02.1	S22 38.6	54 26.8	N 6 00.1	Alphecca	126 14.3	N26 41.1
D 13	240 07.9	339 32.5	00.7	10 15.5	30.7	311 04.1	38.5	69 29.1	6 00.0	Alpheratz	357 46.9	N29 08.6
A 14	255 10.3	354 31.7	00.9	25 16.2	31.2	326 06.2	38.5	84 31.4	5 59.9	Altair	62 11.7	N 8 53.6
Y 15	270 12.8	9 30.8	. . 01.2	40 16.8	. . 31.7	341 08.2	. . 38.4	99 33.6	. . 59.8	Ankaa	353 18.6	S42 15.5
16	285 15.3	24 30.0	01.5	55 17.5	32.2	356 10.2	38.4	114 35.9	59.7	Antares	112 30.9	S26 27.1
17	300 17.7	39 29.2	01.8	70 18.2	32.6	11 12.3	38.3	129 38.1	59.7			
18	315 20.2	54 28.3	S25 02.1	85 18.9	S18 33.1	26 14.3	S22 38.3	144 40.4	N 5 59.6	Arcturus	145 59.2	N19 08.1
19	330 22.7	69 27.5	02.4	100 19.5	33.6	41 16.3	38.2	159 42.6	59.5	Atria	107 36.4	S69 02.8
20	345 25.1	84 26.6	02.7	115 20.2	34.1	56 18.4	38.2	174 44.9	59.4	Avior	234 19.5	S59 31.9
21	0 27.6	99 25.8	. . 02.9	130 20.9	. . 34.5	71 20.4	. . 38.1	189 47.1	. . 59.3	Bellatrix	278 35.5	N 6 21.6
22	15 30.0	114 24.9	03.2	145 21.5	35.0	86 22.4	38.1	204 49.4	59.3	Betelgeuse	271 04.8	N 7 24.7
23	30 32.5	129 24.1	03.5	160 22.2	35.5	101 24.5	38.0	219 51.6	59.2			
6 00	45 35.0	144 23.3	S25 03.8	175 22.9	S18 36.0	116 26.5	S22 38.0	234 53.9	N 5 59.1	Canopus	263 57.4	S52 41.7
01	60 37.4	159 22.4	04.0	190 23.6	36.4	131 28.5	37.9	249 56.1	59.0	Capella	280 39.2	N46 00.4
02	75 39.9	174 21.6	04.3	205 24.2	36.9	146 30.6	37.9	264 58.4	58.9	Deneb	49 34.0	N45 19.0
03	90 42.4	189 20.7	. . 04.6	220 24.9	. . 37.4	161 32.6	. . 37.8	280 00.7	. . 58.9	Denebola	182 37.4	N14 31.3
04	105 44.8	204 19.9	04.9	235 25.6	37.9	176 34.6	37.8	295 02.9	58.8	Diphda	348 59.0	S17 56.2
05	120 47.3	219 19.0	05.1	250 26.2	38.3	191 36.7	37.7	310 05.2	58.7			
06	135 49.8	234 18.2	S25 05.4	265 26.9	S18 38.8	206 38.7	S22 37.7	325 07.4	N 5 58.6	Dubhe	193 55.9	N61 41.9
07	150 52.2	249 17.4	05.7	280 27.6	39.3	221 40.7	37.6	340 09.7	58.5	Elnath	278 16.7	N28 37.0
T 08	165 54.7	264 16.5	05.9	295 28.3	39.7	236 42.8	37.6	355 11.9	58.5	Eltanin	90 48.1	N51 29.4
H 09	180 57.1	279 15.7	. . 06.2	310 28.9	. . 40.2	251 44.8	. . 37.5	10 14.2	. . 58.4	Enif	33 50.5	N 9 55.1
U 10	195 59.6	294 14.8	06.5	325 29.6	40.7	266 46.8	37.5	25 16.4	58.3	Fomalhaut	15 27.5	S29 34.5
R 11	211 02.1	309 14.0	06.7	340 30.3	41.2	281 48.9	37.4	40 18.7	58.2			
S 12	226 04.5	324 13.1	S25 07.0	355 30.9	S18 41.6	296 50.9	S22 37.4	55 20.9	N 5 58.2	Gacrux	172 05.5	S57 09.6
D 13	241 07.0	339 12.3	07.2	10 31.6	42.1	311 52.9	37.3	70 23.2	58.1	Gienah	175 56.2	S17 35.4
A 14	256 09.5	354 11.5	07.5	25 32.3	42.6	326 55.0	37.3	85 25.5	58.0	Hadar	148 53.7	S60 24.9
Y 15	271 11.9	9 10.6	. . 07.8	40 32.9	. . 43.0	341 57.0	. . 37.2	100 27.7	. . 57.9	Hamal	328 04.4	N23 30.5
16	286 14.4	24 09.8	08.0	55 33.6	43.5	356 59.0	37.2	115 30.0	57.8	Kaus Aust.	83 48.7	S34 22.9
17	301 16.9	39 08.9	08.3	70 34.3	44.0	12 01.1	37.1	130 32.2	57.8			
18	316 19.3	54 08.1	S25 08.5	85 34.9	S18 44.4	27 03.1	S22 37.1	145 34.5	N 5 57.7	Kochab	137 20.6	N74 07.0
19	331 21.8	69 07.2	08.8	100 35.6	44.9	42 05.1	37.0	160 36.7	57.6	Markab	13 41.7	N15 15.4
20	346 24.3	84 06.4	09.0	115 36.3	45.4	57 07.1	37.0	175 39.0	57.5	Menkar	314 18.4	N 4 07.7
21	1 26.7	99 05.5	. . 09.3	130 36.9	. . 45.8	72 09.2	. . 36.9	190 41.2	. . 57.4	Menkent	148 12.2	S36 24.8
22	16 29.2	114 04.7	09.5	145 37.6	46.3	87 11.2	36.9	205 43.5	57.4	Miaplacidus	221 40.8	S69 44.9
23	31 31.6	129 03.8	09.8	160 38.3	46.8	102 13.2	36.8	220 45.8	57.3			
7 00	46 34.1	144 03.0	S25 10.0	175 38.9	S18 47.2	117 15.3	S22 36.8	235 48.0	N 5 57.2	Mirfak	308 45.0	N49 53.7
01	61 36.6	159 02.2	10.3	190 39.6	47.7	132 17.3	36.7	250 50.3	57.1	Nunki	76 02.8	S26 17.2
02	76 39.0	174 01.3	10.5	205 40.3	48.2	147 19.3	36.7	265 52.5	57.0	Peacock	53 24.6	S56 42.6
03	91 41.5	189 00.5	. . 10.7	220 40.9	. . 48.6	162 21.3	. . 36.6	280 54.8	. . 57.0	Pollux	243 31.8	N28 00.3
04	106 44.0	203 59.6	11.0	235 41.6	49.1	177 23.4	36.5	295 57.0	56.9	Procyon	245 03.2	N 5 12.2
05	121 46.4	218 58.8	11.2	250 42.3	49.6	192 25.4	36.5	310 59.3	56.8			
06	136 48.9	233 57.9	S25 11.5	265 42.9	S18 50.0	207 27.4	S22 36.4	326 01.6	N 5 56.7	Rasalhague	96 09.9	N12 33.3
07	151 51.4	248 57.1	11.7	280 43.6	50.5	222 29.4	36.4	341 03.8	56.7	Regulus	207 47.3	N11 55.4
08	166 53.8	263 56.2	11.9	295 44.2	51.0	237 31.5	36.3	356 06.1	56.6	Rigel	281 15.1	S 8 11.3
F 09	181 56.3	278 55.4	. . 12.2	310 44.9	. . 51.4	252 33.5	. . 36.3	11 08.3	. . 56.5	Rigil Kent.	139 57.4	S60 52.3
R 10	196 58.8	293 54.5	12.4	325 45.6	51.9	267 35.5	36.2	26 10.6	56.4	Sabik	102 16.8	S15 44.2
I 11	212 01.2	308 53.7	12.6	340 46.2	52.4	282 37.6	36.2	41 12.9	56.3			
D 12	227 03.7	323 52.8	S25 12.9	355 46.9	S18 52.8	297 39.6	S22 36.1	56 15.1	N 5 56.3	Schedar	349 44.3	N56 35.5
A 13	242 06.1	338 52.0	13.1	10 47.6	53.3	312 41.6	36.1	71 17.4	56.2	Shaula	96 27.0	S37 06.7
Y 14	257 08.6	353 51.2	13.3	25 48.2	53.8	327 43.6	36.0	86 19.6	56.1	Sirius	258 36.6	S16 43.5
15	272 11.1	8 50.3	. . 13.5	40 48.9	. . 54.2	342 45.7	. . 36.0	101 21.9	. . 56.0	Spica	158 35.2	S11 12.4
16	287 13.5	23 49.5	13.8	55 49.5	54.7	357 47.7	35.9	116 24.1	56.0	Suhail	222 55.1	S43 27.8
17	302 16.0	38 48.6	14.0	70 50.2	55.1	12 49.7	35.9	131 26.4	55.9			
18	317 18.5	53 47.8	S25 14.2	85 50.9	S18 55.6	27 51.7	S22 35.8	146 28.7	N 5 55.8	Vega	80 41.6	N38 47.7
19	332 20.9	68 46.9	14.4	100 51.5	56.1	42 53.8	35.8	161 30.9	55.7	Zuben'ubi	137 09.6	S16 04.7
20	347 23.4	83 46.1	14.7	115 52.2	56.5	57 55.8	35.7	176 33.2	55.6		SHA	Mer. Pass.
21	2 25.9	98 45.2	. . 14.9	130 52.9	. . 57.0	72 57.8	. . 35.7	191 35.4	. . 55.6		° ′	h m
22	17 28.3	113 44.4	15.1	145 53.5	57.4	87 59.8	35.6	206 37.7	55.5	Venus	98 48.3	14 23
23	32 30.8	128 43.5	15.3	160 54.2	57.9	103 01.8	35.6	221 40.0	55.4	Mars	129 47.9	12 18
Mer. Pass.	h m 20 54.2	v −0.8	d 0.3	v 0.7	d 0.5	v 2.0	d 0.1	v 2.3	d 0.1	Jupiter	70 51.5	16 12
										Saturn	189 18.9	8 19

UT d	UT h	SUN GHA ° ′	SUN Dec ° ′	MOON GHA ° ′	MOON v ′	MOON Dec ° ′	MOON d ′	MOON HP ′
5	00	184 06.2	S15 43.5	102 09.2	12.7	S21 20.3	9.0	54.6
	01	199 06.1	44.2	116 40.9	12.7	21 11.3	9.0	54.7
	02	214 06.1	45.0	131 12.6	12.8	21 02.3	9.1	54.7
	03	229 06.1	. . 45.7	145 44.4	12.9	20 53.2	9.3	54.7
	04	244 06.1	46.5	160 16.3	12.8	20 43.9	9.3	54.7
	05	259 06.1	47.2	174 48.1	13.0	20 34.6	9.4	54.7
WEDNESDAY	06	274 06.0	S15 48.0	189 20.1	12.9	S20 25.2	9.5	54.7
	07	289 06.0	48.8	203 52.0	13.0	20 15.7	9.6	54.8
	08	304 06.0	49.5	218 24.0	13.0	20 06.1	9.7	54.8
	09	319 06.0	. . 50.3	232 56.0	13.1	19 56.4	9.8	54.8
	10	334 06.0	51.0	247 28.1	13.1	19 46.6	9.9	54.8
	11	349 05.9	51.8	262 00.2	13.2	19 36.7	10.0	54.9
	12	4 05.9	S15 52.5	276 32.4	13.2	S19 26.7	10.1	54.9
	13	19 05.9	53.3	291 04.6	13.2	19 16.6	10.2	54.9
	14	34 05.9	54.0	305 36.8	13.3	19 06.4	10.2	54.9
	15	49 05.9	. . 54.8	320 09.1	13.3	18 56.2	10.4	54.9
	16	64 05.8	55.5	334 41.4	13.4	18 45.8	10.4	55.0
	17	79 05.8	56.3	349 13.8	13.3	18 35.4	10.5	55.0
	18	94 05.8	S15 57.0	3 46.1	13.5	S18 24.9	10.6	55.0
	19	109 05.8	57.8	18 18.6	13.4	18 14.3	10.7	55.0
	20	124 05.7	58.5	32 51.0	13.5	18 03.6	10.8	55.1
	21	139 05.7	15 59.3	47 23.5	13.5	17 52.8	10.9	55.1
	22	154 05.7	16 00.0	61 56.0	13.6	17 41.9	10.9	55.1
	23	169 05.7	00.8	76 28.6	13.6	17 31.0	11.1	55.1
6	00	184 05.6	S16 01.5	91 01.2	13.6	S17 19.9	11.1	55.2
	01	199 05.6	02.3	105 33.8	13.7	17 08.8	11.2	55.2
	02	214 05.6	03.0	120 06.5	13.7	16 57.6	11.3	55.2
	03	229 05.5	. . 03.8	134 39.2	13.7	16 46.3	11.3	55.2
	04	244 05.5	04.5	149 11.9	13.8	16 35.0	11.5	55.3
	05	259 05.5	05.3	163 44.7	13.7	16 23.5	11.5	55.3
THURSDAY	06	274 05.5	S16 06.0	178 17.4	13.9	S16 12.0	11.6	55.3
	07	289 05.4	06.7	192 50.3	13.8	16 00.4	11.7	55.3
	08	304 05.4	07.5	207 23.1	13.9	15 48.7	11.8	55.4
	09	319 05.4	. . 08.2	221 56.0	13.9	15 36.9	11.8	55.4
	10	334 05.3	09.0	236 28.9	13.9	15 25.1	12.0	55.4
	11	349 05.3	09.7	251 01.8	13.9	15 13.1	12.0	55.4
	12	4 05.3	S16 10.5	265 34.7	14.0	S15 01.1	12.0	55.5
	13	19 05.3	11.2	280 07.7	14.0	14 49.1	12.2	55.5
	14	34 05.2	11.9	294 40.7	14.0	14 36.9	12.2	55.5
	15	49 05.2	. . 12.7	309 13.7	14.1	14 24.7	12.3	55.6
	16	64 05.2	13.4	323 46.8	14.1	14 12.4	12.4	55.6
	17	79 05.1	14.2	338 19.9	14.0	14 00.0	12.4	55.6
	18	94 05.1	S16 14.9	352 52.9	14.2	S13 47.6	12.6	55.6
	19	109 05.1	15.6	7 26.1	14.1	13 35.0	12.5	55.7
	20	124 05.0	16.4	21 59.2	14.1	13 22.5	12.7	55.7
	21	139 05.0	. . 17.1	36 32.3	14.2	13 09.8	12.7	55.7
	22	154 05.0	17.9	51 05.5	14.2	12 57.1	12.8	55.8
	23	169 04.9	18.6	65 38.7	14.2	12 44.3	12.9	55.8
7	00	184 04.9	S16 19.3	80 11.9	14.2	S12 31.4	12.9	55.8
	01	199 04.9	20.1	94 45.1	14.2	12 18.5	13.0	55.9
	02	214 04.8	20.8	109 18.3	14.2	12 05.5	13.1	55.9
	03	229 04.8	. . 21.5	123 51.5	14.3	11 52.4	13.1	55.9
	04	244 04.7	22.3	138 24.8	14.3	11 39.3	13.2	56.0
	05	259 04.7	23.0	152 58.1	14.2	11 26.1	13.3	56.0
FRIDAY	06	274 04.7	S16 23.7	167 31.3	14.3	S11 12.8	13.3	56.0
	07	289 04.6	24.5	182 04.6	14.3	10 59.5	13.4	56.1
	08	304 04.6	25.2	196 37.9	14.3	10 46.1	13.4	56.1
	09	319 04.6	. . 25.9	211 11.2	14.3	10 32.7	13.5	56.1
	10	334 04.5	26.7	225 44.5	14.3	10 19.2	13.6	56.2
	11	349 04.5	27.4	240 17.8	14.3	10 05.6	13.6	56.2
	12	4 04.4	S16 28.1	254 51.1	14.4	S 9 52.0	13.7	56.2
	13	19 04.4	28.8	269 24.5	14.3	9 38.3	13.7	56.3
	14	34 04.4	29.6	283 57.8	14.3	9 24.6	13.8	56.3
	15	49 04.3	. . 30.3	298 31.1	14.3	9 10.8	13.9	56.3
	16	64 04.3	31.0	313 04.4	14.4	8 56.9	13.9	56.4
	17	79 04.2	31.8	327 37.8	14.3	8 43.0	14.0	56.4
	18	94 04.2	S16 32.5	342 11.1	14.3	S 8 29.0	14.0	56.4
	19	109 04.2	33.2	356 44.4	14.3	8 15.0	14.1	56.5
	20	124 04.1	33.9	11 17.7	14.3	8 00.9	14.1	56.5
	21	139 04.1	. . 34.7	25 51.0	14.3	7 46.8	14.2	56.5
	22	154 04.0	35.4	40 24.3	14.3	7 32.6	14.2	56.6
	23	169 04.0	36.1	54 57.6	14.3	S 7 18.4	14.3	56.6
		SD 16.2	*d* 0.7	SD 15.0		15.1		15.3

Lat. °	Twilight Naut. h m	Twilight Civil h m	Sunrise h m	Moonrise 5 h m	Moonrise 6 h m	Moonrise 7 h m	Moonrise 8 h m
N 72	06 27	07 54	09 33	■	15 52	15 07	14 33
N 70	06 21	07 37	08 58	16 19	15 24	14 53	14 28
68	06 15	07 24	08 34	15 33	15 03	14 42	14 24
66	06 10	07 13	08 15	15 03	14 46	14 33	14 21
64	06 06	07 04	07 59	14 40	14 32	14 25	14 18
62	06 02	06 56	07 47	14 21	14 20	14 18	14 16
60	05 59	06 49	07 36	14 06	14 10	14 12	14 13
N 58	05 56	06 43	07 26	13 53	14 01	14 07	14 11
56	05 53	06 38	07 18	13 42	13 53	14 02	14 10
54	05 50	06 33	07 11	13 32	13 46	13 58	14 08
52	05 48	06 28	07 04	13 23	13 40	13 54	14 07
50	05 45	06 24	06 58	13 15	13 34	13 50	14 05
45	05 40	06 15	06 46	12 58	13 22	13 43	14 02
N 40	05 34	06 07	06 35	12 44	13 12	13 36	14 00
35	05 29	06 00	06 26	12 32	13 03	13 31	13 58
30	05 25	05 53	06 18	12 22	12 55	13 26	13 56
20	05 15	05 41	06 04	12 04	12 42	13 17	13 53
N 10	05 05	05 30	05 52	11 48	12 30	13 10	13 50
0	04 54	05 19	05 40	11 33	12 19	13 03	13 47
S 10	04 41	05 06	05 28	11 19	12 08	12 56	13 44
20	04 25	04 53	05 16	11 03	11 56	12 48	13 42
30	04 05	04 36	05 01	10 44	11 42	12 40	13 38
35	03 53	04 25	04 53	10 34	11 34	12 35	13 36
40	03 37	04 13	04 43	10 21	11 25	12 29	13 34
45	03 18	03 59	04 31	10 07	11 14	12 22	13 32
S 50	02 52	03 40	04 17	09 49	11 01	12 14	13 29
52	02 39	03 31	04 11	09 40	10 55	12 10	13 27
54	02 24	03 21	04 04	09 31	10 48	12 06	13 26
56	02 06	03 10	03 56	09 20	10 41	12 02	13 24
58	01 42	02 57	03 46	09 08	10 32	11 57	13 22
S 60	01 09	02 41	03 36	08 53	10 22	11 51	13 20

Lat. °	Sunset h m	Twilight Civil h m	Twilight Naut. h m	Moonset 5 h m	Moonset 6 h m	Moonset 7 h m	Moonset 8 h m
N 72	13 53	15 32	16 59	■	21 31	23 50	25 59
N 70	14 28	15 49	17 05	19 28	21 57	24 01	00 01
68	14 53	16 02	17 11	20 12	22 17	24 10	00 10
66	15 12	16 13	17 16	20 42	22 32	24 17	00 17
64	15 27	16 22	17 20	21 04	22 45	24 23	00 23
62	15 40	16 30	17 24	21 21	22 55	24 29	00 29
60	15 51	16 37	17 27	21 36	23 04	24 33	00 33
N 58	16 00	16 43	17 30	21 48	23 12	24 37	00 37
56	16 08	16 49	17 33	21 58	23 19	24 41	00 41
54	16 16	16 54	17 36	22 08	23 25	24 44	00 44
52	16 22	16 58	17 39	22 16	23 31	24 47	00 47
50	16 28	17 03	17 41	22 23	23 36	24 50	00 50
45	16 41	17 12	17 47	22 39	23 47	24 55	00 55
N 40	16 52	17 20	17 52	22 52	23 55	25 00	01 00
35	17 01	17 27	17 57	23 03	24 03	00 03	01 04
30	17 09	17 34	18 02	23 12	24 10	00 10	01 08
20	17 23	17 46	18 12	23 28	24 21	00 21	01 14
N 10	17 35	17 57	18 22	23 42	24 31	00 31	01 19
0	17 47	18 09	18 34	23 55	24 40	00 40	01 24
S 10	17 59	18 21	18 47	24 08	00 08	00 49	01 29
20	18 12	18 35	19 02	24 22	00 22	00 59	01 34
30	18 26	18 52	19 23	00 03	00 38	01 10	01 40
35	18 35	19 02	19 35	00 15	00 47	01 16	01 43
40	18 45	19 15	19 51	00 28	00 57	01 23	01 47
45	18 57	19 30	20 11	00 44	01 09	01 31	01 51
S 50	19 11	19 48	20 37	01 03	01 24	01 41	01 56
52	19 17	19 57	20 50	01 12	01 30	01 46	01 59
54	19 25	20 07	21 05	01 22	01 38	01 50	02 01
56	19 33	20 19	21 24	01 33	01 46	01 56	02 04
58	19 43	20 33	21 49	01 46	01 55	02 02	02 07
S 60	19 53	20 49	22 24	02 01	02 06	02 09	02 11

Day d	SUN Eqn. of Time 00^h m s	SUN Eqn. of Time 12^h m s	SUN Mer. Pass. h m	MOON Mer. Pass. Upper h m	MOON Mer. Pass. Lower h m	MOON Age d	MOON %	MOON Phase
5	16 25	16 24	11 44	17 44	05 21	08	44	◐
6	16 23	16 21	11 44	18 29	06 07	09	53	
7	16 20	16 18	11 44	19 13	06 51	10	63	

	UT	ARIES	VENUS −4.0		MARS +1.5		JUPITER −2.1		SATURN +1.1	
		GHA	GHA	Dec	GHA	Dec	GHA	Dec	GHA	Dec
	d h	° ′	° ′	° ′	° ′	° ′	° ′	° ′	° ′	° ′
	8 00	47 33.2	143 42.7	S25 15.5	175 54.8	S18 58.4	118 03.9	S22 35.5	236 42.2	N 5 55.3
	01	62 35.7	158 41.8	15.7	190 55.5	58.8	133 05.9	35.5	251 44.5	55.3
	02	77 38.2	173 41.0	16.0	205 56.1	59.3	148 07.9	35.4	266 46.7	55.2
	03	92 40.6	188 40.1	. . 16.2	220 56.8	18 59.7	163 09.9	. . 35.4	281 49.0	. . 55.1
	04	107 43.1	203 39.3	16.4	235 57.5	19 00.2	178 12.0	35.3	296 51.3	55.0
	05	122 45.6	218 38.4	16.6	250 58.1	00.7	193 14.0	35.2	311 53.5	54.9
	06	137 48.0	233 37.6	S25 16.8	265 58.8	S19 01.1	208 16.0	S22 35.2	326 55.8	N 5 54.9
	07	152 50.5	248 36.7	17.0	280 59.4	01.6	223 18.0	35.1	341 58.0	54.8
S	08	167 53.0	263 35.9	17.2	296 00.1	02.0	238 20.0	35.1	357 00.3	54.7
A	09	182 55.4	278 35.0	. . 17.4	311 00.8	. . 02.5	253 22.1	. . 35.0	12 02.6	. . 54.6
T	10	197 57.9	293 34.2	17.6	326 01.4	03.0	268 24.1	35.0	27 04.8	54.6
U	11	213 00.4	308 33.3	17.8	341 02.1	03.4	283 26.1	34.9	42 07.1	54.5
R	12	228 02.8	323 32.5	S25 18.0	356 02.7	S19 03.9	298 28.1	S22 34.9	57 09.3	N 5 54.4
D	13	243 05.3	338 31.6	18.2	11 03.4	04.3	313 30.2	34.8	72 11.6	54.3
A	14	258 07.7	353 30.8	18.4	26 04.0	04.8	328 32.2	34.8	87 13.9	54.3
Y	15	273 10.2	8 29.9	. . 18.6	41 04.7	. . 05.2	343 34.2	. . 34.7	102 16.1	. . 54.2
	16	288 12.7	23 29.1	18.8	56 05.3	05.7	358 36.2	34.7	117 18.4	54.1
	17	303 15.1	38 28.2	19.0	71 06.0	06.2	13 38.2	34.6	132 20.6	54.0
	18	318 17.6	53 27.4	S25 19.2	86 06.7	S19 06.6	28 40.3	S22 34.6	147 22.9	N 5 54.0
	19	333 20.1	68 26.5	19.4	101 07.3	07.1	43 42.3	34.5	162 25.2	53.9
	20	348 22.5	83 25.7	19.6	116 08.0	07.5	58 44.3	34.5	177 27.4	53.8
	21	3 25.0	98 24.8	. . 19.8	131 08.6	. . 08.0	73 46.3	. . 34.4	192 29.7	. . 53.7
	22	18 27.5	113 24.0	20.0	146 09.3	08.4	88 48.3	34.3	207 32.0	53.6
	23	33 29.9	128 23.1	20.1	161 09.9	08.9	103 50.3	34.3	222 34.2	53.6
	9 00	48 32.4	143 22.3	S25 20.3	176 10.6	S19 09.3	118 52.4	S22 34.2	237 36.5	N 5 53.5
	01	63 34.8	158 21.4	20.5	191 11.2	09.8	133 54.4	34.2	252 38.7	53.4
	02	78 37.3	173 20.6	20.7	206 11.9	10.2	148 56.4	34.1	267 41.0	53.3
	03	93 39.8	188 19.7	. . 20.9	221 12.5	. . 10.7	163 58.4	. . 34.1	282 43.3	. . 53.3
	04	108 42.2	203 18.9	21.1	236 13.2	11.2	179 00.4	34.0	297 45.5	53.2
	05	123 44.7	218 18.0	21.2	251 13.8	11.6	194 02.5	34.0	312 47.8	53.1
	06	138 47.2	233 17.2	S25 21.4	266 14.5	S19 12.1	209 04.5	S22 33.9	327 50.1	N 5 53.0
	07	153 49.6	248 16.3	21.6	281 15.1	12.5	224 06.5	33.9	342 52.3	53.0
	08	168 52.1	263 15.5	21.8	296 15.8	13.0	239 08.5	33.8	357 54.6	52.9
S	09	183 54.6	278 14.6	. . 21.9	311 16.4	. . 13.4	254 10.5	. . 33.8	12 56.8	. . 52.8
U	10	198 57.0	293 13.8	22.1	326 17.1	13.9	269 12.5	33.7	27 59.1	52.7
N	11	213 59.5	308 12.9	22.3	341 17.7	14.3	284 14.6	33.6	43 01.4	52.7
D	12	229 02.0	323 12.1	S25 22.5	356 18.4	S19 14.8	299 16.6	S22 33.6	58 03.6	N 5 52.6
A	13	244 04.4	338 11.2	22.6	11 19.0	15.2	314 18.6	33.5	73 05.9	52.5
Y	14	259 06.9	353 10.4	22.8	26 19.7	15.7	329 20.6	33.5	88 08.2	52.4
	15	274 09.3	8 09.5	. . 23.0	41 20.3	. . 16.1	344 22.6	. . 33.4	103 10.4	. . 52.4
	16	289 11.8	23 08.7	23.1	56 21.0	16.6	359 24.6	33.4	118 12.7	52.3
	17	304 14.3	38 07.8	23.3	71 21.6	17.0	14 26.6	33.3	133 15.0	52.2
	18	319 16.7	53 07.0	S25 23.5	86 22.3	S19 17.5	29 28.7	S22 33.3	148 17.2	N 5 52.1
	19	334 19.2	68 06.1	23.6	101 22.9	17.9	44 30.7	33.2	163 19.5	52.1
	20	349 21.7	83 05.3	23.8	116 23.6	18.4	59 32.7	33.2	178 21.8	52.0
	21	4 24.1	98 04.4	. . 23.9	131 24.2	. . 18.8	74 34.7	. . 33.1	193 24.0	. . 51.9
	22	19 26.6	113 03.6	24.1	146 24.9	19.3	89 36.7	33.0	208 26.3	51.8
	23	34 29.1	128 02.7	24.3	161 25.5	19.7	104 38.7	33.0	223 28.5	51.8
	10 00	49 31.5	143 01.9	S25 24.4	176 26.2	S19 20.2	119 40.7	S22 32.9	238 30.8	N 5 51.7
	01	64 34.0	158 01.0	24.6	191 26.8	20.6	134 42.8	32.9	253 33.1	51.6
	02	79 36.5	173 00.1	24.7	206 27.5	21.1	149 44.8	32.8	268 35.3	51.5
	03	94 38.9	187 59.3	. . 24.9	221 28.1	. . 21.5	164 46.8	. . 32.8	283 37.6	. . 51.5
	04	109 41.4	202 58.4	25.0	236 28.8	21.9	179 48.8	32.7	298 39.9	51.4
	05	124 43.8	217 57.6	25.2	251 29.4	22.4	194 50.8	32.7	313 42.1	51.3
	06	139 46.3	232 56.7	S25 25.3	266 30.1	S19 22.8	209 52.8	S22 32.6	328 44.4	N 5 51.2
	07	154 48.8	247 55.9	25.5	281 30.7	23.3	224 54.8	32.6	343 46.7	51.2
	08	169 51.2	262 55.0	25.6	296 31.3	23.7	239 56.8	32.5	358 48.9	51.1
M	09	184 53.7	277 54.2	. . 25.7	311 32.0	. . 24.2	254 58.9	. . 32.4	13 51.2	. . 51.0
O	10	199 56.2	292 53.3	25.9	326 32.6	24.6	270 00.9	32.4	28 53.5	50.9
N	11	214 58.6	307 52.5	26.0	341 33.3	25.1	285 02.9	32.3	43 55.7	50.9
D	12	230 01.1	322 51.6	S25 26.2	356 33.9	S19 25.5	300 04.9	S22 32.3	58 58.0	N 5 50.8
A	13	245 03.6	337 50.8	26.3	11 34.6	26.0	315 06.9	32.2	74 00.3	50.7
Y	14	260 06.0	352 49.9	26.4	26 35.2	26.4	330 08.9	32.2	89 02.5	50.6
	15	275 08.5	7 49.1	. . 26.6	41 35.8	. . 26.8	345 10.9	. . 32.1	104 04.8	. . 50.6
	16	290 10.9	22 48.2	26.7	56 36.5	27.3	0 12.9	32.1	119 07.1	50.5
	17	305 13.4	37 47.4	26.8	71 37.1	27.7	15 14.9	32.0	134 09.3	50.4
	18	320 15.9	52 46.5	S25 27.0	86 37.8	S19 28.2	30 16.9	S22 31.9	149 11.6	N 5 50.3
	19	335 18.3	67 45.7	27.1	101 38.4	28.6	45 19.0	31.9	164 13.9	50.3
	20	350 20.8	82 44.8	27.2	116 39.1	29.1	60 21.0	31.8	179 16.1	50.2
	21	5 23.3	97 44.0	. . 27.4	131 39.7	. . 29.5	75 23.0	. . 31.8	194 18.4	. . 50.1
	22	20 25.7	112 43.1	27.5	146 40.3	29.9	90 25.0	31.7	209 20.7	50.1
	23	35 28.2	127 42.3	27.6	161 41.0	30.4	105 27.0	31.7	224 22.9	50.0
	Mer. Pass.	h m 20 42.4	v −0.9	d 0.2	v 0.6	d 0.5	v 2.0	d 0.1	v 2.3	d 0.1

STARS

Name	SHA	Dec
	° ′	° ′
Acamar	315 20.4	S40 16.0
Achernar	335 28.5	S57 11.5
Acrux	173 14.1	S63 08.7
Adhara	255 15.1	S28 58.8
Aldebaran	290 53.1	N16 31.8
Alioth	166 23.9	N55 54.5
Alkaid	153 01.9	N49 16.0
Al Na'ir	27 47.8	S46 55.2
Alnilam	275 49.6	S 1 11.6
Alphard	217 59.5	S 8 41.7
Alphecca	126 14.3	N26 41.1
Alpheratz	357 46.9	N29 08.6
Altair	62 11.8	N 8 53.6
Ankaa	353 18.6	S42 15.5
Antares	112 30.9	S26 27.1
Arcturus	145 59.2	N19 08.1
Atria	107 36.5	S69 02.8
Avior	234 19.4	S59 31.9
Bellatrix	278 35.4	N 6 21.6
Betelgeuse	271 04.8	N 7 24.7
Canopus	263 57.3	S52 41.7
Capella	280 39.2	N46 00.4
Deneb	49 34.0	N45 19.0
Denebola	182 37.3	N14 31.3
Diphda	348 59.0	S17 56.2
Dubhe	193 55.9	N61 41.9
Elnath	278 16.7	N28 37.0
Eltanin	90 48.2	N51 29.4
Enif	33 50.5	N 9 55.1
Fomalhaut	15 27.5	S29 34.5
Gacrux	172 05.5	S57 09.6
Gienah	175 56.2	S17 35.4
Hadar	148 53.7	S60 24.9
Hamal	328 04.4	N23 30.5
Kaus Aust.	83 48.7	S34 22.9
Kochab	137 20.6	N74 07.0
Markab	13 41.7	N15 15.4
Menkar	314 18.4	N 4 07.7
Menkent	148 12.2	S36 24.8
Miaplacidus	221 40.7	S69 44.9
Mirfak	308 44.9	N49 53.7
Nunki	76 02.8	S26 17.2
Peacock	53 24.7	S56 42.6
Pollux	243 31.8	N28 00.3
Procyon	245 03.2	N 5 12.2
Rasalhague	96 09.9	N12 33.3
Regulus	207 47.2	N11 55.4
Rigel	281 15.1	S 8 11.3
Rigil Kent.	139 57.4	S60 52.3
Sabik	102 16.8	S15 44.2
Schedar	349 44.3	N56 35.5
Shaula	96 27.0	S37 06.7
Sirius	258 36.6	S16 43.5
Spica	158 35.2	S11 12.4
Suhail	222 55.1	S43 27.8
Vega	80 41.6	N38 47.7
Zuben'ubi	137 09.6	S16 04.7

	SHA	Mer. Pass.
	° ′	h m
Venus	94 49.9	14 27
Mars	127 38.2	12 15
Jupiter	70 20.0	16 02
Saturn	189 04.1	8 08

	UT	SUN GHA	SUN Dec	MOON GHA	v	MOON Dec	d	HP
	d h	° ′	° ′	° ′	′	° ′	′	′
	8 00	184 03.9	S16 36.8	69 30.9	14.3	S 7 04.1	14.3	56.6
	01	199 03.9	37.6	84 04.2	14.3	6 49.8	14.4	56.7
	02	214 03.9	38.3	98 37.5	14.2	6 35.4	14.4	56.7
	03	229 03.8	. . 39.0	113 10.7	14.3	6 21.0	14.5	56.8
	04	244 03.8	39.7	127 44.0	14.2	6 06.5	14.5	56.8
	05	259 03.7	40.5	142 17.2	14.2	5 52.0	14.6	56.8
	06	274 03.7	S16 41.2	156 50.4	14.2	S 5 37.4	14.6	56.9
	07	289 03.6	41.9	171 23.6	14.2	5 22.8	14.6	56.9
S	08	304 03.6	42.6	185 56.8	14.2	5 08.2	14.7	56.9
A	09	319 03.5	. . 43.3	200 30.0	14.1	4 53.5	14.8	57.0
T	10	334 03.5	44.1	215 03.1	14.2	4 38.7	14.7	57.0
U	11	349 03.4	44.8	229 36.3	14.1	4 24.0	14.9	57.1
R	12	4 03.4	S16 45.5	244 09.4	14.0	S 4 09.1	14.8	57.1
D	13	19 03.3	46.2	258 42.4	14.1	3 54.3	14.9	57.1
A	14	34 03.3	46.9	273 15.5	14.0	3 39.4	14.9	57.2
Y	15	49 03.3	. . 47.7	287 48.5	14.0	3 24.5	15.0	57.2
	16	64 03.2	48.4	302 21.5	14.0	3 09.5	15.0	57.3
	17	79 03.2	49.1	316 54.5	14.0	2 54.5	15.0	57.3
	18	94 03.1	S16 49.8	331 27.5	13.9	S 2 39.5	15.1	57.3
	19	109 03.1	50.5	346 00.4	13.9	2 24.4	15.1	57.4
	20	124 03.0	51.2	0 33.3	13.8	2 09.3	15.1	57.4
	21	139 03.0	. . 51.9	15 06.1	13.9	1 54.2	15.2	57.4
	22	154 02.9	52.7	29 39.0	13.7	1 39.0	15.2	57.5
	23	169 02.8	53.4	44 11.7	13.8	1 23.8	15.2	57.5
	9 00	184 02.8	S16 54.1	58 44.5	13.7	S 1 08.6	15.2	57.6
	01	199 02.7	54.8	73 17.2	13.7	0 53.4	15.3	57.6
	02	214 02.7	55.5	87 49.9	13.6	0 38.1	15.3	57.6
	03	229 02.6	. . 56.2	102 22.5	13.6	0 22.8	15.3	57.7
	04	244 02.6	56.9	116 55.1	13.5	S 0 07.5	15.4	57.7
	05	259 02.5	57.6	131 27.6	13.5	N 0 07.9	15.3	57.8
	06	274 02.5	S16 58.3	146 00.1	13.5	N 0 23.2	15.4	57.8
	07	289 02.4	59.1	160 32.6	13.4	0 38.6	15.4	57.8
	08	304 02.4	16 59.8	175 05.0	13.4	0 54.0	15.4	57.9
S	09	319 02.3	17 00.5	189 37.4	13.3	1 09.4	15.5	57.9
U	10	334 02.3	01.2	204 09.7	13.3	1 24.9	15.4	58.0
N	11	349 02.2	01.9	218 42.0	13.2	1 40.3	15.5	58.0
D	12	4 02.1	S17 02.6	233 14.2	13.1	N 1 55.8	15.4	58.0
A	13	19 02.1	03.3	247 46.3	13.1	2 11.2	15.5	58.1
Y	14	34 02.0	04.0	262 18.4	13.1	2 26.7	15.5	58.1
	15	49 02.0	. . 04.7	276 50.5	13.0	2 42.2	15.6	58.2
	16	64 01.9	05.4	291 22.5	12.9	2 57.8	15.5	58.2
	17	79 01.9	06.1	305 54.4	12.9	3 13.3	15.5	58.2
	18	94 01.8	S17 06.8	320 26.3	12.8	N 3 28.8	15.5	58.3
	19	109 01.7	07.5	334 58.1	12.7	3 44.3	15.6	58.3
	20	124 01.7	08.2	349 29.8	12.7	3 59.9	15.5	58.4
	21	139 01.6	. . 08.9	4 01.5	12.6	4 15.4	15.5	58.4
	22	154 01.6	09.6	18 33.1	12.6	4 30.9	15.6	58.4
	23	169 01.5	10.3	33 04.7	12.5	4 46.5	15.5	58.5
	10 00	184 01.4	S17 11.0	47 36.2	12.4	N 5 02.0	15.6	58.5
	01	199 01.4	11.7	62 07.6	12.3	5 17.6	15.5	58.6
	02	214 01.3	12.4	76 38.9	12.3	5 33.1	15.5	58.6
	03	229 01.3	. . 13.1	91 10.2	12.2	5 48.6	15.5	58.6
	04	244 01.2	13.8	105 41.4	12.2	6 04.1	15.6	58.7
	05	259 01.1	14.5	120 12.6	12.0	6 19.7	15.5	58.7
	06	274 01.1	S17 15.2	134 43.6	12.0	N 6 35.2	15.4	58.8
	07	289 01.0	15.9	149 14.6	11.9	6 50.6	15.5	58.8
	08	304 00.9	16.6	163 45.5	11.8	7 06.1	15.5	58.8
M	09	319 00.9	. . 17.3	178 16.3	11.7	7 21.6	15.4	58.9
O	10	334 00.8	18.0	192 47.0	11.7	7 37.0	15.5	58.9
N	11	349 00.7	18.7	207 17.7	11.6	7 52.5	15.4	58.9
D	12	4 00.7	S17 19.4	221 48.3	11.4	N 8 07.9	15.4	59.0
A	13	19 00.6	20.1	236 18.7	11.4	8 23.3	15.3	59.0
Y	14	34 00.5	20.8	250 49.1	11.4	8 38.6	15.4	59.1
	15	49 00.5	. . 21.5	265 19.5	11.2	8 54.0	15.3	59.1
	16	64 00.4	22.2	279 49.7	11.1	9 09.3	15.3	59.1
	17	79 00.3	22.9	294 19.8	11.1	9 24.6	15.2	59.2
	18	94 00.3	S17 23.6	308 49.9	10.9	N 9 39.8	15.3	59.2
	19	109 00.2	24.2	323 19.8	10.9	9 55.1	15.2	59.2
	20	124 00.1	24.9	337 49.7	10.7	10 10.3	15.1	59.3
	21	139 00.1	. . 25.6	352 19.4	10.7	10 25.4	15.2	59.3
	22	154 00.0	26.3	6 49.1	10.6	10 40.6	15.1	59.4
	23	168 59.9	27.0	21 18.7	10.4	N10 55.7	15.0	59.4
		SD 16.2	*d* 0.7	SD 15.6		15.8		16.1

Lat.	Twilight Naut.	Twilight Civil	Sunrise	Moonrise 8	Moonrise 9	Moonrise 10	Moonrise 11
°	h m	h m	h m	h m	h m	h m	h m
N 72	06 39	08 08	09 57	14 33	14 02	13 28	12 40
N 70	06 31	07 49	09 15	14 28	14 05	13 40	13 07
68	06 24	07 35	08 47	14 24	14 08	13 50	13 28
66	06 19	07 23	08 26	14 21	14 10	13 58	13 45
64	06 14	07 12	08 09	14 18	14 12	14 06	13 59
62	06 09	07 04	07 55	14 16	14 14	14 12	14 10
60	06 05	06 56	07 44	14 13	14 15	14 17	14 20
N 58	06 02	06 49	07 33	14 11	14 16	14 22	14 29
56	05 58	06 43	07 25	14 10	14 17	14 26	14 37
54	05 55	06 38	07 17	14 08	14 18	14 30	14 44
52	05 52	06 33	07 10	14 07	14 19	14 33	14 50
50	05 50	06 29	07 03	14 05	14 20	14 36	14 56
45	05 43	06 19	06 50	14 02	14 22	14 43	15 08
N 40	05 37	06 10	06 39	14 00	14 24	14 49	15 18
35	05 32	06 02	06 29	13 58	14 25	14 54	15 27
30	05 27	05 55	06 20	13 56	14 26	14 59	15 35
20	05 16	05 43	06 06	13 53	14 29	15 06	15 48
N 10	05 05	05 31	05 53	13 50	14 30	15 13	16 00
0	04 54	05 19	05 40	13 47	14 32	15 20	16 11
S 10	04 40	05 06	05 28	13 44	14 34	15 27	16 23
20	04 24	04 51	05 15	13 42	14 36	15 34	16 35
30	04 03	04 33	04 59	13 38	14 39	15 42	16 49
35	03 49	04 23	04 50	13 36	14 40	15 47	16 57
40	03 33	04 10	04 40	13 34	14 42	15 52	17 07
45	03 13	03 54	04 28	13 32	14 43	15 59	17 18
S 50	02 46	03 35	04 13	13 29	14 46	16 06	17 32
52	02 32	03 26	04 06	13 27	14 47	16 10	17 38
54	02 16	03 15	03 58	13 26	14 48	16 14	17 45
56	01 55	03 03	03 49	13 24	14 49	16 18	17 53
58	01 29	02 48	03 39	13 22	14 50	16 23	18 02
S 60	00 48	02 31	03 28	13 20	14 52	16 29	18 12

Lat.	Sunset	Twilight Civil	Twilight Naut.	Moonset 8	Moonset 9	Moonset 10	Moonset 11
°	h m	h m	h m	h m	h m	h m	h m
N 72	13 30	15 19	16 48	25 59	01 59	04 13	06 46
N 70	14 12	15 37	16 56	00 01	02 00	04 04	06 21
68	14 40	15 52	17 02	00 10	02 01	03 56	06 03
66	15 01	16 04	17 08	00 17	02 02	03 50	05 48
64	15 18	16 14	17 13	00 23	02 02	03 45	05 35
62	15 32	16 23	17 17	00 29	02 03	03 41	05 25
60	15 43	16 31	17 21	00 33	02 03	03 37	05 17
N 58	15 53	16 37	17 25	00 37	02 04	03 34	05 09
56	16 02	16 43	17 28	00 41	02 04	03 31	05 02
54	16 10	16 49	17 32	00 44	02 05	03 28	04 56
52	16 17	16 54	17 35	00 47	02 05	03 26	04 51
50	16 24	16 59	17 37	00 50	02 05	03 24	04 46
45	16 37	17 09	17 44	00 55	02 06	03 19	04 36
N 40	16 49	17 17	17 50	01 00	02 06	03 15	04 27
35	16 58	17 25	17 55	01 04	02 07	03 11	04 20
30	17 07	17 32	18 01	01 08	02 07	03 08	04 13
20	17 22	17 45	18 11	01 14	02 07	03 03	04 02
N 10	17 35	17 57	18 22	01 19	02 08	02 59	03 53
0	17 47	18 09	18 34	01 24	02 08	02 55	03 44
S 10	18 00	18 22	18 48	01 29	02 09	02 50	03 35
20	18 13	18 37	19 04	01 34	02 09	02 46	03 25
30	18 29	18 55	19 26	01 40	02 10	02 41	03 15
35	18 38	19 06	19 39	01 43	02 10	02 38	03 08
40	18 49	19 19	19 55	01 47	02 10	02 35	03 01
45	19 01	19 34	20 16	01 51	02 11	02 31	02 53
S 50	19 16	19 54	20 44	01 56	02 11	02 26	02 43
52	19 23	20 04	20 58	01 59	02 11	02 24	02 39
54	19 31	20 14	21 15	02 01	02 11	02 22	02 34
56	19 40	20 27	21 35	02 04	02 12	02 19	02 28
58	19 50	20 42	22 03	02 07	02 12	02 17	02 22
S 60	20 01	20 59	22 48	02 11	02 12	02 13	02 16

Day	SUN Eqn. of Time 00^h	SUN Eqn. of Time 12^h	SUN Mer. Pass.	MOON Mer. Pass. Upper	MOON Mer. Pass. Lower	MOON Age	MOON Phase
d	m s	m s	h m	h m	h m	d %	
8	16 16	16 14	11 44	19 58	07 35	11 73	
9	16 11	16 09	11 44	20 43	08 20	12 82	◐
10	16 06	16 03	11 44	21 32	09 07	13 89	

UT d h	ARIES GHA	VENUS −4.0 GHA	VENUS Dec	MARS +1.5 GHA	MARS Dec	JUPITER −2.1 GHA	JUPITER Dec	SATURN +1.1 GHA	SATURN Dec
	° ′	° ′	° ′	° ′	° ′	° ′	° ′	° ′	° ′
11 00	50 30.7	142 41.4	S25 27.7	176 41.6	S19 30.8	120 29.0	S22 31.6	239 25.2	N 5 49.9
01	65 33.1	157 40.5	27.9	191 42.3	31.3	135 31.0	31.6	254 27.5	49.8
02	80 35.6	172 39.7	28.0	206 42.9	31.7	150 33.0	31.5	269 29.7	49.8
03	95 38.1	187 38.8	. . 28.1	221 43.5	. . 32.1	165 35.0	. . 31.4	284 32.0	. . 49.7
04	110 40.5	202 38.0	28.2	236 44.2	32.6	180 37.0	31.4	299 34.3	49.6
05	125 43.0	217 37.1	28.4	251 44.8	33.0	195 39.0	31.3	314 36.6	49.5
06	140 45.4	232 36.3	S25 28.5	266 45.5	S19 33.5	210 41.0	S22 31.3	329 38.8	N 5 49.5
07	155 47.9	247 35.4	28.6	281 46.1	33.9	225 43.1	31.2	344 41.1	49.4
T 08	170 50.4	262 34.6	28.7	296 46.7	34.3	240 45.1	31.2	359 43.4	49.3
U 09	185 52.8	277 33.7	. . 28.8	311 47.4	. . 34.8	255 47.1	. . 31.1	14 45.6	. . 49.2
E 10	200 55.3	292 32.9	28.9	326 48.0	35.2	270 49.1	31.1	29 47.9	49.2
S 11	215 57.8	307 32.0	29.0	341 48.7	35.6	285 51.1	31.0	44 50.2	49.1
D 12	231 00.2	322 31.2	S25 29.1	356 49.3	S19 36.1	300 53.1	S22 30.9	59 52.4	N 5 49.0
A 13	246 02.7	337 30.3	29.3	11 49.9	36.5	315 55.1	30.9	74 54.7	49.0
Y 14	261 05.2	352 29.5	29.4	26 50.6	37.0	330 57.1	30.8	89 57.0	48.9
15	276 07.6	7 28.6	. . 29.5	41 51.2	. . 37.4	345 59.1	. . 30.8	104 59.2	. . 48.8
16	291 10.1	22 27.8	29.6	56 51.8	37.8	1 01.1	30.7	120 01.5	48.7
17	306 12.5	37 26.9	29.7	71 52.5	38.3	16 03.1	30.7	135 03.8	48.7
18	321 15.0	52 26.1	S25 29.8	86 53.1	S19 38.7	31 05.1	S22 30.6	150 06.1	N 5 48.6
19	336 17.5	67 25.2	29.9	101 53.7	39.1	46 07.1	30.5	165 08.3	48.5
20	351 19.9	82 24.3	30.0	116 54.4	39.6	61 09.1	30.5	180 10.6	48.4
21	6 22.4	97 23.5	. . 30.1	131 55.0	. . 40.0	76 11.1	. . 30.4	195 12.9	. . 48.4
22	21 24.9	112 22.6	30.2	146 55.7	40.4	91 13.1	30.4	210 15.1	48.3
23	36 27.3	127 21.8	30.3	161 56.3	40.9	106 15.1	30.3	225 17.4	48.2
12 00	51 29.8	142 20.9	S25 30.4	176 56.9	S19 41.3	121 17.1	S22 30.3	240 19.7	N 5 48.2
01	66 32.3	157 20.1	30.4	191 57.6	41.7	136 19.2	30.2	255 22.0	48.1
02	81 34.7	172 19.2	30.5	206 58.2	42.2	151 21.2	30.1	270 24.2	48.0
03	96 37.2	187 18.4	. . 30.6	221 58.8	. . 42.6	166 23.2	. . 30.1	285 26.5	. . 47.9
04	111 39.7	202 17.5	30.7	236 59.5	43.0	181 25.2	30.0	300 28.8	47.9
05	126 42.1	217 16.7	30.8	252 00.1	43.5	196 27.2	30.0	315 31.0	47.8
06	141 44.6	232 15.8	S25 30.9	267 00.7	S19 43.9	211 29.2	S22 29.9	330 33.3	N 5 47.7
W 07	156 47.0	247 15.0	31.0	282 01.4	44.3	226 31.2	29.9	345 35.6	47.7
E 08	171 49.5	262 14.1	31.1	297 02.0	44.8	241 33.2	29.8	0 37.9	47.6
D 09	186 52.0	277 13.3	. . 31.1	312 02.6	. . 45.2	256 35.2	. . 29.7	15 40.1	. . 47.5
N 10	201 54.4	292 12.4	31.2	327 03.3	45.6	271 37.2	29.7	30 42.4	47.4
E 11	216 56.9	307 11.6	31.3	342 03.9	46.1	286 39.2	29.6	45 44.7	47.4
S 12	231 59.4	322 10.7	S25 31.4	357 04.5	S19 46.5	301 41.2	S22 29.6	60 46.9	N 5 47.3
D 13	247 01.8	337 09.9	31.5	12 05.1	46.9	316 43.2	29.5	75 49.2	47.2
A 14	262 04.3	352 09.0	31.5	27 05.8	47.4	331 45.2	29.5	90 51.5	47.2
Y 15	277 06.8	7 08.2	. . 31.6	42 06.4	. . 47.8	346 47.2	. . 29.4	105 53.8	. . 47.1
16	292 09.2	22 07.3	31.7	57 07.0	48.2	1 49.2	29.3	120 56.0	47.0
17	307 11.7	37 06.5	31.8	72 07.7	48.6	16 51.2	29.3	135 58.3	46.9
18	322 14.2	52 05.6	S25 31.8	87 08.3	S19 49.1	31 53.2	S22 29.2	151 00.6	N 5 46.9
19	337 16.6	67 04.8	31.9	102 08.9	49.5	46 55.2	29.2	166 02.9	46.8
20	352 19.1	82 03.9	32.0	117 09.6	49.9	61 57.2	29.1	181 05.1	46.7
21	7 21.5	97 03.0	. . 32.0	132 10.2	. . 50.4	76 59.2	. . 29.1	196 07.4	. . 46.7
22	22 24.0	112 02.2	32.1	147 10.8	50.8	92 01.2	29.0	211 09.7	46.6
23	37 26.5	127 01.3	32.2	162 11.4	51.2	107 03.2	28.9	226 12.0	46.5
13 00	52 28.9	142 00.5	S25 32.2	177 12.1	S19 51.6	122 05.2	S22 28.9	241 14.2	N 5 46.4
01	67 31.4	156 59.6	32.3	192 12.7	52.1	137 07.2	28.8	256 16.5	46.4
02	82 33.9	171 58.8	32.4	207 13.3	52.5	152 09.2	28.8	271 18.8	46.3
03	97 36.3	186 57.9	. . 32.4	222 14.0	. . 52.9	167 11.2	. . 28.7	286 21.0	. . 46.2
04	112 38.8	201 57.1	32.5	237 14.6	53.3	182 13.2	28.6	301 23.3	46.2
05	127 41.3	216 56.2	32.5	252 15.2	53.8	197 15.2	28.6	316 25.6	46.1
06	142 43.7	231 55.4	S25 32.6	267 15.8	S19 54.2	212 17.2	S22 28.5	331 27.9	N 5 46.0
07	157 46.2	246 54.5	32.6	282 16.5	54.6	227 19.2	28.5	346 30.1	45.9
T 08	172 48.7	261 53.7	32.7	297 17.1	55.0	242 21.2	28.4	1 32.4	45.9
H 09	187 51.1	276 52.8	. . 32.7	312 17.7	. . 55.5	257 23.2	. . 28.4	16 34.7	. . 45.8
U 10	202 53.6	291 52.0	32.8	327 18.3	55.9	272 25.2	28.3	31 37.0	45.7
R 11	217 56.0	306 51.1	32.8	342 19.0	56.3	287 27.2	28.2	46 39.2	45.7
S 12	232 58.5	321 50.3	S25 32.9	357 19.6	S19 56.7	302 29.2	S22 28.2	61 41.5	N 5 45.6
D 13	248 01.0	336 49.4	32.9	12 20.2	57.2	317 31.2	28.1	76 43.8	45.5
A 14	263 03.4	351 48.6	33.0	27 20.8	57.6	332 33.1	28.1	91 46.1	45.5
Y 15	278 05.9	6 47.7	. . 33.0	42 21.5	. . 58.0	347 35.1	. . 28.0	106 48.4	. . 45.4
16	293 08.4	21 46.9	33.1	57 22.1	58.4	2 37.1	27.9	121 50.6	45.3
17	308 10.8	36 46.0	33.1	72 22.7	58.9	17 39.1	27.9	136 52.9	45.2
18	323 13.3	51 45.2	S25 33.2	87 23.3	S19 59.3	32 41.1	S22 27.8	151 55.2	N 5 45.2
19	338 15.8	66 44.3	33.2	102 24.0	19 59.7	47 43.1	27.8	166 57.5	45.1
20	353 18.2	81 43.5	33.2	117 24.6	20 00.1	62 45.1	27.7	181 59.7	45.0
21	8 20.7	96 42.6	. . 33.3	132 25.2	. . 00.5	77 47.1	. . 27.6	197 02.0	. . 45.0
22	23 23.1	111 41.8	33.3	147 25.8	01.0	92 49.1	27.6	212 04.3	44.9
23	38 25.6	126 40.9	33.3	162 26.4	01.4	107 51.1	27.5	227 06.6	44.8
Mer. Pass.	h m 20 30.6	v −0.9	d 0.1	v 0.6	d 0.4	v 2.0	d 0.1	v 2.3	d 0.1

STARS Name	SHA	Dec
	° ′	° ′
Acamar	315 20.4	S40 16.0
Achernar	335 28.6	S57 11.5
Acrux	173 14.0	S63 08.7
Adhara	255 15.0	S28 58.8
Aldebaran	290 53.0	N16 31.8
Alioth	166 23.9	N55 54.5
Alkaid	153 01.9	N49 16.0
Al Na'ir	27 47.8	S46 55.2
Alnilam	275 49.6	S 1 11.6
Alphard	217 59.5	S 8 41.7
Alphecca	126 14.3	N26 41.1
Alpheratz	357 46.9	N29 08.6
Altair	62 11.8	N 8 53.6
Ankaa	353 18.6	S42 15.5
Antares	112 30.9	S26 27.1
Arcturus	145 59.2	N19 08.1
Atria	107 36.5	S69 02.8
Avior	234 19.4	S59 31.9
Bellatrix	278 35.4	N 6 21.6
Betelgeuse	271 04.8	N 7 24.7
Canopus	263 57.3	S52 41.7
Capella	280 39.2	N46 00.4
Deneb	49 34.1	N45 19.0
Denebola	182 37.3	N14 31.3
Diphda	348 59.0	S17 56.2
Dubhe	193 55.9	N61 41.9
Elnath	278 16.7	N28 37.0
Eltanin	90 48.2	N51 29.4
Enif	33 50.5	N 9 55.1
Fomalhaut	15 27.6	S29 34.5
Gacrux	172 05.5	S57 09.6
Gienah	175 56.1	S17 35.4
Hadar	148 53.7	S60 24.9
Hamal	328 04.4	N23 30.5
Kaus Aust.	83 48.7	S34 22.9
Kochab	137 20.6	N74 07.0
Markab	13 41.7	N15 15.4
Menkar	314 18.4	N 4 07.7
Menkent	148 12.2	S36 24.8
Miaplacidus	221 40.7	S69 44.9
Mirfak	308 44.9	N49 53.7
Nunki	76 02.8	S26 17.2
Peacock	53 24.7	S56 42.6
Pollux	243 31.7	N28 00.2
Procyon	245 03.2	N 5 12.2
Rasalhague	96 10.0	N12 33.3
Regulus	207 47.2	N11 55.4
Rigel	281 15.1	S 8 11.3
Rigil Kent.	139 57.4	S60 52.3
Sabik	102 16.8	S15 44.2
Schedar	349 44.3	N56 35.5
Shaula	96 27.0	S37 06.7
Sirius	258 36.5	S16 43.5
Spica	158 35.2	S11 12.4
Suhail	222 55.1	S43 27.8
Vega	80 41.6	N38 47.7
Zuben'ubi	137 09.6	S16 04.7

	SHA	Mer. Pass
	° ′	h m
Venus	90 51.1	14 31
Mars	125 27.1	12 12
Jupiter	69 47.3	15 53
Saturn	188 49.9	7 57

UT		SUN GHA	SUN Dec	MOON GHA	v	MOON Dec	d	HP
d	h	° ′	° ′	° ′	′	° ′	′	′
11	00	183 59.9	S17 27.7	35 48.1	10.4	N11 10.7	15.0	59.4
	01	198 59.8	28.4	50 17.5	10.3	11 25.7	15.0	59.5
	02	213 59.7	29.1	64 46.8	10.1	11 40.7	14.9	59.5
	03	228 59.7	. . 29.8	79 15.9	10.1	11 55.6	14.9	59.5
	04	243 59.6	30.4	93 45.0	10.0	12 10.5	14.8	59.6
	05	258 59.5	31.1	108 14.0	9.8	12 25.3	14.8	59.6
	06	273 59.4	S17 31.8	122 42.8	9.8	N12 40.1	14.7	59.6
	07	288 59.4	32.5	137 11.6	9.6	12 54.8	14.6	59.7
T	08	303 59.3	33.2	151 40.2	9.6	13 09.4	14.6	59.7
U	09	318 59.2	. . 33.9	166 08.8	9.4	13 24.0	14.6	59.7
E	10	333 59.2	34.5	180 37.2	9.3	13 38.6	14.5	59.8
S	11	348 59.1	35.2	195 05.5	9.2	13 53.1	14.4	59.8
D	12	3 59.0	S17 35.9	209 33.7	9.1	N14 07.5	14.4	59.8
A	13	18 58.9	36.6	224 01.8	9.0	14 21.9	14.3	59.9
Y	14	33 58.9	37.3	238 29.8	8.9	14 36.2	14.2	59.9
	15	48 58.8	. . 38.0	252 57.7	8.7	14 50.4	14.1	59.9
	16	63 58.7	38.6	267 25.4	8.7	15 04.5	14.1	60.0
	17	78 58.6	39.3	281 53.1	8.5	15 18.6	14.0	60.0
	18	93 58.6	S17 40.0	296 20.6	8.4	N15 32.6	13.9	60.0
	19	108 58.5	40.7	310 48.0	8.3	15 46.5	13.9	60.1
	20	123 58.4	41.3	325 15.3	8.1	16 00.4	13.8	60.1
	21	138 58.3	. . 42.0	339 42.4	8.1	16 14.2	13.6	60.1
	22	153 58.3	42.7	354 09.5	7.9	16 27.8	13.6	60.2
	23	168 58.2	43.4	8 36.4	7.8	16 41.4	13.5	60.2
12	00	183 58.1	S17 44.0	23 03.2	7.7	N16 54.9	13.5	60.2
	01	198 58.0	44.7	37 29.9	7.6	17 08.4	13.3	60.2
	02	213 57.9	45.4	51 56.5	7.4	17 21.7	13.2	60.3
	03	228 57.9	. . 46.1	66 22.9	7.4	17 34.9	13.1	60.3
	04	243 57.8	46.7	80 49.3	7.2	17 48.0	13.1	60.3
	05	258 57.7	47.4	95 15.5	7.1	18 01.1	12.9	60.3
	06	273 57.6	S17 48.1	109 41.6	6.9	N18 14.0	12.8	60.4
W	07	288 57.5	48.8	124 07.5	6.9	18 26.8	12.8	60.4
E	08	303 57.5	49.4	138 33.4	6.7	18 39.6	12.6	60.4
D	09	318 57.4	. . 50.1	152 59.1	6.5	18 52.2	12.5	60.5
N	10	333 57.3	50.8	167 24.6	6.5	19 04.7	12.4	60.5
E	11	348 57.2	51.4	181 50.1	6.4	19 17.1	12.2	60.5
S	12	3 57.1	S17 52.1	196 15.5	6.2	N19 29.3	12.2	60.5
D	13	18 57.0	52.8	210 40.7	6.1	19 41.5	12.0	60.5
A	14	33 57.0	53.4	225 05.8	5.9	19 53.5	12.0	60.6
Y	15	48 56.9	. . 54.1	239 30.7	5.9	20 05.5	11.8	60.6
	16	63 56.8	54.8	253 55.6	5.7	20 17.3	11.6	60.6
	17	78 56.7	55.4	268 20.3	5.6	20 28.9	11.6	60.6
	18	93 56.6	S17 56.1	282 44.9	5.5	N20 40.5	11.4	60.7
	19	108 56.5	56.8	297 09.4	5.3	20 51.9	11.3	60.7
	20	123 56.5	57.4	311 33.7	5.3	21 03.2	11.1	60.7
	21	138 56.4	. . 58.1	325 58.0	5.1	21 14.3	11.0	60.7
	22	153 56.3	58.8	340 22.1	5.0	21 25.3	10.9	60.7
	23	168 56.2	17 59.4	354 46.1	4.8	21 36.2	10.7	60.8
13	00	183 56.1	S18 00.1	9 09.9	4.8	N21 46.9	10.6	60.8
	01	198 56.0	00.8	23 33.7	4.6	21 57.5	10.4	60.8
	02	213 55.9	01.4	37 57.3	4.5	22 07.9	10.3	60.8
	03	228 55.8	. . 02.1	52 20.8	4.4	22 18.2	10.1	60.8
	04	243 55.8	02.7	66 44.2	4.3	22 28.3	10.0	60.8
	05	258 55.7	03.4	81 07.5	4.2	22 38.3	9.8	60.9
	06	273 55.6	S18 04.1	95 30.7	4.1	N22 48.1	9.7	60.9
T	07	288 55.5	04.7	109 53.8	3.9	22 57.8	9.5	60.9
H	08	303 55.4	05.4	124 16.7	3.8	23 07.3	9.4	60.9
U	09	318 55.3	. . 06.0	138 39.5	3.8	23 16.7	9.2	60.9
R	10	333 55.2	06.7	153 02.3	3.6	23 25.9	9.0	60.9
S	11	348 55.1	07.4	167 24.9	3.5	23 34.9	8.9	60.9
D	12	3 55.0	S18 08.0	181 47.4	3.4	N23 43.8	8.6	61.0
A	13	18 54.9	08.7	196 09.8	3.3	23 52.4	8.6	61.0
Y	14	33 54.9	09.3	210 32.1	3.2	24 01.0	8.3	61.0
	15	48 54.8	. . 10.0	224 54.3	3.1	24 09.3	8.2	61.0
	16	63 54.7	10.6	239 16.4	3.0	24 17.5	8.0	61.0
	17	78 54.6	11.3	253 38.4	2.9	24 25.5	7.8	61.0
	18	93 54.5	S18 11.9	268 00.3	2.8	N24 33.3	7.6	61.0
	19	108 54.4	12.6	282 22.1	2.7	24 40.9	7.5	61.0
	20	123 54.3	13.2	296 43.8	2.6	24 48.4	7.3	61.0
	21	138 54.2	. . 13.9	311 05.4	2.6	24 55.7	7.1	61.0
	22	153 54.1	14.5	325 27.0	2.4	25 02.8	6.9	61.0
	23	168 54.0	15.2	339 48.4	2.4	N25 09.7	6.7	61.1
		SD 16.2	*d* 0.7	SD	16.3	16.5		16.6

Lat.	Twilight Naut.	Twilight Civil	Sunrise	Moonrise 11	Moonrise 12	Moonrise 13	Moonrise 14
°	h m	h m	h m	h m	h m	h m	h m
N 72	06 50	08 22	10 26	12 40	▭	▭	▭
N 70	06 41	08 01	09 33	13 07	11 58	▭	▭
68	06 33	07 45	09 00	13 28	12 52	▭	▭
66	06 27	07 32	08 37	13 45	13 26	12 36	▭
64	06 21	07 21	08 19	13 59	13 51	13 38	▭
62	06 16	07 11	08 04	14 10	14 10	14 13	14 26
60	06 12	07 03	07 51	14 20	14 26	14 39	15 06
N 58	06 08	06 56	07 40	14 29	14 40	14 59	15 33
56	06 04	06 49	07 31	14 37	14 52	15 16	15 55
54	06 00	06 43	07 23	14 44	15 03	15 30	16 13
52	05 57	06 38	07 15	14 50	15 12	15 43	16 28
50	05 54	06 33	07 08	14 56	15 20	15 54	16 41
45	05 47	06 22	06 54	15 08	15 38	16 17	17 09
N 40	05 41	06 13	06 42	15 18	15 53	16 36	17 30
35	05 35	06 05	06 32	15 27	16 05	16 52	17 48
30	05 29	05 58	06 23	15 35	16 16	17 06	18 04
20	05 18	05 44	06 07	15 48	16 35	17 29	18 30
N 10	05 06	05 32	05 54	16 00	16 52	17 50	18 53
0	04 54	05 19	05 41	16 11	17 08	18 09	19 14
S 10	04 40	05 05	05 28	16 23	17 23	18 28	19 36
20	04 22	04 50	05 14	16 35	17 40	18 49	19 59
30	04 00	04 31	04 57	16 49	18 00	19 14	20 26
35	03 47	04 20	04 48	16 57	18 12	19 28	20 42
40	03 30	04 07	04 37	17 07	18 25	19 45	21 00
45	03 08	03 50	04 24	17 18	18 41	20 05	21 22
S 50	02 39	03 30	04 08	17 32	19 01	20 30	21 51
52	02 25	03 20	04 01	17 38	19 10	20 42	22 05
54	02 07	03 09	03 53	17 45	19 21	20 56	22 21
56	01 45	02 55	03 43	17 53	19 33	21 12	22 40
58	01 14	02 40	03 33	18 02	19 47	21 32	23 04
S 60	00 16	02 21	03 21	18 12	20 03	21 57	23 36

Lat.	Sunset	Twilight Civil	Twilight Naut.	Moonset 11	Moonset 12	Moonset 13	Moonset 14
°	h m	h m	h m	h m	h m	h m	h m
N 72	13 02	15 05	16 37	06 46	▭	▭	▭
N 70	13 55	15 26	16 46	06 21	09 26	▭	▭
68	14 27	15 42	16 54	06 03	08 33	▭	▭
66	14 50	15 56	17 01	05 48	08 01	10 56	▭
64	15 09	16 07	17 06	05 35	07 37	09 54	▭
62	15 24	16 16	17 11	05 25	07 18	09 20	11 23
60	15 36	16 25	17 16	05 17	07 03	08 56	10 43
N 58	15 47	16 32	17 20	05 09	06 50	08 36	10 16
56	15 57	16 38	17 24	05 02	06 39	08 20	09 55
54	16 05	16 44	17 27	04 56	06 30	08 06	09 37
52	16 13	16 50	17 31	04 51	06 21	07 54	09 22
50	16 19	16 55	17 34	04 46	06 13	07 43	09 09
45	16 34	17 06	17 41	04 36	05 57	07 21	08 42
N 40	16 46	17 15	17 47	04 27	05 44	07 03	08 21
35	16 56	17 23	17 53	04 20	05 32	06 48	08 03
30	17 05	17 30	17 59	04 13	05 23	06 35	07 48
20	17 21	17 44	18 11	04 02	05 06	06 13	07 23
N 10	17 35	17 57	18 22	03 53	04 51	05 54	07 00
0	17 48	18 09	18 35	03 44	04 37	05 36	06 40
S 10	18 01	18 23	18 49	03 35	04 24	05 19	06 19
20	18 15	18 39	19 06	03 25	04 09	05 00	05 57
30	18 31	18 57	19 28	03 15	03 53	04 38	05 32
35	18 41	19 09	19 43	03 08	03 43	04 26	05 17
40	18 52	19 22	20 00	03 01	03 33	04 11	05 00
45	19 05	19 39	20 21	02 53	03 20	03 54	04 39
S 50	19 21	20 00	20 51	02 43	03 05	03 33	04 13
52	19 29	20 10	21 06	02 39	02 57	03 23	04 00
54	19 37	20 21	21 24	02 34	02 50	03 12	03 46
56	19 46	20 35	21 47	02 28	02 41	02 59	03 29
58	19 57	20 51	22 19	02 22	02 31	02 44	03 09
S 60	20 09	21 10	23 42	02 16	02 19	02 27	02 44

Day	SUN Eqn. of Time 00^h	SUN Eqn. of Time 12^h	SUN Mer. Pass.	MOON Mer. Pass. Upper	MOON Mer. Pass. Lower	MOON Age	Phase
d	m s	m s	h m	h m	h m	d %	
11	16 00	15 56	11 44	22 24	09 57	14 95	○
12	15 53	15 49	11 44	23 22	10 52	15 99	
13	15 45	15 40	11 44	24 24	11 53	16 100	

UT		ARIES	VENUS −4.1		MARS +1.4		JUPITER −2.1		SATURN +1.1	
		GHA	GHA	Dec	GHA	Dec	GHA	Dec	GHA	Dec
d h		° ′	° ′	° ′	° ′	° ′	° ′	° ′	° ′	° ′
14 00		53 28.1	141 40.1	S25 33.4	177 27.1	S20 01.8	122 53.1	S22 27.5	242 08.8	N 5 44.8
01		68 30.5	156 39.2	33.4	192 27.7	02.2	137 55.1	27.4	257 11.1	44.7
02		83 33.0	171 38.4	33.4	207 28.3	02.6	152 57.1	27.3	272 13.4	44.6
03		98 35.5	186 37.5	. . 33.5	222 28.9	. . 03.1	167 59.1	. . 27.3	287 15.7	. . 44.5
04		113 37.9	201 36.7	33.5	237 29.6	03.5	183 01.1	27.2	302 18.0	44.5
05		128 40.4	216 35.8	33.5	252 30.2	03.9	198 03.1	27.2	317 20.2	44.4
06		143 42.9	231 35.0	S25 33.5	267 30.8	S20 04.3	213 05.1	S22 27.1	332 22.5	N 5 44.3
07		158 45.3	246 34.1	33.6	282 31.4	04.7	228 07.1	27.1	347 24.8	44.3
08		173 47.8	261 33.3	33.6	297 32.0	05.2	243 09.1	27.0	2 27.1	44.2
09	F	188 50.3	276 32.4	. . 33.6	312 32.7	. . 05.6	258 11.0	. . 26.9	17 29.3	. . 44.1
10	R	203 52.7	291 31.6	33.6	327 33.3	06.0	273 13.0	26.9	32 31.6	44.1
11	I	218 55.2	306 30.7	33.6	342 33.9	06.4	288 15.0	26.8	47 33.9	44.0
12	D	233 57.6	321 29.9	S25 33.7	357 34.5	S20 06.8	303 17.0	S22 26.8	62 36.2	N 5 43.9
13	A	249 00.1	336 29.0	33.7	12 35.1	07.2	318 19.0	26.7	77 38.5	43.9
14	Y	264 02.6	351 28.2	33.7	27 35.7	07.7	333 21.0	26.6	92 40.7	43.8
15		279 05.0	6 27.3	. . 33.7	42 36.4	. . 08.1	348 23.0	. . 26.6	107 43.0	. . 43.7
16		294 07.5	21 26.5	33.7	57 37.0	08.5	3 25.0	26.5	122 45.3	43.7
17		309 10.0	36 25.6	33.7	72 37.6	08.9	18 27.0	26.5	137 47.6	43.6
18		324 12.4	51 24.8	S25 33.7	87 38.2	S20 09.3	33 29.0	S22 26.4	152 49.8	N 5 43.5
19		339 14.9	66 23.9	33.8	102 38.8	09.7	48 31.0	26.3	167 52.1	43.4
20		354 17.4	81 23.1	33.8	117 39.5	10.2	63 33.0	26.3	182 54.4	43.4
21		9 19.8	96 22.2	. . 33.8	132 40.1	. . 10.6	78 34.9	. . 26.2	197 56.7	. . 43.3
22		24 22.3	111 21.4	33.8	147 40.7	11.0	93 36.9	26.2	212 59.0	43.2
23		39 24.8	126 20.6	33.8	162 41.3	11.4	108 38.9	26.1	228 01.2	43.2
15 00		54 27.2	141 19.7	S25 33.8	177 41.9	S20 11.8	123 40.9	S22 26.0	243 03.5	N 5 43.1
01		69 29.7	156 18.9	33.8	192 42.5	12.2	138 42.9	26.0	258 05.8	43.0
02		84 32.1	171 18.0	33.8	207 43.1	12.6	153 44.9	25.9	273 08.1	43.0
03		99 34.6	186 17.2	. . 33.8	222 43.8	. . 13.0	168 46.9	. . 25.9	288 10.4	. . 42.9
04		114 37.1	201 16.3	33.8	237 44.4	13.5	183 48.9	25.8	303 12.6	42.8
05		129 39.5	216 15.5	33.8	252 45.0	13.9	198 50.9	25.7	318 14.9	42.8
06		144 42.0	231 14.6	S25 33.8	267 45.6	S20 14.3	213 52.8	S22 25.7	333 17.2	N 5 42.7
07	S	159 44.5	246 13.8	33.8	282 46.2	14.7	228 54.8	25.6	348 19.5	42.6
08		174 46.9	261 12.9	33.7	297 46.8	15.1	243 56.8	25.5	3 21.8	42.6
09	A	189 49.4	276 12.1	. . 33.7	312 47.4	. . 15.5	258 58.8	. . 25.5	18 24.1	. . 42.5
10	T	204 51.9	291 11.2	33.7	327 48.1	15.9	274 00.8	25.4	33 26.3	42.4
11	U	219 54.3	306 10.4	33.7	342 48.7	16.3	289 02.8	25.4	48 28.6	42.4
12	R	234 56.8	321 09.5	S25 33.7	357 49.3	S20 16.7	304 04.8	S22 25.3	63 30.9	N 5 42.3
13	D	249 59.3	336 08.7	33.7	12 49.9	17.1	319 06.8	25.2	78 33.2	42.2
14	A	265 01.7	351 07.8	33.7	27 50.5	17.6	334 08.8	25.2	93 35.5	42.2
15	Y	280 04.2	6 07.0	. . 33.7	42 51.1	. . 18.0	349 10.7	. . 25.1	108 37.7	. . 42.1
16		295 06.6	21 06.2	33.6	57 51.7	18.4	4 12.7	25.1	123 40.0	42.0
17		310 09.1	36 05.3	33.6	72 52.3	18.8	19 14.7	25.0	138 42.3	42.0
18		325 11.6	51 04.5	S25 33.6	87 53.0	S20 19.2	34 16.7	S22 24.9	153 44.6	N 5 41.9
19		340 14.0	66 03.6	33.6	102 53.6	19.6	49 18.7	24.9	168 46.9	41.8
20		355 16.5	81 02.8	33.6	117 54.2	20.0	64 20.7	24.8	183 49.2	41.8
21		10 19.0	96 01.9	. . 33.5	132 54.8	. . 20.4	79 22.7	. . 24.8	198 51.4	. . 41.7
22		25 21.4	111 01.1	33.5	147 55.4	20.8	94 24.6	24.7	213 53.7	41.6
23		40 23.9	126 00.2	33.5	162 56.0	21.2	109 26.6	24.6	228 56.0	41.5
16 00		55 26.4	140 59.4	S25 33.4	177 56.6	S20 21.6	124 28.6	S22 24.6	243 58.3	N 5 41.5
01		70 28.8	155 58.6	33.4	192 57.2	22.0	139 30.6	24.5	259 00.6	41.4
02		85 31.3	170 57.7	33.4	207 57.8	22.4	154 32.6	24.4	274 02.9	41.3
03		100 33.8	185 56.9	. . 33.4	222 58.4	. . 22.8	169 34.6	. . 24.4	289 05.1	. . 41.3
04		115 36.2	200 56.0	33.3	237 59.0	23.3	184 36.6	24.3	304 07.4	41.2
05		130 38.7	215 55.2	33.3	252 59.7	23.7	199 38.5	24.3	319 09.7	41.1
06		145 41.1	230 54.3	S25 33.2	268 00.3	S20 24.1	214 40.5	S22 24.2	334 12.0	N 5 41.1
07		160 43.6	245 53.5	33.2	283 00.9	24.5	229 42.5	24.1	349 14.3	41.0
08		175 46.1	260 52.6	33.2	298 01.5	24.9	244 44.5	24.1	4 16.6	41.0
09	S	190 48.5	275 51.8	. . 33.1	313 02.1	. . 25.3	259 46.5	. . 24.0	19 18.8	. . 40.9
10	U	205 51.0	290 51.0	33.1	328 02.7	25.7	274 48.5	24.0	34 21.1	40.8
11	N	220 53.5	305 50.1	33.1	343 03.3	26.1	289 50.4	23.9	49 23.4	40.8
12	D	235 55.9	320 49.3	S25 33.0	358 03.9	S20 26.5	304 52.4	S22 23.8	64 25.7	N 5 40.7
13	A	250 58.4	335 48.4	33.0	13 04.5	26.9	319 54.4	23.8	79 28.0	40.6
14	Y	266 00.9	350 47.6	32.9	28 05.1	27.3	334 56.4	23.7	94 30.3	40.6
15		281 03.3	5 46.7	. . 32.9	43 05.7	. . 27.7	349 58.4	. . 23.6	109 32.6	. . 40.5
16		296 05.8	20 45.9	32.8	58 06.3	28.1	5 00.4	23.6	124 34.8	40.4
17		311 08.3	35 45.1	32.8	73 06.9	28.5	20 02.3	23.5	139 37.1	40.4
18		326 10.7	50 44.2	S25 32.7	88 07.5	S20 28.9	35 04.3	S22 23.5	154 39.4	N 5 40.3
19		341 13.2	65 43.4	32.7	103 08.1	29.3	50 06.3	23.4	169 41.7	40.2
20		356 15.6	80 42.5	32.6	118 08.7	29.7	65 08.3	23.3	184 44.0	40.2
21		11 18.1	95 41.7	. . 32.6	133 09.3	. . 30.1	80 10.3	. . 23.3	199 46.3	. . 40.1
22		26 20.6	110 40.9	32.5	148 10.0	30.5	95 12.3	23.2	214 48.5	40.0
23		41 23.0	125 40.0	32.4	163 10.6	30.9	110 14.2	23.1	229 50.8	40.0
Mer. Pass.		h m 20 18.8	*v* −0.8	*d* 0.0	*v* 0.6	*d* 0.4	*v* 2.0	*d* 0.1	*v* 2.3	*d* 0.1

STARS Name	SHA	Dec
	° ′	° ′
Acamar	315 20.4	S40 16.0
Achernar	335 28.6	S57 11.5
Acrux	173 14.0	S63 08.7
Adhara	255 15.0	S28 58.8
Aldebaran	290 53.0	N16 31.8
Alioth	166 23.9	N55 54.5
Alkaid	153 01.9	N49 16.0
Al Na'ir	27 47.8	S46 55.2
Alnilam	275 49.6	S 1 11.6
Alphard	217 59.5	S 8 41.7
Alphecca	126 14.3	N26 41.1
Alpheratz	357 46.9	N29 08.6
Altair	62 11.8	N 8 53.6
Ankaa	353 18.6	S42 15.5
Antares	112 30.9	S26 27.1
Arcturus	145 59.2	N19 08.1
Atria	107 36.5	S69 02.7
Avior	234 19.4	S59 31.9
Bellatrix	278 35.4	N 6 21.6
Betelgeuse	271 04.8	N 7 24.6
Canopus	263 57.3	S52 41.7
Capella	280 39.1	N46 00.4
Deneb	49 34.1	N45 19.0
Denebola	182 37.3	N14 31.3
Diphda	348 59.0	S17 56.2
Dubhe	193 55.8	N61 41.9
Elnath	278 16.7	N28 37.0
Eltanin	90 48.2	N51 29.4
Enif	33 50.5	N 9 55.1
Fomalhaut	15 27.6	S29 34.5
Gacrux	172 05.4	S57 09.6
Gienah	175 56.1	S17 35.4
Hadar	148 53.7	S60 24.9
Hamal	328 04.4	N23 30.5
Kaus Aust.	83 48.7	S34 22.9
Kochab	137 20.6	N74 07.0
Markab	13 41.7	N15 15.4
Menkar	314 18.3	N 4 07.7
Menkent	148 12.1	S36 24.8
Miaplacidus	221 40.6	S69 44.9
Mirfak	308 44.9	N49 53.7
Nunki	76 02.8	S26 17.2
Peacock	53 24.7	S56 42.6
Pollux	243 31.7	N28 00.2
Procyon	245 03.2	N 5 12.2
Rasalhague	96 10.0	N12 33.3
Regulus	207 47.2	N11 55.4
Rigel	281 15.1	S 8 11.3
Rigil Kent.	139 57.4	S60 52.2
Sabik	102 16.8	S15 44.2
Schedar	349 44.3	N56 35.5
Shaula	96 27.0	S37 06.7
Sirius	258 36.5	S16 43.5
Spica	158 35.2	S11 12.4
Suhail	222 55.0	S43 27.8
Vega	80 41.6	N38 47.7
Zuben'ubi	137 09.6	S16 04.7
	SHA	Mer. Pass.
	° ′	h m
Venus	86 52.5	14 36
Mars	123 14.7	12 09
Jupiter	69 13.7	15 43
Saturn	188 36.3	7 47

UT			SUN GHA	SUN Dec	MOON GHA	v	MOON Dec	d	HP
	d	h	° ′	° ′	° ′	′	° ′	′	′
	14	00	183 53.9	S18 15.8	354 09.8	2.3	N25 16.4	6.5	61.1
		01	198 53.8	16.5	8 31.1	2.2	25 22.9	6.3	61.1
		02	213 53.7	17.1	22 52.3	2.1	25 29.2	6.2	61.1
		03	228 53.6	. . 17.8	37 13.4	2.1	25 35.4	5.9	61.1
		04	243 53.5	18.4	51 34.5	2.0	25 41.3	5.8	61.1
		05	258 53.4	19.1	65 55.5	1.9	25 47.1	5.5	61.1
		06	273 53.3	S18 19.7	80 16.4	1.9	N25 52.6	5.4	61.1
		07	288 53.2	20.4	94 37.3	1.8	25 58.0	5.2	61.1
		08	303 53.1	21.0	108 58.1	1.7	26 03.2	4.9	61.1
F		09	318 53.0	. . 21.7	123 18.8	1.7	26 08.1	4.8	61.1
R		10	333 52.9	22.3	137 39.5	1.6	26 12.9	4.5	61.1
I		11	348 52.8	22.9	152 00.1	1.6	26 17.4	4.4	61.1
D		12	3 52.7	S18 23.6	166 20.7	1.5	N26 21.8	4.2	61.1
A		13	18 52.6	24.2	180 41.2	1.5	26 26.0	3.9	61.1
Y		14	33 52.5	24.9	195 01.7	1.4	26 29.9	3.7	61.1
		15	48 52.4	. . 25.5	209 22.1	1.4	26 33.6	3.6	61.1
		16	63 52.3	26.2	223 42.5	1.3	26 37.2	3.3	61.1
		17	78 52.2	26.8	238 02.8	1.4	26 40.5	3.1	61.1
		18	93 52.1	S18 27.4	252 23.2	1.3	N26 43.6	2.9	61.1
		19	108 52.0	28.1	266 43.5	1.2	26 46.5	2.7	61.1
		20	123 51.9	28.7	281 03.7	1.3	26 49.2	2.5	61.1
		21	138 51.8	. . 29.3	295 24.0	1.2	26 51.7	2.3	61.1
		22	153 51.7	30.0	309 44.2	1.2	26 54.0	2.1	61.0
		23	168 51.6	30.6	324 04.4	1.2	26 56.1	1.8	61.0
	15	00	183 51.5	S18 31.3	338 24.6	1.2	N26 57.9	1.7	61.0
		01	198 51.4	31.9	352 44.8	1.2	26 59.6	1.4	61.0
		02	213 51.3	32.5	7 05.0	1.2	27 01.0	1.2	61.0
		03	228 51.2	. . 33.2	21 25.2	1.2	27 02.2	1.0	61.0
		04	243 51.1	33.8	35 45.4	1.1	27 03.2	0.8	61.0
		05	258 51.0	34.4	50 05.5	1.2	27 04.0	0.6	61.0
		06	273 50.9	S18 35.1	64 25.7	1.2	N27 04.6	0.4	61.0
		07	288 50.8	35.7	78 45.9	1.3	27 05.0	0.2	61.0
S		08	303 50.6	36.3	93 06.2	1.2	27 05.2	0.1	61.0
A		09	318 50.5	. . 37.0	107 26.4	1.3	27 05.1	0.2	60.9
T		10	333 50.4	37.6	121 46.7	1.2	27 04.9	0.5	60.9
U		11	348 50.3	38.2	136 06.9	1.3	27 04.4	0.6	60.9
R		12	3 50.2	S18 38.8	150 27.2	1.4	N27 03.8	0.9	60.9
D		13	18 50.1	39.5	164 47.6	1.4	27 02.9	1.1	60.9
A		14	33 50.0	40.1	179 08.0	1.4	27 01.8	1.3	60.9
Y		15	48 49.9	. . 40.7	193 28.4	1.4	27 00.5	1.5	60.9
		16	63 49.8	41.4	207 48.8	1.5	26 59.0	1.7	60.9
		17	78 49.7	42.0	222 09.3	1.6	26 57.3	2.0	60.8
		18	93 49.5	S18 42.6	236 29.9	1.5	N26 55.3	2.1	60.8
		19	108 49.4	43.2	250 50.4	1.7	26 53.2	2.3	60.8
		20	123 49.3	43.9	265 11.1	1.7	26 50.9	2.5	60.8
		21	138 49.2	. . 44.5	279 31.8	1.7	26 48.4	2.8	60.8
		22	153 49.1	45.1	293 52.5	1.9	26 45.6	2.9	60.8
		23	168 49.0	45.7	308 13.4	1.9	26 42.7	3.2	60.7
	16	00	183 48.9	S18 46.3	322 34.3	1.9	N26 39.5	3.3	60.7
		01	198 48.8	47.0	336 55.2	2.0	26 36.2	3.5	60.7
		02	213 48.6	47.6	351 16.2	2.1	26 32.7	3.8	60.7
		03	228 48.5	. . 48.2	5 37.3	2.2	26 28.9	3.9	60.7
		04	243 48.4	48.8	19 58.5	2.2	26 25.0	4.1	60.6
		05	258 48.3	49.5	34 19.7	2.4	26 20.9	4.3	60.6
		06	273 48.2	S18 50.1	48 41.1	2.4	N26 16.6	4.5	60.6
		07	288 48.1	50.7	63 02.5	2.5	26 12.1	4.7	60.6
		08	303 48.0	51.3	77 24.0	2.6	26 07.4	4.9	60.6
S		09	318 47.8	. . 51.9	91 45.6	2.7	26 02.5	5.1	60.5
U		10	333 47.7	52.5	106 07.3	2.7	25 57.4	5.3	60.5
N		11	348 47.6	53.2	120 29.0	2.9	25 52.1	5.4	60.5
D		12	3 47.5	S18 53.8	134 50.9	3.0	N25 46.7	5.6	60.5
A		13	18 47.4	54.4	149 12.9	3.0	25 41.1	5.8	60.4
Y		14	33 47.2	55.0	163 34.9	3.2	25 35.3	6.0	60.4
		15	48 47.1	. . 55.6	177 57.1	3.3	25 29.3	6.2	60.4
		16	63 47.0	56.2	192 19.4	3.3	25 23.1	6.3	60.4
		17	78 46.9	56.8	206 41.7	3.5	25 16.8	6.6	60.3
		18	93 46.8	S18 57.5	221 04.2	3.6	N25 10.2	6.7	60.3
		19	108 46.6	58.1	235 26.8	3.7	25 03.5	6.8	60.3
		20	123 46.5	58.7	249 49.5	3.8	24 56.7	7.1	60.3
		21	138 46.4	. . 59.3	264 12.3	3.9	24 49.6	7.2	60.2
		22	153 46.3	18 59.9	278 35.2	4.1	24 42.4	7.3	60.2
		23	168 46.2	S19 00.5	292 58.3	4.1	N24 35.1	7.6	60.2
			SD 16.2	d 0.6	SD 16.6		16.6		16.5

Lat.	Twilight Naut.	Twilight Civil	Sunrise	Moonrise 14	Moonrise 15	Moonrise 16	Moonrise 17
°	h m	h m	h m	h m	h m	h m	h m
N 72	07 01	08 36	11 10	□	□	□	□
N 70	06 50	08 13	09 52	□	□	□	□
68	06 42	07 55	09 14	□	□	□	16 39
66	06 35	07 41	08 48	□	□	□	18 02
64	06 28	07 29	08 28	□	□	16 12	18 39
62	06 23	07 18	08 12	14 26	15 19	17 06	19 06
60	06 18	07 10	07 59	15 06	16 05	17 39	19 26
N 58	06 13	07 02	07 47	15 33	16 35	18 03	19 43
56	06 09	06 55	07 37	15 55	16 58	18 22	19 57
54	06 05	06 49	07 28	16 13	17 16	18 38	20 09
52	06 02	06 43	07 20	16 28	17 32	18 52	20 20
50	05 58	06 38	07 13	16 41	17 46	19 04	20 29
45	05 51	06 26	06 58	17 09	18 14	19 29	20 49
N 40	05 44	06 16	06 45	17 30	18 36	19 49	21 05
35	05 37	06 08	06 35	17 48	18 54	20 06	21 19
30	05 31	06 00	06 25	18 04	19 10	20 20	21 31
20	05 19	05 46	06 09	18 30	19 37	20 44	21 51
N 10	05 07	05 33	05 55	18 53	20 00	21 05	22 08
0	04 54	05 19	05 41	19 14	20 21	21 25	22 24
S 10	04 39	05 05	05 27	19 36	20 42	21 44	22 40
20	04 21	04 49	05 13	19 59	21 05	22 05	22 57
30	03 58	04 30	04 56	20 26	21 32	22 29	23 17
35	03 44	04 18	04 46	20 42	21 48	22 43	23 28
40	03 26	04 04	04 34	21 00	22 06	22 59	23 42
45	03 04	03 47	04 21	21 22	22 28	23 19	23 57
S 50	02 33	03 25	04 04	21 51	22 56	23 43	24 16
52	02 17	03 15	03 56	22 05	23 09	23 54	24 24
54	01 58	03 03	03 48	22 21	23 25	24 07	00 07
56	01 33	02 49	03 38	22 40	23 44	24 22	00 22
58	00 57	02 32	03 27	23 04	24 06	00 06	00 40
S 60	////	02 11	03 14	23 36	24 35	00 35	01 02

Lat.	Sunset	Twilight Civil	Twilight Naut.	Moonset 14	Moonset 15	Moonset 16	Moonset 17
°	h m	h m	h m	h m	h m	h m	h m
N 72	12 19	14 52	16 27	□	□	□	□
N 70	13 37	15 15	16 38	□	□	□	□
68	14 14	15 33	16 46	□	□	□	15 55
66	14 40	15 48	16 54	□	□	□	14 31
64	15 00	16 00	17 00	□	□	14 13	13 53
62	15 16	16 10	17 06	11 23	12 50	13 19	13 26
60	15 30	16 19	17 11	10 43	12 04	12 46	13 04
N 58	15 41	16 27	17 15	10 16	11 34	12 21	12 47
56	15 51	16 34	17 20	09 55	11 11	12 02	12 32
54	16 00	16 40	17 23	09 37	10 52	11 45	12 19
52	16 08	16 46	17 27	09 22	10 36	11 31	12 08
50	16 16	16 51	17 30	09 09	10 23	11 18	11 58
45	16 31	17 03	17 38	08 42	09 54	10 53	11 37
N 40	16 43	17 12	17 45	08 21	09 32	10 32	11 20
35	16 54	17 21	17 52	08 03	09 14	10 15	11 05
30	17 04	17 29	17 58	07 48	08 58	10 00	10 52
20	17 20	17 43	18 10	07 23	08 31	09 35	10 31
N 10	17 35	17 57	18 22	07 00	08 08	09 12	10 12
0	17 48	18 10	18 35	06 40	07 46	08 52	09 54
S 10	18 02	18 24	18 50	06 19	07 25	08 31	09 36
20	18 17	18 40	19 08	05 57	07 01	08 09	09 16
30	18 34	19 00	19 31	05 32	06 34	07 43	08 54
35	18 44	19 12	19 46	05 17	06 18	07 28	08 41
40	18 56	19 26	20 04	05 00	06 00	07 10	08 25
45	19 09	19 43	20 27	04 39	05 37	06 48	08 07
S 50	19 26	20 05	20 58	04 13	05 08	06 21	07 44
52	19 34	20 16	21 14	04 00	04 54	06 07	07 33
54	19 43	20 28	21 34	03 46	04 38	05 52	07 20
56	19 53	20 43	21 59	03 29	04 19	05 34	07 06
58	20 04	21 00	22 38	03 09	03 55	05 11	06 49
S 60	20 17	21 21	////	02 44	03 23	04 42	06 28

Day	SUN Eqn. of Time 00^h	SUN Eqn. of Time 12^h	SUN Mer. Pass.	MOON Mer. Pass. Upper	MOON Mer. Pass. Lower	MOON Age	MOON Phase
d	m s	m s	h m	h m	h m	d %	
14	15 36	15 31	11 44	00 24	12 57	17 98	
15	15 26	15 21	11 45	01 30	14 04	18 93	
16	15 16	15 10	11 45	02 37	15 09	19 85	

UT	ARIES	VENUS −4.1		MARS +1.4		JUPITER −2.0		SATURN +1.1	
	GHA	GHA	Dec	GHA	Dec	GHA	Dec	GHA	Dec
d h	° ′	° ′	° ′	° ′	° ′	° ′	° ′	° ′	° ′
17 00	56 25.5	140 39.2	S25 32.4	178 11.2	S20 31.3	125 16.2	S22 23.1	244 53.1	N 5 39.9
01	71 28.0	155 38.3	32.3	193 11.8	31.7	140 18.2	23.0	259 55.4	39.8
02	86 30.4	170 37.5	32.3	208 12.4	32.1	155 20.2	23.0	274 57.7	39.8
03	101 32.9	185 36.6	32.2	223 13.0	32.5	170 22.2	22.9	290 00.0	39.7
04	116 35.4	200 35.8	32.1	238 13.6	32.9	185 24.1	22.8	305 02.3	39.6
05	131 37.8	215 35.0	32.1	253 14.2	33.3	200 26.1	22.8	320 04.6	39.6
06	146 40.3	230 34.1	S25 32.0	268 14.8	S20 33.7	215 28.1	S22 22.7	335 06.8	N 5 39.5
07	161 42.8	245 33.3	31.9	283 15.4	34.1	230 30.1	22.6	350 09.1	39.4
08	176 45.2	260 32.4	31.9	298 16.0	34.5	245 32.1	22.6	5 11.4	39.4
MONDAY 09	191 47.7	275 31.6	31.8	313 16.6	34.9	260 34.0	22.5	20 13.7	39.3
10	206 50.1	290 30.8	31.7	328 17.2	35.3	275 36.0	22.5	35 16.0	39.2
11	221 52.6	305 29.9	31.6	343 17.8	35.6	290 38.0	22.4	50 18.3	39.2
12	236 55.1	320 29.1	S25 31.6	358 18.4	S20 36.0	305 40.0	S22 22.3	65 20.6	N 5 39.1
13	251 57.5	335 28.3	31.5	13 19.0	36.4	320 42.0	22.3	80 22.9	39.1
14	267 00.0	350 27.4	31.4	28 19.6	36.8	335 43.9	22.2	95 25.1	39.0
15	282 02.5	5 26.6	31.3	43 20.2	37.2	350 45.9	22.1	110 27.4	38.9
16	297 04.9	20 25.7	31.3	58 20.8	37.6	5 47.9	22.1	125 29.7	38.9
17	312 07.4	35 24.9	31.2	73 21.4	38.0	20 49.9	22.0	140 32.0	38.8
18	327 09.9	50 24.1	S25 31.1	88 22.0	S20 38.4	35 51.8	S22 21.9	155 34.3	N 5 38.7
19	342 12.3	65 23.2	31.0	103 22.6	38.8	50 53.8	21.9	170 36.6	38.7
20	357 14.8	80 22.4	30.9	118 23.2	39.2	65 55.8	21.8	185 38.9	38.6
21	12 17.3	95 21.6	30.8	133 23.8	39.6	80 57.8	21.8	200 41.2	38.5
22	27 19.7	110 20.7	30.8	148 24.4	40.0	95 59.8	21.7	215 43.5	38.5
23	42 22.2	125 19.9	30.7	163 25.0	40.4	111 01.7	21.6	230 45.7	38.4
18 00	57 24.6	140 19.0	S25 30.6	178 25.6	S20 40.8	126 03.7	S22 21.6	245 48.0	N 5 38.3
01	72 27.1	155 18.2	30.5	193 26.2	41.1	141 05.7	21.5	260 50.3	38.3
02	87 29.6	170 17.4	30.4	208 26.7	41.5	156 07.7	21.4	275 52.6	38.2
03	102 32.0	185 16.5	30.3	223 27.3	41.9	171 09.6	21.4	290 54.9	38.2
04	117 34.5	200 15.7	30.2	238 27.9	42.3	186 11.6	21.3	305 57.2	38.1
05	132 37.0	215 14.9	30.1	253 28.5	42.7	201 13.6	21.2	320 59.5	38.0
06	147 39.4	230 14.0	S25 30.0	268 29.1	S20 43.1	216 15.6	S22 21.2	336 01.8	N 5 38.0
07	162 41.9	245 13.2	29.9	283 29.7	43.5	231 17.5	21.1	351 04.1	37.9
08	177 44.4	260 12.4	29.8	298 30.3	43.9	246 19.5	21.1	6 06.4	37.8
TUESDAY 09	192 46.8	275 11.5	29.7	313 30.9	44.3	261 21.5	21.0	21 08.6	37.8
10	207 49.3	290 10.7	29.6	328 31.5	44.7	276 23.5	20.9	36 10.9	37.7
11	222 51.7	305 09.9	29.5	343 32.1	45.0	291 25.4	20.9	51 13.2	37.6
12	237 54.2	320 09.0	S25 29.4	358 32.7	S20 45.4	306 27.4	S22 20.8	66 15.5	N 5 37.6
13	252 56.7	335 08.2	29.3	13 33.3	45.8	321 29.4	20.7	81 17.8	37.5
14	267 59.1	350 07.4	29.2	28 33.9	46.2	336 31.4	20.7	96 20.1	37.5
15	283 01.6	5 06.5	29.1	43 34.5	46.6	351 33.3	20.6	111 22.4	37.4
16	298 04.1	20 05.7	29.0	58 35.1	47.0	6 35.3	20.5	126 24.7	37.3
17	313 06.5	35 04.9	28.9	73 35.7	47.4	21 37.3	20.5	141 27.0	37.3
18	328 09.0	50 04.0	S25 28.8	88 36.3	S20 47.7	36 39.3	S22 20.4	156 29.3	N 5 37.2
19	343 11.5	65 03.2	28.6	103 36.8	48.1	51 41.2	20.3	171 31.6	37.1
20	358 13.9	80 02.4	28.5	118 37.4	48.5	66 43.2	20.3	186 33.8	37.1
21	13 16.4	95 01.5	28.4	133 38.0	48.9	81 45.2	20.2	201 36.1	37.0
22	28 18.9	110 00.7	28.3	148 38.6	49.3	96 47.2	20.1	216 38.4	37.0
23	43 21.3	124 59.9	28.2	163 39.2	49.7	111 49.1	20.1	231 40.7	36.9
19 00	58 23.8	139 59.0	S25 28.1	178 39.8	S20 50.1	126 51.1	S22 20.0	246 43.0	N 5 36.8
01	73 26.2	154 58.2	27.9	193 40.4	50.4	141 53.1	20.0	261 45.3	36.8
02	88 28.7	169 57.4	27.8	208 41.0	50.8	156 55.0	19.9	276 47.6	36.7
03	103 31.2	184 56.5	27.7	223 41.6	51.2	171 57.0	19.8	291 49.9	36.6
04	118 33.6	199 55.7	27.6	238 42.2	51.6	186 59.0	19.8	306 52.2	36.6
05	133 36.1	214 54.9	27.4	253 42.8	52.0	202 01.0	19.7	321 54.5	36.5
06	148 38.6	229 54.0	S25 27.3	268 43.3	S20 52.3	217 02.9	S22 19.6	336 56.8	N 5 36.5
07	163 41.0	244 53.2	27.2	283 43.9	52.7	232 04.9	19.6	351 59.1	36.4
08	178 43.5	259 52.4	27.0	298 44.5	53.1	247 06.9	19.5	7 01.4	36.3
WEDNESDAY 09	193 46.0	274 51.6	26.9	313 45.1	53.5	262 08.8	19.4	22 03.7	36.3
10	208 48.4	289 50.7	26.8	328 45.7	53.9	277 10.8	19.4	37 06.0	36.2
11	223 50.9	304 49.9	26.6	343 46.3	54.2	292 12.8	19.3	52 08.2	36.1
12	238 53.4	319 49.1	S25 26.5	358 46.9	S20 54.6	307 14.8	S22 19.2	67 10.5	N 5 36.1
13	253 55.8	334 48.2	26.4	13 47.5	55.0	322 16.7	19.2	82 12.8	36.0
14	268 58.3	349 47.4	26.2	28 48.0	55.4	337 18.7	19.1	97 15.1	36.0
15	284 00.7	4 46.6	26.1	43 48.6	55.8	352 20.7	19.0	112 17.4	35.9
16	299 03.2	19 45.8	26.0	58 49.2	56.1	7 22.6	19.0	127 19.7	35.8
17	314 05.7	34 44.9	25.8	73 49.8	56.5	22 24.6	18.9	142 22.0	35.8
18	329 08.1	49 44.1	S25 25.7	88 50.4	S20 56.9	37 26.6	S22 18.8	157 24.3	N 5 35.7
19	344 10.6	64 43.3	25.5	103 51.0	57.3	52 28.6	18.8	172 26.6	35.7
20	359 13.1	79 42.5	25.4	118 51.6	57.7	67 30.5	18.7	187 28.9	35.6
21	14 15.5	94 41.6	25.2	133 52.1	58.0	82 32.5	18.6	202 31.2	35.5
22	29 18.0	109 40.8	25.1	148 52.7	58.4	97 34.5	18.6	217 33.5	35.5
23	44 20.5	124 40.0	24.9	163 53.3	58.8	112 36.4	18.5	232 35.8	35.4
Mer. Pass.	h m 20 07.1	v −0.8	d 0.1	v 0.6	d 0.4	v 2.0	d 0.1	v 2.3	d 0.1

STARS

Name	SHA	Dec
	° ′	° ′
Acamar	315 20.4	S40 16.0
Achernar	335 28.6	S57 11.5
Acrux	173 13.9	S63 08.7
Adhara	255 15.0	S28 58.8
Aldebaran	290 53.0	N16 31.8
Alioth	166 23.9	N55 54.4
Alkaid	153 01.8	N49 15.9
Al Na'ir	27 47.8	S46 55.2
Alnilam	275 49.6	S 1 11.6
Alphard	217 59.4	S 8 41.7
Alphecca	126 14.2	N26 41.0
Alpheratz	357 46.9	N29 08.6
Altair	62 11.8	N 8 53.6
Ankaa	353 18.6	S42 15.5
Antares	112 30.9	S26 27.1
Arcturus	145 59.1	N19 08.1
Atria	107 36.5	S69 02.7
Avior	234 19.3	S59 32.0
Bellatrix	278 35.4	N 6 21.6
Betelgeuse	271 04.7	N 7 24.6
Canopus	263 57.3	S52 41.7
Capella	280 39.1	N46 00.5
Deneb	49 34.1	N45 19.0
Denebola	182 37.3	N14 31.3
Diphda	348 59.0	S17 56.2
Dubhe	193 55.8	N61 41.9
Elnath	278 16.6	N28 37.0
Eltanin	90 48.2	N51 29.4
Enif	33 50.5	N 9 55.1
Fomalhaut	15 27.6	S29 34.6
Gacrux	172 05.4	S57 09.6
Gienah	175 56.1	S17 35.4
Hadar	148 53.7	S60 24.9
Hamal	328 04.4	N23 30.5
Kaus Aust.	83 48.7	S34 22.9
Kochab	137 20.6	N74 07.0
Markab	13 41.7	N15 15.4
Menkar	314 18.3	N 4 07.7
Menkent	148 12.1	S36 24.8
Miaplacidus	221 40.6	S69 44.9
Mirfak	308 44.9	N49 53.7
Nunki	76 02.8	S26 17.2
Peacock	53 24.7	S56 42.6
Pollux	243 31.7	N28 00.2
Procyon	245 03.1	N 5 12.2
Rasalhague	96 10.0	N12 33.2
Regulus	207 47.2	N11 55.4
Rigel	281 15.0	S 8 11.3
Rigil Kent.	139 57.3	S60 52.2
Sabik	102 16.8	S15 44.2
Schedar	349 44.3	N56 35.5
Shaula	96 27.0	S37 06.7
Sirius	258 36.5	S16 43.5
Spica	158 35.2	S11 12.4
Suhail	222 55.0	S43 27.8
Vega	80 41.6	N38 47.6
Zuben'ubi	137 09.6	S16 04.7

	SHA	Mer. Pass.
	° ′	h m
Venus	82 54.4	14 40
Mars	121 00.9	12 06
Jupiter	68 39.1	15 34
Saturn	188 23.4	7 36

UT d	UT h	SUN GHA	SUN Dec	MOON GHA	v	MOON Dec	d	HP
d	h	° ′	° ′	° ′	′	° ′	′	′
17	00	183 46.0	S19 01.1	307 21.4	4.3	N24 27.5	7.6	60.2
	01	198 45.9	01.7	321 44.7	4.4	24 19.9	7.9	60.1
	02	213 45.8	02.3	336 08.1	4.5	24 12.0	8.0	60.1
	03	228 45.7	. . 02.9	350 31.6	4.6	24 04.0	8.2	60.1
	04	243 45.5	03.5	4 55.2	4.7	23 55.8	8.3	60.1
	05	258 45.4	04.1	19 18.9	4.9	23 47.5	8.5	60.0
	06	273 45.3	S19 04.8	33 42.8	5.0	N23 39.0	8.6	60.0
	07	288 45.2	05.4	48 06.8	5.1	23 30.4	8.8	60.0
	08	303 45.0	06.0	62 30.9	5.2	23 21.6	8.9	59.9
M	09	318 44.9	. . 06.6	76 55.1	5.4	23 12.7	9.0	59.9
O	10	333 44.8	07.2	91 19.5	5.5	23 03.7	9.2	59.9
N	11	348 44.7	07.8	105 44.0	5.6	22 54.5	9.4	59.9
D	12	3 44.5	S19 08.4	120 08.6	5.8	N22 45.1	9.5	59.8
A	13	18 44.4	09.0	134 33.4	5.8	22 35.6	9.6	59.8
Y	14	33 44.3	09.6	148 58.2	6.0	22 26.0	9.7	59.8
	15	48 44.2	. . 10.2	163 23.2	6.2	22 16.3	9.9	59.7
	16	63 44.0	10.8	177 48.4	6.2	22 06.4	10.0	59.7
	17	78 43.9	11.4	192 13.6	6.4	21 56.4	10.2	59.7
	18	93 43.8	S19 12.0	206 39.0	6.5	N21 46.2	10.3	59.6
	19	108 43.6	12.6	221 04.5	6.6	21 35.9	10.4	59.6
	20	123 43.5	13.2	235 30.1	6.8	21 25.5	10.5	59.6
	21	138 43.4	. . 13.8	249 55.9	6.9	21 15.0	10.6	59.6
	22	153 43.2	14.3	264 21.8	7.0	21 04.4	10.8	59.5
	23	168 43.1	14.9	278 47.8	7.2	20 53.6	10.8	59.5
18	00	183 43.0	S19 15.5	293 14.0	7.3	N20 42.8	11.0	59.5
	01	198 42.9	16.1	307 40.3	7.4	20 31.8	11.1	59.4
	02	213 42.7	16.7	322 06.7	7.5	20 20.7	11.2	59.4
	03	228 42.6	. . 17.3	336 33.2	7.7	20 09.5	11.4	59.4
	04	243 42.5	17.9	350 59.9	7.8	19 58.1	11.4	59.3
	05	258 42.3	18.5	5 26.7	7.9	19 46.7	11.5	59.3
	06	273 42.2	S19 19.1	19 53.6	8.0	N19 35.2	11.6	59.3
	07	288 42.1	19.7	34 20.6	8.2	19 23.6	11.8	59.2
T	08	303 41.9	20.3	48 47.8	8.3	19 11.8	11.8	59.2
U	09	318 41.8	. . 20.9	63 15.1	8.4	19 00.0	11.9	59.2
E	10	333 41.7	21.4	77 42.5	8.5	18 48.1	12.1	59.1
S	11	348 41.5	22.0	92 10.0	8.7	18 36.0	12.1	59.1
D	12	3 41.4	S19 22.6	106 37.7	8.8	N18 23.9	12.2	59.1
A	13	18 41.2	23.2	121 05.5	8.9	18 11.7	12.3	59.0
Y	14	33 41.1	23.8	135 33.4	9.0	17 59.4	12.4	59.0
	15	48 41.0	. . 24.4	150 01.4	9.2	17 47.0	12.4	59.0
	16	63 40.8	25.0	164 29.6	9.2	17 34.6	12.6	58.9
	17	78 40.7	25.5	178 57.8	9.4	17 22.0	12.6	58.9
	18	93 40.6	S19 26.1	193 26.2	9.5	N17 09.4	12.7	58.9
	19	108 40.4	26.7	207 54.7	9.6	16 56.7	12.8	58.8
	20	123 40.3	27.3	222 23.3	9.8	16 43.9	12.9	58.8
	21	138 40.1	. . 27.9	236 52.1	9.8	16 31.0	12.9	58.8
	22	153 40.0	28.5	251 20.9	10.0	16 18.1	13.1	58.7
	23	168 39.9	29.0	265 49.9	10.0	16 05.0	13.1	58.7
19	00	183 39.7	S19 29.6	280 18.9	10.2	N15 51.9	13.1	58.7
	01	198 39.6	30.2	294 48.1	10.3	15 38.8	13.2	58.6
	02	213 39.4	30.8	309 17.4	10.4	15 25.6	13.3	58.6
	03	228 39.3	. . 31.4	323 46.8	10.5	15 12.3	13.4	58.6
	04	243 39.2	31.9	338 16.3	10.6	14 58.9	13.4	58.5
	05	258 39.0	32.5	352 45.9	10.8	14 45.5	13.5	58.5
	06	273 38.9	S19 33.1	7 15.7	10.8	N14 32.0	13.5	58.5
W	07	288 38.7	33.7	21 45.5	10.9	14 18.5	13.6	58.4
E	08	303 38.6	34.2	36 15.4	11.1	14 04.9	13.7	58.4
D	09	318 38.4	. . 34.8	50 45.5	11.1	13 51.2	13.7	58.4
N	10	333 38.3	35.4	65 15.6	11.2	13 37.5	13.8	58.3
E	11	348 38.2	36.0	79 45.8	11.4	13 23.7	13.8	58.3
S	12	3 38.0	S19 36.5	94 16.2	11.4	N13 09.9	13.9	58.3
D	13	18 37.9	37.1	108 46.6	11.5	12 56.0	13.9	58.2
A	14	33 37.7	37.7	123 17.1	11.7	12 42.1	14.0	58.2
Y	15	48 37.6	. . 38.2	137 47.8	11.7	12 28.1	14.0	58.2
	16	63 37.4	38.8	152 18.5	11.8	12 14.1	14.0	58.1
	17	78 37.3	39.4	166 49.3	11.9	12 00.1	14.1	58.1
	18	93 37.1	S19 40.0	181 20.2	12.0	N11 46.0	14.2	58.1
	19	108 37.0	40.5	195 51.2	12.1	11 31.8	14.1	58.0
	20	123 36.8	41.1	210 22.3	12.1	11 17.7	14.3	58.0
	21	138 36.7	. . 41.7	224 53.4	12.3	11 03.4	14.2	58.0
	22	153 36.5	42.2	239 24.7	12.3	10 49.2	14.3	57.9
	23	168 36.4	42.8	253 56.0	12.4	N10 34.9	14.3	57.9
		SD 16.2	*d* 0.6	SD 16.3		16.1		15.9

Lat.	Twilight Naut.	Twilight Civil	Sunrise	Moonrise 17	Moonrise 18	Moonrise 19	Moonrise 20
°	h m	h m	h m	h m	h m	h m	h m
N 72	07 11	08 50	■	□	18 30	21 38	23 56
N 70	07 00	08 25	10 13	□	19 27	21 57	24 02
68	06 50	08 05	09 29	16 39	20 01	22 12	24 07
66	06 42	07 49	09 00	18 02	20 25	22 24	24 12
64	06 35	07 36	08 38	18 39	20 43	22 34	24 16
62	06 29	07 26	08 21	19 06	20 58	22 42	24 19
60	06 24	07 16	08 06	19 26	21 11	22 49	24 21
N 58	06 19	07 08	07 54	19 43	21 22	22 56	24 24
56	06 14	07 00	07 43	19 57	21 31	23 01	24 26
54	06 10	06 54	07 34	20 09	21 40	23 06	24 28
52	06 06	06 48	07 26	20 20	21 47	23 10	24 30
50	06 02	06 42	07 18	20 29	21 54	23 14	24 31
45	05 54	06 30	07 02	20 49	22 08	23 23	24 35
N 40	05 47	06 20	06 49	21 05	22 20	23 30	24 38
35	05 40	06 11	06 38	21 19	22 29	23 36	24 40
30	05 33	06 02	06 28	21 31	22 38	23 42	24 42
20	05 21	05 47	06 11	21 51	22 53	23 51	24 46
N 10	05 08	05 34	05 56	22 08	23 06	23 59	24 49
0	04 54	05 20	05 42	22 24	23 18	24 07	00 07
S 10	04 39	05 05	05 27	22 40	23 30	24 15	00 15
20	04 20	04 48	05 12	22 57	23 43	24 23	00 23
30	03 57	04 28	04 54	23 17	23 57	24 32	00 32
35	03 41	04 16	04 44	23 28	24 06	00 06	00 37
40	03 23	04 01	04 32	23 42	24 15	00 15	00 43
45	03 00	03 43	04 18	23 57	24 26	00 26	00 50
S 50	02 27	03 21	04 00	24 16	00 16	00 39	00 58
52	02 11	03 10	03 52	24 24	00 24	00 46	01 02
54	01 50	02 57	03 43	00 07	00 34	00 53	01 06
56	01 22	02 42	03 33	00 22	00 45	01 00	01 10
58	00 37	02 24	03 21	00 40	00 58	01 09	01 15
S 60	////	02 02	03 07	01 02	01 13	01 18	01 21

Lat.	Sunset	Twilight Civil	Twilight Naut.	Moonset 17	Moonset 18	Moonset 19	Moonset 20
°	h m	h m	h m	h m	h m	h m	h m
N 72	■	14 39	16 18	□	16 02	14 39	13 59
N 70	13 16	15 05	16 30	□	15 03	14 17	13 49
68	14 01	15 25	16 39	15 55	14 28	14 01	13 41
66	14 30	15 40	16 47	14 31	14 03	13 47	13 35
64	14 52	15 53	16 54	13 53	13 43	13 36	13 29
62	15 09	16 04	17 01	13 26	13 27	13 26	13 24
60	15 24	16 14	17 06	13 04	13 13	13 17	13 20
N 58	15 36	16 22	17 11	12 47	13 01	13 10	13 16
56	15 47	16 30	17 16	12 32	12 51	13 03	13 13
54	15 56	16 36	17 20	12 19	12 42	12 58	13 10
52	16 04	16 42	17 24	12 08	12 34	12 52	13 07
50	16 12	16 48	17 28	11 58	12 26	12 47	13 04
45	16 28	17 00	17 36	11 37	12 10	12 37	12 59
N 40	16 41	17 10	17 43	11 20	11 57	12 28	12 54
35	16 53	17 20	17 50	11 05	11 46	12 20	12 50
30	17 02	17 28	17 57	10 52	11 36	12 14	12 46
20	17 20	17 43	18 10	10 31	11 19	12 02	12 40
N 10	17 35	17 57	18 23	10 12	11 04	11 52	12 34
0	17 49	18 11	18 36	09 54	10 50	11 42	12 29
S 10	18 03	18 26	18 52	09 36	10 36	11 32	12 24
20	18 19	18 42	19 10	09 16	10 21	11 21	12 18
30	18 37	19 03	19 34	08 54	10 03	11 09	12 11
35	18 47	19 15	19 50	08 41	09 53	11 02	12 07
40	18 59	19 30	20 08	08 25	09 41	10 54	12 03
45	19 13	19 48	20 32	08 07	09 27	10 44	11 58
S 50	19 31	20 11	21 05	07 44	09 10	10 33	11 52
52	19 39	20 22	21 22	07 33	09 01	10 27	11 49
54	19 49	20 35	21 43	07 20	08 52	10 21	11 46
56	19 59	20 50	22 12	07 06	08 42	10 14	11 42
58	20 11	21 08	23 02	06 49	08 30	10 07	11 38
S 60	20 25	21 31	////	06 28	08 16	09 58	11 34

Day	SUN Eqn. of Time 00^h	SUN Eqn. of Time 12^h	SUN Mer. Pass.	MOON Mer. Pass. Upper	MOON Mer. Pass. Lower	MOON Age	MOON Phase
d	m s	m s	h m	h m	h m	d %	
17	15 04	14 58	11 45	03 39	16 09	20 76	
18	14 52	14 46	11 45	04 37	17 04	21 65	◑
19	14 39	14 32	11 45	05 30	17 54	22 54	

UT		ARIES	VENUS −4.1		MARS +1.4		JUPITER −2.0		SATURN +1.1		STARS		
		GHA	GHA	Dec	GHA	Dec	GHA	Dec	GHA	Dec	Name	SHA	Dec
d	h	° ′	° ′	° ′	° ′	° ′	° ′	° ′	° ′	° ′		° ′	° ′
20	00	59 22.9	139 39.1	S25 24.8	178 53.9	S20 59.2	127 38.4	S22 18.4	247 38.1	N 5 35.3	Acamar	315 20.4	S40 16.1
	01	74 25.4	154 38.3	24.6	193 54.5	59.5	142 40.4	18.4	262 40.4	35.3	Achernar	335 28.6	S57 11.5
	02	89 27.9	169 37.5	24.5	208 55.1	20 59.9	157 42.3	18.3	277 42.7	35.2	Acrux	173 13.9	S63 08.7
	03	104 30.3	184 36.7	. . 24.3	223 55.7	21 00.3	172 44.3	. . 18.2	292 45.0	. . 35.2	Adhara	255 15.0	S28 58.8
	04	119 32.8	199 35.8	24.2	238 56.2	00.7	187 46.3	18.2	307 47.3	35.1	Aldebaran	290 53.0	N16 31.8
	05	134 35.2	214 35.0	24.0	253 56.8	01.0	202 48.2	18.1	322 49.6	35.0			
	06	149 37.7	229 34.2	S25 23.9	268 57.4	S21 01.4	217 50.2	S22 18.0	337 51.9	N 5 35.0	Alioth	166 23.8	N55 54.4
	07	164 40.2	244 33.4	23.7	283 58.0	01.8	232 52.2	18.0	352 54.2	34.9	Alkaid	153 01.8	N49 15.9
T	08	179 42.6	259 32.6	23.5	298 58.6	02.2	247 54.1	17.9	7 56.5	34.9	Al Na'ir	27 47.9	S46 55.2
H	09	194 45.1	274 31.7	. . 23.4	313 59.1	. . 02.5	262 56.1	. . 17.8	22 58.8	. . 34.8	Alnilam	275 49.5	S 1 11.6
U	10	209 47.6	289 30.9	23.2	328 59.7	02.9	277 58.1	17.8	38 01.0	34.7	Alphard	217 59.4	S 8 41.7
R	11	224 50.0	304 30.1	23.1	344 00.3	03.3	293 00.0	17.7	53 03.3	34.7			
S	12	239 52.5	319 29.3	S25 22.9	359 00.9	S21 03.6	308 02.0	S22 17.6	68 05.6	N 5 34.6	Alphecca	126 14.2	N26 41.0
D	13	254 55.0	334 28.4	22.7	14 01.5	04.0	323 04.0	17.6	83 07.9	34.6	Alpheratz	357 47.0	N29 08.7
A	14	269 57.4	349 27.6	22.6	29 02.1	04.4	338 05.9	17.5	98 10.2	34.5	Altair	62 11.8	N 8 53.6
Y	15	284 59.9	4 26.8	. . 22.4	44 02.6	. . 04.8	353 07.9	. . 17.4	113 12.5	. . 34.4	Ankaa	353 18.7	S42 15.5
	16	300 02.3	19 26.0	22.2	59 03.2	05.1	8 09.9	17.4	128 14.8	34.4	Antares	112 30.9	S26 27.1
	17	315 04.8	34 25.2	22.0	74 03.8	05.5	23 11.8	17.3	143 17.1	34.3			
	18	330 07.3	49 24.3	S25 21.9	89 04.4	S21 05.9	38 13.8	S22 17.2	158 19.4	N 5 34.3	Arcturus	145 59.1	N19 08.1
	19	345 09.7	64 23.5	21.7	104 05.0	06.2	53 15.8	17.2	173 21.7	34.2	Atria	107 36.5	S69 02.7
	20	0 12.2	79 22.7	21.5	119 05.5	06.6	68 17.7	17.1	188 24.0	34.1	Avior	234 19.3	S59 32.0
	21	15 14.7	94 21.9	. . 21.3	134 06.1	. . 07.0	83 19.7	. . 17.0	203 26.3	. . 34.1	Bellatrix	278 35.4	N 6 21.6
	22	30 17.1	109 21.1	21.2	149 06.7	07.4	98 21.7	17.0	218 28.6	34.0	Betelgeuse	271 04.7	N 7 24.6
	23	45 19.6	124 20.2	21.0	164 07.3	07.7	113 23.6	16.9	233 30.9	34.0			
21	00	60 22.1	139 19.4	S25 20.8	179 07.9	S21 08.1	128 25.6	S22 16.8	248 33.2	N 5 33.9	Canopus	263 57.2	S52 41.8
	01	75 24.5	154 18.6	20.6	194 08.4	08.5	143 27.6	16.8	263 35.5	33.8	Capella	280 39.1	N46 00.5
	02	90 27.0	169 17.8	20.4	209 09.0	08.8	158 29.5	16.7	278 37.8	33.8	Deneb	49 34.1	N45 19.0
	03	105 29.5	184 17.0	. . 20.3	224 09.6	. . 09.2	173 31.5	. . 16.6	293 40.1	. . 33.7	Denebola	182 37.3	N14 31.3
	04	120 31.9	199 16.1	20.1	239 10.2	09.6	188 33.4	16.6	308 42.4	33.7	Diphda	348 59.0	S17 56.2
	05	135 34.4	214 15.3	19.9	254 10.7	09.9	203 35.4	16.5	323 44.7	33.6			
	06	150 36.8	229 14.5	S25 19.7	269 11.3	S21 10.3	218 37.4	S22 16.4	338 47.0	N 5 33.5	Dubhe	193 55.7	N61 41.9
	07	165 39.3	244 13.7	19.5	284 11.9	10.7	233 39.3	16.4	353 49.3	33.5	Elnath	278 16.6	N28 37.0
	08	180 41.8	259 12.9	19.3	299 12.5	11.0	248 41.3	16.3	8 51.6	33.4	Eltanin	90 48.2	N51 29.3
F	09	195 44.2	274 12.1	. . 19.1	314 13.0	. . 11.4	263 43.3	. . 16.2	23 53.9	. . 33.4	Enif	33 50.5	N 9 55.1
R	10	210 46.7	289 11.2	18.9	329 13.6	11.8	278 45.2	16.2	38 56.2	33.3	Fomalhaut	15 27.6	S29 34.6
I	11	225 49.2	304 10.4	18.7	344 14.2	12.1	293 47.2	16.1	53 58.5	33.2			
D	12	240 51.6	319 09.6	S25 18.5	359 14.8	S21 12.5	308 49.1	S22 16.0	69 00.8	N 5 33.2	Gacrux	172 05.4	S57 09.6
A	13	255 54.1	334 08.8	18.3	14 15.3	12.8	323 51.1	16.0	84 03.1	33.1	Gienah	175 56.1	S17 35.4
Y	14	270 56.6	349 08.0	18.1	29 15.9	13.2	338 53.1	15.9	99 05.4	33.1	Hadar	148 53.6	S60 24.9
	15	285 59.0	4 07.2	. . 17.9	44 16.5	. . 13.6	353 55.0	. . 15.8	114 07.7	. . 33.0	Hamal	328 04.4	N23 30.5
	16	301 01.5	19 06.4	17.7	59 17.1	13.9	8 57.0	15.8	129 10.0	33.0	Kaus Aust.	83 48.7	S34 22.9
	17	316 03.9	34 05.5	17.5	74 17.6	14.3	23 59.0	15.7	144 12.3	32.9			
	18	331 06.4	49 04.7	S25 17.3	89 18.2	S21 14.7	39 00.9	S22 15.6	159 14.6	N 5 32.8	Kochab	137 20.6	N74 06.9
	19	346 08.9	64 03.9	17.1	104 18.8	15.0	54 02.9	15.6	174 16.9	32.8	Markab	13 41.7	N15 15.4
	20	1 11.3	79 03.1	16.9	119 19.4	15.4	69 04.8	15.5	189 19.2	32.7	Menkar	314 18.3	N 4 07.6
	21	16 13.8	94 02.3	. . 16.7	134 19.9	. . 15.7	84 06.8	. . 15.4	204 21.5	. . 32.7	Menkent	148 12.1	S36 24.8
	22	31 16.3	109 01.5	16.5	149 20.5	16.1	99 08.8	15.4	219 23.8	32.6	Miaplacidus	221 40.5	S69 44.9
	23	46 18.7	124 00.7	16.3	164 21.1	16.5	114 10.7	15.3	234 26.1	32.5			
22	00	61 21.2	138 59.9	S25 16.1	179 21.7	S21 16.8	129 12.7	S22 15.2	249 28.4	N 5 32.5	Mirfak	308 44.9	N49 53.7
	01	76 23.7	153 59.0	15.9	194 22.2	17.2	144 14.6	15.1	264 30.8	32.4	Nunki	76 02.8	S26 17.2
	02	91 26.1	168 58.2	15.7	209 22.8	17.5	159 16.6	15.1	279 33.1	32.4	Peacock	53 24.7	S56 42.6
	03	106 28.6	183 57.4	. . 15.4	224 23.4	. . 17.9	174 18.6	. . 15.0	294 35.4	. . 32.3	Pollux	243 31.7	N28 00.2
	04	121 31.1	198 56.6	15.2	239 23.9	18.3	189 20.5	14.9	309 37.7	32.3	Procyon	245 03.1	N 5 12.2
	05	136 33.5	213 55.8	15.0	254 24.5	18.6	204 22.5	14.9	324 40.0	32.2			
	06	151 36.0	228 55.0	S25 14.8	269 25.1	S21 19.0	219 24.4	S22 14.8	339 42.3	N 5 32.1	Rasalhague	96 10.0	N12 33.2
	07	166 38.4	243 54.2	14.6	284 25.6	19.3	234 26.4	14.7	354 44.6	32.1	Regulus	207 47.1	N11 55.4
S	08	181 40.9	258 53.4	14.4	299 26.2	19.7	249 28.4	14.7	9 46.9	32.0	Rigel	281 15.0	S 8 11.3
A	09	196 43.4	273 52.6	. . 14.1	314 26.8	. . 20.1	264 30.3	. . 14.6	24 49.2	. . 32.0	Rigil Kent.	139 57.3	S60 52.2
T	10	211 45.8	288 51.8	13.9	329 27.4	20.4	279 32.3	14.5	39 51.5	31.9	Sabik	102 16.8	S15 44.2
U	11	226 48.3	303 50.9	13.7	344 27.9	20.8	294 34.2	14.5	54 53.8	31.9			
R	12	241 50.8	318 50.1	S25 13.5	359 28.5	S21 21.1	309 36.2	S22 14.4	69 56.1	N 5 31.8	Schedar	349 44.3	N56 35.5
D	13	256 53.2	333 49.3	13.2	14 29.1	21.5	324 38.2	14.3	84 58.4	31.7	Shaula	96 27.0	S37 06.7
A	14	271 55.7	348 48.5	13.0	29 29.6	21.8	339 40.1	14.2	100 00.7	31.7	Sirius	258 36.5	S16 43.5
Y	15	286 58.2	3 47.7	. . 12.8	44 30.2	. . 22.2	354 42.1	. . 14.2	115 03.0	. . 31.6	Spica	158 35.2	S11 12.4
	16	302 00.6	18 46.9	12.5	59 30.8	22.5	9 44.0	14.1	130 05.3	31.6	Suhail	222 55.0	S43 27.8
	17	317 03.1	33 46.1	12.3	74 31.3	22.9	24 46.0	14.0	145 07.6	31.5			
	18	332 05.6	48 45.3	S25 12.1	89 31.9	S21 23.3	39 47.9	S22 14.0	160 09.9	N 5 31.5	Vega	80 41.6	N38 47.6
	19	347 08.0	63 44.5	11.8	104 32.5	23.6	54 49.9	13.9	175 12.2	31.4	Zuben'ubi	137 09.6	S16 04.7
	20	2 10.5	78 43.7	11.6	119 33.0	24.0	69 51.9	13.8	190 14.5	31.3		SHA	Mer. Pass.
	21	17 12.9	93 42.9	. . 11.4	134 33.6	. . 24.3	84 53.8	. . 13.8	205 16.8	. . 31.3		° ′	h m
	22	32 15.4	108 42.1	11.1	149 34.2	24.7	99 55.8	13.7	220 19.1	31.2	Venus	78 57.4	14 44
	23	47 17.9	123 41.3	10.9	164 34.7	25.0	114 57.7	13.6	235 21.4	31.2	Mars	118 45.8	12 03
		h m									Jupiter	68 03.5	15 24
Mer. Pass.		19 55.3	*v* −0.8	*d* 0.2	*v* 0.6	*d* 0.4	*v* 2.0	*d* 0.1	*v* 2.3	*d* 0.1	Saturn	188 11.2	7 25

UT		SUN GHA	SUN Dec	MOON GHA	v	MOON Dec	d	HP
d	h	° ′	° ′	° ′	′	° ′	′	′
20	00	183 36.3	S19 43.3	268 27.4	12.5	N10 20.6	14.4	57.9
	01	198 36.1	43.9	282 58.9	12.6	10 06.2	14.4	57.8
	02	213 36.0	44.5	297 30.5	12.7	9 51.8	14.4	57.8
	03	228 35.8	. . 45.0	312 02.2	12.7	9 37.4	14.5	57.8
	04	243 35.7	45.6	326 33.9	12.9	9 22.9	14.4	57.7
	05	258 35.5	46.2	341 05.8	12.9	9 08.5	14.5	57.7
	06	273 35.3	S19 46.7	355 37.7	12.9	N 8 54.0	14.6	57.7
	07	288 35.2	47.3	10 09.6	13.1	8 39.4	14.5	57.6
T	08	303 35.0	47.8	24 41.7	13.1	8 24.9	14.6	57.6
H	09	318 34.9	. . 48.4	39 13.8	13.2	8 10.3	14.6	57.6
U	10	333 34.7	49.0	53 46.0	13.2	7 55.7	14.6	57.6
R	11	348 34.6	49.5	68 18.2	13.3	7 41.1	14.7	57.5
S	12	3 34.4	S19 50.1	82 50.5	13.4	N 7 26.4	14.6	57.5
D	13	18 34.3	50.6	97 22.9	13.5	7 11.8	14.7	57.5
A	14	33 34.1	51.2	111 55.4	13.5	6 57.1	14.7	57.4
Y	15	48 34.0	. . 51.8	126 27.9	13.6	6 42.4	14.7	57.4
	16	63 33.8	52.3	141 00.5	13.6	6 27.7	14.7	57.4
	17	78 33.7	52.9	155 33.1	13.7	6 13.0	14.7	57.3
	18	93 33.5	S19 53.4	170 05.8	13.8	N 5 58.3	14.8	57.3
	19	108 33.4	54.0	184 38.6	13.8	5 43.5	14.7	57.3
	20	123 33.2	54.5	199 11.4	13.8	5 28.8	14.8	57.2
	21	138 33.0	. . 55.1	213 44.2	13.9	5 14.0	14.8	57.2
	22	153 32.9	55.6	228 17.1	14.0	4 59.2	14.7	57.2
	23	168 32.7	56.2	242 50.1	14.0	4 44.5	14.8	57.1
21	00	183 32.6	S19 56.7	257 23.1	14.1	N 4 29.7	14.8	57.1
	01	198 32.4	57.3	271 56.2	14.1	4 14.9	14.8	57.1
	02	213 32.3	57.8	286 29.3	14.2	4 00.1	14.8	57.1
	03	228 32.1	. . 58.4	301 02.5	14.2	3 45.3	14.8	57.0
	04	243 31.9	58.9	315 35.7	14.3	3 30.5	14.8	57.0
	05	258 31.8	19 59.5	330 09.0	14.3	3 15.7	14.7	57.0
	06	273 31.6	S20 00.0	344 42.3	14.3	N 3 01.0	14.8	56.9
	07	288 31.5	00.6	359 15.6	14.4	2 46.2	14.8	56.9
	08	303 31.3	01.1	13 49.0	14.5	2 31.4	14.8	56.9
F	09	318 31.1	. . 01.6	28 22.5	14.4	2 16.6	14.8	56.8
R	10	333 31.0	02.2	42 55.9	14.5	2 01.8	14.7	56.8
I	11	348 30.8	02.7	57 29.4	14.6	1 47.1	14.8	56.8
D	12	3 30.7	S20 03.3	72 03.0	14.5	N 1 32.3	14.8	56.8
A	13	18 30.5	03.8	86 36.5	14.6	1 17.5	14.7	56.7
Y	14	33 30.3	04.4	101 10.1	14.7	1 02.8	14.8	56.7
	15	48 30.2	. . 04.9	115 43.8	14.6	0 48.0	14.7	56.7
	16	63 30.0	05.4	130 17.4	14.7	0 33.3	14.7	56.6
	17	78 29.8	06.0	144 51.1	14.8	0 18.6	14.7	56.6
	18	93 29.7	S20 06.5	159 24.9	14.7	N 0 03.9	14.7	56.6
	19	108 29.5	07.1	173 58.6	14.8	S 0 10.8	14.7	56.6
	20	123 29.3	07.6	188 32.4	14.8	0 25.5	14.6	56.5
	21	138 29.2	. . 08.1	203 06.2	14.8	0 40.1	14.7	56.5
	22	153 29.0	08.7	217 40.0	14.9	0 54.8	14.6	56.5
	23	168 28.8	09.2	232 13.9	14.8	1 09.4	14.6	56.5
22	00	183 28.7	S20 09.7	246 47.7	14.9	S 1 24.0	14.6	56.4
	01	198 28.5	10.3	261 21.6	14.9	1 38.6	14.6	56.4
	02	213 28.3	10.8	275 55.5	14.9	1 53.2	14.5	56.4
	03	228 28.2	. . 11.3	290 29.4	15.0	2 07.7	14.5	56.3
	04	243 28.0	11.9	305 03.4	14.9	2 22.2	14.5	56.3
	05	258 27.8	12.4	319 37.3	15.0	2 36.7	14.5	56.3
	06	273 27.7	S20 12.9	334 11.3	15.0	S 2 51.2	14.5	56.3
S	07	288 27.5	13.5	348 45.3	14.9	3 05.7	14.4	56.2
A	08	303 27.3	14.0	3 19.2	15.0	3 20.1	14.4	56.2
T	09	318 27.2	. . 14.5	17 53.2	15.1	3 34.5	14.4	56.2
U	10	333 27.0	15.0	32 27.3	15.0	3 48.9	14.3	56.2
R	11	348 26.8	15.6	47 01.3	15.0	4 03.2	14.4	56.1
D	12	3 26.7	S20 16.1	61 35.3	15.0	S 4 17.6	14.3	56.1
A	13	18 26.5	16.6	76 09.3	15.0	4 31.9	14.2	56.1
Y	14	33 26.3	17.2	90 43.3	15.1	4 46.1	14.2	56.1
	15	48 26.2	. . 17.7	105 17.4	15.0	5 00.3	14.2	56.0
	16	63 26.0	18.2	119 51.4	15.1	5 14.5	14.2	56.0
	17	78 25.8	18.7	134 25.5	15.0	5 28.7	14.1	56.0
	18	93 25.6	S20 19.2	148 59.5	15.0	S 5 42.8	14.1	56.0
	19	108 25.5	19.8	163 33.5	15.1	5 56.9	14.1	55.9
	20	123 25.3	20.3	178 07.6	15.0	6 11.0	14.0	55.9
	21	138 25.1	. . 20.8	192 41.6	15.0	6 25.0	14.0	55.9
	22	153 24.9	21.3	207 15.6	15.0	6 39.0	14.0	55.9
	23	168 24.8	21.9	221 49.6	15.1	S 6 53.0	13.9	55.8
		SD 16.2	*d* 0.5	SD	15.7	15.5		15.3

Lat.	Twilight Naut.	Twilight Civil	Sunrise	Moonrise 20	Moonrise 21	Moonrise 22	Moonrise 23
°	h m	h m	h m	h m	h m	h m	h m
N 72	07 21	09 04	▬	23 56	26 01	02 01	04 07
N 70	07 09	08 36	10 39	24 02	00 02	01 58	03 54
68	06 58	08 15	09 44	24 07	00 07	01 56	03 43
66	06 49	07 58	09 11	24 12	00 12	01 54	03 35
64	06 42	07 44	08 47	24 16	00 16	01 52	03 28
62	06 35	07 32	08 29	24 19	00 19	01 51	03 22
60	06 29	07 22	08 13	24 21	00 21	01 50	03 16
N 58	06 24	07 13	08 00	24 24	00 24	01 49	03 12
56	06 19	07 06	07 49	24 26	00 26	01 48	03 08
54	06 15	06 59	07 39	24 28	00 28	01 47	03 04
52	06 10	06 52	07 31	24 30	00 30	01 46	03 01
50	06 06	06 46	07 23	24 31	00 31	01 45	02 58
45	05 58	06 34	07 06	24 35	00 35	01 44	02 51
N 40	05 50	06 23	06 52	24 38	00 38	01 42	02 46
35	05 42	06 13	06 41	24 40	00 40	01 41	02 41
30	05 35	06 05	06 30	24 42	00 42	01 40	02 37
20	05 22	05 49	06 13	24 46	00 46	01 39	02 31
N 10	05 09	05 35	05 57	24 49	00 49	01 37	02 24
0	04 55	05 20	05 42	00 07	00 53	01 36	02 19
S 10	04 39	05 05	05 28	00 15	00 56	01 35	02 13
20	04 20	04 48	05 12	00 23	00 59	01 33	02 07
30	03 55	04 27	04 53	00 32	01 03	01 32	02 01
35	03 39	04 14	04 42	00 37	01 05	01 31	01 57
40	03 20	03 59	04 30	00 43	01 07	01 30	01 53
45	02 56	03 40	04 15	00 50	01 10	01 29	01 48
S 50	02 22	03 17	03 57	00 58	01 13	01 28	01 42
52	02 04	03 05	03 48	01 02	01 15	01 27	01 39
54	01 41	02 52	03 39	01 06	01 17	01 26	01 36
56	01 10	02 36	03 28	01 10	01 19	01 26	01 33
58	00 00	02 17	03 15	01 15	01 21	01 25	01 29
S 60	////	01 52	03 01	01 21	01 23	01 24	01 25

Lat.	Sunset	Twilight Civil	Twilight Naut.	Moonset 20	Moonset 21	Moonset 22	Moonset 23
°	h m	h m	h m	h m	h m	h m	h m
N 72	▬	14 26	16 09	13 59	13 27	12 57	12 24
N 70	12 53	14 55	16 22	13 49	13 26	13 04	12 39
68	13 47	15 16	16 33	13 41	13 25	13 09	12 52
66	14 20	15 33	16 42	13 35	13 24	13 13	13 02
64	14 44	15 47	16 49	13 29	13 23	13 17	13 11
62	15 02	15 59	16 56	13 24	13 22	13 20	13 18
60	15 18	16 09	17 02	13 20	13 22	13 23	13 25
N 58	15 31	16 18	17 07	13 16	13 21	13 25	13 30
56	15 42	16 26	17 12	13 13	13 20	13 28	13 35
54	15 52	16 33	17 17	13 10	13 20	13 30	13 40
52	16 01	16 39	17 21	13 07	13 20	13 32	13 44
50	16 09	16 45	17 25	13 04	13 19	13 33	13 48
45	16 26	16 58	17 34	12 59	13 18	13 37	13 56
N 40	16 39	17 09	17 42	12 54	13 18	13 40	14 03
35	16 51	17 18	17 49	12 50	13 17	13 43	14 09
30	17 01	17 27	17 56	12 46	13 16	13 45	14 14
20	17 19	17 43	18 10	12 40	13 15	13 49	14 24
N 10	17 35	17 57	18 23	12 34	13 14	13 53	14 32
0	17 50	18 12	18 37	12 29	13 13	13 57	14 39
S 10	18 04	18 27	18 53	12 24	13 13	14 00	14 47
20	18 20	18 44	19 13	12 18	13 12	14 04	14 55
30	18 39	19 06	19 37	12 11	13 10	14 08	15 05
35	18 50	19 18	19 53	12 07	13 10	14 10	15 10
40	19 03	19 34	20 13	12 03	13 09	14 13	15 16
45	19 17	19 52	20 37	11 58	13 08	14 16	15 24
S 50	19 36	20 16	21 12	11 52	13 07	14 20	15 32
52	19 44	20 28	21 30	11 49	13 06	14 22	15 36
54	19 54	20 42	21 53	11 46	13 06	14 24	15 41
56	20 05	20 58	22 26	11 42	13 05	14 26	15 46
58	20 18	21 17	////	11 38	13 05	14 28	15 52
S 60	20 33	21 42	////	11 34	13 04	14 31	15 58

Day	SUN Eqn. of Time 00^h	SUN Eqn. of Time 12^h	SUN Mer. Pass.	MOON Mer. Pass. Upper	MOON Mer. Pass. Lower	MOON Age	MOON Phase
d	m s	m s	h m	h m	h m	d	%
20	14 25	14 18	11 46	06 18	18 41	23	44
21	14 11	14 03	11 46	07 03	19 25	24	33
22	13 55	13 47	11 46	07 46	20 08	25	24

2008 NOVEMBER 23, 24, 25 (SUN., MON., TUES.)

	UT d h	ARIES GHA ° ′	VENUS −4.1 GHA ° ′	VENUS Dec ° ′	MARS +1.4 GHA ° ′	MARS Dec ° ′	JUPITER −2.0 GHA ° ′	JUPITER Dec ° ′	SATURN +1.1 GHA ° ′	SATURN Dec ° ′
	23 00	62 20.3	138 40.5	S25 10.7	179 35.3	S21 25.4	129 59.7	S22 13.6	250 23.8	N 5 31.1
	01	77 22.8	153 39.7	10.4	194 35.9	25.7	145 01.6	13.5	265 26.1	31.1
	02	92 25.3	168 38.9	10.2	209 36.4	26.1	160 03.6	13.4	280 28.4	31.0
	03	107 27.7	183 38.1 . .	09.9	224 37.0 . .	26.4	175 05.5 . .	13.3	295 30.7 . .	30.9
	04	122 30.2	198 37.3	09.7	239 37.6	26.8	190 07.5	13.3	310 33.0	30.9
	05	137 32.7	213 36.5	09.4	254 38.1	27.1	205 09.5	13.2	325 35.3	30.8
	06	152 35.1	228 35.7	S25 09.2	269 38.7	S21 27.5	220 11.4	S22 13.1	340 37.6	N 5 30.8
	07	167 37.6	243 34.9	08.9	284 39.3	27.8	235 13.4	13.1	355 39.9	30.7
	08	182 40.0	258 34.1	08.7	299 39.8	28.2	250 15.3	13.0	10 42.2	30.7
S	09	197 42.5	273 33.3 . .	08.4	314 40.4 . .	28.5	265 17.3 . .	12.9	25 44.5 . .	30.6
U	10	212 45.0	288 32.5	08.2	329 41.0	28.9	280 19.2	12.9	40 46.8	30.6
N	11	227 47.4	303 31.7	07.9	344 41.5	29.2	295 21.2	12.8	55 49.1	30.5
D	12	242 49.9	318 30.9	S25 07.7	359 42.1	S21 29.6	310 23.1	S22 12.7	70 51.4	N 5 30.4
A	13	257 52.4	333 30.1	07.4	14 42.6	29.9	325 25.1	12.6	85 53.7	30.4
Y	14	272 54.8	348 29.3	07.2	29 43.2	30.3	340 27.1	12.6	100 56.1	30.3
	15	287 57.3	3 28.5 . .	06.9	44 43.8 . .	30.6	355 29.0 . .	12.5	115 58.4 . .	30.3
	16	302 59.8	18 27.7	06.6	59 44.3	31.0	10 31.0	12.4	131 00.7	30.2
	17	318 02.2	33 26.9	06.4	74 44.9	31.3	25 32.9	12.4	146 03.0	30.2
	18	333 04.7	48 26.1	S25 06.1	89 45.5	S21 31.7	40 34.9	S22 12.3	161 05.3	N 5 30.1
	19	348 07.2	63 25.3	05.8	104 46.0	32.0	55 36.8	12.2	176 07.6	30.1
	20	3 09.6	78 24.5	05.6	119 46.6	32.3	70 38.8	12.2	191 09.9	30.0
	21	18 12.1	93 23.7 . .	05.3	134 47.1 . .	32.7	85 40.7 . .	12.1	206 12.2 . .	29.9
	22	33 14.5	108 22.9	05.0	149 47.7	33.0	100 42.7	12.0	221 14.5	29.9
	23	48 17.0	123 22.1	04.8	164 48.3	33.4	115 44.6	11.9	236 16.8	29.8
	24 00	63 19.5	138 21.3	S25 04.5	179 48.8	S21 33.7	130 46.6	S22 11.9	251 19.1	N 5 29.8
	01	78 21.9	153 20.5	04.2	194 49.4	34.1	145 48.5	11.8	266 21.4	29.7
	02	93 24.4	168 19.7	04.0	209 49.9	34.4	160 50.5	11.7	281 23.8	29.7
	03	108 26.9	183 18.9 . .	03.7	224 50.5 . .	34.8	175 52.4 . .	11.7	296 26.1 . .	29.6
	04	123 29.3	198 18.1	03.4	239 51.1	35.1	190 54.4	11.6	311 28.4	29.6
	05	138 31.8	213 17.3	03.1	254 51.6	35.4	205 56.3	11.5	326 30.7	29.5
	06	153 34.3	228 16.5	S25 02.9	269 52.2	S21 35.8	220 58.3	S22 11.4	341 33.0	N 5 29.4
	07	168 36.7	243 15.7	02.6	284 52.7	36.1	236 00.3	11.4	356 35.3	29.4
	08	183 39.2	258 15.0	02.3	299 53.3	36.5	251 02.2	11.3	11 37.6	29.3
M	09	198 41.7	273 14.2 . .	02.0	314 53.8 . .	36.8	266 04.2 . .	11.2	26 39.9 . .	29.3
O	10	213 44.1	288 13.4	01.7	329 54.4	37.2	281 06.1	11.2	41 42.2	29.2
N	11	228 46.6	303 12.6	01.4	344 55.0	37.5	296 08.1	11.1	56 44.6	29.2
D	12	243 49.0	318 11.8	S25 01.2	359 55.5	S21 37.8	311 10.0	S22 11.0	71 46.9	N 5 29.1
A	13	258 51.5	333 11.0	00.9	14 56.1	38.2	326 12.0	10.9	86 49.2	29.1
Y	14	273 54.0	348 10.2	00.6	29 56.6	38.5	341 13.9	10.9	101 51.5	29.0
	15	288 56.4	3 09.4 . .	00.3	44 57.2 . .	38.8	356 15.9 . .	10.8	116 53.8 . .	29.0
	16	303 58.9	18 08.6	25 00.0	59 57.7	39.2	11 17.8	10.7	131 56.1	28.9
	17	319 01.4	33 07.8	24 59.7	74 58.3	39.5	26 19.8	10.7	146 58.4	28.8
	18	334 03.8	48 07.1	S24 59.4	89 58.9	S21 39.9	41 21.7	S22 10.6	162 00.7	N 5 28.8
	19	349 06.3	63 06.3	59.1	104 59.4	40.2	56 23.7	10.5	177 03.0	28.7
	20	4 08.8	78 05.5	58.8	120 00.0	40.5	71 25.6	10.4	192 05.4	28.7
	21	19 11.2	93 04.7 . .	58.5	135 00.5 . .	40.9	86 27.6 . .	10.4	207 07.7 . .	28.6
	22	34 13.7	108 03.9	58.2	150 01.1	41.2	101 29.5	10.3	222 10.0	28.6
	23	49 16.1	123 03.1	57.9	165 01.6	41.5	116 31.5	10.2	237 12.3	28.5
	25 00	64 18.6	138 02.3	S24 57.6	180 02.2	S21 41.9	131 33.4	S22 10.2	252 14.6	N 5 28.5
	01	79 21.1	153 01.6	57.3	195 02.7	42.2	146 35.3	10.1	267 16.9	28.4
	02	94 23.5	168 00.8	57.0	210 03.3	42.6	161 37.3	10.0	282 19.2	28.4
	03	109 26.0	183 00.0 . .	56.7	225 03.8 . .	42.9	176 39.2 . .	09.9	297 21.5 . .	28.3
	04	124 28.5	197 59.2	56.4	240 04.4	43.2	191 41.2	09.9	312 23.9	28.3
	05	139 30.9	212 58.4	56.1	255 04.9	43.6	206 43.1	09.8	327 26.2	28.2
	06	154 33.4	227 57.6	S24 55.8	270 05.5	S21 43.9	221 45.1	S22 09.7	342 28.5	N 5 28.2
	07	169 35.9	242 56.9	55.5	285 06.1	44.2	236 47.0	09.6	357 30.8	28.1
T	08	184 38.3	257 56.1	55.2	300 06.6	44.6	251 49.0	09.6	12 33.1	28.0
U	09	199 40.8	272 55.3 . .	54.9	315 07.2 . .	44.9	266 50.9 . .	09.5	27 35.4 . .	28.0
E	10	214 43.3	287 54.5	54.6	330 07.7	45.2	281 52.9	09.4	42 37.7	27.9
S	11	229 45.7	302 53.7	54.3	345 08.3	45.6	296 54.8	09.4	57 40.1	27.9
D	12	244 48.2	317 52.9	S24 53.9	0 08.8	S21 45.9	311 56.8	S22 09.3	72 42.4	N 5 27.8
A	13	259 50.6	332 52.2	53.6	15 09.4	46.2	326 58.7	09.2	87 44.7	27.8
Y	14	274 53.1	347 51.4	53.3	30 09.9	46.6	342 00.7	09.1	102 47.0	27.7
	15	289 55.6	2 50.6 . .	53.0	45 10.5 . .	46.9	357 02.6 . .	09.1	117 49.3 . .	27.7
	16	304 58.0	17 49.8	52.7	60 11.0	47.2	12 04.6	09.0	132 51.6	27.6
	17	320 00.5	32 49.1	52.4	75 11.6	47.5	27 06.5	08.9	147 53.9	27.6
	18	335 03.0	47 48.3	S24 52.0	90 12.1	S21 47.9	42 08.5	S22 08.8	162 56.3	N 5 27.5
	19	350 05.4	62 47.5	51.7	105 12.7	48.2	57 10.4	08.8	177 58.6	27.5
	20	5 07.9	77 46.7	51.4	120 13.2	48.5	72 12.3	08.7	193 00.9	27.4
	21	20 10.4	92 45.9 . .	51.1	135 13.8 . .	48.9	87 14.3 . .	08.6	208 03.2 . .	27.4
	22	35 12.8	107 45.2	50.7	150 14.3	49.2	102 16.2	08.6	223 05.5	27.3
	23	50 15.3	122 44.4	50.4	165 14.9	49.5	117 18.2	08.5	238 07.8	27.3
	Mer. Pass.	h m 19 43.5	v −0.8	d 0.3	v 0.6	d 0.3	v 2.0	d 0.1	v 2.3	d 0.1

STARS

Name	SHA ° ′	Dec ° ′
Acamar	315 20.4	S40 16.1
Achernar	335 28.6	S57 11.6
Acrux	173 13.9	S63 08.7
Adhara	255 14.9	S28 58.8
Aldebaran	290 53.0	N16 31.8
Alioth	166 23.8	N55 54.4
Alkaid	153 01.8	N49 15.9
Al Na'ir	27 47.9	S46 55.2
Alnilam	275 49.5	S 1 11.6
Alphard	217 59.4	S 8 41.7
Alphecca	126 14.2	N26 41.0
Alpheratz	357 47.0	N29 08.7
Altair	62 11.8	N 8 53.6
Ankaa	353 18.7	S42 15.5
Antares	112 30.9	S26 27.1
Arcturus	145 59.1	N19 08.1
Atria	107 36.5	S69 02.7
Avior	234 19.3	S59 32.0
Bellatrix	278 35.4	N 6 21.6
Betelgeuse	271 04.7	N 7 24.6
Canopus	263 57.2	S52 41.8
Capella	280 39.1	N46 00.5
Deneb	49 34.1	N45 19.0
Denebola	182 37.2	N14 31.2
Diphda	348 59.1	S17 56.2
Dubhe	193 55.7	N61 41.9
Elnath	278 16.6	N28 37.0
Eltanin	90 48.2	N51 29.3
Enif	33 50.6	N 9 55.1
Fomalhaut	15 27.6	S29 34.6
Gacrux	172 05.3	S57 09.6
Gienah	175 56.1	S17 35.4
Hadar	148 53.6	S60 24.9
Hamal	328 04.4	N23 30.5
Kaus Aust.	83 48.7	S34 22.9
Kochab	137 20.6	N74 06.9
Markab	13 41.7	N15 15.4
Menkar	314 18.3	N 4 07.6
Menkent	148 12.1	S36 24.8
Miaplacidus	221 40.5	S69 44.9
Mirfak	308 44.9	N49 53.8
Nunki	76 02.8	S26 17.2
Peacock	53 24.8	S56 42.6
Pollux	243 31.6	N28 00.2
Procyon	245 03.1	N 5 12.2
Rasalhague	96 10.0	N12 33.2
Regulus	207 47.1	N11 55.4
Rigel	281 15.0	S 8 11.3
Rigil Kent.	139 57.3	S60 52.2
Sabik	102 16.8	S15 44.2
Schedar	349 44.3	N56 35.5
Shaula	96 27.0	S37 06.7
Sirius	258 36.5	S16 43.5
Spica	158 35.2	S11 12.4
Suhail	222 54.9	S43 27.8
Vega	80 41.7	N38 47.6
Zuben'ubi	137 09.6	S16 04.7

	SHA ° ′	Mer. Pass. h m
Venus	75 01.8	14 47
Mars	116 29.3	12 00
Jupiter	67 27.1	15 15
Saturn	187 59.7	7 14

	UT	SUN GHA	SUN Dec	MOON GHA	*v*	MOON Dec	*d*	HP
	d h	° ′	° ′	° ′	′	° ′	′	′
	23 00	183 24.6	S20 22.4	236 23.7	15.0	S 7 06.9	13.9	55.8
	01	198 24.4	22.9	250 57.7	15.0	7 20.8	13.8	55.8
	02	213 24.2	23.4	265 31.7	14.9	7 34.6	13.8	55.8
	03	228 24.1	. . 23.9	280 05.6	15.0	7 48.4	13.7	55.8
	04	243 23.9	24.4	294 39.6	15.0	8 02.1	13.7	55.7
	05	258 23.7	25.0	309 13.6	14.9	8 15.8	13.7	55.7
	06	273 23.5	S20 25.5	323 47.5	15.0	S 8 29.5	13.6	55.7
	07	288 23.4	26.0	338 21.5	14.9	8 43.1	13.6	55.7
	08	303 23.2	26.5	352 55.4	14.9	8 56.7	13.5	55.6
S	09	318 23.0	. . 27.0	7 29.3	14.9	9 10.2	13.5	55.6
U	10	333 22.8	27.5	22 03.2	14.9	9 23.7	13.4	55.6
N	11	348 22.7	28.0	36 37.1	14.9	9 37.1	13.4	55.6
D	12	3 22.5	S20 28.6	51 11.0	14.8	S 9 50.5	13.3	55.6
A	13	18 22.3	29.1	65 44.8	14.8	10 03.8	13.3	55.5
Y	14	33 22.1	29.6	80 18.6	14.8	10 17.1	13.2	55.5
	15	48 21.9	. . 30.1	94 52.4	14.8	10 30.3	13.2	55.5
	16	63 21.8	30.6	109 26.2	14.7	10 43.5	13.2	55.5
	17	78 21.6	31.1	123 59.9	14.8	10 56.7	13.0	55.4
	18	93 21.4	S20 31.6	138 33.7	14.7	S11 09.7	13.0	55.4
	19	108 21.2	32.1	153 07.4	14.7	11 22.7	13.0	55.4
	20	123 21.0	32.6	167 41.1	14.6	11 35.7	12.9	55.4
	21	138 20.9	. . 33.1	182 14.7	14.6	11 48.6	12.9	55.4
	22	153 20.7	33.6	196 48.3	14.6	12 01.5	12.8	55.3
	23	168 20.5	34.1	211 21.9	14.6	12 14.3	12.7	55.3
	24 00	183 20.3	S20 34.6	225 55.5	14.6	S12 27.0	12.7	55.3
	01	198 20.1	35.1	240 29.1	14.5	12 39.7	12.6	55.3
	02	213 19.9	35.6	255 02.6	14.5	12 52.3	12.5	55.3
	03	228 19.8	. . 36.1	269 36.1	14.4	13 04.8	12.5	55.3
	04	243 19.6	36.6	284 09.5	14.4	13 17.3	12.4	55.2
	05	258 19.4	37.1	298 42.9	14.4	13 29.7	12.4	55.2
	06	273 19.2	S20 37.6	313 16.3	14.4	S13 42.1	12.3	55.2
	07	288 19.0	38.1	327 49.7	14.3	13 54.4	12.3	55.2
	08	303 18.8	38.6	342 23.0	14.2	14 06.7	12.1	55.2
M	09	318 18.6	. . 39.1	356 56.2	14.3	14 18.8	12.1	55.1
O	10	333 18.5	39.6	11 29.5	14.2	14 30.9	12.1	55.1
N	11	348 18.3	40.1	26 02.7	14.2	14 43.0	11.9	55.1
D	12	3 18.1	S20 40.6	40 35.9	14.1	S14 54.9	11.9	55.1
A	13	18 17.9	41.1	55 09.0	14.1	15 06.8	11.9	55.1
Y	14	33 17.7	41.6	69 42.1	14.1	15 18.7	11.7	55.0
	15	48 17.5	. . 42.1	84 15.2	14.0	15 30.4	11.7	55.0
	16	63 17.3	42.6	98 48.2	13.9	15 42.1	11.6	55.0
	17	78 17.1	43.1	113 21.1	14.0	15 53.7	11.5	55.0
	18	93 17.0	S20 43.6	127 54.1	13.9	S16 05.2	11.5	55.0
	19	108 16.8	44.1	142 27.0	13.8	16 16.7	11.4	55.0
	20	123 16.6	44.6	156 59.8	13.8	16 28.1	11.3	54.9
	21	138 16.4	. . 45.1	171 32.6	13.8	16 39.4	11.3	54.9
	22	153 16.2	45.5	186 05.4	13.7	16 50.7	11.1	54.9
	23	168 16.0	46.0	200 38.1	13.7	17 01.8	11.1	54.9
	25 00	183 15.8	S20 46.5	215 10.8	13.6	S17 12.9	11.0	54.9
	01	198 15.6	47.0	229 43.4	13.6	17 23.9	10.9	54.9
	02	213 15.4	47.5	244 16.0	13.6	17 34.8	10.9	54.8
	03	228 15.2	. . 48.0	258 48.6	13.5	17 45.7	10.7	54.8
	04	243 15.1	48.5	273 21.1	13.4	17 56.4	10.7	54.8
	05	258 14.9	48.9	287 53.5	13.4	18 07.1	10.6	54.8
	06	273 14.7	S20 49.4	302 25.9	13.4	S18 17.7	10.5	54.8
	07	288 14.5	49.9	316 58.3	13.3	18 28.2	10.5	54.8
T	08	303 14.3	50.4	331 30.6	13.2	18 38.7	10.3	54.8
U	09	318 14.1	. . 50.9	346 02.8	13.3	18 49.0	10.2	54.7
E	10	333 13.9	51.4	0 35.1	13.1	18 59.2	10.2	54.7
S	11	348 13.7	51.8	15 07.2	13.1	19 09.4	10.1	54.7
D	12	3 13.5	S20 52.3	29 39.3	13.1	S19 19.5	10.0	54.7
A	13	18 13.3	52.8	44 11.4	13.0	19 29.5	9.9	54.7
Y	14	33 13.1	53.3	58 43.4	13.0	19 39.4	9.8	54.7
	15	48 12.9	. . 53.8	73 15.4	12.9	19 49.2	9.7	54.7
	16	63 12.7	54.2	87 47.3	12.9	19 58.9	9.7	54.6
	17	78 12.5	54.7	102 19.2	12.8	20 08.6	9.5	54.6
	18	93 12.3	S20 55.2	116 51.0	12.8	S20 18.1	9.4	54.6
	19	108 12.1	55.7	131 22.8	12.7	20 27.5	9.4	54.6
	20	123 11.9	56.1	145 54.5	12.7	20 36.9	9.2	54.6
	21	138 11.7	. . 56.6	160 26.2	12.7	20 46.1	9.2	54.6
	22	153 11.5	57.1	174 57.9	12.5	20 55.3	9.1	54.6
	23	168 11.3	57.5	189 29.4	12.6	S21 04.4	8.9	54.5
		SD 16.2	*d* 0.5	SD 15.1		15.0		14.9

Lat.	Twilight Naut.	Twilight Civil	Sunrise	Moonrise 23	Moonrise 24	Moonrise 25	Moonrise 26
°	h m	h m	h m	h m	h m	h m	h m
N 72	07 31	09 19	▬	04 07	06 26	▬	▬
N 70	07 17	08 47	11 16	03 54	05 57	08 33	▬
68	07 06	08 24	09 59	03 43	05 35	07 41	▬
66	06 56	08 06	09 23	03 35	05 18	07 09	09 20
64	06 48	07 51	08 57	03 28	05 04	06 45	08 33
62	06 41	07 39	08 37	03 22	04 53	06 27	08 04
60	06 35	07 28	08 20	03 16	04 43	06 12	07 41
N 58	06 29	07 19	08 07	03 12	04 35	05 59	07 23
56	06 24	07 11	07 55	03 08	04 28	05 48	07 08
54	06 19	07 03	07 45	03 04	04 21	05 38	06 55
52	06 15	06 57	07 35	03 01	04 15	05 30	06 43
50	06 10	06 51	07 27	02 58	04 10	05 22	06 33
45	06 01	06 37	07 10	02 51	03 59	05 06	06 12
N 40	05 53	06 26	06 56	02 46	03 49	04 52	05 55
35	05 45	06 16	06 43	02 41	03 41	04 41	05 41
30	05 38	06 07	06 33	02 37	03 34	04 31	05 29
20	05 24	05 51	06 14	02 31	03 22	04 15	05 08
N 10	05 10	05 36	05 58	02 24	03 12	04 00	04 50
0	04 55	05 21	05 43	02 19	03 02	03 47	04 33
S 10	04 39	05 05	05 28	02 13	02 52	03 33	04 16
20	04 19	04 47	05 11	02 07	02 42	03 19	03 58
30	03 54	04 26	04 52	02 01	02 31	03 03	03 38
35	03 37	04 12	04 41	01 57	02 24	02 53	03 26
40	03 18	03 57	04 28	01 53	02 16	02 43	03 13
45	02 52	03 38	04 13	01 48	02 08	02 30	02 57
S 50	02 17	03 13	03 54	01 42	01 57	02 15	02 37
52	01 57	03 01	03 45	01 39	01 52	02 08	02 28
54	01 33	02 47	03 35	01 36	01 47	02 00	02 17
56	00 56	02 30	03 23	01 33	01 41	01 52	02 06
58	////	02 09	03 10	01 29	01 35	01 42	01 52
S 60	////	01 43	02 55	01 25	01 27	01 31	01 36

Lat.	Sunset	Twilight Civil	Twilight Naut.	Moonset 23	Moonset 24	Moonset 25	Moonset 26
°	h m	h m	h m	h m	h m	h m	h m
N 72	▬	14 14	16 01	12 24	11 36	▬	▬
N 70	12 17	14 45	16 15	12 39	12 07	11 04	▬
68	13 34	15 09	16 27	12 52	12 31	11 58	▬
66	14 10	15 27	16 36	13 02	12 49	12 31	11 58
64	14 36	15 41	16 45	13 11	13 04	12 56	12 45
62	14 56	15 54	16 52	13 18	13 16	13 15	13 15
60	15 13	16 05	16 58	13 25	13 27	13 31	13 39
N 58	15 26	16 14	17 04	13 30	13 36	13 45	13 57
56	15 38	16 22	17 09	13 35	13 44	13 56	14 13
54	15 48	16 30	17 14	13 40	13 52	14 07	14 26
52	15 58	16 36	17 19	13 44	13 58	14 16	14 38
50	16 06	16 43	17 23	13 48	14 04	14 24	14 49
45	16 23	16 56	17 32	13 56	14 17	14 42	15 11
N 40	16 38	17 07	17 41	14 03	14 28	14 56	15 28
35	16 50	17 17	17 48	14 09	14 37	15 08	15 43
30	17 01	17 26	17 56	14 14	14 45	15 19	15 56
20	17 19	17 43	18 10	14 24	14 59	15 37	16 19
N 10	17 35	17 58	18 23	14 32	15 12	15 54	16 38
0	17 50	18 13	18 38	14 39	15 23	16 09	16 56
S 10	18 06	18 28	18 55	14 47	15 35	16 24	17 14
20	18 22	18 46	19 15	14 55	15 47	16 40	17 34
30	18 42	19 08	19 40	15 05	16 02	16 59	17 57
35	18 53	19 22	19 57	15 10	16 10	17 10	18 10
40	19 06	19 37	20 17	15 16	16 20	17 23	18 25
45	19 21	19 57	20 42	15 24	16 31	17 38	18 44
S 50	19 40	20 22	21 18	15 32	16 45	17 56	19 07
52	19 50	20 34	21 38	15 36	16 51	18 05	19 18
54	20 00	20 48	22 04	15 41	16 58	18 15	19 30
56	20 11	21 05	22 42	15 46	17 06	18 26	19 45
58	20 25	21 26	////	15 52	17 15	18 39	20 02
S 60	20 41	21 54	////	15 58	17 25	18 54	20 22

Day	SUN Eqn. of Time 00^h	SUN Eqn. of Time 12^h	SUN Mer. Pass.	MOON Mer. Pass. Upper	MOON Mer. Pass. Lower	MOON Age	MOON Phase
d	m s	m s	h m	h m	h m	d %	
23	13 39	13 30	11 46	08 29	20 51	26 16	
24	13 22	13 13	11 47	09 13	21 35	27 10	
25	13 04	12 54	11 47	09 58	22 21	28 5	

	UT	ARIES	VENUS −4.1		MARS +1.4		JUPITER −2.0		SATURN +1.1		STARS		
		GHA	GHA	Dec	GHA	Dec	GHA	Dec	GHA	Dec	Name	SHA	Dec
	d h	° ′	° ′	° ′	° ′	° ′	° ′	° ′	° ′	° ′		° ′	° ′
	26 00	65 17.8	137 43.6	S24 50.1	180 15.4	S21 49.8	132 20.1	S22 08.4	253 10.2	N 5 27.2	Acamar	315 20.4	S40 16.1
	01	80 20.2	152 42.8	49.7	195 16.0	50.2	147 22.1	08.3	268 12.5	27.2	Achernar	335 28.6	S57 11.6
	02	95 22.7	167 42.1	49.4	210 16.5	50.5	162 24.0	08.3	283 14.8	27.1	Acrux	173 13.8	S63 08.7
	03	110 25.1	182 41.3	. . 49.1	225 17.0	. . 50.8	177 26.0	. . 08.2	298 17.1	. . 27.1	Adhara	255 14.9	S28 58.9
	04	125 27.6	197 40.5	48.7	240 17.6	51.2	192 27.9	08.1	313 19.4	27.0	Aldebaran	290 53.0	N16 31.8
	05	140 30.1	212 39.7	48.4	255 18.1	51.5	207 29.8	08.0	328 21.7	27.0			
	06	155 32.5	227 39.0	S24 48.1	270 18.7	S21 51.8	222 31.8	S22 08.0	343 24.1	N 5 26.9	Alioth	166 23.8	N55 54.4
W	07	170 35.0	242 38.2	47.7	285 19.2	52.1	237 33.7	07.9	358 26.4	26.8	Alkaid	153 01.8	N49 15.9
E	08	185 37.5	257 37.4	47.4	300 19.8	52.5	252 35.7	07.8	13 28.7	26.8	Al Na'ir	27 47.9	S46 55.2
D	09	200 39.9	272 36.7	. . 47.1	315 20.3	. . 52.8	267 37.6	. . 07.7	28 31.0	. . 26.7	Alnilam	275 49.5	S 1 11.6
N	10	215 42.4	287 35.9	46.7	330 20.9	53.1	282 39.6	07.7	43 33.3	26.7	Alphard	217 59.4	S 8 41.7
E	11	230 44.9	302 35.1	46.4	345 21.4	53.4	297 41.5	07.6	58 35.6	26.6			
S	12	245 47.3	317 34.3	S24 46.0	0 22.0	S21 53.7	312 43.5	S22 07.5	73 38.0	N 5 26.6	Alphecca	126 14.2	N26 41.0
D	13	260 49.8	332 33.6	45.7	15 22.5	54.1	327 45.4	07.4	88 40.3	26.5	Alpheratz	357 47.0	N29 08.7
A	14	275 52.2	347 32.8	45.3	30 23.1	54.4	342 47.3	07.4	103 42.6	26.5	Altair	62 11.8	N 8 53.6
Y	15	290 54.7	2 32.0	. . 45.0	45 23.6	. . 54.7	357 49.3	. . 07.3	118 44.9	. . 26.4	Ankaa	353 18.7	S42 15.5
	16	305 57.2	17 31.3	44.6	60 24.1	55.0	12 51.2	07.2	133 47.2	26.4	Antares	112 30.9	S26 27.1
	17	320 59.6	32 30.5	44.3	75 24.7	55.4	27 53.2	07.2	148 49.6	26.3			
	18	336 02.1	47 29.7	S24 43.9	90 25.2	S21 55.7	42 55.1	S22 07.1	163 51.9	N 5 26.3	Arcturus	145 59.1	N19 08.1
	19	351 04.6	62 29.0	43.6	105 25.8	56.0	57 57.1	07.0	178 54.2	26.2	Atria	107 36.5	S69 02.7
	20	6 07.0	77 28.2	43.2	120 26.3	56.3	72 59.0	06.9	193 56.5	26.2	Avior	234 19.2	S59 32.0
	21	21 09.5	92 27.4	. . 42.9	135 26.9	. . 56.6	88 00.9	. . 06.9	208 58.8	. . 26.1	Bellatrix	278 35.3	N 6 21.6
	22	36 12.0	107 26.7	42.5	150 27.4	57.0	103 02.9	06.8	224 01.2	26.1	Betelgeuse	271 04.7	N 7 24.6
	23	51 14.4	122 25.9	42.2	165 27.9	57.3	118 04.8	06.7	239 03.5	26.0			
	27 00	66 16.9	137 25.1	S24 41.8	180 28.5	S21 57.6	133 06.8	S22 06.6	254 05.8	N 5 26.0	Canopus	263 57.2	S52 41.8
	01	81 19.4	152 24.4	41.4	195 29.0	57.9	148 08.7	06.6	269 08.1	25.9	Capella	280 39.1	N46 00.5
	02	96 21.8	167 23.6	41.1	210 29.6	58.2	163 10.6	06.5	284 10.4	25.9	Deneb	49 34.1	N45 19.0
	03	111 24.3	182 22.9	. . 40.7	225 30.1	. . 58.6	178 12.6	. . 06.4	299 12.8	. . 25.8	Denebola	182 37.2	N14 31.2
	04	126 26.7	197 22.1	40.4	240 30.7	58.9	193 14.5	06.3	314 15.1	25.8	Diphda	348 59.1	S17 56.2
	05	141 29.2	212 21.3	40.0	255 31.2	59.2	208 16.5	06.3	329 17.4	25.7			
	06	156 31.7	227 20.6	S24 39.6	270 31.7	S21 59.5	223 18.4	S22 06.2	344 19.7	N 5 25.7	Dubhe	193 55.7	N61 41.9
	07	171 34.1	242 19.8	39.3	285 32.3	21 59.8	238 20.3	06.1	359 22.0	25.6	Elnath	278 16.6	N28 37.0
T	08	186 36.6	257 19.0	38.9	300 32.8	22 00.1	253 22.3	06.0	14 24.4	25.6	Eltanin	90 48.2	N51 29.3
H	09	201 39.1	272 18.3	. . 38.5	315 33.4	. . 00.5	268 24.2	. . 06.0	29 26.7	. . 25.5	Enif	33 50.6	N 9 55.1
U	10	216 41.5	287 17.5	38.2	330 33.9	00.8	283 26.2	05.9	44 29.0	25.5	Fomalhaut	15 27.6	S29 34.6
R	11	231 44.0	302 16.8	37.8	345 34.4	01.1	298 28.1	05.8	59 31.3	25.4			
S	12	246 46.5	317 16.0	S24 37.4	0 35.0	S22 01.4	313 30.0	S22 05.7	74 33.6	N 5 25.4	Gacrux	172 05.3	S57 09.6
D	13	261 48.9	332 15.3	37.0	15 35.5	01.7	328 32.0	05.7	89 36.0	25.3	Gienah	175 56.0	S17 35.4
A	14	276 51.4	347 14.5	36.7	30 36.1	02.0	343 33.9	05.6	104 38.3	25.3	Hadar	148 53.6	S60 24.8
Y	15	291 53.9	2 13.7	. . 36.3	45 36.6	. . 02.3	358 35.9	. . 05.5	119 40.6	. . 25.2	Hamal	328 04.4	N23 30.5
	16	306 56.3	17 13.0	35.9	60 37.1	02.7	13 37.8	05.4	134 42.9	25.2	Kaus Aust.	83 48.7	S34 22.9
	17	321 58.8	32 12.2	35.5	75 37.7	03.0	28 39.7	05.4	149 45.3	25.1			
	18	337 01.2	47 11.5	S24 35.2	90 38.2	S22 03.3	43 41.7	S22 05.3	164 47.6	N 5 25.1	Kochab	137 20.6	N74 06.9
	19	352 03.7	62 10.7	34.8	105 38.7	03.6	58 43.6	05.2	179 49.9	25.0	Markab	13 41.7	N15 15.4
	20	7 06.2	77 10.0	34.4	120 39.3	03.9	73 45.6	05.1	194 52.2	25.0	Menkar	314 18.3	N 4 07.6
	21	22 08.6	92 09.2	. . 34.0	135 39.8	. . 04.2	88 47.5	. . 05.1	209 54.5	. . 24.9	Menkent	148 12.1	S36 24.8
	22	37 11.1	107 08.4	33.6	150 40.4	04.5	103 49.4	05.0	224 56.9	24.9	Miaplacidus	221 40.4	S69 44.9
	23	52 13.6	122 07.7	33.2	165 40.9	04.8	118 51.4	04.9	239 59.2	24.8			
	28 00	67 16.0	137 06.9	S24 32.8	180 41.4	S22 05.2	133 53.3	S22 04.8	255 01.5	N 5 24.8	Mirfak	308 44.9	N49 53.8
	01	82 18.5	152 06.2	32.5	195 42.0	05.5	148 55.2	04.8	270 03.8	24.7	Nunki	76 02.8	S26 17.2
	02	97 21.0	167 05.4	32.1	210 42.5	05.8	163 57.2	04.7	285 06.2	24.7	Peacock	53 24.8	S56 42.6
	03	112 23.4	182 04.7	. . 31.7	225 43.0	. . 06.1	178 59.1	. . 04.6	300 08.5	. . 24.6	Pollux	243 31.6	N28 00.2
	04	127 25.9	197 03.9	31.3	240 43.6	06.4	194 01.1	04.5	315 10.8	24.6	Procyon	245 03.1	N 5 12.2
	05	142 28.4	212 03.2	30.9	255 44.1	06.7	209 03.0	04.4	330 13.1	24.6			
	06	157 30.8	227 02.4	S24 30.5	270 44.6	S22 07.0	224 04.9	S22 04.4	345 15.5	N 5 24.5	Rasalhague	96 10.0	N12 33.2
	07	172 33.3	242 01.7	30.1	285 45.2	07.3	239 06.9	04.3	0 17.8	24.5	Regulus	207 47.1	N11 55.4
	08	187 35.7	257 00.9	29.7	300 45.7	07.6	254 08.8	04.2	15 20.1	24.4	Rigel	281 15.0	S 8 11.3
F	09	202 38.2	272 00.2	. . 29.3	315 46.2	. . 07.9	269 10.7	. . 04.1	30 22.4	. . 24.4	Rigil Kent.	139 57.3	S60 52.2
R	10	217 40.7	286 59.4	28.9	330 46.8	08.2	284 12.7	04.1	45 24.8	24.3	Sabik	102 16.8	S15 44.2
I	11	232 43.1	301 58.7	28.5	345 47.3	08.6	299 14.6	04.0	60 27.1	24.3			
D	12	247 45.6	316 57.9	S24 28.1	0 47.8	S22 08.9	314 16.5	S22 03.9	75 29.4	N 5 24.2	Schedar	349 44.4	N56 35.5
A	13	262 48.1	331 57.2	27.7	15 48.4	09.2	329 18.5	03.8	90 31.7	24.2	Shaula	96 27.0	S37 06.7
Y	14	277 50.5	346 56.5	27.3	30 48.9	09.5	344 20.4	03.8	105 34.1	24.1	Sirius	258 36.4	S16 43.5
	15	292 53.0	1 55.7	. . 26.9	45 49.4	. . 09.8	359 22.4	. . 03.7	120 36.4	. . 24.1	Spica	158 35.1	S11 12.5
	16	307 55.5	16 55.0	26.5	60 50.0	10.1	14 24.3	03.6	135 38.7	24.0	Suhail	222 54.9	S43 27.9
	17	322 57.9	31 54.2	26.1	75 50.5	10.4	29 26.2	03.5	150 41.0	24.0			
	18	338 00.4	46 53.5	S24 25.7	90 51.0	S22 10.7	44 28.2	S22 03.5	165 43.4	N 5 23.9	Vega	80 41.7	N38 47.6
	19	353 02.9	61 52.7	25.3	105 51.6	11.0	59 30.1	03.4	180 45.7	23.9	Zuben'ubi	137 09.6	S16 04.7
	20	8 05.3	76 52.0	24.9	120 52.1	11.3	74 32.0	03.3	195 48.0	23.8		SHA	Mer. Pass.
	21	23 07.8	91 51.2	. . 24.4	135 52.6	. . 11.6	89 34.0	. . 03.2	210 50.3	. . 23.8		° ′	h m
	22	38 10.2	106 50.5	24.0	150 53.2	11.9	104 35.9	03.1	225 52.7	23.7	Venus	71 08.3	14 51
	23	53 12.7	121 49.8	23.6	165 53.7	12.2	119 37.8	03.1	240 55.0	23.7	Mars	114 11.6	11 58
		h m									Jupiter	66 49.9	15 06
	Mer. Pass.	19 31.7	v −0.8	d 0.4	v 0.5	d 0.3	v 1.9	d 0.1	v 2.3	d 0.0	Saturn	187 48.9	7 03

UT	SUN GHA	SUN Dec	MOON GHA	v	MOON Dec	d	HP
d h	° ′	° ′	° ′	′	° ′	′	′
26 00	183 11.1	S20 58.0	204 01.0	12.4	S21 13.3	8.9	54.5
01	198 10.9	58.5	218 32.4	12.5	21 22.2	8.7	54.5
02	213 10.7	59.0	233 03.9	12.4	21 30.9	8.7	54.5
03	228 10.5	. . 59.4	247 35.3	12.3	21 39.6	8.6	54.5
04	243 10.3	20 59.9	262 06.6	12.3	21 48.2	8.4	54.5
05	258 10.1	21 00.4	276 37.9	12.2	21 56.6	8.4	54.5
06	273 09.9	S21 00.8	291 09.1	12.2	S22 05.0	8.3	54.5
W 07	288 09.7	01.3	305 40.3	12.1	22 13.3	8.1	54.4
E 08	303 09.5	01.8	320 11.4	12.1	22 21.4	8.1	54.4
D 09	318 09.3	. . 02.2	334 42.5	12.0	22 29.5	7.9	54.4
N 10	333 09.1	02.7	349 13.5	12.0	22 37.4	7.9	54.4
E 11	348 08.9	03.2	3 44.5	12.0	22 45.3	7.7	54.4
S 12	3 08.7	S21 03.6	18 15.5	11.9	S22 53.0	7.6	54.4
D 13	18 08.5	04.1	32 46.4	11.8	23 00.6	7.6	54.4
A 14	33 08.3	04.5	47 17.2	11.8	23 08.2	7.4	54.4
Y 15	48 08.1	. . 05.0	61 48.0	11.7	23 15.6	7.3	54.4
16	63 07.9	05.5	76 18.7	11.7	23 22.9	7.2	54.3
17	78 07.7	05.9	90 49.4	11.7	23 30.1	7.1	54.3
18	93 07.5	S21 06.4	105 20.1	11.6	S23 37.2	6.9	54.3
19	108 07.3	06.8	119 50.7	11.6	23 44.1	6.9	54.3
20	123 07.1	07.3	134 21.3	11.5	23 51.0	6.7	54.3
21	138 06.9	. . 07.8	148 51.8	11.5	23 57.7	6.7	54.3
22	153 06.7	08.2	163 22.3	11.4	24 04.4	6.5	54.3
23	168 06.5	08.7	177 52.7	11.4	24 10.9	6.4	54.3
27 00	183 06.3	S21 09.1	192 23.1	11.3	S24 17.3	6.3	54.3
01	198 06.1	09.6	206 53.4	11.3	24 23.6	6.2	54.3
02	213 05.9	10.0	221 23.7	11.3	24 29.8	6.0	54.2
03	228 05.7	. . 10.5	235 54.0	11.2	24 35.8	6.0	54.2
04	243 05.5	10.9	250 24.2	11.2	24 41.8	5.8	54.2
05	258 05.3	11.4	264 54.4	11.1	24 47.6	5.7	54.2
06	273 05.0	S21 11.8	279 24.5	11.1	S24 53.3	5.6	54.2
07	288 04.8	12.3	293 54.6	11.1	24 58.9	5.5	54.2
T 08	303 04.6	12.7	308 24.7	11.0	25 04.4	5.3	54.2
H 09	318 04.4	. . 13.2	322 54.7	11.0	25 09.7	5.3	54.2
U 10	333 04.2	13.6	337 24.7	10.9	25 15.0	5.1	54.2
R 11	348 04.0	14.1	351 54.6	10.9	25 20.1	5.0	54.2
S 12	3 03.8	S21 14.5	6 24.5	10.9	S25 25.1	4.8	54.2
D 13	18 03.6	15.0	20 54.4	10.8	25 29.9	4.8	54.2
A 14	33 03.4	15.4	35 24.2	10.9	25 34.7	4.6	54.1
Y 15	48 03.2	. . 15.9	49 54.1	10.7	25 39.3	4.5	54.1
16	63 02.9	16.3	64 23.8	10.8	25 43.8	4.4	54.1
17	78 02.7	16.7	78 53.6	10.7	25 48.2	4.3	54.1
18	93 02.5	S21 17.2	93 23.3	10.7	S25 52.5	4.1	54.1
19	108 02.3	17.6	107 53.0	10.6	25 56.6	4.0	54.1
20	123 02.1	18.1	122 22.6	10.6	26 00.6	3.9	54.1
21	138 01.9	. . 18.5	136 52.2	10.6	26 04.5	3.7	54.1
22	153 01.7	18.9	151 21.8	10.6	26 08.2	3.7	54.1
23	168 01.5	19.4	165 51.4	10.5	26 11.9	3.5	54.1
28 00	183 01.2	S21 19.8	180 20.9	10.6	S26 15.4	3.3	54.1
01	198 01.0	20.3	194 50.5	10.5	26 18.7	3.3	54.1
02	213 00.8	20.7	209 20.0	10.4	26 22.0	3.1	54.1
03	228 00.6	. . 21.1	223 49.4	10.5	26 25.1	3.0	54.1
04	243 00.4	21.6	238 18.9	10.4	26 28.1	2.9	54.1
05	258 00.2	22.0	252 48.3	10.4	26 31.0	2.7	54.0
06	273 00.0	S21 22.4	267 17.7	10.4	S26 33.7	2.6	54.0
07	287 59.7	22.9	281 47.1	10.4	26 36.3	2.5	54.0
08	302 59.5	23.3	296 16.5	10.4	26 38.8	2.4	54.0
F 09	317 59.3	. . 23.7	310 45.9	10.3	26 41.2	2.2	54.0
R 10	332 59.1	24.2	325 15.2	10.3	26 43.4	2.1	54.0
I 11	347 58.9	24.6	339 44.5	10.3	26 45.5	2.0	54.0
D 12	2 58.7	S21 25.0	354 13.8	10.3	S26 47.5	1.8	54.0
A 13	17 58.4	25.5	8 43.1	10.3	26 49.3	1.7	54.0
Y 14	32 58.2	25.9	23 12.4	10.3	26 51.0	1.6	54.0
15	47 58.0	. . 26.3	37 41.7	10.3	26 52.6	1.5	54.0
16	62 57.8	26.7	52 11.0	10.3	26 54.1	1.3	54.0
17	77 57.6	27.2	66 40.3	10.2	26 55.4	1.2	54.0
18	92 57.3	S21 27.6	81 09.5	10.3	S26 56.6	1.0	54.0
19	107 57.1	28.0	95 38.8	10.2	26 57.6	1.0	54.0
20	122 56.9	28.4	110 08.0	10.3	26 58.6	0.8	54.0
21	137 56.7	. . 28.9	124 37.3	10.2	26 59.4	0.6	54.0
22	152 56.5	29.3	139 06.5	10.3	27 00.0	0.6	54.0
23	167 56.2	29.7	153 35.8	10.2	S27 00.6	0.4	54.0
	SD 16.2	d 0.4	SD 14.8		14.8		14.7

Lat.	Twilight Naut.	Twilight Civil	Sunrise	Moonrise 26	Moonrise 27	Moonrise 28	Moonrise 29
°	h m	h m	h m	h m	h m	h m	h m
N 72	07 41	09 33	▬	▬	▬	▬	▬
N 70	07 26	08 58	▬	▬	▬	▬	▬
68	07 13	08 33	10 15	▬	▬	▬	▬
66	07 03	08 14	09 34	09 20	▬	▬	▬
64	06 54	07 58	09 06	08 33	10 39	▬	▬
62	06 47	07 45	08 44	08 04	09 41	11 10	12 07
60	06 40	07 34	08 27	07 41	09 08	10 24	11 19
N 58	06 34	07 24	08 13	07 23	08 44	09 55	10 49
56	06 28	07 16	08 00	07 08	08 24	09 32	10 26
54	06 23	07 08	07 50	06 55	08 08	09 14	10 07
52	06 19	07 01	07 40	06 43	07 54	08 58	09 51
50	06 14	06 55	07 32	06 33	07 42	08 44	09 37
45	06 04	06 41	07 14	06 12	07 17	08 17	09 09
N 40	05 56	06 29	06 59	05 55	06 57	07 55	08 47
35	05 47	06 19	06 46	05 41	06 40	07 37	08 29
30	05 40	06 09	06 35	05 29	06 26	07 21	08 13
20	05 26	05 53	06 16	05 08	06 02	06 55	07 47
N 10	05 11	05 37	06 00	04 50	05 41	06 33	07 24
0	04 56	05 22	05 44	04 33	05 21	06 12	07 02
S 10	04 39	05 06	05 28	04 16	05 02	05 51	06 41
20	04 19	04 47	05 11	03 58	04 42	05 28	06 18
30	03 53	04 25	04 52	03 38	04 18	05 02	05 52
35	03 36	04 11	04 40	03 26	04 04	04 47	05 36
40	03 15	03 55	04 27	03 13	03 48	04 29	05 18
45	02 49	03 35	04 11	02 57	03 29	04 08	04 56
S 50	02 12	03 10	03 51	02 37	03 05	03 41	04 28
52	01 51	02 57	03 42	02 28	02 54	03 28	04 14
54	01 24	02 42	03 31	02 17	02 41	03 13	03 58
56	00 41	02 25	03 19	02 06	02 26	02 56	03 40
58	////	02 03	03 06	01 52	02 08	02 35	03 17
S 60	////	01 34	02 49	01 36	01 47	02 08	02 47

Lat.	Sunset	Twilight Civil	Twilight Naut.	Moonset 26	Moonset 27	Moonset 28	Moonset 29
°	h m	h m	h m	h m	h m	h m	h m
N 72	▬	14 02	15 54	▬	▬	▬	▬
N 70	▬	14 36	16 09	▬	▬	▬	▬
68	13 19	15 01	16 21	▬	▬	▬	▬
66	14 01	15 21	16 32	11 58	▬	▬	▬
64	14 29	15 36	16 41	12 45	12 21	▬	▬
62	14 51	15 50	16 48	13 15	13 19	13 35	14 25
60	15 08	16 01	16 55	13 39	13 53	14 21	15 12
N 58	15 22	16 11	17 01	13 57	14 18	14 51	15 42
56	15 35	16 19	17 07	14 13	14 37	15 14	16 05
54	15 45	16 27	17 12	14 26	14 54	15 32	16 24
52	15 55	16 34	17 17	14 38	15 08	15 48	16 40
50	16 03	16 40	17 21	14 49	15 20	16 02	16 53
45	16 22	16 54	17 31	15 11	15 46	16 30	17 21
N 40	16 36	17 06	17 40	15 28	16 07	16 52	17 43
35	16 49	17 17	17 48	15 43	16 24	17 10	18 01
30	17 00	17 26	17 55	15 56	16 38	17 25	18 17
20	17 19	17 43	18 10	16 19	17 04	17 52	18 43
N 10	17 36	17 58	18 24	16 38	17 25	18 15	19 06
0	17 51	18 14	18 39	16 56	17 46	18 36	19 27
S 10	18 07	18 30	18 57	17 14	18 06	18 57	19 48
20	18 24	18 48	19 17	17 34	18 28	19 20	20 11
30	18 44	19 11	19 43	17 57	18 53	19 47	20 37
35	18 56	19 25	20 00	18 10	19 08	20 03	20 52
40	19 09	19 41	20 21	18 25	19 25	20 21	21 10
45	19 25	20 01	20 47	18 44	19 46	20 43	21 31
S 50	19 45	20 27	21 25	19 07	20 12	21 11	21 59
52	19 54	20 40	21 46	19 18	20 25	21 24	22 12
54	20 05	20 55	22 14	19 30	20 40	21 40	22 27
56	20 17	21 13	23 00	19 45	20 57	21 59	22 45
58	20 31	21 35	////	20 02	21 18	22 22	23 06
S 60	20 48	22 05	////	20 22	21 45	22 52	23 34

Day	SUN Eqn. of Time 00^h	SUN Eqn. of Time 12^h	SUN Mer. Pass.	MOON Mer. Pass. Upper	MOON Mer. Pass. Lower	Age	Phase
d	m s	m s	h m	h m	h m	d %	
26	12 45	12 35	11 47	10 45	23 09	29 2	●
27	12 26	12 16	11 48	11 33	23 59	30 0	
28	12 05	11 55	11 48	12 24	24 49	01 1	

UT	ARIES	VENUS −4.2		MARS +1.4		JUPITER −2.0		SATURN +1.1	
d h	GHA ° ′	GHA ° ′	Dec ° ′	GHA ° ′	Dec ° ′	GHA ° ′	Dec ° ′	GHA ° ′	Dec ° ′
29 00	68 15.2	136 49.0	S24 23.2	180 54.2	S22 12.5	134 39.8	S22 03.0	255 57.3	N 5 23.6
01	83 17.6	151 48.3	22.8	195 54.8	12.8	149 41.7	02.9	270 59.7	23.6
02	98 20.1	166 47.5	22.4	210 55.3	13.1	164 43.6	02.8	286 02.0	23.5
03	113 22.6	181 46.8	. . 22.0	225 55.8	. . 13.4	179 45.6	. . 02.8	301 04.3	. . 23.5
04	128 25.0	196 46.1	21.5	240 56.4	13.7	194 47.5	02.7	316 06.6	23.5
05	143 27.5	211 45.3	21.1	255 56.9	14.0	209 49.4	02.6	331 09.0	23.4
06	158 30.0	226 44.6	S24 20.7	270 57.4	S22 14.3	224 51.4	S22 02.5	346 11.3	N 5 23.4
07	173 32.4	241 43.9	20.3	285 57.9	14.6	239 53.3	02.5	1 13.6	23.3
S 08	188 34.9	256 43.1	19.8	300 58.5	14.9	254 55.2	02.4	16 15.9	23.3
A 09	203 37.3	271 42.4	. . 19.4	315 59.0	. . 15.2	269 57.2	. . 02.3	31 18.3	. . 23.2
T 10	218 39.8	286 41.6	19.0	330 59.5	15.5	284 59.1	02.2	46 20.6	23.2
U 11	233 42.3	301 40.9	18.6	346 00.1	15.8	300 01.0	02.1	61 22.9	23.1
R 12	248 44.7	316 40.2	S24 18.1	1 00.6	S22 16.1	315 03.0	S22 02.1	76 25.3	N 5 23.1
D 13	263 47.2	331 39.4	17.7	16 01.1	16.4	330 04.9	02.0	91 27.6	23.0
A 14	278 49.7	346 38.7	17.3	31 01.6	16.7	345 06.8	01.9	106 29.9	23.0
Y 15	293 52.1	1 38.0	. . 16.8	46 02.2	. . 17.0	0 08.8	. . 01.8	121 32.3	. . 22.9
16	308 54.6	16 37.2	16.4	61 02.7	17.3	15 10.7	01.8	136 34.6	22.9
17	323 57.1	31 36.5	16.0	76 03.2	17.6	30 12.6	01.7	151 36.9	22.9
18	338 59.5	46 35.8	S24 15.5	91 03.8	S22 17.9	45 14.6	S22 01.6	166 39.2	N 5 22.8
19	354 02.0	61 35.1	15.1	106 04.3	18.2	60 16.5	01.5	181 41.6	22.8
20	9 04.5	76 34.3	14.6	121 04.8	18.5	75 18.4	01.4	196 43.9	22.7
21	24 06.9	91 33.6	. . 14.2	136 05.3	. . 18.8	90 20.4	. . 01.4	211 46.2	. . 22.7
22	39 09.4	106 32.9	13.8	151 05.9	19.1	105 22.3	01.3	226 48.6	22.6
23	54 11.8	121 32.1	13.3	166 06.4	19.4	120 24.2	01.2	241 50.9	22.6
30 00	69 14.3	136 31.4	S24 12.9	181 06.9	S22 19.6	135 26.2	S22 01.1	256 53.2	N 5 22.5
01	84 16.8	151 30.7	12.4	196 07.4	19.9	150 28.1	01.1	271 55.6	22.5
02	99 19.2	166 30.0	12.0	211 08.0	20.2	165 30.0	01.0	286 57.9	22.4
03	114 21.7	181 29.2	. . 11.5	226 08.5	. . 20.5	180 31.9	. . 00.9	302 00.2	. . 22.4
04	129 24.2	196 28.5	11.1	241 09.0	20.8	195 33.9	00.8	317 02.5	22.3
05	144 26.6	211 27.8	10.6	256 09.5	21.1	210 35.8	00.7	332 04.9	22.3
06	159 29.1	226 27.0	S24 10.2	271 10.1	S22 21.4	225 37.7	S22 00.7	347 07.2	N 5 22.3
07	174 31.6	241 26.3	09.7	286 10.6	21.7	240 39.7	00.6	2 09.5	22.2
08	189 34.0	256 25.6	09.3	301 11.1	22.0	255 41.6	00.5	17 11.9	22.2
S 09	204 36.5	271 24.9	. . 08.8	316 11.6	. . 22.3	270 43.5	. . 00.4	32 14.2	. . 22.1
U 10	219 39.0	286 24.2	08.4	331 12.1	22.6	285 45.5	00.4	47 16.5	22.1
N 11	234 41.4	301 23.4	07.9	346 12.7	22.8	300 47.4	00.3	62 18.9	22.0
D 12	249 43.9	316 22.7	S24 07.5	1 13.2	S22 23.1	315 49.3	S22 00.2	77 21.2	N 5 22.0
A 13	264 46.3	331 22.0	07.0	16 13.7	23.4	330 51.2	00.1	92 23.5	21.9
Y 14	279 48.8	346 21.3	06.6	31 14.2	23.7	345 53.2	00.0	107 25.9	21.9
15	294 51.3	1 20.6	. . 06.1	46 14.8	. . 24.0	0 55.1	22 00.0	122 28.2	. . 21.9
16	309 53.7	16 19.8	05.6	61 15.3	24.3	15 57.0	21 59.9	137 30.5	21.8
17	324 56.2	31 19.1	05.2	76 15.8	24.6	30 59.0	59.8	152 32.9	21.8
18	339 58.7	46 18.4	S24 04.7	91 16.3	S22 24.9	46 00.9	S21 59.7	167 35.2	N 5 21.7
19	355 01.1	61 17.7	04.2	106 16.8	25.1	61 02.8	59.6	182 37.5	21.7
20	10 03.6	76 17.0	03.8	121 17.4	25.4	76 04.7	59.6	197 39.9	21.6
21	25 06.1	91 16.2	. . 03.3	136 17.9	. . 25.7	91 06.7	. . 59.5	212 42.2	. . 21.6
22	40 08.5	106 15.5	02.8	151 18.4	26.0	106 08.6	59.4	227 44.5	21.5
23	55 11.0	121 14.8	02.4	166 18.9	26.3	121 10.5	59.3	242 46.9	21.5
1 00	70 13.5	136 14.1	S24 01.9	181 19.4	S22 26.6	136 12.5	S21 59.2	257 49.2	N 5 21.5
01	85 15.9	151 13.4	01.4	196 20.0	26.9	151 14.4	59.2	272 51.5	21.4
02	100 18.4	166 12.7	00.9	211 20.5	27.1	166 16.3	59.1	287 53.9	21.4
03	115 20.8	181 12.0	. . 00.5	226 21.0	. . 27.4	181 18.2	. . 59.0	302 56.2	. . 21.3
04	130 23.3	196 11.2	24 00.0	241 21.5	27.7	196 20.2	58.9	317 58.5	21.3
05	145 25.8	211 10.5	23 59.5	256 22.0	28.0	211 22.1	58.8	333 00.9	21.2
06	160 28.2	226 09.8	S23 59.0	271 22.6	S22 28.3	226 24.0	S21 58.8	348 03.2	N 5 21.2
07	175 30.7	241 09.1	58.6	286 23.1	28.6	241 25.9	58.7	3 05.6	21.2
08	190 33.2	256 08.4	58.1	301 23.6	28.8	256 27.9	58.6	18 07.9	21.1
M 09	205 35.6	271 07.7	. . 57.6	316 24.1	. . 29.1	271 29.8	. . 58.5	33 10.2	. . 21.1
O 10	220 38.1	286 07.0	57.1	331 24.6	29.4	286 31.7	58.5	48 12.6	21.0
N 11	235 40.6	301 06.3	56.6	346 25.1	29.7	301 33.7	58.4	63 14.9	21.0
D 12	250 43.0	316 05.6	S23 56.1	1 25.7	S22 30.0	316 35.6	S21 58.3	78 17.2	N 5 20.9
A 13	265 45.5	331 04.9	55.7	16 26.2	30.2	331 37.5	58.2	93 19.6	20.9
Y 14	280 48.0	346 04.2	55.2	31 26.7	30.5	346 39.4	58.1	108 21.9	20.9
15	295 50.4	1 03.5	. . 54.7	46 27.2	. . 30.8	1 41.4	. . 58.1	123 24.2	. . 20.8
16	310 52.9	16 02.7	54.2	61 27.7	31.1	16 43.3	58.0	138 26.6	20.8
17	325 55.3	31 02.0	53.7	76 28.2	31.4	31 45.2	57.9	153 28.9	20.7
18	340 57.8	46 01.3	S23 53.2	91 28.8	S22 31.6	46 47.1	S21 57.8	168 31.3	N 5 20.7
19	356 00.3	61 00.6	52.7	106 29.3	31.9	61 49.1	57.7	183 33.6	20.6
20	11 02.7	75 59.9	52.2	121 29.8	32.2	76 51.0	57.6	198 35.9	20.6
21	26 05.2	90 59.2	. . 51.7	136 30.3	. . 32.5	91 52.9	. . 57.6	213 38.3	. . 20.6
22	41 07.7	105 58.5	51.2	151 30.8	32.7	106 54.8	57.5	228 40.6	20.5
23	56 10.1	120 57.8	50.7	166 31.3	33.0	121 56.8	57.4	243 42.9	20.5
Mer. Pass.	h m 19 19.9	v −0.7	d 0.5	v 0.5	d 0.3	v 1.9	d 0.1	v 2.3	d 0.0

STARS Name	SHA ° ′	Dec ° ′
Acamar	315 20.4	S40 16.1
Achernar	335 28.6	S57 11.6
Acrux	173 13.8	S63 08.7
Adhara	255 14.9	S28 58.9
Aldebaran	290 53.0	N16 31.8
Alioth	166 23.8	N55 54.4
Alkaid	153 01.8	N49 15.9
Al Na'ir	27 47.9	S46 55.2
Alnilam	275 49.5	S 1 11.7
Alphard	217 59.3	S 8 41.8
Alphecca	126 14.2	N26 41.0
Alpheratz	357 47.0	N29 08.7
Altair	62 11.8	N 8 53.6
Ankaa	353 18.7	S42 15.5
Antares	112 30.9	S26 27.1
Arcturus	145 59.1	N19 08.0
Atria	107 36.4	S69 02.7
Avior	234 19.2	S59 32.0
Bellatrix	278 35.3	N 6 21.6
Betelgeuse	271 04.7	N 7 24.6
Canopus	263 57.2	S52 41.8
Capella	280 39.0	N46 00.5
Deneb	49 34.2	N45 19.0
Denebola	182 37.2	N14 31.2
Diphda	348 59.1	S17 56.2
Dubhe	193 55.6	N61 41.8
Elnath	278 16.6	N28 37.0
Eltanin	90 48.2	N51 29.3
Enif	33 50.6	N 9 55.1
Fomalhaut	15 27.6	S29 34.6
Gacrux	172 05.3	S57 09.6
Gienah	175 56.0	S17 35.4
Hadar	148 53.5	S60 24.8
Hamal	328 04.4	N23 30.5
Kaus Aust.	83 48.7	S34 22.9
Kochab	137 20.5	N74 06.9
Markab	13 41.7	N15 15.4
Menkar	314 18.3	N 4 07.6
Menkent	148 12.0	S36 24.8
Miaplacidus	221 40.4	S69 44.9
Mirfak	308 44.9	N49 53.8
Nunki	76 02.8	S26 17.2
Peacock	53 24.8	S56 42.6
Pollux	243 31.6	N28 00.2
Procyon	245 03.0	N 5 12.2
Rasalhague	96 10.0	N12 33.2
Regulus	207 47.1	N11 55.4
Rigel	281 15.0	S 8 11.4
Rigil Kent.	139 57.2	S60 52.2
Sabik	102 16.8	S15 44.2
Schedar	349 44.4	N56 35.5
Shaula	96 27.0	S37 06.7
Sirius	258 36.4	S16 43.6
Spica	158 35.1	S11 12.5
Suhail	222 54.9	S43 27.9
Vega	80 41.7	N38 47.6
Zuben'ubi	137 09.5	S16 04.7

	SHA ° ′	Mer. Pass. h m
Venus	67 17.1	14 55
Mars	111 52.6	11 55
Jupiter	66 11.8	14 56
Saturn	187 38.9	6 51

	UT	SUN GHA	SUN Dec	MOON GHA	v	MOON Dec	d	HP
	d h	° ′	° ′	° ′	′	° ′	′	′
	29 00	182 56.0	S21 30.1	168 05.0	10.3	S27 01.0	0.2	54.0
	01	197 55.8	30.5	182 34.3	10.2	27 01.2	0.2	54.0
	02	212 55.6	31.0	197 03.5	10.2	27 01.4	0.0	54.0
	03	227 55.4	. . 31.4	211 32.8	10.2	27 01.4	0.1	54.0
	04	242 55.1	31.8	226 02.0	10.3	27 01.3	0.2	54.0
	05	257 54.9	32.2	240 31.3	10.3	27 01.1	0.4	54.0
	06	272 54.7	S21 32.6	255 00.6	10.2	S27 00.7	0.5	54.0
	07	287 54.5	33.1	269 29.8	10.3	27 00.2	0.7	54.0
S	08	302 54.3	33.5	283 59.1	10.3	26 59.5	0.7	54.0
A	09	317 54.0	. . 33.9	298 28.4	10.3	26 58.8	0.9	53.9
T	10	332 53.8	34.3	312 57.7	10.4	26 57.9	1.0	53.9
U	11	347 53.6	34.7	327 27.1	10.3	26 56.9	1.2	53.9
R	12	2 53.4	S21 35.1	341 56.4	10.3	S26 55.7	1.3	53.9
D	13	17 53.1	35.5	356 25.7	10.4	26 54.4	1.4	53.9
A	14	32 52.9	35.9	10 55.1	10.4	26 53.0	1.5	53.9
Y	15	47 52.7	. . 36.4	25 24.5	10.4	26 51.5	1.7	53.9
	16	62 52.5	36.8	39 53.9	10.4	26 49.8	1.8	53.9
	17	77 52.2	37.2	54 23.3	10.5	26 48.0	1.9	53.9
	18	92 52.0	S21 37.6	68 52.8	10.4	S26 46.1	2.1	53.9
	19	107 51.8	38.0	83 22.2	10.5	26 44.0	2.1	53.9
	20	122 51.6	38.4	97 51.7	10.5	26 41.9	2.3	53.9
	21	137 51.3	. . 38.8	112 21.2	10.6	26 39.6	2.5	53.9
	22	152 51.1	39.2	126 50.8	10.5	26 37.1	2.5	53.9
	23	167 50.9	39.6	141 20.3	10.6	26 34.6	2.7	53.9
	30 00	182 50.6	S21 40.0	155 49.9	10.6	S26 31.9	2.8	53.9
	01	197 50.4	40.4	170 19.5	10.6	26 29.1	3.0	54.0
	02	212 50.2	40.8	184 49.1	10.7	26 26.1	3.0	54.0
	03	227 50.0	. . 41.2	199 18.8	10.7	26 23.1	3.2	54.0
	04	242 49.7	41.6	213 48.5	10.7	26 19.9	3.3	54.0
	05	257 49.5	42.0	228 18.2	10.8	26 16.6	3.5	54.0
	06	272 49.3	S21 42.4	242 48.0	10.8	S26 13.1	3.5	54.0
	07	287 49.0	42.8	257 17.8	10.8	26 09.6	3.7	54.0
	08	302 48.8	43.2	271 47.6	10.9	26 05.9	3.8	54.0
S	09	317 48.6	. . 43.6	286 17.5	10.9	26 02.1	3.9	54.0
U	10	332 48.3	44.0	300 47.4	10.9	25 58.2	4.1	54.0
N	11	347 48.1	44.4	315 17.3	11.0	25 54.1	4.1	54.0
D	12	2 47.9	S21 44.8	329 47.3	11.0	S25 50.0	4.3	54.0
A	13	17 47.7	45.2	344 17.3	11.0	25 45.7	4.4	54.0
Y	14	32 47.4	45.6	358 47.3	11.1	25 41.3	4.6	54.0
	15	47 47.2	. . 46.0	13 17.4	11.1	25 36.7	4.6	54.0
	16	62 47.0	46.4	27 47.5	11.2	25 32.1	4.8	54.0
	17	77 46.7	46.8	42 17.7	11.2	25 27.3	4.9	54.0
	18	92 46.5	S21 47.2	56 47.9	11.2	S25 22.4	5.0	54.0
	19	107 46.3	47.6	71 18.1	11.3	25 17.4	5.1	54.0
	20	122 46.0	47.9	85 48.4	11.3	25 12.3	5.3	54.0
	21	137 45.8	. . 48.3	100 18.7	11.4	25 07.0	5.3	54.0
	22	152 45.6	48.7	114 49.1	11.4	25 01.7	5.5	54.0
	23	167 45.3	49.1	129 19.5	11.5	24 56.2	5.6	54.0
	1 00	182 45.1	S21 49.5	143 50.0	11.5	S24 50.6	5.7	54.0
	01	197 44.9	49.9	158 20.5	11.5	24 44.9	5.8	54.0
	02	212 44.6	50.3	172 51.0	11.6	24 39.1	5.9	54.0
	03	227 44.4	. . 50.7	187 21.6	11.7	24 33.2	6.1	54.1
	04	242 44.1	51.0	201 52.3	11.7	24 27.1	6.1	54.1
	05	257 43.9	51.4	216 23.0	11.7	24 21.0	6.3	54.1
	06	272 43.7	S21 51.8	230 53.7	11.8	S24 14.7	6.4	54.1
	07	287 43.4	52.2	245 24.5	11.8	24 08.3	6.4	54.1
	08	302 43.2	52.6	259 55.3	11.9	24 01.9	6.6	54.1
M	09	317 43.0	. . 52.9	274 26.2	11.9	23 55.3	6.7	54.1
O	10	332 42.7	53.3	288 57.1	12.0	23 48.6	6.9	54.1
N	11	347 42.5	53.7	303 28.1	12.0	23 41.7	6.9	54.1
D	12	2 42.3	S21 54.1	317 59.1	12.1	S23 34.8	7.0	54.1
A	13	17 42.0	54.5	332 30.2	12.1	23 27.8	7.1	54.1
Y	14	32 41.8	54.8	347 01.3	12.2	23 20.7	7.3	54.1
	15	47 41.5	. . 55.2	1 32.5	12.2	23 13.4	7.3	54.1
	16	62 41.3	55.6	16 03.7	12.2	23 06.1	7.5	54.2
	17	77 41.1	56.0	30 34.9	12.4	22 58.6	7.5	54.2
	18	92 40.8	S21 56.3	45 06.3	12.3	S22 51.1	7.7	54.2
	19	107 40.6	56.7	59 37.6	12.4	22 43.4	7.8	54.2
	20	122 40.3	57.1	74 09.0	12.5	22 35.6	7.8	54.2
	21	137 40.1	. . 57.4	88 40.5	12.5	22 27.8	8.0	54.2
	22	152 39.9	57.8	103 12.0	12.6	22 19.8	8.0	54.2
	23	167 39.6	58.2	117 43.6	12.6	S22 11.8	8.2	54.2
		SD 16.2	d 0.4	SD 14.7		14.7		14.7

Lat.	Twilight Naut.	Twilight Civil	Sunrise	Moonrise 29	Moonrise 30	Moonrise 1	Moonrise 2
°	h m	h m	h m	h m	h m	h m	h m
N 72	07 49	09 47	■	■	■	■	■
N 70	07 33	09 09	■	■	■	■	15 14
68	07 20	08 42	10 32	■	■	■	13 57
66	07 09	08 21	09 45	■	■	13 59	13 19
64	07 00	08 05	09 14	■	13 34	13 03	12 52
62	06 52	07 51	08 52	12 07	12 25	12 30	12 31
60	06 45	07 40	08 34	11 19	11 50	12 06	12 14
N 58	06 38	07 29	08 19	10 49	11 24	11 46	12 00
56	06 33	07 20	08 06	10 26	11 04	11 30	11 47
54	06 27	07 12	07 55	10 07	10 47	11 16	11 36
52	06 22	07 05	07 45	09 51	10 33	11 04	11 27
50	06 18	06 58	07 36	09 37	10 20	10 53	11 18
45	06 07	06 44	07 17	09 09	09 54	10 30	11 00
N 40	05 58	06 32	07 02	08 47	09 33	10 12	10 45
35	05 50	06 21	06 49	08 29	09 16	09 57	10 32
30	05 42	06 12	06 38	08 13	09 01	09 43	10 21
20	05 27	05 54	06 18	07 47	08 35	09 20	10 02
N 10	05 13	05 39	06 01	07 24	08 13	09 01	09 45
0	04 57	05 23	05 45	07 02	07 53	08 42	09 29
S 10	04 39	05 06	05 29	06 41	07 32	08 23	09 13
20	04 19	04 47	05 12	06 18	07 10	08 04	08 56
30	03 52	04 24	04 51	05 52	06 45	07 40	08 37
35	03 35	04 10	04 39	05 36	06 30	07 27	08 25
40	03 14	03 54	04 26	05 18	06 12	07 11	08 12
45	02 46	03 33	04 09	04 56	05 51	06 52	07 57
S 50	02 08	03 07	03 49	04 28	05 24	06 29	07 37
52	01 46	02 54	03 39	04 14	05 11	06 17	07 28
54	01 16	02 38	03 29	03 58	04 56	06 04	07 18
56	00 22	02 20	03 16	03 40	04 39	05 49	07 06
58	////	01 56	03 02	03 17	04 17	05 32	06 53
S 60	////	01 25	02 44	02 47	03 50	05 10	06 37

Lat.	Sunset	Twilight Civil	Twilight Naut.	Moonset 29	Moonset 30	Moonset 1	Moonset 2
°	h m	h m	h m	h m	h m	h m	h m
N 72	■	13 50	15 48	■	■	■	■
N 70	■	14 28	16 04	■	■	■	16 23
68	13 05	14 55	16 17	■	■	■	17 39
66	13 52	15 16	16 28	■	■	15 59	18 16
64	14 23	15 32	16 37	■	14 42	16 54	18 42
62	14 45	15 46	16 45	14 25	15 50	17 26	19 02
60	15 04	15 58	16 52	15 12	16 25	17 50	19 18
N 58	15 19	16 08	16 59	15 42	16 51	18 09	19 32
56	15 32	16 17	17 05	16 05	17 11	18 25	19 44
54	15 43	16 25	17 10	16 24	17 27	18 39	19 54
52	15 53	16 32	17 15	16 40	17 42	18 51	20 03
50	16 01	16 39	17 19	16 53	17 54	19 01	20 11
45	16 20	16 53	17 30	17 21	18 20	19 23	20 28
N 40	16 35	17 05	17 39	17 43	18 40	19 40	20 42
35	16 48	17 16	17 47	18 01	18 57	19 55	20 54
30	17 00	17 26	17 55	18 17	19 11	20 08	21 04
20	17 19	17 43	18 10	18 43	19 36	20 29	21 22
N 10	17 36	17 59	18 25	19 06	19 57	20 48	21 37
0	17 52	18 15	18 41	19 27	20 17	21 05	21 51
S 10	18 09	18 31	18 58	19 48	20 37	21 22	22 05
20	18 26	18 50	19 19	20 11	20 58	21 41	22 20
30	18 47	19 14	19 46	20 37	21 22	22 02	22 37
35	18 59	19 28	20 03	20 52	21 36	22 14	22 47
40	19 12	19 44	20 25	21 10	21 52	22 28	22 58
45	19 29	20 05	20 52	21 31	22 12	22 44	23 11
S 50	19 49	20 32	21 31	21 59	22 36	23 05	23 27
52	19 59	20 45	21 54	22 12	22 48	23 15	23 35
54	20 10	21 01	22 24	22 27	23 01	23 25	23 43
56	20 22	21 19	23 24	22 45	23 16	23 38	23 52
58	20 37	21 43	////	23 06	23 34	23 52	24 03
S 60	20 55	22 16	////	23 34	23 57	24 08	00 08

Day	SUN Eqn. of Time 00^h	SUN Eqn. of Time 12^h	SUN Mer. Pass.	MOON Mer. Pass. Upper	MOON Mer. Pass. Lower	MOON Age	MOON Phase
d	m s	m s	h m	h m	h m	d %	
29	11 45	11 34	11 48	13 15	00 49	02 3	
30	11 23	11 12	11 49	14 05	01 40	03 7	
1	11 01	10 49	11 49	14 54	02 30	04 12	

UT	ARIES	VENUS −4.2		MARS +1.3		JUPITER −2.0		SATURN +1.1	
d h	GHA ° ′	GHA ° ′	Dec ° ′	GHA ° ′	Dec ° ′	GHA ° ′	Dec ° ′	GHA ° ′	Dec ° ′
2 00 (TUESDAY)	71 12.6	135 57.1	S23 50.2	181 31.9	S22 33.3	136 58.7	S21 57.3	258 45.3	N 5 20.4
01	86 15.1	150 56.4	49.7	196 32.4	33.6	152 00.6	57.2	273 47.6	20.4
02	101 17.5	165 55.7	49.2	211 32.9	33.8	167 02.5	57.2	288 50.0	20.3
03	116 20.0	180 55.0	. . 48.7	226 33.4	. . 34.1	182 04.5	. . 57.1	303 52.3	. . 20.3
04	131 22.5	195 54.3	48.2	241 33.9	34.4	197 06.4	57.0	318 54.6	20.3
05	146 24.9	210 53.6	47.7	256 34.4	34.7	212 08.3	56.9	333 57.0	20.2
06	161 27.4	225 52.9	S23 47.2	271 34.9	S22 34.9	227 10.2	S21 56.8	348 59.3	N 5 20.2
07	176 29.8	240 52.2	46.7	286 35.4	35.2	242 12.1	56.8	4 01.7	20.1
08	191 32.3	255 51.5	46.2	301 36.0	35.5	257 14.1	56.7	19 04.0	20.1
09	206 34.8	270 50.9	. . 45.7	316 36.5	. . 35.8	272 16.0	. . 56.6	34 06.3	. . 20.0
10	221 37.2	285 50.2	45.2	331 37.0	36.0	287 17.9	56.5	49 08.7	20.0
11	236 39.7	300 49.5	44.7	346 37.5	36.3	302 19.8	56.4	64 11.0	20.0
12	251 42.2	315 48.8	S23 44.2	1 38.0	S22 36.6	317 21.8	S21 56.4	79 13.4	N 5 19.9
13	266 44.6	330 48.1	43.7	16 38.5	36.8	332 23.7	56.3	94 15.7	19.9
14	281 47.1	345 47.4	43.1	31 39.0	37.1	347 25.6	56.2	109 18.0	19.8
15	296 49.6	0 46.7	. . 42.6	46 39.5	. . 37.4	2 27.5	. . 56.1	124 20.4	. . 19.8
16	311 52.0	15 46.0	42.1	61 40.1	37.7	17 29.5	56.0	139 22.7	19.8
17	326 54.5	30 45.3	41.6	76 40.6	37.9	32 31.4	56.0	154 25.1	19.7
18	341 56.9	45 44.6	S23 41.1	91 41.1	S22 38.2	47 33.3	S21 55.9	169 27.4	N 5 19.7
19	356 59.4	60 43.9	40.6	106 41.6	38.5	62 35.2	55.8	184 29.7	19.6
20	12 01.9	75 43.2	40.0	121 42.1	38.7	77 37.1	55.7	199 32.1	19.6
21	27 04.3	90 42.6	. . 39.5	136 42.6	. . 39.0	92 39.1	. . 55.6	214 34.4	. . 19.6
22	42 06.8	105 41.9	39.0	151 43.1	39.3	107 41.0	55.5	229 36.8	19.5
23	57 09.3	120 41.2	38.5	166 43.6	39.5	122 42.9	55.5	244 39.1	19.5
3 00 (WEDNESDAY)	72 11.7	135 40.5	S23 37.9	181 44.1	S22 39.8	137 44.8	S21 55.4	259 41.4	N 5 19.4
01	87 14.2	150 39.8	37.4	196 44.6	40.1	152 46.7	55.3	274 43.8	19.4
02	102 16.7	165 39.1	36.9	211 45.2	40.3	167 48.7	55.2	289 46.1	19.4
03	117 19.1	180 38.4	. . 36.4	226 45.7	. . 40.6	182 50.6	. . 55.1	304 48.5	. . 19.3
04	132 21.6	195 37.8	35.8	241 46.2	40.9	197 52.5	55.1	319 50.8	19.3
05	147 24.1	210 37.1	35.3	256 46.7	41.1	212 54.4	55.0	334 53.2	19.2
06	162 26.5	225 36.4	S23 34.8	271 47.2	S22 41.4	227 56.4	S21 54.9	349 55.5	N 5 19.2
07	177 29.0	240 35.7	34.2	286 47.7	41.6	242 58.3	54.8	4 57.8	19.2
08	192 31.4	255 35.0	33.7	301 48.2	41.9	258 00.2	54.7	20 00.2	19.1
09	207 33.9	270 34.4	. . 33.2	316 48.7	. . 42.2	273 02.1	. . 54.6	35 02.5	. . 19.1
10	222 36.4	285 33.7	32.6	331 49.2	42.4	288 04.0	54.6	50 04.9	19.0
11	237 38.8	300 33.0	32.1	346 49.7	42.7	303 06.0	54.5	65 07.2	19.0
12	252 41.3	315 32.3	S23 31.5	1 50.2	S22 43.0	318 07.9	S21 54.4	80 09.6	N 5 19.0
13	267 43.8	330 31.6	31.0	16 50.7	43.2	333 09.8	54.3	95 11.9	18.9
14	282 46.2	345 31.0	30.5	31 51.2	43.5	348 11.7	54.2	110 14.2	18.9
15	297 48.7	0 30.3	. . 29.9	46 51.7	. . 43.7	3 13.6	. . 54.2	125 16.6	. . 18.8
16	312 51.2	15 29.6	29.4	61 52.3	44.0	18 15.5	54.1	140 18.9	18.8
17	327 53.6	30 28.9	28.8	76 52.8	44.3	33 17.5	54.0	155 21.3	18.8
18	342 56.1	45 28.3	S23 28.3	91 53.3	S22 44.5	48 19.4	S21 53.9	170 23.6	N 5 18.7
19	357 58.6	60 27.6	27.7	106 53.8	44.8	63 21.3	53.8	185 26.0	18.7
20	13 01.0	75 26.9	27.2	121 54.3	45.0	78 23.2	53.7	200 28.3	18.6
21	28 03.5	90 26.2	. . 26.6	136 54.8	. . 45.3	93 25.1	. . 53.7	215 30.7	. . 18.6
22	43 05.9	105 25.6	26.1	151 55.3	45.6	108 27.1	53.6	230 33.0	18.6
23	58 08.4	120 24.9	25.5	166 55.8	45.8	123 29.0	53.5	245 35.4	18.5
4 00 (THURSDAY)	73 10.9	135 24.2	S23 25.0	181 56.3	S22 46.1	138 30.9	S21 53.4	260 37.7	N 5 18.5
01	88 13.3	150 23.6	24.4	196 56.8	46.3	153 32.8	53.3	275 40.0	18.4
02	103 15.8	165 22.9	23.9	211 57.3	46.6	168 34.7	53.2	290 42.4	18.4
03	118 18.3	180 22.2	. . 23.3	226 57.8	. . 46.8	183 36.7	. . 53.2	305 44.7	. . 18.4
04	133 20.7	195 21.6	22.8	241 58.3	47.1	198 38.6	53.1	320 47.1	18.3
05	148 23.2	210 20.9	22.2	256 58.8	47.4	213 40.5	53.0	335 49.4	18.3
06	163 25.7	225 20.2	S23 21.7	271 59.3	S22 47.6	228 42.4	S21 52.9	350 51.8	N 5 18.2
07	178 28.1	240 19.6	21.1	286 59.8	47.9	243 44.3	52.8	5 54.1	18.2
08	193 30.6	255 18.9	20.5	302 00.3	48.1	258 46.2	52.7	20 56.5	18.2
09	208 33.0	270 18.2	. . 20.0	317 00.8	. . 48.4	273 48.2	. . 52.7	35 58.8	. . 18.1
10	223 35.5	285 17.6	19.4	332 01.3	48.6	288 50.1	52.6	51 01.2	18.1
11	238 38.0	300 16.9	18.9	347 01.8	48.9	303 52.0	52.5	66 03.5	18.1
12	253 40.4	315 16.2	S23 18.3	2 02.3	S22 49.1	318 53.9	S21 52.4	81 05.9	N 5 18.0
13	268 42.9	330 15.6	17.7	17 02.8	49.4	333 55.8	52.3	96 08.2	18.0
14	283 45.4	345 14.9	17.2	32 03.3	49.6	348 57.7	52.2	111 10.6	17.9
15	298 47.8	0 14.2	. . 16.6	47 03.8	. . 49.9	3 59.7	. . 52.2	126 12.9	. . 17.9
16	313 50.3	15 13.6	16.0	62 04.3	50.1	19 01.6	52.1	141 15.3	17.9
17	328 52.8	30 12.9	15.4	77 04.8	50.4	34 03.5	52.0	156 17.6	17.8
18	343 55.2	45 12.3	S23 14.9	92 05.3	S22 50.6	49 05.4	S21 51.9	171 19.9	N 5 17.8
19	358 57.7	60 11.6	14.3	107 05.8	50.9	64 07.3	51.8	186 22.3	17.8
20	14 00.2	75 11.0	13.7	122 06.3	51.1	79 09.2	51.7	201 24.6	17.7
21	29 02.6	90 10.3	. . 13.2	137 06.8	. . 51.4	94 11.2	. . 51.7	216 27.0	. . 17.7
22	44 05.1	105 09.6	12.6	152 07.3	51.6	109 13.1	51.6	231 29.3	17.6
23	59 07.5	120 09.0	12.0	167 07.8	51.9	124 15.0	51.5	246 31.7	17.6
Mer. Pass. h m	19 08.1	v −0.7	d 0.5	v 0.5	d 0.3	v 1.9	d 0.1	v 2.3	d 0.0

STARS

Name	SHA ° ′	Dec ° ′
Acamar	315 20.4	S40 16.1
Achernar	335 28.6	S57 11.6
Acrux	173 13.7	S63 08.7
Adhara	255 14.9	S28 58.9
Aldebaran	290 52.9	N16 31.8
Alioth	166 23.7	N55 54.4
Alkaid	153 01.8	N49 15.9
Al Na'ir	27 47.9	S46 55.2
Alnilam	275 49.5	S 1 11.7
Alphard	217 59.3	S 8 41.8
Alphecca	126 14.2	N26 41.0
Alpheratz	357 47.0	N29 08.7
Altair	62 11.8	N 8 53.6
Ankaa	353 18.7	S42 15.5
Antares	112 30.8	S26 27.1
Arcturus	145 59.1	N19 08.0
Atria	107 36.4	S69 02.7
Avior	234 19.2	S59 32.0
Bellatrix	278 35.3	N 6 21.6
Betelgeuse	271 04.6	N 7 24.6
Canopus	263 57.2	S52 41.8
Capella	280 39.0	N46 00.5
Deneb	49 34.2	N45 19.0
Denebola	182 37.2	N14 31.2
Diphda	348 59.1	S17 56.2
Dubhe	193 55.6	N61 41.8
Elnath	278 16.5	N28 37.0
Eltanin	90 48.2	N51 29.3
Enif	33 50.6	N 9 55.1
Fomalhaut	15 27.6	S29 34.6
Gacrux	172 05.2	S57 09.6
Gienah	175 56.0	S17 35.4
Hadar	148 53.5	S60 24.8
Hamal	328 04.4	N23 30.5
Kaus Aust.	83 48.7	S34 22.9
Kochab	137 20.5	N74 06.9
Markab	13 41.7	N15 15.4
Menkar	314 18.3	N 4 07.6
Menkent	148 12.0	S36 24.8
Miaplacidus	221 40.3	S69 44.9
Mirfak	308 44.9	N49 53.8
Nunki	76 02.8	S26 17.2
Peacock	53 24.8	S56 42.6
Pollux	243 31.6	N28 00.2
Procyon	245 03.0	N 5 12.2
Rasalhague	96 09.9	N12 33.2
Regulus	207 47.0	N11 55.3
Rigel	281 15.0	S 8 11.4
Rigil Kent.	139 57.2	S60 52.2
Sabik	102 16.8	S15 44.2
Schedar	349 44.4	N56 35.5
Shaula	96 27.0	S37 06.7
Sirius	258 36.4	S16 43.6
Spica	158 35.1	S11 12.5
Suhail	222 54.9	S43 27.9
Vega	80 41.7	N38 47.6
Zuben'ubi	137 09.5	S16 04.7

	SHA ° ′	Mer. Pass. h m
Venus	63 28.8	14 58
Mars	109 32.4	11 53
Jupiter	65 33.1	14 47
Saturn	187 29.7	6 40

Day	UT (d h)	SUN GHA	SUN Dec	MOON GHA	v	MOON Dec	d	HP
		° ′	° ′	° ′	′	° ′	′	′
2	00	182 39.4	S21 58.6	132 15.2	12.7	S22 03.6	8.3	54.2
	01	197 39.1	58.9	146 46.9	12.7	21 55.3	8.3	54.2
	02	212 38.9	59.3	161 18.6	12.8	21 47.0	8.5	54.3
	03	227 38.7	21 59.7	175 50.4	12.8	21 38.5	8.5	54.3
	04	242 38.4	22 00.0	190 22.2	12.8	21 30.0	8.7	54.3
	05	257 38.2	00.4	204 54.0	13.0	21 21.3	8.7	54.3
	06	272 37.9	S22 00.8	219 26.0	12.9	S21 12.6	8.9	54.3
	07	287 37.7	01.1	233 57.9	13.0	21 03.7	8.9	54.3
T	08	302 37.4	01.5	248 29.9	13.1	20 54.8	9.0	54.3
U	09	317 37.2	. . 01.8	263 02.0	13.1	20 45.8	9.2	54.3
E	10	332 37.0	02.2	277 34.1	13.2	20 36.6	9.2	54.4
S	11	347 36.7	02.6	292 06.3	13.2	20 27.4	9.3	54.4
D	12	2 36.5	S22 02.9	306 38.5	13.3	S20 18.1	9.4	54.4
A	13	17 36.2	03.3	321 10.8	13.3	20 08.7	9.5	54.4
Y	14	32 36.0	03.6	335 43.1	13.3	19 59.2	9.5	54.4
	15	47 35.7	. . 04.0	350 15.4	13.4	19 49.7	9.7	54.4
	16	62 35.5	04.4	4 47.8	13.5	19 40.0	9.8	54.4
	17	77 35.2	04.7	19 20.3	13.5	19 30.2	9.8	54.5
	18	92 35.0	S22 05.1	33 52.8	13.5	S19 20.4	9.9	54.5
	19	107 34.8	05.4	48 25.3	13.6	19 10.5	10.0	54.5
	20	122 34.5	05.8	62 57.9	13.6	19 00.5	10.1	54.5
	21	137 34.3	. . 06.1	77 30.5	13.7	18 50.4	10.2	54.5
	22	152 34.0	06.5	92 03.2	13.7	18 40.2	10.3	54.5
	23	167 33.8	06.8	106 35.9	13.8	18 29.9	10.3	54.5
3	00	182 33.5	S22 07.2	121 08.7	13.8	S18 19.6	10.4	54.6
	01	197 33.3	07.5	135 41.5	13.9	18 09.2	10.6	54.6
	02	212 33.0	07.9	150 14.4	13.9	17 58.6	10.5	54.6
	03	227 32.8	. . 08.2	164 47.3	13.9	17 48.1	10.7	54.6
	04	242 32.5	08.6	179 20.2	14.0	17 37.4	10.8	54.6
	05	257 32.3	08.9	193 53.2	14.0	17 26.6	10.8	54.7
	06	272 32.0	S22 09.3	208 26.2	14.1	S17 15.8	10.9	54.7
W	07	287 31.8	09.6	222 59.3	14.1	17 04.9	11.0	54.7
E	08	302 31.5	10.0	237 32.4	14.1	16 53.9	11.0	54.7
D	09	317 31.3	. . 10.3	252 05.5	14.2	16 42.9	11.2	54.7
N	10	332 31.0	10.7	266 38.7	14.2	16 31.7	11.2	54.7
E	11	347 30.8	11.0	281 11.9	14.3	16 20.5	11.3	54.8
S	12	2 30.5	S22 11.4	295 45.2	14.3	S16 09.2	11.3	54.8
D	13	17 30.3	11.7	310 18.5	14.3	15 57.9	11.5	54.8
A	14	32 30.0	12.0	324 51.8	14.4	15 46.4	11.5	54.8
Y	15	47 29.8	. . 12.4	339 25.2	14.4	15 34.9	11.6	54.8
	16	62 29.5	12.7	353 58.6	14.4	15 23.3	11.6	54.9
	17	77 29.3	13.1	8 32.0	14.5	15 11.7	11.7	54.9
	18	92 29.0	S22 13.4	23 05.5	14.5	S15 00.0	11.8	54.9
	19	107 28.8	13.7	37 39.0	14.5	14 48.2	11.9	54.9
	20	122 28.5	14.1	52 12.5	14.6	14 36.3	11.9	55.0
	21	137 28.3	. . 14.4	66 46.1	14.6	14 24.4	12.0	55.0
	22	152 28.0	14.7	81 19.7	14.6	14 12.4	12.0	55.0
	23	167 27.8	15.1	95 53.3	14.6	14 00.4	12.2	55.0
4	00	182 27.5	S22 15.4	110 26.9	14.7	S13 48.2	12.2	55.0
	01	197 27.3	15.7	125 00.6	14.7	13 36.0	12.2	55.1
	02	212 27.0	16.1	139 34.3	14.8	13 23.8	12.3	55.1
	03	227 26.8	. . 16.4	154 08.1	14.7	13 11.5	12.4	55.1
	04	242 26.5	16.7	168 41.8	14.8	12 59.1	12.5	55.1
	05	257 26.2	17.1	183 15.6	14.8	12 46.6	12.5	55.2
	06	272 26.0	S22 17.4	197 49.4	14.8	S12 34.1	12.5	55.2
T	07	287 25.7	17.7	212 23.2	14.9	12 21.6	12.7	55.2
H	08	302 25.5	18.0	226 57.1	14.9	12 08.9	12.7	55.2
U	09	317 25.2	. . 18.4	241 31.0	14.9	11 56.2	12.7	55.3
R	10	332 25.0	18.7	256 04.9	14.9	11 43.5	12.8	55.3
S	11	347 24.7	19.0	270 38.8	14.9	11 30.7	12.9	55.3
D	12	2 24.5	S22 19.3	285 12.7	15.0	S11 17.8	12.9	55.3
A	13	17 24.2	19.7	299 46.7	14.9	11 04.9	13.0	55.4
Y	14	32 23.9	20.0	314 20.6	15.0	10 51.9	13.0	55.4
	15	47 23.7	. . 20.3	328 54.6	15.0	10 38.9	13.1	55.4
	16	62 23.4	20.6	343 28.6	15.0	10 25.8	13.1	55.4
	17	77 23.2	21.0	358 02.6	15.0	10 12.7	13.2	55.5
	18	92 22.9	S22 21.3	12 36.6	15.1	S 9 59.5	13.3	55.5
	19	107 22.7	21.6	27 10.7	15.0	9 46.2	13.3	55.5
	20	122 22.4	21.9	41 44.7	15.0	9 32.9	13.3	55.5
	21	137 22.1	. . 22.2	56 18.7	15.1	9 19.6	13.4	55.6
	22	152 21.9	22.6	70 52.8	15.1	9 06.2	13.5	55.6
	23	167 21.6	22.9	85 26.9	15.1	S 8 52.7	13.5	55.6
		SD 16.3	*d* 0.3	SD 14.8		14.9		15.1

Lat.	Twilight Naut.	Twilight Civil	Sunrise	Moonrise 2	Moonrise 3	Moonrise 4	Moonrise 5
°	h m	h m	h m	h m	h m	h m	h m
N 72	07 57	10 01	▬	▬	14 23	13 30	12 55
N 70	07 40	09 19	▬	15 14	13 47	13 12	12 47
68	07 26	08 50	10 51	13 57	13 20	12 58	12 41
66	07 15	08 28	09 55	13 19	13 00	12 47	12 35
64	07 05	08 11	09 22	12 52	12 44	12 37	12 30
62	06 57	07 57	08 58	12 31	12 30	12 28	12 26
60	06 49	07 45	08 40	12 14	12 18	12 21	12 23
N 58	06 43	07 34	08 24	12 00	12 08	12 15	12 20
56	06 37	07 25	08 11	11 47	12 00	12 09	12 17
54	06 31	07 16	07 59	11 36	11 52	12 04	12 14
52	06 26	07 09	07 49	11 27	11 45	11 59	12 12
50	06 21	07 02	07 40	11 18	11 38	11 55	12 10
45	06 10	06 47	07 20	11 00	11 24	11 46	12 05
N 40	06 01	06 35	07 05	10 45	11 13	11 38	12 01
35	05 52	06 24	06 52	10 32	11 03	11 31	11 58
30	05 44	06 14	06 40	10 21	10 55	11 25	11 55
20	05 29	05 56	06 20	10 02	10 40	11 15	11 50
N 10	05 14	05 40	06 03	09 45	10 27	11 06	11 45
0	04 58	05 24	05 46	09 29	10 14	10 58	11 41
S 10	04 40	05 07	05 30	09 13	10 02	10 49	11 36
20	04 19	04 48	05 12	08 56	09 49	10 40	11 32
30	03 51	04 24	04 51	08 37	09 33	10 30	11 26
35	03 34	04 10	04 39	08 25	09 25	10 24	11 23
40	03 12	03 53	04 25	08 12	09 14	10 17	11 20
45	02 44	03 32	04 08	07 57	09 02	10 09	11 16
S 50	02 04	03 04	03 47	07 37	08 48	09 59	11 11
52	01 41	02 51	03 37	07 28	08 41	09 55	11 09
54	01 09	02 35	03 26	07 18	08 33	09 50	11 06
56	////	02 15	03 13	07 06	08 25	09 44	11 03
58	////	01 51	02 58	06 53	08 15	09 38	11 00
S 60	////	01 16	02 40	06 37	08 04	09 31	10 57

Lat.	Sunset	Twilight Civil	Twilight Naut.	Moonset 2	Moonset 3	Moonset 4	Moonset 5
°	h m	h m	h m	h m	h m	h m	h m
N 72	▬	13 38	15 42	▬	18 48	21 13	23 19
N 70	▬	14 21	15 59	16 23	19 23	21 28	23 24
68	12 48	14 49	16 13	17 39	19 48	21 40	23 28
66	13 44	15 11	16 24	18 16	20 07	21 50	23 31
64	14 17	15 28	16 34	18 42	20 22	21 59	23 34
62	14 41	15 43	16 43	19 02	20 35	22 06	23 36
60	15 00	15 55	16 50	19 18	20 45	22 12	23 38
N 58	15 16	16 06	16 57	19 32	20 55	22 17	23 40
56	15 29	16 15	17 03	19 44	21 03	22 22	23 42
54	15 41	16 23	17 09	19 54	21 10	22 26	23 43
52	15 51	16 31	17 14	20 03	21 16	22 30	23 44
50	16 00	16 38	17 18	20 11	21 22	22 33	23 46
45	16 19	16 52	17 29	20 28	21 34	22 41	23 48
N 40	16 35	17 05	17 39	20 42	21 44	22 47	23 50
35	16 48	17 16	17 47	20 54	21 53	22 52	23 52
30	17 00	17 26	17 55	21 04	22 01	22 57	23 54
20	17 20	17 44	18 11	21 22	22 14	23 05	23 56
N 10	17 37	18 00	18 26	21 37	22 25	23 12	23 59
0	17 54	18 16	18 42	21 51	22 35	23 18	24 01
S 10	18 10	18 33	19 00	22 05	22 46	23 25	24 03
20	18 28	18 52	19 21	22 20	22 57	23 32	24 06
30	18 49	19 16	19 49	22 37	23 09	23 39	24 08
35	19 01	19 30	20 06	22 47	23 16	23 44	24 10
40	19 15	19 48	20 28	22 58	23 25	23 49	24 11
45	19 32	20 09	20 57	23 11	23 34	23 54	24 13
S 50	19 53	20 36	21 37	23 27	23 45	24 01	00 01
52	20 03	20 50	22 01	23 35	23 51	24 04	00 04
54	20 15	21 06	22 34	23 43	23 56	24 08	00 08
56	20 28	21 26	////	23 52	24 03	00 03	00 11
58	20 43	21 51	////	24 03	00 03	00 10	00 16
S 60	21 01	22 27	////	00 08	00 15	00 18	00 20

Day	SUN Eqn. of Time 00^h	SUN Eqn. of Time 12^h	SUN Mer. Pass.	MOON Mer. Pass. Upper	MOON Mer. Pass. Lower	MOON Age	MOON Phase
d	m s	m s	h m	h m	h m	d %	
2	10 38	10 26	11 50	15 40	03 17	05 19	
3	10 15	10 03	11 50	16 25	04 03	06 27	
4	09 51	09 38	11 50	17 08	04 47	07 36	

UT	ARIES	VENUS −4.2		MARS +1.3		JUPITER −2.0		SATURN +1.1		STARS		
	GHA	GHA	Dec	GHA	Dec	GHA	Dec	GHA	Dec	Name	SHA	Dec
d h	° ′	° ′	° ′	° ′	° ′	° ′	° ′	° ′	° ′		° ′	° ′
5 00	74 10.0	135 08.3	S23 11.4	182 08.3	S22 52.1	139 16.9	S21 51.4	261 34.0	N 5 17.6	Acamar	315 20.4	S40 16.1
01	89 12.5	150 07.7	10.8	197 08.8	52.4	154 18.8	51.3	276 36.4	17.5	Achernar	335 28.7	S57 11.6
02	104 14.9	165 07.0	10.3	212 09.3	52.6	169 20.7	51.2	291 38.7	17.5	Acrux	173 13.7	S63 08.7
03	119 17.4	180 06.4	. . 09.7	227 09.8	. . 52.9	184 22.6	. . 51.1	306 41.1	. . 17.5	Adhara	255 14.9	S28 58.9
04	134 19.9	195 05.7	09.1	242 10.3	53.1	199 24.6	51.1	321 43.4	17.4	Aldebaran	290 52.9	N16 31.8
05	149 22.3	210 05.1	08.5	257 10.8	53.4	214 26.5	51.0	336 45.8	17.4			
06	164 24.8	225 04.4	S23 07.9	272 11.3	S22 53.6	229 28.4	S21 50.9	351 48.1	N 5 17.3	Alioth	166 23.7	N55 54.4
07	179 27.3	240 03.8	07.3	287 11.8	53.9	244 30.3	50.8	6 50.5	17.3	Alkaid	153 01.7	N49 15.8
08	194 29.7	255 03.1	06.8	302 12.3	54.1	259 32.2	50.7	21 52.8	17.3	Al Na'ir	27 47.9	S46 55.2
F 09	209 32.2	270 02.5	. . 06.2	317 12.8	. . 54.4	274 34.1	. . 50.6	36 55.2	. . 17.2	Alnilam	275 49.5	S 1 11.7
R 10	224 34.7	285 01.8	05.6	332 13.3	54.6	289 36.0	50.6	51 57.5	17.2	Alphard	217 59.3	S 8 41.8
I 11	239 37.1	300 01.2	05.0	347 13.8	54.8	304 38.0	50.5	66 59.9	17.2			
D 12	254 39.6	315 00.5	S23 04.4	2 14.3	S22 55.1	319 39.9	S21 50.4	82 02.3	N 5 17.1	Alphecca	126 14.2	N26 41.0
A 13	269 42.0	329 59.9	03.8	17 14.8	55.3	334 41.8	50.3	97 04.6	17.1	Alpheratz	357 47.0	N29 08.7
Y 14	284 44.5	344 59.2	03.2	32 15.3	55.6	349 43.7	50.2	112 07.0	17.1	Altair	62 11.8	N 8 53.6
15	299 47.0	359 58.6	. . 02.6	47 15.8	. . 55.8	4 45.6	. . 50.1	127 09.3	. . 17.0	Ankaa	353 18.7	S42 15.6
16	314 49.4	14 57.9	02.0	62 16.3	56.1	19 47.5	50.1	142 11.7	17.0	Antares	112 30.8	S26 27.1
17	329 51.9	29 57.3	01.4	77 16.8	56.3	34 49.4	50.0	157 14.0	16.9			
18	344 54.4	44 56.7	S23 00.8	92 17.3	S22 56.5	49 51.4	S21 49.9	172 16.4	N 5 16.9	Arcturus	145 59.0	N19 08.0
19	359 56.8	59 56.0	23 00.2	107 17.8	56.8	64 53.3	49.8	187 18.7	16.9	Atria	107 36.4	S69 02.7
20	14 59.3	74 55.4	22 59.6	122 18.3	57.0	79 55.2	49.7	202 21.1	16.8	Avior	234 19.1	S59 32.0
21	30 01.8	89 54.7	. . 59.0	137 18.8	. . 57.3	94 57.1	. . 49.6	217 23.4	. . 16.8	Bellatrix	278 35.3	N 6 21.6
22	45 04.2	104 54.1	58.4	152 19.2	57.5	109 59.0	49.5	232 25.8	16.8	Betelgeuse	271 04.6	N 7 24.6
23	60 06.7	119 53.4	57.8	167 19.7	57.7	125 00.9	49.5	247 28.1	16.7			
6 00	75 09.1	134 52.8	S22 57.2	182 20.2	S22 58.0	140 02.8	S21 49.4	262 30.5	N 5 16.7	Canopus	263 57.1	S52 41.8
01	90 11.6	149 52.2	56.6	197 20.7	58.2	155 04.7	49.3	277 32.8	16.7	Capella	280 39.0	N46 00.5
02	105 14.1	164 51.5	56.0	212 21.2	58.5	170 06.7	49.2	292 35.2	16.6	Deneb	49 34.2	N45 19.0
03	120 16.5	179 50.9	. . 55.4	227 21.7	. . 58.7	185 08.6	. . 49.1	307 37.5	. . 16.6	Denebola	182 37.1	N14 31.2
04	135 19.0	194 50.3	54.8	242 22.2	58.9	200 10.5	49.0	322 39.9	16.6	Diphda	348 59.1	S17 56.2
05	150 21.5	209 49.6	54.2	257 22.7	59.2	215 12.4	48.9	337 42.2	16.5			
06	165 23.9	224 49.0	S22 53.6	272 23.2	S22 59.4	230 14.3	S21 48.9	352 44.6	N 5 16.5	Dubhe	193 55.5	N61 41.8
S 07	180 26.4	239 48.4	53.0	287 23.7	59.6	245 16.2	48.8	7 47.0	16.5	Elnath	278 16.5	N28 37.0
08	195 28.9	254 47.7	52.4	302 24.2	22 59.9	260 18.1	48.7	22 49.3	16.4	Eltanin	90 48.2	N51 29.3
A 09	210 31.3	269 47.1	. . 51.7	317 24.7	23 00.1	275 20.0	. . 48.6	37 51.7	. . 16.4	Enif	33 50.6	N 9 55.1
T 10	225 33.8	284 46.5	51.1	332 25.2	00.3	290 21.9	48.5	52 54.0	16.3	Fomalhaut	15 27.6	S29 34.6
U 11	240 36.3	299 45.8	50.5	347 25.7	00.6	305 23.9	48.4	67 56.4	16.3			
R 12	255 38.7	314 45.2	S22 49.9	2 26.1	S23 00.8	320 25.8	S21 48.3	82 58.7	N 5 16.3	Gacrux	172 05.2	S57 09.6
D 13	270 41.2	329 44.6	49.3	17 26.6	01.0	335 27.7	48.3	98 01.1	16.2	Gienah	175 56.0	S17 35.4
A 14	285 43.6	344 43.9	48.7	32 27.1	01.3	350 29.6	48.2	113 03.4	16.2	Hadar	148 53.5	S60 24.8
Y 15	300 46.1	359 43.3	. . 48.0	47 27.6	. . 01.5	5 31.5	. . 48.1	128 05.8	. . 16.2	Hamal	328 04.4	N23 30.5
16	315 48.6	14 42.7	47.4	62 28.1	01.7	20 33.4	48.0	143 08.2	16.1	Kaus Aust.	83 48.7	S34 22.9
17	330 51.0	29 42.1	46.8	77 28.6	02.0	35 35.3	47.9	158 10.5	16.1			
18	345 53.5	44 41.4	S22 46.2	92 29.1	S23 02.2	50 37.2	S21 47.8	173 12.9	N 5 16.1	Kochab	137 20.5	N74 06.8
19	0 56.0	59 40.8	45.6	107 29.6	02.4	65 39.1	47.7	188 15.2	16.0	Markab	13 41.8	N15 15.4
20	15 58.4	74 40.2	44.9	122 30.1	02.7	80 41.1	47.7	203 17.6	16.0	Menkar	314 18.3	N 4 07.6
21	31 00.9	89 39.6	. . 44.3	137 30.6	. . 02.9	95 43.0	. . 47.6	218 19.9	. . 16.0	Menkent	148 12.0	S36 24.8
22	46 03.4	104 38.9	43.7	152 31.1	03.1	110 44.9	47.5	233 22.3	15.9	Miaplacidus	221 40.3	S69 44.9
23	61 05.8	119 38.3	43.0	167 31.5	03.4	125 46.8	47.4	248 24.7	15.9			
7 00	76 08.3	134 37.7	S22 42.4	182 32.0	S23 03.6	140 48.7	S21 47.3	263 27.0	N 5 15.9	Mirfak	308 44.9	N49 53.8
01	91 10.8	149 37.1	41.8	197 32.5	03.8	155 50.6	47.2	278 29.4	15.8	Nunki	76 02.8	S26 17.2
02	106 13.2	164 36.4	41.2	212 33.0	04.0	170 52.5	47.1	293 31.7	15.8	Peacock	53 24.8	S56 42.6
03	121 15.7	179 35.8	. . 40.5	227 33.5	. . 04.3	185 54.4	. . 47.0	308 34.1	. . 15.8	Pollux	243 31.5	N28 00.2
04	136 18.1	194 35.2	39.9	242 34.0	04.5	200 56.3	47.0	323 36.4	15.7	Procyon	245 03.0	N 5 12.2
05	151 20.6	209 34.6	39.3	257 34.5	04.7	215 58.2	46.9	338 38.8	15.7			
06	166 23.1	224 34.0	S22 38.6	272 35.0	S23 05.0	231 00.1	S21 46.8	353 41.2	N 5 15.7	Rasalhague	96 09.9	N12 33.2
07	181 25.5	239 33.3	38.0	287 35.4	05.2	246 02.1	46.7	8 43.5	15.6	Regulus	207 47.0	N11 55.3
08	196 28.0	254 32.7	37.3	302 35.9	05.4	261 04.0	46.6	23 45.9	15.6	Rigel	281 15.0	S 8 11.4
S 09	211 30.5	269 32.1	. . 36.7	317 36.4	. . 05.6	276 05.9	. . 46.5	38 48.2	. . 15.6	Rigil Kent.	139 57.2	S60 52.2
U 10	226 32.9	284 31.5	36.1	332 36.9	05.9	291 07.8	46.4	53 50.6	15.5	Sabik	102 16.8	S15 44.2
N 11	241 35.4	299 30.9	35.4	347 37.4	06.1	306 09.7	46.4	68 52.9	15.5			
D 12	256 37.9	314 30.3	S22 34.8	2 37.9	S23 06.3	321 11.6	S21 46.3	83 55.3	N 5 15.5	Schedar	349 44.4	N56 35.5
A 13	271 40.3	329 29.7	34.1	17 38.4	06.5	336 13.5	46.2	98 57.7	15.4	Shaula	96 27.0	S37 06.7
Y 14	286 42.8	344 29.0	33.5	32 38.9	06.8	351 15.4	46.1	114 00.0	15.4	Sirius	258 36.4	S16 43.6
15	301 45.2	359 28.4	. . 32.9	47 39.3	. . 07.0	6 17.3	. . 46.0	129 02.4	. . 15.4	Spica	158 35.1	S11 12.5
16	316 47.7	14 27.8	32.2	62 39.8	07.2	21 19.2	45.9	144 04.7	15.3	Suhail	222 54.8	S43 27.9
17	331 50.2	29 27.2	31.6	77 40.3	07.4	36 21.1	45.8	159 07.1	15.3			
18	346 52.6	44 26.6	S22 30.9	92 40.8	S23 07.6	51 23.0	S21 45.7	174 09.5	N 5 15.3	Vega	80 41.7	N38 47.6
19	1 55.1	59 26.0	30.3	107 41.3	07.9	66 25.0	45.7	189 11.8	15.2	Zuben'ubi	137 09.5	S16 04.7
20	16 57.6	74 25.4	29.6	122 41.8	08.1	81 26.9	45.6	204 14.2	15.2		SHA	Mer. Pass.
21	32 00.0	89 24.8	. . 29.0	137 42.3	. . 08.3	96 28.8	. . 45.5	219 16.5	. . 15.2		° ′	h m
22	47 02.5	104 24.2	28.3	152 42.7	08.5	111 30.7	45.4	234 18.9	15.1	Venus	59 43.7	15 01
23	62 05.0	119 23.6	27.7	167 43.2	08.8	126 32.6	45.3	249 21.3	15.1	Mars	107 11.1	11 50
	h m									Jupiter	64 53.7	14 38
Mer. Pass.	18 56.3	*v* −0.6	*d* 0.6	*v* 0.5	*d* 0.2	*v* 1.9	*d* 0.1	*v* 2.4	*d* 0.0	Saturn	187 21.3	6 29

UT		SUN GHA	SUN Dec	MOON GHA	v	MOON Dec	d	HP
d	h	° ′	° ′	° ′	′	° ′	′	′
5 FRIDAY	00	182 21.4	S22 23.2	100 01.0	15.0	S 8 39.2	13.6	55.7
	01	197 21.1	23.5	114 35.0	15.1	8 25.6	13.6	55.7
	02	212 20.8	23.8	129 09.1	15.1	8 12.0	13.6	55.7
	03	227 20.6	. . 24.1	143 43.2	15.1	7 58.4	13.7	55.8
	04	242 20.3	24.4	158 17.3	15.1	7 44.7	13.7	55.8
	05	257 20.1	24.7	172 51.4	15.1	7 31.0	13.8	55.8
	06	272 19.8	S22 25.1	187 25.5	15.1	S 7 17.2	13.8	55.8
	07	287 19.5	25.4	201 59.6	15.0	7 03.4	13.9	55.9
	08	302 19.3	25.7	216 33.6	15.1	6 49.5	13.9	55.9
	09	317 19.0	. . 26.0	231 07.7	15.1	6 35.6	14.0	55.9
	10	332 18.8	26.3	245 41.8	15.1	6 21.6	14.0	56.0
	11	347 18.5	26.6	260 15.9	15.0	6 07.6	14.0	56.0
	12	2 18.2	S22 26.9	274 49.9	15.1	S 5 53.6	14.1	56.0
	13	17 18.0	27.2	289 24.0	15.1	5 39.5	14.1	56.1
	14	32 17.7	27.5	303 58.1	15.0	5 25.4	14.2	56.1
	15	47 17.5	. . 27.8	318 32.1	15.0	5 11.2	14.2	56.1
	16	62 17.2	28.1	333 06.1	15.0	4 57.0	14.2	56.2
	17	77 16.9	28.4	347 40.1	15.0	4 42.8	14.3	56.2
	18	92 16.7	S22 28.7	2 14.1	15.0	S 4 28.5	14.3	56.2
	19	107 16.4	29.0	16 48.1	15.0	4 14.2	14.3	56.3
	20	122 16.1	29.3	31 22.1	14.9	3 59.9	14.4	56.3
	21	137 15.9	. . 29.6	45 56.0	15.0	3 45.5	14.4	56.3
	22	152 15.6	29.9	60 30.0	14.9	3 31.1	14.4	56.4
	23	167 15.4	30.2	75 03.9	14.9	3 16.7	14.5	56.4
6 SATURDAY	00	182 15.1	S22 30.5	89 37.8	14.9	S 3 02.2	14.5	56.4
	01	197 14.8	30.8	104 11.7	14.8	2 47.7	14.5	56.5
	02	212 14.6	31.1	118 45.5	14.8	2 33.2	14.5	56.5
	03	227 14.3	. . 31.4	133 19.3	14.8	2 18.7	14.6	56.5
	04	242 14.0	31.7	147 53.1	14.8	2 04.1	14.6	56.6
	05	257 13.8	32.0	162 26.9	14.7	1 49.5	14.7	56.6
	06	272 13.5	S22 32.3	177 00.6	14.7	S 1 34.8	14.6	56.6
	07	287 13.2	32.6	191 34.3	14.7	1 20.2	14.7	56.7
	08	302 13.0	32.9	206 08.0	14.7	1 05.5	14.7	56.7
	09	317 12.7	. . 33.2	220 41.7	14.6	0 50.8	14.7	56.7
	10	332 12.4	33.5	235 15.3	14.5	0 36.1	14.8	56.8
	11	347 12.2	33.7	249 48.8	14.6	0 21.3	14.8	56.8
	12	2 11.9	S22 34.0	264 22.4	14.5	S 0 06.5	14.8	56.9
	13	17 11.6	34.3	278 55.9	14.5	N 0 08.3	14.8	56.9
	14	32 11.4	34.6	293 29.4	14.4	0 23.1	14.8	56.9
	15	47 11.1	. . 34.9	308 02.8	14.4	0 37.9	14.9	57.0
	16	62 10.8	35.2	322 36.2	14.3	0 52.8	14.8	57.0
	17	77 10.6	35.5	337 09.5	14.3	1 07.6	14.9	57.0
	18	92 10.3	S22 35.7	351 42.8	14.2	N 1 22.5	14.9	57.1
	19	107 10.0	36.0	6 16.0	14.2	1 37.4	14.9	57.1
	20	122 09.8	36.3	20 49.2	14.2	1 52.3	14.9	57.2
	21	137 09.5	. . 36.6	35 22.4	14.1	2 07.2	14.9	57.2
	22	152 09.2	36.9	49 55.5	14.0	2 22.1	15.0	57.2
	23	167 09.0	37.1	64 28.5	14.0	2 37.1	14.9	57.3
7 SUNDAY	00	182 08.7	S22 37.4	79 01.5	14.0	N 2 52.0	15.0	57.3
	01	197 08.4	37.7	93 34.5	13.9	3 07.0	15.0	57.4
	02	212 08.1	38.0	108 07.4	13.8	3 22.0	14.9	57.4
	03	227 07.9	. . 38.3	122 40.2	13.8	3 36.9	15.0	57.4
	04	242 07.6	38.5	137 13.0	13.7	3 51.9	15.0	57.5
	05	257 07.3	38.8	151 45.7	13.7	4 06.9	15.0	57.5
	06	272 07.1	S22 39.1	166 18.4	13.5	N 4 21.9	14.9	57.5
	07	287 06.8	39.4	180 50.9	13.6	4 36.8	15.0	57.6
	08	302 06.5	39.6	195 23.5	13.4	4 51.8	15.0	57.6
	09	317 06.3	. . 39.9	209 55.9	13.4	5 06.8	15.0	57.7
	10	332 06.0	40.2	224 28.3	13.4	5 21.8	15.0	57.7
	11	347 05.7	40.4	239 00.7	13.2	5 36.8	14.9	57.7
	12	2 05.4	S22 40.7	253 32.9	13.2	N 5 51.7	15.0	57.8
	13	17 05.2	41.0	268 05.1	13.1	6 06.7	15.0	57.8
	14	32 04.9	41.3	282 37.2	13.1	6 21.7	14.9	57.9
	15	47 04.6	. . 41.5	297 09.3	12.9	6 36.6	15.0	57.9
	16	62 04.4	41.8	311 41.2	12.9	6 51.6	14.9	57.9
	17	77 04.1	42.0	326 13.1	12.8	7 06.5	14.9	58.0
	18	92 03.8	S22 42.3	340 44.9	12.8	N 7 21.4	14.9	58.0
	19	107 03.5	42.6	355 16.7	12.6	7 36.3	14.9	58.1
	20	122 03.3	42.8	9 48.3	12.6	7 51.2	14.9	58.1
	21	137 03.0	. . 43.1	24 19.9	12.5	8 06.1	14.8	58.2
	22	152 02.7	43.4	38 51.4	12.4	8 20.9	14.9	58.2
	23	167 02.4	43.6	53 22.8	12.3	N 8 35.8	14.8	58.2
		SD 16.3	*d* 0.3	SD 15.3		15.5		15.7

Lat.	Twilight Naut.	Twilight Civil	Sunrise	Moonrise 5	Moonrise 6	Moonrise 7	Moonrise 8
°	h m	h m	h m	h m	h m	h m	h m
N 72	08 04	10 14	■	12 55	12 25	11 54	11 16
N 70	07 47	09 28	■	12 47	12 25	12 02	11 35
68	07 32	08 57	11 13	12 41	12 25	12 08	11 50
66	07 20	08 35	10 05	12 35	12 25	12 14	12 02
64	07 10	08 17	09 30	12 30	12 24	12 18	12 12
62	07 01	08 02	09 05	12 26	12 24	12 22	12 21
60	06 53	07 49	08 45	12 23	12 24	12 26	12 29
N 58	06 47	07 38	08 29	12 20	12 24	12 29	12 35
56	06 40	07 29	08 15	12 17	12 24	12 32	12 41
54	06 35	07 20	08 03	12 14	12 24	12 34	12 47
52	06 29	07 12	07 53	12 12	12 24	12 37	12 52
50	06 24	07 05	07 43	12 10	12 24	12 39	12 56
45	06 13	06 50	07 24	12 05	12 24	12 44	13 06
N 40	06 04	06 37	07 08	12 01	12 24	12 48	13 14
35	05 55	06 26	06 54	11 58	12 24	12 51	13 21
30	05 46	06 16	06 42	11 55	12 24	12 54	13 27
20	05 31	05 58	06 22	11 50	12 24	12 59	13 38
N 10	05 15	05 42	06 04	11 45	12 24	13 04	13 47
0	04 59	05 25	05 47	11 41	12 24	13 08	13 56
S 10	04 41	05 08	05 31	11 36	12 24	13 13	14 05
20	04 19	04 48	05 12	11 32	12 24	13 18	14 15
30	03 51	04 24	04 51	11 26	12 24	13 23	14 26
35	03 33	04 10	04 39	11 23	12 24	13 27	14 33
40	03 11	03 52	04 25	11 20	12 24	13 30	14 41
45	02 42	03 31	04 07	11 16	12 24	13 35	14 49
S 50	02 01	03 03	03 46	11 11	12 24	13 40	15 00
52	01 36	02 49	03 36	11 09	12 24	13 42	15 05
54	01 01	02 32	03 24	11 06	12 24	13 45	15 11
56	////	02 12	03 11	11 03	12 24	13 48	15 17
58	////	01 46	02 55	11 00	12 24	13 51	15 24
S 60	////	01 08	02 37	10 57	12 24	13 55	15 31

Lat.	Sunset	Twilight Civil	Twilight Naut.	Moonset 5	Moonset 6	Moonset 7	Moonset 8
°	h m	h m	h m	h m	h m	h m	h m
N 72	■	13 27	15 37	23 19	25 25	01 25	03 41
N 70	■	14 14	15 55	23 24	25 20	01 20	03 25
68	12 29	14 45	16 10	23 28	25 16	01 16	03 12
66	13 37	15 07	16 22	23 31	25 13	01 13	03 02
64	14 12	15 25	16 32	23 34	25 11	01 11	02 53
62	14 37	15 40	16 41	23 36	25 09	01 09	02 46
60	14 57	15 53	16 49	23 38	25 07	01 07	02 40
N 58	15 13	16 04	16 56	23 40	25 05	01 05	02 34
56	15 27	16 13	17 02	23 42	25 03	01 03	02 29
54	15 39	16 22	17 08	23 43	25 02	01 02	02 25
52	15 49	16 30	17 13	23 44	25 01	01 01	02 21
50	15 59	16 37	17 18	23 46	25 00	01 00	02 17
45	16 19	16 52	17 29	23 48	24 57	00 57	02 10
N 40	16 35	17 05	17 39	23 50	24 55	00 55	02 03
35	16 48	17 16	17 48	23 52	24 54	00 54	01 58
30	17 00	17 26	17 56	23 54	24 52	00 52	01 53
20	17 20	17 44	18 12	23 56	24 49	00 49	01 45
N 10	17 38	18 01	18 27	23 59	24 47	00 47	01 38
0	17 55	18 17	18 43	24 01	00 01	00 45	01 31
S 10	18 12	18 35	19 02	24 03	00 03	00 42	01 24
20	18 30	18 54	19 23	24 06	00 06	00 40	01 17
30	18 51	19 18	19 51	24 08	00 08	00 37	01 09
35	19 04	19 33	20 09	24 10	00 10	00 36	01 04
40	19 18	19 51	20 32	24 11	00 11	00 34	00 59
45	19 35	20 12	21 01	24 13	00 13	00 32	00 53
S 50	19 57	20 40	21 43	00 01	00 15	00 30	00 45
52	20 07	20 55	22 07	00 04	00 16	00 29	00 42
54	20 19	21 11	22 44	00 08	00 18	00 27	00 38
56	20 32	21 32	////	00 11	00 19	00 26	00 34
58	20 48	21 58	////	00 16	00 20	00 25	00 30
S 60	21 07	22 37	////	00 20	00 22	00 23	00 25

Day	SUN Eqn. of Time 00ʰ	SUN Eqn. of Time 12ʰ	SUN Mer. Pass.	MOON Mer. Pass. Upper	MOON Mer. Pass. Lower	MOON Age	MOON Phase
d	m s	m s	h m	h m	h m	d %	
5	09 26	09 14	11 51	17 51	05 29	08 46	◐
6	09 01	08 48	11 51	18 34	06 12	09 56	
7	08 35	08 22	11 52	19 20	06 56	10 67	

UT	ARIES	VENUS −4.2		MARS +1.3		JUPITER −2.0		SATURN +1.1	
	GHA	GHA	Dec	GHA	Dec	GHA	Dec	GHA	Dec
d h	° ′	° ′	° ′	° ′	° ′	° ′	° ′	° ′	° ′
MONDAY 8 00	77 07.4	134 23.0	S22 27.0	182 43.7	S23 09.0	141 34.5	S21 45.2	264 23.6	N 5 15.1
01	92 09.9	149 22.4	26.4	197 44.2	09.2	156 36.4	45.1	279 26.0	15.0
02	107 12.4	164 21.8	25.7	212 44.7	09.4	171 38.3	45.0	294 28.4	15.0
03	122 14.8	179 21.2	. . 25.0	227 45.2	. . 09.6	186 40.2	. . 45.0	309 30.7	. . 15.0
04	137 17.3	194 20.6	24.4	242 45.6	09.8	201 42.1	44.9	324 33.1	15.0
05	152 19.7	209 20.0	23.7	257 46.1	10.1	216 44.0	44.8	339 35.4	14.9
06	167 22.2	224 19.4	S22 23.1	272 46.6	S23 10.3	231 45.9	S21 44.7	354 37.8	N 5 14.9
07	182 24.7	239 18.8	22.4	287 47.1	10.5	246 47.8	44.6	9 40.2	14.9
08	197 27.1	254 18.2	21.7	302 47.6	10.7	261 49.7	44.5	24 42.5	14.8
09	212 29.6	269 17.6	. . 21.1	317 48.1	. . 10.9	276 51.6	. . 44.4	39 44.9	. . 14.8
10	227 32.1	284 17.0	20.4	332 48.5	11.2	291 53.6	44.3	54 47.3	14.8
11	242 34.5	299 16.4	19.8	347 49.0	11.4	306 55.5	44.2	69 49.6	14.7
12	257 37.0	314 15.8	S22 19.1	2 49.5	S23 11.6	321 57.4	S21 44.2	84 52.0	N 5 14.7
13	272 39.5	329 15.2	18.4	17 50.0	11.8	336 59.3	44.1	99 54.3	14.7
14	287 41.9	344 14.6	17.8	32 50.5	12.0	352 01.2	44.0	114 56.7	14.6
15	302 44.4	359 14.0	. . 17.1	47 50.9	. . 12.2	7 03.1	. . 43.9	129 59.1	. . 14.6
16	317 46.9	14 13.4	16.4	62 51.4	12.4	22 05.0	43.8	145 01.4	14.6
17	332 49.3	29 12.8	15.7	77 51.9	12.6	37 06.9	43.7	160 03.8	14.5
18	347 51.8	44 12.2	S22 15.1	92 52.4	S23 12.9	52 08.8	S21 43.6	175 06.2	N 5 14.5
19	2 54.2	59 11.6	14.4	107 52.9	13.1	67 10.7	43.5	190 08.5	14.5
20	17 56.7	74 11.0	13.7	122 53.3	13.3	82 12.6	43.5	205 10.9	14.5
21	32 59.2	89 10.4	. . 13.0	137 53.8	. . 13.5	97 14.5	. . 43.4	220 13.3	. . 14.4
22	48 01.6	104 09.8	12.4	152 54.3	13.7	112 16.4	43.3	235 15.6	14.4
23	63 04.1	119 09.3	11.7	167 54.8	13.9	127 18.3	43.2	250 18.0	14.4
TUESDAY 9 00	78 06.6	134 08.7	S22 11.0	182 55.3	S23 14.1	142 20.2	S21 43.1	265 20.3	N 5 14.3
01	93 09.0	149 08.1	10.3	197 55.7	14.3	157 22.1	43.0	280 22.7	14.3
02	108 11.5	164 07.5	09.7	212 56.2	14.5	172 24.0	42.9	295 25.1	14.3
03	123 14.0	179 06.9	. . 09.0	227 56.7	. . 14.8	187 25.9	. . 42.8	310 27.4	. . 14.2
04	138 16.4	194 06.3	08.3	242 57.2	15.0	202 27.8	42.7	325 29.8	14.2
05	153 18.9	209 05.7	07.6	257 57.7	15.2	217 29.7	42.7	340 32.2	14.2
06	168 21.3	224 05.2	S22 06.9	272 58.1	S23 15.4	232 31.6	S21 42.6	355 34.5	N 5 14.1
07	183 23.8	239 04.6	06.2	287 58.6	15.6	247 33.5	42.5	10 36.9	14.1
08	198 26.3	254 04.0	05.6	302 59.1	15.8	262 35.4	42.4	25 39.3	14.1
09	213 28.7	269 03.4	. . 04.9	317 59.6	. . 16.0	277 37.4	. . 42.3	40 41.6	. . 14.1
10	228 31.2	284 02.8	04.2	333 00.0	16.2	292 39.3	42.2	55 44.0	14.0
11	243 33.7	299 02.3	03.5	348 00.5	16.4	307 41.2	42.1	70 46.4	14.0
12	258 36.1	314 01.7	S22 02.8	3 01.0	S23 16.6	322 43.1	S21 42.0	85 48.7	N 5 14.0
13	273 38.6	329 01.1	02.1	18 01.5	16.8	337 45.0	41.9	100 51.1	13.9
14	288 41.1	344 00.5	01.4	33 02.0	17.0	352 46.9	41.8	115 53.5	13.9
15	303 43.5	358 59.9	. . 00.7	48 02.4	. . 17.2	7 48.8	. . 41.8	130 55.8	. . 13.9
16	318 46.0	13 59.4	22 00.0	63 02.9	17.4	22 50.7	41.7	145 58.2	13.9
17	333 48.5	28 58.8	21 59.3	78 03.4	17.6	37 52.6	41.6	161 00.6	13.8
18	348 50.9	43 58.2	S21 58.6	93 03.9	S23 17.8	52 54.5	S21 41.5	176 02.9	N 5 13.8
19	3 53.4	58 57.6	57.9	108 04.3	18.0	67 56.4	41.4	191 05.3	13.8
20	18 55.8	73 57.1	57.2	123 04.8	18.2	82 58.3	41.3	206 07.7	13.7
21	33 58.3	88 56.5	. . 56.5	138 05.3	. . 18.5	98 00.2	. . 41.2	221 10.1	. . 13.7
22	49 00.8	103 55.9	55.8	153 05.8	18.7	113 02.1	41.1	236 12.4	13.7
23	64 03.2	118 55.4	55.1	168 06.2	18.9	128 04.0	41.0	251 14.8	13.7
WEDNESDAY 10 00	79 05.7	133 54.8	S21 54.4	183 06.7	S23 19.1	143 05.9	S21 40.9	266 17.2	N 5 13.6
01	94 08.2	148 54.2	53.7	198 07.2	19.3	158 07.8	40.9	281 19.5	13.6
02	109 10.6	163 53.7	53.0	213 07.7	19.5	173 09.7	40.8	296 21.9	13.6
03	124 13.1	178 53.1	. . 52.3	228 08.1	. . 19.7	188 11.6	. . 40.7	311 24.3	. . 13.5
04	139 15.6	193 52.5	51.6	243 08.6	19.9	203 13.5	40.6	326 26.6	13.5
05	154 18.0	208 52.0	50.9	258 09.1	20.1	218 15.4	40.5	341 29.0	13.5
06	169 20.5	223 51.4	S21 50.2	273 09.6	S23 20.2	233 17.3	S21 40.4	356 31.4	N 5 13.5
07	184 23.0	238 50.8	49.5	288 10.0	20.4	248 19.2	40.3	11 33.7	13.4
08	199 25.4	253 50.3	48.8	303 10.5	20.6	263 21.1	40.2	26 36.1	13.4
09	214 27.9	268 49.7	. . 48.1	318 11.0	. . 20.8	278 23.0	. . 40.1	41 38.5	. . 13.4
10	229 30.3	283 49.1	47.4	333 11.4	21.0	293 24.9	40.0	56 40.9	13.3
11	244 32.8	298 48.6	46.7	348 11.9	21.2	308 26.8	40.0	71 43.2	13.3
12	259 35.3	313 48.0	S21 45.9	3 12.4	S23 21.4	323 28.7	S21 39.9	86 45.6	N 5 13.3
13	274 37.7	328 47.5	45.2	18 12.9	21.6	338 30.6	39.8	101 48.0	13.3
14	289 40.2	343 46.9	44.5	33 13.3	21.8	353 32.5	39.7	116 50.3	13.2
15	304 42.7	358 46.3	. . 43.8	48 13.8	. . 22.0	8 34.4	. . 39.6	131 52.7	. . 13.2
16	319 45.1	13 45.8	43.1	63 14.3	22.2	23 36.3	39.5	146 55.1	13.2
17	334 47.6	28 45.2	42.4	78 14.7	22.4	38 38.2	39.4	161 57.5	13.1
18	349 50.1	43 44.7	S21 41.6	93 15.2	S23 22.6	53 40.1	S21 39.3	176 59.8	N 5 13.1
19	4 52.5	58 44.1	40.9	108 15.7	22.8	68 42.0	39.2	192 02.2	13.1
20	19 55.0	73 43.6	40.2	123 16.2	23.0	83 43.9	39.1	207 04.6	13.1
21	34 57.5	88 43.0	. . 39.5	138 16.6	. . 23.2	98 45.8	. . 39.0	222 06.9	. . 13.0
22	49 59.9	103 42.5	38.8	153 17.1	23.4	113 47.7	39.0	237 09.3	13.0
23	65 02.4	118 41.9	38.0	168 17.6	23.6	128 49.6	38.9	252 11.7	13.0
Mer. Pass. (h m)	18 44.5	*v* −0.6	*d* 0.7	*v* 0.5	*d* 0.2	*v* 1.9	*d* 0.1	*v* 2.4	*d* 0.0

STARS

Name	SHA	Dec
	° ′	° ′
Acamar	315 20.4	S40 16.1
Achernar	335 28.7	S57 11.6
Acrux	173 13.6	S63 08.7
Adhara	255 14.9	S28 58.9
Aldebaran	290 52.9	N16 31.8
Alioth	166 23.7	N55 54.3
Alkaid	153 01.7	N49 15.8
Al Na'ir	27 48.0	S46 55.2
Alnilam	275 49.5	S 1 11.7
Alphard	217 59.3	S 8 41.8
Alphecca	126 14.2	N26 40.9
Alpheratz	357 47.0	N29 08.7
Altair	62 11.8	N 8 53.6
Ankaa	353 18.7	S42 15.6
Antares	112 30.8	S26 27.1
Arcturus	145 59.0	N19 08.0
Atria	107 36.4	S69 02.6
Avior	234 19.1	S59 32.0
Bellatrix	278 35.3	N 6 21.6
Betelgeuse	271 04.6	N 7 24.6
Canopus	263 57.1	S52 41.9
Capella	280 39.0	N46 00.5
Deneb	49 34.2	N45 18.9
Denebola	182 37.1	N14 31.2
Diphda	348 59.1	S17 56.2
Dubhe	193 55.5	N61 41.8
Elnath	278 16.5	N28 37.0
Eltanin	90 48.3	N51 29.3
Enif	33 50.6	N 9 55.1
Fomalhaut	15 27.6	S29 34.6
Gacrux	172 05.2	S57 09.6
Gienah	175 55.9	S17 35.4
Hadar	148 53.4	S60 24.8
Hamal	328 04.4	N23 30.5
Kaus Aust.	83 48.7	S34 22.9
Kochab	137 20.5	N74 06.8
Markab	13 41.8	N15 15.4
Menkar	314 18.3	N 4 07.6
Menkent	148 12.0	S36 24.8
Miaplacidus	221 40.2	S69 45.0
Mirfak	308 44.9	N49 53.8
Nunki	76 02.8	S26 17.2
Peacock	53 24.8	S56 42.6
Pollux	243 31.5	N28 00.2
Procyon	245 03.0	N 5 12.2
Rasalhague	96 09.9	N12 33.2
Regulus	207 47.0	N11 55.3
Rigel	281 15.0	S 8 11.4
Rigil Kent.	139 57.1	S60 52.2
Sabik	102 16.8	S15 44.2
Schedar	349 44.4	N56 35.6
Shaula	96 27.0	S37 06.7
Sirius	258 36.4	S16 43.6
Spica	158 35.0	S11 12.5
Suhail	222 54.8	S43 27.9
Vega	80 41.7	N38 47.6
Zuben'ubi	137 09.5	S16 04.7

	SHA	Mer. Pass.
	° ′	h m
Venus	56 02.1	15 04
Mars	104 48.7	11 48
Jupiter	64 13.7	14 29
Saturn	187 13.8	6 18

UT	SUN GHA	SUN Dec	MOON GHA	v	MOON Dec	d	HP
d h	° ′	° ′	° ′	′	° ′	′	′
8 00 MONDAY	182 02.2	S22 43.9	67 54.1	12.2	N 8 50.6	14.8	58.3
01	197 01.9	44.1	82 25.3	12.2	9 05.4	14.8	58.3
02	212 01.6	44.4	96 56.5	12.0	9 20.2	14.7	58.4
03	227 01.3	. . 44.7	111 27.5	12.0	9 34.9	14.8	58.4
04	242 01.1	44.9	125 58.5	11.9	9 49.7	14.7	58.4
05	257 00.8	45.2	140 29.4	11.7	10 04.4	14.6	58.5
06	272 00.5	S22 45.4	155 00.1	11.7	N10 19.0	14.7	58.5
07	287 00.2	45.7	169 30.8	11.6	10 33.7	14.6	58.6
08	302 00.0	45.9	184 01.4	11.5	10 48.3	14.6	58.6
09	316 59.7	. . 46.2	198 31.9	11.3	11 02.9	14.5	58.6
10	331 59.4	46.4	213 02.2	11.3	11 17.4	14.5	58.7
11	346 59.1	46.7	227 32.5	11.2	11 31.9	14.5	58.7
12	1 58.9	S22 47.0	242 02.7	11.1	N11 46.4	14.4	58.8
13	16 58.6	47.2	256 32.8	10.9	12 00.8	14.4	58.8
14	31 58.3	47.4	271 02.7	10.9	12 15.2	14.3	58.8
15	46 58.0	. . 47.7	285 32.6	10.8	12 29.5	14.3	58.9
16	61 57.8	47.9	300 02.4	10.6	12 43.8	14.3	58.9
17	76 57.5	48.2	314 32.0	10.5	12 58.1	14.2	59.0
18	91 57.2	S22 48.4	329 01.5	10.4	N13 12.3	14.1	59.0
19	106 56.9	48.7	343 30.9	10.4	13 26.4	14.1	59.1
20	121 56.6	48.9	358 00.3	10.1	13 40.5	14.1	59.1
21	136 56.4	. . 49.2	12 29.4	10.1	13 54.6	14.0	59.1
22	151 56.1	49.4	26 58.5	10.0	14 08.6	13.9	59.2
23	166 55.8	49.7	41 27.5	9.8	14 22.5	13.9	59.2
9 00 TUESDAY	181 55.5	S22 49.9	55 56.3	9.8	N14 36.4	13.8	59.3
01	196 55.3	50.1	70 25.1	9.6	14 50.2	13.7	59.3
02	211 55.0	50.4	84 53.7	9.5	15 03.9	13.7	59.3
03	226 54.7	. . 50.6	99 22.2	9.3	15 17.6	13.6	59.4
04	241 54.4	50.9	113 50.5	9.3	15 31.2	13.6	59.4
05	256 54.1	51.1	128 18.8	9.1	15 44.8	13.4	59.4
06	271 53.9	S22 51.3	142 46.9	9.0	N15 58.2	13.4	59.5
07	286 53.6	51.6	157 14.9	8.8	16 11.6	13.4	59.5
08	301 53.3	51.8	171 42.7	8.8	16 25.0	13.2	59.6
09	316 53.0	. . 52.0	186 10.5	8.6	16 38.2	13.2	59.6
10	331 52.7	52.3	200 38.1	8.5	16 51.4	13.1	59.6
11	346 52.5	52.5	215 05.6	8.3	17 04.5	13.0	59.7
12	1 52.2	S22 52.7	229 32.9	8.3	N17 17.5	12.9	59.7
13	16 51.9	53.0	244 00.2	8.1	17 30.4	12.9	59.8
14	31 51.6	53.2	258 27.3	7.9	17 43.3	12.7	59.8
15	46 51.3	. . 53.4	272 54.2	7.9	17 56.0	12.7	59.8
16	61 51.0	53.7	287 21.1	7.7	18 08.7	12.5	59.9
17	76 50.8	53.9	301 47.8	7.5	18 21.2	12.5	59.9
18	91 50.5	S22 54.1	316 14.3	7.5	N18 33.7	12.4	59.9
19	106 50.2	54.3	330 40.8	7.3	18 46.1	12.3	60.0
20	121 49.9	54.6	345 07.1	7.1	18 58.4	12.1	60.0
21	136 49.6	. . 54.8	359 33.2	7.0	19 10.5	12.1	60.0
22	151 49.4	55.0	13 59.2	6.9	19 22.6	12.0	60.1
23	166 49.1	55.2	28 25.1	6.8	19 34.6	11.8	60.1
10 00 WEDNESDAY	181 48.8	S22 55.5	42 50.9	6.6	N19 46.4	11.7	60.2
01	196 48.5	55.7	57 16.5	6.5	19 58.1	11.7	60.2
02	211 48.2	55.9	71 42.0	6.3	20 09.8	11.5	60.2
03	226 47.9	. . 56.1	86 07.3	6.3	20 21.3	11.4	60.3
04	241 47.7	56.3	100 32.6	6.0	20 32.7	11.2	60.3
05	256 47.4	56.6	114 57.6	6.0	20 43.9	11.2	60.3
06	271 47.1	S22 56.8	129 22.6	5.8	N20 55.1	11.0	60.4
07	286 46.8	57.0	143 47.4	5.6	21 06.1	10.9	60.4
08	301 46.5	57.2	158 12.0	5.6	21 17.0	10.8	60.4
09	316 46.2	. . 57.4	172 36.6	5.4	21 27.8	10.6	60.5
10	331 46.0	57.6	187 01.0	5.2	21 38.4	10.5	60.5
11	346 45.7	57.9	201 25.2	5.2	21 48.9	10.4	60.5
12	1 45.4	S22 58.1	215 49.4	4.9	N21 59.3	10.2	60.5
13	16 45.1	58.3	230 13.3	4.9	22 09.5	10.1	60.6
14	31 44.8	58.5	244 37.2	4.7	22 19.6	10.0	60.6
15	46 44.5	. . 58.7	259 00.9	4.6	22 29.6	9.8	60.6
16	61 44.2	58.9	273 24.5	4.5	22 39.4	9.6	60.7
17	76 44.0	59.1	287 48.0	4.3	22 49.0	9.5	60.7
18	91 43.7	S22 59.3	302 11.3	4.2	N22 58.5	9.4	60.7
19	106 43.4	59.5	316 34.5	4.1	23 07.9	9.2	60.8
20	121 43.1	22 59.8	330 57.6	3.9	23 17.1	9.0	60.8
21	136 42.8	23 00.0	345 20.5	3.8	23 26.1	8.9	60.8
22	151 42.5	00.2	359 43.3	3.7	23 35.0	8.7	60.8
23	166 42.2	00.4	14 06.0	3.6	N23 43.7	8.6	60.9
	SD 16.3	d 0.2	SD 16.0		16.3		16.5

Lat.	Twilight Naut.	Twilight Civil	Sunrise	Moonrise 8	Moonrise 9	Moonrise 10	Moonrise 11
°	h m	h m	h m	h m	h m	h m	h m
N 72	08 11	10 27	■	11 16	10 07	□	□
N 70	07 52	09 36	■	11 35	10 53	□	□
68	07 37	09 04	■	11 50	11 24	10 22	□
66	07 25	08 40	10 14	12 02	11 47	11 22	□
64	07 14	08 22	09 36	12 12	12 05	11 56	11 39
62	07 05	08 06	09 10	12 21	12 20	12 21	12 28
60	06 57	07 53	08 50	12 29	12 33	12 42	13 00
N 58	06 50	07 42	08 33	12 35	12 44	12 58	13 23
56	06 44	07 32	08 19	12 41	12 54	13 12	13 43
54	06 38	07 24	08 07	12 47	13 02	13 25	13 59
52	06 32	07 16	07 56	12 52	13 10	13 36	14 13
50	06 27	07 09	07 47	12 56	13 17	13 45	14 25
45	06 16	06 53	07 27	13 06	13 32	14 06	14 51
N 40	06 06	06 40	07 10	13 14	13 45	14 23	15 11
35	05 57	06 28	06 56	13 21	13 55	14 37	15 28
30	05 48	06 18	06 44	13 27	14 05	14 49	15 43
20	05 32	06 00	06 24	13 38	14 21	15 10	16 08
N 10	05 17	05 43	06 06	13 47	14 35	15 29	16 30
0	05 00	05 26	05 49	13 56	14 49	15 47	16 50
S 10	04 42	05 09	05 32	14 05	15 02	16 04	17 11
20	04 20	04 49	05 13	14 15	15 17	16 23	17 33
30	03 51	04 24	04 52	14 26	15 34	16 45	17 58
35	03 33	04 10	04 39	14 33	15 44	16 58	18 14
40	03 11	03 52	04 24	14 41	15 55	17 13	18 31
45	02 41	03 30	04 07	14 49	16 09	17 31	18 53
S 50	01 58	03 01	03 45	15 00	16 25	17 54	19 20
52	01 33	02 47	03 35	15 05	16 33	18 04	19 33
54	00 55	02 30	03 23	15 11	16 42	18 17	19 48
56	////	02 09	03 09	15 17	16 51	18 31	20 06
58	////	01 42	02 53	15 24	17 03	18 47	20 28
S 60	////	01 00	02 34	15 31	17 16	19 07	20 57

Lat.	Sunset	Twilight Civil	Twilight Naut.	Moonset 8	Moonset 9	Moonset 10	Moonset 11
°	h m	h m	h m	h m	h m	h m	h m
N 72	■	13 18	15 34	03 41	06 37	□	□
N 70	■	14 09	15 52	03 25	05 52	□	□
68	■	14 41	16 07	03 12	05 24	08 23	□
66	13 31	15 04	16 20	03 02	05 02	07 24	□
64	14 08	15 23	16 30	02 53	04 45	06 51	09 18
62	14 35	15 38	16 39	02 46	04 31	06 26	08 29
60	14 55	15 51	16 48	02 40	04 20	06 07	07 58
N 58	15 12	16 03	16 55	02 34	04 09	05 51	07 35
56	15 26	16 12	17 01	02 29	04 01	05 38	07 16
54	15 38	16 21	17 07	02 25	03 53	05 26	07 00
52	15 49	16 29	17 13	02 21	03 46	05 16	06 46
50	15 58	16 36	17 18	02 17	03 40	05 07	06 35
45	16 18	16 52	17 29	02 10	03 26	04 47	06 10
N 40	16 35	17 05	17 39	02 03	03 15	04 32	05 50
35	16 48	17 16	17 48	01 58	03 06	04 19	05 34
30	17 00	17 27	17 56	01 53	02 58	04 07	05 20
20	17 21	17 45	18 12	01 45	02 44	03 48	04 56
N 10	17 39	18 02	18 28	01 38	02 32	03 31	04 35
0	17 56	18 19	18 45	01 31	02 21	03 15	04 16
S 10	18 13	18 36	19 03	01 24	02 09	03 00	03 57
20	18 32	18 56	19 25	01 17	01 57	02 43	03 36
30	18 53	19 21	19 54	01 09	01 43	02 24	03 13
35	19 06	19 36	20 12	01 04	01 36	02 13	02 59
40	19 21	19 53	20 35	00 59	01 27	02 00	02 43
45	19 38	20 15	21 04	00 53	01 16	01 46	02 24
S 50	20 00	20 44	21 48	00 45	01 04	01 28	02 01
52	20 11	20 59	22 14	00 42	00 58	01 19	01 49
54	20 23	21 16	22 53	00 38	00 52	01 10	01 37
56	20 36	21 37	////	00 34	00 44	00 59	01 22
58	20 52	22 05	////	00 30	00 37	00 47	01 05
S 60	21 12	22 47	////	00 25	00 28	00 33	00 44

Day	SUN Eqn. of Time 00^h	SUN Eqn. of Time 12^h	SUN Mer. Pass.	MOON Mer. Pass. Upper	MOON Mer. Pass. Lower	MOON Age	MOON Phase
d	m s	m s	h m	h m	h m	d	%
8	08 09	07 56	11 52	20 08	07 43	11	77
9	07 43	07 29	11 53	21 02	08 34	12	85
10	07 16	07 02	11 53	22 01	09 31	13	93

UT d h	ARIES GHA	VENUS −4.2 GHA	VENUS Dec	MARS +1.3 GHA	MARS Dec	JUPITER −2.0 GHA	JUPITER Dec	SATURN +1.0 GHA	SATURN Dec
	° ′	° ′	° ′	° ′	° ′	° ′	° ′	° ′	° ′
11 00 (Thursday)	80 04.8	133 41.4	S21 37.3	183 18.0	S23 23.7	143 51.5	S21 38.8	267 14.1	N 5 13.0
01	95 07.3	148 40.8	36.6	198 18.5	23.9	158 53.4	38.7	282 16.4	12.9
02	110 09.8	163 40.3	35.9	213 19.0	24.1	173 55.3	38.6	297 18.8	12.9
03	125 12.2	178 39.7	35.1	228 19.5	24.3	188 57.2	38.5	312 21.2	12.9
04	140 14.7	193 39.2	34.4	243 19.9	24.5	203 59.1	38.4	327 23.6	12.8
05	155 17.2	208 38.6	33.7	258 20.4	24.7	219 01.0	38.3	342 25.9	12.8
06	170 19.6	223 38.1	S21 32.9	273 20.9	S23 24.9	234 02.9	S21 38.2	357 28.3	N 5 12.8
07	185 22.1	238 37.5	32.2	288 21.3	25.1	249 04.8	38.1	12 30.7	12.8
08	200 24.6	253 37.0	31.5	303 21.8	25.3	264 06.7	38.0	27 33.1	12.7
09	215 27.0	268 36.4	30.7	318 22.3	25.4	279 08.6	37.9	42 35.4	12.7
10	230 29.5	283 35.9	30.0	333 22.7	25.6	294 10.5	37.9	57 37.8	12.7
11	245 32.0	298 35.3	29.3	348 23.2	25.8	309 12.4	37.8	72 40.2	12.7
12	260 34.4	313 34.8	S21 28.5	3 23.7	S23 26.0	324 14.3	S21 37.7	87 42.6	N 5 12.6
13	275 36.9	328 34.3	27.8	18 24.1	26.2	339 16.2	37.6	102 44.9	12.6
14	290 39.3	343 33.7	27.1	33 24.6	26.4	354 18.1	37.5	117 47.3	12.6
15	305 41.8	358 33.2	26.3	48 25.1	26.6	9 20.0	37.4	132 49.7	12.6
16	320 44.3	13 32.6	25.6	63 25.5	26.7	24 21.9	37.3	147 52.1	12.5
17	335 46.7	28 32.1	24.8	78 26.0	26.9	39 23.8	37.2	162 54.4	12.5
18	350 49.2	43 31.6	S21 24.1	93 26.5	S23 27.1	54 25.7	S21 37.1	177 56.8	N 5 12.5
19	5 51.7	58 31.0	23.3	108 26.9	27.3	69 27.6	37.0	192 59.2	12.5
20	20 54.1	73 30.5	22.6	123 27.4	27.5	84 29.5	36.9	208 01.6	12.4
21	35 56.6	88 30.0	21.9	138 27.9	27.7	99 31.4	36.8	223 03.9	12.4
22	50 59.1	103 29.4	21.1	153 28.3	27.8	114 33.2	36.8	238 06.3	12.4
23	66 01.5	118 28.9	20.4	168 28.8	28.0	129 35.1	36.7	253 08.7	12.4
12 00 (Friday)	81 04.0	133 28.4	S21 19.6	183 29.3	S23 28.2	144 37.0	S21 36.6	268 11.1	N 5 12.3
01	96 06.4	148 27.8	18.9	198 29.7	28.4	159 38.9	36.5	283 13.4	12.3
02	111 08.9	163 27.3	18.1	213 30.2	28.6	174 40.8	36.4	298 15.8	12.3
03	126 11.4	178 26.8	17.4	228 30.7	28.7	189 42.7	36.3	313 18.2	12.3
04	141 13.8	193 26.2	16.6	243 31.1	28.9	204 44.6	36.2	328 20.6	12.2
05	156 16.3	208 25.7	15.9	258 31.6	29.1	219 46.5	36.1	343 22.9	12.2
06	171 18.8	223 25.2	S21 15.1	273 32.1	S23 29.3	234 48.4	S21 36.0	358 25.3	N 5 12.2
07	186 21.2	238 24.6	14.4	288 32.5	29.5	249 50.3	35.9	13 27.7	12.2
08	201 23.7	253 24.1	13.6	303 33.0	29.6	264 52.2	35.8	28 30.1	12.1
09	216 26.2	268 23.6	12.8	318 33.5	29.8	279 54.1	35.7	43 32.5	12.1
10	231 28.6	283 23.1	12.1	333 33.9	30.0	294 56.0	35.6	58 34.8	12.1
11	246 31.1	298 22.5	11.3	348 34.4	30.2	309 57.9	35.5	73 37.2	12.1
12	261 33.6	313 22.0	S21 10.6	3 34.8	S23 30.3	324 59.8	S21 35.5	88 39.6	N 5 12.0
13	276 36.0	328 21.5	09.8	18 35.3	30.5	340 01.7	35.4	103 42.0	12.0
14	291 38.5	343 21.0	09.0	33 35.8	30.7	355 03.6	35.3	118 44.4	12.0
15	306 40.9	358 20.5	08.3	48 36.2	30.9	10 05.5	35.2	133 46.7	12.0
16	321 43.4	13 19.9	07.5	63 36.7	31.0	25 07.4	35.1	148 49.1	11.9
17	336 45.9	28 19.4	06.8	78 37.2	31.2	40 09.3	35.0	163 51.5	11.9
18	351 48.3	43 18.9	S21 06.0	93 37.6	S23 31.4	55 11.2	S21 34.9	178 53.9	N 5 11.9
19	6 50.8	58 18.4	05.2	108 38.1	31.6	70 13.1	34.8	193 56.3	11.9
20	21 53.3	73 17.9	04.5	123 38.5	31.7	85 15.0	34.7	208 58.6	11.8
21	36 55.7	88 17.4	03.7	138 39.0	31.9	100 16.8	34.6	224 01.0	11.8
22	51 58.2	103 16.8	02.9	153 39.5	32.1	115 18.7	34.5	239 03.4	11.8
23	67 00.7	118 16.3	02.2	168 39.9	32.3	130 20.6	34.4	254 05.8	11.8
13 00 (Saturday)	82 03.1	133 15.8	S21 01.4	183 40.4	S23 32.4	145 22.5	S21 34.3	269 08.2	N 5 11.7
01	97 05.6	148 15.3	21 00.6	198 40.9	32.6	160 24.4	34.2	284 10.5	11.7
02	112 08.1	163 14.8	20 59.8	213 41.3	32.8	175 26.3	34.1	299 12.9	11.7
03	127 10.5	178 14.3	59.1	228 41.8	32.9	190 28.2	34.1	314 15.3	11.7
04	142 13.0	193 13.8	58.3	243 42.2	33.1	205 30.1	34.0	329 17.7	11.7
05	157 15.4	208 13.3	57.5	258 42.7	33.3	220 32.0	33.9	344 20.1	11.6
06	172 17.9	223 12.7	S20 56.7	273 43.2	S23 33.4	235 33.9	S21 33.8	359 22.4	N 5 11.6
07	187 20.4	238 12.2	56.0	288 43.6	33.6	250 35.8	33.7	14 24.8	11.6
08	202 22.8	253 11.7	55.2	303 44.1	33.8	265 37.7	33.6	29 27.2	11.6
09	217 25.3	268 11.2	54.4	318 44.5	34.0	280 39.6	33.5	44 29.6	11.5
10	232 27.8	283 10.7	53.6	333 45.0	34.1	295 41.5	33.4	59 32.0	11.5
11	247 30.2	298 10.2	52.9	348 45.5	34.3	310 43.4	33.3	74 34.4	11.5
12	262 32.7	313 09.7	S20 52.1	3 45.9	S23 34.5	325 45.3	S21 33.2	89 36.7	N 5 11.5
13	277 35.2	328 09.2	51.3	18 46.4	34.6	340 47.1	33.1	104 39.1	11.4
14	292 37.6	343 08.7	50.5	33 46.8	34.8	355 49.0	33.0	119 41.5	11.4
15	307 40.1	358 08.2	49.7	48 47.3	34.9	10 50.9	32.9	134 43.9	11.4
16	322 42.6	13 07.7	48.9	63 47.7	35.1	25 52.8	32.8	149 46.3	11.4
17	337 45.0	28 07.2	48.2	78 48.2	35.3	40 54.7	32.7	164 48.7	11.4
18	352 47.5	43 06.7	S20 47.4	93 48.7	S23 35.4	55 56.6	S21 32.6	179 51.0	N 5 11.3
19	7 49.9	58 06.2	46.6	108 49.1	35.6	70 58.5	32.5	194 53.4	11.3
20	22 52.4	73 05.7	45.8	123 49.6	35.8	86 00.4	32.4	209 55.8	11.3
21	37 54.9	88 05.2	45.0	138 50.0	35.9	101 02.3	32.4	224 58.2	11.3
22	52 57.3	103 04.7	44.2	153 50.5	36.1	116 04.2	32.3	240 00.6	11.2
23	67 59.8	118 04.2	43.4	168 51.0	36.3	131 06.1	32.2	255 03.0	11.2
Mer. Pass. (h m)	18 32.7	v −0.5	d 0.8	v 0.5	d 0.2	v 1.9	d 0.1	v 2.4	d 0.0

STARS

Name	SHA	Dec
	° ′	° ′
Acamar	315 20.4	S40 16.1
Achernar	335 28.7	S57 11.6
Acrux	173 13.6	S63 08.7
Adhara	255 14.8	S28 58.9
Aldebaran	290 52.9	N16 31.8
Alioth	166 23.6	N55 54.3
Alkaid	153 01.7	N49 15.8
Al Na'ir	27 48.0	S46 55.2
Alnilam	275 49.5	S 1 11.7
Alphard	217 59.3	S 8 41.8
Alphecca	126 14.2	N26 40.9
Alpheratz	357 47.0	N29 08.7
Altair	62 11.8	N 8 53.6
Ankaa	353 18.7	S42 15.6
Antares	112 30.8	S26 27.1
Arcturus	145 59.0	N19 08.0
Atria	107 36.4	S69 02.6
Avior	234 19.1	S59 32.1
Bellatrix	278 35.3	N 6 21.6
Betelgeuse	271 04.6	N 7 24.6
Canopus	263 57.1	S52 41.9
Capella	280 39.0	N46 00.5
Deneb	49 34.2	N45 18.9
Denebola	182 37.1	N14 31.2
Diphda	348 59.1	S17 56.2
Dubhe	193 55.4	N61 41.8
Elnath	278 16.5	N28 37.0
Eltanin	90 48.3	N51 29.2
Enif	33 50.6	N 9 55.1
Fomalhaut	15 27.7	S29 34.6
Gacrux	172 05.1	S57 09.6
Gienah	175 55.9	S17 35.5
Hadar	148 53.4	S60 24.8
Hamal	328 04.4	N23 30.5
Kaus Aust.	83 48.7	S34 22.9
Kochab	137 20.4	N74 06.8
Markab	13 41.8	N15 15.4
Menkar	314 18.3	N 4 07.6
Menkent	148 11.9	S36 24.8
Miaplacidus	221 40.2	S69 45.0
Mirfak	308 44.9	N49 53.8
Nunki	76 02.8	S26 17.2
Peacock	53 24.8	S56 42.6
Pollux	243 31.5	N28 00.2
Procyon	245 03.0	N 5 12.1
Rasalhague	96 09.9	N12 33.2
Regulus	207 47.0	N11 55.3
Rigel	281 15.0	S 8 11.4
Rigil Kent.	139 57.1	S60 52.2
Sabik	102 16.8	S15 44.2
Schedar	349 44.4	N56 35.6
Shaula	96 26.9	S37 06.7
Sirius	258 36.4	S16 43.6
Spica	158 35.0	S11 12.5
Suhail	222 54.8	S43 27.9
Vega	80 41.7	N38 47.5
Zuben'ubi	137 09.5	S16 04.8

	SHA	Mer. Pass.
	° ′	h m
Venus	52 24.4	15 07
Mars	102 25.3	11 46
Jupiter	63 33.1	14 20
Saturn	187 07.1	6 06

UT	SUN GHA	SUN Dec	MOON GHA	v	MOON Dec	d	HP
d h	° ′	° ′	° ′	′	° ′	′	′
11 00 (THURSDAY)	181 42.0	S23 00.6	28 28.6	3.4	N23 52.3	8.4	60.9
01	196 41.7	00.8	42 51.0	3.3	24 00.7	8.2	60.9
02	211 41.4	01.0	57 13.3	3.2	24 08.9	8.1	60.9
03	226 41.1	. . 01.2	71 35.5	3.1	24 17.0	7.9	61.0
04	241 40.8	01.4	85 57.6	3.0	24 24.9	7.7	61.0
05	256 40.5	01.6	100 19.6	2.8	24 32.6	7.5	61.0
06	271 40.2	S23 01.8	114 41.4	2.8	N24 40.1	7.4	61.0
07	286 39.9	02.0	129 03.2	2.6	24 47.5	7.2	61.1
08	301 39.7	02.2	143 24.8	2.5	24 54.7	7.0	61.1
09	316 39.4	. . 02.4	157 46.3	2.4	25 01.7	6.8	61.1
10	331 39.1	02.6	172 07.7	2.3	25 08.5	6.7	61.1
11	346 38.8	02.8	186 29.0	2.2	25 15.2	6.4	61.1
12	1 38.5	S23 03.0	200 50.2	2.1	N25 21.6	6.3	61.2
13	16 38.2	03.2	215 11.3	2.0	25 27.9	6.0	61.2
14	31 37.9	03.3	229 32.3	1.9	25 33.9	5.9	61.2
15	46 37.6	. . 03.5	243 53.2	1.8	25 39.8	5.7	61.2
16	61 37.3	03.7	258 14.0	1.7	25 45.5	5.5	61.2
17	76 37.1	03.9	272 34.7	1.7	25 51.0	5.3	61.2
18	91 36.8	S23 04.1	286 55.4	1.5	N25 56.3	5.1	61.3
19	106 36.5	04.3	301 15.9	1.5	26 01.4	4.9	61.3
20	121 36.2	04.5	315 36.4	1.3	26 06.3	4.7	61.3
21	136 35.9	. . 04.7	329 56.7	1.3	26 11.0	4.5	61.3
22	151 35.6	04.9	344 17.0	1.3	26 15.5	4.3	61.3
23	166 35.3	05.0	358 37.3	1.1	26 19.8	4.1	61.3
12 00 (FRIDAY)	181 35.0	S23 05.2	12 57.4	1.1	N26 23.9	3.9	61.4
01	196 34.7	05.4	27 17.5	1.1	26 27.8	3.7	61.4
02	211 34.4	05.6	41 37.6	0.9	26 31.5	3.4	61.4
03	226 34.1	. . 05.8	55 57.5	0.9	26 34.9	3.3	61.4
04	241 33.9	06.0	70 17.4	0.9	26 38.2	3.0	61.4
05	256 33.6	06.1	84 37.3	0.8	26 41.2	2.9	61.4
06	271 33.3	S23 06.3	98 57.1	0.7	N26 44.1	2.6	61.4
07	286 33.0	06.5	113 16.8	0.8	26 46.7	2.4	61.4
08	301 32.7	06.7	127 36.6	0.6	26 49.1	2.2	61.4
09	316 32.4	. . 06.9	141 56.2	0.7	26 51.3	2.0	61.4
10	331 32.1	07.0	156 15.9	0.5	26 53.3	1.7	61.5
11	346 31.8	07.2	170 35.4	0.6	26 55.0	1.6	61.5
12	1 31.5	S23 07.4	184 55.0	0.6	N26 56.6	1.3	61.5
13	16 31.2	07.6	199 14.6	0.5	26 57.9	1.1	61.5
14	31 30.9	07.7	213 34.1	0.5	26 59.0	0.9	61.5
15	46 30.6	. . 07.9	227 53.6	0.4	26 59.9	0.7	61.5
16	61 30.4	08.1	242 13.0	0.5	27 00.6	0.5	61.5
17	76 30.1	08.3	256 32.5	0.5	27 01.1	0.2	61.5
18	91 29.8	S23 08.4	270 52.0	0.4	N27 01.3	0.0	61.5
19	106 29.5	08.6	285 11.4	0.5	27 01.3	0.2	61.5
20	121 29.2	08.8	299 30.9	0.4	27 01.1	0.4	61.5
21	136 28.9	. . 08.9	313 50.3	0.5	27 00.7	0.6	61.5
22	151 28.6	09.1	328 09.8	0.5	27 00.1	0.8	61.5
23	166 28.3	09.3	342 29.3	0.5	26 59.3	1.1	61.5
13 00 (SATURDAY)	181 28.0	S23 09.4	356 48.8	0.5	N26 58.2	1.3	61.5
01	196 27.7	09.6	11 08.3	0.5	26 56.9	1.5	61.5
02	211 27.4	09.8	25 27.8	0.5	26 55.4	1.7	61.5
03	226 27.1	. . 09.9	39 47.3	0.6	26 53.7	1.9	61.5
04	241 26.8	10.1	54 06.9	0.6	26 51.8	2.2	61.5
05	256 26.5	10.3	68 26.5	0.7	26 49.6	2.3	61.5
06	271 26.2	S23 10.4	82 46.2	0.7	N26 47.3	2.6	61.5
07	286 25.9	10.6	97 05.9	0.7	26 44.7	2.8	61.5
08	301 25.6	10.7	111 25.6	0.8	26 41.9	3.0	61.5
09	316 25.3	. . 10.9	125 45.4	0.8	26 38.9	3.2	61.5
10	331 25.1	11.0	140 05.2	0.9	26 35.7	3.4	61.5
11	346 24.8	11.2	154 25.1	0.9	26 32.3	3.7	61.4
12	1 24.5	S23 11.4	168 45.0	1.0	N26 28.6	3.8	61.4
13	16 24.2	11.5	183 05.0	1.0	26 24.8	4.1	61.4
14	31 23.9	11.7	197 25.0	1.2	26 20.7	4.2	61.4
15	46 23.6	. . 11.8	211 45.2	1.1	26 16.5	4.5	61.4
16	61 23.3	12.0	226 05.3	1.3	26 12.0	4.6	61.4
17	76 23.0	12.1	240 25.6	1.3	26 07.4	4.9	61.4
18	91 22.7	S23 12.3	254 45.9	1.4	N26 02.5	5.1	61.4
19	106 22.4	12.4	269 06.3	1.5	25 57.4	5.3	61.4
20	121 22.1	12.6	283 26.8	1.6	25 52.1	5.4	61.3
21	136 21.8	. . 12.7	297 47.4	1.7	25 46.7	5.7	61.3
22	151 21.5	12.9	312 08.1	1.7	25 41.0	5.9	61.3
23	166 21.2	13.0	326 28.8	1.9	N25 35.1	6.0	61.3
	SD 16.3	d 0.2	SD 16.7		16.7		16.7

Lat.	Twilight Naut.	Twilight Civil	Sunrise	Moonrise 11	12	13	14
°	h m	h m	h m	h m	h m	h m	h m
N 72	08 16	10 38	■	□	□	□	□
N 70	07 57	09 43	■	□	□	□	□
68	07 42	09 09	■	□	□	□	□
66	07 29	08 45	10 22	□	□	□	14 46
64	07 18	08 26	09 42	11 39	□	□	15 49
62	07 09	08 10	09 15	12 28	12 56	14 22	16 23
60	07 01	07 57	08 54	13 00	13 41	15 01	16 48
N 58	06 53	07 46	08 37	13 23	14 10	15 28	17 08
56	06 47	07 36	08 23	13 43	14 33	15 50	17 25
54	06 41	07 27	08 10	13 59	14 52	16 07	17 38
52	06 35	07 19	07 59	14 13	15 08	16 22	17 51
50	06 30	07 11	07 50	14 25	15 21	16 35	18 01
45	06 18	06 55	07 29	14 51	15 49	17 02	18 24
N 40	06 08	06 42	07 13	15 11	16 11	17 23	18 42
35	05 59	06 31	06 59	15 28	16 30	17 41	18 57
30	05 50	06 20	06 47	15 43	16 46	17 56	19 10
20	05 34	06 02	06 26	16 08	17 12	18 22	19 32
N 10	05 18	05 45	06 07	16 30	17 36	18 44	19 51
0	05 01	05 28	05 50	16 50	17 57	19 05	20 08
S 10	04 43	05 10	05 33	17 11	18 19	19 25	20 26
20	04 20	04 50	05 14	17 33	18 42	19 47	20 45
30	03 52	04 25	04 52	17 58	19 09	20 13	21 07
35	03 33	04 10	04 40	18 14	19 25	20 28	21 19
40	03 11	03 52	04 25	18 31	19 44	20 45	21 34
45	02 41	03 30	04 07	18 53	20 06	21 06	21 51
S 50	01 57	03 01	03 45	19 20	20 35	21 32	22 12
52	01 30	02 46	03 34	19 33	20 49	21 45	22 22
54	00 49	02 29	03 22	19 48	21 05	21 59	22 34
56	////	02 07	03 08	20 06	21 24	22 16	22 46
58	////	01 39	02 52	20 28	21 48	22 36	23 01
S 60	////	00 54	02 32	20 57	22 19	23 01	23 19

Lat.	Sunset	Twilight Civil	Twilight Naut.	Moonset 11	12	13	14
°	h m	h m	h m	h m	h m	h m	h m
N 72	■	13 09	15 31	□	□	□	□
N 70	■	14 05	15 51	□	□	□	□
68	■	14 38	16 06	□	□	□	□
66	13 26	15 03	16 19	□	□	□	13 12
64	14 06	15 22	16 30	09 18	□	□	12 08
62	14 33	15 37	16 39	08 29	10 21	11 18	11 32
60	14 54	15 51	16 47	07 58	09 36	10 38	11 07
N 58	15 11	16 02	16 54	07 35	09 07	10 10	10 46
56	15 25	16 12	17 01	07 16	08 44	09 49	10 29
54	15 37	16 21	17 07	07 00	08 25	09 31	10 15
52	15 48	16 29	17 13	06 46	08 10	09 16	10 02
50	15 58	16 36	17 18	06 35	07 56	09 02	09 51
45	16 18	16 52	17 29	06 10	07 28	08 35	09 28
N 40	16 35	17 05	17 39	05 50	07 06	08 14	09 09
35	16 49	17 17	17 49	05 34	06 48	07 56	08 53
30	17 01	17 27	17 57	05 20	06 32	07 40	08 39
20	17 22	17 46	18 14	04 56	06 06	07 14	08 15
N 10	17 40	18 03	18 30	04 35	05 43	06 51	07 55
0	17 58	18 20	18 46	04 16	05 22	06 29	07 36
S 10	18 15	18 38	19 05	03 57	05 00	06 08	07 16
20	18 34	18 58	19 27	03 36	04 38	05 45	06 55
30	18 56	19 23	19 56	03 13	04 11	05 18	06 31
35	19 08	19 38	20 15	02 59	03 55	05 02	06 17
40	19 23	19 56	20 37	02 43	03 37	04 44	06 00
45	19 41	20 18	21 08	02 24	03 15	04 22	05 40
S 50	20 03	20 47	21 52	02 01	02 48	03 53	05 14
52	20 14	21 02	22 19	01 49	02 34	03 39	05 02
54	20 26	21 20	23 01	01 37	02 19	03 23	04 48
56	20 40	21 41	////	01 22	02 00	03 04	04 32
58	20 56	22 10	////	01 05	01 38	02 40	04 12
S 60	21 16	22 56	////	00 44	01 10	02 09	03 47

Day	SUN Eqn. of Time 00^h	SUN Eqn. of Time 12^h	SUN Mer. Pass.	MOON Mer. Pass. Upper	MOON Mer. Pass. Lower	Age	Phase
d	m s	m s	h m	h m	h m	d	%
11	06 48	06 35	11 53	23 06	10 33	14	98
12	06 21	06 07	11 54	24 13	11 39	15	100 ○
13	05 53	05 38	11 54	00 13	12 47	16	99

UT	ARIES	VENUS −4.3		MARS +1.3		JUPITER −2.0		SATURN +1.0		STARS		
d h	GHA ° ′	GHA ° ′	Dec ° ′	GHA ° ′	Dec ° ′	GHA ° ′	Dec ° ′	GHA ° ′	Dec ° ′	Name	SHA ° ′	Dec ° ′
14 00	83 02.3	133 03.7	S20 42.6	183 51.4	S23 36.4	146 08.0	S21 32.1	270 05.4	N 5 11.2	Acamar	315 20.4	S40 16.2
01	98 04.7	148 03.2	41.8	198 51.9	36.6	161 09.9	32.0	285 07.7	11.2	Achernar	335 28.7	S57 11.6
02	113 07.2	163 02.7	41.0	213 52.3	36.7	176 11.7	31.9	300 10.1	11.2	Acrux	173 13.5	S63 08.7
03	128 09.7	178 02.2	. . 40.2	228 52.8	. . 36.9	191 13.6	. . 31.8	315 12.5	. . 11.1	Adhara	255 14.8	S28 58.9
04	143 12.1	193 01.7	39.5	243 53.2	37.1	206 15.5	31.7	330 14.9	11.1	Aldebaran	290 52.9	N16 31.8
05	158 14.6	208 01.3	38.7	258 53.7	37.2	221 17.4	31.6	345 17.3	11.1			
06	173 17.1	223 00.8	S20 37.9	273 54.1	S23 37.4	236 19.3	S21 31.5	0 19.7	N 5 11.1	Alioth	166 23.6	N55 54.3
07	188 19.5	238 00.3	37.1	288 54.6	37.5	251 21.2	31.4	15 22.0	11.1	Alkaid	153 01.6	N49 15.8
08	203 22.0	252 59.8	36.3	303 55.1	37.7	266 23.1	31.3	30 24.4	11.0	Al Na'ir	27 48.0	S46 55.2
S 09	218 24.4	267 59.3	. . 35.5	318 55.5	. . 37.8	281 25.0	. . 31.2	45 26.8	. . 11.0	Alnilam	275 49.4	S 1 11.7
U 10	233 26.9	282 58.8	34.7	333 56.0	38.0	296 26.9	31.1	60 29.2	11.0	Alphard	217 59.2	S 8 41.8
N 11	248 29.4	297 58.3	33.9	348 56.4	38.2	311 28.8	31.0	75 31.6	11.0			
D 12	263 31.8	312 57.8	S20 33.1	3 56.9	S23 38.3	326 30.7	S21 30.9	90 34.0	N 5 11.0	Alphecca	126 14.1	N26 40.9
A 13	278 34.3	327 57.4	32.3	18 57.3	38.5	341 32.5	30.8	105 36.4	10.9	Alpheratz	357 47.0	N29 08.7
Y 14	293 36.8	342 56.9	31.4	33 57.8	38.6	356 34.4	30.7	120 38.8	10.9	Altair	62 11.8	N 8 53.5
15	308 39.2	357 56.4	. . 30.6	48 58.2	. . 38.8	11 36.3	. . 30.6	135 41.1	. . 10.9	Ankaa	353 18.8	S42 15.6
16	323 41.7	12 55.9	29.8	63 58.7	38.9	26 38.2	30.5	150 43.5	10.9	Antares	112 30.8	S26 27.1
17	338 44.2	27 55.4	29.0	78 59.2	39.1	41 40.1	30.5	165 45.9	10.8			
18	353 46.6	42 55.0	S20 28.2	93 59.6	S23 39.2	56 42.0	S21 30.4	180 48.3	N 5 10.8	Arcturus	145 59.0	N19 08.0
19	8 49.1	57 54.5	27.4	109 00.1	39.4	71 43.9	30.3	195 50.7	10.8	Atria	107 36.3	S69 02.6
20	23 51.6	72 54.0	26.6	124 00.5	39.5	86 45.8	30.2	210 53.1	10.8	Avior	234 19.0	S59 32.1
21	38 54.0	87 53.5	. . 25.8	139 01.0	. . 39.7	101 47.7	. . 30.1	225 55.5	. . 10.8	Bellatrix	278 35.3	N 6 21.6
22	53 56.5	102 53.0	25.0	154 01.4	39.9	116 49.6	30.0	240 57.9	10.7	Betelgeuse	271 04.6	N 7 24.6
23	68 58.9	117 52.6	24.2	169 01.9	40.0	131 51.4	29.9	256 00.2	10.7			
15 00	84 01.4	132 52.1	S20 23.4	184 02.3	S23 40.2	146 53.3	S21 29.8	271 02.6	N 5 10.7	Canopus	263 57.1	S52 41.9
01	99 03.9	147 51.6	22.5	199 02.8	40.3	161 55.2	29.7	286 05.0	10.7	Capella	280 39.0	N46 00.5
02	114 06.3	162 51.1	21.7	214 03.2	40.5	176 57.1	29.6	301 07.4	10.7	Deneb	49 34.2	N45 18.9
03	129 08.8	177 50.7	. . 20.9	229 03.7	. . 40.6	191 59.0	. . 29.5	316 09.8	. . 10.6	Denebola	182 37.1	N14 31.2
04	144 11.3	192 50.2	20.1	244 04.1	40.8	207 00.9	29.4	331 12.2	10.6	Diphda	348 59.1	S17 56.2
05	159 13.7	207 49.7	19.3	259 04.6	40.9	222 02.8	29.3	346 14.6	10.6			
06	174 16.2	222 49.3	S20 18.5	274 05.0	S23 41.1	237 04.7	S21 29.2	1 17.0	N 5 10.6	Dubhe	193 55.4	N61 41.8
07	189 18.7	237 48.8	17.6	289 05.5	41.2	252 06.6	29.1	16 19.4	10.6	Elnath	278 16.5	N28 37.0
08	204 21.1	252 48.3	16.8	304 05.9	41.4	267 08.5	29.0	31 21.8	10.5	Eltanin	90 48.2	N51 29.2
M 09	219 23.6	267 47.8	. . 16.0	319 06.4	. . 41.5	282 10.3	. . 28.9	46 24.1	. . 10.5	Enif	33 50.6	N 9 55.1
O 10	234 26.1	282 47.4	15.2	334 06.8	41.6	297 12.2	28.8	61 26.5	10.5	Fomalhaut	15 27.7	S29 34.6
N 11	249 28.5	297 46.9	14.4	349 07.3	41.8	312 14.1	28.7	76 28.9	10.5			
D 12	264 31.0	312 46.4	S20 13.5	4 07.7	S23 41.9	327 16.0	S21 28.6	91 31.3	N 5 10.5	Gacrux	172 05.1	S57 09.6
A 13	279 33.4	327 46.0	12.7	19 08.2	42.1	342 17.9	28.5	106 33.7	10.5	Gienah	175 55.9	S17 35.5
Y 14	294 35.9	342 45.5	11.9	34 08.7	42.2	357 19.8	28.4	121 36.1	10.4	Hadar	148 53.3	S60 24.8
15	309 38.4	357 45.1	. . 11.1	49 09.1	. . 42.4	12 21.7	. . 28.3	136 38.5	. . 10.4	Hamal	328 04.4	N23 30.5
16	324 40.8	12 44.6	10.2	64 09.6	42.5	27 23.6	28.2	151 40.9	10.4	Kaus Aust.	83 48.7	S34 22.9
17	339 43.3	27 44.1	09.4	79 10.0	42.7	42 25.4	28.1	166 43.3	10.4			
18	354 45.8	42 43.7	S20 08.6	94 10.5	S23 42.8	57 27.3	S21 28.0	181 45.7	N 5 10.4	Kochab	137 20.4	N74 06.8
19	9 48.2	57 43.2	07.7	109 10.9	43.0	72 29.2	27.9	196 48.1	10.3	Markab	13 41.8	N15 15.4
20	24 50.7	72 42.8	06.9	124 11.3	43.1	87 31.1	27.9	211 50.5	10.3	Menkar	314 18.3	N 4 07.6
21	39 53.2	87 42.3	. . 06.1	139 11.8	. . 43.2	102 33.0	. . 27.8	226 52.8	. . 10.3	Menkent	148 11.9	S36 24.8
22	54 55.6	102 41.8	05.2	154 12.2	43.4	117 34.9	27.7	241 55.2	10.3	Miaplacidus	221 40.1	S69 45.0
23	69 58.1	117 41.4	04.4	169 12.7	43.5	132 36.8	27.6	256 57.6	10.3			
16 00	85 00.6	132 40.9	S20 03.6	184 13.1	S23 43.7	147 38.7	S21 27.5	272 00.0	N 5 10.3	Mirfak	308 44.9	N49 53.8
01	100 03.0	147 40.5	02.7	199 13.6	43.8	162 40.6	27.4	287 02.4	10.2	Nunki	76 02.8	S26 17.2
02	115 05.5	162 40.0	01.9	214 14.0	43.9	177 42.4	27.3	302 04.8	10.2	Peacock	53 24.8	S56 42.5
03	130 07.9	177 39.6	. . 01.1	229 14.5	. . 44.1	192 44.3	. . 27.2	317 07.2	. . 10.2	Pollux	243 31.5	N28 00.2
04	145 10.4	192 39.1	20 00.2	244 14.9	44.2	207 46.2	27.1	332 09.6	10.2	Procyon	245 02.9	N 5 12.1
05	160 12.9	207 38.7	19 59.4	259 15.4	44.4	222 48.1	27.0	347 12.0	10.2			
06	175 15.3	222 38.2	S19 58.6	274 15.8	S23 44.5	237 50.0	S21 26.9	2 14.4	N 5 10.1	Rasalhague	96 09.9	N12 33.2
07	190 17.8	237 37.8	57.7	289 16.3	44.6	252 51.9	26.8	17 16.8	10.1	Regulus	207 46.9	N11 55.3
T 08	205 20.3	252 37.3	56.9	304 16.7	44.8	267 53.8	26.7	32 19.2	10.1	Rigel	281 14.9	S 8 11.4
U 09	220 22.7	267 36.9	. . 56.0	319 17.2	. . 44.9	282 55.6	. . 26.6	47 21.6	. . 10.1	Rigil Kent.	139 57.1	S60 52.2
E 10	235 25.2	282 36.4	55.2	334 17.6	45.0	297 57.5	26.5	62 24.0	10.1	Sabik	102 16.8	S15 44.2
S 11	250 27.7	297 36.0	54.3	349 18.1	45.2	312 59.4	26.4	77 26.4	10.1			
D 12	265 30.1	312 35.5	S19 53.5	4 18.5	S23 45.3	328 01.3	S21 26.3	92 28.8	N 5 10.0	Schedar	349 44.4	N56 35.6
A 13	280 32.6	327 35.1	52.7	19 19.0	45.5	343 03.2	26.2	107 31.1	10.0	Shaula	96 26.9	S37 06.7
Y 14	295 35.1	342 34.6	51.8	34 19.4	45.6	358 05.1	26.1	122 33.5	10.0	Sirius	258 36.3	S16 43.6
15	310 37.5	357 34.2	. . 51.0	49 19.9	. . 45.7	13 07.0	. . 26.0	137 35.9	. . 10.0	Spica	158 35.0	S11 12.5
16	325 40.0	12 33.7	50.1	64 20.3	45.9	28 08.8	25.9	152 38.3	10.0	Suhail	222 54.7	S43 27.9
17	340 42.4	27 33.3	49.3	79 20.8	46.0	43 10.7	25.8	167 40.7	10.0			
18	355 44.9	42 32.9	S19 48.4	94 21.2	S23 46.1	58 12.6	S21 25.7	182 43.1	N 5 09.9	Vega	80 41.7	N38 47.5
19	10 47.4	57 32.4	47.6	109 21.6	46.3	73 14.5	25.6	197 45.5	09.9	Zuben'ubi	137 09.4	S16 04.8
20	25 49.8	72 32.0	46.7	124 22.1	46.4	88 16.4	25.5	212 47.9	09.9			
21	40 52.3	87 31.5	. . 45.9	139 22.5	. . 46.5	103 18.3	. . 25.4	227 50.3	. . 09.9			
22	55 54.8	102 31.1	45.0	154 23.0	46.7	118 20.2	25.3	242 52.7	09.9			
23	70 57.2	117 30.7	44.2	169 23.4	46.8	133 22.0	25.2	257 55.1	09.9			
Mer. Pass.	h m 18 20.9	*v* −0.5	*d* 0.8	*v* 0.5	*d* 0.1	*v* 1.9	*d* 0.1	*v* 2.4	*d* 0.0			

	SHA ° ′	Mer. Pass. h m
Venus	48 50.7	15 09
Mars	100 00.9	11 43
Jupiter	62 51.9	14 11
Saturn	187 01.2	5 55

UT d h	Day	SUN GHA ° ′	SUN Dec ° ′	MOON GHA ° ′	v ′	MOON Dec ° ′	d ′	HP ′
14 00		181 20.9	S23 13.2	340 49.7	1.9	N25 29.1	6.3	61.3
01		196 20.6	13.3	355 10.6	2.0	25 22.8	6.4	61.3
02		211 20.3	13.5	9 31.6	2.2	25 16.4	6.6	61.3
03		226 20.0	. . 13.6	23 52.8	2.2	25 09.8	6.8	61.2
04		241 19.7	13.8	38 14.0	2.3	25 03.0	7.0	61.2
05		256 19.4	13.9	52 35.3	2.5	24 56.0	7.2	61.2
06		271 19.1	S23 14.0	66 56.8	2.5	N24 48.8	7.4	61.2
07		286 18.8	14.2	81 18.3	2.7	24 41.4	7.5	61.2
08		301 18.5	14.3	95 40.0	2.7	24 33.9	7.8	61.1
09	S	316 18.2	. . 14.5	110 01.7	2.9	24 26.1	7.9	61.1
10	U	331 17.9	14.6	124 23.6	3.0	24 18.2	8.0	61.1
11	N	346 17.6	14.7	138 45.6	3.1	24 10.2	8.3	61.1
12	D	1 17.3	S23 14.9	153 07.7	3.3	N24 01.9	8.4	61.1
13	A	16 17.0	15.0	167 30.0	3.3	23 53.5	8.6	61.0
14	Y	31 16.7	15.1	181 52.3	3.5	23 44.9	8.7	61.0
15		46 16.4	. . 15.3	196 14.8	3.6	23 36.2	8.9	61.0
16		61 16.1	15.4	210 37.4	3.7	23 27.3	9.1	61.0
17		76 15.8	15.5	225 00.1	3.8	23 18.2	9.2	60.9
18		91 15.5	S23 15.7	239 22.9	4.0	N23 09.0	9.4	60.9
19		106 15.2	15.8	253 45.9	4.1	22 59.6	9.5	60.9
20		121 14.9	15.9	268 09.0	4.2	22 50.1	9.7	60.9
21		136 14.6	. . 16.1	282 32.2	4.4	22 40.4	9.9	60.8
22		151 14.3	16.2	296 55.6	4.5	22 30.5	10.0	60.8
23		166 14.0	16.3	311 19.1	4.6	22 20.5	10.1	60.8
15 00		181 13.7	S23 16.5	325 42.7	4.7	N22 10.4	10.3	60.8
01		196 13.4	16.6	340 06.4	4.9	22 00.1	10.4	60.7
02		211 13.1	16.7	354 30.3	5.0	21 49.7	10.6	60.7
03		226 12.8	. . 16.8	8 54.3	5.2	21 39.1	10.7	60.7
04		241 12.5	17.0	23 18.5	5.2	21 28.4	10.8	60.7
05		256 12.2	17.1	37 42.7	5.5	21 17.6	11.0	60.6
06		271 11.9	S23 17.2	52 07.2	5.5	N21 06.6	11.0	60.6
07		286 11.6	17.3	66 31.7	5.7	20 55.6	11.3	60.6
08		301 11.3	17.4	80 56.4	5.8	20 44.3	11.3	60.5
09	M	316 11.0	. . 17.6	95 21.2	5.9	20 33.0	11.5	60.5
10	O	331 10.7	17.7	109 46.1	6.1	20 21.5	11.6	60.5
11	N	346 10.4	17.8	124 11.2	6.2	20 09.9	11.7	60.4
12	D	1 10.1	S23 17.9	138 36.4	6.4	N19 58.2	11.8	60.4
13	A	16 09.8	18.0	153 01.8	6.5	19 46.4	11.9	60.4
14	Y	31 09.5	18.2	167 27.3	6.6	19 34.5	12.1	60.3
15		46 09.2	. . 18.3	181 52.9	6.7	19 22.4	12.1	60.3
16		61 08.9	18.4	196 18.6	6.9	19 10.3	12.3	60.3
17		76 08.6	18.5	210 44.5	7.0	18 58.0	12.4	60.2
18		91 08.3	S23 18.6	225 10.5	7.2	N18 45.6	12.4	60.2
19		106 08.0	18.7	239 36.7	7.3	18 33.2	12.6	60.2
20		121 07.7	18.8	254 03.0	7.4	18 20.6	12.7	60.1
21		136 07.4	. . 18.9	268 29.4	7.6	18 07.9	12.8	60.1
22		151 07.1	19.1	282 56.0	7.6	17 55.1	12.8	60.1
23		166 06.8	19.2	297 22.6	7.8	17 42.3	13.0	60.0
16 00		181 06.5	S23 19.3	311 49.4	8.0	N17 29.3	13.0	60.0
01		196 06.2	19.4	326 16.4	8.0	17 16.3	13.1	60.0
02		211 05.9	19.5	340 43.4	8.2	17 03.2	13.3	59.9
03		226 05.6	. . 19.6	355 10.6	8.4	16 49.9	13.3	59.9
04		241 05.3	19.7	9 38.0	8.4	16 36.6	13.3	59.9
05		256 05.0	19.8	24 05.4	8.6	16 23.3	13.5	59.8
06		271 04.7	S23 19.9	38 33.0	8.7	N16 09.8	13.5	59.8
07		286 04.4	20.0	53 00.7	8.8	15 56.3	13.6	59.8
08	T	301 04.1	20.1	67 28.5	9.0	15 42.7	13.7	59.7
09	U	316 03.8	. . 20.2	81 56.5	9.0	15 29.0	13.8	59.7
10	E	331 03.5	20.3	96 24.5	9.2	15 15.2	13.8	59.6
11	S	346 03.2	20.4	110 52.7	9.3	15 01.4	13.9	59.6
12	D	1 02.9	S23 20.5	125 21.0	9.4	N14 47.5	13.9	59.6
13		16 02.5	20.6	139 49.4	9.6	14 33.6	14.1	59.5
14	A	31 02.2	20.7	154 18.0	9.7	14 19.5	14.0	59.5
15	Y	46 01.9	. . 20.8	168 46.7	9.7	14 05.5	14.2	59.5
16		61 01.6	20.9	183 15.4	9.9	13 51.3	14.2	59.4
17		76 01.3	21.0	197 44.3	10.0	13 37.1	14.2	59.4
18		91 01.0	S23 21.1	212 13.3	10.1	N13 22.9	14.3	59.3
19		106 00.7	21.2	226 42.4	10.3	13 08.6	14.4	59.3
20		121 00.4	21.3	241 11.7	10.3	12 54.2	14.4	59.3
21		136 00.1	. . 21.4	255 41.0	10.4	12 39.8	14.5	59.2
22		150 59.8	21.4	270 10.4	10.6	12 25.3	14.5	59.2
23		165 59.5	21.5	284 40.0	10.7	N12 10.8	14.5	59.1
		SD 16.3	*d* 0.1	SD 16.6		16.5		16.2

Lat. °	Twilight Naut. h m	Twilight Civil h m	Sunrise h m	Moonrise 14 h m	Moonrise 15 h m	Moonrise 16 h m	Moonrise 17 h m
N 72	08 21	10 48	■	□	□	18 51	21 23
N 70	08 01	09 48	■	□	16 12	19 18	21 33
68	07 45	09 14	■	□	17 08	19 37	21 41
66	07 32	08 49	10 28	14 46	17 41	19 53	21 48
64	07 21	08 29	09 47	15 49	18 05	20 05	21 53
62	07 12	08 13	09 19	16 23	18 24	20 16	21 58
60	07 03	08 00	08 58	16 48	18 40	20 25	22 02
N 58	06 56	07 48	08 40	17 08	18 53	20 32	22 06
56	06 49	07 38	08 26	17 25	19 04	20 39	22 09
54	06 43	07 29	08 13	17 38	19 14	20 45	22 12
52	06 37	07 21	08 02	17 51	19 22	20 51	22 15
50	06 32	07 14	07 52	18 01	19 30	20 56	22 17
45	06 21	06 58	07 32	18 24	19 47	21 07	22 22
N 40	06 10	06 44	07 15	18 42	20 00	21 15	22 26
35	06 01	06 33	07 01	18 57	20 12	21 23	22 30
30	05 52	06 22	06 48	19 10	20 21	21 29	22 33
20	05 36	06 03	06 27	19 32	20 38	21 41	22 39
N 10	05 20	05 46	06 09	19 51	20 53	21 51	22 44
0	05 03	05 29	05 52	20 08	21 07	22 00	22 48
S 10	04 44	05 11	05 34	20 26	21 21	22 09	22 53
20	04 21	04 51	05 15	20 45	21 35	22 19	22 58
30	03 53	04 26	04 53	21 07	21 52	22 30	23 03
35	03 34	04 11	04 40	21 19	22 02	22 36	23 06
40	03 11	03 53	04 25	21 34	22 12	22 44	23 10
45	02 41	03 30	04 07	21 51	22 25	22 52	23 14
S 50	01 56	03 01	03 45	22 12	22 41	23 02	23 19
52	01 28	02 46	03 34	22 22	22 48	23 07	23 21
54	00 44	02 28	03 22	22 34	22 56	23 12	23 24
56	////	02 06	03 08	22 46	23 05	23 17	23 26
58	////	01 37	02 51	23 01	23 15	23 24	23 29
S 60	////	00 49	02 31	23 19	23 27	23 31	23 33

Lat. °	Sunset h m	Twilight Civil h m	Twilight Naut. h m	Moonset 14 h m	Moonset 15 h m	Moonset 16 h m	Moonset 17 h m
N 72	■	13 03	15 30	□	□	13 09	12 21
N 70	■	14 02	15 50	□	13 53	12 41	12 08
68	■	14 37	16 05	□	12 55	12 19	11 58
66	13 23	15 02	16 18	13 12	12 21	12 02	11 49
64	14 04	15 21	16 29	12 08	11 56	11 48	11 41
62	14 32	15 37	16 39	11 32	11 36	11 36	11 35
60	14 53	15 50	16 47	11 07	11 20	11 26	11 29
N 58	15 10	16 02	16 55	10 46	11 06	11 17	11 24
56	15 25	16 12	17 01	10 29	10 54	11 09	11 20
54	15 38	16 21	17 07	10 15	10 43	11 02	11 16
52	15 49	16 29	17 13	10 02	10 34	10 56	11 12
50	15 58	16 37	17 18	09 51	10 25	10 50	11 09
45	16 19	16 53	17 30	09 28	10 07	10 37	11 02
N 40	16 36	17 06	17 40	09 09	09 52	10 27	10 56
35	16 50	17 18	17 50	08 53	09 40	10 18	10 50
30	17 02	17 28	17 58	08 39	09 29	10 10	10 46
20	17 23	17 47	18 15	08 15	09 10	09 56	10 38
N 10	17 42	18 05	18 31	07 55	08 53	09 44	10 30
0	17 59	18 22	18 48	07 36	08 37	09 33	10 23
S 10	18 17	18 40	19 07	07 16	08 21	09 21	10 16
20	18 35	19 00	19 29	06 55	08 04	09 09	10 09
30	18 57	19 25	19 58	06 31	07 44	08 54	10 00
35	19 10	19 40	20 17	06 17	07 32	08 46	09 55
40	19 25	19 58	20 40	06 00	07 19	08 36	09 50
45	19 43	20 21	21 10	05 40	07 03	08 25	09 43
S 50	20 06	20 50	21 55	05 14	06 43	08 11	09 35
52	20 17	21 05	22 23	05 02	06 34	08 05	09 31
54	20 29	21 23	23 08	04 48	06 23	07 58	09 27
56	20 43	21 45	////	04 32	06 11	07 50	09 23
58	21 00	22 15	////	04 12	05 57	07 40	09 17
S 60	21 20	23 03	////	03 47	05 40	07 30	09 12

Day	SUN Eqn. of Time 00^h m s	SUN Eqn. of Time 12^h m s	SUN Mer. Pass. h m	MOON Mer. Pass. Upper h m	MOON Mer. Pass. Lower h m	MOON Age d	%	Phase
14	05 24	05 10	11 55	01 20	13 52	17	95	
15	04 56	04 41	11 55	02 23	14 52	18	89	
16	04 27	04 12	11 56	03 20	15 47	19	80	

Day	UT d h	ARIES GHA ° ′	VENUS −4.3 GHA ° ′	VENUS Dec ° ′	MARS +1.3 GHA ° ′	MARS Dec ° ′	JUPITER −2.0 GHA ° ′	JUPITER Dec ° ′	SATURN +1.0 GHA ° ′	SATURN Dec ° ′
WEDNESDAY	17 00	85 59.7	132 30.2	S19 43.3	184 23.9	S23 46.9	148 23.9	S21 25.1	272 57.5	N 5 09.8
	01	101 02.2	147 29.8	42.5	199 24.3	47.0	163 25.8	25.0	287 59.9	09.8
	02	116 04.6	162 29.4	41.6	214 24.8	47.2	178 27.7	24.9	303 02.3	09.8
	03	131 07.1	177 28.9	40.7	229 25.2	47.3	193 29.6	24.8	318 04.7	09.8
	04	146 09.5	192 28.5	39.9	244 25.6	47.4	208 31.5	24.7	333 07.1	09.8
	05	161 12.0	207 28.1	39.0	259 26.1	47.6	223 33.4	24.6	348 09.5	09.8
	06	176 14.5	222 27.6	S19 38.2	274 26.5	S23 47.7	238 35.2	S21 24.5	3 11.9	N 5 09.7
	07	191 16.9	237 27.2	37.3	289 27.0	47.8	253 37.1	24.4	18 14.3	09.7
	08	206 19.4	252 26.8	36.4	304 27.4	48.0	268 39.0	24.3	33 16.7	09.7
	09	221 21.9	267 26.3	35.6	319 27.9	48.1	283 40.9	24.2	48 19.1	09.7
	10	236 24.3	282 25.9	34.7	334 28.3	48.2	298 42.8	24.1	63 21.5	09.7
	11	251 26.8	297 25.5	33.9	349 28.8	48.3	313 44.7	24.0	78 23.9	09.7
	12	266 29.3	312 25.1	S19 33.0	4 29.2	S23 48.5	328 46.6	S21 23.9	93 26.3	N 5 09.6
	13	281 31.7	327 24.6	32.1	19 29.6	48.6	343 48.4	23.8	108 28.7	09.6
	14	296 34.2	342 24.2	31.3	34 30.1	48.7	358 50.3	23.7	123 31.1	09.6
	15	311 36.7	357 23.8	30.4	49 30.5	48.8	13 52.2	23.6	138 33.5	09.6
	16	326 39.1	12 23.4	29.5	64 31.0	49.0	28 54.1	23.5	153 35.9	09.6
	17	341 41.6	27 22.9	28.7	79 31.4	49.1	43 56.0	23.4	168 38.3	09.6
	18	356 44.0	42 22.5	S19 27.8	94 31.8	S23 49.2	58 57.9	S21 23.3	183 40.7	N 5 09.6
	19	11 46.5	57 22.1	26.9	109 32.3	49.3	73 59.7	23.2	198 43.1	09.5
	20	26 49.0	72 21.7	26.0	124 32.7	49.4	89 01.6	23.1	213 45.5	09.5
	21	41 51.4	87 21.3	25.2	139 33.2	49.6	104 03.5	23.0	228 47.9	09.5
	22	56 53.9	102 20.8	24.3	154 33.6	49.7	119 05.4	22.9	243 50.3	09.5
	23	71 56.4	117 20.4	23.4	169 34.1	49.8	134 07.3	22.8	258 52.7	09.5
THURSDAY	18 00	86 58.8	132 20.0	S19 22.6	184 34.5	S23 49.9	149 09.2	S21 22.7	273 55.1	N 5 09.5
	01	102 01.3	147 19.6	21.7	199 34.9	50.1	164 11.0	22.6	288 57.5	09.5
	02	117 03.8	162 19.2	20.8	214 35.4	50.2	179 12.9	22.5	303 59.9	09.4
	03	132 06.2	177 18.8	19.9	229 35.8	50.3	194 14.8	22.4	319 02.3	09.4
	04	147 08.7	192 18.4	19.1	244 36.3	50.4	209 16.7	22.3	334 04.7	09.4
	05	162 11.2	207 17.9	18.2	259 36.7	50.5	224 18.6	22.2	349 07.1	09.4
	06	177 13.6	222 17.5	S19 17.3	274 37.1	S23 50.6	239 20.5	S21 22.1	4 09.5	N 5 09.4
	07	192 16.1	237 17.1	16.4	289 37.6	50.8	254 22.3	22.0	19 11.9	09.4
	08	207 18.5	252 16.7	15.5	304 38.0	50.9	269 24.2	21.9	34 14.3	09.4
	09	222 21.0	267 16.3	14.7	319 38.5	51.0	284 26.1	21.8	49 16.7	09.3
	10	237 23.5	282 15.9	13.8	334 38.9	51.1	299 28.0	21.7	64 19.1	09.3
	11	252 25.9	297 15.5	12.9	349 39.3	51.2	314 29.9	21.6	79 21.5	09.3
	12	267 28.4	312 15.1	S19 12.0	4 39.8	S23 51.3	329 31.7	S21 21.5	94 23.9	N 5 09.3
	13	282 30.9	327 14.7	11.1	19 40.2	51.5	344 33.6	21.4	109 26.3	09.3
	14	297 33.3	342 14.3	10.2	34 40.7	51.6	359 35.5	21.3	124 28.7	09.3
	15	312 35.8	357 13.9	09.4	49 41.1	51.7	14 37.4	21.2	139 31.1	09.3
	16	327 38.3	12 13.5	08.5	64 41.5	51.8	29 39.3	21.1	154 33.5	09.2
	17	342 40.7	27 13.1	07.6	79 42.0	51.9	44 41.2	21.0	169 35.9	09.2
	18	357 43.2	42 12.7	S19 06.7	94 42.4	S23 52.0	59 43.0	S21 20.9	184 38.3	N 5 09.2
	19	12 45.6	57 12.3	05.8	109 42.8	52.1	74 44.9	20.8	199 40.7	09.2
	20	27 48.1	72 11.9	04.9	124 43.3	52.3	89 46.8	20.7	214 43.2	09.2
	21	42 50.6	87 11.5	04.0	139 43.7	52.4	104 48.7	20.6	229 45.6	09.2
	22	57 53.0	102 11.1	03.1	154 44.2	52.5	119 50.6	20.5	244 48.0	09.2
	23	72 55.5	117 10.7	02.2	169 44.6	52.6	134 52.4	20.4	259 50.4	09.2
FRIDAY	19 00	87 58.0	132 10.3	S19 01.3	184 45.0	S23 52.7	149 54.3	S21 20.3	274 52.8	N 5 09.1
	01	103 00.4	147 09.9	19 00.4	199 45.5	52.8	164 56.2	20.2	289 55.2	09.1
	02	118 02.9	162 09.5	18 59.6	214 45.9	52.9	179 58.1	20.1	304 57.6	09.1
	03	133 05.4	177 09.1	58.7	229 46.3	53.0	195 00.0	20.0	320 00.0	09.1
	04	148 07.8	192 08.7	57.8	244 46.8	53.1	210 01.9	19.9	335 02.4	09.1
	05	163 10.3	207 08.3	56.9	259 47.2	53.2	225 03.7	19.8	350 04.8	09.1
	06	178 12.8	222 07.9	S18 56.0	274 47.7	S23 53.4	240 05.6	S21 19.7	5 07.2	N 5 09.1
	07	193 15.2	237 07.5	55.1	289 48.1	53.5	255 07.5	19.6	20 09.6	09.1
	08	208 17.7	252 07.1	54.2	304 48.5	53.6	270 09.4	19.5	35 12.0	09.0
	09	223 20.1	267 06.7	53.3	319 49.0	53.7	285 11.3	19.4	50 14.4	09.0
	10	238 22.6	282 06.4	52.4	334 49.4	53.8	300 13.1	19.3	65 16.8	09.0
	11	253 25.1	297 06.0	51.5	349 49.8	53.9	315 15.0	19.2	80 19.2	09.0
	12	268 27.5	312 05.6	S18 50.6	4 50.3	S23 54.0	330 16.9	S21 19.1	95 21.7	N 5 09.0
	13	283 30.0	327 05.2	49.7	19 50.7	54.1	345 18.8	19.0	110 24.1	09.0
	14	298 32.5	342 04.8	48.8	34 51.1	54.2	0 20.7	18.9	125 26.5	09.0
	15	313 34.9	357 04.4	47.9	49 51.6	54.3	15 22.5	18.8	140 28.9	09.0
	16	328 37.4	12 04.0	46.9	64 52.0	54.4	30 24.4	18.7	155 31.3	08.9
	17	343 39.9	27 03.7	46.0	79 52.4	54.5	45 26.3	18.6	170 33.7	08.9
	18	358 42.3	42 03.3	S18 45.1	94 52.9	S23 54.6	60 28.2	S21 18.5	185 36.1	N 5 08.9
	19	13 44.8	57 02.9	44.2	109 53.3	54.7	75 30.1	18.4	200 38.5	08.9
	20	28 47.3	72 02.5	43.3	124 53.7	54.8	90 31.9	18.3	215 40.9	08.9
	21	43 49.7	87 02.1	42.4	139 54.2	54.9	105 33.8	18.2	230 43.3	08.9
	22	58 52.2	102 01.8	41.5	154 54.6	55.0	120 35.7	18.1	245 45.7	08.9
	23	73 54.6	117 01.4	40.6	169 55.1	55.1	135 37.6	18.0	260 48.1	08.9
	Mer. Pass.	h m 18 09.1	v −0.4	d 0.9	v 0.4	d 0.1	v 1.9	d 0.1	v 2.4	d 0.0

STARS

Name	SHA ° ′	Dec ° ′
Acamar	315 20.4	S40 16.2
Achernar	335 28.7	S57 11.6
Acrux	173 13.5	S63 08.7
Adhara	255 14.8	S28 59.0
Aldebaran	290 52.9	N16 31.8
Alioth	166 23.6	N55 54.3
Alkaid	153 01.6	N49 15.8
Al Na'ir	27 48.0	S46 55.2
Alnilam	275 49.4	S 1 11.7
Alphard	217 59.2	S 8 41.8
Alphecca	126 14.1	N26 40.9
Alpheratz	357 47.0	N29 08.7
Altair	62 11.8	N 8 53.5
Ankaa	353 18.8	S42 15.6
Antares	112 30.8	S26 27.1
Arcturus	145 59.0	N19 08.0
Atria	107 36.3	S69 02.6
Avior	234 19.0	S59 32.1
Bellatrix	278 35.3	N 6 21.5
Betelgeuse	271 04.6	N 7 24.6
Canopus	263 57.1	S52 41.9
Capella	280 39.0	N46 00.5
Deneb	49 34.2	N45 18.9
Denebola	182 37.0	N14 31.2
Diphda	348 59.1	S17 56.2
Dubhe	193 55.3	N61 41.8
Elnath	278 16.5	N28 37.0
Eltanin	90 48.2	N51 29.2
Enif	33 50.6	N 9 55.1
Fomalhaut	15 27.7	S29 34.6
Gacrux	172 05.0	S57 09.6
Gienah	175 55.9	S17 35.5
Hadar	148 53.3	S60 24.8
Hamal	328 04.4	N23 30.5
Kaus Aust.	83 48.7	S34 22.9
Kochab	137 20.3	N74 06.8
Markab	13 41.8	N15 15.4
Menkar	314 18.3	N 4 07.6
Menkent	148 11.9	S36 24.8
Miaplacidus	221 40.1	S69 45.0
Mirfak	308 44.9	N49 53.8
Nunki	76 02.8	S26 17.2
Peacock	53 24.8	S56 42.5
Pollux	243 31.5	N28 00.2
Procyon	245 02.9	N 5 12.1
Rasalhague	96 09.9	N12 33.1
Regulus	207 46.9	N11 55.3
Rigel	281 14.9	S 8 11.4
Rigil Kent.	139 57.0	S60 52.2
Sabik	102 16.8	S15 44.2
Schedar	349 44.5	N56 35.6
Shaula	96 26.9	S37 06.7
Sirius	258 36.3	S16 43.6
Spica	158 35.0	S11 12.5
Suhail	222 54.7	S43 28.0
Vega	80 41.7	N38 47.5
Zuben'ubi	137 09.4	S16 04.8

	SHA ° ′	Mer. Pass. h m
Venus	45 21.2	15 11
Mars	97 35.7	11 41
Jupiter	62 10.3	14 02
Saturn	186 56.3	5 43

	UT	SUN GHA	SUN Dec	MOON GHA	v	MOON Dec	d	HP
	d h	° ′	° ′	° ′	′	° ′	′	′
WEDNESDAY	17 00	180 59.2	S23 21.6	299 09.7	10.7	N11 56.3	14.6	59.1
	01	195 58.9	21.7	313 39.4	10.9	11 41.7	14.6	59.1
	02	210 58.6	21.8	328 09.3	11.0	11 27.1	14.7	59.0
	03	225 58.3	. . 21.9	342 39.3	11.0	11 12.4	14.7	59.0
	04	240 58.0	22.0	357 09.3	11.2	10 57.7	14.7	58.9
	05	255 57.7	22.1	11 39.5	11.3	10 43.0	14.8	58.9
	06	270 57.4	S23 22.1	26 09.8	11.3	N10 28.2	14.8	58.9
	07	285 57.1	22.2	40 40.1	11.5	10 13.4	14.9	58.8
	08	300 56.8	22.3	55 10.6	11.5	9 58.5	14.8	58.8
	09	315 56.4	. . 22.4	69 41.1	11.7	9 43.7	14.9	58.8
	10	330 56.1	22.5	84 11.8	11.7	9 28.8	15.0	58.7
	11	345 55.8	22.5	98 42.5	11.8	9 13.8	14.9	58.7
	12	0 55.5	S23 22.6	113 13.3	11.9	N 8 58.9	15.0	58.6
	13	15 55.2	22.7	127 44.2	12.0	8 43.9	15.0	58.6
	14	30 54.9	22.8	142 15.2	12.1	8 28.9	15.0	58.6
	15	45 54.6	. . 22.9	156 46.3	12.2	8 13.9	15.1	58.5
	16	60 54.3	22.9	171 17.5	12.2	7 58.8	15.0	58.5
	17	75 54.0	23.0	185 48.7	12.4	7 43.8	15.1	58.4
	18	90 53.7	S23 23.1	200 20.1	12.4	N 7 28.7	15.1	58.4
	19	105 53.4	23.2	214 51.5	12.5	7 13.6	15.1	58.4
	20	120 53.1	23.2	229 23.0	12.5	6 58.5	15.1	58.3
	21	135 52.8	. . 23.3	243 54.5	12.7	6 43.4	15.1	58.3
	22	150 52.5	23.4	258 26.2	12.7	6 28.3	15.2	58.2
	23	165 52.2	23.4	272 57.9	12.8	6 13.1	15.1	58.2
THURSDAY	18 00	180 51.8	S23 23.5	287 29.7	12.9	N 5 58.0	15.2	58.2
	01	195 51.5	23.6	302 01.6	12.9	5 42.8	15.1	58.1
	02	210 51.2	23.6	316 33.5	13.0	5 27.7	15.2	58.1
	03	225 50.9	. . 23.7	331 05.5	13.1	5 12.5	15.1	58.0
	04	240 50.6	23.8	345 37.6	13.1	4 57.4	15.2	58.0
	05	255 50.3	23.8	0 09.7	13.2	4 42.2	15.2	58.0
	06	270 50.0	S23 23.9	14 41.9	13.3	N 4 27.0	15.1	57.9
	07	285 49.7	24.0	29 14.2	13.3	4 11.9	15.2	57.9
	08	300 49.4	24.0	43 46.5	13.4	3 56.7	15.2	57.8
	09	315 49.1	. . 24.1	58 18.9	13.4	3 41.5	15.1	57.8
	10	330 48.8	24.2	72 51.3	13.5	3 26.4	15.2	57.8
	11	345 48.5	24.2	87 23.8	13.6	3 11.2	15.1	57.7
	12	0 48.2	S23 24.3	101 56.4	13.6	N 2 56.1	15.1	57.7
	13	15 47.8	24.3	116 29.0	13.6	2 41.0	15.2	57.6
	14	30 47.5	24.4	131 01.6	13.7	2 25.8	15.1	57.6
	15	45 47.2	. . 24.4	145 34.3	13.8	2 10.7	15.1	57.6
	16	60 46.9	24.5	160 07.1	13.8	1 55.6	15.1	57.5
	17	75 46.6	24.6	174 39.9	13.9	1 40.5	15.1	57.5
	18	90 46.3	S23 24.6	189 12.8	13.9	N 1 25.4	15.1	57.5
	19	105 46.0	24.7	203 45.7	13.9	1 10.3	15.0	57.4
	20	120 45.7	24.7	218 18.6	14.0	0 55.3	15.1	57.4
	21	135 45.4	. . 24.8	232 51.6	14.1	0 40.2	15.0	57.3
	22	150 45.1	24.8	247 24.7	14.0	0 25.2	15.0	57.3
	23	165 44.8	24.9	261 57.7	14.2	N 0 10.2	15.0	57.3
FRIDAY	19 00	180 44.5	S23 24.9	276 30.9	14.1	S 0 04.8	14.9	57.2
	01	195 44.1	25.0	291 04.0	14.2	0 19.7	15.0	57.2
	02	210 43.8	25.0	305 37.2	14.2	0 34.7	14.9	57.2
	03	225 43.5	. . 25.1	320 10.4	14.3	0 49.6	14.9	57.1
	04	240 43.2	25.1	334 43.7	14.3	1 04.5	14.9	57.1
	05	255 42.9	25.2	349 17.0	14.3	1 19.4	14.8	57.0
	06	270 42.6	S23 25.2	3 50.3	14.4	S 1 34.2	14.9	57.0
	07	285 42.3	25.2	18 23.7	14.4	1 49.1	14.8	57.0
	08	300 42.0	25.3	32 57.1	14.4	2 03.9	14.7	56.9
	09	315 41.7	. . 25.3	47 30.5	14.4	2 18.6	14.8	56.9
	10	330 41.4	25.4	62 03.9	14.5	2 33.4	14.7	56.9
	11	345 41.1	25.4	76 37.4	14.5	2 48.1	14.7	56.8
	12	0 40.7	S23 25.5	91 10.9	14.5	S 3 02.8	14.6	56.8
	13	15 40.4	25.5	105 44.4	14.5	3 17.4	14.7	56.8
	14	30 40.1	25.5	120 17.9	14.6	3 32.1	14.5	56.7
	15	45 39.8	. . 25.6	134 51.5	14.5	3 46.6	14.6	56.7
	16	60 39.5	25.6	149 25.0	14.6	4 01.2	14.5	56.7
	17	75 39.2	25.6	163 58.6	14.6	4 15.7	14.5	56.6
	18	90 38.9	S23 25.7	178 32.2	14.7	S 4 30.2	14.5	56.6
	19	105 38.6	25.7	193 05.9	14.6	4 44.7	14.4	56.6
	20	120 38.3	25.7	207 39.5	14.6	4 59.1	14.3	56.5
	21	135 38.0	. . 25.8	222 13.1	14.7	5 13.4	14.4	56.5
	22	150 37.6	25.8	236 46.8	14.7	5 27.8	14.3	56.5
	23	165 37.3	25.8	251 20.5	14.6	S 5 42.1	14.2	56.4
		SD 16.3	*d* 0.1	SD 16.0		15.7		15.5

Lat.	Twilight Naut.	Twilight Civil	Sunrise	Moonrise 17	Moonrise 18	Moonrise 19	Moonrise 20
°	h m	h m	h m	h m	h m	h m	h m
N 72	08 24	10 55	■	21 23	23 35	25 41	01 41
N 70	08 04	09 52	■	21 33	23 34	25 31	01 31
68	07 48	09 17	■	21 41	23 34	25 23	01 23
66	07 35	08 52	10 32	21 48	23 34	25 17	01 17
64	07 24	08 32	09 50	21 53	23 34	25 11	01 11
62	07 14	08 16	09 22	21 58	23 34	25 07	01 07
60	07 06	08 02	09 00	22 02	23 34	25 02	01 02
N 58	06 58	07 51	08 43	22 06	23 34	24 59	00 59
56	06 51	07 41	08 28	22 09	23 34	24 56	00 56
54	06 45	07 31	08 15	22 12	23 34	24 53	00 53
52	06 40	07 23	08 04	22 15	23 34	24 50	00 50
50	06 34	07 16	07 54	22 17	23 34	24 48	00 48
45	06 22	07 00	07 34	22 22	23 34	24 43	00 43
N 40	06 12	06 46	07 17	22 26	23 34	24 39	00 39
35	06 03	06 34	07 03	22 30	23 34	24 35	00 35
30	05 54	06 24	06 50	22 33	23 34	24 32	00 32
20	05 37	06 05	06 29	22 39	23 34	24 26	00 26
N 10	05 21	05 48	06 10	22 44	23 34	24 22	00 22
0	05 04	05 30	05 53	22 48	23 34	24 17	00 17
S 10	04 45	05 12	05 35	22 53	23 34	24 13	00 13
20	04 23	04 52	05 16	22 58	23 34	24 08	00 08
30	03 54	04 27	04 54	23 03	23 34	24 03	00 03
35	03 35	04 12	04 41	23 06	23 34	24 00	00 00
40	03 12	03 53	04 26	23 10	23 34	23 57	24 20
45	02 41	03 31	04 08	23 14	23 34	23 53	24 13
S 50	01 56	03 01	03 46	23 19	23 34	23 49	24 04
52	01 28	02 46	03 35	23 21	23 34	23 46	23 59
54	00 42	02 28	03 23	23 24	23 34	23 44	23 55
56	////	02 06	03 08	23 26	23 34	23 42	23 50
58	////	01 36	02 52	23 29	23 34	23 39	23 44
S 60	////	00 46	02 31	23 33	23 34	23 36	23 38

Lat.	Sunset	Twilight Civil	Twilight Naut.	Moonset 17	Moonset 18	Moonset 19	Moonset 20
°	h m	h m	h m	h m	h m	h m	h m
N 72	■	12 59	15 30	12 21	11 47	11 17	10 45
N 70	■	14 01	15 50	12 08	11 43	11 21	10 57
68	■	14 36	16 06	11 58	11 40	11 24	11 07
66	13 21	15 02	16 19	11 49	11 38	11 27	11 16
64	14 03	15 21	16 30	11 41	11 35	11 29	11 23
62	14 32	15 37	16 39	11 35	11 33	11 31	11 29
60	14 53	15 51	16 48	11 29	11 32	11 33	11 35
N 58	15 11	16 03	16 55	11 24	11 30	11 35	11 40
56	15 25	16 13	17 02	11 20	11 29	11 36	11 44
54	15 38	16 22	17 08	11 16	11 27	11 37	11 48
52	15 49	16 30	17 14	11 12	11 26	11 39	11 51
50	15 59	16 38	17 19	11 09	11 25	11 40	11 54
45	16 20	16 54	17 31	11 02	11 23	11 42	12 01
N 40	16 37	17 07	17 41	10 56	11 21	11 44	12 07
35	16 51	17 19	17 51	10 50	11 19	11 46	12 12
30	17 03	17 30	18 00	10 46	11 18	11 47	12 17
20	17 25	17 49	18 16	10 38	11 15	11 50	12 25
N 10	17 43	18 06	18 32	10 30	11 12	11 52	12 32
0	18 01	18 23	18 49	10 23	11 10	11 55	12 38
S 10	18 18	18 41	19 08	10 16	11 08	11 57	12 45
20	18 37	19 02	19 31	10 09	11 05	11 59	12 52
30	18 59	19 27	20 00	10 00	11 03	12 02	13 00
35	19 12	19 42	20 19	09 55	11 01	12 03	13 04
40	19 27	20 00	20 42	09 50	10 59	12 05	13 09
45	19 45	20 23	21 13	09 43	10 57	12 07	13 16
S 50	20 08	20 53	21 58	09 35	10 54	12 10	13 23
52	20 19	21 08	22 26	09 31	10 53	12 11	13 26
54	20 31	21 26	23 13	09 27	10 51	12 12	13 30
56	20 45	21 48	////	09 23	10 50	12 13	13 34
58	21 02	22 18	////	09 17	10 48	12 15	13 39
S 60	21 23	23 09	////	09 12	10 46	12 16	13 44

Day	SUN Eqn. of Time 00^h	SUN Eqn. of Time 12^h	SUN Mer. Pass.	MOON Mer. Pass. Upper	MOON Mer. Pass. Lower	MOON Age	MOON Phase
d	m s	m s	h m	h m	h m	d %	
17	03 57	03 43	11 56	04 12	16 36	20 70	◑
18	03 28	03 13	11 57	04 59	17 22	21 60	
19	02 58	02 44	11 57	05 44	18 06	22 49	

	UT d h	ARIES GHA ° ′	VENUS −4.3 GHA ° ′	VENUS Dec ° ′	MARS +1.3 GHA ° ′	MARS Dec ° ′	JUPITER −1.9 GHA ° ′	JUPITER Dec ° ′	SATURN +1.0 GHA ° ′	SATURN Dec ° ′
	20 00	88 57.1	132 01.0	S18 39.7	184 55.5	S23 55.2	150 39.5	S21 17.9	275 50.6	N 5 08.9
	01	103 59.6	147 00.6	38.8	199 55.9	55.3	165 41.3	17.8	290 53.0	08.8
	02	119 02.0	162 00.3	37.8	214 56.4	55.4	180 43.2	17.7	305 55.4	08.8
	03	134 04.5	176 59.9	. . 36.9	229 56.8	. . 55.5	195 45.1	. . 17.6	320 57.8	. . 08.8
	04	149 07.0	191 59.5	36.0	244 57.2	55.6	210 47.0	17.5	336 00.2	08.8
	05	164 09.4	206 59.1	35.1	259 57.7	55.7	225 48.8	17.4	351 02.6	08.8
	06	179 11.9	221 58.8	S18 34.2	274 58.1	S23 55.8	240 50.7	S21 17.3	6 05.0	N 5 08.8
	07	194 14.4	236 58.4	33.3	289 58.5	55.9	255 52.6	17.2	21 07.4	08.8
S	08	209 16.8	251 58.0	32.4	304 58.9	56.0	270 54.5	17.1	36 09.8	08.8
A	09	224 19.3	266 57.7	. . 31.4	319 59.4	. . 56.1	285 56.4	. . 17.0	51 12.2	. . 08.8
T	10	239 21.7	281 57.3	30.5	334 59.8	56.2	300 58.2	16.9	66 14.7	08.8
U	11	254 24.2	296 56.9	29.6	350 00.2	56.3	316 00.1	16.8	81 17.1	08.7
R	12	269 26.7	311 56.6	S18 28.7	5 00.7	S23 56.4	331 02.0	S21 16.7	96 19.5	N 5 08.7
D	13	284 29.1	326 56.2	27.8	20 01.1	56.5	346 03.9	16.6	111 21.9	08.7
A	14	299 31.6	341 55.8	26.8	35 01.5	56.6	1 05.8	16.5	126 24.3	08.7
Y	15	314 34.1	356 55.5	. . 25.9	50 02.0	. . 56.7	16 07.6	. . 16.4	141 26.7	. . 08.7
	16	329 36.5	11 55.1	25.0	65 02.4	56.8	31 09.5	16.3	156 29.1	08.7
	17	344 39.0	26 54.7	24.1	80 02.8	56.8	46 11.4	16.2	171 31.5	08.7
	18	359 41.5	41 54.4	S18 23.1	95 03.3	S23 56.9	61 13.3	S21 16.1	186 34.0	N 5 08.7
	19	14 43.9	56 54.0	22.2	110 03.7	57.0	76 15.1	16.0	201 36.4	08.7
	20	29 46.4	71 53.7	21.3	125 04.1	57.1	91 17.0	15.9	216 38.8	08.7
	21	44 48.9	86 53.3	. . 20.4	140 04.6	. . 57.2	106 18.9	. . 15.8	231 41.2	. . 08.6
	22	59 51.3	101 52.9	19.4	155 05.0	57.3	121 20.8	15.7	246 43.6	08.6
	23	74 53.8	116 52.6	18.5	170 05.4	57.4	136 22.7	15.6	261 46.0	08.6
	21 00	89 56.2	131 52.2	S18 17.6	185 05.9	S23 57.5	151 24.5	S21 15.4	276 48.4	N 5 08.6
	01	104 58.7	146 51.9	16.6	200 06.3	57.6	166 26.4	15.3	291 50.8	08.6
	02	120 01.2	161 51.5	15.7	215 06.7	57.7	181 28.3	15.2	306 53.3	08.6
	03	135 03.6	176 51.2	. . 14.8	230 07.1	. . 57.7	196 30.2	. . 15.1	321 55.7	. . 08.6
	04	150 06.1	191 50.8	13.8	245 07.6	57.8	211 32.0	15.0	336 58.1	08.6
	05	165 08.6	206 50.5	12.9	260 08.0	57.9	226 33.9	14.9	352 00.5	08.6
	06	180 11.0	221 50.1	S18 12.0	275 08.4	S23 58.0	241 35.8	S21 14.8	7 02.9	N 5 08.6
	07	195 13.5	236 49.8	11.0	290 08.9	58.1	256 37.7	14.7	22 05.3	08.6
	08	210 16.0	251 49.4	10.1	305 09.3	58.2	271 39.5	14.6	37 07.8	08.5
S	09	225 18.4	266 49.1	. . 09.2	320 09.7	. . 58.3	286 41.4	. . 14.5	52 10.2	. . 08.5
U	10	240 20.9	281 48.7	08.2	335 10.1	58.4	301 43.3	14.4	67 12.6	08.5
N	11	255 23.3	296 48.4	07.3	350 10.6	58.4	316 45.2	14.3	82 15.0	08.5
D	12	270 25.8	311 48.0	S18 06.3	5 11.0	S23 58.5	331 47.1	S21 14.2	97 17.4	N 5 08.5
A	13	285 28.3	326 47.7	05.4	20 11.4	58.6	346 48.9	14.1	112 19.8	08.5
Y	14	300 30.7	341 47.3	04.5	35 11.9	58.7	1 50.8	14.0	127 22.2	08.5
	15	315 33.2	356 47.0	. . 03.5	50 12.3	. . 58.8	16 52.7	. . 13.9	142 24.7	. . 08.5
	16	330 35.7	11 46.7	02.6	65 12.7	58.9	31 54.6	13.8	157 27.1	08.5
	17	345 38.1	26 46.3	01.6	80 13.1	58.9	46 56.4	13.7	172 29.5	08.5
	18	0 40.6	41 46.0	S18 00.7	95 13.6	S23 59.0	61 58.3	S21 13.6	187 31.9	N 5 08.5
	19	15 43.1	56 45.6	17 59.8	110 14.0	59.1	77 00.2	13.5	202 34.3	08.5
	20	30 45.5	71 45.3	58.8	125 14.4	59.2	92 02.1	13.4	217 36.7	08.5
	21	45 48.0	86 45.0	. . 57.9	140 14.9	. . 59.3	107 03.9	. . 13.3	232 39.2	. . 08.4
	22	60 50.5	101 44.6	56.9	155 15.3	59.3	122 05.8	13.2	247 41.6	08.4
	23	75 52.9	116 44.3	56.0	170 15.7	59.4	137 07.7	13.1	262 44.0	08.4
	22 00	90 55.4	131 43.9	S17 55.0	185 16.1	S23 59.5	152 09.6	S21 13.0	277 46.4	N 5 08.4
	01	105 57.8	146 43.6	54.1	200 16.6	59.6	167 11.4	12.9	292 48.8	08.4
	02	121 00.3	161 43.3	53.1	215 17.0	59.7	182 13.3	12.8	307 51.3	08.4
	03	136 02.8	176 42.9	. . 52.2	230 17.4	. . 59.7	197 15.2	. . 12.6	322 53.7	. . 08.4
	04	151 05.2	191 42.6	51.2	245 17.8	59.8	212 17.1	12.5	337 56.1	08.4
	05	166 07.7	206 42.3	50.3	260 18.3	23 59.9	227 18.9	12.4	352 58.5	08.4
	06	181 10.2	221 41.9	S17 49.3	275 18.7	S24 00.0	242 20.8	S21 12.3	8 00.9	N 5 08.4
	07	196 12.6	236 41.6	48.4	290 19.1	00.0	257 22.7	12.2	23 03.3	08.4
	08	211 15.1	251 41.3	47.4	305 19.5	00.1	272 24.6	12.1	38 05.8	08.4
M	09	226 17.6	266 41.0	. . 46.5	320 20.0	. . 00.2	287 26.4	. . 12.0	53 08.2	. . 08.4
O	10	241 20.0	281 40.6	45.5	335 20.4	00.3	302 28.3	11.9	68 10.6	08.4
N	11	256 22.5	296 40.3	44.6	350 20.8	00.3	317 30.2	11.8	83 13.0	08.3
D	12	271 25.0	311 40.0	S17 43.6	5 21.3	S24 00.4	332 32.1	S21 11.7	98 15.4	N 5 08.3
A	13	286 27.4	326 39.7	42.6	20 21.7	00.5	347 33.9	11.6	113 17.9	08.3
Y	14	301 29.9	341 39.3	41.7	35 22.1	00.6	2 35.8	11.5	128 20.3	08.3
	15	316 32.3	356 39.0	. . 40.7	50 22.5	. . 00.6	17 37.7	. . 11.4	143 22.7	. . 08.3
	16	331 34.8	11 38.7	39.8	65 23.0	00.7	32 39.6	11.3	158 25.1	08.3
	17	346 37.3	26 38.4	38.8	80 23.4	00.8	47 41.4	11.2	173 27.5	08.3
	18	1 39.7	41 38.0	S17 37.8	95 23.8	S24 00.8	62 43.3	S21 11.1	188 30.0	N 5 08.3
	19	16 42.2	56 37.7	36.9	110 24.2	00.9	77 45.2	11.0	203 32.4	08.3
	20	31 44.7	71 37.4	35.9	125 24.6	01.0	92 47.1	10.9	218 34.8	08.3
	21	46 47.1	86 37.1	. . 35.0	140 25.1	. . 01.0	107 48.9	. . 10.8	233 37.2	. . 08.3
	22	61 49.6	101 36.8	34.0	155 25.5	01.1	122 50.8	10.7	248 39.7	08.3
	23	76 52.1	116 36.5	33.0	170 25.9	01.2	137 52.7	10.5	263 42.1	08.3
	Mer. Pass. h m	17 57.3	*v* −0.3	*d* 0.9	*v* 0.4	*d* 0.1	*v* 1.9	*d* 0.1	*v* 2.4	*d* 0.0

STARS

Name	SHA ° ′	Dec ° ′
Acamar	315 20.5	S40 16.2
Achernar	335 28.8	S57 11.6
Acrux	173 13.5	S63 08.7
Adhara	255 14.8	S28 59.0
Aldebaran	290 52.9	N16 31.8
Alioth	166 23.5	N55 54.3
Alkaid	153 01.6	N49 15.8
Al Na'ir	27 48.0	S46 55.2
Alnilam	275 49.4	S 1 11.7
Alphard	217 59.2	S 8 41.8
Alphecca	126 14.1	N26 40.9
Alpheratz	357 47.0	N29 08.7
Altair	62 11.8	N 8 53.5
Ankaa	353 18.8	S42 15.6
Antares	112 30.8	S26 27.1
Arcturus	145 58.9	N19 07.9
Atria	107 36.3	S69 02.6
Avior	234 19.0	S59 32.1
Bellatrix	278 35.3	N 6 21.5
Betelgeuse	271 04.6	N 7 24.6
Canopus	263 57.1	S52 41.9
Capella	280 38.9	N46 00.5
Deneb	49 34.2	N45 18.9
Denebola	182 37.0	N14 31.1
Diphda	348 59.1	S17 56.3
Dubhe	193 55.3	N61 41.8
Elnath	278 16.5	N28 37.0
Eltanin	90 48.2	N51 29.2
Enif	33 50.6	N 9 55.1
Fomalhaut	15 27.7	S29 34.6
Gacrux	172 05.0	S57 09.6
Gienah	175 55.8	S17 35.5
Hadar	148 53.3	S60 24.8
Hamal	328 04.4	N23 30.5
Kaus Aust.	83 48.7	S34 22.9
Kochab	137 20.3	N74 06.8
Markab	13 41.8	N15 15.4
Menkar	314 18.3	N 4 07.6
Menkent	148 11.9	S36 24.8
Miaplacidus	221 40.1	S69 45.0
Mirfak	308 44.9	N49 53.8
Nunki	76 02.8	S26 17.2
Peacock	53 24.8	S56 42.5
Pollux	243 31.4	N28 00.2
Procyon	245 02.9	N 5 12.1
Rasalhague	96 09.9	N12 33.1
Regulus	207 46.9	N11 55.3
Rigel	281 14.9	S 8 11.4
Rigil Kent.	139 57.0	S60 52.2
Sabik	102 16.7	S15 44.2
Schedar	349 44.5	N56 35.6
Shaula	96 26.9	S37 06.7
Sirius	258 36.3	S16 43.6
Spica	158 34.9	S11 12.5
Suhail	222 54.7	S43 28.0
Vega	80 41.7	N38 47.5
Zuben'ubi	137 09.4	S16 04.8

	SHA ° ′	Mer. Pass. h m
Venus	41 56.0	15 13
Mars	95 09.6	11 39
Jupiter	61 28.3	13 53
Saturn	186 52.2	5 32

	UT	SUN GHA	SUN Dec	MOON GHA	v	MOON Dec	d	HP
	d h	° ′	° ′	° ′	′	° ′	′	′
	20 00	180 37.0	S23 25.9	265 54.1	14.7	S 5 56.3	14.2	56.4
	01	195 36.7	25.9	280 27.8	14.7	6 10.5	14.2	56.4
	02	210 36.4	25.9	295 01.5	14.7	6 24.7	14.1	56.3
	03	225 36.1	. . 25.9	309 35.2	14.7	6 38.8	14.1	56.3
	04	240 35.8	26.0	324 08.9	14.7	6 52.9	14.1	56.3
	05	255 35.5	26.0	338 42.6	14.7	7 07.0	14.0	56.2
	06	270 35.2	S23 26.0	353 16.3	14.8	S 7 21.0	13.9	56.2
	07	285 34.9	26.0	7 50.1	14.7	7 34.9	13.9	56.2
S	08	300 34.5	26.1	22 23.8	14.7	7 48.8	13.9	56.1
A	09	315 34.2	. . 26.1	36 57.5	14.7	8 02.7	13.8	56.1
T	10	330 33.9	26.1	51 31.2	14.7	8 16.5	13.8	56.1
U	11	345 33.6	26.1	66 04.9	14.7	8 30.3	13.7	56.0
R	12	0 33.3	S23 26.2	80 38.6	14.7	S 8 44.0	13.6	56.0
D	13	15 33.0	26.2	95 12.3	14.7	8 57.6	13.6	56.0
A	14	30 32.7	26.2	109 46.0	14.7	9 11.2	13.6	56.0
Y	15	45 32.4	. . 26.2	124 19.7	14.6	9 24.8	13.5	55.9
	16	60 32.1	26.2	138 53.3	14.7	9 38.3	13.4	55.9
	17	75 31.7	26.2	153 27.0	14.6	9 51.7	13.4	55.9
	18	90 31.4	S23 26.3	168 00.6	14.7	S10 05.1	13.4	55.8
	19	105 31.1	26.3	182 34.3	14.6	10 18.5	13.3	55.8
	20	120 30.8	26.3	197 07.9	14.6	10 31.8	13.2	55.8
	21	135 30.5	. . 26.3	211 41.5	14.6	10 45.0	13.2	55.7
	22	150 30.2	26.3	226 15.1	14.6	10 58.2	13.1	55.7
	23	165 29.9	26.3	240 48.7	14.6	11 11.3	13.0	55.7
	21 00	180 29.6	S23 26.3	255 22.3	14.5	S11 24.3	13.0	55.7
	01	195 29.3	26.3	269 55.8	14.6	11 37.3	13.0	55.6
	02	210 28.9	26.4	284 29.4	14.5	11 50.3	12.9	55.6
	03	225 28.6	. . 26.4	299 02.9	14.5	12 03.2	12.8	55.6
	04	240 28.3	26.4	313 36.4	14.5	12 16.0	12.7	55.6
	05	255 28.0	26.4	328 09.9	14.4	12 28.7	12.7	55.5
	06	270 27.7	S23 26.4	342 43.3	14.5	S12 41.4	12.6	55.5
	07	285 27.4	26.4	357 16.8	14.4	12 54.0	12.6	55.5
	08	300 27.1	26.4	11 50.2	14.3	13 06.6	12.5	55.5
S	09	315 26.8	. . 26.4	26 23.5	14.4	13 19.1	12.4	55.4
U	10	330 26.5	26.4	40 56.9	14.3	13 31.5	12.4	55.4
N	11	345 26.1	26.4	55 30.2	14.3	13 43.9	12.3	55.4
D	12	0 25.8	S23 26.4	70 03.5	14.3	S13 56.2	12.2	55.4
A	13	15 25.5	26.4	84 36.8	14.3	14 08.4	12.2	55.3
Y	14	30 25.2	26.4	99 10.1	14.2	14 20.6	12.1	55.3
	15	45 24.9	. . 26.4	113 43.3	14.2	14 32.7	12.0	55.3
	16	60 24.6	26.4	128 16.5	14.1	14 44.7	11.9	55.3
	17	75 24.3	26.4	142 49.6	14.2	14 56.6	11.9	55.2
	18	90 24.0	S23 26.4	157 22.8	14.1	S15 08.5	11.8	55.2
	19	105 23.7	26.4	171 55.9	14.0	15 20.3	11.7	55.2
	20	120 23.3	26.4	186 28.9	14.0	15 32.0	11.7	55.2
	21	135 23.0	. . 26.4	201 01.9	14.0	15 43.7	11.6	55.1
	22	150 22.7	26.4	215 34.9	14.0	15 55.3	11.5	55.1
	23	165 22.4	26.3	230 07.9	13.9	16 06.8	11.4	55.1
	22 00	180 22.1	S23 26.3	244 40.8	13.9	S16 18.2	11.4	55.1
	01	195 21.8	26.3	259 13.7	13.9	16 29.6	11.2	55.1
	02	210 21.5	26.3	273 46.6	13.8	16 40.8	11.2	55.0
	03	225 21.2	. . 26.3	288 19.4	13.8	16 52.0	11.2	55.0
	04	240 20.8	26.3	302 52.2	13.7	17 03.2	11.0	55.0
	05	255 20.5	26.3	317 24.9	13.7	17 14.2	11.0	55.0
	06	270 20.2	S23 26.3	331 57.6	13.6	S17 25.2	10.8	54.9
	07	285 19.9	26.2	346 30.2	13.7	17 36.0	10.8	54.9
	08	300 19.6	26.2	1 02.9	13.5	17 46.8	10.7	54.9
M	09	315 19.3	. . 26.2	15 35.4	13.6	17 57.5	10.7	54.9
O	10	330 19.0	26.2	30 08.0	13.5	18 08.2	10.5	54.9
N	11	345 18.7	26.2	44 40.5	13.4	18 18.7	10.5	54.8
D	12	0 18.4	S23 26.2	59 12.9	13.4	S18 29.2	10.4	54.8
A	13	15 18.0	26.1	73 45.3	13.4	18 39.6	10.2	54.8
Y	14	30 17.7	26.1	88 17.7	13.3	18 49.8	10.2	54.8
	15	45 17.4	. . 26.1	102 50.0	13.3	19 00.0	10.2	54.8
	16	60 17.1	26.1	117 22.3	13.2	19 10.2	10.0	54.8
	17	75 16.8	26.1	131 54.5	13.2	19 20.2	9.9	54.7
	18	90 16.5	S23 26.0	146 26.7	13.2	S19 30.1	9.9	54.7
	19	105 16.2	26.0	160 58.9	13.1	19 40.0	9.7	54.7
	20	120 15.9	26.0	175 31.0	13.0	19 49.7	9.7	54.7
	21	135 15.5	. . 26.0	190 03.0	13.0	19 59.4	9.6	54.7
	22	150 15.2	25.9	204 35.0	13.0	20 09.0	9.5	54.6
	23	165 14.9	25.9	219 07.0	12.9	S20 18.5	9.3	54.6
		SD 16.3	d 0.0	SD 15.3		15.1		14.9

Lat.	Twilight Naut.	Twilight Civil	Sunrise	Moonrise 20	21	22	23
°	h m	h m	h m	h m	h m	h m	h m
N 72	08 26	10 58	■	01 41	03 55	07 15	■
N 70	08 06	09 55	■	01 31	03 32	05 52	■
68	07 50	09 19	■	01 23	03 14	05 14	08 06
66	07 37	08 54	10 35	01 17	03 00	04 48	06 49
64	07 26	08 34	09 52	01 11	02 48	04 27	06 13
62	07 16	08 18	09 24	01 07	02 38	04 11	05 47
60	07 07	08 04	09 02	01 02	02 30	03 58	05 27
N 58	07 00	07 53	08 45	00 59	02 23	03 46	05 10
56	06 53	07 42	08 30	00 56	02 16	03 36	04 56
54	06 47	07 33	08 17	00 53	02 10	03 28	04 44
52	06 41	07 25	08 06	00 50	02 05	03 20	04 34
50	06 36	07 18	07 56	00 48	02 01	03 13	04 24
45	06 24	07 01	07 35	00 43	01 51	02 58	04 04
N 40	06 14	06 48	07 18	00 39	01 42	02 46	03 48
35	06 04	06 36	07 04	00 35	01 35	02 35	03 35
30	05 56	06 25	06 52	00 32	01 29	02 26	03 23
20	05 39	06 07	06 31	00 26	01 19	02 11	03 04
N 10	05 23	05 49	06 12	00 22	01 09	01 57	02 46
0	05 06	05 32	05 55	00 17	01 01	01 45	02 31
S 10	04 47	05 14	05 37	00 13	00 52	01 32	02 15
20	04 24	04 53	05 18	00 08	00 43	01 19	01 58
30	03 55	04 28	04 56	00 03	00 33	01 04	01 39
35	03 36	04 13	04 43	00 00	00 27	00 56	01 27
40	03 13	03 55	04 28	24 20	00 20	00 46	01 15
45	02 42	03 32	04 10	24 13	00 13	00 34	00 59
S 50	01 57	03 02	03 47	24 04	00 04	00 21	00 41
52	01 29	02 47	03 36	23 59	24 14	00 14	00 32
54	00 41	02 29	03 24	23 55	24 07	00 07	00 23
56	////	02 07	03 09	23 50	23 59	24 12	00 12
58	////	01 37	02 53	23 44	23 50	24 00	00 00
S 60	////	00 45	02 32	23 38	23 40	23 45	23 54

Lat.	Sunset	Twilight Civil	Twilight Naut.	Moonset 20	21	22	23
°	h m	h m	h m	h m	h m	h m	h m
N 72	■	12 58	15 31	10 45	10 03	08 17	■
N 70	■	14 02	15 51	10 57	10 28	09 41	■
68	■	14 37	16 07	11 07	10 48	10 20	09 05
66	13 21	15 03	16 20	11 16	11 04	10 48	10 22
64	14 04	15 22	16 31	11 23	11 16	11 09	10 59
62	14 33	15 39	16 41	11 29	11 27	11 26	11 26
60	14 54	15 52	16 49	11 35	11 37	11 41	11 47
N 58	15 12	16 04	16 57	11 40	11 45	11 53	12 04
56	15 27	16 14	17 03	11 44	11 53	12 03	12 18
54	15 39	16 23	17 10	11 48	11 59	12 13	12 31
52	15 51	16 32	17 15	11 51	12 05	12 21	12 42
50	16 00	16 39	17 21	11 54	12 10	12 29	12 52
45	16 21	16 55	17 32	12 01	12 22	12 45	13 13
N 40	16 38	17 09	17 43	12 07	12 32	12 59	13 29
35	16 52	17 21	17 52	12 12	12 40	13 10	13 44
30	17 05	17 31	18 01	12 17	12 47	13 20	13 56
20	17 26	17 50	18 18	12 25	13 00	13 37	14 17
N 10	17 45	18 07	18 34	12 32	13 11	13 52	14 36
0	18 02	18 25	18 51	12 38	13 22	14 07	14 53
S 10	18 20	18 43	19 10	12 45	13 32	14 21	15 11
20	18 39	19 03	19 32	12 52	13 44	14 36	15 29
30	19 01	19 28	20 02	13 00	13 57	14 54	15 51
35	19 14	19 44	20 20	13 04	14 04	15 04	16 04
40	19 29	20 02	20 44	13 09	14 13	15 16	16 18
45	19 47	20 24	21 14	13 16	14 23	15 30	16 36
S 50	20 10	20 54	22 00	13 23	14 35	15 47	16 58
52	20 20	21 09	22 28	13 26	14 41	15 55	17 08
54	20 33	21 27	23 15	13 30	14 47	16 04	17 20
56	20 47	21 50	////	13 34	14 54	16 15	17 33
58	21 04	22 20	////	13 39	15 02	16 26	17 49
S 60	21 24	23 11	////	13 44	15 12	16 40	18 08

Day	SUN Eqn. of Time 00^h	SUN Eqn. of Time 12^h	SUN Mer. Pass.	MOON Mer. Pass. Upper	MOON Mer. Pass. Lower	MOON Age	MOON Phase
d	m s	m s	h m	h m	h m	d	%
20	02 29	02 14	11 58	06 28	18 49	23	39
21	01 59	01 44	11 58	07 11	19 33	24	30
22	01 29	01 14	11 59	07 56	20 19	25	21

	UT	ARIES	VENUS −4.3		MARS +1.3		JUPITER −1.9		SATURN +1.0	
		GHA	GHA	Dec	GHA	Dec	GHA	Dec	GHA	Dec
	d h	° ′	° ′	° ′	° ′	° ′	° ′	° ′	° ′	° ′
	23 00	91 54.5	131 36.1	S17 32.1	185 26.3	S24 01.3	152 54.6	S21 10.4	278 44.5	N 5 08.3
	01	106 57.0	146 35.8	31.1	200 26.8	01.3	167 56.4	10.3	293 46.9	08.3
	02	121 59.5	161 35.5	30.1	215 27.2	01.4	182 58.3	10.2	308 49.3	08.3
	03	137 01.9	176 35.2	. . 29.2	230 27.6	. . 01.5	198 00.2	. . 10.1	323 51.8	. . 08.3
	04	152 04.4	191 34.9	28.2	245 28.0	01.5	213 02.1	10.0	338 54.2	08.3
	05	167 06.8	206 34.6	27.2	260 28.5	01.6	228 03.9	09.9	353 56.6	08.2
	06	182 09.3	221 34.3	S17 26.3	275 28.9	S24 01.7	243 05.8	S21 09.8	8 59.0	N 5 08.2
	07	197 11.8	236 34.0	25.3	290 29.3	01.7	258 07.7	09.7	24 01.5	08.2
T	08	212 14.2	251 33.7	24.3	305 29.7	01.8	273 09.5	09.6	39 03.9	08.2
U	09	227 16.7	266 33.3	. . 23.4	320 30.2	. . 01.9	288 11.4	. . 09.5	54 06.3	. . 08.2
E	10	242 19.2	281 33.0	22.4	335 30.6	01.9	303 13.3	09.4	69 08.7	08.2
	11	257 21.6	296 32.7	21.4	350 31.0	02.0	318 15.2	09.3	84 11.2	08.2
S	12	272 24.1	311 32.4	S17 20.4	5 31.4	S24 02.0	333 17.0	S21 09.2	99 13.6	N 5 08.2
D	13	287 26.6	326 32.1	19.5	20 31.8	02.1	348 18.9	09.1	114 16.0	08.2
A	14	302 29.0	341 31.8	18.5	35 32.3	02.2	3 20.8	09.0	129 18.4	08.2
Y	15	317 31.5	356 31.5	. . 17.5	50 32.7	. . 02.2	18 22.7	. . 08.9	144 20.9	. . 08.2
	16	332 33.9	11 31.2	16.5	65 33.1	02.3	33 24.5	08.7	159 23.3	08.2
	17	347 36.4	26 30.9	15.6	80 33.5	02.3	48 26.4	08.6	174 25.7	08.2
	18	2 38.9	41 30.6	S17 14.6	95 34.0	S24 02.4	63 28.3	S21 08.5	189 28.1	N 5 08.2
	19	17 41.3	56 30.3	13.6	110 34.4	02.5	78 30.1	08.4	204 30.6	08.2
	20	32 43.8	71 30.0	12.6	125 34.8	02.5	93 32.0	08.3	219 33.0	08.2
	21	47 46.3	86 29.7	. . 11.7	140 35.2	. . 02.6	108 33.9	. . 08.2	234 35.4	. . 08.2
	22	62 48.7	101 29.4	10.7	155 35.6	02.6	123 35.8	08.1	249 37.8	08.2
	23	77 51.2	116 29.1	09.7	170 36.1	02.7	138 37.6	08.0	264 40.3	08.2
	24 00	92 53.7	131 28.8	S17 08.7	185 36.5	S24 02.8	153 39.5	S21 07.9	279 42.7	N 5 08.2
	01	107 56.1	146 28.5	07.7	200 36.9	02.8	168 41.4	07.8	294 45.1	08.2
	02	122 58.6	161 28.2	06.8	215 37.3	02.9	183 43.3	07.7	309 47.5	08.2
	03	138 01.1	176 28.0	. . 05.8	230 37.7	. . 02.9	198 45.1	. . 07.6	324 50.0	. . 08.2
	04	153 03.5	191 27.7	04.8	245 38.2	03.0	213 47.0	07.5	339 52.4	08.1
	05	168 06.0	206 27.4	03.8	260 38.6	03.0	228 48.9	07.4	354 54.8	08.1
	06	183 08.4	221 27.1	S17 02.8	275 39.0	S24 03.1	243 50.7	S21 07.3	9 57.2	N 5 08.1
W	07	198 10.9	236 26.8	01.8	290 39.4	03.2	258 52.6	07.2	24 59.7	08.1
E	08	213 13.4	251 26.5	17 00.8	305 39.8	03.2	273 54.5	07.0	40 02.1	08.1
D	09	228 15.8	266 26.2	16 59.9	320 40.3	. . 03.3	288 56.4	. . 06.9	55 04.5	. . 08.1
N	10	243 18.3	281 25.9	58.9	335 40.7	03.3	303 58.2	06.8	70 07.0	08.1
E	11	258 20.8	296 25.7	57.9	350 41.1	03.4	319 00.1	06.7	85 09.4	08.1
	12	273 23.2	311 25.4	S16 56.9	5 41.5	S24 03.4	334 02.0	S21 06.6	100 11.8	N 5 08.1
S	13	288 25.7	326 25.1	55.9	20 41.9	03.5	349 03.8	06.5	115 14.2	08.1
D	14	303 28.2	341 24.8	54.9	35 42.4	03.5	4 05.7	06.4	130 16.7	08.1
A	15	318 30.6	356 24.5	. . 53.9	50 42.8	. . 03.6	19 07.6	. . 06.3	145 19.1	. . 08.1
Y	16	333 33.1	11 24.2	52.9	65 43.2	03.6	34 09.5	06.2	160 21.5	08.1
	17	348 35.6	26 24.0	51.9	80 43.6	03.7	49 11.3	06.1	175 24.0	08.1
	18	3 38.0	41 23.7	S16 51.0	95 44.0	S24 03.7	64 13.2	S21 06.0	190 26.4	N 5 08.1
	19	18 40.5	56 23.4	50.0	110 44.5	03.8	79 15.1	05.9	205 28.8	08.1
	20	33 42.9	71 23.1	49.0	125 44.9	03.8	94 16.9	05.8	220 31.3	08.1
	21	48 45.4	86 22.8	. . 48.0	140 45.3	. . 03.9	109 18.8	. . 05.6	235 33.7	. . 08.1
	22	63 47.9	101 22.6	47.0	155 45.7	03.9	124 20.7	05.5	250 36.1	08.1
	23	78 50.3	116 22.3	46.0	170 46.1	04.0	139 22.5	05.4	265 38.5	08.1
	25 00	93 52.8	131 22.0	S16 45.0	185 46.5	S24 04.0	154 24.4	S21 05.3	280 41.0	N 5 08.1
	01	108 55.3	146 21.7	44.0	200 47.0	04.1	169 26.3	05.2	295 43.4	08.1
	02	123 57.7	161 21.5	43.0	215 47.4	04.1	184 28.2	05.1	310 45.8	08.1
	03	139 00.2	176 21.2	. . 42.0	230 47.8	. . 04.2	199 30.0	. . 05.0	325 48.3	. . 08.1
	04	154 02.7	191 20.9	41.0	245 48.2	04.2	214 31.9	04.9	340 50.7	08.1
	05	169 05.1	206 20.7	40.0	260 48.6	04.2	229 33.8	04.8	355 53.1	08.1
	06	184 07.6	221 20.4	S16 39.0	275 49.1	S24 04.3	244 35.6	S21 04.7	10 55.6	N 5 08.1
	07	199 10.1	236 20.1	38.0	290 49.5	04.3	259 37.5	04.6	25 58.0	08.1
T	08	214 12.5	251 19.9	37.0	305 49.9	04.4	274 39.4	04.5	41 00.4	08.1
H	09	229 15.0	266 19.6	. . 36.0	320 50.3	. . 04.4	289 41.2	. . 04.4	56 02.9	. . 08.1
U	10	244 17.4	281 19.3	35.0	335 50.7	04.5	304 43.1	04.2	71 05.3	08.1
R	11	259 19.9	296 19.1	34.0	350 51.1	04.5	319 45.0	04.1	86 07.7	08.1
S	12	274 22.4	311 18.8	S16 33.0	5 51.6	S24 04.5	334 46.9	S21 04.0	101 10.2	N 5 08.1
D	13	289 24.8	326 18.5	32.0	20 52.0	04.6	349 48.7	03.9	116 12.6	08.1
A	14	304 27.3	341 18.3	31.0	35 52.4	04.6	4 50.6	03.8	131 15.0	08.1
Y	15	319 29.8	356 18.0	. . 30.0	50 52.8	. . 04.7	19 52.5	. . 03.7	146 17.5	. . 08.1
	16	334 32.2	11 17.8	28.9	65 53.2	04.7	34 54.3	03.6	161 19.9	08.1
	17	349 34.7	26 17.5	27.9	80 53.6	04.7	49 56.2	03.5	176 22.3	08.1
	18	4 37.2	41 17.2	S16 26.9	95 54.1	S24 04.8	64 58.1	S21 03.4	191 24.8	N 5 08.1
	19	19 39.6	56 17.0	25.9	110 54.5	04.8	79 59.9	03.3	206 27.2	08.1
	20	34 42.1	71 16.7	24.9	125 54.9	04.9	95 01.8	03.2	221 29.6	08.1
	21	49 44.6	86 16.5	. . 23.9	140 55.3	. . 04.9	110 03.7	. . 03.1	236 32.1	. . 08.1
	22	64 47.0	101 16.2	22.9	155 55.7	04.9	125 05.6	02.9	251 34.5	08.1
	23	79 49.5	116 16.0	21.9	170 56.1	05.0	140 07.4	02.8	266 36.9	08.1
	Mer. Pass.	h m 17 45.5	v −0.3	d 1.0	v 0.4	d 0.1	v 1.9	d 0.1	v 2.4	d 0.0

STARS

Name	SHA	Dec
	° ′	° ′
Acamar	315 20.5	S40 16.2
Achernar	335 28.8	S57 11.6
Acrux	173 13.4	S63 08.7
Adhara	255 14.8	S28 59.0
Aldebaran	290 52.9	N16 31.7
Alioth	166 23.5	N55 54.3
Alkaid	153 01.6	N49 15.8
Al Na'ir	27 48.0	S46 55.2
Alnilam	275 49.4	S 1 11.7
Alphard	217 59.2	S 8 41.9
Alphecca	126 14.1	N26 40.9
Alpheratz	357 47.1	N29 08.6
Altair	62 11.8	N 8 53.5
Ankaa	353 18.8	S42 15.6
Antares	112 30.7	S26 27.1
Arcturus	145 58.9	N19 07.9
Atria	107 36.2	S69 02.6
Avior	234 19.0	S59 32.1
Bellatrix	278 35.3	N 6 21.5
Betelgeuse	271 04.6	N 7 24.6
Canopus	263 57.1	S52 42.0
Capella	280 38.9	N46 00.5
Deneb	49 34.2	N45 18.9
Denebola	182 37.0	N14 31.1
Diphda	348 59.1	S17 56.3
Dubhe	193 55.3	N61 41.8
Elnath	278 16.5	N28 37.0
Eltanin	90 48.2	N51 29.2
Enif	33 50.6	N 9 55.0
Fomalhaut	15 27.7	S29 34.6
Gacrux	172 04.9	S57 09.6
Gienah	175 55.8	S17 35.5
Hadar	148 53.2	S60 24.8
Hamal	328 04.4	N23 30.5
Kaus Aust.	83 48.6	S34 22.9
Kochab	137 20.3	N74 06.7
Markab	13 41.8	N15 15.4
Menkar	314 18.3	N 4 07.6
Menkent	148 11.8	S36 24.8
Miaplacidus	221 40.0	S69 45.0
Mirfak	308 44.9	N49 53.8
Nunki	76 02.8	S26 17.2
Peacock	53 24.9	S56 42.5
Pollux	243 31.4	N28 00.2
Procyon	245 02.9	N 5 12.1
Rasalhague	96 09.9	N12 33.1
Regulus	207 46.9	N11 55.3
Rigel	281 14.9	S 8 11.4
Rigil Kent.	139 56.9	S60 52.2
Sabik	102 16.7	S15 44.2
Schedar	349 44.5	N56 35.6
Shaula	96 26.9	S37 06.6
Sirius	258 36.3	S16 43.7
Spica	158 34.9	S11 12.5
Suhail	222 54.7	S43 28.0
Vega	80 41.7	N38 47.5
Zuben'ubi	137 09.4	S16 04.8
	SHA	**Mer. Pass**
	° ′	h m
Venus	38 35.2	15 14
Mars	92 42.8	11 37
Jupiter	60 45.8	13 44
Saturn	186 49.0	5 20

UT d h	Day	SUN GHA ° ′	SUN Dec ° ′	MOON GHA ° ′	v ′	MOON Dec ° ′	d ′	HP ′
23 00		180 14.6	S23 25.9	233 38.9	12.9	S20 27.8	9.3	54.6
01		195 14.3	25.8	248 10.8	12.8	20 37.1	9.2	54.6
02		210 14.0	25.8	262 42.6	12.8	20 46.3	9.2	54.6
03		225 13.7	. . 25.8	277 14.4	12.7	20 55.5	9.0	54.6
04		240 13.4	25.7	291 46.1	12.7	21 04.5	8.9	54.6
05		255 13.1	25.7	306 17.8	12.6	21 13.4	8.8	54.5
06		270 12.7	S23 25.7	320 49.4	12.6	S21 22.2	8.7	54.5
07		285 12.4	25.6	335 21.0	12.6	21 30.9	8.6	54.5
08	TUESDAY	300 12.1	25.6	349 52.6	12.5	21 39.5	8.5	54.5
09		315 11.8	. . 25.6	4 24.1	12.4	21 48.0	8.5	54.5
10		330 11.5	25.5	18 55.5	12.4	21 56.5	8.3	54.5
11		345 11.2	25.5	33 26.9	12.4	22 04.8	8.2	54.4
12		0 10.9	S23 25.5	47 58.3	12.3	S22 13.0	8.1	54.4
13		15 10.6	25.4	62 29.6	12.2	22 21.1	8.0	54.4
14		30 10.2	25.4	77 00.8	12.2	22 29.1	7.9	54.4
15		45 09.9	. . 25.3	91 32.0	12.2	22 37.0	7.8	54.4
16		60 09.6	25.3	106 03.2	12.1	22 44.8	7.7	54.4
17		75 09.3	25.2	120 34.3	12.1	22 52.5	7.6	54.4
18		90 09.0	S23 25.2	135 05.4	12.0	S23 00.1	7.5	54.4
19		105 08.7	25.2	149 36.4	12.0	23 07.6	7.4	54.3
20		120 08.4	25.1	164 07.4	11.9	23 15.0	7.2	54.3
21		135 08.1	. . 25.1	178 38.3	11.9	23 22.2	7.2	54.3
22		150 07.8	25.0	193 09.2	11.8	23 29.4	7.1	54.3
23		165 07.4	25.0	207 40.0	11.8	23 36.5	6.9	54.3
24 00		180 07.1	S23 24.9	222 10.8	11.7	S23 43.4	6.8	54.3
01		195 06.8	24.9	236 41.5	11.7	23 50.2	6.8	54.3
02		210 06.5	24.8	251 12.2	11.7	23 57.0	6.6	54.3
03		225 06.2	. . 24.8	265 42.9	11.6	24 03.6	6.5	54.2
04		240 05.9	24.7	280 13.5	11.5	24 10.1	6.4	54.2
05		255 05.6	24.7	294 44.0	11.6	24 16.5	6.2	54.2
06		270 05.3	S23 24.6	309 14.6	11.4	S24 22.7	6.2	54.2
07	WEDNESDAY	285 04.9	24.6	323 45.0	11.5	24 28.9	6.0	54.2
08		300 04.6	24.5	338 15.5	11.4	24 34.9	6.0	54.2
09		315 04.3	. . 24.4	352 45.9	11.3	24 40.9	5.8	54.2
10		330 04.0	24.4	7 16.2	11.3	24 46.7	5.7	54.2
11		345 03.7	24.3	21 46.5	11.3	24 52.4	5.6	54.2
12		0 03.4	S23 24.3	36 16.8	11.2	S24 58.0	5.4	54.2
13		15 03.1	24.2	50 47.0	11.2	25 03.4	5.4	54.2
14		30 02.8	24.2	65 17.2	11.1	25 08.8	5.2	54.1
15		45 02.5	. . 24.1	79 47.3	11.1	25 14.0	5.1	54.1
16		60 02.1	24.0	94 17.4	11.1	25 19.1	5.0	54.1
17		75 01.8	24.0	108 47.5	11.1	25 24.1	4.9	54.1
18		90 01.5	S23 23.9	123 17.6	11.0	S25 29.0	4.7	54.1
19		105 01.2	23.8	137 47.6	10.9	25 33.7	4.7	54.1
20		120 00.9	23.8	152 17.5	10.9	25 38.4	4.5	54.1
21		135 00.6	. . 23.7	166 47.4	10.9	25 42.9	4.4	54.1
22		150 00.3	23.6	181 17.3	10.9	25 47.3	4.2	54.1
23		165 00.0	23.6	195 47.2	10.8	25 51.5	4.2	54.1
25 00		179 59.7	S23 23.5	210 17.0	10.8	S25 55.7	4.0	54.1
01		194 59.3	23.4	224 46.8	10.8	25 59.7	3.9	54.1
02		209 59.0	23.4	239 16.6	10.7	26 03.6	3.8	54.1
03		224 58.7	. . 23.3	253 46.3	10.7	26 07.4	3.6	54.0
04		239 58.4	23.2	268 16.0	10.7	26 11.0	3.5	54.0
05		254 58.1	23.2	282 45.7	10.6	26 14.5	3.4	54.0
06		269 57.8	S23 23.1	297 15.3	10.6	S26 17.9	3.3	54.0
07	THURSDAY	284 57.5	23.0	311 44.9	10.6	26 21.2	3.1	54.0
08		299 57.2	22.9	326 14.5	10.6	26 24.3	3.1	54.0
09		314 56.9	. . 22.9	340 44.1	10.5	26 27.4	2.9	54.0
10		329 56.5	22.8	355 13.6	10.6	26 30.3	2.7	54.0
11		344 56.2	22.7	9 43.2	10.5	26 33.0	2.7	54.0
12		359 55.9	S23 22.6	24 12.7	10.4	S26 35.7	2.5	54.0
13		14 55.6	22.5	38 42.1	10.5	26 38.2	2.4	54.0
14		29 55.3	22.5	53 11.6	10.4	26 40.6	2.2	54.0
15		44 55.0	. . 22.4	67 41.0	10.5	26 42.8	2.2	54.0
16		59 54.7	22.3	82 10.5	10.4	26 45.0	2.0	54.0
17		74 54.4	22.2	96 39.9	10.4	26 47.0	1.9	54.0
18		89 54.1	S23 22.1	111 09.3	10.3	S26 48.9	1.7	54.0
19		104 53.8	22.1	125 38.6	10.4	26 50.6	1.6	54.0
20		119 53.4	22.0	140 08.0	10.3	26 52.2	1.5	54.0
21		134 53.1	. . 21.9	154 37.3	10.4	26 53.7	1.4	54.0
22		149 52.8	21.8	169 06.7	10.3	26 55.1	1.2	54.0
23		164 52.5	21.7	183 36.0	10.3	S26 56.3	1.1	54.0
		SD 16.3	*d* 0.1	SD 14.8		14.8		14.7

Lat. °	Twilight Naut. h m	Twilight Civil h m	Sunrise h m	Moonrise 23 h m	Moonrise 24 h m	Moonrise 25 h m	Moonrise 26 h m
N 72	08 27	10 58	▬	▬	▬	▬	▬
N 70	08 07	09 55	▬	▬	▬	▬	▬
68	07 51	09 20	▬	08 06	▬	▬	▬
66	07 38	08 55	10 36	06 49	▬	▬	▬
64	07 27	08 35	09 53	06 13	08 09	▬	▬
62	07 17	08 19	09 25	05 47	07 24	08 57	10 06
60	07 09	08 06	09 03	05 27	06 54	08 15	09 17
N 58	07 01	07 54	08 46	05 10	06 32	07 46	08 46
56	06 54	07 44	08 31	04 56	06 14	07 24	08 22
54	06 48	07 35	08 18	04 44	05 58	07 06	08 03
52	06 43	07 26	08 07	04 34	05 45	06 51	07 47
50	06 37	07 19	07 57	04 24	05 33	06 38	07 34
45	06 25	07 03	07 37	04 04	05 09	06 11	07 05
N 40	06 15	06 49	07 20	03 48	04 50	05 49	06 43
35	06 06	06 37	07 06	03 35	04 34	05 31	06 25
30	05 57	06 27	06 53	03 23	04 20	05 16	06 09
20	05 40	06 08	06 32	03 04	03 57	04 50	05 43
N 10	05 24	05 51	06 13	02 46	03 37	04 28	05 20
0	05 07	05 33	05 56	02 31	03 18	04 08	04 58
S 10	04 48	05 15	05 38	02 15	02 59	03 47	04 37
20	04 26	04 55	05 19	01 58	02 40	03 25	04 14
30	03 57	04 30	04 57	01 39	02 17	03 00	03 47
35	03 38	04 15	04 44	01 27	02 03	02 45	03 32
40	03 15	03 56	04 29	01 15	01 48	02 27	03 14
45	02 44	03 34	04 11	00 59	01 30	02 07	02 52
S 50	01 58	03 04	03 49	00 41	01 07	01 41	02 24
52	01 31	02 49	03 38	00 32	00 56	01 28	02 10
54	00 44	02 31	03 25	00 23	00 44	01 13	01 55
56	////	02 09	03 11	00 12	00 30	00 57	01 36
58	////	01 39	02 54	00 00	00 14	00 36	01 13
S 60	////	00 48	02 34	23 54	24 11	00 11	00 44

Lat. °	Sunset h m	Twilight Civil h m	Twilight Naut. h m	Moonset 23 h m	Moonset 24 h m	Moonset 25 h m	Moonset 26 h m
N 72	▬	13 02	15 33	▬	▬	▬	▬
N 70	▬	14 04	15 53	▬	▬	▬	▬
68	▬	14 39	16 09	09 05	▬	▬	▬
66	13 24	15 05	16 22	10 22	▬	▬	▬
64	14 06	15 24	16 33	10 59	10 43	▬	▬
62	14 35	15 40	16 42	11 26	11 29	11 39	12 16
60	14 56	15 54	16 51	11 47	11 59	12 22	13 05
N 58	15 14	16 06	16 58	12 04	12 21	12 50	13 36
56	15 29	16 16	17 05	12 18	12 40	13 12	13 59
54	15 41	16 25	17 11	12 31	12 56	13 30	14 18
52	15 52	16 33	17 17	12 42	13 09	13 46	14 34
50	16 02	16 41	17 22	12 52	13 21	13 59	14 48
45	16 23	16 57	17 34	13 13	13 46	14 27	15 16
N 40	16 40	17 10	17 44	13 29	14 06	14 48	15 38
35	16 54	17 22	17 54	13 44	14 22	15 06	15 56
30	17 06	17 33	18 03	13 56	14 37	15 22	16 12
20	17 28	17 52	18 19	14 17	15 01	15 48	16 39
N 10	17 46	18 09	18 35	14 36	15 22	16 11	17 02
0	18 04	18 26	18 52	14 53	15 42	16 32	17 23
S 10	18 21	18 44	19 11	15 11	16 02	16 53	17 44
20	18 40	19 05	19 34	15 29	16 23	17 16	18 07
30	19 02	19 30	20 03	15 51	16 48	17 42	18 33
35	19 15	19 45	20 22	16 04	17 02	17 58	18 49
40	19 30	20 03	20 45	16 18	17 19	18 16	19 07
45	19 48	20 26	21 15	16 36	17 39	18 38	19 29
S 50	20 11	20 55	22 01	16 58	18 05	19 05	19 56
52	20 22	21 10	22 29	17 08	18 17	19 19	20 10
54	20 34	21 28	23 15	17 20	18 31	19 34	20 25
56	20 48	21 51	////	17 33	18 48	19 53	20 44
58	21 05	22 20	////	17 49	19 08	20 16	21 06
S 60	21 25	23 11	////	18 08	19 33	20 45	21 35

Day d	SUN Eqn. of Time 00^h m s	SUN Eqn. of Time 12^h m s	SUN Mer. Pass. h m	MOON Mer. Pass. Upper h m	MOON Mer. Pass. Lower h m	Age d	Phase %
23	00 59	00 44	11 59	08 42	21 06	26	14
24	00 29	00 14	12 00	09 30	21 55	27	8
25	00 01	00 16	12 00	10 20	22 45	28	4

UT d	h	ARIES GHA	VENUS −4.4 GHA	VENUS Dec	MARS +1.3 GHA	MARS Dec	JUPITER −1.9 GHA	JUPITER Dec	SATURN +1.0 GHA	SATURN Dec
d	h	° ′	° ′	° ′	° ′	° ′	° ′	° ′	° ′	° ′
26	00	94 51.9	131 15.7	S16 20.9	185 56.5	S24 05.0	155 09.3	S21 02.7	281 39.4	N 5 08.1
	01	109 54.4	146 15.5	19.9	200 57.0	05.0	170 11.2	02.6	296 41.8	08.1
	02	124 56.9	161 15.2	18.8	215 57.4	05.1	185 13.0	02.5	311 44.2	08.1
	03	139 59.3	176 14.9	. . 17.8	230 57.8	. . 05.1	200 14.9	. . 02.4	326 46.7	. . 08.1
	04	155 01.8	191 14.7	16.8	245 58.2	05.2	215 16.8	02.3	341 49.1	08.1
	05	170 04.3	206 14.5	15.8	260 58.6	05.2	230 18.6	02.2	356 51.5	08.1
	06	185 06.7	221 14.2	S16 14.8	275 59.0	S24 05.2	245 20.5	S21 02.1	11 54.0	N 5 08.1
	07	200 09.2	236 14.0	13.8	290 59.5	05.3	260 22.4	02.0	26 56.4	08.1
	08	215 11.7	251 13.7	12.7	305 59.9	05.3	275 24.2	01.9	41 58.8	08.1
F	09	230 14.1	266 13.5	. . 11.7	321 00.3	. . 05.3	290 26.1	. . 01.7	57 01.3	. . 08.1
R	10	245 16.6	281 13.2	10.7	336 00.7	05.3	305 28.0	01.6	72 03.7	08.1
I	11	260 19.1	296 13.0	09.7	351 01.1	05.4	320 29.8	01.5	87 06.2	08.1
D	12	275 21.5	311 12.7	S16 08.7	6 01.5	S24 05.4	335 31.7	S21 01.4	102 08.6	N 5 08.1
A	13	290 24.0	326 12.5	07.7	21 01.9	05.4	350 33.6	01.3	117 11.0	08.1
Y	14	305 26.4	341 12.2	06.6	36 02.4	05.5	5 35.4	01.2	132 13.5	08.1
	15	320 28.9	356 12.0	. . 05.6	51 02.8	. . 05.5	20 37.3	. . 01.1	147 15.9	. . 08.1
	16	335 31.4	11 11.8	04.6	66 03.2	05.5	35 39.2	01.0	162 18.3	08.1
	17	350 33.8	26 11.5	03.6	81 03.6	05.6	50 41.1	00.9	177 20.8	08.1
	18	5 36.3	41 11.3	S16 02.5	96 04.0	S24 05.6	65 42.9	S21 00.8	192 23.2	N 5 08.1
	19	20 38.8	56 11.1	01.5	111 04.4	05.6	80 44.8	00.7	207 25.7	08.1
	20	35 41.2	71 10.8	16 00.5	126 04.8	05.6	95 46.7	00.5	222 28.1	08.1
	21	50 43.7	86 10.6	15 59.5	141 05.2	. . 05.7	110 48.5	. . 00.4	237 30.5	. . 08.1
	22	65 46.2	101 10.4	58.4	156 05.7	05.7	125 50.4	00.3	252 33.0	08.1
	23	80 48.6	116 10.1	57.4	171 06.1	05.7	140 52.3	00.2	267 35.4	08.1
27	00	95 51.1	131 09.9	S15 56.4	186 06.5	S24 05.7	155 54.1	S21 00.1	282 37.9	N 5 08.1
	01	110 53.5	146 09.7	55.4	201 06.9	05.8	170 56.0	21 00.0	297 40.3	08.1
	02	125 56.0	161 09.4	54.3	216 07.3	05.8	185 57.9	20 59.9	312 42.7	08.1
	03	140 58.5	176 09.2	. . 53.3	231 07.7	. . 05.8	200 59.7	. . 59.8	327 45.2	. . 08.1
	04	156 00.9	191 09.0	52.3	246 08.1	05.8	216 01.6	59.7	342 47.6	08.1
	05	171 03.4	206 08.7	51.3	261 08.5	05.9	231 03.5	59.6	357 50.0	08.1
	06	186 05.9	221 08.5	S15 50.2	276 09.0	S24 05.9	246 05.3	S20 59.4	12 52.5	N 5 08.1
S	07	201 08.3	236 08.3	49.2	291 09.4	05.9	261 07.2	59.3	27 54.9	08.1
	08	216 10.8	251 08.1	48.2	306 09.8	05.9	276 09.1	59.2	42 57.4	08.1
A	09	231 13.3	266 07.8	. . 47.1	321 10.2	. . 06.0	291 10.9	. . 59.1	57 59.8	. . 08.1
T	10	246 15.7	281 07.6	46.1	336 10.6	06.0	306 12.8	59.0	73 02.3	08.1
U	11	261 18.2	296 07.4	45.1	351 11.0	06.0	321 14.7	58.9	88 04.7	08.1
R	12	276 20.7	311 07.2	S15 44.0	6 11.4	S24 06.0	336 16.5	S20 58.8	103 07.1	N 5 08.1
D	13	291 23.1	326 06.9	43.0	21 11.8	06.0	351 18.4	58.7	118 09.6	08.1
A	14	306 25.6	341 06.7	42.0	36 12.3	06.1	6 20.3	58.6	133 12.0	08.1
Y	15	321 28.0	356 06.5	. . 40.9	51 12.7	. . 06.1	21 22.1	. . 58.4	148 14.5	. . 08.1
	16	336 30.5	11 06.3	39.9	66 13.1	06.1	36 24.0	58.3	163 16.9	08.1
	17	351 33.0	26 06.1	38.9	81 13.5	06.1	51 25.9	58.2	178 19.3	08.1
	18	6 35.4	41 05.9	S15 37.8	96 13.9	S24 06.1	66 27.7	S20 58.1	193 21.8	N 5 08.1
	19	21 37.9	56 05.6	36.8	111 14.3	06.2	81 29.6	58.0	208 24.2	08.1
	20	36 40.4	71 05.4	35.7	126 14.7	06.2	96 31.5	57.9	223 26.7	08.2
	21	51 42.8	86 05.2	. . 34.7	141 15.1	. . 06.2	111 33.3	. . 57.8	238 29.1	. . 08.2
	22	66 45.3	101 05.0	33.7	156 15.5	06.2	126 35.2	57.7	253 31.6	08.2
	23	81 47.8	116 04.8	32.6	171 16.0	06.2	141 37.1	57.6	268 34.0	08.2
28	00	96 50.2	131 04.6	S15 31.6	186 16.4	S24 06.2	156 38.9	S20 57.4	283 36.4	N 5 08.2
	01	111 52.7	146 04.4	30.5	201 16.8	06.2	171 40.8	57.3	298 38.9	08.2
	02	126 55.2	161 04.2	29.5	216 17.2	06.3	186 42.7	57.2	313 41.3	08.2
	03	141 57.6	176 03.9	. . 28.5	231 17.6	. . 06.3	201 44.5	. . 57.1	328 43.8	. . 08.2
	04	157 00.1	191 03.7	27.4	246 18.0	06.3	216 46.4	57.0	343 46.2	08.2
	05	172 02.5	206 03.5	26.4	261 18.4	06.3	231 48.3	56.9	358 48.7	08.2
	06	187 05.0	221 03.3	S15 25.3	276 18.8	S24 06.3	246 50.1	S20 56.8	13 51.1	N 5 08.2
	07	202 07.5	236 03.1	24.3	291 19.2	06.3	261 52.0	56.7	28 53.6	08.2
	08	217 09.9	251 02.9	23.2	306 19.6	06.3	276 53.9	56.6	43 56.0	08.2
S	09	232 12.4	266 02.7	. . 22.2	321 20.1	. . 06.3	291 55.7	. . 56.4	58 58.4	. . 08.2
U	10	247 14.9	281 02.5	21.1	336 20.5	06.4	306 57.6	56.3	74 00.9	08.2
N	11	262 17.3	296 02.3	20.1	351 20.9	06.4	321 59.5	56.2	89 03.3	08.2
D	12	277 19.8	311 02.1	S15 19.0	6 21.3	S24 06.4	337 01.3	S20 56.1	104 05.8	N 5 08.2
A	13	292 22.3	326 01.9	18.0	21 21.7	06.4	352 03.2	56.0	119 08.2	08.2
Y	14	307 24.7	341 01.7	16.9	36 22.1	06.4	7 05.0	55.9	134 10.7	08.2
	15	322 27.2	356 01.5	. . 15.9	51 22.5	. . 06.4	22 06.9	. . 55.8	149 13.1	. . 08.2
	16	337 29.7	11 01.3	14.8	66 22.9	06.4	37 08.8	55.7	164 15.6	08.2
	17	352 32.1	26 01.1	13.8	81 23.3	06.4	52 10.6	55.6	179 18.0	08.2
	18	7 34.6	41 00.9	S15 12.7	96 23.7	S24 06.4	67 12.5	S20 55.4	194 20.5	N 5 08.2
	19	22 37.0	56 00.7	11.7	111 24.2	06.4	82 14.4	55.3	209 22.9	08.2
	20	37 39.5	71 00.5	10.6	126 24.6	06.4	97 16.2	55.2	224 25.3	08.3
	21	52 42.0	86 00.3	. . 09.6	141 25.0	. . 06.4	112 18.1	. . 55.1	239 27.8	. . 08.3
	22	67 44.4	101 00.1	08.5	156 25.4	06.4	127 20.0	55.0	254 30.2	08.3
	23	82 46.9	115 59.9	07.5	171 25.8	06.4	142 21.8	54.9	269 32.7	08.3
Mer. Pass.		h m 17 33.7	v −0.2	d 1.0	v 0.4	d 0.0	v 1.9	d 0.1	v 2.4	d 0.0

STARS

Name	SHA	Dec
	° ′	° ′
Acamar	315 20.5	S40 16.2
Achernar	335 28.8	S57 11.6
Acrux	173 13.4	S63 08.7
Adhara	255 14.8	S28 59.0
Aldebaran	290 52.9	N16 31.7
Alioth	166 23.4	N55 54.3
Alkaid	153 01.5	N49 15.7
Al Na'ir	27 48.0	S46 55.2
Alnilam	275 49.4	S 1 11.7
Alphard	217 59.1	S 8 41.9
Alphecca	126 14.1	N26 40.8
Alpheratz	357 47.1	N29 08.6
Altair	62 11.8	N 8 53.5
Ankaa	353 18.8	S42 15.6
Antares	112 30.7	S26 27.1
Arcturus	145 58.9	N19 07.9
Atria	107 36.2	S69 02.6
Avior	234 18.9	S59 32.2
Bellatrix	278 35.2	N 6 21.5
Betelgeuse	271 04.6	N 7 24.6
Canopus	263 57.1	S52 42.0
Capella	280 38.9	N46 00.5
Deneb	49 34.3	N45 18.9
Denebola	182 37.0	N14 31.1
Diphda	348 59.1	S17 56.3
Dubhe	193 55.2	N61 41.8
Elnath	278 16.5	N28 37.0
Eltanin	90 48.2	N51 29.2
Enif	33 50.6	N 9 55.0
Fomalhaut	15 27.7	S29 34.6
Gacrux	172 04.9	S57 09.6
Gienah	175 55.8	S17 35.5
Hadar	148 53.2	S60 24.8
Hamal	328 04.4	N23 30.5
Kaus Aust.	83 48.6	S34 22.9
Kochab	137 20.2	N74 06.7
Markab	13 41.8	N15 15.4
Menkar	314 18.3	N 4 07.6
Menkent	148 11.8	S36 24.8
Miaplacidus	221 40.0	S69 45.0
Mirfak	308 44.9	N49 53.9
Nunki	76 02.8	S26 17.2
Peacock	53 24.9	S56 42.5
Pollux	243 31.4	N28 00.2
Procyon	245 02.9	N 5 12.1
Rasalhague	96 09.9	N12 33.1
Regulus	207 46.8	N11 55.3
Rigel	281 14.9	S 8 11.4
Rigil Kent.	139 56.9	S60 52.2
Sabik	102 16.7	S15 44.2
Schedar	349 44.5	N56 35.6
Shaula	96 26.9	S37 06.6
Sirius	258 36.3	S16 43.7
Spica	158 34.9	S11 12.5
Suhail	222 54.7	S43 28.0
Vega	80 41.7	N38 47.5
Zuben'ubi	137 09.4	S16 04.8

	SHA	Mer. Pass.
	° ′	h m
Venus	35 18.8	15 16
Mars	90 15.4	11 35
Jupiter	60 03.0	13 35
Saturn	186 46.8	5 09

	UT	SUN GHA	SUN Dec	MOON GHA	MOON v	MOON Dec	MOON d	MOON HP
	d h	° ′	° ′	° ′	′	° ′	′	′
	26 00	179 52.2	S23 21.6	198 05.3	10.3	S26 57.4	1.0	54.0
	01	194 51.9	21.5	212 34.6	10.3	26 58.4	0.8	53.9
	02	209 51.6	21.4	227 03.9	10.3	26 59.2	0.7	53.9
	03	224 51.3	. . 21.4	241 33.2	10.3	26 59.9	0.6	53.9
	04	239 51.0	21.3	256 02.5	10.2	27 00.5	0.5	53.9
	05	254 50.7	21.2	270 31.7	10.3	27 01.0	0.3	53.9
	06	269 50.3	S23 21.1	285 01.0	10.3	S27 01.3	0.2	53.9
	07	284 50.0	21.0	299 30.3	10.3	27 01.5	0.1	53.9
	08	299 49.7	20.9	313 59.6	10.3	27 01.6	0.1	53.9
F	09	314 49.4	. . 20.8	328 28.9	10.2	27 01.5	0.2	53.9
R	10	329 49.1	20.7	342 58.1	10.3	27 01.3	0.3	53.9
I	11	344 48.8	20.6	357 27.4	10.3	27 01.0	0.5	53.9
D	12	359 48.5	S23 20.5	11 56.7	10.3	S27 00.5	0.6	53.9
A	13	14 48.2	20.4	26 26.0	10.3	26 59.9	0.7	53.9
Y	14	29 47.9	20.3	40 55.3	10.3	26 59.2	0.8	53.9
	15	44 47.6	. . 20.2	55 24.6	10.3	26 58.4	1.0	53.9
	16	59 47.2	20.1	69 53.9	10.3	26 57.4	1.1	53.9
	17	74 46.9	20.0	84 23.2	10.3	26 56.3	1.3	53.9
	18	89 46.6	S23 19.9	98 52.5	10.4	S26 55.0	1.3	53.9
	19	104 46.3	19.8	113 21.9	10.3	26 53.7	1.5	53.9
	20	119 46.0	19.7	127 51.2	10.4	26 52.2	1.6	53.9
	21	134 45.7	. . 19.6	142 20.6	10.4	26 50.6	1.8	53.9
	22	149 45.4	19.5	156 50.0	10.4	26 48.8	1.9	53.9
	23	164 45.1	19.4	171 19.4	10.4	26 46.9	2.0	53.9
	27 00	179 44.8	S23 19.3	185 48.8	10.5	S26 44.9	2.1	53.9
	01	194 44.5	19.2	200 18.3	10.4	26 42.8	2.3	53.9
	02	209 44.2	19.1	214 47.7	10.5	26 40.5	2.4	53.9
	03	224 43.9	. . 18.9	229 17.2	10.5	26 38.1	2.5	53.9
	04	239 43.5	18.8	243 46.7	10.5	26 35.6	2.6	53.9
	05	254 43.2	18.7	258 16.2	10.6	26 33.0	2.8	53.9
	06	269 42.9	S23 18.6	272 45.8	10.5	S26 30.2	2.9	53.9
	07	284 42.6	18.5	287 15.3	10.6	26 27.3	3.0	53.9
S	08	299 42.3	18.4	301 44.9	10.6	26 24.3	3.2	53.9
A	09	314 42.0	. . 18.3	316 14.5	10.7	26 21.1	3.2	53.9
T	10	329 41.7	18.2	330 44.2	10.7	26 17.9	3.4	53.9
U	11	344 41.4	18.0	345 13.9	10.7	26 14.5	3.5	54.0
R	12	359 41.1	S23 17.9	359 43.6	10.7	S26 11.0	3.7	54.0
D	13	14 40.8	17.8	14 13.3	10.8	26 07.3	3.8	54.0
A	14	29 40.5	17.7	28 43.1	10.8	26 03.5	3.9	54.0
Y	15	44 40.2	. . 17.6	43 12.9	10.8	25 59.6	4.0	54.0
	16	59 39.8	17.4	57 42.7	10.9	25 55.6	4.1	54.0
	17	74 39.5	17.3	72 12.6	10.9	25 51.5	4.3	54.0
	18	89 39.2	S23 17.2	86 42.5	10.9	S25 47.2	4.4	54.0
	19	104 38.9	17.1	101 12.4	11.0	25 42.8	4.5	54.0
	20	119 38.6	17.0	115 42.4	11.0	25 38.3	4.6	54.0
	21	134 38.3	. . 16.8	130 12.4	11.0	25 33.7	4.7	54.0
	22	149 38.0	16.7	144 42.4	11.1	25 29.0	4.9	54.0
	23	164 37.7	16.6	159 12.5	11.2	25 24.1	5.0	54.0
	28 00	179 37.4	S23 16.5	173 42.7	11.1	S25 19.1	5.1	54.0
	01	194 37.1	16.3	188 12.8	11.2	25 14.0	5.2	54.0
	02	209 36.8	16.2	202 43.0	11.3	25 08.8	5.3	54.0
	03	224 36.5	. . 16.1	217 13.3	11.3	25 03.5	5.5	54.0
	04	239 36.2	15.9	231 43.6	11.3	24 58.0	5.6	54.0
	05	254 35.9	15.8	246 13.9	11.4	24 52.4	5.6	54.0
	06	269 35.6	S23 15.7	260 44.3	11.4	S24 46.8	5.8	54.0
	07	284 35.2	15.5	275 14.7	11.5	24 41.0	6.0	54.0
	08	299 34.9	15.4	289 45.2	11.5	24 35.0	6.0	54.0
S	09	314 34.6	. . 15.3	304 15.7	11.5	24 29.0	6.1	54.0
U	10	329 34.3	15.1	318 46.2	11.6	24 22.9	6.3	54.0
N	11	344 34.0	15.0	333 16.8	11.7	24 16.6	6.3	54.1
D	12	359 33.7	S23 14.9	347 47.5	11.7	S24 10.3	6.5	54.1
A	13	14 33.4	14.7	2 18.2	11.7	24 03.8	6.6	54.1
Y	14	29 33.1	14.6	16 48.9	11.8	23 57.2	6.7	54.1
	15	44 32.8	. . 14.5	31 19.7	11.9	23 50.5	6.8	54.1
	16	59 32.5	14.3	45 50.6	11.9	23 43.7	6.9	54.1
	17	74 32.2	14.2	60 21.5	11.9	23 36.8	7.1	54.1
	18	89 31.9	S23 14.0	74 52.4	12.0	S23 29.7	7.1	54.1
	19	104 31.6	13.9	89 23.4	12.0	23 22.6	7.2	54.1
	20	119 31.3	13.7	103 54.4	12.1	23 15.4	7.4	54.1
	21	134 31.0	. . 13.6	118 25.5	12.2	23 08.0	7.4	54.1
	22	149 30.7	13.5	132 56.7	12.1	23 00.6	7.6	54.1
	23	164 30.4	13.3	147 27.8	12.3	S22 53.0	7.6	54.1
		SD 16.3	*d* 0.1	SD 14.7		14.7		14.7

Lat.	Twilight Naut.	Twilight Civil	Sunrise	Moonrise 26	Moonrise 27	Moonrise 28	Moonrise 29
°	h m	h m	h m	h m	h m	h m	h m
N 72	08 27	10 54	▬	▬	▬	▬	▬
N 70	08 07	09 54	▬	▬	▬	▬	▬
68	07 51	09 20	▬	▬	▬	▬	12 27
66	07 38	08 55	10 34	▬	▬	▬	11 37
64	07 27	08 35	09 53	▬	▬	11 19	11 06
62	07 18	08 20	09 25	10 06	10 33	10 41	10 42
60	07 09	08 06	09 04	09 17	09 54	10 13	10 23
N 58	07 02	07 55	08 46	08 46	09 27	09 52	10 07
56	06 55	07 44	08 32	08 22	09 05	09 34	09 54
54	06 49	07 35	08 19	08 03	08 48	09 19	09 42
52	06 43	07 27	08 08	07 47	08 33	09 06	09 32
50	06 38	07 20	07 58	07 34	08 19	08 55	09 22
45	06 27	07 04	07 38	07 05	07 53	08 31	09 03
N 40	06 16	06 50	07 21	06 43	07 31	08 12	08 47
35	06 07	06 39	07 07	06 25	07 13	07 56	08 33
30	05 58	06 28	06 54	06 09	06 58	07 42	08 21
20	05 42	06 09	06 33	05 43	06 32	07 19	08 01
N 10	05 26	05 52	06 15	05 20	06 10	06 58	07 43
0	05 09	05 35	05 57	04 58	05 49	06 39	07 27
S 10	04 50	05 17	05 40	04 37	05 28	06 19	07 10
20	04 27	04 57	05 21	04 14	05 06	05 59	06 52
30	03 58	04 32	04 59	03 47	04 40	05 35	06 31
35	03 40	04 16	04 46	03 32	04 24	05 21	06 19
40	03 17	03 58	04 31	03 14	04 06	05 04	06 05
45	02 46	03 36	04 13	02 52	03 45	04 45	05 49
S 50	02 01	03 06	03 51	02 24	03 17	04 20	05 28
52	01 34	02 51	03 40	02 10	03 04	04 08	05 18
54	00 49	02 33	03 28	01 55	02 49	03 54	05 07
56	////	02 11	03 14	01 36	02 31	03 38	04 54
58	////	01 42	02 57	01 13	02 08	03 19	04 39
S 60	////	00 53	02 37	00 44	01 40	02 56	04 22

Lat.	Sunset	Twilight Civil	Twilight Naut.	Moonset 26	Moonset 27	Moonset 28	Moonset 29
°	h m	h m	h m	h m	h m	h m	h m
N 72	▬	13 09	15 36	▬	▬	▬	▬
N 70	▬	14 08	15 56	▬	▬	▬	▬
68	▬	14 43	16 11	▬	▬	▬	15 02
66	13 29	15 08	16 24	▬	▬	▬	15 52
64	14 10	15 27	16 35	▬	▬	14 30	16 22
62	14 38	15 43	16 45	12 16	13 34	15 09	16 45
60	14 59	15 57	16 53	13 05	14 13	15 36	17 04
N 58	15 16	16 08	17 01	13 36	14 40	15 57	17 19
56	15 31	16 18	17 07	13 59	15 01	16 14	17 32
54	15 44	16 27	17 13	14 18	15 18	16 28	17 43
52	15 55	16 35	17 19	14 34	15 33	16 41	17 53
50	16 04	16 43	17 24	14 48	15 46	16 52	18 01
45	16 25	16 59	17 36	15 16	16 13	17 15	18 20
N 40	16 42	17 12	17 46	15 38	16 34	17 33	18 35
35	16 56	17 24	17 56	15 56	16 51	17 49	18 48
30	17 08	17 34	18 04	16 12	17 06	18 02	18 59
20	17 29	17 53	18 21	16 39	17 31	18 25	19 18
N 10	17 48	18 10	18 37	17 02	17 53	18 44	19 34
0	18 05	18 28	18 54	17 23	18 13	19 02	19 49
S 10	18 22	18 46	19 13	17 44	18 33	19 20	20 04
20	18 41	19 06	19 35	18 07	18 55	19 39	20 20
30	19 03	19 31	20 04	18 33	19 20	20 01	20 38
35	19 16	19 46	20 23	18 49	19 34	20 14	20 49
40	19 31	20 04	20 46	19 07	19 51	20 29	21 01
45	19 49	20 26	21 16	19 29	20 12	20 47	21 15
S 50	20 11	20 56	22 01	19 56	20 37	21 08	21 32
52	20 22	21 11	22 28	20 10	20 49	21 18	21 40
54	20 34	21 29	23 12	20 25	21 03	21 30	21 49
56	20 49	21 51	////	20 44	21 19	21 43	21 59
58	21 05	22 20	////	21 06	21 38	21 58	22 11
S 60	21 25	23 08	////	21 35	22 02	22 17	22 24

Day	SUN Eqn. of Time 00ʰ	SUN Eqn. of Time 12ʰ	SUN Mer. Pass.	MOON Mer. Pass. Upper	MOON Mer. Pass. Lower	MOON Age	MOON Phase
d	m s	m s	h m	h m	h m	d	%
26	00 31	00 45	12 01	11 11	23 36	29	1
27	01 00	01 15	12 01	12 01	24 26	30	0
28	01 30	01 45	12 02	12 50	00 26	01	1

	UT d h	ARIES GHA ° ′	VENUS −4.4 GHA ° ′	Dec ° ′	MARS +1.3 GHA ° ′	Dec ° ′	JUPITER −1.9 GHA ° ′	Dec ° ′	SATURN +1.0 GHA ° ′	Dec ° ′
	29 00	97 49.4	130 59.8	S15 06.4	186 26.2	S24 06.4	157 23.7	S20 54.8	284 35.1	N 5 08.3
	01	112 51.8	145 59.6	05.4	201 26.6	06.5	172 25.6	54.7	299 37.6	08.3
	02	127 54.3	160 59.4	04.3	216 27.0	06.5	187 27.4	54.5	314 40.0	08.3
	03	142 56.8	175 59.2	. . 03.3	231 27.4	. . 06.5	202 29.3	. . 54.4	329 42.5	. . 08.3
	04	157 59.2	190 59.0	02.2	246 27.8	06.5	217 31.2	54.3	344 44.9	08.3
	05	173 01.7	205 58.8	01.2	261 28.2	06.5	232 33.0	54.2	359 47.4	08.3
	06	188 04.2	220 58.6	S15 00.1	276 28.6	S24 06.5	247 34.9	S20 54.1	14 49.8	N 5 08.3
	07	203 06.6	235 58.5	14 59.0	291 29.1	06.5	262 36.8	54.0	29 52.3	08.3
	08	218 09.1	250 58.3	58.0	306 29.5	06.5	277 38.6	53.9	44 54.7	08.3
M	09	233 11.5	265 58.1	. . 56.9	321 29.9	. . 06.5	292 40.5	. . 53.8	59 57.2	. . 08.3
O	10	248 14.0	280 57.9	55.9	336 30.3	06.5	307 42.3	53.6	74 59.6	08.3
N	11	263 16.5	295 57.7	54.8	351 30.7	06.5	322 44.2	53.5	90 02.1	08.3
D	12	278 18.9	310 57.5	S14 53.7	6 31.1	S24 06.5	337 46.1	S20 53.4	105 04.5	N 5 08.3
A	13	293 21.4	325 57.4	52.7	21 31.5	06.5	352 47.9	53.3	120 07.0	08.4
Y	14	308 23.9	340 57.2	51.6	36 31.9	06.5	7 49.8	53.2	135 09.4	08.4
	15	323 26.3	355 57.0	. . 50.6	51 32.3	. . 06.5	22 51.7	. . 53.1	150 11.9	. . 08.4
	16	338 28.8	10 56.8	49.5	66 32.7	06.5	37 53.5	53.0	165 14.3	08.4
	17	353 31.3	25 56.7	48.4	81 33.1	06.4	52 55.4	52.9	180 16.8	08.4
	18	8 33.7	40 56.5	S14 47.4	96 33.5	S24 06.4	67 57.3	S20 52.7	195 19.2	N 5 08.4
	19	23 36.2	55 56.3	46.3	111 33.9	06.4	82 59.1	52.6	210 21.7	08.4
	20	38 38.6	70 56.1	45.2	126 34.3	06.4	98 01.0	52.5	225 24.1	08.4
	21	53 41.1	85 56.0	. . 44.2	141 34.8	. . 06.4	113 02.8	. . 52.4	240 26.6	. . 08.4
	22	68 43.6	100 55.8	43.1	156 35.2	06.4	128 04.7	52.3	255 29.0	08.4
	23	83 46.0	115 55.6	42.0	171 35.6	06.4	143 06.6	52.2	270 31.5	08.4
	30 00	98 48.5	130 55.5	S14 41.0	186 36.0	S24 06.4	158 08.4	S20 52.1	285 33.9	N 5 08.4
	01	113 51.0	145 55.3	39.9	201 36.4	06.4	173 10.3	51.9	300 36.4	08.4
	02	128 53.4	160 55.1	38.8	216 36.8	06.4	188 12.2	51.8	315 38.8	08.4
	03	143 55.9	175 55.0	. . 37.8	231 37.2	. . 06.4	203 14.0	. . 51.7	330 41.3	. . 08.5
	04	158 58.4	190 54.8	36.7	246 37.6	06.4	218 15.9	51.6	345 43.7	08.5
	05	174 00.8	205 54.6	35.6	261 38.0	06.4	233 17.8	51.5	0 46.2	08.5
	06	189 03.3	220 54.5	S14 34.6	276 38.4	S24 06.4	248 19.6	S20 51.4	15 48.7	N 5 08.5
	07	204 05.8	235 54.3	33.5	291 38.8	06.4	263 21.5	51.3	30 51.1	08.5
T	08	219 08.2	250 54.1	32.4	306 39.2	06.3	278 23.3	51.2	45 53.6	08.5
U	09	234 10.7	265 54.0	. . 31.3	321 39.6	. . 06.3	293 25.2	. . 51.0	60 56.0	. . 08.5
E	10	249 13.1	280 53.8	30.3	336 40.0	06.3	308 27.1	50.9	75 58.5	08.5
S	11	264 15.6	295 53.6	29.2	351 40.4	06.3	323 28.9	50.8	91 00.9	08.5
D	12	279 18.1	310 53.5	S14 28.1	6 40.8	S24 06.3	338 30.8	S20 50.7	106 03.4	N 5 08.5
A	13	294 20.5	325 53.3	27.0	21 41.2	06.3	353 32.7	50.6	121 05.8	08.5
Y	14	309 23.0	340 53.2	26.0	36 41.7	06.3	8 34.5	50.5	136 08.3	08.5
	15	324 25.5	355 53.0	. . 24.9	51 42.1	. . 06.3	23 36.4	. . 50.4	151 10.7	. . 08.5
	16	339 27.9	10 52.9	23.8	66 42.5	06.2	38 38.3	50.2	166 13.2	08.6
	17	354 30.4	25 52.7	22.7	81 42.9	06.2	53 40.1	50.1	181 15.6	08.6
	18	9 32.9	40 52.6	S14 21.7	96 43.3	S24 06.2	68 42.0	S20 50.0	196 18.1	N 5 08.6
	19	24 35.3	55 52.4	20.6	111 43.7	06.2	83 43.8	49.9	211 20.6	08.6
	20	39 37.8	70 52.3	19.5	126 44.1	06.2	98 45.7	49.8	226 23.0	08.6
	21	54 40.3	85 52.1	. . 18.4	141 44.5	. . 06.2	113 47.6	. . 49.7	241 25.5	. . 08.6
	22	69 42.7	100 52.0	17.4	156 44.9	06.1	128 49.4	49.6	256 27.9	08.6
	23	84 45.2	115 51.8	16.3	171 45.3	06.1	143 51.3	49.4	271 30.4	08.6
	31 00	99 47.6	130 51.7	S14 15.2	186 45.7	S24 06.1	158 53.2	S20 49.3	286 32.8	N 5 08.6
	01	114 50.1	145 51.5	14.1	201 46.1	06.1	173 55.0	49.2	301 35.3	08.6
	02	129 52.6	160 51.4	13.0	216 46.5	06.1	188 56.9	49.1	316 37.8	08.6
	03	144 55.0	175 51.2	. . 12.0	231 46.9	. . 06.1	203 58.7	. . 49.0	331 40.2	. . 08.7
	04	159 57.5	190 51.1	10.9	246 47.3	06.0	219 00.6	48.9	346 42.7	08.7
	05	175 00.0	205 50.9	09.8	261 47.7	06.0	234 02.5	48.8	1 45.1	08.7
	06	190 02.4	220 50.8	S14 08.7	276 48.1	S24 06.0	249 04.3	S20 48.6	16 47.6	N 5 08.7
W	07	205 04.9	235 50.6	07.6	291 48.5	06.0	264 06.2	48.5	31 50.0	08.7
E	08	220 07.4	250 50.5	06.5	306 48.9	06.0	279 08.0	48.4	46 52.5	08.7
D	09	235 09.8	265 50.4	. . 05.5	321 49.3	. . 05.9	294 09.9	. . 48.3	61 55.0	. . 08.7
N	10	250 12.3	280 50.2	04.4	336 49.7	05.9	309 11.8	48.2	76 57.4	08.7
E	11	265 14.8	295 50.1	03.3	351 50.2	05.9	324 13.6	48.1	91 59.9	08.7
S	12	280 17.2	310 49.9	S14 02.2	6 50.6	S24 05.9	339 15.5	S20 48.0	107 02.3	N 5 08.7
D	13	295 19.7	325 49.8	01.1	21 51.0	05.8	354 17.4	47.8	122 04.8	08.8
A	14	310 22.1	340 49.7	14 00.0	36 51.4	05.8	9 19.2	47.7	137 07.2	08.8
Y	15	325 24.6	355 49.5	. . 13 58.9	51 51.8	. . 05.8	24 21.1	. . 47.6	152 09.7	. . 08.8
	16	340 27.1	10 49.4	57.9	66 52.2	05.8	39 22.9	47.5	167 12.2	08.8
	17	355 29.5	25 49.3	56.8	81 52.6	05.7	54 24.8	47.4	182 14.6	08.8
	18	10 32.0	40 49.1	S13 55.7	96 53.0	S24 05.7	69 26.7	S20 47.3	197 17.1	N 5 08.8
	19	25 34.5	55 49.0	54.6	111 53.4	05.7	84 28.5	47.1	212 19.5	08.8
	20	40 36.9	70 48.9	53.5	126 53.8	05.7	99 30.4	47.0	227 22.0	08.8
	21	55 39.4	85 48.8	. . 52.4	141 54.2	. . 05.6	114 32.3	. . 46.9	242 24.5	. . 08.8
	22	70 41.9	100 48.6	51.3	156 54.6	05.6	129 34.1	46.8	257 26.9	08.8
	23	85 44.3	115 48.5	50.2	171 55.0	05.6	144 36.0	46.7	272 29.4	08.9
	Mer. Pass.	h m 17 21.9	v −0.2	d 1.1	v 0.4	d 0.0	v 1.9	d 0.1	v 2.5	d 0.0

STARS

Name	SHA ° ′	Dec ° ′
Acamar	315 20.5	S40 16.2
Achernar	335 28.8	S57 11.7
Acrux	173 13.3	S63 08.7
Adhara	255 14.8	S28 59.0
Aldebaran	290 52.9	N16 31.7
Alioth	166 23.4	N55 54.3
Alkaid	153 01.5	N49 15.7
Al Na'ir	27 48.0	S46 55.2
Alnilam	275 49.4	S 1 11.7
Alphard	217 59.1	S 8 41.9
Alphecca	126 14.0	N26 40.8
Alpheratz	357 47.1	N29 08.6
Altair	62 11.8	N 8 53.5
Ankaa	353 18.8	S42 15.6
Antares	112 30.7	S26 27.1
Arcturus	145 58.9	N19 07.9
Atria	107 36.2	S69 02.6
Avior	234 18.9	S59 32.2
Bellatrix	278 35.2	N 6 21.5
Betelgeuse	271 04.6	N 7 24.6
Canopus	263 57.1	S52 42.0
Capella	280 38.9	N46 00.5
Deneb	49 34.3	N45 18.9
Denebola	182 36.9	N14 31.1
Diphda	348 59.1	S17 56.3
Dubhe	193 55.2	N61 41.8
Elnath	278 16.5	N28 37.0
Eltanin	90 48.2	N51 29.1
Enif	33 50.6	N 9 55.0
Fomalhaut	15 27.7	S29 34.6
Gacrux	172 04.9	S57 09.6
Gienah	175 55.7	S17 35.5
Hadar	148 53.1	S60 24.8
Hamal	328 04.4	N23 30.5
Kaus Aust.	83 48.6	S34 22.9
Kochab	137 20.2	N74 06.7
Markab	13 41.8	N15 15.4
Menkar	314 18.3	N 4 07.6
Menkent	148 11.8	S36 24.8
Miaplacidus	221 39.9	S69 45.1
Mirfak	308 44.9	N49 53.9
Nunki	76 02.8	S26 17.2
Peacock	53 24.8	S56 42.5
Pollux	243 31.4	N28 00.2
Procyon	245 02.9	N 5 12.1
Rasalhague	96 09.9	N12 33.1
Regulus	207 46.8	N11 55.3
Rigel	281 14.9	S 8 11.4
Rigil Kent.	139 56.9	S60 52.2
Sabik	102 16.7	S15 44.2
Schedar	349 44.5	N56 35.6
Shaula	96 26.9	S37 06.6
Sirius	258 36.3	S16 43.7
Spica	158 34.9	S11 12.6
Suhail	222 54.6	S43 28.0
Vega	80 41.7	N38 47.5
Zuben'ubi	137 09.3	S16 04.8

	SHA ° ′	Mer. Pass h m
Venus	32 06.9	15 16
Mars	87 47.5	11 33
Jupiter	59 19.9	13 26
Saturn	186 45.4	4 57

UT		SUN GHA	SUN Dec	MOON GHA	v	MOON Dec	d	HP
	d h	° ′	° ′	° ′	′	° ′	′	′
MONDAY	29 00	179 30.1	S23 13.2	161 59.1	12.3	S22 45.4	7.8	54.1
	01	194 29.7	13.0	176 30.4	12.3	22 37.6	7.9	54.2
	02	209 29.4	12.9	191 01.7	12.4	22 29.7	7.9	54.2
	03	224 29.1	. . 12.7	205 33.1	12.5	22 21.8	8.1	54.2
	04	239 28.8	12.6	220 04.6	12.5	22 13.7	8.2	54.2
	05	254 28.5	12.4	234 36.1	12.5	22 05.5	8.2	54.2
	06	269 28.2	S23 12.3	249 07.6	12.6	S21 57.3	8.4	54.2
	07	284 27.9	12.1	263 39.2	12.7	21 48.9	8.4	54.2
	08	299 27.6	12.0	278 10.9	12.7	21 40.5	8.6	54.2
	09	314 27.3	. . 11.8	292 42.6	12.7	21 31.9	8.7	54.2
	10	329 27.0	11.7	307 14.3	12.9	21 23.2	8.7	54.2
	11	344 26.7	11.5	321 46.2	12.8	21 14.5	8.9	54.2
	12	359 26.4	S23 11.3	336 18.0	12.9	S21 05.6	8.9	54.2
	13	14 26.1	11.2	350 49.9	13.0	20 56.7	9.0	54.3
	14	29 25.8	11.0	5 21.9	13.0	20 47.7	9.2	54.3
	15	44 25.5	. . 10.9	19 53.9	13.1	20 38.5	9.2	54.3
	16	59 25.2	10.7	34 26.0	13.1	20 29.3	9.3	54.3
	17	74 24.9	10.6	48 58.1	13.2	20 20.0	9.4	54.3
	18	89 24.6	S23 10.4	63 30.3	13.2	S20 10.6	9.5	54.3
	19	104 24.3	10.2	78 02.5	13.3	20 01.1	9.6	54.3
	20	119 24.0	10.1	92 34.8	13.3	19 51.5	9.6	54.3
	21	134 23.7	. . 09.9	107 07.1	13.4	19 41.9	9.8	54.3
	22	149 23.4	09.7	121 39.5	13.4	19 32.1	9.8	54.4
	23	164 23.1	09.6	136 11.9	13.5	19 22.3	9.9	54.4
TUESDAY	30 00	179 22.8	S23 09.4	150 44.4	13.5	S19 12.4	10.1	54.4
	01	194 22.5	09.2	165 16.9	13.6	19 02.3	10.0	54.4
	02	209 22.2	09.1	179 49.5	13.7	18 52.3	10.2	54.4
	03	224 21.9	. . 08.9	194 22.2	13.6	18 42.1	10.3	54.4
	04	239 21.6	08.7	208 54.8	13.8	18 31.8	10.3	54.4
	05	254 21.3	08.6	223 27.6	13.7	18 21.5	10.4	54.4
	06	269 21.0	S23 08.4	238 00.3	13.9	S18 11.1	10.6	54.4
	07	284 20.7	08.2	252 33.2	13.8	18 00.5	10.5	54.5
	08	299 20.4	08.1	267 06.0	14.0	17 50.0	10.7	54.5
	09	314 20.1	. . 07.9	281 39.0	13.9	17 39.3	10.7	54.5
	10	329 19.8	07.7	296 11.9	14.0	17 28.6	10.8	54.5
	11	344 19.5	07.5	310 44.9	14.1	17 17.8	10.9	54.5
	12	359 19.1	S23 07.4	325 18.0	14.1	S17 06.9	11.0	54.5
	13	14 18.8	07.2	339 51.1	14.1	16 55.9	11.0	54.5
	14	29 18.5	07.0	354 24.2	14.2	16 44.9	11.2	54.6
	15	44 18.2	. . 06.8	8 57.4	14.3	16 33.7	11.2	54.6
	16	59 17.9	06.6	23 30.7	14.2	16 22.5	11.2	54.6
	17	74 17.6	06.5	38 03.9	14.4	16 11.3	11.3	54.6
	18	89 17.3	S23 06.3	52 37.3	14.3	S16 00.0	11.4	54.6
	19	104 17.0	06.1	67 10.6	14.4	15 48.6	11.5	54.6
	20	119 16.7	05.9	81 44.0	14.5	15 37.1	11.6	54.6
	21	134 16.4	. . 05.7	96 17.5	14.5	15 25.5	11.6	54.7
	22	149 16.1	05.6	110 51.0	14.5	15 13.9	11.6	54.7
	23	164 15.8	05.4	125 24.5	14.6	15 02.3	11.8	54.7
WEDNESDAY	31 00	179 15.5	S23 05.2	139 58.1	14.6	S14 50.5	11.8	54.7
	01	194 15.2	05.0	154 31.7	14.6	14 38.7	11.9	54.7
	02	209 15.0	04.8	169 05.3	14.7	14 26.8	11.9	54.7
	03	224 14.7	. . 04.6	183 39.0	14.7	14 14.9	12.0	54.8
	04	239 14.4	04.4	198 12.7	14.8	14 02.9	12.1	54.8
	05	254 14.1	04.3	212 46.5	14.8	13 50.8	12.1	54.8
	06	269 13.8	S23 04.1	227 20.3	14.8	S13 38.7	12.2	54.8
	07	284 13.5	03.9	241 54.1	14.8	13 26.5	12.2	54.8
	08	299 13.2	03.7	256 27.9	14.9	13 14.3	12.4	54.8
	09	314 12.9	. . 03.5	271 01.8	15.0	13 01.9	12.3	54.9
	10	329 12.6	03.3	285 35.8	14.9	12 49.6	12.5	54.9
	11	344 12.3	03.1	300 09.7	15.0	12 37.1	12.4	54.9
	12	359 12.0	S23 02.9	314 43.7	15.0	S12 24.7	12.6	54.9
	13	14 11.7	02.7	329 17.7	15.1	12 12.1	12.6	54.9
	14	29 11.4	02.5	343 51.8	15.0	11 59.5	12.6	54.9
	15	44 11.1	. . 02.3	358 25.8	15.1	11 46.9	12.7	55.0
	16	59 10.8	02.1	12 59.9	15.1	11 34.2	12.8	55.0
	17	74 10.5	01.9	27 34.0	15.2	11 21.4	12.8	55.0
	18	89 10.2	S23 01.7	42 08.2	15.2	S11 08.6	12.9	55.0
	19	104 09.9	01.5	56 42.4	15.2	10 55.7	12.9	55.0
	20	119 09.6	01.3	71 16.6	15.2	10 42.8	12.9	55.1
	21	134 09.3	. . 01.1	85 50.8	15.2	10 29.9	13.1	55.1
	22	149 09.0	00.9	100 25.0	15.3	10 16.8	13.0	55.1
	23	164 08.7	00.7	114 59.3	15.3	S10 03.8	13.1	55.1
		SD 16.3	d 0.2	SD 14.8		14.9		15.0

Lat.	Twilight Naut.	Twilight Civil	Sunrise	Moonrise 29	30	31	1
°	h m	h m	h m	h m	h m	h m	h m
N 72	08 25	10 47	■	■	13 02	11 54	11 16
N 70	08 06	09 52	■	■	12 12	11 32	11 05
68	07 51	09 18	■	12 27	11 39	11 15	10 57
66	07 38	08 54	10 31	11 37	11 16	11 01	10 49
64	07 27	08 35	09 51	11 06	10 57	10 50	10 43
62	07 18	08 19	09 24	10 42	10 41	10 40	10 38
60	07 10	08 06	09 03	10 23	10 28	10 31	10 33
N 58	07 02	07 55	08 46	10 07	10 17	10 24	10 29
56	06 56	07 45	08 32	09 54	10 07	10 17	10 25
54	06 50	07 36	08 19	09 42	09 59	10 11	10 22
52	06 44	07 28	08 08	09 32	09 51	10 06	10 19
50	06 39	07 20	07 59	09 22	09 44	10 01	10 16
45	06 27	07 04	07 38	09 03	09 29	09 51	10 10
N 40	06 17	06 51	07 22	08 47	09 16	09 42	10 05
35	06 08	06 40	07 08	08 33	09 06	09 34	10 01
30	05 59	06 29	06 55	08 21	08 56	09 28	09 57
20	05 43	06 11	06 34	08 01	08 40	09 16	09 50
N 10	05 27	05 53	06 16	07 43	08 26	09 06	09 44
0	05 10	05 36	05 59	07 27	08 12	08 56	09 39
S 10	04 52	05 19	05 42	07 10	07 59	08 47	09 33
20	04 29	04 58	05 23	06 52	07 45	08 36	09 27
30	04 00	04 34	05 01	06 31	07 28	08 24	09 20
35	03 42	04 19	04 48	06 19	07 18	08 17	09 16
40	03 19	04 01	04 33	06 05	07 07	08 10	09 12
45	02 49	03 38	04 16	05 49	06 54	08 00	09 06
S 50	02 05	03 09	03 53	05 28	06 38	07 49	09 00
52	01 38	02 54	03 43	05 18	06 31	07 44	08 57
54	00 56	02 37	03 31	05 07	06 22	07 38	08 54
56	////	02 15	03 17	04 54	06 13	07 32	08 50
58	////	01 46	03 00	04 39	06 02	07 25	08 46
S 60	////	01 01	02 40	04 22	05 50	07 16	08 42

Lat.	Sunset	Twilight Civil	Twilight Naut.	Moonset 29	30	31	1
°	h m	h m	h m	h m	h m	h m	h m
N 72	■	13 18	15 40	■	16 04	18 44	20 52
N 70	■	14 14	16 00	■	16 54	19 04	21 00
68	■	14 47	16 15	15 02	17 24	19 19	21 06
66	13 35	15 12	16 28	15 52	17 47	19 31	21 11
64	14 15	15 31	16 39	16 22	18 05	19 41	21 15
62	14 42	15 46	16 48	16 45	18 19	19 50	21 19
60	15 03	16 00	16 56	17 04	18 31	19 57	21 22
N 58	15 20	16 11	17 03	17 19	18 42	20 04	21 25
56	15 34	16 21	17 10	17 32	18 51	20 09	21 28
54	15 46	16 30	17 16	17 43	18 59	20 15	21 30
52	15 57	16 38	17 22	17 53	19 06	20 19	21 32
50	16 07	16 45	17 27	18 01	19 12	20 23	21 34
45	16 27	17 01	17 38	18 20	19 26	20 32	21 38
N 40	16 44	17 14	17 48	18 35	19 37	20 39	21 42
35	16 58	17 26	17 58	18 48	19 47	20 46	21 44
30	17 10	17 36	18 06	18 59	19 55	20 51	21 47
20	17 31	17 55	18 22	19 18	20 10	21 01	21 51
N 10	17 49	18 12	18 38	19 34	20 22	21 09	21 55
0	18 06	18 29	18 55	19 49	20 34	21 17	21 59
S 10	18 24	18 47	19 14	20 04	20 45	21 24	22 02
20	18 42	19 07	19 36	20 20	20 57	21 32	22 06
30	19 04	19 32	20 05	20 38	21 11	21 42	22 10
35	19 17	19 47	20 23	20 49	21 19	21 47	22 13
40	19 32	20 05	20 46	21 01	21 28	21 53	22 15
45	19 50	20 27	21 16	21 15	21 39	22 00	22 18
S 50	20 12	20 56	22 00	21 32	21 52	22 08	22 22
52	20 22	21 11	22 27	21 40	21 57	22 11	22 24
54	20 34	21 28	23 08	21 49	22 04	22 16	22 26
56	20 48	21 50	////	21 59	22 11	22 20	22 28
58	21 05	22 18	////	22 11	22 19	22 25	22 30
S 60	21 24	23 03	////	22 24	22 28	22 31	22 32

Day	SUN Eqn. of Time 00^h	SUN Eqn. of Time 12^h	SUN Mer. Pass.	MOON Mer. Pass. Upper	MOON Mer. Pass. Lower	MOON Age	MOON Phase
d	m s	m s	h m	h m	h m	d	%
29	01 59	02 14	12 02	13 38	01 14	02	4
30	02 28	02 43	12 03	14 23	02 01	03	8
31	02 57	03 12	12 03	15 06	02 45	04	14

EXPLANATION

PRINCIPLE AND ARRANGEMENT

1. *Object.* The object of this Almanac is to provide, in a convenient form, the data required for the practice of astronomical navigation at sea.

2. *Principle.* The main contents of the Almanac consist of data from which the *Greenwich Hour Angle* (GHA) and the *Declination* (Dec) of all the bodies used for navigation can be obtained for any instant of *Universal Time* (UT), or *Greenwich Mean Time* (GMT). The *Local Hour Angle* (LHA) can then be obtained by means of the formula:

$$\text{LHA} = \text{GHA} \begin{matrix} -\text{ west} \\ +\text{ east} \end{matrix} \text{ longitude}$$

The remaining data consist of: times of rising and setting of the Sun and Moon, and times of twilight; miscellaneous calendarial and planning data and auxiliary tables, including a list of Standard Times; corrections to be applied to observed altitude.

For the Sun, Moon, and planets the GHA and Dec are tabulated directly for each hour of UT throughout the year. For the stars the *Sidereal Hour Angle* (SHA) is given, and the GHA is obtained from:

$$\text{GHA Star} = \text{GHA Aries} + \text{SHA Star}$$

The SHA and Dec of the stars change slowly and may be regarded as constant over periods of several days. GHA Aries, or the Greenwich Hour Angle of the first point of Aries (the Vernal Equinox), is tabulated for each hour. Permanent tables give the appropriate increments and corrections to the tabulated hourly values of GHA and Dec for the minutes and seconds of UT.

The six-volume series of *Sight Reduction Tables for Marine Navigation* (published in U.S.A. as Pub. No. 229 and in U.K. as N.P. 401) has been designed for the solution of the navigational triangle and is intended for use with *The Nautical Almanac*.

Two alternative procedures for sight reduction are described on pages 277–318. The first requires the use of programmable calculators or computers, while the second uses a set of concise tables that is given on pages 286–317.

The tabular accuracy is $0'.1$ throughout. The time argument on the daily pages of this Almanac is $12^{h}+$ the Greenwich Hour Angle of the mean sun and is here denoted by UT, although it is also known as GMT. This scale may differ from the broadcast time signals (UTC) by an amount which, if ignored, will introduce an error of up to $0'.2$ in longitude determined from astronomical observations. (The difference arises because the time argument depends on the variable rate of rotation of the Earth while the broadcast time signals are now based on an atomic time-scale.) Step adjustments of exactly one second are made to the time signals as required (normally at 24^{h} on December 31 and June 30) so that the difference between the time signals and UT, as used in this Almanac, may not exceed $0^{s}.9$. Those who require to reduce observations to a precision of better than 1^{s} must therefore obtain the correction (DUT1) to the time signals from coding in the signal, or from other sources; the required time is given by UT1=UTC+DUT1 to a precision of $0^{s}.1$. Alternatively, the longitude, when determined from astronomical observations, may be corrected by the corresponding amount shown in the following table:

Correction to time signals	Correction to longitude
$-0^{s}.9$ to $-0^{s}.7$	$0'.2$ to east
$-0^{s}.6$ to $-0^{s}.3$	$0'.1$ to east
$-0^{s}.2$ to $+0^{s}.2$	no correction
$+0^{s}.3$ to $+0^{s}.6$	$0'.1$ to west
$+0^{s}.7$ to $+0^{s}.9$	$0'.2$ to west

3. *Lay-out.* The ephemeral data for three days are presented on an opening of two pages: the left-hand page contains the data for the planets and stars; the right-hand page contains the data for the Sun and Moon, together with times of twilight, sunrise, sunset, moonrise and moonset.

The remaining contents are arranged as follows: for ease of reference the altitude-correction tables are given on pages A2, A3, A4, xxxiv and xxxv; calendar, Moon's phases, eclipses, and planet notes (i.e. data of general interest) precede the main tabulations. The Explanation is followed by information on standard times, star charts and list of star positions, sight reduction procedures and concise sight reduction tables, tables of increments and corrections and other auxiliary tables that are frequently used.

MAIN DATA

4. *Daily pages.* The daily pages give the GHA of Aries, the GHA and Dec of the Sun, Moon, and the four navigational planets, for each hour of UT. For the Moon, values of *v* and *d* are also tabulated for each hour to facilitate the correction of GHA and Dec to intermediate times; *v* and *d* for the Sun and planets change so slowly that they are given, at the foot of the appropriate columns, once only on the page; *v* is zero for Aries and negligible for the Sun, and is omitted. The SHA and Dec of the 57 selected stars, arranged in alphabetical order of proper name, are also given.

5. *Stars.* The SHA and Dec of 173 stars, including the 57 selected stars, are tabulated for each month on pages 268–273; no interpolation is required and the data can be used in precisely the same way as those for the selected stars on the daily pages. The stars are arranged in order of SHA.

The list of 173 includes all stars down to magnitude 3·0, together with a few fainter ones to fill the larger gaps. The 57 selected stars have been chosen from amongst these on account of brightness and distribution in the sky; they will suffice for the majority of observations.

The 57 selected stars are known by their proper names, but they are also numbered in descending order of SHA. In the list of 173 stars, the constellation names are always given on the left-hand page; on the facing page proper names are given where well-known names exist. Numbers for the selected stars are given in both columns.

An index to the selected stars, containing lists in both alphabetical and numerical order, is given on page xxxiii and is also reprinted on the bookmark.

6. *Increments and corrections.* The tables printed on tinted paper (pages ii–xxxi) at the back of the Almanac provide the increments and corrections for minutes and seconds to be applied to the hourly values of GHA and Dec. They consist of sixty tables, one for each minute, separated into two parts: increments to GHA for Sun and planets, Aries, and Moon for every minute and second; and, for each minute, corrections to be applied to GHA and Dec corresponding to the values of *v* and *d* given on the daily pages.

The increments are based on the following adopted hourly rates of increase of the GHA: Sun and planets, 15° precisely; Aries, 15° 02′.46; Moon, 14° 19′.0. The values of *v* on the daily pages are the excesses of the actual hourly motions over the adopted values; they are generally positive, except for Venus. The tabulated hourly values of the Sun's GHA have been adjusted to reduce to a minimum the error caused by treating *v* as negligible. The values of *d* on the daily pages are the hourly differences of the Dec. For the Moon, the true values of *v* and *d* are given for each hour; otherwise mean values are given for the three days on the page.

7. *Method of entry.* The UT of an observation is expressed as a day and hour, followed by a number of minutes and seconds. The tabular values of GHA and Dec, and, where necessary, the corresponding values of *v* and *d*, are taken directly from the daily pages for the day and hour of UT; this hour is always *before* the time of observation. SHA and Dec of the selected stars are also taken from the daily pages.

The table of Increments and Corrections for the minute of UT is then selected. For the GHA, the increment for minutes and seconds is taken from the appropriate column opposite the seconds of UT; the v-correction is taken from the second part of the same table opposite the value of v as given on the daily pages. Both increment and v-correction are to be added to the GHA, except for Venus when v is prefixed by a minus sign and the v-correction is to be subtracted. For the Dec there is no increment, but a d-correction is applied in the same way as the v-correction; d is given without sign on the daily pages and the sign of the correction is to be supplied by inspection of the Dec column. In many cases the correction may be applied mentally.

8. *Examples.* (a) Sun and Moon. Required the GHA and Dec of the Sun and Moon on 2008 November 6 at $15^h\ 47^m\ 13^s$ UT.

		SUN			MOON			
		GHA	Dec	d	GHA	v	Dec	d
		° ′	° ′	′	° ′	′	° ′	′
Daily page, November $6^d\ 15^h$		49 05·2	S 16 12·7	0·7	309 13·7	14·1	S 14 24·7	12·3
Increments for	$47^m\ 13^s$	11 48·3			11 16·0			
v or d corrections for	47^m		+0·6		+11·2		−9·7	
Sum for November $6^d\ 15^h\ 47^m\ 13^s$		60 53·5	S 16 13·3		320 40·9		S 14 15·0	

(b) Planets. Required the LHA and Dec of (i) Venus on 2008 November 6 at $13^h\ 22^m\ 27^s$ UT in longitude E 79° 48′; (ii) Saturn on 2008 November 6 at $9^h\ 59^m\ 39^s$ UT in longitude W 68° 42′.

		VENUS					SATURN			
		GHA	v	Dec	d		GHA	v	Dec	d
		° ′	′	° ′	′		° ′	′	° ′	′
Daily page, Nov. 6^d	(13^h)	339 12·3	−0·8	S25 07·2	0·3	(9^h)	10 14·2	2·3	N5 58·4	0·1
Increments (planets)	$(22^m\ 27^s)$	5 36·8				$(59^m\ 39^s)$	14 54·8			
v or d corrections	(22^m)	−0·3		+0·1		(59^m)	+2·3		−0·1	
Sum = GHA and Dec.		344 48·8		S25 07·3			25 11·3		N5 58·3	
Longitude	(east)	+ 79 48·0				(west)	− 68 42·0			
Multiples of 360°		−360					+360			
LHA planet		64 36·8					316 29·3			

(c) Stars. Required the GHA and Dec of (i) *Aldebaran* on 2008 November 6 at $9^h\ 59^m\ 39^s$ UT; (ii) *Vega* on 2008 November 6 at $22^h\ 37^m\ 00^s$ UT.

		Aldebaran			*Vega*	
		GHA	Dec		GHA	Dec
		° ′	° ′		° ′	° ′
Daily page (SHA and Dec)		290 53·1	N 16 31.8		80 41·6	N 38 47.7
Daily page (GHA Aries)	(9^h)	180 57·1		(22^h)	16 29·2	
Increments (Aries)	$(59^m\ 39^s)$	14 57·2		$(37^m\ 00^s)$	9 16·5	
Sum = GHA star		486 47·4			106 27·3	
Multiples of 360°		−360				
GHA star		126 47·4			106 27·3	

9. *Polaris (Pole Star) tables.* The tables on pages 274–276 provide means by which the latitude can be deduced from an observed altitude of *Polaris*, and they also give its azimuth; their use is explained and illustrated on those pages. They are based on the following formula:

$$\text{Latitude} - H_O = -p\cos h + \tfrac{1}{2}p\ \sin p\ \sin^2 h\ \tan(\text{latitude})$$

where H_O = Apparent altitude (corrected for refraction)

p = polar distance of *Polaris* = 90° − Dec

h = local hour angle of *Polaris* = LHA Aries + SHA

a_0, which is a function of LHA Aries only, is the value of both terms of the above formula calculated for mean values of the SHA (319° 34′) and Dec (N 89° 18′.2) of *Polaris*, for a mean latitude of 50°, and adjusted by the addition of a constant (58′.8).

a_1, which is a function of LHA Aries and latitude, is the excess of the value of the second term over its mean value for latitude 50°, increased by a constant (0'.6) to make it always positive. a_2, which is a function of LHA Aries and date, is the correction to the first term for the variation of *Polaris* from its adopted mean position; it is increased by a constant (0'.6) to make it positive. The sum of the added constants is 1°, so that:

$$\text{Latitude} = \text{Apparent altitude (corrected for refraction)} - 1° + a_0 + a_1 + a_2$$

RISING AND SETTING PHENOMENA

10. *General.* On the right-hand daily pages are given the times of sunrise and sunset, of the beginning and end of civil and nautical twilights, and of moonrise and moonset for a range of latitudes from N 72° to S 60°. These times, which are given to the nearest minute, are strictly the UT of the phenomena on the Greenwich meridian; they are given for every day for moonrise and moonset, but only for the middle day of the three on each page for the solar phenomena.

They are approximately the Local Mean Times (LMT) of the corresponding phenomena on other meridians; they can be formally interpolated if desired. The UT of a phenomenon is obtained from the LMT by:

$$\text{UT} = \text{LMT} \begin{smallmatrix} + \text{ west} \\ - \text{ east} \end{smallmatrix} \text{ longitude}$$

in which the longitude must first be converted to time by the table on page i or otherwise.

Interpolation for latitude can be done mentally or with the aid of Table I on page xxxii.

The following symbols are used to indicate the conditions under which, in high latitudes, some of the phenomena do not occur:

□ Sun or Moon remains continuously above the horizon;

■ Sun or Moon remains continuously below the horizon;

//// twilight lasts all night.

Basis of the tabulations. At sunrise and sunset 16′ is allowed for semi-diameter and 34′ for horizontal refraction, so that at the times given the Sun's upper limb is on the visible horizon; all times refer to phenomena as seen from sea level with a clear horizon.

At the times given for the beginning and end of twilight, the Sun's zenith distance is 96° for civil, and 102° for nautical twilight. The degree of illumination at the times given for civil twilight (in good conditions and in the absence of other illumination) is such that the brightest stars are visible and the horizon is clearly defined. At the times given for nautical twilight the horizon is in general not visible, and it is too dark for observation with a marine sextant.

Times corresponding to other depressions of the Sun may be obtained by interpolation or, for depressions of more than 12°, less reliably, by extrapolation; times so obtained will be subject to considerable uncertainty near extreme conditions.

At moonrise and moonset allowance is made for semi-diameter, parallax, and refraction (34′), so that at the times given the Moon's upper limb is on the visible horizon as seen from sea level.

11. *Sunrise, sunset, twilight.* The tabulated times may be regarded, without serious error, as the LMT of the phenomena on any of the three days on the page and in any longitude. Precise times may normally be obtained by interpolating the tabular values for latitude and to the correct day and longitude, the latter being expressed as a fraction of a day by dividing it by 360°, positive for west and negative for east longitudes. In the extreme conditions near □, ■ or //// interpolation may not be possible in one direction, but accurate times are of little value in these circumstances.

Examples. Required the UT of (a) the beginning of morning twilights and sunrise on 2008 January 13 for latitude S 48° 55′, longitude E 75° 18′; (b) sunset and the end of evening twilights on 2008 January 15 for latitude N 67° 10′, longitude W 168° 05′.

	(a)	Twilight Nautical	Twilight Civil	Sunrise	(b)	Sunset	Twilight Civil	Twilight Nautical
From p. 19		d h m	d h m	d h m		d h m	d h m	d h m
LMT for Lat	S 45°	13 03 08	13 03 55	13 04 31	N 66°	15 14 21	15 15 41	15 16 52
Corr. to (p. xxxii, Table I)	S 48° 55′	−30	−20	−16	N 67° 10′	−24	−12	−6
Long (p. i)	E 75° 18′	−5 01	−5 01	−5 01	W 168° 05′	+11 12	+11 12	+11 12
UT		12 21 37	12 22 34	12 23 14		16 01 09	16 02 41	16 03 58

The LMT are strictly for January 14 (middle date on page) and 0° longitude; for more precise times it is necessary to interpolate, but rounding errors may accumulate to about 2^{m}.

(a) to January $13^{d} - 75°/360° = $ Jan. $12^{d}_{\cdot}8$, i.e. $\frac{1}{3}(1{\cdot}2) = 0{\cdot}4$ backwards towards the data for the same latitude interpolated similarly from page 17; the corrections are -2^{m} to nautical twilight, -2^{m} to civil twilight and -2^{m} to sunrise.

(b) to January $15^{d} + 168°/360° = $ Jan. $15^{d}_{\cdot}5$, i.e. $\frac{1}{3}(1{\cdot}5) = 0{\cdot}5$ forwards towards the data for the same latitude interpolated similarly from page 21; the corrections are $+7^{m}$ to sunset, $+4^{m}$ to civil twilight, and $+4^{m}$ to nautical twilight.

12. *Moonrise, moonset.* Precise times of moonrise and moonset are rarely needed; a glance at the tables will generally give sufficient indication of whether the Moon is available for observation and of the hours of rising and setting. If needed, precise times may be obtained as follows. Interpolate for latitude, using Table I on page xxxii, on the day wanted and also on the preceding day in east longitudes or the following day in west longitudes; take the difference between these times and interpolate for longitude by applying to the time for the day wanted the correction from Table II on page xxxii, so that the resulting time is between the two times used. In extreme conditions near □ or ■ interpolation for latitude or longitude may be possible only in one direction; accurate times are of little value in these circumstances.

To facilitate this interpolation the times of moonrise and moonset are given for four days on each page; where no phenomenon occurs during a particular day (as happens once a month) the time of the phenomenon on the following day, increased by 24^{h}, is given; extra care must be taken when interpolating between two values, when one of those values exceeds 24^{h}. In practice it suffices to use the daily difference between the times for the nearest tabular latitude, and generally, to enter Table II with the nearest tabular arguments as in the examples below.

Examples. Required the UT of moonrise and moonset in latitude S 47° 10′, longitudes E 124° 00′ and W 78° 31′ on 2008 January 14.

	Longitude E 124° 00′ Moonrise	Longitude E 124° 00′ Moonset	Longitude W 78° 31′ Moonrise	Longitude W 78° 31′ Moonset
	d h m	d h m	d h m	d h m
LMT for Lat. S 45°	14 11 07	14 22 31	14 11 07	14 22 31
Lat correction (p. xxxii, Table I)	+02	−02	+02	−02
Long correction (p. xxxii, Table II)	−27	−07	+18	+04
Correct LMT	14 10 42	14 22 22	14 11 27	14 22 33
Longitude (p. i)	−8 16	−8 16	+5 14	+5 14
UT	14 02 26	14 14 06	14 16 41	15 03 47

ALTITUDE CORRECTION TABLES

13. *General.* In general two corrections are given for application to altitudes observed with a marine sextant; additional corrections are required for Venus and Mars and also for very low altitudes.

Tables of the correction for dip of the horizon, due to height of eye above sea level, are given on pages A2 and xxxiv. Strictly this correction should be applied first and subtracted from the sextant altitude to give apparent altitude, which is the correct argument for the other tables.

Separate tables are given of the second correction for the Sun, for stars and planets (on pages A2 and A3), and for the Moon (on pages xxxiv and xxxv). For the Sun, values are given for both lower and upper limbs, for two periods of the year. The star tables are used for the planets, but additional corrections for parallax (page A2) are required for Venus and Mars. The Moon tables are in two parts: the main correction is a function of apparent altitude only and is tabulated for the lower limb (30′ must be subtracted to obtain the correction for the upper limb); the other, which is given for both lower and upper limbs, depends also on the horizontal parallax, which has to be taken from the daily pages.

An additional correction, given on page A4, is required for the change in the refraction, due to variations of pressure and temperature from the adopted standard conditions; it may generally be ignored for altitudes greater than 10°, except possibly in extreme conditions. The correction tables for the Sun, stars, and planets are in two parts; only those for altitudes greater than 10° are reprinted on the bookmark.

14. *Critical tables.* Some of the altitude correction tables are arranged as critical tables. In these an interval of apparent altitude (or height of eye) corresponds to a single value of the correction; no interpolation is required. At a "critical" entry the upper of the two possible values of the correction is to be taken. For example, in the table of dip, a correction of −4′.1 corresponds to all values of the height of eye from 5·3 to 5·5 metres (17·5 to 18·3 feet) inclusive.

15. *Examples.* The following examples illustrate the use of the altitude correction tables; the sextant altitudes given are assumed to be taken on 2008 November 6 with a marine sextant at height 5·4 metres (18 feet), temperature −3°C and pressure 982 mb, the Moon sights being taken at about 10^h UT.

	SUN lower limb	SUN upper limb	MOON lower limb	MOON upper limb	VENUS	*Polaris*
	° ′	° ′	° ′	° ′	° ′	° ′
Sextant altitude	21 19·7	3 20·2	33 27·6	26 06·7	4 32·6	49 36·5
Dip, height 5·4 metres (18 feet)	−4·1	−4·1	−4·1	−4·1	−4·1	−4·1
Main correction	+13·8	−29·6	+57·4	+60·5	−10·8	−0·8
−30′ for upper limb (Moon)	—	—	—	−30·0	—	—
L, U correction for Moon	—	—	+2·4	+2·2	—	—
Additional correction for Venus	—	—	—	—	+0·1	—
Additional refraction correction	−0·1	−0·6	−0·1	−0·1	−0·5	0·0
Corrected sextant altitude	21 29·3	2 45·9	34 23·2	26 35·2	4 17·3	49 31·6

The main corrections have been taken out with apparent altitude (sextant altitude corrected for index error and dip) as argument, interpolating where possible. These refinements are rarely necessary.

16. *Composition of the Corrections.* The table for the dip of the sea horizon is based on the formula:

$$\text{Correction for dip} = -1'.76\sqrt{(\text{height of eye in metres})} = -0'.97\sqrt{(\text{height of eye in feet})}$$

The correction table for the Sun includes the effects of semi-diameter, parallax and mean refraction.

The correction tables for the stars and planets allow for the effect of mean refraction.

The phase correction for Venus has been incorporated in the tabulations for GHA and Dec, and no correction for phase is required. The additional corrections for Venus and Mars allow for parallax. Alternatively, the correction for parallax may be calculated from $p \cos H$, where p is the parallax and H is the altitude. In 2008 the values for p are:

	Jan. 1		Dec. 5		Dec. 31
Venus		0′.1		0′.2	

	Jan. 1		Feb. 23		Dec. 31
Mars		0′.2		0′.1	

The correction table for the Moon includes the effect of semi-diameter, parallax, augmentation and mean refraction.

Mean refraction is calculated for a temperature of 10°C (50°F), a pressure of 1010 mb (29·83 inches), humidity of 80% and wavelength 0·50169 μm.

17. *Bubble sextant observations.* When observing with a bubble sextant no correction is necessary for dip, semi-diameter, or augmentation. The altitude corrections for the stars and planets on page A2 and on the bookmark should be used for the Sun as well as for the stars and planets; for the Moon it is easiest to take the mean of the corrections for lower and upper limbs and subtract 15′ from the altitude; the correction for dip must not be applied.

AUXILIARY AND PLANNING DATA

18. *Sun and Moon.* On the daily pages are given: hourly values of the horizontal parallax of the Moon; the semi-diameters and the times of meridian passage of both Sun and Moon over the Greenwich meridian; the equation of time; the age of the Moon, the percent (%) illuminated and a symbol indicating the phase. The times of the phases of the Moon are given in UT on page 4. For the Moon, the semi-diameters for each of the three days are given at the foot of the column; for the Sun a single value is sufficient. Table II on page xxxii may be used for interpolating the time of the Moon's meridian passage for longitude. The equation of time is given daily at 00^{h} and 12^{h} UT. The sign is *positive* for unshaded values and *negative* for shaded values. To obtain apparent time add the equation of time to mean time when the sign is *positive*. Subtract the equation of time from mean time when the sign is *negative*. At 12^{h} UT, when the sign is *positive*, meridian passage of the Sun occurs *before* 12^{h} UT, otherwise it occurs *after* 12^{h} UT.

19. *Planets.* The magnitudes of the planets are given immediately following their names in the headings on the daily pages; also given, for the middle day of the three on the page, are their SHA at 00^{h} UT and their times of meridian passage.

The planet notes and diagram on pages 8 and 9 provide descriptive information as to the suitability of the planets for observation during the year, and of their positions and movements.

20. *Stars.* The time of meridian passage of the first point of Aries over the Greenwich meridian is given on the daily pages, for the middle day of the three on the page, to $0^{m}1$. The interval between successive meridian passages is $23^{h}\ 56^{m}1$ (24^{h} less $3^{m}9$) so that times for intermediate days and other meridians can readily be derived. If a precise time is required it may be obtained by finding the UT at which LHA Aries is zero.

The meridian passage of a star occurs when its LHA is zero, that is when LHA Aries + SHA = 360°. An approximate time can be obtained from the planet diagram on page 9.

The star charts on pages 266 and 267 are intended to assist identification. They show the relative positions of the stars in the sky as seen from the Earth and include all 173 stars used in the Almanac, together with a few others to complete the main constellation configurations. The local meridian at any time may be located on the chart by means of its SHA which is 360° – LHA Aries, or west longitude – GHA Aries.

21. *Star globe.* To set a star globe on which is printed a scale of LHA Aries, first set the globe for latitude and then rotate about the polar axis until the scale under the edge of the meridian circle reads LHA Aries.

To mark the positions of the Sun, Moon, and planets on the star globe, take the difference GHA Aries – GHA body and use this along the LHA Aries scale, in conjunction with the declination, to plot the position. GHA Aries – GHA body is most conveniently found by taking the difference when the GHA of the body is small (less than 15°), which happens once a day.

22. *Calendar.* On page 4 are given lists of ecclesiastical festivals, and of the principal anniversaries and holidays in the United Kingdom and the United States of America. The calendar on page 5 includes the day of the year as well as the day of the week.

Brief particulars are given, at the foot of page 5, of the solar and lunar eclipses occurring during the year; the times given are in UT. The principal features of the more important solar eclipses are shown on the maps on pages 6 and 7.

23. *Standard times.* The lists on pages 262–265 give the standard times used in most countries. In general no attempt is made to give details of the beginning and end of summer time, since they are liable to frequent changes at short notice. For the latest information consult Admiralty List of Radio Signals Volume 2 (NP 282) corrected by Section VI of the weekly edition of Admiralty Notices to Mariners.

The Date or Calendar Line is an arbitrary line, on either side of which the date differs by one day; when crossing this line on a westerly course, the date must be advanced one day; when crossing it on an easterly course, the date must be put back one day. The line is a modification of the line of the 180th meridian, and is drawn so as to include, as far as possible, islands of any one group, etc., on the same side of the line. It may be traced by starting at the South Pole and joining up to the following positions:

	°	°	°	°	°	°	°
Lat	S 51·0	S 45·0	S 15·0	S 5·0	N 48·0	N 53·0	N 65·5
Long	180·0	W 172·5	W 172·5	180·0	180·0	E 170·0	W 169·0

thence through the middle of the Diomede Islands to Lat N 68°.0, Long W 169°.0, passing east of Ostrov Vrangelya (Wrangel Island) to Lat N 75°.0, Long 180°.0, and thence to the North Pole.

ACCURACY

24. *Main data.* The quantities tabulated in this Almanac are generally correct to the nearest 0'.1; the exception is the Sun's GHA which is deliberately adjusted by up to 0'.15 to reduce the error due to ignoring the v-correction. The GHA and Dec at intermediate times cannot be obtained to this precision, since at least two quantities must be added; moreover, the v- and d-corrections are based on mean values of v and d and are taken from tables for the whole minute only. The largest error that can occur in the GHA or Dec of any body other than the Sun or Moon is less than 0'.2; it may reach 0'.25 for the GHA of the Sun and 0'.3 for that of the Moon.

In practice it may be expected that only one third of the values of GHA and Dec taken out will have errors larger than 0'.05 and less than one tenth will have errors larger than 0'.1.

25. *Altitude corrections.* The errors in the altitude corrections are nominally of the same order as those in GHA and Dec, as they result from the addition of several quantities each correctly rounded off to 0'.1. But the actual values of the dip and of the refraction at low altitudes may, in extreme atmospheric conditions, differ considerably from the mean values used in the tables.

USE OF THIS ALMANAC IN 2009

This Almanac may be used for the Sun and stars in 2009 in the following manner.

For the Sun, take out the GHA and Dec for the same date but, for January and February, for a time $18^h\ 12^m\ 00^s$ *later* and, for March to December, for a time $5^h\ 48^m\ 00^s$ *earlier* than the UT of observation; in both cases add 87° 00′ to the GHA so obtained. The error, mainly due to planetary perturbations of the Earth, is unlikely to exceed 0'.4.

For the stars, calculate the GHA and Dec for the same date and the same time, but for January and February *add* 44'.0 and for March to December *subtract* 15'.1 from the GHA so found. The error, due to incomplete correction for precession and nutation, is unlikely to exceed 0'.4. If preferred, the same result can be obtained by using a time $18^h\ 12^m\ 00^s$ later for January and February, and $5^h\ 48^m\ 00^s$ earlier for March to December, than the UT of observation (as for the Sun) and adding 86° 59'.2 to the GHA (or adding 87° as for the Sun and subtracting 0'.8, for precession, from the SHA of the star).

The Almanac cannot be so used for the Moon or planets.

LIST I — PLACES FAST ON UTC (mainly those EAST OF GREENWICH)

The times given below should be } *added* to UTC to give Standard Time / *subtracted* from Standard Time to give UTC.

Place	h	m
Admiralty Islands	10	
Afghanistan	04	30
Albania*	01	
Algeria	01	
Amirante Islands	04	
Andaman Islands	05	30
Angola	01	
Armenia*	04	
Australia		
Australian Capital Territory*	10	
New South Wales*[1]	10	
Northern Territory	09	30
Queensland	10	
South Australia*	09	30
Tasmania*	10	
Victoria*	10	
Western Australia*	08	
Whitsunday Islands	10	
Austria*†	01	
Azerbaijan*	04	
Bahrain	03	
Balearic Islands*†	01	
Bangladesh	06	
Belarus*	02	
Belgium*†	01	
Benin	01	
Bosnia and Herzegovina*	01	
Botswana, Republic of	02	
Brunei	08	
Bulgaria*	02	
Burma (Myanmar)	06	30
Burundi	02	
Cambodia	07	
Cameroon Republic	01	
Caroline Islands[2]	10	
Central African Republic	01	
Chad	01	
Chagos Archipelago & Diego Garcia	06	
Chatham Islands*	12	45
China, People's Republic of	08	
Christmas Island, Indian Ocean	07	
Cocos (Keeling) Islands	06	30
Comoro Islands (Comoros)	03	
Congo, Democratic Republic		
Kinshasa, Mbandaka	01	
Haut-Zaire, Kasai, Kivu, Shaba	02	
Congo Republic	01	
Corsica*†	01	
Crete*†	02	
Croatia*	01	
Cyprus†: Ercan*, Larnaca*	02	
Czech Republic*†	01	

Place	h	m
Denmark*†	01	
Djibouti	03	
Egypt, Arab Republic of*	02	
Equatorial Guinea, Republic of	01	
Eritrea	03	
Estonia*†	02	
Ethiopia	03	
Fiji	12	
Finland*†	02	
France*†	01	
Gabon	01	
Georgia	04	
Germany*†	01	
Gibraltar*	01	
Greece*†	02	
Guam	10	
Hong Kong	08	
Hungary*†	01	
India	05	30
Indonesia, Republic of		
Bangka, Billiton, Java, West and Central Kalimantan, Madura, Sumatra	07	
Bali, Flores, South and East Kalimantan, Lombok, Sulawesi, Sumba, Sumbawa, West Timor	08	
Aru, Irian Jaya, Kai, Moluccas, Tanimbar	09	
Iran	03	30
Iraq*	03	
Israel*	02	
Italy*†	01	
Jan Mayen Island*	01	
Japan	09	
Jordan*	02	
Kazakhstan		
Western: Aktau, Uralsk, Atyrau	05	
Eastern: Kzyl-Orda, Astana	06	
Kenya	03	
Kerguelen Islands	05	
Kiribati Republic		
Gilbert Islands	12	
Phoenix Islands[3]	13	
Line Islands[3]	14	
Korea, North	09	
Republic of (South)	09	
Kuril Islands	11	
Kuwait	03	
Kyrgyzstan	06	
Laccadive Islands	05	30
Laos	07	
Latvia*†	02	

* Daylight-saving time may be kept in these places. † For Summer time dates see List II footnotes.

1 Except Broken Hill Area which keeps $09^h 30^m$.

2 Except Pohnpei, Pingelap and Kosrae which keep 11^h and Palau which keeps 09^h.

3 The Line and Phoenix Is. not part of the Kiribati Republic keep 10^h and 11^h, respectively, slow on UTC.

LIST I — (*continued*)

	h	m
Lebanon*	02	
Lesotho	02	
Libya	02	
Liechtenstein*	01	
Lithuania*†	02	
Lord Howe Island*	10	30
Luxembourg*†	01	
Macau	08	
Macedonia*, former Yugoslav Republic	01	
Macias Nguema (Fernando Póo)	01	
Madagascar, Democratic Republic of	03	
Malawi	02	
Malaysia, Malaya, Sabah, Sarawak	08	
Maldives, Republic of The	05	
Malta*†	01	
Mariana Islands	10	
Marshall Islands[1]	12	
Mauritius	04	
Moldova*	02	
Monaco*	01	
Mongolia*	08	
Mozambique	02	
Namibia*	01	
Nauru	12	
Nepal	05	45
Netherlands, The*†	01	
New Caledonia	11	
New Zealand*	12	
Nicobar Islands	05	30
Niger	01	
Nigeria, Republic of	01	
Norfolk Island	11	30
Norway*	01	
Novaya Zemlya	03	
Okinawa	09	
Oman	04	
Pagalu (Annobon Islands)	01	
Pakistan	05	
Palau Islands	09	
Papua New Guinea	10	
Pescadores Islands	08	
Philippine Republic	08	
Poland*†	01	
Qatar	03	
Reunion	04	
Romania*	02	
Russia[2]*		
Zone 1 Kaliningrad	02	
Zone 2 Moscow, St Petersburg, Arkhangelsk, Astrakhan	03	
Zone 3 Samara, Izhevsk	04	
Zone 4 Perm, Amderna, Novyy Port	05	
Zone 5 Omsk, Novosibirsk	06	
Zone 6 Norilsk, Kyzyl, Dikson	07	
Russia (*continued*)		
Zone 7 Bratsk, Irkutsk, Ulan-Ude	08	
Zone 8 Yakutsk, Chita, Tiksi	09	
Zone 9 Vladivostok, Khabarovsk, Okhotsk	10	
Zone 10 Magadan	11	
Zone 11 Petropavlovsk, Pevek	12	
Rwanda	02	
Ryukyu Islands	09	
Sakhalin Island*	10	
Santa Cruz Islands	11	
Sardinia*†	01	
Saudi Arabia	03	
Schouten Islands	10	
Serbia and Montenegro*	01	
Seychelles	04	
Sicily*†	01	
Singapore	08	
Slovakia*†	01	
Slovenia*†	01	
Socotra	03	
Solomon Islands	11	
Somalia Republic	03	
South Africa, Republic of	02	
Spain*†	01	
Spanish Possessions in North Africa*	01	
Spitsbergen (Svalbard)*	01	
Sri Lanka	05	30
Sudan, Republic of	03	
Swaziland	02	
Sweden*†	01	
Switzerland*	01	
Syria (Syrian Arab Republic)*	02	
Taiwan	08	
Tajikistan	05	
Tanzania	03	
Thailand	07	
Timor-Leste	09	
Tonga	13	
Tunisia*	01	
Turkey*	02	
Turkmenistan	05	
Tuvalu	12	
Uganda	03	
Ukraine*	02	
United Arab Emirates	04	
Uzbekistan	05	
Vanuatu, Republic of	11	
Vietnam, Socialist Republic of	07	
Yemen	03	
Zambia, Republic of	02	
Zimbabwe	02	

* Daylight-saving time may be kept in these places. † For Summer time dates see List II footnotes.

[1] Except the Ebon Atol which keeps time 24^h slow on that of the rest of the islands.

[2] The boundaries between the zones are irregular; listed are chief towns in each zone.

LIST II — PLACES NORMALLY KEEPING UTC

Ascension Island	Ghana	Irish Republic*†	Morocco	Sierra Leone
Burkina-Faso	Great Britain†	Ivory Coast	Portugal*†	Togo Republic
Canary Islands†	Guinea-Bissau	Liberia	Principe	Tristan da Cunha
Channel Islands†	Guinea Republic	Madeira*	St. Helena	
Faeroes*, The	Iceland	Mali	São Tomé	
Gambia, The	Ireland, Northern†	Mauritania	Senegal	

* Daylight-saving time may be kept in these places.

† Summer time (daylight-saving time), one hour in advance of UTC, will be kept from 2008 March 30^{d} 01^{h} to October 26^{d} 01^{h} UTC (Ninth Summer Time Directive of the European Union). Ratification by member countries has not been verified.

LIST III — PLACES SLOW ON UTC (WEST OF GREENWICH)

The times given below should be } *subtracted* from UTC to give Standard Time / *added* to Standard Time to give UTC.

	h m
Argentina	03
Austral (Tubuai) Islands[1]	10
Azores*	01
Bahamas*	05
Barbados	04
Belize	06
Bermuda*	04
Bolivia	04
Brazil	
Fernando de Noronha I., Trindade I., Oceanic Is.	02
S and E coastal states*, Goiás*, Brasilia*, Minas Gerais*, Bahia, Tocantins, Para (eastern), N and NE coastal states	03
Mato Grosso do Sul*, Mato Grosso*, Para (western), Roraima, Rondonia, most of Amazonas	04
Amazonas (south western), Acre	05
British Antarctic Territory[2,3]	03
Canada[3]	
Alberta*	07
British Columbia*	08
Labrador*	04
Manitoba*	06
New Brunswick*	04
Newfoundland*	03 30
Nunavut*	
east of long. W. 85°	05
long. W. 85° to W. 102°	06
west of long. W. 102°	07
Northwest Territories*	07
Nova Scotia*	04
Ontario, east of long. W. 90°*	05
west of long. W. 90°	05

	h m
Canada (*continued*)	
Prince Edward Island*	04
Quebec, east of long. W. 63°	04
west of long. W. 63°*	05
Saskatchewan	06
Yukon*	08
Cape Verde Islands	01
Cayman Islands	05
Chile*	04
Colombia	05
Cook Islands	10
Costa Rica	06
Cuba*	05
Curaçao Island	04
Dominican Republic	04
Easter Island (I. de Pascua)*	06
Ecuador	05
El Salvador	06
Falkland Islands*	04
Fanning Island	10
Fernando de Noronha Island	02
French Guiana	03
Galápagos Islands	06
Greenland	
General*	03
Scoresby Sound*	01
Thule, Danmarkshavn, Mesters Vig	00
Grenada	04
Guadeloupe	04
Guatemala*	06
Guyana, Republic of	04
Haiti*	05
Honduras*	06

* Daylight-saving time may be kept in these places.

1 This is the legal standard time, but local mean time is generally used.

2 Stations may use UTC.

3 Some areas may keep another time zone.

LIST III — (*continued*)

	h	m
Jamaica	05	
Johnston Island	10	
Juan Fernandez Islands*	04	
Leeward Islands	04	
Marquesas Islands	09	30
Martinique	04	
Mexico*[1]	06	
Midway Islands	11	
Nicaragua*	06	
Niue	11	
Panama, Republic of	05	
Paraguay*	04	
Peru	05	
Pitcairn Island	08	
Puerto Rico	04	
St. Pierre and Miquelon*	03	
Samoa	11	
Society Islands	10	
South Georgia	02	
Suriname	03	
Trindade Island, South Atlantic	02	
Trinidad and Tobago	04	
Tuamotu Archipelago	10	
Tubuai (Austral) Islands	10	
Turks and Caicos Islands*	05	
United States of America[2]		
Alabama	06	
Alaska	09	
Aleutian Islands, east of W. 169° 30′	09	
Aleutian Islands, west of W. 169° 30′	10	
Arizona[3,4]	07	
Arkansas	06	
California	08	
Colorado	07	
Connecticut	05	
Delaware	05	
District of Columbia	05	
Florida[4]	05	
Georgia	05	
Hawaii[3]	10	
Idaho, southern part	07	
northern part	08	
Illinois	06	

	h	m
United States of America[2] (*continued*)		
Indiana[4]	05	
Iowa	06	
Kansas[4]	06	
Kentucky, eastern part	05	
western part	06	
Louisiana	06	
Maine	05	
Maryland	05	
Massachusetts	05	
Michigan[4]	05	
Minnesota	06	
Mississippi	06	
Missouri	06	
Montana	07	
Nebraska, eastern part	06	
western part	07	
Nevada	08	
New Hampshire	05	
New Jersey	05	
New Mexico	07	
New York	05	
North Carolina	05	
North Dakota, eastern part	06	
western part	07	
Ohio	05	
Oklahoma	06	
Oregon[4]	08	
Pennsylvania	05	
Rhode Island	05	
South Carolina	05	
South Dakota, eastern part	06	
western part	07	
Tennessee, eastern part	05	
western part	06	
Texas[4]	06	
Utah	07	
Vermont	05	
Virginia	05	
Washington D.C.	05	
Washington	08	
West Virginia	05	
Wisconsin	06	
Wyoming	07	
Uruguay*	03	
Venezuela	04	
Virgin Islands	04	
Windward Islands	04	

* Daylight-saving time may be kept in these places.

1 Except the states of Sonora, Sinaloa*, Nayarit*, Chihuahua* and the Southern District of Lower California* which keep 07^h, and the Northern District of Lower California* which keeps 08^h.

2 Daylight-saving (Summer) time, one hour fast on the time given, is kept during 2007 from the March 9 (second Sunday) to November 2 (first Sunday), changing at $02^h\ 00^m$ local clock time.

3 Exempt from keeping daylight-saving time.

4 A small portion of the state is in another time zone.

NORTHERN STARS

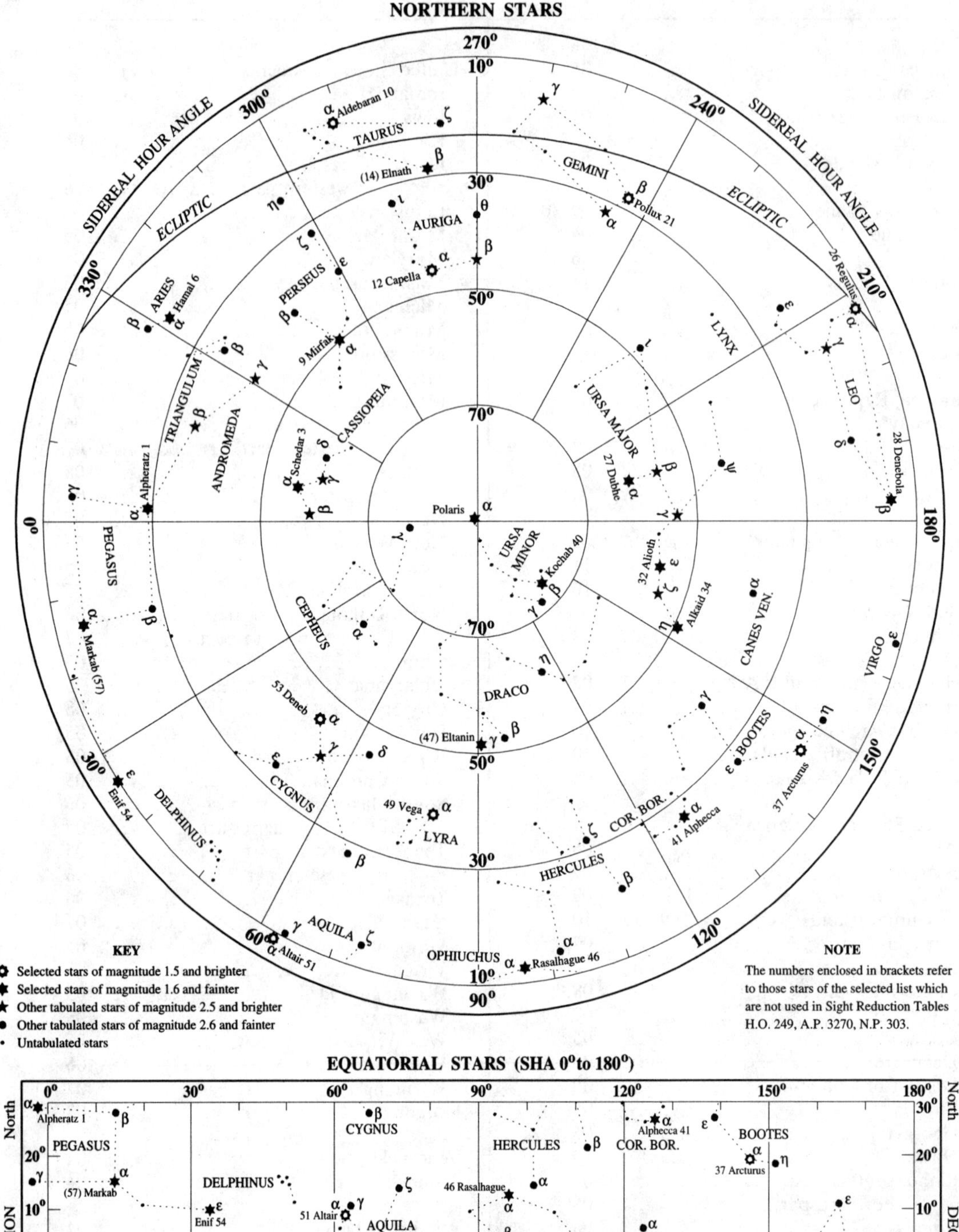

KEY

- Selected stars of magnitude 1.5 and brighter
- Selected stars of magnitude 1.6 and fainter
- Other tabulated stars of magnitude 2.5 and brighter
- Other tabulated stars of magnitude 2.6 and fainter
- Untabulated stars

NOTE

The numbers enclosed in brackets refer to those stars of the selected list which are not used in Sight Reduction Tables H.O. 249, A.P. 3270, N.P. 303.

EQUATORIAL STARS (SHA 0° to 180°)

SOUTHERN STARS

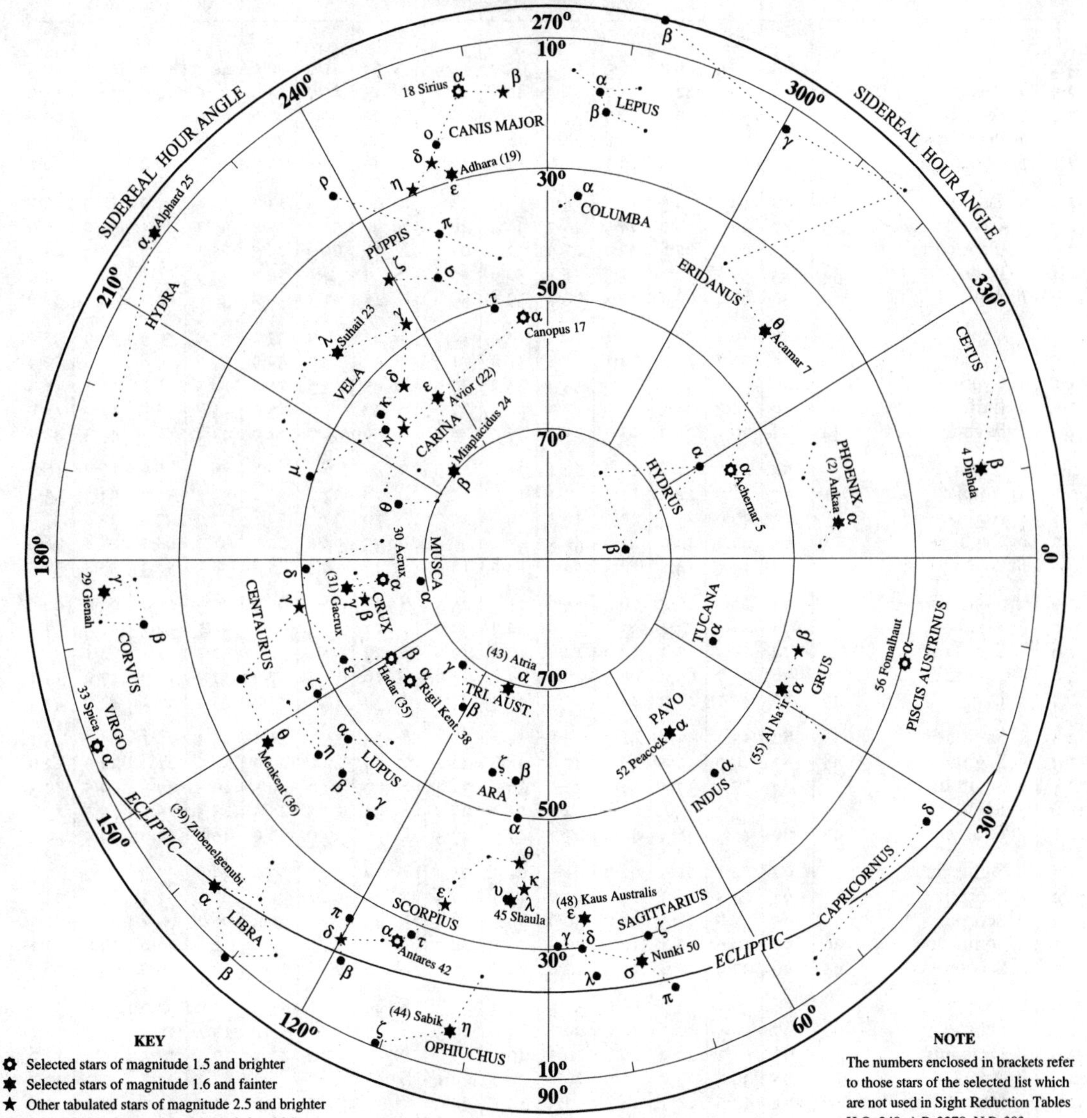

KEY

- ✪ Selected stars of magnitude 1.5 and brighter
- ✸ Selected stars of magnitude 1.6 and fainter
- ★ Other tabulated stars of magnitude 2.5 and brighter
- ● Other tabulated stars of magnitude 2.6 and fainter
- • Untabulated stars

NOTE

The numbers enclosed in brackets refer to those stars of the selected list which are not used in Sight Reduction Tables H.O. 249, A.P. 3270, N.P. 303.

EQUATORIAL STARS (SHA 180° to 360°)

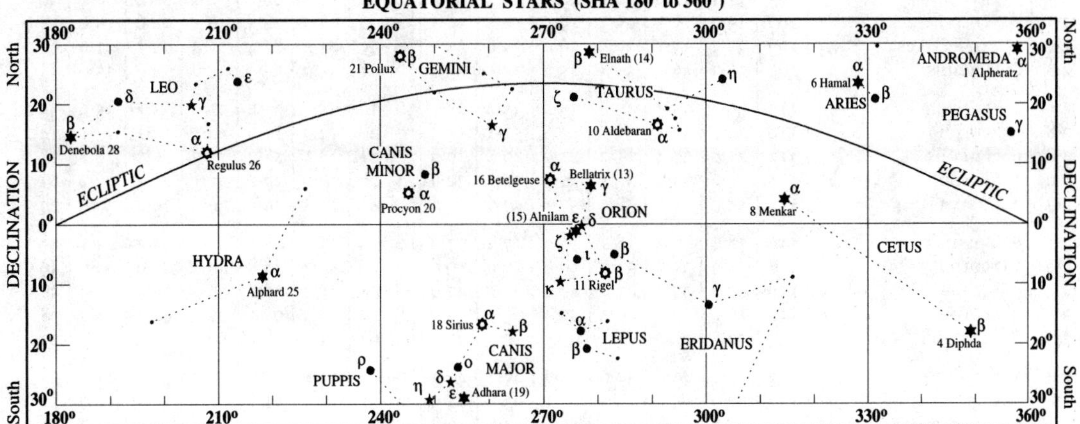

Mag.	Name and Number		SHA							Declination						
				JAN.	FEB.	MAR.	APR.	MAY	JUNE		JAN.	FEB.	MAR.	APR.	MAY	JUNE
			°	′	′	′	′	′	′	°	′	′	′	′	′	′
3·2	γ Cephei		**5**	05·9	06·4	06·6	06·3	05·7	04·9	**N 77**	41·0	40·9	40·7	40·6	40·5	40·5
2·5	α Pegasi	57	**13**	42·7	42·7	42·7	42·5	42·3	42·1	**N 15**	15·0	14·9	14·9	14·9	14·9	15·0
2·4	β Pegasi		**13**	57·7	57·7	57·7	57·6	57·3	57·1	**N 28**	07·7	07·6	07·5	07·5	07·5	07·6
1·2	α Piscis Aust.	56	**15**	28·6	28·6	28·6	28·4	28·2	28·0	**S 29**	34·9	34·9	34·8	34·7	34·6	34·5
2·1	β Gruis		**19**	12·9	12·9	12·8	12·6	12·4	12·1	**S 46**	50·8	50·7	50·5	50·4	50·2	50·2
2·9	α Tucanæ		**25**	14·4	14·5	14·3	14·1	13·7	13·3	**S 60**	13·4	13·2	13·1	12·9	12·8	12·7
1·7	α Gruis	55	**27**	49·0	49·0	48·9	48·7	48·4	48·1	**S 46**	55·5	55·4	55·3	55·1	55·0	55·0
2·9	δ Capricorni		**33**	07·9	07·8	07·7	07·5	07·3	07·1	**S 16**	05·6	05·5	05·5	05·4	05·3	05·3
2·4	ε Pegasi	54	**33**	51·5	51·4	51·3	51·1	50·9	50·7	**N 9**	54·7	54·6	54·6	54·6	54·7	54·8
2·9	β Aquarii		**36**	60·4	60·4	60·3	60·1	59·8	59·6	**S 5**	32·2	32·2	32·2	32·2	32·1	32·0
2·4	α Cephei		**40**	19·2	19·2	19·1	18·7	18·4	18·0	**N 62**	37·3	37·1	37·0	36·9	36·9	37·0
2·5	ε Cygni		**48**	22·3	22·2	22·1	21·8	21·6	21·3	**N 33**	60·0	59·9	59·8	59·8	59·8	59·9
1·3	α Cygni	53	**49**	34·9	34·8	34·6	34·4	34·1	33·8	**N 45**	18·5	18·4	18·3	18·2	18·3	18·4
3·1	α Indi		**50**	28·3	28·1	27·9	27·6	27·3	27·0	**S 47**	15·9	15·8	15·7	15·6	15·6	15·6
1·9	α Pavonis	52	**53**	26·1	25·9	25·7	25·3	24·9	24·5	**S 56**	42·7	42·6	42·4	42·3	42·3	42·3
2·2	γ Cygni		**54**	22·6	22·6	22·4	22·1	21·9	21·6	**N 40**	16·9	16·8	16·7	16·6	16·7	16·8
0·8	α Aquilæ	51	**62**	12·6	12·5	12·3	12·1	11·8	11·6	**N 8**	53·3	53·2	53·2	53·2	53·3	53·4
2·7	γ Aquilæ		**63**	20·6	20·5	20·3	20·1	19·9	19·7	**N 10**	37·9	37·8	37·7	37·8	37·8	37·9
2·9	δ Cygni		**63**	42·1	42·0	41·7	41·5	41·2	41·0	**N 45**	08·9	08·8	08·7	08·7	08·8	08·9
3·1	β Cygni		**67**	14·6	14·5	14·3	14·1	13·8	13·6	**N 27**	58·5	58·4	58·3	58·3	58·4	58·5
2·9	π Sagittarii		**72**	26·6	26·4	26·2	25·9	25·7	25·5	**S 21**	00·8	00·8	00·7	00·7	00·7	00·6
3·0	ζ Aquilæ		**73**	33·5	33·4	33·2	33·0	32·7	32·6	**N 13**	52·4	52·3	52·3	52·3	52·3	52·5
2·6	ζ Sagittarii		**74**	13·4	13·2	12·9	12·7	12·4	12·2	**S 29**	52·2	52·2	52·1	52·1	52·1	52·1
2·0	σ Sagittarii	50	**76**	03·7	03·6	03·3	03·1	02·8	02·6	**S 26**	17·3	17·3	17·3	17·2	17·2	17·2
0·0	α Lyræ	49	**80**	42·2	42·0	41·8	41·5	41·3	41·1	**N 38**	47·3	47·2	47·1	47·1	47·2	47·4
2·8	λ Sagittarii		**82**	53·2	53·0	52·7	52·5	52·2	52·1	**S 25**	25·1	25·1	25·1	25·1	25·1	25·1
1·9	ε Sagittarii	48	**83**	49·6	49·4	49·1	48·8	48·6	48·4	**S 34**	22·9	22·9	22·9	22·9	22·9	22·9
2·7	δ Sagittarii		**84**	37·6	37·4	37·1	36·8	36·6	36·4	**S 29**	49·6	49·5	49·5	49·5	49·5	49·5
3·0	γ Sagittarii		**88**	25·3	25·1	24·8	24·6	24·3	24·2	**S 30**	25·5	25·5	25·5	25·5	25·5	25·5
2·2	γ Draconis	47	**90**	48·5	48·3	48·0	47·7	47·5	47·3	**N 51**	29·0	28·9	28·8	28·9	29·0	29·1
2·8	β Ophiuchi		**94**	02·1	01·9	01·7	01·5	01·3	01·2	**N 4**	33·7	33·6	33·6	33·6	33·6	33·7
2·4	κ Scorpii		**94**	14·5	14·3	14·0	13·7	13·4	13·3	**S 39**	02·1	02·1	02·1	02·1	02·1	02·1
1·9	θ Scorpii		**95**	31·8	31·5	31·2	30·9	30·6	30·4	**S 43**	00·2	00·2	00·2	00·2	00·2	00·3
2·1	α Ophiuchi	46	**96**	10·6	10·4	10·1	09·9	09·7	09·6	**N 12**	33·1	33·0	32·9	33·0	33·0	33·1
1·6	λ Scorpii	45	**96**	27·9	27·6	27·3	27·0	26·8	26·6	**S 37**	06·6	06·6	06·6	06·6	06·7	06·7
3·0	α Aræ		**96**	53·3	53·0	52·6	52·3	52·0	51·8	**S 49**	52·9	52·9	52·9	52·9	53·0	53·1
2·7	υ Scorpii		**97**	10·5	10·3	10·0	09·7	09·5	09·3	**S 37**	18·2	18·2	18·2	18·2	18·2	18·2
2·8	β Draconis		**97**	21·2	20·9	20·6	20·3	20·1	20·0	**N 52**	17·4	17·3	17·3	17·3	17·4	17·6
2·8	β Aræ		**98**	30·8	30·4	30·0	29·6	29·3	29·1	**S 55**	32·2	32·2	32·2	32·2	32·3	32·4
Var.‡	α Herculis		**101**	14·9	14·7	14·5	14·3	14·1	14·0	**N 14**	22·7	22·6	22·5	22·6	22·6	22·7
2·4	η Ophiuchi	44	**102**	17·5	17·3	17·1	16·8	16·7	16·5	**S 15**	44·2	44·2	44·3	44·3	44·3	44·2
3·1	ζ Aræ		**105**	11·0	10·6	10·2	09·8	09·5	09·4	**S 56**	00·1	00·1	00·1	00·2	00·2	00·3
2·3	ε Scorpii		**107**	19·9	19·6	19·3	19·1	18·9	18·7	**S 34**	18·5	18·5	18·5	18·6	18·6	18·6
1·9	α Triang. Aust.	43	**107**	37·7	37·1	36·5	36·0	35·6	35·4	**S 69**	02·4	02·4	02·4	02·5	02·6	02·7
2·8	ζ Herculis		**109**	36·3	36·1	35·8	35·6	35·5	35·4	**N 31**	35·0	34·9	34·9	34·9	35·0	35·2
2·6	ζ Ophiuchi		**110**	36·1	35·8	35·6	35·4	35·2	35·1	**S 10**	35·1	35·2	35·2	35·2	35·2	35·2
2·8	τ Scorpii		**110**	54·4	54·1	53·8	53·6	53·4	53·3	**S 28**	14·0	14·0	14·1	14·1	14·1	14·2
2·8	β Herculis		**112**	21·6	21·4	21·2	21·0	20·8	20·8	**N 21**	28·1	28·0	27·9	28·0	28·1	28·2
1·0	α Scorpii	42	**112**	31·6	31·3	31·1	30·8	30·7	30·6	**S 26**	27·0	27·1	27·1	27·1	27·2	27·2
2·7	η Draconis		**113**	58·8	58·5	58·1	57·8	57·6	57·6	**N 61**	29·4	29·3	29·3	29·4	29·5	29·7
2·7	δ Ophiuchi		**116**	18·6	18·3	18·1	17·9	17·8	17·7	**S 3**	43·1	43·1	43·2	43·2	43·1	43·1
2·6	β Scorpii		**118**	31·5	31·3	31·0	30·8	30·6	30·6	**S 19**	49·7	49·8	49·8	49·9	49·9	49·9
2·3	δ Scorpii		**119**	47·9	47·7	47·4	47·2	47·1	47·0	**S 22**	38·7	38·8	38·8	38·9	38·9	38·9
2·9	π Scorpii		**120**	10·0	09·7	09·5	09·3	09·1	09·0	**S 26**	08·3	08·3	08·4	08·4	08·5	08·5
2·8	β Trianguli Aust.		**121**	02·5	02·0	01·5	01·1	00·8	00·8	**S 63**	27·2	27·2	27·3	27·4	27·5	27·6
2·6	α Serpentis		**123**	50·1	49·8	49·6	49·4	49·3	49·3	**N 6**	23·8	23·7	23·7	23·7	23·8	23·8
2·8	γ Lupi		**126**	04·9	04·6	04·3	04·1	03·9	03·9	**S 41**	11·6	11·6	11·7	11·8	11·9	11·9
2·2	α Coronæ Bor.	41	**126**	14·6	14·4	14·1	13·9	13·8	13·8	**N 26**	41·0	40·9	40·9	40·9	41·0	41·1

‡ 2·9 — 3·6

Mag.	Name and Number		SHA	JULY	AUG.	SEPT.	OCT.	NOV.	DEC.	Declination	JULY	AUG.	SEPT.	OCT.	NOV.	DEC.
			°	′	′	′	′	′	′	°	′	′	′	′	′	′
3·2	γ Cephei		**5**	04·1	03·5	03·3	03·4	03·8	04·4	N **77**	40·6	40·7	40·9	41·1	41·3	41·4
2·5	*Markab*	57	**13**	41·9	41·7	41·6	41·6	41·7	41·8	N **15**	15·1	15·2	15·3	15·4	15·4	15·4
2·4	*Scheat*		**13**	56·8	56·7	56·6	56·6	56·7	56·8	N **28**	07·7	07·9	08·0	08·1	08·1	08·1
1·2	*Fomalhaut*	56	**15**	27·7	27·5	27·4	27·5	27·6	27·7	S **29**	34·4	34·4	34·4	34·5	34·5	34·6
2·1	β Gruis		**19**	11·8	11·5	11·5	11·5	11·7	11·8	S **46**	50·1	50·2	50·3	50·4	50·4	50·4
2·9	α Tucanæ		**25**	12·9	12·7	12·6	12·7	13·0	13·2	S **60**	12·8	12·8	13·0	13·1	13·1	13·1
1·7	*Al Na'ir*	55	**27**	47·8	47·6	47·6	47·7	47·8	48·0	S **46**	54·9	55·0	55·1	55·2	55·2	55·2
2·9	δ Capricorni		**33**	06·8	06·7	06·7	06·8	06·9	06·9	S **16**	05·2	05·2	05·2	05·2	05·2	05·2
2·4	*Enif*	54	**33**	50·5	50·4	50·4	50·4	50·5	50·6	N **9**	54·9	55·0	55·1	55·1	55·1	55·1
2·9	β Aquarii		**36**	59·4	59·3	59·3	59·4	59·5	59·5	S **5**	31·9	31·9	31·8	31·8	31·9	31·9
2·4	*Alderamin*		**40**	17·7	17·6	17·7	18·0	18·3	18·6	N **62**	37·2	37·4	37·6	37·7	37·7	37·7
2·5	ε Cygni		**48**	21·2	21·1	21·2	21·3	21·5	21·6	N **34**	00·1	00·3	00·4	00·4	00·5	00·4
1·3	*Deneb*	53	**49**	33·7	33·6	33·7	33·9	34·1	34·2	N **45**	18·6	18·8	18·9	19·0	19·0	18·9
3·1	α Indi		**50**	26·8	26·6	26·7	26·9	27·0	27·1	S **47**	15·6	15·7	15·7	15·8	15·8	15·8
1·9	*Peacock*	52	**53**	24·3	24·2	24·3	24·5	24·7	24·8	S **56**	42·4	42·5	42·6	42·6	42·6	42·6
2·2	γ Cygni		**54**	21·5	21·4	21·5	21·7	21·9	22·0	N **40**	17·0	17·2	17·3	17·4	17·4	17·3
0·8	*Altair*	51	**62**	11·5	11·5	11·5	11·7	11·8	11·8	N **8**	53·5	53·6	53·6	53·6	53·6	53·5
2·7	γ Aquilæ		**63**	19·5	19·5	19·6	19·7	19·8	19·8	N **10**	38·1	38·1	38·2	38·2	38·2	38·1
2·9	δ Cygni		**63**	40·9	40·9	41·0	41·2	41·4	41·5	N **45**	09·1	09·2	09·3	09·4	09·4	09·3
3·1	*Albireo*		**67**	13·5	13·5	13·6	13·8	13·9	14·0	N **27**	58·7	58·8	58·9	58·9	58·9	58·8
2·9	π Sagittarii		**72**	25·4	25·3	25·4	25·6	25·7	25·7	S **21**	00·6	00·6	00·6	00·6	00·6	00·6
3·0	ζ Aquilæ		**73**	32·5	32·5	32·6	32·7	32·8	32·8	N **13**	52·6	52·7	52·7	52·7	52·7	52·6
2·6	ζ Sagittarii		**74**	12·1	12·0	12·1	12·3	12·4	12·4	S **29**	52·1	52·1	52·1	52·2	52·1	52·1
2·0	*Nunki*	50	**76**	02·5	02·5	02·6	02·7	02·8	02·8	S **26**	17·2	17·2	17·2	17·2	17·2	17·2
0·0	*Vega*	49	**80**	41·1	41·1	41·3	41·5	41·6	41·7	N **38**	47·5	47·6	47·7	47·7	47·7	47·5
2·8	λ Sagittarii		**82**	52·0	52·0	52·1	52·2	52·3	52·3	S **25**	25·1	25·1	25·1	25·1	25·1	25·1
1·9	*Kaus Australis*	48	**83**	48·3	48·3	48·4	48·6	48·7	48·7	S **34**	22·9	22·9	23·0	23·0	22·9	22·9
2·7	δ Sagittarii		**84**	36·3	36·3	36·4	36·6	36·7	36·6	S **29**	49·5	49·6	49·6	49·6	49·5	49·5
3·0	γ Sagittarii		**88**	24·1	24·1	24·2	24·4	24·4	24·4	S **30**	25·5	25·5	25·6	25·5	25·5	25·5
2·2	*Eltanin*	47	**90**	47·4	47·5	47·7	48·0	48·2	48·2	N **51**	29·3	29·4	29·5	29·5	29·4	29·2
2·8	β Ophiuchi		**94**	01·1	01·1	01·3	01·4	01·5	01·4	N **4**	33·8	33·9	33·9	33·9	33·8	33·8
2·4	κ Scorpii		**94**	13·2	13·2	13·4	13·5	13·6	13·6	S **39**	02·2	02·2	02·2	02·2	02·2	02·1
1·9	θ Scorpii		**95**	30·4	30·4	30·6	30·7	30·8	30·8	S **43**	00·3	00·4	00·4	00·4	00·3	00·3
2·1	*Rasalhague*	46	**96**	09·6	09·6	09·7	09·9	10·0	09·9	N **12**	33·2	33·3	33·3	33·3	33·3	33·2
1·6	*Shaula*	45	**96**	26·6	26·6	26·8	26·9	27·0	26·9	S **37**	06·7	06·8	06·8	06·8	06·7	06·7
3·0	α Aræ		**96**	51·8	51·8	52·0	52·2	52·3	52·2	S **49**	53·1	53·2	53·2	53·2	53·1	53·0
2·7	υ Scorpii		**97**	09·2	09·3	09·4	09·6	09·6	09·6	S **37**	18·3	18·3	18·3	18·3	18·3	18·2
2·8	β Draconis		**97**	20·0	20·2	20·5	20·7	20·9	20·9	N **52**	17·8	17·9	17·9	17·9	17·8	17·6
2·8	β Aræ		**98**	29·1	29·2	29·4	29·6	29·7	29·6	S **55**	32·4	32·5	32·5	32·5	32·4	32·3
Var.‡	α Herculis		**101**	14·0	14·1	14·2	14·3	14·4	14·3	N **14**	22·8	22·9	22·9	22·9	22·8	22·7
2·4	*Sabik*	44	**102**	16·5	16·5	16·7	16·8	16·8	16·8	S **15**	44·2	44·2	44·2	44·2	44·2	44·2
3·1	ζ Aræ		**105**	09·3	09·5	09·7	09·9	10·0	09·9	S **56**	00·4	00·5	00·5	00·4	00·4	00·3
2·3	ε Scorpii		**107**	18·7	18·8	18·9	19·1	19·1	19·0	S **34**	18·7	18·7	18·7	18·7	18·6	18·6
1·9	*Atria*	43	**107**	35·4	35·6	36·0	36·3	36·5	36·3	S **69**	02·8	02·9	02·9	02·9	02·7	02·6
2·8	ζ Herculis		**109**	35·4	35·5	35·7	35·9	35·9	35·9	N **31**	35·3	35·4	35·4	35·3	35·2	35·1
2·6	ζ Ophiuchi		**110**	35·1	35·2	35·3	35·4	35·4	35·3	S **10**	35·1	35·1	35·1	35·1	35·1	35·2
2·8	τ Scorpii		**110**	53·3	53·4	53·5	53·6	53·6	53·5	S **28**	14·2	14·2	14·2	14·1	14·1	14·1
2·8	β Herculis		**112**	20·8	20·9	21·0	21·1	21·2	21·1	N **21**	28·3	28·4	28·4	28·3	28·2	28·1
1·0	*Antares*	42	**112**	30·6	30·6	30·8	30·9	30·9	30·8	S **26**	27·2	27·2	27·2	27·2	27·1	27·1
2·7	η Draconis		**113**	57·8	58·0	58·4	58·7	58·9	58·9	N **61**	29·8	29·9	29·9	29·8	29·6	29·4
2·7	δ Ophiuchi		**116**	17·7	17·8	17·9	18·0	18·0	17·9	S **3**	43·0	43·0	43·0	43·0	43·0	43·1
2·6	β Scorpii		**118**	30·6	30·6	30·8	30·9	30·9	30·8	S **19**	49·9	49·9	49·8	49·8	49·8	49·8
2·3	*Dschubba*		**119**	47·0	47·1	47·2	47·3	47·3	47·2	S **22**	38·9	38·9	38·9	38·9	38·8	38·9
2·9	π Scorpii		**120**	09·0	09·1	09·3	09·4	09·3	09·2	S **26**	08·5	08·5	08·5	08·4	08·4	08·4
2·8	β Trianguli Aust.		**121**	00·8	01·0	01·3	01·6	01·6	01·4	S **63**	27·7	27·8	27·7	27·7	27·5	27·4
2·6	α Serpentis		**123**	49·3	49·4	49·5	49·6	49·6	49·5	N **6**	23·9	23·9	23·9	23·9	23·8	23·8
2·8	γ Lupi		**126**	03·9	04·0	04·2	04·3	04·3	04·1	S **41**	12·0	12·0	11·9	11·9	11·8	11·8
2·2	*Alphecca*	41	**126**	13·9	14·0	14·1	14·2	14·3	14·1	N **26**	41·2	41·3	41·2	41·2	41·1	40·9

‡ 2·9 — 3·6

Mag.	Name and Number		SHA °	JAN. ′	FEB. ′	MAR. ′	APR. ′	MAY ′	JUNE ′	Declination °	JAN. ′	FEB. ′	MAR. ′	APR. ′	MAY ′	JUNE ′
3·1	γ Ursæ Minoris		**129**	49·4	48·9	48·4	48·0	47·9	48·1	N **71**	47·9	47·8	47·9	48·0	48·1	48·3
2·9	γ Trianguli Aust.		**130**	05·3	04·7	04·2	03·7	03·5	03·5	S **68**	42·4	42·4	42·5	42·6	42·8	42·9
2·6	β Libræ		**130**	38·4	38·2	37·9	37·8	37·7	37·6	S **9**	24·9	24·9	25·0	25·0	25·0	25·0
2·7	β Lupi		**135**	14·2	13·8	13·5	13·3	13·2	13·2	S **43**	09·9	10·0	10·1	10·2	10·3	10·3
2·8	α Libræ	39	**137**	10·1	09·9	09·6	09·5	09·4	09·4	S **16**	04·6	04·7	04·7	04·8	04·8	04·8
2·1	β Ursæ Minoris	40	**137**	19·8	19·1	18·6	18·2	18·2	18·5	N **74**	06·9	06·9	06·9	07·0	07·2	07·3
2·4	ε Bootis		**138**	39·9	39·6	39·4	39·3	39·2	39·2	N **27**	02·2	02·1	02·1	02·1	02·2	02·3
2·3	α Lupi		**139**	23·1	22·7	22·4	22·2	22·1	22·1	S **47**	25·3	25·3	25·4	25·6	25·7	25·7
−0·3	α Centauri	38	**139**	57·8	57·4	57·0	56·7	56·6	56·7	S **60**	51·9	52·0	52·1	52·2	52·4	52·5
2·3	η Centauri		**140**	59·7	59·4	59·1	59·0	58·9	58·9	S **42**	11·5	11·6	11·7	11·8	11·9	12·0
3·0	γ Bootis		**141**	53·9	53·6	53·4	53·2	53·2	53·2	N **38**	16·0	16·0	16·0	16·1	16·2	16·3
0·0	α Bootis	37	**145**	59·5	59·2	59·0	58·9	58·9	58·9	N **19**	08·2	08·1	08·1	08·1	08·2	08·3
2·1	θ Centauri	36	**148**	12·6	12·3	12·1	11·9	11·9	11·9	S **36**	24·5	24·6	24·7	24·8	24·9	25·0
0·6	β Centauri	35	**148**	54·1	53·7	53·4	53·1	53·1	53·1	S **60**	24·5	24·6	24·8	24·9	25·1	25·2
2·6	ζ Centauri		**150**	59·3	59·0	58·7	58·6	58·5	58·6	S **47**	19·6	19·7	19·8	19·9	20·0	20·1
2·7	η Bootis		**151**	13·9	13·6	13·4	13·3	13·3	13·3	N **18**	21·2	21·1	21·1	21·1	21·2	21·3
1·9	η Ursæ Majoris	34	**153**	02·0	01·6	01·4	01·3	01·3	01·4	N **49**	16·0	16·0	16·0	16·1	16·3	16·4
2·3	ε Centauri		**154**	54·0	53·6	53·3	53·2	53·2	53·2	S **53**	30·3	30·4	30·5	30·7	30·8	30·9
1·0	α Virginis	33	**158**	35·6	35·4	35·2	35·1	35·1	35·1	S **11**	12·3	12·4	12·4	12·5	12·5	12·5
2·3	ζ Ursæ Majoris		**158**	56·0	55·6	55·4	55·3	55·3	55·5	N **54**	52·6	52·6	52·7	52·8	52·9	53·0
2·8	ι Centauri		**159**	44·1	43·9	43·7	43·6	43·6	43·6	S **36**	45·2	45·3	45·5	45·6	45·7	45·7
2·8	ε Virginis		**164**	21·1	20·9	20·8	20·7	20·7	20·7	N **10**	54·8	54·7	54·7	54·7	54·7	54·8
2·9	α Canum Venat.		**165**	53·7	53·4	53·2	53·2	53·2	53·3	N **38**	16·2	16·1	16·2	16·3	16·4	16·5
1·8	ε Ursæ Majoris	32	**166**	23·9	23·6	23·3	23·3	23·3	23·5	N **55**	54·6	54·6	54·7	54·8	54·9	55·0
1·3	β Crucis		**167**	57·0	56·6	56·4	56·3	56·3	56·5	S **59**	43·8	43·9	44·1	44·3	44·4	44·5
2·9	γ Virginis		**169**	28·8	28·6	28·4	28·4	28·4	28·4	S **1**	29·7	29·8	29·9	29·9	29·9	29·9
2·2	γ Centauri		**169**	30·4	30·1	29·9	29·9	29·9	30·0	S **49**	00·1	00·2	00·4	00·5	00·7	00·7
2·7	α Muscæ		**170**	34·9	34·4	34·1	34·0	34·2	34·4	S **69**	10·6	10·7	10·9	11·1	11·2	11·3
2·7	β Corvi		**171**	17·7	17·4	17·3	17·2	17·2	17·3	S **23**	26·5	26·6	26·7	26·8	26·8	26·8
1·6	γ Crucis	31	**172**	05·6	05·3	05·1	05·0	05·1	05·3	S **57**	09·3	09·5	09·6	09·8	09·9	10·0
1·3	α Crucis	30	**173**	14·1	13·7	13·5	13·4	13·5	13·7	S **63**	08·4	08·6	08·8	08·9	09·1	09·1
2·6	γ Corvi	29	**175**	56·5	56·3	56·1	56·1	56·1	56·2	S **17**	35·2	35·3	35·4	35·5	35·5	35·5
2·6	δ Centauri		**177**	48·2	47·9	47·7	47·7	47·8	47·9	S **50**	45·9	46·0	46·2	46·4	46·5	46·5
2·4	γ Ursæ Majoris		**181**	25·7	25·4	25·2	25·3	25·4	25·6	N **53**	38·7	38·7	38·8	38·9	39·0	39·1
2·1	β Leonis	28	**182**	37·6	37·4	37·3	37·3	37·4	37·4	N **14**	31·4	31·4	31·4	31·4	31·5	31·5
2·6	δ Leonis		**191**	21·6	21·4	21·3	21·3	21·4	21·5	N **20**	28·6	28·6	28·6	28·6	28·7	28·7
3·0	ψ Ursæ Majoris		**192**	27·8	27·5	27·4	27·5	27·6	27·7	N **44**	27·0	27·0	27·1	27·2	27·3	27·3
1·8	α Ursæ Majoris	27	**193**	55·9	55·6	55·5	55·6	55·8	56·1	N **61**	42·2	42·2	42·3	42·5	42·6	42·6
2·4	β Ursæ Majoris		**194**	24·5	24·2	24·1	24·2	24·3	24·6	N **56**	20·1	20·1	20·2	20·3	20·4	20·4
2·7	μ Velorum		**198**	12·9	12·7	12·7	12·8	12·9	13·1	S **49**	27·6	27·8	28·0	28·1	28·2	28·2
2·8	θ Carinæ		**199**	10·9	10·7	10·7	10·8	11·1	11·4	S **64**	26·0	26·2	26·4	26·6	26·6	26·7
2·3	γ Leonis		**204**	53·3	53·2	53·1	53·2	53·3	53·4	N **19**	47·9	47·9	47·9	47·9	48·0	48·0
1·4	α Leonis	26	**207**	47·6	47·4	47·4	47·5	47·5	47·6	N **11**	55·6	55·5	55·5	55·5	55·6	55·6
3·0	ε Leonis		**213**	24·9	24·8	24·7	24·8	24·9	25·0	N **23**	44·1	44·1	44·1	44·2	44·2	44·2
3·1	N Velorum		**217**	07·5	07·4	07·5	07·7	08·0	08·2	S **57**	04·1	04·3	04·4	04·5	04·6	04·5
2·0	α Hydræ	25	**217**	59·8	59·7	59·7	59·8	59·9	60·0	S **8**	41·6	41·7	41·8	41·8	41·8	41·8
2·5	κ Velorum		**219**	24·1	24·0	24·1	24·3	24·5	24·7	S **55**	02·6	02·8	02·9	03·0	03·1	03·0
2·2	ι Carinæ		**220**	39·9	39·8	39·9	40·2	40·4	40·7	S **59**	18·4	18·6	18·8	18·9	18·9	18·9
1·7	β Carinæ	24	**221**	40·1	40·0	40·2	40·6	41·0	41·4	S **69**	44·9	45·1	45·2	45·4	45·4	45·4
2·2	λ Velorum	23	**222**	55·2	55·1	55·2	55·3	55·5	55·6	S **43**	27·8	28·0	28·1	28·2	28·2	28·2
3·1	ι Ursæ Majoris		**225**	02·9	02·8	02·8	03·0	03·2	03·3	N **48**	00·5	00·6	00·7	00·7	00·7	00·7
2·0	δ Velorum		**228**	45·6	45·6	45·7	45·9	46·2	46·4	S **54**	44·2	44·4	44·5	44·6	44·6	44·6
1·9	ε Carinæ	22	**234**	19·2	19·2	19·4	19·7	20·0	20·2	S **59**	32·0	32·2	32·4	32·4	32·4	32·4
1·8	γ Velorum		**237**	32·8	32·8	32·9	33·1	33·3	33·5	S **47**	21·6	21·7	21·9	21·9	21·9	21·8
2·8	ρ Puppis		**238**	01·2	01·2	01·3	01·4	01·6	01·6	S **24**	19·6	19·8	19·8	19·9	19·9	19·8
2·3	ζ Puppis		**239**	01·5	01·5	01·6	01·8	02·0	02·1	S **40**	01·5	01·7	01·8	01·8	01·8	01·7
1·1	β Geminorum	21	**243**	32·3	32·3	32·3	32·5	32·6	32·6	N **28**	00·4	00·4	00·4	00·5	00·5	00·5
0·4	α Canis Minoris	20	**245**	03·7	03·6	03·7	03·8	03·9	04·0	N **5**	12·3	12·2	12·2	12·2	12·2	12·2

Mag.	Name and Number		SHA							Declination						
				JULY	AUG.	SEPT.	OCT.	NOV.	DEC.		JULY	AUG.	SEPT.	OCT.	NOV.	DEC.
			°	′	′	′	′	′	′	°	′	′	′	′	′	′
3·1	γ Ursæ Minoris		**129**	48·5	49·0	49·5	49·9	50·1	49·9	N **71**	48·4	48·4	48·3	48·2	48·0	47·8
2·9	γ Trianguli Aust.		**130**	03·6	04·0	04·3	04·6	04·5	04·2	S **68**	43·0	43·0	43·0	42·9	42·7	42·6
2·6	β Libræ		**130**	37·7	37·7	37·9	37·9	37·9	37·7	S **9**	25·0	24·9	24·9	24·9	24·9	25·0
2·7	β Lupi		**135**	13·2	13·4	13·5	13·6	13·6	13·4	S **43**	10·4	10·4	10·3	10·2	10·2	10·1
2·8	*Zubenelgenubi*	39	**137**	09·4	09·5	09·6	09·7	09·6	09·5	S **16**	04·8	04·8	04·7	04·7	04·7	04·8
2·1	*Kochab*	40	**137**	19·0	19·5	20·1	20·5	20·6	20·4	N **74**	07·4	07·4	07·3	07·2	07·0	06·8
2·4	ε Bootis		**138**	39·3	39·4	39·5	39·6	39·6	39·4	N **27**	02·4	02·4	02·4	02·3	02·2	02·0
2·3	α Lupi		**139**	22·2	22·3	22·5	22·6	22·5	22·3	S **47**	25·8	25·8	25·7	25·6	25·5	25·5
−0·3	*Rigil Kent.*	38	**139**	56·8	57·1	57·3	57·5	57·4	57·1	S **60**	52·5	52·5	52·5	52·4	52·2	52·2
2·3	η Centauri		**140**	58·9	59·1	59·2	59·3	59·2	59·0	S **42**	12·0	12·0	11·9	11·8	11·8	11·7
3·0	γ Bootis		**141**	53·3	53·5	53·6	53·7	53·7	53·5	N **38**	16·4	16·4	16·3	16·2	16·1	15·9
0·0	*Arcturus*	37	**145**	59·0	59·1	59·2	59·2	59·2	59·0	N **19**	08·3	08·3	08·3	08·2	08·1	08·0
2·1	*Menkent*	36	**148**	12·0	12·1	12·2	12·2	12·1	11·9	S **36**	25·0	24·9	24·9	24·8	24·8	24·8
0·6	*Hadar*	35	**148**	53·3	53·5	53·8	53·8	53·7	53·4	S **60**	25·2	25·2	25·1	25·0	24·9	24·8
2·6	ζ Centauri		**150**	58·7	58·8	59·0	59·0	58·9	58·6	S **47**	20·1	20·1	20·0	19·9	19·8	19·8
2·7	η Bootis		**151**	13·4	13·5	13·6	13·6	13·5	13·3	N **18**	21·3	21·4	21·3	21·2	21·1	21·0
1·9	*Alkaid*	34	**153**	01·6	01·7	01·9	01·9	01·9	01·7	N **49**	16·4	16·4	16·3	16·2	16·0	15·8
2·3	ε Centauri		**154**	53·4	53·6	53·7	53·7	53·6	53·3	S **53**	30·9	30·9	30·8	30·7	30·6	30·6
1·0	*Spica*	33	**158**	35·2	35·3	35·3	35·3	35·2	35·0	S **11**	12·5	12·4	12·4	12·4	12·4	12·5
2·3	*Mizar*		**158**	55·7	55·9	56·1	56·1	56·0	55·7	N **54**	53·0	53·0	52·9	52·7	52·5	52·4
2·8	ι Centauri		**159**	43·7	43·8	43·9	43·9	43·8	43·5	S **36**	45·7	45·6	45·6	45·5	45·5	45·5
2·8	ε Virginis		**164**	20·8	20·9	20·9	20·9	20·8	20·6	N **10**	54·8	54·8	54·8	54·7	54·6	54·5
2·9	*Cor Caroli*		**165**	53·4	53·5	53·6	53·6	53·5	53·2	N **38**	16·5	16·5	16·4	16·2	16·1	15·9
1·8	*Alioth*	32	**166**	23·7	23·9	24·0	24·0	23·9	23·6	N **55**	55·0	55·0	54·8	54·7	54·5	54·3
1·3	*Mimosa*		**167**	56·7	56·9	57·1	57·0	56·8	56·4	S **59**	44·5	44·4	44·3	44·2	44·1	44·1
2·9	γ Virginis		**169**	28·5	28·6	28·6	28·6	28·4	28·2	S **1**	29·8	29·8	29·8	29·8	29·9	30·0
2·2	*Muhlifain*		**169**	30·1	30·3	30·4	30·3	30·1	29·8	S **49**	00·7	00·6	00·5	00·4	00·4	00·4
2·7	α Muscæ		**170**	34·7	35·1	35·3	35·2	34·9	34·4	S **69**	11·3	11·3	11·1	11·0	10·9	10·9
2·7	β Corvi		**171**	17·4	17·5	17·5	17·5	17·3	17·0	S **23**	26·8	26·8	26·7	26·7	26·7	26·7
1·6	*Gacrux*	31	**172**	05·5	05·6	05·7	05·7	05·4	05·1	S **57**	10·0	09·9	09·8	09·7	09·6	09·6
1·3	*Acrux*	30	**173**	14·0	14·2	14·3	14·3	14·0	13·6	S **63**	09·1	09·1	08·9	08·8	08·7	08·7
2·6	*Gienah*	29	**175**	56·3	56·3	56·4	56·3	56·1	55·9	S **17**	35·5	35·4	35·4	35·4	35·4	35·5
2·6	δ Centauri		**177**	48·1	48·2	48·3	48·2	47·9	47·6	S **50**	46·5	46·4	46·3	46·2	46·1	46·1
2·4	*Phecda*		**181**	25·7	25·9	25·9	25·8	25·6	25·2	N **53**	39·0	38·9	38·8	38·6	38·5	38·3
2·1	*Denebola*	28	**182**	37·5	37·6	37·6	37·5	37·3	37·1	N **14**	31·5	31·5	31·5	31·4	31·3	31·2
2·6	δ Leonis		**191**	21·5	21·6	21·5	21·4	21·2	21·0	N **20**	28·7	28·7	28·6	28·5	28·4	28·3
3·0	ψ Ursæ Majoris		**192**	27·9	27·9	27·9	27·7	27·5	27·2	N **44**	27·3	27·2	27·1	27·0	26·8	26·7
1·8	*Dubhe*	27	**193**	56·3	56·4	56·3	56·2	55·8	55·4	N **61**	42·5	42·4	42·2	42·1	41·9	41·8
2·4	*Merak*		**194**	24·7	24·8	24·7	24·6	24·3	23·9	N **56**	20·4	20·3	20·1	20·0	19·8	19·7
2·7	μ Velorum		**198**	13·2	13·3	13·3	13·1	12·8	12·5	S **49**	28·1	28·0	27·9	27·8	27·8	27·8
2·8	θ Carinæ		**199**	11·6	11·8	11·8	11·6	11·2	10·7	S **64**	26·6	26·5	26·3	26·2	26·2	26·2
2·3	*Algeiba*		**204**	53·4	53·4	53·3	53·2	52·9	52·7	N **19**	48·0	48·0	47·9	47·8	47·7	47·6
1·4	*Regulus*	26	**207**	47·7	47·6	47·6	47·4	47·2	46·9	N **11**	55·6	55·6	55·6	55·5	55·4	55·3
3·0	ε Leonis		**213**	25·0	25·0	24·9	24·7	24·5	24·2	N **23**	44·2	44·2	44·1	44·0	43·9	43·8
3·1	*N* Velorum		**217**	08·3	08·4	08·2	08·0	07·6	07·3	S **57**	04·4	04·3	04·2	04·1	04·1	04·2
2·0	*Alphard*	25	**217**	60·0	60·0	59·9	59·7	59·5	59·2	S **8**	41·7	41·7	41·6	41·6	41·7	41·8
2·5	κ Velorum		**219**	24·8	24·9	24·7	24·5	24·1	23·8	S **55**	02·9	02·8	02·7	02·6	02·6	02·7
2·2	ι Carinæ		**220**	40·8	40·9	40·7	40·4	40·1	39·7	S **59**	18·8	18·6	18·5	18·4	18·4	18·5
1·7	*Miaplacidus*	24	**221**	41·7	41·7	41·6	41·2	40·6	40·1	S **69**	45·3	45·1	45·0	44·9	44·9	45·0
2·2	*Suhail*	23	**222**	55·7	55·7	55·6	55·3	55·0	54·7	S **43**	28·1	28·0	27·8	27·8	27·8	27·9
3·1	ι Ursæ Majoris		**225**	03·3	03·2	03·0	02·8	02·4	02·1	N **48**	00·6	00·5	00·4	00·3	00·2	00·2
2·0	δ Velorum		**228**	46·5	46·4	46·3	46·0	45·6	45·3	S **54**	44·5	44·3	44·2	44·1	44·2	44·3
1·9	*Avior*	22	**234**	20·3	20·3	20·1	19·8	19·4	19·0	S **59**	32·2	32·1	31·9	31·9	31·9	32·1
1·8	γ Velorum		**237**	33·5	33·4	33·2	33·0	32·7	32·4	S **47**	21·7	21·5	21·4	21·4	21·5	21·6
2·8	ρ Puppis		**238**	01·6	01·5	01·4	01·2	00·9	00·7	S **24**	19·7	19·6	19·5	19·5	19·6	19·7
2·3	ζ Puppis		**239**	02·1	02·0	01·8	01·6	01·3	01·1	S **40**	01·6	01·5	01·4	01·3	01·4	01·5
1·1	*Pollux*	21	**243**	32·6	32·4	32·2	32·0	31·7	31·5	N **28**	00·4	00·4	00·3	00·3	00·2	00·2
0·4	*Procyon*	20	**245**	03·9	03·8	03·6	03·4	03·2	02·9	N **5**	12·3	12·3	12·3	12·3	12·2	12·1

Mag.	Name and Number		SHA							Declination						
				JAN.	FEB.	MAR.	APR.	MAY	JUNE		JAN.	FEB.	MAR.	APR.	MAY	JUNE
			°	′	′	′	′	′	′	°	′	′	′	′	′	′
1·6	α Geminorum		**246**	12·7	12·7	12·8	12·9	13·0	13·1	N **31**	52·2	52·3	52·3	52·3	52·3	52·3
3·3	σ Puppis		**247**	37·2	37·2	37·4	37·6	37·8	37·9	S **43**	19·0	19·2	19·3	19·3	19·3	19·2
2·9	β Canis Minoris		**248**	05·7	05·7	05·8	05·9	06·0	06·0	N **8**	16·4	16·4	16·3	16·3	16·4	16·4
2·4	η Canis Majoris		**248**	53·3	53·3	53·4	53·6	53·7	53·8	S **29**	19·1	19·2	19·3	19·3	19·3	19·2
2·7	π Puppis		**250**	38·1	38·1	38·3	38·5	38·6	38·7	S **37**	06·7	06·8	06·9	06·9	06·9	06·8
1·8	δ Canis Majoris		**252**	48·7	48·8	48·9	49·0	49·2	49·2	S **26**	24·3	24·5	24·5	24·5	24·5	24·4
3·0	ο Canis Majoris		**254**	09·1	09·1	09·3	09·4	09·5	09·6	S **23**	50·7	50·8	50·9	50·9	50·8	50·7
1·5	ε Canis Majoris	19	**255**	15·4	15·4	15·5	15·7	15·8	15·9	S **28**	59·0	59·1	59·2	59·2	59·1	59·0
2·9	τ Puppis		**257**	27·4	27·5	27·7	28·0	28·2	28·3	S **50**	37·4	37·6	37·7	37·7	37·6	37·5
−1·5	α Canis Majoris	18	**258**	37·0	37·0	37·1	37·3	37·4	37·4	S **16**	43·6	43·7	43·8	43·8	43·7	43·6
1·9	γ Geminorum		**260**	26·9	26·9	27·0	27·1	27·2	27·2	N **16**	23·6	23·6	23·6	23·6	23·6	23·6
−0·7	α Carinæ	17	**263**	57·5	57·6	57·8	58·1	58·3	58·4	S **52**	42·0	42·2	42·2	42·2	42·1	42·0
2·0	β Canis Majoris		**264**	13·7	13·8	13·9	14·0	14·1	14·1	S **17**	57·6	57·7	57·7	57·7	57·7	57·6
2·6	θ Aurigæ		**269**	55·4	55·4	55·5	55·7	55·8	55·7	N **37**	12·9	12·9	13·0	13·0	12·9	12·9
1·9	β Aurigæ		**269**	57·6	57·6	57·8	57·9	58·0	58·0	N **44**	57·0	57·1	57·1	57·1	57·0	57·0
Var.‡	α Orionis	16	**271**	05·4	05·5	05·6	05·7	05·8	05·7	N **7**	24·6	24·5	24·5	24·5	24·5	24·6
2·1	κ Orionis		**272**	57·5	57·5	57·7	57·8	57·9	57·8	S **9**	40·0	40·1	40·1	40·1	40·0	39·9
1·9	ζ Orionis		**274**	42·1	42·1	42·2	42·4	42·4	42·4	S **1**	56·3	56·3	56·3	56·3	56·3	56·2
2·6	α Columbæ		**275**	00·4	00·5	00·7	00·9	01·0	01·0	S **34**	04·2	04·3	04·4	04·3	04·2	04·1
3·0	ζ Tauri		**275**	27·6	27·7	27·8	27·9	28·0	27·9	N **21**	08·9	08·9	08·9	08·9	08·9	08·9
1·7	ε Orionis	15	**275**	50·2	50·3	50·4	50·5	50·6	50·5	S **1**	11·8	11·8	11·8	11·8	11·8	11·7
2·8	ι Orionis		**276**	02·2	02·2	02·3	02·5	02·5	02·5	S **5**	54·2	54·3	54·3	54·3	54·3	54·2
2·6	α Leporis		**276**	43·3	43·4	43·5	43·6	43·7	43·7	S **17**	49·0	49·1	49·1	49·1	49·0	48·9
2·2	δ Orionis		**276**	53·3	53·3	53·5	53·6	53·6	53·6	S **0**	17·5	17·6	17·6	17·6	17·6	17·5
2·8	β Leporis		**277**	50·7	50·8	50·9	51·1	51·1	51·1	S **20**	45·2	45·3	45·3	45·3	45·2	45·1
1·7	β Tauri	14	**278**	17·5	17·5	17·7	17·8	17·9	17·8	N **28**	37·0	37·0	37·0	37·0	37·0	36·9
1·6	γ Orionis	13	**278**	36·1	36·2	36·3	36·4	36·4	36·4	N **6**	21·5	21·4	21·4	21·4	21·5	21·5
0·1	α Aurigæ	12	**280**	40·1	40·2	40·4	40·6	40·6	40·6	N **46**	00·6	00·6	00·6	00·6	00·5	00·4
0·1	β Orionis	11	**281**	15·7	15·8	15·9	16·0	16·1	16·0	S **8**	11·5	11·6	11·6	11·6	11·5	11·4
2·8	β Eridani		**282**	55·9	56·0	56·1	56·2	56·2	56·2	S **5**	04·5	04·6	04·6	04·6	04·5	04·5
2·7	ι Aurigæ		**285**	36·7	36·8	37·0	37·1	37·1	37·0	N **33**	10·9	10·9	10·9	10·9	10·8	10·8
0·9	α Tauri	10	**290**	53·9	53·9	54·0	54·1	54·2	54·1	N **16**	31·6	31·6	31·6	31·6	31·6	31·6
3·0	γ Eridani		**300**	23·6	23·7	23·8	23·9	23·9	23·8	S **13**	29·1	29·2	29·2	29·1	29·1	28·9
2·9	ε Persei		**300**	23·7	23·8	23·9	24·0	24·0	23·9	N **40**	02·2	02·3	02·2	02·2	02·1	02·1
2·9	ζ Persei		**301**	20·0	20·1	20·3	20·4	20·4	20·2	N **31**	54·7	54·7	54·6	54·6	54·5	54·5
2·9	η Tauri		**303**	00·2	00·3	00·4	00·5	00·5	00·3	N **24**	08·0	08·0	07·9	07·9	07·9	07·9
1·8	α Persei	9	**308**	46·1	46·3	46·5	46·6	46·5	46·3	N **49**	53·7	53·7	53·6	53·6	53·5	53·4
Var.§	β Persei		**312**	49·3	49·4	49·6	49·6	49·6	49·4	N **40**	59·5	59·5	59·4	59·3	59·3	59·2
2·5	α Ceti	8	**314**	19·2	19·3	19·4	19·5	19·4	19·3	N **4**	07·4	07·3	07·3	07·3	07·4	07·4
3·2	θ Eridani	7	**315**	21·2	21·3	21·5	21·6	21·6	21·4	S **40**	16·5	16·5	16·4	16·3	16·2	16·0
2·0	α Ursæ Minoris		**319**	37·6	49·7	60·3	65·9	63·8	55·3	N **89**	18·4	18·4	18·3	18·2	18·0	17·9
3·0	β Trianguli		**327**	29·5	29·6	29·7	29·7	29·6	29·4	N **35**	01·8	01·7	01·7	01·6	01·6	01·6
2·0	α Arietis	6	**328**	05·4	05·5	05·6	05·6	05·5	05·3	N **23**	30·2	30·2	30·1	30·1	30·1	30·1
2·3	γ Andromedæ		**328**	53·9	54·1	54·2	54·2	54·1	53·8	N **42**	22·4	22·3	22·3	22·2	22·1	22·1
2·9	α Hydri		**330**	14·3	14·6	14·8	14·9	14·8	14·6	S **61**	32·1	32·0	31·9	31·7	31·6	31·4
2·6	β Arietis		**331**	13·6	13·7	13·7	13·7	13·6	13·4	N **20**	51·0	51·0	50·9	50·9	50·9	50·9
0·5	α Eridani	5	**335**	29·5	29·7	29·9	30·0	29·9	29·6	S **57**	12·0	11·9	11·8	11·6	11·5	11·3
2·7	δ Cassiopeiæ		**338**	24·8	25·0	25·2	25·2	25·0	24·7	N **60**	17·0	16·9	16·8	16·7	16·6	16·6
2·1	β Andromedæ		**342**	27·2	27·3	27·4	27·3	27·2	27·0	N **35**	40·0	40·0	39·9	39·8	39·8	39·8
Var.‖	γ Cassiopeiæ		**345**	42·1	42·4	42·5	42·5	42·2	41·9	N **60**	46·0	45·9	45·8	45·7	45·6	45·6
2·0	β Ceti	4	**348**	60·0	60·1	60·1	60·1	59·9	59·7	S **17**	56·6	56·6	56·6	56·5	56·4	56·2
2·2	α Cassiopeiæ	3	**349**	45·6	45·8	45·9	45·9	45·6	45·3	N **56**	35·2	35·1	35·0	34·9	34·8	34·8
2·4	α Phœnicis	2	**353**	19·7	19·8	19·8	19·8	19·6	19·3	S **42**	15·9	15·9	15·8	15·6	15·4	15·3
2·8	β Hydri		**353**	27·3	27·8	28·1	28·0	27·6	26·9	S **77**	12·8	12·7	12·5	12·3	12·1	12·0
2·8	γ Pegasi		**356**	35·2	35·3	35·3	35·2	35·1	34·8	N **15**	13·8	13·7	13·7	13·7	13·7	13·8
2·3	β Cassiopeiæ		**357**	36·1	36·3	36·4	36·3	36·0	35·6	N **59**	12·0	11·9	11·7	11·6	11·6	11·6
2·1	α Andromedæ	1	**357**	48·0	48·1	48·1	48·0	47·8	47·6	N **29**	08·3	08·2	08·1	08·1	08·1	08·1

‡ 0·1 — 1·2   § 2·1 — 3·4   ‖ Irregular variable; 2006 mag. 2·1

Mag.	Name and Number		SHA	JULY	AUG.	SEPT.	OCT.	NOV.	DEC.	Declination	JULY	AUG.	SEPT.	OCT.	NOV.	DEC.
			°	′	′	′	′	′	′	°	′	′	′	′	′	′
1·6	*Castor*		**246**	13·0	12·9	12·7	12·4	12·1	11·9	**N 31**	52·2	52·2	52·2	52·1	52·1	52·0
3·3	σ Puppis		**247**	37·9	37·7	37·5	37·3	37·0	36·8	**S 43**	19·0	18·9	18·8	18·8	18·9	19·0
2·9	β Canis Minoris		**248**	05·9	05·8	05·6	05·4	05·2	04·9	**N 8**	16·4	16·4	16·4	16·4	16·4	16·3
2·4	η Canis Majoris		**248**	53·8	53·7	53·5	53·2	53·0	52·8	**S 29**	19·1	19·0	18·9	18·9	19·0	19·1
2·7	π Puppis		**250**	38·7	38·5	38·3	38·1	37·8	37·6	**S 37**	06·7	06·5	06·4	06·4	06·5	06·7
1·8	*Wezen*		**252**	49·2	49·0	48·8	48·6	48·4	48·2	**S 26**	24·3	24·2	24·1	24·1	24·2	24·3
3·0	ο Canis Majoris		**254**	09·5	09·4	09·2	09·0	08·7	08·5	**S 23**	50·6	50·5	50·5	50·5	50·5	50·7
1·5	*Adhara*	19	**255**	15·8	15·7	15·5	15·3	15·0	14·8	**S 28**	58·9	58·8	58·7	58·7	58·8	58·9
2·9	τ Puppis		**257**	28·2	28·1	27·8	27·5	27·2	27·0	**S 50**	37·3	37·2	37·1	37·1	37·2	37·4
−1·5	*Sirius*	18	**258**	37·3	37·2	37·0	36·7	36·5	36·3	**S 16**	43·5	43·4	43·4	43·4	43·5	43·6
1·9	*Alhena*		**260**	27·1	26·9	26·7	26·4	26·2	26·0	**N 16**	23·6	23·6	23·6	23·6	23·6	23·5
−0·7	*Canopus*	17	**263**	58·3	58·2	57·9	57·6	57·3	57·1	**S 52**	41·8	41·7	41·6	41·6	41·7	41·9
2·0	*Mirzam*		**264**	14·0	13·9	13·7	13·5	13·2	13·1	**S 17**	57·5	57·4	57·3	57·3	57·4	57·5
2·6	θ Aurigæ		**269**	55·6	55·4	55·1	54·8	54·5	54·3	**N 37**	12·8	12·8	12·8	12·8	12·8	12·8
1·9	*Menkalinan*		**269**	57·9	57·6	57·3	57·0	56·7	56·5	**N 44**	56·9	56·9	56·8	56·8	56·9	56·9
Var.‡	*Betelgeuse*	16	**271**	05·6	05·4	05·2	05·0	04·8	04·6	**N 7**	24·6	24·7	24·7	24·7	24·6	24·6
2·1	κ Orionis		**272**	57·7	57·5	57·3	57·1	56·9	56·7	**S 9**	39·8	39·8	39·7	39·7	39·8	39·9
1·9	*Alnitak*		**274**	42·3	42·1	41·9	41·6	41·4	41·3	**S 1**	56·1	56·1	56·0	56·1	56·1	56·2
2·6	*Phact*		**274**	60·9	60·7	60·4	60·2	60·0	59·8	**S 34**	04·0	03·8	03·8	03·8	03·9	04·1
3·0	ζ Tauri		**275**	27·8	27·6	27·3	27·1	26·9	26·7	**N 21**	08·9	09·0	09·0	09·0	09·0	09·0
1·7	*Alnilam*	15	**275**	50·4	50·2	50·0	49·8	49·6	49·4	**S 1**	11·7	11·6	11·5	11·6	11·6	11·7
2·8	ι Orionis		**276**	02·4	02·2	01·9	01·7	01·5	01·4	**S 5**	54·1	54·0	54·0	54·0	54·1	54·2
2·6	α Leporis		**276**	43·5	43·3	43·1	42·9	42·7	42·6	**S 17**	48·8	48·7	48·6	48·7	48·8	48·9
2·2	δ Orionis		**276**	53·5	53·3	53·0	52·8	52·6	52·5	**S 0**	17·4	17·4	17·3	17·3	17·4	17·5
2·8	β Leporis		**277**	51·0	50·8	50·6	50·3	50·1	50·0	**S 20**	45·0	44·9	44·8	44·8	44·9	45·1
1·7	*Elnath*	14	**278**	17·6	17·4	17·1	16·9	16·7	16·5	**N 28**	36·9	36·9	36·9	37·0	37·0	37·0
1·6	*Bellatrix*	13	**278**	36·3	36·1	35·8	35·6	35·4	35·3	**N 6**	21·6	21·6	21·6	21·6	21·6	21·6
0·1	*Capella*	12	**280**	40·4	40·1	39·7	39·4	39·1	39·0	**N 46**	00·4	00·4	00·4	00·4	00·4	00·5
0·1	*Rigel*	11	**281**	15·9	15·7	15·5	15·2	15·1	14·9	**S 8**	11·3	11·3	11·2	11·2	11·3	11·4
2·8	β Eridani		**282**	56·1	55·8	55·6	55·4	55·2	55·1	**S 5**	04·4	04·3	04·2	04·3	04·3	04·4
2·7	ι Aurigæ		**285**	36·8	36·6	36·3	36·1	35·8	35·7	**N 33**	10·8	10·8	10·8	10·9	10·9	10·9
0·9	*Aldebaran*	10	**290**	53·9	53·7	53·4	53·2	53·0	52·9	**N 16**	31·7	31·7	31·8	31·8	31·8	31·8
3·0	γ Eridani		**300**	23·6	23·4	23·2	23·0	22·8	22·8	**S 13**	28·8	28·7	28·7	28·7	28·8	28·9
2·9	ε Persei		**300**	23·6	23·3	23·0	22·8	22·6	22·5	**N 40**	02·1	02·1	02·1	02·2	02·3	02·4
2·9	ζ Persei		**301**	20·0	19·7	19·4	19·2	19·1	19·0	**N 31**	54·5	54·6	54·6	54·7	54·7	54·8
2·9	*Alcyone*		**302**	60·1	59·9	59·6	59·4	59·3	59·2	**N 24**	07·9	08·0	08·0	08·1	08·1	08·1
1·8	*Mirfak*	9	**308**	46·0	45·7	45·4	45·1	44·9	44·9	**N 49**	53·4	53·4	53·5	53·6	53·7	53·8
Var.§	*Algol*		**312**	49·1	48·8	48·5	48·3	48·2	48·1	**N 40**	59·3	59·3	59·4	59·5	59·6	59·6
2·5	*Menkar*	8	**314**	19·1	18·8	18·6	18·4	18·3	18·3	**N 4**	07·5	07·6	07·7	07·7	07·7	07·6
3·2	*Acamar*	7	**315**	21·2	20·9	20·7	20·5	20·4	20·4	**S 40**	15·9	15·8	15·8	15·9	16·0	16·2
2·0	*Polaris*		**319**	42·2	27·6	14·7	05·5	01·5	05·6	**N 89**	17·9	17·9	18·0	18·2	18·4	18·5
3·0	β Trianguli		**327**	29·1	28·8	28·6	28·5	28·4	28·4	**N 35**	01·6	01·7	01·8	01·9	02·0	02·0
2·0	*Hamal*	6	**328**	05·1	04·8	04·6	04·5	04·4	04·4	**N 23**	30·2	30·3	30·4	30·4	30·5	30·5
2·3	*Almak*		**328**	53·5	53·2	53·0	52·8	52·8	52·8	**N 42**	22·2	22·3	22·4	22·5	22·6	22·7
2·9	α Hydri		**330**	14·2	13·8	13·5	13·4	13·4	13·5	**S 61**	31·3	31·2	31·3	31·4	31·6	31·7
2·6	*Sheratan*		**331**	13·2	12·9	12·7	12·6	12·6	12·6	**N 20**	51·0	51·1	51·2	51·3	51·3	51·3
0·5	*Achernar*	5	**335**	29·3	28·9	28·6	28·5	28·6	28·7	**S 57**	11·2	11·2	11·2	11·4	11·5	11·6
2·7	*Ruchbah*		**338**	24·2	23·8	23·5	23·4	23·3	23·5	**N 60**	16·6	16·7	16·9	17·0	17·2	17·3
2·1	*Mirach*		**342**	26·7	26·4	26·2	26·1	26·1	26·1	**N 35**	39·9	40·0	40·1	40·2	40·3	40·4
Var.‖	γ Cassiopeiæ		**345**	41·4	41·1	40·8	40·7	40·7	40·8	**N 60**	45·6	45·7	45·9	46·1	46·2	46·3
2·0	*Diphda*	4	**348**	59·5	59·2	59·1	59·0	59·0	59·1	**S 17**	56·1	56·1	56·1	56·1	56·2	56·2
2·2	*Schedar*	3	**349**	44·9	44·6	44·3	44·3	44·3	44·4	**N 56**	34·9	35·0	35·2	35·3	35·5	35·6
2·4	*Ankaa*	2	**353**	19·0	18·8	18·6	18·6	18·6	18·8	**S 42**	15·2	15·2	15·3	15·4	15·5	15·6
2·8	β Hydri		**353**	26·2	25·4	25·0	25·0	25·4	26·0	**S 77**	12·0	12·0	12·1	12·3	12·4	12·5
2·8	*Algenib*		**356**	34·6	34·4	34·3	34·2	34·2	34·3	**N 15**	13·9	14·0	14·1	14·2	14·2	14·2
2·3	*Caph*		**357**	35·2	34·9	34·7	34·7	34·8	34·9	**N 59**	11·6	11·8	12·0	12·1	12·3	12·3
2·1	*Alpheratz*	1	**357**	47·3	47·1	46·9	46·9	46·9	47·0	**N 29**	08·2	08·4	08·5	08·6	08·6	08·7

‡ 0·1 — 1·2 § 2·1 — 3·4 ‖ Irregular variable; 2006 mag. 2·1

POLARIS (POLE STAR) TABLES, 2008

FOR DETERMINING LATITUDE FROM SEXTANT ALTITUDE AND FOR AZIMUTH

LHA ARIES	0° – 9°	10° – 19°	20° – 29°	30° – 39°	40° – 49°	50° – 59°	60° – 69°	70° – 79°	80° – 89°	90° – 99°	100° – 109°	110° – 119°
	a_0	a_0	a_0	a_0	a_0	a_0	a_0	a_0	a_0	a_0	a_0	a_0
°	° ′	° ′	° ′	° ′	° ′	° ′	° ′	° ′	° ′	° ′	° ′	° ′
0	0 27·1	0 22·8	0 19·7	0 17·7	0 17·0	0 17·6	0 19·4	0 22·5	0 26·7	0 31·9	0 37·9	0 44·5
1	26·6	22·5	19·4	17·6	17·0	17·7	19·7	22·9	27·2	32·4	38·5	45·2
2	26·2	22·1	19·2	17·5	17·0	17·9	20·0	23·3	27·7	33·0	39·1	45·9
3	25·7	21·8	18·9	17·4	17·0	18·0	20·2	23·7	28·2	33·6	39·8	46·6
4	25·3	21·4	18·7	17·3	17·1	18·2	20·5	24·1	28·7	34·2	40·4	47·3
5	0 24·8	0 21·1	0 18·5	0 17·2	0 17·1	0 18·4	0 20·8	0 24·5	0 29·2	0 34·8	0 41·1	0 48·0
6	24·4	20·8	18·3	17·1	17·2	18·6	21·1	24·9	29·7	35·4	41·8	48·7
7	24·0	20·5	18·2	17·1	17·3	18·8	21·5	25·3	30·2	36·0	42·4	49·4
8	23·6	20·2	18·0	17·0	17·4	19·0	21·8	25·8	30·8	36·6	43·1	50·1
9	23·2	19·9	17·8	17·0	17·5	19·2	22·2	26·2	31·3	37·2	43·8	50·8
10	0 22·8	0 19·7	0 17·7	0 17·0	0 17·6	0 19·4	0 22·5	0 26·7	0 31·9	0 37·9	0 44·5	0 51·5
Lat.	a_1	a_1	a_1	a_1	a_1	a_1	a_1	a_1	a_1	a_1	a_1	a_1
°	′	′	′	′	′	′	′	′	′	′	′	′
0	0·5	0·5	0·6	0·6	0·6	0·6	0·5	0·5	0·5	0·4	0·4	0·3
10	·5	·6	·6	·6	·6	·6	·6	·5	·5	·4	·4	·4
20	·5	·6	·6	·6	·6	·6	·6	·5	·5	·5	·4	·4
30	·5	·6	·6	·6	·6	·6	·6	·5	·5	·5	·5	·5
40	0·6	0·6	0·6	0·6	0·6	0·6	0·6	0·6	0·6	0·5	0·5	0·5
45	·6	·6	·6	·6	·6	·6	·6	·6	·6	·6	·6	·6
50	·6	·6	·6	·6	·6	·6	·6	·6	·6	·6	·6	·6
55	·6	·6	·6	·6	·6	·6	·6	·6	·6	·6	·6	·7
60	·6	·6	·6	·6	·6	·6	·6	·6	·7	·7	·7	·7
62	0·7	0·6	0·6	0·6	0·6	0·6	0·6	0·7	0·7	0·7	0·7	0·8
64	·7	·6	·6	·6	·6	·6	·6	·7	·7	·7	·8	·8
66	·7	·6	·6	·6	·6	·6	·6	·7	·7	·8	·8	·8
68	0·7	0·7	0·6	0·6	0·6	0·6	0·7	0·7	0·8	0·8	0·9	0·9
Month	a_2	a_2	a_2	a_2	a_2	a_2	a_2	a_2	a_2	a_2	a_2	a_2
	′	′	′	′	′	′	′	′	′	′	′	′
Jan.	0·7	0·7	0·8	0·8	0·8	0·8	0·8	0·8	0·8	0·7	0·7	0·7
Feb.	·6	·7	·7	·8	·8	·8	·9	·9	·9	·9	·9	·8
Mar.	·5	·6	·6	·7	·7	·8	·8	·9	·9	·9	·9	0·9
Apr.	0·4	0·4	0·5	0·6	0·6	0·7	0·8	0·8	0·9	0·9	0·9	1·0
May	·3	·3	·4	·4	·5	·5	·6	·7	·7	·8	·9	0·9
June	·2	·2	·3	·3	·3	·4	·5	·5	·6	·7	·7	·8
July	0·3	0·3	0·3	0·3	0·3	0·3	0·4	0·4	0·4	0·5	0·6	0·6
Aug.	·4	·4	·3	·3	·3	·3	·3	·3	·3	·4	·4	·4
Sept.	·6	·5	·5	·4	·4	·4	·3	·3	·3	·3	·3	·3
Oct.	0·8	0·7	0·7	0·6	0·5	0·5	0·4	0·4	0·3	0·3	0·3	0·3
Nov.	1·0	0·9	0·9	0·8	·7	·7	·6	·5	·4	·4	·3	·3
Dec.	1·1	1·0	1·0	1·0	0·9	0·8	0·7	0·7	0·6	0·5	0·4	0·4

Lat.	AZIMUTH											
°	°	°	°	°	°	°	°	°	°	°	°	°
0	0·4	0·3	0·2	0·1	359·9	359·8	359·7	359·6	359·5	359·4	359·4	359·3
20	0·4	0·3	0·2	0·1	359·9	359·8	359·7	359·6	359·5	359·4	359·3	359·3
40	0·5	0·4	0·2	0·1	359·9	359·8	359·6	359·5	359·4	359·3	359·2	359·1
50	0·6	0·5	0·3	0·1	359·9	359·7	359·5	359·4	359·2	359·1	359·0	359·0
55	0·7	0·5	0·3	0·1	359·9	359·7	359·5	359·3	359·1	359·0	358·9	358·8
60	0·8	0·6	0·4	0·1	359·9	359·6	359·4	359·2	359·0	358·9	358·7	358·6
65	1·0	0·7	0·4	0·2	359·9	359·6	359·3	359·0	358·8	358·6	358·5	358·4

Latitude = Apparent altitude (corrected for refraction) $-1° + a_0 + a_1 + a_2$

The table is entered with LHA Aries to determine the column to be used; each column refers to a range of 10°. a_0 is taken, with mental interpolation, from the upper table with the units of LHA Aries in degrees as argument; a_1, a_2 are taken, without interpolation, from the second and third tables with arguments latitude and month respectively. a_0, a_1, a_2, are always positive. The final table gives the azimuth of *Polaris*.

POLARIS (POLE STAR) TABLES, 2008

FOR DETERMINING LATITUDE FROM SEXTANT ALTITUDE AND FOR AZIMUTH

LHA ARIES	120° – 129°	130° – 139°	140° – 149°	150° – 159°	160° – 169°	170° – 179°	180° – 189°	190° – 199°	200° – 209°	210° – 219°	220° – 229°	230° – 239°
	a_0	a_0	a_0	a_0	a_0	a_0	a_0	a_0	a_0	a_0	a_0	a_0
°	° ′	° ′	° ′	° ′	° ′	° ′	° ′	° ′	° ′	° ′	° ′	° ′
0	0 51·5	0 58·8	1 06·0	1 13·1	1 19·7	1 25·6	1 30·7	1 34·9	1 38·0	1 39·9	1 40·6	1 40·0
1	52·2	0 59·5	06·8	13·7	20·3	26·2	31·2	35·3	38·3	40·0	40·6	39·9
2	53·0	1 00·2	07·5	14·4	20·9	26·7	31·7	35·6	38·5	40·2	40·6	39·8
3	53·7	01·0	08·2	15·1	21·5	27·2	32·1	36·0	38·7	40·3	40·6	39·6
4	54·4	01·7	08·9	15·8	22·1	27·8	32·5	36·3	38·9	40·3	40·5	39·5
5	0 55·1	1 02·4	1 09·6	1 16·4	1 22·7	1 28·3	1 33·0	1 36·6	1 39·1	1 40·4	1 40·5	1 39·3
6	55·9	03·2	10·3	17·1	23·3	28·8	33·4	36·9	39·3	40·5	40·4	39·1
7	56·6	03·9	11·0	17·7	23·9	29·3	33·8	37·2	39·5	40·5	40·3	38·9
8	57·3	04·6	11·7	18·4	24·5	29·8	34·2	37·5	39·6	40·6	40·2	38·7
9	58·1	05·3	12·4	19·0	25·0	30·3	34·5	37·7	39·8	40·6	40·1	38·5
10	0 58·8	1 06·0	1 13·1	1 19·7	1 25·6	1 30·7	1 34·9	1 38·0	1 39·9	1 40·6	1 40·0	1 38·2
Lat.	a_1	a_1	a_1	a_1	a_1	a_1	a_1	a_1	a_1	a_1	a_1	a_1
°	′	′	′	′	′	′	′	′	′	′	′	′
0	0·3	0·3	0·3	0·3	0·4	0·4	0·5	0·5	0·6	0·6	0·6	0·6
10	·3	·3	·4	·4	·4	·5	·5	·6	·6	·6	·6	·6
20	·4	·4	·4	·4	·5	·5	·5	·6	·6	·6	·6	·6
30	·4	·4	·5	·5	·5	·5	·5	·6	·6	·6	·6	·6
40	0·5	0·5	0·5	0·5	0·5	0·6	0·6	0·6	0·6	0·6	0·6	0·6
45	·6	·6	·6	·6	·6	·6	·6	·6	·6	·6	·6	·6
50	·6	·6	·6	·6	·6	·6	·6	·6	·6	·6	·6	·6
55	·7	·7	·7	·6	·6	·6	·6	·6	·6	·6	·6	·6
60	·7	·7	·7	·7	·7	·7	·6	·6	·6	·6	·6	·6
62	0·8	0·8	0·8	0·7	0·7	0·7	0·7	0·6	0·6	0·6	0·6	0·6
64	·8	·8	·8	·8	·7	·7	·7	·6	·6	·6	·6	·6
66	·9	·9	·9	·8	·8	·7	·7	·6	·6	·6	·6	·6
68	0·9	0·9	0·9	0·9	0·8	0·8	0·7	0·7	0·6	0·6	0·6	0·6
Month	a_2	a_2	a_2	a_2	a_2	a_2	a_2	a_2	a_2	a_2	a_2	a_2
	′	′	′	′	′	′	′	′	′	′	′	′
Jan.	0·7	0·6	0·6	0·6	0·5	0·5	0·5	0·5	0·4	0·4	0·4	0·4
Feb.	·8	·8	·7	·7	·6	·6	·6	·5	·5	·4	·4	·4
Mar.	0·9	0·9	0·9	0·8	·8	·7	·7	·6	·6	·5	·5	·4
Apr.	1·0	1·0	1·0	1·0	0·9	0·9	0·8	0·8	0·7	0·6	0·6	0·5
May	0·9	1·0	1·0	1·0	1·0	1·0	0·9	0·9	·8	·8	·7	·7
June	·8	0·9	0·9	0·9	1·0	1·0	1·0	1·0	·9	·9	·9	·8
July	0·7	0·7	0·8	0·8	0·9	0·9	0·9	0·9	0·9	0·9	0·9	0·9
Aug.	·5	·5	·6	·6	·7	·7	·8	·8	·9	·9	·9	·9
Sept.	·3	·4	·4	·5	·5	·6	·6	·7	·7	·8	·8	·8
Oct.	0·3	0·3	0·3	0·3	0·3	0·4	0·4	0·5	0·5	0·6	0·7	0·7
Nov.	·2	·2	·2	·2	·2	·2	·2	·3	·3	·4	·5	·5
Dec.	0·3	0·2	0·2	0·2	0·1	0·1	0·1	0·2	0·2	0·2	0·3	0·4

AZIMUTH

Lat.												
°	°	°	°	°	°	°	°	°	°	°	°	°
0	359·3	359·3	359·3	359·4	359·4	359·5	359·6	359·7	359·8	359·9	0·1	0·2
20	359·3	359·3	359·3	359·3	359·4	359·5	359·6	359·7	359·8	359·9	0·1	0·2
40	359·1	359·1	359·1	359·2	359·3	359·4	359·5	359·6	359·8	359·9	0·1	0·2
50	358·9	358·9	359·0	359·0	359·1	359·2	359·4	359·5	359·7	359·9	0·1	0·3
55	358·8	358·8	358·8	358·9	359·0	359·1	359·3	359·5	359·7	359·9	0·1	0·3
60	358·6	358·6	358·7	358·7	358·9	359·0	359·2	359·4	359·6	359·9	0·1	0·3
65	358·4	358·4	358·4	358·5	358·7	358·8	359·1	359·3	359·6	359·8	0·1	0·4

ILLUSTRATION

)n 2008 April 21 at
3h 18m 56s UT in longitude
V 37° 14′ the apparent altitude
corrected for refraction), H_O, of
olaris was 49° 31′·6

From the daily pages:	° ′
GHA Aries (23h)	195 23·0
Increment (18m 56s)	4 44·8
Longitude (west)	−37 14
LHA Aries	162 54

	° ′
H_O	49 31·6
a_0 (argument 162° 54′)	1 21·4
a_1 (Lat 50° approx.)	0·6
a_2 (April)	0·9
Sum − 1° = Lat =	49 54·5

FOR DETERMINING LATITUDE FROM SEXTANT ALTITUDE AND FOR AZIMUTH

LHA ARIES	240°– 249°	250°– 259°	260°– 269°	270°– 279°	280°– 289°	290°– 299°	300°– 309°	310°– 319°	320°– 329°	330°– 339°	340°– 349°	350°– 359°
	a_0	a_0	a_0	a_0	a_0	a_0	a_0	a_0	a_0	a_0	a_0	a_0
°	° ′	° ′	° ′	° ′	° ′	° ′	° ′	° ′	° ′	° ′	° ′	° ′
0	1 38·2	1 35·2	1 31·1	1 26·1	1 20·2	1 13·7	1 06·7	0 59·4	0 52·1	0 45·1	0 38·4	0 32·4
1	38·0	34·9	30·7	25·5	19·6	13·0	05·9	58·7	51·4	44·4	37·8	31·8
2	37·7	34·5	30·2	25·0	18·9	12·3	05·2	58·0	50·7	43·7	37·1	31·2
3	37·4	34·1	29·7	24·4	18·3	11·6	04·5	57·2	50·0	43·0	36·5	30·7
4	37·2	33·7	29·2	23·8	17·7	10·9	03·8	56·5	49·3	42·3	35·9	30·2
5	1 36·9	1 33·3	1 28·7	1 23·2	1 17·0	1 10·2	1 03·1	0 55·8	0 48·6	0 41·7	0 35·3	0 29·6
6	36·6	32·9	28·2	22·6	16·3	09·5	02·3	55·0	47·9	41·0	34·7	29·1
7	36·2	32·5	27·7	22·0	15·7	08·8	01·6	54·3	47·2	40·3	34·1	28·6
8	35·9	32·0	27·2	21·4	15·0	08·1	00·9	53·6	46·5	39·7	33·5	28·1
9	35·6	31·6	26·6	20·8	14·3	07·4	1 00·1	52·9	45·8	39·0	32·9	27·6
10	1 35·2	1 31·1	1 26·1	1 20·2	1 13·7	1 06·7	0 59·4	0 52·1	0 45·1	0 38·4	0 32·4	0 27·1
Lat.	a_1	a_1	a_1	a_1	a_1	a_1	a_1	a_1	a_1	a_1	a_1	a_1
°	′	′	′	′	′	′	′	′	′	′	′	′
0	0·5	0·5	0·5	0·4	0·4	0·3	0·3	0·3	0·3	0·3	0·4	0·4
10	·6	·5	·5	·4	·4	·4	·3	·3	·4	·4	·4	·5
20	·6	·5	·5	·5	·4	·4	·4	·4	·4	·4	·5	·5
30	·6	·5	·5	·5	·5	·5	·4	·4	·5	·5	·5	·5
40	0·6	0·6	0·6	0·5	0·5	0·5	0·5	0·5	0·5	0·5	0·5	0·6
45	·6	·6	·6	·6	·6	·6	·6	·6	·6	·6	·6	·6
50	·6	·6	·6	·6	·6	·6	·6	·6	·6	·6	·6	·6
55	·6	·6	·6	·6	·6	·7	·7	·7	·7	·6	·6	·6
60	·6	·6	·7	·7	·7	·7	·7	·7	·7	·7	·7	·7
62	0·6	0·7	0·7	0·7	0·7	0·8	0·8	0·8	0·8	0·7	0·7	0·7
64	·6	·7	·7	·7	·8	·8	·8	·8	·8	·8	·7	·7
66	·6	·7	·7	·8	·8	·8	·9	·9	·9	·8	·8	·7
68	0·7	0·7	0·8	0·8	0·9	0·9	0·9	0·9	0·9	0·9	0·8	0·8
Month	a_2	a_2	a_2	a_2	a_2	a_2	a_2	a_2	a_2	a_2	a_2	a_2
	′	′	′	′	′	′	′	′	′	′	′	′
Jan.	0·4	0·4	0·4	0·5	0·5	0·5	0·5	0·6	0·6	0·6	0·7	0·7
Feb.	·3	·3	·3	·3	·3	·4	·4	·4	·5	·5	·6	·6
Mar.	·4	·3	·3	·3	·3	·3	·3	·3	·3	·4	·4	·5
Apr.	0·4	0·4	0·3	0·3	0·3	0·2	0·2	0·2	0·2	0·2	0·3	0·3
May	·6	·5	·5	·4	·3	·3	·3	·2	·2	·2	·2	·2
June	·7	·7	·6	·5	·5	·4	·4	·3	·3	·3	·2	·2
July	0·8	0·8	0·8	0·7	0·6	0·6	0·5	0·5	0·4	0·4	0·3	0·3
Aug.	·9	·9	·9	·8	·8	·8	·7	·7	·6	·6	·5	·5
Sept.	·9	·9	·9	·9	·9	·9	·9	·8	·8	·7	·7	·6
Oct.	0·8	0·8	0·9	0·9	0·9	0·9	0·9	0·9	0·9	0·9	0·9	0·8
Nov.	·6	·7	·8	·8	·9	·9	1·0	1·0	1·0	1·0	1·0	1·0
Dec.	0·5	0·5	0·6	0·7	0·8	0·8	0·9	1·0	1·0	1·0	1·1	1·1
Lat.						AZIMUTH						
°	°	°	°	°	°	°	°	°	°	°	°	°
0	0·3	0·4	0·5	0·6	0·6	0·7	0·7	0·7	0·7	0·6	0·6	0·5
20	0·3	0·4	0·5	0·6	0·7	0·7	0·7	0·7	0·7	0·7	0·6	0·5
40	0·4	0·5	0·6	0·7	0·8	0·9	0·9	0·9	0·9	0·8	0·8	0·7
50	0·4	0·6	0·8	0·9	1·0	1·0	1·1	1·1	1·1	1·0	0·9	0·8
55	0·5	0·7	0·8	1·0	1·1	1·2	1·2	1·2	1·2	1·1	1·0	0·9
60	0·6	0·8	1·0	1·1	1·2	1·3	1·4	1·4	1·4	1·3	1·2	1·0
65	0·7	0·9	1·1	1·3	1·5	1·6	1·6	1·6	1·6	1·5	1·4	1·2

Latitude = Apparent altitude (corrected for refraction) $-1° + a_0 + a_1 + a_2$

The table is entered with LHA Aries to determine the column to be used; each column refers to a range c 10°. a_0 is taken, with mental interpolation, from the upper table with the units of LHA Aries in degrees a argument; a_1, a_2 are taken, without interpolation, from the second and third tables with arguments latitude an month respectively. a_0, a_1, a_2, are always positive. The final table gives the azimuth of *Polaris*.

SIGHT REDUCTION PROCEDURES

METHODS AND FORMULAE FOR DIRECT COMPUTATION

1. *Introduction.* In this section formulae and methods are provided for *calculating* position at sea from observed altitudes taken with a marine sextant using a computer or programmable calculator.

The method uses analogous concepts and similar terminology as that used in *manual* methods of astro-navigation, where position is found by plotting position lines from their intercept and azimuth on a marine chart.

The algorithms are presented in standard algebra suitable for translating into the programming language of the user's computer. The basic ephemeris data may be taken directly from the main tabular pages of a current version of *The Nautical Almanac.* Formulae are given for calculating altitude and azimuth from the *GHA* and *Dec* of a body, and the estimated position of the observer. Formulae are also given for reducing sextant observations to observed altitudes by applying the corrections for dip, refraction, parallax and semi-diameter.

The intercept and azimuth obtained from each observation determine a position line, and the observer should lie on or close to each position line. The method of least squares is used to calculate the fix by finding the position where the sum of the squares of the distances from the position lines is a minimum. The use of least squares has other advantages. For example it is possible to improve the estimated position at the time of fix by repeating the calculation. It is also possible to include more observations in the solution and to reject doubtful ones.

2. *Notation.*

GHA = Greenwich hour angle. The range of *GHA* is from 0° to 360° starting at 0° on the Greenwich meridian increasing to the west, back to 360° on the Greenwich meridian.

SHA = sidereal hour angle. The range is 0° to 360°.

Dec = declination. The sign convention for declination is north is positive, south is negative. The range is from −90° at the south celestial pole to +90° at the north celestial pole.

Long = longitude. The sign convention is east is positive, west is negative. The range is −180° to +180°.

Lat = latitude. The sign convention is north is positive, south is negative. The range is from −90° to +90°.

LHA = *GHA* + *Long* = local hour angle. The *LHA* increases to the west from 0° on the local meridian to 360°.

H_c = calculated altitude. Above the horizon is positive, below the horizon is negative. The range is from −90° in the nadir to +90° in the zenith.

H_s = sextant altitude.

H = apparent altitude = sextant altitude corrected for instrumental error and dip.

H_o = observed altitude = apparent altitude corrected for refraction and, in appropriate cases, corrected for parallax and semi-diameter.

Z = Z_n = true azimuth. Z is measured from true north through east, south, west and back to north. The range is from 0° to 360°.

I = sextant index error.

D = dip of horizon.

R = atmospheric refraction.

HP = horizontal parallax of the Sun, Moon, Venus or Mars.
PA = parallax in altitude of the Sun, Moon, Venus or Mars.
S = semi-diameter of the Sun or Moon.
p = intercept $= H_O - H_C$. Towards is positive, away is negative.
T = course or track, measured as for azimuth from the north.
V = speed in knots.

3. *Entering Basic Data.* When quantities such as GHA are entered, which in *The Nautical Almanac* are given in degrees and minutes, convert them to degrees and decimals of a degree by dividing the minutes by 60 and adding to the degrees; for example, if $GHA = 123° \ 45'\!.6$, enter the two numbers 123 and 45·6 into the memory and set $GHA = 123 + 45{\cdot}6/60 = 123°\!.7600$. Although four decimal places of a degree are shown in the examples, it is assumed that full precision is maintained in the calculations.

When using a computer or programmable calculator, write a subroutine to convert degrees and minutes to degrees and decimals. Scientific calculators usually have a special key for this purpose. For quantities like Dec which require a minus sign for southern declination, change the sign from plus to minus after the value has been converted to degrees and decimals, *e.g.* $Dec = \text{S}\,0° \ 12'\!.3 = \text{S}\,0°\!.2050 = -0°\!.2050$. Other quantities which require conversion are semi-diameter, horizontal parallax, longitude and latitude.

4. *Interpolation of GHA and Dec* The GHA and Dec of the Sun, Moon and planets are interpolated to the time of observation by direct calculation as follows: If the universal time is $a^h \ b^m \ c^s$, form the interpolation factor $x = b/60 + c/3600$. Enter the tabular value GHA_0 for the preceding hour (a) and the tabular value GHA_1 for the following hour ($a + 1$) then the interpolated value GHA is given by

$$GHA = GHA_0 + x(GHA_1 - GHA_0)$$

If the GHA passes through 360° between tabular values add 360° to GHA_1 before interpolation. If the interpolated value exceeds 360°, subtract 360° from GHA.

Similarly for declination, enter the tabular value Dec_0 for the preceding hour (a) and the tabular value Dec_1 for the following hour ($a + 1$), then the interpolated value Dec is given by

$$Dec = Dec_0 + x(Dec_1 - Dec_0)$$

5. *Example.* (a) Find the GHA and Dec of the Sun on 2008 November 6 at $20^h \ 57^m \ 44^s$ UT.

The interpolation factor $x = 57/60 + 44/3600 = 0^h\!.9622$

page 217 $20^h \ GHA_0 = 124° \ 05'\!.0 = 124°\!.0833$

$21^h \ GHA_1 = 139° \ 05'\!.0 = 139°\!.0833$

$20^h\!.9622 \ GHA = 124{\cdot}0833 + 0{\cdot}9622(139{\cdot}0833 - 124{\cdot}0833) = 138°\!.5167$

$20^h \ Dec_0 = \text{S}\,16° \ 16'\!.4 = -16°\!.2733$

$21^h \ Dec_1 = \text{S}\,16° \ 17'\!.1 = -16°\!.2850$

$20^h\!.9622 \ Dec = -16{\cdot}2733 + 0{\cdot}9622(-16{\cdot}2850 + 16{\cdot}2733) = -16°\!.2846$

GHA Aries is interpolated in the same way as GHA of a body. For a star the SHA and Dec are taken from the tabular page and do not require interpolation, then

$$GHA = GHA \text{ Aries} + SHA$$

where GHA Aries is interpolated to the time of observation.

(b) Find the *GHA* and *Dec* of *Vega* on 2008 November 6 at $20^h\ 57^m\ 44^s$ UT.

The interpolation factor $x = 0^h\!.9622$ as in the previous example

page 216 $\quad 20^h\ GHA\ \text{Aries}_0 = 346°\ 24'\!.3 = 346°\!.4050$

$$21^h\ GHA\ \text{Aries}_1 = 1°\ 26'\!.7 = 361°\!.4450 \quad (360° \text{ added})$$

$$20^h\!.9622\ GHA\ \text{Aries} = 346{\cdot}4050 + 0{\cdot}9622(361{\cdot}4450 - 346{\cdot}4050) = 360°\!.8768$$

$$SHA = 80°\ 41'\!.6 = 80°\!.6933$$

$$GHA = GHA\ \text{Aries} + SHA = 81°\!.5702 \quad (\text{multiple of } 360° \text{ removed})$$

$$Dec = \text{N}\,38°\ 47'\!.7 = +38°\!.7950$$

6. *The calculated altitude and azimuth.* The calculated altitude H_C and true azimuth Z are determined from the *GHA* and *Dec* interpolated to the time of observation and from the *Long* and *Lat* estimated at the time of observation as follows:

Step 1. Calculate the local hour angle

$$LHA = GHA + Long$$

Add or subtract multiples of 360° to set *LHA* in the range 0° to 360°.

Step 2. Calculate S, C and the altitude H_C from

$$S = \sin Dec$$
$$C = \cos Dec \cos LHA$$
$$H_C = \sin^{-1}(S \sin Lat + C \cos Lat)$$

where $\sin^{-1}$ is the inverse function of sine.

Step 3. Calculate X and A from

$$X = (S \cos Lat - C \sin Lat)/\cos H_C$$
$$\text{If } X > +1 \quad \text{set} \quad X = +1$$
$$\text{If } X < -1 \quad \text{set} \quad X = -1$$
$$A = \cos^{-1} X$$

where $\cos^{-1}$ is the inverse function of cosine.

Step 4. Determine the azimuth Z

$$\text{If } LHA > 180° \quad \text{then} \quad Z = A$$
$$\text{Otherwise} \quad Z = 360° - A$$

7. *Example.* Find the calculated altitude H_C and azimuth Z when

$$GHA = 53° \quad Dec = \text{S}\,15° \quad Lat = \text{N}\,32° \quad Long = \text{W}\,16°$$

For the calculation

$$GHA = 53°\!.0000 \quad Dec = -15°\!.0000 \quad Lat = +32°\!.0000 \quad Long = -16°\!.0000$$

Step 1. $\quad LHA = 53{\cdot}0000 - 16{\cdot}0000 = 37{\cdot}0000$

Step 2. $\quad S = -0{\cdot}2588$

$$C = +0{\cdot}9659 \times 0{\cdot}7986 = 0{\cdot}7714$$
$$\sin H_C = -0{\cdot}2588 \times 0{\cdot}5299 + 0{\cdot}7714 \times 0{\cdot}8480 = 0{\cdot}5171$$
$$H_C = 31°\!.1346$$

Step 3. $X = (-0{\cdot}2588 \times 0{\cdot}8480 - 0{\cdot}7714 \times 0{\cdot}5299)/0{\cdot}8560 = -0{\cdot}7340$

$A = 137^\circ\!.2239$

Step 4. Since $LHA \leq 180^\circ$ then $Z = 360^\circ - A = 222^\circ\!.7761$

8. *Reduction from sextant altitude to observed altitude.* The sextant altitude H_S is corrected for both dip and index error to produce the apparent altitude. The observed altitude H_O is calculated by applying a correction for refraction. For the Sun, Moon, Venus and Mars a correction for parallax is also applied to H, and for the Sun and Moon a further correction for semi-diameter is required. The corrections are calculated as follows:

Step 1. Calculate dip

$$D = 0^\circ\!.0293\sqrt{h}$$

where h is the height of eye above the horizon in metres.

Step 2. Calculate apparent altitude

$$H = H_S + I - D$$

where I is the sextant index error.

Step 3. Calculate refraction (R) at a standard temperature of 10° Celsius (C) and pressure of 1010 millibars (mb)

$$R_0 = 0^\circ\!.0167/\tan(H + 7{\cdot}32/(H + 4{\cdot}32))$$

If the temperature T° C and pressure P mb are known calculate the refraction from

$$R = fR_0 \qquad \text{where} \qquad f = 0{\cdot}28P/(T + 273)$$

otherwise set $R = R_0$

Step 4. Calculate the parallax in altitude (PA) from the horizontal parallax (HP) and the apparent altitude (H) for the Sun, Moon, Venus and Mars as follows:

$$PA = HP \cos H$$

For the Sun $HP = 0^\circ\!.0024$. This correction is very small and could be ignored.

For the Moon HP is taken for the nearest hour from the main tabular page and converted to degrees.

For Venus and Mars the HP is taken from the critical table at the bottom of page 259 and converted to degrees.

For the navigational stars and the remaining planets, Jupiter and Saturn set $PA = 0$.

If an error of 0′.2 is significant the expression for the parallax in altitude for the Moon should include a small correction OB for the oblateness of the Earth as follows:

$$PA = HP \cos H + OB$$

where $OB = -0^\circ\!.0032 \sin^2 Lat \cos H + 0^\circ\!.0032 \sin(2Lat) \cos Z \sin H$

At mid-latitudes and for altitudes of the Moon below 60° a simple approximation to OB is

$$OB = -0^\circ\!.0017 \cos H$$

Step 5. Calculate the semi-diameter for the Sun and Moon as follows:

Sun: S is taken from the main tabular page and converted to degrees.

Moon: $S = 0^\circ\!.2724HP$ where HP is taken for the nearest hour from the main tabular page and converted to degrees.

Step 6. Calculate the observed altitude

$$H_O = H - R + PA \pm S$$

where the plus sign is used if the lower limb of the Sun or Moon was observed and the minus sign if the upper limb was observed.

9. *Example.* The following example illustrates how to use a calculator to reduce the sextant altitude (H_S) to observed altitude (H_O); the sextant altitudes given are assumed to be taken on 2008 November 6 with a marine sextant, zero index error, at height 5·4 m, temperature −3° C and pressure 982 mb, the Moon sights are assumed to be taken at 10^h UT.

Body limb	Sun lower	Sun upper	Moon lower	Moon upper	Venus —	*Polaris* —
Sextant altitude:						
H_S	21·3283	3·3367	33·4600	26·1117	4·5433	49·6083
Step 1. Dip:						
$D = 0{\cdot}0293\sqrt{h}$	0·0681	0·0681	0·0681	0·0681	0·0681	0·0681
Step 2. Apparent altitude:						
$H = H_S + I - D$	21·2602	3·2686	33·3919	26·0436	4·4752	49·5402
Step 3. Refraction:						
R_0	0·0423	0·2256	0·0251	0·0338	0·1798	0·0142
f	1·0184	1·0184	1·0184	1·0184	1·0184	1·0184
$R = fR_0$	0·0431	0·2298	0·0256	0·0344	0·1831	0·0144
Step 4. Parallax:			(55′.4)	(55′.4)	(0′.1)	
HP	0·0024	0·0024	0·9233	0·9233	0·0017	—
Parallax in altitude:						
$PA = HP \cos H$	0·0022	0·0024	0·7709	0·8296	0·0017	—
Step 5. Semi-diameter:						
Sun : $S = 16{\cdot}2/60$	0·2700	0·2700	—	—	—	—
Moon : $S = 0{\cdot}2724HP$	—	—	0·2515	0·2515	—	—
Step 6. Observed altitude:						
$H_O = H - R + PA \pm S$	21·4894	2·7712	34·3887	26·5872	4·2938	49·5258

Note that for the Moon the correction for the oblateness of the Earth of about $-0^\circ\!.0017 \cos H$, which equals $-0^\circ\!.0014$ for the lower limb and $-0^\circ\!.0015$ for the upper limb, has been ignored in the above calculation.

10. *Position from intercept and azimuth using a chart.* An estimate is made of the position at the adopted time of fix. The position at the time of observation is then calculated by dead reckoning from the time of fix. For example if the course (track) T and the speed V (in knots) of the observer are constant then *Long* and *Lat* at the time of observation are calculated from

$$Long = L_F + t\,(V/60)\sin T/\cos B_F$$
$$Lat = B_F + t\,(V/60)\cos T$$

where L_F and B_F are the estimated longitude and latitude at the time of fix and t is the time interval in hours from the time of fix to the time of observation, t is positive if the time of observation is after the time of fix and negative if it was before.

The position line of an observation is plotted on a chart using the intercept

$$p = H_O - H_C$$

and azimuth Z with origin at the calculated position (*Long*, *Lat*) at the time of observation, where H_C and Z are calculated using the method in section 6, page 279. Starting from this calculated position a line is drawn on the chart along the direction of the azimuth to the body. Convert p to nautical miles by multiplying by 60. The position line is drawn at right angles to the azimuth line, distance p from (*Long*, *Lat*) towards the body if p is positive and distance p away from the body if p is negative. Provided there are no gross errors the navigator should be somewhere on or near the position line at the time of observation. Two or more position lines are required to determine a fix.

11. *Position from intercept and azimuth by calculation.* The position of the fix may be calculated from two or more sextant observations as follows.

If p_1, Z_1, are the intercept and azimuth of the first observation, p_2, Z_2, of the second observation and so on, form the summations

$$A = \cos^2 Z_1 + \cos^2 Z_2 + \cdots$$
$$B = \cos Z_1 \sin Z_1 + \cos Z_2 \sin Z_2 + \cdots$$
$$C = \sin^2 Z_1 + \sin^2 Z_2 + \cdots$$
$$D = p_1 \cos Z_1 + p_2 \cos Z_2 + \cdots$$
$$E = p_1 \sin Z_1 + p_2 \sin Z_2 + \cdots$$

where the number of terms in each summation is equal to the number of observations.

With $G = AC - B^2$, an improved estimate of the position at the time of fix (L_I, B_I) is given by

$$L_I = L_F + (AE - BD)/(G\cos B_F), \qquad B_I = B_F + (CD - BE)/G$$

Calculate the distance d between the initial estimated position (L_F, B_F) at the time of fix and the improved estimated position (L_I, B_I) in nautical miles from

$$d = 60\sqrt{((L_I - L_F)^2\cos^2 B_F + (B_I - B_F)^2)}$$

If d exceeds about 20 nautical miles set $L_F = L_I$, $B_F = B_I$ and repeat the calculation until d, the distance between the position at the previous estimate and the improved estimate, is less than about 20 nautical miles.

12. *Example of direct computation.* Using the method described above, calculate the position of a ship on 2008 July 3 at $21^h\,00^m\,00^s$ UT from the marine sextant observations of the three stars *Regulus* (No. 26) at $20^h\,39^m\,23^s$ UT, *Antares* (No. 42) at $20^h\,45^m\,47^s$ UT and *Kochab* (No. 40) at $21^h\,10^m\,34^s$ UT, where the observed altitudes of the three stars corrected for the effects of refraction, dip and instrumental error, are 27°.4619, 25°.8052 and 47°.5104 respectively. The ship was travelling at a constant speed of 20 knots on a course of 325° during the period of observation, and the position of the ship at the time of fix $21^h\,00^m\,00^s$ UT is only known to the nearest whole degree W 15°, N 32°.

Intermediate values for the first iteration are shown in the table. *GHA* Aries was interpolated from the nearest tabular values on page 132. For the first iteration set $L_F = -15^\circ\!.0000$, $B_F = +32^\circ\!.0000$ at the time of fix at $21^h\ 00^m\ 00^s$ UT.

First Iteration

Body	*Regulus*	*Antares*	*Kochab*
No.	26	42	40
time of observation	$20^h\ 39^m\ 23^s$	$20^h\ 45^m\ 47^s$	$21^h\ 10^m\ 34^s$
H_O	27·4619	25·8052	47·5104
interpolation factor	0·6564	0·7631	0·1761
GHA Aries	232·0854	233·6897	239·9023
SHA (page 132)	207·7950	112·5083	137·3133
GHA	79·8804	346·1980	17·2157
Dec (page 132)	+11·9267	−26·4533	+74·1233
t	−0·3436	−0·2369	+0·1761
Long	−14·9225	−14·9466	−15·0397
Lat	+31·9062	+31·9353	+32·0481
Z	267·1937	151·5051	359·1121
H_C	27·4388	25·4994	47·9105
p	+0·0231	+0·3058	−0·4001

$A = 1{\cdot}7746 \quad B = -0{\cdot}3859 \quad C = 1{\cdot}2254 \quad D = -0{\cdot}6699 \quad E = 0{\cdot}1290 \quad G = 2{\cdot}0257$

$$(A\,E - B\,D)/(G \cos B_F) = -0{\cdot}0172, \qquad (C\,D - B\,E)/G = -0{\cdot}3807$$

An improved estimate of the position at the time of fix is

$$L_I = L_F - 0{\cdot}0172 = -15{\cdot}0172 \quad \text{and} \quad B_I = B_F - 0{\cdot}3807 = +31{\cdot}6193$$

Since the distance between the previous estimated position and the improved estimate $d = 22{\cdot}9$ nautical miles set $L_F = -15{\cdot}0172$, and $B_F = +31{\cdot}6193$ and repeat the calculation. The table shows the intermediate values of the calculation for the second iteration. In each iteration the quantities H_O, *GHA*, *Dec* and *t* do not change.

Second Iteration

Body	*Regulus*	*Antares*	*Kochab*
No.	26	42	40
Long	−14·9401	−14·9640	−15·0568
Lat	+31·5255	+31·5546	+31·6674
Z	267·3816	151·4022	359·1255
H_C	27·4717	25·8268	47·5300
p	−0·0098	−0·0215	−0·0197

$A = 1{\cdot}7727 \quad B = -0{\cdot}3899 \quad C = 1{\cdot}2273 \quad D = -0{\cdot}0003 \quad E = -0{\cdot}0002 \quad G = 2{\cdot}0236$

$$(A\,E - B\,D)/(G \cos B_F) = -0{\cdot}0003, \qquad (C\,D - B\,E)/G = -0{\cdot}0002$$

An improved estimate of the position at the time of fix is

$$L_I = L_F - 0{\cdot}0003 = -15{\cdot}0175 \quad \text{and} \quad B_I = B_F - 0{\cdot}0002 = +31{\cdot}6191$$

The distance between the previous estimated position and the improved estimated position $d = 0{\cdot}02$ nautical miles is so small that a third iteration would produce a negligible improvement to the estimate of the position.

USE OF CONCISE SIGHT REDUCTION TABLES

1. *Introduction.* The concise sight reduction tables given on pages 286 to 317 are intended for use when neither more extensive tables nor electronic computing aids are available. These "NAO sight reduction tables" provide for the reduction of the local hour angle and declination of a celestial object to azimuth and altitude, referred to an assumed position on the Earth, for use in the intercept method of celestial navigation which is now standard practice.

2. *Form of tables.* Entries in the reduction table are at a fixed interval of one degree for all latitudes and hour angles. A compact arrangement results from division of the navigational triangle into two right spherical triangles, so that the table has to be entered twice. Assumed latitude and local hour angle are the arguments for the first entry. The reduction table responds with the intermediate arguments A, B, and Z_1, where A is used as one of the arguments for the second entry to the table, B has to be incremented by the declination to produce the quantity F, and Z_1 is a component of the azimuth angle. The reduction table is then reentered with A and F and yields H, P, and Z_2 where H is the altitude, P is the complement of the parallactic angle, and Z_2 is the second component of the azimuth angle. It is usually necessary to adjust the tabular altitude for the fractional parts of the intermediate entering arguments to derive computed altitude, and an auxiliary table is provided for the purpose. Rules governing signs of the quantities which must be added or subtracted are given in the instructions and summarized on each tabular page. Azimuth angle is the sum of two components and is converted to true azimuth by familiar rules, repeated at the bottom of the tabular pages.

Tabular altitude and intermediate quantities are given to the nearest minute of arc, although errors of 2′ in computed altitude may accrue during adjustment for the minutes parts of entering arguments. Components of azimuth angle are stated to 0°.1; for derived true azimuth, only whole degrees are warranted. Since objects near the zenith are difficult to observe with a marine sextant, they should be avoided; altitudes greater than about 80° are not suited to reduction by this method.

In many circumstances the accuracy provided by these tables is sufficient. However, to maintain the full accuracy (0′.1) of the ephemeral data in the almanac throughout their reduction to altitude and azimuth, more extensive tables or a calculator should be used.

3. *Use of Tables.*

Step 1. Determine the Greenwich hour angle (GHA) and Declination (Dec) of the body from the almanac. Select an assumed latitude (Lat) of integral degrees nearest to the estimated latitude. Choose an assumed longitude nearest to the estimated longitude such that the local hour angle

$$LHA = GHA \;\begin{matrix}-\text{ west}\\+\text{ east}\end{matrix}\; \text{longitude}$$

has integral degrees.

Step 2. Enter the reduction table with Lat and LHA as arguments. Record the quantities A, B and Z_1. Apply the rules for the sign of B and Z_1: B is minus if $90° < LHA < 270°$: Z_1 has the same sign as B. Set $A°$ = nearest whole degree of A and A' = minutes part of A. This step may be repeated for all reductions before leaving the latitude opening of the table.

Step 3. Record the declination Dec. Apply the rules for the sign of Dec: Dec is minus if the name of Dec (*i.e.* N or S) is contrary to latitude. Add B and Dec algebraically to produce F. If F is negative, the object is below the horizon (in sight reduction, this can occur when the objects are close to the horizon). Regard F as positive until step 7. Set $F°$ = nearest whole degree of F and F' = minutes part of F.

Step 4. Enter the reduction table a second time with $A°$ and $F°$ as arguments and record H, P, and Z_2. Set $P° =$ nearest whole degree of P and $Z_2° =$ nearest whole degree of Z_2.

Step 5. Enter the auxiliary table with F' and $P°$ as arguments to obtain $corr_1$ to H for F'. Apply the rule for the sign of $corr_1$: $corr_1$ is minus if $F < 90°$ and $F' > 29'$ or if $F > 90°$ and $F' < 30'$, otherwise $corr_1$ is plus.

Step 6. Enter the auxiliary table with A' and $Z_2°$ as arguments to obtain $corr_2$ to H for A'. Apply the rule for the sign of $corr_2$: $corr_2$ is minus if $A' < 30'$, otherwise $corr_2$ is plus.

Step 7. Calculate the computed altitude H_C as the sum of H, $corr_1$ and $corr_2$. Apply the rule for the sign of H_C: H_C is minus if F is negative.

Step 8. Apply the rule for the sign of Z_2: Z_2 is minus if $F > 90°$. If F is negative, replace Z_2 by $180° - Z_2$. Set the azimuth angle Z equal to the algebraic sum of Z_1 and Z_2 and ignore the resulting sign. Obtain the true azimuth Z_n from the rules

For N latitude, if	$LHA > 180°$	$Z_n = Z$
if	$LHA < 180°$	$Z_n = 360° - Z$
For S latitude, if	$LHA > 180°$	$Z_n = 180° - Z$
if	$LHA < 180°$	$Z_n = 180° + Z$

Observed altitude H_O is compared with H_C to obtain the altitude difference, which, with Z_n, is used to plot the position line.

4. *Example.* (a) Required the altitude and azimuth of *Schedar* on 2008 February 5 at UT 06^h 31^m from the estimated position 5° east, 53° north.

1. Assumed latitude	$Lat =$	53° N		
From the almanac	$GHA =$	222° 19′		
Assumed longitude		4° 41′ E		
Local hour angle	$LHA =$	227		
2. Reduction table, 1st entry				
$(Lat, LHA) = (53, 227)$	$A =$	26 07	$A° = 26$, $A' = 7$	
	$B =$	−27 12	$Z_1 = -49{\cdot}4$,	$90° < LHA < 270°$
3. From the almanac	$Dec =$	+56 35		*Lat* and *Dec* same
Sum $= B + Dec$	$F =$	+29 23	$F° = 29$, $F' = 23$	
4. Reduction table, 2nd entry				
$(A°, F°) = (26, 29)$	$H =$	25 50	$P° = 61$	
			$Z_2 = 76{\cdot}3$, $Z_2° = 76$	
5. Auxiliary table, 1st entry				
$(F', P°) = (23, 61)$	$corr_1 =$	+20		$F < 90°$, $F' < 29'$
Sum		26 10		
6. Auxiliary table, 2nd entry				
$(A', Z_2°) = (7, 76)$	$corr_2 =$	−2		$A' < 30'$
7. Sum = computed altitude	$H_C =$	+26° 08′		$F > 0°$
8. Azimuth, first component	$Z_1 =$	−49·4		same sign as B
second component	$Z_2 =$	+76·3		$F < 90°$, $F > 0°$
Sum = azimuth angle	$Z =$	26·9		
True azimuth	$Z_n =$	027°		N *Lat*, $LHA > 180°$

continued on page 318

SIGHT REDUCTION TABLE

B: (–) for 90° < LHA < 270°
Dec: (–) for Lat. contrary name

Z_1: same sign as B
Z_2: (–) for F > 90°

Lat. / A		0°			1°			2°			3°			4°			5°			Lat. / A	
LHA/F		A/H	B/P	Z_1/Z_2	A/H	B/P	Z_1/Z_2	A/H	B/P	Z_1/Z_2	A/H	B/P	Z_1/Z_2	A/H	B/P	Z_1/Z_2	A/H	B/P	Z_1/Z_2	LHA	
°	°	° ′	° ′	°	° ′	° ′	°	° ′	° ′	°	° ′	° ′	°	° ′	° ′	°	° ′	° ′	°	°	°
0	180	0 00	90 00	90·0	0 00	89 00	90·0	0 00	88 00	90·0	0 00	87 00	90·0	0 00	86 00	90·0	0 00	85 00	90·0	180	360
1	179	1 00	90 00	90·0	1 00	89 00	90·0	1 00	88 00	90·0	1 00	87 00	89·9	1 00	86 00	89·9	1 00	85 00	89·9	181	359
2	178	2 00	90 00	90·0	2 00	89 00	90·0	2 00	88 00	89·9	2 00	87 00	89·9	2 00	86 00	89·9	2 00	85 00	89·8	182	358
3	177	3 00	90 00	90·0	3 00	89 00	89·9	3 00	88 00	89·9	3 00	87 00	89·8	3 00	86 00	89·8	2 59	85 00	89·7	183	357
4	176	4 00	90 00	90·0	4 00	89 00	89·9	4 00	88 00	89·9	4 00	87 00	89·8	3 59	85 59	89·7	3 59	84 59	89·7	184	356
5	175	5 00	90 00	90·0	5 00	89 00	89·9	5 00	88 00	89·8	5 00	86 59	89·7	4 59	85 59	89·7	4 59	84 59	89·6	185	355
6	174	6 00	90 00	90·0	6 00	89 00	89·9	6 00	87 59	89·8	6 00	86 59	89·7	5 59	85 59	89·6	5 59	84 58	89·5	186	354
7	173	7 00	90 00	90·0	7 00	89 00	89·9	7 00	87 59	89·8	6 59	86 59	89·6	6 59	85 58	89·5	6 58	84 58	89·4	187	353
8	172	8 00	90 00	90·0	8 00	88 59	89·9	8 00	87 59	89·7	7 59	86 58	89·6	7 59	85 58	89·4	7 58	84 57	89·3	188	352
9	171	9 00	90 00	90·0	9 00	88 59	89·8	9 00	87 59	89·7	8 59	86 58	89·5	8 59	85 57	89·4	8 58	84 56	89·2	189	351
10	170	10 00	90 00	90·0	10 00	88 59	89·8	10 00	87 58	89·6	9 59	86 57	89·5	9 59	85 56	89·3	9 58	84 55	89·1	190	350
11	169	11 00	90 00	90·0	11 00	88 59	89·8	11 00	87 58	89·6	10 59	86 57	89·4	10 58	85 56	89·2	10 57	84 54	89·0	191	349
12	168	12 00	90 00	90·0	12 00	88 59	89·8	12 00	87 57	89·6	11 59	86 56	89·4	11 58	85 55	89·2	11 57	84 53	88·9	192	348
13	167	13 00	90 00	90·0	13 00	88 58	89·8	13 00	87 57	89·5	12 59	86 55	89·3	12 58	85 54	89·1	12 57	84 52	88·8	193	347
14	166	14 00	90 00	90·0	14 00	88 58	89·8	13 59	87 56	89·5	13 59	86 55	89·3	13 58	85 53	89·0	13 57	84 51	88·8	194	346
15	165	15 00	90 00	90·0	15 00	88 58	89·7	14 59	87 56	89·5	14 59	86 54	89·2	14 58	85 52	88·9	14 56	84 49	88·7	195	345
16	164	16 00	90 00	90·0	16 00	88 58	89·7	15 59	87 55	89·4	15 59	86 53	89·1	15 58	85 50	88·9	15 56	84 48	88·6	196	344
17	163	17 00	90 00	90·0	17 00	88 57	89·7	16 59	87 55	89·4	16 59	86 52	89·1	16 57	85 49	88·8	16 56	84 46	88·5	197	343
18	162	18 00	90 00	90·0	18 00	88 57	89·7	17 59	87 54	89·4	17 58	86 51	89·0	17 57	85 48	88·7	17 56	84 45	88·4	198	342
19	161	19 00	90 00	90·0	19 00	88 57	89·7	18 59	87 53	89·3	18 58	86 50	89·0	18 57	85 46	88·6	18 55	84 43	88·3	199	341
20	160	20 00	90 00	90·0	20 00	88 56	89·6	19 59	87 52	89·3	19 58	86 48	88·9	19 57	85 45	88·5	19 55	84 41	88·2	200	340
21	159	21 00	90 00	90·0	21 00	88 56	89·6	20 59	87 51	89·2	20 58	86 47	88·8	20 57	85 43	88·5	20 55	84 39	88·1	201	339
22	158	22 00	90 00	90·0	22 00	88 55	89·6	21 59	87 51	89·2	21 58	86 46	88·8	21 57	85 41	88·4	21 55	84 37	88·0	202	338
23	157	23 00	90 00	90·0	23 00	88 55	89·6	22 59	87 50	89·2	22 58	86 44	88·7	22 56	85 39	88·3	22 54	84 34	87·9	203	337
24	156	24 00	90 00	90·0	24 00	88 54	89·6	23 59	87 49	89·1	23 58	86 43	88·7	23 56	85 37	88·2	23 54	84 32	87·8	204	336
25	155	25 00	90 00	90·0	25 00	88 54	89·5	24 59	87 48	89·1	24 58	86 41	88·6	24 56	85 35	88·1	24 54	84 29	87·7	205	335
26	154	26 00	90 00	90·0	26 00	88 53	89·5	25 59	87 47	89·0	25 58	86 40	88·5	25 56	85 33	88·1	25 54	84 26	87·6	206	334
27	153	27 00	90 00	90·0	27 00	88 53	89·5	26 59	87 45	89·0	26 58	86 38	88·5	26 56	85 31	88·0	26 53	84 24	87·5	207	333
28	152	28 00	90 00	90·0	28 00	88 52	89·5	27 59	87 44	88·9	27 57	86 36	88·4	27 56	85 28	87·9	27 53	84 20	87·3	208	332
29	151	29 00	90 00	90·0	29 00	88 51	89·4	28 59	87 43	88·9	28 57	86 34	88·3	28 55	85 26	87·8	28 53	84 17	87·2	209	331
30	150	30 00	90 00	90·0	30 00	88 51	89·4	29 59	87 41	88·8	29 57	86 32	88·3	29 55	85 23	87·7	29 52	84 14	87·1	210	330
31	149	31 00	90 00	90·0	31 00	88 50	89·4	30 59	87 40	88·8	30 57	86 30	88·2	30 55	85 20	87·6	30 52	84 10	87·0	211	329
32	148	32 00	90 00	90·0	32 00	88 49	89·4	31 59	87 39	88·8	31 57	86 28	88·1	31 55	85 17	87·5	31 52	84 07	86·9	212	328
33	147	33 00	90 00	90·0	33 00	88 48	89·4	32 59	87 37	88·7	32 57	86 25	88·1	32 55	85 14	87·4	32 52	84 03	86·8	213	327
34	146	34 00	90 00	90·0	34 00	88 48	89·3	33 59	87 35	88·7	33 57	86 23	88·0	33 54	85 11	87·3	33 51	83 59	86·6	214	326
35	145	35 00	90 00	90·0	35 00	88 47	89·3	34 59	87 34	88·6	34 57	86 20	87·9	34 54	85 07	87·2	34 51	83 54	86·5	215	325
36	144	36 00	90 00	90·0	36 00	88 46	89·3	35 58	87 32	88·5	35 57	86 18	87·8	35 54	85 04	87·1	35 51	83 50	86·4	216	324
37	143	37 00	90 00	90·0	37 00	88 45	89·2	36 58	87 30	88·5	36 56	86 15	87·7	36 54	85 00	87·0	36 50	83 45	86·2	217	323
38	142	38 00	90 00	90·0	38 00	88 44	89·2	37 58	87 28	88·4	37 56	86 12	87·7	37 53	84 56	86·9	37 50	83 40	86·1	218	322
39	141	39 00	90 00	90·0	39 00	88 43	89·2	38 58	87 26	88·4	38 56	86 09	87·6	38 53	84 52	86·8	38 49	83 35	86·0	219	321
40	140	40 00	90 00	90·0	40 00	88 42	89·2	39 58	87 23	88·3	39 56	86 05	87·5	39 53	84 47	86·7	39 49	83 29	85·8	220	320
41	139	41 00	90 00	90·0	41 00	88 41	89·1	40 58	87 21	88·3	40 56	86 02	87·4	40 53	84 42	86·5	40 49	83 23	85·7	221	319
42	138	42 00	90 00	90·0	42 00	88 39	89·1	41 58	87 19	88·2	41 56	85 58	87·3	41 52	84 37	86·4	41 48	83 17	85·5	222	318
43	137	43 00	90 00	90·0	43 00	88 38	89·1	42 58	87 16	88·1	42 56	85 54	87·2	42 52	84 32	86·3	42 48	83 11	85·4	223	317
44	136	44 00	90 00	90·0	43 59	88 37	89·0	43 58	87 13	88·1	43 55	85 50	87·1	43 52	84 27	86·1	43 47	83 04	85·2	224	316
45	135	45 00	90 00	90·0	44 59	88 35	89·0	44 58	87 10	88·0	44 55	85 46	87·0	44 52	84 21	86·0	44 47	82 57	85·0	225	315

Lat. / A		0°			1°			2°			3°			4°			5°			Lat. / A	
LHA/F		A/H	B/P	Z_1/Z_2	A/H	B/P	Z_1/Z_2	A/H	B/P	Z_1/Z_2	A/H	B/P	Z_1/Z_2	A/H	B/P	Z_1/Z_2	A/H	B/P	Z_1/Z_2	LHA	
°	°	° ′	° ′	°	° ′	° ′	°	° ′	° ′	°	° ′	° ′	°	° ′	° ′	°	° ′	° ′	°	°	°
45	135	45 00	90 00	90·0	44 59	88 35	89·0	44 58	87 10	88·0	44 55	85 46	87·0	44 52	84 21	86·0	44 47	82 57	85·0	225	315
46	134	46 00	90 00	90·0	45 59	88 34	89·0	45 58	87 07	87·9	45 55	85 41	86·9	45 51	84 15	85·9	45 46	82 49	84·8	226	314
47	133	47 00	90 00	90·0	46 59	88 32	88·9	46 58	87 04	87·9	46 55	85 36	86·8	46 51	84 09	85·7	46 46	82 41	84·7	227	313
48	132	48 00	90 00	90·0	47 59	88 30	88·9	47 58	87 01	87·8	47 55	85 31	86·7	47 51	84 02	85·6	47 46	82 33	84·5	228	312
49	131	49 00	90 00	90·0	48 59	88 29	88·8	48 58	86 57	87·7	48 55	85 26	86·6	48 50	83 55	85·4	48 45	82 24	84·3	229	311
50	130	50 00	90 00	90·0	49 59	88 27	88·8	49 58	86 53	87·6	49 54	85 20	86·4	49 50	83 47	85·2	49 44	82 15	84·1	230	310
51	129	51 00	90 00	90·0	50 59	88 25	88·8	50 57	86 49	87·5	50 54	85 14	86·3	50 50	83 40	85·1	50 44	82 05	83·9	231	309
52	128	52 00	90 00	90·0	51 59	88 23	88·7	51 57	86 45	87·4	51 54	85 08	86·2	51 49	83 31	84·9	51 43	81 55	83·6	232	308
53	127	53 00	90 00	90·0	52 59	88 20	88·7	52 57	86 41	87·3	52 54	85 01	86·0	52 49	83 22	84·7	52 43	81 44	83·4	233	307
54	126	54 00	90 00	90·0	53 59	88 18	88·6	53 57	86 36	87·2	53 54	84 54	85·9	53 49	83 13	84·5	53 42	81 32	83·2	234	306
55	125	55 00	90 00	90·0	54 59	88 15	88·6	54 57	86 31	87·1	54 53	84 47	85·7	54 48	83 03	84·3	54 41	81 20	82·9	235	305
56	124	56 00	90 00	90·0	55 59	88 13	88·5	55 57	86 26	87·0	55 53	84 39	85·6	55 48	82 52	84·1	55 41	81 06	82·6	236	304
57	123	57 00	90 00	90·0	56 59	88 10	88·5	56 57	86 20	86·9	56 53	84 30	85·4	56 47	82 41	83·9	56 40	80 52	82·4	237	303
58	122	58 00	90 00	90·0	57 59	88 07	88·4	57 57	86 14	86·8	57 52	84 21	85·2	57 47	82 29	83·6	57 39	80 38	82·1	238	302
59	121	59 00	90 00	90·0	58 59	88 04	88·3	58 57	86 07	86·7	58 52	84 11	85·0	58 46	82 16	83·4	58 38	80 22	81·7	239	301
60	120	60 00	90 00	90·0	59 59	88 00	88·3	59 56	86 00	86·5	59 52	84 01	84·8	59 46	82 02	83·1	59 37	80 05	81·4	240	300
61	119	61 00	90 00	90·0	60 59	87 56	88·2	60 56	85 53	86·4	60 52	83 50	84·6	60 45	81 48	82·8	60 37	79 46	81·1	241	299
62	118	62 00	90 00	90·0	61 59	87 52	88·1	61 56	85 45	86·2	61 51	83 38	84·4	61 44	81 32	82·5	61 36	79 27	80·7	242	298
63	117	63 00	90 00	90·0	62 59	87 48	88·0	62 56	85 36	86·1	62 51	83 25	84·1	62 44	81 15	82·2	62 35	79 06	80·3	243	297
64	116	64 00	90 00	90·0	63 59	87 43	88·0	63 56	85 27	85·9	63 50	83 11	83·9	63 43	80 56	81·9	63 33	78 43	79·9	244	296
65	115	65 00	90 00	90·0	64 59	87 38	87·9	64 56	85 17	85·7	64 50	82 56	83·6	64 42	80 36	81·5	64 32	78 18	79·4	245	295
66	114	66 00	90 00	90·0	65 59	87 33	87·8	65 55	85 06	85·5	65 49	82 39	83·3	65 41	80 15	81·1	65 31	77 52	78·9	246	294
67	113	67 00	90 00	90·0	66 59	87 27	87·6	66 55	84 54	85·3	66 49	82 22	83·0	66 40	79 51	80·7	66 29	77 23	78·4	247	293
68	112	68 00	90 00	90·0	67 59	87 20	87·5	67 55	84 40	85·1	67 48	82 02	82·6	67 39	79 26	80·2	67 28	76 51	77·8	248	292
69	111	69 00	90 00	90·0	68 59	87 13	87·4	68 55	84 26	84·8	68 48	81 41	82·2	68 38	78 58	79·7	68 26	76 17	77·2	249	291
70	110	70 00	90 00	90·0	69 59	87 05	87·3	69 54	84 10	84·5	69 47	81 17	81·8	69 37	78 27	79·2	69 25	75 39	76·5	250	290
71	109	71 00	90 00	90·0	70 58	86 56	87·1	70 54	83 53	84·2	70 46	80 51	81·4	70 36	77 53	78·5	70 23	74 58	75·8	251	289
72	108	72 00	90 00	90·0	71 58	86 46	86·9	71 54	83 33	83·9	71 46	80 22	80·8	71 35	77 15	77·9	71 20	74 12	75·0	252	288
73	107	73 00	90 00	90·0	72 58	86 35	86·7	72 53	83 11	83·5	72 45	79 50	80·3	72 33	76 33	77·1	72 18	73 20	74·1	253	287
74	106	74 00	90 00	90·0	73 58	86 23	86·5	73 53	82 47	83·1	73 44	79 14	79·7	73 31	75 46	76·3	73 15	72 23	73·1	254	286
75	105	75 00	90 00	90·0	74 58	86 09	86·3	74 52	82 19	82·6	74 43	78 33	78·9	74 29	74 53	75·4	74 12	71 19	72·0	255	285
76	104	76 00	90 00	90·0	75 58	85 52	86·0	75 52	81 47	82·0	75 41	77 47	78·1	75 27	73 53	74·4	75 09	70 07	70·7	256	284
77	103	77 00	90 00	90·0	76 58	85 34	85·7	76 51	81 11	81·4	76 40	76 53	77·2	76 25	72 44	73·2	76 05	68 45	69·3	257	283
78	102	78 00	90 00	90·0	77 58	85 12	85·3	77 50	80 28	80·7	77 38	75 51	76·2	77 22	71 25	71·8	77 01	67 11	67·7	258	282
79	101	79 00	90 00	90·0	78 57	84 46	84·9	78 49	79 38	79·8	78 36	74 39	74·9	78 18	69 52	70·3	77 56	65 22	65·8	259	281
80	100	80 00	90 00	90·0	79 57	84 16	84·3	79 48	78 38	78·8	79 34	73 12	73·5	79 14	68 04	68·4	78 50	63 16	63·7	260	280
81	99	81 00	90 00	90·0	80 57	83 38	83·7	80 47	77 25	77·6	80 31	71 29	71·7	80 09	65 55	66·2	79 43	60 47	61·2	261	279
82	98	82 00	90 00	90·0	81 56	82 51	82·9	81 45	75 55	76·1	81 28	69 22	69·6	81 04	63 19	63·6	80 34	57 51	58·2	262	278
83	97	83 00	90 00	90·0	82 56	81 51	81·9	82 43	74 01	74·1	82 23	66 44	66·9	81 57	60 09	60·4	81 24	54 20	54·6	263	277
84	96	84 00	90 00	90·0	83 55	80 31	80·6	83 41	71 32	71·6	83 18	63 22	63·5	82 48	56 13	56·4	82 12	50 04	50·3	264	276
85	95	85 00	90 00	90·0	84 54	78 40	78·7	84 37	68 10	68·3	84 10	58 59	59·1	83 36	51 16	51·4	82 56	44 53	45·1	265	275
86	94	86 00	90 00	90·0	85 53	75 57	76·0	85 32	63 24	63·5	85 00	53 05	53·2	84 21	44 56	45·1	83 36	38 34	38·7	266	274
87	93	87 00	90 00	90·0	86 50	71 33	71·6	86 24	56 17	56·3	85 45	44 58	45·0	85 00	36 49	36·9	84 10	30 53	31·0	267	273
88	92	88 00	90 00	90·0	87 46	63 26	63·4	87 10	44 59	45·0	86 24	33 40	33·7	85 32	26 31	26·6	84 37	21 45	21·8	268	272
89	91	89 00	90 00	90·0	88 35	45 00	45·0	87 46	26 33	26·6	86 50	18 25	18·4	85 53	14 01	14·0	84 54	11 17	11·3	269	271
90	90	90 00	0 00	0·0	89 00	0 00	0·0	88 00	0 00	0·0	87 00	0 00	0·0	86 00	0 00	0·0	85 00	0 00	0·0	270	270

N. Lat: for LHA > 180° … $Z_n = Z$
for LHA < 180° … $Z_n = 360° - Z$

S. Lat.: for LHA > 180° … $Z_n = 180° - Z$
for LHA < 180° … $Z_n = 180° + Z$

SIGHT REDUCTION TABLE

B: (−) for 90° < LHA < 270°
Dec:(−) for Lat. contrary name

Z_1: same sign as B
Z_2: (−) for F > 90°

Lat. / A		6°			7°			8°			9°			10°			11°			Lat. / A	
LHA/F		A/H	B/P	Z_1/Z_2	A/H	B/P	Z_1/Z_2	A/H	B/P	Z_1/Z_2	A/H	B/P	Z_1/Z_2	A/H	B/P	Z_1/Z_2	A/H	B/P	Z_1/Z_2	LHA	
°	°	° ′	° ′	°	° ′	° ′	°	° ′	° ′	°	° ′	° ′	°	° ′	° ′	°	° ′	° ′	°	°	°
0	180	0 00	84 00	90·0	0 00	83 00	90·0	0 00	82 00	90·0	0 00	81 00	90·0	0 00	80 00	90·0	0 00	79 00	90·0	180	360
1	179	1 00	84 00	89·9	1 00	83 00	89·9	0 59	82 00	89·9	0 59	81 00	89·8	0 59	80 00	89·8	0 59	79 00	89·8	181	359
2	178	1 59	84 00	89·8	1 59	83 00	89·8	1 59	82 00	89·7	1 59	81 00	89·7	1 58	80 00	89·7	1 58	79 00	89·6	182	358
3	177	2 59	84 00	89·7	2 59	82 59	89·6	2 58	81 59	89·6	2 58	80 59	89·5	2 57	79 59	89·5	2 57	78 59	89·4	183	357
4	176	3 59	83 59	89·6	3 58	82 59	89·5	3 58	81 59	89·4	3 57	80 59	89·4	3 56	79 59	89·3	3 56	78 58	89·2	184	356
5	175	4 58	83 59	89·5	4 58	82 58	89·4	4 57	81 58	89·3	4 56	80 58	89·2	4 55	79 58	89·1	4 54	78 58	89·0	185	355
6	174	5 58	83 58	89·4	5 57	82 58	89·3	5 56	81 57	89·2	5 56	80 57	89·1	5 55	79 57	89·0	5 53	78 56	88·9	186	354
7	173	6 58	83 57	89·3	6 57	82 57	89·1	6 56	81 56	89·0	6 55	80 56	88·9	6 54	79 56	88·8	6 52	78 55	88·7	187	353
8	172	7 57	83 56	89·2	7 56	82 56	89·0	7 55	81 55	88·9	7 54	80 55	88·7	7 53	79 54	88·6	7 51	78 54	88·5	188	352
9	171	8 57	83 56	89·1	8 56	82 55	88·9	8 55	81 54	88·7	8 53	80 53	88·6	8 52	79 53	88·4	8 50	78 52	88·3	189	351
10	170	9 57	83 54	88·9	9 55	82 54	88·8	9 54	81 53	88·6	9 53	80 52	88·4	9 51	79 51	88·2	9 49	78 50	88·1	190	350
11	169	10 56	83 53	88·8	10 55	82 52	88·6	10 53	81 51	88·5	10 52	80 50	88·3	10 50	79 49	88·1	10 48	78 48	87·9	191	349
12	168	11 56	83 52	88·7	11 55	82 51	88·5	11 53	81 49	88·3	11 51	80 48	88·1	11 49	79 47	87·9	11 47	78 46	87·7	192	348
13	167	12 56	83 51	88·6	12 54	82 49	88·4	12 52	81 48	88·2	12 50	80 46	87·9	12 48	79 45	87·7	12 45	78 43	87·5	193	347
14	166	13 55	83 49	88·5	13 54	82 47	88·3	13 52	81 46	88·0	13 49	80 44	87·8	13 47	79 42	87·5	13 44	78 40	87·3	194	346
15	165	14 55	83 47	88·4	14 53	82 45	88·1	14 51	81 43	87·9	14 49	80 41	87·6	14 46	79 39	87·3	14 43	78 37	87·1	195	345
16	164	15 55	83 46	88·3	15 53	82 43	88·0	15 50	81 41	87·7	15 48	80 39	87·4	15 45	79 36	87·1	15 42	78 34	86·9	196	344
17	163	16 54	83 44	88·2	16 52	82 41	87·9	16 50	81 38	87·6	16 47	80 36	87·3	16 44	79 33	87·0	16 41	78 31	86·7	197	343
18	162	17 54	83 42	88·1	17 52	82 39	87·7	17 49	81 36	87·4	17 46	80 33	87·1	17 43	79 30	86·8	17 39	78 27	86·5	198	342
19	161	18 54	83 39	87·9	18 51	82 36	87·6	18 48	81 33	87·3	18 45	80 29	86·9	18 42	79 26	86·6	18 38	78 23	86·2	199	341
20	160	19 53	83 37	87·8	19 51	82 33	87·5	19 48	81 30	87·1	19 45	80 26	86·7	19 41	79 22	86·4	19 37	78 19	86·0	200	340
21	159	20 53	83 35	87·7	20 50	82 30	87·3	20 47	81 26	86·9	20 44	80 22	86·6	20 40	79 18	86·2	20 36	78 14	85·8	201	339
22	158	21 52	83 32	87·6	21 50	82 27	87·2	21 46	81 23	86·8	21 43	80 18	86·4	21 39	79 14	86·0	21 35	78 10	85·6	202	338
23	157	22 52	83 29	87·5	22 49	82 24	87·0	22 46	81 19	86·6	22 42	80 14	86·2	22 38	79 09	85·8	22 33	78 05	85·4	203	337
24	156	23 52	83 26	87·3	23 49	82 21	86·9	23 45	81 15	86·5	23 41	80 10	86·0	23 37	79 05	85·6	23 32	77 59	85·1	204	336
25	155	24 51	83 23	87·2	24 48	82 17	86·7	24 44	81 11	86·3	24 40	80 05	85·8	24 36	78 59	85·4	24 31	77 54	84·9	205	335
26	154	25 51	83 20	87·1	25 48	82 13	86·6	25 44	81 07	86·1	25 39	80 00	85·6	25 35	78 54	85·2	25 29	77 48	84·7	206	334
27	153	26 50	83 16	87·0	26 47	82 09	86·4	26 43	81 02	85·9	26 38	79 55	85·4	26 33	78 48	84·9	26 28	77 42	84·4	207	333
28	152	27 50	83 13	86·8	27 46	82 05	86·3	27 42	80 57	85·8	27 38	79 50	85·2	27 32	78 42	84·7	27 27	77 35	84·2	208	332
29	151	28 50	83 09	86·7	28 46	82 01	86·1	28 41	80 52	85·6	28 37	79 44	85·0	28 31	78 36	84·5	28 25	77 28	84·0	209	331
30	150	29 49	83 05	86·5	29 45	81 56	86·0	29 41	80 47	85·4	29 36	79 38	84·8	29 30	78 29	84·3	29 24	77 21	83·7	210	330
31	149	30 49	83 01	86·4	30 45	81 51	85·8	30 40	80 41	85·2	30 35	79 32	84·6	30 29	78 23	84·0	30 22	77 13	83·5	211	329
32	148	31 48	82 56	86·3	31 44	81 46	85·6	31 39	80 35	85·0	31 34	79 25	84·4	31 27	78 15	83·8	31 21	77 05	83·2	212	328
33	147	32 48	82 51	86·1	32 43	81 40	85·5	32 38	80 29	84·8	32 33	79 18	84·2	32 26	78 08	83·6	32 19	76 57	82·9	213	327
34	146	33 47	82 46	86·0	33 43	81 35	85·3	33 37	80 23	84·6	33 32	79 11	84·0	33 25	78 00	83·3	33 18	76 48	82·7	214	326
35	145	34 47	82 41	85·8	34 42	81 29	85·1	34 37	80 16	84·4	34 30	79 03	83·7	34 24	77 51	83·1	34 16	76 39	82·4	215	325
36	144	35 46	82 36	85·7	35 41	81 22	84·9	35 36	80 09	84·2	35 29	78 55	83·5	35 22	77 42	82·8	35 14	76 29	82·1	216	324
37	143	36 46	82 30	85·5	36 41	81 16	84·8	36 35	80 01	84·0	36 28	78 47	83·3	36 21	77 33	82·5	36 13	76 19	81·8	217	323
38	142	37 45	82 24	85·3	37 40	81 09	84·6	37 34	79 53	83·8	37 27	78 38	83·0	37 19	77 23	82·3	37 11	76 09	81·5	218	322
39	141	38 45	82 18	85·2	38 39	81 01	84·4	38 33	79 45	83·6	38 26	78 29	82·8	38 18	77 13	82·0	38 09	75 57	81·2	219	321
40	140	39 44	82 11	85·0	39 39	80 54	84·2	39 32	79 36	83·3	39 25	78 19	82·5	39 16	77 02	81·7	39 07	75 46	80·9	220	320
41	139	40 44	82 04	84·8	40 38	80 46	84·0	40 31	79 27	83·1	40 23	78 09	82·3	40 15	76 51	81·4	40 05	75 33	80·6	221	319
42	138	41 43	81 57	84·6	41 37	80 37	83·7	41 30	79 17	82·9	41 22	77 58	82·0	41 13	76 39	81·1	41 04	75 21	80·3	222	318
43	137	42 42	81 49	84·4	42 36	80 28	83·5	42 29	79 07	82·6	42 21	77 47	81·7	42 12	76 27	80·8	42 02	75 07	79·9	223	317
44	136	43 42	81 41	84·2	43 35	80 19	83·3	43 28	78 57	82·3	43 19	77 35	81·4	43 10	76 14	80·5	43 00	74 53	79·6	224	316
45	135	44 41	81 33	84·0	44 34	80 09	83·1	44 27	78 46	82·1	44 18	77 22	81·1	44 08	76 00	80·1	43 57	74 38	79·2	225	315

Lat. / A		6°			7°			8°			9°			10°			11°			Lat. / A	
LHA/F		A/H	B/P	Z_1/Z_2	A/H	B/P	Z_1/Z_2	A/H	B/P	Z_1/Z_2	A/H	B/P	Z_1/Z_2	A/H	B/P	Z_1/Z_2	A/H	B/P	Z_1/Z_2	LHA	
°	°	° ′	° ′	°	° ′	° ′	°	° ′	° ′	°	° ′	° ′	°	° ′	° ′	°	° ′	° ′	°	°	°
45	135	44 41	81 33	84·0	44 34	80 09	83·1	44 27	78 46	82·1	44 18	77 22	81·1	44 08	76 00	80·1	43 57	74 38	79·2	225	315
46	134	45 41	81 24	83·8	45 34	79 59	82·8	45 26	78 34	81·8	45 16	77 09	80·8	45 06	75 45	79·8	44 55	74 22	78·8	226	314
47	133	46 40	81 14	83·6	46 33	79 48	82·6	46 24	78 21	81·5	46 15	76 56	80·5	46 04	75 30	79·5	45 53	74 05	78·4	227	313
48	132	47 39	81 04	83·4	47 32	79 36	82·3	47 23	78 08	81·2	47 13	76 41	80·1	47 03	75 14	79·1	46 51	73 48	78·0	228	312
49	131	48 38	80 54	83·1	48 31	79 24	82·0	48 22	77 55	80·9	48 12	76 26	79·8	48 01	74 57	78·7	47 48	73 30	77·6	229	311
50	130	49 38	80 43	82·9	49 30	79 11	81·7	49 20	77 40	80·6	49 10	76 09	79·4	48 58	74 40	78·3	48 46	73 10	77·2	230	310
51	129	50 37	80 31	82·6	50 29	78 58	81·4	50 19	77 25	80·2	50 08	75 52	79·1	49 56	74 21	77·9	49 43	72 50	76·7	231	309
52	128	51 36	80 19	82·4	51 27	78 43	81·1	51 18	77 08	79·9	51 06	75 34	78·7	50 54	74 01	77·5	50 40	72 29	76·3	232	308
53	127	52 35	80 06	82·1	52 26	78 28	80·8	52 16	76 51	79·5	52 04	75 15	78·3	51 52	73 40	77·0	51 37	72 06	75·8	233	307
54	126	53 34	79 52	81·8	53 25	78 12	80·5	53 14	76 33	79·2	53 02	74 55	77·8	52 49	73 18	76·6	52 35	71 42	75·3	234	306
55	125	54 33	79 37	81·5	54 24	77 55	80·1	54 13	76 14	78·8	54 00	74 34	77·4	53 47	72 55	76·1	53 31	71 17	74·8	235	305
56	124	55 32	79 21	81·2	55 22	77 37	79·8	55 11	75 54	78·3	54 58	74 11	76·9	54 44	72 30	75·6	54 28	70 50	74·2	236	304
57	123	56 31	79 05	80·9	56 21	77 18	79·4	56 09	75 32	77·9	55 56	73 47	76·5	55 41	72 04	75·0	55 25	70 22	73·6	237	303
58	122	57 30	78 47	80·5	57 19	76 57	79·0	57 07	75 09	77·4	56 53	73 22	75·9	56 38	71 36	74·5	56 21	69 51	73·0	238	302
59	121	58 29	78 28	80·1	58 18	76 35	78·5	58 05	74 44	77·0	57 51	72 54	75·4	57 35	71 06	73·9	57 17	69 19	72·4	239	301
60	120	59 28	78 08	79·7	59 16	76 12	78·1	59 03	74 18	76·4	58 48	72 25	74·8	58 32	70 34	73·3	58 13	68 45	71·7	240	300
61	119	60 26	77 46	79·3	60 14	75 47	77·6	60 01	73 50	75·9	59 45	71 54	74·2	59 28	70 01	72·6	59 09	68 09	71·0	241	299
62	118	61 25	77 23	78·9	61 12	75 21	77·1	60 58	73 20	75·3	60 42	71 21	73·6	60 24	69 25	71·9	60 05	67 31	70·3	242	298
63	117	62 23	76 58	78·4	62 10	74 52	76·5	61 56	72 48	74·7	61 39	70 46	72·9	61 20	68 46	71·2	61 00	66 49	69·5	243	297
64	116	63 22	76 31	77·9	63 08	74 21	76·0	62 53	72 13	74·1	62 35	70 08	72·2	62 16	68 05	70·4	61 55	66 05	68·6	244	296
65	115	64 20	76 02	77·4	64 06	73 48	75·4	63 50	71 36	73·4	63 32	69 27	71·5	63 12	67 21	69·6	62 50	65 18	67·7	245	295
66	114	65 18	75 31	76·8	65 03	73 12	74·7	64 47	70 56	72·6	64 28	68 43	70·6	64 07	66 34	68·7	63 44	64 27	66·8	246	294
67	113	66 16	74 57	76·2	66 01	72 33	74·0	65 43	70 13	71·8	65 23	67 56	69·8	65 02	65 43	67·8	64 38	63 33	65·8	247	293
68	112	67 14	74 20	75·5	66 58	71 51	73·2	66 40	69 26	71·0	66 19	67 05	68·8	65 56	64 48	66·7	65 32	62 35	64·7	248	292
69	111	68 12	73 39	74·8	67 55	71 05	72·4	67 36	68 35	70·1	67 14	66 09	67·8	66 50	63 48	65·7	66 25	61 31	63·6	249	291
70	110	69 09	72 55	74·0	68 51	70 15	71·5	68 31	67 40	69·1	68 09	65 09	66·7	67 44	62 44	64·5	67 17	60 23	62·3	250	290
71	109	70 07	72 06	73·1	69 48	69 20	70·5	69 27	66 39	68·0	69 03	64 03	65·6	68 37	61 34	63·2	68 09	59 10	61·0	251	289
72	108	71 03	71 13	72·2	70 44	68 20	69·4	70 21	65 33	66·8	69 57	62 52	64·3	69 29	60 17	61·9	69 00	57 50	59·6	252	288
73	107	72 00	70 14	71·1	71 39	67 13	68·3	71 16	64 20	65·5	70 50	61 33	62·9	70 21	58 54	60·4	69 50	56 23	58·0	253	287
74	106	72 56	69 08	70·0	72 34	65 59	67·0	72 09	62 59	64·1	71 42	60 07	61·4	71 12	57 24	58·8	70 40	54 49	56·4	254	286
75	105	73 52	67 54	68·7	73 29	64 37	65·5	73 03	61 30	62·6	72 34	58 32	59·7	72 02	55 44	57·1	71 28	53 06	54·5	255	285
76	104	74 48	66 31	67·3	74 23	63 05	64·0	73 55	59 51	60·8	73 24	56 47	57·9	72 51	53 55	55·1	72 16	51 13	52·6	256	284
77	103	75 42	64 57	65·6	75 16	61 22	62·2	74 46	58 00	58·9	74 14	54 51	55·9	73 39	51 55	53·1	73 02	49 10	50·4	257	283
78	102	76 36	63 11	63·8	76 08	59 26	60·2	75 37	55 57	56·8	75 02	52 42	53·6	74 26	49 42	50·8	73 47	46 56	48·1	258	282
79	101	77 29	61 09	61·7	76 59	57 14	57·9	76 26	53 38	54·4	75 49	50 18	51·2	75 11	47 16	48·2	74 30	44 28	45·5	259	281
80	100	78 21	58 49	59·3	77 49	54 44	55·3	77 13	51 01	51·7	76 35	47 38	48·4	75 54	44 34	45·4	75 11	41 47	42·7	260	280
81	99	79 12	56 06	56·6	78 37	51 52	52·4	77 59	48 04	48·7	77 18	44 39	45·4	76 35	41 35	42·4	75 49	38 50	39·7	261	279
82	98	80 01	52 56	53·4	79 23	48 35	49·1	78 42	44 43	45·3	77 59	41 18	41·9	77 13	38 17	39·0	76 26	35 36	36·4	262	278
83	97	80 47	49 13	49·6	80 07	44 47	45·2	79 23	40 56	41·4	78 37	37 35	38·1	77 49	34 39	35·3	76 59	32 05	32·8	263	277
84	96	81 31	44 51	45·2	80 47	40 24	40·8	80 01	36 38	37·1	79 12	33 25	33·9	78 21	30 40	31·2	77 29	28 16	28·8	264	276
85	95	82 12	39 40	39·9	81 24	35 22	35·7	80 34	31 48	32·2	79 43	28 49	29·2	78 50	26 18	26·7	77 56	24 09	24·6	265	275
86	94	82 48	33 34	33·8	81 57	29 36	29·8	81 04	26 24	26·7	80 09	23 46	24·1	79 14	21 35	21·9	78 18	19 44	20·1	266	274
87	93	83 18	26 28	26·6	82 23	23 05	23·3	81 28	20 25	20·6	80 31	18 17	18·5	79 34	16 32	16·8	78 36	15 04	15·4	267	273
88	92	83 41	18 22	18·5	82 43	15 52	16·0	81 45	13 57	14·1	80 47	12 26	12·6	79 48	11 12	11·4	78 49	10 11	10·4	268	272
89	91	83 55	9 26	9·5	82 56	8 05	8·2	81 56	7 05	7·1	80 57	6 17	6·4	79 57	5 39	5·7	78 57	5 08	5·2	269	271
90	90	84 00	0 00	0·0	83 00	0 00	0·0	82 00	0 00	0·0	81 00	0 00	0·0	80 00	0 00	0·0	79 00	0 00	0·0	270	270

N. Lat: for LHA > 180° … $Z_n = Z$
for LHA < 180° … $Z_n = 360° - Z$

S. Lat.: for LHA > 180° … $Z_n = 180° - Z$
for LHA < 180° … $Z_n = 180° + Z$

SIGHT REDUCTION TABLE

B: (−) for 90° < LHA < 270°
Dec:(−) for Lat. contrary name

Z_1: same sign as B
Z_2: (−) for F > 90°

Lat. / A		12°			13°			14°			15°			16°			17°			Lat. / A	
LHA/F		A/H	B/P	Z_1/Z_2	A/H	B/P	Z_1/Z_2	A/H	B/P	Z_1/Z_2	A/H	B/P	Z_1/Z_2	A/H	B/P	Z_1/Z_2	A/H	B/P	Z_1/Z_2	LHA	
°	°	° ′	° ′	°	° ′	° ′	°	° ′	° ′	°	° ′	° ′	°	° ′	° ′	°	° ′	° ′	°	°	°
0	180	0 00	78 00	90·0	0 00	77 00	90·0	0 00	76 00	90·0	0 00	75 00	90·0	0 00	74 00	90·0	0 00	73 00	90·0	180	360
1	179	0 59	78 00	89·8	0 58	77 00	89·8	0 58	76 00	89·8	0 58	75 00	89·7	0 58	74 00	89·7	0 57	73 00	89·7	181	359
2	178	1 57	78 00	89·6	1 57	77 00	89·5	1 56	76 00	89·5	1 56	74 59	89·5	1 55	73 59	89·4	1 55	72 59	89·4	182	358
3	177	2 56	77 59	89·4	2 55	76 59	89·3	2 55	75 59	89·3	2 54	74 59	89·2	2 53	73 59	89·2	2 52	72 59	89·1	183	357
4	176	3 55	77 58	89·2	3 54	76 58	89·1	3 53	75 58	89·0	3 52	74 58	89·0	3 51	73 58	88·9	3 49	72 58	88·8	184	356
5	175	4 53	77 57	89·0	4 52	76 57	88·9	4 51	75 57	88·8	4 50	74 57	88·7	4 48	73 57	88·6	4 47	72 56	88·5	185	355
6	174	5 52	77 56	88·7	5 51	76 56	88·6	5 49	75 56	88·5	5 48	74 55	88·4	5 46	73 55	88·3	5 44	72 55	88·2	186	354
7	173	6 51	77 55	88·5	6 49	76 54	88·4	6 47	75 54	88·3	6 46	74 54	88·2	6 44	73 53	88·1	6 42	72 53	87·9	187	353
8	172	7 49	77 53	88·3	7 48	76 53	88·2	7 46	75 52	88·1	7 44	74 52	87·9	7 41	73 51	87·8	7 39	72 51	87·6	188	352
9	171	8 48	77 51	88·1	8 46	76 51	88·0	8 44	75 50	87·8	8 41	74 49	87·7	8 39	73 49	87·5	8 36	72 48	87·3	189	351
10	170	9 47	77 49	87·9	9 44	76 48	87·7	9 42	75 48	87·6	9 39	74 47	87·4	9 37	73 46	87·2	9 34	72 45	87·0	190	350
11	169	10 45	77 47	87·7	10 43	76 46	87·5	10 40	75 45	87·3	10 37	74 44	87·1	10 34	73 43	86·9	10 31	72 42	86·7	191	349
12	168	11 44	77 44	87·5	11 41	76 43	87·3	11 38	75 42	87·1	11 35	74 41	86·9	11 32	73 40	86·6	11 28	72 39	86·4	192	348
13	167	12 43	77 42	87·3	12 40	76 40	87·0	12 36	75 39	86·8	12 33	74 37	86·6	12 29	73 36	86·4	12 25	72 35	86·1	193	347
14	166	13 41	77 39	87·0	13 38	76 37	86·8	13 35	75 35	86·5	13 31	74 34	86·3	13 27	73 32	86·1	13 23	72 31	85·8	194	346
15	165	14 40	77 35	86·8	14 36	76 33	86·6	14 33	75 32	86·3	14 29	74 30	86·0	14 24	73 28	85·8	14 20	72 26	85·5	195	345
16	164	15 38	77 32	86·6	15 35	76 30	86·3	15 31	75 28	86·0	15 26	74 25	85·8	15 22	73 23	85·5	15 17	72 21	85·2	196	344
17	163	16 37	77 28	86·4	16 33	76 26	86·1	16 29	75 23	85·8	16 24	74 21	85·5	16 19	73 19	85·2	16 14	72 16	84·9	197	343
18	162	17 36	77 24	86·1	17 31	76 21	85·8	17 27	75 19	85·5	17 22	74 16	85·2	17 17	73 13	84·9	17 11	72 11	84·6	198	342
19	161	18 34	77 20	85·9	18 30	76 17	85·6	18 25	75 14	85·2	18 20	74 11	84·9	18 14	73 08	84·6	18 08	72 05	84·3	199	341
20	160	19 33	77 15	85·7	19 28	76 12	85·3	19 23	75 08	85·0	19 17	74 05	84·6	19 12	73 02	84·3	19 05	71 59	83·9	200	340
21	159	20 31	77 10	85·4	20 26	76 07	85·1	20 21	75 03	84·7	20 15	73 59	84·3	20 09	72 56	84·0	20 03	71 52	83·6	201	339
22	158	21 30	77 05	85·2	21 24	76 01	84·8	21 19	74 57	84·4	21 13	73 53	84·0	21 06	72 49	83·6	21 00	71 45	83·3	202	338
23	157	22 28	77 00	85·0	22 23	75 55	84·5	22 17	74 51	84·1	22 10	73 46	83·7	22 04	72 42	83·3	21 56	71 38	82·9	203	337
24	156	23 27	76 54	84·7	23 21	75 49	84·3	23 15	74 44	83·9	23 08	73 39	83·4	23 01	72 34	83·0	22 53	71 30	82·6	204	336
25	155	24 25	76 48	84·5	24 19	75 43	84·0	24 13	74 37	83·6	24 06	73 32	83·1	23 58	72 27	82·7	23 50	71 22	82·2	205	335
26	154	25 23	76 42	84·2	25 17	75 36	83·7	25 10	74 30	83·3	25 03	73 24	82·8	24 55	72 18	82·3	24 47	71 13	81·9	206	334
27	153	26 22	76 35	84·0	26 15	75 28	83·5	26 08	74 22	83·0	26 01	73 16	82·5	25 52	72 10	82·0	25 44	71 04	81·5	207	333
28	152	27 20	76 28	83·7	27 13	75 21	83·2	27 06	74 14	82·7	26 58	73 07	82·2	26 50	72 00	81·7	26 41	70 54	81·2	208	332
29	151	28 18	76 20	83·4	28 11	75 13	82·9	28 04	74 05	82·4	27 55	72 58	81·8	27 47	71 51	81·3	27 37	70 44	80·8	209	331
30	150	29 17	76 13	83·2	29 09	75 04	82·6	29 01	73 56	82·0	28 53	72 48	81·5	28 44	71 41	81·0	28 34	70 33	80·4	210	330
31	149	30 15	76 04	82·9	30 07	74 56	82·3	29 59	73 47	81·7	29 50	72 38	81·2	29 41	71 30	80·6	29 30	70 22	80·0	211	329
32	148	31 13	75 56	82·6	31 05	74 46	82·0	30 57	73 37	81·4	30 47	72 28	80·8	30 37	71 19	80·2	30 27	70 11	79·6	212	328
33	147	32 11	75 47	82·3	32 03	74 37	81·7	31 54	73 27	81·1	31 44	72 17	80·5	31 34	71 07	79·9	31 23	69 58	79·2	213	327
34	146	33 10	75 37	82·0	33 01	74 26	81·4	32 52	73 16	80·7	32 42	72 05	80·1	32 31	70 55	79·5	32 20	69 45	78·8	214	326
35	145	34 08	75 27	81·7	33 59	74 16	81·0	33 49	73 04	80·4	33 39	71 53	79·7	33 28	70 42	79·1	33 16	69 32	78·4	215	325
36	144	35 06	75 17	81·4	34 56	74 04	80·7	34 46	72 52	80·0	34 36	71 40	79·4	34 24	70 29	78·7	34 12	69 18	78·0	216	324
37	143	36 04	75 06	81·1	35 54	73 53	80·4	35 44	72 40	79·7	35 33	71 27	79·0	35 21	70 15	78·3	35 08	69 03	77·6	217	323
38	142	37 02	74 54	80·8	36 52	73 40	80·0	36 41	72 27	79·3	36 29	71 13	78·6	36 17	70 00	77·8	36 04	68 48	77·1	218	322
39	141	38 00	74 42	80·4	37 49	73 27	79·7	37 38	72 13	78·9	37 26	70 59	78·2	37 13	69 45	77·4	37 00	68 32	76·7	219	321
40	140	38 57	74 30	80·1	38 47	73 14	79·3	38 35	71 58	78·5	38 23	70 43	77·7	38 10	69 29	77·0	37 56	68 15	76·2	220	320
41	139	39 55	74 16	79·8	39 44	72 59	78·9	39 32	71 43	78·1	39 19	70 27	77·3	39 06	69 12	76·5	38 51	67 57	75·7	221	319
42	138	40 53	74 02	79·4	40 41	72 45	78·5	40 29	71 27	77·7	40 16	70 10	76·9	40 02	68 54	76·1	39 47	67 38	75·3	222	318
43	137	41 51	73 48	79·0	41 39	72 29	78·2	41 26	71 11	77·3	41 12	69 53	76·4	40 58	68 35	75·6	40 42	67 19	74·7	223	317
44	136	42 48	73 32	78·6	42 36	72 12	77·7	42 23	70 53	76·9	42 09	69 34	76·0	41 54	68 16	75·1	41 38	66 58	74·2	224	316
45	135	43 46	73 16	78·3	43 33	71 55	77·3	43 19	70 35	76·4	43 05	69 15	75·5	42 49	67 56	74·6	42 33	66 37	73·7	225	315

Lat. / A		12°			13°			14°			15°			16°			17°			Lat. / A	
LHA/F		A/H	B/P	Z_1/Z_2	A/H	B/P	Z_1/Z_2	A/H	B/P	Z_1/Z_2	A/H	B/P	Z_1/Z_2	A/H	B/P	Z_1/Z_2	A/H	B/P	Z_1/Z_2	LHA	
°	°	° ′	° ′	°	° ′	° ′	°	° ′	° ′	°	° ′	° ′	°	° ′	° ′	°	° ′	° ′	°	°	°
45	135	43 46	73 16	78·3	43 33	71 55	77·3	43 19	70 35	76·4	43 05	69 15	75·5	42 49	67 56	74·6	42 33	66 37	73·7	225	315
46	134	44 43	72 59	77·8	44 30	71 37	76·9	44 16	70 15	75·9	44 01	68 54	75·0	43 45	67 34	74·1	43 28	66 15	73·2	226	314
47	133	45 40	72 41	77·4	45 27	71 18	76·4	45 12	69 55	75·5	44 57	68 33	74·5	44 40	67 12	73·5	44 23	65 51	72·6	227	313
48	132	46 38	72 23	77·0	46 24	70 58	76·0	46 09	69 34	75·0	45 53	68 11	74·0	45 35	66 48	73·0	45 17	65 27	72·0	228	312
49	131	47 35	72 03	76·5	47 20	70 37	75·5	47 05	69 11	74·4	46 48	67 47	73·4	46 30	66 23	72·4	46 12	65 01	71·4	229	311
50	130	48 32	71 42	76·1	48 17	70 15	75·0	48 01	68 48	73·9	47 44	67 22	72·9	47 25	65 58	71·8	47 06	64 34	70·8	230	310
51	129	49 29	71 20	75·6	49 13	69 51	74·5	48 57	68 23	73·4	48 39	66 56	72·3	48 20	65 30	71·2	48 00	64 05	70·1	231	309
52	128	50 25	70 57	75·1	50 09	69 27	73·9	49 52	67 57	72·8	49 34	66 29	71·7	49 15	65 02	70·6	48 54	63 35	69·5	232	308
53	127	51 22	70 33	74·6	51 06	69 01	73·4	50 48	67 30	72·2	50 29	66 00	71·0	50 09	64 31	69·9	49 48	63 04	68·8	233	307
54	126	52 19	70 07	74·0	52 02	68 33	72·8	51 43	67 01	71·6	51 24	65 30	70·4	51 03	64 00	69·2	50 41	62 31	68·1	234	306
55	125	53 15	69 40	73·5	52 57	68 04	72·2	52 38	66 30	70·9	52 18	64 58	69·7	51 57	63 26	68·5	51 34	61 56	67·3	235	305
56	124	54 11	69 11	72·9	53 53	67 34	71·6	53 33	65 58	70·3	53 12	64 24	69·0	52 50	62 51	67·8	52 27	61 20	66·6	236	304
57	123	55 07	68 41	72·2	54 48	67 02	70·9	54 28	65 24	69·6	54 06	63 48	68·3	53 43	62 14	67·0	53 19	60 42	65·8	237	303
58	122	56 03	68 09	71·6	55 43	66 28	70·2	55 22	64 48	68·8	55 00	63 11	67·5	54 36	61 35	66·2	54 12	60 01	64·9	238	302
59	121	56 59	67 34	70·9	56 38	65 51	69·5	56 16	64 10	68·1	55 53	62 31	66·7	55 29	60 54	65·4	55 03	59 18	64·1	239	301
60	120	57 54	66 58	70·2	57 33	65 13	68·7	57 10	63 30	67·3	56 46	61 49	65·9	56 21	60 10	64·5	55 55	58 33	63·1	240	300
61	119	58 49	66 20	69·4	58 27	64 32	67·9	58 04	62 47	66·4	57 39	61 04	65·0	57 13	59 24	63·6	56 46	57 46	62·2	241	299
62	118	59 44	65 38	68·6	59 21	63 49	67·1	58 57	62 02	65·5	58 31	60 17	64·0	58 05	58 35	62·6	57 36	56 56	61·2	242	298
63	117	60 38	64 55	67·8	60 15	63 03	66·2	59 50	61 13	64·6	59 23	59 27	63·1	58 55	57 43	61·6	58 26	56 03	60·2	243	297
64	116	61 32	64 08	66·9	61 08	62 14	65·2	60 42	60 22	63·6	60 15	58 34	62·0	59 46	56 49	60·5	59 16	55 06	59·1	244	296
65	115	62 26	63 18	66·0	62 01	61 21	64·2	61 34	59 28	62·6	61 06	57 37	61·0	60 36	55 51	59·4	60 05	54 07	57·9	245	295
66	114	63 20	62 25	65·0	62 53	60 25	63·2	62 26	58 30	61·5	61 56	56 37	59·8	61 25	54 49	58·2	60 53	53 04	56·7	246	294
67	113	64 13	61 27	63·9	63 45	59 25	62·1	63 16	57 27	60·3	62 46	55 34	58·6	62 14	53 44	57·0	61 41	51 57	55·4	247	293
68	112	65 05	60 26	62·8	64 37	58 21	60·9	64 07	56 21	59·1	63 35	54 25	57·4	63 02	52 34	55·7	62 27	50 47	54·1	248	292
69	111	65 57	59 20	61·6	65 27	57 13	59·6	64 56	55 10	57·8	64 23	53 13	56·0	63 49	51 20	54·3	63 14	49 32	52·7	249	291
70	110	66 48	58 08	60·3	66 18	55 59	58·3	65 45	53 55	56·4	65 11	51 55	54·6	64 36	50 01	52·9	63 59	48 12	51·2	250	290
71	109	67 39	56 52	58·9	67 07	54 40	56·8	66 33	52 33	54·9	65 58	50 33	53·1	65 21	48 38	51·3	64 43	46 48	49·7	251	289
72	108	68 29	55 29	57·4	67 55	53 14	55·3	67 20	51 06	53·3	66 44	49 04	51·5	66 06	47 08	49·7	65 26	45 18	48·0	252	288
73	107	69 18	53 59	55·8	68 43	51 42	53·7	68 07	49 33	51·6	67 29	47 30	49·8	66 49	45 33	48·0	66 08	43 43	46·3	253	287
74	106	70 06	52 22	54·1	69 30	50 03	51·9	68 52	47 52	49·8	68 12	45 49	47·9	67 31	43 52	46·1	66 49	42 02	44·4	254	286
75	105	70 53	50 36	52·2	70 15	48 16	50·0	69 36	46 04	47·9	68 55	44 00	46·0	68 12	42 04	44·2	67 29	40 15	42·5	255	285
76	104	71 38	48 42	50·2	70 59	46 20	47·9	70 18	44 08	45·9	69 36	42 05	43·9	68 52	40 09	42·1	68 07	38 21	40·5	256	284
77	103	72 23	46 37	48·0	71 42	44 15	45·7	70 59	42 03	43·7	70 15	40 01	41·7	69 30	38 07	39·9	68 43	36 21	38·3	257	283
78	102	73 06	44 22	45·6	72 23	42 00	43·4	71 38	39 49	41·3	70 53	37 49	39·4	70 06	35 57	37·6	69 18	34 13	36·0	258	282
79	101	73 47	41 55	43·1	73 02	39 34	40·8	72 16	37 26	38·8	71 28	35 27	36·9	70 40	33 38	35·2	69 50	31 58	33·6	259	281
80	100	74 26	39 15	40·3	73 39	36 57	38·1	72 51	34 51	36·1	72 02	32 57	34·3	71 12	31 12	32·6	70 21	29 36	31·1	260	280
81	99	75 02	36 21	37·3	74 14	34 07	35·1	73 24	32 06	33·2	72 34	30 17	31·5	71 42	28 37	29·9	70 50	27 06	28·4	261	279
82	98	75 37	33 13	34·1	74 46	31 05	32·0	73 55	29 10	30·2	73 03	27 27	28·5	72 09	25 53	27·0	71 16	24 29	25·7	262	278
83	97	76 08	29 50	30·6	75 16	27 50	28·6	74 23	26 03	26·9	73 29	24 27	25·4	72 34	23 02	24·0	71 39	21 44	22·8	263	277
84	96	76 36	26 11	26·8	75 42	24 22	25·0	74 48	22 45	23·5	73 52	21 19	22·1	72 56	20 02	20·9	72 00	18 53	19·8	264	276
85	95	77 01	22 18	22·8	76 05	20 41	21·3	75 09	19 16	19·9	74 12	18 01	18·7	73 15	16 54	17·6	72 18	15 55	16·7	265	275
86	94	77 22	18 10	18·6	76 25	16 49	17·3	75 27	15 38	16·1	74 29	14 36	15·1	73 31	13 40	14·2	72 33	12 51	13·5	266	274
87	93	77 38	13 50	14·1	76 40	12 46	13·1	75 41	11 51	12·2	74 43	11 03	11·4	73 44	10 21	10·8	72 45	9 43	10·2	267	273
88	92	77 50	9 19	9·5	76 51	8 36	8·8	75 52	7 58	8·2	74 52	7 25	7·7	73 53	6 56	7·2	72 53	6 31	6·8	268	272
89	91	77 58	4 42	4·8	76 58	4 19	4·4	75 58	4 00	4·1	74 58	3 44	3·9	73 58	3 29	3·6	72 58	3 16	3·4	269	271
90	90	78 00	0 00	0·0	77 00	0 00	0·0	76 00	0 00	0·0	75 00	0 00	0·0	74 00	0 00	0·0	73 00	0 00	0·0	270	270

N. Lat: for LHA > 180° … $Z_n = Z$
for LHA < 180° … $Z_n = 360° - Z$

S. Lat.: for LHA > 180° … $Z_n = 180° - Z$
for LHA < 180° … $Z_n = 180° + Z$

SIGHT REDUCTION TABLE

B: (−) for 90° < LHA < 270°
Dec:(−) for Lat. contrary name

Z_1: same sign as B
Z_2: (−) for F > 90°

Lat. / A		18°			19°			20°			21°			22°			23°			Lat. / A	
LHA/F		A/H	B/P	Z_1/Z_2	A/H	B/P	Z_1/Z_2	A/H	B/P	Z_1/Z_2	A/H	B/P	Z_1/Z_2	A/H	B/P	Z_1/Z_2	A/H	B/P	Z_1/Z_2	LHA	
°	°	° ′	° ′	°	° ′	° ′	°	° ′	° ′	°	° ′	° ′	°	° ′	° ′	°	° ′	° ′	°	°	°
0	180	0 00	72 00	90·0	0 00	71 00	90·0	0 00	70 00	90·0	0 00	69 00	90·0	0 00	68 00	90·0	0 00	67 00	90·0	180	360
1	179	0 57	72 00	89·7	0 57	71 00	89·7	0 56	70 00	89·7	0 56	69 00	89·6	0 56	68 00	89·6	0 55	67 00	89·6	181	359
2	178	1 54	71 59	89·4	1 53	70 59	89·3	1 53	69 59	89·3	1 52	68 59	89·3	1 51	67 59	89·3	1 50	66 59	89·2	182	358
3	177	2 51	71 59	89·1	2 50	70 59	89·0	2 49	69 58	89·0	2 48	68 58	88·9	2 47	67 58	88·9	2 46	66 58	88·8	183	357
4	176	3 48	71 58	88·8	3 47	70 57	88·7	3 46	69 57	88·6	3 44	68 57	88·6	3 42	67 57	88·5	3 41	66 57	88·4	184	356
5	175	4 45	71 56	88·5	4 44	70 56	88·4	4 42	69 56	88·3	4 40	68 56	88·2	4 38	67 55	88·1	4 36	66 55	88·0	185	355
6	174	5 42	71 54	88·1	5 40	70 54	88·0	5 38	69 54	87·9	5 36	68 54	87·8	5 34	67 53	87·7	5 31	66 53	87·6	186	354
7	173	6 39	71 52	87·8	6 37	70 52	87·7	6 35	69 52	87·6	6 32	68 51	87·5	6 29	67 51	87·4	6 26	66 51	87·3	187	353
8	172	7 36	71 50	87·5	7 34	70 50	87·4	7 31	69 49	87·2	7 28	68 49	87·1	7 25	67 48	87·0	7 22	66 48	86·9	188	352
9	171	8 33	71 47	87·2	8 30	70 47	87·0	8 27	69 46	86·9	8 24	68 46	86·8	8 20	67 45	86·6	8 17	66 45	86·5	189	351
10	170	9 30	71 44	86·9	9 27	70 44	86·7	9 23	69 43	86·5	9 20	68 42	86·4	9 16	67 42	86·2	9 12	66 41	86·1	190	350
11	169	10 27	71 41	86·6	10 24	70 40	86·4	10 20	69 39	86·2	10 16	68 39	86·0	10 11	67 38	85·8	10 07	66 37	85·7	191	349
12	168	11 24	71 37	86·2	11 20	70 36	86·0	11 16	69 35	85·8	11 12	68 34	85·6	11 07	67 33	85·4	11 02	66 32	85·3	192	348
13	167	12 21	71 33	85·9	12 17	70 32	85·7	12 12	69 31	85·5	12 07	68 30	85·3	12 02	67 29	85·1	11 57	66 28	84·8	193	347
14	166	13 18	71 29	85·6	13 13	70 28	85·4	13 08	69 26	85·1	13 03	68 25	84·9	12 58	67 24	84·7	12 52	66 22	84·4	194	346
15	165	14 15	71 24	85·3	14 10	70 23	85·0	14 05	69 21	84·8	13 59	68 20	84·5	13 53	67 18	84·3	13 47	66 17	84·0	195	345
16	164	15 12	71 19	84·9	15 06	70 18	84·7	15 01	69 16	84·4	14 55	68 14	84·1	14 48	67 12	83·9	14 42	66 10	83·6	196	344
17	163	16 09	71 14	84·6	16 03	70 12	84·3	15 57	69 10	84·0	15 50	68 08	83·7	15 44	67 06	83·5	15 37	66 04	83·2	197	343
18	162	17 05	71 08	84·3	16 59	70 06	84·0	16 53	69 03	83·7	16 46	68 01	83·4	16 39	66 59	83·1	16 32	65 57	82·8	198	342
19	161	18 02	71 02	83·9	17 56	69 59	83·6	17 49	68 57	83·3	17 42	67 54	83·0	17 34	66 52	82·7	17 26	65 49	82·3	199	341
20	160	18 59	70 56	83·6	18 52	69 53	83·2	18 45	68 50	82·9	18 37	67 47	82·6	18 29	66 44	82·2	18 21	65 41	81·9	200	340
21	159	19 56	70 49	83·2	19 48	69 45	82·9	19 41	68 42	82·5	19 33	67 39	82·2	19 24	66 36	81·8	19 16	65 33	81·5	201	339
22	158	20 52	70 41	82·9	20 45	69 38	82·5	20 37	68 34	82·1	20 28	67 31	81·8	20 19	66 27	81·4	20 10	65 24	81·0	202	338
23	157	21 49	70 33	82·5	21 41	69 29	82·1	21 32	68 26	81·7	21 24	67 22	81·4	21 14	66 18	81·0	21 05	65 15	80·6	203	337
24	156	22 45	70 25	82·2	22 37	69 21	81·8	22 28	68 17	81·3	22 19	67 12	80·9	22 09	66 09	80·5	21 59	65 05	80·1	204	336
25	155	23 42	70 17	81·8	23 33	69 12	81·4	23 24	68 07	80·9	23 14	67 03	80·5	23 04	65 58	80·1	22 54	64 54	79·7	205	335
26	154	24 38	70 07	81·4	24 29	69 02	81·0	24 20	67 57	80·5	24 09	66 52	80·1	23 59	65 48	79·6	23 48	64 43	79·2	206	334
27	153	25 35	69 58	81·1	25 25	68 52	80·6	25 15	67 47	80·1	25 05	66 42	79·7	24 54	65 36	79·2	24 42	64 32	78·7	207	333
28	152	26 31	69 48	80·7	26 21	68 42	80·2	26 11	67 36	79·7	26 00	66 30	79·2	25 48	65 25	78·7	25 36	64 19	78·3	208	332
29	151	27 27	69 37	80·3	27 17	68 31	79·8	27 06	67 24	79·3	26 55	66 18	78·8	26 43	65 12	78·3	26 30	64 07	77·8	209	331
30	150	28 24	69 26	79·9	28 13	68 19	79·4	28 01	67 12	78·8	27 50	66 06	78·3	27 37	64 59	77·8	27 24	63 53	77·3	210	330
31	149	29 20	69 14	79·5	29 09	68 07	78·9	28 57	67 00	78·4	28 44	65 53	77·8	28 31	64 46	77·3	28 18	63 39	76·8	211	329
32	148	30 16	69 02	79·1	30 04	67 54	78·5	29 52	66 46	77·9	29 39	65 39	77·4	29 26	64 32	76·8	29 12	63 25	76·3	212	328
33	147	31 12	68 49	78·7	31 00	67 41	78·1	30 47	66 32	77·5	30 34	65 24	76·9	30 20	64 17	76·3	30 05	63 09	75·8	213	327
34	146	32 08	68 36	78·2	31 55	67 27	77·6	31 42	66 18	77·0	31 28	65 09	76·4	31 14	64 01	75·8	30 59	62 53	75·2	214	326
35	145	33 04	68 22	77·8	32 51	67 12	77·2	32 37	66 03	76·5	32 23	64 54	75·9	32 08	63 45	75·3	31 52	62 36	74·7	215	325
36	144	33 59	68 07	77·3	33 46	66 57	76·7	33 32	65 47	76·0	33 17	64 37	75·4	33 01	63 28	74·8	32 45	62 19	74·2	216	324
37	143	34 55	67 52	76·9	34 41	66 41	76·2	34 26	65 30	75·5	34 11	64 20	74·9	33 55	63 10	74·2	33 38	62 01	73·6	217	323
38	142	35 50	67 36	76·4	35 36	66 24	75·7	35 21	65 13	75·0	35 05	64 02	74·4	34 48	62 51	73·7	34 31	61 41	73·0	218	322
39	141	36 46	67 19	76·0	36 31	66 06	75·2	36 15	64 54	74·5	35 59	63 43	73·8	35 42	62 32	73·1	35 24	61 21	72·4	219	321
40	140	37 41	67 01	75·5	37 26	65 48	74·7	37 10	64 35	74·0	36 53	63 23	73·3	36 35	62 12	72·6	36 17	61 01	71·8	220	320
41	139	38 36	66 42	75·0	38 20	65 29	74·2	38 04	64 15	73·4	37 46	63 02	72·7	37 28	61 50	72·0	37 09	60 39	71·2	221	319
42	138	39 31	66 23	74·5	39 15	65 08	73·7	38 58	63 54	72·9	38 40	62 41	72·1	38 21	61 28	71·4	38 01	60 16	70·6	222	318
43	137	40 26	66 03	73·9	40 09	64 47	73·1	39 51	63 33	72·3	39 33	62 18	71·5	39 13	61 05	70·7	38 53	59 52	70·0	223	317
44	136	41 21	65 42	73·4	41 03	64 25	72·5	40 45	63 10	71·7	40 26	61 55	70·9	40 06	60 41	70·1	39 45	59 27	69·3	224	316
45	135	42 16	65 19	72·8	41 57	64 02	72·0	41 38	62 46	71·1	41 19	61 30	70·3	40 58	60 15	69·5	40 37	59 01	68·7	225	315

Lat. / A		18°			19°			20°			21°			22°			23°			Lat. / A	
LHA/F		A/H	B/P	Z_1/Z_2	A/H	B/P	Z_1/Z_2	A/H	B/P	Z_1/Z_2	A/H	B/P	Z_1/Z_2	A/H	B/P	Z_1/Z_2	A/H	B/P	Z_1/Z_2	LHA	
°	°	° ′	° ′	°	° ′	° ′	°	° ′	° ′	°	° ′	° ′	°	° ′	° ′	°	° ′	° ′	°	°	°
45	135	42 16	65 19	72·8	41 57	64 02	72·0	41 38	62 46	71·1	41 19	61 30	70·3	40 58	60 15	69·5	40 37	59 01	68·7	225	315
46	134	43 10	64 56	72·3	42 51	63 38	71·4	42 32	62 21	70·5	42 11	61 05	69·6	41 50	59 49	68·8	41 28	58 34	68·0	226	314
47	133	44 04	64 32	71·7	43 45	63 13	70·8	43 25	61 55	69·9	43 04	60 38	69·0	42 42	59 21	68·1	42 19	58 06	67·3	227	313
48	132	44 58	64 06	71·1	44 38	62 46	70·1	44 18	61 27	69·2	43 56	60 09	68·3	43 33	58 53	67·4	43 10	57 37	66·5	228	312
49	131	45 52	63 39	70·4	45 32	62 18	69·5	45 10	60 59	68·5	44 48	59 40	67·6	44 24	58 22	66·7	44 00	57 06	65·8	229	311
50	130	46 46	63 11	69·8	46 25	61 49	68·8	46 03	60 29	67·8	45 39	59 09	66·9	45 15	57 51	65·9	44 50	56 34	65·0	230	310
51	129	47 39	62 42	69·1	47 17	61 19	68·1	46 55	59 57	67·1	46 31	58 37	66·1	46 06	57 18	65·2	45 40	56 00	64·2	231	309
52	128	48 33	62 11	68·4	48 10	60 47	67·4	47 46	59 25	66·4	47 22	58 03	65·4	46 56	56 44	64·4	46 30	55 25	63·4	232	308
53	127	49 25	61 38	67·7	49 02	60 13	66·6	48 38	58 50	65·6	48 13	57 28	64·6	47 46	56 07	63·6	47 19	54 48	62·6	233	307
54	126	50 18	61 04	67·0	49 54	59 38	65·9	49 29	58 14	64·8	49 03	56 51	63·7	48 36	55 30	62·7	48 08	54 10	61·7	234	306
55	125	51 10	60 28	66·2	50 46	59 01	65·1	50 20	57 36	64·0	49 53	56 12	62·9	49 25	54 50	61·9	48 56	53 30	60·8	235	305
56	124	52 03	59 50	65·4	51 37	58 23	64·2	51 10	56 56	63·1	50 43	55 32	62·0	50 14	54 09	61·0	49 44	52 48	59·9	236	304
57	123	52 54	59 11	64·6	52 28	57 42	63·4	52 00	56 15	62·2	51 32	54 49	61·1	51 02	53 26	60·0	50 32	52 04	59·0	237	303
58	122	53 46	58 29	63·7	53 18	56 59	62·5	52 50	55 31	61·3	52 21	54 05	60·2	51 50	52 41	59·1	51 19	51 18	58·0	238	302
59	121	54 37	57 45	62·8	54 08	56 14	61·5	53 39	54 45	60·4	53 09	53 18	59·2	52 38	51 53	58·1	52 06	50 30	57·0	239	301
60	120	55 27	56 59	61·8	54 58	55 27	60·6	54 28	53 57	59·4	53 57	52 29	58·2	53 25	51 04	57·0	52 52	49 40	55·9	240	300
61	119	56 17	56 10	60·9	55 47	54 37	59·6	55 16	53 06	58·3	54 44	51 38	57·1	54 11	50 12	55·9	53 37	48 48	54·8	241	299
62	118	57 07	55 19	59·8	56 36	53 45	58·5	56 04	52 13	57·2	55 31	50 44	56·0	54 57	49 17	54·8	54 22	47 53	53·7	242	298
63	117	57 56	54 25	58·8	57 24	52 49	57·4	56 51	51 17	56·1	56 17	49 47	54·9	55 42	48 20	53·7	55 06	46 55	52·5	243	297
64	116	58 44	53 27	57·6	58 12	51 51	56·3	57 38	50 18	55·0	57 03	48 48	53·7	56 27	47 20	52·5	55 50	45 55	51·3	244	296
65	115	59 32	52 27	56·5	58 58	50 50	55·1	58 24	49 16	53·7	57 47	47 45	52·5	57 10	46 17	51·2	56 32	44 52	50·0	245	295
66	114	60 19	51 23	55·2	59 45	49 45	53·8	59 09	48 11	52·5	58 32	46 39	51·2	57 53	45 11	49·9	57 14	43 47	48·7	246	294
67	113	61 06	50 15	53·9	60 30	48 37	52·5	59 53	47 02	51·1	59 15	45 30	49·8	58 36	44 02	48·6	57 55	42 38	47·4	247	293
68	112	61 52	49 04	52·6	61 15	47 25	51·1	60 36	45 50	49·8	59 57	44 18	48·4	59 17	42 50	47·2	58 36	41 26	46·0	248	292
69	111	62 37	47 48	51·2	61 58	46 09	49·7	61 19	44 33	48·3	60 39	43 02	47·0	59 57	41 34	45·7	59 15	40 10	44·5	249	291
70	110	63 21	46 28	49·7	62 41	44 48	48·2	62 01	43 13	46·8	61 19	41 42	45·4	60 36	40 15	44·2	59 53	38 52	43·0	250	290
71	109	64 04	45 03	48·1	63 23	43 24	46·6	62 41	41 49	45·2	61 58	40 18	43·9	61 15	38 52	42·6	60 30	37 29	41·4	251	289
72	108	64 45	43 34	46·4	64 04	41 54	44·9	63 21	40 20	43·5	62 37	38 50	42·2	61 52	37 25	40·9	61 06	36 03	39·7	252	288
73	107	65 26	41 59	44·7	64 43	40 20	43·2	63 59	38 46	41·8	63 14	37 18	40·5	62 27	35 53	39·2	61 41	34 34	38·0	253	287
74	106	66 06	40 19	42·9	65 21	38 41	41·4	64 36	37 08	40·0	63 49	35 41	38·7	63 02	34 18	37·4	62 14	33 00	36·3	254	286
75	105	66 44	38 32	40·9	65 58	36 56	39·5	65 11	35 25	38·1	64 23	33 59	36·8	63 35	32 39	35·6	62 46	31 22	34·4	255	285
76	104	67 20	36 40	38·9	66 33	35 05	37·4	65 45	33 37	36·1	64 56	32 13	34·8	64 07	30 55	33·6	63 16	29 41	32·5	256	284
77	103	67 55	34 42	36·8	67 07	33 09	35·3	66 18	31 43	34·0	65 27	30 22	32·8	64 37	29 06	31·6	63 45	27 55	30·6	257	283
78	102	68 29	32 37	34·5	67 39	31 07	33·1	66 48	29 44	31·9	65 57	28 26	30·7	65 05	27 14	29·6	64 13	26 06	28·5	258	282
79	101	69 00	30 25	32·2	68 09	29 00	30·8	67 17	27 40	29·6	66 25	26 26	28·5	65 32	25 17	27·4	64 38	24 12	26·4	259	281
80	100	69 29	28 07	29·7	68 37	26 46	28·4	67 44	25 30	27·3	66 50	24 20	26·2	65 56	23 15	25·2	65 02	22 15	24·3	260	280
81	99	69 57	25 43	27·1	69 03	24 26	25·9	68 09	23 15	24·8	67 14	22 10	23·8	66 19	21 10	22·9	65 23	20 14	22·1	261	279
82	98	70 21	23 11	24·5	69 27	22 00	23·3	68 31	20 56	22·3	67 36	19 56	21·4	66 40	19 00	20·6	65 43	18 09	19·8	262	278
83	97	70 44	20 34	21·7	69 48	19 29	20·7	68 51	18 31	19·7	67 55	17 37	18·9	66 58	16 47	18·1	66 01	16 01	17·4	263	277
84	96	71 03	17 50	18·8	70 07	16 53	17·9	69 09	16 01	17·1	68 12	15 14	16·3	67 14	14 30	15·7	66 16	13 50	15·1	264	276
85	95	71 20	15 01	15·8	70 23	14 12	15·0	69 25	13 28	14·3	68 26	12 48	13·7	67 28	12 10	13·1	66 29	11 36	12·6	265	275
86	94	71 35	12 07	12·8	70 36	11 27	12·1	69 37	10 51	11·6	68 38	10 18	11·0	67 39	9 48	10·6	66 40	9 20	10·1	266	274
87	93	71 46	9 09	9·6	70 46	8 39	9·1	69 47	8 11	8·7	68 48	7 46	8·3	67 48	7 23	8·0	66 49	7 02	7·6	267	273
88	92	71 54	6 08	6·4	70 54	5 47	6·1	69 54	5 29	5·8	68 55	5 12	5·6	67 55	4 56	5·3	66 55	4 42	5·1	268	272
89	91	71 58	3 04	3·2	70 58	2 54	3·1	69 59	2 45	2·9	68 59	2 36	2·8	67 59	2 28	2·7	66 59	2 21	2·6	269	271
90	90	72 00	0 00	0·0	71 00	0 00	0·0	70 00	0 00	0·0	69 00	0 00	0·0	68 00	0 00	0·0	67 00	0 00	0·0	270	270

N. Lat: for LHA > 180° … $Z_n = Z$
for LHA < 180° … $Z_n = 360° - Z$

S. Lat.: for LHA > 180° … $Z_n = 180° - Z$
for LHA < 180° … $Z_n = 180° + Z$

SIGHT REDUCTION TABLE

B: (−) for 90° < LHA < 270°
Dec:(−) for Lat. contrary name

Z_1: same sign as B
Z_2: (−) for F > 90°

Lat. / A		24°			25°			26°			27°			28°			29°			Lat. / A	
LHA/F		A/H	B/P	Z_1/Z_2	A/H	B/P	Z_1/Z_2	A/H	B/P	Z_1/Z_2	A/H	B/P	Z_1/Z_2	A/H	B/P	Z_1/Z_2	A/H	B/P	Z_1/Z_2	LHA	
°	°	° ′	° ′	°	° ′	° ′	°	° ′	° ′	°	° ′	° ′	°	° ′	° ′	°	° ′	° ′	°	°	°
0	180	0 00	66 00	90·0	0 00	65 00	90·0	0 00	64 00	90·0	0 00	63 00	90·0	0 00	62 00	90·0	0 00	61 00	90·0	180	360
1	179	0 55	66 00	89·6	0 54	65 00	89·6	0 54	64 00	89·6	0 53	63 00	89·5	0 53	62 00	89·5	0 52	61 00	89·5	181	359
2	178	1 50	65 59	89·2	1 49	64 59	89·2	1 48	63 59	89·1	1 47	62 59	89·1	1 46	61 59	89·1	1 45	60 59	89·0	182	358
3	177	2 44	65 58	88·8	2 43	64 58	88·7	2 42	63 58	88·7	2 40	62 58	88·6	2 39	61 58	88·6	2 37	60 58	88·5	183	357
4	176	3 39	65 57	88·4	3 37	64 57	88·3	3 36	63 57	88·2	3 34	62 57	88·2	3 32	61 57	88·1	3 30	60 56	88·1	184	356
5	175	4 34	65 55	88·0	4 32	64 55	87·9	4 30	63 55	87·8	4 27	62 55	87·7	4 25	61 55	87·6	4 22	60 54	87·6	185	355
6	174	5 29	65 53	87·6	5 26	64 53	87·5	5 23	63 53	87·4	5 21	62 52	87·3	5 18	61 52	87·2	5 15	60 52	87·1	186	354
7	173	6 24	65 50	87·1	6 20	64 50	87·0	6 17	63 50	86·9	6 14	62 50	86·8	6 11	61 49	86·7	6 07	60 49	86·6	187	353
8	172	7 18	65 47	86·7	7 15	64 47	86·6	7 11	63 47	86·5	7 07	62 46	86·3	7 04	61 46	86·2	6 59	60 46	86·1	188	352
9	171	8 13	65 44	86·3	8 09	64 44	86·2	8 05	63 43	86·0	8 01	62 43	85·9	7 56	61 42	85·7	7 52	60 42	85·6	189	351
10	170	9 08	65 40	85·9	9 03	64 40	85·7	8 59	63 39	85·6	8 54	62 39	85·4	8 49	61 38	85·3	8 44	60 38	85·1	190	350
11	169	10 02	65 36	85·5	9 57	64 35	85·3	9 52	63 35	85·1	9 47	62 34	85·0	9 42	61 33	84·8	9 36	60 33	84·6	191	349
12	168	10 57	65 32	85·1	10 52	64 31	84·9	10 46	63 30	84·7	10 41	62 29	84·5	10 35	61 28	84·3	10 29	60 28	84·1	192	348
13	167	11 52	65 27	84·6	11 46	64 26	84·4	11 40	63 25	84·2	11 34	62 24	84·0	11 27	61 23	83·8	11 21	60 22	83·6	193	347
14	166	12 46	65 21	84·2	12 40	64 20	84·0	12 34	63 19	83·8	12 27	62 18	83·5	12 20	61 17	83·3	12 13	60 16	83·1	194	346
15	165	13 41	65 15	83·8	13 34	64 14	83·5	13 27	63 13	83·3	13 20	62 11	83·1	13 13	61 10	82·8	13 05	60 09	82·6	195	345
16	164	14 35	65 09	83·3	14 28	64 07	83·1	14 21	63 06	82·8	14 13	62 04	82·6	14 05	61 03	82·3	13 57	60 02	82·1	196	344
17	163	15 29	65 02	82·9	15 22	64 00	82·6	15 14	62 59	82·4	15 06	61 57	82·1	14 58	60 56	81·8	14 49	59 54	81·6	197	343
18	162	16 24	64 55	82·5	16 16	63 53	82·2	16 08	62 51	81·9	15 59	61 49	81·6	15 50	60 47	81·3	15 41	59 46	81·0	198	342
19	161	17 18	64 47	82·0	17 10	63 45	81·7	17 01	62 43	81·4	16 52	61 41	81·1	16 42	60 39	80·8	16 33	59 37	80·5	199	341
20	160	18 12	64 39	81·6	18 03	63 36	81·3	17 54	62 34	80·9	17 45	61 32	80·6	17 35	60 30	80·3	17 24	59 28	80·0	200	340
21	159	19 07	64 30	81·1	18 57	63 28	80·8	18 47	62 25	80·4	18 37	61 23	80·1	18 27	60 20	79·8	18 16	59 18	79·5	201	339
22	158	20 01	64 21	80·7	19 51	63 18	80·3	19 41	62 15	80·0	19 30	61 13	79·6	19 19	60 10	79·3	19 08	59 08	78·9	202	338
23	157	20 55	64 11	80·2	20 44	63 08	79·8	20 34	62 05	79·5	20 22	61 02	79·1	20 11	59 59	78·7	19 59	58 57	78·4	203	337
24	156	21 49	64 01	79·7	21 38	62 58	79·3	21 27	61 54	79·0	21 15	60 51	78·6	21 03	59 48	78·2	20 50	58 45	77·8	204	336
25	155	22 43	63 50	79·3	22 31	62 46	78·9	22 19	61 43	78·4	22 07	60 39	78·0	21 55	59 36	77·7	21 42	58 33	77·3	205	335
26	154	23 36	63 39	78·8	23 25	62 35	78·4	23 12	61 31	77·9	22 59	60 27	77·5	22 46	59 24	77·1	22 33	58 20	76·7	206	334
27	153	24 30	63 27	78·3	24 18	62 22	77·8	24 05	61 18	77·4	23 52	60 14	77·0	23 38	59 10	76·5	23 24	58 07	76·1	207	333
28	152	25 24	63 14	77·8	25 11	62 10	77·3	24 57	61 05	76·9	24 44	60 01	76·4	24 29	58 57	76·0	24 15	57 53	75·5	208	332
29	151	26 17	63 01	77·3	26 04	61 56	76·8	25 50	60 51	76·3	25 36	59 47	75·9	25 21	58 42	75·4	25 05	57 38	75·0	209	331
30	150	27 11	62 48	76·8	26 57	61 42	76·3	26 42	60 37	75·8	26 27	59 32	75·3	26 12	58 27	74·8	25 56	57 23	74·4	210	330
31	149	28 04	62 33	76·3	27 50	61 27	75·8	27 35	60 22	75·2	27 19	59 16	74·7	27 03	58 11	74·2	26 46	57 07	73·8	211	329
32	148	28 57	62 18	75·7	28 42	61 12	75·2	28 27	60 06	74·7	28 10	59 00	74·2	27 54	57 55	73·7	27 37	56 50	73·1	212	328
33	147	29 50	62 02	75·2	29 35	60 56	74·7	29 19	59 49	74·1	29 02	58 43	73·6	28 45	57 38	73·0	28 27	56 32	72·5	213	327
34	146	30 43	61 46	74·7	30 27	60 39	74·1	30 10	59 32	73·5	29 53	58 26	73·0	29 35	57 20	72·4	29 17	56 14	71·9	214	326
35	145	31 36	61 28	74·1	31 19	60 21	73·5	31 02	59 14	72·9	30 44	58 07	72·4	30 26	57 01	71·8	30 07	55 55	71·2	215	325
36	144	32 29	61 10	73·5	32 11	60 02	72·9	31 53	58 55	72·3	31 35	57 48	71·7	31 16	56 41	71·2	30 56	55 35	70·6	216	324
37	143	33 21	60 52	73·0	33 03	59 43	72·3	32 45	58 35	71·7	32 26	57 28	71·1	32 06	56 21	70·5	31 46	55 14	69·9	217	323
38	142	34 13	60 32	72·4	33 55	59 23	71·7	33 36	58 15	71·1	33 16	57 07	70·5	32 56	55 59	69·9	32 35	54 53	69·3	218	322
39	141	35 06	60 11	71·8	34 47	59 02	71·1	34 27	57 53	70·5	34 06	56 45	69·8	33 45	55 37	69·2	33 24	54 30	68·6	219	321
40	140	35 58	59 50	71·2	35 38	58 40	70·5	35 17	57 31	69·8	34 56	56 22	69·1	34 35	55 14	68·5	34 12	54 07	67·9	220	320
41	139	36 49	59 28	70·5	36 29	58 17	69·8	36 08	57 08	69·1	35 46	55 59	68·5	35 24	54 50	67·8	35 01	53 42	67·1	221	319
42	138	37 41	59 04	69·9	37 20	57 54	69·2	36 58	56 43	68·5	36 36	55 34	67·8	36 13	54 25	67·1	35 49	53 17	66·4	222	318
43	137	38 32	58 40	69·2	38 11	57 29	68·5	37 48	56 18	67·8	37 25	55 08	67·1	37 02	53 59	66·4	36 37	52 50	65·7	223	317
44	136	39 23	58 15	68·6	39 01	57 03	67·8	38 38	55 52	67·1	38 14	54 41	66·3	37 50	53 32	65·6	37 25	52 23	64·9	224	316
45	135	40 14	57 48	67·9	39 51	56 36	67·1	39 28	55 24	66·3	39 03	54 13	65·6	38 38	53 04	64·9	38 12	51 54	64·1	225	315

Lat. / A		24°			25°			26°			27°			28°			29°			Lat. / A	
LHA/F		A/H	B/P	Z_1/Z_2	A/H	B/P	Z_1/Z_2	A/H	B/P	Z_1/Z_2	A/H	B/P	Z_1/Z_2	A/H	B/P	Z_1/Z_2	A/H	B/P	Z_1/Z_2	LHA	
°	°	° ′	° ′	°	° ′	° ′	°	° ′	° ′	°	° ′	° ′	°	° ′	° ′	°	° ′	° ′	°	°	°
45	135	40 14	57 48	67·9	39 51	56 36	67·1	39 28	55 24	66·3	39 03	54 13	65·6	38 38	53 04	64·9	38 12	51 54	64·1	225	315
46	134	41 05	57 21	67·2	40 41	56 08	66·4	40 17	54 56	65·6	39 52	53 44	64·8	39 26	52 34	64·1	38 59	51 25	63·3	226	314
47	133	41 55	56 52	66·4	41 31	55 38	65·6	41 06	54 26	64·8	40 40	53 14	64·0	40 13	52 04	63·3	39 46	50 54	62·5	227	313
48	132	42 45	56 22	65·7	42 20	55 08	64·9	41 54	53 55	64·0	41 28	52 43	63·2	41 00	51 32	62·5	40 32	50 22	61·7	228	312
49	131	43 35	55 50	64·9	43 09	54 36	64·1	42 43	53 22	63·2	42 15	52 10	62·4	41 47	50 59	61·6	41 18	49 48	60·9	229	311
50	130	44 25	55 17	64·1	43 58	54 02	63·3	43 31	52 49	62·4	43 03	51 36	61·6	42 34	50 24	60·8	42 04	49 14	60·0	230	310
51	129	45 14	54 43	63·3	44 47	53 28	62·4	44 18	52 13	61·6	43 49	51 00	60·7	43 20	49 48	59·9	42 49	48 38	59·1	231	309
52	128	46 03	54 08	62·5	45 35	52 52	61·6	45 06	51 37	60·7	44 36	50 23	59·8	44 05	49 11	59·0	43 34	48 00	58·2	232	308
53	127	46 51	53 30	61·6	46 22	52 14	60·7	45 52	50 59	59·8	45 22	49 45	58·9	44 51	48 32	58·1	44 18	47 21	57·2	233	307
54	126	47 39	52 51	60·8	47 09	51 34	59·8	46 39	50 19	58·9	46 07	49 05	58·0	45 35	47 52	57·1	45 02	46 41	56·3	234	306
55	125	48 27	52 11	59·8	47 56	50 53	58·9	47 25	49 37	58·0	46 53	48 23	57·0	46 19	47 10	56·2	45 46	45 59	55·3	235	305
56	124	49 14	51 28	58·9	48 43	50 11	57·9	48 10	48 54	57·0	47 37	47 40	56·1	47 03	46 27	55·2	46 29	45 15	54·3	236	304
57	123	50 01	50 44	57·9	49 28	49 26	56·9	48 55	48 09	56·0	48 21	46 54	55·0	47 46	45 41	54·1	47 11	44 30	53·3	237	303
58	122	50 47	49 58	56·9	50 14	48 39	55·9	49 40	47 22	54·9	49 05	46 07	54·0	48 29	44 54	53·1	47 53	43 43	52·2	238	302
59	121	51 33	49 09	55·9	50 58	47 51	54·9	50 23	46 34	53·9	49 48	45 18	52·9	49 11	44 05	52·0	48 34	42 54	51·1	239	301
60	120	52 18	48 19	54·8	51 43	47 00	53·8	51 07	45 43	52·8	50 30	44 28	51·8	49 53	43 14	50·9	49 14	42 03	50·0	240	300
61	119	53 02	47 26	53·7	52 26	46 07	52·7	51 49	44 50	51·7	51 12	43 35	50·7	50 33	42 22	49·7	49 54	41 10	48·8	241	299
62	118	53 46	46 31	52·6	53 09	45 12	51·5	52 31	43 54	50·5	51 53	42 39	49·5	51 13	41 27	48·6	50 33	40 16	47·6	242	298
63	117	54 29	45 33	51·4	53 51	44 14	50·3	53 13	42 57	49·3	52 33	41 42	48·3	51 53	40 30	47·3	51 12	39 19	46·4	243	297
64	116	55 12	44 33	50·2	54 33	43 14	49·1	53 53	41 57	48·1	53 13	40 42	47·1	52 31	39 30	46·1	51 49	38 20	45·2	244	296
65	115	55 53	43 30	48·9	55 13	42 11	47·8	54 33	40 55	46·8	53 51	39 40	45·8	53 09	38 29	44·8	52 26	37 19	43·9	245	295
66	114	56 34	42 25	47·6	55 53	41 06	46·5	55 12	39 50	45·4	54 29	38 36	44·4	53 46	37 25	43·5	53 02	36 16	42·6	246	294
67	113	57 14	41 16	46·2	56 32	39 58	45·1	55 50	38 42	44·1	55 06	37 29	43·1	54 22	36 19	42·1	53 37	35 11	41·2	247	293
68	112	57 53	40 05	44·8	57 10	38 47	43·7	56 27	37 32	42·7	55 42	36 19	41·7	54 57	35 10	40·7	54 11	34 03	39·8	248	292
69	111	58 32	38 50	43·3	57 47	37 33	42·2	57 03	36 18	41·2	56 17	35 07	40·2	55 31	33 59	39·3	54 44	32 53	38·4	249	291
70	110	59 09	37 32	41·8	58 24	36 16	40·7	57 38	35 02	39·7	56 51	33 52	38·7	56 04	32 45	37·8	55 16	31 41	36·9	250	290
71	109	59 45	36 11	40·2	58 58	34 55	39·2	58 12	33 43	38·1	57 24	32 35	37·2	56 36	31 29	36·3	55 47	30 26	35·4	251	289
72	108	60 19	34 46	38·6	59 32	33 32	37·6	58 44	32 21	36·5	57 56	31 14	35·6	57 07	30 10	34·7	56 17	29 08	33·8	252	288
73	107	60 53	33 18	36·9	60 05	32 05	35·9	59 16	30 56	34·9	58 26	29 51	34·0	57 36	28 48	33·1	56 46	27 49	32·2	253	287
74	106	61 25	31 46	35·2	60 36	30 35	34·2	59 46	29 28	33·2	58 55	28 25	32·3	58 05	27 24	31·4	57 13	26 26	30·6	254	286
75	105	61 56	30 10	33·4	61 06	29 02	32·4	60 15	27 57	31·4	59 23	26 56	30·5	58 31	25 57	29·7	57 39	25 02	28·9	255	285
76	104	62 26	28 31	31·5	61 34	27 25	30·5	60 42	26 23	29·6	59 50	25 24	28·8	58 57	24 28	28·0	58 04	23 35	27·2	256	284
77	103	62 53	26 48	29·6	62 01	25 45	28·6	61 08	24 46	27·8	60 15	23 49	27·0	59 21	22 56	26·2	58 27	22 05	25·5	257	283
78	102	63 20	25 02	27·6	62 26	24 02	26·7	61 32	23 05	25·9	60 38	22 12	25·1	59 44	21 21	24·4	58 49	20 34	23·7	258	282
79	101	63 44	23 12	25·5	62 50	22 15	24·7	61 55	21 22	23·9	61 00	20 32	23·2	60 05	19 44	22·5	59 09	19 00	21·8	259	281
80	100	64 07	21 18	23·4	63 12	20 25	22·6	62 16	19 36	21·9	61 20	18 49	21·2	60 24	18 05	20·6	59 28	17 24	20·0	260	280
81	99	64 28	19 22	21·3	63 32	18 33	20·5	62 35	17 47	19·9	61 39	17 04	19·2	60 42	16 24	18·6	59 45	15 46	18·1	261	279
82	98	64 47	17 22	19·1	63 50	16 37	18·4	62 53	15 56	17·8	61 56	15 17	17·2	60 58	14 40	16·7	60 01	14 06	16·2	262	278
83	97	65 03	15 18	16·8	64 06	14 39	16·2	63 08	14 02	15·6	62 10	13 27	15·1	61 12	12 55	14·7	60 14	12 24	14·2	263	277
84	96	65 18	13 13	14·5	64 20	12 38	14·0	63 22	12 06	13·5	62 23	11 36	13·0	61 25	11 07	12·6	60 26	10 41	12·2	264	276
85	95	65 31	11 05	12·1	64 32	10 35	11·7	63 33	10 08	11·3	62 35	9 42	10·9	61 36	9 19	10·6	60 37	8 56	10·2	265	275
86	94	65 41	8 54	9·8	64 42	8 30	9·4	63 43	8 08	9·1	62 44	7 48	8·8	61 44	7 28	8·5	60 45	7 10	8·2	266	274
87	93	65 49	6 42	7·3	64 50	6 24	7·1	63 50	6 07	6·8	62 51	5 52	6·6	61 51	5 37	6·4	60 52	5 24	6·2	267	273
88	92	65 55	4 29	4·9	64 56	4 17	4·7	63 56	4 06	4·6	62 56	3 55	4·4	61 56	3 45	4·3	60 56	3 36	4·1	268	272
89	91	65 59	2 15	2·5	64 59	2 09	2·4	63 59	2 03	2·3	62 59	1 58	2·2	61 59	1 53	2·1	60 59	1 48	2·1	269	271
90	90	66 00	0 00	0·0	65 00	0 00	0·0	64 00	0 00	0·0	63 00	0 00	0·0	62 00	0 00	0·0	61 00	0 00	0·0	270	270

N. Lat: for LHA > 180° … $Z_n = Z$
for LHA < 180° … $Z_n = 360° - Z$

S. Lat.: for LHA > 180° … $Z_n = 180° - Z$
for LHA < 180° … $Z_n = 180° + Z$

SIGHT REDUCTION TABLE

B: (−) for 90° < LHA < 270°
Dec:(−) for Lat. contrary name

Z_1: same sign as B
Z_2: (−) for F > 90°

Lat. / A		30°			31°			32°			33°			34°			35°			Lat. / A	
LHA/F		A/H	B/P	Z_1/Z_2	A/H	B/P	Z_1/Z_2	A/H	B/P	Z_1/Z_2	A/H	B/P	Z_1/Z_2	A/H	B/P	Z_1/Z_2	A/H	B/P	Z_1/Z_2	LHA	
°	°	° ′	° ′	°	° ′	° ′	°	° ′	° ′	°	° ′	° ′	°	° ′	° ′	°	° ′	° ′	°	°	°
0	180	0 00	60 00	90·0	0 00	59 00	90·0	0 00	58 00	90·0	0 00	57 00	90·0	0 00	56 00	90·0	0 00	55 00	90·0	180	360
1	179	0 52	60 00	89·5	0 51	59 00	89·5	0 51	58 00	89·5	0 50	57 00	89·5	0 50	56 00	89·4	0 49	55 00	89·4	181	359
2	178	1 44	59 59	89·0	1 43	58 59	89·0	1 42	57 59	88·9	1 41	56 59	88·9	1 39	55 59	88·9	1 38	54 59	88·9	182	358
3	177	2 36	59 58	88·5	2 34	58 58	88·5	2 33	57 58	88·4	2 31	56 58	88·4	2 29	55 58	88·3	2 27	54 58	88·3	183	357
4	176	3 28	59 56	88·0	3 26	58 56	87·9	3 23	57 56	87·9	3 21	56 56	87·8	3 19	55 56	87·8	3 17	54 56	87·7	184	356
5	175	4 20	59 54	87·5	4 17	58 54	87·4	4 14	57 54	87·3	4 12	56 54	87·3	4 09	55 54	87·2	4 06	54 54	87·1	185	355
6	174	5 12	59 52	87·0	5 08	58 52	86·9	5 05	57 52	86·8	5 02	56 51	86·7	4 58	55 51	86·6	4 55	54 51	86·6	186	354
7	173	6 04	59 49	86·5	6 00	58 49	86·4	5 56	57 48	86·3	5 52	56 48	86·2	5 48	55 48	86·1	5 44	54 48	86·0	187	353
8	172	6 55	59 45	86·0	6 51	58 45	85·9	6 47	57 45	85·7	6 42	56 45	85·6	6 38	55 44	85·5	6 33	54 44	85·4	188	352
9	171	7 47	59 42	85·5	7 42	58 41	85·3	7 37	57 41	85·2	7 32	56 40	85·1	7 27	55 40	84·9	7 22	54 40	84·8	189	351
10	170	8 39	59 37	85·0	8 34	58 37	84·8	8 28	57 36	84·7	8 22	56 36	84·5	8 17	55 36	84·4	8 11	54 35	84·2	190	350
11	169	9 31	59 32	84·4	9 25	58 32	84·3	9 19	57 31	84·1	9 13	56 31	84·0	9 06	55 30	83·8	9 00	54 30	83·6	191	349
12	168	10 22	59 27	83·9	10 16	58 26	83·8	10 09	57 26	83·6	10 03	56 25	83·4	9 56	55 25	83·2	9 48	54 24	83·0	192	348
13	167	11 14	59 21	83·4	11 07	58 20	83·2	11 00	57 20	83·0	10 52	56 19	82·8	10 45	55 18	82·6	10 37	54 18	82·5	193	347
14	166	12 06	59 15	82·9	11 58	58 14	82·7	11 50	57 13	82·5	11 42	56 12	82·3	11 34	55 12	82·1	11 26	54 11	81·9	194	346
15	165	12 57	59 08	82·4	12 49	58 07	82·1	12 41	57 06	81·9	12 32	56 05	81·7	12 23	55 04	81·5	12 14	54 04	81·3	195	345
16	164	13 49	59 01	81·8	13 40	57 59	81·6	13 31	56 58	81·4	13 22	55 57	81·1	13 13	54 57	80·9	13 03	53 56	80·7	196	344
17	163	14 40	58 53	81·3	14 31	57 51	81·1	14 21	56 50	80·8	14 12	55 49	80·5	14 02	54 48	80·3	13 51	53 47	80·1	197	343
18	162	15 31	58 44	80·8	15 22	57 43	80·5	15 12	56 42	80·2	15 01	55 40	80·0	14 51	54 39	79·7	14 40	53 38	79·4	198	342
19	161	16 23	58 35	80·2	16 12	57 34	79·9	16 02	56 32	79·7	15 51	55 31	79·4	15 40	54 30	79·1	15 28	53 29	78·8	199	341
20	160	17 14	58 26	79·7	17 03	57 24	79·4	16 52	56 23	79·1	16 40	55 21	78·8	16 28	54 20	78·5	16 16	53 19	78·2	200	340
21	159	18 05	58 16	79·1	17 53	57 14	78·8	17 42	56 12	78·5	17 29	55 11	78·2	17 17	54 09	77·9	17 04	53 08	77·6	201	339
22	158	18 56	58 05	78·6	18 44	57 03	78·2	18 31	56 01	77·9	18 19	55 00	77·6	18 06	53 58	77·3	17 52	52 56	77·0	202	338
23	157	19 47	57 54	78·0	19 34	56 52	77·7	19 21	55 50	77·3	19 08	54 48	77·0	18 54	53 46	76·6	18 40	52 44	76·3	203	337
24	156	20 37	57 42	77·4	20 24	56 40	77·1	20 11	55 38	76·7	19 57	54 36	76·4	19 42	53 34	76·0	19 28	52 32	75·7	204	336
25	155	21 28	57 30	76·9	21 14	56 27	76·5	21 00	55 25	76·1	20 46	54 23	75·7	20 31	53 21	75·4	20 15	52 19	75·0	205	335
26	154	22 19	57 17	76·3	22 04	56 14	75·9	21 49	55 12	75·5	21 34	54 09	75·1	21 19	53 07	74·7	21 03	52 05	74·4	206	334
27	153	23 09	57 03	75·7	22 54	56 00	75·3	22 39	54 57	74·9	22 23	53 55	74·5	22 07	52 52	74·1	21 50	51 50	73·7	207	333
28	152	23 59	56 49	75·1	23 44	55 46	74·7	23 28	54 43	74·3	23 11	53 40	73·8	22 54	52 37	73·4	22 37	51 35	73·0	208	332
29	151	24 50	56 34	74·5	24 33	55 31	74·1	24 17	54 27	73·6	23 59	53 24	73·2	23 42	52 22	72·8	23 24	51 19	72·4	209	331
30	150	25 40	56 19	73·9	25 23	55 15	73·4	25 05	54 11	73·0	24 48	53 08	72·5	24 29	52 05	72·1	24 11	51 03	71·7	210	330
31	149	26 29	56 02	73·3	26 12	54 58	72·8	25 54	53 54	72·3	25 35	52 51	71·9	25 17	51 48	71·4	24 57	50 45	71·0	211	329
32	148	27 19	55 45	72·6	27 01	54 41	72·2	26 42	53 37	71·7	26 23	52 33	71·2	26 04	51 30	70·7	25 44	50 27	70·3	212	328
33	147	28 09	55 27	72·0	27 50	54 23	71·5	27 31	53 19	71·0	27 11	52 15	70·5	26 50	51 12	70·0	26 30	50 08	69·6	213	327
34	146	28 58	55 09	71·4	28 38	54 04	70·8	28 19	53 00	70·3	27 58	51 56	69·8	27 37	50 52	69·3	27 16	49 49	68·8	214	326
35	145	29 47	54 49	70·7	29 27	53 44	70·2	29 06	52 40	69·6	28 45	51 36	69·1	28 24	50 32	68·6	28 01	49 29	68·1	215	325
36	144	30 36	54 29	70·0	30 15	53 24	69·5	29 54	52 19	68·9	29 32	51 15	68·4	29 10	50 11	67·9	28 47	49 07	67·4	216	324
37	143	31 25	54 08	69·4	31 03	53 03	68·8	30 41	51 58	68·2	30 19	50 53	67·7	29 56	49 49	67·2	29 32	48 45	66·6	217	323
38	142	32 13	53 46	68·7	31 51	52 40	68·1	31 28	51 35	67·5	31 05	50 30	66·9	30 41	49 26	66·4	30 17	48 23	65·9	218	322
39	141	33 02	53 23	68·0	32 39	52 17	67·4	32 15	51 12	66·8	31 51	50 07	66·2	31 27	49 03	65·6	31 02	47 59	65·1	219	321
40	140	33 50	53 00	67·2	33 26	51 53	66·6	33 02	50 48	66·0	32 37	49 43	65·4	32 12	48 38	64·9	31 46	47 34	64·3	220	320
41	139	34 37	52 35	66·5	34 13	51 29	65·9	33 48	50 23	65·3	33 23	49 17	64·7	32 57	48 13	64·1	32 30	47 09	63·5	221	319
42	138	35 25	52 09	65·8	35 00	51 03	65·1	34 34	49 56	64·5	34 08	48 51	63·9	33 42	47 46	63·3	33 14	46 42	62·7	222	318
43	137	36 12	51 43	65·0	35 46	50 36	64·3	35 20	49 29	63·7	34 53	48 24	63·1	34 26	47 19	62·5	33 58	46 15	61·9	223	317
44	136	36 59	51 15	64·2	36 33	50 08	63·6	36 06	49 01	62·9	35 38	47 55	62·3	35 10	46 51	61·6	34 41	45 46	61·0	224	316
45	135	37 46	50 46	63·4	37 19	49 39	62·7	36 51	48 32	62·1	36 22	47 26	61·4	35 53	46 21	60·8	35 24	45 17	60·2	225	315

Lat. / A		30°			31°			32°			33°			34°			35°			Lat. / A	
LHA/F		A/H	B/P	Z_1/Z_2	A/H	B/P	Z_1/Z_2	A/H	B/P	Z_1/Z_2	A/H	B/P	Z_1/Z_2	A/H	B/P	Z_1/Z_2	A/H	B/P	Z_1/Z_2	LHA	
°	°	° ′	° ′	°	° ′	° ′	°	° ′	° ′	°	° ′	° ′	°	° ′	° ′	°	° ′	° ′	°	°	°
45	135	37 46	50 46	63·4	37 19	49 39	62·7	36 51	48 32	62·1	36 22	47 26	61·4	35 53	46 21	60·8	35 24	45 17	60·2	225	315
46	134	38 32	50 16	62·6	38 04	49 08	61·9	37 36	48 02	61·2	37 06	46 56	60·6	36 37	45 51	59·9	36 06	44 46	59·3	226	314
47	133	39 18	49 45	61·8	38 49	48 37	61·1	38 20	47 30	60·4	37 50	46 24	59·7	37 19	45 19	59·1	36 48	44 15	58·4	227	313
48	132	40 04	49 13	61·0	39 34	48 05	60·2	39 04	46 58	59·5	38 33	45 51	58·8	38 02	44 46	58·2	37 30	43 42	57·5	228	312
49	131	40 49	48 39	60·1	40 19	47 31	59·4	39 48	46 24	58·6	39 16	45 18	57·9	38 44	44 12	57·2	38 11	43 08	56·6	229	311
50	130	41 34	48 04	59·2	41 03	46 56	58·5	40 31	45 49	57·7	39 59	44 42	57·0	39 26	43 37	56·3	38 52	42 33	55·6	230	310
51	129	42 18	47 28	58·3	41 46	46 20	57·5	41 14	45 12	56·8	40 41	44 06	56·1	40 07	43 01	55·4	39 32	41 57	54·7	231	309
52	128	43 02	46 50	57·4	42 29	45 42	56·6	41 56	44 34	55·9	41 22	43 28	55·1	40 47	42 23	54·4	40 12	41 19	53·7	232	308
53	127	43 46	46 11	56·4	43 12	45 03	55·6	42 38	43 55	54·9	42 03	42 49	54·1	41 28	41 44	53·4	40 52	40 41	52·7	233	307
54	126	44 29	45 31	55·5	43 54	44 22	54·7	43 19	43 15	53·9	42 44	42 09	53·1	42 07	41 04	52·4	41 30	40 01	51·7	234	306
55	125	45 11	44 49	54·5	44 36	43 40	53·7	44 00	42 33	52·9	43 24	41 27	52·1	42 46	40 23	51·4	42 09	39 19	50·7	235	305
56	124	45 53	44 05	53·5	45 17	42 57	52·6	44 40	41 50	51·8	44 03	40 44	51·1	43 25	39 40	50·3	42 46	38 37	49·6	236	304
57	123	46 35	43 20	52·4	45 58	42 11	51·6	45 20	41 05	50·8	44 42	39 59	50·0	44 03	38 55	49·3	43 24	37 53	48·5	237	303
58	122	47 16	42 33	51·3	46 38	41 25	50·5	45 59	40 18	49·7	45 20	39 13	48·9	44 40	38 09	48·2	44 00	37 07	47·5	238	302
59	121	47 56	41 44	50·2	47 17	40 36	49·4	46 38	39 30	48·6	45 58	38 25	47·8	45 17	37 22	47·1	44 36	36 20	46·3	239	301
60	120	48 35	40 54	49·1	47 56	39 46	48·3	47 16	38 40	47·5	46 35	37 36	46·7	45 53	36 33	45·9	45 11	35 32	45·2	240	300
61	119	49 14	40 01	47·9	48 34	38 54	47·1	47 53	37 48	46·3	47 11	36 45	45·5	46 29	35 42	44·7	45 46	34 42	44·0	241	299
62	118	49 53	39 07	46·8	49 11	38 00	45·9	48 29	36 55	45·1	47 46	35 52	44·3	47 03	34 50	43·6	46 19	33 50	42·8	242	298
63	117	50 30	38 11	45·5	49 48	37 04	44·7	49 05	36 00	43·9	48 21	34 57	43·1	47 37	33 57	42·3	46 53	32 57	41·6	243	297
64	116	51 07	37 13	44·3	50 23	36 07	43·4	49 40	35 03	42·6	48 55	34 01	41·8	48 10	33 01	41·1	47 25	32 03	40·4	244	296
65	115	51 43	36 12	43·0	50 58	35 07	42·2	50 14	34 04	41·3	49 28	33 03	40·6	48 43	32 04	39·8	47 56	31 07	39·1	245	295
66	114	52 18	35 10	41·7	51 33	34 06	40·8	50 47	33 04	40·0	50 01	32 04	39·3	49 14	31 05	38·5	48 27	30 09	37·8	246	294
67	113	52 52	34 05	40·3	52 06	33 02	39·5	51 19	32 01	38·7	50 32	31 02	37·9	49 44	30 05	37·2	48 56	29 10	36·5	247	293
68	112	53 25	32 59	38·9	52 38	31 56	38·1	51 50	30 57	37·3	51 02	29 59	36·6	50 14	29 03	35·8	49 25	28 09	35·2	248	292
69	111	53 57	31 50	37·5	53 09	30 49	36·7	52 21	29 50	35·9	51 32	28 53	35·2	50 43	27 59	34·5	49 53	27 06	33·8	249	291
70	110	54 28	30 39	36·1	53 39	29 39	35·2	52 50	28 42	34·5	52 00	27 46	33·8	51 10	26 53	33·1	50 20	26 02	32·4	250	290
71	109	54 58	29 25	34·6	54 08	28 27	33·8	53 18	27 31	33·0	52 28	26 38	32·3	51 37	25 46	31·6	50 46	24 56	31·0	251	289
72	108	55 27	28 09	33·0	54 37	27 13	32·2	53 46	26 19	31·5	52 54	25 27	30·8	52 03	24 37	30·2	51 10	23 49	29·5	252	288
73	107	55 55	26 51	31·4	55 03	25 57	30·7	54 12	25 04	30·0	53 19	24 14	29·3	52 27	23 26	28·7	51 34	22 40	28·1	253	287
74	106	56 21	25 31	29·8	55 29	24 39	29·1	54 36	23 48	28·4	53 43	23 00	27·8	52 50	22 14	27·1	51 57	21 29	26·6	254	286
75	105	56 46	24 09	28·2	55 53	23 18	27·5	55 00	22 30	26·8	54 06	21 44	26·2	53 12	21 00	25·6	52 18	20 17	25·0	255	285
76	104	57 10	22 44	26·5	56 16	21 56	25·8	55 22	21 10	25·2	54 28	20 26	24·6	53 33	19 44	24·0	52 38	19 04	23·5	256	284
77	103	57 33	21 17	24·8	56 38	20 31	24·1	55 43	19 48	23·5	54 48	19 06	23·0	53 53	18 27	22·4	52 57	17 49	21·9	257	283
78	102	57 54	19 48	23·0	56 59	19 05	22·4	56 03	18 24	21·9	55 07	17 45	21·3	54 11	17 08	20·8	53 15	16 32	20·3	258	282
79	101	58 13	18 17	21·2	57 17	17 37	20·7	56 21	16 59	20·1	55 25	16 22	19·6	54 28	15 48	19·2	53 31	15 15	18·7	259	281
80	100	58 32	16 44	19·4	57 35	16 07	18·9	56 38	15 32	18·4	55 41	14 58	17·9	54 44	14 26	17·5	53 47	13 56	17·1	260	280
81	99	58 48	15 10	17·6	57 51	14 36	17·1	56 53	14 03	16·6	55 56	13 33	16·2	54 58	13 03	15·8	54 00	12 36	15·4	261	279
82	98	59 03	13 33	15·7	58 05	13 02	15·3	57 07	12 33	14·9	56 09	12 06	14·5	55 11	11 40	14·1	54 13	11 14	13·8	262	278
83	97	59 16	11 55	13·8	58 18	11 28	13·4	57 19	11 02	13·0	56 21	10 38	12·7	55 22	10 14	12·4	54 24	9 52	12·1	263	277
84	96	59 28	10 16	11·9	58 29	9 52	11·5	57 30	9 30	11·2	56 31	9 09	10·9	55 32	8 49	10·6	54 33	8 29	10·4	264	276
85	95	59 37	8 35	9·9	58 38	8 15	9·6	57 39	7 56	9·4	56 40	7 39	9·1	55 41	7 22	8·9	54 41	7 06	8·7	265	275
86	94	59 46	6 53	8·0	58 46	6 37	7·7	57 47	6 22	7·5	56 47	6 08	7·3	55 48	5 54	7·1	54 48	5 41	7·0	266	274
87	93	59 52	5 11	6·0	58 52	4 59	5·8	57 52	4 47	5·6	56 53	4 36	5·5	55 53	4 26	5·4	54 53	4 16	5·2	267	273
88	92	59 56	3 28	4·0	58 57	3 19	3·9	57 57	3 12	3·8	56 57	3 05	3·7	55 57	2 58	3·6	54 57	2 51	3·5	268	272
89	91	59 59	1 44	2·0	58 59	1 40	1·9	57 59	1 36	1·9	56 59	1 32	1·8	55 59	1 29	1·8	54 59	1 26	1·7	269	271
90	90	60 00	0 00	0·0	59 00	0 00	0·0	58 00	0 00	0·0	57 00	0 00	0·0	56 00	0 00	0·0	55 00	0 00	0·0	270	270

N. Lat: for LHA > 180° … Z_n = Z
for LHA < 180° … Z_n = 360° − Z

S. Lat.: for LHA > 180° … Z_n = 180° − Z
for LHA < 180° … Z_n = 180° + Z

SIGHT REDUCTION TABLE

B: (−) for 90° < LHA < 270°
Dec:(−) for Lat. contrary name

Z_1: same sign as B
Z_2: (−) for F > 90°

Lat. / A		36°			37°			38°			39°			40°			41°			Lat. / A	
LHA/F		A/H	B/P	Z_1/Z_2	A/H	B/P	Z_1/Z_2	A/H	B/P	Z_1/Z_2	A/H	B/P	Z_1/Z_2	A/H	B/P	Z_1/Z_2	A/H	B/P	Z_1/Z_2	LHA	
°	°	° ′	° ′	°	° ′	° ′	°	° ′	° ′	°	° ′	° ′	°	° ′	° ′	°	° ′	° ′	°	°	°
0	180	0 00	54 00	90·0	0 00	53 00	90·0	0 00	52 00	90·0	0 00	51 00	90·0	0 00	50 00	90·0	0 00	49 00	90·0	180	360
1	179	0 49	54 00	89·4	0 48	53 00	89·4	0 47	52 00	89·4	0 47	51 00	89·4	0 46	50 00	89·4	0 45	49 00	89·3	181	359
2	178	1 37	53 59	88·8	1 36	52 59	88·8	1 35	51 59	88·8	1 33	50 59	88·7	1 32	49 59	88·7	1 31	48 59	88·7	182	358
3	177	2 26	53 58	88·2	2 24	52 58	88·2	2 22	51 58	88·2	2 20	50 58	88·1	2 18	49 58	88·1	2 16	48 58	88·0	183	357
4	176	3 14	53 56	87·6	3 12	52 56	87·6	3 09	51 56	87·5	3 06	50 56	87·5	3 04	49 56	87·4	3 01	48 56	87·4	184	356
5	175	4 03	53 54	87·1	3 59	52 54	87·0	3 56	51 54	86·9	3 53	50 54	86·8	3 50	49 54	86·8	3 46	48 54	86·7	185	355
6	174	4 51	53 51	86·5	4 47	52 51	86·4	4 43	51 51	86·3	4 40	50 51	86·2	4 36	49 51	86·1	4 31	48 51	86·1	186	354
7	173	5 39	53 48	85·9	5 35	52 48	85·8	5 31	51 48	85·7	5 26	50 47	85·6	5 21	49 47	85·5	5 17	48 47	85·4	187	353
8	172	6 28	53 44	85·3	6 23	52 44	85·2	6 18	51 44	85·1	6 13	50 44	84·9	6 07	49 43	84·8	6 02	48 43	84·7	188	352
9	171	7 16	53 40	84·7	7 11	52 39	84·6	7 05	51 39	84·4	6 59	50 39	84·3	6 53	49 39	84·2	6 47	48 39	84·1	189	351
10	170	8 05	53 35	84·1	7 58	52 35	83·9	7 52	51 34	83·8	7 45	50 34	83·7	7 39	49 34	83·5	7 32	48 34	83·4	190	350
11	169	8 53	53 30	83·5	8 46	52 29	83·3	8 39	51 29	83·2	8 32	50 29	83·0	8 24	49 29	82·9	8 17	48 28	82·7	191	349
12	168	9 41	53 24	82·9	9 33	52 23	82·7	9 26	51 23	82·5	9 18	50 23	82·4	9 10	49 23	82·2	9 02	48 22	82·1	192	348
13	167	10 29	53 17	82·3	10 21	52 17	82·1	10 13	51 17	81·9	10 04	50 16	81·7	9 55	49 16	81·6	9 46	48 16	81·4	193	347
14	166	11 17	53 10	81·7	11 08	52 10	81·5	10 59	51 10	81·3	10 50	50 09	81·1	10 41	49 09	80·9	10 31	48 09	80·7	194	346
15	165	12 05	53 03	81·0	11 56	52 02	80·8	11 46	51 02	80·6	11 36	50 02	80·4	11 26	49 01	80·2	11 16	48 01	80·0	195	345
16	164	12 53	52 55	80·4	12 43	51 54	80·2	12 33	50 54	80·0	12 22	49 53	79·8	12 11	48 53	79·6	12 00	47 53	79·3	196	344
17	163	13 41	52 46	79·8	13 30	51 46	79·6	13 19	50 45	79·3	13 08	49 45	79·1	12 57	48 44	78·9	12 45	47 44	78·7	197	343
18	162	14 29	52 37	79·2	14 17	51 37	78·9	14 06	50 36	78·7	13 54	49 35	78·4	13 42	48 35	78·2	13 29	47 34	78·0	198	342
19	161	15 16	52 28	78·6	15 04	51 27	78·3	14 52	50 26	78·0	14 39	49 25	77·8	14 27	48 25	77·5	14 13	47 24	77·3	199	341
20	160	16 04	52 17	77·9	15 51	51 16	77·6	15 38	50 16	77·4	15 25	49 15	77·1	15 11	48 14	76·8	14 58	47 14	76·6	200	340
21	159	16 51	52 07	77·3	16 38	51 05	77·0	16 24	50 05	76·7	16 10	49 04	76·4	15 56	48 03	76·1	15 42	47 03	75·9	201	339
22	158	17 39	51 55	76·6	17 24	50 54	76·3	17 10	49 53	76·0	16 56	48 52	75·7	16 41	47 51	75·4	16 25	46 51	75·2	202	338
23	157	18 26	51 43	76·0	18 11	50 42	75·7	17 56	49 41	75·4	17 41	48 40	75·0	17 25	47 39	74·7	17 09	46 38	74·4	203	337
24	156	19 13	51 30	75·3	18 57	50 29	75·0	18 42	49 28	74·7	18 26	48 27	74·3	18 09	47 26	74·0	17 53	46 25	73·7	204	336
25	155	20 00	51 17	74·7	19 44	50 15	74·3	19 27	49 14	74·0	19 10	48 13	73·6	18 53	47 12	73·3	18 36	46 12	73·0	205	335
26	154	20 46	51 03	74·0	20 30	50 01	73·6	20 13	49 00	73·3	19 55	47 59	72·9	19 37	46 58	72·6	19 19	45 57	72·3	206	334
27	153	21 33	50 48	73·3	21 15	49 47	73·0	20 58	48 45	72·6	20 40	47 44	72·2	20 21	46 43	71·9	20 02	45 42	71·5	207	333
28	152	22 19	50 33	72·6	22 01	49 31	72·3	21 43	48 30	71·9	21 24	47 28	71·5	21 05	46 28	71·1	20 45	45 27	70·8	208	332
29	151	23 06	50 17	72·0	22 47	49 15	71·6	22 28	48 14	71·2	22 08	47 12	70·8	21 48	46 11	70·4	21 28	45 11	70·0	209	331
30	150	23 52	50 00	71·3	23 32	48 58	70·8	23 12	47 57	70·4	22 52	46 55	70·0	22 31	45 54	69·6	22 10	44 54	69·3	210	330
31	149	24 37	49 43	70·5	24 17	48 41	70·1	23 57	47 39	69·7	23 36	46 38	69·3	23 14	45 37	68·9	22 52	44 36	68·5	211	329
32	148	25 23	49 25	69·8	25 02	48 23	69·4	24 41	47 21	69·0	24 19	46 19	68·5	23 57	45 18	68·1	23 34	44 17	67·7	212	328
33	147	26 09	49 06	69·1	25 47	48 04	68·7	25 25	47 02	68·2	25 02	46 00	67·8	24 40	44 59	67·3	24 16	43 58	66·9	213	327
34	146	26 54	48 46	68·4	26 32	47 44	67·9	26 09	46 42	67·4	25 45	45 40	67·0	25 22	44 39	66·6	24 58	43 39	66·1	214	326
35	145	27 39	48 26	67·6	27 16	47 23	67·1	26 52	46 21	66·7	26 28	45 20	66·2	26 04	44 19	65·8	25 39	43 18	65·3	215	325
36	144	28 24	48 04	66·9	28 00	47 02	66·4	27 36	46 00	65·9	27 11	44 58	65·4	26 46	43 57	65·0	26 20	42 57	64·5	216	324
37	143	29 08	47 42	66·1	28 44	46 40	65·6	28 19	45 38	65·1	27 53	44 36	64·6	27 27	43 35	64·2	27 01	42 34	63·7	217	323
38	142	29 52	47 19	65·3	29 27	46 17	64·8	29 01	45 15	64·3	28 35	44 13	63·8	28 08	43 12	63·3	27 41	42 12	62·9	218	322
39	141	30 36	46 56	64·5	30 10	45 53	64·0	29 44	44 51	63·5	29 17	43 49	63·0	28 49	42 48	62·5	28 21	41 48	62·0	219	321
40	140	31 20	46 31	63·7	30 53	45 28	63·2	30 26	44 26	62·7	29 58	43 25	62·2	29 30	42 24	61·7	29 01	41 23	61·2	220	320
41	139	32 03	46 05	62·9	31 36	45 03	62·4	31 08	44 01	61·8	30 39	42 59	61·3	30 10	41 58	60·8	29 41	40 58	60·3	221	319
42	138	32 46	45 39	62·1	32 18	44 36	61·5	31 49	43 34	61·0	31 20	42 33	60·5	30 50	41 32	59·9	30 20	40 32	59·4	222	318
43	137	33 29	45 11	61·3	33 00	44 09	60·7	32 30	43 07	60·1	32 00	42 05	59·6	31 30	41 05	59·1	30 59	40 04	58·5	223	317
44	136	34 12	44 43	60·4	33 42	43 40	59·8	33 11	42 38	59·3	32 40	41 37	58·7	32 09	40 36	58·2	31 37	39 36	57·6	224	316
45	135	34 54	44 13	59·6	34 23	43 11	59·0	33 52	42 09	58·4	33 20	41 08	57·8	32 48	40 07	57·3	32 15	39 08	56·7	225	315

Lat. / A		36°			37°			38°			39°			40°			41°			Lat. / A	
LHA/F		A/H	B/P	Z_1/Z_2	A/H	B/P	Z_1/Z_2	A/H	B/P	Z_1/Z_2	A/H	B/P	Z_1/Z_2	A/H	B/P	Z_1/Z_2	A/H	B/P	Z_1/Z_2	LHA	
°	°	° ′	° ′	°	° ′	° ′	°	° ′	° ′	°	° ′	° ′	°	° ′	° ′	°	° ′	° ′	°	°	°
45	135	34 54	44 13	59·6	34 23	43 11	59·0	33 52	42 09	58·4	33 20	41 08	57·8	32 48	40 07	57·3	32 15	39 08	56·7	225	315
46	134	35 35	43 43	58·7	35 04	42 40	58·1	34 32	41 38	57·5	33 59	40 37	56·9	33 26	39 37	56·4	32 53	38 38	55·8	226	314
47	133	36 17	43 11	57·8	35 44	42 09	57·2	35 12	41 07	56·6	34 38	40 06	56·0	34 04	39 06	55·4	33 30	38 07	54·9	227	313
48	132	36 57	42 39	56·9	36 24	41 36	56·2	35 51	40 35	55·6	35 17	39 34	55·0	34 42	38 34	54·5	34 07	37 35	53·9	228	312
49	131	37 38	42 05	55·9	37 04	41 03	55·3	36 30	40 01	54·7	35 55	39 01	54·1	35 19	38 01	53·5	34 43	37 03	53·0	229	311
50	130	38 18	41 30	55·0	37 43	40 28	54·4	37 08	39 27	53·7	36 32	38 27	53·1	35 56	37 27	52·5	35 19	36 29	52·0	230	310
51	129	38 57	40 54	54·0	38 22	39 52	53·4	37 46	38 51	52·8	37 09	37 51	52·1	36 32	36 52	51·6	35 55	35 54	51·0	231	309
52	128	39 36	40 17	53·0	39 00	39 15	52·4	38 23	38 14	51·8	37 46	37 15	51·1	37 08	36 16	50·6	36 30	35 18	50·0	232	308
53	127	40 15	39 38	52·0	39 38	38 37	51·4	39 00	37 36	50·8	38 22	36 37	50·1	37 43	35 39	49·5	37 04	34 42	49·0	233	307
54	126	40 53	38 58	51·0	40 15	37 57	50·4	39 36	36 57	49·7	38 57	35 58	49·1	38 18	35 01	48·5	37 38	34 04	47·9	234	306
55	125	41 30	38 17	50·0	40 52	37 17	49·3	40 12	36 17	48·7	39 32	35 19	48·1	38 52	34 21	47·4	38 11	33 25	46·9	235	305
56	124	42 07	37 35	48·9	41 28	36 35	48·3	40 47	35 36	47·6	40 07	34 38	47·0	39 26	33 41	46·4	38 44	32 45	45·8	236	304
57	123	42 44	36 51	47·9	42 03	35 51	47·2	41 22	34 53	46·5	40 41	33 55	45·9	39 59	32 59	45·3	39 16	32 04	44·7	237	303
58	122	43 19	36 06	46·8	42 38	35 07	46·1	41 56	34 09	45·4	41 14	33 12	44·8	40 31	32 16	44·2	39 48	31 22	43·6	238	302
59	121	43 54	35 20	45·6	43 12	34 21	45·0	42 29	33 24	44·3	41 46	32 27	43·7	41 03	31 32	43·1	40 19	30 39	42·5	239	301
60	120	44 29	34 32	44·5	43 46	33 34	43·8	43 02	32 37	43·2	42 18	31 42	42·5	41 34	30 47	41·9	40 49	29 54	41·3	240	300
61	119	45 02	33 43	43·3	44 18	32 45	42·6	43 34	31 49	42·0	42 49	30 55	41·4	42 04	30 01	40·8	41 18	29 09	40·2	241	299
62	118	45 35	32 52	42·1	44 51	31 55	41·5	44 05	31 00	40·8	43 20	30 06	40·2	42 34	29 14	39·6	41 47	28 22	39·0	242	298
63	117	46 07	32 00	40·9	45 22	31 04	40·3	44 36	30 10	39·6	43 49	29 17	39·0	43 03	28 25	38·4	42 15	27 35	37·8	243	297
64	116	46 39	31 06	39·7	45 52	30 11	39·0	45 06	29 18	38·4	44 18	28 26	37·8	43 31	27 35	37·2	42 43	26 46	36·6	244	296
65	115	47 09	30 11	38·4	46 22	29 17	37·8	45 35	28 25	37·1	44 47	27 34	36·5	43 58	26 44	36·0	43 09	25 56	35·4	245	295
66	114	47 39	29 14	37·1	46 51	28 21	36·5	46 03	27 30	35·9	45 14	26 40	35·3	44 25	25 52	34·7	43 35	25 04	34·2	246	294
67	113	48 08	28 16	35·8	47 19	27 24	35·2	46 30	26 34	34·6	45 40	25 45	34·0	44 50	24 58	33·4	44 00	24 12	32·9	247	293
68	112	48 36	27 17	34·5	47 46	26 26	33·9	46 56	25 37	33·3	46 06	24 50	32·7	45 15	24 03	32·2	44 24	23 19	31·6	248	292
69	111	49 03	26 15	33·1	48 13	25 26	32·5	47 22	24 38	31·9	46 31	23 52	31·4	45 39	23 08	30·8	44 48	22 24	30·3	249	291
70	110	49 29	25 13	31·8	48 38	24 25	31·2	47 46	23 39	30·6	46 55	22 54	30·0	46 03	22 11	29·5	45 10	21 29	29·0	250	290
71	109	49 54	24 08	30·4	49 02	23 22	29·8	48 10	22 37	29·2	47 17	21 54	28·7	46 25	21 12	28·2	45 32	20 32	27·7	251	289
72	108	50 18	23 02	28·9	49 25	22 18	28·4	48 33	21 35	27·8	47 39	20 53	27·3	46 46	20 13	26·8	45 52	19 34	26·3	252	288
73	107	50 41	21 55	27·5	49 48	21 12	26·9	48 54	20 31	26·4	48 00	19 51	25·9	47 06	19 13	25·4	46 12	18 35	25·0	253	287
74	106	51 03	20 47	26·0	50 09	20 06	25·5	49 15	19 26	25·0	48 20	18 48	24·5	47 25	18 11	24·0	46 30	17 36	23·6	254	286
75	105	51 24	19 36	24·5	50 29	18 57	24·0	49 34	18 20	23·5	48 39	17 43	23·1	47 44	17 09	22·6	46 48	16 35	22·2	255	285
76	104	51 43	18 25	23·0	50 48	17 48	22·5	49 52	17 12	22·0	48 57	16 38	21·6	48 01	16 05	21·2	47 05	15 33	20·8	256	284
77	103	52 02	17 12	21·4	51 06	16 37	21·0	50 09	16 04	20·6	49 13	15 31	20·1	48 17	15 00	19·8	47 20	14 31	19·4	257	283
78	102	52 19	15 58	19·9	51 22	15 25	19·5	50 25	14 54	19·0	49 29	14 24	18·7	48 32	13 55	18·3	47 35	13 27	18·0	258	282
79	101	52 35	14 43	18·3	51 37	14 13	17·9	50 40	13 43	17·5	49 43	13 16	17·2	48 46	12 49	16·8	47 48	12 23	16·5	259	281
80	100	52 49	13 27	16·7	51 52	12 59	16·3	50 54	12 32	16·0	49 56	12 06	15·7	48 58	11 42	15·3	48 01	11 18	15·0	260	280
81	99	53 02	12 09	15·1	52 04	11 44	14·7	51 06	11 19	14·4	50 08	10 56	14·1	49 10	10 34	13·8	48 12	10 12	13·6	261	279
82	98	53 14	10 51	13·4	52 16	10 28	13·1	51 18	10 06	12·9	50 19	9 45	12·6	49 20	9 25	12·3	48 22	9 06	12·1	262	278
83	97	53 25	9 31	11·8	52 26	9 11	11·5	51 27	8 52	11·3	50 29	8 34	11·0	49 30	8 16	10·8	48 31	7 59	10·6	263	277
84	96	53 34	8 11	10·1	52 35	7 54	9·9	51 36	7 37	9·7	50 37	7 21	9·5	49 38	7 06	9·3	48 38	6 51	9·1	264	276
85	95	53 42	6 50	8·5	52 43	6 36	8·3	51 43	6 22	8·1	50 44	6 09	7·9	49 44	5 56	7·8	48 45	5 44	7·6	265	275
86	94	53 49	5 29	6·8	52 49	5 17	6·6	51 49	5 06	6·5	50 50	4 55	6·3	49 50	4 45	6·2	48 50	4 35	6·1	266	274
87	93	53 54	4 07	5·1	52 54	3 58	5·0	51 54	3 50	4·9	50 54	3 42	4·8	49 54	3 34	4·7	48 55	3 27	4·6	267	273
88	92	53 57	2 45	3·4	52 57	2 39	3·3	51 57	2 33	3·2	50 57	2 28	3·2	49 58	2 23	3·1	48 58	2 18	3·0	268	272
89	91	53 59	1 23	1·7	52 59	1 20	1·7	51 59	1 17	1·6	50 59	1 14	1·6	49 59	1 11	1·6	48 59	1 09	1·5	269	271
90	90	54 00	0 00	0·0	53 00	0 00	0·0	52 00	0 00	0·0	51 00	0 00	0·0	50 00	0 00	0·0	49 00	0 00	0·0	270	270

N. Lat: for LHA > 180° ... $Z_n = Z$
for LHA < 180° ... $Z_n = 360° - Z$

S. Lat.: for LHA > 180° ... $Z_n = 180° - Z$
for LHA < 180° ... $Z_n = 180° + Z$

SIGHT REDUCTION TABLE

B: (−) for 90° < LHA < 270°
Dec: (−) for Lat. contrary name

Z_1: same sign as B
Z_2: (−) for F > 90°

Lat. / A		42°			43°			44°			45°			46°			47°			Lat. / A	
LHA/F		A/H	B/P	Z_1/Z_2	A/H	B/P	Z_1/Z_2	A/H	B/P	Z_1/Z_2	A/H	B/P	Z_1/Z_2	A/H	B/P	Z_1/Z_2	A/H	B/P	Z_1/Z_2	LHA	
°	°	° ′	° ′	°	° ′	° ′	°	° ′	° ′	°	° ′	° ′	°	° ′	° ′	°	° ′	° ′	°	°	°
0	180	0 00	48 00	90·0	0 00	47 00	90·0	0 00	46 00	90·0	0 00	45 00	90·0	0 00	44 00	90·0	0 00	43 00	90·0	180	360
1	179	0 45	48 00	89·3	0 44	47 00	89·3	0 43	46 00	89·3	0 42	45 00	89·3	0 42	44 00	89·3	0 41	43 00	89·3	181	359
2	178	1 29	47 59	88·7	1 28	46 59	88·6	1 26	45 59	88·6	1 25	44 59	88·6	1 23	43 59	88·6	1 22	42 59	88·5	182	358
3	177	2 14	47 58	88·0	2 12	46 58	88·0	2 09	45 58	87·9	2 07	44 58	87·9	2 05	43 58	87·8	2 03	42 58	87·8	183	357
4	176	2 58	47 56	87·3	2 55	46 56	87·3	2 53	45 56	87·2	2 50	44 56	87·2	2 47	43 56	87·1	2 44	42 56	87·1	184	356
5	175	3 43	47 53	86·6	3 39	46 53	86·6	3 36	45 53	86·5	3 32	44 53	86·5	3 28	43 53	86·4	3 24	42 53	86·3	185	355
6	174	4 27	47 51	86·0	4 23	46 51	85·9	4 19	45 51	85·8	4 14	44 51	85·7	4 10	43 51	85·7	4 05	42 51	85·6	186	354
7	173	5 12	47 47	85·3	5 07	46 47	85·2	5 02	45 47	85·1	4 57	44 47	85·0	4 51	43 47	85·0	4 46	42 47	84·9	187	353
8	172	5 56	47 43	84·6	5 51	46 43	84·5	5 45	45 43	84·4	5 39	44 43	84·3	5 33	43 43	84·2	5 27	42 43	84·1	188	352
9	171	6 41	47 39	84·0	6 34	46 39	83·8	6 28	45 39	83·7	6 21	44 39	83·6	6 14	43 39	83·5	6 07	42 39	83·4	189	351
10	170	7 25	47 34	83·3	7 18	46 34	83·1	7 11	45 34	83·0	7 03	44 34	82·9	6 56	43 34	82·8	6 48	42 34	82·7	190	350
11	169	8 09	47 28	82·6	8 01	46 28	82·4	7 53	45 28	82·3	7 45	44 28	82·2	7 37	43 28	82·0	7 29	42 28	81·9	191	349
12	168	8 53	47 22	81·9	8 45	46 22	81·8	8 36	45 22	81·6	8 27	44 22	81·5	8 18	43 22	81·3	8 09	42 22	81·2	192	348
13	167	9 37	47 16	81·2	9 28	46 15	81·1	9 19	45 15	80·9	9 09	44 15	80·7	8 59	43 15	80·6	8 49	42 16	80·4	193	347
14	166	10 21	47 08	80·5	10 11	46 08	80·3	10 01	45 08	80·2	9 51	44 08	80·0	9 40	43 08	79·8	9 30	42 08	79·7	194	346
15	165	11 05	47 01	79·8	10 55	46 00	79·6	10 44	45 00	79·5	10 33	44 00	79·3	10 21	43 00	79·1	10 10	42 01	78·9	195	345
16	164	11 49	46 52	79·1	11 38	45 52	78·9	11 26	44 52	78·7	11 14	43 52	78·5	11 02	42 52	78·3	10 50	41 52	78·2	196	344
17	163	12 33	46 43	78·4	12 21	45 43	78·2	12 08	44 43	78·0	11 56	43 43	77·8	11 43	42 43	77·6	11 30	41 44	77·4	197	343
18	162	13 17	46 34	77·7	13 04	45 34	77·5	12 51	44 34	77·3	12 37	43 34	77·1	12 24	42 34	76·8	12 10	41 34	76·6	198	342
19	161	14 00	46 24	77·0	13 46	45 24	76·8	13 33	44 24	76·5	13 19	43 24	76·3	13 04	42 24	76·1	12 50	41 24	75·9	199	341
20	160	14 43	46 13	76·3	14 29	45 13	76·1	14 15	44 13	75·8	14 00	43 13	75·6	13 45	42 13	75·3	13 29	41 14	75·1	200	340
21	159	15 27	46 02	75·6	15 12	45 02	75·3	14 56	44 02	75·1	14 41	43 02	74·8	14 25	42 02	74·6	14 09	41 03	74·3	201	339
22	158	16 10	45 50	74·9	15 54	44 50	74·6	15 38	43 50	74·3	15 22	42 50	74·1	15 05	41 50	73·8	14 48	40 51	73·5	202	338
23	157	16 53	45 38	74·1	16 36	44 38	73·9	16 19	43 38	73·6	16 02	42 38	73·3	15 45	41 38	73·0	15 27	40 39	72·8	203	337
24	156	17 36	45 25	73·4	17 18	44 25	73·1	17 01	43 25	72·8	16 43	42 25	72·5	16 25	41 25	72·2	16 06	40 26	72·0	204	336
25	155	18 18	45 11	72·7	18 00	44 11	72·4	17 42	43 11	72·1	17 23	42 11	71·8	17 04	41 12	71·5	16 45	40 12	71·2	205	335
26	154	19 01	44 57	71·9	18 42	43 57	71·6	18 23	42 57	71·3	18 03	41 57	71·0	17 44	40 57	70·7	17 24	39 58	70·4	206	334
27	153	19 43	44 42	71·2	19 24	43 42	70·8	19 04	42 42	70·5	18 43	41 42	70·2	18 23	40 43	69·9	18 02	39 43	69·6	207	333
28	152	20 25	44 26	70·4	20 05	43 26	70·1	19 44	42 26	69·7	19 23	41 27	69·4	19 02	40 27	69·1	18 40	39 28	68·8	208	332
29	151	21 07	44 10	69·6	20 46	43 10	69·3	20 25	42 10	68·9	20 03	41 10	68·6	19 41	40 11	68·3	19 18	39 12	67·9	209	331
30	150	21 49	43 53	68·9	21 27	42 53	68·5	21 05	41 53	68·1	20 42	40 54	67·8	20 19	39 54	67·4	19 56	38 55	67·1	210	330
31	149	22 30	43 35	68·1	22 08	42 35	67·7	21 45	41 36	67·3	21 21	40 36	67·0	20 58	39 37	66·6	20 34	38 38	66·3	211	329
32	148	23 11	43 17	67·3	22 48	42 17	66·9	22 24	41 17	66·5	22 00	40 18	66·2	21 36	39 19	65·8	21 11	38 20	65·4	212	328
33	147	23 53	42 58	66·5	23 28	41 58	66·1	23 04	40 58	65·7	22 39	39 59	65·3	22 14	39 00	65·0	21 48	38 02	64·6	213	327
34	146	24 33	42 38	65·7	24 08	41 38	65·3	23 43	40 39	64·9	23 17	39 40	64·5	22 51	38 41	64·1	22 25	37 42	63·7	214	326
35	145	25 14	42 18	64·9	24 48	41 18	64·5	24 22	40 18	64·1	23 56	39 19	63·7	23 29	38 21	63·3	23 02	37 23	62·9	215	325
36	144	25 54	41 56	64·1	25 28	40 57	63·6	25 01	39 57	63·2	24 34	38 58	62·8	24 06	38 00	62·4	23 38	37 02	62·0	216	324
37	143	26 34	41 34	63·2	26 07	40 35	62·8	25 39	39 35	62·4	25 11	38 37	61·9	24 43	37 38	61·5	24 14	36 41	61·1	217	323
38	142	27 14	41 11	62·4	26 46	40 12	61·9	26 17	39 13	61·5	25 48	38 14	61·1	25 19	37 16	60·7	24 50	36 19	60·3	218	322
39	141	27 53	40 48	61·5	27 24	39 48	61·1	26 55	38 50	60·6	26 25	37 51	60·2	25 55	36 53	59·8	25 25	35 56	59·4	219	321
40	140	28 32	40 23	60·7	28 02	39 24	60·2	27 32	38 25	59·8	27 02	37 27	59·3	26 31	36 30	58·9	26 00	35 32	58·5	220	320
41	139	29 11	39 58	59·8	28 40	38 59	59·3	28 10	38 01	58·9	27 38	37 03	58·4	27 07	36 05	58·0	26 35	35 08	57·6	221	319
42	138	29 49	39 32	58·9	29 18	38 33	58·4	28 46	37 35	58·0	28 14	36 37	57·5	27 42	35 40	57·1	27 09	34 43	56·6	222	318
43	137	30 27	39 05	58·0	29 55	38 06	57·5	29 23	37 08	57·1	28 50	36 11	56·6	28 17	35 14	56·1	27 43	34 18	55·7	223	317
44	136	31 05	38 37	57·1	30 32	37 39	56·6	29 59	36 41	56·1	29 25	35 44	55·7	28 51	34 47	55·2	28 17	33 51	54·8	224	316
45	135	31 42	38 09	56·2	31 08	37 10	55·7	30 34	36 13	55·2	30 00	35 16	54·7	29 25	34 20	54·3	28 50	33 24	53·8	225	315

Lat. / A		42°			43°			44°			45°			46°			47°			Lat. / A	
LHA/F		A/H	B/P	Z_1/Z_2	A/H	B/P	Z_1/Z_2	A/H	B/P	Z_1/Z_2	A/H	B/P	Z_1/Z_2	A/H	B/P	Z_1/Z_2	A/H	B/P	Z_1/Z_2	LHA	
°	°	° ′	° ′	°	° ′	° ′	°	° ′	° ′	°	° ′	° ′	°	° ′	° ′	°	° ′	° ′	°	°	°
45	135	31 42	38 09	56·2	31 08	37 10	55·7	30 34	36 13	55·2	30 00	35 16	54·7	29 25	34 20	54·3	28 50	33 24	53·8	225	315
46	134	32 19	37 39	55·3	31 45	36 41	54·8	31 10	35 44	54·3	30 34	34 47	53·8	29 59	33 51	53·3	29 23	32 56	52·9	226	314
47	133	32 55	37 08	54·3	32 20	36 11	53·8	31 45	35 14	53·3	31 08	34 18	52·8	30 32	33 22	52·4	29 55	32 27	51·9	227	313
48	132	33 31	36 37	53·4	32 55	35 40	52·9	32 19	34 43	52·3	31 42	33 47	51·9	31 05	32 52	51·4	30 27	31 58	50·9	228	312
49	131	34 07	36 05	52·4	33 30	35 08	51·9	32 53	34 11	51·4	32 15	33 16	50·9	31 37	32 21	50·4	30 59	31 27	49·9	229	311
50	130	34 42	35 31	51·4	34 04	34 35	50·9	33 26	33 39	50·4	32 48	32 44	49·9	32 09	31 50	49·4	31 30	30 56	48·9	230	310
51	129	35 17	34 57	50·4	34 38	34 01	49·9	33 59	33 05	49·4	33 20	32 11	48·9	32 40	31 17	48·4	32 00	30 24	47·9	231	309
52	128	35 51	34 22	49·4	35 12	33 26	48·9	34 32	32 31	48·4	33 52	31 37	47·9	33 11	30 44	47·4	32 30	29 52	46·9	232	308
53	127	36 24	33 45	48·4	35 44	32 50	47·9	35 04	31 56	47·3	34 23	31 02	46·8	33 42	30 10	46·3	33 00	29 18	45·9	233	307
54	126	36 57	33 08	47·4	36 17	32 13	46·8	35 35	31 20	46·3	34 54	30 27	45·8	34 12	29 35	45·3	33 29	28 44	44·8	234	306
55	125	37 30	32 30	46·3	36 48	31 36	45·8	36 06	30 43	45·2	35 24	29 50	44·7	34 41	28 59	44·2	33 58	28 08	43·8	235	305
56	124	38 02	31 51	45·2	37 19	30 57	44·7	36 37	30 04	44·2	35 53	29 13	43·6	35 10	28 22	43·2	34 26	27 32	42·7	236	304
57	123	38 33	31 10	44·1	37 50	30 17	43·6	37 06	29 25	43·1	36 22	28 34	42·6	35 38	27 45	42·1	34 53	26 56	41·6	237	303
58	122	39 04	30 29	43·0	38 20	29 36	42·5	37 36	28 45	42·0	36 51	27 55	41·5	36 06	27 06	41·0	35 20	26 18	40·5	238	302
59	121	39 34	29 46	41·9	38 49	28 55	41·4	38 04	28 04	40·9	37 19	27 15	40·4	36 33	26 27	39·9	35 46	25 39	39·4	239	301
60	120	40 04	29 03	40·8	39 18	28 12	40·2	38 32	27 22	39·7	37 46	26 34	39·2	36 59	25 46	38·8	36 12	25 00	38·3	240	300
61	119	40 32	28 18	39·6	39 46	27 28	39·1	38 59	26 39	38·6	38 12	25 52	38·1	37 25	25 05	37·6	36 37	24 20	37·2	241	299
62	118	41 00	27 32	38·5	40 13	26 43	37·9	39 26	25 56	37·4	38 38	25 09	36·9	37 50	24 23	36·5	37 02	23 39	36·0	242	298
63	117	41 28	26 45	37·3	40 40	25 58	36·8	39 52	25 11	36·3	39 03	24 25	35·8	38 14	23 40	35·3	37 25	22 57	34·9	243	297
64	116	41 54	25 58	36·1	41 06	25 11	35·6	40 17	24 25	35·1	39 28	23 40	34·6	38 38	22 57	34·1	37 48	22 14	33·7	244	296
65	115	42 20	25 09	34·9	41 31	24 23	34·4	40 41	23 38	33·9	39 51	22 55	33·4	39 01	22 12	33·0	38 11	21 31	32·5	245	295
66	114	42 45	24 19	33·6	41 55	23 34	33·1	41 05	22 50	32·7	40 14	22 08	32·2	39 23	21 27	31·8	38 32	20 46	31·3	246	294
67	113	43 10	23 28	32·4	42 19	22 44	31·9	41 28	22 02	31·4	40 37	21 21	31·0	39 45	20 40	30·5	38 53	20 01	30·1	247	293
68	112	43 33	22 35	31·1	42 42	21 53	30·6	41 50	21 12	30·2	40 58	20 32	29·7	40 06	19 53	29·3	39 13	19 15	28·9	248	292
69	111	43 56	21 42	29·8	43 04	21 01	29·4	42 11	20 22	28·9	41 19	19 43	28·5	40 26	19 05	28·1	39 33	18 29	27·7	249	291
70	110	44 18	20 48	28·5	43 25	20 08	28·1	42 32	19 30	27·7	41 38	18 53	27·2	40 45	18 17	26·8	39 51	17 41	26·5	250	290
71	109	44 38	19 53	27·2	43 45	19 15	26·8	42 51	18 38	26·4	41 57	18 02	26·0	41 03	17 27	25·6	40 09	16 53	25·2	251	289
72	108	44 58	18 57	25·9	44 04	18 20	25·5	43 10	17 45	25·1	42 16	17 10	24·7	41 21	16 37	24·3	40 26	16 05	24·0	252	288
73	107	45 17	17 59	24·6	44 23	17 24	24·1	43 28	16 51	23·8	42 33	16 18	23·4	41 38	15 46	23·0	40 42	15 15	22·7	253	287
74	106	45 35	17 01	23·2	44 40	16 28	22·8	43 45	15 56	22·4	42 49	15 25	22·1	41 54	14 54	21·7	40 58	14 25	21·4	254	286
75	105	45 53	16 02	21·8	44 57	15 31	21·4	44 01	15 00	21·1	43 05	14 31	20·8	42 09	14 02	20·4	41 12	13 34	20·1	255	285
76	104	46 09	15 02	20·4	45 12	14 33	20·1	44 16	14 04	19·7	43 19	13 36	19·4	42 23	13 09	19·1	41 26	12 43	18·8	256	284
77	103	46 24	14 02	19·0	45 27	13 34	18·7	44 30	13 07	18·4	43 33	12 41	18·1	42 36	12 15	17·8	41 39	11 51	17·5	257	283
78	102	46 38	13 00	17·6	45 40	12 34	17·3	44 43	12 09	17·0	43 46	11 45	16·7	42 48	11 21	16·5	41 51	10 58	16·2	258	282
79	101	46 51	11 58	16·2	45 53	11 34	15·9	44 55	11 11	15·6	43 57	10 48	15·4	43 00	10 26	15·1	42 02	10 05	14·9	259	281
80	100	47 03	10 55	14·8	46 04	10 33	14·5	45 06	10 12	14·2	44 08	9 51	14·0	43 10	9 31	13·8	42 12	9 12	13·6	260	280
81	99	47 13	9 51	13·3	46 15	9 31	13·1	45 16	9 12	12·8	44 18	8 53	12·6	43 19	8 35	12·4	42 21	8 18	12·2	261	279
82	98	47 23	8 47	11·9	46 24	8 29	11·6	45 26	8 12	11·4	44 27	7 55	11·2	43 28	7 39	11·1	42 29	7 24	10·9	262	278
83	97	47 32	7 42	10·4	46 33	7 27	10·2	45 34	7 12	10·0	44 34	6 57	9·9	43 35	6 43	9·7	42 36	6 29	9·5	263	277
84	96	47 39	6 37	8·9	46 40	6 24	8·8	45 41	6 11	8·6	44 41	5 58	8·5	43 42	5 46	8·3	42 42	5 34	8·2	264	276
85	95	47 46	5 32	7·4	46 46	5 20	7·3	45 46	5 09	7·2	44 47	4 59	7·1	43 47	4 49	6·9	42 48	4 39	6·8	265	275
86	94	47 51	4 26	6·0	46 51	4 17	5·9	45 51	4 08	5·7	44 52	3 59	5·6	43 52	3 51	5·6	42 52	3 43	5·5	266	274
87	93	47 55	3 20	4·5	46 55	3 13	4·4	45 55	3 06	4·3	44 55	3 00	4·2	43 55	2 54	4·2	42 56	2 48	4·1	267	273
88	92	47 58	2 13	3·0	46 58	2 09	2·9	45 58	2 04	2·9	44 58	2 00	2·8	43 58	1 56	2·8	42 58	1 52	2·7	268	272
89	91	47 59	1 07	1·5	46 59	1 04	1·5	45 59	1 02	1·4	44 59	1 00	1·4	43 59	0 58	1·4	43 00	0 56	1·4	269	271
90	90	48 00	0 00	0·0	47 00	0 00	0·0	46 00	0 00	0·0	45 00	0 00	0·0	44 00	0 00	0·0	43 00	0 00	0·0	270	270

N. Lat: for LHA > 180° ... $Z_n = Z$
for LHA < 180° ... $Z_n = 360° - Z$

S. Lat.: for LHA > 180° ... $Z_n = 180° - Z$
for LHA < 180° ... $Z_n = 180° + Z$

SIGHT REDUCTION TABLE

B: (−) for 90° < LHA < 270°
Dec:(−) for Lat. contrary name

Z_1: same sign as B
Z_2: (−) for F > 90°

Lat. / A		48°			49°			50°			51°			52°			53°			Lat. / A	
LHA/F		A/H	B/P	Z_1/Z_2	A/H	B/P	Z_1/Z_2	A/H	B/P	Z_1/Z_2	A/H	B/P	Z_1/Z_2	A/H	B/P	Z_1/Z_2	A/H	B/P	Z_1/Z_2	LHA	
°	°	° ′	° ′	°	° ′	° ′	°	° ′	° ′	°	° ′	° ′	°	° ′	° ′	°	° ′	° ′	°	°	°
0	180	0 00	42 00	90·0	0 00	41 00	90·0	0 00	40 00	90·0	0 00	39 00	90·0	0 00	38 00	90·0	0 00	37 00	90·0	180	360
1	179	0 40	42 00	89·3	0 39	41 00	89·2	0 39	40 00	89·2	0 38	39 00	89·2	0 37	38 00	89·2	0 36	37 00	89·2	181	359
2	178	1 20	41 59	88·5	1 19	40 59	88·5	1 17	39 59	88·5	1 16	38 59	88·4	1 14	37 59	88·4	1 12	36 59	88·4	182	358
3	177	2 00	41 58	87·8	1 58	40 58	87·7	1 56	39 58	87·7	1 53	38 58	87·7	1 51	37 58	87·6	1 48	36 58	87·6	183	357
4	176	2 41	41 56	87·0	2 37	40 56	87·0	2 34	39 56	86·9	2 31	38 56	86·9	2 28	37 56	86·8	2 24	36 56	86·8	184	356
5	175	3 21	41 53	86·3	3 17	40 54	86·2	3 13	39 54	86·2	3 09	38 54	86·1	3 05	37 54	86·1	3 00	36 54	86·0	185	355
6	174	4 01	41 51	85·5	3 56	40 51	85·5	3 51	39 51	85·4	3 46	38 51	85·3	3 41	37 51	85·3	3 36	36 51	85·2	186	354
7	173	4 41	41 47	84·8	4 35	40 47	84·7	4 30	39 47	84·6	4 24	38 47	84·5	4 18	37 48	84·5	4 12	36 48	84·4	187	353
8	172	5 21	41 43	84·0	5 14	40 43	83·9	5 08	39 43	83·9	5 01	38 44	83·8	4 55	37 44	83·7	4 48	36 44	83·6	188	352
9	171	6 01	41 39	83·3	5 53	40 39	83·2	5 46	39 39	83·1	5 39	38 39	83·0	5 32	37 39	82·9	5 24	36 40	82·8	189	351
10	170	6 40	41 34	82·5	6 32	40 34	82·4	6 25	39 34	82·3	6 16	38 34	82·2	6 08	37 35	82·1	6 00	36 35	82·0	190	350
11	169	7 20	41 28	81·8	7 11	40 28	81·7	7 03	39 29	81·5	6 54	38 29	81·4	6 45	37 29	81·3	6 36	36 29	81·2	191	349
12	168	8 00	41 22	81·0	7 50	40 22	80·9	7 41	39 23	80·8	7 31	38 23	80·6	7 21	37 23	80·5	7 11	36 24	80·4	192	348
13	167	8 39	41 16	80·3	8 29	40 16	80·1	8 19	39 16	80·0	8 08	38 16	79·8	7 58	37 17	79·7	7 47	36 17	79·6	193	347
14	166	9 19	41 09	79·5	9 08	40 09	79·3	8 57	39 09	79·2	8 45	38 09	79·0	8 34	37 10	78·9	8 22	36 10	78·7	194	346
15	165	9 58	41 01	78·7	9 47	40 01	78·6	9 35	39 02	78·4	9 22	38 02	78·2	9 10	37 02	78·1	8 58	36 03	77·9	195	345
16	164	10 38	40 53	78·0	10 25	39 53	77·8	10 12	38 53	77·6	9 59	37 54	77·4	9 46	36 54	77·3	9 33	35 55	77·1	196	344
17	163	11 17	40 44	77·2	11 04	39 44	77·0	10 50	38 45	76·8	10 36	37 45	76·6	10 22	36 46	76·5	10 08	35 47	76·3	197	343
18	162	11 56	40 34	76·4	11 42	39 35	76·2	11 27	38 35	76·0	11 13	37 36	75·8	10 58	36 37	75·6	10 43	35 38	75·5	198	342
19	161	12 35	40 25	75·6	12 20	39 25	75·4	12 05	38 26	75·2	11 49	37 26	75·0	11 34	36 27	74·8	11 18	35 28	74·6	199	341
20	160	13 14	40 14	74·9	12 58	39 15	74·6	12 42	38 15	74·4	12 26	37 16	74·2	12 09	36 17	74·0	11 53	35 18	73·8	200	340
21	159	13 52	40 03	74·1	13 36	39 04	73·8	13 19	38 04	73·6	13 02	37 05	73·4	12 45	36 06	73·2	12 27	35 08	73·0	201	339
22	158	14 31	39 51	73·3	14 14	38 52	73·0	13 56	37 53	72·8	13 38	36 54	72·6	13 20	35 55	72·3	13 02	34 56	72·1	202	338
23	157	15 09	39 39	72·5	14 51	38 40	72·2	14 33	37 41	72·0	14 14	36 42	71·7	13 55	35 43	71·5	13 36	34 45	71·3	203	337
24	156	15 48	39 26	71·7	15 29	38 27	71·4	15 09	37 28	71·2	14 50	36 30	70·9	14 30	35 31	70·7	14 10	34 33	70·4	204	336
25	155	16 26	39 13	70·9	16 06	38 14	70·6	15 46	37 15	70·3	15 25	36 17	70·1	15 05	35 18	69·8	14 44	34 20	69·6	205	335
26	154	17 03	38 59	70·1	16 43	38 00	69·8	16 22	37 01	69·5	16 01	36 03	69·2	15 39	35 05	69·0	15 18	34 07	68·7	206	334
27	153	17 41	38 44	69·3	17 20	37 46	69·0	16 58	36 47	68·7	16 36	35 49	68·4	16 14	34 51	68·1	15 51	33 53	67·9	207	333
28	152	18 19	38 29	68·4	17 56	37 30	68·1	17 34	36 32	67·8	17 11	35 34	67·5	16 48	34 36	67·3	16 25	33 38	67·0	208	332
29	151	18 56	38 13	67·6	18 33	37 15	67·3	18 09	36 16	67·0	17 46	35 18	66·7	17 22	34 21	66·4	16 58	33 23	66·1	209	331
30	150	19 33	37 57	66·8	19 09	36 58	66·5	18 45	36 00	66·1	18 20	35 03	65·8	17 56	34 05	65·5	17 31	33 08	65·2	210	330
31	149	20 10	37 40	65·9	19 45	36 41	65·6	19 20	35 44	65·3	18 55	34 46	65·0	18 29	33 49	64·7	18 03	32 52	64·4	211	329
32	148	20 46	37 22	65·1	20 21	36 24	64·8	19 55	35 26	64·4	19 29	34 29	64·1	19 02	33 32	63·8	18 36	32 35	63·5	212	328
33	147	21 22	37 03	64·2	20 56	36 06	63·9	20 30	35 08	63·6	20 03	34 11	63·2	19 35	33 14	62·9	19 08	32 18	62·6	213	327
34	146	21 58	36 44	63·4	21 31	35 47	63·0	21 04	34 49	62·7	20 36	33 53	62·3	20 08	32 56	62·0	19 40	32 00	61·7	214	326
35	145	22 34	36 25	62·5	22 06	35 27	62·1	21 38	34 30	61·8	21 10	33 33	61·4	20 41	32 37	61·1	20 12	31 41	60·8	215	325
36	144	23 10	36 04	61·6	22 41	35 07	61·3	22 12	34 10	60·9	21 43	33 14	60·5	21 13	32 18	60·2	20 43	31 22	59·9	216	324
37	143	23 45	35 43	60·8	23 15	34 46	60·4	22 45	33 50	60·0	22 15	32 53	59·6	21 45	31 58	59·3	21 14	31 02	59·0	217	323
38	142	24 20	35 21	59·9	23 49	34 25	59·5	23 19	33 28	59·1	22 48	32 33	58·7	22 16	31 37	58·4	21 45	30 42	58·0	218	322
39	141	24 54	34 59	59·0	24 23	34 02	58·6	23 52	33 07	58·2	23 20	32 11	57·8	22 48	31 16	57·5	22 15	30 21	57·1	219	321
40	140	25 28	34 36	58·1	24 57	33 40	57·7	24 24	32 44	57·3	23 52	31 49	56·9	23 19	30 54	56·5	22 45	30 00	56·2	220	320
41	139	26 02	34 12	57·1	25 30	33 16	56·7	24 57	32 21	56·3	24 23	31 26	56·0	23 49	30 32	55·6	23 15	29 38	55·2	221	319
42	138	26 36	33 47	56·2	26 02	32 52	55·8	25 28	31 57	55·4	24 54	31 02	55·0	24 20	30 08	54·6	23 45	29 15	54·3	222	318
43	137	27 09	33 22	55·3	26 35	32 27	54·9	26 00	31 32	54·5	25 25	30 38	54·1	24 50	29 45	53·7	24 14	28 52	53·3	223	317
44	136	27 42	32 56	54·3	27 07	32 01	53·9	26 31	31 07	53·5	25 55	30 13	53·1	25 19	29 20	52·7	24 43	28 28	52·4	224	316
45	135	28 14	32 29	53·4	27 38	31 35	53·0	27 02	30 41	52·5	26 25	29 48	52·1	25 48	28 55	51·8	25 11	28 03	51·4	225	315

Lat. / A		48°			49°			50°			51°			52°			53°			Lat. / A	
LHA/F		A/H	B/P	Z_1/Z_2	A/H	B/P	Z_1/Z_2	A/H	B/P	Z_1/Z_2	A/H	B/P	Z_1/Z_2	A/H	B/P	Z_1/Z_2	A/H	B/P	Z_1/Z_2	LHA	
°	°	° ′	° ′	°	° ′	° ′	°	° ′	° ′	°	° ′	° ′	°	° ′	° ′	°	° ′	° ′	°	°	°
45	135	28 14	32 29	53·4	27 38	31 35	53·0	27 02	30 41	52·5	26 25	29 48	52·1	25 48	28 55	51·8	25 11	28 03	51·4	225	315
46	134	28 46	32 01	52·4	28 10	31 08	52·0	27 32	30 14	51·6	26 55	29 22	51·2	26 17	28 29	50·8	25 39	27 38	50·4	226	314
47	133	29 18	31 33	51·4	28 40	30 40	51·0	28 02	29 47	50·6	27 24	28 55	50·2	26 46	28 03	49·8	26 07	27 12	49·4	227	313
48	132	29 49	31 04	50·5	29 11	30 11	50·0	28 32	29 19	49·6	27 53	28 27	49·2	27 14	27 36	48·8	26 34	26 46	48·4	228	312
49	131	30 20	30 34	49·5	29 41	29 42	49·0	29 01	28 50	48·6	28 21	27 59	48·2	27 41	27 08	47·8	27 01	26 18	47·4	229	311
50	130	30 50	30 04	48·5	30 10	29 12	48·0	29 30	28 20	47·6	28 49	27 30	47·2	28 08	26 40	46·8	27 27	25 51	46·4	230	310
51	129	31 20	29 32	47·5	30 39	28 41	47·0	29 58	27 50	46·6	29 17	27 00	46·2	28 35	26 11	45·8	27 53	25 22	45·4	231	309
52	128	31 49	29 00	46·4	31 08	28 09	46·0	30 26	27 19	45·6	29 44	26 30	45·2	29 01	25 41	44·8	28 19	24 53	44·4	232	308
53	127	32 18	28 27	45·4	31 36	27 37	45·0	30 53	26 48	44·5	30 10	25 59	44·1	29 27	25 11	43·7	28 44	24 24	43·3	233	307
54	126	32 46	27 53	44·4	32 03	27 04	43·9	31 20	26 15	43·5	30 36	25 27	43·1	29 52	24 40	42·7	29 08	23 53	42·3	234	306
55	125	33 14	27 19	43·3	32 30	26 30	42·9	31 46	25 42	42·4	31 02	24 55	42·0	30 17	24 08	41·6	29 32	23 23	41·2	235	305
56	124	33 42	26 44	42·2	32 57	25 55	41·8	32 12	25 08	41·4	31 27	24 22	41·0	30 41	23 36	40·6	29 56	22 51	40·2	236	304
57	123	34 08	26 07	41·1	33 23	25 20	40·7	32 37	24 34	40·3	31 51	23 48	39·9	31 05	23 03	39·5	30 19	22 19	39·1	237	303
58	122	34 34	25 30	40·1	33 48	24 44	39·6	33 02	23 58	39·2	32 15	23 14	38·8	31 28	22 29	38·4	30 41	21 46	38·0	238	302
59	121	35 00	24 53	39·0	34 13	24 07	38·5	33 26	23 22	38·1	32 39	22 38	37·7	31 51	21 55	37·3	31 03	21 13	37·0	239	301
60	120	35 25	24 14	37·8	34 37	23 30	37·4	33 50	22 46	37·0	33 02	22 03	36·6	32 13	21 20	36·2	31 25	20 39	35·9	240	300
61	119	35 49	23 35	36·7	35 01	22 51	36·3	34 12	22 08	35·9	33 24	21 26	35·5	32 35	20 45	35·1	31 46	20 04	34·8	241	299
62	118	36 13	22 55	35·6	35 24	22 12	35·2	34 35	21 30	34·8	33 45	20 49	34·4	32 56	20 09	34·0	32 06	19 29	33·7	242	298
63	117	36 36	22 14	34·4	35 46	21 32	34·0	34 56	20 51	33·6	34 06	20 11	33·3	33 16	19 32	32·9	32 26	18 53	32·5	243	297
64	116	36 58	21 32	33·3	36 08	20 52	32·9	35 17	20 12	32·5	34 27	19 33	32·1	33 36	18 54	31·8	32 45	18 17	31·4	244	296
65	115	37 20	20 50	32·1	36 29	20 10	31·7	35 38	19 32	31·3	34 47	18 54	31·0	33 55	18 16	30·6	33 03	17 40	30·3	245	295
66	114	37 41	20 07	30·9	36 49	19 28	30·5	35 58	18 51	30·2	35 06	18 14	29·8	34 13	17 38	29·5	33 21	17 02	29·1	246	294
67	113	38 01	19 23	29·7	37 09	18 46	29·4	36 17	18 09	29·0	35 24	17 33	28·6	34 31	16 59	28·3	33 38	16 24	28·0	247	293
68	112	38 21	18 38	28·5	37 28	18 02	28·2	36 35	17 27	27·8	35 42	16 53	27·5	34 48	16 19	27·1	33 55	15 46	26·8	248	292
69	111	38 40	17 53	27·3	37 46	17 18	27·0	36 53	16 44	26·6	35 59	16 11	26·3	35 05	15 38	26·0	34 11	15 07	25·7	249	291
70	110	38 58	17 07	26·1	38 04	16 33	25·7	37 10	16 01	25·4	36 15	15 29	25·1	35 21	14 58	24·8	34 26	14 27	24·5	250	290
71	109	39 15	16 20	24·9	38 20	15 48	24·5	37 26	15 17	24·2	36 31	14 46	23·9	35 36	14 16	23·6	34 41	13 47	23·3	251	289
72	108	39 31	15 33	23·6	38 36	15 02	23·3	37 41	14 32	23·0	36 46	14 03	22·7	35 50	13 34	22·4	34 55	13 07	22·1	252	288
73	107	39 47	14 45	22·4	38 51	14 16	22·1	37 56	13 47	21·8	37 00	13 19	21·5	36 04	12 52	21·2	35 08	12 25	20·9	253	287
74	106	40 02	13 56	21·1	39 06	13 28	20·8	38 10	13 01	20·5	37 13	12 35	20·3	36 17	12 09	20·0	35 21	11 44	19·8	254	286
75	105	40 16	13 07	19·8	39 19	12 41	19·5	38 23	12 15	19·3	37 26	11 50	19·0	36 29	11 26	18·8	35 33	11 02	18·5	255	285
76	104	40 29	12 17	18·5	39 32	11 53	18·3	38 35	11 28	18·0	37 38	11 05	17·8	36 41	10 42	17·6	35 44	10 20	17·3	256	284
77	103	40 41	11 27	17·3	39 44	11 04	17·0	38 47	10 41	16·8	37 49	10 19	16·5	36 52	9 58	16·3	35 54	9 37	16·1	257	283
78	102	40 53	10 36	16·0	39 55	10 15	15·7	38 57	9 54	15·5	38 00	9 33	15·3	37 02	9 14	15·1	36 04	8 54	14·9	258	282
79	101	41 04	9 45	14·7	40 05	9 25	14·4	39 07	9 06	14·2	38 09	8 47	14·0	37 11	8 29	13·9	36 13	8 11	13·7	259	281
80	100	41 13	8 53	13·3	40 15	8 35	13·2	39 16	8 17	13·0	38 18	8 00	12·8	37 19	7 44	12·6	36 21	7 27	12·5	260	280
81	99	41 22	8 01	12·0	40 23	7 45	11·9	39 25	7 29	11·7	38 26	7 13	11·5	37 27	6 58	11·4	36 28	6 43	11·2	261	279
82	98	41 30	7 09	10·7	40 31	6 54	10·5	39 32	6 40	10·4	38 33	6 26	10·3	37 34	6 12	10·1	36 35	5 59	10·0	262	278
83	97	41 37	6 16	9·4	40 38	6 03	9·2	39 39	5 50	9·1	38 39	5 38	9·0	37 40	5 26	8·9	36 41	5 15	8·7	263	277
84	96	41 43	5 23	8·1	40 44	5 12	7·9	39 44	5 01	7·8	38 45	4 50	7·7	37 45	4 40	7·6	36 46	4 30	7·5	264	276
85	95	41 48	4 29	6·7	40 49	4 20	6·6	39 49	4 11	6·5	38 49	4 02	6·4	37 50	3 54	6·3	36 50	3 45	6·3	265	275
86	94	41 52	3 36	5·4	40 53	3 28	5·3	39 53	3 21	5·2	38 53	3 14	5·1	37 53	3 07	5·1	36 54	3 01	5·0	266	274
87	93	41 56	2 42	4·0	40 56	2 36	4·0	39 56	2 31	3·9	38 56	2 26	3·9	37 56	2 20	3·8	36 56	2 16	3·8	267	273
88	92	41 58	1 48	2·7	40 58	1 44	2·6	39 58	1 41	2·6	38 58	1 37	2·6	37 58	1 34	2·5	36 58	1 30	2·5	268	272
89	91	42 00	0 54	1·3	41 00	0 52	1·3	40 00	0 50	1·3	39 00	0 49	1·3	38 00	0 47	1·3	37 00	0 45	1·3	269	271
90	90	42 00	0 00	0·0	41 00	0 00	0·0	40 00	0 00	0·0	39 00	0 00	0·0	38 00	0 00	0·0	37 00	0 00	0·0	270	270

N. Lat: for LHA > 180° … $Z_n = Z$
for LHA < 180° … $Z_n = 360° - Z$

S. Lat.: for LHA > 180° … $Z_n = 180° - Z$
for LHA < 180° … $Z_n = 180° + Z$

SIGHT REDUCTION TABLE

B: (–) for 90° < LHA < 270°
Dec:(–) for Lat. contrary name

Z_1: same sign as B
Z_2: (–) for F > 90°

Lat. / A		54°			55°			56°			57°			58°			59°			Lat. / A	
LHA/F		A/H	B/P	Z_1/Z_2	A/H	B/P	Z_1/Z_2	A/H	B/P	Z_1/Z_2	A/H	B/P	Z_1/Z_2	A/H	B/P	Z_1/Z_2	A/H	B/P	Z_1/Z_2	LHA	
°	°	° ′	° ′	°	° ′	° ′	°	° ′	° ′	°	° ′	° ′	°	° ′	° ′	°	° ′	° ′	°	°	°
0	180	0 00	36 00	90·0	0 00	35 00	90·0	0 00	34 00	90·0	0 00	33 00	90·0	0 00	32 00	90·0	0 00	31 00	90·0	180	360
1	179	0 35	36 00	89·2	0 34	35 00	89·2	0 34	34 00	89·2	0 33	33 00	89·2	0 32	32 00	89·2	0 31	31 00	89·1	181	359
2	178	1 11	35 59	88·4	1 09	34 59	88·4	1 07	33 59	88·3	1 05	32 59	88·3	1 04	31 59	88·3	1 02	30 59	88·3	182	358
3	177	1 46	35 58	87·6	1 43	34 58	87·5	1 41	33 58	87·5	1 38	32 58	87·5	1 35	31 58	87·5	1 33	30 58	87·4	183	357
4	176	2 21	35 56	86·8	2 18	34 56	86·7	2 14	33 56	86·7	2 11	32 56	86·6	2 07	31 56	86·6	2 04	30 56	86·6	184	356
5	175	2 56	35 54	86·0	2 52	34 54	85·9	2 48	33 54	85·9	2 43	32 54	85·8	2 39	31 54	85·8	2 34	30 54	85·7	185	355
6	174	3 31	35 51	85·1	3 26	34 51	85·1	3 21	33 51	85·0	3 16	32 51	85·0	3 11	31 52	84·9	3 05	30 52	84·9	186	354
7	173	4 06	35 48	84·3	4 00	34 48	84·3	3 54	33 48	84·2	3 48	32 48	84·1	3 42	31 48	84·1	3 36	30 49	84·0	187	353
8	172	4 42	35 44	83·5	4 35	34 44	83·4	4 28	33 44	83·4	4 21	32 45	83·3	4 14	31 45	83·2	4 07	30 45	83·1	188	352
9	171	5 17	35 40	82·7	5 09	34 40	82·6	5 01	33 40	82·5	4 53	32 41	82·4	4 45	31 41	82·3	4 37	30 41	82·3	189	351
10	170	5 51	35 35	81·9	5 43	34 35	81·8	5 34	33 36	81·7	5 26	32 36	81·6	5 17	31 36	81·5	5 08	30 37	81·4	190	350
11	169	6 26	35 30	81·1	6 17	34 30	81·0	6 08	33 31	80·8	5 58	32 31	80·7	5 48	31 31	80·6	5 38	30 32	80·5	191	349
12	168	7 01	35 24	80·2	6 51	34 24	80·1	6 41	33 25	80·0	6 30	32 25	79·9	6 20	31 26	79·8	6 09	30 27	79·7	192	348
13	167	7 36	35 18	79·4	7 25	34 18	79·3	7 14	33 19	79·2	7 02	32 19	79·0	6 51	31 20	78·9	6 39	30 21	78·8	193	347
14	166	8 11	35 11	78·6	7 59	34 12	78·5	7 46	33 12	78·3	7 34	32 13	78·2	7 22	31 14	78·1	7 09	30 15	77·9	194	346
15	165	8 45	35 04	77·8	8 32	34 04	77·6	8 19	33 05	77·5	8 06	32 06	77·3	7 53	31 07	77·2	7 40	30 08	77·1	195	345
16	164	9 19	34 56	76·9	9 06	33 57	76·8	8 52	32 58	76·6	8 38	31 58	76·5	8 24	31 00	76·3	8 10	30 01	76·2	196	344
17	163	9 54	34 47	76·1	9 39	33 48	75·9	9 25	32 49	75·8	9 10	31 50	75·6	8 55	30 52	75·5	8 40	29 53	75·3	197	343
18	162	10 28	34 39	75·3	10 13	33 40	75·1	9 57	32 41	74·9	9 41	31 42	74·8	9 25	30 43	74·6	9 09	29 45	74·4	198	342
19	161	11 02	34 29	74·4	10 46	33 30	74·2	10 29	32 32	74·1	10 13	31 33	73·9	9 56	30 35	73·7	9 39	29 36	73·6	199	341
20	160	11 36	34 19	73·6	11 19	33 21	73·4	11 02	32 22	73·2	10 44	31 24	73·0	10 27	30 25	72·8	10 09	29 27	72·7	200	340
21	159	12 10	34 09	72·7	11 52	33 10	72·5	11 34	32 12	72·3	11 15	31 14	72·2	10 57	30 15	72·0	10 38	29 17	71·8	201	339
22	158	12 43	33 58	71·9	12 24	33 00	71·7	12 06	32 01	71·5	11 46	31 03	71·3	11 27	30 05	71·1	11 07	29 07	70·9	202	338
23	157	13 17	33 46	71·0	12 57	32 48	70·8	12 37	31 50	70·6	12 17	30 52	70·4	11 57	29 54	70·2	11 37	28 57	70·0	203	337
24	156	13 50	33 34	70·2	13 29	32 36	70·0	13 09	31 38	69·7	12 48	30 41	69·5	12 27	29 43	69·3	12 06	28 46	69·1	204	336
25	155	14 23	33 22	69·3	14 02	32 24	69·1	13 40	31 26	68·9	13 18	30 29	68·6	12 56	29 31	68·4	12 34	28 34	68·2	205	335
26	154	14 56	33 09	68·5	14 34	32 11	68·2	14 11	31 14	68·0	13 49	30 16	67·8	13 26	29 19	67·5	13 03	28 22	67·3	206	334
27	153	15 29	32 55	67·6	15 06	31 58	67·3	14 42	31 00	67·1	14 19	30 03	66·9	13 55	29 06	66·6	13 31	28 10	66·4	207	333
28	152	16 01	32 41	66·7	15 37	31 44	66·5	15 13	30 47	66·2	14 49	29 50	66·0	14 24	28 53	65·7	14 00	27 57	65·5	208	332
29	151	16 33	32 26	65·8	16 09	31 29	65·6	15 44	30 32	65·3	15 19	29 36	65·1	14 53	28 39	64·8	14 28	27 43	64·6	209	331
30	150	17 05	32 11	65·0	16 40	31 14	64·7	16 14	30 17	64·4	15 48	29 21	64·2	15 22	28 25	63·9	14 55	27 29	63·7	210	330
31	149	17 37	31 55	64·1	17 11	30 58	63·8	16 44	30 02	63·5	16 17	29 06	63·3	15 50	28 10	63·0	15 23	27 15	62·7	211	329
32	148	18 09	31 38	63·2	17 42	30 42	62·9	17 14	29 46	62·6	16 47	28 51	62·3	16 19	27 55	62·1	15 50	27 00	61·8	212	328
33	147	18 40	31 21	62·3	18 12	30 25	62·0	17 44	29 30	61·7	17 15	28 34	61·4	16 47	27 39	61·2	16 17	26 45	60·9	213	327
34	146	19 11	31 04	61·4	18 42	30 08	61·1	18 13	29 13	60·8	17 44	28 18	60·5	17 14	27 23	60·2	16 44	26 29	60·0	214	326
35	145	19 42	30 46	60·5	19 12	29 50	60·2	18 42	28 55	59·9	18 12	28 01	59·6	17 42	27 06	59·3	17 11	26 12	59·0	215	325
36	144	20 13	30 27	59·6	19 42	29 32	59·2	19 11	28 37	58·9	18 40	27 43	58·6	18 09	26 49	58·4	17 37	25 55	58·1	216	324
37	143	20 43	30 07	58·6	20 12	29 13	58·3	19 40	28 19	58·0	19 08	27 25	57·7	18 36	26 31	57·4	18 03	25 38	57·1	217	323
38	142	21 13	29 48	57·7	20 41	28 53	57·4	20 08	27 59	57·1	19 35	27 06	56·8	19 02	26 13	56·5	18 29	25 20	56·2	218	322
39	141	21 43	29 27	56·8	21 10	28 33	56·4	20 36	27 40	56·1	20 03	26 47	55·8	19 29	25 54	55·5	18 55	25 02	55·2	219	321
40	140	22 12	29 06	55·8	21 38	28 13	55·5	21 04	27 20	55·2	20 30	26 27	54·9	19 55	25 35	54·6	19 20	24 43	54·3	220	320
41	139	22 41	28 44	54·9	22 06	27 51	54·5	21 31	26 59	54·2	20 56	26 07	53·9	20 21	25 15	53·6	19 45	24 24	53·3	221	319
42	138	23 10	28 22	53·9	22 34	27 29	53·6	21 58	26 37	53·3	21 22	25 46	52·9	20 46	24 55	52·6	20 10	24 04	52·3	222	318
43	137	23 38	27 59	53·0	23 02	27 07	52·6	22 25	26 15	52·3	21 48	25 24	52·0	21 11	24 34	51·7	20 34	23 43	51·4	223	317
44	136	24 06	27 36	52·0	23 29	26 44	51·7	22 51	25 53	51·3	22 14	25 02	51·0	21 36	24 12	50·7	20 58	23 23	50·4	224	316
45	135	24 34	27 11	51·0	23 56	26 20	50·7	23 17	25 30	50·3	22 39	24 40	50·0	22 00	23 50	49·7	21 21	23 01	49·4	225	315

Lat. / A		54°			55°			56°			57°			58°			59°			Lat. / A	
LHA/F		A/H	B/P	Z_1/Z_2	A/H	B/P	Z_1/Z_2	A/H	B/P	Z_1/Z_2	A/H	B/P	Z_1/Z_2	A/H	B/P	Z_1/Z_2	A/H	B/P	Z_1/Z_2	LHA	
°	°	° ′	° ′	°	° ′	° ′	°	° ′	° ′	°	° ′	° ′	°	° ′	° ′	°	° ′	° ′	°	°	°
45	135	24 34	27 11	51·0	23 56	26 20	50·7	23 17	25 30	50·3	22 39	24 40	50·0	22 00	23 50	49·7	21 21	23 01	49·4	225	315
46	134	25 01	26 47	50·0	24 22	25 56	49·7	23 43	25 06	49·4	23 04	24 17	49·0	22 24	23 28	48·7	21 45	22 39	48·4	226	314
47	133	25 28	26 22	49·1	24 48	25 32	48·7	24 08	24 42	48·4	23 28	23 53	48·0	22 48	23 05	47·7	22 08	22 17	47·4	227	313
48	132	25 54	25 56	48·1	25 14	25 06	47·7	24 33	24 17	47·4	23 53	23 29	47·0	23 11	22 41	46·7	22 30	21 54	46·4	228	312
49	131	26 20	25 29	47·1	25 39	24 40	46·7	24 58	23 52	46·4	24 16	23 05	46·0	23 34	22 17	45·7	22 52	21 31	45·4	229	311
50	130	26 46	25 02	46·0	26 04	24 14	45·7	25 22	23 26	45·3	24 40	22 39	45·0	23 57	21 53	44·7	23 14	21 07	44·4	230	310
51	129	27 11	24 34	45·0	26 28	23 47	44·7	25 45	23 00	44·3	25 02	22 14	44·0	24 19	21 28	43·7	23 36	20 43	43·4	231	309
52	128	27 36	24 06	44·0	26 52	23 19	43·6	26 09	22 33	43·3	25 25	21 48	43·0	24 41	21 03	42·7	23 57	20 18	42·3	232	308
53	127	28 00	23 37	43·0	27 16	22 51	42·6	26 32	22 06	42·3	25 47	21 21	41·9	25 02	20 37	41·6	24 17	19 53	41·3	233	307
54	126	28 24	23 07	41·9	27 39	22 22	41·6	26 54	21 38	41·2	26 09	20 54	40·9	25 23	20 10	40·6	24 37	19 27	40·3	234	306
55	125	28 47	22 37	40·9	28 01	21 53	40·5	27 16	21 09	40·2	26 30	20 26	39·9	25 44	19 43	39·5	24 57	19 01	39·2	235	305
56	124	29 10	22 07	39·8	28 24	21 23	39·5	27 37	20 40	39·1	26 50	19 57	38·8	26 04	19 16	38·5	25 17	18 34	38·2	236	304
57	123	29 32	21 35	38·8	28 45	20 52	38·4	27 58	20 10	38·1	27 11	19 29	37·8	26 23	18 48	37·4	25 35	18 07	37·1	237	303
58	122	29 54	21 03	37·7	29 06	20 21	37·3	28 19	19 40	37·0	27 31	18 59	36·7	26 42	18 19	36·4	25 54	17 40	36·1	238	302
59	121	30 15	20 31	36·6	29 27	19 50	36·3	28 38	19 09	35·9	27 50	18 30	35·6	27 01	17 50	35·3	26 12	17 12	35·0	239	301
60	120	30 36	19 58	35·5	29 47	19 18	35·2	28 58	18 38	34·9	28 09	17 59	34·5	27 19	17 21	34·2	26 29	16 43	34·0	240	300
61	119	30 56	19 24	34·4	30 07	18 45	34·1	29 17	18 06	33·8	28 27	17 29	33·5	27 37	16 51	33·2	26 46	16 14	32·9	241	299
62	118	31 16	18 50	33·3	30 26	18 12	33·0	29 35	17 34	32·7	28 45	16 57	32·4	27 54	16 21	32·1	27 03	15 45	31·8	242	298
63	117	31 35	18 15	32·2	30 44	17 38	31·9	29 53	17 02	31·6	29 02	16 26	31·3	28 10	15 50	31·0	27 19	15 15	30·7	243	297
64	116	31 53	17 40	31·1	31 02	17 04	30·8	30 10	16 28	30·5	29 19	15 53	30·2	28 27	15 19	29·9	27 35	14 45	29·6	244	296
65	115	32 11	17 04	30·0	31 19	16 29	29·7	30 27	15 55	29·4	29 35	15 21	29·1	28 42	14 48	28·8	27 50	14 15	28·5	245	295
66	114	32 29	16 28	28·8	31 36	15 54	28·5	30 43	15 20	28·2	29 50	14 48	28·0	28 57	14 16	27·7	28 04	13 44	27·4	246	294
67	113	32 45	15 51	27·7	31 52	15 18	27·4	30 59	14 46	27·1	30 05	14 14	26·8	29 12	13 43	26·6	28 18	13 13	26·3	247	293
68	112	33 01	15 14	26·5	32 08	14 42	26·3	31 14	14 11	26·0	30 20	13 40	25·7	29 26	13 10	25·5	28 31	12 41	25·2	248	292
69	111	33 17	14 36	25·4	32 23	14 05	25·1	31 28	13 35	24·8	30 34	13 06	24·6	29 39	12 37	24·4	28 44	12 09	24·1	249	291
70	110	33 32	13 57	24·2	32 37	13 28	24·0	31 42	12 59	23·7	30 47	12 31	23·5	29 52	12 04	23·2	28 57	11 37	23·0	250	290
71	109	33 46	13 18	23·1	32 51	12 51	22·8	31 55	12 23	22·6	31 00	11 56	22·3	30 04	11 30	22·1	29 09	11 04	21·9	251	289
72	108	33 59	12 39	21·9	33 04	12 13	21·6	32 08	11 46	21·4	31 12	11 21	21·2	30 16	10 56	21·0	29 20	10 31	20·8	252	288
73	107	34 12	12 00	20·7	33 16	11 34	20·5	32 20	11 09	20·2	31 23	10 45	20·0	30 27	10 21	19·8	29 30	9 58	19·6	253	287
74	106	34 24	11 19	19·5	33 28	10 55	19·3	32 31	10 32	19·1	31 34	10 09	18·9	30 37	9 46	18·7	29 41	9 24	18·5	254	286
75	105	34 36	10 39	18·3	33 39	10 16	18·1	32 42	9 54	17·9	31 44	9 32	17·7	30 47	9 11	17·5	29 50	8 50	17·4	255	285
76	104	34 46	9 58	17·1	33 49	9 37	16·9	32 52	9 16	16·7	31 54	8 56	16·6	30 57	8 36	16·4	29 59	8 16	16·2	256	284
77	103	34 56	9 17	15·9	33 59	8 57	15·7	33 01	8 38	15·6	32 03	8 19	15·4	31 05	8 00	15·2	30 07	7 42	15·1	257	283
78	102	35 06	8 35	14·7	34 08	8 17	14·5	33 10	7 59	14·4	32 11	7 41	14·2	31 13	7 24	14·1	30 15	7 07	13·9	258	282
79	101	35 14	7 54	13·5	34 16	7 37	13·3	33 18	7 20	13·2	32 19	7 04	13·0	31 21	6 48	12·9	30 22	6 32	12·8	259	281
80	100	35 22	7 11	12·3	34 24	6 56	12·1	33 25	6 41	12·0	32 26	6 26	11·9	31 27	6 12	11·7	30 29	5 57	11·6	260	280
81	99	35 29	6 29	11·1	34 30	6 15	10·9	33 32	6 01	10·8	32 33	5 48	10·7	31 34	5 35	10·6	30 35	5 22	10·5	261	279
82	98	35 36	5 46	9·9	34 37	5 34	9·7	33 37	5 22	9·6	32 38	5 10	9·5	31 39	4 58	9·4	30 40	4 47	9·3	262	278
83	97	35 41	5 04	8·6	34 42	4 53	8·5	33 43	4 42	8·4	32 43	4 32	8·3	31 44	4 21	8·2	30 45	4 11	8·2	263	277
84	96	35 46	4 21	7·4	34 47	4 11	7·3	33 47	4 02	7·2	32 48	3 53	7·1	31 48	3 44	7·1	30 49	3 36	7·0	264	276
85	95	35 51	3 37	6·2	34 51	3 30	6·1	33 51	3 22	6·0	32 52	3 14	6·0	31 52	3 07	5·9	30 52	3 00	5·8	265	275
86	94	35 54	2 54	4·9	34 54	2 48	4·9	33 54	2 42	4·8	32 55	2 36	4·8	31 55	2 30	4·7	30 55	2 24	4·7	266	274
87	93	35 57	2 11	3·7	34 57	2 06	3·7	33 57	2 01	3·6	32 57	1 57	3·6	31 57	1 52	3·5	30 57	1 48	3·5	267	273
88	92	35 58	1 27	2·5	34 59	1 24	2·4	33 59	1 21	2·4	32 59	1 18	2·4	31 59	1 15	2·4	30 59	1 12	2·3	268	272
89	91	36 00	0 44	1·2	35 00	0 42	1·2	34 00	0 40	1·2	33 00	0 39	1·2	32 00	0 37	1·2	31 00	0 36	1·2	269	271
90	90	36 00	0 00	0·0	35 00	0 00	0·0	34 00	0 00	0·0	33 00	0 00	0·0	32 00	0 00	0·0	31 00	0 00	0·0	270	270

N. Lat: for LHA > 180° … $Z_n = Z$
for LHA < 180° … $Z_n = 360° - Z$

S. Lat.: for LHA > 180° … $Z_n = 180° - Z$
for LHA < 180° … $Z_n = 180° + Z$

SIGHT REDUCTION TABLE

B: (−) for 90° < LHA < 270°
Dec: (−) for Lat. contrary name

Z_1: same sign as B
Z_2: (−) for F > 90°

Lat. / A		60°			61°			62°			63°			64°			65°			Lat. / A	
LHA/F		A/H	B/P	Z_1/Z_2	A/H	B/P	Z_1/Z_2	A/H	B/P	Z_1/Z_2	A/H	B/P	Z_1/Z_2	A/H	B/P	Z_1/Z_2	A/H	B/P	Z_1/Z_2	LHA	
°	°	° ′	° ′	°	° ′	° ′	°	° ′	° ′	°	° ′	° ′	°	° ′	° ′	°	° ′	° ′	°	°	°
0	180	0 00	30 00	90·0	0 00	29 00	90·0	0 00	28 00	90·0	0 00	27 00	90·0	0 00	26 00	90·0	0 00	25 00	90·0	180	360
1	179	0 30	30 00	89·1	0 29	29 00	89·1	0 28	28 00	89·1	0 27	27 00	89·1	0 26	26 00	89·1	0 25	25 00	89·1	181	359
2	178	1 00	29 59	88·3	0 58	28 59	88·3	0 56	27 59	88·2	0 54	26 59	88·2	0 53	25 59	88·2	0 51	24 59	88·2	182	358
3	177	1 30	29 58	87·4	1 27	28 58	87·4	1 24	27 58	87·4	1 22	26 58	87·3	1 19	25 58	87·3	1 16	24 58	87·3	183	357
4	176	2 00	29 56	86·5	1 56	28 56	86·5	1 53	27 57	86·5	1 49	26 57	86·4	1 45	25 57	86·4	1 41	24 57	86·4	184	356
5	175	2 30	29 54	85·7	2 25	28 54	85·6	2 21	27 55	85·6	2 16	26 55	85·5	2 11	25 55	85·5	2 07	24 55	85·5	185	355
6	174	3 00	29 52	84·8	2 54	28 52	84·7	2 49	27 52	84·7	2 43	26 52	84·6	2 38	25 53	84·6	2 32	24 53	84·6	186	354
7	173	3 30	29 49	83·9	3 23	28 49	83·9	3 17	27 49	83·8	3 10	26 50	83·8	3 04	25 50	83·7	2 57	24 50	83·7	187	353
8	172	3 59	29 45	83·1	3 52	28 46	83·0	3 45	27 46	82·9	3 37	26 46	82·9	3 30	25 47	82·8	3 22	24 47	82·7	188	352
9	171	4 29	29 42	82·2	4 21	28 42	82·1	4 13	27 42	82·0	4 04	26 43	82·0	3 56	25 43	81·9	3 47	24 44	81·8	189	351
10	170	4 59	29 37	81·3	4 50	28 38	81·2	4 41	27 38	81·2	4 31	26 39	81·1	4 22	25 39	81·0	4 13	24 40	80·9	190	350
11	169	5 28	29 33	80·4	5 18	28 33	80·4	5 08	27 34	80·3	4 58	26 34	80·2	4 48	25 35	80·1	4 38	24 36	80·0	191	349
12	168	5 58	29 27	79·6	5 47	28 28	79·5	5 36	27 29	79·4	5 25	26 29	79·3	5 14	25 30	79·2	5 02	24 31	79·1	192	348
13	167	6 27	29 22	78·7	6 16	28 22	78·6	6 04	27 23	78·5	5 52	26 24	78·4	5 40	25 25	78·3	5 27	24 26	78·2	193	347
14	166	6 57	29 15	77·8	6 44	28 16	77·7	6 31	27 17	77·6	6 18	26 18	77·5	6 05	25 20	77·4	5 52	24 21	77·3	194	346
15	165	7 26	29 09	76·9	7 13	28 10	76·8	6 59	27 11	76·7	6 45	26 12	76·6	6 31	25 14	76·5	6 17	24 15	76·4	195	345
16	164	7 55	29 02	76·1	7 41	28 03	75·9	7 26	27 04	75·8	7 11	26 06	75·7	6 56	25 07	75·5	6 41	24 09	75·4	196	344
17	163	8 24	28 54	75·2	8 09	27 56	75·0	7 53	26 57	74·9	7 38	25 59	74·8	7 22	25 00	74·6	7 06	24 02	74·5	197	343
18	162	8 53	28 46	74·3	8 37	27 48	74·1	8 20	26 50	74·0	8 04	25 51	73·9	7 47	24 53	73·7	7 30	23 55	73·6	198	342
19	161	9 22	28 38	73·4	9 05	27 40	73·2	8 48	26 41	73·1	8 30	25 43	72·9	8 12	24 45	72·8	7 55	23 48	72·7	199	341
20	160	9 51	28 29	72·5	9 33	27 31	72·3	9 14	26 33	72·2	8 56	25 35	72·0	8 37	24 37	71·9	8 19	23 40	71·7	200	340
21	159	10 19	28 19	71·6	10 00	27 22	71·4	9 41	26 24	71·3	9 22	25 26	71·1	9 02	24 29	71·0	8 43	23 32	70·8	201	339
22	158	10 48	28 10	70·7	10 28	27 12	70·5	10 08	26 15	70·4	9 48	25 17	70·2	9 27	24 20	70·0	9 07	23 23	69·9	202	338
23	157	11 16	27 59	69·8	10 55	27 02	69·6	10 34	26 05	69·5	10 13	25 08	69·3	9 52	24 11	69·1	9 30	23 14	69·0	203	337
24	156	11 44	27 49	68·9	11 22	26 51	68·7	11 00	25 54	68·5	10 38	24 58	68·4	10 16	24 01	68·2	9 54	23 04	68·0	204	336
25	155	12 12	27 37	68·0	11 49	26 40	67·8	11 27	25 44	67·6	11 04	24 47	67·4	10 41	23 51	67·3	10 17	22 55	67·1	205	335
26	154	12 40	27 26	67·1	12 16	26 29	66·9	11 53	25 33	66·7	11 29	24 36	66·5	11 05	23 40	66·3	10 41	22 44	66·2	206	334
27	153	13 07	27 13	66·2	12 43	26 17	66·0	12 18	25 21	65·8	11 54	24 25	65·6	11 29	23 29	65·4	11 04	22 34	65·2	207	333
28	152	13 35	27 01	65·3	13 09	26 05	65·1	12 44	25 09	64·9	12 18	24 13	64·7	11 53	23 18	64·5	11 27	22 23	64·3	208	332
29	151	14 02	26 48	64·4	13 36	25 52	64·1	13 09	24 56	63·9	12 43	24 01	63·7	12 16	23 06	63·5	11 49	22 11	63·3	209	331
30	150	14 29	26 34	63·4	14 02	25 39	63·2	13 35	24 43	63·0	13 07	23 49	62·8	12 40	22 54	62·6	12 12	21 59	62·4	210	330
31	149	14 55	26 20	62·5	14 28	25 25	62·3	14 00	24 30	62·1	13 31	23 36	61·8	13 03	22 41	61·6	12 34	21 47	61·4	211	329
32	148	15 22	26 05	61·6	14 53	25 11	61·3	14 24	24 16	61·1	13 55	23 22	60·9	13 26	22 28	60·7	12 56	21 35	60·5	212	328
33	147	15 48	25 50	60·6	15 19	24 56	60·4	14 49	24 02	60·2	14 19	23 08	59·9	13 49	22 15	59·7	13 18	21 22	59·5	213	327
34	146	16 14	25 35	59·7	15 44	24 41	59·5	15 13	23 47	59·2	14 42	22 54	59·0	14 11	22 01	58·8	13 40	21 08	58·6	214	326
35	145	16 40	25 19	58·8	16 09	24 25	58·5	15 37	23 32	58·3	15 06	22 39	58·0	14 34	21 47	57·8	14 02	20 54	57·6	215	325
36	144	17 05	25 02	57·8	16 33	24 09	57·6	16 01	23 17	57·3	15 29	22 24	57·1	14 56	21 32	56·9	14 23	20 40	56·6	216	324
37	143	17 31	24 45	56·9	16 58	23 53	56·6	16 25	23 00	56·4	15 51	22 09	56·1	15 18	21 17	55·9	14 44	20 26	55·7	217	323
38	142	17 56	24 28	55·9	17 22	23 36	55·7	16 48	22 44	55·4	16 14	21 53	55·2	15 39	21 01	54·9	15 05	20 11	54·7	218	322
39	141	18 20	24 10	55·0	17 46	23 18	54·7	17 11	22 27	54·4	16 36	21 36	54·2	16 01	20 46	54·0	15 25	19 55	53·7	219	321
40	140	18 45	23 52	54·0	18 09	23 00	53·7	17 34	22 10	53·5	16 58	21 19	53·2	16 22	20 29	53·0	15 46	19 39	52·7	220	320
41	139	19 09	23 33	53·0	18 33	22 42	52·8	17 56	21 52	52·5	17 20	21 02	52·2	16 43	20 13	52·0	16 06	19 23	51·8	221	319
42	138	19 33	23 13	52·1	18 56	22 23	51·8	18 19	21 34	51·5	17 41	20 44	51·3	17 03	19 55	51·0	16 26	19 07	50·8	222	318
43	137	19 56	22 54	51·1	19 18	22 04	50·8	18 40	21 15	50·5	18 02	20 26	50·3	17 24	19 38	50·0	16 45	18 50	49·8	223	317
44	136	20 19	22 33	50·1	19 41	21 44	49·8	19 02	20 56	49·5	18 23	20 08	49·3	17 44	19 20	49·0	17 04	18 33	48·8	224	316
45	135	20 42	22 12	49·1	20 03	21 24	48·8	19 23	20 36	48·6	18 43	19 49	48·3	18 03	19 02	48·1	17 23	18 15	47·8	225	315

Lat. / A		60°			61°			62°			63°			64°			65°			Lat. / A	
LHA/F		A/H	B/P	Z_1/Z_2	A/H	B/P	Z_1/Z_2	A/H	B/P	Z_1/Z_2	A/H	B/P	Z_1/Z_2	A/H	B/P	Z_1/Z_2	A/H	B/P	Z_1/Z_2	LHA	
°	°	° ′	° ′	°	° ′	° ′	°	° ′	° ′	°	° ′	° ′	°	° ′	° ′	°	° ′	° ′	°	°	°
45	135	20 42	22 12	49·1	20 03	21 24	48·8	19 23	20 36	48·6	18 43	19 49	48·3	18 03	19 02	48·1	17 23	18 15	47·8	225	315
46	134	21 05	21 51	48·1	20 25	21 04	47·8	19 44	20 16	47·6	19 04	19 29	47·3	18 23	18 43	47·1	17 42	17 57	46·8	226	314
47	133	21 27	21 30	47·1	20 46	20 43	46·8	20 05	19 56	46·6	19 24	19 10	46·3	18 42	18 24	46·1	18 00	17 39	45·8	227	313
48	132	21 49	21 07	46·1	21 07	20 21	45·8	20 25	19 35	45·6	19 43	18 50	45·3	19 01	18 04	45·1	18 18	17 20	44·8	228	312
49	131	22 10	20 45	45·1	21 28	19 59	44·8	20 45	19 14	44·6	20 02	18 29	44·3	19 19	17 45	44·0	18 36	17 01	43·8	229	311
50	130	22 31	20 22	44·1	21 48	19 37	43·8	21 05	18 52	43·5	20 21	18 08	43·3	19 37	17 24	43·0	18 53	16 41	42·8	230	310
51	129	22 52	19 58	43·1	22 08	19 14	42·8	21 24	18 30	42·5	20 40	17 47	42·3	19 55	17 04	42·0	19 10	16 21	41·8	231	309
52	128	23 12	19 34	42·1	22 28	18 51	41·8	21 43	18 08	41·5	20 58	17 25	41·2	20 13	16 43	41·0	19 27	16 01	40·8	232	308
53	127	23 32	19 10	41·0	22 47	18 27	40·7	22 01	17 45	40·5	21 15	17 03	40·2	20 30	16 21	40·0	19 44	15 41	39·7	233	307
54	126	23 52	18 45	40·0	23 06	18 03	39·7	22 19	17 21	39·4	21 33	16 40	39·2	20 46	16 00	39·0	20 00	15 20	38·7	234	306
55	125	24 11	18 19	39·0	23 24	17 38	38·7	22 37	16 58	38·4	21 50	16 17	38·2	21 03	15 38	37·9	20 15	14 58	37·7	235	305
56	124	24 29	17 54	37·9	23 42	17 13	37·6	22 54	16 34	37·4	22 07	15 54	37·1	21 19	15 15	36·9	20 31	14 37	36·7	236	304
57	123	24 48	17 27	36·9	23 59	16 48	36·6	23 11	16 09	36·3	22 23	15 31	36·1	21 34	14 53	35·8	20 46	14 15	35·6	237	303
58	122	25 05	17 01	35·8	24 17	16 22	35·5	23 28	15 44	35·3	22 39	15 07	35·0	21 49	14 29	34·8	21 00	13 53	34·6	238	302
59	121	25 23	16 34	34·8	24 33	15 56	34·5	23 44	15 19	34·2	22 54	14 42	34·0	22 04	14 06	33·8	21 14	13 30	33·5	239	301
60	120	25 40	16 06	33·7	24 50	15 29	33·4	23 59	14 53	33·2	23 09	14 18	32·9	22 19	13 42	32·7	21 28	13 07	32·5	240	300
61	119	25 56	15 38	32·6	25 05	15 03	32·4	24 15	14 27	32·1	23 24	13 53	31·9	22 33	13 18	31·7	21 42	12 44	31·5	241	299
62	118	26 12	15 10	31·5	25 21	14 35	31·3	24 29	14 01	31·1	23 38	13 27	30·8	22 46	12 54	30·6	21 55	12 21	30·4	242	298
63	117	26 27	14 41	30·5	25 36	14 08	30·2	24 44	13 34	30·0	23 52	13 01	29·8	22 59	12 29	29·5	22 07	11 57	29·3	243	297
64	116	26 42	14 12	29·4	25 50	13 39	29·1	24 57	13 07	28·9	24 05	12 35	28·7	23 12	12 04	28·5	22 19	11 33	28·3	244	296
65	115	26 57	13 43	28·3	26 04	13 11	28·1	25 11	12 40	27·8	24 18	12 09	27·6	23 25	11 39	27·4	22 31	11 09	27·2	245	295
66	114	27 11	13 13	27·2	26 17	12 42	27·0	25 24	12 12	26·8	24 30	11 43	26·6	23 36	11 13	26·4	22 43	10 44	26·2	246	294
67	113	27 24	12 43	26·1	26 30	12 13	25·9	25 36	11 44	25·7	24 42	11 16	25·5	23 48	10 47	25·3	22 54	10 20	25·1	247	293
68	112	27 37	12 12	25·0	26 43	11 44	24·8	25 48	11 16	24·6	24 54	10 48	24·4	23 59	10 21	24·2	23 04	9 55	24·0	248	292
69	111	27 50	11 41	23·9	26 55	11 14	23·7	26 00	10 47	23·5	25 05	10 21	23·3	24 09	9 55	23·1	23 14	9 29	23·0	249	291
70	110	28 01	11 10	22·8	27 06	10 44	22·6	26 11	10 18	22·4	25 15	9 53	22·2	24 20	9 28	22·0	23 24	9 04	21·9	250	290
71	109	28 13	10 39	21·7	27 17	10 14	21·5	26 21	9 49	21·3	25 25	9 25	21·1	24 29	9 01	21·0	23 33	8 38	20·8	251	289
72	108	28 24	10 07	20·6	27 27	9 43	20·4	26 31	9 20	20·2	25 35	8 57	20·0	24 38	8 34	19·9	23 42	8 12	19·7	252	288
73	107	28 34	9 35	19·4	27 37	9 12	19·3	26 41	8 50	19·1	25 44	8 28	18·9	24 47	8 07	18·8	23 50	7 46	18·6	253	287
74	106	28 44	9 03	18·3	27 47	8 41	18·2	26 50	8 20	18·0	25 52	8 00	17·8	24 55	7 39	17·7	23 58	7 19	17·6	254	286
75	105	28 53	8 30	17·2	27 55	8 10	17·0	26 58	7 50	16·9	26 01	7 31	16·7	25 03	7 12	16·6	24 06	6 53	16·5	255	285
76	104	29 01	7 57	16·1	28 04	7 38	15·9	27 06	7 20	15·8	26 08	7 02	15·6	25 10	6 44	15·5	24 13	6 26	15·4	256	284
77	103	29 09	7 24	14·9	28 11	7 06	14·8	27 13	6 49	14·7	26 15	6 32	14·5	25 17	6 16	14·4	24 19	5 59	14·3	257	283
78	102	29 17	6 51	13·8	28 18	6 34	13·7	27 20	6 19	13·5	26 22	6 03	13·4	25 23	5 47	13·3	24 25	5 32	13·2	258	282
79	101	29 24	6 17	12·7	28 25	6 02	12·5	27 27	5 48	12·4	26 28	5 33	12·3	25 29	5 19	12·2	24 31	5 05	12·1	259	281
80	100	29 30	5 44	11·5	28 31	5 30	11·4	27 32	5 17	11·3	26 33	5 03	11·2	25 35	4 50	11·1	24 36	4 38	11·0	260	280
81	99	29 36	5 10	10·4	28 37	4 57	10·3	27 38	4 45	10·2	26 38	4 33	10·1	25 39	4 22	10·0	24 40	4 10	9·9	261	279
82	98	29 41	4 36	9·2	28 41	4 25	9·1	27 42	4 14	9·0	26 43	4 03	9·0	25 44	3 53	8·9	24 44	3 43	8·8	262	278
83	97	29 45	4 01	8·1	28 46	3 52	8·0	27 46	3 42	7·9	26 47	3 33	7·8	25 48	3 24	7·8	24 48	3 15	7·7	263	277
84	96	29 49	3 27	6·9	28 50	3 19	6·9	27 50	3 11	6·8	26 50	3 03	6·7	25 51	2 55	6·7	24 51	2 47	6·6	264	276
85	95	29 52	2 53	5·8	28 53	2 46	5·7	27 53	2 39	5·7	26 53	2 33	5·6	25 54	2 26	5·6	24 54	2 20	5·5	265	275
86	94	29 55	2 18	4·6	28 55	2 13	4·6	27 56	2 07	4·5	26 56	2 02	4·5	25 56	1 57	4·4	24 56	1 52	4·4	266	274
87	93	29 57	1 44	3·5	28 57	1 40	3·4	27 57	1 36	3·4	26 58	1 32	3·4	25 58	1 28	3·3	24 58	1 24	3·3	267	273
88	92	29 59	1 09	2·3	28 59	1 06	2·3	27 59	1 04	2·3	26 59	1 01	2·2	25 59	0 59	2·2	24 59	0 56	2·2	268	272
89	91	30 00	0 35	1·2	29 00	0 33	1·1	28 00	0 32	1·1	27 00	0 31	1·1	26 00	0 29	1·1	25 00	0 28	1·1	269	271
90	90	30 00	0 00	0·0	29 00	0 00	0·0	28 00	0 00	0·0	27 00	0 00	0·0	26 00	0 00	0·0	25 00	0 00	0·0	270	270

N. Lat: for LHA > 180° … $Z_n = Z$
for LHA < 180° … $Z_n = 360° - Z$

S. Lat.: for LHA > 180° … $Z_n = 180° - Z$
for LHA < 180° … $Z_n = 180° + Z$

SIGHT REDUCTION TABLE

B: (−) for 90° < LHA < 270°
Dec:(−) for Lat. contrary name

Z_1: same sign as B
Z_2: (−) for F > 90°

Lat. / A		66°			67°			68°			69°			70°			71°			Lat. / A	
LHA/F		A/H	B/P	Z_1/Z_2	A/H	B/P	Z_1/Z_2	A/H	B/P	Z_1/Z_2	A/H	B/P	Z_1/Z_2	A/H	B/P	Z_1/Z_2	A/H	B/P	Z_1/Z_2	LHA	
°	°	° ′	° ′	°	° ′	° ′	°	° ′	° ′	°	° ′	° ′	°	° ′	° ′	°	° ′	° ′	°	°	°
0	180	0 00	24 00	90·0	0 00	23 00	90·0	0 00	22 00	90·0	0 00	21 00	90·0	0 00	20 00	90·0	0 00	19 00	90·0	180	360
1	179	0 24	24 00	89·1	0 23	23 00	89·1	0 22	22 00	89·1	0 22	21 00	89·1	0 21	20 00	89·1	0 20	19 00	89·1	181	359
2	178	0 49	23 59	88·2	0 47	22 59	88·2	0 45	21 59	88·1	0 43	20 59	88·1	0 41	19 59	88·1	0 39	18 59	88·1	182	358
3	177	1 13	23 58	87·3	1 10	22 58	87·2	1 07	21 58	87·2	1 04	20 58	87·2	1 02	19 58	87·2	0 59	18 59	87·2	183	357
4	176	1 38	23 57	86·3	1 34	22 57	86·3	1 30	21 57	86·3	1 26	20 57	86·3	1 22	19 57	86·2	1 18	18 57	86·2	184	356
5	175	2 02	23 55	85·4	1 57	22 55	85·4	1 52	21 55	85·4	1 47	20 56	85·3	1 42	19 56	85·3	1 38	18 56	85·3	185	355
6	174	2 26	23 53	84·5	2 20	22 53	84·5	2 15	21 53	84·4	2 09	20 54	84·4	2 03	19 54	84·4	1 57	18 54	84·3	186	354
7	173	2 50	23 50	83·6	2 44	22 51	83·6	2 37	21 51	83·5	2 30	20 51	83·5	2 23	19 52	83·4	2 16	18 52	83·4	187	353
8	172	3 15	23 48	82·7	3 07	22 48	82·6	2 59	21 48	82·6	2 52	20 49	82·5	2 44	19 49	82·5	2 36	18 50	82·4	188	352
9	171	3 39	23 44	81·8	3 30	22 45	81·7	3 22	21 45	81·6	3 13	20 46	81·6	3 04	19 46	81·5	2 55	18 47	81·5	189	351
10	170	4 03	23 41	80·8	3 53	22 41	80·8	3 44	21 42	80·7	3 34	20 42	80·7	3 24	19 43	80·6	3 14	18 44	80·5	190	350
11	169	4 27	23 36	79·9	4 17	22 37	79·9	4 06	21 38	79·8	3 55	20 39	79·7	3 45	19 40	79·6	3 34	18 41	79·6	191	349
12	168	4 51	23 32	79·0	4 40	22 33	78·9	4 28	21 34	78·9	4 16	20 35	78·8	4 05	19 36	78·7	3 53	18 37	78·6	192	348
13	167	5 15	23 27	78·1	5 03	22 28	78·0	4 50	21 29	77·9	4 37	20 30	77·8	4 25	19 32	77·8	4 12	18 33	77·7	193	347
14	166	5 39	23 22	77·2	5 25	22 23	77·1	5 12	21 24	77·0	4 58	20 26	76·9	4 45	19 27	76·8	4 31	18 28	76·7	194	346
15	165	6 03	23 16	76·2	5 48	22 18	76·1	5 34	21 19	76·0	5 19	20 21	76·0	5 05	19 22	75·9	4 50	18 24	75·8	195	345
16	164	6 26	23 10	75·3	6 11	22 12	75·2	5 56	21 13	75·1	5 40	20 15	75·0	5 25	19 17	74·9	5 09	18 19	74·8	196	344
17	163	6 50	23 04	74·4	6 34	22 06	74·3	6 17	21 08	74·2	6 01	20 09	74·1	5 44	19 11	74·0	5 28	18 14	73·9	197	343
18	162	7 13	22 57	73·5	6 56	21 59	73·3	6 39	21 01	73·2	6 21	20 03	73·1	6 04	19 06	73·0	5 46	18 08	72·9	198	342
19	161	7 37	22 50	72·5	7 19	21 52	72·4	7 00	20 54	72·3	6 42	19 57	72·2	6 24	18 59	72·1	6 05	18 02	72·0	199	341
20	160	8 00	22 42	71·6	7 41	21 45	71·5	7 22	20 47	71·4	7 02	19 50	71·2	6 43	18 53	71·1	6 24	17 56	71·0	200	340
21	159	8 23	22 34	70·7	8 03	21 37	70·5	7 43	20 40	70·4	7 23	19 43	70·3	7 02	18 46	70·2	6 42	17 49	70·1	201	339
22	158	8 46	22 26	69·7	8 25	21 29	69·6	8 04	20 32	69·5	7 43	19 35	69·3	7 22	18 39	69·2	7 00	17 42	69·1	202	338
23	157	9 09	22 17	68·8	8 47	21 21	68·7	8 25	20 24	68·5	8 03	19 28	68·4	7 41	18 31	68·3	7 19	17 35	68·1	203	337
24	156	9 31	22 08	67·9	9 09	21 12	67·7	8 46	20 16	67·6	8 23	19 19	67·4	8 00	18 24	67·3	7 37	17 28	67·2	204	336
25	155	9 54	21 58	66·9	9 30	21 03	66·8	9 07	20 07	66·6	8 43	19 11	66·5	8 19	18 15	66·3	7 55	17 20	66·2	205	335
26	154	10 16	21 49	66·0	9 52	20 53	65·8	9 27	19 57	65·7	9 02	19 02	65·5	8 37	18 07	65·4	8 12	17 12	65·2	206	334
27	153	10 38	21 38	65·0	10 13	20 43	64·9	9 48	19 48	64·7	9 22	18 53	64·6	8 56	17 58	64·4	8 30	17 03	64·3	207	333
28	152	11 00	21 28	64·1	10 34	20 33	63·9	10 08	19 38	63·8	9 41	18 43	63·6	9 14	17 49	63·5	8 48	16 55	63·3	208	332
29	151	11 22	21 17	63·1	10 55	20 22	63·0	10 28	19 28	62·8	10 00	18 34	62·6	9 33	17 39	62·5	9 05	16 46	62·3	209	331
30	150	11 44	21 05	62·2	11 16	20 11	62·0	10 48	19 17	61·8	10 19	18 23	61·7	9 51	17 30	61·5	9 22	16 36	61·4	210	330
31	149	12 06	20 53	61·2	11 37	20 00	61·1	11 07	19 06	60·9	10 38	18 13	60·7	10 09	17 20	60·5	9 39	16 27	60·4	211	329
32	148	12 27	20 41	60·3	11 57	19 48	60·1	11 27	18 55	59·9	10 57	18 02	59·7	10 27	17 09	59·6	9 56	16 17	59·4	212	328
33	147	12 48	20 29	59·3	12 17	19 36	59·1	11 46	18 43	58·9	11 15	17 51	58·8	10 44	16 58	58·6	10 13	16 06	58·4	213	327
34	146	13 09	20 16	58·4	12 37	19 23	58·2	12 06	18 31	58·0	11 34	17 39	57·8	11 02	16 47	57·6	10 29	15 56	57·5	214	326
35	145	13 29	20 02	57·4	12 57	19 10	57·2	12 24	18 19	57·0	11 52	17 27	56·8	11 19	16 36	56·7	10 46	15 45	56·5	215	325
36	144	13 50	19 49	56·4	13 17	18 57	56·2	12 43	18 06	56·0	12 10	17 15	55·9	11 36	16 24	55·7	11 02	15 34	55·5	216	324
37	143	14 10	19 34	55·5	13 36	18 44	55·3	13 02	17 53	55·1	12 27	17 03	54·9	11 53	16 12	54·7	11 18	15 23	54·5	217	323
38	142	14 30	19 20	54·5	13 55	18 30	54·3	13 20	17 40	54·1	12 45	16 50	53·9	12 09	16 00	53·7	11 34	15 11	53·5	218	322
39	141	14 50	19 05	53·5	14 14	18 15	53·3	13 38	17 26	53·1	13 02	16 37	52·9	12 26	15 48	52·7	11 49	14 59	52·6	219	321
40	140	15 09	18 50	52·5	14 33	18 01	52·3	13 56	17 12	52·1	13 19	16 23	51·9	12 42	15 35	51·7	12 05	14 47	51·6	220	320
41	139	15 29	18 34	51·5	14 51	17 46	51·3	14 14	16 57	51·1	13 36	16 09	50·9	12 58	15 22	50·8	12 20	14 34	50·6	221	319
42	138	15 48	18 18	50·6	15 09	17 30	50·3	14 31	16 43	50·1	13 52	15 55	49·9	13 14	15 08	49·8	12 35	14 21	49·6	222	318
43	137	16 06	18 02	49·6	15 27	17 15	49·4	14 48	16 28	49·2	14 09	15 41	49·0	13 29	14 54	48·8	12 50	14 08	48·6	223	317
44	136	16 25	17 46	48·6	15 45	16 59	48·4	15 05	16 12	48·2	14 25	15 26	48·0	13 45	14 40	47·8	13 04	13 55	47·6	224	316
45	135	16 43	17 29	47·6	16 02	16 42	47·4	15 22	15 57	47·2	14 41	15 11	47·0	14 00	14 26	46·8	13 19	13 41	46·6	225	315

Lat. / A		66°			67°			68°			69°			70°			71°			Lat. / A	
LHA/F		A/H	B/P	Z_1/Z_2	A/H	B/P	Z_1/Z_2	A/H	B/P	Z_1/Z_2	A/H	B/P	Z_1/Z_2	A/H	B/P	Z_1/Z_2	A/H	B/P	Z_1/Z_2	LHA	
°	°	° ′	° ′	°	° ′	° ′	°	° ′	° ′	°	° ′	° ′	°	° ′	° ′	°	° ′	° ′	°	°	°
45	135	16 43	17 29	47·6	16 02	16 42	47·4	15 22	15 57	47·2	14 41	15 11	47·0	14 00	14 26	46·8	13 19	13 41	46·6	225	315
46	134	17 01	17 11	46·6	16 19	16 26	46·4	15 38	15 41	46·2	14 56	14 56	46·0	14 15	14 11	45·8	13 33	13 27	45·6	226	314
47	133	17 18	16 53	45·6	16 36	16 09	45·4	15 54	15 24	45·2	15 12	14 40	45·0	14 29	13 56	44·8	13 46	13 13	44·6	227	313
48	132	17 36	16 35	44·6	16 53	15 51	44·4	16 10	15 08	44·2	15 27	14 24	44·0	14 43	13 41	43·8	14 00	12 58	43·6	228	312
49	131	17 53	16 17	43·6	17 09	15 34	43·4	16 25	14 51	43·2	15 42	14 08	43·0	14 58	13 26	42·8	14 13	12 44	42·6	229	311
50	130	18 09	15 58	42·6	17 25	15 16	42·4	16 41	14 33	42·1	15 56	13 52	41·9	15 11	13 10	41·8	14 27	12 29	41·6	230	310
51	129	18 26	15 39	41·6	17 41	14 57	41·3	16 56	14 16	41·1	16 10	13 35	40·9	15 25	12 54	40·8	14 39	12 14	40·6	231	309
52	128	18 42	15 20	40·5	17 56	14 39	40·3	17 10	13 58	40·1	16 24	13 18	39·9	15 38	12 38	39·7	14 52	11 58	39·6	232	308
53	127	18 57	15 00	39·5	18 11	14 20	39·3	17 24	13 40	39·1	16 38	13 00	38·9	15 51	12 21	38·7	15 04	11 42	38·6	233	307
54	126	19 13	14 40	38·5	18 26	14 01	38·3	17 39	13 22	38·1	16 51	12 43	37·9	16 04	12 05	37·7	15 16	11 26	37·5	234	306
55	125	19 28	14 20	37·5	18 40	13 41	37·3	17 52	13 03	37·1	17 04	12 25	36·9	16 16	11 48	36·7	15 28	11 10	36·5	235	305
56	124	19 42	13 59	36·4	18 54	13 21	36·2	18 06	12 44	36·0	17 17	12 07	35·8	16 28	11 30	35·7	15 40	10 54	35·5	236	304
57	123	19 57	13 38	35·4	19 08	13 01	35·2	18 19	12 25	35·0	17 29	11 49	34·8	16 40	11 13	34·6	15 51	10 37	34·5	237	303
58	122	20 11	13 17	34·4	19 21	12 41	34·2	18 31	12 05	34·0	17 42	11 30	33·8	16 52	10 55	33·6	16 02	10 20	33·5	238	302
59	121	20 24	12 55	33·3	19 34	12 20	33·1	18 44	11 45	32·9	17 53	11 11	32·8	17 03	10 37	32·6	16 12	10 03	32·4	239	301
60	120	20 37	12 33	32·3	19 47	11 59	32·1	18 56	11 25	31·9	18 05	10 52	31·7	17 14	10 19	31·6	16 23	9 46	31·4	240	300
61	119	20 50	12 11	31·2	19 59	11 38	31·1	19 08	11 05	30·9	18 16	10 33	30·7	17 24	10 00	30·5	16 33	9 29	30·4	241	299
62	118	21 03	11 48	30·2	20 11	11 16	30·0	19 19	10 44	29·8	18 27	10 13	29·7	17 35	9 42	29·5	16 42	9 11	29·4	242	298
63	117	21 15	11 26	29·2	20 22	10 54	29·0	19 30	10 24	28·8	18 37	9 53	28·6	17 45	9 23	28·5	16 52	8 53	28·3	243	297
64	116	21 27	11 03	28·1	20 34	10 32	27·9	19 41	10 03	27·7	18 47	9 33	27·6	17 54	9 04	27·4	17 01	8 35	27·3	244	296
65	115	21 38	10 39	27·0	20 44	10 10	26·9	19 51	9 41	26·7	18 57	9 13	26·5	18 03	8 45	26·4	17 10	8 17	26·3	245	295
66	114	21 49	10 16	26·0	20 55	9 48	25·8	20 01	9 20	25·7	19 07	8 52	25·5	18 12	8 25	25·4	17 18	7 58	25·2	246	294
67	113	21 59	9 52	24·9	21 05	9 25	24·8	20 10	8 58	24·6	19 16	8 32	24·5	18 21	8 06	24·3	17 26	7 40	24·2	247	293
68	112	22 09	9 28	23·9	21 14	9 02	23·7	20 19	8 36	23·5	19 24	8 11	23·4	18 29	7 46	23·3	17 34	7 21	23·1	248	292
69	111	22 19	9 04	22·8	21 24	8 39	22·6	20 28	8 14	22·5	19 33	7 50	22·4	18 37	7 26	22·2	17 42	7 02	22·1	249	291
70	110	22 28	8 39	21·7	21 32	8 16	21·6	20 37	7 52	21·4	19 41	7 29	21·3	18 45	7 06	21·2	17 49	6 43	21·1	250	290
71	109	22 37	8 15	20·7	21 41	7 52	20·5	20 45	7 30	20·4	19 48	7 07	20·2	18 52	6 45	20·1	17 56	6 24	20·0	251	289
72	108	22 45	7 50	19·6	21 49	7 28	19·4	20 52	7 07	19·3	19 56	6 46	19·2	18 59	6 25	19·1	18 02	6 04	19·0	252	288
73	107	22 53	7 25	18·5	21 56	7 04	18·4	21 00	6 44	18·2	20 03	6 24	18·1	19 05	6 04	18·0	18 08	5 45	17·9	253	287
74	106	23 01	7 00	17·4	22 04	6 40	17·3	21 06	6 21	17·2	20 09	6 02	17·1	19 12	5 44	17·0	18 14	5 25	16·9	254	286
75	105	23 08	6 34	16·3	22 10	6 16	16·2	21 13	5 58	16·1	20 15	5 40	16·0	19 17	5 23	15·9	18 20	5 06	15·8	255	285
76	104	23 15	6 09	15·3	22 17	5 52	15·2	21 19	5 35	15·1	20 21	5 18	15·0	19 23	5 02	14·9	18 25	4 46	14·8	256	284
77	103	23 21	5 43	14·2	22 23	5 27	14·1	21 24	5 12	14·0	20 26	4 56	13·9	19 28	4 41	13·8	18 30	4 26	13·7	257	283
78	102	23 27	5 17	13·1	22 28	5 03	13·0	21 30	4 48	12·9	20 31	4 34	12·8	19 33	4 20	12·7	18 34	4 06	12·7	258	282
79	101	23 32	4 51	12·0	22 33	4 38	11·9	21 35	4 24	11·8	20 36	4 11	11·8	19 37	3 58	11·7	18 38	3 46	11·6	259	281
80	100	23 37	4 25	10·9	22 38	4 13	10·8	21 39	4 01	10·8	20 40	3 49	10·7	19 41	3 37	10·6	18 42	3 25	10·6	260	280
81	99	23 41	3 59	9·8	22 42	3 48	9·8	21 43	3 37	9·7	20 44	3 26	9·6	19 45	3 16	9·6	18 45	3 05	9·5	261	279
82	98	23 45	3 33	8·7	22 46	3 23	8·7	21 46	3 13	8·6	20 47	3 03	8·6	19 48	2 54	8·5	18 48	2 45	8·5	262	278
83	97	23 49	3 06	7·7	22 49	2 58	7·6	21 50	2 49	7·5	20 50	2 41	7·5	19 51	2 32	7·4	18 51	2 24	7·4	263	277
84	96	23 52	2 40	6·6	22 52	2 32	6·5	21 52	2 25	6·5	20 53	2 18	6·4	19 53	2 11	6·4	18 54	2 04	6·3	264	276
85	95	23 54	2 13	5·5	22 54	2 07	5·4	21 55	2 01	5·4	20 55	1 55	5·4	19 55	1 49	5·3	18 55	1 43	5·3	265	275
86	94	23 56	1 47	4·4	22 56	1 42	4·3	21 57	1 37	4·3	20 57	1 32	4·3	19 57	1 27	4·3	18 57	1 23	4·2	266	274
87	93	23 58	1 20	3·3	22 58	1 16	3·3	21 58	1 13	3·2	20 58	1 09	3·2	19 58	1 05	3·2	18 58	1 02	3·2	267	273
88	92	23 59	0 53	2·2	22 59	0 51	2·2	21 59	0 48	2·2	20 59	0 46	2·1	19 59	0 44	2·1	18 59	0 41	2·1	268	272
89	91	24 00	0 27	1·1	23 00	0 25	1·1	22 00	0 24	1·1	21 00	0 23	1·1	20 00	0 22	1·1	19 00	0 21	1·1	269	271
90	90	24 00	0 00	0·0	23 00	0 00	0·0	22 00	0 00	0·0	21 00	0 00	0·0	20 00	0 00	0·0	19 00	0 00	0·0	270	270

N. Lat: for LHA > 180° ... $Z_n = Z$
for LHA < 180° ... $Z_n = 360° - Z$

S. Lat.: for LHA > 180° ... $Z_n = 180° - Z$
for LHA < 180° ... $Z_n = 180° + Z$

SIGHT REDUCTION TABLE

B: (–) for 90° < LHA < 270°
Dec:(–) for Lat. contrary name

Z_1: same sign as B
Z_2: (–) for F > 90°

Lat. / A		72°			73°			74°			75°			76°			77°			Lat. / A	
LHA/F		A/H	B/P	Z_1/Z_2	A/H	B/P	Z_1/Z_2	A/H	B/P	Z_1/Z_2	A/H	B/P	Z_1/Z_2	A/H	B/P	Z_1/Z_2	A/H	B/P	Z_1/Z_2	LHA	
°	°	° ′	° ′	°	° ′	° ′	°	° ′	° ′	°	° ′	° ′	°	° ′	° ′	°	° ′	° ′	°	°	°
0	180	0 00	18 00	90·0	0 00	17 00	90·0	0 00	16 00	90·0	0 00	15 00	90·0	0 00	14 00	90·0	0 00	13 00	90·0	180	360
1	179	0 19	18 00	89·0	0 18	17 00	89·0	0 17	16 00	89·0	0 16	15 00	89·0	0 15	14 00	89·0	0 13	13 00	89·0	181	359
2	178	0 37	17 59	88·1	0 35	16 59	88·1	0 33	15 59	88·1	0 31	14 59	88·1	0 29	14 00	88·1	0 27	13 00	88·1	182	358
3	177	0 56	17 59	87·1	0 53	16 59	87·1	0 50	15 59	87·1	0 47	14 59	87·1	0 44	13 59	87·1	0 40	12 59	87·1	183	357
4	176	1 14	17 58	86·2	1 10	16 58	86·2	1 06	15 58	86·2	1 02	14 58	86·1	0 58	13 58	86·1	0 54	12 58	86·1	184	356
5	175	1 33	17 56	85·2	1 28	16 56	85·2	1 23	15 57	85·2	1 18	14 57	85·2	1 12	13 57	85·1	1 07	12 57	85·1	185	355
6	174	1 51	17 54	84·3	1 45	16 55	84·3	1 39	15 55	84·2	1 33	14 55	84·2	1 27	13 56	84·2	1 21	12 56	84·2	186	354
7	173	2 09	17 52	83·3	2 03	16 53	83·3	1 56	15 53	83·3	1 48	14 54	83·2	1 41	13 54	83·2	1 34	12 54	83·2	187	353
8	172	2 28	17 50	82·4	2 20	16 51	82·3	2 12	15 51	82·3	2 04	14 52	82·3	1 56	13 52	82·2	1 48	12 53	82·2	188	352
9	171	2 46	17 48	81·4	2 37	16 48	81·4	2 28	15 49	81·3	2 19	14 49	81·3	2 10	13 50	81·3	2 01	12 51	81·2	189	351
10	170	3 05	17 45	80·5	2 55	16 45	80·4	2 45	15 46	80·4	2 35	14 47	80·3	2 24	13 48	80·3	2 14	12 49	80·3	190	350
11	169	3 23	17 41	79·5	3 12	16 42	79·5	3 01	15 43	79·4	2 50	14 44	79·4	2 39	13 45	79·3	2 28	12 46	79·3	191	349
12	168	3 41	17 38	78·6	3 29	16 39	78·5	3 17	15 40	78·5	3 05	14 41	78·4	2 53	13 42	78·3	2 41	12 44	78·3	192	348
13	167	3 59	17 34	77·6	3 46	16 35	77·5	3 33	15 37	77·5	3 20	14 38	77·4	3 07	13 39	77·4	2 54	12 41	77·3	193	347
14	166	4 17	17 30	76·7	4 03	16 31	76·6	3 49	15 33	76·5	3 35	14 34	76·5	3 21	13 36	76·4	3 07	12 38	76·3	194	346
15	165	4 35	17 25	75·7	4 20	16 27	75·6	4 05	15 29	75·6	3 50	14 31	75·5	3 35	13 32	75·4	3 20	12 34	75·4	195	345
16	164	4 53	17 21	74·7	4 37	16 23	74·7	4 21	15 25	74·6	4 05	14 27	74·5	3 49	13 29	74·5	3 33	12 31	74·4	196	344
17	163	5 11	17 16	73·8	4 54	16 18	73·7	4 37	15 20	73·6	4 20	14 22	73·5	4 03	13 25	73·5	3 46	12 27	73·4	197	343
18	162	5 29	17 10	72·8	5 11	16 13	72·7	4 53	15 15	72·7	4 35	14 18	72·6	4 17	13 20	72·5	3 59	12 23	72·4	198	342
19	161	5 46	17 05	71·9	5 28	16 07	71·8	5 09	15 10	71·7	4 50	14 13	71·6	4 31	13 16	71·5	4 12	12 19	71·5	199	341
20	160	6 04	16 59	70·9	5 44	16 02	70·8	5 25	15 05	70·7	5 05	14 08	70·6	4 45	13 11	70·5	4 25	12 14	70·5	200	340
21	159	6 21	16 52	69·9	6 01	15 56	69·8	5 40	14 59	69·7	5 19	14 03	69·7	4 58	13 06	69·6	4 37	12 10	69·5	201	339
22	158	6 39	16 46	69·0	6 17	15 50	68·9	5 56	14 53	68·8	5 34	13 57	68·7	5 12	13 01	68·6	4 50	12 05	68·5	202	338
23	157	6 56	16 39	68·0	6 34	15 43	67·9	6 11	14 47	67·8	5 48	13 51	67·7	5 25	12 56	67·6	5 03	12 00	67·5	203	337
24	156	7 13	16 32	67·1	6 50	15 36	66·9	6 26	14 41	66·8	6 03	13 45	66·7	5 39	12 50	66·6	5 15	11 55	66·5	204	336
25	155	7 30	16 25	66·1	7 06	15 29	66·0	6 41	14 34	65·9	6 17	13 39	65·8	5 52	12 44	65·7	5 27	11 49	65·6	205	335
26	154	7 47	16 17	65·1	7 22	15 22	65·0	6 56	14 27	64·9	6 31	13 32	64·8	6 05	12 38	64·7	5 40	11 43	64·6	206	334
27	153	8 04	16 09	64·1	7 38	15 14	64·0	7 11	14 20	63·9	6 45	13 26	63·8	6 18	12 32	63·7	5 52	11 37	63·6	207	333
28	152	8 20	16 00	63·2	7 53	15 06	63·0	7 26	14 12	62·9	6 59	13 19	62·8	6 31	12 25	62·7	6 04	11 31	62·6	208	332
29	151	8 37	15 52	62·2	8 09	14 58	62·1	7 41	14 05	61·9	7 13	13 11	61·8	6 44	12 18	61·7	6 16	11 25	61·6	209	331
30	150	8 53	15 43	61·2	8 24	14 50	61·1	7 55	13 57	61·0	7 26	13 04	60·9	6 57	12 11	60·7	6 27	11 18	60·6	210	330
31	149	9 09	15 34	60·3	8 40	14 41	60·1	8 10	13 49	60·0	7 40	12 56	59·9	7 09	12 04	59·8	6 39	11 12	59·7	211	329
32	148	9 25	15 24	59·3	8 55	14 32	59·1	8 24	13 40	59·0	7 53	12 48	58·9	7 22	11 56	58·8	6 51	11 05	58·7	212	328
33	147	9 41	15 15	58·3	9 10	14 23	58·2	8 38	13 31	58·0	8 06	12 40	57·9	7 34	11 49	57·8	7 02	10 57	57·7	213	327
34	146	9 57	15 05	57·3	9 25	14 13	57·2	8 52	13 22	57·0	8 19	12 31	56·9	7 46	11 41	56·8	7 14	10 50	56·7	214	326
35	145	10 13	14 54	56·3	9 39	14 04	56·2	9 06	13 13	56·1	8 32	12 23	55·9	7 59	11 33	55·8	7 25	10 43	55·7	215	325
36	144	10 28	14 44	55·4	9 54	13 54	55·2	9 19	13 04	55·1	8 45	12 14	54·9	8 11	11 24	54·8	7 36	10 35	54·7	216	324
37	143	10 43	14 33	54·4	10 08	13 43	54·2	9 33	12 54	54·1	8 58	12 05	53·9	8 22	11 16	53·8	7 47	10 27	53·7	217	323
38	142	10 58	14 22	53·4	10 22	13 33	53·2	9 46	12 44	53·1	9 10	11 55	53·0	8 34	11 07	52·8	7 58	10 19	52·7	218	322
39	141	11 13	14 10	52·4	10 36	13 22	52·2	9 59	12 34	52·1	9 22	11 46	52·0	8 45	10 58	51·8	8 08	10 10	51·7	219	321
40	140	11 27	13 59	51·4	10 50	13 11	51·3	10 12	12 23	51·1	9 35	11 36	51·0	8 57	10 49	50·8	8 19	10 02	50·7	220	320
41	139	11 42	13 47	50·4	11 04	13 00	50·3	10 25	12 13	50·1	9 47	11 26	50·0	9 08	10 39	49·9	8 29	9 53	49·7	221	319
42	138	11 56	13 34	49·4	11 17	12 48	49·3	10 38	12 02	49·1	9 58	11 16	49·0	9 19	10 30	48·9	8 39	9 44	48·7	222	318
43	137	12 10	13 22	48·4	11 30	12 36	48·3	10 50	11 51	48·1	10 10	11 05	48·0	9 30	10 20	47·9	8 49	9 35	47·7	223	317
44	136	12 24	13 09	47·4	11 43	12 24	47·3	11 02	11 39	47·1	10 21	10 55	47·0	9 40	10 10	46·9	8 59	9 26	46·7	224	316
45	135	12 37	12 56	46·4	11 56	12 12	46·3	11 14	11 28	46·1	10 33	10 44	46·0	9 51	10 00	45·9	9 09	9 16	45·7	225	315

Lat. / A		72°			73°			74°			75°			76°			77°			Lat. / A	
LHA/F		A/H	B/P	Z_1/Z_2	A/H	B/P	Z_1/Z_2	A/H	B/P	Z_1/Z_2	A/H	B/P	Z_1/Z_2	A/H	B/P	Z_1/Z_2	A/H	B/P	Z_1/Z_2	LHA	
°	°	° ′	° ′	°	° ′	° ′	°	° ′	° ′	°	° ′	° ′	°	° ′	° ′	°	° ′	° ′	°	°	°
45	135	12 37	12 56	46·4	11 56	12 12	46·3	11 14	11 28	46·1	10 33	10 44	46·0	9 51	10 00	45·9	9 09	9 16	45·7	225	315
46	134	12 51	12 43	45·4	12 08	11 59	45·3	11 26	11 16	45·1	10 44	10 33	45·0	10 01	9 50	44·9	9 19	9 07	44·7	226	314
47	133	13 04	12 30	44·4	12 21	11 47	44·3	11 38	11 04	44·1	10 55	10 21	44·0	10 11	9 39	43·9	9 28	8 57	43·7	227	313
48	132	13 17	12 16	43·4	12 33	11 34	43·3	11 49	10 52	43·1	11 05	10 10	43·0	10 21	9 28	42·9	9 37	8 47	42·7	228	312
49	131	13 29	12 02	42·4	12 45	11 21	42·3	12 00	10 39	42·1	11 16	9 58	42·0	10 31	9 17	41·9	9 46	8 37	41·7	229	311
50	130	13 42	11 48	41·4	12 57	11 07	41·3	12 11	10 27	41·1	11 26	9 46	41·0	10 41	9 06	40·9	9 55	8 26	40·7	230	310
51	129	13 54	11 33	40·4	13 08	10 53	40·3	12 22	10 14	40·1	11 36	9 34	40·0	10 50	8 55	39·8	10 04	8 16	39·7	231	309
52	128	14 06	11 19	39·4	13 19	10 40	39·2	12 33	10 01	39·1	11 46	9 22	39·0	10 59	8 44	38·8	10 13	8 05	38·7	232	308
53	127	14 17	11 04	38·4	13 30	10 26	38·2	12 43	9 47	38·1	11 56	9 10	38·0	11 08	8 32	37·8	10 21	7 55	37·7	233	307
54	126	14 29	10 49	37·4	13 41	10 11	37·2	12 53	9 34	37·1	12 05	8 57	36·9	11 17	8 20	36·8	10 29	7 44	36·7	234	306
55	125	14 40	10 33	36·4	13 51	9 57	36·2	13 03	9 20	36·1	12 14	8 44	35·9	11 26	8 08	35·8	10 37	7 33	35·7	235	305
56	124	14 51	10 18	35·3	14 02	9 42	35·2	13 13	9 07	35·1	12 23	8 31	34·9	11 34	7 56	34·8	10 45	7 21	34·7	236	304
57	123	15 01	10 02	34·3	14 12	9 27	34·2	13 22	8 53	34·0	12 32	8 18	33·9	11 42	7 44	33·8	10 52	7 10	33·7	237	303
58	122	15 12	9 46	33·3	14 21	9 12	33·2	13 31	8 38	33·0	12 41	8 05	32·9	11 50	7 32	32·8	11 00	6 58	32·7	238	302
59	121	15 22	9 30	32·3	14 31	8 57	32·1	13 40	8 24	32·0	12 49	7 51	31·9	11 58	7 19	31·8	11 07	6 47	31·7	239	301
60	120	15 31	9 14	31·3	14 40	8 41	31·1	13 49	8 10	31·0	12 57	7 38	30·9	12 06	7 06	30·8	11 14	6 35	30·6	240	300
61	119	15 41	8 57	30·2	14 49	8 26	30·1	13 57	7 55	30·0	13 05	7 24	29·8	12 13	6 54	29·7	11 21	6 23	29·6	241	299
62	118	15 50	8 40	29·2	14 58	8 10	29·1	14 05	7 40	28·9	13 13	7 10	28·8	12 20	6 41	28·7	11 27	6 11	28·6	242	298
63	117	15 59	8 23	28·2	15 06	7 54	28·0	14 13	7 25	27·9	13 20	6 56	27·8	12 27	6 27	27·7	11 34	5 59	27·6	243	297
64	116	16 08	8 06	27·2	15 14	7 38	27·0	14 21	7 10	26·9	13 27	6 42	26·8	12 34	6 14	26·7	11 40	5 47	26·6	244	296
65	115	16 16	7 49	26·1	15 22	7 22	26·0	14 28	6 55	25·9	13 34	6 28	25·8	12 40	6 01	25·7	11 46	5 34	25·6	245	295
66	114	16 24	7 32	25·1	15 29	7 05	25·0	14 35	6 39	24·9	13 41	6 13	24·7	12 46	5 47	24·6	11 52	5 22	24·6	246	294
67	113	16 32	7 14	24·1	15 37	6 49	23·9	14 42	6 24	23·8	13 47	5 59	23·7	12 52	5 34	23·6	11 57	5 09	23·5	247	293
68	112	16 39	6 56	23·0	15 44	6 32	22·9	14 48	6 08	22·8	13 53	5 44	22·7	12 58	5 20	22·6	12 02	4 57	22·5	248	292
69	111	16 46	6 38	22·0	15 50	6 15	21·9	14 55	5 52	21·8	13 59	5 29	21·7	13 03	5 06	21·6	12 07	4 44	21·5	249	291
70	110	16 53	6 20	20·9	15 57	5 58	20·8	15 01	5 36	20·7	14 05	5 14	20·6	13 08	4 52	20·6	12 12	4 31	20·5	250	290
71	109	16 59	6 02	19·9	16 03	5 41	19·8	15 06	5 20	19·7	14 10	4 59	19·6	13 13	4 38	19·5	12 17	4 18	19·5	251	289
72	108	17 05	5 44	18·9	16 09	5 24	18·8	15 12	5 04	18·7	14 15	4 44	18·6	13 18	4 24	18·5	12 21	4 05	18·4	252	288
73	107	17 11	5 26	17·8	16 14	5 06	17·7	15 17	4 48	17·6	14 20	4 29	17·6	13 23	4 10	17·5	12 25	3 52	17·4	253	287
74	106	17 17	5 07	16·8	16 19	4 49	16·7	15 22	4 31	16·6	14 24	4 13	16·5	13 27	3 56	16·5	12 29	3 38	16·4	254	286
75	105	17 22	4 48	15·7	16 24	4 31	15·7	15 26	4 15	15·6	14 29	3 58	15·5	13 31	3 42	15·4	12 33	3 25	15·4	255	285
76	104	17 27	4 30	14·7	16 29	4 14	14·6	15 31	3 58	14·5	14 33	3 43	14·5	13 35	3 27	14·4	12 36	3 12	14·4	256	284
77	103	17 31	4 11	13·6	16 33	3 56	13·6	15 35	3 41	13·5	14 36	3 27	13·4	13 38	3 13	13·4	12 40	2 58	13·3	257	283
78	102	17 36	3 52	12·6	16 37	3 38	12·5	15 38	3 25	12·5	14 40	3 11	12·4	13 41	2 58	12·4	12 43	2 45	12·3	258	282
79	101	17 39	3 33	11·6	16 41	3 20	11·5	15 42	3 08	11·4	14 43	2 56	11·4	13 44	2 43	11·3	12 45	2 31	11·3	259	281
80	100	17 43	3 14	10·5	16 44	3 02	10·4	15 45	2 51	10·4	14 46	2 40	10·3	13 47	2 29	10·3	12 48	2 18	10·3	260	280
81	99	17 46	2 55	9·5	16 47	2 44	9·4	15 48	2 34	9·4	14 49	2 24	9·3	13 49	2 14	9·3	12 50	2 04	9·2	261	279
82	98	17 49	2 35	8·4	16 50	2 26	8·4	15 50	2 17	8·3	14 51	2 08	8·3	13 52	1 59	8·2	12 52	1 50	8·2	262	278
83	97	17 52	2 16	7·4	16 52	2 08	7·3	15 53	2 00	7·3	14 53	1 52	7·2	13 54	1 44	7·2	12 54	1 37	7·2	263	277
84	96	17 54	1 57	6·3	16 54	1 50	6·3	15 55	1 43	6·2	14 55	1 36	6·2	13 55	1 30	6·2	12 56	1 23	6·2	264	276
85	95	17 56	1 37	5·3	16 56	1 32	5·2	15 56	1 26	5·2	14 56	1 20	5·2	13 57	1 15	5·2	12 57	1 09	5·1	265	275
86	94	17 57	1 18	4·2	16 57	1 13	4·2	15 58	1 09	4·2	14 58	1 04	4·1	13 58	1 00	4·1	12 58	0 55	4·1	266	274
87	93	17 58	0 58	3·2	16 59	0 55	3·1	15 59	0 52	3·1	14 59	0 48	3·1	13 59	0 45	3·1	12 59	0 42	3·1	267	273
88	92	17 59	0 39	2·1	16 59	0 37	2·1	15 59	0 34	2·1	14 59	0 32	2·1	13 59	0 30	2·1	13 00	0 28	2·1	268	272
89	91	18 00	0 19	1·1	17 00	0 18	1·0	16 00	0 17	1·0	15 00	0 16	1·0	14 00	0 15	1·0	13 00	0 14	1·0	269	271
90	90	18 00	0 00	0·0	17 00	0 00	0·0	16 00	0 00	0·0	15 00	0 00	0·0	14 00	0 00	0·0	13 00	0 00	0·0	270	270

N. Lat: for LHA > 180° … $Z_n = Z$
for LHA < 180° … $Z_n = 360° - Z$

S. Lat.: for LHA > 180° … $Z_n = 180° - Z$
for LHA < 180° … $Z_n = 180° + Z$

SIGHT REDUCTION TABLE

B: (−) for 90° < LHA < 270°
Dec: (−) for Lat. contrary name

Z_1: same sign as B
Z_2: (−) for F > 90°

Lat. / A		78°			79°			80°			81°			82°			83°			Lat. / A	
LHA/F		A/H	B/P	Z_1/Z_2	A/H	B/P	Z_1/Z_2	A/H	B/P	Z_1/Z_2	A/H	B/P	Z_1/Z_2	A/H	B/P	Z_1/Z_2	A/H	B/P	Z_1/Z_2	LHA	
°	°	° ′	° ′	°	° ′	° ′	°	° ′	° ′	°	° ′	° ′	°	° ′	° ′	°	° ′	° ′	°	°	°
0	180	0 00	12 00	90·0	0 00	11 00	90·0	0 00	10 00	90·0	0 00	9 00	90·0	0 00	8 00	90·0	0 00	7 00	90·0	180	360
1	179	0 12	12 00	89·0	0 11	11 00	89·0	0 10	10 00	89·0	0 09	9 00	89·0	0 08	8 00	89·0	0 07	7 00	89·0	181	359
2	178	0 25	12 00	88·0	0 23	11 00	88·0	0 21	10 00	88·0	0 19	9 00	88·0	0 17	8 00	88·0	0 15	7 00	88·0	182	358
3	177	0 37	11 59	87·1	0 34	10 59	87·1	0 31	9 59	87·0	0 28	8 59	87·0	0 25	7 59	87·0	0 22	6 59	87·0	183	357
4	176	0 50	11 58	86·1	0 46	10 58	86·1	0 42	9 59	86·1	0 38	8 59	86·0	0 33	7 59	86·0	0 29	6 59	86·0	184	356
5	175	1 02	11 57	85·1	0 57	10 58	85·1	0 52	9 58	85·1	0 47	8 58	85·1	0 42	7 58	85·0	0 37	6 58	85·0	185	355
6	174	1 15	11 56	84·1	1 09	10 56	84·1	1 02	9 57	84·1	0 56	8 57	84·1	0 50	7 57	84·1	0 44	6 58	84·0	186	354
7	173	1 27	11 55	83·2	1 20	10 55	83·1	1 13	9 56	83·1	1 06	8 56	83·1	0 58	7 56	83·1	0 51	6 57	83·1	187	353
8	172	1 39	11 53	82·2	1 31	10 54	82·1	1 23	9 54	82·1	1 15	8 55	82·1	1 07	7 55	82·1	0 58	6 56	82·1	188	352
9	171	1 52	11 51	81·2	1 43	10 52	81·2	1 33	9 53	81·1	1 24	8 53	81·1	1 15	7 54	81·1	1 06	6 55	81·1	189	351
10	170	2 04	11 49	80·2	1 54	10 50	80·2	1 44	9 51	80·1	1 33	8 52	80·1	1 23	7 53	80·1	1 13	6 54	80·1	190	350
11	169	2 16	11 47	79·2	2 05	10 48	79·2	1 54	9 49	79·2	1 43	8 50	79·1	1 31	7 51	79·1	1 20	6 52	79·1	191	349
12	168	2 29	11 45	78·3	2 16	10 46	78·2	2 04	9 47	78·2	1 52	8 48	78·1	1 39	7 50	78·1	1 27	6 51	78·1	192	348
13	167	2 41	11 42	77·3	2 28	10 43	77·2	2 14	9 45	77·2	2 01	8 46	77·2	1 48	7 48	77·1	1 34	6 49	77·1	193	347
14	166	2 53	11 39	76·3	2 39	10 41	76·2	2 24	9 43	76·2	2 10	8 44	76·2	1 56	7 46	76·1	1 41	6 48	76·1	194	346
15	165	3 05	11 36	75·3	2 50	10 38	75·3	2 35	9 40	75·2	2 19	8 42	75·2	2 04	7 44	75·1	1 48	6 46	75·1	195	345
16	164	3 17	11 33	74·3	3 01	10 35	74·3	2 45	9 37	74·2	2 28	8 39	74·2	2 12	7 42	74·1	1 56	6 44	74·1	196	344
17	163	3 29	11 29	73·4	3 12	10 32	73·3	2 55	9 34	73·2	2 37	8 37	73·2	2 20	7 39	73·2	2 03	6 42	73·1	197	343
18	162	3 41	11 26	72·4	3 23	10 28	72·3	3 05	9 31	72·3	2 46	8 34	72·2	2 28	7 37	72·2	2 09	6 40	72·1	198	342
19	161	3 53	11 22	71·4	3 34	10 25	71·3	3 14	9 28	71·3	2 55	8 31	71·2	2 36	7 34	71·2	2 16	6 37	71·1	199	341
20	160	4 05	11 18	70·4	3 45	10 21	70·3	3 24	9 24	70·3	3 04	8 28	70·2	2 44	7 31	70·2	2 23	6 35	70·1	200	340
21	159	4 16	11 13	69·4	3 55	10 17	69·4	3 34	9 21	69·3	3 13	8 25	69·2	2 52	7 28	69·2	2 30	6 32	69·1	201	339
22	158	4 28	11 09	68·4	4 06	10 13	68·4	3 44	9 17	68·3	3 22	8 21	68·2	2 59	7 25	68·2	2 37	6 30	68·1	202	338
23	157	4 40	11 04	67·5	4 17	10 09	67·4	3 53	9 13	67·3	3 30	8 18	67·3	3 07	7 22	67·2	2 44	6 27	67·2	203	337
24	156	4 51	10 59	66·5	4 27	10 04	66·4	4 03	9 09	66·3	3 39	8 14	66·3	3 15	7 19	66·2	2 50	6 24	66·2	204	336
25	155	5 02	10 54	65·5	4 38	9 59	65·4	4 13	9 05	65·3	3 47	8 10	65·3	3 22	7 16	65·2	2 57	6 21	65·2	205	335
26	154	5 14	10 49	64·5	4 48	9 55	64·4	4 22	9 00	64·3	3 56	8 06	64·3	3 30	7 12	64·2	3 04	6 18	64·2	206	334
27	153	5 25	10 43	63·5	4 58	9 50	63·4	4 31	8 56	63·4	4 04	8 02	63·3	3 37	7 08	63·2	3 10	6 15	63·2	207	333
28	152	5 36	10 38	62·5	5 08	9 44	62·4	4 41	8 51	62·4	4 13	7 58	62·3	3 45	7 04	62·2	3 17	6 11	62·2	208	332
29	151	5 47	10 32	61·5	5 18	9 39	61·4	4 50	8 46	61·4	4 21	7 53	61·3	3 52	7 00	61·2	3 23	6 08	61·2	209	331
30	150	5 58	10 26	60·5	5 28	9 33	60·5	4 59	8 41	60·4	4 29	7 49	60·3	3 59	6 56	60·2	3 30	6 04	60·2	210	330
31	149	6 09	10 20	59·6	5 38	9 28	59·5	5 08	8 36	59·4	4 37	7 44	59·3	4 07	6 52	59·2	3 36	6 00	59·2	211	329
32	148	6 20	10 13	58·6	5 48	9 22	58·5	5 17	8 30	58·4	4 45	7 39	58·3	4 14	6 48	58·3	3 42	5 57	58·2	212	328
33	147	6 30	10 06	57·6	5 58	9 16	57·5	5 26	8 25	57·4	4 53	7 34	57·3	4 21	6 43	57·3	3 48	5 53	57·2	213	327
34	146	6 41	10 00	56·6	6 08	9 09	56·5	5 34	8 19	56·4	5 01	7 29	56·3	4 28	6 39	56·3	3 54	5 49	56·2	214	326
35	145	6 51	9 53	55·6	6 17	9 03	55·5	5 43	8 13	55·4	5 09	7 24	55·3	4 35	6 34	55·3	4 00	5 45	55·2	215	325
36	144	7 01	9 45	54·6	6 26	8 56	54·5	5 51	8 07	54·4	5 17	7 18	54·3	4 42	6 29	54·3	4 06	5 40	54·2	216	324
37	143	7 11	9 38	53·6	6 36	8 49	53·5	6 00	8 01	53·4	5 24	7 13	53·3	4 48	6 24	53·3	4 12	5 36	53·2	217	323
38	142	7 21	9 31	52·6	6 45	8 43	52·5	6 08	7 55	52·4	5 32	7 07	52·3	4 55	6 19	52·3	4 18	5 32	52·2	218	322
39	141	7 31	9 23	51·6	6 54	8 35	51·5	6 16	7 48	51·4	5 39	7 01	51·3	5 01	6 14	51·3	4 24	5 27	51·2	219	321
40	140	7 41	9 15	50·6	7 03	8 28	50·5	6 25	7 42	50·4	5 46	6 55	50·3	5 08	6 09	50·3	4 30	5 22	50·2	220	320
41	139	7 50	9 07	49·6	7 11	8 21	49·5	6 32	7 35	49·4	5 53	6 49	49·4	5 14	6 03	49·3	4 35	5 18	49·2	221	319
42	138	8 00	8 59	48·6	7 20	8 13	48·5	6 40	7 28	48·4	6 01	6 43	48·4	5 21	5 58	48·3	4 41	5 13	48·2	222	318
43	137	8 09	8 50	47·6	7 29	8 05	47·5	6 48	7 21	47·4	6 07	6 36	47·4	5 27	5 52	47·3	4 46	5 08	47·2	223	317
44	136	8 18	8 42	46·6	7 37	7 58	46·5	6 56	7 14	46·4	6 14	6 30	46·4	5 33	5 46	46·3	4 51	5 03	46·2	224	316
45	135	8 27	8 33	45·6	7 45	7 50	45·5	7 03	7 06	45·4	6 21	6 23	45·4	5 39	5 41	45·3	4 57	4 58	45·2	225	315

Lat. / A		78°			79°			80°			81°			82°			83°			Lat. / A	
LHA/F		A/H	B/P	Z_1/Z_2	A/H	B/P	Z_1/Z_2	A/H	B/P	Z_1/Z_2	A/H	B/P	Z_1/Z_2	A/H	B/P	Z_1/Z_2	A/H	B/P	Z_1/Z_2	LHA	
°	°	° ′	° ′	°	° ′	° ′	°	° ′	° ′	°	° ′	° ′	°	° ′	° ′	°	° ′	° ′	°	°	°
45	135	8 27	8 33	45·6	7 45	7 50	45·5	7 03	7 06	45·4	6 21	6 23	45·4	5 39	5 41	45·3	4 57	4 58	45·2	225	315
46	134	8 36	8 24	44·6	7 53	7 41	44·5	7 11	6 59	44·4	6 28	6 17	44·4	5 45	5 35	44·3	5 02	4 53	44·2	226	314
47	133	8 45	8 15	43·6	8 01	7 33	43·5	7 18	6 51	43·4	6 34	6 10	43·4	5 51	5 28	43·3	5 07	4 47	43·2	227	313
48	132	8 53	8 06	42·6	8 09	7 25	42·5	7 25	6 44	42·4	6 41	6 03	42·4	5 56	5 22	42·3	5 12	4 42	42·2	228	312
49	131	9 02	7 56	41·6	8 17	7 16	41·5	7 32	6 36	41·4	6 47	5 56	41·4	6 02	5 16	41·3	5 17	4 36	41·2	229	311
50	130	9 10	7 47	40·6	8 24	7 07	40·5	7 39	6 28	40·4	6 53	5 49	40·3	6 07	5 10	40·3	5 21	4 31	40·2	230	310
51	129	9 18	7 37	39·6	8 32	6 58	39·5	7 45	6 20	39·4	6 59	5 42	39·3	6 13	5 03	39·3	5 26	4 25	39·2	231	309
52	128	9 26	7 27	38·6	8 39	6 49	38·5	7 52	6 12	38·4	7 05	5 34	38·3	6 18	4 57	38·3	5 31	4 19	38·2	232	308
53	127	9 33	7 17	37·6	8 46	6 40	37·5	7 58	6 03	37·4	7 11	5 27	37·3	6 23	4 50	37·3	5 35	4 14	37·2	233	307
54	126	9 41	7 07	36·6	8 53	6 31	36·5	8 05	5 55	36·4	7 16	5 19	36·3	6 28	4 43	36·3	5 39	4 08	36·2	234	306
55	125	9 48	6 57	35·6	9 00	6 22	35·5	8 11	5 47	35·4	7 22	5 11	35·3	6 33	4 37	35·3	5 44	4 02	35·2	235	305
56	124	9 56	6 47	34·6	9 06	6 12	34·5	8 17	5 38	34·4	7 27	5 04	34·3	6 38	4 30	34·3	5 48	3 56	34·2	236	304
57	123	10 03	6 36	33·6	9 13	6 03	33·5	8 22	5 29	33·4	7 32	4 56	33·3	6 42	4 23	33·3	5 52	3 50	33·2	237	303
58	122	10 09	6 26	32·6	9 19	5 53	32·5	8 28	5 20	32·4	7 37	4 48	32·3	6 47	4 16	32·3	5 56	3 43	32·2	238	302
59	121	10 16	6 15	31·6	9 25	5 43	31·5	8 34	5 11	31·4	7 42	4 40	31·3	6 51	4 08	31·2	6 00	3 37	31·2	239	301
60	120	10 22	6 04	30·6	9 31	5 33	30·5	8 39	5 02	30·4	7 47	4 32	30·3	6 55	4 01	30·2	6 04	3 31	30·2	240	300
61	119	10 29	5 53	29·5	9 36	5 23	29·5	8 44	4 53	29·4	7 52	4 23	29·3	6 59	3 54	29·2	6 07	3 24	29·2	241	299
62	118	10 35	5 42	28·5	9 42	5 13	28·4	8 49	4 44	28·4	7 56	4 15	28·3	7 04	3 46	28·2	6 11	3 18	28·2	242	298
63	117	10 41	5 31	27·5	9 47	5 03	27·4	8 54	4 35	27·4	8 01	4 07	27·3	7 07	3 39	27·2	6 14	3 11	27·2	243	297
64	116	10 46	5 19	26·5	9 52	4 52	26·4	8 59	4 25	26·3	8 05	3 58	26·3	7 11	3 32	26·2	6 17	3 05	26·2	244	296
65	115	10 52	5 08	25·5	9 57	4 42	25·4	9 03	4 16	25·3	8 09	3 50	25·3	7 15	3 24	25·2	6 20	2 58	25·2	245	295
66	114	10 57	4 56	24·5	10 02	4 31	24·4	9 08	4 06	24·3	8 13	3 41	24·3	7 18	3 16	24·2	6 24	2 52	24·2	246	294
67	113	11 02	4 45	23·5	10 07	4 21	23·4	9 12	3 56	23·3	8 17	3 32	23·3	7 22	3 09	23·2	6 26	2 45	23·2	247	293
68	112	11 07	4 33	22·4	10 11	4 10	22·4	9 16	3 47	22·3	8 20	3 24	22·2	7 25	3 01	22·2	6 29	2 38	22·1	248	292
69	111	11 12	4 21	21·4	10 16	3 59	21·4	9 20	3 37	21·3	8 24	3 15	21·2	7 28	2 53	21·2	6 32	2 31	21·1	249	291
70	110	11 16	4 09	20·4	10 20	3 48	20·3	9 23	3 27	20·3	8 27	3 06	20·2	7 31	2 45	20·2	6 35	2 24	20·1	250	290
71	109	11 20	3 58	19·4	10 24	3 37	19·3	9 27	3 17	19·3	8 30	2 57	19·2	7 34	2 37	19·2	6 37	2 17	19·1	251	289
72	108	11 24	3 45	18·4	10 27	3 26	18·3	9 30	3 07	18·3	8 33	2 48	18·2	7 36	2 29	18·2	6 39	2 10	18·1	252	288
73	107	11 28	3 33	17·4	10 31	3 15	17·3	9 34	2 57	17·2	8 36	2 39	17·2	7 39	2 21	17·2	6 42	2 03	17·1	253	287
74	106	11 32	3 21	16·3	10 34	3 04	16·3	9 37	2 47	16·2	8 39	2 30	16·2	7 41	2 13	16·1	6 44	1 56	16·1	254	286
75	105	11 35	3 09	15·3	10 37	2 53	15·3	9 39	2 37	15·2	8 41	2 21	15·2	7 44	2 05	15·1	6 46	1 49	15·1	255	285
76	104	11 38	2 57	14·3	10 40	2 42	14·3	9 42	2 27	14·2	8 44	2 12	14·2	7 46	1 57	14·1	6 47	1 42	14·1	256	284
77	103	11 41	2 44	13·3	10 43	2 30	13·2	9 44	2 16	13·2	8 46	2 02	13·2	7 48	1 49	13·1	6 49	1 35	13·1	257	283
78	102	11 44	2 32	12·3	10 45	2 19	12·2	9 47	2 06	12·2	8 48	1 53	12·1	7 49	1 40	12·1	6 51	1 28	12·1	258	282
79	101	11 47	2 19	11·2	10 48	2 07	11·2	9 49	1 56	11·2	8 50	1 44	11·1	7 51	1 32	11·1	6 52	1 21	11·1	259	281
80	100	11 49	2 07	10·2	10 50	1 56	10·2	9 51	1 45	10·2	8 52	1 35	10·1	7 53	1 24	10·1	6 54	1 13	10·1	260	280
81	99	11 51	1 54	9·2	10 52	1 45	9·2	9 53	1 35	9·1	8 53	1 25	9·1	7 54	1 16	9·1	6 55	1 06	9·1	261	279
82	98	11 53	1 42	8·2	10 53	1 33	8·1	9 54	1 24	8·1	8 55	1 16	8·1	7 55	1 07	8·1	6 56	0 59	8·1	262	278
83	97	11 55	1 29	7·2	10 55	1 21	7·1	9 55	1 14	7·1	8 56	1 06	7·1	7 56	0 59	7·1	6 57	0 51	7·1	263	277
84	96	11 56	1 16	6·1	10 56	1 10	6·1	9 57	1 03	6·1	8 57	0 57	6·1	7 57	0 50	6·1	6 58	0 44	6·0	264	276
85	95	11 57	1 04	5·1	10 57	0 58	5·1	9 58	0 53	5·1	8 58	0 47	5·1	7 58	0 42	5·0	6 58	0 37	5·0	265	275
86	94	11 58	0 51	4·1	10 58	0 47	4·1	9 59	0 42	4·1	8 59	0 38	4·0	7 59	0 34	4·0	6 59	0 29	4·0	266	274
87	93	11 59	0 38	3·1	10 59	0 35	3·1	9 59	0 32	3·0	8 59	0 28	3·0	7 59	0 25	3·0	6 59	0 22	3·0	267	273
88	92	12 00	0 26	2·0	11 00	0 23	2·0	10 00	0 21	2·0	9 00	0 19	2·0	8 00	0 17	2·0	7 00	0 15	2·0	268	272
89	91	12 00	0 13	1·0	11 00	0 12	1·0	10 00	0 11	1·0	9 00	0 10	1·0	8 00	0 08	1·0	7 00	0 07	1·0	269	271
90	90	12 00	0 00	0·0	11 00	0 00	0·0	10 00	0 00	0·0	9 00	0 00	0·0	8 00	0 00	0·0	7 00	0 00	0·0	270	270

N. Lat: for LHA > 180° … $Z_n = Z$
for LHA < 180° … $Z_n = 360° - Z$

S. Lat.: for LHA > 180° … $Z_n = 180° - Z$
for LHA < 180° … $Z_n = 180° + Z$

SIGHT REDUCTION TABLE

< LHA < 270°
Lat. contrary name

Z_1: same sign as B
Z_2: (–) for F > 90°

LHA/F		84° A/H	84° B/P	84° Z_1/Z_2	85° A/H	85° B/P	85° Z_1/Z_2	86° A/H	86° B/P	86° Z_1/Z_2	87° A/H	87° B/P	87° Z_1/Z_2	88° A/H	88° B/P	88° Z_1/Z_2	89° A/H	89° B/P	89° Z_1/Z_2	Lat. / A LHA	
°	°	° ′	° ′	°	° ′	° ′	°	° ′	° ′	°	° ′	° ′	°	° ′	° ′	°	° ′	° ′	°	°	°
0	180	0 00	6 00	90·0	0 00	5 00	90·0	0 00	4 00	90·0	0 00	3 00	90·0	0 00	2 00	90·0	0 00	1 00	90·0	180	360
1	179	0 06	6 00	89·0	0 05	5 00	89·0	0 04	4 00	89·0	0 03	3 00	89·0	0 02	2 00	89·0	0 01	1 00	89·0	181	359
2	178	0 13	6 00	88·0	0 10	5 00	88·0	0 08	4 00	88·0	0 06	3 00	88·0	0 04	2 00	88·0	0 02	1 00	88·0	182	358
3	177	0 19	6 00	87·0	0 16	5 00	87·0	0 13	4 00	87·0	0 09	3 00	87·0	0 06	2 00	87·0	0 03	1 00	87·0	183	357
4	176	0 25	5 59	86·0	0 21	4 59	86·0	0 17	3 59	86·0	0 13	3 00	86·0	0 08	2 00	86·0	0 04	1 00	86·0	184	356
5	175	0 31	5 59	85·0	0 26	4 59	85·0	0 21	3 59	85·0	0 16	2 59	85·0	0 10	2 00	85·0	0 05	1 00	85·0	185	355
6	174	0 38	5 58	84·0	0 31	4 58	84·0	0 25	3 59	84·0	0 19	2 59	84·0	0 13	1 59	84·0	0 06	1 00	84·0	186	354
7	173	0 44	5 57	83·0	0 37	4 58	83·0	0 29	3 58	83·0	0 22	2 59	83·0	0 15	1 59	83·0	0 07	1 00	83·0	187	353
8	172	0 50	5 57	82·0	0 42	4 57	82·0	0 33	3 58	82·0	0 25	2 58	82·0	0 17	1 59	82·0	0 08	0 59	82·0	188	352
9	171	0 56	5 56	81·0	0 47	4 56	81·0	0 38	3 57	81·0	0 28	2 58	81·0	0 19	1 59	81·0	0 09	0 59	81·0	189	351
10	170	1 02	5 55	80·1	0 52	4 55	80·0	0 42	3 56	80·0	0 31	2 57	80·0	0 21	1 58	80·0	0 10	0 59	80·0	190	350
11	169	1 09	5 53	79·1	0 57	4 55	79·0	0 46	3 56	79·0	0 34	2 57	79·0	0 23	1 58	79·0	0 11	0 59	79·0	191	349
12	168	1 15	5 52	78·1	1 02	4 53	78·0	0 50	3 55	78·0	0 37	2 56	78·0	0 25	1 57	78·0	0 12	0 59	78·0	192	348
13	167	1 21	5 51	77·1	1 07	4 52	77·0	0 54	3 54	77·0	0 40	2 55	77·0	0 27	1 57	77·0	0 13	0 58	77·0	193	347
14	166	1 27	5 49	76·1	1 12	4 51	76·1	0 58	3 53	76·0	0 44	2 55	76·0	0 29	1 56	76·0	0 15	0 58	76·0	194	346
15	165	1 33	5 48	75·1	1 18	4 50	75·1	1 02	3 52	75·0	0 47	2 54	75·0	0 31	1 56	75·0	0 16	0 58	75·0	195	345
16	164	1 39	5 46	74·1	1 23	4 48	74·1	1 06	3 51	74·0	0 50	2 53	74·0	0 33	1 55	74·0	0 17	0 58	74·0	196	344
17	163	1 45	5 44	73·1	1 28	4 47	73·1	1 10	3 50	73·0	0 53	2 52	73·0	0 35	1 55	73·0	0 18	0 57	73·0	197	343
18	162	1 51	5 42	72·1	1 33	4 45	72·1	1 14	3 48	72·0	0 56	2 51	72·0	0 37	1 54	72·0	0 19	0 57	72·0	198	342
19	161	1 57	5 41	71·1	1 38	4 44	71·1	1 18	3 47	71·0	0 59	2 50	71·0	0 39	1 53	71·0	0 20	0 57	71·0	199	341
20	160	2 03	5 38	70·1	1 42	4 42	70·1	1 22	3 46	70·0	1 02	2 49	70·0	0 41	1 53	70·0	0 21	0 56	70·0	200	340
21	159	2 09	5 36	69·1	1 47	4 40	69·1	1 26	3 44	69·0	1 04	2 48	69·0	0 43	1 52	69·0	0 22	0 56	69·0	201	339
22	158	2 15	5 34	68·1	1 52	4 38	68·1	1 30	3 43	68·0	1 07	2 47	68·0	0 45	1 51	68·0	0 22	0 56	68·0	202	338
23	157	2 20	5 32	67·1	1 57	4 36	67·1	1 34	3 41	67·1	1 10	2 46	67·0	0 47	1 50	67·0	0 23	0 55	67·0	203	337
24	156	2 26	5 29	66·1	2 02	4 34	66·1	1 38	3 39	66·1	1 13	2 44	66·0	0 49	1 50	66·0	0 24	0 55	66·0	204	336
25	155	2 32	5 26	65·1	2 07	4 32	65·1	1 41	3 38	65·1	1 16	2 43	65·0	0 51	1 49	65·0	0 25	0 54	65·0	205	335
26	154	2 38	5 24	64·1	2 11	4 30	64·1	1 45	3 36	64·1	1 19	2 42	64·0	0 53	1 48	64·0	0 26	0 54	64·0	206	334
27	153	2 43	5 21	63·1	2 16	4 27	63·1	1 49	3 34	63·1	1 22	2 40	63·0	0 54	1 47	63·0	0 27	0 53	63·0	207	333
28	152	2 49	5 18	62·1	2 21	4 25	62·1	1 53	3 32	62·1	1 24	2 39	62·0	0 56	1 46	62·0	0 28	0 53	62·0	208	332
29	151	2 54	5 15	61·1	2 25	4 23	61·1	1 56	3 30	61·1	1 27	2 37	61·0	0 58	1 45	61·0	0 29	0 52	61·0	209	331
30	150	3 00	5 12	60·1	2 30	4 20	60·1	2 00	3 28	60·1	1 30	2 36	60·0	1 00	1 44	60·0	0 30	0 52	60·0	210	330
31	149	3 05	5 09	59·1	2 34	4 17	59·1	2 04	3 26	59·1	1 33	2 34	59·0	1 02	1 43	59·0	0 31	0 51	59·0	211	329
32	148	3 11	5 06	58·1	2 39	4 15	58·1	2 07	3 24	58·1	1 35	2 33	58·0	1 04	1 42	58·0	0 32	0 51	58·0	212	328
33	147	3 16	5 02	57·1	2 43	4 12	57·1	2 11	3 21	57·1	1 38	2 31	57·0	1 05	1 41	57·0	0 33	0 50	57·0	213	327
34	146	3 21	4 59	56·1	2 48	4 09	56·1	2 14	3 19	56·1	1 41	2 29	56·0	1 07	1 39	56·0	0 34	0 50	56·0	214	326
35	145	3 26	4 55	55·1	2 52	4 06	55·1	2 18	3 17	55·1	1 43	2 27	55·0	1 09	1 38	55·0	0 34	0 49	55·0	215	325
36	144	3 31	4 52	54·1	2 56	4 03	54·1	2 21	3 14	54·1	1 46	2 26	54·0	1 11	1 37	54·0	0 35	0 49	54·0	216	324
37	143	3 36	4 48	53·2	3 00	4 00	53·1	2 24	3 12	53·1	1 48	2 24	53·0	1 12	1 36	53·0	0 36	0 48	53·0	217	323
38	142	3 41	4 44	52·2	3 05	3 57	52·1	2 28	3 09	52·1	1 51	2 22	52·0	1 14	1 35	52·0	0 37	0 47	52·0	218	322
39	141	3 46	4 40	51·2	3 09	3 53	51·1	2 31	3 07	51·1	1 53	2 20	51·0	1 16	1 33	51·0	0 38	0 47	51·0	219	321
40	140	3 51	4 36	50·2	3 13	3 50	50·1	2 34	3 04	50·1	1 56	2 18	50·0	1 17	1 32	50·0	0 39	0 46	50·0	220	320
41	139	3 56	4 32	49·2	3 17	3 47	49·1	2 37	3 01	49·1	1 58	2 16	49·0	1 19	1 31	49·0	0 39	0 45	49·0	221	319
42	138	4 01	4 28	48·2	3 21	3 43	48·1	2 41	2 58	48·1	2 00	2 14	48·0	1 20	1 29	48·0	0 40	0 45	48·0	222	318
43	137	4 05	4 24	47·2	3 24	3 40	47·1	2 44	2 56	47·1	2 03	2 12	47·0	1 22	1 28	47·0	0 41	0 44	47·0	223	317
44	136	4 10	4 19	46·2	3 28	3 36	46·1	2 47	2 53	46·1	2 05	2 10	46·0	1 23	1 26	46·0	0 42	0 43	46·0	224	316
45	135	4 14	4 15	45·2	3 32	3 32	45·1	2 50	2 50	45·1	2 07	2 07	45·0	1 25	1 25	45·0	0 42	0 42	45·0	225	315

Lat. / A		84°			85°			86°			87°			88°			89°			Lat. / A	
LHA/F		A/H	B/P	Z_1/Z_2	A/H	B/P	Z_1/Z_2	A/H	B/P	Z_1/Z_2	A/H	B/P	Z_1/Z_2	A/H	B/P	Z_1/Z_2	A/H	B/P	Z_1/Z_2	LHA	
°	°	° ′	° ′	°	° ′	° ′	°	° ′	° ′	°	° ′	° ′	°	° ′	° ′	°	° ′	° ′	°	°	°
45	135	4 14	4 15	45·2	3 32	3 32	45·1	2 50	2 50	45·1	2 07	2 07	45·0	1 25	1 25	45·0	0 42	0 42	45·0	225	315
46	134	4 19	4 11	44·2	3 36	3 29	44·1	2 53	2 47	44·1	2 09	2 05	44·0	1 26	1 23	44·0	0 43	0 42	44·0	226	314
47	133	4 23	4 06	43·2	3 39	3 25	43·1	2 55	2 44	43·1	2 12	2 03	43·0	1 28	1 22	43·0	0 44	0 41	43·0	227	313
48	132	4 27	4 01	42·2	3 43	3 21	42·1	2 58	2 41	42·1	2 14	2 01	42·0	1 29	1 20	42·0	0 45	0 40	42·0	228	312
49	131	4 31	3 57	41·2	3 46	3 17	41·1	3 01	2 38	41·1	2 16	1 58	41·0	1 31	1 19	41·0	0 45	0 39	41·0	229	311
50	130	4 36	3 52	40·2	3 50	3 13	40·1	3 04	2 34	40·1	2 18	1 56	40·0	1 32	1 17	40·0	0 46	0 39	40·0	230	310
51	129	4 40	3 47	39·2	3 53	3 09	39·1	3 06	2 31	39·1	2 20	1 53	39·0	1 33	1 16	39·0	0 47	0 38	39·0	231	309
52	128	4 43	3 42	38·2	3 56	3 05	38·1	3 09	2 28	38·1	2 22	1 51	38·0	1 35	1 14	38·0	0 47	0 37	38·0	232	308
53	127	4 47	3 37	37·2	3 59	3 01	37·1	3 12	2 25	37·1	2 24	1 48	37·0	1 36	1 12	37·0	0 48	0 36	37·0	233	307
54	126	4 51	3 32	36·1	4 03	2 57	36·1	3 14	2 21	36·1	2 26	1 46	36·0	1 37	1 11	36·0	0 49	0 35	36·0	234	306
55	125	4 55	3 27	35·1	4 06	2 52	35·1	3 17	2 18	35·1	2 27	1 43	35·0	1 38	1 09	35·0	0 49	0 34	35·0	235	305
56	124	4 58	3 22	34·1	4 09	2 48	34·1	3 19	2 14	34·1	2 29	1 41	34·0	1 39	1 07	34·0	0 50	0 34	34·0	236	304
57	123	5 02	3 17	33·1	4 12	2 44	33·1	3 21	2 11	33·1	2 31	1 38	33·0	1 41	1 05	33·0	0 50	0 33	33·0	237	303
58	122	5 05	3 11	32·1	4 14	2 39	32·1	3 23	2 07	32·1	2 33	1 35	32·0	1 42	1 04	32·0	0 51	0 32	32·0	238	302
59	121	5 08	3 06	31·1	4 17	2 35	31·1	3 26	2 04	31·1	2 34	1 33	31·0	1 43	1 02	31·0	0 51	0 31	31·0	239	301
60	120	5 12	3 00	30·1	4 20	2 30	30·1	3 28	2 00	30·1	2 36	1 30	30·0	1 44	1 00	30·0	0 52	0 30	30·0	240	300
61	119	5 15	2 55	29·1	4 22	2 26	29·1	3 30	1 56	29·1	2 37	1 27	29·0	1 45	0 58	29·0	0 52	0 29	29·0	241	299
62	118	5 18	2 49	28·1	4 25	2 21	28·1	3 32	1 53	28·1	2 39	1 25	28·0	1 46	0 56	28·0	0 53	0 28	28·0	242	298
63	117	5 21	2 44	27·1	4 27	2 16	27·1	3 34	1 49	27·1	2 40	1 22	27·0	1 47	0 54	27·0	0 53	0 27	27·0	243	297
64	116	5 23	2 38	26·1	4 30	2 12	26·1	3 36	1 45	26·1	2 42	1 19	26·0	1 48	0 53	26·0	0 54	0 26	26·0	244	296
65	115	5 26	2 33	25·1	4 32	2 07	25·1	3 37	1 42	25·1	2 43	1 16	25·0	1 49	0 51	25·0	0 54	0 25	25·0	245	295
66	114	5 29	2 27	24·1	4 34	2 02	24·1	3 39	1 38	24·1	2 44	1 13	24·0	1 50	0 49	24·0	0 55	0 24	24·0	246	294
67	113	5 31	2 21	23·1	4 36	1 57	23·1	3 41	1 34	23·1	2 46	1 10	23·0	1 50	0 47	23·0	0 55	0 23	23·0	247	293
68	112	5 34	2 15	22·1	4 38	1 53	22·1	3 42	1 30	22·0	2 47	1 07	22·0	1 51	0 45	22·0	0 56	0 22	22·0	248	292
69	111	5 36	2 09	21·1	4 40	1 48	21·1	3 44	1 26	21·0	2 48	1 05	21·0	1 52	0 43	21·0	0 56	0 22	21·0	249	291
70	110	5 38	2 04	20·1	4 42	1 43	20·1	3 46	1 22	20·0	2 49	1 02	20·0	1 53	0 41	20·0	0 56	0 21	20·0	250	290
71	109	5 40	1 58	19·1	4 44	1 38	19·1	3 47	1 18	19·0	2 50	0 59	19·0	1 53	0 39	19·0	0 57	0 20	19·0	251	289
72	108	5 42	1 52	18·1	4 45	1 33	18·1	3 48	1 14	18·0	2 51	0 56	18·0	1 54	0 37	18·0	0 57	0 19	18·0	252	288
73	107	5 44	1 46	17·1	4 47	1 28	17·1	3 49	1 10	17·0	2 52	0 53	17·0	1 55	0 35	17·0	0 57	0 18	17·0	253	287
74	106	5 46	1 40	16·1	4 48	1 23	16·1	3 51	1 06	16·0	2 53	0 50	16·0	1 55	0 33	16·0	0 58	0 17	16·0	254	286
75	105	5 48	1 33	15·1	4 50	1 18	15·1	3 52	1 02	15·0	2 54	0 47	15·0	1 56	0 31	15·0	0 58	0 16	15·0	255	285
76	104	5 49	1 27	14·1	4 51	1 13	14·1	3 53	0 58	14·0	2 55	0 44	14·0	1 56	0 29	14·0	0 58	0 15	14·0	256	284
77	103	5 51	1 21	13·1	4 52	1 08	13·0	3 54	0 54	13·0	2 55	0 41	13·0	1 57	0 27	13·0	0 58	0 13	13·0	257	283
78	102	5 52	1 15	12·1	4 53	1 03	12·0	3 55	0 50	12·0	2 56	0 37	12·0	1 57	0 25	12·0	0 59	0 12	12·0	258	282
79	101	5 53	1 09	11·1	4 54	0 57	11·0	3 56	0 46	11·0	2 57	0 34	11·0	1 58	0 23	11·0	0 59	0 11	11·0	259	281
80	100	5 55	1 03	10·1	4 55	0 52	10·0	3 56	0 42	10·0	2 57	0 31	10·0	1 58	0 21	10·0	0 59	0 10	10·0	260	280
81	99	5 56	0 57	9·0	4 56	0 47	9·0	3 57	0 38	9·0	2 58	0 28	9·0	1 59	0 19	9·0	0 59	0 09	9·0	261	279
82	98	5 56	0 50	8·0	4 57	0 42	8·0	3 58	0 33	8·0	2 58	0 25	8·0	1 59	0 17	8·0	0 59	0 08	8·0	262	278
83	97	5 57	0 44	7·0	4 58	0 37	7·0	3 58	0 29	7·0	2 59	0 22	7·0	1 59	0 15	7·0	1 00	0 07	7·0	263	277
84	96	5 58	0 38	6·0	4 58	0 31	6·0	3 59	0 25	6·0	2 59	0 19	6·0	1 59	0 13	6·0	1 00	0 06	6·0	264	276
85	95	5 59	0 31	5·0	4 59	0 26	5·0	3 59	0 21	5·0	2 59	0 16	5·0	2 00	0 10	5·0	1 00	0 05	5·0	265	275
86	94	5 59	0 25	4·0	4 59	0 21	4·0	3 59	0 17	4·0	3 00	0 13	4·0	2 00	0 08	4·0	1 00	0 04	4·0	266	274
87	93	6 00	0 19	3·0	5 00	0 16	3·0	4 00	0 13	3·0	3 00	0 09	3·0	2 00	0 06	3·0	1 00	0 03	3·0	267	273
88	92	6 00	0 13	2·0	5 00	0 10	2·0	4 00	0 08	2·0	3 00	0 06	2·0	2 00	0 04	2·0	1 00	0 02	2·0	268	272
89	91	6 00	0 06	1·0	5 00	0 05	1·0	4 00	0 04	1·0	3 00	0 03	1·0	2 00	0 02	1·0	1 00	0 01	1·0	269	271
90	90	6 00	0 00	0·0	5 00	0 00	0·0	4 00	0 00	0·0	3 00	0 00	0·0	2 00	0 00	0·0	1 00	0 00	0·0	270	270

N. Lat: for LHA > 180° … $Z_n = Z$
for LHA < 180° … $Z_n = 360° - Z$

S. Lat.: for LHA > 180° … $Z_n = 180° - Z$
for LHA < 180° … $Z_n = 180° + Z$

AUXILIARY TABLE

. F′. *Reverse* sign if $F > 90°$.

Sign for $corr_2$ for A′. ↓

− P°	1 59	2 58	3 57	4 56	5 55	6 54	7 53	8 52	9 51	10 50	11 49	12 48	13 47	14 46	15 45	16 44	17 43	18 42	19 41	20 40	21 39	22 38	23 37	24 36	25 35	26 34	27 33	28 32	29 31	□ 30	− + A′ $Z_2°$
	′	′	′	′	′	′	′	′	′	′	′	′	′	′	′	′	′	′	′	′	′	′	′	′	′	′	′	′	′	′	
1	0	0	0	0	0	0	0	0	0	0	0	0	0	0	0	0	0	0	0	0	0	0	0	0	0	0	0	0	1	1	89
2	0	0	0	0	0	0	0	0	0	0	0	0	0	0	1	1	1	1	1	1	1	1	1	1	1	1	1	1	1	1	88
3	0	0	0	0	0	0	0	0	0	1	1	1	1	1	1	1	1	1	1	1	1	1	1	1	1	1	1	1	2	2	87
4	0	0	0	0	0	0	0	1	1	1	1	1	1	1	1	1	1	1	1	1	1	2	2	2	2	2	2	2	2	2	86
5	0	0	0	0	0	1	1	1	1	1	1	1	1	1	1	1	1	2	2	2	2	2	2	2	2	2	2	2	3	3	85
6	0	0	0	0	1	1	1	1	1	1	1	1	1	1	2	2	2	2	2	2	2	2	2	3	3	3	3	3	3	3	84
7	0	0	0	0	1	1	1	1	1	1	1	1	2	2	2	2	2	2	2	2	3	3	3	3	3	3	3	3	4	4	83
8	0	0	0	1	1	1	1	1	1	1	2	2	2	2	2	2	2	3	3	3	3	3	3	3	3	4	4	4	4	4	82
9	0	0	0	1	1	1	1	1	1	2	2	2	2	2	2	3	3	3	3	3	3	3	4	4	4	4	4	4	5	5	81
10	0	0	1	1	1	1	1	1	2	2	2	2	2	2	3	3	3	3	3	3	4	4	4	4	4	5	5	5	5	5	80
11	0	0	1	1	1	1	1	2	2	2	2	2	2	3	3	3	3	3	4	4	4	4	4	5	5	5	5	5	6	6	79
12	0	0	1	1	1	1	1	2	2	2	2	2	3	3	3	3	4	4	4	4	4	5	5	5	5	5	6	6	6	6	78
13	0	0	1	1	1	1	2	2	2	2	2	3	3	3	3	4	4	4	4	4	5	5	5	5	6	6	6	6	7	7	77
14	0	0	1	1	1	1	2	2	2	2	3	3	3	3	4	4	4	4	5	5	5	5	6	6	6	6	7	7	7	7	76
15	0	1	1	1	1	2	2	2	2	3	3	3	3	4	4	4	4	5	5	5	5	6	6	6	6	7	7	7	8	8	75
16	0	1	1	1	1	2	2	2	2	3	3	3	4	4	4	4	5	5	5	6	6	6	6	7	7	7	7	8	8	8	74
17	0	1	1	1	1	2	2	2	3	3	3	4	4	4	4	5	5	5	6	6	6	6	7	7	7	8	8	8	8	9	73
18	0	1	1	1	2	2	2	2	3	3	3	4	4	4	5	5	5	6	6	6	6	7	7	7	8	8	8	9	9	9	72
19	0	1	1	1	2	2	2	3	3	3	4	4	4	5	5	5	6	6	6	7	7	7	7	8	8	8	9	9	9	10	71
20	0	1	1	1	2	2	2	3	3	3	4	4	4	5	5	5	6	6	6	7	7	8	8	8	9	9	9	10	10	10	70
21	0	1	1	1	2	2	3	3	3	4	4	4	5	5	5	6	6	6	7	7	8	8	8	9	9	9	10	10	10	11	69
22	0	1	1	1	2	2	3	3	3	4	4	4	5	5	6	6	6	7	7	7	8	8	9	9	9	10	10	10	11	11	68
23	0	1	1	2	2	2	3	3	4	4	4	5	5	5	6	6	7	7	7	8	8	9	9	9	10	10	11	11	11	12	67
24	0	1	1	2	2	2	3	3	4	4	4	5	5	6	6	7	7	7	8	8	9	9	9	10	10	11	11	11	12	12	66
25	0	1	1	2	2	3	3	3	4	4	5	5	5	6	6	7	7	8	8	8	9	9	10	10	11	11	11	12	12	13	65
26	0	1	1	2	2	3	3	4	4	4	5	5	6	6	7	7	7	8	8	9	9	10	10	11	11	11	12	12	13	13	64
27	0	1	1	2	2	3	3	4	4	5	5	5	6	6	7	7	8	8	9	9	10	10	10	11	11	12	12	13	13	14	63
28	0	1	1	2	2	3	3	4	4	5	5	6	6	7	7	8	8	8	9	9	10	10	11	11	12	12	13	13	14	14	62
29	0	1	1	2	2	3	3	4	4	5	5	6	6	7	7	8	8	9	9	10	10	11	11	12	12	13	13	14	14	15	61
30	0	1	1	2	2	3	3	4	4	5	5	6	6	7	7	8	8	9	9	10	10	11	11	12	12	13	13	14	14	15	60
31	1	1	2	2	3	3	4	4	5	5	6	6	7	7	8	8	9	9	10	10	11	11	12	12	13	13	14	14	15	15	59
32	1	1	2	2	3	3	4	4	5	5	6	6	7	7	8	8	9	10	10	11	11	12	12	13	13	14	14	15	15	16	58
33	1	1	2	2	3	3	4	4	5	5	6	7	7	8	8	9	9	10	10	11	11	12	13	13	14	14	15	15	16	16	57
34	1	1	2	2	3	3	4	4	5	6	6	7	7	8	8	9	10	10	11	11	12	12	13	13	14	15	15	16	16	17	56
35	1	1	2	2	3	3	4	5	5	6	6	7	7	8	9	9	10	10	11	11	12	13	13	14	14	15	15	16	17	17	55
36	1	1	2	2	3	4	4	5	5	6	6	7	8	8	9	9	10	11	11	12	12	13	14	14	15	15	16	16	17	18	54
37	1	1	2	2	3	4	4	5	5	6	7	7	8	8	9	10	10	11	11	12	13	13	14	14	15	16	16	17	17	18	53
38	1	1	2	2	3	4	4	5	6	6	7	7	8	9	9	10	10	11	12	12	13	14	14	15	15	16	17	17	18	18	52
39	1	1	2	3	3	4	4	5	6	6	7	8	8	9	9	10	11	11	12	13	13	14	14	15	16	16	17	18	18	19	51
40	1	1	2	3	3	4	4	5	6	6	7	8	8	9	10	10	11	12	12	13	13	14	15	15	16	17	17	18	19	19	50

F′ +	1	2	3	4	5	6	7	8	9	10	11	12	13	14	15	16	17	18	19	20	21	22	23	24	25	26	27	28	29	□	− A′
F′ −	59	58	57	56	55	54	53	52	51	50	49	48	47	46	45	44	43	42	41	40	39	38	37	36	35	34	33	32	31	30	+ A′
P°	′	′	′	′	′	′	′	′	′	′	′	′	′	′	′	′	′	′	′	′	′	′	′	′	′	′	′	′	′	′	Z_2°
41	1	1	2	3	3	4	5	5	6	7	7	8	9	9	10	10	11	12	12	13	14	14	15	16	16	17	18	18	19	20	49
42	1	1	2	3	3	4	5	5	6	7	7	8	9	9	10	11	11	12	13	13	14	15	15	16	17	17	18	19	19	20	48
43	1	1	2	3	3	4	5	5	6	7	8	8	9	10	10	11	12	12	13	14	14	15	16	16	17	18	18	19	20	20	47
44	1	1	2	3	3	4	5	6	6	7	8	8	9	10	10	11	12	13	13	14	15	15	16	17	17	18	19	19	20	21	46
45	1	1	2	3	4	4	5	6	6	7	8	8	9	10	11	11	12	13	13	14	15	16	16	17	18	18	19	20	21	21	45
46	1	1	2	3	4	4	5	6	6	7	8	9	9	10	11	12	12	13	14	14	15	16	17	17	18	19	19	20	21	22	44
47	1	1	2	3	4	4	5	6	7	7	8	9	10	10	11	12	12	13	14	15	15	16	17	18	18	19	20	20	21	22	43
48	1	1	2	3	4	4	5	6	7	7	8	9	10	10	11	12	13	13	14	15	16	16	17	18	19	19	20	21	22	22	42
49	1	2	2	3	4	5	5	6	7	8	8	9	10	11	11	12	13	14	14	15	16	17	17	18	19	20	20	21	22	23	41
50	1	2	2	3	4	5	5	6	7	8	8	9	10	11	11	12	13	14	15	15	16	17	18	18	19	20	21	21	22	23	40
51	1	2	2	3	4	5	5	6	7	8	9	9	10	11	12	12	13	14	15	16	16	17	18	19	19	20	21	22	23	23	39
52	1	2	2	3	4	5	6	6	7	8	9	9	10	11	12	13	13	14	15	16	17	17	18	19	20	20	21	22	23	24	38
53	1	2	2	3	4	5	6	6	7	8	9	10	10	11	12	13	14	14	15	16	17	18	18	19	20	21	22	22	23	24	37
54	1	2	2	3	4	5	6	6	7	8	9	10	11	11	12	13	14	15	15	16	17	18	19	19	20	21	22	23	23	24	36
55	1	2	2	3	4	5	6	7	7	8	9	10	11	11	12	13	14	15	16	16	17	18	19	20	20	21	22	23	24	25	35
56	1	2	2	3	4	5	6	7	7	8	9	10	11	12	12	13	14	15	16	17	17	18	19	20	21	22	22	23	24	25	34
57	1	2	3	3	4	5	6	7	8	8	9	10	11	12	13	13	14	15	16	17	18	18	19	20	21	22	23	23	24	25	33
58	1	2	3	3	4	5	6	7	8	8	9	10	11	12	13	14	14	15	16	17	18	19	20	20	21	22	23	24	25	25	32
59	1	2	3	3	4	5	6	7	8	9	9	10	11	12	13	14	15	15	16	17	18	19	20	21	21	22	23	24	25	26	31
60	1	2	3	3	4	5	6	7	8	9	10	10	11	12	13	14	15	16	16	17	18	19	20	21	22	23	23	24	25	26	30
61	1	2	3	3	4	5	6	7	8	9	10	10	11	12	13	14	15	16	17	17	18	19	20	21	22	23	24	24	25	26	29
62	1	2	3	4	4	5	6	7	8	9	10	11	11	12	13	14	15	16	17	18	19	19	20	21	22	23	24	25	26	26	28
63	1	2	3	4	4	5	6	7	8	9	10	11	12	12	13	14	15	16	17	18	19	20	20	21	22	23	24	25	26	27	27
64	1	2	3	4	4	5	6	7	8	9	10	11	12	13	13	14	15	16	17	18	19	20	21	22	22	23	24	25	26	27	26
65	1	2	3	4	5	5	6	7	8	9	10	11	12	13	14	15	15	16	17	18	19	20	21	22	23	24	24	25	26	27	25
66	1	2	3	4	5	5	6	7	8	9	10	11	12	13	14	15	16	16	17	18	19	20	21	22	23	24	25	26	26	27	24
67	1	2	3	4	5	6	6	7	8	9	10	11	12	13	14	15	16	17	17	18	19	20	21	22	23	24	25	26	27	28	23
68	1	2	3	4	5	6	6	7	8	9	10	11	12	13	14	15	16	17	18	19	19	20	21	22	23	24	25	26	27	28	22
69	1	2	3	4	5	6	7	7	8	9	10	11	12	13	14	15	16	17	18	19	20	21	21	22	23	24	25	26	27	28	21
70	1	2	3	4	5	6	7	8	8	9	10	11	12	13	14	15	16	17	18	19	20	21	22	23	23	24	25	26	27	28	20
71	1	2	3	4	5	6	7	8	9	9	10	11	12	13	14	15	16	17	18	19	20	21	22	23	24	25	26	26	27	28	19
72	1	2	3	4	5	6	7	8	9	10	10	11	12	13	14	15	16	17	18	19	20	21	22	23	24	25	26	27	28	29	18
73	1	2	3	4	5	6	7	8	9	10	11	11	12	13	14	15	16	17	18	19	20	21	22	23	24	25	26	27	28	29	17
74	1	2	3	4	5	6	7	8	9	10	11	12	12	13	14	15	16	17	18	19	20	21	22	23	24	25	26	27	28	29	16
75	1	2	3	4	5	6	7	8	9	10	11	12	13	14	14	15	16	17	18	19	20	21	22	23	24	25	26	27	28	29	15
76	1	2	3	4	5	6	7	8	9	10	11	12	13	14	15	16	16	17	18	19	20	21	22	23	24	25	26	27	28	29	14
77	1	2	3	4	5	6	7	8	9	10	11	12	13	14	15	16	17	18	19	19	20	21	22	23	24	25	26	27	28	29	13
78	1	2	3	4	5	6	7	8	9	10	11	12	13	14	15	16	17	18	19	20	21	22	22	23	24	25	26	27	28	29	12
79	1	2	3	4	5	6	7	8	9	10	11	12	13	14	15	16	17	18	19	20	21	22	23	24	25	26	27	27	28	29	11
80	1	2	3	4	5	6	7	8	9	10	11	12	13	14	15	16	17	18	19	20	21	22	23	24	25	26	27	28	29	30	10

For P > 80°, use 80°

For $Z_2 < 10°$, use 10°

USE OF CONCISE SIGHT REDUCTION TABLES (continued)

4. *Example.* (b) Required the altitude and azimuth of *Vega* on 2008 July 29 at UT $04^{h}\ 48^{m}$ from the estimated position 152° west, 15° south.

1. Assumed latitude	$Lat =$ 15° S		
From the almanac	$GHA =$ 99° 54′		
Assumed longitude	151° 54′ W		
Local hour angle	$LHA =$ 308		
2. Reduction table, 1st entry			
$(Lat, LHA) = (15, 308)$	$A =$ 49 34	$A^{\circ} = 50,\ A' = 34$	
	$B = +66$ 29	$Z_1 = +71{\cdot}7,$	$LHA > 270°$
3. From the almanac	$Dec = -38$ 48		*Lat* and *Dec* contrary
Sum $= B + Dec$	$F = +27$ 41	$F^{\circ} = 28,\ F' = 41$	
4. Reduction table, 2nd entry			
$(A^{\circ}, F^{\circ}) = (50, 28)$	$H =$ 17 34	$P^{\circ} = 37$	
		$Z_2 = 67{\cdot}8, Z_2{}^{\circ} = 68$	
5. Auxiliary table, 1st entry			
$(F', P^{\circ}) = (41, 37)$	$corr_1 =$ −11		$F < 90°,\ F' > 29'$
Sum	17 23		
6. Auxiliary table, 2nd entry			
$(A', Z_2{}^{\circ}) = (34, 68)$	$corr_2 =$ +10		$A' > 30'$
7. Sum = computed altitude	$Hc = +17°$ 33′		$F > 0°$
8. Azimuth, first component	$Z_1 = +71{\cdot}7$		same sign as *B*
second component	$Z_2 = +67{\cdot}8$		$F < 90°,\ F > 0°$
Sum = azimuth angle	$Z =$ 139·5		
True azimuth	$Zn =$ 040°		S *Lat*, $LHA > 180°$

5. *Form for use with the Concise Sight Reduction Tables.* The form on the following page lays out the procedure explained on pages 284-285. Each step is shown, with notes and rules to ensure accuracy, rather than speed, throughout the calculation. The form is mainly intended for the calculation of star positions. It therefore includes the formation of the Greenwich hour of Aries (*GHA* Aries), and thus the Greenwich hour angle of the star (*GHA*) from its tabular sidereal hour angle (*SHA*). These calculations, included in step 1 of the form, can easily be replaced by the interpolation of *GHA* and *Dec* for the Sun, Moon or planets.

The form may be freely copied, however, acknowledgement of the source is requested.

Date & UT of observation h m s	Body	Estimated Latitude & Longitude ° ′ ° ′

Step	Calculate Altitude & Azimuth	Summary of Rules & Notes
Assumed latitude	$Lat =$ °	Nearest estimated latitude, integral number of degrees.
Assumed longitude	$Long =$ ° ′	Choose $Long$ so that LHA has integral number of degrees.
1. From the almanac:	$Dec =$ ° ′	Record the Dec for use in Step 3.
GHA Aries h	= ° ′	Needed if using SHA. Tabular value.
Increment m s	= ° ′	for minutes and seconds of time.
SHA	$SHA =$ ° ′	
$GHA = GHA\ Aries + SHA$	$GHA =$ ° ′	Remove multiples of 360°.
Assumed longitude	$Long =$ ° ′	West longitudes are negative.
$LHA = GHA + Long$	$LHA =$ °	Remove multiples of 360°.
2. Reduction table, 1st entry		
$(Lat, LHA) = (\ \ °,\ \ °)$	$A =$ ° ′ $A° =$ °	nearest whole degree of A.
record A, B and Z_1.	$A' =$ ′	minutes part of A.
	$B =$ ° ′	B is minus if $90° < LHA < 270°$.
	$Z_1 =$ °	Z_1 has the same sign as B.
3. From step 1	$Dec =$ ° ′	Dec is minus if contrary to Lat.
$F = B + Dec$	$F =$ ° ′	Regard F as positive until step 7.
	$F° =$ °	nearest whole degree of F.
	$F' =$ ′	minutes part of F.
4. Reduction table, 2nd entry		
$(A°, F°) = (\ \ °,\ \ °)$	$H =$ ° ′ $P° =$ °	nearest whole degree of P.
record H, P and Z_2.	$Z_2 =$ °	
5. Auxiliary table, 1st entry		
$(F', P°) = (\ \ ',\ \ °)$	$corr_1 =$ ′	$corr_1$ is minus if $F < 90°$ & $F' > 29'$,
record $corr_1$		or if $F > 90°$ & $F' < 30'$.
6. Auxiliary table, 2nd entry		$Z_2°$ nearest whole degree of Z_2.
$(A', Z_2°) = (\ \ ',\ \ °)$	$corr_2 =$ ′	$corr_2$ is minus if $A' < 30'$.
record $corr_2$		
7. Calculated altitude =	$Hc =$ ° ′	Hc is minus if F is negative, and
$Hc = H + corr_1 + corr_2$		object is below the horizon.

Step		Summary of Rules & Notes
8. Azimuth, 1st component	$Z_1 =$ °	Z_1 has the same sign as B.
2nd component	$Z_2 =$ °	Z_2 is minus if $F > 90°$. If F is negative, $Z_2 = 180° - Z_2$
$Z = Z_1 + Z_2$	$Z =$ °	Ignore the sign of Z.
		N Lat: If $LHA > 180°$, $Z_n = Z$, or if $LHA < 180°$, $Z_n = 360° - Z$,
		S Lat: If $LHA > 180°$, $Z_n = 180° - Z$, or if $LHA < 180°$, $Z_n = 180° + Z$.
True azimuth	$Z_n =$ °	

For use with *The Nautical Almanac's* Concise Sight Reduction Tables pages 284-318.

NOTES

CONVERSION OF ARC TO TIME

0°–59°		60°–119°		120°–179°		180°–239°		240°–299°		300°–359°			0′·00	0′·25	0′·50	0′·75
°	h m	°	h m	°	h m	°	h m	°	h m	°	h m	′	m s	m s	m s	m s
0	0 00	**60**	4 00	**120**	8 00	**180**	12 00	**240**	16 00	**300**	20 00	**0**	0 00	0 01	0 02	0 03
1	0 04	**61**	4 04	**121**	8 04	**181**	12 04	**241**	16 04	**301**	20 04	**1**	0 04	0 05	0 06	0 07
2	0 08	**62**	4 08	**122**	8 08	**182**	12 08	**242**	16 08	**302**	20 08	**2**	0 08	0 09	0 10	0 11
3	0 12	**63**	4 12	**123**	8 12	**183**	12 12	**243**	16 12	**303**	20 12	**3**	0 12	0 13	0 14	0 15
4	0 16	**64**	4 16	**124**	8 16	**184**	12 16	**244**	16 16	**304**	20 16	**4**	0 16	0 17	0 18	0 19
5	0 20	**65**	4 20	**125**	8 20	**185**	12 20	**245**	16 20	**305**	20 20	**5**	0 20	0 21	0 22	0 23
6	0 24	**66**	4 24	**126**	8 24	**186**	12 24	**246**	16 24	**306**	20 24	**6**	0 24	0 25	0 26	0 27
7	0 28	**67**	4 28	**127**	8 28	**187**	12 28	**247**	16 28	**307**	20 28	**7**	0 28	0 29	0 30	0 31
8	0 32	**68**	4 32	**128**	8 32	**188**	12 32	**248**	16 32	**308**	20 32	**8**	0 32	0 33	0 34	0 35
9	0 36	**69**	4 36	**129**	8 36	**189**	12 36	**249**	16 36	**309**	20 36	**9**	0 36	0 37	0 38	0 39
10	0 40	**70**	4 40	**130**	8 40	**190**	12 40	**250**	16 40	**310**	20 40	**10**	0 40	0 41	0 42	0 43
11	0 44	**71**	4 44	**131**	8 44	**191**	12 44	**251**	16 44	**311**	20 44	**11**	0 44	0 45	0 46	0 47
12	0 48	**72**	4 48	**132**	8 48	**192**	12 48	**252**	16 48	**312**	20 48	**12**	0 48	0 49	0 50	0 51
13	0 52	**73**	4 52	**133**	8 52	**193**	12 52	**253**	16 52	**313**	20 52	**13**	0 52	0 53	0 54	0 55
14	0 56	**74**	4 56	**134**	8 56	**194**	12 56	**254**	16 56	**314**	20 56	**14**	0 56	0 57	0 58	0 59
15	1 00	**75**	5 00	**135**	9 00	**195**	13 00	**255**	17 00	**315**	21 00	**15**	1 00	1 01	1 02	1 03
16	1 04	**76**	5 04	**136**	9 04	**196**	13 04	**256**	17 04	**316**	21 04	**16**	1 04	1 05	1 06	1 07
17	1 08	**77**	5 08	**137**	9 08	**197**	13 08	**257**	17 08	**317**	21 08	**17**	1 08	1 09	1 10	1 11
18	1 12	**78**	5 12	**138**	9 12	**198**	13 12	**258**	17 12	**318**	21 12	**18**	1 12	1 13	1 14	1 15
19	1 16	**79**	5 16	**139**	9 16	**199**	13 16	**259**	17 16	**319**	21 16	**19**	1 16	1 17	1 18	1 19
20	1 20	**80**	5 20	**140**	9 20	**200**	13 20	**260**	17 20	**320**	21 20	**20**	1 20	1 21	1 22	1 23
21	1 24	**81**	5 24	**141**	9 24	**201**	13 24	**261**	17 24	**321**	21 24	**21**	1 24	1 25	1 26	1 27
22	1 28	**82**	5 28	**142**	9 28	**202**	13 28	**262**	17 28	**322**	21 28	**22**	1 28	1 29	1 30	1 31
23	1 32	**83**	5 32	**143**	9 32	**203**	13 32	**263**	17 32	**323**	21 32	**23**	1 32	1 33	1 34	1 35
24	1 36	**84**	5 36	**144**	9 36	**204**	13 36	**264**	17 36	**324**	21 36	**24**	1 36	1 37	1 38	1 39
25	1 40	**85**	5 40	**145**	9 40	**205**	13 40	**265**	17 40	**325**	21 40	**25**	1 40	1 41	1 42	1 43
26	1 44	**86**	5 44	**146**	9 44	**206**	13 44	**266**	17 44	**326**	21 44	**26**	1 44	1 45	1 46	1 47
27	1 48	**87**	5 48	**147**	9 48	**207**	13 48	**267**	17 48	**327**	21 48	**27**	1 48	1 49	1 50	1 51
28	1 52	**88**	5 52	**148**	9 52	**208**	13 52	**268**	17 52	**328**	21 52	**28**	1 52	1 53	1 54	1 55
29	1 56	**89**	5 56	**149**	9 56	**209**	13 56	**269**	17 56	**329**	21 56	**29**	1 56	1 57	1 58	1 59
30	2 00	**90**	6 00	**150**	10 00	**210**	14 00	**270**	18 00	**330**	22 00	**30**	2 00	2 01	2 02	2 03
31	2 04	**91**	6 04	**151**	10 04	**211**	14 04	**271**	18 04	**331**	22 04	**31**	2 04	2 05	2 06	2 07
32	2 08	**92**	6 08	**152**	10 08	**212**	14 08	**272**	18 08	**332**	22 08	**32**	2 08	2 09	2 10	2 11
33	2 12	**93**	6 12	**153**	10 12	**213**	14 12	**273**	18 12	**333**	22 12	**33**	2 12	2 13	2 14	2 15
34	2 16	**94**	6 16	**154**	10 16	**214**	14 16	**274**	18 16	**334**	22 16	**34**	2 16	2 17	2 18	2 19
35	2 20	**95**	6 20	**155**	10 20	**215**	14 20	**275**	18 20	**335**	22 20	**35**	2 20	2 21	2 22	2 23
36	2 24	**96**	6 24	**156**	10 24	**216**	14 24	**276**	18 24	**336**	22 24	**36**	2 24	2 25	2 26	2 27
37	2 28	**97**	6 28	**157**	10 28	**217**	14 28	**277**	18 28	**337**	22 28	**37**	2 28	2 29	2 30	2 31
38	2 32	**98**	6 32	**158**	10 32	**218**	14 32	**278**	18 32	**338**	22 32	**38**	2 32	2 33	2 34	2 35
39	2 36	**99**	6 36	**159**	10 36	**219**	14 36	**279**	18 36	**339**	22 36	**39**	2 36	2 37	2 38	2 39
40	2 40	**100**	6 40	**160**	10 40	**220**	14 40	**280**	18 40	**340**	22 40	**40**	2 40	2 41	2 42	2 43
41	2 44	**101**	6 44	**161**	10 44	**221**	14 44	**281**	18 44	**341**	22 44	**41**	2 44	2 45	2 46	2 47
42	2 48	**102**	6 48	**162**	10 48	**222**	14 48	**282**	18 48	**342**	22 48	**42**	2 48	2 49	2 50	2 51
43	2 52	**103**	6 52	**163**	10 52	**223**	14 52	**283**	18 52	**343**	22 52	**43**	2 52	2 53	2 54	2 55
44	2 56	**104**	6 56	**164**	10 56	**224**	14 56	**284**	18 56	**344**	22 56	**44**	2 56	2 57	2 58	2 59
45	3 00	**105**	7 00	**165**	11 00	**225**	15 00	**285**	19 00	**345**	23 00	**45**	3 00	3 01	3 02	3 03
46	3 04	**106**	7 04	**166**	11 04	**226**	15 04	**286**	19 04	**346**	23 04	**46**	3 04	3 05	3 06	3 07
47	3 08	**107**	7 08	**167**	11 08	**227**	15 08	**287**	19 08	**347**	23 08	**47**	3 08	3 09	3 10	3 11
48	3 12	**108**	7 12	**168**	11 12	**228**	15 12	**288**	19 12	**348**	23 12	**48**	3 12	3 13	3 14	3 15
49	3 16	**109**	7 16	**169**	11 16	**229**	15 16	**289**	19 16	**349**	23 16	**49**	3 16	3 17	3 18	3 19
50	3 20	**110**	7 20	**170**	11 20	**230**	15 20	**290**	19 20	**350**	23 20	**50**	3 20	3 21	3 22	3 23
51	3 24	**111**	7 24	**171**	11 24	**231**	15 24	**291**	19 24	**351**	23 24	**51**	3 24	3 25	3 26	3 27
52	3 28	**112**	7 28	**172**	11 28	**232**	15 28	**292**	19 28	**352**	23 28	**52**	3 28	3 29	3 30	3 31
53	3 32	**113**	7 32	**173**	11 32	**233**	15 32	**293**	19 32	**353**	23 32	**53**	3 32	3 33	3 34	3 35
54	3 36	**114**	7 36	**174**	11 36	**234**	15 36	**294**	19 36	**354**	23 36	**54**	3 36	3 37	3 38	3 39
55	3 40	**115**	7 40	**175**	11 40	**235**	15 40	**295**	19 40	**355**	23 40	**55**	3 40	3 41	3 42	3 43
56	3 44	**116**	7 44	**176**	11 44	**236**	15 44	**296**	19 44	**356**	23 44	**56**	3 44	3 45	3 46	3 47
57	3 48	**117**	7 48	**177**	11 48	**237**	15 48	**297**	19 48	**357**	23 48	**57**	3 48	3 49	3 50	3 51
58	3 52	**118**	7 52	**178**	11 52	**238**	15 52	**298**	19 52	**358**	23 52	**58**	3 52	3 53	3 54	3 55
59	3 56	**119**	7 56	**179**	11 56	**239**	15 56	**299**	19 56	**359**	23 56	**59**	3 56	3 57	3 58	3 59

The above table is for converting expressions in arc to their equivalent in time; its main use in this Almanac is for the conversion of longitude for application to LMT (*added* if *west*, *subtracted* if *east*) to give UT or vice versa, particularly in the case of sunrise, sunset, etc.

0m	SUN PLANETS	ARIES	MOON	v or d	Corrn	v or d	Corrn	v or d	Corrn
s	° ′	° ′	° ′	′	′	′	′	′	′
00	0 00·0	0 00·0	0 00·0	0·0	0·0	6·0	0·1	12·0	0·1
01	0 00·3	0 00·3	0 00·2	0·1	0·0	6·1	0·1	12·1	0·1
02	0 00·5	0 00·5	0 00·5	0·2	0·0	6·2	0·1	12·2	0·1
03	0 00·8	0 00·8	0 00·7	0·3	0·0	6·3	0·1	12·3	0·1
04	0 01·0	0 01·0	0 01·0	0·4	0·0	6·4	0·1	12·4	0·1
05	0 01·3	0 01·3	0 01·2	0·5	0·0	6·5	0·1	12·5	0·1
06	0 01·5	0 01·5	0 01·4	0·6	0·0	6·6	0·1	12·6	0·1
07	0 01·8	0 01·8	0 01·7	0·7	0·0	6·7	0·1	12·7	0·1
08	0 02·0	0 02·0	0 01·9	0·8	0·0	6·8	0·1	12·8	0·1
09	0 02·3	0 02·3	0 02·1	0·9	0·0	6·9	0·1	12·9	0·1
10	0 02·5	0 02·5	0 02·4	1·0	0·0	7·0	0·1	13·0	0·1
11	0 02·8	0 02·8	0 02·6	1·1	0·0	7·1	0·1	13·1	0·1
12	0 03·0	0 03·0	0 02·9	1·2	0·0	7·2	0·1	13·2	0·1
13	0 03·3	0 03·3	0 03·1	1·3	0·0	7·3	0·1	13·3	0·1
14	0 03·5	0 03·5	0 03·3	1·4	0·0	7·4	0·1	13·4	0·1
15	0 03·8	0 03·8	0 03·6	1·5	0·0	7·5	0·1	13·5	0·1
16	0 04·0	0 04·0	0 03·8	1·6	0·0	7·6	0·1	13·6	0·1
17	0 04·3	0 04·3	0 04·1	1·7	0·0	7·7	0·1	13·7	0·1
18	0 04·5	0 04·5	0 04·3	1·8	0·0	7·8	0·1	13·8	0·1
19	0 04·8	0 04·8	0 04·5	1·9	0·0	7·9	0·1	13·9	0·1
20	0 05·0	0 05·0	0 04·8	2·0	0·0	8·0	0·1	14·0	0·1
21	0 05·3	0 05·3	0 05·0	2·1	0·0	8·1	0·1	14·1	0·1
22	0 05·5	0 05·5	0 05·2	2·2	0·0	8·2	0·1	14·2	0·1
23	0 05·8	0 05·8	0 05·5	2·3	0·0	8·3	0·1	14·3	0·1
24	0 06·0	0 06·0	0 05·7	2·4	0·0	8·4	0·1	14·4	0·1
25	0 06·3	0 06·3	0 06·0	2·5	0·0	8·5	0·1	14·5	0·1
26	0 06·5	0 06·5	0 06·2	2·6	0·0	8·6	0·1	14·6	0·1
27	0 06·8	0 06·8	0 06·4	2·7	0·0	8·7	0·1	14·7	0·1
28	0 07·0	0 07·0	0 06·7	2·8	0·0	8·8	0·1	14·8	0·1
29	0 07·3	0 07·3	0 06·9	2·9	0·0	8·9	0·1	14·9	0·1
30	0 07·5	0 07·5	0 07·2	3·0	0·0	9·0	0·1	15·0	0·1
31	0 07·8	0 07·8	0 07·4	3·1	0·0	9·1	0·1	15·1	0·1
32	0 08·0	0 08·0	0 07·6	3·2	0·0	9·2	0·1	15·2	0·1
33	0 08·3	0 08·3	0 07·9	3·3	0·0	9·3	0·1	15·3	0·1
34	0 08·5	0 08·5	0 08·1	3·4	0·0	9·4	0·1	15·4	0·1
35	0 08·8	0 08·8	0 08·4	3·5	0·0	9·5	0·1	15·5	0·1
36	0 09·0	0 09·0	0 08·6	3·6	0·0	9·6	0·1	15·6	0·1
37	0 09·3	0 09·3	0 08·8	3·7	0·0	9·7	0·1	15·7	0·1
38	0 09·5	0 09·5	0 09·1	3·8	0·0	9·8	0·1	15·8	0·1
39	0 09·8	0 09·8	0 09·3	3·9	0·0	9·9	0·1	15·9	0·1
40	0 10·0	0 10·0	0 09·5	4·0	0·0	10·0	0·1	16·0	0·1
41	0 10·3	0 10·3	0 09·8	4·1	0·0	10·1	0·1	16·1	0·1
42	0 10·5	0 10·5	0 10·0	4·2	0·0	10·2	0·1	16·2	0·1
43	0 10·8	0 10·8	0 10·3	4·3	0·0	10·3	0·1	16·3	0·1
44	0 11·0	0 11·0	0 10·5	4·4	0·0	10·4	0·1	16·4	0·1
45	0 11·3	0 11·3	0 10·7	4·5	0·0	10·5	0·1	16·5	0·1
46	0 11·5	0 11·5	0 11·0	4·6	0·0	10·6	0·1	16·6	0·1
47	0 11·8	0 11·8	0 11·2	4·7	0·0	10·7	0·1	16·7	0·1
48	0 12·0	0 12·0	0 11·5	4·8	0·0	10·8	0·1	16·8	0·1
49	0 12·3	0 12·3	0 11·7	4·9	0·0	10·9	0·1	16·9	0·1
50	0 12·5	0 12·5	0 11·9	5·0	0·0	11·0	0·1	17·0	0·1
51	0 12·8	0 12·8	0 12·2	5·1	0·0	11·1	0·1	17·1	0·1
52	0 13·0	0 13·0	0 12·4	5·2	0·0	11·2	0·1	17·2	0·1
53	0 13·3	0 13·3	0 12·6	5·3	0·0	11·3	0·1	17·3	0·1
54	0 13·5	0 13·5	0 12·9	5·4	0·0	11·4	0·1	17·4	0·1
55	0 13·8	0 13·8	0 13·1	5·5	0·0	11·5	0·1	17·5	0·1
56	0 14·0	0 14·0	0 13·4	5·6	0·0	11·6	0·1	17·6	0·1
57	0 14·3	0 14·3	0 13·6	5·7	0·0	11·7	0·1	17·7	0·1
58	0 14·5	0 14·5	0 13·8	5·8	0·0	11·8	0·1	17·8	0·1
59	0 14·8	0 14·8	0 14·1	5·9	0·0	11·9	0·1	17·9	0·1
60	0 15·0	0 15·0	0 14·3	6·0	0·1	12·0	0·1	18·0	0·2

1m	SUN PLANETS	ARIES	MOON	v or d	Corrn	v or d	Corrn	v or d	Corrn
s	° ′	° ′	° ′	′	′	′	′	′	′
00	0 15·0	0 15·0	0 14·3	0·0	0·0	6·0	0·2	12·0	0·3
01	0 15·3	0 15·3	0 14·6	0·1	0·0	6·1	0·2	12·1	0·3
02	0 15·5	0 15·5	0 14·8	0·2	0·0	6·2	0·2	12·2	0·3
03	0 15·8	0 15·8	0 15·0	0·3	0·0	6·3	0·2	12·3	0·3
04	0 16·0	0 16·0	0 15·3	0·4	0·0	6·4	0·2	12·4	0·3
05	0 16·3	0 16·3	0 15·5	0·5	0·0	6·5	0·2	12·5	0·3
06	0 16·5	0 16·5	0 15·7	0·6	0·0	6·6	0·2	12·6	0·3
07	0 16·8	0 16·8	0 16·0	0·7	0·0	6·7	0·2	12·7	0·3
08	0 17·0	0 17·0	0 16·2	0·8	0·0	6·8	0·2	12·8	0·3
09	0 17·3	0 17·3	0 16·5	0·9	0·0	6·9	0·2	12·9	0·3
10	0 17·5	0 17·5	0 16·7	1·0	0·0	7·0	0·2	13·0	0·3
11	0 17·8	0 17·8	0 16·9	1·1	0·0	7·1	0·2	13·1	0·3
12	0 18·0	0 18·0	0 17·2	1·2	0·0	7·2	0·2	13·2	0·3
13	0 18·3	0 18·3	0 17·4	1·3	0·0	7·3	0·2	13·3	0·3
14	0 18·5	0 18·6	0 17·7	1·4	0·0	7·4	0·2	13·4	0·3
15	0 18·8	0 18·8	0 17·9	1·5	0·0	7·5	0·2	13·5	0·3
16	0 19·0	0 19·1	0 18·1	1·6	0·0	7·6	0·2	13·6	0·3
17	0 19·3	0 19·3	0 18·4	1·7	0·0	7·7	0·2	13·7	0·3
18	0 19·5	0 19·6	0 18·6	1·8	0·0	7·8	0·2	13·8	0·3
19	0 19·8	0 19·8	0 18·9	1·9	0·0	7·9	0·2	13·9	0·3
20	0 20·0	0 20·1	0 19·1	2·0	0·1	8·0	0·2	14·0	0·4
21	0 20·3	0 20·3	0 19·3	2·1	0·1	8·1	0·2	14·1	0·4
22	0 20·5	0 20·6	0 19·6	2·2	0·1	8·2	0·2	14·2	0·4
23	0 20·8	0 20·8	0 19·8	2·3	0·1	8·3	0·2	14·3	0·4
24	0 21·0	0 21·1	0 20·0	2·4	0·1	8·4	0·2	14·4	0·4
25	0 21·3	0 21·3	0 20·3	2·5	0·1	8·5	0·2	14·5	0·4
26	0 21·5	0 21·6	0 20·5	2·6	0·1	8·6	0·2	14·6	0·4
27	0 21·8	0 21·8	0 20·8	2·7	0·1	8·7	0·2	14·7	0·4
28	0 22·0	0 22·1	0 21·0	2·8	0·1	8·8	0·2	14·8	0·4
29	0 22·3	0 22·3	0 21·2	2·9	0·1	8·9	0·2	14·9	0·4
30	0 22·5	0 22·6	0 21·5	3·0	0·1	9·0	0·2	15·0	0·4
31	0 22·8	0 22·8	0 21·7	3·1	0·1	9·1	0·2	15·1	0·4
32	0 23·0	0 23·1	0 22·0	3·2	0·1	9·2	0·2	15·2	0·4
33	0 23·3	0 23·3	0 22·2	3·3	0·1	9·3	0·2	15·3	0·4
34	0 23·5	0 23·6	0 22·4	3·4	0·1	9·4	0·2	15·4	0·4
35	0 23·8	0 23·8	0 22·7	3·5	0·1	9·5	0·2	15·5	0·4
36	0 24·0	0 24·1	0 22·9	3·6	0·1	9·6	0·2	15·6	0·4
37	0 24·3	0 24·3	0 23·1	3·7	0·1	9·7	0·2	15·7	0·4
38	0 24·5	0 24·6	0 23·4	3·8	0·1	9·8	0·2	15·8	0·4
39	0 24·8	0 24·8	0 23·6	3·9	0·1	9·9	0·2	15·9	0·4
40	0 25·0	0 25·1	0 23·9	4·0	0·1	10·0	0·3	16·0	0·4
41	0 25·3	0 25·3	0 24·1	4·1	0·1	10·1	0·3	16·1	0·4
42	0 25·5	0 25·6	0 24·3	4·2	0·1	10·2	0·3	16·2	0·4
43	0 25·8	0 25·8	0 24·6	4·3	0·1	10·3	0·3	16·3	0·4
44	0 26·0	0 26·1	0 24·8	4·4	0·1	10·4	0·3	16·4	0·4
45	0 26·3	0 26·3	0 25·1	4·5	0·1	10·5	0·3	16·5	0·4
46	0 26·5	0 26·6	0 25·3	4·6	0·1	10·6	0·3	16·6	0·4
47	0 26·8	0 26·8	0 25·5	4·7	0·1	10·7	0·3	16·7	0·4
48	0 27·0	0 27·1	0 25·8	4·8	0·1	10·8	0·3	16·8	0·4
49	0 27·3	0 27·3	0 26·0	4·9	0·1	10·9	0·3	16·9	0·4
50	0 27·5	0 27·6	0 26·2	5·0	0·1	11·0	0·3	17·0	0·4
51	0 27·8	0 27·8	0 26·5	5·1	0·1	11·1	0·3	17·1	0·4
52	0 28·0	0 28·1	0 26·7	5·2	0·1	11·2	0·3	17·2	0·4
53	0 28·3	0 28·3	0 27·0	5·3	0·1	11·3	0·3	17·3	0·4
54	0 28·5	0 28·6	0 27·2	5·4	0·1	11·4	0·3	17·4	0·4
55	0 28·8	0 28·8	0 27·4	5·5	0·1	11·5	0·3	17·5	0·4
56	0 29·0	0 29·1	0 27·7	5·6	0·1	11·6	0·3	17·6	0·4
57	0 29·3	0 29·3	0 27·9	5·7	0·1	11·7	0·3	17·7	0·4
58	0 29·5	0 29·6	0 28·2	5·8	0·1	11·8	0·3	17·8	0·4
59	0 29·8	0 29·8	0 28·4	5·9	0·1	11·9	0·3	17·9	0·4
60	0 30·0	0 30·1	0 28·6	6·0	0·2	12·0	0·3	18·0	0·5

m 2 s	SUN PLANETS ° ′	ARIES ° ′	MOON ° ′	v or d ′	Corrⁿ ′	v or d ′	Corrⁿ ′	v or d ′	Corrⁿ ′
00	0 30·0	0 30·1	0 28·6	0·0	0·0	6·0	0·3	12·0	0·5
01	0 30·3	0 30·3	0 28·9	0·1	0·0	6·1	0·3	12·1	0·5
02	0 30·5	0 30·6	0 29·1	0·2	0·0	6·2	0·3	12·2	0·5
03	0 30·8	0 30·8	0 29·3	0·3	0·0	6·3	0·3	12·3	0·5
04	0 31·0	0 31·1	0 29·6	0·4	0·0	6·4	0·3	12·4	0·5
05	0 31·3	0 31·3	0 29·8	0·5	0·0	6·5	0·3	12·5	0·5
06	0 31·5	0 31·6	0 30·1	0·6	0·0	6·6	0·3	12·6	0·5
07	0 31·8	0 31·8	0 30·3	0·7	0·0	6·7	0·3	12·7	0·5
08	0 32·0	0 32·1	0 30·5	0·8	0·0	6·8	0·3	12·8	0·5
09	0 32·3	0 32·3	0 30·8	0·9	0·0	6·9	0·3	12·9	0·5
10	0 32·5	0 32·6	0 31·0	1·0	0·0	7·0	0·3	13·0	0·5
11	0 32·8	0 32·8	0 31·3	1·1	0·0	7·1	0·3	13·1	0·5
12	0 33·0	0 33·1	0 31·5	1·2	0·1	7·2	0·3	13·2	0·6
13	0 33·3	0 33·3	0 31·7	1·3	0·1	7·3	0·3	13·3	0·6
14	0 33·5	0 33·6	0 32·0	1·4	0·1	7·4	0·3	13·4	0·6
15	0 33·8	0 33·8	0 32·2	1·5	0·1	7·5	0·3	13·5	0·6
16	0 34·0	0 34·1	0 32·5	1·6	0·1	7·6	0·3	13·6	0·6
17	0 34·3	0 34·3	0 32·7	1·7	0·1	7·7	0·3	13·7	0·6
18	0 34·5	0 34·6	0 32·9	1·8	0·1	7·8	0·3	13·8	0·6
19	0 34·8	0 34·8	0 33·2	1·9	0·1	7·9	0·3	13·9	0·6
20	0 35·0	0 35·1	0 33·4	2·0	0·1	8·0	0·3	14·0	0·6
21	0 35·3	0 35·3	0 33·6	2·1	0·1	8·1	0·3	14·1	0·6
22	0 35·5	0 35·6	0 33·9	2·2	0·1	8·2	0·3	14·2	0·6
23	0 35·8	0 35·8	0 34·1	2·3	0·1	8·3	0·3	14·3	0·6
24	0 36·0	0 36·1	0 34·4	2·4	0·1	8·4	0·4	14·4	0·6
25	0 36·3	0 36·3	0 34·6	2·5	0·1	8·5	0·4	14·5	0·6
26	0 36·5	0 36·6	0 34·8	2·6	0·1	8·6	0·4	14·6	0·6
27	0 36·8	0 36·9	0 35·1	2·7	0·1	8·7	0·4	14·7	0·6
28	0 37·0	0 37·1	0 35·3	2·8	0·1	8·8	0·4	14·8	0·6
29	0 37·3	0 37·4	0 35·6	2·9	0·1	8·9	0·4	14·9	0·6
30	0 37·5	0 37·6	0 35·8	3·0	0·1	9·0	0·4	15·0	0·6
31	0 37·8	0 37·9	0 36·0	3·1	0·1	9·1	0·4	15·1	0·6
32	0 38·0	0 38·1	0 36·3	3·2	0·1	9·2	0·4	15·2	0·6
33	0 38·3	0 38·4	0 36·5	3·3	0·1	9·3	0·4	15·3	0·6
34	0 38·5	0 38·6	0 36·7	3·4	0·1	9·4	0·4	15·4	0·6
35	0 38·8	0 38·9	0 37·0	3·5	0·1	9·5	0·4	15·5	0·6
36	0 39·0	0 39·1	0 37·2	3·6	0·2	9·6	0·4	15·6	0·7
37	0 39·3	0 39·4	0 37·5	3·7	0·2	9·7	0·4	15·7	0·7
38	0 39·5	0 39·6	0 37·7	3·8	0·2	9·8	0·4	15·8	0·7
39	0 39·8	0 39·9	0 37·9	3·9	0·2	9·9	0·4	15·9	0·7
40	0 40·0	0 40·1	0 38·2	4·0	0·2	10·0	0·4	16·0	0·7
41	0 40·3	0 40·4	0 38·4	4·1	0·2	10·1	0·4	16·1	0·7
42	0 40·5	0 40·6	0 38·7	4·2	0·2	10·2	0·4	16·2	0·7
43	0 40·8	0 40·9	0 38·9	4·3	0·2	10·3	0·4	16·3	0·7
44	0 41·0	0 41·1	0 39·1	4·4	0·2	10·4	0·4	16·4	0·7
45	0 41·3	0 41·4	0 39·4	4·5	0·2	10·5	0·4	16·5	0·7
46	0 41·5	0 41·6	0 39·6	4·6	0·2	10·6	0·4	16·6	0·7
47	0 41·8	0 41·9	0 39·8	4·7	0·2	10·7	0·4	16·7	0·7
48	0 42·0	0 42·1	0 40·1	4·8	0·2	10·8	0·5	16·8	0·7
49	0 42·3	0 42·4	0 40·3	4·9	0·2	10·9	0·5	16·9	0·7
50	0 42·5	0 42·6	0 40·6	5·0	0·2	11·0	0·5	17·0	0·7
51	0 42·8	0 42·9	0 40·8	5·1	0·2	11·1	0·5	17·1	0·7
52	0 43·0	0 43·1	0 41·0	5·2	0·2	11·2	0·5	17·2	0·7
53	0 43·3	0 43·4	0 41·3	5·3	0·2	11·3	0·5	17·3	0·7
54	0 43·5	0 43·6	0 41·5	5·4	0·2	11·4	0·5	17·4	0·7
55	0 43·8	0 43·9	0 41·8	5·5	0·2	11·5	0·5	17·5	0·7
56	0 44·0	0 44·1	0 42·0	5·6	0·2	11·6	0·5	17·6	0·7
57	0 44·3	0 44·4	0 42·2	5·7	0·2	11·7	0·5	17·7	0·7
58	0 44·5	0 44·6	0 42·5	5·8	0·2	11·8	0·5	17·8	0·7
59	0 44·8	0 44·9	0 42·7	5·9	0·2	11·9	0·5	17·9	0·7
60	0 45·0	0 45·1	0 43·0	6·0	0·3	12·0	0·5	18·0	0·8

m 3 s	SUN PLANETS ° ′	ARIES ° ′	MOON ° ′	v or d ′	Corrⁿ ′	v or d ′	Corrⁿ ′	v or d ′	Corrⁿ ′
00	0 45·0	0 45·1	0 43·0	0·0	0·0	6·0	0·4	12·0	0·7
01	0 45·3	0 45·4	0 43·2	0·1	0·0	6·1	0·4	12·1	0·7
02	0 45·5	0 45·6	0 43·4	0·2	0·0	6·2	0·4	12·2	0·7
03	0 45·8	0 45·9	0 43·7	0·3	0·0	6·3	0·4	12·3	0·7
04	0 46·0	0 46·1	0 43·9	0·4	0·0	6·4	0·4	12·4	0·7
05	0 46·3	0 46·4	0 44·1	0·5	0·0	6·5	0·4	12·5	0·7
06	0 46·5	0 46·6	0 44·4	0·6	0·0	6·6	0·4	12·6	0·7
07	0 46·8	0 46·9	0 44·6	0·7	0·0	6·7	0·4	12·7	0·7
08	0 47·0	0 47·1	0 44·9	0·8	0·0	6·8	0·4	12·8	0·7
09	0 47·3	0 47·4	0 45·1	0·9	0·1	6·9	0·4	12·9	0·8
10	0 47·5	0 47·6	0 45·3	1·0	0·1	7·0	0·4	13·0	0·8
11	0 47·8	0 47·9	0 45·6	1·1	0·1	7·1	0·4	13·1	0·8
12	0 48·0	0 48·1	0 45·8	1·2	0·1	7·2	0·4	13·2	0·8
13	0 48·3	0 48·4	0 46·1	1·3	0·1	7·3	0·4	13·3	0·8
14	0 48·5	0 48·6	0 46·3	1·4	0·1	7·4	0·4	13·4	0·8
15	0 48·8	0 48·9	0 46·5	1·5	0·1	7·5	0·4	13·5	0·8
16	0 49·0	0 49·1	0 46·8	1·6	0·1	7·6	0·4	13·6	0·8
17	0 49·3	0 49·4	0 47·0	1·7	0·1	7·7	0·4	13·7	0·8
18	0 49·5	0 49·6	0 47·2	1·8	0·1	7·8	0·5	13·8	0·8
19	0 49·8	0 49·9	0 47·5	1·9	0·1	7·9	0·5	13·9	0·8
20	0 50·0	0 50·1	0 47·7	2·0	0·1	8·0	0·5	14·0	0·8
21	0 50·3	0 50·4	0 48·0	2·1	0·1	8·1	0·5	14·1	0·8
22	0 50·5	0 50·6	0 48·2	2·2	0·1	8·2	0·5	14·2	0·8
23	0 50·8	0 50·9	0 48·4	2·3	0·1	8·3	0·5	14·3	0·8
24	0 51·0	0 51·1	0 48·7	2·4	0·1	8·4	0·5	14·4	0·8
25	0 51·3	0 51·4	0 48·9	2·5	0·1	8·5	0·5	14·5	0·8
26	0 51·5	0 51·6	0 49·2	2·6	0·2	8·6	0·5	14·6	0·9
27	0 51·8	0 51·9	0 49·4	2·7	0·2	8·7	0·5	14·7	0·9
28	0 52·0	0 52·1	0 49·6	2·8	0·2	8·8	0·5	14·8	0·9
29	0 52·3	0 52·4	0 49·9	2·9	0·2	8·9	0·5	14·9	0·9
30	0 52·5	0 52·6	0 50·1	3·0	0·2	9·0	0·5	15·0	0·9
31	0 52·8	0 52·9	0 50·3	3·1	0·2	9·1	0·5	15·1	0·9
32	0 53·0	0 53·1	0 50·6	3·2	0·2	9·2	0·5	15·2	0·9
33	0 53·3	0 53·4	0 50·8	3·3	0·2	9·3	0·5	15·3	0·9
34	0 53·5	0 53·6	0 51·1	3·4	0·2	9·4	0·5	15·4	0·9
35	0 53·8	0 53·9	0 51·3	3·5	0·2	9·5	0·6	15·5	0·9
36	0 54·0	0 54·1	0 51·5	3·6	0·2	9·6	0·6	15·6	0·9
37	0 54·3	0 54·4	0 51·8	3·7	0·2	9·7	0·6	15·7	0·9
38	0 54·5	0 54·6	0 52·0	3·8	0·2	9·8	0·6	15·8	0·9
39	0 54·8	0 54·9	0 52·3	3·9	0·2	9·9	0·6	15·9	0·9
40	0 55·0	0 55·2	0 52·5	4·0	0·2	10·0	0·6	16·0	0·9
41	0 55·3	0 55·4	0 52·7	4·1	0·2	10·1	0·6	16·1	0·9
42	0 55·5	0 55·7	0 53·0	4·2	0·2	10·2	0·6	16·2	0·9
43	0 55·8	0 55·9	0 53·2	4·3	0·3	10·3	0·6	16·3	1·0
44	0 56·0	0 56·2	0 53·4	4·4	0·3	10·4	0·6	16·4	1·0
45	0 56·3	0 56·4	0 53·7	4·5	0·3	10·5	0·6	16·5	1·0
46	0 56·5	0 56·7	0 53·9	4·6	0·3	10·6	0·6	16·6	1·0
47	0 56·8	0 56·9	0 54·2	4·7	0·3	10·7	0·6	16·7	1·0
48	0 57·0	0 57·2	0 54·4	4·8	0·3	10·8	0·6	16·8	1·0
49	0 57·3	0 57·4	0 54·6	4·9	0·3	10·9	0·6	16·9	1·0
50	0 57·5	0 57·7	0 54·9	5·0	0·3	11·0	0·6	17·0	1·0
51	0 57·8	0 57·9	0 55·1	5·1	0·3	11·1	0·6	17·1	1·0
52	0 58·0	0 58·2	0 55·4	5·2	0·3	11·2	0·7	17·2	1·0
53	0 58·3	0 58·4	0 55·6	5·3	0·3	11·3	0·7	17·3	1·0
54	0 58·5	0 58·7	0 55·8	5·4	0·3	11·4	0·7	17·4	1·0
55	0 58·8	0 58·9	0 56·1	5·5	0·3	11·5	0·7	17·5	1·0
56	0 59·0	0 59·2	0 56·3	5·6	0·3	11·6	0·7	17·6	1·0
57	0 59·3	0 59·4	0 56·6	5·7	0·3	11·7	0·7	17·7	1·0
58	0 59·5	0 59·7	0 56·8	5·8	0·3	11·8	0·7	17·8	1·0
59	0 59·8	0 59·9	0 57·0	5·9	0·3	11·9	0·7	17·9	1·0
60	1 00·0	1 00·2	0 57·3	6·0	0·4	12·0	0·7	18·0	1·1

4m	SUN PLANETS	ARIES	MOON	v or d	Corrn	v or d	Corrn	v or d	Corrn
s	° ′	° ′	° ′	′	′	′	′	′	′
00	1 00·0	1 00·2	0 57·3	0·0	0·0	6·0	0·5	12·0	0·9
01	1 00·3	1 00·4	0 57·5	0·1	0·0	6·1	0·5	12·1	0·9
02	1 00·5	1 00·7	0 57·7	0·2	0·0	6·2	0·5	12·2	0·9
03	1 00·8	1 00·9	0 58·0	0·3	0·0	6·3	0·5	12·3	0·9
04	1 01·0	1 01·2	0 58·2	0·4	0·0	6·4	0·5	12·4	0·9
05	1 01·3	1 01·4	0 58·5	0·5	0·0	6·5	0·5	12·5	0·9
06	1 01·5	1 01·7	0 58·7	0·6	0·0	6·6	0·5	12·6	0·9
07	1 01·8	1 01·9	0 58·9	0·7	0·1	6·7	0·5	12·7	1·0
08	1 02·0	1 02·2	0 59·2	0·8	0·1	6·8	0·5	12·8	1·0
09	1 02·3	1 02·4	0 59·4	0·9	0·1	6·9	0·5	12·9	1·0
10	1 02·5	1 02·7	0 59·7	1·0	0·1	7·0	0·5	13·0	1·0
11	1 02·8	1 02·9	0 59·9	1·1	0·1	7·1	0·5	13·1	1·0
12	1 03·0	1 03·2	1 00·1	1·2	0·1	7·2	0·5	13·2	1·0
13	1 03·3	1 03·4	1 00·4	1·3	0·1	7·3	0·5	13·3	1·0
14	1 03·5	1 03·7	1 00·6	1·4	0·1	7·4	0·6	13·4	1·0
15	1 03·8	1 03·9	1 00·8	1·5	0·1	7·5	0·6	13·5	1·0
16	1 04·0	1 04·2	1 01·1	1·6	0·1	7·6	0·6	13·6	1·0
17	1 04·3	1 04·4	1 01·3	1·7	0·1	7·7	0·6	13·7	1·0
18	1 04·5	1 04·7	1 01·6	1·8	0·1	7·8	0·6	13·8	1·0
19	1 04·8	1 04·9	1 01·8	1·9	0·1	7·9	0·6	13·9	1·0
20	1 05·0	1 05·2	1 02·0	2·0	0·2	8·0	0·6	14·0	1·1
21	1 05·3	1 05·4	1 02·3	2·1	0·2	8·1	0·6	14·1	1·1
22	1 05·5	1 05·7	1 02·5	2·2	0·2	8·2	0·6	14·2	1·1
23	1 05·8	1 05·9	1 02·8	2·3	0·2	8·3	0·6	14·3	1·1
24	1 06·0	1 06·2	1 03·0	2·4	0·2	8·4	0·6	14·4	1·1
25	1 06·3	1 06·4	1 03·2	2·5	0·2	8·5	0·6	14·5	1·1
26	1 06·5	1 06·7	1 03·5	2·6	0·2	8·6	0·6	14·6	1·1
27	1 06·8	1 06·9	1 03·7	2·7	0·2	8·7	0·7	14·7	1·1
28	1 07·0	1 07·2	1 03·9	2·8	0·2	8·8	0·7	14·8	1·1
29	1 07·3	1 07·4	1 04·2	2·9	0·2	8·9	0·7	14·9	1·1
30	1 07·5	1 07·7	1 04·4	3·0	0·2	9·0	0·7	15·0	1·1
31	1 07·8	1 07·9	1 04·7	3·1	0·2	9·1	0·7	15·1	1·1
32	1 08·0	1 08·2	1 04·9	3·2	0·2	9·2	0·7	15·2	1·1
33	1 08·3	1 08·4	1 05·1	3·3	0·2	9·3	0·7	15·3	1·1
34	1 08·5	1 08·7	1 05·4	3·4	0·3	9·4	0·7	15·4	1·2
35	1 08·8	1 08·9	1 05·6	3·5	0·3	9·5	0·7	15·5	1·2
36	1 09·0	1 09·2	1 05·9	3·6	0·3	9·6	0·7	15·6	1·2
37	1 09·3	1 09·4	1 06·1	3·7	0·3	9·7	0·7	15·7	1·2
38	1 09·5	1 09·7	1 06·3	3·8	0·3	9·8	0·7	15·8	1·2
39	1 09·8	1 09·9	1 06·6	3·9	0·3	9·9	0·7	15·9	1·2
40	1 10·0	1 10·2	1 06·8	4·0	0·3	10·0	0·8	16·0	1·2
41	1 10·3	1 10·4	1 07·0	4·1	0·3	10·1	0·8	16·1	1·2
42	1 10·5	1 10·7	1 07·3	4·2	0·3	10·2	0·8	16·2	1·2
43	1 10·8	1 10·9	1 07·5	4·3	0·3	10·3	0·8	16·3	1·2
44	1 11·0	1 11·2	1 07·8	4·4	0·3	10·4	0·8	16·4	1·2
45	1 11·3	1 11·4	1 08·0	4·5	0·3	10·5	0·8	16·5	1·2
46	1 11·5	1 11·7	1 08·2	4·6	0·3	10·6	0·8	16·6	1·2
47	1 11·8	1 11·9	1 08·5	4·7	0·4	10·7	0·8	16·7	1·3
48	1 12·0	1 12·2	1 08·7	4·8	0·4	10·8	0·8	16·8	1·3
49	1 12·3	1 12·4	1 09·0	4·9	0·4	10·9	0·8	16·9	1·3
50	1 12·5	1 12·7	1 09·2	5·0	0·4	11·0	0·8	17·0	1·3
51	1 12·8	1 12·9	1 09·4	5·1	0·4	11·1	0·8	17·1	1·3
52	1 13·0	1 13·2	1 09·7	5·2	0·4	11·2	0·8	17·2	1·3
53	1 13·3	1 13·5	1 09·9	5·3	0·4	11·3	0·8	17·3	1·3
54	1 13·5	1 13·7	1 10·2	5·4	0·4	11·4	0·9	17·4	1·3
55	1 13·8	1 14·0	1 10·4	5·5	0·4	11·5	0·9	17·5	1·3
56	1 14·0	1 14·2	1 10·6	5·6	0·4	11·6	0·9	17·6	1·3
57	1 14·3	1 14·5	1 10·9	5·7	0·4	11·7	0·9	17·7	1·3
58	1 14·5	1 14·7	1 11·1	5·8	0·4	11·8	0·9	17·8	1·3
59	1 14·8	1 15·0	1 11·3	5·9	0·4	11·9	0·9	17·9	1·3
60	1 15·0	1 15·2	1 11·6	6·0	0·5	12·0	0·9	18·0	1·4

5m	SUN PLANETS	ARIES	MOON	v or d	Corrn	v or d	Corrn	v or d	Corrn
s	° ′	° ′	° ′	′	′	′	′	′	′
00	1 15·0	1 15·2	1 11·6	0·0	0·0	6·0	0·6	12·0	1·1
01	1 15·3	1 15·5	1 11·8	0·1	0·0	6·1	0·6	12·1	1·1
02	1 15·5	1 15·7	1 12·1	0·2	0·0	6·2	0·6	12·2	1·1
03	1 15·8	1 16·0	1 12·3	0·3	0·0	6·3	0·6	12·3	1·1
04	1 16·0	1 16·2	1 12·5	0·4	0·0	6·4	0·6	12·4	1·1
05	1 16·3	1 16·5	1 12·8	0·5	0·0	6·5	0·6	12·5	1·1
06	1 16·5	1 16·7	1 13·0	0·6	0·1	6·6	0·6	12·6	1·2
07	1 16·8	1 17·0	1 13·3	0·7	0·1	6·7	0·6	12·7	1·2
08	1 17·0	1 17·2	1 13·5	0·8	0·1	6·8	0·6	12·8	1·2
09	1 17·3	1 17·5	1 13·7	0·9	0·1	6·9	0·6	12·9	1·2
10	1 17·5	1 17·7	1 14·0	1·0	0·1	7·0	0·6	13·0	1·2
11	1 17·8	1 18·0	1 14·2	1·1	0·1	7·1	0·7	13·1	1·2
12	1 18·0	1 18·2	1 14·4	1·2	0·1	7·2	0·7	13·2	1·2
13	1 18·3	1 18·5	1 14·7	1·3	0·1	7·3	0·7	13·3	1·2
14	1 18·5	1 18·7	1 14·9	1·4	0·1	7·4	0·7	13·4	1·2
15	1 18·8	1 19·0	1 15·2	1·5	0·1	7·5	0·7	13·5	1·2
16	1 19·0	1 19·2	1 15·4	1·6	0·1	7·6	0·7	13·6	1·2
17	1 19·3	1 19·5	1 15·6	1·7	0·2	7·7	0·7	13·7	1·3
18	1 19·5	1 19·7	1 15·9	1·8	0·2	7·8	0·7	13·8	1·3
19	1 19·8	1 20·0	1 16·1	1·9	0·2	7·9	0·7	13·9	1·3
20	1 20·0	1 20·2	1 16·4	2·0	0·2	8·0	0·7	14·0	1·3
21	1 20·3	1 20·5	1 16·6	2·1	0·2	8·1	0·7	14·1	1·3
22	1 20·5	1 20·7	1 16·8	2·2	0·2	8·2	0·8	14·2	1·3
23	1 20·8	1 21·0	1 17·1	2·3	0·2	8·3	0·8	14·3	1·3
24	1 21·0	1 21·2	1 17·3	2·4	0·2	8·4	0·8	14·4	1·3
25	1 21·3	1 21·5	1 17·5	2·5	0·2	8·5	0·8	14·5	1·3
26	1 21·5	1 21·7	1 17·8	2·6	0·2	8·6	0·8	14·6	1·3
27	1 21·8	1 22·0	1 18·0	2·7	0·2	8·7	0·8	14·7	1·3
28	1 22·0	1 22·2	1 18·3	2·8	0·3	8·8	0·8	14·8	1·4
29	1 22·3	1 22·5	1 18·5	2·9	0·3	8·9	0·8	14·9	1·4
30	1 22·5	1 22·7	1 18·7	3·0	0·3	9·0	0·8	15·0	1·4
31	1 22·8	1 23·0	1 19·0	3·1	0·3	9·1	0·8	15·1	1·4
32	1 23·0	1 23·2	1 19·2	3·2	0·3	9·2	0·8	15·2	1·4
33	1 23·3	1 23·5	1 19·5	3·3	0·3	9·3	0·9	15·3	1·4
34	1 23·5	1 23·7	1 19·7	3·4	0·3	9·4	0·9	15·4	1·4
35	1 23·8	1 24·0	1 19·9	3·5	0·3	9·5	0·9	15·5	1·4
36	1 24·0	1 24·2	1 20·2	3·6	0·3	9·6	0·9	15·6	1·4
37	1 24·3	1 24·5	1 20·4	3·7	0·3	9·7	0·9	15·7	1·4
38	1 24·5	1 24·7	1 20·7	3·8	0·3	9·8	0·9	15·8	1·4
39	1 24·8	1 25·0	1 20·9	3·9	0·4	9·9	0·9	15·9	1·5
40	1 25·0	1 25·2	1 21·1	4·0	0·4	10·0	0·9	16·0	1·5
41	1 25·3	1 25·5	1 21·4	4·1	0·4	10·1	0·9	16·1	1·5
42	1 25·5	1 25·7	1 21·6	4·2	0·4	10·2	0·9	16·2	1·5
43	1 25·8	1 26·0	1 21·8	4·3	0·4	10·3	0·9	16·3	1·5
44	1 26·0	1 26·2	1 22·1	4·4	0·4	10·4	1·0	16·4	1·5
45	1 26·3	1 26·5	1 22·3	4·5	0·4	10·5	1·0	16·5	1·5
46	1 26·5	1 26·7	1 22·6	4·6	0·4	10·6	1·0	16·6	1·5
47	1 26·8	1 27·0	1 22·8	4·7	0·4	10·7	1·0	16·7	1·5
48	1 27·0	1 27·2	1 23·0	4·8	0·4	10·8	1·0	16·8	1·5
49	1 27·3	1 27·5	1 23·3	4·9	0·4	10·9	1·0	16·9	1·5
50	1 27·5	1 27·7	1 23·5	5·0	0·5	11·0	1·0	17·0	1·6
51	1 27·8	1 28·0	1 23·8	5·1	0·5	11·1	1·0	17·1	1·6
52	1 28·0	1 28·2	1 24·0	5·2	0·5	11·2	1·0	17·2	1·6
53	1 28·3	1 28·5	1 24·2	5·3	0·5	11·3	1·0	17·3	1·6
54	1 28·5	1 28·7	1 24·5	5·4	0·5	11·4	1·0	17·4	1·6
55	1 28·8	1 29·0	1 24·7	5·5	0·5	11·5	1·1	17·5	1·6
56	1 29·0	1 29·2	1 24·9	5·6	0·5	11·6	1·1	17·6	1·6
57	1 29·3	1 29·5	1 25·2	5·7	0·5	11·7	1·1	17·7	1·6
58	1 29·5	1 29·7	1 25·4	5·8	0·5	11·8	1·1	17·8	1·6
59	1 29·8	1 30·0	1 25·7	5·9	0·5	11·9	1·1	17·9	1·6
60	1 30·0	1 30·2	1 25·9	6·0	0·6	12·0	1·1	18·0	1·7

6^m	SUN PLANETS	ARIES	MOON	v or d	Corr^n	v or d	Corr^n	v or d	Corr^n
s	° ′	° ′	° ′	′	′	′	′	′	′
00	1 30·0	1 30·2	1 25·9	0·0	0·0	6·0	0·7	12·0	1·3
01	1 30·3	1 30·5	1 26·1	0·1	0·0	6·1	0·7	12·1	1·3
02	1 30·5	1 30·7	1 26·4	0·2	0·0	6·2	0·7	12·2	1·3
03	1 30·8	1 31·0	1 26·6	0·3	0·0	6·3	0·7	12·3	1·3
04	1 31·0	1 31·2	1 26·9	0·4	0·0	6·4	0·7	12·4	1·3
05	1 31·3	1 31·5	1 27·1	0·5	0·1	6·5	0·7	12·5	1·4
06	1 31·5	1 31·8	1 27·3	0·6	0·1	6·6	0·7	12·6	1·4
07	1 31·8	1 32·0	1 27·6	0·7	0·1	6·7	0·7	12·7	1·4
08	1 32·0	1 32·3	1 27·8	0·8	0·1	6·8	0·7	12·8	1·4
09	1 32·3	1 32·5	1 28·0	0·9	0·1	6·9	0·7	12·9	1·4
10	1 32·5	1 32·8	1 28·3	1·0	0·1	7·0	0·8	13·0	1·4
11	1 32·8	1 33·0	1 28·5	1·1	0·1	7·1	0·8	13·1	1·4
12	1 33·0	1 33·3	1 28·8	1·2	0·1	7·2	0·8	13·2	1·4
13	1 33·3	1 33·5	1 29·0	1·3	0·1	7·3	0·8	13·3	1·4
14	1 33·5	1 33·8	1 29·2	1·4	0·2	7·4	0·8	13·4	1·5
15	1 33·8	1 34·0	1 29·5	1·5	0·2	7·5	0·8	13·5	1·5
16	1 34·0	1 34·3	1 29·7	1·6	0·2	7·6	0·8	13·6	1·5
17	1 34·3	1 34·5	1 30·0	1·7	0·2	7·7	0·8	13·7	1·5
18	1 34·5	1 34·8	1 30·2	1·8	0·2	7·8	0·8	13·8	1·5
19	1 34·8	1 35·0	1 30·4	1·9	0·2	7·9	0·9	13·9	1·5
20	1 35·0	1 35·3	1 30·7	2·0	0·2	8·0	0·9	14·0	1·5
21	1 35·3	1 35·5	1 30·9	2·1	0·2	8·1	0·9	14·1	1·5
22	1 35·5	1 35·8	1 31·1	2·2	0·2	8·2	0·9	14·2	1·5
23	1 35·8	1 36·0	1 31·4	2·3	0·2	8·3	0·9	14·3	1·5
24	1 36·0	1 36·3	1 31·6	2·4	0·3	8·4	0·9	14·4	1·6
25	1 36·3	1 36·5	1 31·9	2·5	0·3	8·5	0·9	14·5	1·6
26	1 36·5	1 36·8	1 32·1	2·6	0·3	8·6	0·9	14·6	1·6
27	1 36·8	1 37·0	1 32·3	2·7	0·3	8·7	0·9	14·7	1·6
28	1 37·0	1 37·3	1 32·6	2·8	0·3	8·8	1·0	14·8	1·6
29	1 37·3	1 37·5	1 32·8	2·9	0·3	8·9	1·0	14·9	1·6
30	1 37·5	1 37·8	1 33·1	3·0	0·3	9·0	1·0	15·0	1·6
31	1 37·8	1 38·0	1 33·3	3·1	0·3	9·1	1·0	15·1	1·6
32	1 38·0	1 38·3	1 33·5	3·2	0·3	9·2	1·0	15·2	1·6
33	1 38·3	1 38·5	1 33·8	3·3	0·4	9·3	1·0	15·3	1·7
34	1 38·5	1 38·8	1 34·0	3·4	0·4	9·4	1·0	15·4	1·7
35	1 38·8	1 39·0	1 34·3	3·5	0·4	9·5	1·0	15·5	1·7
36	1 39·0	1 39·3	1 34·5	3·6	0·4	9·6	1·0	15·6	1·7
37	1 39·3	1 39·5	1 34·7	3·7	0·4	9·7	1·1	15·7	1·7
38	1 39·5	1 39·8	1 35·0	3·8	0·4	9·8	1·1	15·8	1·7
39	1 39·8	1 40·0	1 35·2	3·9	0·4	9·9	1·1	15·9	1·7
40	1 40·0	1 40·3	1 35·4	4·0	0·4	10·0	1·1	16·0	1·7
41	1 40·3	1 40·5	1 35·7	4·1	0·4	10·1	1·1	16·1	1·7
42	1 40·5	1 40·8	1 35·9	4·2	0·5	10·2	1·1	16·2	1·8
43	1 40·8	1 41·0	1 36·2	4·3	0·5	10·3	1·1	16·3	1·8
44	1 41·0	1 41·3	1 36·4	4·4	0·5	10·4	1·1	16·4	1·8
45	1 41·3	1 41·5	1 36·6	4·5	0·5	10·5	1·1	16·5	1·8
46	1 41·5	1 41·8	1 36·9	4·6	0·5	10·6	1·1	16·6	1·8
47	1 41·8	1 42·0	1 37·1	4·7	0·5	10·7	1·2	16·7	1·8
48	1 42·0	1 42·3	1 37·4	4·8	0·5	10·8	1·2	16·8	1·8
49	1 42·3	1 42·5	1 37·6	4·9	0·5	10·9	1·2	16·9	1·8
50	1 42·5	1 42·8	1 37·8	5·0	0·5	11·0	1·2	17·0	1·8
51	1 42·8	1 43·0	1 38·1	5·1	0·6	11·1	1·2	17·1	1·9
52	1 43·0	1 43·3	1 38·3	5·2	0·6	11·2	1·2	17·2	1·9
53	1 43·3	1 43·5	1 38·5	5·3	0·6	11·3	1·2	17·3	1·9
54	1 43·5	1 43·8	1 38·8	5·4	0·6	11·4	1·2	17·4	1·9
55	1 43·8	1 44·0	1 39·0	5·5	0·6	11·5	1·2	17·5	1·9
56	1 44·0	1 44·3	1 39·3	5·6	0·6	11·6	1·3	17·6	1·9
57	1 44·3	1 44·5	1 39·5	5·7	0·6	11·7	1·3	17·7	1·9
58	1 44·5	1 44·8	1 39·7	5·8	0·6	11·8	1·3	17·8	1·9
59	1 44·8	1 45·0	1 40·0	5·9	0·6	11·9	1·3	17·9	1·9
60	1 45·0	1 45·3	1 40·2	6·0	0·7	12·0	1·3	18·0	2·0

7^m	SUN PLANETS	ARIES	MOON	v or d	Corr^n	v or d	Corr^n	v or d	Corr^n
s	° ′	° ′	° ′	′	′	′	′	′	′
00	1 45·0	1 45·3	1 40·2	0·0	0·0	6·0	0·8	12·0	1·5
01	1 45·3	1 45·5	1 40·5	0·1	0·0	6·1	0·8	12·1	1·5
02	1 45·5	1 45·8	1 40·7	0·2	0·0	6·2	0·8	12·2	1·5
03	1 45·8	1 46·0	1 40·9	0·3	0·0	6·3	0·8	12·3	1·5
04	1 46·0	1 46·3	1 41·2	0·4	0·1	6·4	0·8	12·4	1·6
05	1 46·3	1 46·5	1 41·4	0·5	0·1	6·5	0·8	12·5	1·6
06	1 46·5	1 46·8	1 41·6	0·6	0·1	6·6	0·8	12·6	1·6
07	1 46·8	1 47·0	1 41·9	0·7	0·1	6·7	0·8	12·7	1·6
08	1 47·0	1 47·3	1 42·1	0·8	0·1	6·8	0·9	12·8	1·6
09	1 47·3	1 47·5	1 42·4	0·9	0·1	6·9	0·9	12·9	1·6
10	1 47·5	1 47·8	1 42·6	1·0	0·1	7·0	0·9	13·0	1·6
11	1 47·8	1 48·0	1 42·8	1·1	0·1	7·1	0·9	13·1	1·6
12	1 48·0	1 48·3	1 43·1	1·2	0·2	7·2	0·9	13·2	1·7
13	1 48·3	1 48·5	1 43·3	1·3	0·2	7·3	0·9	13·3	1·7
14	1 48·5	1 48·8	1 43·6	1·4	0·2	7·4	0·9	13·4	1·7
15	1 48·8	1 49·0	1 43·8	1·5	0·2	7·5	0·9	13·5	1·7
16	1 49·0	1 49·3	1 44·0	1·6	0·2	7·6	1·0	13·6	1·7
17	1 49·3	1 49·5	1 44·3	1·7	0·2	7·7	1·0	13·7	1·7
18	1 49·5	1 49·8	1 44·5	1·8	0·2	7·8	1·0	13·8	1·7
19	1 49·8	1 50·1	1 44·8	1·9	0·2	7·9	1·0	13·9	1·7
20	1 50·0	1 50·3	1 45·0	2·0	0·3	8·0	1·0	14·0	1·8
21	1 50·3	1 50·6	1 45·2	2·1	0·3	8·1	1·0	14·1	1·8
22	1 50·5	1 50·8	1 45·5	2·2	0·3	8·2	1·0	14·2	1·8
23	1 50·8	1 51·1	1 45·7	2·3	0·3	8·3	1·0	14·3	1·8
24	1 51·0	1 51·3	1 45·9	2·4	0·3	8·4	1·1	14·4	1·8
25	1 51·3	1 51·6	1 46·2	2·5	0·3	8·5	1·1	14·5	1·8
26	1 51·5	1 51·8	1 46·4	2·6	0·3	8·6	1·1	14·6	1·8
27	1 51·8	1 52·1	1 46·7	2·7	0·3	8·7	1·1	14·7	1·8
28	1 52·0	1 52·3	1 46·9	2·8	0·4	8·8	1·1	14·8	1·9
29	1 52·3	1 52·6	1 47·1	2·9	0·4	8·9	1·1	14·9	1·9
30	1 52·5	1 52·8	1 47·4	3·0	0·4	9·0	1·1	15·0	1·9
31	1 52·8	1 53·1	1 47·6	3·1	0·4	9·1	1·1	15·1	1·9
32	1 53·0	1 53·3	1 47·9	3·2	0·4	9·2	1·2	15·2	1·9
33	1 53·3	1 53·6	1 48·1	3·3	0·4	9·3	1·2	15·3	1·9
34	1 53·5	1 53·8	1 48·3	3·4	0·4	9·4	1·2	15·4	1·9
35	1 53·8	1 54·1	1 48·6	3·5	0·4	9·5	1·2	15·5	1·9
36	1 54·0	1 54·3	1 48·8	3·6	0·5	9·6	1·2	15·6	2·0
37	1 54·3	1 54·6	1 49·0	3·7	0·5	9·7	1·2	15·7	2·0
38	1 54·5	1 54·8	1 49·3	3·8	0·5	9·8	1·2	15·8	2·0
39	1 54·8	1 55·1	1 49·5	3·9	0·5	9·9	1·2	15·9	2·0
40	1 55·0	1 55·3	1 49·8	4·0	0·5	10·0	1·3	16·0	2·0
41	1 55·3	1 55·6	1 50·0	4·1	0·5	10·1	1·3	16·1	2·0
42	1 55·5	1 55·8	1 50·2	4·2	0·5	10·2	1·3	16·2	2·0
43	1 55·8	1 56·1	1 50·5	4·3	0·5	10·3	1·3	16·3	2·0
44	1 56·0	1 56·3	1 50·7	4·4	0·6	10·4	1·3	16·4	2·1
45	1 56·3	1 56·6	1 51·0	4·5	0·6	10·5	1·3	16·5	2·1
46	1 56·5	1 56·8	1 51·2	4·6	0·6	10·6	1·3	16·6	2·1
47	1 56·8	1 57·1	1 51·4	4·7	0·6	10·7	1·3	16·7	2·1
48	1 57·0	1 57·3	1 51·7	4·8	0·6	10·8	1·4	16·8	2·1
49	1 57·3	1 57·6	1 51·9	4·9	0·6	10·9	1·4	16·9	2·1
50	1 57·5	1 57·8	1 52·1	5·0	0·6	11·0	1·4	17·0	2·1
51	1 57·8	1 58·1	1 52·4	5·1	0·6	11·1	1·4	17·1	2·1
52	1 58·0	1 58·3	1 52·6	5·2	0·7	11·2	1·4	17·2	2·2
53	1 58·3	1 58·6	1 52·9	5·3	0·7	11·3	1·4	17·3	2·2
54	1 58·5	1 58·8	1 53·1	5·4	0·7	11·4	1·4	17·4	2·2
55	1 58·8	1 59·1	1 53·3	5·5	0·7	11·5	1·4	17·5	2·2
56	1 59·0	1 59·3	1 53·6	5·6	0·7	11·6	1·5	17·6	2·2
57	1 59·3	1 59·6	1 53·8	5·7	0·7	11·7	1·5	17·7	2·2
58	1 59·5	1 59·8	1 54·1	5·8	0·7	11·8	1·5	17·8	2·2
59	1 59·8	2 00·1	1 54·3	5·9	0·7	11·9	1·5	17·9	2·2
60	2 00·0	2 00·3	1 54·5	6·0	0·8	12·0	1·5	18·0	2·3

8m s	SUN PLANETS ° ′	ARIES ° ′	MOON ° ′	v or d ′	Corrn ′	v or d ′	Corrn ′	v or d ′	Corrn ′
00	2 00·0	2 00·3	1 54·5	0·0	0·0	6·0	0·9	12·0	1·7
01	2 00·3	2 00·6	1 54·8	0·1	0·0	6·1	0·9	12·1	1·7
02	2 00·5	2 00·8	1 55·0	0·2	0·0	6·2	0·9	12·2	1·7
03	2 00·8	2 01·1	1 55·2	0·3	0·0	6·3	0·9	12·3	1·7
04	2 01·0	2 01·3	1 55·5	0·4	0·1	6·4	0·9	12·4	1·8
05	2 01·3	2 01·6	1 55·7	0·5	0·1	6·5	0·9	12·5	1·8
06	2 01·5	2 01·8	1 56·0	0·6	0·1	6·6	0·9	12·6	1·8
07	2 01·8	2 02·1	1 56·2	0·7	0·1	6·7	0·9	12·7	1·8
08	2 02·0	2 02·3	1 56·4	0·8	0·1	6·8	1·0	12·8	1·8
09	2 02·3	2 02·6	1 56·7	0·9	0·1	6·9	1·0	12·9	1·8
10	2 02·5	2 02·8	1 56·9	1·0	0·1	7·0	1·0	13·0	1·8
11	2 02·8	2 03·1	1 57·2	1·1	0·2	7·1	1·0	13·1	1·9
12	2 03·0	2 03·3	1 57·4	1·2	0·2	7·2	1·0	13·2	1·9
13	2 03·3	2 03·6	1 57·6	1·3	0·2	7·3	1·0	13·3	1·9
14	2 03·5	2 03·8	1 57·9	1·4	0·2	7·4	1·0	13·4	1·9
15	2 03·8	2 04·1	1 58·1	1·5	0·2	7·5	1·1	13·5	1·9
16	2 04·0	2 04·3	1 58·4	1·6	0·2	7·6	1·1	13·6	1·9
17	2 04·3	2 04·6	1 58·6	1·7	0·2	7·7	1·1	13·7	1·9
18	2 04·5	2 04·8	1 58·8	1·8	0·3	7·8	1·1	13·8	2·0
19	2 04·8	2 05·1	1 59·1	1·9	0·3	7·9	1·1	13·9	2·0
20	2 05·0	2 05·3	1 59·3	2·0	0·3	8·0	1·1	14·0	2·0
21	2 05·3	2 05·6	1 59·5	2·1	0·3	8·1	1·1	14·1	2·0
22	2 05·5	2 05·8	1 59·8	2·2	0·3	8·2	1·2	14·2	2·0
23	2 05·8	2 06·1	2 00·0	2·3	0·3	8·3	1·2	14·3	2·0
24	2 06·0	2 06·3	2 00·3	2·4	0·3	8·4	1·2	14·4	2·0
25	2 06·3	2 06·6	2 00·5	2·5	0·4	8·5	1·2	14·5	2·1
26	2 06·5	2 06·8	2 00·7	2·6	0·4	8·6	1·2	14·6	2·1
27	2 06·8	2 07·1	2 01·0	2·7	0·4	8·7	1·2	14·7	2·1
28	2 07·0	2 07·3	2 01·2	2·8	0·4	8·8	1·2	14·8	2·1
29	2 07·3	2 07·6	2 01·5	2·9	0·4	8·9	1·3	14·9	2·1
30	2 07·5	2 07·8	2 01·7	3·0	0·4	9·0	1·3	15·0	2·1
31	2 07·8	2 08·1	2 01·9	3·1	0·4	9·1	1·3	15·1	2·1
32	2 08·0	2 08·4	2 02·2	3·2	0·5	9·2	1·3	15·2	2·2
33	2 08·3	2 08·6	2 02·4	3·3	0·5	9·3	1·3	15·3	2·2
34	2 08·5	2 08·9	2 02·6	3·4	0·5	9·4	1·3	15·4	2·2
35	2 08·8	2 09·1	2 02·9	3·5	0·5	9·5	1·3	15·5	2·2
36	2 09·0	2 09·4	2 03·1	3·6	0·5	9·6	1·4	15·6	2·2
37	2 09·3	2 09·6	2 03·4	3·7	0·5	9·7	1·4	15·7	2·2
38	2 09·5	2 09·9	2 03·6	3·8	0·5	9·8	1·4	15·8	2·2
39	2 09·8	2 10·1	2 03·8	3·9	0·6	9·9	1·4	15·9	2·3
40	2 10·0	2 10·4	2 04·1	4·0	0·6	10·0	1·4	16·0	2·3
41	2 10·3	2 10·6	2 04·3	4·1	0·6	10·1	1·4	16·1	2·3
42	2 10·5	2 10·9	2 04·6	4·2	0·6	10·2	1·4	16·2	2·3
43	2 10·8	2 11·1	2 04·8	4·3	0·6	10·3	1·5	16·3	2·3
44	2 11·0	2 11·4	2 05·0	4·4	0·6	10·4	1·5	16·4	2·3
45	2 11·3	2 11·6	2 05·3	4·5	0·6	10·5	1·5	16·5	2·3
46	2 11·5	2 11·9	2 05·5	4·6	0·7	10·6	1·5	16·6	2·4
47	2 11·8	2 12·1	2 05·7	4·7	0·7	10·7	1·5	16·7	2·4
48	2 12·0	2 12·4	2 06·0	4·8	0·7	10·8	1·5	16·8	2·4
49	2 12·3	2 12·6	2 06·2	4·9	0·7	10·9	1·5	16·9	2·4
50	2 12·5	2 12·9	2 06·5	5·0	0·7	11·0	1·6	17·0	2·4
51	2 12·8	2 13·1	2 06·7	5·1	0·7	11·1	1·6	17·1	2·4
52	2 13·0	2 13·4	2 06·9	5·2	0·7	11·2	1·6	17·2	2·4
53	2 13·3	2 13·6	2 07·2	5·3	0·8	11·3	1·6	17·3	2·5
54	2 13·5	2 13·9	2 07·4	5·4	0·8	11·4	1·6	17·4	2·5
55	2 13·8	2 14·1	2 07·7	5·5	0·8	11·5	1·6	17·5	2·5
56	2 14·0	2 14·4	2 07·9	5·6	0·8	11·6	1·6	17·6	2·5
57	2 14·3	2 14·6	2 08·1	5·7	0·8	11·7	1·7	17·7	2·5
58	2 14·5	2 14·9	2 08·4	5·8	0·8	11·8	1·7	17·8	2·5
59	2 14·8	2 15·1	2 08·6	5·9	0·8	11·9	1·7	17·9	2·5
60	2 15·0	2 15·4	2 08·9	6·0	0·9	12·0	1·7	18·0	2·6

9m s	SUN PLANETS ° ′	ARIES ° ′	MOON ° ′	v or d ′	Corrn ′	v or d ′	Corrn ′	v or d ′	Corrn ′
00	2 15·0	2 15·4	2 08·9	0·0	0·0	6·0	1·0	12·0	1·9
01	2 15·3	2 15·6	2 09·1	0·1	0·0	6·1	1·0	12·1	1·9
02	2 15·5	2 15·9	2 09·3	0·2	0·0	6·2	1·0	12·2	1·9
03	2 15·8	2 16·1	2 09·6	0·3	0·0	6·3	1·0	12·3	1·9
04	2 16·0	2 16·4	2 09·8	0·4	0·1	6·4	1·0	12·4	2·0
05	2 16·3	2 16·6	2 10·0	0·5	0·1	6·5	1·0	12·5	2·0
06	2 16·5	2 16·9	2 10·3	0·6	0·1	6·6	1·0	12·6	2·0
07	2 16·8	2 17·1	2 10·5	0·7	0·1	6·7	1·1	12·7	2·0
08	2 17·0	2 17·4	2 10·8	0·8	0·1	6·8	1·1	12·8	2·0
09	2 17·3	2 17·6	2 11·0	0·9	0·1	6·9	1·1	12·9	2·0
10	2 17·5	2 17·9	2 11·2	1·0	0·2	7·0	1·1	13·0	2·1
11	2 17·8	2 18·1	2 11·5	1·1	0·2	7·1	1·1	13·1	2·1
12	2 18·0	2 18·4	2 11·7	1·2	0·2	7·2	1·1	13·2	2·1
13	2 18·3	2 18·6	2 12·0	1·3	0·2	7·3	1·2	13·3	2·1
14	2 18·5	2 18·9	2 12·2	1·4	0·2	7·4	1·2	13·4	2·1
15	2 18·8	2 19·1	2 12·4	1·5	0·2	7·5	1·2	13·5	2·1
16	2 19·0	2 19·4	2 12·7	1·6	0·3	7·6	1·2	13·6	2·2
17	2 19·3	2 19·6	2 12·9	1·7	0·3	7·7	1·2	13·7	2·2
18	2 19·5	2 19·9	2 13·1	1·8	0·3	7·8	1·2	13·8	2·2
19	2 19·8	2 20·1	2 13·4	1·9	0·3	7·9	1·3	13·9	2·2
20	2 20·0	2 20·4	2 13·6	2·0	0·3	8·0	1·3	14·0	2·2
21	2 20·3	2 20·6	2 13·9	2·1	0·3	8·1	1·3	14·1	2·2
22	2 20·5	2 20·9	2 14·1	2·2	0·3	8·2	1·3	14·2	2·2
23	2 20·8	2 21·1	2 14·3	2·3	0·4	8·3	1·3	14·3	2·3
24	2 21·0	2 21·4	2 14·6	2·4	0·4	8·4	1·3	14·4	2·3
25	2 21·3	2 21·6	2 14·8	2·5	0·4	8·5	1·3	14·5	2·3
26	2 21·5	2 21·9	2 15·1	2·6	0·4	8·6	1·4	14·6	2·3
27	2 21·8	2 22·1	2 15·3	2·7	0·4	8·7	1·4	14·7	2·3
28	2 22·0	2 22·4	2 15·5	2·8	0·4	8·8	1·4	14·8	2·3
29	2 22·3	2 22·6	2 15·8	2·9	0·5	8·9	1·4	14·9	2·4
30	2 22·5	2 22·9	2 16·0	3·0	0·5	9·0	1·4	15·0	2·4
31	2 22·8	2 23·1	2 16·2	3·1	0·5	9·1	1·4	15·1	2·4
32	2 23·0	2 23·4	2 16·5	3·2	0·5	9·2	1·5	15·2	2·4
33	2 23·3	2 23·6	2 16·7	3·3	0·5	9·3	1·5	15·3	2·4
34	2 23·5	2 23·9	2 17·0	3·4	0·5	9·4	1·5	15·4	2·4
35	2 23·8	2 24·1	2 17·2	3·5	0·6	9·5	1·5	15·5	2·5
36	2 24·0	2 24·4	2 17·4	3·6	0·6	9·6	1·5	15·6	2·5
37	2 24·3	2 24·6	2 17·7	3·7	0·6	9·7	1·5	15·7	2·5
38	2 24·5	2 24·9	2 17·9	3·8	0·6	9·8	1·6	15·8	2·5
39	2 24·8	2 25·1	2 18·2	3·9	0·6	9·9	1·6	15·9	2·5
40	2 25·0	2 25·4	2 18·4	4·0	0·6	10·0	1·6	16·0	2·5
41	2 25·3	2 25·6	2 18·6	4·1	0·6	10·1	1·6	16·1	2·5
42	2 25·5	2 25·9	2 18·9	4·2	0·7	10·2	1·6	16·2	2·6
43	2 25·8	2 26·1	2 19·1	4·3	0·7	10·3	1·6	16·3	2·6
44	2 26·0	2 26·4	2 19·3	4·4	0·7	10·4	1·6	16·4	2·6
45	2 26·3	2 26·7	2 19·6	4·5	0·7	10·5	1·7	16·5	2·6
46	2 26·5	2 26·9	2 19·8	4·6	0·7	10·6	1·7	16·6	2·6
47	2 26·8	2 27·2	2 20·1	4·7	0·7	10·7	1·7	16·7	2·6
48	2 27·0	2 27·4	2 20·3	4·8	0·8	10·8	1·7	16·8	2·7
49	2 27·3	2 27·7	2 20·5	4·9	0·8	10·9	1·7	16·9	2·7
50	2 27·5	2 27·9	2 20·8	5·0	0·8	11·0	1·7	17·0	2·7
51	2 27·8	2 28·2	2 21·0	5·1	0·8	11·1	1·8	17·1	2·7
52	2 28·0	2 28·4	2 21·3	5·2	0·8	11·2	1·8	17·2	2·7
53	2 28·3	2 28·7	2 21·5	5·3	0·8	11·3	1·8	17·3	2·7
54	2 28·5	2 28·9	2 21·7	5·4	0·9	11·4	1·8	17·4	2·8
55	2 28·8	2 29·2	2 22·0	5·5	0·9	11·5	1·8	17·5	2·8
56	2 29·0	2 29·4	2 22·2	5·6	0·9	11·6	1·8	17·6	2·8
57	2 29·3	2 29·7	2 22·5	5·7	0·9	11·7	1·9	17·7	2·8
58	2 29·5	2 29·9	2 22·7	5·8	0·9	11·8	1·9	17·8	2·8
59	2 29·8	2 30·2	2 22·9	5·9	0·9	11·9	1·9	17·9	2·8
60	2 30·0	2 30·4	2 23·2	6·0	1·0	12·0	1·9	18·0	2·9

m 10 s	SUN PLANETS ° ′	ARIES ° ′	MOON ° ′	v or d ′	Corrⁿ ′	v or d ′	Corrⁿ ′	v or d ′	Corrⁿ ′
00	2 30·0	2 30·4	2 23·2	0·0	0·0	6·0	1·1	12·0	2·1
01	2 30·3	2 30·7	2 23·4	0·1	0·0	6·1	1·1	12·1	2·1
02	2 30·5	2 30·9	2 23·6	0·2	0·0	6·2	1·1	12·2	2·1
03	2 30·8	2 31·2	2 23·9	0·3	0·1	6·3	1·1	12·3	2·2
04	2 31·0	2 31·4	2 24·1	0·4	0·1	6·4	1·1	12·4	2·2
05	2 31·3	2 31·7	2 24·4	0·5	0·1	6·5	1·1	12·5	2·2
06	2 31·5	2 31·9	2 24·6	0·6	0·1	6·6	1·2	12·6	2·2
07	2 31·8	2 32·2	2 24·8	0·7	0·1	6·7	1·2	12·7	2·2
08	2 32·0	2 32·4	2 25·1	0·8	0·1	6·8	1·2	12·8	2·2
09	2 32·3	2 32·7	2 25·3	0·9	0·2	6·9	1·2	12·9	2·3
10	2 32·5	2 32·9	2 25·6	1·0	0·2	7·0	1·2	13·0	2·3
11	2 32·8	2 33·2	2 25·8	1·1	0·2	7·1	1·2	13·1	2·3
12	2 33·0	2 33·4	2 26·0	1·2	0·2	7·2	1·3	13·2	2·3
13	2 33·3	2 33·7	2 26·3	1·3	0·2	7·3	1·3	13·3	2·3
14	2 33·5	2 33·9	2 26·5	1·4	0·2	7·4	1·3	13·4	2·3
15	2 33·8	2 34·2	2 26·7	1·5	0·3	7·5	1·3	13·5	2·4
16	2 34·0	2 34·4	2 27·0	1·6	0·3	7·6	1·3	13·6	2·4
17	2 34·3	2 34·7	2 27·2	1·7	0·3	7·7	1·3	13·7	2·4
18	2 34·5	2 34·9	2 27·5	1·8	0·3	7·8	1·4	13·8	2·4
19	2 34·8	2 35·2	2 27·7	1·9	0·3	7·9	1·4	13·9	2·4
20	2 35·0	2 35·4	2 27·9	2·0	0·4	8·0	1·4	14·0	2·5
21	2 35·3	2 35·7	2 28·2	2·1	0·4	8·1	1·4	14·1	2·5
22	2 35·5	2 35·9	2 28·4	2·2	0·4	8·2	1·4	14·2	2·5
23	2 35·8	2 36·2	2 28·7	2·3	0·4	8·3	1·5	14·3	2·5
24	2 36·0	2 36·4	2 28·9	2·4	0·4	8·4	1·5	14·4	2·5
25	2 36·3	2 36·7	2 29·1	2·5	0·4	8·5	1·5	14·5	2·5
26	2 36·5	2 36·9	2 29·4	2·6	0·5	8·6	1·5	14·6	2·6
27	2 36·8	2 37·2	2 29·6	2·7	0·5	8·7	1·5	14·7	2·6
28	2 37·0	2 37·4	2 29·8	2·8	0·5	8·8	1·5	14·8	2·6
29	2 37·3	2 37·7	2 30·1	2·9	0·5	8·9	1·6	14·9	2·6
30	2 37·5	2 37·9	2 30·3	3·0	0·5	9·0	1·6	15·0	2·6
31	2 37·8	2 38·2	2 30·6	3·1	0·5	9·1	1·6	15·1	2·6
32	2 38·0	2 38·4	2 30·8	3·2	0·6	9·2	1·6	15·2	2·7
33	2 38·3	2 38·7	2 31·0	3·3	0·6	9·3	1·6	15·3	2·7
34	2 38·5	2 38·9	2 31·3	3·4	0·6	9·4	1·6	15·4	2·7
35	2 38·8	2 39·2	2 31·5	3·5	0·6	9·5	1·7	15·5	2·7
36	2 39·0	2 39·4	2 31·8	3·6	0·6	9·6	1·7	15·6	2·7
37	2 39·3	2 39·7	2 32·0	3·7	0·6	9·7	1·7	15·7	2·7
38	2 39·5	2 39·9	2 32·2	3·8	0·7	9·8	1·7	15·8	2·8
39	2 39·8	2 40·2	2 32·5	3·9	0·7	9·9	1·7	15·9	2·8
40	2 40·0	2 40·4	2 32·7	4·0	0·7	10·0	1·8	16·0	2·8
41	2 40·3	2 40·7	2 32·9	4·1	0·7	10·1	1·8	16·1	2·8
42	2 40·5	2 40·9	2 33·2	4·2	0·7	10·2	1·8	16·2	2·8
43	2 40·8	2 41·2	2 33·4	4·3	0·8	10·3	1·8	16·3	2·9
44	2 41·0	2 41·4	2 33·7	4·4	0·8	10·4	1·8	16·4	2·9
45	2 41·3	2 41·7	2 33·9	4·5	0·8	10·5	1·8	16·5	2·9
46	2 41·5	2 41·9	2 34·1	4·6	0·8	10·6	1·9	16·6	2·9
47	2 41·8	2 42·2	2 34·4	4·7	0·8	10·7	1·9	16·7	2·9
48	2 42·0	2 42·4	2 34·6	4·8	0·8	10·8	1·9	16·8	2·9
49	2 42·3	2 42·7	2 34·9	4·9	0·9	10·9	1·9	16·9	3·0
50	2 42·5	2 42·9	2 35·1	5·0	0·9	11·0	1·9	17·0	3·0
51	2 42·8	2 43·2	2 35·3	5·1	0·9	11·1	1·9	17·1	3·0
52	2 43·0	2 43·4	2 35·6	5·2	0·9	11·2	2·0	17·2	3·0
53	2 43·3	2 43·7	2 35·8	5·3	0·9	11·3	2·0	17·3	3·0
54	2 43·5	2 43·9	2 36·1	5·4	0·9	11·4	2·0	17·4	3·0
55	2 43·8	2 44·2	2 36·3	5·5	1·0	11·5	2·0	17·5	3·1
56	2 44·0	2 44·4	2 36·5	5·6	1·0	11·6	2·0	17·6	3·1
57	2 44·3	2 44·7	2 36·8	5·7	1·0	11·7	2·0	17·7	3·1
58	2 44·5	2 45·0	2 37·0	5·8	1·0	11·8	2·1	17·8	3·1
59	2 44·8	2 45·2	2 37·2	5·9	1·0	11·9	2·1	17·9	3·1
60	2 45·0	2 45·5	2 37·5	6·0	1·1	12·0	2·1	18·0	3·2

m 11 s	SUN PLANETS ° ′	ARIES ° ′	MOON ° ′	v or d ′	Corrⁿ ′	v or d ′	Corrⁿ ′	v or d ′	Corrⁿ ′
00	2 45·0	2 45·5	2 37·5	0·0	0·0	6·0	1·2	12·0	2·3
01	2 45·3	2 45·7	2 37·7	0·1	0·0	6·1	1·2	12·1	2·3
02	2 45·5	2 46·0	2 38·0	0·2	0·0	6·2	1·2	12·2	2·3
03	2 45·8	2 46·2	2 38·2	0·3	0·1	6·3	1·2	12·3	2·4
04	2 46·0	2 46·5	2 38·4	0·4	0·1	6·4	1·2	12·4	2·4
05	2 46·3	2 46·7	2 38·7	0·5	0·1	6·5	1·2	12·5	2·4
06	2 46·5	2 47·0	2 38·9	0·6	0·1	6·6	1·3	12·6	2·4
07	2 46·8	2 47·2	2 39·2	0·7	0·1	6·7	1·3	12·7	2·4
08	2 47·0	2 47·5	2 39·4	0·8	0·2	6·8	1·3	12·8	2·5
09	2 47·3	2 47·7	2 39·6	0·9	0·2	6·9	1·3	12·9	2·5
10	2 47·5	2 48·0	2 39·9	1·0	0·2	7·0	1·3	13·0	2·5
11	2 47·8	2 48·2	2 40·1	1·1	0·2	7·1	1·4	13·1	2·5
12	2 48·0	2 48·5	2 40·3	1·2	0·2	7·2	1·4	13·2	2·5
13	2 48·3	2 48·7	2 40·6	1·3	0·2	7·3	1·4	13·3	2·5
14	2 48·5	2 49·0	2 40·8	1·4	0·3	7·4	1·4	13·4	2·6
15	2 48·8	2 49·2	2 41·1	1·5	0·3	7·5	1·4	13·5	2·6
16	2 49·0	2 49·5	2 41·3	1·6	0·3	7·6	1·5	13·6	2·6
17	2 49·3	2 49·7	2 41·5	1·7	0·3	7·7	1·5	13·7	2·6
18	2 49·5	2 50·0	2 41·8	1·8	0·3	7·8	1·5	13·8	2·6
19	2 49·8	2 50·2	2 42·0	1·9	0·4	7·9	1·5	13·9	2·7
20	2 50·0	2 50·5	2 42·3	2·0	0·4	8·0	1·5	14·0	2·7
21	2 50·3	2 50·7	2 42·5	2·1	0·4	8·1	1·6	14·1	2·7
22	2 50·5	2 51·0	2 42·7	2·2	0·4	8·2	1·6	14·2	2·7
23	2 50·8	2 51·2	2 43·0	2·3	0·4	8·3	1·6	14·3	2·7
24	2 51·0	2 51·5	2 43·2	2·4	0·5	8·4	1·6	14·4	2·8
25	2 51·3	2 51·7	2 43·4	2·5	0·5	8·5	1·6	14·5	2·8
26	2 51·5	2 52·0	2 43·7	2·6	0·5	8·6	1·6	14·6	2·8
27	2 51·8	2 52·2	2 43·9	2·7	0·5	8·7	1·7	14·7	2·8
28	2 52·0	2 52·5	2 44·2	2·8	0·5	8·8	1·7	14·8	2·8
29	2 52·3	2 52·7	2 44·4	2·9	0·6	8·9	1·7	14·9	2·9
30	2 52·5	2 53·0	2 44·6	3·0	0·6	9·0	1·7	15·0	2·9
31	2 52·8	2 53·2	2 44·9	3·1	0·6	9·1	1·7	15·1	2·9
32	2 53·0	2 53·5	2 45·1	3·2	0·6	9·2	1·8	15·2	2·9
33	2 53·3	2 53·7	2 45·4	3·3	0·6	9·3	1·8	15·3	2·9
34	2 53·5	2 54·0	2 45·6	3·4	0·7	9·4	1·8	15·4	3·0
35	2 53·8	2 54·2	2 45·8	3·5	0·7	9·5	1·8	15·5	3·0
36	2 54·0	2 54·5	2 46·1	3·6	0·7	9·6	1·8	15·6	3·0
37	2 54·3	2 54·7	2 46·3	3·7	0·7	9·7	1·9	15·7	3·0
38	2 54·5	2 55·0	2 46·6	3·8	0·7	9·8	1·9	15·8	3·0
39	2 54·8	2 55·2	2 46·8	3·9	0·7	9·9	1·9	15·9	3·0
40	2 55·0	2 55·5	2 47·0	4·0	0·8	10·0	1·9	16·0	3·1
41	2 55·3	2 55·7	2 47·3	4·1	0·8	10·1	1·9	16·1	3·1
42	2 55·5	2 56·0	2 47·5	4·2	0·8	10·2	2·0	16·2	3·1
43	2 55·8	2 56·2	2 47·7	4·3	0·8	10·3	2·0	16·3	3·1
44	2 56·0	2 56·5	2 48·0	4·4	0·8	10·4	2·0	16·4	3·1
45	2 56·3	2 56·7	2 48·2	4·5	0·9	10·5	2·0	16·5	3·2
46	2 56·5	2 57·0	2 48·5	4·6	0·9	10·6	2·0	16·6	3·2
47	2 56·8	2 57·2	2 48·7	4·7	0·9	10·7	2·1	16·7	3·2
48	2 57·0	2 57·5	2 48·9	4·8	0·9	10·8	2·1	16·8	3·2
49	2 57·3	2 57·7	2 49·2	4·9	0·9	10·9	2·1	16·9	3·2
50	2 57·5	2 58·0	2 49·4	5·0	1·0	11·0	2·1	17·0	3·3
51	2 57·8	2 58·2	2 49·7	5·1	1·0	11·1	2·1	17·1	3·3
52	2 58·0	2 58·5	2 49·9	5·2	1·0	11·2	2·1	17·2	3·3
53	2 58·3	2 58·7	2 50·1	5·3	1·0	11·3	2·2	17·3	3·3
54	2 58·5	2 59·0	2 50·4	5·4	1·0	11·4	2·2	17·4	3·3
55	2 58·8	2 59·2	2 50·6	5·5	1·1	11·5	2·2	17·5	3·4
56	2 59·0	2 59·5	2 50·8	5·6	1·1	11·6	2·2	17·6	3·4
57	2 59·3	2 59·7	2 51·1	5·7	1·1	11·7	2·2	17·7	3·4
58	2 59·5	3 00·0	2 51·3	5·8	1·1	11·8	2·3	17·8	3·4
59	2 59·8	3 00·2	2 51·6	5·9	1·1	11·9	2·3	17·9	3·4
60	3 00·0	3 00·5	2 51·8	6·0	1·2	12·0	2·3	18·0	3·5

12^m	SUN PLANETS	ARIES	MOON	v or d	Corr^n	v or d	Corr^n	v or d	Corr^n
s	° ′	° ′	° ′	′	′	′	′	′	′
00	3 00·0	3 00·5	2 51·8	0·0	0·0	6·0	1·3	12·0	2·5
01	3 00·3	3 00·7	2 52·0	0·1	0·0	6·1	1·3	12·1	2·5
02	3 00·5	3 01·0	2 52·3	0·2	0·0	6·2	1·3	12·2	2·5
03	3 00·8	3 01·2	2 52·5	0·3	0·1	6·3	1·3	12·3	2·6
04	3 01·0	3 01·5	2 52·8	0·4	0·1	6·4	1·3	12·4	2·6
05	3 01·3	3 01·7	2 53·0	0·5	0·1	6·5	1·4	12·5	2·6
06	3 01·5	3 02·0	2 53·2	0·6	0·1	6·6	1·4	12·6	2·6
07	3 01·8	3 02·2	2 53·5	0·7	0·1	6·7	1·4	12·7	2·6
08	3 02·0	3 02·5	2 53·7	0·8	0·2	6·8	1·4	12·8	2·7
09	3 02·3	3 02·7	2 53·9	0·9	0·2	6·9	1·4	12·9	2·7
10	3 02·5	3 03·0	2 54·2	1·0	0·2	7·0	1·5	13·0	2·7
11	3 02·8	3 03·3	2 54·4	1·1	0·2	7·1	1·5	13·1	2·7
12	3 03·0	3 03·5	2 54·7	1·2	0·3	7·2	1·5	13·2	2·8
13	3 03·3	3 03·8	2 54·9	1·3	0·3	7·3	1·5	13·3	2·8
14	3 03·5	3 04·0	2 55·1	1·4	0·3	7·4	1·5	13·4	2·8
15	3 03·8	3 04·3	2 55·4	1·5	0·3	7·5	1·6	13·5	2·8
16	3 04·0	3 04·5	2 55·6	1·6	0·3	7·6	1·6	13·6	2·8
17	3 04·3	3 04·8	2 55·9	1·7	0·4	7·7	1·6	13·7	2·9
18	3 04·5	3 05·0	2 56·1	1·8	0·4	7·8	1·6	13·8	2·9
19	3 04·8	3 05·3	2 56·3	1·9	0·4	7·9	1·6	13·9	2·9
20	3 05·0	3 05·5	2 56·6	2·0	0·4	8·0	1·7	14·0	2·9
21	3 05·3	3 05·8	2 56·8	2·1	0·4	8·1	1·7	14·1	2·9
22	3 05·5	3 06·0	2 57·0	2·2	0·5	8·2	1·7	14·2	3·0
23	3 05·8	3 06·3	2 57·3	2·3	0·5	8·3	1·7	14·3	3·0
24	3 06·0	3 06·5	2 57·5	2·4	0·5	8·4	1·8	14·4	3·0
25	3 06·3	3 06·8	2 57·8	2·5	0·5	8·5	1·8	14·5	3·0
26	3 06·5	3 07·0	2 58·0	2·6	0·5	8·6	1·8	14·6	3·0
27	3 06·8	3 07·3	2 58·2	2·7	0·6	8·7	1·8	14·7	3·1
28	3 07·0	3 07·5	2 58·5	2·8	0·6	8·8	1·8	14·8	3·1
29	3 07·3	3 07·8	2 58·7	2·9	0·6	8·9	1·9	14·9	3·1
30	3 07·5	3 08·0	2 59·0	3·0	0·6	9·0	1·9	15·0	3·1
31	3 07·8	3 08·3	2 59·2	3·1	0·6	9·1	1·9	15·1	3·1
32	3 08·0	3 08·5	2 59·4	3·2	0·7	9·2	1·9	15·2	3·2
33	3 08·3	3 08·8	2 59·7	3·3	0·7	9·3	1·9	15·3	3·2
34	3 08·5	3 09·0	2 59·9	3·4	0·7	9·4	2·0	15·4	3·2
35	3 08·8	3 09·3	3 00·2	3·5	0·7	9·5	2·0	15·5	3·2
36	3 09·0	3 09·5	3 00·4	3·6	0·8	9·6	2·0	15·6	3·3
37	3 09·3	3 09·8	3 00·6	3·7	0·8	9·7	2·0	15·7	3·3
38	3 09·5	3 10·0	3 00·9	3·8	0·8	9·8	2·0	15·8	3·3
39	3 09·8	3 10·3	3 01·1	3·9	0·8	9·9	2·1	15·9	3·3
40	3 10·0	3 10·5	3 01·3	4·0	0·8	10·0	2·1	16·0	3·3
41	3 10·3	3 10·8	3 01·6	4·1	0·9	10·1	2·1	16·1	3·4
42	3 10·5	3 11·0	3 01·8	4·2	0·9	10·2	2·1	16·2	3·4
43	3 10·8	3 11·3	3 02·1	4·3	0·9	10·3	2·1	16·3	3·4
44	3 11·0	3 11·5	3 02·3	4·4	0·9	10·4	2·2	16·4	3·4
45	3 11·3	3 11·8	3 02·5	4·5	0·9	10·5	2·2	16·5	3·4
46	3 11·5	3 12·0	3 02·8	4·6	1·0	10·6	2·2	16·6	3·5
47	3 11·8	3 12·3	3 03·0	4·7	1·0	10·7	2·2	16·7	3·5
48	3 12·0	3 12·5	3 03·3	4·8	1·0	10·8	2·3	16·8	3·5
49	3 12·3	3 12·8	3 03·5	4·9	1·0	10·9	2·3	16·9	3·5
50	3 12·5	3 13·0	3 03·7	5·0	1·0	11·0	2·3	17·0	3·5
51	3 12·8	3 13·3	3 04·0	5·1	1·1	11·1	2·3	17·1	3·6
52	3 13·0	3 13·5	3 04·2	5·2	1·1	11·2	2·3	17·2	3·6
53	3 13·3	3 13·8	3 04·4	5·3	1·1	11·3	2·4	17·3	3·6
54	3 13·5	3 14·0	3 04·7	5·4	1·1	11·4	2·4	17·4	3·6
55	3 13·8	3 14·3	3 04·9	5·5	1·1	11·5	2·4	17·5	3·6
56	3 14·0	3 14·5	3 05·2	5·6	1·2	11·6	2·4	17·6	3·7
57	3 14·3	3 14·8	3 05·4	5·7	1·2	11·7	2·4	17·7	3·7
58	3 14·5	3 15·0	3 05·6	5·8	1·2	11·8	2·5	17·8	3·7
59	3 14·8	3 15·3	3 05·9	5·9	1·2	11·9	2·5	17·9	3·7
60	3 15·0	3 15·5	3 06·1	6·0	1·3	12·0	2·5	18·0	3·8

13^m	SUN PLANETS	ARIES	MOON	v or d	Corr^n	v or d	Corr^n	v or d	Corr^n
s	° ′	° ′	° ′	′	′	′	′	′	′
00	3 15·0	3 15·5	3 06·1	0·0	0·0	6·0	1·4	12·0	2·7
01	3 15·3	3 15·8	3 06·4	0·1	0·0	6·1	1·4	12·1	2·7
02	3 15·5	3 16·0	3 06·6	0·2	0·0	6·2	1·4	12·2	2·7
03	3 15·8	3 16·3	3 06·8	0·3	0·1	6·3	1·4	12·3	2·8
04	3 16·0	3 16·5	3 07·1	0·4	0·1	6·4	1·4	12·4	2·8
05	3 16·3	3 16·8	3 07·3	0·5	0·1	6·5	1·5	12·5	2·8
06	3 16·5	3 17·0	3 07·5	0·6	0·1	6·6	1·5	12·6	2·8
07	3 16·8	3 17·3	3 07·8	0·7	0·2	6·7	1·5	12·7	2·9
08	3 17·0	3 17·5	3 08·0	0·8	0·2	6·8	1·5	12·8	2·9
09	3 17·3	3 17·8	3 08·3	0·9	0·2	6·9	1·6	12·9	2·9
10	3 17·5	3 18·0	3 08·5	1·0	0·2	7·0	1·6	13·0	2·9
11	3 17·8	3 18·3	3 08·7	1·1	0·2	7·1	1·6	13·1	2·9
12	3 18·0	3 18·5	3 09·0	1·2	0·3	7·2	1·6	13·2	3·0
13	3 18·3	3 18·8	3 09·2	1·3	0·3	7·3	1·6	13·3	3·0
14	3 18·5	3 19·0	3 09·5	1·4	0·3	7·4	1·7	13·4	3·0
15	3 18·8	3 19·3	3 09·7	1·5	0·3	7·5	1·7	13·5	3·0
16	3 19·0	3 19·5	3 09·9	1·6	0·4	7·6	1·7	13·6	3·1
17	3 19·3	3 19·8	3 10·2	1·7	0·4	7·7	1·7	13·7	3·1
18	3 19·5	3 20·0	3 10·4	1·8	0·4	7·8	1·8	13·8	3·1
19	3 19·8	3 20·3	3 10·7	1·9	0·4	7·9	1·8	13·9	3·1
20	3 20·0	3 20·5	3 10·9	2·0	0·5	8·0	1·8	14·0	3·2
21	3 20·3	3 20·8	3 11·1	2·1	0·5	8·1	1·8	14·1	3·2
22	3 20·5	3 21·0	3 11·4	2·2	0·5	8·2	1·8	14·2	3·2
23	3 20·8	3 21·3	3 11·6	2·3	0·5	8·3	1·9	14·3	3·2
24	3 21·0	3 21·6	3 11·8	2·4	0·5	8·4	1·9	14·4	3·2
25	3 21·3	3 21·8	3 12·1	2·5	0·6	8·5	1·9	14·5	3·3
26	3 21·5	3 22·1	3 12·3	2·6	0·6	8·6	1·9	14·6	3·3
27	3 21·8	3 22·3	3 12·6	2·7	0·6	8·7	2·0	14·7	3·3
28	3 22·0	3 22·6	3 12·8	2·8	0·6	8·8	2·0	14·8	3·3
29	3 22·3	3 22·8	3 13·0	2·9	0·7	8·9	2·0	14·9	3·4
30	3 22·5	3 23·1	3 13·3	3·0	0·7	9·0	2·0	15·0	3·4
31	3 22·8	3 23·3	3 13·5	3·1	0·7	9·1	2·0	15·1	3·4
32	3 23·0	3 23·6	3 13·8	3·2	0·7	9·2	2·1	15·2	3·4
33	3 23·3	3 23·8	3 14·0	3·3	0·7	9·3	2·1	15·3	3·4
34	3 23·5	3 24·1	3 14·2	3·4	0·8	9·4	2·1	15·4	3·5
35	3 23·8	3 24·3	3 14·5	3·5	0·8	9·5	2·1	15·5	3·5
36	3 24·0	3 24·6	3 14·7	3·6	0·8	9·6	2·2	15·6	3·5
37	3 24·3	3 24·8	3 14·9	3·7	0·8	9·7	2·2	15·7	3·5
38	3 24·5	3 25·1	3 15·2	3·8	0·9	9·8	2·2	15·8	3·6
39	3 24·8	3 25·3	3 15·4	3·9	0·9	9·9	2·2	15·9	3·6
40	3 25·0	3 25·6	3 15·7	4·0	0·9	10·0	2·3	16·0	3·6
41	3 25·3	3 25·8	3 15·9	4·1	0·9	10·1	2·3	16·1	3·6
42	3 25·5	3 26·1	3 16·1	4·2	0·9	10·2	2·3	16·2	3·6
43	3 25·8	3 26·3	3 16·4	4·3	1·0	10·3	2·3	16·3	3·7
44	3 26·0	3 26·6	3 16·6	4·4	1·0	10·4	2·3	16·4	3·7
45	3 26·3	3 26·8	3 16·9	4·5	1·0	10·5	2·4	16·5	3·7
46	3 26·5	3 27·1	3 17·1	4·6	1·0	10·6	2·4	16·6	3·7
47	3 26·8	3 27·3	3 17·3	4·7	1·1	10·7	2·4	16·7	3·8
48	3 27·0	3 27·6	3 17·6	4·8	1·1	10·8	2·4	16·8	3·8
49	3 27·3	3 27·8	3 17·8	4·9	1·1	10·9	2·5	16·9	3·8
50	3 27·5	3 28·1	3 18·0	5·0	1·1	11·0	2·5	17·0	3·8
51	3 27·8	3 28·3	3 18·3	5·1	1·1	11·1	2·5	17·1	3·8
52	3 28·0	3 28·6	3 18·5	5·2	1·2	11·2	2·5	17·2	3·9
53	3 28·3	3 28·8	3 18·8	5·3	1·2	11·3	2·5	17·3	3·9
54	3 28·5	3 29·1	3 19·0	5·4	1·2	11·4	2·6	17·4	3·9
55	3 28·8	3 29·3	3 19·2	5·5	1·2	11·5	2·6	17·5	3·9
56	3 29·0	3 29·6	3 19·5	5·6	1·3	11·6	2·6	17·6	4·0
57	3 29·3	3 29·8	3 19·7	5·7	1·3	11·7	2·6	17·7	4·0
58	3 29·5	3 30·1	3 20·0	5·8	1·3	11·8	2·7	17·8	4·0
59	3 29·8	3 30·3	3 20·2	5·9	1·3	11·9	2·7	17·9	4·0
60	3 30·0	3 30·6	3 20·4	6·0	1·4	12·0	2·7	18·0	4·1

14ᵐ	SUN PLANETS	ARIES	MOON	v or d	Corrⁿ	v or d	Corrⁿ	v or d	Corrⁿ
s	° ′	° ′	° ′	′	′	′	′	′	′
00	3 30·0	3 30·6	3 20·4	0·0	0·0	6·0	1·5	12·0	2·9
01	3 30·3	3 30·8	3 20·7	0·1	0·0	6·1	1·5	12·1	2·9
02	3 30·5	3 31·1	3 20·9	0·2	0·0	6·2	1·5	12·2	2·9
03	3 30·8	3 31·3	3 21·1	0·3	0·1	6·3	1·5	12·3	3·0
04	3 31·0	3 31·6	3 21·4	0·4	0·1	6·4	1·5	12·4	3·0
05	3 31·3	3 31·8	3 21·6	0·5	0·1	6·5	1·6	12·5	3·0
06	3 31·5	3 32·1	3 21·9	0·6	0·1	6·6	1·6	12·6	3·0
07	3 31·8	3 32·3	3 22·1	0·7	0·2	6·7	1·6	12·7	3·1
08	3 32·0	3 32·6	3 22·3	0·8	0·2	6·8	1·6	12·8	3·1
09	3 32·3	3 32·8	3 22·6	0·9	0·2	6·9	1·7	12·9	3·1
10	3 32·5	3 33·1	3 22·8	1·0	0·2	7·0	1·7	13·0	3·1
11	3 32·8	3 33·3	3 23·1	1·1	0·3	7·1	1·7	13·1	3·2
12	3 33·0	3 33·6	3 23·3	1·2	0·3	7·2	1·7	13·2	3·2
13	3 33·3	3 33·8	3 23·5	1·3	0·3	7·3	1·8	13·3	3·2
14	3 33·5	3 34·1	3 23·8	1·4	0·3	7·4	1·8	13·4	3·2
15	3 33·8	3 34·3	3 24·0	1·5	0·4	7·5	1·8	13·5	3·3
16	3 34·0	3 34·6	3 24·3	1·6	0·4	7·6	1·8	13·6	3·3
17	3 34·3	3 34·8	3 24·5	1·7	0·4	7·7	1·9	13·7	3·3
18	3 34·5	3 35·1	3 24·7	1·8	0·4	7·8	1·9	13·8	3·3
19	3 34·8	3 35·3	3 25·0	1·9	0·5	7·9	1·9	13·9	3·4
20	3 35·0	3 35·6	3 25·2	2·0	0·5	8·0	1·9	14·0	3·4
21	3 35·3	3 35·8	3 25·4	2·1	0·5	8·1	2·0	14·1	3·4
22	3 35·5	3 36·1	3 25·7	2·2	0·5	8·2	2·0	14·2	3·4
23	3 35·8	3 36·3	3 25·9	2·3	0·6	8·3	2·0	14·3	3·5
24	3 36·0	3 36·6	3 26·2	2·4	0·6	8·4	2·0	14·4	3·5
25	3 36·3	3 36·8	3 26·4	2·5	0·6	8·5	2·1	14·5	3·5
26	3 36·5	3 37·1	3 26·6	2·6	0·6	8·6	2·1	14·6	3·5
27	3 36·8	3 37·3	3 26·9	2·7	0·7	8·7	2·1	14·7	3·6
28	3 37·0	3 37·6	3 27·1	2·8	0·7	8·8	2·1	14·8	3·6
29	3 37·3	3 37·8	3 27·4	2·9	0·7	8·9	2·2	14·9	3·6
30	3 37·5	3 38·1	3 27·6	3·0	0·7	9·0	2·2	15·0	3·6
31	3 37·8	3 38·3	3 27·8	3·1	0·7	9·1	2·2	15·1	3·6
32	3 38·0	3 38·6	3 28·1	3·2	0·8	9·2	2·2	15·2	3·7
33	3 38·3	3 38·8	3 28·3	3·3	0·8	9·3	2·2	15·3	3·7
34	3 38·5	3 39·1	3 28·5	3·4	0·8	9·4	2·3	15·4	3·7
35	3 38·8	3 39·3	3 28·8	3·5	0·8	9·5	2·3	15·5	3·7
36	3 39·0	3 39·6	3 29·0	3·6	0·9	9·6	2·3	15·6	3·8
37	3 39·3	3 39·9	3 29·3	3·7	0·9	9·7	2·3	15·7	3·8
38	3 39·5	3 40·1	3 29·5	3·8	0·9	9·8	2·4	15·8	3·8
39	3 39·8	3 40·4	3 29·7	3·9	0·9	9·9	2·4	15·9	3·8
40	3 40·0	3 40·6	3 30·0	4·0	1·0	10·0	2·4	16·0	3·9
41	3 40·3	3 40·9	3 30·2	4·1	1·0	10·1	2·4	16·1	3·9
42	3 40·5	3 41·1	3 30·5	4·2	1·0	10·2	2·5	16·2	3·9
43	3 40·8	3 41·4	3 30·7	4·3	1·0	10·3	2·5	16·3	3·9
44	3 41·0	3 41·6	3 30·9	4·4	1·1	10·4	2·5	16·4	4·0
45	3 41·3	3 41·9	3 31·2	4·5	1·1	10·5	2·5	16·5	4·0
46	3 41·5	3 42·1	3 31·4	4·6	1·1	10·6	2·6	16·6	4·0
47	3 41·8	3 42·4	3 31·6	4·7	1·1	10·7	2·6	16·7	4·0
48	3 42·0	3 42·6	3 31·9	4·8	1·2	10·8	2·6	16·8	4·1
49	3 42·3	3 42·9	3 32·1	4·9	1·2	10·9	2·6	16·9	4·1
50	3 42·5	3 43·1	3 32·4	5·0	1·2	11·0	2·7	17·0	4·1
51	3 42·8	3 43·4	3 32·6	5·1	1·2	11·1	2·7	17·1	4·1
52	3 43·0	3 43·6	3 32·8	5·2	1·3	11·2	2·7	17·2	4·2
53	3 43·3	3 43·9	3 33·1	5·3	1·3	11·3	2·7	17·3	4·2
54	3 43·5	3 44·1	3 33·3	5·4	1·3	11·4	2·8	17·4	4·2
55	3 43·8	3 44·4	3 33·6	5·5	1·3	11·5	2·8	17·5	4·2
56	3 44·0	3 44·6	3 33·8	5·6	1·4	11·6	2·8	17·6	4·3
57	3 44·3	3 44·9	3 34·0	5·7	1·4	11·7	2·8	17·7	4·3
58	3 44·5	3 45·1	3 34·3	5·8	1·4	11·8	2·9	17·8	4·3
59	3 44·8	3 45·4	3 34·5	5·9	1·4	11·9	2·9	17·9	4·3
60	3 45·0	3 45·6	3 34·8	6·0	1·5	12·0	2·9	18·0	4·4

15ᵐ	SUN PLANETS	ARIES	MOON	v or d	Corrⁿ	v or d	Corrⁿ	v or d	Corrⁿ
s	° ′	° ′	° ′	′	′	′	′	′	′
00	3 45·0	3 45·6	3 34·8	0·0	0·0	6·0	1·6	12·0	3·1
01	3 45·3	3 45·9	3 35·0	0·1	0·0	6·1	1·6	12·1	3·1
02	3 45·5	3 46·1	3 35·2	0·2	0·1	6·2	1·6	12·2	3·2
03	3 45·8	3 46·4	3 35·5	0·3	0·1	6·3	1·6	12·3	3·2
04	3 46·0	3 46·6	3 35·7	0·4	0·1	6·4	1·7	12·4	3·2
05	3 46·3	3 46·9	3 35·9	0·5	0·1	6·5	1·7	12·5	3·2
06	3 46·5	3 47·1	3 36·2	0·6	0·2	6·6	1·7	12·6	3·3
07	3 46·8	3 47·4	3 36·4	0·7	0·2	6·7	1·7	12·7	3·3
08	3 47·0	3 47·6	3 36·7	0·8	0·2	6·8	1·8	12·8	3·3
09	3 47·3	3 47·9	3 36·9	0·9	0·2	6·9	1·8	12·9	3·3
10	3 47·5	3 48·1	3 37·1	1·0	0·3	7·0	1·8	13·0	3·4
11	3 47·8	3 48·4	3 37·4	1·1	0·3	7·1	1·8	13·1	3·4
12	3 48·0	3 48·6	3 37·6	1·2	0·3	7·2	1·9	13·2	3·4
13	3 48·3	3 48·9	3 37·9	1·3	0·3	7·3	1·9	13·3	3·4
14	3 48·5	3 49·1	3 38·1	1·4	0·4	7·4	1·9	13·4	3·5
15	3 48·8	3 49·4	3 38·3	1·5	0·4	7·5	1·9	13·5	3·5
16	3 49·0	3 49·6	3 38·6	1·6	0·4	7·6	2·0	13·6	3·5
17	3 49·3	3 49·9	3 38·8	1·7	0·4	7·7	2·0	13·7	3·5
18	3 49·5	3 50·1	3 39·0	1·8	0·5	7·8	2·0	13·8	3·6
19	3 49·8	3 50·4	3 39·3	1·9	0·5	7·9	2·0	13·9	3·6
20	3 50·0	3 50·6	3 39·5	2·0	0·5	8·0	2·1	14·0	3·6
21	3 50·3	3 50·9	3 39·8	2·1	0·5	8·1	2·1	14·1	3·6
22	3 50·5	3 51·1	3 40·0	2·2	0·6	8·2	2·1	14·2	3·7
23	3 50·8	3 51·4	3 40·2	2·3	0·6	8·3	2·1	14·3	3·7
24	3 51·0	3 51·6	3 40·5	2·4	0·6	8·4	2·2	14·4	3·7
25	3 51·3	3 51·9	3 40·7	2·5	0·6	8·5	2·2	14·5	3·7
26	3 51·5	3 52·1	3 41·0	2·6	0·7	8·6	2·2	14·6	3·8
27	3 51·8	3 52·4	3 41·2	2·7	0·7	8·7	2·2	14·7	3·8
28	3 52·0	3 52·6	3 41·4	2·8	0·7	8·8	2·3	14·8	3·8
29	3 52·3	3 52·9	3 41·7	2·9	0·7	8·9	2·3	14·9	3·8
30	3 52·5	3 53·1	3 41·9	3·0	0·8	9·0	2·3	15·0	3·9
31	3 52·8	3 53·4	3 42·1	3·1	0·8	9·1	2·4	15·1	3·9
32	3 53·0	3 53·6	3 42·4	3·2	0·8	9·2	2·4	15·2	3·9
33	3 53·3	3 53·9	3 42·6	3·3	0·9	9·3	2·4	15·3	4·0
34	3 53·5	3 54·1	3 42·9	3·4	0·9	9·4	2·4	15·4	4·0
35	3 53·8	3 54·4	3 43·1	3·5	0·9	9·5	2·5	15·5	4·0
36	3 54·0	3 54·6	3 43·3	3·6	0·9	9·6	2·5	15·6	4·0
37	3 54·3	3 54·9	3 43·6	3·7	1·0	9·7	2·5	15·7	4·1
38	3 54·5	3 55·1	3 43·8	3·8	1·0	9·8	2·5	15·8	4·1
39	3 54·8	3 55·4	3 44·1	3·9	1·0	9·9	2·6	15·9	4·1
40	3 55·0	3 55·6	3 44·3	4·0	1·0	10·0	2·6	16·0	4·1
41	3 55·3	3 55·9	3 44·5	4·1	1·1	10·1	2·6	16·1	4·2
42	3 55·5	3 56·1	3 44·8	4·2	1·1	10·2	2·6	16·2	4·2
43	3 55·8	3 56·4	3 45·0	4·3	1·1	10·3	2·7	16·3	4·2
44	3 56·0	3 56·6	3 45·2	4·4	1·1	10·4	2·7	16·4	4·2
45	3 56·3	3 56·9	3 45·5	4·5	1·2	10·5	2·7	16·5	4·3
46	3 56·5	3 57·1	3 45·7	4·6	1·2	10·6	2·7	16·6	4·3
47	3 56·8	3 57·4	3 46·0	4·7	1·2	10·7	2·8	16·7	4·3
48	3 57·0	3 57·6	3 46·2	4·8	1·2	10·8	2·8	16·8	4·3
49	3 57·3	3 57·9	3 46·4	4·9	1·3	10·9	2·8	16·9	4·4
50	3 57·5	3 58·2	3 46·7	5·0	1·3	11·0	2·8	17·0	4·4
51	3 57·8	3 58·4	3 46·9	5·1	1·3	11·1	2·9	17·1	4·4
52	3 58·0	3 58·7	3 47·2	5·2	1·3	11·2	2·9	17·2	4·4
53	3 58·3	3 58·9	3 47·4	5·3	1·4	11·3	2·9	17·3	4·5
54	3 58·5	3 59·2	3 47·6	5·4	1·4	11·4	2·9	17·4	4·5
55	3 58·8	3 59·4	3 47·9	5·5	1·4	11·5	3·0	17·5	4·5
56	3 59·0	3 59·7	3 48·1	5·6	1·4	11·6	3·0	17·6	4·5
57	3 59·3	3 59·9	3 48·4	5·7	1·5	11·7	3·0	17·7	4·6
58	3 59·5	4 00·2	3 48·6	5·8	1·5	11·8	3·0	17·8	4·6
59	3 59·8	4 00·4	3 48·8	5·9	1·5	11·9	3·1	17·9	4·6
60	4 00·0	4 00·7	3 49·1	6·0	1·6	12·0	3·1	18·0	4·7

16m	SUN PLANETS	ARIES	MOON	v or d	Corrn	v or d	Corrn	v or d	Corrn
s	° ′	° ′	° ′	′	′	′	′	′	′
00	4 00·0	4 00·7	3 49·1	0·0	0·0	6·0	1·7	12·0	3·3
01	4 00·3	4 00·9	3 49·3	0·1	0·0	6·1	1·7	12·1	3·3
02	4 00·5	4 01·2	3 49·5	0·2	0·1	6·2	1·7	12·2	3·4
03	4 00·8	4 01·4	3 49·8	0·3	0·1	6·3	1·7	12·3	3·4
04	4 01·0	4 01·7	3 50·0	0·4	0·1	6·4	1·8	12·4	3·4
05	4 01·3	4 01·9	3 50·3	0·5	0·1	6·5	1·8	12·5	3·4
06	4 01·5	4 02·2	3 50·5	0·6	0·2	6·6	1·8	12·6	3·5
07	4 01·8	4 02·4	3 50·7	0·7	0·2	6·7	1·8	12·7	3·5
08	4 02·0	4 02·7	3 51·0	0·8	0·2	6·8	1·9	12·8	3·5
09	4 02·3	4 02·9	3 51·2	0·9	0·2	6·9	1·9	12·9	3·5
10	4 02·5	4 03·2	3 51·5	1·0	0·3	7·0	1·9	13·0	3·6
11	4 02·8	4 03·4	3 51·7	1·1	0·3	7·1	2·0	13·1	3·6
12	4 03·0	4 03·7	3 51·9	1·2	0·3	7·2	2·0	13·2	3·6
13	4 03·3	4 03·9	3 52·2	1·3	0·4	7·3	2·0	13·3	3·7
14	4 03·5	4 04·2	3 52·4	1·4	0·4	7·4	2·0	13·4	3·7
15	4 03·8	4 04·4	3 52·6	1·5	0·4	7·5	2·1	13·5	3·7
16	4 04·0	4 04·7	3 52·9	1·6	0·4	7·6	2·1	13·6	3·7
17	4 04·3	4 04·9	3 53·1	1·7	0·5	7·7	2·1	13·7	3·8
18	4 04·5	4 05·2	3 53·4	1·8	0·5	7·8	2·1	13·8	3·8
19	4 04·8	4 05·4	3 53·6	1·9	0·5	7·9	2·2	13·9	3·8
20	4 05·0	4 05·7	3 53·8	2·0	0·6	8·0	2·2	14·0	3·9
21	4 05·3	4 05·9	3 54·1	2·1	0·6	8·1	2·2	14·1	3·9
22	4 05·5	4 06·2	3 54·3	2·2	0·6	8·2	2·3	14·2	3·9
23	4 05·8	4 06·4	3 54·6	2·3	0·6	8·3	2·3	14·3	3·9
24	4 06·0	4 06·7	3 54·8	2·4	0·7	8·4	2·3	14·4	4·0
25	4 06·3	4 06·9	3 55·0	2·5	0·7	8·5	2·3	14·5	4·0
26	4 06·5	4 07·2	3 55·3	2·6	0·7	8·6	2·4	14·6	4·0
27	4 06·8	4 07·4	3 55·5	2·7	0·7	8·7	2·4	14·7	4·0
28	4 07·0	4 07·7	3 55·7	2·8	0·8	8·8	2·4	14·8	4·1
29	4 07·3	4 07·9	3 56·0	2·9	0·8	8·9	2·4	14·9	4·1
30	4 07·5	4 08·2	3 56·2	3·0	0·8	9·0	2·5	15·0	4·1
31	4 07·8	4 08·4	3 56·5	3·1	0·9	9·1	2·5	15·1	4·2
32	4 08·0	4 08·7	3 56·7	3·2	0·9	9·2	2·5	15·2	4·2
33	4 08·3	4 08·9	3 56·9	3·3	0·9	9·3	2·6	15·3	4·2
34	4 08·5	4 09·2	3 57·2	3·4	0·9	9·4	2·6	15·4	4·2
35	4 08·8	4 09·4	3 57·4	3·5	1·0	9·5	2·6	15·5	4·3
36	4 09·0	4 09·7	3 57·7	3·6	1·0	9·6	2·6	15·6	4·3
37	4 09·3	4 09·9	3 57·9	3·7	1·0	9·7	2·7	15·7	4·3
38	4 09·5	4 10·2	3 58·1	3·8	1·0	9·8	2·7	15·8	4·3
39	4 09·8	4 10·4	3 58·4	3·9	1·1	9·9	2·7	15·9	4·4
40	4 10·0	4 10·7	3 58·6	4·0	1·1	10·0	2·8	16·0	4·4
41	4 10·3	4 10·9	3 58·8	4·1	1·1	10·1	2·8	16·1	4·4
42	4 10·5	4 11·2	3 59·1	4·2	1·2	10·2	2·8	16·2	4·5
43	4 10·8	4 11·4	3 59·3	4·3	1·2	10·3	2·8	16·3	4·5
44	4 11·0	4 11·7	3 59·6	4·4	1·2	10·4	2·9	16·4	4·5
45	4 11·3	4 11·9	3 59·8	4·5	1·2	10·5	2·9	16·5	4·5
46	4 11·5	4 12·2	4 00·0	4·6	1·3	10·6	2·9	16·6	4·6
47	4 11·8	4 12·4	4 00·3	4·7	1·3	10·7	2·9	16·7	4·6
48	4 12·0	4 12·7	4 00·5	4·8	1·3	10·8	3·0	16·8	4·6
49	4 12·3	4 12·9	4 00·8	4·9	1·3	10·9	3·0	16·9	4·6
50	4 12·5	4 13·2	4 01·0	5·0	1·4	11·0	3·0	17·0	4·7
51	4 12·8	4 13·4	4 01·2	5·1	1·4	11·1	3·1	17·1	4·7
52	4 13·0	4 13·7	4 01·5	5·2	1·4	11·2	3·1	17·2	4·7
53	4 13·3	4 13·9	4 01·7	5·3	1·5	11·3	3·1	17·3	4·8
54	4 13·5	4 14·2	4 02·0	5·4	1·5	11·4	3·1	17·4	4·8
55	4 13·8	4 14·4	4 02·2	5·5	1·5	11·5	3·2	17·5	4·8
56	4 14·0	4 14·7	4 02·4	5·6	1·5	11·6	3·2	17·6	4·8
57	4 14·3	4 14·9	4 02·7	5·7	1·6	11·7	3·2	17·7	4·9
58	4 14·5	4 15·2	4 02·9	5·8	1·6	11·8	3·2	17·8	4·9
59	4 14·8	4 15·4	4 03·1	5·9	1·6	11·9	3·3	17·9	4·9
60	4 15·0	4 15·7	4 03·4	6·0	1·7	12·0	3·3	18·0	5·0

17m	SUN PLANETS	ARIES	MOON	v or d	Corrn	v or d	Corrn	v or d	Corrn
s	° ′	° ′	° ′	′	′	′	′	′	′
00	4 15·0	4 15·7	4 03·4	0·0	0·0	6·0	1·8	12·0	3·5
01	4 15·3	4 15·9	4 03·6	0·1	0·0	6·1	1·8	12·1	3·5
02	4 15·5	4 16·2	4 03·9	0·2	0·1	6·2	1·8	12·2	3·6
03	4 15·8	4 16·5	4 04·1	0·3	0·1	6·3	1·8	12·3	3·6
04	4 16·0	4 16·7	4 04·3	0·4	0·1	6·4	1·9	12·4	3·6
05	4 16·3	4 17·0	4 04·6	0·5	0·1	6·5	1·9	12·5	3·6
06	4 16·5	4 17·2	4 04·8	0·6	0·2	6·6	1·9	12·6	3·7
07	4 16·8	4 17·5	4 05·1	0·7	0·2	6·7	2·0	12·7	3·7
08	4 17·0	4 17·7	4 05·3	0·8	0·2	6·8	2·0	12·8	3·7
09	4 17·3	4 18·0	4 05·5	0·9	0·3	6·9	2·0	12·9	3·8
10	4 17·5	4 18·2	4 05·8	1·0	0·3	7·0	2·0	13·0	3·8
11	4 17·8	4 18·5	4 06·0	1·1	0·3	7·1	2·1	13·1	3·8
12	4 18·0	4 18·7	4 06·2	1·2	0·4	7·2	2·1	13·2	3·9
13	4 18·3	4 19·0	4 06·5	1·3	0·4	7·3	2·1	13·3	3·9
14	4 18·5	4 19·2	4 06·7	1·4	0·4	7·4	2·2	13·4	3·9
15	4 18·8	4 19·5	4 07·0	1·5	0·4	7·5	2·2	13·5	3·9
16	4 19·0	4 19·7	4 07·2	1·6	0·5	7·6	2·2	13·6	4·0
17	4 19·3	4 20·0	4 07·4	1·7	0·5	7·7	2·2	13·7	4·0
18	4 19·5	4 20·2	4 07·7	1·8	0·5	7·8	2·3	13·8	4·0
19	4 19·8	4 20·5	4 07·9	1·9	0·6	7·9	2·3	13·9	4·1
20	4 20·0	4 20·7	4 08·2	2·0	0·6	8·0	2·3	14·0	4·1
21	4 20·3	4 21·0	4 08·4	2·1	0·6	8·1	2·4	14·1	4·1
22	4 20·5	4 21·2	4 08·6	2·2	0·6	8·2	2·4	14·2	4·1
23	4 20·8	4 21·5	4 08·9	2·3	0·7	8·3	2·4	14·3	4·2
24	4 21·0	4 21·7	4 09·1	2·4	0·7	8·4	2·5	14·4	4·2
25	4 21·3	4 22·0	4 09·3	2·5	0·7	8·5	2·5	14·5	4·2
26	4 21·5	4 22·2	4 09·6	2·6	0·8	8·6	2·5	14·6	4·3
27	4 21·8	4 22·5	4 09·8	2·7	0·8	8·7	2·5	14·7	4·3
28	4 22·0	4 22·7	4 10·1	2·8	0·8	8·8	2·6	14·8	4·3
29	4 22·3	4 23·0	4 10·3	2·9	0·8	8·9	2·6	14·9	4·3
30	4 22·5	4 23·2	4 10·5	3·0	0·9	9·0	2·6	15·0	4·4
31	4 22·8	4 23·5	4 10·8	3·1	0·9	9·1	2·7	15·1	4·4
32	4 23·0	4 23·7	4 11·0	3·2	0·9	9·2	2·7	15·2	4·4
33	4 23·3	4 24·0	4 11·3	3·3	1·0	9·3	2·7	15·3	4·5
34	4 23·5	4 24·2	4 11·5	3·4	1·0	9·4	2·7	15·4	4·5
35	4 23·8	4 24·5	4 11·7	3·5	1·0	9·5	2·8	15·5	4·5
36	4 24·0	4 24·7	4 12·0	3·6	1·1	9·6	2·8	15·6	4·6
37	4 24·3	4 25·0	4 12·2	3·7	1·1	9·7	2·8	15·7	4·6
38	4 24·5	4 25·2	4 12·5	3·8	1·1	9·8	2·9	15·8	4·6
39	4 24·8	4 25·5	4 12·7	3·9	1·1	9·9	2·9	15·9	4·6
40	4 25·0	4 25·7	4 12·9	4·0	1·2	10·0	2·9	16·0	4·7
41	4 25·3	4 26·0	4 13·2	4·1	1·2	10·1	2·9	16·1	4·7
42	4 25·5	4 26·2	4 13·4	4·2	1·2	10·2	3·0	16·2	4·7
43	4 25·8	4 26·5	4 13·6	4·3	1·3	10·3	3·0	16·3	4·8
44	4 26·0	4 26·7	4 13·9	4·4	1·3	10·4	3·0	16·4	4·8
45	4 26·3	4 27·0	4 14·1	4·5	1·3	10·5	3·1	16·5	4·8
46	4 26·5	4 27·2	4 14·4	4·6	1·3	10·6	3·1	16·6	4·8
47	4 26·8	4 27·5	4 14·6	4·7	1·4	10·7	3·1	16·7	4·9
48	4 27·0	4 27·7	4 14·8	4·8	1·4	10·8	3·2	16·8	4·9
49	4 27·3	4 28·0	4 15·1	4·9	1·4	10·9	3·2	16·9	4·9
50	4 27·5	4 28·2	4 15·3	5·0	1·5	11·0	3·2	17·0	5·0
51	4 27·8	4 28·5	4 15·6	5·1	1·5	11·1	3·2	17·1	5·0
52	4 28·0	4 28·7	4 15·8	5·2	1·5	11·2	3·3	17·2	5·0
53	4 28·3	4 29·0	4 16·0	5·3	1·5	11·3	3·3	17·3	5·0
54	4 28·5	4 29·2	4 16·3	5·4	1·6	11·4	3·3	17·4	5·1
55	4 28·8	4 29·5	4 16·5	5·5	1·6	11·5	3·4	17·5	5·1
56	4 29·0	4 29·7	4 16·7	5·6	1·6	11·6	3·4	17·6	5·1
57	4 29·3	4 30·0	4 17·0	5·7	1·7	11·7	3·4	17·7	5·2
58	4 29·5	4 30·2	4 17·2	5·8	1·7	11·8	3·4	17·8	5·2
59	4 29·8	4 30·5	4 17·5	5·9	1·7	11·9	3·5	17·9	5·2
60	4 30·0	4 30·7	4 17·7	6·0	1·8	12·0	3·5	18·0	5·3

18m	SUN PLANETS	ARIES	MOON	v or d	Corrn	v or d	Corrn	v or d	Corrn
s	° ′	° ′	° ′	′	′	′	′	′	′
00	4 30·0	4 30·7	4 17·7	0·0	0·0	6·0	1·9	12·0	3·7
01	4 30·3	4 31·0	4 17·9	0·1	0·0	6·1	1·9	12·1	3·7
02	4 30·5	4 31·2	4 18·2	0·2	0·1	6·2	1·9	12·2	3·8
03	4 30·8	4 31·5	4 18·4	0·3	0·1	6·3	1·9	12·3	3·8
04	4 31·0	4 31·7	4 18·7	0·4	0·1	6·4	2·0	12·4	3·8
05	4 31·3	4 32·0	4 18·9	0·5	0·2	6·5	2·0	12·5	3·9
06	4 31·5	4 32·2	4 19·1	0·6	0·2	6·6	2·0	12·6	3·9
07	4 31·8	4 32·5	4 19·4	0·7	0·2	6·7	2·1	12·7	3·9
08	4 32·0	4 32·7	4 19·6	0·8	0·2	6·8	2·1	12·8	3·9
09	4 32·3	4 33·0	4 19·8	0·9	0·3	6·9	2·1	12·9	4·0
10	4 32·5	4 33·2	4 20·1	1·0	0·3	7·0	2·2	13·0	4·0
11	4 32·8	4 33·5	4 20·3	1·1	0·3	7·1	2·2	13·1	4·0
12	4 33·0	4 33·7	4 20·6	1·2	0·4	7·2	2·2	13·2	4·1
13	4 33·3	4 34·0	4 20·8	1·3	0·4	7·3	2·3	13·3	4·1
14	4 33·5	4 34·2	4 21·0	1·4	0·4	7·4	2·3	13·4	4·1
15	4 33·8	4 34·5	4 21·3	1·5	0·5	7·5	2·3	13·5	4·2
16	4 34·0	4 34·8	4 21·5	1·6	0·5	7·6	2·3	13·6	4·2
17	4 34·3	4 35·0	4 21·8	1·7	0·5	7·7	2·4	13·7	4·2
18	4 34·5	4 35·3	4 22·0	1·8	0·6	7·8	2·4	13·8	4·3
19	4 34·8	4 35·5	4 22·2	1·9	0·6	7·9	2·4	13·9	4·3
20	4 35·0	4 35·8	4 22·5	2·0	0·6	8·0	2·5	14·0	4·3
21	4 35·3	4 36·0	4 22·7	2·1	0·6	8·1	2·5	14·1	4·3
22	4 35·5	4 36·3	4 22·9	2·2	0·7	8·2	2·5	14·2	4·4
23	4 35·8	4 36·5	4 23·2	2·3	0·7	8·3	2·6	14·3	4·4
24	4 36·0	4 36·8	4 23·4	2·4	0·7	8·4	2·6	14·4	4·4
25	4 36·3	4 37·0	4 23·7	2·5	0·8	8·5	2·6	14·5	4·5
26	4 36·5	4 37·3	4 23·9	2·6	0·8	8·6	2·7	14·6	4·5
27	4 36·8	4 37·5	4 24·1	2·7	0·8	8·7	2·7	14·7	4·5
28	4 37·0	4 37·8	4 24·4	2·8	0·9	8·8	2·7	14·8	4·6
29	4 37·3	4 38·0	4 24·6	2·9	0·9	8·9	2·7	14·9	4·6
30	4 37·5	4 38·3	4 24·9	3·0	0·9	9·0	2·8	15·0	4·6
31	4 37·8	4 38·5	4 25·1	3·1	1·0	9·1	2·8	15·1	4·7
32	4 38·0	4 38·8	4 25·3	3·2	1·0	9·2	2·8	15·2	4·7
33	4 38·3	4 39·0	4 25·6	3·3	1·0	9·3	2·9	15·3	4·7
34	4 38·5	4 39·3	4 25·8	3·4	1·0	9·4	2·9	15·4	4·7
35	4 38·8	4 39·5	4 26·1	3·5	1·1	9·5	2·9	15·5	4·8
36	4 39·0	4 39·8	4 26·3	3·6	1·1	9·6	3·0	15·6	4·8
37	4 39·3	4 40·0	4 26·5	3·7	1·1	9·7	3·0	15·7	4·8
38	4 39·5	4 40·3	4 26·8	3·8	1·2	9·8	3·0	15·8	4·9
39	4 39·8	4 40·5	4 27·0	3·9	1·2	9·9	3·1	15·9	4·9
40	4 40·0	4 40·8	4 27·2	4·0	1·2	10·0	3·1	16·0	4·9
41	4 40·3	4 41·0	4 27·5	4·1	1·3	10·1	3·1	16·1	5·0
42	4 40·5	4 41·3	4 27·7	4·2	1·3	10·2	3·1	16·2	5·0
43	4 40·8	4 41·5	4 28·0	4·3	1·3	10·3	3·2	16·3	5·0
44	4 41·0	4 41·8	4 28·2	4·4	1·4	10·4	3·2	16·4	5·1
45	4 41·3	4 42·0	4 28·4	4·5	1·4	10·5	3·2	16·5	5·1
46	4 41·5	4 42·3	4 28·7	4·6	1·4	10·6	3·3	16·6	5·1
47	4 41·8	4 42·5	4 28·9	4·7	1·4	10·7	3·3	16·7	5·1
48	4 42·0	4 42·8	4 29·2	4·8	1·5	10·8	3·3	16·8	5·2
49	4 42·3	4 43·0	4 29·4	4·9	1·5	10·9	3·4	16·9	5·2
50	4 42·5	4 43·3	4 29·6	5·0	1·5	11·0	3·4	17·0	5·2
51	4 42·8	4 43·5	4 29·9	5·1	1·6	11·1	3·4	17·1	5·3
52	4 43·0	4 43·8	4 30·1	5·2	1·6	11·2	3·5	17·2	5·3
53	4 43·3	4 44·0	4 30·3	5·3	1·6	11·3	3·5	17·3	5·3
54	4 43·5	4 44·3	4 30·6	5·4	1·7	11·4	3·5	17·4	5·4
55	4 43·8	4 44·5	4 30·8	5·5	1·7	11·5	3·5	17·5	5·4
56	4 44·0	4 44·8	4 31·1	5·6	1·7	11·6	3·6	17·6	5·4
57	4 44·3	4 45·0	4 31·3	5·7	1·8	11·7	3·6	17·7	5·5
58	4 44·5	4 45·3	4 31·5	5·8	1·8	11·8	3·6	17·8	5·5
59	4 44·8	4 45·5	4 31·8	5·9	1·8	11·9	3·7	17·9	5·5
60	4 45·0	4 45·8	4 32·0	6·0	1·9	12·0	3·7	18·0	5·6

19m	SUN PLANETS	ARIES	MOON	v or d	Corrn	v or d	Corrn	v or d	Corrn
s	° ′	° ′	° ′	′	′	′	′	′	′
00	4 45·0	4 45·8	4 32·0	0·0	0·0	6·0	2·0	12·0	3·9
01	4 45·3	4 46·0	4 32·3	0·1	0·0	6·1	2·0	12·1	3·9
02	4 45·5	4 46·3	4 32·5	0·2	0·1	6·2	2·0	12·2	4·0
03	4 45·8	4 46·5	4 32·7	0·3	0·1	6·3	2·0	12·3	4·0
04	4 46·0	4 46·8	4 33·0	0·4	0·1	6·4	2·1	12·4	4·0
05	4 46·3	4 47·0	4 33·2	0·5	0·2	6·5	2·1	12·5	4·1
06	4 46·5	4 47·3	4 33·4	0·6	0·2	6·6	2·1	12·6	4·1
07	4 46·8	4 47·5	4 33·7	0·7	0·2	6·7	2·2	12·7	4·1
08	4 47·0	4 47·8	4 33·9	0·8	0·3	6·8	2·2	12·8	4·2
09	4 47·3	4 48·0	4 34·2	0·9	0·3	6·9	2·2	12·9	4·2
10	4 47·5	4 48·3	4 34·4	1·0	0·3	7·0	2·3	13·0	4·2
11	4 47·8	4 48·5	4 34·6	1·1	0·4	7·1	2·3	13·1	4·3
12	4 48·0	4 48·8	4 34·9	1·2	0·4	7·2	2·3	13·2	4·3
13	4 48·3	4 49·0	4 35·1	1·3	0·4	7·3	2·4	13·3	4·3
14	4 48·5	4 49·3	4 35·4	1·4	0·5	7·4	2·4	13·4	4·4
15	4 48·8	4 49·5	4 35·6	1·5	0·5	7·5	2·4	13·5	4·4
16	4 49·0	4 49·8	4 35·8	1·6	0·5	7·6	2·5	13·6	4·4
17	4 49·3	4 50·0	4 36·1	1·7	0·6	7·7	2·5	13·7	4·5
18	4 49·5	4 50·3	4 36·3	1·8	0·6	7·8	2·5	13·8	4·5
19	4 49·8	4 50·5	4 36·6	1·9	0·6	7·9	2·6	13·9	4·5
20	4 50·0	4 50·8	4 36·8	2·0	0·7	8·0	2·6	14·0	4·6
21	4 50·3	4 51·0	4 37·0	2·1	0·7	8·1	2·6	14·1	4·6
22	4 50·5	4 51·3	4 37·3	2·2	0·7	8·2	2·7	14·2	4·6
23	4 50·8	4 51·5	4 37·5	2·3	0·7	8·3	2·7	14·3	4·6
24	4 51·0	4 51·8	4 37·7	2·4	0·8	8·4	2·7	14·4	4·7
25	4 51·3	4 52·0	4 38·0	2·5	0·8	8·5	2·8	14·5	4·7
26	4 51·5	4 52·3	4 38·2	2·6	0·8	8·6	2·8	14·6	4·7
27	4 51·8	4 52·5	4 38·5	2·7	0·9	8·7	2·8	14·7	4·8
28	4 52·0	4 52·8	4 38·7	2·8	0·9	8·8	2·9	14·8	4·8
29	4 52·3	4 53·1	4 38·9	2·9	0·9	8·9	2·9	14·9	4·8
30	4 52·5	4 53·3	4 39·2	3·0	1·0	9·0	2·9	15·0	4·9
31	4 52·8	4 53·6	4 39·4	3·1	1·0	9·1	3·0	15·1	4·9
32	4 53·0	4 53·8	4 39·7	3·2	1·0	9·2	3·0	15·2	4·9
33	4 53·3	4 54·1	4 39·9	3·3	1·1	9·3	3·0	15·3	5·0
34	4 53·5	4 54·3	4 40·1	3·4	1·1	9·4	3·1	15·4	5·0
35	4 53·8	4 54·6	4 40·4	3·5	1·1	9·5	3·1	15·5	5·0
36	4 54·0	4 54·8	4 40·6	3·6	1·2	9·6	3·1	15·6	5·1
37	4 54·3	4 55·1	4 40·8	3·7	1·2	9·7	3·2	15·7	5·1
38	4 54·5	4 55·3	4 41·1	3·8	1·2	9·8	3·2	15·8	5·1
39	4 54·8	4 55·6	4 41·3	3·9	1·3	9·9	3·2	15·9	5·2
40	4 55·0	4 55·8	4 41·6	4·0	1·3	10·0	3·3	16·0	5·2
41	4 55·3	4 56·1	4 41·8	4·1	1·3	10·1	3·3	16·1	5·2
42	4 55·5	4 56·3	4 42·0	4·2	1·4	10·2	3·3	16·2	5·3
43	4 55·8	4 56·6	4 42·3	4·3	1·4	10·3	3·3	16·3	5·3
44	4 56·0	4 56·8	4 42·5	4·4	1·4	10·4	3·4	16·4	5·3
45	4 56·3	4 57·1	4 42·8	4·5	1·5	10·5	3·4	16·5	5·4
46	4 56·5	4 57·3	4 43·0	4·6	1·5	10·6	3·4	16·6	5·4
47	4 56·8	4 57·6	4 43·2	4·7	1·5	10·7	3·5	16·7	5·4
48	4 57·0	4 57·8	4 43·5	4·8	1·6	10·8	3·5	16·8	5·5
49	4 57·3	4 58·1	4 43·7	4·9	1·6	10·9	3·5	16·9	5·5
50	4 57·5	4 58·3	4 43·9	5·0	1·6	11·0	3·6	17·0	5·5
51	4 57·8	4 58·6	4 44·2	5·1	1·7	11·1	3·6	17·1	5·6
52	4 58·0	4 58·8	4 44·4	5·2	1·7	11·2	3·6	17·2	5·6
53	4 58·3	4 59·1	4 44·7	5·3	1·7	11·3	3·7	17·3	5·6
54	4 58·5	4 59·3	4 44·9	5·4	1·8	11·4	3·7	17·4	5·7
55	4 58·8	4 59·6	4 45·1	5·5	1·8	11·5	3·7	17·5	5·7
56	4 59·0	4 59·8	4 45·4	5·6	1·8	11·6	3·8	17·6	5·7
57	4 59·3	5 00·1	4 45·6	5·7	1·9	11·7	3·8	17·7	5·8
58	4 59·5	5 00·3	4 45·9	5·8	1·9	11·8	3·8	17·8	5·8
59	4 59·8	5 00·6	4 46·1	5·9	1·9	11·9	3·9	17·9	5·8
60	5 00·0	5 00·8	4 46·3	6·0	2·0	12·0	3·9	18·0	5·9

20m	SUN PLANETS	ARIES	MOON	v or d	Corrn	v or d	Corrn	v or d	Corrn
s	° ′	° ′	° ′	′	′	′	′	′	′
00	5 00·0	5 00·8	4 46·3	0·0	0·0	6·0	2·1	12·0	4·1
01	5 00·3	5 01·1	4 46·6	0·1	0·0	6·1	2·1	12·1	4·1
02	5 00·5	5 01·3	4 46·8	0·2	0·1	6·2	2·1	12·2	4·2
03	5 00·8	5 01·6	4 47·0	0·3	0·1	6·3	2·2	12·3	4·2
04	5 01·0	5 01·8	4 47·3	0·4	0·1	6·4	2·2	12·4	4·2
05	5 01·3	5 02·1	4 47·5	0·5	0·2	6·5	2·2	12·5	4·3
06	5 01·5	5 02·3	4 47·8	0·6	0·2	6·6	2·3	12·6	4·3
07	5 01·8	5 02·6	4 48·0	0·7	0·2	6·7	2·3	12·7	4·3
08	5 02·0	5 02·8	4 48·2	0·8	0·3	6·8	2·3	12·8	4·4
09	5 02·3	5 03·1	4 48·5	0·9	0·3	6·9	2·4	12·9	4·4
10	5 02·5	5 03·3	4 48·7	1·0	0·3	7·0	2·4	13·0	4·4
11	5 02·8	5 03·6	4 49·0	1·1	0·4	7·1	2·4	13·1	4·5
12	5 03·0	5 03·8	4 49·2	1·2	0·4	7·2	2·5	13·2	4·5
13	5 03·3	5 04·1	4 49·4	1·3	0·4	7·3	2·5	13·3	4·5
14	5 03·5	5 04·3	4 49·7	1·4	0·5	7·4	2·5	13·4	4·6
15	5 03·8	5 04·6	4 49·9	1·5	0·5	7·5	2·6	13·5	4·6
16	5 04·0	5 04·8	4 50·2	1·6	0·5	7·6	2·6	13·6	4·6
17	5 04·3	5 05·1	4 50·4	1·7	0·6	7·7	2·6	13·7	4·7
18	5 04·5	5 05·3	4 50·6	1·8	0·6	7·8	2·7	13·8	4·7
19	5 04·8	5 05·6	4 50·9	1·9	0·6	7·9	2·7	13·9	4·7
20	5 05·0	5 05·8	4 51·1	2·0	0·7	8·0	2·7	14·0	4·8
21	5 05·3	5 06·1	4 51·3	2·1	0·7	8·1	2·8	14·1	4·8
22	5 05·5	5 06·3	4 51·6	2·2	0·8	8·2	2·8	14·2	4·9
23	5 05·8	5 06·6	4 51·8	2·3	0·8	8·3	2·8	14·3	4·9
24	5 06·0	5 06·8	4 52·1	2·4	0·8	8·4	2·9	14·4	4·9
25	5 06·3	5 07·1	4 52·3	2·5	0·9	8·5	2·9	14·5	5·0
26	5 06·5	5 07·3	4 52·5	2·6	0·9	8·6	2·9	14·6	5·0
27	5 06·8	5 07·6	4 52·8	2·7	0·9	8·7	3·0	14·7	5·0
28	5 07·0	5 07·8	4 53·0	2·8	1·0	8·8	3·0	14·8	5·1
29	5 07·3	5 08·1	4 53·3	2·9	1·0	8·9	3·0	14·9	5·1
30	5 07·5	5 08·3	4 53·5	3·0	1·0	9·0	3·1	15·0	5·1
31	5 07·8	5 08·6	4 53·7	3·1	1·1	9·1	3·1	15·1	5·2
32	5 08·0	5 08·8	4 54·0	3·2	1·1	9·2	3·1	15·2	5·2
33	5 08·3	5 09·1	4 54·2	3·3	1·1	9·3	3·2	15·3	5·2
34	5 08·5	5 09·3	4 54·4	3·4	1·2	9·4	3·2	15·4	5·3
35	5 08·8	5 09·6	4 54·7	3·5	1·2	9·5	3·2	15·5	5·3
36	5 09·0	5 09·8	4 54·9	3·6	1·2	9·6	3·3	15·6	5·3
37	5 09·3	5 10·1	4 55·2	3·7	1·3	9·7	3·3	15·7	5·4
38	5 09·5	5 10·3	4 55·4	3·8	1·3	9·8	3·3	15·8	5·4
39	5 09·8	5 10·6	4 55·6	3·9	1·3	9·9	3·4	15·9	5·4
40	5 10·0	5 10·8	4 55·9	4·0	1·4	10·0	3·4	16·0	5·5
41	5 10·3	5 11·1	4 56·1	4·1	1·4	10·1	3·5	16·1	5·5
42	5 10·5	5 11·4	4 56·4	4·2	1·4	10·2	3·5	16·2	5·5
43	5 10·8	5 11·6	4 56·6	4·3	1·5	10·3	3·5	16·3	5·6
44	5 11·0	5 11·9	4 56·8	4·4	1·5	10·4	3·6	16·4	5·6
45	5 11·3	5 12·1	4 57·1	4·5	1·5	10·5	3·6	16·5	5·6
46	5 11·5	5 12·4	4 57·3	4·6	1·6	10·6	3·6	16·6	5·7
47	5 11·8	5 12·6	4 57·5	4·7	1·6	10·7	3·7	16·7	5·7
48	5 12·0	5 12·9	4 57·8	4·8	1·6	10·8	3·7	16·8	5·7
49	5 12·3	5 13·1	4 58·0	4·9	1·7	10·9	3·7	16·9	5·8
50	5 12·5	5 13·4	4 58·3	5·0	1·7	11·0	3·8	17·0	5·8
51	5 12·8	5 13·6	4 58·5	5·1	1·7	11·1	3·8	17·1	5·8
52	5 13·0	5 13·9	4 58·7	5·2	1·8	11·2	3·8	17·2	5·9
53	5 13·3	5 14·1	4 59·0	5·3	1·8	11·3	3·9	17·3	5·9
54	5 13·5	5 14·4	4 59·2	5·4	1·8	11·4	3·9	17·4	5·9
55	5 13·8	5 14·6	4 59·5	5·5	1·9	11·5	3·9	17·5	6·0
56	5 14·0	5 14·9	4 59·7	5·6	1·9	11·6	4·0	17·6	6·0
57	5 14·3	5 15·1	4 59·9	5·7	1·9	11·7	4·0	17·7	6·0
58	5 14·5	5 15·4	5 00·2	5·8	2·0	11·8	4·0	17·8	6·1
59	5 14·8	5 15·6	5 00·4	5·9	2·0	11·9	4·1	17·9	6·1
60	5 15·0	5 15·9	5 00·7	6·0	2·1	12·0	4·1	18·0	6·2

21m	SUN PLANETS	ARIES	MOON	v or d	Corrn	v or d	Corrn	v or d	Corrn
s	° ′	° ′	° ′	′	′	′	′	′	′
00	5 15·0	5 15·9	5 00·7	0·0	0·0	6·0	2·2	12·0	4·3
01	5 15·3	5 16·1	5 00·9	0·1	0·0	6·1	2·2	12·1	4·3
02	5 15·5	5 16·4	5 01·1	0·2	0·1	6·2	2·2	12·2	4·4
03	5 15·8	5 16·6	5 01·4	0·3	0·1	6·3	2·3	12·3	4·4
04	5 16·0	5 16·9	5 01·6	0·4	0·1	6·4	2·3	12·4	4·4
05	5 16·3	5 17·1	5 01·8	0·5	0·2	6·5	2·3	12·5	4·5
06	5 16·5	5 17·4	5 02·1	0·6	0·2	6·6	2·4	12·6	4·5
07	5 16·8	5 17·6	5 02·3	0·7	0·3	6·7	2·4	12·7	4·6
08	5 17·0	5 17·9	5 02·6	0·8	0·3	6·8	2·4	12·8	4·6
09	5 17·3	5 18·1	5 02·8	0·9	0·3	6·9	2·5	12·9	4·6
10	5 17·5	5 18·4	5 03·0	1·0	0·4	7·0	2·5	13·0	4·7
11	5 17·8	5 18·6	5 03·3	1·1	0·4	7·1	2·5	13·1	4·7
12	5 18·0	5 18·9	5 03·5	1·2	0·4	7·2	2·6	13·2	4·7
13	5 18·3	5 19·1	5 03·8	1·3	0·5	7·3	2·6	13·3	4·8
14	5 18·5	5 19·4	5 04·0	1·4	0·5	7·4	2·7	13·4	4·8
15	5 18·8	5 19·6	5 04·2	1·5	0·5	7·5	2·7	13·5	4·8
16	5 19·0	5 19·9	5 04·5	1·6	0·6	7·6	2·7	13·6	4·9
17	5 19·3	5 20·1	5 04·7	1·7	0·6	7·7	2·8	13·7	4·9
18	5 19·5	5 20·4	5 04·9	1·8	0·6	7·8	2·8	13·8	4·9
19	5 19·8	5 20·6	5 05·2	1·9	0·7	7·9	2·8	13·9	5·0
20	5 20·0	5 20·9	5 05·4	2·0	0·7	8·0	2·9	14·0	5·0
21	5 20·3	5 21·1	5 05·7	2·1	0·8	8·1	2·9	14·1	5·1
22	5 20·5	5 21·4	5 05·9	2·2	0·8	8·2	2·9	14·2	5·1
23	5 20·8	5 21·6	5 06·1	2·3	0·8	8·3	3·0	14·3	5·1
24	5 21·0	5 21·9	5 06·4	2·4	0·9	8·4	3·0	14·4	5·2
25	5 21·3	5 22·1	5 06·6	2·5	0·9	8·5	3·0	14·5	5·2
26	5 21·5	5 22·4	5 06·9	2·6	0·9	8·6	3·1	14·6	5·2
27	5 21·8	5 22·6	5 07·1	2·7	1·0	8·7	3·1	14·7	5·3
28	5 22·0	5 22·9	5 07·3	2·8	1·0	8·8	3·2	14·8	5·3
29	5 22·3	5 23·1	5 07·6	2·9	1·0	8·9	3·2	14·9	5·3
30	5 22·5	5 23·4	5 07·8	3·0	1·1	9·0	3·2	15·0	5·4
31	5 22·8	5 23·6	5 08·0	3·1	1·1	9·1	3·3	15·1	5·4
32	5 23·0	5 23·9	5 08·3	3·2	1·1	9·2	3·3	15·2	5·4
33	5 23·3	5 24·1	5 08·5	3·3	1·2	9·3	3·3	15·3	5·5
34	5 23·5	5 24·4	5 08·8	3·4	1·2	9·4	3·4	15·4	5·5
35	5 23·8	5 24·6	5 09·0	3·5	1·3	9·5	3·4	15·5	5·6
36	5 24·0	5 24·9	5 09·2	3·6	1·3	9·6	3·4	15·6	5·6
37	5 24·3	5 25·1	5 09·5	3·7	1·3	9·7	3·5	15·7	5·6
38	5 24·5	5 25·4	5 09·7	3·8	1·4	9·8	3·5	15·8	5·7
39	5 24·8	5 25·6	5 10·0	3·9	1·4	9·9	3·5	15·9	5·7
40	5 25·0	5 25·9	5 10·2	4·0	1·4	10·0	3·6	16·0	5·7
41	5 25·3	5 26·1	5 10·4	4·1	1·5	10·1	3·6	16·1	5·8
42	5 25·5	5 26·4	5 10·7	4·2	1·5	10·2	3·7	16·2	5·8
43	5 25·8	5 26·6	5 10·9	4·3	1·5	10·3	3·7	16·3	5·8
44	5 26·0	5 26·9	5 11·1	4·4	1·6	10·4	3·7	16·4	5·9
45	5 26·3	5 27·1	5 11·4	4·5	1·6	10·5	3·8	16·5	5·9
46	5 26·5	5 27·4	5 11·6	4·6	1·6	10·6	3·8	16·6	5·9
47	5 26·8	5 27·6	5 11·9	4·7	1·7	10·7	3·8	16·7	6·0
48	5 27·0	5 27·9	5 12·1	4·8	1·7	10·8	3·9	16·8	6·0
49	5 27·3	5 28·1	5 12·3	4·9	1·8	10·9	3·9	16·9	6·1
50	5 27·5	5 28·4	5 12·6	5·0	1·8	11·0	3·9	17·0	6·1
51	5 27·8	5 28·6	5 12·8	5·1	1·8	11·1	4·0	17·1	6·1
52	5 28·0	5 28·9	5 13·1	5·2	1·9	11·2	4·0	17·2	6·2
53	5 28·3	5 29·1	5 13·3	5·3	1·9	11·3	4·0	17·3	6·2
54	5 28·5	5 29·4	5 13·5	5·4	1·9	11·4	4·1	17·4	6·2
55	5 28·8	5 29·7	5 13·8	5·5	2·0	11·5	4·1	17·5	6·3
56	5 29·0	5 29·9	5 14·0	5·6	2·0	11·6	4·2	17·6	6·3
57	5 29·3	5 30·2	5 14·3	5·7	2·0	11·7	4·2	17·7	6·3
58	5 29·5	5 30·4	5 14·5	5·8	2·1	11·8	4·2	17·8	6·4
59	5 29·8	5 30·7	5 14·7	5·9	2·1	11·9	4·3	17·9	6·4
60	5 30·0	5 30·9	5 15·0	6·0	2·2	12·0	4·3	18·0	6·5

22m s	SUN PLANETS ° ′	ARIES ° ′	MOON ° ′	v or d ′	Corrn ′	v or d ′	Corrn ′	v or d ′	Corrn ′
00	5 30·0	5 30·9	5 15·0	0·0	0·0	6·0	2·3	12·0	4·5
01	5 30·3	5 31·2	5 15·2	0·1	0·0	6·1	2·3	12·1	4·5
02	5 30·5	5 31·4	5 15·4	0·2	0·1	6·2	2·3	12·2	4·6
03	5 30·8	5 31·7	5 15·7	0·3	0·1	6·3	2·4	12·3	4·6
04	5 31·0	5 31·9	5 15·9	0·4	0·2	6·4	2·4	12·4	4·7
05	5 31·3	5 32·2	5 16·2	0·5	0·2	6·5	2·4	12·5	4·7
06	5 31·5	5 32·4	5 16·4	0·6	0·2	6·6	2·5	12·6	4·7
07	5 31·8	5 32·7	5 16·6	0·7	0·3	6·7	2·5	12·7	4·8
08	5 32·0	5 32·9	5 16·9	0·8	0·3	6·8	2·6	12·8	4·8
09	5 32·3	5 33·2	5 17·1	0·9	0·3	6·9	2·6	12·9	4·8
10	5 32·5	5 33·4	5 17·4	1·0	0·4	7·0	2·6	13·0	4·9
11	5 32·8	5 33·7	5 17·6	1·1	0·4	7·1	2·7	13·1	4·9
12	5 33·0	5 33·9	5 17·8	1·2	0·5	7·2	2·7	13·2	5·0
13	5 33·3	5 34·2	5 18·1	1·3	0·5	7·3	2·7	13·3	5·0
14	5 33·5	5 34·4	5 18·3	1·4	0·5	7·4	2·8	13·4	5·0
15	5 33·8	5 34·7	5 18·5	1·5	0·6	7·5	2·8	13·5	5·1
16	5 34·0	5 34·9	5 18·8	1·6	0·6	7·6	2·9	13·6	5·1
17	5 34·3	5 35·2	5 19·0	1·7	0·6	7·7	2·9	13·7	5·1
18	5 34·5	5 35·4	5 19·3	1·8	0·7	7·8	2·9	13·8	5·2
19	5 34·8	5 35·7	5 19·5	1·9	0·7	7·9	3·0	13·9	5·2
20	5 35·0	5 35·9	5 19·7	2·0	0·8	8·0	3·0	14·0	5·3
21	5 35·3	5 36·2	5 20·0	2·1	0·8	8·1	3·0	14·1	5·3
22	5 35·5	5 36·4	5 20·2	2·2	0·8	8·2	3·1	14·2	5·3
23	5 35·8	5 36·7	5 20·5	2·3	0·9	8·3	3·1	14·3	5·4
24	5 36·0	5 36·9	5 20·7	2·4	0·9	8·4	3·2	14·4	5·4
25	5 36·3	5 37·2	5 20·9	2·5	0·9	8·5	3·2	14·5	5·4
26	5 36·5	5 37·4	5 21·2	2·6	1·0	8·6	3·2	14·6	5·5
27	5 36·8	5 37·7	5 21·4	2·7	1·0	8·7	3·3	14·7	5·5
28	5 37·0	5 37·9	5 21·6	2·8	1·0	8·8	3·3	14·8	5·6
29	5 37·3	5 38·2	5 21·9	2·9	1·1	8·9	3·3	14·9	5·6
30	5 37·5	5 38·4	5 22·1	3·0	1·1	9·0	3·4	15·0	5·6
31	5 37·8	5 38·7	5 22·4	3·1	1·2	9·1	3·4	15·1	5·7
32	5 38·0	5 38·9	5 22·6	3·2	1·2	9·2	3·5	15·2	5·7
33	5 38·3	5 39·2	5 22·8	3·3	1·2	9·3	3·5	15·3	5·7
34	5 38·5	5 39·4	5 23·1	3·4	1·3	9·4	3·5	15·4	5·8
35	5 38·8	5 39·7	5 23·3	3·5	1·3	9·5	3·6	15·5	5·8
36	5 39·0	5 39·9	5 23·6	3·6	1·4	9·6	3·6	15·6	5·9
37	5 39·3	5 40·2	5 23·8	3·7	1·4	9·7	3·6	15·7	5·9
38	5 39·5	5 40·4	5 24·0	3·8	1·4	9·8	3·7	15·8	5·9
39	5 39·8	5 40·7	5 24·3	3·9	1·5	9·9	3·7	15·9	6·0
40	5 40·0	5 40·9	5 24·5	4·0	1·5	10·0	3·8	16·0	6·0
41	5 40·3	5 41·2	5 24·7	4·1	1·5	10·1	3·8	16·1	6·0
42	5 40·5	5 41·4	5 25·0	4·2	1·6	10·2	3·8	16·2	6·1
43	5 40·8	5 41·7	5 25·2	4·3	1·6	10·3	3·9	16·3	6·1
44	5 41·0	5 41·9	5 25·5	4·4	1·7	10·4	3·9	16·4	6·1
45	5 41·3	5 42·2	5 25·7	4·5	1·7	10·5	3·9	16·5	6·2
46	5 41·5	5 42·4	5 25·9	4·6	1·7	10·6	4·0	16·6	6·2
47	5 41·8	5 42·7	5 26·2	4·7	1·8	10·7	4·0	16·7	6·3
48	5 42·0	5 42·9	5 26·4	4·8	1·8	10·8	4·1	16·8	6·3
49	5 42·3	5 43·2	5 26·7	4·9	1·8	10·9	4·1	16·9	6·3
50	5 42·5	5 43·4	5 26·9	5·0	1·9	11·0	4·1	17·0	6·4
51	5 42·8	5 43·7	5 27·1	5·1	1·9	11·1	4·2	17·1	6·4
52	5 43·0	5 43·9	5 27·4	5·2	2·0	11·2	4·2	17·2	6·5
53	5 43·3	5 44·2	5 27·6	5·3	2·0	11·3	4·2	17·3	6·5
54	5 43·5	5 44·4	5 27·9	5·4	2·0	11·4	4·3	17·4	6·5
55	5 43·8	5 44·7	5 28·1	5·5	2·1	11·5	4·3	17·5	6·6
56	5 44·0	5 44·9	5 28·3	5·6	2·1	11·6	4·4	17·6	6·6
57	5 44·3	5 45·2	5 28·6	5·7	2·1	11·7	4·4	17·7	6·6
58	5 44·5	5 45·4	5 28·8	5·8	2·2	11·8	4·4	17·8	6·7
59	5 44·8	5 45·7	5 29·0	5·9	2·2	11·9	4·5	17·9	6·7
60	5 45·0	5 45·9	5 29·3	6·0	2·3	12·0	4·5	18·0	6·8

23m s	SUN PLANETS ° ′	ARIES ° ′	MOON ° ′	v or d ′	Corrn ′	v or d ′	Corrn ′	v or d ′	Corrn ′
00	5 45·0	5 45·9	5 29·3	0·0	0·0	6·0	2·4	12·0	4·7
01	5 45·3	5 46·2	5 29·5	0·1	0·0	6·1	2·4	12·1	4·7
02	5 45·5	5 46·4	5 29·8	0·2	0·1	6·2	2·4	12·2	4·8
03	5 45·8	5 46·7	5 30·0	0·3	0·1	6·3	2·5	12·3	4·8
04	5 46·0	5 46·9	5 30·2	0·4	0·2	6·4	2·5	12·4	4·9
05	5 46·3	5 47·2	5 30·5	0·5	0·2	6·5	2·5	12·5	4·9
06	5 46·5	5 47·4	5 30·7	0·6	0·2	6·6	2·6	12·6	4·9
07	5 46·8	5 47·7	5 31·0	0·7	0·3	6·7	2·6	12·7	5·0
08	5 47·0	5 48·0	5 31·2	0·8	0·3	6·8	2·7	12·8	5·0
09	5 47·3	5 48·2	5 31·4	0·9	0·4	6·9	2·7	12·9	5·1
10	5 47·5	5 48·5	5 31·7	1·0	0·4	7·0	2·7	13·0	5·1
11	5 47·8	5 48·7	5 31·9	1·1	0·4	7·1	2·8	13·1	5·1
12	5 48·0	5 49·0	5 32·1	1·2	0·5	7·2	2·8	13·2	5·2
13	5 48·3	5 49·2	5 32·4	1·3	0·5	7·3	2·9	13·3	5·2
14	5 48·5	5 49·5	5 32·6	1·4	0·5	7·4	2·9	13·4	5·2
15	5 48·8	5 49·7	5 32·9	1·5	0·6	7·5	2·9	13·5	5·3
16	5 49·0	5 50·0	5 33·1	1·6	0·6	7·6	3·0	13·6	5·3
17	5 49·3	5 50·2	5 33·3	1·7	0·7	7·7	3·0	13·7	5·4
18	5 49·5	5 50·5	5 33·6	1·8	0·7	7·8	3·1	13·8	5·4
19	5 49·8	5 50·7	5 33·8	1·9	0·7	7·9	3·1	13·9	5·4
20	5 50·0	5 51·0	5 34·1	2·0	0·8	8·0	3·1	14·0	5·5
21	5 50·3	5 51·2	5 34·3	2·1	0·8	8·1	3·2	14·1	5·5
22	5 50·5	5 51·5	5 34·5	2·2	0·9	8·2	3·2	14·2	5·6
23	5 50·8	5 51·7	5 34·8	2·3	0·9	8·3	3·3	14·3	5·6
24	5 51·0	5 52·0	5 35·0	2·4	0·9	8·4	3·3	14·4	5·6
25	5 51·3	5 52·2	5 35·2	2·5	1·0	8·5	3·3	14·5	5·7
26	5 51·5	5 52·5	5 35·5	2·6	1·0	8·6	3·4	14·6	5·7
27	5 51·8	5 52·7	5 35·7	2·7	1·1	8·7	3·4	14·7	5·8
28	5 52·0	5 53·0	5 36·0	2·8	1·1	8·8	3·4	14·8	5·8
29	5 52·3	5 53·2	5 36·2	2·9	1·1	8·9	3·5	14·9	5·8
30	5 52·5	5 53·5	5 36·4	3·0	1·2	9·0	3·5	15·0	5·9
31	5 52·8	5 53·7	5 36·7	3·1	1·2	9·1	3·6	15·1	5·9
32	5 53·0	5 54·0	5 36·9	3·2	1·3	9·2	3·6	15·2	6·0
33	5 53·3	5 54·2	5 37·2	3·3	1·3	9·3	3·6	15·3	6·0
34	5 53·5	5 54·5	5 37·4	3·4	1·3	9·4	3·7	15·4	6·0
35	5 53·8	5 54·7	5 37·6	3·5	1·4	9·5	3·7	15·5	6·1
36	5 54·0	5 55·0	5 37·9	3·6	1·4	9·6	3·8	15·6	6·1
37	5 54·3	5 55·2	5 38·1	3·7	1·4	9·7	3·8	15·7	6·1
38	5 54·5	5 55·5	5 38·4	3·8	1·5	9·8	3·8	15·8	6·2
39	5 54·8	5 55·7	5 38·6	3·9	1·5	9·9	3·9	15·9	6·2
40	5 55·0	5 56·0	5 38·8	4·0	1·6	10·0	3·9	16·0	6·3
41	5 55·3	5 56·2	5 39·1	4·1	1·6	10·1	4·0	16·1	6·3
42	5 55·5	5 56·5	5 39·3	4·2	1·6	10·2	4·0	16·2	6·3
43	5 55·8	5 56·7	5 39·5	4·3	1·7	10·3	4·0	16·3	6·4
44	5 56·0	5 57·0	5 39·8	4·4	1·7	10·4	4·1	16·4	6·4
45	5 56·3	5 57·2	5 40·0	4·5	1·8	10·5	4·1	16·5	6·5
46	5 56·5	5 57·5	5 40·3	4·6	1·8	10·6	4·2	16·6	6·5
47	5 56·8	5 57·7	5 40·5	4·7	1·8	10·7	4·2	16·7	6·5
48	5 57·0	5 58·0	5 40·7	4·8	1·9	10·8	4·2	16·8	6·6
49	5 57·3	5 58·2	5 41·0	4·9	1·9	10·9	4·3	16·9	6·6
50	5 57·5	5 58·5	5 41·2	5·0	2·0	11·0	4·3	17·0	6·7
51	5 57·8	5 58·7	5 41·5	5·1	2·0	11·1	4·3	17·1	6·7
52	5 58·0	5 59·0	5 41·7	5·2	2·0	11·2	4·4	17·2	6·7
53	5 58·3	5 59·2	5 41·9	5·3	2·1	11·3	4·4	17·3	6·8
54	5 58·5	5 59·5	5 42·2	5·4	2·1	11·4	4·5	17·4	6·8
55	5 58·8	5 59·7	5 42·4	5·5	2·2	11·5	4·5	17·5	6·9
56	5 59·0	6 00·0	5 42·6	5·6	2·2	11·6	4·5	17·6	6·9
57	5 59·3	6 00·2	5 42·9	5·7	2·2	11·7	4·6	17·7	6·9
58	5 59·5	6 00·5	5 43·1	5·8	2·3	11·8	4·6	17·8	7·0
59	5 59·8	6 00·7	5 43·4	5·9	2·3	11·9	4·7	17·9	7·0
60	6 00·0	6 01·0	5 43·6	6·0	2·4	12·0	4·7	18·0	7·1

24m	SUN PLANETS	ARIES	MOON	v or d	Corrn	v or d	Corrn	v or d	Corrn
s	° ′	° ′	° ′	′	′	′	′	′	′
00	6 00·0	6 01·0	5 43·6	0·0	0·0	6·0	2·5	12·0	4·9
01	6 00·3	6 01·2	5 43·8	0·1	0·0	6·1	2·5	12·1	4·9
02	6 00·5	6 01·5	5 44·1	0·2	0·1	6·2	2·5	12·2	5·0
03	6 00·8	6 01·7	5 44·3	0·3	0·1	6·3	2·6	12·3	5·0
04	6 01·0	6 02·0	5 44·6	0·4	0·2	6·4	2·6	12·4	5·1
05	6 01·3	6 02·2	5 44·8	0·5	0·2	6·5	2·7	12·5	5·1
06	6 01·5	6 02·5	5 45·0	0·6	0·2	6·6	2·7	12·6	5·1
07	6 01·8	6 02·7	5 45·3	0·7	0·3	6·7	2·7	12·7	5·2
08	6 02·0	6 03·0	5 45·5	0·8	0·3	6·8	2·8	12·8	5·2
09	6 02·3	6 03·2	5 45·7	0·9	0·4	6·9	2·8	12·9	5·3
10	6 02·5	6 03·5	5 46·0	1·0	0·4	7·0	2·9	13·0	5·3
11	6 02·8	6 03·7	5 46·2	1·1	0·4	7·1	2·9	13·1	5·3
12	6 03·0	6 04·0	5 46·5	1·2	0·5	7·2	2·9	13·2	5·4
13	6 03·3	6 04·2	5 46·7	1·3	0·5	7·3	3·0	13·3	5·4
14	6 03·5	6 04·5	5 46·9	1·4	0·6	7·4	3·0	13·4	5·5
15	6 03·8	6 04·7	5 47·2	1·5	0·6	7·5	3·1	13·5	5·5
16	6 04·0	6 05·0	5 47·4	1·6	0·7	7·6	3·1	13·6	5·6
17	6 04·3	6 05·2	5 47·7	1·7	0·7	7·7	3·1	13·7	5·6
18	6 04·5	6 05·5	5 47·9	1·8	0·7	7·8	3·2	13·8	5·6
19	6 04·8	6 05·7	5 48·1	1·9	0·8	7·9	3·2	13·9	5·7
20	6 05·0	6 06·0	5 48·4	2·0	0·8	8·0	3·3	14·0	5·7
21	6 05·3	6 06·3	5 48·6	2·1	0·9	8·1	3·3	14·1	5·8
22	6 05·5	6 06·5	5 48·8	2·2	0·9	8·2	3·3	14·2	5·8
23	6 05·8	6 06·8	5 49·1	2·3	0·9	8·3	3·4	14·3	5·8
24	6 06·0	6 07·0	5 49·3	2·4	1·0	8·4	3·4	14·4	5·9
25	6 06·3	6 07·3	5 49·6	2·5	1·0	8·5	3·5	14·5	5·9
26	6 06·5	6 07·5	5 49·8	2·6	1·1	8·6	3·5	14·6	6·0
27	6 06·8	6 07·8	5 50·0	2·7	1·1	8·7	3·6	14·7	6·0
28	6 07·0	6 08·0	5 50·3	2·8	1·1	8·8	3·6	14·8	6·0
29	6 07·3	6 08·3	5 50·5	2·9	1·2	8·9	3·6	14·9	6·1
30	6 07·5	6 08·5	5 50·8	3·0	1·2	9·0	3·7	15·0	6·1
31	6 07·8	6 08·8	5 51·0	3·1	1·3	9·1	3·7	15·1	6·2
32	6 08·0	6 09·0	5 51·2	3·2	1·3	9·2	3·8	15·2	6·2
33	6 08·3	6 09·3	5 51·5	3·3	1·3	9·3	3·8	15·3	6·2
34	6 08·5	6 09·5	5 51·7	3·4	1·4	9·4	3·8	15·4	6·3
35	6 08·8	6 09·8	5 52·0	3·5	1·4	9·5	3·9	15·5	6·3
36	6 09·0	6 10·0	5 52·2	3·6	1·5	9·6	3·9	15·6	6·4
37	6 09·3	6 10·3	5 52·4	3·7	1·5	9·7	4·0	15·7	6·4
38	6 09·5	6 10·5	5 52·7	3·8	1·6	9·8	4·0	15·8	6·5
39	6 09·8	6 10·8	5 52·9	3·9	1·6	9·9	4·0	15·9	6·5
40	6 10·0	6 11·0	5 53·1	4·0	1·6	10·0	4·1	16·0	6·5
41	6 10·3	6 11·3	5 53·4	4·1	1·7	10·1	4·1	16·1	6·6
42	6 10·5	6 11·5	5 53·6	4·2	1·7	10·2	4·2	16·2	6·6
43	6 10·8	6 11·8	5 53·9	4·3	1·8	10·3	4·2	16·3	6·7
44	6 11·0	6 12·0	5 54·1	4·4	1·8	10·4	4·2	16·4	6·7
45	6 11·3	6 12·3	5 54·3	4·5	1·8	10·5	4·3	16·5	6·7
46	6 11·5	6 12·5	5 54·6	4·6	1·9	10·6	4·3	16·6	6·8
47	6 11·8	6 12·8	5 54·8	4·7	1·9	10·7	4·4	16·7	6·8
48	6 12·0	6 13·0	5 55·1	4·8	2·0	10·8	4·4	16·8	6·9
49	6 12·3	6 13·3	5 55·3	4·9	2·0	10·9	4·5	16·9	6·9
50	6 12·5	6 13·5	5 55·5	5·0	2·0	11·0	4·5	17·0	6·9
51	6 12·8	6 13·8	5 55·8	5·1	2·1	11·1	4·5	17·1	7·0
52	6 13·0	6 14·0	5 56·0	5·2	2·1	11·2	4·6	17·2	7·0
53	6 13·3	6 14·3	5 56·2	5·3	2·2	11·3	4·6	17·3	7·1
54	6 13·5	6 14·5	5 56·5	5·4	2·2	11·4	4·7	17·4	7·1
55	6 13·8	6 14·8	5 56·7	5·5	2·2	11·5	4·7	17·5	7·1
56	6 14·0	6 15·0	5 57·0	5·6	2·3	11·6	4·7	17·6	7·2
57	6 14·3	6 15·3	5 57·2	5·7	2·3	11·7	4·8	17·7	7·2
58	6 14·5	6 15·5	5 57·4	5·8	2·4	11·8	4·8	17·8	7·3
59	6 14·8	6 15·8	5 57·7	5·9	2·4	11·9	4·9	17·9	7·3
60	6 15·0	6 16·0	5 57·9	6·0	2·5	12·0	4·9	18·0	7·4

25m	SUN PLANETS	ARIES	MOON	v or d	Corrn	v or d	Corrn	v or d	Corrn
s	° ′	° ′	° ′	′	′	′	′	′	′
00	6 15·0	6 16·0	5 57·9	0·0	0·0	6·0	2·6	12·0	5·1
01	6 15·3	6 16·3	5 58·2	0·1	0·0	6·1	2·6	12·1	5·1
02	6 15·5	6 16·5	5 58·4	0·2	0·1	6·2	2·6	12·2	5·2
03	6 15·8	6 16·8	5 58·6	0·3	0·1	6·3	2·7	12·3	5·2
04	6 16·0	6 17·0	5 58·9	0·4	0·2	6·4	2·7	12·4	5·3
05	6 16·3	6 17·3	5 59·1	0·5	0·2	6·5	2·8	12·5	5·3
06	6 16·5	6 17·5	5 59·3	0·6	0·3	6·6	2·8	12·6	5·4
07	6 16·8	6 17·8	5 59·6	0·7	0·3	6·7	2·8	12·7	5·4
08	6 17·0	6 18·0	5 59·8	0·8	0·3	6·8	2·9	12·8	5·4
09	6 17·3	6 18·3	6 00·1	0·9	0·4	6·9	2·9	12·9	5·5
10	6 17·5	6 18·5	6 00·3	1·0	0·4	7·0	3·0	13·0	5·5
11	6 17·8	6 18·8	6 00·5	1·1	0·5	7·1	3·0	13·1	5·6
12	6 18·0	6 19·0	6 00·8	1·2	0·5	7·2	3·1	13·2	5·6
13	6 18·3	6 19·3	6 01·0	1·3	0·6	7·3	3·1	13·3	5·7
14	6 18·5	6 19·5	6 01·3	1·4	0·6	7·4	3·1	13·4	5·7
15	6 18·8	6 19·8	6 01·5	1·5	0·6	7·5	3·2	13·5	5·7
16	6 19·0	6 20·0	6 01·7	1·6	0·7	7·6	3·2	13·6	5·8
17	6 19·3	6 20·3	6 02·0	1·7	0·7	7·7	3·3	13·7	5·8
18	6 19·5	6 20·5	6 02·2	1·8	0·8	7·8	3·3	13·8	5·9
19	6 19·8	6 20·8	6 02·5	1·9	0·8	7·9	3·4	13·9	5·9
20	6 20·0	6 21·0	6 02·7	2·0	0·9	8·0	3·4	14·0	6·0
21	6 20·3	6 21·3	6 02·9	2·1	0·9	8·1	3·4	14·1	6·0
22	6 20·5	6 21·5	6 03·2	2·2	0·9	8·2	3·5	14·2	6·0
23	6 20·8	6 21·8	6 03·4	2·3	1·0	8·3	3·5	14·3	6·1
24	6 21·0	6 22·0	6 03·6	2·4	1·0	8·4	3·6	14·4	6·1
25	6 21·3	6 22·3	6 03·9	2·5	1·1	8·5	3·6	14·5	6·2
26	6 21·5	6 22·5	6 04·1	2·6	1·1	8·6	3·7	14·6	6·2
27	6 21·8	6 22·8	6 04·4	2·7	1·1	8·7	3·7	14·7	6·2
28	6 22·0	6 23·0	6 04·6	2·8	1·2	8·8	3·7	14·8	6·3
29	6 22·3	6 23·3	6 04·8	2·9	1·2	8·9	3·8	14·9	6·3
30	6 22·5	6 23·5	6 05·1	3·0	1·3	9·0	3·8	15·0	6·4
31	6 22·8	6 23·8	6 05·3	3·1	1·3	9·1	3·9	15·1	6·4
32	6 23·0	6 24·0	6 05·6	3·2	1·4	9·2	3·9	15·2	6·5
33	6 23·3	6 24·3	6 05·8	3·3	1·4	9·3	4·0	15·3	6·5
34	6 23·5	6 24·5	6 06·0	3·4	1·4	9·4	4·0	15·4	6·5
35	6 23·8	6 24·8	6 06·3	3·5	1·5	9·5	4·0	15·5	6·6
36	6 24·0	6 25·1	6 06·5	3·6	1·5	9·6	4·1	15·6	6·6
37	6 24·3	6 25·3	6 06·7	3·7	1·6	9·7	4·1	15·7	6·7
38	6 24·5	6 25·6	6 07·0	3·8	1·6	9·8	4·2	15·8	6·7
39	6 24·8	6 25·8	6 07·2	3·9	1·7	9·9	4·2	15·9	6·8
40	6 25·0	6 26·1	6 07·5	4·0	1·7	10·0	4·3	16·0	6·8
41	6 25·3	6 26·3	6 07·7	4·1	1·7	10·1	4·3	16·1	6·8
42	6 25·5	6 26·6	6 07·9	4·2	1·8	10·2	4·3	16·2	6·9
43	6 25·8	6 26·8	6 08·2	4·3	1·8	10·3	4·4	16·3	6·9
44	6 26·0	6 27·1	6 08·4	4·4	1·9	10·4	4·4	16·4	7·0
45	6 26·3	6 27·3	6 08·7	4·5	1·9	10·5	4·5	16·5	7·0
46	6 26·5	6 27·6	6 08·9	4·6	2·0	10·6	4·5	16·6	7·1
47	6 26·8	6 27·8	6 09·1	4·7	2·0	10·7	4·5	16·7	7·1
48	6 27·0	6 28·1	6 09·4	4·8	2·0	10·8	4·6	16·8	7·1
49	6 27·3	6 28·3	6 09·6	4·9	2·1	10·9	4·6	16·9	7·2
50	6 27·5	6 28·6	6 09·8	5·0	2·1	11·0	4·7	17·0	7·2
51	6 27·8	6 28·8	6 10·1	5·1	2·2	11·1	4·7	17·1	7·3
52	6 28·0	6 29·1	6 10·3	5·2	2·2	11·2	4·8	17·2	7·3
53	6 28·3	6 29·3	6 10·6	5·3	2·3	11·3	4·8	17·3	7·4
54	6 28·5	6 29·6	6 10·8	5·4	2·3	11·4	4·8	17·4	7·4
55	6 28·8	6 29·8	6 11·0	5·5	2·3	11·5	4·9	17·5	7·4
56	6 29·0	6 30·1	6 11·3	5·6	2·4	11·6	4·9	17·6	7·5
57	6 29·3	6 30·3	6 11·5	5·7	2·4	11·7	5·0	17·7	7·5
58	6 29·5	6 30·6	6 11·8	5·8	2·5	11·8	5·0	17·8	7·6
59	6 29·8	6 30·8	6 12·0	5·9	2·5	11·9	5·1	17·9	7·6
60	6 30·0	6 31·1	6 12·2	6·0	2·6	12·0	5·1	18·0	7·7

26^m	SUN PLANETS	ARIES	MOON	v or d	Corr^n	v or d	Corr^n	v or d	Corr^n
s	° ′	° ′	° ′	′	′	′	′	′	′
00	6 30·0	6 31·1	6 12·2	0·0	0·0	6·0	2·7	12·0	5·3
01	6 30·3	6 31·3	6 12·5	0·1	0·0	6·1	2·7	12·1	5·3
02	6 30·5	6 31·6	6 12·7	0·2	0·1	6·2	2·7	12·2	5·4
03	6 30·8	6 31·8	6 12·9	0·3	0·1	6·3	2·8	12·3	5·4
04	6 31·0	6 32·1	6 13·2	0·4	0·2	6·4	2·8	12·4	5·5
05	6 31·3	6 32·3	6 13·4	0·5	0·2	6·5	2·9	12·5	5·5
06	6 31·5	6 32·6	6 13·7	0·6	0·3	6·6	2·9	12·6	5·6
07	6 31·8	6 32·8	6 13·9	0·7	0·3	6·7	3·0	12·7	5·6
08	6 32·0	6 33·1	6 14·1	0·8	0·4	6·8	3·0	12·8	5·7
09	6 32·3	6 33·3	6 14·4	0·9	0·4	6·9	3·0	12·9	5·7
10	6 32·5	6 33·6	6 14·6	1·0	0·4	7·0	3·1	13·0	5·7
11	6 32·8	6 33·8	6 14·9	1·1	0·5	7·1	3·1	13·1	5·8
12	6 33·0	6 34·1	6 15·1	1·2	0·5	7·2	3·2	13·2	5·8
13	6 33·3	6 34·3	6 15·3	1·3	0·6	7·3	3·2	13·3	5·9
14	6 33·5	6 34·6	6 15·6	1·4	0·6	7·4	3·3	13·4	5·9
15	6 33·8	6 34·8	6 15·8	1·5	0·7	7·5	3·3	13·5	6·0
16	6 34·0	6 35·1	6 16·1	1·6	0·7	7·6	3·4	13·6	6·0
17	6 34·3	6 35·3	6 16·3	1·7	0·8	7·7	3·4	13·7	6·1
18	6 34·5	6 35·6	6 16·5	1·8	0·8	7·8	3·4	13·8	6·1
19	6 34·8	6 35·8	6 16·8	1·9	0·8	7·9	3·5	13·9	6·1
20	6 35·0	6 36·1	6 17·0	2·0	0·9	8·0	3·5	14·0	6·2
21	6 35·3	6 36·3	6 17·2	2·1	0·9	8·1	3·6	14·1	6·2
22	6 35·5	6 36·6	6 17·5	2·2	1·0	8·2	3·6	14·2	6·3
23	6 35·8	6 36·8	6 17·7	2·3	1·0	8·3	3·7	14·3	6·3
24	6 36·0	6 37·1	6 18·0	2·4	1·1	8·4	3·7	14·4	6·4
25	6 36·3	6 37·3	6 18·2	2·5	1·1	8·5	3·8	14·5	6·4
26	6 36·5	6 37·6	6 18·4	2·6	1·1	8·6	3·8	14·6	6·4
27	6 36·8	6 37·8	6 18·7	2·7	1·2	8·7	3·8	14·7	6·5
28	6 37·0	6 38·1	6 18·9	2·8	1·2	8·8	3·9	14·8	6·5
29	6 37·3	6 38·3	6 19·2	2·9	1·3	8·9	3·9	14·9	6·6
30	6 37·5	6 38·6	6 19·4	3·0	1·3	9·0	4·0	15·0	6·6
31	6 37·8	6 38·8	6 19·6	3·1	1·4	9·1	4·0	15·1	6·7
32	6 38·0	6 39·1	6 19·9	3·2	1·4	9·2	4·1	15·2	6·7
33	6 38·3	6 39·3	6 20·1	3·3	1·5	9·3	4·1	15·3	6·8
34	6 38·5	6 39·6	6 20·3	3·4	1·5	9·4	4·2	15·4	6·8
35	6 38·8	6 39·8	6 20·6	3·5	1·5	9·5	4·2	15·5	6·8
36	6 39·0	6 40·1	6 20·8	3·6	1·6	9·6	4·2	15·6	6·9
37	6 39·3	6 40·3	6 21·1	3·7	1·6	9·7	4·3	15·7	6·9
38	6 39·5	6 40·6	6 21·3	3·8	1·7	9·8	4·3	15·8	7·0
39	6 39·8	6 40·8	6 21·5	3·9	1·7	9·9	4·4	15·9	7·0
40	6 40·0	6 41·1	6 21·8	4·0	1·8	10·0	4·4	16·0	7·1
41	6 40·3	6 41·3	6 22·0	4·1	1·8	10·1	4·5	16·1	7·1
42	6 40·5	6 41·6	6 22·3	4·2	1·9	10·2	4·5	16·2	7·2
43	6 40·8	6 41·8	6 22·5	4·3	1·9	10·3	4·5	16·3	7·2
44	6 41·0	6 42·1	6 22·7	4·4	1·9	10·4	4·6	16·4	7·2
45	6 41·3	6 42·3	6 23·0	4·5	2·0	10·5	4·6	16·5	7·3
46	6 41·5	6 42·6	6 23·2	4·6	2·0	10·6	4·7	16·6	7·3
47	6 41·8	6 42·8	6 23·4	4·7	2·1	10·7	4·7	16·7	7·4
48	6 42·0	6 43·1	6 23·7	4·8	2·1	10·8	4·8	16·8	7·4
49	6 42·3	6 43·4	6 23·9	4·9	2·2	10·9	4·8	16·9	7·5
50	6 42·5	6 43·6	6 24·2	5·0	2·2	11·0	4·9	17·0	7·5
51	6 42·8	6 43·9	6 24·4	5·1	2·3	11·1	4·9	17·1	7·6
52	6 43·0	6 44·1	6 24·6	5·2	2·3	11·2	4·9	17·2	7·6
53	6 43·3	6 44·4	6 24·9	5·3	2·3	11·3	5·0	17·3	7·6
54	6 43·5	6 44·6	6 25·1	5·4	2·4	11·4	5·0	17·4	7·7
55	6 43·8	6 44·9	6 25·4	5·5	2·4	11·5	5·1	17·5	7·7
56	6 44·0	6 45·1	6 25·6	5·6	2·5	11·6	5·1	17·6	7·8
57	6 44·3	6 45·4	6 25·8	5·7	2·5	11·7	5·2	17·7	7·8
58	6 44·5	6 45·6	6 26·1	5·8	2·6	11·8	5·2	17·8	7·9
59	6 44·8	6 45·9	6 26·3	5·9	2·6	11·9	5·3	17·9	7·9
60	6 45·0	6 46·1	6 26·6	6·0	2·7	12·0	5·3	18·0	8·0

27^m	SUN PLANETS	ARIES	MOON	v or d	Corr^n	v or d	Corr^n	v or d	Corr^n
s	° ′	° ′	° ′	′	′	′	′	′	′
00	6 45·0	6 46·1	6 26·6	0·0	0·0	6·0	2·8	12·0	5·5
01	6 45·3	6 46·4	6 26·8	0·1	0·0	6·1	2·8	12·1	5·5
02	6 45·5	6 46·6	6 27·0	0·2	0·1	6·2	2·8	12·2	5·6
03	6 45·8	6 46·9	6 27·3	0·3	0·1	6·3	2·9	12·3	5·6
04	6 46·0	6 47·1	6 27·5	0·4	0·2	6·4	2·9	12·4	5·7
05	6 46·3	6 47·4	6 27·7	0·5	0·2	6·5	3·0	12·5	5·7
06	6 46·5	6 47·6	6 28·0	0·6	0·3	6·6	3·0	12·6	5·8
07	6 46·8	6 47·9	6 28·2	0·7	0·3	6·7	3·1	12·7	5·8
08	6 47·0	6 48·1	6 28·5	0·8	0·4	6·8	3·1	12·8	5·9
09	6 47·3	6 48·4	6 28·7	0·9	0·4	6·9	3·2	12·9	5·9
10	6 47·5	6 48·6	6 28·9	1·0	0·5	7·0	3·2	13·0	6·0
11	6 47·8	6 48·9	6 29·2	1·1	0·5	7·1	3·3	13·1	6·0
12	6 48·0	6 49·1	6 29·4	1·2	0·6	7·2	3·3	13·2	6·1
13	6 48·3	6 49·4	6 29·7	1·3	0·6	7·3	3·3	13·3	6·1
14	6 48·5	6 49·6	6 29·9	1·4	0·6	7·4	3·4	13·4	6·1
15	6 48·8	6 49·9	6 30·1	1·5	0·7	7·5	3·4	13·5	6·2
16	6 49·0	6 50·1	6 30·4	1·6	0·7	7·6	3·5	13·6	6·2
17	6 49·3	6 50·4	6 30·6	1·7	0·8	7·7	3·5	13·7	6·3
18	6 49·5	6 50·6	6 30·8	1·8	0·8	7·8	3·6	13·8	6·3
19	6 49·8	6 50·9	6 31·1	1·9	0·9	7·9	3·6	13·9	6·4
20	6 50·0	6 51·1	6 31·3	2·0	0·9	8·0	3·7	14·0	6·4
21	6 50·3	6 51·4	6 31·6	2·1	1·0	8·1	3·7	14·1	6·5
22	6 50·5	6 51·6	6 31·8	2·2	1·0	8·2	3·8	14·2	6·5
23	6 50·8	6 51·9	6 32·0	2·3	1·1	8·3	3·8	14·3	6·6
24	6 51·0	6 52·1	6 32·3	2·4	1·1	8·4	3·9	14·4	6·6
25	6 51·3	6 52·4	6 32·5	2·5	1·1	8·5	3·9	14·5	6·6
26	6 51·5	6 52·6	6 32·8	2·6	1·2	8·6	3·9	14·6	6·7
27	6 51·8	6 52·9	6 33·0	2·7	1·2	8·7	4·0	14·7	6·7
28	6 52·0	6 53·1	6 33·2	2·8	1·3	8·8	4·0	14·8	6·8
29	6 52·3	6 53·4	6 33·5	2·9	1·3	8·9	4·1	14·9	6·8
30	6 52·5	6 53·6	6 33·7	3·0	1·4	9·0	4·1	15·0	6·9
31	6 52·8	6 53·9	6 33·9	3·1	1·4	9·1	4·2	15·1	6·9
32	6 53·0	6 54·1	6 34·2	3·2	1·5	9·2	4·2	15·2	7·0
33	6 53·3	6 54·4	6 34·4	3·3	1·5	9·3	4·3	15·3	7·0
34	6 53·5	6 54·6	6 34·7	3·4	1·6	9·4	4·3	15·4	7·1
35	6 53·8	6 54·9	6 34·9	3·5	1·6	9·5	4·4	15·5	7·1
36	6 54·0	6 55·1	6 35·1	3·6	1·7	9·6	4·4	15·6	7·2
37	6 54·3	6 55·4	6 35·4	3·7	1·7	9·7	4·4	15·7	7·2
38	6 54·5	6 55·6	6 35·6	3·8	1·7	9·8	4·5	15·8	7·2
39	6 54·8	6 55·9	6 35·9	3·9	1·8	9·9	4·5	15·9	7·3
40	6 55·0	6 56·1	6 36·1	4·0	1·8	10·0	4·6	16·0	7·3
41	6 55·3	6 56·4	6 36·3	4·1	1·9	10·1	4·6	16·1	7·4
42	6 55·5	6 56·6	6 36·6	4·2	1·9	10·2	4·7	16·2	7·4
43	6 55·8	6 56·9	6 36·8	4·3	2·0	10·3	4·7	16·3	7·5
44	6 56·0	6 57·1	6 37·0	4·4	2·0	10·4	4·8	16·4	7·5
45	6 56·3	6 57·4	6 37·3	4·5	2·1	10·5	4·8	16·5	7·6
46	6 56·5	6 57·6	6 37·5	4·6	2·1	10·6	4·9	16·6	7·6
47	6 56·8	6 57·9	6 37·8	4·7	2·2	10·7	4·9	16·7	7·7
48	6 57·0	6 58·1	6 38·0	4·8	2·2	10·8	5·0	16·8	7·7
49	6 57·3	6 58·4	6 38·2	4·9	2·2	10·9	5·0	16·9	7·7
50	6 57·5	6 58·6	6 38·5	5·0	2·3	11·0	5·0	17·0	7·8
51	6 57·8	6 58·9	6 38·7	5·1	2·3	11·1	5·1	17·1	7·8
52	6 58·0	6 59·1	6 39·0	5·2	2·4	11·2	5·1	17·2	7·9
53	6 58·3	6 59·4	6 39·2	5·3	2·4	11·3	5·2	17·3	7·9
54	6 58·5	6 59·6	6 39·4	5·4	2·5	11·4	5·2	17·4	8·0
55	6 58·8	6 59·9	6 39·7	5·5	2·5	11·5	5·3	17·5	8·0
56	6 59·0	7 00·1	6 39·9	5·6	2·6	11·6	5·3	17·6	8·1
57	6 59·3	7 00·4	6 40·2	5·7	2·6	11·7	5·4	17·7	8·1
58	6 59·5	7 00·6	6 40·4	5·8	2·7	11·8	5·4	17·8	8·2
59	6 59·8	7 00·9	6 40·6	5·9	2·7	11·9	5·5	17·9	8·2
60	7 00·0	7 01·1	6 40·9	6·0	2·8	12·0	5·5	18·0	8·3

28m	SUN PLANETS	ARIES	MOON	v or d	Corrⁿ	v or d	Corrⁿ	v or d	Corrⁿ
s	° ′	° ′	° ′	′	′	′	′	′	′
00	7 00·0	7 01·1	6 40·9	0·0	0·0	6·0	2·9	12·0	5·7
01	7 00·3	7 01·4	6 41·1	0·1	0·0	6·1	2·9	12·1	5·7
02	7 00·5	7 01·7	6 41·3	0·2	0·1	6·2	2·9	12·2	5·8
03	7 00·8	7 01·9	6 41·6	0·3	0·1	6·3	3·0	12·3	5·8
04	7 01·0	7 02·2	6 41·8	0·4	0·2	6·4	3·0	12·4	5·9
05	7 01·3	7 02·4	6 42·1	0·5	0·2	6·5	3·1	12·5	5·9
06	7 01·5	7 02·7	6 42·3	0·6	0·3	6·6	3·1	12·6	6·0
07	7 01·8	7 02·9	6 42·5	0·7	0·3	6·7	3·2	12·7	6·0
08	7 02·0	7 03·2	6 42·8	0·8	0·4	6·8	3·2	12·8	6·1
09	7 02·3	7 03·4	6 43·0	0·9	0·4	6·9	3·3	12·9	6·1
10	7 02·5	7 03·7	6 43·3	1·0	0·5	7·0	3·3	13·0	6·2
11	7 02·8	7 03·9	6 43·5	1·1	0·5	7·1	3·4	13·1	6·2
12	7 03·0	7 04·2	6 43·7	1·2	0·6	7·2	3·4	13·2	6·3
13	7 03·3	7 04·4	6 44·0	1·3	0·6	7·3	3·5	13·3	6·3
14	7 03·5	7 04·7	6 44·2	1·4	0·7	7·4	3·5	13·4	6·4
15	7 03·8	7 04·9	6 44·4	1·5	0·7	7·5	3·6	13·5	6·4
16	7 04·0	7 05·2	6 44·7	1·6	0·8	7·6	3·6	13·6	6·5
17	7 04·3	7 05·4	6 44·9	1·7	0·8	7·7	3·7	13·7	6·5
18	7 04·5	7 05·7	6 45·2	1·8	0·9	7·8	3·7	13·8	6·6
19	7 04·8	7 05·9	6 45·4	1·9	0·9	7·9	3·8	13·9	6·6
20	7 05·0	7 06·2	6 45·6	2·0	1·0	8·0	3·8	14·0	6·7
21	7 05·3	7 06·4	6 45·9	2·1	1·0	8·1	3·8	14·1	6·7
22	7 05·5	7 06·7	6 46·1	2·2	1·0	8·2	3·9	14·2	6·7
23	7 05·8	7 06·9	6 46·4	2·3	1·1	8·3	3·9	14·3	6·8
24	7 06·0	7 07·2	6 46·6	2·4	1·1	8·4	4·0	14·4	6·8
25	7 06·3	7 07·4	6 46·8	2·5	1·2	8·5	4·0	14·5	6·9
26	7 06·5	7 07·7	6 47·1	2·6	1·2	8·6	4·1	14·6	6·9
27	7 06·8	7 07·9	6 47·3	2·7	1·3	8·7	4·1	14·7	7·0
28	7 07·0	7 08·2	6 47·5	2·8	1·3	8·8	4·2	14·8	7·0
29	7 07·3	7 08·4	6 47·8	2·9	1·4	8·9	4·2	14·9	7·1
30	7 07·5	7 08·7	6 48·0	3·0	1·4	9·0	4·3	15·0	7·1
31	7 07·8	7 08·9	6 48·3	3·1	1·5	9·1	4·3	15·1	7·2
32	7 08·0	7 09·2	6 48·5	3·2	1·5	9·2	4·4	15·2	7·2
33	7 08·3	7 09·4	6 48·7	3·3	1·6	9·3	4·4	15·3	7·3
34	7 08·5	7 09·7	6 49·0	3·4	1·6	9·4	4·5	15·4	7·3
35	7 08·8	7 09·9	6 49·2	3·5	1·7	9·5	4·5	15·5	7·4
36	7 09·0	7 10·2	6 49·5	3·6	1·7	9·6	4·6	15·6	7·4
37	7 09·3	7 10·4	6 49·7	3·7	1·8	9·7	4·6	15·7	7·5
38	7 09·5	7 10·7	6 49·9	3·8	1·8	9·8	4·7	15·8	7·5
39	7 09·8	7 10·9	6 50·2	3·9	1·9	9·9	4·7	15·9	7·6
40	7 10·0	7 11·2	6 50·4	4·0	1·9	10·0	4·8	16·0	7·6
41	7 10·3	7 11·4	6 50·6	4·1	1·9	10·1	4·8	16·1	7·6
42	7 10·5	7 11·7	6 50·9	4·2	2·0	10·2	4·8	16·2	7·7
43	7 10·8	7 11·9	6 51·1	4·3	2·0	10·3	4·9	16·3	7·7
44	7 11·0	7 12·2	6 51·4	4·4	2·1	10·4	4·9	16·4	7·8
45	7 11·3	7 12·4	6 51·6	4·5	2·1	10·5	5·0	16·5	7·8
46	7 11·5	7 12·7	6 51·8	4·6	2·2	10·6	5·0	16·6	7·9
47	7 11·8	7 12·9	6 52·1	4·7	2·2	10·7	5·1	16·7	7·9
48	7 12·0	7 13·2	6 52·3	4·8	2·3	10·8	5·1	16·8	8·0
49	7 12·3	7 13·4	6 52·6	4·9	2·3	10·9	5·2	16·9	8·0
50	7 12·5	7 13·7	6 52·8	5·0	2·4	11·0	5·2	17·0	8·1
51	7 12·8	7 13·9	6 53·0	5·1	2·4	11·1	5·3	17·1	8·1
52	7 13·0	7 14·2	6 53·3	5·2	2·5	11·2	5·3	17·2	8·2
53	7 13·3	7 14·4	6 53·5	5·3	2·5	11·3	5·4	17·3	8·2
54	7 13·5	7 14·7	6 53·8	5·4	2·6	11·4	5·4	17·4	8·3
55	7 13·8	7 14·9	6 54·0	5·5	2·6	11·5	5·5	17·5	8·3
56	7 14·0	7 15·2	6 54·2	5·6	2·7	11·6	5·5	17·6	8·4
57	7 14·3	7 15·4	6 54·5	5·7	2·7	11·7	5·6	17·7	8·4
58	7 14·5	7 15·7	6 54·7	5·8	2·8	11·8	5·6	17·8	8·5
59	7 14·8	7 15·9	6 54·9	5·9	2·8	11·9	5·7	17·9	8·5
60	7 15·0	7 16·2	6 55·2	6·0	2·9	12·0	5·7	18·0	8·6

29m	SUN PLANETS	ARIES	MOON	v or d	Corrⁿ	v or d	Corrⁿ	v or d	Corrⁿ
s	° ′	° ′	° ′	′	′	′	′	′	′
00	7 15·0	7 16·2	6 55·2	0·0	0·0	6·0	3·0	12·0	5·9
01	7 15·3	7 16·4	6 55·4	0·1	0·0	6·1	3·0	12·1	5·9
02	7 15·5	7 16·7	6 55·7	0·2	0·1	6·2	3·0	12·2	6·0
03	7 15·8	7 16·9	6 55·9	0·3	0·1	6·3	3·1	12·3	6·0
04	7 16·0	7 17·2	6 56·1	0·4	0·2	6·4	3·1	12·4	6·1
05	7 16·3	7 17·4	6 56·4	0·5	0·2	6·5	3·2	12·5	6·1
06	7 16·5	7 17·7	6 56·6	0·6	0·3	6·6	3·2	12·6	6·2
07	7 16·8	7 17·9	6 56·9	0·7	0·3	6·7	3·3	12·7	6·2
08	7 17·0	7 18·2	6 57·1	0·8	0·4	6·8	3·3	12·8	6·3
09	7 17·3	7 18·4	6 57·3	0·9	0·4	6·9	3·4	12·9	6·3
10	7 17·5	7 18·7	6 57·6	1·0	0·5	7·0	3·4	13·0	6·4
11	7 17·8	7 18·9	6 57·8	1·1	0·5	7·1	3·5	13·1	6·4
12	7 18·0	7 19·2	6 58·0	1·2	0·6	7·2	3·5	13·2	6·5
13	7 18·3	7 19·4	6 58·3	1·3	0·6	7·3	3·6	13·3	6·5
14	7 18·5	7 19·7	6 58·5	1·4	0·7	7·4	3·6	13·4	6·6
15	7 18·8	7 20·0	6 58·8	1·5	0·7	7·5	3·7	13·5	6·6
16	7 19·0	7 20·2	6 59·0	1·6	0·8	7·6	3·7	13·6	6·7
17	7 19·3	7 20·5	6 59·2	1·7	0·8	7·7	3·8	13·7	6·7
18	7 19·5	7 20·7	6 59·5	1·8	0·9	7·8	3·8	13·8	6·8
19	7 19·8	7 21·0	6 59·7	1·9	0·9	7·9	3·9	13·9	6·8
20	7 20·0	7 21·2	7 00·0	2·0	1·0	8·0	3·9	14·0	6·9
21	7 20·3	7 21·5	7 00·2	2·1	1·0	8·1	4·0	14·1	6·9
22	7 20·5	7 21·7	7 00·4	2·2	1·1	8·2	4·0	14·2	7·0
23	7 20·8	7 22·0	7 00·7	2·3	1·1	8·3	4·1	14·3	7·0
24	7 21·0	7 22·2	7 00·9	2·4	1·2	8·4	4·1	14·4	7·1
25	7 21·3	7 22·5	7 01·1	2·5	1·2	8·5	4·2	14·5	7·1
26	7 21·5	7 22·7	7 01·4	2·6	1·3	8·6	4·2	14·6	7·2
27	7 21·8	7 23·0	7 01·6	2·7	1·3	8·7	4·3	14·7	7·2
28	7 22·0	7 23·2	7 01·9	2·8	1·4	8·8	4·3	14·8	7·3
29	7 22·3	7 23·5	7 02·1	2·9	1·4	8·9	4·4	14·9	7·3
30	7 22·5	7 23·7	7 02·3	3·0	1·5	9·0	4·4	15·0	7·4
31	7 22·8	7 24·0	7 02·6	3·1	1·5	9·1	4·5	15·1	7·4
32	7 23·0	7 24·2	7 02·8	3·2	1·6	9·2	4·5	15·2	7·5
33	7 23·3	7 24·5	7 03·1	3·3	1·6	9·3	4·6	15·3	7·5
34	7 23·5	7 24·7	7 03·3	3·4	1·7	9·4	4·6	15·4	7·6
35	7 23·8	7 25·0	7 03·5	3·5	1·7	9·5	4·7	15·5	7·6
36	7 24·0	7 25·2	7 03·8	3·6	1·8	9·6	4·7	15·6	7·7
37	7 24·3	7 25·5	7 04·0	3·7	1·8	9·7	4·8	15·7	7·7
38	7 24·5	7 25·7	7 04·3	3·8	1·9	9·8	4·8	15·8	7·8
39	7 24·8	7 26·0	7 04·5	3·9	1·9	9·9	4·9	15·9	7·8
40	7 25·0	7 26·2	7 04·7	4·0	2·0	10·0	4·9	16·0	7·9
41	7 25·3	7 26·5	7 05·0	4·1	2·0	10·1	5·0	16·1	7·9
42	7 25·5	7 26·7	7 05·2	4·2	2·1	10·2	5·0	16·2	8·0
43	7 25·8	7 27·0	7 05·4	4·3	2·1	10·3	5·1	16·3	8·0
44	7 26·0	7 27·2	7 05·7	4·4	2·2	10·4	5·1	16·4	8·1
45	7 26·3	7 27·5	7 05·9	4·5	2·2	10·5	5·2	16·5	8·1
46	7 26·5	7 27·7	7 06·2	4·6	2·3	10·6	5·2	16·6	8·2
47	7 26·8	7 28·0	7 06·4	4·7	2·3	10·7	5·3	16·7	8·2
48	7 27·0	7 28·2	7 06·6	4·8	2·4	10·8	5·3	16·8	8·3
49	7 27·3	7 28·5	7 06·9	4·9	2·4	10·9	5·4	16·9	8·3
50	7 27·5	7 28·7	7 07·1	5·0	2·5	11·0	5·4	17·0	8·4
51	7 27·8	7 29·0	7 07·4	5·1	2·5	11·1	5·5	17·1	8·4
52	7 28·0	7 29·2	7 07·6	5·2	2·6	11·2	5·5	17·2	8·5
53	7 28·3	7 29·5	7 07·8	5·3	2·6	11·3	5·6	17·3	8·5
54	7 28·5	7 29·7	7 08·1	5·4	2·7	11·4	5·6	17·4	8·6
55	7 28·8	7 30·0	7 08·3	5·5	2·7	11·5	5·7	17·5	8·6
56	7 29·0	7 30·2	7 08·5	5·6	2·8	11·6	5·7	17·6	8·7
57	7 29·3	7 30·5	7 08·8	5·7	2·8	11·7	5·8	17·7	8·7
58	7 29·5	7 30·7	7 09·0	5·8	2·9	11·8	5·8	17·8	8·8
59	7 29·8	7 31·0	7 09·3	5·9	2·9	11·9	5·9	17·9	8·8
60	7 30·0	7 31·2	7 09·5	6·0	3·0	12·0	5·9	18·0	8·9

30m s	SUN PLANETS ° ′	ARIES ° ′	MOON ° ′	v or d ′	Corrn ′	v or d ′	Corrn ′	v or d ′	Corrn ′
00	7 30·0	7 31·2	7 09·5	0·0	0·0	6·0	3·1	12·0	6·1
01	7 30·3	7 31·5	7 09·7	0·1	0·1	6·1	3·1	12·1	6·2
02	7 30·5	7 31·7	7 10·0	0·2	0·1	6·2	3·2	12·2	6·2
03	7 30·8	7 32·0	7 10·2	0·3	0·2	6·3	3·2	12·3	6·3
04	7 31·0	7 32·2	7 10·5	0·4	0·2	6·4	3·3	12·4	6·3
05	7 31·3	7 32·5	7 10·7	0·5	0·3	6·5	3·3	12·5	6·4
06	7 31·5	7 32·7	7 10·9	0·6	0·3	6·6	3·4	12·6	6·4
07	7 31·8	7 33·0	7 11·2	0·7	0·4	6·7	3·4	12·7	6·5
08	7 32·0	7 33·2	7 11·4	0·8	0·4	6·8	3·5	12·8	6·5
09	7 32·3	7 33·5	7 11·6	0·9	0·5	6·9	3·5	12·9	6·6
10	7 32·5	7 33·7	7 11·9	1·0	0·5	7·0	3·6	13·0	6·6
11	7 32·8	7 34·0	7 12·1	1·1	0·6	7·1	3·6	13·1	6·7
12	7 33·0	7 34·2	7 12·4	1·2	0·6	7·2	3·7	13·2	6·7
13	7 33·3	7 34·5	7 12·6	1·3	0·7	7·3	3·7	13·3	6·8
14	7 33·5	7 34·7	7 12·8	1·4	0·7	7·4	3·8	13·4	6·8
15	7 33·8	7 35·0	7 13·1	1·5	0·8	7·5	3·8	13·5	6·9
16	7 34·0	7 35·2	7 13·3	1·6	0·8	7·6	3·9	13·6	6·9
17	7 34·3	7 35·5	7 13·6	1·7	0·9	7·7	3·9	13·7	7·0
18	7 34·5	7 35·7	7 13·8	1·8	0·9	7·8	4·0	13·8	7·0
19	7 34·8	7 36·0	7 14·0	1·9	1·0	7·9	4·0	13·9	7·1
20	7 35·0	7 36·2	7 14·3	2·0	1·0	8·0	4·1	14·0	7·1
21	7 35·3	7 36·5	7 14·5	2·1	1·1	8·1	4·1	14·1	7·2
22	7 35·5	7 36·7	7 14·7	2·2	1·1	8·2	4·2	14·2	7·2
23	7 35·8	7 37·0	7 15·0	2·3	1·2	8·3	4·2	14·3	7·3
24	7 36·0	7 37·2	7 15·2	2·4	1·2	8·4	4·3	14·4	7·3
25	7 36·3	7 37·5	7 15·5	2·5	1·3	8·5	4·3	14·5	7·4
26	7 36·5	7 37·7	7 15·7	2·6	1·3	8·6	4·4	14·6	7·4
27	7 36·8	7 38·0	7 15·9	2·7	1·4	8·7	4·4	14·7	7·5
28	7 37·0	7 38·3	7 16·2	2·8	1·4	8·8	4·5	14·8	7·5
29	7 37·3	7 38·5	7 16·4	2·9	1·5	8·9	4·5	14·9	7·6
30	7 37·5	7 38·8	7 16·7	3·0	1·5	9·0	4·6	15·0	7·6
31	7 37·8	7 39·0	7 16·9	3·1	1·6	9·1	4·6	15·1	7·7
32	7 38·0	7 39·3	7 17·1	3·2	1·6	9·2	4·7	15·2	7·7
33	7 38·3	7 39·5	7 17·4	3·3	1·7	9·3	4·7	15·3	7·8
34	7 38·5	7 39·8	7 17·6	3·4	1·7	9·4	4·8	15·4	7·8
35	7 38·8	7 40·0	7 17·9	3·5	1·8	9·5	4·8	15·5	7·9
36	7 39·0	7 40·3	7 18·1	3·6	1·8	9·6	4·9	15·6	7·9
37	7 39·3	7 40·5	7 18·3	3·7	1·9	9·7	4·9	15·7	8·0
38	7 39·5	7 40·8	7 18·6	3·8	1·9	9·8	5·0	15·8	8·0
39	7 39·8	7 41·0	7 18·8	3·9	2·0	9·9	5·0	15·9	8·1
40	7 40·0	7 41·3	7 19·0	4·0	2·0	10·0	5·1	16·0	8·1
41	7 40·3	7 41·5	7 19·3	4·1	2·1	10·1	5·1	16·1	8·2
42	7 40·5	7 41·8	7 19·5	4·2	2·1	10·2	5·2	16·2	8·2
43	7 40·8	7 42·0	7 19·8	4·3	2·2	10·3	5·2	16·3	8·3
44	7 41·0	7 42·3	7 20·0	4·4	2·2	10·4	5·3	16·4	8·3
45	7 41·3	7 42·5	7 20·2	4·5	2·3	10·5	5·3	16·5	8·4
46	7 41·5	7 42·8	7 20·5	4·6	2·3	10·6	5·4	16·6	8·4
47	7 41·8	7 43·0	7 20·7	4·7	2·4	10·7	5·4	16·7	8·5
48	7 42·0	7 43·3	7 21·0	4·8	2·4	10·8	5·5	16·8	8·5
49	7 42·3	7 43·5	7 21·2	4·9	2·5	10·9	5·5	16·9	8·6
50	7 42·5	7 43·8	7 21·4	5·0	2·5	11·0	5·6	17·0	8·6
51	7 42·8	7 44·0	7 21·7	5·1	2·6	11·1	5·6	17·1	8·7
52	7 43·0	7 44·3	7 21·9	5·2	2·6	11·2	5·7	17·2	8·7
53	7 43·3	7 44·5	7 22·1	5·3	2·7	11·3	5·7	17·3	8·8
54	7 43·5	7 44·8	7 22·4	5·4	2·7	11·4	5·8	17·4	8·8
55	7 43·8	7 45·0	7 22·6	5·5	2·8	11·5	5·8	17·5	8·9
56	7 44·0	7 45·3	7 22·9	5·6	2·8	11·6	5·9	17·6	8·9
57	7 44·3	7 45·5	7 23·1	5·7	2·9	11·7	5·9	17·7	9·0
58	7 44·5	7 45·8	7 23·3	5·8	2·9	11·8	6·0	17·8	9·0
59	7 44·8	7 46·0	7 23·6	5·9	3·0	11·9	6·0	17·9	9·1
60	7 45·0	7 46·3	7 23·8	6·0	3·1	12·0	6·1	18·0	9·2

31m s	SUN PLANETS ° ′	ARIES ° ′	MOON ° ′	v or d ′	Corrn ′	v or d ′	Corrn ′	v or d ′	Corrn ′
00	7 45·0	7 46·3	7 23·8	0·0	0·0	6·0	3·2	12·0	6·3
01	7 45·3	7 46·5	7 24·1	0·1	0·1	6·1	3·2	12·1	6·4
02	7 45·5	7 46·8	7 24·3	0·2	0·1	6·2	3·3	12·2	6·4
03	7 45·8	7 47·0	7 24·5	0·3	0·2	6·3	3·3	12·3	6·5
04	7 46·0	7 47·3	7 24·8	0·4	0·2	6·4	3·4	12·4	6·5
05	7 46·3	7 47·5	7 25·0	0·5	0·3	6·5	3·4	12·5	6·6
06	7 46·5	7 47·8	7 25·2	0·6	0·3	6·6	3·5	12·6	6·6
07	7 46·8	7 48·0	7 25·5	0·7	0·4	6·7	3·5	12·7	6·7
08	7 47·0	7 48·3	7 25·7	0·8	0·4	6·8	3·6	12·8	6·7
09	7 47·3	7 48·5	7 26·0	0·9	0·5	6·9	3·6	12·9	6·8
10	7 47·5	7 48·8	7 26·2	1·0	0·5	7·0	3·7	13·0	6·8
11	7 47·8	7 49·0	7 26·4	1·1	0·6	7·1	3·7	13·1	6·9
12	7 48·0	7 49·3	7 26·7	1·2	0·6	7·2	3·8	13·2	6·9
13	7 48·3	7 49·5	7 26·9	1·3	0·7	7·3	3·8	13·3	7·0
14	7 48·5	7 49·8	7 27·2	1·4	0·7	7·4	3·9	13·4	7·0
15	7 48·8	7 50·0	7 27·4	1·5	0·8	7·5	3·9	13·5	7·1
16	7 49·0	7 50·3	7 27·6	1·6	0·8	7·6	4·0	13·6	7·1
17	7 49·3	7 50·5	7 27·9	1·7	0·9	7·7	4·0	13·7	7·2
18	7 49·5	7 50·8	7 28·1	1·8	0·9	7·8	4·1	13·8	7·2
19	7 49·8	7 51·0	7 28·4	1·9	1·0	7·9	4·1	13·9	7·3
20	7 50·0	7 51·3	7 28·6	2·0	1·1	8·0	4·2	14·0	7·4
21	7 50·3	7 51·5	7 28·8	2·1	1·1	8·1	4·3	14·1	7·4
22	7 50·5	7 51·8	7 29·1	2·2	1·2	8·2	4·3	14·2	7·5
23	7 50·8	7 52·0	7 29·3	2·3	1·2	8·3	4·4	14·3	7·5
24	7 51·0	7 52·3	7 29·5	2·4	1·3	8·4	4·4	14·4	7·6
25	7 51·3	7 52·5	7 29·8	2·5	1·3	8·5	4·5	14·5	7·6
26	7 51·5	7 52·8	7 30·0	2·6	1·4	8·6	4·5	14·6	7·7
27	7 51·8	7 53·0	7 30·3	2·7	1·4	8·7	4·6	14·7	7·7
28	7 52·0	7 53·3	7 30·5	2·8	1·5	8·8	4·6	14·8	7·8
29	7 52·3	7 53·5	7 30·7	2·9	1·5	8·9	4·7	14·9	7·8
30	7 52·5	7 53·8	7 31·0	3·0	1·6	9·0	4·7	15·0	7·9
31	7 52·8	7 54·0	7 31·2	3·1	1·6	9·1	4·8	15·1	7·9
32	7 53·0	7 54·3	7 31·5	3·2	1·7	9·2	4·8	15·2	8·0
33	7 53·3	7 54·5	7 31·7	3·3	1·7	9·3	4·9	15·3	8·0
34	7 53·5	7 54·8	7 31·9	3·4	1·8	9·4	4·9	15·4	8·1
35	7 53·8	7 55·0	7 32·2	3·5	1·8	9·5	5·0	15·5	8·1
36	7 54·0	7 55·3	7 32·4	3·6	1·9	9·6	5·0	15·6	8·2
37	7 54·3	7 55·5	7 32·6	3·7	1·9	9·7	5·1	15·7	8·2
38	7 54·5	7 55·8	7 32·9	3·8	2·0	9·8	5·1	15·8	8·3
39	7 54·8	7 56·0	7 33·1	3·9	2·0	9·9	5·2	15·9	8·3
40	7 55·0	7 56·3	7 33·4	4·0	2·1	10·0	5·3	16·0	8·4
41	7 55·3	7 56·6	7 33·6	4·1	2·2	10·1	5·3	16·1	8·5
42	7 55·5	7 56·8	7 33·8	4·2	2·2	10·2	5·4	16·2	8·5
43	7 55·8	7 57·1	7 34·1	4·3	2·3	10·3	5·4	16·3	8·6
44	7 56·0	7 57·3	7 34·3	4·4	2·3	10·4	5·5	16·4	8·6
45	7 56·3	7 57·6	7 34·6	4·5	2·4	10·5	5·5	16·5	8·7
46	7 56·5	7 57·8	7 34·8	4·6	2·4	10·6	5·6	16·6	8·7
47	7 56·8	7 58·1	7 35·0	4·7	2·5	10·7	5·6	16·7	8·8
48	7 57·0	7 58·3	7 35·3	4·8	2·5	10·8	5·7	16·8	8·8
49	7 57·3	7 58·6	7 35·5	4·9	2·6	10·9	5·7	16·9	8·9
50	7 57·5	7 58·8	7 35·7	5·0	2·6	11·0	5·8	17·0	8·9
51	7 57·8	7 59·1	7 36·0	5·1	2·7	11·1	5·8	17·1	9·0
52	7 58·0	7 59·3	7 36·2	5·2	2·7	11·2	5·9	17·2	9·0
53	7 58·3	7 59·6	7 36·5	5·3	2·8	11·3	5·9	17·3	9·1
54	7 58·5	7 59·8	7 36·7	5·4	2·8	11·4	6·0	17·4	9·1
55	7 58·8	8 00·1	7 36·9	5·5	2·9	11·5	6·0	17·5	9·2
56	7 59·0	8 00·3	7 37·2	5·6	2·9	11·6	6·1	17·6	9·2
57	7 59·3	8 00·6	7 37·4	5·7	3·0	11·7	6·1	17·7	9·3
58	7 59·5	8 00·8	7 37·7	5·8	3·0	11·8	6·2	17·8	9·3
59	7 59·8	8 01·1	7 37·9	5·9	3·1	11·9	6·2	17·9	9·4
60	8 00·0	8 01·3	7 38·1	6·0	3·2	12·0	6·3	18·0	9·5

32m	SUN PLANETS	ARIES	MOON	v or d	Corrn	v or d	Corrn	v or d	Corrn
s	° ′	° ′	° ′	′	′	′	′	′	′
00	8 00·0	8 01·3	7 38·1	0·0	0·0	6·0	3·3	12·0	6·5
01	8 00·3	8 01·6	7 38·4	0·1	0·1	6·1	3·3	12·1	6·6
02	8 00·5	8 01·8	7 38·6	0·2	0·1	6·2	3·4	12·2	6·6
03	8 00·8	8 02·1	7 38·8	0·3	0·2	6·3	3·4	12·3	6·7
04	8 01·0	8 02·3	7 39·1	0·4	0·2	6·4	3·5	12·4	6·7
05	8 01·3	8 02·6	7 39·3	0·5	0·3	6·5	3·5	12·5	6·8
06	8 01·5	8 02·8	7 39·6	0·6	0·3	6·6	3·6	12·6	6·8
07	8 01·8	8 03·1	7 39·8	0·7	0·4	6·7	3·6	12·7	6·9
08	8 02·0	8 03·3	7 40·0	0·8	0·4	6·8	3·7	12·8	6·9
09	8 02·3	8 03·6	7 40·3	0·9	0·5	6·9	3·7	12·9	7·0
10	8 02·5	8 03·8	7 40·5	1·0	0·5	7·0	3·8	13·0	7·0
11	8 02·8	8 04·1	7 40·8	1·1	0·6	7·1	3·8	13·1	7·1
12	8 03·0	8 04·3	7 41·0	1·2	0·7	7·2	3·9	13·2	7·2
13	8 03·3	8 04·6	7 41·2	1·3	0·7	7·3	4·0	13·3	7·2
14	8 03·5	8 04·8	7 41·5	1·4	0·8	7·4	4·0	13·4	7·3
15	8 03·8	8 05·1	7 41·7	1·5	0·8	7·5	4·1	13·5	7·3
16	8 04·0	8 05·3	7 42·0	1·6	0·9	7·6	4·1	13·6	7·4
17	8 04·3	8 05·6	7 42·2	1·7	0·9	7·7	4·2	13·7	7·4
18	8 04·5	8 05·8	7 42·4	1·8	1·0	7·8	4·2	13·8	7·5
19	8 04·8	8 06·1	7 42·7	1·9	1·0	7·9	4·3	13·9	7·5
20	8 05·0	8 06·3	7 42·9	2·0	1·1	8·0	4·3	14·0	7·6
21	8 05·3	8 06·6	7 43·1	2·1	1·1	8·1	4·4	14·1	7·6
22	8 05·5	8 06·8	7 43·4	2·2	1·2	8·2	4·4	14·2	7·7
23	8 05·8	8 07·1	7 43·6	2·3	1·2	8·3	4·5	14·3	7·7
24	8 06·0	8 07·3	7 43·9	2·4	1·3	8·4	4·6	14·4	7·8
25	8 06·3	8 07·6	7 44·1	2·5	1·4	8·5	4·6	14·5	7·9
26	8 06·5	8 07·8	7 44·3	2·6	1·4	8·6	4·7	14·6	7·9
27	8 06·8	8 08·1	7 44·6	2·7	1·5	8·7	4·7	14·7	8·0
28	8 07·0	8 08·3	7 44·8	2·8	1·5	8·8	4·8	14·8	8·0
29	8 07·3	8 08·6	7 45·1	2·9	1·6	8·9	4·8	14·9	8·1
30	8 07·5	8 08·8	7 45·3	3·0	1·6	9·0	4·9	15·0	8·1
31	8 07·8	8 09·1	7 45·5	3·1	1·7	9·1	4·9	15·1	8·2
32	8 08·0	8 09·3	7 45·8	3·2	1·7	9·2	5·0	15·2	8·2
33	8 08·3	8 09·6	7 46·0	3·3	1·8	9·3	5·0	15·3	8·3
34	8 08·5	8 09·8	7 46·2	3·4	1·8	9·4	5·1	15·4	8·3
35	8 08·8	8 10·1	7 46·5	3·5	1·9	9·5	5·1	15·5	8·4
36	8 09·0	8 10·3	7 46·7	3·6	2·0	9·6	5·2	15·6	8·5
37	8 09·3	8 10·6	7 47·0	3·7	2·0	9·7	5·3	15·7	8·5
38	8 09·5	8 10·8	7 47·2	3·8	2·1	9·8	5·3	15·8	8·6
39	8 09·8	8 11·1	7 47·4	3·9	2·1	9·9	5·4	15·9	8·6
40	8 10·0	8 11·3	7 47·7	4·0	2·2	10·0	5·4	16·0	8·7
41	8 10·3	8 11·6	7 47·9	4·1	2·2	10·1	5·5	16·1	8·7
42	8 10·5	8 11·8	7 48·2	4·2	2·3	10·2	5·5	16·2	8·8
43	8 10·8	8 12·1	7 48·4	4·3	2·3	10·3	5·6	16·3	8·8
44	8 11·0	8 12·3	7 48·6	4·4	2·4	10·4	5·6	16·4	8·9
45	8 11·3	8 12·6	7 48·9	4·5	2·4	10·5	5·7	16·5	8·9
46	8 11·5	8 12·8	7 49·1	4·6	2·5	10·6	5·7	16·6	9·0
47	8 11·8	8 13·1	7 49·3	4·7	2·5	10·7	5·8	16·7	9·0
48	8 12·0	8 13·3	7 49·6	4·8	2·6	10·8	5·9	16·8	9·1
49	8 12·3	8 13·6	7 49·8	4·9	2·7	10·9	5·9	16·9	9·2
50	8 12·5	8 13·8	7 50·1	5·0	2·7	11·0	6·0	17·0	9·2
51	8 12·8	8 14·1	7 50·3	5·1	2·8	11·1	6·0	17·1	9·3
52	8 13·0	8 14·3	7 50·5	5·2	2·8	11·2	6·1	17·2	9·3
53	8 13·3	8 14·6	7 50·8	5·3	2·9	11·3	6·1	17·3	9·4
54	8 13·5	8 14·9	7 51·0	5·4	2·9	11·4	6·2	17·4	9·4
55	8 13·8	8 15·1	7 51·3	5·5	3·0	11·5	6·2	17·5	9·5
56	8 14·0	8 15·4	7 51·5	5·6	3·0	11·6	6·3	17·6	9·5
57	8 14·3	8 15·6	7 51·7	5·7	3·1	11·7	6·3	17·7	9·6
58	8 14·5	8 15·9	7 52·0	5·8	3·1	11·8	6·4	17·8	9·6
59	8 14·8	8 16·1	7 52·2	5·9	3·2	11·9	6·4	17·9	9·7
60	8 15·0	8 16·4	7 52·5	6·0	3·3	12·0	6·5	18·0	9·8

33m	SUN PLANETS	ARIES	MOON	v or d	Corrn	v or d	Corrn	v or d	Corrn
s	° ′	° ′	° ′	′	′	′	′	′	′
00	8 15·0	8 16·4	7 52·5	0·0	0·0	6·0	3·4	12·0	6·7
01	8 15·3	8 16·6	7 52·7	0·1	0·1	6·1	3·4	12·1	6·8
02	8 15·5	8 16·9	7 52·9	0·2	0·1	6·2	3·5	12·2	6·8
03	8 15·8	8 17·1	7 53·2	0·3	0·2	6·3	3·5	12·3	6·9
04	8 16·0	8 17·4	7 53·4	0·4	0·2	6·4	3·6	12·4	6·9
05	8 16·3	8 17·6	7 53·6	0·5	0·3	6·5	3·6	12·5	7·0
06	8 16·5	8 17·9	7 53·9	0·6	0·3	6·6	3·7	12·6	7·0
07	8 16·8	8 18·1	7 54·1	0·7	0·4	6·7	3·7	12·7	7·1
08	8 17·0	8 18·4	7 54·4	0·8	0·4	6·8	3·8	12·8	7·1
09	8 17·3	8 18·6	7 54·6	0·9	0·5	6·9	3·9	12·9	7·2
10	8 17·5	8 18·9	7 54·8	1·0	0·6	7·0	3·9	13·0	7·3
11	8 17·8	8 19·1	7 55·1	1·1	0·6	7·1	4·0	13·1	7·3
12	8 18·0	8 19·4	7 55·3	1·2	0·7	7·2	4·0	13·2	7·4
13	8 18·3	8 19·6	7 55·6	1·3	0·7	7·3	4·1	13·3	7·4
14	8 18·5	8 19·9	7 55·8	1·4	0·8	7·4	4·1	13·4	7·5
15	8 18·8	8 20·1	7 56·0	1·5	0·8	7·5	4·2	13·5	7·5
16	8 19·0	8 20·4	7 56·3	1·6	0·9	7·6	4·2	13·6	7·6
17	8 19·3	8 20·6	7 56·5	1·7	0·9	7·7	4·3	13·7	7·6
18	8 19·5	8 20·9	7 56·7	1·8	1·0	7·8	4·4	13·8	7·7
19	8 19·8	8 21·1	7 57·0	1·9	1·1	7·9	4·4	13·9	7·8
20	8 20·0	8 21·4	7 57·2	2·0	1·1	8·0	4·5	14·0	7·8
21	8 20·3	8 21·6	7 57·5	2·1	1·2	8·1	4·5	14·1	7·9
22	8 20·5	8 21·9	7 57·7	2·2	1·2	8·2	4·6	14·2	7·9
23	8 20·8	8 22·1	7 57·9	2·3	1·3	8·3	4·6	14·3	8·0
24	8 21·0	8 22·4	7 58·2	2·4	1·3	8·4	4·7	14·4	8·0
25	8 21·3	8 22·6	7 58·4	2·5	1·4	8·5	4·7	14·5	8·1
26	8 21·5	8 22·9	7 58·7	2·6	1·5	8·6	4·8	14·6	8·2
27	8 21·8	8 23·1	7 58·9	2·7	1·5	8·7	4·9	14·7	8·2
28	8 22·0	8 23·4	7 59·1	2·8	1·6	8·8	4·9	14·8	8·3
29	8 22·3	8 23·6	7 59·4	2·9	1·6	8·9	5·0	14·9	8·3
30	8 22·5	8 23·9	7 59·6	3·0	1·7	9·0	5·0	15·0	8·4
31	8 22·8	8 24·1	7 59·8	3·1	1·7	9·1	5·1	15·1	8·4
32	8 23·0	8 24·4	8 00·1	3·2	1·8	9·2	5·1	15·2	8·5
33	8 23·3	8 24·6	8 00·3	3·3	1·8	9·3	5·2	15·3	8·5
34	8 23·5	8 24·9	8 00·6	3·4	1·9	9·4	5·2	15·4	8·6
35	8 23·8	8 25·1	8 00·8	3·5	2·0	9·5	5·3	15·5	8·7
36	8 24·0	8 25·4	8 01·0	3·6	2·0	9·6	5·4	15·6	8·7
37	8 24·3	8 25·6	8 01·3	3·7	2·1	9·7	5·4	15·7	8·8
38	8 24·5	8 25·9	8 01·5	3·8	2·1	9·8	5·5	15·8	8·8
39	8 24·8	8 26·1	8 01·8	3·9	2·2	9·9	5·5	15·9	8·9
40	8 25·0	8 26·4	8 02·0	4·0	2·2	10·0	5·6	16·0	8·9
41	8 25·3	8 26·6	8 02·2	4·1	2·3	10·1	5·6	16·1	9·0
42	8 25·5	8 26·9	8 02·5	4·2	2·3	10·2	5·7	16·2	9·0
43	8 25·8	8 27·1	8 02·7	4·3	2·4	10·3	5·8	16·3	9·1
44	8 26·0	8 27·4	8 02·9	4·4	2·5	10·4	5·8	16·4	9·2
45	8 26·3	8 27·6	8 03·2	4·5	2·5	10·5	5·9	16·5	9·2
46	8 26·5	8 27·9	8 03·4	4·6	2·6	10·6	5·9	16·6	9·3
47	8 26·8	8 28·1	8 03·7	4·7	2·6	10·7	6·0	16·7	9·3
48	8 27·0	8 28·4	8 03·9	4·8	2·7	10·8	6·0	16·8	9·4
49	8 27·3	8 28·6	8 04·1	4·9	2·7	10·9	6·1	16·9	9·4
50	8 27·5	8 28·9	8 04·4	5·0	2·8	11·0	6·1	17·0	9·5
51	8 27·8	8 29·1	8 04·6	5·1	2·8	11·1	6·2	17·1	9·5
52	8 28·0	8 29·4	8 04·9	5·2	2·9	11·2	6·3	17·2	9·6
53	8 28·3	8 29·6	8 05·1	5·3	3·0	11·3	6·3	17·3	9·7
54	8 28·5	8 29·9	8 05·3	5·4	3·0	11·4	6·4	17·4	9·7
55	8 28·8	8 30·1	8 05·6	5·5	3·1	11·5	6·4	17·5	9·8
56	8 29·0	8 30·4	8 05·8	5·6	3·1	11·6	6·5	17·6	9·8
57	8 29·3	8 30·6	8 06·1	5·7	3·2	11·7	6·5	17·7	9·9
58	8 29·5	8 30·9	8 06·3	5·8	3·2	11·8	6·6	17·8	9·9
59	8 29·8	8 31·1	8 06·5	5·9	3·3	11·9	6·6	17·9	10·0
60	8 30·0	8 31·4	8 06·8	6·0	3·4	12·0	6·7	18·0	10·1

34m s	SUN PLANETS ° ′	ARIES ° ′	MOON ° ′	v or d ′	Corrⁿ ′	v or d ′	Corrⁿ ′	v or d ′	Corrⁿ ′
00	8 30·0	8 31·4	8 06·8	0·0	0·0	6·0	3·5	12·0	6·9
01	8 30·3	8 31·6	8 07·0	0·1	0·1	6·1	3·5	12·1	7·0
02	8 30·5	8 31·9	8 07·2	0·2	0·1	6·2	3·6	12·2	7·0
03	8 30·8	8 32·1	8 07·5	0·3	0·2	6·3	3·6	12·3	7·1
04	8 31·0	8 32·4	8 07·7	0·4	0·2	6·4	3·7	12·4	7·1
05	8 31·3	8 32·6	8 08·0	0·5	0·3	6·5	3·7	12·5	7·2
06	8 31·5	8 32·9	8 08·2	0·6	0·3	6·6	3·8	12·6	7·2
07	8 31·8	8 33·2	8 08·4	0·7	0·4	6·7	3·9	12·7	7·3
08	8 32·0	8 33·4	8 08·7	0·8	0·5	6·8	3·9	12·8	7·4
09	8 32·3	8 33·7	8 08·9	0·9	0·5	6·9	4·0	12·9	7·4
10	8 32·5	8 33·9	8 09·2	1·0	0·6	7·0	4·0	13·0	7·5
11	8 32·8	8 34·2	8 09·4	1·1	0·6	7·1	4·1	13·1	7·5
12	8 33·0	8 34·4	8 09·6	1·2	0·7	7·2	4·1	13·2	7·6
13	8 33·3	8 34·7	8 09·9	1·3	0·7	7·3	4·2	13·3	7·6
14	8 33·5	8 34·9	8 10·1	1·4	0·8	7·4	4·3	13·4	7·7
15	8 33·8	8 35·2	8 10·3	1·5	0·9	7·5	4·3	13·5	7·8
16	8 34·0	8 35·4	8 10·6	1·6	0·9	7·6	4·4	13·6	7·8
17	8 34·3	8 35·7	8 10·8	1·7	1·0	7·7	4·4	13·7	7·9
18	8 34·5	8 35·9	8 11·1	1·8	1·0	7·8	4·5	13·8	7·9
19	8 34·8	8 36·2	8 11·3	1·9	1·1	7·9	4·5	13·9	8·0
20	8 35·0	8 36·4	8 11·5	2·0	1·2	8·0	4·6	14·0	8·1
21	8 35·3	8 36·7	8 11·8	2·1	1·2	8·1	4·7	14·1	8·1
22	8 35·5	8 36·9	8 12·0	2·2	1·3	8·2	4·7	14·2	8·2
23	8 35·8	8 37·2	8 12·3	2·3	1·3	8·3	4·8	14·3	8·2
24	8 36·0	8 37·4	8 12·5	2·4	1·4	8·4	4·8	14·4	8·3
25	8 36·3	8 37·7	8 12·7	2·5	1·4	8·5	4·9	14·5	8·3
26	8 36·5	8 37·9	8 13·0	2·6	1·5	8·6	4·9	14·6	8·4
27	8 36·8	8 38·2	8 13·2	2·7	1·6	8·7	5·0	14·7	8·5
28	8 37·0	8 38·4	8 13·4	2·8	1·6	8·8	5·1	14·8	8·5
29	8 37·3	8 38·7	8 13·7	2·9	1·7	8·9	5·1	14·9	8·6
30	8 37·5	8 38·9	8 13·9	3·0	1·7	9·0	5·2	15·0	8·6
31	8 37·8	8 39·2	8 14·2	3·1	1·8	9·1	5·2	15·1	8·7
32	8 38·0	8 39·4	8 14·4	3·2	1·8	9·2	5·3	15·2	8·7
33	8 38·3	8 39·7	8 14·6	3·3	1·9	9·3	5·3	15·3	8·8
34	8 38·5	8 39·9	8 14·9	3·4	2·0	9·4	5·4	15·4	8·9
35	8 38·8	8 40·2	8 15·1	3·5	2·0	9·5	5·5	15·5	8·9
36	8 39·0	8 40·4	8 15·4	3·6	2·1	9·6	5·5	15·6	9·0
37	8 39·3	8 40·7	8 15·6	3·7	2·1	9·7	5·6	15·7	9·0
38	8 39·5	8 40·9	8 15·8	3·8	2·2	9·8	5·6	15·8	9·1
39	8 39·8	8 41·2	8 16·1	3·9	2·2	9·9	5·7	15·9	9·1
40	8 40·0	8 41·4	8 16·3	4·0	2·3	10·0	5·8	16·0	9·2
41	8 40·3	8 41·7	8 16·5	4·1	2·4	10·1	5·8	16·1	9·3
42	8 40·5	8 41·9	8 16·8	4·2	2·4	10·2	5·9	16·2	9·3
43	8 40·8	8 42·2	8 17·0	4·3	2·5	10·3	5·9	16·3	9·4
44	8 41·0	8 42·4	8 17·3	4·4	2·5	10·4	6·0	16·4	9·4
45	8 41·3	8 42·7	8 17·5	4·5	2·6	10·5	6·0	16·5	9·5
46	8 41·5	8 42·9	8 17·7	4·6	2·6	10·6	6·1	16·6	9·5
47	8 41·8	8 43·2	8 18·0	4·7	2·7	10·7	6·2	16·7	9·6
48	8 42·0	8 43·4	8 18·2	4·8	2·8	10·8	6·2	16·8	9·7
49	8 42·3	8 43·7	8 18·5	4·9	2·8	10·9	6·3	16·9	9·7
50	8 42·5	8 43·9	8 18·7	5·0	2·9	11·0	6·3	17·0	9·8
51	8 42·8	8 44·2	8 18·9	5·1	2·9	11·1	6·4	17·1	9·8
52	8 43·0	8 44·4	8 19·2	5·2	3·0	11·2	6·4	17·2	9·9
53	8 43·3	8 44·7	8 19·4	5·3	3·0	11·3	6·5	17·3	9·9
54	8 43·5	8 44·9	8 19·7	5·4	3·1	11·4	6·6	17·4	10·0
55	8 43·8	8 45·2	8 19·9	5·5	3·2	11·5	6·6	17·5	10·1
56	8 44·0	8 45·4	8 20·1	5·6	3·2	11·6	6·7	17·6	10·1
57	8 44·3	8 45·7	8 20·4	5·7	3·3	11·7	6·7	17·7	10·2
58	8 44·5	8 45·9	8 20·6	5·8	3·3	11·8	6·8	17·8	10·2
59	8 44·8	8 46·2	8 20·8	5·9	3·4	11·9	6·8	17·9	10·3
60	8 45·0	8 46·4	8 21·1	6·0	3·5	12·0	6·9	18·0	10·4

35m s	SUN PLANETS ° ′	ARIES ° ′	MOON ° ′	v or d ′	Corrⁿ ′	v or d ′	Corrⁿ ′	v or d ′	Corrⁿ ′
00	8 45·0	8 46·4	8 21·1	0·0	0·0	6·0	3·6	12·0	7·1
01	8 45·3	8 46·7	8 21·3	0·1	0·1	6·1	3·6	12·1	7·2
02	8 45·5	8 46·9	8 21·6	0·2	0·1	6·2	3·7	12·2	7·2
03	8 45·8	8 47·2	8 21·8	0·3	0·2	6·3	3·7	12·3	7·3
04	8 46·0	8 47·4	8 22·0	0·4	0·2	6·4	3·8	12·4	7·3
05	8 46·3	8 47·7	8 22·3	0·5	0·3	6·5	3·8	12·5	7·4
06	8 46·5	8 47·9	8 22·5	0·6	0·4	6·6	3·9	12·6	7·5
07	8 46·8	8 48·2	8 22·8	0·7	0·4	6·7	4·0	12·7	7·5
08	8 47·0	8 48·4	8 23·0	0·8	0·5	6·8	4·0	12·8	7·6
09	8 47·3	8 48·7	8 23·2	0·9	0·5	6·9	4·1	12·9	7·6
10	8 47·5	8 48·9	8 23·5	1·0	0·6	7·0	4·1	13·0	7·7
11	8 47·8	8 49·2	8 23·7	1·1	0·7	7·1	4·2	13·1	7·8
12	8 48·0	8 49·4	8 23·9	1·2	0·7	7·2	4·3	13·2	7·8
13	8 48·3	8 49·7	8 24·2	1·3	0·8	7·3	4·3	13·3	7·9
14	8 48·5	8 49·9	8 24·4	1·4	0·8	7·4	4·4	13·4	7·9
15	8 48·8	8 50·2	8 24·7	1·5	0·9	7·5	4·4	13·5	8·0
16	8 49·0	8 50·4	8 24·9	1·6	0·9	7·6	4·5	13·6	8·0
17	8 49·3	8 50·7	8 25·1	1·7	1·0	7·7	4·6	13·7	8·1
18	8 49·5	8 50·9	8 25·4	1·8	1·1	7·8	4·6	13·8	8·2
19	8 49·8	8 51·2	8 25·6	1·9	1·1	7·9	4·7	13·9	8·2
20	8 50·0	8 51·5	8 25·9	2·0	1·2	8·0	4·7	14·0	8·3
21	8 50·3	8 51·7	8 26·1	2·1	1·2	8·1	4·8	14·1	8·3
22	8 50·5	8 52·0	8 26·3	2·2	1·3	8·2	4·9	14·2	8·4
23	8 50·8	8 52·2	8 26·6	2·3	1·4	8·3	4·9	14·3	8·5
24	8 51·0	8 52·5	8 26·8	2·4	1·4	8·4	5·0	14·4	8·5
25	8 51·3	8 52·7	8 27·0	2·5	1·5	8·5	5·0	14·5	8·6
26	8 51·5	8 53·0	8 27·3	2·6	1·5	8·6	5·1	14·6	8·6
27	8 51·8	8 53·2	8 27·5	2·7	1·6	8·7	5·1	14·7	8·7
28	8 52·0	8 53·5	8 27·8	2·8	1·7	8·8	5·2	14·8	8·8
29	8 52·3	8 53·7	8 28·0	2·9	1·7	8·9	5·3	14·9	8·8
30	8 52·5	8 54·0	8 28·2	3·0	1·8	9·0	5·3	15·0	8·9
31	8 52·8	8 54·2	8 28·5	3·1	1·8	9·1	5·4	15·1	8·9
32	8 53·0	8 54·5	8 28·7	3·2	1·9	9·2	5·4	15·2	9·0
33	8 53·3	8 54·7	8 29·0	3·3	2·0	9·3	5·5	15·3	9·1
34	8 53·5	8 55·0	8 29·2	3·4	2·0	9·4	5·6	15·4	9·1
35	8 53·8	8 55·2	8 29·4	3·5	2·1	9·5	5·6	15·5	9·2
36	8 54·0	8 55·5	8 29·7	3·6	2·1	9·6	5·7	15·6	9·2
37	8 54·3	8 55·7	8 29·9	3·7	2·2	9·7	5·7	15·7	9·3
38	8 54·5	8 56·0	8 30·2	3·8	2·2	9·8	5·8	15·8	9·3
39	8 54·8	8 56·2	8 30·4	3·9	2·3	9·9	5·9	15·9	9·4
40	8 55·0	8 56·5	8 30·6	4·0	2·4	10·0	5·9	16·0	9·5
41	8 55·3	8 56·7	8 30·9	4·1	2·4	10·1	6·0	16·1	9·5
42	8 55·5	8 57·0	8 31·1	4·2	2·5	10·2	6·0	16·2	9·6
43	8 55·8	8 57·2	8 31·3	4·3	2·5	10·3	6·1	16·3	9·6
44	8 56·0	8 57·5	8 31·6	4·4	2·6	10·4	6·2	16·4	9·7
45	8 56·3	8 57·7	8 31·8	4·5	2·7	10·5	6·2	16·5	9·8
46	8 56·5	8 58·0	8 32·1	4·6	2·7	10·6	6·3	16·6	9·8
47	8 56·8	8 58·2	8 32·3	4·7	2·8	10·7	6·3	16·7	9·9
48	8 57·0	8 58·5	8 32·5	4·8	2·8	10·8	6·4	16·8	9·9
49	8 57·3	8 58·7	8 32·8	4·9	2·9	10·9	6·4	16·9	10·0
50	8 57·5	8 59·0	8 33·0	5·0	3·0	11·0	6·5	17·0	10·1
51	8 57·8	8 59·2	8 33·3	5·1	3·0	11·1	6·6	17·1	10·1
52	8 58·0	8 59·5	8 33·5	5·2	3·1	11·2	6·6	17·2	10·2
53	8 58·3	8 59·7	8 33·7	5·3	3·1	11·3	6·7	17·3	10·2
54	8 58·5	9 00·0	8 34·0	5·4	3·2	11·4	6·7	17·4	10·3
55	8 58·8	9 00·2	8 34·2	5·5	3·3	11·5	6·8	17·5	10·4
56	8 59·0	9 00·5	8 34·4	5·6	3·3	11·6	6·9	17·6	10·4
57	8 59·3	9 00·7	8 34·7	5·7	3·4	11·7	6·9	17·7	10·5
58	8 59·5	9 01·0	8 34·9	5·8	3·4	11·8	7·0	17·8	10·5
59	8 59·8	9 01·2	8 35·2	5·9	3·5	11·9	7·0	17·9	10·6
60	9 00·0	9 01·5	8 35·4	6·0	3·6	12·0	7·1	18·0	10·7

36m s	SUN PLANETS ° ′	ARIES ° ′	MOON ° ′	v or d ′	Corrn ′	v or d ′	Corrn ′	v or d ′	Corrn ′
00	9 00·0	9 01·5	8 35·4	0·0	0·0	6·0	3·7	12·0	7·3
01	9 00·3	9 01·7	8 35·6	0·1	0·1	6·1	3·7	12·1	7·4
02	9 00·5	9 02·0	8 35·9	0·2	0·1	6·2	3·8	12·2	7·4
03	9 00·8	9 02·2	8 36·1	0·3	0·2	6·3	3·8	12·3	7·5
04	9 01·0	9 02·5	8 36·4	0·4	0·2	6·4	3·9	12·4	7·5
05	9 01·3	9 02·7	8 36·6	0·5	0·3	6·5	4·0	12·5	7·6
06	9 01·5	9 03·0	8 36·8	0·6	0·4	6·6	4·0	12·6	7·7
07	9 01·8	9 03·2	8 37·1	0·7	0·4	6·7	4·1	12·7	7·7
08	9 02·0	9 03·5	8 37·3	0·8	0·5	6·8	4·1	12·8	7·8
09	9 02·3	9 03·7	8 37·5	0·9	0·5	6·9	4·2	12·9	7·8
10	9 02·5	9 04·0	8 37·8	1·0	0·6	7·0	4·3	13·0	7·9
11	9 02·8	9 04·2	8 38·0	1·1	0·7	7·1	4·3	13·1	8·0
12	9 03·0	9 04·5	8 38·3	1·2	0·7	7·2	4·4	13·2	8·0
13	9 03·3	9 04·7	8 38·5	1·3	0·8	7·3	4·4	13·3	8·1
14	9 03·5	9 05·0	8 38·7	1·4	0·9	7·4	4·5	13·4	8·2
15	9 03·8	9 05·2	8 39·0	1·5	0·9	7·5	4·6	13·5	8·2
16	9 04·0	9 05·5	8 39·2	1·6	1·0	7·6	4·6	13·6	8·3
17	9 04·3	9 05·7	8 39·5	1·7	1·0	7·7	4·7	13·7	8·3
18	9 04·5	9 06·0	8 39·7	1·8	1·1	7·8	4·7	13·8	8·4
19	9 04·8	9 06·2	8 39·9	1·9	1·2	7·9	4·8	13·9	8·5
20	9 05·0	9 06·5	8 40·2	2·0	1·2	8·0	4·9	14·0	8·5
21	9 05·3	9 06·7	8 40·4	2·1	1·3	8·1	4·9	14·1	8·6
22	9 05·5	9 07·0	8 40·6	2·2	1·3	8·2	5·0	14·2	8·6
23	9 05·8	9 07·2	8 40·9	2·3	1·4	8·3	5·0	14·3	8·7
24	9 06·0	9 07·5	8 41·1	2·4	1·5	8·4	5·1	14·4	8·8
25	9 06·3	9 07·7	8 41·4	2·5	1·5	8·5	5·2	14·5	8·8
26	9 06·5	9 08·0	8 41·6	2·6	1·6	8·6	5·2	14·6	8·9
27	9 06·8	9 08·2	8 41·8	2·7	1·6	8·7	5·3	14·7	8·9
28	9 07·0	9 08·5	8 42·1	2·8	1·7	8·8	5·4	14·8	9·0
29	9 07·3	9 08·7	8 42·3	2·9	1·8	8·9	5·4	14·9	9·1
30	9 07·5	9 09·0	8 42·6	3·0	1·8	9·0	5·5	15·0	9·1
31	9 07·8	9 09·2	8 42·8	3·1	1·9	9·1	5·5	15·1	9·2
32	9 08·0	9 09·5	8 43·0	3·2	1·9	9·2	5·6	15·2	9·2
33	9 08·3	9 09·8	8 43·3	3·3	2·0	9·3	5·7	15·3	9·3
34	9 08·5	9 10·0	8 43·5	3·4	2·1	9·4	5·7	15·4	9·4
35	9 08·8	9 10·3	8 43·8	3·5	2·1	9·5	5·8	15·5	9·4
36	9 09·0	9 10·5	8 44·0	3·6	2·2	9·6	5·8	15·6	9·5
37	9 09·3	9 10·8	8 44·2	3·7	2·3	9·7	5·9	15·7	9·6
38	9 09·5	9 11·0	8 44·5	3·8	2·3	9·8	6·0	15·8	9·6
39	9 09·8	9 11·3	8 44·7	3·9	2·4	9·9	6·0	15·9	9·7
40	9 10·0	9 11·5	8 44·9	4·0	2·4	10·0	6·1	16·0	9·7
41	9 10·3	9 11·8	8 45·2	4·1	2·5	10·1	6·1	16·1	9·8
42	9 10·5	9 12·0	8 45·4	4·2	2·6	10·2	6·2	16·2	9·9
43	9 10·8	9 12·3	8 45·7	4·3	2·6	10·3	6·3	16·3	9·9
44	9 11·0	9 12·5	8 45·9	4·4	2·7	10·4	6·3	16·4	10·0
45	9 11·3	9 12·8	8 46·1	4·5	2·7	10·5	6·4	16·5	10·0
46	9 11·5	9 13·0	8 46·4	4·6	2·8	10·6	6·4	16·6	10·1
47	9 11·8	9 13·3	8 46·6	4·7	2·9	10·7	6·5	16·7	10·2
48	9 12·0	9 13·5	8 46·9	4·8	2·9	10·8	6·6	16·8	10·2
49	9 12·3	9 13·8	8 47·1	4·9	3·0	10·9	6·6	16·9	10·3
50	9 12·5	9 14·0	8 47·3	5·0	3·0	11·0	6·7	17·0	10·3
51	9 12·8	9 14·3	8 47·6	5·1	3·1	11·1	6·8	17·1	10·4
52	9 13·0	9 14·5	8 47·8	5·2	3·2	11·2	6·8	17·2	10·5
53	9 13·3	9 14·8	8 48·0	5·3	3·2	11·3	6·9	17·3	10·5
54	9 13·5	9 15·0	8 48·3	5·4	3·3	11·4	6·9	17·4	10·6
55	9 13·8	9 15·3	8 48·5	5·5	3·3	11·5	7·0	17·5	10·6
56	9 14·0	9 15·5	8 48·8	5·6	3·4	11·6	7·1	17·6	10·7
57	9 14·3	9 15·8	8 49·0	5·7	3·5	11·7	7·1	17·7	10·8
58	9 14·5	9 16·0	8 49·2	5·8	3·5	11·8	7·2	17·8	10·8
59	9 14·8	9 16·3	8 49·5	5·9	3·6	11·9	7·2	17·9	10·9
60	9 15·0	9 16·5	8 49·7	6·0	3·7	12·0	7·3	18·0	11·0

37m s	SUN PLANETS ° ′	ARIES ° ′	MOON ° ′	v or d ′	Corrn ′	v or d ′	Corrn ′	v or d ′	Corrn ′
00	9 15·0	9 16·5	8 49·7	0·0	0·0	6·0	3·8	12·0	7·5
01	9 15·3	9 16·8	8 50·0	0·1	0·1	6·1	3·8	12·1	7·6
02	9 15·5	9 17·0	8 50·2	0·2	0·1	6·2	3·9	12·2	7·6
03	9 15·8	9 17·3	8 50·4	0·3	0·2	6·3	3·9	12·3	7·7
04	9 16·0	9 17·5	8 50·7	0·4	0·3	6·4	4·0	12·4	7·8
05	9 16·3	9 17·8	8 50·9	0·5	0·3	6·5	4·1	12·5	7·8
06	9 16·5	9 18·0	8 51·1	0·6	0·4	6·6	4·1	12·6	7·9
07	9 16·8	9 18·3	8 51·4	0·7	0·4	6·7	4·2	12·7	7·9
08	9 17·0	9 18·5	8 51·6	0·8	0·5	6·8	4·3	12·8	8·0
09	9 17·3	9 18·8	8 51·9	0·9	0·6	6·9	4·3	12·9	8·1
10	9 17·5	9 19·0	8 52·1	1·0	0·6	7·0	4·4	13·0	8·1
11	9 17·8	9 19·3	8 52·3	1·1	0·7	7·1	4·4	13·1	8·2
12	9 18·0	9 19·5	8 52·6	1·2	0·8	7·2	4·5	13·2	8·3
13	9 18·3	9 19·8	8 52·8	1·3	0·8	7·3	4·6	13·3	8·3
14	9 18·5	9 20·0	8 53·1	1·4	0·9	7·4	4·6	13·4	8·4
15	9 18·8	9 20·3	8 53·3	1·5	0·9	7·5	4·7	13·5	8·4
16	9 19·0	9 20·5	8 53·5	1·6	1·0	7·6	4·8	13·6	8·5
17	9 19·3	9 20·8	8 53·8	1·7	1·1	7·7	4·8	13·7	8·6
18	9 19·5	9 21·0	8 54·0	1·8	1·1	7·8	4·9	13·8	8·6
19	9 19·8	9 21·3	8 54·3	1·9	1·2	7·9	4·9	13·9	8·7
20	9 20·0	9 21·5	8 54·5	2·0	1·3	8·0	5·0	14·0	8·8
21	9 20·3	9 21·8	8 54·7	2·1	1·3	8·1	5·1	14·1	8·8
22	9 20·5	9 22·0	8 55·0	2·2	1·4	8·2	5·1	14·2	8·9
23	9 20·8	9 22·3	8 55·2	2·3	1·4	8·3	5·2	14·3	8·9
24	9 21·0	9 22·5	8 55·4	2·4	1·5	8·4	5·3	14·4	9·0
25	9 21·3	9 22·8	8 55·7	2·5	1·6	8·5	5·3	14·5	9·1
26	9 21·5	9 23·0	8 55·9	2·6	1·6	8·6	5·4	14·6	9·1
27	9 21·8	9 23·3	8 56·2	2·7	1·7	8·7	5·4	14·7	9·2
28	9 22·0	9 23·5	8 56·4	2·8	1·8	8·8	5·5	14·8	9·3
29	9 22·3	9 23·8	8 56·6	2·9	1·8	8·9	5·6	14·9	9·3
30	9 22·5	9 24·0	8 56·9	3·0	1·9	9·0	5·6	15·0	9·4
31	9 22·8	9 24·3	8 57·1	3·1	1·9	9·1	5·7	15·1	9·4
32	9 23·0	9 24·5	8 57·4	3·2	2·0	9·2	5·8	15·2	9·5
33	9 23·3	9 24·8	8 57·6	3·3	2·1	9·3	5·8	15·3	9·6
34	9 23·5	9 25·0	8 57·8	3·4	2·1	9·4	5·9	15·4	9·6
35	9 23·8	9 25·3	8 58·1	3·5	2·2	9·5	5·9	15·5	9·7
36	9 24·0	9 25·5	8 58·3	3·6	2·3	9·6	6·0	15·6	9·8
37	9 24·3	9 25·8	8 58·5	3·7	2·3	9·7	6·1	15·7	9·8
38	9 24·5	9 26·0	8 58·8	3·8	2·4	9·8	6·1	15·8	9·9
39	9 24·8	9 26·3	8 59·0	3·9	2·4	9·9	6·2	15·9	9·9
40	9 25·0	9 26·5	8 59·3	4·0	2·5	10·0	6·3	16·0	10·0
41	9 25·3	9 26·8	8 59·5	4·1	2·6	10·1	6·3	16·1	10·1
42	9 25·5	9 27·0	8 59·7	4·2	2·6	10·2	6·4	16·2	10·1
43	9 25·8	9 27·3	9 00·0	4·3	2·7	10·3	6·4	16·3	10·2
44	9 26·0	9 27·5	9 00·2	4·4	2·8	10·4	6·5	16·4	10·3
45	9 26·3	9 27·8	9 00·5	4·5	2·8	10·5	6·6	16·5	10·3
46	9 26·5	9 28·1	9 00·7	4·6	2·9	10·6	6·6	16·6	10·4
47	9 26·8	9 28·3	9 00·9	4·7	2·9	10·7	6·7	16·7	10·4
48	9 27·0	9 28·6	9 01·2	4·8	3·0	10·8	6·8	16·8	10·5
49	9 27·3	9 28·8	9 01·4	4·9	3·1	10·9	6·8	16·9	10·6
50	9 27·5	9 29·1	9 01·6	5·0	3·1	11·0	6·9	17·0	10·6
51	9 27·8	9 29·3	9 01·9	5·1	3·2	11·1	6·9	17·1	10·7
52	9 28·0	9 29·6	9 02·1	5·2	3·3	11·2	7·0	17·2	10·8
53	9 28·3	9 29·8	9 02·4	5·3	3·3	11·3	7·1	17·3	10·8
54	9 28·5	9 30·1	9 02·6	5·4	3·4	11·4	7·1	17·4	10·9
55	9 28·8	9 30·3	9 02·8	5·5	3·4	11·5	7·2	17·5	10·9
56	9 29·0	9 30·6	9 03·1	5·6	3·5	11·6	7·3	17·6	11·0
57	9 29·3	9 30·8	9 03·3	5·7	3·6	11·7	7·3	17·7	11·1
58	9 29·5	9 31·1	9 03·6	5·8	3·6	11·8	7·4	17·8	11·1
59	9 29·8	9 31·3	9 03·8	5·9	3·7	11·9	7·4	17·9	11·2
60	9 30·0	9 31·6	9 04·0	6·0	3·8	12·0	7·5	18·0	11·3

38m	SUN PLANETS	ARIES	MOON	v or d	Corrn	v or d	Corrn	v or d	Corrn
s	° ′	° ′	° ′	′	′	′	′	′	′
00	9 30·0	9 31·6	9 04·0	0·0	0·0	6·0	3·9	12·0	7·7
01	9 30·3	9 31·8	9 04·3	0·1	0·1	6·1	3·9	12·1	7·8
02	9 30·5	9 32·1	9 04·5	0·2	0·1	6·2	4·0	12·2	7·8
03	9 30·8	9 32·3	9 04·7	0·3	0·2	6·3	4·0	12·3	7·9
04	9 31·0	9 32·6	9 05·0	0·4	0·3	6·4	4·1	12·4	8·0
05	9 31·3	9 32·8	9 05·2	0·5	0·3	6·5	4·2	12·5	8·0
06	9 31·5	9 33·1	9 05·5	0·6	0·4	6·6	4·2	12·6	8·1
07	9 31·8	9 33·3	9 05·7	0·7	0·4	6·7	4·3	12·7	8·1
08	9 32·0	9 33·6	9 05·9	0·8	0·5	6·8	4·4	12·8	8·2
09	9 32·3	9 33·8	9 06·2	0·9	0·6	6·9	4·4	12·9	8·3
10	9 32·5	9 34·1	9 06·4	1·0	0·6	7·0	4·5	13·0	8·3
11	9 32·8	9 34·3	9 06·7	1·1	0·7	7·1	4·6	13·1	8·4
12	9 33·0	9 34·6	9 06·9	1·2	0·8	7·2	4·6	13·2	8·5
13	9 33·3	9 34·8	9 07·1	1·3	0·8	7·3	4·7	13·3	8·5
14	9 33·5	9 35·1	9 07·4	1·4	0·9	7·4	4·7	13·4	8·6
15	9 33·8	9 35·3	9 07·6	1·5	1·0	7·5	4·8	13·5	8·7
16	9 34·0	9 35·6	9 07·9	1·6	1·0	7·6	4·9	13·6	8·7
17	9 34·3	9 35·8	9 08·1	1·7	1·1	7·7	4·9	13·7	8·8
18	9 34·5	9 36·1	9 08·3	1·8	1·2	7·8	5·0	13·8	8·9
19	9 34·8	9 36·3	9 08·6	1·9	1·2	7·9	5·1	13·9	8·9
20	9 35·0	9 36·6	9 08·8	2·0	1·3	8·0	5·1	14·0	9·0
21	9 35·3	9 36·8	9 09·0	2·1	1·3	8·1	5·2	14·1	9·0
22	9 35·5	9 37·1	9 09·3	2·2	1·4	8·2	5·3	14·2	9·1
23	9 35·8	9 37·3	9 09·5	2·3	1·5	8·3	5·3	14·3	9·2
24	9 36·0	9 37·6	9 09·8	2·4	1·5	8·4	5·4	14·4	9·2
25	9 36·3	9 37·8	9 10·0	2·5	1·6	8·5	5·5	14·5	9·3
26	9 36·5	9 38·1	9 10·2	2·6	1·7	8·6	5·5	14·6	9·4
27	9 36·8	9 38·3	9 10·5	2·7	1·7	8·7	5·6	14·7	9·4
28	9 37·0	9 38·6	9 10·7	2·8	1·8	8·8	5·6	14·8	9·5
29	9 37·3	9 38·8	9 11·0	2·9	1·9	8·9	5·7	14·9	9·6
30	9 37·5	9 39·1	9 11·2	3·0	1·9	9·0	5·8	15·0	9·6
31	9 37·8	9 39·3	9 11·4	3·1	2·0	9·1	5·8	15·1	9·7
32	9 38·0	9 39·6	9 11·7	3·2	2·1	9·2	5·9	15·2	9·8
33	9 38·3	9 39·8	9 11·9	3·3	2·1	9·3	6·0	15·3	9·8
34	9 38·5	9 40·1	9 12·1	3·4	2·2	9·4	6·0	15·4	9·9
35	9 38·8	9 40·3	9 12·4	3·5	2·2	9·5	6·1	15·5	9·9
36	9 39·0	9 40·6	9 12·6	3·6	2·3	9·6	6·2	15·6	10·0
37	9 39·3	9 40·8	9 12·9	3·7	2·4	9·7	6·2	15·7	10·1
38	9 39·5	9 41·1	9 13·1	3·8	2·4	9·8	6·3	15·8	10·1
39	9 39·8	9 41·3	9 13·3	3·9	2·5	9·9	6·4	15·9	10·2
40	9 40·0	9 41·6	9 13·6	4·0	2·6	10·0	6·4	16·0	10·3
41	9 40·3	9 41·8	9 13·8	4·1	2·6	10·1	6·5	16·1	10·3
42	9 40·5	9 42·1	9 14·1	4·2	2·7	10·2	6·5	16·2	10·4
43	9 40·8	9 42·3	9 14·3	4·3	2·8	10·3	6·6	16·3	10·5
44	9 41·0	9 42·6	9 14·5	4·4	2·8	10·4	6·7	16·4	10·5
45	9 41·3	9 42·8	9 14·8	4·5	2·9	10·5	6·7	16·5	10·6
46	9 41·5	9 43·1	9 15·0	4·6	3·0	10·6	6·8	16·6	10·7
47	9 41·8	9 43·3	9 15·2	4·7	3·0	10·7	6·9	16·7	10·7
48	9 42·0	9 43·6	9 15·5	4·8	3·1	10·8	6·9	16·8	10·8
49	9 42·3	9 43·8	9 15·7	4·9	3·1	10·9	7·0	16·9	10·8
50	9 42·5	9 44·1	9 16·0	5·0	3·2	11·0	7·1	17·0	10·9
51	9 42·8	9 44·3	9 16·2	5·1	3·3	11·1	7·1	17·1	11·0
52	9 43·0	9 44·6	9 16·4	5·2	3·3	11·2	7·2	17·2	11·0
53	9 43·3	9 44·8	9 16·7	5·3	3·4	11·3	7·3	17·3	11·1
54	9 43·5	9 45·1	9 16·9	5·4	3·5	11·4	7·3	17·4	11·2
55	9 43·8	9 45·3	9 17·2	5·5	3·5	11·5	7·4	17·5	11·2
56	9 44·0	9 45·6	9 17·4	5·6	3·6	11·6	7·4	17·6	11·3
57	9 44·3	9 45·8	9 17·6	5·7	3·7	11·7	7·5	17·7	11·4
58	9 44·5	9 46·1	9 17·9	5·8	3·7	11·8	7·6	17·8	11·4
59	9 44·8	9 46·4	9 18·1	5·9	3·8	11·9	7·6	17·9	11·5
60	9 45·0	9 46·6	9 18·4	6·0	3·9	12·0	7·7	18·0	11·6

39m	SUN PLANETS	ARIES	MOON	v or d	Corrn	v or d	Corrn	v or d	Corrn
s	° ′	° ′	° ′	′	′	′	′	′	′
00	9 45·0	9 46·6	9 18·4	0·0	0·0	6·0	4·0	12·0	7·9
01	9 45·3	9 46·9	9 18·6	0·1	0·1	6·1	4·0	12·1	8·0
02	9 45·5	9 47·1	9 18·8	0·2	0·1	6·2	4·1	12·2	8·0
03	9 45·8	9 47·4	9 19·1	0·3	0·2	6·3	4·1	12·3	8·1
04	9 46·0	9 47·6	9 19·3	0·4	0·3	6·4	4·2	12·4	8·2
05	9 46·3	9 47·9	9 19·5	0·5	0·3	6·5	4·3	12·5	8·2
06	9 46·5	9 48·1	9 19·8	0·6	0·4	6·6	4·3	12·6	8·3
07	9 46·8	9 48·4	9 20·0	0·7	0·5	6·7	4·4	12·7	8·4
08	9 47·0	9 48·6	9 20·3	0·8	0·5	6·8	4·5	12·8	8·4
09	9 47·3	9 48·9	9 20·5	0·9	0·6	6·9	4·5	12·9	8·5
10	9 47·5	9 49·1	9 20·7	1·0	0·7	7·0	4·6	13·0	8·6
11	9 47·8	9 49·4	9 21·0	1·1	0·7	7·1	4·7	13·1	8·6
12	9 48·0	9 49·6	9 21·2	1·2	0·8	7·2	4·7	13·2	8·7
13	9 48·3	9 49·9	9 21·5	1·3	0·9	7·3	4·8	13·3	8·8
14	9 48·5	9 50·1	9 21·7	1·4	0·9	7·4	4·9	13·4	8·8
15	9 48·8	9 50·4	9 21·9	1·5	1·0	7·5	4·9	13·5	8·9
16	9 49·0	9 50·6	9 22·2	1·6	1·1	7·6	5·0	13·6	9·0
17	9 49·3	9 50·9	9 22·4	1·7	1·1	7·7	5·1	13·7	9·0
18	9 49·5	9 51·1	9 22·6	1·8	1·2	7·8	5·1	13·8	9·1
19	9 49·8	9 51·4	9 22·9	1·9	1·3	7·9	5·2	13·9	9·2
20	9 50·0	9 51·6	9 23·1	2·0	1·3	8·0	5·3	14·0	9·2
21	9 50·3	9 51·9	9 23·4	2·1	1·4	8·1	5·3	14·1	9·3
22	9 50·5	9 52·1	9 23·6	2·2	1·4	8·2	5·4	14·2	9·3
23	9 50·8	9 52·4	9 23·8	2·3	1·5	8·3	5·5	14·3	9·4
24	9 51·0	9 52·6	9 24·1	2·4	1·6	8·4	5·5	14·4	9·5
25	9 51·3	9 52·9	9 24·3	2·5	1·6	8·5	5·6	14·5	9·5
26	9 51·5	9 53·1	9 24·6	2·6	1·7	8·6	5·7	14·6	9·6
27	9 51·8	9 53·4	9 24·8	2·7	1·8	8·7	5·7	14·7	9·7
28	9 52·0	9 53·6	9 25·0	2·8	1·8	8·8	5·8	14·8	9·7
29	9 52·3	9 53·9	9 25·3	2·9	1·9	8·9	5·9	14·9	9·8
30	9 52·5	9 54·1	9 25·5	3·0	2·0	9·0	5·9	15·0	9·9
31	9 52·8	9 54·4	9 25·7	3·1	2·0	9·1	6·0	15·1	9·9
32	9 53·0	9 54·6	9 26·0	3·2	2·1	9·2	6·1	15·2	10·0
33	9 53·3	9 54·9	9 26·2	3·3	2·2	9·3	6·1	15·3	10·1
34	9 53·5	9 55·1	9 26·5	3·4	2·2	9·4	6·2	15·4	10·1
35	9 53·8	9 55·4	9 26·7	3·5	2·3	9·5	6·3	15·5	10·2
36	9 54·0	9 55·6	9 26·9	3·6	2·4	9·6	6·3	15·6	10·3
37	9 54·3	9 55·9	9 27·2	3·7	2·4	9·7	6·4	15·7	10·3
38	9 54·5	9 56·1	9 27·4	3·8	2·5	9·8	6·5	15·8	10·4
39	9 54·8	9 56·4	9 27·7	3·9	2·6	9·9	6·5	15·9	10·5
40	9 55·0	9 56·6	9 27·9	4·0	2·6	10·0	6·6	16·0	10·5
41	9 55·3	9 56·9	9 28·1	4·1	2·7	10·1	6·6	16·1	10·6
42	9 55·5	9 57·1	9 28·4	4·2	2·8	10·2	6·7	16·2	10·7
43	9 55·8	9 57·4	9 28·6	4·3	2·8	10·3	6·8	16·3	10·7
44	9 56·0	9 57·6	9 28·8	4·4	2·9	10·4	6·8	16·4	10·8
45	9 56·3	9 57·9	9 29·1	4·5	3·0	10·5	6·9	16·5	10·9
46	9 56·5	9 58·1	9 29·3	4·6	3·0	10·6	7·0	16·6	10·9
47	9 56·8	9 58·4	9 29·6	4·7	3·1	10·7	7·0	16·7	11·0
48	9 57·0	9 58·6	9 29·8	4·8	3·2	10·8	7·1	16·8	11·1
49	9 57·3	9 58·9	9 30·0	4·9	3·2	10·9	7·2	16·9	11·1
50	9 57·5	9 59·1	9 30·3	5·0	3·3	11·0	7·2	17·0	11·2
51	9 57·8	9 59·4	9 30·5	5·1	3·4	11·1	7·3	17·1	11·3
52	9 58·0	9 59·6	9 30·8	5·2	3·4	11·2	7·4	17·2	11·3
53	9 58·3	9 59·9	9 31·0	5·3	3·5	11·3	7·4	17·3	11·4
54	9 58·5	10 00·1	9 31·2	5·4	3·6	11·4	7·5	17·4	11·5
55	9 58·8	10 00·4	9 31·5	5·5	3·6	11·5	7·6	17·5	11·5
56	9 59·0	10 00·6	9 31·7	5·6	3·7	11·6	7·6	17·6	11·6
57	9 59·3	10 00·9	9 32·0	5·7	3·8	11·7	7·7	17·7	11·7
58	9 59·5	10 01·1	9 32·2	5·8	3·8	11·8	7·8	17·8	11·7
59	9 59·8	10 01·4	9 32·4	5·9	3·9	11·9	7·8	17·9	11·8
60	10 00·0	10 01·6	9 32·7	6·0	4·0	12·0	7·9	18·0	11·9

40m s	SUN PLANETS	ARIES	MOON	v or d	Corrn	v or d	Corrn	v or d	Corrn
s	° ′	° ′	° ′	′	′	′	′	′	′
00	10 00·0	10 01·6	9 32·7	0·0	0·0	6·0	4·1	12·0	8·1
01	10 00·3	10 01·9	9 32·9	0·1	0·1	6·1	4·1	12·1	8·2
02	10 00·5	10 02·1	9 33·1	0·2	0·1	6·2	4·2	12·2	8·2
03	10 00·8	10 02·4	9 33·4	0·3	0·2	6·3	4·3	12·3	8·3
04	10 01·0	10 02·6	9 33·6	0·4	0·3	6·4	4·3	12·4	8·4
05	10 01·3	10 02·9	9 33·9	0·5	0·3	6·5	4·4	12·5	8·4
06	10 01·5	10 03·1	9 34·1	0·6	0·4	6·6	4·5	12·6	8·5
07	10 01·8	10 03·4	9 34·3	0·7	0·5	6·7	4·5	12·7	8·6
08	10 02·0	10 03·6	9 34·6	0·8	0·5	6·8	4·6	12·8	8·6
09	10 02·3	10 03·9	9 34·8	0·9	0·6	6·9	4·7	12·9	8·7
10	10 02·5	10 04·1	9 35·1	1·0	0·7	7·0	4·7	13·0	8·8
11	10 02·8	10 04·4	9 35·3	1·1	0·7	7·1	4·8	13·1	8·8
12	10 03·0	10 04·7	9 35·5	1·2	0·8	7·2	4·9	13·2	8·9
13	10 03·3	10 04·9	9 35·8	1·3	0·9	7·3	4·9	13·3	9·0
14	10 03·5	10 05·2	9 36·0	1·4	0·9	7·4	5·0	13·4	9·0
15	10 03·8	10 05·4	9 36·2	1·5	1·0	7·5	5·1	13·5	9·1
16	10 04·0	10 05·7	9 36·5	1·6	1·1	7·6	5·1	13·6	9·2
17	10 04·3	10 05·9	9 36·7	1·7	1·1	7·7	5·2	13·7	9·2
18	10 04·5	10 06·2	9 37·0	1·8	1·2	7·8	5·3	13·8	9·3
19	10 04·8	10 06·4	9 37·2	1·9	1·3	7·9	5·3	13·9	9·4
20	10 05·0	10 06·7	9 37·4	2·0	1·4	8·0	5·4	14·0	9·5
21	10 05·3	10 06·9	9 37·7	2·1	1·4	8·1	5·5	14·1	9·5
22	10 05·5	10 07·2	9 37·9	2·2	1·5	8·2	5·5	14·2	9·6
23	10 05·8	10 07·4	9 38·2	2·3	1·6	8·3	5·6	14·3	9·7
24	10 06·0	10 07·7	9 38·4	2·4	1·6	8·4	5·7	14·4	9·7
25	10 06·3	10 07·9	9 38·6	2·5	1·7	8·5	5·7	14·5	9·8
26	10 06·5	10 08·2	9 38·9	2·6	1·8	8·6	5·8	14·6	9·9
27	10 06·8	10 08·4	9 39·1	2·7	1·8	8·7	5·9	14·7	9·9
28	10 07·0	10 08·7	9 39·3	2·8	1·9	8·8	5·9	14·8	10·0
29	10 07·3	10 08·9	9 39·6	2·9	2·0	8·9	6·0	14·9	10·1
30	10 07·5	10 09·2	9 39·8	3·0	2·0	9·0	6·1	15·0	10·1
31	10 07·8	10 09·4	9 40·1	3·1	2·1	9·1	6·1	15·1	10·2
32	10 08·0	10 09·7	9 40·3	3·2	2·2	9·2	6·2	15·2	10·3
33	10 08·3	10 09·9	9 40·5	3·3	2·2	9·3	6·3	15·3	10·3
34	10 08·5	10 10·2	9 40·8	3·4	2·3	9·4	6·3	15·4	10·4
35	10 08·8	10 10·4	9 41·0	3·5	2·4	9·5	6·4	15·5	10·5
36	10 09·0	10 10·7	9 41·3	3·6	2·4	9·6	6·5	15·6	10·5
37	10 09·3	10 10·9	9 41·5	3·7	2·5	9·7	6·5	15·7	10·6
38	10 09·5	10 11·2	9 41·7	3·8	2·6	9·8	6·6	15·8	10·7
39	10 09·8	10 11·4	9 42·0	3·9	2·6	9·9	6·7	15·9	10·7
40	10 10·0	10 11·7	9 42·2	4·0	2·7	10·0	6·8	16·0	10·8
41	10 10·3	10 11·9	9 42·4	4·1	2·8	10·1	6·8	16·1	10·9
42	10 10·5	10 12·2	9 42·7	4·2	2·8	10·2	6·9	16·2	10·9
43	10 10·8	10 12·4	9 42·9	4·3	2·9	10·3	7·0	16·3	11·0
44	10 11·0	10 12·7	9 43·2	4·4	3·0	10·4	7·0	16·4	11·1
45	10 11·3	10 12·9	9 43·4	4·5	3·0	10·5	7·1	16·5	11·1
46	10 11·5	10 13·2	9 43·6	4·6	3·1	10·6	7·2	16·6	11·2
47	10 11·8	10 13·4	9 43·9	4·7	3·2	10·7	7·2	16·7	11·3
48	10 12·0	10 13·7	9 44·1	4·8	3·2	10·8	7·3	16·8	11·3
49	10 12·3	10 13·9	9 44·4	4·9	3·3	10·9	7·4	16·9	11·4
50	10 12·5	10 14·2	9 44·6	5·0	3·4	11·0	7·4	17·0	11·5
51	10 12·8	10 14·4	9 44·8	5·1	3·4	11·1	7·5	17·1	11·5
52	10 13·0	10 14·7	9 45·1	5·2	3·5	11·2	7·6	17·2	11·6
53	10 13·3	10 14·9	9 45·3	5·3	3·6	11·3	7·6	17·3	11·7
54	10 13·5	10 15·2	9 45·6	5·4	3·6	11·4	7·7	17·4	11·7
55	10 13·8	10 15·4	9 45·8	5·5	3·7	11·5	7·8	17·5	11·8
56	10 14·0	10 15·7	9 46·0	5·6	3·8	11·6	7·8	17·6	11·9
57	10 14·3	10 15·9	9 46·3	5·7	3·8	11·7	7·9	17·7	11·9
58	10 14·5	10 16·2	9 46·5	5·8	3·9	11·8	8·0	17·8	12·0
59	10 14·8	10 16·4	9 46·7	5·9	4·0	11·9	8·0	17·9	12·1
60	10 15·0	10 16·7	9 47·0	6·0	4·1	12·0	8·1	18·0	12·2

41m s	SUN PLANETS	ARIES	MOON	v or d	Corrn	v or d	Corrn	v or d	Corrn
s	° ′	° ′	° ′	′	′	′	′	′	′
00	10 15·0	10 16·7	9 47·0	0·0	0·0	6·0	4·2	12·0	8·3
01	10 15·3	10 16·9	9 47·2	0·1	0·1	6·1	4·2	12·1	8·4
02	10 15·5	10 17·2	9 47·5	0·2	0·1	6·2	4·3	12·2	8·4
03	10 15·8	10 17·4	9 47·7	0·3	0·2	6·3	4·4	12·3	8·5
04	10 16·0	10 17·7	9 47·9	0·4	0·3	6·4	4·4	12·4	8·6
05	10 16·3	10 17·9	9 48·2	0·5	0·3	6·5	4·5	12·5	8·6
06	10 16·5	10 18·2	9 48·4	0·6	0·4	6·6	4·6	12·6	8·7
07	10 16·8	10 18·4	9 48·7	0·7	0·5	6·7	4·6	12·7	8·8
08	10 17·0	10 18·7	9 48·9	0·8	0·6	6·8	4·7	12·8	8·9
09	10 17·3	10 18·9	9 49·1	0·9	0·6	6·9	4·8	12·9	8·9
10	10 17·5	10 19·2	9 49·4	1·0	0·7	7·0	4·8	13·0	9·0
11	10 17·8	10 19·4	9 49·6	1·1	0·8	7·1	4·9	13·1	9·1
12	10 18·0	10 19·7	9 49·8	1·2	0·8	7·2	5·0	13·2	9·1
13	10 18·3	10 19·9	9 50·1	1·3	0·9	7·3	5·0	13·3	9·2
14	10 18·5	10 20·2	9 50·3	1·4	1·0	7·4	5·1	13·4	9·3
15	10 18·8	10 20·4	9 50·6	1·5	1·0	7·5	5·2	13·5	9·3
16	10 19·0	10 20·7	9 50·8	1·6	1·1	7·6	5·3	13·6	9·4
17	10 19·3	10 20·9	9 51·0	1·7	1·2	7·7	5·3	13·7	9·5
18	10 19·5	10 21·2	9 51·3	1·8	1·2	7·8	5·4	13·8	9·5
19	10 19·8	10 21·4	9 51·5	1·9	1·3	7·9	5·5	13·9	9·6
20	10 20·0	10 21·7	9 51·8	2·0	1·4	8·0	5·5	14·0	9·7
21	10 20·3	10 21·9	9 52·0	2·1	1·5	8·1	5·6	14·1	9·8
22	10 20·5	10 22·2	9 52·2	2·2	1·5	8·2	5·7	14·2	9·8
23	10 20·8	10 22·4	9 52·5	2·3	1·6	8·3	5·7	14·3	9·9
24	10 21·0	10 22·7	9 52·7	2·4	1·7	8·4	5·8	14·4	10·0
25	10 21·3	10 23·0	9 52·9	2·5	1·7	8·5	5·9	14·5	10·0
26	10 21·5	10 23·2	9 53·2	2·6	1·8	8·6	5·9	14·6	10·1
27	10 21·8	10 23·5	9 53·4	2·7	1·9	8·7	6·0	14·7	10·2
28	10 22·0	10 23·7	9 53·7	2·8	1·9	8·8	6·1	14·8	10·2
29	10 22·3	10 24·0	9 53·9	2·9	2·0	8·9	6·2	14·9	10·3
30	10 22·5	10 24·2	9 54·1	3·0	2·1	9·0	6·2	15·0	10·4
31	10 22·8	10 24·5	9 54·4	3·1	2·1	9·1	6·3	15·1	10·4
32	10 23·0	10 24·7	9 54·6	3·2	2·2	9·2	6·4	15·2	10·5
33	10 23·3	10 25·0	9 54·9	3·3	2·3	9·3	6·4	15·3	10·6
34	10 23·5	10 25·2	9 55·1	3·4	2·4	9·4	6·5	15·4	10·7
35	10 23·8	10 25·5	9 55·3	3·5	2·4	9·5	6·6	15·5	10·7
36	10 24·0	10 25·7	9 55·6	3·6	2·5	9·6	6·6	15·6	10·8
37	10 24·3	10 26·0	9 55·8	3·7	2·6	9·7	6·7	15·7	10·9
38	10 24·5	10 26·2	9 56·1	3·8	2·6	9·8	6·8	15·8	10·9
39	10 24·8	10 26·5	9 56·3	3·9	2·7	9·9	6·8	15·9	11·0
40	10 25·0	10 26·7	9 56·5	4·0	2·8	10·0	6·9	16·0	11·1
41	10 25·3	10 27·0	9 56·8	4·1	2·8	10·1	7·0	16·1	11·1
42	10 25·5	10 27·2	9 57·0	4·2	2·9	10·2	7·1	16·2	11·2
43	10 25·8	10 27·5	9 57·2	4·3	3·0	10·3	7·1	16·3	11·3
44	10 26·0	10 27·7	9 57·5	4·4	3·0	10·4	7·2	16·4	11·3
45	10 26·3	10 28·0	9 57·7	4·5	3·1	10·5	7·3	16·5	11·4
46	10 26·5	10 28·2	9 58·0	4·6	3·2	10·6	7·3	16·6	11·5
47	10 26·8	10 28·5	9 58·2	4·7	3·3	10·7	7·4	16·7	11·6
48	10 27·0	10 28·7	9 58·4	4·8	3·3	10·8	7·5	16·8	11·6
49	10 27·3	10 29·0	9 58·7	4·9	3·4	10·9	7·5	16·9	11·7
50	10 27·5	10 29·2	9 58·9	5·0	3·5	11·0	7·6	17·0	11·8
51	10 27·8	10 29·5	9 59·2	5·1	3·5	11·1	7·7	17·1	11·8
52	10 28·0	10 29·7	9 59·4	5·2	3·6	11·2	7·7	17·2	11·9
53	10 28·3	10 30·0	9 59·6	5·3	3·7	11·3	7·8	17·3	12·0
54	10 28·5	10 30·2	9 59·9	5·4	3·7	11·4	7·9	17·4	12·0
55	10 28·8	10 30·5	10 00·1	5·5	3·8	11·5	8·0	17·5	12·1
56	10 29·0	10 30·7	10 00·3	5·6	3·9	11·6	8·0	17·6	12·2
57	10 29·3	10 31·0	10 00·6	5·7	3·9	11·7	8·1	17·7	12·2
58	10 29·5	10 31·2	10 00·8	5·8	4·0	11·8	8·2	17·8	12·3
59	10 29·8	10 31·5	10 01·1	5·9	4·1	11·9	8·2	17·9	12·4
60	10 30·0	10 31·7	10 01·3	6·0	4·2	12·0	8·3	18·0	12·5

42m	SUN PLANETS	ARIES	MOON	v or d	Corrn	v or d	Corrn	v or d	Corrn
s	° ′	° ′	° ′	′	′	′	′	′	′
00	10 30·0	10 31·7	10 01·3	0·0	0·0	6·0	4·3	12·0	8·5
01	10 30·3	10 32·0	10 01·5	0·1	0·1	6·1	4·3	12·1	8·6
02	10 30·5	10 32·2	10 01·8	0·2	0·1	6·2	4·4	12·2	8·6
03	10 30·8	10 32·5	10 02·0	0·3	0·2	6·3	4·5	12·3	8·7
04	10 31·0	10 32·7	10 02·3	0·4	0·3	6·4	4·5	12·4	8·8
05	10 31·3	10 33·0	10 02·5	0·5	0·4	6·5	4·6	12·5	8·9
06	10 31·5	10 33·2	10 02·7	0·6	0·4	6·6	4·7	12·6	8·9
07	10 31·8	10 33·5	10 03·0	0·7	0·5	6·7	4·7	12·7	9·0
08	10 32·0	10 33·7	10 03·2	0·8	0·6	6·8	4·8	12·8	9·1
09	10 32·3	10 34·0	10 03·4	0·9	0·6	6·9	4·9	12·9	9·1
10	10 32·5	10 34·2	10 03·7	1·0	0·7	7·0	5·0	13·0	9·2
11	10 32·8	10 34·5	10 03·9	1·1	0·8	7·1	5·0	13·1	9·3
12	10 33·0	10 34·7	10 04·2	1·2	0·9	7·2	5·1	13·2	9·4
13	10 33·3	10 35·0	10 04·4	1·3	0·9	7·3	5·2	13·3	9·4
14	10 33·5	10 35·2	10 04·6	1·4	1·0	7·4	5·2	13·4	9·5
15	10 33·8	10 35·5	10 04·9	1·5	1·1	7·5	5·3	13·5	9·6
16	10 34·0	10 35·7	10 05·1	1·6	1·1	7·6	5·4	13·6	9·6
17	10 34·3	10 36·0	10 05·4	1·7	1·2	7·7	5·5	13·7	9·7
18	10 34·5	10 36·2	10 05·6	1·8	1·3	7·8	5·5	13·8	9·8
19	10 34·8	10 36·5	10 05·8	1·9	1·3	7·9	5·6	13·9	9·8
20	10 35·0	10 36·7	10 06·1	2·0	1·4	8·0	5·7	14·0	9·9
21	10 35·3	10 37·0	10 06·3	2·1	1·5	8·1	5·7	14·1	10·0
22	10 35·5	10 37·2	10 06·5	2·2	1·6	8·2	5·8	14·2	10·1
23	10 35·8	10 37·5	10 06·8	2·3	1·6	8·3	5·9	14·3	10·1
24	10 36·0	10 37·7	10 07·0	2·4	1·7	8·4	6·0	14·4	10·2
25	10 36·3	10 38·0	10 07·3	2·5	1·8	8·5	6·0	14·5	10·3
26	10 36·5	10 38·2	10 07·5	2·6	1·8	8·6	6·1	14·6	10·3
27	10 36·8	10 38·5	10 07·7	2·7	1·9	8·7	6·2	14·7	10·4
28	10 37·0	10 38·7	10 08·0	2·8	2·0	8·8	6·2	14·8	10·5
29	10 37·3	10 39·0	10 08·2	2·9	2·1	8·9	6·3	14·9	10·6
30	10 37·5	10 39·2	10 08·5	3·0	2·1	9·0	6·4	15·0	10·6
31	10 37·8	10 39·5	10 08·7	3·1	2·2	9·1	6·4	15·1	10·7
32	10 38·0	10 39·7	10 08·9	3·2	2·3	9·2	6·5	15·2	10·8
33	10 38·3	10 40·0	10 09·2	3·3	2·3	9·3	6·6	15·3	10·8
34	10 38·5	10 40·2	10 09·4	3·4	2·4	9·4	6·7	15·4	10·9
35	10 38·8	10 40·5	10 09·7	3·5	2·5	9·5	6·7	15·5	11·0
36	10 39·0	10 40·7	10 09·9	3·6	2·6	9·6	6·8	15·6	11·1
37	10 39·3	10 41·0	10 10·1	3·7	2·6	9·7	6·9	15·7	11·1
38	10 39·5	10 41·3	10 10·4	3·8	2·7	9·8	6·9	15·8	11·2
39	10 39·8	10 41·5	10 10·6	3·9	2·8	9·9	7·0	15·9	11·3
40	10 40·0	10 41·8	10 10·8	4·0	2·8	10·0	7·1	16·0	11·3
41	10 40·3	10 42·0	10 11·1	4·1	2·9	10·1	7·2	16·1	11·4
42	10 40·5	10 42·3	10 11·3	4·2	3·0	10·2	7·2	16·2	11·5
43	10 40·8	10 42·5	10 11·6	4·3	3·0	10·3	7·3	16·3	11·5
44	10 41·0	10 42·8	10 11·8	4·4	3·1	10·4	7·4	16·4	11·6
45	10 41·3	10 43·0	10 12·0	4·5	3·2	10·5	7·4	16·5	11·7
46	10 41·5	10 43·3	10 12·3	4·6	3·3	10·6	7·5	16·6	11·8
47	10 41·8	10 43·5	10 12·5	4·7	3·3	10·7	7·6	16·7	11·8
48	10 42·0	10 43·8	10 12·8	4·8	3·4	10·8	7·7	16·8	11·9
49	10 42·3	10 44·0	10 13·0	4·9	3·5	10·9	7·7	16·9	12·0
50	10 42·5	10 44·3	10 13·2	5·0	3·5	11·0	7·8	17·0	12·0
51	10 42·8	10 44·5	10 13·5	5·1	3·6	11·1	7·9	17·1	12·1
52	10 43·0	10 44·8	10 13·7	5·2	3·7	11·2	7·9	17·2	12·2
53	10 43·3	10 45·0	10 13·9	5·3	3·8	11·3	8·0	17·3	12·3
54	10 43·5	10 45·3	10 14·2	5·4	3·8	11·4	8·1	17·4	12·3
55	10 43·8	10 45·5	10 14·4	5·5	3·9	11·5	8·1	17·5	12·4
56	10 44·0	10 45·8	10 14·7	5·6	4·0	11·6	8·2	17·6	12·5
57	10 44·3	10 46·0	10 14·9	5·7	4·0	11·7	8·3	17·7	12·5
58	10 44·5	10 46·3	10 15·1	5·8	4·1	11·8	8·4	17·8	12·6
59	10 44·8	10 46·5	10 15·4	5·9	4·2	11·9	8·4	17·9	12·7
60	10 45·0	10 46·8	10 15·6	6·0	4·3	12·0	8·5	18·0	12·8

43m	SUN PLANETS	ARIES	MOON	v or d	Corrn	v or d	Corrn	v or d	Corrn
s	° ′	° ′	° ′	′	′	′	′	′	′
00	10 45·0	10 46·8	10 15·6	0·0	0·0	6·0	4·4	12·0	8·7
01	10 45·3	10 47·0	10 15·9	0·1	0·1	6·1	4·4	12·1	8·8
02	10 45·5	10 47·3	10 16·1	0·2	0·1	6·2	4·5	12·2	8·8
03	10 45·8	10 47·5	10 16·3	0·3	0·2	6·3	4·6	12·3	8·9
04	10 46·0	10 47·8	10 16·6	0·4	0·3	6·4	4·6	12·4	9·0
05	10 46·3	10 48·0	10 16·8	0·5	0·4	6·5	4·7	12·5	9·1
06	10 46·5	10 48·3	10 17·0	0·6	0·4	6·6	4·8	12·6	9·1
07	10 46·8	10 48·5	10 17·3	0·7	0·5	6·7	4·9	12·7	9·2
08	10 47·0	10 48·8	10 17·5	0·8	0·6	6·8	4·9	12·8	9·3
09	10 47·3	10 49·0	10 17·8	0·9	0·7	6·9	5·0	12·9	9·4
10	10 47·5	10 49·3	10 18·0	1·0	0·7	7·0	5·1	13·0	9·4
11	10 47·8	10 49·5	10 18·2	1·1	0·8	7·1	5·1	13·1	9·5
12	10 48·0	10 49·8	10 18·5	1·2	0·9	7·2	5·2	13·2	9·6
13	10 48·3	10 50·0	10 18·7	1·3	0·9	7·3	5·3	13·3	9·6
14	10 48·5	10 50·3	10 19·0	1·4	1·0	7·4	5·4	13·4	9·7
15	10 48·8	10 50·5	10 19·2	1·5	1·1	7·5	5·4	13·5	9·8
16	10 49·0	10 50·8	10 19·4	1·6	1·2	7·6	5·5	13·6	9·9
17	10 49·3	10 51·0	10 19·7	1·7	1·2	7·7	5·6	13·7	9·9
18	10 49·5	10 51·3	10 19·9	1·8	1·3	7·8	5·7	13·8	10·0
19	10 49·8	10 51·5	10 20·2	1·9	1·4	7·9	5·7	13·9	10·1
20	10 50·0	10 51·8	10 20·4	2·0	1·5	8·0	5·8	14·0	10·2
21	10 50·3	10 52·0	10 20·6	2·1	1·5	8·1	5·9	14·1	10·2
22	10 50·5	10 52·3	10 20·9	2·2	1·6	8·2	5·9	14·2	10·3
23	10 50·8	10 52·5	10 21·1	2·3	1·7	8·3	6·0	14·3	10·4
24	10 51·0	10 52·8	10 21·3	2·4	1·7	8·4	6·1	14·4	10·4
25	10 51·3	10 53·0	10 21·6	2·5	1·8	8·5	6·2	14·5	10·5
26	10 51·5	10 53·3	10 21·8	2·6	1·9	8·6	6·2	14·6	10·6
27	10 51·8	10 53·5	10 22·1	2·7	2·0	8·7	6·3	14·7	10·7
28	10 52·0	10 53·8	10 22·3	2·8	2·0	8·8	6·4	14·8	10·7
29	10 52·3	10 54·0	10 22·5	2·9	2·1	8·9	6·5	14·9	10·8
30	10 52·5	10 54·3	10 22·8	3·0	2·2	9·0	6·5	15·0	10·9
31	10 52·8	10 54·5	10 23·0	3·1	2·2	9·1	6·6	15·1	10·9
32	10 53·0	10 54·8	10 23·3	3·2	2·3	9·2	6·7	15·2	11·0
33	10 53·3	10 55·0	10 23·5	3·3	2·4	9·3	6·7	15·3	11·1
34	10 53·5	10 55·3	10 23·7	3·4	2·5	9·4	6·8	15·4	11·2
35	10 53·8	10 55·5	10 24·0	3·5	2·5	9·5	6·9	15·5	11·2
36	10 54·0	10 55·8	10 24·2	3·6	2·6	9·6	7·0	15·6	11·3
37	10 54·3	10 56·0	10 24·4	3·7	2·7	9·7	7·0	15·7	11·4
38	10 54·5	10 56·3	10 24·7	3·8	2·8	9·8	7·1	15·8	11·5
39	10 54·8	10 56·5	10 24·9	3·9	2·8	9·9	7·2	15·9	11·5
40	10 55·0	10 56·8	10 25·2	4·0	2·9	10·0	7·3	16·0	11·6
41	10 55·3	10 57·0	10 25·4	4·1	3·0	10·1	7·3	16·1	11·7
42	10 55·5	10 57·3	10 25·6	4·2	3·0	10·2	7·4	16·2	11·7
43	10 55·8	10 57·5	10 25·9	4·3	3·1	10·3	7·5	16·3	11·8
44	10 56·0	10 57·8	10 26·1	4·4	3·2	10·4	7·5	16·4	11·9
45	10 56·3	10 58·0	10 26·4	4·5	3·3	10·5	7·6	16·5	12·0
46	10 56·5	10 58·3	10 26·6	4·6	3·3	10·6	7·7	16·6	12·0
47	10 56·8	10 58·5	10 26·8	4·7	3·4	10·7	7·8	16·7	12·1
48	10 57·0	10 58·8	10 27·1	4·8	3·5	10·8	7·8	16·8	12·2
49	10 57·3	10 59·0	10 27·3	4·9	3·6	10·9	7·9	16·9	12·3
50	10 57·5	10 59·3	10 27·5	5·0	3·6	11·0	8·0	17·0	12·3
51	10 57·8	10 59·6	10 27·8	5·1	3·7	11·1	8·0	17·1	12·4
52	10 58·0	10 59·8	10 28·0	5·2	3·8	11·2	8·1	17·2	12·5
53	10 58·3	11 00·1	10 28·3	5·3	3·8	11·3	8·2	17·3	12·5
54	10 58·5	11 00·3	10 28·5	5·4	3·9	11·4	8·3	17·4	12·6
55	10 58·8	11 00·6	10 28·7	5·5	4·0	11·5	8·3	17·5	12·7
56	10 59·0	11 00·8	10 29·0	5·6	4·1	11·6	8·4	17·6	12·8
57	10 59·3	11 01·1	10 29·2	5·7	4·1	11·7	8·5	17·7	12·8
58	10 59·5	11 01·3	10 29·5	5·8	4·2	11·8	8·6	17·8	12·9
59	10 59·8	11 01·6	10 29·7	5·9	4·3	11·9	8·6	17·9	13·0
60	11 00·0	11 01·8	10 29·9	6·0	4·4	12·0	8·7	18·0	13·1

44m s	SUN PLANETS ° ′	ARIES ° ′	MOON ° ′	v or d ′	Corrn ′	v or d ′	Corrn ′	v or d ′	Corrn ′
00	11 00·0	11 01·8	10 29·9	0·0	0·0	6·0	4·5	12·0	8·9
01	11 00·3	11 02·1	10 30·2	0·1	0·1	6·1	4·5	12·1	9·0
02	11 00·5	11 02·3	10 30·4	0·2	0·1	6·2	4·6	12·2	9·0
03	11 00·8	11 02·6	10 30·6	0·3	0·2	6·3	4·7	12·3	9·1
04	11 01·0	11 02·8	10 30·9	0·4	0·3	6·4	4·7	12·4	9·2
05	11 01·3	11 03·1	10 31·1	0·5	0·4	6·5	4·8	12·5	9·3
06	11 01·5	11 03·3	10 31·4	0·6	0·4	6·6	4·9	12·6	9·3
07	11 01·8	11 03·6	10 31·6	0·7	0·5	6·7	5·0	12·7	9·4
08	11 02·0	11 03·8	10 31·8	0·8	0·6	6·8	5·0	12·8	9·5
09	11 02·3	11 04·1	10 32·1	0·9	0·7	6·9	5·1	12·9	9·6
10	11 02·5	11 04·3	10 32·3	1·0	0·7	7·0	5·2	13·0	9·6
11	11 02·8	11 04·6	10 32·6	1·1	0·8	7·1	5·3	13·1	9·7
12	11 03·0	11 04·8	10 32·8	1·2	0·9	7·2	5·3	13·2	9·8
13	11 03·3	11 05·1	10 33·0	1·3	1·0	7·3	5·4	13·3	9·9
14	11 03·5	11 05·3	10 33·3	1·4	1·0	7·4	5·5	13·4	9·9
15	11 03·8	11 05·6	10 33·5	1·5	1·1	7·5	5·6	13·5	10·0
16	11 04·0	11 05·8	10 33·8	1·6	1·2	7·6	5·6	13·6	10·1
17	11 04·3	11 06·1	10 34·0	1·7	1·3	7·7	5·7	13·7	10·2
18	11 04·5	11 06·3	10 34·2	1·8	1·3	7·8	5·8	13·8	10·2
19	11 04·8	11 06·6	10 34·5	1·9	1·4	7·9	5·9	13·9	10·3
20	11 05·0	11 06·8	10 34·7	2·0	1·5	8·0	5·9	14·0	10·4
21	11 05·3	11 07·1	10 34·9	2·1	1·6	8·1	6·0	14·1	10·5
22	11 05·5	11 07·3	10 35·2	2·2	1·6	8·2	6·1	14·2	10·5
23	11 05·8	11 07·6	10 35·4	2·3	1·7	8·3	6·2	14·3	10·6
24	11 06·0	11 07·8	10 35·7	2·4	1·8	8·4	6·2	14·4	10·7
25	11 06·3	11 08·1	10 35·9	2·5	1·9	8·5	6·3	14·5	10·8
26	11 06·5	11 08·3	10 36·1	2·6	1·9	8·6	6·4	14·6	10·8
27	11 06·8	11 08·6	10 36·4	2·7	2·0	8·7	6·5	14·7	10·9
28	11 07·0	11 08·8	10 36·6	2·8	2·1	8·8	6·5	14·8	11·0
29	11 07·3	11 09·1	10 36·9	2·9	2·2	8·9	6·6	14·9	11·1
30	11 07·5	11 09·3	10 37·1	3·0	2·2	9·0	6·7	15·0	11·1
31	11 07·8	11 09·6	10 37·3	3·1	2·3	9·1	6·7	15·1	11·2
32	11 08·0	11 09·8	10 37·6	3·2	2·4	9·2	6·8	15·2	11·3
33	11 08·3	11 10·1	10 37·8	3·3	2·4	9·3	6·9	15·3	11·3
34	11 08·5	11 10·3	10 38·0	3·4	2·5	9·4	7·0	15·4	11·4
35	11 08·8	11 10·6	10 38·3	3·5	2·6	9·5	7·0	15·5	11·5
36	11 09·0	11 10·8	10 38·5	3·6	2·7	9·6	7·1	15·6	11·6
37	11 09·3	11 11·1	10 38·8	3·7	2·7	9·7	7·2	15·7	11·6
38	11 09·5	11 11·3	10 39·0	3·8	2·8	9·8	7·3	15·8	11·7
39	11 09·8	11 11·6	10 39·2	3·9	2·9	9·9	7·3	15·9	11·8
40	11 10·0	11 11·8	10 39·5	4·0	3·0	10·0	7·4	16·0	11·9
41	11 10·3	11 12·1	10 39·7	4·1	3·0	10·1	7·5	16·1	11·9
42	11 10·5	11 12·3	10 40·0	4·2	3·1	10·2	7·6	16·2	12·0
43	11 10·8	11 12·6	10 40·2	4·3	3·2	10·3	7·6	16·3	12·1
44	11 11·0	11 12·8	10 40·4	4·4	3·3	10·4	7·7	16·4	12·2
45	11 11·3	11 13·1	10 40·7	4·5	3·3	10·5	7·8	16·5	12·2
46	11 11·5	11 13·3	10 40·9	4·6	3·4	10·6	7·9	16·6	12·3
47	11 11·8	11 13·6	10 41·1	4·7	3·5	10·7	7·9	16·7	12·4
48	11 12·0	11 13·8	10 41·4	4·8	3·6	10·8	8·0	16·8	12·5
49	11 12·3	11 14·1	10 41·6	4·9	3·6	10·9	8·1	16·9	12·5
50	11 12·5	11 14·3	10 41·9	5·0	3·7	11·0	8·2	17·0	12·6
51	11 12·8	11 14·6	10 42·1	5·1	3·8	11·1	8·2	17·1	12·7
52	11 13·0	11 14·8	10 42·3	5·2	3·9	11·2	8·3	17·2	12·8
53	11 13·3	11 15·1	10 42·6	5·3	3·9	11·3	8·4	17·3	12·8
54	11 13·5	11 15·3	10 42·8	5·4	4·0	11·4	8·5	17·4	12·9
55	11 13·8	11 15·6	10 43·1	5·5	4·1	11·5	8·5	17·5	13·0
56	11 14·0	11 15·8	10 43·3	5·6	4·2	11·6	8·6	17·6	13·1
57	11 14·3	11 16·1	10 43·5	5·7	4·2	11·7	8·7	17·7	13·1
58	11 14·5	11 16·3	10 43·8	5·8	4·3	11·8	8·8	17·8	13·2
59	11 14·8	11 16·6	10 44·0	5·9	4·4	11·9	8·8	17·9	13·3
60	11 15·0	11 16·8	10 44·3	6·0	4·5	12·0	8·9	18·0	13·4

45m s	SUN PLANETS ° ′	ARIES ° ′	MOON ° ′	v or d ′	Corrn ′	v or d ′	Corrn ′	v or d ′	Corrn ′
00	11 15·0	11 16·8	10 44·3	0·0	0·0	6·0	4·6	12·0	9·1
01	11 15·3	11 17·1	10 44·5	0·1	0·1	6·1	4·6	12·1	9·2
02	11 15·5	11 17·3	10 44·7	0·2	0·2	6·2	4·7	12·2	9·3
03	11 15·8	11 17·6	10 45·0	0·3	0·2	6·3	4·8	12·3	9·3
04	11 16·0	11 17·9	10 45·2	0·4	0·3	6·4	4·9	12·4	9·4
05	11 16·3	11 18·1	10 45·4	0·5	0·4	6·5	4·9	12·5	9·5
06	11 16·5	11 18·4	10 45·7	0·6	0·5	6·6	5·0	12·6	9·6
07	11 16·8	11 18·6	10 45·9	0·7	0·5	6·7	5·1	12·7	9·6
08	11 17·0	11 18·9	10 46·2	0·8	0·6	6·8	5·2	12·8	9·7
09	11 17·3	11 19·1	10 46·4	0·9	0·7	6·9	5·2	12·9	9·8
10	11 17·5	11 19·4	10 46·6	1·0	0·8	7·0	5·3	13·0	9·9
11	11 17·8	11 19·6	10 46·9	1·1	0·8	7·1	5·4	13·1	9·9
12	11 18·0	11 19·9	10 47·1	1·2	0·9	7·2	5·5	13·2	10·0
13	11 18·3	11 20·1	10 47·4	1·3	1·0	7·3	5·5	13·3	10·1
14	11 18·5	11 20·4	10 47·6	1·4	1·1	7·4	5·6	13·4	10·2
15	11 18·8	11 20·6	10 47·8	1·5	1·1	7·5	5·7	13·5	10·2
16	11 19·0	11 20·9	10 48·1	1·6	1·2	7·6	5·8	13·6	10·3
17	11 19·3	11 21·1	10 48·3	1·7	1·3	7·7	5·8	13·7	10·4
18	11 19·5	11 21·4	10 48·5	1·8	1·4	7·8	5·9	13·8	10·5
19	11 19·8	11 21·6	10 48·8	1·9	1·4	7·9	6·0	13·9	10·5
20	11 20·0	11 21·9	10 49·0	2·0	1·5	8·0	6·1	14·0	10·6
21	11 20·3	11 22·1	10 49·3	2·1	1·6	8·1	6·1	14·1	10·7
22	11 20·5	11 22·4	10 49·5	2·2	1·7	8·2	6·2	14·2	10·8
23	11 20·8	11 22·6	10 49·7	2·3	1·7	8·3	6·3	14·3	10·8
24	11 21·0	11 22·9	10 50·0	2·4	1·8	8·4	6·4	14·4	10·9
25	11 21·3	11 23·1	10 50·2	2·5	1·9	8·5	6·4	14·5	11·0
26	11 21·5	11 23·4	10 50·5	2·6	2·0	8·6	6·5	14·6	11·1
27	11 21·8	11 23·6	10 50·7	2·7	2·0	8·7	6·6	14·7	11·1
28	11 22·0	11 23·9	10 50·9	2·8	2·1	8·8	6·7	14·8	11·2
29	11 22·3	11 24·1	10 51·2	2·9	2·2	8·9	6·7	14·9	11·3
30	11 22·5	11 24·4	10 51·4	3·0	2·3	9·0	6·8	15·0	11·4
31	11 22·8	11 24·6	10 51·6	3·1	2·4	9·1	6·9	15·1	11·5
32	11 23·0	11 24·9	10 51·9	3·2	2·4	9·2	7·0	15·2	11·5
33	11 23·3	11 25·1	10 52·1	3·3	2·5	9·3	7·1	15·3	11·6
34	11 23·5	11 25·4	10 52·4	3·4	2·6	9·4	7·1	15·4	11·7
35	11 23·8	11 25·6	10 52·6	3·5	2·7	9·5	7·2	15·5	11·8
36	11 24·0	11 25·9	10 52·8	3·6	2·7	9·6	7·3	15·6	11·8
37	11 24·3	11 26·1	10 53·1	3·7	2·8	9·7	7·4	15·7	11·9
38	11 24·5	11 26·4	10 53·3	3·8	2·9	9·8	7·4	15·8	12·0
39	11 24·8	11 26·6	10 53·6	3·9	3·0	9·9	7·5	15·9	12·1
40	11 25·0	11 26·9	10 53·8	4·0	3·0	10·0	7·6	16·0	12·1
41	11 25·3	11 27·1	10 54·0	4·1	3·1	10·1	7·7	16·1	12·2
42	11 25·5	11 27·4	10 54·3	4·2	3·2	10·2	7·7	16·2	12·3
43	11 25·8	11 27·6	10 54·5	4·3	3·3	10·3	7·8	16·3	12·4
44	11 26·0	11 27·9	10 54·7	4·4	3·3	10·4	7·9	16·4	12·4
45	11 26·3	11 28·1	10 55·0	4·5	3·4	10·5	8·0	16·5	12·5
46	11 26·5	11 28·4	10 55·2	4·6	3·5	10·6	8·0	16·6	12·6
47	11 26·8	11 28·6	10 55·5	4·7	3·6	10·7	8·1	16·7	12·7
48	11 27·0	11 28·9	10 55·7	4·8	3·6	10·8	8·2	16·8	12·7
49	11 27·3	11 29·1	10 55·9	4·9	3·7	10·9	8·3	16·9	12·8
50	11 27·5	11 29·4	10 56·2	5·0	3·8	11·0	8·3	17·0	12·9
51	11 27·8	11 29·6	10 56·4	5·1	3·9	11·1	8·4	17·1	13·0
52	11 28·0	11 29·9	10 56·7	5·2	3·9	11·2	8·5	17·2	13·0
53	11 28·3	11 30·1	10 56·9	5·3	4·0	11·3	8·6	17·3	13·1
54	11 28·5	11 30·4	10 57·1	5·4	4·1	11·4	8·6	17·4	13·2
55	11 28·8	11 30·6	10 57·4	5·5	4·2	11·5	8·7	17·5	13·3
56	11 29·0	11 30·9	10 57·6	5·6	4·2	11·6	8·8	17·6	13·3
57	11 29·3	11 31·1	10 57·9	5·7	4·3	11·7	8·9	17·7	13·4
58	11 29·5	11 31·4	10 58·1	5·8	4·4	11·8	8·9	17·8	13·5
59	11 29·8	11 31·6	10 58·3	5·9	4·5	11·9	9·0	17·9	13·6
60	11 30·0	11 31·9	10 58·6	6·0	4·6	12·0	9·1	18·0	13·7

46ᵐ	SUN PLANETS	ARIES	MOON	v or d	Corrⁿ	v or d	Corrⁿ	v or d	Corrⁿ
s	° ′	° ′	° ′	′	′	′	′	′	′
00	11 30·0	11 31·9	10 58·6	0·0	0·0	6·0	4·7	12·0	9·3
01	11 30·3	11 32·1	10 58·8	0·1	0·1	6·1	4·7	12·1	9·4
02	11 30·5	11 32·4	10 59·0	0·2	0·2	6·2	4·8	12·2	9·5
03	11 30·8	11 32·6	10 59·3	0·3	0·2	6·3	4·9	12·3	9·5
04	11 31·0	11 32·9	10 59·5	0·4	0·3	6·4	5·0	12·4	9·6
05	11 31·3	11 33·1	10 59·8	0·5	0·4	6·5	5·0	12·5	9·7
06	11 31·5	11 33·4	11 00·0	0·6	0·5	6·6	5·1	12·6	9·8
07	11 31·8	11 33·6	11 00·2	0·7	0·5	6·7	5·2	12·7	9·8
08	11 32·0	11 33·9	11 00·5	0·8	0·6	6·8	5·3	12·8	9·9
09	11 32·3	11 34·1	11 00·7	0·9	0·7	6·9	5·3	12·9	10·0
10	11 32·5	11 34·4	11 01·0	1·0	0·8	7·0	5·4	13·0	10·1
11	11 32·8	11 34·6	11 01·2	1·1	0·9	7·1	5·5	13·1	10·2
12	11 33·0	11 34·9	11 01·4	1·2	0·9	7·2	5·6	13·2	10·2
13	11 33·3	11 35·1	11 01·7	1·3	1·0	7·3	5·7	13·3	10·3
14	11 33·5	11 35·4	11 01·9	1·4	1·1	7·4	5·7	13·4	10·4
15	11 33·8	11 35·6	11 02·1	1·5	1·2	7·5	5·8	13·5	10·5
16	11 34·0	11 35·9	11 02·4	1·6	1·2	7·6	5·9	13·6	10·5
17	11 34·3	11 36·2	11 02·6	1·7	1·3	7·7	6·0	13·7	10·6
18	11 34·5	11 36·4	11 02·9	1·8	1·4	7·8	6·0	13·8	10·7
19	11 34·8	11 36·7	11 03·1	1·9	1·5	7·9	6·1	13·9	10·8
20	11 35·0	11 36·9	11 03·3	2·0	1·6	8·0	6·2	14·0	10·9
21	11 35·3	11 37·2	11 03·6	2·1	1·6	8·1	6·3	14·1	10·9
22	11 35·5	11 37·4	11 03·8	2·2	1·7	8·2	6·4	14·2	11·0
23	11 35·8	11 37·7	11 04·1	2·3	1·8	8·3	6·4	14·3	11·1
24	11 36·0	11 37·9	11 04·3	2·4	1·9	8·4	6·5	14·4	11·2
25	11 36·3	11 38·2	11 04·5	2·5	1·9	8·5	6·6	14·5	11·2
26	11 36·5	11 38·4	11 04·8	2·6	2·0	8·6	6·7	14·6	11·3
27	11 36·8	11 38·7	11 05·0	2·7	2·1	8·7	6·7	14·7	11·4
28	11 37·0	11 38·9	11 05·2	2·8	2·2	8·8	6·8	14·8	11·5
29	11 37·3	11 39·2	11 05·5	2·9	2·2	8·9	6·9	14·9	11·5
30	11 37·5	11 39·4	11 05·7	3·0	2·3	9·0	7·0	15·0	11·6
31	11 37·8	11 39·7	11 06·0	3·1	2·4	9·1	7·1	15·1	11·7
32	11 38·0	11 39·9	11 06·2	3·2	2·5	9·2	7·1	15·2	11·8
33	11 38·3	11 40·2	11 06·4	3·3	2·6	9·3	7·2	15·3	11·9
34	11 38·5	11 40·4	11 06·7	3·4	2·6	9·4	7·3	15·4	11·9
35	11 38·8	11 40·7	11 06·9	3·5	2·7	9·5	7·4	15·5	12·0
36	11 39·0	11 40·9	11 07·2	3·6	2·8	9·6	7·4	15·6	12·1
37	11 39·3	11 41·2	11 07·4	3·7	2·9	9·7	7·5	15·7	12·2
38	11 39·5	11 41·4	11 07·6	3·8	2·9	9·8	7·6	15·8	12·2
39	11 39·8	11 41·7	11 07·9	3·9	3·0	9·9	7·7	15·9	12·3
40	11 40·0	11 41·9	11 08·1	4·0	3·1	10·0	7·8	16·0	12·4
41	11 40·3	11 42·2	11 08·3	4·1	3·2	10·1	7·8	16·1	12·5
42	11 40·5	11 42·4	11 08·6	4·2	3·3	10·2	7·9	16·2	12·6
43	11 40·8	11 42·7	11 08·8	4·3	3·3	10·3	8·0	16·3	12·6
44	11 41·0	11 42·9	11 09·1	4·4	3·4	10·4	8·1	16·4	12·7
45	11 41·3	11 43·2	11 09·3	4·5	3·5	10·5	8·1	16·5	12·8
46	11 41·5	11 43·4	11 09·5	4·6	3·6	10·6	8·2	16·6	12·9
47	11 41·8	11 43·7	11 09·8	4·7	3·6	10·7	8·3	16·7	12·9
48	11 42·0	11 43·9	11 10·0	4·8	3·7	10·8	8·4	16·8	13·0
49	11 42·3	11 44·2	11 10·3	4·9	3·8	10·9	8·4	16·9	13·1
50	11 42·5	11 44·4	11 10·5	5·0	3·9	11·0	8·5	17·0	13·2
51	11 42·8	11 44·7	11 10·7	5·1	4·0	11·1	8·6	17·1	13·3
52	11 43·0	11 44·9	11 11·0	5·2	4·0	11·2	8·7	17·2	13·3
53	11 43·3	11 45·2	11 11·2	5·3	4·1	11·3	8·8	17·3	13·4
54	11 43·5	11 45·4	11 11·5	5·4	4·2	11·4	8·8	17·4	13·5
55	11 43·8	11 45·7	11 11·7	5·5	4·3	11·5	8·9	17·5	13·6
56	11 44·0	11 45·9	11 11·9	5·6	4·3	11·6	9·0	17·6	13·6
57	11 44·3	11 46·2	11 12·2	5·7	4·4	11·7	9·1	17·7	13·7
58	11 44·5	11 46·4	11 12·4	5·8	4·5	11·8	9·1	17·8	13·8
59	11 44·8	11 46·7	11 12·6	5·9	4·6	11·9	9·2	17·9	13·9
60	11 45·0	11 46·9	11 12·9	6·0	4·7	12·0	9·3	18·0	14·0

47ᵐ	SUN PLANETS	ARIES	MOON	v or d	Corrⁿ	v or d	Corrⁿ	v or d	Corrⁿ
s	° ′	° ′	° ′	′	′	′	′	′	′
00	11 45·0	11 46·9	11 12·9	0·0	0·0	6·0	4·8	12·0	9·5
01	11 45·3	11 47·2	11 13·1	0·1	0·1	6·1	4·8	12·1	9·6
02	11 45·5	11 47·4	11 13·4	0·2	0·2	6·2	4·9	12·2	9·7
03	11 45·8	11 47·7	11 13·6	0·3	0·2	6·3	5·0	12·3	9·7
04	11 46·0	11 47·9	11 13·8	0·4	0·3	6·4	5·1	12·4	9·8
05	11 46·3	11 48·2	11 14·1	0·5	0·4	6·5	5·1	12·5	9·9
06	11 46·5	11 48·4	11 14·3	0·6	0·5	6·6	5·2	12·6	10·0
07	11 46·8	11 48·7	11 14·6	0·7	0·6	6·7	5·3	12·7	10·1
08	11 47·0	11 48·9	11 14·8	0·8	0·6	6·8	5·4	12·8	10·1
09	11 47·3	11 49·2	11 15·0	0·9	0·7	6·9	5·5	12·9	10·2
10	11 47·5	11 49·4	11 15·3	1·0	0·8	7·0	5·5	13·0	10·3
11	11 47·8	11 49·7	11 15·5	1·1	0·9	7·1	5·6	13·1	10·4
12	11 48·0	11 49·9	11 15·7	1·2	1·0	7·2	5·7	13·2	10·5
13	11 48·3	11 50·2	11 16·0	1·3	1·0	7·3	5·8	13·3	10·5
14	11 48·5	11 50·4	11 16·2	1·4	1·1	7·4	5·9	13·4	10·6
15	11 48·8	11 50·7	11 16·5	1·5	1·2	7·5	5·9	13·5	10·7
16	11 49·0	11 50·9	11 16·7	1·6	1·3	7·6	6·0	13·6	10·8
17	11 49·3	11 51·2	11 16·9	1·7	1·3	7·7	6·1	13·7	10·8
18	11 49·5	11 51·4	11 17·2	1·8	1·4	7·8	6·2	13·8	10·9
19	11 49·8	11 51·7	11 17·4	1·9	1·5	7·9	6·3	13·9	11·0
20	11 50·0	11 51·9	11 17·7	2·0	1·6	8·0	6·3	14·0	11·1
21	11 50·3	11 52·2	11 17·9	2·1	1·7	8·1	6·4	14·1	11·2
22	11 50·5	11 52·4	11 18·1	2·2	1·7	8·2	6·5	14·2	11·2
23	11 50·8	11 52·7	11 18·4	2·3	1·8	8·3	6·6	14·3	11·3
24	11 51·0	11 52·9	11 18·6	2·4	1·9	8·4	6·7	14·4	11·4
25	11 51·3	11 53·2	11 18·8	2·5	2·0	8·5	6·7	14·5	11·5
26	11 51·5	11 53·4	11 19·1	2·6	2·1	8·6	6·8	14·6	11·6
27	11 51·8	11 53·7	11 19·3	2·7	2·1	8·7	6·9	14·7	11·6
28	11 52·0	11 53·9	11 19·6	2·8	2·2	8·8	7·0	14·8	11·7
29	11 52·3	11 54·2	11 19·8	2·9	2·3	8·9	7·0	14·9	11·8
30	11 52·5	11 54·5	11 20·0	3·0	2·4	9·0	7·1	15·0	11·9
31	11 52·8	11 54·7	11 20·3	3·1	2·5	9·1	7·2	15·1	12·0
32	11 53·0	11 55·0	11 20·5	3·2	2·5	9·2	7·3	15·2	12·0
33	11 53·3	11 55·2	11 20·8	3·3	2·6	9·3	7·4	15·3	12·1
34	11 53·5	11 55·5	11 21·0	3·4	2·7	9·4	7·4	15·4	12·2
35	11 53·8	11 55·7	11 21·2	3·5	2·8	9·5	7·5	15·5	12·3
36	11 54·0	11 56·0	11 21·5	3·6	2·9	9·6	7·6	15·6	12·4
37	11 54·3	11 56·2	11 21·7	3·7	2·9	9·7	7·7	15·7	12·4
38	11 54·5	11 56·5	11 22·0	3·8	3·0	9·8	7·8	15·8	12·5
39	11 54·8	11 56·7	11 22·2	3·9	3·1	9·9	7·8	15·9	12·6
40	11 55·0	11 57·0	11 22·4	4·0	3·2	10·0	7·9	16·0	12·7
41	11 55·3	11 57·2	11 22·7	4·1	3·2	10·1	8·0	16·1	12·7
42	11 55·5	11 57·5	11 22·9	4·2	3·3	10·2	8·1	16·2	12·8
43	11 55·8	11 57·7	11 23·1	4·3	3·4	10·3	8·2	16·3	12·9
44	11 56·0	11 58·0	11 23·4	4·4	3·5	10·4	8·2	16·4	13·0
45	11 56·3	11 58·2	11 23·6	4·5	3·6	10·5	8·3	16·5	13·1
46	11 56·5	11 58·5	11 23·9	4·6	3·6	10·6	8·4	16·6	13·1
47	11 56·8	11 58·7	11 24·1	4·7	3·7	10·7	8·5	16·7	13·2
48	11 57·0	11 59·0	11 24·3	4·8	3·8	10·8	8·6	16·8	13·3
49	11 57·3	11 59·2	11 24·6	4·9	3·9	10·9	8·6	16·9	13·4
50	11 57·5	11 59·5	11 24·8	5·0	4·0	11·0	8·7	17·0	13·5
51	11 57·8	11 59·7	11 25·1	5·1	4·0	11·1	8·8	17·1	13·5
52	11 58·0	12 00·0	11 25·3	5·2	4·1	11·2	8·9	17·2	13·6
53	11 58·3	12 00·2	11 25·5	5·3	4·2	11·3	8·9	17·3	13·7
54	11 58·5	12 00·5	11 25·8	5·4	4·3	11·4	9·0	17·4	13·8
55	11 58·8	12 00·7	11 26·0	5·5	4·4	11·5	9·1	17·5	13·9
56	11 59·0	12 01·0	11 26·2	5·6	4·4	11·6	9·2	17·6	13·9
57	11 59·3	12 01·2	11 26·5	5·7	4·5	11·7	9·3	17·7	14·0
58	11 59·5	12 01·5	11 26·7	5·8	4·6	11·8	9·3	17·8	14·1
59	11 59·8	12 01·7	11 27·0	5·9	4·7	11·9	9·4	17·9	14·2
60	12 00·0	12 02·0	11 27·2	6·0	4·8	12·0	9·5	18·0	14·3

m 48	SUN PLANETS	ARIES	MOON	v or d	Corrⁿ	v or d	Corrⁿ	v or d	Corrⁿ
s	° ′	° ′	° ′	′	′	′	′	′	′
00	12 00·0	12 02·0	11 27·2	0·0	0·0	6·0	4·9	12·0	9·7
01	12 00·3	12 02·2	11 27·4	0·1	0·1	6·1	4·9	12·1	9·8
02	12 00·5	12 02·5	11 27·7	0·2	0·2	6·2	5·0	12·2	9·9
03	12 00·8	12 02·7	11 27·9	0·3	0·2	6·3	5·1	12·3	9·9
04	12 01·0	12 03·0	11 28·2	0·4	0·3	6·4	5·2	12·4	10·0
05	12 01·3	12 03·2	11 28·4	0·5	0·4	6·5	5·3	12·5	10·1
06	12 01·5	12 03·5	11 28·6	0·6	0·5	6·6	5·3	12·6	10·2
07	12 01·8	12 03·7	11 28·9	0·7	0·6	6·7	5·4	12·7	10·3
08	12 02·0	12 04·0	11 29·1	0·8	0·6	6·8	5·5	12·8	10·3
09	12 02·3	12 04·2	11 29·3	0·9	0·7	6·9	5·6	12·9	10·4
10	12 02·5	12 04·5	11 29·6	1·0	0·8	7·0	5·7	13·0	10·5
11	12 02·8	12 04·7	11 29·8	1·1	0·9	7·1	5·7	13·1	10·6
12	12 03·0	12 05·0	11 30·1	1·2	1·0	7·2	5·8	13·2	10·7
13	12 03·3	12 05·2	11 30·3	1·3	1·1	7·3	5·9	13·3	10·8
14	12 03·5	12 05·5	11 30·5	1·4	1·1	7·4	6·0	13·4	10·8
15	12 03·8	12 05·7	11 30·8	1·5	1·2	7·5	6·1	13·5	10·9
16	12 04·0	12 06·0	11 31·0	1·6	1·3	7·6	6·1	13·6	11·0
17	12 04·3	12 06·2	11 31·3	1·7	1·4	7·7	6·2	13·7	11·1
18	12 04·5	12 06·5	11 31·5	1·8	1·5	7·8	6·3	13·8	11·2
19	12 04·8	12 06·7	11 31·7	1·9	1·5	7·9	6·4	13·9	11·2
20	12 05·0	12 07·0	11 32·0	2·0	1·6	8·0	6·5	14·0	11·3
21	12 05·3	12 07·2	11 32·2	2·1	1·7	8·1	6·5	14·1	11·4
22	12 05·5	12 07·5	11 32·4	2·2	1·8	8·2	6·6	14·2	11·5
23	12 05·8	12 07·7	11 32·7	2·3	1·9	8·3	6·7	14·3	11·6
24	12 06·0	12 08·0	11 32·9	2·4	1·9	8·4	6·8	14·4	11·6
25	12 06·3	12 08·2	11 33·2	2·5	2·0	8·5	6·9	14·5	11·7
26	12 06·5	12 08·5	11 33·4	2·6	2·1	8·6	7·0	14·6	11·8
27	12 06·8	12 08·7	11 33·6	2·7	2·2	8·7	7·0	14·7	11·9
28	12 07·0	12 09·0	11 33·9	2·8	2·3	8·8	7·1	14·8	12·0
29	12 07·3	12 09·2	11 34·1	2·9	2·3	8·9	7·2	14·9	12·0
30	12 07·5	12 09·5	11 34·4	3·0	2·4	9·0	7·3	15·0	12·1
31	12 07·8	12 09·7	11 34·6	3·1	2·5	9·1	7·4	15·1	12·2
32	12 08·0	12 10·0	11 34·8	3·2	2·6	9·2	7·4	15·2	12·3
33	12 08·3	12 10·2	11 35·1	3·3	2·7	9·3	7·5	15·3	12·4
34	12 08·5	12 10·5	11 35·3	3·4	2·7	9·4	7·6	15·4	12·4
35	12 08·8	12 10·7	11 35·6	3·5	2·8	9·5	7·7	15·5	12·5
36	12 09·0	12 11·0	11 35·8	3·6	2·9	9·6	7·8	15·6	12·6
37	12 09·3	12 11·2	11 36·0	3·7	3·0	9·7	7·8	15·7	12·7
38	12 09·5	12 11·5	11 36·3	3·8	3·1	9·8	7·9	15·8	12·8
39	12 09·8	12 11·7	11 36·5	3·9	3·2	9·9	8·0	15·9	12·9
40	12 10·0	12 12·0	11 36·7	4·0	3·2	10·0	8·1	16·0	12·9
41	12 10·3	12 12·2	11 37·0	4·1	3·3	10·1	8·2	16·1	13·0
42	12 10·5	12 12·5	11 37·2	4·2	3·4	10·2	8·2	16·2	13·1
43	12 10·8	12 12·8	11 37·5	4·3	3·5	10·3	8·3	16·3	13·2
44	12 11·0	12 13·0	11 37·7	4·4	3·6	10·4	8·4	16·4	13·3
45	12 11·3	12 13·3	11 37·9	4·5	3·6	10·5	8·5	16·5	13·3
46	12 11·5	12 13·5	11 38·2	4·6	3·7	10·6	8·6	16·6	13·4
47	12 11·8	12 13·8	11 38·4	4·7	3·8	10·7	8·6	16·7	13·5
48	12 12·0	12 14·0	11 38·7	4·8	3·9	10·8	8·7	16·8	13·6
49	12 12·3	12 14·3	11 38·9	4·9	4·0	10·9	8·8	16·9	13·7
50	12 12·5	12 14·5	11 39·1	5·0	4·0	11·0	8·9	17·0	13·7
51	12 12·8	12 14·8	11 39·4	5·1	4·1	11·1	9·0	17·1	13·8
52	12 13·0	12 15·0	11 39·6	5·2	4·2	11·2	9·1	17·2	13·9
53	12 13·3	12 15·3	11 39·8	5·3	4·3	11·3	9·1	17·3	14·0
54	12 13·5	12 15·5	11 40·1	5·4	4·4	11·4	9·2	17·4	14·1
55	12 13·8	12 15·8	11 40·3	5·5	4·4	11·5	9·3	17·5	14·1
56	12 14·0	12 16·0	11 40·6	5·6	4·5	11·6	9·4	17·6	14·2
57	12 14·3	12 16·3	11 40·8	5·7	4·6	11·7	9·5	17·7	14·3
58	12 14·5	12 16·5	11 41·0	5·8	4·7	11·8	9·5	17·8	14·4
59	12 14·8	12 16·8	11 41·3	5·9	4·8	11·9	9·6	17·9	14·5
60	12 15·0	12 17·0	11 41·5	6·0	4·9	12·0	9·7	18·0	14·6

m 49	SUN PLANETS	ARIES	MOON	v or d	Corrⁿ	v or d	Corrⁿ	v or d	Corrⁿ
s	° ′	° ′	° ′	′	′	′	′	′	′
00	12 15·0	12 17·0	11 41·5	0·0	0·0	6·0	5·0	12·0	9·9
01	12 15·3	12 17·3	11 41·8	0·1	0·1	6·1	5·0	12·1	10·0
02	12 15·5	12 17·5	11 42·0	0·2	0·2	6·2	5·1	12·2	10·1
03	12 15·8	12 17·8	11 42·2	0·3	0·2	6·3	5·2	12·3	10·1
04	12 16·0	12 18·0	11 42·5	0·4	0·3	6·4	5·3	12·4	10·2
05	12 16·3	12 18·3	11 42·7	0·5	0·4	6·5	5·4	12·5	10·3
06	12 16·5	12 18·5	11 42·9	0·6	0·5	6·6	5·4	12·6	10·4
07	12 16·8	12 18·8	11 43·2	0·7	0·6	6·7	5·5	12·7	10·5
08	12 17·0	12 19·0	11 43·4	0·8	0·7	6·8	5·6	12·8	10·6
09	12 17·3	12 19·3	11 43·7	0·9	0·7	6·9	5·7	12·9	10·6
10	12 17·5	12 19·5	11 43·9	1·0	0·8	7·0	5·8	13·0	10·7
11	12 17·8	12 19·8	11 44·1	1·1	0·9	7·1	5·9	13·1	10·8
12	12 18·0	12 20·0	11 44·4	1·2	1·0	7·2	5·9	13·2	10·9
13	12 18·3	12 20·3	11 44·6	1·3	1·1	7·3	6·0	13·3	11·0
14	12 18·5	12 20·5	11 44·9	1·4	1·2	7·4	6·1	13·4	11·1
15	12 18·8	12 20·8	11 45·1	1·5	1·2	7·5	6·2	13·5	11·1
16	12 19·0	12 21·0	11 45·3	1·6	1·3	7·6	6·3	13·6	11·2
17	12 19·3	12 21·3	11 45·6	1·7	1·4	7·7	6·4	13·7	11·3
18	12 19·5	12 21·5	11 45·8	1·8	1·5	7·8	6·4	13·8	11·4
19	12 19·8	12 21·8	11 46·1	1·9	1·6	7·9	6·5	13·9	11·5
20	12 20·0	12 22·0	11 46·3	2·0	1·7	8·0	6·6	14·0	11·6
21	12 20·3	12 22·3	11 46·5	2·1	1·7	8·1	6·7	14·1	11·6
22	12 20·5	12 22·5	11 46·8	2·2	1·8	8·2	6·8	14·2	11·7
23	12 20·8	12 22·8	11 47·0	2·3	1·9	8·3	6·8	14·3	11·8
24	12 21·0	12 23·0	11 47·2	2·4	2·0	8·4	6·9	14·4	11·9
25	12 21·3	12 23·3	11 47·5	2·5	2·1	8·5	7·0	14·5	12·0
26	12 21·5	12 23·5	11 47·7	2·6	2·1	8·6	7·1	14·6	12·0
27	12 21·8	12 23·8	11 48·0	2·7	2·2	8·7	7·2	14·7	12·1
28	12 22·0	12 24·0	11 48·2	2·8	2·3	8·8	7·3	14·8	12·2
29	12 22·3	12 24·3	11 48·4	2·9	2·4	8·9	7·3	14·9	12·3
30	12 22·5	12 24·5	11 48·7	3·0	2·5	9·0	7·4	15·0	12·4
31	12 22·8	12 24·8	11 48·9	3·1	2·6	9·1	7·5	15·1	12·5
32	12 23·0	12 25·0	11 49·2	3·2	2·6	9·2	7·6	15·2	12·5
33	12 23·3	12 25·3	11 49·4	3·3	2·7	9·3	7·7	15·3	12·6
34	12 23·5	12 25·5	11 49·6	3·4	2·8	9·4	7·8	15·4	12·7
35	12 23·8	12 25·8	11 49·9	3·5	2·9	9·5	7·8	15·5	12·8
36	12 24·0	12 26·0	11 50·1	3·6	3·0	9·6	7·9	15·6	12·9
37	12 24·3	12 26·3	11 50·3	3·7	3·1	9·7	8·0	15·7	13·0
38	12 24·5	12 26·5	11 50·6	3·8	3·1	9·8	8·1	15·8	13·0
39	12 24·8	12 26·8	11 50·8	3·9	3·2	9·9	8·2	15·9	13·1
40	12 25·0	12 27·0	11 51·1	4·0	3·3	10·0	8·3	16·0	13·2
41	12 25·3	12 27·3	11 51·3	4·1	3·4	10·1	8·3	16·1	13·3
42	12 25·5	12 27·5	11 51·5	4·2	3·5	10·2	8·4	16·2	13·4
43	12 25·8	12 27·8	11 51·8	4·3	3·5	10·3	8·5	16·3	13·4
44	12 26·0	12 28·0	11 52·0	4·4	3·6	10·4	8·6	16·4	13·5
45	12 26·3	12 28·3	11 52·3	4·5	3·7	10·5	8·7	16·5	13·6
46	12 26·5	12 28·5	11 52·5	4·6	3·8	10·6	8·7	16·6	13·7
47	12 26·8	12 28·8	11 52·7	4·7	3·9	10·7	8·8	16·7	13·8
48	12 27·0	12 29·0	11 53·0	4·8	4·0	10·8	8·9	16·8	13·9
49	12 27·3	12 29·3	11 53·2	4·9	4·0	10·9	9·0	16·9	13·9
50	12 27·5	12 29·5	11 53·4	5·0	4·1	11·0	9·1	17·0	14·0
51	12 27·8	12 29·8	11 53·7	5·1	4·2	11·1	9·2	17·1	14·1
52	12 28·0	12 30·0	11 53·9	5·2	4·3	11·2	9·2	17·2	14·2
53	12 28·3	12 30·3	11 54·2	5·3	4·4	11·3	9·3	17·3	14·3
54	12 28·5	12 30·5	11 54·4	5·4	4·5	11·4	9·4	17·4	14·4
55	12 28·8	12 30·8	11 54·6	5·5	4·5	11·5	9·5	17·5	14·4
56	12 29·0	12 31·1	11 54·9	5·6	4·6	11·6	9·6	17·6	14·5
57	12 29·3	12 31·3	11 55·1	5·7	4·7	11·7	9·7	17·7	14·6
58	12 29·5	12 31·6	11 55·4	5·8	4·8	11·8	9·7	17·8	14·7
59	12 29·8	12 31·8	11 55·6	5·9	4·9	11·9	9·8	17·9	14·8
60	12 30·0	12 32·1	11 55·8	6·0	5·0	12·0	9·9	18·0	14·9

50m	SUN PLANETS	ARIES	MOON	v or d	Corrn	v or d	Corrn	v or d	Corrn
s	° ′	° ′	° ′	′	′	′	′	′	′
00	12 30·0	12 32·1	11 55·8	0·0	0·0	6·0	5·1	12·0	10·1
01	12 30·3	12 32·3	11 56·1	0·1	0·1	6·1	5·1	12·1	10·2
02	12 30·5	12 32·6	11 56·3	0·2	0·2	6·2	5·2	12·2	10·3
03	12 30·8	12 32·8	11 56·5	0·3	0·3	6·3	5·3	12·3	10·4
04	12 31·0	12 33·1	11 56·8	0·4	0·3	6·4	5·4	12·4	10·4
05	12 31·3	12 33·3	11 57·0	0·5	0·4	6·5	5·5	12·5	10·5
06	12 31·5	12 33·6	11 57·3	0·6	0·5	6·6	5·6	12·6	10·6
07	12 31·8	12 33·8	11 57·5	0·7	0·6	6·7	5·6	12·7	10·7
08	12 32·0	12 34·1	11 57·7	0·8	0·7	6·8	5·7	12·8	10·8
09	12 32·3	12 34·3	11 58·0	0·9	0·8	6·9	5·8	12·9	10·9
10	12 32·5	12 34·6	11 58·2	1·0	0·8	7·0	5·9	13·0	10·9
11	12 32·8	12 34·8	11 58·5	1·1	0·9	7·1	6·0	13·1	11·0
12	12 33·0	12 35·1	11 58·7	1·2	1·0	7·2	6·1	13·2	11·1
13	12 33·3	12 35·3	11 58·9	1·3	1·1	7·3	6·1	13·3	11·2
14	12 33·5	12 35·6	11 59·2	1·4	1·2	7·4	6·2	13·4	11·3
15	12 33·8	12 35·8	11 59·4	1·5	1·3	7·5	6·3	13·5	11·4
16	12 34·0	12 36·1	11 59·7	1·6	1·3	7·6	6·4	13·6	11·4
17	12 34·3	12 36·3	11 59·9	1·7	1·4	7·7	6·5	13·7	11·5
18	12 34·5	12 36·6	12 00·1	1·8	1·5	7·8	6·6	13·8	11·6
19	12 34·8	12 36·8	12 00·4	1·9	1·6	7·9	6·6	13·9	11·7
20	12 35·0	12 37·1	12 00·6	2·0	1·7	8·0	6·7	14·0	11·8
21	12 35·3	12 37·3	12 00·8	2·1	1·8	8·1	6·8	14·1	11·9
22	12 35·5	12 37·6	12 01·1	2·2	1·9	8·2	6·9	14·2	12·0
23	12 35·8	12 37·8	12 01·3	2·3	1·9	8·3	7·0	14·3	12·0
24	12 36·0	12 38·1	12 01·6	2·4	2·0	8·4	7·1	14·4	12·1
25	12 36·3	12 38·3	12 01·8	2·5	2·1	8·5	7·2	14·5	12·2
26	12 36·5	12 38·6	12 02·0	2·6	2·2	8·6	7·2	14·6	12·3
27	12 36·8	12 38·8	12 02·3	2·7	2·3	8·7	7·3	14·7	12·4
28	12 37·0	12 39·1	12 02·5	2·8	2·4	8·8	7·4	14·8	12·5
29	12 37·3	12 39·3	12 02·8	2·9	2·4	8·9	7·5	14·9	12·5
30	12 37·5	12 39·6	12 03·0	3·0	2·5	9·0	7·6	15·0	12·6
31	12 37·8	12 39·8	12 03·2	3·1	2·6	9·1	7·7	15·1	12·7
32	12 38·0	12 40·1	12 03·5	3·2	2·7	9·2	7·7	15·2	12·8
33	12 38·3	12 40·3	12 03·7	3·3	2·8	9·3	7·8	15·3	12·9
34	12 38·5	12 40·6	12 03·9	3·4	2·9	9·4	7·9	15·4	13·0
35	12 38·8	12 40·8	12 04·2	3·5	2·9	9·5	8·0	15·5	13·0
36	12 39·0	12 41·1	12 04·4	3·6	3·0	9·6	8·1	15·6	13·1
37	12 39·3	12 41·3	12 04·7	3·7	3·1	9·7	8·2	15·7	13·2
38	12 39·5	12 41·6	12 04·9	3·8	3·2	9·8	8·2	15·8	13·3
39	12 39·8	12 41·8	12 05·1	3·9	3·3	9·9	8·3	15·9	13·4
40	12 40·0	12 42·1	12 05·4	4·0	3·4	10·0	8·4	16·0	13·5
41	12 40·3	12 42·3	12 05·6	4·1	3·5	10·1	8·5	16·1	13·6
42	12 40·5	12 42·6	12 05·9	4·2	3·5	10·2	8·6	16·2	13·6
43	12 40·8	12 42·8	12 06·1	4·3	3·6	10·3	8·7	16·3	13·7
44	12 41·0	12 43·1	12 06·3	4·4	3·7	10·4	8·8	16·4	13·8
45	12 41·3	12 43·3	12 06·6	4·5	3·8	10·5	8·8	16·5	13·9
46	12 41·5	12 43·6	12 06·8	4·6	3·9	10·6	8·9	16·6	14·0
47	12 41·8	12 43·8	12 07·0	4·7	4·0	10·7	9·0	16·7	14·1
48	12 42·0	12 44·1	12 07·3	4·8	4·0	10·8	9·1	16·8	14·1
49	12 42·3	12 44·3	12 07·5	4·9	4·1	10·9	9·2	16·9	14·2
50	12 42·5	12 44·6	12 07·8	5·0	4·2	11·0	9·3	17·0	14·3
51	12 42·8	12 44·8	12 08·0	5·1	4·3	11·1	9·3	17·1	14·4
52	12 43·0	12 45·1	12 08·2	5·2	4·4	11·2	9·4	17·2	14·5
53	12 43·3	12 45·3	12 08·5	5·3	4·5	11·3	9·5	17·3	14·6
54	12 43·5	12 45·6	12 08·7	5·4	4·5	11·4	9·6	17·4	14·6
55	12 43·8	12 45·8	12 09·0	5·5	4·6	11·5	9·7	17·5	14·7
56	12 44·0	12 46·1	12 09·2	5·6	4·7	11·6	9·8	17·6	14·8
57	12 44·3	12 46·3	12 09·4	5·7	4·8	11·7	9·8	17·7	14·9
58	12 44·5	12 46·6	12 09·7	5·8	4·9	11·8	9·9	17·8	15·0
59	12 44·8	12 46·8	12 09·9	5·9	5·0	11·9	10·0	17·9	15·1
60	12 45·0	12 47·1	12 10·2	6·0	5·1	12·0	10·1	18·0	15·2

51m	SUN PLANETS	ARIES	MOON	v or d	Corrn	v or d	Corrn	v or d	Corrn
s	° ′	° ′	° ′	′	′	′	′	′	′
00	12 45·0	12 47·1	12 10·2	0·0	0·0	6·0	5·2	12·0	10·3
01	12 45·3	12 47·3	12 10·4	0·1	0·1	6·1	5·2	12·1	10·4
02	12 45·5	12 47·6	12 10·6	0·2	0·2	6·2	5·3	12·2	10·5
03	12 45·8	12 47·8	12 10·9	0·3	0·3	6·3	5·4	12·3	10·6
04	12 46·0	12 48·1	12 11·1	0·4	0·3	6·4	5·5	12·4	10·6
05	12 46·3	12 48·3	12 11·3	0·5	0·4	6·5	5·6	12·5	10·7
06	12 46·5	12 48·6	12 11·6	0·6	0·5	6·6	5·7	12·6	10·8
07	12 46·8	12 48·8	12 11·8	0·7	0·6	6·7	5·8	12·7	10·9
08	12 47·0	12 49·1	12 12·1	0·8	0·7	6·8	5·8	12·8	11·0
09	12 47·3	12 49·4	12 12·3	0·9	0·8	6·9	5·9	12·9	11·1
10	12 47·5	12 49·6	12 12·5	1·0	0·9	7·0	6·0	13·0	11·2
11	12 47·8	12 49·9	12 12·8	1·1	0·9	7·1	6·1	13·1	11·2
12	12 48·0	12 50·1	12 13·0	1·2	1·0	7·2	6·2	13·2	11·3
13	12 48·3	12 50·4	12 13·3	1·3	1·1	7·3	6·3	13·3	11·4
14	12 48·5	12 50·6	12 13·5	1·4	1·2	7·4	6·4	13·4	11·5
15	12 48·8	12 50·9	12 13·7	1·5	1·3	7·5	6·4	13·5	11·6
16	12 49·0	12 51·1	12 14·0	1·6	1·4	7·6	6·5	13·6	11·7
17	12 49·3	12 51·4	12 14·2	1·7	1·5	7·7	6·6	13·7	11·8
18	12 49·5	12 51·6	12 14·4	1·8	1·5	7·8	6·7	13·8	11·8
19	12 49·8	12 51·9	12 14·7	1·9	1·6	7·9	6·8	13·9	11·9
20	12 50·0	12 52·1	12 14·9	2·0	1·7	8·0	6·9	14·0	12·0
21	12 50·3	12 52·4	12 15·2	2·1	1·8	8·1	7·0	14·1	12·1
22	12 50·5	12 52·6	12 15·4	2·2	1·9	8·2	7·0	14·2	12·2
23	12 50·8	12 52·9	12 15·6	2·3	2·0	8·3	7·1	14·3	12·3
24	12 51·0	12 53·1	12 15·9	2·4	2·1	8·4	7·2	14·4	12·4
25	12 51·3	12 53·4	12 16·1	2·5	2·1	8·5	7·3	14·5	12·4
26	12 51·5	12 53·6	12 16·4	2·6	2·2	8·6	7·4	14·6	12·5
27	12 51·8	12 53·9	12 16·6	2·7	2·3	8·7	7·5	14·7	12·6
28	12 52·0	12 54·1	12 16·8	2·8	2·4	8·8	7·6	14·8	12·7
29	12 52·3	12 54·4	12 17·1	2·9	2·5	8·9	7·6	14·9	12·8
30	12 52·5	12 54·6	12 17·3	3·0	2·6	9·0	7·7	15·0	12·9
31	12 52·8	12 54·9	12 17·5	3·1	2·7	9·1	7·8	15·1	13·0
32	12 53·0	12 55·1	12 17·8	3·2	2·7	9·2	7·9	15·2	13·0
33	12 53·3	12 55·4	12 18·0	3·3	2·8	9·3	8·0	15·3	13·1
34	12 53·5	12 55·6	12 18·3	3·4	2·9	9·4	8·1	15·4	13·2
35	12 53·8	12 55·9	12 18·5	3·5	3·0	9·5	8·2	15·5	13·3
36	12 54·0	12 56·1	12 18·7	3·6	3·1	9·6	8·2	15·6	13·4
37	12 54·3	12 56·4	12 19·0	3·7	3·2	9·7	8·3	15·7	13·5
38	12 54·5	12 56·6	12 19·2	3·8	3·3	9·8	8·4	15·8	13·6
39	12 54·8	12 56·9	12 19·5	3·9	3·3	9·9	8·5	15·9	13·6
40	12 55·0	12 57·1	12 19·7	4·0	3·4	10·0	8·6	16·0	13·7
41	12 55·3	12 57·4	12 19·9	4·1	3·5	10·1	8·7	16·1	13·8
42	12 55·5	12 57·6	12 20·2	4·2	3·6	10·2	8·8	16·2	13·9
43	12 55·8	12 57·9	12 20·4	4·3	3·7	10·3	8·8	16·3	14·0
44	12 56·0	12 58·1	12 20·6	4·4	3·8	10·4	8·9	16·4	14·1
45	12 56·3	12 58·4	12 20·9	4·5	3·9	10·5	9·0	16·5	14·2
46	12 56·5	12 58·6	12 21·1	4·6	3·9	10·6	9·1	16·6	14·2
47	12 56·8	12 58·9	12 21·4	4·7	4·0	10·7	9·2	16·7	14·3
48	12 57·0	12 59·1	12 21·6	4·8	4·1	10·8	9·3	16·8	14·4
49	12 57·3	12 59·4	12 21·8	4·9	4·2	10·9	9·4	16·9	14·5
50	12 57·5	12 59·6	12 22·1	5·0	4·3	11·0	9·4	17·0	14·6
51	12 57·8	12 59·9	12 22·3	5·1	4·4	11·1	9·5	17·1	14·7
52	12 58·0	13 00·1	12 22·6	5·2	4·5	11·2	9·6	17·2	14·8
53	12 58·3	13 00·4	12 22·8	5·3	4·5	11·3	9·7	17·3	14·8
54	12 58·5	13 00·6	12 23·0	5·4	4·6	11·4	9·8	17·4	14·9
55	12 58·8	13 00·9	12 23·3	5·5	4·7	11·5	9·9	17·5	15·0
56	12 59·0	13 01·1	12 23·5	5·6	4·8	11·6	10·0	17·6	15·1
57	12 59·3	13 01·4	12 23·8	5·7	4·9	11·7	10·0	17·7	15·2
58	12 59·5	13 01·6	12 24·0	5·8	5·0	11·8	10·1	17·8	15·3
59	12 59·8	13 01·9	12 24·2	5·9	5·1	11·9	10·2	17·9	15·4
60	13 00·0	13 02·1	12 24·5	6·0	5·2	12·0	10·3	18·0	15·5

52m s	SUN PLANETS ° ′	ARIES ° ′	MOON ° ′	v or d ′	Corrn ′	v or d ′	Corrn ′	v or d ′	Corrn ′
00	13 00·0	13 02·1	12 24·5	0·0	0·0	6·0	5·3	12·0	10·5
01	13 00·3	13 02·4	12 24·7	0·1	0·1	6·1	5·3	12·1	10·6
02	13 00·5	13 02·6	12 24·9	0·2	0·2	6·2	5·4	12·2	10·7
03	13 00·8	13 02·9	12 25·2	0·3	0·3	6·3	5·5	12·3	10·8
04	13 01·0	13 03·1	12 25·4	0·4	0·4	6·4	5·6	12·4	10·9
05	13 01·3	13 03·4	12 25·7	0·5	0·4	6·5	5·7	12·5	10·9
06	13 01·5	13 03·6	12 25·9	0·6	0·5	6·6	5·8	12·6	11·0
07	13 01·8	13 03·9	12 26·1	0·7	0·6	6·7	5·9	12·7	11·1
08	13 02·0	13 04·1	12 26·4	0·8	0·7	6·8	6·0	12·8	11·2
09	13 02·3	13 04·4	12 26·6	0·9	0·8	6·9	6·0	12·9	11·3
10	13 02·5	13 04·6	12 26·9	1·0	0·9	7·0	6·1	13·0	11·4
11	13 02·8	13 04·9	12 27·1	1·1	1·0	7·1	6·2	13·1	11·5
12	13 03·0	13 05·1	12 27·3	1·2	1·1	7·2	6·3	13·2	11·6
13	13 03·3	13 05·4	12 27·6	1·3	1·1	7·3	6·4	13·3	11·6
14	13 03·5	13 05·6	12 27·8	1·4	1·2	7·4	6·5	13·4	11·7
15	13 03·8	13 05·9	12 28·0	1·5	1·3	7·5	6·6	13·5	11·8
16	13 04·0	13 06·1	12 28·3	1·6	1·4	7·6	6·7	13·6	11·9
17	13 04·3	13 06·4	12 28·5	1·7	1·5	7·7	6·7	13·7	12·0
18	13 04·5	13 06·6	12 28·8	1·8	1·6	7·8	6·8	13·8	12·1
19	13 04·8	13 06·9	12 29·0	1·9	1·7	7·9	6·9	13·9	12·2
20	13 05·0	13 07·1	12 29·2	2·0	1·8	8·0	7·0	14·0	12·3
21	13 05·3	13 07·4	12 29·5	2·1	1·8	8·1	7·1	14·1	12·3
22	13 05·5	13 07·7	12 29·7	2·2	1·9	8·2	7·2	14·2	12·4
23	13 05·8	13 07·9	12 30·0	2·3	2·0	8·3	7·3	14·3	12·5
24	13 06·0	13 08·2	12 30·2	2·4	2·1	8·4	7·4	14·4	12·6
25	13 06·3	13 08·4	12 30·4	2·5	2·2	8·5	7·4	14·5	12·7
26	13 06·5	13 08·7	12 30·7	2·6	2·3	8·6	7·5	14·6	12·8
27	13 06·8	13 08·9	12 30·9	2·7	2·4	8·7	7·6	14·7	12·9
28	13 07·0	13 09·2	12 31·1	2·8	2·5	8·8	7·7	14·8	13·0
29	13 07·3	13 09·4	12 31·4	2·9	2·5	8·9	7·8	14·9	13·0
30	13 07·5	13 09·7	12 31·6	3·0	2·6	9·0	7·9	15·0	13·1
31	13 07·8	13 09·9	12 31·9	3·1	2·7	9·1	8·0	15·1	13·2
32	13 08·0	13 10·2	12 32·1	3·2	2·8	9·2	8·0	15·2	13·3
33	13 08·3	13 10·4	12 32·3	3·3	2·9	9·3	8·1	15·3	13·4
34	13 08·5	13 10·7	12 32·6	3·4	3·0	9·4	8·2	15·4	13·5
35	13 08·8	13 10·9	12 32·8	3·5	3·1	9·5	8·3	15·5	13·6
36	13 09·0	13 11·2	12 33·1	3·6	3·2	9·6	8·4	15·6	13·7
37	13 09·3	13 11·4	12 33·3	3·7	3·2	9·7	8·5	15·7	13·7
38	13 09·5	13 11·7	12 33·5	3·8	3·3	9·8	8·6	15·8	13·8
39	13 09·8	13 11·9	12 33·8	3·9	3·4	9·9	8·7	15·9	13·9
40	13 10·0	13 12·2	12 34·0	4·0	3·5	10·0	8·8	16·0	14·0
41	13 10·3	13 12·4	12 34·2	4·1	3·6	10·1	8·8	16·1	14·1
42	13 10·5	13 12·7	12 34·5	4·2	3·7	10·2	8·9	16·2	14·2
43	13 10·8	13 12·9	12 34·7	4·3	3·8	10·3	9·0	16·3	14·3
44	13 11·0	13 13·2	12 35·0	4·4	3·9	10·4	9·1	16·4	14·3
45	13 11·3	13 13·4	12 35·2	4·5	3·9	10·5	9·2	16·5	14·4
46	13 11·5	13 13·7	12 35·4	4·6	4·0	10·6	9·3	16·6	14·5
47	13 11·8	13 13·9	12 35·7	4·7	4·1	10·7	9·4	16·7	14·6
48	13 12·0	13 14·2	12 35·9	4·8	4·2	10·8	9·5	16·8	14·7
49	13 12·3	13 14·4	12 36·2	4·9	4·3	10·9	9·5	16·9	14·8
50	13 12·5	13 14·7	12 36·4	5·0	4·4	11·0	9·6	17·0	14·9
51	13 12·8	13 14·9	12 36·6	5·1	4·5	11·1	9·7	17·1	15·0
52	13 13·0	13 15·2	12 36·9	5·2	4·6	11·2	9·8	17·2	15·1
53	13 13·3	13 15·4	12 37·1	5·3	4·6	11·3	9·9	17·3	15·1
54	13 13·5	13 15·7	12 37·4	5·4	4·7	11·4	10·0	17·4	15·2
55	13 13·8	13 15·9	12 37·6	5·5	4·8	11·5	10·1	17·5	15·3
56	13 14·0	13 16·2	12 37·8	5·6	4·9	11·6	10·2	17·6	15·4
57	13 14·3	13 16·4	12 38·1	5·7	5·0	11·7	10·2	17·7	15·5
58	13 14·5	13 16·7	12 38·3	5·8	5·1	11·8	10·3	17·8	15·6
59	13 14·8	13 16·9	12 38·5	5·9	5·2	11·9	10·4	17·9	15·7
60	13 15·0	13 17·2	12 38·8	6·0	5·3	12·0	10·5	18·0	15·8

53m s	SUN PLANETS ° ′	ARIES ° ′	MOON ° ′	v or d ′	Corrn ′	v or d ′	Corrn ′	v or d ′	Corrn ′
00	13 15·0	13 17·2	12 38·8	0·0	0·0	6·0	5·4	12·0	10·7
01	13 15·3	13 17·4	12 39·0	0·1	0·1	6·1	5·4	12·1	10·8
02	13 15·5	13 17·7	12 39·3	0·2	0·2	6·2	5·5	12·2	10·9
03	13 15·8	13 17·9	12 39·5	0·3	0·3	6·3	5·6	12·3	11·0
04	13 16·0	13 18·2	12 39·7	0·4	0·4	6·4	5·7	12·4	11·1
05	13 16·3	13 18·4	12 40·0	0·5	0·4	6·5	5·8	12·5	11·1
06	13 16·5	13 18·7	12 40·2	0·6	0·5	6·6	5·9	12·6	11·2
07	13 16·8	13 18·9	12 40·5	0·7	0·6	6·7	6·0	12·7	11·3
08	13 17·0	13 19·2	12 40·7	0·8	0·7	6·8	6·1	12·8	11·4
09	13 17·3	13 19·4	12 40·9	0·9	0·8	6·9	6·2	12·9	11·5
10	13 17·5	13 19·7	12 41·2	1·0	0·9	7·0	6·2	13·0	11·6
11	13 17·8	13 19·9	12 41·4	1·1	1·0	7·1	6·3	13·1	11·7
12	13 18·0	13 20·2	12 41·6	1·2	1·1	7·2	6·4	13·2	11·8
13	13 18·3	13 20·4	12 41·9	1·3	1·2	7·3	6·5	13·3	11·9
14	13 18·5	13 20·7	12 42·1	1·4	1·2	7·4	6·6	13·4	11·9
15	13 18·8	13 20·9	12 42·4	1·5	1·3	7·5	6·7	13·5	12·0
16	13 19·0	13 21·2	12 42·6	1·6	1·4	7·6	6·8	13·6	12·1
17	13 19·3	13 21·4	12 42·8	1·7	1·5	7·7	6·9	13·7	12·2
18	13 19·5	13 21·7	12 43·1	1·8	1·6	7·8	7·0	13·8	12·3
19	13 19·8	13 21·9	12 43·3	1·9	1·7	7·9	7·0	13·9	12·4
20	13 20·0	13 22·2	12 43·6	2·0	1·8	8·0	7·1	14·0	12·5
21	13 20·3	13 22·4	12 43·8	2·1	1·9	8·1	7·2	14·1	12·6
22	13 20·5	13 22·7	12 44·0	2·2	2·0	8·2	7·3	14·2	12·7
23	13 20·8	13 22·9	12 44·3	2·3	2·1	8·3	7·4	14·3	12·8
24	13 21·0	13 23·2	12 44·5	2·4	2·1	8·4	7·5	14·4	12·8
25	13 21·3	13 23·4	12 44·7	2·5	2·2	8·5	7·6	14·5	12·9
26	13 21·5	13 23·7	12 45·0	2·6	2·3	8·6	7·7	14·6	13·0
27	13 21·8	13 23·9	12 45·2	2·7	2·4	8·7	7·8	14·7	13·1
28	13 22·0	13 24·2	12 45·5	2·8	2·5	8·8	7·8	14·8	13·2
29	13 22·3	13 24·4	12 45·7	2·9	2·6	8·9	7·9	14·9	13·3
30	13 22·5	13 24·7	12 45·9	3·0	2·7	9·0	8·0	15·0	13·4
31	13 22·8	13 24·9	12 46·2	3·1	2·8	9·1	8·1	15·1	13·5
32	13 23·0	13 25·2	12 46·4	3·2	2·9	9·2	8·2	15·2	13·6
33	13 23·3	13 25·4	12 46·7	3·3	2·9	9·3	8·3	15·3	13·6
34	13 23·5	13 25·7	12 46·9	3·4	3·0	9·4	8·4	15·4	13·7
35	13 23·8	13 26·0	12 47·1	3·5	3·1	9·5	8·5	15·5	13·8
36	13 24·0	13 26·2	12 47·4	3·6	3·2	9·6	8·6	15·6	13·9
37	13 24·3	13 26·5	12 47·6	3·7	3·3	9·7	8·6	15·7	14·0
38	13 24·5	13 26·7	12 47·9	3·8	3·4	9·8	8·7	15·8	14·1
39	13 24·8	13 27·0	12 48·1	3·9	3·5	9·9	8·8	15·9	14·2
40	13 25·0	13 27·2	12 48·3	4·0	3·6	10·0	8·9	16·0	14·3
41	13 25·3	13 27·5	12 48·6	4·1	3·7	10·1	9·0	16·1	14·4
42	13 25·5	13 27·7	12 48·8	4·2	3·7	10·2	9·1	16·2	14·4
43	13 25·8	13 28·0	12 49·0	4·3	3·8	10·3	9·2	16·3	14·5
44	13 26·0	13 28·2	12 49·3	4·4	3·9	10·4	9·3	16·4	14·6
45	13 26·3	13 28·5	12 49·5	4·5	4·0	10·5	9·4	16·5	14·7
46	13 26·5	13 28·7	12 49·8	4·6	4·1	10·6	9·5	16·6	14·8
47	13 26·8	13 29·0	12 50·0	4·7	4·2	10·7	9·5	16·7	14·9
48	13 27·0	13 29·2	12 50·2	4·8	4·3	10·8	9·6	16·8	15·0
49	13 27·3	13 29·5	12 50·5	4·9	4·4	10·9	9·7	16·9	15·1
50	13 27·5	13 29·7	12 50·7	5·0	4·5	11·0	9·8	17·0	15·2
51	13 27·8	13 30·0	12 51·0	5·1	4·5	11·1	9·9	17·1	15·2
52	13 28·0	13 30·2	12 51·2	5·2	4·6	11·2	10·0	17·2	15·3
53	13 28·3	13 30·5	12 51·4	5·3	4·7	11·3	10·1	17·3	15·4
54	13 28·5	13 30·7	12 51·7	5·4	4·8	11·4	10·2	17·4	15·5
55	13 28·8	13 31·0	12 51·9	5·5	4·9	11·5	10·3	17·5	15·6
56	13 29·0	13 31·2	12 52·1	5·6	5·0	11·6	10·3	17·6	15·7
57	13 29·3	13 31·5	12 52·4	5·7	5·1	11·7	10·4	17·7	15·8
58	13 29·5	13 31·7	12 52·6	5·8	5·2	11·8	10·5	17·8	15·9
59	13 29·8	13 32·0	12 52·9	5·9	5·3	11·9	10·6	17·9	16·0
60	13 30·0	13 32·2	12 53·1	6·0	5·4	12·0	10·7	18·0	16·1

54m s	SUN PLANETS ° ′	ARIES ° ′	MOON ° ′	v or d ′	Corrⁿ ′	v or d ′	Corrⁿ ′	v or d ′	Corrⁿ ′
00	13 30·0	13 32·2	12 53·1	0·0	0·0	6·0	5·5	12·0	10·9
01	13 30·3	13 32·5	12 53·3	0·1	0·1	6·1	5·5	12·1	11·0
02	13 30·5	13 32·7	12 53·6	0·2	0·2	6·2	5·6	12·2	11·1
03	13 30·8	13 33·0	12 53·8	0·3	0·3	6·3	5·7	12·3	11·2
04	13 31·0	13 33·2	12 54·1	0·4	0·4	6·4	5·8	12·4	11·3
05	13 31·3	13 33·5	12 54·3	0·5	0·5	6·5	5·9	12·5	11·4
06	13 31·5	13 33·7	12 54·5	0·6	0·5	6·6	6·0	12·6	11·4
07	13 31·8	13 34·0	12 54·8	0·7	0·6	6·7	6·1	12·7	11·5
08	13 32·0	13 34·2	12 55·0	0·8	0·7	6·8	6·2	12·8	11·6
09	13 32·3	13 34·5	12 55·2	0·9	0·8	6·9	6·3	12·9	11·7
10	13 32·5	13 34·7	12 55·5	1·0	0·9	7·0	6·4	13·0	11·8
11	13 32·8	13 35·0	12 55·7	1·1	1·0	7·1	6·4	13·1	11·9
12	13 33·0	13 35·2	12 56·0	1·2	1·1	7·2	6·5	13·2	12·0
13	13 33·3	13 35·5	12 56·2	1·3	1·2	7·3	6·6	13·3	12·1
14	13 33·5	13 35·7	12 56·4	1·4	1·3	7·4	6·7	13·4	12·2
15	13 33·8	13 36·0	12 56·7	1·5	1·4	7·5	6·8	13·5	12·3
16	13 34·0	13 36·2	12 56·9	1·6	1·5	7·6	6·9	13·6	12·4
17	13 34·3	13 36·5	12 57·2	1·7	1·5	7·7	7·0	13·7	12·4
18	13 34·5	13 36·7	12 57·4	1·8	1·6	7·8	7·1	13·8	12·5
19	13 34·8	13 37·0	12 57·6	1·9	1·7	7·9	7·2	13·9	12·6
20	13 35·0	13 37·2	12 57·9	2·0	1·8	8·0	7·3	14·0	12·7
21	13 35·3	13 37·5	12 58·1	2·1	1·9	8·1	7·4	14·1	12·8
22	13 35·5	13 37·7	12 58·3	2·2	2·0	8·2	7·4	14·2	12·9
23	13 35·8	13 38·0	12 58·6	2·3	2·1	8·3	7·5	14·3	13·0
24	13 36·0	13 38·2	12 58·8	2·4	2·2	8·4	7·6	14·4	13·1
25	13 36·3	13 38·5	12 59·1	2·5	2·3	8·5	7·7	14·5	13·2
26	13 36·5	13 38·7	12 59·3	2·6	2·4	8·6	7·8	14·6	13·3
27	13 36·8	13 39·0	12 59·5	2·7	2·5	8·7	7·9	14·7	13·4
28	13 37·0	13 39·2	12 59·8	2·8	2·5	8·8	8·0	14·8	13·4
29	13 37·3	13 39·5	13 00·0	2·9	2·6	8·9	8·1	14·9	13·5
30	13 37·5	13 39·7	13 00·3	3·0	2·7	9·0	8·2	15·0	13·6
31	13 37·8	13 40·0	13 00·5	3·1	2·8	9·1	8·3	15·1	13·7
32	13 38·0	13 40·2	13 00·7	3·2	2·9	9·2	8·4	15·2	13·8
33	13 38·3	13 40·5	13 01·0	3·3	3·0	9·3	8·4	15·3	13·9
34	13 38·5	13 40·7	13 01·2	3·4	3·1	9·4	8·5	15·4	14·0
35	13 38·8	13 41·0	13 01·5	3·5	3·2	9·5	8·6	15·5	14·1
36	13 39·0	13 41·2	13 01·7	3·6	3·3	9·6	8·7	15·6	14·2
37	13 39·3	13 41·5	13 01·9	3·7	3·4	9·7	8·8	15·7	14·3
38	13 39·5	13 41·7	13 02·2	3·8	3·5	9·8	8·9	15·8	14·4
39	13 39·8	13 42·0	13 02·4	3·9	3·5	9·9	9·0	15·9	14·4
40	13 40·0	13 42·2	13 02·6	4·0	3·6	10·0	9·1	16·0	14·5
41	13 40·3	13 42·5	13 02·9	4·1	3·7	10·1	9·2	16·1	14·6
42	13 40·5	13 42·7	13 03·1	4·2	3·8	10·2	9·3	16·2	14·7
43	13 40·8	13 43·0	13 03·4	4·3	3·9	10·3	9·4	16·3	14·8
44	13 41·0	13 43·2	13 03·6	4·4	4·0	10·4	9·4	16·4	14·9
45	13 41·3	13 43·5	13 03·8	4·5	4·1	10·5	9·5	16·5	15·0
46	13 41·5	13 43·7	13 04·1	4·6	4·2	10·6	9·6	16·6	15·1
47	13 41·8	13 44·0	13 04·3	4·7	4·3	10·7	9·7	16·7	15·2
48	13 42·0	13 44·3	13 04·6	4·8	4·4	10·8	9·8	16·8	15·3
49	13 42·3	13 44·5	13 04·8	4·9	4·5	10·9	9·9	16·9	15·4
50	13 42·5	13 44·8	13 05·0	5·0	4·5	11·0	10·0	17·0	15·4
51	13 42·8	13 45·0	13 05·3	5·1	4·6	11·1	10·1	17·1	15·5
52	13 43·0	13 45·3	13 05·5	5·2	4·7	11·2	10·2	17·2	15·6
53	13 43·3	13 45·5	13 05·7	5·3	4·8	11·3	10·3	17·3	15·7
54	13 43·5	13 45·8	13 06·0	5·4	4·9	11·4	10·4	17·4	15·8
55	13 43·8	13 46·0	13 06·2	5·5	5·0	11·5	10·4	17·5	15·9
56	13 44·0	13 46·3	13 06·5	5·6	5·1	11·6	10·5	17·6	16·0
57	13 44·3	13 46·5	13 06·7	5·7	5·2	11·7	10·6	17·7	16·1
58	13 44·5	13 46·8	13 06·9	5·8	5·3	11·8	10·7	17·8	16·2
59	13 44·8	13 47·0	13 07·2	5·9	5·4	11·9	10·8	17·9	16·3
60	13 45·0	13 47·3	13 07·4	6·0	5·5	12·0	10·9	18·0	16·4

55m s	SUN PLANETS ° ′	ARIES ° ′	MOON ° ′	v or d ′	Corrⁿ ′	v or d ′	Corrⁿ ′	v or d ′	Corrⁿ ′
00	13 45·0	13 47·3	13 07·4	0·0	0·0	6·0	5·6	12·0	11·1
01	13 45·3	13 47·5	13 07·7	0·1	0·1	6·1	5·6	12·1	11·2
02	13 45·5	13 47·8	13 07·9	0·2	0·2	6·2	5·7	12·2	11·3
03	13 45·8	13 48·0	13 08·1	0·3	0·3	6·3	5·8	12·3	11·4
04	13 46·0	13 48·3	13 08·4	0·4	0·4	6·4	5·9	12·4	11·5
05	13 46·3	13 48·5	13 08·6	0·5	0·5	6·5	6·0	12·5	11·6
06	13 46·5	13 48·8	13 08·8	0·6	0·6	6·6	6·1	12·6	11·7
07	13 46·8	13 49·0	13 09·1	0·7	0·6	6·7	6·2	12·7	11·7
08	13 47·0	13 49·3	13 09·3	0·8	0·7	6·8	6·3	12·8	11·8
09	13 47·3	13 49·5	13 09·6	0·9	0·8	6·9	6·4	12·9	11·9
10	13 47·5	13 49·8	13 09·8	1·0	0·9	7·0	6·5	13·0	12·0
11	13 47·8	13 50·0	13 10·0	1·1	1·0	7·1	6·6	13·1	12·1
12	13 48·0	13 50·3	13 10·3	1·2	1·1	7·2	6·7	13·2	12·2
13	13 48·3	13 50·5	13 10·5	1·3	1·2	7·3	6·8	13·3	12·3
14	13 48·5	13 50·8	13 10·8	1·4	1·3	7·4	6·8	13·4	12·4
15	13 48·8	13 51·0	13 11·0	1·5	1·4	7·5	6·9	13·5	12·5
16	13 49·0	13 51·3	13 11·2	1·6	1·5	7·6	7·0	13·6	12·6
17	13 49·3	13 51·5	13 11·5	1·7	1·6	7·7	7·1	13·7	12·7
18	13 49·5	13 51·8	13 11·7	1·8	1·7	7·8	7·2	13·8	12·8
19	13 49·8	13 52·0	13 12·0	1·9	1·8	7·9	7·3	13·9	12·9
20	13 50·0	13 52·3	13 12·2	2·0	1·9	8·0	7·4	14·0	13·0
21	13 50·3	13 52·5	13 12·4	2·1	1·9	8·1	7·5	14·1	13·0
22	13 50·5	13 52·8	13 12·7	2·2	2·0	8·2	7·6	14·2	13·1
23	13 50·8	13 53·0	13 12·9	2·3	2·1	8·3	7·7	14·3	13·2
24	13 51·0	13 53·3	13 13·1	2·4	2·2	8·4	7·8	14·4	13·3
25	13 51·3	13 53·5	13 13·4	2·5	2·3	8·5	7·9	14·5	13·4
26	13 51·5	13 53·8	13 13·6	2·6	2·4	8·6	8·0	14·6	13·5
27	13 51·8	13 54·0	13 13·9	2·7	2·5	8·7	8·0	14·7	13·6
28	13 52·0	13 54·3	13 14·1	2·8	2·6	8·8	8·1	14·8	13·7
29	13 52·3	13 54·5	13 14·3	2·9	2·7	8·9	8·2	14·9	13·8
30	13 52·5	13 54·8	13 14·6	3·0	2·8	9·0	8·3	15·0	13·9
31	13 52·8	13 55·0	13 14·8	3·1	2·9	9·1	8·4	15·1	14·0
32	13 53·0	13 55·3	13 15·1	3·2	3·0	9·2	8·5	15·2	14·1
33	13 53·3	13 55·5	13 15·3	3·3	3·1	9·3	8·6	15·3	14·2
34	13 53·5	13 55·8	13 15·5	3·4	3·1	9·4	8·7	15·4	14·2
35	13 53·8	13 56·0	13 15·8	3·5	3·2	9·5	8·8	15·5	14·3
36	13 54·0	13 56·3	13 16·0	3·6	3·3	9·6	8·9	15·6	14·4
37	13 54·3	13 56·5	13 16·2	3·7	3·4	9·7	9·0	15·7	14·5
38	13 54·5	13 56·8	13 16·5	3·8	3·5	9·8	9·1	15·8	14·6
39	13 54·8	13 57·0	13 16·7	3·9	3·6	9·9	9·2	15·9	14·7
40	13 55·0	13 57·3	13 17·0	4·0	3·7	10·0	9·3	16·0	14·8
41	13 55·3	13 57·5	13 17·2	4·1	3·8	10·1	9·3	16·1	14·9
42	13 55·5	13 57·8	13 17·4	4·2	3·9	10·2	9·4	16·2	15·0
43	13 55·8	13 58·0	13 17·7	4·3	4·0	10·3	9·5	16·3	15·1
44	13 56·0	13 58·3	13 17·9	4·4	4·1	10·4	9·6	16·4	15·2
45	13 56·3	13 58·5	13 18·2	4·5	4·2	10·5	9·7	16·5	15·3
46	13 56·5	13 58·8	13 18·4	4·6	4·3	10·6	9·8	16·6	15·4
47	13 56·8	13 59·0	13 18·6	4·7	4·3	10·7	9·9	16·7	15·4
48	13 57·0	13 59·3	13 18·9	4·8	4·4	10·8	10·0	16·8	15·5
49	13 57·3	13 59·5	13 19·1	4·9	4·5	10·9	10·1	16·9	15·6
50	13 57·5	13 59·8	13 19·3	5·0	4·6	11·0	10·2	17·0	15·7
51	13 57·8	14 00·0	13 19·6	5·1	4·7	11·1	10·3	17·1	15·8
52	13 58·0	14 00·3	13 19·8	5·2	4·8	11·2	10·4	17·2	15·9
53	13 58·3	14 00·5	13 20·1	5·3	4·9	11·3	10·5	17·3	16·0
54	13 58·5	14 00·8	13 20·3	5·4	5·0	11·4	10·5	17·4	16·1
55	13 58·8	14 01·0	13 20·5	5·5	5·1	11·5	10·6	17·5	16·2
56	13 59·0	14 01·3	13 20·8	5·6	5·2	11·6	10·7	17·6	16·3
57	13 59·3	14 01·5	13 21·0	5·7	5·3	11·7	10·8	17·7	16·4
58	13 59·5	14 01·8	13 21·3	5·8	5·4	11·8	10·9	17·8	16·5
59	13 59·8	14 02·0	13 21·5	5·9	5·5	11·9	11·0	17·9	16·6
60	14 00·0	14 02·3	13 21·7	6·0	5·6	12·0	11·1	18·0	16·7

56m	SUN PLANETS	ARIES	MOON	v or d	Corrⁿ	v or d	Corrⁿ	v or d	Corrⁿ
s	° ′	° ′	° ′	′	′	′	′	′	′
00	14 00·0	14 02·3	13 21·7	0·0	0·0	6·0	5·7	12·0	11·3
01	14 00·3	14 02·6	13 22·0	0·1	0·1	6·1	5·7	12·1	11·4
02	14 00·5	14 02·8	13 22·2	0·2	0·2	6·2	5·8	12·2	11·5
03	14 00·8	14 03·1	13 22·4	0·3	0·3	6·3	5·9	12·3	11·6
04	14 01·0	14 03·3	13 22·7	0·4	0·4	6·4	6·0	12·4	11·7
05	14 01·3	14 03·6	13 22·9	0·5	0·5	6·5	6·1	12·5	11·8
06	14 01·5	14 03·8	13 23·2	0·6	0·6	6·6	6·2	12·6	11·9
07	14 01·8	14 04·1	13 23·4	0·7	0·7	6·7	6·3	12·7	12·0
08	14 02·0	14 04·3	13 23·6	0·8	0·8	6·8	6·4	12·8	12·1
09	14 02·3	14 04·6	13 23·9	0·9	0·8	6·9	6·5	12·9	12·1
10	14 02·5	14 04·8	13 24·1	1·0	0·9	7·0	6·6	13·0	12·2
11	14 02·8	14 05·1	13 24·4	1·1	1·0	7·1	6·7	13·1	12·3
12	14 03·0	14 05·3	13 24·6	1·2	1·1	7·2	6·8	13·2	12·4
13	14 03·3	14 05·6	13 24·8	1·3	1·2	7·3	6·9	13·3	12·5
14	14 03·5	14 05·8	13 25·1	1·4	1·3	7·4	7·0	13·4	12·6
15	14 03·8	14 06·1	13 25·3	1·5	1·4	7·5	7·1	13·5	12·7
16	14 04·0	14 06·3	13 25·6	1·6	1·5	7·6	7·2	13·6	12·8
17	14 04·3	14 06·6	13 25·8	1·7	1·6	7·7	7·3	13·7	12·9
18	14 04·5	14 06·8	13 26·0	1·8	1·7	7·8	7·3	13·8	13·0
19	14 04·8	14 07·1	13 26·3	1·9	1·8	7·9	7·4	13·9	13·1
20	14 05·0	14 07·3	13 26·5	2·0	1·9	8·0	7·5	14·0	13·2
21	14 05·3	14 07·6	13 26·7	2·1	2·0	8·1	7·6	14·1	13·3
22	14 05·5	14 07·8	13 27·0	2·2	2·1	8·2	7·7	14·2	13·4
23	14 05·8	14 08·1	13 27·2	2·3	2·2	8·3	7·8	14·3	13·5
24	14 06·0	14 08·3	13 27·5	2·4	2·3	8·4	7·9	14·4	13·6
25	14 06·3	14 08·6	13 27·7	2·5	2·4	8·5	8·0	14·5	13·7
26	14 06·5	14 08·8	13 27·9	2·6	2·4	8·6	8·1	14·6	13·7
27	14 06·8	14 09·1	13 28·2	2·7	2·5	8·7	8·2	14·7	13·8
28	14 07·0	14 09·3	13 28·4	2·8	2·6	8·8	8·3	14·8	13·9
29	14 07·3	14 09·6	13 28·7	2·9	2·7	8·9	8·4	14·9	14·0
30	14 07·5	14 09·8	13 28·9	3·0	2·8	9·0	8·5	15·0	14·1
31	14 07·8	14 10·1	13 29·1	3·1	2·9	9·1	8·6	15·1	14·2
32	14 08·0	14 10·3	13 29·4	3·2	3·0	9·2	8·7	15·2	14·3
33	14 08·3	14 10·6	13 29·6	3·3	3·1	9·3	8·8	15·3	14·4
34	14 08·5	14 10·8	13 29·8	3·4	3·2	9·4	8·9	15·4	14·5
35	14 08·8	14 11·1	13 30·1	3·5	3·3	9·5	8·9	15·5	14·6
36	14 09·0	14 11·3	13 30·3	3·6	3·4	9·6	9·0	15·6	14·7
37	14 09·3	14 11·6	13 30·6	3·7	3·5	9·7	9·1	15·7	14·8
38	14 09·5	14 11·8	13 30·8	3·8	3·6	9·8	9·2	15·8	14·9
39	14 09·8	14 12·1	13 31·0	3·9	3·7	9·9	9·3	15·9	15·0
40	14 10·0	14 12·3	13 31·3	4·0	3·8	10·0	9·4	16·0	15·1
41	14 10·3	14 12·6	13 31·5	4·1	3·9	10·1	9·5	16·1	15·2
42	14 10·5	14 12·8	13 31·8	4·2	4·0	10·2	9·6	16·2	15·3
43	14 10·8	14 13·1	13 32·0	4·3	4·0	10·3	9·7	16·3	15·3
44	14 11·0	14 13·3	13 32·2	4·4	4·1	10·4	9·8	16·4	15·4
45	14 11·3	14 13·6	13 32·5	4·5	4·2	10·5	9·9	16·5	15·5
46	14 11·5	14 13·8	13 32·7	4·6	4·3	10·6	10·0	16·6	15·6
47	14 11·8	14 14·1	13 32·9	4·7	4·4	10·7	10·1	16·7	15·7
48	14 12·0	14 14·3	13 33·2	4·8	4·5	10·8	10·2	16·8	15·8
49	14 12·3	14 14·6	13 33·4	4·9	4·6	10·9	10·3	16·9	15·9
50	14 12·5	14 14·8	13 33·7	5·0	4·7	11·0	10·4	17·0	16·0
51	14 12·8	14 15·1	13 33·9	5·1	4·8	11·1	10·5	17·1	16·1
52	14 13·0	14 15·3	13 34·1	5·2	4·9	11·2	10·5	17·2	16·2
53	14 13·3	14 15·6	13 34·4	5·3	5·0	11·3	10·6	17·3	16·3
54	14 13·5	14 15·8	13 34·6	5·4	5·1	11·4	10·7	17·4	16·4
55	14 13·8	14 16·1	13 34·9	5·5	5·2	11·5	10·8	17·5	16·5
56	14 14·0	14 16·3	13 35·1	5·6	5·3	11·6	10·9	17·6	16·6
57	14 14·3	14 16·6	13 35·3	5·7	5·4	11·7	11·0	17·7	16·7
58	14 14·5	14 16·8	13 35·6	5·8	5·5	11·8	11·1	17·8	16·8
59	14 14·8	14 17·1	13 35·8	5·9	5·6	11·9	11·2	17·9	16·9
60	14 15·0	14 17·3	13 36·1	6·0	5·7	12·0	11·3	18·0	17·0

57m	SUN PLANETS	ARIES	MOON	v or d	Corrⁿ	v or d	Corrⁿ	v or d	Corrⁿ
s	° ′	° ′	° ′	′	′	′	′	′	′
00	14 15·0	14 17·3	13 36·1	0·0	0·0	6·0	5·8	12·0	11·5
01	14 15·3	14 17·6	13 36·3	0·1	0·1	6·1	5·8	12·1	11·6
02	14 15·5	14 17·8	13 36·5	0·2	0·2	6·2	5·9	12·2	11·7
03	14 15·8	14 18·1	13 36·8	0·3	0·3	6·3	6·0	12·3	11·8
04	14 16·0	14 18·3	13 37·0	0·4	0·4	6·4	6·1	12·4	11·9
05	14 16·3	14 18·6	13 37·2	0·5	0·5	6·5	6·2	12·5	12·0
06	14 16·5	14 18·8	13 37·5	0·6	0·6	6·6	6·3	12·6	12·1
07	14 16·8	14 19·1	13 37·7	0·7	0·7	6·7	6·4	12·7	12·2
08	14 17·0	14 19·3	13 38·0	0·8	0·8	6·8	6·5	12·8	12·3
09	14 17·3	14 19·6	13 38·2	0·9	0·9	6·9	6·6	12·9	12·4
10	14 17·5	14 19·8	13 38·4	1·0	1·0	7·0	6·7	13·0	12·5
11	14 17·8	14 20·1	13 38·7	1·1	1·1	7·1	6·8	13·1	12·6
12	14 18·0	14 20·3	13 38·9	1·2	1·2	7·2	6·9	13·2	12·7
13	14 18·3	14 20·6	13 39·2	1·3	1·2	7·3	7·0	13·3	12·7
14	14 18·5	14 20·9	13 39·4	1·4	1·3	7·4	7·1	13·4	12·8
15	14 18·8	14 21·1	13 39·6	1·5	1·4	7·5	7·2	13·5	12·9
16	14 19·0	14 21·4	13 39·9	1·6	1·5	7·6	7·3	13·6	13·0
17	14 19·3	14 21·6	13 40·1	1·7	1·6	7·7	7·4	13·7	13·1
18	14 19·5	14 21·9	13 40·3	1·8	1·7	7·8	7·5	13·8	13·2
19	14 19·8	14 22·1	13 40·6	1·9	1·8	7·9	7·6	13·9	13·3
20	14 20·0	14 22·4	13 40·8	2·0	1·9	8·0	7·7	14·0	13·4
21	14 20·3	14 22·6	13 41·1	2·1	2·0	8·1	7·8	14·1	13·5
22	14 20·5	14 22·9	13 41·3	2·2	2·1	8·2	7·9	14·2	13·6
23	14 20·8	14 23·1	13 41·5	2·3	2·2	8·3	8·0	14·3	13·7
24	14 21·0	14 23·4	13 41·8	2·4	2·3	8·4	8·1	14·4	13·8
25	14 21·3	14 23·6	13 42·0	2·5	2·4	8·5	8·1	14·5	13·9
26	14 21·5	14 23·9	13 42·3	2·6	2·5	8·6	8·2	14·6	14·0
27	14 21·8	14 24·1	13 42·5	2·7	2·6	8·7	8·3	14·7	14·1
28	14 22·0	14 24·4	13 42·7	2·8	2·7	8·8	8·4	14·8	14·2
29	14 22·3	14 24·6	13 43·0	2·9	2·8	8·9	8·5	14·9	14·3
30	14 22·5	14 24·9	13 43·2	3·0	2·9	9·0	8·6	15·0	14·4
31	14 22·8	14 25·1	13 43·4	3·1	3·0	9·1	8·7	15·1	14·5
32	14 23·0	14 25·4	13 43·7	3·2	3·1	9·2	8·8	15·2	14·6
33	14 23·3	14 25·6	13 43·9	3·3	3·2	9·3	8·9	15·3	14·7
34	14 23·5	14 25·9	13 44·2	3·4	3·3	9·4	9·0	15·4	14·8
35	14 23·8	14 26·1	13 44·4	3·5	3·4	9·5	9·1	15·5	14·9
36	14 24·0	14 26·4	13 44·6	3·6	3·5	9·6	9·2	15·6	15·0
37	14 24·3	14 26·6	13 44·9	3·7	3·5	9·7	9·3	15·7	15·0
38	14 24·5	14 26·9	13 45·1	3·8	3·6	9·8	9·4	15·8	15·1
39	14 24·8	14 27·1	13 45·4	3·9	3·7	9·9	9·5	15·9	15·2
40	14 25·0	14 27·4	13 45·6	4·0	3·8	10·0	9·6	16·0	15·3
41	14 25·3	14 27·6	13 45·8	4·1	3·9	10·1	9·7	16·1	15·4
42	14 25·5	14 27·9	13 46·1	4·2	4·0	10·2	9·8	16·2	15·5
43	14 25·8	14 28·1	13 46·3	4·3	4·1	10·3	9·9	16·3	15·6
44	14 26·0	14 28·4	13 46·5	4·4	4·2	10·4	10·0	16·4	15·7
45	14 26·3	14 28·6	13 46·8	4·5	4·3	10·5	10·1	16·5	15·8
46	14 26·5	14 28·9	13 47·0	4·6	4·4	10·6	10·2	16·6	15·9
47	14 26·8	14 29·1	13 47·3	4·7	4·5	10·7	10·3	16·7	16·0
48	14 27·0	14 29·4	13 47·5	4·8	4·6	10·8	10·4	16·8	16·1
49	14 27·3	14 29·6	13 47·7	4·9	4·7	10·9	10·4	16·9	16·2
50	14 27·5	14 29·9	13 48·0	5·0	4·8	11·0	10·5	17·0	16·3
51	14 27·8	14 30·1	13 48·2	5·1	4·9	11·1	10·6	17·1	16·4
52	14 28·0	14 30·4	13 48·5	5·2	5·0	11·2	10·7	17·2	16·5
53	14 28·3	14 30·6	13 48·7	5·3	5·1	11·3	10·8	17·3	16·6
54	14 28·5	14 30·9	13 48·9	5·4	5·2	11·4	10·9	17·4	16·7
55	14 28·8	14 31·1	13 49·2	5·5	5·3	11·5	11·0	17·5	16·8
56	14 29·0	14 31·4	13 49·4	5·6	5·4	11·6	11·1	17·6	16·9
57	14 29·3	14 31·6	13 49·7	5·7	5·5	11·7	11·2	17·7	17·0
58	14 29·5	14 31·9	13 49·9	5·8	5·6	11·8	11·3	17·8	17·1
59	14 29·8	14 32·1	13 50·1	5·9	5·7	11·9	11·4	17·9	17·2
60	14 30·0	14 32·4	13 50·4	6·0	5·8	12·0	11·5	18·0	17·3

58ᵐ s	SUN PLANETS ° ′	ARIES ° ′	MOON ° ′	v or d ′	Corrⁿ ′	v or d ′	Corrⁿ ′	v or d ′	Corrⁿ ′
00	14 30·0	14 32·4	13 50·4	0·0	0·0	6·0	5·9	12·0	11·7
01	14 30·3	14 32·6	13 50·6	0·1	0·1	6·1	5·9	12·1	11·8
02	14 30·5	14 32·9	13 50·8	0·2	0·2	6·2	6·0	12·2	11·9
03	14 30·8	14 33·1	13 51·1	0·3	0·3	6·3	6·1	12·3	12·0
04	14 31·0	14 33·4	13 51·3	0·4	0·4	6·4	6·2	12·4	12·1
05	14 31·3	14 33·6	13 51·6	0·5	0·5	6·5	6·3	12·5	12·2
06	14 31·5	14 33·9	13 51·8	0·6	0·6	6·6	6·4	12·6	12·3
07	14 31·8	14 34·1	13 52·0	0·7	0·7	6·7	6·5	12·7	12·4
08	14 32·0	14 34·4	13 52·3	0·8	0·8	6·8	6·6	12·8	12·5
09	14 32·3	14 34·6	13 52·5	0·9	0·9	6·9	6·7	12·9	12·6
10	14 32·5	14 34·9	13 52·8	1·0	1·0	7·0	6·8	13·0	12·7
11	14 32·8	14 35·1	13 53·0	1·1	1·1	7·1	6·9	13·1	12·8
12	14 33·0	14 35·4	13 53·2	1·2	1·2	7·2	7·0	13·2	12·9
13	14 33·3	14 35·6	13 53·5	1·3	1·3	7·3	7·1	13·3	13·0
14	14 33·5	14 35·9	13 53·7	1·4	1·4	7·4	7·2	13·4	13·1
15	14 33·8	14 36·1	13 53·9	1·5	1·5	7·5	7·3	13·5	13·2
16	14 34·0	14 36·4	13 54·2	1·6	1·6	7·6	7·4	13·6	13·3
17	14 34·3	14 36·6	13 54·4	1·7	1·7	7·7	7·5	13·7	13·4
18	14 34·5	14 36·9	13 54·7	1·8	1·8	7·8	7·6	13·8	13·5
19	14 34·8	14 37·1	13 54·9	1·9	1·9	7·9	7·7	13·9	13·6
20	14 35·0	14 37·4	13 55·1	2·0	2·0	8·0	7·8	14·0	13·7
21	14 35·3	14 37·6	13 55·4	2·1	2·0	8·1	7·9	14·1	13·7
22	14 35·5	14 37·9	13 55·6	2·2	2·1	8·2	8·0	14·2	13·8
23	14 35·8	14 38·1	13 55·9	2·3	2·2	8·3	8·1	14·3	13·9
24	14 36·0	14 38·4	13 56·1	2·4	2·3	8·4	8·2	14·4	14·0
25	14 36·3	14 38·6	13 56·3	2·5	2·4	8·5	8·3	14·5	14·1
26	14 36·5	14 38·9	13 56·6	2·6	2·5	8·6	8·4	14·6	14·2
27	14 36·8	14 39·2	13 56·8	2·7	2·6	8·7	8·5	14·7	14·3
28	14 37·0	14 39·4	13 57·0	2·8	2·7	8·8	8·6	14·8	14·4
29	14 37·3	14 39·7	13 57·3	2·9	2·8	8·9	8·7	14·9	14·5
30	14 37·5	14 39·9	13 57·5	3·0	2·9	9·0	8·8	15·0	14·6
31	14 37·8	14 40·2	13 57·8	3·1	3·0	9·1	8·9	15·1	14·7
32	14 38·0	14 40·4	13 58·0	3·2	3·1	9·2	9·0	15·2	14·8
33	14 38·3	14 40·7	13 58·2	3·3	3·2	9·3	9·1	15·3	14·9
34	14 38·5	14 40·9	13 58·5	3·4	3·3	9·4	9·2	15·4	15·0
35	14 38·8	14 41·2	13 58·7	3·5	3·4	9·5	9·3	15·5	15·1
36	14 39·0	14 41·4	13 59·0	3·6	3·5	9·6	9·4	15·6	15·2
37	14 39·3	14 41·7	13 59·2	3·7	3·6	9·7	9·5	15·7	15·3
38	14 39·5	14 41·9	13 59·4	3·8	3·7	9·8	9·6	15·8	15·4
39	14 39·8	14 42·2	13 59·7	3·9	3·8	9·9	9·7	15·9	15·5
40	14 40·0	14 42·4	13 59·9	4·0	3·9	10·0	9·8	16·0	15·6
41	14 40·3	14 42·7	14 00·1	4·1	4·0	10·1	9·8	16·1	15·7
42	14 40·5	14 42·9	14 00·4	4·2	4·1	10·2	9·9	16·2	15·8
43	14 40·8	14 43·2	14 00·6	4·3	4·2	10·3	10·0	16·3	15·9
44	14 41·0	14 43·4	14 00·9	4·4	4·3	10·4	10·1	16·4	16·0
45	14 41·3	14 43·7	14 01·1	4·5	4·4	10·5	10·2	16·5	16·1
46	14 41·5	14 43·9	14 01·3	4·6	4·5	10·6	10·3	16·6	16·2
47	14 41·8	14 44·2	14 01·6	4·7	4·6	10·7	10·4	16·7	16·3
48	14 42·0	14 44·4	14 01·8	4·8	4·7	10·8	10·5	16·8	16·4
49	14 42·3	14 44·7	14 02·1	4·9	4·8	10·9	10·6	16·9	16·5
50	14 42·5	14 44·9	14 02·3	5·0	4·9	11·0	10·7	17·0	16·6
51	14 42·8	14 45·2	14 02·5	5·1	5·0	11·1	10·8	17·1	16·7
52	14 43·0	14 45·4	14 02·8	5·2	5·1	11·2	10·9	17·2	16·8
53	14 43·3	14 45·7	14 03·0	5·3	5·2	11·3	11·0	17·3	16·9
54	14 43·5	14 45·9	14 03·3	5·4	5·3	11·4	11·1	17·4	17·0
55	14 43·8	14 46·2	14 03·5	5·5	5·4	11·5	11·2	17·5	17·1
56	14 44·0	14 46·4	14 03·7	5·6	5·5	11·6	11·3	17·6	17·2
57	14 44·3	14 46·7	14 04·0	5·7	5·6	11·7	11·4	17·7	17·3
58	14 44·5	14 46·9	14 04·2	5·8	5·7	11·8	11·5	17·8	17·4
59	14 44·8	14 47·2	14 04·4	5·9	5·8	11·9	11·6	17·9	17·5
60	14 45·0	14 47·4	14 04·7	6·0	5·9	12·0	11·7	18·0	17·6

59ᵐ s	SUN PLANETS ° ′	ARIES ° ′	MOON ° ′	v or d ′	Corrⁿ ′	v or d ′	Corrⁿ ′	v or d ′	Corrⁿ ′
00	14 45·0	14 47·4	14 04·7	0·0	0·0	6·0	6·0	12·0	11·9
01	14 45·3	14 47·7	14 04·9	0·1	0·1	6·1	6·0	12·1	12·0
02	14 45·5	14 47·9	14 05·2	0·2	0·2	6·2	6·1	12·2	12·1
03	14 45·8	14 48·2	14 05·4	0·3	0·3	6·3	6·2	12·3	12·2
04	14 46·0	14 48·4	14 05·6	0·4	0·4	6·4	6·3	12·4	12·3
05	14 46·3	14 48·7	14 05·9	0·5	0·5	6·5	6·4	12·5	12·4
06	14 46·5	14 48·9	14 06·1	0·6	0·6	6·6	6·5	12·6	12·5
07	14 46·8	14 49·2	14 06·4	0·7	0·7	6·7	6·6	12·7	12·6
08	14 47·0	14 49·4	14 06·6	0·8	0·8	6·8	6·7	12·8	12·7
09	14 47·3	14 49·7	14 06·8	0·9	0·9	6·9	6·8	12·9	12·8
10	14 47·5	14 49·9	14 07·1	1·0	1·0	7·0	6·9	13·0	12·9
11	14 47·8	14 50·2	14 07·3	1·1	1·1	7·1	7·0	13·1	13·0
12	14 48·0	14 50·4	14 07·5	1·2	1·2	7·2	7·1	13·2	13·1
13	14 48·3	14 50·7	14 07·8	1·3	1·3	7·3	7·2	13·3	13·2
14	14 48·5	14 50·9	14 08·0	1·4	1·4	7·4	7·3	13·4	13·3
15	14 48·8	14 51·2	14 08·3	1·5	1·5	7·5	7·4	13·5	13·4
16	14 49·0	14 51·4	14 08·5	1·6	1·6	7·6	7·5	13·6	13·5
17	14 49·3	14 51·7	14 08·7	1·7	1·7	7·7	7·6	13·7	13·6
18	14 49·5	14 51·9	14 09·0	1·8	1·8	7·8	7·7	13·8	13·7
19	14 49·8	14 52·2	14 09·2	1·9	1·9	7·9	7·8	13·9	13·8
20	14 50·0	14 52·4	14 09·5	2·0	2·0	8·0	7·9	14·0	13·9
21	14 50·3	14 52·7	14 09·7	2·1	2·1	8·1	8·0	14·1	14·0
22	14 50·5	14 52·9	14 09·9	2·2	2·2	8·2	8·1	14·2	14·1
23	14 50·8	14 53·2	14 10·2	2·3	2·3	8·3	8·2	14·3	14·2
24	14 51·0	14 53·4	14 10·4	2·4	2·4	8·4	8·3	14·4	14·3
25	14 51·3	14 53·7	14 10·6	2·5	2·5	8·5	8·4	14·5	14·4
26	14 51·5	14 53·9	14 10·9	2·6	2·6	8·6	8·5	14·6	14·5
27	14 51·8	14 54·2	14 11·1	2·7	2·7	8·7	8·6	14·7	14·6
28	14 52·0	14 54·4	14 11·4	2·8	2·8	8·8	8·7	14·8	14·7
29	14 52·3	14 54·7	14 11·6	2·9	2·9	8·9	8·8	14·9	14·8
30	14 52·5	14 54·9	14 11·8	3·0	3·0	9·0	8·9	15·0	14·9
31	14 52·8	14 55·2	14 12·1	3·1	3·1	9·1	9·0	15·1	15·0
32	14 53·0	14 55·4	14 12·3	3·2	3·2	9·2	9·1	15·2	15·1
33	14 53·3	14 55·7	14 12·6	3·3	3·3	9·3	9·2	15·3	15·2
34	14 53·5	14 55·9	14 12·8	3·4	3·4	9·4	9·3	15·4	15·3
35	14 53·8	14 56·2	14 13·0	3·5	3·5	9·5	9·4	15·5	15·4
36	14 54·0	14 56·4	14 13·3	3·6	3·6	9·6	9·5	15·6	15·5
37	14 54·3	14 56·7	14 13·5	3·7	3·7	9·7	9·6	15·7	15·6
38	14 54·5	14 56·9	14 13·8	3·8	3·8	9·8	9·7	15·8	15·7
39	14 54·8	14 57·2	14 14·0	3·9	3·9	9·9	9·8	15·9	15·8
40	14 55·0	14 57·5	14 14·2	4·0	4·0	10·0	9·9	16·0	15·9
41	14 55·3	14 57·7	14 14·5	4·1	4·1	10·1	10·0	16·1	16·0
42	14 55·5	14 58·0	14 14·7	4·2	4·2	10·2	10·1	16·2	16·1
43	14 55·8	14 58·2	14 14·9	4·3	4·3	10·3	10·2	16·3	16·2
44	14 56·0	14 58·5	14 15·2	4·4	4·4	10·4	10·3	16·4	16·3
45	14 56·3	14 58·7	14 15·4	4·5	4·5	10·5	10·4	16·5	16·4
46	14 56·5	14 59·0	14 15·7	4·6	4·6	10·6	10·5	16·6	16·5
47	14 56·8	14 59·2	14 15·9	4·7	4·7	10·7	10·6	16·7	16·6
48	14 57·0	14 59·5	14 16·1	4·8	4·8	10·8	10·7	16·8	16·7
49	14 57·3	14 59·7	14 16·4	4·9	4·9	10·9	10·8	16·9	16·8
50	14 57·5	15 00·0	14 16·6	5·0	5·0	11·0	10·9	17·0	16·9
51	14 57·8	15 00·2	14 16·9	5·1	5·1	11·1	11·0	17·1	17·0
52	14 58·0	15 00·5	14 17·1	5·2	5·2	11·2	11·1	17·2	17·1
53	14 58·3	15 00·7	14 17·3	5·3	5·3	11·3	11·2	17·3	17·2
54	14 58·5	15 01·0	14 17·6	5·4	5·4	11·4	11·3	17·4	17·3
55	14 58·8	15 01·2	14 17·8	5·5	5·5	11·5	11·4	17·5	17·4
56	14 59·0	15 01·5	14 18·0	5·6	5·6	11·6	11·5	17·6	17·5
57	14 59·3	15 01·7	14 18·3	5·7	5·7	11·7	11·6	17·7	17·6
58	14 59·5	15 02·0	14 18·5	5·8	5·8	11·8	11·7	17·8	17·7
59	14 59·8	15 02·2	14 18·8	5·9	5·9	11·9	11·8	17·9	17·8
60	15 00·0	15 02·5	14 19·0	6·0	6·0	12·0	11·9	18·0	17·9

TABLES FOR INTERPOLATING SUNRISE, MOONRISE, ETC.

TABLE I—FOR LATITUDE

Tabular Interval			Difference between the times for consecutive latitudes															
10°	5°	2°	5^m	10^m	15^m	20^m	25^m	30^m	35^m	40^m	45^m	50^m	55^m	60^m	1^h05^m	1^h10^m	1^h15^m	1^h20^m
° ′	° ′	° ′	m	m	m	m	m	m	m	m	m	m	m	m	h m	h m	h m	h m
0 30	0 15	0 06	0	0	1	1	1	1	1	2	2	2	2	2	0 02	0 02	0 02	0 02
1 00	0 30	0 12	0	1	1	2	2	3	3	3	4	4	4	5	05	05	05	05
1 30	0 45	0 18	1	1	2	3	3	4	4	5	5	6	7	7	07	07	07	07
2 00	1 00	0 24	1	2	3	4	5	5	6	7	7	8	9	10	10	10	10	10
2 30	1 15	0 30	1	2	4	5	6	7	8	9	9	10	11	12	12	13	13	13
3 00	1 30	0 36	1	3	4	6	7	8	9	10	11	12	13	14	0 15	0 15	0 16	0 16
3 30	1 45	0 42	2	3	5	7	8	10	11	12	13	14	16	17	18	18	19	19
4 00	2 00	0 48	2	4	6	8	9	11	13	14	15	16	18	19	20	21	22	22
4 30	2 15	0 54	2	4	7	9	11	13	15	16	18	19	21	22	23	24	25	26
5 00	2 30	1 00	2	5	7	10	12	14	16	18	20	22	23	25	26	27	28	29
5 30	2 45	1 06	3	5	8	11	13	16	18	20	22	24	26	28	0 29	0 30	0 31	0 32
6 00	3 00	1 12	3	6	9	12	14	17	20	22	24	26	29	31	32	33	34	36
6 30	3 15	1 18	3	6	10	13	16	19	22	24	26	29	31	34	36	37	38	40
7 00	3 30	1 24	3	7	10	14	17	20	23	26	29	31	34	37	39	41	42	44
7 30	3 45	1 30	4	7	11	15	18	22	25	28	31	34	37	40	43	44	46	48
8 00	4 00	1 36	4	8	12	16	20	23	27	30	34	37	41	44	0 47	0 48	0 51	0 53
8 30	4 15	1 42	4	8	13	17	21	25	29	33	36	40	44	48	0 51	0 53	0 56	0 58
9 00	4 30	1 48	4	9	13	18	22	27	31	35	39	43	47	52	0 55	0 58	1 01	1 04
9 30	4 45	1 54	5	9	14	19	24	28	33	38	42	47	51	56	1 00	1 04	1 08	1 12
10 00	5 00	2 00	5	10	15	20	25	30	35	40	45	50	55	60	1 05	1 10	1 15	1 20

Table I is for interpolating the LMT of sunrise, twilight, moonrise, etc., for latitude. It is to be entered, in the appropriate column on the left, with the difference between true latitude and the nearest tabular latitude which is *less* than the true latitude; and with the argument at the top which is the nearest value of the difference between the times for the tabular latitude and the next higher one; the correction so obtained is applied to the time for the tabular latitude; the sign of the correction can be seen by inspection. It is to be noted that the interpolation is not linear, so that when using this table it is essential to take out the tabular phenomenon for the latitude *less* than the true latitude.

TABLE II—FOR LONGITUDE

Long. East or West	Difference between the times for given date and preceding date (for east longitude) or for given date and following date (for west longitude)																	
	10^m	20^m	30^m	40^m	50^m	60^m	1^h+ 10^m	20^m	30^m	1^h+ 40^m	50^m	60^m	2^h10^m	2^h20^m	2^h30^m	2^h40^m	2^h50^m	3^h00^m
°	m	m	m	m	m	m	m	m	m	m	m	m	h m	h m	h m	h m	h m	h m
0	0	0	0	0	0	0	0	0	0	0	0	0	0 00	0 00	0 00	0 00	0 00	0 00
10	0	1	1	1	1	2	2	2	2	3	3	3	04	04	04	04	05	05
20	1	1	2	2	3	3	4	4	5	6	6	7	07	08	08	09	09	10
30	1	2	2	3	4	5	6	7	7	8	9	10	11	12	12	13	14	15
40	1	2	3	4	6	7	8	9	10	11	12	13	14	16	17	18	19	20
50	1	3	4	6	7	8	10	11	12	14	15	17	0 18	0 19	0 21	0 22	0 24	0 25
60	2	3	5	7	8	10	12	13	15	17	18	20	22	23	25	27	28	30
70	2	4	6	8	10	12	14	16	17	19	21	23	25	27	29	31	33	35
80	2	4	7	9	11	13	16	18	20	22	24	27	29	31	33	36	38	40
90	2	5	7	10	12	15	17	20	22	25	27	30	32	35	37	40	42	45
100	3	6	8	11	14	17	19	22	25	28	31	33	0 36	0 39	0 42	0 44	0 47	0 50
110	3	6	9	12	15	18	21	24	27	31	34	37	40	43	46	49	0 52	0 55
120	3	7	10	13	17	20	23	27	30	33	37	40	43	47	50	53	0 57	1 00
130	4	7	11	14	18	22	25	29	32	36	40	43	47	51	54	0 58	1 01	1 05
140	4	8	12	16	19	23	27	31	35	39	43	47	51	54	0 58	1 02	1 06	1 10
150	4	8	13	17	21	25	29	33	38	42	46	50	0 54	0 58	1 03	1 07	1 11	1 15
160	4	9	13	18	22	27	31	36	40	44	49	53	0 58	1 02	1 07	1 11	1 16	1 20
170	5	9	14	19	24	28	33	38	42	47	52	57	1 01	1 06	1 11	1 16	1 20	1 25
180	5	10	15	20	25	30	35	40	45	50	55	60	1 05	1 10	1 15	1 20	1 25	1 30

Table II is for interpolating the LMT of moonrise, moonset and the Moon's meridian passage for longitude. It is entered with longitude and with the difference between the times for the given date and for the preceding date (in east longitudes) or following date (in west longitudes). The correction is normally *added* for west longitudes and *subtracted* for east longitudes, but if, as occasionally happens, the times become earlier each day instead of later, the signs of the corrections must be reversed.

INDEX TO SELECTED STARS, 2008

Name	No	Mag	SHA	Dec
			°	°
Acamar	**7**	3·2	315	S 40
Achernar	**5**	0·5	335	S 57
Acrux	**30**	1·3	173	S 63
Adhara	**19**	1·5	255	S 29
Aldebaran	**10**	0·9	291	N 17
Alioth	**32**	1·8	166	N 56
Alkaid	**34**	1·9	153	N 49
Al Na'ir	**55**	1·7	28	S 47
Alnilam	**15**	1·7	276	S 1
Alphard	**25**	2·0	218	S 9
Alphecca	**41**	2·2	126	N 27
Alpheratz	**1**	2·1	358	N 29
Altair	**51**	0·8	62	N 9
Ankaa	**2**	2·4	353	S 42
Antares	**42**	1·0	113	S 26
Arcturus	**37**	0·0	146	N 19
Atria	**43**	1·9	108	S 69
Avior	**22**	1·9	234	S 60
Bellatrix	**13**	1·6	279	N 6
Betelgeuse	**16**	Var.*	271	N 7
Canopus	**17**	−0·7	264	S 53
Capella	**12**	0·1	281	N 46
Deneb	**53**	1·3	50	N 45
Denebola	**28**	2·1	183	N 15
Diphda	**4**	2·0	349	S 18
Dubhe	**27**	1·8	194	N 62
Elnath	**14**	1·7	278	N 29
Eltanin	**47**	2·2	91	N 51
Enif	**54**	2·4	34	N 10
Fomalhaut	**56**	1·2	15	S 30
Gacrux	**31**	1·6	172	S 57
Gienah	**29**	2·6	176	S 18
Hadar	**35**	0·6	149	S 60
Hamal	**6**	2·0	328	N 24
Kaus Australis	**48**	1·9	84	S 34
Kochab	**40**	2·1	137	N 74
Markab	**57**	2·5	14	N 15
Menkar	**8**	2·5	314	N 4
Menkent	**36**	2·1	148	S 36
Miaplacidus	**24**	1·7	222	S 70
Mirfak	**9**	1·8	309	N 50
Nunki	**50**	2·0	76	S 26
Peacock	**52**	1·9	53	S 57
Pollux	**21**	1·1	244	N 28
Procyon	**20**	0·4	245	N 5
Rasalhague	**46**	2·1	96	N 13
Regulus	**26**	1·4	208	N 12
Rigel	**11**	0·1	281	S 8
Rigil Kentaurus	**38**	−0·3	140	S 61
Sabik	**44**	2·4	102	S 16
Schedar	**3**	2·2	350	N 57
Shaula	**45**	1·6	96	S 37
Sirius	**18**	−1·5	259	S 17
Spica	**33**	1·0	159	S 11
Suhail	**23**	2·2	223	S 43
Vega	**49**	0·0	81	N 39
Zubenelgenubi	**39**	2·8	137	S 16

No	Name	Mag	SHA	Dec
			°	°
1	*Alpheratz*	2·1	358	N 29
2	*Ankaa*	2·4	353	S 42
3	*Schedar*	2·2	350	N 57
4	*Diphda*	2·0	349	S 18
5	*Achernar*	0·5	335	S 57
6	*Hamal*	2·0	328	N 24
7	*Acamar*	3·2	315	S 40
8	*Menkar*	2·5	314	N 4
9	*Mirfak*	1·8	309	N 50
10	*Aldebaran*	0·9	291	N 17
11	*Rigel*	0·1	281	S 8
12	*Capella*	0·1	281	N 46
13	*Bellatrix*	1·6	279	N 6
14	*Elnath*	1·7	278	N 29
15	*Alnilam*	1·7	276	S 1
16	*Betelgeuse*	Var.*	271	N 7
17	*Canopus*	−0·7	264	S 53
18	*Sirius*	−1·5	259	S 17
19	*Adhara*	1·5	255	S 29
20	*Procyon*	0·4	245	N 5
21	*Pollux*	1·1	244	N 28
22	*Avior*	1·9	234	S 60
23	*Suhail*	2·2	223	S 43
24	*Miaplacidus*	1·7	222	S 70
25	*Alphard*	2·0	218	S 9
26	*Regulus*	1·4	208	N 12
27	*Dubhe*	1·8	194	N 62
28	*Denebola*	2·1	183	N 15
29	*Gienah*	2·6	176	S 18
30	*Acrux*	1·3	173	S 63
31	*Gacrux*	1·6	172	S 57
32	*Alioth*	1·8	166	N 56
33	*Spica*	1·0	159	S 11
34	*Alkaid*	1·9	153	N 49
35	*Hadar*	0·6	149	S 60
36	*Menkent*	2·1	148	S 36
37	*Arcturus*	0·0	146	N 19
38	*Rigil Kentaurus*	−0·3	140	S 61
39	*Zubenelgenubi*	2·8	137	S 16
40	*Kochab*	2·1	137	N 74
41	*Alphecca*	2·2	126	N 27
42	*Antares*	1·0	113	S 26
43	*Atria*	1·9	108	S 69
44	*Sabik*	2·4	102	S 16
45	*Shaula*	1·6	96	S 37
46	*Rasalhague*	2·1	96	N 13
47	*Eltanin*	2·2	91	N 51
48	*Kaus Australis*	1·9	84	S 34
49	*Vega*	0·0	81	N 39
50	*Nunki*	2·0	76	S 26
51	*Altair*	0·8	62	N 9
52	*Peacock*	1·9	53	S 57
53	*Deneb*	1·3	50	N 45
54	*Enif*	2·4	34	N 10
55	*Al Na'ir*	1·7	28	S 47
56	*Fomalhaut*	1·2	15	S 30
57	*Markab*	2·5	14	N 15

*0·1 — 1·2

App. Alt.	0°–4° Corrⁿ	5°–9° Corrⁿ	10°–14° Corrⁿ	15°–19° Corrⁿ	20°–24° Corrⁿ	25°–29° Corrⁿ	30°–34° Corrⁿ	App. Alt.
′	° ′	° ′	° ′	° ′	° ′	° ′	° ′	′
00	0 34·5	5 58·2	10 62·1	15 62·8	20 62·2	25 60·8	30 58·9	00
10	36·5	58·5	62·2	62·8	62·2	60·8	58·8	10
20	38·3	58·7	62·2	62·8	62·1	60·7	58·8	20
30	40·0	58·9	62·3	62·8	62·1	60·7	58·7	30
40	41·5	59·1	62·3	62·8	62·0	60·6	58·6	40
50	42·9	59·3	62·4	62·7	62·0	60·6	58·5	50
00	1 44·2	6 59·5	11 62·4	16 62·7	21 62·0	26 60·5	31 58·5	00
10	45·4	59·7	62·4	62·7	61·9	60·4	58·4	10
20	46·5	59·9	62·5	62·7	61·9	60·4	58·3	20
30	47·5	60·0	62·5	62·7	61·9	60·3	58·2	30
40	48·4	60·2	62·5	62·7	61·8	60·3	58·2	40
50	49·3	60·3	62·6	62·7	61·8	60·2	58·1	50
00	2 50·1	7 60·5	12 62·6	17 62·7	22 61·7	27 60·1	32 58·0	00
10	50·8	60·6	62·6	62·6	61·7	60·1	57·9	10
20	51·5	60·7	62·6	62·6	61·6	60·0	57·8	20
30	52·2	60·9	62·7	62·6	61·6	59·9	57·8	30
40	52·8	61·0	62·7	62·6	61·6	59·9	57·7	40
50	53·4	61·1	62·7	62·6	61·5	59·8	57·6	50
00	3 53·9	8 61·2	13 62·7	18 62·5	23 61·5	28 59·7	33 57·5	00
10	54·4	61·3	62·7	62·5	61·4	59·7	57·4	10
20	54·9	61·4	62·7	62·5	61·4	59·6	57·4	20
30	55·3	61·5	62·8	62·5	61·3	59·5	57·3	30
40	55·7	61·6	62·8	62·4	61·3	59·5	57·2	40
50	56·1	61·6	62·8	62·4	61·2	59·4	57·1	50
00	4 56·4	9 61·7	14 62·8	19 62·4	24 61·2	29 59·3	34 57·0	00
10	56·8	61·8	62·8	62·4	61·1	59·3	56·9	10
20	57·1	61·9	62·8	62·3	61·1	59·2	56·9	20
30	57·4	61·9	62·8	62·3	61·0	59·1	56·8	30
40	57·7	62·0	62·8	62·3	61·0	59·1	56·7	40
50	58·0	62·1	62·8	62·2	60·9	59·0	56·6	50

HP	L	U	L	U	L	U	L	U	L	U	L	U	L	U	HP
′	′	′	′	′	′	′	′	′	′	′	′	′	′	′	′
54·0	0·3	0·9	0·3	0·9	0·4	1·0	0·5	1·1	0·6	1·2	0·7	1·3	0·9	1·5	54·0
54·3	0·7	1·1	0·7	1·2	0·8	1·2	0·8	1·3	0·9	1·4	1·1	1·5	1·2	1·7	54·3
54·6	1·1	1·4	1·1	1·4	1·1	1·4	1·2	1·5	1·3	1·6	1·4	1·7	1·5	1·8	54·6
54·9	1·4	1·6	1·5	1·6	1·5	1·6	1·6	1·7	1·6	1·8	1·8	1·9	1·9	2·0	54·9
55·2	1·8	1·8	1·8	1·8	1·9	1·8	1·9	1·9	2·0	2·0	2·1	2·1	2·2	2·2	55·2
55·5	2·2	2·0	2·2	2·0	2·3	2·1	2·3	2·1	2·4	2·2	2·4	2·3	2·5	2·4	55·5
55·8	2·6	2·2	2·6	2·2	2·6	2·3	2·7	2·3	2·7	2·4	2·8	2·4	2·9	2·5	55·8
56·1	3·0	2·4	3·0	2·5	3·0	2·5	3·0	2·5	3·1	2·6	3·1	2·6	3·2	2·7	56·1
56·4	3·3	2·7	3·4	2·7	3·4	2·7	3·4	2·7	3·4	2·8	3·5	2·8	3·5	2·9	56·4
56·7	3·7	2·9	3·7	2·9	3·8	2·9	3·8	2·9	3·8	3·0	3·8	3·0	3·9	3·0	56·7
57·0	4·1	3·1	4·1	3·1	4·1	3·1	4·1	3·1	4·2	3·2	4·2	3·2	4·2	3·2	57·0
57·3	4·5	3·3	4·5	3·3	4·5	3·3	4·5	3·3	4·5	3·3	4·5	3·4	4·6	3·4	57·3
57·6	4·9	3·5	4·9	3·5	4·9	3·5	4·9	3·5	4·9	3·5	4·9	3·5	4·9	3·6	57·6
57·9	5·3	3·8	5·3	3·8	5·2	3·8	5·2	3·7	5·2	3·7	5·2	3·7	5·2	3·7	57·9
58·2	5·6	4·0	5·6	4·0	5·6	4·0	5·6	4·0	5·6	3·9	5·6	3·9	5·6	3·9	58·2
58·5	6·0	4·2	6·0	4·2	6·0	4·2	6·0	4·2	6·0	4·1	5·9	4·1	5·9	4·1	58·5
58·8	6·4	4·4	6·4	4·4	6·4	4·4	6·3	4·4	6·3	4·3	6·3	4·3	6·2	4·2	58·8
59·1	6·8	4·6	6·8	4·6	6·7	4·6	6·7	4·6	6·7	4·5	6·6	4·5	6·6	4·4	59·1
59·4	7·2	4·8	7·1	4·8	7·1	4·8	7·1	4·8	7·0	4·7	7·0	4·7	6·9	4·6	59·4
59·7	7·5	5·1	7·5	5·0	7·5	5·0	7·5	5·0	7·4	4·9	7·3	4·8	7·2	4·8	59·7
60·0	7·9	5·3	7·9	5·3	7·9	5·2	7·8	5·2	7·8	5·1	7·7	5·0	7·6	4·9	60·0
60·3	8·3	5·5	8·3	5·5	8·2	5·4	8·2	5·4	8·1	5·3	8·0	5·2	7·9	5·1	60·3
60·6	8·7	5·7	8·7	5·7	8·6	5·7	8·6	5·6	8·5	5·5	8·4	5·4	8·2	5·3	60·6
60·9	9·1	5·9	9·0	5·9	9·0	5·9	8·9	5·8	8·8	5·7	8·7	5·6	8·6	5·4	60·9
61·2	9·5	6·2	9·4	6·1	9·4	6·1	9·3	6·0	9·2	5·9	9·1	5·8	8·9	5·6	61·2
61·5	9·8	6·4	9·8	6·3	9·7	6·3	9·7	6·2	9·5	6·1	9·4	5·9	9·2	5·8	61·5

DIP

Ht. of Eye	Corrⁿ	Ht. of Eye	Ht. of Eye	Corrⁿ	Ht. of Eye
m		ft.	m		ft.
2·4		8·0	9·5		31·5
	−2·8			−5·5	
2·6		8·6	9·9		32·7
	−2·9			−5·6	
2·8		9·2	10·3		33·9
	−3·0			−5·7	
3·0		9·8	10·6		35·1
	−3·1			−5·8	
3·2		10·5	11·0		36·3
	−3·2			−5·9	
3·4		11·2	11·4		37·6
	−3·3			−6·0	
3·6		11·9	11·8		38·9
	−3·4			−6·1	
3·8		12·6	12·2		40·1
	−3·5			−6·2	
4·0		13·3	12·6		41·5
	−3·6			−6·3	
4·3		14·1	13·0		42·8
	−3·7			−6·4	
4·5		14·9	13·4		44·2
	−3·8			−6·5	
4·7		15·7	13·8		45·5
	−3·9			−6·6	
5·0		16·5	14·2		46·9
	−4·0			−6·7	
5·2		17·4	14·7		48·4
	−4·1			−6·8	
5·5		18·3	15·1		49·8
	−4·2			−6·9	
5·8		19·1	15·5		51·3
	−4·3			−7·0	
6·1		20·1	16·0		52·8
	−4·4			−7·1	
6·3		21·0	16·5		54·3
	−4·5			−7·2	
6·6		22·0	16·9		55·8
	−4·6			−7·3	
6·9		22·9	17·4		57·4
	−4·7			−7·4	
7·2		23·9	17·9		58·9
	−4·8			−7·5	
7·5		24·9	18·4		60·5
	−4·9			−7·6	
7·9		26·0	18·8		62·1
	−5·0			−7·7	
8·2		27·1	19·3		63·8
	−5·1			−7·8	
8·5		28·1	19·8		65·4
	−5·2			−7·9	
8·8		29·2	20·4		67·1
	−5·3			−8·0	
9·2		30·4	20·9		68·8
	−5·4			−8·1	
9·5		31·5	21·4		70·5

MOON CORRECTION TABLE

The correction is in two parts; the first correction is taken from the upper part of the table with argument apparent altitude, and the second from the lower part, with argument HP, in the same column as that from which the first correction was taken. Separate corrections are given in the lower part for lower (L) and upper(U) limbs. All corrections are to be **added** to apparent altitude, *but 30′ is to be subtracted from the altitude of the upper limb.*

For corrections for pressure and temperature see page A4.

For bubble sextant observations ignore dip, take the mean of upper and lower limb corrections and subtract 15′ from the altitude.

App. Alt. = Apparent altitude = Sextant altitude corrected for index error and dip.

ALTITUDE CORRECTION TABLES 35°–90°— MOON

App. Alt.	35°–39° Corrⁿ	40°–44° Corrⁿ	45°–49° Corrⁿ	50°–54° Corrⁿ	55°–59° Corrⁿ	60°–64° Corrⁿ	65°–69° Corrⁿ	70°–74° Corrⁿ	75°–79° Corrⁿ	80°–84° Corrⁿ	85°–89° Corrⁿ	App. Alt.
′	° ′	° ′	° ′	° ′	° ′	° ′	° ′	° ′	° ′	° ′	° ′	′
00	35 56·5	40 53·7	45 50·5	50 46·9	55 43·1	60 38·9	65 34·6	70 30·0	75 25·3	80 20·5	85 15·6	00
10	56·4	53·6	50·4	46·8	42·9	38·8	34·4	29·9	25·2	20·4	15·5	10
20	56·3	53·5	50·2	46·7	42·8	38·7	34·3	29·7	25·0	20·2	15·3	20
30	56·2	53·4	50·1	46·5	42·7	38·5	34·1	29·6	24·9	20·0	15·1	30
40	56·2	53·3	50·0	46·4	42·5	38·4	34·0	29·4	24·7	19·9	15·0	40
50	56·1	53·2	49·9	46·3	42·4	38·2	33·8	29·3	24·5	19·7	14·8	50
00	36 56·0	41 53·1	46 49·8	51 46·2	56 42·3	61 38·1	66 33·7	71 29·1	76 24·4	81 19·6	86 14·6	00
10	55·9	53·0	49·7	46·0	42·1	37·9	33·5	29·0	24·2	19·4	14·5	10
20	55·8	52·9	49·5	45·9	42·0	37·8	33·4	28·8	24·1	19·2	14·3	20
30	55·7	52·8	49·4	45·8	41·9	37·7	33·2	28·7	23·9	19·1	14·2	30
40	55·6	52·6	49·3	45·7	41·7	37·5	33·1	28·5	23·8	18·9	14·0	40
50	55·5	52·5	49·2	45·5	41·6	37·4	32·9	28·3	23·6	18·7	13·8	50
00	37 55·4	42 52·4	47 49·1	52 45·4	57 41·4	62 37·2	67 32·8	72 28·2	77 23·4	82 18·6	87 13·7	00
10	55·3	52·3	49·0	45·3	41·3	37·1	32·6	28·0	23·3	18·4	13·5	10
20	55·2	52·2	48·8	45·2	41·2	36·9	32·5	27·9	23·1	18·2	13·3	20
30	55·1	52·1	48·7	45·0	41·0	36·8	32·3	27·7	22·9	18·1	13·2	30
40	55·0	52·0	48·6	44·9	40·9	36·6	32·2	27·6	22·8	17·9	13·0	40
50	55·0	51·9	48·5	44·8	40·8	36·5	32·0	27·4	22·6	17·8	12·8	50
00	38 54·9	43 51·8	48 48·4	53 44·6	58 40·6	63 36·4	68 31·9	73 27·2	78 22·5	83 17·6	88 12·7	00
10	54·8	51·7	48·3	44·5	40·5	36·2	31·7	27·1	22·3	17·4	12·5	10
20	54·7	51·6	48·1	44·4	40·3	36·1	31·6	26·9	22·1	17·3	12·3	20
30	54·6	51·5	48·0	44·2	40·2	35·9	31·4	26·8	22·0	17·1	12·2	30
40	54·5	51·4	47·9	44·1	40·1	35·8	31·3	26·6	21·8	16·9	12·0	40
50	54·4	51·2	47·8	44·0	39·9	35·6	31·1	26·5	21·7	16·8	11·8	50
00	39 54·3	44 51·1	49 47·7	54 43·9	59 39·8	64 35·5	69 31·0	74 26·3	79 21·5	84 16·6	89 11·7	00
10	54·2	51·0	47·5	43·7	39·6	35·3	30·8	26·1	21·3	16·4	11·5	10
20	54·1	50·9	47·4	43·6	39·5	35·2	30·7	26·0	21·2	16·3	11·4	20
30	54·0	50·8	47·3	43·5	39·4	35·0	30·5	25·8	21·0	16·1	11·2	30
40	53·9	50·7	47·2	43·3	39·2	34·9	30·4	25·7	20·9	16·0	11·0	40
50	53·8	50·6	47·0	43·2	39·1	34·7	30·2	25·5	20·7	15·8	10·9	50

HP	L	U	L	U	L	U	L	U	L	U	L	U	L	U	L	U	L	U	L	U	L	U	HP
′	′	′	′	′	′	′	′	′	′	′	′	′	′	′	′	′	′	′	′	′	′	′	′
54·0	1·1	1·7	1·3	1·9	1·5	2·1	1·7	2·4	2·0	2·6	2·3	2·9	2·6	3·2	2·9	3·5	3·2	3·8	3·5	4·1	3·8	4·5	54·0
54·3	1·4	1·8	1·6	2·0	1·8	2·2	2·0	2·5	2·2	2·7	2·5	3·0	2·8	3·2	3·1	3·5	3·3	3·8	3·6	4·1	3·9	4·4	54·3
54·6	1·7	2·0	1·9	2·2	2·1	2·4	2·3	2·6	2·5	2·8	2·7	3·0	3·0	3·3	3·2	3·5	3·5	3·8	3·8	4·0	4·0	4·3	54·6
54·9	2·0	2·2	2·2	2·3	2·3	2·5	2·5	2·7	2·7	2·9	2·9	3·1	3·2	3·3	3·4	3·5	3·6	3·8	3·9	4·0	4·1	4·3	54·9
55·2	2·3	2·3	2·5	2·4	2·6	2·6	2·8	2·8	3·0	2·9	3·2	3·1	3·4	3·3	3·6	3·5	3·8	3·7	4·0	4·0	4·2	4·2	55·2
55·5	2·7	2·5	2·8	2·6	2·9	2·7	3·1	2·9	3·2	3·0	3·4	3·2	3·6	3·4	3·7	3·5	3·9	3·7	4·1	3·9	4·3	4·1	55·5
55·8	3·0	2·6	3·1	2·7	3·2	2·8	3·3	3·0	3·5	3·1	3·6	3·3	3·8	3·4	3·9	3·6	4·1	3·7	4·2	3·9	4·4	4·0	55·8
56·1	3·3	2·8	3·4	2·9	3·5	3·0	3·6	3·1	3·7	3·2	3·8	3·3	4·0	3·4	4·1	3·6	4·2	3·7	4·4	3·8	4·5	4·0	56·1
56·4	3·6	2·9	3·7	3·0	3·8	3·1	3·9	3·2	3·9	3·3	4·0	3·4	4·1	3·5	4·3	3·6	4·4	3·7	4·5	3·8	4·6	3·9	56·4
56·7	3·9	3·1	4·0	3·1	4·1	3·2	4·1	3·3	4·2	3·3	4·3	3·4	4·3	3·5	4·4	3·6	4·5	3·7	4·6	3·8	4·7	3·8	56·7
57·0	4·3	3·2	4·3	3·3	4·3	3·3	4·4	3·4	4·4	3·4	4·5	3·5	4·5	3·5	4·6	3·6	4·7	3·6	4·7	3·7	4·8	3·8	57·0
57·3	4·6	3·4	4·6	3·4	4·6	3·4	4·6	3·5	4·7	3·5	4·7	3·5	4·7	3·6	4·8	3·6	4·8	3·6	4·8	3·7	4·9	3·7	57·3
57·6	4·9	3·6	4·9	3·6	4·9	3·6	4·9	3·6	4·9	3·6	4·9	3·6	4·9	3·6	4·9	3·6	5·0	3·6	5·0	3·6	5·0	3·6	57·6
57·9	5·2	3·7	5·2	3·7	5·2	3·7	5·2	3·7	5·2	3·7	5·1	3·6	5·1	3·6	5·1	3·6	5·1	3·6	5·1	3·6	5·1	3·6	57·9
58·2	5·5	3·9	5·5	3·8	5·5	3·8	5·4	3·8	5·4	3·7	5·4	3·7	5·3	3·7	5·3	3·6	5·2	3·6	5·2	3·5	5·2	3·5	58·2
58·5	5·9	4·0	5·8	4·0	5·8	3·9	5·7	3·9	5·6	3·8	5·6	3·8	5·5	3·7	5·5	3·6	5·4	3·6	5·3	3·5	5·3	3·4	58·5
58·8	6·2	4·2	6·1	4·1	6·0	4·1	6·0	4·0	5·9	3·9	5·8	3·8	5·7	3·7	5·6	3·6	5·5	3·5	5·4	3·5	5·3	3·4	58·8
59·1	6·5	4·3	6·4	4·3	6·3	4·2	6·2	4·1	6·1	4·0	6·0	3·9	5·9	3·8	5·8	3·6	5·7	3·5	5·6	3·4	5·4	3·3	59·1
59·4	6·8	4·5	6·7	4·4	6·6	4·3	6·5	4·2	6·4	4·1	6·2	3·9	6·1	3·8	6·0	3·7	5·8	3·5	5·7	3·4	5·5	3·2	59·4
59·7	7·1	4·7	7·0	4·5	6·9	4·4	6·8	4·3	6·6	4·1	6·5	4·0	6·3	3·8	6·1	3·7	6·0	3·5	5·8	3·3	5·6	3·2	59·7
60·0	7·5	4·8	7·3	4·7	7·2	4·5	7·0	4·4	6·9	4·2	6·7	4·0	6·5	3·9	6·3	3·7	6·1	3·5	5·9	3·3	5·7	3·1	60·0
60·3	7·8	5·0	7·6	4·8	7·5	4·7	7·3	4·5	7·1	4·3	6·9	4·1	6·7	3·9	6·5	3·7	6·3	3·5	6·0	3·2	5·8	3·0	60·3
60·6	8·1	5·1	7·9	5·0	7·7	4·8	7·6	4·6	7·3	4·4	7·1	4·2	6·9	3·9	6·7	3·7	6·4	3·4	6·2	3·2	5·9	2·9	60·6
60·9	8·4	5·3	8·2	5·1	8·0	4·9	7·8	4·7	7·6	4·5	7·3	4·2	7·1	4·0	6·8	3·7	6·6	3·4	6·3	3·2	6·0	2·9	60·9
61·2	8·7	5·4	8·5	5·2	8·3	5·0	8·1	4·8	7·8	4·5	7·6	4·3	7·3	4·0	7·0	3·7	6·7	3·4	6·4	3·1	6·1	2·8	61·2
61·5	9·1	5·6	8·8	5·4	8·6	5·1	8·3	4·9	8·1	4·6	7·8	4·3	7·5	4·0	7·2	3·7	6·9	3·4	6·5	3·1	6·2	2·7	61·5

NOTES

LIN & LARRY PARDEY

CARE & FEEDING OF SAILING CREW

Third Edition, Revised & Expanded

Lin Pardey has incorporated new information on nutrition, on waste disposal, and on current methods for handling finances, officialdom, and the paperwork involved in sailing to new countries. New and expanded sections cover entertaining on board, feeding vegetarian crew, choosing clothing for sailing offshore, and incorporating modern technology in the galley. Her unique guides to reprovisioning as you voyage and buying wines and liquors around the world have been expanded to many off-the-beaten track destinations now attracting intrepid voyagers.

416 pages • ISBN 1-92921-407-3 • Paperback • $24.95

GET READY TO CRUISE

Offshore Sailing - Part One

Join the Pardeys on board *Taleisin*-the boat that has been their home for 65,000 miles of voyaging - they demonstrate galley upgrades and ways to improve ventilation below deck. On deck, learn how sail and ground-tackle handling can be made easier for even the smallest crew member. Incorporates the best ideas from some of their highly praised videos: *Voyaging, Hints for Upgrading Your Cruising Boat,* and *Cruising Coral Seas.*

Run time: 98 minutes • ISBN 1-929214-22-7 • $29.95

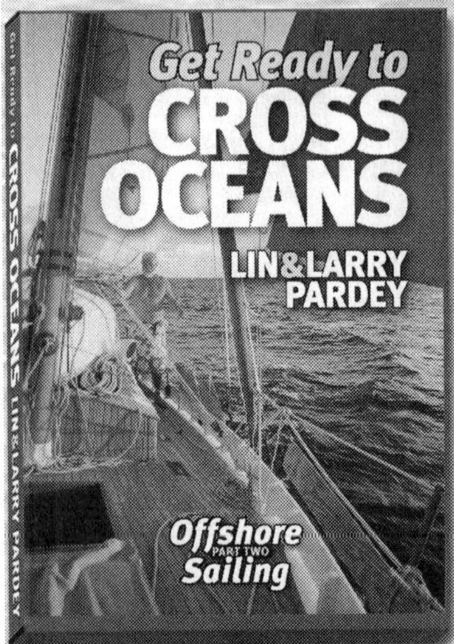

GET READY TO CROSS OCEANS

Join Lin and Larry Pardey as they demonstrate gear storage for offshore voyaging, dinghy choices, proper life-raft storage, storm trysails, sail repairs, and other valuable hints to help you prepare. Then voyage along with them on a classic trade-wind passage across the Indian Ocean toward Africa. Weather planning, landfall considerations, windvanes, sail choices, and crew comfort and more. Incorporates the best ideas from their highly praised videos, including *Cruising with Lin and Larry Pardey* and *The Care and Feeding of Sailing Crew*.

Run time: 98 minutes • ISBN 1-929214-19-7 • $29.95

STORM TACTICS DVD

A PARADISE CAY BESTSELLER 4 YEARS RUNNING!

Learn ways to prepare your crew and your boat to eliminate fear and face heavy weather with a plan; how and when to use the sailors safety valve, heaving to-with or without a para-anchor. Gear and equipment, plus special sails for heavy weather are discussed in detail. This video companion to their highly successful *Storm Tactics Handbook* provides new insights into handling storm sails and para-anchors and is a must for anyone who ventures more than a few miles offshore in a sailboat.

Run time: 84 minutes • ISBN 1-929214-10-3 • $29.95

Paradise Cay Publications, Inc. • P.O. Box 29 • Arcata, CA 95517-0029 •
(800) 736-4509 U.S. • (707) 822-9063 Int. • info@paracay.com • www.paracay.com

PARADISE CAY PUBLICATIONS

The Essentials of Living Aboard a Boat
Mark Nicholas
9780939837663• $17.95

Care and Feeding of Sailing Crew
Lin & Larry Pardey
9781929214075• $24.95

It's Your Boat Too
Suzanne Giesemann
9780939837694• $14.95

Twenty Affordable Sailboats to Take you Anywhere
Gregg Nestor
0939837722• $17.95

American Practical Navigator "Bowditch" (Hardcover)
Nathaniel Bowditch
9780939837542• $49.95

NAUTICAL ALMANAC
2009 COMMERCIAL EDITION
2009

Nautical Almanac 2009 Commercial Edition
HMNAO
(DUE MID 2008)

Celestial Navigation in the GPS Age
John Karl
9780939837155• $24.95

DESIGN AND BUILD YOUR OWN JUNK RIG
DEREK VAN LOAN

The Chinese Sailing Rig
3rd Edition
Derek Van Loan
9780939837700• $18.95

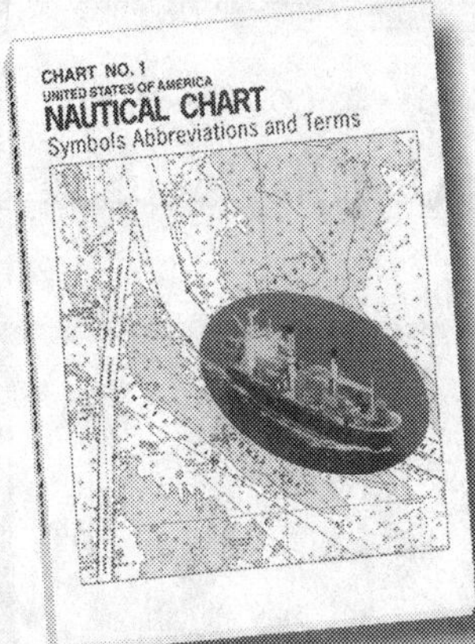

Chart No. 1
Full color illustrations
9780939837564• $9.95

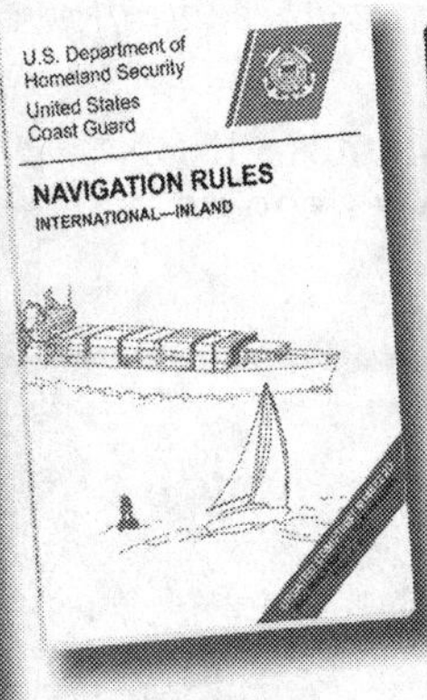

Navigation Rules
updated ed.
Frequently Updated
9780939837496• $10.95

The Great Circle Route, 2nd Ed.
G. Bickley Remmey Jr.
9780939837687• $24.95

Cruising Guide to the Hawaiian Islands
Bob & Carolyn Mehaffy
9780939837731• $29.95

AVAILABLE FROM ROBERT HALE & CO., INC (800) 733-5330 • FAX (425) 881-0731